Congress and the Nation

VOLUME IX   •   1993–1996

Congress and the Nation

VOLUME IX   ·   1993–1996

A REVIEW OF GOVERNMENT AND POLITICS

 CONGRESSIONAL QUARTERLY INC.
WASHINGTON, D.C.

Editors: Ann O'Connor, Jon Preimesberger, David Tarr

Major Contributors: John Cranford, Carolyn Goldinger, Jon Healey,
Ken Jost, Kerry Kern, David Masci, Colleen McGuiness,
Julie Rovner, Andrew Taylor

Contributors: Carroll Doherty, Chris Karlsten, Chris Lawrence,
Mikael McCowan, Ann O'Malley; Jerry Orvedahl, Pat Towell

Composition Specialist: Jessica S. Forman

Index: Jan Danis

Graphics: Deborah Ismond

Library of Congress Catalog Number: 65-22351

ISBN: 1-56802-240-9
ISSN: 1047-1324

Editors' Note

Congress and the Nation Vol. IX continues a series launched by Congressional Quarterly in 1965 with the publication of *Congress and the Nation Vol. I*, a 2,000-page reference book covering national government and politics from 1945 through 1964. Each of the succeeding volumes has covered governmental action during a four-year presidential term: *Congress and the Nation Vol. II, 1965–1968; Congress and the Nation Vol. III, 1969–1972; Congress and the Nation Vol. IV, 1973–1976; Congress and the Nation Vol. V, 1977–1980; Congress and the Nation Vol. VI, 1981–1984; Congress and the Nation Vol. VII, 1985–1988; Congress and the Nation Vol. VIII, 1989–1992.*

With the publication of this volume, librarians, historians, political scientists, journalists and students have nine volumes spanning more than 50 years of Congressional Quarterly's reporting on public policy.

In compiling *Congress and the Nation Vol. IX,* Congressional Quarterly has condensed its legislative, presidential and political coverage during the 1993–1996 period into a 1,300-page volume. Readers are given both an overview of the four-year period and detailed chronologies of governmental action in every major subject area.

This volume chronicles the first presidential term of Bill Clinton. It was an extraordinary four-year period in many ways. With the inauguration of Clinton, the White House and Congress were controlled by the Democratic Party for the first time since the Jimmy Carter presidency 12 years earlier. But the Democrats' unified government was short-lived. Republicans staged a huge upset in the 1994 midterm elections, giving the GOP control of both houses of Congress for the first time in 40 years.

After the pummeling the Democrats took in the 1994 elections, Clinton looked to be a one-term president. But in 1996—with the economy humming, the deficit declining, relative peace abroad and both parties shifting to the political center—the incumbents had the advantage and Clinton and the Republican Congress were reelected.

In the intervening four years, however, neither party had found that its success at the polls translated into easy legislative victories.

The Clinton White House was buffeted by public relations missteps and personnel fiascoes at the outset. The president suffered major defeats on an economic stimulus bill and his effort to lift the ban on homosexuals in the military. And many of his domestic initiatives often were overshadowed by foreign policy crises in Bosnia, Somalia and Haiti. By the end of 1993, however, he had chalked up a string of legislative accomplishments, with big wins on deficit reduction, trade and gun control. Hopes were high that Clinton had hit his stride.

But a combination of bad breaks, questionable decisions and a more aggressive opposition party dealt the president repeated reversals in 1994, none greater than the inglorious demise of his health care plan. Even successes, such as passage of a crime bill, often were clouded by rancorous partisanship.

Public disenchantment with Washington and the White House, among other things, helped seal the Democrats' fate in the 1994 elections.

Republicans took control of the 104th Congress confidant they had been given a mandate for change. But very few of their ideas were enacted in the first session. Instead, their more radical proposals, such as curbing enforcement of key environmental laws, and their hard-charging tactics proved costly for the GOP in public opinion polls. Their chief demand—that Clinton agree to balance the budget in seven years on their terms—ended in a humiliating defeat for the GOP but not before triggering two government shutdowns.

The lesson was learned and confrontation gave way to compromise, as Clinton and Congress worked together to compile a record of legislative achievements that included an overhaul of the nation's welfare system, a rewrite of telecommunications law, new farm policy, an increase in the minimum wage, new standards for drinking water, guaranteed health insurance for workers who lost or left their jobs and a line-item veto for the president.

The four years also saw congressional investigations into various allegations of improprieties by the Clinton White House and some high-ranking members of Congress, including the House Speaker.

Congress made several changes affecting its own operations, including new gift rules and lobby reporting requirements, but an overhaul of the campaign finance law remained elusive.

Congress and the Nation Vol. IX is a record of these and other congressional activities—from momentous events to routine extensions of programs. Researchers can find the pertinent facts on issues and legislation; descriptions of proposals and bills; succinct accounts of legislative, executive and lobbying action; key votes on selected issues; and provisions of legislation.

HOW TO USE THIS BOOK

The **Summary Table of Contents** following this editors' note shows the overall organization of the volume. The detailed **Table of Contents** *(p. ix)* provides an outline of each chapter, as well as a listing of all the stories contained in a particular chapter. For a specific topic within a story, the reader should consult the **Index** *(p. 1213)*. For example, the reader who is interested in congressional action on foreign aid would find in the Table of Contents that stories on this issue are in the

Foreign Policy chapter. A reader who needs more specific information, such as details of executive and legislative action on aid to a particular country or region, could consult the Index and find specific page references under each separate listing of a geographic area.

The first chapter, Politics and National Issues, gives a legislative summary of each session of the 103rd and 104th Congresses and a discussion of the 1994 and 1996 elections. The chapter forms a framework for the legislative chapters that follow.

Note the organization of the legislative chapters—Economic Policy, Foreign Policy, Defense Policy and so on. Each opens with an introduction providing the reader with an overview. That is followed by a chronology of legislative action, divided by Congresses, from 1993 through 1996.

The final chapter discusses the Clinton presidency.

The **Appendix** (*p. 949*) contains a variety of supplementary material, including Senate and House key votes (highlighted in boldface in the legislative chapters) during the four-year period, with charts showing how each member voted; a glossary of congressional terms and an explanation of how a bill becomes law; lists of committee and subcommittee chairmen; biographical data on members of Congress in 1993–1996; profiles of cabinet members and other senior officials; controversial nominations; presidential vetoes; major presidential speeches and messages to Congress; and political charts, including presidential election returns for 1992 and 1996 and House, Senate and gubernatorial returns for 1994 and 1996.

The Editors
February 1998

Summary Table of Contents

Table of Contents

CHAPTER 4 Foreign Policy

CHAPTER 5 Defense Policy

CHAPTER 8   Agricultural Policy

Introduction   479

CHAPTER 9   Health and Human Services

Introduction   509

Health

Human Services

Veterans Affairs

CHAPTER 10   Education Policy

Introduction   607

Congress and the Nation

VOLUME IX · 1993–1996

CHAPTER 1

Politics and National Issues

Politics and National Issues

The period in American politics from 1993 to 1996 was notable for the reversal of fortunes experienced by its main players. When Bill Clinton assumed the presidency, the White House and Congress both came under control of the Democrats for the first time in 12 years. As a result, a slew of legislation that had been blocked by Republicans sailed easily to enactment. However, the Democrats subsequently mishandled the loudly touted health care reform effort, and with it the Clinton presidency seemed to stall. Frustrated and angry voters went to the polls in 1994 and gave the GOP the majority in both houses of Congress for the first time in 40 years. In the heady early days of the 104th Congress, the House Republicans, led by Speaker Newt Gingrich, R-Ga., moved aggressively to enact their conservative agenda. Clinton, meanwhile, appeared to many to be a one-term president. Republican presidential nominee and Senate Majority Leader Bob Dole, R-Kan., believed he could use his powerful perch in Congress to make his case for the presidency, while showing off his legislative and political skills. But, by the end of 1996, the newly reelected Clinton was racking up some of his highest public approval ratings; Dole no longer held elective office; the House Republicans had been successfully branded as extremists; and Gingrich, who soon would be reprimanded and fined by the House for ethical violations, found his Speakership in jeopardy.

THE SPEAKER AND THE HOUSE

From the moment he entered Congress, Gingrich sought to change the GOP's permanent minority status in the House. He spearheaded a two-pronged plan: build up the Republican Party to take over Congress and tear down the Democratic Party that had controlled Capitol Hill for most of the postwar era. He worked to recruit and elect Republicans to Congress. In the late 1980s and early 1990s, he controlled a political action committee called GOPAC, which aimed to cultivate local and state politicians for eventual congressional runs. Gingrich was a chief practitioner of a highly negative brand of politics to wholly discredit the opposition. He led the attack on Democratic Speaker Jim Wright of Texas, who resigned his seat under pressure from an ethics probe instigated by Gingrich and his allies. That the atmosphere in Congress by the 1990s took on a decidedly partisan, acrimonious and uncivil tone could be directly linked to Gingrich.

Gingrich ascended unchallenged to become Speaker of the House in 1995. Unlike his recent predecessors, he was not a patient institutionalist who was lifted slowly to high office by the traditions of the House. He had never chaired a committee or subcommittee during his eight terms in office. Nevertheless,

Gingrich came to the Speakership with a supreme advantage: He had the loyalty of a majority of House Republicans, many of whom felt they owed their elections in part to him. Maximizing both the formal and informal powers at his disposal, Gingrich used his position to consolidate power. Gingrich envisioned the Speakership as a pulpit from which he hoped to displace the president as the primary source of ideas and vision about where the country should be going. "The Congress in the long run can change the country more dramatically than the president," Gingrich said in a 1979 interview. "One of my goals is to make the House the co-equal of the White House."

Seizing the agenda from the president, the Speaker united his troops around the idea of voting on all ten planks of the GOP "Contract with America" in the first 100 days of the 104th Congress. The contract had been drafted to skirt divisive social issues such as abortion and school prayer; it centered instead on politically popular issues about which conservative Republicans had few disagreements, such as balancing the federal budget, reforming welfare and curbing unfunded mandates to the states. By the end of the 100 days, the House had passed nine of the ten items, the proposal imposing congressional term limits being the only failure.

Over time, Gingrich himself increasingly became an issue. Although he may have been considered a savior to House Republicans, Democrats had an entirely different view. Many still harbored deep resentment over his treatment of Wright, and questions regarding Gingrich's ethics were long simmering. At the end of 1995, the House ethics committee announced that it had unanimously found that Gingrich violated House rules governing the proper use of the House floor by touting a college course that he taught called "Renewing American Civilization," by promoting a GOP seminar in floor speeches and by allowing one of his political operatives to interview candidates for congressional staff jobs. The committee also named an outside counsel to investigation charges that Gingrich violated federal tax laws by raising funds for his college course through tax-exempt foundations. However, it dismissed a complaint involving a lucrative book deal Gingrich had signed with HarperCollins two weeks before becoming Speaker.

In addition, Gingrich suffered in the eyes of some of his conservative allies by attempting to find common ground with Clinton and Senate moderates. Intense negotiations on legislative matters among Gingrich, Dole and Clinton forced the Speaker into the unaccustomed role of dealbroker, which sometimes put him at odds with his troops.

The Speaker also proved prone to embarrassing public gaffes. He linked a horrible crime—the purposeful drowning of two boys by their mother—to liberalism and Democratic policies. He said women in the military could not fight in foxholes because they got "infections." And he offered an offhand proposal to help the poor by giving them a tax break to buy laptop computers. His most stunning public stumble came when he revealed that he had forced the first of two government shutdowns in 1995 in part because he felt that Clinton had snubbed him during an overseas diplomatic trip to attend the funeral of Israeli Prime Minister Yitzhak Rabin and had made Gingrich and Dole exit by the rear of the plane. Gingrich said he knew he was being "petty" when he attached tough GOP spending priorities to a stopgap spending bill, which Clinton then vetoed, prompting the shutdown.

The Republicans were just barely able to hang onto their majority status in the House following the 1996 elections. GOP candidates in marginal districts survived by running away from their controversial Speaker and the contract. In a negotiated settlement with the House ethics committee in late 1996, Gingrich said he failed to seek effective legal advice in using tax-exempt foundations to finance the college course he taught. More devastating, he admitted giving the committee false information, although he said he did so inadvertently. In early 1997, the House voted to reprimand Gingrich and to impose a $300,000 penalty on him. Although Gingrich would be reelected Speaker of the 105th Congress, his influence and reputation would be substantially diminished.

THE SENATE

While media attention focused on the House, Republicans also won the Senate in the electoral tide of 1994. Senate action had a profound effect on the progress of the Republican "revolution." Conservatives did not set the agenda in the Senate in the 104th Congress as in the House, because they simply did not have the numbers. Senate Republicans never endorsed the "Contract with America." Most of the contract legislation got bogged down in disagreements with Senate Republican moderates, who opposed many of the proposed policy changes and spending cuts. And, with its six-year terms and unlimited debate, the Senate fulfilled its constitutional role of cooling legislative passions. A determined minority often was enough to block any bill.

Also coloring Senate activity was presidential politics. Dole hoped to use his position as majority leader to showcase his leadership abilities. In a sense, Dole had little choice but to try to harness Congress for his benefit. He was an effective congressional leader who was comfortable dealing with the nuances and the wheeling and dealing of making laws. But he was a lackluster campaigner, a flat and uninspiring orator who had trouble expounding an overarching vision for the country. One way to draw favorable distinctions between himself and Clinton was to pass bills that showed he was a "doer, not a talker," as Dole put it.

But Dole found it nigh impossible to develop a unified message from such a tumultuous institution. At the beginning of 1996, Republicans rallied around Dole to an extraordinary degree, and Gingrich thought that a coordinated campaign strategy with Dole was best. He and Dole discussed ways to develop a common GOP message for the fall congressional and presidential campaigns. But Dole was never able to embrace the Speaker's prescription and was reluctant to commit to a campaign plan not of his making. Furthermore, the House Republicans were demanding faster and more radical changes than Dole was comfortable espousing. As the campaign season unfolded, Dole ran into problems getting fellow Republicans to put aside their priorities in favor of his own. Democrats, meanwhile, made creative use of Senate rules to tie up that chamber. Dole became the target of constant Democratic attempts to embarrass him, for example, by forcing a vote on raising the minimum wage, which the majority leader opposed.

In June 1996, Dole resigned his Senate seat to run full time for president, ending a 35-year congressional career. Presidential politics had less impact on congressional behavior from that point on, and lawmakers of both parties concluded that their electoral interests were best served by getting legislation passed. In addition, Trent Lott, R-Miss., who succeeded Dole as majority leader, had impeccable conservative credentials, which enabled him to strike deals with Democrats without arousing the mistrust of Republicans worried that he had sold out the cause. Republicans from conservatives to moderates gave Lott high marks for his inclusiveness, rapid-fire approach and willingness to tackle problems himself. Given Gingrich's tenuous position, Lott was expected to fill the GOP leadership void in the 105th Congress. He would be helped by the increased number of conservative senators elected in 1996.

THE PRESIDENT

Clinton was not known as the "Comeback Kid" for nothing. Elected as a minority president in 1992 with 43 percent of the vote, Clinton entered the White House with a belief in the good that government could do as well as with big ambitions for change for the country. While he did score impressive legislative successes during his first two years in office—for example, deficit reduction, the North Atlantic Free Trade Agreement and a comprehensive crime bill—the failure of health care reform seemed to spell the failure of his administration. Taking him down further was the steady stream of controversies, regarding, for instance, gays in the military, unacceptable nominees to administration posts, White House travel office personnel firings, FBI background files on former Republican officials, a charge of sexual harassment against Clinton while he was governor and the Clintons' unsuccessful real estate investment known as Whitewater. Furthermore, Republicans came to realize that they could accrue considerable political gains by being obstructionists.

As stunning as the GOP takeover of Congress was as a result of the 1994 elections, no less remarkable was Clinton's return to electoral viability, a testament to his political skills. Clinton effectively established himself as a safeguard against the excesses of the aggressive congressional Republicans, who sought to disband social programs dating from the New Deal era of the 1930s and the Great Society of the 1960s, among other things. Perhaps most damaging to the Republicans was the outcome of the budget battle they engaged in with Clinton in late 1995. The president and congressional Democrats successfully portrayed the Republicans as wanting to cut popular programs such as

Medicare to finance generous tax breaks for upper-income Americans. The showdown with the White House sparked two government shutdowns, which the public, in poll after poll, blamed on the Republicans. Furthermore, despite the naysayers, Clinton seemed to have scored qualified successes in several sticky foreign policy situations, including Haiti and Bosnia, and he presided over a healthy economy. The president also appeared to many to have grown in office. For example, political observers pointed to his measured, solemn yet comforting response to the bombing of a federal building in Oklahoma City, as a sign of Clinton's maturity.

Clinton easily won reelection in 1996. Most voters seemed satisfied with Clinton as an effective check on enthusiastic Republicans and were willing to accept whatever character defects they believed he had. As he began his second term, public support for Clinton remained high even though questions arose about Democratic fund-raising practices, an independent counsel's investigation into Whitewater continued, and the sexual harassment suit was moving forward.

1993

The Legislative Year

The legislative agenda in Congress in 1993 was clearly transformed by having a Democrat in the White House for the first time in 12 years. The year was marked principally by two controversial measures: a deficit-reduction "reconciliation" bill and the North American Free Trade Agreement (NAFTA). Both were triumphs for President Clinton, but they were enacted with enormous difficulty and were not universally popular with voters.

Other laws did not require so much political capital to realize. Congress easily approved a number of bills that had cleared in previous years but had been vetoed or that had languished under veto threats, including measures to guarantee family leave for workers, ease voter registration requirements, expand the political rights of federal workers, reauthorize the National Institutes of Health (NIH) and impose a waiting period for the purchase of a handgun.

Some legislation did bear the stamp of the Clinton era. Impelled largely by the president's desire to portray himself as a new kind of Democrat, Congress cleared a National Service program, and the House passed a package of spending cuts intended to "reinvent" government by streamlining its programs. The deficit-reduction bill reflected Clinton's effort to change the budget priorities of the two previous Republican administrations by raising taxes on the wealthy, cutting the defense budget and increasing funds for some antipoverty programs.

Other legislation reflected changes in Congress itself in the wake of the 1992 elections, which swept in a big new class of reform-oriented freshmen, including unprecedented numbers of women and minorities. Congress took steps toward reworking the campaign finance system, lobbying disclosure law and congressional operations—issues largely promoted by freshmen. However, each initiative fell far short of enactment. Congress

occasionally showed a stronger stomach for cutting popular programs, a trend driven in part by the deficit-conscious freshman class. First-termers threw their weight behind such budget-cutting initiatives as a successful effort to kill the superconducting super collider and an unsuccessful fight for a larger spending cut package than Clinton wanted in his reinventing government initiative.

Issues of special interest to women got increased attention thanks in part to the near-doubling of the number of women in Congress. Both the House and Senate passed legislation to combat violence against women and to make forcibly blocking access to abortion clinics a crime. The new NIH law included provisions to improve biomedical research on women and the diseases that afflicted them.

In the House, the Congressional Black Caucus emerged as a key legislative player regarding, for example, NAFTA, deficit reduction and U.S. policy toward Haiti. Caucus members found strength in numbers: When they threatened to withhold their votes, party vote-counters often came up short. In the end, however, black caucus Democrats proved to be among the most loyal of Democrats.

While Congress cleared plenty of bills with great fanfare, other measures important to Clinton died. Among Clinton's biggest defeats were a package of construction and social service programs intended to stimulate the economy, which was blocked by a Senate filibuster, and an effort to end a prohibition against gays in the military, a campaign promise he dropped in the face of bipartisan opposition on Capitol Hill.

Other casualties included bills of importance to powerful Democratic constituencies whose expectations were raised by the 1992 elections. Despite an influx of new abortion rights advocates into Congress, the Freedom of Choice Act to establish a woman's right to an abortion all but died. And both chambers rejected proposals to allow abortion funding for the poor under Medicaid. Legislation to bar companies from permanently replacing striking workers—a top priority of organized labor—stalled in the Senate. A Senate filibuster also blocked a proposal backed by environmentalists to raise livestock grazing fees. The House rejected statehood for the District of Columbia, a Democratic bastion.

Late in the year, Clinton unveiled his massive plan to reform health care. The effort had been spearheaded by first lady Hillary Rodham Clinton. The president laid out six principles for the plan: security, simplicity, savings, choice, quality and responsibility. His goal was universal health care coverage. Not since Franklin D. Roosevelt made health care security for all Americans a tenet of his "second Bill of Rights" had a president proposed such a grand plan for remaking the country's health system, elevating health care to a civil right. By the end of 1993, the general consensus was that the reputation of the 103rd Congress would rest with the second session, based on what it accomplished on issues such as health care reform.

Congress in general faced continuing public disillusionment with the political process and with both chambers' ethical standards. The Senate spent two wrenching days on topics of sexual misconduct, privacy and improper influence before taking an

CONGRESS IN 1993

The first session of the 103rd Congress ended Nov. 26, 1993, when the House adjourned *sine die* at 10:05 a.m. EST. The Senate had adjourned Nov. 24 at 3:07 p.m.

Convened on Jan. 5, the session lasted 326 days—45 days longer than the last session of the 102nd Congress. The Senate met for 153 days, the House for 142 days.

There were 6,721 bills and resolutions introduced during the 1993 session, compared with 4,258 in 1992 and 7,758 in 1991. A total of 210 bills cleared by Congress in 1993 became public law. President Clinton did not veto a single bill in the first session of the 103rd Congress. (*Public laws, table, p. 14; presidential vetoes, p. 1122*)

During 1993, the House took 597 recorded votes, 124 more than in 1992. The Senate took 395 recorded votes, 125 more than in 1992. (*Recorded votes, table, p. 16*)

apparently unprecedented action by voting to enforce a subpoena against one of its members, Republican Bob Packwood of Oregon, who had been charged with sexual harassment. Meanwhile, the shadow of a federal criminal investigation hung over House Ways and Means Committee Chairman Dan Rostenkowski, D-Ill., for his alleged misdeeds involving the House Post Office.

The Political Year

Following George Bush's 1992 electoral defeat, Republicans were heartened by ballot outcomes in 1993. While voters continued to signal their dissatisfaction with incumbents in general and with governmental business as usual, the main victims of the house-cleaning impulse were Democrats, who lost governorships in New Jersey and Virginia as well as a Senate seat in Texas. However, in all five special elections held to fill House vacancies, the party that had held the seat retained it.

Gubernatorial Races

In New Jersey, Republican Christine Todd Whitman ousted Democratic incumbent governor James J. Florio. In Virginia, former U.S. representative George F. Allen, a Republican, scored a landslide victory over state Attorney General Mary Sue Terry, ending 12 years of Democratic control of the governor's office.

Whitman's election turned less on herself and her plans for the state than on Florio and his record. Six months into his term in 1990, Florio raised taxes by $2.8 billion, including a deeply unpopular increase in the state sales tax. While respected for his intelligence, he paid a price for the abrasive and intense personality that often made him difficult to work with. In a display of his stubborn streak, he insisted that the New Jersey Legislature rush through the tax increases with little public debate. Furthermore, he seemed unable to explain to voters why the increases were needed. Florio's approval ratings plunged as a result of the

tax hike and never fully recovered. He did, however, make something of a comeback in the latter half of his term, largely by stressing toughness on crime and guns.

Whitman's political résumé was slim for a would-be governor. She was a member of the Somerset County Board of Chosen Freeholders, the county's governing body, for five years. She also was appointed to the New Jersey Board of Public Utilities under Florio's predecessor, Republican Thomas H. Kean. She served until 1990. That same year, she was the "sacrificial" Republican chosen to oppose Democrat Bill Bradley, New Jersey's popular senior senator. By running not against Bradley but against Florio and his tax increases, Whitman won 47 percent of the vote and became the front-runner to oppose Florio in 1993.

As a gubernatorial candidate, Whitman found that her inexperience left her vulnerable to mistakes. For example, Whitman attacked Florio's welfare overhaul proposal—which included requiring a woman to name a child's father to become eligible for public assistance and funneling welfare checks to a minor mother through her parents—by comparing some of the plan's requirements with conditions endured by Holocaust survivors. The Florio campaign turned that comment into a public relations bonanza, releasing reactions from Jewish leaders who condemned Whitman's statement, arguing that the comparison belittled the enormity of the Holocaust.

The Florio campaign also made an issue of Whitman's considerable personal wealth. According to 1992 tax returns, the Whitmans earned $3.7 million and took deductions on two farms that they owned. The Florio campaign questioned whether one of the properties was a real working farm. The issue came to a head when Whitman chased off Florio campaign workers who were videotaping her farm for use as a backdrop for a political television advertisement.

When, late in the campaign, Whitman released her proposal to cut income tax rates by 30 percent over three years, she encountered deep voter skepticism. Then, she gave Republican political strategist Edward J. Rollins the reins of her campaign. He reordered her priorities, focusing her stump speeches on Florio's record and playing down her own promises. Whitman also exploited the outsider theme that had worked well for candidates in both parties in the 1990s. On election day, Whitman won 50 percent of the vote; Florio, 48 percent. About a week after the election, Rollins prompted a firestorm of criticism when he told reporters about spreading $500,000 around to suppress African American voter turnout. Rollins later retracted the statement, and Whitman denied that any such tactics were used by her campaign.

In Virginia, Terry was widely expected to cruise to an easy gubernatorial victory over Allen. However, Allen campaigned vigorously while Terry failed to capitalize on her early lead. Allen won 58 percent of the vote in his first statewide bid. Terry's 41 percent was the worst showing by a Democrat since Virginia began popular elections for governor in 1851.

The featured issues of the campaign included crime and gun control. Allen's vow to end parole for violent offenders proved more compelling than Terry's call for a five-day waiting period for handgun purchases. Overriding any issues, however, was the

```
CONGRESSIONAL LEADERSHIP 1993–1996
```

103rd Congress

Senate

President Pro Tempore—Robert C. Byrd, D-W.Va.
Majority Leader—George J. Mitchell, D-Maine
Majority Whip—Wendell H. Ford, D-Ky.
Democratic Conference Secretary—David Pryor, D-Ark.

Minority Leader—Bob Dole, R-Kan.
Assistant Minority Leader—Alan K. Simpson, R-Wyo.
Republican Conference Chairman—Thad Cochran, R-Miss.
Republican Conference Secretary—Trent Lott, R-Miss.

House

Speaker—Thomas S. Foley, D-Wash.
Majority Leader—Richard A. Gephardt, D-Mo.
Majority Whip—David E. Bonior, D-Mich.
Chairman of the Caucus—Steny H. Hoyer, D-Md.

Minority Leader—Robert H. Michel, R-Ill.
Minority Whip—Newt Gingrich, R-Ga.
Chairman of the Conference—Dick Armey, R-Texas
Republican Policy Committee Chairman—Henry J. Hyde, R-Ill.

104th Congress

Senate

President Pro Tempore—Strom Thurmond, R-S.C.
Majority Leader—Bob Dole, R-Kan. [a]
Majority Whip—Trent Lott, R-Miss.
Republican Conference Chairman—Thad Cochran, R-Miss.
Republican Conference Secretary—Connie Mack, R-Fla.

Minority Leader—Tom Daschle, D-S.D.
Minority Whip—Wendell H. Ford, D-Ky.
Democratic Conference Secretary—Barbara A. Mikulski, D-Md.

House

Speaker—Newt Gingrich, R-Ga.
Majority Leader—Dick Armey, R-Texas
Majority Whip—Tom DeLay, R-Texas
Chairman of the Conference—John A. Boehner, R-Ohio
Republican Policy Committee Chairman—Christopher Cox, R-Calif.

Minority Leader—Richard A. Gephardt, D-Mo.
Minority Whip—David E. Bonior, D-Mich.
Chairman of the Caucus—Vic Fazio, D-Calif.

---

difference between Allen's and Terry's campaign styles. Terry was no match for the indefatigable Allen, who appeared genuinely to relish each encounter with voters. Terry was criticized for a manner that many found aloof, while Allen was admired for his "aw shucks" affability.

The theme of Allen's campaign was change. He ran more against the Virginia Democratic establishment than against Terry. For her part, Terry, a moderate from conservative southern Virginia, repudiated some of President Clinton's policies and largely distanced herself from the state's leading Democratic officeholders, Gov. L. Douglas Wilder and Sen. Charles S. Robb. But having twice been elected to statewide office, she found it difficult to convince voters that she did not belong in the same tent as her party's best-known leaders. Terry also was unable to generate excitement among Virginia voters as she sought to become the commonwealth's first female governor

Special Elections

Five House special elections and one Senate special election were held in 1993.

Rep. Leon E. Panetta, D-Calif., resigned his seat to become director of the White House Office of Management and Budget. California state representative Sam Farr, whose Assembly district covered much of Panetta's congressional district, won the

special election with 52 percent of the vote. His Republican challenger, attorney Bill McCampbell, received 42 percent.

In a Michigan contest many considered little more than a formality, Vernon J. Ehlers, a Republican state senator and former physics professor, won the race to succeed the late GOP representative Paul B. Henry. Ehlers took 66 percent of the vote to conservative Democrat Dale R. Sprik's 23 percent.

Democrat Bennie Thompson became the first African American in Mississippi history to be elected on the strength of a district's black majority. Thompson, a county supervisor, and Republican Hayes Dent, an adviser to GOP Gov. Kirk Fordice, faced each other in a runoff to replace Mike Espy, D, who resigned to become agriculture secretary in the Clinton administration. Thompson won 55 percent of the vote; Dent, 45 percent.

Two Cincinnati lawyers vied for the seat vacated by Ohio Republican Bill Gradison, who became president of a health insurance industry group. Republican Rob Portman bested Democrat Lee Hornberger by 70 to 30 percent. Portman had won the right to run by defeating former U.S. representative Bob McEwen (1981–1993) in the GOP primary.

The contest between Democrat Peter W. Barca and Republican Mark W. Neumann in Wisconsin's First District lived up to its billing as the most competitive House special election in 1993: Barca prevailed with a margin of just 675 votes. He succeeded Les Aspin, who resigned to become defense secretary.

After a brief lame duck session to consider the General Agreement on Tariffs and Trade (GATT), the second session of the 103rd Congress ended Dec. 1, 1994, when the Senate adjourned *sine die* at 9:14 p.m. EST. The House had adjourned at 9:10 p.m. on Nov. 29. Before the election, the House had adjourned at 12:05 a.m. on Oct. 8, and the Senate at 5:11 p.m. the same day.

Convened on Jan. 25, the session lasted 311 days—15 days shorter than the first session. The Senate was in session for 138 days, the House for 123 days.

There were 3,103 bills and resolutions introduced during the 1994 session, compared with 6,721 in 1993 and 4,258 in 1992. A total of 255 bills cleared by Congress in 1994 became public law. President Clinton vetoed no bills in 1994, thus becoming the first president since Millard Fillmore in 1851–1853 not to veto a single bill during an entire Congress. *(Public laws, table, p. 14; presidential vetoes, p. 1122)*

During 1994, the House took 497 recorded votes, 100 fewer than in 1993. The Senate took 329 recorded votes, 66 fewer than in 1993. *(Recorded votes, table, p. 16)*

Texas voters confirmed their trend toward the GOP in the only Senate special election held in 1993. Republican Kay Bailey Hutchison soundly defeated—67 to 33 percent—Democratic Sen. Bob Krueger, a state railroad commissioner who had been appointed to the seat vacated by Democrat Lloyd Bentsen. Bentsen retired to become Clinton's Treasury secretary. Hutchison became the first woman from Texas to occupy a U.S. Senate seat. Her triumph gave the GOP control of both Texas Senate seats for the first time since Reconstruction.

1994

The Legislative Year

The centerpiece of a year of legislative setbacks and political fiascoes was the failure of President Clinton's top priority—health care reform. Numerous other measures, some of which began the year with broad bipartisan support, fell victim to partisan disagreement, lack of time for consideration or other problems and had to be abandoned. Among them were bills dealing with campaign finance, lobbying disclosure, telecommunications and toxic waste cleanup. Many smashed into procedural roadblocks erected by Republicans who grew bold in proclaiming the virtues of gridlock.

Clinton and Congress could point to some legislative successes, such as the wide-ranging crime bill, the Goals 2000 measure setting national education standards and an interstate branch banking measure. The 103rd Congress had a three-day lame duck session during which it handed Clinton another belated bipartisan victory, approving a bill to implement a new global trade accord under the General Agreement on Tariffs and Trade (GATT).

Democratic leaders expected to bring the administration's health care initiative to the House and Senate floor by summer of 1994. However, by that time, no committee had produced a bill that could command the necessary votes. Congressional leaders eventually went to the White House to tell Clinton formally that his plan was in trouble and that he would have to make major concessions if he wanted a reform bill. Clinton gave the go-ahead to slow down the pace of the key provisions and to look for common ground, but no legislative breakthrough could be found. The House and Senate majority leaders—Richard A. Gephardt, D-Mo., and George J. Mitchell, D-Maine, respectively—subsequently unveiled their own bills, watered-down versions of the Clinton plan, that inspired little enthusiasm. Senate floor debate on health care reform began in mid-August, but the only votes came on perfunctory matters. Senators then examined a proposed compromise fashioned by a bipartisan group of moderates, which fell far short of Clinton's original demand for universal coverage. In the House, conservative Democrats conspired with moderate Republicans to defeat the leadership's version of health care reform. The leaders postponed bringing the matter to the floor. The stated reason was the need to wait for cost estimates, but the rumors were that the measure did not have the needed votes. The leadership announced that House action on health care would be delayed until September. At the end of August, Mitchell scrapped his reform proposal, conceding that comprehensive action would not come in 1994. He continued intensive talks with the moderates, but their search for an incremental plan proceeded in fits and starts. At the end of September, Mitchell publicly acknowledged that the whole effort was officially dead.

The crime bill was enacted, but in a spirit of rancor. The measure, supported by Clinton and the Democratic congressional leadership, received front-page attention when it was blocked in the House by an odd alliance of conservative pro-gun rights Democrats, antideath penalty liberals and Republicans of every stripe. A new compromise agreement was hammered out after a long, hard week of negotiations. The House passed the bill, which then went to the Senate, where Republicans made a last-ditch effort to kill it on grounds of pork-barrel spending and restrictions on guns. The Senate eventually cleared the bill, but many Republicans insisted that they were fighting a great ideological battle over which party was tougher on crime. However, some conceded that partisan politics was also a motivator.

In the final weeks before Congress recessed for the election, Democratic lawmakers paraded in front of the television cameras announcing the demise of everything from new campaign finance legislation to the rewrite of mining law. Efforts to revise low-income housing programs, revamp the "superfund" hazardous waste cleanup law and reorganize Congress all were moribund. Democrats pinned their hopes for institutional redemption and political survival on a pair of bills that would make their lives tougher: stricter lobbying rules and a bill to apply important labor laws to Congress. Most agreed that if they could pass these measures, they would have some evidence that they had heard the voters' 1992 clarion call for reform.

But Democrats could not get past roadblocks set up by Senate Republicans. In two separate votes, the Senate failed to cut off a GOP-led filibuster against the conference report on the lobbying disclosure bill. The effort to subject Congress to the same labor laws that applied to private sector companies was blocked by a single senator. House Republicans found ways to mimic their Senate colleagues, even though they did not have the power to filibuster legislation. For example, they tied the House in knots, demanding votes on every conceivable procedural question throughout daylong consideration of a bill to protect California desert lands. Democrats worked hard to pass the measure in part to boost the fortunes of Sen. Dianne Feinstein, D-Calif., who was in a close reelection campaign and had been a prime sponsor of the bill. Veteran Democrats complained that GOP leaders had taken partisanship to a new low. Republicans, meanwhile, exulted in their newfound ability to stymie the Democratic majorities in both chambers.

The lame duck session was prompted not by GOP obstructionism but by Senate Commerce, Science and Transportation Committee Chairman Ernest F. Hollings, D-S.C. Hollings announced in late September that he would exercise his right under the rules that governed congressional consideration of trade agreements to hold the bill in his committee for 45 legislative days. Upon hearing of the Senate delay, House Democrats told their leaders that they would prefer postponing the politically sensitive vote until after the election, too. The GATT bill was approved in one of the briefest lame duck sessions on record. Although some members tried to resuscitate other bills in the session, no other significant legislative business was transacted.

Under intense pressure from Republicans, both chambers in 1993 held hearings on the president and his wife's investments in the 1980s in the Whitewater Development Co. in Arkansas, a failed real estate deal, and actions taken by White House officials regarding the affair. No illegalities were uncovered by the congressional probe. A separate investigation was begun by Justice Department special counsel Robert B. Fiske Jr. and then taken up by independent counsel Kenneth W. Starr.

The Political Year

The 1994 elections ushered in a Republican-controlled House and Senate for the first time since 1955. Great partisan shifts in Congress had different origins. Sometimes they were caused by large surges in voter support for one party, sometimes by widespread voter apathy that debilitated the other. The powerful Republican tide of 1994 combined elements of both. Voters flocked to GOP congressional candidates in record numbers in the election that marked the middle of the term Democratic President Clinton had won in 1992. At the same time, the president's party had difficulty motivating its core constituency.

Republicans, whose nationwide vote for House seats had never totaled more than 28 million in a midterm election, won 36.6 million votes in 1994. That was nearly nine million more

---

TERM LIMITS

Although enthusiasm for congressional term limits had waned by the mid-1990s, voters were asked to consider the issue in ballot initiatives in numerous states in 1994. Term limits were on the ballot in eight states and were approved in seven. Alaska, Idaho, Maine, Massachusetts, Nebraska and Nevada all passed limits for their members of Congress, while Colorado tightened the limits it had imposed in 1990 (the first limits for members of Congress in the nation). Utah voters rejected a measure to restrict House members to four terms. Utah previously had adopted limits of six terms for House members and two terms for senators. *(Earlier action, Congress and the Nation Vol. VIII, p. 10)*

Before any member of Congress was hindered by state-passed limitations, however, the U.S. Supreme Court in 1995 in *U.S. Term Limits Inc. v. Thornton* and *Bryant v. Hill,* struck down term limits, ruling that states could not limit congressional terms without amending the Constitution. "Allowing individual states to adopt their own qualifications for congressional service would be inconsistent with the Framers' vision of a uniform National Legislature. . . ." Justice John Paul Stevens wrote for the Court. *(Supreme Court ruling, p. 783)*

Proponents of term limits took a new approach in 1996. Voters in nine states—Alaska, Arkansas, Colorado, Idaho, Maine, Missouri, Nebraska, Nevada and South Dakota—passed measures to ask future candidates in those states to try to enact congressional term limits. Candidates who declined to do so would generally have their positions noted on the ballot the next time they ran. Voters in five states—Montana, North Dakota, Oregon, Washington and Wyoming—rejected the new term limits strategy.

---

than the GOP had won in 1990 and represented the largest midterm-to-midterm increase in one party's vote total in the nation's history. The GOP's 52.4 percent share of the House vote was the party's largest since 1946. It also was the first time since 1946 that GOP House candidates received a majority of the total House vote. Democrats in 1994 drew almost one million fewer votes than in 1990, continuing a general downward slide in their congressional voting strength that had begun in the mid-1980s. In 1982, when recession politics were putting a brake on the popularity of Republican President Ronald Reagan, Democratic candidates for House seats collected more than 35 million votes. In 1994, they drew fewer than 32 million. The combination of shrinking vote totals for Democrats with an exploding GOP vote (nearly one-third larger than in 1990) was unparalleled since the Democrats' growth spurt in the 1930s during the Great Depression and the early days of the New Deal.

The Democratic loss was truly national in scope. In 1992, the Democrats won more House votes than the Republicans in every region of the country. In 1994, the Democrats were outpolled in every region except the East and in every state with at least 10 congressional districts except Massachusetts. In a number of megastates, the GOP edge was substantial. Republicans took 59 percent of the congressional ballots cast in Florida, 58 percent in Ohio, 57 percent in North Carolina, 56 percent in Texas, 54 percent in New Jersey and Pennsylvania and a plurality 49 percent share in California and New York (although Democrats wound up with more seats in California, New York, Pennsylvania and Texas). The Democrats won more House votes than the Republicans in only a dozen small to medium-sized states.

In the Midwest, Republicans picked up 15 House seats, won all four open Senate races, and swept eight of the nine governorships—six of them with more than 60 percent of the vote. The Democrats lost 19 House seats across the South (defined as the 11 states of the Confederacy plus Kentucky and Oklahoma), more than in any other region. Democrats were outpolled by Republican House candidates in every southern state except Mississippi, where most of the Democratic members were so conservative they could just as readily have been Republicans. The Democrats ran no House candidates in 21 southern races, including nine in Florida, five in Texas and three in Virginia. By contrast, the Republicans offered free rides to the Democrats in only four southern districts. The region's lone Democratic senatorial winner was Virginia's Charles S. Robb. And the Democrats took only three gubernatorial contests in the South—Arkansas, Florida and Georgia. The Democrats lost 15 seats in the West, including six in Washington alone. They scored some high-profile victories across the region, however, from Dianne Feinstein's senatorial triumph to gubernatorial wins in Alaska, Colorado, Hawaii, Nevada and Oregon. The Democrats' base in the Northeast was penetrated but not demolished in 1994. Democrats lost only three House seats in the East, retaining a regional majority. Although the GOP picked up governorships in Connecticut, New York, Pennsylvania and Rhode Island, none of those seats was won with a majority of the vote. The only incumbent senator in the East to lose his reelection bid was Democrat Harris Wofford of Pennsylvania.

For a midterm contest, the 1994 turnout was relatively high. In spite of media talk of an electorate turned off by negative campaigning, the number of ballots cast for the House jumped from 61 million in 1990 (which represented 33 percent of the nation's voting-age population) to nearly 70 million in 1994 (36 percent), the highest turnout rate for a midterm election since 1982.

Republicans were the almost exclusive beneficiaries of the increased vote. The total number of votes won by GOP congressional candidates was up dramatically from 1990 in every region of the country—by nearly four million votes in the South, by more than two million in the Midwest, by almost 1.7 million in the West and by 1.3 million in the East. Democratic House candidates in 1994 won nearly 600,000 more votes in the East and 400,000 more in the West than in 1990. However, the number of ballots cast was down by nearly one million from four years earlier in the Midwest and by 800,000 in the South.

The number of votes won by Republican House candidates was higher in 1994 than in 1990 in all but Connecticut, Montana, North Carolina and Rhode Island. The Democratic vote total was down from 1990 in most states. Where Democrats did

show an increase in their vote tally, it was usually dwarfed by the rise in the Republican vote—such as in California, New York and Washington.

Senate Races

After eight years in the minority, Republicans in 1994 captured control of the Senate, 52–48, by sweeping all nine open-seat races and ousting two Democratic incumbents. Adding insult to the Democrats' injury, the day after the general elections, Alabama Sen. Richard C. Shelby announced that he was switching parties, giving the GOP a 53-seat majority to start the 104th Congress.

In the final weeks of the campaign, national Republican strategists became increasingly hopeful that their party could erase its 44–56 deficit in the Senate. Democrats were defending 22 of the 35 seats at stake, and in a dozen of those races, GOP candidates were leading or very competitive. Democrats were making a serious run at a half-dozen seats held by Republicans, and GOP gains were expected to be at least partially offset by Democratic takeaways.

But the 1994 election shattered convention. The GOP did not lose a single seat. The party reelected all 10 of its incumbents, retained the three open seats it was defending, captured six seats of retiring Democratic incumbents and defeated Democrats Jim Sasser of Tennessee and Harris Wofford of Pennsylvania. Republican Senate candidates thrived in every region of the country, taking Democratic seats in the East (Maine and Pennsylvania), the Midwest (Ohio and Michigan), the West (Arizona) and the South (Oklahoma and Tennessee).

Some of the Senate contests stood out as notable voter indictments of the Democratic Party's ruling class in Washington. In Tennessee, the home state of Vice President Al Gore, Democrats lost two Senate seats. The Senate seat that Gore held went by a runaway tally to Republican Fred Thompson, who defeated Democratic Rep. Jim Cooper. Voters dumped three-term veteran Sasser, a leading candidate to be the Senate's Democratic leader in the 104th Congress, for Republican Bill Frist. Sasser's 42 percent of the vote was the worst-ever general election showing by a Tennessee senator. In Pennsylvania, GOP Rep. Rick Santorum ousted Wofford, who had become a national Democratic celebrity with a 1991 special election victory that made health care a marquee issue for the party. To win his first Senate race, Wofford defeated Bush administration attorney general and former Pennsylvania governor Richard L. Thornburgh. And, in Maine, the GOP prevailed in the race to pick a successor to Senate Majority Leader George J. Mitchell, who was retiring. The victor, Republican Olympia J. Snowe, would become the only woman newly elected to the Senate.

Election night was not without Senate Democratic victory celebrations. In Virginia, strong voter turnout helped embattled Sen. Charles S. Robb fend off the fiercely loyal followers of Republican challenger Oliver L. North. In Massachusetts, liberal Democratic icon Sen. Edward M. Kennedy won reelection comfortably over GOP challenger Mitt Romney. And, in California, Democratic Sen. Dianne Feinstein defeated her heavy-spending challenger, GOP Rep. Michael Huffington. In all, 14 Democratic incumbents were reelected.

The incoming Senate freshman class had 11 Republicans and no Democrats. Since 1914, when the popular election of senators began, there had never been an all-GOP Senate freshman class.

House Races

After 40 years of one-party rule in the House of Representatives, Republicans were set to become the majority as a result of the 1994 elections.

A Democratic president held in disfavor and a Democratic-controlled Congress held in disrepute gave Republican candidates a target they could not miss. The GOP also offered the "Contract with America," a list of 10 poll-driven items that Republicans promised to bring to the floor for a vote within the first 100 days of the 104th Congress. More important, Republican candidates reaped the gains they anticipated from redistricting after the 1990 census. The remapping was largely favorable to the GOP.

In addition, money made the difference for some Republican challengers. According to the Federal Election Commission, Republican candidates had an easier time raising money from political action committees and other sources than in previous years. Much of that increase reflected heavy investment from the National Republican Congressional Committee, the Republican National Committee and GOP incumbents who made contributions of their own. Conservative target groups—from the National Rifle Association to term limits advocates—played active roles in several congressional races. And several Republican freshmen were elected with the prominent support of conservative Christian activists.

Georgia Rep. Newt Gingrich was in line to become the first Republican Speaker of the House from the South. His ascendancy accompanied the long-anticipated realignment of the South. For the first time since the end of Reconstruction in the 1870s, Republicans won a majority of the congressional districts in the South.

Another record intact since the Civil War was broken: Thomas S. Foley of Washington became the first sitting House Speaker to lose reelection since Galusha A. Grow of Pennsylvania was defeated in 1862. Foley was not the only venerable House Democrat to fall. Other veterans who lost included 18-term Rep. Dan Rostenkowski of Illinois, the former chairman of the Ways and Means Committee; 21-term Rep. Jack Brooks of Texas, chairman of the Judiciary Committee; and 18-term Rep. Neal Smith of Iowa, chairman of the Appropriations Subcommittee on Labor, Health and Human Services, and Education.

Republicans gained 52 House seats, increasing their number from 178 to 230. The Democratic tally dropped from 256 to 204. For the Republicans, 73 freshmen were elected, 157 incumbents were reelected and no incumbents were defeated. For the Democrats, 13 freshmen were elected, 191 incumbents were reelected and 34 incumbents were defeated. Of the 34 incumbents

who lost, 16 were in their first term. Republicans enjoyed big gains in the 52 open seats, those in which no incumbent was running. Of the 52 open seats, 31 had been held by Democrats and 21 by Republicans. The GOP won 22 Democratic-held open seats and retained 17 Republican-held open seats. The Democrats won four Republican-held open seats and retained nine Democratic-held open seats.

Statehouses

Results of the gubernatorial and state legislature elections were not as dramatic as the congressional elections, but the same general trend was evident. Republicans increased their share of governorships from 19 to 30—their first majority since 1970—and not one of the 10 GOP governors up for reelection lost. As a result of the 1994 elections, Republicans controlled the governor's mansion in four of the five most populous states and eight of the most populous nine. The GOP also had a majority of governorships in each geographic region. Republican gains penetrated the heart of the South, capturing the majority of the governorships there for the first time since Reconstruction.

With no legislative chamber changing hands in favor of the Democrats, the Republicans reached near parity in state legislatures, a status they had not enjoyed since 1968. The GOP won two southern legislative chambers—North Carolina's House and Florida's Senate—for the first time in the twentieth century.

Maine was the only governorship the GOP lost. Independent Angus King bested a four-candidate field that included former Democratic governor Joseph E. Brennan. King succeeded Republican John R. McKernan Jr., who did not run for reelection. Republican John G. Rowland won the governor's seat in Connecticut, which was vacated by the retiring Lowell P. Weicker, an independent. One Republican governor, South Dakota's Walter D. Miller, had been defeated in the primary by Willian J. Janklow, who subsequently won the general election.

Following the 1994 elections, Democrats held 19 governorships. Of the 12 Democratic governors seeking reelection, five were defeated—one in the primary (Rhode Island's Bruce Sundlun) and four in the general election (Alabama's James E. Folsom Jr., New Mexico's Bruce King, New York's Mario M. Cuomo and Texas's Ann W. Richards). The victor of the Rhode Island Democratic primary, state Sen. Myrth York, went on to lose the general election. Six open seats that had been Democratic went Republican: In Idaho, Phil Batt, R, defeated Larry EchoHawk, D, to succeed Cecil D. Andrus, D. In Kansas, Bill Graves, R, won over Jim Slattery, D, to succeed Joan Finney, D. In Oklahoma, Frank Keating, R, beat Jack Mildren, D, to succeed David Waters, D. In Pennsylvania, Tom Ridge, R, topped Mark S. Singel, D, to succeed Robert P. Casey, D. In Tennessee, Don Sundquist, R, defeated Phil Bredesen, D, to succeed Ned McWherter, D. And, in Wyoming, Jim Geringer, R, beat Kathy Karpan, D, to succeed Mike Sullivan, D. The governor's seat in Alaska, which was vacated by independent Walter J. Hickel, was filled by Democrat Tony Knowles.

CONGRESS IN 1995

The first session of the 104th Congress ended Jan. 3, 1996, when the Senate adjourned *sine die* at 12 noon EST. The House had adjourned at 11:59 a.m.

Convened on Jan. 4, 1995, the session lasted 365 days—54 days longer than the second session of the 103rd Congress. The Senate met for 211 days; the House, 168 days.

There were 5,231 bills and resolutions introduced, compared with 3,103 in 1994 and 6,721 in 1993. A total of 88 bills cleared by Congress during the first session became public law, marking the lowest legislative output during a session since 1933, when the Twentieth Amendment was ratified and the starting date of a Congress was moved from March to January. President Clinton vetoed 11 bills; one was overridden—a securities litigation measure (HR 1058). *(Public laws, table, p. 14; presidential vetoes, p. 1122)*

During 1995, the House took 867 recorded votes, 370 more than in 1994. The Senate took 613 recorded votes, 284 more than in 1994. *(Recorded votes, table, p. 16)*

Special Elections

The two House special elections in 1994 replaced a pair of veteran Democrats with younger Republicans, offering a harbinger of the November election.

Republican Frank D. Lucas, a farmer-rancher and state legislator, defeated Democrat Dan Webber Jr., a former congressional staff member, for the Oklahoma seat vacated by 10-term Rep. Glenn English, D, who retired to become head of the National Rural Electric Cooperative Association. Lucas captured 54 percent of the vote; Webber, 46 percent.

Ron Lewis, a Baptist minister and religious bookstore owner, became the first Republican to represent Kentucky's Second District when he defeated former state senator Joseph W. Prather by 55 to 45 percent. Lewis succeeded William H. Natcher, chairman of the House Appropriations Committee, who had died.

1995

The Legislative Year

Roused from decades-old routines by the new Republican majority, Congress in 1995 became an institution more active, more partisan and more willing to defy a president than ever before in the postwar period. Republicans transformed the policy debate, wrestling the agenda-setting role from the White House. But the first year of the Republican "revolution" closed with institutional Washington much the way the GOP majority found it: No federal departments were eliminated, and no long-standing social policies were reshaped. By the ultimate yardstick—legislative enactment—the Republicans scored very few achievements.

In the House, the first 100 days were spent on the "Contract with America," a 10-point manifesto created as a national platform for Republican candidates in the 1994 elections. The House passed eight of the 10 contract planks and the bulk of a ninth, which included a balanced budget constitutional amendment, a line-item veto, changes in the welfare and legal systems, tax cuts and a curb on unfunded mandates. The House failed to pass one plank that called for adopting a constitutional amendment to limit members' terms and dropped a portion of another providing for deployment of an antimissile defense system.

Quick House action on the contract items came, in part, because many of the bills were drawn from legislation that Republicans had introduced in previous Congresses but that had been buried by the Democrats. In some cases, committees took shortcuts to keep on schedule, cutting off debate when amendments were still pending, skipping hearings or subcommittee action or moving a bill to the floor before the report was available. Also, because House Speaker Newt Gingrich, R-Ga., insisted that the specifics were subject to revision, many members were willing to send through bills they conceded were flawed on the assumption that they would be fixed later.

The Senate slowed action on much of the House's priority legislation. Only the bills applying federal labor laws to members of Congress and curbing unfunded mandates to the states made their way through the Senate and were signed into law within the 100 days. (A third measure, to reduce federal paperwork, cleared within the targeted timeframe but was not signed by the president until later.) The slower pace reflected Senate rules, which allowed virtually limitless amendments. It also was a product of the role played by GOP moderates, who did not share the House freshmen's enthusiasm for such planks as a middle-class tax cut and a balanced budget amendment to the Constitution. Moreover, Senate Republicans had never endorsed the contract.

Before the House adjourned for the August recess, it passed a series of sweeping measures to slash spending on education, social programs and environmental programs; deregulate the telecommunications industry; and end U.S. support for the arms embargo against Bosnia. President Clinton began lashing out at the Republican Congress. He used the veto threat to try to reshape the GOP agenda.

By the fall, the Republican fortunes were turning. Democrats defined who and what the Republicans were all about. They effectively painted a picture of the GOP as willing to gut popular government programs such as Medicare and as looking to enhance the benefits accrued to the rich. Republicans also ran up against forces within their party that were less supportive of throwing out the old ways of Washington. For example, efforts to curb government payouts to cotton and rice farmers as part of dismantling costly farm-support programs met with strong resistance from farm-state Republicans on the House Agriculture Committee. The larger problem, however, was posed by the revolutionary vanguard in the House. Gingrich frequently used the intransigence of the highly conservative and assertive freshmen as leverage with the Senate and the administration. But when it came to enacting GOP bills, the freshmen stubbornness became a liability. Many House Republicans preferred to do nothing than to accept softened versions of what they sent to the Senate, where their colleagues were more moderate.

The Republicans' chief demand—that Clinton agree to balance the budget in seven years while also providing major tax cuts—ended in humiliating defeat. Their two key weapons—a willingness to close the government and a threat to provoke federal default by refusing to increase the limit on the national debt—failed to force Clinton to accept their balanced budget plan. Two federal government shutdowns occurred at the end of the year, and, as a result, the congressional majority's standing with the public plummeted. The first shutdown was Nov. 14–19.

Instead of waiting to bargain over their huge budget reconciliation bill, Republicans tried to win major White House budget concessions in exchange for agreeing to temporarily reopen the government. They underestimated Clinton's willingness to take up the fight early. The Democrats, meanwhile, became more aggressive in attacking GOP priorities. They focused on Republican plans for tax cuts for the rich, saying they would come at the expense of medical programs for senior citizens and the poor. They linked the drive to restrain the government's regulatory power with antipathy toward protecting the environment. And they criticized the Republicans for failing to do the basic work of Congress—passing the 13 annual appropriations bills; at the time of the first shutdown, Congress had completed work on just five spending bills.

When the second shutdown began Dec. 16, three spending bills were still pending and three more had been vetoed. Tempers frayed as ongoing budget negotiations between GOP leaders and Clinton stalled. House leaders refused to pass a stopgap spending bill to reopen shuttered agencies temporarily, and only after a protracted delay did the Senate act to ensure that government benefit payments to veterans and welfare recipients would continue. The Senate in late December passed a bill to reopen the government temporarily by designating all workers as essential, but the House took no similar action. The year ended with an unusually high level of animosity and partisan distrust. Myriad factors contributed to the poisoned atmosphere, including the polarization of the parties to their ideological extremes, the difficult transition for the Democrats to second-class minority status, the anti-Washington rhetoric of the large class of Republican newcomers and the Democrats' reported intense dislike of Speaker Gingrich. Stunned that budget blackmail did not work, the Republicans abandoned their government-shutdown strategy Jan. 5, 1996.

Congress left a considerable number of legislative initiatives incomplete at the end of the session, in addition to the appropriations bills and the reconciliation measure. Stalled were bills to put checks on federal agencies' ability to institute and carry out regulations, to place new limits on product liability lawsuits, to provide new financial regulations friendly to banks, to rewrite the nation's telecommunications laws, to update the clean water law, to rewrite the Endangered Species Act, to change federal grazing policy, to overhaul the "superfund" hazardous waste cleanup program and to refashion the way federal campaigns were financed. Action only just began on measures to restrict immigration, to make obtaining abortions more difficult and to reverse provisions in the 1994 crime bill. Attempts to revise agricultural policy by scaling back farm subsidies were put off until the second session. Clinton vetoed a measure including a provision calling for an aggressive missile defense system, saying it would violate existing treaties. And a bill to dismantle the federal welfare program and replace it with block grants to states cleared Congress but was headed for a certain veto.

Amid the rising partisan warfare, the Senate took the extraordinary step of passing a resolution seeking a court order to force the White House to turn over documents related to an investigation into Whitewater, a failed Arkansas land deal involving Clinton and his wife. Although the Democrats held hearings on Whitewater in 1994, Republicans used the power of the majority in 1995 to reopen a congressional probe.

The Political Year

No clear conclusions could be drawn from the results of the elections held in 1995 about voters' opinion of Republicans since their historic electoral gains of 1994. On the one hand, in a California Hose special election, a Republican succeeded in taking a seat that had been held by a Democrat. On the other hand, in the Kentucky gubernatorial contest, the GOP candidate was defeated despite prognostications to the contrary.

Gubernatorial Races

In 1995, Democrats retained the governorships in a closely fought race in Kentucky, Mississippi's first Republican governor since Reconstruction was reelected, and Louisiana chose as governor only the second Republican since Reconstruction.

Kentucky Democratic Lt. Gov. Paul E. Patton defeated Larry Forgy, an attorney and former Republican national committeeman, by 51 to 49 percent. Democratic Gov. Brereton Jones was not allowed to run because he had been elected under the state's former one-term limit. The law was changed in 1992 to allow a governor to seek one additional term.

Both Patton and Forgy stressed conservative themes. Patton supported abortion rights but backed school prayer and some tax cuts. He also stressed his record in office and ideas on economic development and job creation. Forgy campaigned as an economic and social conservative who opposed abortion, saying the state needed a change from Democratic policies.

While the race was too close to call at election time, the Republican was accorded an advantage by many because his party had won two new congressional seats in 1994 and because the base of religious activists and other motivated conservatives was considered likely to vote. But after first trying to make an issue of Forgy's integrity, Patton switched to a strategy of attacking Forgy by linking him to House Speaker Newt Gingrich, R-Ga., and the least popular items on the GOP agenda. Patton characterized proposed reductions in Medicare growth as a cut and attacked the Republican congressional majority for proposing to reduce funds for student loans.

Number of Public Laws Enacted, 1975–1996

Year	Public Laws	Year	Public Laws
1975	205	1986	424
1976	383	1987	242
1977	223	1988	471
1978	410	1989	240
1979	187	1990	410
1980	426	1991	243
1981	145	1992	347
1982	328	1993	210
1983	215	1994	255
1984	408	1995	88
1985	240	1996	245

Forgy's momentum began to slow when Democrats went after a House Republican proposal to sell Army Corps of Engineers reservoirs in Kentucky and other parts of the Southeast. The idea was part of a plan to privatize the Southern Power Administration. Forgy attempted to tie Patton to Clinton's proposals to regulate tobacco and curb teenage smoking. But Patton had immediately criticized the administration's proposal to regulate nicotine as a drug and promised not to support Clinton's reelection if he went through with such a plan.

Mississippi Democratic secretary of state Dick Molpus failed to topple popular Republican Gov. Kirk Fordice. Molpus took 44 percent of the vote; Fordice, 56 percent.

Fordice's main theme was that life in Mississippi had improved on his watch. He touted what he called the "Mississippi miracle," particularly his efforts to bring the state budget into the black and help create 120,000 jobs. He described Molpus, who had served as secretary of state since 1983, as a typical liberal Democrat.

Molpus said most of the jobs created during Fordice's tenure came through the state's gambling industry and were mostly low-wage, dead-end positions. He portrayed Fordice, who was renowned for brash statements, as an embarrassment to the state. Molpus promoted a $25 million plan to curb juvenile crime and accused the governor of ignoring the issue. He also tried to focus on the need to improve education in the state, and he called for cutting the state's sales tax on groceries in half. Fordice favored reducing the state's income tax.

GOP state Sen. Mike Foster easily defeated Democratic Rep. Cleo Fields in the Louisiana gubernatorial runoff. Foster received 64 percent of the vote to Fields's 36 percent. Former governor Buddy Roemer placed fourth in the state's all-party primary.

Foster, whose grandfather served as Louisiana's governor in the 1890s, had inherited land and an interest in several businesses. He added appreciably to his holdings over his career and identified with small business owners around the state. He ventured into politics late in life, winning a seat in the state Senate in 1987. Foster promoted a conservative fiscal and social agenda, stressing his opposition to taxes and regulation as well as to abortion and affirmative action. Foster favored overhauling the welfare system and allowing localities to vote on whether they

wanted gambling. He was the author of a bill that would allow citizens to carry concealed weapons, which passed the legislature but subsequently was vetoed by the governor. Foster financed his gubernatorial campaign largely out of his deep pockets, pouring more than $2 million into the effort, which allowed him to reach many voters via television.

Fields's campaign emphasized improving education in Louisiana, in an effort to reduce crime, create opportunities for youth and enhance economic development. His proposals included ensuring that students had basic learning tools such as books and raising teachers' salaries equal to the average among other southern states. He favored placing a 5 percent tax on the gambling industry and using the proceeds to improve education.

Fields, an African American, steadily maintained that the gubernatorial contest was not about race. But exit polling showed that 96 percent of African American voters chose Fields, while 84 percent of the Caucasian vote went to Foster. Although African American turnout was unusually high, African Americans made up only about 28 percent of Louisiana's voting-age population.

Special Elections

House special elections were held in Illinois and California in 1995, following the resignations of two incumbents.

In Illinois, Democrat Jesse L. Jackson Jr., son of the civil rights leader and two-time Democratic presidential candidate, easily won his first bid for elective office with 76 percent of the vote. Jackson—an executive in the Chicago-based activist organizations founded by his father, Operation PUSH and the National Rainbow Coalition—succeeded former Democratic Rep. Mel Reynolds, who resigned after being convicted on charges of sexual misconduct. Jackson's Republican opponent Thomas "T. J." Somers, a lawyer and former police officer, received 24 percent of the vote.

In California, Republican state Sen. Tom Campbell captured 59 percent of the vote to Democratic stockbroker Jerry Estruth's 36 percent. Campbell succeeded 11-term incumbent Democrat Norman Y. Mineta, who had resigned to become a senior officer at defense contractor Lockheed Martin.

1996

The Legislative Year

Confrontation gave way to compromise in the second session of the 104th Congress, as Republicans abandoned their earlier hard-charging tactics to compile a record of legislative achievements. The pattern was the same on the other end of Pennsylvania Avenue, where President Clinton cooperated with the GOP on a spate of legislation. Congress and the White House agreed on an overhaul of the nation's welfare system, rewrote telecommunications law, remade agriculture policy and increased the minimum wage. They set new standards for safe drinking water, guaranteed health insurance for workers who lost or left their jobs and increased funding for border patrols.

The political landscape was suddenly transformed in May, with the unexpected announcement from Sen. Bob Dole, R-Kan., that he would leave Congress after 35 years of service to devote himself to running full time for president. Dole had gambled that remaining as majority leader would allow him to showcase his leadership skills while he campaigned. But Democrats managed to turn that strategy against him. Instead of using the Senate to challenge Clinton on issues as he intended, Dole was relegated to endless dickering over legislative tactics and parliamentary maneuvering with Senate Minority Leader Tom Daschle, D-S.D. Dole also found himself overshadowed by House Speaker Newt Gingrich, R-Ga., and the tactics of the House conservatives.

Trent Lott, R-Miss., succeeded Dole upon his official resignation in June. Lott's ascendancy was seen as a changing of the guard. Conservative, energetic and ambitious, he was identified with the new generation of Republicans and their guerrilla politics. Upon becoming majority leader, Lott made clear that he intended to get the chamber moving and that he was willing to threaten, cajole and broker deals to make that happen.

In the aftermath of the failed budget strategy, the House Republicans foundered. The once-vaulted leadership team continued to prevail, but on some important votes they were barely able to keep the surly GOP caucus together. Rank-and-file Republicans complained that the leadership lacked direction and focus and that the GOP message was muddled, if it got out at all. The discontent was compounded by election-year pressures, Dole's lackluster presidential campaign, and gloomy polls showing diminished support for Republicans and Dole.

By late July, however, the atmosphere changed. Galvanized by the desire to log major accomplishments in advance of the elections, lawmakers pushed through a remarkable amount of legislation in advance of the August recess and the party conventions. Front and center was legislation ending the 61-year-old federal guarantee of welfare benefits to all eligible low-income mothers and children. Control of the welfare benefits was turned over to the states instead. Congress also cleared a bipartisan bill guaranteeing health insurance for workers who lost or left their jobs; the Democrats' bill raising the minimum wage by 90 cents, coupled with a Republican package of tax breaks for small businesses; a safe drinking water measure; and the agriculture appropriations bill. The obvious winners of the newfound cooperation were incumbents, particularly congressional Republicans and Clinton. Losing out was Dole, who watched as the issues and criticisms he hoped to use against the president vanished. The drive also put to rest a rousing debate among House Republicans over strategy. For weeks, they had argued about whether it was better to compromise with Democrats to get legislation enacted or to simply pass GOP bills and let Clinton veto them as a way of starkly defining the differences between the parties.

The top priority for lawmakers after returning from the August recess was completing the annual appropriations bill, either separately or in catchall legislation. While both parties hoped to

---

CONGRESS IN 1996

The second session of the 104th Congress ended Oct. 4, 1996, when the House adjourned *sine die* at 2:52 p.m. EST. The Senate had adjourned Oct. 3 at 6:54 p.m.

Convened on Jan. 3, the session lasted 276 days—89 days shorter than the first session. The Senate was in session for 132 days and the House for 122.

There were 2,759 bills and resolutions introduced during the 1996 session, compared with 5,231 in 1995 and 3,103 in 1994. A total of 245 bills cleared by Congress in 1996 became public law. President Clinton vetoed six bills; none was overridden. *(Public laws, table, p. 14; presidential vetoes, p. 1122)*

During 1996, the House took 454 recorded votes, 413 fewer than in 1995. The Senate took 306 recorded votes, 307 fewer than in 1995. *(Recorded votes, table, p. 16)*

---

use the remaining weeks of the session to sharpen issues for the campaign, the overriding concern was to finish early and get home. As the endgame approached, the administration upped the ante, demanding an additional $6.5 billion in spending for domestic programs, including $1.1 billion for antiterrorism initiatives. Republican leaders were so anxious to get their troops home to campaign that they were willing to do whatever it took to leave. They mollified their fiscal hard-liners by dangling the prospect of a rescissions bill in 1997 and by reminding them that their primary interest was in holding onto GOP control of Congress so they could fight another day.

In the end, Republicans not only gave Clinton the additional $6.5 billion, but also handed him money that he had not requested. For example, $4.2 billion was earmarked for education ($3.1 billion was sought) and funds were provided for programs such as AmeriCorps, Head Start and the National Endowment for the Arts that Republicans had targeted for elimination or deep cuts.

The omnibus budget package contained provisions of the six unfinished spending measures as well as numerous other measures, large and small. The legislation included proposals to reduce illegal immigration, ban gun sales to people convicted of domestic violence, recapitalize the savings and loan insurance fund, give consumers more protection against erroneous credit reports, crack down on computer-generated child pornography, limit patents on medical activities, reauthorize federal aid to libraries and museums, cut the government's ties to enterprises that helped finance student loans and university improvements, set new federal penalties for counterfeiting state securities, improve accounting by federal agencies, reduce paperwork for mortgages, lighten regulation on some bank functions, improve federal programs for small businesses and authorize several conservation and restoration projects in Oregon.

Part of the Republicans' transformation in the second session from revolutionaries to realists was a cooling of the incendiary rhetoric. Republicans rarely mentioned the "Contract with America," instead using smoothing descriptions of a "com-

Recorded Vote Totals

Following are the recorded congressional vote totals between 1950 and 1996. The figures do not include quorum calls. The 95th Congress (1977–1979) took 2,691 recorded votes, the highest number for an entire Congress. The high for a single year was in 1978, when 1,350 recorded votes were taken. That year also was the high mark for recorded votes in the House—834. The high for the Senate was 688 recorded votes in 1976.

Year	House	Senate	Total
1950	154	229	383
1951	109	202	311
1952	72	129	201
1953	71	89	160
1954	76	171	247
1955	76	87	163
1956	73	130	203
1957	100	107	207
1958	93	200	293
1959	87	215	302
1960	93	207	300
1961	116	204	320
1962	124	224	348
1963	119	229	348
1964	113	305	418
1965	201	258	459
1966	193	235	428
1967	245	315	560
1968	233	281	514
1969	177	245	422
1970	266	422	688
1971	320	423	743
1972	329	532	861
1973	541	594	1,135
1974	537	544	1,081
1975	612	602	1,214
1976	661	688	1,349
1977	706	635	1,341
1978	834	516	1,350
1979	672	497	1,169
1980	604	531	1,135
1981	353	483	836
1982	459	465	924
1983	498	371	869
1984	408	275	683
1985	439	381	820
1986	451	354	805
1987	488	420	908
1988	451	379	830
1989	368	312	680
1990	510	326	836
1991	428	280	708
1992	473	270	743
1993	597	395	992
1994	497	329	826
1995	867	613	1,480
1996	454	306	760

mon-sense agenda." Still, the 104th Congress in the end cleared major elements from the contract: making Congress live under the same labor laws as industry, empowering the president with the line-item veto to kill specific spending items in appropriations bills, limiting death row appeals, making conservative changes in welfare, establishing tax benefits for adoptions, increasing penalties for sex crimes against children, strengthening enforcement of child support orders, expanding individual retirement account savings plans, establishing tax incentives for buying long-term care insurance, increasing first-year deductions for small businesses, reducing unfunded mandates to states, reducing federal paperwork and making it harder for investors to sue companies.

House Speaker Gingrich played a less public role in 1996. Chastened by the budget disaster and a victim of his own gaffes, Gingrich also was the target of an ethics investigation that would lead to the first reprimand of a Speaker.

The Political Year

The political year 1996 was one for the record books: never before had voters reelected a Democratic president and simultaneously entrusted both chambers of Congress to the Republican Party.

President Bill Clinton, who practically was written off after the 1994 midterm elections, scored a remarkable political comeback by handily winning reelection. Clinton began ahead of his GOP challenger and never lost his lead. Republican presidential nominee Bob Dole's campaign was memorable for a series of dramatic thrusts, including his resigning from the Senate. But Dole could never surmount doubts about his age (73) and his communication skills. As election day approached, Dole was left railing against what he saw as a liberal media elite and an incumbent president he intimated was corrupt. "Where's the outrage?" Dole asked plaintively.

The electorate apparently forgave congressional Republicans for their excesses in the 104th Congress. Despite the unpopularity of the federal government shutdowns orchestrated by the GOP and the call to curtail or eliminate favored government programs, voters kept control of both chambers in the hands of the Republicans. The last time the Republicans had returned a majority to the House was following the 1928 election.

Presidential Election

The 1996 presidential election ended with the sense of drama all but gone. While theoretically Dole could have scored the greatest upset since Harry S. Truman was reelected in 1948, Clinton's overall approval rating approached the highest levels of his presidency as election day neared. As a result, the presidential race was not close, not exciting and not as significant as it was expected to be. Not surprisingly, the level of public interest was not high, whether measured quantitatively in the low viewership for the national conventions and the televised debates or measured anecdotally in the absence of the campaign as a conversational staple, even among political aficionados. Fully half of the respondents in a mid-October *New York Times*/CBS News poll described the campaign as "dull."

One of the prime reasons for the lack of interest was the static nature of the race. Clinton enjoyed a large and clear-cut lead over Dole since the early days of the primary season. Clinton ran unopposed on the Democratic side while Dole was skewered as a tax-increasing, Washington insider by his crowded field of Republican rivals. Dole never recovered from the attacks, despite his rapid succession of primary victories in March, his dramatic resignation from the Senate in the spring and the unveiling of his 15 percent tax cut in the summer. Only his choice of former New York representative (1971–1989) and secretary of housing and urban development (1989–1993) Jack Kemp as his running mate on the eve of the GOP convention in August and the convention itself caused an uptick in the polls, but that was canceled by the Democratic convention that followed. Clinton, meanwhile, had a number of assets to work with—a favorable economy, a world generally at peace and a perfect foil in Republican House Speaker Newt Gingrich of Georgia.

The controversial nature of the Republican 104th Congress allowed Clinton to portray himself as the protector of a variety of popular government programs. Just as critical to his success was the perception of a prosperous economy. Presidents who lost their bids for reelection, Jimmy Carter in 1980 and George Bush in 1992, for example, were generally weighed down by the perception of a slumping economy. Clinton was able to run a "good times" campaign.

For his part, Dole tried to gain traction with his tax cut proposal and the character issue, but to no avail. Poll results showed that voters favored deficit reduction over tax cuts and that Clinton was viewed as best able to manage the economy. Regarding Clinton's personal trustworthiness, character as an issue proved of less importance to voters because they had Clinton's performance in office on which to base their judgment of him. Furthermore, some argued that the matter was settled with the 1992 election; voters already knew what they were getting in 1996.

Also dampening voter interest was the pace of the campaign. In the past, campaigns tended to have a continuity to them, from the long primary season in the spring through the summer conventions and into the fall campaign. However, the 1996 campaign was more disjointed. The front-loaded schedule of primaries (most were held in March) and back-loaded conventions (both held in August) left a long intermission in between, with the debates crammed into a 10-day period in October. Many voters not turned off by the start-and-stop nature of the campaign reacted negatively to its heavily scripted nature, most evident at the national conventions where intraparty differences were muted and thematic consistence was demanded of all speakers.

The presence of stark choices could have piqued voter interest. But both Clinton and Republican congressional leaders decided to focus on achieving reelection instead of fashioning a governing mandate for 1997. Clinton was content to stand close to Dole on issues such as crime, welfare and immigration—important wedge issues that the Republicans used effectively against the Democrats in past presidential campaigns. Meanwhile, the unpopularity of the congressional Republican assault

on a variety of government programs prevented the GOP from making the 1996 election the ideological Armageddon that they had hoped it would be.

REPUBLICAN NOMINATION

Former Senate Majority Leader Bob Dole of Kansas was able to reprise the role played by Ronald Reagan in 1980: the aging front-runner who was rocked early in the nominating process but regained his footing to dominate a field of younger Republicans. Dole finished the presidential primary season the choice of 59 percent of all GOP primary voters.

After winning barely 30 percent of the Republican primary vote in February, Dole took 52 percent in the pivotal array of early March primaries dubbed "Junior Tuesday" week, 55 percent in the six southern Super Tuesday primaries a week later, 60 percent in the four industrial midwestern state contests on "Big Ten Tuesday," 65 percent in the late March West Coast primaries and 70 percent in the April, May and June contests that concluded the primary season. Altogether, more than 14 million votes were cast in the Republican presidential primaries, a record number for the party, compared with fewer than 11 million votes on the Democratic side. The 1996 season marked the first time that more votes were cast in the Republican than in the Democratic primaries since 1952, when Dwight D. Eisenhower and Sen. Robert A. Taft of Ohio engaged in a spirited fight for the GOP nomination.

Dole did show some vulnerability in the late primaries, however. When he was drawing three-fourths or more of the vote in a number of states, he only received slightly more than 60 percent in the normally Republican Rocky Mountain states of Idaho and Montana and the battleground state of Pennsylvania. In all three primaries, conservative commentator Patrick J. Buchanan was the primary competitor. Buchanan, who finished a distant second in the GOP presidential primary vote in 1992, railed against insensitive corporate management and the inequities of foreign trade, focusing in particular on the North American Free Trade Agreement (NAFTA). Exit polls showed him drawing disproportionate support from ardent conservatives as well as voters strongly opposed to abortion.

With early caucus victories in Alaska and Louisiana, Buchanan quickly drove Sen. Phil Gramm of Texas from the race and established himself as the champion of the Republican right. And with a strong second-place finish in the Iowa caucuses, Buchanan grabbed the momentum needed to score a narrow victory over a crowded field in New Hampshire. Yet, just when he appeared poised to move to the front of the GOP pack, Buchanan faltered. Instead of moving closer to the center, Buchanan, while campaigning in Arizona, dressed up as a cowboy, complete with six-shooters and a black hat. In South Carolina, he took a protectionist stance on trade and aligned himself with the glories of the Old South. Buchanan lost the South Carolina primary to Dole and never recovered. The only events he could win after that were the low-turnout, first-round caucuses in Missouri. Buchanan finished the GOP primary season overall with 21 percent of the vote and less than 10 percent of the delegates to the Republican convention.

REDISTRICTING CHALLENGES, 1993–1997

Following the 1990 census, numerous states recast congressional district lines under the provisions of the 1965 Voting Rights Act, which required that the interests of minority voters be safeguarded. Districts in which minorities made up a majority of the voting-age population were known as majority-minority districts. In some state legislatures, white Republicans enthusiastically worked to ensure the creation of these districts—at least in part because doing so created corresponding districts that were more white and more Republican. As mapmakers pulled districts this way and that to pick up minority voters, old boundary lines were tugged out of shape. Computer technology, which provided intricate breakdowns of neighborhood demographics, also encouraged more detailed manipulation of district lines. In some states, oddly shaped majority-minority districts, drawn neither compactly nor with respect to community boundaries, emerged. Challenges quickly arose to the new majority-minority districts. *(Voting Rights Act and redistricting, Congress and the Nation Vol. VIII, p. 1164)*

In 1993, the Supreme Court in *Shaw v. Reno,* invited a new round of lawsuits challenging the constitutionality of districts drawn to ensure the election of minorities. In its 5-4 ruling, the Court reinstated a suit by five white North Carolinians who contended that the state's new congressional district map, which created two irregularly shaped majority-black districts, violated their 14th Amendment right to "equal protection under law" by diluting their votes. While the Court did not immediately invalidate North Carolina's map or rule in favor of the plaintiffs' complaint, it did give legal standing to challenges to any congressional map with an oddly shaped majority-minority district that may not be defensible on grounds other than race.

In 1995 the Court, in *Miller v. Johnson,* struck down a Georgia redistricting plan that created three black-majority districts. Moving beyond the question of district shape, the Court cast heavy doubt on any district lines for which race was the "predominant factor." The high court did not spell out how to determine when race was the "predominant" factor instead of one of several. And even districts

where race was a "predominant" concern would be permissible if states could present a compelling justification for them. The thrust of the Court's opinions was a threat to those who defended majority-minority districts as a means of empowering minority voters. But the justices did not make sweeping determinations affecting all such districts; they seemed inclined to chisel out new limits in a sequence of cases, each presenting slightly different circumstances.

Following is a summary of redistricting cases considered in 1993–1997:

Florida. A three-judge panel using the "predominant factor" criterion in 1996 struck down the configuration of Florida's black-majority 3rd District. The state legislature produced a new map that made relatively minor changes to the 3rd District and four adjoining districts. The three-judge panel approved the map, and the Supreme Court declined to review.

Georgia. After the Supreme Court struck down one of the state's three black-majority districts with its 1995 *Miller* decision, a three-judge panel found a second minority district unconstitutional. When the state legislature failed to agree on new districts, a panel of three federal judges in late 1995 imposed a plan that reduced the black population share to about one-third in the two districts. The Supreme Court heard arguments in 1996 in a case challenging that map and in June 1997 ruled in favor of the plan. The high court found that the federal district court had acted permissibly in deciding it could not draw two new black-majority districts without engaging in racial gerrymandering. (In the 1996 congressional elections, all three of Georgia's black Democrats in the House were reelected.)

Illinois. A three-judge panel in Chicago in 1996 said the Hispanic-majority 4th District was "an uncouth configuration" and that "racial considerations predominated" in its drawing. Nonetheless, the panel ruled that the 4th District served a compelling state interest in remedying past discrimination and so "passes constitutional muster." The plaintiffs appealed to the Supreme Court, which sent

REPUBLICAN CONVENTION

National conventions had long been stage-managed affairs, but the 1996 Republican convention in San Diego reached a new level of orchestration. So perfectly timed was the presentation that featured speakers regularly began and finished their remarks within the optimum window of television exposure. The commercial broadcast networks and the convention managers seemingly were collaborators producing a show and were rivals battling over its content. The delegates functioned as a welcoming and well-coached studio audience.

Opening Session

The 1996 Republican platform was formally adopted by voice vote at the San Diego convention's sparsely attended open-

ing session on the morning of Aug. 12. The smooth and swift approval of the platform belied the fierce, prolonged struggle over the plank calling for a constitutional amendment to ban abortion.

During platform deliberations, multiple amendments seeking to soften the abortion plank or acknowledge differing views of the issue within the party were defeated by lopsided votes. Although several party leaders had threatened to carry the fight to the convention floor, by the opening session all such talk had been stilled.

At the urging of the Dole campaign, the platform committee agreed to add the texts of defeated amendments to the document as an appendix.

Without fuss or fanfare, the convention also approved changes in party rules that could significantly modify the GOP

the case back to the panel for further review. In August 1997, the panel again upheld the 4th.

Louisiana. A three-judge panel in 1996 ruled Louisiana's remap with two black-majority districts unconstitutional. The panel imposed a map of its own, leaving the state with one black-majority district. The state legislature codified the panel's plan, and, in light of that action, the Supreme Court dismissed a challenge to the plan as moot.

New York. In August 1997, the New York legislature, acting under orders from a three-judge federal panel, redrew its convoluted, Hispanic-majority 12th District that had joined widely separated Hispanic neighborhoods in New York City. Under the new map, the Hispanic population of the 12th dropped from 58 percent to 45 percent. The change had a ripple affect on five neighboring districts, but alterations in them were less significant. Proponents of an Hispanic-majority 12th District appealed in 1997 to the Supreme Court.

North Carolina. After *Shaw v. Reno*, a lower court upheld the state's two black-majority districts (the 1st and 12th Districts) as constitutional. The Supreme Court, in *Shaw v. Hunt*, reversed the lower court in June 1996 and struck down the 12th District, which aggregated African American voters across a broad swath of the state's urbanized areas. A three-judge federal panel in North Carolina allowed the 1996 election to proceed using the old district lines, but ordered the legislature to draw new lines in 1997. In March 1997, legislators drew a new map for use in the 1998 elections. It refashioned the 12th District to reduce its black population from 57 percent to 46 percent. Changing the shape of the 12th affected the lines of other districts, including the 1st, whose black population dropped from 57 percent to 50 percent of the total. In September 1997, a three-judge federal panel upheld the new district lines that the legislature drew.

Ohio. The Court in 1996 also considered a redistricting case that was not related to race. Former representative Clarence E. Miller (R-Ohio, 1967–1993) filed suit, arguing that Ohio's districts were un-

constitutional because they were drawn to favor one party or the other. A three-judge panel in Ohio rejected the argument, saying the redistricting process was inherently political and that previous court rulings had accepted legislatures' practice of protecting incumbents. The Supreme Court upheld this ruling.

South Carolina. A lawsuit challenging the state's black-majority 6th District was settled in August 1997. Two white plaintiffs had claimed the district was a racial gerrymander that violated their constitutional rights. The plaintiffs dropped their suit in exchange for the state's admission that, in an effort to create a district that was more than 60 percent black, state legislators drew the 6th to connect black voters in four cities.

Texas. A three-judge panel in 1996 not only found three Texas districts unconstitutional—throwing out the map for the three and ten adjoining districts—but the panel also invalidated the 1996 primary results for all affected districts. The Supreme Court let the Texas panel's ruling stand. Open primaries were held in November for the thirteen districts, with only those candidates capturing a majority of the vote winning outright. Special runoff elections were held in December for the top two finishers in the three districts where no candidate received a majority of the vote. An incumbent from one of the adjoining districts subsequently lost his seat—Republican Steve Stockman.

The three-judge federal panel allowed a period of time after the 1996 election for the state legislature to make changes in the map for the 1998 election. But legislators did not act, and in September 1997 the panel upheld the map it had drawn.

Virginia. In February 1997, a federal court held that Virginia's 3rd District, the state's only black-majority district, was a racial gerrymander, and it ordered remapping for the 1998 election. In June, the Supreme Court upheld that ruling. The state legislature was expected to draw a new map when it convened in 1998.

At the end of 1997, a lawsuit challenging the black-majority 7th District was pending in Alabama.

---

presidential nominating process. The aim was to spread out the schedule of Republican primaries. The changes:

• Required all states to submit their delegate-selection plans by July 1, 1999, locking in their primary or caucus dates and potentially preventing the late jockeying that occurred in 1996 among states seeking a high-profile spot near the beginning of the calendar.

• Required that all GOP presidential primaries and caucuses in 2000 be held between the first Monday in February and the third Tuesday in June.

• Provided extra delegate bonuses for states that agreed to move their primary or caucus to a later date in 2000. Those states voting between March 15 and April 14 would get a 5 percent increase in their delegate allocation; between April 15 and May 14, 7.5 percent; and on or after May 15, 10 percent.

• Allowed state parties to refuse to recognize nominees chosen by "broadsheet" primary ballots that listed all parties together and to allow substitute nominees chosen by party conventions. The intent was to prevent non-Republicans from participating in GOP primaries. The rule did not apply to states with "open" primaries, where voters could choose either Democratic or Republican ballots that listed only the candidates of that party.

• Allowed the national party to recognize the winner of a "jungle" primary as the de facto nominee and to contribute resources to the election effort without waiting for primary results. In states with jungle primaries, such as Louisiana, candidates from all parties appeared on a single ballot and a runoff occurred between the two top finishers, regardless of party, if no one won a majority.

Second Session

Former presidents Gerald R. Ford and George Bush spoke to the delegates early in the second session of the convention, which convened in the evening of Aug. 12. Both men attacked the Clinton White House. Ford said, "We desperately need a leader of principled, proven integrity . . . a commander in chief who has earned his salutes." Bush said, "As president, I worked to uphold the dignity and the honor of the presidency. I tried . . . to treat both the White House and the presidency itself with respect. It breaks my heart when the White House is demeaned, the presidency diminished." Bush also said of Dole, his once-bitter rival for the GOP presidential nomination in 1980 and 1988, "He will do us proud."

A videotape tribute to former president Ronald Reagan, who had Alzheimer's disease, was played before former first lady Nancy Reagan addressed the convention. She said Reagan's spirit and optimism were never failing. "He still sees the shining city on the hill," she said, as tears ran down many faces in the hall.

The climactic speech of the night was delivered by the man many would have liked to have seen as the Republican nominee—retired general Colin L. Powell. Sounding the theme of the convention, Powell said the GOP "must always be the party of inclusion." When he stated his support of abortion and of affirmative action, a smattering of boos was heard from the floor. They were quickly lost in an eruption of cheers when Powell added with emphasis that Republicans were "a big enough party and big enough people to disagree on individual issues and still work together for our common goal: restoring the American dream." Powell also used his 20 minutes—by far the longest time allotted in the session—to deliver a personal testimonial for Dole. "In an era of too much salesmanship and too much smooth talking, Bob Dole is a plain-spoken man," Powell said. "He is a man who can bring trust back to government and bring Americans together again."

Another facet of the inclusiveness theme was a speech by acquired immune deficiency syndrome (AIDS) activist Mary Fisher, who had AIDS and who had spoken at the 1992 GOP convention. She said, "We know now that death comes as a consequence of infection, not immorality. And we must act on what we know."

The program also promoted the Republicans as the party of "common-sense" solutions. Haley Barbour, Republican National Committee chairman, told delegates that "common-sense Republican proposals are the first step to restoring the American dream," and New Jersey Gov. Christine Todd Whitman, temporary cochairman of the convention, said the party had grown as people "have flocked to our common-sense approach." The evening's lineup of elected officials was leavened with "mainstream Americans" who talked about local programs in which they were involved, such as an effort in Cincinnati to reduce adolescent drug use.

Third Session

With no official business to conduct, the convention's third session, on Aug. 13, was devoted to showcasing some of the party's rising stars. Delegates also demonstrated their approval for vice presidential pick Jack Kemp, who made his first appearance in the hall, accompanied by Dole's wife, Elizabeth.

The evening began with an assortment of elected officials—mainly governors—and "Main Street Americans" who gave presentations at the podium and via videotape highlighting Republicans' differences with Clinton on small business issues, health care, education, welfare and crime.

Whitman, who was placed on the program to appeal to moderates, gave the first talk in prime time. "For all our differences—whether over choice or national defense—our party is united by this goal: electing Bob Dole the next president of the United States," Whitman said. Texas Sen. Kay Bailey Hutchison made the most excoriating attack on Clinton. Her segment included a video montage of Clinton promising at various times to balance the budget over a period of five, seven, eight, nine or ten years, which the assembled Republicans found amusing.

In an intriguing role reversal, House Speaker Gingrich, who rose to power and controversy as a partisan firebrand, used his time to present a softer, warmer side of the Republican Party. Gingrich was accompanied to the podium by Olympic beach volleyball gold medalist Kent Steffes and talked about the sport as symbolic of opportunity, having grown so fast in popularity since its introduction 40 years ago. Gingrich also told about his volunteer efforts with the Habitat for Humanity organization to build houses for low-income people.

A featured prime-time speaker was Rep. J. C. Watts of Oklahoma, one of two African American Republicans in the House. He was warmly received for his talk about "countless unsung heroes" helping each other instead of relying on government programs. House Budget Committee Chairman John R. Kasich of Ohio also made an appearance before the delegates. He said, "Our budget efforts in Congress have been about sending your power and your money back to you in every city and town across America."

Summing up the party's frontal assault on Clinton was the keynote address delivered by Rep. Susan Molinari of New York. "Americans know that Bill Clinton's promises have the life span of a Big Mac on Air Force One," Molinari said in a two-finger poke at the president's policies and his legendary penchant for fast-food hamburgers. The selection of Molinari, an abortion rights supporter, as the keynoter was meant to signal to moderates that they were welcome in the party. After Molinari capped the proceedings, Kemp began tossing little pink footballs into the crowd.

Fourth Session

The program for the evening began with a series of biographical speeches that portrayed Dole as a man of character and compassion. As Dole's longtime Senate colleague from Kansas, Nancy Landon Kassebaum, spoke, the twin video screens behind her displayed shots of a young Dole and his boyhood home of Russell, Kan. "Duty, honor, commitment—these are the heartland values," Kassebaum said. Sen. Fred Thompson of Tennessee talked of Dole as an effective Senate leader, while Dole's only child, Robin, hailed her father for his "steadiness" and described him as a "man of discipline."

California governor Pete Wilson introduced Elizabeth Dole. Wilson had briefly bid against Dole for the GOP presidential nomination. A supporter of abortion rights, the host governor was abruptly informed just before the convention that he would not receive a prime-time speaking slot. But he was placed back on the program, reportedly at Bob Dole's request.

Elizabeth Dole, as ebullient and polished as a talk-show host, left the podium with a handheld microphone and went to the convention floor to praise her husband's personal and political qualities. Her style of presentation was one she had honed on the campaign trail. As she strolled among the delegates, she introduced people who had touched her husband's life or had been touched by him.

Sen. John McCain of Arizona gave the nominating speech. "In America, we celebrate the virtues of the quiet hero," said McCain. Two Texans—Rep. Henry Bonilla and Wendy Lee Gramm, wife of erstwhile presidential candidate Phil Gramm—delivered brief seconding speeches. They were followed by two young residents of Russell, Kan., who appeared on the video screen before a Dole hometown crowd.

The anticlimactic presidential roll call took about an hour and a half, with the presenter for each state frequently calling Dole a hero or mentioning the amount of money that taxpayers in their state would save with Dole's proposed tax cut. Kansas put its native son over the top. Dole ended up with 1,928 of the 1,990 delegate votes, with Buchanan getting 43 votes, Gramm two votes, and Alan Keyes and Robert Bork one vote each. Not voting or abstaining were 15 delegates.

Immediately after the presidential roll call, New York Gov. George E. Pataki put Kemp's name into nomination for vice president. Kemp's nomination was seconded by Lynne Cheney, wife of former defense secretary Dick Cheney; Ohio state Treasurer J. Kenneth Blackwell; and former education secretary William J. Bennett. Kemp was quickly nominated, and the session ended with a benediction delivered by the Rev. Jerry Falwell.

Closing Session

Dole and Kemp, who would make their acceptance speeches in the convention's closing session, had a unique warm-up act: the "Singing Senators." Four GOP senators who did a barbershop quartet routine as a hobby—Majority Leader Trent Lott of Mississippi, Larry E. Craig of Idaho, James M. Jeffords of Vermont and John Ashcroft of Missouri—took to the stage wearing star-spangled vests and dedicated the song "Elvira" to Elizabeth Dole.

Known as a fervent and enthusiastic promoter of the GOP as the party of opportunity, Kemp delivered a stem-winder, in which he promised Republican policies—including tax cuts and reduced regulations—that would unleash a burst of economic activity benefiting all Americans. One of the few leading conservatives who had been successful at reaching out to minorities, Kemp continued the convention's theme of inclusiveness. "We will carry the word to every man, woman and child of every color and background that today, on the eve of the new American century, it is time to renew the American promise to recapture the American dream," Kemp said.

A smiling Dole made his way through the cramped aisles of the convention floor, shaking hands with the packed-in delegates as he worked his way to the podium. To bring home to the American public his rise from humble beginnings and recovery from devastating war wounds, Dole's speech contained a great deal of personal sentiment. Dole stated that his ability to overcome nearly life-ending injuries suffered in World War II should stand as an example to all that anything was possible in America.

Dole took hard shots at Clinton, blaming him for what Dole called the largest tax increase ever and for failing to stem a tide of violent crime that the Republican nominee said had "paralyzed" the nation. Dole also told the delegates, "It is demeaning to the nation that within the Clinton administration a corps of the elite who never grew up, never did anything real, never sacrificed, never suffered and never learned, should have the power to fund with your earnings their dubious and self-serving schemes." As he strongly emphasized family values, Dole made an oblique criticism of Hillary Rodham Clinton. Although he did not mention her by name, Dole denounced the communitarian concept, embodied in the title of her recent book, that "it takes a village" to raise children. "It takes a family," Dole proclaimed to a roar from the audience.

He attempted to offset the issue of his age with a nostalgic offer of himself as a bridge to an earlier time in America of "tranquility, faith and confidence in action."

Dole made hefty promises of deep cuts in income taxes, a $500-per-child tax credit and a 50 percent cut in capital gains taxes. He pledged to rein in the Internal Revenue Service and to never place U.S. military troops under the command of the United Nations or allow U.S. trade policy to be dictated by the World Trade Organization. The candidate also prescribed racial and ethnic tolerance as a dictum for the party.

DEMOCRATIC PRIMARIES

President Clinton was able to reprise the role played by President Ronald Reagan in 1984, effortlessly dispatching token opposition in the 1996 Democratic primaries while positioning himself strategically for the general election and burnishing his image as president. Clinton had the smoothest path to renomination of any Democratic president since Franklin D. Roosevelt was renominated by acclamation at the Democratic convention in 1936. Clinton drew 88 percent of the overall Democratic vote, the second-best showing during the primary season by any president since the rapid growth of primaries began in the early 1970s.

Despite the absence of competition among Democrats, Democratic voters in most primary states had ways to oppose Clinton's renomination if they wanted to do so—from casting their ballot for political gadfly Lyndon H. LaRouche Jr. to checking an "uncommitted" or "no preference" line that was on the primary ballot in a number of states. However, nearly nine out of every 10 Democratic primary voters cast their ballots for Clinton. The president drew a still higher proportion in the battleground states of the industrial Frost Belt, ranging from 92 percent of the Democratic primary vote in Pennsylvania to 98 percent in Wisconsin. And Clinton's support was similarly monolithic on the Pacific Coast, as he drew 93 percent of the Democratic primary ballots in California, 95 percent in Oregon and 99 percent in Washington.

Yet throughout the primaries, Clinton continued to show relative weakness among Democratic voters in his native South. It was the only region of the country that he had lost to President George Bush in the 1992 general election, and Clinton's comparative weakness in 1996 Democratic primaries across the South presaged the trouble he would have there in the fall. While Clinton regularly surpassed 90 percent of the vote in Democratic primaries in much of the country, he reached that standard in just one contested primary in the South—in Mississippi. He drew a relatively less impressive 81 percent of the Democratic primary vote in North Carolina, Louisiana and Alabama, 77 percent in Kentucky and a nationwide low of 76 percent in Oklahoma and his home state of Arkansas. In Arkansas, 13 percent of the Democratic primary voters cast their ballots for "uncommitted," while another 11 percent voted for either LaRouche or an Illinois woman named Elvena E. Lloyd-Duffie.

DEMOCRATIC CONVENTION

The party in the White House had the traditional privilege of holding its national convention after that of the competition. Often, this allowed the incumbent party to focus on a theme suggested by the challengers. In 1996, the Democrats in Chicago pounced on Republican Bob Dole's offer to be "a bridge to the past" as proof that Dole's party wanted to turn back the clock. Throughout the week, the podium speakers repeatedly sounded a "bridge to the future" theme.

Opening Session

With an incumbent president en route to renomination by acclamation and no major intraparty disputes to resolve, the opening session of the Democratic national convention Aug. 26 aimed for emotional clout. Speakers and videos highlighted the party's racial and ethnic diversity while drawing attention to Clinton's efforts to ease the burdens on middle-class families.

Routine business, such as adoption of the rules committee report and the credentialing of delegates, was dispensed with in a late afternoon session, clearing the prime-time television schedule for speeches by prominent Democrats such as House Minority Leader Richard A. Gephardt, D-Mo., and Senate Minority Leader Tom Daschle, D-S.D., the convention cochairmen. The program also included a video tribute to the late commerce secretary Ronald H. Brown.

The high point of the evening was the appearance of a pair of lifelong Republicans—James S. Brady and his wife, Sarah. After Brady was shot in the head during the attempted assassination of Reagan in 1981 and was left partially paralyzed, the couple campaigned for a new federal law to impose a seven-day waiting period on those seeking to buy a handgun. The so-called Brady bill finally became law in 1994 with the strong backing of Clinton. It had been blocked in Congress for years by pro-gun-rights members backed by the National Rifle Association, and Bush had threatened to veto the legislation. At the convention, the Bradys called for increased efforts to reduce gun violence and praised Clinton for taking on pro-gun interests to get enacted the Brady bill and another anticrime measure banning certain assault weapons.

Actor Christopher Reeve—paralyzed from a horse-riding accident and speaking with difficulty—capped the evening's speeches. He assailed discrimination that prevented disabled individuals from reaching their full potential and shortchanged the society in which they lived.

Clinton, who was making his way to Chicago on a whistle-stop train tour through the Midwest, appeared live on the United Center telescreens from a late-night campaign pep rally in Toledo, Ohio.

Second Session

Two of the Democrats' most skilled orators—civil rights leader Jesse Jackson and former New York governor Mario M. Cuomo—electrified the convention crowd on its second night. Neither was totally uncritical of the president, particularly on the welfare reform legislation that the party's liberal wing strongly opposed, but each provided rousing endorsements of Clinton's reelection campaign, describing it as a bulwark against the extremist policies of the Republican congressional majority. Jackson focused on the need to improve conditions in economically deprived sections of the United States. He ended his speech with chants to "keep that faith" with poor and struggling Americans, which were echoed by the audience. Cuomo stressed the need to elect a Democratic majority to Congress to fend off the GOP conservative agenda.

Perhaps the most highly anticipated speaker of the evening was first lady Hillary Rodham Clinton. The suburban-Chicago native who arrived at the podium as delegates waved signs reading "Welcome Home Hillary" was introduced by Tipper Gore, wife of Vice President Al Gore. Mrs. Clinton's family-centered remarks blended the personal and the professional. She spoke about her husband and their experiences raising their daughter, then applied those anecdotes to societal concerns and family-related programs, such as the Family and Medical Leave Act, that had been embraced by the Clinton administration.

Mrs. Clinton also responded to an oblique attack by Dole, who in his acceptance speech in San Diego had criticized her assertion in a recent book that "it takes a village to raise a child." She said parenting had taught her "that to raise a happy, healthy and hopeful child, it takes a family." But she then listed other crucial influences on a child's life, including teachers and clergy, before adding, "Yes, it takes a village, and it takes a president" who supports communitarian values such as those propounded by President Clinton.

Following the first lady was the keynote speaker, Indiana Gov. Evan Bayh. Coming at the end of an evening filled with strong, often star-powered statements of party policy and principle, Bayh faced an almost impossible task. Though he was widely regarded as a rising Democratic star, his mild presentation made it hard for him to hold the interest of the emotion-drained delegates. Bayh, son of former Indiana senator Birch Bayh, centered his speech on his family and the record of the Clinton administration on issues such as education.

Also speaking during the second session was Rep. Tony P. Hall of Ohio, an abortion rights opponent who took a leading role in successfully urging the addition of "tolerance language" to the Democratic plank on abortion rights, acknowledging differences within the party on the issue. His address held symbolic value because the party had been criticized by social conservatives since antiabortion governor Robert P. Casey of Pennsylvania was not permitted to speak at the 1992 Democratic convention.

Third Session

Wednesday's session lasted more than eight hours. The opening segment focused on Democratic House and Senate candidates, many of whom were challenging high-profile Republican House freshmen or running for open seats.

The focus of prime-time action was an address by the vice president—moved up from its traditional place on the convention's final night. After lauding the Clinton administration's record on domestic and foreign policy, Gore gave a tip of the cap to Dole as "a good and decent man" before dismissing him as a political anachronism. "In his speech from San Diego, Sen. Dole offered himself as a bridge to the past," said Gore. "Tonight, Bill Clinton and I offer ourselves as a bridge to the future." Turning around another of Dole's statements from his acceptance speech—that he was "the most optimistic man in America"—Gore said Dole "voted against the creation of Medicare, against the creation of Medicaid, against the Clean Air Act, against Head Start, against the Peace Corps in the '60s and AmeriCorps in the '90s. He even voted against the funds to send a man to the moon." Gore continued, "If he's the most optimistic man in America, I'd hate to see the pessimists."

Gore depicted Clinton as the last line of defense against a reckless GOP-controlled Congress, along with its interest group allies, which he described as greedy or working against the interests of the American people. "You can judge a president by the enemies he is willing to make," said Gore. In passing, Gore urged the election of a Democratic Congress before ticking off an array of family-friendly actions that the Clinton administration had undertaken. Among them was the crusade to curb teenage smoking, which Gore illustrated with a graphic and tear-provoking story about his older sister, who took up smoking at age 13 and died a painful death from lung cancer in her mid-forties.

Sen. Christopher J. Dodd of Connecticut, the general chairman of the Democratic National Committee, nominated Clinton. Dodd hailed the president for leading the nation into an era of prosperity, while courageously taking on powerful special interests such as the gun lobby and the tobacco industry. To loud applause, he called for civility in the fall campaign. "Stop attacking the president's family," he demanded of Republicans. Clinton's nomination was seconded by Detroit Mayor Dennis W. Archer.

The formality of the presidential roll call capped the evening. Alabama passed to Clinton's home state of Arkansas to begin the balloting. Next, Alaska passed to Gore's home state of Tennessee. The roll call proceeded slowly but was generally good-natured. Mississippi passed to Ohio to put Clinton over the top.

As Clinton waved his thanks on the overhead video screen, Broadway singer Jennifer Holliday came to the podium to sing "This Is the Moment." With delegates streaming out of the hall, the roll call was completed in about 45 minutes. The announced tally was a unanimous 4,289 votes for Clinton, although a dozen votes were not cast during the roll call. Clinton's uneventful nomination came 28 years to the day after the Democrats met in tumultuous, riot-scarred Chicago and nominated an embattled Hubert H. Humphrey for president.

Closing Session

Clinton's crowning day was clouded by the resignation of his chief political adviser, Dick Morris, over allegations of sexual misconduct that threatened to refuel Republicans' attacks on the ethics and morals of the Clinton administration. The incident was surely a distraction for the president, but he did not let it knock him off his stride.

The final day's program on Aug. 29 included more than 35 local, state and federal elected officials and supporters who highlighted Clinton's efforts on a wide range of topics, from crime prevention to education to reducing teenage smoking. Sen. Russell D. Feingold of Wisconsin praised the administration for cutting the budget deficit through its controversial budget package passed in 1993. National Education Association President Keith Geiger told the delegates that Clinton had "stood by education and children again and again and again." Massachusetts Rep. Edward J. Markey discussed the administration's work in helping to reduce children's exposure to violent and sexual programming on television. Rep. Nita M. Lowey of New York talked about how funding for breast cancer research had doubled under Clinton's watch. Peppered throughout the day's speeches were references to how the congressional Democrats had stood with the president in fighting the Republican agenda and calls for a return to Democratic control of Congress.

Liberal lion Sen. Edward M. Kennedy of Massachusetts fired up the delegates with a partisan attack on the records of Dole and congressional Republicans led by House Speaker Gingrich. Kennedy described the GOP agenda as "the radical wish-list of the education-cutting, environment-trashing, Medicare-slashing, choice-denying, tolerance-repudiating, gay-bashing, Social-Security-threatening, assault-rifle-coddling, government-closing, tax-loophole-granting, minimum-wage-opposing Republican majority that dominated the delegations in San Diego."

Al Gore, who had made his major address the night before, offered only brief remarks as he accepted his renomination as vice president.

Clinton's 66-minute acceptance speech was of a length and breadth that had become his trademark. He stressed the centrist themes that had been echoed throughout the convention: "Opportunity for all. Responsibility from all. A strong united American community." He ticked off a list of achievements, saying his administration had created 10 million jobs, placed 100,000 more police officers on the streets through anticrime legislation and moved 1.8 million people off the welfare rolls and into work.

Promising to "build a bridge to the 21st Century," Clinton outlined a series of proposed targeted tax cuts, such as tax credits and deductions for college tuition and tax breaks for first-time home buyers. He then went on to criticize Dole for proposing a 15 percent cut in income taxes, arguing that it would balloon the federal deficit and require deep cuts in popular government programs.

The evening closed with "Only the Beginning" by the rock group Chicago and a blizzard of confetti and red, white and blue balloons, as the first and second families and many supporters joined Clinton on stage.

THE FALL CAMPAIGN

As in 1992, the Clinton-Gore team kicked off the fall campaign with a bus tour. After the Democratic national convention, the president and vice president, along with their spouses, spent two days visiting small towns in Illinois, Kentucky, Missouri and Tennessee. The Dole campaign had a less auspicious start, with the resignation of the candidate's top two media advisers. Staff infighting and the failure to create a strong media image of Dole were blamed.

As had become tradition, a primary focus of the fall campaign was the debates. Negotiations between the Clinton and Dole camps resulted in the scheduling of two presidential debates and one vice-presidential debate. The bipartisan Commission on Presidential Debates had recommended that Reform Party candidate Ross Perot not be invited to take part in the presidential debates because he did not have a "realistic chance to win the election." Dole applauded the commission's recommendation, while Clinton's campaign saw the inclusion of Perot—who had strongly denounced Dole's tax cut proposal—as a potential aid to the president.

The first presidential debate, held Oct. 6 in Hartford, Conn., gave Dole a chance to fashion a more mellow public persona in place of the dour, slash-and-burn partisan that many voters saw in his bids for the vice presidency in 1976 and the GOP presidential nomination in 1988. In many ways, Dole's performance was everything he and his staff had hoped for. He displayed humor, gave voters a glimpse of his life story and frequently smiled. But it was hard for Dole to refurbish his image and attack Clinton at the same time.

With Dole declining to go for the jugular, Clinton seemed unruffled and confident. He painted a picture of a strong economy and a world at peace and silenced differences with Dole on popular issues such as government downsizing and curbing drug use, while accenting what he saw as unpopular excesses of the "Dole-Gingrich" Congress.

Dole saw a world in which America offered uncertain leadership, a nation where two-income families struggled to make ends meet and a Democratic president who took credit for successes that were not his. Dole shied away from overt criticism of Clinton, saying "I don't like to get into personal matters." But he did throw some subtle jabs Clinton's way, noting at one point that "I won't comment on other things that have happened in your administration or your past about drugs." And he compared Clinton to his late brother, Kenny, who Dole said was "a

great talker" but was known in the Dole family as "the great exaggerator." In a reference to Clinton's acceptance speech at the Democratic convention, Dole said, "I want a bridge to the future." He continued, "I also want a bridge to the truth."

On substantive issues, Clinton batted away Dole's assaults. He was dismissive of Dole's repeated efforts to portray him as a big government liberal. "That's what their party always drags out when they get in a tight race," said Clinton. "It's sort of their golden oldie." And to Dole's description of an underfunctioning economy, Clinton responded, "It's not midnight in America, Senator," a reference to Reagan's successful "Morning in America" campaign theme of 1984. Clinton also pounded at the centerpiece of the Dole campaign—the proposed 15 percent income tax cut—that the president repeatedly described as a "$550 billion tax scheme that will blow a hole in the deficit."

In the vice-presidential debate, held Oct. 9 in St. Petersburg, Fla., much of the questioning focused on the economy. Kemp described an overtaxed and overregulated citizenry, who were turned by frustration "into enemies of the U.S. government." He also took aim at the administration's foreign policy, arguing that it was "unbelievable that ambiguity can be called a foreign policy." Gore, meanwhile, more than held his own. He continued the attack on Dole's proposed tax cut. He also calmly pointed out past differences between Dole and Kemp on issues such as affirmative action and tax policy.

Dole made clear in the days before the second presidential debate, held Oct. 16 in San Diego, that he would be sharpening his attacks on Clinton's character. But the congenial "town hall" format, featuring questions from undecided voters, tended to discourage Dole from mounting a sustained attack on Clinton that many thought he would make. Dole began aggressively, concluding his response to the first question on political partisanship by focusing on the possibility that Clinton might pardon his former associates who were convicted in the failed Whitewater land development deal. But none of the questions that followed directly related to the topic, and Dole subsequently made isolated comments about the administration's ethics, from the alleged misuse of FBI files to campaign contributions from foreign nationals. Clinton generally ignored the remarks, seeking to maintain an above-the-fray demeanor.

Dole was compelled to address the "age issue" during the course of the second debate. "Wisdom comes from age, experience and intelligence," he said. "And if you have some of each . . . that adds up to wisdom." Clinton, in response, said, "I don't think Sen. Dole is too old to be president. It is the age of his ideas that I question."

For most of the debate, the candidates sounded familiar themes. Dole emphasized his intention to downsize government and dismissed Clinton as a big-government liberal who was masquerading as a political moderate. Clinton hit Dole for being out of touch with the problems of average Americans. And, as he did in the first debate, Clinton debunked Dole's proposed 15 percent across-the-board tax cut as a "scheme" that would threaten major government programs from Medicare to environmental enforcement. Dole took umbrage at the characterization, promising that his economic plan would "cut taxes and balance the budget" as well as "grow" Medicare and Social Security. "If I have anything in politics," said Dole, "it's my word."

In mid-October, Dole made a serious campaign push in California, with its big electoral-vote prize. His efforts would be to no avail. In an unexpected turn Oct. 23, Dole dispatched his campaign manager to try to persuade Perot to drop out of the race and endorse Dole. Perot rejected the request. The next day, Perot described Dole's entreaty as "weird and inconsequential." In late October, as Dole's prospects for election continued to look dim despite gaining ground in the face of news reports regarding Democratic campaign finance troubles, Republican operatives reportedly were advising GOP candidates to distance themselves from the nominee and to stress the supposed dangers of having a Democratic Congress and Clinton as president. On Nov. 1, Dole began 96 hours of marathon campaigning that brought him to 29 places in 20 states. The tour succeeded in infusing some much-needed enthusiasm into rank-and-file Republicans.

Clinton also finished what he termed the last campaign of his life with a marathon tour: seven days, 20 stops, 15 states. The theme was conciliatory, with the president pledging to find common ground to bring the country together.

Although Dole repeatedly raised the issue of trustworthiness in his campaign, political observers wondered why he did not make more political hay out of Clinton's alleged ethical and moral failings. Americans had become more vocal in their distaste for negative campaigning and the general incivility of political rhetoric, so GOP operatives advised Dole to ease up. More important, however, was a story involving an alleged transgression by Dole himself and the fear of the repercussions if it became public. In August 1996, a woman who said she had an affair with Dole while he was still married to his first wife began talking to the *Washington Post* and *Time* magazine. Dole aides approached both publications to get them to hold the story. According to *Newsweek*, the *Post* "had decided that it would be unfair to print the story." In the end, no major newspaper or television program reported the affair.

Perot's Reform Party candidacy failed to gather as much attention as his independent 1992 presidential bid. In 1992, he benefited from his spot in the debates, unlimited access to his personal fortune and a candidacy seen as new and refreshing. In 1996, however, he was kept out of the debates; could no longer tap his billions at will because federal law restricted personal spending by those who accepted public funds; had trouble buying prime network time for his infomercials, which were increasingly viewed as old hat; and was no longer treated gingerly by the media and the major parties.

ELECTION RESULTS

Clinton in 1996 became the first Democrat since Franklin D. Roosevelt in 1936 to win reelection to a second term. His victory marked the first time since 1960 and 1964 that the Democratic Party won back-to-back presidential elections. And Clinton was only the second of the last five presidents to win reelection; Reagan in 1984 was the other.

Presidential Vote by Region

In winning reelection in 1996, President Bill Clinton ran ahead of Republican Bob Dole in both the popular and electoral vote in three out of the four regions of the country. Clinton made his strongest showing in the East, where he swept all of the states for the second straight election. Like President George Bush in 1992, Dole had the electoral edge only in the South—Dole won the region by only 60,000 votes, however. (Popular vote percentages may not total 100 because of rounding and minor candidate vote.)

| | 1992 | | | | |
| | Popular vote | | | Electoral vote | |
Region	Clinton	Bush	Perot	Clinton	Bush
East	47%	35%	18%	127	0
Midwest	42	37	20	100	29
South	41	43	16	47	116
West	43	34	22	96	23
National	43	37	19	370	168

| | 1996 | | | | |
| | Popular vote | | | Electoral vote | |
Region	Clinton	Dole	Perot	Clinton	Dole
East	55%	34%	9%	127	0
Midwest	48	41	10	100	29
South	46	46	7	59	104
West	48	41	8	93	26
National	49	41	8	379	159

Clinton won a majority of the vote in 18 states and the District of Columbia, representing 230 electoral votes. He won a plurality of the vote in 13 other states with 149 electoral votes. Clinton's total of 47.4 million votes in 1996 was nearly 2.5 million larger than the total he received in 1992 and was a record high for a Democratic nominee. His share of the popular vote rose from 43.0 percent in 1992 to 49.2 percent in 1996.

Republican Dole polled a majority of the vote in six states with 32 electoral votes. He won a plurality in 13 others with 127 electoral votes. Dole drew nearly 100,000 more votes in 1996 than Bush did in 1992, but his total vote of 39.2 million was nearly 10 million below Bush's in 1988 and more than 15 million below Reagan's in 1984. The GOP presidential showing in 1992 and 1996—37.4 percent of the vote and 40.7 percent, respectively—was its weakest back-to-back performance since the 1930s.

Although presidential candidate Ross Perot of the newly founded Reform Party fell far short of the 18.9 percent of the vote he received as an independent in 1992, he and an array of minor party candidates collected a total of about 10 percent of the vote. This was the second consecutive double-digit showing by third-party candidates taken together—the first such showing in back-to-back presidential elections since 1856 and 1860, a turbulent period that gave birth to the Republican Party on the eve of the Civil War. While his 8.4 percent share of the vote was less than half that he received in 1992, Perot, by winning more than 5 percent of the popular vote, ensured that his Reform Party would qualify for federal funding in 2000.

Number of Black Members in Congress, 1947–1997

Listed below by Congress is the number of black members of the Senate and House of Representatives from the 80th Congress through the opening of the 105th Congress. The House figure does not include the nonvoting delegate from the District of Columbia.

Congress		Senate	House
80th	(1947–1949)	0	2
81st	(1949–1951)	0	2
82nd	(1951–1953)	0	2
83rd	(1953–1955)	0	2
84th	(1955–1957)	0	3
85th	(1957–1959)	0	4
86th	(1959–1961)	0	4
87th	(1961–1963)	0	4
88th	(1963–1965)	0	5
89th	(1965–1967)	0	6
90th	(1967–1969)	1	5
91st	(1969–1971)	1	9
92nd	(1971–1973)	1	12
93rd	(1973–1975)	1	15
94th	(1975–1977)	1	16
95th	(1977–1979)	1	16
96th	(1979–1981)	0	16
97th	(1981–1983)	0	17
98th	(1983–1985)	0	20
99th	(1985–1987)	0	20
100th	(1987–1989)	0	22
101st	(1989–1991)	0	24
102nd	(1991–1993)	0	26
103rd	(1993–1995)	1	39
104th	(1995–1997)	1	38
105th	(1997–1999)	1	37

Clinton's reelection raised doubts as to whether the GOP still held an advantage on the electoral college map. Republicans clearly had the upper hand from 1968 through 1988, when they won five of six presidential elections. But for the second straight time, Clinton chewed up the Republican "L," the cornerstone of the recent GOP presidential victories. The L-shaped bloc of states began at the Canadian border, moved south through the Rocky Mountain and Plains states to the Mexican border, then turned east across the South to the Atlantic Ocean. Adding Alaska, which regularly voted Republican in presidential elections, the "L" encompassed 26 states with 223 electoral votes.

When Reagan first won the White House in 1980, he carried every state in the "L" except for President Jimmy Carter's home state of Georgia. In 1984, Reagan swept them all in his landslide victory over Democrat Walter F. Mondale. Bush did the same in 1988, defeating Democrat Michael S. Dukakis. Such dominance freed Republicans to campaign aggressively in California and the vote-rich states of the industrial Frost Belt, while Democrats had to search frantically for toeholds wherever they could find them.

But Clinton made the "L" look like a piece of Swiss cheese, allowing the Democrats to go on the defensive. In 1992, Clinton took nine states in the "L." In 1996, he captured eight: five in the South and three in the Mountain West. Altogether, Clinton's share of electoral votes in the "L" jumped from 67 in 1992 to 76

in 1996. Clinton lost Colorado, Georgia and Montana, all of which he carried in 1992, but he more than compensated by adding Arizona and Florida. Both were states with a Republican heritage in recent presidential voting. Florida had given its electoral votes to only one Democrat since Lyndon B. Johnson—Carter—while the last Democrat for whom Arizona had voted was Truman in 1948.

Dole largely succeeded in defending traditional GOP territory, holding most of the South, most of the Mountain West and all of the Plains states. But just like Bush four years earlier, Dole could take only one state outside the "L": Indiana, in both cases. He failed badly in his eleventh-hour bid to win California.

With Dole giving up early in much of the industrial Frost Belt, Clinton also rolled to victory there. The results underscored a new political reality: The East replaced the South as the Democrats' electoral cornerstone. Not only did Clinton sweep every eastern state for the second straight election, but, with the exception of Pennsylvania, he also won each one in 1996 by at least 10 percentage points. That included historical GOP bastions such as New Hampshire and Vermont.

Senate Elections

The Republicans built on their gains in the Senate from the 1994 elections. For the 105th Congress, the GOP would hold a solid 55–45 majority over the Democrats, up from 53–47 before the 1996 elections. That would be the party's high-water mark in the Senate following any election since 1928.

Most of the nine new Republican members were expected to swell the ranks of their party's conservative wing in the Senate, making the chamber more of an ideological match for the House GOP majority. Three of the new conservative Republican senators—Jeff Sessions of Alabama, Tim Hutchinson of Arkansas and Chuck Hagel of Nebraska—were elected to succeed retiring Democrats. Pat Roberts of Kansas and Gordon H. Smith of Oregon were conservatives who were replacing more moderate retiring senators of their own party. And conservative Rep. Sam Brownback of Kansas won the race to fill the remaining two years of Senate Majority Leader Bob Dole's unexpired term.

Despite the GOP's electoral success, the Democrats did not fare badly at the polls. They held their own in most regions of the country. All seven Democratic incumbents seeking reelection were returned. Democratic Rep. Tim Johnson unseated three-term Republican Larry Pressler of South Dakota, the only incumbent senator defeated in November 1996. (Interim Sen. Sheila Frahm of Kansas, who was appointed to the seat vacated by Dole, had lost the primary for the GOP nomination.) And, unlike in 1994, the freshman Senate class of 1996 would not be confined to Republicans; six Democrats would be taking the oath of office in January 1997.

The relative strengths of the two major political parties varied increasingly by region. The parties controlled swaths of territory with relative ease, while engaging each other primarily at the geographical margins. Republicans were regnant in the South, the lower Plains and the interior West. Democrats took advantage of the different traditions and voter demographics of the East, the Upper Midwest and the Pacific Coast.

Republicans defended eight southern seats, won seats in Alabama and Arkansas that had long been held by Democrats and lost two open seats to Democratic challengers—Mary L. Landrieu in Louisiana and Max Cleland in Georgia. Landrieu's victory left Louisiana the only state in the South with two Democratic senators. Voters in the Midwest states of Nebraska and Kansas elected Republicans who took a harder line on social issues than had been the custom of either the region or the Senate. However, the Upper Midwest rejected GOP Senate hopefuls wholesale, with South Dakota turning out veteran Pressler. The West was split politically, as it was culturally, between coast and interior. Those on the coastal strip from Seattle to San Diego saw the benefits of federal programs—highway and water projects, environmental protections—and tended toward the Democrats. Rural inhabitants of the West resented federal land-use policy and curbs on their personal freedom and tended toward the Republicans. Democrats constructed a new base along the eastern corridor, winning five of the region's seven Senate seats that were up for election. The Democrats' two losses were in Maine (where Republican Susan Collins prevailed over former Democrat governor Joseph E. Brennan) and New Hampshire (where Republican Sen. Robert C. Smith bested former Democratic representative Dick Swett).

House Elections

The Republicans in 1996 won their first back-to-back majority in the House since the 1920s. However, the Democrats managed to cut into the GOP's numbers and disrupt the momentum that had seemed so strong for the Republicans in the elections of 1994. The Democrats gained a net of nine seats, leaving a party breakdown in the House of 227 Republicans and 207 Democrats, with Bernard Sanders of Vermont the lone independent.

National Democratic officials and their House candidates across the country attempted to nationalize the individual House elections just as the Republicans had in 1994. Then, House Republicans produced the agenda-setting "Contract with America" and painted Clinton as a villain. In 1996, Democrats sought to tie their GOP opponents to House Speaker Gingrich, whose brash leadership of the congressional Republican "revolution" made him the most unpopular national political leader, according to public opinion polls.

Democrats tried to tar their Republican challengers for backing the GOP leadership's proposals to reduce the growth in spending on Medicare, Medicaid and education—portrayed in Democratic rhetoric as spending "cuts"—and for supporting efforts to rein in government regulations, which Democrats cast as "antienvironment" and "antisafe." Democrats were aided by the AFL-CIO, which ran a $35 million "educational" campaign, largely attacking GOP incumbents, especially first-termers.

In 1996, a total of 20 incumbents were defeated; all but three were Republicans. By contrast, in 1994, 34 incumbents were swept out of office—every one of them Democrats. The heaviest toll in 1996 was among the mainly conservative and contentious

Number of Women Members in Congress, 1947–1997

Listed below by Congress is the number of women members of the Senate and House of Representatives from the 80th Congress through the opening of the 105th Congress. The figures include women appointed to office as well as those chosen by voters in general elections and special elections. The House figure does not include the nonvoting delegate from the District of Columbia.

Congress		Senate	House
80th	(1947–1949)	1	7
81st	(1949–1951)	1	9
82nd	(1951–1953)	1	10
83rd	(1953–1955)	3	12
84th	(1955–1957)	1	16
85th	(1957–1959)	1	15
86th	(1959–1961)	1	16
87th	(1961–1963)	2	17
88th	(1963–1965)	2	11
89th	(1965–1967)	2	10
90th	(1967–1969)	1	11
91st	(1969–1971)	1	10
92nd	(1971–1973)	2	13
93rd	(1973–1975)	0	16
94th	(1975–1977)	0	19
95th	(1977–1979)	2	18
96th	(1979–1981)	1	16
97th	(1981–1983)	2	21
98th	(1983–1985)	2	22
99th	(1985–1987)	2	23
100th	(1987–1989)	2	24
101st	(1989–1991)	2	29
102nd	(1991–1993)	3	29
103rd	(1993–1995)	7	48
104th	(1995–1997)	8	48
105th	(1997–1999)	9	51

GOP freshman class. Eleven freshman Republicans were defeated.

The GOP salvaged its continuing hold on the House with its performance in open seats, those districts vacated by incumbents who retired, ran for other office or were defeated in their primaries. Of 53 such seats, Republicans won 29, 10 of them given up by Democratic incumbents. Democrats won 24, only four of which had been held by Republicans.

The East proved to be prime Democratic territory. Not only did Democrats hold all their House seats in the region, but they also picked up six seats previously held by Republicans. Republicans offset their eastern setback by expanding their base in the South. They captured seven of the 19 seats vacated by retiring Democrats, while losing only one of their own open seats in the region. Democrats managed to reverse some of the losses they suffered in the Midwest in 1994 by capturing a net gain of four seats. Nonetheless, Republicans scored an upset in Missouri, where 10-term Democratic Rep. Harold L. Volkmer was defeated. Democrats did well along the Pacific Coast, picking up five seats in the three-state region of California, Oregon and Washington. But those gains were mitigated by a GOP pickup of one seat each in Montana and Utah.

Five members of the incoming freshman class had previously served in the House: Republicans Bob Smith of Oregon, Ron

Age Structure of Congress

Listed below are the average ages of members of Congress at the start of every first session from 1949 to 1997.

Year	House	Senate	Congress
1949	51.0	58.5	53.8
1951	52.0	56.6	53.0
1953	52.0	56.6	53.0
1955	51.4	57.2	52.2
1957	52.9	57.9	53.8
1959	51.7	57.1	52.7
1961	52.2	57.0	53.2
1963	51.7	56.8	52.7
1965	50.5	57.7	51.9
1967	50.8	57.7	52.1
1969	52.2	56.6	53.0
1971	51.9	56.4	52.7
1973	51.1	55.3	52.0
1975	49.8	55.5	50.9
1977	49.3	54.7	50.3
1979	49.8	55.5	50.9
1981	48.4	52.5	49.2
1983	45.5	53.4	47.0
1985	49.7	54.2	50.5
1987	50.7	54.4	52.5
1989	52.1	55.6	52.8
1991	52.8	57.2	53.6
1993	51.7	58.0	52.9
1995	50.9	58.4	52.2
1997	51.6	57.5	52.7

Paul of Texas and Wes Watkins of Oklahoma (who served as a Democrat during his earlier House tenure) and Democrats David E. Price of North Carolina and Ted Strickland of Ohio.

State Elections

Party affiliation was not a major factor in the outcomes of either gubernatorial or state legislative contests in 1996. Eleven states held gubernatorial elections. All seven governors seeking reelection—four Democrats and three Republicans—won easily. Two states, Indiana and Washington, replaced retiring Democrats with Democrats. The only state to choose a Democrat to succeed a Republican was the traditionally Republican state of New Hampshire, while the only state to go the opposite way was the equally Democratic West Virginia. The trend left intact the Republican's big majority among governors, 32 to 17, with one independent in Maine.

As a result of the 1996 elections, a record number of states—31—had divided control, with a governor of one party forced to contend with at least one chamber controlled by the other party. Democrats held a small edge in the battle to control state legislatures, regaining some of the ground lost in recent years. However, the GOP consolidated its strengths in other areas.

Democrats won eight chambers that had been under Republican control or where the parties had been tied. They won state houses in California, Illinois, Maine and Michigan and state senates in Maine, Tennessee and Vermont. Democrats captured control of the state house in Nevada, where the parties had been tied, and they won back effective control of the Indiana House.

Republican supremacy in the Florida House meant that the GOP had control of both chambers of the Florida Legislature. It was the first time since Reconstruction that Republicans controlled both houses in a southern state, according to the National Conference of State Legislatures. Republicans also prevailed in the state senates in Iowa and Washington and in such closely contested state houses as North Carolina, Pennsylvania, Ohio and Wisconsin. However, they suffered a bitter blow with the loss of the state Assembly in California. The GOP had gained a majority in that chamber in 1994 after a quarter century in the minority.

Special Elections

One Senate and two House special elections were held and one interim senator was appointed to fill vacancies in 1996.

Democratic Rep. Ron Wyden claimed the Oregon Senate seat vacated by Republican Bob Packwood, defeating GOP state Senate president and wealthy businessman Gordon H. Smith. Packwood had retired in 1995 in the face of almost certain expulsion from the Senate on charges of sexual harassment and other personal misconduct. Official returns gave Wyden 48 percent to 47 percent for Smith. Wyden became the first senator to be elected by mail. Ballots were sent to voters and had to be returned by a specified time. Wyden's win gave Democrats their first victory in an Oregon Senate race since 1962 and their first victory in an open Senate seat contest anywhere in the country since 1992.

Elijah E. Cummings, an African American and the Democratic Speaker pro tem of the Maryland House of Delegates, took 81 percent of the vote to defeat Republican Kenneth Kondner, a Caucasian dental technician. Cummings's victory maintained African American representation for the Maryland congressional district, the population of which was 70 percent African American. Cummings succeeded Democratic Rep. Kweisi Mfume, who resigned to become president of the National Association for the Advancement of Colored People (NAACP).

Democratic California state Rep. Juanita Millender-McDonald won the right to fill the seat vacated by Democratic Rep. Walter R. Tucker III, who resigned in 1995 after a bribery conviction. Millender-McDonald did not face a runoff against a Republican candidate because only Democrats filed for the election to fill the seat. She took 27 percent of the vote, beating eight other Democrats.

Republican Kansas Gov. Bill Graves named Republican Lt. Gov. Shiela Frahm as the interim successor to retiring Republican Senate majority leader Bob Dole. However, Frahm subsequently was soundly defeated in the primary for the GOP nomination to fill the remaining two years of Dole's term. Conservative Rep. Sam Brownback got the nomination and went on to win the Senate seat in November. During her brief stay in the Senate, Frahm and Nancy Landon Kassebaum made history as the first two-woman Republican Senate team from one state, according to the Senate historical office.

CHAPTER 2

Economic Policy

Economic Policy

The perturbations of the U.S. economy have often played havoc with presidential politics, and that clearly was the case in November 1992, when Democrat Bill Clinton rode a wave of recession-induced mistrust and disappointment into the White House over an incumbent president.

Four years later, Clinton claimed credit for the nation's resurgent prosperity, overcoming a challenge from Republican Bob Dole and winning a second term.

To be sure, the country faced long-term concerns over the health of the Social Security and Medicare systems, and shorter-term issues such as how to balance the budget. But in 1996 Clinton could point to a budget deficit that had declined in every year of his presidency and an economy that was generating jobs without any apparent risk of inflation.

The economy, of course, had no partisan affiliation and cast no vote. And often the actions of presidents and Congresses had only the most tangential of effects on economic growth, unemployment and inflation.

Still, voters have been apt to place the blame for bad times on the shoulders of the incumbent president. That was a principal reason why Republican Ronald Reagan so soundly trounced Democrat Jimmy Carter in 1980, after the inflation rate had soared the year before, sending interest rates sky-high and pushing the economy over a cliff.

Likewise, voters have been reluctant to change course when the economy is sailing on an even keel. Hence, Reagan's landslide reelection in 1984 when inflation was falling—by 1986 it had plunged to a 22-year low (even though the reason was falling oil prices that were beyond his control).

Clinton's defeat of Republican George Bush in 1992 could be attributed to many forces—not least of which was that Bush violated a cardinal rule of American politics. He made a promise that he did not keep. "Read my lips, no new taxes," Bush had said in 1988 in accepting the GOP presidential nomination at the party's national convention. Then, he promptly turned around and in 1990 signed into law a tax increase that on the whole was regarded as beneficial to the cause of reducing the federal budget deficit and ultimately adding buoyancy to the economy.

No matter; he had said he would do otherwise. It was also true that Bush was unable to persuade the American public that, at the time of his reelection bid, the recession of 1990–1991 had passed.

Prosperity did not seem just around the corner, even if the economy by then was expanding. As proof of the continued bad times, the unemployment rate climbed steadily in the first six months of 1992 as the lagged effects of the recession worked their way through the economy. Since World War II, no party had retained control of the White House when the unemployment rate rose significantly during an election year. Bush's fate was sealed.

Ironically, in his first year as president, Clinton signed into law a deficit-reduction bill that relied upon a whopping tax increase. He did so after twisting arms and cajoling votes from reluctant members of his own party—not a single Republican voted for the bill. On top of the tax increase, Clinton conveniently put aside his campaign promise of a middle-class tax cut.

Four years later, however, the voters did not hold him accountable for the lapse. The deficit-reduction bill had worked its magic and the government's red ink was shrinking. More critically, the economy was by then humming along in high gear. Unemployment fell to a 23-year low in 1996 and Clinton was given the keys to the White House for four more years.

SIX YEARS AND COUNTING

When Clinton took the oath of office on Jan. 20, 1993, the U.S. economy had enjoyed nearly two years of solid, if not spectacular, growth following the 1990–1991 recession. By the time he took the oath a second time in 1997, the recovery was well-established and the expansion was six years old and showing no signs of coming to an end.

Growth as measured by the gross domestic product (GDP)—the total output of goods and services within the borders of the United States—averaged better than 2.6 percent a year during the four years of Clinton's first term.

That exceeded by a bit the rate of expansion that most economists liked to call "sustainable." Above that level, inflation typ-

REFERENCES

Discussion of economic policy for the years 1945–1964 may be found in *Congress and the Nation Vol. I*, pp. 337–458; for the years 1965–1968, *Congress and the Nation Vol. II*, pp. 119–182, 253–305; for the years 1969–1972, *Congress and the Nation Vol. III*, pp. 53–145; for the years 1973–1976, *Congress and the Nation Vol. IV*, pp. 49–149; for the years 1977–1980, *Congress and the Nation Vol. V*, pp. 205–287; for the years 1981–1984, *Congress and the Nation Vol. VI*, pp. 27–120; for the years 1985–1988, *Congress and the Nation Vol. VII*, pp. 27–136; for the years 1989–1992, *Congress and the Nation Vol. VIII*, pp. 31–161.

GREENSPAN PROVED TO BE A CONSTANT AS CLINTON'S ECONOMIC TEAM EVOLVED

The economic team appointed at the outset of President Clinton's first term distinguished itself by helping orchestrate the administration's message and lobbying successfully for enactment of the fiscal 1994 budget reconciliation bill that led to a succession of declining government deficits.

Still, while most of the faces on that team remained as key members of the administration when Clinton was reelected in November 1996, by then not one was in the same job as in 1993.

Over four years, Clinton was served by two different Treasury secretaries, three directors of the Office of Management and Budget (OMB), two chairmen of the Council of Economic Advisers (CEA) and two chairmen of the National Economic Council—an umbrella organization created by Clinton to coordinate policy making. Seven different people held those four jobs. In the game of musical chairs, two people each held two of the key jobs for a time.

In fact, the only economic policy-making constant during Clinton's first four years in office was the chairman of the Federal Reserve Board, Alan Greenspan. Greenspan was the rock to which U.S. government economic policy had been anchored since 1987. And when Clinton reappointed him in 1996 to a third four-year term as Fed chairman—the third president to give Greenspan the keys to the central bank—it was with the clear understanding that financial markets would accept nothing less. *(Greenspan background, p. 1116)*

Moving to the Center

In December 1992, before his inauguration, Clinton surprised Democrats and Republicans alike by selecting a quartet of economic policy makers regarded as moderates and pragmatists—signaling that he was placing a priority on persuading Congress to reduce the federal budget deficit.

Clinton picked Senate Finance Committee Chairman Lloyd Bentsen, D-Texas, to head the Treasury Department and be the chief spokesman for the administration on economic matters. And he tapped House Budget Committee Chairman Leon E. Panetta, D-Calif., to direct the OMB. *(Bentsen background, cabinet profiles, p. 1114; Panetta background, p. 1116)*

Both men had been highly regarded, were known as advocates of reducing the deficit, and had criticized Clinton's campaign treatise, "Putting People First," for its failure to recognize the need for fiscal prudence. Both were readily confirmed.

Bentsen's nomination sailed through the Finance Committee with unanimous support and the full Senate approved his nomina-

tion him by voice vote on Jan. 20—one of three cabinet members to be confirmed on Inauguration Day.

The Governmental Affairs Committee recommended Panetta's confirmation by voice vote and the Senate confirmed him by voice vote Jan. 21.

The same day, the Senate by voice vote also confirmed Alice M. Rivlin to be Panetta's deputy. Rivlin had been the first director of the Congressional Budget Office (CBO), serving for eight years from its inception in 1975, and was a senior fellow at the Brookings Institution and also teaching at the time Clinton appointed her. At her confirmation hearing, she emphasized her long-held view that the budget deficit was "the greatest long-term threat to the health of our economy." *(Rivlin background, p. 1117)*

Clinton tapped former Wall Street investment banker Robert E. Rubin to head the National Economic Council, a position that did not require Senate confirmation. Rubin, cochairman of Goldman Sachs Corp., had been a latecomer to Clinton's inner circle during the campaign, but was regarded as an "honest broker" among competing interests, a role he was to play at the Council. *(Rubin background, p. 1114)*

A fifth member of Clinton's initial economic team was less well known and regarded as a bit more liberal than the rest. Laura D'Andrea Tyson, an economics professor at the University of California at Berkeley was appointed to head the CEA, which amounted to the administration's private economic think tank. *(Tyson background, p. 1115)*

Known more for her work on trade issues than for broad macroeconomic analysis, Tyson was questioned about her commitment to the role of free markets and her credentials for the job. In an appearance before the Senate Banking Committee, however, she showed a pragmatic side that won her the committee's endorsement by a vote of 18–0 on Feb. 3, and the voice vote approval of the full Senate a day later.

Musical Chairs

That team remained in place through the critical first year, when Clinton won enactment of his centerpiece deficit-reduction bill. Then, after not quite two years, a series of job switches began.

The first of Clinton's economic team to leave was Panetta, who moved in July 1994 from OMB to the White House West Wing to become Clinton's chief of staff. Panetta's departure opened the door for Rivlin, who was elevated to OMB director that fall. She was con-

ically had a tendency to accelerate, though there were few signs of resurgent inflation at the end of Clinton's first four years in the White House.

Over those four years, the economy added more than 11 million jobs, and inflation averaged 2.8 percent a year—the smallest rate of consumer price increases over the four years of a presidential term since John F. Kennedy was in the White House.

Yields on government bonds were falling as Clinton began his second term—a further sign that inflation was so subdued that it played essentially no role in economic decision making by investors, households or corporate chieftains.

Moreover, the prosperity that had helped Clinton sustain his wire-to-wire lead over Republican Dole in 1996 was destined to continue into his second term. Every one of those major economic indicators would show further improvement in 1997:

firmed by the Senate by voice vote on Oct. 7, drawing little opposition.

The following January, Bentsen retired from public life leaving his Treasury post vacant for Rubin, who was by then known as a hard-working, effective advocate on and off Capitol Hill for administration policies. New Senate Majority Leader Bob Dole, R-Kan., called Rubin "an outstanding choice," and the Senate confirmed his nomination by a vote of 99–0 on Jan. 10, 1995.

Soon thereafter, once the coming year's budget request was released in February, Clinton named Tyson to replace Rubin as head of the National Economic Council, which left vacant the CEA chairmanship. And CEA member Joseph E. Stiglitz was elevated to the CEA chair in June 1995. *(Stiglitz background, p. 1116)*

Also in 1995, on Capitol Hill, Republicans tapped a conservative labor economist and Baruch College professor, June O'Neill, to head the CBO. She succeeded Robert D. Reischauer, whose term expired on Jan. 3. She was just the fourth person to head the agency.

One last administration switch occurred in the latter part of 1996. Rivlin left OMB that June to take a seat on the Federal Reserve Board, and Clinton nominated Franklin D. Raines, then vice chairman of the Federal National Mortgage Association (Fannie Mae) to take her place. *(Raines background, p. 1117)*

Raines' nomination first became ensnared in a partisan debate over the reappointment of Greenspan to another term as Fed chairman, and then delayed further by a partisan skirmish over how best to balance the budget. Although the Governmental Affairs Committee endorsed his nomination by voice vote in July, it was not until Sept. 6 that the Senate confirmed him, again by voice vote.

Filling Fed Vacancies

The president's first opportunity to influence monetary policy came in 1994, when Fed Vice Chairman David W. Mullins Jr. stepped down from the central bank's seven-member board of governors. Mullins had been appointed by President George Bush in 1990.

Clinton tapped Alan S. Blinder, a former Princeton professor, who was serving at the time as a CEA member alongside Tyson and Stiglitz. Blinder, who was also named vice chairman of the Fed, defended his economic views during a confirmation hearing before the Senate Banking Committee and countered opponents who criticized him as being "soft on inflation."

The committee approved his appointment to a term that expired Jan. 31, 1996, by a 17–0 vote on May 24, 1994, and the full Senate confirmed him by voice vote on June 24.

Two months later, Clinton had his second nominee on the Fed when the Senate voted 94-6 on Aug. 11 to confirm the appointment of former University of California at Berkeley professor Janet Yellen to an unexpired term that ended Jan. 31, 2000. She replaced Lawrence Lindsay, a Bush appointee from 1991.

In January 1996, Clinton found he had three seats on the Fed to fill. One was Greenspan's seat as chairman; one was the now-expired term that Blinder had filled just a year and a half earlier; one was an unexpired term that ended Jan. 31, 2002 and had been filled by John LaWare, an appointee of President Ronald Reagan in 1988.

Clinton chose to retain Greenspan, both to assuage Wall Street, which was apprehensive in an election year, and because the economy was humming following the 1990–1991 recession and a period in 1994 when some analysts feared it was about to overheat.

To balance Republican Greenspan, he tapped Rivlin to leave OMB and take the vice chairman's seat. And he named one of the nation's most prominent economic forecasters, Laurence H. Meyer, to LaWare's unexpired term as governor.

All three were recommended for confirmation by the Banking Committee on March 27 by 16–0 votes. However, the nominations stalled.

Greenspan's reappointment had come over the complaints of a few Democrats who objected to the Fed's series of seven interest-rate increases in 1994 and early 1995 that were intended to forestall a surge in inflation before it was embedded in the economy—in fact before it was apparent to most observers. The other two nominations were held up by Republicans until an agreement was reached to vote on Greenspan.

"Under the Greenspan Fed, job growth and the living standards of average Americans have been sacrificed in the blind pursuit of inflation control," said Sen. Tom Harkin, D-Iowa, as the Senate finally began debating the chairman's reappointment on June 13.

Most Democrats agreed with Republicans, however, that Greenspan had done well as the economy's most powerful day-to-day steward. He was confirmed 91–7 on June 20.

Rivlin, who had angered some Republicans during protracted partisan battles over balancing the budget, won confirmation the same day by a 57–41 vote. And Meyer was confirmed 98–0, also on June 20.

economists fell over themselves to describe the best-of-all-worlds economy in which the United States was reveling. *(Economy's performance 1980–1996, figures, p. 35)*

The economy in 1997 was to expand at its fastest rate in nine years. Unemployment would fall to a 24-year low. Inflation for the year (as measured by the consumer price index) was the lowest since 1986, and when food and energy costs were excluded, the so-called core CPI rose at the slowest pace since 1965.

The yield on the government's 30-year benchmark bond was to fall toward an all-time low.

The expansion, having reached 67 months by the time Clinton was reelected in November 1996, was already the third longest in U.S. history. And it showed every probability of attaining the second highest spot by continuing to grow throughout 1997 and 1998—surpassing Ronald Reagan's 92-month expansion, the longest in U.S. peacetime. Only the 106-month expansion of 1961–1969 was longer, and it was sustained in part by the Vietnam War buildup. No president since Lyndon Johnson had served without presiding over a recession; Clinton looked as if he just might.

INHERITING A RECOVERY

Some analysts, particularly critics of the Clinton administration, contended that much of this good news simply fell into Clinton's lap. He had taken few steps to use government fiscal policy to stimulate growth—a good thing in the eyes of most economists. In fact, early in his first year, Clinton failed to persuade Congress to enact a supplemental spending bill that was intended to stimulate job growth.

On the other hand, his successful call for deficit-reduction later in that first year in hindsight might have been a critical tonic. Enactment of the deficit-reducing budget reconciliation bill started the federal budget on a path toward balance, and most analysts credited the declining deficit with contributing to sustained economic growth.

The deficit narrowed steadily from $290.4 billion in fiscal 1992—Bush's last year as president—to $107.3 billion in fiscal 1996. When compared with the overall economy, the decline was even more precipitous: the deficit as a percentage of GDP fell from 4.9 percent to 1.4 percent in just four years. In fiscal 1997, the deficit would narrow to just 22.6 billion—the smallest since 1974, amounting to barely 0.3 percent of GDP.

Classical economic theory taught that shrinking government deficits in such a fashion should cause the economy to contract—not expand—as the stimulus of deficit spending was removed.

Clinton and his advisers would later discount that theory. "In the short run, deficit reduction should not cause growth to slow, provided the reduction is credible, financial markets are forward-looking, and the Federal Reserve responds with appropriately accommodative monetary policy," wrote Clinton's Council of Economic Advisers in February 1997.

In fact, the Clinton White House had argued all along that cutting the deficit would allow interest rates to fall, boosting those elements of the economy that relied heavily on borrowed money—housing, for one.

Long-term interest rates did decline over time, aided in no small part by efforts to bring the budget into balance. And that had a salutary effect on growth—and even helped further reduce the deficit—as the cost of borrowing by the federal government declined.

THE ROLE OF THE FED

The path of U.S. interest rates during Clinton's first term was hardly all downhill, however. Barely a year into office, the Federal Reserve's policy-making Open Market Committee voted to increase U.S. borrowing costs to slow a recovery that—the central bank feared—was about to overheat.

It was the sort of action that could have provoked howls of outrage, but instead was later applauded as having done much to keep the economy stable. In 1996, Clinton rewarded Fed Chairman Alan Greenspan with appointment to a third four-year term at the helm of the central bank. That allowed Greenspan to be the only major economic policy maker not to change jobs during the first four years of Clinton's presidency. (Clinton's economic policy team, p. 32)

Greenspan and Clinton both did their best to prepare financial markets for the Fed to raise borrowing costs. In early 1994, Greenspan testified on Capitol Hill that it might be time for the Fed to act, even though the storm clouds of inflation were somewhere over the horizon; Clinton hinted he would not object.

Even so, the Fed caught many investors by surprise on Feb. 4, 1994, when it voted to raise the federal funds target interest rate on overnight loans between banks to 3.25 percent from 3.00 percent. It was the first rate increase by the Fed in five years, and it was to be just one of seven increases in the fed funds target over the ensuing 12 months. By February 1995 the rate on overnight loans was 6.00 percent.

The Fed had waited until 1994 to act, even though the economy's recovery was showing signs of vigor earlier. Central bankers had cut the fed funds rate by a full percentage point in several steps in 1992 to help draw the economy more quickly out of the 1990–1991 recession. Then they waited for the results of that action to take full effect.

Greenspan signaled early in Clinton's presidency that the Fed would be in no hurry to raise rates as long as long-term bond yields—which tend to rise and fall with inflationary expectations—showed investors were sanguine about the possibility of a serious effort by the president and Congress to cut the deficit.

That's exactly what happened. From Election Day 1992 through the fall of 1993, the yield on the Treasury's benchmark 30-year bond fell from about 7.8 percent to 5.8 percent—a drop of two full percentage points.

In that period, Congress passed the 1993 deficit-reduction law and the economy gained a head of steam. Gross domestic product expanded at a 4.8 percent annual rate in the fourth quarter of 1993, about twice as fast as Fed policy makers regarded as "sustainable."

Long-term interest rates then started to rise as the economy gained momentum, and before the Fed acted. Surprisingly, because politicians rarely ever applaud when central bankers raise borrowing costs, Clinton himself and members of his economic team were not critical of the Fed in 1994. After that first move in February 1994, Treasury Secretary Lloyd Bentsen said, "The fundamentals for sustained economic growth are very positive," a signal the administration was content to let the Fed lead.

Greenspan called the 1994 action a "preemptive strike," since there was no evidence at the time inflation was heating up. Years later, in testimony to Congress, he congratulated himself and his colleagues for their foresight. "The preemptive actions of the Federal Reserve in 1994 contained a potentially destabilizing surge in demand, short-circuiting a boom-bust business cycle in the making and keeping inflation low to encourage business innovation."

In fact, the economy performed well in 1995, expanding by 2.0 percent as the unemployment rate continued to decline. Long-term interest rates responded to the Fed's actions as ex-

A Look at the Economy, 1980–1996

Economic Growth...
Annual Percentage Change

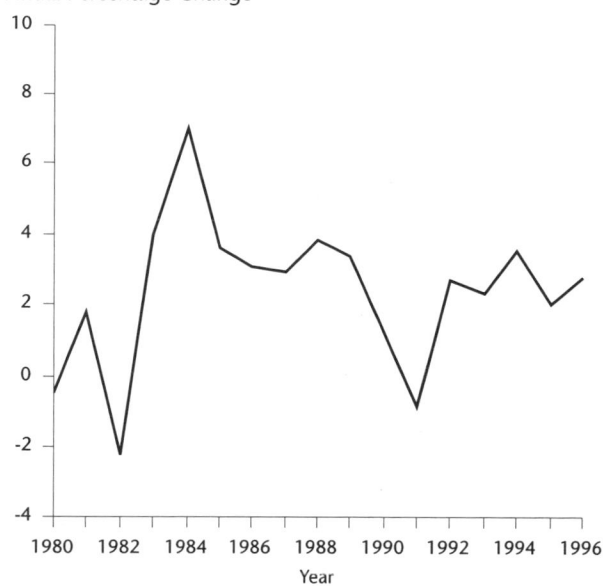

... showed a bigger decline in the 1981–1982 recession than in the shorter 1980 and 1990–1991 recessions. Recovery was weaker immediately following the less-severe downturns, though it was steady during the five years from 1992–1996.

Growth: Annual changes in domestic product, based on constant 1987 dollars.

SOURCE: Commerce Department, Bureau of Economic Analysis.

Inflation...
Annual Percentage Change

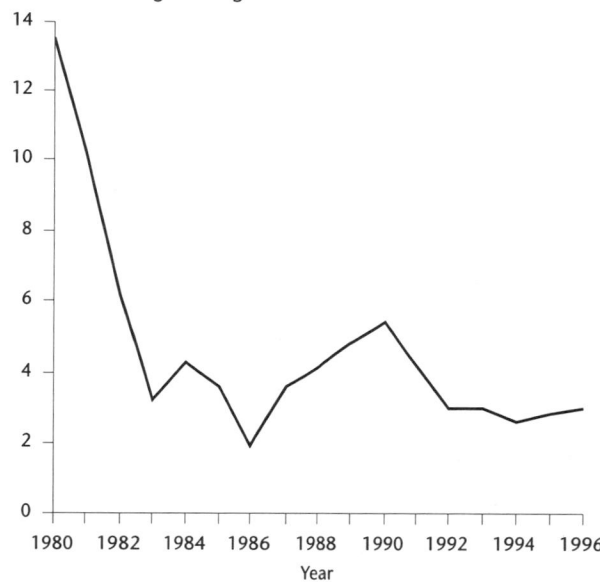

... reached historically high levels before the 1980 and 1981–1982 recessions began. The consumer price index did not hit similar peaks prior to the 1990–1991 recession and has shown tame increases since.

Inflation: Annual change in the consumer price index for all urban consumers, expressed as an annual average rate.

SOURCE: Labor Department, Bureau of Labor Statistics.

Unemployment...
Annual Percentage Average

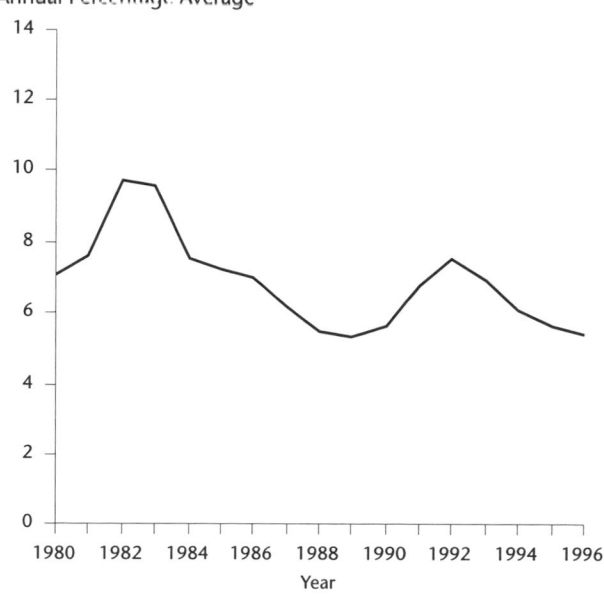

...surged during all three recessions of the past two decades and remained high for a time in the years following each one. Since 1992, the jobless rate has been on a steadily declining path as the economy expanded.

Unemployment: Annual rate of unemployment for all civilian workers (does not include the military).

SOURCE: Labor Department, Bureau of Labor Statistics.

Interest Rates...
Annual Percentage Average

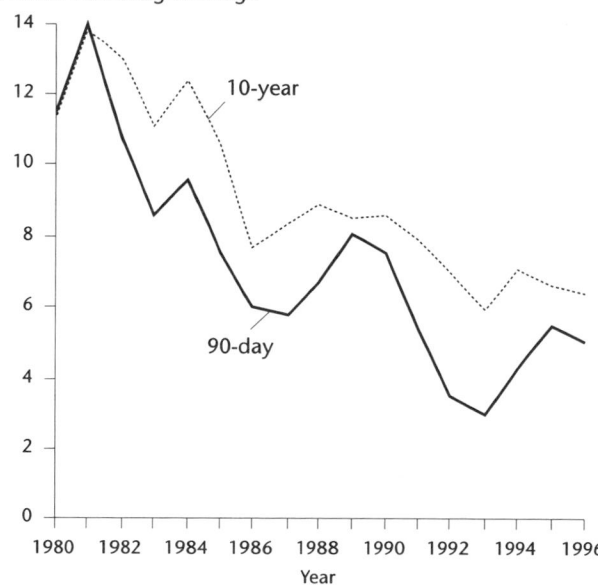

... on long- and short-term Treasury securities fell in 1993 to their lowest levels in almost 20 years, as the economy recovered slowly from the 1990–1991 recession. Since then rates have risen modestly.

Interest rates: Annual average for new issues of 90-day Treasury bills and 10-year Treasury notes, adjusted for constant maturities.

SOURCE: Treasury Department.

pected. Rates rose steadily in 1994 to peak at 8.1 percent in early November.

Even before the Fed's stopped pushing up short-term rates, however, bond yields started falling—a sign investors were confident inflation was not going to become a problem. By early 1996, bond yields were again below 6.0 percent and the Fed had reduced the overnight rate to 5.25 percent, where it would remain for the balance of Clinton's first term.

STORM CLOUDS AHEAD

Although Clinton had offered a means to reducing the federal deficit, the beast had not been fully tamed before the end of Clinton's first term. That would take another concerted effort in Clinton's second term.

And though the economy—with Greenspan's assistance—looked to be on a path of perpetual, sustained growth, few observers truly expected the good times would roll on forever. A recession at some point would be inevitable.

One other problem loomed that posed risks both for the federal budget and the economy on a broader scale. The U.S. population was aging and the Baby Boom generation that Clinton had led into middle age and their prime earning years would some day soon be looking to retire.

It was apparent that social programs aimed at protecting the well-being of the elderly—Social Security and Medicare, in particular—would be stressed in the first decades of the twenty-first century. Moreover, middle-aged earners would become older spenders as they retired and stopped adding to the pool of collective national savings. That pool was not large by any standard, and yet it was critical to the business investment that had fueled growth in the post–World War II period. It would need replenishing.

That said, the burdens that the coming demographic change would impose on the government and the economy were not well understood, nor were Congress and the White House moving forward with plans to cope with them. Policy makers attempted by fits and starts to address the issue, but politics and events blocked progress.

One effort that held promise was a bipartisan commission, created by Clinton in late 1993 and charged with outlining ways to curb the relentless growth in entitlements, which accounted for almost half of all federal spending.

The two moderate senators named to head the commission, Bob Kerrey, D-Neb., and John C. Danforth, R-Mo., outlined their recommendations, which relied chiefly on spending cuts to achieve their goal of preventing runaway growth in entitlements. But the magnitude of proposed Social Security cuts—between 33 percent and 50 percent for future beneficiaries—drew strong protests from interest groups such as organized labor and the American Association of Retired Persons. Other proposals to increase taxes met with a similar fate.

The commission closed shop in December 1994, offering a stern warning about the future of Social Security and Medicare—but no plan of action. Its final product was a report on the problem and a letter urging Congress and the Clinton administration to take a more long-term view of tax and spending proposals.

The report noted that entitlements and interest on the national debt consumed more than 61 cents of every dollar the federal government spent, more than twice the figure of 30 years before. By 2003, this "mandatory" spending was expected to require 72 cents out of every dollar, and if no changes were made before 2012, interest and entitlements would consume all the taxes the federal government collected.

The challenge was daunting; the willingness to confront it was yet to be found.

The Federal Budget

The battle over taming the federal budget deficit came at President Clinton in two waves that defined his first term.

First, in 1993, with Democrats controlling both the White House and Congress for the first time since Jimmy Carter was president, came a politically wrenching effort that was a policy success but political failure. While ultimately successful in its goal of halving the deficit by the end of Clinton's first term, the deficit-cutting drive of Clinton's first year in office contributed to a devastating political loss: the landslide 1994 elections that produced the first GOP Congress in 40 years.

Then, in 1995, with remarkable unity and a boldness that invited a political counterattack, Republicans launched a balanced-budget, tax-cutting drive that overreached and produced a showdown with Clinton that brought his presidency back to life—and helped re-elect a Democratic president for the first time since the 1940s.

Republicans were unsuccessful in forcing Clinton to sign their budget bills, but the battle drew Clinton in their direction and forced him to embrace their budget-balancing goal if not their policies.

Ultimately, negotiations spanning the first several months of Clinton's second term led to a 1997 balanced-budget agreement that was enacted into law, pleasing both sides: Republicans won a taste of the tax cuts they desired, while Clinton signed a budget-reconciliation law that allowed him to claim credit for the first balanced budget since 1969, all the while gaining some modest gains in domestic spending.

That 1997 success was the result of a series of policies spanning nearly 20 years. Despite deficit-cutting efforts in the 1980s, when President Ronald Reagan occupied the White House, including a major 1982 tax increase, the Gramm-Rudman procedural effort and a 1990 budget deal that forced President George Bush to break his "no new taxes" pledge, the newly elected Clinton was presented with an enormous problem. The ballooning budget deficit had risen to a record $290 billion in fiscal 1992—caused in great part by a sluggish economy and deficit figures inflated by the savings and loan debacle.

The new president faced an unappealing bind. Democrats controlled Congress, but the deficit wars of the 1980s and early 1990s had produced a deficit-hawk wing in the party, especially among newer members from swing districts.

At the same time, any successful attack on the deficit had to include tax increases, and the Republican minority had no interest in that.

The driving force in the GOP was no longer Senate Minority leader Bob Dole, D-Kan.—who was a principal engineer of Reagan-Bush endorsed tax increases of the 1980s—but House Minority Whip Newt Gingrich, R-Ga., who opposed those tax increases and viewed the 1993 deficit-cutting plan as an opportunity to lay torpedoes into Clinton's presidency. And that Gingrich did.

SHIFTING ECONOMIC GEARS

Early in his 1992 campaign, candidate Clinton was criticized for promising a middle-class tax cut, but his campaign treatise, "Putting People First" promised new "investment" spending—even as it predicted Clinton's plans would cut the deficit by three-fourths. But most of Clinton's deficit reduction would come via strong economic growth and tax increases on the wealthy.

Shortly after "Putting People First" was published, new predictions from the Congressional Budget Office (CBO)—which forecast a fiscal 1996 deficit $76 billion larger than the previous estimate—rendered Clinton's treatise a work of fiction.

Just before Clinton took office, more bad news arrived from the Bush administration's Office of Management and Budget (OMB). The fiscal 1997 deficit, which Clinton had promised to cut in half, was expected to balloon to $305 billion. If the deficit were not tamed, counseled Clinton budget chief Leon E. Panetta and Federal Reserve Board Chairman Alan Greenspan, long-term interest rates would rise and the stock and bond markets might lose confidence. *(Clinton economic policy team, p. 32)*

All of a sudden, the deficit, on which Clinton had barely focused during the campaign, was front and center. He promised to cut the 1997 deficit roughly in half—to $145 billion.

But the political landscape in Congress was bleak. While Re-

REFERENCES

Discussion of federal budget policy for the years 1945–1964 may be found in *Congress and the Nation Vol. I*, pp. 387–395; for the years 1965–1968, *Congress and the Nation Vol. II*, pp. 127–140; for the years 1969–1972, *Congress and the Nation Vol. III*, pp. 63–75; for the years 1973–1976, *Congress and the Nation Vol. IV*, pp. 57–81; for the years 1977–1980, *Congress and the Nation Vol. V*, pp. 211–230; for the years 1981–1984, *Congress and the Nation Vol. VI*, pp. 33–61; for the years 1985–1988 *Congress and the Nation Vol. VII*, pp. 33–74; for the years 1989–1992, *Congress and the Nation Vol. VIII*, pp. 37–86.

publicans favored cutting the deficit, they were not willing to raise taxes in order to do it.

Simple Democratic Party politics ensured that tax increases, especially on the wealthy, would be part of any deficit reduction plan. At the same time, lacking support from Republicans meant that the Clinton plan would not include cuts in the major entitlement programs such as Social Security, Medicare and Medicaid. For one party alone to have taken such steps would have been politically risky in the extreme.

Clinton's 1993 deficit-reduction bill was crafted to appeal to Democrats—featuring taxes on the wealthy, plus spending restraint from cuts in defense, caps on appropriations and reductions in the growth of Medicare payments to doctors and hospitals.

Still, getting it passed required a full court press from Clinton and his friends on Capitol Hill. Republicans and their outside allies, such as the Christian Coalition, mounted a ferocious campaign against the plan, calling it the biggest tax hike of all time—which was technically true, though it was smaller than Reagan's 1982 tax increase after adjusting for inflation.

The Democratic majority in Congress had long depended on retaining districts that routinely voted Republican for president, and Democrats from such districts were particularly reluctant to embrace the plan. Republicans, meanwhile, predicted the tax-heavy Clinton plan would throw the economy into a tailspin. "This plan is not a recipe for more jobs, it is a recipe for disaster," said House GOP Conference Chairman Dick Armey, R-Texas.

The bill ultimately passed both the House and Senate in by the narrowest possible margins. It took a tie-breaking vote by Vice President Al Gore in the Senate to clear the measure for Clinton's signature. That vote followed a dramatic tally in the House, where the bill passed only after freshman Democrat Marjorie Margolies-Mezvinsky of Pennsylvania broke a promise to her constituents and provided the critical final vote for the plan. She lost her seat in 1994.

While politically devastating, the Clinton plan proved the GOP wrong and contributed to an economy that was beginning to hum impressively at a 3.5 percent rate of growth in 1994, while creating 2.8 million new jobs.

As the economy recovered from the 1990–1991 recession, the resulting deficit reduction was impressive. The potential of chronic $300 billion-a-year deficits that faced Clinton in 1993 had disappeared; the actual deficit shrank to $107.3 billion in fiscal 1996. Clinton had met his goal.

AN ERA OF GOP CONTROL

Republicans swept into power in Congress in the midterm 1994 elections, producing a 52-seat gain for House Republicans and their first majority since Dwight D. Eisenhower was in the White House. The Senate flipped from a 55–45 Democratic majority to a 52-48 GOP majority that later swelled to 54–46 with party switches by two conservative Democrats.

In the early days of GOP rule in 1995, the hard-charging conservatism of the House dominated. The conservative House firebrands set their sights on wholesale spending cuts, tax cuts, and elimination of whole departments of the government—Energy, Education and Commerce.

Early in 1995, House Republicans set about passing the elements of the "Contract with America." One of the most important planks in the contract was a constitutional amendment to require a balanced federal budget by 2002. The House passed the measure easily, but the Senate killed it after a month-long debate that culminated in a wrenching March tally that came up one vote short. Six Democrats who had voted for a virtually identical constitutional amendment less than a year before had switched their votes to "no." But for many conservative Republicans, the focus was on Senate Appropriations Committee Chairman Mark O. Hatfield, R-Ore., who was unwavering in his opposition to the idea. There was even talk of taking away his chairmanship.

The defeat of the amendment was devastating for Republicans, and it could have given them an excuse to adopt a more cautious approach to budget policy. After all, the new chairmen of the Budget committees—Rep. John Kasich, R-Ohio, and Sen. Pete V. Domenici, R-N.M.—understood their task. Both originally spoke of five-year plans that would set the budget on a "glide-path" towards balance.

But House GOP leaders overrode Kasich's objections and declared they wanted to balance the budget outright. The Senate had little choice but to go along.

Republicans would get no help from Clinton, who sent them a budget request in February 1995 that contained few proposals to reduce the deficit below previously set path. The White House knew that what the Contract with America had promised—almost $300 billion in net tax cuts, increasing defense spending and leaving Social Security untouched—could be accomplished only by politically perilous cuts in Medicare and Medicaid, farm subsidies, domestic appropriations and education. White House aides, as well as many longtime budget watchers, did not think Republicans could muster the political will to pass such a plan.

For one thing, the revolutionary fervor of the House, especially the tax-cutting zeal, did not extend to the Senate. Many Senate GOP veterans had a feeling of déjà vu. Cut taxes, increase the Pentagon's budget—all while balancing the budget? For some of the Senate's "old bulls," such as Domenici and Senate Finance Committee Chairman Bob Packwood, R-Ore., the similarity to the Reagan-era policies that had started the deficit spiral were too clear, and they signaled they would not go along with the tax cuts. But in the new political climate, it was too much to expect for a few Senate moderates to stall the GOP budgetary agenda, and it was only a matter of time before they would yield.

Adopting first a budget resolution and then passing a budget-reconciliation bill to implement the GOP's balanced-budget plan took almost all of 1995. Republicans concocted early plans to try to force Clinton into signing their budget bill—knowing he stood prepared to veto it.

The government's authority to borrow money was slated to expire near the end of the year, and Republicans would use the threat of the first-ever default on the national debt—which

Growth of Deficit and Debt

Deficit Rose and Fell...

Deficit as Percentage of GDP

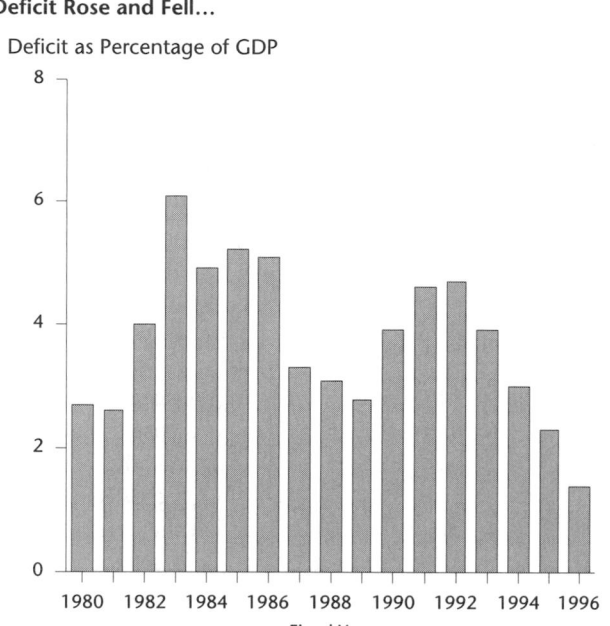

Fiscal Year

...As Debt Rose Steadily

Debt as Percentage of GDP

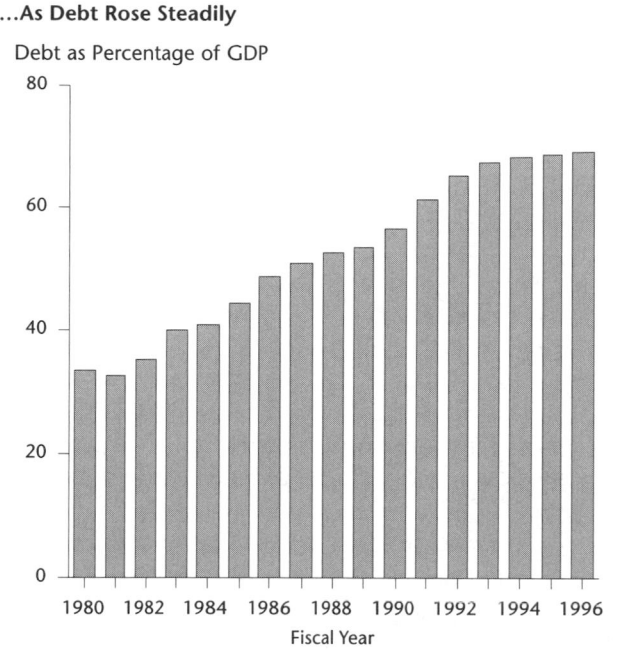

Fiscal Year

The federal deficit responded periodically during the 1980s to efforts to control it. Measured against the performance of the economy as a whole, the deficit rose in the years just after the 1990–1991 recession to 4.7 percent of gross domestic product (GDP). Then, with the economy rebounding and the Clinton administration's budget-cutting efforts having some success, the deficit fell in 1996 to just 1.4 percent of GDP, the lowest it had been in more than 20 years. Meanwhile, the total federal debt (including that portion owed to the Social Security trust funds) rose inexorably—as it would until the government finally balanced its books and began to run surpluses. The debt as a share of the economy more than doubled from about 33 percent of GDP in 1980 to just under 70 percent in 1996.

SOURCE: Office of Management and Budget, *Historical Tables, Budget of the United States Government: Fiscal Year 1998* (Washington, D.C.: U.S. Government Printing Office, 1997), Tables 7.1 and 15.6.

could have devastating effects on financial markets and send interest rates soaring—as leverage to get Clinton to negotiate. The 13 annual appropriations bills might also be withheld, threatening a government shutdown.

"Which of the two of us do you think worries more about the government not showing up?" asked Gingrich, who became House Speaker after the Republican revolution.

Eventually Republicans produced a reconciliation bill that would have reduced Medicare spending by $270 billion, turned Medicaid into a bloc grant program for the states, dramatically overhauled welfare, squeezed $12 billion from farm programs and cut the earned-income tax credit for low-income workers by $32 billion.

The political heat was intense. It had always been easier to attack deficit-reduction packages than to create them and this was no different. Democrats seized on the $270 billion in Medicare cuts and provisions to cut taxes by $245 billion and began their attack: Republicans were slashing Medicare to give tax cuts to the rich.

Meanwhile, the GOP revolution was taking hold in the Appropriations committees, especially in the House, where back-slapping bipartisanship was replaced with budget-cutting fervor and a desire to use the must-pass spending bills as locomotives for policy "riders," such as blocking the Environmental Protection Agency from implementing antipollution laws. This not only created a standoff with Clinton, but also led to intra-party battles that took months to sort out and that delayed all but two of the bills past the Oct. 1 start of fiscal 1996.

All of this built towards a massive collision Nov. 13, when a stopgap spending bill expired. As talks with Clinton went nowhere, and as Treasury Secretary Robert E. Rubin juggled accounts to extend the government's ability to borrow and forestall the need for an increase in the debt limit, Republicans passed a new stopgap spending bill that would have slashed spending on Clinton priorities. Clinton vetoed the measure, calling it blackmail, and a week-long partial shutdown of the government began, sending 800,000 federal workers home.

It was a disaster for the Republicans, but the shutdown ended when Clinton met a key GOP demand to produce a plan to balance the budget in seven years. Another stopgap bill provided time for budget talks between congressional Republicans and the White House. Those talks quickly collapsed, however, amid

Budget Resolution Totals, 1994–1997

(Fiscal years, in billions of dollars)

	1994	1995	1996	1997
Budget Authority	$1,507.1	$1,540.7	$1,591.7	$1,633.3
Outlays	1,495.6	1,513.6	1,587.5	1,622.1
Revenues	1,241.8	1,338.2	1,417.2	1,468.7
Budgeted Deficit	−253.8	−175.4	−170.3	−153.4
Actual Deficit	−203.1	−163.9	−107.3	−22.6

NOTE: For practical purposes, the 1985 Gramm-Rudman antideficit targets (which were revised in 1987 and 1990) no longer applied after 1990. Though overall deficit targets were enacted for fiscal 1994–1995, the 1990 budget reconciliation law (PL 101-508) also created new budget control tools that effectively made the overall targets obsolete.

SOURCES: Congressional budget resolutions; Office of Management and Budget; *Congress and the Nation Vol. VIII.*

bitter recriminations, and, when the temporary spending bill expired Dec. 15, angry Republicans refused to immediately pass another one. A second government shutdown began.

Clinton had vetoed the GOP budget-reconciliation bill on Dec. 7. Eventually it became clear that budget talks between the two parties were futile; it was also apparent that the GOP "train wreck" strategy had backfired badly. Public opinion polls ran 2-1 against Republicans, and many were eager to undo the damage.

A series of stopgap spending bills financed the government until Republicans and Clinton agreed in April 1996 on an omnibus bill to cover the balance of the fiscal year. The frontal attack on the budget by the new GOP majority had been repelled.

THE END GAME

Republicans did manage one significant budgetary victory in 1995-96—enactment of a line-item veto of sorts, long a marquee item on the GOP agenda.

Republicans had always viewed the veto, which would allow presidents to strike individual spending items from appropriations bills without killing the entire measure, as a way for Republican presidents to curb free-spending Democratic Congresses.

Confronted with a Democratic president, however, Republican congressional leaders passed a bill to implement a line-item veto anyway. Passage came only after difficult internal struggles and only after Clinton agreed to delay its effective date to Jan. 1, 1997.

What Republicans could not achieve in their first two years in control of both Houses of Congress—getting Clinton to sign a balanced budget into law on their term—did not mean their efforts had completely failed. In fact, the budget debate had shifted in their direction.

When Clinton submitted the final budget request of his first term in March 1996, he promised a balanced budget by 2002—including almost $100 billion in tax cuts, significant Medicare savings and cuts in discretionary spending.

In many ways it was a campaign document that sought to highlight differences with Republicans. But at the same time, it represented a remarkable break for a sitting Democratic president. It was the first balanced budget submitted in a generation—even if it was looking out over seven years. But in the bitter aftermath of the 1995 budget war and with a tough campaign for Congress and the White House ahead, Republicans rejected the document as a Trojan horse.

As Clinton's first term ended and as he looked forward to a second, conditions were ripe for a historic budget that would actually achieve the balanced-budget promise that had eluded politicians since 1969.

Deficit-reduction bills enacted in 1990 and 1993 had brought the deficit within reach, and the political wars had shifted the debate. The question was no longer whether to balance the budget, but how.

Chronology of Action on Budget Policy

1993–1994

After a six-month process that sometimes resembled a legislative high-wire act, President Clinton won a narrow victory on the fiscal 1994 budget with the aid of his Democratic allies in Congress. The result was the cornerstone of his economic agenda—a deficit-reduction plan that aimed to slice almost $500 billion from the budget deficit over five years.

The tax-heavy plan ensured no Republican support and required a rare tie-breaking vote by Vice President Al Gore to send the deficit-cutting, budget reconciliation bill to the White House for Clinton's signature. A single additional "no" vote would have killed the bill in the House.

Upon entering the White House, Clinton was immediately faced with unexpectedly gloomy deficit projections, and he responded with an economic plan that scrapped election-year promises of tax cuts and instead made taming the widening deficit his top priority.

It was a move fraught with political risk. The country was slowly emerging from a recession and the new tax levies and spending cuts threatened to slow the recovery. But Clinton opted to cut the deficit in the hope that it would keep interest rates and inflation low.

The success of the early 1993 deficit-reduction effort offset Clinton's failure to win enactment of his priorities for spending "investments"—as opposition overwhelmed his proposals in the Senate.

On the other hand, deficit hawks emboldened by their success in early 1993 failed to rally sufficient support for deeper cuts in appropriations later in the year or in the following year. As a result, the fiscal 1995 budget cycle was tame by the standard set the year before.

Fiscal 1994 Budget Resolution

Barely two months into President Clinton's first year, Congress embraced the bulk of his ambitious, five-year deficit-reduction package, adopting a $1.5 trillion budget resolution for fiscal 1994 (H Con Res 64) that called for cutting almost $500 billion from expected federal deficits over five years.

The budget resolution's biggest departure from Clinton's budget request was an additional $50 billion in spending cuts over the period, reflecting conservative pressure for taking a bigger bite out of the deficit.

The budget resolution, a congressional blueprint that did not go to the president for his signature, simply provided the broad guidelines for tax and spending decisions. Controversial details, such as how and whether to adopt an energy tax, were left for a later budget reconciliation bill. (*Fiscal 1994 budget reconciliation, p. 44*)

By administration accounting, the $496 billion in assumed deficit reduction was almost evenly divided between tax increases and spending cuts, though Republicans and even some Democrats argued that a more accurate accounting showed that the plan actually tilted heavily toward higher taxes.

Republicans counted themselves out of the debate at the outset, charging that the plan was far too heavy on taxes and too light on spending cuts. Not a single Republican in either chamber voted for the budget resolution in committee or on the floor. That forced Democrats to get the votes solely from their party, which gave moderate and conservative Democrats leverage to force deeper spending cuts into the package.

Final approval—the House adopted the conference report on H Con Res 64 on March 31 and the Senate followed suit April 1—marked the first time since the 1974 Congressional Budget Act became law that Congress had met the law's April 15 deadline for producing a budget.

The budget resolution bound Congress to reduce the anticipated deficit in two ways:

• **Appropriations.** About a third of the deficit cuts were assigned to the appropriators, who were required to hold discretionary spending to an overall limit for fiscal 1994 that was about $12 billion below the amount of budget authority available under the budget caps set in 1990.

• **Taxes, Entitlements.** The other two-thirds—$343 billion out of the $496 billion—was slated to come from the budget reconciliation bill, a massive measure rolling together hundreds of changes in taxes and entitlement programs (Medicare, Social Security, food stamps and the like) to "reconcile" them with deficit-reduction requirements in the budget resolution.

The budget resolution contained instructions requiring 13 tax-writing and authorizing committees in the House and 12 in the Senate to come up with the necessary savings. Committees could ignore specific directions about how to achieve the savings, but they had to meet the deficit-reduction targets set in the resolution.

Democratic leaders had expected the budget resolution to be the second stage in the process of enacting Clinton's economic package. The first was to be a supplemental appropriations bill aimed at creating jobs and stimulating the economy. But an outcry, particularly from conservative Democrats who were determined to vote first on spending cuts, forced the leadership to call a vote first on the budget resolution. The core of the supplemental died under withering Senate opposition. (*Fiscal 1994 appropriations, p. 56*)

BACKGROUND

Clinton's budgetary task was complicated from the start by the revelation that the expected budget deficit in coming years was bigger than originally thought.

On Jan. 6, 1993, outgoing President George Bush had sent Congress what was described as a "plain vanilla" fiscal 1994 budget. Devoid of policy prescriptions, the document showed what the budget for the next five years would be if existing tax and spending policies remained unchanged. But tucked away in the document were several time bombs for the incoming Clinton administration, the most significant of which was a sharp increase in the projected deficit for fiscal 1994–1997.

The baseline budget, prepared by the Office of Management and Budget (OMB), showed $1.5 trillion in outlays and $1.2 trillion in receipts in fiscal 1994, leaving a projected deficit of $292.4 billion.

Bush White House budget director Richard G. Darman insisted that the budget was a neutral benchmark exercise that was intended to be "helpful" to the incoming administration. But some Democrats painted it as proof that Darman could not resist manipulating the numbers one more time, just to make life difficult for them.

At issue were Darman's 1994–1997 deficit projections, which were much worse than what OMB had forecast the previous summer in the middle of the presidential campaign. Of particular concern to Democrats were Darman's estimates for fiscal 1997, which provided a critical benchmark for a Clinton campaign pledge to cut the deficit in half by the end of his first term.

In July 1992, OMB projected a 1997 deficit of $237 billion; the January 1993 Bush budget figures raised that to $305 billion.

Democrats, including Clinton, insisted the real number was higher yet—as much as $350 billion to $360 billion—due in part to a controversial assumption by Darman that appropriated spending would be frozen after 1995.

Senate Armed Services Committee Chairman Sam Nunn, D-Ga., said the Bush budget underestimated the cost of existing defense programs by a cumulative $50 billion, which meant that the actual deficit would be higher still.

Cutting a 1997 deficit of $360 billion in half would require putting the budget on a fiscal diet radical enough to produce savings of about $180 billion in the fourth year. To get a reduction that big that quickly, spending cuts or revenue increases had to start almost immediately.

CLINTON'S ECONOMIC PLAN

Clinton outlined his economic proposals to a joint session of Congress on Feb. 17, laying out a plan that included deep spending cuts but relied overwhelmingly on tax increases to bring the budget closer to balance. As he promised in his presidential campaign, Clinton proposed sharp new levies on the wealthy, but he also asked middle-income taxpayers and Social Security beneficiaries to shoulder part of the load. Clinton also proposed to boost short-term job creation by pumping billions of dollars in new spending into a wide range of infrastructure, education, health and local development programs.

The Clinton plan received a big political boost when Federal Reserve Board Chairman Alan Greenspan, a Republican, strongly endorsed its outlines.

Clinton's budget-cutting plan was the largest in history, proposing to save $704 billion over five years—$200 billion more than the 1990 budget summit agreement was supposed to save over the same number of years. Of that amount, however, only two-thirds was intended for reducing the deficit; the other third was to be used to pay for increased job creation and long-term investment spending. Net deficit reduction at the end of five years was estimated to be about $473 billion.

At its heart was a five-year proposal to raise $357 billion in new taxes, chiefly by increasing the top rates for individuals and

businesses, imposing a broad new tax on energy, uncapping the Medicare payroll tax and increasing the tax bite on better-off Social Security beneficiaries.

Overall, Clinton's plan included three distinct pieces, only one of which focused on the deficit:

• **Stimulus Package.** This jobs-creation plan involved more than $30 billion, split between $16.3 billion in spending, roughly $12 billion in business tax incentives, and other funds in the form of loans and construction obligation authority.

• **'Investment' Spending.** Clinton proposed more than $230 billion over five years for a combination of spending programs and tax breaks designed to continue stimulating business investment and simultaneously correct an "investment deficit" that Clinton argued had shortchanged infrastructure, education, child care, job training and health care spending over the previous decade.

Key items included $69 billion for spending on infrastructure, environment, housing and technology; $56 billion for education, job training, child nutrition and preschool programs and efforts to convert from a defense-oriented to a peacetime economy; $32 billion to extend unemployment benefits, expand the earned-income tax credit for low-income workers and combat crime; $36 billion for a variety of health, drug treatment and nutrition initiatives; and $28 billion in tax cuts and other incentives for business.

• **Deficit Reduction.** Clinton proposed to cut $704 billion over five years, $375 billion of it coming from spending cuts and $328 billion from tax increases, almost a 1-to-1 ratio. That was much less than the 2-to-1 ratio of spending cuts to taxes advocated by Clinton's budget director Leon E. Panetta (previously a House Democrat from California and Budget Committee chairman) during his Senate confirmation hearings in January.

Clinton chose to cut defense by $112 billion over five years. He elected to save even more than that—about $144 billion over five years—from entitlement programs, including the controversial $29 billion tax increase on Social Security beneficiaries. The entitlement savings also included substantial trims in Medicare, much of it from payments to doctors.

The smallest contribution—$73 billion in cuts over five years—came from a wide range of nondefense programs, an area that Democrats argued had been hard hit during successive Republican administrations.

BUDGET RESOLUTION

After presenting the broad outlines of his economic program in February, Clinton filled in the details April 8 when he sent the House and Senate a $1.52 trillion budget proposal for fiscal 1994. Much of the plan was already known before its release and Congress in the meantime had already completed action on H Con Res 64, the budget resolution which generally followed Clinton's February outline.

Clinton's five-year budget request provided about $678 billion in gross deficit cuts, sharply reducing defense spending, making more modest cuts in domestic spending and levying huge new taxes, much of them on upper-income Americans and corporations.

At the same time, the president proposed spending about a third of those savings—roughly $230 billion—on a variety of new spending and tax-relief initiatives, including wide-ranging "investment" spending.

Clinton's request for $1.52 trillion in outlays, or actual spending, was up just 3.3 percent from 1993, or about the rate of inflation. (The request was for $1,517.2 billion in budget authority, which translated into $1,513.3 billion in outlays.) The budget anticipated revenues of $1.25 trillion, a 9.2 percent increase, reflecting the effect of Clinton's proposed tax increases. The 1994 deficit was pegged at $264.1 billion, down sharply from what was expected to be a record-setting 1993 deficit of $322 billion. Altogether, Clinton proposed to cut the deficit by a net $447.5 billion over five years, down from the $473 billion in deficit reduction projected in his February budget plan.

The arrival of the president's detailed budget proposal a week after Congress completed work on the budget resolution stood the usual procedure on its head. Usually, the president would have delivered his full budget proposal in early February.

But in early February, Clinton had been in office barely two weeks, hardly long enough to work up the enormously detailed document he finally delivered.

Meanwhile, Congress had accelerated its usual budget schedule to get a quick vote on the budget resolution and its promise of broad deficit reduction before turning to Clinton's controversial stimulus spending plan.

Both Clinton's budget and the congressional budget resolution were designed to produce the smallest deficit in fiscal 1997, bringing Clinton close to his campaign promise of cutting the deficit in half in four years. Projections showed the deficit climbing sharply again after that year, driven largely by the increasing costs of the twin health care entitlements, Medicare and Medicaid, and by the rising costs of interest on the nation's accumulated debt.

The White House based its budget proposal on a relatively conservative economic forecast developed by the Congressional Budget Office (CBO), which projected 3.0 percent growth in inflation-adjusted gross domestic product in 1994, slowing to 1.8 percent in 1998, unemployment falling from 7.3 percent in the fourth quarter of 1992 to 5.7 percent in the fourth quarter of 1998, and inflation falling from 2.5 percent in 1993 to 2.2 percent in 1997.

HOUSE ACTION

Rigid Democratic Party discipline rolled over united Republican opposition in back-to-back markup sessions March 10–11 that saw the House and Senate Budget committees approve slightly different versions of a budget resolution on straight party-line votes.

In the House, the Budget Committee voted 27–16 to approve H Con Res 64 (H Rept 103-31) on March 10, after committee leaders added about $63 billion in additional spending cuts to mollify conservative Democrats. All but $8 billion was to come from appropriations. Overall, the measure provided for $510 billion in deficit reduction over five years.

The unity shown by Budget Committee Democrats—they blocked every GOP attempt to make significant changes to the basic Clinton plan—was a departure from the party's liberal-conservative split of recent years.

On March 18, H Con Res 64 came to the House floor, where Democrats steamrollered Republicans and dissenters in their own party, adopting the budget resolution on a largely party-line **key vote of 243–183 (R 0–172, D 242–11, I 1–0).** *(1993 key votes, p. 979)*

Republicans, at the short end of the House's 255–175 Democratic majority, were divided over how best to counter the Clinton juggernaut. With the Democrats enforcing a rule that any substitute had to present detailed cuts, some Republicans worried that a GOP plan would take the focus off Clinton's proposals and make Republicans vulnerable to the same criticism over specifics that they were giving the Democrats. But other Republicans were convinced that they would have no credibility if they did not respond in kind. Neither of the two alternatives that Republicans were allowed to offer won unanimous GOP support.

Top Budget Committee Republican John R. Kasich of Ohio had drafted a detailed package of spending cuts to match Clinton's roughly $500 million in deficit reduction, though with no tax increases. The five-year proposal contained nearly 160 specific cuts, many of them in areas so sensitive—Medicare, veterans' benefits and federal employees' COLAs, for instance—that some Republicans were afraid to go along. The measure failed on a 135–295 vote.

SENATE ACTION

On the other side of the Capitol, the Senate Budget Committee voted 12–9 on March 11 to adopt that panel's version of the budget (S Con Res 18—S Rept 103-19). Like the House measure, it contained $63 billion in extra deficit reduction. But Senate Democrats, unlike their House counterparts, relied on tax increases for about a third of the additional deficit reduction. The rest came in spending cuts, including similarly tight limits on discretionary spending through 1998. Senate budget drafters suggested postponing more than $30 billion of Clinton's $144 billion in investment spending until after 1998 to reduce discretionary spending.

As approved by the committee, the Senate measure trimmed the deficit by a net $516 billion over five years. It contained net new taxes of $295 billion.

Although there were complaints, particularly over the recommendation that Congress go along with Clinton's call for an increase in taxes paid by upper-income Social Security recipients and for a broad energy tax, Budget Chairman Jim Sasser, D-Tenn., tranquilized restive Democrats with reminders that the budget resolution was only a blueprint, and that there was still time to modify the plan during consideration of the coming reconciliation bill.

On the Senate floor, Democrats fought off every substantive change Republicans tried to make and adopted their budget resolution (H Con Res 64) on March 25 on a **key vote of 54–45 (R 0–43; D 54–2).** *(1993 key votes, p. 979)*

The wide-open Senate rules gave Republican tacticians an

opportunity to bring rifle-shot amendments designed to put Democrats on the spot on touchy issues. But Democrats stuck together to vote down amendments that would have stripped out the tax increase for better-off Social Security beneficiaries, knocked out most or all of Clinton's spending and tax increases or restored much of the money Clinton wanted to cut from defense. As in the House, Republicans failed to change a single number in the committee's slightly modified version of Clinton's $1.5 trillion budget.

Throughout the six days of floor debate on the measure, 45 roll call votes and enormous lobbying pressure from their leaders and the president himself, other Senate Democrats frequently seemed sorely tempted to go off the reservation, obviously discomfited by carefully targeted Republican amendments.

The pent-up demand among Democrats for changes in the Clinton plan signaled that there was little chance the president's package would continue unscathed as Congress began putting together a reconciliation bill.

FINAL ACTION

Congress gave its final blessing to Clinton's budget blueprint April 1 after House and Senate conferees agreed to drop as much as $20 billion in deficit reduction that had originally been approved by the separate chambers. As cleared, H Con Res 64 proposed to spend $1.5 trillion in fiscal 1994 and cut $496 billion over five years from the deficit were spending and tax policies not to change.

Congress gave final approval to H Con Res 64 with no Republican votes and almost unbroken Democratic support. The House voted to adopt the conference report on March 31 by a vote of 240–184. Twelve Democrats voted against the measure, just one more than opposed the plan when it originally was adopted by the House.

The Senate adopted the conference report on April 1 by a vote of 55–45, with only two Democrats joining GOP senators in opposition: Bob Krueger of Texas and Richard Shelby of Alabama, the same two who opposed the resolution when the Senate first adopted it in March.

The compromise budget emerged from a House-Senate conference that started with two versions that were not that far apart. The main differences arose from the ways in which the two chambers had added slightly more than $60 billion apiece in deficit reduction to the Clinton plan.

Instead of finding a way to work out their differences while keeping roughly the same amount of deficit reduction, conference negotiators dropped or reduced most of the items that separated them and declined to replace the lost deficit savings.

The Senate dropped its $22 billion in additional taxes. The House agreed to split the difference with the Senate on its extra spending cuts. The House also backed away from more than half its extra cuts in mandatory spending, scaling back the COLA cut for federal retirees and replacing it with one that limited COLAs only for retirees under age 62, and only for one year.

In a bid to hold the support of western and farm-state Democrats for the long-haul fight to enact the Clinton plan, negotiators reduced the spending cuts expected from agriculture programs and dropped plans to increase grazing fees and impose a 12.5 percent royalty on hard-rock mining on public lands. ❑

Fiscal 1994 Budget Reconciliation

With President Clinton's political viability at stake and his party's ability to govern after more than a decade in opposition under attack, congressional Democrats assembled a bare majority in 1993 to clear a massive deficit-reduction bill that made hundreds of changes in the tax code and in mandatory programs such as Medicare and farm price supports.

The budget reconciliation bill was designed to bring tax and spending policy into line with deficit-reduction goals in the previously adopted budget resolution (H Con Res 64) and embodied the heart of Clinton's plan to reshape the nation's economic policy. (*Fiscal 1994 budget resolution, p. 41*)

The fiscal 1994 Omnibus Budget Reconciliation Act (HR 2264—PL 103-66) relied heavily on tax increases to reduce the deficit, making it anathema to Republicans and bitter medicine even for Clinton's own party. The House adopted the conference report on the bill Aug. 5 without a single vote to spare; the Senate cleared the bill the next evening with Vice President Al Gore voting to break a tie. Clinton signed it into law Aug. 10.

The bill had its origins in the economic plan Clinton outlined to Congress on Feb. 17. While Clinton got much of what he asked for, House and Senate negotiators forced him to retreat in several areas.

Although estimates varied, the White House announced that the bill met Clinton's goal of $500 billion in deficit reduction over five years. As Clinton had proposed, most of the new tax revenue came from the wealthiest taxpayers, and the spending cuts resulted largely from cutbacks in defense, overall limits on appropriated spending and reductions in the growth of Medicare payments to doctors and hospitals.

But the battle over the bill forced Clinton to give up other major features—most notably, his proposal for a $71.5 billion tax on almost all forms of energy. The bill also contained less spending than Clinton sought for social programs, such as food stamps and the earned-income tax credit, and for "investment" programs that he hoped would stimulate economic growth.

By embracing the plan, if only barely, congressional Democrats bet that deficit reduction would yield lower interest rates, in turn producing jobs and a healthy economy down the road. If the gamble worked, Democrats could hope to get sole credit: they passed the package without a single Republican vote.

For their part, Republicans gambled that the economy and the deficit would head in the opposite direction. By leaving no fingerprints on the bill, Republicans positioned themselves to disclaim any of the blame if their warnings proved accurate—although the GOP also risked forfeiting an opportunity to claim some of the credit should the Democrats' more upbeat vision of the country's economic future prove closer to the truth.

The solid GOP opposition forced Democrats to rely on their own ranks for majorities in both chambers. That turned the process into a family feud between Democrats who wanted additional spending for social programs and those who wanted fewer tax increases and more spending cuts.

As passed, the bill was expected to cut the deficit by $496 billion over five years—$240 billion of it coming from net tax increases and the rest from spending cuts. The White House Office of Management and Budget (OMB) later revised that estimate, pegging the size of the package at $504.8 billion—$250.1 billion in taxes and other revenue increases and $254.7 billion in spending cuts.

Technically, the bill contained only $71.3 billion worth of net savings, including cuts in Medicare and a variety of user fee increases. But OMB also counted savings that it said the bill would leverage indirectly: $107.7 billion from budget enforcement provisions freezing discretionary appropriations for five years, $59.6 billion from lower interest on the debt as a result of smaller deficits, and $16.4 billion from a Treasury plan to refinance some of the national debt at lower interest rates.

BACKGROUND

During the 1992 presidential campaign, Clinton acknowledged the need to cut the federal deficit, though he placed more emphasis on spending to create jobs and stimulate long-term economic growth. By the time he took office, however, the deficit had begun to crowd out other budget issues.

In drafting the bill, Congress started from a detailed White House plan that relied heavily on taxes. According to the Joint Committee on Taxation, Clinton's budget amounted to a net revenue increase of $242.2 billion over five years ($337.5 billion in new taxes offset by $95.3 billion in tax breaks). *(Clinton's fiscal 1994 budget proposal, p. 42; 1993 tax policy changes, p. 93)*

Most of the new revenue in Clinton's plan came from increases in income taxes for the wealthy, including a new fourth income bracket that increased the top marginal rate to 36 percent for couples with taxable income above $140,000 ($115,000 for individuals).

Other key elements of Clinton's tax plan included: an increase (to 85 percent from 50 percent) in the portion of Social Security benefits subject to taxation for wealthier retirees; a broad-based energy tax affecting industry and consumers, based on the heat content or British thermal units (Btu) of most forms of energy; investment tax credits and a lower capital gains rate for investments in small businesses; a $28.3 billion expansion of the earned-income tax credit, a refundable credit available to poor working families; tax incentives and other federal assistance to spur investment and job creation in impoverished communities.

The Clinton plan also included a $48 billion cut in the growth of Medicare, the federal health insurance program for the elderly and disabled, and a $7.8 billion cut in Medicaid, the state-federal health insurance program for the poor.

Clinton came to the task having suffered an early and humbling defeat over the first piece of his economic plan to go to Congress, an economic stimulus bill that failed in the Senate. The defeat left the impression that the administration lacked the ability to appreciate, or perhaps to manage, challenges in the Senate. *(Fiscal 1994 appropriations, p. 56)*

With their numbers giving them limited influence in Congress, Republicans conducted an intense public campaign, focusing on the effects of the energy tax on the middle class and seeking to mobilize the elderly against the proposed tax increase on Social Security benefits.

The job of drafting the bill fell to 13 tax-writing and authorizing committees in the House and 12 in the Senate, whose deficit-reduction marching orders were contained in the budget resolution. The House Ways and Means Committee and the Senate Finance Committee had by far the biggest assignments.

HOUSE ACTION

The House Ways and Means Committee was responsible for drafting the core of the bill—nearly $300 billion in tax and spending changes. The panel approved its portions of the measure on a 24–14 party-line vote May 13, after making several crucial modifications to shore up business and congressional support.

The committee preserved Clinton's proposals for massive income tax increases on wealthy Americans, a broad-based energy tax and higher taxes on upper-income retirees receiving Social Security benefits. But lawmakers cut in half Clinton's proposed increase in the top corporate income tax rate.

The committee legislation included Medicare spending controls that were expected to save $50.4 billion over five years—the largest chunk of the spending savings in the reconciliation bill.

The committee began marking up the bill May 6, but all of the major decisions were hashed out in a series of closed-door meetings between Chairman Dan Rostenkowski, D-Ill., and committee Democrats.

In major changes to the Clinton tax plan, Ways and Means Democrats decided to: raise the top corporate income tax rate from 34 percent to 35 percent, instead of to 36 percent, as Clinton proposed; allow real estate developers and others working full time in the industry to write off losses on rental property ("passive losses") against ordinary income; and repeal luxury taxes on boats, furs, airplanes and jewelry enacted in 1990.

House Floor Action

The House bill (HR 2264—H Rept 103-111) was assembled by the Budget Committee, combining the Ways and Means package with provisions submitted by the 12 other House committees charged with meeting deficit-reduction targets. The Budget Committee approved the bill on a party-line, 26–17 vote on May 20.

Then, with Democrats teetering uneasily between fear of their constituents and fear of abandoning a Democratic president early in his term, Democratic leaders used everything from sweet persuasion to bare knuckles to assemble the slimmest of majorities behind the bill.

The House passed the bill on May 27 by a razor-thin 219–213 vote, enough to avert what would have been a politically devastating loss for the president.

Republicans without exception opposed the plan, but their numbers and their sharp opposition to tax increases made them virtually irrelevant. At the losing end of the House's 256–176

Democrat-to-Republican margin, GOP members could do little more than register their objections.

Altogether, the five-year House bill contained $496 billion in deficit reduction—about $250 billion in tax increases and $87 billion in entitlement cuts, along with $102 billion in cuts in appropriations and $57 billion in reduced interest payments on the national debt.

In trying to secure a majority for the bill, House Democratic leaders were caught squarely between the two wings of their party, squeezed by conservatives who demanded further spending cuts and in some cases smaller tax increases, and liberals who thought the mix in the bill was about right and warned that they would object to any significant change.

Some deficit hawks were brought on board after winning a provision to guarantee a vote on further cuts in entitlements if the measure did not live up to expectation, and several energy-state Democrats who bitterly opposed Clinton's energy tax won assurances that the tax would be changed, either in the Senate or during the House-Senate conference.

SENATE ACTION

Following the House vote, the debate moved to the Senate Finance Committee, where Democrats approved a package of tax increases and spending cuts on June 18 that retained the basic thrust of Clinton's plan.

The committee approved its recommendations for the reconciliation bill on an 11–9 party-line vote, but only after making further cuts in Medicare spending, trimming tax breaks for businesses and the poor and dropping Clinton's unpopular Btu tax in favor of an increase in the tax on gasoline and other fuels.

For Clinton, the details were less important than simply getting the bill out of committee and to the full Senate. With 11 Democrats and nine Republicans on the committee—and no GOP support for the bill—a single Democratic defection would have crippled the measure.

The compromise approved by the Finance Committee was the product of grinding negotiations during which committee Chairman Daniel Patrick Moynihan, D-N.Y., and Majority Leader George J. Mitchell, D-Maine, worked to patch together a bill that included deeper spending cuts and fewer tax increases than either the House version or Clinton's plan.

A defection by David L. Boren, D-Okla., made committee approval of the Btu tax impossible. That, in turn, left a gaping revenue hole and sharp division within the committee over how to fill it. The compromise bill spread the pain broadly enough to unify the 11 Democrats on the committee and hold Boren in line.

In place of Clinton's proposed energy tax, Democrats agreed on a 4.3-cents-per-gallon increase in the tax on gasoline and other transportation fuels. The fuels tax brought in much less revenue ($24.2 billion over five years) compared to the Btu tax ($71.5 billion), leaving hard bargaining over where to find additional revenue and spending cuts so that the bill achieved at least as much deficit reduction as Clinton's original plan.

Democrats reluctantly cut back Clinton's proposals for tax breaks to help businesses, urban areas and the poor. Additional Medicare cuts of $19 billion over five years were added to the $48 billion Medicare cut in Clinton's plan.

Desperate for revenue, the committee made several other changes, including limiting by $10 billion a proposed increase in the earned-income tax credit. Clinton's plan to establish so-called empowerment zones in depressed urban and rural areas was dropped.

Senate Floor Action

As in the House, the Senate's reconciliation bill was assembled in the Budget Committee. The core provisions came from the Finance Committee; however, 11 others contributed to the measure (S 1134) that went to the Senate floor on June 23.

As in the House, Republican support for the bill was nonexistent and there was sufficient Democratic antagonism to leave passage in doubt. After all amendments to S 1134 were disposed of, the vote to pass came on HR 2264, after the language of S 1134 had been substituted for that of the House-passed version of the bill.

When the final vote came shortly after three o'clock in the morning on June 25, and all senators present had voted, the tally was 49–49. It was up to Gore to cast the tie-breaking vote. HR 2264 passed the Senate on a **key vote of 50–49 (R 0–43, D 49–6).** (*1993 key votes, p. 979*)

The deals that had brought a slim majority of House Democrats together in May were not the same as those that eked out the bare win in the Senate. Even as the Senate voted, House members were already threatening to kill the package if they did not get what they originally voted for.

Of the six Democrats voting against the bill, three were up for reelection in 1994: Richard H. Bryan of Nevada, Dennis DeConcini of Arizona and Frank R. Lautenberg of New Jersey, where taxes had become a lightning-rod issue. The others were J. Bennett Johnston of Louisiana, Sam Nunn of Georgia and Richard C. Shelby of Alabama.

Forced to rely solely on their party in the face of virtually lock-step Republican opposition, Democratic leaders gave up only $17 billion in deficit reduction to buy allegiance from potential renegades, which was regarded as a significant victory. Republicans repeatedly denounced the measure as a job-killer, insisting the tax increases would further weaken an already staggering economy.

Save for a $2.3 billion exemption that protected the troubled airline industry from the transportation fuels tax, a change Democrats supported strongly enough to accept on a voice vote, Republicans failed to make a single significant change in the bill.

The most significant amendment came from liberal Democrats upset with the $19 billion in extra Medicare cuts approved by the Finance Committee. An amendment by Jay Rockefeller, D-W.Va., to reduce the Medicare cuts by $10 billion to $58 billion prompted Tom Harkin, D-Iowa, and others to declare support for the package.

CONFERENCE, FINAL ACTION

Conferees gathered July 15 to begin the arduous task of crafting a compromise bill. To succeed, they had to satisfy two chambers that had passed separate deficit-reduction bills by the barest of margins, found each other's legislation unacceptable and probably would have had trouble passing their own bills a second time.

After an initial, public meeting, the real work began behind closed doors. Scores of senior lawmakers broke into subgroups to work on sections of the massive package. But most of the hard bargaining on taxes and spending was done by Mitchell, Moynihan and Rostenkowski.

The conflicting priorities that had brought the bill close to defeat in the House and Senate were magnified in the conference, which produced a final version of the bill (H Rept 103-213) on Aug. 2.

The pivotal question for the leadership was what form of energy tax to impose and how much revenue it would raise. The far more lucrative House-passed Btu tax was dead, and the main option for replacing much of the lost revenue—a 36 percent top corporate tax rate—was settled in favor of the House's 35 percent rate. Conferees adopted the Senate plan for a 4.3-cents-a-gallon increase in the fuels tax.

In addition, the conference restored some of the extra Medicare cuts approved by the Senate; adopted Clinton's proposal to increase taxes on Social Security benefits for upper-income retirees; accepted the new 35 percent top corporate tax rate; scaled back Clinton's empowerment zone proposal; and expanded both the earned-income tax credit for low-income families and the food stamp program.

With the changes, conferees appeared to fall just short of Clinton's $500 billion deficit reduction goal, though Democrats said the bill cut the deficit by $496 billion over five years. That was virtually the same as the five-year deficit-reduction plan approved in 1990. (*Congress and the Nation Vol. VIII, p. 55*)

Final House Action

Plainly worried and reluctant to take the leap, the House voted on Aug. 5 to adopt the conference report on a **key vote of 218–216 (R 0–175, D 217–41, I 1–0).** With every Republican again voting no, one more Democratic defection would have killed the bill. (*1993 key votes, p. 979*)

In a last-minute effort to win over wavering moderate and conservative Democrats, congressional leaders and Clinton agreed to give Congress another crack at cutting spending. Clinton promised that in the fall he would send Congress a bill to cut fiscal 1994 appropriations further. (*Fiscal 1994 rescissions, p. 59*)

Despite the deal-cutting, by late in the day Aug. 5, vote-counters in the House were still coming up short. The tally seesawed back and forth, but finally freshman Marjorie Margolies-Mezvinsky, D-Pa., and Pat Williams, D-Mont., stepped forward to provide the crucial votes.

Final Senate Action

Twenty-four hours later in the Senate, once more Gore had to break a tie. The conference report was adopted and the bill was cleared on a vote of 51–50.

An air of uncertainty hung over the chamber until shortly before the final balloting. Bob Kerrey, D-Neb., who had voted yes when the Senate passed the bill in June, had criticized the final measure and declined throughout the day to reveal his intentions. When he finally announced his decision to vote yes, a hushed chamber hung on his every word.

Speaking into the TV cameras and directly to Clinton, Kerrey said, "I could not and should not cast the vote that brings down your presidency." Kerrey said the bill "challenges America too little," and he derided the notion that the 4.3-cents-a-gallon gasoline tax increase would hurt the middle class. "If they notice, I'll be surprised; if they complain, I'll be ashamed," he said.

As expected six Democrats voted against the bill: Boren, Bryan, Johnston, Lautenberg, Nunn and Shelby. Boren, whose resistance helped force major changes in the bill when it first came to the Senate, had announced Aug. 1 that he would vote no. That meant that to win enactment, leaders had to convert one of the six Democrats who voted against the bill in June.

Strategists focused on DeConcini as the most likely candidate to save the bill. After four days of feverish wooing from party leaders and Clinton himself, DeConcini finally announced on Aug. 4 his switch from no to yes.

MAJOR PROVISIONS

By White House accounting, the 1993 Omnibus Budget Reconciliation Act (HR 2264—PL 103-66) was to cut the deficit by $504.8 billion in fiscal 1994–1998. It included $250.1 billion in net revenue increases and $254.7 billion in spending cuts. (*Agriculture provisions, p. 486; student loan provisions, p. 626; communications provisions, p. 356; revenue provisions, p. 90; empowerment zones provisions, p. 639*)

As cleared, the bill:

Banking and Housing

- **Depositor Preference.** Required the Federal Deposit Insurance Corporation (FDIC) and the Resolution Trust Corporation (RTC) to give preference to depositors over general creditors and shareholders when they were distributing assets from failed banks or thrifts that had been taken into receivership. The provision increased the amount of money that the FDIC and RTC—which stood in for insured depositors—recovered from failed institutions. Existing law gave the FDIC and the RTC, uninsured depositors and general creditors equal rights.

- **Federal Reserve Surplus.** Required the Federal Reserve to transfer $213 million from its surplus account to the Treasury in 1997–1998.

- **IRS Income Check.** Authorized the Department of Housing and Urban Development (HUD) to use IRS income data to verify applicants' and participants' eligibility for rental assistance programs.

- **REMIC Guarantee Fees.** Authorized the Government National Mortgage Association (Ginnie Mae) to charge guarantee fees on a new class of mortgage-backed securities known as real estate mortgage investment conduits (REMICs). The provision allowed Ginnie Mae to charge a slightly higher annual fee for guaranteeing mortgage-backed securities. The existing limit was the equivalent of 6/100 of one percent of the value of the securities.

• **FHA Premium Refunds.** Required the Federal Housing Administration (FHA) to speed up amortization of mortgage insurance premiums. Under existing law, homeowners paid an upfront premium for mortgages insured by the FHA. If they paid off the mortgage before it came due, they received a partial refund (the portion of the premium that the FHA had not yet earned). The provision accelerated the rate at which HUD earned the premium payment and limited the time frame for premium refunds to seven years.

Employee Benefits

• **ERISA Provisions.** Added several new standards for group health plans governed by the Employee Retirement Income Security Act (ERISA). Federal courts had interpreted ERISA as preempting state laws concerning employee benefits; the bill specified that private group health plans had to comply with state laws requiring them to reimburse the states in cases in which Medicaid was the primary payer but should have acted as a secondary payer because the beneficiary also was covered by a private insurer.

The bill also required group health plans to extend coverage to a child in a case where a parent was required to provide medical child support and required group health plans that covered dependent children to extend coverage to adopted children even if the adoption was not final.

Recreation Fees

• **Admission Fees.** Allowed the Interior and Agriculture secretaries to levy entrance fees at conservation and recreation areas, national monuments, scenic areas and 21 other areas the Agriculture Department managed for outdoor recreation.

• **Golden Age Passports.** Assessed a one-time fee of $10 for "golden age passports" for those 65 or older. The passports allowed holders unlimited entrance to national parks for one year.

• **Recreation User Fees.** Allowed the Interior and Agriculture secretaries to charge visitors for use of such facilities as swimming pools, boat ramps and parking lots at recreation areas the departments managed.

• **Collection Costs.** Permitted the Interior and Agriculture secretaries to keep 15 percent of the cost of collecting recreation or admission fees. The National Park Service collected about $9 million in fees each year, and the Forest Service collected about $2 million.

• **Commercial Tours.** Charged commercial tour companies entrance fees at national parks. Tour vehicles with capacities of up to 25 people were to be charged $25 per vehicle, and those with capacities of 26 people or more were to be charged $50 a vehicle. The fees applied to aircraft used for commercial tours that flew over the Grand Canyon National Park in Arizona, the Haleakala Volcanoes National Park in Hawaii and other national parks that had such tour activities.

• **Golden Eagle Passports.** Allowed businesses, nonprofit groups and other private organizations to sell annual passes to national parks for $25 per person. Such organizations could retain 8 percent of the gross receipts. The Interior and Agriculture

departments were to use the remaining 92 percent of the receipts to pay for resource protection, rehabilitation and conservation projects.

Mining, Mineral Receipts

• **Maintenance Fees.** Extended a $100 fee in fiscal 1994–1998 for maintaining claims to mine such hard-rock minerals as silver and gold from federal lands.

• **Location Fees.** Levied a $25 location fee for new hard-rock mining claims in fiscal 1994–1998.

• **Adjustments.** Directed the Interior secretary to adjust maintenance fees at least every five years. The adjustment was based on the Consumer Price Index, which measured shifts in the retail prices of a set marketbasket of goods and services.

• **Administrative Costs.** Doubled to 50 percent the states' share of the administrative cost of collecting royalties from the onshore mineral leasing program. The change was expected to generate $174 million over five years.

Government Workers

• **Cost of Living Adjustments.** Delayed cost of living adjustments (COLAs) for civilian federal retirees until March 1 in fiscal years 1994, 1995 and 1996. Under existing law, COLAs were effective Dec. 1 of each year.

• **Lump-Sum Retirement Payments.** Prohibited civilian federal retirees, including former State Department and Central Intelligence Agency officials, from taking their retirement benefits in lump-sum payments as of Oct. 1, 1994. Employees with a life-threatening affliction or other critical medical condition could still get a lump-sum payment.

• **Limitation on Physician Fees.** Limited fees for physician and outpatient care for select retirees. Affected were the 220,000 retirees 65 and older who did not participate in the optional portion of Medicare (Medicare Part B) but who were covered by the Federal Employees' Health Benefits Program, the nation's largest health insurance program.

• **Replenishing Civil Service Retirement and Disability Fund.** Required the Postal Service to pay, over fiscal years 1996–1998, $693 million into the Civil Service Retirement and Disability Fund. The Postal Service was required to pay another $348 million into the Employees' Health Benefits Fund. The payments represented what the Postal Service owed for past retiree cost of living adjustments and health benefits.

• **Military Retirees' COLA Delay.** Delayed the annual COLA payments to nondisabled military retirees in 1994–1998. The 1994 COLA was delayed until April 1. COLAs in 1995, 1996, 1997 and 1998 were to be paid Oct. 1. Under existing law, COLAs were paid on Jan. 1 of each year.

Veterans Affairs

• **Copayments for Health Care Benefits.** Extended for one year, to Sept. 30, 1998, a requirement that veterans other than those who were poor or who had major service-connected disabilities pay the Department of Veterans Affairs (VA) $2 for each 30-day supply of medication furnished on an outpatient basis. This requirement was due to expire Sept. 30, 1997.

- **Medical Care Cost Recovery.** Extended until Sept. 30, 1998, the VA's authority to bill private insurers for the reasonable cost of treating veterans for nonservice-connected disabilities. This authority was due to expire Aug. 1, 1994.

- **Pension Limitations.** Extended until Sept. 30, 1998, a $90-per-month limit of the need-based pension paid to veterans and surviving spouses with no dependents who were in nursing homes that participated in the Medicaid program. This authority would have expired Sept. 30, 1997.

- **Defaults on VA-Guaranteed Home Loans.** Extended until Sept. 30, 1998, a provision that allowed the VA to choose the less expensive of two options when a lender foreclosed on a VA-guaranteed mortgage: acquiring and reselling the property or simply paying the amount of the loan that was guaranteed. The authority for this procedure, which saved money, would have expired Oct. 1, 1993.

- **Loan Origination Fees.** Increased the fee charged to most veterans who obtained low-interest VA-guaranteed home mortgages. The existing fee was 1.25 percent of the amount of the loan; it was to increase to 2 percent for loans closed between Oct. 1, 1993, and Sept. 30, 1998. Veterans who previously obtained guaranteed home loans would pay a 3 percent fee for any additional VA-guaranteed loans closed in the same period.

- **COLA Adjustment in Compensation Rates.** Provided that beginning with the cost of living adjustment (COLA) for compensation to disabled veterans and survivors for fiscal 1994, the VA would round monthly payments down to the nearest dollar.

- **Parity in Rates of DIC Benefits.** Sought to create parity in rates for dependency and indemnity compensation (DIC) to surviving spouses and children of veterans who died from service-related causes. Before the enactment of changes in 1992, survivors received benefits based on the rank of the deceased veteran. Under the new law, most survivors of veterans dying Jan. 1, 1993, or after received the same amount—$750 per month—regardless of the rank of the deceased. "Old law" DIC beneficiaries would have their fiscal 1994 COLA halved. "New law" beneficiaries would receive the full COLA, bringing their monthly payments up to $772 per month in fiscal 1994. No DIC beneficiaries, regardless of the date of a veteran's death, would receive less than $772 per month.

- **COLA Limitation for Montgomery GI Bill Benefits.** Eliminated the fiscal 1994 COLA in higher education assistance provided under the Montgomery GI Bill. The COLA was halved for fiscal 1995.

Medicare

- **Hospital Payments/Payment Updates.** Adjusted annual inflation increases for hospitals under Medicare's Prospective Payment System as follows:
  - Urban hospitals in fiscal 1994 and 1995 would receive increases equal to the percentage increase in the "marketbasket" (a measure of goods and services purchased by hospitals) minus 2.5 percentage points. The fiscal 1994 marketbasket increase was 4.2 percent, so beginning Oct. 1, 1993, urban hospitals were to receive inflation increases of 1.7 percent.
  - Rural hospitals, scheduled to receive increases of 6.7 percent in fiscal 1994 (marketbasket plus 1.5 percentage points), were to be subject to a 1 percentage point cut, for a total update of 5.7 percent.
  - Both urban and rural hospitals were to receive updates in fiscal 1996 that were equal to the marketbasket amount minus 2 percentage points. In fiscal 1997 the update would be marketbasket minus 0.5 of a percentage point, and in fiscal 1998 hospitals would receive the full marketbasket update.
  - Specially designated sole community hospitals and Medicare-dependent small rural hospitals (which had been receiving specially augmented rates) were to receive updates of marketbasket minus 2.3 percent in fiscal 1994 and marketbasket minus 2.2 percent in fiscal 1995. Beginning in fiscal 1996, these hospitals were scheduled to receive the same rate of increase as other hospitals.
  - Hospitals exempt from Medicare's Prospective Payment System (including children's hospitals, psychiatric hospitals, rehabilitation hospitals and cancer treatment centers) were to receive increases of the marketbasket percentage minus 1 percentage point for each of fiscal 1994 through 1997 and the full marketbasket update in fiscal 1998. No reduction was to be applied to hospitals whose operating costs exceeded a preset limit in fiscal 1990 by 10 percent or more.

- **Hospital Payments/Capital Costs.** Beginning in fiscal 1994, reduced by 7.4 percent payments to hospitals for capital-related costs (including depreciation, leases and rentals, interest and property taxes). The existing 10 percent reduction was set to expire at the end of fiscal 1995. Medicare capital payments were in the second year of a 10-year phase-in to be fully included in the Prospective Payment System.

- **Hospice Payments.** Increased payment rates for hospice services by the hospital marketbasket increase minus 2 percentage points in fiscal 1994, by marketbasket minus 1.5 percentage points in fiscal 1995 and 1996, by marketbasket minus 0.5 of a percentage point in fiscal 1997 and by the full marketbasket rate in fiscal 1998.

- **Skilled Nursing Facility Payments.** Delayed inflation updates for skilled nursing facilities until fiscal 1996. Beginning Oct. 1, 1993, special payments for "return on equity" for private nursing homes would be eliminated. (Similar payments for hospitals were phased out in the mid-1980s.) The bill also eliminated special payments for excess overhead costs for hospital-based facilities, beginning Oct. 1, 1993.

- **Medicare Hospital Payments/Regional Referral Centers.** Reinstated through Sept. 30, 1994, the 180 large rural hospitals that were designated as regional referral centers as of Sept. 30, 1992. Referral centers were paid at a higher rate than other rural hospitals. The provision also made the facilities eligible for back payments.

- **Medicare Hospital Payments/Small Rural Medicare-Dependent Hospitals.** Continued through fiscal 1994 special payments, on a phased-down basis, for certain small rural hospitals whose caseloads were at least 60 percent Medicare patients.

• **Medicare Hospital Payments/Regional Floor.** Extended through fiscal 1996 a special payment adjustment for hospitals in areas of the country with costs higher than the national average.

• **Part A Premium.** Reduced the premium charged to people 65 and older who did not qualify for Part A benefits but wanted to purchase Part A coverage. The premium was based on the actuarial value of Part A benefits ($221 monthly in 1993). It was to be reduced, on a phased-in basis, for people with credits for 30 or more quarters of taxes paid into the Social Security system and for surviving or divorced spouses of those people. The premium was to be reduced by 25 percent in calendar 1994, and by 45 percent in 1998 and thereafter.

• **Physician Fees: Payment Update.** Reduced the scheduled inflation adjustment in Medicare fees for physician services in fiscal 1994 and 1995. Under the Medicare fee schedule enacted in 1989, physician payments had to be adjusted each year for inflation and for the amount by which all physicians exceeded or failed to reach an aggregate target for the volume of services provided to Medicare beneficiaries.

Because physicians remained far below the volume targets in 1992, under the formula 1994 fees for surgical services would have risen by 12.2 percent, while fees for all other services would have risen by 6.6 percent. Instead, fee increases in 1994 were to be reduced by 3.6 percentage points for surgical services (resulting in an increase of 8.6 percent) and by 2.6 percentage points for all other services except primary care (resulting in an increase of the full 6.6 percent for primary care and 4 percent for all other services.) For 1995, increases for all services except primary care were to be reduced by 2.7 percentage points. Primary care services were to receive the full scheduled update.

• **Physician Fees: Primary Care, Anesthesia Services.** Beginning in fiscal 1994, put primary care in a separate category for the purpose of determining annual increases in physician fees; anesthesia services were put in the surgical services category.

• **Physician Fees: Practice Expenses.** Gradually reduced payments from 1994 to 1997 for the practice expense (overhead) component used to determine fees for individual physician services.

• **Physician Fees: Anesthesia Teams.** Gradually reduced payments to anesthesia care teams (a physician anesthesiologist supervising one or more certified registered nurse anesthetists) so that by 1998, payments to teams would not exceed those that would be made to an anesthesiologist practicing alone in the same locality.

• **Physician Fees: EKG Interpretations.** Repealed a provision of the 1990 reconciliation bill that prohibited separate payments for interpretation of routine electrocardiograms (EKGs) in conjunction with an office visit or consultation. The bill required the Health and Human Services (HHS) secretary to establish fee schedule amounts for such interpretations.

• **Physician Fees: New Physicians.** Repealed provisions in the 1987 and 1990 reconciliation bills that reduced fees for physicians in their first four years of practice.

• **Payment for Allergy Antigens.** Beginning Jan. 1, 1995, provided that payment for antigens used in allergy treatment and related services be made under the Medicare physician fee schedule.

• **Outpatient Hospital Services.** Extended through fiscal 1998 the 10 percent reduction in Medicare payments for capital-related hospital outpatient costs. The reductions were set to expire at the end of fiscal 1995. Sole community hospitals and primary care hospitals remained exempt from the cuts. The bill also continued through fiscal 1998 the 5.8 percent reduction in operating costs payments for hospital outpatient services.

• **Ambulatory Surgical Centers.** Froze the level of fees paid to ambulatory surgical centers for fiscal 1994 and 1995.

• **Intraocular Lenses.** Beginning Jan. 1, 1994, reduced the $200 maximum payment for intraocular lenses used in cataract surgery to $150. The limit was to expire on Jan. 1, 1999.

• **Laboratory Services.** Froze most Medicare payments for laboratory fees for fiscal 1994 and 1995. Beginning in fiscal 1994, the maximum fee was to drop from 88 percent of the national median amount to 76 percent over three years.

• **Durable Medical Equipment.** Set national payment limits for durable medical equipment based on the median of local payment amounts, similar to the limits for laboratory services *(see above)*. For fiscal 1994 and 1995, the bill froze payment levels for orthotics and prosthetics and enteral and parenteral supplies. Payments for transcutaneous electrical nerve stimulation (TENS) devices were reduced by an additional 30 percent.

• **Alzheimer's Demonstration Projects.** Reauthorized for one additional year demonstration projects to provide comprehensive services to Medicare beneficiaries with Alzheimer's disease.

• **Cancer Drugs.** Beginning Jan. 1, 1994, extended Medicare coverage to oral cancer drugs if they were the same chemical entity as anticancer drugs that were covered by Medicare when they were administered intravenously. (Generally, Medicare did not pay for drugs that can be self-administered.) The bill also extended Medicare coverage to off-label uses of anticancer drugs (uses other than those for which a drug originally was approved) in certain specific circumstances.

• **Municipal Health Service Demonstration Projects.** Extended through 1997 four municipal health service demonstration projects.

• **Native American Health Programs.** Extended Medicare coverage to certain programs and facilities operated by Native American tribes under the Indian Self-Determination Act.

• **Certified Nurse Midwife Services.** Clarified that Medicare coverage of certified nurse midwife services was not limited to services provided during pregnancy.

• **Outpatient Physical and Occupational Therapy.** Beginning Jan. 1, 1994, increased from $750 to $900 the annual limit on outpatient physical and occupational therapy services.

• **Graduate Medical Education.** Froze for fiscal 1994 and 1995 the level of Medicare payments made to hospitals to offset the costs of training physicians who treated Medicare patients. Residents in obstetrics and gynecology were exempt from the freeze, as were those in primary care fields, including family medicine, general internal medicine, general pediatrics, preventive medicine, geriatric medicine and osteopathic general practice. Beginning July 1, 1995, the period of eligibility for such "direct" medical education payments was redefined as the minimum number of years before a resident was eligible for board certification in his or her field of specialization.

• **Home Health Services.** From July 1, 1994, to July 1, 1996, eliminated the annual inflation adjustment for the maximum Medicare reimbursement for home health services. Beginning Oct. 1, 1993, special payments to hospital-based home health agencies were eliminated.

• **Medicare Secondary Payer Provisions.** Extended through Sept. 30, 1998, authority for Medicare officials to gain access to the records of the Social Security Administration and the Internal Revenue Service to identify Medicare beneficiaries with other sources of health insurance. By law, Medicare was supposed to be the "secondary payer" for many beneficiaries with other insurance, covering only those costs that were not covered by the primary insurer.

The bill also extended through Sept. 30, 1998, a provision making Medicare the secondary payer for disabled Medicare beneficiaries who were covered by employer health plans in businesses with more than 100 employees, as well as beneficiaries who qualified for Medicare as a result of end-stage renal disease.

• **Physician Referrals.** Extended a ban imposed in the 1989 reconciliation bill on physicians' referring patients to clinical laboratories in which they or their immediate family members had an ownership or investment interest. Beginning Dec. 31, 1994, such self-referrals also were to be banned for physical and occupational therapy services; radiology or other diagnostic services; radiation therapy services; durable medical equipment; parenteral and enteral nutrients, equipment and supplies; orthotic and prosthetic devices; home health services; outpatient prescription drugs; and inpatient and outpatient hospital services.

The bill revised and added a series of exceptions to the ban, including ones for services provided to residents in rural areas, those provided by group practices and those provided by or under the direct supervision of a physician or group of physicians. It also clarified circumstances in which ownership of investment securities constituted a relationship that triggered the referral ban, and it clarified permissible compensation arrangements and definitions of group practices.

• **Immunosuppressive Drugs.** Extended Medicare coverage of outpatient immunosuppressive drugs that were used to prevent rejection in organ-transplant patients. At the time, Medicare covered such drugs for one year following a transplant. Beginning Jan. 1, 1995, coverage was extended to 18 months; beginning Jan. 1, 1996, coverage would continue for 24 months; beginning Jan. 1, 1997, coverage would continue for 30 months; and beginning Jan. 1, 1998, and thereafter, coverage would continue for 36 months.

• **Erythropoietin Payments.** Beginning Jan. 1, 1994, reduced payments for Erythropoietin (an antianemia drug used by dialysis patients in Medicare's end-stage renal disease program) by $1 per 1,000 units. The bill also permitted dialysis patients to administer the drug themselves.

• **Social Health Maintenance Organization Demonstrations.** Continued for two additional years, through Dec. 31, 1997, authority for demonstration programs to offer Medicare beneficiaries integrated health and long-term care services on a prepaid basis.

• **Timing of Claims Payments.** Set new "floors" and "ceilings" for payment of Medicare claims by insurance companies that processed Medicare paperwork. Beginning Oct. 1, 1993, stipulated that "clean" claims (those properly submitted with all necessary information) submitted electronically could not be paid until the 14th day after receipt. (The federal government benefited because it could earn interest on the money in the interim.) Clean claims submitted on paper could not be paid until the 27th day after receipt. However, interest was to be paid to recipients for clean claims not paid within 30 days of receipt.

• **Part B Premium.** Extended through 1998 the requirement that the Medicare Part B premium be calculated to recoup 25 percent of the program's costs. The Treasury would continue to subsidize the remaining 75 percent. Without the change, after 1995 the Part B premium could not rise by more than the Social Security cost of living adjustment.

• **Medicare and Medicaid Coverage Data Bank.** Required the HHS secretary to establish a data bank to help identify and collect from private insurers appropriate reimbursement for services provided to Medicare and Medicaid beneficiaries. Beginning in 1994, employers were required to provide information regarding employee health insurance coverage.

Medicaid

• **Personal Care Services.** Repealed a mandate requiring states to provide personal care services for Medicaid beneficiaries outside the home and clarified that such services could be provided as a state option. (This corrected a drafting error in the 1990 reconciliation bill.)

• **Medicaid Prescription Drug Discount Program.** Permitted states to establish prescription drug formularies (restrictive lists of approved drugs that were to be covered by Medicaid) under certain circumstances. States were allowed to subject drugs to "prior authorization" before they were dispensed to Medicaid recipients—even in the first six months after they were approved by the Food and Drug Administration. Such drugs had been barred from inclusion in prior authorization programs during the first six months.

• **Optional Coverage of TB-Related Services.** Beginning Jan. 1, 1994, allowed states to cover prescribed drugs, directly observed therapy and other services for low-income individuals infected with tuberculosis not otherwise eligible for Medicaid.

• **Emergency Services for Illegal Immigrants.** Stipulated that services related to organ transplant procedures did not qualify as emergencies covered by Medicaid for illegal immigrants.

• **Certified Nurse Midwife Services.** Beginning Oct. 1, 1993, clarified that Medicaid coverage of certified nurse midwife services was not limited to services provided during pregnancy.

• **Transfer of Assets to Facilitate Medicaid Eligibility.** Required a delay in granting eligibility for Medicaid nursing home coverage for institutionalized individuals (or their spouses) who disposed of assets for less than fair market value 36 months before the date they applied for benefits or the date they were institutionalized, whichever was later. Penalties could not be applied to transfers to spouses, to minor or disabled children, or to trusts solely for the benefit of disabled individuals under age 65.

• **Medicaid Estate Recoveries.** Required states to establish programs to recover the cost of long-term care services provided to Medicaid beneficiaries from their estates after their death. Recovery could be waived in cases in which "undue hardship" would result.

• **Disproportionate Share Hospitals.** Tightened conditions under which states could designate hospitals as serving a disproportionate share of low-income individuals (and hence qualifying for higher federal payments). A hospital could not be designated unless at least 1 percent of its inpatients were Medicaid beneficiaries. Special payments were limited to no more than the costs of providing inpatient and outpatient services to Medicaid and uninsured patients, less the amount the hospital received for those patients either from Medicaid or the patients themselves. The bill allowed a transition for high-volume public hospitals.

• **Third-Party Liability Laws.** Required states to enact laws that prohibited insurers, including group health plans under ERISA, from taking an individual's Medicaid eligibility or enrollment into account in enrolling them or paying claims. States also were required to enact laws making it possible to collect payments from group health plans and other private insurers of Medicaid beneficiaries.

• **Medical Child Support Laws.** Beginning April 1, 1994, required states to enact and implement laws to ensure that insurers and employers carried out court or administrative orders for medical child support.

• **Physician Referrals.** Beginning December 1994, applied to Medicaid the rules barring physicians from referring patients to facilities in which they had a financial interest *(see Medicare, above).*

• **State Medicaid Fraud Control.** Beginning Jan. 1, 1995, required states to operate "effective" Medicaid fraud control units that met requirements established by the HHS secretary, unless the state could demonstrate that operating such a unit would not be cost effective and that the state could otherwise protect Medicaid beneficiaries from fraud and neglect.

• **Federal Medicaid Payments to U.S. Territories.** Beginning in fiscal 1994, increased the limit for federal matching payments to Medicaid programs in Puerto Rico, the Virgin Islands, Guam, the Northern Mariana Islands and American Samoa. Beginning in fiscal 1995, the new ceilings were to be adjusted for inflation.

Other Health Provisions

• **Permanent Extension of Vaccine Injury Compensation Trust Fund.** Made permanent the federal program to compensate families of children injured or killed by adverse reactions to vaccines to prevent childhood illnesses. The bill also made permanent the manufacturer's excise tax on certain vaccines that funded the compensation program. Both the tax and the program had expired as of Jan. 1, 1993, but the law provided that children affected after the expiration date would be eligible as if the coverage lapse had not occurred.

• **Immunization Entitlement.** Created a new program under Medicaid designed to guarantee availability of free childhood vaccines to all children eligible for Medicaid, all uninsured children and all Native Americans. Children with health insurance but whose insurance did not cover the cost of vaccines could receive free vaccines at certain federally supported clinics, such as community health centers. The program entitled each state to receive at no charge from the federal government a sufficient supply of vaccine to cover the designated class of children. The state in turn was required to make the vaccines available to all public and private health care providers who were willing to participate in the program and were authorized under state law to administer vaccines. Neither the state nor providers could charge patients for the vaccines, although providers could assess a limited fee for the actual administration. The Health and Human Services secretary was ordered to negotiate with vaccine manufacturers for a bulk purchase price, which also was to be the price at which states could purchase additional amounts of vaccine for children not covered by the mandate. The federal government also was to purchase an emergency stockpile of recommended vaccines as protection against unexpected shortages, such as manufacturing disruptions, or sudden needs, such as an epidemic.

Child Welfare, Adoption

• **Family Preservation.** Created a new capped entitlement for family preservation and family support services in the child welfare services program under Title IV-B of the Social Security Act. The entitlement was authorized to be funded at $60 million in fiscal 1994, $150 million in fiscal 1995, $225 million in fiscal 1996, $240 million in fiscal 1997 and $255 million in fiscal 1998. Allocation of the funds to states was to be based on their relative share of children receiving food stamps. States had to match 25 percent of the federal government's contribution.

• **Funding for State Courts.** Provided $5 million in fiscal 1995 and $10 million in each of the following three years from the new capped entitlement for a grant program for the highest state courts involved in foster care and adoption. The grants would enable the courts to assess their effectiveness in carrying out laws that required court proceedings in foster care placement, ending parental rights, and adoptions. The federal grant had to be matched with 25 percent from states or localities from fiscal 1996 through 1998.

• **Automated Data Systems.** Authorized a 75 percent federal matching rate for state expenses to develop or install a foster care and adoption data collection system. The data system was to be used to provide national information on foster care and adoption. The 75 percent federal matching rate was applicable from fiscal 1994 to 1996; the rate would be 50 percent thereafter.

• **Independent Living Program.** Permanently extended the authorization for the federal-state entitlement program designed to help foster children age 16 and older ease into independent living. The program's authorization expired at the end of fiscal 1992.

• **Training Agency Staff and Foster and Adoptive Parents.** Permanently extended a provision providing 75 percent federal reimbursement to states for training child welfare agency staff as well as foster and adoptive parents. This provision expired at the end of fiscal 1992. The new authorization was effective Oct. 1, 1993.

• **Moratorium on Collection of Disallowances.** Imposed until Oct. 1, 1994, a moratorium preventing the federal government from collecting penalties from states under Title IV-B or IV-E based on reviews of state compliance with foster care protections or financial reviews and audits of foster care and adoption payments. Title IV-B covered child welfare services; Title IV-E covered foster care and adoption.

• **State Paternity Establishment.** Increased the standards states were required to meet in establishing paternity. The new standards required states to establish paternity in 75 percent of out-of-wedlock births, and it set interim improvements that states with lower rates had to meet. States also were required to have laws that promoted voluntary acknowledgment of paternity in hospitals.

Supplemental Security Income (SSI)

• **Federal Administration Fees.** Required the HHS secretary to charge states fees for the federal cost of administering SSI payments. The fees started at $1.67 for each monthly supplemental payment in Fiscal 1994, increasing to $3.33 in fiscal 1995 and to $5 by fiscal 1996. The fee in subsequent years would be $5 or an amount determined by the secretary.

• **State Relocation Assistance.** Permanently excluded from consideration as income or resources any state or local relocation assistance received by SSI beneficiaries. Relocation assistance was paid when a government required individuals to move from their dwellings.

• **Absence Due to Active Military Service.** Prevented SSI benefits from declining when the spouse or parent of a beneficiary was absent from home solely because of active military service. Certain hazardous-duty pay was also excluded from income.

• **Children of Armed Forces Personnel.** Assured that children who were U.S. citizens would remain eligible for SSI when they accompanied their parents on U.S. military assignments to Puerto Rico or to U.S. territories and possessions. The SSI benefits previously continued only if the parents were on military assignments to foreign countries.

• **Income exclusions for Native Americans.** Excluded from determination as income up to $2,000 received by Native Americans that came from leases on individually owned trust or restricted Native American lands. Previously, only income received by Native Americans from tribally owned trust lands had been excluded as income. The change was effective Jan. 1, 1994.

Aid to Families with Dependent Children

• **Federal Match Rate.** Reduced the federal match rate to 50 percent for certain administrative costs for Aid to Families with Dependent Children (AFDC). While the federal government had generally provided a 50 percent match rate for AFDC administrative expenses, it had made exceptions. It had provided 100 percent of expenses to verify the immigration status of aliens, 90 percent for information management and 75 percent for fraud control. The law extended the 50 percent match rate to these three categories, effective with calendar quarters beginning on or after April 1, 1994.

• **Stepparent Income.** Increased the monthly earnings of a stepparent that were excluded from income for purposes of determining eligibility and benefits of AFDC applicants and recipients. The amount to be excluded increased from $75 a month to $90 a month, effective Oct. 1, 1993.

Other Provisions

• **Federal Unemployment Surtax.** Extended the 0.2 percent federal unemployment surtax for two more years, through fiscal 1998. The temporary surtax, on the first $7,000 of wages paid annually to an employee, paid for certain unemployment insurance costs. It was in addition to a permanent 0.6 percent tax.

• **Enterprise Zone Block Grants.** Made available $1 billion in grants to empowerment zones and enterprise communities. The money, provided under Title XX of the Social Security Act, could fund a variety of social services in poor communities targeted for increased federal funding and tax breaks. Each of the six urban empowerment zones to be set up under provisions in the revenue section of this law was eligible for $100 million over two years. Each of the three rural empowerment zones was eligible for $40 million over two years. And each of the 95 enterprise communities was eligible for $2.95 million.

Food Stamps

• **Students' Earnings.** Excluded the income of elementary and secondary school students 21 years of age or under when calculating food stamp eligibility and benefits levels under the food stamps program. Prior law excluded students' earnings until their 18th birthday. The change was effective Sept. 1, 1994.

• **High Shelter Expenses.** Increased the amount households could deduct for high shelter expenses in calculating their income for food stamp purposes. High shelter expenses were housing costs that exceeded 50 percent of a family's net monthly income after other deductions had been taken. For households with elderly or disabled members, there was no dollar limit on the deduction. However, the deduction for other households was capped (at $200 a month at the time). The provision increased the cap to $231 on July 1, 1994, and to $247 on Oct. 1, 1995. The cap was to be eliminated on Jan. 1, 1997.

• **Earned-Income Tax Credits.** Disregarded from food stamp resource calculations any earned-income tax credits received by low-income working families for one year, effective Sept. 1, 1994. The provision applied to families that were continuously enrolled in the food stamps program during the year. The new law was designed to discourage families from spending their tax credits too quickly. Prior law disregarded the tax credits only in the month they were received and in the following month.

• **Homeless Families.** Disregarded from homeless families' income the payments states made to house them in transitional quarters, effective Sept. 1, 1994. Previously, states were able to count part of the value of these payments as income, reducing the amount of food stamps that homeless families were eligible to receive.

• **General Assistance.** Excluded from calculations of households' income certain payments made through state or local General Assistance funds. Such payments for energy or utility costs were to be excluded as income, though payments for general housing expenses could be considered income. The provision was effective Sept. 1, 1994.

• **Continuing Benefits.** Prohibited states from prorating food stamp benefits when a household reapplied after having been off the program for less than one month. Since 1981, new food stamp applicants' first month of benefits had been reduced based on the number of days that had already elapsed in the month. In 1982, this requirement was extended to households reapplying after brief interruptions. The law repealed the 1982 measure, effective Sept. 1, 1994.

• **Child Support Payments.** Gave noncustodial parents a deduction for legally obligated child support payments when determining income for food stamp eligibility and allotment levels. This provision was designed to encourage parents to make child support payments by increasing their food stamp allotment to compensate for the lost income.

• **Child Care.** Increased the limit that certain families with dependent care expenses could deduct from their income when determining food stamp benefits. The $160 monthly deduction was raised to $200 per month for children under 2 and $175 per month for older children, effective Sept. 1, 1994. States also were to be permitted to set the limit for dependent care reimbursements for those participating in food stamp employment and training programs. However, the reimbursement rate could not be above the local market rate as determined for Aid to Families with Dependent Children (AFDC) employment and training programs.

• **Demonstration Projects.** Authorized the Agriculture secretary to conduct demonstration projects that would permit food stamp recipients to save up to $10,000 without losing their food stamp eligibility. These savings were to be used to improve the education or training of household members or to purchase or renovate a home. The demonstration project was to be available to up to 11,000 households over four years.

• **Household Definition.** Revised the definition of a household in determining food stamp eligibility and benefits. Effective Sept. 1, 1994, the law generally permitted people who lived together, but purchased food and prepared meals separately, to apply for food stamps separately.

• **Drug and Alcohol Treatment.** Extended food stamp benefits to children living with their parents in residential treatment centers for drug or alcohol abuse. Previously, the adults entered in such programs were eligible for food stamps, but no provisions were made for their children. The change was effective Sept. 1, 1994.

• **Claims Collection.** Authorized an additional means of recouping overpayments of food stamps resulting from beneficiary error: the reduction of federal pay or pensions. This provision would typically be used after a household had left the food stamps program. The usual way of collecting for overpayments—reducing future food stamp benefits—was not applicable if a household had left the program.

• **Trafficking in Food Coupons.** Strengthened the penalties for trafficking in food stamps. Effective Sept. 1, 1994, those found by a court of law to be trading drugs for food coupons were disqualified from the program for one year; a second violation would draw permanent disqualification. The law also permanently disqualified from the program anyone who was found on the first offense to be trading firearms, ammunition or explosives for food coupons. The existing penalty for trafficking in food stamps was six months disqualification for the first violation, one year for the second violation and permanent disqualification for the third offense.

• **Civil Penalties on Businesses.** Removed the two-year ceiling on civil financial penalties that could be imposed on retailers and wholesalers found to be trafficking in food stamps, including selling firearms, ammunition, explosives or drugs for food coupons. The Agriculture Department could impose a financial penalty in lieu of disqualification on a business that trafficked in food stamps if the ownership and management were unaware of the violation and there was an antifraud policy in place. Previously, the penalty was up to $20,000 per violation, not to exceed $40,000 in a two-year period. The law removed the time limit from the cap, stipulating that a civil money penalty could not exceed $40,000 for all violations occurring during a single investigation. This change ensured that repeated violations were punishable with penalties of up to $40,000 each.

• **Uniform Reimbursement Rates.** Extended the federal government's practice of reimbursing 50 percent of the state and local costs related to administering the food stamps program. The federal government previously increased its 50 percent reimbursement in some instances; for example, paying 63 percent of the costs related to automated data processing systems, 75 percent of the cost of investigating and prosecuting fraud and 100 percent of the cost of verifying the immigration status of aliens applying for benefits. The law reduced the federal share of these activities to 50 percent, beginning with calendar quarters that started on or after April 1, 1994. This provision was part of the Clinton administration's plan to institute a more uniform 50 percent federal matching rate for public assistance programs.

Debt-Limit Increase

• **Permanent Increase.** Raised the permanent limit on the federal debt to $4.9 trillion, an amount estimated to suffice through the end of fiscal 1995. The bill also repealed the temporary debt-limit increase to $4.37 trillion, which was approved by Congress earlier in the year.

Customs and Trade

• **Customs User Fees.** Extended through fiscal 1998 the existing level of fees that the Customs Service charged air and sea passengers, commercial vessels, barges, trucks, rail cars and mail packages. The provision also extended through fiscal 1998 the merchandise processing fee charged on cargo imported from any country other than Canada.

• **General System of Preferences.** Extended through fiscal 1994 the president's authority to grant duty-free treatment to certain products from developing nations under the General System of Preferences (GSP) program. The previous authorization expired July 4, 1993, five weeks before the extension was signed into law, causing some products to be temporarily subject to duties. The provision authorized refunds of those duties, if a request was made by February 1994. The law also eliminated a provision that banned the Union of Soviet Socialist Republics and its successor nations from duty-free treatment under the GSP.

• **Trade Adjustment Assistance.** Extended the Trade Adjustment Assistance Program, which assisted workers and companies hurt by imports that result from trade liberalization, for five years, through fiscal 1998. The program provided cash, job training, moving expenses and other aid to workers displaced by imports, as well as technical assistance to affected companies. The law authorized appropriations for the program for fiscal 1994–1998 but reduced the amount that could be used for training programs in fiscal 1997 by $10 million, to $70 million.

• **Customs Officers' Pay and Benefits.** Reduced some overtime payments, increased the compensation for working the night shift, raised the retirement benefits for officers who worked overtime and authorized a bonus for officers who used foreign-language skills on the job. To pay for these changes in pay and benefits, the Treasury secretary was authorized to take up to $18 million from the user fees collected by the Customs Service.

Budget Process

• **Discretionary Spending Caps.** Extended caps on discretionary spending, which were set in the 1990 budget agreement for fiscal 1991–1995, through fiscal 1998. The bill spelled out the following limits for discretionary spending and continued existing procedures for periodically adjusting those limits and enforcing them through across-the-board spending cuts and points of order.

(amounts in billions of dollars)

	1994	1995	1996	1997	1998
Budget authority	$509.9	517.4	519.1	528.1	530.6
Outlays	$537.3	538.9	547.3	547.3	547.9

• **Pay-as-You-Go Restrictions for Entitlements and Tax Cuts.** Extended through 1998 the existing pay-as-you-go discipline, which required that any tax cuts, new entitlement programs or expansion of existing entitlement benefits be offset by an increase in taxes or a cut in entitlement spending. The bill extended existing enforcement procedures and related points of order through 1998 and it "reset" the pay-as-you-go scorecard

DEBT-LIMIT INCREASE

A small but critically important provision in the 1993 reconciliation bill (HR 2264—PL 103-66) raised the ceiling on the public debt to $4.9 trillion. The increase, which drew virtually no debate, was calculated to allow for all federal government borrowing needs through fiscal 1995.

Treasury Secretary Lloyd Bentsen warned in March 1993 that total federal borrowing—the accumulation of annual budget deficits—would exceed the existing ceiling of $4.145 trillion by April 7.

Congress, which was in the midst of work on Clinton's economic package, passed a bill (HR 1430—H Rept 103-43) to increase the ceiling through Sept. 30 to $4.37 trillion. As the leadership hoped, the short-term bill passed with little fanfare. The House passed the debt-limit bill by a vote of 237–177 on April 2. The Senate cleared the measure by voice vote April 5. Clinton signed it the next day (PL 103-12).

Avoiding Controversial Riders

In previous years, when Republican presidents faced Democratic Congresses, bills raising the debt ceiling had attracted controversial amendments and been subject to lengthy debate. That was because the "must-pass" character of bills increasing the limit on federal borrowing made them engines to carry into law provisions that could not stand on their own.

When the Treasury reached the statutory debt ceiling, Congress had no choice but to raise it; the alternative was to see the federal government run out of cash, fail to pay Social Security benefits to retirees or interest payments to the holders of government bonds, and eventually default on its obligations.

Sen. Phil Gramm, R-Texas, and others warned that in 1993 they would offer major budget-related riders, such as a balanced-budget amendment to the Constitution.

But the Democratic leadership got around those threats by incorporating the debt-limit increase into the reconciliation bill, which was protected by special Senate rules barring filibusters and non-germane amendments.

First, early adoption of the fiscal 1994 budget resolution (H Con Res 64—H Rept 103-48) gave leaders the chance to protect the short-term bill. The budget resolution, completed April 1, included the debt-limit language as part of the instructions directing congressional committees to craft the budget reconciliation bill.

And before the short-term debt-limit bill expired, Congress had passed the omnibus reconciliation bill. The House adopted the conference report on HR 2264 on Aug. 5 and the Senate cleared the bill the next day.

A decade earlier, in August 1982, the ceiling on the debt had stood at $1.389 trillion. In November of that year, it was increased to $1.49 trillion. On 20 occasions since, Congress had acted to increase the debt limit either temporarily or permanently. However, lawmakers had not had to contemplate such a vote since 1990, when Congress set the ceiling high enough to carry the government for more than two years.

to zero to prevent Congress from spending any of the entitlement savings or tax increases it achieved in the reconciliation bill

Miscellaneous

- **Entry Fees at Army Corps of Engineers Recreation Facilities.** Authorized the Army Corps of Engineers to charge entry fees at certain recreation areas, including campsites, swimming beaches and some boat launching ramps. The law set a maximum fee of $3 per day for vehicles carrying no more than eight passengers, including the driver. The law also eliminated a previous requirement that all Army Corps camping facilities provide one free campground.
- **NRC Fees.** Extended through fiscal 1998 the requirement that the Nuclear Regulatory Commission (NRC) charge fees high enough to cover 100 percent of its budget. The change was to cost companies regulated by the NRC, particularly the electric utilities that operated nuclear reactors, almost $1.2 billion. Under prior law, the commission's fees would have dropped to about one-third of their existing level after 1995.
- **Patent and Trademark Fees.** Increased the fees charged by the U.S. Patent and Trademark Office to people who wished to register for and maintain a trademark or patent. The provision was to raise $345 million through fiscal 1998.
- **Merchant Marine Tonnage Duties.** Extended through fiscal 1998 the existing level of duties paid by cargo vessels entering U.S. ports from foreign ports or places. The duties, which were raised 250 percent to 350 percent as part of the 1990 budget agreement, had been scheduled to drop to their original levels after fiscal 1995. Vessels arriving from places in the Western Hemisphere were required to pay 9 cents per ton of cargo capacity; the maximum for a single vessel in a given year was to be 45 cents per ton. Vessels from other foreign countries paid 27 cents per ton, up to a maximum of $1.35 per ton per year.
- **Timber Sales.** Set aside 85 percent of the receipts from the sale of timber on federal lands in Washington, Oregon and northern California counties in fiscal 1994. Counties in those states included large swaths of old-growth forests critical to the survival of the threatened spotted owl and were likely to be hard hit by legal decisions regarding the owl. The pot of funds was to be available to the federal government, the three Northwest states and the affected counties. The amount set aside was to drop by 3 percent each year thereafter until fiscal 2003. To make up for the loss of revenue to the Treasury, the provision eliminated an export subsidy credit for foreign sales of unprocessed logs, which generated about $390 million annually. Northwest timber counties were expected to receive $270 million under the set-aside program and $120 million would go to deficit reduction. ❑

Fiscal 1994 Appropriations

President Clinton came into office in 1993 with ambitious plans to "invest" in a domestic policy agenda that ranged from science, commerce and crime-fighting to education, rural development and highway construction. But he quickly ran up

against an inescapable reality: the $1.5 trillion budget universe was no longer expanding—at least, not that portion the president and his allies in Congress could readily get to from year to year. Strict budgetary limits first enacted in 1990 already were pressing spending downward when Clinton got to the White House, and a Congress with a nervous eye on the 1994 elections accelerated the push.

For fiscal 1994, Democrats managed to find money for much of what they wanted to do—enough, for instance, for above-inflation increases in five of the 13 regular appropriations bills. Among the beneficiaries were many of Clinton's "investment" programs—about 90 separate proposals in education, health, research and development, highways and railroads, housing, environmental protection and other areas. But increases such as these came only after Congress found offsetting reductions in other bills—mainly from defense and foreign aid, but also from other domestic accounts.

The result was evident in the bottom line. Outlays for discretionary spending—the one-third of the federal budget over which Congress had annual discretion—all but stopped growing. The $541.4 billion that was to move out of the Treasury in fiscal 1994 was just $600 million more than was spent in 1993—an increase of one-tenth of 1 percent at a time when inflation was running a little more than 3 percent.

As part of the 1993 budget reconciliation act (HR 2264—PL 103-66), Democrats and Republicans agreed to impose a "freeze" on appropriations outlays through 1998. That was a "hard" freeze, not allowing increases to keep up with inflation, which meant there would not be enough money to cover the same value of services in fiscal 1995 that the government provided in fiscal 1994, much less expand them. *(Fiscal 1994 budget reconciliation, p. 44)*

The result was a tough year for all sorts of spending:

- **Pump-Priming.** Clinton's first appropriations initiative—the $16 billion jobs "stimulus" package that was supposed to be the down payment on his investment agenda—was essentially killed in the Senate when lockstep Republican opposition and a swing group of rebellious Democrats combined to oppose it.
- **Emergency Spending.** Over the summer, a pair of midyear supplemental appropriations bills that would have skated through Congress in previous years suddenly ran into trouble. Lawmakers insisted that the Pentagon find ways to offset part of the cost of the U.S. military deployment to Somalia. And a bill to help victims of devastating Midwestern flooding stalled for five days in the House in a battle over how to pay for it.
- **Big Projects.** Congress killed two projects that had avoided the budget knife for years: the $11 billion superconducting super collider, a Texas-based "big science" project, and the $3.7 billion Advanced Solid Rocket Motor, a NASA project based in Mississippi.
- **Last-Minute Cuts.** Just before adjourning for the year, the House showed its budget-cutting inclinations one last time, voting 429–1 for a bill (HR 3400) to cut $37 billion over the coming five years, mostly from discretionary accounts. About $33 billion of that was supposed to come from adding the force of law to a Clinton administration plan to force the federal work

force to shed 252,000 jobs. The bill died when the Senate failed to act on it. *(Fiscal 1994 rescissions, p. 59)*

REGULAR APPROPRIATIONS

Congress was able to complete action on only two of the 13 regular appropriations bills for fiscal 1994 by the Oct. 1 start of the fiscal year—those for the Legislative Branch (HR 2348—PL 103-69) and Foreign Operations (HR 2295—PL 103-87).

A variety of disputes slowed action: a disagreement between authorizers and appropriators stalled the Transportation measure (HR 2750—PL 103-122) in the House; grazing fees and federal land-use policy held up the Interior bill (HR 2520—PL 103-138) until mid-November; Defense (HR 3116—PL 103-139) was difficult to complete because the parallel authorization bill (HR 2401—PL 103-160) was bogged down over the issues of homosexuals in the military and the U.S. roles in Somalia and Haiti. *(Transportation authorizations, p. 330; grazing rules; p. 413; defense authorization, p. 257)*

Major Battles

The foreign operations appropriations bill (HR 2295) was the scene of a battle over Clinton's $2.5 billion request for aid to the former republics of the Soviet Union. An amendment to cut the aid package by $1.6 billion was defeated June 17 on a **key vote of 140–289 (R 93–79, D 46–210, I 1–0)**. In the Senate, aid for the former Soviet republics advanced as the chamber passed HR 2295 on Sept. 23 on a **key vote of 88–10 (R 36–7, D 52–3)**. *(1993 key votes, p. 979)*

Abortion opponents managed to retain a ban on federally financed Medicaid abortions that had been in place since 1981, despite the turnover in the White House. During debate on the Labor, Health and Human Services and Education spending bill (HR 2518—PL 103-112), the House on June 30 adopted an amendment by Henry Hyde, R-Ill., to ban such abortions except in cases of rape, incest or to save the life of the woman on a **key vote of 255–178 (R 157–16, D 98–161, I 0–1**. In the Senate, a Sept. 28 attempt to strike the Hyde language failed on a **key vote of 40–59 (R 6–38, D 34–21)**.

The massive $11 billion superconducting super collider project got the ax after intense procedural wrangling over the conference report on the Energy and Water appropriations bill (HR 2445—PL 103-126) that contained the giant atom smasher despite a prior House vote to kill it. On a **key vote of 159–264 (R 61–111, D 98–152, I 0–1)**, the House Oct. 19 approved a procedural maneuver (defeating a vote on the previous question) to permit opponents to offer a motion to recommit the conference report (H Rept 103-292) back to a House-Senate conference committee with instructions to scrap the costly project.

In the Senate, support for low grazing fees for Western ranchers using federal land blocked Interior Secretary Bruce Babbitt from increasing grazing fees and tying ranchers' ability to obtain grazing permits to their environmental stewardship records. An amendment to the Interior bill (HR 2520) to impose a one-year moratorium on Babbitt's plan was adopted on a **key vote of 59–40 (R 38–5, D 21–35)**.

Continuing Resolutions

To keep the government in business, Congress had to act on three continuing appropriations resolutions as work progressed on the 13 regular bills.

The first (H J Res 267—PL 103-88) kept money flowing to agencies through Oct. 21, by which time three more regular appropriations bills were enacted—for Agriculture (HR 2493—PL 103-111), Labor, Health and Human Services and Education (HR 2518—PL 103-112) and Military Construction (HR 2446—PL 103-110). The House passed the measure 274–156; the Senate cleared it Sept. 29 by voice vote.

The second continuing resolution (H J Res 281—PL 103-113) cleared Oct. 21 and was good for a week. The House and Senate each approved the measure by voice vote.

By the time it was enacted, three more bills had cleared: Commerce, Justice and State (HR 2519—PL 103-121); Transportation (HR 2750); and Veterans Affairs, Housing and Urban Development, Independent Agencies (HR 2491—PL 103-124).

The third continuing resolution (H J Res 283—PL 103-128), was cleared Oct. 28, by which time the Treasury, Postal Service bill (HR 2401—PL 103-123) and District of Columbia bill (HR 2492—PL 103-127) had cleared.

It provided temporary spending authority until midnight Nov. 10 to give Congress time to complete the Interior and Defense measures, the only ones then outstanding. The House passed the measure 256–157; the Senate cleared it by voice vote.

'STIMULUS' SUPPLEMENTAL

Senate Republicans in April effectively squashed Clinton's first foray into fiscal policy, a $16.3 billion "stimulus package" aimed at creating several hundred thousand temporary jobs.

The idea behind the bill was to provide a shot in the economy's arm in advance of the belt-tightening that would follow with Clinton's deficit-reduction plan. The bill that eventually cleared (HR 1335—PL 103-24) was stripped bare of nearly all of Clinton's initiatives, however.

House Action

The House Appropriations Committee approved the bill virtually unchanged March 9 by voice vote. The bill passed the House March 19 on a 235–190 vote.

Among the most significant provisions contained in the $16.3 billion measure included: $4 billion to extend unemployment benefits; $3 billion for highway and bridge repairs; $2.5 billion in Community Development Block Grants to cities and counties; $1.2 billion for mass transit projects; $1.2 billion for Pell grants to college students; and $1 billion in job training and education for youth.

Before passage, however, House leaders had to overcome a rebellion among conservative Democrats who objected to the size of the package and who wanted to offer spending cuts to offset new spending. Republicans derided the bill as "pork barrel" spending, and House leaders were concerned for a time that the effort might unravel. But Democratic discipline held and the rule that brought the measure to the floor was adopted on a **key vote of 240–185 (R 0–172, D 239–13, I 1–0)**.

Senate Action

The bill stalled in the Senate. First, conservative Democrats slowed it, then Republicans filibustered it, forcing Democrats to strip everything from the package but $4 billion for extended unemployment benefits.

Senate Appropriations Committee Chairman Robert C. Byrd, D-W.Va., brought HR 1335 before his committee on March 23, where it was approved on a 19–10 vote. The divided vote in committee—typically a bipartisan oasis—signaled that the measure faced tough going on the Senate floor.

When the bill came to the floor, Byrd enraged Republicans by using parliamentary maneuvers to thwart their amendments. A GOP filibuster began and Republicans held ranks while Democratic leaders lost a series of cloture votes that would have cut off debate, even after Democrats reduced the bill's price tag by 25 percent and subsequently offered to offset some of the bill with spending cuts.

However, after a debate that spanned three weeks, Republicans had lost interest in compromise.

The last attempt at breaking the filibuster failed on April 21, when a motion to invoke cloture (requiring 60 votes), failed on a **key vote of 56–43 (R 0–42, D 56–1)**.

Democrats then stripped everything from the bill except for $4 billion to extend the unemployment benefits for almost 2 million jobless Americans. The measure passed the Senate by voice vote, and the House cleared it the next day, on a 301–114 vote.

SPRING SUPPLEMENTAL

Congress in 1993 also produced a $3.5 billion supplemental appropriations bill that provided fiscal 1993 money for a broad range of defense and domestic items, but only after appropriators produced a long list of cuts in previously approved spending to offset most of the new money.

The bill (HR 2118—PL 103-50) cleared both House and Senate July 1. The bill financed items such as the U.S. military's Operation Restore Hope in Somalia, a small-business loan program, Pell grants and a cost of living increase for veterans.

But the bill also included about $2.5 billion in offsetting spending cuts, bringing the measure's net spending to just over $1 billion. Included in the bill were a few remnants of Clinton's ill-fated economic-stimulus bill, including some spending for summer jobs and a community police program.

Legislative Action

The House Appropriations Committee approved its version of HR 2118, carrying a $1.8 billion price tag, with bipartisan support on a voice vote May 13. House leaders decided to pair HR 2118 with another bill (HR 2244) that resurrected $931.5 million of Clinton's original stimulus package, including funding for summer jobs and police hiring and wastewater treatment plants. The money was fully offset by cuts in existing programs.

The House passed both bills on May 26; HR 2118 passed by 300–125; HR 2244 passed by 287–140.

The Senate Appropriations Committee rolled the two bills into one, approving HR 2118 on a 26–1 vote and reducing the total tab to $1.9 billion. Most of the reductions came from sharply cutting back on the bits and pieces of Clinton's original stimulus package.

Avoiding the partisan rancor that had doomed Clinton's stimulus package, the Senate on June 22 passed the bill by voice vote after approving a handful of mostly minor amendments.

The final bill was hashed out in a June 29–30 conference. The House approved the conference report on the bill (H Rept 103-165) by a 280–138 vote on July 1. The Senate cleared it by voice vote the same day. Clinton signed the bill into law on July 2.

DISASTER SUPPLEMENTAL

After an unusually bumpy ride for a disaster-aid plan, Congress in August cleared a $5.7 billion supplemental appropriations bill (HR 2667—PL 103-75) to provide financial assistance to the victims of massive floods in the upper Midwest—particularly farmers with crop losses—and other 1993 natural disasters.

HR 2667 was briefly derailed in the House, largely because of concerns about the bill's designation as emergency spending, which allowed Congress and the president to add its full cost directly to the federal budget deficit rather than having to find offsetting spending cuts.

The tab for the bill escalated as the persistent heavy rains in the Midwest steadily grew worse in the summer, and losses mounted.

On July 4, Clinton promised about $900 million in aid. When he sent his proposal to Congress on July 14, the cost was $2.25 billion. By the time the bill reached the House floor, it contained $2.77 billion. The bill eventually swelled to $5.7 billion.

Legislative Action

The bill went directly to the full Appropriations Committee, which approved it without objection July 20.

The atmosphere was sharply different on July 21 when the Rules Committee wrote a rule governing House floor action on HR 2667.

Republicans unsuccessfully pressed to bring the bill to the floor with a rule that would have allowed consideration of GOP-backed "pay-as-you-go" proposals. The Rules Committee also rejected an amendment by Timothy J. Penny, D-Minn., and Jim Nussle, R-Iowa, to pay for the disaster-aid supplemental with offsetting cuts in dozens of other federal programs, rather than by adding its costs to the deficit.

To the surprise of House leaders, the rule went down to defeat July 22, 205–216. That immediately sparked a bitter round of finger-pointing over who was responsible for delaying aid to the flood victims.

Five days later, Democrats reversed the outcome and adopted a nearly identical rule as opposition to the bill evaporated. It passed July 27 on a vote of 400–27.

With the floods growing worse, Clinton requested an additional $1.9 billion two days after the House vote, bringing the total to $4.7 billion. The Senate Appropriations Committee added the money and approved HR 2667 by voice vote on July 30. The price tag for the bill then grew to $5.7 billion on the Senate floor, where it passed by voice vote Aug. 4.

Eager to finish work, the House took up the bill again on Aug. 6, and agreed to the increased spending in the Senate version of the bill. The House also restored $300,000 for the Legal Services Corporation that the Senate had dropped, then passed the bill again by voice vote.

That small change required the Senate to vote again and it did so, clearing the bill Aug. 7 by voice vote. Clinton signed it into law on Aug. 12. ❏

Fiscal 1994 Rescissions

Conservative and moderate Democrats succeeded in November 1993 in pressing the House to vote for an additional $37 billion in spending cuts, though the amount was not as great as they wanted and the effort died in the House.

As passed, the bill (HR 3400—H Rept 103-366, Parts 1–10) would have cut $37.1 billion in outlays through fiscal 1998. The savings would not have been dedicated to deficit reduction, however, so Congress would have been free under the controlling budget resolution (H Con Res 64) to spend it on other programs.

Most of the savings, $32.5 billion in outlays, came from a plan Clinton had announced months before to eliminate 252,000 federal jobs. The other key components were $1.9 billion in rescissions from fiscal 1994 appropriations and $2.7 billion in savings over five years adapted from a proposal by President Clinton and Vice President Al Gore to streamline the federal government.

Before passage, Democratic leaders barely beat back a much more ambitious effort, led by Reps. Tim Penny, D-Minn., and John R. Kasich, R-Ohio, to triple the spending cuts in HR 3400. The bill died at the end of the 103rd Congress when the Senate did not act on it.

BACKGROUND

The rescissions fight was an outgrowth of the bruising battle over the budget reconciliation bill (HR 2264—PL 103-66). In their scramble to win votes to win House adoption of the conference report on HR 2264, House leaders promised Penny and other conservative Democrats a second round of deficit votes in the fall.

To fulfill the promise, Clinton outlined on Oct. 26 a six-year plan to cut spending by $11 billion. The plan added proposed rescissions to pieces of the administration's Gore-led "reinventing government" plan, titled the National Performance Review. That $108 billion collection of budget-saving ideas had been unveiled Sept. 7. As proposed, the elimination of 252,000 federal jobs was not included; Clinton had hoped to make those cuts by executive decision and not been locked into them by statute. ('Reinventing government,' p. 811)

Penny and Kasich, however, thought the administration proposal inadequate and they put together a much more ambitious plan to cut the deficit by $103 billion over five years.

The Penny-Kasich plan would have cut $26 billion from appropriations, $50 billion from Medicare and other entitlement programs and $27 billion from Clinton's plan to trim the federal payroll. Unlike the Clinton plan, all of the savings were to be dedicated to deficit reduction.

LEGISLATIVE ACTION

As introduced, HR 3400 proposed to save $9 billion from the National Performance Review. Those provisions were parceled out to 11 separate committees, which reported them back either intact or rewrote them in various ways.

Meanwhile, the Appropriations Committee Nov. 16 approved a separate bill (HR 3511—H Rept 103-368) that would have rescinded $1.5 billion from enacted fiscal 1994 appropriations for domestic programs, $600 million from defense programs and $450 million from foreign aid.

When HR 3400 came to the House floor, the provisions of HR 3511 were added to it, as was a provision taking credit for the planned job cuts. The change was made by the rule governing floor debate on the bill at the request of the leadership seeking to bolster the claimed savings.

The House passed HR 3400 on Nov. 22 by a 429–1 vote that belied the intensity of the day's action. It took an all-out lobbying blitz by House Democratic leaders and the White House to kill the Penny-Kasich amendment to the bill, which was rejected on a **key vote of 213–219 (R 156–18, D 57–200, I 0–1)**. *(1993 key votes, p. 979)*

Penny and Kasich were beaten by a major effort by the House's old guard. However, 60 percent of the freshman class elected in 1992 voted for their amendment. "There is no question that if this group can stay together, this is the group that is going to write the next budget for the country," Kasich said.

The effort ended there. Senate Appropriations Committee Chairman Robert C. Byrd, D-W.Va., argued that existing budget restraints had already taken a big bite from cherished programs. He declined to act on a draft Senate companion bill devised by Bob Kerrey, D-Neb., and Hank Brown, R-Colo. There was no further action on HR 3400 in the 103rd Congress. ❏

Fiscal 1995 Budget Resolution

After the budget battle of the year before, President Clinton and Congress opted in 1994 to take a year off from further efforts at reducing the federal deficit. Most of the budget action occurred on appropriations bills as Congress came to terms with the first year-to-year drop in real discretionary spending since 1969. With less to spend in fiscal 1995 than in 1994, lawmakers faced the sort of zero-sum game that deficit hawks had long advocated, in which most moves to spend money on new programs required scaling back or killing old ones.

Clinton set the tone in February 1994, when he sent Congress a budget request that mainly sought to rearrange some discretionary spending to make room for about $14 billion in "investments" in such areas as education, job training and health care. Congress largely went along, tinkering a bit with Clinton's investment priorities and approving a fiscal 1995 budget resolution (H Con Res 218) that cut just $13 billion more over five years than the $25 billion Clinton had requested.

That turned out to be the 1994 high-water mark for deficit

reduction. Other efforts, including spending cuts and a balanced-budget constitutional amendment, failed. *(Fiscal 1995 appropriations, p. 61, balanced-budget amendment, p. 62; budget-control efforts, p. 64)*

CLINTON BUDGET REQUEST

President Clinton sent Congress a $1.52 trillion fiscal 1995 budget request on Feb. 7 that was as modest as the preceding year's sweeping economic plan had been ambitious—a follow-up proposal that filled in the outlines of the deficit-reduction plan Congress mandated in 1993 and asked for a second, smaller installment of Democratic "investment" spending.

The White House argued that it was necessary to give the economy time to digest the 1993 package before initiating major new cuts. So, with a politically costly battle looming over health care reform and the deficit looking better than it had in years, Clinton elected to propose no broad new fiscal initiatives and essentially called for no new deficit reduction.

The budget request contained more money for schools, the homeless, children, police, research scientists, highway builders and other programs—but not very much of it. And the projected spending—some $13.4 billion—would be available only if Congress agreed to make room under the tight cap on discretionary spending by cutting other programs.

To pay for its new spending priorities, the administration proposed about $25 billion in one-year spending cuts. The budget called for terminating some 115 federal programs and cutting back another 200 or more, including dozens that immediately provoked opposition from Democrats. Clinton proposed to cut such Democratic standbys as public housing, mass transit operating subsidies and the Low-Income Home Energy Assistance Program (LIHEAP), which helped the poor pay their utility bills.

Carrying out a promise made in his State of the Union address Jan. 25 to "draw the line" against further defense cuts, Clinton requested $263.7 billion in new budget authority for defense. The previous year, the administration had projected $261.1 billion in overall defense spending for fiscal 1995, continuing a long-term reduction.

As part of the fiscal 1994 deficit-reduction bill, Congress tightened the existing budget caps that limited the amount of discretionary appropriations and extended the caps through fiscal 1998. As a result, discretionary spending for fiscal 1995 was set to decline in inflation-adjusted terms for the first time since 1969.

The budget projected a fiscal 1995 deficit of $176.1 billion, the smallest in five years and the third consecutive drop since the record high of $290.4 billion, set in 1992. (The White House predicted an even smaller 1995 deficit—$165.1 billion—if the effects of its health care reform plan were factored in.) Both the White House's Office of Management and Budget (OMB) and the Congressional Budget Office (CBO) ascribed the dramatic drop in the deficit—from a projection of more than $300 billion just a year before—mostly to the tax increases and spending cuts enacted in 1993.

But the good news on the deficit turned sour. The day after

Clinton released his budget, CBO Director Robert D. Reischauer unveiled a long-awaited CBO analysis of the president's health plan. Reischauer said the Clinton proposal held "the promise of reducing the deficit in the long term," but he put the turnaround date much further into the future than Clinton did. *(Health care plan, p. 513)*

While the White House said its health care plan could start cutting the deficit almost immediately, producing $59 billion in savings by 2000, Reischauer said the plan instead would add some $74 billion to the deficit over the same period before finally beginning to cut spending sometime after 2004.

BUDGET RESOLUTION

Congress completed work on its fiscal guidelines for the year on May 12, adopting a hold-the-line fiscal 1995 budget resolution (H Con Res 218—H Rept 103-490) that largely followed the proposal Clinton had submitted in February.

The chief difference between the original House and Senate versions of the $1.5 trillion budget resolution was an extra $26.1 billion in unspecified spending cuts approved by the Senate. In the end, the House and Senate agreed on an extra $13 billion in outlays to be taken out of appropriations over five years—$500 million of it in fiscal 1995.

In the end it would be the appropriators who would have the job of deciding on the program cuts; their only obligation to the budget was to abide by the overall cap.

Under the caps agreed to as part of the fiscal 1994 budget reconciliation bill, discretionary outlays already had been set to decline from $546.8 billion in fiscal 1994 to $541.1 billion in fiscal 1995. The $500 million in additional 1995 cuts required by the budget resolution brought that to $540.6 billion. Accounting for inflation and population growth, that meant fiscal 1995 outlays would fall about $13 billion below the amount needed to keep programs even with 1994. *(Fiscal 1994 budget reconciliation, p. 44)*

Congress's fiscal 1995 blueprint expected a deficit of $175.3 billion—the smallest in dollar terms in six years. Measured against the size of the economy, the projected deficit would amount to 2.5 percent of the gross domestic product (GDP), the lowest in 16 years. The average size of the deficit since 1982 had been 4.4 percent of GDP.

The budget resolution contained no provisions for a new budget reconciliation bill to align taxes and entitlement spending with deficit-reduction goals. It focused instead on rearranging spending within the discretionary part of the budget.

House Committee Action

Voting strictly along party lines, the House Budget Committee on March 3 approved a slightly modified version of Clinton's budget (H Rept 103-428). The vote was 26–17.

The committee tinkered with Clinton's plans to rearrange spending under the fiscal 1995 discretionary limit, imposing some of its own priorities and partially restoring some cuts Clinton had proposed, such as $494 million for the LIHEAP program and $100 million for mass transit operating subsidies.

For the second year in a row, the committee's Republicans, led by John R. Kasich of Ohio, coalesced behind an ambitious alternative budget that included scores of cuts, many of them highly detailed. Kasich said the GOP alternative offered much deeper deficit reduction over five years than Clinton's plan did, while offsetting about a third of the tax increases.

The GOP plan included a tax credit of $500 per child for families with incomes of less than $200,000 a year. Democrats lined up unanimously in the "no" column to defeat the GOP alternative, 17–26.

House Floor Action

The House voted 223–175 on March 11 to adopt the budget resolution as it had been crafted by the committee.

Before adopting H Con Res 218, the House on March 10 rejected a liberal Democratic alternative that would have cut defense appropriations by a relatively modest $2.4 billion in 1995 to pay for additional social spending. Clinton and Democratic leaders opposed the effort, however, and their vigorous lobbying paid off. The amendment was rejected on a **key vote of 105–313 (R 12–160, D 92–153, I 1–0)**. It was the last time a serious attempt was made in the House in 1994 to cut defense spending. (1994 key votes, p. 1003)

The House also rejected a pair of conservative alternatives that called for further deficit reduction.

Senate Committee Action

In the Senate, the Budget Committee voted 13–8 on March 17 in favor of a budget resolution (S Con Res 63—S Rept 103-238) that over five years cut $26.1 billion more in outlays than Clinton requested. One Republican, Charles E. Grassley of Iowa, crossed party lines to vote yes with the Democrats. The budget otherwise largely tracked Clinton's proposal.

Committee Chairman Sasser voted for the committee budget, although he first tried to win support for a stay-the-course draft budget resolution similar to that approved by the House, arguing that Congress had done as much as was prudent in 1993.

But Republicans and a handful of the committee's Democrats disagreed. Kent Conrad, D-N.D., and three other Democrats—Jim Exon of Nebraska, Frank R. Lautenberg of New Jersey and Paul Simon of Illinois—joined the panel's nine Republicans in voting to add cuts to Sasser's draft budget. The committee approved the amendment, offered by Exon and Grassley, by a vote of 13–8.

The committee also voted, 9–12, along party lines to reject a substitute budget offered by ranking Republican Pete V. Domenici of New Mexico that would have cut an additional $322 billion over five years, largely by cutting $180 billion from nondefense appropriations and by using Clinton's proposed savings in Medicare and Medicaid not to pay for health care reform, as Clinton wanted to do, but to reduce the deficit.

As approved by the committee, the budget resolution stuck with Clinton's priorities in most areas. For instance, the panel recommended restoring most cuts Clinton sought in the LIHEAP program and in mass transit operating subsidies.

Senate Floor Action

The full Senate adopted H Con Res 218 by a vote of 57–40 on March 25, after substituting the text of the Budget Committee's measure.

Before the final vote, many senators expressed severe doubts about the additional cuts that had been ordered by the committee, saying that the defense budget would bear the brunt of the cuts. Defense made up about half of all discretionary spending, and Armed Services Committee Chairman Sam Nunn, D-Ga., said he expected that as much as 60 percent of whatever cuts Congress finally accepted would come from the defense budget.

Several attempts to protect defense were soundly defeated, however; alternatives such as cutting Medicare and other entitlement spending could not win a majority.

Conference, Final Action

After weeks of wrangling over the Senate's extra $26.1 billion in spending reductions, House and Senate conferees reached a compromise (H Rept 103-490) early the week of May 2, agreeing to cut $13 billion below the budget caps in stages through 1999.

Before conferees settled down to resolve their differences, the administration engaged in yet another battle over additional spending cuts. Kasich and some Democratic allies in the House tried to win a procedural vote to instruct House conferees to seek deeper cuts. After a vigorous lobbying effort, the House rejected the motion on April 14 on a **key vote of 202–216 (R 159–6, D 43–209, I 0–1)**.

The House adopted the conference report by a vote of 220–183 on May 5. The Senate followed suit May 12, approving the budget on a **key vote of 53–46 (R 2–42, D 51–4)**. The vote on final passage in the Senate was mostly along party lines, though it was notable for its low profile when compared with the intense partisanship over the budget the previous year.

Budget negotiators arranged for the reductions to start gradually, cutting $500 million below the appropriations cap for fiscal 1995. In 1996, however, the cuts were to accelerate dramatically, slicing $5.4 billion from that year's $548.1 billion spending cap. The rest of the cuts—$7.1 billion—were to be taken from the spending limits in 1997–1999. But the budget resolution was only binding for the 1995 cuts. ❑

Fiscal 1995 Appropriations

Congress repeated one of its rarest of accomplishments on Sept. 30, 1994, when it cleared the last of the 13 annual spending bills before the beginning of the new fiscal year Oct. 1. It was only the third time lawmakers had done that since 1948—and as a result 1994 was a rare year that saw Congress take no action on continuing appropriations resolutions.

Appropriators were determined that 1994 would be different, and their unusually quick finish was attributed to several factors:

• Appropriators knew early on how much they could spend. Spending limits set in the fiscal 1991 budget reconciliation bill and extended in the fiscal 1994 budget reconciliation bill (HR

2264—PL 103-66) enabled them to do preliminary work quickly, without waiting for the fiscal 1995 budget resolution to be adopted. (*Congress and the Nation Vol. VIII, p. 55; fiscal 1994 budget reconciliation, p. 44; fiscal 1995 budget resolution, p. 59*)

• There was an early push to get the spending bills out of the way to clear floor debate time in the fall for a sweeping plan to overhaul the nation's health care system. (*Health care overhaul, p. 513*)

• New House Appropriations Chairman David R. Obey, D-Wis., cracked the whip, determined to finish on time in his first year. Senate Appropriations Chairman Robert C. Byrd, D-W.Va., did likewise.

• Individual problems that had slowed bills in the past, such as public lands disputes on the Interior bill, melted away.

The fact that the spending bills were enacted with some dispatch did not mean it was a painless process for Congress. Five years of increasingly tight spending caps dictated by the 1990 budget deal produced a phenomenon lawmakers had not seen in nearly three decades: the first year-to-year drop in actual discretionary spending (outlays) since 1969.

Not counting "emergency spending" outside the budget caps, discretionary outlays were projected to fall from $543.3 billion in fiscal 1994 to $540.1 billion in 1995.

In addition to tight spending caps, appropriators had to cope with an activist president with an aggressive "investment" agenda. President Clinton's fiscal 1995 budget request called for widespread cutbacks and program eliminations to make way for his own spending priorities, which did not always match those long favored by Congress.

The result was the sort of zero-sum game that congressional deficit hawks had long advocated, in which most moves to spend money on new programs required scaling back or killing old ones.

House Appropriations Chairman Obey, who succeeded the late William H. Natcher, D-Ky., in the spring, said appropriators killed 40 programs altogether and cut another 408 below their 1994 spending levels. That allowed the committee to remain under its spending limits while still giving Clinton about 65 percent of the priority spending he asked for.

LEGISLATIVE ACTION

The House adopted the conference reports on the last of the 13 regular appropriations bills on Sept. 29, when it approved the defense appropriations bill (HR 4650—PL 103-335). The Senate cleared 12 of the 13 bills by Sept. 29, and the 13th, for the District of Columbia (HR 4649—PL 103-334), on Sept. 30.

Supplemental Spending

Lawmakers also passed two fiscal 1994 supplemental appropriations bills.

An $11 billion bill (HR 3759—PL 103-211), signed Feb. 12, provided assistance for victims of the January earthquake in California and for other natural disasters, as well as money for U.S. peacekeeping operations and for a variety of other federal programs.

The earthquake supplemental provided a vehicle in the Senate for a bipartisan group to attempt a new round of spending cuts during a year in which Congress was determined that deficit-reduction would take a back seat. (*Fiscal 1995 budget resolution, p. 59; budget-control efforts, p. 64*)

An amendment offered by Bob Kerrey, D-Neb., and Hank Brown, R-Colo., would have cut spending by $94 billion over five years. It was killed on a tabling motion offered by Appropriations Chairman Byrd that was adopted on a **key vote of 65–31 (R 23–19, D 42–12).** (*1994 key votes, p. 1003*)

A second supplemental bill (HR 4568—PL 103-275), enacted July 5, provided just $18.1 million in new spending authority, but it lifted loan ceilings by $93 billion for the Federal Housing Administration and the Government National Mortgage Association.

Critical Fights

Among the most important floor votes during the annual appropriations cycle involved NASA's space station, often criticized for cost overruns. An amendment by Rep. Tim Roemer, D-Ind., to cut $2.1 billion from the space station program was rejected on June 29 during consideration of the Veterans Affairs, Housing and Urban Development and Independent Agencies (VA-HUD) appropriations bill (HR 4624—PL 103-327) on a **key vote of 155–278 (R 40–136, D 114–142, I 1–0).**

In the Senate, opponents of an expected action by Clinton to send military troops into Haiti to stabilize that country tried to amend the foreign operations spending bill (HR 4426—PL 103-306) to block such intervention unless Clinton sought congressional approval or determined that it was necessary to protect U.S. lives or security interests. The amendment, by Judd Gregg, R-N.H., was rejected on a **key vote of 34–65 (R 34–10, D 0–55).**

Finally, an obscure Environmental Protection Agency regulation provoked a major skirmish that pitted farm state senators promoting the use of corn-based ethanol in gasoline against oil state senators and required Vice President Al Gore to cast a tie-breaking vote.

The imbroglio involved an EPA rule under the 1990 Clean Air Act that required, in effect, at least 30 percent of gasoline sold in certain areas to contain ethanol, affecting about 10 percent of the gasoline sold nationwide. Sen. J. Bennett Johnston, D-La., offered an amendment to the VA-HUD bill Aug. 3 to block the regulation by denying the EPA money to carry it out. His amendment was rejected on a **key vote of 51–50 (R 19–25, D 31–25).** ❑

Balanced-Budget Amendment

The Clinton administration and Democratic leaders managed to rally sufficient opposition in 1994 to a proposed balanced-budget amendment to the Constitution to defeat the measure in both the House and Senate.

Proponents had hoped election-year pressures would turn the tide in their favor. However, by raising the specter of cuts to Social Security and giving wavering Democrats enough political cover, opponents managed to defeat the measure.

The proposed constitutional change—sponsored by Paul Simon, D-Ill., in the Senate (S J Res 41) and Charles W. Stenholm, D-Texas, in the House (H J Res 103)—stated that "total outlays for any fiscal year shall not exceed total receipts for that fiscal year" unless three-fifths of the House and Senate voted to lift the requirement.

The requirement would have taken effect in fiscal 1999 at the earliest. Under the Constitution, identical versions of the amendment had to be adopted by two-thirds majorities in both the House and Senate and then be ratified by at least three-fourths of the states (38). The resolution gave the states seven years to complete the task.

The defeat of the amendment was a study in legislative tactics. In each chamber, opponents offered a watered-down version that would have required a balanced budget but effectively put surplus Social Security revenues—which were officially "off budget" but used to calculate whether the budget reached balance—off limits, making it far more difficult to actually achieve balance.

In neither chamber did the alternative amendments come close to passing. But Democrats were able to vote for them and against either the Simon or Stenholm measures and claim they supported a balanced budget. Enough Democrats chose that route that the balanced budget drive failed in both chambers.

BACKGROUND

Growing public concern about the deficit and Congress's perceived inability to address it had made the balanced-budget amendment a popular idea among lawmakers in both parties. Because the amendment required a balanced budget without specifying how that would be achieved, it gave members a chance to vote against the deficit without offending voters by proposing specific spending cuts or tax increases.

In 1992, a similar constitutional amendment fell nine votes short in the House and was blocked by a filibuster in the Senate. Ten years earlier, in 1982, the Senate passed a balanced-budget amendment, only to see it fall 46 votes short in the House. Similar proposals made it to the Senate floor in 1986 and the House floor in 1990, but in both cases failed to win a two-thirds majority. (*Congress and the Nation Vol. VI, p. 52; Congress and the Nation Vol. VII, p. 57; Congress and the Nation Vol. VIII, pp. 75, 84*)

LEGISLATIVE ACTION

The Senate Judiciary Committee had approved Simon's resolution (S J Res 41—S Rept 103-163) by a vote of 15–3 on July 22, 1993. With time growing short at the end of the session, Senate leaders postponed a vote until early in 1994.

Stenholm had introduced the House resolution in February 1993, but it saw no action that year.

Senate Floor Action

The Simon resolution came to the Senate floor for a pair of votes on March 1, 1994.

After first rejecting a substitute amendment sponsored by Harry Reid, D-Nev., by a 22–78 vote, the Senate then rejected Simon's resolution by a **key vote of 63–37 (R 41–3, D 22–34)**—

four votes short of the two-thirds majority needed to adopt the resolution and send it to the states for ratification. (*1994 key votes, p. 1003*)

With a Democrat in the White House who felt his domestic agenda was being threatened, the Senate debate had more overt partisan characteristics than in past years. Opposition was spearheaded by Majority Leader George J. Mitchell, D-Maine, and Appropriations Committee Chairman Robert C. Byrd, D-W.Va. Extensive lobbying by the White House bolstered their efforts.

Reid offered his substitute when opponents to Simon's measure found they were unable to muster the 34 votes needed for its outright defeat. His alternative proved to be a powerful political wedge in the debate.

It included several provisions that would have made it more likely that Congress would continue to run a deficit. Most importantly, the Reid substitute would have exempted Social Security, which meant that the annual surplus in Social Security payroll tax collections could no longer have been counted to reduce the deficit. The Reid amendment also would have allowed the creation of a separate capital budget to permit borrowing for highways and other capital improvements.

The partisan pressure showed in the end as Democrats provided 34 of the 37 votes against Simon's resolution. Four Democrats and one Republican who voted for a similar measure in 1986 changed their positions and opposed the Simon version: Democrats Tom Harkin of Iowa, J. Bennett Johnston of Louisiana, Claiborne Pell of Rhode Island and David Pryor of Arkansas, and Republican Ted Stevens of Alaska.

House Floor Action

The House defeated Stenholm's balanced-budget amendment on March 17 on a **key vote of 271–153: R 172–1; D 99–151 (ND 47–122, SD 59–29); I 0–1.** The tally was 12 votes short of the two-thirds majority needed. And the measure received nine fewer votes than it had in 1992.

Stenholm had forced his proposal to the floor using the same tactic he employed in 1992. First, he introduced his own king-of-the-hill rule (H J Res 103) governing floor action on the constitutional amendment. His rule allowed for floor debate on a series of four alternative balanced-budget amendments; the last version adopted was to be submitted for a final vote, requiring a two-thirds majority.

Next, Stenholm gathered the 218 signatures needed on a discharge petition that allowed him to bypass the Rules Committee and bring the rule and the balanced-budget amendment directly to the floor. The rule was adopted by a 387–22 vote on March 16.

The various alternatives gave lawmakers from both parties plenty of opportunity to go on record in support of the concept of balancing the budget. But it also gave the leadership a vehicle for derailing Stenholm's support.

Only one alternative other than Stenholm's received a majority. A mostly Republican substitute sponsored by Joe L. Barton, R-Texas, and W. J. "Billy" Tauzin, D-La., would have prohibited a deficit but also barred Congress from raising taxes at a rate that exceeded the rate of increase in national income, except by a three-fifths vote of the Congress. The political attractiveness of opposing tax increases was demonstrated when the House endorsed the Barton-Tauzin plan by a 211–204 vote.

Two other alternatives were rejected, including one sponsored by Bob Wise, D-W.Va., that was reminiscent of Reid's Senate substitute and likewise was crafted to give cover to wavering Democrats.

Stenholm's version was then adopted by voice vote, superseding the Barton-Tauzin version and setting up a final vote. On final passage, though, Stenholm's resolution fell short of the necessary two-thirds majority. The Wise amendment siphoned off enough Democratic votes to help ensure Stenholm's defeat. Sixty-four lawmakers, all Democrats, voted for Wise's version and against Stenholm's.   ❑

Budget-Control Efforts

Congress showed little desire in 1994 to make a concerted run at the deficit. So, those members who were most concerned about the issue turned instead to efforts to overhaul the budget process.

A small core of so-called deficit hawks in the House made an unsuccessful run at forcing floor debate and votes on a series of spending cuts—the "A to Z" plan named for its sponsors, Reps. Robert E. Andrews, D-N.J., and Bill Zeliff, R-N.H. They failed to overcome the objections of the Democratic leadership, however, and their parliamentary tactics intended to force the leadership's hand fell short. The floor debate never occurred.

One eventual result of the "A to Z" fight, however, was that the House passed bills to strengthen the president's ability to enact rescissions of already appropriated money, to limit entitlement spending, to bar the use of automatic inflation adjustments when budgeting for the upcoming year and to prohibit Congress from including nonemergency spending in emergency spending bills.

None of these measures received attention from the Senate, however, and they died at the end of the 103rd Congress. Indeed, the Senate was never expected to act, a fact that made the House votes largely symbolic.

'A TO Z' SPENDING CUTS

In June, Democratic leaders quashed the attempt by Andrews and Zeliff to shut down all other business in the House and devote several days to debating and voting on members' proposals for spending cuts. The leadership refused to allow them to bring their plan for spending cuts to the floor, so the sponsors began gathering signatures for a discharge petition that would bypass the Rules Committee and require floor time.

Andrews and Zeliff's petition was for a bill (HR 3266) that was a shell waiting to be filled with spending-cut amendments, accompanied by a rule that provided for 56 hours of floor debate. It contained no specific language on spending cuts.

They said the legislation was an expression of the frustrations they felt at being regularly blocked from offering spending-cut amendments by restrictive floor rules and committee procedures that excluded their proposals.

Zeliff (the original mover behind the plan) and Andrews gathered 204 signatures, 14 short of the 218 needed, before Democratic leaders cut a deal with key Democratic supporters that took the wind out of the plan's sails.

The plan's largely Republican backers (167 of the 204 signers of the discharge petition were Republicans) styled themselves as underdogs fighting an autocratic, out-of-touch House leadership. Conservative commentators such as radio talk show host Rush Limbaugh and the *Wall Street Journal* editorial page actively pushed the idea.

Democratic leaders stopped the plan's progress with an alternative agreed to June 17 by a group of conservative Democrats led by Bill Orton of Utah that repeated a pledge made earlier in the year to Charles W. Stenholm, D-Texas, one his party's most adamant deficit hawks. House Majority Leader Richard A. Gephardt, D-Mo., followed up with a letter stating that the House would hold at least eight votes on spending cuts and budget process changes before the August recess.

BUDGET PROCESS CHANGES

Stenholm had won agreement early in the year from House Democratic leaders to take up bills to change the budget process in exchange for his support of the fiscal 1995 budget resolution (H Con Res 218). *(Fiscal 1995 budget resolution, p. 59)*

In the deal to end the battle over the "A to Z" plan, Gephardt told Orton that budget process votes would occur before the August recess, but that timetable slipped.

Still, by the end of the session, the House had voted on bills to allow for expedited rescissions, to limit entitlements, to restrict automatic inflation adjustments and to constrain emergency spending bills.

Expedited Rescissions

The House voted to strengthen the president's existing authority to propose to rescind, or cut, individual items from appropriations bills. The House passed the expedited rescissions bill (HR 4600—H Rept 103-557, Part 1), known popularly as a modified line-item veto, on July 14 by a vote of 342–69. It was the third time in as many years that the House had endorsed such a bill.

Before passage, the House rejected protests by senior Democrats that it was shifting too much power from Congress to the White House and agreed to stiffen the bill's provisions.

Under existing law, Congress could ignore a presidential request to cancel, or rescind, previously appropriated spending. The request went into effect only if a majority in both chambers approved it; if Congress ignored the request, it expired after 45 days.

As reported by the Rules Committee, HR 4600 would have changed existing law to require Congress to vote on presidential rescissions proposals rather than allowing them to expire. Stenholm offered an amendment to permit the president to reach inside tax bills as well as appropriations bills to pull out targeted tax breaks and ask Congress to cancel them. Stenholm's amendment was adopted by a vote of 298–121.

The House rejected, 205–218, an even stiffer line-item veto

proposal by Gerald B. H. Solomon, R-N.Y., and House Minority Leader Robert H. Michel, R-Ill. Under their amendment, the president's veto of a spending item or a targeted tax break would have gone into effect unless both chambers turned it down.

As it had done twice before, the Senate let the rescissions bill languish without action. The adamant opposition of Senate Appropriations Committee Chairman Robert C. Byrd, D-W.Va., who was unwilling to cede additional authority over spending bills to the White House, was enough to kill the legislation in the 103rd Congress.

Limiting Entitlement Spending

In a series of lopsided votes, the House passed a bill (HR 4604) to set limits on entitlement spending for Medicare, farm programs, welfare, food stamps and the like, and require spending cuts or other action if those ceilings were breached. House members insisted, however, on putting Social Security, which made up 44 percent of all entitlements, strictly off limits.

The House passed the entitlement control measure on July 21 by a vote of 316–107 after first rejecting a substitute plan that would have kept Social Security on the chopping block. The amendment, offered by Stenholm, would have forced real cuts, by capping all entitlement spending at fiscal 1995 levels, with adjustments to allow for increases in the Consumer Price Index and for demographic changes. Proof that Social Security remained a politically untouchable issue on Capitol Hill came on Stenholm's amendment, which was rejected on a **key vote of 37–392 (R 9–165, D 28–226, I 0–1).**

The House also voted to bar Congress from increasing Social Security taxes to offset other entitlement spending. *(1994 key votes, p. 1003)*

The bill would have required the president to set overall targets for fiscal 1994–1997 entitlement spending. If spending exceeded the targets by more than 0.5 percent in any year, the president would have to propose to make up some or all of the gap with spending cuts, tax increases or both.

Alternatively, he could recommend increasing the targets. Congress would have to produce at least as much deficit reduction as the president had, and it would have had to vote separately if it chose to increase the targets.

Baseline Budgeting

On Aug. 12, the House gave voice vote approval to a third budget-process bill (HR 4907) requiring that the amounts budgeted for discretionary spending programs in one fiscal year be compared with the amounts provided the previous year, without adjusting for inflation.

The change was to apply to the annual budgets of both the president and Congress and was at odds with existing practice, which was to compare new budget figures with a "current services" baseline that showed what it would cost to continue a program at its existing level after taking inflation into account.

Emergency Spending Rules

On Aug. 17, the House voted 406–6 to pass a bill (HR 4906) to modify the way Congress handled emergency spending for floods, earthquakes, military actions and the like. The bill barred Congress from mixing emergency spending, which had special treatment under budget rules, with nonemergency add-ons. Critics said the ability to mix the two types of spending encouraged lawmakers to load up fast-moving emergency bills with special interest items in ways that made it impossible to trim the nonemergency spending without voting to kill the entire bill.   ❑

1995–1996

The Republicans' victory at the polls in November 1994 appeared destined to change congressional budget politics for the balance of the 1990s—though not in so profound a fashion as might have been expected.

Balancing the budget had been a Republican goal for more than a decade, but the GOP had never had the clout on Capitol Hill to make the dream a reality. Having won the 1994 elections on the platform of the "Contract with America," House Republicans in particular were energized to press their agenda. And the goal of a balanced budget was suddenly transformed into a mandate.

As it turned out, though, neither President Bill Clinton nor the American public was as certain of that mandate, and 1995 came to a close with a balanced budget nowhere in sight. Bills to change tax and spending policies to achieve that end had been vetoed. And the government was shut down when Republicans decided not to bend to Clinton's demands for compromise. The public blamed the GOP for the shutdowns and in 1996 reelected Clinton, in part on the expectation that he would continue to check the more aggressive impulses of congressional Republicans.

Similarly, the political constraints that had prevented enactment of a constitutional amendment to require a balanced budget were not entirely swept away in the 1994 electoral tide; that effort failed as well, as it had on several occasions in the past.

On the other hand, the debate had changed. Clinton and the Democrats began talking more about the steps that would be needed to balance the budget. And Republicans started considering where they could compromise.

The goal wouldn't be achieved in 1996 either, but the president and Congress continued to move closer together on this critical issue.

Fiscal 1996 Budget Resolution

As the first step in their quest to reshape the federal government, congressional Republicans rallied in 1995 behind a bold seven-year plan to balance the federal budget. The plan sought massive reductions in spending, and still made room for the largest proposed tax cut since Ronald Reagan was president.

The fiscal 1996 budget resolution (H Con Res 67—H Rept 104-159)—a blueprint for congressional spending and tax decisions—won final approval from both chambers on June 29 on virtual party-line votes. The plan was a manifesto of the Republican vision of a government that was far smaller, much cheaper and far less intrusive than the one that then existed.

Their goal was to balance the budget by 2002 while cutting taxes and leaving more than half of all federal spending (Social Security, defense and interest on the debt) untouched.

To meet that goal, GOP budget-cutters called for unprecedented reductions in the growth of the twin health care entitlements: Medicare, the federally subsidized health insurance plan for the elderly, and Medicaid, the government's health insurance program for the poor. They also provided for cutbacks in a variety of programs for veterans, farmers, federal retirees and other traditionally vocal constituencies.

The budget resolution locked Congress into a process that required committees to propose a staggering $894 billion in spending cuts over seven years. The cuts were to be achieved along two separate paths:

• **Budget Reconciliation.** Much of the savings was to come through a budget reconciliation bill; the specific provisions were to be drafted by tax and authorizing committees. The budget resolution's recommended savings included $270 billion from Medicare, $182 billion from Medicaid and $175 billion from other mandatory programs. *(Fiscal 1996 budget reconciliation, p. 68)*

• **Appropriations.** Other savings were to be achieved through cuts in the 13 regular appropriations bills. The budget resolution set new caps on discretionary spending from fiscal 1996 through fiscal 2002, including specific caps for defense and nondefense spending through fiscal 1998. The caps were expected to achieve $190 billion in savings from nondefense discretionary spending, while adding $58 billion for defense. *(Fiscal 1996 appropriations, p. 71)*

Once such savings were achieved, Congress could hand out $245 billion in tax cuts. If it worked—and the plan's success depended heavily on there being no recession before 2002—the budget would be balanced for the first time since 1969.

Democrats savaged the budget resolution as an unconscionable attack on the poor, the elderly and children, but they did not unite behind a comprehensive alternative of their own.

The GOP election triumph seemed to harden Republican attitudes toward what many expected would be a devastating showdown with the president in the fall, when the budget resolution would be translated into the budget reconciliation bill and the 13 potentially difficult appropriations bills, all of which would require the president's signature.

Republicans threatened to raise the ante dramatically by tying some or all of those bills to a must-pass measure to raise the limit on the national debt. Without an increase in the debt limit, the federal government was due to run out of borrowing authority in the fall, a move that could prevent the government from mailing regular monthly Social Security benefits checks and theoretically trigger a default, followed by domestic and international financial chaos. *(Debt-limit increase, p. 76)*

CLINTON'S BUDGET REQUEST

President Clinton on Feb. 6, 1995, sent Congress a $1.6 trillion fiscal 1996 budget request that contained little new deficit reduction and no initiatives on health care or welfare. The message to congressional Republicans—who had made political gains by demonizing Clinton's 1993 deficit-reduction plan—was clear: it's your turn.

Measured against the promises of the Republicans, who had taken over Congress, Clinton's bid was decidedly modest. Clinton proposed middle-class tax cuts of about $63 billion over five years, financed by $144 billion in spending cuts, leaving net deficit reduction of $81 billion—less than one-fifth of the savings that his 1993 budget package produced and nowhere near enough to set the budget on a path toward balance.

Clinton included familiar "investment" spending proposals for priority programs in education, job training, health care and other areas, though it was clear that most or all of them would be discarded by Republicans.

He also called for broad program terminations and consolidations that might have been considered radical in a Democratic-led Congress, but were just a budgetary snack for Republicans who wanted to radically downsize the government.

Clinton's budget called for $1.6 trillion in spending in fiscal 1996, up about 4.8 percent from 1995. Over the following five years, spending was to grow by about 4.3 percent a year, driven by entitlement programs (up about 6.7 percent a year) and net interest on the national debt (up about 4.8 percent a year).

He called for domestic appropriations to drop over the same period, while defense spending was slated to get a boost—but the changes were so small that the effects of inflation would cause both to fall sharply in real terms.

The net effect was to continue the trend in which entitlement spending grew strongly, absorbing a larger and larger share of the budget (rising to about 55 percent by the year 2000), while traditional appropriated spending dropped (from 34 percent of the budget in 1996 to 29 percent four years later).

Clinton proposed to reduce the deficit by $144 billion over five years. The bulk of the savings, about $101 billion, was to come from extending the existing caps on discretionary appropriations. In effect, the White House generated most of the cuts by first projecting what inflation-adjusted spending would be through 2000 and then cutting that spending back to the freeze level that already applied through 1998.

Another $29 billion in savings was to come from mandatory spending, which included the entitlements that all sides agreed must be brought under control if the deficit was ever to be mastered. But the administration got almost half those savings simply by extending expiring money-making provisions, chiefly in Medicare and veterans' benefits. Other major savings were to come from an expanded auction of the broadcast spectrum and sales of government assets.

Clinton's budget also called for ambitious changes in the structure of government spending. Altogether, Clinton called for terminating 131 mostly small programs, cutting 86 and consolidating 271 into 27 programs.

The deficit was expected to rise after three years of decline, but only modestly, to about $197 billion in 1996. After a brief bump up to $213 billion in 1997, the administration projected deficits slightly less than $200 billion through the year 2000.

Republicans sharply criticized the White House for accepting such large deficits, but the administration contended that the deficit, while still a problem, was under control, particularly when compared with the size of the overall economy.

LEGISLATIVE ACTION

As recently as November 1994, the idea that Congress could make a serious run at balancing the budget was dubious. Even early in 1995, the two new Budget committee chairmen—Rep. John R. Kasich, R-Ohio, and Sen. Pete V. Domenici, R-N.M.—worried that rank-and-file Republicans might not have the nerve to make the necessary spending cuts. Domenici advised settling for a "down payment" on a balanced budget.

But the political climate had shifted. Clinton himself jumped in June 13 with a proposal to balance the budget, though with smaller cuts and over a 10-year period, three years longer than the GOP plan. Even liberal Democrats came to concede the goal of balancing the budget, although they differed radically with Republicans over the means.

House Action

The House Budget Committee approved H Con Res 67 (H Rept 104-120) on May 11 by a largely party-line vote of 24–17. (Democrat-later-turned Republican Mike Parker of Mississippi voted with the Republicans.)

The budget resolution promised to cut spending by $1.04 trillion over seven years. However, it also included $287 billion in net tax cuts, which added to the projected deficit. That left a bottom line of $756 billion in deficit reduction over seven years.

The House cuts swept across the budget, touching every major area except defense and Social Security. Even when the absolute dollars in a program were slated to increase, as they were in Medicare, the rate of increase was so much lower than under existing law that the program would have to be overhauled to meet the budget's goals.

The House adopted H Con Res 67 on May 18 by a nearly party-line vote of 238–193. One Republican, Michael Patrick Flanagan of Illinois, voted against the measure, and eight Democrats voted for it.

Senate Action

The Senate Budget Committee adopted its version of the budget resolution (S Con Res 13—S Rept 104-82) on May 11 on a 12–10 party-line vote. The seven-year plan projected a deficit of $157 billion in fiscal 1996, dwindling to $29 billion in fiscal 2001 and a slight surplus of $2 billion in 2002.

To get there, it called for $958 billion in deficit reduction through deep cuts in spending for entitlement programs such as Medicare and Medicaid, and even deeper cuts in appropriations, especially for domestic programs and foreign aid.

At Domenici's insistence, however, the Senate committee budget allowed for tax cuts less than half the size of those in the House budget—$170 billion—and made even that much conditional on enactment first of a deficit-reducing budget reconciliation bill. The Congressional Budget Office (CBO) would have to confirm that the bill was really big enough to balance the budget by 2002 before Congress could go on to pass the tax cuts.

And, while the House had given a quick thumbs-up to its balanced-budget plan, lingering tensions among Senate Republicans over taxes and defense cuts slowed Senate floor action. The Senate debated its measure a week before adopting H Con Res 67 on a 57–42 vote on May 25, after amending it with the text of S Con Res 13. In the end, the plan for $961 billion in deficit reduction adopted by the Senate was virtually identical to that drafted by Domenici.

Three Democratic deficit hawks crossed over to vote for the GOP plan. They were Charles S. Robb of Virginia, whom Democrats had removed from the Budget Committee some years before when he was thought to be too conservative; Bob Kerrey of Nebraska, whose last-minute threat to vote no almost sank Clinton's budget plan in 1993; and Sam Nunn of Georgia, who voted against the 1993 Clinton plan.

After rejecting an alternative by Phil Gramm, R-Texas, to impose stiffer spending cuts and add $312 billion in tax cuts resembling the House plan, the Senate voted, 54–45, to adopt a much weaker fallback plan by Connecticut Democrat Joseph I. Lieberman and Republicans Rod Grams of Minnesota and Spencer Abraham of Michigan.

It changed Domenici's language to say the Senate "shall" rather than "may" alter the budget so that any CBO-approved economic bonus could be used for a tax cut.

Outvoted Democrats could not realistically hope to make major changes to the budget resolution. But they did manage to single out and force Republicans to defend the plan's most politically painful cutbacks in education, Medicare, Medicaid, the earned-income tax credit and other high-profile programs.

The Democrats focused most of their efforts on highlighting GOP tax-cut plans by trying in amendment after amendment to get Republicans to use the $170 billion economic bonus not for a tax cut, but to moderate the cuts in Medicare and other programs.

But Republicans accused Democrats of trying to spend a bonus that Democrats had done nothing to earn, and they held firm in rejecting all major attempts to change the bill.

The only significant changes to Domenici's budget came when Republicans themselves were uncomfortable enough with the tough cuts to seek relief. Olympia Snowe, R-Maine, teamed with Paul Simon, D-Ill., to restore $9.4 billion of the $13.75 billion that was to be cut from student loans; this was to be offset by ending a tax exemption for foreign corporations operating in the United States. The amendment passed, 67–32.

Appropriations Chairman Mark O. Hatfield, R-Ore., managed to restore $7 billion for the National Institutes of Health by taking the money out of other domestic spending programs. Hatfield's amendment passed, 85–14.

Conference, Final Action

Tax cuts were the most contentious issue as House and Senate conferees began working June 8 to craft a compromise budget resolution that could pass both chambers.

In addition to taxes, conferees had to resolve differences over the size of the deficit-reduction package, whether to increase spending for defense, how much to cut Medicare and Medicaid and what agencies to close.

GOP leaders reached their compromise June 22. The budget plan promised to balance the budget by 2002, while giving taxpayers a $245 billion tax cut. Agreement on the seven-year, $894 billion deficit-reduction package came after two weeks of sometimes difficult intraparty negotiations.

Critical elements of the agreement included:

• **Tax Cuts.** The biggest difference between the two chambers was over taxes. House Republican leaders were under pressure from Senate conferees to reduce the size of the cut from $353 billion to $230 billion, but House conferees determined that their bottom line was about $250 billion. If they went much below that, they risked losing their troops. Giving only slightly, they agreed to $245 billion over seven years.

The budget resolution instructed authorizing committees to report enough spending cuts to the Budget committees to balance the budget by the year 2002. CBO would then "score" the resulting bill to ensure the proposed cuts were enough to actually balance the budget. If CBO approved, the Senate Budget Committee could immediately release $245 billion to the Senate Finance Committee for tax cuts. Finance would then have five days to report its tax cuts, which would be packaged with the proposed spending cuts in a single reconciliation bill.

• **Defense Spending.** Conferees agreed to increase defense spending by $33 billion over seven years, far below the increase of $67.8 billion adopted by the House. (The Senate did not include an increase for defense.)

• **Medicare, Medicaid.** In easily the most politically risky element of the plan, conferees agreed to reduce the growth in spending for Medicare by $270 billion over seven years. The House wanted $288 billion in cuts, the Senate $256 billion.

The amount was far greater than what was needed to achieve their most public aim—saving the Medicare trust fund from projected bankruptcy in 2002. Fund trustees had testified that stabilizing the fund would cost about $130 billion to $150 billion over the following seven years.

Medicaid was targeted for $182 billion in savings over seven years. The House had proposed $187 billion; the Senate, $175 billion.

• **Nondefense Discretionary Spending.** The final budget included $190 billion in savings from this category, measured against a freeze at the fiscal 1995 enacted level.

In back-to-back votes June 29, the House voted 239–194 to adopt the conference report on the budget resolution for the seven-year plan, and the Senate quickly followed with a straight, party-line vote of 54–46. Rep. Flanagan, who represented the urban Chicago district he took from Democrat Dan Rostenkowski in the 1994 election, was the only GOP defector.   ❏

Fiscal 1996 Budget Reconciliation

After adopting the fiscal 1996 budget resolution (H Con Res 67), congressional Republicans stuck together in 1995 to do what most budget experts thought could not be done: turn the blueprint into a tough bill to balance the budget, cut taxes and not touch Social Security or defense.

President Clinton, in turn, resisted an escalating series of Republican pressure tactics designed to make him capitulate to the GOP plan. He vetoed the budget reconciliation bill (HR 2491—H Rept 104-350) on Dec. 6, calling it extreme. The bill had passed with such narrow margins in both chambers that there was no chance the veto could be overridden.

The reconciliation bill—the centerpiece of the Republicans' 1995 legislative agenda—promised to balance the federal budget by fiscal 2002. The largest measure of its kind ever passed by Congress, it proposed to cut projected spending by $894 billion and reduce taxes by $245 billion, over seven years.

The GOP plan sought to overhaul social programs that had been mainstays of the Democratic vision of government since the New Deal days of the 1930s and the Great Society era of the 1960s.

It aimed to transform many of the federal safety-net entitlements into block grants and turn them over to the states, ending the long-time guarantee of minimum government assistance for the eligible poor.

The focus on these programs was forced in part because Republicans decided not to cut from Social Security or defense. Moreover, they could do nothing directly to reduce interest payments on the national debt. Together, that took roughly half of all federal spending off the table, leaving Republicans with little choice but to cut projected spending deeply from what was left: nondefense programs and entitlement programs such as Medicare and Medicaid.

HOUSE ACTION

Ten separate House committees approved separate pieces of the reconciliation puzzle between Sept. 13 and Oct. 12. The largest portion of the deficit-cutting package was a proposal to reduce anticipated spending on Medicare by $270 billion over seven years. Proposed cuts in farm subsidies and federal employee pensions were torpedoed in committee by rebellious Republicans.

Three major pieces of what would become the House reconciliation bill were first passed as separate bills:

• **Welfare.** The House on March 24 passed a welfare overhaul bill (HR 4) that proposed to give states broad control over five social services, which the federal government would support with block grants: cash welfare, child care, child protection, school meals, and nutritional aid to low-income pregnant women and their young children. The bill passed on a **key vote of 234–199 (R 225–5, D 9–193, I 0–1)**. *(1995 key votes, p. 1025; welfare, p. 578)*

• **Tax Cuts.** The House also passed on April 5 as a separate bill (HR 1215) a tax cut package that included as centerpieces a $500-per-child tax credit for families earning up to $200,000 a year and a cut in the corporate capital gains tax rate from 35 percent to 25 percent. It passed April 5, on a **key vote of 246–188 (R 219–11, D 27–176, I 0–1)**. *(Taxes, p. 98)*

• **Medicare.** The House passed on Oct. 19 as a separate bill a Medicare overhaul measure (HR 2425) to provide doctors and hospitals smaller than expected increases in payments and require seniors to pay higher premiums for the optional "Part B" insurance that covered doctor care. The measure also promoted less expensive approaches to providing care, such as health maintenance organizations. The House passed the bill on a **key vote of 231–201 (R 227–6, D 4–194, I 0–1).** *(Medicare, p. 554)*

After much additional maneuvering, both at the Budget Committee and behind the scenes, the measure was pulled together. The Budget Committee approved HR 2491—H Rept 104-280) on a 24–16 vote on Oct. 12. The committee also approved a second bill (HR 2459) that contained changes in budget procedures; the provisions of that bill were later rolled into HR 2491 for floor action.

The House then passed HR 2491 on Oct. 26 by a **key vote of 227–203 (R 223–10, D 4–192, I 0–1).** It was a comfortable margin cemented by a series of last-minute changes to accommodate rank-and-file Republicans.

SENATE ACTION

The Senate Budget Committee assembled the pieces of its reconciliation bill (S 1357) that were produced by authorizing committees and approved it on Oct. 23, by a 12–10 party-line vote.

The committee that had the most difficulty meeting its target was Finance, which spent weeks debating Medicare and Medicaid and taxes. The Finance Committee's Medicare proposal was similar to the one passed by the House, although more of its savings were to come from raising the cost to beneficiaries and less from cutting payments to providers.

Finance also proposed to make the $500-per-child tax credit available to families making less than $110,000 a year, not $200,000 as the House proposed. It also called for a smaller cut in corporate capital gains taxes and exchanged the savings to expand individual retirement accounts (IRAs) more than the House and to retain more corporate tax breaks.

Before the Senate bill went to the floor, sponsors spent hours in behind-the-scenes negotiations to appease the moderate wing of the Republican Party and rallied senators behind the reconciliation package.

On Oct. 28, the Senate passed HR 2491 by a **key vote of 52–47 (R 52–1, D 0–46),** after first substituting the text of S 1357.

A series of relatively small changes were made during the sometimes frenetic Senate floor debate, and moderates succeeded in restoring $5.9 billion in subsidies for college loans and about $13 billion in spending for health programs.

Clinton's threat to veto the reconciliation bill ultimately made it easier for some Senate GOP moderates to vote for the bill. John H. Chafee, R-R.I., said moderates were counting on a round of postveto negotiations to soften many of the bill's provisions—and they hoped to produce a bill that Clinton would sign.

CONFERENCE ACTION

Republican leaders made quick work of the House-Senate conference on the sprawling bill. The bill passed by the Senate had much in common with the House bill. Conferees needed less than three weeks to resolve the differences between the two chambers' complex proposals; they sealed the deal on Nov. 15 (H Rept 104-350).

The discussions were moved along in part by political realities: the conferees could not afford to produce a bill that Senate GOP moderates would not support. But also looming over the discussions were two immediate fiscal crises: the need to appropriate money to keep the government operating, and the impending need to raise the statutory debt ceiling. Republicans hoped to use the pending appropriations and debt-limit crises to force Clinton's hand.

Conferees ended up with a package that promised to cut projected spending by $894 billion over seven years and lower taxes by $245 billion. The bill included the following main provisions:

• **Medicare.** Health care providers, not Medicare recipients, were to bear the brunt of the $270 billion in savings. The bill called for providers to receive lower-than-expected rates of increase in their payments, or "reimbursements." It called for better-off seniors to pay more for optional Part B coverage, and it included a House proposal to automatically reduce reimbursements for fee-for-service providers if budget targets were not met through other changes in the bill. Senior citizens were to be offered new options such as coverage by health maintenance organizations and a combination of a medical savings account and a high-deductible insurance policy.

• **Medicaid.** Medicaid, the joint federal-state health insurance program for the poor and disabled, was to be turned over to the states as a block grant—capping the federal government's participation to what had been an open-ended program.

States were to be given great latitude in designing their programs and determining eligibility though states were to be required to cover children and pregnant women who fell below income guidelines. Federal standards for nursing homes were to be retained and families of nursing home residents were allowed to keep some income and assets. Federal spending on Medicaid was to be reduced by $163.4 billion from projected levels over seven years. *(Medicaid, p. 559)*

• **Welfare.** Projected spending for welfare was to be cut by $81.5 billion over seven years. States were to gain broad control only over their cash welfare and child care programs, receiving federal aid in block grants. States that met certain criteria also would have the option of receiving their food stamps in a block grant.

The bill would have limited welfare recipients generally to five years of cash benefits, permitted states to deny welfare checks to unwed teenage mothers, and deterred states from giving additional aid to people who had additional children while on welfare by requiring them to pass legislation permitting such payments.

The final bill also would have denied legal immigrants Supplemental Security Income benefits, which were cash payments to low income aged, blind and disabled.

• **Taxes.** The conference report would have provided a $500-per-child tax credit, limiting eligibility to families with incomes of up to $110,000. The corporate capital gains tax was to drop from 35 percent to 28 percent. The measure would have killed the corporate alternative minimum tax and permitted companies to spend excess funds from their pension plans on other employee benefits.

The bill proposed to cut the earned-income tax credit, which benefited low-income workers, saving $32.4 billion by reducing eligibility for the credit and trimming the amount available to some taxpayers and eliminating the credit for taxpayers without children.

• **Farm Subsidies.** Conferees adopted a modified version of the so-called Freedom to Farm proposal, from the House bill, calling for many farmers to receive fixed but declining subsidy payments for seven years regardless of market conditions. Cotton and rice farmers were to continue to receive lucrative marketing loans, but the maximum loan rates were to be capped at 1995 levels. *(Farm programs, p. 494)*

Because the conferees were unable to reach agreement on changes to the dairy program, their section of the bill proposed to cut agriculture spending by $12.3 billion over seven years, rather than $13 billion as originally required.

• **Banking.** In a provision that aimed to generate $900 million in savings, negotiators from the Banking committees shored up the Savings Association Insurance Fund (SAIF) by requiring thrifts to pay a one-time assessment of slightly less than 1 percent of their deposits to fully capitalize the fund. Banks were to be required to pay assessments of about 2 cents per $100 in deposits to help finance bonds that helped pay for an earlier round of the thrift bailout. The Bank Insurance Fund and the SAIF were to be merged in 1998, but only if a subsequent law was passed to eliminate the thrift charter. *(Deposit insurance funds, p. 131)*

• **Energy/Environment.** The Arctic National Wildlife refuge was to be opened to drilling, raising $1.2 billion. More than 30 million barrels of oil from the Strategic Petroleum Reserve were to be sold to help raise $470 million.

In a bid to settle the long-running dispute over how to overhaul the 1872 mining law, miners were to pay fair market prices for the surface value of their land claims and a 5 percent royalty on the net proceeds of minerals they extracted. Estimated savings: $157 million.

Another $83 million was to be raised by increasing fees at national parks, forests and other recreation sites. Another $82 million was estimated to derive from overhauling the contracting process for operating concessions such as restaurants and lodges at national parks and other facilities.

• **Housing.** The measure would have saved $4.1 billion through noncontroversial changes in housing programs, including an overhaul of the Federal Housing Administration's foreclosure relief program, in which the government helped homeowners avoid foreclosure. About $2.3 billion of the savings came from reductions in scheduled rent increases in Section 8 subsidized housing programs.

• **Student Loans.** Participation in the Direct Student Loan program, which bypassed commercial lenders and sent aid directly to college and graduate school students, was to be cut by roughly two-thirds, saving $1.6 billion. Federal links to the Student Loan Marketing Association (Sallie Mae) were to be cut and federal subsidies for the lenders and loan-guarantee agencies involved in student loans were to be cut to produce $1.0 billion in savings.

• **Veterans Benefits.** Copayments for prescription drugs would have been raised for some veterans by $2 to $4 per prescription, raising $742 million. Cost of living adjustments would have been cut slightly and another $2.5 billion would have been saved by repealing a rule that granted veterans injured in Department of Veterans Affairs health facilities automatic compensation.

• **Spectrum Auctions.** The bill called for raising an estimated $15.3 billion by auctioning 120 megahertz of the communications spectrum, drawing 20 megahertz allocated to federal agencies and another 100 megahertz allocated by the Federal Communications Commission via public and private sources. *(Spectrum auctions, p. 396)*

FINAL ACTION/BUDGET NEGOTIATIONS

Undeterred by Clinton's threat to veto the bill, the House and Senate wasted little time in adopting the conference report.

The House adopted the conference report on Nov. 17 on a 237–189 vote. The Senate then used procedural rules to knock two minor provisions out of the conference report before adopting it later that day on a 52–47 vote. The House cleared the revised conference report on Nov. 20 by a 235–192 vote.

By the time the House and Senate acted on the conference report, Republicans had stepped up the pressure on Clinton. They had already forced a government shutdown and threatened to let the government default on its debt unless Clinton capitulated to their reconciliation package.

The GOP leadership shipped the president a short-term continuing appropriations resolution and a short-term borrowing extension for the Treasury, both with poison pills Clinton had signaled for days he would reject. Clinton vetoed both bills. *(Fiscal 1996 appropriations, p. 71; debt-limit increase, p. 76)*

The tactics did not lead Clinton to sign the reconciliation bill, but they did prompt him to agree in principle to the idea of balancing the budget. As part of another continuing appropriations resolution (H J Res 122—PL 104-56) that ended the Nov. 14–19 government shutdown, Clinton agreed to language committing him to sign legislation in 1995 that would balance the federal budget in seven years, using updated economic projections from the Congressional Budget Office (CBO).

The resolution also mandated, however, that the balanced-budget plan reflect Clinton's priorities—providing adequate funding for Medicaid, education and the environment, for example.

On Nov. 28, the long-delayed budget negotiations began between the White House and top congressional leaders. They quickly stalled two days later, however, after producing little more than accusations of bad faith. Clinton refused to submit a seven-year balanced budget plan at the start of the talks.

Clinton then vetoed the budget reconciliation bill Dec. 6. In his veto message, he blasted the Republican majority for taking an "extreme" approach that would "hurt average Americans and help special interests."

The next day, the president laid out his own plan for the budget, his third of 1995. Unlike his previous proposals, the one he released Dec. 7 proposed to balance the budget in seven years—but based on the economic assumptions of the White House's Office of Management and Budget, not CBO as Republicans demanded.

A CBO analysis of the reconciliation bill and Clinton's Dec. 7 proposal found the two sides $365 billion apart—the Republicans saving almost $500 billion more through spending reductions, and Clinton proposing $137 billion less in tax cuts. CBO also calculated that Clinton's plan was $115 billion to $175 billion short of a balanced budget.

Rather than breathing new life into the budget talks, the proposal seemed to make Republicans angrier. They saw it as little more than political posturing and denounced Clinton for using economic projections they said were phony.

The White House made a new offer Dec. 15, the day the latest stopgap spending bill was due to run out. But Republicans denounced the offer, and talks collapsed. With six of the regular appropriations bills still not enacted, much of the government shut down again Dec. 16, idling some 260,000 federal workers.

Talks between Clinton and senior Republicans began in earnest at the White House on Dec. 22 and continued off and on through Dec. 31. Participants said the two sides outlined their positions in detail and made progress, though little real bargaining was done.

When Republican lawmakers returned the first week of January, their strategy quickly collapsed. Senate Majority Leader Bob Dole, R-Kan., who had been openly pushing to reopen the government, got a condition-free stopgap spending bill through the Senate Jan. 2.

Torn between bewilderment at Clinton's ability to shrug off the "leverage" that they thought the shutdown had given them, and rage at what they claimed was his obstinate refusal to bargain honestly, House Republicans abruptly abandoned their strategy and agreed to bring federal employees back to work.

By the end of January, Republicans had given up on their larger goal, done in by their own and Clinton's calculation that it was better to stick with principles than compromise enough to get a deal.   ❑

Fiscal 1996 Appropriations

A protracted battle between Congress and the White House over Republican efforts to shrink the size and power of the federal government began in 1995 and finally concluded in late April 1996, when negotiators reached a deal on an omnibus spending bill for the fiscal year that was already half over (HR 3019—PL 104-134).

The final fiscal 1996 appropriations bill ended a watershed appropriations season that saw Republicans make the largest cutbacks in nondefense discretionary programs since President Ronald Reagan's first term. That process resulted in $22 billion in cuts from the fiscal 1995 levels set by the previous Democratic Congress; HR 3019 accounted for roughly half of those reductions.

The battle over the spending bills featured huge fights over spending levels and GOP-driven policy "riders," and the process dragged almost seven months past the nominal deadline—the Oct. 1, 1995, start of the fiscal year.

All told, it took 14 stopgap spending measures and that final omnibus bill to wrap up the year. Two politically debilitating government shutdowns took much of the starch out of the Republican revolution and by the end of the process, President Clinton had won at least partial funding for all of his priorities.

REGULAR APPROPRIATIONS

When fiscal 1996 began just after midnight Sept. 30, Congress had sent Clinton just two spending bills for the coming year—those for Military Construction (HR 1817—PL 104-32) and for the Legislative Branch (HR 1854—vetoed Oct. 3). That necessitated the first of 14 stopgap spending bills to keep the remaining government agencies operating just as a huge fight loomed on the separate budget reconciliation bill (HR 2491).

In the first round, congressional Republicans and Clinton agreed to give themselves a six-week extension to complete work on the remaining spending bills.

The result was a continuing resolution (H J Res 108—PL 104-31) that provided appropriations through Nov. 13 for programs financed by unfinished spending bills. The House adopted the interim measure by voice vote Sept. 28; the Senate cleared it by voice vote the next day; and Clinton signed it Sept. 30.

The spending battle got off to a late start thanks to the House's preoccupation with the "Contract with America" and the duel over fiscal 1995 spending cuts. So it was not surprising that the conclusion did not come until the fiscal year was more than half over.

Compounding the problem was the House GOP leadership's insistence that spending bills carry contentious policy riders to reverse or weaken laws that conservatives opposed. In the end, virtually all of these riders were blocked not only by Clinton and congressional Democrats, but also by Senate and moderate House Republicans.

For example, the bill for Veterans Affairs, Housing and Urban Development and Independent Agencies (HR 2099) had included proposals to curtail some of the Environmental Protection Agency's regulatory power. The conservative-backed riders were stripped from the bill in the House on July 28 on a **key vote of 212–206 (R 51–175, D 160–31, I 1–0.)** (1995 key votes, p. 1025)

The riders were later restored to the bill on a House revote that followed strenuous arm-twisting by House leaders, but they ran into further trouble in the Senate and even after they had been modified, the VA-HUD bill faced a veto threat. In the end, all of the disputed riders were dropped.

At the end of the calendar year, only six of the 13 regular appropriations bills had been signed into law: Military Construction; Agriculture (HR 1976—PL 104-37); Energy and Water Development (HR 1905—PL 104-46); Legislative Branch (second bill: HR 2492—PL 104-53); Transportation (HR 2002—PL 104-50); and Treasury, Postal Service (HR 2020—PL 104-52).

A seventh bill, for Defense (HR 2126—PL 104-61), became law without the president's signature. The bill provided about $7 billion more than Clinton had requested, though the total was still below an amount sufficient to account for inflation—thereby pitting defense hawks against deficit hawks in both chambers.

The Senate passed its version of the Defense bill (S 1087) on Sept. 5 by a **key vote of 62–35 (R 48–4, D 14–31).** In the House, the conference report on the bill was adopted on Nov. 16 by a **key vote of 270–158 (R 195–37, D 75–120, I 0–1).**

Three other regular appropriations bills were sidelined by vetoes: Commerce, Justice, State (HR 2076); Interior (HR 1977); and VA-HUD.

Finally, three bills were simply bogged down in Congress: District of Columbia (HR 2548, S 1244); Foreign Operations (HR 1868); and Labor, Health and Human Services, Education (HR 2127).

Agencies financed under those bills that had not been enacted were dependent on the successive short-term continuing resolutions. Twice, from Nov. 14–19 and from Dec. 16 to Jan. 6, 1996, those agencies were shut down, with all "nonessential" employees sent home. The longest previous government shutdown had lasted only three days.

GOVERNMENT SHUTDOWNS

The first shutdown occurred when Republicans tried to turn up the heat on Clinton at the time the first continuing resolution expired at midnight Nov. 13.

At the time, only three of the 13 regular spending bills had been signed and Clinton had vetoed the Legislative Branch, saying Congress should not take care of its own business before paying for other parts of the government.

By this point, there was widespread talk of a coming "train wreck." Under this scenario, Clinton would receive and veto several more spending bills, along with the budget reconciliation bill, which included a critical extension of the federal debt limit. *(Fiscal 1996 budget reconciliation, p. 68; debt-limit increase, p. 76)*

At that point, the massive collision—with a threat of a government shutdown and default on the debt—would force both sides to finally sit down and work out a comprehensive budget deal.

But with their own work behind schedule, Republicans tried to force Clinton to bend to their key budget demands as the price simply for buying a little more time. With the reconciliation bill unfinished and half the appropriations bills still on Capitol Hill, they shipped the president a new stopgap continuing resolution and a short-term borrowing extension for the Treasury, both with added provisions that Clinton had signaled for days he would reject.

Republicans had made the new short-term bill (H J Res 115) tougher to raise pressure on Clinton to come to terms on the unfinished appropriations bills, several of which he had threatened to veto, and also to satisfy GOP conservatives who were spoiling for a fight.

The House passed H J Res 115 on Nov. 10 by a vote of 224–172. The Senate cleared the measure by voice vote Nov. 13. That same day, Clinton vetoed it, along with the short-term extension of the debt limit (HR 2586), which included several riders he refused to accept. Much earlier than expected and sooner than either side might have wished, the fight was on.

The impasse precipitated a government shutdown, as fiscal 1995 funding for most departments ran out at midnight Nov. 13. Almost 800,000 "nonessential" federal workers were ordered home. Polls quickly punished the Republicans, who were blamed almost two-to-one over Clinton for the shutdown. But Republicans vowed not to budge until Clinton agreed to a plan to balance the budget.

Three days into the shutdown, on Nov. 16, the House passed a new continuing resolution (H J Res 122) that dropped a controversial Medicare proposal but included the balanced-budget condition. Democrats started peeling off and 48 House Democrats supported the new bill. The bill passed the House by 277–151; seven Senate Democrats backed the measure when the Senate passed it the next day, 60–37.

The two sides announced a truce on Sunday night, Nov. 19, sending federal employees back to work Monday morning and giving themselves four more weeks to reach a budget deal. Both sides agreed they would craft a plan that would balance the budget in seven years.

H J Res 122 was rewritten to include the terms of the deal. The Senate voted to wipe out its previous vote passing H J Res 122 and passed the revised version by voice vote on Nov. 19. The House cleared it Nov. 20 by a near-unanimous **key vote of 421–4 (R 227–2, D 193–2, I 1–0).** Clinton signed the measure the same day (PL 104-56).

The new stopgap bill was good through Dec. 15. But by the time it ran out, budget talks had collapsed in angry recriminations, triggering the second partial government shutdown of the year and sending nearly 300,000 federal employees home 10 days before Christmas. This second shutdown lasted for 21 days.

By the time lawmakers returned in January 1996, it was clear that holding the government hostage had not only failed to produce a balanced-budget deal, but had tarnished the Republican revolution and obscured its message.

Dole openly broke with House Republicans, saying "enough is enough." With solidarity among House Republicans coming unglued, Gingrich on Jan. 5 told a GOP conference meeting the time had come to end the shutdown. Later that day, Congress cleared the first of a series of stopgap spending bills (HR 1643—PL 104-92; HR 1358—PL 104-91) that fully reopened the federal government.

The sentiment to pass HR 1643 and end the shutdown was overwhelming. The House passed the bill on a **key vote of 401–17 (R 214–15, D 186–2, I 1–0).** The Senate cleared the bill by voice vote. *(1996 key votes, p. 1047)*

In mid-January, House GOP leaders abandoned their strategy in the face of a public backlash against the government shutdowns. Conceding defeat on the balanced-budget bill, top Republicans agreed to a stopgap bill that financed unappropriated programs through March 15. The bill (HR 2880—PL 104-99), which the Senate cleared January 26, also financed foreign-aid programs through the end of fiscal 1996.

Several additional short-term spending bills were still needed between mid-March and late April. The appropriations impasse finally came to an end on April 26, 1996, when Clinton signed the omnibus bill (HR 3019) that carried into law all or part of the last five unfinished 1996 spending bills: Commerce-Justice-State; Labor-HHS-Education; Interior; VA-HUD-Independent Agencies; and District of Columbia.

PEACEKEEPING SUPPLEMENTAL

Before the battle over fiscal 1996 appropriations, 1995 started placidly enough as Congress cleared on April 6 a $3.1 billion supplemental appropriations bill to pay for unbudgeted military operations in Haiti, the Persian Gulf, the former Yugoslavia and elsewhere. President Clinton signed the bill into law April 10 (HR 889—PL 104-6).

The Pentagon had warned for months that, unless the bill was enacted by the beginning of April, the armed services would have to begin canceling scheduled training exercises and maintenance work. Money budgeted for those activities had been "borrowed" to cover the cost of the unbudgeted deployments.

The bill included $2.5 billion to cover the cost in fiscal 1995 of peacekeeping and humanitarian operations. It also provided the Pentagon with an additional $561 million, most of it to cover a 2.6 percent military pay raise that Congress had approved for fiscal 1995, and to cover an increase in the cost of overseas operations due to the dollar's decline in value against key foreign currencies.

Those appropriations were more than offset by provisions rescinding $2.36 billion in defense appropriations and $1.12 billion in nondefense appropriations that were not yet spent. Overall, the bill reduced fiscal 1995 appropriations by a net total of $746 million.

The bill also earmarked $360 million received from allied governments and from the United Nations to help pay for the deployments.

The House passed the bill (H Rept 104-29) on Feb. 22 by a vote of 262–165. The Senate passed its version (S Rept 104-12) on March 16 by a 97–3 margin.

House and Senate conferees agreed on the compromise bill April 5 (H Rept 104-101). The House adopted the conference report April 6 by a vote of 343–80, and the Senate cleared the bill by voice vote later the same day.

EMERGENCY SUPPLEMENTAL, RESCISSIONS

Congress and Clinton had a much more difficult time in 1995 agreeing on a bill that combined $16.3 billion in rescissions from prior appropriations with $7.2 billion in emergency spending, mostly for disaster relief.

The bulk of the cuts came from housing programs, unused airport grants, school and job training programs, aid for water-treatment plants and federal building projects. The emergency funding went primarily to disaster relief in California, debt relief for Jordan and help for agencies affected by the April 19 Oklahoma City bombing.

Clinton signed the bill into law July 27 (HR 1944—PL 104-19), after having vetoed an earlier version. It was the first bill he had vetoed as president.

As passed by the House in March, the original version of the bill (HR 1158) targeted some of Clinton's top social-welfare priorities. Deep cuts were proposed in home energy subsidies, job training programs, housing subsidies, the recently enacted Goals 2000 program to improve schools, and Clinton's National Service initiative. The House-passed bill also contained changes to several environmental policies opposed by Republican conservatives, including the regulation of automobile emissions and the sale of timber on federal lands.

Conferees produced a report that moderated some of the largest cuts in social spending. But the House still won deep cuts in such Democratic staples as worker training programs, school aid and National Service.

The House and Senate approved the conference report on votes that followed party lines in May, and Clinton carried out his veto threat on June 7.

After a week of trading barbs and threats with the White House, top House and Senate appropriators fashioned a new bill (HR 1944) that restored almost $800 million to programs favored by the administration while proposing almost $1 billion in new cuts.

The new bill contained $16.3 billion in rescissions and $7.2 billion in new spending, including $6.6 billion in disaster assistance, $290 million for the effects of the April 19 Oklahoma City bombing and $275 million in debt relief for Jordan.

The House passed HR 1944 on June 29 by a vote of 276–151; the Senate cleared the bill by a vote of 90–7 on July 21.   ❏

Fiscal 1997 Budget Resolution

Softening the edges of their vetoed 1995 effort, congressional Republicans in June 1996 adopted a new plan to balance the federal budget by 2002. Their effort was abetted in part by President Clinton, who had offered his own plan to achieve a balanced budget in seven years, adhering to the strict accounting standards demanded by Republicans.

Still, there was little expectation that the goals of the non-binding budget resolution would be etched into law; rather, the budget was expected to be one basis for the election-year battles for Congress and the White House.

Adoption of the $1.6 trillion fiscal 1997 budget resolution (H Con Res 178—H Rept 104-612) was delayed by internal Republican disputes and by efforts to clean up unfinished fiscal 1996 business, including nearly half the regular appropriations bills. (Fiscal 1996 appropriations, p. 71)

At the same time, the budget edged closer to Clinton's position on such politically sensitive programs as Medicaid—calling for savings of $72 billion by 2002, instead of the $85 billion proposed in a final round of budget talks with Clinton the previous January. It also called for a net $122 billion in tax cuts, rather than the $177 billion January figure and the $245 billion over seven years in the fiscal 1996 budget resolution. (Fiscal 1996 budget resolution, p. 65)

Also, at the Senate's insistence, Republicans included an extra $4 billion for domestic appropriations, essentially freezing them at fiscal 1996 levels, rather than insisting on another round of deep cuts as originally planned. The extra money was intended to placate both Senate GOP appropriators and Clinton, who had made the appropriators miserable the year before by vetoing bills and dragging out the process to extract additional money from the Republican Congress.

Nonetheless, the extra money for appropriations provoked a rebellion by GOP hard-liners in the House that almost killed the budget resolution conference report in that chamber.

The budget resolution called for such changes in tax and entitlement programs to be broken into three budget reconciliation bills.

That strategy was designed less to balance the budget than to focus attention on specific issues and raise the political stakes when Clinton vetoed the separate bills, as Republicans expected he would.

The first reconciliation bill was to contain major changes in welfare and Medicaid, the federal-state health care program for the poor and disabled.

The second reconciliation bill was to make major changes to Medicare, the federal health care program for the elderly. The third was to include a package of tax cuts, possibly reviving the 1995 proposals for a $500-per-child tax credit for families and for capital gains relief.

The plan proved overly ambitious—given the work needed to enact appropriations, the upcoming elections and little incentive to revisit the draining battles of the previous year's reconciliation fight. *(Fiscal 1996 budget reconciliation, p. 68)*

The proposed welfare-Medicaid bill became a welfare-only bill (HR 3734—PL 104-193), though one hardly considered inconsequential. The tax and Medicare bills never materialized. *(Welfare overhaul, p. 578)*

CLINTON BUDGET REQUEST

Clinton on March 19 sent Congress a $1.64 trillion budget request for fiscal 1997. Though clearly a political document in an election year, Clinton's budget was nevertheless a remarkable manifesto for a Democrat—proof of how far the Republicans had moved the president and the budget debate since sweeping into control of Congress in 1995. It was the first balanced budget submitted by a president to Congress in a generation.

Only a year earlier, the White House had drawn up a budget that assumed deficits of $200 billion or more a year well into the future. This time, Clinton proposed to balance the federal budget by 2002, using strict Congressional Budget Office (CBO) forecasts rather than somewhat more optimistic White House projections. That had been the Republicans' demand for more than a year, and it made Clinton the first president in a generation to send Congress a balanced budget.

The proposal called for huge out-year cuts in discretionary spending, the appropriations Democrats had used for decades to build the programs and the bureaucracy that congressional Republicans wanted to dismantle. But Clinton also asked for more money in the short run for priorities such as education, job training and the environment.

The budget's March 19 submission date came more than a month after the statutory deadline, which required the White House to produce its budget by the first Monday in February. Delayed by efforts to settle the fiscal business left over from the previous year, Clinton offered a "placeholder" budget outline Feb. 5—a thin, 20-page elaboration of the last balanced-budget offer he had made before budget negotiations broke down in early January. Republicans threw in the towel Jan. 24.

The deficit had dropped steadily since Clinton took office, falling three times in a row for the first time since 1949. The deficit was expected to fall for a fourth straight year in fiscal 1996 to about $146 billion. Measured against the size of the economy, that amounted to 1.9 percent of the gross domestic product, the lowest level since 1979.

Despite the shrinking deficit, Republicans had so radically remade deficit politics that Clinton pushed for even deeper cuts. He proposed to reduce projected spending for Medicare, the federal health insurance program for the elderly and disabled, and Medicaid, the federal-state health insurance program for the poor. And he offered to squeeze money out of welfare and even from the earned-income tax credit (EITC) for the working poor, which he had worked with congressional Democrats to raise in 1993.

Clinton's biggest proposed cuts were unrealistic whacks in discretionary appropriations, where anything not on the White House priority list faced reductions of somewhere between a fifth and a third in the final years.

At the same time, Clinton offered about $120 billion in tax cuts, most of it for middle-class taxpayers in the form of child tax credits, tuition tax deductions and expanded Individual Retirement Accounts. Almost half of that was to be paid for by cutting back on "corporate welfare"—chiefly limiting various business tax breaks.

Based on the White House's interpretation of CBO scorekeeping (CBO did its own estimate later), Clinton's budget promised $593 billion in savings over seven years from 1996 to 2002, enough to produce a bare, $8 billion surplus in fiscal 2002, the final year. Scored on the basis of OMB's more optimistic projections, the budget produced surpluses in both 2001 and 2002.

To get additional money for dozens of his priority programs in fiscal 1997, Clinton proposed to carve about $5 billion out of nondefense programs and about $9 billion from defense.

Clinton's proposed spending increases were mostly familiar from his earlier budgets. For example, he asked for a 37 percent increase from fiscal 1996 for summer youth employment and training programs that Republicans had tried to kill. He sought a 17 percent increase for AmeriCorps, which was high on the GOP target list.

Clinton also sought significant increases in other education and training programs, crime programs, technology and research and numerous environmental programs, including a 9 percent increase for Environmental Protection Agency operations.

BACKGROUND

Republicans unveiled their own budget proposal only after weeks of internal struggle between House and Senate leaders for dominance in the second round of a fight that had ended in disaster the previous year—with vetoes and government shutdowns that mostly were blamed by the public on GOP congressional leaders.

Senate Republicans who felt they had been forced to knuckle under to House Republicans' wrongheaded confrontational strategy in 1995 demanded more say in the decision-making this time around.

Even after they had agreed on a plan, the duel continued—evidenced in a call by House Budget Committee Chairman John R. Kasich, R-Ohio, for more tax cuts than had been agreed to and a decision by Senate Budget Chairman Pete V. Domenici, R-N.M., to add another $5 billion for domestic appropriations on the Senate floor.

The agreement by conferees to accept much of Domenici's add-on was an additional sign of retreat by Republicans from their original plan to keep making deeper and deeper cuts in discretionary spending.

LEGISLATIVE ACTION

Both the House and Senate Budget committees voted along party lines in early May to approve slightly different versions of the GOP plan. The Senate Budget Committee approved its version of the budget resolution (S Con Res 57—S Rept 104-271) on the evening of May 9 by a vote of 13–11. The House Budget Committee followed shortly after 1 a.m. on May 10 with a 23–18 vote to approve its budget resolution (H Con Res 178—H Rept 104-575).

The most dramatic and internally contentious change to the GOP budget came from the Republicans' decision to slash their proposed tax cut from a net of $177 billion proposed in January to $122 billion. Senate Republicans in particular were determined not to leave themselves open again to Democrats' politically devastating accusations that the GOP was cutting Medicare spending to provide tax cuts for the rich.

The only tax cut that lawmakers initially identified was a $500-per-child tax credit for couples earning up to $110,000 per year.

The House did not stick with the script, however. Budget Chairman Kasich immediately promised that Republicans would produce as much as $180 billion in total tax cuts, including a capital gains cut and other items. He said the amount above the agreed-upon $122 billion in net cuts would be offset by extending expiring taxes and closing "corporate welfare" loopholes.

The House and Senate also differed over whether to keep trying to kill off Cabinet departments, a high priority goal for House Republicans that fizzled in the Senate in 1995. Kasich's budget explicitly called for closing the Commerce and Energy departments, a demand that did not appear in the Senate proposal.

While the two budget resolutions otherwise set largely similar priorities, they contained a few significant differences. House budget-writers, for instance, wanted to spend about $1.6 billion more on defense in fiscal 1997 and $900 million less on domestic appropriations than their Senate counterparts.

House Floor Action

Republican leaders pushed H Con Res 178 through the House after brisk debate May 15 and 16. The largely party-line vote on May 16 to adopt the budget resolution was 226–195.

Senate Floor Action

After slogging through more than 50 amendments, the Senate on May 23 adopted H Con Res 178 on a party-line vote of 53–46, after substituting the text of S Con Res 57.

Before the budget was adopted, Domenici surprised House budget leaders by proposing to increase nondefense appropriations by $5 billion. The amendment, which abrogated a House-Senate agreement on discretionary spending limits, was adopted by a vote of 76–24, with the support of 30 of the chamber's 53 Republicans.

Domenici acted when he saw how House appropriators planned to split the agreed-upon domestic spending allocation among their various subcommittees. And among the panels that was expected to take a big hit was the energy-water appropriations bill that was the purview of an Appropriations subcommittee that Domenici also chaired in his dual role as an appropriator. Hard-liners were angry at the retreat.

Although most of the Senate floor votes were cast along party lines, one centrist alternative budget—offered by a bipartisan group of moderates led by John H. Chafee, R-R.I., and John B. Breaux, D-La.—failed on a surprisingly close, bipartisan **key vote of 46–53 (R 22–30, D 24–23),** which showed the growing strength of moderates of both parties in the Senate. *(1996 key votes, p. 1047)*

The Chafee-Breaux plan proposed to balance the budget with slightly shallower spending cuts than the main GOP proposal, along with a net $105 billion in tax cuts. But it contained a controversial provision to legislatively adjust the consumer price index downward by 0.5 percent, which would result in lower cost of living increases in entitlement programs.

Conference, Final Action

GOP budget negotiators ended testy House-Senate talks June 6 and agreed to give the Senate most of the extra domestic spending it wanted, cutting defense to help make room.

The conference agreement on the budget resolution included $4 billion of the extra budget authority the Senate had demanded for domestic appropriations above the House-passed level. The House also agreed to cut defense appropriations by $1.6 billion in budget authority to match the Senate-approved level.

The House adopted the conference report June 12, by a narrow 216–211 vote. Nineteen Republicans openly defied their leadership to vote no—by far the largest number to defect on a key budget or reconciliation vote since Republicans took over Congress in 1995.

Speaker Newt Gingrich, R-Ga., and his lieutenants came excruciatingly close to failure. With all time expired for the vote tally, the budget was losing, 201–212. GOP fiscal hard-liners, most of them freshman members, were in open revolt, unhappy that the budget drove the deficit up temporarily in 1997 and 1998 before forcing it down to zero in 2002. They were also enraged at Senate Republicans for adding more domestic spending and angry with their leaders for going along.

The GOP leadership frantically scoured the floor in a search for votes to turn the tide, and it held the vote open long enough to secure a victory. At the last possible minute, leaders had persuaded four GOP "nays" to switch to "yea"—Wayne Allard of Colorado, Wes Cooley of Oregon, Barbara Cubin of Wyoming and Jack Metcalf of Washington.

Final action in the Senate the following day, June 13, was anticlimactic. Twenty-three conservative Republicans originally had opposed Domenici's call for additional appropriations. None thought it important enough to oppose the conference agreement, which the Senate adopted on a party-line, 53–46 vote. ❏

Fiscal 1997 Appropriations

Congressional Republicans took a mostly accommodating approach to fiscal 1997 appropriations after engaging in protracted warfare with President Clinton over the previous year's spending bills that dragged into April of 1996.

Fiscal 1997 began on Oct. 1, 1996, with all appropriations bills enacted and no need for a temporary spending bill. It was only the fourth time that had happened since modern federal budgeting began in 1974.

Driven by rank-and-file desperation to adjourn Congress and go home to campaign, GOP leaders resisted most of the controversial policy riders they had encouraged the year before and repeatedly sought middle-ground compromises with the White House on spending levels.

REGULAR APPROPRIATIONS BILLS

The willingness of Republicans to compromise brought peace on seven of the 13 regular fiscal 1997 spending bills.

Those seven bills were cleared and signed into law by Sept. 30: Agriculture (HR 3603—PL 104-180); District of Columbia (HR 3845—PL 104-194); Energy and Water Development (HR 3816—PL 104-206); Legislative Branch (HR 3754—PL 104-197); Military Construction (HR 3715—PL 104-196); Transportation (HR 3675—PL 104-205); and Veterans Affairs, Housing and Urban Development and Independent Agencies (HR 3666—PL 104-204).

OMNIBUS APPROPRIATIONS

Persistent disputes—chiefly a split between the Republicans and Clinton over how much money to spend on domestic programs—left six bills unfinished as the end of the fiscal year approached in late September.

When endgame negotiations began, Clinton demanded a total of $6.5 billion in extra spending for his priorities in education, the environment and other areas. GOP negotiators had only one demand of their own: that talks be wrapped up quickly. The desire to leave Washington to campaign and hold their congressional majorities was stronger than the need to bargain over a few billion dollars.

That virtual GOP surrender on most money and policy items allowed talks to conclude in time to get all appropriations enacted before the midnight Sept. 30 deadline.

That was accomplished by wrapping the five unfinished measures—Commerce-Justice-State (HR 3814); Foreign Operations (HR 3540); Interior (HR 3662); Labor-Health and Human Services-Education (HR 3755); and Treasury-Postal Service (HR 3756)—into the conference agreement on what had been the Defense appropriations bill, and thereby converting it into an omnibus fiscal 1997 bill (HR 3610—PL 104-208).

The House adopted the conference report on HR 3610 on Sept. 28 on a **key vote of 370–37 (R 202–24, D 167–13, I 1–0)**. *(1996 key votes, p. 1047)*

The Senate cleared the measure Sept. 30 by voice vote after first passing an identical bill (HR 4278) by a vote of 84–15. Passing the separate bill preserved the right of senators to offer amendments, which were not in order on the conference agreement; no senator did so, however. Clinton signed the bill the same day.

To finance the additional spending demanded by Clinton, Republicans and the administration agreed on offsets that struck some budget experts as gimmickry.

For example, a plan to shore up the deposit insurance fund for the thrift industry was attached to HR 3610 because it resulted in expected savings of $3.1 billion. Appropriators got credit for another $2.9 billion in auctions of the electromagnetic spectrum, but the actual auctions generated far less cash. *(Deposit insurance funds, p. 131; spectrum auctions, p. 396)*

The omnibus package provided roughly $380 billion in discretionary spending and more than $600 billion overall, counting mandatory spending that flowed through the appropriations process.

Total discretionary spending for fiscal 1997 for all 13 regular bills was $510 billion in new discretionary budget authority and $549 billion in outlays, or actual spending.

Sensitive to suggestions that they had caved in, Republicans said that since taking control of Congress in 1995, they had cut more than $50 billion from projected nondefense discretionary spending. The calculation was conservative; it measured from a freeze at the level enacted by the last Democratic Congress in 1995, not from the inflation-adjusted "baseline" that was often used to make such savings appear larger.

Still, in an indication of tensions among Republicans on Pentagon spending, the House on June 13 rejected an amendment by liberal GOP deficit hawk Christopher Shays of Connecticut and Democrat Barney Frank of Massachusetts to deviate from the GOP budget resolution (H Con Res 178) and trim about $1.9 billion from the fiscal 1997 defense appropriations bill to freeze the defense budget at fiscal 1996 levels. The amendment was rejected on a **key vote of 194–219 (R 60–161, D 133–58, I 1–0)**. ❏

Debt-Limit Increase

After months of threatening President Clinton with the nation's first-ever government default if he failed to agree to their plans for balancing the budget, Republican lawmakers backed down in early 1996 and voted overwhelmingly to raise the statutory ceiling on the national debt.

The bill (HR 3136—PL 104-121), which cleared March 28 and was signed into law the next day, raised the limit on the accumulated federal debt from $4.9 trillion to $5.5 trillion. The new ceiling was expected to cover the government's borrowing needs through October 1997.

Immediately after Clinton signed the bill, the Treasury Department announced it would auction more than $50 billion in notes on April 1 and 2 to raise needed cash to keep the government in business. Treasury Secretary Robert E. Rubin had been juggling accounts since November 1995 to avoid default. But after a few months, Rubin had run out of wiggle room.

Republican leaders in Congress had blinked, knowing that the public had blamed them for the debacle of two government shutdowns in late 1995 that stemmed from budgetary confrontations between the GOP and Clinton.

On Feb. 1 and again on March 7, Congress passed short-term increases in the debt limit, chiefly to assure that Social Security recipients and other beneficiaries of government programs would receive their checks on time.

Then in late March, Republican leaders decided to pass a permanent increase in the government's borrowing authority. To ensure that it would pass the House, they packaged it with a widely popular provision to increase the Social Security earnings limit and another that increased the ability of small businesses to challenge federal regulations in court.

Moving in tandem with the debt-limit bill was the conference report on a bill (S 4—PL 104-130) to give the president enhanced rescissions authority—tantamount to a line-item veto. That bill became law separately. (*Enhanced rescissions, p. 78*)

The packaging was necessary to win the votes of GOP conservatives who were reluctant to vote for the debt-limit increase unless they could point to something attached to it that guaranteed further cuts in the deficit.

BACKGROUND

Although raising the debt ceiling was nothing more than fiscal housekeeping to allow the government to pay bills incurred under previously enacted legislation, it was traditionally one of the most difficult and least popular votes for members.

The debt limit set a ceiling on the amount that the government could legally borrow to pay interest owed to government bondholders, to redeem and refinance government bonds when they matured and to pay beneficiaries of government trust funds that were invested in government bonds.

The debt ceiling had last been raised in August 1993, to $4.9 trillion, as part of that year's budget reconciliation bill (PL 103-66). The increase was generally expected to cover Treasury borrowing through September or October of 1995. (*Fiscal 1994 budget reconciliation, p. 44*)

At the start of the 104th Congress in 1995, GOP strategists began talking about using the need for a higher borrowing limit that fall to force Clinton to accede to their plan for balancing the budget in seven years—and without making major concessions to the White House.

It was a high-stakes strategy, and ultimately Clinton refused to yield. The showdown came in November 1995, when Republicans sent him a short-term debt-limit extension (HR 2586). Tacked on to the bill were provisions to limit death penalty appeals, require federal agencies to conduct risk-assessment and cost-benefit analyses on new regulations, and bar Treasury from juggling accounts to put off default in the absence of a permanent debt-ceiling extension.

Clinton vetoed the bill Nov. 13, 1995, and Republicans watched in frustration as Rubin undertook a series of maneuvers that forestalled default and enabled the White House to resist their budget demands.

Eventually, March 1, 1996, loomed as the date by which Rubin would run out of options.

LEGISLATIVE ACTION

Temporary Debt-Limit Extensions

After several weeks of indecision in early 1996, Republicans were fearful they would be attacked by Democrats during the February congressional recess for jeopardizing delivery of March 1 Social Security checks.

So the GOP leadership quickly crafted a bill (HR 2924—PL 104-103) to authorize the Treasury Department to borrow enough to cover the estimated $30 billion in March Social Security payments, temporarily exempting those obligations from the debt limit.

The House passed the measure on a 396–0 vote Feb. 1, and the Senate cleared it the same day on a voice vote. Clinton signed it Feb. 8. That debt-limit extension was to run out March 15.

A second short-term extension bill (HR 3021—PL 104-115)—enough to cover government obligations through March 29—was passed March 7, as GOP leaders worked on a strategy to enact a permanent debt-ceiling increase.

The House voted 362–51 in favor of the second short-term extension. A few hours later, the Senate passed it by voice vote after defeating on a party-line vote, 43–47, an amendment by Daniel Patrick Moynihan, D-N.Y., that would have extended the debt limit through March 1997. Clinton signed the second temporary extension on March 12.

Permanent Debt-Limit Extension

Having decided to move ahead with a permanent extension of the debt ceiling, GOP leaders agreed to add sweeteners to the bill to win votes from their membership. Although the votes existed within the Senate to pass a "clean" debt-limit increase, consensus was anything but close in the House.

Several factions developed among Republicans including: those who thought significant entitlement savings could be attached to the debt-limit bill; those who wanted to cut Republican losses, pass a narrowly crafted measure and move on to other issues; and those who wanted to use the debt-ceiling bill as leverage to force Clinton to accept other GOP agenda items that had drawn veto threats.

Republicans abandoned their strategy to use the debt limit to force Clinton to agree to their plans to cut taxes, balance the budget, or at least take major steps toward reducing the deficit.

Instead, they agreed that HR 3136—the long-term extension—would carry two other provisions: an increase in the amount of income seniors could earn without losing Social Security earnings and opening federal regulations to court challenge on the basis that the regulations were made without sufficiently considering their impact on small business.

GOP tacticians also decided to send the enhanced rescissions bill to the president simultaneously, and the White House approved the strategy.

HR 3136 passed both chambers on March 28. The House passed it on a **key vote of 328–91 (R 201–30, D 127–60, I 0–1).** The Senate cleared it by voice vote. *(1996 key votes, p. 1047)*

To ensure that S 4, the enhanced rescissions bill, and the debt-limit increase went to the president at the same time, GOP leaders directly linked the two measures until action by the Senate—where opposition to enhanced rescissions raised doubt about its enactment.

Before the House took up HR 3136, the Senate voted to adopt the conference report on enhanced rescissions (H Rept 104-491), and notified the House of that action.

Under the rule governing House floor debate on the debt limit bill, the conference report on S 4 had been attached to HR 3136 until the Senate acted. At that point, the enhanced rescissions language was deleted from the debt-limit bill and was deemed to have been adopted by the House as a stand-alone conference report.

MAJOR PROVISIONS

Major provisions of the debt-limit bill included:

• **Debt Limit.** An increase in the federal statutory debt limit from $4.9 trillion to $5.5 trillion.

• **Social Security Earnings Limit.** Targeting seniors ages 65 to 69, the provisions—to be phased in over seven years—allowed the working elderly to earn up to $30,000 and continue to receive their full Social Security benefits.

Under existing law, Social Security recipients ages 65 to 69 could earn up to $11,520 and continue to receive their full Social Security benefits. For every $3 earned over the limit, a recipient lost $1 in benefits.

The provision raised the maximum earnings threshold to $12,500 in 1996. It then would go up $1,000 a year until it hit $15,500 in 1999, after which it would jump to $17,000 in 2000, $25,000 in 2001 and $30,000 in 2002.

The earnings limit increase was expected to cost $7 billion over seven years. It was offset by eliminating supplemental security insurance benefits to alcoholics and drug addicts and by eliminating Social Security payments to stepchildren unless they were dependent on their stepparents.

• **Small Business.** Three key provisions were designed to help small businesses deal with regulatory agencies:

• Business owners could recover attorneys' fees and related costs in civil and administrative actions between businesses and federal agencies.

• Small businesses were allowed to file lawsuits to compel federal agencies to comply with the Regulatory Flexibility Act. The bill required that agencies take into account the special needs of small businesses and farmers when they issued federal rules.

In addition, the Environmental Protection Agency and the Occupational Safety and Health Administration, as part of their rule-making processes, were required to collect advice and recommendations from small businesses to improve their analyses of the impact of proposed regulations.

• A Small Business and Agriculture Regulatory Enforcement Ombudsman was to be appointed to work with each regulatory agency to ensure that small businesses had a way to comment on regulatory enforcement. ❏

Enhanced Rescissions

In March 1996, Congress cleared and President Clinton signed a bill (S 4—PL 104-130) to give the president new authority to cancel, or rescind, previously enacted spending provisions—roughly equivalent to a line-item veto.

The new law, creating so-called enhanced rescissions authority, was intended to strengthen the hand of the president in his budget dealings with Congress by making it easier to strike out individual spending items from appropriations bills and narrowly targeted provisions in tax bills.

Granting the president something akin to the long-sought line-item veto (which would require a constitutional amendment for enactment) was one of the very few issues on which Clinton and the GOP revolutionaries who wrote the "Contract with America" wholeheartedly agreed.

Still, enactment of the new law did not come easily. Republicans in control of Congress opted not to give the power to Clinton—a Democrat—during his first term, which ended in January 1997.

And late-stage resistance among some Senate GOP opponents was broken chiefly by appeals from Senate Majority Leader Bob Dole, R-Kan., who needed results for his 1996 presidential campaign against Clinton. Dole was forced repeatedly to intervene to whip Republicans into line.

Moreover, the law's eventual success was uncertain. It was not to take effect until January 1997, so it was not tested right away. And soon after it took effect, Sen. Robert C. Byrd, D-W.Va., a long-standing opponent, moved to challenge its constitutionality.

Byrd and five other members of Congress filed a lawsuit claiming that the new law gave the president the authority to amend a law. Under the Constitution, the president only had the authority to sign a bill into law, veto it or let it become law without his signature.

Federal District Court Judge Thomas P. Jackson agreed with Byrd and declared the law unconstitutional on April 10, 1997, saying it "effectively permits the President to repeal duly enacted provisions of federal law. This he cannot do."

However, on June 26, 1997, the Supreme Court reversed Jackson, and ruled that Byrd and his fellow plaintiffs did not have sufficient standing to sue because they had not been concretely injured by the law. Other legal challenges were pending.

BACKGROUND

Under prior law, the president could single out items in already enacted appropriations bills for proposed cuts. However, Congress was free to ignore these so-called rescissions requests, and often did. Bill supporters argued that the president needed stronger authority to curb Congress's propensity to slip wasteful pork barrel projects into appropriations bills that he had little choice but to sign.

And amending the Constitution to give the president a true line-item veto—the power to strike individual lines or groups of lines from appropriations bills before he signed them—was regarded as an essentially impossible task. So, the House and Senate bills sought instead to provide the power by legislative fiat.

The House had on several prior occasions passed bills to improve the odds that Congress would act on rescissions, though the Senate largely ignored these bills. In 1994, the House had passed what was called an expedited rescissions bill (HR 4600), but it died without further action. (Budget-control efforts, p. 64)

With Republicans in control of both houses of Congress at the beginning of 1995, though, and with support from Clinton, the odds greatly improved.

LEGISLATIVE ACTION

Enactment capped a very difficult legislative drive. The House had easily passed its version of the bill in the opening weeks of the 1995 session. But action in the Senate required tortuous negotiations between such "Old Bulls" as Budget Committee Chairman Pete V. Domenici, R-N.M., and deficit hawks such as John McCain, R-Ariz., the top Senate sponsor.

Domenici was among a small group of Senate Republicans who disliked the enhanced rescissions idea that had gained support in the House because it would have shifted too much power to the president, in his view. Eventually, Domenici and Ted Stevens, R-Alaska, another reluctant convert, agreed to the version that passed the House and was championed in the Senate by McCain.

House Action

The House bill (HR 2—H Rept 104-11, Parts 1 and 2) won quick acceptance in committee. The Government Reform Committee approved it by a 30–11 vote on Jan. 25, as part of the "Contract with America" drive. The Rules Committee followed suit the next day, approving the bill 9–4.

The full House passed HR 2 on Feb. 6 by 294–134, with 71 Democrats joining all but four Republicans in supporting the measure.

Under the House bill, the president was permitted to submit a package of rescissions for each enacted appropriations bill. The cuts would become law automatically unless both chambers passed a bill to reject them. It was assumed the president would veto any such "disapproval bill," requiring a two-thirds vote to override.

In addition to specific cuts, the president could have proposed reductions in overall spending, giving him great flexibility in shaping the budget. The rescissions authority was also to apply to any tax bill that contained certain special interest tax breaks; it would not apply to entitlements.

Before passage, the House rejected an amendment by Rep. Bob Wise, D- W.Va., that would have substituted a version of the previously passed expedited rescissions language. Wise and other argued that it would increase the president's leverage by forcing Congress to act on rescissions requests, but not go so far as requiring affirmatively to reject the president's proposed cuts. The Wise amendment failed, 167–246.

Senate Action

In the Senate, the House-style enhanced rescissions bill (S 4) sponsored by McCain had considerable GOP support, but it encountered stiff resistance from several senior Republicans who contended it would transfer too much power to the president.

With Republicans deeply split, the Senate Budget Committee approved both bills without recommending which one should pass on the floor. The two roll call votes followed a tense markup session Feb. 14, in which S 4 was approved 12–10 (S Rept 104-9) and S 14 was approved 13–8 (S Rept 104-8).

Domenici had postponed the markup twice, convening it only after winning assurances from Republican conservatives that they would vote for his bill, even though they preferred McCain's.

The Governmental Affairs Committee, which shared jurisdiction over the legislation, followed the path set by the Budget Committee and voted March 2 to report both bills without recommendation. The vote on Domenici's bill was 13–2 (S Rept 104-14). McCain's bill was approved by voice vote (S Rept 104-13).

To avert an intraparty floor fight that might have scuttled the entire effort, Dole offered yet another alternative that called for "separate enrollment" of each item in an appropriations bill—essentially creating a bundle of hundreds or thousands of mini-bills that would be passed en bloc under tightly restricted rules and sent to the president. The president could then veto any individual bill, with a two-thirds majority required to overrule him.

The same rules would have applied to targeted tax breaks or new entitlement spending; the new authority was to expire in 2000.

The Senate then passed S 4 on March 23 by a **key vote of 69–29 (R 50–2, D 19–27),** after substituting Dole's alternative separate enrollment language.

Several Democratic opponents blasted Dole's alternative as a poorly drafted and hastily debated measure that would produce a logistical nightmare. Byrd said if it had been in place the previous year, the 13 fiscal 1995 appropriations bills would have been broken up into almost 10,000 "billettes or actlettes or public lawlettes." As Congress neared the start of the new fiscal year, he said, there would be no way to process that many bills in time.

And while the separate enrollment idea eased passage in the Senate, it was strongly opposed by the House, which regarded it as far too cumbersome a process. This was tacitly acknowledged by Senate supporters, and it slowed conference negotiations.

Conference, Final Action

After a delay of six full months, House and Senate conferees officially opened talks on the bill Sept. 27.

Little progress was made at the initial meeting Sept. 27, but on Nov. 8 Stevens, a key negotiator, said a majority of Senate GOP conferees were willing to accept the House's enhanced rescissions approach. He warned, however, that he remained committed to the Senate-passed provision that would terminate the new authority in 2000. Dropping that provision would threaten Senate adoption of the conference report, Stevens said. Many other differences over details—as well as lingering reluctance by Domenici and Stevens—slowed the conference further.

By March 1996, the demands of Dole's presidential campaign added a political imperative to the bill's prospects and Dole ordered negotiators to strike a deal.

In addition, House GOP leaders were eager to find conservative agenda items to attach to a must-pass bill to raise the federal debt limit (HR 3136). *(Debt-limit increase, p. 76)*

In the end, the conference adopted the House bill's framework and kept the Senate's "sunset" provision, extending it to 2003. Dole and Clinton agreed to remove the presidential campaign overlay from action on the bill by delaying the effective date to Jan. 1, 1997. Conferees approved S 4 on March 21 (H Rept 104-491).

To ensure that S 4, the enhanced rescissions bill, and the debt-limit increase (HR 3136) went to the president at the same time, House GOP leaders directly linked the two measures until action by the Senate on the enhanced rescissions conference report.

The Senate adopted the conference report by a 69–31 vote on March 27. Under the rule governing House floor debate on the debt limit bill, the conference report on S 4 had been attached to HR 3136 until the Senate acted. After the Senate vote, the enhanced rescissions language was deleted from the debt-limit bill and the conference report was deemed to have been adopted by the House. Clinton signed the bill April 9. ❏

Balanced-Budget Amendment

Proponents of amending the Constitution to require a balanced federal budget thought 1995 would be their year.

Early vote counts seemed to show that, after years of coming up short—most recently in 1994—they would finally get the two-thirds majority needed in both chambers to send the amendment to the states for ratification.

Adoption in the House was practically a foregone conclusion after Republicans took control of the chamber and a tide of incoming GOP freshmen swelled the ranks of amendment supporters.

The amendment (H J Res 1) was adopted overwhelmingly on Jan. 26 on a **key vote of 300–132 (R 228–2, D 72–129, I 0–1).** Even so, Republican leaders first had to drop a provision dear to conservatives that would have required a three-fifths majority vote in Congress to raise taxes. *(1995 key votes, p. 1025)*

But supporters' hopes were dashed in the Senate, where the amendment was rejected on March 2 by a **key vote of 65–35 (R**

51–2, D 14–33), two votes short of the 67 needed. Senate supporters in fact had 66 votes, but Majority Leader Bob Dole, R-Kan., switched his vote in a procedural move that allowed him to call for a revote at any time.

In the end, the measure actually lost ground in the midst of the 1996 presidential fight. When Dole brought it back to the Senate floor on June 6, 1996, it was killed on a **key vote of 64–35 (R 52–1, D 12–34).** *(1996 key votes, p. 1047)*

BACKGROUND

The debate over amending the Constitution to require a balanced budget followed years of frustration over the seemingly permanent federal deficit that had ballooned during the 1980s.

And, although the Senate had adopted a balanced-budget amendment by the necessary two-thirds majority in 1982, the House fell well short. Throughout the rest of the decade, Senate supporters tried in vain to revive the amendment, seeing it rejected again in 1986 and failing in most years even to get a measure to the floor. *(Congress and the Nation Vol. VI, p. 52; Congress and the Nation Vol. VII, p. 57)*

With growing concern about the intractability of the deficit, supporters gained ground in the 1990s. In 1990, 1992 and 1994, the House came within a dozen votes or less of adopting an amendment sponsored by Rep. Charles W. Stenholm, D-Texas. *(Congress and the Nation Vol. VIII, pp. 75, 84)*

In 1994, the amendment fell just four votes short in the Senate in the face of a hard-fought campaign by the Clinton administration and Senate opponents led by Appropriations Chairman Robert C. Byrd, D-W.Va., and Majority Leader George J. Mitchell, D-Maine. *(1994 balanced-budget amendment, p. 62)*

Supporters argued that without a constitutional requirement to balance the budget, politically popular entitlement programs such as Medicare, Medicaid and Social Security would remain virtually impossible to cut. The amendment, they said, also would force other difficult cuts from appropriated programs such as farm subsidies, highway programs and entrenched bureaucracies.

Opponents responded that the amendment itself would have no impact on the deficit: the actual cuts would still have to be made through legislation. They said it was better for Congress and the president to roll up their sleeves and pass a binding budget resolution that actually required that the budget be placed on a path towards balance.

On Sept. 27, 1994, House Republicans unveiled their "Contract with America," a 10-point plan that they vowed to act on in the first 100 days of the 104th Congress. The first item was passage of a balanced-budget amendment that included a provision requiring a three-fifths majority of the full membership of each chamber to approve any tax increase. When Republicans won control of the House in November, the contract was transformed from a campaign platform into an agenda for the next Congress.

Of all the items in the document, the balanced-budget amendment was thought to present the incoming House GOP leadership with its easiest job.

LEGISLATIVE ACTION

As 1995 opened, supporters offered competing versions of the constitutional amendment. The Senate version (S J Res 1), introduced by Dole, would have required the president to submit, and Congress to pass, a balanced federal budget each year by 2002 or two years after ratification of the amendment by the states.

A three-fifths vote in both chambers would have been required to run a deficit, except in times of war or serious military threats. A three-fifths vote also would be required to raise the statutory limit on the national debt.

In the House, Joe L. Barton, R-Texas, introduced a more stringent proposal (H J Res 1). Based on the Contract with America, it included the controversial requirement that any increase in taxes be approved by a three-fifths majority of each chamber.

Stenholm, joined by Dan Schaefer, R-Colo., introduced a measure (H J Res 28) identical to Dole's. Deficit hawks from both parties had rallied around that version of the amendment for years, and even supporters of the stricter resolution acknowledged that it was the only one with a chance to ultimately pass.

Rather than attacking the amendment head-on, the Clinton administration tried to undercut support by calling on Republicans to spell out exactly how they planned to balance the budget.

Public opinion polls indicated that the White House strategy might resonate with voters. A CBS News/New York Times poll released Dec. 14, 1994, showed 81 percent of Americans favored amending the Constitution. But that support slipped to 30 percent or less when respondents were told that cuts in Social Security, Medicare and education might be required.

House Action

Consideration began Jan. 11 in a fractious session of the House Judiciary Committee, which approved Barton's more stringent version by a party-line vote of 20–13 (H Rept 104-3).

The markup lasted almost nine hours, with Republicans easily rejecting more than a dozen Democratic amendments, most significantly a move by Barney Frank, D-Mass., to build a constitutional wall between Social Security and the rest of the budget.

Barton's tax language was controversial enough that Republican leaders then crafted a rule for floor debate on H J Res 1 that allowed preliminary votes on several alternatives. In addition to Barton's, the House was also allowed a vote on the Stenholm-Schaefer version. The version adopted by the largest majority would then be presented for a vote on final passage.

The leadership took that course because it was clear that Barton's version could not attract the minimum 60 Democratic votes that were needed to reach the two-thirds mark (290 votes if all members were present and voting). In fact, Barton's version drew just a 253–173 majority in a preliminary vote.

Republicans then rallied behind the Stenholm-Schaefer alternative, adopting it by a preliminary vote of 293–139. To prevail, though, House Republican leaders first had to put out a brush fire among GOP freshmen upset over having to settle for the less stringent version.

"We all saw clearly at the end of this day we had to have a balanced-budget amendment," said Majority Leader Dick Armey, R-Texas. And H J Res 1, amended to reflect the Stenholm-Schaefer alternative, was adopted by a 300–132 vote and sent on to the Senate.

In the end, 72 Democrats and all but two Republicans, John Hostettler and Mark E. Souder, both freshmen from Indiana, voted for the amendment.

Senate Action

The Senate Judiciary Committee approved S J Res 1 (S Rept 104-5) on Jan. 18 by a vote of 15–3.

During the markup, the Republican majority rejected a handful of Democratic amendments, most importantly one by Dianne Feinstein, D-Calif., to remove the Social Security trust funds from deficit calculations.

Feinstein said her amendment was critical to prevent future Congresses from raiding Social Security to balance the budget. Republicans countered that it would create a giant loophole that would allow Congress to avoid closing the deficit.

Feinstein's amendment was tabled (killed) by a 10–8 vote, but the issue was gaining resonance among Democrats who had previously voted for the underlying measure. That would prove to provide the critical margin for defeat.

The Senate took up H J Res 1 (which was identical to S J Res 1) on Jan. 30, kicking off a debate that consumed the entire month of February. In the end, backers fell one vote short of the 67 needed to send the constitutional amendment to the states for approval. And after Dole switched to "no" to preserve his ability to call for a revote later in the 104th Congress, the measure failed on March 2 on a 65–35 vote.

From the opening speech to the final hours of debate, it was clear that the vote would be a cliffhanger. That put the spotlight on a small but potentially pivotal group of Democrats who had previously voted for the constitutional amendment but who now said they were undecided.

Many in that group said they would vote for the measure if it were changed to prevent Social Security surpluses from being used to hide the budget deficit. The idea would have required the federal government to run an overall surplus.

On Feb. 14, however, the Senate voted 57–41 to table (kill) an amendment by Harry Reid, D-Nev., to exclude Social Security trust funds from deficit calculations.

Democrats permitted the debate to come to a close on Feb. 28, and with the end in sight, the drama over the ever-shifting vote tally grew increasingly intense.

Vote counters tallied 52 Republicans—everyone but Appropriations Chairman Mark O. Hatfield of Oregon—for the amendment. That meant supporters had to win the votes of 15 Democrats, while only 10 were considered solid "yes" votes. Two Democrats who voted for the amendment in 1994—Minority Leader Tom Daschle of South Dakota and Jeff Bingaman of New Mexico—announced Feb. 16 that they would reverse course and vote "no."

In the final days, four undecided Democrats came off the fence and announced their support—but the fifth proved elusive. Dole permitted the climactic vote, knowing the amendment would go down to defeat. Six Democrats who voted against the amendment—saying it did not adequately protect Social Security—had supported virtually the same language in 1994.

Just before the tally closed, with the vote at 66–34, Dole changed his vote to "no," a parliamentary move that enabled him to call the measure for a revote at any time.

Then, 15 months later—after Dole had clinched the GOP nomination for president—he brought the amendment back for another vote.

But Dole had lost ground. Senate newcomer Ron Wyden, D-Ore., who replaced "aye" vote Bob Packwood, a Republican, voted "no." And longtime amendment supporter Jim Exon, D-Neb., switched his vote after decrying the politics driving Dole's move for a revote and his embrace of tax cuts.

On June 6, 1996, H J Res 1 was rejected again 64–36, failing once more to get a two-thirds majority. ❑

Tax Policy

Democratic presidential candidate Bill Clinton in 1992 joined the chorus of those advocating a tax cut for the middle class, who were feeling increasingly anxious about stagnant real wages. After winning the election, however, Clinton abandoned the idea of a middle-class tax cut.

Faced with a federal budget more unbalanced than anticipated, he instead decided to concentrate on reducing the federal budget deficit. The 1993 budget reconciliation bill would turn out to be a defining piece of legislation for the Clinton presidency. The measure cleared Congress without a single Republican vote, and it included one of the largest tax increases in the history of the United States. Most important, Clinton's actions served as a signal to Wall Street that he was serious about bringing down the deficit and that he was willing to make tough decisions and expend precious political capital to do so.

In the ensuing years, the economy would strengthen as inflation stayed low, interest rates and unemployment fell, the deficit shrank and the stock market boomed. Clinton's reelection in 1996 was attributed in no small part to the economy's vigor.

Republicans found considerably less success in the area of tax policy after they took control of Congress as a result of the 1994 elections. The 1995 budget reconciliation bill reflected the GOP's long-time push for substantive tax cuts. Believing they could carry the day on their own, the Republicans made little or no effort to court Democratic support in the formulation of the reconciliation bill.

The strategy worked insofar as they had the votes to pass the bill they wanted. That was not enough when Clinton vetoed the bill and Republicans were unable to muster enough Democratic votes to override. That defeat, together with the forced government shutdowns that proved devastatingly unpopular, resulted in subdued GOP behavior in 1996 regarding tax and budget issues.

1993 DEFICIT-REDUCTION BILL

A central element of putting President Clinton's budget into effect was enactment of a budget reconciliation measure that called for far-reaching tax changes as well as significant government program spending cuts. The hefty tax increases on the wealthy proposed by Clinton in the 1993 deficit-reduction bill were the opposite remedy for the nation's ills that were proposed by his White House Republican predecessors—namely, large tax cuts.

About half the deficit reduction was to come from $240 billion in new taxes, mostly concentrated on upper-income individuals. But for a 4.3-cents-per-gallon increase in the federal excise tax on gasoline, middle-income taxpayers were mostly spared. And poor families—even those who owed no tax—were to benefit from an increase in the earned income tax credit, a tax break for the working poor.

Although many elements of the massive reconciliation bill were a source of conflict, the spotlight was on the tax increases it contained. Democrats used traditional arguments of fairness and progressivity to make the case for dramatic increases in taxes on wealthy individuals. Republicans countered that spending cuts were far better for the economy and that tax increases would cost jobs, particularly in small businesses. When the conference report on the deficit-reduction bill was completed, which contained a retroactive tax increase for the wealthy, Republicans screamed even louder.

The reconciliation package was nearly brought down in its early stages by a Clinton-proposed, $72 billion tax on energy consumption—dubbed a Btu tax for the method of calculating the levy on heat content of fuels as measured in British thermal units. One argument in support of the Btu tax was the environmental benefits of reduced consumption of energy. Another selling point was that a Btu tax was broad-based and thus its cost would be shared widely. But that argument became the principal objection to the tax. Because of the way it was to be levied, the tax would have raised the cost of producing goods, thereby adding to inflation and, critics said, costing jobs.

Over the vigorous protests of Democrats from oil- and natural gas-producing states, the original House-passed version of the bill contained the Btu tax. Some voted for the bill only reluctantly, after winning assurances that the tax would be changed later—though it was unclear how at the time. The Btu tax was killed in the Senate. In need of votes, Senate leaders compromised and pushed for an increase in the gasoline tax,

REFERENCES

Discussion of tax policy for the years 1945–1964 may be found in *Congress and the Nation Vol. I*, pp. 397–442; for the years 1965–1968, *Congress and the Nation Vol. II*, pp. 141–182; for the years 1969–1972, *Congress and the Nation Vol. III*, pp. 77–96; for the years 1973–1976, *Congress and the Nation Vol. IV*, pp. 83–106; for the years 1977–1980, *Congress and the Nation Vol. V*, pp. 231–251; for the years 1981–1984, *Congress and the Nation Vol. VI*, pp. 63–82; for the years 1985–1988, *Congress and the Nation Vol. VII*, pp. 75–107; for the years 1989–1992, *Congress and the Nation Vol. VIII*, pp. 87–112.

which was estimated to raise about a third of the revenue of a Btu tax but would spare the natural gas industry. The gas tax provision survived in the final bill.

In 1994, the Clinton administration held its fire on taxes and the budget. The deficit-reduction bill enacted in 1993 had set a course for the future that a year later was considered acceptable—and economically prudent—by both the administration and Democratic congressional leaders. Mostly, they found it convenient to adhere to a budget blueprint that required no additional difficult choices in an election year.

GOP TAX PLANS

The roots of the Republicans' tax-cutting fervor in the 1994 congressional campaign and in the Congress they later controlled could be found in the 1992 presidential election. After Clinton, upon assuming the presidency, dropped his campaign promise of a middle-class tax cut, House GOP leaders picked up the theme. They proposed in their 1994 campaign tract, the "Contract with America," a list of tax cuts to aid families and senior citizens and to promote economic growth.

In particular, the contract proposed to provide income tax credits of $500 for each child or dependent parent or grandparent; give a $5,000 tax credit to families who adopted a child; eliminate the marriage penalty; reduce the tax rate on capital gains; create an individual retirement account that taxed money before it was contributed to the account, not when it was withdrawn; cut taxes on Social Security benefits; and provide tax breaks for the purchase of long-term care insurance.

The 1995 budget reconciliation bill carried much of the GOP economic agenda, including a sizable tax cut for investors, corporations, and families with children. The central purpose of the overall Republican economic program was to balance the federal budget by fiscal 2002. Tax relief was designed to soften the impact of the deficit-shrinking spending cuts and to build support for those cuts from an array of interest groups. The GOP thinking was that even if the groups disliked some of the spending cuts, they would support the overall budget reconciliation bill to get the tax benefits.

The reconciliation bill would have provided an annual tax credit of $500 per child to families with incomes of up to $110,000, a reduction in capital gains taxes, an end to the corporate alternative minimum tax, lower taxes on estates, new deductions for individual retirement accounts, and an array of tax breaks for small businesses. It also would have reduced the earned income tax credit by $32 billion.

As the tax cut proposal progressed through the legislative process, it encountered a swirl of forces—deficit hawks who opposed all tax cuts, Democrats who blasted the proposal as class warfare, moderate Republicans and Democrats who favored limited tax cuts tied to the elimination of the deficit, tax-cut hardliners who wanted a deep cut in time for the 1996 elections, and leaders of both parties caught up in presidential politics.

Still, pushed steadily by House Republican leaders, the tax cut advanced. Without their prime source of leverage—the threat of a Senate filibuster, which was not possible on the budget resolution or the reconciliation bill—the minority Demo-

crats were essentially powerless in the congressional debate until the president stepped up with his veto pen.

In the end, the Republicans were unable to overcome the veto and force the bill into law. One reason was they had ignored or overrun most Democratic objections to their fiscal policies, resulting in a bill that was uniquely Republican. Thus, when Clinton vetoed the measure, Republicans could not attract the Democratic votes they needed for an override.

Despite the outcome, Republicans had a gleeful moment when Congress was considering the 1995 reconciliation measure. Clinton made news Oct. 18 when he told political supporters in Texas that he had raised taxes too much in the 1993 budget reconciliation bill. "Probably there are people in this room still mad at me about that budget because you think I raised your taxes too much," Clinton said. "It might surprise you to know that I think I raised them too much, too."

Senate Finance Committee Chairman William V. Roth Jr., R-Del., invoked Clinton's name in support of the GOP tax cut plan every chance he got. Democrats looked uncomfortable and appeared unable to believe that the president could have made such a statement. "The president may in retrospect think that he made a mistake. I think we did the right thing," said ranking Finance Committee Democrat Daniel Patrick Moynihan of New York. Other Democrats felt that Clinton was abandoning them after they had gone out on a limb to vote for the 1993 bill.

Clinton attempted to retract his statements the following day, saying, "If anything I said was interpreted by anybody to imply that I am not proud of that program, proud of the people who voted for it, that I don't believe it was the right thing to do, then I shouldn't have said that because I am very proud of it."

Although most of the Republican tax-cutting agenda was attached to the budget reconciliation bill, Congress in 1995 moved one small piece separately: a proposal to renew the partial deduction for health insurance premiums paid by the self-employed. Moreover, in renewing the tax break, Congress struck the first blow in the larger GOP drive to scale back federal affirmative action programs: It canceled a tax break for companies that sold broadcast stations or cable systems to minority-owned businesses.

ELECTION YEAR 1996

Congressional Republicans scored no big victories on the fiscal policy front in 1996—no balanced budget deal, no sweeping tax cuts. Such victories eluded the majority in part because the GOP did not want to repeat the knock-down, drag-out budget fight that had consumed much of the 1995 session. Lawmakers did not want to spend the time or the political capital needed to wage such a battle, let alone win it.

GOP leaders did not try to enact the tax cut proposed by the budget resolution. A major hurdle was the budget rule that effectively required the tax cut to be financed by a tax increase or a cut in federal benefit programs. The former was a nonstarter for the GOP and their political allies. The latter was a trade-off that Democrats had accused the Republicans of making in 1995, hurting the GOP at the polls.

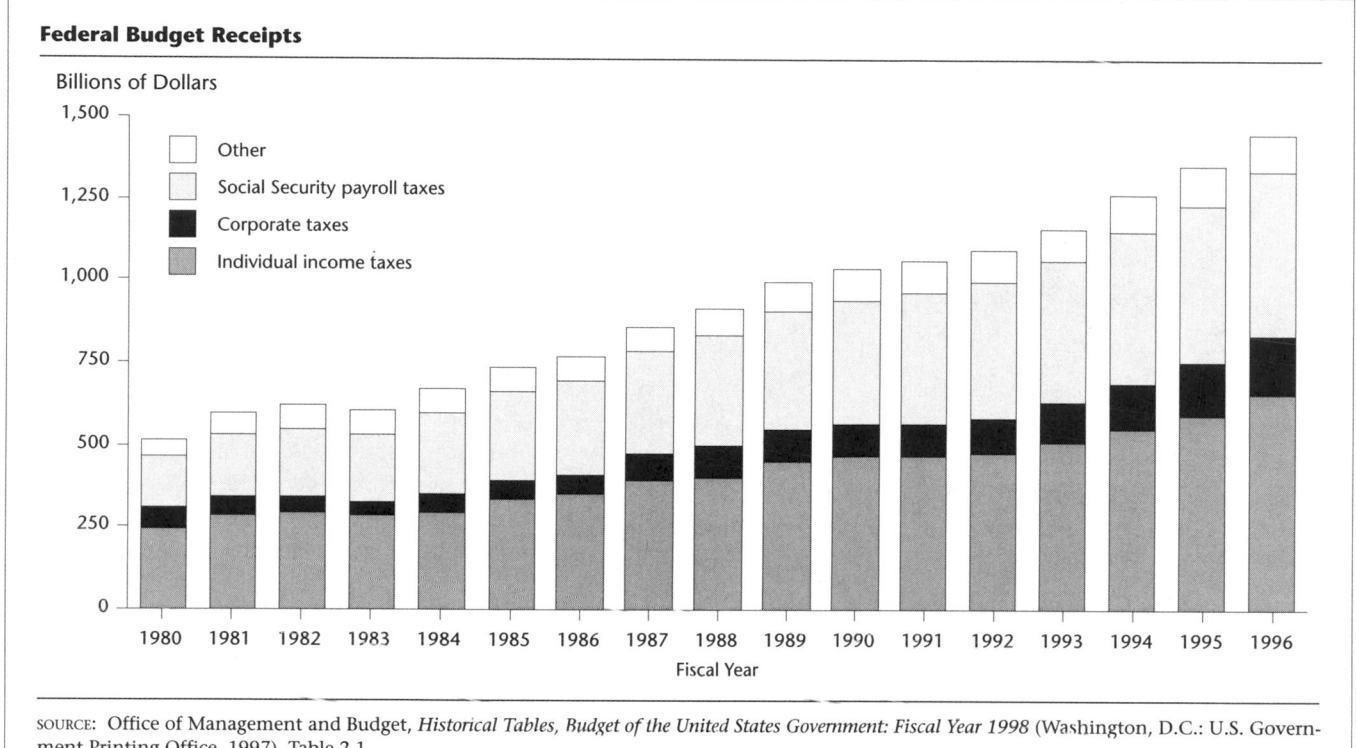

Federal Budget Receipts

Billions of Dollars

Legend:
- Other
- Social Security payroll taxes
- Corporate taxes
- Individual income taxes

Fiscal Year: 1980 1981 1982 1983 1984 1985 1986 1987 1988 1989 1990 1991 1992 1993 1994 1995 1996

SOURCE: Office of Management and Budget, *Historical Tables, Budget of the United States Government: Fiscal Year 1998* (Washington, D.C.: U.S. Government Printing Office, 1997), Table 2.1.

In place of a major tax cut, the Republicans tried to repeal the only tax increase in Clinton's 1993 deficit-reduction plan that had not been targeted at the wealthy: the 4.3-cents-per-gallon increase in the tax on motor fuels. The idea came from Senate Majority Leader Bob Dole, R-Kan., who was on his way to becoming the 1996 Republican presidential nominee to run against Clinton.

Given budgetary constraints, the repeal would have been temporary, but long enough to last through the elections. The proposed repeal appeared to be a sure thing—even Clinton said he would support it. The measure became entangled in other partisan maneuvering, however, and it slipped beneath the surface not long after Dole resigned from the Senate to run for president full time.

Congress did enact a number of targeted tax breaks as part of a legislative package that otherwise had little appeal among Republicans. A bill to increase the minimum wage was made more palatable for the GOP with the addition of $20 billion in tax breaks for businesses, retirement plans and adoptive parents.

In search of a winning economic theme for the 1996 presidential campaign, Republican candidates explored the appeal of a simple, if untested, idea: the flat tax. The main difference between a flat tax and the existing income tax was that a single tax rate would replace the several brackets currently in the code, as well as the vast majority of exemptions, credits and deductions. The renaissance of interest in revamping the income tax echoed the period before the 1986 tax overhaul, when flat tax proposals also were put forth. Those ideas eventually evolved into an over-

hauled tax code that eliminated many tax breaks and reduced the number of tax brackets.

Most GOP politicians found that the concept of a flat tax had great appeal, particularly because it reinforced the party's theme of shrinking government. Several Republican presidential hopefuls in 1996 endorsed different versions of the flat tax. Malcolm S. "Steve" Forbes Jr. based his campaign on the flat tax—a 17 percent rate with no deductions. Sen. Phil Gramm of Texas favored a flat rate of 16 percent, but he would preserve the tax deductions for mortgage interest and charitable donations.

Dole, the eventual GOP nominee, said he favored a "flatter" tax but steered clear of endorsing any specific proposal during the Republican primaries. He also made clear that he was sensitive to the warnings of economists that a flat tax could fall heavily on the middle class.

In January 1996, the National Commission on Economic Growth and Tax Reform issued its long-awaited report on the flat tax. Commission Chairman and Republican Party luminary Jack F. Kemp offered a warm endorsement of the principle. "We believe with all our hearts that if the rate were low and single, with full deductibility of the payroll tax and a large exemption for the poor and low-income Americans, it would create a doubling of the rate of growth of the U.S. economy," he said. Dole would tap Kemp as his vice-presidential running mate in August 1996.

Several members of Congress also had espoused versions of a flat tax, the best known advanced by House Majority Leader Dick Armey, R-Texas. Armey's plan had a 20 percent rate for the first two years, dropping to 17 percent thereafter.

Taxes and Other Revenues as Percentage of GDP

Fiscal year	Individual income	Corporate income	Social insurance	Excise	Other	Total
1935	0.7	0.8	—	2.0	1.5	5.1
1940	0.9	1.2	1.8	2.0	0.7	6.7
1945	8.5	7.4	1.6	2.9	0.5	20.8
1950	5.8	3.8	1.6	2.8	0.5	14.5
1955	7.3	4.5	2.0	2.3	0.5	16.5
1960	7.9	6.0	2.8	2.3	0.8	17.8
1965	7.1	3.7	3.2	2.1	0.8	17.0
1970	9.0	3.3	4.4	1.6	0.9	19.1
1975	7.9	2.6	5.4	1.1	1.0	18.0
1980	9.0	2.6	5.8	0.9	1.0	19.0
1981	9.4	2.0	6.0	1.3	0.9	19.7
1982	9.3	1.5	6.3	1.1	1.0	19.2
1983	8.4	1.1	6.1	1.0	0.9	17.6
1984	7.8	1.5	6.3	1.0	0.9	17.5
1985	8.2	1.5	6.5	0.9	0.9	17.9
1986	8.0	1.4	6.5	0.8	0.9	17.6
1987	8.5	1.8	6.6	0.7	0.9	18.6
1988	8.1	1.9	6.7	0.7	0.9	18.4
1989	8.3	1.9	6.7	0.6	0.9	18.5
1990	8.2	1.6	6.7	0.6	1.0	18.2
1991	8.0	1.7	6.8	0.7	0.9	18.0
1992	7.7	1.6	6.7	0.7	0.9	17.8
1993	7.9	1.8	6.6	0.7	0.8	17.8
1994	8.0	2.1	6.8	0.8	0.9	18.4
1995	8.2	2.2	6.7	0.8	0.9	18.8
1996	8.8	2.3	6.8	0.7	0.8	19.4

NOTE: The Social Insurance category includes Social Security, Medicare, railroad and other retirement programs, and unemployment insurance. The Other category principally includes estate and gift taxes and customs duties.

SOURCE: Office of Management and Budget.

Some economists noted that a flat tax potentially would be a far more complex system than most politicians would acknowledge. "If a flat tax is enacted without a firm grasp of the goal, you'll rapidly end up with a system that's just as complicated as what we've got now," said David Bradford, an economist at Princeton University and a former member of President George Bush's Council of Economic Advisers. Bradford said that the flat tax rate might have to be as high as 25 percent or 30 percent to accommodate popular deductions and collect roughly as much money as the existing income tax system did. That was far higher than the 17 percent rate promised by flat tax proponents on the campaign trail and in Congress.

Proponents of the flat tax cited three major benefits. First, they argued that, by eliminating the distorting effect of an array of tax benefits and the multiple layers of taxation of income from capital investment, it would generate more economic growth, potentially even doubling the gross domestic product. Currently, income is taxed when it is earned. Then, if it is invested in stocks or bonds, the dividends are taxed. Moreover, when the investment is sold, the profit—or capital gain—is taxed. Eliminating this overlap in taxation, it was said, would encourage investment and raise the country's long-term growth rate.

Second, many economists agreed that the proposed elimination of deductions under a flat tax would make the code fairer for lower-income and middle-income taxpayers. Third, proponents said another advantage of a flat tax was its potential to reduce administrative burdens because it would eliminate many of the highly complex deductions, exemptions, credits and depreciation schedules in the existing system.

But opponents of the flat tax pointed to studies that suggested its impact on economic growth was highly questionable. "The estimates are all over the map," noted Randall D. Weiss, a partner at the accounting firm Deloitte and Touche and a former deputy staff director of the Joint Committee on Taxation. By most estimates, flat tax plans such as Armey's would have been revenue losers, which means they would fuel the federal deficit and undermine the goal of achieving a balanced budget.

And a flat tax also could ultimately cause a shift in the distribution of the tax burden so that low- and middle-income taxpayers pay more because they would lose their deductions. Over time, many perceived inequities might be ironed out, especially if the flat tax had the positive effect on the economy forecast by its proponents. But that could take years, and there was no guarantee the public or the politicians who represented them would have the patience to wait.

Chronology of Action on Taxes

1993–1994

Congressional Democrats and President Clinton were successful in 1993 in pushing through—with no Republican help—a far-reaching budget reconciliation measure that counted heavily on tax increases for well-to-do Americans to reduce the federal deficit.

A tax simplification plan passed the House in 1994 but stalled in the Senate.

1993 Deficit-Reduction Bill

Democrats in 1993 assembled a bare majority to clear a massive deficit-reduction bill (HR 2264—PL 103-66) that made hundreds of changes in the tax code and in spending for government programs. (*Reconciliation, legislative history, provisions, p. 44*)

According to the Sept. 1, 1993, Office of Management and Budget estimate, HR 2264 would cut the deficit by $504.8 billion in fiscal 1994–1998—$250.1 billion in net revenue increases and $254.7 billion in spending cuts.

ADMINISTRATION PLAN

In drafting the reconciliation bill, Congress started from a detailed White House plan that relied heavily on taxes. According to the Joint Committee on Taxation, President Clinton's budget amounted to a net revenue increase of $242.2 billion over five years ($337.5 billion in new taxes offset by $95.3 billion in tax breaks). Most of the new revenue in the administration's plan came from increases in income taxes for the wealthy, including a fourth income bracket that increased the top marginal rate to 36 percent for couples with taxable income above $140,000 ($115,000 for individuals).

Other key tax elements of Clinton's plan included:

• **Social Security.** An increase—to 85 percent from 50 percent—in the portion of Social Security benefits subject to taxation for individuals who made $25,000 or more and couples who made $32,000 or more.

• **Btu Tax.** A broad-based energy tax affecting industry and consumers, based on the heat content or British thermal units (Btu) of most forms of energy.

• **Investment.** Investment incentives, including two tax credits—a temporary credit for all businesses in 1993–1994 and a permanent credit for smaller businesses—and a lower capital gains rate for investments in small businesses.

• **Social Programs.** A $28.3 billion expansion of the earned income tax credit (EITC), a refundable credit available to poor working families; and tax incentives and other federal assistance to spur investment and job creation in impoverished communities. (*Enterprise zones, p. 639*)

• **Medicare.** Elimination of the cap on wages ($135,000 in 1993) subject to Medicare tax.

HOUSE COMMITTEE ACTION

The House Ways and Means Committee preserved Clinton's plan for massive income tax increases on wealthy Americans, a broad-based energy tax and higher taxes on upper-income retirees receiving Social Security benefits. But the committee cut in half the administration's proposed increase in the corporate tax rate. It also rejected a Jim Bunning, R-Ky., amendment to drop the Social Security tax increase and use part of the revenue to extend a 25 percent deduction for the health insurance costs of the self-employed. Clinton had proposed to extend the deduction, which expired in 1992, through the end of 1993.

Much of the negotiation focused on efforts to protect specific regions and industries from the effects of the proposed Btu tax. The administration agreed to a number of changes and exemptions, although it rejected a suggestion that electric utilities across the country pay a uniform tax on every kilowatt-hour of energy sold. The White House insisted that the tax vary depending on the mix of fuels the utility used as an incentive for companies to burn the cleanest fuels.

Bill Brewster, D-Okla., won agreement that the tax would be collected directly from the consumer. Clinton originally planned to impose the tax on energy producers and distributors, assuming they would pass it along to consumers, but utilities had complained that state regulations might prevent them from passing along the tax. Under Brewster's plan, the utilities could make the energy tax a separate line on customers' electric and gas bills, bypassing state regulators entirely.

To shore up farm-state support, the committee added a partial exemption—worth 34.2 cents per million Btu—for diesel fuel and gasoline used in farming operations. However, the committee took away another exemption important in farm country, for ethanol and methanol, which the administration had endorsed under pressure from several Democratic senators. Other committee changes included an exemption worth roughly $700 million a year for electricity used as a feedstock in the production of aluminum, chlorine and similar industrial products. The Northeast won an expanded exemption for heating oil used commercially. The administration previously had agreed to an exemption for exported fuels, which primarily applied to the coal industry.

To pay for the exemptions, the committee boosted the basic energy tax rate to 26.8 cents per million Btu, 1.1 cents higher than Clinton had proposed, and added a new tax equivalent to the domestic Btu rate on imported goods if more than 2 percent of their value was from energy costs.

The committee rejected an amendment offered by ranking Republican Bill Archer of Texas to drop the Btu tax and offset the revenue loss by eliminating the investment tax credit and the proposed $28.3 billion expansion in the EITC.

In other changes to the Clinton tax plan, Ways and Means Democrats decided to:

• **Corporate Rate.** Raise the corporate income tax rate from 34 percent to 35 percent, instead of to 36 percent, as Clinton proposed.

• **Investment Incentives.** Drop the investment tax credits, which had virtually no support on the committee or in the business community. To satisfy the administration's demand for some investment incentives to help the economy, the committee substituted provisions to increase to $25,000 from $10,000 the amount that small businesses could write off for the cost of machinery and equipment in the year it was purchased.

• **Social Security.** Require that the $32 billion in new revenue from Clinton's proposed increase in the portion of Social Security benefits subject to taxation be deposited into general government coffers, instead of the Social Security Trust Fund. The administration had said that the Social Security revenues would be earmarked for the trust funds to prevent future shortfalls.

• **Real Estate.** Expand several tax incentives proposed for the real estate industry. The committee adopted a Michael A. Andrews, D-Texas, amendment to allow real estate developers and others working full time in the industry to write off losses on rental property ("passive losses") against ordinary income. Clinton had proposed allowing the write-off, but only against real estate income.

• **Luxury Taxes.** Repeal luxury taxes on boats, furs, airplanes and jewelry that were enacted in 1990. In addition, the committee agreed that the luxury tax on automobiles costing more than $30,000 would be indexed for inflation.

• **Empowerment Zones.** Expand the tax incentives and other government benefits that Clinton proposed for impoverished urban and rural areas, bringing the total cost of the zones to $5.2 billion over five years.

• **Intangibles.** Attach a plan offered by Ways and Means Chairman Dan Rostenkowski, D-Ill., to require businesses that acquired intangible assets, such as customer lists and franchise rights, to write off the cost of the purchase over a period of 14 years. Existing law specified no write-off period for intangible assets.

HOUSE FLOOR ACTION

The administration and House Democratic leaders made a no-holds-barred lobbying effort to gather the necessary votes to pass HR 2264. Republicans without exception opposed the plan. John R. Kasich of Ohio, ranking Republican on the House Budget Committee, offered a substitute reconciliation package that would more than match the deficit reduction in the Democratic plan without tax increases. The House rejected the amendment 138–295 on May 27, 1993.

As a result of one of the many lobbying campaigns, several energy-state Democrats who bitterly opposed Clinton's energy tax won assurances that the plan would be changed, either in the Senate or during the House-Senate conference. A specific change sought by members with petrochemical plants in their districts was a rebate in the tax for energy-intensive or energy-dependent products such as petrochemicals or aluminum.

SENATE COMMITTEE ACTION

The Senate Finance Committee retained the basic thrust of Clinton's plan to concentrate the tax increases on upper-income earners and, to a lesser extent, on corporations. But major changes saved additional money by trimming tax breaks for businesses and the poor as well as dropped the unpopular Btu tax in favor of a regressive increase in the tax on gasoline and other fuels. Overall, the committee version included deeper spending cuts and fewer tax increases than either the House-passed bill or the administration's plan.

In place of Clinton's proposed energy tax, Democrats agreed on a 4.3-cents-per-gallon increase in the tax on gasoline and other transportation fuels. The fuels tax was expected to bring in $24.2 billion over the next five years, compared with $71.5 billion for the Btu tax. Most of the hard bargaining focused on what rate to set for the fuels tax and where to find additional revenue and spending cuts so that the bill achieved at least as much deficit reduction as Clinton's original plan.

Max Baucus, D-Mont., insisted that Democrats hold the increase in the fuels tax below 5 cents a gallon. To make up part of the revenue, Baucus and Kent Conrad, D-N.D., favored raising the top corporate income tax rate another percentage point above the 35 percent the House had approved. But that ran into opposition from senators who wanted lower taxes. Democrats reluctantly turned to a money-saving approach suggested by Bill Bradley, D-N.J.—cutting back the administration's proposals for tax breaks to help businesses, urban areas and the poor.

To shore up support on the Senate floor and to mute opposition from the elderly, committee Democrats reduced the impact of Clinton's proposed tax increase on Social Security benefits by applying it to individuals who made $32,000 and to couples who made $40,000 (as opposed to $25,000 and $32,000, respectively, under Clinton's plan).

The committee made the following changes to raise revenue:

• **Business Breaks.** Much of what remained of Clinton's plan for stimulating the economy through business tax breaks was scaled back or dropped. For example, while the House had increased the small business write-offs for equipment purchases to $25,000, Senate Finance provided for only $15,000. The committee also rejected Clinton's proposal to make the research and development tax credit permanent, opting instead to extend it until July 1994, which "saved" $8.4 billion under government accounting rules. In addition, the panel dropped the administration proposal to give a capital gains tax break to investors in certain small companies.

• **EITC.** The committee reduced the proposed increase in the earned income tax credit by $10 billion.

• **Empowerment Zones.** Clinton's plan to establish empowerment zones in depressed urban and rural areas was dropped.

• **Capital Gains.** The panel made capital gains subject to the new 10 percent surtax on income above $250,000 a year.

Among the tax-related amendments offered by Republicans and rejected by the committee were those:

• By John H. Chafee of Rhode Island to strike the transfer of 2.5 cents a gallon in motor fuels taxes to the Highway Trust Fund.

• By Chafee to strike the provision prohibiting businesses from deducting executive salaries above $1 million in the absence of explicit performance standards approved by an outside board of directors and stockholders.

• By Chafee to replace the provision limiting the executive salary deduction with one limiting deductibility for all individuals who were paid more than $1 million, including, for example, professional athletes.

• By John C. Danforth of Missouri to exempt jet fuel used in commercial airlines and cargo planes from the new fuel tax if such a tax would adversely affect the airline industry's financial health.

• By William V. Roth Jr. of Delaware, on behalf of Malcolm Wallop of Wyoming, to exempt small businesses such as sole proprietorships, partnerships and subchapter S corporations from the increase in individual income tax rates.

• By Roth to sunset all tax increases in the bill at the end of 1998.

• By ranking member Bob Packwood of Oregon, on behalf of Orrin G. Hatch of Utah, to strike a provision reducing the business meal deduction.

• By Minority Leader Bob Dole of Kansas to increase the percentage of amortized intangibles to 100 percent.

SENATE FLOOR ACTION

Although the Finance Committee reshaped the heart of the reconciliation bill more to the liking of Senate moderates and conservatives, individual senators found much to oppose in the measure. Probusiness moderates were upset that business investment incentives were dealt away to help pay for the downsizing of the energy tax. Liberals were angry that Medicare spending cuts were increased for the same reason. Democratic leaders, forced to rely solely on their party in the face of virtually lockstep Republican opposition, gave up $17 billion in deficit reduction to buy allegiance from the potential renegades, shrinking the $516 billion package that came to the floor down to the $499 billion package that eventually passed. The Senate rejected a Dole substitute designed to achieve roughly $411 billion in deficit reduction over five years but with none of the Democrats' tax increases.

The Senate voted on a number of other tax-related amendments:

• **Business Tax Incentives.** To appease some moderate Democrats, Majority Leader George J. Mitchell, D-Maine, proposed to add $3.6 billion in tax breaks to benefit small business, including a targeted capital gains tax cut and a bigger write-off for equipment purchases. Bradley, who argued that the proposal was a giveaway and would have little economic benefit, and four other Democrats joined the Republicans to kill the amendment, 54–44 on June 23, 1993. The amendment required a three-fifths majority because of a procedural motion.

Mitchell then offered a redesigned amendment that dropped the capital gains break and substituted a $3.6 billion provision to expand to $20,500 the amount that small businesses could write off their taxes for purchases of equipment and machinery. (Existing law allowed $10,000; the original Senate bill allowed $15,000.) No longer subject to the procedural hurdle, the amendment was adopted 93–5 on June 24.

• **Tax Exemption for Small Business.** Roth offered an amendment to exempt small businesses and family farms from a portion of the higher taxes in the bill. The amendment needed a two-thirds majority for a waiver of the budget rules. It fell short, 56–42 on June 24.

• **Transportation Tax.** The Senate tabled (killed) a Don Nickles, R-Okla., amendment to drop the 4.3-cents-per-gallon increase in fuel taxes on a 50–48 vote June 24. Adopted by voice vote was a Slade Gorton, R-Wash., amendment to give the airline industry a $2.3 billion exemption from the tax on jet fuel beginning after 1993.

• **Social Security.** Trent Lott, R-Miss., offered an amendment to eliminate the increase in taxes on Social Security benefits for upper-income recipients. The amendment was defeated 51–46 on June 24 on a tabling motion.

CONFERENCE, FINAL ACTION

As the reconciliation bill headed for conference, the pivotal question for the leadership was what form of energy tax to impose and how much revenue it would raise. The far more lucrative House-passed Btu tax appeared dead; a large contingent of Democrats wanted to drop the idea of an energy tax altogether, arguing that the Senate version was too small and not worth the political pain. It was the one tax in the bill that was aimed at the middle class, and Republicans were using it to bash the Democrats. But Democratic leaders said that killing the tax would make it almost impossible to reach a compromise that fulfilled Clinton's goal for deficit reduction and paid for the many expensive tax breaks sought mainly by the House. In a maneuver that foiled those seeking to scrap the energy levy, Rostenkowski and Senate Finance Committee Chairman Daniel Patrick Moynihan, D-N.Y., eliminated the main option for replacing much of the lost revenue: they won early approval for a 35 percent top corporate rate, killing energy tax opponents' hopes of tapping a bigger, 36 percent top rate. Rostenkowski and Moynihan tried without success to come up with a compromise energy tax that split the difference between the revenue raised by a Btu tax and that raised by the Senate's fuels tax. With nowhere else to go for the money, conferees adopted the Senate plan for a 4.3-cents-a-gallon increase in the fuels tax.

The conferees made other tax-related decisions regarding the reconciliation bill:

• **Individual Tax Rates.** Both chambers had approved a new top marginal rate of 36 percent, along with a 10 percent surtax on taxable income above $250,000. In a last-minute move that maximized revenue collections but provoked intense controversy, negotiators kept a House-passed provision making the increase retroactive to Jan. 1, 1993. The Treasury Department announced Aug. 4, 1993, that taxpayers would have up to three years to pay any back taxes resulting from the change and would face no late penalties.

• **Social Security.** The conferees adopted Clinton's proposal to raise the portion of Social Security benefits subject to taxation from 50 percent to 85 percent for upper-income retirees. But they set a higher threshold than was found in either the House- or Senate-passed bill. The change applied to individuals earning at least $34,000 a year and couples making $44,000 a year.

• **Corporate Income Tax.** Conferees stuck with the new 35 percent top corporate rate approved by both chambers, resisting calls to go to 36 percent to help offset added social spending or replace the energy tax. Both chambers had made the new corporate rate retroactive to Jan. 1, 1993.

• **Small Business Incentives.** Conferees limited the increased write-off for equipment and machinery purchased by small businesses to $17,500. Both chambers originally were more generous: the House had approved a $25,000 write-off; the Senate had reduced that to $20,500.

• **Empowerment Zones.** Conferees scaled back Clinton's empowerment zones, providing $1 billion in grants and $2.5 billion in tax incentives. The bill authorized nine empowerment zones that would qualify for federal tax breaks and other assistance and awarded lesser benefits to 95 other communities. Clinton had asked for $4.1 billion for 10 empowerment zones and 100 additional communities. The House had increased the funds to $5.2 billion.

• **EITC.** The conference expanded the earned income tax credit for low-income families, including some families with no children, at a cost of $20.8 billion over five years. Clinton had requested and the House had approved a larger, $28.3 billion expansion.

Before adopting the conference report on HR 2264, the Senate rejected 44–56 on Aug. 6 a GOP effort to strip the bill of provisions making tax increases retroactive as a violation of the Constitution.

MAJOR PROVISIONS

As cleared, the tax provisions of the 1993 Omnibus Reconciliation Act (HR 2264—PL 103-66):

Individual Taxes

• **Individual Rates.** Imposed a fourth tax bracket, increasing the top marginal rate to 36 percent for individuals with taxable income above $115,000, joint filers with taxable income above $140,000 and heads of households with taxable income above $127,000. A 10 percent surtax was imposed on taxable income above $250,000, creating an effective top rate of 39.6 percent for these taxpayers.

These provisions took effect retroactively, beginning Jan. 1, 1993. Taxpayers could choose to pay additional taxes for 1993 that were attributable to the rate increase in three annual installments, beginning on the due date for the taxpayer's 1993 taxes. Taxpayers were not subject to penalties for underpaying estimated taxes attributable to these changes. The law made permanent the limitation on itemized deductions and the phaseout of the personal exemption for upper-income taxpayers, which were scheduled to expire in 1996 and 1997, respectively.

• **Alternative Minimum Tax.** Created a two-tier rate structure for the alternative minimum tax (AMT), which was designed to ensure that individuals who claimed numerous deductions and other tax breaks paid a minimum tax. Under the new structure, a 26 percent rate applied to the first $175,000 of a taxpayer's income subject to the AMT, and a 28 percent rate applied above $175,000.

The law increased the amount of income exempt from the AMT from $40,000 to $45,000 for married couples filing jointly, and from $30,000 to $33,750 for individuals.

• **Anticonversion Rules.** Imposed rules to prevent taxpayers from converting ordinary income to capital gains income to take advantage of the lower, 28 percent top rate on capital gains. With certain exceptions, capital gains or profits earned from the sale or trade of appreciated property that was part of a so-called conversion transaction were taxed as ordinary income. The law authorized the secretary of the Treasury to issue regulations defining such transactions.

• **Payroll Taxes.** Subjected all wages and self-employment income to the hospital insurance payroll tax, which went to finance Medicare. Under existing law, only the first $135,000 earned was subject to the tax. The provision was effective Jan. 1, 1994.

• **Estate Taxes.** Made permanent the top tax rates on estates (property transferred at death) and gifts (property transferred while the owner was alive). The rates were 53 percent for taxable transfers worth $2.5 million to $3 million, and 55 percent for taxable transfers over $3 million. The provision was retroactive to Jan. 1, 1993.

• **Business Meals.** Reduced the deductible portion of business meals and entertainment expenses from 80 percent to 50 percent.

• **Club Dues.** Eliminated the existing deduction for dues paid to any club organized for business, pleasure, recreation or other social purpose.

• **Moving Expenses.** Scaled back the existing deduction for moving expenses associated with taking a new job. The law barred taxpayers from claiming the deduction for nontransportation costs, such as meals, the cost of selling a residence and house-hunting trips.

Taxpayers could not exclude moving expenses from gross income for tax purposes if the expenses were paid by an employer. Moving expenses could be deducted if they were not paid for by an employer.

The law also required that, to claim a moving expense deduction, a taxpayer's new principal place of work had to be at least 50 miles farther from his former residence than was his former place of work. The previous minimum was 35 miles.

• **Estimated Taxes.** Liberalized estimated tax rules. Under prior law, individual taxpayers were subject to a penalty in some cases if they underpaid their estimated taxes. To avoid the penalty, taxpayers had to pay in advance (by such means as withholding or quarterly estimated payments) either 100 percent of their previous year's tax or 90 percent of what they owed for the current year. However, for taxpayers whose adjusted gross income exceeded $75,000 and was $40,000 more than it was the previous year, paying 90 percent of their current tax was the only way to avoid penalty.

The law allowed those taxpayers to use the 100 percent of previous-year taxes option, though it required individuals whose adjusted gross income in the previous year exceeded $150,000 to pay 110 percent, instead of 100 percent, effective Jan. 1, 1994.

• **Social Security.** Raised the portion of Social Security benefits subject to taxation from 50 percent to 85 percent for some upper-income retirees. Beginning in 1994, individuals making more than $34,000 a year and couples making more than $44,000 a year were to be subject to the provision. The definition of income included adjusted gross income, tax-exempt interest, foreign-source income and one-half of the taxpayer's Social Security benefits. The provision also applied to Railroad Retirement Tier 1 benefits.

• **Travel Expenses.** Prohibited taxpayers from deducting travel expenses associated with a spouse, dependent or other person accompanying them on business travel, unless the person's presence was business-related.

• **Bonuses.** Increased the withholding rate on wages paid as bonuses from 20 percent to 28 percent.

Business Taxes

• **Corporate Income Tax.** Imposed a new fourth bracket, increasing the top marginal rate to 35 percent for corporate taxable income in excess of $10 million. A corporation with taxable income of more than $15 million was required to pay an additional amount—either $100,000 or 3 percent of the amount by which its taxable income exceeded $15 million, whichever was lower. The provision was designed to phase out the benefits of the 34 percent rate for affected corporations. The rate increase was retroactive to Jan. 1, 1993.

• **Lobbying Expenses.** Prohibited companies from taking a deduction for lobbying expenses. The provision, effective Jan. 1, 1993, specified that no deduction was allowed for any amount paid in connection with an attempt to influence federal or state legislation or any communication with certain covered federal executive branch officials, including the president, vice president, cabinet member and other senior White House officials.

The law also prohibited a deduction for the portion of membership dues paid to a tax-exempt organization that went toward funding lobbying activities.

• **Executive Pay.** Limited the ability of companies to deduct compensation, including benefits, paid to top executives. Publicly traded companies could not deduct salaries in excess of $1 million for each of their top five executives. Exceptions were provided for pay earned from commissions and other performance-based compensation and for pay provided under a contract that was in effect Feb. 17, 1993. In addition, companies could continue to claim a deduction for benefits paid to executives if the employee could deduct the benefit from gross income.

• **Retirement Plans.** Reduced the amount of compensation that could be taken into account under a qualified retirement plan to $150,000 from $235,840 for 1994. The limit was used in determining the amount the employer could deduct for contributions to the plan as well as determining the participant's benefits. The limit was indexed to increase with inflation in $10,000 increments. The limit could force employers to reexamine defined contribution plans to ensure they did not discriminate against lower-paid employees.

• **'Mark-to-Market' Securities Rules.** Revised rules governing the tax treatment of securities held by dealers for sale to customers. Under the so-called mark-to-market rules in the law, a security that was held as inventory by a securities dealer had to be reported at its fair market value. In addition, a security that was not in inventory and was held at the end of a taxable year was treated as sold for its fair market value; any gain or loss was to be reflected in gross income. The law specified several exceptions. For example, the mark-to-market rules did not apply to any security that was held for investment.

• **Special Savings and Loan Tax Benefit.** Clarified that a special tax benefit that had been granted to purchasers of failed savings and loan institutions, and repealed effective May 10, 1989, could no longer be used for transactions completed before that date. Before 1989, buyers of failed thrifts often received guarantees of tax-exempt cash payments from the Federal Savings and Loan Insurance Corporation to cover losses on bad assets acquired in the purchase of failed institutions. The tax code also permitted deductions from income for those same losses. Following repeal of this "double dip," the Treasury Department ruled that assistance payments from thrift sales that were concluded before the repeal would no longer be tax exempt, but it asked Congress to clarify whether that had been the intent of the 1989 repeal. The provision was effective for income on losses recorded after March 4, 1991, the date of the Treasury ruling.

• **Estimated Taxes.** Tightened corporate estimated tax rules. Under prior law, corporations could avoid the penalty for underpaying their estimated taxes if they made timely estimated payments totaling 97 percent of their tax liability for the current year (91 percent after 1996). The provision required corporations with taxable income of more than $1 million to make estimated payments that fully covered their current year taxes. Corporations with less than $1 million in taxable income had the option of paying 100 percent of their prior-year tax, as they did under prior law.

• **Debt Provisions.** Repealed the so-called stock-for-debt exception, which provided favorable tax treatment for bankrupt companies that gave creditors stock to retire debt.

• **Puerto Rico.** Scaled back an existing credit, called the Section 936 tax credit, which was intended to attract businesses to locate in Puerto Rico. As under prior law, the provision allowed companies in Puerto Rico to claim a tax credit based on their profits, but in 1994 the credit was to be limited to 60 percent of what was allowed under existing law, declining to 40 percent in 1998. The law also gave companies the option of claiming a scaled-back credit based on investment and wages, instead of on profits.

• **Foreign Taxes.** Repealed parts of a provision of the tax code allowing companies to defer paying taxes on earning accumulated in foreign subsidiaries. In general, the new law required U.S. shareholders to include the undistributed earnings of a foreign subsidiary in its income to the extent that the subsidiary sheltered its income in "excess passive assets."

• **Research and Experimentation.** Required that U.S. multinational companies allocate 50 percent of their research and development expenses to U.S.-source income for tax purposes; the other half was to be allocated to foreign-source income. The provision was effective only in 1994.

- **Intangibles.** Allowed companies to write off over 15 years the cost of acquiring most intangible assets, including the value of the company as an ongoing concern, workforce know-how, licenses and permits, covenants not to compete and other similar arrangements, and franchises, trademarks and trade names. The law provided more generous tax treatment for purchased mortgage servicing rights, which could be written off over nine years.

Energy Taxes

- **Transportation Fuels.** Imposed a permanent 4.3-cents-per-gallon excise tax beginning Oct. 1, 1993, on most transportation fuels, including motor fuels, aviation gasoline, diesel fuels used in trains, fuels used in inland waterway transportation, compressed natural gas used in highway motor vehicles, and jet fuel used in noncommercial aviation. Gasoline and jet fuel used in commercial aviation were subject to the tax beginning Oct. 1, 1995. Revenue raised by the tax was to be deposited into the general fund of the Treasury.

The law also extended through 1999 a 2.5-cents-per-gallon increase in the motor fuels tax that was enacted in 1990 and was scheduled to expire in 1995. The revenues were to go into the Highway Trust Fund. The provision included a 1.25-cents-per-gallon tax on diesel fuel used in trains, with those revenues going into the general fund.

- **Motorboard Fuel.** Imposed a new tax of 20.1 cents per gallon on noncommercial use of diesel fuel in boats. Revenues were to go to the general fund.

Training and Investment

- **Educational Assistance.** Extended until Dec. 31, 1994, a provision that allowed employees to exclude from their taxable income up to $5,250 in educational assistance provided by their employer. The provision, which expired July 1, 1992, was renewed retroactively to that date.

- **Targeted Jobs.** Extended the targeted jobs tax credit, which gave employers a tax break—generally up to $2,400 per employee—for hiring certain hard-to-employ individuals. The provision was made effective retroactively for individuals who began work after June 30, 1992, and on or before Dec. 31, 1994. The credit had expired June 30, 1992.

- **Research and Development.** Extended for three years the research and development (R&D) tax credit, beginning retroactively on July 1, 1993, through June 30, 1995. The credit provided a tax break equal to 20 percent of the amount by which a company's qualified research expenditures exceeded a base amount determined by its previous expenditures on R&D. It also applied to university basic research. The law contained new rules for calculating the R&D base for new companies without a history of R&D expenditures.

- **Orphan Drugs.** Extended until Dec. 31, 1994, a 50 percent tax credit for qualified clinical testing of certain drugs for rare diseases, generally referred to as orphan drugs. The extension was retroactive to July 1, 1992, when the provision expired.

- **Small Business Investment.** Allowed investors who purchased newly issued stock in small companies to exclude from their income 50 percent of the gain when they sold the stock as long as it was held for at least five years. The amount of the gain eligible for the break was limited to $10 million per shareholder or 10 times the taxpayer's basis in the stock, whichever was greater.

For stock to qualify for the break, the company had to have less than $50 million in gross assets, meaning cash and other assets held by the company.

- **AMT Relief.** Gave capital intensive companies tax relief by eliminating the so-called adjusted existing earnings test, which required them to add back in certain deductions when calculating what they owed under the alternative minimum tax.

- **Small Business Expenses.** Beginning Jan. 1, 1993, increased from $10,000 to $17,500 the amount that small businesses could write off on the cost of equipment and machinery in the year it was purchased. The maximum was available only to businesses that invested less than $210,000 in depreciable property a year.

- **Tax-Exempt Bonds.** Permanently extended authority for state and local governments to issue qualified small-issue bonds, which were used to finance purchases of manufacturing facilities and farm property. The law also contained an exclusion from state volume caps for bonds issued to finance high-speed rail projects, as long as the property was to be owned by a government entity.

- **Mortgage Revenue Bonds.** Permanently extended authority for local housing agencies to issue qualified mortgage bonds, which are used to finance the purchase or rehabilitation of single-family, owner-occupied residences through subsidized mortgages. The law made the bond authority retroactive to July 1, 1992. It had expired June 30, 1992. The same was true for mortgage credit certificates, which provided income tax credits based on interest paid on mortgage loans.

- **Low-Income Housing.** Made permanent the low-income housing tax credit, which gave developers a tax break for rehabilitating rental housing for the poor. The credit, which expired the previous year, was made permanent beginning on July 1, 1992. It had expired June 30, 1992.

- **Real Estate Incentives.** Allowed real estate developers and others in the industry to deduct so-called passive losses on rental property against ordinary income. To qualify for the deduction, an individual had to spend at least 750 hours a year in real estate activities, and more than half the personal services performed by the taxpayer had to involve real estate transactions.

The law also modified the tax code to permit pension funds to invest in real estate.

The law increased the depreciation period for nonresidential real estate from 31.5 years to 39 years, a change that would increase federal revenue by spreading out deductions over a longer period.

Earned Income Tax Credit

- Expanded the earned income tax credit (EITC), a program to help poor working families, including those who owed no taxes and could receive the credit as a check from the government. For eligible families with one child, the EITC was 26.3 percent of the first $7,750 of earned income in 1994, for a maximum credit of $2,038. For 1995, the credit rate increased to 34 percent on earned income of up to $6,170.

For eligible families with two or more children, the credit was increased to 30 percent of the first $8,425 of earned income in 1994, for a maximum credit of $2,527. The credit rate increased to 36 percent in 1995 and 40 percent in 1996 and thereafter.

Taxpayers earning more than $11,000 a year were eligible for a partial credit. The EITC was not available to families with one child that were making more than $23,760 or to families with two or more children making more than $27,000.

Childless workers over age 25 and below 65 qualified for a modest credit of 7.65 percent of the first $4,000 in income, for a maximum credit of $306 in 1994. No one making more than $9,000 a year qualified for the childless worker credit.

Empowerment Zones

• **Creation of Zones, Communities.** Provided for the creation of nine enterprise zones in economically distressed areas of the country—six in urban areas and three in rural areas. The zones were eligible for special tax benefits and other federal assistance aimed at creating jobs and encouraging economic development. The secretary of housing and urban development was to select the urban areas and the secretary of agriculture was to select the rural areas, based on size and other criteria.

In addition, 95 other areas—65 of them urban and 30 rural—were to be designated as enterprise communities and would be eligible for more limited tax benefits.

• **Tax Incentives.** Created a 20 percent tax credit for the first $15,000 of wages and certain training that a business provided to each employee who lived and worked in an empowerment zone. Businesses within the zone were also allowed to write off a maximum of $37,500 in investments in depreciable property in the first year, compared with $17,500 elsewhere.

The law created a new category of tax-exempt bonds to promote economic development within the zones and communities. An enterprise zone business was limited to issuing bonds with an aggregate face value of $3 million per zone or community, and $20 million for all zones and communities.

• **Block Grant.** Created a new social services block grant worth $1 billion over two years. The urban zones would get $100 million each, the rural zones would get $40 million each and the enterprise communities would get $2.95 million each.

• **Native American Reservations.** Provided certain tax incentives for Native American reservations, although no reservations were designated as enterprise zones. Businesses qualified for a shorter depreciation period for property used in connection with a trade or business on a Native American reservation. A 20 percent credit against income tax liability was provided to reservation employers for wages and health insurance costs paid to members of Native American tribes living on or near a reservation. The credit was available for the first $20,000 in wages or benefits paid to each qualified employee.

Miscellaneous Tax Provisions

• **Luxury Taxes.** Repealed the 10 percent excise tax on yachts, aircraft, jewelry and furs that was enacted in 1990. The tax on the portion of the price of an automobile that exceeded $30,000 was retained, but the threshold above which the tax applied was to increase with inflation in $2,000 increments.

• **Charitable Donations.** Made permanent an exemption from the alternative minimum tax (AMT) for gifts of appreciated tangible property, such as artwork, and extended it to real estate and securities. Donors could deduct the market value of contributions from their taxable income without having to add the appreciated value back in when calculating their liability under the AMT. The provision was retroactive to July 1, 1992.

• **Self-Employed Health Benefits.** Extended the 25 percent deduction for the cost of health insurance for self-employed workers and their spouses and dependents. The provision, which expired July 1, 1992, was extended retroactively to that date through Dec. 31, 1993.

• **Vaccine Excise Tax.** Made permanent the excise taxes imposed on certain vaccines, which were used to finance the Vaccine Injury Compensation Trust Fund.

• **Disaster Relief.** Provided tax breaks for individuals whose homes and property were damaged in a presidentially declared disaster zone. Taxpayers would have an additional two years to use insurance proceeds to purchase a replacement home without incurring tax on any gain. In addition, tax treatment of insurance proceeds was liberalized.

• **Presidential Campaign Checkoff.** Increased from $1 to $3 the amount individual taxpayers could earmark for the presidential campaign fund on their tax returns. The amount for joint filers was increased from $2 to $6. The change was intended to ensure that the fund did not run out of money before the 1996 campaign.

• **Tips.** Provided restaurant owners and other taxpayers with a dollar-for-dollar credit for federal payroll taxes paid on tips earned by their employees. After the bill cleared the Treasury Department indicated it would interpret the change to apply only to income earned in 1994 and after.

• **Group Health Plans.** Required that, as a condition of an employer's tax deduction for health care expenses, group health plans continued to reimburse for inpatient hospital services provided in the state of New York at the rate required under New York's all-payer system.

Dropped from the bill were five states' waivers from the requirements of the federal Employee Retirement Income Security Act (ERISA). The waivers would have allowed Hawaii, Maryland, Minnesota, New York and Oregon to proceed with health care reform plans.   ❑

Tax Simplification

The House, by voice vote May 17, 1994, passed a bill (HR 3419) to simplify the tax filing process for both taxpayers and the Internal Revenue Service (IRS) by making more than 100 changes to the tax code. HR 3419 died upon adjournment, because the Senate did not act on it.

Tax simplification legislation dated to 1990, when the House Ways and Means Committee launched an effort to simplify the tax code. The initiative stalled in 1992, when President George Bush vetoed two tax bills that contained the bulk of the panel's proposals.

The provision in HR 3419 with the broadest potential impact on consumers was a plan to permit taxpayers to pay their taxes with credit cards. Congress paved the way for this change with a provision included in a separate bill (HR 5116—PL 103-394) that specified that tax debts, unlike other charges on credit cards, could not be erased through bankruptcy. *(Bankruptcy rewrite, p. 347)*

The House Ways and Means Committee reported HR 3419 (H Rept 103-353) on Nov. 10, 1993. During markup, the committee adopted a technical amendment offered by Bill Brewster, D-Okla., to preserve a special tax treatment that Congress created in 1987 for retirement plans for football coaches. Because the provision was placed in the wrong section of the tax code, Brewster said, the IRS planned to end the tax preference at the end of 1993.

The committee also sparred over a provision in the budget reconciliation bill (HR 2264—PL 103-66) that granted restaurants a tax credit for the payroll taxes they paid on their employees' tip income; the budget bill left the effective date unclear. Gerald D. Kleczka, D-Wis., urged the committee to clarify that restaurants could use the credit only for tips earned beginning in 1994. Although the committee declined to make the change, Kleczka said after hearing from a Treasury Department official during the markup that, when Treasury implemented the provision, it would apply only to income beginning in 1994.

HR 3419 also included provisions to:

• Eliminate an existing law provision that permitted people who received their pensions in one lump sum to average the lump-sum payment over five years for income tax purposes.

• Simplify the administration of pension plans by changing rules preventing employers from contributing more to the pension plans of high-salaried employees than to those of lower-paid employees.

• Allow tax-exempt corporations to set up 401(k) accounts for their employees. In 401(k) accounts, employees set aside part of their salaries in tax accounts to be withdrawn after they turned 59 years old.

The Joint Committee on Taxation estimated that, overall, the tax simplification and technical corrections in HR 3419 would cost $467 million over five years. To offset the revenue loss, the bill included provisions to:

• Impose tax withholding on gambling winnings from bingo and keno when the winnings exceeded $10,000, raising $208 million over five years.

• Eliminate, with narrow exceptions, an exemption that permitted owners who rented homes or apartments for fewer than 15 days to avoid declaring the proceeds as taxable income, raising $97 million over five years.

• Change the rules for tax-exempt entities such as charities or pension trusts to treat certain income from foreign corporations as unrelated business taxable income, raising $98 million over five years.

• Require thrift institutions to take net operating loss carryovers into account when calculating bad debt reserves, raising $64 million over five years.

• Require multiemployer pension plans to follow the same guidelines for vesting enrolled employees as other employer plans. Under existing law, employees were vested—meaning they became eligible for at least part of their pension—in five years. Under multiemployer plans, workers had to wait 10 years to become eligible.   ❑

1995–1996

The GOP's dream to deeply cut individual and corporate taxes went largely unfulfilled in the 104th Congress. However, lawmakers did enact legislation providing modest tax breaks for businesses, making permanent a health insurance deduction for self-employed persons, barring states from taxing the retirement income of former residents and empowering taxpayers in their dealings with the Internal Revenue Service.

A politically motivated move to repeal a gas tax provided for in the 1993 deficit-reduction bill failed, as did efforts to adopt a constitutional amendment requiring a "supermajority" to pass a tax increase, to close a loophole allowing wealthy Americans to avoid paying taxes by giving up their U.S. citizenship, and to stop tax increases from being imposed retroactively.

1995 Deficit-Reduction Bill

Republicans took control of the 104th Congress with sweeping plans to reduce family and corporate taxes. While the House passed a separate bill (HR 1215) to highlight its commitment to broad tax cuts, the GOP proposals were eventually incorporated in the fiscal 1996 budget reconciliation bill (HR 2491). However, the Republicans' tax cutting agenda was left unfulfilled, when President Clinton vetoed HR 2491 and the veto stood. *(GOP tax plan, p. 98; reconciliation, legislative history, provisions, p. 44)*

The tax cut package was an emblem of the GOP budget balancing plan. Previous big deficit-reduction bills had relied heavily on tax increases. A portion of the cost of the cuts was to be offset by a series of revenue raisers. But the amount of the proposed tax cuts meant that Republicans had to reduce spending much more than otherwise would have been necessary to reach the reconciliation bill's central goal of balancing the budget in seven years. For many conservatives, that was the point: tax cuts were key to shrinking the federal government.

From the outset, the House Republicans drove the tax cut bandwagon. The House April 5, 1995, passed HR 1215, which promised to cut taxes by $353 billion over seven years. The Senate, skeptical of tax cuts and preferring to focus on reducing the deficit, provided little encouragement at first. The Senate eventually joined the crusade, however. House Republicans' enthusiasm proved catching. Furthermore, the rivalry between Senate Majority Leader Bob Dole, R-Kan., and Sen. Phil Gramm,

R-Texas, both vying for the 1996 GOP presidential nomination, put added pressure on that chamber.

BUDGET RESOLUTION

The fiscal 1996 budget resolution (H Con Res 67), which did not have the force of law, set the parameters for the budget reconciliation bill as well as the appropriations measures. *(Budget resolution, p. 65)*

By the time the House Budget Committee began work on H Con Res 67, the House had already passed HR 1215. As a result, the committee simply incorporated the bill's tax cuts into its version of the budget resolution.

By contrast, the Senate Budget Committee started with a budget resolution that assumed no tax cuts. But the Senate was under pressure to accommodate the tax-cutting fever in the House, so Budget Chairman Pete V. Domenici, R-N.M., struck a compromise. While the Senate budget resolution did not include a tax cut, it did provide that if the deficit-reduction plan was enacted and the Congressional Budget Office (CBO) certified that it would balance the budget, then Congress could use a $170 billion "economic bonus" that CBO said would result from balancing the budget to offset an equal amount of tax cuts over seven years.

When Domenici's budget resolution reached the Senate floor, Gramm tried to add $312 billion in House-passed tax cuts. The amendment failed 31–69 on May 23, 1995. Instead, the Senate adopted, 54–45 on May 25, an amendment by Joseph I. Lieberman, D-Conn., Spencer Abraham, R-Mich., and Rod Grams, R-Minn., that changed Domenici's language to say the Senate version "shall," not "may," use a CBO-certified economic bonus to offset a tax cut.

The dispute over taxes dominated the House-Senate conference on the budget resolution. The bigger the tax cut, the deeper conferees had to go to reduce spending. Clinton had repeatedly said he would not accept cuts in programs such as Medicare and Medicaid to pay for the kind of tax cuts the House had endorsed.

The Budget conferees agreed to instruct the tax-writing committees to come up with $245 billion in tax cuts over seven years as part of the reconciliation bill, but only if CBO first certified that congressional committees had produced enough spending cuts to balance the budget by 2002. The tax cuts were to be paid for in part with the $170 billion economic bonus. Tax-writing committees could make up the remaining $75 billion by raising other taxes, cutting more entitlement spending or letting deficits rise in the early years of the plan.

HOUSE ACTION

House GOP leaders decided to fold the tax cut bill—HR 1215—into their version of the reconciliation bill and wait until conference to determine how to stay within the budget resolution's $245 billion limit. The only task left for the House Ways and Means Committee was to put together a set of revenue raising provisions to offset a portion of the proposed cuts.

Ways and Means signed off Sept. 19, 1995, on a plan to increase net federal revenues by $38.7 billion over seven years. The provisions were to be inserted into the House version of the reconciliation bill along with the language of HR 1215. The plan would:

• Raise $30.2 billion over seven years by ending or phasing out a number of corporate tax benefits.

• Raise $23.2 billion over seven years by sharply limiting tax credits available to the working poor under the earned income tax credit (EITC).

• Extend several expiring tax benefits at a cost of $14.4 billion.

• Create tax-sheltered medical savings accounts for people with high-deductible health insurance. *(Medical savings accounts, p. 551)*

The proposed revenue-raising changes in corporate tax law included the following:

• **Excess Pension Funds.** The biggest of the revenue raisers was a proposal to ease pension rules so that companies could remove "excess" money from their pension funds. Excess funds were defined as 125 percent of current liabilities.

Under existing law, companies could transfer out excess funds, but unless the transfers were for certain limited purposes, such as providing medical benefits to retirees, they were subject to steep excise taxes of 20 percent to 50 percent. In addition, the company had to pay income tax on the amount removed.

The committee bill would do away with the excise tax entirely until July 1, 1996, and then levy a 6.5 percent excise tax. Companies would still pay income tax on the amount withdrawn. The Joint Committee on Taxation estimated that doing away with the punitive excise tax would give companies such a strong incentive to dip into pension funds that $30 billion to $40 billion would be withdrawn almost immediately. That would raise about $9.5 billion in additional revenue for the Treasury because the companies would pay income tax on the withdrawals.

An amendment by Gerald D. Kleczka, D-Wis., to strike the provision was rejected. A second Democratic attempt to require companies to notify pension plan participants if the company was taking out excess funds also failed.

• **Corporate Life Insurance.** Existing law gave companies an incentive to purchase life insurance contracts instead of investing in other assets, because of interest deductions and exclusions permitted for life insurance policyholders. Ways and Means proposed to eliminate the availability of the deduction for an estimated revenue increase of $7 billion.

• **Section 936 Repeal.** The plan proposed to phase out, over 10 years, an existing tax preference that exempted U.S. companies doing business in Puerto Rico from paying income tax on most of their operations there. The main beneficiaries of the tax break included pharmaceutical, electronic and soft drink companies. The estimated revenue increase was $3.1 billion.

• **Low-Income Housing Credit.** The credit, which was supposed to encourage builders to construct low-income housing, would be allowed to expire in 1997, bringing in $3.5 billion in added revenue.

• **Ethanol.** The tax credit for blenders of synthetic fuels, such as ethanol, would be reduced, increasing revenues by $1.8 billion.

- **Expatriate Taxes.** A plan to impose a tax on wealthy expatriates was expected to bring in $1.4 billion. *(Expatriate taxation, p. 105)*

Republicans' proposals to scale back the EITC drew sharp attacks from Democrats, who defined the action as a tax increase on working families. Ways and Means Chairman Bill Archer, R-Texas, disputed that view, noting that when Republicans took over Congress he promised to comb the tax code for provisions that were no longer achieving the goal Congress had intended.

Under existing law, the maximum credit, about $3,600, was available to families with two or more children earning less than $11,600 annually. The eligibility gradually decreased to zero for families earning more than $28,553 a year. About 19 million workers were expected to claim the credit in 1996.

House Republicans proposed to reduce or eliminate the credit for 14 million workers by curtailing eligibility and reducing the size of the credit that millions more would receive. Childless, low-income workers no longer would receive the credit; all families earning more than $11,600 a year would receive less from the credit than they did under existing law; and the eligibility of older workers with income from Social Security would be curtailed because such outside income would be counted when determining income eligibility.

Democrats supported a provision aimed at tightening the administration of the EITC.

Democratic attempts to strike the three major changes in eligibility failed, as did an amendment to delete all but the administrative changes.

The expiring tax benefits that were extended included:

- **Research.** The research and experimentation credit, which was especially beneficial to biotechnology and pharmaceutical companies.
- **Targeted Jobs.** A new version of the targeted jobs tax credit, which was available to employers who hired economically disadvantaged workers such as people trying to get off welfare. It would be worth up to $1,500 per worker.
- **Education.** A tax deduction for employer-provided assistance of up to $5,250 available only for undergraduate education.
- **Aviation Fuel.** An exemption from the 4.3-cents-per-gallon fuel tax for airplane fuel, benefiting the commercial airline industry.

Other revenue-losing provisions included medical savings accounts for the nonelderly, projected to lose $1.8 billion. The proposal also included 116 changes in the tax code for a net loss of $4.7 billion. Many had no cost, some would save money and some would create new tax breaks for corporations and individuals.

Additional amendments offered to the bill were:

- By Charles B. Rangel, D-N.Y., to restore funding for the low-income housing tax credit, which was rejected.
- By Pete Stark, D-Calif., to strike the medical savings account provision and replace it with an increase in the tax deduction for health insurance for the self-employed, which was rejected.

- By Barbara B. Kennelly, D-Conn., to reward people who helped the Internal Revenue Service detect and punish fraud, which was adopted.
- By Mel Hancock, R-Mo., to undo a 1992 deal to fund health care for working and retiring coal miners by requiring companies that were, or were at one time, in the coal business to contribute to their care, which was adopted.

SENATE ACTION

The Senate Finance Committee approved its version of the tax provisions Oct. 19, 1995. The package contained $245 billion in tax cuts for families and businesses over seven years as allowed in the budget resolution; the short-term extension of a number of expiring tax benefits at a cost of $6.1 billion; and $21 billion in revenue raisers, mainly targeting corporations. The bill also proposed a number of new tax breaks to benefit specific industries or interest groups. The Senate reconciliation package was introduced as S 1357.

The key elements of the Senate Finance Committee's tax package were as follows:

- **Child Tax Credit.** The committee limited the $500-per-child tax credit to couples with adjusted gross incomes of up to $110,000 per year, or individuals with adjusted gross incomes of up to $75,000. Taxpayers could earn an additional $20,000 for each additional child and still receive the credit. As in the House bill, the credit would not be refundable, meaning that families who paid little or no taxes would not receive it.

The committee rejected two proposals by Chairman William V. Roth Jr., R-Del., to phase out the child tax credit in 1999 and to convert the existing personal exemption for dependents into a credit, which would have helped lower-income families.

- **Tuition Tax Credit.** Parents with dependent children in postsecondary schools would be eligible for a tax credit worth 20 percent of the interest on their student loans. The maximum credit would be capped at $500 per year per borrower. This provision was not in the House bill

- **Individual Retirement Accounts.** Individuals earning up to $85,000 and couples earning up to $100,000 would be eligible to defer taxes on contributions to an individual retirement account (IRA). In addition, the proposal included a new "backloaded" IRA. People would pay taxes on the money when they put it into the savings account, but they would be able to withdraw it after five years without paying taxes on the interest. Tax-free and penalty-free withdrawals would be permitted for first home purchases, medical expenses, periods of unemployment and higher education expenses.

- **Estate Tax.** The first $1.5 million resulting from the sale of a family-owned business would be exempt from the tax, and the tax rate on the next $3.5 million would be cut by 50 percent. Under existing law, only the first $600,000 was exempt.

- **Capital Gains.** Individuals would be allowed to exclude 50 percent of their capital gains from taxation, reducing the effective top rate to 19.8 percent from 28 percent. The corporate capital gains tax rate would drop from 35 percent to 28 percent. The committee did not include the House proposal to index gains for inflation. The effective date was to be Oct. 13, 1995.

• **Expiring Provisions.** The plan included the extension of several expiring tax benefits, among them the targeted jobs tax credit; the deduction for employer-provided educational assistance; the research and experimentation tax credit; the exemption for aviation fuel; and the tax credit for nonconventional fuels produced from biomass and coal.

• **Revenue Raisers.** The committee proposed to change 27 tax rules affecting corporations and individuals to raise revenues and defray the cost of the tax cut. The changes included allowing companies to shift excess money from their pension funds to other employee benefit programs, such as health benefits, child care benefits or other pension plans. Another provision would phase out over seven years the tax credit for U.S. companies doing business in Puerto Rico.

• **EITC.** The credit would be phased out more quickly than by the House, producing $43.2 billion in savings over seven years.

• **Social Security Tax.** The plan did not include a House proposal to repeal a 1993 provision that imposed taxes on 85 percent of the Social Security benefits of the better-off elderly.

Finance Committee Democrats offered dozens of amendments aimed at striking the tax cuts or targeting them to lower- and middle-income families. The committee adopted a proposal by David Pryor, D-Ark., to add a pension simplification package to the bill. The committee rejected a Bill Bradley, D-N.J., amendment to reduce the amount of the tax cuts to $170 billion and use the savings to restore spending for the EITC and for a more targeted child tax credit. Also rejected was a similar amendment by Max Baucus, D-Mont., and John B. Breaux, D-La., to make the family tax credit refundable and to change the credit for higher education into a tax deduction.

On the floor, the Senate adopted by 94–5 on Oct. 27, 1995, an amendment by Edward M. Kennedy, D-Mass., and Nancy Landon Kassebaum, R-Kan., to strike the provision allowing companies to tap into excess corporate pension funds and use the money for other employee benefits. On a 99–0 vote Oct. 26, the Senate adopted a Pryor and Christopher S. Bond, R-Mo., amendment to expand the tax deduction for health insurance for the self-employed from 30 percent to 35 percent. An attempt by Breaux to target the $500-per-year child tax credit to lower-income families by making it refundable and by starting to phase it out for those making more than $60,000 a year, instead of $75,000, was killed, 53–46 on Oct. 26, on a tabling motion offered by Domenici.

CONFERENCE ACTION

House and Senate conferees on the reconciliation bill compromised on more than 200 tax code changes, producing a plan to cut taxes by $245 billion over seven years. Overall, 69 percent of the tax cuts were aimed at families and couples. The biggest benefit was the child credit, which was expected to cost $147.6 billion over seven years. The balance of the tax cuts was for business, with the benefits divided among small businesses, Wall Street firms, and the manufacturing and oil production sectors. Small businesses were earmarked with an $8.7 billion package of tax cuts. About $62 billion of the tax cuts were offset by revenue increases, split roughly half and half between corporate revenue raisers and cuts in the EITC.

The issues settled by the reconciliation conferees included the following:

• **Child Tax Credit.** The toughest issue for conferees was structuring the politically sensitive $500-per-child tax credit. The House eventually accepted the Senate's $110,000 income threshold. However, both chambers wanted to make the credit retroactive; otherwise, taxpayers would not see it on their returns until 1997. Conferees agreed to delay the House-passed proposal to index capital gains for inflation and use the savings to pay for the retroactive tax credit. Even then, they could only afford to make the credit retroactive to Oct. 1, 1995, meaning that in 1996 families would receive one-quarter of the credit, an amount equal to $125 per child.

• **EITC.** Conferees agreed on savings of $32.4 billion from cutting back the earned income tax credit. They tried to soften the impact by providing that workers too poor to pay income taxes would not be affected by the changes.

• **IRAs.** Conferees agreed to gradually make tax-deferred IRAs available to couples earning up to $100,000 per year. Spouses would be allowed to save up to $2,000 in traditional IRAs. The final version also included the new, "back-loaded" IRAs. The estimated cost was $11.8 billion over seven years.

• **Estate and Gift Taxes.** Estates would be exempt from taxation if they were worth $750,000 or less, compared with a threshold of $600,000 under existing law. For small businesses or family farmers attempting to pass on a business to an heir, the first $1 million of the business or farm would be exempt from taxation and only 50 percent of the next $1.5 million would be subject to taxation. The projected cost was $11.9 billion over seven years.

• **Marriage Penalty.** Conferees agreed to increase the standard deduction for married taxpayers filing jointly to $6,800 in 1996, rising to $10,800 in 2005, at an expected cost of $8 billion.

• **Medical Savings Accounts.** The conference agreement provided for new tax-deductible accounts for medical expenses that would allow taxpayers to save up to $2,000-a-year per individual ($4,000-a-year per couple) to defray the cost of routine medical expenses.

However, taxpayers could only maintain a medical savings account if they bought a high deductible, catastrophic health plan. Money could be withdrawn only for medical expenses other than health insurance premiums; long-term care insurance premiums; health care continuation coverage for individuals who lost employer-provided coverage; and coverage while the individual was receiving unemployment compensation. The estimated seven-year cost was $2.1 billion.

• **Capital Gains.** The effective top rate on capital gains would be reduced to 19.8 percent for individuals and 28 percent for corporations. The reduced rate would be retroactive, applying to assets sold after Dec. 31, 1994.

• **Other Family Benefits.** Also included were a $5,000 credit for adoption expenses for couples earning less than $75,000 and a $1,000-a-year deduction for families caring for an elderly relative in their home.

• **Expiring Provisions.** Conferees agreed to extend through 1996 the targeted jobs credit, the deduction for employer-provided education, the research credit, the orphan drug credit and the deduction for the appreciated value of stock donated to private foundations. In addition, conferees agreed to extend the aviation fuel exemption through Sept. 30, 1997, and end the low-income housing credit after Dec. 31, 1997.

• **Alternative Minimum Tax.** The final bill eliminated the depreciation adjustment used in calculating both the individual and corporate alternative minimum tax (AMT). The change would be especially beneficial for manufacturers, oil companies and other industries that were capital intensive.

• **Pension Funds.** Employers could withdraw excess monies from their employee pension funds, which would be defined as the amount of money needed to terminate the pension fund or the fund's accrued liability, whichever was greater. The money could be used only for employee benefits, such as health benefits or disability benefits.

Conferees dropped House-passed provisions to repeal the tax on 85 percent of the Social Security benefits on the affluent elderly and to raise the amount from $11,280 to $30,000 that the elderly could earn annually without losing their full Social Security benefits.   ❑

GOP Tax Plan

The House April 5, 1995, passed a bill (HR 1215) that called for $188.8 billion in tax cuts for families and businesses over five years, growing to $353 billion over seven years. House Speaker Newt Gingrich, R-Ga., called the legislation the "crowning jewel" of the Contract with America, the conservative agenda drawn up by Republicans as part of their 1994 campaign to win control of the House. *(Contract with America, box, p. 885)*

Republicans said the tax cuts would be paid for with $100 billion of unspecified reductions in domestic spending programs, plus cuts in spending on Medicare, the government-subsidized health insurance program for the elderly, and an increase in pension contributions from federal employees. They also anticipated cuts in welfare and food stamp programs. None of the spending cuts was provided for in HR 1215, however.

The GOP tax bill, unveiled March 9, 1995, by House Ways and Means Committee Chairman Bill Archer, R-Texas, was a slightly modified version of the proposals in the contract. Several changes, which reduced some business taxes and made families too poor to pay taxes ineligible for the family tax breaks, reduced the five-year cost by $7.5 billion, from $196.3 billion in the contract version.

Sixty percent of the tax relief was aimed at families, with another 16 percent directed at senior citizens; the rest was for businesses. Initially, business interests, especially manufacturers, had expressed little enthusiasm over many of the contract's tax provisions.

Furthermore, the tax cuts did not have universal support from House Republicans. Among the critics were GOP moderates, deficit hawks and members of the Appropriations Committee, who worried that they would be forced to find a large chunk of the money to pay for the tax cuts from programs in their jurisdiction. But the leadership stood firmly behind the bill, and the House Republicans generally were determined to remain united behind the contract.

From the outset, the House tax cuts clearly were not intended to be enacted as a stand-alone bill. Instead, they were to be folded into a deficit-reduction bill that Republicans planned to use later in the year as a key tool in their drive to balance the budget. Because many Senate Republicans were far less enthusiastic than their House colleagues about making tax cuts a priority, the size of the final cuts was expected to be pared back through negotiations. The early vote, however, enabled House Republicans to build momentum for big tax cuts at a time when many senators and outside economists were advocating delay. By its very size, the bill raised the bar for any future talks on tax reductions.

House Republicans subsequently incorporated the $353 billion seven-year cost of the cuts into their version of the fiscal 1996 budget resolution (H Con Res 67), which set the parameters for the later budget reconciliation bill. The Senate version of the budget resolution included less than half that—$170 billion in tax reductions—and made them conditional on passage of a reconciliation bill that the Congressional Budget Office (CBO) said would balance the budget. The final budget resolution allowed $245 billion in tax cuts over seven years once CBO assured the Senate Budget Committee that the rest of the reconciliation bill would balance the budget by 2002. *(Budget resolution, p. 73)*

Instead of rewriting their tax-cut package to conform to the requirements of the final budget resolution, House Republicans folded HR 1215 into their version of the reconciliation bill (HR 2491), along with a set of revenue raisers that was crafted separately. They left to the House-Senate conferees the task of trimming the total in tax reduction to meet the $245 billion limit. *(Reconciliation, p. 68)*

HOUSE ACTION

The House Ways and Means Committee reported HR 1215 (H Rept 104-84) on March 21, 1995. Democrats offered only one amendment—to end the tax cuts after five years; it was rejected. Instead, they concentrated their efforts during markup on painting the Republicans as intent on aiding the wealthy at the expense of the poor.

Democrats cited a Treasury Department analysis that concluded the tax reductions overall would disproportionately benefit wealthier families, with 51 percent of the benefits going to families earning $100,000 or more a year. Treasury said the programs that would have to be cut to pay for the tax reductions would disproportionately affect those at the bottom of the economic ladder.

Republicans responded that the bill would help middle-income Americans who deserved a break, and they emphasized that it would be paid for with spending cuts.

The House passed HR 1215 on a **key vote of 246–188 (R 219–11; D 27–176; I 0–1),** with 27 Democrats voting for the measure and 11 Republicans voting against it. One provision that was added shortly before the bill came to the floor required that before any tax cuts were enacted, a budget resolution and budget reconciliation bill would have to put the deficit on the path to zero. The change was aimed at appeasing moderates who wanted more emphasis on deficit reduction. *(1995 key votes, p. 1025)*

Democratic leaders could persuade only a little more than half their members to vote for a substitute prepared by Minority Leader Richard A. Gephardt, D-Mo. The substitute, to cut $31.6 billion in taxes over five years, was rejected 119–313 on April 5.

MAJOR PROVISIONS

HR 1215 as passed by the House included provisions to:

Individual and Family Tax Provisions

• **Child Tax Credit.** Provide a $500-per-child tax credit for each child younger than 18, with the credit phased out for families earning more than $200,000 a year. The credit would not be available to low-income families that paid no taxes.

• **Marriage Penalty.** Provide a tax credit of up to $145 to married couples who, under existing law, paid more if they filed jointly than if they filed singly.

• **Individual Retirement Accounts.** Allow individuals to deposit up to $2,000 annually into a new type of individual retirement account (IRA), which Republicans dubbed the "American Dream Savings Account." Deposits would not be deductible, but after five years, funds could be withdrawn without paying taxes on interest or principal. To make tax-free withdrawals, the individual would have to be 59-1/2 years old or the money would have to be used for such purposes as buying a first home, college expenses, medical expenses or long-term care.

Also, nonworking spouses would be able to contribute up to $2,000 a year to a traditional IRA. This provision, which was not in the Contract with America, was added at the behest of women lawmakers in both parties.

• **Adoption Tax Credit.** Provide a $5,000 tax credit for families earning less than $60,000 a year who adopted a child. The credit, intended to help pay adoption expenses, would be phased out for families earning more than $100,000.

• **Elderly Care Credit.** Provide a $500 annual tax credit for taxpayers who cared for a mentally or physically disabled relative in the taxpayer's home.

• **Capital Gains Tax Cut.** Lower, from 28 percent to 19.8 percent, the top rate on individual capital gains—profits from the sale of assets such as stocks, real estate or artwork. Gains also could be indexed to eliminate the effects of inflation.

• **Tax on Social Security Benefits.** Allow elderly taxpayers who earned more than $25,000 annually if filing singly, or more than $32,000 annually if filing jointly, to pay taxes on 50 percent of their Social Security benefits instead of 85 percent, as in existing law. The higher rate was enacted in 1993 (HR 2264—PL 103-66). *(1993 action, p. 91)*

Business Tax Provisions

• **Capital Gains Tax Cut.** Offer corporations a choice of paying the existing corporate capital gains tax (35 percent for most

companies) or an alternative capital gains tax rate of 25 percent. Capital gains could be indexed.

• **Alternative Minimum Tax Repeal.** Phase out the corporate alternative minimum tax (AMT) over five years. The AMT, put in place in 1986 (PL 99-514), was designed to ensure that companies that might otherwise pay little or no tax because of deduction and depreciation would pay some taxes. The existing AMT rate was 20 percent, lower than the top regular corporate rate of 35 percent. *(1986 action, Congress and the Nation Vol. VII, p. 79)*

• **Small Business Expensing.** Allow businesses to write off up to $35,000 a year in new equipment costs—twice what was allowed under existing law.

• **Accelerated Depreciation.** Allow businesses to accelerate the rate of depreciation on equipment to account for inflation. Because the provision would allow a business to deduct more than the original value of the equipment, it was expected to spur equipment purchases and was scored as a revenue raiser in the first five years.

FLAT TAX

The National Commission on Economic Growth and Tax Reform issued its report on Jan. 17, 1996, recommending flatter tax rates. The commission, which was established by the Republican congressional leadership in May 1995, was chaired by former secretary of housing and urban development (1989–1993) and former representative (R-N.Y., 1971–1989) Jack F. Kemp, who became the 1996 Republican nominee for vice president.

The commission shied away from endorsing a specific flat tax plan, offering instead what Kemp called "a road map" to overhauling the income tax code. In its purest form, a flat tax would have one rate, no deductions and a filing form the size of a post card. However, the commission raised red flags about the political viability of flat tax proposals. And it sounded warnings about the risks of eliminating deductions, including those for mortgage interest and charitable contributions.

The commission's main recommendations included:

• A single flat tax rate of not more than 20 percent, with a "generous"—but unspecified—personal exemption that would reduce or eliminate taxes for low-income Americans.

• Elimination of taxes on capital gains, dividends and inheritances.

• Continued tax deductibility of mortgage interest and charitable donations and the addition of deductions for individuals of Social Security and Medicare payroll taxes.

While the idea of a flat tax gained the greatest mileage among Republicans, some GOP members were skeptical of the commission's report. House Ways and Means Committee Chairman Bill Archer, R-Texas, criticized it for failing to recommend a sufficiently radical change in the tax code. Archer said, "I am disappointed the commission failed to recommend consideration of a tax on the consumption of goods and services as an alternative to taxing people's work."

Business Tax Breaks

Despite grander GOP plans, the only substantive tax measure enacted in 1996 was a modest package of business tax breaks attached to a bill (HR 3448) that increased the federal minimum wage. The tax provisions were projected to cost $20 billion over 10 years. *(Minimum wage, p. 666)*

Bill sponsors argued the tax breaks offered businesses a way to recoup some of the costs of paying employees the higher minimum wage and gave conservatives who opposed the wage increase a reason to vote for the legislation. Several of the tax provisions had been part of the House Republicans' Contract with America. *(Contract with America, box, p. 885)*

HOUSE ACTION

The House Ways and Means Committee reported HR 3448 (H Rept 104-586) on May 20, 1996. The measure, drafted by Chairman Bill Archer, R-Texas, proposed $7.05 billion in tax cuts over eight years but was expected to grow in the Senate.

Most of the provisions were aimed at small businesses, which would be most affected by the minimum wage increase. The bill contained proposals to increase first-year write-offs for equipment and create a new type of simpler pension plan for companies with 100 or fewer employees. It proposed to relax tax rules that governed so-called subchapter S corporations, a form of business organization that had tax advantages and was frequently used by small businesses and family-owned firms.

The measure also sought to extend several tax benefits that helped big and midsize businesses, such as the targeted jobs tax credit for companies that hired disadvantaged workers and the exclusion for employer-paid tuition assistance. Also included was a provision to repeal an existing tax on excess passive assets held by foreign subsidiaries of U.S. companies. The repeal was important to large, high-tech companies.

In addition, HR 3448 contained numerous special interest provisions to help a variety of businesses and investors—restaurants that delivered meals, small wineries, racehorse owners, football coaches and multinational firms that did business in foreign countries.

The bill proposed to offset the revenue loss by ending a tax credit for U.S. manufacturing companies that did business in Puerto Rico and other U.S. territories, and by ending a tax exclusion for financial institutions that made loans to employee stock ownership plans. The bill also proposed to tax punitive damages received from personal-injury lawsuits or nonlitigated settlements.

The committee debate over HR 3448 was at times acrimonious. For example, Sander M. Levin, D-Mich., offered an amendment to renew the employer-paid tuition exclusion with coverage of graduate as well as undergraduate studies. The expired provision covered graduate studies, but the Republicans planned to renew it only for undergraduate work.

Levin proposed to offset the greater revenue loss under his amendment with a provision, sought by banks and financial institutions, to facilitate the pooling of consumer debt. Shortly after Levin's amendment was adopted, GOP committee aides talked to each Republican who had voted for it. They argued that the Levin language would put the bill out of balance by $13 million over five years, although it would be in the black again over eight years—the full life of the bill. Under budget rules, a bill had to be in balance in the first year and over five years after its passage. Levin offered an alternative offset, but to no avail.

The biggest uproar during the markup was over a GOP decision to overturn a Treasury Department regulation that limited a credit used by restaurant owners to offset some of their cost in paying payroll taxes on waiters' tips. The Joint Committee on Taxation originally supported the Treasury regulation, but with the Republicans in the majority, the panel reversed that position, saying no revenue effect would be felt. The about-face infuriated Gerald D. Kleczka, D-Wis., who charged that someone had a concealed motive for seeking the change. His attempt to strike the provision failed.

In one of the most bipartisan votes of the year, the House 414–10 on May 22, 1996, passed HR 3448. A separate bill (HR 1227) to increase the minimum wage by 90 cents was appended to the tax bill the following day, and the combined measure was sent to the Senate with the tax bill's number.

Despite the overall House support for HR 3448, several urban Democrats with large Puerto Rican constituencies were vocal in their opposition to phasing out the tax credit for businesses with operations on the island. Their chief criticism was that none of the savings from the repeal would be put back into Puerto Rico in the form of health care spending, education or other investment. The Clinton administration objected to repealing the Puerto Rico tax credit, too. Instead, the administration favored a partial repeal that would continue to help companies that created jobs in Puerto Rico. The administration also objected to repealing the tax on excess passive assets.

SENATE ACTION

The Senate Finance Committee on June 18, 1996, reported (S Rept 104-281) a greatly expanded package of tax breaks. Chairman William V. Roth Jr., R-Del., won bipartisan support by altering the House version of HR 3448 to accommodate the interests of both Democrats and Republicans. In the process, the bill's eight-year cost grew by about $4 billion to about $11 billion. However, the revenue losses were to be offset by terminating a number of existing corporate tax benefits.

Roth eased Treasury Department concerns by omitting the repeal of taxes on passive assets invested abroad by U.S.-based multinational corporations. And he softened the House provision on the Puerto Rico tax credit. Under the Finance-approved bill, companies that received the credit based on the number of jobs they created would continue to get a scaled-back credit. Roth pleased members of both parties by including the revival of two expired tax credits: one for research and experimentation costs, and the other for clinical tests associated with the production of orphan drugs.

The Finance Committee allowed employer-provided tuition credit not only for college and trade school education, as the House had, but also for graduate school. The Senate committee version also excluded from taxation damages recovered from lawsuits except for punitive damages; the House bill also included noneconomic damages.

The Senate passed HR 3448 by 74–24 on July 9. The Senate's tax provisions offered as much tax relief to big companies as to small businesses. The Senate bill was estimated to cost almost twice as much as the House's: $13 billion over eight years, ballooning to $19 billion over 11 years. All of the tax cuts were offset by ending existing tax benefits and by renewing expired taxes.

The Senate adopted, 96–2 on July 9, a Roth amendment that lengthened the proposed extensions for the orphan drug credit (to Dec. 31, 1997), the airline ticket tax (to April 15, 1997) and the research and experimentation credit (to Dec. 31, 1997); and added a package of pension simplification proposals.

FINAL ACTION

House and Senate conferees on HR 3448 quickly settled their disagreements over tax provisions, the only differences between the two versions of the bill. The final cost of the package of tax cuts was $10.1 billion over five years and $20 billion over 10 years.

In resolving their differences, the conferees:

• Accepted the Senate proposal to renew the research and experimentation tax credit, but for a shorter time—11 months. The House version did not include the renewal.

• Accepted the Senate extension for the orphan drug credit, for 11 months instead of 18 months. The House did not seek to renew the credit.

• Agreed with the Senate to include graduate tuition in employer-provided educational assistance, but only through June 30, 1996. After that, the exclusion would cover only undergraduate education. The provision would expire after May 31, 1997.

• Included a Roth plan to allow nonworking spouses to save up to $2,000 a year in tax-deferred individual retirement accounts (IRAs).

• Accepted most of the House proposals on the Section 936 tax credit for companies doing business in Puerto Rico and other U.S. possessions. The credit would be phased out over 10 years; during that time, companies with existing operations could continue to use the credit. The Senate had voted to grandfather many existing claimants permanently.

• Accepted the Senate plan to pay for some of the tax cuts by extending through the end of 1996 the 10 percent surcharge on domestic airline tickets and a $6-per-ticket tax on international departures. The House had not sought to renew the airline ticket tax, and the airlines were deeply opposed to its reinstatement.

The final bill also included an array of changes in pension law that were strongly supported by business but drew criticism from pension right groups and concern from the Clinton administration. Critics said they would make it easier for higher-wage employees to save for retirement at the expense of lower-wage workers. However, lobbyists for business owners and trade groups said pension laws were too complex and discouraged companies, especially smaller ones, from creating pension plans at all.

In the final hours of the conference, Archer and Roth agreed to use HR 3448 as a vehicle for several other pieces of unfinished tax and trade legislation, including a bill that gave a $5,000 tax credit to offset the cost of adoption, which was included in the Contract with America. Also added was an extension of the Generalized System of Preferences, which allowed products from developing countries to enter the United States duty-free.

The House agreed to the conference report (H Rept 104-737) by 354–72 on Aug. 2, 1996. The Senate voted 76–22 the same day, completing congressional action.

MAJOR PROVISIONS

The major tax provisions of HR 3448, as signed into law (PL 104-188) on Aug. 20, 1996, would:

Business Tax Benefits

• **Expensing for Small Businesses.** Gradually increase the amount of equipment purchases that small businesses could deduct in the first year instead of having to depreciate over the life of the equipment. The amount was to increase from $17,500 under existing law to $25,000 in 2003. The estimated revenue loss was $1.6 million over five years.

• **Pension Law Changes.** Create a new type of pension plan, known as SIMPLE (Savings Incentive Match Plan for Employees), for businesses with fewer than 100 workers. Under the plan, an employee could contribute up to $6,000 annually into an individual retirement account or other tax-deferred pension plan. Employers had to match that contribution up to 3 percent of the worker's salary. The amount contributed was deductible for the employer, while workers could exclude their contributions from their taxable income.

Larger firms won a provision relaxing rules that tied the size of tax-deferred retirement plans that were available to higher paid workers to the level of participation by lower paid workers.

The bill also protected the pensions of 16 million state and local government employees if a government declared bankruptcy.

For all pension provisions, the estimated revenue loss was $1.6 billion over five years, more than tripling to $6 billion over 11 years.

• **Subchapter S Corporations.** Relax the requirements for forming subchapter S corporations, a form of business organization frequently used by small businesses and family-owned firms. Previously, companies with 35 or fewer shareholders could organize as subchapter S corporations; that increased to 75 shareholders under the bill. The estimated revenue loss was no more than $396 million over five years, $932 million over 10 years.

• **Tax Credit for Tips.** Expand the tip credit, which accrued to employers. Under prior law, owners of bars and restaurants paid Social Security taxes on servers' tips as well as on their salaries, but they could only receive a credit for the taxes paid on tips paid while the servers were on the premises. Under the bill, the tips of workers who delivered food such as pizza also became eligible for the credit.

The bill also overturned a Treasury Department rule that limited the applicability of the tip credit to taxes paid after Dec. 31, 1993, on tips received after that date. The Treasury regulation also limited the credit to tips reported by the employee to the employer. The bill allowed employers to collect the tip credit regardless of whether the tips were reported by the employee and prior to the date that the tip credit provision went into effect. The estimated revenue loss was $68 million over five years, $165 million over 10 years.

- **Accelerated Depreciation for Gas Station/Convenience Stores.** Reduce from 39 years to 15 years the length of time over which a convenience store that also sold gasoline could depreciate the cost of the store. The estimated revenue loss was $209 million over five years.

- **Excess Passive Assets Overseas.** Repeal a tax on excess passive assets held by foreign subsidiaries of U.S. companies. Under prior law, foreign subsidiary profits above a certain level were taxed if they were put in a bank account or other financial instrument. The only way to avoid the tax was to invest the money in active business ventures overseas. The estimated revenue loss was $139 million over five years, $427 million over 10 years.

Renewal of Expired Provisions

- **Employer-Provided Educational Assistance.** Extend through May 31, 1997, the tax exclusion of up to $5,250 for workers who received employer-provided educational assistance. The exclusion was retroactive to Dec. 31, 1994, when it had last expired. The renewal covered graduate and undergraduate education from the provision's expiration through June 30, 1996. After that, only undergraduate education would qualify. The estimated revenue loss was $1 billion over the period.

- **Research and Experimentation Tax Credit.** Extend from July 1, 1996, through May 31, 1997, the tax credit for research and experimentation. The credit had expired June 30, 1995; it was not reinstated retroactively. The estimated revenue loss was $1.6 billion for the extension period.

- **Orphan Drug Tax Credit.** Extend from July 1, 1996, through May 31, 1997, the tax credit for qualified clinical testing associated with the development of drugs for rare diseases. The credit had expired Dec. 31, 1994. The estimated revenue loss was $20 million over the extension period.

- **Federal Unemployment Tax Exemption for Alien Agricultural Workers.** Extend permanently the exemption from federal unemployment taxes for employers of seasonal immigrant agricultural workers. The estimated revenue loss was $15 million.

- **Work Opportunity Tax Credit.** Modify the tax credit for employers who hired workers from disadvantaged groups—formerly known as the targeted jobs tax credit—and extend it temporarily. The credit had expired Dec. 31, 1994; the renewal covered only the period from Sept. 30, 1996, through Sept. 30, 1997. The estimated revenue loss was $383 million for the period of the extension.

Trade

- **Generalized System of Preferences.** Reauthorize the Generalized System of Preferences (GSP), which gave duty-free treatment to goods from developing countries. The previous authorization had expired July 31, 1995. The renewal was good from Oct. 1, 1996, through May 3, 1997, but the bill also included relief for many goods that had entered the country during the expiration period. The estimated revenue loss was $817 million for the extension period.

Family Tax Breaks

- **Adoption Tax Credit.** Provide adoptive parents a nonrefundable, $5,000 tax credit to offset the costs of domestic and foreign adoptions. The credit was to expire on Dec. 31, 2001. The bill also included a permanent $6,000 tax credit for domestic special-needs adoptions such as those of disabled children. The full credit was available to parents whose adjusted gross income was less than $75,000. The estimated revenue loss was $1.28 billion over five years.

- **Spousal IRAs.** Allow nonworking spouses to save up to $2,000 a year in tax-deferred individual retirement accounts (IRAs). The estimated revenue loss was $810 million over five years, $2.1 billion over 10 years.

Revenue Raisers

- **Puerto Rico Tax Credit.** Phase out over 10 years the Section 936 tax credit for companies doing business in Puerto Rico and other U.S. possessions. During the 10 years, companies with existing operations in Puerto Rico could continue to receive the credit, which erased any taxes on income from activities in Puerto Rico. The estimated revenue increase was $2.9 billion over five years, $10.6 billion over 10 years.

- **Airport and Airway Trust Fund Taxes.** Renew the five Airport and Airway Trust Fund excise taxes at pre-1996 rates for the period beginning seven days after enactment and running through Dec. 1, 1996. Included were a 10 percent surcharge on domestic airline tickets and a $6-per-ticket tax on international departures. The taxes had expired Dec. 31, 1995. The estimated revenue increase was $1.5 billion for the extension period.

- **Interest Income on Loans to Employee Stock Ownership Plans.** Repeal an existing law that made it easier for financial institutions to make loans to employee stock ownership plans by allowing the institutions to exclude 50 percent of the interest received on those loans. The repeal affected loans made after June 10, 1996. The estimated revenue increase was $715 million over five years, $2.3 billion over 10 years.

- **Tax on Damages Recovered in Lawsuits.** Remove the existing tax exclusion from gross income for punitive damages and nonphysical economic damages, such as those for pain and suffering. The estimated revenue savings were $289 million over five years.

- **Savings and Loan Debt Deduction.** Repeal special bad-debt deduction rules for thrift institutions. The estimated revenue increase was $1.2 billion over five years. ❑

Health Insurance Deduction

Congress in 1995 made permanent a popular tax provision allowing self-employed people to deduct part of the cost of their health insurance premiums from their taxable income. The bill (HR 831—PL 104-7) increased the deduction from 25 percent to 30 percent starting in fiscal 1995.

The GOP-led Congress opted to pay for the deduction in part by ending a tax break for companies that sold broadcast properties to minority investors. HR 831 also tightened eligibility rules to keep wealthy taxpayers from receiving the earned income tax credit (EITC), a refundable credit for the working poor. Over five years, repealing the minority tax break was expected to yield $1.4 billion; tightening the EITC rules was estimated to bring in $2 billion.

BACKGROUND

Before it expired Dec. 31, 1993, the health insurance tax break had allowed self-employed taxpayers to deduct 25 percent of the cost of their premiums from their taxable income. The Treasury Department estimated that about 3.2 million people used the deduction, and according to internal House Ways and Means Committee staff estimates, 70 percent of those taxpayers earned less than $75,000 a year.

The deduction was estimated to cost the government $487 million a year in lost revenue. The White House and lawmakers of both parties proposed expanding the break as part of 1994 health care reform, but no such legislation was enacted.

The break for minority broadcasters, known as a minority preference, allowed a company to defer paying tax on the profits of the sale of a radio or television station if it was sold to a firm that was partially owned by a minority. The program, which was run by the Federal Communications Commission (FCC), was started in 1943 to give tax certificates to aid companies that were forced to sell off stations to comply with FCC rules prohibiting ownership of more than one station in a city. The certificates deferred the seller's taxes on the profit from the sale.

In 1978, the FCC broadened the program into an affirmative action tool by granting tax certificates to companies that sold to minority broadcasters. At the time, only a tiny fraction—about one-half of 1 percent—of all radio and television stations were owned by minorities. The underlying purpose of the program, which had since been extended to cable systems, was both to help minority businesses and to increase the likelihood that programs reflecting minority views would be on the air.

Since 1978, the FCC had issued 330 certificates in sales involving African American, Hispanic and Asian buyers. Over the same period, minority ownership had risen to nearly 3 percent of all stations.

The tax certificate program was open to abuse because it was possible for a media company to find a minority broadcaster to front for a larger, nonminority-owned company. In such cases, the seller could get the tax break, even if the minority owner had little involvement in the broadcast work of the company. The interest in repealing the minority break was piqued by a $2.3 billion sale by entertainment giant Viacom Inc. in January 1995. Viacom sold its cable systems to a partially minority-owned company, a transaction that was expected to net Viacom a $400 million to $600 million tax break under existing law.

HOUSE ACTION

The House Ways and Means Committee decision to pay for the health insurance extension in part by ending the tax prefer-

ence for minority broadcasters sparked an acrimonious debate in which members of the Congressional Black Caucus leveled charges of racism at the Republican majority.

Charles B. Rangel, D-N.Y., a senior member of the caucus who led the opposition, saw the termination of the tax break as the opening salvo in a GOP effort to dismantle all affirmative action policies. However, in the end, the philosophy articulated by Ways and Means Chairman Bill Archer, R-Texas, carried the day. "It is unwise to have in the code anything related to race, color or creed," he said.

During the markup, an amendment by Jim McDermott, D-Wash., to narrow the minority preference instead of repealing it was rejected, along with about a dozen other Democratic amendments to limit the preference or to substitute another funding source to pay for the health insurance tax break.

The committee-approved bill was retroactive to Jan. 17, 1995, to ensure that the Viacom deal was covered and that the company would not gain from the minority preference. As reported by Ways and Means (H Rept 104-32) on Feb. 14, 1995, HR 831 also would make EITC eligibility rules more restrictive.

The rule governing floor debate allowed McDermott to offer an amendment to finance the tax deduction for health insurance by levying a punitive tax on wealthy people who gave up their U.S. citizenship to avoid taxes and by revising the rules governing foreign trusts as well as making changes in the EITC. Instead of ending the tax preference for minority broadcasters, McDermott proposed to limit its use to halt abuses. He called for making it available only for transactions worth less than $50 million and requiring the minority business to hold the properties for at least three years. The amendment was rejected 191–234 on Feb. 21.

The House passed HR 831 by 381–44 on Feb. 21.

SENATE ACTION

Republicans on the Senate Finance Committee made the tax deduction in HR 831 more generous and Democrats won approval of a Clinton administration plan to block wealthy Americans from evading taxes by renouncing their citizenship. The bill was formally reported (S Rept 104-16) on March 20.

Expansion of the health insurance deduction came on an amendment by William V. Roth Jr., R-Del., which increased the amount that self-employed individuals could deduct from their taxable income to 30 percent, starting with their 1995 returns. The amendment was expected to bring the cost of the deduction to about $3.4 billion over five years. Like the House, the Senate committee agreed to partially finance the deduction for the self-employed by terminating the minority tax preference. The panel also preserved a House provision making the repeal retroactive and applying it to the Viacom deal.

The Senate version toughened the House EITC provisions, denying the tax credit to wealthy taxpayers whose income from interest, dividends, rental properties and royalties was greater than $2,500 annually. The House version covered only interest and dividends.

In an attempt to save some of the minority tax preferences, ranking Democrat Daniel Patrick Moynihan of New York proposed financing the health insurance deduction in part with the $500 million in additional revenue that was expected to come from the tougher EITC provision. Republicans rejected Moynihan's amendment, but appropriated his idea—using the $500 million to help finance the increase in the health insurance deduction. The committee rejected a Bill Bradley, D-N.J., amendment to dedicate the $500 million to the federal deficit.

The committee also rejected a Moynihan amendment to finance the health insurance deduction in part by closing the expatriate tax loophole. The committee subsequently adopted this language separately when it was offered by Bradley as a way to reduce the deficit. Moynihan's amendment also would have repealed the minority broadcasting tax break for two years, instead of eliminating it permanently. Moynihan said that would provide time to develop ways to reform the program.

The Senate passed the revised bill by voice vote March 24.

FINAL ACTION

The House adopted the conference report on HR 831 (H Rept 104-92) by voice vote March 30. The Senate followed suit April 3, completing congressional action. As cleared, the bill:

• Extended the 25 percent health insurance deduction for the 1994 tax year and increased it to 30 percent starting in 1995.

• Terminated the tax preference for minority broadcasters, raising an expected $1.4 billion over five years.

• Tightened eligibility requirements for the EITC, raising $2 billion over five years. The bill barred people earning more than $2,350 a year in interest income, rents and royalties from using the EITC. It was expected to affect about 500,000 people.

• Dropped the Senate provision that would have taxed the assets of wealthy individuals who gave up their U.S. citizenship to avoid paying taxes. The provision would have raised an estimated $1.4 billion over five years.

Most of the Senate debate, led by Edward M. Kennedy, D-Mass., focused on the deleted expatriate provision. After an 83–0 cloture vote on the conference report April 3, Kennedy agreed to drop his objections and the Republican leadership promised that the tax loophole would be dealt with later in the year. (*Expatriate taxation, p. 106*)

In one last flare-up, Democrats asked President Clinton to veto the bill to protest an exemption inserted in the conference report by Carol Moseley-Braun, D-Ill. The provision aimed to help a partnership of the Tribune Company and African American music producer Quincy Jones complete a contract to buy two television stations. One was a Fox station in Atlanta, Ga., owned by media magnate Rupert Murdoch, who stood to gain tens of millions of dollars. However, Clinton signed the bill into law April 11, 1995. ❑

Retirement Income

President Clinton on Jan. 10, 1996, signed into law a bill (HR 394—PL 104-95) that barred states from imposing taxes on the retirement income of former residents. HR 394 was a boon to senior citizens who had built up tax-deferred pensions and retirement accounts during careers in states with high taxes, then retired to states without income taxes.

High-tax states, such as California and New York, had long complained that they lost revenue from an exodus of retirees to states with no income tax, such as Florida and Nevada. California, Oregon and other states had reserved the right to tax the pension income of nonresidents.

Bill sponsor Rep. Barbara F. Vucanovich, R-Nev., and other proponents said it was unfair to force seniors to pay taxes in a state where they no longer received services, calling it taxation without representation. Critics, such as Rep. Jerrold Nadler, D-N.Y., argued that the bill was an unfunded mandate designed to provide a tax loophole for highly paid executives who would be able to receive tax-supported government services while shielding their pension funds from taxation and leaving just when they were about to start paying taxes on their accumulated retirement income.

The House Judiciary Subcommittee on Commercial and Administrative Law adopted a Jack Reed, D-R.I., amendment to require recipients of certain "golden parachute" retirement plans to receive payments over their lifetimes, or at least 10 years, instead of in one lump sum. Such payments would be taxable in the retiree's new state.

The full committee adopted a Nadler amendment to allow states to tax the pension benefits of those who left the country and renounced their U.S. citizenship to avoid taxation. The committee rejected an amendment by ranking Democrat John Conyers Jr. of Michigan to allow states to tax the pension income of former residents in excess of $100,000.

The House Judiciary Committee reported HR 394 (H Rept 104-389) on Dec. 7, 1995. The House passed the measure by voice vote Dec. 18. The Senate followed suit Dec. 22, completing congressional action.

The House in 1994 had passed a less far-reaching bill to cap the income that retirees could shield at $30,000. (*Taxes on pension benefits, p. 665*) ❑

'Taxpayer Bill of Rights II'

A politically popular bill giving taxpayers greater rights in battles with the Internal Revenue Service (IRS) was signed into law July 30, 1996 (HR 2337—PL 104-168).

Treasury Secretary Robert E. Rubin said that 17 of the 41 steps required by HR 2337 had already been carried out administratively. But he and President Clinton said the law, which followed the 1988 "Taxpayers' Bill of Rights" (PL 100-647), mandated additional changes that were welcome. (*1988 taxpayer bill of rights, Congress and the Nation Vol. VII, p. 105*)

The bill, sponsored by Rep. Nancy L. Johnson, R-Conn., allowed taxpayers to make delinquent tax payments of less than $100,000 without interest up to 21 days after a deadline. The interest-free period for late payments had been 10 days. HR 2337 also replaced the IRS ombudsman with an office of "taxpayer advocate," appointed by, and reporting directly to, the IRS commissioner. And it dramatically raised—from $100,000 under existing law to $1 million—the maximum penalty that the IRS could face in court if one of its employees recklessly or intentionally disregarded the law or IRS regulations when dealing with a taxpayer.

Key provisions of the law, dubbed the "Taxpayer Bill of Rights II," had been contained in the budget reconciliation bill (HR 2491), which was vetoed in 1995.

The House Ways and Means Committee reported HR 2337 (H Rept 104-506) on March 28, 1996. The House passed the measure, 425–0 under suspension of the rules, on April 16. The Senate passed HR 2337 by voice vote July 11, clearing the bill. ❑

Gas Tax Repeal

An election-year proposal to repeal a 1993 increase in the federal gasoline tax was passed by the House (HR 3415) in 1996, but the effort stalled in the Senate.

BACKGROUND

The 4.3-cents-a-gallon addition to the federal gasoline tax, provided for in the 1993 deficit-reduction package (PL 103-66), was crafted by congressional Democrats as a replacement for President Clinton's original proposal—a much broader and more unpopular energy tax based on the heat content or British thermal units (Btu) of most forms of energy.

The gasoline tax wound up being the only direct tax hit on the middle class in the $500 billion deficit-reduction package. The rest of the 1993 law's taxes fell chiefly on upper-income individuals and on corporations. But in political terms, having a gas tax increase left Democrats open to attacks—often deliberately misleading—that the entire budget reconciliation package would whack the middle class. The legislation did not get a single GOP vote. *(1993 deficit-reduction bill, p. 87)*

Unlike most previous federal gasoline tax increases, revenue from the 4.3-cent increase was devoted to deficit reduction via the Treasury Department's general fund, not earmarked for highway construction as part of the Highway Trust Fund.

The gas tax increase was barely noticeable at the pump because it was lost in much larger gasoline price fluctuations caused by ordinary swings in supply and demand. The price of gasoline was actually lower one year after Congress agreed to impose the tax. However, between February and April 1996, gasoline prices at the pump jumped an average of 20 cents per gallon nationwide.

In the midst of the 1996 presidential campaign, Senate Majority Leader Bob Dole of Kansas, who was seeking the Republican presidential nomination, decided to make the spike in gasoline prices a political issue. On April 26, he called for repeal of the tax increase. In response, on April 29, Clinton authorized the sale of about 12 million barrels of oil from the nation's strategic petroleum reserves, a move aimed at driving down prices by increasing supply. He also directed Energy Secretary Hazel R. O'Leary to report within 45 days on what caused the sudden price increases. On April 30, Attorney General Janet Reno said the Justice Department's antitrust division had started looking into whether an illegal price gouging was behind the price increases.

Meanwhile, virtually every oil industry expert said the price jump had nothing to do with the 1993 tax increase and everything to do with gyrations involving the supply of crude oil,

gasoline refinery capacity, and, in the critical presidential election state of California, clean air laws requiring the reformulation of gasoline.

Most congressional Republicans eagerly embraced the idea of repeal, even though the cost of such an action would threaten their ability to balance the budget or finance other tax cuts. Permanent repeal of the tax would cost $33.9 billion over seven years, according to the Joint Committee on Taxation. Dole and House Speaker Newt Gingrich, R-Ga., initially opted for a seven-month rollback spanning Memorial Day 1996 through Jan. 1, 1997, which would cost $2.9 billion.

Deficit hawks on both sides of the aisle were opposed to repeal. Some Democrats defended the 1993 increase for helping reduce the deficit, and they said no guarantee existed that any repeal would be passed along to consumers. Other Democrats signaled that they would not conduct a frontal assault to preserve the 1993 increase. Instead, many appeared content to score a few political points of their own. The top targets were oil companies and the seemingly naked politics driving the rollback effort—as well as Dole's long history of supporting gasoline tax increases.

Dole had orchestrated a 5-cents-per-gallon increase in 1982 as chairman of the Senate Finance Committee and played a key role in another 5-cents-per-gallon increase included in the 1990 budget deal; an earlier Dole-supported deal that failed in the House would have added 10 cents per gallon. Furthermore, Dole in 1993 appeared to be on record in support of the 4.3-cents-per-gallon tax.

The White House strategy was not to rule out the idea of the repeal proposal but to try to shift the focus toward a potential balanced budget agreement. "I think to sort of out of the blue say we're going to add $30 billion to the deficit, instead of talking about what the best kind of tax relief for America's families is, and how we're going to do it in the context of balancing the budget, is not a responsible thing to do," said Clinton on May 2.

HOUSE ACTION

The House Ways and Means Committee reported HR 3415 (H Rept 104-576, Part I) on May 15, 1996. The bill would repeal 4.3 cents of the 18.3-cents-per-gallon federal gas tax from Memorial Day to Dec. 31, 1996. The GOP majority on the committee rejected a Charles B. Rangel, D-N.Y., amendment that aimed to guarantee that the tax repeal would be passed along to consumers instead of being pocketed by oil companies.

Provisions to offset the $2.9 billion cost of the seven-month repeal were added by the House Rules Committee. The cost was to be covered by auctioning 35 megahertz of the "nontelevision" portion of the broadcast spectrum and by cutting $578 million from the Energy Department budget over the next six years. Those offsets had first been identified by Dole and members of the Senate Finance Committee.

The House passed HR 3415 by 301–108 on May 21. Opponents of repeal, for the most part, did not rush to defend the tax, which was the most regressive tax provision in the 1993 reconciliation bill. Given the small size of the temporary cut provided for in HR 3415—it could award a typical motorist perhaps $20 over its lifetime, if passed on to consumers—Republicans did not make great claims for it.

Roughly half of the Democrats, including all the senior members of the leadership, supported the temporary tax cut. But most of the Democrats who participated in the debate blasted the maneuver as political gamesmanship. Republican John Edward Porter of Illinois said publicly what many of his colleagues admitted privately—that the repeal would harm long-term deficit-cutting efforts and that the motivation behind it was purely political.

SENATE ACTION

The gas tax repeal was taken to the Senate floor as an amendment to a bill (HR 2937) to provide relief to fired White House travel office chief Billy Dale. However, on May 9, Senate Minority Leader Tom Daschle, D-S.D., lodged a point of order against it because the proposed offsets did not raise enough in fiscal 1996. Waiving the budget rules required 60 votes.

Dole countered with a plan to use as the offset a measure to shore up the Savings Association Insurance Fund (SAIF). Though controversial with banks, it was a top Clinton administration priority. Dole brandished letters from the White House and the Treasury Department asking for its passage—but those letters did not ask that it be linked to repeal of the gas tax.

Senate Democrats then vowed to try to attach their proposal for an increase in the minimum wage to the gas tax repeal bill, and a threatened filibuster caused Dole to pull it from the floor May 14. Clinton said he would sign the repeal bill if demands on the minimum wage increase were met.

After Dole resigned from the Senate in June, little talk was heard of reviving the repeal measure. By the end of summer, the pump price of gasoline dropped, just as industry experts and the Energy Department had predicted in the spring. ❑

'Supermajority' Amendment

The House on April 15, 1996, rejected a proposed constitutional amendment (H J Res 159) to require a "supermajority"— a two-thirds vote in both the House and Senate—to raise taxes. The 243–177 vote was 37 votes short of the two-thirds majority needed to pass a constitutional amendment.

In a departure from usual procedure, H J Res 159 was not marked up by the House Judiciary Committee, which usually had jurisdiction over constitutional amendments. Instead, it went straight to the Rules Committee with language that had been negotiated by Joe L. Barton, R-Texas, the amendment's chief sponsor, and Bill Archer, R-Texas, chairman of the Ways and Means Committee, which had jurisdiction over taxes.

The measure would have required two-thirds of House members and senators present and voting to pass any bill that "increases the internal revenues" of the country "by more than a de minimis amount." The only exceptions would be if the country was at war or in a military conflict that was a threat to national security.

Opponents cited two chief concerns: the potential impact of the amendment on deficit reduction, and the precedent of alter-

ing the Constitution on the issue of supermajorities. The Constitution called for supermajorities in five specific instances, each of them involving a rare situation such as presidential impeachment. A number of legislators said they did not think the Constitution should control decisions about ordinary legislative policy such as taxation.

In addition, opponents pointed out that the proposed amendment would make it almost impossible for Congress to eliminate corporate tax benefits as a way to reduce the budget deficit. The effect of such an amendment on the basic tenet of majority rule also bothered some; that is, the power of a minority would be enhanced by the supermajority requirement.

The Clinton administration opposed the amendment.

Barton conceded that he and other supporters did not expect to prevail. But they said they wanted to give lawmakers a chance to highlight their position on tax increases.

The supermajority amendment was not a new idea for the 104th Congress. In their Contract with America, House Republicans had proposed requiring a three-fifths vote for tax increases as part of a balanced budget constitutional amendment. House leaders ultimately dropped the controversial provision. (Contract with America, box, p. 885; balanced budget amendment, p. 80)

The House in 1995 had adopted a rule requiring a three-fifths to raise income tax rates. The action was challenged in court by a group arguing that the rule was unconstitutional. (Rule change, p. 888; tax rule challenge, box, p. 107) ❑

Expatriate Taxation

The House Ways and Means Committee June 16, 1995, reported a bill (HR 1812—H Rept 104-145) aimed at wealthy Americans who gave up their U.S. citizenship to avoid paying taxes. No further action was taken on the bill and it died at the end of the 104th Congress.

A version of the legislation had also been included in the 1995 budget reconciliation bill (HR 2491), which was vetoed. And the Senate had included similar language in a bill (HR 831) to make permanent a tax deduction for self-employed individuals, but the provision was dropped in conference. The Senate April 6, 1995, by 96–4, adopted an Edward M. Kennedy, D-Mass., amendment to the fiscal 1995 supplemental appropriations and rescissions bill (HR 1158) expressing the sense of the Senate that Congress should close the loophole, effective Feb. 6, 1995. (1995 reconciliation, p. 131; health insurance deduction, p. 102; appropriations, p. 61)

The use of the tax loophole first came to public attention in a *Forbes* magazine cover story entitled "The New Refugees," published Nov. 21, 1994. The article described super-rich individuals with assets generally in the hundreds of millions, if not billions, of dollars who gave up their U.S. citizenship to escape taxes. A study by the Treasury Department found that 10 very wealthy individuals had expatriated in 1994. But because officials believed that they had not counted everyone who used the loophole, they estimated that approximately two dozen very wealthy individuals probably expatriated for tax purposes annually.

The Clinton administration proposed closing the loophole as part of its 1996 budget request. Even so, Ways and Means Chairman Bill Archer, R-Texas, resisted pressure for several months to move an expatriate taxation bill, giving ammunition to Democrats who were painting Republicans as defenders of the wealthy. In June 1995, the Joint Committee on Taxation issued a 300-plus-page study of the problem, one of the most comprehensive studies it had issued in several years. Soon after, Archer introduced HR 1812.

The rationale behind requiring former citizens to pay taxes when they left the country was that they made their money while in the United States and should have to pay taxes on their gains, just as citizens who stayed in the country did. Archer's bill assumed that everyone who had a net worth of more than $500,000 and expatriated did so to avoid paying taxes. Those people would be required to continue paying taxes on their so-called domestic-source income, such as dividends from shares of U.S. companies or capital gains from U.S. real estate, for 10 years. People would have the opportunity to prove that they had expatriated for other reasons. The Archer bill also proposed to close a commonly used loophole that allowed people to transfer domestic assets easily into foreign holdings to avoid taxation.

During committee markup, Treasury officials raised questions about HR 1812. Assistant Secretary for Tax Policy Leslie Samuels said it would allow "patient expatriates" to avoid taxes by waiting the 10 years before liquidating their assets. In addition, Samuels said, a number of ways existed to switch domestic assets into foreign assets that Archer did not seek to curtail. Samuels also charged that the bill would be nearly impossible for the Internal Revenue Service (IRS) to enforce because it would mean the IRS would have to track financial transactions of individuals living in foreign jurisdictions. But Joint Tax Committee lawyers disagreed, saying they did not think people would fail to pay their taxes. ❑

Retroactive Tax Increases

The Senate Governmental Affairs Committee Aug. 27, 1996, reported a bill (S 94—S Rept 104-354) to erect a new parliamentary barrier against legislation that would increase taxes retroactively. No further action was taken on the bill and it died at the end of the 104th Congress.

S 94, sponsored by Paul Coverdell, R-Ga., would amend the Congressional Budget and Impoundment Control Act of 1974 (PL 93-344) to create a new point of order on the Senate floor; 60 votes were required to waive a point of order. The bill was a response to provisions in the 1993 budget reconciliation law (PL 103-66) that raised tax rates for more than a million high-income taxpayers retroactive to Jan. 1, 1993. The law also reinstated expired taxes on the estates of people who died after Dec. 31, 1992. *(1974 law, Congress and the Nation Vol. IV, p. 71; 1993 reconciliation, p. 44)*

S 94 would have defined a tax increase as any change in a tax, deduction, exemption, credit, exclusion or other action that resulted in a larger tax burden.

TAX RULE CHALLENGE

The U.S. District Court of the District of Columbia on Aug. 23, 1995, upheld a House rule, adopted Jan. 4, 1995, that required any bill that would increase income tax rates to receive the support of at least three-fifths of the members of the House to pass. The ruling was appealed to the U.S. Court of Appeals for the District of Columbia Circuit. *(Rule change, p. 888)*

A group led by Rep. David E. Skaggs, D-Colo., and including twenty-six other members of Congress, six private citizens, and the League of Women Voters filed suit Feb. 8, 1995. *Skaggs v. Carle* charged that the "supermajority" rule violated the Constitution's principle of majority rule.

The Constitution specifically required supermajorities of two-thirds to overcome a presidential veto, expel a member, and ratify treaties. Skaggs said the framers considered and rejected proposals to require a supermajority to pass bills of particular content. But the defenders argued that nothing explicit in the Constitution prohibited Congress from requiring a supermajority for whatever measures it chose. They argued that Congress's power to decide its own rules, granted by the Constitution, extended to allowing Congress to decide whether certain measures should require a supermajority.

Robin Carle, the clerk of the House and the official defendant in the case, said that Skaggs and his colleagues had not been injured by the new rule and so technically had no grounds for their lawsuit. Skaggs replied that the change in the rules diluted representatives' ability to pass a certain kind of legislation and thereby already had diminished their power. Though not emphasized by either side, the three-fifths rule was largely symbolic. At any time, the House could vote by a simple majority to waive the rule, allowing it to pass a tax increase without a three-fifths majority.

However, the precedent-setting nature of the House rule led to criticism from Democrats as well as Republicans who considered it a misguided limit on congressional freedom and a dangerous new practice. A 1995 attempt to have the three-fifths tax requirement included in a proposed constitutional amendment to require a balanced budget failed, and the House in 1996 rejected a proposed constitutional amendment to require a supermajority to raise taxes. *(Balanced-budget amendment, p. 80; supermajority amendment, p. 106)*

The committee adopted an amendment by Chairman Ted Stevens, R-Alaska, to make the effective date of the bill Jan. 1, 1997. The committee also adopted a William V. Roth Jr., R-Del., amendment that he said would give tax-writing committees some flexibility to set retroactive effective dates to avoid "abusive tax situations" by those who would try to avoid a potential tax burden before a proposed change is enacted.

The Constitution, Federalism, and Property Rights Subcommittee of the Senate Judiciary Committee approved the bill on July 30, 1996. The Senate Budget Committee, which also shared jurisdiction over S 94, was discharged Oct. 3, 1996. ❑

Financial Regulation

Congress during the early 1990s—whether controlled by Democrats or Republicans—displayed little enthusiasm for wading back into the troubled waters of banking law that had swallowed two prior efforts to overhaul statutes that many regarded as obsolete. At the same time, lawmakers faced none of the financial crises requiring their attention that had plagued the late 1980s. Unlike President George Bush—who twice had to step in and push politically explosive bills to shore up the federal system of deposit insurance—President Clinton inherited a banking industry that had begun to earn record profits and a smaller thrift industry that had regained its health.

Wall Street continued to enjoy the good times of a bull market that had begun a decade earlier—the "crash" of 1987 was barely a distant memory. Mutual funds boomed, putting more of the benefits of the market's gains into the pockets of ordinary people, not just high-rolling investors.

For the most part, the instinct was to leave well enough alone. Instead of seeking legislative fixes to help them reach new markets or protect their turf, most financial services companies—including banks and thrifts, securities firms, insurance companies and diversified conglomerates—were content to take a breather and let the marketplace evolve.

To be sure, Congress made occasional forays into the morass of banking law, with mixed success. In more than a decade of trying, Congress had not shown an ability to lead the way in modernizing the nation's financial services framework—at least not without creating trouble along the way. Instead, legislative changes had come mostly in the form of crisis intervention—the savings and loan salvage operation being the most apparent—or reaction to changing conditions in the marketplace. That pattern largely repeated itself during Clinton's first term.

When Clinton's presidency began in January 1993, the experience of past failures was fresh in the minds of lawmakers, administration officials and industry groups alike. In 1991, responding to a wave of bank failures that had weakened the deposit insurance system, Congress and the Bush administration tried to make the industry more profitable by overhauling decades-old banking laws. But interest groups fought pitched battles, congressional titans protected their turf and the entire effort tied Congress in knots. Almost everyone involved wanted a break.

Luckily for Clinton, he inherited an economy that was beginning to rebound from the 1990–1991 recession, if slowly. The banking industry in particular was coming back to health, helped greatly by a big 1992 cut in short-term interest rates by the Federal Reserve that widened loan spreads and sweetened profits for lenders. A "credit crunch" caused by the early 1990s recession began to ease as well.

Clinton's financial services policy advisers took a cautious tack as they oversaw the growing and diverse industry. Banks continued to make considerable progress with their regulators, who decided it should be easier for banks to sell insurance and who were poised to give banks greater access to the lucrative securities market.

These advances on the regulatory front contributed both to success and failure in Congress. The changing financial landscape made it easy for Congress to agree that banks should be able to operate freely across state lines.

At the same time, banks' regulatory success led to the demise of the most ambitious financial services bill of Clinton's first term: a House GOP drive to repeal the Glass-Steagall Act, a steadily eroding Depression-era law that barred banks from fully engaging in the securities business. In the end, banks refused to accept curbs on their ability to sell insurance in return for the promise of lucrative fees from new powers to underwrite and sell securities.

Banks were getting most of what they wanted on the securities and insurance fronts from their regulators. Accepting legislative constraints was not a necessary part of the bargain, they reasoned.

CLINTON'S INITIATIVES

For his part, Clinton pursued a piecemeal agenda, sometimes leading Congress, sometimes being dragged along. Battle scars from the thrift bailout and prior attempts to update bank-

REFERENCES

Discussion of financial regulation legislation for the years 1945–1964 may be found in *Congress and the Nation Vol. I*, pp. 337–386; for the years 1965–1968, *Congress and the Nation Vol. II*, pp. 253–279; for the years 1969–1972, *Congress and the Nation Vol. III*, pp. 135–145; for the years 1973–1976, *Congress and the Nation Vol. IV*, pp. 107–117; for the years 1977–1980, *Congress and the Nation Vol. V*, pp. 253–265; for the years 1981–1984, *Congress and the Nation Vol. VI*, pp. 83–93; for the years 1985–1988, *Congress and the Nation Vol. VII*, pp. 109–136; for the years 1989–1992, *Congress and the Nation Vol. VIII*, pp. 113–161.

ing law had long meant that banking bills rarely took priority—a sentiment shared both by Congress and the White House.

Clinton's first major task was to persuade Congress to write one final taxpayer check for the thrift bailout of the 1980s. The bill passed, though the arduous process took most of 1993 to accomplish and that for a bill that was, all along, a must-pass measure.

His only true banking initiative was to make good on a campaign promise. Clinton had given short shrift to financial services issues during his 1992 presidential quest. He did, however, call for creation of a network of 100 community development banks to pump loans into capital-starved inner cities and poor rural areas.

Clinton was impressed by the example of Chicago's South Shore Bank, a for-profit institution with a community development mission that had helped rebuild crumbling neighborhoods.

Two years later, he signed into law on the South Lawn of the White House a bill to give subsidies to a fledgling network of community development lenders. The bill failed to create the 100 new lenders and was able to be enacted even in its meager form because it was sweetened by industry-sought provisions to ease regulatory "red tape."

In fact, that the banking lobby made such a big issue of "regulatory relief" during the years 1993–1996 was an indication of the industry's modest agenda.

Moving in tandem with the community development bill was the widely backed measure to allow banks to set up nationwide branch networks. Again, though, that effort largely ratified marketplace and regulatory changes that had permitted banks to travel far down the road to nationwide banking.

REPUBLICANS TAKE CHARGE

When the Republican revolution swept over Congress in 1995, the legislative dynamic changed—but only slightly. House Banking Committee Chairman Jim Leach, R-Iowa, immediately announced plans to repeal the Glass-Steagall Act, but his bill never gained enough momentum to reach the House floor.

House Republicans also pressed an ambitious—and easy-to-veto—regulatory relief bill that attacked the core of consumer and community protections in existing banking law, especially the 1977 Community Reinvestment Act (CRA), which required regulators to grade banks' efforts to serve the entire community in which they did business. Veto threats and promises of Senate filibusters easily derailed the House GOP's effort.

In the end, a modest regulatory bill became law that had the blessing of the Clinton administration—and carried with it some new safeguards for consumers in their dealings with lenders and credit reporting agencies. Existing consumer protections escaped essentially unscathed. That measure was accompanied by provisions to require banks to help pay to shore up lingering problems in the insurance fund that protected thrift deposits.

The impact of these legislative efforts was modest compared to the ongoing evolution in the financial services industry. Investment banks and securities firms earned big new fees by devising and marketing a complex and highly volatile class of investments known as "derivatives."

A wave of mergers and consolidations continued to shrink the banking and thrift industries. Banks looked for business beyond traditional commercial and consumer lending. With the permission of regulators and courts—if not Congress—they made inroads into markets from mutual funds to insurance to securities underwriting. The age of at-home computer banking began.

By the end of Clinton's first term, Treasury Department officials were looking to craft an ambitious financial services modernization plan to try to rationalize the archaic but rapidly crumbling regulatory and statutory barriers that confined the entire financial services industry. The plan would likely seek to repeal Glass-Steagall and eliminate the thrift industry. It eventually might permit banks to affiliate with any commercial entity.

The success of such an endeavor was far from assured.

Chronology of Action on Financial Regulation

1993–1994

The first two years after President Clinton's election proved to be a busy time for banking and financial regulatory issues. A number of items of unfinished business from prior years were resolved, such as a bill to permit banks to operate freely across state lines, and another to conclude the salvaging of failed savings and loan associations.

Clinton also persuaded Congress to create a network of community lenders to provide credit to fledgling businesses and nonprofit organizations that had difficulty gaining credit from traditional lenders. This was the one banking agenda item carried over from the 1992 presidential election campaign, though the outcome fell short of what Clinton had proposed.

Interstate Branching and Banking

The U.S. banking industry won a long-sought victory in 1994 as the 103rd Congress cleared a bill to permit banking companies to set up nationwide networks of branch banks without having to form separate banks in each state.

President Clinton, for whom the bill never seemed a priority, signed it into law on Sept. 29 (HR 3841—PL 103-328). The new law capped years of lobbying by the nation's bigger banking companies, which had long sought the freedom to open branches across state lines without having to set up separately capitalized and managed subsidiaries as required under existing law.

The Clinton administration was slow to endorse the effort and made it clear that it was willing to invest little effort toward advancing the bill. Instead, the administration was focused on winning enactment of a bill (HR 3474) to provide federal help to a fledgling network of community development banks. *(Community development banks, p. 116)*

Interstate branching had been a widely backed element in a broad—though not entirely successful—effort to overhaul banking law in 1991. That year, Congress enacted a major bill to shore up the federal deposit insurance system. Lawmakers pitched overboard significant, though highly controversial, pieces of that bill aimed at updating U.S. banking laws that were generally seen as obsolete. *(Congress and the Nation Vol. VIII, p. 136)*

The new law enacted in 1994 allowed multistate bank holding companies to merge their subsidiary banks into branches of a single bank as of June 1, 1997; it also lifted the few remaining obstacles to interstate purchases of whole banks by bank holding companies.

The effect was to accelerate an existing trend toward consolidation in the industry. Under the bill, so-called super-regional banking companies, such as North Carolina's NationsBank Corp., were unchained from laws that had required them to maintain separate banks in each state in which they did busi-

ness. The idea was to create conditions for a more efficient and profitable banking industry and, it was hoped, to pass along savings to consumers as banks jockeyed for customers in the new nationwide market.

But the bill's path into law—despite sweeping support for it on Capitol Hill—was not easy. Small banks generally opposed the measure and the potent insurance agents lobby threatened to hold the bill hostage as a vehicle for an agent-backed provision to scale back banks' ability to sell insurance.

The insurance agents' stance was a key reason why neither the House nor Senate Banking committees acted on the interstate banking and branching issue in 1993; the prospect of tough votes that would have forced members to choose between the rival banking and insurance lobbies was not pleasant, nor was it helpful for campaign fund-raising.

The Clinton administration finally entered the fight in October 1993, endorsing an interstate banking and branching bill. But in an Oct. 25 speech, Treasury Secretary Lloyd Bentsen urged Congress to move slowly and finish other items on the banking agenda first—such as replenishing the fund created to finance salvage operations on hundreds of failed and failing savings and loan associations and providing assistance to community development lenders. *(RTC financing, p. 122)*

The administration also indicated privately that it did not see the point in investing political energy into the branching effort given the likelihood that the insurance powers controversy would doom the bill.

In February 1994, however, the tide changed. Sen. Christopher J. Dodd, D-Conn.—the principal advocate for insurance agents in Congress—announced he would not attempt to pair the bank insurance powers rollback with the interstate branching bill. He feared to do so would sink the interstate bill of which he was also a principal booster. By withdrawing his support for the agents' provision, the way was cleared to enactment.

HOUSE COMMITTEE ACTION

The interstate banking and branching bill began its advance in the House, winning approval from the Banking Subcommittee on Financial Institutions on Feb. 3 by a 29–0 vote. Subcommittee Chairman Stephen L. Neal, D-N.C., was the premier advocate of interstate branch banking in the House; his state of North Carolina was home to NationsBank Corp., the fourth largest bank in the country and the loudest industry voice for interstate branching.

Neal's bill largely mirrored an interstate branching bill that won a test floor vote in 1991. (The underlying bill failed to pass, however, and was subsequently scaled back to remove the interstate language.) The draft measure contained the following basic provisions:

• **Interstate Banking.** Repeal of the Douglas Amendment to the 1956 Bank Holding Company Act to allow a banking company to purchase banks located in other states, one year after enactment, without limitation.

• **Interstate Branching.** Eighteen months after enactment, bank holding companies that owned multistate branch net-

LEVITT, TIGERT APPOINTED

President Clinton in the first year of his presidency tapped a prominent Democratic fund-raiser to head the Securities and Exchange Commission (SEC) and the first woman to head the Federal Deposit Insurance Corporation (FDIC).

SEC chairman

By voice vote July 26, 1993, the Senate confirmed Arthur Levitt Jr., former chairman of the American Stock Exchange, to fill the SEC post, replacing Richard C. Breeden, a Republican popular on Capitol Hill.

A New Yorker who raised money for Clinton's presidential campaign, Levitt had built a small brokerage house into the giant that later became Shearson Lehman Bros. Inc. He headed the American Stock Exchange during the 1987 market crash.

The Senate Banking Committee approved Levitt's nomination by 19–0 on July 22, 1995.

FDIC chairman

The Senate on Oct. 4, 1994, voted 90–7 to confirm Ricki R. Tigert as chairman of the FDIC, which managed the funds that insured bank depositors. Tigert replaced William Taylor, who died in August 1992. The agency had been without a chairman in the intervening two years.

Tigert was a Washington lawyer with experience at both the Treasury Department and the Federal Reserve Board. Clinton, who had a close relationship with Tigert, nominated her in November 1993.

The Senate Banking Committee had voted 16–1 on Feb. 10, 1994, to recommend Tigert's confirmation.

After winning easy committee approval, Tigert's nomination was held up by Republicans who said her relationship with the Clintons posed a potential conflict of interest, since the FDIC was one agency that would be looking into the Whitewater affair and the failure of Madison Guaranty Savings and Loan, which also had ties to the Clintons.

Tigert wrote to Banking Committee members and promised to recuse herself from any decisions involving Whitewater or Madison. Ultimately, seven Republicans voted with Democrats on a 63–32 vote to end the Senate floor filibuster holding up the confirmation.

works could consolidate them into branches of a single bank. Three years after enactment, banks could open new interstate branches by purchasing banks and converting them into branches. States were given three years to "opt out" of branching by passing laws to bar it.

• **De Novo Branching.** Banks could branch across state lines without acquiring and converting an existing bank only in states that "opted in" by enacting state laws to permit such "de novo" branching.

• **State Laws.** Another provision required interstate branches of federally chartered out-of-state banks to follow state consumer protection, fair lending and community reinvestment laws as if the branches were state-chartered banks.

• **Foreign Banks.** The bill allowed foreign banks, which operated so-called "wholesale branches" not subject to deposit insurance premiums or community reinvestment requirements, to open such branches nationwide.

• **Community Reinvestment.** The measure also required state-by-state Community Reinvestment Act (CRA) evaluations of institutions with multistate branch networks. One of the provisions of the 1977 CRA law required federal regulators to determine whether a bank served the credit and banking services needs of the community in which it operated before approving bank applications to merge with other banks or open and close branches.

Neal's bill (HR 3841—H Rept 103-448) sailed through the full House Banking Committee on March 9 on an overwhelming 50–1 vote.

The committee rejected two consumer-backed amendments. One, offered by Kweisi Mfume, D-Md., would have required banks wishing to take advantage of the new powers to pledge to make loans and offer banking services in poor neighborhoodsand other underserved banking markets. It failed on a 17–34 vote.

Another amendment, offered by Cleo Fields, D-La., would have required interstate branch banks to provide basic banking and government check-cashing services.

HOUSE FLOOR ACTION

The bill came to the House floor with an unusual degree of dispatch for an important banking bill. It passed the House by voice vote under suspension of the rules, an expedited procedure that limited debate and barred amendments.

SENATE COMMITTEE ACTION

Three weeks after Dodd announced he would not use the bill to roll back the ability of banks to sell insurance, the Senate Banking Committee Feb. 23 easily approved its version of the interstate bill, 19–0.

Supporters of the bill (S 1963—S Rept 103-240) managed to keep the scope of the measure narrow, free of controversy and unwelcome amendments.

The Senate bill generally mirrored the House version. It also contained language to repeal the Douglas Amendment and permit full interstate bank ownership one year after enactment. Banks could consolidate interstate branch networks two years after enactment. Language on "de novo" branching and the Community Reinvestment Act was similar to that in the House bill.

The Senate committee-reported bill differed in two significant ways from the House measure. First, federally chartered banks that were converted into branches would not have been subject to state laws. This was important for branches in such states as California and New York where consumer protection regulations were broader than under federal law.

Also, the Senate bill contained a provision authored by Wendell H. Ford, D-Ky., to allow a foreign bank to take advantage of the new branching powers only if it established or acquired an insured U.S. bank and then created networks of branches from that bank.

SENATE FLOOR ACTION

As in the House, consideration of the interstate bill did not generate the controversy it had in 1991. The Senate passed HR 3841 by voice vote April 26, after substituting the text of S 1963, as amended.

Not a single Senate amendment triggered a roll-call vote, and possible amendments requiring banks to offer basic, low-cost services, which could have created controversy, were quietly abandoned.

The Senate did adopt by voice votes amendments to give states additional time to "opt out" of interstate branching and to preserve state authority to tax banks.

But the most significant amendment, offered by Howard M. Metzenbaum, D-Ohio, and adopted by voice vote, sought to extend the federal statute of limitations to restore $1.6 billion in Federal Deposit Insurance Corporation (FDIC) and Resolution Trust Corporation (RTC) lawsuits against officials of failed banks and thrifts. Court rulings had jeopardized the claims by applying state statutes of limitations to federal suits.

The administration, the FDIC and the RTC all wanted the changes, which were designed to extend the statute of limitations for fraud and negligent behavior to five years from the time when regulators took over an institution.

CONFERENCE, FINAL ACTION

The core of the House and Senate bills—interstate banking and branching—were fairly easy to reconcile by conferees on the bill. A variety of lesser provisions required lengthy behind-the-scenes talks, however.

In addition, the interstate bill's fate became intertwined with Clinton's community development bank bill. Conference meetings on both bills began the week of July 18.

Conferees agreed that state banking laws would apply equally to state-chartered banks and to branches of national banks. But the Office of the Comptroller of the Currency, the chief regulator of national banks, was empowered to preempt state laws that discriminated against national banks or conflicted with federal law.

Metzenbaum's statute of limitations language was watered down to apply only to cases of fraud or intentional misconduct that resulted in "unjust enrichment," a much more difficult standard to prove than simple negligence.

And conferees dropped Ford's amendment to require foreign banks to set up subsidiary banks if they wanted to open new branches.

After the conference wrapped up July 25, the measure quickly headed to the full House, which adopted the conference re-

port by voice vote Aug. 4. The Senate cleared the measure Sept. 13 by a 94–4 vote.

MAJOR PROVISIONS

As cleared, the interstate banking and branching bill (HR 3841—PL 103-328):

Interstate Banking

• **Bank Acquisitions.** Permitted adequately capitalized and managed bank holding companies to acquire banks in any state one year after enactment of the legislation (Sept. 29, 1995). State laws that limited holding company acquisitions to banks that had been in existence for a specified period of time, though not to exceed five years, were preserved. Under prior law, acquisitions were allowed when states had enacted reciprocal laws permitting them. Every state but Hawaii permitted interstate purchases of whole banks, though about a dozen states limited such purchases along regional lines.

• **Concentration Limits.** Barred interstate acquisitions if they resulted in the bank holding company controlling more than 10 percent of U.S. bank and thrift deposits or more than 30 percent of the deposits in the home state of the bank to be acquired. State legislatures or regulators could waive the 30 percent limit. These concentration limits did not apply to the initial entry into a state by a bank holding company. States could stipulate that any bank targeted for acquisition had to have been in existence for a specified period not to exceed five years; this was aimed at preventing the formation of new banks simply for the purpose of selling them to an out-of-state holding company.

• **CRA Compliance.** Required the Federal Reserve Board, the primary regulator of bank holding companies, to examine the Community Reinvestment Act (CRA) evaluation of any holding company (and its affiliated institutions) before approving an acquisition. This was a restatement of existing law. The 1977 Community Reinvestment Act required banks and thrifts to demonstrate that they were attempting to meet the credit and bank service needs of the entire community in which they did business. The Fed also was required to take into account an institution's compliance with state community reinvestment laws before approving interstate bank acquisitions; under existing procedures, the Fed considered state CRA evaluations but was not officially required to do so.

• **Affiliated Banks.** Permitted bank subsidiaries of an interstate bank holding company to act as agents for each other for certain banking activities: receiving deposits, renewing time deposits, closing loans, servicing loans and receiving payments on loans and other obligations for other affiliated institutions. Insured savings and loans that were affiliated with banks as of July 1, 1994, subject to certain conditions, were allowed to act as agents for such banks.

Affiliated banks could act as agents for one another regardless of whether the institutions were in the same or different states.

Interstate Branching

• **Interstate Mergers.** Permitted adequately capitalized and managed banks to merge with out-of-state subsidiary banks and convert each branch office into a branch of the resulting bank, starting June 1, 1997. The bank could subsequently establish additional branches in the host state.

The law preserved state laws that required out-of-state banks or bank holding companies to merge with or acquire banks that had been in existence for a specified minimum period of time (not to exceed five years). Banks were allowed to set up branches across state lines via the purchase of individual branches only if permitted by state laws.

- **State Opt-Out/Opt-In.** Gave states until June 1, 1997, to enact laws to block out-of-state banks from establishing branches in the state. The process was called "opting out." Banks headquartered in any state that opted out of interstate branching would not be allowed to participate in any interstate merger transaction. States also could enact laws to permit ("opt into") interstate branching before June 1, 1997.

- **De Novo Branching.** Permitted banks to open branches in a state without first acquiring and converting an existing bank only if the state enacted a law to permit such "de novo" branching. Once a bank established a de novo branch in a host state, the bank could freely establish and acquire additional branches at any location in the host state in accordance with federal and state laws.

- **Concentration Limits.** Prohibited mergers if the resulting bank would control more than 10 percent of deposits of insured depository institutions in the United States or 30 percent or more of the deposits in any state. The provision, however, contained significant exemptions. States were permitted to waive the 30 percent limit, and the concentration limits did not apply to mergers of existing subsidiary banks, nor did they apply to a bank's initial entry into a state. State concentration caps applied to initial entries.

- **State Taxation Authority.** Preserved the rights of states to tax banks and bank holding companies. The provision meant that when a bank in a state was converted to a branch of an out-of-state bank, state and local governments retained the right to tax the branch, using their own taxation methods. The bill specifically allowed state and local governments to impose a shares tax on a portion of a bank's stock.

- **State Laws.** Applied host-state laws governing community reinvestment, consumer protection and usury, fair lending and intrastate branching to any branch of a federally chartered bank, including branches of banks headquartered out of state. The Office of the Comptroller of the Currency (OCC), which regulated national banks, was made responsible for enforcing such state laws. As under existing law, federal law could preempt state laws in certain circumstances. Generally, state law applied to national banks unless it was in direct conflict with or an obstacle to accomplishing the purposes of a federal law, or the federal law was comprehensive enough to demonstrate congressional intent concerning a given subject area.

Because some members of Congress believed that the OCC had overreached in its use of preemption power, particularly in a case in which it ruled that federally chartered banks in New Jersey did not have to comply with New Jersey's basic checking account law, the bill added procedural requirements onto the federal government's ability to preempt state laws. Before preempting state law, the comptroller had to publish the proposed ruling with a 30-day comment period; the OCC had to consider the comments it received before making final judgment.

For state-chartered banks, host state banking laws applied to branches of out-of-state banks. State bank regulators were permitted to examine branches of banks chartered in another state; state regulators had the same enforcement authority over such branches as they had for banks chartered by their state.

- **CRA Evaluations.** Modified the Community Reinvestment Act (CRA) to adapt it to interstate banks. Generally, under existing law, individual banks were given CRA evaluations during annual examinations. Regulators (the Federal Deposit Insurance Corporation, the Federal Reserve and the OCC) assessed how well the bank was meeting the credit and bank service needs of the community in which it did business, including low- and moderate-income neighborhoods.

Regulators were required to take these CRA evaluations into account when the bank filed any application to the regulator, including applications by the bank or its holding company to establish or close branches or merge with another bank.

The bill updated the CRA to adapt it to the new rules of interstate banking and branching. It required bank regulators to prepare one overall evaluation of an institution's compliance with the CRA, as well as separate state-by-state evaluations in each state in which it maintained branches. The state-by-state evaluations had to include separate CRA evaluations to measure performance in each city in which the bank had a branch; a separate CRA evaluation was required for each rural area in which the bank had a branch.

Federal banking regulators also were required to take into account banks' CRA performance ratings when considering interstate branching applications from banks desiring to merge and consolidate their out-of-state bank operations. An institution's CRA performance in each state in which it maintained branches had to be considered.

The existing law governing interstate acquisitions of whole banks was the Bank Holding Company Act, enforced by the Federal Reserve Board as the regulator of bank holding companies. Bank mergers were carried out under the Bank Merger Act. The Federal Reserve Board's CRA regulations and practices for interstate bank acquisitions were somewhat more stringent than the CRA rules and practices governing intrastate bank mergers.

When a bank made its initial entry into a state in which it had no banks or affiliates, the bill required that the CRA be applied to such future interstate banking activities in a fashion that paralleled the approach taken by the Federal Reserve. For all other interstate merger applications, existing regulations and practices governing bank mergers were to apply.

- **30-Mile Rule.** Barred banks from using the so-called 30-mile rule to evade the provisions of the bill and branch into states that did not permit interstate branching. Under a provision in the Civil War-era National Bank Act, a federally chartered bank was permitted to move its headquarters 30 miles, even across state lines. This provision had been used as a means to branch interstate in advance of the new banking and branching law, because banks were permitted to retain branches in the original state after they moved the headquarters across state lines.

- **Texas Home Equity Loans.** Overturned a federal court decision (*First Gibraltar Bank v. Morales*) that held that the Office of Thrift Supervision had the authority to preempt a homestead protection provision in the Texas Constitution. Texas was the only state that did not permit lenders to foreclose on borrowers' homes; as a result, it was the only state in which consumers could not borrow against the equity that had built up in their homes. The provision, added by House Banking Committee Chairman Henry B. Gonzalez, D-Texas, as his price for letting the bill pass, reinforced the Texas Constitution and continued to block home equity lending in the Lone Star State.

- **Coordinated Examinations.** Permitted state banking regulators to examine branches of out-of-state banks for safety and soundness and to ensure compliance with state banking community reinvestment, fair lending and consumer protection laws.

If a host-state examiner discovered that an out-of-state branch was in an unsafe or unsound condition or detected violations of state banking laws, it could take enforcement actions equal to those it could take against a bank chartered in the host state.

State regulators were permitted to enter into cooperative agreements to facilitate supervision of state banks operating interstate. Nothing in this provision affected the authority of federal banking agencies to examine branches of insured depository institutions.

- **Branch Closures.** Required that whenever a bank proposed to close a branch in a low- or moderate-income area, the appropriate federal bank regulator upon request by the community consult with community representatives to explore alternative means to meet the community's needs. Such options could include seeking ways to attract or establish a new branch of another bank, chartering a new bank or thrift, or establishing a community development credit union.

Under the 1991 banking law (PL 102-242), notices of branch closures had to be mailed to customers; the bill required that such notices include the address of the bank's regulator and inform consumers that they could file comments with the agency. Notwithstanding these consultations, nothing in the provision was to affect the authority of a bank to close a branch, or affect the timing of such closures. (*1991 law, Congress and the Nation Vol. VIII, p. 136*)

- **Bank Fees Study.** Required the Federal Reserve to conduct an annual survey of the fees charged by banks for retail banking services. Each report was required to describe national and state trends in the cost and availability of bank services. Reports were required for seven years.

- **Deposit Production Ban.** Barred banks from using interstate branches to siphon deposits from the community in which the branch was located to other states. By June 1, 1997, banking regulators were required to draw up regulations to prohibit such so-called deposit production offices. If an out-of-state bank lent less than half as much as the average in-state bank, regulators

would be required to examine the bank's loan portfolio to determine whether the bank was reasonably fulfilling the credit needs of the community in the host state. If not, the regulators would be authorized to close the branch and bar the bank from opening new branches in that state.

Foreign Banks

- **Branching.** Enacted a delicately negotiated compromise on rules governing establishment of wholesale branches by foreign banks. The Senate-passed bill contained a provision that would have required foreign banks to establish a U.S. subsidiary bank in order to branch across state lines. The House-passed bill would have provided foreign banks with branching powers that mirrored the powers given to U.S. banks (that is, requiring them to purchase a U.S. bank and convert it to a branch).

The final bill generally accepted the House position, though with several modifications aimed at addressing concerns that foreign banks' wholesale branches might obtain a competitive advantage over U.S. banks. The provision was supported by Democratic Sens. Donald W. Riegle Jr., Mich., and Wendell H. Ford, Ky., who said that uninsured wholesale branch operations of foreign banks that took large deposits and made loans to big corporate customers had a competitive advantage over U.S. banks because they were exempt from CRA lending and record-keeping requirements and did not pay deposit insurance premiums.

The bill permitted a foreign bank to establish and operate wholesale bank branches, either de novo or by acquisition and merger, in states other than their home states, to the same extent that a U.S. bank (state- or federally chartered) headquartered in the foreign bank's home state was allowed to establish such branches.

- **CRA Requirements.** Continued to subject branches of foreign banks established through the acquisition of existing banks or branches to CRA requirements. Banks that did not accept domestic deposits were not subject to the CRA.

- **Wholesale Deposits.** Capped at 1 percent, instead of 5 percent as under existing law, the total amount of so-called retail deposits that could be held by a wholesale branch of a foreign bank. In addition, bank regulators were directed to revise regulations under the International Banking Act to make sure that they did not favor foreign banks over U.S. banks. Under existing law, foreign wholesale bank branches were barred from taking retail deposits of less than $100,000 that required deposit insurance. This effectively required foreign banks to establish a U.S. subsidiary bank in order to take deposits of less than $100,000.

Exceptions were made for foreign businesses and governments, foreign citizens not residing in the United States, and U.S.-based foreign employees of foreign banks, businesses, governments and international organizations. The bill directed bank regulators to consider whether to restrict classes of customers who were permitted to make retail deposits of less than $100,000.

- **Capital Requirements.** Permitted, but not require, the Federal Reserve or the OCC to require a foreign bank to establish a separate U.S. subsidiary bank in order to engage in interstate branching if the Fed or the OCC determined that it was the only way to verify that a foreign bank adhered to capital requirements that were equivalent to those applicable to a U.S. bank engaged in interstate branching.

• **Offshore Shell Branches.** Prohibited foreign banks from using offshore "shell" branches of its U.S. subsidiaries to conduct banking and financial activities that foreign branches of U.S. banks were not permitted to conduct.

• **Consumer Protection Laws.** Clarified that U.S. consumer protection laws applied to foreign banks, affirming the longtime regulatory interpretation of the Federal Reserve Board, which regulated foreign banks. The provision specified the following laws: Electronic Funds Transfer Act, Equal Credit Opportunity Act, Expedited Funds Availability Act, Fair Credit Billing Act, Fair Credit Reporting Act, Fair Debt Collection Practices Act, Home Mortgage Disclosure Act, Real Estate Settlement Procedures Act, Truth in Leasing Act, Truth in Lending Act and Truth in Savings Act.

• **Foreign Bank Examination Fees.** Provided a three-year moratorium on a provision of the 1991 banking law that required the Federal Reserve Board and other bank regulators to impose fees to cover the cost of examinations of a branch, agency or representative office of a foreign bank. The moratorium was to begin in July 1995; regulators had delayed implementing the fees because corresponding fees had not been imposed on U.S. banks.

General Provisions

• **Statute of Limitations.** Extended the statute of limitations to permit the Federal Deposit Insurance Corporation (FDIC) and the Resolution Trust Corporation (RTC) to "revive" lawsuits that had expired under state statutes of limitation. The purpose was to give federal banking regulators additional time to sue officers and directors of failed institutions for actions that contributed to an institution's failure, including fraud, intentional misconduct resulting in unjust enrichment and intentional misconduct resulting in substantial loss to the institution. Examples of such misconduct included self-dealing that resulted in unjust enrichment or a substantial loss to the institution, falsifying financial records to disguise increased financial loss and conspiracy to violate banking rules or regulations.

A proposal to extend the statute of limitations in cases of negligence or gross negligence was dropped in conference. The FDIC or the RTC, as conservator or receiver of a failed depository institution, could revive such claims within five years of the appointment of the conservator or receiver.

• **Coin Bills.** Directed the U.S. Mint to issue several new commemorative coins. Profits derived from sales of the coins were to be used to support the events or institutions to be commemorated. Coins were to be minted to support the following: the 1995 Special Olympics World Games; the National Community Service Trust; the endowment of the Robert F. Kennedy Memorial; the Bicentennial of the United States Military Academy in 2002; and the United States Botanic Garden.

• **Financial Services Commission.** Required a study of the United States financial services system conducted by the Treasury Department in consultation with an Advisory Commission on Financial Services (to be named by the secretary of the Treasury) and other enumerated federal agencies.   ❏

Community Development Banks

The 103rd Congress cooperated to give President Clinton a partial victory in his attempt to create and finance a network of community lenders to supplement banks and more traditional sources of credit for startup enterprises and nonprofit organizations.

Late in 1994 Congress cleared a bill (HR 3474—PL 103-325) to establish a new federal fund to provide subsidies to alternative "community development financial institutions" (CDFIs), such as credit unions and loan funds, that provided capital to borrowers considered "unbankable" by mainstream lenders.

During the 1992 presidential election campaign, Clinton had promised to seek creation of 100 such alternative lenders. It was the new president's sole banking initiative. Faced with less-than-wholehearted congressional support, constraints on cost and other limitations, Clinton was forced to scale back his proposal.

The bill that finally became law did not establish 100 new community development banks, though it did authorize spending of up to $382 million over four years to assist new and existing lenders whose principal focus was local community development.

Along the way, the bill also served as a magnet for a banking industry-led drive to curb regulations on financial institutions as well as a plan to overhaul the federal government's flood insurance program.

In the end, Clinton was able to declare a measure of victory and bankers got some of what they wanted in the process.

BACKGROUND

Impressed by the example of Chicago's South Shore Bank, a for-profit institution dedicated to developing Chicago's poor and lower-middle-class neighborhoods, Clinton vowed during the 1992 campaign to create similar banks using federal government assistance.

But after hearings in 1993 by the House and Senate Banking committees, the idea of 100 new community development banks was dropped as too costly and unrealistic. Instead, Clinton in July 1993 sent Congress a plan to establish the Community Development Banking and Financial Institutions Fund to provide up to $5 million in federal subsidies to specially designated CDFIs.

Under the Clinton plan, only institutions whose "primary mission" was community development would be eligible for the federal aid. That ruled out participation by conventional lending institutions.

To be eligible for a subsidy, insured financial institutions (credit unions, for instance) were required to match the federal money with private capital on a one-to-one basis. The plan required nontraditional lenders that received federal aid (chiefly community development corporations) to attract private money, though they would not have to provide a one-to-one match. The new CDFI fund could also provide grants for technical assistance to help CDFIs get started or expand existing operations.

HOUSE COMMITTEE ACTION

The House Banking Committee approved the core of Clinton's plan by voice vote Nov. 10, 1993, after giving it a makeover that pleased the banking industry. The committee agreed to an amendment, offered by Floyd H. Flake, D-N.Y., and Tom Ridge, R-Pa., that set aside a third of the money that would be authorized by the bill to reward commercial banks and thrifts for loans made in distressed communities.

The committee sent the Clinton plan to the floor as part of a bill (HR 3474) to provide modest regulatory burden relief to banks and thrifts.

Adoption of the Flake-Ridge amendment, which prevailed on a 36–14 vote, capped years of effort by the two men to find new ways to encourage lending in inner city and low income communities. In 1991, as part of a measure (PL 102-242) that overhauled the federal deposit insurance system, they had won inclusion of a provision to authorize deposit insurance premium rebates for banks and thrifts that made loans in poor neighborhoods. But Congress had yet to appropriate any money for the program. (*Congress and the Nation Vol. VIII, p. 136*)

Their 1993 effort required that one-third of the money appropriated to fund the Clinton plan—up to $127 million—be earmarked to finance the 1991 deposit insurance rebate initiative. The two congressmen, whose plan was opposed by the White House, said their idea would prod mainstream banks to lend more money in poor neighborhoods than alternative lenders possibly could.

Opponents countered that federal law already required banks to make loans in underdeveloped communities and that commercial banks, which were making record profits, did not deserve any federal subsidies.

Also included in the bill were about 40 modest "regulatory relief" provisions drawn from HR 962—a more ambitious deregulatory bill that had strong industry support.

HOUSE FLOOR ACTION

The combination of the watered-down Clinton proposal and the regulatory relief provisions was potent enough that there was effectively little opposition to the bill.

Those who had wanted more out of the community development program understood that backing from the banking industry for HR 3474 was critical to its passage. The House passed HR 3474 by voice vote Nov. 21, as Congress was preparing to adjourn for the year.

SENATE COMMITTEE ACTION

The Senate Banking Committee strongly endorsed a bill embodying Clinton's plan (S 1275—S Rept 103-169) on Sept. 21, 1993, by an 18–1 vote.

As in the House, Senate committee leaders added several unrelated provisions to attract support for the measure, including provisions to encourage a secondary market for small business loans, to curb abusive treatment of minority borrowers by home equity lenders and to ease banks' paperwork burdens.

Committee Chairman Donald W. Riegle Jr., D-Mich., and top panel Republican Alfonse M. D'Amato of New York teamed up to deflect more ambitious banking provisions that might have bogged the measure down and invited fights among competing interest groups.

For example, Christopher J. Dodd, D-Conn., at first indicated an interest in adding provisions to allow banks to open branches across state lines and scale back the ability of banks to sell insurance. Eventually, a separate interstate branching bill (HR 3841) was enacted, though its fate and that of the community development bill became linked toward the end. *Interstate branching and banking, p. 111)*

SENATE FLOOR ACTION

Congress adjourned in 1993 before the full Senate could consider S 1275. The bill came to the Senate floor in March 1994, where it proved to be an attractive magnet for several provisions that fell within the jurisdiction of the Banking Committee but were unable to advance on their own.

The Senate debated and amended S 1275. Then the Senate substituted the text of HR 3474 with the redrawn text of S 1275, and passed the amended version of HR 3474 by voice vote March 17.

On the floor, the Senate agreed to amendments making the following additions to the community development bill:

• **Fair Trade in Financial Services.** The most significant addition was language adapted from a bill proposing the so-called Fair Trade in Financial Services Act.

This widely backed plan would have allowed the Treasury Department to block foreign banks and securities firms from expanding existing operations in the United States or starting new ones if their home countries discriminated against U.S. banks and securities firms.

The amendment, offered by Riegle and D'Amato, was drawn from a bill (S 1527) that had been approved by the Banking Committee on Feb. 10. Similar bills had passed the House and Senate on several occasions, but never been enacted. (*Congress and the Nation Vol. VIII, pp. 187, 198*)

• **Regulatory Changes.** Richard C. Shelby, D-Ala., and Connie Mack, R-Fla., won adoption of several additional regulatory changes sought by banks.

Under the expanded Shelby-Mack plan added on the floor, a greater number of small institutions were made eligible to be scrutinized by federal bank examiners every 18 months instead of each year. Well-capitalized banks with assets of $250 million or less faced the 18-month exam cycle; existing law applied to banks with less than $100 million in assets.

In addition, a provision was added to reduce the number of currency transaction reports that banks had to file to comply with anti–money-laundering laws. The language was similar to a bill (HR 3235) that passed the House March 21 by voice vote.

• **Flood Insurance.** The Senate adopted, by voice vote, an amendment by John Kerry, D-Mass., to shore up the federal government's troubled flood insurance program. The amendment required homeowners who lived in flood plains to purchase federal flood insurance and authorized federal grants for communities that took action to mitigate potential flood hazards. *(Flood insurance, p. 643)*

CONFERENCE, FINAL ACTION

Following Senate passage of HR 3474, it took conference committee members nearly five months to convene, as negotiations lagged. The fate of the community development lending bill became linked to the future of the interstate banking and branching bill (HR 3841), which was generally more popular with the banking industry and its GOP allies.

Congressional Democrats made it clear that they would not finish work on the interstate banking and branching bill unless the community development bill passed as well.

So conferees considered the two bills in tandem, completing work on the two bills July 25.

The House easily adopted the conference report on the bill (H Rept. 103-652) on Aug. 4 by a 410–12 vote. The Senate cleared the bill by voice vote Aug. 9.

The chief sticking point in conference was whether to include the Senate's Fair Trade in Financial Services provisions.

The Fair Trade bill was strongly supported by the Senate conferees, as well as by most conferees drawn from the House Banking Committee. But the effort ran into opposition from the Ways and Means Committee, which argued it would have fractured U.S. trade policy by shifting at least some authority from the Office of the U.S. Trade Representative to Treasury. Conferees from the House Energy and Commerce Committee lined up with Ways and Means and the Senate language was dropped.

Conferees also adopted D'Amato's provisions relaxing certain federal regulations and capital rules to make it easier for the private sector to develop a secondary market for small business loans. They accepted Senate language requiring that consumers be given more information about high-cost home equity loans and they agreed to Senate language to shore up the federal flood insurance program.

MAJOR PROVISIONS

As cleared, the community development financial institutions bill (HR 3474—PL 103-325):

Community Development Fund

• **CDFI Fund.** Established the Community Development Financial Institutions (CDFI) Fund, a wholly owned government corporation, to provide financial and technical assistance to CDFIs. To be eligible for assistance, CDFIs had to have community development as their primary mission, serve communities in need of economic assistance and provide development services to complement their lending activities. State and local government agencies were not eligible.

The CDFI Fund was authorized to receive up to $382 million in appropriations over fiscal 1995–1998. The fund was to be managed by an administrator and overseen by a 15-person board, whose membership was to include several Cabinet secretaries, the administrator of the Small Business Administration and nine private citizens with community development experience. The fund was to provide financial assistance, including equity investments, grants, loans, credit union shares and deposits. It also could provide technical assistance and establish a training program.

No CDFI could receive more than $5 million in aid over any three-year period, though an exception could be made for an institution that sought to establish a subsidiary or affiliate in another state. Institutions receiving federal assistance had to match federal money on a dollar-for-dollar basis, though the matching requirements could be waived for CDFIs that were particularly cash-strapped. Each CDFI receiving assistance was required to issue an annual report to the fund.

• **Community Partnerships.** Allowed community development financial institutions to form partnerships with mainstream banks and bank holding companies, credit unions, nonprofit organizations, state or local government agencies, and investment companies. A community partnership was defined as an agreement between a CDFI and a mainstream institution to provide development services, loans or investments in an underdeveloped area. These combinations were eligible for federal assistance, though any federal funds could be disbursed only to the CDFI.

• **Bank Enterprise Act.** Provided a financing mechanism for the Bank Enterprise Act (BEA), which was designed to give incentives to mainstream banks and thrifts to make loans and provide banking services in distressed communities. One-third of the money appropriated to the CDFI Fund, up to $127 million, was to finance cash rebates to banks under the Bank Enterprise Act program.

The aim of the BEA program, originally established in the 1991 banking law (PL 102-242), was to use federal money to leverage private capital into underdeveloped communities; the administrator of the federal CDFI Fund also was to oversee BEA-related activities. But Congress had never appropriated money to implement the law. *(1991 banking law, Congress and the Nation Vol. VIII, p. 136)*

To receive a rebate, banks and thrifts had to apply to the fund. The administrator was required to rank the applicants according to several criteria, foremost being the extent to which they made equity investments in CDFIs. Other criteria included the extent to which a bank made loans in distressed neighborhoods, participated in community development ventures and provided basic banking services. Insured CDFIs were to have an advantage in the competition for the BEA rebates.

• **Performance Report.** Required the General Accounting Office (GAO), the investigative arm of Congress, to issue a progress report on the CDFI program 30 months after the CDFI administrator was named.

• **Credit Unions.** Authorized additional appropriations of $10 million over fiscal 1995–1998 for the Community Development Credit Union Revolving Loan Fund, an existing fund operated by the National Credit Union Administration.

Home Equity Loan Abuses

- **Reverse Redlining.** Curbed the practice of "reverse redlining," in which nonbank lenders targeted low- and moderate-income homeowners, minorities and the elderly for home equity loans on abusive terms. Typically, such second mortgages had large upfront fees and high interest rates. Repayment terms could be such that homeowners were unable to keep up and ended up losing their homes.

The bill imposed several new disclosure requirements for such high-cost loans to give consumers a better understanding of their terms, including a warning that people could lose their homes if they defaulted. The measure amended the Truth in Lending Act (PL 101-73), a 1989 law that required uniform loan terms and disclosures, to provide additional disclosures for high-cost mortgage loans. Such loans were defined as loans with interest rates higher than 10 percentage points over comparable Treasury securities (the Federal Reserve could adjust this requirement after September 1996) or transactions in which upfront points and fees totaled more than 8 percent of the loan, or $400, whichever was greater.

Such loans were not barred, but creditors (such as finance and mortgage companies) were required to provide borrowers with a special, simplified disclosure notice three days before settlement. The creditor was required to disclose that the consumer could lose his or her home for failure to meet the terms of the loan and that the person still had time to back away from the loan.

In addition, the lender had to reveal the annual percentage rate of the loan and what the monthly payments would be. If a high-cost mortgage (as defined by the law) was made without the required disclosures, the borrower would have three years to rescind the transaction.

- **Prohibited Practices.** Banned several high-cost mortgage lending practices. Consumers had the right to rescind any loan (which met the criteria for a high-cost mortgage loan as defined by the bill) that included the following terms or practices:

- **Prepayment Penalties.** Such loans could not contain prepayment penalties. However, the prohibition applied only to cases in which consumers were carrying heavy debt burdens (a 50 percent debt-to-income ratio, including the loan in question). Prepayment penalties had been used to trap borrowers in abusive mortgages by making it prohibitively expensive to pay off their loans early.

- **Limitations after Default.** Creditors could not charge a higher interest rate after a borrower defaulted than the rate prior to default.

- **Balloon Payments.** High end-of-loan balloon payments—which often misled borrowers by making the loan appear less expensive than it really was—generally were barred when the length of the loan was less than five years.

- **Negative Amortization.** Negative amortization, which occurred when monthly loan payments did not cover the interest due, was barred. Previously, under such terms, the amount owed grew over the life of the loan.

- **Prepaid Payments.** Prepaid payments—periodic loan payments that were consolidated and paid in advance from loan proceeds that otherwise would have gone to the borrower—also were barred.

- **Disregard of Ability to Pay.** Creditors could not extend high-cost mortgage loans unless they had given consideration to a consumer's ability to repay the loans. In determining the ability to pay, creditors were required to evaluate existing or expected income, existing obligations, repayment capacity or employment.

- **Payments to Contractors.** Loan proceeds could not be given directly to home improvement contractors, though they could be extended jointly to the borrower and a contractor. The Federal Reserve retained flexibility to exempt certain mortgage loans from these prohibitions if it determined the exemption to be in the public interest, for example, in the case of certain short-term construction loans that might be covered by the measure. On the other hand, the Federal Reserve was required to prohibit acts and practices that it found unfair, deceptive and aimed at evading the restrictions of the bill.

- **Civil Liability.** Borrowers were given the right to sue creditors who failed to provide adequate disclosures or made loans on prohibited terms. Such civil liability was to equal all finance charges and fees paid by the consumer. State attorneys general had the right to bring actions in federal district courts to enforce the antireverse redlining provisions of the bill for up to three years after violations occurred. This provision was designed to strengthen regulation of finance companies, which were only loosely regulated by the federal government under existing law. The state had to notify the appropriate federal agency responsible for enforcement, and the agency had the right to intervene.

- **Purchaser Liability.** Purchasers of high-cost mortgage loans were subject to any claims that could be raised against the original lender. This provision sought to curb the secondary market in abusive mortgage loans by making them less desirable to purchase. Any seller of a high-cost mortgage was required to provide a notice of potential liability to the purchaser.

Small-Business Loans

- **Secondary Market.** Relaxed capital requirements and other regulations to encourage the private sector secondary market for small-business loans. The idea was to encourage banks to make loans to small businesses by making it easier for them to turn around and sell the loans to Wall Street investment firms, which would package them into securities backed by the loans. The measure removed impediments in existing law that blocked securitization of small-business loans and leases. A new class of "small-business related securities" was created.

The provision was based on the Secondary Mortgage Market Enhancement Act of 1984 (PL 98-440), which had helped pump money into the housing market by removing regulatory impediments to a private sector secondary market in home mortgages. Securities laws governing margin and securities delivery requirements were eased to permit issuers more time to pool and sell small-business related securities.

Small-business securities were considered acceptable investments for banks, thrifts and credit unions, though regulators were authorized to issue rules to ensure safety and soundness of the institution. State and local governments also were authorized to invest in small-business related securities.

Securities and Exchange Commission (SEC) securities registration rules were relaxed to permit issuers of small-business securities to file a single registration form with the SEC rather than separate ones with each state.

• **Capital Requirements.** Changed existing regulations that required banks to maintain capital reserves against loans they sold. (When an institution sold a loan, purchasers usually insisted that the bank retain part of the risk and remain responsible for part of the loan should a borrower default. This was known as selling a loan with "recourse." Under existing rules, banks had to hold 8 percent capital on the total amount of a loan, even if they sold almost all of it.)

The bill changed recourse rules so that banks had to maintain capital reserves only against the portion of loan risk they retained. Only well-capitalized banks were eligible to use the new rules. The total amount of recourse retained by an institution was limited to 15 percent of the institution's risk-based capital reserves, though regulators could increase the limit.

• **Commercial Real Estate Loan Securitization.** In a provision added during Senate floor consideration of the bill and modified in conference, similar regulatory treatment was given to "commercial mortgage related securities." In essence, the regulatory benefits provided under the Secondary Mortgage Market Enhancement Act to home mortgages (and, under this bill, to small-business related securities) also were accorded to securities derived from commercial real estate loans. This provision was designed to shore up the troubled commercial real estate market.

However, the new capital rules that applied to small-business loans regarding recourse on sold loans did not apply to commercial real estate loans.

• **Impact Study.** Directed the Federal Reserve and the SEC to study the impact of small-business and commercial real estate loan securitization on the credit and securities markets. The study was to evaluate the impact of these provisions on business and commercial credit, especially on firms in low- and moderate-income areas, minority- and women-owned businesses, community development programs and community development financial institutions. The study also was to focus on the markets that evolved for securities backed by small business and commercial real estate loans.

• **Capital Access Program.** Authorized $50 million to provide federal grants to state capital access programs. Such programs encouraged banks to make small-business loans that were somewhat riskier than conventional commercial loans, without posing a threat to the safety and soundness of the bank. In a capital access program, banks, borrowers and states contributed to a loss reserve fund that covered losses from loans made under the program. The administrator of the new federal Community Development Financial Institutions Fund was to run the program.

Regulatory Burden Relief

The bill contained more than 50 provisions to reduce bank regulatory burden and paperwork requirements established under recent banking laws. Obtaining this "regulatory relief" was a top priority for bank and thrift lobbyists during the 103rd Congress. The most significant of these provisions:

• **Regulatory Burden Evaluation.** Required bank regulators to consider the burdens and benefits of new banking regulations, especially on smaller banks. New regulations were to take effect on the first day of a calendar quarter.

• **Streamlining Regulations.** Required each federal banking regulator to review and streamline its regulations within two years and eliminate inconsistent, outmoded or duplicative rules. When different regulatory agencies enforced the same laws, they were required to implement the rules in a uniform fashion.

• **Duplicative Filings.** Required bank regulators to work together to curb duplicative reporting requirements.

• **Coordinated Examinations.** Required regulators to coordinate their examinations and, within two years, create a system in which one regulator would take the lead in a unified examination of a bank or thrift and its affiliates.

• **18-Month Examinations.** Raised the asset threshold for eligibility for an 18-month exam cycle from $100 million to $250 million for well-capitalized and well-managed institutions with "outstanding" CAMEL ratings. (CAMEL stood for capital adequacy, asset quality, management, earnings and liquidity; essentially it was a composite rating that signified how strong a bank was.) Existing law required on-site examinations of insured depository institutions every 12 months.

The 18-month exception was broadened to apply to institutions with "good" CAMEL ratings and assets of less than $100 million. After two years, the asset cap could be raised to $175 million for such institutions.

• **Call Report Simplification.** Directed banking agencies to develop a single report of condition (call report) for the filing of core information to regulators. Banks also were permitted to file call reports electronically, and the public was to have electronic access to the information. Banks no longer were required to publish condition reports in local newspapers.

• **Appeals Process.** Required all federal banking agencies and the National Credit Union Administration Board within six months to establish an internal process under which the financial institutions they regulated could appeal regulatory decisions. Each regulator was required to create an ombudsman's office and develop a pilot program to encourage alternative ways such as mediation and arbitration to resolve disputes between institutions and regulators.

• **Currency Transaction Reports.** Permitted banks and thrifts to file currency transaction reports (which detailed cash transactions of $10,000 or more) by electronic means.

• **RESPA Exemptions.** Exempted residential real estate loans for business purposes from coverage under the Real Estate Settlement Procedures Act (RESPA), which required extensive paperwork disclosures at settlement. Also, RESPA mortgage disclosure rules were modified to require that lenders provide a statement indicating whether the bank had sold loans in the past, rather than an analysis of the percentage of loans sold, as required under existing law.

• **Local Boards of Directors.** Required that a majority, rather than two-thirds, of the board of directors of a federally chartered bank reside in the area in which the bank was located.

• **Audit Requirements.** Allowed banks and thrifts with total assets of more than $9 billion and CAMEL ratings of 1 or 2 that were subsidiaries of holding companies to meet independent audit requirements at the holding company level.

• **Real Estate Appraisals.** Encouraged states to enter into reciprocity agreements so that appraisers licensed or certified by one state could perform appraisals in other states. States could not impose excessive fees or burdensome requirements on out-of-state appraisers engaged in temporary practice.

• **Liability on Foreign Accounts.** Provided that domestic banks were not required to repay deposits made at foreign branches in cases of a sovereign action by that country or in cases of war, insurrection or civil strife.

• **Capital Standards Study.** Required the Treasury Department to conduct a study of the effect of risk-based capital standards on the safety and soundness of insured depository institutions, economic growth and the availability of credit, particularly for individuals and small businesses.

• **Interest on Reserves.** Required the Federal Reserve to study the monetary policy and banking implications of whether financial institutions should receive interest on cash reserves kept at the Fed. The Office of Management and Budget and the Congressional Budget Office were to report on the budgetary impact of such interest payments.

• **Consumer Credit Study.** Required the Treasury Department to conduct a study of ways to streamline the consumer lending process.

• **Regulatory Autonomy.** Clarified the degree of autonomy of the Office of the Comptroller of the Currency (OCC) and the Office of Thrift Supervision (OTS) as bureaus of the Treasury Department. The OCC and the OTS were responsible for supervising and regulating national banks and thrift institutions, which held nearly two-thirds of the total assets in U.S. depository institutions. Regulations developed by the OCC and the OTS no longer were to be subject to Treasury Department review or clearance. The FDIC, OCC and Federal Reserve were also authorized to conduct litigation through their own attorneys.

• **Check Hold Study.** Required the Federal Reserve to study whether the existing one-day hold on local checks under the Expedited Funds Availability Act should be extended to two days as a means to combat check fraud.

• **Insider Lending.** Permitted institutions to make a loan to a bank officer without prior approval of the board of directors, provided the loan was secured by the insider borrower's residence. Such loans remained subject to the individual and aggregate insider lending limits. The Federal Reserve also was permitted to exempt officers and directors of nonbank subsidiaries (who were not involved in bank policy-making) from insider lending limits.

• **Radio Advertising.** Streamlined truth-in-lending requirements for radio advertising to permit radio advertisers to reduce the amount of information that had to be disclosed. Additional

information would have to be made available through use of a toll-free telephone number.

• **Management Interlocks.** Allowed individuals who served on boards of directors of more than one bank to apply for a five-year extension of rules barring such "management interlocks." Some individuals had been "grandfathered" repeatedly since laws barring such interlocks took effect in 1978.

• **Fair Credit Reporting Act Amendments.** Required credit bureaus to disclose to consumers more specific information (dates, original payees and amounts) of any checks that formed the foundation for a negative characterization of a consumer.

• **Nonfederally Insured Institutions.** Eased rules that required nonfederally insured institutions to obtain written customer acknowledgment that they knew the institution was not federally insured. In cases of existing customers of the institution, the requirement could be met through mailed notices to the depositor.

• **Application Deadlines.** Required banking regulators to complete action on bank applications within one year of receipt.

• **Right of Rescission.** Directed the Federal Reserve Board to study whether waiving or modifying a consumer's right to rescind a loan within three days—only in cases of loan transactions involving a refinancing or consolidation of existing loans—would benefit consumers.

• **Nonbanking Activities.** Replaced the existing application process for bank holding companies to engage in nonbanking activities with a 60-day-notice procedure. The provision was aimed at simplifying and speeding up the approval process.

• **State Examinations.** Required the Federal Financial Institutions Examination Council to develop standards for state examinations of banks that were also subject to federal exams. Under a provision of the 1991 deposit insurance overhaul law, which required annual bank exams, the federal banking agencies (the FDIC and the Federal Reserve system) could alternate responsibility for such annual examinations. The provision was aimed at spurring federal regulators to allow state authorities to conduct the alternating examinations by establishing federal guidelines for such exams.

• **Revision of Recourse Rules.** Required all federal bank regulators to review and revise their regulations and policies regarding loans sold with recourse. (Recourse occurred when the institution that originally made the loan sold the loan but retained a portion of the responsibility should the borrower default. Banks said existing recourse rules were too stringent because they required banks to hold capital against the entire amount of a loan sold with recourse, even if they had sold almost the entire loan.)

The bill required that financial institutions hold capital only to the amount of retained risk of loans sold with recourse. For example, existing rules required banks to hold 8 percent capital on the total amount of a loan.

If the bank retained recourse of only 5 percent, it would be required to retain 5 percent in capital reserves. Bank regulators could permit institutions to hold less capital than the amount at risk in appropriate situations.

Money Laundering

- **Currency Transaction Reports.** Required the Treasury Department to develop ways to substantially reduce (by 30 percent) the number of currency transaction reports (CTRs) filed by depository institutions under the Bank Secrecy Act. Generally, CTRs had to be filed for every cash transaction of $10,000 or more. This reduction in paperwork was to be accomplished by exempting routine cash transactions between banks and their customers from CTR filing requirements.

- **Exemptions.** Required the Treasury Department to exempt the following from CTR filing requirements: transactions between depository institutions; bank transactions with federal, state and local governments, as well as quasi-governmental entities; and transactions between depository institutions and businesses where the CTRs had little or no value for law enforcement purposes.

  Treasury also was given discretion to exempt transactions between depository institutions and their qualified business customers, though such customers had to be approved by the department.

- **Civil Penalties.** Allowed Treasury to delegate authority to assess civil penalties for violations of the Bank Secrecy Act to the appropriate federal bank regulator. (Treasury's Office of Financial Enforcement had such authority, but it had been criticized for failing to process cases in a timely manner.)

- **State Exemptions.** Permitted the Treasury Department to exempt classes of transactions within a state from Bank Secrecy Act reporting requirements should those transactions fall under state requirements that were substantially similar to federal ones. This could apply, for example, to state-regulated casinos.

- **Money Transmitters.** Required check cashing companies, currency exchanges and other so-called money transmitters to register with the Treasury Department as a way to curb money laundering by entities outside the regulated financial services sector. The aim of the provision was to promote Treasury Department enforcement of money laundering laws and to better educate money transmitters about their responsibilities under the law. The bill expressed the sense of Congress that states should adopt uniform laws to license and regulate money transmitting businesses.

- **Ratzlaf Decision.** Responded to a Supreme Court decision (*Ratzlaf v. U.S.*), which required that the government prove that a defendant not only tried to evade reporting requirements for large currency transactions but also knew such conduct to be against the law. The provision removed the requirement, established by the Court, that the government prove that the defendant knew his or her conduct was illegal.

RTC Financing

A priority for the Clinton administration and its Democratic allies at the start of the 103rd Congress was to finish cleaning up the remnants of the savings and loan debacle of the 1980s.

The need to write the final taxpayer check for the salvage operation was anything but popular. For one thing, with Democrats in control of both the White House and Congress, it soon became clear that most Republicans were not interested in lending their support to the unpopular measure.

In the end, Democrats mustered sufficient votes to pass the bill (S 714—PL 103-204), but only after paring down the administration's $45 billion request by more than half.

Final approval for the $18.3 billion measure came Nov. 23 as the House cleared the conference report on the bill (H Rept 103-380) on a 235–91 vote; the Senate had adopted the conference report three days earlier, 54–45.

President Clinton signed the bill into law Dec. 17, eight months after Treasury Secretary Lloyd Bentsen came before the House and Senate Banking Committees to request $45 billion to finish the thrift salvage job. Of that request, $28 billion was desired for the Resolution Trust Corp. (RTC), the agency charged with closing down failing thrifts, paying off depositors and selling the assets of closed thrifts. Bentsen also requested $17 billion to capitalize the Savings Association Insurance Fund (SAIF), which was scheduled under existing law to take over responsibility for protecting thrift depositors in October 1993.

As the legislation moved through Congress, members proved unwilling to finance the full request, which represented Treasury's worst-case projections of failures. Congress not only cut back the request for the RTC, it refused to provide any money for the SAIF.

The $18.3 billion that was finally sent to the much-criticized cleanup agency came from a previous infusion of cash that reverted to the Treasury on April 1, 1992, when the money was not used by the deadline imposed when Congress appropriated $25 billion in 1991. Essentially, the bill rescinded the prior deadline and restored the money to the RTC. (*1991–1992 thrift bailout efforts, Congress and the Nation Vol. VIII, p. 150*)

The law gave the RTC additional time to take over failing thrifts—from October 1993 to July 1995—which at the same time gave the SAIF an opportunity to collect insurance premiums from healthy thrifts and build a cushion against future failures.

To build support among Democrats, the bill contained provisions that increased the number of RTC contracts awarded to minority businesses and imposed reforms on the troubled agency.

BACKGROUND

Congress had never found it easy to vote to finance the thrift cleanup, which cost taxpayers an estimated $150 billion or more by 1996. The job was so distasteful that as 1993 began, the agency had been left without cash for almost a year. The RTC was created in 1989 under the huge thrift bailout law and received $50 billion initially. The RTC received another $30 billion in the spring of 1991 and $25 billion in November of that year. However, the agency could only spend the money provided in November until April 1, 1992. On that date, $18.3 billion in unspent funds reverted to the Treasury.

Lawmakers tried and failed to pass another financing bill in 1992 when an insufficient number of Republican members pledged to support the Bush administration request. Congressional leaders of both parties had previously passed RTC financing bills by obtaining votes from a majority of both parties.

Without cash, the agency could not close down failing thrifts but instead had to operate the institutions it took over at a loss—costing taxpayers at least $1.1 billion in additional cleanup costs.

SENATE ACTION

On March 25, two weeks after Bentsen came before the Senate Banking Committee to request the full $45 billion, the panel voted 16–3 for a draft bill (eventually reported as S 714—S Rept 103-36) to provide the money—though not without attaching a few strings. Feeling pressure from freshman Democrats, Banking Chairman Donald W. Riegle, D-Mich., pushed through amendments to require Treasury to certify that administrative changes were in place to improve RTC operations before more than $10 billion of the money could be used.

By the time the bill came to the Senate floor May 12, enough pressure had built to cut the bill's pricetag, as well as to attach more strings. Riegle and top Banking Committee Republican Alfonse M. D'Amato, N.Y., offered most of the changes through a substitute amendment adopted by voice vote.

The Senate passed S 714 on May 13 by a bipartisan 61–35 vote after the administration and Banking Committee leaders from both parties agreed to cut $15.2 billion from the administration's revised $42 billion request.

The revised bill directly provided $18.3 billion for the RTC and $8.5 billion for the SAIF, which coincided with the administration's best guess of how much money would actually be needed. The Senate made it clear that the Treasury could not count on receiving enough money to cover a worst-case scenario.

Provisions taken from a companion House bill were included on the Senate floor to improve the RTC's performance in selling off assets from failed thrifts, to prevent fraud and abuse by agency contractors and to give more business opportunities to small businesses, minorities and women. Other changes included limiting bonuses paid to RTC executives and giving federal employees additional whistleblower protections when they reported mismanagement at the RTC and the Federal Deposit Insurance Corporation (FDIC).

Another provision, added by Howard M. Metzenbaum, D-Ohio, sought to rebuild the agency's professional liability section by appointing a new assistant general counsel to shore up the office, which he said fell into disarray under the Bush administration. Metzenbaum also won a 63–32 vote to extend from three to five years the time the RTC had to sue thrift officials after the agency had taken over a failed thrift.

HOUSE ACTION

The House Banking Financial Services Subcommittee approved its version of the bill by voice vote April 12 after cutting the administration's request to $30.3 billion—$18.3 billion for the RTC and $12 billion for the SAIF.

The pressure to reduce the funding levels came as the General Accounting Office (GAO) issued revised estimates that, under favorable conditions, the RTC might need as little as $7 billion to finish the job.

Panel members also significantly restricted the $12 billion in SAIF financing, providing the money only if thrift regulators certified that the industry could not support the fund on its own through premium payments.

The subcommittee bill also contained language, approved on a party-line vote, to set specific quotas for distributing RTC contracts among minorities and women.

The full Banking Committee approved the bill (HR 1340—H Rept 103-103, Part 1) by a 36–16 vote May 6. Before acting, the committee cut the bill's price tag by another $12 billion, eliminating the money for the SAIF altogether, but substituting language authorizing a separate appropriation later. Several committee Democrats agreed with Republicans that the proposed infusion into the thrift insurance fund amounted to a subsidy of the industry.

That language was a part of a compromise worked out with top committee Republican Jim Leach of Iowa, whose vote and help Democrats needed. Other elements of the compromise pared back the subcommittee-approved minority contracting requirements slightly. The most significant provisions required minority subcontractors on agency contracts of $500,000 or more, and gave preference to minorities in bidding for failed institutions located in black and Hispanic neighborhoods. An amendment by Joseph P. Kennedy II, D-Mass., to extend the statute of limitations for RTC lawsuits against officials of failed thrifts from three to five years was adopted by a single vote.

The bill moved to the House Judiciary Committee, which approved it by voice vote June 10 (H Rept 103-103, Part 2), after revising the statute of limitations provision to limit the extension to cases of fraud or "intentional misconduct" in which thrift executives unjustly enriched themselves. Both committees would extend the statute of limitations in cases in which it had already expired.

House leaders delayed bringing the bill to the floor for weeks as they shored up a precarious vote count. Finally, on Sept. 14, a newly revised version passed on a **key vote of 214–208 (R 24–148; D 190–59; I 0–1)**. *(1993 key votes, p. 979)*

Subsequently, the House passed S 714 by voice vote after substituting the text of the House-passed bill. The final House-passed version reduced the authorization for the SAIF from $16 billion to $8 billion and postponed the date when the SAIF was to take over responsibility for failed thrifts for 18 months, to March 31, 1995, in order to give the insurance fund additional time to build up its reserves from deposit insurance premiums.

CONFERENCE, FINAL ACTION

Two months of negotiations by aides produced a House-Senate compromise that conferees agreed to on Nov. 18. The dollar amounts—$18.3 billion in previously appropriated money for the RTC and an authorization of $8 billion for future appropriations to the SAIF—were embodied in the House bill and the result of lengthy negotiations before the conference began.

The final bill extended the statute of limitations for lawsuits against thrift officials, but only in cases of fraud and gross negligence, not simple negligence as under the Senate bill. Also, House-passed provisions requiring minority subcontracts for RTC contracts in excess of $500,000 were modified slightly.

The conference report squeaked through the Senate on Nov. 20 on a 54–45 vote that required Majority Leader George J. Mitchell, D-Maine, to prevail upon several Democrats to switch their votes to yes.

In the House, the Democratic leadership had been skittish throughout the year about bringing the bill to the floor. With a Democrat in the White House, Republicans essentially considered themselves off the hook.

That meant scores of reluctant Democrats had to be cajoled into voting for the unpopular bill. But House members generally did not get any criticism at home after voting for the measure the first time around. In the end, the conference report was cleared by the House on Nov. 23 by 235–91—a relatively wide margin.

MAJOR PROVISIONS

As cleared, the RTC financing bill (S 714—PL 103-204):

RTC Financing

• Appropriated $18.3 billion to the RTC to cover depositor losses in failed thrifts. The money was provided by removing the April 1, 1992, deadline for using $25 billion appropriated in 1991 (PL 102-233). Only $6.7 billion of that appropriation was used by the prior law deadline. $10 billion could be used immediately; the remaining $8.3 billion could be used after the secretary of the Treasury certified that the RTC was complying with "management reforms" mandated under the bill.

RTC Termination

• Set Dec. 31, 1995, as the termination date for the RTC, instead of Dec. 31, 1996, as under prior law. The Federal Deposit Insurance Corporation (FDIC) was to assume responsibility for all RTC activities, including sales of remaining thrift assets.

In addition, the period during which the RTC was to be appointed conservator or receiver of failed thrifts was extended. The agency's responsibility for such institutions expired Sept. 30, 1993; it was extended to a date to be determined by the secretary of the Treasury between Jan. 1 and July 1, 1995. The extension provided additional time for deposit insurance premiums to flow into the undercapitalized Savings Association Insurance Fund (SAIF), to better capitalize it for resolving failed institutions.

Savings Association Insurance Fund

• **SAIF Financing.** Reduced the authorization for future SAIF appropriations from $32 billion to $8 billion and limited the use of such money to losses incurred by the SAIF in fiscal 1994–1998. The SAIF was the thrift industry's new insurance fund, and was operated by the FDIC. The SAIF was to assume from the RTC responsibility for thrifts that failed after the RTC's authority to take institutions into conservatorship or receivership lapsed in 1995.

The requirement under prior law that the Treasury capitalize the SAIF to $8.8 billion by fiscal 1999 was repealed.

Any money transferred to the SAIF that was not needed to pay off depositors reverted to the Treasury.

Any RTC money remaining after that agency finished its portion of the cleanup could be turned over to the SAIF, starting at the end of 1995. The money was subject to certification requirements outlined below.

• **Certification.** Required the chairman of the FDIC to certify to Congress each fiscal year that several conditions were met before any appropriated money flowed to the SAIF. Among the conditions were requirements that the money was needed to cover losses expected in the coming year and that an increase in thrift deposit insurance premiums would have been detrimental to the industry's financial health and led to additional thrift failures.

The FDIC was given flexibility to extend the 15-year schedule under which the SAIF was to be fully capitalized, thereby allowing the FDIC to reduce deposit insurance premiums. Such action could only be taken if the FDIC determined that such a move increased SAIF revenue by allowing more institutions to remain viable to pay premiums.

RTC Management Reforms

Required the RTC to adopt a series of management reforms, including:

• Development of a comprehensive business plan for the balance of the cleanup.

• Creation of a small investor program under which the RTC was generally required to sell real property assets on an individual basis for 120 days after acquiring such assets.

• Appointment of a chief financial officer, deputy chief executive officer and assistant general counsel for the agency.

• Strengthening of its system for awarding and overseeing contracts, including those for legal services.

• Reduction of the cost of the RTC's legal services by using staff attorneys whenever they could provide the same quality legal services as outside counsel at the same or lower cost.

• Creation of a "client responsiveness" unit at every RTC regional office.

• Establishment of a process for business and commercial borrowers to appeal lending decisions made by the RTC when it managed failed thrifts.

Minority Contracting

Required the RTC to implement provisions designed to improve the agency's record in providing business opportunities to minorities and women when issuing RTC contracts or selling assets. In implementing these provisions, the RTC was required to continue to conduct the bailout in a manner that resulted in the least cost to taxpayers.

The RTC was required to:

• **Division of Minority and Women's Programs.** Create and maintain a Division of Minorities and Women's Programs.

• **Basic Ordering Agreements.** Take greater steps to ensure that lists of eligible contractors (basic ordering agreements) contained as many minority- and women-owned businesses as possible.

- **Parity Guidelines.** Establish guidelines that did not have the force of law for achieving the goal of a reasonably even distribution of contracts awarded to minority- and women-owned businesses and law firms among various subgroups such as women, blacks, Hispanics and Asian Americans.

- **Subcontracting Requirements.** Require any contractor that received an RTC contract worth $500,000 or more for services (such as accounting or legal services) to subcontract with minority- or women-owned businesses unless no such subcontractor was available. This provision did not apply if such subcontracting significantly increased the cost of the contract or hindered the ability of the contractor to fulfill the contract.

- **Sanctions.** Draft sanctions, including contract penalties and suspensions for contractors who did not comply with joint venturing and minority subcontracting rules.

- **Minority Preference in Acquisition of Institutions.** Give priority to minorities and minority-owned businesses that bid for thrifts in RTC conservatorship or receivership that were in minority neighborhoods, provided that such a sale did not result in greater cost to the taxpayer than would nonminority offers.

RTC-FDIC Transition

Extended to the FDIC a series of RTC regulations concerning management practices. The provisions:

- **Conflict of Interest.** Required the FDIC to issue regulations governing agency employees or contractors regarding conflict of interest, ethical responsibilities and the use of confidential information by independent contractors.

- **Restrictions on Asset Sales.** Barred those who had engaged in questionable or illegal practices from buying assets from the FDIC.

- **Asset Disposition Division.** Established a new and separate Division of Asset Disposition within the FDIC, effective July 1, 1995, to conduct the agency's liquidation of insured banks and thrifts and disposition of their assets. The provision merged the asset disposition functions of the SAIF and the BIF.

Affordable Housing

- **Housing Stock.** Expanded the existing affordable housing programs of the RTC and the FDIC by broadening the potential affordable housing stock of the two agencies. Under the programs, the RTC and the FDIC sold such housing at market or below-market prices and provided loans at market or below-market rates to individuals and groups to purchase housing stock from failed thrifts and banks.

The limit for RTC-eligible single-family properties was raised from $67,500 to $101,250, but money to cover the cost had to be separately appropriated.

- **Information.** Required the FDIC and RTC to provide additional information on the availability of residential properties to agencies and housing groups.

- **Joint Management.** Unified the management of the RTC and FDIC affordable housing programs to run the programs more efficiently and save administrative costs.

- **Property Sales.** Gave tenants of residential properties acquired by the RTC and the FDIC right of first refusal to purchase the properties. Groups that housed the homeless were given preference in buying RTC and FDIC properties, provided that the revenue from such sales was substantially similar to other sales under the affordable housing program.

- **Housing Opportunity Hotline.** Required each of the Federal Home Loan Banks to establish a toll-free hotline to provide information on federally owned and controlled single-family homes to prospective buyers. Properties held by the Farmers Home Administration, the FDIC, the Federal National Mortgage Association, the Federal Home Loan Mortgage Corporation, the GSA, the Department of Housing and Urban Development, the RTC and the Department of Veterans Affairs were to be covered.

Legal Liabilities

- **Statute of Limitations.** Increased the statute of limitations on RTC civil lawsuits from three years to five, or to the period provided in state law, whichever was longer, to give agency lawyers additional time to sue thrift officials for negligence and fraud.

In cases in which the statute of limitations already had expired, claims could be revived for fraud and intentional misconduct resulting in unjust enrichment or substantial loss to the thrift. Such offenses typically were not covered by liability insurance policies purchased for thrift officers and directors.

If the statute of limitations had not yet expired, it was extended for a wider set of offenses, including gross negligence.

Miscellaneous

- **Whistleblower Protection.** Expanded whistleblower protections to include RTC employees and contractors who reported agency problems to authorities. The measure protected those who reported possible violations of laws or regulations by RTC officials, gross mismanagement and abuses of authority. Prior law applied whistleblower protections only to those who reported "violations of law or regulation."

- **BIF Moratorium.** Continued an existing moratorium on SAIF members converting to BIF membership until the SAIF had attained its designated reserve ratio of 1.25 percent. This provision reflected concerns that thrifts would be tempted to convert to banks in order to elude higher deposit insurance premiums.

- **Shareholder Protection.** BIF and SAIF money could be used only to protect insured depositors and not to benefit shareholders of insured institutions in any manner. ❑

Securities Market Regulation

Congress in November 1993 cleared a bill to strengthen regulation of the nation's $2.3 trillion market in U.S. Treasury securities. The effort followed a 1991 scandal involving Salomon Brothers Inc. and came only after the Clinton administration and key House members reached a compromise that ended a fight among the Treasury Department, the Securities and Exchange Commission (SEC) and competing House committees over how much new authority to give the SEC.

The bill grew out of a 1991 bid-rigging scandal in which Salomon Brothers bought larger-than-permitted stakes in government bonds. A prior effort to beef up oversight collapsed in 1992 amid a jurisdictional and procedural fight between the House Energy and Commerce and Banking committees. *(Congress and the Nation Vol. VIII, p. 158)*

The bill (S 422—PL 103-202) permanently renewed the 1986 Government Securities Act, which gave Treasury authority to issue rules on government bond auctions and set capital levels for bond traders.

The new law gave the SEC new access to the transaction records of securities dealers to make it easier for the agency to investigate allegations of illegal trading activity. It also gave Treasury authority to require dealers with large holdings of federal debt to report such positions in an effort to improve oversight of the market.

The Senate approved the bill Nov. 22 by voice vote; the House cleared it the next day, also by voice vote.

BACKGROUND

The 1986 Government Securities Act had expired in 1991 and had been on its way to routine reauthorization that year when the loosely regulated government securities market was rocked by the Salomon Brothers scandal. The Wall Street firm was the largest of about 40 so-called primary dealers in government bonds—firms that bought government securities from the Federal Reserve Bank of New York. Salomon was found to have purchased larger-than-allowed stakes at government auctions.

Treasury had already taken steps to curb the potential for abuses in the market, but senior members of the House Energy and Commerce Committee pushed an ambitious effort in 1992 to give the SEC authority over the secondary market, where banks and securities firms sold government debt to individual and institutional investors.

The 1992 effort would have given the SEC unprecedented authority over the activities of banks. The bill died when the Energy and Commerce Committee tried to bring it to the House floor, and House Banking Committee members joined with the Bush administration Treasury Department and the Federal Reserve Board to oppose it.

SENATE ACTION

The Senate acted first, passing S 422 on July 22 by voice vote. The Banking Committee had approved the bill by a vote of 19–0 on May 27 (S Rept 103-109).

The bill, as passed by the Senate, permanently extended the Treasury's regulatory authority over the market. The bill also required federal banking regulators to write sales practice rules for banks that dealt in government securities. It required the National Association of Securities Dealers (NASD) to write rules for securities brokers, subject to SEC approval. Unlike the House approach from a year earlier, the SEC was not to have authority over the secondary market in government bonds.

HOUSE ACTION

The House Energy and Commerce Subcommittee on Telecommunications and Finance approved its version (HR 618) by voice vote on July 22. It was nearly identical to the panel's 1992 bill, but Chairman Edward J. Markey, D-Mass., was already negotiating changes with Treasury, the SEC and bipartisan committee leaders.

A compromise was reached in early August, and the full committee approved the amended version of the bill on Sept. 14 by voice vote (H Rept 103-255).

The new bill provided the framework for the final measure: Bank regulators won regulatory authority over banks that marketed securities and the SEC retained authority over nonbank securities broker-dealers.

The House passed HR 618 Oct. 5 by voice vote after minor changes were made to incorporate input from the Banking and Ways and Means committees. Subsequently, the House passed S 422 by voice vote after substituting the language of HR 618.

The version of S 422 that was signed into law hewed closely to the House-passed bill. Several minor changes were made through informal negotiations and without holding a conference. Instead, on Nov. 22, the Senate agreed by voice vote to the House amendments to S 422 (the text of the House-passed bill) with further amendments incorporating the negotiated changes.

One of those changes was to add language imposing regulatory conditions on so-called limited partnership roll-ups. *(Partnership roll-ups, p. 127)*

The House agreed to the Senate amendments by voice vote the next day, clearing the bill for President Clinton. He signed it into law Dec. 17.

As cleared, the government securities regulation provisions of the bill (S 422—PL 103-202):

• Permanently extended Treasury's regulatory authority over capital and recordkeeping requirements for dealers of government securities.

• Authorized the Securities and Exchange Commission (SEC) to demand the records of securities brokers to make it easier for the agency to reconstruct trades when making an investigation. The SEC was not given comparable authority over commercial banks.

• Authorized the Treasury Department to require banks, Wall Street firms and others with large positions in government securities to report their holding to the Federal Reserve Bank of New York to make it easier for regulators to monitor the market. The information had to be provided to the SEC.

• Required securities brokers and dealers to establish internal policies to prevent and detect fraud and market manipulation by their employees, subject to oversight by Treasury and the SEC.

• Authorized the appropriate regulatory agency to issue rules governing sales practices for financial institutions that dealt in government securities and authorized the National Association of Securities Dealers to regulate its members' transactions in government securities. ❑

Partnership Roll-ups

After a three-year debate prompted by horror stories of investor losses, Congress cleared legislation on Nov. 23, 1993, aimed at curbing abusive "roll-ups" of limited partnerships.

The measure gave investors new tools to fight roll-up deals, which occurred when limited partnerships were converted into publicly traded corporations, often leaving some investors holding stock in the new corporation that had no value. The measure became law after its provisions were incorporated into an unrelated bill (S 422—PL 103-202) to strengthen regulation of the market in U.S. government securities (*Government securities regulation, p. 125*)

BACKGROUND

Limited partnerships typically were long-term, nontraded investments in oil and gas or real estate ventures, in which the investors pooled their money under the management of a general partner. These partnerships were designed to be held for a fixed term and then liquidated.

In a roll-up, general partners typically combined several partnerships into a single public company and the investors received stock in exchange for their partnership shares. Often the roll-up left limited partner investors with a loss, even as the managing partners got rich through the roll-up. Almost all investors in a roll-up lost money, bill sponsors said, as the new stock plummeted from its promised value.

Some members of Congress, particularly Sen. Phil Gramm, R-Texas, argued that roll-ups offered a way out of a failing venture. (Many limited partnerships had invested in the lagging oil and gas and real estate industries.)

Congress first began to look at the issue in 1991, when the House passed a bill to require that stock prospectuses for roll-ups be written more clearly, to make it easier for limited partners to communicate with each other to fight a roll-up, and to bar the practice of paying proxy solicitors only for votes in favor of a roll-up. (*Congress and the Nation Vol. VIII, p. 158*)

Gramm had single-handedly blocked action in the 102nd Congress; however, when the 103rd Congress opened, he was ready to make a deal. The ideas included in the 1991 effort had already been implemented through regulations by the Securities and Exchange Commission (SEC) and the National Association of Securities Dealers (NASD).

HOUSE ACTION

Bill sponsors wanted to codify and move beyond the SEC and NASD rules. In addition, they wanted to offer partners who opposed a roll-up so-called dissenting rights—the option to receive different compensation, such as cash or a bond, instead of the stock issue.

Action started in the House, which passed the bill (HR 617—H Rept 103-21) on March 2 by a 408–6 vote. The Energy and Commerce Committee had approved the bill by voice vote Feb. 23; the panel's Telecommunications and Finance Subcommittee had given the bill voice vote approval five days earlier.

As passed by the House, the bill required roll-up sponsors to provide an independent "fairness opinion" of proposed roll-ups and to protect "dissenter's rights." It also codified the SEC and NASD roll-up rules.

SENATE ACTION

The Senate Banking Committee had approved its own roll-up bill (S 424—S Rept 103-121) by an 18–0 vote June 29, after a deal between Gramm and Sen. Christopher J. Dodd, D-Conn., broke a two-year impasse on the issue within the committee. The Senate passed the bill by voice vote Aug. 6.

The Senate bill was similar to the House measure in some respects, though it did not require that investors receive an independent evaluation of a roll-up and it contained provisions to make it easier for roll-ups deemed nonabusive to go forward.

FINAL ACTION

Gramm had allowed S 424 to pass the Senate, but he balked at allowing the bill to go to conference with the House on HR 617, where his leverage might be lessened.

Instead, the House and Senate reached a compromise that included key elements of the Gramm-Dodd deal. The Senate attached the compromise language to a separate measure (S 422) to beef up regulation of the government securities market, which it passed by voice vote Nov. 22. The House cleared S 422 by voice vote Nov. 23.

PROVISIONS

As cleared, the roll-up provisions of the securities bill (S 422—PL 103-202):

• **Fairness Opinion.** Deleted a House provision to require "fairness opinions" of proposed roll-ups, but it encouraged them to do so. Any roll-up sponsor who did not provide such an independent opinion had to say why. Any such opinions had to disclose whether the author had access to all of the relevant books or had a financial stake in the roll-up.

• **Exemptions.** Included Senate language exempting several types of nonabusive roll-ups from the new law. "Arm's-length" transactions proposed by third parties were allowed, provided they were approved by two-thirds of the partnership and did not provide special compensation to the general partners. Also exempted were roll-ups that offered investors seasoned securities with an easy-to-ascertain value or those approved by three-fourths of the limited partners.

• **Dissenters' Rights.** Included House language to require investors to receive dissenters' rights such as cash or retention of the original investment instead of the stock issue.

• **Regulatory Changes.** Codified into law the regulatory changes previously made by the Securities and Exchange Commission and the National Association of Securities Dealers. ❏

Credit Reporting Requirements

A widely backed bid to beef up the law governing companies that compiled and furnished credit information died at the end of the 103rd Congress in the face of opposition from a single Senate Republican.

The House and Senate each passed by sweeping margins bills to update and tighten the 1970 Fair Credit Reporting Act, which set rules for the booming market for consumer credit information.

Generally, the bills sought to make it easier for consumers to get access to their credit reports and challenge erroneous information. Strengthening the law was a top priority for consumer groups hoping to capitalize on the Democratic takeover of the White House.

The House and Senate considered several bills that would have restricted the circumstances under which consumer credit reports were released, made it easier for consumers to challenge mistakes in credit reports and placed banks and certain other businesses under the law for the first time.

The Senate overwhelmingly passed its bill (S 783) in May 1994. And the House passed different versions of the Senate bill and two House bills (HR 1015, HR 5178) in June, September and October of that year, each by voice votes.

But Sen. Phil Gramm, R-Texas, a foe of the bill, placed a procedural "hold" on further Senate action on any of the measures and the overhaul effort died at the end of the 103rd Congress.

BACKGROUND

Since the Fair Credit Reporting Act was enacted in 1970, the credit reporting industry had grown enormously, and computerization had made it much easier to collect and disseminate information about consumers' credit histories. This explosive growth had been accompanied by major problems, as mistakes in credit reports resulted in consumers being denied mortgages and other credit.

An effort to revise the law foundered in 1992 as supporters shelved the measure after losing a House floor vote on an amendment that would have permitted states to preserve stricter credit reporting standards than would have been imposed by federal law. *(Congress and the Nation Vol. VIII, p. 157)*

Still, there was widespread support for the underlying proposal, both among consumer groups that wanted to curb abuses and among many companies that stood to gain the ability to share consumer credit information with their affiliates and gain a marketing boost.

SENATE ACTION

The Senate Banking Committee, working along bipartisan lines, approved S 783 (S Rept 103-209) by a 15–4 vote on Oct. 28, 1993, with conservative Republicans casting the "nays."

The Senate measure's framework generally resembled the 1992 House effort, but in deference to consumer groups, bill sponsors Richard H. Bryan, D-Nev., and Christopher S. Bond, R-Mo., eventually agreed to drop the so-called preemption language that would have replaced tougher state laws with a uniform federal standard. In exchange, they also dropped a provision that would have required credit bureaus to give free credit reports to consumers who requested them.

The Senate bill would have required credit bureaus to reinvestigate information in credit reports that was challenged by consumers. It would have required banks, retailers and other furnishers of credit information to clean up their files to ensure such data were correct. And it would have required credit bureaus to set up toll-free telephone lines to make it easier for consumers to challenge errors in their reports.

The Senate passed S 783 May 4, 1994 by a 87–10 vote, after adopting several changes aimed at placating business interests.

Under the amended bill, lenders and other suppliers of credit could have been fined by the Federal Trade Commission (FTC) for providing bad information to credit bureaus only if they violated FTC cease and desist orders; the committee-approved bill would have permitted fines for lesser offenses.

The Senate-passed bill also would have permitted credit bureaus to charge $3 for credit reports with a maximum $3 fee. Its preemption of state laws would have expired after six years. And, in a win for business groups, existing restrictions on the use of credit information for direct marketing purposes would have been relaxed.

HOUSE ACTION

A more partisan atmosphere characterized House consideration of the proposal. By a party-line 17–12 vote, the House Banking Subcommittee on Consumer Credit approved its bill (HR 1015) on Nov. 19, 1993.

HR 1015 contained no state-law preemption; it would have required free reports on request; and, in a provision that ensured stout industry opposition, it would have allowed consumers to sue businesses that negligently furnished inaccurate credit information to credit bureaus.

Subcommittee member Larry LaRocco, D-Idaho, was poised to offer the significantly narrower language of the Senate committee bill as a substitute amendment, but he fell just shy of rounding up enough votes. Instead, Joseph P. Kennedy II, D-Mass., the subcommittee's chairman, agree to draw up an amendment for full committee consideration that would make a few changes, among them to make it easier for credit information to be used for direct marketing. The close call in subcommittee had made it clear that business-friendly changes had to be made if the bill was going to pass the House.

Some of those changes were made to HR 1015 during a short but rancorous markup by the full Banking Committee on March 3, 1994. The committee approved the bill by a party-line 29–20 vote (H Rept 103-486). The committee had previously met on Feb. 9 in a contentious session where the necessary quorum evaporated and House Banking Committee Chairman Henry B. Gonzalez, D-Texas, was forced to adjourn the session.

The most contentious debate by the full Banking Committee involved allowing affiliated companies—banks, other lenders and credit card companies, for example, that were jointly owned—to share credit information about their clients.

After much debate, the committee ultimately settled precariously on a provision, offered by Richard H. Baker, R-La., and Cal Dooley, D-Calif., to permit increased information sharing, provided that lenders told their customers of the practice and received explicit permission to share the information. The Baker-Dooley language was adopted by a 30–19 vote on Feb. 9.

Further revisions to the affiliate sharing language that would have given consumers additional rights were outlined in a tentative compromise between Kennedy and Baker just prior to the March 3 markup. The deal collapsed in full public view when Baker pulled out after seeing the legislative language.

When the House took up HR 1015, on June 13, it had been revised to appease Republican opponents and the rancor was gone; Kennedy had agreed to remove several provisions objectionable to business. The House passed the bill by voice vote under suspension of the rules.

The bill, as passed, now generally hewed closely to S 783, which had already passed the Senate. Removed were provisions permitting consumers and consumer groups to sue furnishers of credit information. The compromise version also required consumers to pay a $3 fee to obtain a credit report. Federal law would have preempted state credit reporting laws for eight years.

FINAL ACTION

Informal negotiations between the House and Senate—rather than a formal conference—produced yet another compromise that was embodied in a new version of S 783 that the House passed by voice vote on Sept. 27.

The revised bill generally mirrored the House- and Senate-passed versions; the main element of the compromise was to leave to the courts the question of whether credit information could be used in lists sold to direct marketing companies. The Senate bill had permitted such information to be used in limited ways for marketing purposes; the House bill preserved existing law that generally barred the practice.

Resistance remained in the Senate, however, and Gramm refused to allow the House-passed compromise version of S 783 to come to the floor for a last vote that would have cleared it for the president. He not only opposed the credit reporting changes; he had been unsuccessful in attaching an unrelated provision to override a Texas state law that essentially prohibited home equity loans. Gonzalez had fought to preserve the Texas law.

In a final, desperate attempt to enact the credit bill before adjournment, the House by voice vote on Oct. 5 passed a new bill (HR 5178) that incorporated the compromise from S 783 plus several nongermane sweeteners aimed at Gramm's Senate colleagues. Gramm did not budge, however, and the bills died. ❏

Insurance Redlining

Concluding a fight chiefly among Democrats, the House in 1994 passed a bill (HR 1188) aimed at fighting insurance "redlining," the practice of refusing to sell policies in poor or minority neighborhoods.

The action featured a fight between liberal Democrats on the Banking Committee—who wanted insurance companies to meet tougher rules—and the more pro-industry Democrats on the Energy and Commerce Committee, who eventually seized control over the process.

By the time the bill reached the floor, the jurisdictional fight took on larger proportions than the substantive debate.

On July 20, 1994, the House passed the Energy and Commerce version of HR 1188 by voice vote. The vote came a year after the two committees began wrestling with the issue and over which panel should have jurisdiction over it. The Senate took no action on HR 1188 and had no companion bill, so the effort died at the end of the 103rd Congress.

The House-passed bill required all but the smallest insurance companies that wrote home and automobile policies in the nation's 25 largest urban areas to report information on the types and number of policies issued, broken out by five-digit ZIP code. The reporting requirements were to begin in 1995 and last for five years, with a possible two-year extension.

The bill was patterned after the Home Mortgage Disclosure Act, a 1975 law that required mortgage lenders to report loan data; the law had proven successful in documenting lending discrimination and had prompted regulators to crack down.

Supporters from both committees cited evidence that insurance companies frequently refused to sell property and casualty insurance policies in black and Hispanic inner-city neighborhoods. Consumer advocates supported the effort; Republicans and the insurance industry generally opposed it as too burdensome.

During floor debate, the Banking Committee was beaten soundly in its attempts to require that insurance companies make available to regulators and citizens precise information regarding insurance sales within smaller geographic areas than ZIP codes.

HOUSE SUBCOMMITTEE ACTION

The House Energy and Commerce Subcommittee on Commerce, Consumer Protection and Competitiveness approved HR 1188 by voice vote on July 28, 1993. To win approval, Subcommittee Chairman Cardiss Collins, D-Ill., had to make concessions to the insurance lobby.

Collins circulated a version of the bill that would have required companies to disclose how many policies they sold and how many agents they employed in each city. The information was to be broken down by census tract and was required of the 150 largest cities.

Two of Collins's Democratic colleagues—Jim Slattery of Kansas and J. Roy Rowland of Georgia—were set to side with Republicans, however, and to support an industry-supported GOP amendment to sharply scale back the bill's data reporting requirements.

Collins agreed to changes that were adopted by voice vote to limit reporting areas to five-digit ZIP codes instead of the more precise census tract; to limit the bill's scope to the 25 largest metropolitan areas; and to cap the bill's lifespan at five years.

The following day, the House Banking Subcommittee on Consumer Credit and Insurance approved HR 1257—a bill that was much tougher on the insurance industry—on a party-line 19–12 vote, with Independent Bernard Sanders of Vermont siding with Democrats.

The subcommittee was stocked with urban liberal Democrats, and Joseph P. Kennedy II, D-Mass., the subcommittee's chairman and the bill's sponsor, had little difficulty in staving off industry-backed amendments.

Kennedy's bill contained many provisions included in Collins's original measure: It applied to 150 cities, required data to be collected by census tract and required companies to report how much they paid in claims to specific neighborhoods, to allow analysts to determine whether higher premiums to minority neighborhoods were merited.

HOUSE COMMITTEE ACTION

The full Energy and Commerce Committee approved HR 1188 by voice vote on Sept. 14 (H Rept 103-270). Even though Republicans generally disliked the bill, they generally cooperated in moving it along because they did not want the pending Banking Committee bill to be the only option available for floor debate.

The Banking Committee approved HR 1257 on Sept. 22 by a party-line 30–19 vote (H Rept 103-302, Part 1). Banking Committee sponsors said the Clinton administration backed its tougher measure. That whipped up the turf battle with Energy and Commerce, whose chairman, John D. Dingell, D-Mich., complained that the administration had taken sides in a jurisdictional fight.

The issue fell to the House parliamentarian, who agreed with Dingell that Energy and Commerce had primary jurisdiction over the issue and awarded Energy and Commerce jurisdiction over Banking's bill but not vice versa. Energy and Commerce then approved an amended version of HR 1257 (H Rept 103-302, Part 2), which was identical to HR 1188.

With Republicans complaining that there was no evidence of a national problem for the bill to address, HR 1188 finally came to the House floor on July 20, 1994. A series of amendments intended to move the bill back in the direction of the Banking Committee's version were overwhelmingly rejected. The House eventually passed the bill by voice vote, but there was no action in the Senate and it died. ❑

Single Bank Regulator

The Clinton administration in late 1993 unveiled a plan to create a single bank regulator to regulate the banking and thrift industries, but the idea faced strong opposition from the Federal Reserve Board and was shelved a few months later.

Treasury Secretary Lloyd Bentsen on Nov. 23 proposed the measure, which would have created a single Federal Banking Commission to take over the supervisory functions of the four bank and thrift regulators—the Federal Reserve, the Federal Deposit Insurance Corporation (FDIC), the Office of the Comptroller of the Currency (OCC) and the Office of Thrift Supervision (OTS). The plan was similar to bills (HR 1214; S 1633) backed by Rep. Henry B. Gonzalez, D-Texas, and Sen. Donald W. Riegle Jr., D-Mich., the chairmen of the House and Senate Banking committees.

Bentsen said the plan would have streamlined the system and eliminated "a spider's web of overlapping jurisdictions" that required most banks to answer to more than one regulator.

Under the proposal, the FDIC and the Federal Reserve would have largely lost their supervisory roles. The FDIC would have continued to provide deposit insurance to banks and savings and loan associations, and the Fed would have continued to conduct monetary policy. The functions of the OCC and the OTS would have been melded into the new agency. The administration's plan outlined a five-person board: three presidentially appointed members, including a chairman whose four-year term coincided with the president's, plus the secretary of the Treasury and a member of the Federal Reserve Board.

But the administration's plan immediately drew fire from the Fed, which said that for the central bank to keep a "hands-on role in banking supervision is essential to carrying out the Federal Reserve's responsibilities for the stability of the financial system."

As the Senate Banking Committee held hearings on the plan in early March 1994, it was apparent that the Clinton plan was in deep trouble, mostly as a result of the Fed's aggressive lobbying.

Shortly after, the Clinton Treasury pulled the plug, concluding that opposition from the Fed and the nation's banks, many of which expressed concern about having to report to a monolithic regulator instead of the existing four-regulator system. State-chartered banks, in particular—most of which were overseen by the FDIC—said they were worried that a single regulator would have reined in the innovative impulses of the state banking system.

After it became clear that Treasury's original plan was dead, representatives from the administration and the Fed came up with a potential compromise. Under their tentative deal, the new Federal Banking Commission was to assume the regulatory duties of the OCC, which supervised federally chartered banks, the OTS and the FDIC. The Fed was to retain regulatory authority over the largest bank holding companies as well as the 950 or so state-chartered banks it supervised under existing law.

The proposed compromise might have eased the Fed's objections sufficiently for the legislation to move. But Gonzalez and Riegle, the top supporters of the single regulator plan, gave the proposal a cool reception, and the idea died.

1995–1996

The first two years of a Republican-controlled Congress in two generations might have been expected to result in bold changes in banking and securities laws. In fact, the 1994 elections did little to change the playing field for financial regulation on Capitol Hill.

Once more, legislators had to resolve issues stemming from the savings and loan debacle of the late 1980s, as the costs of the thrift salvage operation continued to bedevil lawmakers.

Once more, Congress failed to navigate a lobbying minefield to find a way to overhaul the Depression-era law that segregated commercial banking from securities underwriting and dealing.

Congress did manage in those two years to make detailed changes in securities and banking laws in an effort to eliminate regulations deemed overly burdensome and unnecessary. These changes, though, were not entirely front-page material and did not attract much notice outside the House and Senate

Banking and House Commerce committees, or from the public at large.

Deposit Insurance Funds

Congress in 1996 enacted a controversial plan to shore up the insurance fund that protected thrift deposits, driven by two compelling concerns.

First, the Savings Association Insurance Fund (SAIF), which was to take responsibility for protecting thrift deposits from the Resolution Trust Corporation (RTC) in 1995, was far undercapitalized. Second, Congress needed to find budget "offsets" for new spending programs requested by the Clinton administration, and one method of financing the SAIF would look on the government's books like a budgetary windfall.

The measure that was enacted required thrifts to pay a large one-time assessment into the SAIF. It also required banks to pick up a share of the cost of financing the thrift salvage operations of the late 1980s and 1990s. The upshot of those cash flows was a bit of budget legerdemain that allowed the proposal to be counted as a budget savings of $3.1 billion.

The SAIF measure never moved as a free-standing bill; its budgetary effects made it too valuable as a device to offset the cost of spending increases.

Sponsors won enactment of the SAIF provisions by including them in an omnibus spending bill for fiscal 1997 (HR 3610—PL 104-208). That bill, passed at the end of September 1996, wrapped together six of the 13 regular appropriations bills for the year. *(Fiscal 1997 appropriations, p. 76)*

Before the victory, however, came two setbacks. Sponsors first chose to attach the SAIF language to the 1995 budget reconciliation bill (HR 2491), which died following President Clinton's veto Dec. 6, 1995. The SAIF measure was then attached to a one-day emergency spending bill in April 1996. The House Rules Committee knocked the language out, however, before the emergency bill went to the floor.

Once included in the end-of-year omnibus bill, the SAIF provisions served as a magnet that attracted other elements of the banking agenda and guided them into law also as part of PL 104-208. *(Bank regulatory relief, p. 136)*

BACKGROUND

The SAIF was established under the 1989 bailout law (PL 101-73) to assume responsibility for protecting thrift deposits after the RTC concluded its salvage operations for the industry. *(Congress and the Nation Vol. VIII, p. 117)*

The thrift bailout law established a requirement that the SAIF reach a "reserve ratio" or capital cushion of 1.25 percent of SAIF-protected deposits. Once that reserve ratio was established, the Federal Deposit Insurance Corporation (FDIC), which operated the SAIF, could reduce thrift deposit insurance premiums.

The healthy portion of the thrift industry was hamstrung in its efforts to build up the SAIF's reserves. Thrifts also had to finance annual payments of about $780 million to cover payments on bonds used in the late 1980s to pay part of the cost of the thrift bailout. Those annual payments in effect came from thrift deposit insurance premiums that were supposed to build up the SAIF.

At the same time, the companion Bank Insurance Fund (BIF) was flush with cash, and the FDIC in September 1995 cut deposit insurance premiums for banks to essentially zero. Premiums for most thrifts remained at 23 cents per $100 of deposits. The disparity in insurance costs for banks and thrifts further harmed the ability of the thrift industry to recover, prosper and hold onto its customers by paying competitive interest rates to depositors.

Working closely with top leaders of the Senate Banking Committee, including Chairman Alfonse M. D'Amato, R-N.Y., the Clinton administration developed a plan to shore up the SAIF.

The Clinton plan, released in July 1995, contained the same basic elements that eventually became law: a one-time assessment on SAIF-insured deposits to capitalize the thrift fund; charging banks as well as thrifts a portion of the cost to pay off some bonds used to finance the thrift bailout; and eventually merging the SAIF and BIF into a single deposit insurance fund.

The strategy was to include the proposal in the budget reconciliation bill, where it would have political and procedural protection to carry it past opposition from the banking lobby.

The banking industry opposed the plan from the start and focused much of its lobbying behind a move to eliminate the thrift industry altogether. Under federal and state laws, thrifts had certain advantages over banks—generally tax benefits and access to low-cost loans from the Federal Home Loan Bank System that were tied to the industry's historic role as a source of home mortgage financing. Those same laws also required thrifts to focus their business on mortgage lending, an area where increased competition cut their market share by more than half from the preceding decade.

1995 BUDGET RECONCILIATION

D'Amato opted to address the issue within the budget reconciliation process that got under way in September 1995. Budget calculations showed that the financing arrangements produced long-term budget savings.

Calculations were extremely complicated, but basically the plan derived its savings by shoring up the thrift deposit base, which would in turn increase revenues in the form of increased deposit insurance premiums. Though the one-time assessment on thrift deposits raised revenue in the short term, it did not by itself produce long-term savings.

Committee Action

The House Banking Committee approved its version of the plan Sept. 19 on a party-line, 26–20 vote, after a lengthy and partisan markup. Chairman Jim Leach, R-Iowa, presented the panel with a comprehensive approach, proposing to not only fix the SAIF's financial problems but also to eliminate the federal savings and loan charter by 1998 and to require all federally chartered thrifts to convert to a national bank or state-chartered bank.

The House plan would have preserved for five years thrift powers in areas such as insurance, securities and real estate activities. State chartered thrifts would have been allowed to retain some of their thrift powers when they converted to state banks, though it wasn't clear that state laws would permit that.

Leach's proposal also included a hotly contested plan to permit small banks to "self-certify" that they were complying with the Community Reinvestment Act, a 1977 law that required banks to demonstrate their efforts to lend in the neighborhoods in which they did business.

The Senate Banking Committee, working in a bipartisan fashion, quickly approved a more narrow version of the plan by voice vote Sept. 20. The Senate version closely mirrored the administration's proposal and did not address the issue of revoking or changing the thrift charter. Under Senate rules, provisions of reconciliation bills that did not involve the budget were subject to challenges and could be easily stricken; that left charter issues especially vulnerable.

The Senate committee did agree to an amendment by Bill Frist, R-Tenn., to block the merger of the bank and thrift insurance funds until enactment of a bill to eliminate the thrift industry.

The House Banking Financial Institutions Subcommittee convened on Sept. 27 and approved on a 15–1 vote a separate draft bill that that addressed SAIF financing and thrift charter issues. The action signaled that the House knew its more comprehensive approach for the reconciliation bill was about to fall prey to the Senate's rules.

Floor, Conference Action

The House and Senate committee recommendations were incorporated into the reconciliation bills for floor debate in both chambers, and the provisions survived floor action.

In conference on HR 2491, Leach argued for the House's broader language. In the end, however, the Senate prevailed. D'Amato said at the initial Nov. 1 conference meeting that the Senate could not accept the House framework until it had held hearings on the charter issue.

In ceding to Senate, Leach insisted that the conference retain the Frist amendment to block merger of the BIF and SAIF funds until Congress voted to eliminate the thrift charter.

With Clinton's veto of HR 2491, the SAIF financing plan died for 1995.

1996 ACTION

Both congressional leaders and top Clinton administration officials argued that Congress had to act in 1996 to shore up the SAIF, though they conceded that the measure could not pass on its own. Once again, Republican congressional leaders looked for a larger legislative vehicle to carry the measure into law.

House GOP leaders rebuffed a request from supporters of the plan to attach it to a must-pass bill to raise the debt limit (HR 3136—PL 104-122).

Then, the proposal came very close to being inserted into a series of stopgap spending bills for fiscal 1996. As a bill wrapping up fiscal 1996 omnibus appropriations (HR 3019—PL 104-134) moved towards final action in late April, the SAIF proposal was suggested as an amendment. Reflecting the continued opposition from the banking lobby, about two dozen House members threatened to vote against the underlying spending bill if the SAIF language were included.

To avoid risking that bill's success, the SAIF provisions were included in a stop-gap continuing resolution that financed federal operations for only one day, April 25. That measure was required as negotiations on the broader spending bill reached the final stages.

The plan unraveled when the House Rules Committee voted to strip out the SAIF language, defying instructions from the GOP leadership to leave it in the bill. A brief but strong lobbying campaign by banks led to the uproar, which was the first time in memory that the leadership-driven Rules Committee—whether under GOP or Democratic control—had so directly contravened a leadership order.

Banking Committee Rewrite

As the year progressed, Leach convened his House Banking Committee again on July 25 to redraw the SAIF measure in an attempt to salvage it.

Officially, the markup session was intended to draft the committee's contribution to a 1996 budget reconciliation bill, even though House leaders had already called off drafting a reconciliation bill following the previous year's veto. Leach hoped to build consensus behind a modified SAIF plan that banks would not oppose so vehemently.

Leach's renewed push on the SAIF measure came just after Leach pulled the plug on an 18-month-long effort to repeal the Glass-Steagall Act. He was eager to come up with a new banking bill that would combine the deposit insurance fund provisions with other pieces of the banking agenda, including a stalled "regulatory relief" bill (HR 1858).

Leach devised a new SAIF measure that drew a new cast of opponents. He proposed requiring the politically potent and highly profitable duo of the Federal National Mortgage Association (Fannie Mae) and the Federal Home Loan Mortgage Corp. (Freddie Mac)—two government-sponsored corporations that fueled the home mortgage market—to pay half of the annual $780 million bond obligation from the thrift bailout and require banks to contribute less.

A bipartisan group of senior committee members responded with a plan to require banks and thrifts to pay unequal shares of the bond burden, and leave Fannie Mae and Freddie Mac out of the picture. Thrifts were to pay five times the assessment rate as banks for the bond payments until 2000, when banks and thrifts were to pay equal rates.

By voice vote, the committee adopted the bipartisan plan. But the committee never completed the markup, and there was no ready legislative vehicle to carry the provisions.

As the congressional leadership began looking for ways to finish its appropriations work for fiscal 1997, it needed to offset the cost of $6.5 billion in spending initiatives that was Clinton's price for cooperating on appropriations.

The SAIF financing plan, which was a priority for the administration and the leadership of the House and Senate Banking committees, proved useful because it brought with it $3.1 billion in "savings" that appropriators could use to offset Clinton administration priorities.

High-level negotiations in late September between Clinton administration officials and House and Senate leaders resulted in a compromise covering six unfinished appropriations bills. The compromise included the language on financing the SAIF that had been worked out by the House Banking Committee (and informally with the Senate Banking Committee).

At the same time, the banking lobby successfully pressed to have elements of their regulatory relief agenda made a part of the compromise.

The compromise was incorporated into the conference report on the defense appropriations bill (HR 3610—H Rept 104-863), which the House adopted Sept. 28 on a **key vote of 370–37 (R 202–24; D 167–13)**. The Senate cleared the bill Sept. 30 by voice vote, and Clinton signed it the same day.

PROVISIONS

As enacted, the thrift deposit insurance fund–related provisions of PL 104-208:

• **SAIF Recapitalization.** Required the Federal Deposit Insurance Corporation (FDIC) to impose a one-time special assessment on Savings Association Insurance Fund (SAIF)-insured deposits to bring the thrift fund to the 1.25 percent of insured deposits required under existing law. (The FDIC set the assessment to reach the required "designated reserve ratio" at 65.7 cents per $100 in deposits.)

• **Oakar Banks.** Reduced the special assessment on so-called Oakar banks—commercial banks that acquired thrift deposits or a thrift—by 20 percent. Only banks whose deposits were insured by the Bank Insurance Fund (BIF) on June 30, 1995, were eligible for this reduction.

• **FICO Bonds.** Required banks to pay assessments on BIF-insured deposits to finance a portion of the $780 million annual interest payment on Financing Corporation (FICO) bonds issued during an earlier round of the thrift salvage operation in 1987. These payments previously were solely the responsibility of thrifts through the SAIF. *(FICO, Congress and the Nation Vol. VII, p. 120)*

FICO assessments on banks (BIF-insured deposits) were one-fifth the rate imposed on thrifts (SAIF-insured deposits) until Dec. 31, 1999. Banks paid about 1.3 cents per $100 for FICO bonds and thrifts paid 6.4 cents per $100. Beginning Jan. 1, 2000, banks and thrifts were to share the FICO assessment at approximately 2.4 cents per $100.

• **Deposit Shifting.** Required bank regulators to take actions to block thrifts and banks and their holding companies from "facilitating or encouraging the shifting" of SAIF-insured deposits to the BIF in order to evade higher SAIF deposit insurance premiums. However, actions undertaken in the ordinary course of business and not aimed at depositors of an affiliated bank or thrift were not affected.

• **BIF/SAIF Merger.** Required the merger of the BIF and SAIF into a single deposit insurance fund on Jan. 1, 1999, but only if no savings associations existed at that time. The intent of the limitation was to block the BIF/SAIF merger until Congress acted separately to eliminate the thrift charter and force all thrifts to convert to banks.

• **Treasury Charter Study.** Required the Treasury Department to study elimination of separate bank and thrift charters and creation of a single common charter for all insured depository institutions. Treasury was to report to Congress by March 31, 1997.

• **Assessment Refunds.** Required the FDIC to refund balances in any deposit insurance fund when the reserve ratio exceeded 1.25 percent. The FDIC was prohibited from setting insurance assessments that would cause a fund to exceed the 1.25 percent reserve ratio. ❑

Glass-Steagall Repeal

An ambitious GOP-driven plan to tear down Depression-era walls that prevented banks from offering a full range of financial services collapsed in 1996 amid the same interest group warfare that had blocked similar efforts in 1991 and 1988.

House Banking Committee Chairman Jim Leach, R-Iowa, drove the 1995–1996 effort to update federal banking laws. He was especially interested in repealing key portions of the 1933 Glass-Steagall Act, which erected an extensive, though imperfect, barrier between commercial banking and underwriting and sales of stocks and nongovernment bonds.

The effort unraveled because competing financial services interest groups, particularly banks and insurance agents, battled for competitive advantage in the postrepeal period. Failing to put together a coalition that could support repeal, Leach pulled the plug in July 1996. In the Senate, Banking Committee Chairman Alfonse M. D'Amato, R-N.Y., took no steps towards advancing a bill to repeal Glass-Steagall.

Leach crafted repeated rewrites of a draft repeal bill in his attempt to find the right balance to satisfy the various interest groups. Still, three separate House Banking Committee markups on all or part of the legislation failed to produce a bill that House leaders were comfortable bringing to the floor.

At the core of Leach's effort was a bill (HR 1062) to allow banking companies and securities firms to enter each other's markets under the umbrella structure of a financial services holding company. Such holding companies would have been allowed to offer both retail and wholesale banking services and engage in the full scope of securities activities.

During much of the 18-month period he pursued Glass-Steagall repeal, Leach paired his overhaul bill with a measure (HR 1858) to provide "regulatory relief" to banks. The combined Glass-Steagall and regulatory relief bill was introduced as HR 2520, but much of the debate involved unnumbered drafts.

The provisions of the regulatory relief bill ultimately became law at the end of the 104th Congress by catching a ride on an omnibus spending bill (HR 3610—PL 104-208). That bill, passed at the end of September 1996, wrapped together six of the 13 regular appropriations bills for fiscal 1997. *(Bank regulatory relief, p. 136; fiscal 1997 appropriations, p. 76)*

A key reason the Glass-Steagall repeal bid failed was that House Speaker Newt Gingrich, R-Ga., had instructed Leach to include a provision—sought by the insurance agents lobby—to block the principal regulator for nationally chartered banks from allowing those banks to make further inroads into the insurance business. When that language was inserted into the Glass-Steagall bill, banks turned against the measure.

Moreover, the resolve of the banking industry stiffened after it won a critical Supreme Court case, *Barnett Banks v. Nelson,* that affirmed the right of banks based in small towns to conduct widespread sales of insurance, free of interference from state insurance regulators.

BACKGROUND

It was clear from the beginning that Leach's effort to repeal Glass-Steagall would be an uphill battle. Congress had rarely shown the ability to lead in modernizing the nation's financial services framework.

Most previous changes in banking law—the 1989 thrift cleanup and a 1991 overhaul of the deposit insurance system, for example—had come in response to crises. Other successful legislative endeavors, such as the 1994 law to permit banks to set up interstate branch networks, came after court decisions and regulatory actions had already transformed the marketplace.

The Glass-Steagall Act looked to be ripe for an overhaul in the same vein as the interstate branching law. Glass-Steagall was enacted in the midst of a banking crisis that had shuttered most of the nation's banks and resulted in losses by millions of depositors.

It was intended to keep banks out of the securities business. Over the previous decade, decisions by regulators and in the courts had permitted some banking companies to create separate affiliates that could underwrite and sell securities. Those regulatory changes prompted two prior efforts, in 1988 and 1991, to repeal Glass-Steagall's barriers and place Congress's imprint on the marketplace. *(Congress and the Nation Vol. VII, p. 114; Congress and the Nation Vol. VIII, p. 136)*

However, resistance to repealing Glass-Steagall among key segments of the industry, especially securities firms and small banks—combined with aggressive demands by insurance agents for separate legislation to limit banks' inroads into the insurance business—worked to sink prior attempts.

Almost every participant in the debate agreed that Glass-Steagall was out of date and that banks and securities firms should have the right to enter each others' business, with appropriate safeguards to the deposit insurance system. But the central question—the extent to which banks, securities firms, insurance companies and commercial firms—could affiliate with each other invited intense controversy.

Generally, larger banks and securities firms desired a broadly written bill that would permit, for example, a banking company to sell insurance, serve as a stockbroker and underwriter as well as offer traditional banking services. Because many securities firms had affiliations with insurance companies and nonfinancial subsidiaries, they generally desired sweeping Glass-Steagall repeal.

Pressure for a broad bill was countered by small banks and insurance companies and agents, each of which sought to keep competitors at bay.

Financial services–related bills had earned a reputation for putting members in uncomfortable positions from which they had to choose between competing interest groups. As the 1995 debate opened, everyone involved wanted to avoid the experience of 1991, when two major banking bills blew up on the House floor.

Since 1991, continued evolution in the marketplace had resulted in banks and securities firms making further inroads into each other's traditional lines of business. But among those wanting the most for Congress to act were insurance agents, whose turf was being invaded by banks, with the acquiescence of regulators and the courts.

Banks had benefited from sympathetic rulemaking by the Office of the Comptroller of the Currency (OCC), the chief regulator of national banks, which aggressively interpreted an obscure Civil War–era provision of banking law to make it easy for banks with operations in small towns to sell insurance.

Insurance agents hoped to stop the banks in their tracks.

Meanwhile, while only a few large banking companies were truly agitating for Glass-Steagall repeal, all of the nation's 12,000 or so banks wanted legislation to peel back a layer of banking regulations that they viewed as needlessly expensive and restrictive. Any legislative effort that promised to provide regulatory relief would have the support of the banking industry.

HOUSE ACTION

Leach drafted a narrow bill (HR 1062) patterned after the 1988 Senate effort to repeal Glass-Steagall. The measure would have permitted banks and securities firms to affiliate under the umbrella of a "financial services holding company" and offer a full range of retail and wholesale services in both banking and securities underwriting and sales.

The measure also proposed to create an alternative "investment bank holding company" framework that would allow largely unfettered ties between securities companies and "wholesale" banks that accepted only large deposits that were not protected by the federal deposit insurance safety net.

The draft bill retained existing barriers that prevented banks from affiliating with insurance companies and nonfinancial businesses. This narrow scope would have blocked many securities firms and other diversified financial services providers—which had ties with insurance companies and commercial firms—from being able to take full advantage of the bill's proposed new corporate structures.

Banking Committee Action

The House Banking Committee easily approved HR 1062 on May 11, 1995, by a sweeping 38–6 vote (H Rept. 104-127, Part 1).

As soon as the final gavel dropped, the insurance agents' lobby, which had pledged neutrality, announced its opposition to the measure. The agents were satisfied that the legislation preserved certain constraints from existing law on bank insurance activities. However, they wanted the bill to include language from a separate bill (HR 1317) that would have permitted state insurance regulators to roll back bank insurance powers.

Beyond opposition from insurance agents, the Clinton Treasury Department expressed its reservations the night before the markup. In a letter to Leach, the administration outlined its general support for the bill, but said the draft bill, which had been written with much help from the Federal Reserve, would shift too much supervisory authority to the Fed and away from other regulators.

Commerce Committee Action

As the bill headed toward markup in the Commerce Committee, which shared jurisdiction in the House, a round of talks seeking to settle the insurance controversy began.

Commerce Chairman Thomas J. Bliley Jr., R-Va., first tried to expand the bill to permit affiliations between national banks and insurance companies, subject to state regulation, but he dropped that idea on June 8 amid opposition from the insurance agents' lobby.

House GOP leaders met four days later on June 12 with Leach, Bliley and Rules Committee Chairman Gerald B. H. Solomon, R-N.Y., and agreed to marry Leach's Glass-Steagall bill with a bank-friendly bill to peel back bank regulations that was about to be marked up by the Banking Committee.

In deference to insurance agents, a newly drawn provision to impose a moratorium on the OCC's authority to give banks new insurance powers was to be added to the regulatory relief bill during the upcoming markup.

By voice vote, the Commerce Committee approved Leach's bill unchanged on June 16 (H Rept 104-127, Part 3).

Leadership Plan Unravels

When the Banking Committee marked up the bank regulatory relief bill (HR 1858—H Rept 104-193) the leadership plan came undone. The committee approved the bill, 27–23, on June 29.

However, under intense pressure from banking and securities interests, the committee turned the insurance compromise on its head. The panel accepted with reluctance the moratorium on the OCC's ability to expand bank insurance powers, but it also voted 36–12 to adopt an amendment by Richard H. Baker, R-La., to permit banks to affiliate with insurance companies, subject to state law.

The change built support for the bill among banks and securities firms, but it drew a furious response from insurance agents and some insurance companies, as well as from smaller banks.

Prospects for the bill were increasingly uncertain, but Leach kept working through the summer. And the leadership was beginning to tire of the issue, not wanting to put GOP members through wrenching floor votes that would force them to choose between their friends in the warring banking and insurance industries.

Floor Action Stalls

Under pressure from Leach, a plan for floor consideration was agreed to on Sept. 27. Under the compromise, the Glass-Steagall repeal bill (HR 1062) and the regulatory relief bill (HR 1858) were to be merged; the Baker bank-insurance affiliations language was to be dropped; and the OCC moratorium was to be capped after five years.

The new plan did not go over well either, however. The redrawn and combined bill (HR 2520) was scheduled for floor consideration the week of Oct. 23, but with banks badly divided and a potential revolt brewing among probank members of the Rules Committee, House Republican leaders postponed action. House Majority Leader Dick Armey, R-Texas, announced the postponement on Oct. 19, hours after the American Bankers Association announced it would oppose the bill because of the provision that would freeze bank insurance powers.

In the end, the banking lobby decided that the OCC moratorium was too much to accept. Expanded insurance sales powers were too important a line of business to give up.

Moreover, the Supreme Court had announced in September that it would hear arguments in *Barnett Banks v. Nelson,* which bankers were confident they would win, thereby permitting them insurance sales powers free of interference from state regulators.

The bill was clearly stalled. And when the Court decided unanimously in March 1996 to uphold the banks' side in the *Barnett* case, the political landscape had shifted sharply in favor of the banking lobby.

By this time, Leach was seemingly the only one fighting to advance the Glass-Steagall overhaul. He declined entreaties to separate the regulatory relief provisions from HR 2520 and embarked on a lengthy series of negotiations between banks and the insurance industry.

In the end, he produced insurance language that would have permitted banks and insurance companies to affiliate subject to state law, but also would have required employees of national banks to obtain state insurance licenses to sell insurance. That compromise was rejected by many state banking trade associations who, because of nuances in state laws, believed it would hurt banks in their states to compete in the insurance market.

In the end, the compromise collapsed, despite an extraordinary move in the summer of 1996 by Leach to bring the Glass-Steagall and insurance portions of the bill back before the Banking Committee for a revote.

Committee members balked. Democrats had by now completely deserted Leach, blasting him for not consulting with them. And some Republicans were poised to vote against the measure because of the insurance language.

It had also become clear that there was no way that House leaders would schedule the measure for a floor vote, given the lateness of the session and a presumption that the Senate had no intention of acting on the measure.

On July 11, Leach called off the new markup and gave up on the Glass-Steagall bill. Other elements of the agenda would later advance on the end-of-session omnibus spending bill. ❑

Bank Regulatory Relief

The banking industry succeeded in 1996 in winning enactment of a package of revisions to bank regulations that satisfied some industry concerns that banking law changes of the early 1990s went too far.

As enacted, the measure also included a long-sought provision to protect banks and other lenders from being assessed the costs of cleaning up hazardous waste sites, unless they had played a role in managing the property at the time it became an environmental hazard.

And it served as a vehicle to carry into law changes to the Fair Credit Reporting Act—some sought by lenders and some sought by consumers.

These provisions followed a tortured path to enactment. There were unsuccessful efforts to move the regulatory relief provisions as a free-standing bill in both the House and the Senate. And there were failed attempts to win enactment as part of a bill to roll back Depression-era restrictions on securities underwriting and dealing by banks.

Sponsors succeeded in getting the regulatory relief measure into law by including its provisions in an omnibus spending bill for fiscal 1997 (HR 3610—PL 104-208). That bill, passed at the end of September 1996, wrapped together six of the 13 regular appropriations bills for the year.

The bill also carried into law another central piece of the banking agenda for the 104th Congress, a measure to shore up the deposit insurance fund for savings and loan institutions. *(Fiscal 1997 appropriations, p. 76; deposit insurance funds, p. 131)*

The banking industry was unhappy with the deposit insurance measure, because it called on banks to pay a portion of the cost of the savings and loan salvage operation of the late 1980s. The regulatory relief language was added to the appropriations bill as a sort of palliative for the industry.

Even so, the changes that were enacted paled when compared to the industry's wish list at the beginning of the 104th Congress or to the early efforts of the House Banking Committee. The Clinton administration resolutely blocked Republican plans to roll back not only red tape but decades' worth of proconsumer laws.

BACKGROUND

Bankers started their antiregulatory push in 1992, protesting in particular new layers of regulations imposed under a 1991 law to shore up the deposit insurance system. *(Congress and the Nation Vol. VIII, p. 136)*

Banks, especially smaller ones with few employees, said the regulations were stifling productivity and cutting profits. Consumer advocates countered that the industry was enjoying record profits and seeking to eliminate critical consumer protections.

The Clinton administration supported some changes and took administrative steps to streamline bank examinations and permit lending based on an applicant's character, not on strict underwriting standards. Also, in 1994, about 50 noncontroversial changes were attached to the community development bank bill. *(Community development banks, p. 116)*

More significantly, the administration in 1995 overhauled the way in which the Community Reinvestment Act (CRA) was implemented to make it easier for banks to comply with the law.

But with Republicans in control of Congress and in a distinctly antiregulatory mood, the industry pressed for much more. They sought to gut the 1977 CRA , which required banks and thrifts to serve the entire community in which they did business and face sanctions if they failed to do so. And they sought virtual repeal of the 1991 Truth-in-Savings Act (enacted as part of the broader deposit insurance bill of that year) that required banks to disclose to consumers clearly and accurately the fees charged and interest earned on their savings.

The administration's veto threats prevailed, however, and the bill as enacted did not touch the CRA and made minor changes in the Truth-in-Savings law.

HOUSE COMMITTEE ACTION

The House Banking Committee's Financial Institutions Subcommittee approved a regulatory relief bill (HR 1362) sponsored by Doug Bereuter, R-Neb., on June 15, 1995, by an almost party-line 13–6 vote.

The bill would have exempted 90 percent of the nation's banks from coverage under the CRA and in so doing curbed the ability of activists to pressure banks to lend in inner cities and other areas traditionally avoided by banks.

Small banks and thrifts with assets of less than $250 million would be able to "self-certify" that they were obeying the law. Banks with assets of less than $100 million would be exempt altogether. The bill would have given a "safe harbor" to banks that had previously earned satisfactory CRA grades. Bank regulators would not be able to deny merger or branching applications from such institutions. Protests by community groups could not be considered until the bank's next exam.

The bill proposed to roll back parts of the 1968 Truth-in-Lending Act to allow greater tolerance of inaccurate disclosures of loan finance charges, thereby limiting a borrower's right to cancel loan agreements. The bill aimed to remedy a situation that had evolved since a 1994 federal appeals court decision *(Rodash v. AIB Mortgage Co.)* held that small and technical violations of the law could be used to rescind a loan.

The bill also sought to repeal the bulk of the Truth-in-Savings law. Bankers complained that most institutions had to conduct a costly overhaul of their operations in order to comply with the law.

After a contentious markup that lasted four days spread over two weeks, the full Banking Committee approved a revised version of the subcommittee bill on June 29, 1995, by a vote of 27–23 (HR 1858—H Rept 104-193).

The committee worked from a fresh bill introduced by Chairman Jim Leach, R-Iowa, which included controversial language—mandated by House Speaker Newt Gingrich, R-Ga., in deference to the potent insurance agent's lobby—to block the Office of the Comptroller of the Currency (OCC) from issuing regulations to allow banks greater access to the insurance market.

However, ignoring the wishes of the chairman and House GOP leaders, the committee turned the leadership insurance compromise on its head, voting instead to allow banks to affiliate with insurance companies under limited conditions.

The change built additional support for the bill from the banking and securities industries, and the measure was expected to be incorporated with the provisions of Leach's bill (HR 1062) to repeal the 1933 Glass-Steagall Act that restrained banks from engaging in securities activities.

At the same time, the bill drew immediate fury from lobbyists for insurance agents and smaller banks. Given the leadership's desire to avoid difficult floor votes, it also postponed floor action.

Democrats teamed with Leach to strip out a few of the provisions they considered most odious. But they continued to charge that the measure would go too far. In a June 29 letter to committee members, Treasury Secretary Robert E. Rubin said he would recommend that President Clinton veto the bill because of its assault on consumer protections.

For example, the committee adopted, 25–17, an amendment by Bill McCollum, R-Fla., to eliminate the enforcement system for the CRA. Under the amendment, community groups' protests could no longer hold up or block bank applications for expansion. The effect was to further extend the "safe harbor" already provided by the bill to banks and thrifts with failing CRA grades.

The committee also added a provision, long sought by banks, to protect lenders who took possession of an environmentally hazardous property or waste site by reducing their liability under the superfund hazardous waste law, provided they did not contribute to releases of hazardous wastes. The section was added by voice vote on an amendment by John J. LaFalce, D-N.Y.

SENATE COMMITTEE ACTION

The Senate Banking Committee approved a much more restrained regulatory relief bill by voice vote Sept. 27, 1995 (S 650—S Rept 104-185). The bill had been substantially reworked to address the concerns of panel Democrats and the Clinton administration.

Even though Chairman Alfonse M. D'Amato, R-N.Y., failed to get the bill to the Senate floor on its own, it provided the blueprint for the regulatory relief package that became law.

The bill would have eliminated some disclosure requirements under the Truth-in-Lending Act and the Real Estate Settlement Procedures Act. It would have taken away consumers' rights to sue under the Truth-in-Savings Act, leaving enforcement to bank regulators. However, Democrats succeeded in blocking a wholesale repeal of the law, which D'Amato had first proposed and which the House bill called for.

Other provisions sought to ease per-branch capital requirements to make it easier for banks to take advantage of the interstate branching law enacted in 1994; permit more small banks to be examined every 18 months instead of once a year; and provide the Federal Reserve Board greater authority to allow foreign banks to enter the U.S. market. *(Interstate branching and banking, p. 111)*

D'Amato appeared to bend over backward to accommodate Democrats, who praised him for producing a bill that would reduce regulations on banks without broadly attacking consumer and community lending laws. In the most significant change from his original draft, D'Amato dropped a controversial provision that would have given small banks a sweeping exemption from the CRA. D'Amato said he supported changes to CRA, but had decided to scrap the proposed exemptions because of Clinton's veto threat.

And in an ironic move that promised banks and other lenders increased regulation, the committee folded into the bill language from a separate bill to overhaul the Fair Credit Reporting Act (S 709), which proposed to make it easier for consumers to correct errors in their credit reports.

Efforts to overhaul the credit reporting law had failed in 1992 and again in 1994, as opposition—particularly from Sen. Phil Gramm, R-Texas—proved insurmountable. *(Credit reporting requirements, p. 127; Congress and the Nation Vol. VIII, p. 157)*

The series of compromises reflected in the Senate bill created a final product that the Treasury Department regarded as relatively innocuous. At the same time, some panel Republicans grumbled that the bill was too watered down. And bank lobbyists—who had drafted much of D'Amato's original draft—were disappointed that the measure did not provide as much regulatory relief as they had hoped.

But D'Amato said it was more important to craft a bill that could pass.

The Senate regulatory relief effort quickly stalled, however, as Banking Committee members, who dominated the ranks of the special Whitewater Committee, turned their attention to that matter. *(Whitewater investigation, p. 942)*

FINAL ACTION

Pushed hard by Leach, top House Republican leaders agreed Sept. 27, 1995—the same day the Senate Committee acted—on a plan to bring the regulatory relief bill to the House floor with some significant changes. It was combined with HR 1062, Leach's Glass-Steagall repeal bill, as a new measure (HR 2520) and was to come to the House floor the week of Oct. 23.

Two key changes were made in the regulatory relief bill: the provision to permit affiliation between banks and insurance companies was replaced with a limited bar on the OCC from allowing banks broader insurance powers through regulation. And the sweeping CRA exemption for small banks, which had drawn a veto threat, was dropped.

The changes left the banking industry divided. So, facing a potential revolt among probank members of the Rules Committee, the leadership pulled the bill. House Majority Leader Dick Armey, R-Texas, announced Oct. 19 that the bill would not come to the floor until a "date to be determined later." His announcement came only hours after the American Bankers Association, the top lobby for the industry, told lawmakers that it would oppose the bill over the provision to freeze bank insurance powers.

In late September 1995, the Supreme Court had agreed to accept the case of *Barnett Bank v. Nelson,* which raised directly the issue of the OCC granting banks broad insurance powers. Banks were generally confident that the high court would overturn a lower court's ruling and permit them sweeping access to the lucrative insurance market.

The bill stalled as all sides awaited the outcome of the *Barnett* case. In March 1996, the Supreme Court unanimously confirmed the ability of banks to sell insurance in small towns free of interference from state regulators. The effect was to stiffen the resolve of banks to keep the bill free of provisions that would impede their ability to get into the insurance business.

In the summer of 1996, Leach attempted but failed to find a compromise that could pass on the House floor and D'Amato had showed no interest in attempting to repeal Glass-Steagall. Pressure built in the House to split the two bills and move the regulatory relief bill on its own.

Leach then worked to redraw the regulatory relief bill and combine it with the bill to shore up the deposit insurance fund for the thrift industry. Many of the controversial regulatory provisions opposed by Democrats were to be dropped.

In September 1996, plans took shape to add the deposit insurance provisions to the omnibus appropriations bill (HR 3610); the regulatory relief provisions were expected to move with them. That ended any attempt to move a free-standing regulatory bill.

With the two major banking bills of the 104th Congress attached to the end-of-session omnibus spending bill, the administration gained leverage. Moreover, the administration had been engaged in bipartisan negotiations with the Senate for some time and had largely agreed on a tentative framework for the regulatory provisions that was modeled on the Senate committee-approved bill.

After several rounds of negotiation among the House, Senate and the White House, a narrowly drawn set of provisions was added to HR 3610. The compromise carried the imprint of the Clinton Treasury Department and congressional Democrats, who combined to preserve long-standing consumer protection laws. In fact, the entire spending bill was held up for hours on Saturday, Sept. 28, as Rep. David R. Obey of Wisconsin, top Democrat on the House Appropriations Committee, insisted on blocking a Senate attempt to permit credit bureaus to sell consumer credit information to direct marketing companies.

The compromise was incorporated into the conference report on the defense appropriations bill (HR 3610—H Rept 104-863), which the House adopted Sept. 28 on a **key vote of 370–37 (R 202–24; D 167–13; I 1–0).** The Senate cleared the bill Sept. 30 by voice vote, and Clinton signed it the same day.

PROVISIONS

As enacted, the bank regulatory provisions of PL 104-208:

Fair Credit Reporting Act

Updated the 1971 Fair Credit Reporting Act, the federal law governing the credit reporting industry. Generally, the law balanced provisions to give consumers new powers to correct errors in their credit reports with business-sought provisions designed to make it easier to use credit information for marketing purposes and for prescreened credit offers. The changes generally took effect Sept. 30, 1997.

• **Prescreening and Direct Marketing.** Permitted prescreening, the practice of a lender, such as a credit card company, establishing a set of criteria and receiving from a credit bureau a roster of potential customers who met those criteria.

The act did not previously address the practice and the Federal Trade Commission (FTC) allowed it, although under conditions that some credit-grantors found too restrictive.

Credit bureaus were required to set up a toll-free telephone number for consumers to call if they wished to be excluded from prescreened lists. By Sept. 30, 1997, each credit bureau that sold prescreened lists had to publish an annual notice stating that fact and include the address and telephone number available to opt out of prescreening.

• **Affiliate Sharing.** Permitted affiliated companies within a holding company or other corporation to share information (including specific transactions and experiences, such as credit applications and reports) with each other without falling under the Fair Credit Reporting Act. (The FTC had interpreted prior law to bar such "affiliate sharing" of credit information.)

The federal affiliate sharing standard preempted state laws through Jan. 1, 2004.

• **Consumer Disclosures.** Required credit bureaus to provide greater disclosure to consumers of information contained in credit reports and required such disclosures be made in writing. When use of a consumer's credit report resulted in an "adverse action," such as being denied credit or insurance, the consumer was to be notified and given the address and toll-free telephone number of the credit bureau that supplied the report.

The term "adverse action" was broadened to include other areas such as denial of insurance, reducing insurance coverage or canceling an insurance policy; denying employment or taking any unfavorable action such as denying a promotion to an existing employee; and other "business transactions," such as an apartment rental or automobile lease.

Consumers denied credit had to be provided a summary of their rights under the act, including their right to a free copy of their credit report and to dispute information contained in it. Information about which federal agencies to contact to report violations was also required to be provided. Credit bureaus also had to provide detailed information to consumers of companies that obtained their credit information, as well as those that obtained their names via prescreening.

Credit bureaus could no longer bar lenders or other users of credit reports from showing them to consumers if the report has led to an adverse action against the consumer, such as being denied a loan.

• **Disputed Information.** Provided strengthened rights to consumers who dispute the accuracy of information in their credit reports. Credit bureaus were required to reinvestigate within 30 calendar days information that a consumer said was inaccurate. The information had to be deleted if it was inaccurate or could not be confirmed. Credit bureaus were required to notify furnishers of credit information within five days of a consumer's dispute.

If disputed information was reinserted, the consumer was to be notified. Credit bureaus and credit furnishers were required to establish procedures such as computer upgrades to ensure erroneous information was not reinserted.

Credit bureaus that bought and resold credit reports had to take steps to ensure that resold reports were used only for permissible purposes; they were required to verify the identity of the user of the report and certify the purpose for which the report was obtained and also certify that it would not be used for any other purpose.

• **Contents of Reports.** Clarified and tightened requirements about certain information contained in credit reports. In cases of bankruptcy, a consumer's credit report was required to detail what type of bankruptcy (such as Chapter 7 versus Chapter 13). Former restrictions on obsolete information—information that was seven years old—were tightened. For example, when an account was 180 days past due, that information could be reported for seven years and then was considered obsolete and could be reported no longer. Former law permitted that seven-year window to be reopened if the debt were charged off or placed with a collection agency, or if the consumer made some effort to repay the debt.

If a consumer closed an account voluntarily, that had to be noted in the credit report. Finally, if an item was disputed by a consumer, that dispute had to be disclosed in the credit report.

• **Credit Information Furnishers.** Imposed new responsibilities on banks, retailers and other companies that furnished information to credit bureaus. Credit information furnishers were barred from supplying information to credit reporting agencies that they knew (or consciously avoided knowing) was inaccurate. Unlike other elements of the act, consumers could not sue credit information furnishers for violating the law; enforcement of this provision was to be the responsibility of the FTC, banking regulators and the states.

If a credit information furnisher discovered that it had given incomplete or inaccurate information to a credit bureau, it was to promptly notify the credit bureau and make sure that the erroneous information was not resupplied.

Consumers could dispute information provided by credit information furnishers, and if they notified the furnisher, the furnisher may not supply the information to a credit bureau unless it told the credit bureau that the information was disputed.

Credit bureaus were required to inform furnishers of credit information within five business days that a consumer disputed the information; the furnisher had to investigate the dispute and report the results to both the credit bureau and the consumer. If such disputed information was, in fact, inaccurate, the furnisher was required to notify all credit bureaus to which the information was supplied.

• **Charges for Credit Reports.** Required credit bureaus to make credit reports available to consumers for a fee not to exceed $8; this was to be adjusted for inflation.

The bill also made it somewhat easier for consumers to obtain a free copy of their credit report, which formerly was to be provided only after an applicant was denied credit. Consumers could obtain free copies after use of their report results in an "adverse action," such as denying or canceling an insurance policy, any adverse action by an employer, as well as being refused other business transactions such as a checking account or lease.

Annual free reports were required to be provided upon request to unemployed persons, welfare recipients and those who believed their reports contained inaccurate information due to fraud.

• **Use of Credit Reports by Employers.** Required employers who used credit reports in employment decisions, such as hiring job applicants or retaining existing employees, to notify all applicants or employees. Before a credit bureau could release a credit report for employment purposes, the applicant or employee had to authorize the release. An employer could require that information be released as a condition of employment, but when taking any "adverse action" against an applicant or employee, it was required to provide a copy of the credit report to the individual and a notice of his or her rights under the act.

• **Unauthorized Use of Credit Reports.** Made it illegal for those who obtained a credit report to use it for purposes not permitted by the act; users of reports were required to certify that it would be used for permitted activities such as evaluating credit, insurance and rental applications, by employers or for court-approved investigations.

The intent was to curb use of credit reports by private investigators, political campaigns and others by making them liable to lawsuits and federal and state enforcement actions.

• **Credit Repair Organizations.** Imposed new restrictions on the activities of "credit repair" firms, which were paid to clear out negative information from consumers' credit reports.

• **Medical Information.** Barred credit reporting agencies from releasing medical information without a consumer's permission.

• **Preemption of State Law.** Preempted state credit reporting laws in several areas, replacing them with a uniform federal statute through Jan. 1, 2004.

Federal preemption applied to: use of credit reports for prescreened offers of credit or insurance; time limits on reporting obsolete information (existing state laws grandfathered); time limits for reinvestigation (state laws grandfathered); credit bureau responsibilities after taking an adverse action against a consumer; responsibilities placed on furnishers of credit information; and the text of the summary of rights that must be provided to consumers.

After Jan. 1, 2004, states could enact laws to provide consumer protection that went beyond the federal statute.

• **Enforcement.** Permitted individuals to sue anyone for violations of the act, although credit information furnishers were exempt. Minimum damages of $100 to $1,000 were imposed for "willful noncompliance." Individuals who obtained credit reports under false pretenses or knowingly for an impermissible purpose were liable for at least $1,000. Plaintiffs who filed lawsuits in bad faith or to harass the defendant could be found liable for the defendant's legal fees.

Banking agencies were provided authority to enforce compliance with the act by insured banks and thrifts, though only after a complaint was filed or if they otherwise had knowledge of violations.

The FTC was given new authority to impose fines of up to $2,500 per violation for a knowing violation which constituted a pattern or practice of violations of the act. (Prior law permitted FTC fines only for violation of agency orders.)

States were permitted to enforce the act after notifying the FTC or the appropriate banking agency. They could bring suit in behalf of their residents, provided a federal enforcement action was not in progress; a ceiling of $1,000 per violation applied. Unlike individuals, states could sue furnishers of credit information for supplying inaccurate information to credit bureaus, but only for violating injunctions.

Environmental Liability

• **Lender Liability.** Limited the liability of banks, other lenders and fiduciaries under the 1980 Superfund law and the storage tank provisions of the Solid Waste Disposal Act, provided they played no role in causing environmental problems on properties obtained through foreclosure.

The superfund law contained a "safe harbor" for lenders who foreclosed on contaminated properties, but recent court decisions held lenders liable for cleanup costs on foreclosed properties because of their ability to influence management of such properties.

The bill clarified that lenders were not liable unless they participated in management of contaminated property. Also, lenders who did not participate in management and acquire a property through foreclosure were not liable if they disposed of it properly or prepared it for sale at the earliest practicable time on commercially reasonable terms. The bill limited liability for fiduciaries to the assets held in their fiduciary capacity and clarified the law so that several fiduciary actions did not create liability. Also, it reinstated a 1992 Environmental Protection Agency rule that set forth the safe harbor for lenders.

Regulatory 'Relief'

• **RESPA/Truth-in-Lending.** Made multiple changes to the Real Estate Settlement Procedures Act (RESPA) and the Truth-in-Lending Act. (Truth-in-Lending required lenders to provide specific and accurate disclosures of the terms of credit extended to consumers; RESPA required lenders to provide estimates of settlement costs at the time of closing.)

The Department of Housing and Urban Development (HUD), which enforced RESPA, and the Federal Reserve, which enforced the Truth-in-Lending Act, were required by March 31, 1997, to simplify and improve the laws' disclosure requirements and provide a single format for these disclosures.

The bill delayed implementation of a pending HUD anti-kickback rule under RESPA until July 31, 1997. The rule placed strict limits on employer compensation of employees who made mortgage referrals to its affiliates.

The law authorized the Federal Reserve to exempt additional credit transactions from Truth-in-Lending disclosure requirements, provided that the disclosures offered no meaningful benefit to consumers or involved wealthy individuals who waived the disclosure in writing.

It relaxed regulations on lenders by requiring that they provide a statement to borrowers that the loan may be sold; prior law required that lenders inform borrowers of the percentage of loans made over three prior years that had been sold.

The law exempted most business loans from RESPA.

And it permitted lenders under Truth-in-Lending to provide a less detailed disclosure of potential payment fluctuations for adjustable-rate mortgages.

• **Truth-in-Savings Act.** As of Sept. 30, 2001, civil liability for violations of the Truth-in-Savings Act was repealed. The law required clear and accurate disclosures of fees and interest rates on deposits.

• **Home Mortgage Disclosure Act.** The 1975 Home Mortgage Disclosure Act (HMDA) required thrifts, banks and other mortgage lenders to report data on the geographic and demographic characteristics of their lending patterns, permitting regulators to track discriminatory lending practices. Prior law exempted depository institutions with less than $10 million in assets from the law. Under HR 3610, the exemption was to be adjusted annually for inflation, including a one-time increase to about $28 million in assets.

• **Self Testing.** Encouraged lenders to "self test" for compliance with the Equal Credit Opportunity Act and the Fair Housing Act by barring the results of such tests from being used in agency enforcement actions or in civil lawsuits, as permitted under prior law. The Federal Reserve Board and HUD were directed to establish rules governing self testing. Self tests were protected only if they met the new standards and if the lender took steps to correct any discriminatory practices it found.

• **Nonbanking Activities.** Created a new expedited procedure that allowed well-capitalized and well-managed bank holding companies to engage in nonbanking activities, provided the transaction was below a certain size. Qualified banking companies were permitted to engage in any activity permitted under Federal Reserve Regulation Y without prior notice; they were required to notify the Fed within 10 days. For non-Regulation Y activities, or for acquisitions of nonbanking companies, a holding company was required to inform the Fed 12 days before beginning the activity.

Prior law required that bank holding companies wait 60 to 90 days for Federal Reserve Board approval before engaging in routine nonbanking activities or acquiring a nonbanking company.

• **Bank Holding Companies/Thrift Ownership.** Eliminated a requirement that bank holding companies that owned thrifts also be regulated as savings and loan holding companies, which subjected them to different and sometimes conflicting rules. Required the Federal Reserve and the Office of Thrift Supervision to coordinate regulation of such holding companies as well as acquisition of thrifts by bank holding companies.

• **Consumer Leasing.** Required the Federal Reserve Board to issue regulations governing consumer leases, with the intent of providing consumers with simplified, meaningful disclosures of the terms of a lease. The Fed also was to issue model disclosure forms, and any lessor who used such forms was to be deemed in compliance with the law's disclosure requirements.

Rules governing consumer lease advertisements were modified to require clear and conspicuous disclosure of the fact that the advertised transaction was a lease; the total number of payments required at or before consummation of the lease; any security deposit requirement; the number and timing of payments; and the possibility of additional end-of-lease charges.

The changes were intended to make the Consumer Leasing Act consistent with other consumer laws such as the Truth-in-Lending Act.

• **Debt Collection.** Modified the Fair Debt Collection Practices Act to require that debt collectors inform consumers only in their initial communication that the collector was trying to collect a debt. Prior law required disclosure in all communications—whether with the debtor or any other individual contacted regarding the debt. However, in all communications with the debtor, they still were required to be notified that the communication is from a debt collector.

• **Stored Value Cards.** Blocked the Federal Reserve from finalizing proposed rules to require some sophisticated "stored value" cards be regulated under the Electronic Funds Transfer Act (EFTA). The Fed was required to conduct a study and report to Congress by March 30, 1997, on the feasibility of applying some of the provisions of the EFTA to stored value cards, while exempting others.

• **Retirement CD.** Made the so-called retirement certificate of deposit—a controversial tax-deferred annuity product offered by a small bank in Montana—ineligible for deposit insurance.

• **GSE-Sponsored Credit Unions.** Prohibited government-sponsored enterprises such as the Farm Credit System from sponsoring credit unions.

• **ATMs/Branch Closings.** Permitted banks and thrifts to remove automated teller machines without having to notify customers 90 days in advance as required for branch closings. Permitted branch relocations within the same neighborhood without triggering the 90-day notice requirement. Clarified that ATMs were not a branch for purposes of federal interstate branching laws and therefore were not subject to application requirements or geographic restrictions that applied to branching activities.

• **Per Branch Capital.** Eliminated the obsolete requirement that national and state member banks maintain capital for their branches as if each branch were a separately chartered bank.

• **Bank Fees Study.** Required the annual Federal Reserve study of bank fees to describe trends in bank fees in each state, metropolitan area and nationally; the study also had to highlight trends in the availability of banking services related to the size of the institution and whether it was a multistate institution.

• **Management Interlocks.** Eased restrictions on officers and directors of banks and thrifts from participating in the management of an unaffiliated institution. Asset thresholds that permitted smaller banks and thrifts to have such "management interlocks" were raised. Grandfathered interlocks were contin-

ued indefinitely, and bank regulators were given greater latitude to waive the restrictions.

• **Foreign Banks.** Eased requirements on foreign banks trying to open U.S. offices or branches. Prior law permitted the Federal Reserve—which regulated foreign banks operating in the United States—to terminate foreign bank operations if it found that the institution was not subject to rigorous worldwide supervision. Under the new law, those operations could not be terminated if the host country was preparing a supervisory framework or making "demonstrable progress" toward doing so. The Fed could approve applications for new offices so long as the home country was taking such steps toward establishing a supervisory framework.

The Fed also was required to act on applications from foreign banks within 180 days (a 180-day extension is allowed), and the requirement that foreign banks pay examination fees was repealed as long as exam fees were not paid by state member banks.

• **Nonbank Banks.** Lifted an annual 7 percent growth cap on grandfathered "nonbank banks," which were otherwise banned in 1987. This permitted the diversified financial services firms that owned these remaining hybrid institutions to make greater use of them.

• **Qualified Thrift Investments.** Made it easier for thrifts to meet the "qualified thrift lender" test, which required that 65 percent of a thrift's assets be qualified thrift investments (generally real estate–related assets) by counting small business, credit card and student lending toward the 65 percent cap. Other personal, family and household loans up to 20 percent of the thrift's assets could be used to meet the QTL test, dropping a 10 percent restriction.

• **Edge Act Corporations.** Permitted the Federal Reserve to increase the investment by banks in Edge Act and Agreement corporations from 10 percent to 20 percent. Such subsidiaries were offshore entities that had powers similar to foreign branches of U.S. banks and operated in the United States.

• **Independent Auditor Requirements.** Eliminated a requirement that an independent auditor attest whether a financial institution is within FDIC regulations on insider lending and dividend limits. In addition, regulators could waive under limited circumstances a requirement that all members of an institution's independent audit committee be unaffiliated with the institution, provided that outside directors formed a majority of the committee.

• **FDIC Board of Directors.** Required at least one member of the Federal Deposit Insurance Corporation board of directors to have experience supervising state banks.

• **Small Bank Examinations.** Permitted bank and thrift regulators to examine more small banks and thrifts every 18 months, instead of annually as most institutions are. Prior law permitted institutions with $175 million in assets that received good but not excellent supervisory ratings to receive on-site examinations every 18 months. The new law raises that cap to $250 million.

• **Agency Reports.** Eliminated a requirement that the Federal Reserve collect data each year on the availability of credit to small farms and small and minority-owned businesses. Repealed a requirement that bank regulators report annually to Congress on enforcement actions as well as on troubled foreign loans held by U.S. banks.

- **Regulatory Review.** Required regulators to review all banking regulations every 10 years and eliminate outdated or otherwise unnecessary rules.
- **Insider Lending.** Permitted the Fed under certain conditions to allow preferential "insider loans" to officers and directors of affiliates, provided the insider does not have a significant management role at the depository institution. The affiliate cannot be controlled by another company or exceed 10 percent of holding company assets.

Securities Fraud Lawsuits

A bipartisan Congress voted in December 1995 to override President Clinton's surprise veto of a widely backed bill to change the playing field for securities fraud lawsuits. It was the only successful veto override of Clinton's first term.

The bill (HR 1058—PL 104-67) was intended to block attorneys from launching what sponsors said were frivolous class-action lawsuits against publicly traded companies whose stock had lost substantial value.

Clinton had not raised the threat of a veto during the year-long debate on the measure, which was a low profile but heavily lobbied part of the House GOP's "Contract with America." Clinton's Dec. 19 veto stunned bill sponsors, including Sen. Christopher J. Dodd, D-Conn.

Dodd then out-lobbied the president to reverse the veto, an effort that was made easier because both the House and Senate had passed the bill by sweeping margins.

BACKGROUND

Supporters of the measure said it was aimed mostly at thwarting a small group of attorneys who made a cottage industry of watching for a company whose stock dropped suddenly, scouring the company's records for optimistic projections and suing on the grounds that the statements had misled and defrauded shareholders. Especially vulnerable to such lawsuits—and therefore supporting the bill—were high technology companies, whose shares tended to be volatile and which often settled such cases out of court.

Opponents acknowledged some lawyers abused the system, but they contended the effect of the measure would go beyond curtailing the 250 or so class-action shareholder suits filed each year. They said the measure would roll back more than a half-century's worth of laws designed to protect investors from fraud in the securities markets.

The measure contained numerous provisions to deter meritless lawsuits. It established new rules to give plaintiffs rather than lawyers greater control over the lawsuit. For instance, it required judges to allow the largest investor to be the lead plaintiff in any suit.

Plaintiffs were required to cite specific facts to support their claims when filing a suit, and judges were permitted to penalize those filing lawsuits found to be frivolous. The bill barred lawyers from paying investors to attach their names to a lawsuit and modified the system for paying attorney's fees in order to ensure that investors got their fair share of damages.

The most bitterly fought provision created a "safe harbor" to protect corporations from liability for erroneous projections of future company performance. It allowed companies to make projections that turned out to be wrong, provided the projections were accompanied by cautionary statements that warned that the projections might be inaccurate. Critics said the "safe harbor" would permit corporations to make knowingly false and fraudulent statements to stockholders without having to worry about being sued.

Another controversial provision established a system of "proportionate liability" under which defendants generally would be liable only for the share of liability for which they are found responsible, as determined by a judge or jury. Under the existing system of joint and several liability, a defendant who was only partly responsible for defrauding investors could be held responsible for all damages if other defendants could not pay. That gave attorneys an incentive to target deep-pocketed defendants who play a small role in a fraudulent action.

HOUSE ACTION

The House Commerce Subcommittee on Telecommunications and Finance took the first action on the measure, approving a draft version on Feb. 14 by voice vote.

The full Commerce Committee approved the bill (HR 1058) on Feb. 16 by a 33–10 vote. The committee's Republicans were joined in support of the bill by eight Democrats.

The original GOP plan—derived from the structure of the Contract with America—was to include the shareholder lawsuit provisions in a broader bill to curb all civil lawsuits. The shareholder provisions were broken into a separate bill so that no single element of the larger package would threaten enactment of the others.

The House committee–approved bill went much further than the measure that was eventually enacted, containing a controversial "loser pays" provision to require that a losing plaintiff pay attorneys' fees unless the court determined the plaintiff had a justifiable reason for bringing the suit. Opponents said this provision would have scared off small investors with legitimate claims.

The House passed HR 1058 by a 325–99 vote on March 8. Before passage, the House agreed, 252–173, to an amendment by sponsor Christopher Cox, R-Calif., clarifying the "safe harbor" provision to exempt from liability only companies that did not "deliberately" mislead investors. The House rejected, 167–254, an amendment from Thomas J. Manton, D-N.Y., that would have restricted the "loser pays" provision to cases where the plaintiff's arguments were deemed to be frivolous.

SENATE ACTION

The Senate Banking Committee approved its version of the bill (S 240—S Rept 104-98) on May 25, by an 11–4 vote, with four Democrats joining all but one Republican in support.

The bill was largely the product of negotiations between committee Chairman Alfonse M. D'Amato, R-N.Y., and Dodd. It contained some of the same provisions as the House bill, but did not include the "loser pays" language passed by the House.

The committee-approved bill permitted the largest investor to be the lead plaintiff in any suit, established proportional liability for plaintiffs and established a "safe harbor" for earnings forecasts or other predictions, so long as there was no intent to deceive investors. Those who knowingly made fraudulent statements with the intent of misleading investors could still be sued, but top committee Democrat Paul S. Sarbanes of Maryland said that standard was much too high, and would permit companies to make false and reckless statements without being liable for them.

On the Senate floor the bill withstood most of a barrage of Democratic amendments. After debating and amending S 240, the Senate substituted the text of HR 1058 with that of the Senate bill. The Senate passed the amended version of HR 1058 by 70–29 on June 28.

Among the amendments rejected during floor debate was one by Sarbanes to deny "safe harbor" protections for false statements. A motion to table, or kill, Sarbanes's amendment was agreed to, 50–48.

The Senate also rejected, 43–56, a Sarbanes amendment to give the Securities and Exchange Commission (SEC) authority to craft "safe harbor" regulations instead of enforcing the provision as designed by Congress.

CONFERENCE, FINAL ACTION

The bill lingered in conference until November, as House and Senate negotiators slowly worked out their differences. It represented one of the few instances of bipartisan congressional cooperation in 1995, but it was clear that for a bill to become law, it would have to closely mirror the more tame Senate version.

House and Senate conferees approved a final version of the bill Nov. 28, endorsing a compromise that had been worked out in advance in unofficial talks.

The Senate adopted the conference report on Dec. 5 by a 65–30 vote. The following day, the House cleared the measure by a 320–102 vote.

The final bill generally resembled the Senate version. It dropped the "loser pays" language, though a judge would be permitted to determine that a lawsuit was frivolous and order plaintiffs to pay defendant's fees and expenses.

The final bill also included a modified "safe harbor" for false "forward-looking" statements if they were accompanied by "meaningful cautionary statements" that included specific information that could affect stock prices. (The conference agreement was reached after SEC Chairman Arthur Levitt—reportedly after pressure from Dodd and D'Amato—indicated that his agency supported the "safe harbor" language, though it did not explicitly say the agency supported the bill.)

VETO AND OVERRIDE

Throughout the year, the White House had objected to parts of the bill, but Clinton had not given any indication that he would veto the bill. Critics on both sides of the issue were frustrated by Clinton's lack of engagement on the issue.

Clinton vetoed the bill Dec. 19 just hours before the bill would have become law without his signature. In his veto message, Clinton said the bill made it too difficult for plaintiffs to bring legitimate lawsuits, and he objected to language that treated plaintiffs more harshly than defendants for violating federal rules against filing frivolous suits.

Barely 13 hours after Clinton's veto, the House voted 319–100 to override on a **key vote of 319–100 (R 230–0; D 89–99; I 0–1)**. *(1995 key votes, p. 1025)*

The Senate overrode the veto on Dec. 22 on a **key vote of 68–30 (R 48–4; D 20–26)**. *(1995 key votes, p. 1025)*

Clinton concentrated his anti-override effort on the Senate, but Dodd worked hard to out-lobby Clinton. Not a single senator switched his vote. Many Democrats were angered at the way Clinton handled the matter. They were dismayed that he directed his veto at issues the administration had not previously raised. And they complained that he showed his hand too late, making it politically difficult if not impossible for senators to switch their positions. ❑

Securities Law Overhaul

Congress in 1996 cleared a bill to strip away duplicative regulation of the securities and mutual fund industries, reauthorize the activities of the Securities and Exchange Commission (SEC) and overhaul the financing of the SEC.

As enacted, the bill (HR 3005—PL 104-290) was significantly scaled back from what sponsors initially proposed. President Clinton signed the bill into law Oct. 11, 1996.

The measure streamlined the often overlapping regulation of mutual funds, stock offerings and investment advisers by the states and the SEC essentially by preempting state regulation. It had widespread backing from the securities industry and benefited from an especially powerful push from the mutual fund industry, which was largely freed from a patchwork quilt of state registration requirements. The bill also gradually reduced SEC stock registration fees.

The new law made changes to the 1933 Securities Act, the 1934 Securities Exchange Act, the 1940 Investment Advisers Act and the 1940 Investment Company Act.

Supporters, led by Jack Fields, R-Texas, chairman of the House Commerce Subcommittee on Telecommunications and Finance, had to overcome resistance from state securities regulators, whose turf would have been trampled under an earlier draft of the bill.

Fields initially proposed to preempt most state securities laws and regulations, allow stockbrokers to more freely pitch risky investments to institutional clients, repeal major portions of a law that helped companies detect hostile takeovers and permit stockbrokers to sell newly issued securities to clients who had not received prospectuses.

Just before a subcommittee markup in March 1996, Fields and his ranking Democrat, Edward J. Markey of Massachusetts, met and agreed to scrap the more controversial provisions. A redrafted version (HR 3005) sailed through the House and that action prompted the Senate to begin work in earnest.

The Senate bill, which passed June 27, was substantially similar to the House bill, which made it relatively easy to find a conference compromise. One issue remained troublesome, though: how to overhaul regulation of the booming investment adviser industry. A long-standing House-Senate disagreement over the issue was resolved as Congress was preparing to adjourn for the year, allowing the bill to be enacted.

BACKGROUND

The effort began in 1995 as part of a Republican drive to relax regulations and make it easier for corporations to raise capital; however, the first draft of the House bill (HR 2131) came under attack from critics who said it would have recklessly eroded decades' worth of laws designed to protect investors.

HR 2131 would have preempted most state securities laws and regulations. Supporters argued that myriad state laws cost corporations and securities firms hundreds of millions of dollars in compliance expenses. Opponents countered that state regulators were often the first to spot new schemes aimed at ripping off investors.

Emasculating state regulators—many of whom were armed with tougher laws than the SEC—promised to let many wrongdoers get away, while shifting a huge enforcement burden to the federal agency, critics said.

The bill also would have eliminated key elements of the Williams Act, a 1968 law that required companies to make disclosures when they bought large blocks of a company's stock to give companies and investors notice of takeover attempts. Supporters said that complying with the law cost corporations too much in lawyers' fees.

Securities and Exchange Commission Chairman Arthur Levitt Jr. opposed most of the measure's major provisions, though he took pains not to blast the bill too forcefully. "HR 2131 contributes some provocative ideas," Levitt said at a Nov. 30, 1995 hearing. However, he added, "Our markets are so good, so vital, so strong, that any changes must be done with the greatest of care and the greatest of caution."

Fields acknowledged that the bill was a "work in progress." His subcommittee had a history of bipartisan cooperation when advancing securities-related legislation. Typically, it gave great deference to the SEC.

In the wake of criticism from Levitt and others, Fields negotiated with other senior panel members to produce a compromise.

HOUSE ACTION

The Telecommunications and Finance Subcommittee approved Fields's revised bill (HR 3005) by a vote of 25–0 on March 7 after a round of negotiations that involved Fields, Commerce Chairman Thomas J. Bliley Jr., R-Va., John D. Dingell, D-Mich., the ranking member of the full committee, and Markey.

The compromise bill laid out most of the framework for what eventually became law. Gone was a provision to eliminate for large institutional clients a requirement that brokers offer only investments deemed "suitable." Also dropped was a provision to repeal key elements of the Williams Act.

In addition, the new draft did not attack the authority of state regulators as much as did the original Fields bill, though it eliminated many duplications between state and federal regulations governing mutual funds and other securities activities.

The most significant feature of the bill was the end of state oversight of mutual funds, leaving such regulation to the SEC. This promised to make it easier for mutual fund sponsors to get new funds to the market.

Another major provision significantly scaled back state regulation of securities offerings, though state regulators were to retain authority over stock offerings by companies with assets of less than $10 million as well as much of their power to police fraud and sales abuses by brokers.

Another provision permitted securities firms to borrow from insurance companies, pension funds and other lenders and therefore save millions through lowered borrowing costs to finance securities trades. Previously, such financing had to be obtained from commercial banks.

House Committee Action

Two months later, after negotiations to fine-tune the measure, HR 3005 sailed through the full House Commerce Committee May 15 by unanimous voice vote (H Rept 104-622).

Deferring to state securities regulators, the panel agreed to preserve state authority in several areas, including issues of penny stocks, enforcement against fraud and collection of fees on new stock issues.

The effort earned praise from Levitt and Wall Street. It won the endorsement of trade groups representing the mutual fund and securities industries. Criticism from state securities regulators was muted.

House Floor Action

The House passed HR 3005 on June 19 by a 407–8 vote. However, the measure lost the backing of the Clinton administration because Bliley added to the bill the text of a separate measure to reauthorize the SEC's budget.

The SEC authorization bill (HR 2972) had passed the House in March, but it was not supported by the White House because it proposed to leave the watchdog agency at the mercy of appropriators, instead of being financed through the fees it collected on securities filings and transactions.

The authorization provisions added to HR 3005 proposed to reduce or eliminate various SEC fees over five years, losing $680 million in revenue. The potential revenue loss complicated prospects for enactment, but it also forced the administration and Congress to negotiate over the agency's budget, which had bedeviled Congress for years.

SEC fees were to be reduced to an amount equal to the agency's budget, but the money was no longer to be earmarked for the agency. Instead, the SEC was to be made subject to appropriations. That prospect caused anxiety within the Clinton administration, which worried about the revenue loss and the prospect of the SEC competing with other popular programs financed under the annual Commerce-Justice-State spending bill.

SENATE ACTION

The Senate Banking Committee released a draft bill at the same time the draft House committee bill was circulating for comment. The Senate draft, written by Senate Banking Securities Subcommittee Chairman Phil Gramm, R-Texas, generally mirrored the House measure, with a few additions.

Gramm's draft included language to authorize $16 million in 1997 and 1998 to regulate investment advisers, while transferring to the states sole responsibility for regulating smaller advisers. The House measure contained no language on the regulation of investment advisers.

The Senate draft also contained a provision to gradually reduce SEC stock registration fees from 1/29 of 1 percent of the value of a stock offering to 1/50 of 1 percent. That mirrored the fee provisions of HR 2972 that were added to HR 3005 on the House floor.

Another provision in Gramm's draft was derived from a bill that passed the Senate in 1993 and promised to ease restrictions on the ability of investment companies to invest in the stocks of small corporations.

Senate Committee Action

Gramm's bill (S 1815—S Rept 104-293) won unanimous 16–0 Banking Committee approval on June 19, the same day the House passed HR 3005.

Like the House bill, it contained broadly supported provisions to eliminate much of the ability of the states to regulate large securities offerings and mutual funds. It also contained language virtually identical to the House plan to overhaul the 1940 Investment Company Act, which governed the booming market in mutual funds.

In addition to preempting state regulation of mutual funds, the measure sought to simplify the way mutual funds calculated and paid registration fees to the SEC, to permit funds to include more information in advertisements and to make it easier for mutual funds to invest in other mutual funds.

Due to opposition from the Clinton administration, language in Gramm's earlier draft to cut SEC stock registration fees was not included.

Senate Floor Action

The Senate passed HR 3005 on June 27 by voice vote during a late-night "mop-up" session prior to the July Fourth holiday. The principals were not present and their statements were inserted into the Congressional Record.

Before passing the bill, the text S 1815 as approved by the Senate Banking Committee was substituted for the text of HR 3005 as it passed the House.

CONFERENCE, FINAL ACTION

The biggest issues that faced House-Senate conference negotiators involved SEC fees and the regulation of investment advisers.

Negotiations between House Commerce Committee Chairman Bliley and Sen. Ernest F. Hollings, D-S.C., culminated in agreement Sept. 9 on the SEC fee question. Hollings was the top Democrat on the Senate Commerce, Justice and State Appropriations Subcommittee—which oversaw the agency's budget—and he had supported the administration.

Under their compromise, SEC fees for stock registration were to slide from 1/29 of 1 percent of the value of the stock to 1/50 of 1 percent over 10 years—and then drop to 1/150 of 1 percent in 2007.

In addition, over-the-counter stock exchanges were to pay the same 1/300 of 1 percent fee on every stock trade that the New York and American exchanges paid. That fee was slated to drop in 2007 to 1/800 of 1 percent. The reduced fees were to produce about $850 million less in revenues over 10 years.

Disagreements over regulation of investment advisers between the House and Senate—chiefly between Markey and Gramm—threatened to derail the effort, however.

Prior Congresses had killed efforts to beef up oversight of investment advisers. Gramm played a central role in killing House efforts, which were shaped largely by Markey and then-Energy and Commerce Committee Chairman Dingell. (*Congress and the Nation Vol. VIII, p. 159*)

A flurry of offers and counteroffers were exchanged as Congress was about to adjourn in late September 1996, but the impasse continued into the very latest stages of the legislative process—the last day (Sept. 28) that the House was in regular session.

Longtime adversaries Gramm and Markey each gave ground in the end. Gramm successfully blocked new fees on the industry and prevailed on his provision to lift state regulation of larger adviser firms. Markey preserved the ability of states to oversee small-client investment advisers and won inclusion of a provision to make it easier for investors to call a toll-free telephone number to find out whether their advisers had been disciplined by regulators.

The deal was reached only hours before members were set to go home for the year. The House adopted the conference report by voice vote on Sept. 28; the Senate cleared the bill by voice vote on Oct. 1. President Clinton signed it into law on Oct. 11.

PROVISIONS

As cleared, the securities law overhaul and Securities and Exchange Commission authorization bill of 1996 (HR 3005—PL 104-290):

Capital Markets

• **Securities Registration.** Preempted, or blocked, state regulation of "covered securities," including those listed on national exchanges such as the New York Stock Exchange, American Stock Exchange and NASDAQ, as well as other exchanges with standards that were substantially similar. Also covered: securities (mutual funds) issued by registered investment companies; securities sold to "qualified purchasers" as defined by the Securities and Exchange Commission (SEC); certain secondary market transactions; unsolicited customer trades by brokers; government securities, commercial paper and other securities issued under section 3(a) of the Securities Act (except for securities of nonprofit organizations, intrastate transactions and municipal bonds); and private placements.

Many states already exempted many of these types of securities under prior law.

States were also preempted from regulating prospectuses, proxy statements, annual reports or disclosure documents.

State authority was preserved in several areas: enforcement of laws regarding fraud, deceit and unlawful conduct. States could also continue to collect securities registration fees. As under prior practice, states could not impose registration fees on stocks listed on national exchanges.

States retained fee and regulatory authority over "small-cap" NASDAQ offerings and securities traded on regional exchanges.

• **Broker-Dealer Regulation.** Preempted certain state laws that regulated broker-dealers differently than federal law did. State laws that imposed financial responsibility, bonding, reporting and margin or custody requirements inconsistent with or exceeding the Exchange Act were preempted. In other words, broker-dealers were no longer subject to differing state net capital and recordkeeping requirements.

Stockbrokers were permitted to execute, subject to certain requirements, a de minimis number of transactions for customers vacationing in a state where the broker is not licensed.

• **Margin Lenders.** Permitted broker-dealers to borrow from sources other than banks (such as insurance companies or pension funds) to meet margin requirements. Margin requirements were made more flexible for brokers to finance market-making and underwriting positions.

• **SEC Flexibility.** Granted the SEC additional regulatory flexibility by providing general authority to the agency to exempt firms, securities and types of transactions from the Securities Act and the Exchange Act and any regulations issued under those laws, provided the exemption was necessary or appropriate in the public interest and did not harm investors. The idea behind the provision was to give the SEC greater flexibility to modernize securities registration and regulation without having to rely on sometimes tortured interpretations of existing law.

• **SEC Mission.** Directed the agency to consider "efficiency, competition and capital formation" when issuing regulations or reviewing self-regulatory organizations, such as the National Association of Securities Dealers, provided the public interest was served and investors protected.

• **Privatization of "EDGAR."** Required the agency to examine proposals to privatize the Electronic Data Gathering And Retrieval (EDGAR) system, which permitted securities issuers to file reports via computer and makes that information and other SEC data available to investors, analysts and other individuals.

• **Examination Coordination.** Required the SEC and self-regulatory organizations (SROs) to share information and work in a coordinated fashion to eliminate burdensome duplication in the examination process. The SEC and the SROs were already working toward this goal.

• **Foreign News Conferences.** Required the SEC—which had already proposed a rule in this area—to make it easier for

U.S. journalists to gain access to offshore news conferences and materials without violating the Securities Act.

Mutual Funds

• **General Rules.** Overhauled the Investment Company Act, the law governing investment companies that principally offered mutual funds. Generally, the bill simplified the process for registering mutual funds, eased rules on advertising, permitted so-called funds of funds and made it easier for sophisticated investors to invest in private investment funds, many of which are known as "hedge funds."

• **Funds of Funds.** Relaxed restrictions on so-called funds of funds—mutual funds that invested in other funds—provided these new funds of funds invested only in affiliated funds within the same corporate "family," something the SEC had allowed on a limited, case-by-case basis. The agency was given authority to permit funds to invest in nonaffiliated funds.

• **Flexible Registration of Securities.** Simplified the system under which mutual funds calculated and paid registration fees under the Securities Act. (Mutual funds were continuously in registration, which complicated the registration process.)

Mutual funds were permitted to pay registration fees to the SEC within 90 days after the end of their fiscal year, based upon net sales for that year.

• **Fund Advertising.** Provided mutual funds with more flexibility to advertise by removing restrictions that limited mutual fund ads to information contained in official prospectuses. The new flexibility permitted mutual funds to issue an "advertising prospectus" that could contain other information, such as up-to-the-present details about fund performance.

• **Variable Insurance Contracts.** Permitted more flexibility in the regulation of variable insurance contracts. Prior limits on the amount, type and timing of fees were replaced with a requirement that aggregate charges be "reasonable."

• **Reports to the SEC and Shareholders.** Broadened SEC authority to permit the agency to require investment companies to file reports to the agency more frequently than on a quarterly basis. The agency could require reporting of such information as it deemed necessary to keep "reasonably current," including investment activities and performance results. Such additional information was to be provided to shareholders.

• **Books, Records and Inspections.** Expanded the SEC's regulatory authority to permit the agency to require mutual fund and investment companies to keep any records that the SEC deems "necessary or appropriate in the public interest or for the protection of investors," instead of only records related to an investment company's financial statement as required under existing law.

• **Misleading Fund Names.** Expanded SEC rulemaking authority to permit the agency to block mutual funds from using deceptive or misleading words or phrases in naming mutual funds or other securities.

• **Exempted Investment Companies.** Exempted a number of entities from regulation under the Investment Company Act, including dealers in interest rate and currency "swaps."

In addition, private investment pools whose securities were

held by "qualified purchasers," namely wealthy individuals and institutional investors, were exempted from the Investment Company Act, which had limited such entities to 100 or fewer investors.

(Qualified purchasers primarily included individuals with investments of at least $5 million and institutions with investments of at least $25 million.)

The most significant effect of the provision was to permit "hedge" funds to sell securities to more than 100 investors. Such privately traded funds typically invested in riskier investments such as options and derivatives than did publicly traded mutual funds.

The prior 100-investor exemption to the act for private investment pools was further streamlined.

The SEC was given authority to define additional persons as qualified investors and was required to define what constitutes an "investment" for purposes of meeting the $5 million and $25 million caps for eligibility to participate in a hedge fund.

• **Performance Fees.** Exempted investment advisers to hedge funds and other qualified purchaser pools from the Investment Advisers Act's general prohibition on fees based on investment performance. Such performance fees were also permitted for offshore clients of investment advisers and for advice provided to sophisticated investors.

Investment Advisers

• **General Rules.** Overhauled the Investment Advisers Act, which governed the booming market in financial planning. Smaller investment adviser firms were to be regulated by the states; the SEC was to regulate and examine larger investment adviser firms.

• **SEC Funding.** Authorized $20 million in both fiscal 1997 and 1998 for additional scrutiny of investment advisers, or financial planners. (None of this money was appropriated for fiscal 1997.)

• **Federal/State Regulation.** Divided regulatory responsibility for advisers between the SEC and the states, based generally upon assets under management.

Investment advisers with assets of $25 million or more (or such higher figure set by the SEC) were required to register and be regulated by the SEC, as were investment advisers that service investment companies registered with the SEC or that were not regulated by their home states. (Four states did not regulate the industry.) The SEC anticipated regulating 28 percent of all advisers, representing 96 percent of assets under management by advisers.

All other advisers, those with less than $25 million in assets, were required to register with the state in which they maintained their principal place of business.

States were preempted from regulating investment adviser firms registered with the SEC or their supervised persons, including employees who did not have contact with customers.

States also retained authority to receive filings and existing registration fees from SEC-registered and regulated advisers and retained antifraud authority over all advisers.

States could register "investment adviser representatives"—as later defined by the SEC—of SEC-registered advisers, such as certain contract workers, if those representatives had a place of business in the state.

• **State Uniformity.** In cases in which advisers were state-registered, the home state determined capital, bonding and recordkeeping requirements. States were prohibited from requiring registration or licensing of out-of-state investment advisers that had six or fewer clients within the state.

• **Convicted Felons.** Permitted the SEC to revoke registration and licenses of persons convicted of all felonies, not just ones involving financial crimes.

• **Investor Access to Information.** Required the SEC to establish and maintain a readily accessible telephonic or other electronic process (intended to be a toll-free number) to enable investors to obtain information regarding disciplinary actions and proceedings against investment advisers.

SEC Authorization/Fees

• **SEC Authorization.** Authorized fiscal 1997 appropriations of $300 million for the SEC.

• **Securities Registration Fees.** Reduced future SEC registration fees from 1/29th of 1 percent in fiscal 1996 to 1/50th of 1 percent in 2006, and then 1/150th of 1 percent in 2007 and subsequent years. (The statutory limit in the Securities Act was 1/50th of 1 percent, but prior appropriations bills had raised the fees.)

Fees in excess of 1/50th of 1 percent could be used as "offsetting collections" to directly fund the agency, subject to approval of congressional appropriators; in the event of a lapse in appropriations, the agency could continue to collect fees at the level of the prior year.

• **Transaction Fees.** Imposed transaction fees of 1/300th of 1 percent on the aggregate dollar amount of each stock trade through 2007, when they were to be reduced to 1/800th of 1 percent. Prior law imposed the 1/300th of 1 percent fee on stocks traded on exchanges but not for the NASDAQ over-the-counter market.

As with the above registration fees, the transaction fees could be used as offsetting collections.

Miscellaneous

• **Economic, Business and Development Companies.** Exempted a new class of investment companies—those whose activities were limited to economic, business or industrial development in the same state—from the Investment Company Act. (The effect was to exempt them from SEC regulation.) Such companies were aimed at stimulating local economies by providing direct investment and lending, as well as managerial assistance, to state and local businesses.

For a company to qualify for the exemption, at least 80 percent of its securities had to be sold to state residents. Only accredited investors could purchase the securities, which could not be redeemed before the maturity date.

• **Intrastate Closed-End Investment Companies.** Provided the SEC greater flexibility to exempt from regulation closed-end funds that issued securities only within a particular state by increasing the aggregate amount of securities that could be offered from $100,000 to $10,000,000.

• **Business Development Companies.** Modified existing law to lift certain restrictions on "business development companies," which were closed-end funds that invested in small and developing businesses and, unlike traditional mutual funds, were required to provide managerial assistance to the businesses in which they invested.

Most significantly, the class of businesses eligible to receive investments and managerial help ("small eligible company") from business development companies was broadened to include a new class: those with assets of less than $4 million and capital and surplus of at least $2 million. Business development companies were permitted to invest in, but not provide managerial assistance to, these new eligible portfolio companies.

• **Church Employee Pension Plans.** Exempted from most federal securities laws any church employee pension plan and preempted state regulation of such plans. None of the assets in such plans may be diverted to any other use but to benefit employees, who had to be notified that the plan was not regulated.

• **Studies and Reports.** Required the SEC to conduct a number of studies, including: the need for international accounting standards; impact of technological advances; shareholder proposals; the practice of giving preference to some customers when executing stock trades; and ways to develop uniform state broker-dealer licenses.

CHAPTER 3

Trade Policy

Trade Policy

In his first two years in office, President Clinton brought to fruition two landmark trade initiatives begun by his Republican predecessors: the North American Free Trade Agreement (NAFTA) and the Uruguay Round of the General Agreement on Tariffs and Trade (GATT). These pacts, however, represented the high-water mark for free trade and multilateralism in the mid-1990s, as shifting political winds caused Congress and the administration to change their trade priorities.

The emotional NAFTA debate was a defining moment for Clinton and Congress both. More than any previous trade agreement, NAFTA brought home the risks as well as the benefits of the long-standing U.S. preference for free trade. The abstract notion of lower tariffs suddenly became very real to mainstream Americans—either as a threat to their jobs or as the promise of a new and growing market close at hand.

Some key Democratic constituencies crusaded against the agreement, and they had formidable allies in Congress, particularly among northeastern Democrats. Clinton, however, took up the free-trade mantle of such Democratic presidents as Franklin D. Roosevelt, John F. Kennedy and Lyndon B. Johnson, all of whom viewed trade as an engine of economic growth.

Clinton was not a purist on trade, however. Adopting some of the "fair trade" rhetoric of congressional Democrats, Clinton frequently threatened the nation's trading partners with retaliatory sanctions if they did not import more U.S. products or correct other perceived problems. He also tried to use NAFTA to improve environmental and labor conditions in Mexico as well as lower trade barriers, helping to ease some Democratic concerns.

Still, NAFTA needed strong Republican support to overcome the entrenched opposition of liberal Democrats. Clinton proved for the first time in his presidency that he could join forces with congressional Republicans, assembling a wholly new coalition to win approval for NAFTA.

The negotiation and implementation of a new GATT, while not as hard-fought as NAFTA, was a larger victory for U.S. free-traders. Bringing seven years of difficult negotiations to a largely successful conclusion, the revised GATT was a major step toward lower trade barriers around the globe.

The dominion of the free-traders was short-lived. When a new Republican majority took control of Congress in 1995, GOP leaders tried to assert U.S. national interests more aggressively. Trade became subservient to foreign policy on a number of fronts, and others Republicans were less inclined to give Clinton the leeway he sought to negotiate new agreements.

The support for free trade diminished further in 1996 as Republican Pat Buchanan, a self-styled populist and NAFTA bash-er, rang up victories in the early GOP presidential primaries. Both Clinton and his main GOP rival, Senate Majority Leader Bob Dole of Kansas, toughened their rhetoric about America's trading partners. The atmosphere was so charged, free-trade advocates in Congress decided to set aside most of their trade bills rather than risk having them defeated or turned into protectionist vehicles.

TRADE DEFICIT CLIMBS

The growing hostility toward free trade was fueled in part by the steadily deepening trade deficit. Although the United States had for years been importing more goods than it exported, the merchandise trade deficit burgeoned in the 1980s, growing to $160 billion in 1987. The deficit narrowed during the Bush administration, in part because of the Gulf War and in part because of a recession that dampened demand for imported goods. But it started growing again after 1991, and the trend continued through 1996. From a low of $74 billion in 1991, the merchandise trade deficit grew to $133 billion by the end of 1993 and an estimated $191 billion by the end of 1996.

U.S. exports rose steadily, even robustly, throughout the period. Imports grew as well, however, despite a decline in the value of the dollar. The currency's decline was not as steep as the 40 percent drop in the mid-1980s, yet it still alarmed some analysts. In 1994, the dollar reached its lowest value against the Japanese yen since World War II, prompting the previously hands-off Treasury Department to order the Federal Reserve to buy dollars on the Asian market. By the end of the first Clinton term, the dollar had returned to its level at the end of the Bush administration, when measured against the trade-weighted average of foreign currencies.

REFERENCES

Discussion of trade action for the years 1945–1964 may be found in *Congress and the Nation Vol. I,* pp. 187–207; for the years 1965–1968, *Congress and the Nation Vol. II,* pp. 49–116; for the years 1969–1972, *Congress and the Nation Vol. III,* pp. 119–134; for the years 1973–1976, *Congress and the Nation Vol. IV,* pp. 125–137; for the years 1977–1980, *Congress and the Nation Vol. V,* pp. 267–276; for the years 1981–1984, *Congress and the Nation Vol. VI,* pp. 95–112; for the years 1985–1988, *Congress and the Nation Vol. VII,* pp. 139–166; for the years 1989–1992, *Congress and the Nation Vol. VIII,* pp. 165–200.

Trade Balance

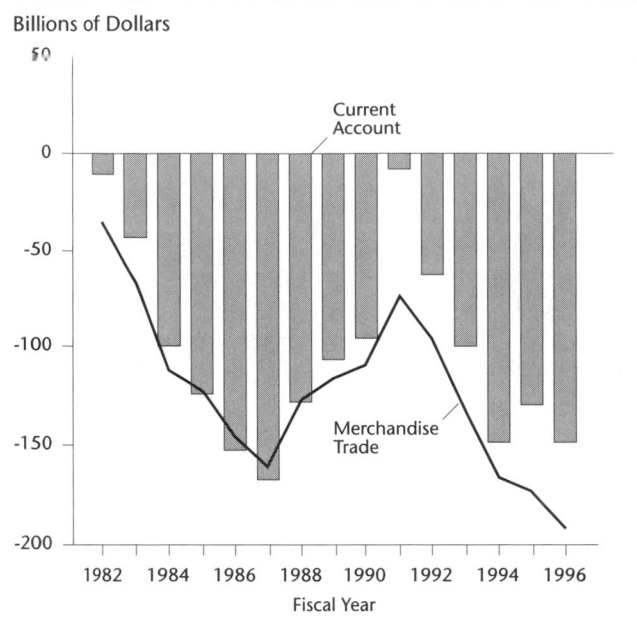

Billions of Dollars

SOURCES: Office of Management and Budget, *Economic Report of the President 1997* (Washington, D.C.: U.S. Government Printing Office, 1997), Tables B-101 and B-103; Commerce Department, Bureau of Economic Analysis.

The deficit in investments also grew during the first Clinton term. The value of U.S.-owned assets abroad first exceeded the value of foreign-owned assets in the United States in 1988; by 1996, the gap had widened to almost $10 billion.

One area where the United States continued to lead its trading partners was in services, where exports exceeded imports by a growing margin. Still, the merchandise trade deficit far outweighed the services surplus. The overall trade deficit in goods, services, investment income and monetary transfers—the so-called balance on current account—was $62.6 billion in 1992, George Bush's last year in office, and it grew to an estimated $148 billion in 1996. (The record trade imbalance was the $167 billion set in 1987 during the Reagan era.)

Thus, although Clinton's negotiating strategies on currency and trade may have helped continue the growth of U.S. exports, on balance they did not stem the tide of rising trade deficits. That increase, in turn, spelled trouble for trade legislation in the second half of Clinton's first term.

THE NAFTA ORDEAL

Clinton took office at a time when the Democratic Party, after a decade of bashing Republican presidents' trade policies, found itself needing—and lacking—a policy of its own. The major fault line was between the old-line free-traders, such as Ways and Means Committee Chairman Dan Rostenkowski, D-Ill., and those who wanted a more aggressive, retaliatory posture, led by House Majority Leader Richard A. Gephardt, D-Mo.

Clinton's choice for U.S. trade representative was a neutral pick: Mickey Kantor, a lobbyist and Democratic Party insider with no track record on international trade. As a negotiator, Kantor would prove to be very formidable—the proverbial tough cop with a holster full of punitive tariffs and import quotas. First, however, Clinton and Kantor had to deal with NAFTA, the trade pact they had inherited from President Bush.

During the presidential campaign, Clinton had given NAFTA a late and tepid endorsement, stressing the need to attend to labor and environmental issues. Organized labor, environmental groups and consumer activists—three core Democratic constituencies—were fiercely opposed to NAFTA, arguing that U.S. corporations would flock to Mexico for its cheap labor and lax environmental standards. The main beneficiaries of the deal would be corporate shareholders, they argued, while U.S. blue-collar workers and border communities would pay the price.

After winning the presidency, Clinton's options were limited. If he tried to renegotiate the pact, he risked damaging U.S. credibility in other trade negotiations. On the other hand, the administration had some leverage over Mexico because the Mexican government was eager for a deal. So the administration extracted from Mexico a series of side agreements addressing some of the concerns about wage differentials, environmental standards and import surges.

This linkage of trade with social issues would recur often in the Clinton administration. Still, in selling NAFTA to the public, the administration's main argument was the free-traders' pitch that trade was critical to the country's economy. For example, in a nationally televised debate with Texas billionaire Ross Perot, a leading NAFTA critic and patron of a nascent independent political party, Vice President Al Gore likened NAFTA's opponents to the sponsors of the 1930 Tariff Act of 1930 (PL 71-361). Better known as the Smoot-Hawley Act, the law boosted tariffs on more than 20,000 items, triggering an international wave of protectionism that economists have since blamed for prolonging the global depression.

Selling NAFTA to Congress, and to the House in particular, was another story. The administration struck a whirl of deals aimed at addressing Democrats' concerns about the pact's effect on their districts. To bolster Republican support, Clinton blasted the labor unions and pledged to defend any member of either party who voted for the pact. Administration officials also argued that defeating NAFTA would cripple Clinton's efforts to bring the GATT talks to a successful conclusion.

Although NAFTA's opponents howled at the dealmaking, it helped carry the day for Clinton in November 1993. Critical support in the House came from members representing the western and southern border states, the southeastern Sunbelt, and the wheat-growing Midwest. Opposition came largely from areas high in blue-collar workers, import-sensitive manufacturers (such as clothing and shoe makers) and non-Mexican immigrants.

By endorsing NAFTA, Congress moved beyond the debate of the previous decade, when free-trade forces found themselves on the defensive, parrying efforts to protect particular industries from foreign competition. Significantly, it was the first time the United States had agreed to take down all economic walls guarding it from a country whose economy was as poor and as different from its own as Mexico's.

Next on the trade agenda was GATT. Negotiations had begun in Uruguay in 1986, but they had stalled repeatedly over the issue of agriculture subsidies. The United States originally sought to eliminate all farm subsidies by the year 2000, but later focused on subsidies paid to purchasers of agricultural exports. European negotiators resisted until a compromise was struck in 1992. Even then, though, several stubborn issues remained, such as how quickly to end tariffs on apparel and textile imports. There, U.S. industries pleaded for a lengthy phaseout, while negotiators for developing countries argued for a swift one.

Hoping to push the negotiations to a conclusion in 1993, Clinton sought and Congress provided only a temporary extension for the "fast-track" procedures under which Congress would consider a new trade pact. The legislation effectively set a deadline of December 1993 for the GATT talks to conclude, and negotiators just beat the deadline.

The debate over the new GATT was less heated than the one over NAFTA, even though the issues were similar. One factor was the support for GATT from a broader array of industries, particularly high-technology companies and service. A single, powerful Senate opponent of the pact, Democrat Ernest F. Hollings of South Carolina, used his leverage as chairman of the Senate Commerce Committee to delay a vote on the GATT implementing bill until after the 1994 elections. House and Senate leaders refused to let the measure wait for the 104th Congress, however; they convened a lame duck session and pushed the bill through by a wide margin.

THE TIDE TURNS

The Republican sweep in November 1994 turned the leadership of the House Ways and Means and the Senate Finance committees over to Republicans who were at least as committed to free-trade principles as their Democratic predecessors, if not more so. But the new Congress also brought in a host of freshmen who were committed to reasserting American interests around the globe, as well as reestablishing Republican priorities in Washington. Trade legislation thus ran into conflicting political and philosophical currents.

On the one hand, the Republican majority was responsive to corporate America, which strongly favored free trade in most areas. On the other hand, Republicans cast a suspicious eye on Clinton's trade initiatives, such as his move to bail out the Mexican peso in March 1995. They also were willing to impose punitive trade barriers to achieve other national goals.

The congressional agenda in 1995 was focused on the House Republicans' "Contract with America" and the GOP efforts to balance the federal budget, leaving little room for trade issues. Lawmakers did tuck into the fiscal 1996 budget reconciliation bill (HR 2491) a proposal to renew the duty-free treatment for most imports from developing countries, but the measure was killed by a presidential veto.

More significant were two bills that used trade sanctions to advance U.S. policy toward Cuba, Iran and Libya. The Cuba measure, also known as the Helms-Burton Act, tried to discourage foreign investment in Cuba by allowing U.S. nationals to sue the foreign companies that bought or improved property confiscated by the Cuban government. The other measure proposed to ban trade with foreign companies that invested in the Iranian or Libyan oil industries. *(Cuba sanctions, p. 237; Iran, Libya sanctions, p. 239)*

The bills drew howls from the United States' trading partners, who accused Congress of trying to bully them. Clinton objected to the bills, too, but events and election-year pressures led him to sign them both.

Early in 1996, Republican presidential candidate Buchanan campaigned on an "America First" platform, decrying NAFTA in particular and free-trade deals in general. He hammered away at populist-sounding themes, arguing that free trade benefited corporate fat cats at the expense of the working class. Voters in the early GOP primaries were surprisingly supportive, helping Buchanan to score a stunning victory over Dole in the New Hampshire primary.

Although he soon lost momentum, Buchanan caused Dole and the Clinton administration to move in his direction rhetorically and strike their own populist chords. For example, Dole said on Feb. 29 that he would not vote for NAFTA again unless changes were made, and Kantor signaled a more confrontational posture toward trading partners.

As Dole and Buchanan were testing their messages in South Carolina in February, key lawmakers met behind closed doors on Capitol Hill and quietly agreed to shelve most of the year's free-trade agenda. The legislative atmosphere, they concluded, had been poisoned.

Another factor in the dearth of trade legislation was the split between Clinton and the more purely free-trade Republicans on the House Ways and Means Committee, led by Texas Republican Bill Archer. Clinton asked Congress to revive the fast-track procedures so that the administration could negotiate a free-trade pact with Chile. The Ways and Means panel, however, proposed to rewrite the fast-track ground rules so that they would apply only to policies and practices directly related to trade. The change would have prevented fast-track consideration of a trade agreement that included such things as labor or environmental riders. The administration objected, and the legislation never reached the House floor.

Congress did take up one trade agreement in 1996: a pact to eliminate subsidies for shipyards. After five years of hard bargaining, U.S. trade negotiators had convinced Japan, Korea and the major European shipbuilding nations in December 1994 to phase out their shipbuilding subsidies. Those subsidies made it harder for U.S. yards to compete in the global market for cargo and cruise vessels because the yards received no direct subsidies from the U.S. government. When a bill to implement the pact reached Congress, however, the shipyards' allies would not allow it to pass without an amendment preserving the loan guarantees and other indirect aid that Congress provided for the yards. The resulting controversy sank the implementing bill.

THE CHINA PROBLEM

The shift in rhetoric during the 104th Congress raised the stakes in the annual battle over China's trade status. As in previous years, however, Clinton renewed China's most-favored-nation (MFN) designation, allowing its goods to enter the United States at normal tariff levels, and Congress affirmed his decision.

Clinton's position on China evolved significantly in his first two years as president. Initially he joined a coalition of liberal Democrats and conservative Republicans who argued that China's MFN designation should be tied to its record on human rights, intellectual property and other benchmarks. In 1994, however, Clinton settled into the stance taken by his Republican predecessors, saying that maintaining trade relations with China was key to improving the Chinese government's behavior. His switch raised hackles in the House, yet a resolution to block the MFN renewal was easily defeated.

Meanwhile, the trade deficit with China soared. A mere $10 million in 1985, the deficit reached $34 billion in 1995 despite the rapid growth of U.S. exports to China. Some U.S. industries also complained about rampant, government-sanctioned theft of intellectual property in China. Such piracy cost U.S. companies an estimated $2.3 billion in 1995.

The administration tried taking a harder line with China early in 1995, pledging to impose $2 billion in punitive tariffs unless Beijing cracked down on software and compact disc pirates. After an exchange of threats, the Chinese government promised an ambitious effort to shut down pirate factories. The administration was not impressed with the results, and it renewed the threat of sanctions in 1996. More intense negotiations ensued, resulting in the closure of 15 factories and a suspension of the sanctions.

The debate over China's trade status was unusually mild in 1995 as most House Republicans favored a bill calling for diplomatic initiatives, rather than trade sanctions, to mend China's ways. The Senate did not act on the issue.

The following year, China's provocative actions in the arenas of weapons proliferation, human rights and relations with Taiwan reinvigorated the anti-MFN forces. Still, the House refused to block the MFN designation. While many rank-and-file conservative Republicans opposed MFN,

Dole joined House Speaker Newt Gingrich, R-Ga., and Clinton in supporting China's trade privileges. Dole's endorsement took the issue out of the crucible of presidential politics and made it more difficult for the conservatives to attack the president. With their close links to business, Republicans also were particularly sensitive to the argument that ending MFN would effectively freeze the United States out of China for years to come.

Chronology of Action on Trade

1993–1994

In the 103rd Congress, lawmakers put the finishing touches on two epic trade pacts: the North American Free Trade Agreement (NAFTA), a Bush administration initiative, and a new General Agreement on Tariffs and Trade (GATT), which had been in negotiation for the better part of a decade.

The emotional debate over NAFTA dominated the trade agenda in 1993, with lawmakers split into two camps: those who saw NAFTA as an opportunity to expand U.S. investment and exports in Mexico, and those who believed it would launch an exodus of jobs out of the United States. The debate over GATT the following year was not as highly charged, yet it covered much of the same ground.

Two other long-running efforts to open markets and promote exports—one dealing with financial services, the other with high-technology products that had potential military uses—were again stymied. Opponents of trade with China tried, for the fourth and fifth consecutive year, to impose higher tariffs on imports from that country. Their attempts to link tariffs to human rights issues failed, as even President Clinton—an ally in principle in 1993—took the position that human rights concerns should not influence decisions about trade with China.

NAFTA Implementation

Overcoming fierce opposition from organized labor and its populist allies, President Clinton won congressional approval in November 1993 for the North American Free Trade Agreement (NAFTA), a pact designed to phase out tariffs and trade barriers among the United States, Mexico and Canada.

Clinton had inherited NAFTA from his predecessor, Republican President George Bush, who signed the agreement with the presidents of Mexico and Canada shortly before leaving office. The pact was opposed by some of the Democratic Party's most loyal constituencies, yet Clinton staked the prestige of his presidency on winning its approval.

Before NAFTA could go into effect, Congress had to pass a bill (HR 3450) implementing the pact. The main battleground proved to be the House, where Clinton prevailed on Nov. 17 with the strong support of Republicans—the first time that the GOP had rallied behind the Democratic president on a major issue. The Senate cleared the implementing legislation three days later, and Clinton signed it into law Dec. 8 (PL 103-182).

The agreement extended to Mexico the principles embodied by the U.S.-Canada Free Trade Agreement, which Congress had approved in 1988. Among other things, NAFTA phased out over 15 years the tariffs on goods shipped across the U.S.-Mexican border, provided more protection for U.S. investment and intellectual property in Mexico, and mandated that the United States, Mexico and Canada work toward common environmen-

tal and food-safety standards. *(Highlights, Congress and the Nation Vol. VIII, p. 188; Canada free-trade agreement, Congress and the Nation Vol. VII, p. 159)*

The proposal sparked an intense, emotional debate about the U.S. economy, jobs, imports, exports, environment and foreign competition. The main criticism came from groups who feared that NAFTA would cause U.S. investment and jobs to migrate south while cheap Mexican products flowed north. A free-trade pact made sense only if the countries involved were economic peers, these critics argued; otherwise, the trade deal would cause companies in the more developed nation to shift their operations into the less developed one just as surely as water ran downhill.

The opposition forces were led by labor unions and their Democratic allies in Congress, most notably northern Democrats in the House. They were joined by self-styled populists such as Ross Perot, a billionaire who had run for president as an independent in 1992; Pat Buchanan, a Republican conservative and unsuccessful candidate for the GOP presidential nomination; and Ralph Nader, a liberal consumer advocate.

Some environmental groups also blasted the pact, arguing that it would weaken U.S. pollution controls. Other opponents included farmers who grew fruits, vegetables and flowers, who feared a flood of inexpensive Mexican imports.

Supporters included many U.S. manufacturers and midwestern grain producers, who argued that NAFTA would boost sales to and investment opportunities in Mexico. Advocates also contended that NAFTA would help Mexico's economy grow, which they said was the best way to raise Mexican wages, improve its environment and boost its demand for American goods and services.

Clinton argued that the agreement was an important leg of his plan to create more high-skill, high-wage jobs. But as the vote neared, Clinton also issued dire warnings about the consequences of rejecting free trade with Mexico: Illegal immigration from Mexico would rise, he said, and Japan and Germany were poised to infiltrate the Mexican market if the United States passed up the opportunity.

Pleading, pushing and bargaining his way, Clinton won a bipartisan come-from-behind victory that had looked nearly impossible when he began the battle in September. Clinton called the victory "a defining moment for our nation," and he lauded Congress for recognizing that "change is the only constant."

While economists generally expected the pact to have slight, though generally positive, overall consequences in the United States because of Mexico's small economy, Clinton and other NAFTA supporters clearly exposed themselves to political risks by backing NAFTA to the hilt. Some jobs and some factories were certain to move to Mexico—as opponents of the agreement warned—and those who backed NAFTA would have to answer for those losses, even if the trade pact were not directly responsible.

"There will be three votes on this agreement," Perot said before the Senate cleared the implementing bill. "This is the first one. The second vote will be in '94, and the third one will be in '96."

BACKGROUND

Though politicians in the United States credited—or blamed—Bush for originating NAFTA, the trade pact came to fruition only because of extraordinary changes in Mexico. In less than a decade Mexico, first under President Miguel de la Madrid and then under President Carlos Salinas de Gortari, had transformed its economy from one of the most tightly controlled in Latin America to one of the most open. NAFTA was the capstone of that effort.

It was a strategy born out of desperation following an economic crisis triggered in the early 1980s by the plummeting price of oil, Mexico's largest export. With the country reeling from high inflation, a $100 billion foreign debt, rising unemployment and a 1987 stock market crash, Salinas stepped up the pace of economic liberalization after winning the presidency by a razor-thin majority in 1988. Trade and other import barriers came down on many products, and Mexico signed onto the General Agreement on Tariffs and Trade (GATT). Salinas bargained for some debt relief from the United States and sold off many government-owned enterprises.

By 1989, the Mexican economy was growing, imports were soaring, and foreign capital again was flowing to Mexico. In the spring of 1990, Salinas broached the idea of a free-trade agreement with the United States, arguing that Mexico's continued recovery depended on capital and greater access to the vast U.S. market. It was an enormous risk for a politician in a country that had felt exploited by the behemoth to the north.

The Bush administration, which was focusing on the latest round of GATT talks, responded coolly at first to Mexico's overture. Bush warmed to the idea, however, in part because it was popular in his home state of Texas. The free-trade pact also provided an important political opportunity for Bush as the GATT talks deadlocked and the U.S. economy cooled. Europe and Asia seemed to be coalescing into regional trading blocs, giving the United States more incentive to forge closer trade ties on its continent.

In September 1990 Bush announced that he would begin negotiations with Mexico. After an acrimonious debate, Congress in 1991 agreed to give fast-track consideration to any agreement Bush signed—a concession that was critical to the negotiations going forward. Bush and Salinas initialed a free-trade pact in August 1992, and the final agreement with Mexico and Canada was signed on Dec. 17, 1992. *(Fast-track background, Congress and the Nation Vol. VIII, p. 189)*

Clinton, who inherited the task of convincing Congress to implement the pact, had been a lukewarm supporter of NAFTA during the campaign. He belatedly endorsed the agreement but promised to seek more protections for U.S. jobs, the environment and worker safety. Those protections took the form of side deals that the Clinton administration negotiated with Mexico and Canada over the course of 1993.

One side deal attempted to protect U.S. industries from unforeseen surges in exports from Canada and Mexico. Two other deals, which were more contentious, tried to ensure that each country complied with its labor and environmental regulations.

The United States had sought the right to impose trade sanctions against Mexico or Canada if either country did not comply with its laws governing pollution and working conditions, but Canada balked. The three countries eventually agreed to create joint commissions to deal with labor and environmental disputes. If a dispute between Mexico and the United States could not be resolved there, it would be forwarded to an arbitration panel with the power to recommend trade sanctions. Unresolved complaints against Canada would be referred to the Canadian court system.

Hours after the deals were announced on Aug. 13, 1993, a coalition of labor union spokesmen, consumer advocates and environmental groups accused Clinton of backing down on campaign promises to get stronger labor and environmental provisions. "The side agreements would relegate worker rights and the environment to commissions with no real enforcement mechanisms, no power to impose trade sanctions and no effective remedies," said AFL-CIO President Lane Kirkland.

While the administration was negotiating the side deals, opponents of NAFTA were campaigning in Congress and at the grass roots. Their main argument was that NAFTA would induce U.S. industries to move their plants into Mexico, where labor was cheap and environmental regulations were lax. The result, they argued, would be the loss of hundreds of thousands of American jobs. Perot stressed these points in an anti-NAFTA book, "Save Your Job, Save Our Country," which he promoted with a series of television and radio appearances.

Two environmental groups and one of Nader's consumer groups also tried to slow down the pact in the courts. The three groups filed a lawsuit arguing that the administration had to prepare an analysis of NAFTA's environmental impact. They won the first round on June 30, 1993, when U.S. District Judge Charles R. Richey ruled that the 1970 National Environmental Policy Act required such a study. A federal appeals court reversed that ruling on Sept. 24, saying that the president was not covered by the environmental law.

Support for NAFTA seemed solid in the Senate, but the picture was far less clear in the House. The House Democratic leadership was deeply split on NAFTA, with Whip David E. Bonior, a prolabor Democratic liberal from Michigan, using all the tools of his office to defeat the pact. Majority Leader Richard A. Gephardt, D-Mo., also lined up against the pact and the side deals, saying they did not provide enough protection against U.S. jobs moving south of the border.

That left only Speaker Thomas S. Foley, D-Wash., among the top House leadership supporting NAFTA, and even he appeared lukewarm at times. He said the vote would be like those on gun control and abortion—issues on which the party leadership largely withdrew, leaving members to vote their consciences.

The White House effort to sell the trade pact did not get under way in earnest until Congress returned from its August recess. Clinton launched his campaign Sept. 14 in a White House ceremony to sign the NAFTA side deals. Flanked by three former presidents—Gerald R. Ford, Jimmy Carter and George Bush—Clinton made an impassioned speech that left no doubt that he was putting his prestige on the line. "In a fundamental sense," Clinton said, "this debate about NAFTA is a debate about whether we will embrace change and create the jobs of tomorrow, or try to resist those changes, hoping we can preserve the economic structure of yesterday." Clinton's strong performance seemed to reassure Republicans, whose support for NAFTA had softened during the congressional recess amid doubts about Clinton's commitment and the barrage of organized opposition.

LEGISLATIVE ACTION

The implementing legislation for NAFTA was subject to the fast-track rules of the 1988 Trade Act (PL 100-418), meaning that it could not be amended after it was introduced. For that reason, the legislative give-and-take occurred during a quirky mock markup process that took place before Clinton sent the NAFTA bill to Capitol Hill for introduction. Although the president did not have to incorporate all the congressional proposals into the implementing bill, the mock drafting process allowed the administration to strike deals with concerned members to secure their support. *(1988 Trade Act, Congress and the Nation Vol. VII, p. 148)*

In particular, the deals tried to allay the concerns of border-state House members about pollution, job losses and a surge in imports. Opponents of the trade pact decried this as an excess of dealmaking at the expense of U.S. workers and others whom the accord would affect, but supporters said it was no different from the horse-trading over any significant and controversial bill.

As the draft implementing bill made its way through the House Ways and Means, Senate Finance, and House Agriculture committees in September and October, it picked up riders renewing the reciprocal trade penalties against countries that barred U.S. products and protecting U.S. peanut and sugar producers, among other provisions. As the process was winding up in the last two weeks of October, the administration brought new proposals to the table on the following issues:

• **Worker Retraining.** For workers who lost their jobs as a result of NAFTA, the administration proposed cash benefits, retraining programs and help in finding new jobs. The benefits would be extended to any workers who lost their jobs because their employer moved to Mexico or their industry was undermined by imports. The administration estimated that as many as 22,500 workers could lose their jobs in the 18 months after NAFTA went into effect, with half of the workers qualifying for benefits under the new program. The combined cost of the training and unemployment benefits in that period was projected to be $90 million to $141 million.

The administration was not counting on its proposal to change many minds: Those who were inclined to vote against NAFTA were apt to consider the retraining benefits too paltry to ameliorate what they argued would be widespread job loss. But Labor Secretary Robert B. Reich told reporters that the plan might be sufficient to solidify the votes of members leaning in favor of NAFTA.

• **Financing.** To cover the estimated $2.7 billion cost of the worker training program and tariff cuts, the administration first proposed to double the duties and customs fees paid by planes, trains, cruise ships and trucks entering the United States. This

proposal caused quavering within the all-important bloc of Republican NAFTA supporters, 27 of whom—including House Minority Whip Newt Gingrich, R-Ga.—threatened in writing to withdraw their support. The administration scaled back its proposal, dropping the entry fees on trucks and trains and seeking only a 30 percent increase for international plane and cruise-ship passengers. It also proposed to speed the collection of tax withholding payments, boost Customs Service enforcement, and recalculate future farm-subsidy payments.

Under House rules, the NAFTA implementing bill had to contain enough spending cuts or revenue increases to offset the projected cost of the bill over five years.

• **Environmental Cleanup.** To help border communities combat pollution and adjust to NAFTA, the administration proposed $8 billion in spending from a variety of sources. Among these were two new entities, a North American Development Bank and a Border Environment Cooperation Commission. The development bank, referred to as NADBank, was to receive $450 million over four years in start-up capital—half from the United States, half from Mexico—to support at least $2 billion in loans and loan guarantees for borrowers in the two countries.

Although most NADBank loans were to be used for environmental improvement projects in the border region, 10 percent of its lending capacity was reserved to spur economic recovery in communities hurt by NAFTA. The latter provision was included to win the support of Rep. Esteban E. Torres, D-Calif., and other members of the Congressional Hispanic Caucus. Many of their Hispanic constituents were industrial or farm workers who feared that NAFTA would shift working-class jobs from the United States to Mexico.

Before sending the implementing bill to Congress, Clinton wrung some last-minute concessions from Mexico in an effort to win more votes. Mexico agreed not to substitute corn sweeteners for Mexican-grown sugar in domestic products, averting a potential increase in Mexican sugar exports to the United States. This pledge was intended to mollify members of Congress from sugar-producing states, such as Louisiana.

To build support among Florida lawmakers, the Clinton administration won the right to reimpose tariffs on Mexican orange juice concentrate if the price of domestic orange juice concentrate fell below a certain level on the New York Commodity Exchange. Similarly, the tariffs on Mexican vegetables, including tomatoes, were to be reinstated faster in case of a flood of imports.

Mexico also agreed to begin negotiations soon after NAFTA took effect on a faster phaseout of tariffs on such products as flat glass, wine, appliances and bedding. U.S. manufacturers had complained that the agreement retained Mexican tariffs on those products for as long as 10 years.

The deals and concessions helped move more undecided lawmakers into the pro-NAFTA column, but supporters still believed in early November that they were 30 to 40 House votes short of the 218 needed for passage. Bonior, meanwhile, said in late October that 209 House members had committed to voting against the pact.

House Action

Clinton sent the long-awaited implementing bill to Congress on Nov. 3, including in the text his proposals for worker retraining, the NADBank, and other provisions negotiated with lawmakers. He also submitted the side agreements and a statement describing what actions the administration would take to put the agreement into effect. House Ways and Means Committee Chairman Dan Rostenkowski, D-Ill., introduced the measure (HR 3450) the following day, starting a statutory fast-track clock that ensured a floor vote Nov. 17.

Three House committees gave pro forma consideration to the bill the week of November 8. On Nov. 15, Ways and Means reported the bill favorably, Banking reported it unfavorably, and Energy and Commerce reported it without recommendation (H Rept 103-361, Parts I, II and III).

In the days leading up to the vote on the House floor, the White House tried again to sway uncommitted members by offering last-minute deals on a range of issues, some relating to the Mexico trade agreement and some not. For example, on Nov. 16 Clinton pledged to Florida lawmakers that he would toughen safeguards against a flood of tomato imports from Mexico, helping to secure most of the Florida delegation's votes.

After announcing his support for the NAFTA bill, Floyd H. Flake, D-N.Y., got a call from Clinton telling him that a Small Business Administration pilot program would be located in his Queens district. The White House also agreed to let a dredging project go forward at Jones Beach on Long Island in response to a request by NAFTA backer Peter T. King, R-N.Y.

Some delegations asked for too much. Lawmakers from North Carolina tried to win a reduction in a 75-cents-a-pack tax on cigarettes that the administration had proposed to finance its

health care overhaul bill, slated for action the following year. The administration refused, but eight out of 12 North Carolina members voted for the trade pact anyway.

The spate of deals infuriated NAFTA critics, who accused the White House of buying off the opponents. But the White House responded that most of the deals involved trade issues and represented concessions to satisfy lawmakers with legitimate concerns about NAFTA. The deals, officials said, were a substitute for amendments to the implementing bill, which the fast-track rules did not permit.

Lawmakers on the receiving end took a more pragmatic view of the deal-cutting. "It's not a question of buying votes," said Glenn English, D-Okla. "This is the only way we could have supported the agreement."

Clinton and Vice President Al Gore also helped the cause among Republicans with strong performances in the media. Gingrich said the turning point in the effort to round up GOP votes came when Clinton denounced organized labor for its "muscle-bound" tactics. "It said to a lot of our guys that, if he's going to take that kind of risk in taking on labor unions, how can I turn my back on him?" Gingrich said. Gore also deflated Perot's efforts by outperforming him in a nationally televised debate on Nov. 9.

After 11 hours of debate on Nov. 17, the House passed HR 3450 on a **key vote of 234–200 (R 132–43, D 102–156, I 0–1).** Support was strong from Republicans even in the districts where Perot had performed best in the 1992 election. *(1993 key votes, p. 979; Bill provisions, p. 159)*

By the end of the debate, there was little mystery or passion left: Both sides knew the White House had won, and it showed in different ways. Marcy Kaptur, D-Ohio, who had crusaded against NAFTA, wiped away tears listening to Bonior give one of the closing speeches. Minority Leader Robert H. Michel, R-Ill., brought down the House when he referred to NAFTA foes Perot, Buchanan and Nader as the "Groucho, Chico and Harpo of NAFTA politics."

Senate Action

As in the House, Senate committee action on the measure was routine and largely inconsequential. Six different Senate panels—Finance; Agriculture, Nutrition, and Forestry; Commerce, Science, and Transportation; Governmental Affairs; Judiciary; and Foreign Relations—met formally Nov. 18 to consider S 1627, a NAFTA-implementing bill identical to HR 3450. The six reported the bill jointly without recommendation later the same day (S Rept 103-189).

On Nov. 20, the Senate approved HR 3450 on a **key vote of 61–38 (D 27–28; R 34–10).** The vote reflected the same divisions that had made NAFTA such a tough sell in the House, in particular the strong opposition from organized labor. Opponents argued that the agreement would lead to job losses and downward pressure on U.S. wages, while supporters took a more long-range view. "This agreement will define the American role in the global economy and in world affairs well into the 21st century," said Senate Majority Leader George J. Mitchell, D-Maine. *(1993 key votes, p. 979)*

The margin of victory in the Senate was larger in part because senators were less susceptible to the pressures that caused many House members to vote no. Most states were expected to derive some benefit from free trade with Mexico; that was certainly not the case with every House district. For example, two of labor's strongest Democratic allies—Edward M. Kennedy of Massachusetts and Tom Harkin of Iowa—backed the agreement because Mexico offered export opportunities for their states' high-technology or agricultural exports.

Many of the opponents were from states whose manufacturers had cut employment sharply or whose industries were vulnerable to increased competition from Mexico. "This is a jobs program for Mexico, and, my Lord, we need a jobs program for America," said Democrat Donald W. Riegle Jr. of Michigan.

Some conservative opponents said they feared that the pact would erect a powerful trinational bureaucracy. "The United States should seriously reconsider any agreement which gives up sovereignty to any multinational group that will place the needs of international trade over the interests of the American people," said Dirk Kempthorne, R-Idaho.

Opponents tried once to amend the agreement—a step prohibited under fast-track rules—but they were rebuffed on a procedural ruling. The amendment by Ted Stevens, R-Alaska, sought to strike provisions relating to side agreements with Mexico, but the attempt was blocked on a 73–26 vote.

MAJOR PROVISIONS

HR 3450 conformed U.S. laws with NAFTA but did not contain the text of the agreement. As enacted, the measure:

• **Entry into Force.** Authorized the president to exchange notes with the governments of Canada and Mexico providing for entry into force of the agreement on or after Jan. 1, 1994.

• **State Law.** Established a federal-state consultative process for the purpose of bringing state laws into conformity with the agreement. Only the federal government could challenge a state law on the grounds that it was inconsistent with the agreement.

• **Private Right of Action.** Denied individuals the right to sue on the grounds that any action or inaction by federal, state or local government was inconsistent with the trade agreement or the side agreements on labor and the environment.

• **NAFTA Secretariat.** Authorized the president to establish a United States section of the secretariat created under the agreement. For the secretariat, which was to oversee implementation of the agreement, the measure authorized $2 million in fiscal 1994 or such sums as necessary, whichever was smaller.

• **Tariff Modifications.** Gave the president authority to make the tariff changes provided in the agreement and required him to remove Mexico from eligibility for the Generalized System of Preferences, a program that gave preferential access to the U.S. market to certain developing countries.

The president was not allowed to accelerate duty reductions for articles whose phaseout period was longer than 10 years and for which a request for acceleration had been denied in the preceding three years.

• **Rules of Origin.** Established a set of rules for determining whether a good originated in one of the three NAFTA countries and therefore qualified for duty-free treatment under the agreement. In general, a good qualified if it was produced entirely in one or more of the NAFTA countries, or if each nonoriginating material used in the good underwent a change in tariff classification as a result of production in one or more NAFTA countries.

Certain goods, including automobiles, footwear and chemicals, were subject to stricter rules. These goods had to contain at least half and in certain cases more than 60 percent North American content to move duty-free across borders. Duty-free textile and apparel goods would have to be manufactured in North America with fabric and yarn made in one of the three countries. Exceptions were provided for nonindigenous fabrics, such as silk. Changes to the textile rule of origin would have to be approved by Congress.

• **Duty Drawback.** Defined the goods that would be subject to duty drawback, a program that provided for refunding duties paid on imported goods when they were reexported or incorporated into another good for export. Duties had to be paid within 60 days of export. For goods traded between NAFTA countries, the duty amount was equal to duties owed on components initially imported, or the total amount of customs duties paid to another NAFTA country on the exported good, whichever was less. The measure prohibited drawbacks on certain cathode-ray television picture tubes and on materials used in ocean vessels. It did not permit refund, waiver or reduction of countervailing or antidumping duties imposed on an imported good.

• **Country-of-Origin Marking.** Specified exemptions to a requirement that goods carry a country-of-origin marking, by which the buyer "reasonably knows" that they were NAFTA-origin goods. The exemption applied to works of art, ceramic bricks, semiconductor devices and integrated circuits. Certain pipes, fittings, compressed gas cylinders and manhole covers were provided possible exceptions.

• **Emergency Import Relief.** Established a mechanism for providing relief for U.S. producers from a flood of imports from Mexico and made some changes to the safeguards provided by the U.S.-Canada Free Trade Agreement. A petition requesting relief had to be filed with the International Trade Commission (ITC) by an industry group. The ITC had to begin an investigation within 120 days. In the case of Mexican imports, the ITC would determine whether the imports caused serious injury or the threat of serious injury to the domestic industry. Within 30 days after receiving the ITC report, the president had to provide whatever relief he deemed necessary, if any.

In general, the president was authorized to suspend further scheduled tariff reductions on the affected good or to restore tariffs to the level provided to countries with most-favored-nation trading status. The relief could not exceed three years unless the article was among a group of export-sensitive products. In that case, relief could be extended for up to one additional year. Limits on relief did not apply to textile or apparel articles. The measure also provided safeguards in cases when a NAFTA country contributed to an import increase from many foreign countries.

The measure also created a special expedited mechanism to restore tariffs temporarily on orange juice concentrate imported from Mexico. This so-called snapback provision would be triggered if the U.S. price dropped below a rolling average of the daily closing price on the New York Commodity Exchange, and if certain volume levels were exceeded. Expedited relief was also provided for certain other perishable agricultural products.

• **Agriculture.** Amended the Meat Import Act of 1979 to remove Mexican meat from its jurisdiction. Previous law specified the maximum amount of meat that could be imported before import quotas were triggered.

The measure gave the president authority to exempt from quantitative limits or fees certain agricultural commodities imported from Mexico, according to the provisions of the agreement. The trade agreement laid out penalties for handlers who exported peanuts, then brought them back into the United States in commercial quantities.

The measure also required the secretary of Agriculture to begin a program to require importers of wheat and barley from certain countries to specify how the commodities were to be used. These so-called end-use certificates were to be required for imports from countries that employed end-use certificates on imported U.S. wheat and barley. The provision was designed to respond to Canada's system of end-use certificates.

• **Standards.** Liberalized many U.S. agricultural standards, bringing them into conformity with the agreement. Certain inspections were not to be required on a variety of agriculture products if the secretary of Agriculture determined that Canada or Mexico met standards, such as being disease-free. The measure allowed the secretary of Agriculture to lift certain requirements on imports if Mexico and Canada certified that the level of protection for humans provided by their standards was equivalent to that provided by standards in U.S. law. The measure required that imported peanut butter and peanut paste be processed from peanuts that met U.S. quality standards.

The measure liberalized U.S. government procurement, making some government contracts available to Mexican bidders in conformity with the agreement. It also allowed automobiles manufactured in Mexico or Canada to qualify as domestically produced for the purpose of federal fuel efficiency standards if 75 percent of the cost of an automobile was attributable to value added in North America. This exception did not apply in some cases, including when an automobile was assembled in Canada or Mexico and not imported to the United States within 30 days after the model year expired.

• **Dispute Settlement.** Established procedures for settling cases when a dispute arose between the United States and another NAFTA country over antidumping and countervailing duty actions.

In general, the process closely followed the procedures established by the U.S.-Canada Free Trade Agreement. Panels to hear and resolve the dispute were to be created with representatives from both affected countries. The measure required that U.S. members of the panels to the fullest extent possible be judges and former judges.

The measure created an extraordinary challenge procedure for appealing a decision from a binational panel. It specified

that changes to U.S. law necessary to implement NAFTA did not apply to binational panel reviews under way with Canada.

The measure also required the administration to seek elimination of subsidies provided to foreign industries in future trade negotiations.

• **Worker Assistance.** Established a temporary program to provide income payments and retraining to workers who lost their jobs as a result of NAFTA. Workers were to be eligible for benefits if a significant number in a company or division of a company were laid off or were threatened with layoffs because of imports from Mexico or Canada.

The secretary of labor was required to make a preliminary determination about eligibility within 30 days of receiving a petition from a group of workers. Certified workers were to receive help finding new jobs, payments of up to $30,000 a year for retraining, and income-support payments. To qualify for benefits, a worker would have to be enrolled in a training program within 16 weeks of first drawing unemployment compensation or within six weeks of being certified for the program. The program was authorized through Sept. 30, 1998.

• **Cultural Industries.** Required the United States trade representative (USTR) to monitor Canada's treatment of so-called cultural industries (including production, distribution and sale of film, video and printed material). The USTR was required annually to identify any act, policy or practice adopted or expanded after Dec. 17, 1992, that unfairly discriminated against U.S. cultural exports, unless the issue had already been addressed in separate negotiations.

• **Western Hemispheric Trade.** Authorized $10 million in fiscal 1994 to establish a Center for the Study of Western Hemispheric Trade in Texas.

• **Financing.** Increased the fee imposed on each passenger arriving in the United States on a commercial vessel or commercial airliner from $5 to $6.50 through fiscal 1997. The measure also authorized disclosure of tax return information to the Customs Service that would enable quicker and more complete recovery of duties, taxes and fees owed the federal government. The secretary of the Treasury was required to establish a system providing for electronic transfers that would enable the IRS to collect payroll taxes more quickly. These changes were intended to generate revenue to offset the amount lost due to NAFTA's tariff reductions.

• **Side Agreements.** Authorized $5 million in fiscal years 1994 and 1995 for the U.S. contribution to the Commission for Environmental Cooperation, established under a NAFTA side agreement to monitor compliance with environmental laws. The measure authorized $2 million in fiscal years 1994 and 1995 for the U.S. contribution to the Commission for Labor Cooperation, established under a NAFTA side agreement to monitor compliance with labor laws. The measure authorized $5 million a year for the U.S. contribution to the Border Environment Cooperation Commission, established to oversee pollution cleanup along the U.S.-Mexico border.

• **North American Development Bank.** Authorized participation by the United States in the North American Development Bank, which was to finance border cleanup and economic development projects. The measure authorized appropriations of $1.5 billion for the bank, of which $225 million was to be used for paid-in capital of the bank and $1.3 billion was to be used for so-called callable capital. For fiscal 1995, the paid-in capital payment was capped at $56.2 million. Ten percent of that amount could be transferred to the president to pay for development projects. In fiscal 1995, the callable capital provided to the bank by the United States was limited to $318 million.

• **Customs Modernization.** Authorized the Customs Service to establish a program allowing importers to transmit documents electronically for the purpose of clearing goods into the United States. Filers could elect to transmit documents electronically from a location other than the goods' point of entry. The program was set to terminate in 1997 unless reauthorized.

The measure made other changes in customs laws designed to modernize procedures. For example, it lifted a requirement that customs officials take unentered merchandise into their custody and send it to an unbonded warehouse. Under the measure, carriers were required to notify a bonded warehouse of unentered merchandise, and the warehouse was to arrange for transport of the goods. Customs was allowed to dispose of seized merchandise when the cost of storing the merchandise exceeded the value of storing it. The secretary of the Treasury was authorized to contract with private collection agencies to recover unpaid customs duties.   ❑

GATT Implementation

In the second major trade victory for the Clinton administration, Congress cleared legislation in a lame duck session late in 1994 to implement a global pact slashing tariffs and other trade barriers.

The new General Agreement on Tariffs and Trade (GATT) was less contentious but potentially more significant than the North American Free Trade Agreement, which Congress had approved the year before. The most sweeping change in the world trading system since the original GATT in 1947, the revised GATT cut tariffs worldwide by almost 40 percent, clamped down on protectionist practices, provided more protection for intellectual property, and promoted trade in services and farm products.

The agreement also created the World Trade Organization (WTO), an international panel to resolve disputes over trade. Previous efforts to give an international body jurisdiction over trade fights had been blocked by Congress, in part because of concerns about U.S. sovereignty. *(GATT history, p. 167)*

Both the House and Senate approved the implementing legislation (HR 5110—PL 103-465) by wide margins, yet the administration's victory was hard-won. Led by Sen. Ernest F. Hollings, D-S.C., opponents prevented Congress from voting on HR 5110 before the 1994 elections, necessitating a lame duck session.

As was the case with NAFTA, Clinton's main allies in the GATT fight were Republicans and his main foes were Democrats. The opponents spanned the ideological spectrum, howev-

er; among them were labor unions, environmentalists, self-styled populists, "America First" conservatives and import-sensitive manufacturers, such as textile and apparel companies.

One of the opponents' main criticisms was that the United States had more to lose from the agreement than it could gain. Free trade, they contended, aided developing nations and multinational corporations at the expense of industrialized nations, their workers, and their manufacturing base.

Conservatives blasted the proposed World Trade Organization as a threat to U.S. laws and trade policies. Opponents also said the implementing legislation relied on accounting gimmickry to offset the loss of some $12 billion in tariffs over five years.

Clinton and other proponents responded that the new GATT would boost the U.S. economy by opening new markets to U.S. exports. The president's Council of Economic Advisers estimated that annual U.S. national income would increase by $100 billion to $200 billion within 10 years of the new GATT's implementation, an amount equal to 1.5 percent to 3 percent of the existing gross domestic product.

"It is the largest world trade agreement in history," Clinton told a congressional delegation at the White House Sept. 20. "It will provide a global tax cut of $740 billion, reducing tariffs worldwide by more than a third."

One of the biggest projected gains for the U.S. economy was expected to come from the extension of GATT to include intellectual property rights. Companies and individuals in such U.S. industries as computer software, motion pictures, music and publishing hailed this portion of the agreement. They hoped it would force other nations to crack down on the piracy of their products and ideas, which they said cost them hundreds of millions of dollars each year in lost income.

The new agreement also brought trade in such services as business accounting, construction, computer services and tourism under the system of multilateral trade rules. The United States, already the world's leading exporter of such services, stood to benefit from freer international trade, GATT supporters said.

A third area being brought under the trade rules for the first time was agriculture. Administration officials argued that the pact would make U.S. farmers more competitive overseas because it reduced the long-standing, politically sacrosanct subsidies and import protections for farmers in Europe, among other regions. They estimated that the pact would boost U.S. farm exports by $1.6 billion to $4.7 billion a year by 2000.

The GATT proposal did not raise passions as high as NAFTA did, in part because it was viewed as an extension of the United States' longtime efforts to open markets overseas. NAFTA, on the other hand, was considered groundbreaking because it set up a free-trade regime with a country far less developed than the United States.

Clinton's task was eased by the support of some key Democrats who usually were aligned with organized labor, such as Majority Leader Richard A. Gephardt of Missouri, a NAFTA opponent. In addition, the U.S. business community was overwhelmingly in favor of the pact.

GATT ACCORD HIGHLIGHTS

On April 15, 1994, top international trade officials signed a 550-page agreement revising the General Agreement on Tariffs and Trade (GATT). Once implemented by the 117 signatories, the agreement would sharply reduce international trade barriers, including tariffs, import quotas and export subsidies.

The pact was scheduled to take effect July 1, 1995, but the participating nations agreed informally to put the terms into effect by Jan. 1, 1995. Key elements of the agreement included changes in the following areas:

• **Tariffs.** Tariffs were to be cut on approximately 85 percent of world trade and eliminated or significantly reduced on a broad range of products, including construction and agricultural equipment, pharmaceuticals, paper and steel. Tariffs on industrial goods were to drop from an average of about 5 percent to an average of 3 percent. Some cuts were to occur immediately, and most were to take full effect over five years, although sensitive industries such as textiles were given 10-year phaseouts.

The U.S. objective of complete duty elimination on wood products, electronics, distilled spirits, nonferrous metals and oilseeds and oilseed products was not achieved. President Clinton notified Congress in 1994 that further negotiations on those products would be sought.

• **World Trade Organization.** The Geneva-based GATT organization was to be replaced by the World Trade Organization (WTO), a permanent body with greater authority to force member nations to comply with the Uruguay Round agreements.

Like the existing GATT system, the WTO would require member nations to seek consensus on trade disputes. But under the old GATT, "consensus" was interpreted to mean that all nations—including the one accused of unfair trade practices—had to agree to a GATT ruling. This allowed countries found guilty of unfair trade practices to block adverse GATT rulings unilaterally.

Under the WTO, "consensus" meant that a ruling would go into effect unless all member nations opposed it. The WTO also would set the amount of compensation, either in the form of trade restrictions on the defendant country or trade concessions on the complaining country, to offset the economic effect of the unfair trade practice. If no settlement was possible under the dispute resolution system, WTO members could vote on the issue in a body, similar to the United Nations General Assembly, in which each member nation would have one vote.

• **Agriculture.** The agreement brought the production and export of farm commodities under GATT for the first time. Governments agreed to reduce agriculture subsidies by an average of 24 to 36 percent and to cut the amount of exports eligible for subsidies by 14 to 21 percent.

The agreement required the conversion of all nontariff trade barriers, including import quotas, variable duties and minimum import prices, to tariff equivalents, a process known as "tariffication." Those items also would be subject to the overall tariff cuts.

The bill established a category of "green box" farm subsidies, allowable under the new GATT, most of which were used in the United States. These included government spending for agricultural research, inspection, marketing, promotion, extension and advisory services; public warehousing for food security purposes; domestic food aid; income "safety nets" for farmers; crop insurance/disaster relief; environmental and conservation programs and regional assistance programs.

A second round of multilateral agriculture negotiations was scheduled to ensue five years after the new GATT went into force.

• **Textiles.** The signatories agreed to phase out the Multi-Fiber Arrangement (MFA), under which industrial nations had imposed quotas on textile imports from developing countries for more than 30 years. The MFA was to be phased out over 10 years.

Each participating country was required to declare those textile and clothing products it chose to integrate into the GATT, using three phases (immediately after the new agreement went into effect, after three years and after seven years). All such textile and clothing

---

By wide margins, the House approved the GATT implementing bill Nov. 29, and the Senate cleared it Dec. 1. Clinton signed the bill Dec. 8.

FAST-TRACK PROCEDURES

The negotiations over a new GATT began with a 74-nation trade conference in Punta del Este, Uruguay, in September 1986. The talks proceeded fitfully, stalling periodically over disputes involving agriculture, films and textiles, among other issues.

Hoping to spur the negotiations to a conclusion, Clinton asked Congress to give him only until the end of 1993 to reach a new GATT deal in order to qualify for fast-track consideration. Established in the 1988 Trade Act (PL 100-418), the fast-track procedures helped assure foreign trade negotiators that any deal struck by the White House would not be rewritten by Congress.

The procedures required Congress to vote on trade agreements within 90 days, with no amendments allowed to the implementing legislation submitted by the president.

In response, the House Ways and Means Committee reported a bill (HR 1876—H Rept 103-128, Part I) on June 14 that extended fast-track authority only for GATT, and only from June 1, 1993, through April 15, 1994. The bill also required Clinton to notify Congress by Dec. 15, 1993, if he intended to sign a new GATT pact, effectively making that date the deadline for an agreement.

The House Rules Committee reported the bill two days later (H Rept 103-128, Part II), and the House passed the measure, 295–126, on June 22. After the Senate Finance Committee reported an identical measure (S 1003—S Rept 103-66) on June 23, the Senate cleared HR 1876 on June 30, 76–16. Clinton signed the bill July 2 (PL 103-49).

products were to be covered by the end of the 10-year period. After a product was integrated, the country could not impose import quotas on it.

- **Dumping.** The United States and Europe preserved their existing authority to use domestic antidumping laws to impose fines or countervailing duties against countries that exported goods at prices below cost, with some changes. Among these were new standards for minimum dumping margins, requirements that cost calculations be adjusted appropriately for start-up operations, and the establishment of a five-year review for antidumping orders.

The agreement incorporated the U.S. practice of "cumulating" imports from several foreign countries, rather than just individual countries, in order to prove injury to a domestic industry because of dumping.

- **Subsidies.** In a big win for the U.S. aerospace industry, the pact included civil aircraft products, a leading U.S. export, under new rules restricting government industrial subsidies. That paved the way for lower subsidies to the European Airbus consortium, a major competitor of the Boeing Co.

The agreement tightened the restrictions on export subsidies and other trade-distorting government benefits to domestic industries. Under the existing GATT, only 24 nations participated in the agreement to limit trade-distorting subsidies. Under the new GATT, the Subsidies Agreement applied to all member countries. The administration described this expansion as "one of most significant U.S. achievements" in the Uruguay Round negotiations.

The new Subsidies Agreement prohibited export subsidies based on domestic content; required all developing countries (other than least developed) to phase out export subsidies and import substitution subsidies; and applied the WTO dispute resolution mechanism so that a subsidizing country could not unilaterally block adoption of panel reports.

The agreement set up three categories of subsidies: prohibited "red light" subsidies; GATT-legal "green light" subsidies; and "yellow light" subsidies, which technically were legal under GATT but could be challenged in WTO dispute resolution proceedings and be subject to domestic countervailing duties. The permitted subsidies included those to develop an early prototype of a new technology, aid industries in disadvantaged regions, or help industries meet new environmental standards.

The agreement allowed the United States and other member nations to continue to apply countervailing duties when it was determined that a nation was providing its exporting industries with trade-distorting subsidies.

- **Intellectual Property.** GATT rules were extended to protect from piracy such intellectual property as computer programs, semiconductor chip designs, books, films and music. Developing countries had 10 years before they would have to honor patents on drugs.

The agreement also required members to provide for seizures of counterfeit and pirated goods at the border and to institute criminal penalties for willful copyright piracy and trademark counterfeiting on a commercial scale.

- **Services.** Applying GATT rules to the world market in services, valued at almost $1 trillion annually, was a key goal of U.S. negotiators. However, multilateral agreements to open markets in specific service sectors, such as shipping, banking, securities and insurance, proved elusive.

- **Safeguards.** The new GATT established rules under which member nations were permitted to impose import restrictions, or "safeguards," when import surges caused or threatened to cause serious injury to a domestic industry. Few conforming changes to U.S. laws were necessary, as those laws served as the model for the new GATT safeguard rules.

For textile and apparel products, as an example, countries could apply temporary quotas on a product-by-product and country-by-country basis. The quotas could not be lower than the actual import level during a recent 12-month period and could remain in effect for up to three years.

Trade negotiators barely met the fast-track deadline, and Clinton announced his support for the new agreement on Dec. 15, 1993. Top trade officials from the 117 nations participating in the talks signed the accord in Marrakesh, Morocco, on April 15, 1994.

The agreement did not require signatories to implement its provisions until July 1995, but Clinton was determined to have Congress enact GATT legislation by the end of the 1994 session. In fact, he joined with leaders of the other major industrialized nations in pledging to implement the agreement by the beginning of 1995. Clinton wanted both to assert the United States' leadership on world trade issues and to demonstrate, as he had done with NAFTA, that he was an internationalist who would fight protectionists at both ends of the political spectrum.

In constructing the implementing bill, however, the administration had to resolve a number of thorny issues with different factions in Congress. The process was time-consuming and, at times, plodding. By the time Clinton sent the final bill to Capitol Hill in late September, only a week and a half remained before Congress' planned adjournment—a situation that Hollings exploited to throw the process into chaos.

LEGISLATIVE ACTION

Because the fast-track procedures did not allow Congress to amend the GATT implementing bill after it was introduced, the administration and lawmakers negotiated behind the scenes for months before the bill was submitted.

One of the most significant disputes concerned the World Trade Organization and the United States' ability to pursue independent economic and trade policies. Beginning in the 1950s, the GATT system had operated solely by consensus. Although specially appointed panels could make rulings on trade disputes and recommend sanctions, a country could block an adverse ruling simply by disagreeing with it.

The new GATT pact turned the consensus concept on its head. The WTO's ruling on a dispute would be binding unless all the nations involved disagreed. If a country refused to change a trade practice found to be in violation of the GATT, the WTO could authorize retaliatory trade sanctions.

U.S. Trade Representative Mickey Kantor and other officials hailed the new system, noting that the U.S. negotiators had pressed for a tough enforcement mechanism. The United States had frequently brought trade discrimination complaints to GATT panels and won, only to see the offending country ignore the ruling.

But GATT opponents insisted that U.S. participation in the WTO would lead to a degradation, and perhaps outright violation, of U.S. sovereignty. Critics on the left, including environmental and consumer activists, argued that U.S. health, safety and environmental protections could be undermined by the WTO because the protections applied to imported products. Critics on the right said that Clinton was turning over control of U.S. foreign policy to multinational bodies—something Clinton had also been accused of doing on United Nations peacekeeping missions.

The WTO provisions raised fears among state officials, too. Under the GATT agreement, national governments were required to ensure that their political subdivisions abided by the terms of the pact. Thus, the federal government could end up pursuing legal action to force states to revoke laws put into place to encourage economic growth within their borders.

Administration officials insisted these concerns were overblown. The WTO, they said, could not overturn any federal or state law. If U.S. officials felt strongly enough, these laws would stay on the books, albeit at the risk of sanctions authorized by the WTO.

Conservative radio talk show hosts eventually started a drumbeat of criticism against the WTO, generating some grassroots activism against the implementing bill. They found an ally in Senate Minority Leader Bob Dole, R-Kan., who withheld his support for HR 5110. In addition to concerns about the WTO, Dole wanted Clinton to cut the tax on capital gains in exchange for Dole supporting the GATT bill.

After weeks of bargaining, Dole and Clinton reached an arrangement Nov. 23, 1994, aimed at settling the Republican leader's qualms. The agreement centered on a "three strikes" proposal that enabled the United States to withdraw from the WTO under certain conditions. A panel of U.S. judges would review all decisions of the new body. If the panel found that the WTO had acted arbitrarily against U.S. interests in three cases, lawmakers could propose a joint resolution instructing the president to withdraw from the WTO. The joint resolution would have to be signed into law or enacted over the president's veto to take effect.

"We've resolved concerns about the WTO," said Dole, announcing his support for GATT at a Rose Garden ceremony attended by Clinton and key administration officials. Dole also agreed to drop his bid to link the capital gains cut to the GATT bill.

A second dispute concerned the fast-track procedures. Clinton wanted to extend the procedures to cover future trade agreements, such as one integrating Chile into NAFTA. Responding to pressure from organized labor and its Democratic allies in the House, Clinton proposed to add a requirement that the principal negotiating objectives for future trade talks include the protection of workers' rights and the environment.

This provision alienated many free-trade Republicans, who wanted negotiating objectives limited to trade issues. They argued that requiring other countries to adhere to an international standard for worker rights or the environment would restrain trade.

In its preliminary work on the implementing bill, the Senate Finance Committee dropped the proposed extension of fast-track authority. The House Ways and Means Committee, meanwhile, included a fast-track extension without the provision on labor and environmental objectives.

On Sept. 13, Kantor announced that the administration would drop the fast track extension from the final bill in exchange for a commitment from Finance Committee Chairman Daniel Patrick Moynihan, D-N.Y., and Ways and Means Committee acting Chairman Sam M. Gibbons, D-Fla., that Congress would take up a fast-track renewal bill early in 1995. The administration had little choice, as the stalemate over the issue threatened to stall the GATT legislation.

A third problem for the administration was finding a way to pay for the loss of $12 billion in tariff revenue over five years. Republicans made it clear that they would not support a bill with tax increases, so the administration's options were limited.

Some Democratic and many Republican GATT supporters contended that no offsets were needed because the pact would generate a huge upswing in domestic economic activity, bringing in more than enough tax revenue to offset the loss of tariffs. The administration avoided this tack for two reasons: it did not want to signal any retreat from its efforts to cut the deficit, and it did not want to support such supply-side economics.

Instead, the administration offered a five-year package that combined a handful of real offsets and a roster of bookkeeping maneuvers. These included $1.7 billion in savings from reduced farm subsidy payments, $1 billion in savings from an overhaul of the Pension Benefit Guaranty Corporation, and more than $1 billion in revenues from auctioning parts of the broadcast spectrum.

Much of the financing package was made up of what Kantor himself referred to as "compliance and timing devices," such as advancing the date on which businesses were required to remit their tax payments. The implementing bill also required that parents obtain Social Security numbers for their infant children right after birth, rather than at age one, to combat fraud.

Such gimmicks had been banned from recent deficit-reduction packages because they only worked once. "A date shift is a cheap way of making money," said Rep. Bill Thomas, R-Calif., a member of the Ways and Means Committee's Trade Subcommittee. "You can't have a 13-month year every year. You can do it once and then you've got to pay for it."

The financing package left the plan open to a point of order in the Senate that it violated budget rules. Senate rules required that legislation pay for any proposed reductions in revenue for 10 years after enactment, not five years as required by the House. The projected 10-year cost of the GATT bill was $30 billion, a daunting sum. Rather than trying to find $30 billion in offsets, supporters concentrated on lining up the 60 Senate votes needed to overcome a point of order.

Implementing Bill

As part of the preliminary work on HR 5110, several House and Senate committees held mock markups on a draft version of the implementing bill. The main action fell to the two panels with primary responsibility for trade and tax policy: Senate Finance and House Ways and Means.

The Finance Committee gave tentative approval to an implementing bill Aug. 2, but the panel left out several provisions sought by the White House, most notably the fast-track extension. The Ways and Means panel wrapped up its work on the legislation Aug. 17 after dropping a provision that would have changed the tax rules for inventory accounting by retailers.

Negotiators for the two chambers held a mock conference, reaching agreement by Sept. 20. However, they left it to the administration to resolve four sticky issues in the final version of the GATT bill.

The first issue was whether to reenact the so-called Super 301 authority, a version of the Section 301 provision of the Trade Act of 1974. Super 301 required the president to name countries that maintained unfair trade practices against the U.S. goods and services and to explore retaliatory sanctions. The statutory authority for Super 301 lapsed in 1990, but Clinton had renewed it by executive order in March 1994.

While numerous Democrats backed the provision as an important market-opening tool, many Republicans and free-trade Democrats opposed Super 301 as a protectionist device that exacerbated economic tensions between the United States and its trading partners. The Senate Finance Committee favored reenactment, the House Ways and Means Committee did not.

Clinton, who did not address the issue in his original proposal, included a provision codifying Super 301 in the final GATT bill.

The second issue was rules of origin. The House had included a provision to require, after a one-year transition period, that apparel items imported into the United States be labeled as having originated in the country in which they were assembled, rather than where they were cut. The requirement was aimed particularly at manufacturers in Hong Kong and several other Asian nations that cut their material at home but sent the pieces to be assembled in China, where wages were lower. The Senate proposed to require the change in labeling after five years.

The measure was strongly opposed by many clothing retailers, who feared it would reduce imports of inexpensive clothing items from the Far East and raise prices for consumers. Nevertheless, Clinton included language in the final bill requiring the labeling as of July 1, 1996.

The third issue was imports from nations in the Caribbean region. The House version temporarily gave developing Caribbean nations apparel import preferences equal to those provided to Mexico under NAFTA. Proponents said this would stem the flow of factory jobs to Mexico from the Caribbean nations, which threatened to undercut the economic development goals of a U.S. program known as the Caribbean Basin Initiative (CBI).

The Senate negotiators opposed the provision, and Clinton did not include it in the final bill.

The final issue was tobacco tariffs. The 1993 budget reconciliation bill (PL 103-66) required U.S. tobacco companies to certify that 75 percent of the tobacco in their products came from U.S. growers, but a GATT administrative panel ruled that the requirement was a barrier to trade. In response, the House version of the draft GATT bill would have authorized the president to increase tariffs on foreign tobacco to protect domestic growers from a flood of low-cost imports.

The Senate negotiators objected to the tariff proposal, and opponents argued that it could subject other U.S. industries to retaliation by tobacco-exporting countries under the new GATT agreement. Clinton, however, included the tariff increase in his GATT bill.

Clinton submitted the final version of his bill to Congress on Sept. 27, and it was introduced as HR 5110 and S 2467. The delay in submitting the bill, however, enabled Hollings to prevent it from coming to a vote in the Senate before the elections. The chairman of the Senate Commerce Committee, Hollings announced on Sept. 28 that he was holding onto the bill for 45 days—the maximum allowed by the fast-track rules—in order to conduct hearings.

The House Ways and Means Committee and Energy and Commerce Committee went ahead with their markups, reporting the bill on Oct. 3. (H Rept 103-826, Parts I and II). The Senate Finance Committee unanimously approved an identical Senate bill on Sept. 29, but the committee waited until Nov. 22 to issue a joint report with the Governmental Affairs and Agriculture, Nutrition and Forestry committees (S Rept 103-412).

Hollings hoped that he could force the leadership to put off consideration of GATT until the new Congress convened in January 1995, potentially resulting in an even longer delay that might have killed the bill. The textile and apparel industries, which were major employers in Hollings' native South Carolina, opposed the new GATT because it would phase out the high U.S. tariffs on textile and apparel imports faster than the industries wanted.

Although he had long been the textile industry's leading advocate in the Senate, Hollings said his actions were spurred by a broader concern about U.S. free-trade policies, which he said had badly damaged the nation's industrial economy. "I'm not shilling for a single industry," he said. "I'm shilling for the United States of America."

Hollings' attempt to scuttle the bill for 1994 was foiled by Senate Majority Leader George J. Mitchell, D-Maine, and Minority Leader Dole, both GATT supporters, who agreed to schedule a rare, two-day lame duck session, beginning Nov. 30, solely to debate and vote on the GATT bill.

In the House, Speaker Thomas S. Foley, a Democrat from Washington who was a strong GATT supporter, was eager to avoid a lame duck session. He ran into an unexpected problem in September, however, when controversy flared over one of the financing provisions in the GATT bill submitted by Clinton. This provision, which had not been in the preliminary versions of the bill, proposed to raise at least $534 million in license fees from three telecommunications companies that had pioneered a technology called personal communications systems, or PCS.

The three companies—American Personal Communications Inc., an affiliate of the Washington Post Co.; Cox Enterprises Inc., a branch of the company that also owned the Atlanta Journal & Constitution newspaper; and the Colorado-based Omnipoint Communications Inc.—had received licenses for PCS services free of charge in 1992 from the Federal Communications Commission (FCC) as part of an initiative to encourage speculative investments in new technology. The licenses allowed the companies to provide service in three of the nation's largest markets: southern California, the New York metropolitan area, and the Washington, D.C., region.

At the time, the FCC was not charging anyone for licenses—it was awarding them by lottery. The next year, however, Congress ordered the FCC in 1993 to start auctioning off PCS and other communications licenses to the highest bidder. The FCC decided to charge the three pioneers a fee equal to 90 percent of the average winning bid in the 10 next-largest markets.

The three companies sued, arguing that the FCC had no authority to charge fees retroactively. Fearing that the federal government would lose the suit and get nothing, House Energy and Commerce Committee Chairman John D. Dingell, D-Mich., proposed legislation to settle the issue by requiring the companies to pay lower fees, at a rate of 85 percent of the average fees in the next 20 largest markets.

The administration included Dingell's proposal in the GATT bill. The proposal drew fire from some of the pioneers' competitors and federal budget watchdogs, however, who argued that the three companies would receive too deep a discount. The most telling blow was struck by the Pacific Telesis telecommunications company, which ran an advertisement in The Washington Post accusing the administration of slipping in a $1 billion "sweetheart deal" for The Post and other companies connected with the pioneers. The accusation set off a brush fire among House members, particularly Republicans, who warned that they would block consideration of the GATT bill if the issue was not explained to their satisfaction.

Foley tried to keep the GATT vote on schedule, but a series of party caucuses and leadership meetings on Oct. 5 convinced him to wait until after the elections. That evening he struck a deal with Minority Leader Robert H. Michel, R-Ill., putting off the GATT debate until a one-day lame duck session Nov. 29.

Lame Duck Session

The delay gave GATT opponents a chance to breathe new life into what had been a low-profile campaign against the implementing bill. With all other legislative business done for the year, they hoped to focus public attention on what they saw as the flaws of the GATT agreement and the implementing legislation. They highlighted the threat to U.S. sovereignty supposedly presented by the WTO, the failure of the bill to pay for the tariff losses over the full 10 years required by the Senate, and the fact that the bill would be considered by dozens of retired or defeated members of the 103rd Congress in a lame duck session.

Hollings, as promised, held a series of Commerce Committee hearings dominated by his severe critique of U.S. free-trade policy. The hearings featured a parade of GATT opponents who confirmed Hollings' views, and only a handful of GATT supporters.

Still, support for GATT in the House was bipartisan and strong. The four-hour House debate was routine and one-sided, most notable for the valedictory speeches of Foley, who was defeated in the GOP landslide, and Michel, who was retiring after 40 years in the House. "I believe no single measure, public or private, offers such a potential for economic progress," said Foley. Michel called upon his colleagues to "have the political courage and the national confidence to proclaim to the world that we are for GATT because we are Americans and we can compete with anyone at any time in every field in free and open competition."

The opponents struck a populist tone. "Working people in America, there is nothing in this GATT for you and your family," said Marcy Kaptur, D-Ohio, a strong supporter of the labor unions that put up a solid front against the agreement. But they had no chance.

The House passed HR 5110 on Nov. 29 by a lopsided vote of 288–146, a margin of nearly two-to-one.

The Senate spent 10 hours debating the bill on Nov. 30 and Dec. 1, with Hollings leading the outnumbered opponents. "What has been going on is that we are in a disastrous decline," he argued.

On the other hand, many members who typically sided with labor, including some who voted against NAFTA, accepted the administration's promises of booming U.S. export and job growth resulting from the new GATT pact. "For my home state right now, the key to the future is export jobs," said self-described "blue-collar senator" Barbara A. Mikulski, D-Md. "The world is changing and a new economy is about to be born. I do not want the United States of America to be left behind."

The only suspense in the Senate's debate was whether GATT supporters would have the 60 votes needed to overcome a budget point of order against HR 5110. The bill passed that test easily on Dec. 1, when the Senate voted 68–32 to waive the budget rules. The Senate then cleared the bill, 76–24.

MAJOR PROVISIONS

As enacted, the GATT implementing bill contained provisions to:

World Trade Organization

- **U.S. Sovereignty.** Specify that U.S. law would prevail in instances when there was a conflict between a United States law

HISTORY OF GATT

U.S. participation in the 1994 General Agreement on Tariffs and Trade (GATT) agreement marked the culmination of a free-trade policy that had been evolving for more than 60 years. Early in the century, as the United States grew into the world's leading economic power, it set high tariffs to protect its manufacturing industries. Its trading partners responded in kind, resulting in a protectionist duel that many economists and historians say was a key factor in the global economic collapse in the 1930s.

The U.S. strategy started to change in 1934, when it began striking bilateral deals with other nations to reduce tariffs. After World War II, multilateral talks sought to establish an International Trade Organization that would oversee international trade. The U.S. Congress balked at the proposal and similar ones that followed, but the United States did join 22 other nations in adopting the original GATT in 1947.

Over the next 19 years, the United States took part in five additional "rounds" of negotiations to expand the GATT and further reduce tariffs. The seventh or Tokyo Round of negotiations, which lasted from 1973 to 1979, took GATT in a new direction. Although tariff reduction was still a goal, the participating nations also tried to address a novel and growing impediment to trade: nontariff barriers, such as subsidies, countervailing duties, import licensing procedures, government procurement, customs valuation and antidumping measures.

The Tokyo Round resulted in a series of agreements, or codes of conduct, which set rules for addressing nontariff barriers to trade. However, the agreements contained many loopholes, and members were not required to adhere to all the negotiated "codes."

The eighth round, the Uruguay Round, began in 1986 and aimed to fix some of these problems. With the strong backing of President Ronald Reagan, U.S. negotiators sought to lower tariff barriers, place enforceable sanctions against many nontariff barriers and bring a number of economic sectors not previously covered under the GATT umbrella.

Most major issues were resolved by the time Reagan left office, leaving President George Bush with one substantial stumbling block: agricultural subsidies. European Union nations in general, and France in particular, took a hard line against reducing politically popular farm export subsidies. After almost four years of difficult negotiations, the Bush administration helped orchestrate the Blair House Accord, in which the United States and the European Union resolved major agricultural disputes and gave the stalled talks new life.

The negotiations received another boost in July 1993, when the United States, the European Community, Japan and Canada reached a major agreement on lowering industrial tariffs. The Uruguay Round negotiations were concluded Dec. 15, 1993, and signing ceremonies were held the following April.

---

and a provision of the trade agreement. Unless specifically provided for, nothing in the implementing bill amended or modified any U.S. law relating to protection of human, animal or plant life or health, environmental protection or worker safety. Nor did it limit any authority conferred under any U.S. law, including Section 301 of the 1974 Trade Act, which allowed the president to take retaliatory action against a nation that restricted imports of U.S. goods.

However, if the United States were to decline to revoke a law that was ruled by the WTO to create an unfair trade practice, it might face economic penalties. Such penalties would be in the form of trade restrictions or concessions, not cash payments from the U.S. Treasury.

To prevent WTO dispute resolution panels from being stacked against U.S. interests, the bill required the administration to review membership of such panels annually and ensure that the members were qualified. It also required the United States Trade Representative (USTR) to seek establishment of conflict-of-interest rules for WTO panel members.

• **State Sovereignty.** Require the federal government to get a state law overturned, either through consultation or judicial action, if the WTO ruled that the state law violated a GATT commitment.

The bill required the USTR to set up a federal-state consultation process on GATT issues. Whenever another WTO member nation questioned or challenged a state or local law as conflicting with GATT, the USTR was to consult with the state's gover-

nor and chief legal officer of the affected jurisdiction in developing a U.S. position in the dispute.

If the WTO ruled against a state law, the USTR would have to consult with state officials to develop a mutually agreeable response. The only way a state law could be declared invalid for violating the GATT agreement was if the federal government were to pursue a successful lawsuit for such purposes. Only the United States would have legal standing to sue states or localities over GATT issues. No individual or foreign government could sue on such grounds.

• **Congressional and Public Consultation.** Require the USTR to consult with appropriate congressional committees before any WTO vote on an action that could affect U.S. rights or obligations under the WTO agreement or potentially require a change in federal or state law.

Whenever the United States was a party before a WTO dispute settlement panel, the USTR would have to consult with congressional committees and relevant private sector advisory committees concerning the issue.

The USTR would have to make U.S. written statements to WTO panels available to the public, request the other party in the dispute to do the same and make each WTO report available to the public promptly after it was circulated to WTO members. If other parties did not release their confidential submissions, the USTR would request nonconfidential summaries of them.

In the event of an adverse WTO ruling, no federal regulation could be changed until congressional committees were informed, the USTR sought advice from private-sector advisory committees, and public comment was solicited through the Federal Register. No final rule could take effect until 60 days after consultations with congressional committees began; during that period, the House Ways and Means Committee or Senate Finance Committee could hold a nonbinding vote on the proposed rule.

The USTR would have to report to the Ways and Means and Finance committees at least 30 days before bringing a legal action to declare invalid a state law that was ruled inconsistent with the GATT and would have to consult with the committees before the action was brought.

By March 1 of each year beginning in 1996, the USTR would have to submit a report to Congress detailing the WTO bureaucratic structure, including how much the United States and other countries contributed to its budget, any WTO dispute settlement action that affected federal or state law, and what progress was made in achieving greater openness ("transparency") of WTO proceedings.

Within 90 days of receiving the first USTR report after the fifth anniversary of U.S. entry into the WTO, and every fifth year thereafter, Congress could withdraw the United States from the WTO by enacting a joint resolution. Relevant committees would have up to 45 days to review a proposed joint resolution.

• **Entry into Force.** Specify that U.S. commitments under the new GATT would take effect when the president determined that a sufficient number of countries—including the countries of the European Union, Japan, Canada and Mexico—had accepted the obligations of the agreement to ensure adequate benefits to the United States.

The bill authorized appropriations for U.S. payment of its share of WTO expenses.

• **Extended Negotiations.** Call for the United States to pursue its market-opening goals in some industry sectors for which agreements could not be concluded during the Uruguay Round of GATT negotiations—specifically including financial services and basic telecommunications services.

U.S. Trade Retaliation (Section 301)

• **Imposition of Duties.** Eliminate the requirement under Section 301 of the Trade Act of 1974 that the USTR always give priority to the imposition of import duties as the preferred U.S. action to retaliate against another country's unfair trade practices.

• **Super 301.** Amend the Super 301 provision of the 1988 trade law (PL 100-418) by requiring the USTR to report to the Ways and Means and Finance committees within 180 days after publication of the 1995 National Trade Estimate report on "priority" foreign country trade barriers, the removal of which were likely to have the greatest potential to increase U.S. trade. Within 21 days of the submission of that report, the USTR was required to initiate Section 301 investigations of any identified priority practices.

• **Congressional Consultation.** Require the USTR to consult periodically with appropriate congressional committees concerning foreign trade barriers and how best to address them.

Safeguards

• **Provisional Relief.** Allow U.S. industries to continue to apply to the federal government for provisional "critical circumstances" relief from import surges and expedite the process for providing such relief. The International Trade Commission (ITC) would have up to 60 days from the filing of the petition to decide whether to recommend such relief; if it did, the president would have to decide whether to act within 30 days. Deadlines under previous law were 120 days for the ITC and seven days for the president. Provisional relief was limited to 200 days.

• **Regular Safeguards.** Allow an initial safeguard period of up to four years if the president determined that an industry required ongoing safeguard protection. Protection could be extended for an additional four years after public proceedings.

• **Quota Levels.** Require that any safeguard quota be at least the average quantity or value of such articles imported into the United States in the most recent representative three years unless the president found that importation of different quantity or value was justified. Safeguards would have to be phased down at regular intervals.

Environment, Workers' Rights

• **Environment.** Require the inclusion of nongovernmental environmental and conservation organizations on the federal advisory committee that issued opinions on the impact of trade agreements on the environment.

• **Workers' Rights.** Require the president to seek the establishment within WTO of a working party on the linkage between trade and internationally recognized workers' rights, and to report to Congress within a year of enactment on progress toward establishing the working party.

Tariffs

• **Presidential Authority.** Authorize the president to modify or add import duties as necessary to carry out U.S. obligations under the GATT and to make technical corrections as necessary.

• **Tariffs on Nonsignatories.** Authorize the president to increase tariffs on a foreign country that was not a member of the WTO and was not providing adequate trade benefits to the United States. The provision was intended to end the problem, common under the previous GATT system, of "free rider" countries that took advantage of U.S. trade benefits provided under most-favored-nation rules while not joining GATT or providing reciprocal benefits to the United States.

Textiles and Clothing

• **Publication of U.S. Obligations.** Within 120 days of the new agreement's taking effect, the U.S. secretary of Commerce was to publish in the Federal Register a notice of those textile and apparel products to be integrated during each stage. Within 30 days of publication, the secretary was to notify the WTO Textile Monitoring Body of the lists.

- **Country of Origin.** Require the U.S. secretary of the Treasury, no later than July 1, 1995, to produce regulations for enforcing country-of-origin rules aimed at preventing other countries from circumventing U.S. quotas by mislabeling or transshipping goods through other countries, during the quota phaseout period.

Country of origin was defined as that country in which the textile or apparel product was wholly assembled; where the most important assembly or manufacturing process occurred; or the last country in which important assembly or manufacturing process occurred. Exceptions were provided to those products cut in the United States, assembled overseas, then returned to the United States; products covered by the U.S.-Israel Free Trade Agreement; and products knit to shape.

The rules applied to goods that entered or were withdrawn from a warehouse in the United States on or after July 1, 1996, except that the rules would not apply until Jan. 1, 1998, for those goods covered by a contract entered into before July 20, 1994.

The bill also authorized the Treasury secretary to publish in the Federal Register the names of individuals and companies outside the United States that had provided false documentation of country of origin, used counterfeit documents, falsely labeled items, or abetted the transshipment of products in a manner that concealed country of origin or evaded quotas.

The president was authorized to publish in the Federal Register, after consulting with the secretaries of Commerce and Treasury and other relevant officials, the names of countries that had failed to make good-faith efforts to stop illegal country-of-origin or transshipment activities.

Dumping

- **Measuring Dumping.** Provide that in determining whether a good was being dumped in the United States below normal value, U.S. investigators would measure sales of the good in the exporter's home market against sales in the United States. Under previous law, home market sales were measured against the quantities of the good sold to countries other than the United States.

If the home market sales of the good were less than 5 percent of the aggregate of sales to the United States, they would instead be compared with sales of that good to a country other than the United States. Third-country sales would have to be based on a single country, rather than multiple countries as under previous law.

In calculating the normal value of a foreign-made good, a deduction would be made for indirect taxes imposed on the product or component that had been rebated or not collected.

- **Start-up Costs.** Make allowance for a company's unusually high costs in starting up a new product or product facility; such costs could temporarily inflate the home market price of a good, making it appear that ensuing export sales were being made below cost. The Commerce Department, which oversaw antidumping regulations, could make adjustments for start-up costs only if a company was using new production facilities or making a new product requiring substantial additional investment, and production levels were limited by technical factors as-

sociated with the initial phase of commercial production. Start-up cost adjustments would not be applied to routine model year changes of existing plants or improvements to basic products.

The start-up period was considered ended when a level of commercial production characteristic of the merchandise, producer or industry was reached.

- **Country of Origin.** Allow an exception to the usual practice of treating an intermediary country as the country of origin for purposes of antidumping investigations when an item was exported to an intermediate country and then reexported to the United States. The original exporter would be regarded as the country of origin when the producer knew the merchandise was destined for reexportation; when the merchandise was simply transshipped; when not enough of the good was sold in the intermediate country to make possible the calculation of normal value; or the product was not produced in the intermediate country.

- **De Minimus Standards.** The dumping margin (that is, the ratio of the U.S. price of the imported good against the home market value of that good) of exports from each country to the United States had to reach a minimum (de minimus) threshold to fall under the provisions of U.S. antidumping law. To conform with the standard set in the new GATT, the bill required that the weighted average dumping margin of any producer or exporter that was less than 2 percent ad valorem be treated as de minimus. (The previous U.S. de minimus standard was 0.5 percent.)

- **Assisting Third Countries to Fight Dumping.** Allow the Commerce Department or the ITC to take antidumping actions on behalf of a third country when the petitioning country could prove that imported goods being sold in the United States were being sold for less than fair value and were doing material damage to an industry in the petitioning country. Previous law allowed the USTR to ask other countries to take action against dumping that damaged U.S. exporters, but not to take action on behalf of other governments.

- **Captive Production.** Provide standards for situations in which a U.S. company made a product that was then used by the same producer in the manufacture of a distinct product (for example, raw steel, which was then incorporated into a consumer product by the same manufacturer). For the purposes of antidumping investigations, authorities would compare the imports of the foreign version of the original component product rather than those of the value-added "downstream" product.

- **Measuring "Negligible" Imports.** Treat imports as negligible for antidumping purposes if they accounted for less than 3 percent of all such merchandise imported in the most recent 12-month period for which data were available. Exceptions would be made when imports that otherwise would be classified as negligible were included with other countries for which investigations were filed on the same day, and the cumulative imports were more than 7 percent of the total imports of that good. The ITC was to terminate investigations if it determined imports were negligible.

- **Industry Support.** Require that, before pursuing an antidumping investigation, U.S. authorities determine whether there was sufficient support within the domestic industry for such an action.

Industry support was to be measured as sufficient when a petition supporting an antidumping investigation was backed by domestic producers or workers who accounted for at least 25 percent of the total production of the domestic product and who accounted for more than 50 percent of the production of the domestic product by that portion of the industry expressing an opinion for or against the petition.

"Industry support" could be expressed by either management or workers within the affected industry.

If a petition did not establish majority support, Commerce would poll the industry or, if there were many producers, use any statistically valid sampling method.

In cases of an industry defined as a "regional industry," support would be established only in that region, not the United States as a whole.

The bill allowed interested parties to comment on the issue of industry support. It added trade associations of producers, exporters or importers and the government of the exporting country to the previous list of interested parties.

Industrial users of the merchandise and consumer groups were to be given the opportunity to provide relevant information but would not automatically gain interested-party status.

• **Provisional Measures.** Specify that provisional antidumping measures would not apply until 60 days after initiation of an investigation. Provisional measures were limited to four months, except the Commerce Department could extend them to six months if it was requested by exporters representing a significant percentage of the exported product.

• **Terminating Penalties.** Require parties seeking revocation of an antidumping order or a countervailing duty to show that such termination would not lead to continuance or recurrence of material injury against a domestic industry.

• **Sunset Provision.** Require automatic five-year reviews of antidumping duty orders, countervailing duties or injury determinations.

Subsidy Restrictions

• **Injury Test.** Repeal a provision of U.S. law that excluded some countries from an "injury test" used to determine whether to apply countervailing duties. Under previous law, countervailing duties could be applied to most members of the Subsidies Agreement only if the ITC first found that a domestic industry had been materially injured by subsidized imports. The new GATT required that this injury test be applied to all member nations.

• **De Minimus Standards.** Require U.S. authorities to ignore de minimus subsidies, defined as less than 1 percent ad valorem, 2 percent for developing countries and 3 percent for least-developed countries. The developing-countries standard expired in eight years.

• **U.S. Actions Against Illegal Subsidies.** Put the Commerce Department in charge of coordinating subsidies enforcement efforts for the U.S. government. If Commerce determined that a GATT-actionable subsidy was in place, it was to inform the USTR, which then could take action under Section 301. If a U.S. industry believed there had been a violation of the green-light standards, it could request that Commerce investigate.

The USTR would determine appropriate retaliatory action under Section 301 if a foreign country failed to observe a recommendation by the WTO Subsidies Committee within six months of its issuance.

• **Congressional Oversight.** Require that the USTR promptly inform the Ways and Means, Finance and other appropriate committees on WTO Subsidies Committee actions. The USTR and the Commerce Department were required to report to Congress by Feb. 1 every year beginning in 1996 on subsidy practices of major U.S. trading partners and USTR monitoring and enforcement activities.

The WTO Subsidies Committee would review provisions of the Subsidies Agreement after five years to determine whether to extend the agreement. Even if this action was taken, the implementing bill contained a sunset provision ending U.S. participation under the Subsidies Agreement unless Congress passed a law to extend it.

Agriculture

• **Presidential Authority.** Provide the president with broad authority to take action as necessary to ensure that imports under tariff-rate quotas did not disrupt the orderly marketing of commodities in the United States.

Under certain circumstances, such as natural disaster, disease or major domestic marketing disruption, the president could temporarily increase the quantity of an imported product subject to regular import duties when that product was not available to U.S. consumers at a reasonable price.

The bill authorized the president to implement special agricultural-product safeguard provisions of the GATT by publishing in the Federal Register the list of safeguarded goods and the level of imports that would trigger the safeguards.

• **Export Enhancement Program.** Reauthorize the Export Enhancement Program, which was scheduled to expire in 1995, until 2001, while committing to adjust the program to meet U.S. obligations under GATT. The bill ended the previous requirement that the program be used only to discourage unfair trade practices because other countries did not impose a similar restriction on their export programs.

• **Market Promotion Program.** Drop the previous requirement that Market Promotion Program funding be directed against unfair practices of U.S. trading partners because other countries did not place such limitations on their export programs.

• **Section 22.** Amend Section 22 of the Agriculture Adjustment Act to bar imposition of quantitative import restrictions or fees on WTO members. The change was waived until Sept. 11, 1995, to allow imposition of fees on Canadian wheat exports to the United States under a one-year Memo of Understanding between the two nations. The president could continue to take Section 22 actions against non-WTO members.

• **Dairy.** Extend the Dairy Export Incentive Program, authorized through 1995, to 2001.

The bill gave the secretary of Agriculture the option to sell for export certain minimum levels of dairy products from government-owned stocks. Previous law had made such sales mandatory.

- **Tobacco.** Authorize the president to proclaim tariff increases on certain tobacco products of up to 350 percent ad valorem over rates in effect on Jan. 1, 1975. The language effectively replaced a provision of the 1993 budget-reconciliation bill that placed a 75 percent domestic tobacco content requirement on U.S. cigarettes. Should the president proclaim a tariff-rate quota for these products, the domestic content requirement—which had been ruled in violation of world trade rules by a GATT panel—would expire at the end of 1994.

- **Meat Imports.** Repeal the Meat Import Act of 1979 and replace quantitative limitations on meat imports with tariff-rate quotas.

- **Food Aid.** Reaffirm the U.S. commitment to provide food aid to developing and least-developed nations.

- **Additional Funding.** Authorize the federal government to spend additional funds from the Commodity Credit Corporation (CCC) for export promotion and development, credit financing and development of alternative uses for agricultural products. These additional funds were to be credited to the CCC in amounts equaling the fiscal 1995 pay-as-you-go savings or the five-year pay-as-you-go savings resulting from the enactment of the Crop Insurance Reform Act of 1994.

- **Sanitary and Phytosanitary Standards.** Require the standards information center in the Department of Commerce to make information available to the public on federal and other sanitary and phytosanitary standards and methodology and participation in international and regional systems and organizations.

The new GATT agreement explicitly acknowledged that nations and their governing bodies had a legitimate need to maintain sanitary and phytosanitary standards for farm imports. But it sought to ensure that such standards were based on actual risk and were not disguised trade barriers. It suggested that each nation harmonize its laws with international standards but did not bar higher standards as long as they had a scientific basis.

Administration officials insisted that because most U.S. sanitary and phytosanitary standards were science-based, the new GATT would leave them safe from challenge.

The bill also barred federal agencies from certifying that a sanitary measure of an exporting country was equivalent to the U.S. standard unless it provided at least the same sanitary protection as the comparable U.S. measure. It required the president to authorize an agency to issue an annual public report on international sanitary standard-setting activities.

Intellectual Property

- **Patents.** Set the term of patent protection at 20 years from the date on which the patent application was filed. Previous law set the period as 17 years from date on which the patent was granted.

The extension from 17 to 20 years could benefit applicants for patents on conventional items that were routinely approved

by the U.S. Patent Office. However, the change in the start of the term—from "time of patent approval" as under previous law to "time of filing"—was highly worrisome to patent applicants from cutting-edge, science-based industries such as microbiology. They said their complicated patent applications often took 10 or more years to be approved. With the new provision starting the patent clock at the time of application, these researchers could find their period of effective patent protection greatly truncated.

The bill provided for an extension of patent protection for up to five years when a patent process had been delayed by interventions by competing patent applicants or other parties, or when an adverse patent decision had been overruled on appeal or by a federal court.

The bill sought to aid U.S. inventors in establishing priority on inventions by allowing them to file provisional applications for a $150 fee. Applicants then would have up to 12 months to file formal applications, the period of which would not be included in calculation of the patent term.

- **Copyrights.** Create new federal civil and criminal penalties for bootlegging of sound recordings of live performances "knowingly and for purposes of commercial advantage or private gain."

It provided for the restoration of copyright protection to foreign works that had fallen into public domain in the United States but were not in the public domain in their country of origin. This would apply even to works that, for technical reasons, never obtained copyright protection in the United States. Protection would exist for the remainder of the term that otherwise would have been granted.

The bill revoked the sunset provision of Computer Software Rental Amendments Act of 1990, thus making computer software rental rights permanent.

- **Trademarks.** Declare that a trademark be considered abandoned after nonuse of three years; under previous law, the period of nonuse was two years.

The bill barred the registration of trademarks for wines or spirits containing misleading geographical indications (such as "champagne" or "burgundy") if they were first used after the new GATT had been in effect for one year. Existing trademarks of this kind were not affected.

Generalized System of Preferences

- **Nine-Month Extension.** Renew the Generalized System of Preferences (GSP), which provided trade benefits and concessions to developing countries, until July 31, 1995, and provide for refunds on duties paid between Sept. 30, 1994, and the date of enactment of the bill. The law authorizing the GSP had expired Sept. 30, 1994.

Customs Fees

- **Merchandise Processing Fees.** Increase Customs Service merchandise processing fees from 0.17 percent to 0.21 percent ad valorem. The bill also raised the maximum filing fee for a formal entry from $400 to $485 and the minimum fee from $21 to $25, effective Jan. 1, 1995.

Financing Provisions

• **Indian Casino Profits.** Change the rules for Indian tribes, which were allowed under previous law to make taxable distributions to their members of proceeds from tribe-run or tribe-licensed gambling activities. The bill required tribes to deduct and withhold from such payments a tax in an amount equal to such payment's proportionate share of the individual's annualized tax. Effective Dec. 31, 1994. (Projected five-year revenue increase: $71 million.)

• **Withholding on Certain Federal Payments.** Require that recipients of taxable federal payments for Social Security, crop disaster relief, farm program loans and other payments specified by the secretary of the Treasury be given the option of having federal income taxes withheld from the payments. A taxpayer could request withholding rates of 7 percent, 15 percent, 28 percent or 31 percent. Recipients of unemployment benefit recipients were allowed to have federal income taxes withheld at a 15 percent rate. States could, but were not required to, allow recipients to have state and local income taxes withheld. Effective for payments made after Dec. 31, 1996. (Projected five-year revenue increase: $221 million for federal payments withholding; $156 million for unemployment compensation.)

• **Estimated Taxes.** Require taxpayers to include subpart F income and Section 936 intangible property income when calculating their quarterly estimated tax payments. The bill provided "safe harbor" protections from penalties for underpayment of estimated tax on subpart F or Section 936 income if those amounts equaled at least 115 percent of such income for the relevant prior year for corporations, and 100 percent of such payments for individual taxpayers. Effective after Dec. 31, 1994. (Projected five-year revenue increase: $1.4 billion.)

• **Federal Excise Taxes.** Move due dates for August and September semimonthly payments of federal excise taxes from October to Sept. 29, thus enabling such payments to be recorded in the earlier fiscal year. Effective Jan. 1, 1995, except for commercial air passenger and freight excise taxes, for which the provision was effective Jan. 1, 1997. (Projected five-year revenue increase: $1.2 billion.)

• **Interest on Corporate Tax Overpayments.** Reduce the interest rate that the Internal Revenue Service paid to corporations on tax overpayments in excess of $10,000. The new interest formula was the federal short-term rate plus one-half of a percentage point, down from the previous formula of the federal short-term rate plus 2 percentage points. Effective Dec. 31, 1994. (Projected five-year revenue increase: $800 million.)

• **Earned-Income Tax Credit.** Bar nonresident aliens from claiming the earned-income tax credit on their annual tax returns unless they were married and agreed to subject all of their income to U.S. income tax, regardless of the country in which it was earned. Net revenues from this provision were reduced somewhat by an amendment that made U.S. military personnel stationed overseas eligible for the earned-income tax credit. Effective Dec. 31, 1994. (Projected five-year revenue increase: $299 million.)

The bill also removed income received for work done while an inmate in a penal institution from definition of earned income. Effective Dec. 31, 1993. (Projected five-year revenue increase: $14 million.)

• **Excess Pension Assets.** Extend for five years, until Dec. 31, 2000, a provision in previous law that allowed employers to transfer excess taxable pension plan assets to cover nontaxable contributions to a retiree health benefit plan established under section 401(h) rules. The provision reduced the amount of assets eligible to be transferred by a percentage equal to the amount of money previously set aside for future retiree health liabilities divided by the present value of all future retiree health liabilities. (Projected five-year revenue increase: $399 million.)

• **Rounding Rules on COLAs.** Establish new rounding rules for cost of living adjustments (COLAs) to the dollar limit for maximum benefits under defined benefit pension plans. For such plans, COLA increases to the benefit ceiling would be made in increments of $5,000; limits on elective deferrals under a qualified cash or deferred arrangement would be rounded to increments of $500; and the minimum compensation limit for simplified employee pension participation would be rounded to increments of $50. Effective Dec. 31, 1994. (Projected five-year revenue increase: $395 million.)

• **Tax on Social Security Benefits to Nonresidents.** Increase to 85 percent from 50 percent the amount of Social Security or railroad retirement benefits that nonresident aliens were required to include as gross income in determining their taxes. Effective Dec. 31, 1994. (Projected five-year revenue increase: $303 million.)

• **Partnership Distribution of Marketable Securities.** Require that when a business partner exchanged appreciated partnership assets for an increased share in the partnership's marketable securities, those securities be treated as cash for tax purposes. This was aimed at closing a loophole that allowed partners to make such potentially lucrative exchanges tax-free. Generally effective as of date of enactment. (Projected five-year revenue increase: $211 million.)

• **Taxpayer Identification Number at Birth.** Require taxpayers to obtain taxpayer identification numbers (TINs) for any children, including newborns, whom the taxpayers claimed as dependents for tax exemption purposes. Previous law required TINs for all children older than age 1. This was aimed at reducing fraudulent claiming of dependents. To be phased into effect beginning with tax year 1995. (Projected five-year revenue increase: $94 million.)

• **IRS User Fees.** Extend for five years, until Sept. 30, 2000, the user fees charged by the IRS for written responses to questions relating to tax status or to the effects of particular transactions on tax liability. (Projected five-year revenue increase: $124 million.)

• **Underpayment Penalty for Tax Shelter Participants.** Require individual taxpayers to include tax shelter income in calculating whether their total income tax was substantially understated, even if there was substantial legal authority for the tax shelter item and the taxpayer reasonably believed that the claimed treatment was proper. Effective date of enactment of the implementing bill. (Projected five-year revenue increase: $95 million.)

- **Savings Bond Interest Rates.** Repeal a requirement that Series E savings bonds pay investment yields of at least 4 percent per year, allowing the Treasury secretary to set market-rate yields. (Projected five-year revenue increase: $122 million.)
- **"Pioneer Preferences."** Require the recipients of "pioneer" licenses from the Federal Communications Commission to pay the higher of $400 million plus interest or 85 percent of the average per capita bids for comparable personal communications system licenses. (Expected to raise at least $534 million.) ❏

China Trade

President Clinton in 1993 announced a new approach to trade relations with the People's Republic of China, tamping down what had been a fiery dispute with Congress. One year later, however, Clinton reversed himself and adopted the approach taken by his Republican predecessors, triggering a new battle with lawmakers.

At issue was whether China should continue to trade with the United States on a most-favored-nation (MFN) basis. Almost all of the United States' trading partners had MFN status, which assured them the lowest available tariffs on exports to the United States. Countries that were not most favored nations were subject to tariffs up to 10 times as high.

A number of lawmakers from both parties opposed MFN for China because of the country's record on human rights, intellectual property, weapons sales and trade barriers, among other issues. Proponents of MFN status acknowledged China's often hostile actions but argued that trade was the best way to bring about change in the underdeveloped giant.

U.S. presidents had renewed China's MFN status every year since 1980, despite growing opposition in Congress. In renewing China's trade status in 1993, Clinton announced that he would not do so again unless China stopped producing exports with prison labor and made "overall significant progress" on human rights issues. The move effectively ended a three-year effort by Congress to limit the president's discretion over China's MFN status.

The following year, Clinton acknowledged that China had not met the human rights benchmarks he had set in 1993. Nevertheless, he renewed the country's trading status and said that there should be no link between MFN and human rights, echoing his GOP predecessors.

The move angered the band of MFN opponents in Congress, but they did not have the votes to stop the renewal.

BACKGROUND

China first gained MFN status with the United States as part of a trade agreement completed in 1980. That status came up for renewal each year, as required by the Jackson-Vanik amendment to the 1974 Trade Act (PL 93-618), which governed trade relations with communist countries. If the president decided to renew China's MFN status, the renewal took effect automatically on July 3 unless Congress voted to reject it. (*1974 act, Congress and the Nation Vol. IV, p. 131*)

While Congress had never rejected the president's decision,

the opposition to MFN status grew significantly after the Chinese government cracked down on prodemocracy demonstrators in Tienanmen Square in 1989. The House passed bills in 1990 to end the MFN status and put restrictions on future renewals, but the Senate did not act on either proposal. In 1992, Congress cleared two bills that would have barred MFN renewals unless China made significant progress on human rights. Both were vetoed by President Bush, and although the House voted to override the vetoes, the Senate sustained them. (*1990 action, Congress and the Nation Vol. VIII, p. 173; 1992 action, Congress and the Nation Vol. VIII, p. 190*)

During the 1992 campaign, Clinton took issue with Bush's approach to the China trade issue. China's trade status, Clinton argued, should be contingent on respect for human rights in China and Tibet, responsible conduct on weapons deals, and more open markets for U.S. goods. That was the approach Clinton took the first time he reviewed China's trade status, in 1993.

LEGISLATIVE ACTION

On May 28, 1993, Clinton notified Congress that he planned to renew China's MFN status for the year. At the same time, he signed an executive order tying the next renewal to China's performance on a series of issues. In particular, the renewal would depend on whether China complied with a 1992 agreement not to use prison labor to produce exports, released and accounted for political and religious prisoners, ensured humane treatment of other prisoners, protected Tibet's religious and cultural heritage, and permitted international radio and television broadcasts into China.

The executive order also stipulated that the United States would vigorously enforce laws barring unfair trading practices and weapons proliferation—two areas where China's actions had been sharply criticized. But Clinton did not explicitly tie renewal of MFN to evidence that China was opening its markets or refraining from shipments of missile and other technology to third countries.

Echoing his predecessor, Clinton said, "I don't want to isolate China. I want to do what's good for the Chinese people." But by placing conditions on trade with China, Clinton departed sharply from Bush's policy.

Clinton's approach satisfied two Democratic leaders of the anti-MFN forces, Senate Majority Leader George J. Mitchell, D-Maine, and Rep. Nancy Pelosi, D-Calif. They announced that they would not move forward with the legislation they had introduced to place conditions on China's trade status.

Republican Rep. Gerald B. H. Solomon of New York, who had sponsored previous efforts to revoke China's MFN status, was not willing to wait. Solomon introduced a resolution to block the renewal (H J Res 208) on June 8. The House Ways and Means Committee, which overwhelmingly favored the renewal, reported Solomon's resolution unfavorably on July 1 (H Rept 103-167). The Jackson-Vanik amendment required the full House to vote on resolutions of disapproval, however, and Solomon had his chance on July 20.

In an about-face for many members who had backed Solomon's bill in prior years, the House rejected the bill by a

ROMANIA TRADE STATUS

After a one-year delay, Congress late in 1993 bestowed most-favored-nation (MFN) status on Romania, the only nation in eastern Europe that did not hold the MFN designation.

Romania had been designated a most favored nation from 1975 until 1988, when then-President Nicolae Ceausescu renounced it. At the time, Congress was poised to revoke Romania's MFN status because of the government's human rights violations.

The resolution granting MFN status (H J Res 228—PL 103-133) put into effect a U.S.-Romania trade agreement that had been signed in 1992 by President George Bush. Although Bush had asked Congress in June 1992 to upgrade Romania's status, lawmakers had balked out of concern over the pace of economic and democratic reforms in the country. *(Congress and the Nation Vol. VIII, p. 194)*

One of Romania's leading advocates was House Ways and Means Committee Chairman Dan Rostenkowski, D-Ill. "Romania is a country that suffered for years under a crushing dictatorship," Rostenkowski told his House colleagues. "The new leadership of Romania deserves any leg up that the United States can provide them in their long climb back to the community of democratic, free-market societies."

The Ways and Means Committee had reported the resolution on Oct. 7, 1993 (H Rept 103-279), and the House passed it by voice vote five days later. The Senate Finance Committee approved the resolution by voice vote Oct. 14 but did not formally report it; the full Senate cleared the measure by voice vote Oct. 21. President Clinton signed the legislation on Nov. 2.

The resolution mandated that Romania's trade status come up for renewal each year. The MFN designation could not be renewed unless the president certified to Congress that the Romanian government was assuring free emigration and other human rights.

He also outlined a new strategy to maintain pressure on Chinese authorities, relying on quieter diplomacy and less brinkmanship. One element was a modest set of sanctions that would ban imports of Chinese-made guns and ammunition.

A small group of Democratic legislators, led by Mitchell, Pelosi and other China critics, broke with Clinton over China policy. On June 16 they introduced legislation (HR 4590) that would have punished Beijing with trade sanctions for failing to improve its treatment of dissidents and for other human rights shortcomings.

In order to spare China's growing free enterprise sector as much as possible, HR 4590 provided for higher tariffs only on products made by the Chinese army, defense trading companies and selected state-owned enterprises. Mitchell said the bill would affect about $5 billion in Chinese exports to the United States, which totaled $31 billion in 1993. Over the same period, U.S. exports to China totaled $8 billion. "Obviously, China needs our market more than we need theirs," Mitchell said.

Solomon also introduced another resolution to revoke China's MFN status (H J Res 373). Again, the Ways and Means Committee was overwhelmingly opposed, reporting the resolution unfavorably on June 30, 1994 (H Rept 103-575). The committee reported HR 4590 unfavorably on Aug. 1 (H Rept 103-640, Part I).

The full House easily defeated Solomon's resolution on Aug. 9, 75–356. The same day, it adopted a substitute version of HR 4590 by Lee H. Hamilton, D-Ind., chairman of the Foreign Affairs Committee, that essentially codified Clinton's executive order extending China's low-tariff trade status. The vote on the Hamilton substitute was 280–152.

Pelosi then offered her original language as a substitute to the Hamilton version. The House rejected her effort, 158–270, and passed the Hamilton version by voice vote.

With the House having rejected the effort to relink China's trade status with its human rights record, Senate sponsors had no reason to take further action on HR 4590. It advanced no further.   ❑

wide margin, 105–318. The vote assured that China's MFN designation would survive for another year, rendering moot any action by the Senate. "It's very important to get a big vote behind the president so a very clear message is sent to the Chinese government that unless these conditions are met, no kidding, next year MFN is revoked," Pelosi said.

Less than a year later, Clinton made an about-face of his own. While acknowledging that China had not made "overall significant progress" on human rights, Clinton nonetheless renewed China's MFN status, arguing that remaining engaged in the country was a better policy than cutting off billions of dollars in trade.

In announcing his decision on May 26, 1994, Clinton said that linking China's trade status to human rights criteria had "reached the end of [its] usefulness." It was a frank acknowledgment that his previous policy had not worked and that he deemed the economic consequences for both countries to be too severe to carry out the threat.

Export Controls

Efforts to update the cold war–era restrictions on technology exports were stymied in 1993 and 1994, as lawmakers were unable to reconcile the conflicting goals of boosting high-tech exports and curbing the global arms race.

The Export Administration Act (PL 96-72), the federal law governing civilian exports, restricted the sales of computers and other high-technology devices to communist countries. The last permanent authorization expired in 1990, but President Bush and Clinton kept the restrictions in place by executive order.

Congress cleared temporary extensions of the restrictions in 1993 and 1994 while lawmakers wrangled over bills (HR 3937, S 1902) to overhaul the act. The bills would have made it easier to export "dual use" goods—items with civilian and military applications—while also increasing sanctions against countries that exported the technologies used in weapons of mass destruction.

The legislation never reached the floor in either the House or the Senate. The House approved one more temporary extension late in the 1994 session, but the Senate did not act on the bill (HR 5108).

BACKGROUND

The United States began controlling civilian exports after World War II as part of a multinational effort to deny new technologies to the Soviet Union, the Warsaw Pact, China and other communist countries. Starting with the Export Control Act of 1949 and continuing with the Export Administration Act of 1979, the government barred companies from exporting some sensitive items to cold war enemies, and it required companies to obtain export licenses for other dual-use goods.

The Commerce Department, in consultation with the Pentagon and other agencies, maintained the list of controlled dual-use goods and handled applications for export licenses. The Commerce, Defense, State, and Energy departments, among other agencies, jointly reviewed applications to determine whether the proposed export posed a risk to U.S. interests.

As the Warsaw Pact and the Soviet Union dissolved, the goal of the NATO allies shifted from waging economic war to promoting economic growth and stability in the emerging democracies. Concerns about the misuse of U.S. technology remained, but the threat shifted from cold war enemies to rogue states and terrorist hotbeds, such as Libya, Iraq and Syria.

Pressure to update the export law started to mount in the late 1980s. Business groups clamored for passage of a comprehensive rewrite of the act, arguing that the outdated restrictions were hindering their entry and growth in global markets. They were joined by lawmakers concerned about weapons proliferation, who argued that the export law no longer targeted the right countries.

Congress cleared legislation in 1990 to overhaul the act, but President Bush pocket-vetoed the bill because of provisions restricting foreign aid to countries involved in the production of chemical weapons. The measure would have shortened the Commerce Department's list of controlled exports and accelerated the granting of licenses. (*Congress and the Nation Vol. VIII, p. 175*)

Similar legislation nearly cleared in 1992, but end-of-session delaying tactics killed the bill in the House. Opponents objected to a provision that would have reduced the Defense Department's power to block sensitive exports. (*Congress and the Nation Vol. VIII, p. 195*)

LEGISLATIVE ACTION

The efforts to update the law heated up again in 1994, when four House committees and a Senate committee approved competing proposals. In each chamber, however, disputes between business advocates and Defense Department allies stymied the legislation.

In the House, the Foreign Affairs Committee moved first, reporting HR 3937 on May 25, 1994 (H Rept 103-531, Part I). Intent on reducing the restrictions on exporters, the committee proposed to eliminate controls on most dual-use items, require the automatic granting of any license application not rejected within 30 days, and give the Defense Department less say over whether to reject an export license. The bill also called for punitive trade sanctions on countries that exported component parts of biological, chemical and nuclear weapons.

The Ways and Means Committee reported a similar version of the bill on June 17 (H Rept 103-531, Part III). The Armed Services Committee, however, proposed to give the Defense Department more power to stop dual-use exports that could aid the weapons programs of unfriendly nations. It also proposed to give the government 50 days to review license applications. The committee reported its version of the bill June 17 (H Rept 103-531, Part IV).

The Intelligence Committee, which had jurisdiction over only a portion of the bill, reported its proposed changes on June 16 (H Rept 103-531, Part II). It proposed that the government study how its export controls were affecting U.S. computer software manufacturers.

Foreign Affairs Chairman Lee H. Hamilton, D-Ind., and Armed Services Chairman Ronald V. Dellums, D-Calif., attempted to broker a compromise, but they fell short of a deal. A single sticking point reportedly remained outstanding: how to handle some goods that were considered both munitions and dual-use items.

Under existing law, dual-use items came under the control of the Export Administration Act while munitions were regulated by the State Department under the Arms Export Control Act. HR 3937 would have required that items be classified as either munitions or dual-use products, not both, to keep exporters from having to undergo two reviews. But lawmakers were not able to agree on where to put some items, and the bill never came up for a vote in the House.

The Senate Banking Committee approved yet another proposal (S 1902) on May 24; the vote was 19–0. The bill sought to loosen restrictions on the export of some items to nations that were no longer considered a threat to the United States. At the same time, it proposed to tighten controls on the export of weapons and other technologies that could be used against the United States in terrorist attacks or during a war. The bill would have authorized the president to impose sanctions on countries that exported such technologies.

The committee added an amendment by Patty Murray, D-Wash., to require a study on the impact on U.S. companies of unilateral export controls on computer software. The issue was an important one for companies such as Seattle-based Microsoft Corp., which made business software. By law, U.S. software companies could not export software containing strong encryption, a form of coding used to thwart computer hackers and other unauthorized users.

Murray and panel members from California, Massachusetts and Utah wanted to see such unilateral restrictions lifted. They argued that because such software was already available overseas, the U.S. restrictions did not effectively protect U.S. interests. The National Security Agency, however, opposed decontrolling software.

The committee never reported S 1902 to the Senate.

SHORT-TERM EXTENSIONS

To keep the statutory restrictions in place pending an overhaul, Congress twice cleared temporary extensions of the Export Administration Act. By a 330–54 vote, the House passed a bill (HR 750) on Feb. 16, 1993, to reauthorize the act through June 30, 1994.

The Senate cleared the bill by voice vote March 11, and President Clinton signed it March 27 (PL 103-10). The measure made no substantive changes to the law.

Just before the authorization expired, Congress cleared a stop-gap extension through Aug. 20, 1994. The bill (HR 4635—PL 103-277) passed the House by voice vote June 27 and cleared the Senate by voice vote June 30. President Clinton signed it July 5.

When the overhaul legislation stalled, the House Foreign Affairs Committee gave voice-vote approval to a bill (HR 5108) that would have kept the act in force for one more year. The House passed the bill Oct. 4, 1994, 407–4, but the measure died in the Senate Banking Committee. ❑

Financial Services Trade

The Senate and House each passed bills in 1994 to help U.S. banks and/or securities firms in foreign markets, but neither measure made it into law. The bills were the third and fourth "Fair Trade in Financial Services" proposals since 1990 to fall short of enactment after passing one chamber.

The Senate measure, which was included in a community banking bill (HR 3474), would have given U.S. trade negotiators new tools to pressure foreign governments into opening their markets for U.S. financial-services companies. It had widespread support in the House, especially within the Banking Committee.

The Clinton administration, which sought the legislation to shore up its negotiating position in ongoing trade talks, pleaded for its passage. But stout opposition from the House Ways and Means Committee killed the proposal.

The House bill (HR 4926) was a watered-down version of the Senate provisions, applying only to banks and wielding less clout. It passed the House in the final days of the 1994 session but was not taken up by the Senate.

The measures responded to concerns that U.S. companies were being frozen out of financial services markets, particularly in the Pacific Rim, while foreign banks were grabbing a large share of the U.S. market. The Senate proposal would have authorized the administration to block foreign banks and securities firms from expanding their U.S. operations if the Treasury Department uncovered discrimination against U.S. financial-services companies in the foreign firms' home countries.

Members of Ways and Means and the House Energy and Commerce Committee opposed the Senate language because they believe it would give the Treasury Department too much power over the domain of the Office of the U.S. Trade Representative and the Securities and Exchange Commission, which fell under their respective jurisdictions.

BACKGROUND

Under the International Banking Act of 1978 (PL 95-369), foreign banks and securities firms were given the same rights to operate in the United States as their U.S. counterparts. This standard, known as "national treatment," was established even though some other countries imposed tighter controls on U.S. companies than they did on domestic firms. (*Congress and the Nation Vol. V, p. 259*)

Previous Fair Trade in Financial Services bills had tried to establish a new set of ground rules, "reciprocal national treatment." Under that approach, banks and securities firms from countries that did not provide national treatment to U.S. companies would be subject to discriminatory treatment in the United States.

In 1990, the House approved the proposal as part of a conference report on an unrelated defense measure. The Senate opposed the defense provisions, however, and the proposal sank. In 1992, the Senate attached the proposal to a new version of the defense measure, but it was dropped in the face of opposition from the House conferees. (*1990 action, Congress and the Nation Vol. VIII, p. 187; 1992 action, p. 198*)

LEGISLATIVE ACTION

The Senate Banking Committee reported another Fair Trade in Financial Services bill (S 1527) on March 15, 1994 (S Rept 103-235). In light of the recently concluded negotiations over a new General Agreement on Tariffs and Trade (GATT), the bill barred sanctions against firms from nations that had agreed during the GATT talks to open their financial markets.

Two days later, the Senate agreed by voice vote to add the provisions of S 1527 to a House-passed community-development banking bill (HR 3474). The expanded bill then passed the Senate by voice vote.

In conference, negotiators from the House and Senate Banking committees agreed to the following procedure for imposing sanctions on foreign financial-services companies: If the Treasury Department determined that U.S. firms were being harmed by discriminatory treatment in a foreign country, it would try to solve the problem by negotiating with that country. If the negotiations did not bear fruit, the department would order sanctions against the corresponding foreign companies that sought to start or expand operations in the United States. The sanctions would not have to be imposed, however, if regulators found that the penalties would harm the U.S. financial system or securities markets, or if they violated an existing trade agreement.

When leaders of the Ways and Means Committee resisted the proposal, Energy and Commerce Chairman John D. Dingell, D-Mich., proposed to shift the sanctions authority from the Treasury Department to the U.S. Trade Representative—an approach that Ways and Means had endorsed three years before. The compromise did not satisfy Ways and Means this time, however, and the provisions were dropped from the conference report.

The House Banking Committee had given voice-vote approval March 9 to a more limited measure (HR 3248), covering the treatment of banks but not securities firms. That measure never reached the House floor. The committee tried again on Sept. 19, reporting a new and far less ambitious bill (H.R. 4926—H Rept 103-727). HR 4926 would have allowed, but not required, federal regulators to consider how U.S. firms were treated overseas when deciding whether to allow a foreign bank to start or expand operations in the United States.

To keep the bill out of Ways and Means, the Banking Committee dropped provisions that would have let the Treasury Department impose sanctions on trading partners that discriminated against U.S. banks. By applying the measure only to banks, the committee also avoided a referral to Energy and Commerce.

The measure passed the House by voice vote Sept. 30, but the Senate did not take it up. ❏

Financing Defense Exports

Congress cleared a bill in October 1994 to help U.S. defense contractors sell more products in commercial civilian markets overseas.

The measure (HR 4455—PL 103-428) authorized the Export-Import Bank to provide financing for defense exports if it determined that the products or services were nonlethal and intended primarily for civilian use. For example, the change allowed the bank to finance the purchase of a U.S. radar system for an airport primarily used by civilian aircraft.

Previous law had forbidden the Ex-Im Bank, which provided loans and loan guarantees to foreign entities purchasing U.S. goods, to finance defense exports unless the goods or services were used primarily for antinarcotics activities. Defense exports were classified as any item listed on the State Department's Munitions List.

The House Banking, Finance and Urban Affairs Committee reported the bill Aug. 8, 1994 (H Rept 103-681), after adding a requirement that the Ex-Im Bank give Congress 15 days notice before financing a defense item unrelated to narcotics. The House passed the bill by voice vote later that day under suspension of the rules.

The Senate passed a slightly modified version of the bill by voice vote Oct. 5, making more specific a House provision to encourage environmentally beneficial exports. The House cleared the Senate version on Oct. 7, and President Clinton signed it Oct. 31. ❏

OPIC Reauthorization

After striking a compromise on the scope of the legislation, Congress cleared a bill in October 1994 to reauthorize the Overseas Private Investment Corporation (OPIC) for two years. President Clinton signed the bill (HR 4950—PL 103-392) on Oct. 22.

OPIC's mission was to promote economic growth in developing countries, particularly those converting to market-oriented economies. It helped U.S. investors find investment opportunities overseas, provided insurance to protect those investments,

and made loans and loan guarantees to help finance projects abroad.

The previous authorization for OPIC, enacted in 1992, expired Sept. 30, 1994. A proposal to reauthorize OPIC for an additional year passed the House in June 1993 as part of HR 2404, an omnibus foreign aid authorization bill, but that legislation died in the Senate. *(1992 action, Congress and the Nation Vol. VIII, p. 199; foreign aid bill, p. 202)*

On Sept. 19, 1994, the House Foreign Affairs Committee reported a version of HR 4950 (H Rept 103-726) that would have reauthorized OPIC for three years and made a number of changes in its operations, such as extending its programs to investments in Northern Ireland. The bill also included the text of HR 3813, a proposal to promote the export of U.S. environmental technologies, products and services. Foreign Affairs had reported HR 3813 on April 18, 1994 (H Rept 103-478), and the House passed it the same day, 416–0, but the Senate had not acted on it.

The House passed HR 4950 by voice vote on Sept. 19. The Senate Foreign Relations Committee countered with a simple one-year reauthorization bill (S 2438), which it reported on Sept. 22. After inserting the text of S 2438 into HR 4950, the Senate passed the House bill by voice vote Sept. 30.

House-Senate conferees agreed to reauthorize OPIC for two years, through Sept. 30, 1996. The conference report (H Rept 103-834), filed Oct. 4, also included the provisions promoting environmental-oriented exports and extending OPIC benefits to Ireland and Northern Ireland.

Other provisions of the conference report raised the limit on the total amount of insurance and financial assistance provided by OPIC; ordered the Agency for International Development to provide a training program for foreign officials in the protection of intellectual property; and reauthorized for two years a number of export-promotion programs.

The Senate approved the conference report by voice vote Oct. 6. The House did the same the next day, clearing the bill. ❏

1995–1996

Aside from the annual proposals to end China's most-favored-nation (MFN) status, few trade bills reached the floor of the House or Senate in the 104th Congress. The drop-off in activity was not surprising, given the major accomplishments of 1993 and 1994. The GOP agenda focused on other issues, and the Clinton administration did not put forward any major new proposals. Nor did Congress agree to give fast-track consideration to any new trade deals, effectively forestalling negotiations to extend NAFTA to more countries.

The main action in 1995 and 1996 was on tariffs and duties. China's MFN designation was preserved, Cambodia attained MFN status for the first time, and two former Warsaw Pact nations were granted MFN status on a permanent basis. Preferential duties for developing nations were renewed, and tariffs were phased out on imports from areas governed by the Palestinian Authority.

Fast-Track Rules

Lawmakers in the 104th Congress declined to extend the so-called fast-track rules that required expedited congressional consideration of trade agreements. The lack of action stemmed at least in part from a dispute between Republican leaders and the administration over the scope of trade talks.

The House Ways and Means Committee reported a bill (HR 2371—H Rept 104-285, Part I) on Oct. 20, 1995, to extend the fast-track rules through 1999, but the measure advanced no further. Similar language was included in an early version of the fiscal 1996 budget-reconciliation bill (HR 2491) in October 1995, but House GOP leaders dropped the provisions before the bill reached the floor in response to complaints from Republican members opposed to fast-track procedures.

First authorized in the Trade Act of 1974, the fast-track rules aimed to assure foreign trade negotiators that Congress would not rewrite any deals struck with the White House. The law provided that the rules would renew automatically every two years unless Congress intervened. *(1974 law, Congress and the Nation Vol. IV, p. 131)*

Under fast-track rules, the president was required to notify and consult with Congress while negotiating eligible trade agreements; in exchange, Congress agreed to vote on the implementing bill within 90 legislative days of its submission by the president. The bill was subject only to an up or down vote, and no amendments were allowed. To give Congress an opportunity for input, lawmakers conducted a series of mock markups to refine the legislation before the president formally submitted it.

In 1993, Congress extended the rules only for six months and only for the negotiations over a new General Agreement on Tariffs and Trade. The rules then lapsed, meaning that no agreement entered into after Dec. 15, 1993, was eligible for fast-track consideration. *(1993 action, p. 162)*

The bill approved by the Ways and Means Committee in 1995 would have extended fast-track procedures to trade pacts negotiated by Dec. 31, 1999. It would have permitted an additional two-year extension if the president requested it and Congress did not pass a resolution of disapproval.

The measure was more than a simple extension of the rules, however—it also included a direct attack on Clinton's approach to trade talks. In particular, the free-trade-oriented Republicans on Ways and Means objected to the administration making an issue of wage rates, worker safety, environmental protection and related topics during trade negotiations.

The bill proposed to narrow the negotiating objectives for the U.S. trade representative, removing references to "worker rights" and "developing countries" in existing law and mandating that the talks deal with "policies and practices directly related to trade." It also would have limited the president's discretion in drafting legislation to implement a trade agreement.

The administration wanted the fast-track procedures continued so it could conduct talks aimed at bringing Chile into NAFTA. But it objected to the "directly related to trade" provision, arguing that wage rates and environmental enforcement were key issues when lowering trade barriers with developing countries.

"The president is committed to addressing labor and environmental issues in the context of trade agreements," U.S. Trade Representative Mickey Kantor said. "Why limit our potential?"

The dispute over negotiating goals had its roots in the 1992 NAFTA debate, when many congressional Democrats refused to vote for the agreement until concerns about Mexico's low wages and weak environmental protections were addressed. Although Clinton took office after NAFTA negotiations were complete, he reopened talks with Mexico, winning enough concessions in labor and environment and other areas to shore up votes in Congress for the final deal. *(NAFTA implementation, p. 155)*

At its markup session on Sept. 21, 1995, the Ways and Means Committee rejected, 12–21, a Democratic alternative that was favored by the administration. It then approved the bill by voice vote, but the House never took up the measure. ❑

Bilateral Trade Relations

The 104th Congress renewed the most-favored-nation (MFN) designations for the People's Republic of China, Romania and Bulgaria while bestowing it for the first time on Cambodia. Only China's MFN status generated any real controversy, as opponents of China's communist regime continued their annual efforts to impose economic sanctions.

The United States gave all but a handful of countries MFN status, ensuring the lowest available tariffs on their exports to the United States. Under the Jackson-Vanik amendment to the 1974 Trade Act (PL 93-618), China and other communist countries received the MFN designation only on a year-by-year basis. The amendment, which penalized nations that did not allow free emigration, was intended to pressure the Soviet Union to let Jews leave the country. *(1974 act, Congress and the Nation Vol. IV, p. 131)*

Reflecting the routine nature of the MFN label, the Senate passed a bill in 1996 to change the designation to having "normal trade relations" with the United States. The House did not act on the measure, however.

CHINA

Relations with China grew increasingly tense over the course of 1995. To force China to combat copyright violations, the United States threatened to impose punitive tariffs on $1 billion worth of Chinese goods early in February. China responded in kind, but the threats were dropped when China signed an agreement pledging to crack down on compact-disc piracy and other thefts of intellectual property.

Bowing to congressional pressure, the State Department granted a visa in May to Taiwanese President Lee Teng-hui, prompting China to recall its ambassador to the United States in June. Later that month, China detained a Chinese-American human rights activist, Harry Wu.

Renewing MFN Status in 1995

Against this backdrop, President Clinton announced on June 2 that he was renewing China's MFN status. Opponents of the move, led by Reps. Frank R. Wolf, R-Va., and Nancy Pelosi, D-

Calif., quickly introduced a resolution (H J Res 96) to block Clinton. The House Ways and Means Committee, which had long been dominated by free-traders, reported the resolution adversely on July 17 (H Rept 104-188). To mollify the anti-China faction, however, Rep. Doug Bereuter, the Nebraska Republican who chaired the Foreign Relations Subcommittee on Asia, introduced a bill (HR 2058) calling for "intensified diplomatic initiatives" to address a number of concerns about Beijing.

The eight objectives laid out by Bereuter's bill included gaining the release of Wu and other political prisoners, halting the export of missile technology and nuclear weapons to Iran and Pakistan, ending coercive abortion practices, allowing freedom of speech and religion, reducing tensions with Taiwan and stopping the export of goods made with prison labor. The president would have been required to report to Congress every six months on the actions taken to achieve those goals, and a new Radio Free Asia would have been required to broadcast into China within three months.

At the request of House Speaker Newt Gingrich, R-Ga., Bereuter, Wolf and Pelosi worked together before the issue came to the House floor. The result was an unexpected motion by Wolf on July 20 to table (kill) the disapproval resolution that he had introduced. Wolf said he had come to believe that Bereuter's approach would send a clearer message to China on behalf of human rights.

A number of members decried Wolf's decision, saying Bereuter's bill was a hollow threat. "This bill will not free one dissident, it will not close one prison camp," said David Funderburk, R-N.C. "China's abysmal human rights record has not earned any special kind of treatment," said Jim Bunning of Kentucky, who led the GOP opposition. Bunning cited the arrest and beating in April of Chinese Christians conducting an Easter Mass as evidence of China's continuing human rights abuses.

Wolf responded with an impassioned plea that members take Bereuter's legislation seriously. "Believe me, I know the Chinese are worse than many of you even think they are. . . . But I have talked with Chinese dissidents, with Christians in China about this bill, and they said if we could get a good strong vote for this, [it would] for the first time [put] Congress on record," said Wolf. "This will help the democracy movement in China."

Ways and Means Chairman Bill Archer, R-Texas, Jennifer Dunn, R-Wash., and Robert T. Matsui, D-Calif., also argued forcefully that only through engagement would the United States have any leverage over China's political policies. The House on July 20 passed HR 2058, 416–10, and tabled H J Res 96, 321–107. The Senate, which traditionally had been more supportive of China's MFN status than the House, did not take up HR 2058.

Renewing MFN Status in 1996

Tensions between the United States and China continued to increase in late 1995 and early 1996. In addition to menacing Taiwan with provocative military maneuvers, China was accused of selling nuclear-weapons components to Pakistan and violating its agreement to protect U.S. intellectual property, among other transgressions. "Since the MFN debate last year, I

can't see any hard evidence that China is mending its ways," said Bunning. "It puts a twist on the old saying, the more things change the more they get worse."

Nevertheless, Clinton announced on May 31, 1996, that he was renewing China's MFN status for another year. The growing anti-MFN faction responded not only with a resolution to block the renewal (H J Res 182), but also a number of proposals aimed at changing China's behavior. For example, Rules Committee Chairman Gerald B. H. Solomon, R-N.Y., a longtime opponent of China's MFN status, introduced a bill (HR 3577) to cut funding for the World Bank and other international entities that lent money to China. International Relations Committee Chairman Benjamin A. Gilman, R-N.Y., proposed legislation (HR 3684) to prohibit imports by Chinese companies controlled by the People's Liberation Army.

The MFN opponents wanted to bring the sanctions bills to the House floor at the same time as the MFN resolution, but the GOP leadership would not agree. Nor would the leadership grant the opponents' request to delay the MFN vote until after the July 4th recess. The rush to the floor enraged many MFN opponents, who bitterly complained that Gingrich and other GOP leaders had caved in to pressure from U.S. corporations. Pelosi delivered a lengthy tirade against the leadership at a late-night Rules Committee meeting June 25, which set the procedures for floor action.

"It's an act of cowardice," Pelosi said the next day. "The Republican leadership mugged us."

The House took up H J Res 182 on June 27. The three-hour debate was punctuated by fierce attacks on China's policies on trade, human rights and other issues, with MFN opponents homing in on the United States' $34 billion trade deficit with China. "The debate is not about free trade, it is about fair trade," said House Minority Whip David E. Bonior, D-Mich. "It is about whether we are going to use the leverage we have as a nation to open up markets in a way that is fair to American workers."

Supporters of MFN argued that, despite the deficit, trade with China represented an important source of jobs for their states and districts. They also argued that cutting off MFN would only serve to antagonize China and deny U.S. businesses a chance to compete in the world's hottest export market. "A decision to revoke MFN and isolate China would eliminate whatever modest influence we have now on Chinese behavior," said Lee H. Hamilton of Indiana, ranking Democrat on the International Relations Committee.

Most proponents of unconditional China trade repeatedly made the point that they were not endorsing the Beijing regime.

"These Chinese, these communist bums, shot me over there in 1950," said New York Democrat Charles B. Rangel, a veteran of the Korean War. "I do not like any communists. . . . But I do not know whether the United States of America has to have a litmus test with who we trade with."

Clinton was aided on the issue by his Republican opponent in the 1996 presidential race, former Senate Majority Leader Bob Dole, R-Kan., who called for the MFN status to be renewed. Corporate lobbyists also pointed to the Boeing Co.'s troubles in China as an example of how American industries suffered when

U.S.-China trade relations become unstable. Earlier in the year, when tensions were near their peak, China passed over Boeing and placed a huge aircraft order with Airbus Industrie, a European consortium.

The House defeated the resolution, 141–286, allowing China's trade status to be maintained. As a partial consolation to the MFN opponents, however, the House then adopted a nonbinding resolution (H Res 461) by Christopher Cox, R-Calif., calling for hearings and possible legislation to punish China for various misdeeds. The vote was 411–7.

Cox's resolution contained nine pages of detailed allegations against China's government. It directed four committees—International Relations, National Security, Ways and Means, and Banking and Financial Services—to hold hearings and report "appropriate" legislation by the end of the year targeting objectionable Chinese activities. The resolution did not require action by the four committees, however, and they took none.

BULGARIA AND ROMANIA

Congress cleared legislation in 1996 that authorized the president to grant permanent MFN status to Bulgaria and Romania. The bills allowed the president to take the two countries off the list of current or former communist regimes whose trade status was subject to annual review.

Bulgaria had been granted MFN status annually since 1991, and the proposal to authorize a permanent MFN designation (HR 2853) moved swiftly through Congress. The House Ways and Means Committee reported the bill Feb. 29, 1996 (H Rept 104-466), and the House passed it by voice vote March 5. The Senate Finance Committee reported the bill without amendment on May 9 (S Rept 104-265), and the Senate cleared it by voice vote June 28.

President Clinton signed the measure on July 18 (PL 104-162).

Romania had received MFN status from 1975 to 1988, and it regained the designation in 1993 (PL 103-133). On May 14, 1996, the Ways and Means Committee reported a bill (HR 3161—H Rept 104-629) to authorize permanent MFN treatment for Romania. Unlike the proposal for Bulgaria, however, HR 3161 generated some sparks on the House floor.

Opponents of the bill, including David Funderburk, R-N.C., a former ambassador to Romania, alleged that the government under Romanian President Ion Iliescu was a "crypto-communist" system that continued to abuse human rights, impede the press and commit other abuses. Before granting permanent MFN status, the opponents wanted to wait for the results of Romania's second national election, scheduled for November 1996.

Supporters argued that granting MFN status would encourage Romania's transition to democracy and a free economy. The country already had undertaken significant economic reforms, was rapidly privatizing industry and agriculture, and was fostering a swift growth in trade with the United States, according to the bill's sponsors.

The House passed the bill on July 17, 334–86. The Senate cleared the measure July 19 by voice vote, and Clinton signed it Aug. 3 (PL 104-171).

CAMBODIA

Congress cleared legislation in 1996 to give the MFN designation to Cambodia, one of the seven communist nations denied MFN status under the 1988 Omnibus Trade Act (PL 100-418). As a prerequisite, however, lawmakers required that Cambodia and the United States reach a trade agreement giving U.S. exports the lowest available tariffs in Cambodia.

President Clinton signed the bill (HR 1642—PL 104-203) on Sept. 25.

Lawmakers had reservations about the change, given reports of government repression and growing corruption in Cambodia. Still, sponsors viewed the MFN designation as a way to help Cambodia make the transition to a free-market economy, promote democracy, advance human rights and boost U.S. exports in the rapidly growing southeast Asian market.

The House Ways and Means Committee reported the bill on June 27, 1995 (H Rept 104-160), and the House passed it by voice vote without amendment on July 11, 1995. The Senate Finance Committee reported the bill (S Rept 104-264) on May 9, 1996, after adding language to encourage democratic reforms. The Senate passed the amended measure by voice vote July 25, and the House cleared the bill Sept. 12.

RENAMING MFN

The Senate approved a bill in 1996 to redesignate "most favored" nations as nations having "normal trade relations" with the United States, but the House would not endorse the change. The bill was cosponsored by every member of the Senate Finance Committee. According to Daniel Patrick Moynihan, D-N.Y., the ranking member of the Finance Committee, the MFN label first appeared in treaties written in the 17th century, and it was a misnomer even then. "There is . . . no single most-favored nation," he said. "The vast majority of our trading partners receive treatment equal to all others—not most-favored treatment, but normal treatment."

The Senate passed the bill by voice vote Sept. 10, but the House did not act on it. Later that month the Finance Committee added a similar proposal to a House-passed bill (HR 3815) of largely technical corrections to trade laws, but the committee dropped the provision before reporting the bill to avoid a fight with the House. (*Trade technical corrections, p. 183*) ❑

Other Tariff Legislation

Congress cleared legislation in 1996 to give preferential treatment to products from the West Bank, the Gaza Strip and developing countries. A similar effort targeted at the Caribbean basin stalled in the House Ways and Means Committee, however.

DEVELOPING COUNTRIES

After a few false starts, Congress in 1996 renewed the Generalized System of Preferences (GSP) through May 31, 1997. The GSP allowed products from most developing countries to enter the United States duty-free, provided that similar U.S. products were not "import sensitive."

The renewal was included in HR 3448 (PL 104-188), a bill to raise the minimum wage.

First enacted as part of the Trade Act of 1974 (PL 93-618), the GSP stemmed from a United Nations initiative to promote economic development and diversification in the world's poorest regions. Approximately 4,500 products from 148 countries and territories received duty-free treatment from the United States through the GSP. Unlike other trade programs, the GSP was unilateral: it cut duties on imports without requiring similar treatment of U.S. exports.

Congress had last renewed the GSP in 1994 as part of the bill to implement the new General Agreement on Tariffs and Trade (PL 103-465). That renewal expired on July 31, 1995. *(GATT implementation, p. 161)*

The House Ways and Means Subcommittee on Trade started work on renewing the GSP in early 1995, proposing to extend the preferences through 2000 and streamline administration of the program. The subcommittee's bill (HR 1654), approved 13–0 on May 18, 1995, went no further, however.

Instead, the full Ways and Means Committee proposed on Sept. 13, 1995, to insert a similar proposal into the fiscal 1996 budget reconciliation bill. The House Budget Committee concurred, including the proposal in the reconciliation bill (HR 2491) that it reported on Oct. 17 (H Rept 104-280). The proposal won approval from the full House and Senate, but it died when President Clinton vetoed the reconciliation bill on Dec. 6, 1995. *(Budget reconciliation, p. 68)*

The following year, the Senate Finance Committee proposed to extend the GSP through June 30, 1997, as part of a bill (HR 3074) authorizing the president to lift tariffs on imports from the West Bank and Gaza Strip. The bill stalled short of the Senate floor, however, because of opposition to an unrelated provision on shipbuilding subsidies. *(Story, below)*

The GSP extension then found another vehicle, a bill (HR 3448) to raise the minimum wage and cut taxes. Conferees on HR 3448 agreed to include provisions similar to HR 1654 in their report, which was filed on Aug. 1 (H Rept 104-737). On Aug. 2, the House approved the report, 354–72, and the Senate followed suit, 76–22, clearing HR 3448. Clinton signed the legislation on Aug. 20 (PL 104-188).

In addition to extending the GSP through May 31, 1997, HR 3448 authorized the president to give duty-free treatment to more products from the poorest nations, provided that similar U.S.-made goods were not vulnerable to imports. It also set tougher criteria for countries and products to qualify for the GSP, including lower limits on per-capita income and exports to the United States.

WEST BANK AND GAZA STRIP

After shedding a contentious amendment on shipbuilding subsidies, Congress cleared a bill (HR 3074) in September 1996 to let the president lift tariffs on imports from the newly self-governing West Bank and Gaza Strip. President Clinton signed the measure on Oct. 2 (PL 104-234).

The measure implemented a free-trade deal that the U.S. trade representative reached on Oct. 17, 1995, with representa-

tives of Israel and the Palestinian Authority. The deal was an extension of the 1985 U.S.-Israel Free Trade Agreement that phased out tariffs between the United States and Israel over 10 years. The 1985 agreement had not covered the West Bank or the Gaza Strip.

In exchange for an end to U.S. tariffs, the Palestinian Authority agreed to give U.S. products duty-free access to the West Bank and the Gaza Strip, to prevent goods from being funneled through those regions to escape U.S. duties, and to help end the Arab economic boycott of Israel. The goal of the agreement was to promote peace in the region by aiding the Palestinian economy.

The House Ways and Means Committee moved quickly on the issue. On Oct. 20, 1995, it reported a bill (HR 2371—H Rept 104-285, Part I) to extend the fast-track rules for trade agreements, including a provision to let the president waive the tariffs on Palestinian goods. The bill advanced no further, however. *(Fast-track rules, p. 178)*

The committee tried again on March 25, 1996, reporting a bill (HR 3074—H Rept 104-495) to authorize the lifting of tariffs. The House passed the bill by voice vote on April 16. The Senate Finance Committee, however, amended the bill in May to include provisions extending the Generalized System of Preferences and implementing an international agreement barring subsidies for shipyards. The committee reported the amended bill on May 13 (S Rept 104-270). *(Shipbuilding subsidies, p. 372)*

Allies of the U.S. shipyards objected to the bill, causing it to bog down short of the Senate floor. On Sept. 27, the Senate dropped the Finance Committee amendment and passed the House bill by voice vote, clearing it for the president.

As enacted, HR 3074 allowed the president to give equal treatment to products from Israel, the West Bank, the Gaza Strip and qualifying industrial zones at the Israel-Jordan and Israel-Egypt borders. The reduction in tariffs was expected to have a negligible impact on U.S. revenues because U.S. Customs collected less than $1,000 annually in tariffs on goods from the West Bank, the Gaza Strip and the industrial zones.

CARIBBEAN BASIN

Legislation to shield nations in the Caribbean basin from the possible detrimental effects of the North American Free Trade Agreement (NAFTA) stalled in the House Ways and Means Committee in 1995. Congress had been trying for more than a decade to promote stability and economic growth in Caribbean nations by giving their exports preferential treatment. Starting with the Caribbean Basin Economic Recovery Act of 1983 (PL 98-67), also known as the Caribbean Basin Initiative (CBI), the federal government had lifted duties and expanded quotas on numerous products from 27 countries in the Caribbean and Central America. *(CBI, Congress and the Nation Vol. VI, p. 106)*

Supporters of the CBI feared that the free-trade zone created by NAFTA would drain jobs and investment from the Caribbean nations. On March 29, 1995, the Ways and Means Subcommittee on Trade approved a bill (HR 553), 11–3, that would have placed the same quotas and tariffs on Caribbean

ENCRYPTION

Lawmakers introduced similar bills in the House and Senate in 1996 to allow the export of more data-scrambling products, but strong opposition from the administration and top law enforcement officials helped bottle up the measures in committee.

The federal government classified most "encryption" devices and software as munitions and banned their export. The goal was to keep terrorists, crime syndicates and other hostile foreign entities from escaping detection by concealing their communications in unbreakable codes.

The U.S. computer industry and their allies in Congress argued that the export restrictions did not stop the spread of encryption around the world because such products were available from foreign sources. Instead, these critics said, the restrictions harmed U.S. manufacturers by forcing them to surrender much of the encryption market overseas to foreign companies. Indeed, a Commerce Department study in 1996 found that the restrictions cost U.S. computer industry $60 billion in potential 1995 exports.

Worse yet, computer industry officials argued that the limits discouraged U.S. companies from developing encryption products for the U.S. market, even though there was no law against domestic sales. Foreign software companies thus enjoyed a potential advantage with U.S. customers who wanted their software enhanced by encryption.

Picking up on a Bush administration initiative, the Clinton administration proposed in February 1994 to allow exports of encryption based on a code developed by the National Security Agency, with the code's keys being held by the federal government.

After this "clipper chip" proposal was shunned by industry, the administration came up with a variation in October 1996 that would have allowed other forms of encryption to be exported if law enforcement agents were guaranteed access to the decoding keys. This proposal was endorsed by a few major companies, such as IBM, but otherwise found little favor outside the administration.

The House bill (HR 3011) and its Senate counterpart (S 1587) would have legalized the export of an encryption product if a comparable product were available in the United States from a foreign supplier. Unlike the administration's proposal, the two bills would not have mandated that decoder keys for exported encryption products be made available to law enforcement, or even that the products have decoder keys. However, the bills would have continued to bar encryption exports to countries that sponsored international terrorism, such as Libya, and those subject to U.S. or international trade embargoes, such as North Korea.

Civil libertarians and computer user groups, who vehemently opposed the administration's initiative, remained wary of the two bills. They argued that the bills proposed to give the government too much access to private information.

The House Judiciary Committee held a hearing on HR 3011 on Sept. 25, 1996, but the bill did not advance. The sponsors of the Senate measure, Democrat Patrick J. Leahy of Vermont and Republican Conrad Burns of Montana, tried for several weeks to come up with a compromise acceptable to the administration and industry, but the late-session efforts bore no fruit.

---

products as NAFTA placed on Mexican goods. The measure was seen as a first step toward including the CBI countries into NAFTA or a similar free-trade agreement; its provisions would have expired after 10 years.

Because many Caribbean products already were exempt from tariffs, the main effect of the bill would have been on the products not granted duty-free treatment by the CBI: textiles and apparel, footwear, handbags, luggage, flat goods, work gloves, leather apparel, canned tuna, petroleum and petroleum products, and certain watches. The U.S. manufacturers of these products, however, strongly opposed legislation that could lead to more imports.

The full House Ways and Means Committee never took up HR 553.   ❏

Export Controls

The long-running efforts to update cold war–era restrictions on civilian exports bore no fruit in the 104th Congress, despite the broad support in the House for a major rewrite.

At issue was the Export Administration Act of 1979 (PL 96-72), the federal law governing the export of "dual use" products—civilian goods that had military applications, such as computers. Lawmakers had tried for the previous three con-

gresses to update the act, to no avail. The provisions of the act had expired in 1994, but President Clinton kept many of the export controls in effect by executive order. *(Congress and the Nation Vol. V, p. 274; background, p. 174)*

Critics of the original act said its focus on the Soviet Union and eastern Europe rendered it obsolete. Domestic companies also complained that U.S. export restrictions were tougher and more cumbersome than those in other countries, punishing U.S. industries without necessarily controlling the proliferation of sensitive technology.

The critics found many sympathetic ears in Congress. However, the main hurdle for the legislation in the 104th Congress, as in previous years, was the conflict between lawmakers who wanted to loosen the restraints on high-technology exports and those who wanted to preserve the Pentagon's authority to keep potentially lethal tools out of the wrong hands. Although the House International Relations Committee was able to find a compromise approach in 1996 that most members supported, the committee's bill (HR 361) reached the Senate too late for a similar consensus to be developed.

LEGISLATIVE ACTION

HR 361 attempted to streamline and accelerate the granting of export licenses for sensitive technology while strengthening the protections against weapons proliferation and terrorism. It would have required the Commerce Department to create a central index of all products covered by export controls, making it easier for companies to know which shipments required licenses. The bill also would have set tight deadlines for the department to grant or deny a license application.

The Commerce Department would have been required to consult with U.S. industry representatives about the items restricted and the nature of the controls. To reduce the competitive disadvantage for U.S. companies, the bill emphasized a multilateral approach to export controls and limited the president's ability to impose unilateral restrictions. Except in emergency situations, the bill stated, U.S. export controls had to be based on those provided in existing multilateral agreements.

The bill also would have required the Commerce Department to review regularly whether products restricted by the United States were available from foreign sources. Foreign or domestic companies that knowingly helped rogue nations develop weapons of mass destruction would have been barred temporarily from shipping goods into the United States or entering into procurement contracts with the U.S. government.

To combat terrorism, the bill would have barred dual-use exports and reexports to countries known to support terrorism. It also would have urged the administration to seek international support for such restrictions.

The bill would have prohibited U.S. companies from participating in foreign-led boycotts against U.S. allies and trading partners, a restriction aimed mainly at the Arab boycott of Israel. The provision was ironic, given that Congress had cleared two other bills in 1996 to penalize foreign companies that did not adhere to U.S. trade embargoes of Cuba, Iran and Libya. (Cuba sanctions, p. 237; Iran, Libya sanctions, p. 239)

To satisfy leaders of the House National Security Committee, the International Relations Committee amended HR 361 on March 29, 1996, to require the Defense Department's approval before export controls were lifted on items that were available from foreign sources. The amendment by bill sponsor Toby Roth, R-Wis., also eliminated a proposal to let U.S. companies petition for an end to export controls on items soon to be available overseas.

Connecticut Democrat Sam Gejdensen said it would be a "great step backward" to give so much power to the Defense Department, which traditionally opposed licenses for sensitive exports. Roth, however, said that the Pentagon already had a say over export licenses. Without the amendment, he added, the National Security Committee would have asserted jurisdiction over the bill, hurting the bill's chances. The committee adopted the amendment, 19–16, and approved the bill by voice vote. The committee reported the bill on June 5, and the House Ways and Means Committee reported the portion under its jurisdiction on June 27 (H Rept 104-605, Parts I and II).

On the House floor July 16, Republicans hailed the bill as a major step forward for U.S. exporters, while Democrats complained that the measure did not go far enough in enabling exporters to compete internationally. Nevertheless, the House passed the bill that day by voice vote.

The Senate Banking, Housing and Urban Affairs Subcommittee on International Finance held a hearing on the bill later that month. Subcommittee Chairman Christopher S. Bond, R-Mo., said there was not enough time left in the session to have the committee produce a new version of the measure; the only hope for passage was if senators agreed to take the bill directly to the floor without amendment. No subsequent action was taken on the bill.

Technical Corrections

Congress in 1996 enacted a package of narrowly drawn trade proposals, ranging from purely technical changes in law to duty suspensions for specific products.

One of the main purposes of the bill (HR 3815—PL 104-295) was to make technical corrections and adjustments to existing trade laws, such as the Customs and Trade Act of 1990 and the implementing legislation for the North American Free Trade Agreement (PL 103-182). Lawmakers also studded the measure with special-interest provisions aimed at lowering costs for their constituents in an election year. (NAFTA implementation, p. 155)

For example, Sen. Larry Pressler, R-S.D., inserted a provision waiving the $35,000 duty on a Swedish-made mobile bison slaughter unit, which Indian tribes in South Dakota planned to purchase to make buffalo steaks. Lawmakers from California added a six-month duty exemption for three chemicals used in the development of AIDS drugs. And Rep. Jon Christensen, R-Neb., slipped in a waiver to help a leather-products manufacturing company in his district avoid paying $24,852 in duties on leather from Thailand.

The bill also included provisions to:

• Exempt coffee products, tea and spices from a requirement that they reveal their country of origin. A similar proposal to exempt bulk pharmaceuticals from country-of-origin labeling was abandoned before the bill reached the Senate floor, however.

• Require the International Trade Commission to study how the cattle and beef trade were affected by the North American Free Trade Agreement and the latest General Agreement on Tariffs and Trade.

• Limit duties on cars manufactured in U.S. foreign trade zones, exported to Canada or Mexico and later reimported into the United States. Under this provision, only the foreign content of such cars was to be charged duties.

• Allow participants in the 1998 Goodwill Games and their families to bring their equipment and personal effects into the United States without paying duties.

• Bar the president from waiving the duties on products imported from a developing country if that country had repeatedly supported international terrorism.

• Allow repair and maintenance workers to bring their professional books and tools back into the United States duty-free after taking them temporarily out of the country.

• Waive the duties on certain telescope parts used by the Gemini Telescopes Project in Mauna Kea, Hawaii, and the Steward Observatory at the University of Arizona.

The House Ways and Means Committee included an early version of the legislation in its recommendations for the fiscal 1996 budget-reconciliation bill (HR 2491), which the committee reported to the House Budget Committee on Sept. 13, 1995. The proposals were dropped in the House-Senate conference, however, because they violated a Senate rule against extraneous provisions on reconciliation bills.

Ways and Means revived the proposals the following year as part of HR 3815, which it reported on July 29 (H Rept 104-718). The House passed the bill by voice vote July 30.

To assure the bill's passage, the Senate Finance Committee dropped several potentially controversial provisions. One House-passed provision would have temporarily barred the U.S. Customs Service from changing the required country-of-origin markings on hand tools and metal forgings. Supporters of the provision contended that the Customs Service had been too aggressive in requiring every imported article to be marked with the name of the country in which its parts were made. But some Democrats argued that the provision was geared toward special interests, particularly The Stanley Works, based in Connecticut.

The committee also dropped a House provision that would have required the administration to give Congress advance notice of any change in policy on rules of origin or country-of-origin markings. A Senate proposal to change the designation "most favored nation" to "normal trade relations" was abandoned, too. (Bilateral trade relations, p. 178)

The Finance Committee reported the revised bill on Sept. 25 (S Rept 104-393), and the Senate passed it on Sept. 28 by voice vote. The House cleared the bill the same day by voice vote, and President Clinton signed the measure on Oct. 11. ❑

Agricultural Imports

The Senate passed a bill (S 1463) in 1996 to help U.S. tomato growers and other producers of perishable goods win protection against a flood of Mexican imports, but the House refused to take up the measure. The House Ways and Means Committee held a hearing on a similar House proposal (HR 2795), but did not advance it.

Sponsored by Sen. Bob Graham, D-Fla., S 1463 addressed a problem encountered by Florida vegetable farmers in the wake of the North American Free Trade Agreement (NAFTA). Faced with an increase in imports from Mexico, the winter tomato growers in Florida asked the International Trade Commission (ITC) in 1995 to put import restrictions on Mexican tomatoes. The ITC considered the winter growers part of a national, year-round tomato industry, however, and refused to provide any relief.

Graham argued that Florida growers should not be lumped together with California farmers, who produced tomatoes in the summer. "While the product may be the same," he said, "it is a fact that the market, the competition and the trade involved are totally separate." His bill would have allowed seasonal producers of perishable farm goods to seek relief from the ITC separately from their industries as a whole.

The Senate passed the bill by voice vote on Jan. 26, 1996. On April 16, the House sent the bill back to the Senate without acting on it because it violated the Constitutional requirement that all revenue bills originate in the House. ❑

Customs Service Reauthorization

The House Ways and Means Committee approved a bill in 1995 to reauthorize the U.S. Customs Service, the International Trade Commission (ITC) and the Office of the U.S. Trade Representative (USTR) for fiscal 1996 and 1997. The legislation advanced no further, however.

The bill (HR 1887) would have authorized $1.45 billion each year for the Customs Service, $44.5 million annually for the ITC, and $20.9 million annually for the USTR. Authorization for the three agencies had lapsed at the end of fiscal 1992. The bill would have authorized the amounts requested by the administration for the Customs Service and the USTR, while freezing the ITC's budget instead of granting the slight increase sought by the administration.

The legislation also would have eliminated the requirement that the administration track and periodically report the impact of trade pacts with Caribbean nations and former East Bloc states, and it would have restored the Customs Service's authority to support federal, state and local law enforcement and humanitarian efforts.

The committee reported the bill on June 27, 1995 (H Rept 104-161), but the House did not take it up for a vote. Despite the lack of authorization, the Customs Service, the ITC, and the USTR continued to receive funding from Congress in fiscal 1996 and 1997 through annual appropriations bills. ❑

CHAPTER 4

Foreign Policy

Foreign Policy

As the first president elected in the post–cold war era, Bill Clinton struggled with a range of nettlesome and complex international crises, from a bitter ethnic conflict in the heart of Europe to dire humanitarian catastrophes that threatened millions of lives in Africa.

By the end of his first term, Clinton could boast that his policies had achieved progress in several areas. U.S. military missions brought a measure of peace and stability to Bosnia, which had been torn apart by war, and to Haiti, whose people suffered for decades under the yoke of brutal dictatorships.

U.S. relations with Russia stayed on an even keel, the Middle East peace process made significant progress and the administration's nuclear agreement with North Korea reduced tensions on the Korean peninsula.

But Clinton's foreign policy, particularly early in his presidency, was also plagued by missteps and miscalculations, several of which proved disastrous. Public and congressional support for the administration's handling of international affairs hit rock bottom in October 1993, when 18 U.S. Army Rangers were killed in a futile effort to capture a Somali warlord.

The president's performance gradually improved after the Somalia debacle, although Republican critics continued to lambaste Clinton for taking an overly reactive approach to overseas crises and failing to devote sufficient time and attention to foreign policy.

And as Clinton prepared to take the oath of office for a second time in January 1997, the administration's ballyhooed foreign policy success stories—Bosnia and the Middle East—were in danger of unraveling.

The president had predictably tense relations with congressional Republicans, who as a result of the 1994 elections seized control of both chambers of Congress. Republicans challenged the president's policies on a wide ranges of issues, from Sino-American relations to the U.S. role in the United Nations. Congress also forced significant reductions in the administration's requests for international spending.

Senate Foreign Relations Committee Chairman Jesse Helms, R-N.C., embarked on a crusade to eliminate a trio of cold war–era foreign affairs agencies—the Agency for International Development, the Arms Control and Disarmament Agency and the United States Information Agency.

Clinton responded by branding his GOP critics as isolationists who were bent on undermining his capacity to conduct diplomacy. The president used his veto pen to prevent a scaled-back version of Helms's proposal from becoming law.

But gradually, the two sides forged an uneasy modus vivendi. Under pressure from Congress, Clinton reined in his ambitious plans to expand U.S. involvement in U.N. peacekeeping missions. The president eventually came up with his own foreign affairs reorganization proposal, which was strikingly similar to Helms's plan.

In spite of vehement objections raised by many Republicans to Clinton's deployment of U.S. troops to both Bosnia and Haiti, Congress nonetheless rejected GOP-backed attempts to deny funding for those operations.

BRAVE NEW WORLD

Clinton was not alone in having difficulty formulating and implementing a grand strategy for the post–cold war world. President George Bush, the man Clinton defeated in the election of 1992, was far better versed in foreign affairs and promoted a new vision of global peace and stability under the banner of a "new world order."

But Bush's idealistic vision for a more peaceful, stable world was never realized. He made no headway in ending the war in Bosnia, which was perhaps the toughest foreign policy challenge of the new era. In Bosnia, well-armed Serbs were accused of carrying out a genocidal campaign of "ethnic cleansing" against Muslims.

During the campaign, Clinton had chided Bush for failing to stop the slaughter, but once in office he proved no more successful than his predecessor in bringing the war to a close. Clinton's difficulties in dealing with Bosnia and other global hot spots were complicated by his promise to devote most of his time and attention to the nation's economic woes.

With the demise of communism, Clinton expected he would be free to spend more time on domestic concerns than recent presidents. He vowed to focus "like a laser" on the stagnant economy. But the world's problems clearly would not go away.

REFERENCES

Discussion of foreign policy for the years 1945–1964 may be found in *Congress and the Nation Vol. I*, pp. 91–232; for the years 1965–1968, *Congress and the Nation Vol. II*, pp. 49–116; for the years 1969–1972, *Congress and the Nation Vol. III*, pp. 853–948; for the years 1973–1976, *Congress and the Nation Vol. IV*, pp. 847–912; for the years 1977–1980, *Congress and the Nation Vol. V*, pp. 31–95; for the years 1981–1984, *Congress and the Nation Vol. VI*, pp. 123–197; for the years 1985–1988, *Congress and the Nation Vol. VII*, pp. 169–251; for the years 1989–1992, *Congress and the Nation Vol. VIII*, pp. 203–297.

Outlays for International Affairs

Billions of Dollars

NOTE: Data for 1997 are estimated.

SOURCE: Office of Management and Budget, *Historical Tables, Budget of the United States Government: Fiscal Year 1998* (Washington, D.C.: U.S. Government Printing Office, 1997), Table 3.2.

The administration's first year was marred by a series of well-publicized setbacks. First, Secretary of State Warren M. Christopher failed in an attempt to persuade European allies to adopt a more muscular approach in Bosnia—by ending the U.N. arms embargo against the Muslims and launching air strikes against the Serbs.

The administration was harshly criticized for failing to do more to stop the bloodshed. However, while the American people were horrified by the violence, little public support was evident for a major commitment of U.S. ground forces to Bosnia.

While the crisis in Bosnia gave the administration fits, the president and his senior aides largely overlooked the rising dangers to U.S. peacekeeping troops in Somalia. That was to prove perhaps the costliest error of Clinton's first term.

In one of his last acts as president, Bush had deployed U.S. troops to the east African nation to join a U.N. peacekeeping force that was distributing food there. Somalia had been devastated by drought and famine. The wrenching television images of starving Somalis had created pressure on Bush to act.

The mission initially had broad public and congressional support. But the scope of the operation changed dramatically in June 1993, after forces loyal to warlord Mohammed Farah Aidid ambushed a U.N. peacekeeping contingent, killing 23 Pakistani troops.

The administration went along with a U.N. plan to capture Aidid. But Congress grew increasingly restive over the operation, particularly after U.S. forces began assuming the role of combatants.

Then came the botched raid on Aidid's headquarters, which

resulted in the highest casualty rate for a single American unit in combat since the Vietnam War: 18 dead and nearly 80 wounded. An immediate clamor arose from Congress for Clinton to withdraw all U.S. forces from Somalia.

The president refused. But, facing a rebellion that included many members of his party, he promised that most U.S. troops would be pulled out of Somalia by March 31, 1994. In an unmistakable demonstration of dissatisfaction with the administration's handling of foreign policy, Congress enacted legislation cutting off funds for the operation after the deadline.

Memories of the policy breakdown in Somalia continued to plague the administration for the remainder of Clinton's first term. For instance, the United States refrained from sending combat troops to prevent tribal genocide in Rwanda, although the magnitude of the catastrophe there might have exceeded what occurred in Somalia.

BOSNIA CONUNDRUM

On Bosnia, no one seemed to have any easy answers for how to end the war. Many in Congress contended that the United States had a moral obligation to intervene. Others argued, just as passionately, that such a course would trap the United States in a Vietnam-style spiral of military escalation in the Balkans.

U.S. allies in Europe had supplied the troops for the U.N. peacekeeping mission in Bosnia. The operation failed abysmally at forging peace, but European officials worried that taking a harder line militarily against the Serbs would expose their soldiers to retaliatory strikes.

As the carnage continued, Clinton faced fierce congressional pressure to end the long-standing U.N. arms embargo against the Muslims. The embargo had been slapped on all parties in the conflict, but many lawmakers claimed the arms ban worked to the advantage of the better-armed Serbs, who were widely seen as the aggressors.

In 1995, as efforts to resolve the war seemed to be going nowhere, the House and Senate passed legislation lifting the arms ban. Clinton, mindful of the allies' objections, vetoed the measure. Then, in August, the debate in Washington was overshadowed by dramatic developments in the region.

First, a lightning military offensive by neighboring Croatia against the Bosnian Serbs punctured the myth of Serb military invincibility. Then, Clinton and North Atlantic Treaty Organization (NATO) allies in Europe finally took an aggressive stance against the Serbs, launching coordinated air strikes to pressure them into peace negotiations with the Muslims and Croats.

The strategy worked, and the three warring parties embarked upon a tortuous path to peace, with constant prodding by Assistant Secretary of State Richard C. Holbrooke. After weeks of exhaustive negotiations—with the final, decisive rounds held in Dayton, Ohio—the Serbs, Muslims and Croats Nov. 21, 1995, forged an agreement to end the war.

But that proved to be a mixed blessing for Clinton, who had previously promised to provide U.S. ground troops to help police the peace. As long as the fighting raged on, few Americans paid much attention to Clinton's pledge. But shortly after the accord was reached, about 20,000 American troops began preparing to take up positions in war-torn Bosnia. Clinton's commitment suddenly became a big deal.

Determined efforts were made in the House and Senate to cut off funds for the deployment. Several lawmakers warned that the United States was stepping into a quagmire. But Congress grudgingly acquiesced in the decision made by the commander in chief. In the Senate, the president won important backing from Majority Leader Bob Dole, R-Kan.—the man who would challenge Clinton for the presidency in 1996—and Arizona Republican John McCain, who was once a prisoner of war in Vietnam.

On one level, the operation exceeded the expectations of administration officials. Defying the dire predictions of many lawmakers, from 1995 to 1996 it proved to be almost a casualty-free mission.

But it soon became clear that, without the presence of U.S. and other NATO forces, Bosnia would likely revert to violence. As Clinton's second term began, widespread congressional skepticism existed that the president would meet his objective of withdrawing all U.S. forces from Bosnia by June 1998.

FROM PORT-AU-PRINCE TO PYONGYANG

The administration's foreign policy was marked by a major paradox. Despite the end of the cold war, and Clinton's own lack of military experience, he deployed troops abroad with surprising frequency.

Aside from the military operations in Bosnia and Somalia, the president in 1994 dispatched troops to Haiti to oust the ruling junta and restore democracy to that benighted nation.

The prospect of invasion spawned considerable anxiety in Congress, as many members feared for the worst. Virtually the administration's only support came from a small group of Democratic liberals and members of the Congressional Black Caucus. But as with the Bosnia mission, the United States suffered no combat casualties in Haiti. Violence was averted when a high-level delegation appointed by Clinton to negotiate a diplomatic resolution of the crisis—led by former president Jimmy Carter—won a commitment from Haiti's military leaders that they would relinquish power.

When U.S. troops began arriving peacefully in the Haitian capital of Port-au-Prince on Sept. 19, they were greeted by throngs of Haitian citizens. The operation restored Jean-Bertrand Aristide, Haiti's democratically elected president, to power. But the country continued to be ravaged by political violence and grinding poverty.

The administration also launched a high-stakes diplomatic initiative in 1994 to try to put the brakes on North Korea's nuclear weapons program. The stakes were enormous. The communist government in Pyongyang was among the most isolated, heavily armed regimes in the world. Poised across the demilitarized zone in South Korea were 37,000 U.S. troops, who would be in mortal peril if North Korea attacked the South.

After intense negotiations, the administration struck a deal under which North Korea would abandon its nuclear weapons program. In return, the United States and its allies agreed to provide North Korea with economic assistance, including new, light-water reactors to be funded by South Korea and Japan.

Many Republicans decried the agreement as a giveaway to a brutal, unstable regime. Still, the accord held through the end of 1996, although North Korea's deteriorating economy triggered concerns over the country's viability.

CHANGING COURSE

Just as Clinton criticized Bush's Bosnia policy during the 1992 presidential campaign, so, too, did he blast the incumbent's approach to China. Candidate Clinton said the United States should be more willing to challenge China's aging dictators on sensitive issues such as human rights and Tibet.

As president, Clinton adopted a far more pragmatic approach. In 1994, he called for delinking China's human rights record from the annual debate over China's most-favored-nation (MFN) trading status. The decision did not sit well with the legion of congressional critics of Beijing, but Clinton contended it would help the United States maintain a more stable relationship with China.

That did not occur, however, as Sino-American relations reeled from crisis to crisis over the next two years. Angered by Clinton's decision to invite Taiwanese President Lee-Teng-hui to the United States, China stepped up its campaign of military intimidation against Taiwan, which Beijing has long regarded as a renegade province.

Tensions neared the breaking point in the spring of 1996, when China conducted threatening military exercises near Taiwan. The administration responded by dispatching a pair of aircraft carrier battle groups to the western Pacific. The crisis ended peacefully, as China gradually reduced its military pressure on Taiwan. Congress was disturbed by the incident but did not reverse Clinton's decision to renew Beijing's MFN status.

While Clinton was accused of vacillating on China policy, his administration steered a steadier course in relations toward Russia. Soon after taking office, Clinton made support for Russian President Boris N. Yeltsin a major priority. In 1993, he persuaded Congress to approve a massive $2.5 billion aid package for Russia and the other former Soviet republics.

Progress toward economic reform and democratization remained fitful, however. In addition, Yeltsin's health problems and Russia's heavy-handed military campaign to quell a pro-independence uprising in the border republic of Chechnya created uncertainty over the future course of U.S.-Russia relations.

CLINTON AND CONGRESS

Upon taking control of Congress, Republicans approved deep cuts in foreign aid and forced Clinton into concessions on several significant issues. But on the major questions—particularly those involving the deployment of troops—the president prevailed.

In 1994, the final year Democrats held majorities in the House and Senate, Congress appropriated about $13.8 billion in foreign assistance, U.S. contributions to international banks and subsidies for export programs. In the fiscal 1996 legislation, which was delayed for months by a dispute over abortion, the GOP-led Congress provided only $12.1 billion, a reduction of about 12 percent.

Helms wanted to save even more money by merging the three independent foreign affairs agencies with the State Department. Early in 1995, Secretary of State Christopher floated a similar plan, but it was scuttled after a fierce interagency battle. Subsequently, the administration and congressional Democrats waged a concerted effort to block Helms's proposal.

Senate Democrats stalled Helms's bill with a filibuster. But the North Carolina Republican responded by bringing his committee to a standstill, stalling ambassadorial nominees and treaties.

The bitter impasse was finally broken in December, when Democrats agreed to permit a vote on a scaled-backed reorganization plan that did not require any of the entities to be eliminated. The Senate approved the legislation, and a House-Senate conference backed a provision mandating that one of the agencies be merged. But Clinton staunchly opposed the modified bill, which he vetoed in April 1996.

Congress had greater success with a pair of sanctions bills intended to slow the flow of foreign investment in Cuba, Iran and Libya. Helms cosponsored the Cuba sanctions bill along with Indiana Republican Rep. Dan Burton. The measure, which won strong backing from conservative Cuban American groups, permitted U.S. citizens to sue foreign companies or individuals using their confiscated property in Cuba.

In addition, the legislation prevented foreign executives found to be "trafficking" in expropriated property from entering the United States and codified all existing economic sanctions against Fidel Castro's regime, including the long-standing trade embargo.

U.S. trading partners in Europe and elsewhere raised strong objections to the bill, as did the administration.

At the end of 1995, Senate opponents appeared to block the bill with a filibuster, but it received new life in February 1996, when Cuban MiG fighters shot down two U.S. civilian aircraft, killing four members of a Miami-based anti-Castro organization.

Clinton's objections melted away in the furor sparked by the downing. Administration officials managed to win a significant concession from House and Senate negotiators on the bill by persuading them to include language permitting the president to waive the so-called "lawsuits" provision. But even with that change, European nations, Canada and Mexico—which maintain economic ties with Castro's regime—protested the bill.

Many of those same nations also were outraged when Clinton signed bipartisan legislation punishing foreign companies investing in the energy sectors of Iran and Libya. Like the Cuba bill, that measure had strong backing from an influential domestic lobby, in this case American Jewish organizations.

Chronology of Action on Foreign Policy

1993–1994

Throughout the tenure of the 103rd Congress, official Washington struggled with the question of what the United States' role should be in the post–cold war era. Old assumptions as to what constituted the national interest no longer applied. Instead of dealing with one known enemy and well-defined spheres of interest, the United States faced hot spots flaring up around the globe, each with its own set of geographic, ethnic and military circumstances and risks.

Bill Clinton had assumed the presidency confident that he could avoid the clashes with Congress over foreign policy that had plagued his Republican predecessors. After a generation of ideological conflict with GOP presidents, congressional Democrats eagerly accepted Clinton's pledge of cooperation.

Before long, however, Clinton found himself replicating battles with Congress that President Ronald Reagan had waged a decade earlier. The venues shifted from Central America and Lebanon to Somalia, Bosnia and Haiti, but the rhetoric in Washington was strikingly familiar. When Congress demanded a voice, Clinton protected his powers as fiercely as Reagan and George Bush had.

The most intense foreign policy debate on Capitol Hill in 1993 centered on the U.S. role in Somalia. The United States' once peaceful humanitarian mission to help feed starving Somalians gradually turned into more of a military operation after the command was turned over to the United Nations. When 18 American soldiers were killed in a battle with a local warlord, an outraged Congress pressured Clinton into agreeing to set a date for the withdrawal of U.S. troops from the peacekeeping force. Congress wrote the pullout date into law and then—for the first time since the Vietnam War—mandated an end to funding for the operation after that date. The Somalian experience sharpened congressional antipathy toward the United Nations and multinational peacekeeping missions.

Washington and its North Atlantic Treaty Organization (NATO) allies grappled with the question of what role to play in ending the civil war in the former Yugoslavian republic of Bosnia-Herzegovina, as reports of atrocities and "ethnic cleansing" weighed heavily on their collective conscience. The debate on Capitol Hill was dominated by the issue of whether the United Nations should lift its embargo on arms sales to the former Yugoslavian republics. The ban had greatly benefited the already well-armed Serbs, while putting the besieged Muslim-led government forces at a serious disadvantage. Clinton, who was opposed to any unilateral action by the United States, managed to fend off mandatory amendments to lift the embargo, but Congress in 1994 did succeed in forcing him to take steps in that direction.

Closer to home, the Clinton administration struggled with the problem of how to end military rule in Haiti and restore its democratically elected president to power. Despite members' widespread opposition to military action in Haiti, Congress backed away from imposing restraints on the president's constitutional powers as commander in chief. After the junta agreed to step down in the face of an imminent U.S. military invasion, Clinton—without prior congressional approval—ordered a peaceful deployment of 20,000 U.S. troops to oversee the transfer of power.

The 103rd Congress and President Clinton did find common ground on other issues. Congress gave the president a major foreign policy victory when it approved his $2.5 billion aid request for the former Soviet Union in 1993. Additional aid was approved the next year as well. Both Congress and the White House shared in the jubilation over the historic 1993 agreement between Israel and the Palestine Liberation Organization (PLO) on Palestinian self-rule.

Somalia Peacekeeping Mission

Congress in 1993 initially supported the use of U.S. troops to protect deliveries of humanitarian aid in Somalia, a country on the east coast of Africa devastated by famine and civil war. Both chambers passed S J Res 45, authorizing U.S. participation in the Somalia mission. But lawmakers subsequently became wary of continued U.S. involvement in the turbulent country, as the once peaceful humanitarian effort of the United States turned into an increasingly bloody operation under United Nations command. Members never took final action on the joint resolution.

With the military and civilian casualties in Somalia mounting, Congress, in a nonbinding amendment to the fiscal 1994 defense authorization bill (HR 2401—PL 103-160), called on the Clinton administration to clarify U.S. objectives and seek congressional authorization for continued participation in the mission. Following the deaths of 18 U.S. soldiers in a battle with a local warlord in October, an outraged Congress pressured President Clinton to agree to withdraw most U.S. forces from Somalia by March 31, 1994. In an amendment to the fiscal 1994 defense appropriations bill (HR 3116—PL 103-139), Congress endorsed that timetable and asserted ultimate control of overseas interventions—the power of the purse—by explicitly cutting off funding for the Somalia mission after the March 31 deadline.

BACKGROUND

After its repressive leader of 22 years, Mohammed Siad Barre, was driven from power in early 1991, Somalia disintegrated into warring factions loosely organized along clan lines and armed with the vast stockpiles of weapons Barre had acquired first from Moscow and then, beginning in 1978, from Washington.

The civil war, coupled with a prolonged drought, triggered famine as food distribution networks collapsed and hundreds of thousands of refugees assembled in camps. Television newscasts with wrenching images of the suffering in Somalia attracted international attention.

With an estimated 30 percent of the Somali population facing starvation, the United Nations Security Council approved an emergency airlift of relief supplies in mid-1992. On Dec. 4, 1992, acting under the authority of a Security Council resolution adopted the previous day, President George Bush announced that as many as 28,000 U.S. troops would be sent to Somalia to join in a U.N. peacekeeping force to help distribute food. At the United States' insistence, U.S. troops, which made up the largest share of the force, were under U.S. command. *(1992 action, Congress and the Nation Vol. VIII, p. 278)*

Most congressional leaders of both parties, as well as President-elect Clinton, praised Bush's initial decision to commit U.S. troops. Although Republicans later argued that Bush had set a carefully circumscribed mission for the U.S. forces, signs of uncertainty were present from the beginning. U.N. Secretary General Boutros Boutros-Ghali asserted even at the mission's start that the humanitarian efforts in Somalia could not succeed unless the international peacekeepers disarmed the warring clans. And defense experts had questioned the administration's optimistic assessments of how quickly U.S. troops could come home. Bush spoke at one point of ending the mission, called Operation Restore Hope, before Clinton's inauguration on Jan. 20, 1993. Pentagon officials talked only slightly more cautiously of "an operation that will take two or three months."

The operation went well initially, and by spring the United States had begun withdrawing troops. The United States transferred the mission to the United Nations on May 4, 1993. About 3,000 U.S. combat supply troops remained in Somalia, reporting to the U.N. operation commander, Turkish Gen. Cevik Bir, through Bir's deputy, U.S. Army Major Gen. Thomas M. Montgomery. Although noncombatant forces had served in the past under the U.N. flag, the Somalia contingent was the first combat-capable unit to operate outside the U.S. chain of command. Montgomery had sole command over a rapid response combat unit composed of 1,300 troops that was stationed offshore.

Operations in Somalia became increasingly violent. On June 5, troops loyal to Somali warlord Mohammed Farah Aidid ambushed Pakistani peacekeeping soldiers, killing 23 and wounding nearly 60 others. After that bloody clash, the U.N. mission became largely a military manhunt for Aidid. The U.N. Security Council unanimously adopted a resolution June 6 condemning the attack and calling for the "arrest and detention for prosecution, trial and punishment" of the perpetrators. Administration officials later acknowledged that, having turned over the operation to the U.N., they had failed to appreciate the ramifications of the changed mission.

The violence continued to escalate as U.N. troops hunted for Aidid, culminating in the Oct. 3 botched raid on a suspected Aidid compound. The 18 Americans killed and nearly 80 wounded were the highest casualty rates for a single unit in combat since the Vietnam War. The Army Rangers were pinned down by hostile fire for a reported 16 hours before fellow peacekeepers could reach them. An injured U.S. helicopter pilot was captured and held hostage by Aidid's forces.

In the aftermath, Clinton, under pressure from Congress, pledged in a nationally televised address Oct. 7 that most U.S. forces would be pulled out by March 31, 1994. In a bow to critics who charged that the United Nations had become preoccupied with capturing Aidid, Clinton said U.S. forces were not in Somalia to "personalize the conflict." The president's decision to play down the campaign to capture Aidid led to a de facto truce in the fighting and to the release of the injured pilot.

The political impact of the botched raid played out for months, becoming a factor in the forced resignation in December of Defense Secretary Les Aspin. The secretary became the target of fierce criticism when it was learned he had denied a request in September from U.S. commanders in Somalia for armored reinforcements. *(Aspin resignation, p. 259)*

SOMALIA RESOLUTION

Congress in 1992 had already adjourned when Bush announced that he was sending U.S. troops to Somalia. Most individual members in both chambers were supportive of the intervention, but nearly two months would pass and a new administration would succeed to office before any formal congressional action was taken on the Somalia mission.

The Senate on Feb. 4, 1993, approved by voice vote a measure (S J Res 45) authorizing the use of force in support of the U.N.-sponsored operation to establish a "secure environment" for delivery of relief supplies to Somalia. The resolution urged the transfer of the mission to a U.N.-led force "at the earliest possible date." At that time, no fixed date was set for the withdrawal of U.S. troops.

S J Res 45 languished for nearly four months before the House, 243–179, passed its version on May 25, several weeks after the operation had been transferred to the United Nations. The House Foreign Affairs Committee had reported the measure on May 11 (H Rept 103-89). The House version authorized U.S. participation for up to a year after the measure's enactment. It also authorized retroactively the initial U.S.-led food distribution mission.

House debate on the resolution revived the long-running dispute over the War Powers Resolution of 1973 (PL 93-148), which demanded that a president seek formal congressional approval within 60 days whenever U.S. troops were sent into a situation in which they faced "imminent involvement in hostilities." The Senate version of S J Res 45 had sidestepped the disputed war powers law by stating that the Somalia resolution was "consistent with" the law's terms. But, because of sporadic incidents of violence, the House version granted authority for the operation under the war powers law. An amendment, offered by Benjamin A. Gilman of New York, ranking Republican on House Foreign Affairs, to delete the reference to the War Powers Resolution and to set a six-month authorization period was rejected, 179–248, on May 25. Members also rejected, 127–299 on May 25, a Toby Roth, R-Wis., amendment to cut off the troop authorization and funding for the Somalia mission by June 30. *(PL 103-148, Congress and the Nation Vol. IV, p. 849)*

DEFENSE AUTHORIZATION

As the United Nations took a more aggressive role in Somalia and clashes with Aidid forces escalated, members of Congress increasingly questioned U.S. participation. By a vote of 90–7, the Senate on Sept. 9 adopted a nonbinding amendment to the

Senate's fiscal 1994 defense authorization bill (S 1298), requiring the president to report to Congress on the deployment in Somalia by Oct. 15 and to obtain congressional authorization for the mission by Nov. 15. The amendment had been crafted by Senate Majority Leader George J. Mitchell, D-Maine, and Minority Leader Bob Dole, R-Kan. *(Defense authorization, p. 257)*

The Senate vote came on the bloodiest day yet of U.S. involvement in Somalia, when U.S. and Pakistani forces fired into an attacking mob, killing up to 100 Somalis, including women and children. "We went to Somalia to keep people from starving to death. Now we are killing women and children because they are combatants," said Sen. John McCain, R-Ariz.

But many senators from both sides of the aisle seemed ambivalent. "No one wants to leave that country in shambles. No one wants to set up a situation where they go right back into the same kind of despair they had before," said Armed Services Committee Chairman Sam Nunn, D-Ga. "But neither do we want to set up a situation where the United States has committed its military to a mission that is very broad and basically has no end point and really no definition."

Virtually all members agreed on two points: that congressional debate on the issue was long overdue and that the president needed to better explain what the United States hoped to achieve by staying in Somalia. Sen. Robert C. Byrd., D-W.Va., who forced the Senate debate by proposing an even stronger amendment that would have cut off funding for the Somalia mission within a month of enactment unless Congress explicitly continued the deployment, said: "The United Nations' mandate to disarm the warlords and rebuild a civil society in Somalia, approved by the U.N. Security Council, was never addressed, never debated or never approved by this body."

The House on Sept. 28 accepted an identical amendment to its version of the defense authorization bill (HR 2401) by a vote of 406–26. The amendment was cosponsored by House Majority Leader Richard A. Gephardt, D-Mo., and Gilman. A Republican motion to recommit the bill to the Armed Services Committee with instructions to add a provision limiting future deployments of U.S. troops under foreign commanders was rejected 192–238 on Sept. 29.

Even as Congress was moving to place some limits on U.S. involvement in Somalia, the administration had begun a retreat from its earlier commitment to aggressive international peacekeeping, in Somalia and elsewhere. On Sept. 27, Clinton cautioned the U.N. General Assembly that "the United Nations simply cannot become engaged in every one of the world's conflicts." Edging away from past Somalia policy, Clinton downgraded the objective of capturing Aidid. And he moved toward putting a deadline on what had been an open-ended Somalia mission, saying that it was necessary to establish "a date certain" for withdrawal in every peacekeeping mission.

DEFENSE APPROPRIATIONS

The bloody clash on Oct. 3 crystallized opposition to the Somalia operation. Congress and the American public were galvanized by graphic television pictures of the captured pilot and of a dead American being dragged through the streets of the capi-

---

FOREIGN POLICY LEADERSHIP

Warren Christopher was confirmed as President Clinton's secretary of state on Jan. 20, 1993, by a voice vote of the Senate. Christopher, a Los Angeles corporate lawyer who had served as deputy secretary of state in the Carter administration, endured two grueling days of testimony before the Senate Foreign Relations Committee. He repeatedly addressed the issue of where and how U.S. military force should be used, and Jesse Helms, R-N.C., exhumed the Carter foreign policy record to question Christopher at length on everything from the Iranian hostage crisis to the Panama Canal treaties. *(Cabinet profiles, p. 1113)*

CIA Director

The Senate on Feb. 3, 1993, easily confirmed by voice vote R. James Woolsey for director of central intelligence. During confirmation hearings a day earlier, Intelligence Committee members applauded the former arms negotiator for the Reagan and Bush administrations as someone who would advise them on how to balance the need for budget cuts against emerging demands for intelligence on a range of issues, from obscure ethnic conflicts to economic and environmental threats. Woolsey had served as general counsel to the Senate Armed Services Committee in the early 1970s and was an undersecretary of the Navy during the Carter administration. *(Woolsey profile, p. 1115)*

But Woolsey's stewardship of the CIA was hobbled by the light punishments he handed out for the Aldrich H. Ames espionage case and his increasingly strained relationship with the White House and Congress. *(Ames espionage case, p. 217)*

Woolsey stepped down Jan. 9, 1995. Clinton on Feb. 8 tapped retired Air Force Gen. Michael P. C. Carns to succeed Woolsey, but Carns on March 10 withdrew his name amid revelations that he had broken immigration laws. Clinton then prevailed upon Deputy Defense Secretary John M. Deutch to take the job. Deutch, who had turned down the job earlier, agreed after Clinton acceded to his demand that the CIA director be promoted to cabinet rank. That step troubled lawmakers, who feared that, as a member of the cabinet, the CIA director would succumb to policy-making and fail to provide the unfettered information required of the spy chief. But the Senate put aside its reservations and confirmed Deutch May 9 by a vote of 98-0.

U.N. Representative

Madeleine K. Albright's nomination as permanent representative to the United Nations was approved by the Senate on a voice vote Jan. 26, 1993. President Clinton boosted the prestige of the post by according it cabinet-level status. He also signed an order making Albright, who served as an aide to national security adviser Zbigniew Brzezinski during the Carter administration, a member of the National Security Council.

---

tal city of Mogadishu. With a fury that neither administration officials nor their own leaders seemed able to control, lawmakers angrily clamored for Clinton to bring home U.S. forces.

WAR POWERS DEBATE

As the first president elected in the post–cold war era, Bill Clinton assumed office in 1993 confident that he could avoid the clashes with Congress over the power to commit U.S. troops abroad that had bedeviled his Republican predecessors. Indeed, the Clinton administration briefed Congress so regularly and solicited guidance so deferentially on intervention abroad that in some cases lawmakers questioned whether the administration had a position of its own. After a generation of ideological conflict with GOP presidents, congressional Democrats eagerly accepted Clinton's pledge of cooperation.

At first, the White House and Congress brushed aside long-standing, unresolved questions over the validity of the War Powers Resolution of 1973 (PL 93-148), which purported to set deadlines for presidents to obtain congressional approval whenever troops were sent into likely conflict. But before the end of his first year in office, Clinton found himself replicating battles with Congress that President Ronald Reagan had waged a decade earlier. *(1973 act, Congress and the Nation Vol. IV, p. 849)*

This time, some Republicans abandoned their previous defense of presidential prerogatives, demanding advance congressional approval for U.S. deployments to Haiti and Bosnia and for any dispatch of combat forces under the United Nations flag. In November 1993, some House Republicans even invoked provisions of the war powers law, which they had long rejected as unconstitutional, to force expedited House action on a resolution that would have required U.S. forces to be withdrawn from Somalia more quickly than the administration had planned. *(Details, p. 192)*

For his part, Clinton protected his powers as fiercely as had Reagan and President George Bush. In the end, Clinton survived a series of votes in the Senate in 1993 over intervention abroad with his executive powers intact. As previously, lawmakers ultimately proved reluctant to impose statutory restrictions on the president. But the experience reminded lawmakers that changes in the world had done nothing to resolve the constitutional struggle between the White House and Congress over who should have war-making authority.

Background

The War Powers Resolution, which grew out of the conflicts over the Vietnam War, was enacted over President Richard M. Nixon's veto on Nov. 7, 1973. But it came to be so widely regarded as unworkable that it was seldom invoked even by those lawmakers who demanded a greater voice in foreign policy.

The law provided that, in the absence of a formal declaration of war, the president had to report to Congress within 48 hours of introducing U.S. forces "into hostilities or into situations where imminent involvement in hostilities is clearly indicated by the circumstances." The troops had to be withdrawn—generally within 60 days, although the president could extend the period for as much as 30 days—unless Congress voted to extend the period or "declared war or enacted a specific authorization for such use of United States armed forces." But Clinton's predecessors had resisted sharing the responsibility for sending troops into battle, questioning the constitutionality of the law, and most lawmakers seemed relieved to hand such politically explosive decisions to the executive branch.

When he entered office, Clinton appeared to support the law, but by the end of 1993, he had adopted the same linguistic straddle used by his predecessors: He described his reports on the use of U.S. armed forces abroad as "consistent with" the war powers law—a phrase chosen to indicate that he was not seeking a confrontation over the statute but neither was he conceding its constitutionality.

A group of 142 House Republicans sent Clinton a letter Oct. 6 insisting that he pull out U.S. forces. The United States, they said, could not afford an "indecisive and naive" foreign policy. Initial administration efforts at damage control only seemed to make matters worse. With the policy in danger of unraveling, congressional leaders from both parties sought to cool the overheated atmosphere. Senate leaders provided breathing space for the administration by delaying consideration of the fiscal 1994 defense appropriations bill (HR 3116). *(Defense appropriations, p. 267)*

Facing calls from Capitol Hill for an immediate withdrawal, Clinton pledged in his Oct. 7 address that most U.S. forces would be pulled out by March 31. But the president also announced that in the meantime he was sending more troops into Somalia so that the United States could leave "on our terms." Clinton's policy met with broad, bipartisan opposition, but no consensus emerged as to whether the United States should pull out instantly or within months. Congress ultimately endorsed the president's timetable.

On Oct. 15, the Senate agreed 61–38 to table (kill) an amendment by McCain to HR 3116 that would have repudiated Clinton's Somalia plan by requiring a "prompt" withdrawal of U.S. forces. Then the Senate, in a **key vote of 76–23 (R 24–20; D 52–3)**, adopted a compromise, offered by Byrd, that effectively endorsed Clinton's plan, by cutting off funding for the Somalia operation after March 31. The Senate action marked the first time since the closing phase of the Vietnam War that either chamber had voted to terminate funding for an overseas military mission. The provision authorized self-defense and keeping open communications lines as the only legitimate U.S. military aims in Somalia. While the Senate vote showed a solid win for Clinton, the debate surrounding it reflected unease—bordering on contempt—toward the administration's performance in international peacekeeping. *(1993 key votes, p. 979; U.N. peacekeeping missions, p. 200)*

Although the House accepted the Senate provision when it adopted the conference report on HR 3116 (H Rept 103-339) on Nov. 10, House members had sent conflicting signals just a day earlier during consideration of a nonbinding resolution (H Con Res 170) endorsing Clinton's March 31 deadline. As originally introduced by Gilman, the resolution urged Clinton to bring U.S. troops home two months earlier. Concerned that Democratic leaders would block the measure, Gilman invoked in his resolution a section of the war powers law providing for expedited committee and floor consideration of such a measure.

The House Foreign Affairs Committee reported H Con Res 170 (H Rept 103-329) on Nov. 5, after voting 22–21 to modify the resolution to endorse the March 31 deadline. When the resolution reached the floor, the full House at first backed the resolution's original wording by adopting, 224–203, on Nov. 9 a Gilman amendment calling on Clinton to pull U.S. forces out of Somalia by Jan. 31.

But the administration escaped more serious embarrassment when the House reversed course an hour later and adopted a Lee H. Hamilton, D-Ind., amendment supporting Clinton's March 31 pullout date, by a **key vote of 226–201 (R 2–170; D 224–30; I 0–1).** Under the "king of the hill" procedures that the Rules Committee set for the debate, the second amendment prevailed. The zigzagging votes were purely symbolic but underscored congressional divisions over Clinton's policies. Lawmakers went on to approve H Con Res 170 by voice vote. *(War Powers, box, p. 194)* ❑

Haiti Intervention

Despite widespread opposition on Capitol Hill and among the American people, President Clinton in 1994 dispatched nearly 20,000 soldiers to Haiti to oversee the return of democracy to that troubled Caribbean nation. Eleventh-hour negotiations between Haitian military leaders and a U.S. delegation led by former president Jimmy Carter averted a full-scale military invasion. The peaceful occupation and the restoration of Haiti's democratically elected government gave the Clinton administration a much-needed foreign policy success.

Several attempts had been made in the Senate in 1993 and 1994 to force Clinton to seek congressional authorization before deploying forces to Haiti, but those efforts were defeated. The votes reflected senators' reluctance to tie the hands of the commander in chief on crucial national security issues, not enthusiasm for military action in Haiti. Congress had gone on record urging the president to come to Congress before launching any military action in Haiti.

Almost immediately after the U.S. troops arrived, some lawmakers began demanding a deadline for terminating the operation. But, with the deployment going smoothly and many members fearful of jeopardizing the safety of American soldiers, momentum in favor of setting a deadline quickly evaporated. Instead, Congress cleared a joint resolution (S J Res 229) that did little more than require the president to provide detailed reports on the mission.

BACKGROUND

Haiti was the poorest nation in the Western Hemisphere. Its history had been one of political and economic turmoil, and the previous decade had been no exception. With the end of the rule of father-and-son dictators François "Papa Doc" Duvalier

and Jean-Claude "Baby Doc" Duvalier in 1986, the first free elections in 30 years were scheduled the following year but were canceled when violence broke out. On Dec. 16, 1990, Jean-Bertrand Aristide, a leftist Roman Catholic priest, was elected president, but he was ousted by a military coup Sept. 30, 1991.

In the midst of this turmoil, Haitians increasingly fled by boat for the United States and elsewhere, with many landing in Florida. President Ronald Reagan began a policy of intercepting Haitian "boat people" and returning those who did not qualify for political asylum, on the premise that most Haitians were fleeing their economic circumstances instead of political persecution. When the number of boat people surged following Aristide's ouster and exile, President George Bush on May 24, 1992, ordered that all boat people be returned to their point of origin without first screening them to see if they qualified for political asylum. Bush established procedures for Haitians to apply for political asylum in Port-au-Prince, Haiti's capital.

The policy was criticized by some as inhumane and racist. Presidential candidate Bill Clinton was among the critics but, as inauguration day approached, he reversed himself. Faced with the prospect of a massive exodus of boat people headed to the United States to take advantage of a more hospitable U.S. policy, Clinton on Jan. 14, 1993, in a move coordinated with Aristide, told Haitians in a radio address that he would continue the practice of summarily returning boat people to the island. Explaining his decision to reporters the next day, Clinton said the procedure would be a temporary one designed to protect the lives of Haitians, who might otherwise drown. He pledged to improve procedures for Haitians to apply for political asylum from within Haiti.

Clinton's decision won applause in some quarters, including from many Florida lawmakers who had feared a huge influx of Haitian boat people. Some Democratic members who had strongly attacked the Bush repatriation policy generally refrained from criticizing Clinton's decision. They appeared reluctant to criticize a new Democratic president, and many were encouraged by what they saw as a new commitment to resolve Haiti's problems.

But their hopes—and Clinton's—for a quick solution were not realized, and patience with the administration's policies soon wore thin among some on Capitol Hill. Although Clinton's policy toward Haitian boat people was upheld by the Supreme Court in an 8–1 decision (*Sale v. Haitian Centers Council Inc.*) on June 21, 1993, it irritated relations between the White House and the initially restrained Congressional Black Caucus. *(Court decision, p. 790)*

The administration had high hopes that U.N. sanctions would pressure the military government in Haiti to step down. The U.N. Security Council on June 16 unanimously adopted an oil, arms and financial embargo against Haiti. The increased pressure seemed to have accomplished its purpose when Aristide and Haitian coup leader Lt. Gen. Raoul Cédras reached a compromise on July 3. The U.N.-brokered agreement set out steps to restore democratic government in Haiti, lift international economic sanctions and return Aristide to power by Oct. 30.

But on Oct. 11, armed Haitians prevented the U.S.S. *Harlan County* from landing with about 200 U.S. and Canadian engineers who were supposed to aid in rebuilding the strife-torn island nation, as part of the July 3 agreement. About 600 lightly armed U.S. military construction troops had been slated to participate in rebuilding efforts. Three days later, assassins killed Justice Minister Guy Malary, a leading supporter of Aristide, in a daylight public shoot-out in Port-au-Prince. The violence left the July 3 agreement in tatters and the United States humiliated. On Oct. 15, Clinton ordered a flotilla of Navy warships to waters off the Haitian coast to enforce U.N. economic sanctions.

U.S. INTERVENTION

The Clinton White House continued to struggle with its policy toward Haiti in 1994, as it came under increasingly harsh attack from African American leaders and other supporters of Haiti.

After months of internal debate, the administration adopted a new strategy of applying increased economic pressure on the Haitian military. The U.N. Security Council approved a U.S.-backed resolution May 6, 1994, that imposed a near-total trade embargo on Haiti. On May 8, Clinton replaced the summary forced repatriation of boat people with a new policy that called for hearings aboard U.S. ships or in a third country. Clinton also appointed former representative William H. Gray III (D-Pa., 1979–1991) as special envoy to Haiti.

The Haitian military junta responded by installing an elderly judge as a figurehead president, thus signaling its determination to ride out the toughened U.N. economic sanctions. That fueled new demands from a disparate coalition of some Congressional Black Caucus members, a few other liberal Democrats and some Florida lawmakers that Clinton consider using force to remove the Haitian military.

But congressional opposition to an invasion was extraordinarily broad. Although conservative Republicans, who branded Aristide as a mentally unstable radical, had been the most vocal critics of restoring him to power, the opposition included lawmakers from every point on the political spectrum. Sen. William V. Roth Jr., R-Del., seemed to capture the restive congressional mood during a Sept. 14 debate, when he said: "I would like to take this opportunity to send a succinct message to President Clinton concerning the projected invasion of Haiti: Don't do it." Many critics suggested that Clinton's Haiti policies had been dictated more by domestic political concerns—placating the Black Caucus and staving off an unpopular refugee influx—than by U.S. security interests.

Despite the pounding from liberals and conservatives alike, Clinton moved toward military intervention in Haiti. At the administration's request, the U.N. Security Council on July 31 voted to authorize the use of force against Haiti. Clinton appeared on national television Sept. 15 to issue a blunt warning to Haiti's military leaders. "The message of the United States is clear," he said. "Your time is up—leave now or we'll force you from power." The president seemed intent on using the speech to answer the congressional critics who charged that the United States did not have any interests in Haiti to justify placing troops in harm's way. Clinton listed several justifications for the mission: to stop human rights abuses by Haiti's military; to restore Aristide to power; to prevent a new wave of refugees; and to uphold the international credibility of the United States.

In a last-ditch attempt to resolve the situation without bloodshed, Clinton Sept. 16 dispatched a high-level delegation to Haiti to persuade Cédras and his allies to step down voluntarily. The group—consisting of former president Carter, former Joint Chiefs of Staff chairman Gen. Colin L. Powell Jr. and Senate Armed Services Committee Chairman Sam Nunn, D-Ga.—was successful in reaching an agreement with the military leaders and staving off an invasion. U.S. troops began arriving peacefully in Port-au-Prince on Sept. 19. The soldiers easily neutralized Haitian military and police forces, and Aristide returned to power on Oct. 15.

PRIOR APPROVAL AMENDMENTS

Clinton's October 1993 decision to dispatch Navy warships to Haitian waters set off a heated battle in the Senate over the ground rules for U.S. intervention abroad, but the Senate drew back from a constitutional challenge over war-making powers, as it did in debates on Haiti policy in 1994.

The Senate on Oct. 21, 1993, during consideration of the fiscal 1994 defense appropriations bill (HR 3116), rejected 19–81 an amendment by Jesse Helms, R-N.C., that would have required prior congressional authorization to send U.S. forces into Haiti except to protect and evacuate U.S. citizens. The Senate then adopted, 98–2, a nonbinding amendment sponsored by Majority Leader George J. Mitchell, D-Maine, and Minority Leader Bob Dole, R-Kan. It expressed the sense of Congress that the U.S. military should not operate in Haiti unless Congress granted prior approval or the president sent Congress a detailed report before the deployment. The House accepted the nonbinding amendment when it approved the conference report on HR 3116 (H Rept 103-339) Nov. 10. The Senate cleared the bill later that day, and Clinton signed it into law (PL 103-139) on Nov. 11. (*Defense appropriations, p. 267*)

In 1994, as President Clinton seemed to be moving inexorably toward ordering a military invasion of Haiti, concern intensified on Capitol Hill. On May 24, moderate and conservative lawmakers from both parties in the House supported a nonbinding amendment to the House fiscal 1995 defense authorization bill (HR 4301) opposing the use of force in Haiti. The amendment, offered by Porter J. Goss, R-Fla., was adopted 223–201. But the statement was nullified when the House voted on the question a second time June 9 and rejected it, 195–226.

Several attempts in 1994 by Senate Republicans to force Clinton to seek prior authorization proved unsuccessful. The Senate on June 29 rejected, in a **key vote of 34–65 (R 34–10; D 0–55),** an amendment offered by Judd Gregg, R-N.H., to the fiscal 1995 foreign operations appropriations bill (HR 4426) that would have barred U.S. military intervention in Haiti unless the president first sought congressional approval or determined that intervention was necessary to protect U.S. citizens or security interests. Instead, the Senate voted 93–4 in favor of a milder, nonbinding Mitchell amendment urging the president to seek congressional approval before committing troops to Haiti. *(1994 key votes, p. 1003)*

In a later round on HR 4426, the Senate on July 14 agreed 57–42 to table (kill) an amendment offered by Dole that would have established a bipartisan commission of senior lawmakers to assess and report to Congress within 45 days on conditions in Haiti and options available to the United States with respect to Haiti. The real objective of Dole's amendment, in the view of members on both sides of the aisle, was to slow momentum toward an invasion. Opponents successfully argued that it would undercut international pressure on the military rulers.

On Aug. 5, the Senate voted 63–31 to table an Arlen Specter, R-Pa., amendment to the fiscal 1995 Labor, Health and Human Services and Education appropriations bill (HR 4606) that would have prohibited Clinton from deploying U.S. troops in Haiti to restore Aristide to power without the consent of Congress, unless it was vital to national security interests or to protect lives of U.S. citizens. Two days earlier, the Senate had adopted, 100–0, a nonbinding Dole amendment to the fiscal 1995 appropriations bill for the departments of Veterans Affairs and Housing and Urban Development and independent agencies (HR 4624) that expressed the sense of the Senate that the July 31 U.N. Security Council resolution did not constitute authorization for the deployment of U.S. forces in Haiti under the U.S. Constitution or the War Powers Resolution of 1973.

DEPLOYMENT RESOLUTIONS

In an immediate response to the Haiti intervention, both houses adopted nonbinding resolutions supporting the U.S. forces in Haiti and urging a prompt withdrawal. The House adopted, 353–45, its resolution (H Con Res 290) on Sept. 19, and the Senate adopted, 94–5, its resolution (S Res 259) on Sept. 21.

Several weeks later, after an exhaustive, sometimes rancorous, debate on the Haiti deployment, Congress did little more. The Senate by a vote of 91–8 on Oct. 6 approved S J Res 229 calling for a "prompt and orderly withdrawal" of U.S. forces from Haiti and chiding Clinton for failing to seek congressional authorization of the operation. The measure also required Clinton to make detailed reports on the intervention. The House approved, 236–182, an identical resolution (H J Res 416—H Rept 103-819, Part I) on Oct. 7 (in the session that began Oct. 6). That same day, the House by voice vote passed S J Res 229, and the president signed it into law Oct. 25 (PL 103-423).

No serious effort was made in either chamber to set a withdrawal date for U.S. troops. During consideration of H J Res 416 on Oct. 6, the House rejected on a **key vote of 205–225 (R 173–1; D 32–223; I 0–1)** a GOP substitute amendment, offered by Benjamin A. Gilman of New York, harshly criticizing the Haiti operation, calling for a pullout "as soon as possible in a manner consistent with the safety of the forces" and setting up expedited procedures for considering a resolution to terminate the operation when the 104th Congress convened in January 1995. The House then handily adopted, 258–167, an amendment by Ronald V. Dellums, D-Calif., that mirrored the resolution the Senate had adopted a few hours earlier. The House next rejected, 27–398, a Robert G. Torricelli, D-N.J., amendment that

would have set a March 1, 1995, withdrawal date unless the president certified that the mission was in the national interest or was necessary to protect U.S. citizens.

The lowest-common-denominator approach to the crisis attracted broad, if not enthusiastic, support. But it outraged longtime defenders of Congress's foreign policy prerogatives. "We have not approved of the policy, we have not disapproved of the policy," said House Foreign Affairs Committee Chairman Lee H. Hamilton, D-Ind. "We simply default." On the Senate side, Appropriations Committee Chairman Robert C. Byrd, D-W.Va., characterized congressional action as a "shrug of the shoulders in terms of any real assertion of the constitutional role of Congress." ❑

Bosnia Policy

The bloody civil war in the former Yugoslav republic of Bosnia-Herzegovina dragged on for a second year and then a third, defying a horrified outside world to find a solution to the centuries-old enmity that existed among the ethnic groups involved—the Serbs, the Muslims and the Croats.

The Clinton administration's policy vacillated between assertiveness and restraint. The White House at times advocated airstrikes against Serb-held positions, arguing that the United States had a stake in stopping the war from spreading. At other times, the administration acquiesced in the more conciliatory approach taken by North Atlantic Treaty Organization (NATO) allies who opposed military measures.

Congress was no more decisive on Bosnia than the president. Some lawmakers favored bombing raids to halt Serb aggression, but many others had reservations about ensnaring the United States in a civil war where no clear U.S. interests were at stake. Some worried that without bold action by the United Nations and NATO, the West would look impotent in the face of regionally spawned threats to peace, fostering a cycle of instability in the post–cold war era. But other members warned of getting trapped in a Vietnam-like spiral of military escalation in the Balkans.

The one option a majority on Capitol Hill could agree on was a lifting of the United Nations arms embargo against the Bosnian Muslims. The ban had greatly benefited the already well-armed Serbs, while putting the besieged Muslim-led government forces at a serious disadvantage. Ending the embargo against the Muslims was seen by many members as the best way of stopping Serbian aggression without involving U.S. troops in the war. The Clinton administration agreed that the embargo should be lifted but opposed unilateral action by the United States. The president argued that such action would encourage other nations to violate international sanctions that the United States supported, such as trade sanctions against Iraq. And the chances of a multilateral lifting of the embargo appeared slim, given the strong opposition of the NATO allies who feared that any widening of the war would endanger their peacekeeping troops on the ground in Bosnia.

Congress in 1993 and 1994 approved nonbinding provisions urging President Clinton to lift the embargo. Both chambers in

1994 originally approved amendments requiring the president to break the embargo, but the administration successfully lobbied against the provisions. Instead, under intense congressional pressure, Clinton accepted a compromise in the fiscal 1995 defense authorization bill (S 2182—PL 103-337) that urged him to introduce a U.N. Security Council resolution to lift the embargo and that cut off funds for U.S. enforcement of the arms ban by Nov. 15, unless the Security Council adopted such a resolution by that date or the Serbs agreed to internationally mediated peace terms. Because neither happened, the United States found itself in the position of no longer participating militarily in the enforcement of the embargo while still participating in the embargo itself.

BACKGROUND

By the calendar, the civil war in Bosnia had been going on since 1992, but by the history books, it was the newest chapter in a centuries-old story of ethnic and communal hatreds. This recent conflict had erupted with the fall of communism and the breakup of the former Yugoslavia into feuding republics. Four of the six republics—including Bosnia-Herzegovina—declared their independence in 1991 and 1992. What remained of Yugoslavia was controlled by Serbia, which fought for territory and dominance with neighboring Croatia and Bosnia-Herzegovina. Open warfare broke out in Bosnia following a March 1992 referendum in which voters reaffirmed their 1991 declaration of independence. The Serbian minority in Bosnia, with the aid of the largely Serbian Yugoslav army, went on the offensive and laid siege to Muslim-populated areas.

The international community imposed an arms embargo on the former Yugoslavia republics in 1991 and sent in U.N. peacekeeping forces but beyond that seemed unable to agree on how to respond to the increasingly brutal conflict. Stories of Serbian-run detention camps and a Serbian military strategy of "ethnic cleansing," involving the systematic use of murder and rape against Muslims, weighed heavily on the outside world.

As a presidential candidate, Bill Clinton criticized President George Bush's policy toward the conflict, saying the United States should consider bombing Serbian targets in Bosnia to ensure delivery of U.N. relief supplies. But once in office, Clinton largely abandoned tough campaign talk in favor of international mediation, a position favored by the United States' NATO allies.

In February 1993, the administration unveiled a policy of increased diplomatic and economic pressure on the combatants. Clinton's plan called for U.S. participation in multilateral efforts to enforce a peace accord, including possible U.S. military action. The initiative won broad congressional backing, although some Republicans were wary of any troop involvement. Congress also lent bipartisan support when Clinton announced plans for airdrops of desperately needed humanitarian aid to Bosnia. But the move again stoked the concerns of some Republicans that the administration had started down a path that would result in full-scale U.S. military intervention in Bosnia. Twice in 1993 Clinton moved close to taking military action but did not.

The United States in May 1993 joined Russia and European allies in an interim plan to contain the war by creating six Muslim enclaves that the allies would protect—a strategy that later fell apart. In another attempt to contain the war, the United States announced in June that it would send a small contingent of troops to Macedonia to join U.N. forces already on the ground in that former Yugoslav republic. Even some lawmakers who openly opposed intervening in Bosnia agreed that U.S. interests required action to prevent a broader regional conflict.

In February 1994, the United States won NATO approval for airstrikes against Serb forces. Faced with the NATO threat, Serbian forces stopped their bombardment of the Bosnia capital of Sarajevo and largely withdrew their heavy weapons. In the meantime, the diplomatic momentum picked up, with the announcement of new talks aimed at a union between the Muslims and Croats in Bosnia.

The climate of success created an opening for discussion about the possible commitment of U.S. ground troops to enforce a Bosnia peace accord. The administration promised to seek congressional approval before deploying forces to Bosnia and to subject the operation to tough conditions in line with the administration's new, scaled-back approach to multilateral peacekeeping. The United States, alone, would command its forces abroad, correcting what many felt was the fatal error of Somalia, where U.S. forces operated under a U.N. mandate. And the president would lay out an "exit strategy" for concluding the operation. Clinton said that the United States could not afford to ignore problems in Europe and that it had a stake in preventing the conflict from spreading on the continent. (*Somalia mission, p. 191; peacekeeping, p. 200*)

But most members of Congress remained skeptical. Despite efforts by Democratic allies of the White House, Congress declined to go on record with a resolution backing the NATO strategy of threatening airstrikes.

The first limited airstrikes came in April to halt attacks on the besieged enclave of Gorazde. Congressional leaders generally supported the airstrikes, but many rank-and-file lawmakers expressed concern that the United States might be drawn into an open-ended military campaign.

Clinton called for expanded airstrikes, but he was unable to convince NATO allies and by late 1994 had once again acquiesced in their more conciliatory approach. In early December, the administration said it was prepared to dispatch U.S. ground forces to help rescue 24,000 U.N. peacekeepers who had come increasingly under attack by the Serbs. Lawmakers from both parties set aside their differences to offer qualified support for the announcement.

Shortly before Christmas, former president Jimmy Carter, with the wary support of the Clinton White House, went to Bosnia to attempt to negotiate a cease-fire agreement. Carter was successful, and the Muslims and Serbs signed a four-month cessation-of-hostilities accord on Dec. 31. The Croat faction joined in the truce on Jan. 2, 1995. (*1995–1996 action, p. 224*)

1993 LEGISLATIVE ACTION

In the first congressional action on Bosnia in Clinton's term, the House Foreign Affairs Committee voted, 24–15, on June 8, 1993, to authorize the president to spend up to $200 million arming Bosnia's Muslim-dominated government forces—even if the United Nations declined to lift the embargo. The provision, sponsored by Henry J. Hyde, R-Ill., was added to the fiscal 1994 foreign aid authorization bill (HR 2404), which the House passed by voice vote June 16. Committee approval had come over administration objections, even though the panel had amended the proposal so that the action would not be forced on the president. The Senate Foreign Relations Committee voted, 14–5, for a similar nonbinding amendment, offered by Richard G. Lugar, R-Ind., to its foreign aid authorization, which the panel reported Sept. 16 (S 1467—S Rept 103-144). No further action was taken on either bill.

The fiscal 1994 foreign aid appropriations bill (HR 2295—PL 103-87), which cleared Congress Sept. 30, allowed the president to provide up to $50 million in military equipment to Bosnia's government if the international arms embargo were lifted. *(Foreign aid bills, pp. 203, 204)*

Clinton in late September set out more specific—and restrictive—criteria for U.S. participation in any international effort to police a peace agreement in Bosnia. He said he would want a NATO commander to head the operation, a clear timetable for review of the mission and for U.S. withdrawal, and support from Congress.

But those conditions were not enough to forestall the congressional debate over involvement in Bosnia—as well as Somalia and Haiti—that erupted during Senate consideration of the fiscal 1994 defense appropriations bill (HR 3116). During four days of debate, criticism of the administration's foreign policy performance could be heard on both sides of the aisle. Senators on Oct. 20 adopted 99–1 a nonbinding amendment, sponsored by Majority Leader George J. Mitchell, D-Maine, and Minority Leader Bob Dole, R-Kan., which stated the sense of Congress that no funds in the defense bill should be used for deployments to enforce a peace settlement in Bosnia unless Congress authorized the intervention in advance. Dole had led an unsuccessful push for binding restrictions on the president's power to intervene. Clinton previously had promised to seek congressional authorization. In other action on HR 3116, the Senate on Oct. 19 rejected 33–65 a Don Nickles, R-Okla., amendment to require the president to obtain prior congressional approval to place troops under a foreign officer in any conflict. Senators then adopted 96–2 a nonbinding amendment by Armed Services Committee Chairman Sam Nunn, D-Ga., urging the same course of action. The House accepted the Senate's Bosnia language when it adopted the conference report (H Rept 103-339) on Nov. 10. The Senate cleared the measure later that day, and it was signed into law on Nov. 11 (PL 103-139). *(Defense appropriations, p. 193)*

1994 LEGISLATIVE ACTION

The debate in 1994 repeatedly returned to the issues of whether airstrikes would work to deter Serbian aggression and whether the United States should act unilaterally to lift the arms embargo. In the end, Congress neither went on record with a vote explicitly supporting or opposing the administration on the issue of airstrikes nor did it order the unilateral lifting of the embargo, although it did set a deadline for the United States to cease enforcing the embargo.

Renewed violence in Sarajevo early in the year prompted Congress to act on the Bosnian issue. On Jan. 27, the Senate voted, 87–9, to adopt a nonbinding amendment, offered by Dole, to its fiscal 1994–1995 State Department authorization bill (S 1281) urging a lifting of the embargo against Bosnia. The provision was included in the final bill (HR 2333—PL 103-236). *(State Department authorization, p. 212)*

Though the Senate heaped blame on the administration for an unfocused policy in the war, its vision was no clearer, as evidenced by two votes on May 12 on a Bosnia bill (S 2042). The Senate adopted, 50–49, a tough amendment, offered by Dole, requiring the president to terminate the embargo. But, much to the administration's relief, the Senate earlier had approved by another 50–49 vote a much weaker nonbinding amendment, sponsored by Mitchell, urging Clinton to seek a U.N. resolution lifting the embargo, but, failing that, the president was required only to consult with Congress on the prospects of ending the arms ban unilaterally. The two amendments carried equal weight in S 2042, which the Senate subsequently approved by voice vote that same day. The bill saw no further action.

The House took the first decisive action toward arming the Muslims. On June 9, the House voted to force Clinton to unilaterally abandon the U.N. embargo. The **key vote of 244–178 (R 127–45; D 117–132; I 0–1)** came on an amendment offered by Frank McCloskey, D-Ind., and House Democratic Whip David E. Bonior of Michigan to the House version of the 1995 defense authorization bill (HR 4301). The House rejected, 181–242, a more moderate, administration-backed amendment offered by Lee H. Hamilton, D-Ind., urging the president to seek NATO and U.N. backing for lifting the embargo. *(1994 key votes, p. 1003)*

When the Senate took up its defense authorization (S 2182), vigorous lobbying by Clinton and top administration officials paid off in a narrow but important tactical victory July 1, as the Senate stopped one vote short of ordering the president to ship arms to Bosnia's Muslims. The Senate rejected, on a **key vote of 50–50 (R 37–7; D 13–43)**, an amendment sponsored by Dole and Connecticut Democrat Joseph I. Lieberman that would have required the weapons shipments in defiance of the U.N. embargo. Before that vote, the Senate adopted 52–48 an administration-backed amendment, sponsored by Nunn and Virginia Republican John W. Warner, urging the president to seek a multilateral end to the embargo if Serbian forces derailed efforts to negotiate a peace settlement.

Nunn engineered a compromise in the conference version of S 2182 (H Rept 103-701) that was meant to satisfy Clinton's goals and to quiet the Dole forces, which had been growing steadily. Nunn's proposal prodded Clinton toward a more active approach without imposing a deadline for unilateral action. But it also forced the administration to make significant concessions. If the United Nations failed to lift the embargo by Nov. 15—and the Serbs continued to reject an internationally brokered peace agreement—the administration would have to stop militarily enforcing the arms ban. While Nunn's compromise did not eliminate the prohibition on shipments of U.S. weapons to the Muslims, it would stop U.S. ships and planes in the region from blocking arms shipments by other countries. Both chambers approved the conference report, and the president signed the bill into law on Oct. 5 (PL 103-337). *(Defense authorization, p. 192)*

Bosnian policy was also debated during Senate action on the companion fiscal 1995 defense appropriations bill (HR 4650). Nunn's compromise was offered as an alternative to a Dole-Lieberman amendment forcing the administration to terminate the embargo by Nov. 15. On Aug. 11, the Senate first adopted the Nunn amendment, 56–44, and then approved the Dole-Lieberman amendment, 58–42. The provisions were deleted in conference.

Under mounting pressure from Congress, Clinton on Aug. 10 had vowed to introduce and support a U.N. resolution scrapping the embargo. In his letter, the president was cool toward the unilateral approach. If the Security Council did not go along with the administration's promised lift-the-embargo resolution, he vowed only to consult with Congress about acting alone to break the arms ban.

In November, the Bosnian government changed the terms of the embargo debate when it backed off its long-standing demand for an immediate termination of the ban and instead declared it would accept a six-month deadline for ending the embargo. When the congressionally mandated Nov. 15 deadline arrived, the United States officially ceased to participate in enforcing the embargo, though its NATO allies continued to do so. ❏

U.N. Peacekeeping Missions

U.S. participation in United Nations peacekeeping missions generated heated debate in the 103rd Congress. Initial wariness about the Clinton administration's plans for a multilateral approach to peacekeeping turned into highly vocal opposition as the United States became increasingly involved in such operations. The 1993 debacle in Somalia, in which 18 U.S. soldiers participating in a U.N. operation were killed in a street battle with a local warlord, came to symbolize for critics the price of indiscriminate U.S. participation in the peculiar local problems of countries with violent histories. *(Somalia, p. 191)*

Congress appropriated $402 million for U.N. peacekeeping operations in fiscal 1994 (HR 2519—PL 103-121). Lawmakers the following year approved another $670 million for fiscal 1994 and $510 million for fiscal 1995 (HR 2333—PL 103-236; HR 4603—PL 103-317). A number of restrictions were attached to the use of these funds.

BACKGROUND

With the end of the cold war, the United Nations appeared ready and able to step into a power vacuum. No longer stalemated at every turn by the U.S.-Soviet competition for power and influence, the world organization could attempt to become the exemplar and enforcer of world peace that some of its founders envisioned after the Second World War. Clinton had campaigned on a platform of active U.S. participation in a standing U.N. peacekeeping force, and his foreign policy deputies began 1993 with an expansive vision of a new "assertive multilateralism."

Many on Capitol Hill initially welcomed the prospect of a more muscular United Nations as a way to ease the burdens that the United States had inherited as the sole surviving superpower. But several concerns arose as well: That the United States would have to give up a good measure of its authority in international affairs. That Americans would have to continue to pay nearly a third of the rapidly growing bill for U.N. operations around the world. And, perhaps most emotional of all, that U.S. peacekeeping troops might have to serve under U.N. command, a break with tradition.

Something of a role reversal also was evident in Congress. Some liberal Democrats who had objected to U.S. military intervention during the cold war and had opposed the Persian Gulf War were disposed to support military missions in the name of international peacekeeping, as conservatives drew back from their previous willingness to intervene.

During 1993, widespread criticism of Clinton's peacekeeping policies emerged on Capitol Hill. By late in the year, Clinton himself seemed to be espousing a policy that was neither very assertive nor consistently multilateral. On Sept. 27, even before the deaths of the U.S. soldiers in Somalia, Clinton used his first speech to the U.N. General Assembly to circumscribe the limits of U.S. support for multinational missions. "The United Nations simply cannot become engaged in every one of the world's conflicts," Clinton said. "If the American people are to say yes to U.N. peacekeeping, the United Nations must know when to say no." For critics of the administration's emphasis on multilateralism, the president's cautious tone was a welcome change. *(Text, p. 1130)*

After the deaths of the U.S. soldiers in Somalia, sharply contrasting views on multilateralism could be heard on Capitol Hill. "Creeping multilateralism died on the streets of Mogadishu. . . . This is not just about Somalia. This is about how we should operate in the post–cold war world," said Sen. Mitch McConnell, R-Ky.

But other senators lamented the backlash against U.S. participation in collective military actions. "Do we really think we can ask other countries to bear the burden . . . while we remain at home? . . . Let's not condemn the whole concept of multilateral action because mistakes were made in Somalia and Haiti," said Patrick J. Leahy, D-Vt.

Clinton in a May 1994 policy directive imposed new conditions on direct participation by U.S. troops in U.N. peacekeeping missions. The president would no longer relinquish command authority over U.S. forces participating in any U.N. mission. And the administration would thoroughly review any new missions—even those that did not involve U.S. forces—to determine whether a clear "exit strategy" existed to conclude the operation.

After the November 1994 elections, Republicans, who were poised to take control of both chambers for the first time in 40 years, increased the pressure on the White House to restrict peacekeeping ventures. House Republicans drafted legislation barring placement of U.S. troops under foreign command and ordering that Pentagon costs for U.N. missions be deducted from U.S. payments to the United Nations. *(1995–1996 action, p. 236)*

1993 LEGISLATIVE ACTION

Congress agreed to appropriate $402 million for the U.S. contribution to international peacekeeping efforts—$240 million less than Clinton requested—as part of the fiscal 1994 appropriations bill for the departments of Commerce, Justice and State and the federal judiciary, which was signed into law Oct. 27 (HR 2519—PL 103-121). The House had passed HR 2519 (H Rept 103-157) on July 20 by a vote of 327–98, and the Senate had passed its version (S Rept 103-105) on July 29, 87–13. The conference report (H Rept 103-293) was adopted by the House, 303–100, Oct. 19 and by the Senate, 90–10, Oct. 21.

House-Senate conferees on HR 2519 called on the administration to notify Congress of new or changed peacekeeping missions whenever possible. Conferees also asked the president to notify the United Nations that the United States would not pay more than 25 percent of the costs of any new or expanded peacekeeping commitments. The United States at the time was paying close to 32 percent of the cost of U.N. peacekeeping troops. According to the bill's conference report, the United States' projected contributions far exceeded even Clinton's funding request. With the addition of three new missions for U.N. troops in Haiti, Liberia and Rwanda, the U.S. obligation was estimated at nearly $1.3 billion for peacekeeping activities in fiscal 1994.

Congress also used the appropriations bill to signal its concern over allegations of mismanagement and corruption within the United Nations. Lawmakers instructed the administration to withhold 10 percent of U.S. dues until the organization appointed an inspector general or equivalent watchdog for spending.

Legislation authorizing the peacekeeping funds was not enacted in 1993. The House June 22 passed a bill (HR 2333) authorizing $598 million for fiscal 1994 peacekeeping costs, but companion legislation stalled in the Senate and a final bill did not clear Congress until April 1994. *(State Department authorization, p. 212)*

The U.N. peacekeeping issue was raised during consideration of other legislation. The final version of the fiscal 1994 defense appropriations bill (HR 3116—PL 103-139) included a nonbinding amendment offered by John P. Murtha, D-Pa., urging the president to deploy U.S. forces for humanitarian or peacekeeping missions only after providing Congress with a detailed assessment of the mission, funding and time limit at least 15 days before the deployment. A provision that would have mandated such a report had been removed from the House bill on a point of order that it violated the House rule barring legislation on an appropriations bill.

Also included in the final defense funding bill was a Senate provision urging the president to get prior congressional approval before placing U.S. troops under command of a foreign officer in a United Nations operation. The Senate on Oct. 19 had adopted the Sam Nunn, D-Ga., amendment, 96–2, after re-

jecting, 33–65, a Don Nickles, R-Okla., amendment that would have mandated prior approval. *(Defense appropriations, p. 193)*

During debate on the fiscal 1994 defense authorization bill (HR 2401—PL 103-160), the House on Sept. 13 rejected two amendments to set aside Pentagon funds for peacekeeping efforts even though the sponsors had argued that the purpose was to prevent such operations from diverting funds that would otherwise go to readiness programs such as troop training. The first, offered by Norman Sisisky, D-Va., and rejected 199–211, would have set aside $30 million as a Defense Response Fund to cover the cost of deploying U.S. forces for international peacekeeping operations and other large-scale emergency missions. The second, by Sisisky and rejected 199–210, would have earmarked $10 million to create a U.N. peacekeeping command post and to train other nations' troops in peacekeeping operations. It also would have set aside $23 million for efforts to instill deference to civil authority in the military personnel of emerging democracies.

Just before the defense authorization bill passed, the House Sept. 29 rejected, 192–238, a Republican motion to recommit the measure to the Armed Services Committee with instructions to add a provision to limit future deployments of U.S. troops under foreign commanders. The provision would have allowed such an operation only if the president certified to Congress 30 days in advance that such a deployment would protect vital U.S. security interests and accompanied that certification with a detailed report on the size, cost and withdrawal timetable for the U.S. force. *(Defense authorization, p. 192)*

1994 LEGISLATIVE ACTION

In February 1994, Clinton requested an additional $670 million in peacekeeping money for fiscal 1994 as part of a supplemental appropriations bill (HR 3759—PL 103-211) intended for disaster relief, but the Senate Appropriations Committee scuttled that idea.

Congress did authorize the $670 million for fiscal 1994, along with $510 million for fiscal 1995, in the fiscal 1994–1995 State Department authorization bill (HR 2333—PL 103-236). House-Senate conferees attached a long list of conditions to their approval of the funds, although most appeared to be in line with the administration's revamped policy toward peacekeeping. Only half of the $670 million would be provided immediately, with the rest becoming available only when the United Nations established a separate office of inspector general. The conference bill also prohibited the United States from paying for more than 25 percent of U.N. peacekeeping operations beginning in fiscal 1996.

The full $1.2 billion requested for fiscal years 1994–1995 was included in the fiscal 1995 appropriations bill for the departments of Commerce, Justice and State and the judiciary, which was signed into law Aug. 26 (HR 4603—PL 103-317). Conferees dropped a Senate amendment to shift $350 million from the peacekeeping account to reimburse states for the costs of incarcerating illegal aliens. That amendment, offered by Minority Leader Bob Dole, R-Kan., had been adopted by voice vote in the Senate on July 22, after a motion to table (kill) it had failed,

44–52. An attempt in the House by Harold Rogers, R-Ky., to shift some of the peacekeeping funds to crime-fighting efforts had failed on a 178–228 vote June 27. The House passed HR 4603 (H Rept 103-552) June 28 by a vote of 286–112, and the Senate passed an amended version (S Rept 103-309) July 22 by voice vote. The House adopted, 322–98, the conference report (H Rept 103-708) Aug. 18, and the Senate approved it the next day, 88–10.

During debate June 9 on the fiscal 1995 defense authorization bill (HR 4301), House Republicans were rebuffed in a bid to place constraints on putting U.S. troops under foreign command in multilateral peacekeeping missions. The House rejected the motion to recommit the bill to the Armed Services Committee on a near party-line vote of 185–237. Following the lead of the House, House-Senate conferees on the defense authorization bill rejected Clinton's request that the Pentagon pay $300 million of the U.S. government's assessment for U.N. peacekeeping operations. In the past, such costs had been funded from the State Department budget. *(Defense authorization, p. 192)*   ❑

Israeli-PLO Agreement

Just as with the fall of the Soviet Union less than two years earlier, the dramatic peace agreement between Israel and the Palestine Liberation Organization (PLO) signed in 1993 forced lawmakers to seek a new approach for a region where U.S. policy had not substantially changed for a generation.

Israel and the PLO, after months of secret negotiations mediated by Norway, on Sept. 9 declared an end to a quarter-century of violence, agreeing to recognize each other's right to exist. The PLO formally renounced its long-standing commitment to terrorism and Israel's destruction. That paved the way for a White House ceremony Sept. 13 at which Israeli Prime Minister Yitzhak Rabin and PLO Chairman Yasir Arafat signed an agreement—formally called the Declaration of Principles—laying the foundation for Palestinian self-rule in the Gaza Strip and the Jericho area of the West Bank, which had been occupied by Israel since 1967. It was the most significant moment in Middle East diplomacy since the 1978 Camp David accords between Israel and Egypt. *(Camp David accords, Congress and the Nation Vol. V, p. 106)*

The emotional high point came after the signing, when Rabin and Arafat shook hands, as former presidents, foreign dignitaries and members of Congress looked on. They heard President Clinton marvel at "an extraordinary act in one of history's defining dramas," at "this brave gamble that the future can be better than the past." They heard Rabin and Arafat plead eloquently for reconciliation and an end to the violence that had long wracked the Middle East.

For U.S. lawmakers, the sense of history in the making was tempered by the realization that peace had a price and that the United States would probably be asked to help foot the bill in an era of declining funds for foreign aid. An even more significant issue was the psychological barrier that lawmakers were being asked to cross in accepting the legitimacy of the PLO, long regarded by the United States as a terrorist organization.

Congress responded cautiously to the agreement, passing legislation temporarily allowing the president to waive some of the restrictions on PLO activities. But Clinton declined to use this authority in 1993 because of the fitful progress of Israel-PLO negotiations on implementing the broad, even vague, terms of their agreement. And Congress approved no significant aid for the Palestinians for fiscal 1994.

LEGISLATIVE ACTION

Congress cleared legislation (S 1487—PL 103-125) lifting, until Jan. 1, 1994, provisions of law that prohibited the PLO from operating an office in the United States and that barred U.S. funds from going to international organizations that provided money to the PLO. The Senate Foreign Relations Committee reported S 1487 on Sept. 28, and the Senate passed it by voice vote the next day. The House Foreign Affairs Committee reported its version (H Rept 103-283, Part I) on Oct. 12, and the House passed it later that day by voice vote. The Senate accepted the House version on Oct. 15, clearing the bill for the president. It was signed into law Oct. 28.

S 1487 set the Jan. 1 time restriction partly to pressure the Senate to take up a State Department authorization (S 1281) that was expected to extend the waiver. When the State Department bill stalled, Congress cleared another bill (S 1667—PL 103-166) extending to July 1, 1994, the president's authority to lift the restrictions. The Senate passed S 1667 by voice vote Nov. 17, and the House passed it the next day, also by voice vote. The president signed the measure Dec. 2.

The conference agreement (H Rept 103-267) on the fiscal 1994 foreign aid appropriations bill (HR 2295—PL 103-87) also included a provision waiving the ban on U.S. funds for international organizations that gave money to the PLO. When the fiscal 1994–1995 State Department authorization (HR 2333—PL 103-236) finally cleared Congress in April 1994, it, too, contained a waiver of various restrictions on PLO activities.

As they moved to lift restrictions, lawmakers criticized Arab League nations for failing to drop their long-standing boycott of any company that did business with Israel. The Senate Foreign Relations Committee on Nov. 18 reported a nonbinding resolution (S Con Res 50) condemning the boycott. The Senate adopted the resolution by voice vote on Nov. 20. The House approved the measure under suspension of the rules, 425–1, on Nov. 21.

In response to the founding of Israel, the Arab League in 1948 had begun a boycott of all companies dealing with the Jewish state. Later, the league expanded the boycott to cover companies that did business with other businesses working in or for Israel. Egypt was the only member of the league not participating in the boycott; Saudi Arabia and Kuwait actively enforced it.   ❑

1994 Aid Authorization

Congress in 1993 failed to enact a bill to authorize U.S. foreign aid programs in fiscal 1994. Although the House passed a $9.3 billion authorization bill (HR 2404), a $12 billion companion bill (S 1467) never got beyond committee approval in the Senate.

It was the eighth year in a row in which Congress had failed to clear an authorization bill. Efforts in previous years had been doomed by such factors as traditional congressional hostility to foreign assistance and the failure of committee leaders to circumvent divisive foreign policy issues. As a result, the foreign policy committees in both chambers had become increasingly irrelevant in this area, as the Appropriations committees effectively assumed sole jurisdiction over the aid program.

The situation was much the same in 1993. Senate leaders apparently did not want to risk a divisive floor debate over a bill that was no longer viewed as indispensable. In a time of considerable resistance to spending scarce funds abroad, the leaders concentrated on winning enactment of the annual foreign operations appropriations bill that provided foreign aid funds. The final version of the appropriations bill (HR 2295—PL 103-87) included a blanket authorization of the programs funded by the measure. *(1994 aid appropriations, p. 204)*

No authorization bill was passed in 1994 either, leaving foreign aid once again to be provided solely through the foreign operations appropriations bill (HR 4426—PL 103-306). *(1995 aid appropriations, p. 209)*

HOUSE ACTION

In a determined effort to win passage of the fiscal 1994 foreign aid authorization bill, the new House Foreign Affairs Committee chairman, Lee H. Hamilton, D-Ind., established a task force of senior members to prevent the legislation from becoming a magnet for controversial policy amendments. Over the years, the Foreign Affairs subcommittees frequently produced contentious proposals that made gaining votes for the unpopular foreign aid bill more difficult. With each panel acting more or less on its own, the draft bill would grow dramatically and become more complex by the time it was considered by the full committee.

Delivering on Hamilton's promise, the House Foreign Affairs Committee on June 11 reported a bill (HR 2333—H Rept 103-126) with little resemblance to authorization bills from years past. It contained few new initiatives and in most instances merely authorized spending at the approximate levels requested by the administration or included in the foreign operations appropriations bill that the House passed June 17.

Moreover, Hamilton combined the foreign aid bill with the less controversial State Department authorization in an effort to overcome traditional congressional hostility to foreign assistance. But Democratic leaders separated the two bills at the insistence of committee Republicans, who were concerned that the unpopular aid bill would drag down the State Department legislation. The aid bill arrived on the House floor as HR 2404.

The committee's consideration of the bill reflected a dramatically different political environment from the one that existed during the previous 12 years: Committee Democrats found themselves in the unfamiliar position of defending an administration's foreign policy.

But the panel did break with Clinton on the topic of Bosnia. Over administration objections, the panel voted 24–15 to authorize the president to provide up to $200 million in military

equipment to Bosnian government forces, despite a U.N. embargo that barred weapons shipments to any of the warring parties in the former Yugoslavia. The vote, on an amendment by Henry J. Hyde, R-Ill., was the first congressional action on Bosnia since Clinton took office. *(Bosnia, p. 197)*

The House easily passed the $9.3 billion authorization by voice vote June 16, after overwhelmingly defeating, 118–317, an amendment by Jon Kyl, R-Ariz., to delete $704 million of the $904 million in the bill for economic and technical assistance for Russia and the other former Soviet republics. *(Aid to Russia, box, p. 206)*

Republicans Benjamin A. Gilman of New York and John R. Kasich of Ohio offered an amendment to shut down the Agency for International Development (AID)—the lead agency in delivering foreign aid—by the end of fiscal 1994 in response to allegations of corruption and mismanagement at the agency. But, with lawmakers largely split along party lines, the House on June 16 voted 246–186 in favor of a Hamilton substitute amendment to continue AID but terminate the $1.3 billion development assistance account—which also had been roundly criticized—by the end of fiscal 1995.

In other action during the June 16 debate, the House rejected, 201–233, a Dan Burton, R-Ind., amendment attaching stiff restrictions on development assistance to India. But lawmakers vented their concerns over alleged human rights violations in India by adopting by voice vote an amendment, by Vic Fazio, D-Calif., setting human rights conditions on military training assistance for that country. After a contentious debate, the House rejected, 191–236, a Christopher H. Smith, R-N.J., amendment barring aid to the U.N. Population Fund unless the president certified that China's population control program was not coercive or that the U.N. fund withdrew from China.

SENATE ACTION

The Senate Foreign Relations Committee on Sept. 16 reported a $12 billion aid authorization (S 1467—S Rept 103-144), but no further action was taken on the bill. Like the companion House bill, S 1467 authorized up to $200 million in military equipment and training for Bosnian government forces. The panel had adopted the provision, offered by Richard G. Lugar, R-Ind., 14–5.

In other action, the committee, after hours of debate, modified or defeated several amendments aimed at attaching conditions to the $904 million aid package for the former Soviet Union. For example, a Jesse Helms, R-N.C., amendment that proposed to link assistance to Russia to its termination of subsidized trade with China was rejected. A sense-of-the-Senate resolution, offered by Larry Pressler, R-S.D., calling on Clinton to lift the long-standing U.S. trade embargo against Vietnam was narrowly defeated, 7–9. *(Vietnam, p. 246)* ❑

Aid Authorization Reform

An effort to rewrite the law that governs the U.S. foreign aid program began with much fanfare early in 1994. But the proposal never got further than Senate subcommittee approval, a victim of a crowded legislative session and disagreements over how the program should be revamped.

The legislation—a cornerstone of the administration's foreign policy—would have scrapped the 1961 law governing foreign aid (PL 87-195), which had become encrusted with scores of outdated provisions and numerous congressionally mandated objectives and accounts. In its place, the administration proposed to link foreign assistance more closely to clearly identifiable goals—such as promoting peace and democracy—that mirrored President Clinton's overall foreign policy objectives. *(1961 law, Congress and the Nation Vol. I, p. 181)*

But the administration encountered a host of procedural and political difficulties in trying to move the legislation through Congress, which had not enacted a foreign aid authorization bill since 1985. Since that time, all foreign aid had been provided through the companion foreign operations appropriations bills.

Virtually no one on Capitol Hill disputed the argument that the 33-year-old foreign assistance law was hopelessly out of date and that the aid program had been adrift for years without a compelling rationale. But the reform effort had much working against it. The legislative session was a busy one, and lawmakers were preoccupied with domestic issues. The task of rewriting the statute hardly approached the sense of urgency of reforming the nation's health care system or welfare programs.

The bill's chances were also weakened by election-year pressures. Most members of Congress customarily took a dim view of anything associated with foreign aid, even legislation that purported to improve the program's efficiency. And few Democrats were eager to take up legislation that would give Republicans another chance to bash Clinton's handling of foreign policy.

Moreover, members could not agree on a new approach to foreign aid, and they strongly resisted proposals that would reduce their own power to channel foreign aid to favored programs. Where the administration saw reform, many lawmakers saw a potential raid on their authority in foreign policy and on their power of the purse.

The reform effort was also hurt by weak lobbying on the part of the administration. Clinton did not weigh in on the issue, and his top foreign policy advisers were preoccupied with high-stakes international crises, such as the nuclear weapons program in North Korea. Consequently, the lobbying effort fell largely on the shoulders of the Agency for International Development, which engendered scant congressional support or loyalty.

The only congressional action taken on the proposal came in the Senate Foreign Relations Subcommittee on International Economic Policy, which on June 15 approved a draft reform bill that scrapped most of the provisions of the 1961 law but retained some restrictions favored by Congress and added some new ones. The bill also would have authorized $10.9 billion in fiscal foreign assistance spending.

Because no authorization measure was enacted in 1994, foreign aid once again was provided solely through the foreign operations appropriations bill (HR 4426—PL 103-306). *(1995 aid appropriations, p. 209)*

BACKGROUND

For decades, U.S. aid had been apportioned largely to advance U.S. interests in ideological, economic and military competition against the Soviet Union, a goal that had been overtaken by events.

The 1961 foreign aid law had also become loaded with aid accounts and programs and with scores of congressional mandates and policy recommendations. For instance, 28 sections in the law dealt with development assistance, aid targeted at the poorest countries, covering everything from the importance of protecting endangered species to the need to integrate women into national economies. Language also promoted the use of vaccines for immunization and salts for oral rehydration as the best means to improve the health of poor children. The chapter even distinguished between "least developed" and "relatively least developed" countries.

The administration's blueprint for revamping the foreign aid law was formally introduced in the House on Feb. 2, 1994. The bill (HR 3765) was similar to a "discussion draft" the administration had sent to Congress in November 1993. HR 3765 proposed to de-emphasize traditional country-to-country, or bilateral, aid programs in favor of funding to advance six broad goals: promoting democracy, promoting peace, providing humanitarian aid, promoting growth through trade and investment, advancing diplomacy and promoting sustainable development.

Mindful that several previous foreign aid authorization bills had died in the Senate, House Democrats delayed action on HR 3765 until they received assurances that any reform measure voted out of the Senate Foreign Relations Committee would be considered by the full Senate. But with the summer's crowded legislative calendar, Senate Democrats were never able to provide such a commitment.

The Clinton administration was not the first to find it virtually impossible to translate a broad, bipartisan desire to reform foreign aid into law. Reform efforts in 1989 and 1991 also failed. *(1989, 1991 action, Congress and the Nation Vol. VIII, pp. 227, 267)* ❏

1994 Aid Appropriations

Congress in 1993 cleared a $14.6 billion foreign operations appropriations bill (HR 2295—PL 103-87) for fiscal 1994, which had a $2.5 billion aid package for the former Soviet Union as its centerpiece. Inclusion of that aid in the bill, in spite of the political chaos that was gripping Russia and its neighbors at the time, represented a major foreign policy victory for President Clinton.

Facing a taut foreign aid budget, lawmakers were forced to draw $1.6 billion of the aid for the former Soviet republics from unexpended fiscal 1993 defense and foreign aid funds. That funding was attached to the bill as a supplemental appropriation for fiscal 1993.

The regular fiscal 1994 measure provided $13 billion, a reduction of $1.4 billion from the administration's request. But the cuts could have been worse for the White House. The legislation closely followed funding levels included in the more generous House bill, which provided nearly $500 million more than the Senate version.

More than half the bill's funding—$7.6 billion—went to a handful of recipients. Congress earmarked $3 billion in military and economic aid for Israel and $2.1 billion for Egypt in addition to the $2.5 billion provided for Russia and the other former Soviet republics.

While most foreign aid accounts were reduced, Congress was particularly rough on U.S. support for international financial institutions, such as the World Bank and the International Monetary Fund, slashing about $450 million from the administration's nearly $2 billion request. A combination of stiff competition for scarce resources and congressional anger at reported financial abuses by one multilateral lender, the European Bank for Reconstruction and Development, caused the shortfall. The reduction left the United States $819 million behind in promised contributions to those institutions.

Final action on the aid bill came as Russia's political crisis became more ominous and nationalist violence intensified elsewhere in the former Soviet empire. In spite of the turmoil, the dominant sentiment in Congress seemed to be that the United States had little choice but to extend strong support for the political and economic changes being pursued by Russian President Boris N. Yeltsin. The formula for aiding the former Soviet republics through a combination of fiscal 1993 and 1994 funds grew out of an intensive series of meetings among senior administration officials and members of the House leadership, as well as House Foreign Operations Subcommittee Chairman David R. Obey, D-Wis., and other members of the Appropriations Committee. Highlighting the importance of the effort to the administration, Office of Management and Budget Director Leon E. Panetta took time out from lobbying for the president's economic plan to work on the package. (*Aid to Russia, box, p. 206*)

Congress failed to enact a foreign aid authorization in 1993. HR 2295 included a blanket authorization of the programs funded by the bill. (*1994 aid authorization, p. 202*)

HOUSE ACTION

Overcoming its traditional reluctance to vote for foreign aid, the House on June 17 passed the $14.6 billion funding bill by a vote of 309–111. HR 2295 had been reported by the House Appropriations Committee on June 10 (H Rept 103-125).

During the June 17 floor debate on the bill, a disparate alliance of some conservative Republicans and some members of the Congressional Black Caucus, motivated by an array of cost and foreign policy concerns, joined forces to back an amendment to strip from the bill the $1.6 billion fiscal 1993 supplemental for aid to the former Soviet Union. But the amendment, offered by Sonny Callahan, R-Ala., was rejected by a **key vote of 140–289 (R 93–79; D 46–210; I 1–0)**. The strong backing provided by leading Republicans accounted for the convincing victory. (*1993 key votes, p. 979*)

The bipartisan spirit evaporated, however, when John R. Kasich of Ohio, the ranking Republican on the Budget Committee,

offered an amendment to eliminate the nearly $56 million U.S. contribution to the World Bank. Kasich said the institution had squandered massive sums on ill-considered projects and extravagant perquisites for senior officials. The amendment was narrowly rejected, 210–216 on June 17. But providing funds for international financial institutions was clearly a sensitive issue for many lawmakers.

Indiana Republican Dan Burton failed in an attempt to strike $41 million from the bill, the amount requested for development assistance for India. Burton had long crusaded against such aid because of atrocities committed by Indian security forces in Kashmir and Punjab. The House June 17 voted 425–0 to adopt an Obey substitute amendment, which cut only $4.1 million in development aid.

Reflecting Obey's determination to provide the new Clinton administration broad latitude in allocating foreign aid, the House-passed bill was free of all earmarks—congressionally mandated spending levels for certain programs favored by lawmakers, including popular earmarks for Israel and Egypt. The latter was not challenged in committee because of a tacit understanding that aid for the Middle East allies would be earmarked in the final version of the bill and because of administration assurances that no cuts would be made in 1993 in U.S. aid to the two countries.

The House bill fell short of Clinton's $2 billion request for international financial institutions by more than $450 million. Outraged by news reports that the European Bank for Reconstruction and Development had diverted millions of dollars to build an opulent headquarters, the Foreign Operations Subcommittee had eliminated all of the $70 million that the administration sought for the bank. The bill also reduced funding for the World Bank to protest its recent loans to Iran.

SENATE ACTION

Acting against a backdrop of political upheaval in Russia, the Senate on Sept. 23 overwhelmingly approved a $14.1 billion foreign operations appropriations bill containing the $2.5 billion aid package for the former Soviet Union. Senate Foreign Operations Subcommittee Chairman Patrick J. Leahy, D-Vt., had warned that bringing the bill to the Senate floor was chancy while Russia was teetering on the brink of political collapse. But the measure passed on a **key vote of 88–10 (R 36–7; D 52–3)**.

HR 2295 had been reported by the Senate Appropriations Committee on Sept. 14 (S Rept 103-142) after committee members overcame several funding snags. Senate Defense Appropriations Subcommittee Chairman Daniel K. Inouye, D-Hawaii, and other pro-Pentagon senators balked at the plan to tap unused defense funds for aid to the former Soviet Union. But after personal lobbying by Clinton, Inouye signed on to the deal and other senators fell into line. A second funding snag was overcome by evading a requirement of the Congressional Budget Office that $170 million in outlays be set aside to protect against a possible default by Israel in a program that provided guarantees for up to $10 billion in loans over five years. In essence, the bill treated any costs associated with the loan guarantee program as an off-budget expense.

CONGRESS AGREES TO PROVIDE MASSIVE AID DESPITE TURMOIL IN FORMER SOVIET UNION

Voting for a massive aid program for the former Soviet Union was not easy for lawmakers in the mid-1990s. Spending for domestic programs was becoming increasingly tight, making it more difficult to persuade members to overcome their antipathy to foreign aid and vote to send more tax dollars abroad. At the same time, the news from Moscow was troubling, as Russian President Boris N. Yeltsin resorted to undemocratic means to crush his hard-line opponents in the worst political violence in Russia in seventy years. Congress nonetheless agreed with President Clinton that Yeltsin was democracy's best hope in Russia.

Congress approved a $2.5 billion aid package in 1993 (HR 2295—PL 103-87) and another $850 million in 1994 (HR 4426—PL 103-306). Congress also appropriated $400 million for each of fiscal years 1994 and 1995 to assist the former Soviet republics in dismantling nuclear and chemical weapons arsenals (HR 3116—PL 103-139; HR 4650—PL 103-335).

Lawmakers in 1993 cleared legislation (HR 3000—PL 103-199) to remove statutory vestiges of the cold war. In 1994, Clinton moved further toward fully normalizing trade relations with Russia and the two countries made further progress on arms control.

1993 Aid Package

In a series of announcements in April 1993, Clinton proposed a total of $4.5 billion in aid to Russia and its neighbors: $1.6 billion in food credits and aid, all of it from previously appropriated funds; $2.5 billion in new grants and other aid; and $400 million to help dismantle the nuclear arsenal of the former Soviet Union.

Leaders in Congress were generally supportive of Clinton's aid proposals, echoing the administration's rationale that the United States had a huge stake in seeing democracy take hold in Russia. But key members expressed anxiety about the difficulties of winning passage of so much aid—particularly because they assumed it would require a separate supplemental appropriations bill.

With a strong push from the leadership of both parties, a $2.5 billion aid package sailed through the House in June as part of the fiscal 1994 foreign operations appropriations bill (HR 2295).

To finesse congressional resistance to passing a separate fiscal 1993 supplemental, the single measure incorporated two ways of funding the aid to the former Soviet republics: about $900 million in regular fiscal 1994 foreign aid funds, and about $1.6 billion from unspent fiscal 1993 funds ($630 million from foreign aid and $979 million from defense) provided through a supplemental appropriation that was attached to the foreign aid bill. *(1994 aid appropriations, p. 204)*

The Senate began consideration of HR 2295 on Sept. 22, just one day after Yeltsin threw his nation into turmoil by disbanding the parliament and calling for December elections. Yeltsin's move prompted the opposition to impeach Yeltsin and establish a parallel government under the hard-line vice president, Aleksandr V. Rutskoi. The opposition forces hunkered down in the parliament building—the so-called White House.

Clinton moved quickly to express his full support for Yeltsin while attempting to put the Russian president's actions—which clearly violated the existing Soviet-era constitution—in a broader context. "There is no question that President Yeltsin acted in response to a constitutional crisis that had reached a critical impasse and had paralyzed the political process," Clinton said in a Sept. 21 statement.

A few senators raised concerns over Yeltsin's decision. But in the end the Senate followed Clinton's lead in rallying around the Russian president and passing the aid package.

Final action on the aid bill came as Russia's crisis grew more ominous and nationalist violence intensified elsewhere in the former Soviet empire. In spite of the turmoil, the dominant sentiment in Congress seemed to be that the United States had little choice but to extend strong support for the political and economic changes being pursued by the Russian president.

The two-week standoff between Russia's president and his hard-line opponents ended Oct. 4 with an assault on parliament by troops loyal to Yeltsin. A worldwide television audience witnessed Russian tanks shelling the parliament building in Moscow. The next day, Yeltsin instituted the first widespread censorship of the Russian news media since the Soviet era. Although he subsequently rescinded the censorship order, a handful of opposition newspapers remained closed.

At least in the short run, the violence in Russia did nothing to undercut the strong support in Washington for Yeltsin's government. In the view of Clinton and many members of Congress, Yeltsin had been forced to resort to extreme measures.

In the aftermath, Yeltsin vowed in a conversation with Clinton to go ahead with Dec. 12 elections for a new parliament. For his part, Clinton pledged to move quickly to provide the economic assistance approved by Congress. But the administration was careful to emphasize on Capitol Hill that U.S. aid was intended to support the process of reform, not a single individual or policy.

Results of the December elections only raised new questions about Russia's future—and Yeltsin's—because the new parliament appeared as conservative as the one that had been forcibly disband-

The Senate bill appropriated about $500 million less than the House-passed version. In another striking contrast, the Senate measure was studded with statutory earmarks. The bill set spending levels for several development accounts as well as for aid to the Middle East and much of the assistance for the former Soviet Union.

In floor action on the bill, the Senate addressed the changed political environment in the Middle East by adopting by voice vote a pair of amendments, cosponsored by Leahy and Mitch McConnell, R-Ky., lifting long-standing restrictions on the PLO. The Senate easily disposed of several amendments aimed at attaching conditions to aid for Moscow that reflected concerns over various Russian policies.

But, for all the concern over the Russian aid package, the de-ed. And the largest bloc of votes went to ultranationalists led by Vladimir V. Zhirinovsky, a far-rightist given to anti-Semitic statements and casual threats to use Russia's nuclear arsenal.

Additional Aid

Congress in 1994 agreed to appropriate $850 million in fiscal 1995 economic assistance to Russia and the other former Soviet republics, despite lawmakers' anger over the Aldrich H. Ames spy scandal and rising concern over Russia's new assertiveness in foreign affairs. Ames had pleaded guilty in May to selling top-secret information to the Soviet Union and subsequently to Russia from 1985 until his arrest in February. The $850 million in HR 4426 was just $50 million less than Clinton had requested. *(1995 aid appropriations, p. 209; Ames spy case, p. 219)*

Congress added conditions to the aid, including a requirement that Russia abide by agreements to remove its forces from the Baltic nations to get the money but the president could waive the provision if he determined it was in the national security interest. The Senate's original language had required Moscow to fulfill its longstanding pledge to withdraw Russian forces from the Baltic nations by Aug. 31.

The amendment had come in response to a July 10 statement by Yeltsin that he did not intend to withdraw about two thousand troops still stationed in Estonia by the deadline. The Senate amendment was toned down in conference after Moscow had agreed to withdraw the remaining troops.

Congress also provided $400 million in the Pentagon's fiscal 1994 appropriations (HR 3116) and again in its 1995 appropriations (HR 4650) for the so-called Nunn-Lugar program to assist former Soviet republics in dismantling nuclear and chemical weapons arsenals. The program, named after its sponsors, Sens. Sam Nunn, D-Ga., and Richard G. Lugar, R-Ind., was established in 1991.

Cold War Vestiges

Congress handed Clinton a modest victory by clearing a measure (HR 3000) eliminating scores of largely symbolic cold war–era constraints on relations with Russia and the other former Soviet republics. The House passed HR 3000 (H Rept 103-297, Part I) by voice vote on Nov. 15, and the Senate followed suit Nov. 22. The House cleared the bill for the president Nov. 23. He signed the measure Dec. 17.

Some of the anti-Soviet provisions dated back four decades. For instance, the bill repealed most sections of the Internal Security Act of 1950, which required registration of communist front organiza-

tions and created the Subversive Activities Control Board. The final bill also included an amendment, offered by Sen. Jesse Helms, R-N.C., authorizing a privately funded but official memorial in Washington, D.C., to the "victims of communism."

Clinton had wanted the legislation in hand before meeting with Yeltsin in Moscow in January 1994. As enacted, however, the bill did not address several economic provisions that Yeltsin had urged be lifted, in particular, the Jackson-Vanik amendment to the 1974 Trade Act (PL 93-618), which denied most-favored-nation (MFN) trading status to countries with nonmarket economies unless the president certified that its government allowed free emigration. *(1974 law, Congress and the Nation Vol. IV, p. 131)*

Despite its name, MFN status was the norm, not the exception, for U.S. trading partners; nearly all nations were accorded such treatment. U.S. Jewish organizations had long viewed Jackson-Vanik—named for sponsors, Sen. Henry M. Jackson, D-Wash. (House 1941–1953; Senate 1953–1983) and Rep. Charles A. Vanik, D-Ohio (1955–1981)—as a tool to ensure that Moscow lived up to its commitment to free emigration for Jews. Goods from Russia had received MFN treatment since 1992, but only because Presidents George Bush and Clinton had provided annual waivers from the Jackson-Vanik requirement.

In preparation for a September summit meeting with Yeltsin in Washington, Clinton submitted a letter to Congress stating that Russia was in compliance with the Jackson-Vanik amendment. During the summit, Yeltsin asked legislators to go further and remove Russia from the roster of countries subject to Jackson-Vanik, but Congress was not ready to take that step.

Washington Summit

After riding a roller coaster for two years, U.S.-Russian relations appeared to be on a more solid footing as Yeltsin arrived in Washington for the September summit. While the meeting produced significant advances on a range of arms control and national security issues, the absence of a crisis mentality might have been its most salient feature.

Clinton and Yeltsin announced a new deal to possibly speed up the timetable for deactivating nuclear warheads established by the 1993 strategic arms reduction talks (START II) treaty. It would not, however, take effect until START II was ratified. Both countries had been slow to act because other former Soviet republics were delaying the implementation of the original START treaty, which had laid the groundwork for the START II pact. *(Arms control agreements, p. 292)*

bate was dominated by other issues. In the most closely contested Senate vote, the Senate on Sept. 23 agreed 55–44 to table (kill) a Hank Brown, R-Colo., amendment to cut the bill's $28 million appropriation for the World Bank. An amendment by Robert C. Smith, R-N.H., to cut $200 million from the bill and use the money to support defense conversion programs was tabled, 64–35.

Conferees on HR 2295 rushed to complete their work by midnight Sept. 30, the last day of the fiscal year. After that date, the $1.6 billion in fiscal 1993 funds in the former Soviet Union aid package would no longer be available. The deadline was met. The House voted 321–108 to adopt the conference report (H Rept 103-267) on Sept. 29. The Senate approved the conference report 88–11 the next day, clearing the bill for the president's signature later that day.

The conference on the measure went smoothly, unlike previous years when the annual funding bill often became embroiled in foreign policy disputes. Most of the four-hour conference was spent in debate over earmarks. Conferees backed a compromise offered by Obey, which eliminated many of the spending mandates but spared the politically popular earmarks for aid to Egypt and Israel, along with earmarks of $80 million for an assistance program for Jewish immigrants to Israel and $15 million for Cyprus.

Senate conferees were more aggressive in defending earmarks in the aid to the former Soviet republics package. McConnell argued strenuously for his amendment requiring the administration to provide at least $300 million to Ukraine. Conferees agreed on a compromise calling on the administration to provide that amount but allowed some of the money to be drawn from a fund for dismantling weapons in the former Soviet Union.

Conferees took a similar tack for the rest of the aid package, agreeing not to earmark the aid but including extensive guidance and numerous recommendations on how the money should be spent.

The most hotly contended issue was a Senate amendment, sponsored by Connie Mack, R-Fla., that required the president to certify that Russia had cut off support to Cuba as a condition of aid to Moscow. McConnell proposed a compromise allowing the president to waive the restriction if he determined it to be in the "national security interest." But House conferees insisted that the waiver be allowed if the president determined that it was in the "national interest," an easier standard to meet. The conference endorsed several other conditions on assistance to the former Soviet Union and other nations, though most provided some sort of waiver authority for the president.

Conferees also reached agreement on numerous other restrictions on foreign assistance, many of which initially were proposed by Sen. Jesse Helms, R-N.C. His concerns ranged from weighty policy issues, such as aid to Nicaragua, to more mundane tiffs over deadbeat foreign embassies that did not pay their parking tickets.

MAJOR PROVISIONS

The final version of the foreign operations appropriations bill (HR 2295—PL 103-87) provided $14.6 billion—$1.6 billion in supplemental appropriations for fiscal 1993 and $13 billion in regular fiscal 1994 funds. The fiscal 1994 funds included $1.87 billion for multilateral aid, $7.04 billion for bilateral aid, $3.04 billion for military aid and $1.03 billion for export assistance.

HR 2295 also:

Former Soviet Republics

Provided $2.5 billion in assistance to Russia and the other former republics of the Soviet Union. Of the total, $1.6 billion was in unexpended defense and foreign aid balances from fiscal 1993 and about $900 million in fiscal 1994 appropriations.

The bill did not earmark spending in the aid package but did include extensive guidance and numerous recommendations. It stated that Ukraine should receive no less than $300 million but stipulated that some of the money could be drawn from the Pentagon budget's so-called Nunn-Lugar funds—named for Sens. Sam Nunn, D-Ga., and Richard G. Lugar, R-Ind.—for dismantling weapons in the former Soviet Union. The final bill urged the administration to provide no less than one-third of the aid package to countries other than Russia and recommended that $18 million in humanitarian aid be provided to Armenia.

Congress included detailed recommendations on the types of projects the aid should support, which were roughly in line with the administration's plans for the package:

• Nearly $900 million for private sector development, through technical assistance and the establishment of enterprise funds;

• $125 million for the U.S. share of a special multilateral privatization fund;

• $470 million to underwrite loans and loan guarantees and provide technical assistance for the energy and environmental sectors, with a particular emphasis on projects aimed at upgrading nuclear safety;

• $295 million to support exchange programs and other prodemocracy initiatives;

• $190 million to provide more housing for Russian officers in an effort to facilitate their withdrawal from the Baltics and other countries;

• $239 million for humanitarian assistance, including support for establishment of a pharmaceutical industry in the former Soviet Union.

Israel, Egypt

Earmarked $1.2 billion in economic aid and $1.8 billion in military aid for Israel. The aid was to be fully disbursed in cash by Oct. 31, allowing the government of Israel to invest the cash and thereby earn tens of millions of dollars in interest income.

• Earmarked $815 million in economic aid and $1.3 billion in military aid for Egypt.

Military Sales

Required the Pentagon to solicit the views of foreign governments and U.S. defense contractors before making any change in the existing policy that allowed Israel and several other countries to negotiate arms sales deals directly with arms manufacturers instead of going through the U.S. government.

Refugee Assistance

Provided $720 million for migration and refugee assistance programs, of which $80 million was earmarked to support resettlement of refugees in Israel.

AID

Provided $502 million for the Agency for International Development's operating expenses but barred the agency from spending that money after March 31, 1994, unless it had begun to implement the recommendations of Vice President Al Gore's

National Performance Review. That report called for the number of AID overseas missions to be reduced by more than half—from 105 to 50. The bill required AID to close 12 missions during fiscal 1994. (In November 1993, the agency announced the closing of 21 AID missions—nine of which were in Africa—over the next three fiscal years.)

Cyprus

Earmarked $15 million in economic aid to Cyprus.

North Atlantic Treaty Organization (NATO) Countries

Set a ceiling in the military assistance program of $284 million in loans for Greece, $81 million for Portugal and $405 million for Turkey. The three countries, which previously had received grants or low-interest loans, were to receive only market-based loans in fiscal 1994. The bill continued the long-standing custom of providing military aid for the historic adversaries of Greece and Turkey in a 7:1 ratio.

International Financial Institutions

Provided $1.5 billion for multilateral financial institutions, along with $4.1 billion in callable capital, which the United States would pay only if a development bank faced default—an extremely unlikely event. As a result, the $4.1 billion did not translate into any outlays.

• Provided $55.8 million in paid-in capital and $1.8 billion in callable capital for the International Bank of Reconstruction and Development (IBRD or World Bank). The amounts represented a reduction of $14 million in paid-in capital and of $463 million in callable capital pledged by the United States, an amount equal to loans the bank had made to Iran. The bill specified that the Treasury could not make periodic disbursements of the IBRD contribution unless the secretary of the Treasury certified that no further loans had been made to Iran since Oct. 1, 1993, or the president certified that disbursement was in the national interest.

U.N. Population Fund

Provided $40 million of the $50 million requested for the U.N. Population Fund. HR 2295 required the administration to report to Congress on the agency's budget for its activities in China. Any amount above the $10 million that the agency intended to spend in China was to be deducted from the U.S. contribution. (U.N. Population Fund, box, this page) ❑

1995 Aid Appropriations

Congress in 1994 cleared a $13.8 billion fiscal 1995 foreign operations appropriations bill (HR 4426—PL 103-306). The final bill was about $247 million less than President Clinton's request.

HR 4426 endorsed the status quo in most programs, which enabled skittish lawmakers to justify a vote for sending aid abroad in an election year. As in previous years, much of the funding was reserved for two countries: $3 billion for Israel and $2.1 billion for Egypt.

U.N. POPULATION FUND

In one of his first acts in the White House, President Clinton on Jan. 22, 1993, signed an executive order overturning the so-called Mexico City policy, a Reagan-era prohibition on funding for international organizations offering abortion-related services. Soon after, the administration lifted an eight-year-old ban on U.S. assistance for the U.N. Population Fund, which provided family planning aid in more than one hundred developing nations.

The United States had helped set up the U.N. program in 1969 and for a decade had been the agency's largest contributor. But controversy erupted in 1985, when reports emerged that China's one-child per family policy included forced sterilizations, abortions and even infanticide. China denied condoning such actions, and the U.N. population agency denied supporting abortion as a method of family planning. But the Reagan administration withheld from the program fiscal 1985 funds equal to the agency's program in China. (1985 action, Congress and the Nation Vol. VII, p. 193)

Congress subsequently enacted legislation that led to a total funding cutoff. An amendment to a fiscal 1985 supplemental appropriations bill (PL 99-88) prohibited funding of any organization that supported programs that included forced abortions or involuntary sterilizations. The provision also stated that the determination was up to the president or the secretary of state.

Attempts to resurrect the funding failed until the Clinton administration came into office. Clinton in 1993 requested $50 million for the U.N. Population Fund as part of the fiscal 1994 foreign appropriations bill (HR 2295—PL 103-87). But renewed reports of brutality in China's population program spurred controversy even among supporters of the U.N. agency, and Congress cut $10 million out of the $50 million request, the estimated amount that would have been spent in China. The provision also required reducing the $40 million for the U.N. fund by any amount in excess of $10 million that it budgeted for activities in China. (Failed funding attempts, Congress and the Nation Vol. VIII, pp. 228, 269, 271)

The bill also included $850 million for the former Soviet republics—just $50 million less than Clinton had requested but a significant reduction from the $2.5 billion in aid Congress voted in fiscal 1994. The legislation required that Russia abide by agreements to remove its forces from the Baltic nations to get the U.S. aid, although the provision could be waived if the president determined it was in the national security interest.

International financial institutions, such as the World Bank and International Monetary Fund, were big winners in the bill. After slashing the funding request the previous year, Congress in 1994 restored most of the reduction, providing $1.9 billion of the administration's $2.1 billion request.

HR 4426 included two supplemental appropriations for fiscal 1994 in response to a last-minute administration request to provide up to $220 million in debt relief for Jordan, which had just agreed to cease hostilities with Israel, and emergency aid for refugees from Rwanda, which had been devastated by bloody tribal conflict that had cost an estimated 500,000 lives. The bill provided $99 million for the Jordanian debt relief, along with $50 million in emergency funds for Rwanda.

HOUSE ACTION

The House passed a $13.8 billion foreign aid funding bill on May 25 by a vote of 337–87. The bill had been reported by the House Appropriations Committee May 23 (H Rept 103-524).

For the second straight year, the House Appropriations Foreign Operations Subcommittee, desiring to give the administration as much latitude as possible, had produced a bill that was free of earmarks—requirements that the administration provide a minimum level of funding for a program. It was assumed, however, that the president's $900 million request for the former Soviet republics would be fully funded and that Israel would continue to receive $3 billion and Egypt, $2.1 billion.

Despite anger over the Aldrich H. Ames spy scandal, the House on May 25 rejected 144–286 an amendment offered by Sonny Callahan, R-Ala., to cut $348 million from the administration's $390 million aid proposal for Russia, leaving only $42 million in humanitarian aid. Callahan had argued that Russia had made little progress in moving toward free markets, but that brought a heated rejoinder from his fellow Republican Robert L. Livingston of Louisiana. "The cold war ended three years ago," said Livingston. "We can't expect miracles, but if this amendment passes we won't get one." Foreign Affairs Committee Chairman Lee H. Hamilton, D-Ind., and other lawmakers who previously had expressed concern over the aid program voiced similar sentiments. Callahan had offered a similar amendment to the fiscal 1994 foreign operations bill and had been defeated by almost the same margin, 140–289. *(1994 aid bill, p. 202; Ames spy scandal, p. 219)*

With some last-minute maneuvering, Callahan did manage to win House approval by voice vote of a plan that trimmed about $25 million in aid for Russia and the other former republics, bringing the total down to $875 million.

The generally amicable floor debate on the bill turned bitter when Dan Burton, R-Ind., offered an amendment to freeze fiscal 1995 aid to the new government of South Africa at fiscal 1994 levels—about $80 million instead of the $206 million in aid and credits planned for fiscal 1995. Burton protested that several members of President Nelson Mandela's cabinet were communists and urged the administration to expand trade and investment in South Africa instead of increasing direct aid. Members of the Congressional Black Caucus and other lawmakers from both parties denounced the proposal, which was defeated 103–321 on May 25.

The House that same day rejected 54–371 an Anthony C. Beilenson, D-Calif., amendment to add $100 million for population programs to the $450 million already in the bill through a 0.75 percent across-the-board reduction from other accounts in the bill. Because the bill contained no earmarks, opponents argued that the amendment would force cuts in important programs such as aid to Israel and Egypt.

SENATE ACTION

The Senate passed a $13.7 billion version of HR 4426 on July 15 by a vote of 84–9. The Senate Appropriations Committee had reported the bill on June 16 (S Rept 103-287).

The Senate bill generally endorsed the funding blueprint contained in the House-passed version. However, the Senate Appropriations Subcommittee on Foreign Operations loaded the measure with earmarks.

Senate floor debate on the bill, which had begun June 29 but had been delayed by a crowded calendar before the July 4 recess, gave Republicans an opportunity to criticize the administration's policy on Haiti and other issues. But only a handful of the scores of amendments adopted by the Senate appeared to create significant problems for the administration. The big-ticket items in the bill were left untouched.

Freshman Republican Judd Gregg ignited the Haiti debate June 29, offering an amendment to require that the president seek congressional authorization before ordering military action against Haiti. The president could waive the requirement under certain circumstances. After sparring over the administration's policy toward Haiti and over whether Gregg's amendment went too far in tying the president's hands, the Senate rejected the amendment by a **key vote of 34–65 (R 34–10; D 0–55).** The Senate then adopted 93–4 a nonbinding amendment offered by Majority Leader George J. Mitchell, D-Maine, urging the president to seek congressional approval. On July 14, the Senate agreed 57–42 to table (kill) an amendment offered by Minority Leader Bob Dole, R-Kan., to establish a bipartisan commission of senior lawmakers to assess diplomatic and policy conditions in Haiti. *(Haiti policy, p. 195; 1994 key votes, p. 1003)*

The Senate backed several Republican-sponsored amendments aimed at establishing new conditions on U.S. economic assistance to Russia, which the Senate bill set at $839 million. An amendment by Mitch McConnell, R-Ky., requiring Russia to fulfill its long-standing pledge to withdraw all troops from the Baltic nations by Aug. 31, 1994, to receive U.S. economic aid was adopted 89–8 on July 13. The amendment was in response to a July 10 statement by Russian President Boris N. Yeltsin that he did not intend to withdraw about 2,000 troops still stationed in Estonia by the deadline. The president could waive the condition if it was in the national security interest. Senators adopted by voice vote an amendment by Jesse Helms, R-N.C., to prohibit aid to Russia unless the president certified that Moscow was committed to complying with treaties barring the export of chemical and biological weapons. The Senate on July 15 backed, 56–38, an amendment by Pete V. Domenici, R-N.M., and Dole authorizing the president to tap the aid to Moscow provided in the foreign operations bill to dismantle nuclear weapons in the former Soviet Union. Funds for the Nunn-Lugar program—named for its original sponsors, Sam Nunn, D-Ga., and Richard G. Lugar, R-Ind.—previously had come from the Pentagon's budget.

In other action, the Senate agreed 59–35 on June 29 to table (kill) language inserted by the Senate Appropriations Committee that would have barred Indonesia from using in East Timor any military equipment purchased from the United States. Controversy had surrounded the issue of military aid to Indonesia since 1991 when as many as 100 civilians had been massacred by Indonesian forces on the island of East Timor. Congress in 1992 had terminated military training assistance to Indonesia, but, in a move that outraged some members of Congress, the administration had allowed Indonesia to pay for continued training. The committee provision in HR 4426 had drawn strong opposition from the Pentagon, the State Department and some large U.S. corporations with operations in Indonesia. Several senators hammered away at the economic argument, asserting that the restriction on arms sales would insult an important U.S. trading partner.

The Senate on July 15 adopted, 95–0, an amendment by Dole and Frank H. Murkowski, R-Alaska, to bar any U.S. aid for North Korea unless the president certified that Pyongyang did not posses nuclear weapons and had not exported weapons-grade plutonium. *(North Korea, p. 221)*

By voice vote June 29, the Senate significantly weakened a Senate subcommittee provision that would have barred arms sales to Greece unless Athens agreed that the equipment would not be used in violation of the U.N. embargo against Serbia. Instead, the Senate acted to require that the State Department report on how U.S. aid "is promoting respect for principles and obligations" under the U.N. sanctions against Serbia.

The Senate also put more pressure on the administration to support North Atlantic Treaty Organization (NATO) membership for several eastern European countries. Senators on July 14 voted 76–22 to adopt an amendment offered by Hank Brown, R-Colo., to expand defense cooperation with Poland, Hungary and the Czech Republic. The proposal, which the administration opposed, broadened the terms of a similar amendment that Brown had attached to the defense authorization bill. The Senate July 14 agreed 53–44 to table (kill) a McConnell amendment that would have required the administration to spell out criteria for admitting several eastern European nations to NATO. But the substantial vote in favor of the proposal meant the issue almost certainly would resurface.

CONFERENCE, FINAL ACTION

The House adopted the conference report on HR 4426 (H Rept 103-633) on Aug. 4 by a vote of 341–85. The Senate adopted the conference report Aug. 10 on an 88–12 vote, clearing the bill. Clinton signed the measure Aug. 23.

The 12-hour conference saw a long tug of war over the Senate earmarks. A good measure of partisan sparring also took place over the administration's handling of foreign policy.

David R. Obey, D-Wis., who took over the reins of the full House Appropriations Committee in March 1994, waged a largely successful campaign against Republican-backed policy amendments and a number of senators' earmarks for individual countries. For example, conferees accepted an Obey alternative that urged—but did not require—the administration to provide

$150 million for Ukraine, $75 million for Armenia and $50 million for the republic of Georgia. The conference committee replaced Sen. McConnell's amendment barring aid to Russia unless Russian troops were out of the Baltics by Aug. 31 with a milder substitute that set no specific deadline for troop withdrawals. Opponents argued that McConnell's amendment had been made moot by a recent agreement by Moscow to withdraw its troops from Estonia.

A Senate amendment aimed at expanding NATO military contacts with eastern European nations also fell. In addition, conferees modified Helms's amendment linking aid for Moscow to its commitment to comply with chemical and biological weapons treaties by requiring a report on the matter instead of cutting off aid. Conferees also removed the Senate amendment on North Korea.

Although the administration got most of what it wanted from the conference, not everything went according to plan. A Senate amendment to tighten existing restrictions on aid to the Palestine Liberation Organization (PLO)—a provision that caught many lawmakers unaware—was adopted by the conference committee. The restrictions were intended to ensure that the PLO lived up to its peace agreement with Israel. The amendment eliminated language in existing law that allowed the president to waive the conditions if he determined it to be in the national interest. But language in the conference report reaffirmed the president's option to use other statutory authority to waive the restriction.

Compromises were reached on aid to Indonesia, Greece and Turkey.

At the administration's request, conferees agreed to include in the bill supplemental fiscal 1994 funds for Jordan and Rwanda. Although the requests came too late for appropriators in either chamber to consider them in committee or on the floor, conferees approved them without much dissent.

MAJOR PROVISIONS

The final version of the fiscal 1995 foreign operations appropriations bill (HR 4426—PL 103-306) provided $13.8 billion. This included $2.30 billion for multilateral aid, $7.61 billion for bilateral aid, $3.03 billion for military aid and $734 million for export assistance, as well as supplemental appropriations for fiscal 1994 of $99 million to provide up to $220 million in debt relief for Jordan and $50 million in emergency assistance to Rwanda.

In addition, the conference committee authorized the president to tap the Pentagon's stocks of excess military equipment to provide light weaponry to Jordan.

HR 4426 also:

Former Soviet Republics

• Provided $850 million in aid for the former Soviet republics. From this, the bill urged the administration to provide $150 million for Ukraine, $75 million for Armenia and $50 million for the republic of Georgia.

• Required that Russia abide by agreements to remove its forces from the Baltic states as a condition of U.S. aid, but no specific deadline was set. The president could waive the provision if he determined it was in the national security interest.

• Required the administration to submit a report on Russia's commitment to chemical and biological weapons treaties.

Israel, Egypt

Earmarked $1.2 billion in economic aid and $1.8 billion in military aid for Israel and $815 million in economic aid and $1.3 billion in military aid for Egypt. Continued the requirement for early disbursal of Israel's assistance.

Refugee Assistance

Provided $671 million in migration and refugee aid, of which $80 million in refugee assistance was earmarked for Israel.

Cyprus

Earmarked $15 million in aid for Cyprus.

U.N. Sanctions

Barred aid to countries that violated U.N. Security Council sanctions against Serbia and Montenegro.

North Korea

Barred the use of aid appropriated under the bill for North Korea.

PLO

Eliminated language in existing law that allowed the president to waive conditions on aid to the PLO if he determined it to be in the national interest.

Greece, Turkey

Included $255 million in military loans to Greece and $365 million in military loans to Turkey, in keeping with the long-standing practice of providing $7 in military aid to Greece for each $10 provided to Turkey. Ten percent of the money for Turkey was to be withheld until the administration reported on alleged abuses by Turkish military forces against Kurdish civilians. Ten percent of the funding for Greece was to be withheld until the administration submitted a report on alleged Greek violations of international sanctions against Serbia.

Indonesia

Barred sales of light arms to Indonesia until the secretary of state reported that the Indonesian government had made "significant progress" in eliminating human rights abuses by security forces in East Timor. (Existing administration policy denied small arms sales to Jakarta.) Sales of major weapons were not affected. The bill prohibited the use of U.S. aid to underwrite Pentagon training for Indonesian officers, but Jakarta could still pay for the training itself.

International Financial Institutions

Provided $1.9 billion for the international banks, including $25 million for the International Monetary Fund's Enhanced Structural Adjustment Facility, a program of debt relief for poor countries.

U.N. Population Fund

Provided $50 million of the administration's $60 million request for the U.N. Population Fund and continued existing conditions on the funding. *(Population fund, box, p. 209)* ❑

State Department Authorization

Congress in 1994 cleared legislation (HR 2333—PL 103-236) authorizing $13.5 billion for the State Department, the United States Information Agency (USIA) and related agencies for fiscal 1994 and 1995, as well as revamping the foreign policy bureaucracy. Congress had begun work on the bill nearly a year earlier, but a dispute in the Senate over foreign broadcasting provisions delayed approval.

As in the past, the State Department bill served as an important barometer of congressional sentiment on controversial foreign policy issues. Over the strong objections of the administration, the bill urged President Clinton to provide weapons to the forces of Bosnia's beleaguered Muslim-led government despite the United Nations embargo on arms to the region. The bill also contained a nonbinding Senate provision calling on Clinton to end economic sanctions against Vietnam, a step the president took shortly after the Senate acted.

Another important nonbinding provision supported arms sales to Taiwan. As a result of negotiations on that provision, the administration signaled it would approve new sales of advanced military electronics to Taiwan.

HR 2333 authorized the administration's long-sought $670 million supplemental request for fiscal 1994 U.N. peacekeeping contributions but set restrictions on U.S. support for peacekeeping. The final bill also imposed stiff sanctions on nations engaged in the trade of nuclear weapons parts or weapons-related materials.

In a signing statement reminiscent of those issued by his Republican predecessors, Clinton complained that several sections of the law interfered with the discharge of his constitutional responsibilities and said that he would regard those sections as "precatory"—in essence, congressional entreaties—instead of as requirements. Clinton was particularly troubled by the bill's comprehensive sanctions on companies engaging in nuclear proliferation. He called the sanctions "essentially unworkable," adding, "I have been assured that this provision will be corrected."

HOUSE ACTION

The House passed its $14.9 billion version of HR 2333 on June 22, 1993, by a vote of 273–144. The bill had been reported by the House Foreign Affairs Committee on June 11 (H Rept 103-126).

The House measure generally stuck to the so-called core issues—the organizational structure of the State Department, U.S.-backed broadcasting services and international scholarship programs. The biggest controversy during floor action came when the House, with backing from Republicans and freshmen from both parties, voted 243–181 on June 22 to cut off funding for the National Endowment for Democracy (NED), a nonprofit corporation that supported prodemocracy activities in scores of countries. The vote was a blow to Clinton's plans to expand financial support to promote democracy abroad. Support for the amendment, which was offered by Paul E. Kanjorski, D-Pa., was said to have come from lawmakers weary of supporting international programs. In addition, the administration, which appeared to underestimate the strength of that sentiment, had scaled back its lobbying presence on the State Department bill.

The House rejected, 184–235 on June 22, a Gerald B. H. Solomon, R-N.Y., amendment to require random drug testing for State Department employees.

SENATE ACTION

The Senate passed a $12.4 billion version of the State Department bill by a vote of 92–8 on Feb. 2, 1994, after substituting the text of its own bill (S 1281). The Senate Foreign Relations Committee had reported S 1281 on July 23, 1993 (S Rept 103-107).

The committee bill had languished for months, largely because of a dispute over an administration proposal to overhaul government-sponsored international broadcasting programs, placing them under the USIA. Sen. Joseph R. Biden Jr., D-Del., objected strongly to the plan but failed to add an amendment to maintain the independent status of two cold war–era networks, Radio Free Europe and Radio Liberty. Just before the end of the 1993 session, the administration reached a compromise with Biden, acquiescing in his demand that the two radio networks retain their status as independent, government-funded contractors. That freed the bill for floor action in 1994.

Senate floor consideration of the bill turned out to be relatively tame when compared with the highly charged policy debates of previous years. The Senate did adopt amendments urging administration action on issues ranging from nuclear proliferation in North Korea to preferential trade status for China. But few posed any real threat to the administration's policies.

Most significant, perhaps, the Senate went on record Jan. 27 in favor of lifting the U.S. economic embargo against Vietnam. The **key vote of 62–38 (R 20–24; D 42–14),** on an amendment sponsored by John Kerry, D-Mass., and John McCain, R-Ariz., provided Clinton with the political equivalent of a flak jacket. Just a week later, he formally ended 18 years of trade sanctions that were imposed at the conclusion of the Vietnam War. *(1994 key votes, p. 1003; Vietnam policy, box, p. 214)*

The historic action on Vietnam overshadowed the scores of other foreign policy issues addressed in the bill. The Senate overwhelmingly supported nonbinding language, offered by Minority Leader Bob Dole, R-Kan., urging the president to unilaterally lift the international arms embargo that barred weapons shipments to the Bosnian government, but the 87–9 vote on Jan. 27 belied deep reservations over direct U.S. military intervention in Bosnia and divisions over how the United States should proceed. *(Bosnia policy, p. 197)*

By voice vote, the Senate adopted a sense of the Congress amendment, by McCain, calling on Clinton to seek an international consensus to isolate North Korea economically until it had halted its nuclear program. *(North Korea policy, p. 221)*

Several GOP amendments were toned down considerably before being approved. A sweeping Dole amendment on international peacekeeping that would have limited the president's power to commit U.S. troops to peacekeeping operations was watered down significantly before being adopted by voice vote. Similarly, a nonbinding proposal by Jesse Helms, R-N.C., explicitly linking the renewal of China's nondiscriminatory most-favored-nation trade status to its performance on human rights and proliferation issues was replaced by a far milder substitute amendment by Kerry on a 61–39 vote on Feb. 1. The Senate on Jan. 27 adopted 94–3 a nonbinding amendment offered by Mitch McConnell, R-Ky., urging "prompt"—instead of "immediate," as it was originally worded—admission to the North Atlantic Treaty Organization (NATO) for qualified European nations.

In other action on the many amendments offered, the Senate adopted by voice vote a John Glenn, D-Ohio, amendment requiring the United States to impose sanctions on nations engaging in nuclear proliferation and to punish private companies that sold nuclear material that could be used in making weapons. The president could waive the sanctions under certain circumstances. By a 93–0 vote on Jan. 28, the Senate approved a Hank Brown, R-Colo., amendment barring arms sales to countries that participated in the boycott of U.S. companies doing business with Israel, unless the president certified that it was in the national interest.

An attempt to table (kill) a Dale Bumpers, D-Ark., amendment trimming the NED authorization from $50 million to $35 million (the amount already appropriated for fiscal 1994) was rejected 41–59 on Jan. 27. The amendment was then adopted by voice vote.

CONFERENCE, FINAL ACTION

The House approved the conference report (H Rept 103-482) by voice vote April 28. A Republican-led effort in the House to return the legislation to conference to remove the Vietnam provision fell short, 195–209 on April 28.

The House vote cleared the bill for the president. The Senate had agreed two days earlier to deem the legislation cleared as soon as it was approved by the House, a step that ensured that the funeral of former president Richard M. Nixon, which interrupted the Senate schedule, would not delay enactment of the bill past April 30, the expiration date for the waiver allowing the programs covered by the bill to receive fiscal 1994 appropriations even though they had not been reauthorized. Clinton signed the measure April 30. Just prior to adjournment, Congress cleared a technical corrections bill (HR 5034—PL 103-415) making mostly minor changes in the legislation. The president signed HR 5034 on Oct. 25.

MAJOR PROVISIONS

As cleared, HR 2333 (PL 103-236):
• **Funding.** Authorized $13.5 billion for the State Department, USIA and related agencies for fiscal years 1994 and 1995.

VIETNAM TRADE EMBARGO

In a simple executive action that followed years of difficult and often emotionally charged congressional investigations into the fate of missing servicemen from the Vietnam War, President Clinton on Feb. 3, 1994, lifted what had been an 18-year U.S. trade embargo against Vietnam.

Clinton's executive order came a week after the Senate, in a **key vote of 62–38 (R 20–24; D 42–14),** urged the president to lift the embargo. The Jan. 27 Senate vote was on a nonbinding amendment to the fiscal 1994–1995 State Department authorization bill (S 1281). *(1994 key votes, p. 1003)*

The embargo, which had been in place since the end of the Vietnam War, had been maintained under Presidents Jimmy Carter, Ronald Reagan, George Bush and Clinton largely to pressure the Vietnamese government to turn over all available information about U.S. servicemen listed as missing in action during the war. A sensitive political and social subject, the POW-MIA (prisoners of war-missing in action) issue resonated in the public and on radio talk shows. It had been fanned by charges from some Vietnam veterans groups that U.S. soldiers were detained well into the late 1980s and that the Defense Department was covering up information about POW-MIA cases.

1993 Steps Toward Normalization

The Senate in August 1991 had created a select committee to study the question of the approximately 2,200 American soldiers who never came home from the Vietnam War. On Jan. 13, 1993, after 15 months of investigation, the Senate Select Committee on POW-MIA Affairs issued a final report that concluded that "no compelling evidence" existed that any U.S. soldiers were held against their will in Vietnam at the time of the committee's investigation. It did, however, hold open the possibility that some soldiers had languished in captivity after the hostilities ended and after Hanoi said it had returned all POWs. *(Committee investigation, Congress and the Nation Vol. VIII, p. 288)*

Broad interest in the issue was renewed by the February 1993 discovery in Moscow of a 20-year-old military document quoting a Vietnamese general as confiding that his country held more than 1,200 American prisoners in 1972, at a time when it told the United States it held 368. But after an April visit to Vietnam, retired Gen. John W. Vessey, the U.S. envoy to Vietnam on POW questions, claimed that the document, while authentic, was also thoroughly inaccurate.

On Memorial Day, May 30, Clinton signed an executive order calling for the declassification by Veterans Day, Nov. 11, of the government's remaining files relating to the POWs and MIAs. His ac-

tion bolstered an executive order issued in 1992 by President Bush by setting a deadline for release of the material. The government had already declassified about 800,000 pages of documents out of about 1.5 million that were expected to be made public.

On July 2, Clinton announced the United States was dropping its long-standing opposition to loans to Vietnam from such international institutions as the World Bank and International Monetary Fund. On Sept. 13, Clinton renewed the trade embargo against Vietnam, but he relaxed it slightly to allow U.S. companies to bid on multimillion-dollar contracts in Vietnam financed by the World Bank and the Asian Development Bank.

Clinton's decision was greeted with general approval on Capitol Hill by lawmakers who said that U.S. business should be able to profit from the large-scale development projects planned in Vietnam.

But some members warned that, with each step the White House took toward normalizing relations, leverage might be lost in the search for long-missing U.S. soldiers.

1994 Lifting of Embargo

Clinton's decision to lift the embargo was influenced by Hanoi's cooperation in 1993 in helping resolve some of the MIA cases. But it was the Senate's Jan. 27 vote on the amendment to the State Department bill that provided Clinton with the political cover to end the embargo. The Senate amendment was written by John Kerry, D-Mass., a decorated Vietnam veteran who had chaired the Senate Select Committee on POW-MIA Affairs, and John McCain, R-Ariz., a committee member who had spent nearly six years as a POW in Vietnam.

The Senate the same day rejected, 42–58, an amendment by Robert C. Smith, R-N.H., and Minority Leader Bob Dole, R-Kan., that would have conditioned the lifting of the embargo on the president's certification that the U.S. intelligence community was satisfied that Vietnam was providing the fullest accounting possible. Smith, the vice chairman of the select committee, contended that the intelligence community was convinced that Vietnam was not fully forthcoming on the POW issue.

Some members were deeply critical of the decision to end the embargo, saying it removed the last best lever to force more information from the Vietnamese government. Representatives of the American Legion and the Veterans of Foreign Wars lobbied against the Kerry amendment. Behind the scenes, however, lawmakers had been lobbied by Mobil, Amoco, the U.S. Chamber of Commerce and other interests that saw rich potential in Vietnam's oil reserves and economic development.

● **Vietnam.** Called on the administration, in a nonbinding provision, to lift the U.S. economic embargo against Vietnam.

● **Bosnia.** Urged the White House, in a nonbinding provision, to provide weapons to the besieged Muslim-led government in Bosnia despite a U.N. embargo barring weapons to combatants in the former Yugoslavia.

● **China.** Asserted, in a provision made nonbinding by conferees, that the 1979 Taiwan Relations Act (PL 96-8) providing for unlimited transfers of defensive arms to Taiwan took precedence over a 1982 U.S.-China communiqué, in which the United States agreed to gradually reduce arms sales to Taiwan. *(U.S.-China communiqué, Congress and the Nation Vol. VI, p. 154)*

- **Peacekeeping Funds.** Authorized $670 million in supplemental funding for fiscal 1994 and $510 million for fiscal 1995 for U.N. peacekeeping contributions. Set new restrictions on U.S. support for peacekeeping and withheld half the $670 million until the United Nations established an independent inspector general. Prohibited the United States from paying for more than 25 percent of U.N. peacekeeping operations beginning in fiscal 1996.

- **Reorganization of State, International Broadcasting.** Provided for the establishment of a new undersecretary of global affairs. Preserved a separate post of coordinator for counterterrorism for a year after enactment, instead of merging the State Department's office of counterterrorism with the new global affairs section as proposed by the administration.

  Consolidated all U.S.-funded international broadcasting—the Voice of America, Radio Free Europe, Radio Liberty and Radio and TV Marti—under a single broadcasting board of governors. Also authorized creation of a new Radio Free Asia to provide uncensored news to China and other totalitarian states in Asia.

- **Cuba.** Expanded the range of cultural and educational materials available for export to Cuba and other countries that were subject to U.S. economic sanctions. Urged the president, in a nonbinding provision, to seek a U.N. trade embargo against Cuba.

- **Nuclear Proliferation.** Imposed stiff economic sanctions on companies and countries that assisted in the spread of nuclear arms and weapons-related materials. The sanctions could be waived under certain circumstances.

- **PLO.** Extended a waiver of various statutory restrictions on the Palestine Liberation Organization (PLO) until one year after enactment of the bill.

- **Arab Boycott.** Prohibited U.S. arms sales to countries that upheld the Arab economic boycott of companies that did business with Israel. The provision was to go into effect one year after enactment of the bill. The president could waive the restriction if he determined that to be in the national interest.

- **NED.** Authorized $35 million for the National Endowment for Democracy. ❏

1994 Intelligence Authorization

With the cold war becoming a faded memory, Congress in 1993 continued its clampdown on intelligence costs by imposing a freeze on spending for intelligence activities in the fiscal 1994 intelligence authorization bill (HR 2330—PL 103-178). Although the intelligence budget officially was classified, the final bill was widely reported to provide $28 billion—the same amount as in fiscal 1993 and $1 billion less than President Clinton had requested. With no additional funds to cover inflation, the bill amounted to a slight cut in spending power.

The administration had lobbied vigorously for its full request but Congress resisted, as it faced the challenge of allocating funds in a period of tight budgets to a legion of intelligence agencies that were searching to define their purpose and opponents after the breakup of the Soviet Union.

Sen. Dennis DeConcini, D-Ariz., and Rep. Dan Glickman, D-Kan., made sharp first impressions as the new chairmen of the Intelligence committees by attempting to improve the intelligence community's relationship with Congress and the public. DeConcini and Glickman held open meetings and encouraged the new director of central intelligence, R. James Woolsey, to be more forthcoming about intelligence activities with members. *(Woolsey nomination, p. 193)*

Despite those moves, neither Congress nor the Clinton administration wanted the trend toward openness to go so far as to put on the record the total amount spent on intelligence activities, even though that was the nation's worst-kept intelligence secret. A nonbinding Senate amendment to HR 2330 asking the executive branch to reveal the total was dropped in conference.

LEGISLATIVE ACTION

HR 2330 was reported by the House Select Intelligence Committee on June 29 (H Rept 103-162, Part I) and the House Armed Services Committee on July 21 (H Rept 103-162, Part II). The House passed the bill on Aug. 4 by a vote of 400–28.

Clinton reluctantly went along with the spending freeze in the Intelligence Committee bill but vowed to fight moves to cut deeper. House members agreed, soundly defeating proposals for further reductions. The House on Aug. 3 rejected, 104–323, a 10 percent cut in funding proposed by Bernard Sanders, I-Vt. The next day, the House rebuffed, 134–299, an amendment by Barney Frank, D-Mass., to cut the bill's authorization by $500 million.

Glickman's support from Democrats came in part from his moves to make intelligence matters less secret and more accessible to members. The House bill formalized the new openness by requiring the CIA director to submit an annual unclassified report describing the intelligence community's "successes and failures" for the previous fiscal year. But the desire for openness did not extend to proposals to make public the total spending in the bill. The House on Aug. 4 rejected, 169–264, an amendment by Frank to reveal the total.

Porter J. Goss, R-Fla., revived a GOP proposal from 1991 to require House members to sign an oath promising not to disclose classified intelligence information and acknowledging that a violation could bring censure or expulsion. His amendment was adopted, 341–86, on Aug. 4, but only after Glickman won approval, 262–171, of language expanding the oath-taking requirement to all members of the Senate and executive branch. *(1991 action, Congress and the Nation Vol. VIII, p. 281)*

The Senate Intelligence Committee reported its fiscal 1994 intelligence authorization bill (S 1301—S Rept 103-115) on July 28. The Senate Armed Services Committee reported the bill (S Rept 103-155) on Oct. 5. The Senate passed HR 2330 by voice vote Nov. 10, after substituting the text of S 1301.

The Senate-passed bill froze spending at fiscal 1993 levels and carried the same price tag as the House-passed version. The bill also included a nonbinding provision asking the executive branch to make public the aggregate amount spent to fund the intelligence agencies. The amendment, offered by Howard M.

CIA RETIREMENT

Congress in 1993 cleared legislation (HR 1723—PL 103-36) to provide lump sum payments of up to $25,000 to unneeded CIA employees who took early retirement. The early retirement incentive was to be offered to CIA employees in certain specialties or locations that were designated as overstaffed by the director of central intelligence.

Congress had mandated in the fiscal 1993 intelligence authorization bill (PL 102-496) that the agency reach a 17.5 percent reduction in its workforce by 1997. House Intelligence Committee Chairman Dan Glickman, D-Kan., said HR 1723 was "a tool in not only shrinking the size of the CIA but in reorienting it from its cold war focus and methods." The measure's advocates also made clear that the incentive payments were devised in part to reduce the risk of forced layoffs that could produce disgruntled—and disloyal—former employees. The measure prohibited a CIA employee who took the early retirement bonus from being rehired by the agency or working for it under contract for a year. *(PL 102-496, Congress and the Nation Vol. VIII, p. 283)*

The House Intelligence Committee reported HR 1723 on May 24 (H Rept 103-102) and the full House passed it later that day by voice vote. Two days later, the Senate passed the bill by voice vote, clearing it. The president signed the measure June 8. The Senate Intelligence Committee had reported a similar bill (S 647—S Rept 103-43) on May 5.

Metzenbaum, D-Ohio, was adopted 52–48, on Nov. 10 after a motion to table (kill) the amendment narrowly lost, 49–51. Opponents argued that revealing the number could start the government down a slope that eventually would lead to making public an agency-by-agency breakdown of spending. Such details, they said, would aid foreign spy agencies in their efforts to figure out the U.S. intelligence community's programs and objectives. But supporters of Metzenbaum's amendment countered that excess secrecy acted as a shield to protect agencies from public scrutiny and proper congressional oversight.

FINAL BILL

The House and Senate adopted the conference report on HR 2330 (H Rept 103-377) by voice votes on Nov. 20.

Conferees deleted several contentious Senate amendments, including Metzenbaum's language urging the administration to make public the amount spent annually on intelligence activities. According to the conference report, members removed the provision because the House had defeated an attempt to make the number public. But the report warned that both the House and Senate Intelligence committees would hold hearings on the topic in 1994. In another signal that the issue would not go away anytime soon, House Speaker Thomas S. Foley, D-Wash., Senate Majority Leader George J. Mitchell, D-Maine, and 10 other senior members—including DeConcini and Glickman—on Nov. 22 wrote to Clinton asking him to reveal the intelligence budget total. In the letter, the members said that, with the end of the

cold war, they could no longer "rely upon unquestioning public support for secret operations or for the budgets to support them." The president agreed to review the issue.

Conferees also dropped the House-passed provision requiring members of Congress and the executive branch to sign an oath promising not to disclose classified intelligence information.

Conferees included a provision requiring the head of the intelligence community to release an unclassified annual report detailing intelligence successes and failures during the previous year. The final bill authorized $120 million for the National Security Trust Fund, a scholarship program for college and graduate-level students, $5 million less than the Senate had approved. The House had sought to cancel the program. Also included in the final bill was a House provision providing retirement and survivor benefits to former spouses of CIA employees who were divorced before Dec. 4, 1991.

Clinton signed HR 2330 on Dec. 3.

1995 Intelligence Authorization

Congress in 1994 cleared a fiscal 1995 intelligence authorization (HR 4299—PL 103-359) that kept overall funding for the nation's intelligence agencies relatively constant. But HR 4299 contained changes with potentially sweeping consequences for the nation's intelligence community. Over the objections of the Clinton administration, the bill effectively put the FBI in charge of counterintelligence and established a 17-member blue-ribbon panel to carry out a wholesale review of the mission and conduct of the CIA and the other intelligence agencies.

The aggregate funding level in the bill was classified, as were the figures for the CIA, Defense Intelligence Agency, National Security Agency and other government bureaus with intelligence-gathering functions. But the total for fiscal 1994 was reportedly about $28 billion, similar to the level approved for fiscal 1994. *(1994 intelligence authorization, p. 215)*

The policy changes came in the wake of revelations of perhaps the worst case ever of espionage against the United States. In February 1994, longtime CIA official Aldrich H. Ames and his wife were arrested for having sold top-secret information to the Soviet Union and, subsequently, to Russia from 1985 until their arrest. Ames's revelations to Soviet officials had led to the execution of at least 10 Soviet sources of the CIA and FBI and the imprisonment of others. *(Ames spy case, p. 219)*

The intelligence bill also reflected a general concern in Congress that predated the Ames scandal over the size, management and focus of the nation's intelligence establishment in the aftermath of the cold war.

BACKGROUND

Debate on the fiscal 1995 intelligence authorization bill took place in the shadow of the Ames spy case. Ames's ability to escape detection for nearly nine years led both the Clinton administration and key members of Congress to conclude that the government's spy-catching structure was badly in need of redesign. In particular, action was needed to end turf fights and lack of communication between the CIA, which conducted foreign intelligence and counterintelligence activities, and the FBI, which handled counterespionage investigations within the United States. FBI officials told Congress that the CIA's failure to share its early suspicions might have delayed Ames's detection and arrest.

But each branch had its own idea of how to reform the system. Taking the traditional position that intelligence policy making was an executive branch function, the administration opposed locking new arrangements into law, arguing instead for the greater flexibility of executive orders.

Clinton laid down his marker May 3, signing a presidential directive that set up a policy board to coordinate the government's counterespionage efforts and improve information-sharing arrangements between the CIA and FBI. The directive created a new National Counterintelligence Policy Board, made up of representatives of the CIA, FBI, National Security Council and the departments of State, Defense and Justice. A National Counterintelligence Operations Board and a National Counterintelligence Center were established under the board. The directive gave the FBI greater prominence and access to CIA information. An FBI official was to head the Counterintelligence Center for its first four years and was always to serve either as chief or deputy chief. Also, a senior executive from the FBI was to be put in charge of the CIA's counterespionage group; in turn, CIA officials were to be placed in the FBI's national security division.

But Congress disagreed with the administration's approach. Senate Intelligence Committee Chairman Dennis DeConcini, D-Ariz., cited a series of failed attempts over the years to coordinate the counterintelligence bureaucracy through executive action and said legislation was needed to correct the problem.

The government's system for classifying documents also received new attention as a result of the Ames case. Intelligence officials were under increasing pressure to end what critics called the unnecessary classification of millions of less critical documents and records. In March 1994, DeConcini and Dan Glickman, D-Kan., chairman of the House Intelligence Committee, introduced parallel bills to create statutory standards for classifying government documents. The two lawmakers said that millions of classified documents had little bearing on national security while draining money and resources from more crucial efforts, such as improving supervision of intelligence personnel. Advocates for revamping the system also argued that the lack of a uniform set of classification procedures administered by a single federal official had led to weak control over who was authorized to classify documents and who got access to them.

The intelligence community agreed in principle but opposed efforts to write reforms into law. The administration told lawmakers that the standards should be revamped through a new executive order that was being drafted.

In a report delivered to CIA Director R. James Woolsey and Defense Secretary William J. Perry on March 1, a panel made up of former defense and intelligence officials described the existing classification system as "overkill." The report called for a sin-

gle subcommittee of the National Security Council to oversee clearance procedures.

LEGISLATIVE ACTION

The House Intelligence Committee reported HR 4299 (H Rept 103-541, Part I) on June 9. The House passed the bill July 20 by a 410–16 vote.

The House bill was said to authorize about $28 billion. But an amendment offered by Glickman to be more precise in the future and declassify the aggregate intelligence budget total as of fiscal 1996 was defeated, 194–221, on July 19. A coalition of liberal Intelligence Committee members staged an effort to cut the overall spending by 10 percent below the fiscal 1994 level, but their amendment was rejected, 106–315, that same day.

The House-passed bill included provisions to increase federal investigators' access to the financial records of potential espionage suspects by waiving privacy law protections for many intelligence community employees. Another provision required intelligence agencies to set aside 2 percent of the money they received for security-related activities to plan for the phased declassification of government documents.

The Senate Intelligence Committee reported its version of the legislation (S 2082—S Rept 103-256) on May 5. The bill was reported by Senate Armed Services on June 30 (S Rept 103-295). The Senate on Aug. 12 passed HR 4299, by a vote of 97–2, after substituting the text of S 2082.

Before passing the bill, the Senate defied the Clinton administration and adopted an amendment tacitly placing the FBI in charge of counterespionage investigations. The amendment, offered by DeConcini and adopted by voice vote, appended the text of a bill reported by the Senate Intelligence Committee June 30 (S 2056—S Rept 103-296). That bill included provisions creating a National Counterintelligence Policy Board made up of the heads of various agencies with counterintelligence responsibilities, including the FBI, CIA, Defense Department, State Department and National Security Council, but the bill still made the FBI the lead agency on all counterespionage probes. DeConcini's amendment required the FBI to keep relevant agencies informed of its own counterintelligence investigations and allowed the president to waive the requirement that the FBI be informed immediately of suspected spying if it was determined that withholding the information was in the interest of national security. The amendment also included provisions from S 2056 aimed at giving spycatchers greater access to the financial records of espionage suspects.

In other action, the Senate on Aug. 12 adopted 99–0 an amendment by John W. Warner, R-Va., and Bob Graham, D-Fla., to establish a presidential commission to examine the roles and missions of the intelligence agencies in the post–cold war era.

Responding to a flap over the cost of the new headquarters complex for the National Reconnaissance Office (NRO), the Senate that same day adopted, 99–0, a DeConcini amendment capping the project's cost at $310 million and requiring the CIA and Defense Department to review the project and report back to Congress. *(NRO, box, p. 218)*

NATIONAL RECONNAISSANCE OFFICE

The $300-million-plus price tag for the construction of a head-quarters complex for the super-secretive National Reconnaissance Office (NRO) seemed like something that would be hard to hide. But senators' claims that they had been kept in the dark about the extent of the building project in Chantilly, Va., created a flap in 1994.

The mystery was how senators with responsibility for overseeing the nation's intelligence agencies could have failed to notice that the NRO, which developed and operated the nation's spy satellites, was building a four-office-tower headquarters complex, with nearly a fifth of the space of the Pentagon, in plain sight in the suburban Washington countryside near Dulles International Airport.

Senate Intelligence Committee members accused the NRO of failing to inform them about the size and cost of the building project. But their counterparts on the House Intelligence Committee claimed that they had been sufficiently informed of the building plans. Some House committee members accused the senators of trumping up charges of subterfuge to cover their own failure to keep up with the project. Even as he excoriated intelligence officials, Senate Intelligence Committee Chairman Dennis DeConcini, D-Ariz., conceded that his panel had not asked the right questions about the project.

The idea of consolidating the NRO's widely scattered office facilities in a single complex originally emanated from Congress in 1989. The agency notified Congress in September 1990 of its intention to purchase land and begin site planning. But DeConcini and other senators said they did not know that the NRO was nearing completion of the immense and costly compound until the Senate committee staff turned it up in an audit begun in April 1994.

Instead of breaking out the building project as a line item in its annual budget requests, NRO officials had included the cost in an unitemized "base" budget that was supposed to cover expenses that sustained the agency's base level of services. CIA Director R. James Woolsey and other officials explained that the procedure was a legacy of the deeply covert nature of the NRO, the very existence of which was classified until 1992. Even the land deal for the project was conducted as a cover operation, with a division of Rockwell International, a major defense contractor, making the purchase.

Intelligence officials gave lawmakers and reporters loose-leaf binders containing excerpts from twenty-two documents and briefings on the project that they said had been provided over the years to members and their staffs. In response, several senators complained that the information was provided in jigsaw puzzle-type fashion, not in a single, easily digestible document. They said congressional committees lacked the personnel to pull together such disparate clues and relied on the good faith of the agency officials to spell out where the money was going. But House members pointed to passages that indicated efforts by NRO officials to inform Congress and that implied a tacit, if not express, congressional authorization for the project.

The Senate reacted quickly on the issue. On Aug. 10, it amended the fiscal 1995 defense spending bill, requiring a specific line item for any intelligence agency building project costing more than $300,000 and barring new contracts for the NRO project until it had been fully investigated by Congress. The final version of the bill (HR 4650—PL 103-335) deleted the prohibition on the NRO project but included the language requiring a specific line item for each building request.

The final version of the fiscal 1995 intelligence authorization (HR 4299—PL 103-359) included a Senate amendment capping the project at $310 million and requiring the CIA and the Defense Department to review the project and report back to Congress. HR 4299 also required all intelligence agencies to get specific authorization from Congress for any building that would cost $750,000 or more.

FINAL BILL

The House and Senate adopted the conference report on HR 4299 (H Rept 103-753) by voice votes Sept. 30. The final bill, according to Glickman, authorized 2 percent less in overall spending than Clinton had requested and was appropriated in fiscal 1994.

House-Senate conferees agreed to accept the Senate amendments effectively placing the FBI in charge of all counterespionage investigations. (In return for the House's agreement to the FBI provision, Senate conferees dropped their objections to a satellite project that was backed by House members.) The conference bill required all intelligence agencies to report immediately to the FBI any suspected leaks of classified information and to give the FBI access to relevant agency and employee files.

The bill also included provisions from both earlier versions requiring executive branch employees who had access to classified information to consent to the disclosure of their financial and credit records.

The bill created a new Commission on the Role and Capabilities of the United States Intelligence Community to explore everything from the roles and missions of the intelligence agencies to which operations were run best and what management structure was most effective. The commission was to report its recommendations to Congress by March 1, 1996. At least nine of the commission's 17 members were not to have held leadership positions in the intelligence community, although this definition did not exclude current and past members of Congress who had had oversight responsibility for intelligence. The president was to appoint nine commission members, with the other eight appointments divided between the Senate and House. Of the eight appointed by Congress, four were to be members and four were to be private citizens. To maintain independence from the intelligence community, all but three of the commission's staff members were to be private citizens with no links to the community.

HR 4299 required the president to issue an executive order within 90 days of enactment establishing uniform standards for classifying government documents. Intelligence agencies that received more than $1 million for security were required to allocate 2 percent to develop a phased plan for declassifying documents.

The bill provided for a $1,000 fine or imprisonment for more than one year, or both, for people who knowingly removed classified documents with the intent to keep them in an unauthorized place.

The conference bill included the provision capping spending for the NRO complex at $310 million. It also required all intelligence agencies to get specific authorization from Congress for any building that would cost $750,000 or more.

HR 4299 lifted the ban on intelligence relations with South Africa.

Omitted from the final bill were House provisions that would have made permanent the positions of inspector general at the Defense Intelligence Agency and National Security Agency.

Clinton signed HR 4299 on Oct. 14.   ❏

Ames Spy Scandal

Lawmakers were outraged by revelations in 1994 that CIA employee Aldrich H. Ames had gone undetected for nine years while he acted as a double agent, selling critical U.S. secrets to the Soviet Union and later to the Russians.

Ames, a 31-year CIA employee, and his wife, Maria del Rosario Casas Ames, were arrested Feb. 21 and charged with taking $1.5 million from the Soviets in exchange for classified information. Ames pleaded guilty to espionage and was sentenced to life in prison. His wife was sentenced to 63 months on Oct. 21. Their actions resulted in the execution of 10 CIA and FBI sources in the Soviet Union and the imprisonment of untold others.

Congressional criticism—which grew increasingly harsh as details of the scandal emerged—focused on three issues: the CIA's failure to detect and stop the massive security breach, despite obvious signs of trouble and Ames's own clumsiness; the lack of an aggressive response to the scandal by CIA Director R. James Woolsey; and the discovery that the CIA had failed repeatedly to notify lawmakers of intelligence compromises in the mid-1980s, which were later linked to Ames.

The Senate and House Intelligence Committees each produced public reports on the case. The reports came in a congressional climate increasingly critical of the intelligence agency, with some lawmakers pushing to reduce the CIA's budget and others suggesting that the agency be folded into the Defense Department.

Congress authorized the creation of a 17-member blue-ribbon commission to review the CIA's role in the post–cold war era as part of the fiscal 1995 intelligence authorization bill (HR 4299—PL 103-359). In the same bill, lawmakers required the CIA to begin coordinating with the FBI on counterintelligence cases, with the FBI in the lead. *(1995 intelligence authorization, p. 216)*

SENATE REPORT

The Senate Select Committee on Intelligence issued a scalding appraisal of the CIA on Nov. 1. The report, the first formal response by Congress to the Ames debacle, was a 116-page indictment of an institution slack in its security, seemingly oblivious to serious personal problems among its employees and unwilling to come to grips with the possibility of a "mole" in its midst.

The intelligence panel called Ames's betrayal "the most egregious in American history" and identified seven major agency failures that were exploited by a bungling spy with a drinking problem. The CIA, the panel said, was guilty of "gross negligence—both individually and institutionally—in creating and perpetuating the environment in which Ames was able to carry out his espionage activities for nine years without detection."

The report listed 23 steps to rectify problems, including random polygraph tests and listing personal problems on official employee records. The committee stressed that it regarded the agency's response to be of "special oversight interest" and requested a progress report by Sept. 1, 1995.

Senators also expressed deep dissatisfaction with the disciplinary steps taken by CIA Director Woolsey in response to the Ames case. They noted that the agency's own inspector general recommended that 23 current and former CIA employees be held accountable for the Ames fiasco. Woolsey instead issued letters of reprimand to four current and seven retired agency employees. "All committee members believe that the director's disciplinary actions in this case are seriously inadequate and disproportionate to the magnitude of the problems identified in the inspector general's report," the intelligence panel said.

The committee withheld judgment on Woolsey's attempts to fix the agency's problems, including measures to shore up the counterintelligence unit, a review of the polygraph system, the initiation of random package searches and the creation of evaluation boards for promotions.

The Senate panel's richly detailed report offered new revelations about the case.

More than 100 intelligence operations of allied nations, the CIA, the FBI and the U.S. military were compromised, as were countless other operations that Ames said he did not specifically recall. The compromises during the 1985–1986 period "resulted in a virtual collapse of CIA's Soviet operations at the height of the Cold War," the report said. Ames also gave thousands of classified documents to the KGB, removing some of them in shopping bags from CIA offices.

The report painted a portrait of a mediocre CIA employee who rose through the ranks despite a chronic drinking problem, security lapses and several evaluations that categorized his work as poor. Ames's plans to marry a foreign national—Maria del Rosario Casas, a Colombian—raised security questions for some officials, but no steps were taken to implement the recommendation that he be assigned to a less sensitive job. Ames's lifestyle—he owned two Jaguars, purchased an expensive home in cash and ran up exorbitant credit card bills—was lavish beyond his salary of roughly $70,000 a year and eventually proved to be his downfall.

The report described an agency that responded tentatively to a significant number of deaths of Soviet agents and failed to launch a full-blown investigation. Perhaps the CIA's most serious failing was an inability to fathom the possibility of a traitor in its ranks. Institutional myopia allowed even a clumsy spy like Ames to operate unchallenged for years, the Senate panel concluded.

The report faulted the CIA leadership from 1986 to 1991, which included former directors William J. Casey and William H. Webster and former deputy directors Robert M. Gates and Richard J. Kerr.

HOUSE REPORT

In a report issued Nov. 30, the House Intelligence Committee ordered the CIA to explain why it failed to tell the panel about an unusually high number of deaths and disappearances of agents spying for the United States in the Soviet Union. Angry members of the House Intelligence Committee accused the agency of remaining silent although it had several opportunities to notify Congress of intelligence compromises in the mid-1980s, which had since been linked to Ames.

The 79-page committee report was highly critical of both the CIA and the FBI. The panel said that, despite repeated and pointed questions to the agency from its members about rumors of lost intelligence agents, the CIA was mum. It also found that the FBI was "inexplicably passive" in the Ames's espionage case despite access to CIA files.

Committee members said they were determined to find out whether the CIA's failure to notify oversight committees as required by law was a blatant disregard of the 1947 National Security Act or incompetence by senior intelligence officials. They instructed Woolsey to submit a written report by Dec. 31, which was to include all corrective steps under consideration.

The National Security Act required the CIA to keep congressional committees informed of all intelligence activities, including "any significant intelligence failures." The House committee's report said, "While there is rarely a reluctance to provide information when there is an intelligence success, the committee's experience when there is bad news has been uneven at best. Notification, however, is not discretionary."

In a last-minute addition to the report reflecting the committee's determination to shore up the disclosure process, the panel recommended that the CIA and FBI directors provide a written report to the intelligence committees twice a year on all counterintelligence and counterespionage investigations.

The House report also pointed to weaknesses in the CIA system, including a breakdown in communications in which investigators failed to apprise senior officials of information that could have led to Ames's arrest several years earlier. It was less harsh than the Senate report in its assessment of Woolsey's directorship, faulting him for giving senior officials the benefit of the doubt.   ❑

South Africa Sanctions

Congress in 1993 cleared legislation (HR 3225—PL 103-149) to remove the last of the U.S. economic sanctions imposed on South Africa by the 1986 Comprehensive Anti-Apartheid Act. HR 3225 repealed bans on the import of South African products, removed South Africa from a list of nations that were ineligible for most-favored-nation trade status and authorized the president to make foreign aid available to support the country's transition to a nonracial democracy.

The 1986 act (PL 99-440) was enacted by Congress over the veto of President Ronald Reagan in protest over apartheid, South Africa's institutionalized system of racial discrimination against its black majority. The law had imposed a series of sanctions, such as barring importation of South African coal, steel and agricultural products, and it had ended landing rights in the United States for the government-owned South African Airways. Supporters had argued that the only way to break the system of apartheid was to isolate South Africa and its economy from the rest of the world. Opponents had countered that sanctions would hurt the very people they were designed to help by making the poor in South Africa even poorer. *(1986 law, Congress and the Nation Vol. VII, p. 180)*

Changes in South Africa led President George Bush to lift some of the sanctions in 1991. In subsequent years, South Africa made dramatic progress toward dismantling apartheid. In 1993, African National Congress President Nelson Mandela and South African President F. W. de Klerk shared the Nobel Peace Prize for their efforts to bring about change peaceably in South Africa. On Nov. 18, 1993, the two leaders signed an agreement calling for a multiparty transitional government that would rule for five years, based on an election to be held April 27, 1994. It was to be the first general election in which the black majority in South Africa was to be permitted to vote. *(1991 action, Congress and the Nation Vol. VIII, p. 294)*

1993 LEGISLATIVE ACTION

The Senate passed legislation (S 1493) repealing the remaining U.S. economic sanctions against South Africa by voice vote Sept. 24, hours after Mandela urged the international community to drop all sanctions in recognition of South Africa's progress toward democracy.

The House passed its version (HR 3225) by voice vote Nov. 19. The measure had been put together by four House committees. It was reported by Foreign Affairs Oct. 15 (H Rept 103-296, Part I); Public Works and Transportation Nov. 8 (Part II); Banking, Finance and Urban Affairs Nov. 15 (Part III); and Ways and Means Nov. 17 (Part IV). The Senate approved the House bill on Nov. 20, completing congressional action. President Clinton signed the measure Nov. 23.

1994 DEVELOPMENTS

Mandela won the election in 1994 and was inaugurated May 10 as South Africa's first black president. Responding to the historic multiracial elections, Clinton on May 5 promised $600 million in assistance to South Africa over the following three years, including a doubling of aid in fiscal 1994 to $206 million. Clinton called Mandela's landslide election a "miracle" that occurred in part because of steadfast U.S. support for majority rule. "Now we must not turn our backs," Clinton said.

Mandela addressed a joint meeting of Congress on Oct. 6, saying that raising living standards for South Africa's vast underclass should be considered essential to the national interest of prosperous democracies such as the United States. The previous day, Clinton announced $100 million in new economic aid for southern Africa, about half to go to South Africa.   ❑

North Korea Nuclear Capacity

In contrast to the highly vocal, public positions it took on other trouble spots around the world, Congress was wary and cautious about North Korea, one of the most isolated, formidably armed regimes in the world.

With an army nearly twice the size of South Korea, the hard-line communist country represented a serious military threat to South Korea and the 37,000 U.S. troops stationed there. And that threat escalated dramatically when North Korea announced in 1993 that it planned to withdraw from a 1968 treaty intended to limit the spread of nuclear weapons.

The crisis continued throughout much of 1994 but seemed to be defused with the signing of a U.S.-North Korean nuclear power agreement late in the year.

1993 DEVELOPMENTS

R. James Woolsey, director of central intelligence, told the Senate Governmental Affairs Committee on Feb. 24, 1993, that the U.S. government believed that North Korea was rapidly gaining the ability to assemble a nuclear weapon.

North Korea's announcement on March 12 that it planned to withdraw from the 1968 nuclear nonproliferation treaty and its subsequent refusal to allow officials from the International Atomic Energy Agency to make complete inspections of nuclear development sites fanned suspicions that North Korea had violated the treaty by covertly extracting from its reactor enough plutonium to build one or two nuclear weapons. North Korea maintained that its nuclear research program was conducted for peaceful purposes, as allowed by the treaty. *(1968 treaty, Congress and the Nation Vol. II, p. 104)*

1994 DEVELOPMENTS

Beyond the nuclear threat, North Korea appeared increasingly bellicose toward South Korea in 1994. One North Korean official threatened to turn the South Korean capital of Seoul into a "sea of fire."

The House weighed in on the deepening crisis on June 8, when it adopted a pair of noncontroversial, nonbinding amendments to the fiscal 1995 defense authorization bill (HR 4301). By a vote of 415–1, the House approved a Gerald B. H. Solomon, R-N.Y., amendment calling for international sanctions against North Korea if it did not allow inspections of a nuclear facility. A John R. Kasich, R-Ohio, amendment calling on the president to urge South Korea to upgrade its military readiness was adopted 414–3.

The Senate overwhelmingly adopted, 93–3, a nonbinding amendment by John McCain, R-Ariz., to an unrelated airport improvement bill (S 1491) June 16 urging President Clinton to "take all necessary and prudent actions" to deter a potential North Korean attack and enhance the safety of U.S. troops in South Korea. The Pentagon had dispatched Patriot air defense missiles to South Korea, but critics called that hopelessly inadequate.

At the same time as the Senate was acting, former president Jimmy Carter was in North Korea negotiating an agreement with that nation's 82-year-old leader, Kim Il Sung, to seek a diplomatic solution to the stalemate.

The July 8 death of Kim Il Sung and the ascension to power of his son Kim Jong II forced a delay in the U.S.-North Korean negotiations and sparked new worries over North Korea's nuclear weapons program. The Senate weighed in again on Korea policy July 15, when it voted 95–0 on a Mitch McConnell, R-Ky., amendment to bar any U.S. aid to North Korea unless the president certified that it did not possess nuclear weapons, had halted its nuclear weapons program and had not exported weapons-grade plutonium. The Senate amendment, attached to the fiscal 1995 foreign operations appropriation bill (HR 4426), was opposed by the administration as a potential stumbling block in negotiations with North Korea. The ban, which would have barred aid from other statutes as well as HR 4426, was stripped from the bill in conference. North Korea, however, was included on a list of countries barred from receiving the aid appropriated by HR 4426.

The high-level talks resumed and an agreement was signed Oct. 21. Under the pact, North Korea would abandon its effort to develop nuclear power plants based on "graphite-moderated" reactors, from which it was relatively easy to remove plutonium for use in nuclear weapons. In return, the United States would help North Korea acquire two power plants based on "light water" reactors, from which administration officials maintained it was harder to extract weapons-quality plutonium. Pending completion of the new reactors, the United States would supply North Korea with fuel oil for power plants that would substitute for the mothballed reactors. North Korea was to allow inspections only after construction was well along on the new reactors—probably not for several years.

Some critics complained that the United States had made too many concessions, but the administration contended that the accord would restrict North Korea's nuclear war-making potential more stringently than had the nonproliferation treaty because it would immediately padlock the reactors and nuclear-handling facilities that were allowed under the 1968 treaty. The October agreement did not require congressional approval.

U.S.-North Korean relations were exacerbated and ongoing nuclear talks threatened in the closing weeks of 1994 when a U.S. Army reconnaissance helicopter was downed several miles into North Korean territory. One pilot was killed and a second captured in the Dec. 17 incident. The diplomatic crisis was eased with the Dec. 30 release of the second pilot.   ❑

Iran-Contra Probe

Independent counsel Lawrence E. Walsh concluded his seven-year investigation into the Iran-contra affair in 1994. In his long-anticipated final report, released Jan. 18, Walsh exonerated former president Ronald Reagan of criminal culpability in the affair even as he bluntly accused the former president of creating a climate in which his senior aides felt free to violate the law. "They skirted the law, some of them broke the law, and almost all of them tried to cover up the president's willful activities," the report said.

Walsh also sharply disputed former president George Bush's repeated assertions that, as Reagan's vice president, he was "out of the loop" during the arms-for-hostages dealings with Iran. But Walsh also said he found no evidence of criminal wrongdoing by Bush.

The Iran-contra scandal had erupted with the stunning disclosure Nov. 25, 1986, that some of the proceeds from secret arms sales to Iran had been diverted to help the Nicaraguan contras. This took place at a time when the United States had declared an embargo on direct U.S. arms sales to Iran and Congress had restricted aid to contra rebels attempting to overthrow the communist Sandinista government of Nicaragua.

A series of investigations ensued. Reagan appointed a board of inquiry chaired by former Republican senator John Tower of Texas. Walsh, a retired federal judge and an Oklahoma Republican, was appointed independent counsel on Dec. 19, 1986. And Congress established select Iran-contra investigating committees. With the board of inquiry and investigating committees having issued their reports in 1987, Walsh's report represented the last official word on the scandal. (*Background, earlier action, Congress and the Nation Vol. VII, p. 253; Congress and the Nation Vol. VIII, pp. 238, 240, 284*)

WALSH'S REPORT

The 566-page final report painted a damning portrait of the Reagan administration, which Walsh said was bent on covering up the secret policies. The report's main conclusion differed significantly from the one reached by the select congressional committees, which alleged that the scheme had been carried out largely by a "cabal of zealots" in the middle reaches of the Reagan administration. By contrast, Walsh said Reagan and his entire foreign policy team knowingly pursued secret programs that directly contravened the U.S. embargo on arms sales to Iran and the congressional restrictions on aid to the contras.

The report said, "Congress was defrauded. Its appropriations restrictions having been circumvented, Congress was led to believe that the administration was following the law." Moreover, Walsh alleged that cabinet-level officials deliberately attempted to make "scapegoats" of a handful of staff members of the National Security Council.

Despite the gravity of the charges against Reagan and his top lieutenants, Walsh achieved negligible prosecutorial success after an investigation that cost about $38 million. None of the high-level officials alleged to have been responsible for the scandal was brought to trial.

Walsh's investigation was stymied by several factors, including the controversial decision by Congress's Iran-contra committees to grant immunity to key players in the scandal and Bush's post-election pardon in 1992 of six Iran-contra defendants.

Just as the high-profile congressional probe of Iran-contra eventually triggered a powerful backlash, Walsh wrapped up his inquiry with his reputation tarnished. Walsh's long-standing Republican credentials did not protect him from the charge, made repeatedly by many congressional Republicans, that the investigation amounted to little more than a high-priced fishing expedition intended to sully the reputations of a pair of GOP presidents.

That line of attack resurfaced with a vengeance in the scorching written responses to Walsh's findings. The responses ran 1,150 pages and were included as part of the three-volume final report.

Reagan and Bush denied wrongdoing and denounced the investigation, as did most of the other former officials named by Walsh.

ADVICE TO CONGRESS

Walsh offered some parting advice to Congress, urging lawmakers to think carefully before granting immunity to secure the testimony of any witness. Appellate courts threw out Walsh's most important convictions, those of National Security Council staff aide Oliver L. North and Reagan national security adviser John M. Poindexter, on grounds that trial witnesses had been tainted by their exposure to the immunized congressional testimony of the two men.

Walsh said he accepted Congress's need to investigate high-profile cases quickly and thoroughly. But he warned that "if it wants to compel testimony by granting immunity, it has to realize that the odds are very strong that it's going to kill any resulting criminal prosecution."

He also expressed frustration with the section of the independent counsel law that essentially gave the attorney general the final say over the release of classified material in cases brought by independent counsels. "That gives [the attorney general] the power to kill the prosecution of an independent counsel," Walsh said.   ❑

Iraqi Asset Claims

The House in 1994 easily passed legislation (HR 3221) to set up a system to distribute approximately $1.2 billion in Iraqi assets that the United States froze when Iraq invaded Kuwait in August 1990. But the measure, sought by the Clinton administration, stalled in the Senate, where key senators objected that the House-passed bill gave insufficient priority to the claims of U.S. businesses and private citizens. Without legislative action, the funds remained frozen.

The House bill authorized the U.S. Foreign Claims Settlement Commission to use the frozen assets to pay long-standing private and government claims brought against the government of Iraq. HR 3221 gave the president the right to claim about 40 percent of the $1.2 billion for the government. Iraq owed the U.S. government about $2 billion; private claims accounted for about $3 billion.

Preference was to be given to the claims of U.S. soldiers injured during the 1991 Persian Gulf War and in the 1987 Iraqi missile attack on the U.S.S. *Stark,* as well as the relatives of those killed. Once all claimants were paid $10,000 each, members of these preferred groups would have gotten an additional $90,000. *(Persian Gulf War, Congress and the Nation Vol. VIII, p. 299; 1987 attack, Congress and the Nation Vol. VII, p. 315)*

The House passed HR 3221 on April 28, 1994, by a vote of 398–5, after a brief but intense debate over allowing former Iraqi soldiers to immigrate to the United States. The bill had been reported by the House Foreign Affairs Committee on Nov. 20, 1993 (H Rept 103-396, Part I). The bill did not get beyond the hearing stage in the Senate. ❏

Air Strikes on Iraq

A decision by Clinton to launch cruise missiles at an intelligence center in Baghdad on June 26, 1993, won wide support from lawmakers, but it also reopened a long-running debate over White House consultations with Congress and over war-making authority.

Clinton ordered the attack in response to what he called "compelling evidence" that Iraq had attempted to assassinate George Bush when the former president visited Kuwait in April. Sixteen suspects in the alleged attack, several of whom were said to have confessed to involvement in a plot to kill Bush, were facing charges in Kuwait.

The administration maintained that it had the right to act unilaterally under provisions of the U.N. charter that permitted nations to act in self-defense. Madeleine K. Albright, the U.S. envoy to the United Nations, reported to the Security Council on June 27 about evidence linking Iraq to the botched assassination attempt, including photos of a Toyota Land Cruiser filled with explosives said to be clearly of Iraqi design.

Members of Congress traditionally had ceded to a president the right to order lightning strikes that did not risk entangling U.S. forces in lengthy conflicts. But the Iraq attack became a first test of whether the Clinton administration would consult—or simply notify—Congress when it decided to use force. In this case, the administration attempted to notify congressional leaders shortly before the weekend attack. Officials did not consult Congress on the specific course of action, but the White House apparently sounded out some senior members about the possibility of a military response.

On June 28, Clinton sent a letter to Congress formally notifying members of the weekend's events. As Republican presidents before him had, he described the letter as "consistent with the War Powers Resolution" of 1973, a formulation designed to sidestep the question of whether that law was constitutional. *(War powers, box, p. 194)* ❏

Americans Missing in Cyprus

In 1994, Congress cleared a bill (HR 2826—PL 103-372) providing for the State Department to hunt for five Americans who had vanished in 1974 during a bloody conflict between Greeks and Turks on the Mediterranean island of Cyprus. Four of the missing Americans were elderly people who had retired to

the island and the fifth was a 17-year-old visiting Cyprus with his family.

The war had begun when the Greek-controlled military overthrew the elected government of Cyprus. Five days later, armed forces from Turkey invaded on behalf of the Turkish minority on the island. The interim military-led government fell and the elected government was restored, except in the northern third of the country, which was controlled by Turkey. Over the years, U.N. efforts to look for missing people on Cyprus had bogged down, and little was accomplished.

The House first passed the bill by voice vote Aug. 1, calling for a much broader investigation into the disappearances of 1,600 Greeks who remained unaccounted for, as well as 800 Turks who disappeared during Greek control of the island from 1963 to 1974. The State Department objected to the House-passed bill, saying that three years and an additional 12 employees would be required to conduct such an investigation.

The Senate passed a scaled-down version by voice vote Oct. 3. The House agreed to the Senate changes by voice vote Oct. 5, clearing the bill. President Clinton signed HR 2826 on Oct. 19. ❏

Treaty on Women

Fourteen years after President Jimmy Carter pledged U.S. support for a treaty designed to eliminate discrimination against women, the Senate Foreign Relations Committee approved ratification of the pact (Exec Rept, 96-2) by a vote of 13–4. The panel reported the treaty on Oct. 3, 1994 (Exec Rept 103-38), but the full Senate did not take it up before adjourning.

The United States had signed the treaty on July 17, 1980. Lack of support from both the Reagan and Bush administrations was the primary reason the treaty, known as the Convention on the Elimination of All Forms of Discrimination Against Women, had languished so long. The Clinton administration, however, asked the Senate to approve its ratification.

The accord, which had been ratified by 136 nations, set out a long list of goals for the women of the world, such as making sure that they had equal opportunities to work, draw benefits and earn the same pay as men. It also required signatories to set national minimum ages for marriage. Because of the potentially broad interpretation of some of these provisions, the State Department drew up a set of "reservations" to U.S. ratification that, among other things, explicitly said the treaty did not include a right to an abortion. ❏

Biodiversity Treaty

The Senate Foreign Relations Committee in 1994 recommended that the Senate approve ratification of a treaty to preserve diversity among the world's plant and animal species, despite concerns among some senators about the treaty's cost to the United States. The committee formally reported the Convention on Biological Diversity (Treaty Doc 103-20—Exec Rept 103-30) on July 11, 1994. The treaty, however, never was taken up by the full Senate during the 103rd Congress.

The treaty represented a multinational commitment to protecting the Earth's diverse species. President George Bush had opposed the treaty when it was signed by other nations in June 1992 at the U.N. Conference of Environment and Development in Rio de Janeiro, Brazil. But President Clinton supported it, and the United States signed it in June 1993. (*Environment summit, Congress and the Nation Vol. VIII, p. 528*)

In addition to approving the treaty's ratification, the Foreign Relations Committee adopted a nonbinding resolution, by Hank Brown, R-Colo., calling on Clinton to make an annual report to Congress on the treaty's costs and other effects, which critics said were too open-ended and uncertain. The resolution also urged the president to ensure that the costs of U.S. participation not exceed $100 million a year and that other U.S. interests were protected. ❑

1995–1996

Conflicts over foreign policy issues continued unabated in the 104th Congress. President Clinton's various foreign policy missteps during the first two years of his tenure—especially the peacekeeping mission in Somalia and his shifts on Bosnia—had opened the door to increased congressional activism on foreign affairs. The Republican takeover of the House and Senate as a result of the 1994 elections heightened the clashes between the White House and Capitol Hill and brought out Clinton's veto pen.

Bosnia overtook all other foreign policy issues in significance in the 104th Congress. It was an issue fraught with dangers and ripe for policy confrontations. Congress spent much of 1995 trying to legislate an end to U.S. participation in the United Nations-mandated arms embargo on the former Yugoslav republics. For the first time, members cleared antiembargo legislation, only to see it fall to a presidential veto.

But the arms embargo issue paled in comparison with the controversy that arose about the commitment of 20,000 U.S. ground troops as part of a North Atlantic Treaty Organization (NATO) force to police a U.S.-brokered peace agreement in Bosnia. Most Republicans and many Democrats opposed the deployment, but they lacked the votes needed to override an inevitable veto. The deployment proved to be a qualified success. U.S. and NATO troops achieved their primary goals of pacifying the country and separating the warring parties. But civil reconstruction and political unification lagged badly, necessitating the continued deployment of NATO troops. Clinton's announcement that a partial deployment would continue for 18 months beyond the one-year mission he had promised set off another round of criticism, but, again, no action was taken to stop it.

Other high-profile conflicts included a State Department authorization bill containing a series of challenges to Clinton's foreign policies that was vetoed after a bitter yearlong battle. The bill would have reorganized the foreign affairs bureaucracy and reversed a number of Clinton's policies on Asia.

Republicans took frequent shots at Clinton's peacekeeping policies. In the end, Congress reduced funding for U.N. peacekeeping missions and set some restrictions on U.S. participation.

GOP initiatives aimed at isolating Cuba, Iran and Libya by deterring foreign companies from investing there were enacted. Foreign governments and corporations, particularly in Europe, blasted the legislation as heavy-handed attempts to dictate their trade and investment decisions. Clinton balked at some of the bills' provisions as well, but election-year politics, two deadly aviation incidents and a compromise over wording convinced the administration to drop its objections.

By contrast, Congress refused to disrupt U.S. trade relations with China, despite members' outrage over some of China's policies and actions.

The Senate easily approved the second Strategic Arms Reduction Talks (START II) treaty. But action on a chemical weapons treaty was put off until the next Congress.

An attempt to make sweeping changes in the intelligence bureaucracy produced only modest results. The fiscal 1997 intelligence authorization bill left the Pentagon in charge of defense-related intelligence agencies instead of expanding the authority of the CIA director, as reformers had proposed.

Bosnia Policy

For most of 1995, debate on Bosnia followed the well-worn ruts of earlier battles over breaking the U.N.-mandated arms embargo on the former Yugoslav republics. Many on Capitol Hill wanted to lift the embargo so the Bosnian Muslim government could obtain weapons to offset the heavily armed forces of the country's ethnic Serb community. President Clinton had managed to stave off previous congressional attempts to clear antiembargo legislation but in 1995 had to veto one such effort (S 21).

But the battle over Bosnia policy took a sharp turn in a different direction late in the year when U.S.-brokered peace talks among the warring Yugoslav factions produced a peace agreement. Clinton previously had pledged to police a peace with 20,000 U.S. ground troops as part of a North Atlantic Treaty Organization (NATO) force. In a televised speech on Nov. 27, Clinton touted the peace agreement and outlined his reasons for deploying U.S. troops to enforce it.

The deployment was vehemently opposed by most Republicans and many Democrats, particularly in the House. But Congress clearly lacked the votes to block the planned deployment, so each chamber took a series of votes that added up to a murky signal of support for the troops (though not for the commander in chief) and grudging acquiescence in the deployment.

Clinton had pledged that U.S. troops would be out of Bosnia within a year but in late 1996 announced that they would remain another 18 months. Republicans were infuriated by the extension but took no action.

Away from the military front, GOP leaders in the House and Senate launched investigations of a secret White House decision in 1994 not to interfere with the shipment of arms from Iran to Muslim forces in Bosnia by way of neighboring Croatia. (*Box, p. 226*)

BACKGROUND

A cease-fire agreement reached at the end of 1994 produced a winter that was relatively peaceful by the bloody standards of the region. *(Background, 1993–1994 action, p.198)*

But the three-year-old conflict grew more violent in the early spring of 1995, with Serb forces overrunning U.N.-designated "safe areas." Troops serving in the United Nations Protection Force proved increasingly ineffectual—and were threatened themselves. More than 400 peacekeepers were held hostage by Serb forces at one point.

In a May 31 commencement speech at the U.S. Air Force Academy, Clinton said that, to save the U.N. peacekeeping forces, the United States should be prepared to join with its NATO allies to strengthen those forces—and, if necessary, to relocate them to more defensible positions. He said the administration would participate in such an operation only if NATO received a request for assistance and "after consultation with the Congress."

Two days later, on June 2, a U.S. F-16 fighter jet was shot down over northern Bosnia, heightening fears on Capitol Hill that the administration was on an unalterable course toward a much broader role in the conflict. Pilot Scott F. O'Grady was rescued after six days on the ground, having survived on insects and grass.

The developments sparked renewed efforts to lift the arms embargo, which had been imposed by the United Nations Sept. 25, 1991, on all the warring factions in what was then Yugoslavia. The embargo had benefited the better-armed Serbs and put the Bosnian Muslims at a serious disadvantage.

ARMS EMBARGO ISSUE

On June 8, 1995, the same day that pilot O'Grady was rescued, the House voted overwhelmingly to require Clinton to end the embargo upon receiving a request for military assistance from the Bosnian Muslims. However, the 318–99 vote was tempered by the fact that it was a rider to the foreign aid and State Department authorization bill (HR 1561), which Clinton had already pledged to veto.

Meanwhile in the Senate, Majority Leader Bob Dole, R-Kan., who had been urging an end to the arms embargo for two years, worked to craft a resolution authorizing the use of U.S. ground forces to assist in the withdrawal of U.N. peacekeepers from Bosnia, then requiring an end to the arms embargo against the Muslims. The NATO allies had opposed the lifting of the embargo because they feared for the safety of their peacekeeping troops in Bosnia.

While Republicans argued among themselves and with the administration over Dole's proposal, the debate shifted again. On June 16, the U.N. Security Council unanimously approved a resolution creating a "Rapid Reaction Force" to help protect U.N. personnel in case of attack and prevent a replay of the taking of U.N. peacekeepers as hostages. The administration gave its blessing to the plan in hopes that, by reinforcing the U.N. peacekeepers, it could avoid the possibility of having to go in and extricate them. But the day before the U.N. vote, Republican leaders wrote to Clinton expressing deep skepticism about providing U.S. troops or financing for the new force.

In a clear attempt to avoid a battle on Capitol Hill, Clinton planned to support the new force through the use of special drawdown and waiver authorities that did not require congressional approval. GOP leaders accused the president of trying an end run by failing to seek an appropriation for the aid package.

On July 26, the Senate gave overwhelming support to S 21, a bill sponsored by Dole and Joseph I. Lieberman, D-Conn., requiring an end to the embargo. Despite last-minute lobbying by the president, the Senate passed the bill by a **key vote of 69–29 (R 48–5; D 21–24),** two votes more than needed to override a veto with all senators voting. The bill required the president essentially to end the arms embargo after the U.N. troops were withdrawn or 12 weeks after the Bosnian government requested the force to leave. The president could extend the 12-week time frame for successive one-month periods to provide a safe withdrawal of U.N. forces. The bill included no direct military aid for the Muslims, but the hope was that, once the United States broke the embargo, other countries would follow suit and provide arms to the Bosnian Muslims. *(1995 key votes, p. 1025)*

Before final passage of S 21, the Senate July 26 adopted a pair of amendments aimed at ensuring that the president would seek multilateral backing for lifting the embargo before taking that step on his own. The Senate voted 75–23 to adopt an amendment by Sam Nunn, D-Ga., requiring that, once conditions were met to trigger a unilateral termination of the embargo, the president sponsor a resolution in the U.N. Security Council to end the arms ban. The Senate adopted, 57–41, a William S. Cohen, R-Maine, amendment calling for a U.N. General Assembly vote on ending the embargo if the Security Council failed to adopt the resolution called for under Nunn's proposal.

The administration warned that lifting the embargo would force the withdrawal of U.N. troops from Bosnia, in turn forcing Clinton to make good on his pledge to deploy U.S. ground troops to help in the withdrawal. But the argument was to no avail, as the House approved S 21 by a 298–128 vote on Aug. 1.

Clinton vetoed S 21 on Aug. 11, calling its mandate "the wrong step at the wrong time." Although the Senate and House had passed the bill by more than enough votes to override the president, Clinton possessed many advantages, not the least of which was Congress's hesitancy to take the reins of foreign policy. With a four-week August recess looming before Congress would vote on overriding the veto, the president also had more time to make his case.

TROOP DEPLOYMENT ISSUE

Once again, however, events overtook the debate. An allied bombing campaign during August pounded Serb military targets and ultimately brought them to the negotiating table.

With negotiations under way, the administration began efforts to sell Congress on the need for a U.S. role in a Balkan peacekeeping force. For their part, lawmakers became more insistent in their demand that Clinton go beyond consulting with Congress and seek formal congressional authorization for any Bosnian mission, in the way that President George Bush sought Congress's authorization before the 1991 Persian Gulf War. *(Gulf War Resolution, Congress and the Nation Vol. VIII, p. 309)*

CONGRESSIONAL PANELS PROBE U.S. ROLE IN IRANIAN ARMS SHIPMENTS TO BOSNIA

Republican leaders in 1996 launched a high-profile investigation of reports that President Clinton had given a green light in April 1994 to secret Iranian arms shipments to Bosnia through Croatia. Those signals had come at the same time the administration was lobbying Congress against unilaterally lifting the international arms embargo on Bosnia. The White House had not notified Congress about the secret policy.

Senate Majority Leader Bob Dole, R-Kan., compared the Iran-Bosnia arms deal with the Iran-contra scandal under President Ronald Reagan and charged that the Clinton administration had opened the door to Iranian involvement in the Balkans, thereby heightening the risk for U.S. troops in Bosnia. Republicans also charged that the Iranian shipments made a mockery of the administration's high-profile commitment to uphold the arms embargo, and they challenged the administration's decision not to notify Congress of its actions regarding the Iranian arms shipments. *(1993–1994 Bosnia policy, p. 197; Iran-contra affair, Congress and the Nation Vol. VII, p. 253)*

President Clinton denied any wrongdoing. The administration indicated that it did not object to the Iranian arms shipments because it wanted to aid Bosnia's Muslims in their struggle against the far better-armed Serbs—a goal that nearly everyone, including Dole, endorsed. Democrats saw the GOP probe as election-year politics and an attempt to get even for Democratic congressional investigations of Republican Presidents Reagan and George Bush.

Background

The flurry of interest in the 1994 events was triggered by an April 1996 story in the *Los Angeles Times* indicating U.S. diplomats had told Croatia that the United States would not object to the establishment of an arms pipeline for Iranian weapons to flow to Bosnia. A similar report had appeared in the *Washington Post* nearly a year earlier, but no one in Congress had paid much attention to the story then.

When the issue resurfaced, the White House dismissed it as old news. But Dole said the *Los Angeles Times* story added an important new element by showing that Clinton was directly involved in the decision to turn a blind eye to the Iranian shipments.

Under existing law, the president was required to send Congress a "finding," or formal policy justification, for every covert action. A 1991 law (PL 102-88) defined a covert action as "an activity or activities of the United States government to influence political, economic or military conditions abroad, where it is intended that the role of the United States government will not be apparent or acknowledged publicly."

The White House asked the Intelligence Oversight Board, a small, presidentially appointed panel responsible for investigating wrongdoing in the intelligence community, to review the administration's decision to allow the Iranian arms shipments to see if a finding should have been issued. The board concluded that the Iranian arms shipments did not meet the legal definition of a covert action and thus did not require a presidential finding.

However, the White House denied a request by Senate Intelligence Committee Chairman Arlen Specter, R-Pa., for access to the board's secret report on the grounds that it needed to protect confidential policy discussions. That amounted to a claim of "executive privilege," and it further infuriated Republicans.

Congressional Investigations

The House created a select subcommittee of the International Relations Committee to investigate. A resolution (H Res 416—H Rept 104-551) establishing the subcommittee was reported by the House Rules Committee May 2 and passed by the full House, 224–187,

On Sept. 29, the Senate voted, 94–2, to call on the president to seek advance approval for deploying forces to Bosnia, except for a temporary mission to evacuate U.N. peacekeepers. The sense-of-the-Senate provision, offered by Judd Gregg, R-N.H., was an amendment to the State Department appropriations bill (HR 2076). Administration officials, protective of the president's foreign policy prerogatives, would not agree to submit such a request. But an acknowledgment existed that Congress would be asked to write the check for the deployment.

Planning for a NATO-led peacekeeping mission took on increased urgency after Bosnia's warring parties agreed to a cease-fire Oct. 11. On Oct. 26, 50 Senate Republicans and Wisconsin Democrat Herb Kohl sent Clinton a letter urging him to request congressional authorization in advance of any deployment.

On Oct. 30, just two days before the U.S.-brokered peace talks began at Wright-Patterson Air Force Base near Dayton, Ohio, the House adopted, 315–103, a nonbinding resolution (H Res 247) expressing the sense of the House that a successful outcome for the peace talks should not assume the deployment of

U.S. troops and that any deployment should be authorized by Congress. Hours before the vote, the chief U.S. mediator, Assistant Secretary of State Richard C. Holbrooke, had warned that approval of the resolution could undermine U.S. efforts to secure an agreement. The administration argued that the talks would not have begun and could not produce results without the assurance that U.S. troops would help enforce an agreement. Their arguments did not sway votes, but a follow-up effort by GOP conservatives to pass binding legislation to restrict funds for a deployment was deferred.

Hoping to forestall more embarrassing votes, Clinton said Oct. 31 that he expected to consult "intensely" with the leaders of Congress. Democrats who supported Clinton's position urged him to assure Congress that, between the conclusion of a peace agreement and the deployment of combat units, members would have enough time to conduct an informed debate on the specific deployment plan.

Clinton and other top officials attempted to offer Congress that assurance, but House Republicans refused to believe them.

May 8. A resolution (H Res 417—H Rept 104-559) to provide $995,000 to finance the inquiry was reported by the House Oversight Committee May 6 and passed by the House, 225–203, on May 8.

The subcommittee, chaired by Henry J. Hyde, R-Ill., also consisted of Republicans Doug Bereuter of Nebraska, Dan Burton of Indiana, Cass Ballenger of North Carolina and Sam Brownback of Kansas; and Democrats Lee H. Hamilton of Indiana, Howard L. Berman of California and Alcee L. Hastings of Florida.

Hearings were held by both the Senate Intelligence and House International Relations committees.

During the week of May 20, former assistant secretary of state Richard C. Holbrooke and Deputy Secretary of State Strobe Talbott testified before the Senate Intelligence Committee on whether the administration's decision not to object to Iran's arms shipments met the legal definition of a covert action. The two described the policy decision as a risky but necessary diplomatic maneuver that did not constitute a covert action.

The administration's approach was ultimately vindicated, they said, by the peace agreement signed in Dayton in December 1995. Yet their testimony and information released by Specter showed that the White House had been acutely aware of the political sensitivity of appearing to acquiesce in Iran's military role in Bosnia. National Security Adviser Anthony Lake ordered that no written report be made of the decision, according to Specter's information. *(1995–1996 Bosnia policy, p. 224)*

Testimony by Peter Galbraith, ambassador to Croatia, and Charles E. Redman, former special envoy for the Balkans crisis, before the House International Relations Committee on May 30 generally affirmed previous testimony and news accounts.

Galbraith detailed the subtle diplomatic signals he sent to Croatian leaders indicating that the United States would not protest the shipping of Iranian arms through Croatia to neighboring Bosnia. A former Democratic staffer for the Senate Foreign Relations Committee, Galbraith testified that in calls to his former Senate colleagues to lobby against a unilateral lifting of the arms embargo he had made clear that arms were going through and the United States was not objecting. He added that, when asked, he would tell people which nations were providing the weapons. But the two diplomats said the administration had not asked third parties to approach the Croatians. "This was indeed a Croatian idea," Redman said.

Select Subcommittee Report

Hyde's special subcommittee wrapped up its investigation Oct. 10, 1996, with a 200-page report charging that "several administration officials gave false testimony to Congress on the development and implementation of the Iranian green light policy." But Hyde stopped well short of pointing the finger at anyone in the administration. "We do not accuse anyone or any institution of criminality. We simply say we did not receive candid testimony," Hyde said.

The report said that several senior officials, including Lake, gave statements that contradicted Galbraith's sworn congressional testimony. The subcommittee referred the matter to the Justice Department for criminal investigation.

Administration officials joined congressional Democrats in denouncing the report as an election-eve attempt to tarnish the president. "It is our belief that no laws were broken, no wrongdoing occurred, no covert actions took place, no false statements given, no U.S. interests harmed," said a statement by the subcommittee's Democratic members.

Hyde said that the subcommittee was unable to provide evidence to back up its charges because the administration dragged its feet in declassifying key documents.

On Nov. 8, the House Republican conference overwhelmingly approved a resolution calling for "prompt" House action to block any deployment. On Nov. 17, the House passed, by a **key vote of 243–171 (R 214–12; D 28–159; I 1–0),** a bill (HR 2606), drafted by Joel Hefley, R-Colo., to block deployment unless Congress approved funds for it.

Before the Senate took up HR 2606, a peace agreement was reached. After three weeks of intensive negotiations, the weary leaders of the warring parties initialed a package of military, economic and political understandings on Nov. 21.

Efforts on Capitol Hill to keep U.S. troops out of Bosnia quickly collapsed, underscoring the reality that a president enjoyed wide discretion in deciding whether to deploy U.S. forces on risky missions abroad, no matter the vehemence of congressional opponents. Clinton had presented Congress with a fait accompli. He had staked the U.S. government's credibility abroad on a U.S.-brokered deal that was guaranteed for about a year by a NATO-led force that would include a substantial U.S. ground contingent. Moreover, given that Congress had no practical way to bar Clinton from sending the troops, members faced the possibility that any effort to compel a withdrawal by cutting off funds would put the troops at greater risk.

In a round of hearings at the end of November, administration officials told congressional panels that, in addition to the 20,000 troops in Bosnia, the operation would require support from 5,000 U.S. troops stationed in neighboring Croatia and 7,000 in Italy, Hungary and other countries. The total cost was estimated at $2 billion. The need to cover those costs convinced Clinton to let the fiscal 1996 defense appropriations bill (HR 2126—PL 104-61) become law without his signature on Dec. 1, despite his objection that it contained $7 billion more than he had requested. *(1996 defense appropriations, p. 301)*

With advance units already on the ground in Bosnia, Congress shied away from cutting off funds. One the eve of the Dec. 14 signing in Paris of the Balkan peace accord, the Senate brushed aside HR 2606 by a vote of 22–77. The House later Dec. 13 rejected a second bill (HR 2770) to deny funds for the mission, but the vote was surprisingly close—210–218.

After rejecting the funding cutoff, each chamber took several symbolic votes on the mission. The Senate Dec. 13 adopted, 69–30, a bipartisan measure (S J Res 44) saying that the president could fulfill his commitment to send troops, provided he also promised to begin building up the armed forces of Bosnia's Muslim-led government. Earlier the same day, the Senate rejected, 47–52, a resolution (S Con Res 35) that would have objected to Clinton's policy but expressed support for the troops.

Also on Dec. 13, the House approved, 287–141, a resolution (H Res 302) that disowned the deployment decision, supported the troops, but insisted that the United States remain scrupulously neutral among Bosnia's contending parties. Then early Dec. 14, the House rejected, 190–237, a resolution (H Res 306) that would have declared support for the troops without slamming Clinton's policy.

DEPLOYMENT EXTENSION

Early indications that U.S. troops would not be leaving Bosnia by Dec. 20, 1996, the one-year anniversary of the deployment, as promised by the Clinton administration, drew sharp GOP criticism. The official announcement of an 18-month extension came on Nov. 15.

Clinton told a White House press conference that the initial deployment of 20,000 U.S. troops, as part of a 60,000-member force, had met its principal goal of ending the open warfare among Bosnia's ethnic factions. But he said the parallel, civilian-led effort to reconstruct Bosnia's economy and civil society had lagged behind and would progress only if NATO-led troops remained behind for a while. This smaller, reorganized NATO-led force at the outset was to include 8,500 Americans among its 31,000 troops in Bosnia. A reserve multilateral force of 5,000 would be stationed outside the country.

Many Republicans who had opposed the U.S. Bosnia mission in the first place contended that the extended deployment confirmed their fears that U.S. forces would slip into an open-ended commitment in an unending ethnic struggle. But no action was taken to end the deployment.

OTHER ISSUES

Congress in 1996 agreed to foot the bill for the Bosnian deployment, though not before complaining about Clinton's plan to use $200 million from the defense budget for aid and reconstruction in Bosnia.

The overall price tag for U.S. participation in the NATO military operation was estimated at $1.9 billion for fiscal 1996. Of that total, $1.3 billion was to come from savings from lower-than-expected inflation and cuts in unspecified accounts. The administration requested $820 million in supplemental appropriations for fiscal 1996 to cover $620 million in military expenses and $200 million in aid to Bosnia. This portion was to be financed by rescinding funds previously appropriated for the National Reconnaissance Office, an agency found to be hoarding money in a secret account. *(NRO, 1996 intelligence authorization, p. 242)*

The $200 million for civilian assistance, not the military expenses, triggered criticism on Capitol Hill. No one denied that Bosnia needed a massive infusion of outside aid, but many members objected to using Pentagon funds for activities they saw as only marginally related to national security. They thought the money should come out of the State Department budget. (In addition to the $200 million, the State Department did plan to shift about $330 million from foreign assistance accounts to underwrite various reconstruction and humanitarian projects in Bosnia.)

Clinton's full request was included in an omnibus appropriations bill for fiscal 1996 (HR 3019—PL 104-134), which was signed into law April 26, 1996, but the final bill included two Senate-approved amendments placing restrictions on the $200 million in reconstruction aid. The amendments, sponsored by Dole and Mitch McConnell, R-Ky., had been adopted by voice vote March 13. The first was in response to persistent reports that Bosnia's Muslim-led government was dragging its feet in ejecting Iranian forces, as required by the 1995 Dayton peace accords. It barred use of the funds until Clinton certified that all foreign military forces except the NATO-led force had left Bosnia and that Bosnia officials had ceased collaborating with Iranian officials on intelligence matters. The second amendment required that the funds be used in the area controlled by U.S. troops or in the Bosnian capital of Sarajevo. Expenditure of the money was to be cut off within three months unless bilateral contributions from all other countries matched the U.S. total aid package of $532 million.

The omnibus fiscal 1997 appropriations bill (HR 3610—PL 104-208), signed into law Sept. 30, 1996, also included restrictions on Bosnia aid, withholding half the funds until the president certified that Iranian troops had withdrawn and intelligence collaboration with Iran had ceased.

In other action, Congress in 1996 cleared legislation (HR 2778—PL 104-117) exempting from income taxes the full pay of enlisted personnel and some of the pay for officers stationed in Bosnia, Croatia and Macedonia as part of the U.N. peacekeeping force. Most of the tax breaks were standard fare for troops stationed in combat zones, but troops in the Bosnian conflict could not qualify for those benefits unless Congress passed separate legislation because Clinton had not declared the operation a combat mission.

HR 2778 had been reported (H Rept 104-465) by the House Ways and Means Committee Feb. 29, 1996, and was passed by the House, 416–0, March 5. The Senate cleared the bill by voice vote March 6, and it was signed into law March 20.   ❑

State, Aid Authorizations

Congress in 1996 cleared a $13 billion fiscal 1996–1997 State Department authorization bill after a bitter yearlong battle. The bill (HR 1561), which would have downsized the foreign affairs bureaucracy and reversed a number of administration policies on Asia, was vetoed by President Clinton. An attempt in the House to override the veto failed.

The bill contained a scaled-back version of a plan devised by Senate Foreign Relations Committee Chairman Jesse Helms, R-N.C., to abolish three foreign affairs agencies and merge them with the State Department. A House-Senate conference committee had modified Helms's proposal by requiring Clinton to eliminate just one of the three: the Agency for International Development (AID), the Arms Control and Disarmament Agency (ACDA) or the United States Information Agency (USIA).

The changes adopted in conference did not soften the deep-seated opposition of the White House, which declared that the consolidation would infringe on the president's prerogatives. In addition, the administration strongly objected to several provisions aimed at boosting relations with Taiwan. Administration officials feared that enactment of the bill would increase tensions with China, which regarded Taiwan as a breakaway province. Objections were raised to other foreign policy provisions as well.

HR 1561, as originally passed by the House, had also included authorizations for the foreign assistance program. But foreign aid authorizations were not included in the Senate version of HR 1561 or in the conference bill. A foreign aid authorization bill had not been enacted since 1985. *(1994 aid authorization, p. 202)*

BACKGROUND

Hoping to preempt congressional Republicans' plans to make deep cuts in its budget, the State Department began 1995 by pushing its own proposal to shrink the size of the foreign policy bureaucracy. The plan—which the State Department presented Jan. 5 as a follow-up to Vice President Al Gore's campaign to "reinvent government"—called for absorbing AID, the lead agency for providing foreign assistance; ACDA, which provided arms control advice to the cabinet; and USIA, which managed a host of international broadcasting and exchange programs.

But Gore announced Jan. 27 that his National Performance Review staff had concluded that AID, ACDA and USIA should remain as separate agencies under the overall policy guidance of the State Department. Gore directed the State Department and the three agencies to streamline their administrative services and eliminate duplicative functions, estimating that they could save $5 billion over five years.

The ill-fated State Department proposal, however, inadvertently gave Helms an opening to try to rewrite the organizational chart for the foreign policy agencies. On March 15 he released a foreign policy plan that included, among other things, consolidation of AID, ACDA and USIA within the State Department. Helms also called for "privatizing" foreign assistance through the creation of a quasi-private international development foundation to take over AID's role in providing economic aid to poor countries.

HOUSE ACTION

Divided sharply along partisan lines and under the threat of a presidential veto, the House passed HR 1561 June 8 by a vote of 222–192. It had been reported by the House International Relations Committee on May 19 (H Rept 104-128, Part I).

HR 1561, which contained authorizations for both the State Department and foreign aid accounts, authorized $16.5 billion in fiscal 1996 and $15.3 billion in fiscal 1997. The administration had requested $18.2 billion for fiscal 1996.

The House bill, like Helms's plan, proposed to fold the three independent agencies into an expanded State Department. Republicans insisted that the reorganization would streamline a foreign policy bureaucracy that had grown unchecked for decades, while Democrats argued that the consolidation would save no money and would result in a bloated State Department.

The bill mandated deep cuts in aid for Africa and other poor nations, while leaving the politically popular assistance programs for Israel and Egypt untouched. The bill also contained a number of policy provisions affecting specific countries, including Cuba, North Korea, Russia, China, Turkey, Pakistan and Northern Ireland. *(North Korea, p. 236)*

Early floor action was dominated by consideration of an antiabortion amendment offered by Christopher H. Smith, R-N.J. The amendment sought to reinstitute restrictions on aid for international family planning programs that had been imposed during the Bush and Reagan administrations. It would have cut off aid for the U.N. Population Fund unless that agency shut down its activities in China, which had been condemned for using coercive methods to limit population growth. After an emotional debate, the House adopted the amendment, 240–181, on May 24. A similar amendment had stalled the fiscal 1996 foreign operations appropriations bill (HR 1868) for months. *(1996 aid appropriations, p. 231)*

Smith was also at the center of an immigration debate because of the language he had inserted in the original bill barring the forced repatriation of certain high-risk refugees from Laos, Cambodia or Vietnam, such as those who had served with U.S. forces in Vietnam, and authorizing $30 million to help resettle thousands of them in the United States. Opponents charged that the funding would raise false hopes among the refugees that they ultimately would be granted asylum in the United States. Doug Bereuter, R-Neb., offered an amendment to strip the provision, but the House on May 24 adopted, 266–156, a modified Smith amendment that set no specific authorization level for the resettlement program.

The latter phase of the House debate was dominated by the related issues of Bosnia policy and Congress's role in sending troops into combat.

In a sharp rejection of the administration's approach toward the war in the former Yugoslavia, the House voted overwhelmingly to require the president to lift the three-year-old U.N. arms embargo against Bosnia's Muslims. The amendment, by Democrat Steny H. Hoyer of Maryland, was approved, 318–99, on June 8. *(Bosnia policy, p. 224)*

Anxious over the prospects that U.S. ground troops might soon be deployed to Bosnia, the House rejected a Republican-led effort to repeal the 1973 War Powers Resolution (PL 93-148). The amendment, proposed by Henry J. Hyde, R-Ill., would have scrapped the controversial law, which required that the president withdraw U.S. forces from overseas military missions within 60 days unless Congress authorized their deployment. The president could extend the deadline another 30 days in emergency situations. Hyde's proposal would have retained the law's reporting requirements. Despite an appeal from House Speaker Newt Gingrich, R-Ga., the House voted 201–217 to defeat the amendment on June 7. *(War Powers Resolution, box, p. 194)*

In other action, the House May 23 adopted, 276–134, a Sam Brownback, R-Kan., amendment slashing $478 million in fiscal 1997. But an amendment by Dan Burton, R-Ind., to cut AID's operating expenses by about $69 million in fiscal 1996 and $22 million more in fiscal 1997 was turned back, 182–236, on June 8.

SENATE ACTION

The Senate dealt with the State Department and foreign aid authorizations in separate bills.

Foreign Aid

The Senate Foreign Relations Committee reported a fiscal 1996–1997 foreign aid authorization bill (S 961—S Rept 104-99) on June 23. The bill, which would have authorized about $9 billion for foreign aid in fiscal 1996 and $8.7 billion in fiscal 1997, was not taken up on the floor.

The committee bill, among other things, would have authorized funding for the U.N. Population Fund, eased sanctions on aid to Pakistan, denied aid to Turkey unless it lifted its blockade of Armenia, and cut off aid to Russia if it followed through on a planned sale of nuclear power plants to Iran.

State Department

The Senate Foreign Relations Committee had reported a State Department authorization bill June 9 (S 908—S Rept 104-95). The Senate passed HR 1561 by a vote of 82–16 on Dec. 14, after substituting a revised version of S 908.

The committee bill, containing Helms's plan to disband AID, ACDA and USIA, was reported on a 10–8 party-line vote. Partisan divisions continued when the bill reached the floor, delaying final action for more than six months.

The Senate took some early action on the bill, adopting, 94–2, on July 31 an amendment by Helms to cut $10 million in funding from the fiscal 1996 U.S. contribution to the United Nations unless the U.N. secretary general helped resolve debts owed to U.S. businesses by what Helms called the United Nations' "deadbeat diplomats." The Senate also adopted by voice vote an amendment by Helms and John Kerry, D-Mass., that included some concessions to the administration. The amendment eliminated the bill's restrictions on funding for liaison offices with North Korea and extended the president's authority to provide aid to the Palestinian Authority. Despite that, the administration and Senate Democrats remained adamantly opposed to the bill.

Helms was given a shot at passing S 908 on Aug. 1, but in a pair of votes, Republicans failed to muster the 60 votes needed to cut off a Democratic filibuster. Both GOP attempts to invoke cloture fell short on 55–45 near party-line splits. Majority Leader Bob Dole, R-Kan., then halted debate, although he left the bill on the calendar.

Helms retaliated over the next several months by holding up 18 ambassadorial nominees and a pair of important arms control treaties—the Strategic Arms Reduction Talks (START II)

treaty and the Chemical Weapons Convention. The stalled envoys included Clinton's designees for postings in Bosnia and several former Soviet republics. The most prominent nominee was former senator Jim Sasser (D-Tenn., 1977–1993), who was waiting to take up his post as ambassador to China. *(START II, p. 320; Chemical Weapons Convention, p. 321)*

When the fiscal 1996 foreign aid appropriations bill (HR 1868) reached the floor Sept. 20, Helms attempted to attach a scaled-back version of his State Department proposal that would have eliminated two of the three agencies. He also indicated that under the right circumstances he might accept a vote on legislation abolishing one, to be chosen by the administration. Kerry expressed interest, but the administration dug in its heels, and Helms withdrew the amendment.

After three more months of hardball tactics and tortuous negotiations, Helms and Kerry finally reached an agreement Dec. 7 on a greatly watered-down version of Helms's original reorganization plan. Instead of forcing the elimination of the three agencies, the legislation mandated that the administration come up with $1.7 billion in spending cuts from those agencies and the State Department over five years, with the bulk of the cuts to come from salaries and other administrative expenses. However, the deal apparently would result in the merger of at least one of the agencies with the State Department because cuts to State's administrative accounts were limited to 15 percent of the total.

Several other changes were made in the bill. Helms agreed to drop a pet provision to grant asylum in the United States to refugees from regimes with coercive population control policies. The final version also softened sections aimed at limiting U.S. participation in the United Nations, including easing proposed restrictions on sharing intelligence data with the United Nations to allow the president greater latitude.

The agreement ended the logjam over Clinton's ambassadorial appointments and the arms control agreements, as well as unrelated bills that had been caught up in the dispute, including a constitutional amendment on flag burning and a bill to stiffen economic pressure on Cuba. *(Flag burning, p. 754; Cuba sanctions, p. 237)*

CONFERENCE

The House agreed to the conference report on HR 1561 (H Rept 104-478) by a vote of 226–172 on March 12, 1996. The Senate approved it by a vote of 52–44 on March 28, clearing the bill.

House-Senate conferees agreed to provide about $13 billion in spending for the State Department and other foreign policy agencies—$6.5 billion for fiscal 1996 and $6.5 billion for fiscal 1997.

The bill called for abolishing all three of the foreign policy agencies on Helms's original list but gave the president the option of waiving the requirement for two of the three, meaning that just one would have to go.

The final bill also was laden with proposals addressing important and obscure overseas issues.

The measure included a series of China-related provisions, reflecting GOP concerns over China's increasingly aggressive military and diplomatic posture. Democrats complained that the provisions would provoke Beijing at a time when Sino-American relations had been buffeted by disputes over Taiwan, trade and nuclear proliferation. *(U.S.-China relations, p. 240)*

Democrats were particularly exercised over provisions aimed at signaling U.S. support for Taiwan. One would have asserted the primacy of the 1979 Taiwan Relations Act (PL 96-8) over the 1982 joint communiqué between the United States and China. The somewhat arcane proposal was intended to ensure that the United States provided Taipei with a steady supply of defensive weapons, as stipulated in the 1979 law. The communiqué, concluded three years later by Chinese leaders and President Ronald Reagan, called for the United States to gradually reduce its weapons sales to Taiwan. *(1979 law, Congress and the Nation Vol. V, p. 65; joint communiqué, Congress and the Nation Vol. VI, p. 154)*

Conferees also included a sense-of-Congress provision stating that the president of Taiwan should be allowed to visit the United States in 1996. Clinton's decision in 1995—made under congressional pressure—to grant Taiwan President Lee Teng-Hui a visa to visit the United States had badly strained U.S.-China relations.

The legislation urged the president to appoint a special envoy to Tibet, which had been occupied by China for decades. It also called on the president not to visit China until a marked improvement was seen in the human rights situation in China and Tibet. And the bill would have made it easier for victims of regimes practicing coercive population policies to seek political asylum in the United States, a provision clearly aimed at China's one-child-per-family policy.

The bill also would have prevented the president from expanding the U.S. diplomatic mission in Vietnam unless he certified that its government was cooperating in efforts to recover U.S. servicemen still missing from the war in Southeast Asia. Many Republicans had not forgiven Clinton for restoring diplomatic ties with Vietnam in 1995. *(Vietnam policy, p. 246)*

The measure banned funding for the repatriation of Vietnamese, Laotians and Cambodians unless they had been given a fair hearing by U.S. immigration officers and unless those having refugee status under U.S. law had been offered resettlement outside their native countries. The controversial provision had been blamed for causing riots in refugee camps in Hong Kong, when residents of the camps apparently believed they could avoid being returned to Vietnam.

The bill also contained a provision to prohibit U.S. aid to nations that blocked delivery of shipments of U.S. humanitarian aid to other countries. The prohibition, designed to punish Turkey for its blockade of Armenia, could be waived by the president in the interest of national security.

VETO, OVERRIDE ATTEMPT

Clinton vetoed HR 1561 on April 12. The president primarily criticized its foreign policy provisions, particularly the proposals intended to boost military ties with Taiwan and impose restrictions on funds for normalizing diplomatic relations with Vietnam. Clinton also charged that, by mandating the elimina-

tion of one of the three agencies, the bill "would seriously impede the president's authority to organize and administer foreign affairs agencies to best serve the nation's interests and the administration's foreign policy priorities."

A House attempt on April 30 to override the veto failed. The House voted 234–188 in favor of overriding the veto, 48 votes short of the two-thirds needed to accomplish that objective.

The bill's demise marked a bitter defeat for Senate Foreign Relations Committee Chairman Helms, who had been on a quest to scale back the foreign affairs bureaucracy almost since taking the chairmanship in 1995. ❑

1996 Aid Appropriations

Congress in early 1996 cleared a $12.1 billion fiscal 1996 foreign operations appropriations bill (HR 1868). The bill, which had been stalled for months by a dispute over international family planning programs, was first attached to a temporary spending bill signed into law Jan. 26, 1996 (HR 2880—PL 104-99). HR 1868 was signed into law a second time—this time as a free-standing bill—on Feb. 12 (PL 104-107).

The foreign aid bill—which funded nearly all U.S. bilateral aid, support for international financial institutions, and subsidies for American exporters—had enjoyed broad bipartisan backing. But a House-passed provision reimposing Reagan-era restrictions on overseas population programs proved intractable during conference negotiations. A compromise passing off the dispute to the House International Relations and Senate Foreign Relations committees permitted the bill to move forward. Prospects for a resolution in the authorizing committees appeared slim, however, given that no foreign aid authorization bill had become law in a decade and the fiscal 1996 bill (HR 1561) under consideration was loaded with GOP proposals opposed by the administration. *(1996 foreign aid authorization, p. 228)*

HR 1868 cut President Clinton's $14.8 billion request by $2.7 billion. But a number of popular items—such as aid to the Middle East nations—were untouched by the GOP budget-cutters. The legislation provided $3 billion in aid for Israel and $2.1 billion for Egypt, the same levels as in recent years.

Many of the reductions in Clinton's request fell on programs for the poorest countries, reflecting deep Republican skepticism toward such programs. Arguing that such countries benefited more from private investment than from traditional bilateral aid, Republicans moved to increase guarantees for export assistance programs. Funding for the Overseas Private Investment Corporation (OPIC) guaranteed loan program was nearly tripled, from $26 million in fiscal 1995 to $68 million.

The bill included a number of policy changes sought by the administration, including the easing of long-standing restrictions on aid to Pakistan and Azerbaijan. It extended the president's authority to provide assistance to the Palestinian Authority and provided funds to underwrite a U.S. nuclear agreement with North Korea. *(Palestinian aid, box, p. 232; U.S.-Korea agreement, p. 221, p. 247)*

The final bill also contained a one-year ban on U.S. use of antipersonnel mines. The ban had originally been attached by

PALESTINIAN AID

Five times in 1995, Congress passed short-term extensions of the Middle East Peace Facilitation Act, the 1994 law (PL 103-236) that granted the president authority to waive a host of long-standing statutes barring aid and diplomatic contacts with the Palestinians. The act initially expired on July 1, 1995. *(Israeli-PLO agreement, p. 202; 1994–1995 State Department authorization, p. 212)*

An 18-month extension of the act was included in the fiscal 1995 foreign operations appropriations bill (HR 1868), which cleared in early 1996. *(1996 foreign aid appropriations, p. 231)*

In the meantime, Congress passed a series of stopgap bills extending the waiver authority:

- S 962, cleared June 29, 1995, ran until Aug. 15 (PL 104-17).
- HR 2161, cleared Aug. 11, ran until Oct. 1 (PL 104-22).
- HR 2404, cleared Sept. 29, ran until Nov. 1 (PL 104-30). (A delay in its consideration caused some embarrassment during Palestine Liberation Organization leader Yasir Arafat's visit to Washington to sign a Sept. 28 agreement ending Israel's military occupation of much of the West Bank.)
- HR 2589, cleared Nov. 9, ran until Dec. 31 (PL 104-47).
- HR 2808, cleared Dec. 31, ran until March 31, 1996 (PL 104-89).

the Senate to the fiscal 1996 defense authorization bill (HR 1530), but the Pentagon vehemently opposed the provision and it had been dropped in conference. Then, with no fanfare, Senate sponsor Patrick J. Leahy, D-Vt., had inserted the provision into HR 1868. The Pentagon remained opposed, arguing that a blanket prohibition on the use of land mines would impede military effectiveness.

HOUSE ACTION

The House passed HR 1868 on July 11, 1995, by a vote of 333–89. The $11.9 billion appropriations bill had been reported by the House Appropriations Committee June 15 (H Rept 104-143).

The committee bill reflected the limited agenda of Sonny Callahan, R-Ala., who had become chairman of the Foreign Operations Subcommittee of the House Appropriations Committee with the Republican takeover of the 104th Congress. In writing his first foreign operations bill, Callahan wanted to substantially reduce spending, carve out some extra aid for U.S. exporters and provide the administration with maximum flexibility in managing the foreign aid program. He succeeded in committee on all three counts, while managing to produce a bill that won the acceptance of his immediate predecessor, David R. Obey, D-Wis., and other Democrats. The legislation included no specific spending mandates, known as earmarks, and the report accompanying the measure was largely devoid of foreign policy statements and recommendations.

The bill passed with some changes in Callahan's plan, after a delay stemming from a partisan scrap over an unrelated matter.

During an all-night session June 28–29, the House took up some of the most important amendments.

By a vote of 247–155 in the session that began June 28, the House adopted an amendment by John Edward Porter, R-Ill., to cap economic aid for Turkey at $21 million, a reduction of $25 million from the $46 million originally included in the bill. The strong vote reflected the growing congressional distaste for Turkey's harsh campaign against the Kurds and the clout of the Greek American and Armenian American communities, which bitterly recalled Turkey's historical treatment of Greece and Armenia.

In a related move, the House gave voice vote approval to an amendment by Peter J. Visclosky, D-Ind., to retain a ban on direct aid to Azerbaijan, which had been locked in a bitter conflict with Armenia over the enclave of Nagorno-Karabakh. The committee bill, at the request of the State Department, would have softened a 1992 ban (PL 102-511) on all U.S. aid to Azerbaijan to allow for humanitarian and "democracy-building" assistance. Visclosky's amendment had been defeated during committee consideration. *(1992 law, Congress and the Nation Vol. VIII, p. 266)*

Reflecting the increasing strength of antiabortion forces in the House, lawmakers voted 243–187 on June 28 to reinstate the so-called Mexico City policy, Reagan-era restrictions that barred U.S. aid to international organizations that performed or "actively promoted" abortions. The amendment, sponsored by Christopher H. Smith, R-N.J., also prohibited aid to the United Nations Population Fund unless it withdrew from China or China stopped coercive abortions. Smith's amendment represented a direct challenge to Clinton, who had signed an executive order scrapping the Mexico City policy and other abortion-related federal policies soon after taking office. *(U.N. Population Fund, box, p. 209)*

After a sharp partisan debate on June 28, the House adopted, 252–164, a GOP-backed proposal by Porter J. Goss, R-Fla., to bar aid to Haiti unless that nation held free presidential balloting later in the year. A Democratic proposal, offered by Carrie P. Meek of Florida, that would have weakened the conditions on aid for Haiti had been rejected earlier June 28 by a vote of 189–231.

Aside from those amendments, the compromise fashioned by the Foreign Operations Subcommittee held, for the most part, throughout the marathon floor debate. Most proposals to cut spending were rejected or modified.

SENATE ACTION

The Senate passed its $12.4 billion version of HR 1868 on Sept. 21 by a 91–9 vote. The Senate Appropriations Committee had reported the bill Sept. 14 (S Rept 104-143).

The Senate committee bill bore the strong imprint of Mitch McConnell, R-Ky., chairman of the Appropriations Subcommittee on Foreign Policy. A sharp critic of the administration's policy toward the former Soviet Union, McConnell included several restrictions on aid to Russia and other former Soviet republics. The bill, for example, tied aid to Russia to a certification by the president that Moscow had canceled plans to sell nuclear technology to Iran. The bill also included a series of detailed ear-marks.

The Senate committee bill dropped the House provisions re-instituting the Mexico City policy and restricting aid to Turkey.

Senate passage came after Jesse Helms, R-N.C., withdrew a proposal aimed at folding at least two independent foreign poli-cy agencies into the State Department. Stymied in his effort to move a separate bill (S 908) to reorganize the foreign affairs bu-reaucracy, Helms attempted to attach it to the foreign aid bill. But when it became clear that his effort would derail the appro-priations bill, he backed down. (*Reorganization, p. 230*)

The most significant step taken during floor debate was an endorsement of a shift in U.S. nuclear nonproliferation policy. After a lobbying push from the Clinton administration, the Sen-ate Sept. 21 adopted, 55–45, a Hank Brown, R-Colo., amend-ment providing the first direct economic aid to Pakistan since 1990, when assistance was cut off because of that nation's nu-clear program. The proposal also freed up $368 million in mili-tary equipment paid for by Pakistan but never delivered.

Brown's proposal did not seek to repeal the so-called Pressler amendment, a 1985 law (PL 99-83) named for South Dakota Republican Sen. Larry Pressler that barred aid to Pakistan unless the president certified that Islamabad did not possess a "nuclear explosive device." Instead, it proposed to waive the Pressler re-strictions so the administration could provide Pakistan with aid to fight terrorism and drug-trafficking. Military and economic aid to the country had been frozen since 1990, when President George Bush declined to make the certification required by the Pressler amendment.

Brown defended his amendment as a modest step intended to bring some fairness to U.S. relations with Pakistan, a close U.S. ally in the struggle against communism. Critics—led by John Glenn, D-Ohio, and Pressler himself—charged that the proposal would undermine the U.S. commitment to nonprolif-eration. (*Pakistan policy, Congress and the Nation Vol. VII, p. 225; Congress and the Nation Vol. VIII, p. 232*)

Senators dealt antiabortion forces a setback Sept. 21 by re-jecting, 43–57, an amendment by Helms to reinstitute the Mexi-co City policy. Helms's amendment was identical to the one ap-proved by the House.

With no debate, the Senate adopted by voice vote a wide-ranging en bloc amendment that addressed U.S. policy toward several nations, including North Korea, Myanmar (the former Burma) and Bosnia. The amendment softened restrictions on aid to North Korea that McConnell had inserted in the bill, in-corporated tough trade sanctions against Myanmar, and autho-rized—but did not require—$100 million in military aid to Bosnia.

The Senate adopted by voice vote an amendment by Majori-ty Leader Bob Dole, R-Kan., mirroring a House-passed provi-sion to deny military and economic aid to countries that blocked shipments of humanitarian assistance to other nations. Dole left no doubt that the proposal was aimed at Turkey and its blockade against Armenia. The president could waive the re-strictions on national security grounds. But the Senate, tradi-tionally more supportive of Turkey than the House, voted 60–36

on Sept. 20 to table (kill) an Alfonse M. D'Amato, R-N.Y., amendment to cap economic aid to Ankara at $21 million.

In the first test of Senate sentiment on Clinton's decision to normalize U.S. relations with Vietnam, the Senate Sept. 20 re-jected, 39–58, a Robert C. Smith, R-N.H., amendment to restrict future U.S. trade ties with that country unless the president cer-tified that Hanoi was providing greater cooperation in resolving cases of Americans missing from the Vietnam War and was making substantial progress on human rights. (*Vietnam policy, p. 246*)

CONFERENCE, FINAL ACTION

House-Senate conferees worked out a compromise $12.1 bil-lion appropriations bill. They agreed to ease long-standing re-strictions on aid to Pakistan and Azerbaijan; extended the presi-dent's waiver authority on aid to the Palestinian Authority, though under tight conditions; modified Senate conditions on aid for Russia; boosted funding for hard-hit programs such as the In-ternational Development Association, the World Bank affiliate that made loans to the world's poorest countries; and dropped the Senate's harsh sanctions against Myanmar.

But the conferees could not bridge the gap over the abortion-related restrictions on aid to international family planning orga-nizations. In an effort to break the deadlock, Rep. Smith agreed to slightly ease the restrictions he put in the House bill, but the proposal was rejected by Senate conferees. As a result, the con-ferees reported that they were in disagreement on the provision, setting the stage for a new round of floor fights.

The House on Oct. 31 first adopted the conference report, 351–71, and then backed Smith's modified amendment, 232–187. The next day the Senate adopted the report, 90–6, but rejected Smith's proposal, 53–44.

The stalemate continued for months. The House on Nov. 15 again voted to stick by its position, 237–183. That same day the Senate voted 54–44, to table (kill) both Smith's language and a Senate provision endorsing the Clinton administration's inter-national family planning policy. On Dec. 13, the House adopted, 226–201, a Callahan motion to drop the Smith provision but withhold all family planning assistance—an estimated $400 million in fiscal 1996—unless it was explicitly authorized. Abor-tion rights supporters strongly opposed the proposal, claiming it was a back-door effort to end funding for population pro-grams. The Senate's first effort to gain unanimous consent to bring Callahan's proposal up for a vote failed Dec. 15, and the year ran out without an agreement.

A compromise was reached early in the next session. Under the agreement, funds for family planning programs would be reduced by 35 percent from the fiscal 1995 level of $548 million unless a separate bill authorizing those programs became law by July 1, 1996.

The conference report on HR 1868—along with the family planning compromise—then was attached to a temporary spending bill that would keep the government open through March 15 (HR 2880). The House passed HR 2880 Jan. 25 on a 371–42 vote. The Senate endorsed it, 82–8, the next day, sending it to the president. Clinton signed the measure that same day.

The resolution of the abortion dispute also cleared HR 1868 and, on Feb. 12, the president took the unusual step of signing it as well. His action, which surprised many lawmakers who believed the appropriations bill had already been enacted as part of HR 2880, tied up any loose ends and assured funding for foreign aid programs through the end of the fiscal year.

MAJOR PROVISIONS

As signed into law, the fiscal 1996 foreign operations appropriations bill provided $12.1 billion. This included $1.44 billion in multilateral aid, $6.83 billion in bilateral economic aid, $3.16 billion in bilateral military aid and $678 million in export assistance.

Major provisions of the bill:

• **Middle East.** Earmarked $3 billion in economic and military aid to Israel and $2.1 billion to Egypt.

The bill extended the president's authority to waive certain provisions of law to provide aid to the Palestinian Authority for up to 18 months, provided the president certified to Congress that the Palestinians had met certain conditions. These included taking specific steps to halt terrorism and providing no funds for a Palestinian Authority presence in Jerusalem unless established by agreement with Israel.

• **Pakistan.** Permitted Pakistan to receive $368 million in withheld military equipment.

• **Azerbaijan.** Allowed limited refugee aid to Azerbaijan.

• **Former Soviet Union.** Provided $641 million in economic aid to Russia and the former Soviet republics, about $147 million below the administration's request. The bill included some of the Senate-backed earmarks, such as $225 million for Ukraine and $85 million for Armenia.

• **North Korea.** Provided $22 million to underwrite a U.S. nuclear agreement with North Korea.

• **Export Assistance.** Provided $68 million for the Overseas Private Investment Corporation's guaranteed loan program, nearly triple the previous year's appropriation.

• **Family Planning.** Reduced family planning programs by 35 percent from the fiscal 1995 level of $548 million, unless a separate bill authorizing those programs became law by July 1, 1996. If no authorization bill was enacted by that date, population programs would receive $356 million, to be disbursed in monthly installments over a 15-month period.

• **Haiti.** Barred aid to Haiti after March 1, 1996, unless its government was elected in democratic elections and in compliance with the 1987 Constitution of Haiti.

• **Land Mine Moratorium.** Imposed a one-year ban on U.S. use of antipersonnel mines, except along international borders or in demilitarized zones that were marked. The ban was to take effect three years after enactment. ❏

1997 Aid Appropriations

Congress in 1996 appropriated $12.3 billion for fiscal 1997 foreign operations as part of an omnibus spending measure (HR 3610—PL 104-208). President Clinton had requested $12.9 billion for multilateral, bilateral and export assistance programs.

Both chambers had passed a free-standing appropriations bill (HR 3540), but a stubborn dispute over abortion delayed the bill for so long that it was ultimately folded into the catchall measure with five other appropriations bills.

In final negotiations on HR 3610, the Clinton administration managed to wring a number of concessions on foreign aid from Republican leaders, including an increase in overall spending, more funding for energy aid to North Korea, and authorization for U.S. participation in a new Middle East Development Bank. (*U.S.-North Korea agreement, p. 248*)

While Republicans agreed to drop a House-passed provision that would have placed abortion-related restrictions on international family planning aid, they succeeded in imposing tight funding limits on the program. A similar battle had delayed the fiscal 1996 foreign operations bill (HR 1868—PL 104-107). (*1996 aid appropriations, p. 231*)

HOUSE ACTION

The House passed an $11.9 billion version of HR 3540 by a vote of 366–57 on June 11, 1996. The House Appropriations Committee had reported the bill on May 29 (H Rept 104-600).

For the second year in a row, Republicans had fashioned a huge bipartisan vote for the bill by cutting funding for most programs and placing tough conditions on controversial ones, while preserving politically popular accounts.

Floor action was dominated by debate over aid for Turkey. The committee bill included a provision barring assistance to Turkey unless it lifted its blockade of humanitarian aid to Armenia. On June 5, the House adopted, 301–118, an amendment by Indiana Democrat Peter J. Visclosky to close a loophole that would have allowed the president to waive that restriction and provide $25 million in economic aid to Turkey. The House June 5 also adopted, 268–153, an amendment by George P. Radanovich, R-Calif., to cap economic aid to Turkey at $22 million unless the government formally acknowledged that the Armenian population of the Ottoman Empire was subjected to genocide between 1915 and 1923. The amendments triggered sharp protests from Ankara and a denial of the genocide allegation.

The House bill also eliminated the president's authority to send humanitarian aid directly to Azerbaijan. A ban on all aid had been imposed in 1992 because of Azerbaijan's blockade of neighboring Armenia, but that ban had been softened in the fiscal 1996 foreign operations bill to permit refugee aid. HR 3540 allowed indirect aid only through private humanitarian groups in proportional amounts to Azeri and Armenian refugees.

International family planning programs continued to be among the most controversial ones in the bill. The House version would have funded those programs at the fiscal 1996 level of approximately $356 million. It would have required recipients to pledge not to use their own funds to perform abortions overseas and not to lobby against foreign abortion laws. Otherwise, they would face a 50 percent cut in aid.

Among the most popular items in the annual appropriations bill were the aid programs for Israel and Egypt. While the House measure contained no earmarks, it continued the practice of providing $3 billion for military and economic aid to Israel and $2.1 billion for Egypt. Assistance for those nations accounted for 42 percent of the bill's total.

Many other countries, however, faced aid reductions, including Russia and the other former Soviet republics. The House bill also would have nearly halved a $25 million request for the Korean Peninsula Energy Development Organization (KEDO) to implement a deal in which North Korea agreed to freeze its nuclear weapons program in exchange for shipments of heavy fuel oil.

Substantial cuts were also made in multilateral assistance accounts. Members were particularly incensed by procurement restrictions at the World Bank's International Development Association (IDA), which made interest-free loans to the world's poorest nations. The United States had fallen badly behind in its promised payments to the IDA, and other donor nations had established an interim fund to bridge the gap until a new round of fund-raising was completed. U.S. firms were barred from bidding on contracts underwritten by the interim fund. An angry House Appropriations Subcommittee on Foreign Operations included in the bill $525 million for the IDA, $410 million less than requested, and prohibited the expenditure of the money until the Treasury Department reported to Congress on steps it had taken to challenge the procurement decision.

Most of the hot-button issues were glossed over during floor action and, aside from the battle over aid to Turkey, debate on the bill went smoothly.

SENATE ACTION

The Senate passed a $12.29 billion version of HR 3540 on July 26 by a vote of 93–7. The bill had been reported by the Senate Appropriations Committee on June 27 (S Rept 104-295).

The Senate bill contained about $300 million more for foreign aid programs than the House-passed version. It also was closer to the administration on several contested points.

The House language conditioning aid to Turkey on that country's policy toward Armenia was dropped. The Senate bill boosted overall family planning aid to $410 million and contained no new abortion-related restrictions. The Senate panel went along with the House decision to cut the KEDO request to $13 million, but the full Senate on July 26 adopted, 73–27, a Joseph I. Lieberman, D-Conn., amendment to raise the funding to the full $25 million requested.

Funding for the World Bank's IDA was boosted to $626 million by the Senate Appropriations Committee and then to $700 million by a voice vote of the full Senate. Aid to the former Soviet Union was also hiked, but a number of conditions and directions as to how that aid should be spent were attached.

The full Senate softened committee provisions imposing sweeping new sanctions against the government of Myanmar (formerly Burma) whose political repression and links to the heroin trade had made it a target in Congress. The committee-added restrictions drew protests from the administration, which objected to Congress imposing unilateral sanctions, and by U.S. oil companies that were exploring business opportunities in Myanmar. William S. Cohen, R-Maine, offered an alternative

that barred most direct aid to Myanmar and replaced it with milder restrictions. The Senate on July 25 rejected an effort to table (kill) Cohen's amendment on a 45–54 vote that cut across partisan and ideological divisions. It then adopted the amendment on a voice vote.

The Senate bill earmarked $3 billion for Israel and $2.1 billion for Egypt. The legislation also raised the sensitive question of the status of Jerusalem by requiring that all U.S. government publications refer to Jerusalem as the capital of Israel. In 1995, a law (S 1322—PL 104-45) was enacted without the president's signature requiring that the U.S. Embassy be relocated from Tel Aviv to Jerusalem by mid-1999. Since then, proponents had complained that the administration was dragging its feet in implementing the law. (U.S. Embassy in Jerusalem, p. 249)

During floor consideration, the Senate adopted by voice vote an amendment to provide $52.5 million to establish the new Middle East Development Bank, an administration priority. The House had not included funds for the proposed bank, which was intended to fund cooperative ventures involving Israelis and Arabs.

The Senate bill also proposed barring payment of a salary to Export-Import Bank President Martin A. Kamarck unless he was confirmed by the Senate. Kamarck, a recess appointment of the president's, had drawn criticism over reports that he approved excessive bonuses to senior Ex-Im officials.

HR 3540 included $60 million in military aid for Poland, Hungary and the Czech Republic to help speed their entry into the North Atlantic Treaty Organization (NATO). After a brief debate on the floor July 25, senators agreed, 81–16, to a Hank Brown, R-Colo., amendment authorizing the $60 million and naming those three countries plus Slovenia as participants eligible for NATO membership.

In other action, the Senate July 25 adopted, 51–46, a Paul Coverdell, R-Ga., amendment increasing funding for international narcotics law enforcement to the administration's request of $213 million. The House bill had included $150 million.

CONFERENCE, FINAL ACTION

By mid-September, House-Senate conferees had resolved all issues except family planning assistance. With time running out in the session, leaders of the Appropriations committees abandoned hope of enacting a stand-alone foreign operations bill.

Conferees initially agreed on a $12.1 billion bill, with a $140 million rescission from aid already appropriated but not yet disbursed. In a bow to the administration, they stripped the House-passed restriction on economic aid for Turkey and agreed to fund the IDA at the Senate-approved level of $700 million.

But they also endorsed provisions that were less to the administration's liking—including one forcing a modest funding reduction, from the $25 million Clinton request to $23 million, in energy aid to Korea. Administration officials were concerned that even a modest funding reduction would call into question the U.S. commitment to the agreement with North Korea. Another provision would have barred U.S. participation in the new Middle East Development Bank. Conferees also included the Senate provision requiring confirmation of Ex-Im President Kamarck and the requirement that all government documents refer to Jerusalem as Israel's capital.

When conferees failed to resolve their disagreement over family planning assistance, the bill became part of the negotiations on the omnibus appropriations package.

This shift benefited Clinton. With Republicans anxious to adjourn and concentrate on campaigning, the administration won a number of new concessions from GOP leaders. These included increased funds for energy aid to North Korea and authorization for U.S. participation in the new Middle East Development Bank. The Senate provision on Jerusalem was dropped. Overall spending for foreign operations was increased by $143 million, and the $140 million rescission was eliminated.

International family planning lived up to its advance billing as one of the most intractable issues in the budget talks. After intensive negotiations, Republicans agreed to drop the House-passed provision imposing abortion-related restrictions and provide $385 million for family planning programs. But tough conditions were attached.

The House adopted the conference report on the omnibus bill (H Rept 104-863) on Sept. 28 by a vote of 370–37. The Senate cleared it by voice vote Sept. 30. Clinton signed the legislation into law the same day.

MAJOR PROVISIONS

As signed into law, HR 3610 appropriated $12.3 billion for fiscal 1997 foreign operations. This included $1.16 in multilateral aid, $7.29 billion in bilateral economic aid, $3.23 billion in bilateral military aid and $635 million in export assistance.

Major provisions of the bill:

• **Middle East.** Earmarked $3 billion in aid for Israel and $2.1 billion for Egypt.

The bill authorized U.S. participation in the new Middle East Development Bank, which was to fund cooperative ventures between Israelis and Arabs, but included no funding.

• **North Korea.** Included the administration's full request of $25 million for the Korean Peninsula Energy Development Organization.

• **Former Soviet Union.** Provided $625 million of the $640 million requested for Russia and other ex-Soviet republics. This included an earmark of $225 million for Ukraine.

The bill retained the ban on aid to the government of Azerbaijan until it had taken steps to cease all blockades and other uses of force against Armenia and the enclave of Nagorno-Karabakh.

• **NATO.** Earmarked $30 million in military assistance grants, $20 million in loans and $10 million for military training to help Poland, Hungary and the Czech Republic become members of NATO. In addition, the legislation included the NATO Enlargement Facilitation Act, which urged the speedy admission of Eastern European nations into NATO. (*NATO expansion, p. 319*)

• **Turkey.** Capped economic aid to Turkey at $22 million.

• **Family Planning.** Included $385 million for international family planning programs, but none of the funds could be spent until July 1, 1997, unless both chambers voted to release the aid

by Feb. 28—which they subsequently did. The funds then could be disbursed at a maximum rate of only 8 percent per month.

• **Ex-Im President.** Cut off Export-Import Bank President Martin A. Kamarck's salary by July 21, 1997, unless he had been confirmed by the Senate.

• **OPIC.** Included $72 million to support the Overseas Private Investment Corporation (OPIC) direct and guaranteed loan programs for U.S. exporters. This was significant because, only days before, the House had rejected a bill to reauthorize OPIC. That bipartisan rebuke of taxpayer-subsidized programs for business was made somewhat easier by the assumption that the appropriators would, nevertheless, keep the programs going. (*OPIC, p. 177*)

• **Narcotics Control.** Included the full $213 million request for antinarcotics programs. ❏

U.N. Peacekeeping Missions

After winning control of Congress in 1994, Republicans in the 104th Congress sharply attacked President Clinton's global peacekeeping policies. But they had limited success in trying to change those policies.

The GOP's "Contract with America," which had been used by Republicans in the 1994 congressional elections, had called for tough new restrictions on the president's ability to deploy U.S. troops to multinational peacekeeping operations. The debate over limiting such operations involved several issues. (*GOP contract proposals, p. 315*)

Probably the most emotional and heated battle was fought over the question of assigning U.S. forces to serve under U.N. command. The 1993 killings of 18 U.S. servicemen under U.N. command in Somalia provided the backdrop. The House approved a number of provisions that would have permanently limited the president's authority to place U.S. soldiers under U.N. command, only to see the proposals die in the Senate or fall to President Clinton's veto. But both the fiscal 1996 (HR 3019—PL 104-134) and fiscal 1997 (HR 3610—PL 104-208) omnibus appropriations bills included temporary bans on funding for such operations unless the president notified Congress that it was in the national security interest. (*U.N. command of U.S. troops, p. 318; Somalia peacekeeping mission, p. 191*)

Arguing that the United States was paying more than its fair share of U.N. peacekeeping operations, members also pushed for deep cuts in that funding. In fiscal 1990, Congress had appropriated just $81 million for its peacekeeping bills, known in U.N. parlance as assessments. The administration asked for $445 million for those assessments in fiscal 1996, plus an additional $672 million in fiscal 1995 supplemental funds for peacekeeping dues the United States owed the United Nations. (*1993–1994 action, p. 200*)

But Congress included only $225 million for U.N. peacekeeping in the conference version of the fiscal 1996 appropriations bill for the departments of Commerce, Justice and State (HR 2076). That was the amount approved by the Senate; the House had approved $425 million. Clinton vetoed HR 2076 on

Dec. 19, 1995, for a variety of reasons, including the cuts in his peacekeeping request. Fiscal 1996 funding for Commerce-Justice-State programs ultimately was included in HR 3019. The omnibus appropriations bill upped the U.N. peacekeeping account to $359 million.

Congress included fiscal 1997 Commerce-State-Justice funding in HR 3610. The omnibus appropriations bill appropriated $352 million of the $425 million requested for peacekeeping contributions. That was $20 million more than the House level and nearly $70 million more than the Senate. The bill also provided $50 million to pay peacekeeping arrearages but included tough conditions on use of the money. To disburse the funds, the secretary of state had to certify that U.N. agencies had achieved major budget savings or had made substantial cuts in staff.

Both omnibus appropriations bills contained provisions requiring the administration to give Congress 15 days' notice before voting at the United Nations Security Council for a new or expanded peacekeeping mission, except in emergencies. The House and Senate Appropriations committees had to be informed of the estimated cost and length of the mission, the "vital national interest" to be served, and the plan for ending the U.S. troops' involvement. If those conditions were not met, each bill stated, none of its funds could be used for that mission.

Members rejected administration proposals to use Defense Department funds to pay for U.N. missions. Already concerned over the costs of unilateral U.S. peacekeeping operations and their impact on military readiness, they insisted that funding for U.N. missions come out of the State Department budget. Congress turned down administration requests for U.N. peacekeeping funds in the fiscal 1996 defense authorization (S 1124—PL 104-106) and appropriations (HR 2126—PL 104-61) bills. (Congress in 1995 did approve a fiscal 1995 defense supplemental appropriations bill (HR 889) for peacekeeping, but it was to pay for the unbudgeted costs of U.S. military operations in Haiti, the Persian Gulf, the former Yugoslavia and elsewhere.) *(1996 defense authorization, p. 294; 1996 defense appropriations, p. 301; 1995 defense supplemental, p. 304)* ❑

Cuba Sanctions

Outraged by Cuba's downing of two U.S. civilian planes, Congress cleared a bill in 1996 to deter foreign individuals and companies from investing in Cuba. The measure (HR 927—PL 104-114) was the second bill in four years that tried to tighten the long-standing U.S. embargo against Cuba.

A top priority for GOP leaders and politically formidable Cuban-American groups, the so-called Helms-Burton bill—named for cosponsors Senate Foreign Relations Committee Chairman Jesse Helms, R-N.C., and Rep. Dan Burton, R-Ind.—foreclosed any possibility of normalizing relations with Cuba as long as Fidel Castro remained in power. " 'Farewell Fidel,' that's the message of this bill," Helms declared after House and Senate negotiators reached agreement with the White House on a final version of the legislation. President Clinton had previously opposed the bill, but his opposition melted away in the furor over the downing of the planes.

The bill authorized U.S. nationals whose property had been confiscated by Cuba to sue any foreign government, company, or individual who bought, sold or improved the property. Foreigners who were subject to those claims were barred from entering the United States under most circumstances, as were their families. The goal was to hurt Cuba by stopping new foreign commercial investment, which had become a crucial source of hard currency for Castro's government.

Equally important, the measure put into law all existing sanctions against Cuba, including the comprehensive trade embargo that had been a cornerstone of U.S. policy since 1962. Previously, the embargo had been imposed by executive orders and regulations, which meant the president could lift or ease it without congressional approval. The new law took that decision, a jealously guarded presidential prerogative, out of the hands of the White House and gave it to Congress.

U.S. trading partners blasted the bill as a heavy-handed attempt to force the rest of the world to toe the U.S. line on Cuba. Some countries threatened to retaliate, and officials from Canada and Mexico said they would try to suspend enforcement of the measure because it violated the North American Free Trade Agreement. Opponents in Congress also warned that the bill would flood the U.S. court system with new claims.

Both chambers passed bills in 1995, but the legislation stalled in conference early in 1996. The logjam was broken on Feb. 24, 1996, when Cuban MiG fighters shot down two unarmed Cessna aircraft operated by an anti-Castro group, killing the four Cuban-Americans aboard. Within four days, the White House and congressional negotiators had agreed to a bill that was tougher than either the House or the Senate bill, neither of which sought to codify the economic embargo of Cuba. Both chambers quickly adopted the conference report, and President Clinton signed the bill on March 12.

Clinton, who had vigorously opposed the bill's lawsuit provision, won a key concession in conference that allowed him to delay the onset of lawsuits indefinitely. In August he imposed a six-month delay, saying he would use the time to build international support for increased economic pressure on the Castro government.

BACKGROUND

The U.S. government had been trying to topple Castro ever since he seized power in 1959, with the overt efforts focused on isolating Cuba's economy from the rest of the world. The United States first imposed a unilateral trade embargo in 1962. The U.S. embargo had limited effect, however, because of the assistance extended by Cuba's communist allies in the 1960s, 1970s and 1980s.

The fall of communism in Eastern Europe and the Soviet Union, combined with the latter's economic problems, cut Castro's lifeline and put Cuba's economy into a tailspin. Hoping to hasten the end of communism in Cuba, Congress tightened the economic sanctions in 1992 as part of the fiscal 1993 defense authorization bill (PL 102-484). The measure barred the foreign subsidiaries of U.S. companies from engaging in new trade with Cuba and temporarily denied vessels entry into U.S. ports if they had shipped goods or passengers to or from Cuba. *(Congress and the Nation Vol. VIII, p. 295)*

Castro made the next move, announcing in August 1994 that he would not block people attempting to leave the island by sea. Thousands of refugees joined the exodus, evoking painful memories of the 1980 Mariel boat lift and raising fears that Florida's social services would be overwhelmed.

The United States had routinely admitted Cuban refugees since Castro assumed power. The Clinton administration, however, announced on Aug. 18, 1994, that it would not admit the boat people but would detain them indefinitely at the U.S. Naval Air Station at Guantanamo Bay, Cuba. The exodus continued nonetheless, causing dangerous overcrowding at Guantanamo. After a round of secret, high-level talks with Cuba, the administration announced on May 2, 1995, that it would allow the 20,000 detainees in Guantanamo to enter the United States but would intercept future refugees at sea and return them to Cuba.

The deal angered Cuban-Americans, a crucial voting bloc in Florida and New Jersey, and their friends in Congress, who demanded a more confrontational approach to Castro. Early in 1995, Helms and Burton, the chairman of the House International Relations Subcommittee on Western Hemisphere Affairs, introduced bills to pressure foreign companies and executives into joining the U.S. embargo.

The bills (HR 927, S 381) gained momentum in the fall, when Clinton unveiled a new approach to Cuba. In addition to tightening the enforcement of the economic embargo, Clinton said he would permit increased academic and cultural exchanges with the country. He also allowed U.S. news organizations to open bureaus in Cuba and permitted Cuban exiles to send money to the relatives they left behind.

LEGISLATIVE ACTION

The original Burton bill bogged down briefly in the House International Relations Committee in June 1995. The administration and its allies on the committee, led by ranking Democrat Lee H. Hamilton of Indiana, objected to the property-claims and visa provisions. Hamilton also noted that the bill had drawn complaints from some U.S. companies that had lost property in Cuba, which worried that the bill would dramatically expand the pool of potential claimants and reduce their chance of ever being reimbursed.

But the committee rejected Hamilton's proposal to drop the provision on property claims. It reported the measure to the House on July 24, 1995 (H Rept 104-202, Part I).

Despite a veto threat from the administration, the House easily passed HR 927 on Sept. 21 by a vote of 294–130—a margin wide enough to override a veto. Sentiment in favor of the bill was so strong, lawmakers even rejected an amendment—offered by Washington Democrat Jim McDermott, a physician—to allow U.S. companies to sell medicine and staple foods to Cuba, 138–283 on Sept. 21.

In the Senate, Majority Leader Bob Dole, R-Kan., took a modified version of Helms's bill (S 381) to the floor in October, bypassing the Foreign Relations Committee. The new version was milder in several respects than the House bill; for example,

it did not include any restrictions on visas for the executives of foreign companies.

Still, Helms had not retreated on the property-claims provision, which drew opposition on both sides of the aisle. Critics argued that the provision would overburden the courts, strain relations with U.S. allies and trigger a backlash against U.S. companies abroad. According to Sen. Christopher J. Dodd, D-Conn., the bill would expand the number of potential claims for expropriated property from 6,000 to 430,000.

Two attempts to cut off debate on the bill failed to attract the 60 votes needed to invoke cloture—the first failed on Oct. 12 by a vote of 56–37 and the second on Oct. 17 by a vote of 59–36. With Republican moderates Nancy Landon Kassebaum of Kansas and James M. Jeffords of Vermont joining most Democrats in opposition to the bill, Dole and Helms were unable to overcome the filibuster until they agreed to drop the section on lawsuits against foreign companies in U.S. courts. After making that change, the Senate passed the bill, 74–24, on Oct. 19. Before final passage, the Senate Oct. 19 had tabled (killed) a Paul Simon, D-Ill., amendment to lift U.S. restrictions on travel to Cuba by a vote of 73–25 and a Dodd amendment to strike from the bill conditions on aid to a post-Castro transitional government by a vote of 64–34.

The conference was delayed for two months by a dispute between Helms and Senate Democrats over ambassadorial nominations and the foreign policy bureaucracy. Conferees then tussled with the administration over the House-passed property-claims provision, which lawmakers wanted to preserve but the administration wanted to gut.

The February 1996 downing of the two Cessnas operated by Brothers to the Rescue, a U.S.-based anti-Castro group, cut the legs out from under Clinton's position. "President Castro created a veto-proof majority for the Helms-Burton bill," said Richard A. Nuccio, Clinton's special adviser for Cuba.

Clinton responded quickly to the attack by announcing a series of steps designed to ratchet up the pressure on Castro, including a ban on U.S. charter flights and a somewhat vague commitment to find common ground with Congress on the sanctions bill. But those moves opened the president to a fusillade of criticism from the Cuban-American community and political opponents such as Dole, who accused Clinton of "coddling" Castro.

Rep. Robert Menendez, D-N.J., a Cuban-American lawmaker who played a key role in brokering the agreement, said Clinton had shown interest in fashioning a deal on the Helms-Burton bill well before the shootdown. But the attack, and the bipartisan desire to punish Castro, forced the president's hand.

The Clinton administration was able to water down the property-claims provision in conference in exchange for allowing other sections of the bill to be toughened. The final version allowed the president to postpone the filing of lawsuits for six months at a time, with an unlimited number of postponements.

The legislation also took the decision on whether to lift the embargo away from Clinton. To some GOP critics, the bill provided an insurance policy against Clinton normalizing relations with Cuba as he had with Vietnam.

Several of the bill's opponents blasted the conference bill as a thinly disguised attempt to curry favor with Cuban-American voters in an election year. Still, the Senate overwhelmingly approved the conference report (H Rept 104-468) on March 5, 1996, by a **key vote of 74–22 (R 47–4; D 27–18),** and the House cleared the bill the next day, 336–86. *(1996 key votes, p. 1047)*

MAJOR PROVISIONS

As signed into law, HR 927, the so-called Cuba Libertad bill:

• **Property Claims.** Created a "right of action," enabling U.S. nationals whose property had been confiscated by Castro's government to sue foreign governments, companies and individuals who "trafficked" in the property.

The bill defined trafficking as buying, selling, transferring, profiting from or even improving expropriated property that once belonged to a current U.S. national. For example, if a Canadian businessman bought a factory that a U.S. citizen had lost through expropriation, the Canadian could be sued. If the businessman had bought the factory before the bill's enactment, he still could be sued if he sought to expand it or perform anything other than "routine maintenance."

The provision was scheduled to go into effect August 1, although the bill allowed the president to delay implementation indefinitely, six months at a time, if doing so would be in the national interest and would facilitate Cuba's transition to democracy.

• **Denial of Entry.** Barred foreigners and their families entry into the United States if they had trafficked in expropriated property claimed by a U.S. national. Exceptions were provided only for entries to obtain medical treatment or to contest an expropriation lawsuit.

• **Codification of the Embargo.** Put into law all existing economic sanctions against Cuba, including the original embargo imposed by President John F. Kennedy in 1962, until a "democratic transition" was under way in Cuba.

Under the embargo, U.S. companies were forbidden to trade with Cuba and their foreign subsidiaries were barred from engaging in new commerce with the country. Travel to Cuba was allowed only for government or international officials on business, people with family emergencies, and journalists.

HR 927 laid out 12 separate criteria for determining whether the Cuban government was making the transition to democracy, including a commitment to hold free elections. One key criterion was that a transitional government could not include Fidel Castro or his brother Raul, the head of Cuba's armed forces. Other criteria included the establishment of an independent judiciary and trade unions.

• **Foreign Aid Cuts.** Reduced U.S. aid to Russia by $200 million because of its support of an intelligence facility at Lourdes, Cuba. The president was allowed to waive the provision on national security grounds if he received assurances from Moscow that Russia was not sharing intelligence with Cuba. The legislation also reduced aid to foreign governments by the amount of support they had provided for the Cuban nuclear facility at Juragua.

• **Other Provisions.** Directed the Treasury Department to continue voting against Cuban participation in international financial institutions and to reduce U.S. payments to an institution by the amount of any loan or aid to Cuba approved over U.S. opposition.

The bill authorized aid for prodemocracy activities in Cuba.

The bill also called for TV Marti, the controversial U.S. broadcasting service to Cuba, to switch broadcast frequencies from VHF to UHF channels, which backers said would be harder to jam. At the time, TV Marti, which had an annual budget of $11 million, was routinely blocked by Cuban jammers and effectively had no audience.   ❏

Iran, Libya Sanctions

Trying to put teeth into a U.S.-orchestrated embargo, Congress cleared a bill in 1996 to penalize foreign firms that assisted the oil industries of Iran or Libya. Proponents of the measure cited the two countries' continuing practice of sponsoring terrorism and their efforts to manufacture weapons of mass destruction as the main reasons for the bill.

The measure (HR 3107—PL 104-172) was Congress's second effort in 1996 to isolate hostile states by imposing sanctions on friendly ones. The first (HR 927—PL 104-114) created penalties for companies that bought or improved certain properties in Cuba. *(Cuba sanctions, p. 237)*

The White House was not pleased with the Iran-Libya bill, just as it had balked at the Cuba measure. However, facing election-year pressure to take a hard line against a pair of nations closely linked with international terrorism, President Clinton signed HR 3107 on Aug. 5.

The new law required the president to impose two of six possible sanctions on foreign companies that invested at least $40 million in the oil industries of Iran or Libya within a 12-month period. The same penalties were required for foreign companies that sold weapons, aviation equipment or petroleum-related goods and technology to Libya in violation of United Nations Security Council resolutions.

The penalties included denial of Export-Import Bank financing; denial of licenses for sensitive U.S. exports; a ban on loans by U.S. financial institutions in excess of $10 million per year; prohibition against serving as a primary dealer in U.S. government bonds; prohibition against serving as a repository for U.S. government funds; and a ban on U.S. government procurement of the sanctioned firm's goods and services.

The sanctions were to last for two years or until the president certified that the company had ceased the sanctioned actions, if that came sooner. The president could waive any sanction, if he determined that doing so was in the national security interest of the United States.

The legislation was strongly backed by the influential American Israel Public Affairs Committee (AIPAC) and other groups that viewed Iran as the main threat to Middle East stability.

Critics of the bill noted that the United States had protested in the 1970s and 1980s when the Arab League used secondary boycotts against U.S. companies that traded with Israel. In HR

3107 and the Cuba bill, the United States seemed to be adopting the very policies it criticized in the past, they said.

One official at the Canadian embassy said HR 3107 appeared to be part of a worrisome trend. "We don't like to be told who to trade with," the official said. "We don't approve of the extension of United States law outside its borders; we think the proper place for multilateral action against Libya and Iran should be the United Nations."

BACKGROUND

The United States had long tried to isolate Iran and Libya, which were viewed as rogue regimes hostile to U.S. interests. In Iran's case, backers of Israel sought to tighten the economic noose because of the Iranian government's efforts to develop nuclear warheads and other weapons of mass destruction. In Libya's case, the United States had repeatedly clashed with the regime of Col. Muammar el-Quaddafi over his reputed support for terrorist attacks against U.S. citizens.

The U.S. government had already imposed the strictest unilateral sanctions possible on the two countries, barring all U.S. companies from trading with them. Other industrialized nations maintained their ties to Iran and Libya, however, undercutting the U.S. efforts. Foreign companies—most notably German, Asian and French firms—invested heavily in oil exploration and production in Iran and Libya. Supporters of HR 3107 argued that they were indirectly providing the funds that helped finance terrorist activities and the military buildup in those two countries.

Libya had been targeted by the U.N. Security Council for some limited economic sanctions, including a cutoff of commercial air links and a ban on some sales of oil equipment. U.S. efforts to broaden the embargo to cover Libyan oil, however, had met with stiff resistance from U.S. allies in Europe, many of whom relied on Libya's high-quality crude.

The U.N. sanctions stemmed from the 1988 bombing of Pan Am Flight 103 over Lockerbie, Scotland, an incident that claimed the lives of 189 Americans. In 1991, two mid-level Libyan intelligence officials were charged by U.S. and British authorities in connection with the bombing, but Qaddafi refused to hand over the men for trial. The Security Council sanctions may have encouraged Libya to become less active in its support for terrorism, U.S. officials said, but they did not cause Qaddafi to turn over the suspects.

Iran, meanwhile, badly needed foreign investment to modernize its oil industry. Clinton issued an executive order prohibiting U.S. companies from investing in Iran's oil industry, but administration officials and lawmakers were concerned that foreign corporations would fill the void when U.S. capital withdrew.

LEGISLATIVE ACTION

The Senate Banking Committee moved first, reporting a bill (S 1228—S Rept 104-187) on Dec. 15, 1995, that would have imposed sanctions on foreign companies that invested in the Iranian oil industry. Responding to White House concerns about violating the General Agreement on Tariffs and Trade (GATT), the panel dropped provisions that would have banned imports from sanctioned companies.

The Senate quickly passed the bill on Dec. 18 by voice vote, then recalled it the next day to consider an amendment by Edward M. Kennedy, D-Mass. Kennedy, a longtime advocate for the Lockerbie victims' relatives, offered an amendment to extend the penalties to foreign companies that invested in Libya's oil industry. The Senate adopted the amendment by voice vote Dec. 20, then passed the bill by voice vote.

The House International Relations Committee reported a more far-reaching measure (HR 3107—H Rept 104-523, Part I) on April 17, 1996. The committee's bill proposed sanctions on foreign companies that exported petroleum-related equipment and technology to Iran or Libya as well as those that invested in their oil industries.

The House Ways and Means Committee then struck a new deal with the administration, coming up with a significantly weaker version. In the case of Iran, mandatory sanctions would be triggered only by investments in the oil sector, not by sales of goods and technology. In the case of Libya, the reverse would be true: the penalties would be triggered by sales of petroleum-related goods and technology, not by investment. Existing contracts would be exempt from possible sanctions. Reported by Ways and Means on June 14 (H Rept 104-523, Part II), that version of HR 3107 won the House's unanimous approval on June 19, 415–0.

Despite the overwhelming support in both chambers, the bill was nearly snagged by a last-minute dispute over the Libya sanctions. When the Senate took up the House version of the bill July 16, it added by voice vote a Kennedy amendment restoring the mandatory penalties against companies investing in Libya's oil industry. The Senate approved the modified version that day by voice vote.

The House had dropped those sanctions largely because of complaints from European allies and foreign multinationals. The Senate's move raised concerns among some probusiness House members, including Ways and Means Chairman Bill Archer, R-Texas.

Any opposition to the bill vanished, however, in the aftermath of the July 17 explosion of TWA Flight 800 over the Atlantic Ocean, which killed all 230 people aboard. Although federal officials could not pinpoint the cause of the explosion, the frightening parallels to the bombing of Pan Am Flight 103 made lawmakers want to pass the strongest possible bill. The House cleared the measure, including Kennedy's amendment, on July 23 by voice vote. ❑

U.S.-China Relations

Diplomatic relations between the United States and China sank in 1995–1996 to their lowest level since the Chinese army brutally crushed prodemocracy demonstrators at Tiananmen Square in 1989. A series of actions and policies by China triggered widespread outrage in the 104th Congress, but in neither 1995 nor 1996 did Congress block the Clinton administration's renewal of China's most-favored-nation trade status, which allowed China's goods to enter the United States at low, nondiscriminatory tariff rates. Congress did, however, pressure the administration to take action in other areas. *(China trade, p. 178)*

Taiwan policy proved to be one of the most enduring sore points between the United States and China. Relations also were strained by China's human rights and trade practices.

TAIWAN

Officially, the United States acknowledged the Chinese position that there was only one China and that Taiwan was a part of China. But, after establishing diplomatic ties with Beijing in 1979, the United States still maintained an unofficial relationship with Taiwan. And Taiwan enjoyed deep support on Capitol Hill. Trade between the United States and Taiwan was booming, and members of Congress were eager to broaden formal contacts with that nation.

The House and Senate in 1995 approved a resolution (H Con Res 53) calling on Clinton to allow Taiwanese President Lee Teng-hui to pay an unofficial visit to the United States. The House adopted the resolution May 2 by a 396–0 vote, and the Senate adopted it, 97–1, on May 9. Senate Foreign Relations Committee Chairman Jesse Helms, R-N.C., went further, slipping language to require that the administration allow Lee into the country into the draft bill aimed at reorganizing the State Department (S 908).

The administration opposed the trip out of concern that it would strain U.S. relations with China. But, yielding to the pressure from Capitol Hill, the State Department announced that Lee would be granted a visa for a private visit.

While Congress applauded the administration's decision, China registered its displeasure by ordering home a military delegation that had been visiting the United States and then recalling its ambassador to the United States.

Despite the flap Lee's visit caused in 1995, Congress included in the fiscal 1996–1997 State Department authorization bill (HR 1561) a sense-of-Congress provision stating that Lee should be allowed to visit the United States again in 1996.

HR 1561 included other controversial provisions related to Taiwan. One declared that the 1979 Taiwan Relations Act (PL 96-8)—which guaranteed Taiwan a steady supply of defensive weapons—superseded the 1982 joint communiqué between the United States and China—which called for the United States to gradually reduce its weapons sales to Taiwan. Another provision, clearly aimed at China, made it easier for victims of regimes practicing coercive population policies to seek political asylum in the United States. Other provisions urged the appointment of a special envoy to Tibet, which had been occupied by China for decades, and called on the president not to visit China until a marked improvement had taken place in the human rights situation in China and Tibet. Clinton vetoed the bill, in part because of the China provisions. *(1996–1997 State Department authorization, p. 228)*

In March 1996, just weeks before the State Department bill veto, the administration had rushed naval forces to the waters off Taiwan. The move was in response to Chinese threats against the island, an attempt to influence the outcome of the March 23 Taiwanese elections. Once the voting was over, tensions subsided. Both the House and Senate passed versions of a nonbinding resolution (H Con Res 148) urging the United States to defend Taiwan against military attack, but the differing versions were never reconciled. The House adopted H Con Res 148 on March 19 by a vote of 369–14; the Senate approved an amended version March 21, 97–0.

ACTIVIST'S ARREST

Still simmering over the U.S. decision to grant Taiwan's president a visa, Beijing in June 1995 detained a Chinese-American human rights activist, Harry Wu. China further strained relations on Aug. 2, when it expelled two U.S. military officers on espionage charges. Both actions drew stern U.S. protests.

Wu's imprisonment gave new ammunition to critics of a United Nations women's conference that China had won the right to host Sept. 4–15. Both the full House and the Senate Foreign Relations Committee adopted in their versions of the State Department authorization bill language aimed at ensuring that China opened the international conference to its political opponents. Besides objecting to the location of the conference, lawmakers and conservative women's organizations also voiced concerns over a draft version of the conference platform.

Despite such opposition, the Clinton administration reaffirmed its intention to send a U.S. delegation to the conference. But the question of whether First Lady Hillary Rodham Clinton would lead the delegation as originally planned was left up in the air.

Mrs. Clinton did go to Beijing as honorary chairman of the U.S. delegation, but only after Wu was freed. After charging Wu with espionage and sentencing him to 15 years in prison, China expelled him on Aug. 24.

Foes of Mrs. Clinton's attendance were largely silent after the first lady bluntly criticized China's human rights policies in two speeches there on Sept. 5 and 6. Sensitive to the rocky relations between Beijing and Washington, President Clinton attempted to set some distance between his wife's remarks and U.S. policy. "There was no attempt to single any country out," the president said Sept. 6.

AMBASSADOR SASSER

Relations began to improve following the women's conference. In a series of carefully choreographed steps, China raised the possibility that its ambassador would be returned to Washington. And on Sept. 22, 1995, the State Department announced that Chinese officials had agreed to the appointment of former senator Jim Sasser, a Tennessee Democrat who had lost his bid for reelection in 1994, as U.S. ambassador to China.

Sasser's confirmation hearings were held in October, but the nomination was stalled until December, while Helms used it—and 17 other nominations—as leverage in his battle with Democrats over his State Department reorganization plan. The Senate Foreign Relations Committee finally reported Sasser's nomination favorably Dec. 12. He was confirmed by the full Senate on Dec. 14 by voice vote.

DISSIDENT PROTESTS

Even as Sasser was being confirmed, Congress and the Clinton administration were condemning the 14-year prison sentence handed to a leading Chinese dissident. Wei Jingsheng, regarded as the father of China's modern democracy movement, was convicted of conspiring to subvert the government after a one-day trial Dec. 13.

Anticipating the outcome, the House on Dec. 12 adopted, 409–0, a resolution (H Con Res 117) calling for Wei's immediate release. A similar resolution (S J Res 43) was reported by the Senate Foreign Relations Committee Dec. 12 and adopted by voice vote of the full Senate the next day.

OTHER ISSUES

Reports in 1996 that China had sold nuclear weapons machinery to Pakistan led the administration to delay $10 billion in Export-Import Bank loans. The 1994 Nuclear Proliferation Prevention Act, enacted as part of the fiscal 1994–1995 State Department authorization (PL 103-236) and permanently authorized by legislation enacted in 1996 (PL 104-164), denied Export-Import Bank loans and credits to countries that traded in material and technology used to develop nuclear weapons, unless waived by the president. But the White House reopened the pipeline on May 10 after announcing that it had determined that Chinese government leaders did not know of the sales. Beijing promised not to allow further such sales. (1994–1995 State Department authorization, p. 212)

An outright trade war with China was averted June 17 when the administration announced that Beijing had agreed to further steps to control the piracy of U.S.-made compact discs, computer software and other intellectual property. Both sides had announced a list of punitive tariffs. ❏

1996 Intelligence Authorization

Congress in 1995 cleared a fiscal 1996 intelligence authorization bill (HR 1655—PL 104-93) that protected much of the overall spending for the nation's spy agencies from the budget ax, a reflection of the new Republican majority's desire for robust spending on national security-related operations. Although its funding levels were classified, the bill reportedly provided $28 billion for the CIA as well as the counterintelligence and foreign intelligence programs of the Defense Department, National Security Agency, FBI, State Department and several other government agencies.

The final bill contained hard-fought compromises creating a special fund to finance future U.S. covert operations in Iran and adopting a go-slow approach in purchasing small spy satellites.

Congress flexed its oversight muscle, slowing an attempt by Director of Central Intelligence John M. Deutch and Defense Secretary William J. Perry to consolidate imagery and mapping operations until lawmakers had had an opportunity to review and comment on the plan.

Congress also took steps in HR 1655, as well as in the fiscal 1996 defense appropriations bill (HR 2126—PL 104-61), to punish the National Reconnaissance Office (NRO) for reportedly hoarding more than $1 billion, while still seeking more money from Congress. The NRO, which oversaw the nation's spy satellites, had run into trouble in 1994 over the cost of its new office complex. HR 1655 required a review of NRO operations, and HR 2126 reduced its accounts by more than $900 million. (NRO, box, p. 218)

The fallout from the 1994 Aldrich H. Ames espionage case also lingered in 1995 as lawmakers gave additional power to the FBI for its counterintelligence investigations. (Ames spy case, p. 219)

BACKGROUND

Congress crafted the fiscal 1996 intelligence authorization bill as the CIA struggled to carve out a post-cold war direction without a permanent director for four months and as the intelligence community continued to assess the damage from the Ames fiasco.

R. James Woolsey stepped down as CIA director in January 1995, a victim of his decision to hand out light punishments for the Ames case as well as his troubled relationship with the White House and Congress. President Clinton's first nominee for CIA director, retired Gen. Michael P. C. Carns, was forced to withdraw amid allegations of immigration law violations. The president finally convinced Deputy Defense Secretary Deutch to take the helm of the besieged agency. (Foreign policy leadership, box, p. 193)

Deutch faced stiff competition from Congress in shaping a post–cold war CIA. Both the House and Senate oversight committees embarked on far-reaching reviews of the nation's intelligence-gathering apparatus, with plans to incorporate their recommendations into fiscal 1997 legislation.

The Ames case also continued to torment the intelligence community. The CIA's final report on the damage from the spy scandal concluded that Ames's treachery allowed tainted information from cold war double agents to reach the top echelons of the U.S. government. Deutch apprised the oversight committees of the report Oct. 31, 1995.

LEGISLATIVE ACTION

HR 1655 was reported by the House Select Intelligence Committee on June 14, 1995, and by the House Government Reform and Oversight Committee on July 19 (H Rept 104-138, Parts I and II). It was passed by a voice vote of the House on Sept. 13.

HR 1655 reportedly provided nearly $30 billion. During the Sept. 13 debate, the House voted 154–271 to reject a proposal by Barney Frank, D-Mass., that would have disclosed the exact overall amount. The House also rejected, 162–262, a second amendment by Frank that would have imposed a 3 percent across-the-board cut in the intelligence budget with an exemption for the CIA's retirement and disability fund.

A provision—added after prodding from the CIA and State Department—to allow the president to delay the imposition of economic sanctions raised concerns among some members. Responding to those reservations, the House approved by voice vote an amendment by House Intelligence Committee Chair-

CLASSIFIED INFORMATION DISCLOSURE

Disclosure in 1995 of explosive allegations of a CIA link to the death of an American living in Guatemala and the disappearance of a rebel leader nearly cost Rep. Robert G. Torricelli, D-N.J., his seat on the House Permanent Select Committee on Intelligence. But the House Committee on Standards of Official Conduct ultimately concluded that the ambiguity of a new House secrecy oath precluded punishing Torricelli, who said he had received the classified information from outside sources instead of Intelligence Committee briefings.

In a letter to President Clinton on March 22, 1995, that he also sent to the *New York Times,* Torricelli had claimed that a paid CIA informant in Guatemala ordered the killings of U.S. citizen Michael DeVine, an innkeeper, in 1990 and rebel leader Efrain Bamaca Velasquez in 1992. Velasquez's case attracted widespread attention when his wife, American lawyer Jennifer Harbury, waged a hunger strike after his disappearance. Torricelli's revelations touched off a furor in Congress that prompted House Speaker Newt Gingrich, R-Ga., to demand the Democrat's ouster from the intelligence panel.

Following a four-month inquiry, the House ethics committee concluded July 12 that while a secrecy breach had occurred based on its interpretation of the oath, the oath's lack of clarity prevented further action against Torricelli.

The oath—Rule 43, clause 13, adopted by the House on Jan. 4, 1995—required each member, officer and employee to swear that he or she "will not disclose any classified information received in the course of my service with the House of Representatives, except as authorized by the House of Representatives or in accordance with its rules."

The committee found varying interpretations of the language. Some members believed it applied only to classified information received in an official House proceeding, while others thought it applied to any information a member obtained. For future reference, the panel released a two-page memorandum describing the rule, the possible confusion and the best intent of the oath. The panel also said that, if in doubt, a member was required to make a good faith effort to determine whether the material was classified by contacting either the intelligence panel or other relevant committees.

In regard to Torricelli, the ethics panel said that the events in Guatemala contained "elements of both deep personal tragedy and possible government wrongdoing" and that the lawmaker had strong views on the matter. "The release of much of the information in question was clearly within Mr. Torricelli's prerogatives as a member of Congress," the committee said.

In a rare open hearing April 5, the Senate Select Committee on Intelligence had taken the CIA to task for failing to inform the congressional oversight panels of evidence implicating a paid CIA informant in the murder of a U.S. citizen by Guatemalan military personnel. Acting CIA Director William O. Studeman admitted that the agency should have notified the panels in October 1991 that it had potentially incriminating information about the informant but said the failure was an oversight rather than intentional deception.

In September, CIA Director John M. Deutch punished nine former and present CIA employees for unprofessional behavior and failure to inform Congress of human rights abuses in Guatemala.

---

man Larry Combest, R-Texas, to limit a presidential stay of sanctions to 120 days, require the president to report promptly to Congress if he took such a step, and end the provision after three years.

The bill slashed from $17.6 million to $5 million Clinton's request for funding for the administration's Environmental Task Force, which made environmental information obtained from intelligence gathering more readily available to the public. It also ordered each agency of the National Foreign Intelligence Program to spend no more than $2.5 million to carry out an April 17, 1995, executive order requiring the declassification of documents 25 or more years old.

The Senate Select Intelligence Committee reported its version of the intelligence bill (S 922—S Rept 104-97) on June 14. The Senate Armed Services Committee reported the bill Aug. 4 (S Rept 104-127). The Senate passed HR 1655 by voice vote Sept. 29 after substituting the text of S 922.

In the aftermath of reports about the NRO's $1 billion cache, Arlen Specter, R-Pa., chairman of the Senate Intelligence panel, offered an amendment to cap the NRO's ability to hold unspent funds to an amount equal to one month's operating expenses. The amendment, which was adopted by voice vote, also recommended a joint investigation of the fund by the inspectors gen-

eral of the CIA and the Pentagon, a step Deutch and Perry had announced in September, and the appointment of a financial control officer for the NRO.

The bill included a provision, pushed by the FBI, allowing the agency to obtain credit reports for counterintelligence investigations.

FINAL BILL

The House agreed to the conference report (H Rept 104-427) by voice vote Dec. 21, and the Senate followed suit later that day, clearing the bill for the president's signature Jan. 6, 1996.

Negotiators took nearly three months to complete the bill as they worked to resolve the disputes over the Iran covert fund and small spy satellites.

Newt Gingrich, R-Ga., who as House Speaker was an ex officio member of the House Intelligence Committee, sought to establish an $18 million fund for a future U.S. intelligence mission designed to aid in the overthrow of the Iranian regime. The proposal touched off fierce debate within the House and Senate Intelligence committees over the significant step of writing executive policy into the bill. The final bill authorized $2 million for traditional covert activities in Iran and $18 million in a conditional fund to be used as the administration determined.

House Intelligence Chairman Combest had pushed for the NRO to move quickly in buying 2,000-pound satellites, but several House Democrats and a bipartisan group on the Senate panel expressed reservations about rushing to purchase unproven technology. The final bill allowed Deutch to appoint a special panel that would recommend how to proceed in acquiring small satellites.

Responding to the administration's objections, the final bill provided $25 million for all intelligence agencies to declassify documents that were at least 25 years old. Citing varying cost estimates, conferees required the president to include the specific cost for declassification in his fiscal 1997 through fiscal 2000 budget requests.

The final bill provided $15 million for the Environmental Task Force, a $10 million increase over the House-passed level. The bill included the House provision allowing the president to delay imposition of economic sanctions, but the authority was to last only one year instead of three.

Conferees agreed to include the Senate provision amending the Fair Credit Reporting Act to allow the FBI the right to obtain credit reports for counterintelligence investigations. Under the bill, the FBI could obtain a court order to gain access to consumer credit reports and find the names and addresses of the financial institutions where an individual had an account. All parties would face civil penalties if the FBI effort were disclosed.

Conferees tempered the punishment for the NRO. The bill required a review of the NRO by the CIA and Defense Department inspectors general, a step the administration had already taken. After the review, the CIA director was to notify Congress before reprogramming, reallocating or rescinding any NRO money. The president was required to report to Congress by Jan. 30, 1996, on a plan for increased executive branch oversight of the intelligence budget, including the possibility of a new chief financial officer for the NRO. The report was to include an analysis of the Senate's initial plan to limit the NRO's ability to carry money over from one month to the next, but conferees abandoned the notion of imposing the more stringent cap.

House and Senate negotiators also tacked onto the conference report a provision prohibiting the CIA and Defense Department from using fiscal 1996 funds and previous-year dollars to create the National Imagery and Mapping Agency until Congress had a chance to receive, review and comment on the plan. Deutch and Perry had planned to consolidate the imagery and mapping operations on Oct. 1, 1996. ❑

1997 Intelligence Authorization

Congress in 1996 cleared a fiscal 1997 intelligence authorization bill (HR 3259—PL 104-293) that left the intelligence community's budget intact and made modest changes in the spy agencies' organization.

Unlike many other government programs, the intelligence budget came through the budget process unscathed. Although the overall figure was classified, it was widely reported that HR 3259 authorized about $30 billion—a 4.2 percent increase over the previous fiscal year and a 2.3 percent increase over the president's request. Renewed efforts to have the exact total made public failed once again.

Action on the annual authorization had been overshadowed by simultaneous efforts to overhaul the way the intelligence community was organized. Ambitious reorganization proposals in the House—which would have given the CIA director increased oversight of Defense Department intelligence agencies—never made it to the floor, and a greatly weakened version of the overhaul was passed in the Senate as part of HR 3259.

The final authorization bill included provisions aimed at helping the director of central intelligence keep a closer watch over the intelligence community by creating new positions to take on the day-to-day management of the CIA and other issues. That and a few other changes were all that survived of a two-year effort to revamp the intelligence community. *(Intelligence reorganization, p. 245)*

LEGISLATIVE ACTION

HR 3259 was passed by voice vote of the House on May 22, 1996. The House Intelligence Committee had reported the bill May 15 (H Rept 104-578, Part I).

House liberals strongly objected to giving the CIA and other intelligence agencies more money at a time when social welfare programs faced deep cuts, but two attempts to reduce the overall funding were defeated on May 22 before final passage. One amendment, by Bernard Sanders, I-Vt., was rejected 115–311. The second amendment, by Barney Frank, D-Mass., was rejected 192-235.

In other action on May 22, an attempt by Patricia Schroeder, D-Colo., to reduce the budget of the National Reconnaissance Office (NRO) to its fiscal 1996 level was rejected, 137–292. The NRO, whose very existence had been classified until 1992, had gotten into trouble in 1994 when the Senate Intelligence Committee alleged that it had not been informed of the agency's construction of a headquarters complex costing more than $300 million. It was back in hot water in 1995, when it was reported that the agency had hoarded more than $1 billion in unspent funds while still seeking additional money. Estimates of the size of the cache grew in 1996, reaching nearly $4 billion in May. CIA Director John M. Deutch had fired the NRO's top two officials in February, and the House declined to punish the agency further. *(NRO, box, p. 218; 1996 intelligence authorization, p. 242)*

House members May 22 also defeated a proposal by John Conyers Jr., D-Mich., to reveal the overall amount in the intelligence budget. The effort, which had become routine during annual consideration of the intelligence bill, was easily defeated, 176–248.

The Senate passed its version of HR 3259 by voice vote Sept. 17. The bill provided for a reported $30 billion for intelligence activities and called for the bottom line number to be made public.

The Senate Intelligence Committee on April 30 had reported legislation combining the annual intelligence authorization with sweeping proposals to overhaul the intelligence community (S 1718—S Rept 104-258). But the bill, which would have given the director of central intelligence more authority over Defense Department intelligence agencies, drew strong opposition from the Pentagon and from the Senate Armed Services Committee. A watered-down version was reported by the Armed Services panel June 6 (S Rept 104-277). The Senate Governmental Affairs Committee reported the bill July 29 (S Rept 104-337).

The Armed Services Committee prevailed on the Senate floor, when the Senate passed HR 3259, after substituting a version of S 1718 reflecting the panel's priorities.

FINAL BILL

The House adopted the conference report on HR 3259 (H Rept 104-832) by voice vote Sept. 25. The Senate followed suit a few hours later, also by voice vote, clearing the bill for the president. The bill was signed into law Oct. 11.

Conferees dropped the Senate-passed provision requiring the president to disclose the total amount spent annually on intelligence-related activities. The idea was strongly opposed by Larry Combest, R-Texas, chairman of the House Intelligence Committee.

The legislation addressed the thorny issue of whether the CIA should be barred from using journalists as spies. The House measure had included a fairly sweeping prohibition against the practice, although it allowed the president to waive the restriction in the interest of national security. Conferees also gave the director of central intelligence authority to waive the provision.

The measure prohibited former senior CIA personnel from accepting employment with foreign governments for three years (not five years, as called for in the Senate version) after their retirement, although the president could also waive that prohibition.

The final bill also included the changes in the organization of the intelligence community. *(Details, p. 246)*   ❑

Intelligence Community Overhaul

Attempts in 1996 at sweeping reform of the intelligence community resulted in minor changes. The modest reforms were included in the fiscal 1997 intelligence authorization bill (HR 3259—PL 104-293).

Proponents of ambitious reform proposals had called for expanding the power of the director of central intelligence. In particular, they wanted the Pentagon to cede some of its authority over spy programs to a strengthened Central Intelligence Agency. But the Pentagon and prodefense lawmakers succeeded in blocking any changes that would have diluted the defense secretary's control over Pentagon agencies. An ambivalent stance by the Clinton administration also helped doom the proposals.

In the end, the legislation not only allowed the defense secretary to retain ultimate control over defense-related intelligence agency budgets and appointments but also went a step further and strengthened the role of the Defense Department. Instead of losing some of its turf, the Pentagon was put in charge of a new National Imagery and Mapping Agency, which was to con-

solidate and manage all high-tech imagery and mapping operations, including programs that had been run by the CIA.

The intelligence director was given more help in managing the intelligence community, but it was help he did not want. Director of Central Intelligence John M. Deutch strongly objected to new positions created by the bill, and President Clinton vowed to seek changes in the next Congress.

Foreign policy analysts who participated in studies of the intelligence community believed that Congress missed a golden opportunity to refocus the bureaucracy—still largely oriented to deal with cold war military threats—to address such challenges as terrorism, crime and drug-trafficking.

BACKGROUND

Rocked by the devastating 1994 Aldrich Ames spy scandal and embarrassed by revelations that the National Reconnaissance Office (NRO) had amassed more than $1 billion in unspent funds, the intelligence community began 1996 as a prime candidate for a major makeover by Congress. *(Ames spy scandal, p. 219; NRO, 1996 intelligence authorization, p. 242)*

The congressional debate kicked off March 1, 1996, with the widely anticipated release of a report by a presidential commission on intelligence. The bipartisan panel, chaired by former Carter administration defense secretary Harold Brown, had been created by Congress in 1994 to "review the efficacy and appropriateness" of U.S. intelligence activities in the post–cold war era. *(1995 intelligence authorization, p. 216)*

Despite its broad mandate, the Brown commission rejected radical changes that had been proposed by members of Congress over the years. For example, the panel opposed creating an intelligence "czar."

To relieve some of the burden on the director of central intelligence, the panel recommended creating another deputy position. Having one deputy for the CIA's day-to-day operations and another responsible for the intelligence community, the commission argued, would give the intelligence director more time to oversee the sprawling intelligence bureaucracy.

The commission endorsed a CIA-Defense Department plan to consolidate imagery and mapping operations under a National Imagery and Mapping Agency. It also supported plans for greater coordination between intelligence activities and law enforcement to meet post–cold war threats posed by the proliferation of weapons of mass destruction, foreign terrorism, international organized crime and drug-trafficking. Since March 1995, the deputy intelligence director and the deputy attorney general had cochaired a board for this purpose.

Other recommendations included making public the annual budget figure for intelligence activities and eliminating the eight-year limits for members on the two intelligence committees to improve congressional oversight.

HOUSE ACTION

House Intelligence Committee Chairman Larry Combest, R-Texas, put forward a legislative proposal (HR 3237) that went much further than the Brown commission report. His plan would have created what he called a "truly corporate" intelligence community by enhancing the role of the central intelligence director and abolishing several defense intelligence agencies.

The House Intelligence Committee reported a watered-down version of HR 3237 on June 13, 1996 (H Rept 104-620, Part I). To win committee approval, Combest had agreed to substantially tone down his bill by removing many of the sweeping structural changes and providing instead for continued studies on consolidating agencies and offices. But even with those changes, Democrats objected that the committee was going too far and not considering the Clinton administration's concerns.

Combest's efforts to soften the bill could not hold off the defense establishment. The House National Security Committee reported an even more pared-back version on July 23 (H Rept 104-620, Part II). As expected, the committee came down squarely on the Pentagon's side in the long-running turf war over reorganizing intelligence agencies. The panel eliminated from the bill nearly all the provisions aimed at increasing the authority of the director of central intelligence over military-related intelligence.

The intercommittee battle was so intense that Combest did not press to bring the bill to the floor.

SENATE ACTION

On the Senate side, the process unfolded in a more contentious fashion, but the outcome was essentially the same: what began as a sweeping proposal to overhaul the intelligence community was transformed by prodefense lawmakers into a set of modest changes that left the Pentagon's authority intact.

The Senate Intelligence Committee on April 30 reported an overhaul proposal authored by its chairman, Arlen Specter, R-Pa., as part of the fiscal 1997 intelligence authorization bill (S 1718—S Rept 104-258). The measure included provisions to give the intelligence director more authority over the budgets of three Pentagon agencies—the National Security Agency, the NRO and the new National Imagery and Mapping Agency—as well as veto power over the appointment of the heads of those three agencies. The bill also endorsed the idea of making public the total amount spent on intelligence activities. (*1997 intelligence authorization, p. 244*)

The bill drew strong opposition from the Pentagon and from the Senate Armed Services Committee. Armed Services Chairman Strom Thurmond, R-S.C., and senior Democrat Sam Nunn of Georgia asked Specter to hold off action until the following year, but Specter refused. The Armed Services panel delayed action on the bill for a month, while the two committees tried unsuccessfully to work out a compromise.

Finally, Armed Services abandoned the effort and reported its own version of the bill June 6 (S Rept 104-277), calling for leaving the secretary of defense in charge of defense intelligence budgets and personnel. The Senate Governmental Affairs Committee then sat on the bill for a while, before essentially endorsing the Armed Services version in its July 29 report (S Rept 104-337).

No further action was taken on S 1718. Instead, the Senate took up HR 3259, the House-passed fiscal 1997 intelligence au-

thorization bill. The Senate passed HR 3259 by voice vote Sept. 17, after substituting a version of S 1718 that reflected the Armed Services Committee's priorities. The fate of one Intelligence Committee proposal was indicative of the destiny of the broader reorganization agenda. The panel had proposed dropping the Senate rule that restricted service on the Intelligence Committee to eight consecutive years and thus limited the ability of committee members to build seniority and expertise. When the Senate created the Intelligence Committee in 1976, that rule was one of several intended to hobble the new panel and thus protect the jurisdiction of Armed Services and other committees. Faced with opposition from other senators, Specter had to drop the provision when the Senate took up the bill.

FINAL BILL

The House adopted the conference report on HR 3259 (H Rept 104-832) by voice vote Sept. 25, and the Senate did the same a few hours later, clearing the bill for the president's signature Oct. 11.

The final bill contained a Senate-passed provision intended to give the intelligence director more help in managing the intelligence community. A new position of deputy director for community management was established, along with three assistant directors to oversee collection, analysis and administration. The Senate was to confirm appointments to those posts. CIA Director Deutch opposed the three new assistant positions, arguing that they would not significantly enhance the director's ability to manage the intelligence community. Clinton said he would support Deutch's efforts to seek repeal or modifications of the provision in the 105th Congress.

The bill authorized the intelligence director to help draw up budgets for defense-related intelligence agencies and required the secretary of defense to consult with the intelligence chief before appointing directors to those agencies. But the defense secretary retained the final say over those budgets and appointments. Control of the new National Imagery and Mapping Agency was given to the Defense Department.

Conferees dropped the Senate provision requiring the president to disclose the total amount spent annually on intelligence-related activities. Combest strongly opposed the idea, although it had won support from the administration and many of the blue-ribbon commissions that had studied intelligence operations.

Vietnam Policy

President Clinton normalized diplomatic relations with Vietnam on July 11, 1995, a bold move that drew the wrath of some in Congress but was widely accepted by much of the nation 20 years after the United States' inglorious defeat at the hands of the communists. The Southeast Asian nation was seen as fertile territory for U.S. business investments and a diplomatic opportunity to bolster a challenger to China.

Seventeen months earlier, on Feb. 3, 1994, Clinton had ended the ban on trade with Vietnam that had been in place since the Vietnam War. (*Vietnam trade embargo, box, p. 214*)

When the embargo lifting failed to generate the political fallout that many had feared, several lawmakers pushed for the further step of normalizing U.S. relations with Vietnam. The backing of Republican and Democratic members who had survived the war provided political cover for Clinton, who continued to be dogged by his decision while in college to avoid military service in Vietnam.

Key support came from Sens. John McCain, R-Ariz., a former Navy fighter pilot who spent nearly six years in Vietnamese prisons, and John Kerry, D-Mass., a decorated veteran of the war. Citing assessments from the military, the lawmakers argued that Vietnam had been cooperative in helping the United States determine the fate of missing U.S. servicemen.

U.S. businesses—among them, oil companies, telecommunications firms and airplane manufacturers—also urged Clinton to act, envisioning a financial boon through investment and development of oil-rich Vietnam.

But others in Congress—including Senate Majority Leader Bob Dole, R-Kan., a World War II veteran and the leading contender for the 1996 GOP presidential nomination, and Sen. Robert C. Smith, R-N.H., a Vietnam veteran—said the Clinton administration had acted hastily. They charged that Vietnam had not provided a full accounting of missing Americans.

On Nov. 13, 1995, the Pentagon released a report concluding that 567 of the 2,202 cases of U.S. military personnel unaccounted for in Southeast Asia would never be fully resolved. In those cases, the Americans were killed in explosions that destroyed their remains, were lost at sea when their aircraft went down or were buried on river beds that had since eroded or been swept away by flooded rivers. The report, a 10-page summary of a yearlong review, said that 1,476 other cases warranted additional inquiry and 159 cases should be deferred as the government awaited new leads. The review had been conducted by 58 analysts from the Defense POW-MIA Office in Washington, the Joint Task Force for Full Accounting in Hawaii, and the Central Identification Laboratory, also in Hawaii.

OTHER ACTION

In other Vietnam-related action:

• Congress in 1995 imposed procedural restrictions on the Pentagon's ability to declare dead those personnel missing in action (MIA). Included in the fiscal 1996 defense authorization bill (HR 1530) was a 37-page provision that called for the creation of a new, centralized office in the Defense Department to handle the POW-MIA issue and imposed requirements on commanders in the field. Field commanders were to make a preliminary assessment on a missing service member and forward that report to a theater commander within 48 hours. Within 14 days, the theater commander was to determine whether the individual was a POW or MIA and relay that information to the service secretary or defense secretary. Robert K. Dornan, R-Calif., chairman of the House National Security Military Personnel Subcommittee and a critic of Clinton administration policy toward Vietnam, was the driving force behind the provisions. *(1996 defense authorization, p. 294)*

However, at the Pentagon's request, Congress in 1996 repealed several of the provisions, as part of the fiscal 1997 defense authorization bill (HR 3230). For instance, unit commanders were given 10 days to report any MIA to the service secretary, eliminating the theater commander from the reporting chain. Although the bill did not repeal as much as the Senate had proposed, Dornan still declared that the conference report had gutted the original package. *(1997 defense authorization, p. 306)*

• The fiscal 1996 appropriations bill for the departments of Commerce, Justice and State (HR 2076) would have barred U.S. dollars for an embassy in Vietnam unless the president certified that Vietnam had been "fully cooperative" on POW-MIA issues. President Clinton vetoed the bill for a number of reasons, including the Vietnam provision.

• The fiscal 1996–1997 State Department authorization bill (HR 1561) would have restricted the president from normalizing relations with Vietnam unless he certified that Hanoi was cooperating in accounting for U.S. servicemen still listed as missing in action from the war in Southeast Asia. This provision was one of the reasons cited by Clinton for his veto of the bill.

HR 1561 also would have prohibited the use of U.S. dollars for the repatriation of Vietnamese, Cambodians or Laotians, without a fair hearing and unless those eligible were offered resettlement outside their native countries. *(1996–1997 State Department authorization, p. 228)*

• The Senate in September 1996 put off until 1997 consideration of the nomination of Rep. Pete Peterson, D-Fla., to be U.S. ambassador to Vietnam. Senior Republicans on the Senate Foreign Relations Committee contended that the appointment of Peterson, a former prisoner of war in Vietnam, would violate a clause of the Constitution barring members of Congress from serving in offices created during their terms. (Peterson's nomination was not confirmed by the Senate until April 10, 1997.) ❑

North Korea Nuclear Agreement

Members of the 104th Congress made sporadic attempts to block or modify the 1994 nuclear agreement between the United States and North Korea, but in the end Congress provided the funding needed to implement the deal.

Under the agreement, the United States and its allies promised to provide Pyongyang with oil and safe nuclear energy in exchange for North Korea's commitment to freeze its nuclear weapons program. The United States agreed to supply the North Koreans with $4.7 million worth of fuel oil to compensate them for shutting down an existing reactor, which they claimed was needed to supply energy. The United States also joined a multinational consortium that was to supply additional oil pending completion of new reactors, at an estimated cost to taxpayers of between $20 million and $30 million a year over 10 years. *(Agreement, p. 221)*

Congress appropriated a requested $22 million to underwrite the agreement in the fiscal 1996 foreign operations appropriations bill (HR 1868—PL 104-107) and $25 million in the fiscal 1997 bill (HR 3610—PL 104-208), despite efforts in the

House to nearly halve the request. *(1996 foreign aid appropriations, p. 231; 1997 foreign aid appropriations, p. 234)*

In January 1996, the chairmen of three Senate committees—Energy and Natural Resources, Foreign Relations and Intelligence—demanded that the agreement be redefined as a formal treaty, which would mean that it would require the advice and consent of the Senate. The Clinton administration refused, characterizing the arrangement as an "agreed framework," which was less binding than a formal treaty and gave the United States more flexibility in monitoring North Korea's compliance.

The House had included in its version of the ill-fated foreign aid and State Department authorization bill (HR 1561), which it passed in June 1995, a provision calling for stricter terms for the deal with North Korea. Among other steps, it urged that South Korea be declared "the only acceptable source" for the light water reactors that were to be provided to North Korea. It also would have required that Congress be notified of any reprogramming of funds within accounts that already were authorized and appropriated by Congress for implementing the deal.

On Sept. 18, 1995, the House had approved by voice vote a resolution (H J Res 83) that was virtually identical to the amendment added to HR 1561, except that it dropped the reporting requirement because of objections from the administration.

Despite the nuclear agreement, North Korea continued to be regarded as a tinderbox. Its situation became increasingly precarious in 1996, as famine, fuel shortages and a moribund economy took a devastating toll. Impoverished and armed to the teeth, North Korea seemed to grow more desperate by the day. The country's decision to dispatch a submarine in a clumsy attempt to infiltrate the South fanned already high tensions on the peninsula and alienated potential donors of food. ❏

Mexico Loan Guarantees

Amid echoes of the rancorous 1993 debate over the North American Free Trade Agreement (NAFTA), lawmakers tried but failed to block an economic bailout of Mexico in early 1995. It was President Clinton's first major foreign policy test in the Republican-led 104th Congress.

Mexico seemed on the verge of a financial collapse after a panic followed the abrupt devaluation of the peso on Dec. 20, 1994. Mexican President Ernesto Zedillo issued a desperate plea for help. Without U.S. intervention, Mexican officials warned, their government would not be able to pay off some $40 billion in short-term obligations that would come due over the first half of 1995.

Clinton administration officials said a default by Mexico could have a ripple effect throughout Latin America and lead to a surge of illegal immigration into the United States. They devised a plan to help stabilize Mexico's economy by offering up to $40 billion in U.S.-backed loan guarantees.

The proposal won strong backing from GOP congressional leaders, most of whom had supported NAFTA. But rank-and-file lawmakers of both parties immediately raised questions. They were taken aback by the size of the package and were con-

cerned about the risk of a Mexican default on the U.S.-backed loans. *(NAFTA, p. 155)*

Comparisons to U.S. loan guarantees for Israel, assurances that the guarantees would be backed up by Mexican oil revenues, and strong lobbying by the administration failed to assuage members' fears. Liberal Democrats who had led the unsuccessful bid to defeat NAFTA joined forces with a group of isolationist-leaning conservatives in opposing the deal. The revolt was fueled by charges that the loan guarantees would be a taxpayer-financed bailout of not only the unstable Mexican government but also the U.S. financial institutions that had extended Mexico billions of dollars in credit.

With even supporters pushing for adding conditions to the package, the administration put together an alternative plan that would not require congressional approval. It included:

• $20 billion in credits from the Treasury Department's Exchange Stabilization Fund. Clinton signed an executive order authorizing those credits Jan. 31.

• $17.8 billion in credits from the International Monetary Fund.

• $10 billion in credits from the Bank for International Settlements.

With Canada and several Latin American countries also pitching in, the package totaled about $50 billion.

The immediate reaction from most lawmakers was relief at being spared a vote on the loan guarantees. But some opponents of the original plan blasted Clinton for bypassing Congress and tapping Treasury's Exchange Stabilization Fund, whose primary purpose was to stabilize the value of the dollar. Treasury Secretary Robert E. Rubin acknowledged that the administration's plan represented a unique use of the fund.

The critics continued to skirmish with the administration for weeks. The heat was turned up after U.S. and Mexican officials signed an implementing agreement Feb. 21.

The House Banking and Financial Services Committee Feb. 27 reported a resolution of inquiry (H Res 80—H Rept 104-53) requesting that scores of documents on the U.S. deal with Mexico and on the overall health of the Mexican economy be turned over within 14 days. The full House passed H Res 80 on March 1 by a vote of 407–21.

When the White House said it would not be able to provide all of the information for two months, a rebellious group of House members pushed to block the administration package but not enough support could be mustered for that move.

Several Senate committees also requested more information. The Senate Foreign Relations Committee April 4 reported a bill (S 384) requiring monthly reports on loan guarantees and other aid to Mexico. Senate Banking, Housing, and Urban Affairs Committee Chairman Alfonse M. D'Amato, R-N.Y., proposed limiting use of the Exchange Stabilization Fund but eventually withdrew his amendment to a fiscal 1995 rescissions package (HR 1158).

In a surprise move on April 5, conferees on a supplemental defense appropriations bill (HR 889) added a provision to block new loans to Mexico unless the administration produced all documents requested under H Res 80. Critics of the rescue package immediately proclaimed victory and said that all new credits had to stop as soon as the president signed the bill. But that did not occur because the provision left it to the president to certify compliance. The White House provided some 2,300 documents to the House Banking Committee on April 5 and proclaimed that it was in "substantial compliance" on April 6. Officials said the remaining documents would be delivered as soon as the House established procedures for handling the classified information covered by the resolution.

House Speaker Newt Gingrich, D-Ga., charged in a May 4 letter to Clinton that the administration had not abided by the terms of the document disclosure provision and that $3 billion in loans extended to Mexico since he signed HR 889 April 10 were "a direct violation of federal law." The White House called the allegation baseless.   ❏

U.S. Embassy in Israel

Congress in 1995 cleared legislation (S 1322—PL 104-45) aimed at forcing the administration to relocate the U.S. Embassy in Israel from Tel Aviv to Jerusalem by mid-1999. Facing veto-proof majorities in both chambers, Clinton—who had warned that enacting the bill would jeopardize the Middle East Peace process—let the measure become law Nov. 8 without his signature. But the president vowed: "I will use the legislation's waiver authority to avoid damage to the peace process."

Like most other nations, the United States maintained its embassy in Tel Aviv, although Israel considered Jerusalem the country's capital. The State Department had taken the position that the status of Jerusalem should be determined by Israelis and Arabs in a final resolution of their conflict.

But Israel's supporters on Capitol Hill disagreed and pushed ahead with legislation. S 1322, introduced by Senate Majority Leader Bob Dole, R-Kan., required that the United States move its embassy by May 31, 1999. The bill earmarked $25 million for the project from the State Department's buildings and maintenance account in fiscal 1996 and $75 million in fiscal 1997. It further specified that, in fiscal 1999, 50 percent of the money in the account would be withheld until the secretary of state affirmed that the new embassy had opened. But the president could waive the funding limitation for indefinite six-month periods if he determined that such action was warranted by national security interests.

The bill was passed by the Senate on Oct. 24 by a vote of 93–5. The House cleared it the same day, 374–37.

Israeli Prime Minister Yitzhak Rabin warmly thanked Congress for passing the legislation at an elaborate ceremony held Oct. 25 to commemorate the 3,000th anniversary of King David's entry into Jerusalem. Rabin told the audience of lawmakers, Jewish leaders and other dignitaries gathered in the Capitol Rotunda that Jerusalem "was ours, is ours and will be ours forever."

RABIN ASSASSINATION

Less than two weeks later, Rabin was dead. He was shot by a right-wing Israeli law student Nov. 4 after giving a speech to a peace rally. Rabin's successor, Shimon Peres, appeared before a joint meeting of Congress on Dec. 12 and used his speech to make a dramatic appeal to Syria for resumption of peace talks.

1996 JERUSALEM PROVISION

The Senate in 1996 included in its version of the fiscal 1997 foreign operations appropriations bill (HR 3540) a provision requiring that all U.S. government documents refer to Jerusalem as the capital of Israel. The controversial provision—which the administration said was "ill-advised" and "may raise serious separation-of-power issues"—was dropped in conference. (1997 foreign aid appropriations, p. 234)   ❏

Jordan Debt Relief

Congress provided $275 million in debt relief for Jordan, as part of a rescissions bill (HR 1944—PL 104-19) enacted in 1995. President Clinton had requested the debt relief to reward Jordan for signing a peace agreement with Israel. (Rescissions package, p. 73)

The provision had originally been attached to a fiscal 1995 defense supplemental appropriations bill (HR 889). But it was dropped in conference and attached instead to HR 1158, thus giving Clinton additional incentive not to veto that measure.

The House had approved $50 million, but the Senate had gone along with the requested $275 million. Conferees agreed on the Senate provision.   ❏

Iraq Resolution

The Senate became ensnared in election-year politics as it struggled to come up with a response to President Clinton's missile strikes against Iraq in September 1996. After intense negotiations, Senate Democrats and Republicans finally agreed on a cautiously worded resolution (S Res 288) that praised actions taken by the U.S. armed forces "under the direction of the commander in chief." But the president was not mentioned by name.

Clinton unleashed the two missile strikes against Iraq Sept. 3 after Saddam Hussein's forces moved against a protected Kurdish enclave in northern Iraq. The measured U.S. attacks, involving a total of 44 cruise missiles, targeted military installations in southern Iraq, hundreds of miles from the area under Iraqi attack. The president also greatly expanded the "no-fly zone" in southern Iraq to deny Iraqi military flights from the border with Kuwait north to the suburbs of Baghdad.

Buoyed by the apparent success of the operation and their rising political fortunes, Senate Democrats had wanted to express support not only for the military operation but also for the president who ordered it.

Republicans bristled at lauding the president, arguing that a string of administration diplomatic blunders forced Clinton to resort to the military option. Republicans also expressed concern over the lack of international support for the mission and the breakdown in unity among Iraq's Kurds, which provided Saddam an opening to dispatch his forces into the north. Republicans were also deeply dissatisfied with the administration's failure to provide advance notice to key lawmakers of the president's decision to launch the missiles.

Democrats countered that with 1996 GOP presidential nominee Bob Dole lagging badly behind Clinton in the polls, Republicans were simply unwilling to credit the president on his handling of foreign policy, an area that Dole considered his strong suit.

After a bipartisan negotiating group cobbled together S Res 288, a politically neutral resolution designed to offend no one, the Senate adopted it, 96–1, on Sept. 5. The House, where partisan tensions typically ran even higher, did not try to move a similar resolution. ❑

Haiti Policy Documents

Political skirmishing between the Clinton administration and House Republicans over Haiti escalated dramatically with President Clinton's refusal Sept. 23, 1996, to release 47 of 51 documents on Haiti policy that had been subpoenaed by the House International Relations Committee.

The panel's Republicans, who had sharply criticized the administration's handling of Haiti policy, demanded the documents as part of a yearlong probe into political violence there. But Clinton declined to release them, invoking the constitutional doctrine of executive privilege.

Republicans alleged that the administration was trying to cover up embarrassing information showing the complicity of the U.S. backed Haitian government in political murders. Democrats countered that the GOP was engaged in an election-year effort to tarnish Clinton's success in restoring democratic rule to Haiti. The White House said the documents being withheld included confidential memoranda on conversations with foreign leaders and deliberations by the president's national security advisers.

An aide to House International Relations Committee Chairman Benjamin A. Gilman, R-N.Y., said insufficient time remained in the 104th Congress to attempt to obtain the documents by threatening a contempt of Congress citation. ❑

Colombia Decertification

The Clinton administration announced March 1, 1996, its determination that Colombia had failed to stem illicit narcotics-trafficking. The president was required by law to determine whether major drug-producing or conduit countries were cooperating in the war on drugs. Its decision to decertify Colombia required the administration to cut off financing from the Export-Import Bank and most direct aid and to oppose loans to Colombia by international financial institutions.

Senate Foreign Relations Committee Chairman Jesse Helms, R-N.C., had repeatedly demanded that President Clinton decertify Colombia. Helms and other lawmakers had raised similar questions concerning Mexico, but Clinton spared that country from punishment. ❑

CHAPTER 5

Defense Policy

Defense Policy

Bill Clinton got clobbered on a defense issue in the first big political battle of his presidency: within days of his taking office, his campaign pledge to eliminate the Pentagon regulation barring gays and lesbians from the armed services clearly was doomed by the adamant opposition of Republicans, led by Senate GOP Leader Bob Dole, Kan.; conservative Democrats, led by Senate Armed Services Committee Chairman Sam Nunn, Ga.; and the military, led by Joint Chiefs of Staff Chairman Gen. Colin Powell. The early debacle was widely seen as proof that Clinton's personal history of trying to avoid military service during the Vietnam War left him hopelessly disadvantaged in dealing with hawkish critics of his defense program.

But less than four years later, the Republican-led Congress scurried out of Washington in the run-up to the 1996 elections, after a truncated defense debate that Clinton had effortlessly dominated. To be sure, Congress cleared in 1996—and Clinton signed—annual authorization and appropriations bills for fiscal 1997 that slightly increased the defense budget the president had sent Congress at the start of the year. But the added funds were shotgunned across the sprawling procurement and research budgets, adding up to relatively minor increases to hundreds of programs. In effect, the additions reaffirmed Clinton's overall defense program by modestly enhancing it, instead of challenging it in any fundamental respect.

The only defense issue on which Republicans seemed able to work up a good head of steam—the effort to accelerate deployment of a nationwide antimissile defense—was deliberately spun out of the annual defense funding bills in 1996, relegated to separate legislation that had no chance of becoming law. Three major factors contributed to this striking transformation of defense politics during Clinton's first term in the White House:

• After half a century in which the looming Soviet threat had preempted a large slice of the U.S. public's attention, that public had become largely disengaged from the outside world, partly because the Soviet threat had suddenly collapsed and partly because the national political system was focused on a raft of domestic issues. The public did not become isolationist—at least no more so than usual. If anything, it seemed to become more receptive to the argument that U.S. military force remained essential, partly because the Persian Gulf conflict of 1990–1991 dulled the euphoria about a possible "new world order" that had bloomed in the immediate aftermath of the Soviet empire's collapse.

A sense that the post-Soviet world remained a dangerous place provided strong political underpinnings for a relatively robust defense budget even as the rest of the federal budget was being sliced in real terms. The practical result was that Clinton, aligned with a majority of congressional Republicans and defense-minded Democrats, repeatedly brushed aside legislative initiatives that would have significantly reduced the administration's Pentagon spending plans.

• Against that background, the first big change in the political dynamic of the 1993–1996 defense debate was Clinton's. Over the course of his first 12 to 18 months in office, he abandoned a handful of symbolically charged stances on national security issues—the gay ban was one, deference to the United Nations was another—that had marked him as a liberal instead of as the centrist "new Democrat" he had claimed to be in his election campaign. Partly because Clinton shifted ground, GOP attacks aimed at some of his more liberal early initiatives missed their mark.

• But most important, when the Republicans got control of the defense budget in 1995–1996, having won control of Congress in the 1994 elections, they were unable to present to the country a coherent, alternative national security policy that differed in any significant respect from Clinton's. One reason for this failure was the profound differences, running deep in the GOP political community, over the proper degree of U.S. engagement with the outside world and with allies. But another was that, particularly for the large class of House Republican freshmen elected in 1994, defense issues—like all other policy questions—ranked far down on their list of priorities, below the near-sovereign goal of slicing the size of the federal budget.

So, even before GOP defense hawks had to weigh the likelihood that Clinton would veto an increase in Pentagon spending that he deemed too large, they faced an equally fundamental

REFERENCES

Discussion of defense policy for the years 1945–1964 may be found in *Congress and the Nation Vol. I*, pp. 237–334; for the years 1965–1968, *Congress and the Nation Vol. II*, pp. 827–890; for the years 1969–1972, *Congress and the Nation Vol. III*, pp. 191–252; for the years 1973–1976, *Congress and the Nation Vol. IV*, pp. 153–197; for the years 1977–1980, *Congress and the Nation Vol. V*, pp. 125–176; for the years 1981–1984, *Congress and the Nation Vol. VI*, pp. 201–257; for the years 1985–1988, *Congress and the Nation Vol. VII*, pp. 273–340; for the years 1989–1992, *Congress and the Nation Vol. VIII*, pp. 335–412.

National Defense (Budget Authority)

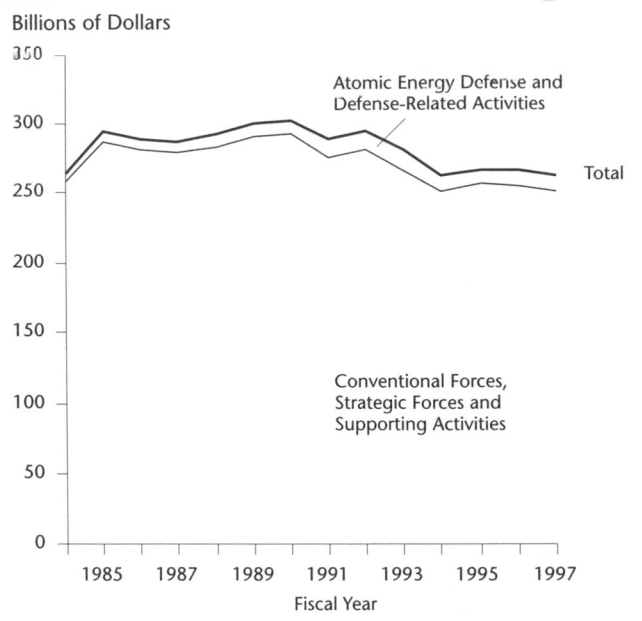

Billions of Dollars

NOTE: Data for 1997 are estimated.

SOURCE: Office of Management and Budget, *Historical Tables, Budget of the United States Government: Fiscal Year 1998* (Washington, D.C.: U.S. Government Printing Office, 1997), Table 5.1.

political problem: the Republican deficit hawks would not allow them as large an increase in Clinton's defense budgets as the defense hawks had hoped for. The party tried to finesse this problem with a couple of issues they hoped would pack a symbolic wallop, in addition to being substantively important: antimissile defense was preeminent among these. But none of those hot-button issues gained traction outside the ranks of Republican loyalists, either during the 1995–1996 legislative battles or during Dole's ill-fated presidential campaign in 1996. The antimissile defense campaign underscored the Republicans' intramural rift, foundering twice because too many GOP conservatives were leery of its potential cost.

The upshot was that, apart from a rough patch in his first 18 months in the White House, Clinton secured from Congress essentially the defense program he wanted and he used U.S. forces basically as he wished, regardless of strong congressional opposition to many of the missions.

THE OPENING ROUNDS

An accidental quality existed to the emergence of the Pentagon's gay ban as first big defense policy battle of Clinton's presidency. Clinton had said as early as October 1991 that he would eliminate the Pentagon policy, a commitment he reiterated whenever he was asked about it during the presidential campaign. Although Clinton openly courted the support of gay and lesbian political activists, his stand on the military policy never became a focal point of debate, partly because President George Bush and his aides were wary of recalling the harsh, antigay rhetoric of the 1992 Republican Convention.

So when Clinton won the election, he was solidly on record behind a potentially controversial policy that had not been seriously tested in the political marketplace. Almost immediately, the issue burst into the center of the political arena.

One reason for its sudden prominence was that Clinton's pledge to eliminate the gay ban was one of the few concrete and controversial stands he took during the campaign that he had not either dropped or fobbed off onto a study committee by the time he began organizing his administration. Another reason was that it rekindled critics' contention that Clinton's avoidance of the draft reflected not only a lack of empathy with the American military but also an ideologically rooted contempt for it on the part of the man who now was its commander in chief.

Clinton defenders blamed Defense Secretary Les Aspin for catalyzing the rapid coalescence of opposition to Clinton's effort to drop the gay ban: during a televised interview program, Aspin had noted that Congress could stymie any effort by Clinton to unilaterally change the policy. But this claim assumed that Clinton's leading opponents on the issue—Dole, Nunn and Powell, three of the most politically astute players in Washington—needed a nudge from Aspin to remind them of the many levers the Senate could use against unpopular presidential initiatives.

Clinton's plan was foredoomed by the intense opposition of the military. The president strung out the battle for six months until late July, when he announced to an audience of senior officers a compromise that made only minor changes in the existing policy. In his speech, Clinton forcefully stated his case for a more liberal policy than the military would accept. But his comments also were laced with expressions of deference to military expertise, which became a more prominent feature of the administration's public stands on defense issues.

FROM ASPIN TO PERRY

Because the outcome of the gay ban debate was seen by gay activists as a betrayal, Clinton's dogged refusal to abandon a lost cause had little practical effect except to occupy during the administration's first six months a large part of the time and energy of Aspin and the top aides he had brought to the Pentagon from the House Armed Services Committee, which he had chaired.

That was only one of the obstacles Aspin had to surmount in formulating a defense policy for the first Democratic administration in a dozen years—and the first one since the Soviet Union's demise. Another set of problems—the most daunting—was Aspin's shortcomings as Pentagon chief, including his penchant for prolonged and sometimes public rumination on issues, and his aggressively casual personal style, which grated on military sensibilities.

Then, too, Aspin's Pentagon, like the other agencies in Clinton's administration, limped along for months after the inauguration while key senior jobs went unfilled as White House political operatives tried to balance contending claims based on expertise, social diversity and political loyalty to Clinton.

For all that, Aspin did for Clinton during 1993 what he had done as Armed Services Chairman for House Democrats during the Bush administration: he put Clinton's name on a relatively coherent defense program that was widely supported within his party and buffered Democrats against the charge of being "soft" on defense, which had been the party's bugaboo for two decades. The Democratic program Chairman Aspin had unveiled in 1991 was built on the premise that U.S. forces should be large enough to win two major regional wars. According to Aspin's analysis, this could be done with an active-duty force of 1.4 million, a reduction of some 300,000 troops. In addition to providing a rallying point for House Democrats during the balance of the Bush administration, Aspin's analysis provided the basis for Clinton's pledge during the 1992 campaign to cut $60 billion from Bush's long-range Pentagon spending plan.

As Clinton's Pentagon chief, Aspin presided over a "bottom-up review" of future U.S. defense needs, which, in September 1993, recommended a slightly modified version of the force that resulted from Aspin's Armed Services Committee analysis.

Aspin thus set the terms of the mainstream defense debate for the balance of Clinton's first term. Republican critics attacked his defense program on grounds that it was too meager to meet the two-war strategy. But no significant challenge to the two-war goal ever gained political traction. Aspin had hoped to similarly shape the national debate on the conditions under which U.S. forces should be deployed overseas in the post-Soviet era. His own views, outlined in a September 1992 speech, were decidedly interventionist and critical of the idea—widely associated with Powell—that U.S. forces should be committed to potentially dangerous situations only if they had an explicitly defined mission and robust political support at home.

Aspin, who had been a leading supporter of war with Iraq in 1991, contended that precision-guided "smart" bombs allowed limited attacks that were finely calibrated to achieve enough leverage to make an adversary comply with U.S. demands. He also hinted that, unless the U.S. military demonstrated that it could perform missions that were less cataclysmic—but much more likely—than winning a war with Iraq, public support would wane for annual defense budgets that were on the order of a quarter of a trillion dollars.

But Aspin's perspective on the use-of-force issue was quickly overshadowed by other voices within the Clinton administration that stressed reliance on multilateral organizations—preeminently, the United Nations—as the channels through which U.S. force would be used to shape the international environment.

The administration's insistent discussion of the United States as one nation among many, instead of one that pursued uniquely justifiable goals, grated on public sensibilities. But GOP claims that Clinton was subordinating U.S. interests to shadowy international bureaucrats began to gain momentum when U.N. forces in Somalia—including a large U.S. contingent—got into waters that were clearly over the head of many of the U.N. leaders and non-Western military forces involved.

The issue came to a head on Oct. 3, 1993, when U.S. troops trying to apprehend a local warlord in Mogadishu got into a brutal firefight in which 18 Americans were killed and nearly 80 wounded. Subsequent critiques quickly focused on Aspin's decision weeks before the incident not to dispatch to Somalia some tanks the U.S. commander on the scene had requested. The commander later said that the presence of the tanks probably would not have prevented most of the U.S. casualties. And some analysts contended that the can-do ethos of an elite U.S. unit involved in the operation had contributed to the disaster. But whatever Aspin's true role in the events leading up to the incident, his handling of the political backlash was ruinous: In a closed-door briefing, he shocked members of Congress who were demanding answers about the U.S. mission in Somalia by asking them what they thought should be done.

In December 1993, less than a year after he took office, Aspin announced his resignation. For its part, the Clinton administration learned that the only way to sustain at least a modicum of public support for sending U.S. troops on such nontraditional missions, and the only way to get the missions accomplished, was to insist that the U.S. forces take the lead in such operations.

Aspin's successor as Pentagon chief was William J. Perry, the soft-spoken technocrat who had been Aspin's deputy secretary. A kingpin of the military-technology establishment since the Carter administration, when he was the Pentagon's research chief, Perry was known for his aptitude as a manager and for his commitment to the development of high-tech weaponry. But within months of taking over as defense secretary, he demonstrated a striking commitment to maintaining the combat-readiness of the forces and to boosting service members' quality-of-life as one component of readiness. That commitment was starkly highlighted by Perry's calls on two tough budget issues:

• Though he had been a prime mover behind development of the B-2 stealth bomber during the Carter administration, he now opposed congressional efforts to buy more of the costly planes, insisting that the limited defense budgets in prospect could not accommodate the cost.

• At the same time, he publicly pressed the White House to give service members annual pay hikes that would keep pace with inflation.

THE REPUBLICAN CRACKUP

Late in 1994, as Republicans organized to take over both sides of Capitol Hill for the first time in decades, the party's traditional defense hawks laid plans to, at a minimum, halt the steady drop in Pentagon purchasing power, which had declined in inflation-adjusted terms since 1985. Moreover, they were confident they had some potent political ammunition for their contention that Clinton not only was short-changing the force with too stringent budgets but also was siphoning funds out of Pentagon coffers to pay for nondefense projects. They also thought they had evidence that the forces were losing their edge because Clinton was wearing them out on peacekeeping missions that were peripheral at best to core U.S. security needs.

In addition, although they had not noticeably damaged Clinton with the antimissile defense issue during his first two years, conservative activists remained convinced that their demand that the nation be physically protected from missile attack as soon as possible would be politically irresistible, now that they could use their control of Congress to force the topic onto the public agenda.

But the Republican defense crusade started to come apart quickly, and on perhaps the most basic point: by April of 1995, deficit hawks clearly were ascendant in the party's congressional councils and they would allow a much smaller increase over Clinton's projected budgets than many defense hawks had called for.

On top of that, Pentagon officials—including top military officers—insisted that the readiness problems that had surfaced in the fall of 1994 reflected short-term cash flow problems rather than a fundamental erosion of combat preparedness. To be sure, the cash flow problems resulted in part from some of the peacekeeping deployments the conservatives so loathed—to Rwanda and to Haiti. But another big contributor to the Pentagon's money crunch—which had forced the cancellation of many training exercises—was the speedy dispatch of troops, ships and planes to the Persian Gulf in August 1994, when Iraqi Army units made threatening moves toward neighboring Kuwait. The only role Congress played in this situation was to replenish budget accounts that had been drawn on to pay for the unanticipated deployments. This gave the critics no leverage over the peacekeeping missions, because refusal to provide the funds merely would have left the delayed training undone.

The nondefense spending issue also proved a bust, politically. Administration critics cited totals of more than $10 billion annually for activities that, they insisted, either were political pork or belonged in some domestic agency's budget. But that total was misleading: it included upwards of $5 billion for environmental cleanup at military bases and at the Energy Department's complex of nuclear weapons plants and nearly $1 billion for programs designed to ease the transition to nondefense work of military personnel and civilian Pentagon employees as the defense establishment rapidly contracted.

All those programs proved politically bulletproof. The more dubious programs featured in "pork-busters" press releases, such as funds for military personnel to staff international athletic events, amounted to a few tens of millions of dollars here and there—a pittance, in the quarter-trillion dollar annual defense budget. That left the antimissile defense issue, and the Republicans played it to the hilt in 1995.

Ultimately, they included in the fiscal 1996 defense authorization bill a provision mandating deployment by 2003 of a "thin" antimissile defense that would protect all 50 states. Administration officials insisted the policy would require violation of the 1972 treaty limiting the deployment of antimissile defenses, and it was one of the major reasons Clinton vetoed the authorization bill.

Because no such language was included in the companion defense appropriations measure, the committees responsible for the authorization bill—Senate Armed Services and House National Security—faced the prospect that they would lose any impact on the fiscal 1996 defense program. So, after the House sustained Clinton's veto early in 1996, the authorization panels abandoned the missile defense provision as well as other provisions that were aimed at constraining Clinton's assignment of U.S. forces to nontraditional missions and particularly to U.N.-commanded peacekeeping operations.

Congress quickly passed and Clinton signed the stripped down bill. As whipped as congressional Republicans were after their showdown with Clinton over the shutdown of the federal government at the start of fiscal 1996, the defense authorizing committees were even more gun-shy of confrontation with him, after almost losing their bill in the veto fight. The antimissile advocates' only real effort in 1996 was to make their cause an issue in the GOP presidential campaign. However, it drew as little voter attention as did every other defense and foreign policy issue.

Chronology of Action on Defense

1993–1994

The 103rd Congress generally gave President Clinton what he wanted in his defense budget. But that support came grudgingly. Liberals had expected deeper cuts in defense spending after the breakup of the Soviet Union. They tagged some programs as "cold war relics" and periodically made attempts—albeit unsuccessful ones—to legislate defense reductions.

More worrisome for the administration were the conservative and centrist members of Congress who argued that Clinton's projected budgets were inadequate to meet U.S. defense needs. Among the leading critics was the powerful, well-respected chairman of the Senate Armed Services Committee, Sam Nunn, D-Ga.

Clinton's credentials in the area of defense were somewhat shaky from the outset because of his youthful attempts to avoid military service during the Vietnam War era. He did little to improve his stance among the armed services with his proposal to lift the ban on gays serving in the military, an initiative that the uniformed military abhorred and that they and their congressional allies stopped cold. The controversial issue sidetracked Clinton's defense team for the first six months of his administration until agreement was reached on a modest revision of existing policy.

Once that issue was put to rest, policy makers could focus on broader defense issues. Under the direction of Clinton's first secretary of defense, former House Armed Services Committee chairman Les Aspin, the administration reexamined U.S. interests with a bottom-up review of the Pentagon's mission and machinery. Aspin's long-awaited study, released in September 1993, reduced spending for defense programs but less than experts had expected. Administration officials said that the changes would be enough to meet Clinton's budget targets—cuts estimated at nearly $123 billion over five years—while allowing for a more flexible fighting force.

Policy makers also grappled with the role the United States should play in a changed world. No longer facing a clearly defined military threat such as the Soviet Union had posed, the United States found itself being drawn into murky, ambiguous conflicts in places such as Somalia, Haiti and Bosnia. Opinions ranged widely on when, where and how force should be used. Critics charged that peacekeeping deployments diverted defense money from needed projects and damaged combat readiness. The one point on which most members seemed to agree is that they wanted to be consulted about overseas troop commitments.

Despite the increasingly severe budget crunch, Congress cut little in Clinton's overall defense budgets. Less than $3 billion was cut from Clinton's fiscal 1994 budget request—and that was largely because of budgeting technicalities—and only $1 billion the following year.

But Congress did not function as a rubber stamp. The issue of military pay raises provided one of the clearest examples of Congress putting its mark on the Clinton budgets. Members insisted on higher raises than Clinton proposed and in the end won over the administration, especially Aspin's successor as defense secretary, William J. Perry, to their view.

Late in 1994, Pentagon officials estimated that their budget plan fell short of the amount needed to pay for Clinton's program. Clinton announced that he was adding $25 billion to the $1.5 trillion projected budget for the next six fiscal years to allow the Pentagon to raise military pay, improve combat readiness and make a raft of quality-of-life improvements for military personnel and their families.

In a move earlier in the year to contain defense costs, Secretary Perry had called for radical, cost-saving changes in the way the Pentagon bought weapons. He said it was necessary to stretch the defense budget enough to pay for an upturn in weapons procurement slated to begin in 1997. He also argued that a more businesslike purchasing system was essential so the armed services could acquire cutting-edge technologies being developed by commercial companies that refused to bid for government business under the complex and rigid rules then in effect. Legislation ultimately enacted in 1994 simplified the procurement process for commercial purchases and promised a substantial reduction in overhead costs. *(Federal procurement, p. 812)*

1994 Defense Authorization

Congress in 1993 cleared a $261 billion fiscal 1994 defense authorization. The legislation (HR 2401—PL 103-160) backed the essentials of President Clinton's budget request, from his efforts to revamp research into antimissile defenses to his proposals to continue work on a new generation of combat planes.

Lawmakers sliced about $2.6 billion from the Clinton request, which in turn was $12 billion less than former president George Bush had proposed in a skeletal budget request that he had prepared before leaving office. The $2.6 billion reduction largely was made to comply with budget limits and technical assumptions made by the Congressional Budget Office (CBO).

Although liberal members argued for deeper defense cuts to reflect the end of the cold war arms race, other members in both chambers expressed concern that Clinton's long-range defense plans would cut too fast and too deep and would risk the nation's military capabilities. Those warnings were conveyed by leaders of the Armed Services committees and the Defense Appropriations subcommittees in both chambers.

Congress also asserted its own priorities in the bill, spurning Clinton's request for a governmentwide wage freeze to approve a 2.2 percent pay raise for military personnel.

Action on the defense authorization bill was delayed for months beyond the customary congressional schedule to avoid embroiling the measure in a fierce dispute over Clinton's campaign promise to eliminate the military's long-standing ban on homosexuals. Ultimately, Clinton settled for a slight easing of the ban, but lawmakers, led by Senate Armed Services Committee Chairman Sam Nunn, D-Ga., insisted on adding a provision to the authorization bill that attempted to ensure the ban's permanence by sealing it into law. *(Gays in the military, p. 284)*

Other controversial issues, including congressional resistance to U.S. involvement in U.N. peacekeeping operations in Somalia and elsewhere, played out partly on the companion defense appropriations bill (HR 3116—PL 103-139). *(1994 defense appropriations, p. 267)*

CLINTON BUDGET

Clinton's fiscal 1994 budget request, formally submitted on April 8, 1993, called for $263.4 billion in new budget authority for defense-related programs. The proposed defense budget maintained most major weapons programs to preserve the administration's options pending Defense Secretary Les Aspin's sweeping bottom-up review of U.S. defense requirements in the post–cold war world. *(Defense review, p. 290)*

But even before Clinton formally submitted his budget, key members of the Armed Services committees questioned the cuts that Clinton had promised in his presidential campaign and that Aspin—the former chairman of the House Armed Services Committee—set out to impose in his new role as Pentagon chief.

On Feb. 17, the president had announced that he would seek to cut defense spending by at least $88 billion from Bush's projected budgets for fiscal 1994–1997. This included the $60 billion that Clinton had pledged to cut during his presidential campaign, plus $18 billion that would be saved from the defense payroll by freezing federal pay in fiscal 1994 and limiting raises thereafter.

In addition, Aspin held out the prospect of deeper cuts—$10 billion or more—if needed to compensate for what some Pentagon officials viewed as unrealistic assumptions of costs and savings in Bush's plan. Administration officials also spoke of another $42 billion that could be trimmed because of lower inflation estimates than Bush's plan had anticipated; a figure of only $27 billion was later settled upon.

Coupled with the $7.4 billion that Congress had sliced from the fiscal 1993 budget, the projected cuts for fiscal 1993–1997 added up to $122.6 billion, more than twice the cuts Clinton had promised in his campaign.

As the Senate geared up to debate the budget proposals, Nunn called on administration and congressional budget writers to buffer the Pentagon from unanticipated increases in costs. With his expertise on military affairs and his centrist politics, Nunn typically played a pivotal role in Senate debates on defense policy.

In a March 5 speech, Nunn portrayed the added cuts beyond the $60 billion pledged in the campaign as reasonable, if somewhat optimistic. However, Nunn insisted that future Pentagon budgets should be increased if the projected cost reductions did not materialize. Otherwise, Nunn argued, the Defense Department would have to make unacceptably large cutbacks in the number and readiness of its forces.

Although Congress seemed likely from the start to go along with the basics of Clinton's fiscal 1994 defense budget, some staunch Pentagon allies on Capitol Hill rebelled at the administration's intention to postpone tough decisions on which expensive weapons programs to winnow out. The strategy of marking time until Aspin finished his review met with strong criticism from both the Senate and House Armed Services committees.

BUDGET RESOLUTION

Congress completed action on H Con Res 64, its blueprint for fiscal 1994 spending and tax decisions, on April 1. The budget resolution allocated $263.4 billion for national defense. *(Budget resolution, p. 41)*

The House-passed version had included $263.2 billion for defense. The only House vote on the budget resolution specifically relating to defense spending came March 18, 1993, on an amendment embodying the Congressional Black Caucus's budget proposal, which would have cut defense spending and increased taxes to devote more funds to domestic programs. It was rejected 87–335.

In its version, the Senate had approved $263.5 billion. During floor action on March 23, the Senate adopted nonbinding amendments offered by Nunn. One amendment, adopted 69–30, expressed the sense of the Senate that allowances for defense and unspecified other parts of the budget should be increased if inflation were higher than anticipated and that pay increases for the Defense Department should be allowed if Congress did not enact Clinton's pay freeze. The other, adopted 56–43, expressed the view that, if Congress cut Clinton's defense budget request, the savings should be used solely to reduce the deficit.

Among the amendments rejected by the Senate was one sponsored by Pete V. Domenici, R-N.M., that would have reduced Clinton's long-term cuts in the Bush administration defense budget plan to the $60 billion Clinton had proposed in the presidential campaign; it was tabled (killed) 58–41, on March 23.

SENATE COMMITTEE ACTION

The Senate Armed Services Committee moved to cut back radically the Pentagon's plans for a new generation of combat jets when the panel reported a $262 billion fiscal 1994 defense authorization on July 27 (S 1298—S Rept 103-112).

Rejecting the plans for new tactical aircraft as too expensive, the committee ordered the Air Force and Navy to scrap two costly aircraft programs. Anticipating a decision that Clinton would soon announce, the committee denied $399 million requested to develop the long-range Navy ground attack plane designated A/F-X, ordering the service instead to adapt the Air Force's new F-22 fighter to carry bombs. And it ordered the Air Force to drop plans to develop a small fighter (designated MRF for Multi-Role Fighter) to replace existing F-16s early in the twenty-first century. *(Combat aircraft, box, p. 260)*

The fighter plane decisions were among the most significant elements of the bill. For some other controversial weapons programs—including the C-17 cargo plane, the B-2 stealth bomber and the antimissile defense program formerly known as the Strategic Defense Initiative—the committee approved all or most of the funds that Clinton requested. But in each case, the panel stipulated that the funds could not be spent unless the program satisfied various criteria. *(C-17, box, p. 275; antimissile defense, box, p. 262)*

DEFENSE LEADERSHIP

The Senate Jan. 20, 1993, gave voice vote approval to the nomination of Wisconsin Democratic Rep. Les Aspin as President Clinton's first secretary of defense. Aspin, who had chaired the House Armed Services Committee since 1985, was lavishly praised for his mastery of defense-related issues. The Senate Armed Services Committee had approved Aspin's nomination earlier Jan. 20. *(Background, cabinet profiles, p. 1110)*

But Aspin's expertise failed to translate into an effective stewardship at the Pentagon. Until becoming defense secretary, Aspin had never run anything larger than the staff of House Armed Services. His lack of administrative experience became a chronic problem, and he frequently became bogged down in controversies. At the Pentagon, Aspin's quest for the political clout to implement his views was handicapped by his penchant for prolonged—and sometimes public—rumination before he reached a decision. Furthermore, early in his tenure, Aspin was sidelined for weeks with a heart ailment that required the implanting of a pacemaker.

Aspin was thwarted as defense secretary by Clinton's agenda. For example, for six months, the secretary and his senior aides were occupied trying to salvage some shard of Clinton's fiercely disputed campaign pledge to lift the armed services' ban on gay and lesbian members. *(Gays in the military, p. 284)*

Aspin became the chief lightning rod for broader dissatisfaction with Clinton's difficulty in defining U.S. security needs in the post–cold war world. On Aspin's watch, this ambivalence played out most dramatically in the U.S. involvement in Somalia. After 18 U.S. soldiers were killed in a firefight in October 1993, it was revealed that Aspin had denied requests to reinforce the U.S. contingent in Somalia with tanks and other equipment. His backers contended that the criticism was unjustified because military planners wanted to use the tanks for purposes different from the deadly firefight. But Aspin acknowledged his regret at failing to send the armor, and the issue became one more item on the list of his political liabilities. *(Somalia, p. 323)*

Aspin resigned on Feb. 2, 1994. His bottom-up review of the defense establishment may prove his most enduring legacy. The review was quintessential Aspin—typical of his success over the previous decade in shaping debate on defense policy and in pushing the Democratic Party toward more hawkish stands. *(Defense Department review, p. 290)*

On Dec. 16, 1993, Clinton named retired admiral Bobby Ray Inman to succeed Aspin. A highly regarded intelligence specialist, Inman was expected to be easily confirmed. However, Inman stunned the administration and Congress on Jan. 18, 1994, when he abruptly withdrew his nomination. *(Controversial nominations, p. 1119)*

On Jan. 24, 1994, Clinton named Deputy Defense Secretary William J. Perry to take over the Pentagon's top civilian post. The nomination was approved by the Senate Armed Services Committee Feb. 3 by a vote of 22–0 and by the full Senate by a 97–0 vote later that day. The Senate's swift and unanimous action on the Perry nomination underscored the extraordinarily high regard that Democrats and Republicans alike had for Perry, a mathematician and defense technologist who had served as Aspin's deputy, as well as the Pentagon's research and engineering chief during the Carter administration. *(Background, cabinet profiles, p. 1111)*

Army Gen. John M. Shalikashvili won Senate confirmation by voice vote Oct. 5, 1993, to serve as chairman of the Joint Chiefs of Staff, succeeding Gen. Colin L. Powell Jr. The Polish-born Shalikashvili had been commander in chief since June 1992 of U.S. forces in Europe and of the North Atlantic Treaty Organization (NATO) military forces.

The Senate Armed Services Committee held up Shalikashvili's nomination briefly, but only because it was unwilling to see him leave his post as NATO commander until a successor had been named. The hold was lifted when Clinton nominated Gen. George A. Joulwan. An Army officer who had been commander in chief of the U.S. Southern Command, Joulwan was confirmed by the Senate by voice vote on Oct. 7.

The committee bill incorporated a modified version of the policy on gay military personnel that Clinton announced July 19. It would also repeal the statutory ban on the assignment of women to combat ships. *(Women in the military, p. 291)*

Rejecting Clinton's recommendation of a pay freeze for civilian and military federal employees, the committee approved a 2.2 percent pay increase for military personnel.

To fit the spending within the limit on defense outlays set by the congressional budget resolution, S 1298 cut $1 billion from the total defense budget authority that Clinton had requested and that the congressional budget resolution allowed. And Nunn warned that a technical dispute between the administration and CBO might force a much larger cut in budget authority.

HOUSE COMMITTEE ACTION

The defense authorization measure reported by the House Armed Services Committee July 30 (HR 2401—H Rept 103-

200) followed the Clinton administration's lead, both in its major decisions and its overall caution in waiting until the administration review was completed.

The committee bill included provisions to cancel development of the A/F-X bomber, to repeal the statutory ban against assigning women to combat vessels and to deny $206 million of the $428 million requested for the underground nuclear test program. But in each of those instances, the House panel either was tracking a decision that Clinton previously had announced or—in the case of the A/F-X cancellation—anticipating a decision.

The bill's highest profile provision used language borrowed from the Senate Armed Services version of the defense bill codifying the Pentagon's ban on homosexual conduct.

The House committee sliced nearly $1 billion from the administration's $3.76 billion request to develop defenses against missile attack. The Senate panel had cut the program by $553 million. In both bills, part of the reduction resulted from the

CONGRESS, WHITE HOUSE AGREE TO CUT BACK PLANS FOR NEW GENERATION OF COMBAT PLANES

The Clinton administration and the Appropriations and Armed Services committees of the House and Senate agreed in 1993 on the basic outline of a pared-down program to develop a new generation of combat planes for the Navy and Air Force.

Despite the broad accord, lingering differences existed over the specific goals and funding of some programs. And the agreement came only after Congress prodded the new administration to begin making some tough choices. That pressure contributed to the Pentagon's decision to abandon plans for a new carrier-based stealth bomber that would have been called the A/F-X.

Background

Officially, Pentagon plans inherited by the Clinton administration called for spending more than $150 billion over the next 20 years—and tens of billions more thereafter—to buy more than 4,000 new combat planes. The menu of planned aircraft had ranged from enlarged versions of existing F/A-18s to the futuristic A/F-X attack plane that was still on the drawing boards.

But most defense specialists across the political spectrum contended that these planes were too expensive for the shrinking defense budgets that were expected following the end of the cold war.

And some critics argued that the Pentagon was pushing too hard at the frontiers of combat aircraft technology, considering that no opponent was on the horizon who could rival the prowess displayed by U.S. air squadrons during the 1991 Gulf War. In particular, some skeptics questioned the price the Pentagon was willing to pay for planes that were stealthy—built of expensive and exotic materials and with carefully calibrated contours so that they would be hard to spot and shoot down.

The military services responded that they needed to develop the planes that they would buy in 10 years and fly for 20. Given the rapid proliferation of high-technology equipment, they warned, it would be dangerous to count on maintaining the U.S. advantages in air power without such new aircraft.

Debate also arose over the competing—and some said redundant—plans of the various services.

The Air Force was equipped with the high-end F-15 fighter; the smaller, much less expensive F-16 that could be used as either a fighter or an attack plane; and three types of long-range attack planes packed with target-finding electronics for all-weather combat: the F-15E, the stealthy F-117 and the Vietnam War-era F111.

The Air Force's priority was to develop a top-of-the-line jet fighter that would give U.S. pilots early in the twenty-first century the unquestioned aerial supremacy that the 1970s-vintage F-15 had guaranteed at the start of the 1990s. The Air Force held a competition between two advanced fighters, picking the Lockheed F-22 in 1991.

The Navy, too, already had a high-end fighter—the F-14, with its powerful radar and long-range Phoenix missiles, which had been designed to fend off swarms of Soviet antiship missiles. It also had a smaller swing fighter, the F/A-18, designed to handle both fighter and attack missions. And it had a major, imminent problem: the aging A-6Es that made up its force of long-range, all-weather attack planes. The wings of these 1970s-vintage planes were wearing out, requiring a costly and technically difficult effort to replace them. More fundamentally, the design, dating from the late 1950s, made the plane relatively slow and anything but stealthy, compared with other frontline jets.

The Navy's plans for the future initially included the A-12, a stealthy flying wing design, reminiscent of the larger B-2 stealth bomber. But in 1991, the Bush administration canceled the A-12, citing rising costs, slipping schedules and technical difficulties with the

shifting of $253 million requested to develop the Brilliant Eyes missile detection satellite to another program. Contending that the Pentagon was trying to fund too many similar systems, the panels had lumped funding for several systems—including Brilliant Eyes—into one fund and ordered the Defense Department to thin out the field. *(Antimissile defense system, box, p. 262)*

Like the Senate committee, the House panel approved substantial additional funding for the C-17 cargo jet but ordered the Pentagon to consider alternatives before spending the money on a project with a history of cost increases and technical problems.

The House panel, like its Senate counterpart, also added a 2.2 percent pay raise for all military personnel.

SENATE FLOOR ACTION

After five days of debate that lacked much of the intensity and drama that permeated defense debates in the 1980s, the Senate approved a $261 billion version of the defense authorization bill (S 1298) Sept. 14 by a vote of 92–7.

Only the issue of homosexuals in the military stirred much emotion, and that fight had been all but settled before S 1298 reached the Senate floor. The bill basically sought to codify the existing prohibition against openly gay armed services personnel. Senators on Sept. 9 defeated, by a **key vote of 33–63 (R 3–38; D 30–25),** an amendment by Barbara Boxer, D-Calif., that would have struck the committee provisions on gays in the military and explicitly ceded the issue to the president. *(1993 key votes, p. 979)*

The Senate's most dramatic departure from the administration's funding proposals came Sept. 9, when senators, in a **key vote of 50–48 (R 6–36; D 44–12)** on an amendment offered by Jim Sasser, D-Tenn., approved only $2.8 billion for antimissile defenses, $400 million less than Senate Armed Services had recommended. Neither figure included the separate funding of $253 million for the Brilliant Eyes missile detection satellite, which had been transferred to another account. Clinton had requested nearly $3.8 billion for the program, including Brilliant Eyes.

In a move indicative of growing congressional unease over the continued deployment of U.S. troops in Somalia, the Senate on Sept. 9 voted, 90–7, to add to the bill a nonbinding amendment offered by Robert C. Byrd, D-W.Va., urging Clinton to ob-

design. The Navy solicited proposals for a replacement for the A-12, ultimately settling on the equally ill-fated A/F-X.

Administration Plans

The fiscal 1994 Pentagon request that President Clinton sent to Congress in March 1993 essentially continued the Bush administration's plans for combat aircraft, earmarking $4.1 billion to develop the new planes. It included requests for the F-22, F/A-18 E and F, the new A/F-X and upgrades of the F-14. Clinton's plan included two changes made by Bush at the last minute: it dropped the Air Force's Multi-Role Fighter, a relatively inexpensive plane to replace F-16s, and accelerated the timetable for retiring A-6Es, slating the last squadron to leave service in 1999.

The administration's failure to cut back the services' array of combat aircraft caused grumbling in Congress, but Defense Secretary Les Aspin said such decisions would be put off until completion of a comprehensive bottom-up review of defense policy. *(Defense review, p. 290)*

By June, however, reports were published that the Pentagon would recommend canceling the A/F-X and proceeding with the other aircraft. The cancellation of the A/F-X was not formally announced until the release of the defense review on Sept. 1. But lawmakers were well aware of that outcome when they crafted the defense authorization and appropriations bills, leaving out the $399 million originally requested for the plane.

Congressional Action

The final versions of the fiscal 1994 defense authorization bill (HR 2401—PL 103-160) and the companion defense appropriations bill (HR 3116—PL 103-139) reflected the fundamentals of the Clinton administration's plans for combat planes.

- **A/F-X.** The bills provided no funds for the canceled A/F-X.
- **F-22.** The authorization bill backed the administration's full $2.25 billion request to develop the Air Force's F-22 fighter to replace the F-15 as the service's most sophisticated fighter. The appropriations bill funded the F-22 program at $2.09 billion.

Conferees on the authorization bill dropped the $50 million that the Senate had added to begin work on a variation of the F-22 that could operate from aircraft carriers.

- **F/A-18 E and F.** Of the $1.49 billion requested, Congress authorized $1.46 billion and appropriated $1.47 billion to develop the enlarged E and F versions of the Navy's F/A-18.
- **F-16s.** The authorization bill approved $400 million for 12 final Air Force F-16s plus $71 million to terminate that contract. This was half the number requested for the last batch.
- **F-14s.** The biggest unresolved difference concerned improvements for the Navy's F-14 fighter. Congress agreed to appropriate the $188 million requested to develop and install modifications to the F-14, partly to adapt the plane as an interim replacement for the A-6E. But the appropriators objected to the emphasis of the Navy's upgrade program, arguing that equipping the plane with more powerful engines was more important than equipping it to serve as a bomber. By contrast, the authorization bill contained $315 million for F-14 upgrades, focusing on equipping the planes—which could fly faster than the enlarged F/A-18s—to drop smart bombs.

The debate over combat aircraft in 1993 did not directly address two additional planes that were on Pentagon drawing boards as eventual complements to the F-22 and the F/A-18 E and F. One was a relatively low-cost fighter to replace the F-16, just as the F-22 was slated to replace the larger F-15. The other plane was a long-range, carrier-based bomber as a full replacement for the A-6E. *(1994 defense authorization, p. 257; 1994 defense appropriations, p. 267)*

tain by Nov. 15 congressional authorization for the deployment. *(Somalia, p. 323)*

The largest single group of amendments considered by the Senate during debate on the defense bill dealt with the base-closing process, which called for another round of politically agonizing cutbacks in 1995. On Sept. 10, the Senate brushed aside, 18–79, the most controversial of these, an amendment by Dianne Feinstein, D-Calif., that would have delayed the 1995 round of closings until 1997. *(Base closings, p. 288)*

In the area of arms control, Tom Harkin, D-Iowa, offered an amendment to delete from the bill $10 million earmarked to develop an antisatellite (ASAT) missile. By a vote of 90–10 on Sept. 14, the Senate gutted Harkin's amendment by adopting a modification by Richard C. Shelby, D-Ala., providing that the ASAT funds could be spent once the Pentagon adopted a formal statement of requirements for the program. But then, by a 40–60 vote, the Senate rejected even that watered-down version of the Harkin amendment.

The Senate also adopted by voice vote an amendment to cut the amount authorized for the Energy Department to maintain

its capability to conduct nuclear testing. Harkin offered an amendment to cut the administration's $428 million request for testing funds to $222.4 million, the same amount included in the House bill. But senators approved by voice vote a substitute amendment offered by Jim Exon, D-Neb., setting the funding at $375 million. Clinton in July had extended a moratorium on underground nuclear tests that had been imposed by Congress in 1992 (PL 102-377). Both the House and Senate defense authorization bills sought to terminate a 30-year-old program intended to preserve the option of resuming above-ground tests that were banned by a 1963 treaty. *(Nuclear test ban, box, p. 293)*

HOUSE FLOOR ACTION

The House on Sept. 29 passed a $263 billion version of the defense bill (HR 2401) by a vote of 268–162. Armed Services Committee Chairman Ronald V. Dellums, D-Calif., known as one of the most liberal members of Congress, voted "yea" on a defense bill for the first time in his 23 years in the House.

HR 2401 included language identical to that in the Senate version to codify the military's ban on gay personnel. The provi-

ANTIMISSILE DEFENSE PROGRAM

The Clinton administration in 1993 renamed the Strategic Defense Initiative (SDI), endorsed a less ambitious focus for the antimissile defense program and dramatically reduced its projected funding.

But the rechristened Ballistic Missile Defense program was not scaled back enough for Congress. The $2.8 billion included in the fiscal 1994 defense authorization bill (HR 2401—PL 103-160) and the $2.64 billion in the fiscal 1994 defense appropriations bill (HR 3116—PL 103-139) were significantly less than the average annual budget of $3.6 billion that Defense Secretary Les Aspin had outlined for the Clinton administration's approach to antimissile defenses.

Background

President Ronald Reagan established SDI in 1983 with a vision of rendering nuclear missiles "impotent and obsolete." The program's original goal was to deploy a shield of antimissile defenses, including futuristic space-based weapons, that could make the United States impregnable to an all-out attack by the Soviet Union.

The program was embraced by conservatives as the key to future defense policy, ridiculed by liberals as "Star Wars" and accepted with caveats and some skepticism by many centrists.

Through 1986, most congressional debate over the program centered on funding, with Congress routinely slicing Reagan's requests but rejecting calls for even deeper cuts that would have limited the effort to laboratory research.

From 1987 to 1991, the SDI debate turned largely on the role of space-based weapons, which conflicted with the 1972 U.S.-Soviet treaty limiting antiballistic missile (ABM) systems.

Republican conservatives fought for a network of space-based interceptor missiles that could destroy attacking Soviet weapons in the first few minutes of flight, before they could swamp the defense with multiple warheads and swarms of decoys. But prominent centrist Democrats—such as Senate Armed Services Chairman Sam Nunn, D-Ga., and Aspin, who was then chairman of the House Armed Services Committee—challenged that goal as technically dubious and gratuitously provocative.

The two Democrats proposed a more modest goal of protecting U.S. territory, allies and forces abroad against limited missile attacks by a third world country such as Iraq or a renegade military unit. From 1987 onward, Congress repeatedly insisted that the antimissile program be subordinated to the ABM Treaty.

Without abandoning the long-term goal of a defense of the continental United States, President George Bush in 1991 made SDI's priority a program called GPALS, or global protection against limited strikes. It was envisioned as a combination of space-based Brilliant Pebbles missile interceptors and ground-based defensive missiles.

The same year, Congress went further by ordering that SDI be recast to focus on near-term, ground-based defenses and antitheater (shorter-range) missile programs.

Clinton Stance

In 1993, President Clinton reined in SDI, eliminating large budget increases that Bush had planned for the program. For fiscal 1994, Clinton requested $3.8 billion—including $121 million for procurement—instead of the $6.3 billion that Bush had projected.

Clinton also reshaped the antimissile work along the lines mandated by Congress in 1991, placing more emphasis on early deployment of ground-based defenses against attacks by a small number of intercontinental-range ballistic missiles or theater missiles.

Aspin announced that he had changed not only the Strategic Defense Initiative's priorities but also its name, which became the Ballistic Missile Defense program.

In another move away from Reagan's vision of SDI, the Clinton administration told Congress in July that it would not support Reagan's loose interpretation of the ABM Treaty and instead would hew to a traditional or narrow interpretation of the treaty, which sharply limited the testing and deployment of antimissile defenses. The Reagan administration in 1985 had proposed a broad interpretation of the ABM Treaty that would have allowed testing of space-based ABM weapons for SDI. But Congress later blocked the Reagan and Bush administrations from acting on that new interpretation.

Legislative Action

The final version of the fiscal 1994 defense authorization bill authorized $2.8 billion of the $3.8 billion requested for the Ballistic Missile Defense program. The amount authorized did not include the $253 million requested for Brilliant Eyes, which the legislation had consolidated with other missile-tracking satellites in another account. *(1994 defense authorization, p. 257)*

The final version of the companion defense appropriations bill provided $2.64 billion for the Ballistic Missile Defense program. *(1994 defense appropriations, p. 267)*

sion, sponsored by Ike Skelton, D-Mo., was adopted by the House Sept. 28 by a vote of 301–134. Earlier the same day, it rejected 144–291 an amendment by Duncan Hunter, R-Calif., that would have made the ban tougher by ordering the Pentagon to resume the practice—suspended by Clinton in January 1993—of asking recruits to disclose whether they were homosexual.

Also rejected that day, by a **key vote of 169–264 (R 11–163; D 157–101; I 1–0)**, was an amendment backed by opponents of the gay ban. Similar to a proposal rejected by the Senate, this

amendment, offered by Martin T. Meehan, D-Mass., would have deleted from the defense bill any reference to the issue, explicitly leaving the policy in the hands of the president.

The House also debated a number of amendments that reflected congressional concern about the budgetary costs and military risks of growing U.S. involvement in international peacekeeping missions.

Reflecting widespread congressional frustration over the continued deployment of U.S. troops in Somalia, the House, by a 406–26 vote on Sept. 28, added to the defense bill a nonbinding amendment requesting that Clinton obtain congressional authorization by Nov. 15 if he wanted to continue the deployment in Somalia. The resolution, offered by Richard A. Gephardt, D-Mo., was identical to one attached by the Senate to its defense bill.

Just before passing HR 2401, the House rejected, 192–238, a Republican motion to recommit the bill to the Armed Services Committee with instructions that it add a provision to limit future deployments of U.S. troops under foreign commanders. In previous debate on the bill, Republicans on Sept. 13 spearheaded the defeat of two amendments offered by Norman Sisisky, D-Va., that would have provided defense funds for peacekeeping efforts. (*U.N. peacekeeping missions, p. 200*)

The House stuck with the antimissile defense funding approved by the Armed Services Committee—$2.76 billion, plus $253 million for the separate but related Brilliant Eyes satellite program. Lawmakers on Sept. 8 rejected two liberal amendments to cut deeper and a conservative effort to match the Senate Armed Services Committee's recommended figure of $3.46 billion, including the funding for Brilliant Eyes. Dellums's proposal to cut $1.5 billion from the program was rejected 160–272. An amendment by Patricia Schroeder, D-Colo., to shift $200 million from the program to defense conversion efforts failed more narrowly, 202–227.

The amendment to increase the funding level by $467 million, proposed by Joel Hefley, R-Colo., was soundly rejected, 118–312.

A Dellums amendment to eliminate $1.1 billion for the procurement of Trident II submarine-launched missiles after fiscal 1993, with half of the savings going to defense conversion programs, was rejected 183–240 on Sept. 9. Also rejected, 188–240, was an amendment by Neil Abercrombie, D-Hawaii, to eliminate funding for the missiles after fiscal 1994.

Two Republican attempts to reduce spending for defense conversion programs—programs to help businesses and workers convert from defense to civilian work—were rejected. But the House Sept. 9 adopted, 256–160, an amendment, offered by Thomas H. Andrews, D-Maine, banning the use of conversion funds to finance foreign arms sales.

As in previous years, the House debated burden-sharing amendments that sought to force allies to contribute more toward the cost of U.S. troops stationed abroad. Barney Frank, D-Mass., offered an amendment that would have cut funding for U.S. forces in Europe by $1 billion, reducing troop levels unless allies picked up the tab. On Sept. 9 Frank's amendment, opposed by the administration, was narrowly rejected, 210–216. Also rejected, 195–231, was an amendment by John Bryant, D-Texas, to withdraw all U.S. troops from North Atlantic Treaty Organization (NATO) countries, Japan and South Korea unless those countries assumed the costs of stationing them abroad by the end of fiscal 1996.

But the House adopted, 424–0, an amendment by Marilyn Lloyd, D-Tenn., to reduce operation and maintenance funding for overseas bases by $580 million. And members adopted, 286–137, a Schroeder amendment requiring the 1995 Base Closure and Realignment Commission to include foreign bases in its closure recommendations.

CONFERENCE ACTION

The Senate passed an amended version of HR 2401 by voice vote Oct. 6. The bill then went to conference.

The House adopted the conference report (H Rept 103-357) Nov. 15 by a vote of 273–135; the Senate approved it Nov. 17 by a vote of 77–22, clearing HR 2401 for the president.

Conferees did not have to address the emotional issue of homosexuals in the military, because both chambers had passed bills with identical language codifying the long-standing ban on gay military personnel.

But the mostly pro-Pentagon members of the Armed Services committees had the uncomfortable task of cutting Clinton's request even though they generally agreed that the president already was cutting defense too deeply.

In large measure, the cuts in the bill resulted from a technical disagreement between CBO and the Office of Management and Budget (OMB) over how to estimate the fiscal 1994 outlays that would result from Clinton's defense budget request. The upshot was that the conferees had to slice the defense bill's projected outlays by $2 billion from the level Congress had approved in its annual budget resolution.

Beyond the reductions forced by the dispute between CBO and OMB, some Republicans and centrist Democrats warned that defense spending was being cut too much by the bill—and by Clinton's long-range defense plan, on which the bill was to be a first installment.

The conference report on the measure conveyed a warning on that score. It came in the form of a provision barring any further reduction in the Army's personnel ceiling below the level of 540,000 set by the bill. Though the administration had not announced how much more it planned to cut the Army, there were reports that its goal was a force of about 500,000 soldiers.

The conference provision was sponsored by Skelton, chairman of the House Armed Services Subcommittee on Military Forces and Personnel. In an unusual move, Skelton set the stage by holding a hearing on Army manpower levels Oct. 27, in the midst of conference negotiations on the authorization bill. In a display of political solidarity, senior members of the House Defense Appropriations Subcommittee joined Armed Services members at Skelton's hearings to inveigh against cuts in the Army roster.

When the conference report came to the Senate floor for approval, Nunn warned, "Readiness . . . is beginning to be threatened by disproportionate cuts in the defense budget. We must either adjust our defense resources or our expectations of what our military will be able to do because the two are going in opposite directions."

The $261 billion defense bill supported—or made only minor reductions in—the major elements of Clinton's budget request, including funding three new Navy destroyers ($2.8 billion) and continuing development of the Army's Comanche helicopter ($367 million) and the Air Force's F-22 fighter ($2.3 billion).

The final bill authorized $2.8 billion for antimissile defenses, not including $253 million for the Brilliant Eyes satellite. For the controversial C-17 cargo jet, the bill left open the possibility of ultimately providing as much as $2.2 billion of the $2.32 billion Clinton requested to buy six planes, although the bill earmarked exclusively for C-17s only enough to buy four planes.

The bill authorized a 2.2 percent increase in military pay.

MAJOR PROVISIONS

As signed into law Nov. 30, HR 2401 authorized $261 billion in defense spending for fiscal 1994, $2.6 billion less than requested. The Senate version had authorized $261 billion and the House version, $263 billion.

In final action, Congress in HR 2401:

Strategic Arms

Approved Clinton's request for $604 million in procurement funds related to the 20 B-2 stealth bombers that were previously authorized.

Congress had barred the Air Force from paying for the last five planes until the Pentagon certified that prototypes had passed certain tests. That certification was made, and the conference report lifted the restriction. But it also reaffirmed the statutory provisions allowing deployment of no more than 20 B-2s at a total cost of no more than $29 billion in fiscal 1981 dollars.

• Reconciled diametrically opposite approaches to equipping the long-range bomber fleet for nonnuclear missions. The House insisted that the older B-1s be modified, while the Senate insisted the upgrades be limited, at least initially, to the B-2.

At issue were two types of bombs designed to be dropped from high altitudes and to use extremely precise data from satellites to steer themselves toward preselected targets. In contrast to many smart bombs used during the 1991 war with Iraq, the new systems would not require that a laser be kept trained on the target by the bomber pilot.

While imposing a variety of funding restrictions, the conference report authorized the Air Force to equip the B-2 with the first of the new bombs—an interim system designated GATS/GAM—and to test the feasibility of installing that system on the B-1. The report also authorized modifying the B-1 to carry the second, more sophisticated system, designated JDAM, which was originally intended for B-2s.

• Required the Air Force to test under realistic conditions its claim that B-1 squadrons could keep 75 percent of their planes mission-ready for several months, provided they were given larger stocks of spare parts and maintenance equipment.

• Authorized the $983 million requested for 24 additional Trident II submarine-launched missiles. The conferees also approved the $145 million requested for components that would be used in missiles requested in future budgets. The Senate had recommended an additional $25 million for these long lead-time components to provide the option of accelerating missile production.

• Included a modified form of a House provision requiring the Pentagon to report on alternative ways of meeting a limit on submarine-launched missile warheads that would be set by the second U.S.-Russian Strategic Arms Reduction Talks (START II) treaty, which awaited ratification.

To meet the limit, the Pentagon planned to deploy Trident IIs carrying only four warheads apiece, instead of the eight they could carry. Some critics favored buying fewer missiles but loading them with eight warheads.

• Reflecting Clinton's decision to continue a moratorium on underground nuclear tests, authorized only $211 million of the $428 million requested to keep the nuclear testing infrastructure ready to resume testing. The measure also ended a 30-year-old program intended to preserve the capability of testing nuclear weapons in the atmosphere.

Antimissile and Space Programs

Authorized $2.8 billion of the $3.8 billion requested for antimissile defenses being developed by the Ballistic Missile Defense program, previously called the Strategic Defense Initiative.

The $2.8 billion did not include $253 million requested to develop the Brilliant Eyes satellite, intended to detect and track incoming missiles. The conferees treated this issue separately.

The $2.8 billion included $1.45 billion to develop defenses against relatively short-range (theater) ballistic missiles, such as the Soviet-designed Scuds fired by Iraq in 1991; $121 million to buy Patriot missiles modified to intercept theater missiles; $650 million to develop a system to defend U.S. territory against a small number of missile warheads; and $538 million to develop more sophisticated defenses for possible future deployment and to cover overhead costs.

• Ordered the administration to determine whether several key antitheater missile devices were consistent with the 1972 U.S.-Soviet treaty limiting antiballistic missile (ABM) systems.

Weeks after the conferees wrote that provision, the administration reportedly proposed easing ABM Treaty standards to allow tests of an antitheater missile designated THAAD. Arms control advocates warned that the new standard would dangerously blur the line between permitted and prohibited weapons.

In their report, conferees complained that the antimissile effort remained too unfocused. "Future program plans, timetables for deployment, testing plans and missile defense architectures are incompletely defined, providing little basis thus far for congressional support of higher funding levels," they said.

• Authorized $3.8 million requested by the Air Force to test the effectiveness of laser-armed airplanes to intercept theater missiles.

• Authorized $10 million to develop an antisatellite weapon. However, the companion defense appropriations bill denied the funds.

• For the Brilliant Eyes satellite, combined that request with three other programs to develop and procure missile attack warning systems for which the administration had requested a total of $1.05 billion. The conferees authorized $802 million, which the Pentagon was permitted to allocate among the four programs.

• Authorized $1 billion to develop and purchase satellite launch rockets: $801 million, as requested, for the large Titan

IVs and $202 million—$2 million less than was requested—for the smaller Atlas IIs and Delta IIs.

But conferees turned a skeptical eye toward Pentagon plans to develop an array of future launch vehicles. "The administration must stop trying to keep multiple space launch programs alive despite ever dwindling resources," they complained. "The administration must focus scarce resources to achieve any success at all."

The bill authorized none of the $54 million requested for a National Launch System for heavy payloads. Conferees also rejected the administration's request for $43 million to continue developing an experimental prototype of the so-called X-plane, a hypersonic aerospace plane designed to take off like an airplane and soar into orbit, but they did authorize $40 million to experiment with hypersonic technology. They also approved $35 million for space launch modernization, including the $5 million requested to develop a single-stage, reusable launch vehicle.

Ground Combat

To accelerate modernization of early model M-1 tanks into A2 models, with larger cannons and nightvision electronics, authorized $97 million for the program instead of the $80 million requested.

- Authorized the $192 million requested to begin upgrading early model Bradley armored troop carriers. But conferees rejected a House initiative to add $33 million to the bill to develop still more sophisticated electronics for the Bradley.

- Authorized the $8 million requested to continue buying a small number of lightweight tanks for air-mobile Army divisions.

- Added to the request $150 million for 10 Apache missile-armed attack helicopters, intended to keep that production line in operation until its scheduled use for a major upgrade of the Apache fleet.

- Authorized $278 million to continue developing the Longbow modification, a program to equip Apaches with target-finding radar.

- Authorized $258 million to modernize 18 scout helicopters with missiles and target-finding electronics.

- Authorized $367 million to continue developing the new Comanche scout helicopter.

- Added funds to accelerate the Army's plan to achieve horizontal integration of combat units by digital data links that could transmit among its units information about the location of both U.S. and enemy units.

In the final bill, the conferees approved $8 million for the project. But they complained that the Army's plan would install the data links only in several thousand tanks, armored troop carriers and attack helicopters, and only gradually, as part of more extensive upgrades of those vehicles that were scheduled to stretch well into the twenty-first century.

Citing the importance of such equipment to prevent accidental friendly fire attacks by U.S. units against their own side, the conferees urged the Army to install the data links in all air and land vehicles likely to wind up near the front lines and to complete the project in half the planned time.

- Authorized $547 million of the $629 million requested to develop and gear up for production of a 300-mile-range stealth missile designated TSSAM, canceling the Army's participation in the triservice project. But the conferees approved $146 million—only $7 million less than requested—to continue production of the ATACMS bombardment missile, with a range of less than 100 miles.

- Rejected the Army's plan to shut down for two years the production line for smaller, 20-mile-range MLRS rockets and then reopen the line to build a longer-range version of those missiles. To keep the factory running—and thus, the conferees argued, to save money in the long run—they added $45 million to buy 12,000 additional rockets.

- Authorized $110 million of the $117 million requested to continue developing BAT warheads, intended to be scattered from TSSAM, ATACMS and MLRS missiles and to home in on enemy tanks.

- Authorized $477 million for two JSTARS radar planes—intended to find targets for bombardment rockets far behind enemy lines—instead of the $282 million requested for one of the converted jetliners.

- To modernize the Army's artillery, authorized $172 million, as requested, to upgrade existing self-propelled cannons; $19 million, as recommended by the House, to equip those artillery vehicles with a cannon that could shoot much farther; and $148 million, as requested, to develop a new self-propelled cannon and an armored ammunition carrier to accompany it.

Tactical Air Combat

Agreed with the administration, in both the House and Senate versions of the bill, on the blueprint to develop a new generation of combat jets for the Navy and Air Force.

- Authorized $2.25 billion to continue development of the Air Force's F-22 fighter, intended to supplant the 1970s-vintage F-15 as the service's most sophisticated fighter. The conferees dropped $50 million the Senate had added to begin work on a variation of the F-22 to operate from aircraft carriers.

- Authorized $1.46 billion, only $27 million less than requested, to develop enlarged E and F models of the Navy's F/A-18. The new planes were to replace aging A-6E carrier-based bombers, though they could not fly as far. Anticipating the administration's cancellation of the stealthy, carrier-based A/F-X, which the Navy had planned as a replacement for the A-6E, both chambers denied the $399 million request for the project.

To keep U.S. air squadrons up to date for the following 10 to 15 years, before new planes entered service in large numbers, the bill:

- Authorized $400 million for 12 Air Force F-16s plus $71 million to terminate that contract. This was half the number requested, but the administration had planned to buy no more after fiscal 1994.

- Authorized $1.49 billion for 36 of the current model F/A-18s, as requested, plus $113 million for components to be used in future production, a cut of $139 million from the request.

- Authorized $130 million, as requested, to refurbish and upgrade four Harrier vertical takeoff jets used by the Marines.

• Authorized $315 million to upgrade the Navy's F-14 fighter and ordered the Navy to reorient the program so that at least some of the F-14s—which could fly farther than the enlarged F/A-18 models that were being developed—could attack ground targets with smart bombs. The administration had requested $188 million for the project.

Naval Combat

Authorized $2.64 billion, as requested, for three *Arleigh Burke*-class destroyers, equipped with the Aegis long-range anti-aircraft system. It provided $373 million—$19 million more than requested—for a program intended to link the radars of several types of ships and aircraft so a fleet could protect itself more effectively against high-speed missiles.

• Turned down a House initiative that would have added to the bill $20 million to test a large blimp as an airborne radar station that could detect approaching missiles much sooner than ship-borne radars. But the conference report urged the Navy to study how a radar blimp might fit into the new fleet radar network.

• Authorized, as requested, $215 million for 220 Standard long-range missiles and $58 million for 240 short-range RAM missiles.

• Authorized $25 million—$7.5 million more than requested—to test methods of equipping warships with either guns or missiles that could bombard distant shore targets to support ground troops. One option being studied was equipping ships to launch Army ATACMS missiles.

• Authorized $240 million, as requested, to develop a new nuclear submarine, designated *Centurion*, which was intended to be less expensive than the two *Seawolf*-class ships under construction. The administration planned to buy only one more *Seawolf* because of the ship's high cost.

• Adopted some House initiatives intended to accelerate a change in focus of the Navy's submarine-hunting efforts from finding Soviet nuclear-powered subs in the ocean depths to finding the smaller, nonnuclear-powered subs operated by other countries in relatively shallow water.

In some respects, the new problem was more complex: Modern conventional subs running submerged on battery power were quieter than some nuclear ships. And shallow seas often had high levels of background noise.

Following the House's lead, the bill included $50 million to adapt for existing *Los Angeles*-class subs a sonar system designed for the new *Seawolf* class.

It also added to the budget $10 million to test the ability of powerful computers to make existing sonars on some older ships more effective in detecting subs in shallow water.

But the bill authorized $125 million of the $134 million requested to develop a portable network of listening gear that could be deployed quickly near a distant trouble spot. The reduction was intended to slow the project pending the completion of certain tests.

Conferees approved $100 million requested for large Mark 48 homing torpedoes, carried by submarines. But they also added $21 million to begin adapting for shallow water operation the smaller Mark 46 homing torpedoes that were already in the inventory.

Air and Sea Transport

Authorized Clinton's request for $2.32 billion for C-17 long-range cargo jets and stipulated that the funding could be used to buy as many as six planes. But the bill specified that the administration could do so only if the trouble-plagued plane satisfied certain schedule and testing requirements.

In any case, the bill required the Air Force to come up with an off-the-shelf alternative—either modified commercial cargo jets or newly built Air Force C-5 planes—that could replace some of the 120 C-17s that were planned. Later, Defense Secretary Les Aspin announced that the Pentagon was considering buying only 40 C-17s.

Specifically, the bill provided $1.9 billion for four C-17s; $100 million to buy alternative planes; and $300 million that could be used either for two additional C-17s or for additional alternative planes.

• Authorized the $894 million requested for a helicopter carrier the size of a medium-size aircraft carrier. The ship was designed to carry 2,000 Marines plus helicopters and barges to haul them ashore.

Personnel Issues

Authorized a ceiling of 1,623,500 active-duty personnel in fiscal 1994, which allowed the services to keep 2,900 more members on the rolls than Clinton proposed.

• Authorized a 2.2 percent military pay raise to take effect Jan. 1, 1994, thus rejecting Clinton's planned freeze on all federal pay.

• Extended the Pentagon's expiring authorization to pay various bonuses intended to encourage the enlistment or reenlistment of personnel in certain essential job specialities.

• Expanded the pool of service members eligible to receive either a lump-sum payment or a multiyear annuity if they left the service after completing more than 15 years of duty but less than the 20 years that was needed to qualify for a military pension.

• Backed Clinton's proposal to repeal the statutory ban on assigning women to combat vessels. The conference report also required the Pentagon to give Congress 90 days' notice before announcing a change in the ban on assigning women to ground combat units and 30 days' notice before opening to women any combat unit or ship from which they had been barred.

• Added to Clinton's research and development request $20 million to establish a center for medical research related to women in the services. Another provision expanded the definition of medical services to which women in the military and female dependents were entitled to include mammograms, treatment for pregnancy and infertility and other gynecological procedures.

• Included a House provision authorizing $1.2 million to study the possible health effects of exposure to low levels of oil smoke and other chemicals on veterans of the 1991 Persian Gulf War. The report also included $1.7 million for a five-year study of the medical effects of contact with depleted uranium darts fired by U.S. tank guns. The mildly radioactive metal was used because its great density helped penetrate enemy tank armor.

Conferees rejected a Senate provision earmarking $2 million to study the claims of some veterans that they might have been exposed to chemical or biological weapons during the Gulf War. Although insisting they did not take those claims lightly, the conferees contended that focusing on suspected chemical and biological weapons effects would be unwise while ignoring the possibility that the symptoms resulted from the troops' exposure to other toxic substances, such as the pervasive smoke from thousands of sabotaged oil wells in Kuwait.

• Sealed into law, with only slight modifications, the Pentagon's longtime ban on homosexual conduct by military personnel. The definition of "conduct" was sufficiently broad to include the private disclosure to a friend of one's homosexual orientation.

Guard and Reserves

Trimmed 55,580 members from National Guard and reserve units, setting the ceiling at 1,039,400. Clinton had proposed a cut of nearly 68,000.

The bill did not include two Clinton proposals intended to make easier the mobilization of Guard and reserve units in conflicts short of all-out war. The conferees balked at expanding the president's call-up authority without first studying the impact of any change on employers' support for the reserves.

• Authorized $990 million, not requested by the administration, for equipment to be allocated to Guard and reserve units.

• Accepted a House provision ordering the Army to test a new approach to the round-out policy that used National Guard units to bolster active-duty combat forces. In several active-duty Army divisions, a Guard brigade had been designated since the mid-1970s as one of the three brigades forming the unit. But when three of these divisions were deployed to the Persian Gulf in 1991, they left behind the round-out brigades, contending they were not ready for combat.

The conferees ordered the Army to test the round-out idea on a smaller scale, by assigning a National Guard unit as one of the three battalions—each with several hundred members—in an active-duty brigade and assigning a Guard company as one of the several companies constituting some active-duty battalions.

To further bolster the combat-readiness of Guard and reserve units, the bill included provisions requiring the Army to establish two units to provide training support to reserve forces and demonstrate, in effect, that active-duty officers assigned to duties in support of the reserves had at least as good a chance of promotion as officers assigned to other duties.

• Elevated the status of the Army Reserve Command in the Army's hierarchy.

• Required the secretary of defense to report to Congress on Air Force plans to turn over some B-1 bombers to Air National Guard and Air Force Reserve units.

Operations and Maintenance

Authorized a total of $87.4 billion for operations and maintenance programs, $2.1 billion less than Clinton's request.

• Allowed the Pentagon to designate unanticipated missions as national contingency operations, thus exempting the services from having to reimburse other Pentagon agencies for transportation, supplies and services worth up to $300 million. This was intended to reduce the pressure on the services to skimp on training and maintenance to fund unexpected operations such as the deployment of forces to Somalia.

In such cases, however, the secretary of defense was required to submit a plan to pay the deferred costs through reprogramming, supplemental appropriations or allied contributions.

• Authorized $400 million, as requested, to help Russia and its neighbors dismantle the former Soviet nuclear arsenal.

• Authorized $1.96 billion to clean up toxic and hazardous waste on current or former military bases, $347 million less than Clinton requested.

Burden-Sharing

Ordered the Pentagon to spend nearly $600 million less than the $17.5 billion it requested to operate overseas bases. The withheld funds were to be channeled instead toward covering the operating costs of bases in the United States. However, the secretary of defense could waive this requirement if he gave Congress 15 days' notice. The provision was intended to beef up the administration's effort to get host countries to pick up a larger share of the cost of stationing U.S. forces abroad.

Economic Conversion

Authorized $2.55 billion for programs aimed at helping government and private sector defense workers, defense contractors and their communities adapt to a long-term retrenchment in defense spending.

The lion's share ($2.22 billion) was to help defense firms reorient themselves toward finding commercial markets. This included $624 million—$300 million more than Clinton requested—for dual-use partnerships to help small- and medium-size firms develop technologies that had military applications and that could provide a foothold in the commercial arena.

The bill also included $197 million to help domestic shipbuilding companies become competitive in the construction of commercial ships. And it had several provisions intended to speed the search for new job-producing uses for abandoned military bases. ❑

1994 Defense Appropriations

Congress in 1993 cleared a $240.5 billion fiscal 1994 defense appropriations bill. The bill (HR 3116—PL 103-139) represented 92 percent of the total amount that Congress provided for fiscal 1994 defense-related activities. An additional $10.1 billion came in the military construction bill (HR 2446—PL 103-110) and most of the rest of the nation's defense budget was made up of $10.9 billion included in the energy and water development appropriations bill (HR 2445—PL 103-126).

As was typical of defense funding bills, HR 3116 mirrored in most respects the companion fiscal 1994 defense authorization bill (HR 2401—PL 103-160). The defense bills generally followed the outlines of President Clinton's budget request and only slightly accelerated the cuts in Pentagon spending that had been planned by President George Bush following the collapse of the Soviet military threat. *(1994 defense authorization, p. 257)*

HR 3116 added to Clinton's request nearly $1.05 billion to provide a 2.2 percent pay raise for military personnel that Clinton had sought to postpone and $1.2 billion to buy equipment for National Guard and reserve units.

While appropriators were working within rigid spending ceilings set by the authorization bill, they still managed to accommodate billions of dollars' worth of spending that was of particular interest to individual members of Congress—especially to members of the Defense Appropriations subcommittees.

The appropriators achieved the spending cuts and paid for the members' add-ons in part by outright cuts from programs requested by the Pentagon. A handful of large slashes were made in individual programs, such as $1 billion from Clinton's request for antimissile defense research. But most of the cuts were relatively modest reductions made to hundreds of programs, mostly in research and development. The appropriators displayed their usual prowess in wringing from the budget request hundreds of millions of dollars that the subcommittees insisted reflected outdated economic assumptions and thus could be cut with no impact on Pentagon operations.

Highlights of the bill included:

• A reduction of nearly 105,000 in active-duty personnel, 97 percent of the cut Clinton proposed. But the bill added to the budget the 2.2 percent pay raise for the 1.6 million who remained in the service.

• Maintaining the existing tempo of operations for major combat units. To pay for those activities, the bill included $205 million more than Clinton requested.

• Continued production of several major weapons, such as the Navy's *Arleigh Burke*-class Aegis destroyer and the Air Force's C-17 cargo plane, and added funds to continue production of Army combat helicopters and missiles that Clinton's request would have let lapse.

• Continued development of a new generation of high-tech weaponry, including the Army's Comanche scout helicopter, the Navy's *Centurion*-class submarine and enlarged F/A-18 fighter-attack jet, and the Air Force's F-22 fighter jet.

HOUSE ACTION

The House passed a $239.4 billion funding bill (HR 3116) on Sept. 30 by a vote of 325–102. The bill had been reported by the House Appropriations Committee on Sept. 22 (H Rept 103-254).

Both committee and floor action on the bill featured debates over militarily risky humanitarian missions abroad. As reported by the House Appropriations Committee, the bill provided $383 million of the $448 million requested by Clinton to cover some of the costs of unanticipated deployments for natural disaster relief or multilateral peacekeeping operations. But it barred use of funds provided in the bill for humanitarian interventions other than natural disaster relief, unless the president gave Congress 15 days' notice of the mission accompanied by an analysis of its timetable and budget.

The House eliminated the notification provision on a point of order on the grounds that it violated the House rule barring legislation on an appropriations bill. Subsequently, the House adopted by voice vote an amendment offered by John P. Murtha, D-Pa., eliminating the $383 million earmarked for humanitarian missions.

Also dropped on a point of order was a provision earmarking $1 billion to begin work on a new aircraft carrier, which the Clinton administration planned to request in the fiscal 1995 budget.

The Rules Committee, which set the parameters for floor debate on the bill, could have protected the provisions with a rule that waived points of order against them. Instead, the panel agreed on a rule that provided no such protection, leaving the provisions vulnerable to challenge. When the House took up the rule (H Res 263) Sept. 29, Republicans objected, contending that it would deprive Congress of an opportunity to head off any prospect that Clinton might commit U.S. forces in Bosnia. But the House adopted the rule on a 254–176 vote, thus dooming the two provisions. Members split almost entirely along party lines.

In other action on the bill Sept. 30, the House rejected, 178–248, an amendment by Timothy J. Penny, D-Minn., that would have eliminated $1.1 billion for continued production of Trident II submarine-launched missiles.

SENATE ACTION

After seven days of debate, the Senate on Oct. 21 approved by voice vote a $238.8 billion version of the defense spending bill. The Senate Appropriations Committee had reported the bill on Oct. 4 (S Rept 103-153).

Concern over the direction of U.S. foreign policy surfaced in the Senate debate, as it had in the House. Floor action on the bill became bogged down over questions about U.S. policies in such hot spots as Haiti, Bosnia and Somalia, contributing to the need for another continuing resolution to keep the government running while the Senate worked on the bill.

Despite days of talk about the U.S. role in the world, the Senate changed little of the underlying spending bill. Members rejected all amendments that would have cut funds.

Armed Services Committee Chairman Sam Nunn, D-Ga., and Pete V. Domenici, R-N.M., offered—but eventually withdrew—an amendment intended to underscore their opposition to cutting defense too deeply. The amendment would have reinstated a prohibition on transferring money from defense to other domestic programs, rebuilding the budgetary walls that had stood for three years under a 1990 budget deal between President Bush and Congress. But the amendment ran into strong objections from Budget Committee Chairman Jim Sasser, D-Tenn., and was withdrawn because Nunn and Domenici said they lacked the 60 votes needed to alter budget rules.

The agreement between Congress and the administration on

ending the U.S. deployment in Somalia was provided for in a Robert C. Byrd, D-W.Va., amendment to HR 3116, which was adopted Oct. 15 (in the session that began Oct. 14) by a **key vote of 76–23 (R 24–20; D 52–3).** The compromise endorsed Clinton's March 31, 1994, pullout date but cut off most U.S. funds after that. An amendment offered by John McCain, R-Ariz., to prohibit funding of U.S. military operations in Somalia except for the withdrawal of all U.S. troops had been tabled (killed) by an earlier vote of 61–38. *(1993 key votes, p. 979; Somalia, p. 191)*

An amendment offered by Don Nickles, R-Okla., to prohibit funding for U.S. forces under the command of U.N. foreign officers unless authorized by Congress or waived by the president was rejected, 33–65, on Oct. 19. Instead, the Senate the same day adopted, 96–2, a sense-of-Congress amendment proposed by Nunn that the president should consult with Congress before placing combat troops under foreign command. *(U.N. peacekeeping missions, p. 200)*

On Oct. 20, the Senate voted 99–1 for a nonbinding amendment offered by Senate Majority Leader George J. Mitchell, D-Maine, urging the administration not to send U.S. forces to Bosnia without first obtaining congressional approval. *(Bosnia, p. 197)*

The Senate also weighed in on U.S. policy toward Haiti. The Senate on Oct. 21 rejected, 19–81, a Jesse Helms, R-N.C., amendment that would have prohibited funding for U.S. military operations in Haiti unless Congress authorized it or the president certified that U.S. citizens in Haiti were in imminent danger. Instead, the Senate adopted, 98–2, a Mitchell sense-of-Congress amendment that Congress should authorize U.S. military operations in Haiti under most circumstances. *(Haiti, p. 195)*

By voice vote, the Senate on Oct. 20 accepted an amendment by McCain and Jeff Bingaman, D-N.M., that they said was intended to crack down on the practice of earmarking funds in the defense bill to circumvent competitive procedures in awarding contracts and research grants. But the amendment was accepted only after being shorn of a broad policy statement and reworded to apply to authorization bills as well as appropriations.

As it had before, the Senate rejected a move by Dale Bumpers, D-Ark., to end production of the Trident II missile. By a vote of 63–34, the Senate on Oct. 14 gutted Bumpers's amendment by adding to it a provision allowing the president to waive the Trident II production prohibition if he deemed it contrary to U.S. national security interests. The amended provision then was adopted by voice vote.

The Senate on Oct. 14 tabled (killed), 52–47, a McCain amendment that would have blocked Clinton's decision to build a third *Seawolf*-class submarine. By voice vote, the Senate adopted another McCain amendment that capped at $4.7 billion the total that could be spent to complete work on the first two *Seawolf*-class subs.

In other action, the Senate on Oct. 14 tabled (killed), 64–35, a Bumpers amendment to cut $400 million from the secret amount—reportedly $17 billion—earmarked for national intelligence activities. A Sasser amendment to require other coun-

tries to provide 20 percent of the cost of developing defenses against short-range (or theater) ballistic missiles, unless waived by the president on national security grounds, was tabled, 54–42, earlier that day. On Oct. 20, the Senate tabled, 80–20, an amendment by Bill Bradley, D-N.J., that would have eliminated $150 million that the appropriators had added to buy small transport planes for the National Guard.

CONFERENCE

Both chambers adopted the conference report on HR 3116 (H Rept 103-339) on Nov. 10. The House approved it by voice vote; the Senate, by a vote of 88–9.

In its final form, the $240.5 billion defense bill included $1.1 billion more than the House-passed version of the bill and $1.7 billion more than the Senate-passed version.

The conference report included no funds to accelerate work on the nuclear-powered aircraft carrier that was slated for inclusion in the 1995 budget request. Proponents, including Republican Sen. John W. Warner and Democratic Rep. Norman Sisisky, both of Virginia, where the ship was to be built, argued that the Navy would save $200 million if it funded the ship a year earlier than scheduled. Moreover, Clinton and senior administration officials backed the funding speedup. But House Armed Services Committee Chairman Ronald V. Dellums, D-Calif., objected strenuously to appropriating the funds before his committee reviewed the project as part of an authorization bill. Conferees included in the bill $1.5 billion to buy high-speed cargo ships instead of the $291 million requested, saying that $1.2 billion of the sealift funds could be shifted to the carrier project if that course was approved by a supplemental authorization bill.

The conference report included several provisions intended to assert Congress's right to be consulted by the president before he committed U.S. military forces to conflicts in which U.S. interests were uncertain or ambiguous.

The bill sliced $1 billion from Clinton's request for Ballistic Missile Defense, leaving $2.6 billion for the antimissile program. Clinton's antimissile defense budget channeled a much larger share of funds toward systems that could defend U.S. forces or allies overseas against shorter-range ballistic missiles, such as the Soviet-designed Scuds used by Iraq in the 1991 Persian Gulf War. Conferees steered the program even more toward theater defenses at the expense of defenses for U.S. territory, cutting Clinton's $1.2 billion request for a nationwide antimissile defense nearly in half, to $650 million, but approving $1.4 billion of the $1.6 billion requested for theater defense. *(Antimissile defense, box, p. 262)*

MAJOR PROVISIONS

As signed into law Nov. 11, HR 3116 endorsed March 31, 1994, as the deadline for pulling U.S. troops out of Somalia and cut off most funds after that date. The bill included nonbinding sense-of-Congress declarations that the president should seek congressional approval before placing U.S. forces under command of a foreigner in a United Nations operation; sending forces into Haiti; and deploying troops in Bosnia, consultation that Clinton previously had promised.

The conference report also included a nonbinding provision by Murtha, who had vigorously opposed the Somalia deployment, expressing the sense of Congress that the president should commit U.S. forces to humanitarian or peacekeeping missions only after providing Congress with a detailed assessment of the mission, funding and time limit at least 15 days in advance of the deployment.

HR 3116 appropriated:

• $61.2 billion for pay and benefits for 1.62 million active-duty service members, including $919 million added by Congress for the military pay raise that President Clinton had wanted to forgo. The size of the active-duty payroll would be as requested except for the addition of 2,900 Marines. The bill provided $9.4 billion for 1.02 million members of the reserve and National Guard units, 5,300 more than Clinton had requested, and for Reserve Officers Training Corps stipends. The reserve and Guard funding included $126 million for their share of the 2.2 percent military pay hike.

• $76.6 billion for operations and maintenance, including funding for operating forces, mobilization, training and recruiting, and administration and other costs. This title of the bill covered most of the day-to-day costs of military operations, including most of the $41.5 billion for the nearly 919,000 civilians employed by the Pentagon.

• $2.2 billion to purchase six C-17 cargo jets, plus so-called long lead-time components for future purchases. To put competitive pressure on the McDonnell-Douglas Corp., builder of the C-17, the bill also provided $100 million to begin buying a modified version of an existing wide-body cargo jet, either a plane in commercial service or the Air Force's C-5. The bill also provided $180 million for continued development of the C-17.

• $735 million largely for equipment used to maintain and operate the 96 B-1 bombers already in service and the 20 B-2s previously authorized by Congress. The bill included $790 million to continue development of the B-2.

• $1.52 billion for 36 Navy F/A-18s (plus $128 million for long-lead funding) and $1.47 billion to continue developing an enlarged version of the fighter; $130 million to rebuild four of the Marine Corps's Harrier vertical takeoff jets (plus $15 million for long-lead funding); $400 million for a final production run of 12 Air Force F-16s; and $2.1 billion for continued development of the F-22 fighter plane.

• $437 million for two JSTARS radar planes and $289 million for continued development; $408 million for 60 Blackhawk helicopters for the Army (plus long-lead time items) and $131 million for six Blackhawks for the Navy; $292 million for 12 Marine Corps CH-53E helicopters (plus long-lead items); $339 million for 15 Navy Seahawks (plus long-lead); $168 million for 10 Army Apache helicopters; $144 million for 12 Marine Cobra helicopters; $367 million for development of the Army's Comanche helicopter; and $278 million to develop the Army's Longbow project, a target-finding radar coupled with a radar-guided version of the Hellfire antitank missile.

• $97 million to upgrade 72 older M-1 tanks to M-1A1s; $160 million to modernize self-propelled 155 mm howitzers;

and $192 million to maintain the production line for Bradley armored troop carriers so it would be available when the Army wanted to begin upgrading its early-model Bradleys.

• $2.6 billion for three *Arleigh Burke*-class destroyers equipped with the Aegis antiaircraft system of powerful radars and missiles; $894 million for a *Wasp*-class helicopter carrier and $50 million, unrequested, for long-lead time funding for another ship of the same type; and $240 million for continued development of the new *Centurion* nuclear submarine.

• $1.5 billion for high-speed cargo ships, $1.2 billion beyond what was requested. The extra money could be used to expedite work on a new nuclear-powered aircraft carrier if Congress passed a supplemental bill authorizing the shift. Otherwise, the entire $1.5 billion was to be spent on cargo ships.

• $1.14 billion to buy 24 Trident II submarine-launched missiles (plus long lead-time components); $248 million for 216 of the Navy's Tomahawk cruise missiles; nearly $370 million for Army artillery rockets, including the ATACMS missile; more than $400 million for short-range guided missiles; $621 million for antiaircraft weapons; $339 million for air-to-ground missiles, including the stealth TSSAM missile (the amount appropriated for the TSSAM missile was secret but various sources reported it to be $548 million, including $161 million for procurement and $387 million for development); $549 million for nearly 800 AMRAAM radar-guided air-to-air missiles used by Air Force, Navy and Marine Corps fighters; and $234 million for homing torpedoes and related equipment.

• $2.6 billion for the antimissile defense program formerly known as the Strategic Defense Initiative (SDI) and renamed the Ballistic Missile Defense program.

• Nearly $1.44 billion for space satellites and related equipment, including $471 million for Titan IV launch rockets and $360 million for satellites that could detect missile launches. The bill included $273 million to continue development of the Titan IV; $250 million to develop new types of satellites that could detect attacking missiles; and $932 million to continue developing the Milstar communications satellite.

• $1.2 billion added by Congress for equipment to be issued to National Guard and reserve units.

• $2.49 billion for economic conversion programs to help Pentagon workers, defense contractors, employees of those firms and their localities retool for nondefense business as the defense budget continued to shrink. This amount included $474 million to fund the federal government's share of so-called dual-use partnerships, projects to develop technologies that promised to be useful both in military applications and in commercial products.

FISCAL 1993 SUPPLEMENTAL

Before Congress took up its fiscal 1994 defense spending bill, it had to take care of some unfinished business from the previous year. On July 1, 1993, both chambers signed off on a fiscal 1993 supplemental appropriations bill, which provided $3.5 billion for a broad range of defense and domestic items, including the U.S. military's Operation Restore Hope in Somalia. The legislation (HR 2118—PL 103-50) was signed into law the next day.

The question of where the more than $1.2 billion in defense spending in the bill would come from produced heated debate. In the end, House-Senate conferees agreed on a compromise that rescinded enough spending from lower-priority defense programs to cover $973.5 million of the Pentagon money while allowing an additional $326 million to count against the defense spending available under the budget caps for 1993.

FISCAL 1994 SUPPLEMENTAL

An emergency fiscal 1994 supplemental appropriations bill (HR 3759—PL 103-211) was signed into law on Feb. 12, 1994. Although rushed through to provide disaster relief for the victims of a major earthquake in Los Angeles, the $11 billion appropriations measure included funds for, among other things, U.S. peacekeeping operations abroad. The bill appropriated the nearly $1.2 billion President Clinton requested, but it stipulated that the money could be used for ongoing U.S. operations in Somalia, Bosnia, Iraq and Haiti only and not for any new missions or changes in existing missions.

To offset some of the costs of the bill, Congress ordered $3.25 billion in rescissions. Those affecting the Defense Department were $89.8 million from the Pentagon's procurement budget; $160.5 million from research and development; $93.5 million from military construction; $507.7 million from funds for the third phase of base closures; and $122.3 million from the Army Corps of Engineers.

1994 Military Construction

Congress in 1993 cleared a $10.1 billion fiscal 1994 military construction appropriations bill. Although the size of the U.S. military was declining, the price tag on the legislation (HR 2446—PL 103-110) was $1.7 billion more than was approved for fiscal 1993. HR 2446 cut President Clinton's request by $729 million.

The military construction appropriations bill covered the annual cost of building U.S. bases around the world, including everything from houses, shops and recreation centers to infrastructure needs such as roads, utilities, hospitals and schools. Since 1989, the bill also had paid for the cost of cleaning up and closing surplus military bases.

For a measure that cost the government more than $10 billion and affected about 1.6 million active-duty personnel and their dependents, the bill generated remarkably little controversy. As in the past, debate in the committees and on the floor rarely lasted longer than a few minutes. But even as the military grappled with the problems of a 25 percent, five-year force reduction and a continually shrinking budget, military construction remained expensive—$3.88 billion for new base facility projects; $3.5 billion to construct, operate and maintain housing; and $2.68 billion to close bases.

LEGISLATIVE ACTION

The House passed a $10.3 billion military construction bill on June 23 by a vote of 347–67. The bill had been reported by the House Appropriations Committee on June 17 (H Rept 103-136).

Although the House bill cut the administration's original request by $521 million, it added more than 100 domestic spending projects not requested by the Pentagon. A proposed amendment to eliminate $520 million for 143 projects that the committee had added or expanded in the bill never came to a vote because Harris W. Fawell, R-Ill., leader of a group of self-styled porkbusters, left the floor in the middle of what turned out to be a brief debate on the measure.

As usual, the construction bill was laden with projects in the states and districts of Appropriations Committee members. High on the winners' list were Texas and California.

The Senate passed a $9.8 billion version of the construction bill by voice vote on Sept. 30. Floor action on the bill was handled without roll-call votes or debate. The bill had been reported by the Senate Appropriations Committee on Sept. 23 (S Rept 103-148).

In a move reflecting reluctance to spend scarce funds on overseas bases, the Appropriations panel had sidestepped the administration's $240 million request for the North Atlantic Treaty Organization (NATO) infrastructure fund. Instead of trimming the request, as the House had, Senate appropriators voted to establish a $300 million special account for both NATO and U.S. overseas bases. The panel said the administration's request for the two items was more than $450 million.

During floor action, the Senate adopted without debate an amendment by Frank R. Lautenberg, D-N.J., that held hostage $120 million of the $300 million account. The money was not to be spent until the secretary of defense certified that negotiations were under way—and making progress—for host nations to pick up more of the costs of U.S. military operations overseas.

CONFERENCE, MAJOR PROVISIONS

The House approved the conference report (H Rept 103-278) on the $10.1 billion measure by voice vote Oct. 13. The Senate adopted the conference report, 94–5, on Oct. 19, completing congressional action. HR 2446 was signed into law Oct. 21.

Funding for military construction projects totaled almost $3.9 billion for fiscal 1994. The administration had requested $4 billion. Big winners were the politically well-connected National Guard and reserve forces, which garnered $752 million, more than twice the requested $352 million. Conferees agreed to the House decision to provide $140 million for the controversial NATO infrastructure fund.

The Defense Department received $3.5 billion of the $3.76 billion that the administration sought for family housing. The final bill cut requested levels for family housing for all three branches of the military. The Army received $1.30 billion of its requested $1.34 billion; the Navy received $1.10 billion of its $1.21 billion request; and the Air Force received $923 million of its requested $1.03 billion.

W. G. "Bill" Hefner, D-N.C., chairman of the House Military Construction Appropriations Subcommittee, said the bill included $500 million for a Pentagon initiative to upgrade and replace "antiquated World War II barracks" and to "repair and replace housing that is substandard and dangerous to the health of families because of the presence of asbestos and lead-based paint."

The $2.68 billion for base realignment and closing was a cut from the $3.03 billion requested by the administration but an increase over the $2.03 billion appropriated for fiscal 1993.

SUBSEQUENT RESCISSIONS

A fiscal 1994 emergency supplemental appropriations bill (HR 3759—PL 103-211) cleared by Congress in early 1994 ordered a number of rescissions—cuts in already appropriated spending—to offset part of its cost.

The fiscal 1994 rescissions included $93.5 million in military construction funds and $507.7 million in funds for the third phase of base closures and realignments. *(1994 supplemental appropriations, p. 271)* ❑

1995 Defense Authorization

Congress in 1994 cleared a $263.8 billion fiscal 1995 defense authorization. The legislation (S 2182—PL 103-337) closely followed President Clinton's defense budget request of $263.7 billion.

The administration request amounted to an inflation-adjusted reduction of less than 1 percent from the previous year's spending level. Liberals had wanted bigger cuts in Pentagon spending, and conservatives had wanted less retrenchment.

On the festering question of whether the United States should break the U.N.-sponsored arms embargo against the out-gunned Muslim forces in Bosnia, the bill urged—but did not require—the president to seek a U.N. Security Council resolution to lift the embargo. But a compromise, engineered by Senate Armed Services Chairman Sam Nunn, D-Ga., did cut off funds for U.S. enforcement of the arms ban by Nov. 15, 1994, unless the Security Council adopted such a resolution by that date or the Serbs agreed to internationally mediated peace terms. Neither happened. *(Bosnia, p. 197)*

On a major weapons procurement matter, the measure ordered a high-level Pentagon review of whether the Air Force needed more long-range bombers than projected budgets would allow. The bill earmarked up to $125 million to study options for acquiring additional bombers and to keep intact for one year critical parts of the network of companies that built and equipped such planes. This formulation sidestepped the long-running dispute over whether to keep building the B-2 stealth bomber. *(B-2 bomber, box, p. 277)*

The Bosnia embargo and B-2 production were among the most contentious issues confronting the defense authorization conferees. On most big-ticket items in the bill, the Senate and House were in substantial agreement, including authorization for a new nuclear-powered aircraft carrier requested by Clinton and for a 2.6 percent pay raise for military personnel instead of the 1.6 percent raise proposed by Clinton.

CLINTON BUDGET

The budget request that Clinton presented on Feb. 7, 1994, was the first installment of a five-year, $1.3 trillion defense pro-

gram that rested on a complex budgetary gamble: It assumed that inflation would boost future Pentagon expenses more slowly than forecast, thus cutting budgetary requirements by at least $20 billion. And it assumed that the Pentagon would be able to trim its annual costs significantly by revamping the way it bought weapons and managed its financial affairs and by disposing of unneeded facilities.

Some combination of lower inflation and cost-cutting reforms had to yield tens of billions of dollars in net savings for the Pentagon over the next five years. Otherwise, Clinton's projected budgets would be too small to cover an upturn in weapons procurement funding slated to come in fiscal 1998, when the large inventories of modern weaponry amassed during the flush years of the 1980s would have been used up. The projected resurgence in procurement spending was a key element of Clinton's plan to maintain a force of 1.4 million active-duty military personnel, all combat-ready and equipped with high-tech weaponry.

The president's plan faced criticism from liberals, who found his goal of a 1.4 million personnel force unduly ambitious and favored deeper cuts in spending. But Clinton had pledged in his State of the Union speech on Jan. 25 to hold the line against liberals who might cut deeper: "The budget I send to Congress draws the line against further defense cuts. . . . We must not cut defense further."

At least initially, however, the more vocal criticism came from conservatives who accepted Clinton's defense goals but faulted his budget as inadequate to the purpose. *(Box, p. 273)*

BUDGET RESOLUTION

Congress allocated $263.8 billion for defense in its fiscal 1995 budget resolution (H Con Res 218). Action on the resolution was completed May 12. *(Budget resolution, p. 273)*

Ignoring Clinton's call for no further defense cuts, House liberals had proposed a $2.4 billion cut in fiscal 1995 defense budget authority. They theorized that the president would not fight hard to fend off the cuts because, in part, the defense budget was virtually the only source from which Congress could squeeze funds to pay for new domestic initiatives. But Clinton, his top aides and the House Democratic leadership lobbied vigorously against the Barney Frank, D-Mass., amendment, which went down to defeat on March 10 by a **key vote of 105–313 (R 12–160; D 92–153; I 1–0).** *(1994 key votes, p. 1003)*

When the Senate Budget Committee wrote a resolution making $26 billion in additional cuts over the next five years, Pentagon supporters scrambled to shield the defense budget from the cuts, but none of their proposals came close to approval during Senate floor action.

The House, haunted by fears of further defense reductions and pushed hard by the White House to say no, set the stage for a conference battle when it rejected by a **key vote of 202–216 (R 159–6; D 43–209; I 0–1)** on April 14 a nonbinding motion that would have told House negotiators to go along with the Senate's additional cuts. After weeks of wrangling, conferees agreed to $13 billion in cuts, which were to start gradually with a first installment of just $500 million in fiscal 1995.

CLINTON DEFENSE PROJECTIONS

Although Congress in 1994 essentially gave President Clinton what he wanted in his defense budget, there was an uneasiness about Clinton's long-range defense projections, as seen in the debate over the conference report on the fiscal 1995 defense authorization bill (S 2182).

In the House, Armed Services Committee Chairman Ronald V. Dellums, D-Calif., said Clinton's effort to maintain a force capable of fighting two major wars was too rich a goal. Meanwhile, many Republicans and conservative Democrats decried both the bill and Clinton's request as dangerously lean. These critics argued that Clinton's planned force was too small to begin with and that his budget was inadequate to fund it. They also warned that shortages of money and manpower were exacerbated when Clinton spent Pentagon money on nondefense projects at the same time that he deployed U.S. forces for a wide array of humanitarian missions.

In the Senate, Armed Services Committee Chairman Sam Nunn, D-Ga., warned that Clinton's projected funding levels "will not be adequate to maintain the current readiness of our forces, provide for their needed modernization and still support the force structure necessary."

The concerns about a coming crunch were underscored by an Aug. 18 memo written by Deputy Defense Secretary John M. Deutch. He directed the armed services to prepare alternative budget plans that would fund the higher military pay raises on which Congress had insisted—and which Defense Secretary William J. Perry had come to embrace. Deutch's memo instructed the services to consider budget alternatives that would cancel, postpone or slow production of nine major weapons, including the F-22 fighter and the Comanche helicopter. Deutch insisted that the ad-

ministration likely would propose only a handful of the potential cutbacks.

Late in the year, Pentagon officials estimated that their six-year budget plan fell $49 billion short of the amount needed to pay for Clinton's program. Half of the shortfall was expected to be made up by canceling or stretching out weapons programs and by lower inflation than anticipated.

Clinton announced on Dec. 1 that the remaining $25 billion would be added to the $1.5 trillion the Pentagon planned to seek from Congress in the next six fiscal years (1996–2001). And on Dec. 9, the Pentagon announced plans to save $7.7 billion in that same period by slowing production of several major weapons, canceling the TSSAM stealth missile and indefinitely delaying production of the Comanche helicopter.

Critics of Clinton's defense budget had acquired potent rhetorical ammunition in mid-November, when the Pentagon announced that three of the Army's 12 combat divisions had reported significant limitations in their ability to carry out the full range of their potential combat missions. They welcomed Clinton's announcement as a vindication of their position that the president's Pentagon budgets were too small to begin with and that he was diverting billions from those budgets for nondefense programs. Moreover, they argued, Clinton had worn out combat units with frequent overseas deployments to places such as Haiti and Somalia where, they contended, no vital U.S. interests were at stake.

For his part, Clinton insisted that the services' current readiness problems resulted from the costs of unanticipated operations in Haiti, Kuwait and other areas, and not from any fundamental weakness in his approach.

HOUSE COMMITTEE ACTION

The House Armed Services Committee reported a $263.3 billion authorization bill (HR 4301—H Rept 103-499) on May 10.

On most issues, the committee bill adhered to the administration's budget request, although it did make some cuts—in the requests for the Ballistic Missile Defense and C-17 programs, for example, and in the cancellation of the short-range, stealth TSSAM missile—and some additions—such as an increased military pay raise and six additional Apache helicopters.

Most members of the House panel regarded Clinton's long-term plans for defense spending as too stingy and underscored that view with provisions such as nonbinding language urging a larger Army than the administration planned. But the concern over cuts did not play out in the bottom line. A Republican amendment, offered by Duncan Hunter of California, to increase the total authorization by $6.8 billion—a purely symbolic move because the budget resolution would have blocked appropriation of the additional funds—was rejected on a party-line vote of 22–34.

Besides blasting Clinton's budget as too small, committee Republicans hammered at the theme that core defense programs

were being cut even more deeply than it appeared because Pentagon funds were being earmarked for new missions, such as cleaning up toxic waste on abandoned military bases and helping former republics of the Soviet Union dismantle the nuclear weapons they inherited. The committee scotched one such plan: Clinton's proposal to earmark $300 million in defense funds to pay the U.S. share of certain U.N. peacekeeping costs previously paid from the State Department's budget. The funds were earmarked instead to pay for unanticipated deployments involving peacekeeping, humanitarian assistance or disaster relief. The committee included in its report on the bill a statement strongly opposing the use of Pentagon funds to pay U.N. assessments.

HOUSE FLOOR ACTION

The House passed HR 4301, 260–158, on June 9. In preparation for conference, the House agreed July 25 by voice vote to pass the Senate bill (S 2182), after substituting the text of HR 4301.

Before passing the $263.3 billion bill, lawmakers on June 9 defied the administration on foreign policy by adopting, by a **key vote of 244–178 (R 127–45; D 117–132; I 0–1),** an amendment to force the United States to break the U.N. embargo against arming the combatants in the former Yugoslavia so that weapons could be provided to Bosnia. The amendment was sponsored by Frank McCloskey, D-Ind., and House Democratic Whip David E. Bonior of Michigan. The House June 9 then rejected, 181–242, a more moderate, administration-backed amendment, crafted by House Foreign Affairs Committee Chairman Lee H. Hamilton, D-Ind., that urged the president to seek multilateral support for lifting the ban. *(1994 key votes, p. 1003)*

The House also backed the Armed Services Committee decision to scuttle administration plans to tap defense funds to pay assessed contributions for U.N. peacekeeping operations. It was included along with other proposals in a single amendment, which the House adopted en bloc by voice vote. Also included in the en bloc amendment was an earmark of $400 million of the funds in the bill to assist former Soviet states in disposing of the nuclear and chemical weapons they inherited.

The House June 9 rejected, 185–237, a Republican-led move to impose stiff conditions on the deployment of U.S. forces under foreign command in multilateral missions.

On a nuts-and-bolts defense spending issue, the House on May 20 rejected, 166–229, an amendment by Timothy J. Penny, D-Minn., to eliminate from the bill funding for continued production of the Trident II (D-5) long-range, submarine-launched nuclear missile. The House on May 20 had adopted, 226–169, a Norm Dicks, D-Wash., amendment allowing the Pentagon discretion to waive a committee provision that would have prohibited installing Trident IIs in the eight oldest subs, a move expected to cost about $3 billion.

By a comfortable margin, the House on May 18 rejected, 155–271, a Martin T. Meehan, D-Mass., amendment that would have sliced an additional $200 million from the $2.7 billion approved by the Armed Services panel for ballistic missile defenses. Clinton requested $3.25 billion for the program.

On May 24, the House voted decisively, 330–100, to stand by Clinton's full request for six C-17 planes, spurning a plan by the Armed Services Committee to limit the purchases to four of the controversial transport planes. The amendment was sponsored by Jane Harman, D-Calif.

Only on the issue of burden-sharing—pressuring U.S. allies to pay more of the cost of stationing U.S. forces overseas—did the proponents of deeper cuts draw blood from the committee bill. By a hefty margin, the House on May 19 adopted, 268–144, an amendment to reduce the number of U.S. personnel stationed in Europe by up to 75,000 if European allies were not paying 75 percent of the nonsalary costs of their deployment by the end of fiscal 1998. The amendment, which could be waived by the president in an emergency, was strongly opposed by the administration. But cosponsors Barney Frank, D-Mass., and Christopher Shays, R-Conn., prevailed, tapping into the deeply rooted belief on Capitol Hill that many wealthy allies—who were also commercial competitors—underspent on their own military. The House the previous day had rejected, 163–260, a more radical proposal by Texas Democrat John Bryant that would have required a pullout of all troops by 2000 if the allies did not begin paying all costs of overseas U.S. forces.

The House first opposed U.S. intervention in Haiti, but later, in a symbolic victory for Clinton, reversed itself. The first vote came May 24, when the House adopted, 223–201, a sense-of-Congress amendment offered by Porter J. Goss, R-Fla., urging the president not to invade Haiti unless he first certified that a clear and present danger existed to U.S. citizens in that country. The amendment also urged the administration to use an island off the Haitian coast as a safe haven for Haitian refugees. On June 9, the House took another vote on the amendment, rejecting it 195–226. *(Haiti, p. 195)*

In other action, the House on May 24 rejected, 68–362, an amendment by James V. Hansen, R-Utah, to delay until 1997 the 1995 round of military base closings. *(Base closings, p. 288)*

SENATE COMMITTEE ACTION

The Senate Armed Services Committee reported its $263.3 billion defense authorization bill (S 2182—S Rept 103-282) June 14.

The most hotly contested issue was something Clinton did not request: $150 million added by the committee to preserve the option of buying additional B-2 stealth bombers. The money was intended to keep the B-2 production network alive for one more year. The House-passed version of the bill limited the B-2 force to the 20 planes previously authorized. *(B-2 bomber, box, p. 277)*

The committee endorsed other initiatives to beef up the bomber force, including ordering the Air Force to keep in active service the 95 B-1s and 95 B-52s that were in its inventory and approving $488 million of the $604 million requested for the TSSAM missile, which the House version of the bill sought to cancel.

The bill essentially embraced all the major weapons programs that Clinton requested, although it made some cuts in funding for such programs as the C-17 and antimissile defenses. Additions to Clinton's request included funding for the 2.6 percent military pay raise and for National Guard and reserve unit equipment.

SENATE FLOOR ACTION

The Senate passed a $263.1 billion version of S 2182 by voice vote on July 1.

Members handed Clinton a narrow but tactical victory earlier that day by stopping one vote short of approving an amendment that would have ordered the president to permit arms to flow to Bosnia's Muslim forces.

The Senate rejected, on a **key vote of 50–50 (R 37–7; D 13–43),** an amendment sponsored by Minority Leader Bob Dole, R-Kan., and Joseph I. Lieberman, D-Conn., that would have mandated the weapons shipments in defiance of the U.N. arms embargo.

Before that vote, the Senate approved, 52–48, an administration-backed amendment sponsored by Nunn and Virginia Republican John W. Warner. Their nonbinding amendment urged Clinton to seek a multilateral end to the embargo if the Serbian forces battling the Bosnian government derailed efforts to negotiate a peace settlement.

C-17 PROGRAM

Even as U.S. military strategy placed increased emphasis on deploying troops and equipment rapidly to distant trouble spots, the Clinton administration and Congress faced continuing problems with the C-17 cargo jet, which was intended to be the new workhorse of the military's airlift. Costs for the plane had increased and schedules had slipped, partly because of design flaws revealed by prototype planes and partly because the plane's manufacturer, McDonnell Douglas Corp., had problems managing the program and manufacturing the aircraft.

As the troubles mounted, so, too, did the criticism on Capitol Hill, even among the Pentagon's staunchest supporters. Citing repeated Air Force assurances in recent years that the program had "turned the corner" as a result of some change in its budget, schedule or organization chart, Rep. Gene Taylor, D-Miss., asked at House Armed Services subcommittee hearings in 1993, "How many corners are there in this program?"

Taylor's colleague, John Tanner, D-Tenn., contended that the program's travails made it difficult to lobby other members to support defense requests. "When we can't convincingly [explain] to people what we're trying to get them to vote for . . . this is a very serious matter," he said. "I'm about out of ammunition on this one."

House Defense Appropriations Subcommittee Chairman John P. Murtha, D-Pa., put it more bluntly, telling reporters in 1993 that the C-17 program was "one of the most screwed-up programs we've ever seen. . . . Our patience is very thin on this issue."

Although some lawmakers called for outright cancellation of the C-17 program, a majority accepted the administration's argument that the cargo jet was too important to the nation's mobilization plans to abandon.

Congress in 1993 authorized and appropriated funding for six of the jets. But strings were attached to require certain schedule and testing standards and to prod the Pentagon to develop alternatives in case the C-17 continued to falter. *(1994 defense authorization, p. 257; 1994 defense appropriations, p. 267)*

In 1994, Congress agreed to purchase another six planes. Lawmakers also approved a deal negotiated between the Pentagon and the plane manufacturer to settle several contract disputes. *(1995 defense authorization, p. 272; 1995 defense appropriations, p. 280)*

Background

Like the huge C-5 cargo jet that was its predecessor, the C-17 had a cavernous belly that could haul outsize items too bulky for other cargo planes—such as M-1 tanks, Patriot antimissile batteries and Bradley armored troop carriers. Unlike commercial wide-body jets, the C-17 and C-5 had low-slung fuselages from which vehicles could quickly be driven on and off the aircraft.

The C-17 was smaller than the C-5 and more agile on the ground. Thus a fleet of C-17s was supposed to be able to deliver more cargo faster and make use of runways too short to accommodate the C-5. The newer plane was also designed to cost much less to operate, partly because it was to have a crew of three, compared with the C-5's six-member crew.

But the C-17 program encountered a number of problems, and, by the fall of 1993, those problems had been compounded by a welter of contending legal claims by the government and McDonnell Douglas. Senior administration officials were speaking openly of terminating the program.

Contract Disputes Deal

In December 1993, the Pentagon and McDonnell Douglas struck a tentative agreement to resolve their differences. Under the package deal:

• The government and the contractor would abandon certain pending and prospective legal claims.

• Each would invest several hundred million additional dollars in the C-17 program.

• The Pentagon would slightly reduce the plane's specifications for range and payload weight.

• The Pentagon would buy a total of 14 additional C-17s in fiscal 1995–1996. That would bring the total number of operational planes to 40, the smallest fleet that would be militarily useful, according to the Pentagon.

• Depending on how well McDonnell Douglas met its budget, schedule and performance specifications through fiscal 1996, the Defense Department would decide how many additional C-17s to budget for.

Pentagon plans originally had called for a total of 120 C-17s, both to replace some older cargo jets and to expand its transoceanic (or strategic) airlift fleet. But, depending on the company's performance, as many as 80 of the McDonnell Douglas planes could be replaced by other wide-body jets, such as the C-5s built by Lockheed or Boeing 747s.

President Clinton asked Congress for legislation to waive any provisions that would obstruct the proposed deal. Congress approved the deal as part of the fiscal 1995 defense authorization bill (S 2182—PL 103-337).

Senators earlier handed Nunn a victory by rejecting, 45–55, an amendment by Carl Levin, D-Mich., to delete the $150 million he wanted to set aside to preserve the option of building more B-2 bombers.

By a vote of 32–66 on June 22, the Senate rejected an amendment intended to scrap a deal between the Pentagon and McDonnell Douglas Corp., builder of the C-17 cargo jet. The amendment by Charles E. Grassley, R-Iowa, would have eliminated a provision of the bill authorizing the deal, which was negotiated in response to a raft of troubles bedeviling the wide-body jet. *(C-17, box, this page)*

The Senate tabled (killed), by a vote of 72–24 on June 23, an amendment by Russell D. Feingold, D-Wis., that would have barred work on a new nuclear-powered aircraft carrier, for which the bill authorized $3.65 billion.

That same day the Senate rejected, 35–61, a Dirk Kempthorne, R-

Idaho, amendment that would have nullified a provision earmarking $300 million to pay the U.S. share of U.N. peacekeeping operations. The amendment would have used that money instead to beef up the training and maintenance of U.S. forces.

Also on June 23, the Senate, 71–27, tabled (killed) an amendment by Arlen Specter, R-Pa., that would have given federal courts limited power to intervene in the process that Congress had created to permit the closing of excess military bases. (*Judicial review, box, p. 289*)

By a vote of 88–12 on July 1, the Senate accepted a Warner amendment to accelerate the 1995 cost-of-living increase for military pensions by six months so that it would occur April 1. That was the date that civil service retirees were slated to receive their cost-of-living adjustment. Appropriations Committee Chairman Robert C. Byrd, D-W.Va., and Armed Services Chairman Nunn argued against the amendment, which was expected to cost $376 million in outlays and would have to be offset by reductions in other parts of the defense budget.

CONFERENCE ACTION

The House on Aug. 17 adopted the conference report (H Rept 103-701) on S 2182, 280–137. The Senate adopted the report Sept. 13 by a vote of 80–18, clearing the bill for the president.

Although Congress generally followed Clinton's requests, the final bill boosted funding in certain areas: It approved a 2.6 percent military pay raise instead of the 1.6 percent proposed by the president, and it authorized $125 million to study the options for acquiring additional long-range bombers.

On most big-ticket items, the Senate and House were in substantial agreement. For instance, both chambers backed Clinton's request for an aircraft carrier, approving $2.4 billion in new budget authority plus $1.2 billion transferred from the fiscal 1994 budget.

The artful compromises that deferred final decisions on the contentious issues of Bosnia and continued production of the B-2 bomber allowed Senate-House conferees to knit together the compromise bill.

The bill also resolved members' disagreement over the C-17 cargo jet. Both chambers had approved the request for six planes, but only the Senate had endorsed a contract modification that was negotiated to settle several legal issues in dispute between the Pentagon and McDonnell Douglas Corp. The conference report approved the contract settlement.

Following the lead of the House, the conferees rejected Clinton's request that the Pentagon pay $300 million of the U.S. government's assessment for U.N. peacekeeping operations. In the past, such costs had been funded from the State Department budget.

Floor debate on the conference report underscored the unresolved dispute over whether Clinton was spending too much on defense—or failing to provide the resources to back up his purported defense strategy. (*Box, p. 273*)

MAJOR PROVISIONS

As signed into law Oct. 5, S 2182 authorized $263.8 billion in defense spending for fiscal 1995, $100 million more than re-

quested. The Senate version had authorized $263.1 billion and the House version, $263.3 billion.

In final action on S 2182, conferees:

Strategic Arms

Deadlocked over a Senate provision that would have earmarked $150 million to preserve the option of buying additional B-2 stealth bombers in future budgets. They ordered the Pentagon to review whether the Air Force needed more long-range bombers than projected budgets would pay for. And they added to the bill $125 million that could be used to study options for buying additional bombers and to keep intact the critical nodes in the network of companies that built such aircraft.

Some of the $125 million could go to B-2 subcontractors, but none of it could be used to buy components in anticipation that they would be used to build additional B-2s.

• Prohibited the retirement of any bomber in service, and added $23 million to keep operating 24 B-52s that the budget had slated for retirement.

• Approved the $641 million requested for 18 additional Trident II submarine-launched ballistic missiles. Of the 18 Trident submarines in service or under construction, 10 were slated to each carry 24 of the 4,000-mile range Trident IIs, which carried eight nuclear warheads apiece. The conferees added a House provision barring conversion of the eight oldest of the subs to carry Trident IIs instead of the less powerful Trident Is on board. The defense secretary could waive the prohibition on grounds of being a significant national security risk.

• Included $305 million of the $604 million requested for the TSSAM stealth missile, another potential victim of Deputy Defense Secretary John M. Deutch's budget review. More than half the budget request was earmarked to begin TSSAM production. By summer, however, the Air Force conceded that more bugs had to be wrung out of the new missile. The conference report funded the Air Force's revised TSSAM program. (The missile was canceled in December 1995.)

• Boosted funding for precision-guided smart bombs, adding more than $120 million to accelerate the deployment of various weapons. The bill authorized $26 million, added to the request, to buy 36 Israeli-designed Have Nap missiles to be carried by some B-52s; $128 million, an increase of $17 million over the request, to accelerate development of a one-ton bomb designated JDAM; $78 million, added to the bill, to develop various kinds of interim smart bombs that could be used until JDAM was ready for service; and $160 million, as requested, to develop a glider bomb designated JSOW, so planes could attack targets from beyond the reach of their antiaircraft missiles.

Antimissile Program

$2.80 billion of the $3.25 billion requested for antimissile defenses. The final amount:

• Included $400 million of the $587 million requested for work on components of a national defense of U.S. territory against missile attack. The conferees' reduction included $120 million that had been earmarked to develop the Brilliant Eyes

B-2 BOMBER PRODUCTION

Proponents of the B-2 stealth bomber had mixed success in a last-ditch effort to preserve the option of buying additional copies of the bomber in future years.

Since 1990, the radar-evading B-2 had been the focus of vigorous debate. The bomber's price tag of several hundred million dollars per plane made such battles inevitable. But the B-2 also took on a symbolic aspect. Designed for nuclear strikes against the Soviet Union, the plane seemed a perfect target for those who insisted that the demise of the Soviet state permitted dramatic cuts in Pentagon spending. B-2 supporters, however, contended that, equipped with super-accurate smart bombs, it would be an invaluable example of the high-tech weaponry that would give U.S. forces the edge over enemy forces in nonnuclear combat.

In 1993, Congress gave final approval to building the last five of the 20 authorized B-2s in the fiscal 1994 defense authorization bill (HR 2401—PL 103-160). The measure also reaffirmed the 1992 agreement between Congress and the Bush administration to limit the B-2 force to those 20 planes. *(1994 defense authorization, p. 257; Congress and the Nation Vol. VIII, box, p. 398)*

But in 1994, Northrop-Grumman Corp., the prime contractor, and some Air Force personnel began lobbying to add $150 million to the fiscal 1995 budget to keep intact some parts of the B-2 production network that otherwise would begin to wind down during work on the final five planes.

The notion of building more B-2s was vehemently opposed by House Armed Services Committee Chairman Ronald V. Dellums, D-Calif., and committee member John R. Kasich, R-Ohio. So B-2 proponents made no effort to add funds for future B-2 production to the House version of the defense authorization bill.

Instead, the initiative was launched on the Senate side, where the B-2 had a powerful advocate in Armed Services Committee Chairman Sam Nunn, D-Ga. Although President Clinton had not requested the money, Nunn's committee added $150 million to the Senate version of the fiscal 1995 defense authorization (S 2182).

Nunn pointed out that the administration's bottom-up review of U.S. defenses had concluded that at least 185 long-range bombers, equipped to carry nonnuclear smart bombs, would be needed to meet the goal of a force that could fend off two virtually simultaneous attacks. Because of budgetary limitations, however, the administration planned to reduce the active force to about 100 planes. Nunn said half the $150 million would be used to accelerate the acquisition of spare parts that were slated for later purchase even if no additional bombers were bought. He called the remaining $75 million "an insurance policy."

House-Senate conferees who negotiated the final version of S 2182 (PL 103-337) reaffirmed the 20-plane limit on the B-2 force but also directed the defense secretary to review the need for additional bombers and authorized $125 million to support that review. The conference version also earmarked funds for various other projects to beef up the bomber force. *(1995 defense authorization provisions, p. 272)*

The fiscal 1995 defense appropriations bill (HR 4650—PL 103-335) provided $125 million specifically to preserve the B-2 industrial base. *(1995 defense appropriations, p. 280)*

---

missile detection satellite. That project was not killed but was made independent of the antimissile defense program.

- Included $273 million, as requested, to begin buying defenses against theater-range missiles, such as the Soviet-designed Scuds used by Iraq in the Persian Gulf War. The bulk of this money was to buy a new version of the Patriot missile.

- Included $1.69 billion of the $1.73 billion earmarked to develop antitheater missile defenses. This included $285 million to develop a replacement for the Patriot, designated ERINT; $496 million to develop a longer-range interceptor, designated THAAD; and $140 million to modify the Aegis antiaircraft system on some Navy ships to intercept theater-range missiles.

- Included $433 million of the $624 million requested for support activities and program management.

In addition to the antimissile defense funds, the conference report approved a total of $365 million—$19 million more than requested—for three projects intended to develop more effective satellites to detect missile launches. Included in the $365 million was the $120 million for Brilliant Eyes.

Ground Combat

Authorized the $525 million requested to continue developing the Army's Comanche scout helicopter, one of nine major weapons programs that Deputy Defense Secretary Deutch placed under review in August for possible cutbacks to fund higher military pay raises.

- Authorized $309 million, as requested, to gear up for equipping larger Apache attack helicopters with the Longbow target-finding radar and other upgrades.

- Authorized $72 million, not requested, to buy six additional Apaches, so that the production line would be intact when the time came to begin the Longbow modifications.

- Authorized $150 million, not requested, to upgrade 24 small Kiowa helicopters with antitank missiles and target-finding electronics.

- Authorized $96 million—$20 million more than requested—to accelerate the digitization program and insisted that the Army include Marine Corps ground units in the program. The digitization program, a key part of the Army's plan to make its forces more agile on battlefields, sought to provide all major combat vehicles and helicopters with radio links so that all the elements of a combat force could share information about their locations and those of enemy units.

- Boosted funding for M-1 upgrades to $318 million, including an addition of $108 million to modify 24 extra tanks that were to be transferred to the Marine Corps Reserve. The administration had requested $175 million to upgrade M-1 tanks, not only to keep the tank production line intact, but also to equip the tanks with digital links and other improvements.

- Authorized the $145 million requested to modify Bradley armored troop carriers. As with the M-1 modification, this program served the dual purposes of preserving an industrial base for armored vehicles and equipping vehicles already in service with digital communications and other improvements.

- Authorized $239 million, $12 million more than requested, to continue developing a new mobile cannon that would use liquid fuel instead of gunpowder to fire shells. But conferees added $18 million to continue developing more conventional alternatives.

The new cannon, designated AFAS, was another potential target of Deutch's memo. One alternative to it was for the Army to expand a plan to upgrade some of its artillery with digital communications and other equipment to allow more mobile operations. The conferees approved $218 million of the $238 million requested for this program, which was called Paladin.

- Authorized slightly more than requested to develop two kinds of smart munitions intended to destroy enemy tanks at ranges of 10 miles or more. The conference report recommended $72 million for a coffee can-sized warhead designated SADARM, designed to be scattered from cannon shells over an enemy column. The budget request initially earmarked the entire amount to continue developing the weapon. But by April 1994, successful weapons tests had persuaded the Army to ask that $30 million of the funds be earmarked instead to start production.

Conferees also recommended $119 million, $10 million more than requested, to continue developing BAT, a yard-long glider designed to be scattered from missiles to home in on the noise and heat of enemy vehicles.

- Authorized the $56 million requested to continue developing a longer-range version of the MLRS artillery rocket (which already had a range of 20 miles) and added $26 million to keep the production line running and to speed up, if possible, the start of production of the longer-range missile.

- Authorized more antitank missiles and small arms than the administration requested, including $127 million to buy more than 1,200 helicopter-launched Hellfires, compared with the budget request of $121 million for 830 missiles; $28 million to continue buying smaller TOW missiles (the administration had requested that amount to shut down the TOW production line); $214 million for nearly 900 shoulder-fired Javelins, compared with the administration request of $131 million for fewer than 400 Javelins; and $94 million, nearly four times the amount requested, to buy machine guns, rifles, mortars and other small arms.

Tactical Air Combat

Authorized Clinton's request for $2.46 billion to continue development of the Air Force's F-22 fighter, slated for production beginning in 1998. In addition, the conferees approved $10 million to begin developing a version of the plane that could operate off Navy carriers. The F-22 was the most expensive of the programs that Deutch's memo called into question.

- Authorized $1.02 billion for 24 F/A-18s, used by the Navy and Marines as both fighters and bombers. This was $98 million less than the budget requested.

- Authorized $1.35 billion, as requested, to develop larger E and F models of the F/A-18.

- Authorized $130 million, as requested, to rebuild four Harrier vertical takeoff jets used by the Marines as bombers.

- Approved $158 million, as requested, to modernize some of the Navy's F-14 fighters. But the conferees rejected a House proposal that would have earmarked $142 million to equip some late-model F-14s to carry large payloads of smart bombs and electronics capable of finding ground targets at night or in bad weather.

- Authorized the $230 million requested for a joint Navy-Air Force project to develop prototypes of a combat plane that could enter service toward the end of the next decade and a prototype of a new vertical takeoff jet with hotter performance than the Harrier.

- Included $108 million of the $123 million requested to buy the first three of a new type of basic training plane, designated JPATS, intended for use by both the Navy and Air Force. But Deutch directed the Navy and Air Force to examine the alternatives of either delaying JPATS production for seven years or buying the planes at a slower annual rate than was planned.

- Approved $26 million to modify the midair refueling equipment on Air Force tankers so they could refuel Navy planes.

- Added to the bill $100 million to return to service three aircraft from the Air Force's fleet of SR-71 high-speed reconnaissance planes, which were retired in 1990 because of their high operating cost.

- Authorized $445 million, as requested, for two additional JSTARS radar planes, intended to locate ground targets far behind enemy lines. Following the Senate's lead, conferees also added to the bill $100 million to buy used Boeing jetliners for future conversion into JSTARS planes.

Naval Combat

Approved the administration plan to provide nearly $3.7 billion for construction of a nuclear-powered aircraft carrier. The conferees, like the Senate, agreed to fund the ship the way the administration requested: $2.46 billion in new budget authority plus $1.2 billion previously appropriated as part of the fiscal 1994 budget.

- Included the $2.7 billion request for three additional *Arleigh Burke*-class destroyers equipped with the Aegis system of powerful, computer-controlled radars and antiaircraft missiles. However, Deutch ordered the Navy to consider buying the new destroyers at a slower rate.

- Approved the amounts requested for shipborne antiaircraft missiles: $258 million for 202 long-range Standards and $64 million for 240 short-range RAM missiles.

- Approved $398 million—$24 million more than requested—for a set of programs intended to develop better antiaircraft defenses for ships not equipped with the Aegis system. And $7 million was added to test a blimp as a radar picket for a fleet.

• Approved the $507 million requested to continue developing a new class of nuclear-powered submarine.

• Endorsed a Senate proposal earmarking $5 million to speed the process of modifying Navy ships to provide separate quarters for women. Also approved was the $54 million requested to modernize two supply ships. The latter were to get new machinery and more spacious quarters so they could be operated by largely civilian crews that would be much smaller—and thus less expensive—than all-Navy crews.

• Approved a total of $352 million, as requested, to buy nuclear reactor components and modify the power plants on nuclear-powered ships.

Air and Sea Transport

Trimmed $304 million from the budget request for six C-17 wide-body cargo jets, approving $2.17 billion, plus $190 million, as requested, for components that would be used in eight additional planes slated for funding in the fiscal 1996 budget.

The bill also authorized a package deal under which the government and C-17 contractor McDonnell Douglas Corp. were to abandon legal claims against each other and the Pentagon was to slightly relax the plane's contract schedule and performance specifications.

Conferees also approved the $104 million requested to test off-the-shelf wide-body cargo planes as supplements to the C-17.

• Added $50 million to the budget request in hopes of accelerating construction of a large helicopter carrier intended to deploy 2,000 Marines and the aircraft to haul them ashore. The Navy planned to fund the ship in its fiscal 2000 budget.

• Approved the request for $497 million to continue developing the Marine Corps's V-22 Osprey, a hybrid airplane-helicopter that Congress kept alive during the Bush administration despite efforts by then-Defense Secretary Dick Cheney to kill it on grounds that it was too expensive. The V-22 was also on Deutch's list as a potential target to be cut.

• Approved $30 million, $4 million more than requested, to continue development of another of Deutch's potential targets, the AAAV, a high-speed amphibious tractor designed to carry nearly 20 Marines toward shore at triple the 10 mph pace of the personnel carriers already in service.

• Approved the request for $601 million to buy two so-called RO/RO cargo ships, vessels with large ramps over which an Army division's tanks and other vehicles could quickly "roll on" at a U.S. port and "roll off" at a distant trouble spot.

• Approved a Senate initiative adding to the bill $220 million to buy two additional ships for conversion to floating depots that would carry tanks and other equipment for a Marine brigade.

Personnel Issues

Approved an active-duty personnel ceiling of 1,525,692 as requested—a reduction of more than 85,000 from fiscal 1994.

• Included the 2.6 percent military pay increase that both chambers had approved instead of the 1.6 percent Clinton proposed.

DRAFT REGISTRATION

Both chambers in 1994 rejected efforts to end registration for the military draft, during debate on the fiscal 1995 defense authorization bill (S 2182—PL 103-337). The House on May 23 turned back, 125–273, a proposal by Armed Services Committee Chairman Ronald V. Dellums, D-Calif. The Senate on July 1 voted 50–30 to table (kill) a similar amendment offered by Bill Bradley, D-N.J.

In 1993, the House had attempted to end the Selective Service System by slashing its funding in the fiscal 1994 spending bill for the departments of Veterans Affairs, Housing and Urban Development and related agencies (HR 2491—PL 103-124). But Senate conferees resisted, and in the end the House on Oct. 19, 1993, voted 236–194 to accept the Senate's appropriation of $25 million for Selective Service.

Under the system, men were required to register with the Selective Service within 30 days of their eighteenth birthday, filling out the forms at a post office or by mail. They were dropped from the active rolls when they turned 26.

Supporters of the system argued that, for a modest expense, Selective Service gave the United States a hedge in an unstable world. The agency said it could have the first draftees in uniform within 13 days. Without registration, the agency said it could get the first men in uniform in 42 days, if the agency remained fully staffed.

Opponents said that registration and a well-staffed Selective Service System were wasteful in light of the breakup of the Soviet Union and the Warsaw Pact. A 13-day mobilization was an unnecessary luxury when any sort of massive military buildup by an enemy would give the United States ample time to react, they said.

• Required the Pentagon to adopt a policy for processing complaints of sexual harassment or discrimination.

• Earmarked funds for several high-profile medical projects, including $40 million for work on health care issues affecting women in the military and $20 million for research into the so-called Persian Gulf syndrome afflicting veterans of the 1990–1991 deployment to the Persian Gulf region. The bill also included provisions establishing policies intended to improve medical treatment of Persian Gulf War veterans.

• Extended the period after a service member's death during which his or her survivors remained eligible for housing and medical benefits.

• Mandated that military retirees receive cost-of-living increases in their pensions at the same time that civilian federal retirees received their annual pay increases. Raises for military retirees had been delayed by the previous year's budget-reconciliation process.

Guard and Reserves

Recommended a personnel ceiling for National Guard and reserve units of 989,247—a level more than 3,000 above the budget request, but still a reduction of more than 45,000 compared with the fiscal 1994 Guard and reserve manpower. The customary add-on to the budget request for equipment earmarked for Guard and reserve units amounted to $640 million.

Clinton had requested two changes of law to make it easier for the president to mobilize Guard and reserve units. One would have doubled to 12 months the period for which he could call up as many as 200,000 personnel; the other would have allowed the president to delegate to the secretary of defense authority to mobilize up to 25,000 reservists for up to 90 days. But conferees agreed only to increase to nine months the period for which the president could call up large numbers of reservists without a declaration of war or national emergency.

Operations and Maintenance

Authorized $91.5 billion for operations and maintenance costs, a net reduction of $1.38 billion from the budget request.

• Approved the $400 million requested to help former Soviet republics dispose of the nuclear weapons they inherited.

• Included a provision blocking the administration's proposal to close the armed services' medical school in Bethesda, Md.

• Earmarked $10 million for Pentagon support of the 1996 Olympic Games in Atlanta and $3 million for support of the 1995 Special Olympics.

Burden-Sharing

Authorized $8.2 billion of the $8.6 billion requested to operate U.S. bases overseas, shifting $400 million to the budget for domestic base operations. However, the secretary of defense could waive the reduction if the overseas cuts mandated by the conferees could not be made.

• Required the president to attempt to revise the bilateral agreements under which U.S. forces were stationed in the territory of other NATO members so that those countries would pay 37.5 percent of the nonpayroll costs of U.S. installations in Europe. By the Pentagon's calculation, the allies were covering 36 percent of such costs.

Bipartisan resentment over the much lower defense budgets of most U.S. allies made burden-sharing a politically explosive issue. But in their report, the conferees argued that some allies bore heavy shares of the burden of collective security in ways that were not reflected by the size of their military budgets. They cited NATO troop deployments as part of the U.N. peacekeeping force in the former Yugoslavia and Germany's expenditures to reconstruct the states of eastern Europe and the former Soviet Union.

• Approved $119 million of the $219 million requested for the annual U.S. contribution to NATO's infrastructure fund for building facilities for common use. One reason they cited for that cut was to offset $35 million they added to the budget request to improve the living quarters for U.S. troops stationed in South Korea.

Economic Conversion

Approved a total of $3.09 billion for programs intended to help displaced military personnel, defense contractors and their communities adjust to the decline in defense spending. This in-

cluded $2.19 billion to help small and midsize companies develop new technologies and dual-use products having both military and commercial application; $188 million for community assistance programs; and $715 million for severance bonuses, job retraining and other personnel transition programs.

An additional $392 million in the fiscal 1995 budget, which did not require authorization by S 2182, was to go to fund early pensions. Some military personnel were being allowed to retire on a reduced pension after 15 years of service instead of the usual 20 years.

Other Provisions

Approved a total of $86 million to cover the cost of humanitarian and disaster relief operations. Of this amount, $20 million was earmarked for clearing land mines, which claimed a large and gruesome toll of civilian victims long after the end of the wars during which the mines were laid.

• Authorized supplemental appropriations for fiscal 1994 to cover the cost of humanitarian operations: $1.2 billion to cover Somalia, Bosnia, Southwest Asia and Haiti, and $270 million to cover Rwanda. But the conferees could not agree on rules governing the use of $300 million the administration requested as a contingency fund to cover U.N. peacekeeping operations. The House was adamant that such payments should continue to come out of the State Department's budget, so the funds were dropped.

• Urged the president to introduce and support a U.N. Security Council resolution to lift the arms embargo against Bosnia. The bill mandated the cut off of funds for U.S. enforcement of the arms ban by Nov. 15, 1994, unless the Security Council had adopted a resolution lifting the embargo by that date or the Serbs had agreed to internationally mediated peace terms.

• Prohibited the award of any grant or contract to a college that had a policy of barring military recruiters from its campus. The provision was aimed at schools that barred representatives of the armed services on grounds that the services' ban on gay and lesbian conduct was a form of discrimination. ❏

1995 Defense Appropriations

Congress in 1994 cleared a $243.7 billion fiscal 1995 defense appropriations bill. Despite attacks from both the left and the right, the bill (HR 4650—PL 103-335) represented a reduction of less than 1 percent in the president's request of $244.7 billion.

Funding provided in other bills, mainly for military construction (HR 4453—PL 103-307) and defense-related nuclear programs conducted by the Energy Department (HR 4506—PL 103-316), brought the total amount appropriated for national defense in fiscal 1995 to nearly $263 billion. (*1995 military construction, p. 283*)

HR 4650 generally supported the force size, tempo of operations and weapons procurement plans in Clinton's budget. It funded a new aircraft carrier, continued production of the controversial C-17 cargo jet and maintained development of new generations of combat helicopters for the Army and jet fighters for the Navy and Air Force.

The bill also incorporated several significant congressional initiatives contained in the fiscal 1995 defense authorization bill (S 2182—PL 103-337), such as a higher military pay raise than requested and funds to preserve the option of buying additional B-2 stealth bombers in the future. *(1995 defense authorization, p. 272)*

Defense appropriators, many of them promilitary conservatives, did what they could within tight spending limits to reverse what they said were signs of decline in the military's combat readiness and morale. They argued that the dollars being invested in defense were not sufficient to support the administration policy of maintaining a defense establishment capable of fighting two major regional wars simultaneously. And lawmakers increasingly questioned the president's use of scarce defense dollars for nontraditional military missions such as humanitarian relief to Rwanda and the prodemocracy mission in Haiti. As cleared, HR 4650 included $299 million in supplemental funding for fiscal 1994 to reimburse the Defense Department for some of the costs of the operations in Rwanda and for the care of refugees from Cuba.

House appropriators contemplated cutting a major weapons program such as the Air Force's F-22 fighter to illustrate the point that something had to give, but they decided against it. In a symbolic move, however, they lopped off $900 million in politically popular university research grants. Most of the research money was later restored in the Senate.

Congress did shift funds within the budget to put more emphasis on combat readiness. And it warned the Pentagon to rein in certain projected costs, such as those of a new nuclear-powered submarine and for satellite launchers.

Despite the tight budget, lawmakers also found room for several initiatives beneficial to the constituencies of House and Senate defense appropriators.

HOUSE ACTION

The House passed a $243.6 billion defense appropriations bill on June 29 by a vote of 330–91. The House-passed bill was nearly identical to the version reported by the House Appropriations Committee on June 27 (H Rept 103-562).

Most battles over defense spending in the House had already been fought during the writing of the authorization bill. Liberals had failed in attempts to block the Navy's nuclear carrier project, to scale back spending on antimissile defenses and to discontinue the Trident II missile.

By contrast, John P. Murtha, D-Pa., chairman of the House Defense Appropriations Subcommittee, whisked the appropriations bill through the House, with just 15 minutes lapsing between the time the House took up the measure and when it started the roll call on passage. Only two minor amendments were considered.

The House bill gave Clinton most of what he sought for major weapons, including funding for a new nuclear-powered aircraft carrier for the Navy, continued development of the Army's Comanche helicopter and purchase of six C-17 cargo jets.

But House appropriators added nearly $3.2 billion to redress what they called early signs of a decline in combat readiness.

And they added $995 million to pay for a 2.6 percent raise for military personnel and a 2 percent raise for civilians, instead of the 1.6 percent Clinton had proposed.

Partly to offset the funds added for readiness and partly to dramatize the budget squeeze, appropriators made their $900 million cut in university research. It was the kind of draconian move Murtha had used successfully in the past to establish a bargaining position with the executive branch.

When the subcommittee's initial draft had exceeded by roughly $700 million the limit on outlays imposed by the full Appropriations Committee, Murtha had pressed the Pentagon to sacrifice a major weapons program. Slowing or axing a program such as the F-22 or one of the other weapons he suggested to save money, Murtha argued, was one of the few options the government had for averting a $20 billion to $40 billion shortfall over five years. But the Pentagon in the end persuaded the subcommittee to cut the $700 million elsewhere in the budget, mostly in personnel.

The House bill denied requests for $400 million to continue the so-called Nunn-Lugar program (named for Sens. Sam Nunn, D-Ga., and Richard G. Lugar, R-Ind.) to help dismantle nuclear weapons in the former Soviet Union and for $300 million to pay the U.S. share of certain United Nations peacekeeping costs previously paid from the State Department's budget.

SENATE ACTION

After four days of debate, the Senate on Aug. 11 passed a $243.4 billion spending bill by a vote of 86–14. The Senate Appropriations Committee had reported a $243.6 billion version on July 29 (S Rept 103-321).

In subcommittee, senators restored $821 million of the $900 million that the House had cut from Pentagon-sponsored research programs. Panicked universities had lobbied furiously to restore the lucrative grants.

The Senate bill endorsed much of Clinton's budget, but it included several significant departures. Appropriators added $150 million to preserve the option of buying additional B-2 bombers. Although House appropriators had urged the administration to keep open the option of building additional B-2s, they had included no funds in their version for that purpose.

The committee also added $380 million to move up by six months the annual cost-of-living (COLA) increases for military retirees so that they would receive their pay adjustments at the same time as civilian federal retirees. House appropriators endorsed the idea of redressing the inequity but believed that the military retirement fund could and should cover the COLA acceleration.

The panel denied Clinton's request for $300 million to use for the U.S. share of U.N. peacekeeping operations.

Senators also used HR 4650 to express unhappiness with aspects of the president's foreign policy. The committee bill included $170 million of the administration's $270 million last-minute request for aid to Rwandan relief and Cuban refugee operations. But the bill restricted U.S. forces in Rwanda to humanitarian relief missions, barring them from participating in military operations without congressional approval.

Floor debate on the bill provided a chance for the Senate to weigh in on another foreign policy matter—whether Congress should force Clinton to break the U.N.-mandated arms embargo against outgunned Muslim forces in Bosnia. As it often had done in the past in the foreign policy realm, where presidential prerogatives traditionally dominated, the Senate equivocated.

On a vote of 58–42, the Senate on Aug. 11 adopted an amendment by Minority Leader Bob Dole, R-Kan., and Joseph I. Lieberman, D-Conn., to require the president to end the embargo by Nov. 15, 1994. But earlier that day the Senate also approved, 56–44, an amendment by Armed Services Committee Chairman Nunn and Majority Leader George J. Mitchell, D-Maine, to urge, but not require, the president to seek international agreement to end the embargo if Serbian forces refused to accept an internationally sponsored settlement of the Bosnian civil war. The amendment, however, also would have barred the United States from militarily enforcing the embargo if it was not lifted by Nov. 15, 1994. *(Bosnia, p. 197)*

The Senate on Aug. 10 rejected three amendments that would have significantly altered the Appropriations Committee's funding recommendations for major weapons programs.

By 38–62, it rejected a proposal by Dale Bumpers, D-Ark., to stop deployment of the Milstar communications satellite and force the Pentagon to find a less expensive replacement. Bumpers called Milstar a "cold war relic" designed in the early 1980s to survive a prolonged U.S.-Soviet nuclear war. But supporters successfully argued that the satellite had been stripped of some of its nuclear war-oriented features and given capacity to transmit military communications in conventional warfare.

Another Bumpers amendment, rejected 40–60, would have eliminated funds for the Trident II submarine-launched missile.

By a vote of 38–60, the Senate rejected an amendment by Malcolm Wallop, R-Wyo., that would have boosted from $18 million to $120 million funds to equip Navy warships to intercept short-range, theater ballistic missiles at a great distance.

In addition to the Bosnia provisions, the Senate tacked several other foreign policy amendments onto the defense bill. Among these was an amendment by Dirk Kempthorne, R-Idaho, adopted 54–44 on Aug. 10, to require the withdrawal by Oct. 1, 1994, of the small U.S. security force stationed in Somalia.

The Senate also approved by voice votes two amendments relating to a controversial office complex being built for the National Reconnaissance Office. *(NRO, box, p. 218)*

FINAL ACTION

The House agreed to the conference report on HR 4650 (H Rept 103-747) by a vote of 327–86 on Sept. 29. Later that day, the Senate adopted it by voice vote, clearing the bill for the president.

The final bill appropriated $243.7 billion, of which $299 million was in fiscal 1994 emergency supplemental funding.

The bill, which provided only $1 billion less than had been requested, generally supported both the thrust and the specifics of Clinton's proposal. But it also incorporated significant congressional initiatives, including the 2.6 percent military pay raise; $100 million to put back in service three ultra-high-speed

SR-71 reconnaissance jets; and $125 million to preserve the option of buying additional B-2 stealth bombers. While approving the president's $500 million request to continue building a new type of nuclear-powered sub, conferees, at the same time, called on the Navy to try to ratchet down the price to $1.2 billion from $1.5 billion. The bill appropriated the $382 million requested by Clinton to continue buying Titan IV rockets used to launch big military satellites but included a slightly modified version of a House provision barring the Pentagon from buying more than 47 of the Titan IVs. Conferees also earmarked $40 million to develop new, less expensive satellite launchers.

Conferees deleted the Senate-passed provisions on Bosnia. The Nunn-Mitchell compromise amendment was included in S 2182, the companion defense authorization bill.

MAJOR PROVISIONS

As signed into law Sept. 30, HR 4650 appropriated:

• $70.4 billion for pay and benefits for a 1.53 million-member active-duty force and a National Guard and reserve force slightly larger than the roster of 978,997 requested by the president.

The bill endorsed a 2.6 percent military pay raise in fiscal 1995 but provided only $186 million of the $465 million needed for the increase. Conferees directed the Defense Department to find the remaining funds elsewhere in its fiscal 1995 appropriation.

The bill accelerated by six months a COLA increase for military retirees in fiscal 1995, nullifying a provision of the 1993 budget-reconciliation bill (HR 2264—PL 103-66) that required military retirees to get their pay increase six months later than civilian federal retirees. The cost of the change was $376 million.

• $80.9 billion for operations and maintenance. This included congressional additions of $350 million for the overhaul of ships, planes and vehicles and $200 million for the maintenance and repair of facilities, initiatives aimed at improving military readiness.

The bill added $67 million to pay for actions already taken to reinforce U.S. forces in South Korea, including the deployment of a Patriot missile battalion and a battalion of missile-armed helicopters.

The bill incorporated a Senate initiative adding $16 million to fund Defense Secretary William J. Perry's order to expand the Air Force's pool of trained crew members for AWACS radar planes. A Pentagon investigation cited overworked AWACS crew members as a factor in the accidental downing of two U.S. Army helicopters by U.S. jets over Iraq in April 1994.

The measure included the $400 million requested by the administration and approved by the Senate to help the former Soviet Union dismantle its nuclear arsenal.

• $2.17 billion to purchase six additional C-17 long-range cargo jets. The bill also included $190 million to continue flight-testing the plane and $190 million for components to be used in eight additional planes slated for funding in fiscal 1996. But it dropped $104 million requested to test the feasibility of buying existing wide-body jets off the shelf, possibly including commercial aircraft, to complement the C-17 force.

• $125 million in unrequested funding to preserve the option of buying additional B-2 stealth bombers in the future. It also added $60 million to keep in service 10 B-52 bombers the administration had planned to retire. And it contained a provision barring the Pentagon from retiring any long-range bombers during fiscal 1995. Conferees ordered the Pentagon to do an elaborate analysis of the fleet of F-111 long-range ground attack planes, which many Air Force officers wanted to retire to cut costs.

The bill included $100 million to put back in service three SR-71 reconnaissance jets, which the Air Force had retired in 1990 to save money.

• $934 million to buy about 24 of the Navy's F/A-18 fighters; $42 million to modify the Navy's F-14 fighter; $123 million to continue rebuilding the Marines' fleet of Harrier vertical-takeoff bombers; $2.35 billion to continue development of the Air Force's F-22 fighter; $1.34 million to continue work on an enlarged version of the F/A-18; and $186 million to develop prototypes of combat jets slated to be in service at the end of the next decade.

• $95 million to continue developing a new smart bomb called JDAM and $172 million to continue development of a super-accurate glide-bomb designated JSOW. Because of technical glitches in the development of the TSSAM missile, conferees provided only $222 million of the $604 million requested. (In December 1994, the Pentagon canceled the TSSAM program altogether in a cost-saving move.)

• $495 million to develop the Army's Comanche helicopter. (In another cost-saving move, Defense Secretary Perry announced in December 1994 that no Comanches beyond the two planned prototypes would be built.) The bill included $251 million to continue developing the Longbow target-finding radar modification for the Army's Apache helicopter, as well as $78 million to buy six additional Apaches that had not been requested.

• $175 million requested to upgrade M-1 tanks, plus $108 million added by the Senate and approved by the conferees to upgrade 24 additional M-1s; and $84 million for digitization, intended to give all elements of a U.S. force a view of their own locations and those of the enemy.

• $2.28 billion for construction of a new nuclear-powered aircraft carrier; $500 million to continue development of a new nuclear-powered submarine (but conferees insisted that the Navy bring the estimated $1.5 billion cost for each ship down to $1.2 billion); $2.66 billion for three destroyers equipped with the Aegis missile defense system; and $458 million to develop a more effective defense against high-speed cruise missiles for ships not equipped with the Aegis system.

• $546 million to buy two new so-called RO/RO (roll on/roll off) ships, cargo ships with ramps so that Army vehicles could quickly roll on at a U.S. port and roll off near a distant trouble spot; $110 million for another large cargo ship used by the Marines as floating depots near potential trouble spots; and $467 million for continued development of the V-22 Osprey, a hybrid airplane-helicopter designed for the Marines as a troop carrier.

• $616 million to purchase 18 Trident II submarine-launched missiles.

• $2.8 billion to develop and buy antiballistic missile defenses and $120 million to develop missile detection satellites dubbed Brilliant Eyes.

• $382 million to continue buying the big Titan IV rocket used to launch the largest military satellites. However, conferees included a slightly modified version of a House provision barring the purchase of more than 47 Titan IVs. They also earmarked $40 million for the development of new, less expensive satellite launchers.

• $9.9 billion for medical care of active-duty personnel, their dependents and retirees.

• $3.3 billion for defense conversion efforts aimed at helping military personnel, contractors, and their employees and communities adjust to big drops in defense spending.

• $299 million in supplemental funding for fiscal 1994 to reimburse the Defense Department for some of the costs of humanitarian relief operations in Rwanda and for emergency migrant processing and safe haven costs for refugees from Cuba. The bill barred U.S. forces in Rwanda from participating in anything other than a relief mission without congressional approval.

• The final bill cut $200 million from Pentagon-sponsored university research. Clinton's total request for research earmarks was estimated to be between $1.5 billion and $1.8 billion.   ❏

1995 Military Construction

Congress in 1994 cleared an $8.84 billion military construction appropriations bill for fiscal 1995. Lawmakers rejected sharp cutbacks in President Clinton's $8.35 billion request, but the legislation (HR 4453—PL 103-307) still provided $628 million less than was available for fiscal 1994 after rescissions. (*1994 military construction, p. 271*)

HR 4453 provided $3.52 billion for family housing on military bases; $2.65 billion for military construction and renovation projects; and $2.68 billion for the expensive process of cleaning up and closing down unneeded bases so that they could be sold or converted to other uses.

National Guard and reserve unit facilities fared well under the bill, receiving $574 million for construction projects. Senate lawmakers, in particular, said these military services had received short shrift in the Clinton budget, which had recommended $171 million for facility construction.

LEGISLATIVE ACTION

The House passed an $8.82 billion military construction spending bill on May 24 by a vote of 380–42. HR 4453 had been reported by the House Appropriations Committee on May 19 (H Rept 103-516).

As usual, sponsors worked hard to keep the bill free of controversy and little debate took place on the bill in committee or on the floor. In what also had become routine, the bill provided an opportunity for lawmakers to lobby for hometown projects; the House version contained 132 domestic construction projects that had not been requested by the president.

The House bill included $119 million, $100 million less than requested, for the North Atlantic Treaty Organization (NATO) infrastructure fund, the pooled contributions that paid for improvements to bases used by NATO. This line item had been controversial in the past, with Congress asking host nations to pay a greater share.

The Senate passed an $8.84 billion version of the bill July 15 by a vote of 84–2. The Senate Appropriations Committee had reported the measure the previous day (S Rept 103-312).

An amendment adopted by voice vote on the Senate floor took aim at the bill's reputation as a repository of pork-barrel projects for members' districts. The language, sponsored by John McCain, R-Ariz., expressed the sense of the Senate that any military construction projects that had not been authorized by the Senate had to meet specific criteria of need and national security importance before they could be included in the appropriations bill.

Unlike the House bill, the version in the Senate would have fully funded the president's request for NATO's infrastructure fund.

The Senate bill called for $533 million for construction projects for the National Guard and reserves, as compared with $452 million in the House version. Both were a substantial jump over the president's request.

CONFERENCE, MAJOR PROVISIONS

The House adopted the conference report on the $8.84 billion military construction appropriations bill (H Rept 103-624) by voice vote Aug. 1. The Senate approved the report Aug. 10 by a vote of 95–5, clearing the bill. The president signed HR 4453 on Aug. 23.

The final bill provided $490 million more than Clinton requested. That increase, combined with reductions in various Clinton requests, paid for a rise of nearly $700 million in funding for domestic construction, from the requested $2.2 billion to $2.9 billion.

More than half the increase for domestic construction projects—nearly $400 million—was earmarked for dozens of National Guard and reserve facilities, most of which were relatively minor projects costing less than $10 million apiece.

House and Senate conferees went with the House in slicing $100 million from the $219 million request for NATO's infrastructure fund.

The final bill provided $2.65 billion for military construction, an increase over the president's request of $2.24 billion. Funding for two of the largest projects requested by the Clinton administration—Army demilitarization facilities in Arkansas and Oregon intended to dismantle chemical weapons and neutralize their toxic ingredients—was all but eliminated.

HR 4453 provided $3.52 billion for family housing, as compared with Clinton's $3.44 billion request. Of that, $2.81 billion was for operations and maintenance of existing housing, with only $714 million allocated for new construction.

The conference bill provided all of the $2.68 billion requested for base closure costs, as had both the House and Senate versions.   ❑

Gays in the Military

Debate over defense policy in the early months of the Clinton administration was consumed by a searingly emotional conflict over the new president's campaign promise to lift the military's longtime ban on homosexuals.

During the 1992 election campaign, Bill Clinton promised to eliminate the prohibition against gay service members. But most senior military personnel vehemently opposed the shift, and they were supported by many conservative members of Congress and the powerful chairman of the Senate Armed Services Committee, Sam Nunn, D-Ga.

Ultimately, Clinton in 1993 settled for a modest revision of the policy under which homosexual conduct still would be prohibited, but recruits no longer would be asked if they were gay. In addition, under the new policy, investigations of suspected homosexuals could be initiated only by a senior officer acting on the basis of credible information.

Equally important, Congress sealed the ban, which had been a military regulation, into law as a provision of the fiscal 1994 defense authorization bill (HR 2401). *(1994 defense authorization, p. 257)*

BACKGROUND

Under the policy that Clinton inherited, the military could discharge through an expedited administrative process any member found to have engaged in homosexual actions, including simply declaring his or her homosexual orientation. In addition, specific homosexual acts prohibited by military law, the Uniform Code of Military Justice, could result in court-martial or other disciplinary actions. The Defense Department's prohibition was embodied in Directive 1332.14, issued on Jan. 28, 1982, during the Reagan administration. A 1992 General Accounting Office study found that the military dismissed an average of 1,500 people a year for homosexuality from fiscal 1980 through fiscal 1990.

The first major party presidential nominee to openly seek gay support, Clinton had pledged months before he secured the Democratic nomination that he would eliminate the military ban on homosexuals. Though Clinton repeated the promise several times during the campaign, it never became a focal point of the Democratic message, and President George Bush's reelection campaign did little to highlight it.

By the time Clinton won the election, he was solidly on record in favor of a controversial policy that had not been seriously tested in the political arena. Furthermore, the issue exposed a deep divide between Clinton, who had sidestepped military service during the Vietnam War, and the military establishment. It raised tensions between the new administration and Congress. And it put a man who ran as a centrist Democrat in the position of defending one of his party's most liberal positions during his first full week in office.

The vast majority of senior military personnel, including Gen. Colin L. Powell Jr., then chairman of the Joint Chiefs of Staff, strongly opposed lifting the ban on homosexuals, arguing that the esprit de corps that was crucial to morale and unit cohesion would be undermined if heterosexuals were forced to live with homosexuals in the close quarters of military life. The courts repeatedly had upheld the military's broad authority to set regulations that it deemed necessary to maintain a well-disciplined fighting force.

If the religious right and the gay and lesbian community agreed on anything, it was that the issue was far more than a debate over whether homosexuals should be allowed in the military. They said that it went to the heart of what role homosexuals would have in American society.

DECISION POSTPONED

The issue erupted within days of Clinton's January 1993 inauguration, with conservatives in Congress from both parties threatening to write the military's regulation barring homosexuals into law unless the president retreated from his campaign pledge.

Following hours of meetings, dozens of news conferences by lawmakers and thousands of phone calls to the Capitol from angry citizens, Clinton on Jan. 29 announced a compromise: a six-month delay in lifting the ban. Defense Secretary Les Aspin, who had recommended the delay from the outset, was directed to review the ban and then prepare a draft executive order by July 15, 1993.

In the meantime, the military's existing policy remained in effect except that recruits were not to be questioned about their sexual orientation; the Justice Department sought court continuances in pending cases involving former service members who had been discharged solely on the basis of being homosexual; dismissal proceedings continued against service members charged with homosexual conduct; dismissal of service members solely on the basis of their homosexuality was to be blocked by the attorney general, although they could be removed from active duty and placed in Selected Reserve, which meant no pay or benefits; and commanding officers were permitted to reassign accused or acknowledged homosexuals.

DEBATE ON CAPITOL HILL

Armed politically with their compromise with Clinton, Senate Democrats on Feb. 4 decisively rebuffed a Republican amendment that would have locked into law the military's pre-Clinton version of the ban on homosexuals and would have required Clinton to seek congressional approval before lifting the ban by executive order. The Senate voted 62–37 to table (kill) the amendment, which was offered by Minority Leader Bob Dole, R-Kan., during debate on a popular family leave measure (S 5). *(Family leave, p. 665)*

Before rejecting Dole's proposal, the Senate approved by voice vote a nonbinding resolution, criticized as a "political fig leaf" by Republican opponents, calling on the Pentagon and Congress to review existing policy regarding homosexuals in the military. In an attempt to undermine the significance of the vote, Dole and other Republicans joined Democrats to defeat a motion by Dole to table (kill) the resolution, 1–98, on Feb. 4.

Most Democrats clung to the position staked out by Nunn. Few wanted to be viewed as being in favor of wide-ranging

probes to root out homosexuals from the military, but a widespread reluctance also existed to join in Clinton's call for an executive order lifting the military's ban. For conservative Republicans, the issue was far less complicated. Many charged angrily that Clinton's approach sprang from deep-seated hostility toward those in uniform. Yet Republicans, too, were divided on questions of philosophy and political tactics.

Clinton's January compromise bought the administration six months to cool off tempers while Pentagon task forces attempted to reach some resolution of the issue. For Congress, the issue moved from floor debate to committee hearing rooms.

The focus remained on the Senate side, where Nunn promised to conduct "fair, thorough and objective" hearings. But gay rights groups protested throughout that his hearings were stacked against their cause, and Nunn made clear from the start that the sessions he chaired would spotlight not broad issues of civil liberties but the minute complexities of allowing acknowledged homosexuals in a military environment.

Nunn created a stir just before the March 29 start of the hearings by suggesting that the interim arrangements worked out by Congress and the White House to defuse the crisis—which he termed a "don't ask, don't tell" approach—might serve as a basis for compromise. Over the following weeks, lawmakers and Pentagon officials attempted to define an arrangement in which the military would no longer ask its recruits or personnel about their sexual orientation ("don't ask"), and homosexuals in the military would be permitted to stay so long as they refrained from homosexual activity and kept their sexual orientation private ("don't tell").

On the House side, the House Armed Services Committee put off action on the annual defense authorization bill, customarily considered in late May, to late July. The move was partly to prevent Republicans from forcing an early vote on Clinton's plan.

Although the liberal new House Armed Services Committee chairman, Ronald V. Dellums, D-Calif., went on record in favor of lifting the ban, he showed little inclination to press the matter in a committee where the majority in both parties held views far more conservative than his. But Dellums did convene a hearing on the issue May 4 that proved a far livelier exchange than the carefully orchestrated and largely circumscribed discussions held by Nunn's Senate panel.

Rep. Barney Frank, D-Mass., one of two openly gay members of Congress, shook up the debate by proposing a variation on the "don't ask, don't tell" compromise. He dubbed it "don't ask, don't tell, don't listen and don't investigate." In essence, according to Frank's plan, homosexuals in the military would be allowed to be open about their orientation—but only when they were off duty and off base. The compromise was criticized as a capitulation by some gay leaders and as unacceptable by conservatives.

CLINTON'S DECISION

On July 19, Clinton announced his long-promised policy in the form of a Pentagon directive. It was intended to take effect Oct. 1, although that was later delayed by court rulings.

The fundamental premise of Clinton's new version of the ban was that people could neither be barred from joining the armed services nor discharged solely because of their homosexuality. The plan barred the Pentagon from asking gays to disclose their sexual orientation. And it reeled in the dragnets sometimes cast by Pentagon investigators in an effort to catch closeted homosexuals.

At the same time, however, the new policy reaffirmed the Pentagon's strict proscription of homosexual conduct. And the sphere of prohibited conduct was defined very broadly, encompassing all three types of activity that were prohibited by the previous Pentagon policy: homosexual acts, statements by a member that he or she was homosexual, and marriage or attempted marriage to a person of the same sex. "From the point of view of homosexuals who wish to serve honorably," Clinton said, "I think it was a substantial advance."

But as Defense Secretary Aspin told the Senate Armed Services Committee on July 20, "Homosexual members will have to play by the rules." And the burden of rules that precluded any sexual self-expression was compounded by an institutional culture that remained unapologetically hostile. "If a person is homosexual, they would be much more comfortable pursuing a different profession," Aspin said.

Clinton's compromise evoked powerful—and largely hostile—reactions. Gay rights advocates blasted the move as a betrayal of his campaign pledge to a constituency that generously supported him with votes and cash. Social conservatives, including many congressional Democrats from southern and border states, were disturbed by one of several administration moves—including the nomination of openly gay officials to domestic policy posts—that appeared to weaken traditional moral sanctions against homosexuality. Some Republicans cited Clinton's initiative as one more indicator that he did not understand the armed forces.

Although Clinton's plan drew few enthusiastic backers and a bevy of critics, it gained considerable political momentum largely because it carried the endorsement of the Joint Chiefs of Staff. General Powell called Clinton's July 19 policy "an honorable compromise" and praised the administration's extensive consultations with the chiefs.

After committee hearings on July 21 and 22, Nunn said the chiefs had been "effective and persuasive" in arguing that Clinton's policy could be implemented. But Nunn also insisted that lawmakers had a constitutional duty to act on the issue, despite Clinton's stated preference that they not lock provisions on gays into law.

CONGRESSIONAL ACTION

Congress wrote a tougher-toned version of the ban into the fiscal 1994 defense authorization bill. The provision withstood challenges on the floor of both chambers and became law when Clinton signed the defense authorization bill Nov. 30 (HR 2401—PL 103-160). *(HR 2401, p. 257)*

The language, proposed by Senate Armed Services Chairman Nunn, did not directly overturn any element of Clinton's plan, but it sealed what had been a military regulation into the law—

and framed it in tough terms intended to provide a clear rationale for the inevitable court challenges.

Ignoring Clinton's policy statement that "homosexual orientation is not a bar to service," the provision stated that those who "demonstrate a propensity or intent to engage in homosexual acts would create an unacceptable risk" to morale, discipline and cohesion.

The Senate Armed Services Committee approved, 17–5, Nunn's language on July 23, only four days after Clinton announced his plan. On July 27, the House Armed Services Committee approved an identical provision by voice vote.

The full Senate stood by Nunn's provision, rebuffing an effort Sept. 9 to cede the explosive issue to the president. Senators defeated, by a **key vote of 33–63 (R 3–38; D 30–25),** an amendment by Barbara Boxer, D-Calif., that would have struck the Nunn language from the defense authorization bill (S 1298). Nunn maintained that under the amendment Congress would give up its right to have a say on the matter as well as its constitutional duty to act. *(1993 key votes, p. 979)*

The House on Sept. 28 adopted, on a 301–134 vote, an amendment by Ike Skelton, D-Mo., reaffirming the gay ban language in its version of the defense authorization measure (HR 2401). That same day, the House rejected, 144–291, a Duncan Hunter, R-Calif., amendment to order the Pentagon to resume the practice of asking recruits to disclose their sexual orientation.

Also rejected, by a **key vote of 169–264 (R 11–163; D 157–101; I 1–0),** was a Martin T. Meehan, D-Mass., amendment that, like Boxer's amendment in the Senate, would have deleted from the defense bill any reference to the issue, leaving the policy in the hands of the president.

Because the House and Senate bills contained identical language on gays in the military, the issue was not debated in the conference committee that crafted the final version of the bill.

PROVISIONS

The language on gays in the military that Congress adopted as part of HR 2401 was stern in rejecting homosexual conduct in the armed forces. Unlike the Clinton administration's regulations, the congressional version offered no words of tolerance toward homosexuals.

The provisions incorporated into the defense bill superseded the Pentagon rules wherever the two versions conflicted. Mostly, however, the congressional language allowed the specifics of the Clinton plan to take effect while locking into law a broad policy statement rejecting the notion of accepting gays in the military.

Congress's Authority

In a matter that the White House had sought to resolve solely by executive order, the provisions reasserted that "it lies within the discretion of the Congress to establish qualifications for and conditions of service in the armed forces." The measure cited Article I, Section 8 of the Constitution, which gave Congress exclusive power to "make rules for the government and regulation of the land and naval forces."

The Rationale

Setting forth a rationale—and a legal defense—for continued rejection of gays in the military, the provisions maintained that "there is no constitutional right to serve in the armed forces." The bill asserted that "the conduct of military operations requires members . . . to make extraordinary sacrifices, including the ultimate sacrifice," and that "the military society is characterized by its own laws, rules, customs and traditions, including numerous restrictions on personal behavior, that would not be acceptable in civilian society."

"The prohibition against homosexual conduct is a longstanding element of military law that continues to be necessary in the unique circumstances of military service," the provisions said. They added, "The presence in the armed forces of persons who demonstrate a propensity or intent to engage in homosexual acts would create an unacceptable risk to the high standards of morale, good order and discipline and unit cohesion that are the essence of military capability."

The Ban

The provisions stated that the armed forces, under regulations set out by the secretary of defense, were to dismiss a member who was found to have engaged in, attempted to engage in or solicited a homosexual act; married or tried to marry a person of the same sex; or stated that he or she was homosexual, unless such a member could show that "he or she has not engaged in or attempted to engage in homosexual acts and did not have a propensity or intent to engage in such acts."

A One-Time Exception

The provisions revived from past Pentagon policy an exemption that appeared aimed at protecting "straight" soldiers who might give in just once to a passionate urge or to youthful experimentation. It provided that a service member who committed a homosexual act need not be dismissed if he or she could demonstrate that "such conduct is a departure from the member's usual and customary behavior" and, "under all the circumstances, is unlikely to recur."

Asking Recruits

In a sense-of-Congress statement, the provisions gave a cautious go-ahead to the military's practice since January 1993 of no longer asking applicants to military service whether they were homosexual. It said the suspension "should be continued, but the secretary of defense may reinstate that questioning . . . if the secretary determines that it is necessary to do so."

What Was Missing

The congressional measure did not address—and thus left intact—the portion of Aspin's order that curbed dragnet-style investigations of suspected gays. Under Aspin's order, a commanding officer could begin an inquiry or request a criminal investigation of a service member only on the basis of "credible information" of homosexual conduct.

The congressional codification did not extend any words of support or tolerance for homosexuals who stayed chaste or in the closet. By contrast, Aspin's directive said that the Department of Defense "recognizes that individuals with a homosexual orientation have served with distinction in the armed services" and specified that "homosexual orientation is not a bar to service entry or continued service unless manifested by homosexual conduct."

Also conspicuously missing from the congressional language was Aspin's order that commanders "will investigate allegations of violations of the Uniform Code of Military Justice in an even-handed manner without regard to whether the conduct alleged is heterosexual or homosexual or whether it occurs on-base or off-base."

COURT ACTION

Despite the flurry of administration and congressional activity, the gay ban was in limbo at the end of 1993 as a result of a series of court rulings.

On July 27, the American Civil Liberties Union and the Lambda Legal Defense and Education Fund asked the U.S. District Court for the District of Columbia to block it. The plaintiffs argued that the ban was a violation of the First Amendment guarantee of free speech and association and of the Equal Protection Clause of the Fourteenth Amendment.

In October, the Pentagon suspended enforcement of its ban while preparing to appeal a California judge's ruling. Acting in the case of Keith Meinhold, a Navy sonar specialist who had been discharged from the service after acknowledging on national television that he was homosexual, U.S. District Judge Terry Hatter Jr. of Los Angeles had issued a sweeping order Sept. 30 banning discrimination against homosexuals in the military. The U.S. Court of Appeals for the Ninth Circuit declined to block the decision. On Oct. 29, the Supreme Court granted a request from the Clinton administration for an emergency stay of Hatter's ruling.

Another ruling against the gay ban came Nov. 16 from a panel of the U.S. Court of Appeals for the District of Columbia. In a unanimous decision, a three-judge panel headed by Chief Judge Abner J. Mikva ordered the Navy to give an officer's commission to Joseph C. Steffan, who had been forced to resign as a midshipman in 1987, just six weeks before he would have graduated from the U.S. Naval Academy, after disclosing that he was gay. Steffan was accused of no homosexual conduct beyond revealing his sexual orientation.

Mikva wrote that the policy that drove Steffan from the service was based on the assumption that other military personnel would be offended by having to serve with homosexuals. "The Constitution does not allow government to subordinate a class of persons simply because others do not like them," Mikva wrote.

In the past, federal courts had given the armed services wide leeway to depart from generally applicable standards of civil liberties in deference to the requirements of military life. They also had held that the military services need not assume that an avowed homosexual would abstain from disruptive conduct. But Mikva argued that the gay ban went too far. "There is no 'military exception' to the Constitution," he said.

The broader issue of the military treatment of homosexuals was left to the Supreme Court to resolve. ❑

Military Base Closings

Congress in 1993 accepted the recommendation that 35 major military installations and 95 minor ones be closed. Another 45 bases—27 major and 18 minor—were slated for cutbacks. It was the third time in five years that Congress had agreed to close unneeded military bases and realign others.

On July 1, the Defense Base Closure and Realignment Commission recommended closing or realigning the facilities. President Clinton quickly accepted the recommendations, which the commission estimated would save $2.3 billion annually after 1999, and forwarded the list to Congress.

On Sept. 20, the Senate defeated a resolution that would have blocked the closures. The House never took up the matter because any action it took would have been moot under a base closure law that required both chambers to act to block the closing list from taking effect.

The closures were scheduled to take place over the following five years. Among the bases to be closed were the huge Navy complexes in Charleston, S.C., and Alameda, Calif., and K. I. Sawyer Air Force Base in Michigan.

The deliberation process in 1993 had been a politically painful one for the members of Congress and communities affected by the decisions, as it had been during previous rounds of closings.

It was for this reason that Congress in 1990 had designed an all-or-nothing base closing process that would thwart efforts by members to block closure of individual bases. An attempt to allow for judicial review of base closing decisions was rejected by the Supreme Court in 1994. *(Box, p. 289)*

BACKGROUND

The 1993 action was the second round of closures approved under the 1990 law (PL 101-510). The first round had taken place in 1991, when members voted to close 34 military installations—25 of them major—and realign 37 others. Under slightly different procedures, Congress had voted in 1989 to close or cut back operations at 91 bases. *(Congress and the Nation VIII, pp. 353, 393)*

A third round of closings under PL 101-510 was to take place in 1995. *(1995 action, p. 319)*

Under the 1990 law, the president (with bipartisan input from House and Senate leaders) appointed an eight-member commission to handle each round of base closings, subject to confirmation by the Senate. The commission would weigh base closings recommended by the Defense Department. In considering the Pentagon's recommendations, the commission was to evaluate whether the Pentagon had met or substantially deviated from eight criteria set in the 1990 law.

To determine the military value of a base, the Pentagon was to look at:

• How the base affected mission requirements (both existing and future) and the readiness of U.S. forces.

• How easily the base could expand into adjacent land if needed and the condition of that land.

• How the base could accommodate mobilization and other future force structure requirements.

• The cost and manpower implications of closing the base.

The Pentagon also considered:

• How much money could be saved by closing the base.

• The economic impact on local communities, including the cumulative economic impact.

• The ability of bases receiving additional forces to accommodate them in terms of schools, roads and other facilities.

• The environmental impacts.

The commission would conduct public hearings to elicit the views of affected communities, members of Congress and other interested parties. It then would send a revised list to the president, who had to accept or reject it unchanged. If the president rejected the revised list, the process for that year stopped. If he approved it, the decisions took effect automatically. Congress could stop the closings by acting within 45 legislative days to pass a bill blocking the entire list.

1993 ACTION

President George Bush appointed the eight-member commission for the 1993 round on Jan. 8, sparing Clinton the task. The Senate confirmed the eight on March 4. (After commissioner Arthur Levitt Jr. was nominated to head the Securities and Exchange Commission, he resigned from the base closing commission and was not replaced.) James A. Courter, former Republican House member from New Jersey (1979–1991), was to chair the commission as he had in 1991.

Defense Secretary Aspin on March 12 released a list recommending 31 major domestic military bases for closure. On March 15, the commission began its work, first hearing from the Pentagon and then the communities affected. In addition to a series of regional hearings, every military base that was on the list received a visit by at least one commission member.

The commission added 47 bases to the Pentagon's list of candidates for closure. Most of the bases were offered as possible alternatives to those selected by the Pentagon.

In the end, the commissioners accepted many of Aspin's recommendations, including his call to close the Charleston shipyard. But the commission spared five installations that were on Aspin's list and voted to close three facilities that Aspin had wanted to keep open—Plattsburgh Air Force Base in upstate New York, Agana Naval Air Station in Guam and the Portsmouth Naval Electronics Systems Engineering Center in Virginia.

The commission estimated that its recommendations would require a one-time expenditure of $7.4 billion, then would save about $2.3 billion each year after 1999.

Less than 24 hours after receiving the commission's list, Clinton announced July 2 that he had accepted the panel's recommendations. He promised that he would take steps to reduce the economic pain of the closings.

Clinton said the moves would include appointing a single federal coordinator to work with each affected community, offering grants averaging $1 million to help plan new uses for

JUDICIAL REVIEW OF BASE CLOSINGS

The Supreme Court in 1994 ruled that the 1990 law (PL 101-510) that established the process for closing unneeded military facilities was not subject to judicial review.

On May 23, the Supreme Court unanimously ruled in *Dalton v. Specter* that President George Bush had acted within his powers in 1991 when he accepted the recommendation of the base closure commission to close the Philadelphia Naval Shipyard. *(Case summary, p. 787)*

Sen. Arlen Specter, R-Pa., argued the case before the high court March 2, the first sitting member of Congress to appear before the Court since 1972.

Specter had been fighting the case for the Philadelphia Naval Shipyard since its closure was approved. The base was slated to close in mid-1995, and several thousand workers already had been let go in preparation. Specter and other elected officials from New Jersey, Pennsylvania and Delaware sued the government in July 1991, claiming that the Navy and the base closure commission had violated the law's detailed procedures for closure decisions.

A U.S. District Court threw out the case, saying that the base closure law prohibited judicial review. The 3rd U.S. Circuit Court of Appeals reversed that decision, ruling that the law prohibited judicial review only of certain aspects of the process. Courts, it said, could assess whether the commission and the Defense Department followed statutory guidelines.

The government appealed to the Supreme Court. Had Specter prevailed, it could have opened the gates for lawsuits by cities and states fighting to keep their bases open.

In oral arguments, the Clinton administration urged the high court to stay out of the complicated process for closing domestic military bases. Solicitor General Drew S. Days III told the justices that the statute did not provide for judicial review and that Congress did not intend to allow it. Moreover, he said, the Administrative Procedures Act of 1946 (PL 79-404), which allowed judicial review of final agency actions, did not apply in this case because the final action was taken by the president, who was not subject to that law.

Specter countered that "the courts must always be able to review the delegation of authority by Congress." He further argued that the base-closure commission made the final decision, because the president could not add or subtract a base from the closure list.

Chief Justice William H. Rehnquist wrote the main opinion, saying Specter and other plaintiffs could not challenge the commission's recommendation under the Administrative Procedures Act because the president, not the commission, made the actual determination to close the bases.

Rehnquist said Congress gave the president ample discretion to accept or reject the commission's recommendations. "How the President chooses to exercise the discretion Congress had granted him is not a matter for our review," he wrote.

In a concurring opinion joined by Justices Harry A. Blackmun, Ruth Bader Ginsburg and John Paul Stevens, Justice David H. Souter said that Congress did not want to provide judicial review for provisions of the base closing law. "The very reasons that led Congress by this enactment to bind its hands from untying a package, once assembled, go far to persuade me that Congress did not mean the courts to have any such power through judicial review," Souter wrote.

A month later, on June 23, during consideration of the fiscal 1995 defense authorization bill (S 2182), Specter offered an amendment that would have allowed people affected by base closures to obtain a judicial review if they could show relevant information was fraudulently concealed from the base closure commission. The amendment was tabled (killed) on a 71–27 vote.

---

bases, speeding the cleanup of pollution that tainted many of the bases and changing federal rules so that closed bases could be sold at a discount for new commercial uses that create jobs.

Clinton spoke of a $5 billion program over five years, half of it for environmental cleanup; Aspin confirmed that the money would come mostly from previously proposed spending.

With timing that appeared aimed at underscoring the need for military belt-tightening, Aspin on July 1 announced plans to close or reduce 92 overseas bases. These closures did not require congressional approval.

The Senate on Sept. 20 dealt the final blow to the bases on the commission's list. By a vote of 12–83, the Senate rejected a resolution (S J Res 114) that would have overturned the work of the panel and kept the bases open. The Senate Armed Services Committee had reported the resolution adversely on July 30 (S Rept 103-118).

1994 ACTION

With the next scheduled round of base closings a year away, Congress was not required to approve any shutdowns in 1994.

However, several base closing matters did come up during the year:

• The Supreme Court ruled that the 1990 base closure law was not subject to judicial review. *(Box, this page)*

• On May 24, the day after the Supreme Court ruling, the House rejected, 68–362, an amendment to its version of the fiscal 1995 defense authorization bill (HR 4301) that would have delayed until 1997 the round of base closings scheduled for 1995. Armed Services Committee member James V. Hansen, R-Utah, the amendment's sponsor, argued that a two-year pause would allow time for the defense budget to catch up with the enormous costs of base closings and for communities to make necessary economic adjustments. The administration had also broached the idea of adding a round of closures in 1997 to delay some of the pain until after the 1996 elections. But, with even some of the most ardent GOP critics of Clinton's defense cutbacks arguing that additional bases had to be closed, the full Senate voted against the proposal.

• The Senate set the 1995 round of base closings in motion by approving by voice vote Oct. 7 the nomination of former

1993 Military Bases Closure List

Following are the major military bases on the Defense Base Closure and Re-alignment Commission's closure list in 1993, as well as the Pentagon's estimate of the number of military and civilian personnel employed at each facility:

Base	Employees	
	Military	Civilian
Mobile Naval Station, Ala.	524	126
Mare Island Naval Shipyard, Calif.	1,963	7,567
Alameda Naval Aviation Depot, Calif.	376	2,672
Alameda Naval Air Station, Calif.	10,586	556
Treasure Island Naval Station, Calif.	637	454
Oakland Naval Hospital, Calif.	1,472	809
San Diego Naval Training Center, Calif.	5,186	402
El Toro Marine Corps Air Station, Calif.	5,689	979
Port Hueneme Naval Civil Engineering Lab, Calif.	17	384
Public Works Center, Calif.	10	1,834
Orlando Naval Training Center, Fla.	8,727	753
Pensacola Naval Aviation Depot, Fla.	297	3,107
Pensacola Naval Supply Center, Fla.	20	245
Cecil Field Naval Air Station, Fla.	6,833	995
Orlando Naval Hospital, Fla.	759	352
Barbers Point Naval Air Station, Hawaii	3,534	618
Glenview Naval Air Station, Ill.	1,833	389
O'Hare Airport Air Force Reserve Station, Ill.	5	757
K. I. Sawyer Air Force Base, Mich.	2,354	788
Detroit Naval Air Facility, Mich.	523	24
Trenton Naval Air Warfare Center, N.J.	8	448
Staten Island Home Port, N.Y.	1,773	1,001
Plattsburgh Air Force Base, N.Y.*	2,009	304
Newark Air Force Base, Ohio	92	1,760
Defense Electronics Supply, Dayton, Ohio	93	2,804
Philadelphia Defense Clothing Factory, Pa.	2	1,235
Philadelphia Defense Personnel Support, Pa.	78	3,878
Charleston Naval Station, S.C.	8,634	1,194
Charleston Naval Shipyard, S.C.	74	4,837
Dallas Naval Air Station, Texas	1,374	268
Vint Hill Farms Station, Va. (defense intelligence)	407	1,472
Norfolk Naval Aviation Depot, Va.	104	4,295
Portsmouth Naval Electronic Systems Engineering Center, Va.*	12	413
Naval Electronic Security System Engineering Center, Washington, D.C.	515	636
Agana Naval Air Station, Guam*	2,920	391

* These bases were added by the commission to those originally proposed by Defense Secretary Les Aspin.

NOTE: This list is based on the commission's definition of a major base, which differed from the definition used in Aspin's initial list.

SOURCES: Defense Base Closure and Realignment Commission; Defense Department.

senator Alan J. Dixon (D-Ill., 1981–1993) to be chairman of the Defense Base Closure and Realignment Commission. At the confirmation hearing, senators raised concerns ranging from the estimated costs of environmental restoration at bases that were being shut to the Pentagon's methodology for calculating the military worth of a base.

• Congress cleared legislation (S 2534—PL 103-421) to make it easier for local communities to get land from bases that were being closed. The measure added an exemption for mili-tary bases to the 1987 McKinney Act (PL 100-77), which had required that underutilized federal facilities be used to assist the homeless. Although advocates for the homeless no longer could claim first rights to use closed military bases, the bill created a strong incentive for homeless advocates and local officials to negotiate reuse plans taking into account both economic factors and the needs of the homeless. The Senate and House passed S 2534 by voice vote Oct. 6 and Oct. 7, respectively. The president signed the measure into law Oct. 25. ❑

Defense Department Review

Les Aspin began his tenure as defense secretary in January 1993 by announcing that the Defense Department would reexamine its mission in a world that had grown uncertain since the cold war ended and the Soviet Union broke up, leaving the United States without the main target of its strategic defenses.

From January through August, teams within the Pentagon examined every facet of their operations—from rules governing weapons purchases to the number and structure of the troops.

On Sept. 1, Aspin released the results of his bottom-up review of the Pentagon's mission and machinery. The plan cut less than experts had expected, but administration officials said the changes would reduce defense spending enough to meet President Clinton's budget targets while still allowing for a more flexible fighting force.

Although no specific cost analysis was released, Deputy Defense Secretary William J. Perry said that the cost estimates were in the ballpark of the nearly $123 billion that Clinton had planned to cut from the defense budget.

The plan was intended as a blueprint for the new administration's defense policy, a set of decisions and priorities that would guide year-to-year defense spending and provide broad outlines for military strategy in the aftermath of the cold war.

Key lawmakers began to use the report as a frame of reference as well, questioning whether the spending, force levels and weaponry sought by the administration were sufficient to meet the announced standard: the ability to simultaneously fight and win two major regional wars. For example, the Aspin force structure was designed to allow the United States to deploy troops rapidly to the Middle East in the event of an Iraqi invasion of Kuwait and still have sufficient troops and weapons to begin deploying to the Korean Peninsula if North Korea prepared to invade South Korea at roughly the same time.

Many of the immediate steps recommended by Aspin were incorporated in the fiscal 1994 defense authorization bill (HR 2401—PL 103-160). *(1994 defense authorization, p. 257)*

KEY ELEMENTS OF THE PLAN

The plan was designed to cut active-duty forces from the existing level of about 1.7 million to 1.4 million. It hit the Army hardest, providing for 10 active divisions in place of the existing 14 divisions, with about five National Guard units, down from 10 in fiscal 1990.

The Air Force also was set to lose strength, going from 16 active-duty fighter wings to 13 and losing five reserve wings.

The Marine Corps was the only force to get a reprieve of sorts. The Pentagon decided to reduce the Corps by 8,000, to 174,000 active-duty Marines. The Marine Corps had found its services much in demand for the new missions facing the armed services, such as the U.N. humanitarian relief effort in Somalia.

The existing 443-ship Navy was to be reduced to 346, a larger fleet than many analysts had predicted. The number of attack submarines was to be reduced from 88 to 55. The fleet of aircraft carriers was to be reduced from 13 to 12: 11 active-duty carriers and an additional one for training. Aspin said 10 carriers would have been enough to fight a two-pronged war effort but an additional ship was needed to allow the Navy to station carriers around the world as visible reminders to other countries of U.S. interests and capabilities.

The decision to build another aircraft carrier was also motivated by a desire to keep at least part of the carrier industry in business. Similarly, it was decided that a third unneeded *Seawolf*-class submarine should be built at a cost of at least $1 billion to keep one of the country's two nuclear submarine-building companies up and running until the United States decided to proceed with a new line of attack submarines, called the *Centurion* class.

These handouts to defense industries were also potential methods of easing the economic strain imposed on various parts of the country by the massive and relatively rapid downsizing of U.S. forces. The Clinton administration was sensitive to that issue, especially with the large number of bases likely to close on its watch. *(Base closings, p. 288)*

Unlike the shipbuilding business, the aerospace industry had too many companies competing for too few Pentagon contracts. The Aspin plan gave the go-ahead to only two major aircraft purchases: the F-22 stealth fighter and the E and F versions of the F-18 fighter. As expected, Aspin decided to terminate the Navy's A/F-X and the development of the Air Force's Multi-Role Fighter. *(Combat planes, box, p. 260)*

The Aspin plan backed the need for a heavy-lift plane, such as the troubled C-17 cargo program, but it did not specifically endorse that project. *(C-17, box, p. 275)*

The fleet of B-1B and B-2 stealth bombers would be reconfigured to attack major enemy targets, such as communications centers, with nonnuclear payloads, Aspin said. The remainder of the bombing would be left to the smaller planes.

As part of the review, Aspin announced that the Strategic Defense Initiative would be renamed the Ballistic Missile Defense program, which was expected to cost $18 billion over the next five years. That was $21 billion less than the antimissile program envisioned by President George Bush but roughly the same funding level as in the Clinton administration's previously announced fiscal 1994 budget. *(Missile defense program, box, p. 262)* ◻

Women in the Military

Congress and the Pentagon took important steps during the 103rd Congress to expand combat roles for women in the military. They also dealt with the explosive issue of sexual harassment in the armed forces.

WOMEN IN COMBAT

Defense Secretary Les Aspin in 1993 called for opening to women opportunities to serve on combat aircraft and on warships. And in early 1994 the Pentagon chief ordered a policy change that allowed women to apply for combat support positions in the Army and Marine Corps.

1993 Action

Aspin on April 28, 1993, ordered the military services to allow women aviators to compete for coveted assignments to fly fighters, bombers and armed helicopters in combat squadrons. Inspired by the role of women just behind the front lines of the Persian Gulf War, Congress in 1991 had repealed a law that had prevented women in the military from flying combat missions. The change, part of the fiscal 1992 defense authorization bill (PL 102-190), did not force the armed services to open combat pilot positions to women; instead it left the military with discretion on whether to maintain the ban. A sharply divided presidential advisory commission in 1992 recommended that the ban on female combat pilots and flight crews be continued. *(Congress and the Nation Vol. VIII, p. 374)*

While Aspin had the authority to open the doors to women pilots, he needed congressional action to repeal a provision of law barring women on combat vessels. Congress went along with the administration's request and repealed the combat exclusion for women on ships as a part of the fiscal 1994 defense authorization (HR 2401—PL 103-160), which was signed into law Nov. 30, 1993. The conference report accompanying the bill required the Pentagon to notify Congress 90 days before announcing a change in the ban on assigning women to ground combat units and provided 30 days' notice before allowing women to join any combat unit or ship from which they had been barred. *(1994 defense authorization, p. 257)*

1994 Action

In one of his last acts before leaving office, Aspin on Jan. 13, 1994, scrapped the Pentagon's so-called risk rule under which the services had barred women from certain types of noncombat units solely on the basis that personnel in such units routinely incurred a significant risk of being killed, wounded or captured by enemy forces.

Under the new policy, women could only be excluded outright from units that were primarily intended to engage in "direct combat," which was defined as "engaging an enemy on the ground with . . . weapons, while being exposed to hostile fire and to a high probability of direct physical contact with" enemy troops.

The services could request permission from the defense secretary to exclude women from units under certain other conditions, such as when those units routinely were located alongside ground combat units.

The new policy was expected to open about 18,000 Army positions to women.

SEXUAL HARASSMENT

The advancements for women shared the spotlight with the damaging revelations of the Navy's so-called Tailhook scandal and other instances of sexual harassment.

1993 Action

On April 23, 1993, the Pentagon's inspector general released a report that found that 83 women and seven men had been subjected to "indecent assaults" during a three-day meeting of the Tailhook Association in Las Vegas in September 1991. The Tailhook Association was a private club of Navy and Marine Corps aviators that had worked closely with the Navy hierarchy.

The report concluded that 117 officers were "implicated in one or more incidents of indecent assault, indecent exposure, conduct unbecoming an officer or failure to act in a proper leadership capacity. . . . Some of the Navy's most senior officers were knowledgeable as to the excesses . . . and, by their inaction, these officers served to condone and even encourage the type of behavior that occurred."

Attempts to prosecute the cases ran into problems of evidence and witnesses. Most of the cases ultimately were dropped for lack of evidence. Some of the accused received nonjudicial punishments, which effectively ended some military careers. Only a handful of the cases ever reached the court-martial stage, and those were at the request of the accused.

Navy Secretary H. Lawrence Garrett III and two admirals who had conducted the initial probe of the incident resigned, and dozens of other officers were fined or disciplined. John H. Dalton, Garrett's successor as Navy secretary, argued unsuccessfully for the dismissal of Chief of Naval Operations Adm. Frank B. Kelso II for failing to exercise leadership in dealing with the scandal. Aspin Oct. 4 rejected the recommendation, saying it would unfairly subject Kelso to a different standard than the one applied to other senior officers at the meeting. The issue of Kelso's leadership during the scandal reemerged in 1994, during a heated debate in the Senate over the rank at which Kelso would retire from the Navy.

1994 Action

The House Armed Services Committee on March 9, 1994, held a hearing on the military's treatment of four women who reported instances of sexual harassment. The witnesses, one from each of the four services, said the retribution exacted upon them for complaining of sexual harassment was worse than the original offense.

Members of both parties hinted that Congress might force changes through legislation if the Pentagon failed to act. Congress included a provision requiring the Pentagon to adopt a policy for processing complaints of sexual harassment or discrimination in the fiscal 1995 defense authorization (S 2182—PL 103-337).   ❑

Arms Control Agreements

Major arms control treaties to reduce the number of strategic nuclear warheads and eliminate chemical weapons were signed in 1993, but neither agreement came to a vote during the 103rd Congress.

Congress in 1993 did approve the ratification of a treaty binding the United States, Russia and other European countries to allow reciprocal reconnaissance overflights.

START II TREATY

President George Bush and Russian President Boris N. Yeltsin signed the second Strategic Arms Reduction Talks (START II) treaty on Jan. 3, 1993. President Bill Clinton and Yeltsin announced at their September 1994 summit meeting agreement on possibly accelerating the START II timetable for deactivating nuclear warheads, once START II had been ratified.

But neither side had ratified START II by the end of 1994 because other former Soviet republics were delaying the implementation of the original START treaty, which laid the groundwork for the second agreement.

The START II treaty, which fleshed out a broad agreement signed by Yeltsin and Bush in June 1992, called for slashing the number of U.S. and Russian nuclear warheads to no more than 6,500. The treaty thus promised to remove from service more than two-thirds of the nearly 24,000 warheads that had been deployed as of 1990 by the United States and the Soviet Union. That cutback would eliminate from service all weapons carried by multiple-warhead, land-based missiles, which U.S. officials long had regarded as the most threatening type in the former Soviet arsenal. (*Congress and the Nation Vol. VIII, p. 390*)

On Sept. 22, 1994, Defense Secretary William J. Perry announced that the Clinton administration planned to reduce the number of nuclear armed bombers and submarines in service, but that it would not cut the number of nuclear warheads that U.S. forces could deliver below levels previously agreed upon. Under the new policy, the U.S. arsenal was to decline to 3,500 weapons by 2003, the ceiling set by START II.

START I ROADBLOCK

The initial START treaty had been ratified by the Senate on Oct. 1, 1992, only to become stalled by the complexities of post-Soviet geopolitics. (*Congress and the Nation Vol. VIII, p. 387*)

START I, negotiated between the United States and the Soviet Union, was supposed to reduce strategic warhead inventories by about one-third. But after the Soviet Union disintegrated, that pact had to be recast with a series of negotiated appendices to bind the four former Soviet republics that controlled parts of the former Soviet nuclear force.

START I, in its final form, required that the three republics other than Russia—Ukraine, Belarus and Kazakhstan—eliminate all nuclear weapons under their control and seal that commitment by signing the 1968 nuclear nonproliferation treaty. The Russian government announced that it would not begin implementing START I reductions until the other three republics followed through on those requirements.

The Clinton administration initially took the stand that the Senate should move ahead with START II, instead of waiting until conflicts over its predecessor treaty were resolved. But the treaty did not advance, and the administration did not continue to lobby for action.

CHEMICAL WEAPONS TREATY

During a three-day meeting in Paris that began Jan. 13, 1993, the United States, Russia, China and more than 120 other countries signed a treaty that sought to eliminate chemical weapons within 20 years. The Senate Foreign Relations Committee held hearings on the 450-page Chemical Weapons Convention (Treaty Doc. 103-21) in 1994, but because of objections from several committee members, it did not vote on the treaty before the 103rd Congress adjourned.

The far-reaching treaty banned the development, production, use or stockpiling of chemical weapons. It required that such weapons be destroyed and their production facilities dismantled or converted to other uses within 10 years, although a country could request a five-year extension. It was to take effect two years after the signing ceremony or six months after 65 countries ratified it, whichever came first.

Negotiations for the total elimination of chemical weapons had begun in Geneva in 1968. The 1991 Persian Gulf War and Iraqi President Saddam Hussein's threat to use chemical weapons was the galvanizing force needed to conclude the treaty.

The treaty would set up some of the most intrusive verification measures ever included in an arms control agreement. It provided for the creation of an international monitoring agency to conduct both scheduled and surprise inspections of chemical plants and other companies that used chemicals covered by the treaty. Some U.S. companies were concerned about the costs of such inspections. The Office of Technology Assessment had estimated that a one-time inspection of a large, complex facility that used many chemicals in its products could cost as much as $500,000. The U.S. government had no plans to reimburse businesses for these expenses.

Even more troubling to companies than the costs were fears that business secrets might be disclosed either by a bad faith inspector or through an insecure computer data bank.

Critics of the treaty argued that it had little value because several nations suspected of having chemical weapons—Iraq, Libya, Syria and North Korea—had not signed it. The Clinton administration called it one of its top priorities, although trouble spots such as Haiti, Cuba and Bosnia kept the president's team focused elsewhere.

Regardless of what happened to the Chemical Weapons Convention, both the United States and the former Soviet Union had pledged to destroy the majority of their chemical weapons stockpiles. (The Russian Federation had taken over Soviet obligations agreed to in a 1990 U.S.-Soviet accord.) The two, however, were encountering problems carrying out their commitment as they discovered how expensive a process it was and how strong public resistance was to their proposed disposal methods. (*Congress and the Nation Vol. VIII, p. 366*)

OPEN SKIES TREATY

The Senate on Aug. 6, 1993, approved an international pact, known as the Open Skies Treaty, that allowed signatories to

---

NUCLEAR TEST BAN EXTENSION

Responding to pressure from Congress, the Clinton administration announced July 3, 1993, that it would not resume nuclear testing for at least 15 months if no other nation broke the worldwide moratorium on testing. If another country did break the moratorium, Clinton said that he would direct the Department of Energy to prepare to conduct additional tests, while seeking congressional approval to do so.

Three months later, on Oct. 5, the Chinese government detonated an 80- to 90-kiloton nuclear bomb at the Lop Nur underground test site in northwest China. Lawmakers again urged Clinton not to resume testing, and Clinton agreed, although he ordered the Energy Department to be ready in case he decided to conduct tests in 1994. The president, however, did not ask Congress to approve new testing. The White House said the president was not committed to the resumption of testing but was keeping options open to allow for a test at a later date.

Congress had imposed a nine-month testing moratorium in October 1992 as part of the fiscal 1993 energy and water development appropriations act (PL 102-377). The law allowed up to 15 underground detonations of nuclear warheads from July 1, 1993, to Sept. 30, 1996, but none thereafter unless another country conducted tests. The law also required the president to notify Congress 90 legislative days in advance of the first detonation. (*Congress and the Nation Vol. VIII, p. 392*)

A number of Pentagon and Energy Department officials had urged the new administration early in 1993 to resume testing and to continue testing through the end of the twentieth century. In addition to the tests specifically allowed by the appropriations act, they wanted to conduct test detonations with small warheads after 1996. Supporters of the proposal said it would help test trigger systems and retain valuable nuclear scientists at Energy Department laboratories.

In protest of the proposal, 26 senators and 38 House members had sent letters to the administration. Many of the lawmakers also had urged the administration not to resume testing at all, saying that new tests would hurt U.S. efforts to stop nuclear proliferation.

---

fly unarmed reconnaissance planes over each other's territories.

The treaty had been signed March 24, 1992, by President George Bush, along with the leaders of the 15 other NATO countries, the five surviving members of the Warsaw Pact and four former Soviet republics: Russia, Belarus, Ukraine and Georgia. (*Congress and the Nation Vol. VIII, p. 390*)

The pact (Treaty Doc. 102-37), approved by the requisite two-thirds of senators on a standing vote, assigned each country an annual quota of overflights that it had to accept. Quotas ranged from a high of 42, the number assigned to the United States and the combined quota for Russia and Belarus, to Portugal's two annual overflights. After giving 72 hours' notice, the planes could use photography and infrared devices to look for troop or equipment movements.

U.S. and Russian satellites routinely provided more detailed information than did the sensors that the Open Skies Treaty mandated for these overflights. But the Bush and Clinton administrations, in mutual support of the treaty, argued that the pact would reassure other European countries.

The resolution of ratification approved by the Senate required the president to:

• Give the Senate 30 days' notice of any proposed change in the aerial sensors.

• Estimate, after the treaty had been in effect for one year, the annual number of U.S. flights to be conducted under the treaty and the number of specially equipped planes required.

The Senate Foreign Relations Committee had approved the Open Skies Treaty by voice vote May 20 with no discussion.   ❑

1995–1996

The GOP victory in the 1994 congressional elections heightened the debate over President Clinton's defense policies. From the vantage point of their newly won majority status and their leadership positions, Republicans challenged the president on everything from basic defense tenets to timetables and dollar amounts.

In the end, though, their electoral victory failed to translate into substantial revisions in Clinton's blueprint for the military. The Republicans managed to increase defense spending substantially, but it was spending for programs that were still basically Clinton's.

The GOP "Contract with America," which Republicans used in their 1994 campaigns, had two primary defense and foreign policy goals: "No U.S. troops under U.N. command and restoration of the essential parts of our national security funding to strengthen our national defenses and maintain our credibility around the world." More specifically, Republicans wanted to limit, though not prohibit, the placement of U.S. troops under United Nations command; reduce U.S. contributions for U.N. peacekeeping; set a timetable for expanding the North Atlantic Treaty Organization (NATO); require deployment of a national antimissile defense system; and increase defense spending.

Republicans vigorously pursued their defense agenda throughout the 104th Congress. Their greatest successes came in increasing the defense budget totals. About $7 billion was added in fiscal 1996 and $11 billion in fiscal 1997, with the bulk of the money going for military procurement and research.

But attempts to push other issues on their agenda either stalled in the Senate, fell to a presidential veto, or produced limited results. GOP efforts to speed development of antimissile defenses was a prime example. Demands for larger budgets and a firmer deployment timetable than the administration was willing to commit to yielded a significant increase in antimissile funding but left Clinton's deployment plan essentially untouched.

Republicans sharply attacked Clinton's global peacekeeping policies but had limited success in trying to change those policies. Although they managed to win cutbacks in U.S. funding

for U.N. peacekeeping missions, they won only temporary, not permanent, limits on the president's ability to place U.S. troops under U.N. command.

Both Congress and the White House agreed on the goal of expanding NATO into former communist states in Central and Eastern Europe, but, here again, they differed over specifics. Clinton supported legislation promoting NATO expansion but only after it was watered down to allow him to decide how and when to do so.

The two branches suffered through another round of painful base closings. President Clinton was particularly incensed at the base closing commission's addition of maintenance depots in the vote-rich states of California and Texas to the Pentagon's original list. He acquiesced but first ordered the Pentagon to devise a plan to privatize the maintenance work at or near the bases.

Conservatives blocked Senate consideration in 1996 of a multilateral treaty to ban the development, production, use or stockpiling of chemical weapons. Many of these same conservatives opposed a treaty signed by Clinton in September 1996 to ban test explosions of nuclear weapons. But the Senate did approve the second Strategic Arms Reduction Talks (START II) treaty early in the year, three years after its signing.

1996 Defense Authorization

Congress in early 1996 cleared a $265.3 billion defense authorization for fiscal 1996. The legislation (S 1124—PL 104-106) provided about $7 billion more than President Clinton had requested, of which more than $5 billion was to go for weapons development and procurement.

The final bill, however, was shorn of several GOP-backed provisions that had triggered a presidential veto of an earlier version (HR 1530). Republicans had to make significant concessions to the Democratic president on the contentious issues of deployment of missile defenses at home and of control over peacekeeping missions abroad.

The veto was one of a number of obstacles the legislation had faced along its bumpy route to enactment. The Senate and House had passed versions with major differences on such issues as ballistic missile defenses, the B-2 stealth bomber and the *Seawolf* submarine. Negotiations dragged on for weeks and then months before a conference report was finally assembled and the bill cleared. Then, as promised, Clinton vetoed the measure. After a House override attempt failed, a compromise version was worked out and the final bill cleared in January 1996.

The delays and difficulties on the authorization bill had some observers wondering whether they might signal a shift of power from defense authorizers to their colleagues on the Appropriations committees.

As cleared, S 1124 still included provisions Clinton strongly opposed, such as ones related to acquired immune deficiency syndrome (AIDS) and abortion. But it also contained several important provisions that were not controversial, such as a 2.4 percent military pay raise and a Pentagon initiative to encourage private financing for military family housing.

Though Clinton objected to the $7 billion increase in funding and much of the added weapons money in the bill had been earmarked for items built in leading Republicans' districts, Defense Secretary William J. Perry said he had no trouble with most of those initiatives because they simply accelerated the purchase of items the Pentagon planned to buy in future years. The most conspicuous exception was the authorization of additional B-2 stealth bombers, beyond the 20 planes already authorized. Perry and nearly all other Pentagon officials insisted that future defense budgets would not be able to pay for more B-2s.

CLINTON BUDGET

The fiscal 1996 budget Clinton submitted to Congress on Feb. 6, 1995, called for $246 billion in budget authority for the Defense Department, a $6.6 billion cut in Pentagon funding compared with the previous year. In addition, Clinton sought $11.2 billion for nuclear weapons programs managed by the Department of Energy. Clinton's overall request was the first installment of a six-year budget plan to provide $1.6 trillion for defense through 2001.

The figures reflected revisions made in December 1994 in the administration's projected defense budgets to meet an anticipated $49 billion shortfall in funding the administration's goal of fielding a force capable of winning two major regional wars that occurred nearly simultaneously. *(1994 action, p. 258)*

Clinton's budget plan hinged on several critical assumptions. It depended on the cost of weapons going down as a result of a 1994 law (PL 103-355) aimed at making federal purchasing more businesslike. It assumed that closing unneeded military bases would trim the services' annual operating costs, although the initial costs of earlier base closings had far outstripped the expected savings. And it assumed that the Pentagon's annual budget would start growing in 1998 after cuts of $6.6 billion in 1996 and an additional $3.2 billion in 1997. *(Government procurement, p. 850; military base closings, pp. 288, 319)*

But Republican defense hawks wanted to go further to remedy what they saw as serious flaws in Clinton's spending blueprint for the military. They argued that the Pentagon's aging weapons stockpile should be replaced at a faster rate than called for in Clinton's six-year budget plan. And they said the president's overall plan for the military was based on forecasts that even top Pentagon officials considered debatable.

The GOP critics initially hoped to boost the fiscal 1996 defense budget by $12 billion to $15 billion to cover the costs of inflation and keep defense spending level year-to-year. It rapidly became clear, however, that they were not going to be able to add that kind of money to Clinton's plan.

BUDGET RESOLUTION

In May 1995, the House adopted a budget resolution (H Con Res 67) that recommended adding nearly $68 billion over seven years to Clinton's budget request for defense. However, the Senate version (S Con Res 13) included a cap on defense appropriations that matched Clinton's request. The Senate on May 23 rejected, 40–60, an amendment by Senate Armed Services Committee Chairman Strom Thurmond, R-S.C., to boost the defense cap to match the House figure. A compromise version of H Con Res 67 allowed for an increase of $40 billion in budget authority and $58 billion in outlays for national defense over seven years. The resolution called for $264.7 billion in budget authority and $263.1 billion in outlays for defense in fiscal 1996. *(1996 budget resolution, p. 65)*

HOUSE COMMITTEE ACTION

The House National Security Committee reported its version of the defense authorization bill (HR 1530—H Rept 104-131) on June 1, 1995. The bill authorized a $267 billion defense budget—about $9.5 billion more than Clinton proposed—as called for in the House-passed budget resolution. The lion's share of the increase, more than $6 billion, was to speed up weapons-development programs, especially for antimissile defense, and to add more weapons to the force.

The committee bill included nearly $3.8 billion for antimissile work, an increase of $763 million—or about 25 percent—over Clinton's request. The bill also contained provisions intended to promote the GOP's case for greatly liberalizing, or scrapping, the 1972 Antiballistic Missile (ABM) Treaty. *(Antimissile defense background, box, p. 262; 1995–1996 summary, p. 294)*

Added weapons included a third Navy destroyer, on top of two Clinton requested; a new amphibious landing ship; 12 Air Force fighter jets; two high-speed cargo ships, in addition to two Clinton requested; and components for two additional B-2 stealth bombers that would have to be funded in fiscal 1997. *(B-2 background, box, p. 277)*

The committee faulted Clinton's Army modernization budget from both short- and long-term perspectives. It said the president's plan would mortgage the Army's future by delaying deployment of the Comanche helicopter, which officials described as the quarterback of the fast-moving and lethal forces they planned to field in the next decade. The panel added $100 million to the Pentagon's $199 million request for building prototypes of the Comanche. The panel also contended that Clinton's budget would buy neither enough planes nor the kind of highly sophisticated weapons that would be needed to fend off attacks on distant allies.

The committee rejected Clinton's $1.5 billion request to build a third nuclear-powered submarine of the *Seawolf* class, instead proposing a complex package of sub-related construction and development projects aimed at keeping the Navy's two submarine suppliers in business so they could compete for contracts to build a future class of subs.

The bill repudiated an array of administration-backed programs that Republicans contended were diverting Pentagon resources to purposes that were peripheral to defense needs. Among these was the Nunn-Lugar program—named for Senate sponsors Sam Nunn, D-Ga., and Richard G. Lugar, R-Ind.—to assist the former Soviet republics in dismantling the nuclear and chemical weapons arsenals they inherited. The committee sliced $171 million of the $371 million requested for the program. The panel also proposed to kill the Technology Reinvestment Program, a Clinton initiative intended to fund dual-use technologies that had both military and commercial applications, and cut more than $900 million from the request for funds to clean up toxic and hazardous waste at existing or former defense installations.

The committee struck a distinctly conservative tone on some questions that reflected broader social issues. Provisions requiring that military personnel with HIV, the virus that causes AIDS, be discharged and barring female service members or dependents from obtaining abortions in U.S. military hospitals abroad, even if they paid for them, provoked the angriest exchanges between Democrats and Republicans during committee markup. Attempts to strike the controversial provisions failed.

While challenging many Clinton policies head-on, the committee did endorse a series of organizational reforms favored by the Pentagon, including a Perry proposal for pilot programs to persuade private companies to build or renovate housing for military families.

HOUSE FLOOR ACTION

The House passed its $267.3 billion defense authorization bill on June 15 by a vote of 300–126. GOP members of the National Security Committee fended off nearly every challenge, finally defeating a motion to recommit the bill, 188–239.

The House rejected efforts to eliminate two of the committee's largest add-ons—$763 million to accelerate deployment of antimissile defenses and $553 million to resume production of the B-2 stealth bomber.

Democratic attacks on the funding and policy aspects of the bill's missile defense initiative were handily beaten on June 14 by nearly solid GOP majorities and a small number of Democratic defectors. An amendment by Peter A. DeFazio, D-Ore., which was rejected, 178–250, would have sliced $628 million from the missile defense authorization and used those funds to increase various housing allowances for military personnel. An amendment by John M. Spratt Jr., D-S.C., stipulating that no provision of the bill would violate the ABM Treaty was rejected by a **key vote of 185–242 (R 7–221; D 177–21; I 1–0)**. *(1995 key votes, p. 1025)*

The B-2 showdown came June 13 on an amendment offered by Budget Committee Chairman John R. Kasich, R-Ohio, and Ronald V. Dellums, D-Calif., the two who had led the successful 1992 effort to cap B-2 production at 20 planes. The House rejected, 203–219, their amendment to delete the $553 million for components for two additional B-2s, if the craft got funded in the fiscal 1997 budget. *(1992 action, Congress and the Nation Vol. VIII, p. 398)*

By a vote of 244–180, the House June 13 adopted an amendment that seemed almost certain to interrupt the Nunn-Lugar program. The amendment by Robert K. Dornan, R-Calif., required the president to certify that Russia had terminated its biological weapons program before spending any of the $200 million authorized by the bill for the arms-dismantling program.

Over the objections of National Security Committee Chairman Floyd D. Spence, R-S.C., the House agreed to a so-called burden-sharing amendment, intended to make U.S. allies in Europe pay by the end of the 1990s for most of the cost of stationing U.S. forces on their soil. The amendment, adopted 273–156 on June 14, was offered by Christopher Shays, R-Conn., Barney Frank, D-Mass., Elizabeth Furse, D-Ore., and Fred Upton, R-Mich.

The House backed the committee's stance on abortions at overseas military facilities. An attempt by Rosa DeLauro, D-Conn., to strike from the bill the provision reviving an administrative order barring most abortions at U.S. military medical facilities overseas, even if they were privately financed, failed by a vote of 196–230 on June 15. Such privately paid abortions had been allowed between 1973 and 1988 on grounds that abortions were illegal or that local medical services were substandard in many countries that hosted U.S. forces. In 1988, President Ronald Reagan banned most such abortions, except in the case of rape, incest or to save a woman's life. Women stationed overseas could fly back to the United States free of charge to obtain abortions. Clinton removed the ban in 1993 in one of his first acts as president.

A proposal by Spence and William F. Clinger, R-Pa., chairman of the Committee on Government Reform and Oversight, to give federal contracting officers wider latitude in deciding how to solicit bids for federal purchases was killed when the House June 14 adopted, 213–207, an amendment by Cardiss Collins, D-Ill., to reaffirm the existing rules.

SENATE COMMITTEE ACTION

The Senate Armed Services Committee reported a $264.7 billion defense authorization bill (S 1026—S Rept 104-112) on July 12. S 1026 added $7 billion to Clinton's request.

Like the House bill, most of the additional funding was for weapons procurement and development programs. However, the House and the Senate committees split sharply over some major programs. Projects approved by the Senate panel but not by the House included the *Seawolf* sub; $1.3 billion for a large helicopter carrier to transport 2,000 Marines and the helicopters to ferry them ashore; and 12 F/A-18 Navy fighters, in addition to the dozen requested.

The Senate committee rejected House proposals to fund additional B-2 stealth bombers, F-15 and F-16 Air Force fighter jets and the proposed LPD-17 cargo ship, which would be smaller than the Senate's helicopter carrier but also was intended to carry an amphibious landing force.

The committee's emphasis on weaponry over diplomacy was reflected in a nonbinding provision added to the bill declaring it to be U.S. policy to deploy by 2003 an antimissile defense system located at more than one U.S. site. The ABM Treaty required that any defense of U.S. or Russian territory consist of no more than 100 interceptor missiles located at a single site. The bill added $770 million to Clinton's request for antimissile programs, roughly the same increase as the House.

The bill also called on the Energy Department, which oversaw the U.S. nuclear weapons stockpile, to keep in readiness a much larger nuclear arsenal than the Strategic Arms Reduction Talks (START II) agreement would allow. And it ordered the Energy Department to prepare to conduct small "subnuclear" test explosions to ensure that aging weapons had not lost their punch, a move that critics warned would undermine efforts to conclude a multilateral treaty banning nuclear test explosions.

In other differences with the House, the Senate panel approved $365 million of the $371 million requested for the Nunn-Lugar program, compared with $200 million in the House bill; $238 million of the $500 million requested for the Technology Reinvestment Program, which the House had proposed to kill; and virtually the entire $1.6 billion requested to clean up military installations, a request nearly halved by the House.

Senate authorizers agreed with their House counterparts that Clinton's budget would not adequately fund key elements in the military's planning. For example, they, too, complained that the budget did not reflect the importance of the Comanche helicopter to Army planning. The panel recommended $373 million instead of the $199 million requested to continue developing the craft, and it ordered the Army to begin buying Comanches in 2001 and to put them in service starting in 2003. And, like the House National Security Committee, the Senate panel maintained that Clinton's budget would not support the pivotal role that Clinton's defense strategy assigned to long-range bombers in assisting allies in distant conflicts.

SENATE FLOOR ACTION

The Senate passed HR 1530 by a vote of 64–34 on Sept. 6, after inserting the text of S 1026. The bill authorized $265.3 billion.

The Senate had debated the measure under the threat of a presidential veto. The administration objected to the bill's antimissile defense language and its $7 billion in add-ons, among other provisions.

But early attempts to make the bill more palatable to the White House went nowhere. For example, on Aug. 4, the Senate voted, 51–46, to table (kill) an amendment by Herb Kohl, D-Wis., to cut $7 billion from the bill and bring it back into line with Clinton's original request. A day earlier, the Senate had tabled, 51–48, an amendment by Byron L. Dorgan, D-N.D., to cut the bill's national missile defense authorization by $300 million, to $371 million, the amount Clinton had requested.

Attempts to fashion a compromise on missile defense language went on for weeks. In the meantime, the Senate on Aug. 3 adopted, 69–26, a William S. Cohen, R-Maine, amendment expressing the sense of Congress that the multisite deployment policy could be carried out through means consistent with the ABM Treaty, including amendments. Cohen's proposal urged the president to begin negotiations with the Russians and, if they failed, to consult with the Senate on possible withdrawal from the ABM Treaty.

A compromise was finally hammered out by senior members of the Armed Services Committee. On Sept. 6, the Senate adopted, 85–13, a Nunn amendment calling for the military to be ready to deploy by the end of 2003 a national missile defense system to counter a limited, accidental or unauthorized ballistic missile attack. The compromise required that, before a decision to deploy a national missile defense was made, Congress was to review the system to ensure that it was affordable and operationally effective. It retreated from a commitment to a multisite system but mandated that the ground-based interceptors be capable of deployment at several sites. The compromise urged negotiations with Russia to pursue changes to the ABM Treaty to allow deployment of a national missile defense system.

While the Pentagon viewed the missile defense compromise as a major improvement from the original bill, the administration remained opposed to several other provisions in the legislation.

In other action, the Senate on Aug. 3 rejected, 30–70, an amendment offered by John McCain, R-Ariz., to delete the $1.5 billion authorization for the third and last *Seawolf* submarine.

By a vote of 70–26 on Aug. 4, the Senate tabled an amendment by Tom Harkin, D-Iowa, to greatly reduce the number of U.S. troops stationed in Europe, unless the NATO allies began paying a much larger proportion of the cost of their deployment.

The Senate on Aug. 4 adopted, 67–27, a Patrick J. Leahy, D-Vt., amendment to impose a one-year moratorium on U.S. forces' use of antipersonnel land mines. The Pentagon vehemently opposed the provision.

The Senate on Aug. 4 tabled, 56–44, a Jim Exon, D-Neb., amendment to strip from the bill a $50 million authorization to conduct small hydronuclear tests to determine the reliability of the U.S. nuclear stockpile. After Clinton on Aug. 11 endorsed a continued moratorium on U.S. nuclear testing, including the small hydronuclear tests, Exon revisited the issue. On Sept. 5, the Senate adopted by voice vote Exon's amendment stating that nothing in the bill should be viewed as authorization to conduct hydronuclear tests or construed as amending or repealing the 1992 law (PL 102-377) that banned all nuclear test explosions after Sept. 30, 1996. *(1992 law, Congress and the Nation Vol. VIII, p. 392)*

Despite protests from some lawmakers about spending on projects the administration never requested, the Senate approved by voice vote a Thurmond amendment adding $228 million for military construction. To offset those projects, the Senate on Sept. 5 adopted an amendment by Thurmond to cut several projects.

James M. Inhofe and Don Nickles, both Oklahoma Republicans, won voice vote approval for an amendment requiring a General Accounting Office review of a Clinton proposal to privatize depot maintenance work at two Air Force bases slated for closure. The proposal worried lawmakers whose states were home to the Air Force's three other depots, which had been the likely recipients of work from the two shuttered facilities. *(Maintenance depots, box, p. 310)*

CONFERENCE ACTION

House and Senate conferees held their first meeting in September but did not complete their work for more than three months. The disagreements over social issues—abortion and HIV—were part of the problem. But the bigger factor in the delay was the GOP plan to accelerate deployment of a nationwide antimissile defense.

Antimissile Defenses

The $265.3 billion defense authorization bill added $854 million to the president's request for antimissile defenses. The sticking point between Clinton and congressional Republicans was not the amount of money, however, but the legislative provisions defining the program's goals.

The conference report required that the Pentagon deploy by 2003 a system that could protect the United States, including Alaska and Hawaii, against a relatively small number of attacking warheads, such as might be fired by a Third World country. It also called for the United States to make a unilateral distinction between systems to defend national territory—severely limited by the ABM Treaty—and so-called theater defenses intended to protect U.S. allies and forces in the field against shorter-range missiles.

The issue of where to draw the line between the two types of antimissile systems was under negotiation with Russia. Conservatives warned that the Clinton administration might agree to Russian demands that would hamstring promising theater defense programs, particularly the long-range, ship-launched Navy Upper Tier system.

Administration officials countered that the Russian government could view the controversial antimissile provisions as inconsistent with the 1972 ABM Treaty and respond by shelving ratification of the START II treaty. The White House and Democratic congressional defense experts led by Nunn also contended that the bill's requirement to deploy by 2003 was premature, given that no missile threat to U.S. territory was in the offing.

GOP-led conferees insisted on the missile defense provisions, partly at the urging of Senate Majority Leader Bob Dole, R-Kan. Early deployment of antimissile defenses and elimination of the ABM Treaty were the top defense priorities of conservative activists, whom Dole was courting in his bid for the 1996 GOP presidential nomination.

Other Issues

There were other issues as well to resolve. On two of the most contentious ones—procurement of additional B-2 stealth bombers and submarines—the conferees fashioned elaborate compromises.

They added $493 million to Clinton's request for B-2 production funds but deliberately left unsettled the question of how the money was to be spent. The House had voted to resume production of B-2s, while the Senate had voted against building any more than the 20 planes already authorized.

As for submarine construction, both chambers rejected the Navy's plan to award contracts for the first two of a new class of smaller, cheaper subs to General Dynamics' Electric Boat Division in Groton, Conn., and then to allow Electric Boat and Tenneco-owned Newport News (Va.) Shipbuilding to compete for subsequent contracts. Conferees agreed to the basic outline of the Senate bill's plan to provide funding to continue work on the third and last *Seawolf*-class sub at Groton, to begin work at Groton on the first of a new class of subs and to begin buying components for the second ship of the new class to be built at Newport News. The report ordered the Navy to budget two more subs: one to be built in 2000 (at Groton) and another in 2001 (at Newport News). The four subs would each test differ-

ent design features, which would determine the design to be used for future subs.

In other action, the conferees dropped the Senate bill's one-year moratorium on antipersonnel land mines. However, with no fanfare, sponsor Leahy inserted the core provision of his land-mine ban into the fiscal 1996 foreign operations appropriations bill (HR 1868), which was attached to a stopgap spending bill (HR 2880—PL 104-99). *(1996 aid appropriations, p. 231)*

Conferees approved $300 million for the Nunn-Lugar program and revised House-passed restrictions on the use of the funds.

Conferees wrangled for weeks over a House section on the handling of missing-in-action (MIA) cases. They finally agreed on a 37-page provision that called for the creation of a new, centralized office in the Defense Department to handle such cases and imposed requirements on commanders in the field. Sponsor Dornan and his allies contended that the changes were necessary to force the Pentagon to place a higher priority on resolving the status of MIAs and to protect missing persons and their families from arbitrary or politically motivated Pentagon decisions. The Defense Department vigorously opposed the provisions.

Final Action

The House adopted the conference report (H Rept 104-406) Dec. 15 by a vote of 267–149.

The Senate agreed to the report, 51–43, on Dec. 19, clearing the bill. Notably, Nunn voted against the report—the first he had opposed in his 23 years in the Senate—because of the missile defense language, among other provisions. "This is taking probably the most gigantic step backwards in arms control that we've taken in years," he said.

VETO, OVERRIDE ATTEMPT

After the conference report cleared, GOP defense specialists went into high gear to try to dissuade Clinton from vetoing the bill. They vehemently denied the Democrats' claim that the bill's antimissile provisions would conflict with the ABM Treaty. And they argued that if Clinton did not sign it, he would be depriving the military of the 2.4 percent pay raise authorized by the bill.

But on Dec. 28, Clinton made good on his threat. In his veto message, Clinton singled out as particularly objectionable provisions of the bill that mandated deployment by 2003 of a missile defense that would protect all 50 states. The administration contended that such a system would have to be deployed at more than one site. "By setting U.S. policy on a collision course with the ABM Treaty," Clinton said, "the bill would jeopardize continued Russian implementation of the START I Treaty as well as Russian ratification of the START II Treaty."

Aside from the missile defense language, other sections cited by Clinton in his veto message included provisions requiring the president to report to Congress when he placed U.S. military forces under U.N. command and requiring the president to seek a supplemental appropriation to cover any unplanned overseas deployment costing more than $100 million. Clinton also objected to the bill's requirement that HIV-positive military personnel be discharged, a ban on most abortions in U.S. military hospitals overseas, and limitations on the use of Nunn-Lugar funds.

On Jan. 3, 1996, the House tried unsuccessfully to override Clinton's veto. A majority of House members again voted in favor of the bill, by a **key vote of 240–156 (R 206–16; D 34–139; I 0–1),** but that was short of the required two-thirds majority (264 in this case). *(1996 key votes, p. 1047)*

Because the defense appropriations bill (HR 2126—PL 104-61) had become law on Dec. 1, 1995, the administration was under little pressure to accept the authorization bill. The only "must-have" provision was the military pay raise.

An attempt to enact a freestanding pay raise bill proved futile. The Senate on Dec. 30 passed by voice vote a bill (S 1514) to put the higher pay rates in effect through April 2, 1996. But key House Republicans were loath to separate the pay-raise provisions from the authorization bill because they were among its most popular features. An attempt to bring S 1514 to the House floor was spiked on procedural grounds immediately after the unsuccessful override attempt. National Security Chairman Spence, however, said he would take steps to ensure passage of the pay raise, if a new version of the authorization bill was not completed by the end of January. *(1996 defense appropriations bill, p. 301)*

SECOND AUTHORIZATION BILL

Once the House sustained Clinton's veto, leaders of the two defense committees agreed to convene a handful of senior members in a rump conference that would try to salvage the bill by accommodating Clinton's bottom-line demands.

The Senate-House conferees approved a revised version Jan. 19, 1996, that eliminated entirely the antimissile defense and U.N. command provisions and that changed to a nonbinding sense-of-Congress declaration the requirement for a supplemental appropriations request for certain overseas deployments. But other provisions Clinton had objected to—although in less strenuous terms—remained for the most part, including the HIV, abortion and Nunn-Lugar language.

Conferees incorporated the revised version of HR 1530 into S 1124, a bill the Senate had passed to hedge against precisely what had happened. Following a pattern set years ago, immediately after the Senate passed its version of the defense authorization bill Sept. 6, 1995, it passed S 1124, which had been reported by the Senate Armed Services Committee Aug. 7, and two other bills, each of which contained a section of HR 1530. This created a fleet of legislative vehicles that could be used to quickly form a new Senate-House conference report should it be necessary. S 1124 was passed by a voice vote of the House Jan. 5, 1996, and then sent to conference.

The House adopted the new conference report (H Rept 104-450) on Jan. 24 by a vote of 287–129. The Senate followed suit Jan. 26 by a vote of 56–34, clearing the bill. President Clinton signed it into law Feb. 10.

MAJOR PROVISIONS

As signed into law Feb. 10, 1996, S 1124 authorized $265.3 billion in defense spending for fiscal 1996, $7 billion more than requested. The Senate version had authorized $265.3 billion; the House version, $267.3 billion.

Major provisions of the final bill:

Strategic Arms

Added $493 million to the $904 million Clinton had requested to continue testing and building the 20 B-2 stealth bombers already authorized.

But conferees deliberately left unsettled the question of how the money was to be spent. The House had voted to use the money to buy components for use in fiscal 1997 to resume B-2 production, while the Senate had voted against building any more B-2s. The conference report stated that Senate conferees believed the added funds should be used only for "components, upgrades and modifications that would be of value for the existing fleet of B-2s."

Antimissile Program

Added $854 million to Clinton's $2.9 billion request for antimissile defenses.

The add-ons included a $170 million increase over Clinton's $30 million request for a long-range, ship-based missile defense system, designated the Navy Upper Tier system. The bill required initial deployment of the Army's ground-based Theater High-Altitude Air Defense (THAAD) system by 2000 and of the Upper Tier system by 2001. *(Antimissile defenses, p. 297)*

Ground Combat

Added more than $1.5 billion to Clinton's budget request for Army equipment, spreading the funds across programs ranging from the most mundane trucks to the most sophisticated helicopters.

• Called for accelerating upgrades of key weaponry with new target-finding electronics and other improvements. Additions to Clinton's budget included $140 million to modernize 20 older scout helicopters and arm them with guided missiles; $76 million, in addition to the $342 million requested, to equip missile-armed Apache helicopters with Longbow radars; and $110 million, in addition to the $474 million requested, to upgrade M-1 tanks. The added M-1 funds would pay for 24 more conversions than were planned.

• Ordered the Army to give the Marine Corps 24 unmodified tanks.

• Added $100 million to the $199 million requested to continue developing the new Comanche helicopter.

• Authorized the $336 million requested to buy 60 Blackhawk troop-carrying helicopters.

However, while the administration had planned to buy no more of these craft, the bill included $70 million for components to be used in fiscal 1997 to build an additional 36 Blackhawks.

• Called for accelerating production of several categories of Army equipment, adding to the request $78 million for three types of antitank missiles; $111 million for artillery rockets and their launchers; $440 million for ammunition; $91 million for rifles, pistols and machine guns; and $327 million for new and reconditioned trucks, ranging from jeep-like "Humvees" to huge, "low-boy" tractor-trailers that could carry a 70-ton tank.

Tactical Air Combat

Added to the budget request nearly $1 billion for tactical combat aircraft, which was spread across every major program to buy or upgrade combat jets already in service.

• Authorized $81 million to rebuild four Harrier vertical takeoff jets used by the Marines, in addition to the $148 million requested for four of the planes.

• Authorized $213 million for six Navy F/A-18s, in addition to the $610 million requested for 12 of them.

• Added $311 million for six Air Force F-15Es and $50 million for components to buy six more in fiscal 1997.

• Added $159 million for six Air Force F-16s.

• Added $165 million to upgrade the fleet of Navy radar-jamming planes and to expand that force by modernizing older planes, thus offsetting the planned retirement of Air Force jammer planes.

• Authorized $121 million, $17 million more than requested, to convert F-14 Navy fighters into ground attack planes.

• Authorized the amounts requested for two new planes slated to begin entering service by the end of the decade: $1.1 billion to gear up for production of an enlarged version of the Navy's F/A-18 and $2.1 billion for the Air Force's F-22 fighter.

• Included only $200 million of the $331 million originally requested for the so-called Joint Advanced Strike Technology program, an umbrella project under which the Air Force and Navy were trying to develop a generation of planes to succeed the F-22, beginning in about 2010. The reduction was consistent with a change in the Pentagon's plans.

• Added $145 million to buy various types of super-accurate "smart" missiles; added $66 million to the $282 million requested to develop two new types.

Naval Combat

Authorized $700 million of the $1.5 billion requested to continue work on the third and last *Seawolf*-class sub at General Dynamics' Electric Boat Division in Groton, Conn. The bill also authorized $704.5 million, as requested, to begin work at Groton on the first of a new class of subs, which was to be fully funded in the fiscal 1998 budget.

The bill included $100 million, added to the budget request, to begin buying components for the second ship of the new class, to be fully funded in the fiscal 1999 budget and slated for construction at Tenneco-owned Newport News (Va.) Shipbuilding.

Conferees ordered the Navy to budget one additional sub each in 2000 (at Groton) and 2001 (at Newport News) as well as required the Navy to exploit new technologies to make each of the four post-*Seawolf* subs cheaper and more effective than the one before and to award all subsequent sub-building contracts on the basis of price competition.

• Authorized the Navy to contract in fiscal 1996 for three more destroyers equipped with the Aegis antiaircraft system and

for three additional ships in fiscal 1997. But it authorized only $2.2 billion, the amount requested to buy two of the ships in fiscal 1996. The conferees ordered the Navy to split the six new ships between the Maine and Mississippi shipyards that had built earlier ships of the class.

• Added $20 million to buy the 14th ship in a class of 170-foot patrol vessels built in Louisiana, and $18 million to buy two smaller, high-speed patrol boats.

Air and Sea Transport

Authorized the $2.4 billion requested to buy eight additional C-17 long-range cargo jets.

• Added $1.3 billion for the seventh in a class of large helicopter carriers built by Litton Industries in Pascagoula, Miss. These ships, designated LHDs, could carry nearly 2,000 Marines plus helicopters and landing barges to haul them ashore. The Navy had planned to fund the ship in its budget for fiscal 2000.

• Added $974 million for the first of a new class of slightly smaller amphibious landing transports, designated LPDs.

Personnel Issues

Authorized $69.2 billion for military personnel expenses. The president's budget had included $68.7 billion.

• Approved the administration's request for a ceiling of nearly 1.49 million active-duty personnel and a National Guard and reserve ceiling of 938,844 personnel.

• Authorized a 2.4 percent military pay raise, as requested.

• Included a Pentagon initiative intended to encourage private financing for military family housing.

Authorized $92.6 billion for operations and maintenance costs. The budget request was $91.6 billion.

Nontraditional Programs

Included $300 million of the $371 million requested for the Nunn-Lugar program to assist the former Soviet republics in dismantling their nuclear and chemical arsenals. The conference bill required the president to certify that Russia had terminated its biological weapons program before $60 million could be used for strategic weapons destruction in Russia. In the absence of such a certification, the money could be used for weapons destruction in Ukraine, Kazakhstan or Belarus. The provision also barred the obligation of more than half the funds authorized for chemical weapons destruction-related activities in Russia, pending a presidential certification that Russia had met certain conditions.

• Authorized $195 million of the $500 million requested for the Technology Reinvestment Program, Clinton's initiative to develop dual-use technologies.

• Authorized $1.4 billion, $200 million less than requested, to clean up toxic and hazardous waste at military installations.

• Authorized $5.55 billion of the $6 billion requested to clean up Energy Department nuclear weapons facilities.

• Authorized $50 million of the $80 million requested for overseas disaster relief and humanitarian assistance.

Other Provisions

Required that military personnel who tested positive for the AIDS virus be discharged or retired within six months. No one would be discharged who was within two years of completing the 20 years of services needed to qualify for retirement. Those forced out before retirement would remain eligible for military medical care.

• Barred female service members or dependents from obtaining abortions in U.S. military hospitals overseas, even if they paid for the procedure, unless the pregnancy endangered the woman's life or was the result of rape or incest.

• Created a new, centralized office in the Pentagon to handle missing-in-action (MIA) cases; required the commander of any combat unit to report to the senior U.S. commander in the region, within 48 hours, any MIA personnel; required the senior, or "theater," commander, within two weeks of being notified, to report any MIA case to the secretary of the appropriate armed service; required a board of inquiry to be convened every three years to review each MIA case; and made it a criminal offense for an official wrongfully to conceal from an MIA's family any information that bore on his or her status. ❑

1996 Defense Appropriations

Congress in 1995 cleared a $243.3 billion fiscal 1996 defense appropriations bill. Objecting to a number of costly add-ons, President Clinton allowed the legislation (HR 2126—PL 104-61) to become law without his signature.

HR 2126 contained $6.9 billion more than requested. The new Republican majority in Congress was committed to reversing what it saw as a precipitous decline in U.S. military strength. Republican defense specialists contended that they needed to add funds to bolster an administration budget that was too anemic.

The president was especially troubled by HR 2126's additional funding for B-2 stealth bombers, the Air Force's F-22 fighter and missile defense. But Congress sent the bill to the White House in late November 1995 at the same time U.S. forces were about to be deployed to Bosnia to enforce a peace agreement brokered by the Clinton administration. The president needed a source of funds to cover the estimated $1.5 billion cost of the peacekeeping mission. Clinton, therefore, backed away from his veto threat, claiming that he had obtained an implicit agreement from GOP leaders that funds for the Bosnia mission could be drawn from the defense bill. GOP leaders, however, denied a firm agreement. *(Bosnia, p. 225)*

Reversing a historical trend, the defense appropriations bill cleared weeks before work was completed on the fiscal 1996 defense authorization bill (HR 1530). *(1996 defense authorization, p. 294)*

In addition to HR 2126 funds, most of the rest of the defense budget was made up of $11.2 billion in the fiscal 1996 military construction appropriations bill (HR 1817—PL 104-32) and $10.6 billion contained in the fiscal 1996 energy and water development appropriations bill (HR 1905—PL 104-46).

The House passed HR 2126 on Sept. 7, 1995, by a vote of 294–125. The House Appropriations Committee had reported the bill (H Rept 104-208) on July 27.

As passed, HR 2126 appropriated $244.1 billion, $7.8 billion more than Clinton had requested. In general, the bill tracked the House-passed authorization bill in most of its major additions to Clinton's budget. That included $493 million to set the stage for building additional B-2 stealth bombers beyond the 20 planes already approved (the authorization included $60 million more) and $600 million in addition to the $2.9 billion requested for antimissile defenses. *(B-2 background, box, p. 277; antimissile defenses, box, p. 262)*

But the appropriators also added some of their own initiatives, such as an extra $647 million to cover the cost of ongoing military operations in northern and southern Iraq and $200 million, in addition to the $2.3 billion requested, for development of the Air Force's F-22 fighter plane. The F-22 was slated to replace the F-15 as the front-line air-combat jet beginning around the turn of the century.

The bill matched the authorization bill in many of its proposed cuts to Clinton's budget, denying the $65 million requested to pay the U.S. share of U.N. peacekeeping costs and the $500 million requested for the Technology Reinvestment Program to develop so-called dual-use technologies with commercial and military applications. Reflecting the tighter budget ceiling, however, the bill did not go along with the House-passed authorization bill's extra funding for development of the Army's Comanche helicopter and for an additional Aegis destroyer.

House passage of HR 2126 had come after considerable wrangling over controversial amendments earlier on Sept. 7. The House narrowly turned back, 210–213, an amendment offered by John R. Kasich, R-Ohio, to eliminate the $493 million added to continue production of the B-2 bomber.

Robert K. Dornan, R-Calif., proposed an amendment to reinstate a ban on service personnel and military dependents' obtaining abortions at overseas military facilities, unless the life of the woman was endangered. Clinton had signed an executive order Jan. 22, 1993, ending a version of the ban that had been in place since 1988. An amendment by Rosa DeLauro, D-Conn., to revise the Dornan proposal to allow women to have abortions if they reimbursed the government for any costs associated with the procedure failed, 194–224. The House then adopted the Dornan amendment, 226–191.

With air strikes by North Atlantic Treaty Organization (NATO) forces on Bosnian Serb military targets having forced the warring sides to the negotiating table, lawmakers limited the number of Bosnia-related amendments that they had planned to offer to the spending bill. The lone exception was an amendment offered by Mark W. Neumann, R-Wis., to bar funds for U.S. troop deployments in Bosnia for any type of operation other than the removal of allies' peacekeeping forces, unless the president obtained congressional authorization. The House adopted the amendment by voice vote.

The House initially adopted by voice vote but then rejected Sept. 7 on a 182–238 roll call an amendment by Patricia Schroeder, D-Colo., to bar defense contractors from using money in the defense bill to lobby.

In other action, the House rejected, 126–293, a David R. Obey, D-Wis., amendment to cut $1 billion from the $2.3 billion earmarked for development of the F-22. Also rejected, 124–296, was a Schroeder amendment to reduce the overall bill by 3 percent across-the-board to bring it in line with Clinton's original request.

SENATE ACTION

The Senate passed its $242.7 billion version of the defense funding bill (S 1087) on Sept. 5 by a **key vote of 62–35 (R 48–4; D 14–31)**. In preparation for a conference with the House, the Senate on Sept. 8 passed HR 2126 by voice vote, after substituting the text of S 1087. *(1995 key votes, p. 1025)*

The Senate bill had been reported by the Senate Appropriations Committee (S Rept 104-124) on July 28, but final floor action was delayed until a deadlock over provisions relating to antimissile defense programs in the companion defense authorization bill (S 1026) could be resolved.

S 1087 would have appropriated $6.4 billion more than Clinton requested. Add-ons included $300 million more than the $371 million Clinton requested for development of a national missile defense, $70 million to resuscitate efforts to develop a laser-armed antimissile satellite and $1.4 billion more than requested for Aegis guided-missile destroyers.

Unlike the House bill, S 1087 included no additional funds for the B-2 bomber. Instead, the Senate bill added funds for F-15E and F-16 fighter planes and for C-17 transport planes. The Senate bill did not include funding for military operations in northern and southern Iraq, as the House bill had. The Senate included $238 million for dual-use technologies, while the House bill denied funding for the program. But the Senate agreed with the House decision to deny the $65 million request for international peacekeeping operations.

During floor action on Aug. 10, the Senate reaffirmed the additional funds for antimissile defenses and antisatellite weapons. By a vote of 45–54, the Senate rejected an amendment by Byron L. Dorgan, D-N.D., to eliminate the $300 million added for a national missile defense. An amendment by Tom Harkin, D-Iowa, to eliminate the $70 million added for development of the laser-armed antimissile satellite was tabled (killed), 57–41. Another Harkin amendment, to eliminate funds to resume development of an antisatellite missile, was tabled, 57–41, as well.

Also tabled, 67–31 on Aug. 11, was an amendment by Dale Bumpers, D-Ark., to cut from the bill $120 million earmarked to begin adapting four of the oldest Trident nuclear missile subs to carry the Trident II missile.

The Senate also turned back challenges to some priorities of the Appropriations Committee that differed from those of the Pentagon. By a vote of 73–26 on Aug. 10, the Senate tabled a Jeff Bingaman, D-N.M., amendment to eliminate the $1.3 billion the Senate bill added for a helicopter carrier and add $1.1 billion to pay for ongoing operations around Iraq, Bosnia and the Caribbean.

Other proposals rejected by the Senate included a Paul Wellstone, D-Minn., amendment to cut $3.2 billion from bill, which was tabled, 56–42, on Aug. 10. A John Kerry, D-Mass., amendment to instruct the Appropriations Committee to cut the bill by $6.4 billion, bringing it to the amount requested by Clinton, was tabled, 60–38, on Aug. 11.

CONFERENCE ACTION

As House and Senate negotiators hammered out a compromise bill, Clinton made clear in a letter the additions and provisions that would draw a veto. He singled out House-passed provisions on the B-2 bomber, abortion and deployment of troops to Bosnia.

Conferees produced a bill (H Rept 104-261) that was nearly $7 billion more than the president had requested and still contained items certain to draw Clinton's opposition. These included funding to continue production of the B-2 bomber, increased funds for antimissile defenses, and funds for unrequested F-15 and F-16 jet fighters, as well as reductions in the requests for the Technology Reinvestment Program, the *Seawolf*-class submarine, and the Nunn-Lugar program—named for Senate sponsors Sam Nunn, D-Ga., and Richard G. Lugar, R-Ind.—to help the former Soviet republics dismantle their nuclear and chemical weapons.

The bill also would have reversed administration policy by reinstating the ban on service personnel and military dependents obtaining abortions at overseas military facilities, even if they used their own money to pay for the procedure. But in one of their final steps, the conferees added the proviso that the ban would take effect only if it was enacted as part of the defense authorization bill.

Conferees watered down the restrictive House-approved provision on deployment of troops to Bosnia to make it a nonbinding sense-of-Congress statement that the president should seek congressional approval before deploying troops to Bosnia.

In a Sept. 29 letter, Office of Management and Budget Director Alice M. Rivlin told the House leadership that Clinton would veto the defense bill as a matter of overall budget priorities.

But that same day House members stunned GOP leaders by rejecting the conference report by a vote of 151–267. It went down in the face of an alliance between conservatives who were angry that conferees had attempted to forestall a presidential veto by watering down House-backed positions—especially the abortion ban—and liberals who wanted to spend less on defense.

A new conference was convened. The logjam over the abortion issue was broken when the Senate conferees offered—and the House conferees finally accepted—a provision to allow privately funded abortions overseas in cases of rape or incest or to save the life of the woman. It omitted a House-proposed requirement that the rape or incest had to have been reported to military authorities.

The House adopted the new conference report (H Rept 104-344) on Nov. 16 by a **key vote of 270–158 (R 195–37; D 75–120;**

I 0–1). The Senate agreed to the report a few hours later by a vote of 59–39, clearing the bill.

Except on abortion policy, the conference report was nearly identical to the version the House rejected.

Clinton's veto threat disappeared in the wake of the peace agreement among the warring factions from Bosnia, which was reached Nov. 21 in Dayton, Ohio. After several days of talks, the White House and leaders of the House and Senate Appropriations committees emerged with a tacit understanding that the defense spending bill would be a source for financing the Bosnia operation.

The White House went so far as to suggest in a statement that an agreement had been reached with congressional leaders to use money in the bill for troop deployment. House Appropriations Committee Chairman Robert L. Livingston, R-La., denied any such agreement but indicated that the Pentagon, without congressional approval, could borrow from its operational accounts to fund U.S. troops in Bosnia. The White House then would have to get Congress to accept a rescissions package to replenish that account.

MAJOR PROVISIONS

IIR 2126, which became law on Dec. 1 without President Clinton's signature, appropriated $243.3 billion for fiscal 1996 Defense Department programs, about $800 million less than the House bill and about $600 million more than the Senate version.

Appropriations

HR 2126 appropriated:

• $69.1 billion for salaries and benefits, $357 million more than requested. The amount was intended to pay for an active-duty force of 1.49 million members, which was slightly larger than was requested but amounted to a reduction of nearly 38,000 from the fiscal 1995 force.

It also was expected to support a force of more than 930,000 reservists and National Guard members, about 3,300 more than Clinton requested but nearly 35,000 fewer than were on the rolls in fiscal 1995.

• $81.6 billion for operations and maintenance, $752 million more than requested.

Following the House's lead, conferees added $647 million to cover the anticipated cost in fiscal 1996 of two military operations in Iraqi territory: Provide Comfort, which supported Kurdish communities in northern Iraq; and Southern Watch, the enforcement of a "no-fly" zone for Iraqi planes in southern Iraq. Critics complained that the two operations in Iraq, which had been under way since the 1991 Persian Gulf War, showed no sign of ending and should be budgeted for as routine activities, not as contingencies. The added funds could not be spent unless the administration included the operations' cost in its fiscal 1997 budget request.

• $3.43 billion for antimissile defense, nearly 20 percent more than Clinton's $2.9 billion request. The most dramatic change was in the funding for national missile defense. The $746 million in the bill for defense systems intended to protect U.S. territory against missile attack was more than double Clinton's request.

Conferees also boosted by $170 million, to $200 million, the amount provided for the Navy's Upper Tier system, a very long-range interceptor missile designed to be launched from warships.

In addition to increasing funds for antimissile projects, the bill added $135 million to accelerate development of "Brilliant Eyes" satellites, intended to detect approaching missiles.

The bill also included a $30 million Senate initiative to develop an antisatellite missile, a program that liberal arms control activists had spiked in the mid-1980s.

• $1.3 billion for a Senate-approved helicopter carrier, LPD-7, the seventh in a class of ships built in Pascagoula, Miss., and $974 million for the slightly smaller LPD-17, a House initiative. These two ships, which were designed to transport Marine combat units to distant trouble spots and land them on a hostile shore, accounted for nearly one-third of the net addition to Clinton's budget request.

• $700 million to continue work on the third submarine of the *Seawolf* class, $705 million for the first of a new class of smaller, cheaper subs, and $100 million for components that would be used to build the second. The administration had requested $1.5 billion to complete construction of the third *Seawolf* sub and an additional $705 million to buy components to be used to build the first of the new subs. The Senate bill had included $700 million for the *Seawolf*, while the House bill had included nothing for the sub.

The conference report was silent on the rationale for the submarine package, but it funded the Senate plan that had been incorporated in the final version of the companion defense authorization bill. The plan was designed to guarantee future contracts to both of the companies that built nuclear-powered subs: General Dynamics' Electric Boat Division in Groton, Conn., and Tenneco-owned Newport News (Va.) Shipbuilding.

• $2.16 billion requested for two destroyers equipped with the Aegis antiaircraft system.

• $493 million added by the House to continue production of the B-2 bomber beyond the 20 planes already authorized and deemed sufficient by the Pentagon.

• $311 million in unrequested funding for six F-15E Air Force bombers and an unrequested $50 million for components for future planes; $229 million to modernize eight Harrier vertical takeoff jets used by the Marines as bombers, compared with a $148 million budget request to rebuild four planes; $159 million for six F-16 Air Force fighters, which were not requested; $823 million for 18 F/A-18 Navy fighters, compared with a budget request of $610 million for 12 of the planes; $2.2 billion—$100 million more than requested—to continue development of the Air Force's F-22 fighter; and $200 million of the $331 million initially requested for the Joint Advanced Strike Technology (JAST) program, intended to develop several new types of combat planes to replace existing models in about 2010 (conferees said the reduction reflected a revision of the program's schedule).

• $299 million to continue developing the Comanche scout helicopter, $100 million more than requested; $140 million to continue equipping existing scout helicopters with new target-finding electronic gear, a program for which the budget included no funds; and $418 million, $76 million more than requested, to begin equipping the Army's larger Apache helicopters with Longbow radar, designed to find targets in fog and rain that would blind the Apache's existing target-finding gear.

• $1.4 billion of the $1.6 billion requested for environmental cleanup of toxic and hazardous waste at military installations; $300 million of the $371 million requested for the Nunn-Lugar program, intended to help former Soviet states dismantle their nuclear and chemical arsenals; and $195 million of the $500 million requested for the Technology Reinvestment Program, which promoted the use of defense technology in the commercial sector. The bill provided none of the $65 million requested to pay for part of the U.S. assessment for U.N. peacekeeping operations.

Republicans criticized these nontraditional programs as no more than marginally related to the Pentagon's core mission.

Other Provisions

HR 2126 also:

• Allowed service personnel and military dependents to have privately funded abortions at overseas military facilities in cases of rape or incest or to save the life of the woman.

• Expressed the sense of Congress that the president should seek congressional authorization before deploying U.S. troops in Bosnia for any type of operation other than the evacuation of allies' peacekeeping forces. ❑

1996 Military Construction

Congress in 1995 cleared an $11.2 billion fiscal 1996 military construction appropriations bill. The legislation (HR 1817—PL 104-32) exceeded President Clinton's request by $479 million and was $2.4 billion more than Congress had appropriated the previous year. *(1995 military construction, p. 283)*

HR 1817 included $2.97 billion for military construction projects, $4.3 billion for family housing on military bases and $3.9 billion for the costs of closing unneeded military bases and realigning others.

LEGISLATIVE ACTION

The House passed an $11.2 billion appropriations bill on June 21 by a vote of 319–105. HR 1817 had been reported by the House Appropriations Committee on June 13 (H Rept 104-137).

Several lawmakers attempted to cut back spending in the bill, particularly for members' projects that, as usual, had crept in without a request from the Pentagon. But in the end, only two amendments prevailed: one offered by Wally Herger, R-Calif., to eliminate $14 million to buy land for an Army museum, adopted 261–137 on June 16, and a second amendment proposed by Mark W. Neumann, R-Wis., to reduce funds for Air Force family housing by $7 million, approved 266–160 on June 20.

The Senate passed its $11.2 billion version of HR 1817 on July 21 by an 84–10 vote. The Senate Appropriations Committee had reported the bill on July 19 (S Rept 104-116).

The lone amendment on the floor came from Jeff Bingaman, D-N.M., who sought to cut $300 million from military con-

struction and family housing. Bingaman criticized the committee for adding $774 million in projects the Clinton administration had not requested, though he targeted less than half of that amount. Opponents saw the amendment as an attack on prized National Guard and reserve projects. The Senate appropriation of $445 million for those projects was $263 million more than requested and $160 million more than in the House bill. Senators voted 77–18 on July 21 to table (kill) the amendment.

CONFERENCE, MAJOR PROVISIONS

The House adopted the conference report (H Rept 104-247) by a vote of 326–98 on Sept. 20. The Senate agreed to the report, 86–14, on Sept. 22, clearing the bill. It was signed into law on Oct. 3.

The final bill's appropriation of $2.97 billion for military construction projects was nearly $300 million more than requested. The appropriation for the construction projects of the National Guard and reserves jumped from Clinton's request of $182 million to nearly $430 million in the final bill.

The conference bill provided $179 million more than Clinton requested for family housing, bringing the total appropriation to $4.3 billion. The final bill, like the House and Senate versions, provided exactly the $3.9 billion Clinton had requested for base closure and realignment, including $457 million for environmental cleanup at the facilities.

When the administration objected to the bill's overall total, David R. Obey, D-Wis., mounted an effort to cut it by $80 million, with an exemption for family housing and quality of life programs. But conferees rejected Obey's proposal.

A significant number of members' projects inserted into the bill survived the conference process. For example, a $10 million appropriation for a new runway at the Barstow-Daggett Airfield in California remained in the final bill, despite the Army's objections and the Senate's deletion of the money in its version. The new runway was to be used for troops rotating through the National Training Center at Fort Irwin. Two days before the negotiators completed the bill, Army Secretary Togo D. West Jr. told Congress that a review concluded that the preferred airfield for rotating the troops was Edwards Air Force Base. Nonetheless, the money remained in the bill for the project, which was scheduled to begin in 1997 and expected to cost $32 million.

Among the winning states in the final bill's funding were Montana, Hawaii and Nevada. All three states were well represented among appropriators: The Senate Appropriations Military Construction Subcommittee was chaired by Conrad Burns, R-Mont., and included Harry Reid, D-Nev., and Daniel K. Inouye, D-Hawaii. The chair of the House Appropriations Military Construction Subcommittee was Barbara F. Vucanovich, R-Nev. Kansas, home of Republican Majority Leader Bob Dole, also did well. ❑

1995 Supplemental Appropriations

Congress averted a crisis in the combat-readiness of U.S. forces by clearing in early April 1995 a $3.1 billion fiscal 1995 defense supplemental appropriations bill. The legislation (HR

889—PL 104-6) was to pay for unbudgeted military operations in Haiti, the Persian Gulf, the former Yugoslavia and elsewhere.

The Pentagon had warned for months that, unless the bill was enacted by the beginning of April, the armed services would have to begin canceling scheduled training exercises and maintenance work. Funds for those activities had been "borrowed" to cover the cost of the unbudgeted deployments.

The appropriations in the bill—$2.5 billion to cover peacekeeping and humanitarian operations and $561 million to fully fund a 2.6 percent military pay raise approved for fiscal 1995—were more than offset by rescissions in both defense and nondefense accounts.

Some in the new Republican majority in Congress used the bill to begin a furious debate over President Clinton's defense policies, including complaints that he had deployed troops to intervene in situations that were hardly crucial to U.S. interests. Their frustration was reflected in the conference report on HR 889, which stated: "Military deployments in support of peacekeeping or humanitarian objectives both merit and require advance approval by the Congress."

LEGISLATIVE ACTION

As part of his fiscal 1996 budget, submitted Feb. 6, 1995, Clinton asked Congress for a $2.56 billion peacekeeping supplemental. The proposed defense supplemental included $1.04 billion for operations in or near Iraq, $595 million for the U.S. occupation of Haiti, $367 million for costs related to Cuban and Haitian refugees and $312 million for operations in the former Yugoslavia. The administration asked for authorization to rescind $703 million in unspecified prior-year appropriations to partially offset the additional spending.

The House Appropriations Subcommittee on National Security acted even before Clinton submitted his request, approving a $3.2 billion version of the legislation in late January. The full House Appropriations Committee reported HR 889 on Feb. 10 (H Rept 104-29).

The bill allocated $2.54 billion for unbudgeted military operations and $670 million to further bolster readiness, while rescinding $1.8 billion in prior defense appropriations. The rescissions included programs canceled by the Pentagon as well as cuts in funding for such White House priorities as environmental cleanup at defense facilities and the Technology Reinvestment Program to develop dual-use technologies with both commercial and military applications. The bill also proposed rescissions in funding for the Nunn-Lugar program—a program named for Senate sponsors Sam Nunn, D-Ga., and Richard G. Lugar, R-Ind., that was aimed at eliminating the threat of nuclear and chemical weapons arsenals in the former Soviet Union—but the panel insisted that the cuts would not affect actual weapons dismantlement.

The House Appropriations Committee reported a second bill on Feb. 10 (HR 845—H Rept 104-30) rescinding an additional $1.4 billion in nondefense appropriations.

The House passed the $3.2 billion measure Feb. 22 by a vote of 262–165, after incorporating into the bill the cuts in HR 845, bringing the rescission total to $2.86 billion. Democratic at-

tempts to reduce spending in the bill and to require the rescissions to come entirely from the defense budget were rejected during House debate.

The Senate passed its version of HR 889 March 16 by a vote of 97–3. The bill, which had been reported by the Senate Appropriations Committee March 2 (S Rept 104-12), appropriated $1.94 billion in spending—less than two-thirds the amount approved by the House.

Senate appropriators insisted on offsetting all the additional defense spending by eliminating funds from the Pentagon's own accounts, instead of cutting domestic programs. A separate portion of the bill did rescind $1.5 billion from nondefense programs, but those savings were directed to deficit reduction.

Because the measure was considered a must-pass bill, it became a magnet in the Senate for unrelated issues ranging from strikers' rights to endangered species to debt relief for Jordan. The bill stalled for more than a week while Republicans maneuvered to use the legislation to overturn White House policies. *(Striker replacement, p. 672; endangered species, p. 458; Jordan debt relief, p. 249)*

The only amendment that would have substantially changed the bill was a proposal by John McCain, R-Ariz., to restore the funds cut by the House for environmental cleanup of defense facilities and to cut all funding for the Technology Reinvestment Program. The Senate rejected the amendment, 22–77, on March 7 and approved instead, by voice vote, a Jeff Bingaman, D-N.M., amendment endorsing the dual-use technology program.

CONFERENCE, MAJOR PROVISIONS

The House adopted the conference report (H Rept 104-101) on April 6 by a vote of 343–80, and the Senate cleared the bill by voice vote later the same day.

As signed into law April 10, HR 889:

• Included the entire $2.48 billion the Pentagon said was needed to pay for the unbudgeted peacekeeping and humanitarian operations in fiscal 1995. (Because of updated cost estimates, this was less than the original request.)

• Appropriated an additional $561 million for the Pentagon, most of it to fully fund the cost of the military pay raise, and to cover an increase in the cost of overseas operations as a result of the dollar's decline in value against key foreign currencies.

• Contained rescissions that more than offset the cost of the bill, reducing fiscal 1995 appropriations by a net total of $746 million. The final bill rescinded $2.36 billion from defense programs, including $300 million from the Technology Reinvestment Program and $20 million from the Nunn-Lugar program. The bill also rescinded $1.12 billion from nondefense programs, including $142 million from foreign aid projects and $200 million for environmental cleanup of nuclear weapons facilities managed by the Energy Department.

• Earmarked $360 million received from or promised by allied governments and the United Nations to help pay for the deployments.

• Prohibited any new credits to Mexico until the administration provided a broad array of documents to Congress. However, the language left it to the president to certify compliance. *(Mexico loan guarantees, p. 248)* ❏

1997 Defense Authorization

Congress in 1996 cleared a $265.6 billion fiscal 1997 defense authorization bill (HR 3230—PL 104-201). The bill added $11.2 billion to President Clinton's budget request, $8.6 billion of which was to go to military procurement and research accounts.

Unlike past bills that had become battlegrounds over the direction of U.S. defense policy and specific weapons systems, HR 3230 essentially provided more generous funding for Clinton's defense program. The more notable additions included increases in funding for antimissile defense and for programs to forestall terrorist attacks using chemical, biological or nuclear weapons.

Controversial issues that had doomed the previous year's defense authorization—deployment of an antimissile defense system by 2003 and limits on the president's authority to place U.S. troops under foreign command—were raised in separate bills. Republican leaders chose this strategy to highlight the issues without risking the authorization bill. *(Antimissile defenses, p. 316; U.N. command, p. 318)*

Despite earlier veto threats over the increased funding, Clinton signed HR 3230 into law. This was attributed, in part, to election-year politics: Much of the added weapons funding would go to the vote-rich states of Texas and California, plus vetoing a defense bill might have given Republicans an opportunity to draw attention to Clinton's past clashes with the military establishment, including his avoidance of military service during the Vietnam War.

Conferees also made the final bill more palatable to the administration by dropping several GOP-sponsored social policy initiatives, including provisions dealing with HIV-positive and gay service members. But conferees dropped an abortion provision supported by Clinton.

The final bill also included a 3 percent military pay raise, as requested.

CLINTON BUDGET

In the budget he submitted to Congress on March 19, 1996, Clinton requested $254.4 billion in new budget authority—the amount appropriated—for defense in fiscal 1997. This represented an inflation-adjusted decline of about 6 percent from the fiscal 1996 level.

The vast bulk of the request—$243.4 billion—was earmarked for military operations of the Defense Department. Another $10.9 billion was requested for defense-related programs conducted by the Energy Department, most of which dealt with nuclear weapons, nuclear power plants for warships, and environmental cleanup at defense nuclear facilities. The balance of the national defense budget request was for miscellaneous programs.

The Defense Department request was part of Clinton's six-year plan to appropriate $1.6 billion for Pentagon activities in fiscal 1997–2002. That plan would end the contraction of the U.S. defense establishment that began in 1989, leaving a force of about 1.4 million active-duty personnel—roughly two-thirds as large as the force was at its cold war peak. The administration contended that this smaller force, provided it was kept combat-ready and equipped with modern weapons, could meet the goal of winning two regional wars that broke out several weeks apart in areas that were distant from each other and from the United States.

After dropping 6 percent in fiscal 1997, Clinton's plan called for the Pentagon budget to drop in real terms by an additional 0.2 percent in 1998 and hold constant in 1999. Pentagon purchasing power then would increase at a slow pace: up 0.5 percent in fiscal 2000, 0.6 percent in 2001 and 0.2 percent in 2002.

Many congressional Republicans maintained that Clinton's plan would shrink the military too much and that the out-year increases would never materialize. Moreover, top Pentagon officials and some defense-minded Democrats wondered whether the plan could survive the pressure for deficit reduction.

Prominent defense specialists in both parties wanted to see the past decade's sharp drop in weapons spending quickly reversed. Joint Chiefs of Staff Chairman Gen. John M. Shalikashvili called for the annual procurement budget to rise to $60 billion by fiscal 1998, three years before Clinton's plan would hit that benchmark.

BUDGET RESOLUTION

Congressional Republicans had hoped to add as much as $13 billion to Clinton's proposed budget but in the end settled for the $11.2 billion increase.

Congress in June approved a fiscal 1997 budget resolution (H Con Res 178) calling for $265.6 billion in budget authority for defense. The House adopted the conference report (H Rept 104-612) on June 12, and the Senate agreed to it the next day. *(1997 budget resolution, p. 73)*

HOUSE COMMITTEE ACTION

The House National Security Committee reported a $266.7 billion authorization bill (HR 3230—H Rept 104-563) on May 7, 1996.

The Republican majority blasted Clinton's defense budget as being dangerously stingy on several fronts: eroding morale by stinting on quality-of-life improvements, undermining combat-readiness, and risking the technological edge that U.S. forces enjoyed over potential adversaries.

The bulk of the increase approved by the committee—$7.5 billion—was to go toward procuring weapons and other hardware. The rest of the increased funding would be spread across several accounts, including military housing.

In its report on the bill, the House committee charged that the president's $39 billion budget for procurement was the lowest in nearly 50 years. To beef up weapons programs, the National Security Committee in general boosted the amounts Clinton had budgeted to develop a new generation of equipment and to update existing hardware with new technologies, but it also added funds to buy more copies of weapons already in service.

The Army's helicopter programs typified this approach. The House panel added $50 million to Clinton's $289 million request for a new generation of Army helicopters, the Comanche scout, which had a "stealth" design intended to evade radar detection. It also provided $260 million to buy 12 new upgraded Apache helicopters, in addition to Clinton's request for $379 million to modify 26 existing Apaches with the Longbow radar. Longbow was intended to find targets in rain or fog that would blind the Apache's infrared TV camera. Another $181 million was added to upgrade 24 of the Army's older scout helicopters with guided missiles and target-finding electronics, pending deployment of the Comanche sometime in the next decade. Both the Bush and Clinton administrations had tried unsuccessfully to terminate this upgrade program.

The House committee significantly increased spending on missile defense programs. The administration had requested $2.8 billion, to which the panel added $725 million. Funds were also authorized for two additional F-15 and two more F-16 fighters beyond the four of each requested.

But defense spending issues were nearly eclipsed by social issues. The committee attached to HR 3230 two amendments sought by Robert K. Dornan, R-Calif. One would have required that service members with less than 15 years of service who had HIV, the virus that causes acquired immune deficiency syndrome (AIDS), be discharged from the military. The same provision had been included in the fiscal 1996 defense authorization (S 1124) but repealed as part of a fiscal 1996 omnibus appropriations bill (HR 3019—PL 104-134), which cleared April 25. The second Dornan amendment included in HR 3230 would have overturned the policy prohibiting homosexual conduct by military personnel but preventing recruiters from asking service applicants if they were gay—the "don't ask, don't tell" policy—and replaced it with an outright ban. *(1996 defense authorization, p.294; gays in the military, p. 284)*

The committee bill also barred the sale of "lascivious" magazines or videotapes on U.S. military bases.

HOUSE FLOOR ACTION

The House passed HR 3230 on May 15 by a vote of 272–153, after a brief debate. The $266.7 billion bill would have added $12.4 billion to Clinton's request, prompting a veto threat from the Office of Management and Budget.

But National Security Committee Chairman Floyd D. Spence, R-S.C., and his allies brushed aside the administration's warnings, contending that Clinton was making the Pentagon do too much with too little, thus undermining its ability to deal with potentially serious threats on the horizon. They hammered away at General Shalikashvili's call for a substantially higher procurement budget than Clinton had proposed.

The rule governing debate disallowed consideration of five amendments that would have reduced the bill's overall authorization, and no amendments challenging the bill's additions to specific programs were offered.

The most contentious issue during the floor debate was whether female service members and military dependents stationed overseas should be allowed to have abortions in U.S. military hospitals, provided they paid for the procedure. A ban on such abortions, which had been in effect from 1988 until Clinton rescinded it in 1993 in one of his first official acts as president, had been reinstated and written into permanent law by the fiscal 1996 defense authorization bill. The House on May 14 rejected by a vote of 192–225 an amendment to HR 3230 by Rosa DeLauro, D-Conn., that would have repealed the ban.

On May 15, the House rejected, 202–220, an amendment by Gerald B. H. Solomon, R-N.Y., that would have effectively barred assistance to Russia and Belarus under the Nunn-Lugar program, which was intended to help former Soviet states dismantle their nuclear, chemical and biological weapons establishments. The program was named for Sens. Sam Nunn, D-Ga., and Richard G. Lugar, R-Ind. After defeating the Solomon amendment, the House May 15 adopted, 249–171, an amendment by Benjamin A. Gilman, R-N.Y., that would have barred Nunn-Lugar recipient countries from using any appropriated funds for the conversion of defense plants in former Soviet states to civilian production.

The House adopted, 353–62, on May 14 an amendment by a bipartisan group led by Christopher Shays, R-Conn., to direct the president to try to make U.S. allies in Europe pay a larger share of the cost of mutual defense efforts. Unlike previous burden-sharing amendments adopted by the House, this version would not have required the president to reduce the number of U.S. troops deployed in any country that did not comply with the request and would have allowed an allied country to meet the amendment's goal by increasing its contribution to U.N. peacekeeping operations or to foreign aid.

Among several en bloc amendments adopted on the floor was one by Edward J. Markey, D-Mass., expressing the sense of Congress that Clinton should have invoked economic sanctions against China because it sold nuclear weapons-related equipment to Pakistan. *(China policy, p. 178)*

SENATE COMMITTEE ACTION

The Senate Armed Services Committee reported a $267.3 billion defense authorization bill (S 1745—S Rept 104-267) on May 13. The bill was reported by the Senate Intelligence Committee on June 11 (S Rept 104-278).

The committee bill increased overall defense spending by nearly $13 billion, $7.7 billion of which would go toward procuring weapons and other hardware. Like its House counterpart, the Senate panel took the general approach of boosting funding for new equipment and upgrades, as well as for more copies of existing weapons. The Senate bill, for example, added $100 million for the Comanche scout helicopter and $183 million for six additional upgraded Apaches, along with $158 million to continue upgrading the existing scout helicopter force.

The bill added $856 million to the administration's request for antimissile defense. The Armed Services Committee authorized the administration's $3.4 billion request for four of the Navy's *Arleigh Burke*-class destroyers, as the House committee had, but the Senate panel also added another $750 million for advance procurement of more destroyers in future years. The committee funded eight Air Force F-16 fighters—two more than the House committee approved and four more than requested. Unlike the House measure, the Senate bill added $234 million for six Navy F/A-18C/D fighters, although the administration requested none of the planes.

The Senate Armed Services Committee took a far less confrontational approach on social issues, either ignoring them entirely or preempting provisions approved by the House panel. For instance, the committee approved language mandating that HIV-positive personnel be treated in the same manner as other service personnel with medical conditions that prevented them from being deployed.

The Senate bill repealed, as requested, many of the provisions of the fiscal 1996 defense bill that made it more difficult to declare dead those military personnel missing in action (MIA). The House bill contained no such provision. The 1996 provisions were rooted in allegations by family members that the Pentagon was improperly withholding information about MIAs.

SENATE FLOOR ACTION

S 1745 was passed by a vote of 68–31 on July 10. The Senate then passed HR 3230 by voice vote, after substituting the provisions of S 1745.

The Senate-passed bill authorized $265.6 billion for defense programs, $1.7 billion less than approved in committee. By a vote of 100–0 on June 26, the Senate had approved that reduction in an amendment by Armed Services Committee Chairman Strom Thurmond, R-S.C., to bring the bill in line with the ceiling set by the congressional budget resolution (H Con Res 178). Three other amendments that would have made larger reductions in the authorization were rejected.

The Senate avoided a clash over antiballistic missile (ABM) defenses, when it adopted by voice vote two amendments, offered by Majority Leader Trent Lott, R-Miss., containing a delicate compromise diluting Republican restrictions on ABM negotiations with Russia. One GOP provision would have stipulated rules for distinguishing between missiles designed to defend national territory—severely limited by the 1972 ABM Treaty—and theater defenses to protect forces in the field. Some Republican leaders warned that Clinton might make concessions that would impede development of some U.S. theater-defense weapons. The second provision would have barred the administration from agreeing to make Belarus, Ukraine and Kazakhstan parties to the ABM Treaty unless the Senate approved the change, which would have required a two-thirds majority. Republicans, intent on amending the ABM pact to liberalize some of its restrictions on antimissile deployments, feared that the addition of other countries would make it harder to negotiate those changes.

In return, Democrats agreed to end a filibuster and let the Senate debate a GOP bill mandating deployment by 2003 of a nationwide antimissile defense system. Democrats also won assurances from Lott that the Senate would act on a treaty to outlaw chemical weapons. *(Antimissile defense legislation, p. 316; chemical weapons treaty, p. 321)*

In other action on antimissile defense, the Senate on June 19 rejected, 44–53, a Byron L. Dorgan, D-N.D., amendment to eliminate $300 million added in committee to the $508 million Clinton requested to develop an antimissile defense system for U.S. territory. By a vote of 52–46 that same day, the Senate tabled (killed) a Jeff Bingaman, D-N.M., amendment eliminating committee provisions intended to mandate development of an antisatellite missile.

The Senate on June 26 tabled, by a vote of 53–45, an amendment by Jon Kyl, R-Ariz., and Harry Reid, D-Nev., that would have extended the president's authority to order some underground nuclear weapons tests until a test-ban treaty, under negotiation at that time, went into effect. His authority for the tests was to expire Sept. 30, 1996.

On June 27, two days after a truck bomb killed 19 Americans at a Saudi Arabian air base, the Senate adopted 96–0 an amendment aimed at preventing terrorist assaults in the United States with nuclear, chemical or biological weapons and at helping cities deal with such attacks if they occurred. The amendment, sponsored by Nunn, Lugar and Pete V. Domenici, R-N.M., provided $235 million for counterterrorism. It authorized the Defense and Energy departments, under some circumstances, to respond to a domestic terrorist attack that employed weapons of mass destruction and to spend up to $80 million to help police, fire and emergency medical service agencies prepare for such an attack. House conservatives had knocked a similar provision out of antiterrorism legislation (PL 104-132) enacted earlier in 1996. The amendment also permitted $94 million to be spent to expand the scope of the Nunn-Lugar program to include activities such as disposing of spent nuclear fuel from Russian warships and rebuilding some nuclear power plants so they could not produce radioactive material for use in weapons production. *(Antiterrorism bill, p. 727; Saudi Arabia bombing, p. 323)*

By a vote of 97–0, the Senate on June 28 approved another Nunn amendment, requiring the president to report on the costs and benefits of extending North Atlantic Treaty Organization (NATO) membership to Eastern European states formerly part of the Soviet Union.

Abortion rights proponents won a round June 19 when the Senate rejected, 45–51, a motion to table an amendment by Patty Murray, D-Wash., to repeal the ban on most abortions at military hospitals overseas. Murray's amendment was then adopted by voice vote.

Two amendments adopted by voice vote resolved, at least temporarily, hard-fought battles that crossed party and ideological lines. One amendment by Idaho Republican Larry E. Craig, adopted June 20, would have speeded the opening of the Waste Isolation Pilot Project (WIPP), a huge, underground storage site in New Mexico intended to hold radioactive waste from the Energy Department's nuclear weapons plants.

The other amendment, offered by Thurmond and adopted June 26, marked a truce in a months-long turf battle between the Senate Armed Services and Select Intelligence committees. The Intelligence panel had recommended giving the director of central intelligence more authority over intelligence organizations within the Defense Department. The compromise, instead, left the secretary of defense in charge of those organizations but allowed the director of central intelligence to have a say in the annual evaluations of the directors of those agencies. It also created a new National Imagery and Mapping Agency, consolidating mapmaking and satellite photo-interpretation jobs being performed by several agencies. *(Intelligence community overhaul, p. 245)*

In other action, the Senate by a vote of 100–0 on June 25 approved a Joseph I. Lieberman, D-Conn., amendment establishing a commission to study national security needs.

CONFERENCE ACTION

The House adopted the conference report on HR 3230 (H Rept 104-724) Aug. 1 by a vote of 285–132. The Senate adopted it Sept. 10 by a vote of 73–26, clearing the bill for the president.

The final bill reflected both a GOP determination to increase Clinton's defense budget and a broader, bipartisan consensus that any increase should be used to speed the production of existing weapons and to develop new ones.

Conferees added $914 million to Clinton's $2.8 billion funding request for antimissile defenses. The authorization to develop a national defense system intended to protect U.S. territory against a small number of ballistic missiles was increased from the $508 million requested to $858 million. The report also increased funding for two long-range defenses against theater missiles fired at U.S. troops or allies abroad.

Conferees dropped provisions intended to force the president to seek Senate approval, with a two-thirds majority, before agreeing to two modifications to the ABM Treaty, changes under negotiation with Russia and other former Soviet states. One of those changes would have specified "demarcation" rules for distinguishing between national missile defenses, which were stringently limited by the treaty, and theater defenses, which were not. The other change would have made Belarus, Ukraine and Kazakhstan parties to the treaty in addition to Russia, which at that time was the only former Soviet republic recognized to have inherited Soviet obligations under the treaty. In explaining their decision to drop the ABM Treaty provisions, conferees argued that administration officials had, in effect, conceded that the Senate would have to approve any demarcation agreement. And they also included in the report an extended argument that Clinton already was legally required to obtain Senate approval for any agreement that would extend the treaty to cover former Soviet states other than Russia.

Conferees jettisoned several contentious social policies from the defense bill, among them the House initiative that would have required the discharge of most service personnel testing positive for the AIDS virus and another that would have repealed the "don't ask, don't tell" policy toward homosexuals in the armed services. Also dropped was the Senate provision repealing the abortion ban.

However, conferees left in the bill a few politically charged policy initiatives, including an authorization for military forces to respond to domestic terrorist attacks under certain circumstances, a ban on the sale of erotic magazines and videos on military bases, and the repeal of several provisions of law imposing

procedural restrictions on the Pentagon's ability to declare dead those personnel missing in action.

Conferees rejected a Senate provision to increase from 40 percent to 50 percent the proportion of major equipment overhauls that could be performed by private contractors instead of government-owned repair depots. Proponents of the public depots were hopeful that the conference action would block an administration plan for a major shift of overhaul work to outside contractors. *(Maintenance depots, box, p. 310)*

MAJOR PROVISIONS

As signed into law Sept. 23, HR 3230 authorized $265.6 billion in defense spending for fiscal 1997, $11.2 billion more than requested. The House version had authorized $266.7 billion; the Senate version, $265.6 billion.

Major provisions of the final bill:

Antimissile Defenses

Authorized $3.7 billion for antimissile defenses, compared with the $2.8 billion requested by Clinton. The plan included the development of a national defense system that could be in place by 2003 to protect U.S. territory from a limited number of attacking missiles. The bill provided $858 million for this system, compared with $508 million requested by Clinton.

• Increased the authorization for two long-range defenses against theater missiles fired at U.S. troops or allies abroad, adding $140 million to the $482 million requested for the Army's Theater High-Altitude Air Defense (THAAD) program and $246 million to the $58 million requested for the Navy's Upper Tier system.

Ground Combat

Authorized $339 million, $50 million more than requested, to continue developing the missile-armed Comanche scout helicopter.

• Authorized $464 million, as requested, to upgrade existing M-1 tanks with digital communications and electronics for night fighting. The bill also earmarked $10 million to develop an auxiliary power unit so the tank's crew could use the electronic gear without running the vehicle's fuel-guzzling turbine engine.

• Authorized $192 million to speed up the modification of Bradley armored troop carriers with digital links and night-vision gear, instead of the $134 million requested.

• Authorized $162 million, as requested, plus an additional $34 million to accelerate the production of Javelin shoulder-fired antitank missiles.

• Authorized $162 million, instead of the $93 million requested, to continue production of ATACMS artillery rockets, with a range of upwards of 100 miles.

• Authorized $146 million, $83 million more than requested, to equip National Guard units with shorter-range MLRS rockets; and $106 million, an increase of $31 million, to supply them with the Paladin cannon.

• Authorized $79 million instead of the $28 million requested for rifles, machine guns and grenade launchers.

MAINTENANCE DEPOTS

A Pentagon plan to rely more on private companies for routine maintenance of vehicles and equipment ran into vehement opposition in 1996 from members of Congress representing areas with large government-owned depots.

Of the roughly $13 billion worth of depot maintenance the Pentagon would pay for in fiscal 1997—top-to-bottom overhauls of ships, planes, vehicles, engines and electronic equipment—about two-thirds of the work was performed by some 89,000 public employees in 17 large depots and several smaller sites. The balance of the work was contracted out to some 1,300 private companies of various sizes.

Under the proposed policy change, announced April 4, 1996, the public and private sectors would have roughly equal shares of the workload by fiscal 2001. Anticipated savings from the change were a key element in Defense Secretary William J. Perry's plan to squeeze money out of other parts of the Pentagon budget so he could boost by nearly 50 percent spending for new weapons.

Before the Pentagon could reallocate its overhaul work as planned, Congress had to repeal two laws:

• One required that no less than 60 percent of each year's depot-maintenance workload be performed by federal employees.

• The other required competitive bidding between a private firm and a government depot for any package of overhaul work worth more than $3 billion. The Pentagon insisted that such public-private competitions were inherently biased toward public facilities, because they enjoyed various subsidies that were costs to the government even though they did not show up in the bottom line of a depot's contract bid.

Although Congress had strongly supported the general thrust of Pentagon hopes to rely more on outside contractors, depot maintenance was a tougher issue, politically. Existing government depots were vital to local economies and were represented by members of Congress who sat on committees that oversaw the Pentagon budget.

Critics of the Pentagon plan warned that private companies might not be responsive to military exigencies or could be disrupted by labor disputes or bankruptcies. They also cautioned that the process could be tailored to political ends, citing President Clinton's response to the Base Realignment and Closure Commission's 1995 decision to eliminate Air Force depots in California and Texas. Instead of shuttering the two bases and transferring their work to other depots, Clinton told the Pentagon to encourage private contractors to bid on the work at or near the bases, potentially saving jobs in the two vote-rich states. *(Military base closings, p. 319)*

During consideration of the fiscal 1997 defense authorization bill (HR 3230), the Senate Armed Services and House National Security committees squared off over the issue. The Senate panel approved legislation that, instead of repealing the so-called 60-40 requirement, amended the law to require that at least 50 percent of the work would go to public depots. This would have given the Pentagon roughly enough leeway to carry out its proposed shift. The House committee, a bastion of support for the public depots, sustained the 60-40 rule, rejecting the proposed repeal by a margin of more than two-to-one. The House position prevailed, when conferees dropped the Senate provision from the final version of the bill.

• Authorized $149 million, in addition to the $493 million requested, for trucks and jeep-like "Humvees."

• Authorized $67 million, on top of the $112 million requested, for night-vision equipment.

• Added funds to research programs aimed at problems that were drawing increased attention in the post-cold war world. For instance, $29 million was added to the $44 million requested to develop improved land mine detection equipment.

Air Combat

Both chambers had approved, essentially unchanged, the amounts requested for new types of combat jets:

• Authorized $2.2 billion for the first dozen production-line copies of a new version of the Navy's F/A-18, enlarged to give it longer range.

• Authorized $2 billion to continue development of the Air Force's F-22 fighter.

• Authorized $602 million to develop the Joint Strike Fighter.

• Added $234 million to buy six of the existing model F/A-18s, to bolster the force pending arrival of various new types of combat jets.

• Authorized $257 million for six F-15s, an increase of two planes ($71 million).

• Authorized $155 million for six F-16s, an increase of two planes ($49 million).

• Authorized $373 million to equip 12 of the Marine Corps Harrier vertical takeoff jets with radars and more powerful engines, an increase of two planes ($68 million).

• Authorized $234 million to rebuild Prowler electronic warfare planes and develop new radar jammers for them, an addition of $133 million.

• Added 100 weapons ($22 million) to the administration's request for $227 million to buy more than 1,400 super-accurate "smart bombs." The bill also added $114 million for 275 air-launched guided missiles of various types with ranges of up to several hundred miles.

• Authorized $166 million to upgrade B-1 bombers, an increase of $82 million, and $740 million to develop modifications for B-2 stealth bombers, an increase of $212 million. Conferees had complained that the Pentagon was moving too slowly in adapting long-range bombers, designed to carry nuclear weapons, to carry smart bombs instead.

• Authorized $89 million, as requested, for 120 additional Tomahawk long-range, ship-launched cruise missiles. The bill also added $55 million to renovate older Tomahawks already in the inventory.

Naval Combat

Authorized the $699 million requested to complete the third and last *Seawolf*-class sub.

• Authorized $997 million for components to be used in the first two ships of a new class of smaller, cheaper subs. The administration had requested $296 million of that and planned to request about $2 billion more for the first of these new subs in fiscal 1998. But the bill had added the extra $701 million for advance parts to be used in a second sub of the new class scheduled for the fiscal 1999 budget. The bill also added $98 million to develop new technologies that could be incorporated into the first four ships of the new class.

• Authorized the $3.4 billion requested for four destroyers equipped with the Aegis system. But the bill also added $525 million to buy components for 12 more ships, to be bought at a rate of three per year in fiscal 1998–2001.

• Authorized, as requested, $25 million to begin work on a new type of warship, a highly automated missile carrier called an arsenal ship.

• Added $12 million to modify shipborne radars to better detect planes flying at low altitude over nearby land; $98 million beyond the $71 million requested, for various submarine detection devices; $26 million, added to $23 million requested, to upgrade minesweeping ships; and added $10 million to the $15 million requested to conduct a competition between systems for a helicopter-borne laser to detect underwater mines.

• Added $99 million for two oceanographic research ships.

Electronic Links

A prime beneficiary of the bill's added funding was the Pentagon's effort to leverage its high-tech weaponry by plugging combat units into a dense electronic information web. The goal was to give U.S. forces superior "battlefield awareness"—a shared image of friendly and enemy forces that U.S. commanders could use to strike an enemy's weakest points. The largest single addition in this category was $210 million for a third Joint STARS radar plane, in addition to the two requested. The Air Force had listed a second pair as its top priority for any congressional funding increases. The conferees authorized only one of those two additional planes.

Other reconnaissance aircraft programs accounted for a large slice of the congressional largess, including additions of:

• $93 million to replace the engines on AWACS radar planes, which were designed to locate distant aerial targets.

• $204 million, on top of $65 million requested, for electronic eavesdropping planes. The additional funds would buy one more jetliner to be converted to this role and begin replacing engines on the planes already in service.

• $108 million, in addition to the $759 million requested, to develop and procure other types of spy planes, including drones.

Other related additions included:

• $12 million, in addition to the $110 million requested, to develop the Army's network of digital communication links among front-line units.

• $20 million, in addition to the $48 million requested, to equip Army units with radios that automatically reported their position to headquarters.

• $35 million, in addition to the $174 million requested, for the Navy's counterpart of Army "digitization"—a system that would allow any ship or plane in a fleet to shoot accurately at a target detected by the radar of any one of them.

Air and Sea Transport

Authorized $2.38 billion for the C-17 transport program. This included $234 million for a ninth plane, in addition to the $2.14 billion requested to buy eight C-17s, support equipment and components that would be used in planes to be bought later.

• Authorized $660 million for 13 C-130 Hercules cargo planes of various models, compared with the $63 million requested for one C-130. The planes, built in Georgia by Lockheed-Martin, had been the mainstay of the Pentagon's medium-range airlift fleet for nearly 40 years. Four of the added planes were earmarked for the Air National Guard, part of a $780 million package of equipment the conferees added to the bill for the politically influential Guard and reserve forces. That total did not include $114 million added for artillery rockets and cannon that would go to the Guard.

• Authorized $1.47 billion for development and purchase of the V-22 Osprey. The administration requested $501 million to buy four Ospreys and $58 million for components to be used in future purchases. The conferees added $232 million for two additional aircraft and another $70 million for components.

• Added $20 million to the $40 million requested to develop for the Marine Corps an armored troop carrier that could "swim" ashore from transport ships at upwards of 25 mph, three times the speed of its existing troop carrier.

• Authorized $604 million, as requested, for two large cargo ships to haul the tanks and other heavy equipment of an Army division from U.S. ports to distant trouble spots. The conferees also approved $240 million to either build two similar ships to carry Marine Corps equipment or buy two commercial ships and modify them for the Marines.

Personnel Issues

Authorized $70 billion for military personnel expenses. The president's budget had included $69.8 billion.

• Approved the administration's request for a ceiling of 1.46 million active-duty personnel. It barred some proposed reductions in the size of Air National Guard and Navy air squadrons and, accordingly, approved a Guard and reserve ceiling of about 911,000 personnel, slightly higher than was requested.

• Included Clinton's proposed 3 percent military pay raise and a 4.6 percent increase in the tax-free allowance paid to service members who did not live in government housing.

Operations and Maintenance

Authorized $89.9 billion, $1 billion more than requested, for operations and maintenance costs.

Other Provisions

Limited government reimbursement of companies' executive compensation to $250,000 per executive. The provision was included over the objections of the Pentagon and defense contractors.

• Allowed the Pentagon, in many cases, to waive "buy America" laws so it could buy equipment manufactured in allied countries.

• Added $201 million to beef up Pentagon programs designed to forestall terrorist attacks using chemical, biological or nuclear weapons. Military forces were authorized, under certain circumstances, to respond to a domestic terrorist attack that employed weapons of mass destruction.

• Repealed several provisions of the fiscal 1996 defense authorization bill (S 1124—PL 104-106) that imposed procedural restrictions on the Pentagon's ability to declare dead those personnel missing in action (MIA). The bill repealed a requirement for a triennial board of inquiry and the imposition of criminal penalties for withholding information. The bill also gave a unit commander 10 days to report any MIA to the service secretary, eliminating the theater commander from the reporting chain.

• Barred the sale of erotic magazines and videos on military bases.   ❑

1997 Defense Appropriations

Congress in 1996 cleared a $244.3 billion fiscal 1997 defense appropriations bill (HR 3610—PL 104-208). Despite veto threats over the bill's $9.7 billion addition to the administration's budget request, President Clinton signed the bill.

HR 3610 closely tracked the fiscal 1997 defense authorization bill (HR 3230—PL 104-201). Except for an effort to speed deployment of some antimissile defenses, most of the added funds were spread across a wide range of weapons procurement and research and development programs. *(1997 defense authorization, p. 306)*

In the rush to adjourn so members could go home to campaign for the November elections, HR 3610 was transformed into an omnibus appropriations bill. Five other appropriations bills, plus an immigration bill and miscellaneous spending, were folded into the defense bill's conference report before it cleared. *(Omnibus appropriations bill, p. 76)*

In addition to the defense funding in HR 3610, the fiscal 1997 defense budget also included nearly $10 billion in the fiscal 1997 military construction appropriations bill (HR 3517—PL 104-196) and $11.3 billion in the fiscal 1997 energy and water appropriations bill (HR 3816—PL 104-206) for defense-related nuclear programs. *(1997 military construction appropriations, p. 314)*

HOUSE ACTION

The House passed HR 3610 on June 13, 1996, by a vote of 278–126. The bill had been reported by the House Appropriations Committee on June 11 (H Rept 104-617).

The House-passed bill appropriated $245.2 billion for defense programs, $10.6 billion more than Clinton had requested. As in the companion defense authorization bill, most of the additional funds were earmarked to speed up production of weapons and other equipment and were allocated largely in accord with the armed services' recommendations as to how additional money should be spent.

In its report accompanying the bill, the Appropriations Committee contended that its increase simply made up some of the shortfall in Clinton's budget. The committee thought that Clinton underfunded the services even as he sent U.S. forces on nontraditional missions, covering the funding gap by stinting on weapons programs that the troops would depend on a decade from then.

Among the bill's major add-ons was $704 million for missile defense; Clinton had requested $2.8 billion. Within that total, the House added $350 million to develop a system that could be deployed by 2003 to protect U.S. territory against a limited number of attacking missiles. Authorization for the stepped-up program was included in the defense authorization bill and in separate legislation (HR 3144). *(Antimissile defense bill, p. 316)*

The only major weapons program to be significantly cut was the Navy's $3.4 billion request for four destroyers, from the which the House sliced one ship ($750 million).

During June 13 floor action, the House voted 396–25 to adopt an amendment by National Security Appropriations Subcommittee Chairman C. W. Bill Young, R-Fla., to cut $508 million from the bill, to bring it in line with the defense ceiling set by the fiscal 1997 budget resolution (H Con Res 178). *(1997 budget resolution, p. 73)*

But an attempt to freeze defense spending at the level of the fiscal 1996 defense appropriations bill (PL 104-61)—approximately $243 billion—was rejected June 13 by a **key vote of 194–219 (R 60–161; D 133–58; I 1–0)**. The amendment, offered by Connecticut Republican Christopher Shays and Massachusetts Democrat Barney Frank, had supporters on both sides of the aisle who warned that protecting the Pentagon from the budget squeeze that was hitting all other federal programs would undermine Congress's ability to deal with the more immediate threat of the deficit. *(1996 key votes, p. 1047)*

Appropriations Committee Chairman Robert L. Livingston, R-La., however, insisted that his committee's increase was an essential correction to Clinton's too-stingy request. By accelerating planned purchases, the Appropriations panel argued, some of its add-ons would allow contractors to build equipment at more efficient production rates, thus reducing costs in the long run.

Most other attempts to cut back on the bill's appropriations were defeated as well. The House June 13 rejected, 148–265, an amendment by Patricia Schroeder, D-Colo., that would have sliced $6.5 billion from the bill, reducing it to the level of defense spending recommended by the "Blue Dog" coalition of fiscally conservative Democrats. Senior House Appropriations Committee Democrat David R. Obey of Wisconsin was rebuffed on a series of amendments he offered to cut specific programs.

By a vote of 190–208, the House June 13 rejected an amendment by Peter A. DeFazio, D-Ore., stipulating that none of the $858 million included in the bill to develop an antimissile defense of U.S. territory could be used for space-based antimissile weapons. Before it was voted on, the proposal was amended by Norm Dicks, D-Wash., to specify that the ban applied only to the procurement of space weapons and would not interfere with research.

SENATE ACTION

The Senate passed HR 3610 on July 18 by a vote of 72–27, after substituting the text of its version (S 1894). The Senate Appropriations Committee had reported S 1894 on June 20 (S Rept 104-286).

Although some of the provisions the administration found objectionable in the House-passed bill were dropped, the Senate's $244.7 billion bill was still more than $10 billion higher than Clinton's request. The lion's share of the increased funding was steered to procurement and research accounts, as it was in the House version and the companion defense authorization. Like the House, the Senate disregarded veto threats from the Office of Management and Budget and passed its bill.

For procurement and development related to antimissile defenses, the bill provided $3.65 billion—$856 million more than Clinton requested. Within this, the Senate added $300 million for a national defense system that could be deployed by 2003. The Senate bill also restored the funding for a fourth Navy destroyer, which the House bill had cut, and added $525 million for components to be used in destroyers that would be requested in future budgets.

During floor action, the Senate rejected the only two amendments that would have significantly trimmed major additions to the bill. By a vote of 58–41 on July 18, the Senate tabled (killed) a Carl Levin, D-Mich., amendment to cut from the bill $48 million for two F-16 fighters. The budget requested four of the planes and the Air Force had asked for two more, but the Senate appropriated (and authorized) eight. By a vote of 44–56, the Senate on July 17 rejected a Dale Bumpers, D-Ark., amendment to cut $234 million for six of the 12 F/A-18 Navy and Marine fighters the bill would add. None was requested, but six were approved in the Senate authorization bill.

With the Pentagon scrambling to better protect U.S. troops overseas from terrorism—particularly in the wake of a June 25 terrorist attack in Saudi Arabia that killed 19 U.S. service members—the Senate on July 17 added a wide range of antiterrorist initiatives to the bill. By voice vote, the Senate approved amendments by John McCain, R-Ariz., and Levin that required a security audit of all U.S. bases and earmarked $14 million for stepped-up protection measures. By a vote of 100–0, the Senate adopted an amendment by Sam Nunn, D-Ga., Richard G. Lugar, R-Ind., and Pete V. Domenici, R-N.M., that earmarked $150 million for initiatives designed to prevent terrorist attacks in the United States with nuclear, chemical or biological weapons and to help U.S. cities cope with such attacks if they occurred. The amendment funded the Pentagon's share of programs authorized by a Nunn-Lugar-Domenici amendment to

the Senate's defense authorization bill. *(Saudi Arabia bombing, p. 323)*

CONFERENCE ACTION

The House agreed to the conference report on HR 3610 (H Rept 104-863) on Sept. 28 by a vote of 370–37. The Senate adopted the report by voice vote on Sept. 30.

Although Senate-House conferees had finished hammering out a compromise version of HR 3610 in mid-September, they waited more than two weeks before filing the conference report. By the time it was filed, it had become the legislative vehicle on which the White House and congressional leaders piled five other unfinished appropriations bills, among other items.

In the course of those negotiations, the White House pressed Congress to shift at least $1 billion from the defense side of the ledger to the domestic programs for which Clinton was demanding more funds. Ultimately, the defense portion of the conference report remained essentially intact. But within the budget resolution's overall limit on appropriations, some spending room was—in effect—transferred from defense to domestic programs, without any defense programs being significantly cut. These shifts included:

• Nearly $700 million, the amount by which the conference report fell short of the ceiling on defense spending set by the budget resolution (H Con Res 178).

• $137 million appropriated in previous defense bills that had not been spent.

In addition, the conference report levied a 2 percent across-the-board cut on all research and development programs except those related to antimissile defense, thus reducing the cost of the bill by $681 million. The bill also included $352 million for the Pentagon's share of an antiterrorism package Clinton unveiled Sept. 9. The initiative's cost was covered by another across-the-board cut that deducted $231 million from all programs in the bill and by rescinding $123 million in unspent prior-year appropriations. *(Antiterrorism, p. 727)*

This maneuvering resulted in a $244.3 billion bill instead of the $245 billion measure initially approved by conferees.

MAJOR PROVISIONS

As signed into law Sept. 30, HR 3610 appropriated $244.3 billion, about $900 million less than approved by the House and $400 million less than approved by the Senate. Funding included:

• $70 billion for military personnel costs. The bill funded an active-duty force of 1.46 million members, which was a reduction of about 24,000 members from the fiscal 1996 level, only 366 more personnel than requested. It also funded a National Guard and reserve force of nearly 903,000 members, which was almost 1,900 members more than the administration proposed.

The bill funded the 3 percent military pay raise Clinton proposed, which would cost approximately $1.6 billion.

• Nearly $79.2 billion for operations and maintenance, $701 million more than requested. Included in that was $1.14 billion for ongoing military missions over Iraq and in Bosnia, an increase of $148 million over the budget request.

• $3.65 billion for antimissile defenses, a 31 percent increase over Clinton's $2.8 billion request. Within this, slightly more than a quarter was for systems to defend forces in the field against relatively short-range missiles ($311 million for the Navy's Lower Tier system and $597 million for the Army's Patriot system upgrade, as requested), another quarter was for more sophisticated antimissile weapons to protect against advanced missiles flying farther and faster than existing types ($622 million for the Army's THAAD program—$140 million more than requested—and $304 million for the Navy's Upper Tier system—$246 million more than requested), slightly less than a quarter was to develop a national missile defense system ($833 million, $325 million more than requested), slightly less than 15 percent for other theater defenses ($526 million) and the remaining 10 percent was for basic research, including exploration of more futuristic antimissile technologies such as a satellite-borne antimissile laser ($367 million, $140 million more than requested).

In addition to the $3.65 billion appropriated for the Pentagon's Ballistic Missile Defense Organization, other funding in the bill included $249 million—more than double the $120 million requested—to develop missile detection satellites; $57 million requested to develop an antimissile laser to be carried by a jumbo jet; and $50 million, unrequested, to develop an antisatellite missile.

• $464 million requested to upgrade existing M-1 tanks and $235 million—$101 million more than requested—to upgrade Bradley armored troop carriers; $339 million—$50 million more than requested—to continue development of the Comanche helicopter; the $383 million requested to equip Apache helicopters with Longbow target-finding radars; and an unrequested $190 million to continue production of the small scout helicopters the Comanche eventually would supplant.

• $979 million to accelerate the conversion of B-1 and B-2 bombers to carry nonnuclear weapons, especially precision-guided smart bombs, an increase of $145 million over the request. The budget requested $95 million to buy smart bombs, but the bill approved $196 million.

Compared with the request, the bill boosted by more than 80 percent funding for combat jets then in production, including $275 million for six F-15s, an increase of $90 million for two planes; $155 million for six F-16s, an increase of $49 million for two planes; $279 million, not requested, for six F/A-18s; and $345 million to rebuild 12 Marine Corps Harrier vertical takeoff jets, an increase of $63 million and two planes.

The bill also provided $1.91 billion of the $2 billion requested to continue development of the F-22 fighter, $1.84 billion as requested for the first dozen of an enlarged version of the F/A-18, and $599 million ($10 million more than requested) to develop the so-called Joint Strike Fighter, intended to enter service late in the next decade as a replacement for several jets.

• $3.4 billion for four destroyers (the House had approved only three), plus an add-on of $225 million to buy components that would be used to build future ships; $649 million of the $699 million requested to complete work on the third and last submarine of the *Seawolf*-class; $296 million requested to buy components for the first ship of a new class of smaller subs, along with an unrequested $501 million toward a second of the smaller subs; $1.9 billion as requested for eight C-17 cargo jets; and $621 million for the Marine Corps' first five production-run V-22 Ospreys, as compared with a $501 million budget request for four.

• $780 million in unrequested funding for equipment earmarked for National Guard and reserve units. ❑

1997 Military Construction

Congress in 1996 cleared a nearly $10 billion fiscal 1997 military construction appropriations bill (HR 3517—PL 104-196). Despite administration complaints about the bill's addition of $850 million to the president's $9.1 billion budget request, President Clinton signed the bill into law on Sept. 16.

HR 3517 included nearly $3.4 billion for military construction projects, $4.1 billion for family housing and $2.5 billion for military base closing and realignment costs.

LEGISLATIVE ACTION

The House passed a $10 billion military construction bill on May 30, 1996, by a vote of 369–43. The House Appropriations Committee had reported the bill on May 23 (H Rept 104-591).

The House bill included $900 million more than requested, with the lion's share of the increase—$670 million—for building and renovating barracks, family housing and child care centers. Although the administration had declared such "quality of life" projects a high priority, the House Appropriations Committee decided that the administration had not requested enough.

Since the end of conscription in 1973, the armed services had had to raise their pay and standards of living to attract enough volunteers willing to accept the rigors of military life. This adaption was complicated by changes in the services' demographics.

The percentage of married personnel, single parents and service members whose spouses were employed all had increased since 1974, as had the number of preschool-aged children belonging to service members. These changes led to an unprecedented demand on the Pentagon to ensure the availability of family housing and child care within financial reach of even junior enlisted personnel. The problem was compounded by the location of many large military installations in isolated areas where the housing market might be small or in coastal ports where housing prices typically ran high. Further problems were posed by the growing numbers of aging family housing units and spartan barracks in need of repair or replacement.

The House bill also provided the requested $2.5 billion to carry out the recommendations of the Base Closure and Realignment commissions that met in 1991, 1993 and 1995. The funds were to be used to move units out of bases being closed, to build new facilities at bases where they were going and to clean up hazardous waste they had left behind. (Military base closings, pp. 288, 319)

The Senate passed a $9.8 billion version of HR 3517 on June 26 by voice vote. The Senate Appropriations Committee had reported the bill on June 20 (S Rept 104-287).

The Senate's $700 million increase over the budget request included the addition of $189 million to Clinton's $3.86 billion request for family housing. The Senate also added $370 million to the $194 million Clinton requested for National Guard and reserve facilities.

The Appropriations Committee complained that the Defense Department historically underfunded Guard and reserve projects, expecting Congress to step in.

CONFERENCE, MAJOR PROVISIONS

The House agreed to the conference report (H Rept 104-721) on Aug. 1 by a vote of 396–26, and the Senate followed suit on Sept. 5 by a vote of 92–6, clearing the bill.

Of the $850 million the $9.98 billion conference bill added to the budget request, more than half was for housing and family assistance facilities ($344 million) and for installations used by the politically influential National Guard and reserve forces ($191 million).

Clinton had requested $562 million to build or modernize barracks complexes, but the congressional panels said that amount would set too slow a pace for the barracks replacement project. The conference added $178 million. It also included $5 million, not requested, for a pilot program of direct loans, loan guarantees, and leasing arrangements to induce private developers to build and renovate barracks.

The administration had requested $714 million to build or renovate nearly 6,400 family housing units. The conference report added $257 million for 3,900 more units. It also included $25 million, instead of the $20 million requested, for a pilot program to induce private developers to build and renovate military family housing.

The final bill included the $2.51 billion requested to shut down or realign military bases.

HR 3517 appropriated $172 million of the $197 million requested for the annual U.S. contribution to the North Atlantic Treaty Organization (NATO) infrastructure fund—a kitty to which all members of the alliance contributed and which was used to build facilities for common use.

The bill also included the $82 million requested to build, in an undisclosed country near the Persian Gulf, a compound of climate-controlled warehouses to store tanks, trucks, ammunition and other supplies for Army and Air Force units that would be flown to the scene in case of a crisis. The Senate version of the bill had included only $7 million of this amount. ❏

'GOP Contract' Proposals

A bill containing the defense and foreign policy proposals from the House Republicans' "Contract with America"—dubbed the National Security Revitalization Act (HR 7)—was passed by the House in early 1995 but was never taken up in the Senate. A hearing was held on a separate bill in the Senate (S 5), but it was not acted upon.

The GOP contract laid out two primary defense and foreign policy goals: "No U.S. troops under U.N. command and restoration of the essential parts of our national security funding to strengthen our national defenses and maintain our credibility around the world." *(Contract, box, p. 885)*

In writing legislation to carry out the contract, House GOP lawmakers turned that simple statement into an omnibus bill addressing the nuances of defense strategy, the U.S. relationship with the United Nations, and the future of the North Atlantic Treaty Organization (NATO). At the heart of the bill were provisions dealing with peacekeeping operations. Other sections concerned the expansion of NATO, accelerating defense spending, and development of an antimissile defense system.

After some initial hesitation, the administration weighed in strongly against HR 7. Secretary of State Warren Christopher objected to a proposal to reduce U.S. funding for the United Nations. Secretary of Defense William J. Perry opposed a provision requiring the establishment of an independent commission to review military readiness. The nation's military leaders, including Joint Chiefs Chairman Gen. John M. Shalikashvili, raised stern objections to the original bill's specific timetable for NATO expansion, a provision dropped in committee.

Although HR 7 never got beyond the House floor, portions reappeared elsewhere. The bill's antimissile-defense provisions were debated as part of the fiscal 1996 defense authorization bill, though ultimately abandoned to secure President Clinton's signature. But the debate continued in the next session, as did the effort to limit placing troops under foreign command. Restrictions on U.S. support for international peacekeeping missions were included in ill-fated bills to authorize foreign aid and finance State Department operations. Language promoting the expansion of NATO into Central and Eastern Europe was included in the fiscal 1997 foreign operations appropriations bill. *(1996 defense authorization, p. 294; antimissile defenses, p. 316; U.S. troops under U.N. command, p. 318; State Department authorization, p. 228; U.N. peacekeeping missions, p. 236; NATO expansion, p. 319)*

LEGISLATIVE ACTION

After two days of bitterly partisan floor debate, the House passed HR 7 on Feb. 16, 1995, by a vote of 241–181. As they had on most other contract-inspired bills, House Republicans gave it near solid support. Democrats, who were almost as solidly opposed, blasted the bill as an isolationist screed.

HR 7 had been reported on Feb. 6 by the House National Security, International Relations, and Intelligence committees (H Rept 104-18, Parts I-III).

Antimissile Defense

Despite their unity on final passage, Republicans during floor debate suffered defections on the issue of antimissile defense, giving GOP leaders their first major defeat on a contract-related vote. On Feb. 15, the House voted 218–212 to strike a provision calling for the Pentagon to deploy a nationwide antimissile defense as soon as "practical." The amendment, by John M. Spratt Jr., D-S.C., stipulated instead that combat-readiness, weapons modernization, and the development of defenses against short-range missiles such as the Scuds that Iraq had used in the 1991 Persian Gulf War should have a higher priority than deployment of missile defenses for U.S. territory. Many of the Republicans who supported Spratt's amendment did so because of budget concerns.

Later that day, the House adopted, 221–204, an amendment by House National Security Committee Chairman Floyd D. Spence, R-S.C., to allow a higher budget for nationwide missile defense in fiscal 1996 than in the previous year and to declare that both a nationwide defense and a theater-missile defense system were essential to U.S. national security.

U.N. Peacekeeping Costs

Given the unpopularity of foreign aid in general and the dubious results of many U.N.-sponsored operations, Democratic leaders saw no chance of eliminating a provision in the bill to reduce the U.S. share of U.N. peacekeeping costs. The bill required that, before paying its annual assessment for U.N. peacekeeping, the United States deduct the cost of U.S. military operations in support of U.N. goals.

Nearly all U.S. experts agreed that the United States was footing too much of the world organization's annual bill. The administration insisted that it was making every effort to reduce the U.S. share. Although the assessments came due for 31.7 percent of each mission, the administration paid only 30.4 percent. In addition, the administration, under pressure from Congress, announced that it would pay only 25 percent beginning in fiscal 1996. By voice vote, the House adopted an amendment by James A. Traficant Jr., D-Ohio, to lower the limit to 20 percent, although the president could retain the 25 percent ceiling simply by sending Congress a report justifying it.

U.S. Peacekeeping Role

By voice vote, the House adopted an amendment by Doug Bereuter, R-Neb., striking a provision that would have prohibited the president from assigning U.S. forces to any U.N. peacekeeping operation without prior congressional approval.

Democrats offered criticism but did not try to change the provision barring the placement of U.S. forces under the command of a non-U.S. officer in a U.N. peacekeeping operation. The provision allowed the president to waive the ban if he certified to Congress that placing U.S. troops under a foreign commander was essential to U.S. national security interests and provided a detailed report on the mission of the U.S. force, the command arrangements and the anticipated cost.

Defense Commission

The Clinton administration and most Democrats vigorously opposed the bill's proposal for a blue-ribbon defense commission as an infringement on the responsibilities of the administration and of Congress itself. Republican supporters scoffed that Democrats had shown no hesitation about creating similar commissions to second-guess Republican administrations on defense policy.

Warning that the commission's $1.5 million cost would be siphoned out of readiness funds, Democrats backed an amendment by Jane Harman, D-Calif., to eliminate the provision from the bill. But on Feb. 16 the House instead adopted, 211–180, a

Joel Hefley, R-Colo., amendment requiring that the commission be paid out of the budget of the office of the secretary of defense. The Harman amendment was then rejected, 207–211.

NATO Expansion

During committee action on the bill, Robert G. Torricelli, D-N.J., had led a successful effort to eliminate from the bill a January 1999 deadline for inviting Poland, Hungary, the Czech Republic and Slovakia to join NATO. But on the floor Feb. 16, a Torricelli amendment to weaken a requirement for an aid program to ease the transition of former communist nations to NATO membership, by leaving it to the discretion of the president, was rejected 191–232.

In other action, the House adopted by voice vote a Richard J. Durbin, D-Ill., amendment making more explicit the possibility that countries other than the four that were named could become eligible for NATO membership. ❑

Antimissile Defenses

Congressional Republicans failed in the 104th Congress to secure enactment of one of their key defense initiatives—a commitment to early deployment of a nationwide defense against ballistic missiles. But they did win sizable increases in funding for antimissile defenses.

After their efforts in 1995 to require deployment of a national defense system by 2003 led to the veto of the fiscal 1996 defense authorization bill (HR 1530), Republicans tried a different approach in the second session: They isolated the issue in separate legislation. The idea was to spotlight GOP differences with President Clinton on the issue without slowing down or risking vital legislation.

But the separate bills (HR 3144, S 1635) never got to the floor of either chamber and Clinton's deployment plan was left essentially untouched. Moreover, though GOP activists continued to tout the effort as a political trump in the presidential election year, it failed to resonate with the public, partly because Clinton claimed that his program, too, could field an antimissile defense by 2003 but that a decision to meet that deadline could be deferred to see whether new missile threats materialize.

BACKGROUND

Antimissile defense was the salient military issue dividing the two parties in the 104th Congress.

National Defense

A key component in the debate was Clinton's decision to develop pieces of a national defense system but to defer until 1999 the question of whether to deploy such a system by 2003.

Emphasizing the prospect that Third World states might acquire ballistic missiles armed with nuclear, chemical or biological warheads, Republicans wanted a commitment for more rapid deployment. And they insisted that any U.S. defense cover all 50 states, including Alaska and Hawaii.

Most Democrats, however, argued that such a commitment would be premature, because no missile threat to U.S. territory was in the offing. They also contended that the United States should take seriously Russia's insistence that any deployments conform to the 1972 treaty limiting antiballistic missile (ABM) weapons. The ABM Treaty, which could be amended, provided that neither the United States nor Russia could deploy more than 100 interceptor missiles—all located at a single site—to protect its territory against longer-range, or strategic, missiles. Democrats said that a system protecting all 50 states probably would require the deployment of interceptor rockets at several sites. Republicans rejected this contention, citing Army and Air Force proposals for single-site nationwide defenses.

The administration was anxious to avoid inflaming nationalist forces in Russia and Joint Chiefs of Staff Chairman Gen. John M. Shalikashvili warned that violation of the ABM Treaty might induce the Russians not to ratify the Strategic Arms Reduction Talks (START II) agreement, which required the retirement of thousands of nuclear warheads.

Theater Defenses

Also at issue in the antimissile defense debate were theater defenses, so-called because they were intended to protect U.S. forces or allies in distant theaters of military operations instead of protecting U.S. territory. The ABM Treaty did not limit defenses against theater missiles, but it also did not define the distinction between those exempt defenses and strategic defenses. The United States and Russia were attempting to negotiate a "demarcation" agreement on these defenses.

Theater defenses ranged from less-advanced systems designed to protect against short-range missiles—such as the Patriot missiles, which intercepted the Scuds fired by Iraq during the 1991 Persian Gulf War—to more sophisticated systems being developed to intercept missiles traveling farther and faster—such as the Army's Theater High-Altitude Air Defense (THAAD) and the Navy's Upper Tier system. Some arms control specialists contended that both THAAD and the Upper Tier systems would violate the ABM Treaty because, under certain circumstances, either could intercept some Russian missiles aimed at U.S. territory.

But Republicans, citing reports—disputed by the administration—that North Korea was rushing development of a missile that could reach Alaska, pushed for accelerated development of the two more advanced programs.

MANDATED DEPLOYMENT BILLS

In 1995, during debate on the bill embodying the defense-related provisions of the House GOP's "Contract with America" (HR 7), the House voted to eliminate a provision calling for the Pentagon to deploy a nationwide antimissile defense as soon as "practical." *(GOP contract bill, p. 315)*

But advocates of antimissile defense regained the initiative during consideration of the fiscal 1996 defense authorization bill (HR 1530). The conference version required the Pentagon to aim at deploying a national defense system protecting all 50 states by 2003. President Clinton objected to various sections of HR 1530, but the missile defense provisions were the principal reason for his veto of the bill.

The mandated deployment provision was eliminated entirely from S 1124, the new version of the fiscal 1996 defense authorization bill signed into law in early 1996 (PL 104-106).

Proponents of antimissile defenses turned to freestanding bills in 1996 to avoid a repeat of the previous year's stalemate over critical legislation. A "Defend America Act" (HR 3144, S 1635) was introduced in each chamber. The act would have required deployment by 2003 of a system that could protect all 50 states from a relatively small number of missiles—the kind of attack that might be launched by a rogue state such as North Korea or by a renegade military commander. To that extent, the program tracked Clinton's.

But the legislation stipulated that the system to be deployed by 2003 subsequently would be expanded to deal with a larger and more sophisticated missile attack. The legislation allowed the president a year to negotiate changes in the ABM Treaty. If those negotiations were unsuccessful, the act called for U.S. consideration of withdrawal from the treaty.

The House National Security Committee reported HR 3144 May 16 (H Rept 104-583, Part I). The Senate Armed Services Committee reported S 1635 that same day. But the bills went no further.

House action had been slated for the following week but was canceled after Congressional Budget Office cost estimates ranging to $60 billion alarmed some deficit-minded conservative lawmakers.

In the Senate, Democrats blocked Republican efforts to debate S 1635. A June 4 attempt to invoke cloture over a procedural motion and begin debate on the bill was rejected 53–46, falling short of the 60 votes needed. A compromise allowing the Senate to debate the bill at a later time was reached during consideration of the fiscal 1997 defense authorization (HR 3230—PL 104-201), but the bill still never made it to the floor.

LARGER BUDGETS

Although in the end they were unable to dictate specific policy, antimissile advocates did succeed in adding substantial sums to Clinton's budget requests.

S 1124, the fiscal 1996 defense authorization bill, added $854 million to the president's antimissile defense request of $2.9 billion. The fiscal 1996 defense appropriations bill (HR 2126—PL 104-61) included $3.4 billion for antimissile defenses. The two bills added $170 million to Clinton's $30 million request for the Upper Tier system. *(1996 defense authorization, p. 294; 1996 defense appropriations, p. 301)*

Moreover, S 1124 contained language requiring initial deployment of THAAD by 2000 and of the Navy weapon by 2001. However, shortly after the authorization was enacted in 1996, the administration said it did not intend to meet those deadlines. Instead, it proposed trimming funding for the THAAD and Upper Tier programs and shifting the emphasis of the theater defense program to the more quickly deployable short-range defenses. Clinton had the support on this of senior military leaders, who were desperate to pry out of the antimissile program funds for additional ships, planes, trucks and tanks, and who saw the near-term missile threat as the more urgent problem.

Forty-one Republicans then went into federal court to seek a court order to force Clinton and Defense Secretary William J. Perry to follow the requirements of S 1124 and accelerate the two antimissile programs. A federal district court dismissed the suit on Oct. 9. However, while Judge Stanley Sporkin declined to rule on the dispute at the time, he insisted that a president could not simply disregard an explicit law and indicated that the court might weigh in later.

The fiscal 1997 defense authorization bill (HR 3230—PL 104-201) added $914 million to Clinton's $2.8 billion request for the antimissile programs. The companion defense appropriations bill (HR 3610—PL 104-208) added $855 million to Clinton's request, bringing the final total to $3.65 billion. Ignoring Clinton's proposed cuts in the programs, both bills added $140 million to the $482 million requested for the THAAD program and $246 million to the $58 million requested for the Upper Tier system. *(1997 defense authorization, p. 306; 1997 defense appropriations, p. 312)* ❑

U.N. Command of U.S. Troops

The 104th Congress enacted temporary restrictions on the president's authority to place troops under United Nations command as part of the fiscal 1996 and 1997 omnibus appropriations bills (HR 3019—PL 104-134 and HR 3610—PL 104-208). But House Republican attempts to push through permanent limits either died in the Senate or were killed by President Clinton's veto. One such proposal was a factor in Clinton's veto in 1995 of the fiscal 1996 defense authorization bill (HR 1530). Another proposal was included in legislation encompassing the House GOP's "Contract with America" (HR 7), which passed the House in 1995 but got no further. A new attempt in 1996 (HR 3308) suffered the same fate.

BACKGROUND

Republicans were deeply critical of what they regarded as the Clinton administration's dangerous overreliance on the United Nations and multilateral diplomacy. They were particularly incensed by the idea of placing U.S. soldiers under the command of foreign officers.

The issue had emerged in 1993 after 18 U.S. soldiers under U.N. command in Somalia were killed in a bloody battle with a Somalian warlord. Members of both parties were enraged that a once peaceful humanitarian effort of the United States had turned into an increasingly bloody military operation under U.N. command. *(Somalia peacekeeping mission, p. 191)*

Although noncombatant U.S. soldiers had previously served under U.N. command, the Somalia contingent was the first combat-capable unit to serve outside the U.S. chain of command. The debacle triggered efforts to limit such deployments in the future.

LEGISLATIVE ACTION

Congress barred the use of funds in HR 3019 and HR 3610 for peacekeeping operations in which U.S. troops were placed under U.N. command, unless the president notified Congress

that top military advisers had found it to be in the national security interest. The restrictions were to expire at the end of the fiscal years covered by each bill. *(Omnibus appropriations bills, p. 236)*

Republicans tried several different avenues to legislate a permanent limit on the president's authority to place U.S. forces under the command of foreign officers. It was part of the defense section of the GOP contract that was used in the successful campaigns of House Republicans in the 1994 elections.

From there, it went into HR 7, a bill expanding on the contract's defense and foreign policy goals. Passed by a vote of 241–181 on Feb. 16, 1995, HR 7 barred the placement of U.S. forces under the command of a non-U.S. officer in a U.N. peacekeeping operation. The provision allowed the president to waive the ban if he certified to Congress that placing U.S. troops under a foreign commander was essential to U.S. national security interests and provided a detailed report on the mission of the U.S. force, the command arrangements and the anticipated cost. During the House debate, Democrats offered criticism but did not attempt to change the provision. The Senate did not act on the bill. *(GOP Contract proposals, p. 315)*

The House included a similar provision in the ill-fated fiscal 1996 defense authorization. When Clinton vetoed HR 1530, he cited three key objections to the bill, one of which was the provision requiring the president to submit various reports to Congress when he placed U.S. military forces under U.N. command. The authorization bill ultimately enacted (S 1124—PL 104-106) contained no such provision. *(1996 defense authorization, p. 294)*

But during the Jan. 24, 1996, debate on the revised defense authorization, House National Security Committee Chairman Floyd D. Spence, R-S.C., predicted that the issue would come back to haunt Clinton. Critics contended that the administration was badly out of step with the public on the issue.

The issue did return in the second session of the 104th Congress but advanced no further than previous attempts. This time it was showcased in a freestanding bill (HR 3308). Republicans chose this separate-bill approach as a way of highlighting the issue without jeopardizing more significant legislation such as an authorization bill.

The House passed HR 3308 on Sept. 5, 1996, by a 299–109 vote, as 81 Democrats joined 218 Republicans in supporting the measure. The bill had been reported by the House National Security Committee on June 27 (H Rept 104-642, Part I).

HR 3308 would have denied funding for U.S. participation in any U.N. military operation unless Congress authorized such a mission or the president declared in advance that it was in the interest of national security. The requirement could have been waived if the president certified that an emergency precluded advance notice and if he also submitted to Congress a detailed report within 48 hours.

The only major amendment approved by the House underscored the near-contempt in which many members, particularly Republicans, held the United Nations. The amendment, offered by Roscoe G. Bartlett, R-Md., and adopted Sept. 5 on a 276–130 vote, would have prevented the Pentagon from requiring U.S.

troops to wear U.N. uniforms without prior approval by Congress. The proposal stemmed from the case of Army Specialist Michael New, who became something of a folk hero for conservatives by refusing to wear U.N. insignia on his uniform when he was part of a U.S. unit deployed to the U.N. peacekeeping mission in Macedonia.

The administration staunchly opposed HR 3308. In a letter to House Democrats, Secretary of Defense William J. Perry called the bill a "significant intrusion upon the constitutional prerogatives of the Commander-in-Chief" and said he would recommend a veto. The bill, however, never got to that point because the Senate did not take it up.   ❑

NATO Expansion

Congress in 1996 approved legislation to promote, but not require, the expansion of the North Atlantic Treaty Organization (NATO) to include former communist states in central and eastern Europe. The provisions were included in the final version of the fiscal 1997 foreign operations appropriations bill, which was enacted into law as part of an omnibus appropriations bill (HR 3610—PL 104-208).

The expansion of NATO had bipartisan support. It was a goal of President Clinton. It was included in the Republicans' "Contract with America" and was promoted by Bob Dole, R-Kan., in one of his last official acts as majority leader before resigning from the Senate. It had strong backing from groups representing Americans who traced their heritage to central and eastern Europe. But differences emerged over the details of such a move. *(GOP contract proposals, p. 315)*

The White House agreed to support the legislation in 1996 after sponsors watered it down to give the president wide leeway in deciding how and how quickly to pursue expanding the alliance. Such a step, likely to include Poland, Hungary and the Czech Republic, would have a profound impact on the future of Europe and could antagonize Russia, which sharply opposed NATO's eastward expansion. It would oblige the United States to defend those nations if they were attacked, just as it was committed to come to the defense of existing NATO members such as France and Germany.

LEGISLATIVE ACTION

The House passed the NATO expansion legislation as a free-standing bill (HR 3564) on July 23 by a vote of 353–65. The House bill did not call for any country to be admitted to the alliance but would have authorized $60 million in grants, loans and training for former Warsaw Pact nations to assist their eventual entry into NATO. It expressed the sense of Congress that, among those states, Poland, Hungary and the Czech Republic had made the most progress toward meeting NATO's membership criteria, including a demonstrated commitment to democracy, human rights and civilian control of the military.

Nearly identical provisions were adopted by the Senate, 81–16, on July 25 as an amendment, offered by Colorado Republican Hank Brown, to the fiscal 1997 foreign operations appropriations bill (HR 3540). Slovenia was added to the list of favored states as a floor amendment, at the insistence of Delaware Democrat Joseph R. Biden Jr. The Senate passed HR 3540 by a vote of 93–7 on July 26.

The language in both the House and Senate bills had been diluted to win the support of the Clinton administration, which was leery of provoking nationalist sentiment in Russia. For instance, the provisions did not specifically call for granting NATO membership to any state, nor did it set a timetable for the alliance to make such a decision.

During Senate action, Georgia Democrat Sam Nunn had threatened to filibuster Brown's amendment unless it was watered down. Nunn had authored an amendment to the fiscal 1997 defense authorization bill requiring the president to report on the costs and benefits of expanding NATO. *(1997 defense authorization, p. 306)*

FINAL ACTION

As signed into law Sept. 30, HR 3610 urged the speedy admission of central and eastern European nations into NATO. The bill earmarked $30 million in military assistance grants, $20 million in loans and $10 million for military training to help Poland, Hungary and the Czech Republic become members of NATO. The legislation provided that Slovenia and other countries could become eligible for assistance when they met certain criteria.   ❑

Military Base Closings

Congress in 1995 endorsed plans to shut down 79 unneeded U.S. military installations and scale back 26 others at an estimated savings of $19.3 billion over 20 years. A resolution in the House (H J Res 102) to block the closings was easily defeated.

The list of bases to be closed originated in the Pentagon and was modified by the Defense Base Closure and Realignment Commission. President Clinton had reluctantly accepted the commission's recommendations but only after the Pentagon devised a plan to privatize depot work at two bases slated to be closed—McClellan Air Force Base near Sacramento, Calif., and Kelly Air Force Base in San Antonio, Texas. The two maintenance depots had not been on the Pentagon's original list.

The 1995 round of base closures was the fourth in seven years and the third under a special process set up by a 1990 law (PL 101-510) to shut down military facilities no longer needed in the post–cold war era. Lawmakers had designed the base-closing process to avoid the parochialism that was likely to thwart any attempt initiated by Congress to close unneeded bases that were key to local economies. *(Background, p. 288)*

RECOMMENDATIONS

Under the 1990 law, the president was to appoint and the Senate confirm an eight-member commission to review the Pentagon's list of proposed closings and draw up its recommendations. The commission's list could be rejected by the president and returned for revisions or accepted and forwarded to Congress. Congress could only accept or reject the list in its entirety; no changes could be made.

1995 Military Bases Closure List

Following are military bases on the Defense Base Closure and Realignment Commission's 1995 closure list that would lose 500 or more jobs. Included are Pentagon estimates of the number of military and civilian personnel employed at each facility:

Base	Employees	
	Military	Civilian
Fort McClellan, Ala.	10,163	1,115
Adak Naval Air Facility, Alaska	1,044	75
Long Beach Naval Shipyard, Calif.	263	3,443
McClellan Air Force Base, Calif.	2,757	8,828
Naval Fleet & Industrial Supply Center, Oakland, Calif.	307	1,052
Oakland Army Base, Calif.	52	673
Fitzsimons Army Medical Center, Colo.	1,303	1,601
Ship repair facility, Guam	26	660
Naval Air Warfare Center-Aircraft Division, Indianapolis, Ind.	36	2,011
Naval Surface Warfare Center, Crane Division Detachment, Louisville, Ky.	15	1,292
Fort Ritchie, Md.	991	918
South Weymouth Naval Air Station, Mass.	691	210
Bayonne Military Ocean Terminal, N.J.	161	1,794
Memphis Defense Distribution Depot, Tenn.	11	1,289
Kelly Air Force Base, Texas	10,093	13,661
Red River Army Depot, Texas	13	2,380
Reese Air Force Base, Texas	1,090	442

SOURCES: Defense Base Closure and Realignment Commission; Defense Department

The nomination of former senator Alan J. Dixon (D-Ill., 1981–1993) to chair the commission had been approved by voice vote of the Senate on Oct. 7, 1994. The Senate approved the remaining members of the commission by voice vote March 2, 1995.

The Pentagon had begun the base-closing process only days earlier, on Feb. 28, with the release of a list of recommended closures and realignments affecting 146 domestic bases. Although the Defense Department had initially vowed that the 1995 round would be the largest ever, the list was significantly smaller than the final 1993 list, which slated 130 bases for closure and 45 for cutbacks.

Several Republican lawmakers accused the Pentagon of allowing presidential politics to determine the scope of the list. But Defense Secretary William J. Perry defended the list, arguing that the military was still trying to manage the effects of the previous base closure rounds. He also said that the up-front costs of shutting many of the facilities proved to be too high.

Absent from the Pentagon's list were all five of the Air Force maintenance depots, despite reports that the service had recommended closing some of the facilities because of excess capacity. Congressional and commission sources said that the military groups reviewing the bases had recommended closing McClellan and Kelly, but an 11th-hour decision spared the facilities.

McClellan and Kelly were not spared, however, from the base-closing commission's list, which was sent to the president [Jul]y 1, after months of hearings and visits to bases.

California, which benefited from the defense buildup of the 1980s but paid the price with base closings in the 1990s, took a major hit as the commission voted to close Long Beach Naval Shipyard, the Army base and Naval Fleet & Industrial Supply Center in Oakland, and McClellan—a loss of about 16,000 jobs. Texas was slated to lose more than 25,000 jobs with the closure of Kelly, the Red River Army Depot and Reese Air Force Base.

Clinton wrestled with the recommendations for nearly two weeks before forwarding the list to Congress on July 13. Initially, the administration—furious with the commission's action and facing the wrath of California lawmakers—had considered asking the panel to reconsider Kelly and McClellan. But that drew immediate resistance, leading the White House to craft its privatization plan for the two maintenance depots. The plan called for the Pentagon to pursue private companies to perform the maintenance work at or near McClellan and Kelly, for an estimated savings of 8,700 jobs at McClellan and 16,000 at Kelly. The plan worried lawmakers representing the Air Force's three remaining depots, which had been the likely recipients of the work from McClellan and Kelly.

CONGRESSIONAL ACTION

Clinton's delay in accepting the list and indications that the White House was allowing presidential politics to seep into the process caused consternation on Capitol Hill. Members on both sides of the aisle urged Clinton to accept the commission's recommendations. Republicans warned against politicizing the base-closing process.

The House on Sept. 8 sealed the fate of the installations targeted for closure. By a vote of 75–343, the House rejected a resolution of disapproval. The House National Security Committee had voted 43–10 on July 26 to endorse the commission's recommendations.

No resolution of disapproval was offered in the Senate. The House action effectively set the wheels in motion to close the bases over five years, because both chambers had to disapprove the list to block the closures. ◻

Arms Control Agreements

The Senate in 1996 gave its approval to the second Strategic Arms Reduction Talks (START II) treaty, which had been signed in 1993. But action on another treaty concluded in 1993—the Chemical Weapons Convention—was put off.

Also in 1996 President Clinton signed a treaty to ban test explosions of nuclear weapons.

START II

Three years after President George Bush and Russian President Boris N. Yeltsin signed the START II agreement, the Senate on Jan. 26, 1996, approved the pact (Treaty Doc. 103-1) by a vote of 87–4. A two-thirds majority was required.

START II would slash the number of long-range U.S. and Russian nuclear weapons deployed to no more than 6,500 weapons—3,500 for the United States and 3,000 for Russia [by] 2003, or by the end of 2000 if the United States ha[d]

the dismantling of Russian weapons. That was less than one-third of the nearly 24,000 U.S. and Soviet warheads deployed in 1990. (*Table, this page*)

Realizing a long-standing goal of U.S. arms control policy, it would eliminate all land-based intercontinental ballistic missiles equipped with multiple warheads. Such weapons—equipped with multiple independently targeted reentry vehicles (MIRVs), each of which could be aimed at a different target—made up the backbone of the Russian nuclear arsenal.

To meet Russian demands for reductions in sub-launched missiles, which made up the largest part of the U.S. force, the treaty would allow no more than 1,750 warheads on sub-launched weapons. That would require cuts of about 50 percent in the planned U.S. force of sub-launched warheads, to be achieved by removing four of the 18 Trident submarines from service and deploying each Trident II missile with only four of the eight warheads it could carry.

START II extended the logic of the preceding nuclear arms reduction pact, START I, signed in 1991 by Bush and Soviet President Mikhail S. Gorbachev, which mandated a reduction of about one-third in the deployed U.S. and Soviet nuclear arsenals. (*START I, Congress and the Nation Vol. VIII, p. 387*)

Ratification of START II had been delayed by the failure of several of the former Soviet states to comply with START I's requirement that they eliminate all nuclear weapons. (Under START I, Russia was the only former Soviet republic entitled to have nuclear weapons.) Russian nationalists also vigorously opposed the START II treaty. Russia had not ratified the treaty by the end of 1996. (*1993–1994 action, p. 292*)

In the United States, the treaty generated scant opposition and enjoyed strong bipartisan support on Capitol Hill. To answer some conservative GOP members' concerns about the administration's nuclear reduction policy, the Senate by voice vote attached to the resolution of ratification a package of eight declarations and one condition, the latter requiring the president to consult the Senate if START II did not take effect and the president decided to reduce the number of U.S. nuclear weapons unilaterally. The declarations, while not binding, indicated some skepticism over whether Russia would comply with the treaty.

The resolution of ratification had been unanimously approved by the Senate Foreign Relations Committee on Dec. 12, 1995.

CHEMICAL WEAPONS TREATY

The Senate in 1996 postponed floor action on a treaty requiring signatories to eliminate within 10 years all chemical weapons and all facilities for their development or manufacture. The Chemical Weapons Convention (Treaty Doc. 103-21) was concluded in 1993 and by 1996 had been signed by 160 countries. (*1993 action, p. 293*)

The Senate Foreign Relations Committee, by a vote of 13–5 on April 25, 1996, had approved the treaty with seven conditions and 11 declarations. The treaty was reported on Sept. 11 (Exec. Rept 104-33) but it went no further in the 104th Congress.

Warheads Decline

	1990	START I	START II
Total Warheads			
United States	12,646	8,556	3,500
Soviet Union/Russia	11,012	6,163	3,000
Total Warheads on Land-Based Missiles			
United States	2,450	1,400	500
Soviet Union/Russia	6,612	3,153	504
Total Warheads on Multiple-Warhead, Land-Based Missiles			
United States	2,000	1,100	0
Soviet Union/Russia	5,958	2,460	0

Conservatives mounted a vigorous attack on the agreement, which had been negotiated by Presidents Ronald Reagan and Bush, signed by Bush as one of his last presidential initiatives, and enjoyed the strong support of the Clinton administration. After GOP presidential candidate Bob Dole announced his objections to the treaty Sept. 11, the Clinton administration and Senate supporters of the agreement concluded that they would fall short of a two-thirds Senate majority, which the Constitution required for approval of a treaty. The administration and Majority Leader Trent Lott, R-Miss., agreed to defer Senate action on the pact indefinitely.

Senate Foreign Relations Committee Chairman Jesse Helms, R-N.C., and other leading treaty foes, such as Arizona Republican Sen. Jon Kyl and former Reagan Pentagon official Frank J. Gaffney Jr., saw the treaty as fatally flawed. They contended that the few states that posed the most plausible chemical-weapons threat to U.S. interests were unlikely to submit to the treaty. Opponents also warned that the pact would foster a false sense of security in members of Congress and would sap their will to finance necessary defenses against chemical weapons.

Critics opposed the treaty's procedures for verification as well. To ensure compliance, the treaty would have established a wide-ranging system of international inspections that would be applied not only to acknowledged chemical weapons sites, but also to a large number of factories that processed—or could readily be adapted to process—substances that could be used to make chemical weapons. Opponents contended that the provisions would require thousands of U.S. firms to meet onerous reporting requirements and would allow foreign bureaucrats to pry into their business and perhaps steal trade secrets. Moreover, they warned, for all the treaty's verification provisions, the prospects for catching highly motivated cheaters were slim, partly because some hideously lethal chemicals could be manufactured in a very small space.

Supporters of the treaty conceded that no way existed to ensure 100 percent compliance with the treaty, but they argued that ratification of the pact would give U.S. officials a much stronger hand in trying to eliminate potential chemical weapons threats. For one thing, they contended, approval of the pact would turn up the political pressure on some countries to abolish their chemical weapons programs. For another, it would lend moral authority to Washington's demands for concerted international action against countries that violated an international norm that proscribed chemical weapons. Supporters also argued that the treaty's web of verification requirements would help expose likely violators of the chemical weapons prohibition.

The treaty had appeared to have much going for it. With its roots in Republican administrations and strong support from the current Democratic White House, it had impeccably bipartisan credentials. Moreover, because existing law (PL 99-145, PL 102-484) required the elimination of virtually all U.S. chemical weapons by 2004, the treaty would have had little practical impact on the U.S. defense establishment.

The pact had been vigorously endorsed by senior military leaders and many national security specialists in the Senate, as well as by major chemical companies. Top executives of 53 large chemical companies summed up their support for the treaty in an Aug. 29 letter, in which they warned that, if the United States did not ratify the pact, they could lose hundreds of millions of dollars in overseas sales because the treaty required that signatory countries bar transactions in certain chemicals with nonsignatories.

But on the opponents' side were four top officials from the Reagan administration and Dick Cheney, who was secretary of defense under Bush. They were among more than 50 former officials and military officers who attacked the treaty in a Sept. 6 letter. And in a Sept. 9 letter, the National Federation of Independent Business, a small business lobby, warned that its members might incur steep costs complying with the treaty's reporting requirements.

TEST BAN TREATY

President Clinton signed a treaty Sept. 24, 1996, to ban test explosions of nuclear weapons. However, the Comprehensive Test Ban Treaty faced opposition from many of the same conservative Republicans who had derailed administration efforts to ratify the treaty banning chemical weapons earlier that month.

Existing treaties barred nuclear test explosions above ground, underwater and in outer space and limited underground tests to those with an explosive force equivalent to no more than 150,000 tons of TNT. The test ban treaty would bar even those underground tests, using an international network of monitoring sites to verify compliance. The treaty would allow tests of nuclear weapons components—including the high explosives used to trigger weapons—so long as no nuclear energy was released.

Critics of the treaty contended that occasional, full-scale nuclear explosive tests were essential to maintain confidence in the nation's dwindling nuclear arsenal and to attract and retain talented scientists. But the country's three nuclear weapons laboratories had agreed to support the pact. A new, $20 billion science program, designed to replace nuclear testing with supercomputer simulations, powerful laser blasts and high-explosive tests, finally convinced the labs of the alternatives to testing.

The test ban treaty, which climaxed four decades of intermittent efforts to negotiate such a ban, would not take effect for two

years at the earliest and, in any case, not until 44 countries that had nuclear research and power reactors had signed. One of that group, India, had refused to sign the treaty until the countries that already had nuclear weapons agreed to a timetable for eliminating them.

Pending resolution of India's status, countries that had ratified the pact were prohibited by international law from conducting any test explosions. Before the treaty was approved Sept. 10 by a vote of 158–3 in the United Nations General Assembly (Libya, India and Bhutan voted against the accord), the five countries that acknowledged possession of nuclear arms—the United States, Russia, France, Great Britain and China—each had declared a unilateral test moratorium.

Congress had voted in 1992 (PL 102-377) to halt U.S. nuclear test explosions for nine months and ban them permanently after Sept. 30, 1996, unless another country conducted such tests. Clinton had endorsed the moratorium in July 1993 and continued it since then in hopes of concluding a permanent test ban treaty. *(1992 action, Congress and the Nation Vol. VIII, p. 392; 1993 action, box, p. 293)* ❑

Sexual Harassment Cases

Allegations that Army drill sergeants at several training bases pressured female recruits for sex surfaced late in the 104th Congress. House Speaker Newt Gingrich, R-Ga., on Nov. 20, 1996, directed the House National Security Committee to conduct a review of each armed services efforts to prevent such abuse.

The Army on Nov. 7 had disclosed several alleged instances of sexual abuse at a training base in Aberdeen, Md. Criminal investigations were being conducted by the Army.

Though deeply disturbed by the Aberdeen cases and by subsequent, similar allegations at other training facilities, National Security panel members praised the Army for moving quickly to disclose the alleged incidents and prosecute wrongdoers. The speed and candor of the Army's investigation stood in contrast to the Navy's apparent reluctance to deal with a series of sexual abuse scandals, most notably the assaults on dozens of women and a few men at the 1991 Tailhook conference for naval aviators. *(Tailhook scandal, p. 292)*

House committee members said they would try to find out why the network of Army policies intended to prevent the harassment of recruits broke down and why some victims were slow to report the incidents. ❑

Defense Production Act

Congress in 1995 cleared legislation (HR 2204—PL 104-64) extending the Defense Production Act of 1950 through Sept. 30, 1998.

The Korean War-era statute granted the president sweeping authority over defense-related industries if emergency production was necessary for national security. It also gave the president extra power to mobilize responses to national disasters, such as earthquakes, floods and hurricanes. The act, which had last been reauthorized in 1992, was due to expire Sept. 30, 1995. *(1992 action, Congress and the Nation Vol. VIII, p. 412)*

In response to complaints that parts of the act were outdated, HR 2204 called for a study of its implementation, with a final report due Sept. 30, 1997.

HR 2204 passed by voice vote of the House Nov. 13, 1995. The Senate cleared it by voice vote Dec. 5. It was signed into law Dec. 18. A companion bill (S 1147—S Rept 104-134), reported by the Senate Banking, Housing, and Urban Affairs Committee Aug. 10, and passed by voice vote of the Senate Sept. 28.   ❏

Somalia Report

Two years after 18 U.S. soldiers died in a battle with forces of a Somalia warlord, the Senate Armed Services Committee on Sept. 29, 1995, issued a report that faulted former defense secretary Les Aspin for turning down a request by military leaders that U.S. troops be reinforced with tanks and armored troop carriers.

The U.S. casualties, which occurred Oct. 3–4, 1993, sparked a public uproar that intensified congressional demands that U.S. forces be withdrawn from Somalia. Aspin's refusal to send the tanks became one factor in President Clinton's decision to oust the former House Armed Services Committee chairman from the Pentagon's top job. *(Somalia peacekeeping mission, p. 191; Aspin, box, p. 259)*

Aspin had said he turned down the request—which had come from U.S. commanders on the scene and had been approved by then Joint Chiefs of Staff Chairman Gen. Colin L. Powell—on grounds that the shipment of tanks would have boosted dramatically the prominence of the U.S. role in the U.N.-sponsored effort to pacify Somalia's warring factions. The administration's policy at the time was both to reduce the U.S. military role in Somalia and to use forces already in the country to bolster the U.N. effort.   ❏

Saudi Arabia Bombing

A terrorist bombing that killed 19 U.S. service members in Dhahran, Saudi Arabia, on June 25, 1996, sparked Senate hearings that focused on whether U.S. officials had tried hard enough to improve security at the housing complex following a November 1995 bombing in Riyadh that killed five Americans.

Defense Secretary William J. Perry told the Senate Armed Services Committee July 9, 1996, that a number of antiterrorist measures had been taken following the Riyadh attack. However, he acknowledged that officials had not focused on the possibility that installations used by Americans might be attacked with a truck bomb as powerful as the 5,000-pound device used in the Dhahran attack.

Perry confirmed that Saudi officials had rebuffed at least two requests by U.S. officers to move the security fence around the Dhahran billet so it would be 400 feet from the building, instead of only 100 feet. The impasse was not reported to Gen. J. H. Binford Peay III, the commander-in-chief of U.S. forces in the Middle East, or to the Pentagon. Perry said that, had he known, he would have weighed in with Saudi officials at the highest level to secure the relocation of the fence. However, Perry and Peay both insisted that the local U.S. commander's decision to continue pressing Saudi officials for the relocation, instead of bucking the request to a higher level, had been reasonable.

Perry told the panel that U.S. personnel were being moved out of Saudi cities and into more isolated bases, which could more easily be protected by wide buffer zones.   ❏

Arms Transfers

Congress in 1996 cleared legislation (HR 3121—PL 104-164) setting new limits on the transfer of excess military equipment to U.S. allies. The bill increased the annual limit on military equipment transfers from $250 million to $350 million but eliminated a variety of existing loopholes, sponsors said.

Other provisions of the bill gave Congress a means of disapproving third-country transfers of U.S. equipment and defense manufacturing agreements with overseas firms; authorized the transfer of 10 U.S. naval vessels—eight by sale to Egypt, Mexico, New Zealand, Taiwan and Thailand, one by lease to Taiwan, and one by grant to Portugal; and renewed for four years an existing requirement that grants of excess military equipment to Greece and Turkey be offered on a 7–1 ratio.

HR 3121 also permanently authorized the 1994 Nuclear Proliferation Prevention Act, enacted as part of the fiscal 1994–1995 State Department authorization (PL 103-236), which denied Export-Import Bank loans and credits to countries that traded in material and technology used to develop nuclear weapons.

That law gave the Clinton administration headaches in early 1996 when China transferred nuclear weapons-related equipment to Pakistan. In May, the administration decided not to impose the stiff penalties required by the statute, after Chinese leaders agreed not to make such sales in the future. *(1994–1995 State Department authorization, p. 212; U.S.-China relations, p. 240)*

HR 3121 was reported by the House International Relations Committee April 16, 1996 (H Rept 104-519, Part I) and passed by voice vote of the House that same day. The Senate Foreign Relations Committee reported an amended version June 26, and the full Senate passed it the next day. The House agreed to the Senate amendments July 9, clearing the bill. The president signed it July 21.   ❏

CHAPTER 6

Transportation, Commerce and Communications

Transportation, Commerce and Communications

Although the 103rd and 104th Congresses worked on many of the same issues in the fields of transportation, commerce and communications, there were sharp differences in approach and emphasis. President Clinton had sought to boost federal spending on transportation and technology in his first two years in office, arguing that such spending was an investment, not an expense. Few of the proposals were enacted, however. In some cases, lawmakers could not reconcile their differences over such side issues as liability or special projects. In other cases, deficit-conscious Republicans balked at the increase in federal outlays.

After Republicans gained the majority of both chambers in the 1994 elections, Congress took control of the agenda and pursued a more deregulatory course. For example, instead of increasing Amtrak funding, the GOP sought to wean the railroad from federal assistance. The more dramatically the GOP tried to shift course, however, the less likely the legislation was to succeed. The main legislative accomplishments in the 104th Congress were made after Republicans' lowered their deregulatory sights enough to win Democratic support.

TRANSPORTATION INFRASTRUCTURE

When Clinton took office, state and local transportation officials had reason to believe that their ship had come in. After all, one of Clinton's campaign themes had been "rebuilding America," which raised the prospect of new spending programs on highways, mass-transit systems and other infrastructure.

Clinton came out early in 1993 with a request for $16.3 billion in supplemental appropriations to stimulate the economy, including $3 billion for highway projects, $1.2 billion for mass-transit and passenger railroads, and $4.8 billion for miscellaneous construction and maintenance projects. In a preview of things to come, however, the stimulus package was stymied by Republican opposition in the Senate. None of the supplemental money for infrastructure was provided. The administration went on to propose several other costly transportation initiatives in the 103rd Congress, only to meet repeatedly with failure.

In 1995, the new GOP majority in Congress sought to roll back numerous federal regulations on transportation, arguing that the freedom would allow agencies to do more with less money. These included proposals to pare back the federal rules protecting mass-transit and Amtrak workers and eliminate a number of mandates on highway programs.

These proposals met with mixed success. The most significant victory for Republicans was the elimination of federal speed limits and a motorcycle helmet mandate, and in those cases the GOP was backed by numerous Democrats.

The GOP agenda also differed from the previous Congress in that it included few new safety initiatives. Aside from taking steps to beef up airport security and restrict child pilots, Congress did little in 1995 and 1996 to improve transportation safety. By contrast, bills to reduce accidents involving high-risk drivers, railroads, barges, recreational boaters and ruptured pipelines all advanced in 1993 and 1994, although most ultimately were not enacted.

Like the Democrat leaders who preceded them, though, Republicans worked to keep the spigot of federal dollars open for transportation projects. For example, the Senate stayed in session several extra days in 1996 in order to renew a federal grant program for airports. Although overall spending on transportation programs declined from the levels set during the 103rd Congress, spending from the transportation trust funds climbed as lawmakers boosted capital spending, particularly on highway programs.

The 104th Congress picked up where the previous session left off on cargo-vessel subsidies, enacting a new program with a projected cost of $1 billion over 10 years. Unlike the previous proposal, though, the enacted subsidies were financed by taking money from other federal programs, not by raising the duties on vessels entering U.S. ports. The subsidies thus did not require an increase in spending.

COMPETITIVENESS AND COMMERCE

Clinton's early initiatives in the arena of commerce met the same fate as his transportation proposals. In 1993, Clinton sought a major expansion of the Commerce Department programs aimed at helping U.S. industries develop and commer-

REFERENCES

Discussion of transportation and commerce policy for the years 1945–1964 may be found in *Congress and the Nation Vol. I*, pp. 517–562, 1159–1185; for the years 1965–1968, *Congress and the Nation Vol. II*, pp. 227–251, 281–305, 779–823; for the years 1969–1972, *Congress and the Nation Vol. III*, pp. 147–187, 659–700; for the years 1973–1976, *Congress and the Nation Vol. IV*, pp. 146–147, 433–451, 505–555; for the years 1977–1980, *Congress and the Nation Vol. V*, pp. 291–362; for the years 1981–1984, *Congress and the Nation Vol. VI*, pp. 261–286, 289–329; for the years 1985–1988, *Congress and the Nation Vol. VII*, pp. 357–413; for the years 1989–1992, *Congress and the Nation Vol. VIII*, pp. 415–464.

Outlays for Transportation

Billions of Dollars

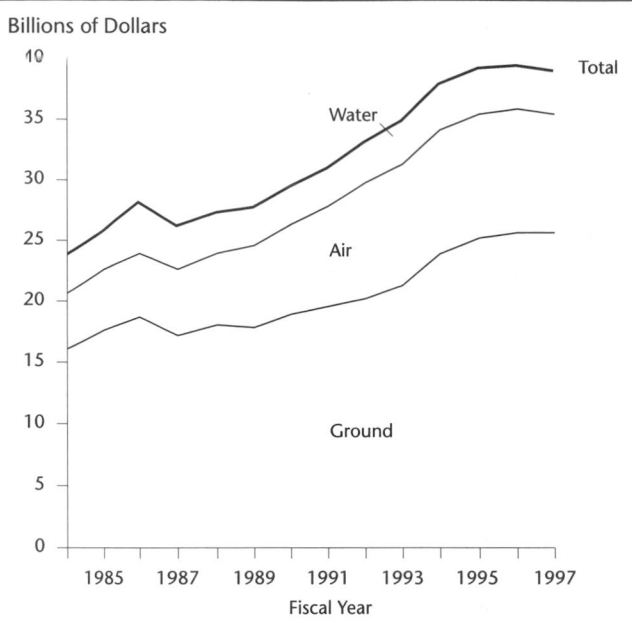

NOTE: Data for 1997 are estimated.

SOURCE: Office of Management and Budget, *Historical Tables, Budget of the United States Government: Fiscal Year 1998* (Washington, D.C.: U.S. Government Printing Office, 1997), Table 3.2.

cialize new technologies. His Democratic allies in Congress proposed hundreds of millions of dollars in subsidies for high-tech manufacturers, hoping to boost U.S. competitiveness in the global marketplace.

Republicans resisted the proposal, calling it corporate welfare. They successfully forced the spending level to be cut in the Senate, and the bill later died in conference. The measure had included one of Vice President Al Gore's top priorities, a proposal to boost spending on advanced communications and computer networks.

Democrats also pushed a number of bills to protect consumers, including measures to improve toy safety and crack down on telemarketing fraud. The most significant enactment aided consumers and businesses alike by overhauling bankruptcy law to speed up the process and make it more fair.

When they assumed the majority, Republicans sought to pare back the powers of the government and the courts. For example, freshmen Republicans pushed to eliminate the Commerce Department and terminate subsidies for technology development. Those proposals were stymied in the face of opposition from the White House and some senior Senate Republicans.

The Republican majority's dislike of subsidies even extended to popular Small Business Administration (SBA) programs. Congress enacted legislation in 1995 and in 1996 to reduce the amount of subsidy involved in the SBA loan programs, and it moved in 1996 to reduce the subsidies involved in the SBA's venture-capital programs.

The GOP did succeed in eliminating the Interstate Commerce Commission, the oldest federal regulatory body. The commission had lost most of its power over the years, so the move was more symbolic than substantive.

Congress also cleared a major bill to limit product-liability lawsuits after conservative Republicans abandoned their efforts to limit all civil claims. The measure had long been a top priority for manufacturers and insurance companies, which argued that lawsuits were raising costs and deterring innovation. The measure was killed by a veto, however, as Clinton sided with the trial lawyers and consumer advocates who opposed the bill.

COMMUNICATIONS LEGISLATION

For more than 20 years, lawmakers had sought to adapt the Communications Act of 1934 to the technology-driven changes in the communications industry. The issue was so complex, however, that Congress could only address pieces of the puzzle, such as cable television regulations and satellite transmissions. Meanwhile, a 1982 consent decree that broke up AT&T made the federal courts the actual regulators of the telephone industry.

In 1994, leading House Democrats and Republicans came up with a compromise plan to overhaul the Communications Act and open the telephone and cable television markets to competition. Backed by almost all segments of the industry, the legislation swept through the House with only a handful of dissenting votes. A competing Senate proposal drew more complaints from industry, however, and it ran into insurmountable hurdles in that chamber. The main opponents were the regional Bell telephone companies and their Republican allies, who argued that the proposal was too regulatory.

In 1995, Republican leaders put a deregulatory spin on the previous year's bill. The central purpose of the legislation remained the same—moving the industry from monopoly to competition—but companies were given more control over their own destinies. Regulators were given less time and discretion, and more of the existing rules on broadcasters, phone companies and cable operators were discarded.

To win the support of the White House, however, GOP leaders had to make numerous concessions in conference. These changes left more power in the hands of regulators than Republicans had sought, limiting the freedom granted to industry. Still, the final version of the bill, which Clinton signed in February 1996, placed more faith in market forces and less in government controls than the 1994 legislation had proposed.

In addition to laying the groundwork for the final telecommunications bill, the 103rd Congress enacted two significant measures affecting the communications industry. One called for the government to make a sizable amount of the electromagnetic spectrum available for wireless communications technologies, such as portable phones. Breaking sharply from past practice, however, Congress ordered the frequencies to be auctioned off to the highest bidder, not handed out free by lottery. Congress also ordered the local phone companies in 1994 to adapt their networks so that the advances in technology would not frustrate court-ordered wiretaps. The move set the stage for future battles over how to pay for the changes that the FBI and other agencies demanded.

Chronology of Action on Transportation, Commerce and Communications

1993–1994

In keeping with the thrust of his 1992 campaign, President Clinton sent Congress a number of ambitious proposals in 1993 to promote transportation and high-technology industries. In virtually every case, however, lawmakers rejected the president's plan or stopped far short of his mark.

Clinton led off in 1993 by proposing to spend $4.2 billion on highway and mass-transit projects as part of a $16.3 billion "economic stimulus" package. The transportation funding was blocked in the Senate after Republicans, who had not been consulted on what to put in the package, refused to allow so large an increase in deficit spending. (*'Stimulus' supplemental, p. 57*)

In a similar vein, Congress rejected initiatives by Transportation Secretary Federico F. Peña to revive the maritime industry with $1 billion in new subsidies, promote high-speed rail with $1.3 billion in federal grants, and revitalize the aviation industry by freeing the air-traffic control system from federal regulations. An administration push to provide $17 billion in subsidies and tax breaks for high-tech companies also fell flat.

Congress was more receptive to proposals that involved no federal dollars, particularly if they were limited in scope. Trucking companies won freedom from most federal and state economic regulations, although safety and insurance rules remained intact. A major bill to limit product liability lawsuits died in the Senate, but a modest bill to limit such claims against the manufacturers of small planes made its way into law.

Transportation safety measures had a mixed record, with Congress reauthorizing existing programs but shying away from most new ones. Lawmakers were late in reauthorizing the airport improvement grants program, costing airports hundreds of millions of dollars in aid. And when Congress tried to designate routes for a major new highway system ahead of schedule, the legislation died in a dispute over lawmakers' pet projects.

The most significant piece of commercial legislation enacted in the 103rd Congress may have been a bill to make federal bankruptcy proceedings more expeditious and fair to all parties. Despite its broad reach, however, the bill was more a compendium of small changes than an overhaul of the bankruptcy system.

For consumers, Congress approved new protections against unfair advertising, hazardous toys and telemarketing scams. The small businesses that operated gas stations for the oil companies also won more protection against having their franchises unfairly revoked.

In the field of telecommunications, lawmakers came closer than ever before to rewriting the 1934 Communications Act and taking control over the phone networks back from the federal courts. Although the legislation died in the Senate late in 1994, it laid the groundwork for a successful effort in the 104th Congress.

The telecommunications bill died largely because the local phone companies contended it was too burdensome. Phone company lobbyists made a similar argument against a bill to ensure that police could tap and trace calls on the increasingly sophisticated telephone networks. Their complaints could not stop the bill from becoming law, however, largely because FBI Director Louis J. Freeh pushed relentlessly for the measure.

Airlines' Revitalization

Alarmed by the multibillion-dollar losses of U.S. airlines but uncertain how to address them, Congress quickly cleared legislation (HR 904—PL 103-13) in 1993 to accelerate a study mandated the year before. The results of the study landed with a thud four months later, generating little interest and no tangible results.

The aviation industry had a history of slumps and rallies, but it went into an unusually long and steep tailspin from 1990 to 1992. The industry posted some $10 billion in losses during that period, and its hard times continued in early 1993.

Late in 1992, Congress created a national commission to examine the plight of the airlines as part of a reauthorization bill (PL 102-581) for the Federal Aviation Administration (FAA). The seven-member National Commission to Ensure a Strong Competitive Airline Industry was given six months to complete its work but no money. Although President Bush filled his one appointment, Congress did not name the remaining six members and the commission did not begin its work.

When Federico F. Peña, took over as secretary of the Transportation Department in early 1993, he announced that revitalizing the aviation industry was one of his top priorities. On his request, Congress wasted little time enacting a bill to put the study commission back on a fast track. The final version of the measure passed the Senate by voice vote March 17, 1993, and cleared the House by voice vote March 23.

As signed into law by President Clinton on April 7, the measure expanded the study commission to 15 voting and 11 nonvoting members, shortened its deadline to 90 days, provided $750,000 for staff and allowed the president to appoint one-third of its members instead of one-seventh.

The commission released its report Aug. 19, 1993, calling for the government to spin off the air-traffic control system into an independent government corporation. The commission reasoned that government procurement and personnel regulations were hindering the badly needed modernization of the air-traffic control system, which in turn was causing costly delays for the airlines. The commission also urged the government to limit the cost of federal regulations on airlines, negotiate more landing rights overseas, cut taxes on the industry and its customers, and allow greater foreign investment in U.S. air carriers.

The report drew at best a lukewarm response, not even generating any hearings in 1993. Although the Clinton administration embraced the commission's call for an independent air-traffic control corporation, key lawmakers blasted the idea. On the second-to-last day of the 1994 session, the chairmen of the House and Senate aviation subcommittees introduced bills (HR 5274, S

2546) with a competing proposal: making the FAA independent from the Transportation Department. The sponsor of the Senate bill, Democrat Wendell H. Ford of Kentucky, said the purpose of the bills was to establish a starting point for discussion on the issue in the 104th Congress. *(FAA overhaul, p. 361)* ❑

FAA Reauthorization

Congress in 1994 cleared a bill (HR 2739—PL 103-305) to reauthorize the Federal Aviation Administration (FAA) and an airport grants program after resolving a long series of messy policy disputes over liability, landing fees and other issues. The eight-month delay resulted in a sharp cut in grants to airports, a reduction that would carry over into future appropriations bills.

Some lawmakers had hoped to use HR 2739 to address the flagging fortunes of the U.S. airline industry, but they were deterred by the lack of consensus. Instead, the legislation made only incremental changes in policy.

LEGISLATIVE ACTION

Congress in 1992 had reauthorized most FAA programs through fiscal 1995 (PL 102-581). The main exception was the Airport Improvement Program, which was reauthorized only through fiscal 1993 because of a dispute over compensation for victims of air terrorism. *(Congress and the Nation Vol. VIII, p. 446)*

The Airport Improvement Program, which supported construction projects, runway maintenance and equipment purchases, had to be reauthorized by Oct. 1, 1993, to keep federal money flowing to airports. Congress did not come close to meeting that deadline.

The House passed HR 2739, a three-year reauthorization bill for the airport grants and other FAA programs, by a vote of 384–42 on Oct. 13, 1993. The House Public Works and Transportation Committee had reported the bill (H Rept 103-240) on Sept. 14.

The Senate on Oct. 21 cleared a transportation spending bill for fiscal 1994 (HR 2750—PL 103-122) that made $1.69 billion available for airport grants once Congress reauthorized the program.

The Senate Commerce, Science and Transportation Committee reported a one-year reauthorization bill (S 1491—S Rept 103-181) on Nov. 12, but the bill bogged down late in 1993. First, Sen. Nancy Landon Kassebaum, R-Kan., threatened to attach a controversial measure (S 1458) limiting the liability of small-plane manufacturers whose products crashed. Then the bill was snared in a dispute between airports and airlines over landing fees. The Supreme Court had ruled on Jan. 24, 1994, in *Northwest Airlines Inc. v. Kent County, Mich.,* that airports had wide latitude to set landing fees and rents, but the airlines wanted the fees to be limited in recognition of the money airports were making off of parking, gift shops and other concessions. *(Aircraft liability, p. 347; Supreme Court decision, p. 765)*

The Senate finally passed HR 2739 by voice vote June 16, 1994, after substituting the text of S 1491. The bill included a series of riders addressing unrelated issues, ranging from the

Whitewater imbroglio to North Korean aggression to state regulation of certain interstate trucking companies. The latter issue stalled the bill for weeks. *(Trucking regulation, p. 333)*

The House finally adopted the conference report to HR 2739 (H Rept 103-677) by voice vote on Aug. 8, and the Senate cleared the bill by voice vote later the same day.

MAJOR PROVISIONS

As signed into law Aug. 23, the bill authorized the FAA to award $2.1 billion in airport-improvement grants in fiscal 1994, $2.2 billion in fiscal 1995 and $2.2 billion in fiscal 1996. The long delay, however, prompted appropriators to restrict the FAA to spending only $1.45 billion in fiscal 1995 and 1996—a drop of $350 million, or almost 20 percent, from fiscal 1993.

The FAA administrator was given a five-year term, a move aimed at promoting stability in aviation policy. Previous administrators had served at the president's discretion, leading the average FAA leader to stay at the helm for only two years.

The measure did not require airports to consider their concession revenue when setting landing fees, as the airlines had sought. Instead, it set up a way for the Transportation Department to resolve disputes over landing fees speedily and toughened the rules against local officials using airport revenues for nonaviation purposes.

Other main provisions of the law required air carriers to give 45 days' notice before terminating service to airports that were not hubs; barred the use of gambling devices on international flights; ordered the FAA to study the effectiveness and cost of child-restraint systems on aircraft; and required the FAA to consider allowing airlines to test fewer employees for illegal drug use—a costly burden that the airlines wanted to lighten.

TEMPORARY RELIEF

While the reauthorization bill was still bogged down in the Senate, its sponsor, Democrat Wendell H. Ford of Kentucky, steered a stopgap airport-grants measure (S 2024—PL 103-260) through Congress. S 2024 initially passed the Senate April 19, 1994, and the House May 3, by voice votes. The final version of the bill passed the Senate by voice vote May 12, cleared the House by voice vote May 17, and was signed into law by President Clinton May 26.

The measure allowed the FAA to award up to $800 million in airport grants by June 30. The minimum grant for small airports was raised from $400,000 to $500,000, and the FAA was given discretion over no less than $325 million in annual airport-improvement grants. ❑

Smoking Ban on Flights

The House passed a bill (HR 4495) late in the 1994 session to ban smoking on the American segments of international flights, but the measure saw no action in the Senate.

Congress in 1987 had banned smoking on short domestic flights, and it extended the ban in 1989 to all flights of six hours or less within the continental United States. HR 4495 proposed to ban smoking on any international flight segment that started or ended anywhere in the United States, whether the airline was domestic or foreign.

At the House Public Works and Transportation Committee markup, an amendment to postpone the ban until July 1, 1996, was rejected, 20–42. The later date would have coincided with the goal set by the International Civil Aviation Organization for banning smoking on all international flights. The panel reported HR 4495 (H Rept 103-771) on Oct. 3 and the full House passed the bill by voice vote the next day.

No action was taken in the Senate, in part because the chairman of the Commerce Committee Subcommittee on Aviation, Democrat Wendell H. Ford of Kentucky, opposed airline smoking restrictions.   ❏

National Highway System

A disagreement between the House and Senate over pork-barrel projects spelled doom in 1994 for a bill (S 1887) to designate routes for a new National Highway System (NHS).

The ostensible purpose of the bill was to comply with the 1991 surface transportation act (PL 102-240), which created the NHS. That law gave Congress until Sept. 30, 1995, to identify routes for the new system. (Congress and the Nation Vol. VIII, p. 437)

The House version of the bill (HR 4385), however, included $2 billion worth of new road and mass transit projects as well as a slew of proposed changes to the 1991 law. The Senate Environment and Public Works Committee balked at the projects, and the bill died without a conference convening.

The demise of the bill did not have any immediate effect on state highway programs, which suffered no loss in federal highway grants. Key lawmakers noted that the deadline for designating the routes would not arrive until well into the 104th Congress, adding that the lack of time pressure contributed to the stalemate between the two chambers.

Indeed, Congress did not manage to clear a bill designating the routes until late 1995, several weeks after the deadline passed. (1995 action, p. 363)

Senate and House committees also had far different motivations in pursuing the legislation. Leaders of the House Public Works and Transportation Committee had gone through a bruising turf battle over highway projects with the House Appropriations Transportation Subcommittee in 1993, and they wanted to reassert themselves in that arena. Leaders of the Senate Environment and Public Works Committee, on the other hand, had no such problem with their appropriators. They also felt less pressure from their colleagues to direct money to specific projects. (Box, p. 332)

BACKGROUND

The 1991 law established the NHS as a successor to the interstate highway system, which was scheduled to be completed in 1996. The goal was to direct about 30 percent of the federal highway aid to the roads most important to interstate commerce, national defense, tourism and transportation centers, such as airports and train stations.

TRANSPORTATION, COMMERCE LEADERSHIP

Ronald H. Brown won confirmation as secretary of commerce by voice vote Jan. 21, 1993, after quieting concerns about his past lobbying activities, including his representation of former Haitian dictator Jean-Claude "Baby Doc" Duvalier and U.S. subsidiaries of Japanese electronics firms. A longtime Washington insider and Democratic operative, Brown had been the first African American to run a major U.S. political party. Brown worked as commerce secretary both to restructure the department and to boost U.S. companies in developing countries. Although the business community lauded him for his work on its behalf, Republicans blasted Brown for some questionable financial deals. Brown was killed in a plane crash on April 3, 1996, while on a business trip to Croatia. (Background, cabinet profiles, p. 1110)

Brown was succeeded by Mickey Kantor, the U.S. trade representative. Avoiding a debate over the fate of the Commerce Department, the chairman of the Senate Commerce, Science and Transportation Committee decided not to hold hearings on Kantor's nomination to replace Brown. President Clinton picked Kantor to lead the Commerce Department on April 12, nine days after Brown's death. Because the appointment was made while the Senate was in recess, Kantor did not have to be confirmed until the end of 1997. Commerce Committee Chairman Larry Pressler, R-S.D., said in mid-June 1996 that the committee was simply too busy to hold hearings on Kantor, who had gone through the Senate confirmation process in 1993 as Clinton's choice to be trade representative. (Background, cabinet profiles, p. 1110)

Clinton's choice to lead the Transportation Department, Federico F. Peña, easily won confirmation early in 1993. His nomination was approved by voice vote Jan. 21. One of two Hispanics in Clinton's original cabinet, Peña came to Washington from Denver, where he had been mayor from 1983 to 1991 and a lawyer and investment adviser after that. Peña had little success with Congress, which largely ignored his attempts to lead on transportation funding, air-traffic-control modernization, highway safety and high-speed rail. Congress did agree to renew and overhaul the subsidies for merchant ships in 1996, but it did not provide the dedicated funding mechanism that Peña advocated. (Background, cabinet profiles, p. 1114)

On July 26, 1993, the Senate by voice vote easily confirmed Arthur Levitt Jr., the former chairman of the American Stock Exchange, to become the chairman of the Securities and Exchange Commission. He succeeded Richard C. Breeden, a Republican who was popular on Capitol Hill, as the nation's top securities regulator. A New Yorker who helped raise big money for Clinton, Levitt had broad experience in the markets. He built a small brokerage house into the giant that later became Shearson Lehman Bros. Inc. He also guided the American Stock Exchange through the 1987 stock market crash.

After consulting with state transportation officials, the Transportation Department proposed roughly 160,000 miles of routes for the NHS in December 1993. The routes, the vast ma-

SPECIAL HIGHWAY PROJECTS

In another chapter in a long-running turf war between authorizers and appropriators, the House Public Works and Transportation Committee held off two attempts by the House Appropriations Transportation Subcommittee in 1993 to steer money to unauthorized road and bridge projects. The projects had been attached to the transportation spending bill for fiscal 1994 (HR 2750—PL 103-122).

The appropriators, usually in consultation with the Public Works panel, traditionally had steered money from the general Treasury to lawmakers' pet projects, while the authorizing committee had funneled money from the Highway Trust Fund to similar ventures. The main difference was timing: the appropriators acted every year, while authorization bills came along once every four to six years.

The start of the 103rd Congress ushered in new chairmen at the Public Works Committee, Democrat Norman Y. Mineta of California, and at the Appropriations Transportation Subcommittee, Democrat Bob Carr of Michigan. Carr announced early in 1993 that the subcommittee would try to break from the past practice of choosing projects based on their importance to lawmakers and instead use a new set of "investment criteria" to judge the economic and transportation value of lawmakers' requests.

Using those criteria, Carr's subcommittee twice tried to spend some $300 million out of the Highway Trust Fund on projects not fully authorized by Congress as part of the transportation spending bill for fiscal 1994. The first effort (HR 2490—H Rept 103-149) was pulled off the floor by the House leadership on July 22 in the face of a Public Works Committee revolt.

When the subcommittee returned with a bill (HR 2750—H Rept 103-190) little different from the first, the leadership-controlled House Rules Committee proposed to leave the projects open to procedural attack by Public Works members on the House floor. The appropriators were not able to stop the House from adopting the rule Sept. 22, 257–163. Mineta subsequently knocked the disputed projects out of the bill by invoking a House rule against ap-

propriating money for unauthorized programs, although the House later agreed to provide $33.8 million out of the general Treasury for four of the projects.

The victory for the Public Works Committee was complete, and Carr did not attempt to restore funding for any of the other projects in conference. Still, Carr's move had a clear effect on Mineta's panel. Before the appropriators released their transportation spending bill for fiscal 1995, the Public Works Committee rushed a bill (HR 4385) through the House authorizing a raft of new highway projects. And those projects were judged, in part, according to a list of "investment criteria" modeled after Carr's. *(National Highway System, p. 331)*

Fiscal 1995 Fight

In 1994, the House appropriators toed the line drawn by Public Works. Their bill for fiscal 1995 (HR 4556) included slightly under $300 million for special highway projects, all of them authorized or included in HR 4385. The Senate came up with its own proposal for $352 million in special projects; in conference on Sept. 22, negotiators for the two chambers agreed to split the larger Senate pot roughly down the middle.

A new dispute over special projects emerged at that point. The top Republican on Carr's subcommittee, Frank R. Wolf of Virginia, objected to the $90 million that the Senate conferees had steered to a single project in West Virginia, home of the venerable Senate Appropriations Committee chairman, Democrat Robert C. Byrd. Wolf threatened to call for a recorded vote on the project on the House floor unless the Senate trimmed the grant—a highly unusual demand, given the appropriators' tradition of letting each chamber distribute its share of the dollars for special projects as it saw fit.

Still, it would have been difficult for the West Virginia project to survive such a vote. With time running down in the session, Byrd agreed to a far smaller grant—$35 million—to avoid a stalemate between the chambers over the final version (PL 103-331).

jority of which had already been built, carried 40 percent of the nation's drivers and 75 percent of its commercial traffic. Included in the list were all the interstates, the Defense Department's Strategic Highway Network, and 21 "high priority corridors" named by Congress in 1991.

Leaders of the House Public Works Committee agreed to advance an NHS bill that would not only designate the routes recommended by the Transportation Department but also authorize numerous new transportation projects favored by lawmakers. Their hand had been forced to some degree by the appropriators, who had tried to authorize $300 million in special projects in 1993 only to be blocked in a rules fight.

By early 1994, the committee had received more than 900 proposals totaling $32.4 billion. Committee leaders, meanwhile, had identified $1.15 billion that had been awarded from the Highway Trust Fund but not yet spent, including funds for dor-

mant or underused highway safety and high-speed rail programs. They also proposed authorizing some $900 million from the general Treasury for projects over the following three years.

That left the leadership with about $2 billion for projects, or $1 for every $16 in requests. Chairman Norman Y. Mineta, D-Calif., assigned about 60 percent of the money to projects sought by Democrats, particularly those who had supported the Democratic leadership on tough votes in 1993. Mineta let the committee's top Republican, Bud Shuster of Pennsylvania, parcel out the rest to projects sought by Republicans.

One other element included in the original House measure was a so-called technical corrections bill (HR 3276) that proposed dozens of changes to the 1991 law. The bill had been reported by the House Public Works Committee (H Rept 103-337) and passed by a voice vote of the full House Nov. 8, 1993, but the Senate had taken no action on it.

Although many of the changes proposed by HR 3276 were truly technical, some were more substantive in nature. For example, the measure would have given states an additional year to mandate the use of seat belts and motorcycle helmets before they risked losing highway construction aid. It also would have dictated or altered the path of numerous highway projects funded by the 1991 law.

LEGISLATIVE ACTION

The House Public Works Committee put HR 4385 on a fast track in May, reporting it May 19 (H Rept 103-519). The full House approved it on May 25 by a vote of 412–12.

At every step toward passage, the bill's sponsors added more special projects. The final tally for the House version: 287 road and bridge projects worth $1.4 billion and 65 transit projects worth $605 million.

Virtually all the discussion of projects occurred behind closed doors, and only Rep. Jon Kyl, R-Ariz., opposed them publicly. In a statement inserted into the *Congressional Record,* Kyl said, "The problem with earmarking is that funds are allocated, not necessarily according to merit or which projects will help the United States of America most, but rather according to how well connected politically the project sponsors are. Fifty-five percent of the total funding earmarked in HR 4385 goes to 10 states which just happen to be represented by 36 of the 64 Public Works Committee members."

Most of the debate over the bill during committee consideration concerned whether to repeal the penalties that the 1991 law imposed on states that did not require motorcyclists to wear helmets or highway contractors to use recycled rubber in a portion of their paving projects. As passed by the House, the bill weakened the mandate to use recycled rubber but did not change the motorcycle helmet provision.

Leaders of the Senate Environment and Public Works Committee responded with a "clean" NHS bill (S 1887—S Rept 103-357), which the committee reported Aug. 23. The bill would have designated the NHS routes recommended by the Transportation Department and allowed the department to add routes at the states' request without congressional approval.

With committee chairman Max Baucus, D-Mont., holding firm against special projects, the Senate passed the bill by voice vote Sept. 23 without amendment and virtually without debate. The House took up the bill six days later, substituted the contents of HR 4385, and passed the amended bill by voice vote.

Baucus had said that he would not go to conference unless the House dropped the special projects and "technical corrections" from the bill. Committee staff members also said that the funding mechanism in the House bill would not pass the Senate's budget rules, necessitating large-scale cuts in other highway programs in future years.

With time running out on the session, Baucus offered to accept some of the House projects on one condition: that the money for each state's projects come out of that state's annual allocation from the Highway Trust Fund. Mineta initially said he could accept the proposal, but other members of his committee insisted on raising the money for the new projects by

canceling old ones. Unable to narrow their differences, Mineta and Baucus decided not to convene a conference and the legislation died.   ❏

Seismic Retrofits

Spurred by a Jan. 17, 1994, earthquake in Southern California, Congress cleared a bill to let states use federal bridge-repair grants to gird their bridges against future tremors. President Clinton signed the measure into law March 17, 1994 (S 1789—PL 103-220).

The Federal Highway Administration had allowed federal bridge repair dollars to be used for "seismic retrofits" only on bridges that were damaged or structurally deficient. This policy prevented states like California from using federal dollars to pay for preventative measures on healthy bridges.

House Public Works Committee Chairman Norman Y. Mineta, D-Calif., had introduced a bill (HR 1435) in March 1993 to overturn the highway administration's policy. Sen. Barbara Boxer, D-Calif., introduced a similar proposal (S 1789) eight days after the earthquake collapsed several highway overpasses around Los Angeles. The Senate Environment and Public Works Committee reported the bill Feb. 4 and the Senate passed it by voice vote Feb. 7.

The House approved Boxer's version by voice vote March 2. As signed into law, the measure allowed states to use bridge repair dollars for seismic retrofits on bridges not otherwise in need of repair, with no loss in future bridge repair dollars.   ❏

Trucking Regulation

The 103rd Congress swept away years of regulation on trucking companies, although the change occurred more by happenstance than design. Lawmakers first settled a long-running dispute over interstate trucking prices by retroactively nullifying one set of federal rules. Then they removed most of the remaining federal controls on interstate trucking as well as key state regulations on trucking within their borders.

SHIPMENT UNDERCHARGES

Rolling over the objections of organized labor, Congress cleared a bill (S 412—PL 103-180) late in 1993 to limit the amount that creditors of bankrupt trucking companies could collect from shippers who had paid rates below the ones on file with the Interstate Commerce Commission (ICC).

The dispute over undercharges was a byproduct of the last round of trucking deregulation, in 1980 (PL 96-296), when Congress ended the ICC's power to decide which companies served which routes. Companies were still required to file their rates with the ICC and offer equivalent rates to customers making equivalent shipments. The increase in competition spawned by deregulation, however, led many companies to vie for valuable customers by offering discounts well below the rates on file.

The competition also led to a wave of bankruptcies. The bankrupt companies' creditors—most notably the International

Brotherhood of Teamsters, the AFL-CIO and other representatives of the employees who had lost their jobs, pensions and other benefits—responded by suing the shippers to collect the difference between the discounted rates and the rates on file.

After the Supreme Court in 1990 upheld the creditors' right to sue, a coalition of shippers and trucking companies appealed to Congress for help. Lobbyists for the coalition argued that the creditors were trying to renege on deals that had been negotiated in good faith. Union lobbyists responded by blaming the undercharges for the bankruptcies. They also argued that the shippers' money was needed to pay the wages and benefits owed to workers, but the coalition's allies countered that only a small percentage of the money won in undercharge lawsuits had made its way to the employees.

Sen. Jim Exon, D-Neb., tried in vain to overturn the court's ruling in 1990, then pushed a bill through the Senate in 1992 to allow shippers to settle undercharge lawsuits by paying a small percentage of the amount claimed. The bill stalled in the House, however, after intense lobbying by the Teamsters. *(Congress and the Nation Vol. VIII, p. 445)*

Exon tried again in 1993. A nearly identical proposal (S 412—S Rept 103-79) was reported by the Senate Commerce, Science and Transportation Committee June 29 and was passed by voice vote of the full Senate July 1. The main difference was that S 412 exempted charitable organizations from having to pay undercharge claims.

On Nov. 15, the House Public Works and Transportation Committee reported and the full House approved, 292–116, a bill (HR 2121—H Rept 103-359) that called for shippers to pay a higher percentage on undercharge claims but exempted more shipments. The House inserted its language into the text of S 412 by voice vote that same day, and the Senate cleared the modified bill by voice vote Nov. 19.

As signed into law Dec. 3, the measure allowed shippers to settle undercharge claims by paying 15 percent of the claim for shipments larger than 10,000 pounds, 20 percent for smaller ones. No payment was required for undercharge claims on shipments made before Oct. 1, 1990—an exemption that wiped out 90 to 95 percent of all claims, critics said. Small businesses, charitable organizations and recyclers also were exempted from undercharge claims.

FEDERAL REGULATIONS

Congress ensured in 1994 that there would be no repeat of the undercharge dispute, passing legislation eliminating the need for trucking companies to file rates with the Interstate Commerce Commission (ICC).

The change was included in a bill (HR 2178—PL 103-311) to reauthorize federal safety programs for the transportation of hazardous materials. It was prompted less by the undercharge legislation, however, than by the growing number of lawmakers who favored eliminating the ICC.

The House fired the first shot, adopting by a vote of 234–192 on June 16, 1994, an amendment by John R. Kasich, R-Ohio, to eliminate funding for the ICC in the fiscal 1995 transportation spending bill (HR 4556—PL 103-331). Although conferees on

that bill later restored most of the funding for the ICC, Sens. Jim Exon, D-Neb., and Bob Packwood, R-Ore., advanced a bill (S 2275) to shrink the ICC by eliminating the remainder of its power over interstate trucking companies.

The Senate attached the Exon-Packwood proposal to the House-passed hazardous materials bill by voice vote Aug. 11, before passing the bill by another voice vote. The House agreed to the amendment on Aug. 16, clearing HR 2178. President Clinton signed the bill 10 days later. *(Hazardous shipments, p. 336)*

The measure ended for all trucking companies—except household-goods movers and bus lines—the requirement to file interstate rates with the ICC. It also simplified the process of getting a license for interstate service, requiring companies to show only that they met federal safety and insurance standards. The ICC previously had required companies to demonstrate that "public convenience and necessity" justified the service.

STATE REGULATIONS

Shortly before it eliminated most interstate trucking regulations, Congress extinguished much of the states' regulatory power over trucking companies.

As part of a bill to reauthorize federal aviation programs (HR 2739—PL 103-305), Congress preempted all state economic regulation of trucking companies. The preemption barred states from controlling prices and routes, but it did not affect safety regulations, size and weight limits, insurance requirements, uniform business rules or regulations on household-goods movers. *(FAA reauthorization, p. 330)*

The idea started with a bid by Sen. Wendell H. Ford, D-Ky., to help United Parcel Service (UPS) compete with Federal Express. Ford's provision would have exempted all package delivery services from state trucking regulations, giving UPS the same relief that Federal Express had won through the courts in 1991.

The exemption grew on the Senate floor during debate over the Senate version of the aviation bill (S 1491), covering an increasing number of trucking companies. Then, in conference on HR 2739, House negotiators proposed that the exemption apply to all trucking companies, and the Senate accepted. The only exception made was for truckers in Hawaii, which the bill kept under state regulation for three years after enactment.

The House approved the final version of the bill by voice vote Aug. 8, and the Senate cleared it by voice vote the same day. President Clinton signed the measure into law Aug. 23.

Near the end of the 1994 session, the House and Senate each passed versions of a bill to let states keep in effect all their regulations on tow trucks and wreckers. The Senate version of the bill (HR 5123), which passed by voice vote Oct. 6, went farther than the House version, which passed by voice vote Sept. 29—the Senate bill also would have preserved state and local control over garbage haulers and curbside recycling programs. The differences could not be reconciled before Congress adjourned, but a compromise version was enacted in 1995 as part of a bill eliminating the ICC. *(1995 action, p. 381)*

High-Speed Rail

The Clinton administration's proposed foray into high-speed passenger rail lines foundered in the 103rd Congress, unable to overcome opposition from freight railroads and transportation unions.

Congress eventually authorized $184 million through fiscal 1997 to help states plan high-speed rail corridors and develop the technology. By contrast, Transportation Secretary Federico F. Peña had proposed a five-year, $1.3 billion program in April 1993 that would have started building high-speed rail projects.

The authorization was part of HR 4867 (PL 103-440), a bill that also reauthorized federal railroad safety programs. As signed into law Nov. 2, 1994, the measure authorized the Transportation Department to cover up to half of the planning costs of a new publicly financed high-speed rail corridor. It also required the department to develop safety regulations for high-speed services. *(Railroad safety, p. 337)*

The administration's push for high-speed rail began with an April 28, 1993, press conference on the Capitol lawn, where Peña laid out an ambitious plan for bringing futuristic rail service to the United States. Top Democrats on the House and Senate authorizing committees quickly introduced legislation to carry out Peña's plan, and the measures slowly picked up steam.

The House Energy and Commerce Committee approved its version (HR 1919—H Rept 103-258) on July 27, 1993, 28–16, and reported it Sept. 28. The bill would have authorized $1.2 billion over five years to cover up to half the cost of designing, acquiring and building high-speed rail corridors. The Senate Commerce, Science and Transportation Committee approved a competing proposal (S 839—S Rept 103-208) by voice vote Nov. 9 and reported it Nov. 23. The Senate version would have authorized $982 million over five years. Both measures also proposed to authorize $75 million to develop related technology.

The measures soon ran into separate but equally intractable problems.

The House bill, which guaranteed 18 months of pay and benefits for transportation workers displaced by new high-speed rail lines, was opposed by transportation union lobbyists who wanted more protection against job losses. The freight railroads also demanded protection against liability in the event of accidents involving high-speed trains on their tracks.

Republicans also objected to a provision of the bill that would have applied the 1931 Davis-Bacon Act to contracts funded by the high-speed rail program. That law required federal contractors to pay the prevailing local wage, which typically was the local union wage.

The Senate bill proposed to make the agency receiving the high-speed rail grant obtain $500 million in liability insurance for itself, the operator of the high-speed train and the owner of the tracks. That provision would have imposed a financial hurdle, however, for states looking to launch a high-speed line.

The Senate bill did not include any of the House bill's protections for transportation labor, drawing opposition from union lobbyists. The unions also wanted the bill to require compliance with the Davis-Bacon Act, a provision that would have drawn stiff Republican opposition.

Sponsors of HR 1919 pulled the plug on the bill in August 1994, turning instead to the much less ambitious designs of HR 4867, which was reported by the House Energy and Commerce Committee Aug. 10 (H Rept 103-692). Because HR 4867 did not include any money to build high-speed routes, it did not need to address the issues of job losses, liability or Davis-Bacon.

The House passed HR 4867 on Aug. 16, 281–103, and the Senate passed an amended version by voice vote the next day. By voice votes, the House approved another version on Oct. 7 and the Senate cleared the bill Oct. 8.   ❑

Amtrak Reauthorization

Bills to authorize a significant increase in funding for financially troubled Amtrak, the national railroad corporation, failed to reach the floor in either chamber in 1994.

The House Energy and Commerce Committee on Aug. 11, 1994, reported a bill (HR 4111—H Rept 103-698) that would have authorized $878 million in fiscal 1995 and $890 million in fiscal 1996 for Amtrak's operations, capital improvements and retirement obligations, up from $790 million in fiscal 1994. An additional $250 million would have been authorized each year for the Northeast Corridor, the high-speed line Amtrak was developing from Washington, D.C., to Boston. The bill also proposed to require states to pick up a larger share of the cost of routes that Amtrak served on their request.

On Sept. 28, the Senate Commerce, Science and Transportation Committee reported its own Amtrak bill (S 2002). That proposal would have authorized $788 million in fiscal 1995 and $895 million in fiscal 1996 for the railroad, plus $250 million in fiscal 1995 and $275 million in fiscal 1996 for the Northeast Corridor.

Neither measure advanced further. Despite the lack of authorization, appropriators provided $772 million for Amtrak's operations, capital improvements and retirement obligations in the transportation spending bill for fiscal 1995 (HR 4556—PL 103-331). The measure also provided $40 million to begin work on a new Amtrak station in New York City, but the grant was rescinded early the next year in a supplemental spending bill for the Pentagon (PL 104-6). *(Supplemental appropriation, p. 304)*

Late in 1994, Amtrak announced that it would cut service by one-fourth, mainly by curtailing its expensive long-distance routes. Amtrak officials said that years of inadequate appropriations from Congress, particularly the sharp cuts for capital improvements in the 1980s, forced them to make the cuts.   ❑

Transportation Safety

Lawmakers reauthorized a series of transportation safety programs during the 103rd Congress, including the National Transportation Safety Board and oversight programs for railroads and shipments of hazardous materials. They also considered new safety initiatives aimed at railroad crossings, high-risk drivers and underground pipelines, but only the railroad measure made it into law.

NTSB REAUTHORIZATION

In a bid to boost aviation safety, Congress cleared a bill in 1994 to expand the jurisdiction of the National Transportation Safety Board (NTSB) and authorize more spending.

As signed by President Clinton Oct. 25, 1994, the measure (HR 2440—PL 103-411) required certain nonmilitary government aircraft to meet federal safety regulations. The requirement applied to the federal, state and local government aircraft used to transport passengers, such as a governor's official plane, not to the aircraft used to carry out safety, regulatory or law enforcement duties.

The law also gave the NTSB authority to investigate accidents involving government-owned aircraft other than military aircraft. These provisions were championed by Sen. Larry Pressler, R-S.D., in the wake of a plane crash that claimed the life of South Dakota Gov. George S. Mickelson, R, and seven others in 1993.

Created in 1966 as part of the Transportation Department and made an independent agency in 1974, the five-member NTSB investigated accidents in most forms of transportation and made nonbinding recommendations for improving safety. The measure authorized a 19 percent hike in the NTSB's budget, to $44 million in fiscal 1995 and $45.1 million in fiscal 1996. By the time the bill cleared, however, Congress had already approved a transportation spending bill for fiscal 1995 (HR 4556—PL 103-331) that increased the NTSB's funding less than 1 percent, to $37.4 million.

The original version of HR 2440 was reported by the House Public Works and Transportation Committee on Sept. 14, 1993, and by the House Energy and Commerce Committee Nov. 3 (H Rept 103-239, Parts I and II). It passed the House, 353–49, on Nov. 8. The Senate added the Pressler provisions on May 12, 1994, and approved the bill by voice vote. The House made technical changes to the bill on Oct. 4, and the Senate gave its final approval two days later.

HAZARDOUS SHIPMENTS

After resolving a number of contentious, unrelated issues, Congress in 1994 reauthorized for four years the federal programs governing the transportation of hazardous goods.

As signed into law Aug. 26, 1994, the bill (HR 2178—PL 103-311) authorized a total of $75.3 million in fiscal 1994 through fiscal 1997 for the programs established by the Hazardous Materials Transportation Act (PL 93-633). Those programs aimed to increase the safety and accountability of hazardous shipments, help states respond to toxic spills, and pay for cleanups in the event of a mishap. The act had last been reauthorized in 1990 (PL 101-615). *(PL 93-633, Congress and the Nation Vol. IV, p. 527; PL 101-615, Congress and the Nation Vol. VIII, p. 422)*

The measure also required the Transportation Department to study how new communications technologies could promote safer shipments of hazardous materials.

The House passed its version of the bill by voice vote Nov. 21, 1993, after the authorizing committees dropped contentious

proposals to allow more billboards along scenic highways and reconsider the ban on radar detectors in commercial vehicles. The House Energy and Commerce Committee had reported HR 2178 (H Rept 103-336, Part I) on Nov. 8. The Public Works and Transportation Committee the next day approved a larger bill (HR 3460) containing the controversial provisions but that bill was never reported out of committee.

The Senate passed HR 2178 by voice vote Aug. 11, 1994, after inserting a provision that eliminated much of the Interstate Commerce Commission's authority over interstate trucking. The House accepted the Senate version by voice vote Aug. 16, clearing the bill for President Clinton. *(Trucking regulation, p. 333)*

In a related action, the Senate gave voice-vote approval Oct. 8, 1994, to a bill (S 2559) ordering federal agencies not to treat vegetable oils and animal fats the same as petroleum-based products when implementing the Oil Pollution Act of 1990 (PL 101-380). The measure was intended to stop the Transportation Department from treating shipments of vegetable oils and animal fats as hazardous materials covered by the liability provisions of the 1990 law. The House took no action on the bill, however.

HIGH-RISK DRIVERS

The Senate and House approved similar bills in the 103rd Congress to deter unsafe driving by youths and repeat traffic offenders, but the measures died in end-of-session maneuvering.

The proposals (S 738, HR 5248) would have provided grants to states that adopted increasingly stringent laws for drivers, particularly in regard to youths and alcohol. The Senate proposal would have authorized $100 million in grants over five years, while the House would have authorized $114 million.

Among the steps encouraged by the bills were establishing a "zero tolerance" policy for drinking by drivers less than 21 years old; allowing minors to obtain only provisional drivers licenses; banning the possession of open containers of alcohol in a vehicle; and confiscating the vehicles of drivers convicted two or more times in five years of driving under the influence of drugs or alcohol. They also would have required the Transportation Department to study the abilities of older drivers and examine ways to limit but not prohibit their driving.

S 738 was reported by the Senate Commerce, Science and Transportation Committee (S Rept 103-199) and passed by voice vote of the Senate on Nov. 20, 1993, but the House Public Works Committee did not act on it. The Senate tried again the following year, approving the measure by voice vote Oct. 6 as part of a bill reauthorizing federal rail safety programs (HR 4545). *(Railroad safety, p. 337)*

The next day, the House included a similar high-risk driver proposal in a bill it passed by voice vote to protect underground pipelines from being ruptured by construction crews (HR 5248). Although the new version was embraced by the Senate sponsors, they could not obtain the unanimous consent needed to bring the bill to the floor before the Senate adjourned.

PIPELINE RUPTURES

Legislation to stop construction crews from inadvertently slicing through underground pipelines passed the House twice in October 1994 but died in the Senate on the final day of the session.

The bills (HR 4394, HR 5248) were spurred by the rupture of a natural gas pipeline in Edison, N.J., on March 23, 1994, that destroyed an apartment complex. The rupture was believed to have been caused by excavation work—the same cause as in 60 percent of all pipeline accidents, bill supporters said.

HR 4394, which passed the House by voice vote Oct. 3, would have authorized $4 million in grants to help states start or improve "one call" notification systems based on a model to be developed by the Transportation Department. The systems would enable construction crews to determine the location of all underground pipelines in their work area by calling a single number in each state. HR 4394 had been reported by the House Energy and Commerce Committee Sept. 29 and the House Public Works and Transportation Committee Sept. 30 (H Rept 103-765, Parts I and II).

The House again passed the provisions of HR 4394 on Oct. 7 as part of a bill (HR 5248) that also urged states to crack down on high-risk drivers. The bill was blocked in the Senate the next day, however. (High-risk drivers, p. 336)

RAILROAD SAFETY

Congress established new safety rules for railroad crossings and rail passenger cars in 1994 as part of a measure to authorize spending on high-speed rail projects (HR 4867—PL 103-440).

The measure ordered the Transportation Department to establish, on an experimental basis, a toll-free number for the public to call when railroad gates malfunctioned. It also mandated that locomotives sound their horns when approaching highway crossings that lacked certain safety features.

Other provisions of the bill authorized $316.7 million through fiscal year 1998 for more than 40 programs run by the Federal Railroad Administration related to research, development and safety. The department was instructed to set minimum safety standards for railroad passenger cars, step up its efforts against safety-threatening vandalism, promote new technologies to avert railroad collisions and establish an Institute for Railroad Safety, among other safety-related actions.

The measure also allowed freight railroads and their unions to experiment with schedules that did not comply with federal limits on work shifts if the Transportation Department approved.

The House approved an early version of the bill (HR 4545) by a vote of 395–0 on Aug. 8. The bill had been reported by the House Energy and Commerce Committee Aug. 3 (H Rept 103-655). The Senate passed a competing version of HR 4545 by voice vote Oct. 6 after adding the contents of S 738, a bill to crack down on high-risk drivers. (High-risk drivers, p. 336)

The House did not act on the amended version of HR 4545. Instead, it took its original reauthorization proposal, along with the Senate provisions on railroad crossings and railroad passenger car safety, and attached them to HR 4867, the high-speed rail bill. That measure passed by voice votes in the House Oct. 7 and the Senate Oct. 8. President Clinton signed it into law Nov. 2. (High-speed rail, p. 335) ❑

Merchant Marine Subsidies

Legislation to provide a new, leaner round of subsidies for U.S. cargo ships died in the Senate late in 1994, blocked mainly by a handful of farm-state lawmakers who had long opposed maritime subsidies that raised shipping costs.

The defeat was a blow to Transportation Secretary Federico F. Peña, who had fought hard to win the administration's support for subsidies. It also was a stinging loss for U.S. shipping lines, which had threatened to register their oceangoing vessels under foreign flags if the new subsidies were not approved.

BACKGROUND

The federal government had long supported U.S. shipping lines and shipyards. In the 1920 Jones Act, Congress required all ships carrying cargo between U.S. ports to be built, owned and registered in the United States. And in the 1936 Merchant Marine Act, Congress provided cash subsidies to U.S. ships engaged in international trade. The stated purpose was to ensure that U.S. ships and crews would be available to carry U.S. cargo in peacetime and military equipment in wartime.

The subsidies initially covered the difference between a U.S. vessel's labor costs and those on foreign vessels (the "operating differential") as well as the difference in construction costs (the "construction differential"). In 1981, however, Congress barred new construction differential subsidies in a budget-cutting move. (Congress and the Nation Vol. VI, p. 299)

Operating subsidies reached a similar point in the 103rd Congress, when they were supporting about 75 vessels. Most of the subsidy contracts were set to expire between 1993 and 1997, and Congress had not authorized any new contracts.

The shipping lines argued that the loss of subsidies would be disastrous to the shrinking U.S. merchant fleet because their operating costs were far above those of foreign vessels. They blamed U.S. laws and regulations for inflating their costs by requiring them to use U.S. crews, pay U.S. wages, comply with more costly safety standards and use vessels built in more expensive U.S. shipyards.

Signaling their dissatisfaction, the two largest lines—Sea-Land Service Inc. and American President Lines Ltd.—applied for permission in 1993 to shift 20 of their vessels to foreign registries. The chief executives of the companies told a House Merchant Marine Committee panel that year that the U.S.-flag shipping industry was in a state of "orderly liquidation."

The Bush administration proposed a new subsidy program in 1992 that would have made fixed, lower payments to U.S. vessels, and Peña championed a modified version in 1993. The Clinton administration's National Economic Council, an interagency group formed by Clinton to help set domestic policy, initially rejected the subsidy proposal, but Clinton later endorsed subsidies in response to appeals from Peña, AFL-CIO President Lane Kirkland and congressional leaders.

LEGISLATIVE ACTION

The House Merchant Marine and Fisheries Committee approved a trio of bills aimed at revitalizing the maritime industry.

One, HR 2547, reported Feb. 9, 1994 (H Rept 103-420, Part I), proposed $200 million in subsidies and loan guarantees for US shipyards. The House Armed Service Committee incorporated three of the bill's provisions—the ones regarding loan guarantees for ship purchases, loans for shipyard modernization and the development of shipbuilding technology—into the defense authorization bill for fiscal 1994 (HR 2401—PL 103-160). The appropriators followed suit, providing $50 million for loan programs and $30 million for technology development as part of the fiscal 1994 defense spending bill (HR 3116—PL 103-139).

A second Merchant Marine proposal, HR 2152, reported July 27, 1993 (H Rept 103-194, Part I), proposed tax breaks to encourage shipping lines to buy or lease new vessels built in U.S. shipyards. The bill quickly stalled in the House Ways and Means Committee and advanced no further.

The third bill, HR 2151, reported Sept. 22, 1993 (H Rept 103-251), proposed a subsidy program for shipping lines costing roughly $2 billion over 10 years. Subsidies of at least $2.1 million per vessel would be paid annually to shipping lines that pledged to aid the military in times of war or national emergency. Unlike the expiring subsidies, the new ones would not vary according to a vessel's labor costs and they would not be limited to ships built in the United States.

The Merchant Marine panel approved the bill after adding a provision, originally in HR 2547, calling for direct subsidies to U.S. shipyards that built commercial vessels. The House overwhelmingly approved the bill Nov. 4, 347–65, but the Senate Commerce Committee did not act on it because the House had not proposed a way to pay for the subsidies. HR 2151 was subsequently incorporated into a bill to raise tonnage fees (HR 4003). (Tonnage fees, below)

Foreign Shipyard Subsidies

The Ways and Means Subcommittee on Trade took a different approach to helping U.S. shipyards. It approved a bill (HR 1402) by voice vote Nov. 9, 1993, that called for high duties and entry restrictions on vessels built in subsidized foreign yards.

The bill was similar to one that Subcommittee Chairman Sam M. Gibbons, D-Fla., had pushed through the House in 1992. Answering complaints from the administration and shippers, Gibbons dropped a provision that would have imposed heavy duties on companies that used foreign-subsidized yards to build or repair their vessels. (Congress and the Nation Vol. VIII, p. 449)

Gibbons said his main goal was to give the United States more leverage in international negotiations to end shipbuilding subsidies, which had been going on for several years. Although his bill moved no further in the 103rd Congress, trade representatives for the industrialized nations agreed in July 1994 to a treaty phasing out shipyard aid.

Tonnage Fees

After several months of negotiations, proponents of the merchant marine won the administration's support in March 1994 for financing vessel subsidies with a $1 billion increase in ton-

nage fees on cargo and cruise ships entering U.S. ports. The Merchant Marine Committee went further, reporting on June 13, 1994, a bill (HR 4003—H Rept 103-544, Part I) that would have raised tonnage fees by $1.7 billion over 10 years to pay for the vessel and shipyard subsidies in HR 2151.

The Ways and Means Committee cut the proposed increase sharply, calling instead for a mixture of higher tonnage fees and excise taxes, with no subsidies for shipyards in the version it reported July 29 (H Rept 103-544, Part II). On Aug. 2, the House voted 268–153 in favor of an amendment offered by Gerry E. Studds, D-Mass, and Jack Fields, R-Texas, calling for a $1.35 billion increase in tonnage duties, providing $1 billion to subsidize vessels and $350 million to aid shipyards. The House then passed HR 4003, including the provisions of HR 2151, 294–122.

The bill drew stiff opposition from coal and grain shippers, who argued that the increase in tonnage fees would cripple their exports. The chief Senate supporters of the measure—John B. Breaux, D-La., and Trent Lott, R-Miss.—agreed to scale back the increase to $1 billion and exempt shipments of grain, coal and other dry bulk cargo. Unsatisfied, Sen. Larry Pressler, R-S.D., invoked a rarely used procedural rule to block the Senate Commerce Committee from advancing HR 4003 in the waning days of the session.

Even if Pressler had allowed the bill to move forward, the measure may never have reached the Senate floor. Senate Majority Leader George J. Mitchell, the Democrat from Maine who controlled the Senate's schedule, told Breaux that he wanted subsidies for shipping yards—something Breaux said he could not provide in light of the pending international agreement. ◻

Other Maritime Bills

A long list of bills to authorize or continue federal maritime programs passed the House during the 103rd Congress, but most sank in the Senate in the wake of the dispute over merchant marine subsidies. The exceptions included a one-year reauthorization bill for the Coast Guard and the five noncontroversial measures that were attached to it, which cleared on the last day of the 1993 session.

The successful initiatives also included one extending federal safety standards to more charter vessels. The measures that died in the Senate included proposals to bring U.S. Coast Guard regulations into line with less costly international standards for vessel safety, toughen the safety standards for barges and recreational boaters, and guard U.S. waters against the introduction of potentially harmful foreign species, such as zebra mussels.

1994 COAST GUARD AUTHORIZATION

Congress cleared a bill late in 1993 to authorize $3.6 billion for the Coast Guard in fiscal 1994. The measure (HR 2150—PL 103-206) included $2.6 billion for operations and $418 million to purchase vessels, aircraft and other equipment.

The total was about 4 percent above the fiscal 1993 spending level and $40 million more than the appropriators provided in the fiscal 1994 transportation spending bill (HR 2750—PL 103-122). The bill raised the limit on the number of commissioned, active-duty Coast Guard officers from 6,000 to 6,200 and targeted new or improved facilities to several lawmakers' districts.

The House Merchant Marine and Fisheries Committee reported the bill on June 21, 1993 (H Rept 103-146). It passed the House by voice vote July 30. The Senate Commerce, Science and Transportation Committee reported its own version of the Coast Guard bill (S 1052—S Rept 103-198) on Nov. 20. Committee leaders rolled the bill into HR 2150 and pushed it through the Senate by voice vote Nov. 22, the last full day of the 1993 session, after attaching several other pieces of legislation that had won approval from their committee, the House or the House Merchant Marine panel. The expanded measure then cleared the House by voice vote in the early morning hours of Nov. 23. It was signed into law Dec. 8.

Included among the items added by the Senate were provisions related to:

• **Atlantic Coast Fisheries.** Based on a bill (S 1126—S Rept 103-201) reported by the Senate Commerce Committee Nov. 20, this provision gave the federal government and the states more power to regulate fishing along the Atlantic coast. The House had passed a similar bill (HR 2134) by voice vote Aug. 2. *(Details, p. 427)*

• **Charter Boat Safety.** Based on a bill (HR 1159—H Rept 103-99) reported by the House Merchant Marine Committee May 19, 1993, and passed by the full House June 9, 409–4, this provision closed a loophole in marine safety laws that had allowed some boat owners to rent out their vessels to groups without complying with Coast Guard safety regulations. Under these "bareboat charters," boat owners would rent out their vessels without providing a crew, temporarily making the renters liable for anything that happened on the boat while it was in their possession.

The new legislation empowered the Coast Guard to inspect any bareboat charter, as well as larger boats chartered with crews and submersible vessels that carried passengers. As a result, supporters of the bill said, an estimated 500 to 700 boat operators would be forced to make their vessels safer. For passenger vessels not subject to inspection, the Transportation Department was ordered to require additional safety equipment.

• **Fishermen's Access.** Based on a bill (HR 3509—H Rept 103-382) reported by the Merchant Marine Committee Nov. 19, 1993, this provision extended until May 1, 1994, an agreement between the United States and Russia allowing fishermen from each nation access to waters controlled by the other.

1995 COAST GUARD AUTHORIZATION

The House twice passed bills in 1994 to reauthorize the Coast Guard for fiscal 1995. The bills were heavily laden with other maritime provisions, however, and both sank despite a late-session flurry of activity.

The initial bill (HR 4422—H Rept 103-706), reported by the House Merchant Marine and Fisheries Committee Aug. 16, 1994, would have authorized $3.7 billion for the Coast Guard, including $2.6 billion for operations, $439 million for vessels and other equipment, and $21 million for drug interdiction. The measure would have required the Coast Guard to dedicate

no less than 9.5 percent of its operating budget to drug interdiction.

Passed on Sept. 22 by a vote of 402–13, the bill also included the contents of five bills to improve barge and recreational boat safety, reduce regulations on cargo ships and encourage construction of cruise ships in U.S. yards.

That same day the Senate Commerce, Science and Transportation Committee reported its own Coast Guard reauthorization bill (S 2373—S Rept 103-372), proposing $3.7 billion for the Coast Guard in fiscal 1995. Neither that bill nor HR 4422 proceeded to the Senate floor, however.

Instead, House and Senate negotiators put together an even larger package of maritime bills (HR 4852) that they hoped to speed through both chambers in the final legislative days. At the center were the Coast Guard reauthorization provisions from HR 4422, which had strong bipartisan support.

The expanded bill ran into unexpected problems on the House floor, however, forcing some of the add-ons to be scrapped. A modified version finally passed by voice vote late on Oct. 7, but there was not enough time left to clear the measure in the Senate.

Despite the lack of authorizing legislation, the appropriators provided almost $3.7 billion for the Coast Guard as part of the fiscal 1995 transportation spending bill (HR 4556—PL 103-331). The total was $68 million below the amount called for in the authorization bills.

Earlier Provisions

The ill-fated omnibus bill included proposals from the earlier Coast Guard bill related to:

• **Barge Safety.** Based on a bill (HR 3282) approved by the House Merchant Marine Committee on Sept. 21, 1994, the provision would have promoted safer operations of river barges by mandating up-to-date navigational and safety equipment and more proficient crews.

The measure had been prompted by two major mishaps in 1993 involving barges that collided with bridges. One of the collisions caused an Amtrak train to derail and plunge into a murky bayou, killing 47 people.

The most contentious provision of the bill, added by the committee at the behest of Chairman Gerry E. Studds, D-Mass., would have required all unlicensed crewmen to have Coast Guard-issued merchant mariner documents. The requirement, similar to one passed by the House in 1992, would have forced workers to submit to drug testing and background checks. The proposal drew objections from rural lawmakers, however, who argued that it would impose a heavy and needless burden on those workers who had to travel far to obtain documents. *(Congress and the Nation Vol. VIII, p. 450)*

When Studds tried to bring the omnibus bill to the House floor by unanimous consent Oct. 7, Rep. W. J. "Billy" Tauzin, D-La., objected and demanded that the documentation requirement be removed. Studds complied, leaving the remaining barge safety provisions in the bill.

• **Recreational Boating Safety.** Prompted by a July 1993 river boating accident in Arkansas that claimed the lives of seven family members, this provision would have required all children under 13 years of age to wear life jackets or other flotation devices when on the deck of any recreational boat no larger than 26 feet long. Also included were incentives for states that adopted tougher laws against boating while intoxicated.

The provision was based on a bill (HR 3786—H Rept 103-445) reported by the House Merchant Marine panel on March 21, 1994, and passed by a voice vote of the House that same day.

• **Boating Safety Grants.** This provision would have provided money for state boating safety programs by transferring up to $59 million from a sport fish restoration trust fund in fiscal years 1995 through 1999. It also would have authorized federal grants for boat ramps and related public facilities.

Based on bill (HR 4477—H Rept 103-849) reported Oct. 7, 1994, by the House Merchant Marine Committee, the provision responded to a Clinton administration proposal to cut funding for boating safety grants.

• **Maritime Regulations.** This provision would have brought Coast Guard regulations, which applied only to U.S.-flag vessels, into line with the less stringent international construction and safety standards that foreign ships had to meet. Based on a bill (HR 4959) approved Sept. 21, 1994, by the House Merchant Marine Committee, it also would have reduced the number of mandatory Coast Guard inspections on vessels and allowed some self-inspections.

• **Cruise Ship Construction.** Based on a bill (HR 3821) approved Aug. 11, 1994, by the House Merchant Marine Committee, this provision would have allowed a foreign-built cruise vessel to carry passengers between U.S. ports if its owner agreed to build another ship in U.S. yards. The foreign vessels would have been required to register in the United States, however, and hire U.S. crews.

New Provisions

The omnibus bill also contained a number of provisions that were not in the previous Coast Guard authorization bill, including ones related to:

• **Zebra Mussels.** This provision would have authorized $2 million over two years to study ways to prevent vessels from releasing potentially harmful foreign species when they dumped their ballast water. It was culled from a bill (HR 3360—H Rept 103-440) that had been reported by the House Merchant Marine Committee on March 21, 1994, and passed by voice vote of the House the same day.

Ships took on ballast water in foreign ports to balance the weight of their cargo, and they dumped the water at their destination port as they unloaded the cargo. A number of harmful foreign species had been introduced into U.S. waters that way; one, the notorious zebra mussel, had caused an estimated $3.4 billion in damage since arriving in 1986.

• **Biotechnology Development.** Based on a bill (HR 1916) that the House had passed July 13, 1993, this provision would have established a marine biotechnology program at selected colleges and universities. *(Biotechnology grants, p. 431)*

• **Fishing Restrictions.** This provision would have penalized foreign and U.S. vessels that harvested fish in the Peanut Hole of the Sea of Okhotsk. The restriction had won voice-vote approval from the House on Nov. 2, 1993, as HR 3188. *(Fishing limits, p. 427)*

• **Reimbursing Fishermen.** This section would have reauthorized the 1967 Fishermen's Protective Act (PL 90-482), which allowed the government to reimburse commercial fishermen for fines paid to foreign countries when their catches and boats were seized. It also would have allowed fishermen to be reimbursed for fees that Canada imposed on U.S. fishing vessels that passed through Canadian waters between Washington and Alaska in mid-1994.

The House passed a bill (HR 3817) by voice vote July 12 to reauthorize the 1967 law and reimburse fishermen for the fees. HR 3817, as reported earlier that day by the House Merchant Marine panel (H Rept 103-585), also included a provision that would have barred some Canadian fishermen from entering western U.S. waters unless they paid a fee equal to the one levied on U.S. boats. The Senate passed its own reauthorization bill (S 2243) by voice vote on July 1, also proposing to reimburse fishermen for the fees but not attempting to restrict Canadian vessels.

The provision in HR 4852 would have reimbursed U.S. fishermen for the Canadian fees and required U.S. agencies to impose reciprocal fees or restrictions on vessels from any country that imposed improper fees or restrictions on U.S. vessels. A similar provision was enacted in 1995 as part of an omnibus fisheries bill. *(Fishermen's Protective Act, p. 374)*

MARITIME HERITAGE PROGRAM

The one maritime-related measure that cleared in 1994 was a modest bill (HR 3059—PL 103-451) to fund maritime preservation and education projects. Moving separately from the omnibus package, it passed the House by voice vote Oct. 5, cleared the Senate by voice vote Oct. 8 and was signed into law Nov. 2.

The legislation created a National Maritime Heritage Program to support maritime exhibits, vessel-building and sailing programs, underwater archaeological work, historic vessel repairs and similar projects by states, local governments and nonprofit agencies. The measure directed that the heritage program receive 25 percent of the proceeds when ships were scrapped from the National Defense Reserve Fleet, a collection of government-owned cargo vessels maintained by the Maritime Administration. The rest of the proceeds were reserved for upgrading vessels in the fleet and aiding state maritime academies.

MARITIME ADMINISTRATION

A bill to reauthorize the Maritime Administration for fiscal 1994 passed the House easily in July 1993 but made no headway in the Senate. The measure (HR 1964—H Rept 103-182), reported July 19 by the House Merchant Marine and Fisheries Committee, would have authorized $621 million for the Maritime Administration and related programs, including $54 million for a loan guarantee program that would support the purchase of up to $1 billion in commercial vessels from U.S. shipyards.

The Maritime Administration conducted research on shipbuilding and ship operations, helped secure financing for new vessels, maintained a reserve fleet for use in times of war or emergency, and operated the U.S. Merchant Marine Academy in Kings Point, N.Y.

On the House floor July 29, lawmakers adopted, 388–41, an amendment by Merchant Marine Committee Chairman Gerry E. Studds, D-Mass., barring any U.S. shipping line from moving its vessels to foreign registries in 1993 or 1994. The amended bill passed later that day, 372–48, but the Senate Commerce Committee took no action on it in part because of opposition to the Studds amendment.

In 1994, the Merchant Marine Committee proposed to authorize $613 million for the Maritime Administration in fiscal 1995 as part of HR 4003, the maritime subsidies bill. The proposal passed the House but died in the Senate. *(Tonnage fees, p. 338)*

EXTENDING U.S. LABOR LAWS

The House Education and Labor Committee advanced a bill in 1994 to apply U.S. minimum wage and overtime laws to certain foreign-flagged vessels, but the measure never reached the House floor.

The bill (HR 1517—H Rept 103-818), which the committee reported Oct. 3, targeted cargo, cruise and fishing vessels that registered in foreign countries to avoid having to comply with costly U.S. labor laws. While U.S.-flagged vessels had to employ U.S. crews and meet U.S. wage standards, foreign-flagged vessels often hired crews from developing countries and paid minimal wages.

The bill would have required certain foreign vessels to meet U.S. wage standards if their owners and at least half of their crew were not citizens of the country in which the vessels were registered.

The bill would have applied only to vessels that regularly engaged in business at U.S. ports or that made or processed goods on board for sale in the United States.

Opponents of the measure included lawmakers allied with U.S. cruise lines, who argued that it would force those lines to move their operations overseas.

CRUISES TO NOWHERE

Overcoming objections from allies of the cruise industry, the House approved a bill (HR 1250) late in 1993 to bar foreign-flagged vessels from operating excursions that began and ended in the same U.S. port. The Senate, however, took no action on the bill.

The bill was a direct attack on the foreign cruise ships that dominated the "cruise to nowhere" business. Although U.S. law required ships traveling between U.S. ports to be built, owned and registered in the United States, it imposed no such requirement on ships that started at a U.S. port, sailed into international waters and then returned to the same port. Foreign vessels thus could operate gambling, sightseeing or dinner cruises without having to comply with costly U.S. labor, safety and hiring requirements.

The bill, which was reported by the House Merchant Marine and Fisheries Committee Oct. 26 (H Rept 103-307) and won voice-vote approval of the full House Nov. 20, would have eliminated that loophole. Its opponents—including foreign cruise lines, selected U.S. port authorities and lawmakers from port cities—were able to freeze the bill in the Senate Commerce, Science and Transportation Committee, however, just as they had stopped a similar bill that the House passed in 1992. *(Congress and the Nation Vol. VIII, p. 450)*

SEAMEN REEMPLOYMENT

For the third consecutive year, the House in 1993 passed a bill to provide reemployment rights for workers who left their jobs to serve on merchant marine ships during a war, national emergency or maritime mobilization. The measure (HR 1109) met the same fate as its two predecessors: it died in the Senate.

The bill would have given civilian sailors substantially the same reemployment rights as members of the armed forces reserves. It won unanimous approval from the House on March 16, 1993, 403–0, but the Senate Commerce Committee took no action on it. Similar language had passed the House in 1991 and 1992 as part of bills to reauthorize the Maritime Administration, but neither measure reached the Senate floor. *(1995–1996 action, p. 371)*

PANAMA CANAL COMMISSION

The House passed a bill in 1993 to reauthorize the Panama Canal Commission for fiscal 1994, but the Senate took no action on it. The legislation (HR 1522) would have authorized the commission to spend as much as on its operations as it collected in tolls, which was estimated to be $542 million in fiscal 1994. Established by the Panama Canal Treaty of 1977, the commission was responsible for operating and maintaining the canal until the United States finished transferring ownership of the canal to Panama in 2000.

HR 1522 was reported by the House Merchant Marine and Fisheries Committee on June 24 (H Rept 103-154) and passed by voice vote of the House on July 13.

FEDERAL MARITIME COMMISSION

The Senate took no action in 1994 on a House-passed bill (HR 4391—H Rept 103-716) to reauthorize the Federal Maritime Commission for fiscal 1995 and set a minimum compensation level for all freight forwarding companies.

The bill would have authorized $18.9 million for the commission, which regulated domestic and international shipping in U.S. waters. The amount was the same as authorized in fiscal 1994 but roughly $200 million more than the administration requested.

Included in the bill, which the House Merchant Marine and Fisheries Committee reported (H Rept 103-716) and the House passed by voice vote Sept. 12, 1994, was a requirement that shipping lines carrying U.S. imports or exports pay freight forwarders at least 1.25 percent of the revenue associated with the cargo provided by the forwarders. Freight forwarders reserved space on cargo vessels for shippers.   ❑

Transportation Taxes, Fees

The 1993 budget reconciliation bill (HR 2264—PL 103-66) included two significant tax and fee changes affecting the transportation industries in addition to the 4.3-cents-per-gallon hike in the excises taxes on most motor fuels.

The tonnage fees paid by cargo vessels entering U.S. ports, which had been scheduled to drop significantly after fiscal 1995, were instead maintained at the level set in 1990 as part of the massive budget agreement (PL 101-508). The extension was projected to cost shippers $205 million from fiscal 1996 through fiscal 1998.

The fees had been raised 250 percent to 350 percent in 1990. Vessels arriving from countries in the Western Hemisphere paid 9 cents per ton, and vessels arriving from other countries paid 27 cents per ton. The fees could be imposed no more than five times per vessel each year.

The reconciliation measure also ended the exemption that recreational boaters had enjoyed from taxes on diesel fuel, which increased from 20.1 cents per gallon to 24.4 cents on Jan. 1, 1994. The change was projected to cost boaters $148 million over five years.

Congress did not remove the diesel-tax exemption for boats used for commercial fishing, transportation for hire or other commercial purposes.

The House-passed version of the reconciliation bill would have increased registration fees for the owners of noncommercial aircraft from a flat, one-time fee of $5 to annual weight-based fees of $40 to $1,000. The provision, which would have raised an estimated $140 million over five years, was dropped in the Senate in the face of stiff opposition from the influential Aircraft Owners and Pilots Association. ❑

High-Tech Competitiveness

Spurred by the Clinton administration, the House and Senate passed bills in the 103rd Congress to boost U.S. competitiveness in the global marketplace by authorizing more federal aid for high-technology companies. The legislation died in 1994, however, when negotiators for the two chambers were unable to resolve their differences over three contentious provisions.

A similar legislative effort had produced the same result in 1992, when the House and Senate each passed competitiveness bills but could not reconcile their differences before adjourning. (Congress and the Nation Vol. VIII, p. 891)

The bills in the 103rd Congress (HR 820, S 4) would have authorized a vast increase in federal grants, loans and research subsidies to help small and midsized U.S. businesses develop and deploy new technologies. Although Democratic supporters said the legislation would help U.S. manufacturers meet the increasing global competition, Republican critics said that such governmental involvement was inappropriate, unneeded and unwanted by industry.

Indeed, the legislation lacked the sense of urgency needed to propel a major authorization bill through Congress. Signaling the lack of interest outside Washington, the bills bogged down on the House and Senate floors in weeks of debate that often ranged far from the issue of competitiveness.

The battle over government support for technology was joined again in the 104th Congress as House Republicans sought to eliminate the Commerce Department and its Advanced Technology Program (ATP). The Senate stymied the efforts to end the department, and President Clinton used his veto pen to keep the ATP alive. (1995–1996 action, p. 381)

BACKGROUND

Reflecting Vice President Al Gore's interest in technology, President Clinton unveiled a four-year plan on Feb. 22, 1993, to provide $17 billion in subsidies and tax breaks for high-technology research and development. The plan emphasized joint efforts between government and industry, and it called for the government to induce more private investment in targeted technologies.

The initiative was one of the cornerstones of Clinton's economic plan. A sharp shift in approach, it proposed to funnel money into "applied" research—work aimed at specific technologies or processes—instead of "basic" research—fundamental scientific inquiries relevant to a broad range of industries.

Previous Republican administrations had balked at such efforts, contending that the market alone should determine winners and losers in the business world. Clinton, however, argued that more government help was needed to counter the increasingly aggressive foreign competition. Basic research was leading to new technologies, Clinton administration officials said, but the fruits of that investment were being harvested in some cases by foreign companies, not American ones.

HOUSE ACTION

The House Science, Space and Technology Committee on May 3, 1993, reported a pared down version of the original HR 820 (H Rept 103-77). The bill proposed to authorize a total of $1.5 billion in fiscal 1994 and 1995 for the ATP, the National Institute of Standards and Technology (NIST), the National Science Foundation and a technical outreach program at the Commerce Department modeled after the Agriculture Department's extension centers.

A slightly modified version of the bill passed the House, 243–167, on May 19, 1993, after three weeks of intermittent debate. That measure proposed $1.5 billion over two years, including $731.5 million for ATP, $722 million for NIST and $50 million for the National Science Foundation. The NIST total included $186 million for the manufacturing extension centers.

As they had done in committee, Republicans tried in vain on the House floor to reduce the spending levels and eliminate specific programs from the bill. The most significant change was an amendment by Thomas J. Manton, D-N.Y., to bar aid to the U.S. subsidiaries of foreign-owned companies unless the government in the parent company's home country provided similar aid. The amendment was adopted by voice vote May 6 after the powerful chairman of the Energy and Commerce Committee, Democrat John D. Dingell of Michigan, weighed in on Manton's behalf.

SENATE ACTION

The Senate Commerce, Science and Transportation Committee reported its own competitiveness bill (S 4—S Rept 103-113) July 28, 1993. The bill proposed to authorize nearly $2.4 billion for high-tech programs in fiscal years 1994 and 1995.

The main difference between the House version and the Senate committee bill was that S 4 proposed to authorize a $380 million increase in spending on research into high-performance computing and computer networks in fiscal 1994 and 1995. The research was aimed at linking libraries, schools, health care facilities and manufacturing centers to the national communications and computing network, better known as the "information superhighway." The House had proposed $1 billion over five years for these efforts as part of a separate measure (HR 1757) passed on July 26, 1993. *(National Information Infrastructure, p. 357)*

On the Senate floor in March 1994, Commerce Committee Chairman Ernest F. Hollings, D-S.C., offered a substitute to S 4 that changed the authorization levels and added funding for fiscal 1996. The new version proposed to authorize roughly $2.8 billion for fiscal 1995 and 1996. It quickly became snarled in a series of debates over airplane manufacturers' liability limits, pesticide regulations, espionage and the Whitewater scandal, among other unrelated matters.

On the issue of competitiveness, Republicans tried to knock out some of the specific subsidies and to substitute their own proposal, which would have reduced regulatory burdens on businesses and entrepreneurs. They did not have the votes to make such sweeping changes—their substitute amendment offered by Alan K. Simpson, R-Wyo., was tabled (killed) on a 56–42 vote March 10. Their threat to filibuster, however, forced the bill's sponsors to roll back the authorized amount to $1.9 billion. That change cleared the way for the Senate to approve HR 820 on March 16, 59–40, after inserting the amended version of S 4.

The sponsors made no effort to reconcile the $1.9 billion limit with the individual authorization levels in the bill, which for fiscal 1995 and 1996 alone included $1.05 billion for the ATP, $170 million for manufacturing extension programs, $670 million for other NIST science and technology research programs, and $150 million for National Science Foundation manufacturing programs. The revised version also proposed a $359 million increase in the authorization for computer-network-related projects in fiscal 1995 and 1996.

CONFERENCE IMPASSE

House negotiators accepted the Senate provision authorizing $359 million for computing projects. Two other amendments added by the Senate proved problematic, however. One, sponsored by Republican Malcolm Wallop of Wyoming, proposed to let small businesses challenge in court any federal regulations that were difficult or costly to meet. A second, by Republican Don Nickles of Oklahoma, would have required the Congressional Budget Office to estimate the economic impact of all federal regulatory or legislative proposals.

Another troublesome provision was the House proposal to exclude many foreign-owned U.S. companies from the programs authorized by the bill.

With negotiators unable to resolve their differences over these items, the legislation died in conference. ❑

Competitiveness Council

The House passed a bill in 1993 to rename the independent Competitiveness Policy Council and reauthorize it for four years, but the measure advanced no further.

The bill (HR 2960), which passed the House by voice vote Nov. 21, would have changed the council's name to the National Competitiveness Commission and cut its authorization in half, from $5 million annually to $2.5 million.

The council was created as part of an omnibus trade law in 1988 (PL 100-418) and was charged with recommending policies to restore U.S. competitiveness in the world economy. It was a bipartisan body whose 12 members were chosen by Congress and the president from industry, government, labor and public interest groups. ❑

Joint Production Ventures

Congress cleared legislation in 1993 to encourage more joint efforts by the nation's manufacturers to produce innovative goods and services. President Clinton supported the bill (HR 1313—PL 103-42) as part of his drive to make U.S. companies more competitive in world markets.

HR 1313 expanded the protections provided by Congress in a 1984 law (PL 98-462), which gave joint research and development ventures limited protection against antitrust claims. As enacted, HR 1313 made it easier for companies engaged in a joint production venture to defend against an antitrust lawsuit, and it eliminated the possibility of triple damages even if the lawsuit were successful. It also allowed courts to find that joint production ventures were reasonable given the existing competitive climate. *(1984 law, Congress and the Nation Vol. VI, p. 706)*

Supporters of the bill said it eliminated a deterrent to joint production ventures by removing the threat of triple damages. Opponents argued that there was no evidence of joint production ventures being deterred by the antitrust laws.

The House Judiciary Committee approved HR 1313 March 24 and reported it May 18 (H Rept 103-94). The Senate Judiciary Committee approved a similar bill (S 574—S Rept 103-51) March 25 and formally reported it June 7. Both bills proposed to relax antitrust restrictions against joint ventures involving cooperative research, development and production agreements among competing companies, but they differed on the issue of foreign participation.

Instead of heading to the floor with their competing bills, the House and Senate sponsors reached a compromise limiting the antitrust protection to production facilities located in the United States. The companies also had to be owned by U.S. residents or by companies from countries that did not discriminate against U.S. participants in joint ventures abroad.

The compromise version of HR 1313 passed the House by voice vote May 18 and cleared the Senate by voice vote May 28. President Clinton signed the bill June 10.

Similar legislation had won overwhelming approval from the Senate in 1992, but it died in the House amid a dispute over foreign participation. *(Congress and the Nation Vol. VIII, p. 890)* ❑

Economic Development

Opposition in the Senate again stalled legislation to reauthorize the Economic Development Administration (EDA) and the Appalachian Regional Commission in the 103rd Congress. The rural lawmakers who led the congressional Appropriations committees remained strongly supportive of the two programs, however, keeping them well funded.

Seeking to stimulate growth and employment, the EDA was created in 1965 (PL 89-136) to provide technical assistance and grants for public works projects to governmental and nonprofit organizations in economically distressed areas. The Appalachian Regional Commission similarly was created in 1965 (PL 89-4) to finance public works and other development projects. The program in time included 399 economically blighted counties in the 13 Appalachian states.

Both programs had gone unauthorized since the end of fiscal 1982. Although the House had passed reauthorization bills every Congress since then, the measures routinely died in the Senate. The programs were sustained by the annual appropriations bills, despite the efforts of Presidents Ronald Reagan and George Bush to phase them out.

In May 1994, the House approved a bill (HR 2442) to authorize the EDA and the Appalachian Regional Commission for fiscal 1994 through fiscal 1996. The measure called for the EDA's funding to increase from $313 million in the first year to $386 million thereafter, and for the commission's funding to drop from $249 million in fiscal 1994 to $214 million the following two years.

The funding levels represented a compromise between the House Banking, Finance and Urban Affairs Committee, which sought larger increases for the EDA, and the House Public Works and Transportation Committee. The compromise version also attempted to ensure that the money went to only the neediest areas. HR 2442 was reported by the Public Works panel Feb. 10, 1994, and the Banking Committee April 26 (H Rept 103-423, Part I and II).

On the House floor May 11 and 12, lawmakers defeated a series of attempts by Republicans to cut or eliminate funding for the programs. The bill passed May 12 with bipartisan support, 328–89.

On Sept. 30, the Senate Environment and Public Works Committee reported a bill (S 2257—S Rept 103-391) authorizing $295 million annually for the EDA in fiscal years 1995 through 1997. The bill also would have authorized $120 million in fiscal 1995 and an unlimited sum in the following two years for EDA projects to help communities adapt to the closure of military bases. Like the House bill, the Senate measure sought to target federal aid to the communities most in need. It would

have required the EDA to allocate grants based on the level of distress, rather than giving preference to certain geographic areas or types of distress.

The full Senate did not take up S 2257. One opponent, Republican Alan K. Simpson of Wyoming, said that the EDA provided aid that industry could easily obtain from private sources, and that it no longer tried to link industries with their communities and local governments.

The House attempted to salvage the legislation on Oct. 7, giving voice-vote approval to a bill (HR 5243) based on S 2257. The Senate did not act on that bill, either.

Ignoring the lack of authorization, Congress appropriated $249 million in fiscal 1994 and $282 million in fiscal 1995 for the Appalachian Regional Commission as part of the spending bills for energy and water programs (HR 2445—PL 103-126 and HR 4506—PL 103-316). The amounts were sharp increases from the $190 million appropriated in fiscal 1993.

Congress also appropriated $351 million in fiscal 1994 and $440 million in fiscal 1995 for the EDA as part of the spending bills for the Commerce, Justice and State departments (HR 2519—PL 103-121 and HR 4603—PL 103-317). Those totals were down from the $444 million appropriated in fiscal 1993. ❑

Small Business Legislation

After allowing a popular loan guarantee program for small businesses to run out of money early in 1993, Congress cleared three bills in 1993 and 1994 to extend and expand aid to small businesses. Other measures to ease securities regulation on small businesses and help minority-owned businesses died in the House in 1994 after winning Senate approval.

SMALL BUSINESS LOANS

The 103rd Congress endorsed a major expansion in the loan guarantees provided by the Small Business Administration (SBA). In addition to authorizing more guarantees, lawmakers made the SBA's main loan program less profitable for lenders and less risky for the taxpayers.

The SBA's 7(a) program helped small businesses obtain loans from banks and other commercial lenders by guaranteeing to repay 70 to 90 percent of loan if the borrower defaulted. With a credit crunch boosting demand for the guarantees, the program ran out of funding in late April 1993, five months before the end of the fiscal year.

The administration proposed $181 million for the program as part of a $16.3 billion "economic stimulus" package (HR 1335), but that proposal and most other elements of the bill were blocked in April 1993 by a Senate GOP filibuster. On July 1, Congress cleared a less controversial, $3.5 billion supplemental spending bill (HR 2118—PL 103-50) that provided $175 million to restart the 7(a) program.

Fees and Guarantee Levels

One month later, Congress cleared a bill (S 1274—PL 103-81) allowing the SBA to collect fees from lenders that sold SBA-guaranteed loans on the secondary market to private investors.

The measure ordered that the fees be plowed back into the 7(a) program, enabling the SBA to issue loan guarantees to more small businesses.

The bill, which was reported by the Senate Small Business Committee July 28, 1993, also allowed the SBA to reduce the maximum guarantees provided by the 7(a) program by 5 to 10 percentage points on selected loans, a move that sponsors said would yield more loan guarantees and less risk for the government. The SBA's authority to reduce guarantees and impose fees expired at the end of fiscal 1996.

Other provisions of the bill authorized increases in the SBA's "certified development company" loan guarantee program, which helped small businesses obtain long-term loans for new construction and equipment. The authorization was boosted by $125 million in fiscal 1993, to $900 million, and by $375 million in fiscal 1994, to $1.2 billion.

The Senate had approved an early version of the bill by voice vote July 30. The House amended and passed the bill by voice vote Aug. 4, substituting provisions from four related bills (HR 2746, HR 2747, HR 2748, HR 2766) that the House had passed by voice vote Aug. 2. This version called for a smaller increase in the 7(a) program and only a temporary change in fees and guarantee levels, with the SBA studying the impact of the changes on small businesses.

The Senate cleared the House version by voice vote Aug. 5, and President Clinton signed the measure into law Aug. 13.

Construction and Equipment Loans

In 1994, Congress authorized another increase in the SBA's certified development company program. The measure (HR 4322—PL 103-282) raised the authorized level in fiscal 1994 from $1.2 billion to $1.5 billion.

The bill's sponsor, Rep. John J. LaFalce, D-N.Y., said the increase was needed to keep up with surging demand for the loan guarantees. The SBA was expected to use $1.5 million from other programs to pay for the increase in loan guarantees.

The measure also allowed SBA employees to remain in the field on disaster-relief projects for up to one year, a six-month increase. The House Small Business Committee reported HR 4322 (H Rept 103-572) June 30 and the full House approved the bill by voice vote July 19. The Senate cleared it by voice vote the next day and President Clinton signed it July 22.

Higher Authorization Levels

Late in 1994, Congress authorized major increases in the 7(a) program, loan guarantees for defense-conversion projects, venture capital for small businesses and the certified development company program. The bill (S 2060—PL 103-403) also made it less expensive for businesses to refinance loans at lower interest rates.

As signed into law Oct. 22, S 2060 boosted the authorization for 7(a) loan guarantees from $7.2 billion in fiscal 1994 to $9.2 billion in fiscal 1995, $10.5 billion in fiscal 1996 and $13.1 billion in fiscal 1997. An additional $7.5 billion over three years was authorized for loan guarantees on defense-conversion projects, a previously unfunded effort to help communities adapt to the

closure of military bases, and $8.15 billion was authorized over three years for the certified development company program.

The authorized levels of the Small Business Investment Company and Specialized Small Business Investment Company, two programs that provided venture capital, were boosted from $504 million in fiscal 1994 to $667 million in fiscal 1995, $930 million in fiscal 1996 and $1.2 billion in fiscal 1997. The increase was still well below the level sought by the administration, mainly because Republicans considered the programs too risky for so great a federal commitment.

To aid very small businesses, the bill authorized $758 million over three years for direct loans of up to $25,000 and $90 million for a new program of loan guarantees. It also promoted efforts within the SBA and the executive branch to assist female business owners.

Finally, the measure ordered the SBA to spend $30 million from its fiscal 1995 appropriation to reduce the penalty that small businesses had to pay when refinancing SBA-guaranteed loans at a lower interest rate. The House had sought to reduce the penalties for refinancing as part of the previous SBA reauthorization bill in 1990 (PL 101-574), but opposition from the Senate forced the proposal to be dropped. (*Congress and the Nation Vol. VIII, p. 435*)

The Senate Small Business Committee reported S 2060 (S Rept 103-332) on Aug. 11 and the full Senate passed it by voice vote Aug. 18. The House Small Business Committee on July 21 had reported a companion bill (HR 4801—H Rept 103-616), which the House passed Sept. 21, 370–48. The House then passed S 2060 by voice vote, after substituting the text of HR 4801. The House adopted a conference report on the bill (H Rept 103-824) by voice vote Oct. 4, and the Senate followed suit the next day, clearing the bill.

The increases authorized in S 2060 were not matched by the dollars Congress actually provided, at least not in fiscal 1995. The fiscal 1995 appropriations bill that covered the SBA (HR 4603—PL 103-317) not only failed to meet the increases called for in S 2060, it provided less for SBA loan guarantees than had been authorized in fiscal 1994.

FEDERAL CONTRACTING

The House Small Business Committee approved a bill (HR 4263) in 1994 to help small businesses gain more government contracts. Although the bill advanced no further, some of its provisions became law as part of legislation (S 1587—PL 103-355) to overhaul government procurement procedures. (*Procurement, p. 812*)

HR 4263 was formally reported (H Rept 103-606, Part I) July 14. It had been approved June 29, 26–19, despite the opposition of every Republican present and one Democrat. Among other disputed provisions, it would have eliminated the requirement that minority business owners prove that they were economically disadvantaged in order to participate in SBA programs designed to help minority-owned businesses secure government contracts.

One widely supported provision of the bill called for federal agencies to give small businesses the first crack at all contracts worth $100,000 or less, up from $25,000. Another provision urged all federal agencies to steer at least 5 percent of their contract dollars to businesses owned by women and minorities. Versions of both proposals were included in the final procurement bill.

SMALL BUSINESS SECURITIES

The House Energy and Commerce Committee and the full Senate approved similar bills to stimulate investment in small businesses by easing regulations on their securities. The legislation never reached the House floor, however.

The bills (S 479, HR 4858) would have allowed small businesses to sell up to $10 million in securities without having to register their offerings with the Securities and Exchange Commission. Existing law required companies to register sales of more than $5 million in securities. The bills also included a proposal to exempt from federal regulation certain investment funds that backed small businesses.

The Senate Banking, Housing and Urban Affairs Committee reported S 479 (S Rept 103-166) on Oct. 26, 1993, and the full Senate approved it by voice vote Nov. 2. The House Energy and Commerce Committee approved HR 4858 by voice vote Aug. 5, 1994, but never formally reported the bill. No further action was taken on either bill.

MINORITY-OWNED BUSINESSES

The Senate passed a bill near the end of the 1994 session to address complaints about the SBA's 8(a) program, a training and assistance program for minority-owned businesses. The action came too late, however, for the measure to be considered by the House.

The bill (S 2478) attempted to improve the long-term prospects of companies in or graduating from the 8(a) program by encouraging new enterprises to team up with established minority-owned businesses, giving companies access to more capital, and lifting some of the restrictions on government contracts. It also attempted to curb abuses of the program by ineligible companies that masqueraded as minority-owned businesses while broadening participation by legitimate minority-owned enterprises.

The Senate passed the bill by voice vote Oct. 7, but it advanced no further. ❏

Product Liability

A long-running effort to protect the business community against product liability lawsuits was thwarted again in the 103rd Congress, blocked by a Senate filibuster.

Lobbyists for manufacturers, insurers and other business groups had been pressing Congress for 17 years to limit the damages that could be awarded in lawsuits involving defective products. They were opposed by a coalition of consumer advocates and trial lawyers, who argued that such damages were a critical deterrent against irresponsible, profit-driven corporations.

The opponents prevailed in the Senate in 1994, but just barely. After the Senate Commerce, Science and Transportation Committee reported a bipartisan product liability bill (S 687—S Rept 103 203) Nov. 20, 1993, the bill was met on the Senate floor by a filibuster the following June. Opponents of the legislation defeated two efforts to curtail debate, effectively killing the bill.

While the broad product liability bill was stymied, a measure targeted at the aviation industry won approval after an eight-year lobbying effort. The bill (S 1458—PL 103-298) was limited in scope, barring product liability claims only if they involved small planes more than 18 years old. *(Aircraft manufacturers' liability, p. 347)*

Advocates of product liability limits for all manufacturers pledged to renew their efforts in the 104th Congress, and they did so with greater success. Congress cleared a bill in 1996 similar to the one that stalled in 1994, but the legislation was killed by a presidential veto. *(1995–1996 action, p. 376)*

The central question in the debate over S 687 was whether the federal government should replace a patchwork of state tort laws with a single national standard for claims involving products that injured or killed their users.

The Senate proposal, sponsored by Democrat John D. Rockefeller IV of West Virginia and Republican Slade Gorton of Washington, would have made it harder to collect punitive damages, ended joint liability for noneconomic damages such as pain and emotional distress, absolved sellers from liability in most cases, cut off lawsuits involving old machinery and barred damages for people whose use of drugs or alcohol had helped to cause their injuries.

The bill also would have promoted pretrial settlements by requiring the claimant in some cases to pay the defendant's legal fees, and vice versa. And to help people with valid claims, the bill would have extended the time limit for filing product liability lawsuits to two years after an injury and its cause were discovered, as opposed to the existing limit of two years after an injury occurred.

The Senate Commerce Committee had approved a similar bill in 1991. When sponsor Bob Kasten, R-Wis., tried to bring it to the floor in September 1992, however, he fell two votes short of the 60 needed to cut off a filibuster. *(Congress and the Nation Vol. VIII, p. 462)*

In 1994, opponents no longer had the votes to keep the product liability bill off the floor, and debate began June 24. When Rockefeller tried to curtail debate on June 28, however, he fell six votes short, 54–44.

Hoping to sway senators, Rockefeller and Gorton pledged to remove a controversial provision barring punitive damages against companies whose products had been approved by the Food and Drug Administration or the Federal Aviation Administration. On June 29, however, the Senate again declined to limit debate on a **key vote of 57–41 (R 38–6; D 19–35).** *(1994 key votes, p. 1003)*

Rockefeller conceded defeat at that point, having agreed to try no more than twice to cut off the filibuster. The defeat led the advocates of product liability limits in the House to abandon a similar bill (HR 1910) in the Energy and Commerce Committee. ❏

Aircraft Manufacturers' Liability

After eight years of trying, supporters of U.S. airplane manufacturers pushed a bill through Congress to limit lawsuits against the makers of small, noncommercial planes.

The bill (S 1458—PL 103-298) barred product liability lawsuits once an airplane had been in service for more than 18 years. The cut-off applied to any airplane built to carry fewer than 20 passengers.

The measure was championed by two Kansans—Republican Sen. Nancy Landon Kassebaum and Democratic Rep. Dan Glickman—whose state was home to three of the largest manufacturers of small planes. Those manufacturers blamed rising liability insurance costs for the sharp decline in aircraft production and jobs, and one pledged to open a new production line if the bill became law.

To reduce opposition, Kassebaum did not include in S 1458 several controversial provisions from bills she had offered previously, including proposals to limit punitive damages and end joint liability for noneconomic damages. The changes helped the bill win approval from the Senate Commerce, Science and Transportation Committee, which reported it on Nov. 20, 1993 (S Rept 103-202). Still, Kassebaum did not secure a spot on the Senate floor until she threatened in early 1994 to attach her measure to bills reauthorizing federal aviation and airport-improvement programs (HR 2739) and promoting U.S. manufacturing competitiveness (S 4). (FAA reauthorization, p. 330; High-tech competitiveness, p. 342)

Her threat led to a deal with the bill's chief Senate opponent, Democrat Howard M. Metzenbaum of Ohio, that freed S 4 and averted a filibuster on S 1458. Kassebaum agreed to increase the cut-off age for aircraft from 15 years to 18 years and add exceptions for lawsuits where there was clear and convincing evidence of fraud, when people in other planes or on the ground were injured, or when the crash involved patients being transported for emergency medical treatment.

The revised bill passed the Senate March 16, 91–8, and headed to the House Judiciary Committee, where it faced a formidable obstacle: Chairman Jack Brooks, D-Texas, a foe of all product liability legislation. Brooks was under pressure to release the bill, however, because Glickman had obtained more than 300 cosponsors for his own aircraft liability proposal (HR 3087). The House Public Works and Transportation Committee also had thrown its support behind S 1458, reporting it May 24 (H Rept 103-525, Part I).

On June 24, the House Judiciary Committee reported a compromise version (H Rept 103-525, Part II) backed by Brooks that set the cut-off age at 15 to 22 years, depending on the type of engine. The new version also assured the Judiciary Committee continued jurisdiction with the Public Work Committee over aviation liability law. It passed the House by voice vote June 27 under suspension of the rules, a procedure reserved for noncontroversial measures.

The Senate approved the modified bill by voice vote Aug. 2 with one last change, returning the cut-off age to 18 years for all small planes. The House cleared that version of the bill Aug. 3 by voice vote, and President Clinton signed it into law Aug. 17.

Bankruptcy Overhaul

Congress enacted a slew of changes in federal bankruptcy law late in the 1994 session, aiming to make the process faster and fairer for everyone involved.

The legislation (HR 5116—PL 103-394) gave judges more flexibility in handling bankruptcy cases, which had often turned into lengthy ordeals. In addition to streamlining the process of settling claims, it attempted to block some common tactics used by debtors to delay or evade claims. It also gave debtors more opportunity to reorganize their assets and repay their creditors, rather than forcing them into liquidation.

In crafting the original Senate bill (S 540) and HR 5116, lawmakers sought to address a laundry list of complaints about the existing bankruptcy code as opposed to making fundamental changes. Thus, the measures read like a disjointed series of revisions without a unifying theme.

The legislation laid the groundwork for a sweeping overhaul, however, by establishing a nine-member National Bankruptcy Review Commission. The commission, whose members were to be appointed by Congress, the president and the chief justice of the Supreme Court, was to recommend additional legislation within two years.

Prime Senate sponsor Howell Heflin, D-Ala., said that the bankruptcy laws were due for an update in part because of the rapid growth in bankruptcy filings since 1978, the last time the law was rewritten. Bankruptcy filings rose from roughly 350,000 in 1982 to almost 920,000 in 1993, making up about 75 percent of all federal court cases. Individual bankruptcies, spurred by the proliferation of credit and the declining stigma of bankruptcy, accounted for more than 90 percent of the filings.

LEGISLATIVE ACTION

The Senate Judiciary Committee reported an early version of S 540 (S Rept 103-168) on Oct. 28, 1993, after adding a provision to clear the way for people to pay their income taxes with a credit card, as recommended in Vice President Al Gore's reinventing government proposal. The provision called for individuals who had paid their federal income taxes with a credit card and then declared bankruptcy to pay their tax liabilities even if their other credit card debt was erased.

The Senate approved S 540 on April 21, 1994, 94–0, after lawmakers removed two contentious provisions with potentially far-reaching impact. One would have created a new category of bankruptcies for small businesses, which critics said would have allowed companies to write off many debts while staying in business.

The other disputed provision, which stalled the bill for two days on the Senate floor, would have required bankrupt companies that were reorganizing under Chapter 11 to pay their retired employees' health care costs before any other expenses. Opponents said the provision would have made it harder for companies to work their way out of bankruptcy. Its author,

Democrat Howard M. Metzenbaum of Ohio, agreed to strike the provision after organized labor groups said it would pit a company's current employees against its retirees.

The House Judiciary Committee took no action on the legislation until late in September 1994, when House and Senate Judiciary Committee aides worked out a mutually acceptable bill. That measure, reported on Oct. 4 by the House panel (HR 5116—H Rept 103-835), hewed closely to S 540 to avoid raising hackles in the Senate, where a single disgruntled senator could sink virtually any bill late in the session.

Among other Senate provisions added to the House bill, the negotiators agreed to insert language creating the bankruptcy review commission and speeding resolution of bankruptcies involving single pieces of commercial property.

With little debate, the full House passed the bill by voice vote Oct. 5. The Senate cleared the bill early in the morning of Oct. 7, and President Clinton signed it into law Oct. 22.

MAJOR PROVISIONS

As signed into law, HR 5116:

Creditors

Included a number of provisions aimed at helping creditors and reducing delays in bankruptcy proceedings. Among them were provisions that:

• Allowed creditors to appeal immediately a court order extending the 180-day deadline for debtor companies to file acceptable reorganization plans under Chapter 11. Creditors complained that such extensions were often used by debtors to delay reorganizing and repaying.

• Required courts to rule on automatic-stay requests within 60 days after a debtor filed for bankruptcy. Such requests allowed debtors to avoid foreclosure on cars, property and other assets.

• Required debtors in Chapter 11 to file an acceptable reorganization plan within 90 days if their only asset was one piece of commercial property. Previously, debtors with "single asset real estate" were able to use automatic stays to stave off creditors.

• Gave sellers more time (20 days instead of 10) to reclaim goods sold on credit to a company, usually a retailer, that had filed for bankruptcy.

• Required airlines that filed for bankruptcy under Chapter 11 to honor lease and conditional sales contracts while reorganizing.

• Allowed creditors to keep assets or payments received from a company more than 90 days before it filed for bankruptcy, unless they were corporate insiders. Some courts had required payments and assets to be returned if they had been collected up to one year before a bankruptcy filing.

• Gave independent sales representatives of a bankrupt company the same standing as employees when seeking to recover wage and benefit payments, provided that the representatives earned at least 75 percent of their income from the company.

Debtors

Included provisions to aid debtors that:

• Required federal and state governments, when acting as creditors, to honor automatic stays and other bankruptcy procedures.

• Enabled small businesses with less than $2 million in debts to reorganize more quickly under Chapter 11.

• Allowed buyers to return goods purchased before they filed for bankruptcy, if they obtained the bankruptcy court's approval within 120 days of filing for bankruptcy.

• Allowed a municipality to file for bankruptcy so long as it was eligible to do so under state law.

• Protected bankrupt companies that had established trust funds for asbestos liability claims from having those funds tapped to pay new creditors. The provision codified court rulings in the 1982 Johns-Manville bankruptcy case.

Personal Bankruptcies

Included a number of provisions aimed at personal bankruptcies. Among them were ones that:

• Raised the amount of debt an individual could have and still file for bankruptcy under Chapter 13, which allowed debtors to work out repayment schedules with creditors. The threshold was raised from $100,000 to $250,000 in unsecured debt and from $350,000 to $750,000 in secured debt. The provision was intended to encourage individuals to file under Chapter 13 instead of Chapter 7, which would liquidate their assets.

• Required bankruptcy trustees in Chapter 7 cases to explain in full to a debtor the option to file for reorganization under Chapter 13 as well as the long-term ramifications of liquidating debts under Chapter 7.

• Gave a debtor who was under Chapter 13 protection more time to cure (resolve) a home mortgage default before losing the property. Such debtors were given until the foreclosure sale was completed, or longer if provided by state law.

• Classified alimony and child support payments as priority debt, making it more difficult to use a bankruptcy filing to avoid these obligations.

• Made it more difficult for a divorced person to evade, through bankruptcy, the marital debts that person had assumed in exchange for a reduction in alimony or child support. Such maneuvering had enabled some bankrupt individuals to throw their debts back on their ex-spouses.

• Prohibited the discharge through bankruptcy of loans used to pay federal taxes. This provision was designed to allow the use of credit cards to pay taxes.

• Prohibited individuals who restructured their debts under Chapter 13 from discharging criminal fines.

• Prohibited individuals from being denied student loans because they had a history of bankruptcy that included the failure to pay off a previous student loan.

Other Provisions

Included provisions that:

• Established a nine-member National Bankruptcy Review Commission to recommend additional changes to the Bankruptcy Code within two years. Four members were to be appointed by Congress, three by the president and two by the chief justice of the United States.

• Spelled out new requirements for people (other than attorneys) who prepared bankruptcy petitions and set stiff penalties for negligent or fraudulent filings. The provision was aimed at fee-seeking "bankruptcy typing mills" that preyed upon immigrants and the poor.

• Set criminal penalties for those who declared bankruptcy with fraudulent intent.

• Authorized bankruptcy judges to conduct jury trials with the consent of all parties involved.

• Authorized panels of bankruptcy judges to hear bankruptcy appeals in place of U.S. District Court judges.   ❑

Insurance Antitrust Exemption

House Judiciary Committee Chairman Jack Brooks's crusade to apply federal antitrust laws to the insurance industry continued in the 103rd Congress but came no closer to succeeding, despite the newfound support of some insurance industry groups.

Brooks, D-Texas, had been trying for several years to overturn at least part of the McCarran-Ferguson Act (PL 79-15), a 1945 law that exempted the insurance industry from antitrust restraints. According to Brooks, the industry had taken advantage of the exemption to fix prices and avert competition. (McCarran-Ferguson background, Congress and the Nation Vol. I, p. 454)

Although Brooks had been able to move several bills through his committee to amend the McCarran-Ferguson Act, his opponents stopped them well short of passage. They argued that insurance companies needed antitrust immunity to pool data and set accurate rates— a process, they said, that had produced the best rates for consumers and insurers alike. (Congress and the Nation Vol. VIII, p. 435, p. 463)

In 1994, Brooks won support from some insurance lobbyists by dropping provisions from his bill (HR 9) that would have barred companies from sharing data on previous losses, making joint fire inspections and using uniform policy forms. He also added a provision allowing insurance companies to provide agents with common tables for calculating rates.

The revised bill still would have exposed insurance companies to antitrust enforcement if they fixed prices or imposed regional monopolies. It also would have curtailed the long-standing practice of sharing the "trending" information used to project future costs and calculate prices, requiring companies within three years to do their own projections or obtain them from consultants.

The bill was approved by the Judiciary Committee Economic and Commercial Law Subcommittee July 19 on a party-line, 9–6 vote. The full Judiciary Committee followed suit July 22 by a vote of 20–15, with one Democrat joining 14 Republicans in opposition.

The new version was backed by the American Insurance Association, a major trade group representing property and casualty insurance providers, and the Independent Insurance Agents of America, a trade group mainly for the agents representing small insurance companies. Other insurance groups continued to oppose the bill, however, arguing that it would raise costs and make it harder for small companies to compete with large insurers.

HR 9 was formally reported Oct. 7 (H Rept 103-853), but the full House never took up the bill. In the meantime, the Judiciary Committee on Aug. 2 voted 20–15 to tack the bill onto the massive health care reform legislation (HR 3600) that was moving through House committees, but that measure never reached the floor either.   ❑

Petroleum Franchise Protection

Congress cleared a bill in 1994 to stop oil companies from turning independent franchises involuntarily into company-owned ones.

The measure (HR 1520—PL 103-371) expanded on the 1978 Petroleum Marketing Practices Act (PL 95-297), which set a single set of rules for oil company franchise agreements. The service stations' lobbyists argued that the 1978 law was not protecting franchise operators from improper terminations and abusive requirements designed to make them go out of business. (1978 act, Congress and the Nation Vol. V, p. 490)

As signed into law Oct. 19, HR 1520 barred oil companies from terminating franchises for the sole purpose of converting the stations into company-owned outlets. It also barred companies from imposing conditions on franchises that violated state law.

States were allowed to regulate some franchise terms, such as the required hours of operation. They could not require an oil company, however, to pay a station operator for the intangible value ("goodwill") of a franchise that was terminated or not renewed.

Disputes between oil companies and franchises grew in the late 1980s, prompting states to intervene and Congress to take another look at the 1978 act. Negotiators for the oil companies and the franchises finally reached a compromise in 1992 that called for new protections for franchise operators and new limits on state intervention, but the legislation did not reach the House or Senate floor. (Congress and the Nation Vol. VIII, p. 530)

Lawmakers tried to enact the compromise again in the 103rd Congress. The House Energy and Commerce Committee approved an early version of HR 1520 on June 8, 1993, but the bill was stymied for more than a year by opposition from three major oil companies—Texaco, Shell Oil Co. and Mobil Corp. The dissenters wanted more power to stop franchises from buying gasoline from a competitor.

A new compromise was reached in September 1994, clarifying that states could not stop a company from terminating a franchise whose operator violated basic agreements. The House Energy and Commerce Committee reported the modified version of HR 1520 on Sept. 22 (H Rept 103-737). The Senate Energy and Natural Resources Committee approved its version of the compromise bill (S 338—S Rept 103-387) on Sept. 29. The House passed HR 1520 on Oct. 4, 413–0, and the Senate cleared the bill by voice vote the next day.   ❑

Telemarketing Scams

Congress omitted new protections against deceptive and abusive telephone sales techniques in 1994, expanding on legislation adopted in the 102nd Congress.

The measure (HR 868—PL 103-297) required federal regulators to ban telemarketing scams, such as offering bogus oil leases and land deals over the phone. It also called for rules against abusive phone sales practices, such as repeatedly disturbing individuals with unsolicited calls.

The Federal Trade Commission (FTC) was ordered to adopt rules by August 1995 to implement the law. The Securities and Exchange Commission (SEC) and the Commodities Futures Trading Commission (CFTC) were given an additional six months to adopt any rules necessary to bar deceptive telemarketing practices by brokers or dealers.

To boost enforcement of the new rules, the law authorized state attorneys general to file federal lawsuits against telemarketers preying on their residents, even if the telemarketers were outside of their state's borders. Individuals were authorized to file similar lawsuits if they suffered more than $50,000 in damages. Such lawsuits would be easier to win than a criminal prosecution because they would have to show only that a telemarketer had deceived customers, not that the telemarketer had a criminal intent to deceive.

Finally, the law expanded the ban on false advertisements to cover claims related to services. Previous law had banned false advertisements only if they related to food, drugs, devices or cosmetics.

Consumer advocates and state prosecutors had been pushing Congress for six years to crack down on telemarketing scam artists, whose fly-by-night operations had largely evaded prosecution. Although Congress had enacted more protections for consumers against unsolicited sales calls and facsimiles in 1992 (PL 102-243), legislation targeted at telemarketing scams died at the end of the 1992 session. *(Congress and the Nation Vol. VIII, p. 459)*

The House Energy and Commerce Committee reported an early version of HR 868 (H Rept 103-20) on Feb. 24, 1993. The full House passed it on March 2, 411–3. The Senate responded on June 30, 1993, by giving voice-vote approval to an amended version of HR 868, based on a bill (S 568—S Rept 103-80) reported by the Senate Commerce, Science and Transportation Committee the day before.

The bill then stalled while House and Senate negotiators worked out their differences over a related measure (HR 2243), a bill to reauthorize the Federal Trade Commission (FTC) *(Story, this page)*

A compromise version of HR 868 was worked out by the House and Senate. The final bill dropped all references to "fraud," clarifying that a state could win a court order to stop a scam without having to prove that the telemarketer intended to defraud consumers.

The amended version passed the House by voice vote July 25, 1994, and cleared the Senate by voice vote Aug. 2. President Clinton signed the bill into law Aug. 16.

SCAMS ON THE ELDERLY

The Senate passed a bill in 1993 to expand the penalties for telemarketing scams on the elderly, but the House took no action on it. The bill (S 557), which was reported by the Senate Judiciary Committee July 22 and passed by voice vote of the Senate July 30, would have provided longer prison terms for telemarketers who committed fraud, particularly if the victims were over age 55. The bill also would have authorized rewards for those who helped convict telephone scam artists, training programs to help federal agents combat the scams, and a national toll-free hotline to report scams. ❑

FTC Reauthorization

After settling a decade-long dispute over advertising regulations, Congress cleared a bill in 1994 to reauthorize the Federal Trade Commission (FTC) and restore some of its power to protect consumers.

The measure (HR 2243—PL 103-312) authorized a total of $294 million for the commission through fiscal 1996. It also allowed the FTC, under certain conditions, to issue industrywide rules against unfair advertising practices. Advertisements were considered unfair if they took advantage of vulnerable audiences, such as children or the elderly.

Congress had not reauthorized the FTC since 1980, mainly because of the dispute between the House and Senate over rules on unfair advertising. The 1980 law barred the FTC from issuing industrywide rules against such advertisements, leaving the commission to try to stop unfair practices by bringing lawsuits against individual companies. *(Congress and the Nation Vol. V, p. 847)*

Antismoking groups, consumer advocates and state attorneys general urged Congress to restore the FTC's rulemaking power, and their position was supported by Rep. John D. Dingell, D-Mich., the powerful chairman of the House Energy and Commerce Committee. Advertising firms and their clients argued that such rules were vague and possibly unconstitutional, and some key senators agreed.

The initial House version of HR 2243 (H Rept 103-138), reported by the House Energy and Commerce Committee June 17, 1993, and passed by voice vote of the full House June 21, would have restored the commission's rulemaking power. The Senate version, S 1179 (S Rept 103-130), which was reported by the Senate Commerce, Science and Transportation Committee Aug. 24, 1993, would have left the ban in place. The Senate passed HR 2243 by voice vote Sept. 22, after substituting the text of its own bill.

House and Senate negotiators reached a compromise allowing the FTC to bar unfair advertising practices by rule or by lawsuit only under three conditions: the advertisement caused or was likely to cause substantial injury to consumers; the injury was neither avoidable nor outweighed by benefits to consumers or competition; and public policy considerations were not the primary basis for finding the advertisement to be unfair. It also limited the commission's authority over deceptive advertisements, allowing rules against such misleading or exaggerated claims only if they were widespread in an industry.

The compromise was included in a conference report (H Rept 103-617) adopted by voice votes in the House July 25, 1994, and the Senate Aug. 11. President Clinton signed it into law Aug. 26. *(1996 action, p. 387)* ❑

Warning Labels on Toys

Hoping to promote child safety, Congress approved two new mandates in 1994: warning labels on toys that posed a choking hazard, and performance standards for bicycle helmets. The mandates were included in a bill (HR 965—PL 103-267) that President Clinton signed into law June 16.

The measure required children's toys and games with small detachable parts, small balls, marbles and balloons sold in the United States after Jan. 1, 1995, to carry a specific warning label stating that the product could choke small children. The warning label had to be placed prominently on the product's package.

Balls intended for children under age three were banned unless they were larger than 1.75 inches in diameter, making them too big to be swallowed. State safety regulations on the issue were preempted.

The measure also required the Consumer Product Safety Commission to develop minimum safety standards for bicycle helmets, replacing the voluntary standards observed by industry. And it authorized the National Highway Traffic Safety Administration to issue $9 million in grants from fiscal 1995 through fiscal 1997 to help states encourage riders less than 16 years old to wear helmets.

At the time, about 3,200 children a year were being treated in hospital emergency rooms for toy-related ingestion and aspiration injuries, according to the Consumer Product Safety Commission. Between 1980 and 1991, 186 children choked to death on balloons, marbles and small balls.

Many toy manufacturers were voluntarily placing labels on toy packages indicating the age group for which the toys were intended. According to the bill's supporters, however, parents often mistakenly interpreted the labels as measuring a toy's sophistication, not warning about a safety hazard.

The House passed an early version of the bill on March 16, 1993, 362–38. The bill had been reported by the House Energy and Commerce Committee March 10 (H Rept 103-29). The Senate approved HR 965 by voice vote Nov. 20, after substituting the text of a similar bill (S 680—S Rept 103-195) reported by the Senate Commerce, Science and Transportation Committee the previous day.

The conference report (H Rept 103-500) dropped a disputed Senate provision, that would have required warning labels on household buckets. The Consumer Product Safety Commission later announced that it still intended to require the labels, which would alert parents to the danger of toddlers drowning in even a small amount of water in the bucket.

The House approved the conference report by voice vote May 23, 1994, and the Senate cleared it by voice vote two days later. ❑

Protections for Car Buyers

Bills to protect automobile buyers against undisclosed vehicle damage and to increase the strength of vehicle bumpers advanced in the Senate in the 103rd Congress but did not become law.

On Nov. 20, 1993, the Senate Commerce, Science and Transportation Committee reported and the full Senate gave voice-vote approval to a bill (S 431—S Rept 103-197) to require automobile titles to disclose all previous, major damage to a car. The bill aimed to outlaw "title washing," the practice of selling used cars without disclosing that they had been extensively rebuilt after an accident.

The bill also would have required that automobile titles indicate if the car had been repurchased under a state "lemon" law. Such laws required car dealers to buy back cars that were plagued with multiple defects.

The House Energy and Commerce Committee did not act on the bill.

On Aug. 22, 1994, the Senate Commerce Committee reported a second measure (S 1848—S Rept 103-353) to require that bumpers on new cars and minivans withstand collisions of at least 5 miles per hour with minimal damage. The bill also would have required manufacturers to put a label on new cars indicating whether they met the standard.

No bumper standards had ever been applied to minivans. Automobile bumpers had to meet the 5-miles-per-hour standard from 1980 to 1982, but the National Highway Traffic Safety Administration reduced the standard in 1982 to 2.5 miles per hour. The reduction was made for the sake of reducing vehicle weight, which increased fuel economy.

The Senate adjourned without acting on the bill. Similar measures had passed the Senate in 1987, 1989 and 1991, but none had ever made it through the House. ❑

Made in America Hotline

The House passed a bill in 1994 to establish a toll-free number that consumers could call to find out about products made in the United States. The measure advanced no further, however.

The bill (HR 3342) called for the Commerce Department to establish the telephone hotline as a three-year pilot project. Companies that made products worth $250 or more, using at least 90 percent U.S.-made parts and U.S. labor, could pay to have those goods featured on the hotline.

Supporters of the bill said that consumers could not rely on the "made in America" labels on products because many of those goods had been built largely from foreign parts and labor. HR 3342 was reported by the House Energy and Commerce Committee on Aug. 3 (H Rept 103-660) and was passed by voice vote of the House on Aug. 8. ❑

Baseball Antitrust Exemption

Despite a protracted strike that wiped out the World Series, lawmakers refused to scale back the antitrust exemption for major league baseball. Labor's allies tried to move a baseball bill (S 500) in the Senate Judiciary Committee in June 1994, seven weeks before the strike began. But the committee defeated the proposal, which would have lifted baseball's antitrust exemption only in regard to labor-management relations. The vote on June 23 was 7–10.

On Sept. 29, a month and a half into the strike, the House Judiciary Committee took a more favorable stance toward the players' union, when it approved a bill (HR 4994) to let players sue the team owners on antitrust grounds if the owners unilaterally imposed certain conditions, such as a salary cap. HR 4994 was formally reported Nov. 29 (H Rept 103-871). The full House did not act on the bill.

On Sept. 30, the sponsor of the Senate bill, Howard M. Metzenbaum, D-Ohio, tried to attach the provisions of HR 4994 to the fiscal 1995 spending bill for the District of Columbia (HR 4649). He withdrew the amendment later that day, however, to avoid a fight that would have delayed funding for the District.

Opponents of the antitrust exemption, which the Supreme Court established in 1922, said that it prolonged baseball's labor disputes. Players in other professional sports—none of which were exempt from the antitrust laws—had used the courts to help avoid lengthy contract fights, but baseball players had no such power.

The team owners and their allies in Congress made two main arguments for preserving the exemption. They contended that ending the exemption would threaten minor league baseball by endangering the reserve clause, a provision in minor league contracts that binds young players to teams for six years. They also said that Congress should not meddle in a labor dispute that posed no threat to national security or the national economy. ❑

Boxing Safety

The Senate Commerce, Science and Transportation Committee approved a bill late in 1994 to keep professional boxers out of the ring while injured or suspended, but the measure advanced no further before Congress adjourned. A related measure cleared in the 104th Congress. *(Boxing safety, p. 386)*

The bill (S 1991) would have required state boxing officials to report the results of professional fights and the names of suspended fighters to a national registry. Before any fight, officials would have been required to check the registry to ensure that boxers were not listed as injured or suspended.

Reported by the Commerce Committee Sept. 28, the bill also would have required state boxing commissions to supervise all bouts and register all fighters. ❑

Telecommunications Overhaul

A threatened filibuster by three Senate Republicans late in the 103rd Congress sank a bill to rewrite federal communications law, despite the overwhelming support that sponsors had built for competing legislation in the House.

The bills (HR 3626, S 1822) would have removed barriers to competition in local telephone and cable TV service, opening the door to no-holds-barred competition throughout the telecommunications industry. The Senate bill, however, was opposed by several of the powerhouse regional Bell operating companies, which argued that it would put them at a competitive disadvantage.

The legislation would have set new conditions on the Bells' entry into long-distance service, equipment manufacturing and other lines of business that the courts and Congress had kept off-limits. Although the Bells wanted Congress to shift control over their actions away from the courts, they did not want their fates left to the discretion of federal bureaucrats while competitors gobbled up their most lucrative local-phone customers.

Other segments of the industry were unhappy with elements of the Senate bill, too, as were consumer advocates. The sheer scope and complexity of the measure made it difficult for lawmakers to balance all the competing interests and achieve consensus in the industry.

Nevertheless, the pressure on Congress to update the federal Communications Act of 1934 was intense and growing. When Senate Commerce Committee Chairman Ernest F. Hollings, D-S.C., pulled the plug on S 1822 in September 1994, supporters and opponents alike knew that the fight had merely been interrupted, not ended.

Indeed, a more deregulatory version of the legislation started moving in the Senate shortly after the 104th Congress convened. After an intense, yearlong series of negotiations among Republican and Democratic lawmakers, industry lobbyists and the White House, a major telecommunications overhaul cleared the Senate in February 1996. *(1995–1996 action, p. 387)*

BACKGROUND

Since Alexander Graham Bell's first telephone patents expired in the 1890s, thousands of companies had vied for pieces of the telephone market. Still, the dominant players had always been the Bell companies and their erstwhile parent, AT&T. By the time Congress took up the issue in 1934, the AT&T family controlled about two-thirds of the local phone business in the United States and all of the long-distance market.

Adopted at a time when powerful corporations were viewed with deep suspicion, the Communications Act of 1934 called for strict federal regulation of interstate phone service instead of a direct assault on the AT&T monopoly. The states, meanwhile, were adopting similar laws for the regulation of local phone service by AT&T's Bell subsidiaries and neighboring companies.

One effect of the regulation was to assure that the monopolies in long-distance and local service would be preserved. In exchange, the companies were required to provide phone lines at affordable rates to rural, remote and other high-cost areas—a policy known as universal service.

The playing field started shifting in the post–World War II years. New technologies, many of them developed by AT&T's engineers, made competition in long-distance service and phone equipment economically feasible. The Federal Communications Commission (FCC)—an independent regulatory body created in 1934—and the courts began in the late 1950s and 1960s to open the door to competition in niches of AT&T's empire.

Lawmakers sympathetic to AT&T tried in the mid-1970s to roll back the clock, preserving the company and its affiliates' monopoly over the telephones on customers' desks and everything that connected them. Another group of lawmakers moved in the opposite direction, pushing legislation to promote competition by carving AT&T into segments.

With Congress stymied by the lack of consensus over the amount and pace of competition, the telephone industry was reworked in the courts. In 1974, the U.S. Department of Justice had accused AT&T of violating federal antitrust laws by improperly trying to stave off competition in long-distance service and telephone equipment. AT&T settled the suit in 1982, agreeing to break into eight pieces as of Jan. 1, 1984: seven regional Bells, which would be restricted to local phone service, and AT&T, which would provide long-distance service and manufacture telecommunications equipment. The Bells thus were excluded from competitive markets and AT&T from monopoly markets.

As approved by U.S. District Judge Harold H. Greene, the consent decree allowed a Bell to offer long-distance service, manufacture telecommunications equipment or provide information services (such as automated stock quotes over the phone) only if Greene found that there was "no substantial possibility" of the Bell impeding competition in the market it was entering. This provision was section 8(c) of the consent decree, and so it became known as "the 8(c) test."

The Bells, which chafed at the restrictions imposed by the consent decree, soon began pressing Congress to retake control of the industry from Greene. They had allies on both sides of the aisle, including Hollings and two leading Senate Republicans, Bob Dole of Kansas and Bob Packwood of Oregon, as well as House Energy and Commerce Committee Chairman John D. Dingell, D-Mich.

The Bells also had powerful opponents, however, as evidenced by the competing bills that advanced in the 102nd Congress. The Senate passed a Hollings bill in 1991 to let the Bells manufacture telecommunications equipment in the United States, with safeguards to guard against the Bells imposing unfair terms on other phone companies or using local phone revenues to subsidize their manufacturing operations. The House Judiciary Committee countered the following year with a bill to codify the court-imposed restrictions on the Bells and reverse a 1991 appeals court ruling that allowed the Bells to offer information services. (Congress and the Nation Vol. VIII, p. 461)

HOUSE ACTION

The legislative logjam in the House broke in 1993, when Dingell and House Judiciary Committee Chairman Jack Brooks, D-Texas, agreed to a compromise approach toward the Bells' entry into new markets. Their legislative muscle, combined with a near-united front of industry support, pushed the bill through the House virtually without dissent.

The Brooks-Dingell bill (HR 3626) would have allowed the Bells into the interstate long-distance and equipment markets as soon as the FCC and the Justice Department approved. The Justice Department would have applied the 8(c) test when judging a Bell's application, while the FCC was charged with determining whether the Bell's expansion was in the public interest. The Bells' entry into in-state long-distance markets would have been controlled by state regulators.

The bill also would have set restrictions on the Bells' entry into information services, such as electronic publishing. The Bells would have been required to enter the market through a separate subsidiary or joint venture, although that provision would have expired after four years.

The measure swept through the Judiciary and Energy and Commerce Committees by voice vote March 16, 1994, with few changes. The changes were significant enough, however, to force Dingell and Brooks to hammer out one final compromise on two issues: the Justice Department's role over in-state long-distance service and the Bells' ability to use long-distance lines for "incidental" services.

The compromise, announced June 23, left state regulators in control over the Bells' ability to carry in-state long-distance calls, but it gave the Justice Department 90 days to file suit to block any state decision it opposed. The new version of the bill also would have freed the Bells to cross their local boundaries in order to offer audio and video programming, interactive services, cable television, mobile telephone services and voice mail.

The two chairmen modified the bill further to address a smattering of concerns voiced by the administration and other lawmakers. One new provision, sought by the administration, would have nullified a proposed requirement that the Bells do their manufacturing within the United States if the requirement violated U.S. trade agreements. Two others aimed to protect telephone answering services and providers of "enhanced" services, such as Internet access, from unfair tactics by competing local phone companies.

HR 3626 was formally reported by the Energy and Commerce Committee and the Judiciary Committee on June 24 (H Rept 103-559, Parts I and II).

The Brooks-Dingell bill represented only half of the communications overhaul. The other piece of the package was a bill (HR 3636) by Edward J. Markey, D-Mass., chairman of the Energy and Commerce Subcommittee on Telecommunications and Finance, and Jack Fields, R-Texas, the subcommittee's ranking member.

This measure would have opened local telephone markets to competition by requiring the local monopolies to share their networks with competitors. It also would have allowed local phone companies to enter the local cable TV business through separate subsidiaries once they opened their networks to competition, repealing a restriction in the 1984 cable television deregulation law (PL 98-549).

The Markey-Fields bill had a rockier path to the House floor, undergoing numerous changes in the sponsors' panel and the full Energy and Commerce Committee. Among the additions were provisions that would have limited Bell price increases, slowed the phone companies' move into cable TV, added safeguards against Bell cross-subsidies and price discrimination, and given the TV broadcasters more freedom in the use of their transmission frequencies.

When the dust settled on March 16, the amended Markey-Fields bill had the unanimous support of the Energy and Commerce Committee—a remarkable feat for such complex and far-reaching legislation. It was approved, 44–0. HR 3636 was reported by the panel on June 24 (H Rept 103-560).

On June 28, both bills went to the House floor under suspension of the rules, an expedited procedure usually reserved for minor or noncontroversial bills. That tactic barred amendments, but it also required a two-thirds vote for passage.

Testifying to Brooks's and Dingell's power as well as their thoroughness in addressing members' concerns, HR 3626 passed on a **key vote of 423–5 (R 173–1; D 249–4; I 1–0).** The Markey-Fields bill passed by a similar margin, 423–4. Afterwards, the provisions of the Markey-Fields bill were inserted into the Brooks-Dingell measure, and the expanded version of HR 3626 was sent to the Senate. *(1994 key votes, p. 1003)*

The margins would not have been so wide, however, had the only segment of the telecommunications industry opposed to the bill—the long-distance companies—put up a fight. Those companies decided instead to concentrate their efforts on the Senate, where Hollings, along with the top Republican on the Commerce Committee, John C. Danforth of Missouri, and the chairman of the Communications Subcommittee, Democrat Daniel K. Inouye of Hawaii, had introduced a bill much more to the long-distance companies' liking.

SENATE ACTION

More detailed and demanding than the House bill, the Senate proposal (S 1822) would have required local phone companies to take specific technical steps to share their network with competitors, such as allowing people to change phone companies without changing phone numbers. The Bells also would have been required to win approval from the FCC and the Justice Department before they could enter the long-distance, equipment or cable TV markets. No Bell would have been allowed to enter those markets for 21 months or until the FCC had adopted new rules for preserving universal service, whichever came first.

The original version of the bill was even tougher on the Bells, requiring them to face "actual and demonstrable competition" in the local phone business before they could enter new markets. In a hard-fought deal with the Bells and the long-distance companies, however, Hollings dropped that provision in favor of the checklist of competition-promoting steps.

The change was one of many Hollings made in his effort to get the bill through his committee. The bill almost doubled in length as provision after provision was added to address the scattershot concerns of industry lobbyists and lawmakers. For example, Hollings agreed to let states determine whether competition would be allowed for local phone service in rural areas. That modification had been sought by aides to a group of rural-state senators, dubbed the Farm Team.

Hollings also included a provision requiring any phone company receiving universal-service subsidies to provide discounted service to schools, libraries, health care facilities and other public institutions. The FCC would have been required to encour-age the companies to provide advanced services, such as high speed links to the Internet web of computer networks. The provision reflected the Clinton administration's push to connect public institutions to the emerging "information superhighway." *(National Information Infrastructure, p. 357)*

The changes helped the bill win approval from the Commerce Committee on Aug. 11, 18–2, but they did not unite industry behind the legislation. Most notably, the Bells were galled by the amount of regulation that the bill proposed at the behest of their future competitors, as well as the head start that cable TV companies would enjoy in any head-to-head competition.

The committee had tried to mollify the Bells on the cable issue, adopting an amendment that would have allowed the Bells to enter the cable television market sooner if they won permission from a federal court. All of the Bells were trying to have the 1984 ban on cross-ownership of telephone and cable companies struck down as unconstitutional, and two had already won rulings to that effect. Still, the Bells were far from satisfied.

The Bells' cause was taken up by Dole, Packwood and John McCain, R-Ariz., who called on Hollings to lighten the Bells' regulatory load. Packwood and McCain favored giving the Bells a date certain for entry into new markets, as proposed in a bill (S 2111) cosponsored by Packwood and Democrat John B. Breaux of Louisiana. Dole's 30-page draft bill proposed a date certain for the Bells, an end to federal regulation of the cable TV industry and lighter regulation on the broadcasters. *(Background on cable regulation, Congress and the Nation Vol. VIII, p. 451)*

At the same time, the changes made to satisfy the Farm Team drew fire from consumer advocates. The consumer groups' main Senate ally, Democrat Howard M. Metzenbaum of Ohio, also threatened to filibuster unless the original bill's proposed restrictions on the Bells were restored.

In fact, virtually every segment of the industry was calling for changes as time ran down in the session. Hollings tried to make peace with Dole to clear a path to the Senate floor for S 1822, which had been formally reported on Sept. 14 (S Rept 103-367). When Dole's staff demanded changes that would have undone the deal that Hollings had struck over the Bells' entry into long distance, allowing the Bells a quicker entry, Hollings decided the time had come to call a halt.

Hollings announced on Sept. 23 that the legislation was dead for the year, and he blamed three of the Bells for its demise: Ameritech of Chicago, BellSouth of Atlanta and US West of Denver. The Bells made a last-ditch effort to revive the measure, but their efforts proved futile. ❑

Wiretapping Capabilities

In a major victory for top law enforcement officials and a bitter defeat for privacy advocates, the Senate cleared a bill late in the 1994 session to help police wiretaps keep pace with advancing telephone technology.

The measure (HR 4922—PL 103-414) gave telephone companies four years to adapt their networks and services to ensure the success of court-ordered wiretaps. In particular, investigators had to be able to record, track and trace any call in secret from a remote site. However, law enforcement officials were not allowed to dictate what communications technologies could be used or introduced.

In a nod to the local phone companies, the taxpayers were required to pay the first $500 million of the cost to upgrade existing telephone equipment and services. Because the measure did not actually provide the money, opponents renewed their fight in the 104th Congress by trying to prevent any of the funds from being appropriated. *(1995–1996 action, p. 395)*

The FBI had been urging Congress for several years to require more wiretap-friendly phone networks, arguing that criminals were using mobile phones and call-forwarding services to evade their pursuers. New digital, wireless and cellular technologies could route calls around the points that investigators traditionally used to place wiretaps, obscure the source or destination of intercepted calls, or make it impossible to tap a single line.

FBI Director Louis J. Freeh led the push for legislation in the 103rd Congress, proposing that phone companies be given three years to guarantee that calls could be tapped or tracked. The police did not need more wiretapping authority, Freeh said, they simply needed to be sure that their existing authority was not undermined by the new technologies.

Privacy advocates and phone companies resisted the FBI's proposal, saying the phone networks should be designed with privacy in mind, not wiretaps. Still, Freeh won grudging support from two Democrats who usually sided with the civil libertarians: Sen. Patrick J. Leahy of Vermont and Rep. Don Edwards of California, chairmen of the Senate and House Judiciary Committee panels that had jurisdiction over the proposal.

After lengthy negotiations with the FBI, telephone company lobbyists and privacy advocates, Leahy and Edwards introduced identical bills on Aug. 9, 1994, to require wiretap-friendly phone networks within four years. The bills contained several new privacy protections, including provisions barring police from obtaining e-mail addresses or pinpointing the location of mobile phones without a court order. They also proposed to bar the deliberate interception of calls made on cordless telephones.

As the bills moved to the House and Senate floor, Leahy and Edwards added several provisions to help the phone companies. One allowed the companies not to upgrade their existing networks if the federal government failed to provide the initial $500 million. Another required the government to cover the cost of any required increase in network capacity—a key point for wireless carriers.

A third provision, added at the behest of the House Energy and Commerce Committee, let companies appeal to the Federal Communications Commission (FCC) any change that law enforcement officials demanded in a future network or service. If the FCC found the cost to be unreasonable, the government would have to foot the bill or allow the company not to make the change.

The House Judiciary Committee reported HR 4922 (H Rept 103-827, Part I) Oct. 4. The bill passed the full House by voice vote the next day.

The Senate Judiciary Committee had reported a nearly identical version of the bill (S 2375—S Rept 103-402) on Sept. 28. But Leahy struggled to bring the legislation to the floor during the Senate's final week of legislating. The bill was blocked first by senators seeking leverage on unrelated issues, then by Republican Malcolm Wallop of Wyoming—a conservative who made an unlikely ally for the American Civil Liberties Union and the Electronic Privacy Information Center.

Wallop argued that the bill was an infringement on privacy, but he dropped his objection late in the evening of Oct. 7 after being lobbied by a succession of law enforcement officials and Senate colleagues. The Senate passed S 2375 and then cleared HR 4922 by voice vote. President Clinton signed the measure into law on Oct. 25.   ❑

Spectrum Auctions

Ending the traditional practice of awarding frequencies for free, Congress ordered the Federal Communications Commission (FCC) in 1993 to start auctioning portions of the electromagnetic spectrum to the highest bidder.

The shift to auctions was part of the budget reconciliation bill (HR 2264—PL 103-66) that President Clinton signed into law Aug. 10, 1993. It was projected to raise $7.2 billion for the federal Treasury over five years. *(Budget reconciliation, p. 44)*

The measure required the FCC to use auctions through fiscal 1998 to award any licenses for wireless phone companies, paging systems and other businesses that sold direct access to the airwaves. It did not affect the licenses obtained by broadcasters, electric utilities or other companies that did not depend on the airwaves for subscriptions.

Another provision of the law required 200 megahertz of spectrum controlled by the government to be made available gradually to private industry, starting by February 1995. The House had approved a bill in 1991 with a similar goal, but it stalled when President Bush demanded that the frequencies be auctioned instead of awarded by lottery. *(Congress and the Nation Vol. VIII, p. 459)*

The final bill barred states from adopting new price controls on mobile telephone service. The 19 states that already regulated mobile-phone rates were required to drop their controls after one year unless the FCC agreed to leave them in effect.

HR 2264 also required broadcasters and other users of the spectrum to pay annual fees ranging from $6 to $18,000. This provision was expected to raise $100 million a year to support the FCC's work.

The move to auctions had been opposed by key House Democrats before the 103rd Congress, but they climbed on board after Clinton included auctions in his deficit-reduction plan in early 1993. Licenses for wireless phones and pagers had previously been awarded by lottery, a system that enabled license speculators to buy out other applicants and then sell their frequencies to the highest bidder.

The first round of auctions was expected to control licenses for personal communications services—a new, digital form of wireless phones and pagers. Although various factions urged lawmakers to reserve licenses for rural areas and new entrants, Congress left these decisions largely to the FCC. It did require the commission, however, to ensure that licenses were distributed geographically and that small businesses, rural phone companies and minority-owned businesses had the chance to win some of the licenses.

MAJOR PROVISIONS

As signed into law, the communications provisions of HR 2264:

Radio Spectrum Transfer

• **Planning.** Required the chairman of the Federal Communications Commission (FCC) and the assistant commerce secretary for telecommunications to meet at least biannually to plan the management of the radio spectrum.

• **Identification of Frequencies.** Required the commerce secretary within 18 months to submit a report recommending which radio frequencies used by the federal government could be turned over to the private sector.

The selected frequencies were to have the largest potential for public benefit and productive use. The secretary was to choose at least 200 megahertz of radio spectrum for reassignment, all located below 5 gigahertz (the highest end of the usable spectrum). Of that amount, 100 megahertz was to reside in the portion of the spectrum below 3 gigahertz.

The secretary was required to consider the following factors when identifying which government frequencies should be offered to the private sector: whether the frequency was commercially available; whether reassigning the frequency promoted sharing of frequencies and the development of new communications technologies; and whether the shift would seriously harm federal services, impose excessive federal costs or disrupt the use of government frequencies by amateur radio licensees.

The secretary was to assume that the assignments would be made within 15 years.

• **Power Agency Exemptions.** Exempted the Tennessee Valley Authority, the Bonneville Power Administration and the Western, Southwestern, Southeastern and Alaska power administrations from having the radio band they used offered for use by the public sector. Those agencies were required to share their frequencies with commercial users where possible.

• **Procedures for Identifying Spectrum.** Required that, within six months, the commerce secretary submit a preliminary list of radio bands that met the criteria for reassignment. The public was to be given 90 days to comment, and the FCC was then to have 90 days to analyze the recommendations. The secretary was urged to encourage discussions among commercial users and government users. The secretary then was to issue a timetable. No less than 50 megahertz was to be reassigned immediately after the preliminary report was issued.

• **Presidential Review.** Allowed the president, within six months of receiving the secretary's report, to make changes in the plan. The president could substitute an alternative frequency, while stating the reasons for doing so to the FCC and Congress. The president could retain the frequencies for govern-ment use when the reallocation stood to jeopardize national defense or public health or safety, result in excessive costs, eliminate a use uniquely suited to the government or disrupt the use of a government-held band of frequencies by amateur radio licensees.

• **Award of Frequencies.** Required the FCC to parcel out the reassigned frequencies in three stages. Within 18 months, the commission had to identify which communications services would be allowed to use the initial 50-megahertz block of frequencies reassigned by the commerce secretary. At the same time, it had to propose regulations for assigning those frequencies to specific users. One year after that, the FCC had to submit a plan for allocating and assigning the remaining 150 megahertz of reassigned frequencies. That plan was to provide for the gradual allocation and assignment of many of the frequencies over the subsequent 10 years, with a "significant portion" of the frequencies being reserved for allocation and assignment at the end of that period. The plan had to ensure that enough frequencies would be available to support new technologies and services as well as public safety communications. The plan could be changed over time, and it would not preclude the FCC from allocating and assigning other frequencies.

• **Presidential Authority.** Allowed the president to reclaim frequencies allocated to the private sector in the future, as long as the president allowed for an orderly transition. The provision required the president to estimate the cost of displacing spectrum users should the government take back control of the frequencies.

• **Transfer Authority.** Declared that nothing in the law prevented shifting more of the radio band from the government's use to the private sector.

Competitive Bidding

• **Competitive Bidding.** Gave the FCC authority to use competitive bidding to grant some radio licenses. The initiative overturned a long-standing policy of awarding radio licenses free through lottery or merit review.

The provision affected only businesses that sold direct access to the airwaves, such as cellular phone companies. Other radio licensees, such as broadcasters and cable systems, were not affected.

• **Fair Auctions.** Required the FCC to design a competitive bidding system for each class of radio license or permit affected. The agency was required to design and test alternative ways of conducting the auctions. The provision put in place safeguards to protect the public interest; to spur the development of new communications services, including those for people living in rural areas; to promote economic opportunity and competition by disseminating licenses among a variety of applicants, including small businesses, rural telephone companies and businesses owned by minorities and women; to require that auctions earn for taxpayers a portion of the value of the radio band being put up for auction and that the auctions avoid "unjust enrichment"; and to ensure the efficient use of the electromagnetic spectrum.

• **Content of Regulations.** Required the FCC to include the following when devising auction regulations: alternative payment schedules for those who won bids for licenses, including lump-sum or installment payments, royalty payments or other methods that would promote competition and economic opportunity; performance requirements, such as deadlines and penalties, to ensure prompt delivery of service to rural areas, to prevent the hoarding of spectrum by licensees and to promote investment in and rapid deployment of new technologies; equitable geographic distribution of spectrum assignments that also provided the widest possible economic opportunity to small businesses, rural telephone companies and businesses owned by minorities and women; assurances that small businesses, rural telephone companies, minority groups and women, by use of tax certificates, bidding preferences and other means, were given a chance to participate in the auctions; and requirements for disclosure of license transfers, antitrafficking rules and payment schedules to prevent the unjust enrichment of bidders as a result of the auction system.

• **Public Interest.** Barred the FCC from citing the government's need to raise revenues as a rationale for granting a license or permit. The provision did not, however, bar the FCC from considering consumer demand for spectrum-based services.

• **Treatment of Revenues.** Required that all receipts from auctions be deposited in the Treasury. Revenues also were to be used to offset the FCC's costs of carrying out the auctions.

• **Auction Timetable.** Stated that the FCC's authority to grant a license or permit by competitive bidding would expire Sept. 30, 1998. The commission was required to issue a report to Congress examining the auction program no later than Sept. 30, 1997.

Mobile Communications

• **Commercial Mobile Services.** Stated that any person engaged in a commercial mobile communications service be treated as a "common carrier." The designation meant that the FCC could require that competitors be allowed to connect with the service. The FCC had to list in its annual report the number of competitors in various mobile commercial services, determine whether there was effective competition and whether any competitors had a dominant share of the market.

The FCC could ease some of these requirements and drop the common carrier status only if they were unnecessary to ensure that the service's rates, practices and rules were reasonable and nondiscriminatory, and to protect consumers.

• **Private Mobile Services.** Stated that private mobile services, such as radio dispatch services used by delivery companies, should not be treated as common carriers, nor should companies provide dispatch service on any frequencies allocated for common carriers, except those already licensed as such before Jan. 1, 1982.

State preemption. Prohibited state or local governments from regulating the rates or entry of any commercial or private mobile service. Sates could regulate other terms and conditions of commercial services, however, The provision did not affect any state requirements that aimed to ensure telecommunications services at affordable rates and widespread availability.

A state could petition the FCC for authority to regulate the rates for any commercial mobile service. Within nine months, the FCC was to grant the petition if a state demonstrated that market conditions failed to protect subscribers from unjust, unreasonable or discriminatory rates, or that wireless services were replacing a "substantial portion" of the land-based telephone exchange. In the interim, the state retained its rate-setting powers.

States that had in effect on June 1, 1993, any regulation concerning the rates of any commercial mobile service could within one year ask the FCC to continue the regulations. The agency had to act on the petition within one year. Should the rate-setting authority be allowed to continue, private parties could later petition the agency to reverse the decision.

• **Communications Fees.** Directed the FCC to collect regulatory fees from all licensees to recover the costs of the agency's activities. The law set exact fees for each type of licensee for fiscal 1994. They ranged from $6 for a small-sized satellite television programmer to $600 for a medium-sized FM radio station and $18,000 for a large-market VHF television station. The provision directed that future fees be based on a combination of factors, including the number of FCC workers it took to perform various duties and the public benefit of those duties.

The total amount collected annually was to equal the amount appropriated for that fiscal year for those FCC activities. The schedule of fees was to be revised annually. Licensees who did not pay in time faced a 25 percent penalty. The money was to be used to offset appropriations used to carry out the functions of the commission.   ❑

National Information Infrastructure

Prodded by the Clinton administration, the House passed a pair of bills in 1993 to promote the development and use of a nationwide grid of high-speed communications networks, formally known as the National Information Infrastructure (NII) but commonly dubbed the "information superhighway." The Senate in 1994 incorporated NII-related proposals into major bills aimed at U.S. competitiveness and telecommunications competition, but none of the measures made it into law.

The first House bill (HR 1757), which passed in July 1993, would have authorized $1 billion in fiscal 1994 through 1998 for a multiagency effort to expand the availability and applications of the nation's high-speed computer networks. The second bill (HR 2639), which passed in November 1993, would have authorized $250 million over two years to help local governments, universities, hospitals and other public institutions hook into the information superhighway.

BACKGROUND

The federal government had played a role in computer networking since 1969, when the Defense Department first linked two distant computers over telephone lines. By 1993, that network had grown into an unregulated, worldwide web of computer systems known as the Internet. Its backbone was the National Science Foundation's network, known as NSFNET, which linked about 1,000 colleges and universities.

In 1991 Congress cleared legislation (PL 102-194), sponsored by then-Sen. Al Gore, D-Tenn., to merge the patchwork of agency initiatives into one high-performance computing and networking program. The 1991 law, which focused on linking high-performance supercomputers to sophisticated research projects, quickly illustrated how small amounts of federal spending promised to leverage significant private-sector investment. *(1991 law, Congress and the Nation Vol. VIII, p. 889)*

In a comprehensive technology policy statement issued Feb. 22, 1993, President Clinton called for linking more schools, libraries, hospitals and businesses through an information superhighway. Just as the interstate highway system had fostered decades of economic growth, Clinton's plan was intended to spawn a new era in technology.

The plan, which was included in Clinton's fiscal 1994 budget, called for about $1 billion to be spent on finding better ways for doctors, educators and manufacturers to use computer networks. Another $1 billion was to go toward grants to help schools, libraries and other public institutions tap into the 10,000 computer networks that already were linked worldwide. The government investment was intended to spur private companies to complete the information superhighway—a task that was estimated to cost as much as $400 billion.

The goal was to link public and private institutions—and eventually households—to a communications network capable of transmitting vast amounts of text and video data at lightning speed. Much of the network already had been built by telephone and cable companies, although it operated at slower speeds.

LEGISLATIVE ACTION

HR 1757 would have given the federal high-performance computing program an additional function: developing ways to use computer network technologies to improve schools, create digital libraries, expand the reach of hospitals and increase access to government records. A total of $829 million would have been authorized over five years for such projects, plus $81 million for research to improve computer-network security, privacy and ease of use.

The bill would have authorized an additional $95 million over three years to help develop local computer networks linking government agencies, schools, libraries and museums. Those funds also could have been used to cover 75 percent of the cost of the equipment and services needed to connect local institutions to the Internet.

The House Science, Space and Technology Committee reported HR 1757 July 13 (H Rept 103-173). The House passed it July 26, 326–61.

HR 2639 would have created a new grants program to cover up to half the cost of linking schools, hospitals, libraries, museums, research facilities and government agencies to the information superhighway. The bill would have authorized $100 million for the grants in fiscal 1995 and $150 million in fiscal 1996.

An additional $70 million would have been authorized over two years for planning and construction grants to expand the reach of public broadcasting stations. The bill also would have created clearinghouses for information on distance learning and telemedicine programs, which used computer networks to bring educational and medical services to remote or rural areas.

The House Energy and Commerce Committee reported HR 2639 (H Rept 103-325) Nov. 3. The measure passed the House by voice vote Nov. 8.

The Senate did not act on either bill. Provisions similar to HR 2639 were included in the Senate-passed version of the competitiveness bill (HR 820), which died in conference at the end of the 103rd Congress. The Senate telecommunications bill (S 1822) would have encouraged telephone companies to give schools, hospitals and other public institutions access to advanced telecommunications services like the Internet, but the bill was stopped short of the Senate floor. *(High-tech competitiveness, p. 342; telecommunications overhaul, p. 352)* ❑

Satellite TV Transmissions

Congress cleared a bill in 1994 to ensure that satellite dish owners would continue receiving network television broadcasts, although possibly at a higher cost. The bill (S 2406—PL 103-369) allowed satellite-based television services to retransmit the programs carried by the networks and so-called superstations through 1999. Had Congress not acted, that retransmission authority would have expired at the end of 1994.

Satellite dishes were used by an estimated 4.5 million households, most of them in isolated rural areas out of the reach of broadcast signals. Federal law barred satellite systems from transmitting network programs to customers who could receive clear signals from their local broadcasters.

The legislation was stalled for several months by a dispute over how much the satellite companies would have to pay for the programs. The proposal reported by the Senate Judiciary Committee May 5, 1994 (S 1485—S Rept 103-407), which the satellite companies supported, would have maintained the existing system. The bill the House Judiciary Committee reported Aug. 16 (HR 1103—H Rept 103-703), which was backed by the networks and Hollywood studios, would have required the fee to reflect the fair market value of the programs.

House and Senate lawmakers eventually agreed to have the existing arbitration panel set fees that reflected fair market value, taking into consideration the fees that the cable companies paid for similar retransmission rights, among other factors.

The compromise was attached to a bill (S 2406), passed by the Senate Aug. 18, that required cable TV systems to carry the signals from certain Fox Broadcasting Network stations and other local, low-power broadcasters. The revised bill also set a new procedure for resolving complaints by broadcasters that satellite companies were serving ineligible customers.

The modified bill passed the House Sept. 20 by voice vote, and the Senate cleared it by voice vote Oct. 4. President Clinton signed the bill Oct. 18. ❑

FCC Reauthorization

The House passed a bill late in the 1994 session to authorize a significant increase in spending by the Federal Communicaions Commission (FCC), but the measure was blocked in the Senate.

The bill (HR 4522) called for a 16 percent increase in FCC spending in fiscal 1995, to $186 million. Most of the money would have come from fees paid by broadcasters, wireless phone companies and other licensed users of the radio spectrum.

Also included were proposals to eliminate a number of obsolete FCC regulations, such as the requirement that recreational boaters and aviators obtain licenses for their two-way radios.

HR 4522 was reported by the House Energy and Commerce Committee Oct. 6 (H Rept 103-844) and was passed by voice vote of the full House the next day. Leaders of the Senate Commerce Committee tried to bring the bill to the Senate floor Oct. 8, but they were not able to obtain the unanimous consent needed to proceed. They also were blocked from bringing to the Senate floor a revised version of a two-year FCC reauthorization proposal (S 2336) that had not been acted on by the committee.

The FCC received much of the proposed increase anyway, courtesy of the fiscal 1995 appropriations bill for the Commerce, Justice and State departments (HR 4603—PL 103-317). That measure gave the FCC authority to spend $185.2 million.   ❏

1995–1996

Responding to their core constituencies in the business community, Republicans in the 104th Congress sought to cut federal regulatory power over numerous aspects of commerce and transportation.

Their initiatives included proposals to wipe out much of the regulation on cable television franchises, broadcasters and local telephone companies; overhaul the air traffic control system and Amtrak, the national passenger rail system; deregulate ocean shipping and other forms of freight hauling; limit federal rule-making power over pipelines for oil and natural gas; remove federal mandates on state highway programs; and limit the damages that could be recovered from the manufacturers of faulty products.

Most of the proposals were fought by Democrats in Congress and the White House, who had less faith in market forces to protect consumers and workers. Intra-industry battles also helped sink some of the initiatives, as small and midsized companies argued that deregulation would help their largest competitors more than it would aid them.

Still, the GOP scored some notable victories in areas where it scaled back its deregulatory ambitions and forged a consensus with the Democrats. Topping the list of accomplishments was a bill to rewrite the 62-year-old federal communications act, a New Deal-era law that members had been trying to update for two decades. The new measure, which President Clinton signed into law in February 1996, sought to bring competition into the local telephone and cable television markets while easing regulation on all segments of the communications industry.

A bipartisan group of lawmakers also pushed through a measure to limit product liability lawsuits after Republicans gave up on provisions to curb all civil claims. The victory was short-lived, however; President Clinton vetoed the bill, and the House could not override him.

Some of the most dramatic Republican proposals were opposed by lawmakers from both parties. For example, House Republican freshmen sought to eliminate the Commerce Department, saying the agency promoted corporate welfare and unwarranted government intrusion in the market. The House twice passed proposals to disband the department, but the measures were scuttled by bipartisan opposition in the Senate.

The most significant transportation bill to clear in the 104th Congress was a measure designating routes for a new National Highway System. Backed by conservative Democrats, Republicans used the bill to repeal an assortment of federal transportation mandates, including the federal speed limit. The effect was to shift regulatory power over highway safety from Washington to the state capitals.

The driving force behind the highway bill was money: unless the routes were designated, states stood to lose billions of federal highway dollars. Similarly, a bill to reauthorize federal aviation programs was propelled by lawmakers' desire to keep money flowing to airport improvement projects.

Indeed, transportation was one field where Republicans rarely sought to slash spending. The House went so far as to pass a bill in 1996 that would have allowed Congress to spend down the multibillion-dollar balances in four transportation trust funds, but the measure was blocked in the Senate by deficit-conscious members.

Even Amtrak, long a bane of some Republican budget-cutters, would have benefited from a new stream of subsidies under a proposal endorsed by the Senate Commerce, Science and Transportation Committee. That bill foundered, however, as did a House proposal to relieve Amtrak of some costly federal regulations.

FAA Reauthorization

Congress cleared in 1996 a $19.5 billion bill to reauthorize the Federal Aviation Administration (FAA) and related programs for two years. The legislation (HR 3539—PL 104-264) was critical to the continued operation of the Airport Improvement Program, whose authorization had expired on Sept. 30, 1996. Although Congress had approved more than $1.4 billion for the airport grants as part of the fiscal 1997 transportation appropriations bill (HR 3675—PL 104-205), not a penny could be spent for the popular grants for airport construction and security projects until the program was reauthorized.

The measure included numerous provisions to boost safety and airport security, a top priority for lawmakers at a time of heightened public concern about flying. The year had seen at least two fiery plane crashes that claimed hundreds of lives: the plunge of ValuJet Flight 592 into the Florida Everglades in May and the mid-air explosion of TWA Flight 800 over the Atlantic Ocean in July.

Among the safety-related provisions were three House-passed bills to aid the families of crash victims, restrict child pilots and mandate more extensive background checks on commercial pilots. Senate conferees agreed to their addition to HR 3539.

Almost all the elements of HR 3539 had broad, bipartisan support. The one exception was a provision added to the final version of the bill in late September by Sen. Ernest F. Hollings, D-S.C. The provision, which was inserted during the House-Senate conference, made it harder for truck drivers at the Federal Express Corp. to unionize.

Labor's allies in the Senate launched a filibuster, demanding that the Federal Express provision be dropped from the conference report. Senate GOP leaders stood behind the Hollings provision, vowing to keep the chamber in session until the bill was cleared. The Senate voted to cut off the filibuster on Oct. 3, and the Senate cleared the conference report later that day.

Although President Clinton had opposed the Hollings provision, he signed the bill into law on Oct. 9.

LEGISLATIVE ACTION

The dispute over Federal Express nearly caused a replay of the previous FAA reauthorization debate, in the 103rd Congress. A series of disputes had held up passage of the legislation in 1993 and 1994, causing the Airport Improvement Program to shut down for eight months. The appropriators later responded by cutting $240 million from the program. *(1993–1994 action, p. 330)*

On July 26, 1996, the House Transportation and Infrastructure Committee and the Senate Commerce, Science and Transportation Committee reported competing bills to reauthorize the aviation programs. The House committee's bill (HR 3539—H Rept 104-714, Part I) proposed to authorize $29.7 billion in spending over three years for the FAA. The bill also proposed to adjust airport funding formulas, increasing the amount that all airports received by formula and reducing the amount that the FAA awarded at its discretion.

The Senate committee's bill (S 1994—S Rept 104-333) proposed to authorize $9.3 billion in spending on FAA programs in fiscal 1997. Unlike the House bill, S 1994 would have left the airport funding formula basically the same. Also included in the Senate bill were provisions to give the FAA more autonomy. These provisions had been drawn from S 1239, an FAA restructuring bill that had stalled short of the Senate floor. *(FAA overhaul, p. 361)*

The House overwhelmingly approved HR 3539 on Sept. 11, 398–17. The Senate followed suit on Sept. 18, voting 99–0 in favor of a new version of HR 3539 based on S 1994.

Before approving the bill, the Senate added a series of antiterrorism provisions that had been recommended by a special administration commission on airport security. These included a proposal to mandate criminal background checks on airport security personnel.

In conference, House and Senate negotiators agreed to Hollings's proposal to insert the phrase "express company" into labor law. That provision benefited a single company—Federal Express, based in Memphis, Tenn.—by requiring its truck drivers to organize nationally when trying to form a union, rather than organizing one workplace at a time.

Hollings said the provision was nothing more than a technical correction to an earlier bill (HR 2539—PL 104-88) that had deleted the "express company" phrase when terminating the Interstate Commerce Commission (ICC). But labor allies, including Democratic Sen. Edward M. Kennedy of Massachusetts, denounced it as a special-interest provision that would set back the rights of working men and women.

After a fierce, partisan debate, the House adopted, 218–198, the conference report (H Rept 104-848) on Sept. 27. Kennedy and other liberals in the Senate then launched an end-of-session filibuster against the measure, demanding the removal of the Federal Express provision. Rather than adjourn as scheduled without clearing the FAA bill, Senate Majority Leader Trent Lott, R-Miss., decided to keep the Senate in session, file a cloture petition and try to curtail debate.

Provision supporters argued that lawmakers were obligated to restore the phrase because Congress had never meant to change Federal Express's status under labor law. Both Democratic and Republican staff members who helped draft the ICC legislation said they had merely been trying to delete outdated provisions from the statute books, not to affect Federal Express. *(ICC elimination, p. 381)*

In the months since the ICC bill was signed into law, however, Federal Express truck drivers in Pennsylvania had started trying to form unions at their job sites. Changing the company's status again would derail the drivers' efforts, making it seem as if Congress was union-busting.

Ending a filibuster required 60 votes, a threshold that other union-opposed measures had not been able to meet in the 104th Congress. Nevertheless, supporters of the bill were able on Oct. 3 to cut off debate, 66–31, having convinced a number of labor's usual allies that the disputed provision was truly a correction of an inadvertent error. The Senate then cleared the measure, 92–2.

MAJOR PROVISIONS

As signed into law, HR 3539:

• **FAA Funding Levels.** Authorized almost $5.2 billion in fiscal 1997 and more than $5.3 billion in fiscal 1998 for FAA operations. An additional $2.1 billion was authorized for FAA equipment purchases in each of the two years, plus $208 million for research in fiscal 1997.

• **Airport Improvement Grants.** Reauthorized the Airport Improvement Program at just under $2.3 billion in fiscal 1997 and just above $2.3 billion in fiscal 1998. It also changed the formula for distributing grants, guaranteeing more money to each airport while reducing the amount to be awarded at the FAA's discretion.

• **FAA Mission.** Narrowed the FAA's mandate, ending its duty to promote the airline industry and making the agency responsible only for aviation safety. The change had been sought by critics of the FAA, who said the conflicting missions had allowed ValuJet to remain in operation until shortly after the May crash despite its safety problems. The proposal to make safety the FAA's top priority had come from a separate omnibus science bill (HR 3322—H Rept 104-550, Part I), which had been reported by the House Science Committee May 1, 1996, and passed by the House by voice vote May 30.

- **Airport Security.** Adopted several of the counterterrorism proposals from Vice President Al Gore's commission on aviation safety. These included a study of the potential cost and benefits of bomb-detection devices at major U.S. airports, mandatory criminal background checks for airport security officers and baggage employees, more unannounced security inspections by the FAA and improved screening of baggage and air cargo.
- **FAA Restructuring.** Gave the FAA more independence from the Transportation Department when making purchases, managing its staff and issuing regulations. It also called on the agency to improve the management of the air traffic control system, with an advisory council established to offer guidance from outside the government.
- **Airport Privatization.** Created a pilot program to privatize up to five airports, one fewer than the House proposed. To answer objections from the Senate, the bill placed additional restrictions on the diversion of revenues from federally subsidized airports. That restriction limited the ability of private airports to obtain federal grants.

SAFETY RIDERS

The House passed three other aviation measures in 1996 in response to plane crashes or safety concerns. All were incorporated into HR 3539.

- **Families of Crash Victims.** The bill required the National Transportation Safety Board to appoint a liaison to help family members get information quickly from airlines and government agencies after an airline disaster. It also prohibited attorneys from soliciting cases from the victims' families or survivors of airline accidents within 30 days of the incident.

The provision was drawn from HR 3923, which was reported by the House Transportation and Infrastructure Committee on Sept. 17, 1996 (H Rept 104-793), and passed by the House the next day, 401–4. Transportation Committee Chairman Bud Shuster, R-Pa., said families of crash victims had complained in recent years that airlines kept them in the dark for an agonizingly long period after an accident.

- **Child Pilots.** The reauthorization bill prohibited a person without a valid pilot's license from operating an airplane for the purpose of breaking a record or accomplishing some other aeronautical feat. The FAA also was ordered to study whether an age requirement should be necessary to obtain a pilot's license and whether other license restrictions should be changed.

The provision came from HR 3267, which was reported by the Transportation and Infrastructure Committee on July 17, 1996 (H Rept 104-683), and passed by the House July 22, 395–5. The measure responded to the death of seven-year-old Jessica Dubroff, her father and a flight instructor in an April crash that cut short Jessica's efforts to become the youngest person to fly a plane across the country. The text of HR 3267 had been added to HR 3539 before the FAA reauthorization was brought to the floor.

- **Pilot Applicants.** The FAA bill required airlines to perform background checks on prospective pilots, including re-

Congress allowed the taxes that fund most Federal Aviation Administration (FAA) programs to expire at the end of 1995. The taxes later were renewed for only five months, raising the possibility that the programs would run out of money sometime in 1997.

The taxes, which had produced about $5 billion in annual revenue for the FAA, included a 10 percent tax on tickets for domestic flights, a $6-per-passenger tax on international flights, and various fuel and cargo taxes. All of the levies expired on Dec. 31, 1995.

A proposal to renew the taxes was included in the fiscal 1996 budget reconciliation bill (HR 2491) that Congress cleared in November 1995, but Clinton vetoed the bill Dec. 6. Congress tried again the following year, proposing to renew the ticket taxes through Dec. 31, 1996, as part of a bill to raise the minimum wage (HR 3448). That measure was signed by Clinton Aug. 20, putting the taxes back into effect. *(Minimum wage, p. 666)*

The temporary restoration of the ticket taxes was expected to raise $1.5 billion for the Airport and Airway Trust Fund, which financed much of the FAA's operations as well as the federal grant program for airports. That amount was not expected to sustain the trust fund beyond July 1997.

The airlines were united in opposing the taxes but divided over the issue of whether the levies should be restructured. The seven largest airlines—American, Continental, Delta, Northwest, TWA, United and USAir—urged Congress to replace the 10 percent ticket tax with charges per passenger, per seat and per mile traveled. This proposal was opposed by the smaller airlines, which argued that the change would shift the tax burden away from high-priced tickets and hub-and-spoke routes onto the discount airlines and direct routes.

In November 1995, the Senate Commerce, Science and Transportation Committee approved a proposal to replace the existing aviation taxes with a new system of user fees for using FAA services, such as the air traffic control system and airplane inspections. The proposal was included in a bill to revamp the FAA (S 1239), which never reached the Senate floor. *(FAA overhaul, this page)*

views of motor vehicle driving records and medical examinations. Airlines were also ordered to share such information with each other.

The provision was drawn from HR 3536, which was reported by the Transportation and Infrastructure Committee on July 17, 1996 (H Rept 104-684), and passed by the House July 22, 401–0. To protect pilot privacy, airlines were required to destroy the records or return them to the FAA when they no longer were needed. The text of HR 3536 also had been added to HR 3539 before the House acted on the FAA bill.

FAA Overhaul

House and Senate committees sought to overhaul the Federal Aviation Administration (FAA) and give the agency a new source of funding, but those efforts bore little fruit in the 104th Congress.

Lawmakers did exempt the FAA from most federal procurement and personnel regulations in a bid to make the agency more efficient and able to cope with funding cuts. Those provisions, which had been sought by the FAA, were attached to the transportation spending bill for fiscal 1996 (HR 2002—PL 104-50).

The House also sought to transform the FAA into an independent federal agency, while the Senate called for an overhaul of the excise taxes that supported the air-traffic control system and airport construction projects. Only a fraction of those proposals made it into law, however, as part of an FAA reauthorization bill (HR 3539—PL 104-264).

Lawmakers had long been critical of the FAA, blaming the agency for exacerbating the financial problems of the airline industry. They were particularly frustrated with the FAA's efforts to modernize the air-traffic control system, whose antiquated equipment contributed to costly delays at the nation's airports and raised safety questions among passengers.

The multiyear effort to upgrade air-traffic control equipment and the communications links between towers had been plagued by delays and cost overruns in the billions. Because of the slow progress of the modernization, lawmakers said, the FAA remained the world's largest buyer of vacuum tubes and, in some cases, still used card-punch computer technology.

Similar problems beset the FAA's efforts to improve weather-detection, runway-traffic management and communications equipment at the airports.

A congressionally mandated study commission came up with a list of recommendations in 1993 for improving the FAA. The most significant was a proposal to shift air-traffic control operations into an independent government corporation, free from most federal regulations. *(1993 action, p. 329)*

The proposal was embraced by the Clinton administration, but leaders of the House and Senate aviation panels reacted coolly. In 1995, those panels advanced their own, competing remedies for the FAA's ailments.

LEGISLATIVE ACTION

The first step taken by Congress came on the transportation spending bill that the Senate Appropriations Committee reported Aug. 4, 1995 (S Rept 104-126). The committee proposed in its version of HR 2002 to exempt the FAA from most federal personnel and procurement rules, a change intended to speed the FAA's acquisition of high technology and make more efficient use of air-traffic controllers.

Leaders of the Senate Governmental Affairs Committee tried to remove the provisions, arguing that the rules protected taxpayers, small businesses and federal workers against wasteful, unfair and unethical practices. But the amendment by Chairman William V. Roth, R-Del., was killed on a tabling motion Aug. 10, 59–40. The Senate then passed the bill, 98–1.

House and Senate negotiators included the exemption in the conference report on HR 2002 (H Rept 104-286), with minor modifications. The House agreed to the report Oct. 25, 393–29,

and the Senate did the same Oct. 31, 87–10, clearing the bill. As signed into law Nov. 15, the bill ordered the FAA administrator to develop and implement the new procurement and personnel systems by April 1, 1996.

The House Transportation and Infrastructure Committee backed a different approach, proposing to make the FAA an independent federal agency managed by a three-member board of presidential appointees. Supporters of the bill (HR 2276) argued that it would give the FAA the autonomy it needed to streamline and improve its operations.

The bill also proposed to move the aviation trust fund out of the unified federal budget, exempting it from the annual spending caps and other budget rules. Such a move would have allowed Congress to spend more than $5 billion that had accumulated in the trust fund.

The committee approved the measure by voice vote on Nov. 1, 1995, but did not report the bill until March 7, 1996 (H Rept 104-475, Part I). The delay was caused in part by the trust-fund provision, which was bitterly opposed by leaders of the Budget and Appropriations committees. The provision was dropped when the bill reached the House floor March 12, and the bill passed by voice vote. *(Transportation trust funds, p. 367)*

The measure died in the Senate Commerce, Science and Transportation Committee, which had thrown its support behind an alternative proposal (S 1239) to give the FAA more autonomy without removing it from the Transportation Department.

The legislation proposed to shift control over more aviation regulations and FAA operations from the Secretary of Transportation to the FAA administrator. Its most controversial element called for the four excise taxes on airline tickets and aviation fuel to be replaced by new users' fees that would go directly to the FAA, rather than to a trust fund limited by the appropriators.

The Commerce Committee approved a modified version of the bill Nov. 9, 1995. The measure was not reported until April 10, 1996 (S Rept 104-251), and the full Senate never acted on it. Instead, a version of the bill without the fee proposals was included in the Senate-passed version of HR 3539, an FAA reauthorization measure that the Senate passed on Sept. 18, 1996. *(FAA reauthorization, p. 359)*

The final version of HR 3539, which cleared the Senate on Oct. 3, 1996, included provisions shifting authority from the secretary of transportation to the FAA administrator. It also called for an independent review of the FAA's procurement system, and it required the FAA to cancel any purchases that were beset by serious cost-overruns, delays or shortfalls in performance.

The bill made only one change in the FAA's finances, ordering new fees on foreign aircraft that flew over the United States but did not land there. Those fees could raise no more than $100 million in fiscal 1997.

The bill also mandated an independent study of the agency's financial needs through 2002. The Senate Commerce Committee was ordered to act on the recommendations from that study by early 1998.   ❏

Washington Airports

Responding to a Supreme Court ruling from early 1995, Congress in 1996 agreed to relinquish its grip over the two northern Virginia airports serving metropolitan Washington, D.C. Congress long had struggled to preserve some degree of control over National and Dulles airports, which were owned by the federal government but operated by a regional airport authority. The Supreme Court twice ruled, however, that lawmakers had overstepped their authority.

The House Transportation and Infrastructure Committees tried a new tack in 1995, proposing that the airport authority alert Congress before taking major actions. That proposal eventually was abandoned, however; instead, Congress agreed to add two more presidential appointees to the airport authority, giving a greater voice to representatives of the national interest.

BACKGROUND

The federal government turned over the operation of National and Dulles to a new Metropolitan Washington Airports Authority in 1986, allowing the airports to be expanded and upgraded in ways that the federal government could not afford. Lawmakers were concerned about turning over all control to local officials, however, so the Metropolitan Washington Airports Act of 1986 (PL 99-591) created a congressional review board with veto power over major financial, planning and personnel decisions made by the authority. The board consisted of seven members of Congress, most of them members of the transportation authorizing committees. (*Congress and the Nation Vol. VII, p. 368*)

The Supreme Court struck down part of the law in 1991, ruling that the review board violated the constitutional doctrine of separation of powers (*Metropolitan Washington Airports Authority v. Citizens for the Abatement of Aircraft Noise*). (*Congress and the Nation Vol. VIII, p. 834*)

Congress responded by eliminating the review board's veto power as part of the 1991 surface transportation law (PL 102-240). Instead, the board was allowed to make nonbinding recommendations on a wider range of actions by the authority. If the authority did not follow the board's recommendations, the disputed action would be delayed for 60 legislative days while Congress considered whether to block it.

The changes did not satisfy the Supreme Court, which ruled on Jan. 23, 1995, that the review board's power to delay actions by the airports authority amounted to an agent of Congress usurping executive-branch functions. The ruling (*Hechinger v. Metropolitan Washington Airports Authority*) was made effective March 31, 1995, giving Congress two months to amend the law.

LEGISLATIVE ACTION

The House Transportation and Infrastructure Committee approved a bill (HR 1036) March 1, 1995, to transform the review board into an advisory commission. The bill would have required the airports authority to notify the commission and Congress 60 days before any major action, except in "urgent or compelling circumstances." It also would have expanded the authority's board of directors to 15 members by adding four presidential appointees, giving nonlocal interests one-third of the votes on the board. The bill was not reported until May 29, 1996 (H Rept 104-596), delayed in part by protests from the airports authority.

The Senate Commerce, Science and Transportation Committee on March 28, 1995, approved a far different bill (S 288), proposing simply to eliminate the review board and add two presidential appointees to the authority's board of directors. The measure was not reported (S Rept 104-166) until Nov. 2, 1995, and it progressed no further.

For a year and a half, the authority went without the power to adopt a budget, issue bonds, issue airport regulations or award certain contracts while it waited for Congress to resolve the review board problem. Finally, on Oct. 3, 1996, Congress cleared a Federal Aviation Administration reauthorization bill (HR 3539—PL 104-264) that included a modified version of S 288. In addition to eliminating the review board and adding two presidential appointees to the board of directors, the bill barred the authority from obtaining new airport-improvement grants or imposing a new surcharge on passengers until the presidential appointees arrived.   ❑

National Highway System

After adding a dose of deregulation, Congress cleared legislation in November 1995 to designate routes for a new National Highway System (NHS).

The routes—more than 160,000 miles of highways, most of them already built—were never in dispute. Instead, the main points of contention in the NHS bill (S 440—PL 104-59) were provisions that rolled back federal mandates on states and the transportation industry. The most notable of those provisions eliminated the federal speed limit, leaving states to decide how fast drivers could travel on their highways. As predicted by critics of the bill, many states moved quickly after the new law took effect to raise the speed limit on interstates and other highways.

In general, though, lawmakers did not use the NHS bill to make sweeping changes in federal highway policy. That job was left for 1997, when the highway programs were due for reauthorization. Nor did House members try to authorize a host of new highway and mass-transit projects, as they had in an ill-fated NHS bill in 1994. The bill gave its blessing to only one new project: a replacement for the Woodrow Wilson bridge in Washington, D.C. (*1993–1994 action, p. 331*)

Still, the bill contained enough controversial provisions, particularly in the arena of safety regulations, that its Senate sponsors tried to abandon it in conference. Their efforts to move a "clean" NHS bill were blocked by the House leadership, which backed the deregulatory thrusts of S 440.

The maneuvering delayed the final passage of the bill until almost two months into fiscal 1996, causing a brief interruption in the flow of federal NHS aid to the states. A handful of states ran into problems as a result, but none suffered any irreparable harm.

Congress had established the National Highway System in 1991 as part of the Intermodal Surface Transportation Efficiency Act (PL 102-240). That law gave Congress until Sept. 30, 1995, to designate routes for the NHS, giving preference to the roads most important to interstate commerce, national defense, tourism, and other forms of transportation. The law set aside $6.5 billion in annual federal highway aid for the NHS and ordered the money withheld from states if Congress did not designate the routes on time. *(Congress and the Nation Vol. VIII, p. 437)*

Acting on recommendations from the various state and local transportation agencies, the Transportation Department proposed roughly 160,000 miles of routes for the NHS in December 1993. Except for a handful of minor changes, that list of routes remained unchanged throughout the deliberations by Congress.

SENATE ACTION

Introduced as a simple bill to designate the NHS routes recommended by the Transportation Department, S 440 became the battleground for a fight over federal transportation mandates. The opening salvos came in the Senate Environment and Public Works Committee, which reported a significantly expanded bill on May 22, 1995 (S Rept 104-86).

One of the most controversial provisions was an amendment by Republican Lauch Faircloth of North Carolina, a former state highway commissioner, to eliminate the federal limits on highway speeds. Begun in 1973 in the wake of an embargo by foreign oil exporters, the federal speed limit in 1995 was 65 miles per hour on four-lane divided highways in rural areas, 55 miles per hour on all other routes.

Although the limit was designed to conserve fuel, not lives, the number of highway fatalities dropped dramatically after it took effect in 1974. Still, lawmakers from sparsely populated and remote areas argued that the limit was an improper intrusion on state authority.

The Faircloth amendment drew a quick rebuke from Advocates for Highway and Auto Safety, a group that promoted ways to reduce traffic accidents. According to the group's president, Judith Lee Stone, 2,500 more people were likely to die in traffic accidents each year if states raised speed limits to pre-1974 levels.

The amendment was narrowed a bit on the Senate floor June 20. By a vote of 51–49, lawmakers approved a proposal by Harry Reid, D-Nev., to leave the federal speed limit in place for commercial vehicles, such as trucks or tour buses. They soundly rejected, however, a proposal by Frank R. Lautenberg, D-N.J., and Mike DeWine, R-Ohio, to restore the speed limit for all vehicles. Their amendment was tabled (killed) on a 65–35 vote.

The Senate also weakened two mandates in the 1991 surface transportation law that encouraged the use of seat belts in automobiles and helmets on motorcycles. Under that law, states that did not require the use of seat belts and motorcycle helmets had to spend a portion of their federal highway aid on safety programs.

Senators agreed by voice vote June 21 to an Olympia J. Snowe, R-Maine, amendment lifting the penalties related to motorcycle helmets. Proponents argued that state officials could

be trusted to do what was best for their residents; opponents said that the move would only result in more injuries and higher health care bills, a portion of which would have to be borne by the taxpayers.

The Senate stopped short of eliminating the penalties for states that did not require the use of seat belts outright, but it did approved by voice vote a break for Maine and New Hampshire, the two states that had not adopted such laws. If seat belt use in those states rose to 50 percent by the end of fiscal 1995 and 1996 and to the national average in subsequent years, the states would not be penalized. The amendment was authored by New Hampshire Republicans Robert C. Smith and Judd Gregg.

Senators set aside their concerns about states' rights long enough to adopt one significant new safety-related mandate: a requirement that states adopt tough new laws against driving by underage drinkers. The mandate was added to the bill on the Senate floor June 21, 64–36. The amendment, sponsored by Democrat Robert C. Byrd of West Virginia, called for states to lose a portion of their highway aid if they did not adopt a "zero tolerance" policy toward underage drinkers. Under such a policy, it would be illegal for drivers less than 21 years old to have a blood-alcohol content of .02 or above.

Environmental and Labor Rules

Two federal environmental mandates also came under attack in the bill. A subcommittee amendment proposed to repeal a 1991 requirement that states use recycled rubber in a portion of their highway paving projects. The requirement was aimed at the mounting waste-disposal problem posed by used tires, but many state transportation officials argued that it was an expensive and unproven approach.

The full Senate also agreed by voice vote June 20 to an amendment by Gregg and Christopher S. Bond, R-Mo., barring the Environmental Protection Administration (EPA) from enforcing for one year a regulation on motor vehicle emissions. The regulation, which was based on federal clean air laws, compelled states to adopt a specific, centralized testing regimen for such emissions.

One other deregulatory thrust was blunted before the bill reached the Senate floor.

On an 8–7 party-line vote May 10, the Environment and Public Works Committee had adopted an amendment by John Warner, R-Va., exempting highway projects from the 1931 Davis-Bacon Act. The law, which required federal contractors to pay the prevailing local wage (often union rates), was blamed by conservative Republicans for artificially boosting construction costs.

The Davis-Bacon provision drew a filibuster from a group of Democratic senators when Senate Majority Leader Bob Dole, R-Kan., tried to bring S 440 to the Senate floor on June 15. Led by Edward M. Kennedy, D-Mass., supporters of Davis-Bacon argued that the act needed to be reformed, not repealed.

After nearly two days of behind-the-scenes negotiating and vote counting, Warner agreed to drop the controversial provision. Kennedy and his allies, in turn, agreed to end the filibuster.

Money Shifts

Much of the ensuing action on the Senate floor concerned the flow of federal highway dollars to the states. Warner and Democrat Max Baucus of Montana, the ranking member of the Environment and Public Works Committee, successfully discouraged lawmakers from trying to authorize new spending or designate additional NHS routes.

Instead, lawmakers settled for redirecting federal dollars from old transportation projects to new ones. For example, highway and mass-transit dollars in at least nine states were shuffled, making a number of new projects eligible for money that Congress had already authorized to be spent.

The one exception to the ban on new spending was a provision authorizing $97.6 million to replace the Woodrow Wilson Bridge, an aging and overused span at the southern tip of Washington, D.C. The provision, tacked onto the bill in subcommittee by Warner, was particularly beneficial to Warner's constituents in northern Virginia who commuted to work in the District.

On another money-related issue, the Senate agreed to let states use a portion of their highway aid on Amtrak service—an unprecedented diversion of highway funds that was strenuously opposed by the road-builders and the highway-users lobby. The amendment, offered by Delaware Republican William V. Roth Jr., was approved by voice vote June 21 after an attempt to kill it was defeated, 36–64.

The highway-users lobby won on another disputed issue, tolls on interstate highways. A provision that would have let states impose tolls on Interstates to help raise money for road projects was stricken by voice vote June 21.

The Senate ultimately approved the modified version of the bill June 22 by voice vote.

Deadline Worries

Supporters of the NHS bill had hoped for quick action by the House in light of the Sept. 30 deadline for designating NHS routes. As the weeks passed without action by the House Transportation and Infrastructure Committee, however, Warner, Baucus, and Senate Environment and Public Works Chairman John H. Chafee, R-R.I., started looking for alternative routes to passage.

They settled on the transportation spending bill for fiscal 1996 (HR 2002), which reached the Senate floor in early August. They offered a stripped-down version of S 440 as an amendment to that bill, and it was adopted by voice vote Aug. 9. The amendment proposed to designate the NHS routes recommended by the Transportation Department and give the department authority to modify the routes at states' request. It also proposed to delay the deadline for designating the routes until Sept. 30, 1997.

The tactic was particularly appealing to Chafee and Senate Appropriations Chairman Mark O. Hatfield, R-Ore., who supported the NHS but opposed several of the safety-related provisions of S 440.

The House appropriators, on the other hand, were far less eager to encroach on the Transportation and Infrastructure Committee's jurisdiction. The House had a long history of bruising turf fights between the transportation appropriators and authorizers, and the appropriators had been on the losing end in recent years. *(1993–1994 action, p. 332)*

HOUSE ACTION

Transportation and Infrastructure Committee Chairman Bud Shuster held off action on the NHS issue as he tried to maneuver one of his top priorities through the House: a proposal to remove the transportation trust funds from the unified federal budget (HR 842). Because it was a must-pass bill, the NHS legislation was Shuster's ace in the hole: any member seeking to authorize a project or change federal highway policy could be asked, in exchange, to support the trust-fund bill. *(Transportation trust funds, p. 367)*

House appropriators and Budget Committee members strongly opposed the trust-fund proposal, however, and Shuster was making little headway as the NHS deadline approached. With time running out, Shuster introduced his own NHS bill (HR 2274) on Sept. 7, and the Transportation and Infrastructure Committee reported it one week later (H Rept 104-246).

In addition to designating the NHS routes recommended by the Transportation Department, Shuster's bill proposed to circumvent a limit on federal highway spending that Congress adopted as part of the 1991 surface transportation law. That cap threatened to quash up to $2.7 billion in aid that states were authorized to receive in fiscal 1996. Shuster's bill proposed to get around the cap by canceling some older projects and allowing states to use federal money that they had been allocated but not permitted to spend. The most controversial element of Shuster's plan would have let states build roads with money that had been pegged for alternative uses, such as reducing traffic congestion and smog.

As in the Senate measure, Shuster's bill had a number of deregulatory elements. These included provisions to end the requirement that commercial drivers, pilots and air-traffic controllers be tested before they were hired for alcohol use; ease the ban on highway billboards along scenic routes; and remove the mandates that states use recycled tires in a portion of their paving projects and that they install highway signs with metric measurements.

The Transportation and Infrastructure Subcommittee on Surface Transportation added a provision Sept. 7 eliminating the federal speed limit for all vehicles. The amendment, offered by Democrat Bill Brewster of Oklahoma, survived an impassioned challenge by senior Democrats the next day in the full committee.

The full committee also voted to eliminate the penalties for states that did not require motorcycle helmets. And it agreed to exempt some truck drivers from the federal limits on hours spent behind the wheel. The exemption applied to drivers transporting agricultural commodities or farm supplies during harvest or planting seasons as well as the drivers of ground water well-digging rigs, construction industry trucks and utility service vehicles.

Although the safety-related proposals were contentious, it was a financial provision that threatened to cause the most trouble for the bill. The Surface Transportation Subcommittee had tacked on an amendment moving the Highway, Airport and Airway, Inland Waterways and Harbor Maintenance trust funds out of the unified federal budget, as Shuster had proposed in HR 842. The amendment was dropped on the House floor, however, in the face of stiff opposition from leaders of the Budget and Appropriations committees.

The House approved a modified version of HR 2274 on Sept. 20, 419–7, after lawmakers easily defeated Democratic efforts to preserve the federal speed limit and motorcycle helmet laws. While proponents said that speed limits and helmet mandates were critical to saving lives, opponents argued that they were an affront to states' rights. Two amendments by Nick J. Rahall II, D-W.Va., to preserve federal speed limits were rejected 112–313 and 133–291, and a Mike Ward, D-Ky., amendment to continue penalties for states without helmet mandates was rejected by voice vote.

As in the Senate, however, the House's enthusiasm for states' rights waned on the subject of underage drinking. By a vote of 223–203, the House adopted a proposal by Nita M. Lowey, D-N.Y., to penalize states that did not adopt a zero-tolerance policy toward drinking by drivers less than 21 years old. Like Byrd's amendment in the Senate, Lowey's amendment proposed to reduce the federal highway grants to states that did not comply.

CONFERENCE, FINAL ACTION

Negotiations over a final version of the bill took almost two months as House and Senate conferees battled over numerous differences.

The Sept. 30 deadline, once seemingly inviolable, lost much of its teeth as the bill's supporters cooled their rhetoric about the 1991 law. No longer did they warn of states losing highway money if the deadline were missed; instead, they talked merely of delays.

A major problem for the negotiations was that some top Senate conferees had little enthusiasm for the bill, particularly the safety provisions. Chafee in particular wanted to let the appropriators designate the NHS routes in the transportation spending bill, a move that would have cut the legs out from under S 440.

Shuster, however, had extracted a promise from the House Republican leadership that his turf would not be violated. The leadership had pledged that the NHS routes would be designated through S 440, not the appropriations bill. Rep. Frank R. Wolf, the Virginia Republican who chaired the House Appropriations Transportation Subcommittee, honored the leadership's promise to Shuster. The Senate appropriators eventually backed down, putting the NHS squarely back in the authorizers' court.

A second point of contention was the House's efforts to circumvent the cap on highway spending. Metropolitan planning associations and environmental groups fought the House's proposal, saying it would promote road building at the expense of cities and urban problems. On the other side were highway user groups, contractors and state transportation departments with ambitious road construction plans. The conferees eventually agreed to modify the House proposal to address the cities' concerns.

Another issue that pitted some of the same groups against each other was the Senate proposal to let highway trust fund money be spent on Amtrak. Allied with the highway-user groups, Shuster ultimately convinced the conferees to reject the Senate Amtrak proposal. They did allow Rhode Island and Pennsylvania, however, to spend some of their federal highway aid on improvements to freight rail lines.

Conferees snagged on the issue of speed limits, too. The Senate had voted to retain federal limits for trucks and other commercial vehicles, while the House had voted to give states complete discretion over speed limits. The House position ultimately prevailed.

The final differences were not reconciled until Nov. 15, when the conferees agreed to their report (H Rept 104-345). The Senate adopted the conference report, 80–16, on Nov. 17. The House cleared it by voice vote the next day, during a rare Saturday session.

President Clinton signed the bill Nov. 28 despite the concerns some Transportation Department officials voiced about the weakened federal safety laws.

MAJOR PROVISIONS

As signed into law, S 404:

• Designated almost 161,000 miles of NHS routes, as recommended by the Transportation Department. The department was authorized to make changes to the routes on a state's request.

• Eliminated the federal maximum speed limits. Governors were allowed to retain the federal limits temporarily, however, to give state legislatures a chance to adopt new limits. The measure also required a study of the costs and benefits of removing the federal limits.

• Eliminated the penalties for states that did not mandate motorcycle helmets.

• Waived sanctions against New Hampshire and Maine for not mandating seat belts if usage in each state increased.

• Exempted metropolitan areas that had not experienced transportation-related smog or ozone problems from some pollution-reducing requirements of the 1990 Clean Air Act Amendments (PL 101-549). (*Congress and the Nation Vol. VIII, p. 473*)

• Repealed the federal requirement that certain transportation employees be tested for alcohol use before employment.

• Barred the EPA from requiring states to adopt a specific, centralized approach to testing motor vehicle emissions. Unlike the Senate's proposed one-year moratorium, the final version called for a permanent ban. The EPA was required to evaluate alternative approaches to reducing tailpipe emissions, rather than automatically requiring states to do more to reduce air pollution.

• Eliminated the requirement that states use recycled tires in a portion of their paving projects.

• Eliminated the mandate that states use metric measurements on highway signs, and delayed at least until fiscal year

2001 any requirement that states use metric measurements in their planning and engineering documents.

• Waived or eased the limits on certain truck drivers' hours.

• Waived federal safety regulations for selected companies transporting nonhazardous materials, provided that they maintained a good safety record.

• Required states to adopt a zero-tolerance policy toward drinking by drivers less than 21 years old. The bill also authorized a study of state laws allowing health care providers to disclose excessive blood-alcohol levels in patients who had been involved in traffic accidents.

• Required the Transportation Department to demonstrate ways to improve the performance of elderly drivers and other "special driver groups."

• Allowed states to permit billboards along specially designated scenic corridors in areas that did not meet the state's criteria for such corridors. Intended to codify the Transportation Department's policy, the provision let states decide whether to allow billboards on scenic highways in commercial or industrial zones.

• Circumvented the cap on highway aid to states. States were allowed to use some of the aid they previously received but had not been able to spend. However, states were not allowed to shift money out of congestion relief, smog reduction and other alternative transportation programs unless it was the last resort for funding a project.

• Made preventative maintenance projects eligible for federal highway aid.

• Allowed states to experiment with infrastructure banks, which would develop new ways to finance transportation projects. The proposal had originated in the Senate version of the transportation spending bill for fiscal 1996 (HR 2002—PL 104-50), but had been dropped by the conferees on that bill.

• Authorized $90 million for a new Amtrak station in New York City and related improvements. The appropriators were given control, however, over whether any of that money would actually be provided. The bill also included $26 million in aid for the project that was to be provided automatically, without action by the appropriators.

• Authorized the federal government to pay the entire cost of a replacement for the Woodrow Wilson Memorial Bridge. The conferees agreed to provide $97.5 million to design the new bridge and make interim repairs to the existing span. ❏

Mexican Trucks

The Senate Commerce, Science and Transportation Committee approved a bill (S 981) in July 1995 to prevent the Clinton administration from allowing Mexico to send tractor-trailers longer than 53 feet across the U.S. border. The bill was reported Feb. 20, 1996 (S Rept 104-235) but went no further.

The North American Free Trade Agreement (NAFTA) called for the United States to open its borders to Mexican trucks by December 1995. The pact also required the two countries to discuss common standards for truck weights, dimensions and operating procedures.

At the time, no federal law or regulation controlled the length of tractor-trailers. One of the four border states—California—had a 53-foot limit, while the other three states—Arizona, New Mexico and Texas—allowed longer trailers.

S 981 would have barred the administration from agreeing to a limit longer than 53 feet as part of the NAFTA talks. In December 1995, the administration announced that it would not open the border to Mexican trucks on schedule because of lingering disagreements about safety measures. The impasse continued through the rest of the 104th Congress. ❏

Transportation Trust Funds

Transportation industry lobbyists scored a stunning victory in 1996, winning House approval for legislation that would have allowed a multibillion-dollar increase in spending on transportation programs. Industry lobbyists had no such success in the Senate, however, and the measure advanced no further.

The bill (HR 842) was part accounting maneuver, part jurisdictional power play. It proposed to remove the four main transportation trust funds from the unified federal budget, exempting them from the annual limits on spending and other budget rules.

Proponents, led by House Transportation and Infrastructure Chairman Bud Shuster, R-Pa., said the measure was needed to stop Congress from hoarding transportation funds. Because Congress frequently spent less out of the trust funds than it collected in transportation taxes, the four funds had accumulated roughly $31 billion in unspent balances by late 1994.

Leaders of the Appropriations and Budget committees, on the other hand, argued that taking the trust funds out of the unified budget would lead to disproportionate cuts in other programs. If Congress wanted to eliminate the deficit, any increase in transportation spending would have necessitated offsetting cuts elsewhere.

The four funds at issue were the Highway Trust Fund, which included separate accounts for road projects and mass-transit systems; the Airport and Airway Trust Fund; the Harbor Maintenance Trust Fund; and the Inland Waterways Trust Fund. Money in the funds came from taxes on gasoline, airplane tickets and cargo, which amounted to user fees on the nation's highways, airports, harbors and canals.

By law, money in the trust funds could be spent only on transportation projects. Thus, in theory, the trust funds had large balances reflecting the amounts collected but not spent in prior years, plus interest.

In practice, however, the balances existed only on paper. Congress had spent every dollar coming into the federal Treasury and then some, leaving the trust funds with IOUs instead of cash. In order to cash those IOUs and spend the trust-fund balances, the government would have to borrow more money from somewhere else.

Still, Shuster and his allies argued that it was unjust, even immoral, for Congress not to spend the money it collected for transportation projects. And Shuster's argument resonated among members, who relished the thought of divvying up more money for projects in their districts.

LEGISLATIVE ACTION

Shuster's committee gave speedy approval to a modified version of HR 842 on May 3, 1995. Shuster tried first to have the measure incorporated into the fiscal 1996 budget resolution (H Con Res 67), but was stopped by opposition from the Budget Committee. Instead, House GOP leaders assembled a task force to look for "budget-neutral" ways to increase spending from the trust funds.

When the task force got off to a slow start, Shuster attached the trust-fund provisions to a must-pass bill designating routes for a new National Highway System (HR 2274). That move drew fierce opposition from leaders of the Budget and Appropriations committees, however, and Shuster dropped the trust-fund provisions from the highway bill when it reached the House floor. *(National Highway System, p. 363)*

After Shuster threatened to put the trust-fund provisions in a must-pass bill to reauthorize the Federal Aviation Administration (HR 2276), the leadership agreed to give him a vote on HR 842. By that time, Shuster had lined up 224 cosponsors for his bill—six more than a majority of the House.

The Transportation and Infrastructure Committee reported HR 842 on March 27, 1996, and the House Budget Committee reported it unfavorably two days later (H Rept 104-499, Parts I and II). The measure reached the House floor on April 17, backed by a powerful alliance of about 100 transportation, business and labor organizations and an array of local government groups.

Supporters contended that each $1 billion in highway spending would support 42,100 full-time jobs. With the nation's highways needing an estimated $315 billion in repairs and upgrades, and airports needing an estimated $10 billion annually to keep pace with increasing traffic, Shuster said the time had come to free the funds from budget constraints.

Opponents responded that money in the funds was being spent promptly. They said that Highway Trust Fund spending had exceeded fee collections in 12 of the previous 15 years, although some interest had built up. What the bill really represented, they said, was a bid by transportation interest groups for a greater slice of the budgetary pie.

The appropriators already had limited control over spending from the trust funds. The transportation authorizing committees drew up the formulas and earmarks used to divide the funds among the states; the appropriators could do little more than limit the total spent from each fund. The limits were often set below the authorized level in order to leave room under the annual spending caps for other transportation priorities, such as Amtrak operations and aviation safety inspectors.

If the trust funds were moved off-budget, the appropriators would have no grounds to set limits on the trust-fund spending. Thus, the authorizing committees would be left in complete control over the funds.

The bill drew an unusual warning from Federal Reserve Board Chairman Alan Greenspan, who said it "could weaken the ability of the Congress to prioritize and control spending effectively." Also weighing in against the measure were the Concord Coalition and other budget watchdog groups.

President Clinton did not explicitly threaten a veto, but the White House Office of Management and Budget (OMB) said on April 15 that the administration strongly opposed HR 842. Moving the four trust funds off budget could force the government to cut other programs by as much as $50 billion to balance the budget by 2002, OMB estimated.

Still, opponents could not overcome the election year allure of increased spending for projects in lawmakers' districts. Indeed, the House easily rejected a proposal by deficit hawks to end the Highway Trust Fund's off-budget treatment if any of its funds were earmarked for transportation projects—something Shuster's committee had done in the 1991 highway authorization bill and was expected to do again in the 1997 reauthorization. That amendment by David Minge, D-Minn., was rejected, 129–298, on April 17.

The final vote on the bill that day was 284–143, with 162 Republicans, 121 Democrats and Independent Bernard Sanders of Vermont voting in favor. In an unusual twist, almost as many Democrats as Republicans voted against the potential increase in spending.

Two leading Senate transportation policy makers, Majority Leader Trent Lott, R-Miss., and Max Baucus, D-Mont., had introduced a similar measure (S 729) in 1995. But no action was taken on that bill or HR 842 after the House vote. With key senators in opposition, such as Environment and Public Works Committee Chairman John H. Chafee, R-R.I., the Senate could not afford the time to debate the measure, Lott said. ❑

Transit Labor Protections

Allies of organized labor soundly defeated an effort by Republican House appropriators in 1995 to wipe out labor protections for mass-transit workers.

At issue was section 13(c) of the Federal Transit Act (originally the Urban Mass Transportation Act of 1964—PL 88-365), which required each mass-transit agency to obtain the U.S. Department of Labor's approval before spending a federal grant. The department reviewed the agency's plans to ensure that the agency's employees would not be made worse off by the federal aid.

The roots of the protection went back to 1964, when Congress first offered local governments money to take over financially beleaguered private bus and rail lines. Because many states barred public employees from being unionized or bargaining collectively, Congress enacted section 13(c) to ensure that transit workers who were unionized did not lose their bargaining rights when they moved to the public sector.

The House Appropriations Committee reported a fiscal 1996 transportation spending bill (HR 2002—H Rept 104-177) on July 11, 1995, that proposed to eliminate section 13(c). Rep. Frank R. Wolf, R-Va., chairman of the Appropriations Subcommittee on Transportation, argued that 13(c) imposed costly delays in funding for the agencies. Ending the Labor Department reviews, he said, was critical to helping the transit agencies make do with fewer federal dollars.

The proposal epitomized the efforts by the House GOP leadership in 1995 to repeal some of the Republicans' least favorite policies through the annual spending bills. The move amounted to an end-run around the House Transportation and Infrastructure Committee, where a majority of the members were friendly to organized labor.

The leadership also tried to rig the contest on the House floor, proposing a rule for debate on HR 2002 that effectively allowed only an all-or-nothing vote on 13(c). The rule, which was narrowly adopted July 21 after a raucous debate, prevented Democrats from offering an alternative that would have left 13(c) in place but required speedier reviews by the Labor Department.

When debate on 13(c) resumed on July 25, Democrat Ronald D. Coleman of Texas and Republican Bob Ney of Ohio led a bipartisan push against the labor provision. They argued that it would cause thousands of blue-collar transit workers to lose their right to collective bargaining.

The faction favoring repeal, led by Wolf, countered that 13(c) was responsible for inflated wages for transit workers, outrageous benefits and costly delays in obtaining federal transit aid. Wolf said eliminating 13(c) would help transit agencies cut costs in the lean times to come. Although he could not gauge the total impact, he said the Chicago Regional Transit Authority alone estimated that it could save $96 million in 1996 by privatizing if the labor protections were eliminated.

Section 13(c) did not specifically bar privatization, however. Instead, the Labor Department's oversight effectively required transit agencies to negotiate with their unions before making any major changes that affected employees.

Wolf tried to head off Coleman and Ney with an amendment that said the repeal of 13(c) would not abrogate the collective bargaining rights of transit workers under state laws. Union officials had lobbied hard against the Wolf amendment, however, arguing that many state laws protecting transit workers' rights would either be repealed or cease to be effective as soon as Congress eliminated 13(c). The House defeated the Wolf amendment, 201–224. It then voted 233–186 in favor of an amendment by Coleman and Ney striking the labor provision.

The battle over 13(c) provided a rare glimpse of Republican disunity, as 44 Republicans—mainly from northern cities—joined most Democrats in backing the Coleman-Ney amendment. It also was an unexpected victory for the unions in one of the first major labor battles of the 104th Congress.

The 13(c) proposal did not resurface in later versions of HR 2002 or any other legislation that moved in the 104th Congress. The Senate cleared the final version of HR 2002 on Oct. 31, 1995, and President Clinton signed it into law Nov. 15.   ❑

Amtrak Subsidies

Allies of Amtrak, the national passenger rail corporation, pushed a bill through the House in 1995 to help wean the beleaguered railroad from federal operating subsidies. The legislation died in the Senate, however, after a dispute erupted over liability limits.

Long plagued by money-losing routes and aging equipment, Amtrak officials had urged lawmakers in 1995 to help them cut costs and find a more stable source of funding. In particular, they asked for Congress to ease labor mandates, limit the damages that could be recovered by people injured in train wrecks, and provide a large, steady stream of money for capital improvements.

Although the House and Senate authorizing committees were sympathetic to most of Amtrak's requests, lawmakers were not able to settle a dispute between allies and opponents of the trial lawyers' lobby. The demise of the legislation left Amtrak unauthorized, as it had been since the end of fiscal 1994. The service was kept alive by the annual appropriations bills, which provided a shrinking pot of dollars—further compounding Amtrak's financial problems.

Amtrak had been on shaky fiscal ground since it was created by Congress in the Rail Passenger Service Act in 1970 (PL 91-518). Amtrak began operating one year later, and passenger rail quickly proved to be no more profitable under federal control than it had been in private hands. *(Congress and the Nation Vol. III, p. 161)*

The rail system hit the wall in 1994 as its operating deficit climbed near $200 million. Amtrak cut back service by 17 percent and laid off 2,000 workers, or 8 percent of its staff. The steady losses had led some conservative Republicans to call on Congress to abandon its support for Amtrak. When the GOP took control of Congress in 1995, pressure mounted to curb the railroad's subsidies and force it to live or die on its own.

Top Amtrak officials did not try to dissuade the Republicans, telling Congress that their goal was to survive without operating subsidies by 2002. The Republicans' budget resolution for fiscal 1996 (H Con Res 67) incorporated that goal, phasing out Amtrak's operating assistance over seven years.

HOUSE ACTION

The House Transportation and Infrastructure Committee reported a bill to revamp Amtrak (HR 1788—H Rept 104-299) on Oct. 30, 1995, after a protracted and bitter fight between rail labor's allies and the committee's Republican leaders. Committee Chairman Bud Shuster, R-Pa., and Railroads Subcommittee Chairman Susan Molinari, R-N.Y., wanted to sweep away two significant elements of rail law: the guarantee of up to six years of severance benefits for laid-off Amtrak workers and the restrictions on Amtrak contracting out work. Their proposal would have abrogated existing Amtrak contracts with the labor unions.

The unions' allies blocked those provisions in committee, causing Shuster to threaten to cut off all of Amtrak's funds. A compromise finally was reached in September, calling for the existing rules on severance benefits and contracting to stay in place for 254 days while a new Amtrak board of directors negotiated new contracts with the unions.

The bill also proposed to start cutting Amtrak's operating subsidies deeply in fiscal 1999 and to limit damages against Amtrak for injuries suffered in train wrecks.

On Nov. 30, the House voted 406–4 to approve the bill after soundly rejecting, 164–239, a bid by Cardiss Collins, D-Ill., to remove some of the proposed limits on damages. The bill's easy passage had been assured by the deal on labor protections, which appeared to pacify both sides without making either particularly happy.

SENATE ACTION

Unlike the House panel, the Senate Commerce, Science and Transportation Committee tried to give Amtrak a new source of revenue to take the place of its federal operating subsidies. The committee's bill was reported on Oct. 12, 1995 (S 1318—S Rept 104-157).

The measure would have required Amtrak to develop a plan to break even without federal subsidies after five years and, if it did not keep pace with that plan, to be liquidated after three years. To help the railroad survive, the bill would have reserved for Amtrak's capital improvements a portion of the federal tax on motor fuels. The money—one-half of a cent on every gallon sold, or more than $660 million annually—would have come out of a fund reserved for mass-transit agencies.

Amtrak previously received no gas-tax revenues, mainly because trucking companies and other highway users did not want gasoline taxes spent on railroads.

Other provisions of the bill would have cut the maximum severance pay for laid-off Amtrak workers from six years to six months and lifted the ban on contracting out work. The bill also proposed to let Amtrak enter contracts with its passengers to limit its liability in the case of accidents.

On Nov. 2, 1995, the Senate Finance Committee reported an amended version of S 1318 that had no tax provisions. It also reported a new bill (S 1395—S Rept 104-168) on Nov. 3 to dedicate a portion of the tax on motor fuels to Amtrak from Jan. 1, 1996, to Sept. 30, 2000.

The main problem with S 1395 was that it violated the constitutional requirement that tax bills originate in the House. Proponents planned to attach its provisions to the next tax bill sent over by the House, but the opportunity never arose.

Senate leaders tried to bring the truncated version of S 1318 to the floor in early 1996, but they were stopped by a lingering dispute over liability limits. Although those limits were endorsed by the Railroad Passengers Association of America, the main advocacy group for Amtrak customers, they were vehemently opposed by the trial lawyers' lobby and other consumer advocates.

Majority Leader Trent Lott, R-Miss., agreed to drop the liability provision from S 1318, but allies of the trial lawyers did not want the bill to pass the Senate until a deal had been struck with the House. But House Republicans had strongly backed a series of proposals to limit liability claims, and Shuster was not willing to concede on that point. As a consequence, the Senate never voted on the Amtrak legislation.

A SHRINKING POT

While the authorizing committees were struggling to aid Amtrak, the appropriators were trying to cut its budget. The transportation spending bill for fiscal 1996 (HR 2002—PL 104-50) provided only $750 million for Amtrak and its Northeast Corridor high-speed rail project, or $244 million less than the previous year.

The transportation appropriations bill for fiscal 1997 (HR 3675—PL 104-205) provided $565 million for Amtrak operations and capital improvements, down $70 million from fiscal 1996, and $115 million for the Northeast Corridor project, the same as the year before. An additional $80 million, however, was provided to help Amtrak buy high-speed engines for the Northeast Corridor.

Not satisfied with that amount, the White House, key Senate Democrats and even some top Republicans successfully pressed for more Amtrak funds as part of the omnibus spending bill for fiscal 1997 (HR 3610—PL 104-208). That measure provided an additional $60 million for the Northeast Corridor and $22.5 million to keep five money-losing Amtrak routes open for six months.

The additional money still left Amtrak with less for its operations than it received in fiscal 1996. Three months later, Amtrak officials disclosed that they would have to borrow up to $70 million to stay afloat.   ❏

Maritime Subsidies

Coming to the rescue of a dying American industry, Congress cleared a bill in 1996 to authorize a new subsidy program for merchant ships that sailed under the U.S. flag.

The measure (HR 1350—PL 104-239) continued the support for U.S. cargo vessels that Congress had begun in 1936, albeit at a diminished level. Aid per vessel was trimmed from an average of more than $3 million per year to a maximum of $2.3 million in fiscal 1996 and $2.1 million in fiscal years 1997 through 2005. Overall, the bill authorized $100 million per year for fiscal 1996–2005.

Authorization for the previous subsidy program had already expired, preventing the Commerce Department from renewing any of the subsidy contracts it had with U.S.-flagged vessels. Unless subsidies were continued, supporters of the maritime industry had warned, U.S. cargo vessels were likely to shift to foreign registries.

Allies of the industry had pushed a subsidy bill through the House in 1994, arguing that the measure was vital to U.S. military and economic security. The measure died in the Senate, however, in part because farm-state lawmakers objected to its cost. The bill would have guaranteed funding for the subsidies by sharply increasing the duties on vessels entering U.S. ports. The funding mechanism had been vehemently opposed by shippers who would have borne the higher duties, however, and the dispute had helped to sink the bill. (1994 action, p. 337)

In 1995, the House National Security Committee tried a different approach. The new bill (HR 1350—H Rept 104-229), reported Aug. 3, authorized up to $100 million in subsidies to be paid each year, but did not guarantee that the subsidies would be provided. Instead, the subsidy program was to depend on annual appropriations, competing for funds each year with other federal programs. The House approved a modified version of the bill by voice vote December 6.

The Senate Commerce, Science and Transportation Committee had reported a similar bill on Nov. 2 (S 1139—S Rept 104-167). Chairman Larry Pressler, a South Dakota Republican who had helped to kill the previous year's bill on behalf of grain shippers in his state, said he supported the new version because it did not raise duties.

The legislation then idled in the Senate for more than nine months. Rather than trying to move S 1139, the maritime industry's allies brought HR 1350 to the Senate floor in mid-September 1996 and urged that it be passed without amendments. That way the bill could go straight to President Clinton, not back to the House or to conference.

Republican Charles E. Grassley of Iowa, a longtime opponent of the maritime subsidies, led efforts to change the bill. He started on Sept. 20 with an amendment to cut the taxpayer bonuses received by merchant mariners when they were called to duty in national emergencies. Grassley argued that merchant mariners received hazardous duty bonuses that were up to 15 times larger than the bonuses given to military service personnel. Opponents, who argued that the higher bonuses were justified because the mariners received none of the other benefits available to military personnel, killed the amendment through a tabling motion, 77–16.

Another Grassley amendment nearly succeeded on Sept. 24. That proposal, which would have barred ship owners from using federal dollars to lobby or make political donations, was killed on a tabling motion, 50–48. The Senate then cleared the bill, 88–10.

MAJOR PROVISIONS

As signed into law Oct. 8, the bill limited subsidies to militarily useful ships that the owners agreed to make available to the Pentagon in the event of war or national emergency. The ships had to be carrying cargo to and from foreign countries, and in most cases had to be less than 15 years old.

Instead of basing the subsidies on the difference between a vessel's labor costs and the average foreign ship's costs, as in the previous program, the measure provided a single, lower subsidy rate for all eligible vessels. The idea, supporters said, was to give owners and their crews an incentive to reduce labor costs.

In another change from the previous program, the subsidies were not confined to U.S.-built and U.S.-flagged ships, although those ships received preference for the aid. No subsidies were provided directly to U.S. shipyards, but the bill did extend federal loan guarantees for the first time to foreign citizens ordering ships from U.S. yards—a change intended to boost ship sales.

The measure also imposed more obligations on subsidized shipping lines than in the past. Vessel owners were required to make available to the military not only their ships but also associated transportation services, such as terminals and equipment.

The bill was expected to provide subsidies to as many as 47 merchant ships. If Congress failed to appropriate enough money to pay subsidies to all the vessels in the program, the bill stated that the owners would be free to move their ships to one of the foreign registries approved by the Transportation Department.

In fiscal 1997, the subsidy program cost well below the authorized amount. The fiscal 1997 omnibus appropriations bill (HR 3610—PL 104-208) included $54 million for the new subsidies, in addition to $148 million for the remaining subsidy contracts under the old program.

The Congressional Budget Office estimated that the full $100 million in subsidies would not be needed until fiscal 1998.

Also included in HR 1350 was a provision giving merchant seamen the same reemployment rights as members of the armed forces reserves. The protection was offered to seamen who worked on commercial or National Defense Reserve Fleet vessels put into service by the Defense Department during a war or national emergency. Similar provisions had passed the House in 1991, 1992 and 1993, only to die in the Senate. *(1993 action, p. 341)* ❑

Coast Guard Reauthorization

A bill to reauthorize the Coast Guard became the vehicle for a number of deregulatory initiatives aimed at U.S. shipping lines, petroleum companies and cruise lines.

The measure (S 1004—PL 104-324), which cleared in 1996, authorized $2.6 billion for Coast Guard operations in fiscal 1996 and 1997. An additional $1 billion to $1.1 billion was authorized for acquisitions, research, construction and retirement pay in each year.

Unlike the far-reaching reauthorization package that died in 1994, S 1004 included few new safety mandates. It did, however, make it more difficult for the Coast Guard to carry out its plan to close almost two dozen rescue stations.

LEGISLATIVE ACTION

The House Transportation and Infrastructure Committee reported an early version of the legislation (HR 1361—H Rept 104-106) on May 1, 1995, proposing to authorize nearly $3.7 billion for the Coast Guard in fiscal 1996.

To lower the shipping industry's compliance costs, the measure proposed to reduce Coast Guard inspections of most commercial vessels and allow the use of safety equipment that met less rigorous international standards. Similar provisions had been included in the previous year's Coast Guard bill. *(1994 action, p. 338)*

The bill also sought to lift state barriers to gambling on cruise ships if the vessels entered international waters and stopped at multiple states or countries. The provision had been sought by cruise lines serving California, which were barred by state law from offering gambling on certain portions of their cruises to Mexico and Canada.

One other regulation-easing provision lowered from $150 million to $35 million the amount of insurance that offshore oil and gas wells were required to maintain. Small wells and marinas were exempted entirely from the insurance requirement, which Congress had imposed in the Oil Pollution Act of 1990

SHIPBUILDING SUBSIDIES

An international agreement to end shipbuilding subsidies did not pass muster with Congress, as lawmakers were not ready to swear off all support for U.S. shipyards. At issue were subsidies for the construction and repair of large vessels—those weighing at least 100 gross tons. About 80 percent of the vessels that carried cargo and passengers internationally fell into that category.

U.S. trade negotiators had spent five years trying to convince representatives from the other industrialized nations to abandon their shipyard subsidies. Finally, in December 1994, the world's major shipbuilding nations—Japan, South Korea, the European Union, Finland, Sweden, Norway and the United States—signed onto a pact to terminate the subsidies.

The sticking point for Congress was that the agreement ruled out indirect subsidies as well as direct aid. Some allies of U.S. shipyards were not willing to end one such indirect subsidy—loan guarantees for the purchase of U.S. built vessels—and they blocked legislation in the Senate to implement the agreement.

The United States had ended its direct subsidies for shipyards in 1981, a budget-cutting move that allies of the shipyards likened to unilateral disarmament. While some lawmakers proposed to resume the direct aid to U.S. yards, free-trade-oriented members of the House Ways and Means Committee tried to pressure foreign governments to end their subsidies. *(Background, Congress and the Nation Vol. VIII, p. 449; 1993–1994 action, p. 337)*

The free-traders appeared to have been granted their wish in 1994 with the agreement to end subsidies. The pact called for the signatories to implement the agreement in July 1996, giving Congress until June 1996 to pass the necessary legislation.

The Ways and Means Committee reported an implementing bill (HR 2754—H Rept 104-524, Part I) on April 18, 1996. The bill would have authorized the government to impose financial penalties on companies that sold foreign-built vessels to U.S. buyers at a subsidized price. Offending vessels also could have been denied entry into U.S. ports for up to four years.

As approved by the committee, the bill barred direct and indirect subsidies for U.S. shipyards. It also lifted the existing 50 percent duty on repairs made to U.S. vessels overseas, provided that the work was done in a country that had signed the agreement.

The House National Security Committee threw a wrench in the works the following month. On May 30, it reported a new version of HR 2754 (H Rept 104-524, Part II) that continued loan guarantees for U.S. shipbuilders through 1998 and allowed direct U.S. subsidies to resume if other signatories did not comply with the agreement.

Those changes were temporarily set aside when HR 2754 reached the House floor June 13. By a vote of 278–149, however, the House adopted an amendment by Herbert H. Bateman, R-Va., to retain the loan guarantees through 1998. The amendment also carved out an exemption for ships in the U.S. military reserve fleet and vessels that carried cargo or passengers between U.S. ports.

Ways and Means Trade Subcommittee Chairman Philip M. Crane, R-Ill., warned that unless the amendment was taken out in conference with the Senate, the agreement would collapse. Still, the House approved the modified bill, 325–100, on June 13.

The Senate never took up the bill. Instead, the Senate Finance Committee tucked language to implement the shipbuilding agreement into a bill (HR 3074) giving Palestinian imports the same preferential treatment as products from Israel. The committee reported the modified bill May 13 (H Rept 104-270). When the measure reached the Senate floor Sept. 27, however, the provisions to implement the shipbuilding agreement were stripped by voice vote before the bill was passed. *(West Bank and Gaza Strip, p. 181)*

(PL 101-380). Supporters of the provision said that the annual cost of oil spills from all offshore wells had never reached $35 million.

The bill stirred an emotional debate over the Coast Guard's plan to consolidate its rescue operations and close 23 small boat rescue stations. The Coast Guard estimated that the plan would save it $6 million, but it also projected that two additional deaths might result each year because search-and-rescue boats would have to travel farther to reach some victims.

James A. Traficant Jr., D-Ohio, tried in vain at the committee markup April 5 to keep all of the small-boat rescue stations open. Instead, the committee voted 30–23 to allow stations to be closed if the transportation secretary certified that it would not harm public safety. Traficant offered his amendment again on the House floor May 9, 1995, but was rebuffed, 146–272. The House passed the bill shortly thereafter, 406–12.

Instead of taking up the House bill, the Senate Commerce, Science and Transportation Committee reported its own, $3.7 billion proposal (S 1004—S Rept 104-160) on Oct. 19, 1995. This measure, which contained many of the elements of the House bill, passed with minor changes by voice vote of the Senate Nov. 17, 1995.

The Senate measure did not include three House proposals to limit lawsuits against the owners of commercial vessels. One would have prohibited foreign crew members from filing suit in U.S. courts for injuries suffered on a foreign-owned vessel. A second would have enabled cruise ship owners to prevent their passengers from filing lawsuits for emotional distress except when the crew's intentional or negligent conduct inflicted or nearly inflicted injuries. The third provision would have extended state limits on medical-malpractice awards to cases where a cruise ship brought a passenger to shore for medical treatment. Under previous law, if the passenger was the victim of malpractice on shore, the vessel owner was vicariously liable for an unlimited amount of damages.

The Senate bill also included a safety provision that the House had not included in HR 1361: a requirement that children age six or younger wear Coast Guard-approved life preservers whenever they were on the open deck of a recreational boat less than 26 feet long. A similar requirement had been included in the previous year's Coast Guard authorization bill.

The House passed a new version of S 1004 by voice vote on Feb. 29, 1996, after replacing the Senate-passed text with HR 1361. In September, conferees agreed to drop the provision barring lawsuits by foreign crew members and requiring life preservers for young boaters. The conferees retained the other liability limits from the House bill, however.

The conference report (H Rept 104-854) received voice-vote approval from the House Sept. 27 and the Senate Sept. 28. President Clinton signed the measure into law Oct. 19.

MAJOR PROVISIONS

The final version of the bill authorized the Transportation Department to turn over vessel inspection and certification duties to qualified third parties, such as the "classification societies" that examined vessels for insurance purposes. The change helped cargo and cruise vessels avoid duplicate and potentially conflicting inspections.

The frequency of inspections also was reduced. The bill required most vessels to be inspected once every five years, not every two years as in previous law.

The bill permitted vessels to use safety equipment and materials that complied with international standards, which generally were less demanding than those imposed by the Coast Guard. Lifesaving equipment that met a foreign country's standards also could be used if that country gave reciprocal treatment to U.S.-approved equipment.

On the issue of station consolidation, the bill barred the Transportation Department from closing any small-boat rescue stations unless it held a public hearing and determined that safety would be maintained, Coast Guard search and rescue response-time standards would still be met, and local weather and marine conditions did not require the station to remain open.

Other provisions of the bill affected the following issues:

• **Gambling on Cruise Ships.** The bill preempted a California law that barred gambling on cruise ships traveling between ports in that state. The provision allowed gambling to occur in international waters along every coastal state except Hawaii as long as the cruise traveled to more than one state or country.

The bill also allowed gambling on ships in Lake Michigan that were in the territorial waters of the state of Indiana, and on certain cruises within Alaskan territorial waters.

• **Insurance Requirements.** Large offshore wells were required to maintain $10 million or $35 million in insurance, depending on their proximity to the shore. The president was allowed to require up to $150 million in insurance if justified by the environmental or health risks.

• **Deepwater Ports.** The bill eased federal restrictions, regulations and antitrust scrutiny on deepwater ports, which the petroleum industry used as transportation hubs for crude oil recovered from the outer continental shelf. The stated purpose was to "eliminate, for as long as a port remains subject to effective competition, unnecessary federal regulatory oversight or involvement in the . . . business and economic decisions" of the port.

• **Towing Vessel Safety.** The bill required single-hulled oil barges or the vessels that towed them to have additional safety equipment to prevent runaway barges. ❏

Maritime Administration Reauthorization

The House National Security Committee approved bills in 1995 and 1996 to reauthorize the Maritime Administration and related programs, but the measures advanced no further.

An agency of the Transportation Department, the Maritime Administration maintained a reserve fleet of cargo vessels for military use, conducted research on shipbuilding and maritime operations, helped secure financing for shipbuilding, and operated the U.S. Merchant Marine Academy in Kings Point, N.Y.

Both bills would have authorized funding for Maritime Administration and a variety of state maritime training programs. They also would have authorized funding for federal loan guarantee programs that aided U.S. shipyards.

The first bill, HR 1347, would have authorized almost $82 million for the agency and maritime training programs, $52 million for loan guarantees, and almost $163 million for existing cargo-vessel subsidy contracts in fiscal 1996. The committee approved a modified version of the bill May 24, 1995, but never reported it to the full House.

The second bill, HR 3281, would have authorized $69.5 million for the agency and the training programs, plus $40 million for loan guarantees. The committee approved a modified version of the bill by voice vote May 1, 1996, but the committee did not report it to the House.

Despite the lack of authorization, Maritime Administration and related programs were kept alive through the annual appropriations bills for fiscal 1996 and 1997. The omnibus appropriations bill for fiscal 1996 (HR 3019—PL 104-134) provided $66.6 million for agency operations and training programs, $43.5 million for the loan-guarantee program, and $163 million for existing subsidy contracts. The omnibus appropriations bill for fiscal 1997 (HR 3610—PL 104-208) provided $65 million for agency operations and training programs, just under $37.5 million for loan guarantees, and $148 million for existing subsidy contracts. ❏

Shipping Deregulation

A House-passed bill to deregulate the ocean shipping industry died in the Senate in the face of opposition from unions, ports and small shippers. The measure (HR 2149) would have weakened the control that international shipping conferences wielded over rates and contracts. It would have permitted importers and exporters to negotiate confidential, discounted rates with individual shipping lines, encouraging the lines to act independently.

Ocean shipping was the last mode of transportation still subject to strict federal regulation. For routes between U.S. and foreign ports, federal law required the shipping lines to file their rates with the Federal Maritime Commission (FMC) and offer the same price to all "similarly situated" customers.

Those rates generally were set by international shipping conferences. Members of the conferences were allowed to offer discounts from the rates only if they gave advance notice to other members. Such price-fixing would have been illegal in other industries, but Congress had exempted the shipping conferences from most U.S. antitrust law since 1916. As long as shipping lines were not required to join, conferences could agree on the prices charged for each route with little fear of violating U.S. law.

Allies of the shipping lines argued that the conferences helped protect U.S. lines from being underpriced by foreign vessels with lower labor and construction costs. But the lines' major U.S. customers—represented by the National Industrial Transportation League, a trade group for large commercial shippers—argued that the policy rewarded inefficiency and hurt consumers.

In 1995, the shippers and the U.S. lines came up with a compromise proposal to phase out U.S. regulation and encourage one-on-one negotiating. Introduced as HR 2149, the bill would have ended on June 1, 1997, the requirement that shipping lines file their prices with the federal government. The FMC would have been disbanded at the end of fiscal 1997.

As of Jan. 1, 1998, the bill would have enabled shippers and lines to bargain confidentially for discounts. Instead of having to make their rates public, shipping lines would have been required only to offer a standard list of prices to customers upon request.

The measure did not propose to end the conferences' exemption from antitrust law or their ability to set rates. However, by freeing shipping lines to strike deals independently with customers, the bill was expected to make the conferences' prices increasingly irrelevant to the market.

LEGISLATIVE ACTION

The House Transportation and Infrastructure Committee approved HR 2149 on Aug. 2 without amendment. Sponsored by committee Chairman Bud Shuster, R-Pa., the bill was cosponsored by the committee's top Democrats, reflecting the new unity between the shippers and the shipping lines.

Rather than reporting the bill, the committee first tried to append HR 2149 onto the massive fiscal 1996 budget reconciliation bill (HR 2491) that Republicans pushed through the House on Oct. 26, 1995. The Senate dropped the shipping provisions from its version of the bill, however, and they were not included in the conference report (H Rept 104-347).

Opposition to the proposal came mainly from maritime labor unions and the American Association of Port Authorities, whose members feared it would increase port expenses and cause layoffs. They worried that permitting shipping rates to be set privately would allow the biggest shippers and carriers to underbid their competitors and consolidate an industry that was largely immune from antitrust laws.

Small and midsized shippers also raised concerns about the bill. They argued that the bill would put them at a competitive disadvantage by allowing large shippers to negotiate better discounts than they could command.

The Transportation panel reported HR 2149 on Nov. 1 (H Rept 104-303). As Shuster prepared to take it to the House floor the following May, top Democrats on the committee withdrew their support. The ranking member of the committee, Democrat James L. Oberstar of Minnesota, led efforts to bar confidential discounts.

On the floor May 1, 1996, Republican leaders rallied their troops against an Oberstar amendment requiring the shipping rates to remain public. The vote appeared to hinge in part on Republican anger at the AFL-CIO and its president, John J. Sweeney, who was waging a $35 million campaign to unseat House members, mostly Republicans, the union regarded as antilabor.

The Oberstar amendment failed, by a vote of 197–224, with just 15 Republicans and 10 Democrats crossing party lines. The House then passed HR 2149 with only minor modifications, 239–182.

The bill was stalled in the Senate by powerful coastal lawmakers from both parties, including Republican Trent Lott of Mississippi, who became Senate Majority Leader in June, and Democrat John B. Breaux of Louisiana. These lawmakers feared that the measure would hurt smaller ports and shippers.

Supporters of the legislation worked through the end of the session to fashion a compromise acceptable to the ports and small shippers. Although progress was made toward a deal, the session ended without further action on the legislation. ❑

Fishermen's Protective Act

Congress in 1995 cleared legislation aimed at reimbursing U.S. fishermen who had been caught the year before in a costly dispute between the United States and Canada.

The measure (HR 716—PL 104-43) reauthorized and expanded the 1967 Fishermen's Protective Act (PL 90-482), which allowed the government to reimburse commercial fishermen who had been charged fees or had equipment seized while traveling through the waters of a foreign country, if the U.S. government considered it a violation of international law. The bill also contained provisions to conserve fish stocks worldwide through international agreements, research and conservation projects. *(Omnibus fishing bill, p. 467)*

The House and Senate had passed competing bills in 1994 to reauthorize and expand the Fishermen's Protective Act, but the differences could not be reconciled before the session ended. *(1994 action, p. 340)*

As signed into law Nov. 3, HR 716 broadened the 1967 law to allow U.S. fishermen to be reimbursed for fees they paid to cross foreign waters en route from one part of the United States to another. It authorized the secretary of state to seek repayment from the nation that charged the fee, and it permitted the United States to impose retaliatory fees or restrictions on vessels from the offending nation.

The provisions were aimed at Canada, which had charged U.S. vessels $1,100 in 1994 to pass through Canadian waters en route from Washington state and Alaska. The fee, which was suspended after raising roughly $285,000, was meant to jump-start talks between the United States and Canada on a treaty to limit salmon fishing.

The House Resources Committee had reported an early version of the bill Feb. 23, 1995 (H Rept 104-47). On April 3, the House passed the bill without amendment, 384–0.

The Senate Commerce, Science and Transportation Committee reported a broader bill (S 267—S Rept 104-91) on May 26, 1995. The Senate approved HR 716 by voice vote on June 30, after substituting the text of S 267, and the House cleared that version of the bill Oct. 24.　　　　　　　　　　　❏

Transportation Safety

The 104th Congress cleared legislation to require cost-benefit analysis of underground pipeline safety regulations. It also reauthorized the National Transportation Safety Board and cleared a bill to exempt nontoxic oils from regulations on the transportation of petroleum-based oils.

PIPELINE SAFETY

Congress cleared a bill late in the 1996 session to forbid new safety regulations for underground pipelines unless they produced benefits greater than the costs they imposed.

The measure (S 1505—PL 104-304) represented one small victory for conservative lawmakers in their battle to rein in federal regulators. Their more far-reaching efforts—legislation to make all federal rules subject to cost-benefit analysis—died at the hands of Democrats in the Senate. (Regulatory overhaul, p. 842)

Environmentalists had opposed the pipeline bill, too, arguing that it would eliminate important safety regulations. But the federal Office of Pipeline Safety supported it because it authorized substantially more spending than earlier proposals.

The pipelines covered by the bill carried natural gas and hazardous liquids, such as petroleum. The safety programs were funded by fees on pipeline operators and the petroleum industry.

The bill did not go as far as a proposal backed by two House committees (HR 1323), which would have made it even more difficult for the government to impose new safety rules. The House bill would have rolled back funding and forced the Office of Pipeline Safety to lay off newly hired inspectors.

The issue came up in part because the authorization for pipeline safety programs was due to expire in September 1995, and in part because of complaints from the pipeline industry. The fees on the industry had nearly doubled in 1994 when Congress boosted pipeline safety programs to $37.4 million. The $18 million increase, which came in response to two major pipeline accidents, allowed the government to add 33 new safety inspectors to the 27 already employed. One of the accidents, a pipeline rupture in Edison, N.J., had left an estimated 2,000 people homeless.

Legislative Action

The industry's allies tried early in 1995 to reverse the increase in fees. House Transportation and Infrastructure Committee

Chairman Bud Shuster, R-Pa., introduced HR 1323 in March, proposing to authorize less than $21 million for pipeline programs in fiscal 1996. The bill would have required new pipeline safety standards or regulations to pass a cost-benefit test if they were projected to cost the industry more than $25 million per year. This cost-benefit analysis, the bill stated, had to be based on objective scientific and economic studies.

Shuster's committee reported a modified version of the bill on May 1, 1995, and the House Commerce Committee reported a slightly different version on June 1 (H Rept 104-110, Parts I and II). The Commerce Committee rejected proposals by Democrats to delete the cost-benefit analyses, authorize more spending, and deter industry officials from serving on the advisory panels that were to review proposed safety rules.

The House took no action on the bill. Instead, the focus shifted to S 1505, which the Senate Commerce, Science and Transportation Committee reported on July 26, 1996 (S Rept 104-334). Sponsored by Senate Majority Leader Trent Lott, R-Miss., S 1505 proposed to authorize much more spending than the House bill—$34 million in fiscal 1997, increasing to $37.5 million by fiscal 2000. Like the House bill, however, it required new safety standards to pass a cost-benefit test, although the test was less rigorous than the one in the House bill.

S 1505 also proposed to repeal a federal requirement that all individuals responsible for the operation and maintenance of pipeline transportation facilities be tested to assure they were qualified. Instead, the bill simply required that the individuals be qualified.

The bill included a number of the regulatory relief provisions from the House proposal, eliminating the requirement for biennial pipeline inspections among other mandates. But it also required pipeline operators to use remotely controlled valves to halt the flow of natural gas through a ruptured pipeline, if they proved to be feasible and effective. The House Commerce Committee had rejected a similar provision.

One other provision called for the department to experiment with risk-management programs that allowed pipeline operators to demonstrate new, less costly ways to reduce the risk of accidents. This provision had been sought by the department as a way to cut enforcement costs.

Industry representatives praised the bill for allowing companies and regulators to develop safety standards suited for individual pipelines. This change made sense, they said, because most of the 48 interstate pipelines performed different tasks and were distinctively constructed.

Environmental activists, citing a pair of damaging pipeline ruptures in 1996, complained that S1505 would make it tougher to tighten safety standards. They could not stop the Senate from passing the bill, however, which it did by voice vote Sept. 26. The House cleared the bill the next day, 276–125, and President Clinton signed it on Oct. 12.

While the reauthorization bills were making their way through the chambers, Congress enacted a pair of transportation spending bills that curbed spending on pipeline safety. The measure for fiscal 1996 (HR 2002—PL 104-50) provided $31.4 million, a decrease of $6 million. Although the cut was deep, the

Office of Pipeline Safety received almost all of the money it requested for personnel.

The bill for fiscal 1997 (HR 3675—PL 104-205) provided $31 million for pipeline safety programs, down $460,000 from the year before. A cut in research and development spending accounted for the decrease.

NTSB REAUTHORIZATION

Congress cleared legislation (HR 3159—PL 104-291) in 1996 to reauthorize the National Transportation Safety Board (NTSB) through fiscal 1999 and clarify liability for overweight truck shipments.

The NTSB was responsible for investigating fatal accidents in all modes of transportation, conducting safety studies, and evaluating other federal agencies' transportation safety programs. The board had no regulatory power over the transportation industry, however, and its recommendations were not binding.

HR 3159 authorized $42.4 million for the NTSB in fiscal 1997, $44.4 million in fiscal 1998, and $46.6 million in fiscal 1999. It also permitted the board to raise money for its training programs by opening them to nonemployees and charging fees.

The measure ordered the safety board not to make public for up to two years any information obtained when investigating plane crashes in other countries. This provision brought U.S. law more into line with an international aviation agreement that gave foreign countries control over investigations within their jurisdictions. Another confidentiality provision applied to safety-related information that companies submitted voluntarily to the NTSB, not in response to an accident. The bill prohibited the board from disclosing such information if doing so would discourage companies from sharing it. Both provisions overrode the Freedom of Information Act, which had barred the board from withholding much of the information it collected.

The House Transportation and Infrastructure Committee approved an early version of the bill May 9, 1996, after rejecting, 26–27, a Democratic proposal to authorize more spending and more investigators. The committee reported the bill July 17 (H Rept 104-682) and the House passed it July 22, 400–0.

The Senate Commerce, Science and Transportation Committee had reported a competing bill (S 1831—S Rept 104-324) July 19, proposing to authorize more for the board than the House approved. The Senate passed HR 3159 on Sept. 18 by voice vote, after substituting the text of its own bill. The House cleared the modified bill Sept. 26. President Clinton signed it into law Oct. 11.

Overweight Containers

The Senate also added provisions to HR 3159 modifying a 1992 law (PL 102-548) on "intermodal" cargo containers, or containers transported from railroads or ships to trucks en route to their destinations.

The 1992 law, which the Transportation Department had not yet implemented, required shippers to disclose to freight companies the weight and content of intermodal containers weighing more than 10,000 pounds. The measure was aimed at help-ing truckers avoid violating highway weight limits when accepting containers directly from railroads and cargo ships, which were not subject to such limits.

By voice vote Sept. 18, the Senate adopted an amendment to HR 3159 making it easier for shippers to notify transportation companies when their containers threatened to violate highway weight limits. The amendment, which required notice only for preloaded containers weighing more than 29,000 pounds, held the shippers liable for any highway weight penalties if they failed to provide notice to the first company that transported the container.

The provisions were similar to a bill (HR 4040) that the House passed the same day by voice vote. HR 4040 had been reported by the House Transportation Committee Sept. 17 (H Rept 104-794).

NONTOXIC OIL SHIPMENTS

Congress in 1995 cleared a bill (HR 436—PL 104-55) that required federal agencies to differentiate between nontoxic, biodegradable oils and petroleum-based oils when writing transportation regulations.

HR 436 ensured that the owners and operators of vessels carrying animal fats and vegetable oils, such as those made from peanuts, olives and corn, were not required to meet the same environmental regulations as those that transported petroleum oil. In 1993, the Department of Transportation had issued regulations under the 1990 Oil Pollution Act (PL 101-380) classifying such products as hazardous materials. A 1994 attempt to exempt them from the oil pollution law had failed. *(1994 action, p. 336)*

HR 436 was reported by the House Agriculture and House Commerce committees on Sept. 27, 1995 (H Rept 104-262, Parts I and II). The House passed it by voice vote Oct. 10. By voice votes, the Senate passed an amended version Nov. 2 and the House agreed to it Nov. 7, clearing the bill for the president's signature Nov. 20. ❑

Product Liability

After almost 20 years of frustration, lawmakers aligned with manufacturers and insurance companies finally pushed a bill through Congress in 1996 to limit lawsuits based on defective products. President Clinton vetoed the bill (HR 956), however, siding with the trial lawyers and consumer advocates who opposed even a watered-down version of the measure.

At issue was the patchwork of state tort laws that governed claims against the makers or vendors of defective products. Although a number of state legislatures had passed "tort reform" laws to limit such claims, business groups pressed Congress for limits that would apply nationally.

Manufacturers and insurance companies argued that excessive claims and jury awards were harming U.S. competitiveness, raising the price of goods, and keeping new products off the market. Their opponents countered that the threat of lawsuits helped deter irresponsible manufacturers from cutting corners on safety to increase profit.

OTHER LIABILITY LEGISLATION

Bills to deter frivolous lawsuits and restrict malpractice claims stalled in the 104th Congress as lawmakers focused on limiting product-liability awards.

The measures attracted the same allies and enemies as the product-liability bill (HR 956): the business community and insurance companies were strongly in favor, while the trial lawyers' lobby and consumer activists were vehemently opposed.

'Loser Pays'

The measure on frivolous claims grew out of the "tort reform" plank of the House Republicans' "Contract with America," which proposed to let judges order the losers in lawsuits to pay the lawyers' fees of both sides. Advocates said that the change would discourage frivolous lawsuits and promote pretrial settlements. Critics said it would deter valid claims by people with few resources.

The proposal was first included in HR 10, a bill carrying all of the tort reform proposals from the GOP contract. A watered-down version was later introduced as HR 988, which was weakened again by the House Judiciary Committee in February 1995.

Under a compromise offered by Republican Robert W. Goodlatte of Virginia, if either side rejected a settlement and went on to win something less at trial, that side would have been liable for the attorney's fees incurred after the other side made its final settlement offer. The idea was to encourage both sides to settle and avoid trial.

As reported March 1 (H Rept 104-62), HR 988 also was limited to "diversity" cases, a small class of suits that fell under federal jurisdiction because the parties were from different states. Other provisions of the bill would have required penalties on attorneys involved in frivolous court tactics and barred expert witnesses from having a financial stake in the outcome of the trial.

On the House floor March 6, lawmakers further reduced the amount of attorney's fees that could be awarded. They adopted, 317–89, a Goodlatte amendment that required payment only for fees incurred after both sides had made their final settlement offers—a change intended to spur negotiations.

After rejecting eight attempts to narrow the measure and limit attorneys fees, the House approved the bill, 232–193, on March 7.

The bill did not advance in the Senate. During the debate over product-liability legislation (HR 956), senators on April 26 voted 56–37 in favor of a Hank Brown, R-Colo., amendment to require sanctions against parties that filed frivolous claims or motions. That section was dropped from the bill, however, as part of the efforts to overcome a filibuster.

Medical Malpractice

Proposals to limit medical malpractice claims made it through the House and onto the Senate version of the product-liability bill, only to be abandoned in the face of the Senate filibuster.

The House proposal, which was appended to the product-liability bill on the House floor, would have capped awards for pain, emotional distress and other noneconomic losses at $250,000 in health care liability cases. Sponsored by Republican Christopher Cox of California, the amendment to HR 956 was approved March 9, 1995, 247–171.

The Senate Commerce Committee had stripped those provisions from its version of the bill. On May 2, however, the Senate approved an amendment by Republican Mitch McConnell of Kentucky to cap punitive damages and end joint liability for punitive and noneconomic damages in health care liability cases. Adopted by a vote of 53–47, the amendment also proposed to set a strict deadline for filing claims, reduce awards to reflect a claimant's insurance coverage, limit attorney's fees and make it harder to obtain punitive damages.

The amendment mirrored a bill that McConnell had introduced (S 454), which the Senate Labor and Human Resources Committee had modified substantially before approving by a party-line vote of 9–7 on April 25. The committee had proposed to drop the limits on punitive damages, allow states to opt out of almost all of the bill's provisions, and require the reimbursement of attorney's fees in some cases.

McConnell largely ignored the committee's changes when he offered his amendment to HR 956. The malpractice provisions helped strengthen a filibuster by opponents of the product-liability bill, however, and they were stripped from the bill before the Senate passed it on May 10.

The final version of the bill contained only one restriction on health care liability: a ban on most claims against the suppliers of parts and raw materials for medical devices.

The Labor and Human Resources Committee reported S 454 May 16 (S Rept 104-83), but the Senate took no action on it.

The opponents had enough strength in the Senate to block a sweeping proposal in 1995 to limit damage awards in all civil cases. They did not have the votes, however, to stop a milder, bipartisan proposal to curtail product liability claims.

As cleared in March 1996, HR 956 would have imposed national standards on several elements of product liability claims. The bill focused on limiting punitive damages, which juries awarded in some cases to punish deliberate misdeeds, and compensation for noneconomic losses, such as pain and emotional distress.

President Clinton vetoed the measure May 2, saying that he could sign a product liability bill but not one that was so tilted against consumers. The veto doomed the legislation, as supporters did not have enough votes in either chamber to override Clinton.

BACKGROUND

Product liability law held manufacturers and, in some cases, vendors responsible for the injuries caused by products that proved faulty. Under the doctrine of strict liability, a manufacturer had to pay for the injuries caused by defective products even if it had not been negligent.

Bills to limit liability for faulty products were debated in committee or on the floor in almost every session of Congress in the 1980s and 1990s. Although the legislation seemed to have the support of a majority of the members, the bills were blocked by filibusters in the Senate or influential committee chairmen in the House.

As a result, neither the House nor the Senate had even voted on a product liability bill before 1995. The only victory for the "tort reform" forces came in 1994, when Congress cleared a narrowly drawn bill to shield the manufacturers of small airplanes from some lawsuits. *(1994 action, p. 346)*

After yet another product liability bill was stymied in the Senate in 1994, House Republican leaders decided to take the issue to the voters. One plank of their "Contract with America," a manifesto for the 1994 campaign, called for noneconomic and punitive damages to be limited in product liability and medical malpractice cases.

The contract also called for an end to joint liability, a long-standing doctrine that held each of the parties being sued liable for the full amount of damages awarded by the jury. Joint liability effectively shifted responsibility from the party most at fault to the party with the largest amount of insurance.

The Republican takeover of the House and Senate gave proponents of the legislation new hope in the 104th Congress, particularly with House GOP leaders committed to fulfilling the promises in their contract. Their prospects were further boosted in the House by the defeat of Democrat Jack Brooks of Texas, the former chairman of the House Judiciary Committee and a powerful foe of tort reform. Brooks was replaced as chairman by Henry J. Hyde, R-Ill., a supporter of the legislation.

In the Senate, where product liability legislation had long been stymied by filibusters, four Republicans arrived to take the seats of Democrats allied with the trial lawyers. The shift seemed to assure enough votes to defeat a filibuster.

HOUSE ACTION

The legislation moved first in the House, where the Judiciary Committee approved a broad bill (HR 956) on Feb. 23, 1995, to limit claims and damage awards. The vote was 21–11, with only Democrat Rich Boucher of Virginia crossing party lines to vote for the bill.

Later that day, the House Commerce Committee approved a more narrow product liability bill (HR 917), 26–17, with the support of three Democrats long sympathetic to the tort-reform movement.

Both bills proposed to require "clear and convincing" evidence before awarding punitive damages and to cap punitive damages at $250,000 or three times the amount awarded for the injured party's economic losses, whichever was greater. The Judiciary Committee bill would have applied the cap to all lawsuits, while the Commerce Committee bill applied it only to product liability cases.

Other provisions of both bills would have ended joint liability for noneconomic damages in product liability cases, barred lawsuits for most injuries caused by products more than 15 years old, prohibited claims by people whose injuries were caused primarily by their own drug or alcohol use, and protected the sellers of defective products against most claims.

The committees fended off numerous amendments by Democrats to weaken the restrictions on claims and damage awards. These opponents argued to no avail that the bills were tilted in favor of the wealthy and would work against women, children and working-class Americans.

Hyde and Commerce Committee Chairman Thomas J. Bliley Jr., R-Va., produced a compromise bill (HR 1075) on Feb. 28 that combined elements from the two committees' proposals. Closer in scope to the Judiciary Committee's bill, the new measure proposed to cap punitive damages in all lawsuits, not just product liability cases. HR 917 was reported March 1 (H Rept 104-63, Part I), and HR 956 was reported the next day (H Rept 104-64, Part I). HR 956 went to the House floor March 9, with the text of HR 1075 substituted for the committee-approved provisions.

On the House floor March 9, lawmakers approved a series of amendments greatly expanding the bill. These included a Christopher Cox, R-Calif., amendment limiting awards for noneconomic damages in medical malpractice cases to $250,000, adopted 247–171; a Michael G. Oxley, R-Ohio, amendment barring punitive damages against most products that had been approved by the Food and Drug Administration, adopted by voice vote; a Cox amendment ending joint liability for noneconomic damages in all lawsuits involving interstate commerce, adopted 263–164; and a Pete Geren, D-Texas, amendment shielding rental and leasing companies from liability for most defective products, adopted by voice vote. Another Democratic amendment to be approved was a John Conyers Jr., D-Mich., proposal to allow foreign manufacturers to be sued in federal courts if the companies knew their products were sold or used in the United States, adopted 258–166.

The House rejected six Democratic proposals to trim the bill, including amendments to raise or remove the cap on punitive damages and drop the requirement for "clear and convincing evidence," preserve joint liability for noneconomic damages in all cases, and repeal the bill after five years unless product liability insurance rates had declined at least 10 percent in real terms.

The modified version of HR 956 passed the House March 10, 265–161.

SENATE ACTION

On April 18, 1995, the Senate Commerce, Science and Transportation Committee reported a bipartisan bill (S 565—S Rept 104-69) that hewed closely to the measure it had endorsed in 1994. If anything, the bill was less ambitious than its predecessors.

Sponsored by Slade Gorton, R-Wash., and John D. Rockefeller IV, D-W.Va., the bill proposed the same cap on punitive damages as the House bill but applied it only to product liability cases. It would have barred lawsuits against products that had been in service more than 20 years, not the 15 years proposed by the House, and it waived the time limit for toxic materials, commercial trains and airplanes.

The measure included only one provision related to health care: a shield against lawsuits for the suppliers of parts and raw materials for medical devices. It also proposed to give consumers more time to sue the manufacturer of a harmful product, changing the statute of limitations from two years after the date of injury to two years after the discovery of the injury's cause.

Gorton and Rockefeller dropped two proposals that had helped stall the bill the year before: a provision barring punitive damages against companies whose products had been approved by the FDA, and a requirement that litigants pay their opponents' legal fees if they turned down a pretrial settlement more favorable than the eventual verdict.

The full Senate began debating HR 956 on April 24, using the Commerce Committee's alternative as its starting point. Prodded by Majority Leader Bob Dole, R-Kan., conservative Republicans quickly moved to broaden the bill, hoping to make it as far-reaching as the House-passed version.

The Senate agreed to a Hank Brown, R-Colo., amendment to add penalties for frivolous claims, by a 56–37 vote on April 26; a revised Mitch McConnell, R-Ky., amendment to limit liability for medical malpractice, by a 53–47 vote on May 2; a Dole amendment to extend the limit on punitive damages to all civil cases, by a 51–49 vote on May 3; and a Mike DeWine, R-Ohio, amendment to lower the cap on punitive damages for small businesses and charities, by voice vote on May 3.

These provisions proved too great a load. When proponents of the bill tried to curtail debate on May 4, they were defeated twice by stunning margins: first by a vote of 46-53 and then by a **key vote of 47–52 (R 45–9; D 2–43),** far short of the 60 votes needed. Four days later, after Dole dropped many of the add-ons, the Senate again voted 43–49 against limiting debate. The three votes amounted to a stinging rebuke of Dole's ambition to push a sweeping bill through the Senate. *(1995 key votes, p. 1025)*

With the expanded bill floundering, Gorton and Rockefeller started pushing a scaled-back compromise modeled after the committee-approved bill. Their efforts paid off on May 9, when the Senate cut off the filibuster, 60–38, and adopted the Gorton-Rockefeller compromise by voice vote. The modified bill passed the following day, 61–37.

One of the main differences between the Senate-passed bill and the committee proposal was in the cap on punitive damages in product liability cases. The cap in the Senate-passed bill was $250,000 or twice the amount of other damages awarded by the jury, whichever was greater. A lower cap—the lesser of $250,000 or twice the other damages—was set for small businesses, small towns and individuals whose net worth was less than $500,000.

Judges also would have been allowed to increase a punitive award against large manufacturers or municipalities whose conduct was egregious. This provision had been demanded by Senate Democrats as a way to protect consumers.

CONFERENCE AGREEMENT

House Republican leaders held off the conference for six months in a futile attempt to convince the Senate to support a far-reaching bill. When the conferees finally met Dec. 15, they tentatively agreed to accept major several elements from the Senate's version. The deals included dropping the House provisions on medical malpractice.

Even after agreeing in principle to lower their sights, the House negotiators pushed for tougher limits on liability than the Senate proposed. In particular, they opposed the Senate provision allowing judges to lift the cap on punitive-damage awards in cases they deemed to be egregious.

The Senate negotiators held firm, however, and the bruising defeats that the GOP suffered in the budget battle eventually convinced House negotiators to settle on March 13, 1996, for a bill that closely tracked the more modest Senate proposal.

Affecting only product liability lawsuits, the bill included the Senate provisions limiting punitive damages, ending joint liability for noneconomic losses, barring most claims against the suppliers of parts and raw materials for medical devices, allowing claims against product sellers only if the manufacturer was unable to pay the damages, and giving injured parties more time to file claims.

Also included was a provision backed by both chambers to bar claims by people whose injuries were caused primarily by their own drug or alcohol use.

The main difference between the conference report and the Senate-passed bill was in the proposed statute of repose, or time limit for liability on durable equipment. The Senate had proposed to cut off claims 20 years after the equipment was delivered, but the conferees went with the House proposal of 15 years.

The statute of repose also was extended to more products, such as handguns. And the conferees dropped a Senate provision that would have prevented injured parties from losing the right to sue because a manufacturer filed for bankruptcy.

PRESIDENTIAL POLITICS

Both supporters and opponents of the conference report offered personal and emotion-laden arguments during the House and Senate debates. Supporters argued that costly litigation stifled innovation and prevented manufacturers from bringing to market safe products that would benefit consumers. Opponents sounded populist themes, saying the bill would aid corporate titans at the expense of the vulnerable consumer.

In mapping out a public position on the bill, Clinton appeared to send conflicting signals. He made clear in a March 16 letter to congressional leaders that he objected to major provisions of the measure, such as the limits on punitive damages. Yet he told reporters March 21 that he could accept a bill if some "relatively modest" changes were made, possibly after the veto.

The lead Senate sponsors—Rockefeller and Gorton—were skeptical that Clinton really wanted to strike a deal. They said they had offered to make several changes, such as lengthening the statute of repose to 18 years instead of 15, but the White House had rebuffed every overture.

When Dole brought the conference report to the Senate floor in March, opponents mounted another filibuster. With Clinton threatening a veto and personally urging senators to sustain the filibuster, the issue was transformed into a partisan battle between the incumbent president and Dole, his expected Republican challenger. And Republicans were not about to let their man lose.

Republicans also wanted to force Clinton's hand on the veto threat. Although they knew they would have a hard time overriding a veto, they believed a veto would hurt Clinton in the campaign by painting him as a captive of special interests.

The Senate GOP succeeded in curtailing debate on March 20 by a vote of 60–40, with the help of 12 Senate Democrats. The report was approved the next day on a **key vote of 59–40 (R 47–6; D 12–34).** *(1996 key votes, p. 1047)*

The House adopted the conference report March 29, 259-158, clearing the bill. Clinton vetoed it May 2, citing the proposals to eliminate joint liability for noneconomic damages, cap punitive damages, set a 15-year statute of repose, and allow bankrupt companies to escape some claims, as well as the bill's general approach to preempting state tort laws.

The House tried to override Clinton's veto May 9 but failed on a **key vote of 258–163 (R 225–5; D 33–157; I 0–1)**—23 short of the two-thirds majority needed for an override. ◻

Commerce Department Elimination

A drive by freshmen Republicans to eliminate the Commerce Department stalled in the face of opposition from senior Senate Republicans and the business community.

Instead, the freshmen had to settle for cutting the department's budget from $4.2 billion in fiscal 1995 to $3.8 billion in fiscal 1997. The cuts were not as deep as opponents of the department had sought, however, nor were they as permanent.

The Commerce Department came under fire both for policy reasons and for political ones. Republican critics argued that the department's work on behalf of U.S. companies smacked of corporate welfare and government interference in the free market. They also were eager to eliminate cabinet departments as a symbol of their commitment to shrinking the federal bureaucracy, and Commerce was the least controversial target.

Indeed, the 73 House GOP freshmen had started the 104th Congress looking to scuttle four departments: Energy, Education, Housing and Urban Development, and Commerce. By mid-1995 it was clear that the first three agencies had too much support in Congress to be axed, leaving only the Commerce Department on the chopping block.

The department was saved in part by the smooth salesmanship of Commerce Secretary Ronald H. Brown, who argued that eliminating the department would be "tantamount to unilateral disarmament in the global marketplace." Noting that the department was already being trimmed as part of the government-wide cuts ordered by Congress and the administration, Brown and his Democratic allies argued that the Republican proposal would only result in a fragmented group of smaller bureaucracies.

More important, Commerce Department officials said, was the quiet lobbying of corporations who benefited from the department's export promotion programs, technology development efforts, and economic analyses and forecasting. It was slow developing, but by November 1995, the "Ad Hoc Industry Coalition" brought to the department's defense 65 businesses and industry groups, including AT&T, the Boeing Co., General Electric Co. and IBM Corp.

That same month, two major Republican stalwarts, the U.S. Chamber of Commerce and the National Association of Manufacturers, informed GOP lawmakers they did not relish losing their voice in the executive branch.

The department also performed a number of functions that even its critics admitted were essential, such as conducting the decennial census, monitoring the weather, issuing patents, analyzing the economy and representing the United States in trade negotiations. Several House committees produced competing proposals for preserving or extinguishing the roughly 100 Commerce Department programs, causing a jurisdictional tangle.

The final blow to the GOP efforts came April 3, 1996, when Brown and 34 others died in a plane crash on a trade mission to Croatia. The crash led the House GOP leadership to cancel an April 29 vote on legislation to dismantle the department, and later plans to revive the legislation never were carried out.

LEGISLATIVE ACTION

Congress pasted a bull's eye on the Commerce Department in the fiscal 1996 budget resolution (H Con Res 67), which recommended that the department be eliminated. The final version of the resolution passed both chambers in June 1995.

One month later, House Majority Leader Dick Armey, R-Texas, and House Speaker Newt Gingrich, R-Ga., pledged to incorporate legislation dismantling the Commerce Department into the deficit-reducing budget reconciliation bill for fiscal 1996 (HR 2491). The pledge, made in a July 25 letter to House Government Reform and Oversight Committee Chairman William F. Clinger, R-Pa., kept the freshmen from offering amendments to slash the department's funding during the debate over fiscal 1996 spending bills.

Meanwhile, House committees began hearings on HR 1756, a bill by freshman Dick Chrysler, R-Mich., to eliminate the Commerce Department. Eleven panels shared jurisdiction over the measure because they all oversaw portions of the department.

In September, the committees began marking up the bill. The original version would have ended only six Commerce Department programs; dozens of others would have been turned into private entities or transferred to other federal agencies over three years. A new agency would have managed the transition for three years, then closed its doors.

The measure changed dramatically as it struggled through a series of House committees, several of which wanted to create new agencies instead of transferring Commerce functions to existing departments. Some lawmakers complained that the goal of the measure was being lost as committee members tried to preserve turf.

The House Resources Committee agreed Sept. 13 to transform the National Oceanic and Atmospheric Administration (NOAA)—the largest segment of the department—into an independent agency rather than parceling its pieces among existing agencies and the private sector. The committee then approved the bill by voice vote.

The same day, the Ways and Means Committee amended the bill to create a U.S. Trade Administration to house all federal trade functions. The committee approved its version of the bill by a party-line 22–14 vote and reported it Sept. 21 (H Rept 104-260, Part I).

On Sept. 14, the House Science Committee agreed by voice vote to its version, which created a new U.S. Science and Technology Administration to take over the Commerce Department's efforts in those areas. Also on Sept. 14, the Transportation and Infrastructure Committee agreed by voice vote to a version creating several new regional commissions and an Office of Economic Development to carry on the functions of the Economic Development Administration.

On Sept. 19, the Commerce Committee voted 25–18 in favor of a substitute version of the Commerce Department bill, which it included in its budget reconciliation recommendations. The committee called for the census activities and economic analyses to be continued in a new Federal Statistics Administration.

Selecting bits and pieces from the other panels' proposals, the Government Reform and Oversight Committee approved its own version of HR 1756 on Sept. 21, 28–16.

The GOP leadership tabbed Clinger to stitch together a compromise proposal from the various committee drafts. That version was attached to the reconciliation bill just before it went to the House floor on Oct. 26.

The revised proposal would have eliminated six major Commerce agencies, established two new agencies to take over federal trade and scientific functions, and created a government corporation to issue patents and trademarks. The rest of the department's functions would have been privatized or parceled out to existing agencies within three years.

HR 2491 passed the House as amended on Oct. 26, 227–203. The Senate version of the bill, however, included no Commerce Department language—in part because of a rule barring provisions that did not have a significant impact on the deficit. With this procedural problem in mind, the House-Senate conferees on the reconciliation bill dropped the Commerce Department proposal from the final version. The bill ultimately was killed by a presidential veto. *(Budget reconciliation, p. 68)*

On Nov. 9, the House attached the Commerce Department provisions to a bill temporarily raising the federal debt ceiling (HR 2586). The move was intended to mollify House conservatives, who had refused to vote for an increase in the ceiling unless it included some budget-cutting provisions.

The provisions triggered a revolt by moderate Senate Republicans, however, who wanted a bill free of legislative riders. The Senate dropped the provisions by voice vote later that day, and the House agreed to the Senate version of the bill. That measure also was killed by a presidential veto. *(Debt limit, p. 76)*

A Senate bill similar to Chrysler's proposal made it through the Governmental Affairs Committee in September 1995 but progressed no further. The bill (S 929) would have dismantled the Commerce Department, terminated a half-dozen Com-

merce programs, spun off NOAA and the patents office into independent agencies, assigned the census to the Labor Department, and created an agency to handle federal trade functions. It also would have established a bipartisan, nine-member commission to recommend how to eliminate three more federal departments.

Backed strongly by Chairman William V. Roth Jr., R-Del., the Governmental Affairs committee approved the bill, 5–3, on Sept. 7. Shortly thereafter, however, Roth moved to the helm of the Finance Committee and was replaced as chairman by Alaska Republican Ted Stevens, no great fan of the bill. The committee reported the bill Oct. 20 (S Rept 104-164), but it moved no further.

BUDGET CUTS

While the efforts to eliminate the department were struggling to overcome Republican divisions, GOP appropriators were united in their desire to end some of the department's functions. The fiscal 1996 spending bill for the departments of Commerce, Justice and State (HR 2076), which cleared on Dec. 7, 1995, would have provided less than $3.4 billion for the department—a 19 percent cut. The largest savings would have come from eliminating the Advanced Technology Program, which aimed to help industry develop cutting-edge technologies. It was one of President Clinton's favorite programs.

Clinton vetoed the bill Dec. 19. The department was kept operating by stop-gap spending bills until April 1996, when Congress approved an omnibus spending bill (HR 3019—PL 104-134) that provided $3.6 billion for Commerce. Included was $221 million for the Advanced Technology Program, only enough to complete work on existing projects.

The administration was able to squeeze out a few more dollars for the department in the omnibus appropriations bill for fiscal 1997 (HR 3610—PL 104-208). The measure provided $3.8 billion for the department, including $225 million to keep the Advanced Technology Program alive.

ICC Elimination

Congress in 1995 moved to abolish the Interstate Commerce Commission (ICC), a regulatory agency that already had lost much of its power to regulate.

The elimination had been sought by House Republicans, who argued that the commission was obsolete. Legislation to disband the ICC (HR 2539—PL 104-88) moved swiftly through Congress in November and December 1995, slowed only by disputes over labor protections for freight rail workers.

In particular, lawmakers clashed over how much severance pay to guarantee rail workers laid off in mergers. Congress ultimately agreed to cut the guaranteed pay sharply for many workers, although it took steps to preserve collective-bargaining rights.

BACKGROUND

The nation's oldest independent regulatory authority, the ICC was founded by Congress in 1887 mainly to regulate the powerful railroad monopolies. Its mandate was to ensure that the public had an adequate, efficient transportation system for moving goods.

The ICC's oversight eventually extended to interstate shipping and trucking companies as well as railroads. Among other things, the commission had power over which companies entered the market, the rates they charged, the routes they served, the agreements they entered with labor, and the mergers they proposed.

The commission's power waned as Congress freed the rail and truck industries from regulation. The last major deregulation came in 1994, when Congress eliminated much of the ICC's control over interstate trucking rates and licenses. *(1994 action, p. 333)*

House Republicans had long sought to eliminate the ICC and end its remaining regulatory power, but they had little success until 1994. That year, in a move that caught appropriators by surprise, the House voted to eliminate funding for the ICC in the transportation spending bill for fiscal 1995 (HR 4556—PL 103-331). The final version of the spending bill restored much of the commission's funding, but it was clear that the ICC's days were numbered—particularly after Republicans took control of Congress in 1995. Sure enough, the fiscal 1996 transportation spending bill (HR 2002—PL 104-50) provided no money for the ICC or its 417 employees after Dec. 31, 1995, except closeout funding.

LEGISLATIVE ACTION

Divided largely along party lines, the House Transportation and Infrastructure Committee approved HR 2539, 36–22, on Nov. 1, 1995. As reported Nov. 6 (H Rept 104-311), the bill proposed to eliminate or modify a host of regulations on shipping, truck and rail companies, such as the requirement that railroads file their rates with the ICC.

Tasks that the committee deemed indispensable were to be continued by other transportation agencies and a new, three-member Surface Transportation Board within the Transportation Department. The Surface Transportation Board was to focus on railroad issues, such as preventing strikes and setting maximum rates for rail monopolies.

Most of the committee's Democrats opposed the bill out of concern over labor protections. The federal government provided special protections for rail workers—such as a six-year guarantee of severance pay in the event of layoffs—because it did not permit them to strike. The bill proposed to leave existing protections in place for workers at railroads earning more than $250 million annually, but it would have guaranteed only 30 days of pay and benefits for workers at smaller railroads that merged or sold lines.

That issue sparked a sharp debate on the House floor Nov. 14. Rep. Edward Whitfield, R-Ky., proposed an amendment to guarantee one year's severance for workers at smaller railroads under certain conditions. The guarantee applied only to layoffs that resulted when two midsized railroads merged or a midsized line merged with a small railroad. Whitfield's amendment also proposed to bar midsized railroads—those with annual rev-

enues between $20 million and $250 million—from using a merger to shift work from unionized labor to nonunionized workers.

Transportation and Infrastructure Committee Chairman Bud Shuster, R-Pa., said the Whitfield amendment would impose such high costs on small railroads, it would drive many out of business. "It we want to see the wholesale abandonments [of rail lines], particularly in rural America, this is the amendment," Shuster said.

Still, the amendment attracted the support of 50 Republicans and virtually all Democrats. It was adopted, 241–184, on Nov. 14. The modified bill passed the House later that day, 417–8.

The Senate Commerce, Science and Transportation Committee reported a competing ICC bill (S 1396—S Rept 104-176) on Nov. 18. The Senate bill would have eliminated both the ICC and the Federal Maritime Commission, which oversaw international cargo vessels. A new Intermodal Surface Transportation Board would have been created to take over some of the functions of the two commissions.

Another key difference from the House bill was in labor protections. S 1396 would have guaranteed one year of severance pay and benefits for laid-off workers from any railroad, regardless of size.

The Senate passed HR 2539 by voice vote Nov. 28 after substituting a modified version of S 1396. The main debate was over a proposal by two Midwestern senators—Byron L. Dorgan, D-N.D., and Christopher S. Bond, R-Mo.—to require railroad mergers to comply with the Clayton Antitrust Act, not the more permissive Interstate Commerce Act. Their amendment was made retroactive so that it would apply to a proposed merger between two rail giants, Union Pacific and Southern Pacific.

Proponents of the amendment said it would help protect consumers against higher costs and abandoned routes. Critics countered that it would be a mistake to rewrite decades of rail transportation policy after an hour of debate. The opponents prevailed, killing the amendment on a tabling motion, 62–35.

In conference, House and Senate negotiators agreed to drop the Senate proposal to eliminate the Federal Maritime Commission. They included most of the House provisions on labor protections, but gave midsized railroads a new option when merging with another midsized or small railroad: they could give workers six years of severance benefits and preserve collective-bargaining agreements, or they could provide one year of severance benefits and abrogate the agreements.

The conferees agreed to their report (H Rept 104-422) on Dec. 16. Days later the White House threatened a veto, citing the labor protections, among other issues.

Armed with the veto threat, labor's allies successfully pressed the House GOP leadership to abandon the offending provision. By Dec. 21, the two sides agreed on a resolution (S Con Res 37) to amend the conference report. The final version guaranteed that workers affected by a merger between midsized railroads or between a midsized and a small railroad would receive severance benefits for one year, with no loss of collective-bargaining rights. It also barred midsized railroads from using a merger to shift work away from their unionized force to nonunionized workers of the company they purchased.

The Senate approved the resolution and the conference report by voice votes Dec. 21, and the House did the same the next day. Although several of his objections had not been addressed, President Clinton still signed the bill on Dec. 29.

TOW TRUCKS

The final version of HR 2539 also restored the authority of state and local governments to regulate the prices charged for towing. The provision, which was championed by Rep. Nick J. Rahall II, D-W.Va., applied only to tows done without the prior authorization of the car owner or driver.

Such price controls were preempted by Congress in 1994 as part of legislation to reauthorize federal aviation programs (PL 103-305). That measure barred state and local governments from imposing any economic regulations on the trucking industry, but Rahall said that lawmakers had not intended to deregulate tow trucks and wreckers. *(1994 action, p. 334)*

HR 2539 left towing companies free from regulation on routes, services and prices charged for consensual tows. ❑

Small Business Programs

Congress cleared three measures in 1995 and 1996 aimed at reducing the cost of federal aid to small businesses.

Although the Small Business Administration (SBA) aid programs were popular in Congress, leaders of the House and Senate Small Business committees had grown concerned about the increasing cost to the Treasury. The demand for SBA assistance had increased rapidly in the 1990s, requiring repeated cash infusions from Congress. *(1993–1994 action, p. 344)*

Concerned that the SBA's appropriations could not continue to grow in a time of increasingly tight budgets, lawmakers enacted a bill in 1995 to help the SBA provide more financial assistance with fewer tax dollars. When that measure did not reduce subsidy rates as expected, lawmakers acted again in 1996 to control the SBA's costs.

At issue were two of the main financial tools that the SBA used to help small businesses: the 7(a) program and the 504 program. The 7(a) program provided loan guarantees to support long-term loans, which private lenders otherwise were reluctant to give to small businesses. The 504 program established "certified development companies" that, in partnership with private lenders, helped small businesses finance construction projects and major purchases.

Lawmakers also took steps in 1996 to reduce the costs and financial risk of the SBA's venture capital program.

CUTTING SUBSIDY RATES

With the 7(a) and development company programs running short of funds, Congress cleared a bill in 1995 to reduce the maximum loan guaranteed by the SBA and increase the fees paid by lenders and borrowers.

Signed into law Oct. 12, the bill (S 895—PL 104-36) capped the 7(a) guarantees at 80 percent of the value of loans up to $100,000 and 75 percent of the value of larger loans. Previous law had capped the guarantee at 90 percent for loans up to $155,000 and 85 percent for loans up to $750,000.

The measure did not change the guarantee fee for 7(a) loans of $100,000 or less. For larger loans, it increased the initial guarantee fee from 2 percent of the guaranteed portion of a loan to 3 percent of the first $250,000 guaranteed, 3.5 percent of the next $250,000, and 3.9 percent for the rest. Lenders were allowed to pass these fees on to the borrowers.

A new, annual fee also was established that 7(a) lenders were required to pay out of their own pockets, rather than passing on to the borrowers. The fee was set at 0.5 percent of the outstanding principle of the guaranteed portion of the loan. The same fee applied to guaranteed loans sold on the secondary market, an increase from the previous 0.4 percent fee.

Finally, the bill imposed an annual fee of 0.125 percent on the outstanding balance of guaranteed loans made through the 504 program.

The Senate Committee on Small Business reported an early version of the bill on Aug. 5, 1995 (S Rept 104-129), and the Senate passed a slightly modified version by voice vote Aug. 11.

The House Small Business Committee on Sept. 6 reported a similar bill (HR 2150—H Rept 104-239), which sailed through the House on Sept. 12, 405–0. Its provisions then were inserted into S 895, which the House passed by voice vote. The conferees quickly resolved the largely technical differences between the House and Senate bills. The Senate adopted the conference report (H Rept 104-269) by voice vote without debate on Sept. 28. The House did the same the next day.

The bill was projected to lower the subsidy rate of the 7(a) program—the percentage of loan costs covered by the taxpayers, not the borrowers—from 2.74 percent to 1.06 percent. The fees on the 504 program were expected to cover all the costs of development-company loans, reducing the subsidy rate from 0.57 percent to zero.

A SECOND TRY

The House Small Business Committee proposed more revisions to SBA programs in 1996, after learning that S 895 had not reduced the subsidy rates on SBA loans. In fact, the subsidy for the 504 program, which was supposed to have been eliminated, shot up to almost 7 percent.

The committee contended that the programs were poorly managed by the SBA, resulting in a declining recovery of loans. It reported a bill (HR 3719—H Rept 104-750) on Aug. 2, 1996, to reduce reimbursement of 7(a) lenders, give preferred lenders more freedom, and require higher fees and down payments on development-company loans.

The bill also would have raised the interest rate on disaster-relief loans from half of the rate on similar Treasury Department securities to three-quarters of the rate. Another provision would have reauthorized SBA programs for fiscal 1998 at the same level as in fiscal 1997.

The House approved a slightly modified version of the bill Sept. 5, 1996, 408–0. Leaders of the Senate Small Business Committee agreed on a new version of the bill later that month, but they were blocked from bringing the bill to the Senate floor by an objection from the Democratic leadership. Conferees on the omnibus appropriations bill for fiscal 1997 (HR 3610) included provisions similar to HR 3719 in their conference report (H Rept 104-863). The House approved the conference report later on Sept. 28, 370–37, and the Senate cleared the bill by voice vote Sept. 30. President Clinton signed the measure a few hours later (PL 104-208).

The final version of the bill dropped the proposed increase in disaster-loan interest rates and the reauthorization of SBA programs. It also added provisions requiring the SBA to use the fees, interest payments and profits it received on the loan programs to lower the subsidy rate, rather than spending the money as it had been on salaries and expenses.

Other provisions in the final version:

• Raised the down payment that certain small businesses were required to make on 504 loans from 10 percent to 15 percent or 20 percent. The provision applied to start-up small businesses and those financing a single-purpose building, such as a car wash. The bill also raised the fee that all borrowers were required to pay for 504 loans in fiscal 1997 from 0.125 percent of the outstanding balance to a maximum of 0.9375 percent.

• Imposed a new fee for one year on lenders and development companies involved in 504 loans. The fee on lenders was set at 0.5 percent of its portion of the loan, and the fee on development companies was set at 0.125 percent of its portion.

• Lowered the amount of interest that lenders could collect from the government when a small business defaulted on a guaranteed 7(a) loan. The interest rate was set at 1 percentage point below the rate charged on the loan.

• Gave preferred lenders the power to liquidate defaulted 7(a) loans without SBA approval. The SBA was ordered to let some development companies liquidate defaulted 504 loans after an expedited review.

• Required the SBA to start foreclosing on development-company borrowers if they were more than 65 days late on their payments.

• Required the SBA to develop rules allowing banks to sell the unguaranteed portion of 7(a) loans on the secondary market.

• Created a data base to track problems in SBA loan underwriting, collections, recovery and liquidation.

• Mandated an independent assessment of the 7(a) and development-company loan programs.

• Allowed disaster loans for small businesses hurt by the closure of commercial fisheries.

• Required the SBA to hire private firms to service 30 percent of its disaster loans.

• Continued indefinitely the requirement that lenders pay the SBA a fee for the 7(a) loans they sold on the secondary market.

SMALL BUSINESS SECURITIES

A similar concern about subsidy levels and SBA management led the Senate to pass a bill (S 1784) in July 1996 to modify the SBA's Small Business Investment Company (SBIC) program, which provided venture capital to small businesses. A modified version of the bill was signed into law as part of HR 3610, the omnibus appropriations bill for fiscal 1997.

Congress established the program in 1958 to create privately funded companies to provide venture capital to small businesses. The SBA matched the money raised by the SBICs with funds guaranteed by the taxpayers. The SBICs helped small businesses, in turn, by buying equity in the company ("participating security") or providing unsecured long-term loans ("debentures").

HR 3610 doubled the amount of private funds that companies had to raise in order to become SBICs: $5 million for debenture SBICs and $10 million for participating security SBICs. Although SBA regulations had already imposed these standards on new SBICs, previous federal law had not.

The measure also increased the fees that SBICs paid the SBA in order to reduce the subsidy level; required SBICs to make at least 20 percent of its financings to businesses worth less than $6 million; eliminated a specialized category of SBICs for minority businesses, transforming the existing ones into ordinary SBICs; and barred new SBICs from being managed by the same people who owned them.

The Senate Small Business Committee reported an early version of S 1784 on June 25, 1996. The Senate slightly modified the bill before passing it by voice vote July 25, and this version was included in HR 3610 with little change. ❑

Small Business Rules

Congress gave small businesses more power to challenge federal regulators as part of a bill enacted in 1996 to raise the federal debt ceiling.

The main purpose of the measure (HR 3136—PL 104-121) was to keep the federal government from running out of borrowing authority and defaulting on its debts. To help attract Republican votes, GOP leaders included a provision amending the Regulatory Flexibility Act of 1980 (PL 96-354) to let small businesses sue agencies that adopted rules without considering or endorsing less costly alternatives.

The Regulatory Flexibility Act required agencies to determine whether a proposed rule would have a significant economic impact on a substantial number of small businesses. If so, the agency had to consider alternatives that minimized the impact on small businesses and, if the alternatives were not adopted, release a statement explaining its decision. *(1980 law, Congress and the Nation Vol. V, p. 850)*

LEGISLATIVE ACTION

House and Senate committees had approved regulatory-flexibility bills for small business in 1995, but the proposals foundered in disputes over other deregulatory initiatives.

The House Small Business Committee moved first, reporting a regulatory-flexibility bill (HR 937—H Rept 104-49, Part I) on Feb. 23, 1995. The same day the House Judiciary Committee reported a similar proposal as part a bill (HR 926—H Rept 104-48) to require elaborate cost-benefit analyses before federal agencies adopted major new rules. The House did not act on

HR 937. It passed HR 926 on March 1, 1995, by an overwhelming, 415–15 vote, but the bill did not advance in the Senate.

Instead, the Senate GOP leadership included regulatory-flexibility provisions in a far-reaching regulatory-overhaul bill (S 343) by Majority Leader Bob Dole, R-Kan. That measure was blocked on the Senate floor in July 1995 by a Democratic filibuster. (*Regulatory overhaul, p. 842*)

The House GOP leadership revived the regulatory flexibility proposal in early 1996, including it in a modified version of a bill (HR 994) requiring federal agencies to review all their regulations. Earlier versions of the bill had been reported by the Government Reform and Oversight Committee Oct. 19, 1995, and the Judiciary Committee Nov. 7 (H Rept 104-284, Parts I and II).

House GOP leaders planned to bring the bill to the floor March 5, 1996, but they changed their minds in the face of opposition from both wings of their party. Conservatives argued that the bill did not go far enough, and moderates contended that the proposed regulatory reviews would swamp agencies in paperwork.

On March 6, the Senate Committee on Small Business reported a bill (S 942) with regulatory-flexibility provisions and a series of proposals aimed at helping small companies comply with federal rules. After a brief procedural wrangle on the Senate floor, a modified version of the bill passed on March 19, 100–0.

Instead of requiring agencies to review their regulations, as HR 994 proposed, S 942 called for major new rules to be delayed 45 days so that Congress would have a chance to repeal them before they went into effect. The proposal was a variation on a bill (S 219) that the Senate passed in March 1995. Although S 219 had won bipartisan support in the Senate, it stalled when the House passed a substitute version establishing a moratorium on new regulations. (*Regulation moratorium, p. 847*)

Republican leaders then attached a modified version of S 942 to the debt-ceiling bill, which swept through both chambers on March 28, 1996—the day before the government was due to run out of borrowing authority. The House passed the bill 328–91, and the Senate cleared it by voice vote. President Clinton signed HR 3136 on March 29. (*Debt limit, p. 76*)

MAJOR PROVISIONS

As signed into law, HR 3136 let small businesses take federal agencies to court if they did not comply with relevant provisions of the 1980 Regulatory Flexibility Act. HR 3136 allowed the courts to review an agency's rulemaking record to determine whether the agency made any procedural missteps. It also allowed the court to second-guess an agency's determination that a proposed rule would not have a significant economic impact on a substantial number of small businesses. If a court ruled against the agency and the agency failed to take corrective action within 90 days, the bill allowed the court to suspend the regulation.

Other provisions of the bill:

• Gave small businesses more input into proposed rules before they were finalized.

• Allowed small business owners to collect attorney fees when an administrative law judge or court found that regulators had made substantially excessive or unreasonable demands.

• Required agencies to publish clear, jargon-free guides to help small businesses comply with any new rule that was expected to have a significant impact on a substantial number of them. Agencies also were instructed to set up programs to answer small businesses' questions about rules.

• Directed federal agencies to reduce or waive fines for violations by small businesses, if the circumstances were appropriate.

• Required the Small Business Administration (SBA) to establish an ombudsman to hear confidential complaints from small businesses about audits, inspections and other enforcement actions.   ❏

Baseball Antitrust Exemption

A protracted strike by major league baseball players prompted lawmakers to introduce at least 11 bills in early 1995 to expose the league to federal antitrust enforcement. The end of the strike in April 1995 took the urgency out of the legislation, however, and none of the bills reached the floor in either chamber.

The Supreme Court exempted the league owners from antitrust laws in 1922 (*Federal Baseball Club v. National League*), and the exemption endured despite periodic challenges by disgruntled lawmakers. A new round of legislative attacks began in 1994, when the owners attempted to impose a cap on players' salaries. (*1994 action, p. 351*)

The players went out on strike in August 1994, a work stoppage that caused the World Series to be canceled for the first time in 90 years. Money was the crux of the conflict, with many team owners arguing for a salary cap to halt the escalation of player contracts.

In the first three months of the 104th Congress, 11 lawmakers introduced bills to end the owners' exemption from antitrust laws or invoke binding arbitration to end the strike. Opponents of the antitrust exemption argued that it allowed owners to impose unfair labor conditions collusively and unilaterally, undermining the players' collective-bargaining rights.

The owners and their allies in Congress, however, said that the exemption was appropriate because the teams were not competitors in business—they were competitors only on the field. The Supreme Court had ruled the league exempt because the sport was not an essential part of interstate commerce and, as such, not covered by laws designed to protect competition.

In February 1995, President Clinton tried to end the impasse by calling a White House meeting between the owners, players and federal mediator Bill Usery Jr. When that gambit failed, Clinton urged Congress to intervene.

The courts moved before Congress did, however. In March a federal judge issued an injunction restoring the terms of baseball's collective bargaining agreement, as the union had sought, and the players called off their strike.

Still, Senate Judiciary Committee Chairman Orrin Hatch, R-Utah, moved forward with his bill to pare back the owners' antitrust exemption. The measure (S 627) proposed to make the owners vulnerable to antitrust lawsuits if they colluded to cap players' salaries or otherwise interfered with normal marketplace conditions. It did not apply to minor league operations, negotiations over broadcasting rights, or decisions about franchise location.

The bill narrowly won the Judiciary Committee's endorsement, 9–8, on Aug. 3, 1995, and was reported Feb. 6, 1996 (S Rept 104-231). It advanced no further, however, in part because of the determined opposition of Democrats Dianne Feinstein of California and Paul Simon of Illinois.

House Judiciary Committee Chairman Henry J. Hyde, an Illinois Republican who had opposed previous efforts to end the antitrust exemption, announced in 1995 that he would not take up any of the House baseball bills unless the Senate passed S 627. Six bills died in his committee, and a seventh was buried in the House Economic and Educational Opportunities Committee. ❑

Sports Franchises

Legislation to help cities hold onto or regain major league sports franchises won the endorsement of one House committee in 1996 but died in another.

The bill (HR 2740) was sponsored by Republican Martin R. Hoke of Ohio, whose district once was home to the Cleveland Browns of the National Football League (NFL). The Browns' owner moved the team to Baltimore after the 1995–1996 season after failing to resolve a dispute with Cleveland officials over a new stadium.

As approved by the House Judiciary Committee, the bill would have required the NFL, the National Basketball Association and the National Hockey League to offer an expansion franchise to any city whose team moved more than 25 miles away, provided that city officials had lined up a qualified investor. The city would have been given three years to find an investor, and once it had, the league would have been given 12 months to provide a franchise.

If a league failed to provide a franchise, a federal court could have awarded the city up to three times the purchase price of a team or the market value, whichever was greater. The court also could have suspended for one season the antitrust exemption that allowed each league to pool its broadcasting rights and revenues.

The bill proposed to give the three leagues an expanded exemption from antitrust law so that league members could bar a franchise from leaving a city. To deter a team from moving, the bill would have required owners who broke a lease on their city- or state-owned facilities to repay all the financial assistance they received. Teams that violated this requirement would have been liable for triple damages.

Finally, the bill would have required the leagues to hold at least two public hearings before permitting a team to move.

When the Judiciary Committee took up the bill in April 1996, the debate largely was driven by parochial concerns about impending or rumored moves. The opposition was led by Rep. Ed Bryant, R-Tenn., who likened the bill to an unfunded government mandate and argued that it ultimately would prevent teams from moving. The Houston Oilers football team was considering a move to Bryant's state by 1999. The panel rejected a substitute that would have given cities or individuals 14 days to sue a league that allowed a franchise to move, as well as an amendment that would have given Major League Baseball expanded power over franchise relocations.

The committee reported a modified version of the bill June 27 (H Rept 104-656, Part I), but the measure languished in the House Commerce Committee the rest of the session. ❑

Boxing Safety

After three decades of failed efforts, Congress cleared a bill in 1996 to set minimum safety standards for boxers and require bouts to be sanctioned by state authorities. The measure (HR 4167—PL 104-272) made it harder for fighters to get back into the ring after injuries or a string of losses. It also required fighters to register with state boxing commissions, undergo medical examinations before a fight and be insured against injuries sustained in the bout.

The boxing industry had been under congressional scrutiny since the 1960s because of its alleged ties to organized crime and its disregard for the health and livelihood of fighters. Lawmakers were particularly concerned about journeymen boxers who traveled from state to state, often steered into mismatches for the sake of bettors.

Critics said that the bill left too much power in the hands of state commissions. Supporters, however, argued that more prescriptive proposals to clean up boxing had never made it through Congress.

The Senate Commerce, Science and Transportation Committee had approved a similar bill late in 1994, but it advanced no further. *(1994 action, p. 352)*

The Senate Commerce panel reported a new bill (S 187—S Rept 104-159) on Oct. 19, 1995, proposing to bar boxing matches that had not been approved by the state boxing commission or, if the state did not have its own commission, by one from another state.

The Senate approved the bill by voice vote Oct. 31, 1995, but the House Commerce Committee did not act on it. Instead, the House panel reported a similar bill (HR 1186—H Rept 104-833, Part I) on Sept. 24, 1996. House leaders then brought an identical bill (HR 4167) to the floor, where it passed by voice vote Sept. 25 without amendment. The gesture was a tribute to HR 4167 sponsor Pat Williams, D-Mont., a longtime advocate of boxing regulation who was retiring after 18 years in the House. The Senate cleared the bill by voice vote Sept. 27.

As signed into law Oct. 9, the measure barred fights unless a state commission had approved them, a doctor had certified that the boxers were physically fit to compete, and a doctor was present at ringside. Each boxing commission was required to report promptly to other state commissions the results of all fights they sanctioned and any suspensions they imposed. Grounds for suspension included a recent knockout, multiple losses in succession, an injury or a failed drug test.

Fighters who had been suspended in one state were forbidden to fight in any other, although state commissions could make exceptions under certain circumstances. To prevent suspended fighters from entering the ring under a different name, boxers were required to obtain identification cards from state commissions and renew them every three years.

The measure imposed criminal penalties on boxers, promoters and managers who violated the law. ❏

Tourism Promotion

Congress set up a private organization in 1996 to promote the United States as a vacation site and shut down a Commerce Department agency that had coordinated the federal government's role in international tourism.

The legislation (HR 2579—PL 104-288) established the U.S. National Tourism Organization to promote international tourism in the United States. Although the organization was given no formal power, leaders of the Commerce and State Departments, the U.S. Trade Representative and other federal officials were instructed to give priority to the organization's recommendations.

The organization was to be governed by a 47-member board, whose members represented an array of travel and tourism industries. No federal funds were authorized by the bill.

HR 2579 also eliminated authorization for the Commerce Department's Tourism and Travel Administration, which had coordinated federal actions on international tourism. The department had already started dismantling the agency because Congress had eliminated its $16.3 million budget in fiscal 1996.

The legislation was prompted by concerns about the United States' share of the global tourism market, which had shrunk from its peak of 19.3 percent in 1992 to 15.7 percent by the end of 1994. Supporters of the bill argued that because travel and tourism was the nation's second largest service and retail industry, it merited a federally sanctioned effort to increase the U.S. share of international vacationers.

The Senate Commerce, Science and Transportation Committee moved first, reporting its own version of the legislation (S 1735—S Rept 104-341) on July 31, 1996. The Senate passed that bill by voice vote Aug. 2, but the House did not act on it. Instead, the House Commerce Committee reported HR 2579 on Sept. 25 (H Rept 104-839, Part I), and the House approved it by voice vote the next day. The Senate cleared the House bill by voice vote Sept. 28, and President Clinton signed it Oct. 11. ❏

FTC Reauthorization

Congress cleared a bill (HR 3553—PL 104-216) in 1996 to reauthorize the Federal Trade Commission (FTC) for two years at its existing level of activity.

Principally a law enforcement agency, the FTC carried out federal consumer protection and antitrust laws. Its main activities included guarding consumers against unfair or deceptive claims and reviewing proposed mergers to ensure that they would not impede competition.

Although the agency received an annual appropriation from Congress, more than half its budget was derived from the fees collected from the corporations it regulated. HR 3553 authorized Congress to appropriate $107 million for the commission in fiscal 1997 and $111 million in fiscal 1998, enough to maintain the existing services.

The bill made no changes in FTC policy or programs, unlike the reauthorization measure in 1994 that had altered the commission's rulemaking power. The 1994 legislation settled a protracted dispute over advertising regulations, clearing the way for a simple reauthorization bill like HR 3553. *(1994 action, p. 350)*

The House Commerce Committee reported the bill on Aug. 2, 1996 (H Rept 104-754), two days after the Senate Commerce, Science and Transportation Committee had reported a virtually identical proposal (S 1840—S Rept 104-342). The House passed HR 3553 by voice vote Sept. 4, the Senate cleared it by voice vote Sept. 13, and President Clinton signed it into law Oct. 1. ❏

Telecommunications Overhaul

Culminating three years of intense work and two decades of debate, Congress cleared a bill in 1996 to rewrite the nation's 62-year-old communications law and usher in a new era of competition in telephone, video and data services.

The Telecommunications Act of 1996 (S 652—PL 104-104) was hailed by lawmakers from both parties as a great leap forward, clearing out the legal and regulatory restrictions that were hindering U.S. companies in the Information Age. It aimed to break up the local telephone and cable TV monopolies, expand competition in long-distance telephone service, create incentives for the development of the so-called information superhighway and lighten the regulatory load on all telecommunications companies.

The disparate threads of the legislation shared a common purpose: to create one giant marketplace for telecommunications services with evenly matched competitors. Advances in digital technology were bringing voice, video and data services into convergence, but their markets had remained segmented by federal and state laws, regulations and federal court orders restraining the regional Bell telephone companies and AT&T.

Lawmakers agreed that the Communications Act of 1934 had to be updated to reflect the new realities of digital communications. The main disputes were over how quickly to remove the restraints on the powerhouse Bells and how large a role to give the federal government in the transition from regulation to competition.

The most deregulatory-minded Republicans wanted to entrust as much as possible to the free market. They argued for a speedy end to the Bell restrictions, cable TV price controls, broadcast ownership rules and all other restraints on communications companies.

Liberal Democrats, on the other hand, called for the federal government to retain strong regulatory powers to ensure that real competition developed in all markets. They also wanted the government to ensure that the information superhighway did not bypass rural and poor communities, as market forces might otherwise dictate.

Between those two poles stood much of the communications industry. Although the companies all wanted to shed as much regulation as possible, they also wanted restraints to remain on their potential competitors.

What united lobbyists and lawmakers alike was a conviction that the legal barriers between industry segments were a detriment to the economy and had to be removed. That core belief pushed Republicans and Democrats to find common ground between the free market and regulatory extremes.

The resulting legislation was the first major bill promoted by the Republican leadership in the 104th Congress that had been crafted with the help of moderate and liberal Democrats. Symbolically, it cleared just after Republicans conceded defeat on their deficit-reducing budget reconciliation bill (HR 2491), which had been formulated without Democratic input. *(Budget reconciliation, p. 68)*

The final version of the bill mixed nuggets of regulatory relief with new regulatory burdens in an effort to balance the competitive power of Bells, long-distance carriers, wireless companies, cable TV operators, broadcasters and satellite companies. The balance had been adjusted repeatedly en route to passage as lawmakers tried to ensure that no player would get too great a head start in the race to compete—a race that had no clear start, no certain entrants and no obvious route.

The impact of the legislation was not expected to be felt immediately because the Federal Communications Commission (FCC) had to adopt a host of implementing regulations, among other reasons. The impact was further delayed in October 1996, when a federal court blocked the FCC's regulations on local telephone competition. A second federal panel also barred enforcement of a provision restricting the flow of indecent material over the Internet and other interactive computer networks.

SENATE COMMITTEE ACTION

The groundwork for the Telecommunications Act of 1996 was laid in 1993 and 1994. Leaders of the House Judiciary Committee and the House Energy and Commerce Committee were able to unite much of the communications industry behind legislation to unleash the Bells while spawning competition in the local phone and cable TV markets.

The long-distance companies, which had not signed off on the House proposal, threw their support behind a competing bill by Sen. Ernest F. Hollings, D-S.C., that would have explicitly required the Bells to face competition in local phone service before entering any new markets. That measure died short of the Senate floor, largely because of opposition from a few of the Bells and then-Minority Leader Bob Dole, R-Kan. *(Background and 1994 action, p. 352)*

Despite their demise, the 1994 bills helped sketch a rough outline of a bill that would be acceptable to all parties. In particular, they established the principle that the Bells could not expect to enter the long-distance business as long as they retained a monopoly over local service.

Republicans signaled early on that they were eager to enact a bill, although not necessarily one that picked up where the Hollings bill left off. New Senate Commerce, Science and Transportation Committee Chairman Larry Pressler, R-S.D., got the process going before the 104th Congress even convened, bringing committee Republicans together with Dole to start hashing out the outlines of a bill.

Pressler's immediate challenge was finding a way to bridge the gap between two Republican camps: those who favored aggressively deregulating and quickly unleashing the Bells, and those who wanted to restrain the Bells until the local telephone markets were open to competition. The former group consisted of Dole, Bob Packwood of Oregon and John McCain of Arizona, all of whom vigorously opposed the bill developed in 1994 by Hollings and former Sen. John C. Danforth, R-Mo. The latter group, which included Pressler, Trent Lott of Mississippi and Ted Stevens of Alaska, had supported the measure.

By the end of January, the Republicans had united behind a sketchy draft bill that proposed a date certain for the Bells to enter the long-distance market, stiff penalties for local phone companies that did not open their networks to competition, and the elimination of many federal regulations on cable-TV prices, phone company profits and broadcast station ownership.

Two weeks later the Democrats on the committee, led by Hollings, responded with their own proposal that hewed more closely to the previous year's bill. Aides for the two sides then began hammering out a compromise bill, a process that took six weeks of almost daily meetings.

The critical moment came March 22, 1995, the day before the Commerce Committee was scheduled to mark up the bill. Republicans circulated a draft bill that was more favorable to the Bells in several respects than the two sides had negotiated, outraging Democrats and threatening to sink the measure in a partisan standoff.

To quell the disturbance, Pressler disavowed the preliminary draft and sought peace with Hollings. They struck a deal that night, hours before the markup was to begin. The deal drew Pressler away from McCain and Packwood, while pulling Hollings away from the administration and some liberal Democrats.

Melding elements of the Republican and Democratic drafts, the compromise proposed a host of new regulations to guide the transition to full-blown competition in phone and video services. It also proposed to ease some existing rules on phone company profits, cable TV prices, foreign investment in U.S. telecommunications companies, and broadcast ownership, while promising to eliminate more rules after competition broke up the existing monopolies.

The bill would have required local phone companies to share their networks with would-be competitors upon request. To give fledgling companies a chance to compete, the bill included a series of specific requirements for the local phone incumbents, such as enabling customers to change phone companies without changing phone numbers ("number portability") and allowing their competitors' customers to make local calls without having to dial extra digits ("dialing parity").

It would not have set a date certain for the Bells to enter long distance, as the Bells and their GOP allies had sought. Nor would it have required the Justice Department to approve any Bell move into long distance, as AT&T and its Democratic allies had sought. Instead, a Bell would have been allowed to offer long-distance service once it complied with a list of network-sharing requirements and the Federal Communications Commission approved.

Other provisions of the bill would have allowed the Bells to manufacture phone equipment, offer alarm services and engage in electronic publishing under certain conditions; allowed power companies to offer telephone service, in some cases through a separate subsidiary; and required the FCC to identify and eliminate outdated regulations every two years.

One of the most controversial provisions of the draft was added during the March 23 markup with little debate and no recorded vote. Offered by Jim Exon, D-Neb., and Slade Gorton, R-Wash., it proposed to expand the prohibitions against obscene, indecent and harassing phone calls so that they would apply to all forms of electronic communications. The committee had included similar language in the previous year's bill, at Exon's request.

The committee's quiet acceptance of the proposal contrasted with the fierce opposition from a coalition of electronic information services, computer manufacturers and users, civil libertarians and some communications companies. The prohibition on making indecent material available to minors was unconstitutionally vague, they argued, and would inhibit the flow of information over computer networks like the Internet.

The committee also adopted, 10–8, an amendment by Olympia J. Snowe, R-Maine, John D. Rockefeller IV, D-W.Va., Exon and Bob Kerrey, D-Neb., to give schools, nonprofit hospitals and libraries advanced telecommunications services at a discount. The amendment, Rockefeller said, was critical to the quality of education in rural areas.

The Senate Commerce Committee then approved the draft bill, 17–2. The draft was introduced as S 652 and reported March 30 (S Rept 104-23).

In the weeks following the committee's vote, Pressler, Packwood and McCain vied behind the scenes for Dole's support. Packwood and McCain wanted to speed the Bells' entry into the long-distance market, scale back the subsidies for local phone service in rural areas, and delete the Snowe-Rockefeller amendment, among other changes. Pressler wanted to push the bill through without major changes as quickly as possible.

The Clinton administration, meanwhile, lined up opposition to several key elements of the Pressler-Hollings compromise. Its goals included leaving cable price controls in place until competition took hold, giving the Justice Department veto power over any Bell move into long distance, preventing an undue concentration of media control, and limiting the ability of local telephone and cable companies to join forces rather than competing.

A key question was how much deregulation Dole would demand as a price for bringing the bill to the floor. Pressler and Hollings ultimately agreed to a swap: Dole would add a package

that stopped well short of the changes sought by McCain and Packwood, and Minority Leader Tom Daschle, D-S.D., would add provisions reining in some of the bill's deregulatory elements.

SENATE FLOOR ACTION

Backed by their parties' leadership, Pressler and Hollings were able to steer their compromise through the Senate largely intact. The Senate approved S 652 by a **key vote of 81–18 (R 51–2; D 30–16)** on June 15, after making only two major changes during the weeklong debate. *(1995 key votes, p. 1025)*

The first was a wide-ranging amendment by Dole and Daschle, adopted June 9 by a vote of 77–8. Dole's contribution was a grab bag of deregulatory benefits for broadcasting, cable and telephone companies, while Daschle's proposed to scale back some of the telephone and cable deregulation called for by the bill.

The main elements of the Dole-Daschle amendment proposed to remove all ownership limits on radio stations, with the FCC retaining the power to prevent "undue concentration of control"; allow television networks to own an unlimited number of stations, provided that their signals reached no more than 35 percent of all households; lift most federal price controls on small cable franchises; relieve telephone companies of some accounting regulations; bar healthy telephone and cable companies in the same market from joining forces, except in rural areas with fewer than 50,000 residents; and remove a loophole in the committee-approved version of the bill that could have allowed unlimited, steady rate increases by large cable companies.

The other major change came on June 13, when the Senate unexpectedly voted to require television programs to be rated for violence and other objectionable content.

Ironically, Dole set the stage for the amendment, which was sponsored by Democrats Joseph I. Lieberman of Connecticut and Kent Conrad of North Dakota. Although he had often said that he did not favor government intervention in programming, Dole recently had excoriated Time Warner and other entertainment companies for their sale of violent and lewd material.

Lieberman and Conrad took Dole's refrain further, saying that parents needed Congress's help to keep objectionable television programs away from their children. They offered a pair of amendments to require stations to broadcast ratings along with their programs. Also, the amendments called for new television sets to contain special circuitry, called a "V-chip," that could be programmed to block out programs carrying certain ratings. The senators' amendment gave the television and cable companies one year to come up with their own rating system. If the industry did not produce, the amendment called for a five-member panel appointed by the president to establish a ratings system.

Supporters of the chip said there was an apparent disconnection between market forces, which seemed to favor graphic and violent programs, and family values. They also cited studies showing the damaging effect that televised violence seemed to be having on youth.

The networks and the National Association of Broadcasters opposed the proposal, arguing that ratings were too subjective to be effective. They also said the system would have a disproportionate effect on broadcasters by reducing advertising revenue, which mattered far more to broadcasters than to other video services.

The Senate defeated Pressler's attempt to kill the Conrad-Lieberman package, voting 26–73 against the tabling motion, and adopted the package by voice vote.

Senators offered a flurry of amendments aimed at aiding particular elements of the industry or consumers. The bill's managers, however, managed to defeat the ones that threatened to tip the regulatory scales or disturb the Pressler-Hollings compromise.

For example, McCain began the debate on June 8 by proposing to eliminate the FCC's discretion over the Bells' entry into long distance and manufacturing. His amendment would have forced the FCC to let the Bells into new markets as soon as they met the bill's specific requirements for sharing their networks with competitors, rather than allowing the FCC to determine whether the move would be in the public's interest. Pressler's tabling motion killed the amendment, 68–31.

The administration and its allies were similarly frustrated in their efforts to beef up the Justice Department's power over the Bells, keep the existing cable price controls in place and set lower limits on broadcast-station ownership.

For instance, Byron L. Dorgan, D-N.D., and Strom Thurmond, R-S.C., offered an amendment to let the Justice Department block a Bell's move into long distance if it would "substantially lessen competition or . . . create a monopoly in any line of commerce in any section of the country." The amendment was killed, 57–43, on a tabling motion by Pressler June 13.

On cable rates, Lieberman proposed to retain much of the price regulation that Congress had imposed in the 1992 Cable Act (PL 102-385). Opponents argued that the amendment would make it harder for cable companies to compete with the Bells and that the bill would drive down the price of video programming by spurring competition. The amendment was killed June 15 on a tabling motion by Pressler, 67–31.

On Exon's decency provision, Patrick J. Leahy, D-Vt., proposed a Justice Department study of existing laws and technological solutions in lieu of new criminal penalties. Instead, however, the Senate voted 84–16 on June 14 in favor of a tougher version of the original Exon amendment. Sponsored by Exon and Daniel R. Coats, R-Ind., it removed a section that would have shielded the operators of computer networks and Internet access services from prosecution if they exercised no editorial control over the information available there.

Kerrey tried to add a number of provisions aimed at increasing competition and protecting consumers. The most significant of these would have required each Bell to face competition from more than one local phone company capable of serving a substantial number of business and residential customers before it could offer long distance. This requirement, which could have forced the Bells to lose more of their local business before offering long distance, was killed on a tabling motion June 14, 79–21.

The ability of Pressler and Hollings to keep their deal intact reflected not only their face-to-face work with their colleagues but also the behind-the-scenes efforts of key allies such as Lott and Daschle and the vigorous lobbying of industry leaders. The Commerce Committee's version included much of what the companies had argued was necessary to support competition, giving virtually every segment of the industry something to gain from the passage of S 652.

HOUSE COMMITTEE ACTION

Unlike their Senate counterparts, leaders of the House Commerce Committee tried a bipartisan approach from the outset. The resulting bill (HR 1555), which was unveiled May 3, 1995, had the backing of the committee's senior Democrat, John D. Dingell of Michigan, among other members of the minority.

To help move the bill through the committee, GOP leaders doled out legislative plums to broadcasters, phone companies and cable operators. They also kept Republicans united against efforts by liberal Democrats to roll back the bill's proposals to deregulate broadcast ownership and cable prices.

Still, Telecommunications and Finance Subcommittee Chairman Jack Fields, R-Texas, and Committee Chairman Thomas J. Bliley, Jr., R-Va., struggled to find a competitive balance in the bill. Under heavy lobbying pressure from the Bells, the long-distance companies and other opposing forces in the industry, they adjusted the bill's central provisions repeatedly after it was unveiled.

The committee ultimately approved the bill, 38–5, on May 25 after two days of debate and 36 amendments. The dissenters were led by the top Democrat on the Telecommunications and Finance Subcommittee, Edward J. Markey of Massachusetts, the coauthor of the House-passed measure in 1994 to let the phone and cable companies enter each other's markets. HR 1555 was reported on July 24 (H Rept 104-204, Part I).

With committee leaders focused on addressing the industry's concerns, administration officials and consumer advocates were left feeling frustrated and ignored on the sidelines. Complained Larry Irving, the administration's top telecommunications official: "It's an inside-the-Beltway game, a wise guy's game."

The bill had the same goals as the Senate proposal but differed on many key details. As approved by the committee, the bill would have kept each Bell out of the long-distance market until it faced a qualifying "facilities-based" competitor—that is, a competitor that had its own network separate from the Bell's wires. To qualify, the competitor had to offer residential and business service "comparable in price, features and scope" to the Bell's.

This condition was far more onerous to the Bells than the Senate proposal because it would have kept the Bells out of the long-distance market until they lost a significant share of their core local business. The main proponent was Bliley, whose district was home to hundreds of AT&T employees.

The bill also demanded that the Bells provide their services to competitors at prices low enough to make resale a viable business. This requirement also favored AT&T, which planned to enter the local-phone market as a reseller.

On cable TV rates, the bill proposed to lift price controls on all cable companies' equipment, installation and "expanded basic" programs after no more than 15 months. In the interim, it would raise substantially the number of complaints required to trigger an FCC review of "expanded basic" prices. As in the Senate proposal, the bill would have lifted price controls immediately on most services offered by small cable operators, although the exemption would have covered far more companies than the Senate had proposed.

The bill also went further than the Senate proposed in lifting limits on TV station ownership. Networks would have been allowed after one year to control stations reaching half of all U.S. households, and broadcasters would have been permitted to own two stations in a single market if the FCC did not object.

The measure would have eliminated the ban on television broadcasters owning the newspaper or cable system in their markets, too, although the FCC could block the acquisition of three or more local media outlets to prevent "an undue concentration of media voices."

In a nod to major electronic-equipment retailers, the bill would have required cable converter boxes and similar "set top" controls to be available through retail outlets. This provision, championed by Bliley and Markey, would have allowed consumers to escape the equipment-rental fees charged by cable and other subscription services by purchasing the necessary devices.

Finally, the bill included provisions similar to the Senate proposals for allowing more foreign investment in U.S. telephone companies, letting the Bells into new markets, eliminating unneeded FCC regulations, permitting radio networks to own an unlimited number of stations, making it easier for broadcasters to renew licenses and ending state regulation of telephone company profits.

House Judiciary Committee

Before the full Commerce Committee could act on HR 1555, the House Judiciary Committee overwhelmingly approved a measure (HR 1528) that would have required the Bells to obtain the Justice Department's permission before offering long distance, equipment manufacturing or alarm-monitoring services.

The committee's 29–1 vote on May 18 set up a clash with the Commerce Committee, whose leaders strongly opposed any Justice Department control over the Bells. Unlike its Senate counterpart, the House Commerce Committee proposed no role at all for the Justice Department in a Bell's application to enter new markets.

The two House committees parted company in determining what constituted the end of a Bell monopoly over local phone service and who should make that judgment. Instead of requiring a facilities-based competitor, the bill by Judiciary Committee Chairman Henry J. Hyde, R-Ill., would have allowed a Bell into a new market as soon as the Justice Department found no "dangerous probability" of the Bell using its local dominance to substantially impede competition in that market. And instead of having federal and state regulators judge a Bell's application, Hyde's bill would have given that job to the Justice Department's antitrust division.

Hyde wanted to graft his bill onto HR 1555, giving the Bells a choice of routes into the long-distance market. The idea generated little enthusiasm in the industry, however, and Hyde was forced to abandon much of his legislation. The compromise he struck with Bliley called only for the FCC to consult with the Justice Department before deciding whether to grant a Bell's application to offer long-distance service.

The Judiciary Committee reported HR 1528 on July 24 (H Rept 104-203, Part I), and it moved no further.

COURTING GINGRICH

Hoping to outflank Bliley before HR 1555 reached the House floor, the Bells stepped up their lobbying of committee members and the House GOP leadership. In the latter arena, they had three key allies: Dennis Hastert of Illinois, the chief deputy whip; Bill Paxon of New York, the chairman of the National Republican Congressional Committee; and Speaker Newt Gingrich, whose district in Georgia was home to many employees of BellSouth, the Atlanta-based Bell. The leadership took up the Bells' cause, instructing Bliley and Fields to make the bill as deregulatory as possible and to justify any new regulations proposed.

After more than a month of behind-the-scenes negotiations, Bliley agreed to make changes easing the Bells' entry into the long-distance market and reducing their competitors' leverage. The changes included dropping the requirement that a Bell face competition "comparable in price, features and scope" from a company using an entirely separate network before offering long-distance service; speeding up the FCC's regulations on interconnection to hasten the Bells' entry into long distance; and requiring local phone companies to provide their services to competitors at a standard wholesale discount, not at a discount deep enough to make resale "economically feasible."

The long-distance companies denounced the changes, saying they would let a Bell offer long distance while preserving much of its monopoly over local phone service.

The Bells' allies were only one of many groups that Bliley sought to mollify before taking HR 1555 to the floor. Other disputes raged over efforts to limit Internet indecency and television violence, expand the broadcast networks' holdings and deregulate cable rates.

The negotiations over these issues and the busy House floor schedule held up the bill for two months. Bliley circulated a 66-page "manager's amendment" in late July, proposing more than 40 changes to the committee-approved bill.

On Aug. 1, 1995, as the Rules Committee was considering Bliley's request to restrict debate on the bill, President Clinton blasted the measure and pledged to veto it unless fundamental changes were made. In particular, Clinton said the bill went too far in easing the limits on broadcast ownership; permitting the Bells to offer long distance service before competition took hold in local markets; not giving the Justice Department veto power over a Bell's entry into new markets; allowing telephone companies and cable operators to team up rather than compete; lifting price controls on cable service before consumers were protected by competition; and preempting too much state regulation of phone companies. He also criticized sponsors for not having a version of the Senate's V-chip proposal.

HOUSE FLOOR ACTION

Unfazed by a threatened veto, the House hurriedly passed an amended version of HR 1555 on Aug. 4. The **key vote of 305–117 (R 208–18; D 97–98; I 0–1)** represented a partial defeat for the administration and a total rejection of the long-distance companies' position. *(1995 key votes, p. 1025)*

Although the debate reflected the differences in the two parties' political philosophies and desire to deregulate, it did not divide neatly along party lines. Constituent concerns played a major role, resulting in numerous Democrats siding with the Bells and some Republicans aligning with long-distance companies.

The House Republican leadership sent the bill to the floor Aug. 2 under a rule that allowed only eight amendments, with 10 to 30 minutes of debate on each. The debate was accelerated because the bill's sponsors and the House leadership badly wanted to get the bill passed before House members began their five-week summer recess. That way, members would not have been subject to intense industry lobbying during the break.

The leadership also planned to conduct the entire debate over the telecommunications bill in the dead of night Aug. 2 and Aug. 4. However, Democrats used a combination of delaying tactics and threats to move the bulk of the debate to the morning of Aug. 4, well after the sun rose.

After winning approval for the manager's amendment, 256–149, Bliley and Fields successfully held off several administration-backed amendments. A John Conyers, Jr., D-Mich., amendment to give the Justice Department veto power over a Bell's move into new markets was rejected, 151–271. An amendment, offered by Markey and Christopher Shays, R-Conn., to leave price controls on cable TV in place until competition arrived was rejected, 148–275.

The administration won two other battles, though, with the help of Markey and a shifting coalition of members from both parties.

Markey challenged the bill's provisions on broadcast ownership, arguing that they would allow single companies to control much of the media in a community. By a vote of 228–195, the House adopted Markey's amendment to bar broadcasters from joining forces with the local cable system and limit network-owned stations' reach to 35 percent of the viewers—up from 25 percent under existing rules. The amendment not only addressed an administration concern, but it also tapped into a long-standing power struggle between TV networks and the affiliates they did not own. The affiliates contended that raising the audience cap to 50 percent, as the bill had proposed to do, would let the networks bully their affiliates, shifting control over programming from local communities to network headquarters in New York or Los Angeles.

Markey, who was one of the first lawmakers to advocate the V-chip, then teamed with conservative Republican Dan Burton of Indiana to add a milder variation of the Senate's V-chip proposal to the House bill. The four main TV networks tried to head off the V-chip by announcing Aug. 1 that they had created a $2 million fund to develop blocking technology for parents. They also backed an alternative amendment offered by Tom Coburn, R-Okla., that would have encouraged the television and video industries to develop blocking technology.

With the GOP leadership strongly opposing the V-chip, the House voted, 222–201, to substitute the Coburn proposal for the Markey-Burton amendment. Markey then used a procedural tactic to force a vote on the V-chip proposal, and he prevailed, 224–199.

On another issue affecting the content of communications networks, the House voted, 420–4, in favor of a proposal by Christopher Cox, R-Calif., and Ron Wyden, D-Ore., to combat indecency on the Internet through technology. Billed as a better approach than the Exon language, the amendment proposed to remove some of the legal impediments to computer networks using technology to filter out material they considered objectionable. The provision already had been adopted as part of the Bliley amendment, but Cox and Wyden wanted to buttress their case against Exon before going into conference with the Senate. Still, the vote was misleading because the Cox-Wyden proposal did not supplant the Exon-like language in the House bill. The Bliley amendment had also included a proposal by Hyde to create criminal penalties for transmitting indecent material across state lines to minors via the Internet or other computer network.

The House took up S 652 on Oct. 12, agreeing by voice vote to insert the text of HR 1555 and to pass the amended version of the bill. The House also appointed conferees; the Senate followed suit the next day.

CONFERENCE, FINAL ACTION

In conference—an intense, staff-driven exercise that stretched from early October to Christmas—the Republicans' deregulatory initiatives were again tempered. Democrats used the threat of a Senate filibuster or a veto to force the conferees to address their major concerns and those voiced by the Clinton administration.

The GOP negotiators made concessions on numerous fronts. The Bells were required to meet the most demanding conditions from both bills before offering long-distance service in their regions or manufacturing equipment. Most of the existing barriers to a company owning multiple media outlets in a market were left in place. Price controls were not eliminated for large and midsized cable systems until April 1999 or until the local phone companies started offering a comparable video service in their market, whichever came first. And a version of the V-chip proposal was retained, despite strong opposition from the TV broadcasters.

Even the proposal to allow greater foreign ownership of U.S. telephone companies, which the two chambers had adopted in varying forms, was dropped when Hollings could not reach agreement with House negotiators. So, too, were provisions in both bills to end state regulation of telephone company profits.

One issue that dragged out the conference was Internet decency, which conferees ultimately settled by including virtually every element of the competing proposals. The conferees adopted Exon's proposal to make it a crime to use an interactive computer service knowingly to send indecent material to minors or display it in a way that minors could view it. They also included Hyde's proposal to clarify that the federal laws against trafficking in obscene material applied to computer networks. And they added the Cox-Wyden proposal to allow network operators to filter out or block potential offensive items without becoming legally responsible for all the material posted on their systems.

The four top Republican and Democratic conferees reached a tentative agreement on Dec. 20. Their draft report was immediately embraced by Vice President Al Gore, but several influential House Republicans and Dole stopped the report from moving forward.

The dissident House Republicans groused that the Democrats had too much input into the final House-Senate compromise. The conference report was not "Republican" enough, they said; it was too much like the legislation that Democrats had championed in 1994. For example, Fields held out for changes that would ease the ownership limits on TV broadcasters. And Rep. Michael G. Oxley, R-Ohio, pressed the conferees to restore his proposal allowing greater foreign investment in U.S. telecommunications companies.

Dole also wanted a few more deregulatory elements in the bill. His main goal, though, was to bar the FCC from handing out valuable frequencies in the broadcast spectrum to television stations for advanced, digital broadcasting. To Dole, the FCC's plan to award 6 megahertz of additional spectrum to each station was corporate welfare on a grand scale. His proposal to auction the spectrum was fiercely resisted by the broadcasters, however, who wielded great power in Congress.

Late in January 1996, while Dole was out of Washington campaigning for the GOP presidential nomination, top House and Senate Republicans agreed to let the conference report go to the floor without major changes. A key figure in the negotiations was Lott, who had played the role of telecommunications middleman between conservative Republicans and Democrats throughout the process.

Dole, who had sent Lott in his place, did not come away empty handed. In a letter to Dole, FCC Chairman Reed Hundt pledged that no frequencies would be awarded for advanced television service before 1997, giving Dole plenty of time to push for auctions through separate legislation. Dole left the Senate in June without succeeding on that front, however.

The revised conference report (H Rept 104-458) then raced through both chambers on Feb. 1, 1996. The House adopted it after a perfunctory debate on a **key vote of 414–16 (R 236–0; D 178–15; I 0–1),** and the Senate quickly followed suit on a **key vote of 91–5 (R 51–1; D 40–4).** President Clinton signed the bill Feb. 8. *(1996 key votes, p. 1047)*

MAJOR PROVISIONS

As signed into law, the main elements of S 652:
• **Local Telephone Service.** Preempted state and local laws that prohibited local phone competition. The local phone monopolies were ordered to allow competitors to interconnect with and lease portions of their networks at a reasonable price.

They also were required to make their services available to resellers at a wholesale price. Consumers who switched to a competing local phone company had to be able to keep their phone number, if technically feasible ("number portability"), and to make calls without dialing extra digits ("dialing parity").

Electric, gas, water and steam utilities were allowed to offer local phone service and other telecommunications services, subject to regulation by the FCC and state public service commissions.

• **FCC Interconnection Standards.** Gave the FCC until Aug. 8, 1996, to set standards for the interconnection services and prices that local phone companies had to offer their competitors. The FCC issued those standards one week ahead of schedule, but they were quickly blocked by the federal courts in response to a lawsuit by several local phone companies. The FCC appealed the ruling to the Eighth Circuit Court of Appeals, where the case remained at the end of 1996.

• **Universal Service.** Gave the FCC, advised by a joint board of state and federal regulators, until May 8, 1997, to adopt rules for making affordable local phone service available to all, a policy known as universal service. All competing telecommunications companies in a market were required to contribute to the cost of universal service.

The FCC was ordered to determine which services should be made available to all, a list that had to be updated periodically as technology changed. Schools, libraries and rural health care facilities were made eligible for discounts on more advanced services.

Universal service subsidies were limited to companies that made their service available to every customer in their markets, starting when the FCC's regulations took effect. In areas where no company was willing to provide universal service, the law ordered that service be provided by whatever carriers were best qualified.

• **Exemptions for Rural and Small Phone Companies.** Waived the interconnection requirements for rural telephone companies unless state regulators found that a competitor's proposal for interconnection or resale was technically feasible, was not economically burdensome and would not reduce the availability of phone service.

In lieu of waiving the interconnection requirements, states were allowed to require would-be competitors in rural areas to agree to make their service available to all customers in that area.

• **Public Rights of Way.** Did not affect the authority of state and local governments to manage public rights of way. State and local governments also were allowed to continue imposing fees for using the rights of way, provided that the fees did not favor or discriminate against individual companies. The fees had to be made public.

• **Long-Distance Telephone Service.** Allowed each regional Bell to offer long-distance service immediately to customers outside its region. A Bell could do so inside its region only after opening its network to competition and, if a competitor emerged, implementing a network-sharing agreement that met minimum federal standards. The minimum standards were laid out in a 14-point checklist, covering such items as the prices charged for interconnection and the services provided.

The FCC could not give a Bell permission to offer long-distance service in its region unless it found, after consulting with the Justice Department, that the service was in the public interest. For the first three years after winning the FCC's approval, the Bell was required to use a separate affiliate to sell its long-distance service.

- **Simultaneous Competition in Telephone Service.** Barred the largest long-distance companies from selling a package of local and long-distance services that used a Bell's local wires. The ban was to be lifted in three years or when the Bell had gained entry to the long-distance market, whichever came first.

States also were barred from requiring a Bell to provide dialing parity for short-distance toll calls, one of the most lucrative portions of the Bells' markets, for three years or until that Bell had gained entry into the long-distance market. In a concession to state officials and long-distance companies, however, the bill exempted sparsely populated states and states that had already ordered dialing parity—roughly 22 states in all.

- **Long-Distance Prices in Rural Areas.** Barred long-distance companies from charging higher rates in rural and high-cost areas than in urban areas. The law also barred them from charging customers in one state higher rates than the customers in other states paid.

- **Unauthorized Changes in Phone Companies.** Prohibited telecommunications carriers from switching a phone line from one company's service to another unless the change was verified by the customer in accordance with FCC rules. The provision was aimed at "slamming," an unscrupulous practice used by some long-distance companies to take over service on lines without a customer's knowledge.

- **Bell Entry into Other Markets.** Allowed the Bells to manufacture telephone equipment once they had been cleared to offer long-distance service. The manufacturing had to be done through a separate affiliate for three years. They were permitted to engage in electronic publishing and other information services immediately, although a separate affiliate was required until Feb. 8, 2000. The Bells were not allowed to provide alarm-monitoring services until Feb. 8, 2001. The ban did not apply to Ameritech, the Bell based in Chicago, which had already established an alarm-monitoring business.

- **Cable Television.** For midsized and large cable systems, lifted price controls on cable television services beyond the basic package of local and educational channels after March 31, 1999. Cable systems with less than 50,000 subscribers had their price controls lifted immediately, and larger systems would have all price controls removed as soon as a telephone company began offering a comparable video service.

- **Spreading the Cost of New Equipment.** Allowed cable companies, when charging customers for services beyond the basic tier, to include a portion of the cost of all customers' equipment. This provision authorized what amounted to an internal cross-subsidy for new equipment that was being introduced one neighborhood at a time, such as the expensive set-top boxes required for digital transmissions.

- **Video Programming by Telephone Companies.** Repealed the ban on telephone companies offering video services. Federal courts across the country had already found the ban unconstitutional, but their rulings had been stayed pending Supreme Court review. The legislation allowed companies to choose the degree of regulation, depending on the degree of control they exerted over programming on their systems. A new and less regulated category, "open video systems," was created for companies that made at least two-thirds of their channels available to unaffiliated programmers.

Local phone and cable companies were barred from merging unless the cable system served a rural community with less than 35,000 residents.

- **Retail Sale of Set-Top Boxes.** Ordered the FCC to give consumers the chance to buy set-top boxes for their cable TV and other multichannel video services at outlets not tied to the company providing the video service. The FCC had to waive its rules temporarily if needed to help new or improved subscription services or technology.

- **Broadcast Licenses, Ownership.** Extended licenses for television and radio stations to eight years. The law also made it far easier for broadcasters to renew their licenses, barring the FCC from considering competing applications unless it found that a broadcaster had not served the public interest or had seriously violated the law and/or FCC regulations.

Radio broadcasters were permitted to own an unlimited number of stations nationwide, as long as they did not violate a new set of limits on the number of stations owned locally. Television broadcasters also could own an unlimited number of stations, provided that their signals did not reach more than 35 percent of the nation's households. The law ordered the FCC to reconsider its limits on the ownership of multiple local television stations, but it did not eliminate any of the FCC's restrictions. It did, however, remove the statutory prohibition on a cable operator owning a television station in the same market, and vice versa.

- **Internet Indecency.** Banned the transmission of obscene material over any form of telecommunications, including computer networks. It also ordered that indecent material not be made available to minors. Interactive computer services were required to make a good faith effort to prevent any indecent material on their networks from being obtained by minors. An exemption was provided for companies that merely provided access to the Internet without supplying any content.

In June 1996, a federal appeals court ruled that the restriction on indecency was unconstitutional. The decision was appealed to the Supreme Court, with a ruling expected sometime in 1997.

- **Scrambling Video Programs.** Required cable, wireless cable and other multichannel video services to scramble or block their adult channels so that nonsubscribers did not receive either the video or audio portion. Until a video service complied with this requirement, it was permitted to broadcast indecent programs only during the hours that they were not likely to be seen by a significant number of children, as determined by the FCC. This provision was to take effect March 9, 1996.

Cable companies also were ordered to scramble, without charge, the audio and video portions of a channel for any subscriber who requested the scrambling.

• **Refusal to Carry.** Allowed cable operators to drop any program on a channel reserved for public access, schools, local government or unaffiliated programmers if the program contained obscenity, indecency or nudity. Previous law did not allow cable companies to refuse any programs on those channels.

• **Television Violence.** Required, starting on a date to be determined by the FCC and the electronics industry, television sets built in the United States or transported across state lines to include circuitry (the "V-chip") capable of screening out programs according to their rating. The law did not require broadcasters to rate programs, but it did require them to transmit any ratings that had been assigned voluntarily.

Cable and broadcasting companies were given until Feb. 8, 1997, to develop their own system for rating programs. If the industry did not comply, the FCC was to establish ratings guidelines with the help of a panel of parents and industry representatives.

• **Licenses for Advanced Services.** Instructed the FCC, if it decided to issue licenses for advanced TV service, to limit the initial eligibility to existing TV stations. Advanced TV was defined as digital broadcasts, in contrast with the existing analog transmissions.

As a condition for receiving a license for advanced TV frequencies, stations had to agree to give back these frequencies at some unspecified date or surrender the ones they already had. The intent was to give stations a limited time to broadcast in both formats while digital sets gradually replaced analog ones in homes.

Broadcasters were permitted to use any advanced TV frequencies they received for other, unrelated services that were consistent with the public interest and compatible with digital TV transmissions. If they charged for those services, however, they were required to pay the FCC a special fee.

• **Regulatory Relief.** Ordered the FCC not to enforce a law or regulation if it was no longer needed to protect consumers or competitors. Every two years the commission had to identify and eliminate regulations that competition had rendered unnecessary, starting in 1998. Companies also were allowed to petition the FCC to stop enforcing regulations that were no longer needed to protect the public.

• **Privacy.** Required all phone companies to use the information they collected from customers only to provide the services requested by those customers.

• **Toll-Free Scams.** Barred companies with toll-free lines from transferring callers to pay-per-minute lines. The law also made it harder for information services to charge callers for services provided over toll-free lines.

• **Access by the Disabled.** Required manufacturers of telecommunications equipment and providers of telecommunications service to make their products accessible to the disabled if readily achievable. If not, they had to make their equipment or services compatible with existing devices used by the disabled, if readily achievable.

Companies providing video programs were required to add closed captions for the deaf, provided that it did not pose an undue burden.

• **Antenna Siting.** Prohibited state and local governments, when considering applications for telecommunications antennas, from blocking a wireless service, imposing unreasonable delays and discriminating unreasonably between competitors. In all other respects, local governments retained their traditional zoning authority over antenna towers and wireless communications facilities.

• **Funding for Telecommunications Ventures.** Created a quasi-governmental Telecommunications Development Fund to help finance the telecommunications ventures of small businesses. It also authorized federal agencies to give money to the National Education Technology Funding Corporation, a nongovernmental organization designed to promote advanced communications facilities in schools and libraries. ❑

Wiretap Fund

Under pressure from the administration, Congress agreed in 1996 to provide $60 million to help telephone companies make their networks more accommodating to police wiretaps. The money was included in HR 3610 (PL 104-208), the omnibus appropriations bill for fiscal 1997.

Congress had ordered the phone companies in 1994 to adapt their networks and services to ensure the success of court-ordered wiretaps within four years. The measure (PL 103-414), a top priority for FBI Director Louis J. Freeh, required the federal government to pay the first $500 million of the cost to upgrade existing equipment and services. *(1994 action, p. 354)*

Having lost their fight to stop the 1994 bill, privacy advocates shifted their efforts in 1995 to stopping the $500 million. They were aided by conservative House Republicans, who distrusted federal law enforcement agencies and opposed any expansion of wiretapping powers.

The administration first proposed to raise the $500 million through a temporary 40 percent surcharge on fines levied by federal agencies. In October 1995, the proposal was included in HR 2517, an intermediate draft of the House GOP's deficit-reducing budget reconciliation bill. But opponents of the provision, led by Republican freshman Richard M. Burr of North Carolina, persuaded the House GOP leadership to abandon the surcharge just before the reconciliation bill reached the House floor on Oct. 26.

The House Judiciary Committee had included a similar surcharge in an antiterrorism bill that it approved June 20, 1995, and reported Dec. 5 (HR 1710—H Rept 104-383). Opposition from conservative Republicans scuttled the bill, however, and the surcharge was not included in a compromise version that emerged in December (HR 2703).

The administration then asked appropriators to provide $100 million for a Telecommunications Carrier Compliance Fund in the fiscal 1997 spending bill for the Departments of Commerce, Justice and State (HR 3814). The fund was to pay for upgrades to the local phone networks.

The House and Senate Appropriations Subcommittees on Commerce, Justice and State both balked at the administration's request. Although they endorsed the idea of a fund, they proposed that it be financed through transfers from the budgets of federal law enforcement and intelligence agencies. An early version of HR 3814 was reported by the House Appropriations Committee on July 16, 1996 (H Rept 104-676) and passed by the House on July 24, 246–179. The Senate Appropriations Committee reported its version on Aug. 27 (S Rept 104-353).

The appropriators argued that the administration's request was premature because the telecommunications industry and the FBI remained deeply split over the changes needed to assure the success of wiretaps. For example, while the FBI predicted that its needs could be met for less than $500 million, the industry said that the FBI's demands for wiretapping capacity and capability would cost as much as $1.8 billion.

After HR 3814 stalled in the Senate, its provisions were folded into the omnibus bill (HR 3610) in September 1996. Conferees on the omnibus bill agreed not only to create the fund as had been proposed in the earlier versions of the bill but also to provide $60 million in start-up dollars for the fund. That money was to help the industry develop the technology necessary to meet the requirements of law enforcement.

The conference report on HR 3610 also required the Justice Department to submit an implementation plan to the appropriators and the congressional Judiciary committees before spending any of the money in the fund. The plan had to lay out the needs of law enforcement, including the maximum number of simultaneous wiretaps or traces expected in each county, and the estimated cost of the modifications to telephone company facilities and services. ❑

Spectrum Auctions

Looking for ways to balance the budget by fiscal 2002, Republican lawmakers toyed with the idea of auctioning off a large chunk of the radio spectrum and even considered selling some of the frequencies reserved for TV broadcasters.

By the end of the 1996 session, however, only one small band of frequencies was ordered up for sale. And the purpose of the sale was not to reduce the deficit but to allow more spending on social programs.

Spectrum auctions were a recent and lucrative innovation by Congress, launched in 1993 as part of the Democrats' deficit-reducing budget reconciliation law (PL 103-66). Before that, the Federal Communications Commission (FCC) had dispensed licenses for free to companies chosen by lottery or through hearings. (1993 action, p. 355)

In 1995, the Republicans' budget reconciliation bill (HR 2491) called for the government to raise $15.3 billion over seven years by auctioning 120 megahertz of the spectrum. The bill specified that 20 megahertz be auctioned from frequencies reserved for government use, with the remaining 100 megahertz coming from unspecified frequencies outside the bands reserved for TV broadcasters.

The House Commerce Committee on Sept. 13, 1995, had proposed the auctions, as part of its budget reconciliation recommendations. Senate Commerce, Science and Transportation Committee Chairman Larry Pressler, R-S.D., floated an alternative proposal to auction the frequencies reserved for digital TV broadcasts, but the idea was quickly shot down by allies of the powerful National Association of Broadcasters. The Senate Commerce Committee instead endorsed an auctions plan on Sept. 28, 10–9, that was nearly identical to the House proposal.

The auctions sank when President Clinton vetoed HR 2491 on Dec. 6, 1995. The following June, the Republican-penned budget resolution for fiscal 1997 (H Con Res 178) again called for $15.3 billion in revenue from spectrum auctions. No effort was made to implement that recommendation, however.

Senate Majority Leader Bob Dole, R-Kan., made three runs at the spectrum issue in 1996 but was stymied each time.

After House and Senate conferees reached tentative agreement on a major telecommunications bill (S 652) late in December 1995, Dole complained that its provisions on advanced TV frequencies amounted to a multibillion-dollar giveaway to the broadcasters. Those provisions called for current TV stations to have the first crack at any licenses that the FCC issued for advanced TV, a digital form of broadcasting.

After putting a temporary hold on the conference report, Dole relented when FCC Chairman Reed Hundt pledged that the FCC would not award any licenses for advanced TV broadcasts before 1997. The conference report breezed through both chambers on Feb. 1, and the measure was signed into law Feb. 8 (PL 104-104). (Telecommunications overhaul, p. 387)

Later that month, Dole circulated a proposal to auction the frequencies that the FCC had reserved for advanced TV as well as the 120 megahertz targeted by the 1995 budget reconciliation bill. His proposal, which was to be offered to a bill raising the debt limit, never came up for a vote, however.

Dole made a less ambitious auction proposal in May, calling for 25 megahertz of the nontelevision portion of the spectrum to be auctioned to offset the cost of a temporary reduction in the federal gasoline tax. The gas tax proposal stalled in a partisan fight over the minimum wage, and the legislation was dropped after Dole left the Senate in June.

Senate Democrats resuscitated the auction proposal as a way to pay for $3.1 billion in additional spending on education and training programs. The frequencies at issue had been reserved for Digital Audio Radio Satellite service, or DARS, an advanced form of radio that relied on satellite transmissions.

Their idea was adopted by conferees on the fiscal 1997 omnibus appropriations bill (HR 3610—PL 104-208), which provided funds for the Department of Education and eight other federal departments. The estimated revenue from the auction of the two 15-megahertz bands of frequencies was $2.9 billion. ❑

Public Broadcasting

Once seemingly destined for financial exile, the Corporation for Public Broadcasting (CPB) emerged from the 104th Congress with reduced but steady funding.

Numerous GOP conservatives had hoped to cut off federal funding for the CPB, which Congress created in 1967 (PL 90-129) to support public radio and TV stations. The corporation collected $285 million from the federal taxpayers in fiscal 1995, or 14 percent of its $2 billion budget. *(1967 law, Congress and the Nation Vol. II, p. 297)*

Critics of the corporation said that its programming was elitist and biased in favor of liberal causes. If the public really wanted such programs, the market would support them without the need for subsidies, they said.

Defenders countered that the federal support was critical to maintaining the noncommercial nature of public broadcasting. They also argued that small broadcasting stations, which relied more heavily on federal aid than large stations, would be hard pressed to survive a funding cut.

Still, the GOP-controlled Appropriations committees moved early in 1995 to trim the corporation's budget, which Congress funded three years in advance. The House proposed to cancel a total of $141 million from the CPB's grants for fiscal 1996 and 1997 as part of a massive rescissions bill (HR 1158—H Rept 104-70) passed on March 16.

The Senate called for a far smaller reduction, and the two sides ultimately agreed to rescind a total of $92 million in the final version of the legislation (HR 1944—PL 104-19). The rescission canceled the increases that the CPB had been slated to receive, lowering its funding instead to $275 million in fiscal 1996 and $260 million in fiscal 1997.

In August 1995, during consideration of a fiscal 1996 Labor, Health and Human Services and Education appropriations bill (HR 2127), freshman Rep. Peter Hoekstra, R-Mich., proposed to eliminate all the corporation's funding in fiscal 1998. Backed by the GOP leadership, Hoekstra argued that the corporation should not receive that money until it was reauthorized. The last CPB bill enacted by Congress (PL 102-356) authorized the corporation only through the end of fiscal 1996. Democrats flailed Hoekstra's proposal as an attack on such popular programs as *Sesame Street*. And on Aug. 3, the amendment was trounced, 136–286, with 96 Republicans joining 189 Democrats and one Independent in opposition. *(1992 law, Congress and the Nation Vol. VIII, p. 457)*

The appropriators ultimately provided $250 million for the corporation in fiscal 1998, despite the lack of authorization, as part of an omnibus spending bill for fiscal 1996 (HR 3019—PL 104-134). They provided the same amount for fiscal 1999 as part of an omnibus spending bill for fiscal 1997 (HR 3610—PL 104-208).

Neither the House nor Senate Commerce committees acted on a reauthorization bill for the CPB in 1996. Senate Commerce, Science and Transportation Committee Chairman Larry Pressler, R-S.D., tried to drum up support in 1995 for privatizing the CPB, but the idea never caught on. Instead, it raised hackles in some rural areas of his home state that were underserved by commercial radio and TV broadcasters.

Rep. Jack Fields, a Texas Republican who led the House Commerce Subcommittee on Telecommunications and Finance, introduced a reauthorization bill (HR 2979) that would

have established a $1 billion trust fund for public broadcasting in lieu of annual subsidies. It also would have lifted a number of prohibitions on public broadcasters to help them raise more money from corporate sources. Although the CPB had embraced the idea of a trust fund, critics of Fields's proposal said it would not have provided enough money. They added that the public did not want the kind of commercialization that his bill would have promoted.   ❏

TV Violence

The Senate Commerce, Science and Transportation Committee endorsed bills in 1995 to restrict the broadcast of violent television shows and to measure the violent content of network programming, but the legislation never reached the floor.

The bills reflected the complaints about violence on television that lawmakers had been making since the early 1950s. Their power to restrict the airwaves, however, was limited by the First Amendment's guarantee of free speech.

Both measures were approved by wide margins in the committee on Aug. 10, 1995. A third initiative against TV violence—the "V-chip"—had already been included in the House and Senate bills to overhaul telecommunications law but had not yet been signed into law. *(Telecommunications overhaul, p. 387)*

The first bill (S 470—S Rept 104-171), reported Nov. 9, 1995, would have authorized the Federal Communications Commission (FCC) to bar violent TV programs during the hours that children were likely to be watching. The definition of what constituted violence would have been left to the FCC.

Although the FCC's time restrictions on indecent broadcasts had been upheld by the Supreme Court, the American Civil Liberties Union (ACLU) argued that similar restrictions on violent broadcasts would not pass constitutional muster. If the FCC defined what constituted violence not fit for the eyes of children, it would end up censoring far more than what many people would consider dangerous material, said Dan Katz, a fellow at the ACLU.

The second bill (S 772—S Rept 104-234), reported Feb. 9, 1996, would have commissioned a private, nonprofit group to issue quarterly reports on the violent content of television programs.

Neither measure was brought up for a vote in the Senate. Instead, a modified version of the V-chip proposal was included in the final version of the telecommunications bill (S 652—PL 104-104), which President Clinton signed into law Feb. 8, 1996. That legislation called for a rating system to be developed for television and cable programs and for broadcasters to transmit any ratings that had been assigned to shows, although there was no requirement that programs be rated. It also required that TV manufacturers include "V-chip" circuitry in new sets so that viewers could screen out programs with ratings they did not consider suitable.

A HISTORY OF EFFORTS

An increase in delinquency and crime by youths in the 1950s prompted Congress to hold its first hearings on the influence that violent radio and television broadcasts exerted on children. Lawmakers were not the only ones who suspected such a link; over the years, as many as 3,000 studies were conducted on the issue.

One of the most controversial, a 1972 report by the U.S. surgeon general, concluded that there is a causal relationship between TV violence and acts of violence, but only in children presupposed to be aggressive. Other, more recent studies found broader links between TV and actual violence.

Still, Congress did not legislate on the issue until 1990. That year, Congress granted industry executives a three-year exemption from antitrust laws so they could discuss ways to reduce violence on television. The exemption was included in a bill to create more federal judgeships (PL 101-650). *(Congress and the Nation Vol. VIII, p. 428)*

The legislation did not bear fruit until late in 1992, shortly before the House was scheduled to hold more hearings on TV violence. On Dec. 11, the three major networks released a joint policy on violence and agreed to hold an industrywide conference. Six months later the four main TV networks—ABC, NBC, CBS and Fox—announced that they would air parental advisories before broadcasting programs that they deemed violent. The following month, 15 major cable networks announced that they would join in the policy.

The networks' gesture did not deter lawmakers in both chambers from continuing to press for restrictions on violent programming. On Feb. 1, 1994, the networks made a further concession, agreeing to commission an independent, annual study of program content. Cable programmers had already made a similar announcement. ❏

FCC Reorganization

Efforts to overhaul the Federal Communications Commission (FCC) fell short in the 104th Congress, as one faction of lawmakers sought to phase out the commission and another called for its expansion.

An independent agency created by Congress in 1934, the FCC oversaw broadcasting, cable TV, satellite communications, and wireless and long-distance telephone services. Among other activities, it managed the use of the radio spectrum to guard against interference, auctioned frequencies for mobile phone service, and regulated the price of cable television subscriptions.

In 1995, deregulatory-minded Republicans in the House leadership and on the House and Senate Commerce committees called for a sharp reduction in the FCC's duties. Pointing to the computer industry as a model for the benefits of deregulation,

they argued that the FCC's rules and standards did more harm to the public than good.

Democrats and the Clinton administration, in turn, argued that the FCC needed more resources to meet the demands of a new, competition-promoting telecommunications bill (S 652—PL 104-104) that was moving through Congress. Designed to reduce regulation in the long run, the legislation called for a host of new rulemakings to guide the transition from regulation to competition. *(Telecommunications overhaul, p. 387)*

The chairman of the House Commerce Subcommittee on Telecommunications and Finance, Republican Jack Fields of Texas, convinced his colleagues to hold their fire on the FCC until work was finished on the telecommunications bill. In the meantime, Fields proposed to authorize $186 million for the FCC in fiscal 1996, roughly the same amount as the commission received in fiscal 1995.

That proposal passed the House as part of HR 2491, the fiscal 1996 budget reconciliation bill, but it was dropped by the Senate. The appropriators ultimately provided just under $186 million for the FCC in an omnibus spending bill for fiscal 1996 (HR 3019—PL 104-134). Of that amount, $126 million was to come from fees on companies regulated by the FCC.

The major overhaul contemplated by Fields never emerged. Instead, in August 1996 Fields introduced a modest bill (HR 3957) to eliminate several outdated FCC duties and have the commission draw up a plan for its own streamlining. The goal of the bill, Fields said, was to clear out "regulatory underbrush" and prepare for the competitive communications marketplace of the near future.

At the subcommittee markup on Sept. 12, however, Fields's Republican colleagues had more far-reaching designs. Over the objections of many Democrats on the panel, they resurrected two proposals that had been dropped from the telecommunications overhaul bill in conference. One amendment would have allowed companies with foreign officers or major foreign investors to own U.S. telephone and broadcasting companies unless the FCC ruled it was not in the public interest. Another proposal would have declared that the FCC had no jurisdiction or authority over the Internet or other interactive computer services. The subcommittee approved the bill by voice vote, but it advanced no further.

The appropriators continued to hold the FCC's funding roughly level in fiscal 1997, providing more than $189 million in a year-end omnibus spending bill (HR 3610—PL 104-208). To reduce the cost to taxpayers, however, the appropriators called for the FCC to raise almost $153 million through fees on the industry, $26 million more than in fiscal 1996. ❏

CHAPTER 7

Environment and Energy

Environment and Energy

The Democratic-controlled 103rd Congress could claim only one significant accomplishment in the area of environment and energy—passage of a bill to protect a vast portion of California desert. The Republican-controlled 104th Congress improved on that record, but not by much. It counted three environmental victories—a rewrite of the Safe Drinking Water Act, an overhaul of pesticide regulations and a revamping of the management of the nation's fisheries.

The list of unfinished business was far longer—the superfund toxic waste cleanup program, Endangered Species Act, clean water act, grazing rights on western lands, mining law, national park and public land issues, solid waste management and nuclear waste disposal, to name the major ones.

The expectations of both parties had been far higher. For the Democratic 103rd, having a Democrat in the White House for the first time in 12 years, especially one perceived as friendly to the environment, seemed to put the environmentalists' broad agenda within reach. For the Republican 104th, the stunning GOP victory in the November 1994 elections was perceived by many of the victors as a mandate to turn the tide on government regulation, particularly environmental regulation.

But on issue after issue, congressional leaders found it increasingly difficult to bridge the differences between warring factions of environmentalists and allies of industry, as well as combatants in both chambers. The parties were splintered on many issues, and the bipartisan coalitions needed for passage proved to be a rarity.

There were ample reasons for this. Budgets were tighter, and the signals on the environment coming from the public and their representatives in Congress were mixed. Gone—at least for the time being—were the days of cries to protect the bald eagle or the fears sparked by the toxic waste of a Love Canal. Many voters favored protecting the environment but were skittish about regulations that went too far or meant personal sacrifice, such as spending hours in line at car emissions testing centers. A growing consensus emerged that regulations needed to be more flexible and that regulators should be given more authority to weigh costs and benefits in writing regulations.

But translating such principles into action was a delicate balancing act that neither the 103rd nor the 104th Congress seemed to be able to put together very often. Both parties registered stunning successes and colossal failures at appealing to the competing impulses.

The volatility of the issues was vividly illustrated at times. In 1994, westerners hung in effigy President Clinton's interior secretary, Bruce Babbitt, over a grazing rights decision that pleased many environmentalists but angered ranchers. And less than a year after Republicans rode the 1994 wave of antigovernment anger to majority status in Congress, Senate Majority Leader Bob Dole, R-Kan., was vilified on editorial pages as a protector of polluters because of his effort to move legislation that would have eased regulatory policy.

ONETIME BIPARTISAN ISSUE

This ambivalence on environmental regulation was relatively new. For many years, environmental issues enjoyed great bipartisan support. Until well into the last half of the 20th century, pollution had been widely tolerated as the price of progress, which had led to the emergence of the United States as the world's economic and industrial giant. But, in the 1960s, public concern about pollution had been raised by a confluence of events. The mass media focused attention on Los Angeles and other smog-choked cities and on waste-clogged waterways, among them Cleveland's Cuyahoga River, where a slick of industrial pollutants caught fire in 1969. Books, such as Rachel Carson's *Silent Spring*, warned of dire consequences to man and nature from air, water and soil contamination, as did a number of scientific studies.

What had been mainly a localized, grassroots movement became a large-scale national campaign, culminating in the first Earth Day activities in April 1970. Membership in environmental groups exploded. The perceived public demand for pollution cleanup and prevention made environmentalism a bipartisan cause in Washington. Although Democrats controlled Congress through much of the ensuing period, environmental laws were regularly passed with substantial Republican support. Many of the nation's fundamental environmental statutes—including the National Environmental Policy Act of 1970, the Coastal

REFERENCES

Discussion of energy and environmental policy for the years 1945–1964 may be found in *Congress and the Nation Vol. I*, pp. 771–1095; for the years 1965–1968, *Congress and the Nation Vol. II*, pp. 463–528; for the years 1969–1972, *Congress and the Nation Vol. III*, pp. 745–849; for the years 1973–1976, *Congress and the Nation Vol. IV*, pp. 201–320; for the years 1977–1980, *Congress and the Nation Vol. V*, pp. 451–530, 533–597; for the years 1981–1984, *Congress and the Nation Vol. VI*, pp. 333–400, 403–482; for the years 1985–1988, *Congress and the Nation Vol. VII*, pp. 417–495; for the years 1989–1992, *Congress and the Nation Vol. VIII*, pp. 467–532.

Outlays for Natural Resources and Environment

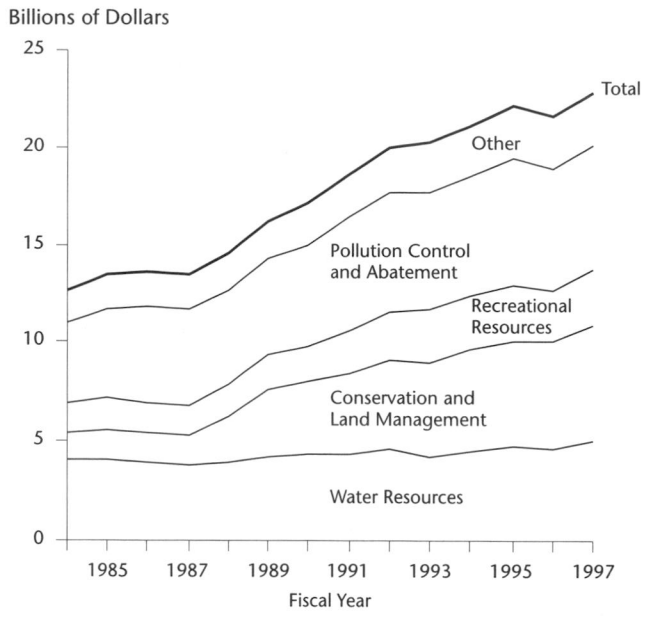

NOTE: Data for 1997 are estimated.

SOURCE: Office of Management and Budget, *Historical Tables, Budget of the United States Government: Fiscal Year 1998* (Washington, D.C.: U.S. Government Printing Office, 1997), Table 3.2.

Zone Management Act of 1972, the Endangered Species Act of 1973 and the Safe Drinking Water Act of 1974—were signed into law by Republican President Richard M. Nixon, who also created the Environmental Protection Agency (EPA).

Revelations of health-endangering industrial carelessness continued to drive the environmental agenda. The discovery of toxic chemical wastes buried at the Love Canal in Niagara Falls, N.Y., spurred a federally financed evacuation of a community and led to the enactment in 1980 of the Comprehensive Environmental Response, Compensation, and Liability Act, better known as the superfund law.

The potential for a backlash against the growth of federal environmental regulation was nonetheless present. Industries warned of job losses stemming from the high costs of government requirements for the installation of pollution-abatement equipment and the production of more environmentally friendly products. In the late 1970s, western conservatives, harboring a historic resentment over federal ownership of much of their region's land, sparked a "Sagebrush Rebellion" to demand greater access to public lands for natural resource development and livestock grazing.

Ronald Reagan, the Republican who capitalized on anti-Washington sentiment to win the presidency in 1980, appointed two veterans of the Sagebrush Rebellion to key environmental policy positions: James G. Watt as interior secretary and Anne Gorsuch Burford as administrator of the EPA. But Watt's bold talk of selling off public lands and Burford's efforts to slash EPA's enforcement of regulations turned into great fund-raising tools for environmentalist groups, who succeeded in labeling them as

extremists. By the end of his presidency, Reagan had signed a pair of bills approved by a Republican-controlled Senate that resulted in a multibillion-dollar effort by localities to remove asbestos from public school buildings.

Reagan's GOP successor, George Bush, ran in 1988 on a pledge to be the "environmental president." In 1990, Bush signed a revision of the Clean Air Act that sought to greatly reduce smokestack emissions that could cause acid rain and to clamp down on pollution caused by automobiles.

ANTIREGULATORY REBELLION

But, by the early 1990s, signs became evident of growing dissatisfaction with the continual extension of environmental regulation. Big business complained that federal regulators set super-clean standards that required expenditures disproportionate to the risks involved. Small-business owners saw their livelihoods threatened by regulatory and paperwork burdens. State and local officials said their coffers were being depleted by unfunded mandates issued under federal environmental laws.

The reaction to federal regulation contained several ingredients. One factor was the increase in economic uncertainty among American workers. During the early days of the environmental era, the post-World War II growth period was ongoing, and regulatory costs were widely regarded as sustainable. But, beginning in the 1970s, as a shrinkage in the blue-collar job base was followed by white-collar "down-sizings," an increasing number of Americans started to question the costs of environmental protection.

Another aspect was what critics described as regulators' demand for environmental perfection. It was widely accepted that the major environmental laws had cleaned up much of the nation's gross pollution problems and dramatically improved air, water and soil quality. But some said the push to remove all residual pollutants had diverted resources from greater environmental risks and other pressing social problems.

Furthermore, maintaining public support for environmental regulation was easier when most of the direct impact was on industry smokestacks and water discharge pipes. As the environmental statutes succeeded in cleaning up many of these "point sources," lawmakers and regulators turned their attention to "non-point source" pollution, such as generalized water runoff from lawns, roadways, farm fields and other surfaces. Efforts to reduce pollution from these sources affected individuals, farmers and small-business owners, some of whom rebelled against the imposition of costs or lifestyle restrictions threatened by new regulations.

But the most politically explosive element of the regulatory regime was its impact on private property use. Regulatory restrictions on land uses under such laws as the Endangered Species Act and the wetlands provisions of the Clean Water Act spurred the rapid development of a "private property rights" movement. This movement in turn generated much of the grassroots support for what became known as "takings" legislation, which was based on the guarantee of the Fifth Amendment of the Constitution of "just compensation" for private property owners if their property was "taken" for public use. Recent court decisions had expanded the definition of a "taking" to include a loss in the value of private property resulting from regulation. Property-rights advocates wanted to ensure that landowners who lost their livelihoods or whose property values decreased because of federal regulations were compensated by the federal government.

While this new wave of conservative populism was blossoming, the environmental community, according to some observers, allowed its own grass roots to wither. Its efforts were said to have become too focused on shaping legislative policy with an amenable Democratic-controlled Congress and less on working with everyday people.

103RD STALEMATE

Activists had expectations of an environmental heyday when Clinton took office in January 1993. The environment had long been a trademark issue for Vice President Al Gore, whose 1992 book, *Earth in the Balance,* called for a new era of government policy centered on the goal of "sustainable development."

The Democratic-controlled 103rd Congress that came to town with Clinton and Gore advanced an ambitious agenda reflecting the goals of environmentalists. The main legislative proposals were largely extensions of the prevailing philosophy of strong regulation. For example, a Democratic bill to reauthorize the clean water act would have required states to institute mandatory programs to control non-point source pollution and would have allowed citizens to sue for damages resulting from past pollution. Bills to update the superfund law, the Safe Drinking Water Act and other environmental statutes sought to maintain a strong role for federal "command and control" policies. The EPA would have become the Department of the Environment, with cabinet status.

The 103rd Congress, however, turned out to be a major disappointment for environmentalists. A large minority of Republicans and conservative Democrats acted assertively to restrict the bills' regulatory requirements or block their passage. And when this coalition appeared poised to attach provisions to several bills requiring regulators to employ cost-benefit and risk analyses in writing new regulations, environmentalists drew back their support for legislative action. In the end, the bill to designate large tracts of the California desert as wilderness became the major environmental legislation enacted during the 103rd Congress.

When evaluating the 103rd, environmentalists put a share of the blame on Clinton. Although Clinton supported a long list of environmental initiatives, in his first two years in office he did not focus on any one of them long enough to overcome opposition forces in Congress. By the end of the Congress, Clinton was avoiding politically divisive fights that frequently pitted producer against environmental interests and were difficult for the White House to mediate.

For example, in his first year, Clinton and Babbitt infuriated environmentalists when they abandoned efforts to pass legislation raising grazing fees on federally owned western rangeland. Opposition from western Democrats in the Senate and the

Outlays for Energy

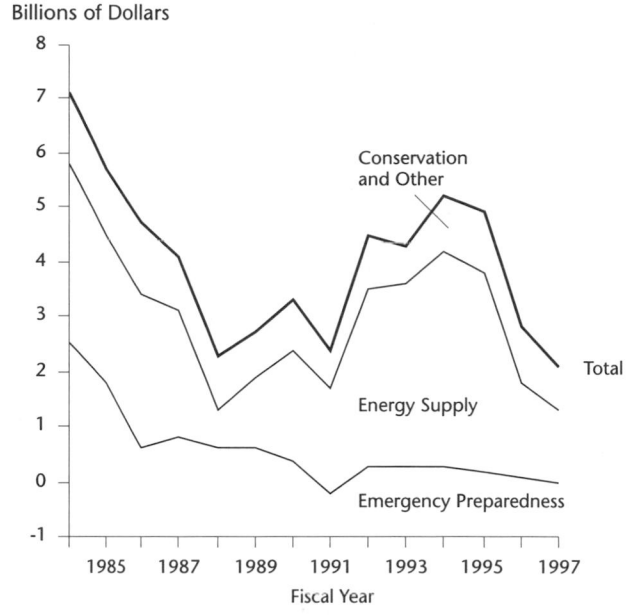

Billions of Dollars

NOTE: Data for 1997 are estimated.

SOURCE: Office of Management and Budget, *Historical Tables, Budget of the United States Government: Fiscal Year 1998* (Washington, D.C.: U.S. Government Printing Office, 1997), Table 3.2.

ranching industry doomed the legislation. In 1994, facing much the same array of opposition to legislation that would have raised royalties paid by hard-rock miners in the West, Clinton and Babbitt made little public effort to save the bill. It died late in the year, but Clinton avoided a messy, public fight.

REPUBLICAN STRATEGY

Once it gained control of Congress, the GOP made clear its intention to rewrite many of the nation's major environmental laws to provide regulatory relief to businesses and individuals. Republican strategists contended that the 1994 elections provided a mandate to reduce environmental regulation. The House GOP campaign platform, the "Contract with America," included a commitment to overhaul the federal regulatory structure.

Just as vigorously, environmental activists disagreed that the 1994 elections warranted such a transformation in policy. They noted that the contract never specifically mentioned environmental issues and insisted that the public consensus in favor of environmental regulation, which they traced to at least that first Earth Day in 1970, remained strong.

The Republican-led effort to revamp environmental regulation was based on three by-now-familiar tenets:

• **Justifying Regulations.** The deregulatory coalition wanted to force federal agencies to go to greater lengths to defend new regulations. Their proposals required agencies to conduct detailed analyses of the environmental risks that the proposed regulations sought to address and then to quantify that the benefits of the regulations would exceed the economic costs to individuals and society.

• **Protecting Property Rights.** Advocates of reducing regulation said government officials had been overzealous in declaring landowners' properties off-limits to development under such statutes as the Endangered Species Act and the wetlands provisions of the clean water act. They wanted "takings" legislation to compensate landowners when their property values declined because of federal regulations.

• **Relaxing Federal Control and Privatizing Responsibility.** They proposed to give states and localities more leeway in waiving certain environmental requirements or in promoting market-based pollution reduction programs, provided that the result was a "net benefit" to the environment.

GOP MISSTEPS

At the beginning of the 104th Congress, Republicans showed few signs of division over environmental regulation. The House quickly and easily passed an omnibus regulatory overhaul bill. Although it would have covered a number of federal agencies, the bill was aimed largely at those that regulated the environment. It would have restricted federal regulation by forcing agencies to perform scientific risk assessments and cost-benefit analyses on most proposed rules. It also would have required compensation to landowners when federal action reduced the value of their property or when the federal government occupied their property. The proposals were passed by the House as separate bills, as well.

Similar ease was seen in the passage of legislation to curb unfunded federal mandates, those requirements that Congress or federal agencies imposed on state and local governments without providing the money to pay for them. The clean water act—cited by officials as by far the most costly federal statute for states and localities—imposed billions of dollars in costs on jurisdictions that operated water and sewage treatment works.

But the display of unity was short-lived. The first hint of division emerged in May 1995 when the House passed a major rewrite of the clean water act. Some House Republicans took a lashing back home for supporting the bill, exposing the party's vulnerability on environmental issues. The opposition of Democrats, moderate Republicans and environmentalists to the bill planted a seed for future battles.

The divisions among Republicans soon surfaced on other bills. A major battle was fought in the House over appropriations riders that would have curbed the EPA's regulatory authority. The two sides were also at odds over such issues as allowing low-cost mining claims on federal land and on opening the Arctic National Wildlife Refuge to oil exploration.

Even in cases when they succeeded in moving legislation through the House, GOP leaders faced trouble in the Senate. A version of the House regulatory bill ran aground in the Senate after stinging attacks from most Democrats and a handful of Republicans who argued that the measure would undo needed regulation. Majority Leader Dole, sponsor of the bill, suspended action after failing to cut off a Democratic filibuster.

As they fought over legislation, Republicans were embroiled in a public relations battle as well. They were hampered by the fact that the Democrats were most closely identified in the public's mind as the party of clean air and clean water. The GOP was unable to develop a message that rebutted the opposition's claim that they had no sympathy for the environment.

Even senior Republicans sometimes played into the Democrats' tactics. In a March 6, 1995, *Wall Street Journal* profile, House Majority Whip Tom DeLay, R-Texas, a prominent opponent of government regulations, was asked whether there was any regulation he would keep on the books. "I can't think of one," he replied and later compared the EPA to the Gestapo.

In May, when the House passed the clean water act revisions, the bill was attacked by Democrats as "the dirty water act." In July, Dole was skewered in a widely distributed editorial cartoon that portrayed him as a black-hatted witch stirring up a noxious "Dole stew," when he pushed his regulatory overhaul bill. Over the summer, Republicans proposed riders to several appropriations bills that were aimed at rolling back the enforcement of environmental laws. Clinton seized the opening, exploiting the Republicans' credibility gap to tar them as "extremists" and positioning himself as the chief protector of the environment.

GOP REGROUPS

In March 1996, after months of taking a beating on environmental issues, House Speaker Newt Gingrich, R-Ga., appointed a House GOP Task Force on the Environment. Headed by Sherwood Boehlert, R-N.Y., and Richard W. Pombo, R-Calif., it was charged with bridging ideological and regional differences within the party and developing an environmental agenda.

From the outset, the task force's first job was clear. House leaders could not hope to force a new direction in environmental policy without first establishing peace between warring factions within the House Republican Conference. Boehlert and his Eastern Republican allies had repeatedly battled with Pombo and other conservative Westerners and Southerners over environmental legislation.

The public fights had cast a media spotlight on the intraparty conflict. But even more troubling for the party, the disagreements created an opening for the White House, congressional Democrats and the environmental community to portray House Republicans as a reactionary band of marauders out to roll back popular environmental protections.

On May 15, 1996, the task force released a one-page vision statement and principles approved by the entire Republican Conference. Over the next few months, Congress, with strong bipartisan support, cleared major environmental bills overhauling pesticide regulations, the safe drinking water law and management of the nation's fisheries.

But the deep divisions among Republicans remained, and moderates such as Boehlert repeatedly intervened to help block moves by hardliners to take broad swipes at environmental regulations. Although the broad attacks on environmental laws failed in the 104th Congress and significant legislation was enacted, the middle ground on numerous issues remained elusive. The search for a way to translate the growing consensus on the need for more flexible and cost-conscious regulation into concrete pieces of legislation was far from over.

Chronology of Action
on Environment and Energy

1993–1994

At the beginning of the 103rd Congress, the outlook for environmental issues was promising. A number of important issues were on the table, and broad agreement was apparent on all sides on the need for some major revisions in existing programs. Democrats, traditionally sympathetic toward environmental causes, controlled both the White House and Congress for the first time in some years. And the Clinton administration was espousing the seemingly practical view that environmental laws could be rewritten to impose lower costs and less regulatory red tape on state and local governments but still leave them the tools to do the job.

Nonetheless, things went badly for environmentalists. Only one major environmental bill—legislation to protect a vast portion of California's fragile desert—was signed into law in 1993–1994. Administration attempts to raise grazing fees and impose tough environmental standards on the use of federal rangelands was thwarted by western senators. Legislation to make the Environmental Protection Agency a cabinet-level department only made it through one chamber. A reauthorization of the Safe Drinking Water Act died in conference. Proposals to overhaul the "superfund" hazardous waste cleanup law never got beyond committee approval. Irreconcilable differences sealed the fate of efforts to rewrite an 1872 mining law. And the list of unfinished business went on, including, the Clean Water Act, the Endangered Species Act and waste disposal legislation.

The low success rate for environmental initiatives was blamed, in part, on a popular perception that government regulation was becoming too invasive. Environmental groups and lawmakers in both parties contended the backlash against environmental regulation reflected a growing anger about what many people saw as heavy-handed rules striking increasingly close to their daily lives—whether the regulations affected the cars people drove or the land they made their living from or the chemicals that kept their golf courses lush.

At the center of this mounting confrontation over environmental legislation were three explosive issues: risk assessment and cost-benefit analysis of regulations, private property rights and unfunded mandates. The three emerged repeatedly in environmental debates in the 103rd Congress.

California Desert Protection

An eight-year battle to protect a huge swath of California's fragile desert culminated in enactment of the California Desert Protection Act (S 21—PL 103-433) in 1994, giving environmentalists their only major victory in the 103rd Congress. S 21 was the largest land protection measure adopted by Congress since the 1980 Alaska Lands Act (PL 96-487).

The measure protected as wilderness about 7.5 million acres, stretching from the Sierra Nevada to the U.S.-Mexico border,

and elevated national monument areas in Death Valley and at Joshua Tree to national parks. As a concession to hunters, the centerpiece Mojave area was designated a national preserve—a notch below the more restrictive national park status.

S 21 survived intense lobbying and bitter partisan battles. With control of the Senate up for grabs in 1994, some Republicans tried to deny sponsor Dianne Feinstein, D-Calif., who was in a tight Senate reelection race, and President Clinton an environmental victory. But the appeal of keeping an area larger than the state of Maryland away from developers, combined with lawmakers' desire to get out of town for the campaign season, won out over the opposition.

BACKGROUND

Legislation to protect the California desert had been hotly debated since 1986, when Sen. Alan Cranston, D-Calif. (1969–1993), introduced a bill to include California desert land in the nation's park and wilderness system. But its path in the Senate had been blocked by California Republican senators—Pete Wilson (1983–1991) and Wilson's successor, John Seymour (1991–1992)—who prevented the legislation from even coming to a vote in committee. Republicans had opposed the proposal because it would add millions of acres to the financially strapped national park system. Off-road enthusiasts, miners, ranchers and the National Rifle Association had argued that the legislation would emphasize conservation over commercial and recreational uses of the land.

The House had passed a desert protection bill in 1991, but Seymour had blocked it in the Senate. The legislation's fortunes improved dramatically in 1992 with the election of two Democratic senators from California, Feinstein and Barbara Boxer, effectively ending partisan squabbling among California senators. Bill Clinton's election gave the measure White House backing for the first time. (*Congress and the Nation Vol. VIII, p. 522*)

SENATE ACTION

The Senate passed the bill April 13, 1994, by a vote of 69–29. S 21 had cleared a major hurdle the previous October, when it was approved by the Senate Energy and Natural Resources Committee. The bill was formally reported Oct. 26, 1993 (S Rept 103-165). Although Feinstein was not a member of the panel, she sat in on markup sessions and negotiated changes. To get the measure onto the Senate floor, Feinstein brokered more than 50 specific modifications to make it more acceptable to commercial users of the desert.

Once the bill was on the Senate floor, Feinstein and Energy Chairman J. Bennett Johnston, D-La., were able to show that it had overwhelming support. Intent on proving to colleagues that the bill would protect more than a vast, parched space void of anything but sand, Feinstein displayed numerous pictures of the area, which included the world's largest forest of cactus-like Joshua trees, 90 mountain ranges, the only known dinosaur tracks in California and more than 760 wildlife species, such as the threatened desert tortoise. "This is a unique and fragile piece of Americana," Feinstein said.

Few senators quibbled with her assertion that the resources needed protection. But Malcolm Wallop, R-Wyo., ranking member of the Energy Committee, led a chorus of senators who charged that the National Park Service could not afford to operate three new parks when it already was cutting back on operations and maintenance of existing facilities. Interior Secretary Bruce Babbitt, however, said his department had the resources and personnel to implement the bill.

The Senate took up a number of amendments April 12. Wallop tried to amend the bill to give the Mojave a national monument designation, a less protective and less expensive status, but was defeated, 35–62. Also rejected, 34–64, was an amendment by Robert F. Bennett, R-Utah, to set a 10-year limit for the federal government to pay for 90 percent of the private lands it needed to create the three national parks.

Johnston won voice vote approval for an amendment to incorporate provisions creating a historical park commemorating New Orleans as the birthplace of jazz. The Senate also adopted amendments allowing use of some areas for law enforcement purposes and for livestock grazing.

HOUSE ACTION

The House passed, 298–128, a companion bill (HR 518) on July 27, after a protracted and bitter floor debate. The House then called up S 21, amended it with the text of HR 518 and passed it by voice vote.

The Natural Resources Committee had reported HR 518 on May 10 (H Rept 103-498). Committee Republicans, whose attempts to rein in the far-reaching bill had been unsuccessful, voted unanimously against the bill.

The 298–128 vote on passage belied the difficulty Natural Resources Committee Chairman George Miller, D-Calif., had in steering the bill through a crowded legislative calendar that frequently bumped the bill for other business, as well as past a barrage of amendments and drawn-out discussions by Republican opponents. Republicans were able to win concessions on hunting and private property appraisals but failed to reduce the bill's size and scope dramatically.

On July 12, the House adopted an amendment by Larry LaRocco, D-Idaho, to allow hunting to continue on 1.5 million acres of the Mojave desert. Approval came on a **key vote of 239–183 (R 146–26; D 92–157; I 1–0)**. The amendment altered the protected status of the Mojave, designating it as a national preserve instead of a national park. The two labels offered virtually the same protections, but the preserve designation explicitly allowed hunting as long as the natural values of an area were not harmed. LaRocco had the support of the Congressional Sportsmen's Caucus, a bipartisan group that advocated hunting and trapping and had about 180 members in the House. (1994 key votes, p. 1003)

On July 14, the House overwhelmingly adopted, 281–148, an amendment by W. J. "Billy" Tauzin, D-La., aimed at increasing the value of private land in the desert that contained endangered species. Specifically, the amendment called for the federal government to ignore any endangered species or land-use restrictions, such as local zoning laws, when appraising privately owned property for wilderness designation. Tauzin said the provision would allow desert landowners to sell their property to the federal government at a higher price. He had won a similar battle in 1993 on a measure (HR 1845) to authorize the National Biological Survey. (National Biological Survey, p. 418)

The House overwhelmingly adopted several other amendments, including one on June 13 by a 360–0 vote that gave the state of California the authority to protect fish and wildlife in federally protected desert areas and allow state agencies to use motorized vehicles to gain access to those public lands. An attempt to clarify a federal agency's role in protecting fish and wildlife in the California desert was rejected, 183–189, the same day.

The House rejected amendments that would have allowed off-road vehicle riders to continue to use nearly 200 roads in the desert, by 169–191 on June 10; phased out grazing on federal land in the proposed Death Valley National Park, by 190–207 on July 12; prohibited the government from acquiring private land for the proposed Mojave park by condemnation, by 145–274 on July 12; and delayed the effective date of the bill until the National Park Service had reduced its backlog of land acquisition, construction and park operations by 50 percent, by 138–288 on July 27.

CONFERENCE, FINAL ACTION

The road to enactment grew rougher as the bill moved toward conference, buffeted by deepening partisanship and election fever. GOP delaying tactics—a filibuster in the Senate and the use of arcane procedural rules in the House—underscored the zeal of Republicans in both chambers to deny Feinstein a legislative victory before she headed home to campaign to retain her Senate seat against a surprisingly strong challenge from Rep. Michael Huffington, R-Calif. The stakes were high: Republicans saw the California seat as a key element in their drive to take control of the Senate.

But once the legislation got past Republican roadblocks and to conference, agreement was quickly reached on a compromise bill. Committee chairmen Johnston and Miller and their staffs had been meeting privately for weeks to resolve differences. And even before the conference began, Feinstein said she was ready to accept the House-passed language on hunting and preserve status for the Mojave. She said the House vote was too strong to ignore. In return, Feinstein got the House to agree to a Senate-passed package providing for roads for motorized vehicles. Senate conferees went along with the Tauzin amendment as well.

The House adopted the conference report (H Rept 103-832) by voice vote Oct. 7. About 10 hours after the House had closed up shop until after the November elections, the Senate on Oct. 8, by a **key vote of 68–23 (R 14–23; D 54–0)**, shut off debate on the bill and then gave final voice vote approval to the conference report. The Senate adjourned later that day.

The vote, while providing its own moments of high drama, represented a key concession by opponents, who agreed late Oct. 7 to forgo the two-day layover allowed them under Senate rules for a motion to invoke cloture, thereby limiting debate. After forcing the bill to be read line-by-line and trying to remove visiting Interior Secretary Babbitt from the Senate floor, Wallop and other Republicans consented to let the cloture vote take place first thing Saturday morning, instead of at 12:01 a.m. Sunday, as Majority Leader George J. Mitchell, D-Maine, had threatened.

The importance of the vote was underscored by an extraordinary effort to get bill supporters to the chamber on Saturday. Mindful of the wishes of some senators to be at home campaigning but needing every Democratic vote possible that Saturday, Mitchell even arranged for a private plane to ferry one senator back to Washington. Once the pivotal sixtieth vote to invoke cloture showed up with only minutes to spare, some of the bill's GOP supporters, who had been nervously holding back, quickly cast "yea" votes.

MAJOR PROVISIONS

As signed into law Oct. 31, major provisions of S 21:

• Created the largest wilderness area outside Alaska, two new national parks in Death Valley and Joshua Tree and a national preserve in the Mojave Desert.

Overall, the bill designated 69 wilderness areas covering 3.5 million acres, scattered from the Sierra Nevada to the U.S.-Mexico border and protected about 4 million acres inside the two parks and preserve as wilderness. The measure allowed hunting of small game to continue within the 1.4 million-acre Mojave National Preserve.

• Authorized $300 million for land acquisition and $36 million over five years for park operations. (The Congressional Budget Office estimated that acquiring the land would cost between $100 million and $300 million.)

• Required the federal government to appraise private property needed for wilderness and national parks as though it did not contain endangered or threatened species.

• Set aside desert lands within the China Lake Naval Weapons Center and Chocolate Mountain Aerial Gunnery Range for 20 years for use by the military for overflights and training.

• Included unrelated Senate-passed provisions to establish a national historical park to commemorate New Orleans as the birthplace of jazz and to authorize several studies in the Lower Mississippi Delta aimed at sparking economic development in the impoverished region.   ❏

EPA Cabinet Status

Legislation to make the Environmental Protection Agency (EPA) the fifteenth cabinet-level department was one of President Clinton's and environmentalists' top goals for the 103rd Congress. The proposal won the backing of the Senate (S 171) in 1993, but the House version (HR 3425) fell victim to the politically explosive issues of risk assessment and cost-benefit analysis in 1994 and never reached the House floor.

When HR 3425 stalled in the House, a last-ditch attempt was made in the Senate to revive the issue by attaching the EPA cabinet language to unrelated legislation (S 2019), but that bill also failed to clear Congress.

ENVIRONMENT, ENERGY LEADERSHIP

Bruce Babbitt was confirmed by voice vote of the Senate Jan. 21, 1993, to be secretary of interior. Babbitt—a committed environmentalist as well as a member of one of Arizona's oldest ranching families—had served as governor of Arizona and was a 1988 Democratic presidential contender. (Background, cabinet profiles, p. 1113)

Carol M. Browner was also confirmed by voice vote on Jan. 21, 1993, to be administrator of the Environmental Protection Agency. Browner, who had served as Vice President Al Gore's legislative director for several years when he was in the Senate, was secretary of the Florida Department of Environmental Regulation. (Background, p. 1116)

The Senate by voice vote Jan. 21, 1993, confirmed Hazel R. O'Leary as energy secretary. O'Leary, an executive with an electric and gas utility in Minnesota, previously had served in energy-related positions in the Gerald Ford and Jimmy Carter administrations. (Background, cabinet profiles, p. 1112)

BACKGROUND

The creation of the EPA in 1970 marked the beginning of the federal government's increased involvement in writing rules and enforcing laws devoted to protecting the environment. Beginning in 1989, members of Congress tried to boost that commitment by proposing legislation to elevate the EPA to the cabinet. Supporters said that cabinet status would give the agency additional lobbying clout during the budget season, provide its secretary with more management flexibility and strengthen EPA's hand in international negotiations.

The proposal enjoyed bipartisan support. But some lawmakers used the widespread appeal of the proposal to try to reinvent the agency through a vast array of provisions that went beyond granting the EPA a formal seat at the cabinet table. As a result, no legislation was enacted during the Bush administration. (Congress and the Nation Vol. VIII, pp. 498, 529)

When Clinton came into office, he vowed to add the EPA to his cabinet and in the meantime gave EPA Administrator Carol M. Browner an informal seat at the cabinet table. But he angered environmentalists and key lawmakers by proposing to abolish the Council on Environmental Quality (CEQ), the White House office charged with ensuring that other federal agencies conducted environmental impact studies before undertaking actions that could harm the environment. Clinton's plan called for the transfer of CEQ functions to the new Department of the Environment. Clinton established a smaller White House Office of Environmental Policy to advise him and coordinate the federal government's response to environmental problems.

Opponents of Clinton's proposal to abolish CEQ argued that it would weaken the administration's ability to enforce environmental initiatives. CEQ had been a frequent target of Republicans who wanted to ease regulations. In the fall of 1993, after intenoe lobbying from John D. Dingell, D-Mich., the House Energy and Commerce Committee chairman, and Gerry E. Studds, D-Mass., the House Merchant Marine and Fisheries Committee chairman, Clinton agreed to keep a smaller version of the council in the White House. Once the EPA bill was dead, Clinton announced plans to merge the White House Office of Environmental Policy and CEQ.

SENATE ACTION

The Senate passed S 171 on May 4, 1993, by a vote of 79–15. The bill had been reported by the Governmental Affairs Committee on March 31 (S Rept 103-38) and by the Environment and Public Works Committee on April 15 (S Rept 103-39).

The two-year authorization contained $5 million for the new department and added to its duties, including creating a Bureau of Environmental Statistics to compile and publish data on the environment and an Office of Environmental Justice to document environmental problems in poor neighborhoods. The bill designated one assistant secretary to oversee environmental concerns on Indian lands and created an ombudsman for small business and local government concerns. It also provided for the abolition of the Council on Environmental Quality.

Before passing S 171, the Senate considered a handful of amendments. On April 29, it adopted, 95–3, an amendment offered by J. Bennett Johnston, D-La., requiring the new department to analyze the risks addressed by newly proposed regulations and the cost of implementing them as well as to certify that benefits to human health and the environment justified the regulations.

That same day, the Democratic leadership reached an agreement with Republicans that limited further debate. The agreement eliminated a major threat to the bill—a proposed amendment by Minority Leader Bob Dole, R-Kan., that would have required the government to compensate private property owners for land taken from them through new land-use regulations. A similar Senate-approved amendment had contributed to the demise of an EPA bill in the House in 1991.

HOUSE ACTION

The House Government Operations Committee Nov. 10, 1993, reported legislation (HR 3425—H Rept 103-355) that did little more than designate the EPA as a cabinet-level department and correct some management problems. It provided for the creation of several new subagencies within the department, including a Bureau of Environmental Statistics, an Office of Environmental Justice and an advisory committee to deal with human environmental health risks. Agreement was reached with the administration to keep a smaller version of the Council on Environmental Quality in the White House. (The CEQ compromise was incorporated into separate legislation (HR 3512), which the House passed by voice vote Nov. 20, 1993. The Senate took no action on the bill.)

A number of Democrats had hoped to use HR 3425 to overhaul the agency and broadly rewrite environmental policy, but they had to give up on those goals to move the bill forward.

However, the bill did not move forward. Floor action was postponed in 1993 after bill opponent William F. Clinger, R-Pa., was hospitalized at the end of the session and could not attend the debate. And in 1994 opponents succeeded in preventing the bill from coming to the floor by defeating the rule (H Res 312—H Rept 103-372) governing debate on the bill on a **key vote of 191–227 (R 5–167; D 185–60; I 1–0).** Opponents rejected the rule Feb. 2 because it did not allow freshmen John L. Mica, R-Fla., and Karen L. Thurman, D-Fla., to offer an amendment requiring cost-benefit analysis and risk assessment. Their proposal was identical to the Johnston amendment adopted by the Senate in 1993. *(1994 key votes, p. 1003)*

The Democratic-controlled Rules Committee had voted Nov. 17, 1993, against allowing the amendment on grounds that it was a policy issue not germane to the bill, which was concerned solely with the structure of the agency. The Clinton administration and bill sponsors argued that the amendment would amount to a one-size-fits-all policy that would put economic concerns above the health of the public and the environment. The EPA said that it already used both risk assessment and cost-benefit analysis and that the amendment was unnecessary.

But the issues were high on the agendas of lawmakers who believed the EPA wielded too heavy a hand when issuing environmental standards and mandates on state and local governments and the public. Vice President Al Gore and EPA Administrator Browner met with freshman Democrats to urge them to support the rule. Ultimately, 64 members of the freshman class voted against the rule, including 15 Democrats.

SENATE SALVAGE ATTEMPT

With the House bill stalled, Senate supporters began looking for ways to get the initiative moving again. Governmental Affairs Committee Chairman John Glenn, D-Ohio, in 1994 included the text of the Senate's EPA bill in an unrelated bill (S 2019) to reauthorize the 1974 Safe Drinking Water Act. The House and Senate failed to agree on a final version of the drinking water bill, however, and it, too, died at the end of the Congress. *(Drinking water, this page)*   ❑

Safe Drinking Water

Despite nearly unanimous agreement that the Safe Drinking Water Act needed fixing, the 103rd Congress proved not up to the task. Both chambers passed bills (S 2019, HR 3392) aimed at making federal drinking water rules more flexible and less costly for state and local governments. But attempts to resolve differences between the two versions during Congress's final days were unsuccessful. The biggest sticking points involved three major, unrelated provisions attached to the Senate version but rejected by House negotiators. They dealt with cabinet status for the Environmental Protection Agency (EPA), risk assessment studies and the protection of private property rights.

BACKGROUND

An outbreak of waterborne diseases in the 1960s and early 1970s spurred Congress to pass the 1974 Safe Drinking Water

Act (PL 93-523). By the time the act expired in 1986, the drinking water supplied by cities and towns was virtually free of bacteria, but chemicals had begun to contaminate ground water, the nation's primary source of drinking water. The 1986 revisions to the act (PL 99-339) provided tougher requirements for the testing and monitoring of contaminants and new provisions to protect ground water supplies. The law's authority to award grants to states and cities for drinking water programs expired in 1991 and had been kept alive with annual appropriations. *(1974 act, Congress and the Nation Vol. IV, p. 293; 1986 revisions, Congress and the Nation Vol. VII, p. 433)*

Driving the reauthorization effort were governors, mayors and operators of small water systems, who held up the safe drinking water law as a primary example of stringent federal regulations that were unaccompanied by sufficient funds to carry them out.

To address this concern, the Clinton administration on Sept. 8, 1993, called on Congress to make complying with major environmental mandates easier and less costly for state and local officials. Key administration proposals included a new five-year, $4.6 billion revolving loan fund for states to help pay for improvements to drinking water systems and an end to a provision in the drinking water act that required the EPA to set standards for 25 new contaminants every three years.

While the nation's drinking water supply was considered among the world's safest, a 1993 outbreak of waterborne diseases in Milwaukee that contributed to the deaths of 103 people and a breakdown at the facility that supplied drinking water to Washington, D.C., added to the pressure for changes in the law.

1993 LEGISLATIVE ACTION

Legislation to authorize a new revolving loan fund to help states pay for improvements to drinking water systems got caught in a turf battle between two House committees in 1993.

The House Energy and Commerce Committee on May 27, 1993, reported legislation (HR 1701—H Rept 103-114) providing for a new, federally financed revolving fund that states could draw on to issue loans to local communities to build drinking water treatment plants or to make improvements to older plants. HR 1701 amended the Safe Drinking Water Act, which was under Energy and Commerce's jurisdiction. But because the bill authorized money for the building of new public water treatment plants, Public Works Committee Chairman Norman Y. Mineta, D-Calif., argued that his committee also had jurisdiction.

Not waiting for a parliamentary ruling on the referral issue, Public Works reported its own bill (HR 1865—H Rept 103-115), also on May 27. HR 1865 provided for a state-run revolving fund for the purpose of financing the construction of new water supply systems and improvements to existing systems. The bill also covered loans for the treatment of pollutants from navigable waters to make such water usable by water supply systems.

No further action was taken on the two House bills. Related legislation in the Senate (S 1547) never got beyond the hearing stage in 1993.

1994 LEGISLATIVE ACTION

Both chambers passed reauthorization bills in 1994, only to see them die in the final hours of the 103rd Congress, casualties of major environmental controversies.

The Senate on May 19 passed S 2019 by an overwhelming 95–3 vote. The bill had been reported by the Senate Environment and Public Works Committee (S Rept 103-250) on April 14. S 2019 authorized $6.6 billion over seven years for a new state revolving loan fund to allow state and local communities to improve drinking water quality. (Of this, $600 million had already been appropriated for fiscal 1994.)

To win the support of wavering senators, Environment Committee Chairman Max Baucus, D-Mont., brokered several deals. One of those allowed the EPA to lower existing standards for contaminants that were rarely found in drinking water to save money if the changes would not endanger human health. The committee bill had allowed the EPA to lower standards, but only for cancer-causing agents, not all contaminants. While the compromise gained crucial support from the coalition led by the National Governors' Association, it angered major environmental groups, such as the Natural Resources Defense Council, which charged that the deal would weaken public health safeguards.

The Senate also agreed by voice vote to add to the bill the key provisions of a separate but controversial measure (S 171) to elevate the EPA to cabinet-level status. The amendment was sponsored by John Glenn, D-Ohio. *(EPA cabinet status, p. 407)*

Two other explosive issues were added to S 2019. Minority Leader Bob Dole, R-Kan., won voice vote approval May 18 for a sweeping amendment to require that all federal agencies complete a taking impact analysis when issuing any regulation or policy that was likely to affect private property values. A growing number of lawmakers were urging that the government compensate private property owners whose land had been devalued or whose use of their land had been limited by federal regulations.

Senate Energy and Natural Resources Committee Chairman J. Bennett Johnston, D-La., led the Senate into another political quagmire when he offered an amendment to require the EPA and other federal agencies to conduct cost, benefit and risk analyses on environmental regulations that cost businesses or individuals $100 million or more per year to implement. The Senate approved the amendment by a **key vote of 90–8 (R 41–3; D 49–5)** on May 18. *(1994 key votes, p. 1003)*

HR 3392 sailed through the House Sept. 27 on a voice vote under a rule that prohibited amendments—an expedited procedure usually reserved for noncontroversial bills. HR 3392 had been reported by the House Energy and Commerce Committee (H Rept 103-745, Part I) on Sept. 23 with bipartisan support after sometimes tense negotiations brokered by Health and the Environment Subcommittee Chairman Henry A. Waxman, D-Calif. HR 3392 provided for a new revolving loan fund, authorized at $3.6 billion for four years, to provide money to states and local governments to improve drinking water treatment plants. The bill garnered the support of a broad range of interest groups, including the National Governors' Association and the Natural Resources Defense Council.

The Senate and House bills shared much common ground. Both bills, for example, called for an end to the existing requirement that the EPA regulate 25 contaminants every three years. Instead, they required the EPA to develop a list of at least 12 unregulated contaminants every four years and then issue standards for those contaminants that occurred most frequently in water supplies and posed the greatest risk to human health.

Among the differences between the two bills was that the House bill allowed the EPA to weigh the costs and benefits only for new drinking water regulations. The Senate bill provided for cost-benefit analysis of existing regulations as well. House negotiators had settled on their provisions after months of give-and-take with members who had wanted to cover existing regulations, too.

But the biggest problems in conference negotiations were posed by the Senate's add-ons—the EPA cabinet bill, Johnston's risk assessment provisions and Dole's amendment on private property rights. When the conference reached an impasse, Sen. Baucus on Oct. 7 attempted to bring a clean bill to the Senate floor that would strip out the controversial provisions. But Dole and Johnston objected and put holds on the bill, blocking it from reaching the floor. Even if those issues had been resolved, however, floor action would likely have been prevented by a GOP filibuster on the California desert protection bill (S 21), which took up Congress's final hours. ❑

'Superfund' Overhaul

A proposal to overhaul the nation's troubled hazardous waste cleanup program—the "superfund" program—died in the final weeks of the 103rd Congress, derailing one of the Clinton administration's top environmental initiatives. Although the legislation (HR 3800, S 1834) won bipartisan approval from five committees, no superfund bill got to the floor of either chamber. Instead, the legislation fell victim to a combination of partisan politics, disputes over labor and tax provisions, and a final rush to adjournment.

The Clinton administration's proposal was designed to institute an arbitration process that would put an end to the protracted litigation that had snarled the superfund cleanup effort. In contrast to existing law, under which a single party could be held liable, the proposal also sought to spread cleanup costs among the companies responsible for polluting a site.

An unusual coalition of polluters, insurers and environmentalists, bound together by a mutual concern over skyrocketing litigation costs, backed the legislation.

But several key issues stalled action on the bills. Small and medium-size insurers protested a provision in both the House and Senate versions that would have levied $8.1 billion in new commercial liability insurance taxes, a dispute that delayed action for several critical weeks in August and September 1994 while the administration tried to work out a compromise. A controversial House provision on wages to be paid superfund workers was strongly opposed by businesses and effectively prevented the legislation from reaching the floor of the House. Disagreements over cleanup standards—the Senate bill contained more stringent standards than did the House bill—also posed obstacles to forging a compromise in the contentious final days of the 103rd Congress.

BACKGROUND

The legislation was designed to overhaul the 1980 Comprehensive Environmental Response, Compensation and Liability Act (PL 96-510), known as the superfund law. Written in the wake of public outrage over chemical dumping in the Love Canal subdivision of Niagara Falls, N.Y., the law required polluters to pay to clean up the worst hazardous waste sites or reimburse the Environmental Protection Agency (EPA) for the cost of doing the job. To finance such cleanups, the law established the superfund, which was fed primarily by a tax on oil and chemical manufacturers and an environmental tax on companies. These taxes were due to expire at the end of 1995. (*Congress and the Nation Vol. V, p. 583*)

Superfund originally was envisioned as a five-year, $1.6 billion program to clean up Love Canal and about 400 other toxic waste sites. But the effort quickly became mired in litigation, and relatively few sites were cleaned up. By the beginning of 1994, the federal government, polluters, insurers and the states had spent roughly $13 billion on the superfund program since its inception, but only 256 of 1,345 priority toxic waste sites so far identified by the EPA had been cleaned up; 168 more were in the final stages of cleanup. A study by the Congressional Budget Office released Jan. 31, 1994, estimated that it could take $75 billion to clean up a total of about 4,500 sites that were in need of work.

Deciding which companies or individuals were responsible for cleaning up hazardous waste sites had been one of the biggest failures of the superfund program. Polluters often went to court to find other polluters—such as municipalities that hauled household garbage to toxic waste sites—to share the cleanup costs. EPA Administrator Carol M. Browner said it could take as long as 15 years to traverse a maze of litigation and clean up a toxic waste site.

On Feb. 3, 1994, Browner unveiled the administration plan, which was quickly characterized as a fragile compromise. The plan retained the backbone of the superfund law: the principle that polluters should pay to clean up their own waste sites. But the proposal abandoned the existing policy that allowed the EPA to track down a single polluter—regardless of how much waste was disposed of—and force that polluter to pay all the costs. It was that policy that created the incentive for polluters to try to force their insurers or other responsible parties to share in the expense—leading to thousands of lawsuits and little cleanup.

The liability of polluters that had contributed only incidentally to a hazardous waste site was to be limited. All other polluters were to be given incentives to join an arbitration process to determine how to allocate costs. Polluters that refused to submit to such negotiations would be liable for the entire cleanup costs, as they were under existing law, even if they only marginally contributed to the hazardous waste.

The proposal called for setting aside $300 million a year to pay so-called orphan cleanup costs incurred by polluters that either could not be identified by the government or that were defunct or insolvent.

The Clinton plan also called for a new trust fund to be made up of taxes levied on property and casualty insurers. The goal was to raise $3 billion over five years and $8 billion over 10 years to settle old insurance claims stemming from toxic waste problems on a superfund site before 1986, the year insurance companies began writing new hazardous waste policies that more accurately estimated the high cost of cleaning up sites. Companies identified as polluters would apply to the fund for money instead of suing their insurers to pay for cleanups.

The Clinton plan also attempted to make cleanup standards more flexible by allowing the future use of a site to be taken into consideration. Potential home sites, for example, would have to meet more stringent standards than would land slated for shopping malls or industrial centers. The issue was a continuing source of conflict throughout the year, with environmentalists wanting uniform standards to be set for all sites across the country and industry wanting more flexibility.

The plan also called for citizens who lived near toxic waste sites to have a say in deciding how far to clean up their neighborhoods before such jobs began—a provision that many environmental groups welcomed. The EPA estimated that about 73 million people lived near toxic waste sites.

LEGISLATIVE ACTION

Both the House and Senate bills largely reflected the administration's proposal.

The Energy and Commerce Committee was the first of three House panels with jurisdiction to take up the superfund legislation. The panel reported HR 3800 (H Rept 103-582, Part I) on June 30, 1994.

The House Public Works and Transportation Committee reported its version (H Rept 103-582, Part II) on Aug. 8. The panel changed several liability provisions in the bill, but its most controversial amendment was offered by Nick J. Rahall II, D-W.Va., to require most superfund contractors who received federal money to pay their workers the prevailing local wage, often set by union contracts, as called for by the Davis-Bacon Act of 1931. The amendment drew opposition from Republicans, southern Democrats and businesses, who argued that such a change in the law would be so expensive that it would almost outweigh any savings gained from reducing the amount of superfund litigation.

After a protracted debate over who should pay how much to clean up hazardous waste sites, the House Ways and Means Committee on Aug. 26 reported the bill (H Rept 103-582, Part III) with a compromise package that included $8.1 billion in retrospective and prospective insurance taxes. Disputes over the tax issue had delayed committee action on the bill for weeks. Large insurance companies that wrote the superfund-related liability policies of the 1970s and early 1980s did not want to be taxed retroactively, but insurers who had had little to do with such policies resisted a prospective tax that would put some of

the superfund burden on them. At a series of meetings during the week of Aug. 15, the Treasury Department struck a deal with a large segment of the insurance industry, agreeing to raise about half the money from taxes retroactive to 1968 and half from taxes that would take effect after the bill's enactment. Not all groups were pleased with the compromise, including reinsurers, who covered various commercial liability policies and were taxed under the proposal.

After winning approval from the three committees with jurisdiction over the superfund law, HR 3800 died in the Rules Committee, which failed to issue a rule to govern debate on the bill. With the House deeply divided, the Rules Committee was unable to resolve differences over the Rahall prevailing wages amendment, as well as an amendment offered by John L. Mica, R-Fla., requiring the EPA to do a cost-benefit analysis before setting a cleanup standard. Risk assessment amendments such as Mica's had snarled other environmental legislation in the 103rd Congress, including an overhaul of the 1974 Safe Drinking Water Act.

On the Senate side, the Environment and Public Works Committee reported S 1834 (S Rept 103-349) on Aug. 19. With the support of moderate Republicans considered critical to the bill's prospects in the Senate, Environment Chairman Max Baucus, D-Mont., won them over by compromising on the bill's ground water cleanup requirements.

The last panel to vote on the superfund overhaul was the Senate Finance Committee, which reported the bill (S Rept 103-389) on Sept. 30 after a bipartisan group of panel members beat back a series of amendments that could have stalled the bill.

With just one week left before Congress's targeted Oct. 7 adjournment and with a backlog of bills awaiting action, the prospects for getting the superfund bill through both chambers, a conference committee and final passage were nil. Senate Minority Leader Bob Dole, R-Kan., a critic of the bill's liability provisions, was threatening to unleash a series of floor amendments that could play havoc with the Senate's schedule. Dole's end-of-session delaying tactics had stymied other Democratic initiatives, such as campaign finance reform.

Moreover, many Democrats facing tough reelection campaigns, including House Speaker Thomas S. Foley, D-Wash., were eager to wrap up the session and get back to the campaign trail as soon as possible. At an Oct. 5 strategy session, supporters agreed reluctantly that the time to give up had come. ❑

Mining Law

A two-year effort to impose royalties and new environmental standards on companies that extracted gold, silver and other hard-rock minerals from public lands in the West ended in failure in 1994, when the Senate and House were unable to reconcile differences in bills passed the previous year (S 775, HR 322).

Attempts to overhaul the 1872 Mining Law had become a perennial battle, pitting western lawmakers whose states were heavily dependent on the mining industry against environmentalists who wanted more protection for federal lands and policy

advocates who wanted more money from those who used feder
al land for commercial enterprises.

When negotiations for a compromise bill reached an impasse, Congress enacted a temporary change in the mining law as part of the fiscal 1995 Interior appropriations bill (HR 4602—PL 103-332). The spending bill imposed a one-year moratorium on new mining patent applications, aimed at stopping the inexpensive sale of mineral-rich lands.

BACKGROUND

The 1872 Mining Law was among the last of the homesteading measures enacted to attract settlers to the western frontier. The law did not charge royalties for the extraction of gold, silver, copper, platinum, zinc and other hard-rock minerals from federal lands. Miners were allowed to buy or patent claims on federal lands for as little as $2.50 an acre. The law also had few environmental standards or requirements for the restoration of lands damaged by hard-rock mining, and it presumed that mining was acceptable on virtually any federal parcel.

Many lambasted the frontier-era law as a federal giveaway program. Mining companies were extracting an estimated $1.2 billion worth of minerals annually from federal lands.

Lawmakers had tried since 1987 to revamp the mining law. But as with other natural resource and public lands issues, western senators had long managed to outmuscle their House colleagues, and the effort to change the law had remained at a virtual standstill. Prospects for an overhaul seemed to improve in 1993, however. Led by Interior Secretary Bruce Babbitt, the new Clinton administration put a priority on preservation of federal land. And concern about the budget deficit prompted a review of what industry was charged for using federal resources. Babbitt and environmentalists wanted the law changed to provide a greater return to taxpayers for the commercial use of federal lands, to impose tough reclamation standards to protect water supplies and to give the secretary more authority to declare some parcels off-limits to hard-rock mining.

Opponents argued that overhauling the law threatened to force mines to close, put thousands of workers out of jobs and encourage U.S. mining companies to set up operations overseas—where the environmental laws were looser and royalty payments less burdensome. Industry officials did not oppose paying a royalty but wanted to be able to deduct the costs of production and development first. The industry also argued that existing state laws were sufficient to repair damaged lands and that new federal regulations were unnecessary.

President Clinton initially had planned to include a new 12.5 percent royalty on hard-rock mineral sales as part of his proposed 1993 deficit reduction package. Before submitting his plan, however, he bowed to western lawmakers and dropped the royalty, though he promised to push the fee as part of separate legislation. Although the administration never proposed separate legislation, Babbitt voiced support for a tough bill (S 257) sponsored by Sen. Dale Bumpers, D-Ark., and for HR 322, the House measure.

LEGISLATIVE ACTION

The Senate on May 25, 1993, passed by voice vote a lean, industry-backed mining bill (S 775). The bill had been reported by the Senate Energy and Natural Resources Committee on May 19 (S Rept 103-45).

Committee Chairman J. Bennett Johnston, D-La., said the bill represented "a ticket to conference committee" with the House. Fearing that a stronger bill would never get past the western-dominated Energy Committee, Johnston moved S 775 swiftly through committee and onto the Senate floor without amendments. Bumpers, the Senate's most ardent advocate of mining reform, agreed with Johnston's strategy and stopped pushing his own tougher bill.

S 775, sponsored by Larry E. Craig, R-Idaho, included a 2 percent royalty on the extraction of hard-rock minerals but allowed miners to deduct more development, exploration and production costs. The bill eliminated the practice of selling federal lands cheaply and required miners to pay the fair market value of the land's surface—not including the value of the underground minerals.

S 775 required a $25 location fee, but it limited annual maintenance fees to $100. The maintenance fee was to be waived for miners with 10 claims or fewer, and miners with 10 to 50 claims were to pay $25 a year to maintain each claim. Craig's bill required miners to comply with state laws for reclamation, which varied widely in their stringency. It did not set up a fund to pay for the repair of abandoned mines.

In contrast, the House passed a tough bill that represented an environmentalists' wish list. Despite strong opposition from western Republicans, the House passed HR 322 on Nov. 18, 1993, by a **key vote of 316–108 (R 70–102; D 245–6; I 1–0).** The bill, written by Nick J. Rahall II, D-W.Va., with the aid of Natural Resources Committee Chairman George Miller, D-Calif., and Energy and Mineral Resources Subcommittee Chairman Richard H. Lehman, D-Calif., had been reported by the Natural Resources Committee Nov. 9 (H Rept 103-338). *(1993 key votes, p. 979)*

HR 322 imposed an 8 percent royalty on the extraction of hard-rock minerals but allowed miners to deduct the costs of smelting and shipping. It also required miners to pay a $25 location fee for each claim, a $100 annual fee to maintain existing claims and a $200 annual fee for new claims. The size of a mining claim increased from 20 acres to 40 acres under the bill. Small mining operations with 10 claims or fewer were exempt from the maintenance fees, although they were required to perform $100 worth of work annually to keep their claims active.

Under the House bill, all revenue from royalties and fees was to be placed in a new fund to pay for the cleanup of abandoned mines damaged by past mining operations. The bill included stricter rules for mining operations, aimed at making them more environmentally sensitive. And it gave the interior secretary the authority to declare certain federal lands unsuitable for mining operations.

During floor consideration of various amendments, HR 322's managers worked hard to maintain the bill's balance. Bill opponents questioned whether miners would be able to meet the bill's requirement that their parcels be restored to the uses they were capable of supporting before the mining. An amendment by Barbara F. Vucanovich, R-Nev., to add to this provision the phrase "to the maximum extent practicable" was rejected on a 149–278 vote on Nov. 16. But bill proponents earlier that day also beat back, 199–232, an amendment by Peter A. DeFazio, D-Ore., to allow the interior secretary to declare lands unsuitable for mining if mining activities would cause significant damage (the bill specified "significant, permanent and irreparable" damage). Lehman said DeFazio's amendment threatened to "lock up far more land than is necessary."

CONFERENCE STALEMATE

House and Senate conferees began formal negotiations to resolve their differences on the mining overhaul in late June 1994. It was a multisided affair with Johnston in the middle. A consummate deal-maker who relished the role, Johnston quickly found himself trying to placate six constituencies: industry; environmentalists; House Natural Resources Committee Chairman Miller and the House; western Republicans on the Senate Energy Committee; Babbitt and the Clinton administration; and western Democrats such as Sen. Harry Reid of Nevada, whose votes were needed to block the GOP.

A flurry of proposals, eight by Johnston's count, went back and forth among the key players over a period of five months. None of the negotiating was done in public. Johnston's final offer, made late Sept. 28, included a 3.5 percent royalty, relatively tame provisions for the interior secretary to block mining on fragile lands and a crucial concession by environmentalists that the federal government would not impose new water quality standards for mining. The proposal also included expanded authority for citizens to sue for violations of the law, a provision sought by environmentalists and opposed by industry.

But the industry balked at the proposal and Miller said it was unacceptable to the House. Negotiations came to an end on Sept. 29, when environmentalists and the mining industry acknowledged they could not reconcile their differences.

The defeat of the mining law overhaul was a stinging blow to Babbitt. Already chastened by a bitter fight over grazing fees and suffering from a White House seemingly more concerned about maintaining its western support than in land reform, Babbitt had kept a low profile during the mining law debate. Environmentalists and industry privately criticized the secretary for not weighing in earlier or more forcefully in what was deemed by both groups to be an achievable goal for the session. (Grazing fees, this page)

INTERIOR APPROPRIATIONS BILL

When negotiations for a compromise bill reached an impasse, Ralph Regula, R-Ohio, ranking member of the House Interior Appropriations Subcommittee, succeeded in winning a temporary change in the mining law as part of the fiscal 1995 Interior appropriations bill (HR 4602), which cleared Congress on Sept. 28, 1994. The spending bill imposed a one-year moratorium on new mining patent applications.

Regula had included the moratorium in his chamber's Interior spending bill every year since 1991, but western senators had never agreed to it. The House in 1994 again included the provision in its version of the appropriations legislation as a way to put pressure on the mining bill conferees and as an insurance policy in case those talks failed. To show just how serious they were, House members on Sept. 13 agreed 318–64 to a nonbinding motion instructing their conferees on HR 4602 to keep the moratorium in the final spending bill.

Senate conferees did not want to hold up the spending bill and reluctantly agreed to a compromise with the House. Under the deal, no new mining applications would be accepted for one year, although more than two-thirds of the more than 600 pending applications—those that were halfway through the years-long review process—would be allowed to proceed.

The mining industry said it had essentially been operating under a patent moratorium for at least a year, because Babbitt had halted a Bush administration practice that expedited the review of mining patent applications. Barrick Goldstrike Mines Inc., a Canadian company developing a gold mine in Nevada, sued Babbitt for the delay and eventually won the legal battle. On May 16, 1994, Babbitt held a news conference to sign seven deeds to Barrick that allowed the company to buy about 1,950 acres of public land—believed to contain an estimated $10 billion in gold—for less than $10,000. Babbitt had used the occasion to underscore the need for mining law reform. ❑

Grazing Rules

The Clinton administration's plans to raise grazing fees and impose tough environmental standards on federal rangelands was stopped cold in the 103rd Congress by the opposition of western senators.

When legislative action appeared unlikely, Interior Secretary Bruce Babbitt in 1993 attempted to take administrative steps to impose grazing policy changes. But the Senate moved quickly to bar spending of any money to implement the proposed changes, as part of the fiscal 1994 Interior appropriations bill (HR 2520—PL 103-138). Although House-Senate conferees on HR 2520 worked out a grazing fee compromise, a Senate filibuster forced supporters to drop the conference language before the funding bill could clear.

BACKGROUND

Critics had long contended that federal grazing fees amounted to a subsidy for 27,000 western ranchers—dubbed "welfare cowboys" by Rep. Mike Synar, D-Okla.

The existing grazing fee rate, based on a formula established by a 1985 executive order issued by President Ronald Reagan, was $1.86 per animal unit month—enough forage to feed one cow and calf, five sheep or one horse for a month. That was about one-fifth the amount charged on private lands, although ranchers contended that the lower fee was justified because they had to pay for improvements such as fences and stock ponds that were normally provided on higher-priced private lands.

Environmentalists also warned that the low fees had led to years of overgrazing on once-verdant ranges and grasslands.

But western ranchers, portraying themselves as the backbone of the Old West, countered that increased federal fees would drive many of them out of business. They had been aided by western senators, who for years had succeeded in blocking attempts to raise grazing fees substantially. *(Congress and the Nation Vol. VIII, p. 518)*

ADMINISTRATION PROPOSALS

President Clinton vowed in early 1993 to overhaul grazing policy as part of the budget reconciliation process. Although the Senate on March 23 tabled (killed), 59–40, an amendment to its fiscal 1994 budget resolution (S Con Res 18) that would have cut out most of Clinton's proposed increases for public land usage, the administration clearly faced a tough battle. Just a week after the vote, western senators successfully lobbied Clinton to reverse his budget proposals. Because congressional approval was not needed to implement higher grazing fees, Clinton instead sought to pursue grazing policy changes by executive order.

Secretary Babbitt on Aug. 9 announced administrative steps to impose higher grazing fees and tough environmental standards for federal rangeland. He said grazing fees would increase to $4.28 over three years from the existing $1.86. The Bureau of Land Management (BLM) was to retain the rights to water, even after ranchers built water facilities on public lands, making its policy consistent with U.S. Forest Service standards. Babbitt also proposed levying steep fees to discourage subletting of grazing permits and tying the duration of a grazing permit to a rancher's environmental stewardship.

LEGISLATIVE ACTION

Before Babbitt's August announcement, Synar and Ralph Regula, R-Ohio, had introduced a bill (HR 643) to change the formula used to calculate the grazing fees and to eventually increase the fees to more than $5 a month. HR 643 was never acted on. Synar and Regula had planned to offer the same language as an amendment to BLM reauthorization legislation (HR 2530), but they held off after the administration's action. A Regula amendment to increase grazing fees by 33 percent was added to the fiscal 1994 Interior funding bill (HR 2520), by a House subcommittee, but the amendment was killed on the House floor July 14 on a procedural vote because it violated rules against legislating on an appropriations bill. *(BLM reauthorization, p. 429)*

The Senate on Sept. 14 defined its opposition to grazing policy overhaul, when it adopted, by a **key vote of 59–40 (R 38–5; D 21–35)**, a Pete V. Domenici, R-N.M., amendment to HR 2520 that would bar Babbitt from spending any money in the bill to implement his grazing proposals for one year. *(1993 key votes, p. 979)*

Fearing that past House support for higher grazing proposals could lead to a stalemate over the Senate amendment, Sen. Harry Reid, D-Nev., sought a compromise in conference with Synar and other House Democrats. The legislators agreed to language

that would increase the fees to $3.45 over three years; after fiscal 1996, any increase or decrease in the fee would be limited to 15 percent annually. The compromise codified most of Babbitt's land management proposals, including:

- Prohibiting those who received new permits to graze cattle on federal land from claiming rights to water and water facilities. Existing permit holders would be allowed to retain rights to water and facilities.
- Allowing permits to be suspended if ranchers violated environmental safeguards.
- Imposing a 20 percent surcharge on ranchers who subleased the land for grazing.
- Abolishing grazing advisory boards dominated by ranchers and herders and replacing them with panels that included environmentalists, wildlife managers and fisheries experts as well as ranchers.

Babbitt agreed to hold off on other rangeland proposals for one year, including a plan to issue comprehensive environmental and management guidelines for federal rangeland.

The House accepted the compromise Oct. 20 on a 317–106 vote. But when the final version of the spending bill came to the Senate floor, most of the western legislators balked, contending that the land management proposals were far too sweeping. After the leadership failed three times to get the 60 votes needed to cut off debate—cloture votes failed 53–41 on Oct. 21, 51–45 on Oct. 26 and 54–44 on Oct. 28—both sides agreed to drop all grazing fee provisions from the bill, as well as Domenici's one-year moratorium. The western senators then ended their filibuster, and the Senate adopted the conference report (H Rept 103-299), 91–9, on Nov. 9. The House accepted the change and cleared the bill by voice vote that same day.

POSTSCRIPT

The final agreement on the Interior spending bill left Babbitt free to pursue his grazing proposals. But the maneuverings in Congress had altered the political climate considerably. Babbitt appeared far more conciliatory toward the concerns of ranchers and their allies in the Senate than he had when the legislative tug of war began.

And, by late 1994, he seemed even more resigned to political reality. In a Dec. 21, 1994, printed statement, Babbitt said he would defer to Congress on the issue. He agreed to give Congress six months to review the environmental portions of his proposed grazing plan before issuing a final rule. His announcement came after receiving a Dec. 6 letter from Sens. Domenici and Larry E. Craig, R-Idaho, that warned Congress could use "all possible means" to stop the regulations unless there was more congressional and public input.

The battle was renewed in the 104th Congress, when Babbitt finally put into effect new regulations for grazing lands. *(1995–1996 action, p. 455)* ❑

Clean Water

Like many of the other environmental bills that came before the 103rd Congress, efforts to overhaul and reauthorize the nation's clean water law fell victim to changing agendas and conflicting goals. A bill (S 2093) was reported out of committee in the Senate in 1994, but companion legislation in the House (HR 3948) drew a bipartisan challenge and never reached the markup stage.

The driving force behind the reauthorization effort had been the impending expiration of the Clean Water Act's revolving loan fund, which helped local communities build sewage treatment plants. Although the reauthorization legislation died, appropriators continued to provide money for the fund after it expired on Sept. 30, 1994.

BACKGROUND

Almost a quarter century had passed since Ohio's once heavily polluted Cuyahoga River ignited for a third time, mobilizing Congress to pass in 1972 the nation's first sweeping clean water law. Designed to reduce the dumping of raw industrial sewage into rivers and streams by regulating the discharge of pollutants and the overflow from sewers, the Federal Water Pollution Control Act Amendments of 1972 (PL 92-500) was credited with dramatically improving water quality in many of the nation's lakes, rivers and streams. (Congress and the Nation Vol. III, p. 792)

The original law provided federal grants to help communities build sewage treatment plants and other pollution-control projects. Congress eliminated the grant program in 1987, the last time the law was reauthorized (PL 100-4), and replaced it with a state revolving loan fund. Under the 1987 rewrite, the federal government provided seed money to states, which in turn made low-interest loans to local communities to help build or refurbish sewage treatment plants. (Congress and the Nation Vol. VII, p. 454)

The pool of funds was divided among the states based on a 1976 formula that took into account the sewage treatment needs of communities in a particular state as well as other factors, including population. Senators from small states or from those whose population had grown considerably since 1976 wanted to ensure that their states would receive a fair share of the funds.

In addition to the funding formula, lawmakers were faced with the problem of coping with a new generation of pollution not addressed under the 1972 statute. Known as non-point source pollution, it came from water that had drained from such places as farmland, asphalt roads, construction sites, and treated lawns and golf courses. Because the origins of the pollution could not be linked to a single pipe or source, it was the most difficult water problem to trace or to regulate.

Another highly controversial issue was the protection of wetlands. There were an estimated 104 million acres of wetlands in the lower 48 states and 170 million acres in Alaska. In the mid-1980s, those wetlands were disappearing at a rate of nearly 300,000 acres each year. Environmentalists wanted to protect the fragile ecosystems, citing their role as a critical habitat for wildlife. Wetlands also were used to control floods and maintain water quality. At the same time, farmers and developers were seeking more flexibility in managing wetlands.

The Clinton administration on Aug. 24, 1993, offered a series of administrative and legislative recommendations aimed at protecting wetlands. The plan was designed to give farmers and developers more flexibility to comply with federal regulations. It also called on Congress to give states and local governments financial incentives to protect wetlands.

A further wrinkle in the debate was the burgeoning interest in private property rights. Advocates of property rights were watchful for provisions that would limit landowners' use of their land or that would not ensure proper compensation if the government took control of the land or limited its uses.

LEGISLATIVE ACTION

Bills to reauthorize the Clean Water Act and to protect wetlands never got beyond the hearing stage in 1993.

The bipartisan leadership of the Senate Environment and Public Works Committee—Chairman Max Baucus, D-Mont., and ranking member John H. Chafee, R-R.I.—made reauthorization of the Clean Water Act their top legislative priority for the 103rd Congress. The panel on May 10, 1994, reported S 2093 (S Rept 103-257), which was aimed at giving states more flexibility to address water pollution problems. It also sought to ease regulatory burdens on farmers and developers who wanted to build on wetlands, while strengthening protections on more environmentally sensitive areas.

S 2093 included a controversial new formula for allocating funds from the revolving fund, based on population and water quality needs. The formula tended to favor heavily populated states, and members from states with smaller populations promised a floor fight over it.

But the bill never made it to the Senate floor. Baucus decided to wait for the House to mark up its bill first; meanwhile, an agricultural coalition raised concerns that the bill would be too burdensome for farmers. They argued that some of the issues should be put off until 1995, when Congress was expected to write a comprehensive farm bill.

A House Public Works and Transportation Committee subcommittee held hearings in May on HR 3948, a bill sponsored by panel Chairman Norman Y. Mineta, D-Calif. The bill was generally in line with the administration's recommendations, including provisions to deal with agricultural runoff, protection of key watersheds and no net loss of wetlands. But a bipartisan group on the House panel objected to the bill and offered its own draft proposal that did not address pollution caused by agricultural runoff, made watershed protection plans voluntary, extended deadlines under the existing law and scaled back protections for wetlands.

Further dimming the bill's chances was a shift of emphasis in the environmental community, with the focus being placed on other issues such as the "superfund" overhaul. ('Superfund,' p. 410)

Pesticide Regulation

No agreement was reached in the 103rd Congress on major revisions to the nation's pesticide laws. Legislative attempts—

only one of which made it as far as subcommittee approval—fell victim to the long-standing stalemate between propesticide interests and those who wanted tighter restrictions on the use of potentially hazardous farm chemicals.

In related action, the House approved a bill to keep less profitable pesticides on the market and Congress cleared legislation to postpone some pesticide regulations.

DELANEY CLAUSE

At issue in the 103rd Congress was a controversial clause of the 1938 Federal Food, Drug and Cosmetic Act. While the law permitted raw food products to contain infinitesimal residues of pesticides that had been scientifically determined to be potentially cancer-causing, a provision known as the Delaney Clause prohibited any trace of carcinogenic residue in processed food. When the provision was enacted in 1958, chemical analysts were able to detect pesticide traces in parts per million. By the early 1990s, technology had advanced to the point that incredibly minute traces were detectable in parts per trillion. Advocates of pesticide use worried that such exacting technological capabilities would uncover chemical traces in practically all processed foods and would therefore lead to the wholesale banning of certain pesticides. *(Congress and the Nation Vol. I, p. 1176)*

Because the Delaney Clause had such a broad effect, the Environmental Protection Agency (EPA) had rarely enforced it in recent years. But a 1992 federal court ruling in a suit brought by certain environmental activists required its enforcement. Despite this legal action, even some environmentalists viewed the Delaney Clause's total ban on pesticide residues as too extreme. They proposed a more moderate but still stringent standard. Their proposal was still too tough for pesticide makers and users, who favored a much looser standard. *(Congress and the Nation Vol. VIII, p. 522)*

Pressure to rewrite the pesticide laws mounted with the release in June 1993 of a National Academy of Sciences report on toxicity in children's diets. The report concluded that there should be different standards for measuring the pesticide tolerances of children and adults, which was not the case under existing regulations. It also recommended that scientists take into account the cumulative amount of pesticides in children's diets.

Three major legislative proposals to replace the Delaney Clause with a single standard to govern both raw and processed foods were put forward in the 103rd Congress. But they differed significantly on how stringent to make the new standard. A House Agriculture subcommittee approved one of them, HR 1627, in July 1994 but the bill went no further.

Major pesticide legislation was finally enacted in 1996. *(1995–1996 action, p. 446)*

MINOR-USE PESTICIDES

With no sign that the 103rd Congress was going to enact a sweeping overhaul of the nation's pesticide use laws, the House in 1994 passed a more limited bill (HR 967) aimed at keeping less profitable "minor-use" pesticides—those used on fruits and vegetables—on the market. But in the Senate, those eager to address broader pesticide control issues in a single bill were unwilling to act on HR 967.

Congress in 1988 had passed legislation requiring all pesticides to be reviewed and "reregistered" by the EPA by 1997. Manufacturers complained that the cost of the extensive testing of minor-use pesticides outstripped their sales revenues. As a result, many manufacturers were opting not to make the minor-use pesticides at all. That brought protests from farmers, who said these chemicals were often the only pesticides that effectively protected a particular crop against a specific pest.

HR 967, which provided several incentives to encourage chemical companies to continue production, was reported by the House Agriculture Committee (H Rept 103-784) on Oct. 3, 1994, and passed by the full House the next day by a 334–80 vote.

PESTICIDE REGULATIONS DELAY

Congress in 1994 cleared legislation (S 1913—PL 103-231) that postponed implementation of certain pesticide safety training and labeling requirements under the 1947 Federal Insecticide, Fungicide and Rodenticide Act.

The bill put off the effective date of select EPA regulations from April 15, 1994, until Jan. 1, 1995, in order to give the agency more time to provide necessary training, education and compliance information to farmers and regulators.

The bill, however, did not postpone pesticide safety protections for farm workers. Indeed, it required that pesticide users comply with all the provisions for worker protection that appeared directly on the label of pesticides.

The Senate passed S 1913 by voice vote on March 9, 1994, and the House passed an amended version by voice vote March 17. The Senate cleared the bill by voice vote March 24. It was signed into law April 6. ❑

Endangered Species

Hearings were held in the House and Senate in 1994 on reauthorization of the 1973 Endangered Species Act, but Congress was focused on other environmental issues and there was no further action. The controversial law—a target of advocates of private property rights—expired in 1992; annual appropriations had kept enforcement alive.

The law (PL 93-205) made it illegal to kill, injure, trap, harass or otherwise take any animal or plant that was deemed endangered or threatened. It also established a comprehensive process for designating an endangered or threatened species and required a plan for its recovery. Among its success stories was the American bald eagle, taken off the endangered list July 4, 1994, and bumped down to a less restrictive category. *(PL 93-205, Congress and the Nation Vol. IV, p. 289)*

In recent years, however, the law had been criticized for ignoring economic interests and had sparked an intense debate about balancing the needs of landowners with the goals of environmentalists. The law also was criticized for emphasizing the protection of single species, instead of ecosystems where several species might be in danger.

Interior Secretary Bruce Babbitt announced changes June 14 to make the law more flexible and easier to understand for landowners. On Aug. 11, Babbitt pledged that the administration would make no further demands on property owners after they obtained approval for a plan to protect endangered species on their land.

A key critic of the law in the House was W. J. "Billy" Tauzin, D-La., who wanted to make sure that landowners who lost their livelihoods or whose property values decreased because of regulations were compensated by the federal government. Environmentalists feared that Tauzin's proposals would weaken the law.

Tauzin and his supporters had used several land and conservation bills as vehicles to attack the law. In 1993, the House restricted access to private property by federal scientists as part of a bill (HR 1845) to formally authorize a new research agency to study the nation's plants and animals. Tauzin also won approval in 1994 for an amendment to the California desert bill (S 21—PL 103-433) to require the federal government to appraise private property needed for wilderness and national parks as though it did not contain endangered species. The intent was to raise property values. But Tauzin lost on an amendment to compensate landowners as part of a bill (HR 5044) to designate American Heritage areas. (*National Biological Survey, p. 418; California desert protection, p. 405; American Heritage areas, p. 422*)   ❑

Pacific Northwest Forests

The 103rd Congress remained mostly on the sidelines as the White House and the federal court system attempted to resolve the long-running legal dispute over how to protect the threatened northern spotted owl and its old-growth forest habitat without jeopardizing timber jobs in the already economically depressed Pacific Northwest. The issue was finally resolved in late 1994 when a federal judge accepted President Clinton's forest management plan.

Congress, in the meantime, took action on a variety of bills designed to boost the area's timber-dependent economy and employment prospects.

BACKGROUND

The federal government had been caught up since 1989 in a protracted legal battle over timber harvests in the Pacific Northwest. The issue became more heated in 1990, when the spotted owl, which inhabited old-growth forests in Washington, Oregon and northern California, was declared threatened under the 1973 Endangered Species Act (PL 93-205). Most old-growth forests were on federal land.

In 1991, U.S. District Judge William Dwyer of Seattle halted logging on public lands, ruling that the government was violating environmental laws by overharvesting. The Bush administration convened a high-level committee—known as the God squad—which voted in May 1992 to suspend the Endangered Species Act and allow logging on 13 of 44 disputed tracts of timberland that were home to the spotted owl. But court injunctions prevented the action from taking effect, and Congress in 1992 failed to enact any compromise logging plan. (*Congress and the Nation Vol. VIII, p. 520*)

President Clinton announced a forest management plan on July 1, 1993. Clinton's proposal called for an annual timber harvest of 1.2 billion board feet, about half the amount cut before the federal court imposed the logging ban. (A board foot was one foot square by one inch thick.) The plan reserved areas for the spotted owl in which logging was to be greatly restricted. (An estimated 3,600 pairs of birds remained in 1993.) It also set aside 10 areas for ecological experiments and watershed protections. To help workers and families in the region, Clinton proposed spending $1.2 billion over five years for a new Northwest Economic Adjustment Fund to support retraining and activities such as cleaning up logging roads.

The plan was immediately assailed from all sides. Environmentalists said it did not go far enough to block logging activity or preserve fragile ecosystems. Timber groups contended that the plan threatened the future of their industry and thousands of jobs. Home builders warned that fewer new houses would be built, because less timber would be available.

To win over environmentalists and strengthen its case in court, the administration scaled back the logging proposal on Feb. 23, 1994. The revised plan called for harvests of 1.1 billion board feet of timber annually over 10 years, one-fifth the amount cut during peak years in the mid-1980s. The plan would establish reserves of old-growth forests to protect the owl's breeding grounds, as well as protect key watersheds and streams. An estimated 9,500 jobs would be lost under the plan. Despite the changes, environmentalists and the timber industry challenged the plan and filed separate lawsuits in May.

But on Dec. 21, Judge Dwyer declared that the administration plan, which was known as Option 9, was legal. The court ruled that the plan met the requirements of the Endangered Species Act and forestry management laws.

LEGISLATIVE ACTION

The lengthy legal action left Congress to focus on less sweeping steps, including allocating money to the region—a key element of Clinton's plan to resolve the long-stalled issue.

Budget Reconciliation Bill. Congress set up a long-term funding mechanism to provide economic development for the Pacific Northwest as part of the budget reconciliation bill (HR 2264—PL 103-66) enacted in 1993. The bill set aside 85 percent of the receipts from the sale of timber on federal lands in the Pacific Northwest in fiscal 1994 for economic development in the region. After fiscal 1994, the amount dropped by 3 percent per year until fiscal 2003. The receipts were to be shared by the federal government, the three Northwest states and the affected counties. Previously, the amount set aside for the region from the timber receipts had fluctuated.

To make up for the loss in revenue to the Treasury, the bill eliminated an export subsidy for foreign sales of unprocessed logs, generating about $390 million in savings annually. Of that amount, about $270 million was earmarked for the timber communities and the remainder was to go for deficit reduction. (*Budget reconciliation bill, p. 44*)

Congress in 1994 cleared legislation (HR 5161—PL 103-443) making technical corrections to PL 103-66 and clarifying how the timber receipts were to be distributed. The House passed HR 5161 by voice vote Oct. 5; the Senate followed suit Oct. 8. The president signed the measure Nov. 2.

Interior Appropriations Bills. Congress in 1993 cleared a fiscal 1994 Interior appropriations bill (HR 2520—PL 103-138) containing $69.5 million for various forestry, wildlife and park programs in the Pacific Northwest.

The following year Congress included in the fiscal 1995 Interior appropriations bill (HR 4602—PL 103-332) about $169 million to allow timber sales proposed in the administration's plan to proceed and to pay for watershed assessment and restoration projects and ongoing economic development projects.

Export Ban. Congress in 1993 cleared legislation (HR 2343—PL 103-45) aimed at boosting employment in the timber-processing industry by restoring an export ban on raw logs from state-owned and other public lands that had been enacted as part of the 1990 Customs and Trade Act (PL 101-382). A federal court had ruled that a provision of the 1990 law requiring governors to come up with plans to implement part of the log ban was unconstitutional because it required states to regulate trade, a power that the Constitution delegated to Congress. *(PL 101-382, Congress and the Nation Vol. VIII, p. 180)*

HR 2343 circumvented the problem by making the commerce secretary responsible for implementing regulations, though states could voluntarily submit their own plans. House sponsor Jolene Unsoeld, D-Wash., said that exporting unprocessed timber made no sense when there was a shortage of logs for mills in the Northwest—a situation that had caused job loss in the industry. By voice votes, the House passed the bill on June 14 and the Senate cleared it June 17. Clinton signed the measure into law on July 1.

Community Assistance. The House on Oct. 6, 1993, cleared by voice vote legislation (S 1508—PL 103-115) amending the 1990 farm bill (PL 101-624) to provide economic development assistance and diversification programs for communities in the region that were economically dependent on timber from national forests. The Senate had passed the bill, which clarified and broadened eligibility standards, by voice vote on Sept. 30. S 1508 was signed into law on Oct. 26. *(1990 farm bill, Congress and the Nation Vol. VIII, p. 537)*

Rural Development Aid. The Senate by voice vote on Oct. 6, 1994, cleared a bill (HR 4196—PL 103-427) authorizing water and sewer grants to timber-dependent communities of up to 25,000 in population in the areas affected by logging restrictions. Previously, the grants had been available for towns of 10,000 or fewer. The House had passed the bill by voice vote on Sept. 29. Clinton signed HR 4196 on Oct. 31.   ❑

National Biological Survey

After lengthy debates on property rights issues, the House in 1993 passed legislation (HR 1845) to authorize an inventory of all plant and animal species in the United States. The Senate took no action on the bill.

The National Biological Survey was a priority of Interior Secretary Bruce Babbitt, who envisioned it as a way of heading off conflicts in the implementation of the 1973 Endangered Species Act (PL 93-205). For example, a protracted battle was taking place in the Pacific Northwest, where efforts to protect the threatened northern spotted owl had collided with the needs of the timber industry. By taking inventory of the nation's biological resources, he said, the government would have a better chance of preventing a species from becoming endangered. *(Pacific Northwest timber feud, p. 417)*

Babbitt used administrative authority to shift funds from an array of programs under eight different branches of the Interior Department to pay about 1,600 workers—1,400 of them scientists—to conduct the survey. But he wanted to make the survey permanent and sought help from some of Congress's key environmentalists to pass authorizing legislation.

Some critics feared that the survey would create even more endangered species controversies. The bill encountered strong opposition from conservatives in the House who argued that it would inspire regulatory decisions that would trample the rights of private property owners. They won a key amendment requiring that the federal government obtain written permission before entering private property.

Although HR 1845 was not enacted, the survey was funded in the fiscal 1994 and 1995 Interior appropriations bills.

LEGISLATIVE ACTION

After two days of debate, the House on Oct. 26 passed HR 1845 by a vote of 255–165. The bill had been reported by the Merchant Marine and Fisheries Committee on July 27 (H Rept 103-193, Part I) and the Natural Resources Committee on Sept. 9 (Part II). The bill provided for the creation of an office within the Interior Department to undertake the survey and supply information on all species. The measure also authorized the creation of a policy board to advise the survey's director and a science council to work with other governmental agencies and private groups.

The bill's supporters had only partial success in fighting off amendments aimed at watering down the legislation. They were on the losing end of votes on two amendments backed by conservatives who said the survey would cause landowners to be blocked from using their land as they wished. The first vote was on an amendment by Charles H. Taylor, R-N.C., requiring that survey workers obtain written permission from landowners before entering private property. The House adopted the amendment on Oct. 6 by a **key vote of 309–115 (R 171–3; D 138–111; I 0–1).** On a closer 217–212 vote that same day, the House adopted a W. J. "Billy" Tauzin, D-La., amendment barring the survey from enlisting the support of volunteers to help collect information. Tauzin argued that untrained or overly pro-environment volunteers would produce tainted data. While these amendments did not cripple the bill, they served as significant portents for more ambitious environmental bills, such as rewrites of the Endangered Species Act and the Clean Water Act. *(1993 key votes, p. 979)*

Two other weakening amendments were deflected on the

grounds that the provisions were not germane because they strayed outside the purview of the biological survey. One, by Tauzin, would have compensated owners of private property that had been devalued by environmental restrictions, and the other, also by Tauzin, would have authorized the director of the survey to consider the economic impact of the work. A Tauzin amendment that won voice vote approval prohibited other federal agencies from using information collected under the survey until it had been disclosed to the landowner.

SURVEY FUNDING

The fiscal 1994 Interior appropriations bill (HR 2520—PL 103-138), which cleared Nov. 9, 1993, provided $163.5 million for the survey. At the behest of Republican conferees, the language of the Taylor amendment was inserted into the final version of the bill. But conferees resisted pressure to include amendments barring the use of volunteers for the survey and forcing the government to disclose survey findings to private property owners.

The fiscal 1995 Interior appropriations bill (HR 4602— PL 103-332), which cleared Sept. 28, 1994, provided $167.2 million for the survey. During House action on the bill June 22, an amendment by Wayne Allard, R-Colo., that would have killed funding for the survey was rejected, 169–259.   ❑

Solid Waste Management

Legislation that would have partially overruled several Supreme Court decisions by giving state and local governments more authority over shipments of solid waste died at the end of the 103rd Congress.

The bill (S 2345) would have allowed states to control the receipt of out-of-state garbage. And, as amended by the House, it included a separate proposal (HR 4683) to allow local governments to direct waste to publicly operated waste disposal facilities. Local governments wanted this so-called flow-control authority to guarantee a revenue stream for the facilities.

Although the House easily endorsed a compromise that included both pieces of legislation, attempts to bring it up in the Senate failed.

BACKGROUND

Municipal solid waste—which included everything from household garbage to nonhazardous industrial wastes—was a growing problem that had given rise to bitter interstate battles. As disposal costs rose and landfills reached their capacity, the issue had pitted major garbage exporters such as New York and New Jersey against states such as Pennsylvania and Indiana that were the destinations of such shipments.

At least 37 states had enacted laws to restrict or otherwise treat out-of-state garbage differently from wastes generated within the state. But, in 1992, the Supreme Court ruled that states did not have the right to ban or place restrictions on the import of out-of-state garbage (*Fort Gratiot Landfill Inc. v. Michigan Department of Natural Resources* and *Chemical Waste Management v. Hunt*). The Court reiterated that the Constitution prohibited states and localities from discriminating against the commerce of another state unless authorized to do so by Congress.

Congressional efforts in 1992 to address the problem failed. (*Congress and the Nation Vol. VIII, p. 523*)

INTERSTATE SOLID WASTE SHIPMENTS

Over the objections of members from major waste-producing states, the House on Sept. 28, 1994, passed a bill (HR 4779) allowing state and local governments to restrict interstate shipments of municipal solid waste. The vote was 368–55, with almost every New York and New Jersey representative voting "nay." HR 4779 had been reported by the Energy and Commerce Committee (H Rept 103-720) on Sept. 16.

The Senate approved companion legislation (S 2345) by voice vote on Sept. 30. The Environment and Public Works Committee had reported the bill (S Rept 103-322) Aug. 1.

'FLOW-CONTROL' LEGISLATION

With adjournment just days away, House and Senate negotiators worked frantically to strike a compromise melding HR 4779 and S 2345, as well as the separate flow-control bill. That bill, HR 4683, had been reported by the Energy and Commerce Committee (H Rept 103-738) on Sept. 22, 1994, and passed by voice vote of the House on Sept. 29.

HR 4683, which would have allowed local governments to specify where their solid waste was to be dumped, had also been inspired by a Supreme Court decision. At least 35 states had laws authorizing some or all municipalities to adopt flow-control ordinances, which required that solid waste be disposed of at designated sites, usually a landfill or incinerator in which the local government had a financial stake. Municipalities argued that flow control made it easier for them to invest in a landfill because they knew it would handle enough volume to recoup an investment. But the Supreme Court ruled May 16, 1994, that flow-control ordinances unlawfully restricted interstate commerce and prevented competition for local waste management contracts (*C&A Carbone v. Town of Clarkstown*). That set Congress in action on the issue. (*Case summary, p. 784*)

Municipalities feared that without flow-control legislation, their bond ratings could be downgraded, which could mean higher financing costs on future projects. But waste haulers and small business owners argued that the legislation would create local monopolies by giving elected officials total authority over solid waste. Adding to the controversy were environmentalists' concerns that flow-control measures could lead to the building of more municipal-owned incinerators.

The House passed HR 4683 by voice vote Sept. 29, after turning back, 161–244, an amendment by Bill Richardson, D-N.M., to ban any future flow control authority, while grandfathering existing facilities that were built on the assumption that they would receive guaranteed waste flows.

COMPROMISE BILL

Negotiators agreed on a compromise that allowed governors to curb interstate shipments to new landfills, but not to landfills that accepted such shipments in 1993. It allowed local govern ments to continue their existing flow-control policies but not to create new ones.

On Oct. 7, the House amended S 2345 to reflect the compromise and passed the bill by voice vote. But on the Senate side, John H. Chafee, R-R.I., criticized some of the bill's provisions as overly broad and blocked the Senate from taking up the legislation in the final hours of the session.   ❑

National Park System

The 103rd Congress considered a series of bills aimed at reorganizing the management of the national park system and boosting national park revenue, but the measures died in the crush of business at the end of the session.

Since the designation of Yellowstone as the first national park in 1872 and the creation of the National Park Service in 1916, the national park system had grown to 367 sites covering 80 million acres in 49 states, the District of Columbia and the U.S. territories. The park system—including preserves, monuments, historic sites, seashores and battlefields in addition to national parks—attracted more than 268 million visitors annually.

Despite the parks' popularity, their operating budgets had not kept pace. The demand for more national parks and the upkeep of the federal lands, especially the recreation areas found in nearly every state and county, was an expensive proposition. Congress allocated about $1.1 billion for park operations in fiscal 1994. But the National Park Service estimated that it would cost at least $2 billion—almost double the agency's budget—to repair a host of facilities and reduce a long list of maintenance projects.

PARK SYSTEM REORGANIZATION

With the national park system facing shrinking budgets and increasing demands for expansion, the House passed legislation (HR 4476) to overhaul management of the system and to establish criteria for adding or removing parks from the system. Separate legislation (S 471) was reported in the Senate but never reached the floor because of the attention being given the California desert bill (S 21).

HR 4476 was reported by the House Natural Resources Committee (H Rept 103-725) on Sept. 19, 1994, and passed by the full House on Sept. 28 by a vote of 421–0. Responding to criticism that the existing review and designation system for the National Park Service failed to plan and prioritize potential system additions, HR 4476 required the Interior Department to submit to Congress a comprehensive plan for the park system within three fiscal years. The plan was to include a list of parks that should be modified or removed from the system. If the list was not submitted to Congress within a year of completion of the overall plan, the bill provided for the establishment of a seven-member commission to determine which park facilities, if any, should be closed.

In contrast, S 471, reported by the Senate Energy and Natural Resources Committee on Sept. 27, would have established at the outset a seven-member commission to review the park system. Under the bill, the interior secretary was also to submit to Congress within three years a national park system plan. Park service officials opposed the creation of an external panel to survey the agency's progress before they had had an opportunity to do so themselves.

PARK CONCESSIONS

In 1994, both the Senate and House passed legislation to force businesses that wanted to provide food, lodging and recreation in national parks to compete for that right. But the measure (S 208) died at the end of the session.

Background

In the 20 years before 1994, national parks had become a prime tourist destination. But critics said that private concessionaires, not the government, had reaped much of the benefits.

The 1965 Concessions Policy Act (PL 89-249) regulated how the Interior Department awarded and managed concession contracts. Private companies that operated concessions were essentially allowed to renew their contracts automatically without regard to their performance. Although each contract stipulated how much money should be paid to the government for the privilege of operating a concession, in practice these franchise fees had been waived or reduced by the Interior Department in exchange for the private company's paying for a capital improvement, such as a new building, at the facility.

As a result, only a fraction of the money made from national park concessions were returned to the Treasury. In 1991, about 660 concessionaires grossed about $618 million and paid the federal government $18.1 million, or roughly 2.9 percent, in franchise fees.

Concessionaires and their supporters in Congress argued that the concessions provided vital services to the public that the government otherwise would have to supply at a substantial cost to taxpayers. They said many concessionaires had made major investments in buildings, equipment and maintenance that benefited the government.

Legislative Action

The Senate Energy and Natural Resources Committee reported S 208 (S Rept 103-226) on Feb. 11, and the bill was passed by the full Senate on March 22 by a vote of 90–9. The House Natural Resources Committee reported its version of the bill (H Rept 103-571) on June 30, and the House passed it July 28 by a 386–30 vote. The Senate never acted on the measure as amended by the House.

Both the Senate and House versions would have eliminated the preferential right of renewal for the roughly 20 percent of concession holders that grossed more than $500,000 a year, requiring instead a competitive bidding process. The maximum term of a contract was to be limited to 10 years, although the interior secretary would have the authority under special circumstances to sign a 20-year contract.

After the bill's enactment, new concessionaires who owned possessory interests—ownership rights to structures built on federal lands—would be reimbursed for improvements at their depreciated value when their contracts expired, instead of at the current market value as under existing law. The bill allowed for any existing concession operator to be reimbursed for the full value of any improvement made before the bill's enactment.

In a key difference with the Senate-passed bill, the House version required competitive bidding for outfitters and guides. The Senate measure gave the interior secretary the authority to set fees for those types of concessions. Supporters of the Senate position argued that outfitters and guides were engaged in a uniquely competitive and dangerous business that required preferential treatment to attract qualified and safe operators.

PARK FEES

Legislation to permit the National Park Service to increase fees for park users (HR 4533) fell victim in 1994 to an end-of-session Republican strategy of slowing the Democratic-controlled House to a halt. A companion Senate bill (S 2121) was reported out of committee but went no further.

Congress had last approved an increase to park entrance fees in 1987. Since then, lawmakers had been reluctant to raise the fees, choosing instead in the 1993 Omnibus Budget-Reconciliation Act (HR 2264—PL 103-66) to expand the Interior and Agriculture departments' authority to assess and collect fees from other recreational activities and facilities, such as boat ramps and swimming areas. *(Budget reconciliation, p. 11)*

The House Natural Resources Committee reported HR 4533 (H Rept 103-793) on Oct. 3, 1994. The House tried twice to pass the bill under suspension of the rules, which did not permit amendments, but was unable to attract the two-thirds majority needed to pass a bill under the expedited procedure. The first vote on Oct. 4 was 238–174, and the second vote the next day was 242–174. No time was left in the session to bring the bill back a third time.

S 2121 was reported from the Energy and Natural Resources Committee (S Rept 103-422) on Sept. 27 but did not make it to the floor, largely because senators were focused on clearing the California Desert Protection Act.

HR 4533 allowed Congress to retain its authority to set national park fees, instead of giving broad discretion to the interior secretary to increase or reduce park fees, as had been requested by the administration. The bill provided for an increase in the cap on entrance fees from $3 to $6 per person, and from $5 to $20 per vehicle. The House bill also would have allowed the park service, beginning in fiscal 1996, to keep 100 percent of the revenue generated by the increase in fees, for resource protection, interpretation programs, research and maintenance. The Clinton administration and the Senate bill both called for half of the new fees collected to remain in the parks for building improvements. ❑

Presidio Park Management

With the historic Presidio military post in San Francisco slated to become a national park, the House twice in 1994 passed legislation to provide for its management and operation. An amended version of one of the bills was reported in the Senate, but the legislation never made it to the Senate floor.

BACKGROUND

The Presidio, established as a Spanish colonial military settlement in 1776, was the oldest continually operating military post in the nation. Located at the foot of the Golden Gate Bridge, the 1,480-acre complex with its 870 buildings was a scenic attraction marked by forests, grasslands and coastal bluffs.

A law enacted in 1972 (PL 92-589) mandated that, if the Defense Department ever decided that it no longer needed the base, the army facility would be shifted to the National Park Service and become part of the Golden Gate National Urban Recreation Area. In 1988, the Presidio was included in the list of unneeded facilities targeted for shutdown by the Base Realignment and Closure Commission. In 1993, the commission modified its recommendation to allow the continued presence of the 6th U.S. Army Headquarters at the Presidio.

The Presidio was slated to be converted to Interior Department control on Oct. 1, 1994. The General Accounting Office estimated that it would cost $700 million to $1.2 billion over 15 years to complete the transfer.

The park service planned to restore and adapt for new uses about 475 historic buildings on the Presidio lands; it planned to tear down most of the others to create additional open space.

LEGISLATIVE ACTION

The House passed its first bill, HR 3433, on Aug. 18, 1994, by a vote of 245–168, after defeating two Republican amendments aimed at limiting the Presidio's costs. HR 3433 provided for the creation of the Presidio Trust, a government corporation within the Interior Department, to manage the facility. The trust would be allowed to borrow up to $150 million at any one time directly from the Treasury. The Appropriations Committee was to allocate any of the funds that would be lent. HR 3433 had been reported by the House Natural Resources Committee on July 21 and by Ways and Means on Aug. 9 (H Rept 103-615, Parts I and II).

The Senate Energy and Natural Resources Committee reported a revised version of HR 3433 on Sept. 22 (S Rept 103-429). The Senate committee-approved bill also set up a government corporation. However, unlike the House-passed bill, which made financing for the trust subject to annual appropriation, the Senate version allowed the trust to incur as public debt the proceeds from the sale of up to $150 million worth of securities.

On Oct. 7, the House gave voice vote approval to a fresh bill (HR 5231) that was identical to the House-passed version of HR 3433. With the initial measure amended and bogged down in the Senate, sponsors hoped to free up the legislation and win quick Senate passage. The Senate, however, did not act on HR 5231.

LEASING THE PRESIDIO

In related action, the House passed legislation (HR 3286) by voice vote on Nov. 15, 1993, aimed at paving the way for private companies to lease buildings on the grounds of the mothballed Presidio Army Base in San Francisco. The Senate did not act on the bill.

Under HR. 3286, which had been reported Nov. 15 by the House Natural Resources Committee (H Rept 103-363), the Interior Department was to be allowed to lease out a 50-building complex at the Presidio that included a hospital and biological research institute. Bill sponsor Nancy Pelosi, D-Calif., whose House district included the Presidio, said leasing out the hospital would help speed up the facility's conversion to a national park. ❑

American Heritage Areas

The House in 1994 passed a bill (HR 5044) authorizing the Interior Department to designate 10 American Heritage areas that had historical, natural or cultural significance in their communities but did not reach national park status. There was no action in the Senate.

The House Natural Resources Committee had reported an earlier version of the legislation (HR 3707—H Rept 103-570) on June 30, 1994. The House passed HR 5044, which incorporated parts of HR 3707, on Oct. 5 by a 281–137 vote.

House passage had come over the objections of property rights advocates, who argued that the bill would permit local governments to include private lands within the boundaries of the heritage areas and establish bicycle and hiking trails on the land without an owner's consent. They had succeeded in blocking HR 5044 when it was first brought up Sept. 27 under suspension of the rules—an expedited procedure that allowed no amendments and required a two-thirds vote for passage. The vote was 273–150, nine votes short.

The property rights debate resurfaced when the bill was taken up again on Oct. 5. W. J. "Billy" Tauzin, D-La., who had led the charge to add protections for property owners on numerous bills, had hoped to add two amendments to the legislation: the first would have required local governments to obtain a landowner's consent before including land in a heritage area; the second would have required that landowners be compensated if their property values declined as a result of being included without their consent.

Instead, the House voted 222–202 to add language by Ralph Regula, R-Ohio, to require county governments, not individual property owners, to consent to inclusion of land in a heritage area. Lawmakers also adopted, 234–187, an amendment by Nick J. Rahall III, D-W.Va., to require that landowners be told how to seek compensation if their property was included in a heritage area. ❑

Steamtown Historic Site

The House in 1994 passed legislation (HR 3708) to scale back funding for the controversial Steamtown National Historic site in Scranton, Pa., but the full Senate did not act on the measure.

Since its inception in 1986, Steamtown, a museum designed to memorialize the age of steam-powered locomotion, had been characterized by critics as a quintessential "pork-barrel" project. They raised questions about its historical value and objected that lawmakers had appropriated $01 million for the site even though it had never been authorized.

A procedure existed for designating a national park: the interior secretary, with help from an advisory board, was asked by Congress for recommendations on proposed additions to the system. But lawmakers had bypassed that process, in essence, sanctioning new national parks through appropriations, as they had in the case of Steamtown.

The House on July 12, 1994, passed by voice vote HR 3708, which was aimed at changing the rules governing the operation, maintenance and development of Steamtown. The bill had been reported by the Natural Resources Committee (H Rept 103-588) earlier that day. The Senate Energy and Natural Resources Committee on Sept. 27 reported an amended version of HR 3708, but the Senate took no further action on it. ❑

Colorado Wilderness

Congress in 1993 cleared legislation (HR 631—PL 103-77) designating 611,730 acres in Colorado as wilderness and setting aside 174,510 acres in a less protective management area.

Passage of the Colorado wilderness protection bill ended a 13-year impasse over the issue of water rights on the lands. In the past, House leaders had strongly opposed Senate water rights language because it differed from wilderness laws that gave the federal government the right to water found within wilderness areas. Key House lawmakers and environmentalists feared that if water rights were not given to the federal government, state water authorities would be more likely to rule in favor of the water claims of landowners or municipalities, possibly threatening preservation of wilderness areas dependent upon scarce water resources.

Those opposed to federal control included property owners living upstream from the wilderness areas, who were concerned that they might lose their access to water. The dispute doomed legislation as recently as 1992. *(Congress and the Nation Vol. VIII, p. 526)*

HR 631 did not assert any federal waters rights in the protection area. The bill was silent on the controversial issue, but it did not allow anyone to claim a reserved water right in court or through any administrative proceeding. The bill also prohibited construction of new or expanded water projects on the lands.

Lawmakers pointed out that the water rights issue might no longer be a serious concern because the land designated as wilderness in HR 631 was limited to headwaters areas. Headwaters were the streams that were the sources of a river, and in most wilderness areas they originated on federal lands. Previous versions of the legislation had included a wilderness area that received its water from a stream that began outside the area.

HR 631 had been reported by the House Natural Resources Committee on July 19, 1993 (H Rept 103-181) and was passed by the House by voice vote that same day. The Senate Energy and Natural Resources Committee reported the measure Aug. 3 (S Rept 103-123) and the Senate passed it by voice vote Aug. 4. President Clinton signed HR 631 on Aug. 13. ❑

Montana, Idaho Wilderness

Legislation (HR 2473) to bar timber, mining and recreational development on millions of acres of Montana wilderness won House approval in 1994 but was never taken up in the Senate. A wilderness protection bill (HR 3732) for Idaho never got beyond House subcommittee approval.

Montana and Idaho were the only two states without congressionally approved, statewide wilderness plans.

BACKGROUND

Congress had embarked in 1964 on a course to preserve the country's last remaining wilderness, with passage of the Wilderness Act (PL 88-577). The goal was to establish a national wilderness preservation system for all regions of the country.

As of June 1994, the system covered slightly more than 4 percent of the land in the United States—including national parks, forests, wildlife refuges and acreage overseen by the Bureau of Land Management. But pressure to develop wilderness areas commercially made it increasingly difficult to pass this type of conservation legislation.

Rep. Pat Williams, D-Mont., had spent nearly 16 years trying to craft a bill for his home state. Legislators from Idaho—which had the largest amount of roadless national forestlands in the nation outside of Alaska—had tried for 14 years to enact a wilderness protection bill.

MONTANA BILL

The House passed HR 2473 on May 17, 1994, by a 308–111 vote. The bill had been reported by the House Natural Resources Committee on April 28 and by the Agriculture Committee on May 10 (H Rept 103-487, Parts I and II). HR 2473 aimed to prevent development on 3 million acres in Montana—1.7 million of it to be designated as wilderness and 1.3 million acres to be set aside under less restrictive classifications. The bill would have opened to development and motorized recreation another 3 million acres of roadless forest that had been considered for wilderness designation.

But disagreements between environmental interests that wanted to preserve the pristine wilderness areas and commercial interests that wanted more land available for logging and mining—and between Montana's two senators, Republican Conrad Burns and Democrat Max Baucus—doomed the bill in the Senate. Western Democrats in particular were reluctant to act on wilderness bills that did not have the full support of a state's congressional delegation.

Baucus urged Burns to join him in reintroducing a compromise bill that they had crafted in the 102nd Congress, but Burns instead introduced legislation (S 2125) that was more development-oriented. Baucus went ahead and introduced the compromise bill (S 2137). The Senate acted on neither measure. *(Congress and the Nation Vol. VIII, p. 526)*

IDAHO WILDERNESS

The House Natural Resources Subcommittee on National Parks, Forests and Public Lands on June 23, 1994, gave voice vote approval to a bill (HR 3732) to classify 1.36 million acres in Idaho as protected wilderness and to release 2.8 million acres of roadless forestland for multiple uses such as logging, mining and motor vehicles.

But HR 3732 went no further. The bill, which addressed only half the state and did not have the support of the rest of the Idaho congressional delegation, had virtually no chance of enactment in 1994.

In other action, the House passed by voice vote Oct. 7, 1994, a pared-down bill (S 2100) to continue an ecosystem management program in Idaho. The Senate, which had passed by voice vote on May 10 a broader version of the bill that would have applied to a number of states, took no action on the revised legislation, and it died. Under the program, the Forest Service tested ways to improve wildlife habitats, watersheds, fisheries, timber stands and reforestation to find the best ways to protect forest ecosystems across the country.   ❑

Montana Land Swap

Congress in 1993 cleared legislation (HR 873—PL 103-91) to use land exchanges to acquire about 80,000 acres north of Yellowstone National Park in Montana, consolidating ownership of private land into federal hands to protect parts of the Gallatin National Forest from development. The land was home to the nation's largest elk herd and the endangered grizzly bear.

HR 873 had been reported by the House Natural Resources Committee (H Rept 103-82, Part I) on May 6, 1993, and passed by the House by a vote of 317–101 on May 20. An attempt on May 11 to pass the bill under suspension of the rules had failed on a 262–140 vote, six short of the two thirds majority needed.

The House bill authorized $3.4 million to pay for the acquisitions. Republicans opposed the bill, citing Congressional Budget Office estimates that the land could cost as much as $20 million if the exchanges were not successful. But an attempt to send the bill back to committee failed.

An amended version of HR 873 was reported by the Senate Energy and Natural Resources Committee on Aug. 3 (S Rept 103-122) and was passed by voice vote the next day. The Senate version eliminated the $3.4 million authorization, leaving the Big Sky lands to be acquired only through land swaps. It also removed nonprofit land trusts from having a role in facilitating the land exchanges authorized by the bill.

The House accepted the Senate's changes, clearing HR 873 on Sept. 13. President Clinton signed the measure into law on Oct. 1.   ❑

New Mexico Cave Protection

Congress in 1993 cleared a bill (HR 698—PL 103-169) to protect Lechuguilla Cave in Carlsbad Caverns National Park in New Mexico. Proposals to drill for oil and gas on federal lands next to the national park had raised concerns about Lechuguilla, which was the nation's deepest cave, extending for more than 60 miles, and which contained such rare features as gypsum chandeliers.

Under HR 698, the interior secretary was prohibited from issuing new leases for drilling or allowing new mineral exploration on federal lands. Development was restricted on existing leases in the Dark Canyon area of Lechuguilla Cave, along the northern boundary of Carlsbad Caverns National Park.

HR 698 had been reported by the House Natural Resources Committee on May 11 (H Rept 103-86) and was passed by the House that same day by voice vote. An amended version was reported by the Senate Energy and Natural Resources Committee Nov. 17 (S Rept 103-213) and was passed by the Senate by voice vote Nov. 19. The House cleared the bill Nov. 21, after accepting Senate amendments clarifying access to rights of way and the authority of the interior secretary to cancel any existing mineral or geothermal lease. President Clinton signed HR 698 on Dec. 2. ❑

New Mexico Recreation Area

Congress in 1993 cleared legislation establishing the Jemez National Recreation Area in New Mexico to protect one of the nation's richest ancient Indian settlements. The bill (HR 38—PL 103-104) created a 57,000-acre recreation area for the 300,000 visitors who trekked to the lands each year for sightseeing, camping, hunting and other activities.

HR 38 was reported by the House Natural Resources Committee (H Rept 103-58) on April 20, 1993, and was passed by the House on April 21 by a 363–57 vote. An amended version was reported by the Senate Energy and Natural Resources Committee (S Rept 103-139) on Sept. 14 and was passed by the Senate Sept. 22 by voice vote. The House cleared HR 38 on Sept. 29. The president signed the measure Oct. 12.

In other action, Congress cleared a bill (HR 328—PL 103-132) directing the Forest Service to transfer control of Old Taos Ranger Station and Warehouse to Taos, N.M. The city was to pay $18,000 each year for 20 years for the land. The bill was reported by the House Natural Resources Committee (H Rept 103-60) on April 20, 1993, and was passed 420–0 the next day. The Senate passed HR 328 by voice vote Oct. 20, completing congressional action. The bill was signed into law Nov. 2. ❑

Idaho Bird Refuge

A compromise bill that set aside nearly a half-million acres around Idaho's Snake River as a federally protected conservation area cleared in 1993. The bill (HR 236—PL 103-64) protected lands that stretched about 30 miles south of Boise and supported one of North America's densest populations of eagles, hawks and owls.

The Snake River Birds of Prey Natural Conservation Area had been a refuge since 1980, but that status had been scheduled to expire in 2000. The bill established new standards for compatible use of the area by visitors, the military and ranchers.

The House Natural Resources Committee reported HR 236 (H Rept 103-80, Part I) on May 6, 1993, and the House passed it by voice vote May 11. The Senate Energy and Natural Resources Committee reported the bill (S Rept 103-108) on July 23, and

the Senate passed it by voice vote July 28. Clinton signed HR 236 on Aug. 4. ❑

Guam Park

Congress cleared legislation (HR 1944—PL 103-197) in 1993 authorizing $8 million to develop a national park in the U.S. territory of Guam and build a memorial there. The memorial was to be dedicated to the U.S. forces who liberated Guam during World War II and to the people of Guam who suffered under the Japanese occupation from Dec. 8, 1941, to Aug. 10, 1944. The goal was to have the monument completed by July 21, 1994, the fiftieth anniversary of the Marianas Campaign, in which U.S. forces liberated Guam.

HR 1944 was reported by the House Natural Resources Committee (H Rept 103-145) on June 21, 1993, and was passed by the House by voice vote later that day. An amended version was reported by the Senate Energy and Natural Resources Committee (S Rept 103-98) on July 16 and passed by voice vote of the Senate July 21. The House approved a compromise version by voice vote on Nov. 21, and the Senate cleared the bill the next day. President Clinton signed the measure Dec. 17. ❑

Everglades Protection

Congress in 1994 cleared legislation (HR 3617—PL 103-219) authorizing the interior secretary to spend $17.4 million to purchase land needed to improve water flow through the Everglades into Florida Bay. The funds were to be transferred from an Army Corps of Engineers flood control and pump station project.

The House passed the bill by voice vote on Nov. 23, 1993. Identical language had been included in a separate bill (HR 2530) to reauthorize the Interior Department's Bureau of Land Management (BLM), which the House had passed on Sept. 13, 1993, but the Senate did not act on. (BLM, p. 429)

HR 3617 was reported by the Senate Energy and Natural Resources Committee (S Rept 103-224) on Feb. 7, 1994, and was cleared by the Senate Feb. 10. The president signed the measure March 9. ❑

Outer Continental Shelf

Congress in 1994 cleared legislation (HR 3678—PL 103-426) authorizing the interior secretary to negotiate agreements for the use of outer continental shelf resources. The bill was aimed at making it easier for coastal states to use outer continental shelf resources such as sand or shells for beach and barrier island restoration projects. It allowed the interior secretary to waive fees for sand and gravel resources used in coastal management programs that were funded with at least 50 percent federal funds. Under existing law, the federal government was required to lease such rights, a process that bill supporters argued had allowed commercial interests to outbid government entities seeking the same rights.

HR 3678 was reported by the House Natural Resources Committee (H Rept 103-817, Part I) on Oct. 3 and was passed by the full House later that day by voice vote. The Senate passed the measure Oct. 6 by voice vote, completing congressional action. The president signed HR 3678 on Oct. 31.   ❑

Protecting Old Faithful

The House in 1993 passed a bill (HR 1137) to protect Old Faithful and other geysers at Yellowstone National Park from being developed as energy sources by surrounding landowners. An amended version was reported in the Senate in 1994, but there was no further action.

Under the bill, future geothermal development was to be banned within a 15-mile area surrounding the park. The interior secretary was restricted from issuing any leases for tapping into the energy sources on nearby federal land. HR 1137, which amended the 1970 Geothermal Steam Act (PL 91-581), also clarified the water rights of the federal government and Montana. It directed the interior secretary to research the potential impact of full development of the geothermal resources.

HR 1137 was reported by the House Natural Resources Committee (H Rept 103-364) on Nov. 15, 1993, and was passed by a voice vote of the full House that same date. The Senate Energy and Natural Resources Committee reported its version (S Rept 103-431) on Sept. 28, 1994.   ❑

Urban Recreation

The House passed by a vote of 361–59 on March 22, 1994, a bill (HR 4034) to direct more funding toward recreational programs in urban areas as a way of fighting juvenile crime. HR 4034 had been reported by the Natural Resources Committee (H Rept 103 444) the previous day. The Senate never acted on the bill, but portions of it were included in the omnibus crime bill signed into law by President Clinton on Sept. 13 (HR 3355—PL 103-322). *(Crime bill, p. 683)*   ❑

Six Rivers National Forest

The House passed 288–133 on Sept. 21, 1994, a bill (HR 2866) allowing the government to add 44,000 acres of redwood forest to the Six Rivers National Forest in northern California. The Senate did not act on the bill.

Supporters said HR 2866, which had been reported by the House Natural Resources Committee on Aug. 4 and the Agriculture Committee on Aug. 16 (H Rept 103-667, Parts I and II), would provide a management plan and protection from accelerated logging. They were particularly concerned about 3,000 acres known as the Headwaters Forest—the nation's largest privately owned tract of ancient redwoods—which was to be included as federally protected wilderness. Logging was to be banned in the Headwaters Forest, which had never been logged and was home to some endangered species, and in about 2,000 surrounding acres but could continue under tighter regulation in the rest of the forest. Opponents said the bill would infringe on the rights of private landowners by allowing the presence of endangered species or old-growth forest to devalue the land.   ❑

Conservation at Military Bases

The House passed a bill (HR 3300) Sept. 12, 1994, by voice vote aimed at improving the Defense Department's protection of fish and wildlife at its military installations. But the measure, which would have reauthorized a 1960 law known as the Sikes Act (PL 86-797) through 1997, never got to the Senate floor. It had been reported by the House Merchant Marine and Fisheries Committee (H Rept 103-718) on Sept. 12 and by the Senate Environment and Public Works Committee on Oct. 5.   ❑

Wheeling Heritage Area

The House on April 13, 1994, rejected a bill (HR 2843) that would have created a national heritage area in Wheeling, W.Va. The vote was 264–154, 15 short of the two-thirds majority needed to pass under the expedited procedure known as suspension of the rules. The bill had been reported by the Natural Resources Committee (H Rept 103-471) the previous day.

Provisions of HR 2843 were included in a House-passed bill (HR 5044) authorizing funds for the designation of 10 American Heritage areas, but the Senate did not act on the measure. *(American Heritage areas, p. 422)*   ❑

Alaskan Park Fishing

The House Merchant Marine and Fisheries Committee Aug. 2, 1993, reported a bill (HR 704—H Rept 103-201, Part I) to allow fishing in Glacier Bay National Park in Alaska to continue at its existing level with these restrictions: no new types of equipment; no fishing in wilderness areas; and, for each species, no catches larger than the average number of fish or crabs caught per season over the previous 10 years. Roughly 400 boats were licensed to fish commercially in the bay, with the primary catches being salmon and crabs.

The Clinton administration and some environmental groups that wanted to reduce fishing in the bay opposed the bill. The National Park Service had proposed prohibiting all commercial fishing in the park after 1997.

There was no further action on HR 704.   ❑

Marine Mammal Protection

Congress in 1994 cleared a six-year reauthorization of the 1972 Marine Mammal Protection Act that lawmakers said would reduce the accidental killing of marine mammals without harming the economic well-being of commercial fishermen.

The measure (S 1636—PL 103-238) was hailed as a compromise between environmentalists and the $10 billion-a-year fishing industry, which had been at odds since Congress first voted to protect marine mammals.

BACKGROUND

The Marine Mammal Protection Act (PL 92-522) was enacted to ensure that marine mammals such as whales, dolphins, sea otters, seals, walruses, manatees and polar bears stayed at or returned to healthy population levels. The act banned the intentional killing or capture of marine mammals and prohibited the importation of mammal skins or products made from them. It included highly regulated exceptions for incidental taking, or killing, of certain marine mammals by commercial fishermen. *(1972 act, Congress and the Nation Vol. III, p. 812)*

But a 1987 court ruling blocked the National Marine Fisheries Service from issuing permits for some fishermen to accidentally harm marine mammals. The fishing industry argued that the ruling had the potential to shut down U.S. commercial fishing operations. In response, Congress in 1988 cleared a five-year exemption (PL 100-711) allowing permits for the commercial fishing industry, while government agencies studied the problem and came up with a long-term solution. The plan those agencies sent to Congress in November 1992 drew criticism from the fishing industry and the scientific and environmental communities. A coalition of interested parties came up with a compromise plan in June 1993. *(1988 law, Congress and the Nation Vol. VII, p. 466)*

LEGISLATIVE ACTION

In the meantime, the five-year exemption from the ban on killing marine mammals and the underlying law were set to expire Oct. 1, 1993. Congress on Sept. 22, 1993, cleared legislation (HR 3049—PL 103-86) extending the exemption for six months, giving lawmakers until April 1, 1994, to negotiate protections acceptable to conservationists and the fishing industry. A second stopgap measure (HR 4122—PL 103-228) with a 30-day extension was cleared March 25, 1994, after negotiations on the long-term extension bogged down.

The Senate Commerce, Science and Transportation Committee had reported a five-year reauthorization (S 1636—S Rept 103-220) on Jan. 25, 1994. The House Merchant Marine and Fisheries Committee reported a six-year reauthorization (HR 2760—H Rept 103-439) on March 21.

Hurrying to make the April 1 deadline, the House and Senate passed their respective bills by voice vote March 21. Negotiators came to an agreement the same night, without a formal conference, and the House passed a compromise version of S 1636 by voice vote March 22. But the Senate approved another version by voice vote two days later, as the bill became hung up over two issues.

The first was a House provision lifting the ban on the import of polar bear skins, which was vehemently opposed by animal protection groups. Specifically, it allowed sport hunters who killed polar bears in Canada to bring back their trophies, usually the animal's hide, to the United States. House Merchant Marine and Fisheries Chairman Gerry E. Studds, D-Mass., said the change would not lead to the killing of more polar bears, because Canada had a quota on how many animals could be hunted annually. Permits, which were sold to sport hunters for $15,000 to $20,000 each, were issued based on that quota.

Although the provision was not in the original Senate bill, Sen. John Kerry, D-Mass., the bill's sponsor, went along. But Kerry amended the House version to call for a two-year study tracking the health of the Canadian polar bear sleuth and to allow the revoking of trophy permits if the study found negative effects on the sleuth.

The Senate also removed a provision from the House version that would have expanded the bill's definition of "takings" of animals to include actions that would "harm" a mammal population. The timber industry was fearful that expanding the definition would disrupt the use of private property.

To satisfy environmentalists, the final bill made explicit that the secretaries of interior and commerce had the authority to protect marine mammal habitat.

The back and forth between the two chambers, particularly over the definition of takings, stalled the bill long enough that members saw a need to clear the second interim measure, HR 4122.

The House passed S 1636 a final time by voice vote April 26. The Senate cleared the bill the same day, also by voice vote.

FINAL PROVISIONS

As signed into law April 30, S 1636 retained the goal of the 1972 Marine Mammal Protection Act to reduce the accidental killing of marine mammals to insignificant levels, meaning as close to zero as possible. The bill authorized $20 million annually in fiscal years 1994–1999 to carry out conservation measures.

The bill explicitly outlawed the intentional killing of marine mammals by commercial fishermen. However, it allowed the intentional killing of nuisance seals and sea lions that had been eating endangered and threatened fish stocks at dams. It included regulations for the public display of marine mammals in zoos, aquariums and theme parks.

The bill included the controversial provision lifting a ban on importing trophies, typically skins, of polar bears that were legally hunted in Canada. But it also required a study on Canada's polar bear stock and allowed the interior secretary to revoke permits for importing trophies if the study found negative effects.

The final bill authorized the secretaries of interior and commerce to protect marine mammal habitat, including feeding grounds, rookeries, nursery grounds and migration paths. ❑

Fishing Regulation

The 103rd Congress considered numerous bills regarding fishing regulation.

FISHERY CONSERVATION, MANAGEMENT

Legislation to reauthorize the nation's primary fishing law went no further than subcommittee approval in the House in 1994.

Gerry E. Studds, D-Mass., chairman of the House Merchant Marine and Fisheries Committee, on Sept. 28, 1994, said not enough time was available to reach consensus on a bipartisan bill (HR 780) to reauthorize the 1976 Magnuson Fishery Conservation and Management Act (PL 94-265). Studds pointed to wide disagreement on controversial issues such as privatizing fisheries and imposing fishing fees.

The 1976 law was designed to halt overfishing by foreign fleets and to bolster the domestic fishing industry. It gave the United States sole management authority of all resources within 200 miles of its shores. The law created eight regional management councils charged with developing plans to allocate fishing rights for species within their jurisdictions. But the councils were filled with commercial and recreational fishing experts, sparking charges of conflicts of interest.

While the Magnuson Act was credited with boosting U.S. access to ocean fisheries, it had not been as successful in ensuring there were enough fish to keep recreational and commercial fishing operations in business. More than half the nation's 213 most commercially harvested fish species were severely depleted, according to the National Marine Fisheries Service.

As approved by a House Merchant Marine subcommittee in August 1994, HR 780 emphasized the protection of fish habitat, attempted to reduce overfishing and the catching of young or unwanted fish, and addressed the possible conflicts of interest in the councils. But the panel deflected decisions on such issues as user fees and fishing quotas for the full committee—which never acted.

Under the Magnuson Act, the federal government collected fees from the issuance of six to eight different fishing permits. President Clinton proposed new user fees to raise $82 million for fishery management and conservation programs. But appropriators balked at the new fees. The fiscal 1995 spending bill for the departments of Commerce, Justice and State (HR 4603—PL 103-317) instead allowed the National Oceanic and Atmospheric Administration, which oversaw fishing programs, to expand existing fees to raise $35 million.

ATLANTIC MARINE PROTECTIONS

Congress cleared legislation in 1993 giving federal and state governments more power to regulate fishing along the Atlantic coast. The provisions, aimed at renewing the marine life of several Atlantic coast fisheries, were folded into a bill reauthorizing the Coast Guard (HR 2150—PL 103-206). (Coast Guard provisions, p. 338)

HR 2150 established a procedure under which the secretary of commerce could impose a federal fishing moratorium on Atlantic states that violated coastal fishery management plans. The bill called on the Atlantic States Marine Fishery Commission to develop management plans for each dwindling species of fish. The federal government could bar fishermen in a state that did not implement or enforce the plan from catching that species until their state came into compliance. The bill authorized funding for the fisheries commission at $3 million for fiscal 1994, $5 million for fiscal 1995 and $7 million for fiscal 1996.

The fish conservation provisions had begun as a separate bill (S 1126—S Rept 103-201), which had been reported by the Senate Commerce, Science and Transportation Committee on Nov. 20, 1993. A similar bill had been reported by the House Merchant Marine and Fisheries Committee (HR 2134—H Rept 103-202) on Aug. 2 and passed by a voice vote of the House later that day.

The Senate attached the fishing provisions to HR 2150 and passed the bill by voice vote Nov. 22. The House cleared it by voice vote the next day. The president signed the measure Dec. 20.

FISHING LIMITS

Congress in 1993 considered several other measures aimed at reviving marine life in the Atlantic Ocean and parts of the Pacific Ocean. The legislation pressed U.S. fisheries to stem pollock and bluefin tuna harvests in international waters and encouraged other nations to follow suit.

The House on Nov. 2, 1993, passed by voice vote HR 3188, adding new fishing restrictions to a 1992 law (PL 102-582) that penalized both foreign and U.S. ships that harvested fish in a part of the Bering Sea called the Donut Hole.

The bill, reported by the House Merchant Marine and Fisheries Committee Nov. 2 (H Rept 103-316), imposed similar punishments for U.S.-flag ships in the nearby Peanut Hole in the Sea of Okhotsk, where pollock fishing had migrated. HR 3188 also granted the United States authority to participate in the enactment of a 10-year-old Northwest Atlantic Fisheries Organization treaty governing fishing in international waters near Canada and the United States. There was no Senate action on HR 3188.

The House also on Nov. 2 adopted by voice vote H Con Res 135 expressing congressional support for negotiators urging China, Korea, Poland and Japan to join the United States and Russia in developing permanent limits on pollock fishing in the Central Bering Sea. The resolution had been reported by the Merchant Marine and Fisheries Committee (H Rept 103-317) earlier that day. There was no Senate action.

Again on Nov. 2, the House approved by voice vote H Con Res 169, a nonbinding resolution expressing congressional support for Atlantic tuna conservation rules. It urged U.S. delegates to an upcoming conservation meeting to win pledges from other delegates to comply with international limits on bluefin tuna harvests. The resolution had been reported by Merchant Marine and Fisheries (H Rept 103-318) earlier on Nov. 2. This time the Senate did act, adopting H Con Res 169 by voice vote Nov. 16.

STRIPED BASS

The House on July 12, 1994, passed by voice vote a bill (HR 4504) to reauthorize a law designed to protect striped bass—a popular sport fish also known as rockfish—on the Atlantic Coast from overfishing and water pollution. The Senate did not act on the bill.

The measure, which was reported by the House Merchant Marine and Fisheries Committee (H Rept 103-584) on July 12, proposed to extend through fiscal 1996 the Atlantic Striped Bass Conservation Act of 1984 (PL 98-613).

The bill also proposed to reauthorize a related law passed in 1979 (PL 96-118) that required the interior secretary to cooperate with states and private groups that researched striped bass populations. (1984 law, Congress and the Nation Vol. VI, p. 481)

FISH AND WILDLIFE FOUNDATION

Congress in 1994 cleared legislation (S 476—PL 103-232) reauthorizing the National Fish and Wildlife Foundation, a nonprofit organization that funded natural resources conservation and environmental education projects with a combination of donations from private contributors and federal dollars.

The measure reauthorized the foundation through fiscal 1998 and authorized $25 million annually to be used for projects administered by the National Oceanic and Atmospheric Administration and the U.S. Fish and Wildlife Service. It also included provisions to expand the foundation's board and to honor former House Merchant Marine Committee chairman Walter B. Jones, D-N.C., who died in 1992.

The legislation began in the House, which approved its own bill (HR 2684) on Nov. 3, 1993, by a vote of 368–59. HR 2684 had been reported by the Merchant Marine and Fisheries Committee on Sept. 21 (H Rept 103-249). On March 8, 1994, the Senate by voice vote passed its bill, S 476, which had been reported by the Environment and Public Works Committee (S Rept 103-225) on Feb. 10. The House passed an amended version of S 476 by voice vote on March 21, and the Senate cleared the bill on March 25. President Clinton signed S 476 on April 11.

RUSSIAN RIVER

The House Merchant Marine and Fisheries Committee on Aug. 11, 1994, approved a bill (HR 4408) calling for the restoration of the fisheries and riverbed of northern California's Russian River, once home to a bounty of steelhead trout. But the bill was never formally reported by the committee, and there was no further action in either chamber.

FISHING VESSEL REGISTRATION

The Senate in 1994 approved ratification of a 1993 international agreement (Treaty Doc 103-24) intended to prevent fishermen from reflagging their vessels to evade prosecution for violating conservation measures while fishing on the high seas. Legislation (S 2455) to implement the agreement was reported out of committee in the Senate but never reached the floor.

Under the terms of the agreement, which was adopted at a Rome, Italy, conference of the United Nations Food and Agriculture Organization in November 1993, each participating nation was obligated to develop a system for licensing fishing boats that carried its flag on the high seas. With the world's fish stocks dwindling, global and regional fisheries management organizations had responded by adopting more stringent conservation measures. But commercial fishing vessels circumvented these restrictions by reflagging—flying the flag of a nation that did not belong to a regional fish management organization.

The Senate Foreign Relations Committee reported the treaty (Exec Rept 103-32) Sept. 26, 1994, and the full Senate approved its ratification by a division vote on Oct. 6.

The Senate Commerce, Science and Transportation Committee reported S 2455 on Sept. 28, 1994. Among other things, the bill sought to implement the terms of the Rome agreement by requiring all U.S. fishing vessels operating on the high seas to register with the Commerce Department. ❑

Radioactive Waste Dumping

The House in 1994 passed a bill (HR 3982) aimed at bringing the United States in line with an expanded international accord that barred the dumping of all radioactive waste in the ocean. The House tried to move the legislation again at the end of the session, attaching it to an unrelated maritime bill (HR 3664), which became a vehicle for a number of environmental bills languishing at the end of the session. Neither HR 3982 nor HR 3664 became law.

The legislation amended the 1972 Marine Protection, Research and Sanctuaries Act (PL 92-532), which had been enacted to bring U.S. law into conformity with the London Convention, an international agreement that banned ocean dumping of high-level radioactive waste. The 1972 law allowed the U.S. government to dump low-level radioactive waste into the ocean with specific congressional approval of each instance. In practice, however, the United States stopped dumping all radioactive waste in 1970 and had never used the authority granted to it under the 1972 ocean dumping law.

In 1993, the London Convention was expanded to include low-level waste, following the revelation that Russia had dumped and had been storing large amounts of high- and low-level radioactive waste in the ocean. The new agreement took effect Feb. 20, 1994.

HR 3982 was reported by the House Merchant Marine Committee (H Rept 103-522) on May 23, 1994, and passed by a voice vote of the House that same day. When the Senate failed to act on HR 3982, the House made another attempt to win Senate approval by rolling the ocean dumping provisions into the unrelated HR 3664. Both chambers already had passed HR 3664—the House on March 21 and the Senate on Sept. 21—but they had not reconciled their differences. The House approved its amended version of HR 3664—with the provisions of HR 3882 attached—by voice vote on Oct. 7, but the Senate took no further action. ❑

Environmental Technology R&D

The Senate and House in 1994 passed separate bills (S 978, HR 3870) aimed at helping bring to market innovative technologies to prevent, reduce or clean up environmental pollution—or "green" technologies. But the two chambers did not reconcile their differences on the legislation, which died at the end of the 103rd Congress.

The federal government spent about $4 billion annually for research and development (R&D) of environmental technologies to help reduce pollution and clean up hazardous wastes. The demand for such technologies was increasing, with the global market expected to reach an estimated $300 billion by 2000. The bills sought to codify a Clinton administration plan to develop an interagency strategy to guide the federal government's future spending on research and development of such environmental technologies. The aim was to help ensure that U.S. companies kept pace with foreign competitors.

S 978 was reported by the Senate Environment and Public Works Committee (S Rept 103-156) on Oct. 5, 1993, and was passed by the Senate May 11, 1994, by a vote of 85–14. The Senate bill called for the creation of a technology panel under the White House's Office of Science and Technology Policy (OSTP) and a separate environmental technology information office at the Environmental Protection Agency (EPA).

The House Merchant Marine and Fisheries Committee had reported a similar bill (HR 2112—H Rept 103-214, Part I) on Aug. 4, 1993, but there was no further action. The House Science, Space and Technology Committee reported HR 3870 (H Rept 103-536) on June 8, 1994, and the full House passed the bill by voice vote July 26. HR 3870 required the OSTP to coordinate research efforts among the Commerce Department, EPA and other federal agencies. It also sought to improve access to information about environmental technology.

Before passing HR 3870, the House July 26 adopted, 286–139, an amendment offered by Robert S. Walker, R-Pa., to establish legislative criteria and guidelines for environmental risk assessments, after rejecting, 202–225, an amendment by George E. Brown Jr., D-Calif., giving the White House science adviser the power to set such guidelines. Walker argued that, because the bill instructed the administration to develop priorities for environmental technology research according to assessments of risk, the bill should establish guidelines for making such judgments.

Both bills authorized funding for grant programs to support research and development of such technologies.

There was no further action on the R&D bills. However, provisions promoting U.S. exports of environmental technology were included in a House-passed bill (HR 3813) regarding "green" exports and cleared as part of a bill reauthorizing the Overseas Private Investment Corporation (OPIC, HR 4950—PL 103-392). ('Green' exports, p. 432; OPIC, p. 177) ❏

Environmental Research

The House on Nov. 20, 1993, passed by voice vote a bill (HR 1994) authorizing $475.4 million in fiscal 1994 for Environmental Protection Agency (EPA) research and development programs. But there was no Senate action, and the bill died at the end of the Congress.

The bill, which was reported by the House Science, Space and Technology Committee on Nov. 18 (H Rept 103-376), was intended to improve the quantity and quality of the EPA's scientific research projects. It required the EPA administrator to support research programs that ensured that the agency's environmental regulations were based on sound science. For example, bill supporter Tom Lewis, R-Fla., said during floor debate that the EPA had determined after spending billions of dollars that a $20 billion program to remove asbestos from public buildings created more health risk from asbestos dust than was caused by leaving the material in place. Lewis said more rigorous scientific

risk assessment promised to avoid such policy decisions. (Risk assessment, below)

The Office of Research and Development had been operating without an authorization since 1982, but it had continued to receive annual appropriations. The office employed about 1,900 people and administered 17 laboratories nationwide. ❏

Risk Assessment

A bill (HR 4306) to establish a comprehensive risk assessment program at the Environmental Protection Agency (EPA) won committee approval in the House in 1994 but went no further.

Risk assessment had become a hot-button issue in the 103rd Congress. Under existing law, the EPA assessed risks to human health and safety and issued regulations to combat those risks. But critics said the process was alarmist and vulnerable to political manipulation. By revising the process, they hoped to force the EPA to conduct more analysis of economic and social factors before issuing regulations that could be costly to industry and local governments.

HR 4306, reported Oct. 7 by the House Science, Space and Technology Committee (H Rept 103-857), provided for the establishment of an office and a director of risk assessment at the EPA to ensure that state-of-the-art scientific methods were the basis for any agency risk assessment guidelines. The bill also provided for a pilot program to compare and rank the severity of various environmental hazards, and it required the White House Office of Science and Technology Policy to coordinate risk research among federal agencies. ❏

BLM Reauthorization

The House by voice vote Sept. 13, 1993, approved a two-year renewal for programs under the Interior Department's Bureau of Land Management (BLM), but the measure died when the Senate failed to act on it.

The bill (HR 2530) reauthorized the agency's activities but remained silent on a trio of controversial issues targeted in earlier versions of the bill—grazing fees, timber clear-cutting in the Pacific Northwest and access for aircraft over federal parks.

As the nation's chief landlord, BLM received $1 billion a year to oversee about 270 million acres of federal land, mostly in the West. The bureau's vast terrain covered about 13 percent of the United States. The bureau also leased more than 300 million acres that contained a wealth of hard-rock minerals beneath their surface. About 4.3 million head of cattle grazed on bureau lands, and timber was harvested from 4 million acres of its forests.

Although the BLM authorization had expired at the end of fiscal 1982, the land agency had continued to receive funding through annual appropriations bills, which in effect provided temporary authorization. But pressure to pass a BLM reauthorization bill mounted in 1993, when the House on July 14 stripped from its fiscal 1994 Interior appropriations bill (HR 2520) funding for BLM's land management programs after members objected that it represented legislating on an appropriations bill—action that violated House rules. The funding, however, was restored in conference on HR 2520.

HR 2530 had been reported by the House Natural Resources Committee on July 13 (H Rept 103-171). Floor action was delayed when it appeared controversial amendments would jeopardize passage. The bill was finally passed under special procedures that allowed no amendments.

The House had passed bills reauthorizing BLM during the previous two Congresses, but the Senate failed to act on the legislation. *(Congress and the Nation Vol. VIII, pp. 499, 520)* ❏

Subsurface Mining Rights

President Clinton on April 16, 1993, signed into law a bill (HR 239—PL 103-23) requiring mining companies eyeing or holding subsurface mineral rights to notify ranchers and farmers who used the same land of their intention to prospect the area.

Under the 1916 Stock Raising Homestead Act, which HR 239 amended, subsurface minerals such as gold and silver remained federal property, subject to claim, even after ranchers obtained title to the surface lands. The surface rights to 68 million acres of western lands were transferred to private hands under the 1916 law. But the law gave miners precedence over ranching and farming operations, and throughout the years this had sparked tensions.

HR 239 required miners to notify ranchers of their intent to prospect on such lands. In the event a miner decided to develop and mine a claim, he first had to seek permission of the surface owner. If permission was denied, an operator had to submit to the Interior Department a plan aimed at minimizing disruption of grazing and farming operations.

The bill also required mining companies to restore the land to approximately its original condition and pay a fee to the surface owner for damage or any income lost due to the mining or mineral exploration.

The House on March 30, 1993, passed HR 239 on a vote of 421–1. The House Natural Resources Committee had reported the bill (H Rept 103-44) on March 29. The Senate on April 1 passed HR 239 by voice vote, thus clearing the measure, and then indefinitely postponed action on a companion bill, which had been reported by the Senate Energy and Natural Resources Committee on March 17 (S 336—S Rept 103-21).

The 102nd Congress had failed to clear similar legislation. *(Congress and the Nation Vol. VIII, p. 531)* ❏

Flood Victims Assistance

In the aftermath of summer floods that inundated 17,000 square miles and destroyed thousands of homes in the Midwest, Congress in 1993 cleared legislation (S 1670—PL 103-181) to encourage flood victims to move out of danger instead of rebuilding in the flood plain. The aim was to reduce the likelihood that they would need disaster assistance again. The bill's provisions applied to victims of future floods as well as to those hit by the 1993 disaster.

The bill allowed the Federal Emergency Management Agency (FEMA) to use 15 percent of all its appropriated disaster assistance funds to aid people who wished to relocate outside flood plains. Under existing law, FEMA was limited to using 10 percent of only the portion of its funds dedicated to community assistance disaster funding for relocation, or hazard mitigation, activities. The bill also increased from 50 percent to 75 percent the share of relocation activity costs that the federal government would pick up.

A House-passed provision requiring the Army Corps of Engineers to report to Congress by June 30, 1995, on flood control policy was dropped from the final bill. But funding for the study was provided in the fiscal 1994 appropriations bill for energy and water development (HR 2445—PL 103-126).

The House version of the relocation bill was reported by the Public Works and Transportation Committee (HR 3445—H Rept 103-358) on Nov. 15, 1993, and was passed by a voice vote of the House later that day. The Senate passed its version (S 1670) by voice vote on Nov. 20. The House passed S 1670 by voice vote that same day, clearing the measure. President Clinton signed the bill into law Dec. 3.

In separate action, the House on Nov. 23, 1993, passed by voice vote a bill (HR 3583) to make it easier for individuals to obtain federal assistance to repair flood-damaged levees that were not built by the federal government. The Senate, however, did not act on the measure.

Neither S 1670 nor HR 3583 authorized the expenditure of any new disaster aid funds by the federal government. Each placed new claims, however, on a $5.7 billion pool of disaster assistance funds that Congress approved in a supplemental appropriations bill (HR 2667—PL 103-75) enacted in August 1993. *(Disaster assistance, p. 490)* ❏

Corps of Engineers Projects

Legislation (HR 4460) to authorize $1.3 billion over two years for Army Corps of Engineers water projects was approved by a voice vote of the House on Oct. 3, 1994, but it died in the Senate.

HR 4460 would have authorized funding for dams, levees and locks and other corps projects in 14 states, the District of Columbia and Puerto Rico. It had been reported by the Public Works and Transportation Committee on Sept. 30 (H Rept 103-770).

On the Senate side, Max Baucus, D-Mont., chairman of the Environment and Public Works Committee, blocked a companion measure (S 2233) in committee because of a controversy with Republicans over a separate flood control bill (S 2418). Baucus wanted to include provisions from S 2418, which recommended that the corps abandon its preference for dams and levees in preventing floods and instead promote the evacuation of risky flood plains and the restoration of natural flood cycles. The recommendations came from a government task force that had been set up in response to the 1993 Midwest floods.

But opponents to Baucus's plan argued that it would radically reorder the priorities of river management without adequate debate. Critics charged that it would devastate transportation of crops on the rivers in the middle of harvest season and would add to the flood risk by making recreation in upstream states a higher priority than flood control in the downstream states.   ❑

Rhino, Tiger Fund

Congress in 1994 cleared legislation aimed at halting the poaching of rhinoceroses and tigers. The measure (HR 4924—PL 103-391) authorized $10 million annually in fiscal years 1996–2000 for a new Rhinoceros and Tiger Conservation Fund, to be administered by the interior secretary. The fund was to make grants to foreign governments and nonprofit groups that were trying to conserve the rare animals in their home countries.

Scientists estimated that at the beginning of the twentieth century there were about 1 million rhinos and 100,000 tigers worldwide, but poaching and destruction of their habitat had reduced the numbers to fewer than 11,000 rhinos and 6,000 tigers in the wild.

HR 4924 was reported by the House Merchant Marine and Fisheries Committee (H Rept 103-748) on Sept. 26, 1994, and was passed by a voice vote of the House the next day. When the Senate did not act on the HR 4924, House lawmakers on Oct. 7 attached it to an unrelated maritime bill (HR 3664). After that measure stalled, the Senate on Oct. 8 passed HR 4924, clearing the legislation. President Clinton signed HR 4924 on Oct. 22.   ❑

Wetlands Protection

President Clinton on Oct. 19, 1994, signed legislation (HR 4308—PL 103-375) extending a program to protect and restore wetlands in the United States, Canada and Mexico. The measure authorized grants of $20 million annually in fiscal years 1995–1996 and $30 million annually in fiscal years 1997–1998.

The North American Wetlands Conservation Act (PL 101-233) had been credited with protecting more than 1.2 million acres of wetlands in the United States and Canada since its inception in 1989. The law used federal money to get matching funds from private sources for wetlands protection, restoration and management projects. (Congress and the Nation Vol. VIII, p. 494)

HR 4308 was reported by the House Merchant Marine and Fisheries Committee (H Rept 103-717) on Sept. 12, 1994, and was passed by the House Sept. 13 by a vote of 368–5. The Senate Environment and Public Works Committee reported a similar bill (S 1857—S Rept 103-326) on Aug. 5. Instead of taking up that bill, the Senate passed HR 4308 by voice vote Oct. 4, clearing the measure.   ❑

Water Bank Extension

Congress in 1994 cleared a one-year extension (HR 5053—PL 103-393) of water bank agreements that were due to expire at the end of 1994. The 24-year-old Water Bank Program provided 10-year agreements for farmers to preserve and restore an estimated 60,000 acres of wetlands.

The House passed HR 5053 by voice vote Oct. 4, 1994; the Senate followed suit Oct. 7. The president signed the measure into law Oct. 22.   ❑

Indoor Air

Both chambers passed legislation (S 656) designed to improve the quality of indoor air, but time ran out in the 103rd Congress before differences could be settled.

The legislation would have required the Environmental Protection Agency (EPA) to study indoor air pollution and develop guidelines aimed at reducing potential health hazards. S 656 authorized up to $48.5 million per year in fiscal years 1994–1998 for research, grants to states and the assessment of "sick" buildings that had a high concentration of indoor air pollutants. The House version replaced some of the Senate bill's proposed mandates with voluntary programs in an attempt to ease industry concerns and win Republican votes.

The EPA considered indoor air pollution a top environmental health threat. Indoor air was believed to be up to 1,000 times more polluted than outdoor air, and medical and scientific studies showed that constant exposure could lead to cancer, respiratory diseases and headaches.

The Senate Environment and Public Works Committee reported S 656 (S Rept 103-161) on Oct. 21, 1993, and the full Senate passed it by voice vote Oct. 29. The House Energy and Commerce Committee reported its version (HR 2919—H Rept 103-719) on Sept. 13, 1994, and the House passed it by voice vote Oct. 3. The House then inserted the text of its bill into S 656 and passed that bill by voice vote Oct. 3. The Senate did not take up the amended bill.   ❑

Marine Biotechnology Grants

The House on July 13, 1993, passed by voice vote a bill (HR 1916) to establish a marine biotechnology program at selected colleges and universities.

The bill, which was reported by the House Merchant Marine and Fisheries Committee (H Rept 103-170) on July 13, authorized $90 million in grants over four years to support research into genetically modified marine organisms. Those grants were in addition to the roughly $44 million being spent each year under a federal program for marine biotechnology.

Proponents said the research held great promise for food production, pharmaceuticals, industry and environmental cleanups. They also said the United States needed to increase such research to keep pace with efforts in Japan and other Pacific Rim competitors.

The Senate took no action on HR 1916. A companion measure (S 1517—S Rept 103-219) was reported by the Senate Commerce, Science and Transportation Committee Dec. 9, 1993.   ❑

Fountain Darter

The House on Nov. 20, 1993, passed by voice vote a bill (HR 3402) to help boost the population of the endangered fountain darter, an inch-long fish found in the San Antonio, Texas, region. The Senate took no action on the measure.

The bill established a captive breeding program at the San Marcos National Fish Hatchery and Technology Center and authorized $1 million annually during fiscal 1994–1998. An estimated 1,000 fountain darters remained in the San Marcos River and in Comal Springs, which fed from Edwards Aquifer, the primary source of water for San Antonio. The aquifer had been drying up rapidly. According to a Fish and Wildlife Service report, 100,000 fish had been in the habitat in 1975. ❏

NOAA Reauthorization

The House on Nov. 20, 1993, passed by voice vote a bill (HR 2811) to reauthorize National Oceanic and Atmospheric Administration (NOAA) weather, satellite and atmospheric research programs for six years. The Senate did not act on the measure.

HR 2811, which was reported by the House Science, Space and Technology Committee on Sept. 21 and the Merchant Marine and Fisheries Committee on Oct. 22 (H Rept 103-248, Parts I and II), authorized $1 billion in fiscal 1994, $1.2 billion in fiscal 1995 and $543 million in fiscal years 1996–1999 for the programs.

The measure sought to ensure continued operation of all National Weather Service offices and to help modernize satellites and facilities used by the service. The weather service's flood forecasting system also was to be improved in response to the flooding in the Midwest in 1993. ❏

Lead Use Restrictions

The Senate passed legislation (S 729) in 1994 to reduce the use of lead in consumer products such as paint, toys, plumbing systems and gift wrap, but companion legislation in the House (HR 4882) never got beyond subcommittee approval.

Lead poisoning was the most common disease among children, according to the Centers for Disease Control and Prevention. Sen. Harry Reid, D-Nev., had tried since 1990 to win approval of a comprehensive lead restriction bill, but the Senate had never voted on his proposals because of opposition from manufacturers, who were concerned about a provision that would have required them to get permission from the Environmental Protection Agency (EPA) before they made or modified a new product containing lead. That provision was not included in S 729.

The bill proposed to restrict the use of lead in a number of products. It required the EPA to develop an inventory of products that contained lead and establish a list of uses that posed a health risk. Manufacturers would have to notify the EPA when new lead uses were developed. In addition, the bill required labeling for products containing lead, recycling of lead-acid batteries and state inspections for lead hazards at schools and day-care centers. The bill authorized funds to implement its provisions.

S 729 was reported by the Environment and Public Works Committee (S Rept 103-152) on Oct. 4, 1993, and passed by the Senate on May 25, 1994, by a vote of 97–1. HR 4882 was approved by the House Energy and Commerce Subcommittee on Transportation and Hazardous Materials on Aug. 1, but there was no further action. ❏

'Green' Exports

The House in 1994 passed a bill (HR 3813) aimed at preserving the U.S. edge in exports of environmental—or "green"—technologies. Although the Senate did not act on the measure, the text of HR 3813 was ultimately included in legislation reauthorizing the Overseas Private Investment Corporation (OPIC), which cleared Congress Oct. 7, 1994 (HR 4950—PL 103-392). *(OPIC, p. 177)*

Exports of products and services that helped to reduce pollution or clean up existing problems had produced a $4 billion trade surplus for U.S. companies in 1990. Although U.S. companies held about 40 percent of the market, bill sponsors warned that other countries were catching up.

HR 3813, reported by the House Foreign Affairs Committee (H Rept 103-478) on April 18, 1994, and passed by the House the next day by a vote of 416–0, provided for the creation of an Environmental Technologies Trade Advisory Committee to guide the federal environmental export promotion. It required the administration to identify each year the five countries most in need of environmental technology and then work to increase U.S. exports to those nations. The commerce secretary was to offer matching grants to fund regional centers that promoted such exports. The bill also authorized international initiatives to encourage other countries to adopt U.S.-style environmental standards. ❏

Radon Risk Disclosure

The House in 1994 passed a bill (HR 2448) to require real estate agents and home sellers to inform prospective buyers of the risk of radon in a house and to disclose the results of any known radon tests. The Senate did not act on the bill, however, and it died at the end of the session.

According to the surgeon general and other health authorities, exposure to radon, an odorless, colorless radioactive gas, was the second-leading cause of lung cancers in the United States, after cigarette smoking. Radon became a risk to people when it seeped from soil into cracks in buildings and home foundations. According to government figures, radon exceeded safe levels in about 6 million homes. Some states had required home sellers to disclose such information, but there was no federal requirement.

HR 2448 was reported by the House Energy and Commerce Committee (H Rept 103-574) on June 30, 1994. The House passed the bill on July 28 by a vote of 255–164, after rejecting, 193–227, an amendment by Michael G. Oxley, R-Ohio, that would have deleted all requirements that homeowners disclose radon information. Among other provisions of the bill were requirements for the Environmental Protection Agency to take steps to control radon in high-risk areas.

In related action, the Senate Environment and Public Works Committee on Nov. 10, 1993, reported a bill (S 657—S Rept 103-176) requiring testing for radon gas in federally owned buildings and housing, as well as in schools in high-risk areas. But no further action was taken on that bill either. ❑

Strategic Petroleum Reserve

Congress in 1994 cleared a narrow reauthorization of the nation's oil stockpile, the Strategic Petroleum Reserve, after House and Senate negotiators failed to agree on a more far-ranging alternative. The bare-bones bill (S 2466—PL 103-406), which the Senate passed Sept. 30, 1994, and the House passed Oct. 7, reauthorized the reserve through fiscal 1996 without making any changes in its operations. President Clinton signed S 2466 on Oct. 22.

The reserve, which in 1994 held 600 million barrels in underground storage areas in Louisiana, was the nation's main insurance against oil supply and price disruptions. By the end of fiscal 1994, it was to hold an estimated 68 days of import oil protection. The 1992 Energy Policy Act (PL 102-486) required that the reserve be expanded to one billion barrels as soon as possible. (Congress and the Nation Vol. VIII, p. 500)

The House on Aug. 8 had passed by voice vote a five-year reauthorization bill (HR 4752) that proposed to soften the requirement for one billion barrels. The bill, which had been reported by the House Energy and Commerce Committee (H Rept 103-663) on Aug. 3, allowed oil to be bought and stored in the reserve as funds were made available. It also extended U.S. participation in the International Energy Agency and reauthorized two state conservation programs along with federal assistance for renewable energy plants.

The Senate version of the bill (S 2251), which was reported by the Senate Energy and Natural Resources Committee (S Rept 103-334) on Aug. 12, 1994, and passed by voice vote of the full Senate Sept. 30, reauthorized the Strategic Petroleum Reserve without changing its mandate. It did, however, eliminate a requirement that the Energy Department go before Congress whenever it wanted to lease oil.

During floor debate on S 2251, Senate Energy and Natural Resources Chairman J. Bennett Johnston, D-La., tacked on two amendments that House negotiators subsequently refused to accept. The first, contained in a separate bill passed by the Senate Nov. 20, 1993 (S 473), would have fostered cooperation between Energy Department laboratories and private companies and would have provided the laboratories with specific research missions. The second, contained in a separate bill also passed by the Senate Nov. 20 (S 991—S Rept 103-187), would have provided education and job opportunities in the seven-state lower Mississippi Delta region, stretching from southern Illinois to the Gulf of Mexico. (Energy laboratories, p. 343)

Neither of these add-ons had made it through the House as stand-alone bills. The Mississippi Delta grants seemed to attract the particular ire of some House members, who viewed then as unwarranted, "pork-barrel" spending. House and Senate negotiators were also at odds over the one billion barrel requirement

and over how often the Energy Department should submit reports to Congress. As a result, they were unable to agree on a final bill. ❑

Ethanol Use

Congress in 1994 rejected efforts to block a proposed Environmental Protection Agency (EPA) rule requiring that corn-based ethanol be used in reformulated, or cleaner-burning, gasoline. The battle over the rule—fought during consideration of the fiscal 1995 appropriations bill for the departments of Veteran Affairs (VA), Housing and Urban Development (HUD) and related agencies (HR 4624—PL 103-327)—pitted farm states, which supported the EPA rule as a boon to corn products, against oil-producing states, which opposed the rule.

The ethanol controversy stemmed from the 1990 rewrite of the Clean Air Act (PL 101-549), which required that in 1995 nine cities with poor air quality begin selling gasoline reformulated to increase oxygen content—and thereby decrease carbon monoxide pollution. The act left it up to the marketplace to determine how to reformulate the gasoline. (Congress and the Nation Vol. VIII, p. 473)

In a rule proposed in December 1993 and issued June 30, 1994, the EPA required that at least 30 percent of the gasoline sold in those markets contain a renewable oxygenate. That meant ethanol or its derivative, thus effectively requiring about one-tenth of all gasoline sold in the United States to contain ethanol. The EPA concluded that the use of ethanol would cut dependence on foreign oil and that it would reduce emissions that could cause global warming.

The National Corn Growers Association welcomed the proposal, saying it would generate sales of an additional 250 million to 500 million bushels of corn, reduce farm subsidies and stimulate economic growth in rural America. But the petroleum industry objected strongly, saying that fuels such as methanol, propane or compressed natural gas were superior alternatives to the corn-based products. The American Petroleum Institute said ethanol could increase pollution largely because so much energy was needed to harvest the corn and operate ethanol distilleries.

During House Appropriations consideration of HR 4624, an amendment that would have blocked the EPA rule was withdrawn when it appeared to face defeat.

On the Senate side, Democrat J. Bennett Johnston, from oil-rich Louisiana, succeeded in amending the bill to block the EPA rule during subcommittee consideration. But when key opponents threatened to delay the work of the full Appropriations Committee, the amendment was removed and the battle taken to the floor. On Aug. 3, with Vice President Al Gore casting the deciding vote, the Senate by a **key vote of 51–50 (R 19–25; D 31–25)** tabled (killed) an amendment—offered by Johnston and Democrat Bill Bradley, whose state of New Jersey was home to many oil refineries—to deny the EPA the funding to carry out the rule. Midwestern farm-state senators were backed by powerful agriculture companies, most notably the Archer-Daniels-Midland Corp., in their fight against the amendment. (1994 key votes, p. 1003) ❑

Foreign Refiners

Congress in 1994 agreed to block a proposed Environmental Protection Agency (EPA) rule that would have given foreign refiners more flexibility to certify that their gasoline was reformulated, or cleaner-burning. An amendment blocking the rule was included in the final version of the fiscal 1995 appropriations bill for the departments of Veterans Affairs (VA), Housing and Urban Development (HUD) and related agencies (HR 4624— PL 103-327).

The dispute grew out of a provision of the 1990 Clean Air Act amendments (PL 101-549) that required reformulated gasoline to burn 15 percent more cleanly than conventional 1990 fuels. To determine the 1990 baseline, an EPA rule issued in December 1993 required each U.S. refiner to be guided by its 1990 average of pollutants. However, because of the difficulty of tracking and verifying data from foreign sources, the baseline for foreign refiners was set at the 1990 average for all U.S. refiners. (*Congress and the Nation Vol. VIII, p. 473*)

Venezuela, one of the largest suppliers of foreign oil to the United States, objected, saying the rule treated foreign suppliers differently from domestic refineries, violating the General Agreement on Tariffs and Trade. At Venezuela's behest, the EPA proposed to amend the rule to allow foreign refiners to be guided by their individual 1990 baseline for pollutants if their baseline could be verified.

Lawmakers who opposed the revised rule predicted that it would result in job losses in the U.S. oil and gas industry because of the increased foreign competition. They said the original rule would keep Venezuela and other foreign refiners from exporting dirtier gasoline than domestic refiners would have to manufacture. Efforts to stop the revision were supported by big domestic oil and gasoline companies, as well as some environmental groups.

Those who defended the revision said it would treat foreign refiners the same as domestic. To do otherwise, they said, would risk gasoline shortages, higher gasoline prices and retaliatory trade practices. They also denied that the reformulated gasoline from foreign refineries such as those in Venezuela would be any dirtier than that from U.S. refineries.

The Senate included in its version of HR 4624 a provision barring the EPA from using funds in the bill to carry out its proposed rule. House conferees, however, insisted that it was not an appropriations matter and refused to go along. The issue was sent back to the two chambers for a vote. The House on Sept. 12, 1994, voted 222–148 to accept the Senate amendment blocking the proposed rule. HR 4624 cleared Congress on Sept. 27.   ❑

Energy Research

The Senate, by voice vote June 29, 1993, passed a bill (S 646) to require the Energy Department to devise a research plan for harnessing magnetic fusion energy. The House, by voice vote Aug. 19, 1994, passed a related bill (HR 4908) to authorize a variety of energy research programs, including fusion and high-

energy physics research. The two chambers could not resolve their differences, and both measures died.

Senate Energy and Natural Resources Committee Chairman J. Bennett Johnston, D-La., whose panel had reported the bill (S Rept 103-62) on June 22, said S 646 would help the Energy Department prepare for its next big science project—the international thermonuclear experimental reactor. Bill supporters said they hoped the reactor, which was in its infancy, eventually would let scientists sustain magnetic fusion reactions long enough to produce power that could be used commercially. Scientists were studying the use of magnetic fields to contain hot gases that reacted to produce energy. S 646 authorized about $350 million for fiscal 1994 but required the energy secretary to direct all research toward development of the new reactor.

HR 4908, which had been reported (H Rept 103-674) by the House Science, Space and Technology Committee on Aug. 5, 1994, authorized $1.3 billion for fusion research through fiscal 1997 and $4.3 billion through fiscal 1999 for high-energy and nuclear physics programs at the Department of Energy. In an attempt to provide direction for the Energy Department's program, the bill called for demonstrating the potential commercial application of fusion by 2010 and commercial production by 2040. The measure also reinforced the U.S. commitment to participate in a joint project with Japan, Russia and host of European nations to build the experimental reactor. The goal was for the reactor to be fully operational by 2005.

HR 4908 also included provisions to authorize and provide direction for Department of Energy high-energy and physics programs. Research in these areas had helped spur advances in cancer therapy, radioactive isotope production, high-speed data acquisition and computer development. The bill authorized $695.4 million in fiscal 1996, $719.7 million in fiscal 1997, $744.9 million in fiscal 1998 and $713.6 million in fiscal 1999 for high-energy physics. It also authorized $337.1 million in fiscal 1996 for nuclear physics, increasing to $373.7 million by fiscal 1999. That money was to provide for the construction of the Relativistic Heavy Ion Collider at Brookhaven National Laboratory outside Chicago.   ❑

Energy Research Labs

The 103rd Congress tried to define a new, post–cold war mission for the Department of Energy's research laboratories, but lawmakers could not agree on how far the laboratories should be required to go in forging new partnerships with private industry.

The Senate Energy and Natural Resources Committee on June 24, 1993, reported S 473 (S Rept 103-69), which required some Energy Department laboratories to set aside 20 percent of their budgets for partnerships with industry. The legislation served as a jurisdictional marker for Committee Chairman J. Bennett Johnston, D-La., who wanted to ensure that the department laboratories remained in his panel's domain despite their increasingly commercial mission. As of 1993, the laboratories had entered into more than 500 cooperative research and development agreements worth more than $700 million.

On Sept. 9, the Senate by voice vote added most of the provisions of S 473 to its version of the fiscal 1994 defense authorization bill (S 1298, subsequently HR 2401). The amendment expanded the mission of the laboratories to include research, development and commercial application of industrial technologies. It also removed paperwork roadblocks that often inhibited partnerships between government and the private sector and took steps to encourage a range of partnership arrangements. However, the House rejected the addition of the language to the defense authorization bill. The Senate subsequently passed S 473 by voice vote Nov. 20.

The House Energy and Commerce Committee on July 19, 1994, reported a revised version of S 473 (H Rept 103-611, Part I). The bill aimed to shift the Energy Department laboratories' focus from national security to industrial competitiveness. It proposed to expand efforts to find commercial applications for such laboratory technologies as pollution reduction and waste disposal, as well as research and development.

The committee rejected a contentious amendment that would have set aside specific targets for federal spending cuts at Energy Department laboratories over the following three fiscal years and established a commission to find ways to reduce funding for the laboratories. Those members instead adopted an amendment calling for the Energy Department to implement cost-saving measures at the laboratories over the following four years.

A compromise bill (HR 1432) was reported by the House Armed Services Committee April 26 and by the House Science, Space and Technology Committee May 19 (H Rept 103-484, Parts I and II). The bill preserved nuclear weapons research and supervision as the first of three missions for the laboratories. The other missions were research into energy supply and the environmental impacts of producing energy. The compromise was aimed at resolving the dispute over the missions of the three defense laboratories—the Sandia and Los Alamos facilities in New Mexico and the Lawrence Livermore laboratory in California. The two House committee versions differed slightly because of amendments adopted by the Science Committee.

Several Republicans announced plans to offer more significant amendments when the full House considered the bill. However, neither HR 1432 nor S 473 made it to the House floor before adjournment.   ❑

Nuclear Research Projects

After granting a last-minute reprieve in 1993, Congress in 1994 agreed to terminate a controversial nuclear power reactor that was designed to recycle used nuclear materials, such as plutonium, from atomic weapons and power plants and use them to generate electricity. The fate of the Advanced Liquid Metal Reactor was sealed by the fiscal 1995 energy and water development appropriations bill (HR 4506—PL 103-316).

Critics said that the reactor would pose environmental and proliferation risks, while supporters said that the project was worth funding and that ending it would cost almost as much as continuing it.

The House had attempted to kill the project in 1993, during consideration of the fiscal 1994 energy and water development appropriations bill (HR 2445—PL 103-126). The House on June 24, 1993, voted 267–162 to terminate the project, but the Senate on Sept. 30 rejected a similar amendment, 53–45. The Senate position prevailed during the conference on the bill.

But in 1994, when the same scenario unfolded, House conferees on the fiscal 1995 funding bill refused to budge on the issue. The version of HR 4506 passed by the House on June 14, 1994, had included funds to shut down the project. The conference confrontation was set up when the Senate on June 30 voted 52–46 to table (kill) an amendment to terminate the project. But this time the House position prevailed, and $84 million to terminate the project was included in the final bill, which cleared Congress Aug. 11.

Space-Based Reactor. In other action in 1993 on HR 2445, Congress included in the final bill $25 million for a space-based nuclear reactor program. The House had voted 333–98 on June 24 to cancel funding for the project, which aimed to develop a nuclear-based power source for use in outer space.

Helium Reactor. Conferees on HR 2445 also agreed to keep funds in the bill for more research into a gas-turbine helium reactor, also known as the high-temperature gas reactor, aimed at eventually developing a nuclear reactor impervious to meltdown. The Senate on Sept. 30, 1993, had agreed by voice vote to an amendment to kill the project.

During action on HR 4506 in 1994, an attempt in the House to kill the helium reactor was rejected by a vote of 188–241 on June 14, although the administration had urged lawmakers not to finance the reactor.

Tokamak Reactor. In 1994, Congress included $42 million in HR 4506 to design a new experimental fusion reactor, known as Tokamak, in Princeton, N.J. But appropriators agreed not to allocate funds for construction until Congress had authorized the project. The project was intended to provide scientists with a research tool as a step toward development of a commercially successful fusion plant by the middle of the twenty-first century. Some scientists contended that fusion would offer an energy source that was more economical and environmentally sound than provided by traditional nuclear fission reactors.   ❑

Weatherization Program

The House by voice vote on Aug. 8, 1994, passed legislation (HR 4751) to reauthorize the federal weatherization assistance program for two years, but the Senate did not take up the bill. The program, a block grant administered through state community action agencies and energy offices, funded insulation and home energy efficiency repairs for schools, hospitals and low-income families.

The House Energy and Commerce Committee, which reported the bill (H Rept 103-662) on Aug. 3, reduced the authorization from five to two years to pressure the Energy Department into revising the formula that it used to allocate money under the program. Southern lawmakers, who argued that extreme heat was as dangerous to a person's health as extreme cold, had long complained that the formula heavily favored northern and rural states.   ❏

Nuclear Regulatory Commission

The Senate Environment and Public Works Committee approved two bills in 1994 related to the Nuclear Regulatory Commission (NRC), but neither saw floor action in the 103rd Congress.

S 2313 would have reauthorized NRC operations at $530.2 million in fiscal 1994 and $541.4 million in fiscal 1995. The money for the NRC, whose reauthorization ran out in 1985, came entirely from fees paid by its licensees. The bill included new penalties for wrongdoing at nuclear facilities and authorized the NRC to obtain a warrant from a federal judge to search unlicensed facilities, such as parts suppliers, without giving advance notice. The committee reported the measure on July 25 (S Rept 103-319).

The committee on Aug. 11 reported S 1165 (S Rept 103-331) allowing people to petition the NRC for sanctions against an operating nuclear facility and providing for court review of the NRC's response to such petitions.   ❏

Helium Sales

The House Natural Resources Committee on Aug. 3, 1994, reported legislation (HR 3967—H Rept 103-661) to take the federal government out of the business of selling helium, but the full House did not take up the bill. The panel approved HR 3967 in the wake of widespread criticism of the Bureau of Mines' helium program, which had racked up a $1.3 billion debt and drawn bipartisan charges that it was costly and inefficient. The committee bill required that the federal government cease refining and producing helium but allowed it to continue monitoring domestic resources and conducting some associated research. The government would also sell its 32 billion cubic-foot helium stockpile.   ❏

Multistate Utility Companies

The Senate Energy and Natural Resources Committee on Aug. 22, 1994, reported a bill (S 544—S Rept 103-351) aimed at resolving a complex dispute over the regulation of public utility holding companies that operated in a number of states. The measure went no further in the 103rd Congress. Some provisions were included in a bill to rewrite the rules of competition in the telecommunications industry (S 1822), but that measure also died.

S 544 continued the division of regulatory authority over the holding companies between the Securities and Exchange Commission (SEC) and the Federal Energy Regulatory Commission. But it restored the energy commission's latitude in setting wholesale electricity rates for utilities affiliated with the holding companies. The energy commission's discretion had been limited by a 1992 ruling by the U.S. Court of Appeals for the District of Columbia Circuit, which held that the SEC had sole authority to regulate the costs of goods and services provided under contracts between multistate utility holding companies and their affiliates.   ❏

Alternative Energy

The House Energy and Commerce Committee on Aug. 8, 1994, reported a bill (HR 4866—H Rept 103-684) aimed at facilitating the development of alternative energy sources. HR 4866 would have extended for two years an existing provision of law that allowed solar, wind, waste and geothermal power plants larger than 80 megawatts to benefit from certain exemptions to the regulatory requirements under the Public Utility Regulatory Policies Act of 1978 (PL 95-617). Because HR 4866 saw no further action, the exemption for plants larger than 80 megawatts, which had been included in the 1990 Solar, Wind and Geothermal Power Production Incentives Act (PL 101-575), expired Dec. 31. *(Congress and the Nation Vol. VIII, p. 486)*   ❏

1995–1996

The Republican-controlled 104th Congress chalked up some major victories on environmental legislation, despite initial missteps that energized opposition to their efforts to rollback regulations.

Republican leaders rewrote the Safe Drinking Water Act, overhauled pesticide regulations and revamped management of the nation's fisheries. A number of other GOP environmental initiatives languished, however, particularly those backed by conservatives and westerners but opposed by GOP environmentalists and many Democrats. They included efforts to rewrite the 1973 Endangered Species Act and to overturn administration rules for grazing on public lands. Also abandoned was legislation to rewrite the nation's superfund hazardous waste law. The GOP was forced to drop a handful of controversial environment-related riders attached to spending bills as well.

Efforts to go beyond specific issues to overhaul the regulatory process itself also stalled. The House passed sweeping legislation that, in part, would have boosted private property rights when they conflicted with government regulations and would have required scientific risk assessments and cost-benefit analyses on most proposed rules. Although the bill would have covered a number of federal agencies, it was aimed largely at those that regulated the environment. But the legislation died in the Senate. A House-passed bill to halt the implementation of new regulations, while Congress worked on overhauling the regulatory process, suffered the same fate. One of the few items on the GOP agenda to be enacted into law was a curb on unfunded federal mandates, requirements that Congress imposed on state and local governments without providing the money to pay for them. *(Regulatory overhaul, p. 842; unfunded mandates, p. 837)*

In their eagerness to rewrite environmental law, Republican leaders made some serious mistakes. They rushed ahead with various legislative proposals without uniting their party behind them or developing a coherent political message to counter Democratic claims that they were extremists with no sympathy for the environment. The GOP had to do considerable fence-mending to achieve the victories it did in the second session.

Safe Drinking Water

Congress in 1996 cleared a major, bipartisan rewrite of the nation's safe drinking water law aimed at streamlining federal health regulations to focus on contaminants that posed the greatest health risk and upgrading local water plants. Republican leaders, stung by a political backlash against their environmental record, had pushed hard for the legislation (S 1316—PL 104-182).

Central to the measure was a new $7.6 billion fund to help local water systems improve drinking water facilities. In addition, the bill gave the Environmental Protection Agency (EPA) more flexibility in setting drinking water standards, required that water systems provide more information for consumers and permitted small systems to choose alternative technologies.

Several factors helped make bipartisan accord on the bill possible. For one thing, the legislation provoked little of the ideological and industry infighting seen on other bills. The drinking water issue largely affected publicly administered water systems and state governments, which could only gain from the multimillion-dollar state-administered loan fund. Moreover, the bill's popularity put pressure on Republicans and Democrats, alike, to support it. Democrats supported the bill even though some acknowledged privately that doing so went against their election-year goal of highlighting environmental differences between the two parties.

Environmentalists did not endorse the final product, in part because of the last-minute addition of millions of dollars in grants at the behest of the House Transportation and Infrastructure Committee. Many environmentalists saw the grants as drawing funds away from drinking water improvement programs. But they also saw much in the bill to make them happy, including a strong section on consumer information.

Among its key elements, the bill:

• **Federal Grants.** Authorized $7.6 billion through fiscal 2003 for federal grants to states that established drinking water revolving loan funds. States were to use the funds to provide low-cost financing to water systems for infrastructure and other activities needed to comply with the provisions of the bill. States were required to provide a 20 percent match and could transfer money between drinking water revolving funds and wastewater funds.

• **Drinking Water Standards.** Repealed an existing requirement that the EPA set standards for 25 new contaminants every three years. Instead, the bill gave the EPA the option of issuing regulations for at least five contaminants every five years. It required the EPA to consider risk and cost-benefit analyses in setting new standards. Use of drinking water disinfectants such as chlorine and efforts to eliminate biological organisms such as cryptosporidium were specifically exempted from the cost-benefit mandate.

• **Arsenic, Radon and Sulfates.** Required the EPA to set a drinking water standard for arsenic by 2000; issue within three years two radon standards for states to choose from; and study the health effects of sulfate before issuing a final ruling on that substance.

• **Consumer Notification.** Required water systems to notify customers within 24 hours of failing to comply with any drinking water standard, and to publish detailed annual water reports that included information on contaminant levels in the system's water and the health effects of contaminants that exceeded standards.

• **Small Systems.** Allowed small systems to use the best available, affordable technology to treat their drinking water.

• **Monitoring Relief.** Permitted water systems to reduce their monitoring of a contaminant that was not detected or was found only at very low levels.

• **Bottled Water.** Required bottled water to meet the same standards that the EPA set for tap water.

BACKGROUND

The 1974 Safe Drinking Water Act (PL 93-523) sprang from the modern environmental movement and was pushed through the legislative process in response to revelations about cancer-causing chemicals and other suspect substances found in the nation's drinking water. Passage of the act, however, did not fully address health concerns, and Congress in 1986 enacted a set of revisions aimed at tightening EPA oversight of the nation's drinking water (PL 99-339). *(1974 act, Congress and the Nation Vol. IV, p. 293; 1986 revisions, Congress and the Nation Vol. VII, p. 433)*

Since the act's inception, the EPA had regulated only about two dozen of the more than 600 contaminants found in drinking water; the 1986 amendments required the agency to establish standards for a list of 83 contaminants by 1989. The EPA was further directed to come up with 25 additional contaminants to regulate every three years, a schedule that soon proved unrealistic.

The 1986 revisions were criticized as being so restrictive as to be unworkable. Carol M. Browner, EPA administrator in the Clinton administration, said the revised act denied the agency flexibility, compelling it to focus on a list of contaminants instead of identifying those that posed the greatest risk to public health and targeting limited resources accordingly.

For the 185,000 water systems regulated by the EPA, the law was full of equally problematic provisions. Water systems often had to test for substances unlikely to be found in their water, thus diverting financial resources that otherwise could have been used to maximize health protections.

A series of health crises and equally disturbing studies spurred public demands for a new federal response. One of the most high-profile and deadly incidents was the outbreak in 1993 of cryptosporidium in Milwaukee's drinking water supply, which resulted in more than 100 deaths. A 1994 Centers for Disease Control and Prevention study estimated that 900,000 people became ill annually, 900 of them dying, as a result of dangerous organisms in drinking water.

Both the House and Senate passed safe drinking water bills in 1994, but conference negotiations reached an impasse over unrelated Senate add-ons. *(1993–1994 action, p. 408)*

SENATE, HOUSE ACTION

The Senate passed S 1316 on Nov. 29, 1995. The bill proved so popular that the chamber endorsed it 99–0. S 1316 had broad backing from the water systems and the Clinton administration, although environmentalists were opposed, saying it would not go far enough in regulating substances such as radon and arsenic.

Drafted by Senate Environment and Public Works Chairman John H. Chafee, R-R.I., and many of his Democratic colleagues, S 1316 had been reported by Chafee's committee Nov. 7 (S Rept 104-169).

Before passage, the Senate had adopted by voice vote a Chafee amendment to delete language that would have given the EPA authority to study and rank the nation's environmental health risks. J. Bennett Johnston, D-La., complained that the wording of the bill would have granted EPA too broad an authority. Chafee promised to schedule a committee hearing on the issue.

The only roll-call vote taken was on a motion to table (kill) a Barbara Boxer, D-Calif., amendment that would have required local water systems to provide all of their customers with comprehensive lists of drinking water contaminants, including those that met federal safety standards. The bill's sponsors argued that the bill required water suppliers to inform customers of any violation of drinking water standards and did not preclude states from imposing tougher requirements on their own, as California did. The motion was agreed to, 59–40, on Nov. 29.

After its unanimous send-off from the Senate, the drinking water legislation slowed down in the House. Speaker Newt Gingrich, R-Ga., gave marching orders to House Commerce Committee Chairman Thomas J. Bliley Jr., R-Va., to produce a bipartisan bill that would win administration support and avoid the bitter environmental fights of the previous year.

To get such a bill required months of behind-the-scenes negotiations. In the initial rounds, Republicans won agreement on GOP-favored provisions. But the Democrats' leverage increased, as the Republicans' desire to get a drinking water bill grew. GOP leaders were under pressure to get the measure signed by Aug. 1 to get $725 million provided in the 1996 omnibus appropriations bill (HR 3019—PL 104-134) for the state loan fund.

The House Commerce Committee finally reported its version on June 24, 1996 (HR 3604—H Rept 104-632, Part I). The bill went to the floor with the enthusiastic backing of the House Republican leadership and support from environmentalists and allies of industry.

The House passed HR 3064 by voice vote June 25, but last-minute opposition from Commerce Committee Democrats erupted when Republicans added language from a separate bill (HR 2747—H Rept 104-515), which had been reported by the House Transportation and Infrastructure Committee March 29. Under a deal the GOP leadership made to avert a standoff with Transportation Committee Chairman Bud Shuster, R-Pa., a new title was added authorizing $50 million annually in fiscal years 1997 to 2003 for water infrastructure grants, along with several less controversial provisions.

The new money was to be available each year only if 75 percent of the money authorized for the state loan fund was appropriated. The Transportation Committee was to have oversight of the loan fund—and the power to authorize millions of dollars in grants for localities—along with a seat in the House-Senate conference on the drinking water bill. Democrats attacked the grants as pork and said the deal violated the spirit of bipartisan cooperation that had made the bill possible. Ultimately, the Democrats allowed the bill to go through on a voice vote, but the dispute did little to build trust between the parties.

CONFERENCE, FINAL ACTION

The conference on S 1316 was delayed by continuing turf fights in the House, which did not agree to go to conference until July 17, the day it passed S 1316 by voice vote after substituting the text of its own bill.

Partisan conflicts, particularly between House Democrats and the Senate conferees, slowed the talks once the bill got to conference. As a result of the delays, GOP leaders missed the Aug. 1 deadline for getting the $725 million for the state loan fund under the omnibus appropriations bill.

The House adopted the conference report (H Rept 104-741) by a vote of 392–30 on Aug. 2. Hours later, the Senate concurred, 98–0, clearing the bill for the president.

Under pressure from environmentalists and the White House, conferees generally adopted House language requiring community water systems to inform the public about contaminants in drinking water. The Senate version had not had that requirement.

Despite environmentalists' opposition, negotiators agreed to a two-standard system for radon in air and water: the House bill's more stringent standard set by the EPA or a more relaxed standard under state programs.

Both the House and Senate versions included some reduced standards for smaller water systems that might not have the money to buy the best available technology. Conferees split the difference on the size of such systems.

In a victory for environmentalists, conferees generally agreed to House language requiring water systems to be operated by certified operators, with the EPA issuing regulations for state certification programs. The Senate would have required only those systems receiving federal aid to meet the certification requirement.

A stubborn dispute broke out among conferees over the $50 million in grants added on the House floor. The conference committee agreed to subject half of the grant money to the requirement that at least 75 percent of the funds authorized for the state revolving fund be appropriated before the infrastructure money could be released. The other half was made available without conditions.

The House proposed to require states to identify watershed boundaries of drinking water sources and track the origins of contaminants. The Senate had a somewhat similar requirement and proposed creating a voluntary program of partnerships among interested parties to protect drinking water sources from contamination. Conferees adopted provisions from both versions. They kept the House language on state requirements, while also allowing community-based partnerships to petition states for funding for projects to protect water sources.

MAJOR PROVISIONS

Following are the major provisions of S 1316, as signed into law Aug. 6, 1996:

Regulatory Process

• **New Regulations.** As a general rule, the bill required the Environmental Protection Agency (EPA) to establish regulations for contaminants in two stages. First, the agency was to establish the maximum safe exposure level, or "maximum contaminant level goal," for the substance. Second, the EPA was to set a regulation for the contaminant that was as close to the maximum contaminant level goal as feasible.

In establishing the regulation, the EPA was required to determine that the contaminant affected public health, that it was present in drinking water or was very likely to be present, and that the regulation would meaningfully reduce health risks.

• **Timetables.** After deciding to regulate a contaminant, the EPA had two years to propose a maximum contaminant level goal and a drinking water regulation. The EPA had another 18 months within which to establish the goal and issue the new regulation. The deadline could be extended for up to nine months through a notice published in the *Federal Register*.

• **Effective Date.** The bill specified that national drinking water regulations should take effect three years after being issued, unless an earlier date was considered practical. A water system could be granted up to two additional years to comply if extra time was needed for capital improvements.

• **Occurrence Data Base.** Within three years, the EPA was required to assemble and maintain a data base on the occurrence of contaminants in public water systems. The EPA was to use the list to determine the substances that posed health threats and should be subject to regulations. Recommendations were to be solicited from the National Academy of Sciences and from the states. The public could also make recommendations. To be listed, the contaminant had to at least be likely to be found in drinking water and pose a public health risk.

The data base had to include information on the detection of regulated contaminants. For unregulated contaminants, it had to include monitoring results from systems serving more than 10,000 people, a representative sample of all other systems, and any other "reliable and appropriate" information on the occurrence of unregulated substances.

Selecting Contaminants to Regulate

• **Unregulated Contaminants.** The EPA was required to publish a master list of unregulated contaminants no later than 18 months after enactment, and every five years thereafter. The list was to be developed in consultation with scientists, after the public was allowed to comment and after a review of the Occurrence Data Base of possible contaminants.

At a minimum, the EPA had to consider listing substances cataloged in a section of the 1980 superfund hazardous waste law and pesticides registered under the Federal Insecticide, Fungicide, and Rodenticide Act. EPA's decision to list a substance was not subject to legal challenge.

• **Determination to Regulate.** No later than five years after enactment, and every five years after that, the EPA was required to make a decision on whether or not to regulate at least five of the contaminants on the master list. The decision to regulate, which was subject to public comment, had to be based on a number of factors, including health effects and the presence of the contaminant in drinking water.

A contaminant that was not on the master list could be considered for regulation so long as the EPA made its decision based on the enumerated factors. A determination not to regulate was considered a final agency action, but it was subject to legal challenge.

• **Priorities.** In choosing the contaminants to place on the master list, the EPA was required to select substances that posed the greatest public health concern. In particular, the agency had to pay attention to the health effects of these substances on the most vulnerable groups, such as infants, pregnant women and the elderly, when those groups ran a greater risk from those contaminants than did the general population.

• **Urgent Threats.** The EPA could issue an interim regulation, sidestepping many of the requirements for permanent standards, to address an "urgent threat" to public health. The standard could be issued only after consultation with the secretary of the Health and Human Services Department, acting through the director of the Centers for Disease Control and Prevention or the director of the National Institutes of Health. Within three years of issuing the interim regulation, the EPA had to publish an analysis that included such factors as costs and benefits and effects. The regulation had to be reissued or revised within five years of taking effect.

• **Health Advisories.** The EPA could publish health advisories or take other appropriate action for contaminants that were not subject to drinking water regulations.

• **Disinfectants.** The bill endorsed the negotiated rule making on disinfectants and their byproducts, such as chlorine, being carried out by the EPA in conjunction with industry, water systems and environmentalists. The bill specifically exempted disinfectants and their byproducts from the cost-benefit analysis provisions. But the bill authorized EPA to consider the same factors in setting the final regulations that it used in setting the proposed rule. It gave the EPA flexibility to avoid maximizing one health benefit if doing so would counteract another. For example, the agency would not be required to reduce chlorine if it would increase the risk of contamination from dangerous organisms.

New Regulations

Risk Assessment

• **Use of Science.** The EPA was directed to use the best available science and the most up-to-date data in determining the costs and benefits of drinking water regulation and the maximum safe exposure levels.

• **Public Information.** The bill required the EPA to publish a report explaining the health effects and risks of a regulation, including information on the people affected by the regulation, possible risks to this group, an examination of the uncertainties associated with the regulation, and studies that shed light on the public health threat.

• **Cost Analysis.** The bill directed the EPA to publish an analysis of the costs and benefits for most of the regulations it proposed. The analysis was to include the health benefits of the regulation, as well as how the regulation was likely to reduce health risks from unregulated contaminants affected by the rule.

Other areas of study included compliance costs, costs and benefits of alternative exposure levels considered during rule making, and effects of the contaminant on vulnerable populations. In addition, any increased health risk that might result because of compliance was to be factored in. The EPA had some flexibility to identify other costs and benefits, including the willingness of consumers to defray compliance costs.

• **Authorization.** The bill authorized annual appropriations of $35 million in fiscal years 1996 to 2003 to develop methods for conducting cost-benefit studies.

Standard Setting

• **Safe Levels.** When proposing a regulation, the EPA was required to publish a conclusion on whether the health effects of the safe exposure level included in the regulation justified the costs.

• **Additional Health Risks.** The EPA could set drinking water standards at other than "feasible" levels in cases where the treatment technology would increase overall health risks by raising the concentration of other contaminants in drinking water or by interfering with the efficiency of compliance with other drinking water regulations.

• **Cost-Benefit Test.** The EPA could set a standard below the "feasible" level if it determined, based on the bill's cost-benefit test, that the benefits of the higher standard would not justify the costs. The EPA could then issue a standard at a level that maximized health protections at a cost that was justified by the benefits.

• **Review and Revision.** Every six years, the EPA was to review and revise drinking water standards, where appropriate. Any revision would have to maintain or provide for greater protection of public health and comply with the act's standard-setting requirements.

Small System Technologies

• **EPA Role.** The EPA was directed to help small systems comply with regulations by publishing a list of affordable technology and treatment techniques within two years for three categories of small systems. The categories included systems that served populations between 3,300 and 10,000, 500 and 3,300, and 25 and 500. After it was issued, the list could be supplemented with new treatment techniques for regulated contaminants.

• **Surface Water.** Within one year, the EPA had to list technologies to meet surface water treatment rules.

• **Variances.** Smaller water systems could use the next best affordable technology when the technology needed to comply with the law was too expensive. When issuing a regulation, the EPA was required to list such alternative methods for the small systems, if the alternatives would protect public health. Technologies for regulations on the books before enactment had to be issued within two years. The treatments were to be reviewed at least every seven years.

Alternative to Filtration

The bill allowed for a limited alternative to filtration for public water systems that had an undeveloped and uninhabited watershed and had control over access and activities in the area. The watershed land had to be owned by a single entity. The state, acting with approval from the EPA, had to ensure that any alternative treatment plan would be more effective than running the water through a filter or disinfecting it with chlorine.

Arsenic

• **Study Plan.** Within 180 days of enactment, the EPA was to develop a plan to study health risks associated with exposure to low levels of arsenic, a known carcinogen linked to skin cancer and vascular diseases. In carrying out the plan, the EPA was to consult with the National Academy of Sciences, federal agencies and interested members of the public. In executing the study, the EPA could enter into cooperative agreements with other federal agencies, state and local governments, and the interested public.

• **Deadline.** The EPA was to propose a standard by 2000, and a final regulation by 2001 after a public comment period.

• **Authorization.** The bill authorized $2.5 million annually in fiscal 1997 to 2000 to carry out the arsenic studies.

Sulfate

• **Study Plan.** The EPA and the Centers for Disease Control were directed to conduct a joint study on the health effects of sulfate in drinking water, including groups at particular risk. Sulfate, which could occur naturally and as a waste product of steel and metal manufacturing, could result in acute but temporary bouts of diarrhea, particularly among newborns. The study was to be carried out in consultation with interested states and according to the best available science, and it was to be completed 30 months after enactment.

• **Determination.** The EPA was required to determine whether to regulate sulfate within five years of enactment. As a possible substitute for traditional treatment, a regulation had to include options for providing alternative water supplies to at-risk populations to comply with the rule.

Radon

• **Timetable.** The EPA was directed to withdraw any radon standard proposed before enactment and offer a new standard within three years. A final regulation was to be proposed 12 months later. Radon, an odorless, naturally occurring gas, was the second leading cause of lung cancer; it was found in tap water and released when the water ran.

• **Risk Assessment.** Before proposing a new standard, the EPA was directed to arrange with the National Academy of Sciences or another designated scientific group to evaluate the risks of radon in drinking water and to prepare an analysis of the costs and health benefits for the maximum safe exposure levels under consideration for radon. The studies had to take into account radon from sources other than tap water. The academy also was to evaluate different methods to reduce indoor radon exposure. The final rule had to be based on the cost-benefit study.

The EPA was directed to publish the study within 30 months after enactment.

• **Alternatives.** If the EPA proposed a standard more stringent than the rules for outdoor exposure, it also had to propose an alternative standard equal to outdoor exposure. A state could comply with the alternative standard if it developed a mitigation program approved by the EPA that included public education, testing and other measures and was as protective of public health as the more stringent standard. The program had to be reviewed at least every five years.

• **Exceptions for Systems.** If a state was not granted an exception, a water system could apply for one on its own.

Estrogen

• **Screening Program.** The bill directed the EPA to establish a screening program for pesticides and other chemicals that could behave similar to estrogen or have estrogenlike effects on the body's hormones, raising potential cancer risks. A major goal of the study was to identify estrogenlike chemicals found in drinking water. The EPA was required to report the results of the study within four years of enactment.

Bottled Water

• **Standards.** The bill gave the Food and Drug Administration (FDA) specific deadlines for issuing regulations for bottled water. Under existing law, the FDA was required to issue regulations for the contaminants in bottled water based on EPA regulations for contaminants in tap water. The new law required the FDA to issue the equivalent regulation for bottled water within 180 days before the effective date of a drinking water standard. Otherwise, the tap water standard would automatically apply to bottled water.

• **Right to Know.** The bill required the FDA, working with the EPA, to publish a study on how to inform the public on the contents of bottled water. A draft was to be published within 18 months of enactment, with the final study due 30 months after enactment.

State Role

• **Primacy.** The bill specified that states could run state drinking water programs if they adopted regulations at least as stringent as federal standards. A state-run program generally had two years to bring a standard into line with a federal regulation, although additional two-year extensions could be granted

if "necessary and justified." The states had interim enforcement authority after they submitted a regulation.

• **Federal Role.** For states that did not operate their own programs, the EPA was required to set aside an amount equal to the allotment that would have otherwise been used to fund the loan and grant fund for the state. The money was to be used by the EPA to supervise the drinking water program in the state.

Notification and Enforcement
Public Notification

• **General Rule.** The bill required public water systems to alert their customers if they failed to comply with safe levels of exposure to contaminants or failed to follow the proper treatment or testing technique as defined by regulation. If the system was operating under a special exception, or "variance," to a regulation, it had to so inform the public and tell the public of any failure to comply with the variance. In some circumstances, information also was to be provided on unregulated contaminants.

• **Adverse Health Effects.** A public water system that was responsible for a violation that had the potential of a serious impact on public health because of a short-term exposure had to follow special procedures. Within 24 hours of the violation, the water system had to distribute a notice that included the violation, the potential effects on human health, the steps being taken to correct the problem and the need to switch to other water supplies while the problem was being fixed. Notification had to be provided to the appropriate agency and made available through television or radio, a local newspaper or, as an alternative, door-to-door posting

• **Annual Reports.** By 1998, states that ran their own programs were required to publish an annual report on violations of drinking water standards. By July 1, 1998, the EPA had to publish the first annual report summarizing and evaluating the results. The report was to include information on water systems that served Native American tribes and recommendations on how to comply with the act.

• **EPA Regulation.** The EPA was directed to develop a regulation on public notification, taking into account such factors as the frequency of violations and seriousness of health effects. A state could also develop its own requirements if they were at least as stringent as the federal rule.

• **Consumer Confidence Reports.** The EPA had 24 months to issue regulations requiring community water systems to mail annual reports on water quality. The regulations were to include plainly worded definitions of the terms used in the act (such as "maximum contaminant level goal"), health problems associated with regulated contaminants, and a toll-free information hotline.

At a minimum, the annual reports had to include the source of the water, definitions of terms, safe levels for contaminants, a statement of health concerns for violations, whether the system was operating under a variance, and levels of some unregulated contaminants, including cryptosporidium and radon. The report also was to include a statement that the presence of contaminants in drinking water did not necessarily pose a health risk and that more information could be obtained from the EPA hotline.

- **Exceptions.** A governor could allow a system serving fewer than 10,000 customers to skip mailing the report. But the system had to notify the public that it would not be mailing the report, make it available on request and publish it in a local paper. Systems serving fewer than 500 persons that were granted an exception were required at least to prepare the report and notify the public once a year that it was available upon request.

Enforcement

- **Sanctions.** The EPA was authorized to take legal or administrative actions against a water system if a state with primary enforcement responsibilities did not take action to enforce certain provisions of the Safe Drinking Water Act. The EPA would have to provide notice and opportunity for a public hearing before issuing a civil fine.
- **Incentive for Consolidation.** A system could be allowed to merge with another water system to avoid a fine or other enforcement action. The merger plan would have to be approved by the EPA or by the state if it ran its own program.
- **Federal Compliance.** The federal government was required, as a general rule, to comply with the Safe Drinking Water Act. Any fines collected by state-run programs from federal agencies were to be used to protect the environment or enforce environmental laws, unless state law in effect on the day of enactment or the state constitution specified otherwise. No penalties assessed on the Washington, D.C., water system could be passed on by the Army Corps of Engineers to taxpayers.

Small System Variances

- **General Rule.** Systems serving fewer than 3,300 people were eligible for a variance from a safe level or treatment technique prescribed in a drinking water regulation. With approval from the EPA, such an exception could be granted for systems serving between 3,300 and 10,000 people.
- **Conditions.** An exception could be made if the EPA identified a treatment technology that was compatible with the size and quality of a system's source water, the technology was installed and operated correctly, and the system met the conditions for obtaining the variance.

The system had to qualify for an exception on grounds that it could not afford to comply with a particular regulation and that the variance would safeguard public health. A system generally had three years to comply with the conditions of a variance, although it could have up to two additional years if capital improvements were necessary or financing from the state or federal government was outstanding. The variance had to be reviewed by the state or federal government every five years.

- **Exceptions.** Variances could not be issued for a safe level or treatment technique contained in a regulation that was on the books before 1986. Also, no variance could be granted for microbial contaminants such as cryptosporidium.
- **Regulations.** The bill gave the EPA two years to put into effect a rule on variances. The regulation was to contain the procedures for approving variances, requirements for installing and operating treatment equipment, eligibility for variance regarding each drinking water regulation and the amount of information that had to be included on variance applications.

- **EPA Oversight.** The EPA was directed to make periodic reviews of state programs, including whether the variances complied with the affordability standards administered by the state. The EPA was to notify the state if variances were out of compliance. In addition, the EPA could object within 90 days to any variance proposed by a state, and it had the right to overturn the variance if not in compliance. A person served by the system had 30 days to raise an objection to a variance to the EPA, which had 60 days to respond.

General Drinking Water Provisions
Lead Plumbing and Pipes

- **General Prohibition.** No person could use any pipe, fitting, fixture, solder or flux after June 19, 1986, that was not "lead-free" as defined by law in the installation or repair of any public water system or facility providing drinking water. The prohibition did not apply to leaded joints used in the repair of cast iron pipes.
- **Unlawful Acts.** Within two years, marketing any non-lead-free pipe, fitting or fixture would be illegal unless it was used in manufacturing or industrial processing. A person supplying plumbing goods, other than a manufacturer, could not legally sell or market solder or flux that contained lead unless it bore a label stating that it was against the law to use the material for drinking water plumbing.
- **Standards.** The EPA was required to provide information and technical assistance to qualified, independent inspectors involved in developing a voluntary standard for lead leaching from new plumbing fittings and fixtures intended for tap water. If a voluntary standard was not established, the EPA had to set a mandatory standard, which would be in effect five years after it was issued.

If no mandatory regulation had been proposed and no voluntary regulation had taken effect five years after enactment, a prohibition would automatically be put in place barring a person from importing, manufacturing, processing or distributing a new fitting or fixture that contained more than 4 percent lead, as measured by dry weight.

Capacity Development

- **New Systems.** The states were required to have the legal authority in place to ensure that all new community water systems that began operations after Oct. 1, 1999, demonstrated technical expertise, managerial competence and financial resources to comply with all drinking water regulations when they opened for business. The state would lose 20 percent of its allotment under the federally funded, but state-administered, loan fund if it failed to comply with this requirement.
- **Significant Noncompliance.** Each state was to prepare and submit to the EPA a list of systems that had a history of being out of compliance with financial, technical and managerial requirements. The submission was due within a year of enactment. Within five years of enactment, states were required to

provide a status report on enforcement actions and efforts to bring the systems in compliance.

• **Sanctions.** Each state had to develop and implement a strategy to assist public water systems in acquiring and maintaining technical, managerial and financial resources. A state that failed to comply with the conditions would receive 10 percent less in 2001 from the loan fund, 15 percent less in 2002 and 20 percent less in future years.

• **Federal Role.** Within 180 days of enactment, the EPA was required to review state efforts and publish information to assist the states. In issuing a regulation, the EPA was to include an analysis of the impact on the technical, financial and managerial resources of water systems. The EPA was also authorized to make grants to colleges and universities to establish training and technology assistance centers.

Operator Certification

• **Minimum Standards.** The bill required the EPA to publish guidelines in the *Federal Register* within 30 months of enactment outlining minimum standards for certifying the operator of a water system, taking into account existing state programs and costs. Two years after publishing the guidelines, the EPA was required to withhold 20 percent of a state's loan fund if an approved certification program was not in place.

A state could run its own certification program if it was "substantially equivalent" to the EPA guidelines. States had 18 months after publication of the guidelines to submit a program to the EPA for approval, and six additional months for revisions if the EPA rejected the program.

• **Reimbursement.** Small systems serving fewer than 3,300 people were eligible to be reimbursed for training costs.

Monitoring

• **General Rule.** All water systems were required to keep records on and test for regulated substances to assist the EPA in determining whether the system was in compliance. A person could be required to turn over records to the EPA to determine whether he or she was acting in compliance. Within two years, the EPA was to review monitoring requirements for at least 12 contaminants and modify the requirements where appropriate.

• **Interim Relief.** Systems serving fewer than 10,000 people in states that ran their own programs could be excused on a stopgap basis from monitoring for substances. Certain conditions would have to be met, however. First, microbial contaminants such as cryptosporidium, disinfectants and their byproducts, and corrosion byproducts could not be included in the exemption. Second, the system could be excused only if the contaminant was not detected and was unlikely to be found in the drinking water supply. Interim relief would expire three years after enactment or when a permanent exemption was granted, whichever was earlier.

• **Permanent Relief.** A state that ran its own program could develop its own monitoring program as long as it complied with EPA guidelines and assured compliance with federal drinking water regulations. The program could not apply to regulated microbial contaminants, disinfectants and their byproducts or corrosion byproducts. A governor in a state that did not run its own program could request the EPA to modify monitoring requirements.

• **EPA Guidelines.** EPA guidelines for alternative monitoring had to protect public health and require that a state program assess each contaminant on a case-by-case basis. States had to require a system seeking an exemption to demonstrate that a contaminant was not present in drinking water or was below levels considered safe. If a contaminant in question was detected at unsafe levels after an exemption was granted, the system would have to either demonstrate that the contaminant had been removed or resume testing for the contaminant under the applicable regulation.

• **Unregulated Contaminants.** The EPA was directed to establish a regulation on the criteria used for testing for unregulated contaminants. The rule had to take into account the system size, the water source and the contaminants likely to be found. Only a "representative sample" of systems serving fewer than 10,000 people could be included in a monitoring program. A state could develop its own monitoring program, but it had to be representative of the different sizes, types and locations of the systems.

Water systems were required to make data on unregulated contaminants available to states that ran their own programs or to the federal government. Customers had to be notified that results were available.

Within three years, and every five years after that, the EPA was required to issue a list of no more than 30 unregulated contaminants that had to be monitored by public water systems. The list was to be included in the national Occurrence Data Base.

In most cases, the EPA was required to list an unregulated contaminant if seven governors signed a petition recommending it; however, the EPA could make an exception to the rule if listing the substance would prevent the inclusion of a substance that posed a greater health concern.

State Loan Fund

• **Authorization.** The bill authorized $599 million for fiscal 1994 and $1 billion annually from fiscal 1995 to 2003 for a state loan fund. The EPA was required to reserve $10 million of this amount for health studies, with priority given to studies on cryptosporidium, disinfection byproducts and arsenic. Up to 2 percent of the funds appropriated in fiscal 1997–2003 could be reserved for technical assistance for small systems, but the amount could not exceed $15 million a year.

• **Eligibility.** To be eligible to receive federal payments, states first had to establish a state-administered revolving loan fund. Federal money deposited in the fund could be used for loans to facilitate compliance with the law or protection of public health, such as building new treatment plants. The funds could not be used for operational and maintenance expenses or to acquire property, unless the project was central to safeguarding drinking water and a willing seller existed. Fifteen percent of the annual allotment to a state had to be reserved for systems serving fewer than 10,000 people.

- **Limitations.** No assistance could be provided to a public water system that lacked the technical, managerial and financial resources to comply with regulations or that was in "significant" noncompliance with a regulation. But broad exceptions were available. An errant system could continue to receive assistance if the money would ensure that it had proper resources and if the system made state-mandated changes needed to comply with the act.

- **Intended Use Plan.** Each state that agreed to receive funds had to develop a plan on how the money would be used—including a list of projects that were to receive assistance, the criteria used to distribute money, and the financial status of the fund, as well as short-term and long-term goals. Priority had to be given to projects that addressed the most serious health threats and were necessary to comply with the law as well as to systems that served needy communities. Each state was required to publish a list of projects eligible for assistance and the priority and funding schedules assigned to them.

- **Disadvantaged Communities.** States were allowed to subsidize loans made to disadvantaged communities, including lifting the requirement that principal be repaid. Subsidies in a given year could not exceed 30 percent of the allotment for the loan fund.

- **State Contribution.** States were generally required to provide a match equal to 20 percent of their federal allotment, although matching money for fiscal years 1994–1997 had to be deposited before Sept. 30, 1999.

- **Conditions.** Loans made from a state fund had to meet certain conditions: the interest rate had to be less than or equal to market rates; payments had to begin no more than one year after completion of the project; and loans had to be paid off within 20 years. Disadvantaged communities could have up to 30 years to pay off a loan if the loan did not exceed the lifespan of a project. Other uses included refinancing or buying out loans to municipalities agreed to before July 1, 1993, and purchasing insurance if this would improve access to credit markets or reduce interests rates.

- **Administration.** A state could consolidate administration of the loan fund with other similar state loan funds. Drinking water money had to be accounted for separately by the agency that was responsible for oversight and setting priorities for loans. Four percent of the annual federal allotment could be used to cover administration costs of the fund. An additional 10 percent of the fund could be used for activities including source water protection, capacity development strategy and operator certification if the state met the requirement to provide an equal match. An additional 2 percent of the funds could be used to provide technical help to systems serving fewer than 10,000 people.

- **Exceptions.** Loan funds could not be used for enforcement actions.

- **Guidance and Regulations.** The EPA was directed to publish guidelines and regulations necessary to carry out the provisions of the loan fund, including guidance on avoiding waste, fraud and abuse. Each state that administered a loan fund was required to publish and submit to the EPA a report on its activities every two years. The EPA had to conduct audits of the state administered funds.

- **Needs Survey.** The EPA was directed to conduct an assessment of the infrastructure needs of the nation's water systems, make a report to Congress within 180 days of enactment, and then issue a report every four years after that.

- **Native American Tribes.** The EPA could use 1.5 percent of the annual federal appropriation for the state loan funds to make grants to Native American tribes and Alaska Native villages that had not otherwise received grants or loans. The funds were to be used to address the most significant health threats in public water systems that served Native American tribes. For Alaska Native villages, the EPA was also authorized to make grants to the state. In addition, the EPA was required to study the needs of drinking water treatment facilities that served tribes.

- **Other Expenditures.** The total amount of assistance for the following activities could not exceed 15 percent of the loan fund, or 10 percent for any one activity: acquiring land or conservation easements; funding to implement voluntary, incentive-based source water protection; assistance related to capacity development; assessing or delineating source water protection areas; and establishing or implementing well head safeguards.

- **Evaluation.** The EPA was directed to conduct an evaluation of the effectiveness of the loan fund through fiscal 2001 and submit the report to Congress at the same time as the president's budget request for fiscal 2003.

- **Transfer.** States were permitted to reserve up to one-third of their annual allotment and use this money in conjunction with funds provided under the clean water act. The same rule applied in reverse to allotments made under the clean water act. A report to Congress on the transfer program was required within four years of enactment. Transfer funds could not be used as matching dollars under either law.

Water Infrastructure Grants

- **Authorization.** The EPA was authorized to make the grants for construction, rehabilitation and improvement of water systems. The bill authorized $25 million annually for fiscal 1997 to 2003. In addition, an annual authorization of $25 million for fiscal 1997–2003 was provided on the condition that at least 75 percent of the annual authorization for the revolving loan fund was appropriated.

- **Conditions.** The grants had to be consistent with management programs established under the clean water act for pollution arising from multiple sources and source water quality protection programs that addressed pollutants in navigable waters that produced drinking water. No more than 30 percent of the appropriations for the grants could be used for source water quality. The federal match was 50 percent.

- **Land Acquisition.** The grants could be used to acquire land from a willing seller.

- **Earmarks.** Report language directed the EPA to give priority to more than 20 projects in New York, Pennsylvania, Washington and other states.

Groundwater Protection

• **Grants.** The EPA was authorized to make grants to a state for the development and implementation of a state program to protect groundwater. The bill authorized $15 million annually for fiscal 1997–2003. The agency had to publish guidelines within a year, and every year after that, spelling out the application process. The EPA was required to submit a report to Congress on groundwater quality and protection programs every three years.

• **Conditions.** Grants were to be awarded based on the amount of groundwater in a state and the likelihood that the grant would result in "sustained and reliable" protection of groundwater. They were to be awarded as well for "innovative" programs proposed by a state to prevent groundwater contamination, although no grant money could be used to clean up already existing groundwater contamination.

• **Limits.** The EPA was required to send at least 1 percent of the annual appropriation for the grant program to each state that had an approved application. Grants could not be used for more than 50 percent of program costs, and states were required to cover at least half of the costs.

Miscellaneous Provisions

Source Water Assessments

• **Guidance.** Within 12 months after enactment, the EPA was required to publish guidelines for states that ran their own programs to study local drinking water sources, such as lakes, rivers and tributaries. The EPA was required to conduct a demonstration project to examine the best means for assessing and protecting source water serving large metropolitan areas and located on federal land.

• **Requirements.** The programs had to map the boundaries of watersheds that supplied tap water and identify regulated contaminants in the area. States also could identify any unregulated contaminants that they determined posed a health threat. If practical, the source of the contaminants also had to be identified to determine threats to water supplies. The results of the study were to be available to the public.

• **Approval.** A state program had to be submitted for approval within 18 months of the date the guidelines were issued and approved within nine months. The program was to begin as soon as it was approved. The approval of a state program was to include a timetable, established in consultation with the state, allowing not more than two years for completion, although the EPA could extend the deadline for an additional 18 months. State tap water programs had the flexibility to use other state programs to avoid overlap, including programs under the clean water act. Permanent monitoring relief authority was contingent upon completion of the source water assessment.

Source Water Petitions

• **General Rule.** States could allow owners or operators of public water systems or local governments to petition for state assistance to create partnerships to improve water quality at its source. The partnerships had to be voluntary and based on incentives for action, not regulation. Their purpose was to reduce regulated contaminants and other substances that posed health threats in source water and obtain technical or financial assistance for source water protection.

• **Petition Contents.** At a minimum, petitions had to include: boundaries of the watershed in question; origins of contaminants; any lack of information that could hamper protection efforts; details of how the partnership was established; and broad participation from governments, water systems and other parties likely to be affected by the partnership's actions. The petition also had to take into account other water quality programs being considered in the area and specify the technical, financial or other assistance needed from the state.

• **Approval.** States had to approve or disapprove a petition in whole or part within 120 days of its submission. The notice of approval was to include some basic information, such as state assistance and other assistance available through federal programs. A petition that was disapproved could be resubmitted if new information became available, conditions affecting source water changed and modifications were made to the assistance requested.

• **Federal Role.** States with approved partnership programs were eligible for EPA grants of up to 50 percent of the cost of administering the program. The EPA also was required to publish guidelines within a year to help states develop programs and to help potential members of a partnership participate. The guidelines also had to make recommendations on procedures for approving partnerships, submission of petitions, and federal and state programs that could be of assistance to partnerships. The annual authorization was $5 million for fiscal 1997–2003.

Water Conservation

• **Guidelines.** Within two years, the EPA was required to publish in the *Federal Register* guidelines for water conservation plans, one version for systems serving fewer than 3,300 people, another for systems serving between 3,300 and 10,000 people, and a third for all other systems. The guidelines had to take into consideration such factors as availability of water and climate.

• **Requirements.** Within a year after the guidelines were published, a state program could require a conservation plan consistent with EPA guidelines as a condition for receiving money from the state-administered loan and grant fund.

Community Programs

• **New York Watershed.** The EPA was authorized to provide $15 million per year in fiscal 1997–2003 to New York for demonstration programs aimed at protecting the drinking water supply for New York City.

• **Border Communities.** The EPA was authorized to make grants to protect drinking water to needy communities along the Mexico border. The bill authorized $25 million annually for fiscal 1997–1999, as well as $25 million annually in the same period for treatment of wastewater.

• **Alaska Native American Villages.** The EPA was authorized to provide grants to Native American villages in Alaska to cover costs of the development and construction of water and wastewater systems as well as training, technical and other assistance. The annual authorization was $15 million for fiscal 1997–2000.

• **Washington, D.C.** The federally run water system that served the District of Columbia and some surrounding communities was required to transfer title within three years to an operator other than the federal government.

Drinking Water Studies

• **General Rule.** The bill required the EPA to conduct studies to identify groups at greater risk from drinking water contaminants and what the risks were, including elevated cancer rates. Among the groups to be included were infants, children, pregnant women, the elderly and the seriously ill. A report was to be made to Congress within four years and periodically thereafter when significant new information became available. Toxicological and other studies were called for in connection with three major standards: the enhanced surface water treatment rule, the disinfectant byproducts standard and the groundwater disinfection rule.

• **Biomedical Studies.** The EPA was required to conduct studies to determine how chemical contaminants were absorbed, distributed, metabolized and eliminated from the body. The studies also were to look at how chemicals caused adverse health effects, such as infectious diseases, with a particular focus on vulnerable groups. In a bow to a growing body of evidence on the dangers of exposure to a combination of chemicals, instead of a single contaminant, a study was mandated to develop new approaches to studying chemicals and microbes that act in concert.

• **Waterborne Disease Study.** The Centers for Disease Control and Prevention and the EPA were required within two years after enactment to conduct pilot studies of waterborne diseases for five major cities and report on the findings within five years. ❑

Pesticide Regulation

Congress in 1996 cleared a major, bipartisan rewrite of federal pesticide law. The legislation (HR 1627—PL 104-170) created a unified health standard for both raw and processed foods, with guidelines to protect children.

The bill's quick passage was a remarkable achievement. Industry and environmental supporters had deadlocked repeatedly since the last major pesticide overhaul in 1978. HR 1627 had stalled in the House for more than a year because of disputes over proposals to relax regulations.

But, by 1996, its time had come. Congress was spurred into action, in part, by a court ruling that had interpreted pesticide regulations so strictly that the Environmental Protection Agency (EPA) would otherwise have had to begin canceling the use of some common chemicals.

In addition, GOP lawmakers were anxious for an election-year environmental bill, after coming under fire in 1995 for repeatedly attempting to scale back environmental regulations. Finally, lobbyists on opposing sides of the pesticide issue were tired of fighting the same battle year after year.

As signed into law, HR 1627 imposed a safety standard to ensure that pesticide residues on both raw and processed foods posed no reasonable risk of harm, meaning no more than a one in-a-million chance existed that the residue would cause cancer. Special attention was to be given to the food children frequently consumed and the effect of pesticides on children.

The bill streamlined EPA approval of certain chemicals and allowed for the emergency suspension of a pesticide's use. It authorized EPA to collect millions of dollars in fees to help expedite the pesticide approval process. It also restricted the ability of states to pass laws stricter than federal regulations and contained provisions to educate the public about both the risks and benefits of agricultural chemicals.

BACKGROUND

For the better part of two decades, lawmakers had wrestled in vain with proposals to overhaul pesticide regulations, stymied by stubborn disputes among farmers, industry officials, environmentalists and public health advocates.

At issue was a complicated body of laws. Two major statutes governed pesticide usage: the 1947 Federal Insecticide, Fungicide, and Rodenticide Act (FIFRA), which set the standards for assessing the safety of pesticides before they could be "registered" with the federal government and put on the market, and the 1938 Federal Food, Drug, and Cosmetic Act, which set the level of pesticide residues allowed in food.

FIFRA

The last sweeping revisions of FIFRA, enacted in 1978 (PL 95-396), had left intact the law's basic philosophy that the public should be protected from harmful poisons. But it allowed the EPA to simplify the registration of pesticides, thereby clearing the chemicals for use. At the time, the EPA was drowning in data on the 35,000 pesticides on the market and failing to meet statutory deadlines for assessing their safety. *(Congress and the Nation Vol. V, p. 568)*

But the registration process still moved slowly, and Congress came under renewed pressure to rewrite pesticide laws in the mid-1980s.

Congress scored a partial breakthrough in 1988, clearing a bill (PL 100-532) to speed the testing of hundreds of pesticides already on the market to see whether they caused cancer, birth defects or other health problems. The bill set a nine-year timetable for the EPA to finish tests of some 600 pesticide-active ingredients to determine whether they met modern health standards and therefore could be reregistered and allowed to stay on the market. The agency had been moving at a pace that would have taken it until 2024 to complete the testing. *(Congress and the Nation Vol. VII, p. 458)*

But the bill did not address many controversial issues, such as federal preemption of state pesticide standards and protections for farmers from liability for pesticide pollution.

Delaney Clause

The food and drug act had its own set of problems. The law allowed infinitesimal residues of potentially cancer-causing pesticides in raw food. But a provision enacted in 1958, the so-called Delaney Clause, barred processed food from containing even the most minute traces of a chemical that had been shown to cause cancer in humans or in test animals. The provision was named for Rep. James J. Delaney, D-N.Y. (1945–1947, 1949–1978), who in the 1950s chaired a select investigating committee on the use of chemicals in food. *(Congress and the Nation Vol. I, p. 1176)*

When the provision was enacted, food pesticide residues were detectable in parts per million. But by 1996, scientists often could detect pesticides in parts per billion or trillion, meaning that minuscule concentrations fell under the ban even though they might not pose a danger.

Based on a study by the National Academy of Sciences, the EPA had tried applying a single standard of negligible risk—defined as a one-in-a-million chance of causing cancer—to residues in both raw and processed foods. But a July 8, 1992, decision by the U.S. Court of Appeals for the Ninth Circuit required the EPA to strictly enforce the Delaney Clause. This would have meant canceling use of many common pesticides. *(Congress and the Nation Vol. VIII, p. 522)*

The American Farm Bureau Federation warned that the cancellations would affect farmers of virtually every crop, including California grapes, Florida tomatoes, North Dakota wheat, Texas soybeans, Vermont apples and Virginia peanuts.

Environmentalists, however, objected to proposals to codify the "negligible risk standard," saying it would leave national health standards to the vagaries of politicians, because each EPA administrator could have a different definition of "negligible risk."

LEGISLATIVE ACTION

The House Agriculture Committee in 1995 approved sections of HR 1627 aimed at expediting government decision making on pesticide use. But the panel postponed further work on the measure pending action in the House Commerce Committee, which had jurisdiction over a controversial provision to allow traces of cancer-causing substances in processed foods. The Commerce Committee took no action in 1995.

On July 11, 1996, the Agriculture panel formally reentered the fray, reporting sections of HR 1627 aimed at revising EPA's ground rules for registering pesticides (H Rept 104-669, Part I). The bill sought to streamline the registration of several classifications of chemicals, including minor use, antimicrobial and public health pesticides. It allowed EPA to issue an emergency order suspending the sale of a chemical, as long as within 90 days it issued a notice of intent to cancel the chemical's registration. On an issue that had been subject to continuing negotiations, the bill proposed to give the EPA the authority to collect $14 million annually from pesticide companies until 2001 to fund the reregistration of chemicals and to require an annual audit of the handling of those fees.

Moving with rare dispatch, the House Commerce Committee reported its portion of HR 1627 on July 23 (H Rept 104-669, Part II). But the swift action came only after key Republicans and Democrats resolved contentious issues in closed-door meetings. Overall, their compromise sought to protect people from dangerous levels of cancer-causing pesticides in food,

while allowing some chemical residues in food so farmers could continue using many pesticides.

The bill required the EPA to replace the zero tolerance of the Delaney Clause with a tolerance level that would ensure that people who ate either raw or processed food had a "reasonable certainty of no harm." That was generally interpreted to mean that no more than a one-in-a-million chance existed that the pesticide residues in the food would cause cancer. Under certain circumstances, such as the threat of a significant disruption in domestic food supply, the EPA could allow higher pesticide residues in food but the lifetime risk could not be more than a two-in-a-million risk of cancer. The bill also required EPA, when setting health standards, to take into account foods children ate in large quantities (such as apples) and which pesticides were known to severely affect children.

The House suspended its rules and passed the compromise measure July 23 by a **key vote of 417–0 (R 229–0; D 187–0; I 1–0)**. The unanimous vote on the House floor was a surprise, coming in the midst of one of the most unrelentingly partisan sessions in memory. *(1996 key votes, p. 1047)*

Not wanting to lose momentum, the Senate Agriculture, Nutrition, and Forestry Committee amended the companion Senate bill (S 1166) the following day to make it identical to the House language. Just hours later, the full Senate passed HR 1627 by voice vote, clearing the measure. President Clinton signed it into law Aug. 3.

MAJOR PROVISIONS

Following are major provisions of HR 1627, as enacted into law:

Changes to the Federal Food, Drug, and Cosmetic Act

Tolerance Levels

Under the new law, pesticide residues in processed foods were no longer regulated under the Delaney Clause, which had set a zero-tolerance standard. Instead, the Environmental Protection Agency (EPA) in most cases was directed to establish a tolerance level to ensure that people who ate both raw and processed foods would have a "reasonable certainty of no harm" from pesticide residues.

When establishing such a tolerance level, the EPA administrator was required to consider the risks of aggregate exposure to the residue, including all anticipated dietary exposures and any other exposure for which reliable information was available.

The "reasonable certainty" standard was generally interpreted to mean that no more than a one-in-a-million lifetime chance existed that the residue would cause cancer. The bill's report language called on the EPA administrator to continue to follow such an interpretation or adopt a different interpretation by regulation that was "at least equally protective of public health."

A tolerance level could be changed or revoked upon the EPA administrator's own initiative or in response to a petition. The administrator was required to modify or revoke a tolerance level that was found to be unsafe.

• **Exemptions.** A pesticide could be exempt from a tolerance level standard if the administrator determined that such an exemption was "safe," meaning that aggregate exposure to the residue would result in a reasonable certainty of no harm. Such exemptions could apply to previous pesticide uses that the government regarded as "generally recognized as safe." Any exemption could be modified or revoked.

Generally, the EPA was required to apply the tolerance levels and exemptions established for residues of a parent pesticide to residues of the pesticide's breakdown products unless the established tolerance level specifically excluded breakdown products. If a pesticide residue on raw food was within permitted levels, that residue could also be on processed food, so long as it was below the raw food tolerance level.

Relaxing the Standards

• **Exceptions.** The law allowed the EPA to relax the reasonable certainty standard in particular cases. For example, the standard could be pared back if the consumption of food without a pesticide would pose a greater risk than the consumption of such food with a pesticide. (A pesticide, for instance, might be necessary to minimize dietary risk from a fungus or other crop condition.)

In addition, the standard could be relaxed if using the pesticide would avoid a significant disruption in the domestic food supply production.

In no case, however, could the EPA permit the annual risk to be more than 10 times higher than the safe annual tolerance standard or twice the safe lifetime risk. Furthermore, any tolerance level had to be safe for children.

In cases of relaxed standards, the EPA was required to review the need for the pesticide use and the risks every five years to determine whether to leave the standard in place. Without such a review, the relaxed standard would automatically expire. If the pesticide no longer met the conditions required for a relaxed standard, the EPA had to modify or revoke the tolerance within 180 days.

Infants and Children

• **Health Effects.** Whenever establishing or changing a tolerance level, the EPA was required to take into account the health effects on infants and other children. The administrator was directed to consider children's consumption patterns, as well as their special susceptibility to chemical residues and the cumulative effects that residues might have on children. Also to be considered were the effects of in utero exposure to pesticide chemicals.

The agency had to ensure that tolerance levels posed a "reasonable certainty of no harm" to infants and children. It was directed to publish a specific determination regarding the safety of a pesticide residue for consumption by infants and children.

When data regarding the health effects of residues on infants and children were incomplete, the administrator was required to apply an additional tenfold margin of safety. However, the administrator could apply a different margin if data showed that it would be safe for infants and children.

The secretaries of agriculture and health and human services, in consultation with the EPA administrator, were to conduct surveys on the diets of infants and children.

Estrogenic Effects

• **Tests and Screening.** When the EPA established, modified or revoked a pesticide tolerance level, it was required to consider whether the pesticide caused health effects that were similar to naturally occurring estrogen, which had been linked to increased breast cancer levels. It also had to consider other endocrine effects, meaning effects on humans similar to naturally occurring hormones.

The EPA, in consultation with the Health and Human Services Department, was required to develop a screening program within two years to evaluate whether certain substances caused such estrogen or endocrine effects. After an additional year following a public comment period, the EPA was required to implement such a screening program. The agency was to report to Congress within four years on its findings from the screening program and could make recommendations for additional testing and action.

The screening program was to include tests on all pesticide chemicals. The agency also could test other substances (described in report language as "environmental contaminants") that produced effects similar to pesticides, although substances that were not likely to produce estrogenic effects would be exempt.

The EPA administrator was directed to notify pesticide manufacturers and importers of the screening process and direct them to conduct certain estrogenic tests. To the extent practicable, the agency was to avoid duplicative tests and keep business information confidential. It was to develop an equitable way to share test costs.

The EPA was required to suspend the sale or distribution of a substance if the registrant failed to comply with a test order, after issuing a 30-day notice of the pending suspension. It would reinstate the sale or distribution once the registrant complied with the test order.

The law provided for a hearing process to determine whether the registrant was in compliance and also allowed court appeals. A manufacturer or registrant who was not in compliance could face up to $25,000 in fines per day. A person who intentionally violated a test order could face up to one year in prison.

Pesticide Tolerance Factors

Additional Factors. In addition to estrogenic effects, the EPA was required to consider the following factors when examining pesticide tolerances:

• The reliability of available data on the pesticide and its residue.

• The nature of any toxic effect caused by the pesticide.

• Patterns of dietary consumption.

• The cumulative effects of residues and certain other substances.

• The aggregate exposure levels of consumers to the residues and related substances.

• Information about the varying sensitivities of various consumer subgroups.

• Safety factors generally recognized as appropriate for the use of animal experimentation data.

The agency could not establish a tolerance unless a practical method existed for measuring the residue levels on or in food.

If the agency established a tolerance based on anticipated residues, it had to require evidence within five years that actual residue levels had not increased above the anticipated levels used to set the tolerance. If such evidence was not submitted, or if the levels had sharply increased, the EPA would have to modify or revoke the tolerance.

When setting a tolerance for a pesticide, the EPA could take into account the percentage of food treated with the pesticide. However, the administrator had to ensure that such a method did not understate the exposure for a population subgroup.

International Standards

• **Tolerance Levels.** When determining tolerance levels, the EPA was required to consider any maximum residue level established by the international Codex Alimentarius Commission. (The commission, sponsored by the United Nations Food and Agriculture Organization and the World Health Organization, negotiated international standards for food.) If the EPA established a standard that was different from a Codex standard, it had to publish a notice explaining the departure.

Petition Procedures

• **Requests.** Any person could file with the EPA a petition proposing a regulation to establish, modify or revoke a tolerance level for a pesticide residue or to exempt the residue from regulation. (The EPA administrator also had the authority to establish a tolerance or exemption without any outside request.)

The petition, which could be published in a proposed or final regulation, had to contain the name and composition of the pesticide residue as well as the chemical that produced the residue. It also had to include information on the application and safety of the residue, methods of detecting the residue, the amount of residue likely to remain on or in food, and ways of removing some of that residue.

The administrator was to publish a notice of the petition filing within 30 days. The administrator could then issue a proposed or final regulation that agreed with, or varied from, the petition, or the administrator could deny the petition.

Priority would be given to petitions to establish tolerances for pesticide residues that might be safer than existing residues. In such a case, the EPA had to act on the petition within one year.

Additional Data

• **Manufacturer Reporting.** The EPA could require pesticide companies to submit additional data on a pesticide, if such information was needed to support the continuation of a tolerance or exemption. The administrator could, after setting a 60-day notice and comment period, publish an order in the *Federal Register* describing the data needed, as well as the reports that would be prepared from the data.

If the requested data were not submitted, the administrator was authorized to modify or revoke the tolerance in question.

Appeals

• **Affected People.** As under existing law, any person adversely affected by a new regulation had 60 days to file an objection and request a public hearing. As soon as practicable after the hearing, the administrator was to proceed with the regulation or revise the regulation based only on substantial evidence presented at the hearing.

Any person adversely affected by a new regulation or order also could petition a federal court to set it aside. The court had exclusive jurisdiction to affirm or set aside the regulation or order, in part or in whole.

Confidentiality

• **Disclosure Rules.** As under existing law, all records submitted to the EPA in support of a tolerance or an exemption were to be considered confidential until the publication of a regulation. Some information, at the administrator's discretion, could be disclosed to authorized federal employees and contractors who were safeguarding public health. However, the intent of lawmakers, according to report language, was that the EPA issue regulations to protect confidential business information.

Lawful Applications

• **Revocation.** Even if a tolerance or exemption for a pesticide residue was revoked, the residue was allowed on foods if it was legally sanctioned at the time that it was applied and if it did not exceed the previously authorized tolerance. The EPA had the authority to order the food destroyed, but only after determining that such legally treated food posed an unreasonable dietary risk. The provision allowed for the continued use of existing food stocks that were treated with a lawful pesticide.

In addition, the administrator was authorized to establish tolerances for unavoidably persistent residues of canceled or suspended pesticides on food.

Fees

• **Assessment.** The EPA was directed to assess fees to cover various costs, including the costs of accepting petitions, writing regulations, accepting objections and certifying and filing court transcripts. The administrator could waive or refund fees, if done equitably.

State Preemption

• **Standards.** The law generally preempted state and local governments from imposing stricter tolerances than those established by the EPA. A state could not enforce its own regulations on the production, processing, shipping or other handling of a food because it contained a pesticide residue. However, a state could impose a stricter standard temporarily until the EPA revised tolerances under the new law.

In addition, states could refuse to follow the EPA's lead in relaxing standards. For example, if the EPA relaxed a tolerance because it was concerned about a disruption to domestic food supply, a state could continue to impose the "reasonable risk of no harm" standard.

In addition, a state could petition the EPA for permission to impose a stricter tolerance. Such a petition had to include scientific data about the pesticide, including the exposure of state residents to the chemical. The administrator could grant such permission if the proposed state regulation was justified by compelling local conditions and if it would not cause any food to be in violation of federal law.

• **Expedited Petition.** The law also provided for an urgent petition procedure, if a state demonstrated that consumption of a food would pose a significant public health threat. If the administrator did not grant or deny the request within 30 days, the state could establish temporary regulations curbing the residue. The administrator would then have to validate or terminate the temporary regulation.

States retained the right to require warning labels on foods with certain pesticide residues.

Consumer Right-to-Know

• **Publication of Information.** The law required the EPA, beginning by August 1998, to publish and distribute to large retail grocers a list of information about pesticide residues. That information had to be publicly displayed in grocery stores.

The information had to be conveyed in a format easily understandable to a layperson. It was to include a discussion of the risks and benefits of pesticide residues in or on food bought by consumers, a list of actions taken to relax tolerances, and recommendations on reducing exposures to pesticide residues.

Retail grocers could provide additional information.

Schedule for Review

• **Time Frame.** As expeditiously as possible, the EPA was required to review tolerances and exemptions for pesticide residues that were in use before enactment of the law. Within a year of the law's enactment, the agency was to publish a schedule of the review.

The law required that the EPA review 33 percent of the tolerances and exemptions within three years of enactment, review another 33 percent in the next three years, and complete its review of all the tolerances and exemptions within 10 years of enactment.

Priority in the review process was to be given to those tolerances or exemptions that appeared to pose the greatest public health risk.

A tolerance or exemption that did not meet the standards of the new law had to be modified or revoked.

As under existing law, the agency could issue temporary tolerances or exemptions for the use of pesticides under certain experimental conditions.

Authorization for Monitoring

• **FDA Scrutiny.** The law authorized a total of $12 million from fiscal 1997 to fiscal 1999 for increased monitoring by the Food and Drug Administration of pesticide residues in both domestic and imported food.

Penalties

• **Fines.** The law provided for civil fines against people who engaged in the interstate commerce of food that was unlawfully adulterated with a pesticide chemical residue. The fines were up to $50,000 per individual and $250,000 per corporation for each violation but could not exceed a total of $500,000 in a single legal proceeding.

People who were fined could not face criminal penalties, and the government could not seize the adulterated food as an additional punishment.

The growers of the adulterated food were exempt from the fines.

Changes to the Federal Insecticide, Fungicide, and Rodenticide Act

Procedure

The EPA was required to regularly review the registrations of pesticides. The administrator had to set up a procedure so that every registration was reviewed every 15 years.

Both the old and new laws required a pesticide to be registered for specific uses. In most cases, pesticide manufacturers, processors or distributors applied for registration.

Emergency Suspension

• **Notices.** As under existing law, the EPA had to issue a notice of cancellation before suspending use of a pesticide. But the new law gave broader power to the EPA, enabling it to issue an emergency order to immediately suspend or change the use of a pesticide. The agency would then have 90 days to issue a formal notice of cancellation, or the emergency order would expire.

'Minor Use Pesticides'

• **Definition.** The law made numerous changes to regulations of "minor use pesticides," usually defined as chemicals used for fruits, vegetables and other specialty crops that did not generate sufficient revenue to cover the costs of registration. (Generally, chemicals used on the "major" crops, such as wheat, corn, soybeans, cotton and rice, did not fall into the minor use category.) The EPA administrator, in consultation with the agriculture secretary, was given some leeway when defining minor use pesticides.

• **Review.** The law required the EPA to act as expeditiously as possible on an application to register a minor use pesticide. The agency was supposed to complete its review within 12 months, although failure to do so would not subject the agency to court action.

• **Cancellation.** The EPA could take up to 180 days to respond to a request to voluntarily cancel a pesticide use—a period twice as long as past law—if such a cancellation would adversely affect the availability of a pesticide.

• **Exclusive Use.** In certain cases, the law guaranteed pesticide manufacturers the exclusive use of data they submitted when applying to register a pesticide for up to 13 years, instead of the existing 10 years. The extended period would be granted if the pesticide had few alternative uses or if the pesticide was important to the public health or for pest management.

• **Deadline Extension.** The law also allowed manufacturers and importers, under certain circumstances, to request deadline extensions for submitting residue chemistry data to support the registration or reregistration of a pesticide. However, such extensions could neither lead to unreasonable environmental damage nor delay the EPA's decision on the registration.

• **Waivers.** The EPA could waive some data requirements if it determined that the data were not needed to assess the risk of a minor use pesticide.

• **EPA Program.** The EPA administrator was directed to establish a minor use program within the EPA Office of Pesticide Programs to coordinate the development of minor use pesticide programs and policies and consult with growers on minor use issues. The Office of Pesticide Programs was to issue a report within three years on the progress in registering minor uses.

• **Registration Assistance.** The agriculture secretary was directed to establish a minor use grant program to help private companies and individuals develop data in support of minor use pesticide registrations. Priority was to be given to applicants who would not directly profit from the sales of the pesticide. The law authorized a total of $10 million annually for the program, with the amount of each grant to be capped at one-half the cost of the project. The resulting data would be jointly owned by the Agriculture Department and the grantee.

Antimicrobial Pesticides

• **Definition.** The law generally defined antimicrobial pesticides as pesticides that disinfected, sanitized or reduced the growth of microbiological organisms. The definition excluded wood preservatives, agricultural fungicide products and aquatic herbicide products.

• **Registration and Review.** The EPA administrator was to evaluate proposals to expedite the antimicrobial registration process. The aim would be to reduce the review period to no more than: 540 days for a new antimicrobial active ingredient pesticide registration; 270 days for a new antimicrobial use; 120 days for any other new antimicrobial product; 90 days for a substantially similar or identical antimicrobial product; 90 days for an amendment to an existing registration that did not require a scientific review of data; 90 to 180 days for an amendment that did require a scientific review.

Within 270 days of enactment, the administrator was to publish in the *Federal Register* proposed rules to expedite reviews of antimicrobial products to the extent practicable. Within 240 days after the close of a comment period, the EPA was to issue final rules on the expedited reviews. If the rules failed to meet the review period goals, the administrator would have to explain why those goals could not be met and identify future steps to achieve them.

If the final rules were not in effect within 630 days of enactment, the law included specified time periods for reviews until those final rules took effect. The time periods ranged from two years for a new active pesticide ingredient to 90 days for a substantially similar or identical product.

Until the new goals were met, the agency had to submit a report every March 1 to the House Agriculture Committee and the Senate Agriculture, Nutrition, and Forestry Committee on measures taken to reduce the backlog of pending registration applications.

The agency generally had to review wood preservative registration applications within the same time periods as those established for antimicrobial pesticides, if the preservative contained an antimicrobial pesticide.

The EPA was directed to work toward standardizing federal and state data requirements for antimicrobial pesticide applications.

The law prohibited false or misleading labels. The registrant of an antimicrobial pesticide was allowed to change the label to include information about product efficacy, container composition and other details.

Public Health Pesticides

• **Definition.** The law generally defined public health pesticides as any minor use pesticide used to prevent or control viruses, bacteria and other microorganisms that could threaten the public health. The pesticides could also be used against insects that spread diseases.

• **Risks and Benefits.** The administrator had to consider the risks and benefits of public health pesticides separately from the risks and benefits of other pesticides and had to weigh the risks of using such a pesticide against the public health risk of the organism that it would control.

• **Waivers.** The administrator could waive registration and reregistration fees for a public health pesticide if the sales of the pesticide would not cover the cost of the fees.

The administrator was to identify pests of "significant public health importance" and develop and implement programs to combat and control such pests.

Before publishing a regulation for a public health pesticide, the EPA administrator was required to solicit the views of the health and human services secretary.

• **Authorization.** The law authorized up to $12 million in appropriations to carry out public health pesticide programs.

Fees

• **Registration.** With the EPA facing long delays in processing and reregistering pesticide uses, the law authorized the agency to collect $14 million annually in fees from pesticide registrants through the end of fiscal 2001 to help pay for expediting the process. To help address backlogged case studies and related reviews, the law also authorized the agency to collect a total of $6 million in additional fees—$2 million annually in fiscal years 1998, 1999 and 2000.

• **Spending Rules.** Before spending any money derived from the fees, the EPA had to adopt cost accounting rules and procedures approved by the General Accounting Office and the EPA inspector general.

The spending rules were meant to ensure that the funds were spent only on the costs of reregistration and the expedited processing of applications and that they did not exceed appropriated levels. The EPA was barred from spending the funds in other ways.

The EPA could contract with outside vendors if necessary to conduct reviews of reregistration studies.

The law directed the EPA to hold down personnel and facility costs.

• **Audits.** The law required an annual audit of the Federal Insecticide and Rodenticide Fund. The EPA inspector general was required to conduct, or contract out, an audit of the maintenance fees and EPA's handling of reregistration and expedited processing of applications. The audit was to be funded by the maintenance fees. Audit results were to be reported to Congress.

Each year, the EPA was required to publish in the *Federal Register* a report on performance measures and goals, including action on pesticide registrations and the projected year when reregistrations would be completed.

Miscellaneous

• **Reduced Risk Pesticides.** The law authorized the EPA to set up an expedited review process for reduced risk pesticides. Such a review process was authorized, generally, if use of the pesticide could reduce pesticide risks to public health or lessen damage to the environment.

The law did not establish specific time periods for the expedited reviews, other than to require the EPA to notify a registration applicant within 30 days if the application was incomplete.

• **Science Review Board.** The law created a Science Review Board, consisting of 60 scientists, to assist the EPA's independent Scientific Advisory Panel in reviewing pesticides.

• **Training.** The law authorized states to require minimum training requirements for various workers who used pesticides such as janitors, groundskeepers and pest control specialists. The training had to include instructions on the safe and effective handling of pesticides.

People who applied ready-to-use consumer pesticides were excluded from such training requirements.

• **Data Collection.** The agriculture secretary was directed to collect data of statewide or regional importance on the use of pesticides and to consult with the health and human services secretary and EPA administrator to ensure that the data were relevant.

• **Integrated Pest Management.** The agriculture secretary, in cooperation with the EPA, was to conduct research, demonstration and education programs to support integrated pest management efforts, which used biological and other approaches to control pests while minimizing environmental risks. Federal agencies were directed to use integrated pest management techniques in carrying out pest management activities.   ❏

Fishery Conservation, Management

Congress in 1996 cleared a major rewrite of the 1976 Magnuson Fishery Conservation and Management Act. The reauthorization measure (S 39—PL 104-297) called for tougher conservation measures to protect the nation's fisheries, many of which were in critical condition because of overfishing.

Passage of S 39 provided the Republican leadership with a big victory on a landmark environmental bill just as the 104th

Congress was ending. The bill had attracted broad support from both environmental groups and allies of the fishing industry as well as from a wide spectrum of members of Congress.

The backing reflected a newfound acknowledgment that the economic interests of fishing communities were inextricably linked to safeguards against overfishing. In the past, fishing communities often had perceived efforts to curb harvesting in the name of conservation as a direct threat to their livelihood.

BACKGROUND

The Magnuson Act (PL 94-265) had been the nation's principal offshore fisheries conservation policy since it was enacted in 1976. The law had two main goals: defending U.S. coastal fisheries against foreign competition and protecting them against overfishing.

The act established a 200-mile zone off the U.S. coastline that sharply curtailed foreign fishing. It also provided loan guarantees and other financial incentives to bolster the U.S. fishing fleet. Those efforts had succeeded in limiting foreign competition and building up the nation's fleet, particularly the factory trawlers capable of catching and processing large quantities of fish.

But while the law had been highly successful in limiting foreign competition, it had not prevented domestic industries from fishing some species to near extinction.

Under the act, eight regional councils had been set up to manage the nation's fisheries. The councils set the rules—from harvest quotas and season length to restrictions on fishing gear—under which the fishing industry operated. But the councils were dominated by the domestic fishing industry and were often loath to limit fishing by U.S. vessels, even when faced with evidence that fish stocks were being reduced below sustainable levels. According to National Marine Fisheries Service estimates, 40 percent of the nation's fish species were overfished.

The authorization for the Magnuson Act had expired in 1993, but reauthorization legislation never got beyond subcommittee approval in the 103rd Congress. The law had been sustained through the appropriations process. *(1994 action, p. 426)*

LEGISLATIVE ACTION

The House passed its version of the legislation (HR 39) on Oct. 18, 1995, by an overwhelming vote of 388–37. The bill had been reported by the House Resources Committee on June 30 (H Rept 104-171).

The House measure was designed to bolster efforts to limit the harvesting of fish that fishermen caught but did not intend to use. Other proposed steps to limit harvests included requiring enforceable management plans in overfished areas. The bill also sought to reduce conflicts of interest on regional councils.

The Senate Commerce, Science, and Transportation Committee reported a companion bill (S 39—S Rept 104-276) on May 23, 1996. But the full Senate did not act on the bill until September because of a high-stakes regional dispute that pitted Washington state fishing operations against those of Alaska.

At issue was a requirement that crabbers in Washington state and elsewhere set aside 7.5 percent of their catch for economically distressed Alaskan fishing communities. Proponents said the program would ensure that the communities were treated fairly and that their rights were protected under the Magnuson Act's mandate to provide opportunities to all U.S. fishermen. But Washington crabbers, who harvested most of the crab catch off Alaska waters in the Bering Sea, argued that the proposal was comparable to a social welfare program and that they were being pushed out despite having risked capital to build up their fleets.

Another point of controversy was a program to limit harvesting by awarding vessels individual fishing quotas, instead of allowing unlimited access to fisheries. Fish processing plants operating in Alaska wanted a moratorium on the program, fearing that such quotas would give a competitive advantage to the Washington-based industrial trawlers that processed fish onboard.

Washington and Alaska senators spent months working out a compromise. They finally agreed that Washington crabbers would have to provide the amount required for the Alaska communities, but it would be phased in over three years, instead of taking effect in the first year of the program. They also agreed that the moratorium on issuing new quotas for fish that could be caught in designated areas would be shortened from five to four years.

After settling other issues, including a dispute over limiting lobster harvests in New England, the Senate passed the compromise bill on Sept. 19 by a vote of 100–0.

The Senate bill departed from the House-passed bill in several key respects, including the fishing quotas and community development provisions that were the centerpiece of the Washington-Alaska deal. Key backers of the House bill were less supportive of using quotas to try to control overfishing, and the House bill would have scaled back the ability of the regional councils to use such quota programs.

But, with the 104th Congress nearing adjournment, no time was left for a House-Senate conference. Moreover, the Washington senators—Republican Slade Gorton and Democrat Patty Murray—made it clear that, if the House significantly amended the bill and returned it to the Senate, they would filibuster and kill it.

House leaders chose to go along with the Senate bill. The House passed S 39 Sept. 27 by a vote of 384–30, clearing it for the president, who signed it into law Oct. 11.

MAJOR PROVISIONS

As signed into law, major provisions of S 39:

• **Management Plans.** Required the eight regional fishery management councils to put in place plans that restored fish populations to "sustainable" levels and minimized the incidental kill of unwanted fish and other marine life. Fish caught but discarded accounted for 20 percent of the nation's fish harvest, and scientists said such "bycatch" depleted fish populations.

Also required were management plans to promote safety at sea, which critics said was sometimes sacrificed in the rush to scoop up diminishing fish supplies.

• **Fishing Quotas.** Imposed a moratorium on new fishing quota programs before Oct. 1, 2000, and required the National

Academy of Science to submit a report on the programs by Oct. 1, 1998. Quotas—essentially assigning to some fishing operations a permanent share of the market—had been one of the approaches the regional councils had used to guard against overharvesting. But, depending on how the quota program was structured, it could benefit one group of fishermen over another. Fishermen, as well as environmentalists, were divided over how beneficial the controversial approach was. S 39 allowed for the cooling-off period to assess the approach.

• **Community Quotas.** Phased in over three years a program that would require crabbers in Washington state and elsewhere to set aside a percentage of their catch for economically distressed Alaska fishing communities. The program had been approved in 1995 by the North Pacific Council, the regional council that oversaw Alaskan waters. S 39 required that 3.5 percent be set aside in 1998, 5 percent in 1999 and 7.5 percent in 2000.

• **Conflict of Interest.** Barred regional council members from voting on issues that would have a "significant and predictable" positive financial outcome for them. A council member could be removed for failing to adhere to the standard or if he or she knowingly or willingly failed to disclose or falsely disclosed a financial interest.

• **Authorization.** Authorized $612 million through fiscal 1999 to implement programs under the Magnuson Act.   ❑

Superfund Overhaul

After more than a year of trying to forge a compromise, Republican leaders in 1996 abandoned efforts to overhaul the superfund hazardous waste cleanup program. Like their Democratic predecessors in the 103rd Congress, they were unable to resolve key disputes that for years had thwarted attempts to correct glaring problems in the superfund law.

The rewrite effort suffered from a host of maladies that included partisan sniping, division among business groups, and strong ideological splits on how to overhaul the program. Topping the list was a seemingly intractable dispute over who should pay to clean up the nation's worst toxic waste sites.

Republicans and some Democrats wanted to at least partially repeal "retroactive liability" provisions in the superfund law that could hold a company responsible for cleaning up waste dumped legally before superfund was enacted in 1980. They argued that it was unfair to tag businesses for the costs of cleaning up waste that had been dumped legally. And they said that easing the liability standards would lead to the cleanup of more sites because it would help clear up the tangle of litigation that had drastically slowed cleanups and contributed to the program's problems.

But relieving companies of liability would have forced the government to pick up more of the tab. Congressional Budget Office (CBO) estimates for some of the proposals ran as high as nearly $3 billion a year.

Many Democrats argued that, if polluters were let off the hook, their responsibilities would be shifted to the taxpayers. A central principle of the superfund program was that the polluter should foot the bill.

A federal court weighed in May 20, 1996, ruling in *U.S. v. Olin Corp.*, a case involving an Alabama chemical plant, that the superfund law could not be applied to waste dumped before the law's enactment in 1980.

Republicans hoped the court action would increase pressure for a bipartisan agreement. But despite months of talks, neither side could come up with a formula to bridge their differences. With an already crowded fall agenda and plans to adjourn in early October 1996, Senate and House Republicans signaled in mid-July that time had run out and the superfund effort was dead for the year.

Failure to get a bill through Congress left the program in partial limbo. One key issue left unresolved was the future of the taxes that helped pay for the program. The taxes had expired at the end of 1995. However, the program's trust fund had a surplus, and CBO estimated that enough money was in the fund to cover the program's costs through fiscal 2000.

BACKGROUND

The superfund program charged the Environmental Protection Agency (EPA) with identifying hazardous waste sites in need of cleanup, and it allowed the government to tap a single deep-pocketed polluter to pay the entire costs of the cleanup, even if many individuals or businesses were responsible for the pollution.

Instead of living up to its promise, the program had long been bogged down by a flood of litigation, as polluters who were targeted sued others to help defray the cleanup costs. Largely as a result, relatively few sites had been cleaned up.

Congress came close to rewriting the law in 1994. Although the measure had bipartisan support and the backing of the Clinton administration, it died in the final weeks of the 103rd Congress. The 1994 bill had focused on replacing protracted litigation with a process for arbitration, instead of retroactive liability, and on spreading the cost of cleanup among the parties responsible for polluting a site, instead of holding a single party liable. *(Superfund background, 1994 action, p. 410)*

LEGISLATIVE ACTION

The high-water mark for efforts to rewrite the superfund law in the 104th Congress came late in 1995, when Republicans pushed a bill (HR 2500) through a House Commerce subcommittee over strong Democratic opposition.

The bill contained provisions aimed at exempting municipalities and small businesses from paying cleanup costs. For other businesses, it called for a government rebate, paid out of the program's trust fund, for up to 50 percent of cleanup costs for waste dumped before 1987. Michael G. Oxley, R-Ohio, who chaired the Commerce Subcommittee on Commerce, Trade, and Hazardous Materials, said the relief was intended to encourage private parties to clean up sites and avoid litigation.

Oxley, who led the superfund overhaul effort in the House, had initially presented a far more sweeping plan that would have fully repealed pre-1980 liability and shielded insurance companies from liability for waste dumped before 1987. But confronted with the high cost—Oxley had put it at $300 million

to $800 million a year, while CBO estimates for the pre-1987 repeal were as high as $1.6 billion a year—the Ohio lawmaker modified the bill before the markup. Democrats nevertheless lambasted the measure as a polluters' bailout that would shift the cost of cleaning up superfund sites to taxpayers. The Republican leadership, meanwhile, still wanted full repeal.

Senate sponsor Robert C. Smith, R-N.H., in 1995 similarly modified his initial proposal for full repeal of retroactive liability, calling instead for a tax credit equal to 50 percent of the cost for companies that had to pay for waste dumped before 1980. The bill (S 1285) did not include Oxley's proposals for a rebate on cleanup costs or an exemption for small businesses that dumped waste at municipal landfills.

Smith's plan also ran into opposition from his chamber's leadership. Majority Leader Bob Dole, R-Kan., wanted at least partial repeal of retroactive liability and expressed concern over the bill's tax credit funding mechanism.

No committee or floor action took place in either chamber on the superfund overhaul in 1996. But that fact belied considerable behind-the-scenes maneuvering and fitful negotiations between the White House and Congress during the year.

In the House, Commerce Committee Chairman Thomas J. Bliley Jr., R-Va., negotiated with John D. Dingell of Michigan, the panel's ranking Democrat, in hopes of securing Democratic backing and avoiding potential floor fights. Speaker Newt Gingrich, R-Ga., had warned panel Republicans that the bill had to gain wide support before it could be considered on the floor. A broader version of the bill—exempting an estimated 90 percent of the parties facing cleanup costs from liability—was proposed, but bipartisan agreement was not reached.

On the Senate side, the Environment and Public Works Committee on April 23, 1996, opened long-delayed hearings on a much-revised version of S 1285. Led by committee Chairman John H. Chafee, R-R.I., negotiators on both sides of the aisle had been meeting behind closed doors for weeks trying to broker a compromise that could win the support of some Senate Democrats and the White House.

Under Chafee's version, parties that deposited small quantities of waste before superfund was enacted would be totally relieved from paying. Bigger polluters, such as waste haulers, would have to enter into a government allocation system to determine their share of cleanup costs. Once these were determined, the program's trust fund, paid for by taxes on potential polluting companies, would be used to pay for cleanup, relieving businesses of directly footing the tab. The intent of the allocation system was to reduce the litigation that had tied up the program.

Chafee's plan faced several obstacles, not the least of which was opposition from the administration. EPA Administrator Carol M. Browner said S 1285 would delay cleanups, shift costs to federal and state governments, and let polluters off the financial hook. She said preliminary administration estimates were that the bill would cost from $2.6 billion to $2.8 billion a year. The superfund appropriation was about $1.5 billion annually.

Democrats on the Senate panel and the administration countered with a proposal to exempt a number of small businesses and limit the liability of about 500 municipalities that owned and operated landfills. The plan was expected to boost the program's annual cost to about $2 billion. House Democrats floated a similar proposal.

But no plan won enough support to move forward, and Republicans pronounced the rewrite dead for the year in July.

In the meantime, Browner had announced June 4 several administrative changes, including the appointment of an ombudsman in all 10 EPA regions to oversee community relations and to increase the number of small businesses and municipalities no longer responsible for cleanup costs. ❑

Grazing Rights

A bill aimed at overturning Clinton administration rules for grazing livestock on public lands passed the Senate and was approved, with slight modification, by a House committee in 1996. But the legislation (S 1459) ran up against a veto threat and opposition in the House from a coalition of deficit hawks and environmentalists, and it died at the end of the 104th Congress.

S 1459 sought to roll back rules put on the books in August 1995 by Interior Secretary Bruce Babbitt. The rules set minimum national standards for rangeland management and integrated environmentalists' viewpoints into the process. western ranchers contended that they were top-notch stewards of the land and that the new regulations would put them out of business.

The ranchers backed S 1459, which would have given them more influence in federal decision making about public rangeland and imposed a modest increase of about 50 cents in grazing fees. They were willing to accept the increase in the hope that it would forestall bigger fees from the Interior Department.

When S 1459 stalled in the House, conservative westerners in that chamber tried to fold the measure into an omnibus parks bill (HR 1296). They later dropped that strategy in the face of a veto threat and possible Senate filibuster.

BACKGROUND

Babbitt had been locked in a dispute with western lawmakers over public rangelands since he became interior secretary in 1993. Much of the rancor had focused on his 1993 attempt to raise grazing fees.

The grazing fees were set and adjusted according to a complex formula. In 1996, the fee was $1.35 per animal unit month (AUM), the amount of forage a cow and a calf typically consumed in a month.

The fees to graze livestock on private land were much higher, often topping $10 per AUM, but ranchers argued that the public lands tended to be of lower quality for grazing and that they lacked improvements, generally provided on private lands. Environmentalists and some deficit hawks, however, argued that low federal grazing fees not only amounted to big federal subsidies to ranchers but also encouraged ranchers to increase the sizes of their herds on public lands, resulting in overgrazing and environmental damage.

In 1993, Babbitt had tried to use administrative action to raise grazing fees to $4.28 per AUM over three years, but he had

been forced to back down by a rebellion from western senators, led by Pete V. Domenici, R-N.M. *(1993–1994 action, p. 413)*

Hoping to avoid a repeat of the 1993 controversy, Babbitt omitted the fee issue from the new Interior Department regulations. But the rules, first announced in February 1995 and put in place on Aug. 21, 1995, still contained much that angered western ranching interests. Offending provisions included a requirement that all rangeland areas meet minimal federal standards, the creation of regional resource advisory councils on which interested environmentalists would be guaranteed a place, limitation of the right of ranchers to appeal Bureau of Land Management decisions reducing the number of animals they could graze, and provisions under which the federal government could claim title to all land improvements and water developments made by ranchers on public lands.

LEGISLATIVE ACTION

Hoping to preempt Babbitt, the Senate Energy and Natural Resources Committee on July 28, 1995, reported a bill (S 852—S Rept 104-123) that proposed to increase grazing fees slightly and create locally appointed boards of ranchers to monitor rangeland activities.

Unable to assemble enough votes to break a near-certain filibuster on the Senate floor, the committee reported a revised bill (S 1459—S Rept 104-181) on Dec. 7. Responding to criticism that S 852 would have established livestock grazing as a dominant use of public lands to the detriment of other activities, the bill left intact existing use and access to public lands for hunting, fishing and other pursuits. It also proposed expanding the advisory councils to include nongrazing interests. Grazing fees were to be increased by 30 percent.

In the months that followed, Domenici and others negotiated with Republicans and some Democrats to win support for S 1459. They came up with a substitute amendment.

Under Babbitt's regulations, resource councils—made up of commodity users, conservation interests and other stakeholders, and appointed by the interior secretary—offered recommendations on issues of public lands management. The aim was to empower local officials to broker competing demands on the land. Domenici proposed to retain the councils but narrow their influence and to create grazing advisory councils made up of ranchers, landowners affected by bureau decisions, and elected local officers.

According to the new rules, the "interested public" could weigh in on specific grazing decisions by writing to an authorized official. Ranchers argued that the provision would permit citizens in such far-flung locations as New York to have a say. Domenici proposed to drop the "interested public" category and require the secretary to provide for public participation and comment on land use plans and standards. Opponents contended that the provisions were intended to shut out the public by narrowing and abbreviating opportunities for public comment.

Under Babbitt's rules, approved permit holders could hold land for conservation for 10 years without paying fees and without losing rights to the land in the future. Under Domenici's plan, the Interior Department would be required to establish guidelines for rangeland health. But provisions on holding land for conservation for 10 years would be dropped.

Babbitt's rules gave the federal government title to new, permanent range improvements. The Domenici proposal provided for government and private interests to share the title, according to their contribution.

Under Babbitt's rules, new water rights remained with the federal government; existing permit holders were not affected. Domenici's bill would only allow federal water rights to be acquired under state laws.

The Senate adopted Domenici's substitute amendment by voice vote, before passing S 1459 on March 21, 1996, by a vote of 51–46. But the measure appeared to have little chance of being enacted.

The day before the Senate voted, the administration threatened a veto, saying the bill would undermine environmental protection, limit public involvement in decision making, emphasize ranching over recreation and other uses of the land, and impose red tape and administrative burdens on land managers.

Opposition to the bill during the March 21 floor debate had come from two main camps—those who wanted a big increase in grazing fees and others, mostly western Democrats, who sought a compromise between Domenici and Babbitt. An amendment by Dale Bumpers, D-Ark., calling for increased grazing fees was tabled (killed) by a vote of 52–47. A substitute amendment by Jeff Bingaman, D-N.M., which backers said would maintain public input while providing land managers the authority they needed to make decisions, was tabled by a vote of 57–40.

The House Resources Committee reported an amended version of S 1459 on July 12 (H Rept 104-674, Part I), but it never reached the House floor. Although many Democrats agreed that the bill was a big improvement over the version of the bill (HR 1713) approved by a House Resources subcommittee in September 1995, they said they still could not support it. HR 1713, written along the lines of the original Senate bill (S 852), had been rolled into the 1995 deficit reduction bill (HR 2491), but the provisions had been dropped before the bill cleared. *(Deficit reduction bill, p. 94)*

With the grazing bill languishing in the House, James V. Hansen, R-Utah, and other House Republicans tried for months to fold the text into the omnibus parks package (HR 1296). But the effort was abandoned in September, when it became obvious that the Clinton administration was unlikely to accept any new grazing bill and that pushing forward would carry a political price.

The parks bill, which contained more than 50 separate measures, had too many election-year implications for members to let it go down over the grazing issue. Hansen, who chaired the western-dominated House Resources Subcommittee on National Parks, Forests, and Lands, said it did not make political sense for ranchers who favored the parks bill to "burn up their chits" in drumming up support for a bill that would face a sure veto. For similar reasons, he said he had ruled out a stand-alone vote on a grazing bill on the House floor. *(Omnibus parks bill, p. 461)*

In early August, Rep. Sherwood Boehlert, R-N.Y., had announced a compromise intended to allow S 1459 to be brought up independently. The Boehlert compromise would not have changed the proposed grazing fee increase but would have expanded public participation in the appeals process and made other changes. It was coolly received, however, both by environmentalists, who said it would roll back protection for the land, and key deficit hawks, who argued that it would sustain a subsidized industry. ❑

Clean Water

The House in 1995 passed a sweeping overhaul of the federal clean water act. But the bill (HR 961) faced vigorous opposition and advanced no further.

Its passage had been hailed as a harbinger by most congressional Republicans and some conservative Democrats who advocated easing environmental regulation. They hoped the rapid House action to overhaul the nation's major water pollution law would spur a flurry of efforts to change environmental statutes they regarded as placing unwarranted economic hardship on businesses and individuals.

Instead, the clean water bill stalled in the face of opposition from a resurgent environmental community—which portrayed the bill as an effort to roll back public health and safety protections—and its most crucial Republican ally, Senate Environment and Public Works Committee Chairman John H. Chafee, R-R.I. It also drew a veto threat from President Clinton.

HR 961 would have reauthorized the Federal Water Pollution Control Act of 1972 (PL 92-500) at about $20.3 billion over five years. *(Background, p. 437)*

As passed by the House, the bill contained provisions to ease, overhaul or revoke a number of existing pollution-control requirements, provided that such actions were not deemed damaging to the environment, and to sharply restrict the ability of federal agencies to declare wetlands off-limits to development.

The bill included proposals to:

• Allow federal, state and local officials to waive or ease a number of regulatory requirements for "point sources"—individual industrial or municipal facilities that discharged wastes into waterways—provided that the actions did not harm the environment.

• Allow states to use voluntary or incentive-based approaches, instead of enforceable regulatory programs and standards, to reduce "non-point source" pollution. Non-point source pollution—runoff of polluted water from diffuse sources, such as farmland and city streets—was widely regarded as the biggest problem yet to be addressed under the clean water act.

States were to develop programs that provided for "reasonable further progress" toward attaining federal water quality standards within 15 years. Existing law required states to implement non-point source programs based on the use of "best management practices" to control polluted runoff at the earliest practicable date.

• Repeal a requirement that industrial facilities and municipalities obtain federal permits to discharge polluted storm water into waterways. The bill proposed to designate storm water as a non-point source, instead of a point source, pollutant.

• Require risk assessment and cost-benefit analyses for many water pollution regulations.

• Require the classification of wetlands based on their ecological importance, relax regulatory requirements for development on less essential wetlands, and require federal agencies to compensate any landowner whose property values declined by 20 percent or more because of federal wetlands regulation.

Advocates said the bill would achieve the goals of the clean water act at a lower cost while reversing what they saw as excessive federal regulation that caused undue hardship for industry, state and local governments, and individuals. They insisted that no action would be taken under the bill unless it provided net environmental benefits.

Opponents argued that the measure was full of loopholes and waivers that would increase pollution and return the nation to the days when rivers and lakes were clogged with industrial wastes and sewage. Their description of the bill as "the dirty water act" was trumpeted by environmental activists and by Clinton, who accused the Republican majority of waging a "war on the environment."

On the Senate side, Chafee, a moderate on environmental issues, agreed that some regulations under the act were excessive and needed changing but said he opposed the kind of sweeping measure passed by the House. He did not make an overhaul of the law a priority, and the bill never moved out of his committee.

House supporters of the bill in the meantime tried to force the issue by way of the fiscal 1996 appropriations bill for the Departments of Veterans Affairs (VA) and Housing and Urban Development (HUD) and for independent agencies (HR 2099). The House version of the VA-HUD bill contained language barring the Environmental Protection Agency (EPA) from spending money to implement most major provisions of the clean water act pending its reauthorization. But the House kept that language in the bill only after a bitter floor fight and by the barest of margins, and opponents later won a vote instructing House conferees to accept the Senate position stripping it from the bill. The language was dropped in conference. *(VA-HUD bill, p. 459)*

BACKGROUND

With the Republican takeover in the 104th Congress, the debate over the Federal Water Pollution Control Act was turned on its head. The emphasis in previous Democratic-controlled Congresses had been on stiffening the law's regulatory requirements. By contrast, the goal of HR 961 was to provide regulatory "relief" to private and public sector entities that said they were overburdened by the law's mandates.

Even in the Democrat-controlled 103rd Congress, however, signs were evident that the times were changing. The Senate Environment and Public Works Committee reported a bill in 1994 that would have eased the law's requirements somewhat. And, on the House side, a bill easing some regulations appeared to have bipartisan majority support on the House Public Works

and Transportation Committee, although no formal action was taken on it. *(1993–1994 action, p. 409)*

HOUSE ACTION

HR 961 was reported (H Rept 104-112) by the House Transportation and Infrastructure Committee May 3, 1995, with the support of some conservative and moderate Democrats.

The bipartisan support in committee undercut efforts by environmental stalwarts to characterize the bill as a GOP effort to gut the clean water act at the behest of their big business allies. So did the strong support for most bill provisions voiced by representatives of state and local government officials. While some environmental laws mainly affected private industry, the clean water act imposed billions of dollars in costs on jurisdictions that operated water and sewage treatment works. During debate on a separate bill to curb unfunded federal mandates (S 1—PL 104-4), officials had listed the clean water law as by far the most costly federal statute for states and localities. *(Unfunded mandates, p. 837)*

Much of the committee markup had focused on the legislation's extensive wetlands sections. Its provisions were intended to replace the brief, vaguely worded language in the existing law about dredging and filling of waterways. Federal agencies had interpreted that language to allow them to limit land-use activities in wetlands through a restrictive permit process. Critics said regulators had been overzealous, declaring areas of marginal or no ecological value off-limits and causing economic hardship for individual and corporate landowners. HR 961 included new, more stringent criteria for defining an area as a wetland.

The House easily passed HR 961 on May 16 by a **key vote of 240–185 (R 195–34; D 45–150; I 0–1)**, after soundly defeating amendments aimed at highlighting provisions Democrats claimed would "turn back the clock" to the days of widespread water pollution. *(1995 key votes, p. 1025)*

Debate on the bill was contentious, with each side attempting to make a villain of the other. Supporters of the bill portrayed the opposition as Washington insiders who ignored the demands of the public for regulatory reform. Opponents charged that the bill was an extreme measure that would give polluters free rein as they had had before the enactment of the clean water act.

Democratic opponents chose not to offer a comprehensive substitute, a task that fell instead to centrist Republicans Sherwood Boehlert of New York and H. James Saxton of New Jersey. Their substitute would have stricken many of the bill's waivers and other provisions that eased regulations for industrial and municipal facilities that discharged point-source waste, eliminated requirements that private and public sector facilities obtain federal permits to discharge storm water into combined drainage systems, relaxed federal wetlands regulations, required compensation for landowners whose property values declined 20 percent or more because of wetlands regulations, and eliminated the Coastal Zone Management Act's non-point source pollution program. The amendment was rejected May 10 on a 184–242 vote.

The House adopted, 209–192, on May 12 a Steve Largent, R-Okla., amendment to eliminate a new $500 million state revolving loan program for non-point source pollution added by Boehlert in committee and to reduce funding for the existing state water pollution control revolving funds.

The House rejected, 185–242, on May 16 another Boehlert proposal to revise the bill's wetlands provisions. His amendment would have substituted language based on a proposal by the National Governors' Association. A Wayne T. Gilchrest, R-Md., amendment to eliminate the bill's wetlands classification process and instead have the Army Corps of Engineers develop regulations based on the best available science was then rejected, 180–247.

On another key issue, the House on May 10 adopted, 224–199, a Boehlert amendment to strike a provision from the bill that would have eliminated the mandatory federal Coastal Zone Management program for controlling non-point source pollution. The program had been established in the 1990 reauthorization (PL 101-508) of the 1972 Coastal Zone Management Act (PL 92-583). A modifying amendment, offered by Tom Petri, R-Wis., and adopted by voice vote May 16, gave states a choice between that program and a voluntary non-point source program approved by the EPA. *(1990 bill, Congress and the Nation Vol. VIII, p. 63)*

Among the Democratic proposals rejected by the House were a series of amendments offered by Norman Y. Mineta of California, ranking Democrat on the Transportation Committee. A Mineta proposal to strike provisions relaxing regulation of point-source polluters was rejected May 10, 166–260. His amendment to continue existing permit requirements for storm water discharge by industrial operations, while retaining the bill's provisions relaxing storm water regulations on municipalities, was defeated May 11, 159–258. Another Mineta amendment requiring the EPA to conduct risk-assessment and cost-benefit analyses of certain waivers of regulatory requirements allowed by the bill was rejected May 11, 152–271. A proposal to delay certain risk-assessment and cost-benefit analysis requirements and revise criteria under which the analysis would be carried out was rejected May 11, 157–262. ❏

Endangered Species

An effort to rewrite the 1973 Endangered Species Act never got beyond House committee approval in the 104th Congress.

The law (PL 93-205) had become a lightning rod for conservatives eager to relax federal environmental regulations. But proposals to revise it faced the same split—between conservatives and westerners determined to scale back federal land-use policy and GOP environmentalists and many Democrats who favored a more cautious approach—that hampered other environmental legislation.

House Speaker Newt Gingrich, R-Ga., who was preoccupied with the budget and other issues in 1995, had pledged to move a strong endangered species reauthorization bill in 1996. But no floor action took place on the House bill (HR 2275) as Republicans sought to improve their image among environmentalists before the 1996 election.

While awaiting action on a reauthorization bill, species law

critics took some preliminary steps. A moratorium on new federal listings of species as endangered or threatened was enacted in April 1995, although Congress in 1996 allowed President Clinton to lift it.

BACKGROUND

The Endangered Species Act had long been one of the nation's most popular environmental laws, widely viewed as at least partially responsible for the survival of such nationally symbolic but dwindling species as the bald eagle and the grizzly bear.

But in recent years, the law had come under fire from property-rights activists and their allies in Congress, mainly Republicans and conservative Democrats. These critics argued that federal regulators often implemented the law in an extreme fashion, barring individuals and businesses from otherwise lawful economic uses of their private property to protect a variety of lesser-known birds, rodents and insects.

The 1973 law made it illegal to kill, harm, capture, harass or otherwise "take" any animal or plant that was listed by the Interior Department's Fish and Wildlife Service as endangered or threatened. It also established a comprehensive process for designating an endangered or threatened species and required a plan for its recovery.

Demands for major revisions by critics of the act took on added urgency June 29, 1995, when the Supreme Court ruled against them on a key provision of the law. The case of *Babbitt v. Sweet Home Chapter of Communities for a Greater Oregon* involved the language barring any act that "harmed" an endangered species. *(Court ruling, p. 784)*

Since 1975, the Fish and Wildlife Service had defined "harm" to include any land modification that destroyed the actual or potential habitat of an endangered species. The plaintiffs, a coalition of Oregon foresters, argued that the interpretation was too broad and that the term "harm" should be limited to actions that directly hurt or killed a member of an endangered species. The Supreme Court, by a 6–3 vote, sided with the Interior Department.

Supporters of the act voiced concern that the debate was being driven by conservative activists and business interests that wanted to hamstring or even eliminate the law. But some of its strongest supporters conceded that the statute needed to be re-examined. "The time is ripe," Interior Secretary Bruce Babbitt told lawmakers March 7, 1995.

Authorization for the endangered species law had expired in 1992, and programs under the act had been kept alive since then through the annual appropriations process.

Hearings had been held in 1994, but there had been no action to reauthorize the law. Critics, however, had used other legislation to attack it. *(1993–1994 action, p. 416)*

LEGISLATIVE ACTION

The House Resources Committee reported HR 2275 on Sept. 9, 1996 (H Rept 104-778, Part I).

The bill proposed to greatly restrict the government's ability to bar development within animal and plant habitats. It would have narrowed the definition of "harm" to those direct actions that killed or injured a member of an endangered or threatened species. To protect broad areas of habitat on private land, federal officials would have had to enter into cooperative management agreements with landowners, provide compensation to landowners when a regulatory action caused a property to lose 20 percent or more of its value, or provide financial incentives, such as grants or tax breaks, to encourage individuals' participation in species protection activities. The bill would have required peer review of the scientific information used to determine whether to protect a species and consultation with local officials before adding a species to the endangered list. It also proposed to set aside certain public lands to encourage biodiversity.

Two endangered species bills (S 768, S 1364) were introduced in the Senate in 1995, but neither measure was acted upon.

RELATED ACTION

Critics found other ways to attack the endangered species law. A six-month moratorium on new federal listings of species as endangered or threatened was enacted in April 1995 as part of a fiscal 1995 defense supplemental spending bill (HR 889—PL 104-6). During Senate action, Texas Republican Kay Bailey Hutchison had won voice vote approval for an amendment imposing the moratorium. A motion to table Hutchison's amendment, offered by Max Baucus, D-Mont., had been defeated, 38–60, on March 16. The provision was kept in the conference version. Congress attempted to extend the moratorium for one year or until enactment of an overhaul bill, whichever came first, as part of the fiscal 1996 appropriations bill for the Interior Department (HR 1977). The moratorium extension had been endorsed by both chambers. But Clinton vetoed the bill.

The fiscal 1996 omnibus appropriations bill (HR 3019—PL 104-134)—legislation containing five unfinished fiscal 1996 spending bills, including the Interior Department bill—kept the moratorium largely intact, except for limited activities such as emergency listings. But in a major concession to the White House, the omnibus bill gave the president the authority under certain conditions to lift the moratorium—which Clinton did April 26, 1996, the day he signed HR 3019 into law.

In other action, the House on March 3, 1995, passed an omnibus bill (HR 9) to overhaul the federal regulatory process, which contained provisions to require federal officials to compensate private landowners whose property values diminished by 20 percent or more because of regulatory action taken under the Endangered Species Act, as well as the wetlands provisions of the clean water law and the 1985 farm bill, and certain laws pertaining to western water rights. The property rights portion of HR 9 also was passed as separate legislation (HR 925). But neither bill went any further. A broader property rights bill (S 605) was reported in the Senate in late 1995 but never reached the Senate floor. *(Regulatory overhaul, p. 842)*   ❏

EPA Regulatory Authority

An attempt by House conservatives in 1995 to limit the regulatory authority of the Environmental Protection Agency (EPA) dominated the debate over the fiscal 1996 appropriations bill for Veterans Affairs (VA), Housing and Urban Development (HUD) and independent agencies (HR 2099).

Seventeen provisions limiting the EPA's ability to regulate such things as emissions from industrial facilities and oil refineries, raw sewage overflows, arsenic and radon in drinking water and traces of cancer-causing substances in processed food were added during House consideration but nearly all were removed from the final bill.

HR 2099, however, made deep cuts in housing and environmental programs, triggering a veto. EPA funding would have been cut 21.1 percent, to $5.7 billion. Among the EPA accounts that would have been hit the hardest were the superfund toxic waste cleanup program and loans to states for waste-water treatment and safe drinking water projects.

After the veto, the bill's funding was added to a fiscal 1996 omnibus appropriations bill (HR 3019—PL 104-134). That bill, which was signed into law April 26, 1996, increased EPA funding to $6.5 billion and included none of the controversial restrictions on the agency.

VA-HUD BILL

The House VA-HUD Appropriations Subcommittee approved a 33 percent cut in EPA funding, to $4.9 billion. Republicans on the subcommittee also sought to use the spending bill as a vehicle to make substantive changes in environmental policy. With environmental authorization bills facing an uncertain future, they attached their set of 17 legislative provisions to HR 2099. Attempts to delete the provisions were turned back during full committee consideration.

During floor action, environmentalists scored a surprising victory by striking the 17 EPA restrictions, only to suffer a stunning reversal after conservatives threatened to vote against the whole bill.

A large group of moderate Republicans joined with a majority of the Democrats on July 28 to strike the EPA provisions. Most of these Republicans were from Florida and northeastern and Great Lakes states. The amendment, offered by Louis Stokes, D-Ohio, and cosponsored by moderate Republican Sherwood Boehlert of New York, was adopted by a **key vote of 212–206 (R 51–175; D 160–31; I 1–0)**. During the two-hour debate on the amendment, its supporters warned of an environmental disaster if Congress prevented the EPA from enforcing key regulations. They also said that such sweeping policy changes should be debated by the authorizing committees after a series of public hearings, instead of being added to appropriations bills. *(1995 key votes, p. 1025)*

But several chairmen of authorizing committees, including Agriculture Committee Chairman Pat Roberts, R-Kan., Resources Chairman Don Young, R-Alaska, and Commerce Chairman Thomas J. Bliley Jr., R-Va., said the provisions would cement some changes that the House had approved in other bills. Veteran conservatives such as Roberts said they would vote against the bill unless it put curbs on the EPA.

On July 31, the House reconsidered the vote. After a bitter floor vote, the House voted to reject the Stokes amendment and thus retain the EPA provisions. The 210–210 vote hinged largely on absentees.

That same day the House rejected, 188–228, a Richard J. Durbin, D-Ill., amendment to waive any provision in the bill that would limit EPA's ability to protect people from exposure to arsenic, benzene, dioxin, lead or any known carcinogen. A motion to return the bill to the Appropriations Committee with instructions to amend it with the Durbin amendment was rejected, 198–222. An amendment by Michigan Democrat John D. Dingell, to increase the superfund appropriation was rejected, 155–261.

The Senate Appropriations Committee approved $5.7 billion for the EPA and included only one of the controversial House provisions, to prevent the EPA from requiring states to adopt a centralized inspection and maintenance program under the Clean Air Act. However, the Senate bill did include other, narrower provisions aimed at constraining the EPA. For example, it proposed to prohibit the agency from vetoing decisions made by the Army Corps of Engineers regarding development permits for wetlands.

Senate Democrats' attempts to reshape the bill's environmental provisions during floor debate failed. The Senate on Sept. 27 rejected, 45–54, a procedural motion to allow consideration of a Frank R. Lautenberg, D-N.J., amendment to boost environmental funding. That same day senators rejected, 39–61, a Max Baucus, D-Mont., amendment to enable the EPA administrator to disregard any provision in the bill that would weaken environmental protection or public health.

On Nov. 2, before the bill went to conference, the House dropped its support for the controversial EPA provisions in its bill. The House first voted, 231–195, to end debate on a motion by Stokes to strike the EPA provisions, thereby blocking a substitute motion that would have instructed House conferees simply to study each of the EPA provisions individually for its merit. The House then approved Stokes's motion, 227–194.

Afterward, Stokes and Boehlert attributed the outcome in part to strong public opposition to the provisions. Environmental activists had delivered bags full of petitions to Congress the day before, saying that they contained the signatures of 1.2 million people opposed to the proposals.

In the end, conferees dropped nearly all of the House-passed EPA provisions, except a directive to prevent the agency from issuing a rule for the maximum allowable level of radon in drinking water. They also retained five Senate riders, including the one on wetlands.

Clinton vetoed the bill Dec. 18, in part because the bill would "threaten public health and the environment."

OMNIBUS BILL, 1997 BILL

VA-HUD funding was included in the fiscal 1996 omnibus appropriations bill signed into law on April 26, 1996. Gone from HR 3019 were the last of the environmental riders, including the wetlands provision. The EPA's $6.5 billion appropriation was $757 million more than in the bill Clinton had vetoed.

The partisan rancor was absent when Congress considered the fiscal 1997 VA-HUD funding bill (HR 3666—PL 104-

201). The bill, which provided $6.7 billion for the EPA, was free of controversial legislative riders.

A House attempt to make $861 million of the bill's $2.2 billion for the superfund hazardous waste cleanup program subject to future appropriation was dropped in conference. The provision had been largely designed to pressure lawmakers to enact separate legislation to reauthorize the superfund program. The final bill provided more than $1.3 billion for the program. *(Superfund, p. 453)* ❑

Solid Waste Management

The House in 1996 overwhelmingly rejected a Senate-passed bill (S 534) that would have allowed municipalities with big investments in solid waste management and disposal facilities to continue directing waste to those sites. S 534 also would have given states new authority to keep out unwanted garbage, while at least partially accommodating the needs of other states in search of a home for their waste.

The vote ended efforts in the 104th Congress to blunt the effects of a pair of Supreme Court decisions that prevented local governments from requiring that waste go to specific incinerators, landfills or dumps and that barred states from banning the importation of waste from outside their jurisdiction.

BACKGROUND

Numerous states had laws authorizing flow control ordinances, under which local governments could require that municipal solid waste be managed, stored and disposed only at designated sites. Local governments used flow control to ensure that the amount of waste sent to a waste management or disposal facility was sufficient to produce enough revenue to repay the bonds issued to finance it. However, in 1994, the Supreme Court ruled in *C&A Carbone v. Town of Clarkstown* that flow control ordinances were an unconstitutional restriction of interstate commerce and prevented competition. *(Court ruling, p. 784)*

Two years earlier, in 1992, the Supreme Court had ruled that attempts by states to limit outside waste by charging higher fees or banning the waste outright was also an unlawful restriction on interstate commerce. The Court, for example, struck down a Michigan law allowing limits on the importation of waste in *Fort Gratiot Sanitary Landfill v. Michigan Department of Natural Resources. (1992 ruling, Congress and the Nation Vol. VIII, p. 831)*

A House attempt in 1994 to overturn these decisions was blocked in the Senate by John H. Chafee, R-R.I., who criticized the legislation as overly broad. Chafee objected that the legislation favored states that imported garbage over those, such as his own, that exported it. *(1994 action, p. 419)*

LEGISLATIVE ACTION

In 1995, Chafee, who had become the chairman of the Senate Environment and Public Works Committee, worked to fashion a compromise on the issue. As reported by Chafee's committee on April 18 (S Rept 104-52), S 534 allowed towns and cities to continue guaranteeing a flow of business to select dump sites if they had flow control laws before May 15, 1994, and had made commitments before that date to build a facility to receive the waste. These exceptions were to expire after 30 years. The bill also gave states new authority to keep out unwanted garbage from other states and to charge higher fees for such waste disposal under certain circumstances.

The Senate passed S 534 May 16 by a vote of 94–6, after adopting compromise language to allow a handful of states that imported more than 750,000 tons of garbage, including Indiana, Michigan, Ohio and Pennsylvania, to impose additional limits.

The Senate had begun work on the bill May 10, but action was stalled by a flood of amendments, mostly to add new protections for specific states and communities. An attempt to end debate May 12 failed, 50–47; 60 votes were needed.

Companion legislation languished in the House Commerce Committee, after running into long-standing conflicts between lawmakers from waste-exporting states and those whose states wanted to ban out-of-state garbage. After seven months of wrangling, House leaders tried to bypass the Commerce Committee and bring S 534 directly to the floor. But the measure died when the House on Jan. 31, 1996, refused to consider it under expedited procedures. The vote was 150–271 on a motion to suspend the rules and agree to a resolution (H Res 349) to pass and ask for a conference on an amended version of S 534 dealing with only the flow control issue.   ❑

Omnibus Parks Bill

Congress cleared a popular omnibus parks and lands bill (HR 4236—PL 104-333) as the 104th Congress neared adjournment. The massive bill contained more than 100 parks, lands and rivers provisions, including such high-profile items as a plan to preserve the Presidio, a former military base in San Francisco, and a plan to buy land in the Sterling Forest, a vital watershed and ecosystem on the New York and New Jersey border.

HR 4236 commanded broad bipartisan support, and Republican leaders had put a priority on getting it through. But doing that proved to be no easy task. The bill became a magnet for contentious riders—from grazing rules to Utah wilderness provisions—as individual lawmakers looked for a vehicle to carry proposals too controversial to pass on their own. Removing the deal-breaking provisions without losing their sponsors' support for the bill was a painstaking process that dominated action on the parks bill for most of 1996. The package teetered on the brink of collapse in the final hours of the·104th Congress, as the bill's fate turned on a provision affecting a single logging company in southeast Alaska.

LEGISLATIVE ACTION

The bill began in 1995 as a relatively noncontroversial proposal (HR 1296) to create a public-private Presidio Trust to help manage the hundreds of historic buildings that covered more than 1,400 acres at the foot of the Golden Gate Bridge.

First established as a Spanish colonial military settlement in 1776, the Presidio had been the oldest continuously operated U.S. Army base before it closed in 1994. It then became part of the Golden Gate National Recreation Area. But the Presidio, with an annual operating budget of about $25 million, had become one of the federal government's most expensive sites, with many of its structures requiring continuous maintenance.

HR 1296 called for the trust to rent space to government agencies and private companies as a way to raise revenue to pay for the upkeep of the facility. Similar legislation had been passed by the House in the 103rd Congress but was killed in the Senate by Republicans who argued that the Park Service could not afford to take on the new duties prescribed in the bill. *(1993–1994 action, p. 420)*

HR 1296 (H Rept 104-234) was reported by the House Resources Committee Aug. 4, 1995, and passed by the full House on Sept. 19 by a vote of 317–101.

The Senate Energy and Natural Resources Committee reported a slightly revised version of HR 1296 (S Rept 104-202) on Dec. 22. But by the time HR 1296 was passed by voice vote of the Senate May 1, 1996, the bill had been expanded to carry nearly 60 parks and lands bills that had stalled as stand-alone measures. The bill passed only after Energy and Natural Resources Committee Chairman Frank H. Murkowski, R-Alaska, who had engineered the expansion of the bill, had agreed to jettison the most controversial provisions.

The rider that drew the greatest outcry was a Utah lands bill (S 884, HR 1745), which had been approved by committees in both chambers in 1995. The proposal set aside nearly 2 million acres in Utah as wilderness but precluded the government's remaining 20 million acres in Utah from being managed as wilderness unless Congress designated them as such. Environmentalists feared the provisions would set a precedent that could make it far more difficult to protect sensitive lands, and they had made defeat of the Utah bill a top priority. *(Utah wilderness, p. 464)*

Democrats, led by Bill Bradley, D-N.J., launched a filibuster when Murkowski brought the expanded bill to the floor. They also used the opportunity to try to force a vote on the politically charged issue of raising the minimum wage. Majority Leader Bob Dole, R-Kan., pulled the bill from the floor after two votes to cut off debate failed. *(Minimum wage, p. 666)*

To save the rest of the bill, Murkowski ultimately agreed to drop the Utah provisions. Also dropped from the Senate version was language to allow the purchase of more than 17,000 acres for the Sterling Forest. The initiative itself was not especially controversial, but it was important to Bradley and other East Coast senators.

CONFERENCE, FINAL ACTION

House and Senate conferees began work in May, but it took them months to agree on which of the Senate provisions to include in a final parks bill. One of the biggest sticking points was an attempt by some House Republicans to add the text of another controversial bill—this one (S 1459) aimed at overturning Clinton administration rules for grazing livestock on public lands. The standoff was finally broken in early September, when western GOP House members gave up trying to add the grazing provisions. *(Grazing rights, p. 455)*

Next came a move by Murkowski to use the conference report as a vehicle for a 15-year contract extension for the Ketchikan Pulp Co., the largest remaining logging operator in the Tongass National Forest, a temperate rainforest in southeast Alaska. Under a lucrative 50-year contract, due to expire in 2004, Ketchikan was able to log in the Tongass as long as it operated a pulp mill, where most of its employees worked. Murkowski's provision, opposed by the White House and environmentalists who had made preservation of the Tongass a top priority, would have allowed the company to close the money-losing mill, shift operations to its profitable Tongass sawmills, and still log in the Tongass. (*Tongass National Forest, p. 463*)

Murkowski and his House counterpart, Resources Committee Chairman Don Young, R-Alaska, included the Tongass provision in the conference report (H Rept 104-836), along with a number of hot-button environmental provisions. The report faced opposition from Democrats and moderate Republicans and a veto threat from the White House. Adding to its troubles was a tax provision included as part of an Alaska-land exchange proposal. The tax provision originated in the Senate, instead of the House as required by the Constitution, leaving House leaders little choice but to pull the report from floor consideration.

With the bill collapsing and attempts being made to add some of its provisions to the nearly completed fiscal 1997 omnibus appropriations bill (HR 3610), House authorizers went back to work. They dumped the conference report and created yet another version of the parks bill, dropping Murkowski's favored Alaska provision and most other controversial items. The Sterling Forest provisions were included.

The House passed the new bill (HR 4236) Sept. 28 by a vote of 404–4. The Senate went along, after Murkowski made a deal with the White House allowing the Alaskan company to close its pulp mill and still get a two-year supply of federal timber if it reached an agreement with the administration to sever its 50-year contract. The Senate passed HR 4236 by voice vote Oct. 3, completing congressional action.

MAJOR PROVISIONS

As signed into law Nov. 12, HR 4236 authorized scores of new preserves, land exchanges and boundary adjustments in about 130 parks projects in 41 states. Major provisions of the bill:

• **Presidio.** Established a public-private trust to manage and preserve the hundreds of historic buildings at the Presidio.

• **Tallgrass Prairie.** Established the Tallgrass Prairie National Preserve in the Flint Hills of Kansas southwest of Topeka through a private-public partnership. The bill provided for 180 acres of land to be donated to the federal government; 10,700 acres would be owned by the National Park Trust, a private conservation group.

• **Sterling Forest.** Authorized the federal government to provide $17.5 million to buy land in the Sterling Forest along the New York and New Jersey border. The forest—a vital watershed for northern New Jersey and a valued greenspace for the metropolitan region—was to be managed by the congressionally chartered Palisades Interstate Park Commission. The fiscal 1997 omnibus appropriations bill (HR 3610 – PL 104-208) provided $9 million, or a little more than half the authorization, for land purchase. The proposal had also been considered as separate legislation. (*Sterling Forest, p. 466*)

• **Bay Delta.** Authorized $430 million to clean up the California Bay Delta, a vital watershed and ecosystem near San Francisco. Authorizing language also was included in the omnibus appropriations bill.

• **Civil Rights Tail.** Created a historic trail commemorating the Selma-to-Montgomery route used by the Rev. Dr. Martin Luther King Jr., in a civil rights march.

• **Florida Barrier Islands.** Provided federal flood insurance to condominiums and other developments on Florida's barrier islands. Proponents prevailed on the argument that the provision was a technical correction that would provide flood insurance to 36.4 acres of land mistakenly included in the coastal barriers resources systems, which discouraged development.

• **Utah Olympics.** Authorized a land swap to provide federal land to a private company, which proponents said was necessary for the Winter Olympics to be held in Utah in 2002. The provision had begun as separate legislation. (*Utah land swap, p. 466*)

• **Ski Fees.** Restructured fees charged to ski operators using U.S. Forest Service land. The provision had begun as separate legislation. (*Ski fees, p. 465*)

• **Employee Housing.** Permitted the Interior and Agriculture departments to use private contractors to build and maintain housing for forest rangers, park rangers and other federal land management employees. The provision had begun as separate legislation. (*Employee housing, p. 465*) ❑

Timber Issues

Environmentalists and timber industry supporters clashed a number of times in the 104th Congress over the issue of logging on federal land.

TIMBER-SALVAGE PROVISION

A controversial provision to allow timber companies to expedite logging in old-growth forests was included in a fiscal 1995 rescissions bill (HR 1944—PL 104-19). Environmentalists in Washington and Oregon contended that it would lead to damaging overharvesting, and President Clinton later said he regretted signing it into law. But subsequent efforts to repeal it failed.

The original House bill (HR 1158) would have mandated that the federal government sell more than 6 million board feet of timber in two years, following expedited procedures that would streamline environmental reviews, waive administrative appeals and limit court challenges. The requirement would not have applied to federal lands that had been formally designated as wilderness, to selected roadless areas that had been proposed for designation as wilderness, or to lands where all timber harvesting was outlawed.

Sponsor Charles H. Taylor, R-N.C., said his proposal was designed to recover timber in burned, diseased or otherwise threatened forest areas. Opponent Sidney R. Yates, D-Ill., attacked the proposed sales as a "grab for government property." But a Yates amendment to strip the timber salvage program from the bill was rejected, 150–275, on March 15, 1995.

Taylor's provision was modified during Senate Appropriations Committee consideration to remove the requirement that more than 6 million board feet be sold in two years. During floor action March 30, a Patty Murray, D-Wash., amendment to restore some of the environmental reviews that the bill sought to suspend was tabled (killed) by a vote of 48–46.

House-Senate conferees dropped the House sales target of 6 million board feet, but they did agree to speed approval of a proposed rule to let private landowners sell timber in regions inhabited by threatened and endangered species. The rule was exempted from an environmental-impact review.

Clinton vetoed HR 1944 for a number of reasons, including the timber provision. The president asked Congress to remove the proposal from the bill. During negotiations on a replacement bill (HR 1944), the administration and the appropriators worked out an agreement on a new version that terminated the expedited sale procedures on Dec. 31, 1996, not Sept. 30, 1997, and gave more weight to existing management plans that restricted timber harvests on federal lands. *(1995 rescissions bill, p. 78)*

Clinton pushed for repeal of the provision in the fiscal 1996 omnibus appropriations bill (HR 3019—PL 104-134), which was signed into law April 26, 1996, but the logging language remained unchanged.

An Elizabeth Furse, D-Ore., amendment to repeal the provision was only narrowly defeated, 209–211, on June 20, 1996, during House consideration of a fiscal 1997 funding bill for the Interior Department and other agencies (HR 3662).

TONGASS NATIONAL FOREST

Congress included in its final version of the fiscal 1996 Interior appropriations bill (HR 1977) provisions to greatly increase the amount of timber available for cutting in the Tongass National Forest, a temperate rainforest in southeast Alaska. This, along with other controversial issues, triggered a presidential veto. A compromise on the Tongass issue was reached during negotiations on a fiscal 1996 omnibus appropriations bill (HR 3019—PL 104-134).

As cleared Dec. 14, 1996, HR 1977 would have allowed the Forest Service to sell as much as 418 million board feet of Tongass timber per year in line with a management plan known as "Alternative P," favored by timber interests and opposed by environmentalists who said the plan would lead to overharvesting. The bill also included a two-year moratorium on a new Forest Service Tongass management plan.

Alternative P had been selected in 1991 by Bush administration Forest Service officials as their preferred Tongass land-use plan, but it was shelved by the Clinton administration on the grounds that it would not sufficiently protect the forest's fish and wildlife. Sen. Ted Stevens, R-Alaska, sponsor of the effort to resurrect the plan, accused the administration of dragging its feet and costing jobs for his state.

The Tongass language went through several rounds of revisions. The House rejected two conference reports, in part be-

cause of the timber provisions. An attempt in the House to strike compromise language from the third and final conference report on HR 1977 (H Rept 104-402) was rejected, 187–241, on Dec. 13, 1995. The bill was vetoed on Dec. 18.

The Clinton administration denounced the Tongass provision, saying it would lead to overharvesting and undermine a fragile ecosystem. In a compromise reached on the fiscal 1996 omnibus funding bill, language was added to clarify that the legislation did not mandate clear-cutting. In addition, negotiators agreed to allow Clinton to suspend the provisions if he determined that such a decision would be in the public's interest. The president did so April 26, 1996, the day he signed HR 3019 into law.

To mollify Stevens and the Alaska congressional delegation, the bill provided $110 million in grants to employ former timber workers and for community development if the harvesting was suspended.

During conference action on the fiscal 1997 omnibus appropriations bill (HR 3610—PL 104-208), appropriators agreed to drop a Senate provision requiring the General Accounting Office (GAO) to review whether the Forest Service was abiding by the law in developing a management plan. Stevens argued that the language should provoke little controversy because it simply requested a GAO review. But after the White House disputed this, contending that the GAO report would be used to thwart administration policy, he backed off.

Logging in the Tongass also provoked controversy during consideration of an omnibus parks and lands bill (HR 4236—PL 104-333). *(Omnibus parks bill, p. 461)*

FOREST HEALTH ISSUE

The Senate Energy and Natural Resources Committee on July 16, 1996, reported a bill (S 391—S Rept 104-321) aimed at streamlining and expediting the sale of dead, diseased or dying trees on federal land. But the proposal set off a rhetorical war between environmental groups and timber companies and, as a result, went no further.

Bill sponsor Larry E. Craig, R-Idaho, and other supporters argued that existing management practices often prevented federal forest managers from offering salvage lumber for sale before it decayed beyond productive use, thus denying the U.S. Treasury profits.

In addition, Craig argued that the management practices had fueled a health crisis in the nation's forests, apparent in the rash of fires seen across the West during the spring.

But environmentalists, who strongly opposed the bill, contended that Craig and his supporters had manufactured a forest health crisis to mask the true aim of his bill: expediting logging to benefit timber companies. More than 100 scientists had gone on record in opposition to the bill, arguing that dead and dying trees were often critical to protecting the habitats of species, safeguarding water quality and guarding against pests. In a June 19 letter to President Clinton, they wrote that Craig's bill could worsen the health of the nation's forests, noting problems in forests caused by road building and poor management practices. ❑

National Park System

Bills to overhaul various aspects of the national park system were considered in the 104th Congress. But they shared the same fate as similar bills in the previous Congress: none was enacted into law.

PARK SYSTEM REORGANIZATION

The House in 1995 rejected a proposal (HR 260) to require a comprehensive review of National Park Service sites. A subsequent attempt to include the plan in the deficit reduction budget reconciliation bill (HR 2491) was rejected by GOP leaders.

HR 260, reported by the House Resources Committee June 7 (H Rept 104-133), called for the interior secretary to submit to Congress within two fiscal years a long-range management plan for the national park system. The secretary would have been required to establish criteria for adding new sites to the park system, establish a National Park System Review Commission, and require the commission to develop a list of insignificant or undesirable park sites. The commission would have had two years to recommend the closure of some parks or their transfer to state or private management. Such actions would have required the approval of Congress.

Supporters said lawmakers had focused more on adding coveted sites in their districts to the park system than on properly maintaining the facilities already within the system. The Interior Department's National Park Service faced a multibillion-dollar backlog in repairs and maintenance at many of the nation's most popular sites, including Yellowstone National Park and Independence Hall in Philadelphia.

Foes of the bill succeeded in branding it a "park-closing" bill, and the House rejected it by a vote of 180–231 on Sept. 19, under suspension of the rules. Later that day the House Resources panel added the provisions of HR 260 to its section of the budget reconciliation package, but the park system reorganization plan was dropped before the reconciliation bill reached the floor. Republican leaders said the plan had become controversial both for its content and the way it had been attached to HR 2491.

A reorganization plan had been approved by the House in 1994 but died in the Senate. *(1994 action, p. 420)*

PARK CONCESSIONS

The House Resources Subcommittee on National Parks, Forests, and Lands on April 10, 1996, approved a bill (HR 2028) to overhaul management of federal park concessions, amid Democratic criticism that the bill favored corporations at the expense of small operators. The bill, which would have opened their contracts to free-market competition, went no further.

In 1994, both chambers passed versions of a bill that would have forced businesses to bid competitively for the right to operate concessions in the national parks. But the bill was never cleared. *(1994 action, p. 420)*

PARK FEES

The House Resources Committee on Sept. 4, 1996, reported legislation to create a new fee system for visitors to most national parks and forests. The bill (HR 2107—H Rept 104-757), however, went no further.

HR 2107 proposed to expand the authority of Interior and Agriculture department agencies to collect fees for the use of facilities such as camping and swimming areas, hiking trails, boat-launching areas and parking lots. It also called for removing existing caps on admission fees and allowing individual parks and forests to set their own fees.

Bill sponsor James V. Hansen, R-Utah, chairman of the Resources Subcommittee on National Parks, Forests, and Lands, said the measure would increase funding for parks to 125 percent of the fiscal 1995 level by using a combination of increased recreation and admission fees and appropriations. Republicans estimated that the bill would generate more than $300 million for parks, forests and refuges over seven years.

Ranking subcommittee Democrat Bill Richardson of New Mexico strongly opposed the bill, arguing that the increases would disproportionately hurt poor families, senior citizens and children. But Richardson's attempts to amend the bill were rejected by the full committee.

Congress had last approved an increase to park entrance fees in 1987. As part of the 1993 budget reconciliation bill (PL 103-66), lawmakers expanded the Interior and Agriculture departments' authority to assess and collect fees from other recreational activities and facilities. Legislation to increase park user fees stalled in both chambers in 1994. *(Budget reconciliation bill, p. 44; 1994 action, p. 421)* ❑

Utah Wilderness

A plan to designate as wilderness 1.8 million acres owned by the federal government in Utah and release an additional 20 million acres for potential development won approval from House and Senate committees in 1995. Proponents claimed—and opponents feared—that the legislation (HR 1745, S 884) would set a precedent for greater constraints on federal land management.

Utah's congressional delegation and many western and conservative lawmakers said the proposal balanced the goals of protecting the environment and preserving the potential for economic development. Opponents, including the Wilderness Society and other environmental groups, contended that Utah's GOP congressional delegation was pushing a bill that favored developers and amounted to a federal land giveaway.

The measure also included a state-federal land swap that some critics asserted would be a "sweetheart deal" for the mining industry and the state. About 200,000 acres of federal land was to be transferred to the state in exchange for state-owned parcels within the designated wilderness area. The exchange was to be on an acre-by-acre, instead of an equal value, basis, and Utah stood to get federal land that held billions of tons of recoverable coal.

HR 1745 was reported by the House Resources Committee on Dec. 11, 1995 (H Rept 104-396). The Senate Energy and Natural Resources Committee reported S 884 (S Rept 104-192) on Dec. 19.

But the bills went no further. An attempt to attach the proposal to an omnibus parks bill (HR 1296) failed as well. *(Omnibus parks bill, p. 461)* ❏

Wildlife Refuges

The House passed legislation in 1996 to overhaul the nation's wildlife refuge system for the first time since 1966, but it died at the end of the 104th Congress. The Senate offered no companion legislation.

The bill (HR 1675) would have required the Interior Department to set a uniform mission statement for the 91.7 million-acre National Wildlife Refuge System that included hunting and fishing. The two activities would generally have been allowed unless the Interior Department found they would be incompatible with a particular refuge or would threaten public safety.

Supporters said that the intent was to codify existing practices and that the bill would not change the overall management of the areas. The bill had strong support from the 205-member bipartisan sportsmen's caucus.

But environmentalists contended that elevating hunting and fishing would compromise protections of sensitive habitats and undermine the refuges' historic mission of protecting threatened wildlife. The administration also raised objections to the bill.

To avoid a bitter fight and bring Republican environmentalists on board, supporters of the bill backed an amendment by Sherwood Boehlert, R-N.Y., aimed at ensuring that hunting and fishing did not supersede conservation goals. After adopting the Boehlert amendment by voice vote, the House easily passed HR 1675 by a vote of 287–138 on April 24, 1996. The bill had been reported by the House Resources Committee on July 31, 1995 (H Rept 104-218). ❏

Conte Wildlife Refuge

Congress in 1996 cleared legislation (HR 2909) that would have barred the U.S. Fish and Wildlife Service from forcing people to give up land along the Connecticut River in New England to add lands to the Silvio O. Conte wildlife refuge. But President Clinton vetoed the bill on the ground that it was an infringement on the federal government's constitutionally bestowed authority of eminent domain.

The Silvio O. Conte National Fish and Wildlife Refuge—named for the late Republican representative from Massachusetts (1959–1991)—was established in 1991 to protect the habitat along the river. Under existing law, the Fish and Wildlife Service could buy, trade or take land under eminent domain to add to the refuge. The wildlife service, however, said it did not want to use those powers in this case.

HR 2909, which would have allowed acquisition of land for the project only with the consent of the landowner, was reported (H Rept 104-579) by the House Resources Committee May 16, 1996, and passed by voice vote of the House June 11. The Senate Environment and Public Works Committee reported the bill July 24, and the Senate passed it by voice vote Sept. 18. Clinton vetoed the bill Oct. 2. ❏

Virginia Parks

The House passed legislation (HR 1091) to authorize the establishment of a 1,860-acre Shenandoah Valley Battlefields National Historic Park in Virginia to commemorate key Civil War battles in 1862 and 1864. The new park would be based on sites identified in a 1992 National Park Service study of important Civil War battlefields in the area.

The bill also redefined the boundaries of the Shenandoah National Park and the Richmond National Battlefield, shrinking them to conform to land that the federal government owned or planned to acquire in the near future. Bill sponsor Thomas J. Bliley Jr., R-Va., voiced concern that, if the existing boundaries remained authorized for an area far greater than the land owned and managed by the park service, "these two parks can expand whenever they want, without congressional approval or a fair representation of local communities' concerns."

HR 1091 was reported (H Rept 104-176) by the House Resources Committee July 11, 1995, and passed by a 377–31 vote of the full House Sept. 19. The Senate Energy and Natural Resources Committee reported (S Rept 104-389) an amended version Sept. 16, 1996. There was no further action. ❏

Ski Fees

The House in 1996 passed a bill to overhaul the fees charged to ski operators using U.S. Forest Service land. The measure (HR 1527) was later enacted as part of an omnibus parks and lands bill signed into law Nov. 12 (HR 4236—PL 104-333).

At the time, there were 143 ski areas on federal forest land used by tens of millions of skiers annually, including such well-known Colorado locations as Vail, Steamboat Springs and Aspen. Under the existing system, which critics said was overly complex, ski operators paid about $19 million to the federal government in 1995—about 2 percent of their gross revenues.

The new structure required ski companies to pay according to their revenue. Companies with gross revenues of more than $50 million were to pay 4 percent of their revenues to the Forest Service; companies with revenues between $3 million and $50 million, from 2.5 percent to 2.75 percent; and companies with less than $3 million, 1.5 percent.

The bill included language requiring the agriculture secretary to report to Congress within three years on whether the new fee structure was achieving a fair market return. The administration expressed concern in an April 30 statement that the revised structure would not ensure a fair return.

HR 1527 was reported (H Rept 104-516, Part I) by the House Resources Committee April 15, 1996, and passed by voice vote of the House April 30. Companion legislation had been reported (S 907—S Rept 104-183) by the Senate Energy and Natural Resources Committee Dec. 8, 1995. ❏

Federal Employee Housing

The House in 1996 passed a bill (HR 2941) aimed at improving the living quarters of forest rangers, park rangers and other federal land management employees. The measure was subsequently incorporated into an omnibus parks bill signed into law Nov. 12 (HR 4236—PL 104-333).

HR 2941 allowed the Interior and Agriculture departments to use private contractors to build and maintain housing for land management employees. Under existing law, the agency responsible for the land had to build and maintain the housing.

HR 2941, which also allowed federal employees and their families to buy homes on public lands, had been reported (H Rept 104-802, Part I) by the House Resources Committee Sept. 17, 1996, and passed by voice vote of the House that same day. ❏

Utah Land Swap

Congress in 1996 agreed to allow a Utah land swap to help accommodate downhill skiing events in the 2002 Winter Olympics in that state. Originally considered as separate legislation, the proposal was cleared as part of an omnibus parks bill signed into law Nov. 12 (HR 4236—PL 104-333).

Under the legislation, the Forest Service was allowed to transfer 1,320 acres of federal land in the Cache National Forest to the owner of the Snowbasin Ski Resort near Salt Lake City. In return, the Sun Valley Co., which owned the resort, was to transfer land of equal value and similar characteristics to the U.S. Forest Service within one year.

Supporters said the transfer was necessary to build the new facilities needed to support the Olympic events. Opponents said it was aimed at privatizing the land for development under the guise of a politically acceptable purpose such as the Olympics.

The Senate Energy and Natural Resources Committee reported a Utah land swap bill on Jan. 3, 1996 (S 1371—S Rept 104-201). The House Resources Committee first approved the land swap in a bill reported Dec. 15, 1995 (HR 2402—H Rept 104-409). Because a quorum had not been present when HR 2402 was approved, the panel reported an identical bill March 25, 1996 (HR 2824—H Rept 104-493).

The House combined the Utah land swap with a proposal to purchase land in the Sterling Forest along the New York and New Jersey border in a bill (HR 3907) it passed by voice vote July 30, 1996. Both proposals were approved in the final omnibus parks bill. (Sterling Forest, below) ❏

Sterling Forest

The House in 1996 passed a bill (HR 3907) to permit the acquisition of land in the 17,500-acre Sterling Forest along the New York-New Jersey border. The proposal was included in the final omnibus parks bill signed into law Nov. 12 (HR 4236—PL 104-333).

The Sterling Forest was home to part of the Appalachian Trail and to numerous threatened species. It included a drinking water source for one-fourth of New Jersey residents. The land was owned by private landholders who were planning to build a large commercial and residential development. The developers announced an agreement in May to sell 15,800 acres of the tract for $55 million to the congressionally chartered Palisades Inter-

state Park Commission. Private contributors donated $7.5 million for the purchase, and New York and New Jersey agreed to put up $10 million each but looked to Congress for the additional money.

Lawmakers hoping to protect the Sterling Forest tried various legislative vehicles. The Senate initially included the acquisition authority in its version of HR 1296, an omnibus parks and lands bill, but then dropped the provision before passage, at least in part because of an intraparty struggle between northeastern Republicans and some of their western colleagues. (Omnibus parks bill, p. 461)

The House then approved the Sterling Forest provision as part of a separate bill. HR 3907, which also included a Utah land swap proposal, was passed by voice vote of the House July 30, 1996. (Utah land swap, this page)

The acquisition authority was finally included in HR 4236, a new version of the omnibus parks bill, which replaced HR 1296. HR 4236 authorized $17.5 million for the Sterling Forest purchase. The fiscal 1997 omnibus appropriations bill (HR 3610—PL 104-208) provided $9 million. ❏

Mining Patent Moratorium

The 104th Congress agreed to extend a moratorium on new applications for the low-cost purchase by miners of the federal lands on which they prospected for hard-rock mineral deposits, such as gold and silver. Extensions were included in both the fiscal 1996 and 1997 funding bills for the Interior Department and related agencies.

Originally intended to promote the settlement of the West, the 1872 Mining Law allowed prospectors to obtain "patents"—essentially ownership claims on federal lands—for as little as $2.50 an acre and charged them no royalties for the minerals they extracted. Critics called it a rip-off of taxpayers, while western members said they were distorting the issue. In 1994, Congress had agreed to a one-year freeze on issuing new mining patents after it became clear that congressional efforts to agree on a broad rewrite of the 1872 statute were foundering. The moratorium was enacted as part of the fiscal 1995 Interior appropriations bill (PL 103-332). (Mining law, p. 411)

Congress included a one-year extension in a fiscal 1996 Interior appropriations bill (HR 1977) that ultimately was vetoed for other reasons. The House Interior Appropriations Subcommittee had called for ending the moratorium, but the full House on July 18, 1995, voted, 271–153, to adopt a Scott L. Klug, R-Wis., amendment to extend it for one year.

The Senate Interior Appropriations Subcommittee included a provision to end the moratorium in its version of HR 1977. A Dale Bumpers, D-Ark., amendment to remove that language from the bill was rejected, 46–51, on Aug. 8. As an alternative, Larry E. Craig, R-Idaho, proposed to drop the moratorium provision and replace it with a requirement that miners pay fair market prices for land patents based on the surface value of the land and not the value of the minerals under the soil. An attempt to table (kill) Craig's amendment failed, 46–53, on Aug. 8. The Senate then passed the Craig amendment by voice vote.

The House Sept. 8 by voice vote instructed its conferees on HR 1977 to insist on extending the moratorium. But the House conferees instead agreed to accept the Senate position. Most Democrats, as well as a coalition of GOP environmentalists and deficit hawks, opposed the conferees' decision. Two conference reports were rejected in large part because of the moratorium issue—one would have ended the moratorium (H Rept 104-259) and the other would have extended it but with conditions and exceptions (H Rept 104-300). The House finally agreed to a third conference report (H Rept 104-402) Dec. 13 that extended the moratorium without conditions. But President Clinton vetoed HR 1977 because the bill still contained much that the White House opposed.

Fiscal 1996 Interior appropriations were then included in an omnibus appropriations bill (HR 3019—PL 104-134). HR 3019 extended the mining patent moratorium, as did the fiscal 1997 omnibus appropriations bill (HR 3610—PL 104-208). ❑

Bureau of Land Management

Legislation (HR 1077) to reauthorize the Bureau of Land Management (BLM) received House committee approval in 1995 but advanced no further. The bureau, which managed about 270 million acres of federal land, primarily in the West, had been operating without authorization since 1982.

HR 1077, which would have reauthorized BLM through fiscal 2001 at unspecified levels of spending, was reported by the House Resources Committee on June 22, 1995 (H Rept 104-155).

The House had last attempted to reauthorize the bureau in 1993, when it passed a two-year authorization bill. But the measure died in the Senate. *(1993 action, p. 429)* ❑

International Fishing

Congress in 1995 cleared an omnibus fish management and conservation bill (HR 716—PL 104-43), aimed at implementing a set of international agreements to conserve fish stocks worldwide and at providing relief to U.S. fishermen caught in a dispute between the United States and Canada.

Major provisions of HR 716:

• Provided for the establishment of a system for licensing, reporting and regulating U.S. vessels fishing on the high seas in accordance with an agreement reached by the United Nations Food and Agriculture Organization in 1993 to reserve global fish resources. *(Fishing vessel registration, p. 428)*

• Reauthorized the 1967 Fishermen's Protective Act (PL 90-482), which allowed the federal government to reimburse owners of U.S. fishing vessels for fines they paid to foreign countries that seized their boats and catches, if the U.S. government considered the fees a violation of international law. HR 716 added provisions relating to a 1994 dispute over fees imposed by Canada on U.S. vessels passing through Canadian waters between Washington and Alaska. *(Details, p. 374)*

• Expanded the Central Bering Sea Fisheries Enforcement Act of 1992 to prohibit U.S. vessels or citizens from fishing in an area of the Sea of Okhotsk known as the "Peanut Hole." Similar legislation had been reported separately by the House Resources Committee Feb. 21 (HR 715—H Rept 104-42) and passed by voice vote of the House March 14. *(1993 action, p. 427*

• Reauthorized U.S. participation in the International Commission for the Conservation of Atlantic Tunas through fiscal 1998 and provided for development of a research and monitoring program for bluefin tuna and other wide-ranging Atlantic fish stocks. Similar legislation had been reported separately by the House Resources Committee May 1, 1995, and the House Ways and Means Committee June 27 (HR 541—H Rept 104-109, Parts I and II). *(1993 action, p. 426)*

• Authorized U.S. participation in the Northwest Atlantic Fisheries Organization, an international body established in 1978 to oversee certain fisheries in the northwest Atlantic beyond the 200-mile territorial seas of the United States, Canada and Greenland. Although the United States had signed the 1978 Convention on Future Multilateral Cooperation in the Northwest Atlantic Fisheries, Congress had never passed implementing legislation. Under a treaty adopted by the United Nations in 1993, U.S. vessels could not fish in the affected area unless the United States participated in the convention.

The House on March 28, 1995, had passed by voice vote a bill (HR 622) to authorize U.S. participation in the organization. HR 622 had been reported by the House Resources Committee Feb. 21 (H Rept 104-41).

• Barred the United States from making any international agreement that would violate the international moratorium on large-scale drift-net fishing.

LEGISLATIVE ACTION

The House passed HR 716 by a vote of 384-0 on April 3, 1995. The bill, which had been reported by the House Resources Committee Feb. 23 (H Rept 104-47), focused on reauthorizing the Fishermen's Protective Act and expanding it to include provisions related to the dispute with Canada.

The Senate Commerce Committee reported a broader bill (S 267—S Rept 104-91) on May 26, 1995. The full Senate passed HR 716 by voice vote June 30, after substituting the text of S 267. The House accepted the Senate changes Oct. 24, thus clearing the bill. The president signed HR 716 on Nov. 3. ❑

'Dolphin-Safe' Tuna

The House in 1996 passed legislation (HR 2823) that would have implemented an international agreement to change the definition of "dolphin-safe" tuna in U.S. law, thereby allowing imports into the United States of tuna caught with nets that also encircled dolphins. However, opposition in the Senate prevented the measure from being brought to the floor in that chamber, and the bill died at the end of the 104th Congress.

BACKGROUND

Under U.S. law, only tuna determined to be dolphin-safe could be imported into the United States, and tuna could be labeled dolphin-safe only if it was caught using fishing methods that did not harm dolphins. This prohibition grew out of an effort to protect dolphins in the eastern tropical Pacific Ocean where, for reasons not fully understood, schools of dolphins regularly swam above schools of large yellowfin tuna. In the late 1950s, commercial fishermen began harvesting the tuna swimming below the dolphins by deploying large purse-seine nets around the dolphins. During this process, dolphins often became trapped in the nets and drowned. It was estimated that more than 6 million dolphins had been killed that way since 1959.

Congress in 1992 cleared legislation (PL 102-523) prohibiting U.S. tuna companies from claiming that tuna caught in the eastern tropical Pacific was dolphin-safe, if purse-seine nets were used to encircle dolphins. It also barred the import into the United States of tuna that was not considered dolphin-safe. (1992 law, Congress and the Nation Vol. VIII, p. 528)

That same year, foreign nations that fished the eastern tropical Pacific met in La Jolla, Calif., and agreed to modify their purse-seine net fishing practices to reduce dolphin mortalities and convince the United States to end its embargo. Dolphin kills dropped dramatically, and in 1995, the United States and 11 other nations signed the Declaration of Panama, whereby each agreed to continue using the La Jolla dolphin protection fishing practices. They established an initial annual limit of 5,000 dolphins that could be killed during such fishing.

In return, the United States agreed to allow the import of all tuna caught in compliance with the agreement by member nations of the Inter-American Tropical Tuna Commission. It also agreed to redefine dolphin-safe tuna to include tuna caught in purse-seine nets in which no dolphin mortalities were seen.

LEGISLATIVE ACTION

The House passed the implementing legislation on July 31 by a vote of 316–108. HR 2823 had been reported by the House Resources Committee July 10 and by the Ways and Means Committee July 23 (H Rept 104-665, Parts I and II).

But on Sept. 28, when Senate Majority Leader Trent Lott, R-Miss., sought unanimous consent to consider the House bill, Barbara Boxer, D-Calif., objected, thereby killing the bill for the year. Boxer argued that the measure would significantly weaken protections for dolphins and "gut" the integrity of the dolphin-safe label and that the Declaration of Panama agreement was not a binding legal agreement on the United States.

The Senate Commerce, Science, and Transportation Committee reported companion legislation on Sept. 30 (S 1420—S Rept 104-373), but there was no further action on that bill either. ❑

Fishing Regulation

The 104th Congress considered several bills regarding fishing regulation.

FISH HATCHERIES

Three bills were enacted in 1995 directing the secretary of the interior to transfer control of federally owned fish hatcheries to the states in which they were located.

In all three cases, the legislation enabled the states to make capital improvements to the aging facilities. State officials said they wanted to modernize the hatcheries but had trouble getting funding for the projects without title to the property. The bills provided that the properties would revert to federal control if the states used them for anything but fisheries activities.

The bills, which were handled as a group, transferred:

• Corning National Fish Hatchery to the state of Arkansas (HR 535—PL 104-23);

• Fairport National Fish Hatchery to the state of Iowa (HR 584—PL 104-24); and

• New London National Fish Hatchery to the state of Minnesota (HR 614—PL 104-25).

The bills had been reported by the House Resources Committee Feb. 15, 1995 (H Rept 104-34, H Rept 104-35 and H Rept 104-36, respectively) and passed by voice vote of the House June 7. The Senate Environment and Public Works Committee reported the bills Aug. 7 (S Rept 104-130, S Rept 104-131 and S Rept 104-132, respectively), and the Senate passed them by voice vote Aug. 9. President Clinton signed the bills Sept. 6.

STRIPED BASS

The House in 1995 and again in 1996 passed legislation to reauthorize the 1984 Atlantic Striped Bass Conservation Act (PL 98-613). Similar legislation won committee approval in the Senate but advanced no further.

Efforts to protect the striped bass, also known as the rockfish, had been so successful that the Atlantic States Marine Fisheries Commission declared that stocks of the fish had recovered as of Jan. 1, 1995. The commission had been formed to develop an interstate management plan for striped bass. Anadromous fish, including striped bass, swam primarily in coastal waters but returned to rivers and bays to spawn.

In 1995, a bill (HR 1139) to reauthorize the striped bass act through 1998 was reported by the House Resources Committee May 1 (H Rept 104-105) and passed by voice vote of the House May 9. A Senate bill (S 776) to extend the striped bass act, as well as the 1965 Anadromous Fish Conservation Act (PL 89-304), was reported by the Senate Commerce, Science, and Transportation Committee Dec. 7 (S Rept 104-182) and by the Environment and Public Works Committee Dec. 19.

In 1996, the House April 23 passed 406–0 a bill (HR 2160) to extend the anadromous fish act. HR 2160 had been reported by House Resources April 15 (H Rept 104-517). A bill (HR 4139) to reauthorize both the striped bass and anadromous fish acts was passed by voice vote of the House Sept. 27.

A 1994 attempt to extend the striped bass act also never got beyond House passage. (1994 action, p. 427) ❑

Coastal Zone Management

Congress agreed in 1996 to extend through fiscal 2000 a program of grants to states that had federally approved management plans for their coastal regions. The legislation (HR 1965—PL 104-150) authorized $289 million for activities under the 1972 Coastal Zone Management Act (PL 92-583).

States with approved management plans for their coastal areas were eligible for grants under the act. By 1996, 29 of the nation's 35 coastal states and territories had management plans for nearly 95,000 miles of coastline, representing almost 95 percent of the nation's total. States participated on a voluntary basis and had to match the full amount of the federal grant. Grant amounts were determined by a state's coastal population and the length of its shoreline. States with approved plans could also apply for grants under the act to protect and restore wetlands, control the impact of development, increase access to public beaches, and clean up marine debris.

Congress enacted the 1972 legislation because population densities along the Atlantic and Pacific oceans, the Gulf of Mexico and the Great Lakes coasts were growing rapidly, with significant potential impact on water quality, coastal ecosystem and wildlife. The act was last reauthorized as part of the 1990 budget reconciliation bill (PL 101-508). The five-year reauthorization expired Sept. 30, 1995. (Congress and the Nation Vol. VIII, p. 63)

HR 1965 authorized $245 million over five years for federal grants to states for the implementation of federally approved coastal zone management programs. The bill also authorized $1.1 million for grants to states to develop coastal zone programs; however, it provided for such grants to be abolished after fiscal 1999. Another $22.5 million was authorized over five years for grants for the protection and study of estuaries.

HR 1965 was reported (H Rept 104-521) by the House Resources Committee April 16, 1996, and passed by a 407–0 vote of the full House April 23. The Senate passed the bill May 21, clearing it. The president signed the measure June 3. ❏

Corps of Engineers Projects

Congress in 1996 cleared a $4.5 billion water projects measure (S 640—PL 104-303) for flood-control, navigation and dredging projects of the U.S. Army Corps of Engineers. Of the $4.5 billion, $3.8 billion would be in federal spending and the rest would be funded by state and local governments.

The bill increased the cost to state and local governments of future flood-control projects, raising the nonfederal share from 25 percent to 35 percent. The hope was that a larger local price tag would discourage development on vulnerable flood plains. The administration had proposed passing 50 percent of the costs on to state and local governments.

Of the federal spending, $890 million was earmarked for environmental and ecosystem restoration projects. The bill included $75 million to implement the Clinton administration's effort to restore the Everglades in South Florida, plus $200 million to improve two Everglades canals.

Still, environmental groups expressed disappointment in the bill, not only because its cost-sharing fell short of their wishes but also because they said its sheer size sent the signal that development of the nation's rivers and coastlines could continue in an era of austere federal budgets.

Water authorization bills typically passed every other year and averaged about $2 billion. Sponsors said the 1996 bill was significantly larger because Congress had failed to pass a water bill in 1994. (1994 action, p. 414)

The Senate passed S 640 by voice vote July 11, 1996, after accepting an amendment by Environment and Public Works Committee Chairman John H. Chafee, R-R.I., increasing the bill's proposed cost to the federal government by $2 billion, bringing it to $3.3 billion. Chafee's committee had reported the bill Nov. 9, 1995 (S Rept 104-170). Additions to the bill included projects helpful to incumbent Republicans, as well as White House requests that included the Everglades project.

The House on July 30, 1996, passed by voice vote a $5.9 billion version of S 640, after substituting the text of its own bill, HR 3592. The House had passed HR 3592 by voice vote earlier that day. Of the $5.9 billion, $4.5 billion was to be federal spending. HR 3592 had been reported by the House Transportation and Infrastructure Committee on July 22 (H Rept 104-695), after an impassioned debate that had ended in defeat for proponents of a controversial $949 million dam. The Auburn Dam, a giant flood-control project on the American River, about 40 miles upstream from Sacramento, Calif., had first been authorized in 1965, but the project was halted in 1975, when the site was rattled by a 5.7 magnitude earthquake. The dam came back to life in 1986, after flooding swamped the area. But the project became a target for national environmental and taxpayer groups, which painted it as an enormous, destructive boondoggle.

House and Senate conferees compromised on a $3.8 billion authorization. Chafee initially expressed misgivings about enlarging the bill further to accommodate the House. But the final version included nearly all the projects approved by the House, though some authorizations were cut back slightly. Conferees dropped two House provisions opposed by some environmentalists and budget hawks. One would have extended the shipping navigation season on the upper Missouri River, and another would have prohibited the planned closure of the Corps of Engineers' North Central Division office in Chicago.

The House adopted the conference report (H Rept 104-843) by voice vote Sept. 26. The Senate cleared it the following day, also by voice vote. Clinton signed the bill into law Oct. 12. ❏

Radioactive Waste Disposal

The House in 1995 rejected a bill (HR 558) that would have given congressional consent to an agreement among Maine, Texas and Vermont to deposit their low-level radioactive waste at a yet-to-be-built facility in Texas.

Maine and Vermont would each have paid Texas $25 million for hosting the disposal facility, expected to be located in Sierra Blanca, about 15 miles from the Rio Grande. Texas would have been able to exclude radioactive waste from other states.

Under 1985 amendments (PL 99-240) to the 1980 Low-Level Radioactive Waste Policy Act (PL 96-573), Congress required states to open their own waste-disposal sites or make arrangements to use facilities in other states. The regional compacts that resulted from these negotiations were subject to congressional approval. The waste consisted mostly of irradiated uniforms, tools and trash from nuclear power plants and medical laboratories. (1985 law, Congress and the Nation Vol. VII, p. 449; 1980 law, Congress and the Nation Vol. V, p. 521)

The House rejected the bill Sept. 19 by a vote of 176–243, after a storm of opposition from a sizable portion of the Texas congressional delegation. Opponents argued that the proposed location of the site would pose an environmental hazard, including concerns that the area was in an earthquake zone. They also complained that the bill would unfairly compel Texas to accept waste from out of state.

A Senate version of the bill (S 419) had been reported by the Judiciary Committee May 18 but went no further. ❑

California Desert

Congress cleared a fiscal 1996 funding bill for the Interior Department and other agencies (HR 1977) that included language that would have thwarted a major provision of the 1994 California Desert Protection Act (PL 103-433). The 1994 statute shifted management of the 1.4 million-acre East Mojave National Scenic Area from the Bureau of Land Management (BLM) to the National Park Service. HR 1977 included House language to shift management back to the BLM, though it contained $500,000 for the park service to develop a management plan for the area. (California desert law, p. 405)

President Clinton objected to the provision, among others, and vetoed HR 1977. Fiscal 1996 funding was then incorporated into an omnibus appropriations bill (HR 3019—PL 104-134), as were compromises on controversial issues. Under HR 3019, the park service retained management of the preserve. But the bill required it to manage the preserve under the less-restrictive guidelines of the BLM, which allowed multiple uses from mountain biking to mining, a key Republican concern. The bill allowed Clinton to suspend those management guidelines, if he determined that doing so would be in the public interest. The president suspended them on April 26, 1996, the day he signed HR 3019 into law. ❑

National Biological Service

Congress agreed in the fiscal 1996 omnibus appropriations bill (HR 3019—PL 104-134) to eliminate the National Biological Service as a separate agency and transfer most of its functions to the U.S. Geological Survey. HR 3019 was signed into law April 26, 1996.

Established administratively in 1993 as the National Biological Survey, the agency studied and inventoried animal and plant populations. Supporters said its mission was strictly scientific, but conservatives saw it as a base for those advocating additions to the endangered species list. (National Biological Survey, p. 418)

The provision to eliminate the survey had been part of the fiscal 1996 funding bill for the Interior Department and other agencies (HR 1977) that President Clinton vetoed. The proposal had originated in the House. The Senate version would have taken a softer swipe at the service, allowing it to remain as a separate entity, renamed the Natural Resources Science Agency. Conferees agreed with the House position. ❑

Carpooling Mandate

Congress in 1995 cleared legislation (HR 325—PL 104-70) to lift a federal requirement that employers in high pollution zones reduce the number of car trips that their workers made in commuting to and from work. The bill left it up to the states to decide whether to enforce the mandate, which was part of the 1990 amendments to the Clean Air Act (PL 101-549), or come up with alternative methods of meeting pollution-reduction standards.

Under the amendments, employers with 100 or more employees had been required to reduce car trips to and from work by at least 25 percent when air quality levels reached "severe" or "extreme" levels. Originally meant to promote carpooling, the requirement appeared to have done little to reduce pollution and had caused headaches for many companies.

HR 325 was reported (H Rept 104-387) by the House Commerce Committee Dec. 6, 1995, and passed by voice vote of the House Dec. 12. The Senate passed the bill the next day. It was signed into law Dec. 23. ❑

Antarctica Protection

Congress in 1996 cleared a bill to implement a 1991 multilateral treaty increasing protections for Antarctica's environment while allowing scientific research to go forward. The legislation (HR 3060—PL 104-227) brought U.S. law into conformity with the 1991 Protocol on Environmental Protection to the Antarctic Treaty of 1959.

HR 3060 banned development of mineral resources in Antarctica and required environmental impact statements on all human activities. It imposed strict limits on pollutants—for example, barring the introduction of petroleum products to the continent—and prohibited practices such as the open burning of waste and the disposal of waste onto ice-free lands and into fresh waters. The bill also barred introduction of any nonnative species to the continent and required scientists to obtain a permit to kill any native Antarctic species for research purposes.

Legislation to implement the treaty was considered in the 102nd Congress, but the bill never got beyond House committee approval. (Congress and the Nation Vol. VIII, p. 529)

HR 3060 was reported (H Rept 104-593, Part I) by the House Science Committee May 23, 1996, and passed by a vote of 352–4 of the full House June 10. The Senate Commerce, Science, and Transportation Committee reported a nearly identical bill July 24 (S 1645—S Rept 104-332). The Senate passed HR 3060 by voice vote Sept. 4, after inserting the text of S 1645. Before passage, the Senate had adopted by voice vote a Ted Stevens, R-Alaska, amendment requiring the National Science Foundation to report to Congress on the implementation of environmental protections for the Arctic. The House cleared HR 3060, as amended, by voice vote Sept. 10. President Clinton signed the bill Oct. 2. ❑

EPA Exemptions

Congress in 1996 cleared legislation (HR 2036—PL 104-119) authorizing the Environmental Protection Agency (EPA) to grant two exemptions from environmental requirements for landfills.

The bill reinstated a 1991 EPA rule that exempted landfills in remote or dry areas from certain EPA groundwater monitoring standards. The exemption had been overturned by a 1993 court decision. The bill also exempted small landfills that disposed of less than 20 tons of waste per day if no evidence existed of groundwater contamination. Communities surrounding the landfill were also exempt from the law if no other realistic waste management option was available.

HR 2036 was reported (H Rept 104-454) by the House Commerce Committee Jan. 30, 1996, and passed by a House vote of 402–19 the next day. The Senate passed the bill by voice vote Feb. 20, after adopting an amendment to strengthen protections for human health. The House agreed to the changes by voice vote March 7, clearing the bill. The president signed it March 26. ❑

Batteries

Congress in 1996 cleared legislation (HR 2024—PL 104-142) to phase out the use of mercury in batteries and establish new labeling requirements for rechargeable batteries.

More than 2.5 billion dry cell batteries were disposed of in the United States each year. Common household batteries generally were made of alkaline-manganese and zinc-carbon, but some, such as ones used in medical, military or computer equipment, also contained mercury. When disposed of in a landfill, the mercury broke down and polluted groundwater; if incinerated, it produced toxic emissions. Rechargeable batteries contained heavy metal nickel-cadmium or lead, also known pollutants.

HR 2024 phased out the use of mercury in most batteries manufactured one year after enactment. It also required manufacturers, within one year of enactment, to label rechargeable batteries as recyclable. After one year, the bill specifically prohibited the sale of rechargeable batteries that did not conform to the standard.

HR 2024 was reported (H Rept 104-530) by the House Commerce Committee April 23, 1996, and passed by voice vote of the House that same day, as part of the GOP's "Earth Week" effort.

The Senate passed the bill April 25, completing congressional action. The president signed the measure May 13. Companion legislation (S 619—S Rept 104-136) had been reported by the Senate Environment and Public Works Committee Aug. 30, 1995, and passed by voice vote of the Senate Sept. 21, 1995. ❑

Conservation on Military Bases

The House on July 11, 1995, passed by voice vote a bill aimed at improving conservation of natural resources at 900 military facilities across the country. The bill (HR 1141) would have reauthorized the Sikes Act for fiscal 1995–1998 at $13.5 million annually.

The Sikes Act of 1960 authorized the Defense and Interior departments to develop plans to manage natural resources at military bases. Under HR 1141, those management plans would have been required, instead of "authorized," and they would have been expanded to include all natural resource management activities, such as restoring and protecting wetlands. The bill also would have required the secretary of defense to submit annual reports to Congress on how well the plans were being carried out.

HR 1141 was reported by the House Resources Committee on May 1, 1995, and by the House National Security Committee on June 1 (H Rept 104-107, Parts I and II). The Senate took no action on the bill. ❑

Underground Storage Tanks

The House passed a bill (HR 3391) in 1995 to expedite federal funding of state efforts to clean up leaking underground storage tanks. HR 3391 proposed to increase the amount of money disbursed by the federal government to the states from the Leaking Underground Storage Tank Trust Fund.

The fund had been established in 1986 to ensure a source of federal assistance to clean up underground tanks that were leaking or had leaked gasoline and other toxic substances. Such leakage could contaminate groundwater and soil, potentially causing substantial health risks. The fund was financed by a 0.1-cent-per-gallon gasoline tax that expired Dec. 1, 1995.

Supporters of the bill said that only $600 million of the $1.7 billion collected since the fund was created had been spent on the program—in part because many states were unaware that the program existed. HR 3391 contained provisions to require the Environmental Protection Agency to give states at least 85 percent of the funds that were annually appropriated to the agency from the trust fund. Other provisions dealt with the allocation and use of the funds.

HR 3391 was reported (H Rept 104-822, Part I) by the House Commerce Committee Sept. 24, 1996, and passed by voice vote of the House the next day. The Senate did not act. ❑

Alaska Oil Exports

Congress agreed to lift a 22-year ban on the export of oil from Alaska's North Slope in legislation cleared in 1995 (S 395—PL 104-58). The bill also required the federal government to sell the Alaska Power Administration, one of five regional authorities that sold electricity generated by federal hydroelectric power plants to public utilities and municipalities. In addition, S 395 exempted certain oil producers from paying royalties in the Gulf of Mexico.

The bill was backed by a broad coalition of Republicans and Democrats who said that lifting the ban on North Slope oil would spur domestic oil production and bring economic relief to a sagging industry. It was also a big win for Alaska's three-member congressional delegation, which had made passage of the legislation a priority.

BACKGROUND

The ban on Alaska oil exports was first enacted in 1973, after an embargo by oil-exporting countries created oil shortages, a loap in gaoolino prioos, and long linoo at gaooline pumps. The ban was put in place to protect domestic supplies and limit U.S. dependence on foreign oil. (*Congress and the Nation Vol. IV, p. 206*)

In recent years, however, there had been a relative glut on the international oil market, leading to lower prices and greater use of foreign oil. In 1994, for the first time, imports met more than half of U.S. domestic demand. The Energy Information Administration forecast that, by 2000, the portion would rise to two-thirds.

In the meantime, production on Alaska's North Slope had entered a period of sustained decline, with flow on the Trans-Alaska pipeline dropping from 2.2 million barrels a day in 1989 to about 1.5 million. Supporters of S 395 said the bill would open markets overseas, creating more demand for Alaska oil and boosting U.S. oil production.

But opponents strongly opposed the bill on the grounds that it would lead to greater dependence on foreign oil, price increases at the pump, and job losses at West Coast refineries that would no longer process Alaskan oil.

Critics also argued that the bill was a first step toward opening the Coastal Plain of Alaska's Arctic National Wildlife Refuge to oil exploration. But such a move was strongly opposed by environmentalists, and the proposal was one of the reasons President Clinton vetoed the 1995 budget reconciliation bill (HR 2491). (*Arctic drilling plan, this page*)

LEGISLATIVE ACTION

The Senate Energy and Natural Resources Committee reported S 395 on April 27, 1995 (S Rept 104-78). As reported, the bill lifted the ban on exporting Alaska North Slope oil and required the sale of the power administration.

The Senate passed the bill, 74–25, on May 16 after adopting by voice vote an amendment by J. Bennett Johnston, D-La., to allow exemptions from government royalties for companies drilling in more than 200 meters, or about 600 feet, in the Gulf of Mexico. To qualify, companies would have to demonstrate that they found it too costly to produce oil without the suspension of royalty payments. The amendment was expected to lead to development of two new fields in the gulf, resulting in approximately 150 million barrels of oil.

The House Resources Committee on June 15 reported a bill to lift the export ban on North Slope oil (HR 70—H Rept 104-139, Part I). The panel on July 13 reported a bill to authorize the sale of the power administration (HR 1122—H Rept 104-187, Part I).

HR 1122 did not come up on the House floor, but the House passed HR 70 on July 24 by a vote of 324–77. During floor action, the House rejected, 95–301, a George Miller, D-Calif., amendment to limit exports of oil to the amount that was being produced at that time but not used by West Coast states and Hawaii. On July 25, the House inserted the text of HR 70 into S 395 and then passed S 395 by voice vote. That same day, the House agreed, 261–161, to a motion by Miller to instruct House conferees not to accept the Senate's royalty exemption for drilling in the Gulf of Mexico.

CONFERENCE, FINAL ACTION

House-Senate conferees agreed on a final bill containing provisions lifting the export ban and providing for the sale of the power administration. The bill also included the controversial provision for royalty exemptions in the Gulf of Mexico, but in a concession to the Florida congressional delegation, the exemption did not apply to drilling off the Gulf Coast of Florida.

When the House took up the conference report Nov. 8 (H Rept 104-312), Miller tried to strip the royalty exemption language from the bill, but his motion was rejected, 160–261. The House then adopted the conference report by a vote of 289–134. The Senate on Nov. 14 approved it, 69–29, clearing the bill. President Clinton signed S 395 into law Nov. 28. ❑

Arctic Drilling Plan

Congress included in the 1995 budget reconciliation bill (HR 2491) a controversial proposal to open a 1.5 million-acre swath of wilderness in the Arctic National Wildlife Refuge (ANWR) to oil and gas drilling. President Clinton vetoed the measure for a number of reasons, including the ANWR provision.

Proponents had been fighting for 15 years to allow drilling in the 75-mile strip along the Alaskan coast, and they thought they had their best chance in years to prevail. Clinton adamantly opposed opening the area of wilderness, known as the Coastal Plain. Even before the reconciliation bill was written, the administration warned that the drilling proposal would provoke a presidential veto.

But Republicans refused to back down and included plans to open the area to drilling in the reconciliation bill. In vetoing the bill, Clinton cited the ANWR proposal among other key objections, saying it would threaten "a unique, pristine ecosystem" that should be preserved permanently.

BACKGROUND

The 19 million-acre Arctic National Wildlife Refuge was created by Congress in 1960. Oil companies and state officials in Alaska had fought for years to open the area to drilling, but environmentalists had prevailed in all previous battles.

In 1980, Congress passed the Alaska National Interest Lands Conservation Act (PL 96-487), which assigned the Interior Department to study exploration and left it to future Congresses to decide about drilling in the Coastal Plain. The rest of the refuge was put off-limits. (*Congress and the Nation Vol. V, p. 577*)

Over the years, proponents of development tried to pass legislation to allow exploration, but they were repeatedly rebuffed by a coalition of Democrats and some Republicans who opposed drilling because of environmental concerns.

The Interior Department sought to open ANWR land for oil drilling in 1987, during the Reagan administration, provoking an outcry from environmentalists and a rebuff from Congress both that year and in 1988. (*Congress and the Nation Vol. VII, p. 476*)

A bill to authorize ANWR drilling suffered the same fate in 1990, and a drilling proposal killed a Senate omnibus energy bill in 1991. (*Congress and the Nation Vol. VIII, pp. 499, 512*)

LEGISLATIVE ACTION

In 1995, unlike in past sessions, the chief GOP proponents of drilling were in positions of power. In the Senate, Frank H. Murkowski, R-Alaska, chaired the Energy and Natural Resources Committee, while in the House, Alaska's Don Young chaired the Resources Committee.

The House Resources Committee on Sept. 19 approved its section of the budget reconciliation bill, including provisions to open the Coastal Plain to oil production. Two days later, the Senate Energy and Natural Resources Committee approved its recommendations, which also included the ANWR provisions.

Republican environmentalists actively lobbied House leaders to take out the provisions before the bill went to the floor. But leaders took a sounding and found that few if any of the Republicans who wanted ANWR out considered it a killer issue by itself. The provisions remained in the bill.

Drilling proponents also defeated an effort to delete the ANWR language from the Senate version of the bill. The Senate voted 51–48 on Oct. 27 to table (kill) an amendment offered by Max Baucus, D-Mont., that would have removed the provision.

The Senate leadership had little flexibility. They needed virtually every Republican to pass the bill, and Murkowski and Ted Stevens, the other GOP senator from Alaska, said they would not vote for a final reconciliation bill that did not contain the drilling language.

Drilling proponents hoped that the ANWR proposal would survive as part of the reconciliation bill. But Clinton vetoed HR 2491 on Dec. 6. *(1995 budget reconciliation bill, p. 68)*   ❏

Nuclear Waste Storage

The Senate in 1996 voted to construct a temporary dump for the nation's high-level radioactive waste in Nevada, but that state's four-member congressional delegation managed to stall the legislation (S 1936) long enough to block final action in the 104th Congress. Companion legislation (HR 1020) had been reported in the House in 1995.

The legislation would have instructed the Department of Energy to establish an interim nuclear waste storage site at the former nuclear testing grounds next to Yucca Mountain, an arid ridge about 100 miles northwest of Las Vegas. Proponents, especially the nuclear energy industry, said building a temporary waste dump was the only way the federal government could meet its obligation to begin disposing of spent nuclear fuel from 110 utility reactors by 1998. A permanent waste repository under study for the same Nevada site, if approved, was not expected to be ready until at least 2010.

The bill had the strong support of the nuclear power industry but was just as adamantly opposed by national environmental groups, as well as Nevadans. Moreover, President Clinton vowed to veto the bill.

Proponents of the interim storage dump were hopeful that Clinton would change his position in the 105th Congress, once the 1996 presidential election was over and Nevada's four Electoral College votes were no longer at stake. But the Energy Department and the White House maintained that no interim site could be approved until scientific studies determined the viability of Yucca Mountain as a long-term waste dump.

Placing a temporary dump there would undermine the integrity of ongoing studies, according to the White House. Should the studies come out in favor of Yucca Mountain as the long-term waste site, the White House argued, opponents would charge that federal scientists were pressured to reach that verdict by the presence of as much as 60,000 metric tons of nuclear waste already on-site. That would make obtaining a license from the Nuclear Regulatory Commission that much more difficult. Already, the Energy Department expected licensing to take years.

BACKGROUND

The 1982 Nuclear Waste Policy Act (PL 97-425) established a national nuclear waste disposal system, giving the Energy Department until 1998 to open a permanent underground repository for high-level nuclear waste. The measure also established the Nuclear Waste Fund, fed by fees imposed on the electricity produced by nuclear utilities, to pay for the project. *(Congress and the Nation Vol. VI, p. 361)*

By the late 1980s, the Energy Department had narrowed its search for a permanent site to three western states: Nevada, Texas and Washington. But with prominent voices in Congress at the time—including House Speaker Jim Wright, D-Texas, and Majority Leader Thomas S. Foley, D-Wash.—Texas and Washington were excluded as possibilities. In 1987, Congress amended the 1982 act, directing the Energy Department to study a single site at Yucca Mountain as a permanent repository. Equally important, the 1987 compromise (PL 100-203) dropped a requirement of the 1982 law that a second repository be built in the East. Even supporters of the deal conceded that Nevada had been a casualty in a raw power play. *(Congress and the Nation Vol. VII, p. 483)*

The 1987 amendments also directed the Energy Department to develop a temporary repository to store nuclear waste until a permanent site was ready. It barred making Nevada the site of both the permanent and interim facilities.

ARGUMENTS PRO AND CON

Proposals put forward in the 104th Congress to build a temporary storage site at Yucca Mountain drew strong opposition from Nevada's congressional delegation, who feared that pressure would only increase for it to become the permanent repository. They pointed to questionable geology and the risk of earthquakes in the Yucca Mountain area. A geological formation, known as the Ghost Dance Fault, was located at the site, although proponents asserted it posed no risk. Opponents also argued that it would be much more prudent to store the waste product on the sites where it was generated, instead of transporting deadly waste to Nevada.

Meanwhile, nuclear utilities insisted that the nation needed to manage nuclear waste at a single, central location. They argued that the viability of the whole industry was at stake because the permanent repository was taking too long to create. They said the mounting costs of dealing with the problem threatened to make nuclear power uncompetitive in the energy market.

Companies with nuclear reactors and rate payers whose electricity was generated through nuclear power had already contributed nearly $12 billion to the Nuclear Waste Fund by 1996, according to the Nuclear Energy Institute. Although $5 billion had been spent on the project, it was well behind schedule. And the companies still had to store their waste.

Most of the waste in question was stored at pools of water at the 110 plants. But by 1998, 26 reactors were expected to have run out of pool space, and by 2001 that number was expected to grow to 80. When those ponds filled up, the waste had to be carefully loaded into casks and stored on sites that were basically parking lots.

LEGISLATIVE ACTION

The House Commerce Committee reported HR 1020 Sept. 20, 1995 (H Rept 104-254, Part I). The bill proposed to amend the Nuclear Waste Policy Act to require the Energy Department to build and open a temporary storage facility at Yucca Mountain by 1998, while proceeding to develop and build a permanent repository there by 2010, generally following a timetable set by the department in 1994. The bill also proposed to create a more stable funding source by replacing the Nuclear Waste Fund with an annual user fee on utilities that would be adjusted to match annual appropriations.

The Senate Energy and Natural Resources Committee reported a nuclear waste storage bill (S 1271—S Rept 104-248) on March 29, 1996. The committee bill provided for Yucca Mountain to become an interim storage site, even if the secretary of energy determined it would never become the permanent repository.

Nevada's Democratic senators—Richard H. Bryan and Harry Reid—waged an often lonely battle for more than three months to keep the legislation off the floor. But the Senate voted 65–34 on July 16 to break the Nevadans' filibuster and take up a revised bill (S 1936).

The Senate passed S 1936 on July 31 by a vote of 63–37. The new bill included changes to accommodate some criticisms of S 1271, as well as provisions aimed at matching language in the companion House bill in hopes of speeding final action.

As a concession to opponents, S 1936 proposed to delay construction of the temporary site at Yucca Mountain until Dec. 31, 1998, the date by which the 1982 law stipulated that the federal government had to assume control of spent fuel rods from the civilian reactors. Under the new version, the energy secretary could halt construction of the temporary site if the president determined that Yucca Mountain was unsuitable for a long-term storage site.

Further concessions were made in a substitute amendment, offered by Senate Energy Committee Chairman Frank H. Murkowski, R-Alaska, and adopted July 31 by a vote of 86–12. The amendment stipulated that nuclear waste shipping routes avoid heavily populated and environmentally sensitive areas. It also gave the Environmental Protection Agency authority to protect the public from radiation releases and instructed the Energy Department to draft an environmental impact statement on the project.

The bill included a provision that said the bill would preempt any law with which it conflicted, a provision critics said would effectively gut environmental protections. A Bryan amendment to require compliance with all federal laws and regulations in development of the temporary site and to strike from the bill language specifying that the environmental review should not examine any alternative waste sites or means of disposing of nuclear waste was tabled (killed), 73–27 on July 31. Murkowski had warned senators that a comprehensive review would force the Energy Department to study shipping the waste to their states.

Senators July 31 also easily tabled, 83–17, an amendment by Paul Wellstone, D-Minn., to force nuclear utilities to bear all the costs of disposing of waste, unless public health and safety were at risk.

In the waning days of the 104th Congress, House Republican leaders decided against taking up S 1936. The legislation had been expected to pass the House easily, but the 63 votes for passage in the Senate was well short of a veto-proof margin. With the president standing firmly against it, House leaders decided the political costs were not worth passing a symbolic bill. Moreover, by the time bill supporters finagled a vote for Senate passage, little time was left to put the bill on the House floor, much less to try to override a veto. ❑

Energy Department

The Energy Department survived a push by House Republicans in the 104th Congress to close it down. Agency critics proposed to privatize, consolidate or eliminate the department's programs. But Democratic and Republican defenders of the department argued that the concept of centering the government's oversight of the nation's energy policy in a single agency made sense.

The original fiscal 1996 House budget resolution (H Con Res 67) presumed elimination of the department, and House freshmen June 8, 1995, unveiled a proposal to eliminate the department over three years. The proposal drew the immediate support of Senate Majority Leader Bob Dole, R-Kan., House Majority Leader Dick Armey, R-Texas, and House Budget Committee Chairman John R. Kasich, R-Ohio.

But the plan was opposed by appropriators such as John T. Myers, R-Ind., the chairman of the House Appropriations Subcommittee on Energy and Water Development, and Senate Budget Committee Chairman Pete V. Domenici, R-N.M. The department also enjoyed strong support among Democrats, who saw everything from its nuclear waste cleanup programs to its energy research as valuable government functions.

BACKGROUND

First created in 1977 under President Jimmy Carter in the wake of the 1970s energy crisis, the department's mission often appeared unfocused and its management subject to widespread criticism. *(Congress and the Nation Vol. V, p. 459)*

During the 1980 presidential campaign, Ronald Reagan pledged to eliminate the agency only a few years after its birth. Reagan specifically wanted to dismantle the bureaucracy, move most of its functions elsewhere and save money. But his 1982 attempt to carry out the proposal was sidetracked by Congress. *(Congress and the Nation Vol. VI, p. 397)*

More recently, the Clinton administration floated a plan to eliminate the department in the wake of the Republican victory in the 1994 midterm elections. In the end, the administration backed away, proposing instead in its fiscal 1996 budget plan to sell off key programs and scale back funding for others such as the nuclear waste cleanup program.

LEGISLATIVE ACTION

During House action on the fiscal 1996 energy and water appropriations bill (HR 1905—PL 104-46), the GOP freshmen decided to hold their fire because they had not had enough time to work out the details of what to do with programs that should be moved to other agencies.

The department, however, did not emerge unscathed. The final bill provided about $15.4 billion of the nearly $16.5 billion requested for the agency. This was approximately $650 million more than in the House bill and $850 million less than in the Senate version. Deep cuts were made in the energy supply, research, and development account, with the final bill providing $2.7 billion of the $3.4 billion requested.

In the fiscal 1997 energy and water development appropriations bill (HR 3816—PL 104-206), Congress increased Energy Department funding to $15.8 billion. President Clinton had requested $16.2 billion. ❑

Helium Reactor

Congress in 1995 voted to eliminate the gas turbine modular helium reactor, an experimental alternative to conventional nuclear reactors, during action on the fiscal 1996 energy and water development appropriations bill (HR 1905—PL 104-46).

The Energy Department, which had opposed the reactor, estimated that taxpayers had spent more than $900 million in the past 25 years in unsuccessful attempts to develop a technology that would burn excess weapons-grade plutonium.

The House on July 11, 1995, voted 306–121 for a Scott L. Klug, R-Wis., amendment to eliminate funding for the reactor. The Senate on Aug. 1 adopted, 62–38, a Dale Bumpers, D-Ark., amendment to terminate the project.

During the 103rd Congress, the Senate had attempted to kill the project but the House had saved it. *(1993 action, p. 435)* ❑

Hydrogen Research

Congress in 1996 cleared legislation (HR 4138—PL 104-271) to boost spending for research into the use of hydrogen as an alternative energy source. The bill called for $164.5 million in spending for hydrogen research over six years, up from an an-

nual level of $10 million. The proposed amounts were $14.5 million in fiscal 1996, $20 million in fiscal 1997, $25 million for fiscal 1998, $30 million for fiscal 1999, $35 million for fiscal 2000 and $40 million for fiscal 2001.

HR 4138 also authorized a total of $50 million for fiscal years 1997 and 1998 to fund projects to prove the feasibility of integrating fuel cells with hydrogen production systems. At least 50 percent of the funding for a demonstration project was to come from nonfederal sources, although the energy secretary could waive the requirement.

The House passed HR 4138 by voice vote Sept. 26, 1996, and the Senate followed suit Sept. 28, clearing the bill. The president signed it Oct. 9.

An earlier version (HR 655—H Rept 104-95) had been reported by the House Science Committee March 30, 1995, and passed by voice vote of the full House May 2. The Senate Energy and Natural Resources Committee reported an amended bill Sept. 13, 1996. HR 655 would have authorized $100 million over three years, while freezing authorizations for a number of other energy supply research programs. ❑

U.S. Enrichment Corporation

The House Commerce Committee on March 23, 1995, reported a bill to allow the sale of the United States Enrichment Corporation (HR 1216—H Rept 104-86). The wholly owned government corporation supplied enriched uranium for use in civilian nuclear power plants in the United States and 11 foreign countries, as well as for other government needs, including defense.

No further action was taken on HR 1216. But provisions of the bill were included in the package of tax cuts (HR 1215) passed by the House April 5. Similar language was subsequently included in the budget reconciliation bill (HR 2491) that President Clinton vetoed Dec. 6. *(Tax bill, p. 98; reconciliation bill, p. 68)*

The 1992 Energy Policy Act (PL 102-486) that established the corporation created a framework for its privatization by the late 1990s. Clinton backed such a sale, calling in his budget for privatizing the corporation in fiscal 1996 at an estimated gain to the government of $1.5 billion. The proposal also drew support from Republican leaders, who were eager to privatize a number of government programs. *(1992 act, Congress and the Nation Vol. VIII, p. 508)* ❑

Nuclear Weapons Waste

The House Commerce Committee on April 25, 1996, reported legislation (HR 1663—H Rept 104-540, Part I) designed to speed up the opening of the Waste Isolation Pilot Plant (WIPP) in Carlsbad, N.M., to store nuclear waste from the nation's weapons industry. The bill, however, advanced no further.

HR 1663 sought to remove some of the regulatory hurdles that had kept the WIPP closed four years after its completion. It included provisions to exempt the site from disposal regulations with regard to low-level transuranic waste found at defense plants that could be absorbed into gloves, clothing and machinery.

To head off opposition from Democrats concerned that the bill was an attempt to circumvent environmental laws, HR 1663 was amended to give the Environmental Protection Agency a greater role in certifying health and safety requirements at the facility. The original bill would have given virtually all such functions to the Energy Department.

Electric Power Deregulation

Members of Congress and the White House in 1996 began gearing up for what was expected to be the next big deregulatory fight: reshaping the electric power industry, the last major government-sanctioned monopoly.

Opponents argued that no public clamor existed for a radical overhaul of the nation's power system, which they considered the best in the world. But economists, power producers and many energy experts viewed competition as the key to lower energy costs and efficiency improvements at complacent utilities. Large industrial users who paid a significant price for their electrical power stood to benefit hugely.

Talk of introducing competition into the electricity industry had been around since the 1970s. The idea caught fire after the Federal Energy Regulatory Commission (FERC), the regulatory body responsible for monitoring interstate electricity transmission, on April 24, 1996, issued a landmark ruling (Order 888) requiring public utilities to open their power lines to any electric generating company willing to pay a fair transmission cost. That cleared the major technical impediment to true competition. States quickly began to act. As a result, state legislators confronted federal impediments to their efforts.

More than half a dozen bills to partially deregulate electricity and introduce retail competition were offered in the 104th Congress. At stake was the fate of a $208 billion electric generating transmission and marketing industry, larger than the automotive industry, larger than telecommunications.

The Public Utilities Holding Company Act of 1935, enacted to prevent the U.S. power supply from being concentrated in a few corporate hands, hamstrung the ability of major investor-owned utilities to compete in a free market. The Public Utility Regulatory Policies Act of 1978, designed to spark the development of alternative energy supplies, saddled utilities with unprofitable generating facilities. A federal role was still likely to be needed to govern competitive interstate electricity transmission

and to monitor pricing. Moreover, whether states could order retail competition in their electricity markets was not legally clear. Some utilities, seeking to block or slow state efforts, contended that FERC's transmission access ruling gave federal regulators control over all electricity distribution.

The Energy Department began a series of public meetings Oct. 10, 1996, to prepare to draft the administration's restructuring legislation. The White House also wanted to ensure that the development of renewable energy resources, such as solar and wind power, would continue, that deregulation would not trigger increased air pollution, and that low-income Americans would be protected.

The Energy Department did not want a mandate on states to open their markets to competition, but providing such a mandate appeared to be the GOP bottom line. For example, HR 3790, introduced by House Commerce Subcommittee on Energy and Power Chairman Dan Schaefer, R-Colo., would give the states until Dec. 15, 2000, to implement retail competition. If they failed, FERC would do it for them. HR 4297, sponsored by Majority Whip Tom DeLay, R-Texas, would move that deadline forward to Jan. 1, 1998.

The only electric power deregulation bill that moved in the 104th Congress was one pushed by the utilities. The Senate Banking, Housing, and Urban Affairs Committee Sept. 9, 1996, reported S 1317 (S Rept 104-365) to free utilities to enter new energy markets while maintaining their monopoly over electricity consumers. S 1317, sponsored by Committee Chairman Alfonse M. D'Amato, R-N.Y., called for repealing the 1935 law, which restricted investment activity by multistate utility companies and was enforced by the Securities and Exchange Commission (SEC). Bill supporters said the evolution of the utility industry and increased regulation by FERC and state public utility commissions had rendered the 1935 law obsolete. Repealing it, they said, would give public utility holding companies more flexibility to invest in other companies and respond to changing consumer demands and market conditions.

The bill would transfer primary responsibility for regulating utilities from the SEC to FERC and state public utility commissions. To protect consumers, FERC and state regulators would get the authority to review all the records of a public utility holding company to ensure that rates were set fairly and that consumers did not foot the bill for the company's investment ventures. Senate Banking amended the bill to delay the implementation until 18 months after enactment, instead of one year after enactment. ❑

CHAPTER 8

Agricultural Policy

Agricultural Policy

Change in U.S. agricultural policy began slowing during Bill Clinton's first year at the White House. Signs had been evident that some change was in the offing. Congress had steadily nicked away at agriculture funding in deficit-reduction measures and in the previous two omnibus farm bills. As a result, farm spending had declined an average of 9 percent annually since 1985.

In 1993 the Clinton administration convinced Congress to go along with further reductions in spending and the curtailment of the smallest farm subsidy programs—for honey, wool and mohair producers—that had been widely criticized as boondoggles benefiting handfuls of commodity producers. Congress also agreed to cut some price supports for wheat and feed grain, and reduce low-cost electrification loans to farmers in rural areas.

In 1994 the White House lead again by applying the administration's "reinventing government" plan to the U.S. Department of Agriculture (USDA)—long criticized as the most bloated and inefficient in the federal bureaucracy. Congress enacted landmark legislation to restructure the department by cutting thousands of staff positions, by combining or eliminating redundant programs and by cutting or merging more than 1,000 of the department's field offices across the country.

In 1995 and 1996, however, the initiative on agricultural policy passed to the other end of Pennsylvania Avenue as the 104th Congress worked on legislation to reverse long-standing New Deal-era farm policies. In 1996 Congress passed, and Clinton reluctantly signed, the omnibus farm bill—historic legislation that greatly deregulated farm programs and replaced the existing system of government subsidies with fixed but declining payments.

FREEDOM TO FARM

"Freedom to Farm" was the name given to the historic legislation that allowed farmers to plant what they wanted and as much as they wanted, while still receiving government payments. The concept sounded simple and straightforward enough. But, it was radical, reversing decades-old policies of protective intervention by the federal government.

The Republican victory in the 1994 congressional elections made sweeping change possible. The new House majority leader, Dick Armey, R-Texas, was a leading critic of government intervention in the farm economy. Richard G. Lugar, R-Ind., the new Senate Agriculture Committee chairman and a farm manager, and Pat Roberts, R-Kan., new chairman of the House Agriculture Committee, also believed that farmers would be better off without government regulations. And many in the Republi-

can rank and file said they preferred to let the free market work its will in agricultural America.

Farm programs still had staunch defenders in Congress. Many Democrats were fierce advocates of the government's traditional safety net for farmers. The Republicans, however, had the votes.

DEBATE OVER NEW DEAL-ERA PROGRAMS

The goal of the farm policies was to shield farmers from the vagaries of weather and the marketplace, thereby keeping them in business and assuring the country of a stable food supply. Nonetheless, by the 1990s, analysts were debating whether the programs still were doing much good.

On the positive side, the programs had helped make commodities so accessible that Americans paid only about 10 percent of their disposable income for food. That was virtually the lowest rate of any nation in the world, although part of the reason was the high level of American income, instead of the low cost of food, according to the Congressional Research Service.

Growers, aided by government-sponsored research and more consolidated farm operations, were becoming increasingly efficient. Each farmer and rancher produced enough food and fiber by the mid-1990s to feed 129 other people, compared with just 19 in 1940.

The United States was expected to export nearly $50 billion in agricultural products by the mid-1990s, generating an estimated $20 billion trade surplus. In addition, the government was spreading goodwill by donating food to famine-ravaged countries.

The farm economy, which suffered wild swings and massive bankruptcies in the early and mid-1980s, was back on solid

REFERENCES

Discussion of agricultural policy for the years 1945–1964 may be found in *Congress and the Nation Vol. I*, pp. 665–767; for the years 1965–1968, *Congress and the Nation Vol. II*, pp. 555–597; for the years 1969–1972, *Congress and the Nation Vol. III*, pp. 331–352; for the years 1973–1976, *Congress and the Nation Vol. IV*, pp. 717–740; for the years 1977–1980, *Congress and the Nation Vol. V*, pp. 365–395; for the years 1981–1984, *Congress and the Nation Vol. VI*, pp. 485–516; for the years 1985–1988, *Congress and the Nation Vol. VII*, pp. 499–539; for the years 1989–1992, *Congress and the Nation Vol. VIII*, pp. 535–557.

Outlays for Agriculture

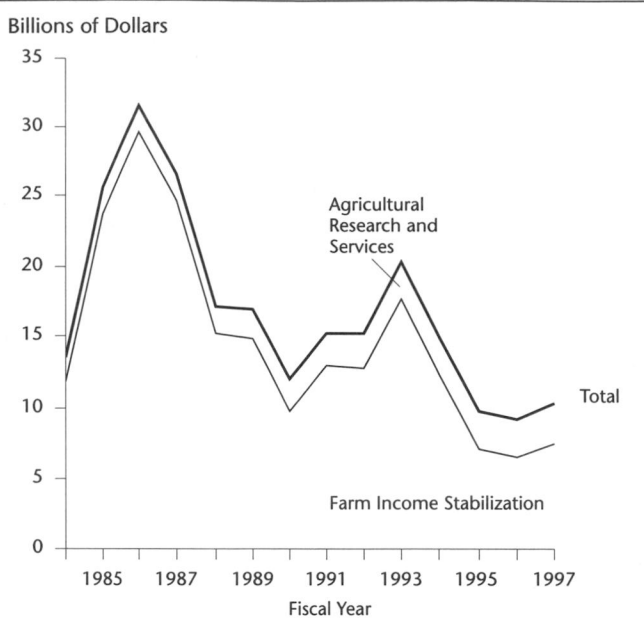

Billions of Dollars

Agricultural Research and Services

Total

Farm Income Stabilization

Fiscal Year

1985 1987 1989 1991 1993 1995 1997

NOTE: Data for 1997 are estimated.

SOURCE: Office of Management and Budget, *Historical Tables, Budget of the United States Government: Fiscal Year 1998* (Washington, D.C.: U.S. Government Printing Office, 1997), Table 3.2.

footing. Between 1985 and 1994, total farm equity reached $772 billion, an increase of about 30 percent. Armed with such statistics, backers strongly praised the farm programs. Agriculture Secretary Dan Glickman in 1995 characterized them as "the extraordinary success story of American agriculture."

But a downside attracted the attention of powerful business groups, government auditors and members of Congress. Critics said that, far from helping family farmers, the programs had squeezed them to the point where farmers constituted less than 2 percent of the population in the 1990s, compared with 25 percent in the 1930s.

The subsidies primarily benefited large landowners, some of whom exploited loopholes to earn hundreds of thousands of dollars in government payments every year, according to groups such as the Progressive Foundation, a public policy center affiliated with moderate Democrats. This had the effect of distorting land values, enriching farmers who already had an average net worth of $300,000 or more, and undermining the family farmers who were the original beneficiaries of the depression-era programs.

Furthermore, the programs were driving up the price of commodities such as peanuts and sugar, according to General Accounting Office estimates. As a result, taxpayers, already footing the bill for federal farm programs, were getting hit a second time at the supermarket checkout line.

Analysts with the U.S. Chamber of Commerce also warned that the programs were undercutting American exports by requiring farmers to set aside land and plant the rest with crops supported by government programs, instead of those that were in demand overseas.

Even though consumer advocates and urban liberals heaped scorn on the farm programs, perhaps the harshest rhetoric of all came from free-market conservatives. House Majority Leader Armey in 1995 denounced the "staggering waste and inefficiency" of the programs, likening them to failed Soviet attempts to control supply and demand.

RADICAL OVERHAUL

By the mid-1990s, because of a chance combination of poor weather in the Midwest and conservatism in Washington, the payment scheme was facing a radical overhaul. Much of the country's agricultural heartland had been plagued with devastating weather in 1995, including frosts in early spring, flooding during the traditional late spring planting period and an abnormally dry summer. The resulting poor yields had sent commodity prices skyrocketing because supplies were unusually low. Yet many farmers had too little grain to make a profit from the markets. Far from getting any money from the government, the farmers would have to repay advance deficiency payments that they had received in the spring, when analysts predicted lower market prices.

The situation was feeding farmer discontent with government programs, which already had come under criticism for restricting planting flexibility. At the same time, free-market conservatives in Congress such as Armey were trying to scale back the subsidies. To spur their budget-cutting efforts, they also insisted that any future subsidies be capped if commodity prices plunged dramatically.

To satisfy both farmers and congressional conservatives, Roberts introduced the Freedom to Farm Act in August 1995. In general, his bill proposed to guaranteed payments, on a gradually diminishing scale, to farmers regardless of market conditions or planting decisions. The bill also proposed to end the practice of encouraging farmers to idle land. Congress attempted to incorporate Roberts's plan in 1995 deficit reduction legislation, but that bill fell to President Clinton's veto.

Roberts and his supporters renewed their efforts in the next session. Congress was under enormous pressure to pass a farm bill because programs authorized by the 1990 farm bill had started to expire and laws from the 1930s and 1940s that were still on the books were about to become the law of the land once again. Congress moved quickly and, with the support of many farmers and agribusiness interests, the 1996 Freedom to Farm bill was enacted into law.

Many Democrats denounced the new system, insisting that the fixed payments would award farmers too much in flush times, while unraveling the traditional safety net when prices dropped. They also argued that the bill would help well-moneyed grain traders, at the expense of small farmers, by boosting commodity supplies and reducing prices. President Clinton signed the bill but said he would propose legislation to strengthen the farm safety net. And Democratic opponents vowed to repeal the bill when they won enough seats in Congress.

Chronology of Action on Agriculture

1993–1994

Congress typically revisits the complex and arcane agricultural laws every five years, but the off-years of 1993 and 1994 brought several significant changes in agricultural policy.

Congress signaled that popular and well-protected farms programs were not sacrosanct. With the mounting budget crisis, members realized that farm programs could no longer be funded as generously as they had been. The change in attitudes helped give impetus to President Clinton's proposals to reduce agriculture spending. While lawmakers did not go along with all of his suggestions, Clinton enjoyed more success in this area than his two predecessors, Ronald Reagan and George Bush. By the end of 1993, members had agreed to cut some price supports to wheat and feed grain farmers, reduce low-cost electrification loans to farmers in rural areas, abolish price supports for honey and kill the subsidies for wool and mohair production.

The Clinton administration and the 103rd Congress also tackled the formidable job of fixing a U.S. Department of Agriculture (USDA) bureaucracy that had been widely criticized as one of the most overgrown and redundant in the federal government. Landmark legislation was enacted to realign and downsize USDA. The measure was based on an administration proposal promoted as the first sweeping effort to reform a cabinet department under the "reinventing government" plan.

A Clinton-proposed bill to remake the Federal Crop Insurance Corporation, the Agriculture Department agency that provided subsidized policies to farmers to cover catastrophic crop losses, was also enacted into law. Its aim was to increase farmer participation in the program and reduce the need for ad hoc federal disaster assistance, such as that provided in 1993 to aid victims of massive flooding in the upper Midwest.

These major reforms were shepherded through the legislative process by Clinton's first secretary of agriculture, Mike Espy. But Espy had little time to savor his legislative victories. Under investigation on charges of financial irregularities, he resigned at the end of 1994.

USDA Reorganization

Congress in 1994 cleared legislation (HR 4217—PL 103-354) to streamline and reduce the size of the U.S. Department of Agriculture (USDA). The overhaul provisions, modeled closely after a Clinton administration proposal introduced more than a year earlier, required wholesale changes in the operations of one of the largest and most criticized departments in the federal government.

The bill wrote into law Agriculture Secretary Mike Espy's goal of eliminating 7,500 USDA staff positions within five years and specifically authorized the agriculture secretary to eliminate or merge more than 1,000 of the department's field offices across the country.

The centerpiece of the bill's farm-related provisions was the creation of a Consolidated Farm Service Agency through the merger of the department's major farm subsidy, farm lending and crop insurance programs. The goal in creating this omnibus agency was to provide one-stop shopping for farmers who previously had to visit separate agency offices to participate in Agriculture Department programs.

The final bill consolidated most of the department's conservation programs into a new Natural Resources Conservation Service. But to placate members who feared that the plan would give environmentalists too much influence over conservation policy and result in new, burdensome restrictions on farmers' land use, the bill also required cost-benefit analyses of proposed USDA regulations with an expected national economic impact of more than $100 million annually.

The changes in the bill were hailed by government watchdog groups, deficit hawks and agricultural organizations, which said that the department had grown too cumbersome and difficult for farmers and agribusiness companies to work with. With cost savings and government streamlining on the minds of both parties in Congress, the bill's enactment had been widely anticipated.

Yet the dispute over merging the conservation programs stalled the reorganization plan for months, and the bill's path was so convoluted that it ended up being cleared as part of separate legislation that contained another of the administration's top agriculture policy priorities: an overhaul of the federal crop insurance program. (*Crop insurance overhaul, p. 483*)

BACKGROUND

From its founding in 1862 until the 1930s, the Agriculture Department was a relatively small cabinet department that focused its efforts on research and on providing information to farmers on the latest agricultural techniques and technology.

But the 1930s brought the Great Depression and President Franklin D. Roosevelt's New Deal programs to provide farmers with an economic safety net. Over the ensuing 60 years, Agriculture expanded into a huge bureaucracy that not only issued income and price-support subsidies to farmers but also managed a variety of soil, water and forest conservation programs; provided food and nutrition support for millions of low-income Americans; and promoted the use of U.S. farm commodities in both domestic and foreign markets.

By the early 1990s, the Agriculture Department had an annual budget of more than $60 billion and more than 111,000 employees, who were located in its hulking headquarters facility that spanned Constitution Avenue in downtown Washington, dozens of other facilities in the Capital region and thousands of field offices, with at least one located in nearly every county in the United States.

The department also faced a growing number of critics who said it was overgrown with too many employees, underused facilities and "alphabet soup" agencies with overlapping jurisdictions that created confusion for citizens participating in the department's farm or food subsidy programs. The General Accounting Office (GAO) issued a report in 1991 calling for a complete overhaul of the department. The *Kansas City Star* won a Pulitzer Prize that same year for uncovering instances of waste, fraud, abuse and discrimination in department activities.

Proposals for streamlining the department emerged on Capitol Hill and within the Bush administration, but, with the turnover in the White House, the issue was left to the Clinton administration to resolve. (*Congress and the Nation Vol. VIII, box, p. 556*)

When Vice President Al Gore on Sept. 7, 1993, unveiled the administration's overall plan to "reinvent government," Secretary Espy was the only cabinet chief ready with a comprehensive reorganization plan. (*'Reinventing government,' p. 811*)

ADMINISTRATION PROPOSAL

Espy's plan called for eliminating and merging more than a dozen Agriculture Department agencies, reducing the total from 43 to 30 or fewer. Espy said the plan would result in budget savings—mainly from his projected 7,500-person work force reduction—of $2.3 billion over five years.

Espy called for the creation of a Farm Service Agency, merging the farm subsidy programs of the department's Agricultural Stabilization and Conservation Service, the farm-lending programs of the Farmers Home Administration and the disaster assistance programs of the Federal Crop Insurance Corporation. He said the change would make the department more farmer-friendly by providing a single office to handle multiple programs.

He also proposed to create a Natural Resources Conservation Service to consolidate environmental conservation programs, which were managed mainly by the Agricultural Stabilization and Conservation Service and the Soil Conservation Service. This new agency and the Forest Service were to be overseen by an assistant secretary for natural resources and environment.

Espy sought to merge the county committees that carried out the farm subsidy and lending programs at the local level. He also proposed giving the agriculture secretary authority to appoint some of the members of what were then farmer-elected committees, to bring in people with expertise in areas such as law and science, as well as to increase the committees' racial and gender diversity.

SENATE ACTION

The Senate easily approved legislation (S 1970) tailored after Espy's plan. S 1970 was reported by the Senate Agriculture, Nutrition and Forestry Committee (S Rept 103-241) on March 24, 1994, and was passed by a 98–1 vote of the full Senate on April 13.

The Senate bill proposed to consolidate all USDA conservation programs into a new service, but it left the local management of the programs to the county committees that would also oversee the farm subsidy programs. The bill upheld the status quo by maintaining separate committees to oversee the farm subsidy and lending programs and rejected as well Espy's proposal to allow the agriculture secretary to appoint members.

HOUSE ACTION

In contrast to the Senate, House action was delayed for months. The House Agriculture Subcommittee on Department Operations and Nutrition initially approved a bill (HR 3171) on Feb. 8, 1994, but the full committee did not report the measure (H Rept 103-714) until Aug. 23. A supplemental report (H Rept 103-714, Part II) was filed on Sept. 21, and the full House passed the bill by voice vote Sept. 28. The House then inserted its text into S 1970 and passed the amended Senate bill by voice vote.

The proposal to merge most USDA conservation programs disrupted the Agriculture Committee's usually strong bipartisan consensus concerning farms issues. The administration aimed to increase the efficiency of and eliminate duplication in department activities. But some members feared that the proposed office would become a mini-Environmental Protection Agency within the Agriculture Department that would exacerbate the regulatory burden on farmers.

House Agriculture Committee Chairman E. "Kika" de la Garza, D-Texas, delayed action in hopes of finding a compromise but went ahead with markup when efforts at a compromise failed. The committee rejected a Wayne Allard, R-Colo., proposal to place the Soil Conservation Service within the Farm Service Agency instead of the new conservation service, but it did agree to an amendment offered by Gary A. Condit, D-Calif., to require the Agriculture Department to set up an agency to conduct cost-benefit analyses of any proposed regulation affecting health, safety or the environment.

Condit's amendment had significance beyond the Agriculture reorganization bill. Conservative Republicans and Democrats had argued for years that federal agencies failed to measure the expected benefits of a regulation against the costs that the regulation imposed on individuals, businesses and the economy in general. During the 103rd Congress, this coalition fought on several fronts to get legislation enacted that would require bureaucrats to do cost-benefit calculation.

The inclusion of Condit's amendment in turn caused a reaction among environmentalist members, who viewed the cost-benefit issue as a scheme by prodevelopment members to bog down the regulatory process and place a spurious price tag on human life, health and safety. Their opposition again delayed progress on the bill until close to the end of the 103rd Congress.

Months of additional negotiations on the conservation issue produced a compromise that was largely a victory for those who wanted to require cost-benefit analyses. The language of the Condit provision was modified to apply only to regulations that were expected to have a national economic impact of more than $100 million annually. The agreement allowed the House to pass the bill.

The only other significant change made to HR 3171 during House floor debate dealt with the department's county committees. The House approved an amendment by de la Garza to bar the agriculture secretary from merging farmer-elected county committees unless the local farmers voted for such a merger. An identical amendment had been rejected in committee.

In its only recorded vote during consideration of the bill, the House on Sept. 28 rejected, 177–247, an Allard amendment that would have blocked the creation of a new Agriculture Service Agency to consolidate the USDA crop subsidy, farm lending and crop insurance programs.

FINAL ACTION

While the reorganization bill was stalled in the House, Senate supporters grew increasingly concerned about the legislation's prospects. Seeking to get the attention of their House counterparts, they attached S 1970 to a separate bill (HR 4217) to overhaul the federal crop insurance program. The action was approved by the Senate Aug. 25 by voice vote, as was HR 4217 as a whole.

Although the House finally passed S 1970 on Sept. 28, Congress moved ahead on the Agriculture reorganization and crop insurance bill, HR 4217.

With barely a week left before the planned adjournment date of Oct. 7, leaders of the House and Senate Agriculture committees held an informal conference to resolve differences between the two chambers' reorganization bills. The House approved the revised HR 4217 by voice vote Oct. 3. The Senate followed suit, also by voice vote, clearing the bill the next day.

MAJOR PROVISIONS

As signed into law on Oct. 13, the reorganization portion of HR 4217:

• Placed most land and water conservation programs under a new Natural Resources Conservation Service. It required cost-benefit analyses of proposed Agriculture Department regulations with an expected national economic impact of more than $100 million annually.

• Created a Consolidated Farm Service Agency by merging the agencies that had managed the USDA major farm subsidy, farm lending and crop insurance programs.

• Required the Agriculture Department to reduce total employment by 7,500 staff positions over the ensuing five years.

• Specifically authorized the agriculture secretary to close or consolidate more than 1,000 Agriculture Department field offices.

• Required that staff reductions be proportionately higher in the Washington department headquarters than in the field offices.

• Separated the department's meat inspection and food safety responsibilities from its food marketing functions, and elevated the prominence of the inspection activities by placing them under the new position of undersecretary for food safety.

• Established a National Appeals Division to handle appeals by farm program participants of decisions by Agriculture Department agencies.

• Gave the agriculture secretary full authority to merge existing county committees. The bill also directed the department to encourage ethnic, gender and racial diversity on the county committees, and the bill required the GAO to study whether minority group members were underrepresented on those committees.   ❑

AGRICULTURE LEADERSHIP

The Senate confirmed former Democratic representative Mike Espy of Mississippi as secretary of agriculture by voice vote on Jan. 21, 1993. Espy, who had served for six years in the House (1987–1993), was the first African American and the first person from the Deep South to head the Agriculture Department. *(Background, cabinet profiles, p. 1109)*

But Espy's tenure lasted only long enough for him to see Congress approve his main legislative handiwork, an omnibus bill that combined reorganization of the Agriculture Department with an overhaul of the federal crop insurance program (HR 4217). On Oct. 3, 1994, Espy announced that he would resign his position before the end of 1994, amid an ongoing investigation by an independent counsel and by the White House into his professional conduct. Espy had been shadowed since early in 1994 by allegations that he had accepted trips, sporting tickets and other benefits from agriculture interests regulated by the Agriculture Department, including Arkansas-based Tyson Foods Inc., one of the nation's largest poultry producers.

Espy strongly denied suggestions that his acceptance of small corporate gifts influenced his actions as secretary, including an allegation that he had delayed changes to poultry inspection procedures while pushing for immediate improvement of other meat inspection programs. Nonetheless, the Justice Department in September 1994 had appointed Donald C. Smaltz as an independent counsel to investigate the allegations. Espy left office Dec. 31.

Espy was succeeded by his former House colleague Dan Glickman, a nine-term Democratic representative from Kansas (1977–1995) who had been defeated for reelection in 1994. Glickman was confirmed as secretary of agriculture on March 30, 1995, by a 94–0 vote of the Senate. *(Background, cabinet profiles, p. 1109)*

Crop Insurance Overhaul

Congress in 1994 cleared legislation to overhaul the federal crop insurance program. The bill (HR 4217—PL 103-354) closely followed a Clinton administration proposal, which had drawn widespread, bipartisan praise.

The crop insurance program had suffered from persistent financial losses. Farmers generally had eschewed paying what they regarded as high premiums for the federal subsidized insurance and had relied instead on the government to come through with ad hoc disaster relief payments when major crop losses occurred.

Under HR 4217, the revised program eliminated premiums for basic catastrophic-loss coverage, charging each farmer only a processing fee, and gave the government added muscle to get farmers to join the program. At the same time, the bill revoked Congress's authority to enact disaster aid bills without fully funding them.

The final version of HR 4217 contained not only the crop insurance provisions but also language to reorganize the Agriculture Department. Originally proposed separately, the measures—the top two agriculture policy priorities for the Clinton administration and Congress in 1994—were merged to expedite their enactment before the end of the session. *(Agriculture reorganization, p. 481)*

BACKGROUND

The federal crop insurance program was founded in 1938 as a reaction to the devastating Dust Bowl drought, which ruined many farmers. Part of President Franklin D. Roosevelt's New Deal agenda, the program was aimed at providing a financial safety net that would allow farmers to keep their land even in the face of massive crop losses.

Despite its good intentions, the crop insurance program never lived up to its billing. Only about a third of eligible farmers participated in the insurance program. Most farmers said it provided too few benefits at too high a premium cost. Also, Congress showed a tendency that increased over the years to pass supplemental spending bills that provided special aid to farmers who suffered catastrophic crop losses—whether or not they had participated in the crop insurance program.

Congress in 1980 sought to boost program participation by enacting legislation (PL 96-365) that increased crop insurance subsidies to farmers and private insurance companies. But most farmers continued to view the premiums as too high relative to the potential benefits and opted to gamble on Congress providing special assistance when disaster hit. *(Congress and the Nation Vol. V, p. 391)*

As a result, the program turned into a consistent money-loser for the federal government, with benefits paid to insured farmers exceeding the relatively small pool of premiums in most years. On top of those losses, the federal government regularly paid out large sums in supplemental disaster aid. In August 1993, for example, Congress provided $1.1 billion to pay farmers for crop losses as part of a disaster aid supplemental spending bill (HR 2667—PL 103-75) that added $5.7 billion to the federal deficit. *(Disaster aid, p. 490)*

ADMINISTRATION PLAN

Agriculture Secretary Mike Espy on March 3, 1994, outlined the administration's plan to greatly increase farmer participation in the crop insurance program, sharply reduce ad hoc disaster aid spending and restore actuarial soundness to the insurance program. Under the plan, the federal government would ease some of the costs to farmers who signed up for the program but would require farmers receiving federal crop subsidies to take part.

Key to the plan was congressional acceptance of the administration's position that added costs for subsidies and insurance payments under the expanded program would be more than offset by reductions in emergency disaster aid payments, resulting in a net federal savings of $750 million over the new program's first five years.

The funding plan was critical because Congress's budget rules required increased spending in any program to be fully funded. If lawmakers rejected Espy's speculative projection of disaster aid savings as a spending cut, they would have to find

some other way to offset the increased cost of the crop insurance program.

LEGISLATIVE ACTION

The House Agriculture Committee reported a bill (HR 4217—H Rept 103-649) closely following the administration's proposal on Aug. 1, 1994. The House passed the crop insurance bill by voice vote Aug. 5.

House consideration of HR 4217 was dominated by the issue of finances. Debate was precipitated by a separate decision made by the House and Senate Appropriations committees. Although crop insurance payments came out of mandatory spending accounts, the money for salaries and administrative expenses was discretionary spending. To meet their own tight requirements for fiscal 1995, appropriators had slashed that discretionary spending. Because the money was primarily to reimburse the private insurance companies that administered the program, funds had to be found to cover the shortfall or the program would be shut down.

The House Agriculture Committee solved the problem for fiscal 1995 by classifying the spending as mandatory and paying for it with savings from the elimination of emergency disaster aid bills. Appropriators were to finance future administrative expenses out of discretionary spending.

But Timothy J. Penny, D-Minn., proposed to offset the entire cost of administrative expenses, estimated at $586 million over five years, by reducing reimbursements to private insurance agents and lowering the percentage of crop value that would be covered under the basic insurance package. Penny argued that a failure to designate a definite funding source for the administrative costs of the program would leave appropriators with two unfavorable choices in future years: not providing the money, thus killing the program, or making deep cuts in other vital programs.

Penny lost his battle both in committee and on the floor. The House instead on Aug. 5 adopted, 253–156, a substitute amendment offered by Agriculture Committee Chairman E. "Kika" de la Garza, D-Texas, that proposed to pay for crop insurance from mandatory accounts over the first three years after enactment. Although the funding source for the ensuing two years was left uncertain, de la Garza pledged that he would not allow the program to shift back to discretionary accounts. De la Garza's amendment also included provisions aimed at achieving budget savings. The Penny amendment, as amended by the de la Garza substitute, was adopted, 401–1.

The Senate Agriculture, Nutrition and Forestry Committee reported its version of the crop insurance bill (S 2095—S Rept 103-301) on July 1. The full Senate on Aug. 25 passed HR 4217 by voice vote after substituting the text of S 2095.

Unlike the House, the Senate spent little time worrying about the financial aspects of the bill. It readily accepted the administration's position that any additional costs under the bill would be offset by savings in special disaster aid.

But the bill was delayed in the Senate for weeks by Jesse Helms, R-N.C., as he sought to reverse an Agriculture Department decision to demote an employee for publicly denouncing the department's gay rights policies. Helms eventually relented, but he won an amendment barring preemptory removal of any Agriculture employee for comments in opposition to the department's policy on homosexuals and effectively returning the employee in question to his original job. Helms also raised the issue during Senate consideration of the fiscal 1995 agricultural appropriations bill (HR 4554—PL 103-330).

Before passing HR 4217, the Senate attached the text of a separate bill it had passed to reorganize the Agriculture Department (S 1970), in hopes of spurring House action on that matter.

The House concurred with the Senate action to merge the crop insurance and Agriculture reorganization bills into a single measure. House and Senate committee leaders met privately in an informal conference to resolve the few differences between the bills, which were both closely modeled on administration proposals. The negotiators settled on a financing plan for the program that tracked that in the House version.

The House approved the final bill by voice vote Oct. 3. The Senate followed suit the next day, clearing the bill.

MAJOR PROVISIONS

As signed into law on Oct. 13, the crop insurance portion of HR 4217:

• Made participation in the federal crop insurance program mandatory for farmers who took part in federal price-support programs for such major crops as wheat, feed grains, rice, cotton, tobacco, peanuts, oilseed and sugar.

• Barred Congress from designating ad hoc disaster aid bills for crop losses as emergency spending, thereby requiring lawmakers to offset the spending instead of simply adding it to the deficit.

• Provided premium-free basic catastrophic coverage to farmers of major crops. Farmers were to pay only an administrative fee of $50 per crop per county farmed, with maximums of $200 per producer per county and $600 regardless of how many counties the producer farmed.

• Provided for insurance benefits to be paid on crop losses in excess of 50 percent of normal yield at a rate of 60 percent of the expected market price for the crop. The price coverage rate was scheduled to drop to 55 percent beginning with the 1999 crop year.

• Encouraged farmers to purchase additional coverage by increasing subsidies for buy-up policies.

• Allowed farmers to purchase basic catastrophic policies through either private insurers or the Agriculture Department's Federal Crop Insurance Corporation (FCIC). But buy-up policies could be purchased only through private insurers that were reinsured by the FCIC.

• Set up a permanent Agriculture Department disaster aid program for other crops, with an identical benefit formula for the basic catastrophic policy.

• Required a reduction over five years in federal reimbursements to private insurance companies and agents that participated in the crop insurance program. The rate was scheduled to fall from 31 percent in 1995 to 27.5 percent in 1999.

• Provided funding from mandatory spending accounts to cover the crop insurance program's administrative activities in 1995, 1996 and half of 1997, but the bill left uncertain the funding source for activities beyond that point. ❑

Agriculture Program Cuts

Congress included $3.2 billion in cuts to Agriculture Department programs in the 1993 budget reconciliation bill (HR 2264—PL 103-66). President Clinton had recommended $3.8 billion in cuts.

The single largest agriculture savings in HR 2264—$586 million over five years—stemmed from a provision limiting the ability of the agriculture secretary to boost price-support payments as a bargaining chip in negotiations aimed at strengthening the General Agreement on Tariffs and Trade (GATT).

In addition, lawmakers agreed to reduce subsidies paid to farmers who agreed not to plant certain grain crops; to reform crop insurance to reduce fraud and abuse; and to reduce participation in a conservation program that paid farmers not to plant on erodible land.

CLINTON'S PROPOSAL

Clinton called for an end to government subsidies for farmers who earned more than $100,000 in nonfarm income—effectively converting farm programs from universal entitlements to means-tested welfare programs, an idea that was anathema to independent-minded farmers. The administration said the change would save $470 million by fiscal 1997.

Clinton also proposed lopping $2 billion from the $10 billion to $13 billion annual cost of farm subsidies, including cutting the amount of acreage eligible for some crop subsidies for wheat, feed grains, cotton and rice; eliminating a program that paid farmers to idle most or all of their land; and increasing the assessments on farmers of nongrain crops, such as soybeans, sugar and tobacco, which did not qualify for subsidies but were protected through price-support loans.

Many of Clinton's cost-saving proposals hewed closely to ideas that were proposed during the Reagan and Bush administrations—and that were routinely ignored by Congress. For example, Clinton wanted to revamp the Rural Electrification Administration (REA) loan program so that the REA would charge its borrowers usual Treasury Department interest rates instead of rates as low as 2 percent.

LEGISLATIVE ACTION

Democratic members of the House and Senate Agriculture committees found themselves caught between the need to help Clinton find the savings he needed to get his proposals through Congress and their longtime loyalty to the farming community.

When the House Agriculture Committee marked up the legislation May 13, 1993, members rejected the most controversial cost-cutting suggestions in Clinton's plan and opted instead for a $3 billion deficit-reduction package designed to avoid hitting farmers' pocketbooks directly. The House later approved the agriculture provisions, unchanged, when it passed the budget reconciliation bill, 219–213, on May 27. *(1994 budget reconciliation, p. 44)*

The bulk of the savings in the House bill came from expanding the triple-base program, which limited the land on which farmers could grow the major subsidized crops of wheat, corn, cotton and feedgrains, while still protecting a farmer's base acreage for future planting decisions. Under the program, farmers could plant a portion of the idled land (so-called flex-acres) with other nonsubsidized crops that were in demand at no penalty if they wanted to return the flex-acres to subsidized crops in future years. The flex-acre option was expected to induce farmers to forgo planting subsidized crops on those acres, thus reducing the subsidy cost to the government.

Other provisions in the House bill included changes in the Conservation Reserve Program, which paid farmers not to plant crops on land vulnerable to erosion; policy changes to the REA, including higher loan costs; a Clinton administration proposal to increase spending for the federal food stamp program by $7.29 billion over five years; and a reauthorization of all commodity programs through fiscal 1998.

The Senate Agriculture Committee approved a $3.2 billion package of spending cuts, which the full Senate incorporated into its version of the budget reconciliation bill (S 1134). The Senate passed HR 2264, 50–49, on June 25 (in the session that began June 24), after substituting the text of S 1134.

The largest single component of savings in the Senate-passed measure came from eliminating a provision of law that permitted the agriculture secretary to boost price-support payments to grain farmers should European and other nations refuse to cooperate on reducing farm subsidies as part of the GATT talks. The Congressional Budget Office estimated that, if the Agriculture Department used its authority once in the following four years, the cost in additional corn subsidies would be $586 million.

The Senate achieved savings in commodity programs by reducing the size of payments to farmers who agreed not to plant certain subsidized grain crops. Under the so-called 0/92 program—designed to control the supply of grains—farmers were paid 92 percent of their allotted subsidies if they decided not to plant. The Senate measure reduced payments to wheat and feed grain farmers to 85 percent of their expected subsidies.

The Senate bill required cigarette manufacturers to report their use of imported tobacco and to institute a fee for cigarette manufacturers who used more than 25 percent imported tobacco in their products. The committee version would have imposed a one-year moratorium on sales of milk from cows that had been injected with bovine somatotropin (bST), a synthetic growth hormone, but on June 24 the full Senate voted 38–60 on a procedural motion to strip the bovine hormone provision from the bill.

FINAL ACTION

House and Senate conferees on HR 2264 (H Rept 103-213) generally followed the Senate's lead in cutting agriculture programs. They reduced payments to wheat and feed grain farmers under the 0/92 program, saving an estimated $300 million over

five years, and opted against the House changes to the triple base program. Conferees also agreed with the Senate's proposals to eliminate the so-called GATT trigger and to institute a fee for cigarette manufacturers who used imported tobacco. The final bill barred manufacturers of bST from marketing the hormone for 90 days after any Food and Drug Administration (FDA) approval of the chemical. (The FDA approved bST for use later in the year.)

The conference bill limited enrollment in the Conservation Reserve Program, as both the House and Senate bills had. It also included a Senate-backed plan to tighten fraud controls and administrative oversight of the Federal Crop Insurance Program.

One of the toughest battles came over House changes to the REA. Conferees adopted a compromise designed by Rep. Glenn English, D-Okla., that allowed rural electric cooperatives to continue providing utility service to rural areas even if those areas were annexed by a nearby municipality that ran its own utility. The language subsequently was stripped from the conference report because of concern that it would spark a procedural challenge in the Senate. Later in 1993, Congress cleared a separate REA bill (HR 3123—PL 103-129). *(REA bill, p. 489)*

A few commodity programs were reauthorized through 1998, though many were not because of fears that the reauthorization provisions would violate the same Senate procedural rules at issue in the REA language.

The final bill expanded the food stamp program at a cost of $2.5 billion over five years, substantially less than the amount approved in the original House bill. *(Food stamp program, p. 575)*

PROVISIONS

As signed into law Aug. 10, the agriculture provisions of HR 2264:

Commodity Programs

• **Cotton: Reauthorization.** Reauthorized certain provisions of the price support programs for upland cotton through the 1997 crop year. The reauthorization excluded cotton skip-row practices, extra-long staple cotton, cottonseed and cottonseed oil support, preliminary allotments for the 1998 cotton crop, suspension of marketing quotas and acreage allotments, and the suspension of parity-based price supports, which had to be addressed in 1995. Other commodity programs also had to be reauthorized in 1995.

• **Cotton: Deficiency Payments.** Pared a program that paid farmers to limit their crops to help the government control supply. The so-called 50/92 and 0/92 programs guaranteed farmers 92 percent of their annual deficiency payments or subsidies when producers opted to set aside all or half of their acreage for some alternative crops or conservation steps. As a cost-saving measure, the program was trimmed to guarantee farmers only 85 percent of their deficiency payments when they devoted all or half their land to such other uses. The revised programs, to be known as the 50/85 and 0/85, applied to 1994 and 1995 crops.

The 92 percent deficiency payment was maintained for specified cases: Farmers who certified early in the summer that weather or other factors had killed their crop, or who opted to plant alternative crops such as sunflowers on their acreage, would still receive 92 percent of their deficiency payments.

• **Cotton: Surplus Crops.** Required the agriculture secretary to reduce the amount of cotton planted by setting a lower surplus stock target. To do so, the secretary was required to change the acreage reduction program under which farmers were required to idle land in order to qualify for price supports. Surplus stock targets were part of the formula used by the agriculture secretary to determine how much land farmers had to idle to qualify for deficiency payments. Under the bill, the surplus stock target fell from 30 percent to 29.5 percent for the 1995 and 1996 crop years and 29 percent for the 1997 crop year.

• **Wheat and Feed Grains: Deficiency Payments.** Reduced the so-called 0/92 program for wheat and feed grains so that farmers were paid 85 percent of their deficiency payments, rather than 92 percent, if they opted to devote none of their acreage to wheat and feed grains.

• **Rice: Deficiency Payments.** Cut the so-called 50/92 program for rice, so that farmers were paid 85 percent of their deficiency payments, rather than 92 percent, when they planted rice on less than 50 percent of their land.

• **Dairy: Butter.** Continued the system of government purchases of surplus milk products in order to guarantee a minimum price to producers during periods of oversupply. But the provision lowered the price the government could pay to purchase surplus butter from 76 cents per pound to a maximum of 65 cents per pound. The move was expected to boost commercial butter sales and thus reduce butter surpluses and government costs.

• **Dairy: Nonfat Dry Milk.** Increased the minimum price the government could pay for surplus nonfat dry milk to $1.03 per pound from 97 cents per pound.

• **Dairy: Assessments.** Continued assessments levied on milk producers to help offset the cost of the dairy price support program and lower the federal deficit. Under the 1990 budget reconciliation act (PL 101-508), the assessment was collected by lowering by 11.25 cents per hundredweight the price milk producers received from the federal government for their milk. The assessment was slated to expire in 1995, but the provision extended it through 1996 at a lower rate. It required that dairy producers get 10 cents per hundredweight less from the federal government for their milk.

• **Dairy: Reauthorization.** Reauthorized certain provisions of the dairy price support program through 1996. Reauthorization excluded programs relating to transfer of dairy products to military and veterans hospitals, the dairy indemnity program, the dairy export incentive program, and provisions dealing with the export sales of dairy products.

• **Dairy: Bovine Growth Hormone.** Prohibited the sale of bovine growth hormone for 90 days after the date on which the Food and Drug Administration first approved the sale of the hormone. The hormone, an artificial drug that increased milk production in cows, was expected to be approved for sale within the following 12 months. During the 90-day moratorium, marketing assessments on milk producers were to be reduced by 10 percent.

• **Tobacco: Import Fees.** The 1990 budget reconciliation act required that producers of domestic tobacco pay a fee equal to 1 percent of their government loans, with the revenue going to deficit reduction. This law imposed a similar assessment on purchasers of imported tobacco. The new assessment was calculated by multiplying the number of pounds of imported tobacco by the sum of the per pound marketing assessment imposed on purchasers of domestic tobacco.

• **Tobacco: Domestic Content.** Required domestic cigarette manufacturers to certify the total amount of U.S.-produced tobacco used in their cigarettes.

• **Tobacco: Import Curbs.** Imposed a penalty on cigarette manufacturers who used less than 75 percent domestically grown tobacco in their tobacco products. The provision also required that such manufacturers purchase from tobacco cooperative marketing associations an amount of domestic tobacco equal to the amount they imported. The associations were industry groups that aided in marketing domestic tobacco.

• **Tobacco: Tracking Imports.** Required U.S. tobacco manufacturers to keep adequate records to help officials determine the amount of foreign grown and domestically grown tobacco used in cigarette manufacturing. Manufacturers who failed to provide required information faced federal criminal sanctions.

• **Tobacco: Assessment.** Imposed a fee on tobacco importers to go toward the tobacco marketing associations or to the federal government to make the tobacco program a no-cost program to the Treasury.

• **Tobacco: User Fees.** Imposed user fees on tobacco importers to pay for inspection of foreign-grown tobacco that was used in U.S.-manufactured tobacco products.

• **Tobacco: Quota Floors.** Extended floors on reductions that could be made in burley and flue-cured tobacco marketing quotas for the 1995 and 1996 crop years. Flue-cured and burley tobacco were the most common types of tobacco grown in the United States. Growers were limited in the amount they could produce by government-imposed quotas. The provision gave the secretary the right to waive the floors if the tobacco stocks were excessive.

• **Sugar: Marketing Fees.** Increased the marketing fee that sugar growers paid in fiscal years 1995 through 1998. For raw cane sugar the fee was an amount equal to 1.1 percent of the loan level for raw cane sugar and 1.1794 percent of the loan level per pound of beet sugar. The bill authorized penalties against sugar producers who knowingly violated the marketing allocations set by the 1990 farm law.

• **Sugar: Price Supports.** Continued the sugar price support program through the 1997 crop year.

• **Oilseeds: Soybeans.** Reduced the loan rates for soybeans to $4.92 per bushel from $5.02 per bushel through 1997. The provision lowered the loan rates for minor oilseeds to 9 cents per pound from $4.09 per pound through 1997.

• **Oilseeds: Loan Origination Fees.** Eliminated the fees loan applicants had to pay for oilseed crop loans in the 1994 crop year. The provision also required that such loans matured nine months after the application was made, or in no case later than the last day of the fiscal year in which they were made.

- **Peanuts: Marketing Fees.** Increased the marketing fees paid by peanut producers by 10 percent beginning with the 1994 crop. The provision raised the marketing fee by an additional 10 percent in each of the 1996 and 1997 crop years.

- **Honey: Loan Rate.** Ratcheted down the minimum price-support loan rate for honey beginning in the 1994 crop year and extending through 1998. The existing rate was 53.8 cents per pound. It dropped to 50 cents in 1994 and 1995, 49 cents in 1996, 48 cents in 1997 and 47 cents in 1998. The provision also tightened limits on the total amount of payments an individual honey producer could receive under the program from $125,000 in the 1994 crop year to $100,000 in 1995, $75,000 in 1996, and $50,000 in 1997 and 1998.

- **Honey: Reauthorization.** Reauthorized the honey price support program through the 1997 crop year.

- **Honey: User Fees.** Eliminated user fees paid to honey marketing associations.

- **Wool and Mohair: Incentive Payments.** Limited the amount of incentive payments for individual wool and mohair producers to $125,000 per farmer in the 1994 marketing year, $100,000 in the 1995 marketing year, $75,000 in the 1996 marketing year and $50,000 in the 1997 marketing year.

- **Wool and Mohair: Producer Prices.** Altered the way the Agriculture Department calculated the average price producers got for their wool in an effort to trim the cost of the program. The provision prohibited the agriculture secretary from deducting certain marketing charges when determining net sales proceeds for shorn wool and shorn mohair.

- **Wool and Mohair: Reauthorization.** Reauthorized the price support program through the 1997 marketing year.

Rural Electrification

- **Loan Programs.** Amended the Rural Electrification Act of 1936 to allow borrowers of funds from the Federal Financing Bank, which coordinated federal agency borrowing, to refinance their loans at existing interest rates or prepay the loans. The provision authorized certain penalties to be assessed on borrowers who opt for refinancing or prepayment.

Agricultural Trade

- **GATT.** Eliminated the authority of the agriculture secretary to waive minimum levels of acreage that had to be retired by wheat and corn producers under the so-called GATT trigger provisions of the 1990 budget reconciliation act. The waiver authority had been included in the 1990 budget agreement to give the agriculture secretary more leverage in negotiations as part of the Uruguay Round of the General Agreement on Tariffs and Trade (GATT). This provision was a savings device: Removing the GATT trigger eliminated its potential for increasing government payments to producers.

- **Sorghum.** Abolished minimum acreage reduction requirements for grain sorghum and barley set by the 1990 budget reconciliation law.

- **Market Promotion.** Amended the Agricultural Trade Act of 1978 (PL 95-501) to limit spending on the market promotion program, which subsidized overseas marketing of U.S. agricultural products, to $110 million a year beginning in fiscal 1994 through fiscal 1997. The provision capped fiscal 1993 spending at $148 million.

- **Unfair Trade Practices.** Directed the agriculture secretary to provide marketing assistance to counter or offset unfair trade practices of a foreign country. Redirected spending for the market promotion program to small-sized firms.

- **Brand-Name Promotion.** Limited promotion assistance for any brand name to five years. The provision banned the use of the market promotion program to promote foreign sales of U.S. tobacco.

Restructuring the REA

Congress in 1993 cleared legislation (HR 3123—PL 103-129) making far-reaching changes in the Rural Electrification Administration (REA) lending programs for rural electric and telephone cooperatives. The changes were largely the result of work that had been done earlier in the year on the budget reconciliation bill (HR 2264) but were stripped out at the last minute because of procedural complications.

Later in 1993, Congress cleared another bill (HR 3514—PL 103-201) clarifying REA's regulatory authority.

BACKGROUND

Critics had argued for years that the REA had outlived its usefulness. When President Franklin D. Roosevelt created the agency in 1935, just 10 percent of America's rural areas had access to electricity. By 1993, the Agriculture Department reported that 99 percent of the country's 2.3 million farms had electricity, and 97 percent had telephones.

Both the Reagan and Bush administrations had tried to do away with the REA and found Congress unwilling to change a program that had such strong support among rural populations. When President Clinton came into office and proposed cutting $545 million from the REA budget over five years, REA supporters and rural cooperatives began negotiating with the administration on options for saving money while preserving the REA.

Members of Congress, the administration and the National Rural Electric Cooperative Association reached agreement on a plan to increase the rates for REA loans and fold the agency into the Agriculture Department's Rural Development Administration. Lawmakers envisioned the agency as becoming a main source of funding for rural water and sewer systems, many of which were in need of renovation and modernization. The change promised to give rural electric cooperatives, the main recipients of REA loans, the chance to play a larger role in rural development.

LEGISLATIVE ACTION

The interest rate proposal was included in the House- and Senate-passed versions of HR 2264, the omnibus budget reconciliation bill. The two chambers disagreed over a House-passed limitation on the ability of cities and towns to annex territory served by rural electric cooperatives. In the end, conferees on HR 2264 agreed to allow rural electric cooperatives to continue to provide utility service to rural areas even if those areas were annexed by a nearby municipality that ran its own utility. As part of the compromise, House conferees agreed to drop language in their version making the REA part of the Rural Development Agency.

Despite the lengthy debate that went into the REA restructuring, all provisions related to the REA were stripped from the final reconciliation bill before the conference report was sent to the floor. Senate Agriculture Committee members were concerned that the entire bill might be endangered if a point of order was raised on the floor that the REA language violated a Senate rule barring extraneous provisions from a reconciliation bill.

House and Senate lawmakers moved quickly to pass a version of the REA language as a stand-alone bill. HR 3123 was passed by voice vote of the House on Sept. 28, 1993, and cleared by voice vote of the Senate Oct. 4. Because of some wording differences, a concurrent resolution (H Con Res 160) was passed by voice votes in the House Oct. 6 and the Senate Oct. 18.

MAJOR PROVISIONS

As signed into law Nov. 1, HR 3123 included the lending structure worked out by the reconciliation bill conferees for both rural electric and rural telephone cooperatives. It did not contain the controversial provisions on annexing territory or incorporating the REA into the Agriculture Department.

Under the bill, low-cost loans, formerly available to some rural electric cooperatives at 2 percent interest, were eliminated and replaced with a new three-tiered interest rate system. Rural cooperatives that had electric rates 20 percent higher than the statewide average and whose consumers earned less than the state average income were eligible for loans at a subsidized interest rate of 5 percent. Most other rural cooperatives that had more than 5.5 people per mile of electric utility line or whose electric rates and local income were lower than the state average could borrow money at the same rate available to municipalities up to a maximum rate of 7 percent. Rural telephone cooperatives were eligible for similar rates. Those utilities, local government groups and rural cooperatives that did not fit into these two tiers could borrow from the Treasury with an REA guarantee of repayment but at the same rate as the government's cost of borrowing.

Rural electric cooperatives were given additional access to water and sewage improvement grants and loans administered by the Rural Development Administration, and states were required to submit plans to modernize rural telephone systems if they wished to be eligible for REA loans.

CLARIFYING LEGISLATION

Later in 1993, Congress cleared HR 3514 to clarify a provision in HR 3123 that prohibited the REA from imposing restrictions on or delaying a loan to any borrower with a net worth exceeding 110 percent of the outstanding principal of all loans made or guaranteed to the borrower by the REA. Officials at REA had complained that the provision was too broad.

HR 3514 revised the provision to allow the REA to issue regulations on such borrowers based on the practices of private lenders, while meeting the original provision's goal of minimizing regulatory controls. The new legislation also authorized the REA administrator to ensure that adequate security was provided for any loan or guarantee made by the agency and stated that nothing in the provision limited the authority of the REA administrator to invoke terms and conditions relating to how the borrower might use the money.

HR 3514 was reported by the House Agriculture Committee (H Rept 103-381) on Nov. 19, 1993, and passed by a voice vote of the House later that day. The Senate cleared the bill by voice vote Nov. 22. Clinton signed it Dec. 17. ❑

Honey, Wool, Mohair Subsidies

Congress in 1993 acted to eliminate honey subsidies in the fiscal 1994 agriculture appropriations bill (HR 2493—PL 103-111). Lawmakers also ended wool and mohair subsidies in separate legislation (S 1548—PL 103-130).

The subsidy programs were ripe targets for members looking for ways to cut federal spending. For years, Congress's fiscal watchdogs had described the programs as boondoggles that had outlived their justifications. The honey program was created in the late 1940s to provide income security to beekeepers, who had increased honey production during World War II but faced a drop in demand and prices after the war. The wool and mohair program was founded in the wake of the Korean War to create a stockpile of wool for military uniforms.

President Clinton proposed to eliminate the honey subsidy program in his fiscal 1994 budget request. The administration gave a further boost to the programs' opponents when it targeted the wool and honey subsidies for elimination as part of its "reinventing government" effort. *('Reinventing government,' p. 811)*

HONEY SUBSIDIES

During consideration of HR 2493, the Senate July 26, 1993, adopted by voice vote a Hank Brown, R-Colo., amendment to limit honey subsidies to individual farmers under the price-support program to a maximum of $50,000 a year. Brown said most of the spending for the program ($17 million in fiscal 1992) went to a small number of participants and cited instances of beekeepers who received as much as $191,000 from the government in a single year. Supporters of the program argued that many of the subsidized beekeepers provided valuable pollination services to crop farmers.

House conferees on HR 2493 readily agreed to the Senate-passed provision. But when the conference report (H Rept 103-212) came before the full House, members, by a vote of 344–60 on Aug. 6, added an amendment that its sponsor Harris W. Fawell, R-Ill., believed would end federal payments to honey producers altogether. The Agriculture Department, however, said that while the amendment barred subsidy payments to honey producers, it left in place an alternative loan forfeiture program that could have entitled honey producers to millions more dollars in federal funds than they would have received under the program Fawell was seeking to eliminate.

Before approving the conference report on Sept. 23, the Senate agreed by voice vote to a Brown amendment that adapted Fawell's amendment to expressly bar expenditures for loan forfeitures as well as payments to honey producers. The House Sept. 30 voted 430–0 to accept the Senate amendment. The provision was included in the final version of the conference report. HR 2493 cleared Oct. 15 and was signed into law Oct. 21.

WOOL, MOHAIR SUBSIDIES

Sen. Richard H. Bryan, D-Nev., offered an amendment to HR 2493 that eliminated wool and mohair subsidies for fiscal 1994. The Senate adopted it by voice vote July 26 and the next day voted, 63–36, to table (kill) a motion to recommit the bill to the Appropriations Committee with instructions to delete the Bryan language.

The provision, however, was dropped in conference after considerable debate. Supporters of the subsidies described the program as a crucial economic aid to producers who had to compete with a large volume of imported wool. They also argued that the subsidies were financed by tariffs collected on wool imports. Defenders of the Bryan amendment maintained that the subsidies went mainly to large ranching interests, some of them owned by corporations. They also pointed out that the wool tariff long predated the domestic subsidy program, so sheep and goat ranchers were benefiting from tariff revenues that otherwise would go to the federal Treasury.

During Senate consideration of the conference report, Bryan again offered his amendment barring all spending on the wool and mohair subsidy program. The Senate adopted it by voice vote Sept. 23, after rejecting a motion, 41–56, to table (kill) the amendment.

The House Sept. 30 modified the Senate wool amendment to require the government to finish paying subsidies to sheep and goat ranchers for the 1993 marketing year; funding would end in the 1994 calendar year. Dispute over the wool and mohair subsidies held up the bill until Oct. 15, when subsidy opponents agreed to continue fully funding the program in fiscal 1994 at $190 million.

As a compromise, the Senate passed by voice vote legislation (S 1548) on Oct. 15 that reduced the subsidies in fiscal 1995 and 1996, leading to their elimination in fiscal 1997. The House passed the bill later that day by voice vote, completing congressional action. Clinton signed it Nov. 1.   ❑

Disaster Assistance

Congress in 1993 cleared a $5.7 billion supplemental appropriations bill (HR 2667—PL 103-75) to provide financial assistance to the victims of massive floods in the upper Midwest and other presidentially declared 1993 natural disasters.

The flooding of the Mississippi, Missouri and dozens of tributary rivers and streams was the nation's worst in at least a century. It caused widespread damage to thousands of homes, farms, businesses, roads, bridges, railways and public facilities.

By July 4, damages were assessed at $10 billion and growing. President Clinton initially requested $2.24 billion but twice asked for more money as the bill moved through Congress. The House approved $2.8 billion in spending. Clinton asked the Senate for $4.7 billion and later went along with its final figure of $5.7 billion.

LEGISLATIVE ACTION

While most disaster aid bills sail through Congress, HR 2667 had a bumpy ride. The bill proposed to add billions of dollars to the federal deficit under emergency spending rules and for that reason got caught in the then-raging battle over Clinton's budget reconciliation package.

HR 2667 was reported by the House Appropriations Committee on July 20, 1993 (H Rept 103-184). That version included an additional $501 million that Clinton requested on the eve of the committee's markup of the bill. Fiscal conservatives were planning to offer on the floor a proposal by Timothy J. Penny, D-Minn., and Jim Nussle, R-Iowa, and another by Jim Slattery, D-Kan., to offset the disaster spending with cuts elsewhere in the federal budget. However, the Democratic leadership blocked their moves by adopting a rule limiting floor amendments. The Rules Committee stirred further controversy when it included in the rule a self-enacting clause, not subject to amendment, authorizing stipends for participants in a low-income youth job training and counseling services program.

When the bill came to the floor, it was quickly derailed by an uprising of fiscal conservatism and GOP opposition to the stipends clause. Democratic deficit hawks joined a solid bloc of Republicans and narrowly defeated the rule (H Res 220) governing floor debate on a 205–216 vote July 22. But on July 27 the leadership marshaled its forces and got another rule (H Res 226) passed, 224–205. Deficit dissidents, however, exacted a promise from House Speaker Thomas S. Foley, D-Wash., to establish a bipartisan task force to examine ways to fund future disaster relief efforts. After an attempt to kill the stipend clause failed and with few members willing to vote against providing the disaster aid, the $2.77 billion bill passed by the overwhelming vote of 400–27 that same day.

Two days after the House vote, Clinton requested an additional $1.94 billion, bringing the total to $4.7 billion. The Senate Appropriations Committee included the request in the version of HR 2667 it reported on July 30.

In contrast to the House, the Senate focused its debate on more aid instead of how to pay for it. A coalition of flood-state senators, led by Tom Harkin, D-Iowa, and Christopher S. Bond, R-Mo., complained that a formula included in the bill by Clinton and adopted by the House would provide farmers with about 21 cents on the dollar to cover crop losses, a figure they said would drive some to economic ruin. Harkin persuaded the White House to support doubling the crop-loss payments, thus bringing it back up to the 42-cents-on-the-dollar formula set in the 1990 farm bill (PL 101-624) as the standard for crop-loss payments. Harkin's amendment was adopted 68–32 on Aug. 4. An earlier Harkin amendment that would have provided full formula funding not only for 1993 crop losses but also retroactively for 1991 and 1992 disasters—when a 50 percent cut in the formula was imposed because of fiscal restraints—was ruled nongermane on a 46–54 vote.

Harkin's amendment increased the cost of the bill by $900 million, which was to be counted as fiscal 1994 borrowing authority for the Commodity Credit Corporation. Attempts to offset the bill's spending with cuts in other programs were rejected before the Senate passed its $5.7 billion version by voice vote on Aug. 4.

The House on Aug. 6 approved by voice vote the Senate version while restoring $300,000 for the Legal Services Corporation that the Senate had cut and making several other minor technical changes. An administration pledge to implement by administrative action the controversial youth stipend program, which the Senate had dropped from its version, took that issue off the table.

The Senate accepted the House modifications and cleared the bill by voice vote in the early morning hours of Aug. 7 (in the session that began Aug. 6). Clinton signed it Aug. 12.

In other action related to the Midwest floods, Congress cleared legislation (S 1670—PL 103-181) to encourage victims to move out of flood plains. *(Flood victims assistance, p. 430)*

FISCAL 1994 SUPPLEMENTAL

Congress in 1994 cleared an emergency supplemental appropriations bill (HR 3759—PL 103-211) in response to a major earthquake that struck the Los Angeles area in January. The $11 billion appropriations bill also included $685.5 million for flood control and repairs related to the 1993 Midwest flood and other disasters. An additional $550 million was made available to the president for unforeseen needs stemming from the earthquake and the Midwest floods.

GATT Agricultural Provisions

Congress in 1994 cleared a bill (HR 5110—PL 103-465) to implement the new General Agreement on Tariffs and Trade (GATT), which had been signed earlier in the year. The worldwide trade pact lowered tariffs and other trade barriers on agricultural products and thus required changes to some U.S. farm trade laws. The changes were embodied in HR 5110. *(GATT, p. 161)*

The new GATT agreement brought agricultural production and export subsidies under international trade disciplines for the first time. This was a leading goal of the United States when it entered the negotiations, which began in Punta del Este, Uruguay, in 1986. Although the United States had its own set of farm subsidies and import restrictions, many other countries maintained even higher barriers that handicapped efforts to increase U.S. farm exports.

Under the agreement, economically developed nations were required to reduce tariffs on agricultural goods by 36 percent over six years. Developing countries had to reduce their tariffs by 24 percent over 10 years. Tariff reductions were waived only for the least developed countries. Government subsidies for the export of farm products would also have to be reduced.

The agreement required reductions in certain support payments to farmers. However, the Clinton administration said that the United States had already made such reductions in the 1985 (PL 99-198) and 1990 (PL 100-624) farm bills and would not have to make further cuts.

The biggest change required by the GATT agreement's agriculture provisions dealt with nontariff trade barriers. The agreement required that farm import quotas be converted to tariff equivalents, a process known as tariffication, to make nations' trade restrictions on farm goods more readily comparable. As a result of this provision, Congress was required to eliminate quantitative import restrictions under Section 22 of the Agriculture Adjustment Act of 1933. The move provoked some opposition among farm-state members, who regarded Section 22 as the nation's only effective tool to retaliate against countries that dumped their farm products into the United States at below-market prices.

Strong opposition to the GATT bill also came from some dairy-state members, who said the tariff and import quota reductions for dairy products under the GATT agreement would result in a flood of foreign competition for the domestic industry.

However, the Clinton administration's claims that the agreement would increase U.S. farm exports by $1.6 billion to $4.7 billion a year by 2000 swayed most farm-state members, who joined in the wide House and Senate majorities that passed the implementing bill.

Grain Inspection Fees

Congress in 1993 cleared legislation (S 1490—PL 103-156) extending the authority of the Federal Grain Inspection Service to collect fees for weighing and inspecting marketed grain through Sept. 30, 2000.

Before clearing the bill, the Senate yielded on the most controversial issue, agreeing to drop a provision that banned the use of water on stored grain. Some companies used water to suppress grain dust, which could explode if allowed to accumulate in high concentrations. But foreign importers of U.S. grain complained that some exporters added water to increase the weight, and therefore the price, of the grain. A provision banning the use of water had been dropped from the House version of the legislation (HR 2689) during committee consideration.

HR 2689 was reported by the House Agriculture Committee (H Rept 103-265) on Sept. 28, 1993, and passed by a voice vote of the full House later that day. The Senate passed S 1490 by voice vote on Sept. 29. The House on Nov. 4 passed an amended version of S 1490, a seven-year authorization without the watering ban, which the Senate cleared on Nov. 11. It was signed into law Nov. 24.

Market Promotion Programs

Congress in 1993 cleared several bills affecting Agriculture Department market-promotion programs—industry-financed programs through which growers and producers collectively promoted their specific products. The boards were operated out of the Agriculture Department, but producers paid for advertisements.

All four bills were passed by the Senate on Nov. 20, 1993, and by the House the next day. The bills were signed into law Dec. 14:

• S 994 (PL 103-190) established a program to promote sales of fresh-cut flowers and greenery. The bill had been reported by the Senate Agriculture, Nutrition and Forestry Committee (S Rept 103-229) on Nov. 19.

• S 717 (PL 103-188) increased the cost for participants in the existing egg research and marketing program and required the Egg Board to allocate a proportion of future funds for research. The bill had been reported by Senate Agriculture on Nov. 19.

• S 778 (PL 103-189) expanded the watermelon marketing program to Alaska, Hawaii and the District of Columbia, and exempted watermelon growers with 10 acres or fewer from program assessments.

• S 1766 (PL 103-194) changed the lime marketing program so that it applied to seedless limes and not seeded limes, and exempted producers of up to 200,000 pounds of limes a year from assessments. ❑

Plant Variety Protection

Congress in 1994 cleared legislation implementing a 1991 international agreement reinforcing patentlike protection for developers of new plant varieties. The bill (S 1406—PL 103-349), which brought the Plant Variety Protection Act of 1970 (PL 91-577) into agreement with the Convention of the International Union for the Protection of New Varieties, generally made only modest changes in U.S. law. For example, it extended the period of patentlike protection for new plant varieties from 18 years to 20 years.

The Senate passed S 1406 by voice vote on May 25, 1994. The House passed the bill by voice vote Aug. 12, after substituting the text of its version, which had been reported by the House Agriculture Committee earlier that day (HR 2927—H Rept 103-699). The Senate agreed by voice vote Sept. 21 to accept the House version, clearing S 1406. It was signed into law Oct. 6.

The easy passage contrasted with an unusually divisive battle that had taken place in the House Agriculture Committee over a provision of the bill barring farmers from selling to each other leftover seeds from a protected plant variety without compensating the plant breeder who developed the variety. Supporters of selling the leftover seeds argued that they enabled farmers to stretch their incomes and even helped neighbors in financial distress with low-cost seed. But plant breeders said the sales of saved seeds denied them the return on their work that they needed to sustain further research into new varieties of plants. The international convention barred unauthorized saved-seed sales. The House Agriculture Committee narrowly affirmed the provision. ❑

Vegetable Oil-Based Ink

Congress in 1994 cleared legislation (S 716—PL 103-348) to require the federal government to use ink made from vegetable oil for much of its lithographic printing. The bill, designed to help domestic farmers and improve the environment, mandated that the government use soybean and other vegetable oils and materials derived from renewable resources when technologically feasible.

S 716 set varying thresholds for different types of government printing and required that the government's cost of using vegetable oil-based ink remain competitive with printing costs using the more common petroleum-based inks. Specific printing jobs were exempted from these requirements if the head of the agency determined that vegetable oil ink was unsuitable.

Many government documents already were printed with soy oil-based ink. Inks based on vegetable oils were less likely to rub off on a reader's fingers, and they created fewer environmentally harmful byproducts.

S 716 was reported by the Senate Rules and Administration Committee (S Rept 103-178) on Nov. 10, 1993, and was passed by a voice vote of the full Senate on Nov. 19. An amended version was reported by the House Government Operations Committee (H Rept 103-625, Part I) on July 28, 1994, and passed by a voice vote of the House on Sept. 20. The Senate cleared the bill on Sept. 27. It was signed into law Oct. 6. ❑

Dispute Resolution Fees

Congress in 1994 cleared legislation (HR 4581—PL 103-276) that allowed the Agricultural Marketing Service to temporarily charge a fee to parties filing complaints with a dispute-resolution service administered by the agency. The service was used by farmers, food brokers, wholesalers and retailers who were unable to resolve disputes about produce quality, grading and other contractual matters.

The agency was supposed to be fully funded by licensing fees paid by participating businesses, but the program was running into a budget shortfall that threatened its continuation. HR 4581 gave the service authority to charge $60 for informal complaints and $300 for formal complaints in fiscal years 1995 and 1996. A fee could be incorporated into the damage award if the complaint was upheld by the dispute-resolution mediator.

The House had included a similar fee provision in its version of the fiscal 1995 agriculture appropriations bill (HR 4554), but the language subsequently was struck.

The House passed HR 4581 by voice vote June 16, and the Senate followed suit June 28. It was signed into law July 5. ❑

Farm Credit System

Congress in 1994 cleared legislation (HR 4379—PL 103-376) that gave the quasi-federal Farm Credit System greater ability to finance foreign purchases of U.S. agricultural products. HR 4379 was expected to boost exports of hops, tallow, pork and cattle.

The measure lifted restrictions that previously had limited financing by system banks to products (mostly bulk grains) grown by agricultural cooperatives. The bill allowed the banks to participate in financing arrangements with other domestic or foreign-owned businesses to promote the export of U.S. agriculture commodities. It also allowed system banks to finance joint ventures and partnerships in which farm cooperatives participated.

The House passed HR 4379 by voice vote Sept. 29, 1994; the Senate, Oct. 5. The bill was signed into law Oct. 19.   ❏

Farmers Home Administration Loans

Congress in 1994 cleared legislation (S 1930—PL 103-248) that gave the agriculture secretary authority to hire private lawyers, as well as Justice Department and Agriculture Department litigators, to pursue government claims against individuals who were delinquent on Farmers Home Administration (FmHA) loans. The legislation was aimed at reducing a backlog of more than 4,000 pending foreclosures involving $4.2 billion in bad debts on FmHA loans.

Congressional action had been spurred by a front-page exposé published in the *Washington Post* on Jan. 28, 1994, that described how a number of wealthy part-time farmers had gone unpunished for reneging on large FmHA loans.

The Senate passed the bill March 24 and the House cleared it April 21, both by voice votes. President Clinton signed the measure into law May 11.   ❏

Disaster Aid Tax Relief

The Senate Finance Committee on April 5, 1994, reported a bill (S 1814—S Rept 103-244) to amend the tax code to allow farmers to declare crop insurance and disaster aid payments either in the year in which the losses occurred or in the year in which payments were received. No further action was taken on the bill.

Many farmers who suffered losses in the 1993 floods that devastated the Midwest did not receive their federal disaster aid checks until 1994, which caused some of them to report—and pay taxes on—unusually high incomes for the year. S 1814 would have allowed farmers to declare their disaster payments on their 1993 returns—thereby allowing many of them to write off the payments against their disaster losses. The bill would have applied to future farm disasters as well.   ❏

Dairy Compact

Lawmakers in both chambers in 1994 considered legislation (HR 4560, S 2069) aimed at empowering a six-state compact in New England to increase the federally mandated milk price in that region. Neither bill got to the floor.

The price paid dairy farmers for their product was set by a complex formula called the milk marketing system. Under the system, the nation was divided into several regions. Every farmer in a region was paid the same amount for his cows' milk. Prices varied from region to region and had fluctuated from quarter to quarter, influenced by the availability of milk and other economic factors. Many dairy farmers in the Midwest and Northeast complained that the price was set so low and had fluctuated so much that it was driving them out of business.

The problem had led six states—Connecticut, Maine, Massachusetts, New Hampshire, Rhode Island and Vermont—to draw up a compact for their region, with a commission that could increase the price paid to farmers for milk they sold in the region.

Under existing law, states could increase the federal milk price. But individual New England states had not done so because milk was sold across many borders in that region. The compact, which needed congressional approval to go into effect, was intended to supplant the existing state authority.

The Senate Judiciary Committee reported its version (S 2069—S Rept 103-333) on Aug. 12, 1994, but objections from other farm-state senators kept the bill from coming to the floor. The House Judiciary Subcommittee on Administrative Law and Governmental Relations voted on Oct. 4 to send HR 4560 to the full committee without recommendation, but the full committee did not act on the bill.   ❏

1995–1996

The 104th Congress took a historic step with the passage of the 1996 omnibus farm bill. The legislation reversed decades-old policies and moved farm programs toward a free-market approach.

The farm bill rewrote the rules for farm subsidies, essentially ending a system that dated back to the New Deal. Instead of giving subsidies—or "deficiency payments"—to planters when markets dropped, under the new plan the government would sign contracts with farmers to issue fixed, declining payments over seven years regardless of market conditions. The legislation also gave farmers broad planting flexibility and did away with policies that required subsidized farmers to idle land.

Adoption of the so-called "Freedom to Farm" plan was a resounding victory for free-market Republicans. Many Democrats, not unexpectedly, denounced the plan and vowed to reverse it when they had the votes. President Clinton signed the bill into law, albeit reluctantly.

The farm bill was nearly a year in the making. Congress had cleared the Freedom to Farm plan in 1995 as part of a deficit-reducing budget reconciliation bill. Clinton vetoed that bill for a number of reasons, the prime ones being changes to Medicare and Medicaid but the agricultural provisions also were cited.

With farm programs starting to expire and farmers preparing to plant without clear guidelines from Washington, a sense of urgency surrounded the farm bill. Lawmakers went back to work on farm policy in January 1996 and over the course of just a few months managed to resolve major disputes. The bill was signed into law in early April.

The acrimony that surrounded the farm bill seemed to evaporate when Congress turned to another topic of interest to the agricultural community: pesticide legislation. Breaking a logjam that had lasted for nearly two decades, lawmakers easily cleared a major, bipartisan rewrite of federal pesticide regulations in July 1996. *(Pesticide regulation, p. 446)*

Omnibus Farm Bill

After a prolonged battle that split lawmakers along both regional and partisan lines, Congress in 1996 cleared a landmark, seven-year farm bill to undo New Deal-era farm programs and move agriculture partially to the free market. Despite misgivings that the legislation could unravel the federal safety net for farmers, President Clinton signed it into law (HR 2854—PL 104-127).

The new law did away with the decades-old policies of issuing subsidies when market prices dropped and requiring farmers to plant the same commodities every year. Instead, it guaranteed farmers fixed, declining federal payments regardless of market prices. By removing government planting restrictions, it allowed farmers to rotate their crops to take advantage of weather conditions and market prices. In addition, under the new law, the government could no longer require that subsidized farmers idle a portion of their land.

HR 2854 authorized an estimated $56 billion over seven years for farm and forestry programs, with additional money for nutrition programs. Of that amount, $45.3 billion was for the Commodity Credit Corporation, which funded most major farm programs, including direct payments to producers. The bill was expected to save $2.1 billion compared with previous farm programs, according to the Congressional Budget Office (CBO).

Enactment was a triumph for free-market Republicans, who for years had criticized policies such as requiring subsidized farmers to idle land.

But Democrats denounced the new system of fixed, declining payments. They were critical of the bill for providing an estimated $5 billion in additional payments in 1996 and 1997, when market prices were expected to be high, and lower payments later in the decade, even if market prices dropped. Democrats also argued that the bill would help well-moneyed grain traders, at the expense of small farmers, by boosting commodity supplies and reducing prices. Many Democrats opposed the Freedom to Farm bill so strongly that they vowed to revisit the issue in future years.

Congress originally had planned to put new farm laws on the books by the fall of 1995, when key provisions of the 1990 farm act were to expire and the underlying 1949 farm act would surface as the law of the land. But instead of working on a stand-alone omnibus farm bill, lawmakers ended up adding agriculture provisions to the budget reconciliation bill (HR 2491), which was vetoed in December.

In January 1996, members tried again, taking up the farm bill as separate legislation. After difficult battles in the House and Senate, HR 2854 cleared in late March, in time to avoid the chaos that had been expected to result from the expiration of temporary amendments to decades-old farm laws.

BACKGROUND

The federal government's farm programs dated to Franklin D. Roosevelt's New Deal, when protective intervention was deemed essential to shore up farm income. During the Great Depression commodity prices were in a disastrous slump and farm income averaged about half that of nonfarm families. Starting with the Agriculture Adjustment Act of 1933, Washington began to prop up prices by cutting supplies of basic commodities. At the time, Agriculture Secretary Henry A. Wallace wrote that government intervention was "but a temporary method for dealing with an emergency."

But getting out of the farm business proved more difficult than getting into it. The Agricultural Adjustment Act of 1938, which established the basic price-support and production-control system for nonperishable agricultural commodities, remained in existence more than 50 years later. *(Congress and the Nation Vol. I, p. 682)*

The Agricultural Act of 1949 (PL 81-439) revised the system by giving the secretary of agriculture more flexibility in setting price-support levels. The revisions in effect reflected a middle position in the debate that Congress would revisit time and again between those who favored government management of farm prices and those who advocated a free market for agricultural products. *(Congress and the Nation Vol. I, p. 690)*

In the decades that followed, Congress passed a series of major farm bills—but always as temporary amendments to the permanent 1938 and 1949 laws.

Key revisions included:

• The Agricultural Act of 1970 (PL 91-524), enacted under President Richard M. Nixon, maintained the system of crop and price controls but added a "set-aside" program that required farmers to take a portion of their land out of production to qualify for price supports. The farmers would be compensated for setting aside acreage, and they could raise whatever they wanted on the remaining land. *(Congress and the Nation Vol. III, p. 336)*

• The Agriculture and Consumer Protection Act of 1973 (PL 93-86) replaced the old support prices for the major commodities of cotton, wheat, corn and other feed grains with lower "target prices" that reimbursed farmers only in the event of sharp market-price drops. *(Congress and the Nation Vol. IV, p. 719)*

• The 1981 farm bill (PL 97-98), crafted by Congress and signed by President Ronald Reagan, maintained price supports and even added a new support program for sugar. *(Congress and the Nation Vol. VI, p. 487)*

• The 1985 farm bill (PL 99-198) was enacted during a devastating farm depression that had forced the government to buy up huge amounts of surplus commodities and support farmers' incomes with artificially high prices—at a final, four-year cost of $54.7 billion. The 1985 law lowered those prices but kept a lifeline to struggling farmers through massive income-support payments. The bill probably did more to nurse agriculture back to health than any collection of government programs since the

Great Depression—but again, at a high cost: $68.6 billion over five years. *(Congress and the Nation Vol. VII, p. 501)*

• The 1990 farm bill (PL 101-624) aimed to reduce the projected cost of federal subsidies by nearly $14 billion over five years. Although it did not reduce subsidy levels, the bill froze farm price- and income-support rates at existing levels. Most of the savings came from putting into law the triple base acreage-reduction plan. Under the plan, 15 percent of farmland was ineligible for crop subsidy payments, though farmers could grow other crops on the land and take those crops to market. *(Congress and the Nation Vol. VIII, p. 537)*

• The fiscal 1994 budget reconciliation bill (PL 103-66) contained another round of cuts for farmers, reducing Agriculture Department programs by $3.2 billion. The bill also included provisions reforming crop insurance to reduce fraud and abuse, decreasing participation in the Conservation Reserve Program, and cutting the size of payments to farmers who agreed not to plant certain subsidized grain crops. *(Fiscal 1994 bill, p. 44)*

By the 1990s the government remained as deeply involved as ever in curtailing supplies of commodities to control the market. Since the Great Depression, the scope of farm legislation had also expanded beyond basic commodities to include nutrition and conservation programs. The total agriculture budget in 1995 was $63 billion, of which $8 billion to $10 billion went for farm subsidies and related programs depending on market conditions.

PUSH FOR CHANGE

The Republican takeover of Congress at the beginning of the 104th Congress appeared to foreshadow major changes in farm programs. Many Republicans believed that farmers would be better off without government regulations telling them what they could and could not plant. Even some farm organizations, such as the National Corn Growers Association, thought the time had come for wholesale changes in farm policy.

Some of the most heated criticism of farm programs was aimed at the long-standing government policy of requiring subsidized farmers to idle, or set aside, a portion of their land. The drive to stop rewarding farmers for cutting production came from both conservatives who wanted an agricultural free market and urban liberals who wanted to do away with costly farm subsidies. Fanning the flames, a powerful coalition of agribusiness companies, including major grain elevators, processors and exporters, said land-idling programs should be done away with to increase production for export. In 1995, the programs had set aside an estimated 53 million acres out of the nation's 435 million acres of cropland. The Clinton administration favored retaining the authority to order set-asides, although it said the president was unlikely to exercise that authority anytime soon.

Many farmers, including corn and soybean growers, wanted to do away with government requirements that they plant the same crops year after year to keep receiving subsidies. They argued that they should be free to plant for booming overseas markets, thereby spurring agricultural exports. The administration supported somewhat more flexibility, although not as

much as some wanted. Cotton and rice farmers, however, feared increased competition and generally favored the existing planting restrictions.

Among the farm programs under the most political pressure were price supports for sugar and peanut growers. Although the programs cost little government money, they were under fire from corporate users because they limited the supply of commodities and increased prices. Environmentalists, consumer advocates and free-market conservatives also criticized the program. But sugar and peanut lobbyists had the backing of powerful southern lawmakers.

The Republican focus on balancing the budget, more than any other issue, promised to dominate the farm debate. Farm subsidies were projected to cost $56.6 billion over seven years, a large pot of money for conservatives to target.

1996 BUDGET RECONCILIATION BILL

Congress in 1995 cleared a plan to cut federal spending on farm programs by $12.3 billion over seven years, with wholesale changes in the nation's system of crop subsidies and price supports. But the proposal was part of HR 2491, the massive budget reconciliation bill that Clinton vetoed Dec. 6, largely because of cuts in Medicare and Medicaid; he also cited the farm provisions. *(Fiscal 1996 budget reconciliation, p. 68)*

With the 1990 farm bill due to expire in 1995, members of Congress had expected to spend the year working on new omnibus farm legislation. But when the new Republican majority turned its attention to cutting the deficit, lawmakers split the farm legislation into two pieces. It put provisions governing controversial crop subsidies, which usually cost $6 billion or more yearly, into the seven-year budget reconciliation bill. Then it tried to put other, less politically sensitive issues, such as research and credit, into a slimmed-down farm bill. Most of the latter provisions did not progress far in the first session.

The Clinton administration played a relatively minor role in the farm debate during the early part of the year, with the president vowing to resist wholesale cuts to farm programs. His first budget plan called for $1.5 billion in unspecified agriculture cuts over five years. Later, Clinton called for about $4 billion in cuts over seven years, mostly by increasing the amount of acreage ineligible for subsidies.

House Action

The House Agriculture Committee ran into roadblocks as soon as the panel began voting on plans to cut farm programs by as much as $13.4 billion over seven years, the amount recommended in the budget resolution (H Con Res 67) adopted by both houses of Congress June 29. *(Budget resolution, p. 65)*

The committee on Sept. 20 rejected, 22–27, a proposal by Chairman Pat Roberts, R-Kan., that would have replaced traditional subsidies with a system of fixed but declining payments, regardless of market conditions or planting decisions. Four Cotton Belt Republicans refused to go along with their chairman's plan. Before rejecting Roberts's so-called Freedom to Farm Act (HR 2195), the panel also turned down two rival plans offered as substitute amendments.

With his panel unable to reach a consensus, Roberts adjourned the markup and turned the issue over to the Budget Committee and House leaders. House Speaker Newt Gingrich, R-Ga., and his lieutenants backed Roberts's bill. But some rural southern lawmakers, concerned that the proposal would end the lucrative marketing loan program for cotton and rice, refused to support the plan. A coalition of northeastern and southeastern Republicans also threatened to vote against the budget reconciliation bill because of provisions that would end dairy price supports. Finally, Gingrich promised disaffected members during a series of meetings in late October that their concerns would be addressed in conference, and most rural Republicans voted for the budget reconciliation bill. The House passed HR 2491 on Oct. 26, 227–203.

The Freedom to Farm plan inserted in the reconciliation bill would have saved the required $13.4 billion. Farmers were to be allowed to enter into seven-year contracts with the federal government that guaranteed continued subsidies regardless of market conditions or their planting decisions. The dairy price-support program, which propped up shelf prices of dairy products, and the federal milk marketing orders, a controversial program that subsidized fluid milk producers according to region, were to be terminated, while the peanut and sugar price-support programs were reauthorized. In addition, the bill would have allowed farmers to terminate their contracts to take environmentally sensitive land out of production and would have established a commission to study farm policy.

Senate Action

Like its House counterpart, the Senate Agriculture, Nutrition, and Forestry Committee had a hard time agreeing on a farm plan but, in the end, it succeeded. After weeks of grueling behind-the-scene negotiations, committee Chairman Richard G. Lugar, R-Ind., on Sept. 28 rallied just enough support for a plan aimed at cutting farm programs by up to $13.6 billion over seven years. Of the total savings, however, about $900 million would have been added back for new conservation and other programs.

A free-market conservative, Lugar backed off from earlier proposals to greatly scale back the peanut and sugar price-support programs, but he insisted on provisions giving farmers greater planting flexibility and terminating many decades-old farm laws. Most of the savings were to come from doubling the amount of farmland ineligible for subsidies, to 30 percent.

Farm programs sparked little controversy after the committee markup. The Senate approved the budget reconciliation bill, with the farm cuts, on Oct. 28 by a vote of 52–47. The one significant farm amendment concerned dairy programs. Offered Oct. 27 by James M. Jeffords, R-Vt., and Thad Cochran, R-Miss., and adopted by voice vote, the amendment sought to establish a farmer-financed price-support program for dry milk and butter to replace the government subsidies that were to be phased out under the Senate plan. It also ratified the Northeast Interstate Dairy Compact, which allowed six New England states to raise the consumer price of locally produced milk and send the additional money back to local farmers to help them stay in business. *(Dairy compact, p. 500)*

Conference

Meeting in November, agriculture conferees were under pressure to come to terms to avoid delaying final passage of the bill. To hasten the negotiations, Speaker Gingrich and Senate Majority Leader Bob Dole, R-Kan., chaired some of the negotiations.

The conferees quickly agreed to end deficiency payments provided to farmers when domestic market prices fell below target prices and instead to guarantee farmers fixed but declining payments over seven years regardless of market conditions, as in the House plan. Farmers were given flexibility in choosing which crops to plant, and the acreage set-aside program was to be eliminated. The marketing loan program was continued, as the Senate had proposed, with maximum loan rates to be capped at 1995 levels.

Considerable negotiating was necessary before conferees agreed to reauthorize both the sugar and peanut price-support programs for seven years, with some changes.

But the most intractable issue proved to be the House provision to eliminate the government's regional milk marketing orders. Although widely criticized as outdated in an era of rapid transportation and refrigerated freight cars, the orders had long proved resistant to legislative change, because they boosted dairy producers in the East. GOP leaders finally booted dairy provisions out of the bill, altogether, losing about $700 million in potential savings over several years.

As a result, the House and Senate conferees had to get a waiver from the Budget committees that reduced their savings target to about $12.3 billion over seven years, instead of the $13 billion target that budget writers had agreed to just a few weeks earlier. The original budget resolution recommendation of $13.4 billion had been worn down by resistance from powerful farm lobbies.

Presidential Veto

HR 2491 cleared on Nov. 20, and Clinton vetoed it on Dec. 6. Although the cuts in Medicare and Medicaid were the prime reason for the veto, the president also criticized the farm provisions. "The agriculture provisions would eliminate the safety net that farm programs provide for U.S. agriculture," Clinton wrote. "[They] would provide windfall payments to producers when prices are high, but not protect family farm income when prices are low."

1995 FARM BILLS

While most major farm issues were debated in the context of the budget reconciliation bill in 1995, lawmakers had begun work on several other proposals that were expected to become part of an omnibus farm bill.

The Senate Agriculture Committee in July approved relatively noncontroversial, discretionary provisions of four titles in the farm bill—credit, trade, research and rural development—but took no further action on the authorizing legislation. A House Agriculture subcommittee in November approved a plan (HR 2542) to pare back farmland conservation regulations, intended to be included in the farm bill, but that proposal also went no further.

The House Agriculture Committee in December approved two bills (HR 2130 and HR 2029) to ease regulations on the Farm Credit System and expand the authority of the Federal Agricultural Mortgage Corporation, or Farmer Mac. The bills were subsequently merged in the Senate and enacted into law in early 1996 (HR 2029—PL 104-105). *(Farm credit, p. 504)*

1996 LEGISLATIVE ACTION

When the 104th Congress reconvened in January 1996, the pressure was on to move quickly on agricultural legislation. Key provisions of the 1990 farm act had begun to expire in late 1995 and the underlying Agricultural Act of 1949 was taking effect. That gave lawmakers about four months to pass new commodity programs or extend the expired ones. Otherwise, the winter wheat harvest at the end of April 1996 would take place under permanent farm law, which would triple government loan rates for some commodities and create upheaval in the commodity markets. And that was only the first of far more drastic consequences expected under the permanent law, particularly when cotton, sugar and dairy programs expired in 1997 and 1998. Farm analysts argued that shrewd rural lawmakers had kept the old law on the books over the decades precisely to force Congress to regularly update farm programs.

The conventional wisdom in early 1996 held that Congress would be unable to make substantial changes to farm policy in an election year and, instead, would simply reauthorize programs with changes for one year.

But a looming economic disaster in the heartland drove farm policy in another direction. Production had been down for months across much of the Great Plains, due to a severe drought. As a result of the low output, commodity prices began spiraling up sharply.

The combination of low yields and high prices threatened to ruin many farmers. That was because, at the same time that little produce was available to sell, market prices were too high for the government to issue subsidy checks under the old farm programs. A number of farmers faced the prospect of having to repay the government for advance payments that had been issued when economists forecast lower commodity prices.

This unusual economic situation gave a critical boost to Roberts's Freedom to Farm plan. Powerful rural organizations, such as the American Farm Bureau Federation, endorsed the proposal because it would give farmers high subsidies in 1996 and 1997, even though market prices were cresting. It also would allow farmers considerable flexibility to plant crops that grew better in dry conditions.

In addition, rural constituents were complaining that they did not know what kind of seeds and fertilizer to buy for the spring planting season, because they did not know what sort of farm program would be in effect.

House Action

The issue quickly picked up momentum in the House. The House Agriculture Committee Feb. 9 reported HR 2854 (H Rept 104-462, Part I), which was based on the farm provisions in the 1995 budget reconciliation bill. Committee Chairman Roberts said he wanted to quickly clear a bill to revamp subsidies and price supports before taking up legislation to reauthorize less controversial agricultural issues such as credit and trade.

The House committee version, a narrowly focused bill to establish fixed, declining payments, was projected to cost roughly $44 billion over seven years. The bill retained sugar and peanut price-support programs. It included a dairy title ending price-support programs for butter and nonfat dry milk and requiring the Agriculture Department to consolidate the system of milk marketing orders within two years. The bill also proposed to repeal much of the 1949 farm law.

The House passed HR 2854 Feb. 29 by a **key vote of 270–155 (R 216–19; D 54–135; I 0–1)**. During floor action, lawmakers added trade provisions and about $2.3 billion in conservation spending. Rural members of both parties banded together to stave off contentious amendments that would have phased out the peanut and sugar price-support programs, but they were unable to preserve provisions that called for immediate changes to dairy programs. *(1996 key votes, p. 1047)*

The first major clash erupted over an amendment by Christopher Shays, R-Conn., and others to phase out the peanut program by 2002. The decades-old program boosted prices through a combination of government loans and production limits, and it was opposed by consumer groups and manufacturers. But southern lawmakers rallied to the program's defense, and the House on Feb. 28 defeated the amendment, 209–212, in a dramatic vote that split across regional instead of party lines.

The close vote set the stage for the day's main event: the vote on an amendment by Dan Miller, R-Fla., to phase out the sugar program over five years. After a tense debate, the House rejected the amendment, 208–217. The vote capped a year-long, multimillion-dollar advertising and lobbying battle that pitted well-heeled sugar cane and beet planters against a powerful coalition of manufacturers, consumer groups and environmentalists.

In a somewhat anticlimatic sequel, lawmakers then fought over regionally divisive dairy provisions. The House adopted, 258–164, an amendment by Rules Committee Chairman Gerald B. H. Solomon, R-N.Y., to retain dairy price supports and milk marketing orders for five years.

On Feb. 29, the House adopted by a vote of 372–37 an amendment by Sherwood Boehlert, R-N.Y., to add about $2.1 billion for conservation programs and by a vote of 299–124 an amendment by Mark Foley, R-Fla., to authorize $210 million to help restore the Florida Everglades. During the two-day debate, the House also adopted by voice vote a Toby Roth, R-Wis., amendment to reauthorize trade programs.

Among amendments rejected was a Charles W. Stenholm, D-Texas, amendment to delete the bill's provisions repealing the 1949 law, add funding for a variety of farm programs, and increase the loan rate for oilseeds. It was rejected, 163–258, on Feb. 29.

Senate Action

The Senate gave bipartisan approval to an expanded version of the farm bill (S 1541) on Feb. 7 by a **key vote of 64–32 (R 44–6; D 20–26)**. The bill was passed a full three weeks before the

House voted on its version, after Senate Agriculture Committee Chairman Lugar decided to bypass formal committee action and take the bill directly to the floor. Senate approval capped more than a week of intense maneuvering.

Overall, the Senate measure, like the House bill, proposed to replace traditional crop subsidies with a system of fixed, declining payments through 2002. It contained provisions to eliminate acreage reduction programs and give subsidized farmers the flexibility to plant a variety of crops. It proposed to reauthorize the sugar and peanut price-support programs, with some modifications, for seven years.

In contrast to HR 2854, the Senate bill neither proposed major changes to dairy price supports nor called for a commission to make recommendations on future government involvement in agriculture. But S 1541 had a much broader scope than the House bill. It included titles to reauthorize nutrition, trade, credit and other programs, which brought the total authorization to $50 billion—about $3 billion more than the House version. The primary spending differences were in conservation and rural development programs, as well as rice and oilseed subsidies.

Lugar had made considerable concessions in his attempts to ward off a Democratic filibuster. He proposed both his original version of S 1541, which was based on the Freedom to Farm initiative, and a draft bill backed by Patrick J. Leahy of Vermont, the committee's senior Democrat. Leahy's bill not only included the Freedom to Farm plan for fixed payments but also expanded conservation programs, reauthorized nutrition programs, such as food stamps, and sanctioned the Northeast Interstate Dairy Compact. Despite the changes, most Democrats still opposed the bill and insisted that Republicans back off from their fixed payment proposal.

An attempt to cut off debate on the original Lugar plan failed on a mostly party-line vote of 53–45 on Feb. 1, seven votes short of the 60 needed to invoke cloture. When a Democratic attempt to come up with an alternative plan stalled, Republicans focused on picking up support for the Lugar-Leahy plan. An attempt to cut off debate on that substitute failed on Feb. 6 by a vote of 59–34, just one vote short. But seven senators, including five Republicans, were out of town.

Certain to lose a cloture vote once the Senate was at full strength, Democratic leaders agreed to limit debate and bring the farm bill to a final vote on Feb. 7. But in exchange for dropping a series of amendments, they wrung a key concession from Republicans—the retention of permanent farm law.

During the Feb. 7 floor action, the Senate adopted, 50–46, a Herb Kohl, D-Wis., amendment to strip the provision calling for the Northeast Interstate Dairy Compact. The vote divided along regional lines, with midwesterners voting in favor of the amendment and northeasterners opposing it.

The Senate adopted by voice vote an amendment by Senate Minority Leader Tom Daschle, D-S.D., and Wendell H. Ford, D-Ky., to authorize $300 million over three years for rural development projects such as water and sewage grants. The Fund for Rural America was a top administration priority.

In the closest vote of the debate, the Senate rejected, 48–48, an amendment by Byron L. Dorgan, D-N.D., that would have required farmers to plant a government-subsidized crop to receive the fixed payments. Democrats, who backed the amendment without a single dissenter, said that under the bill a farmer could take an overseas vacation and still get a government check. Lugar, however, said that it would defy common sense for a farmer to let productive land lie fallow.

A proposal by Judd Gregg, R-N.H., to strip out provisions extending the sugar price-support program was rejected, 35–61. An amendment by Rick Santorum, R-Pa., to cut the peanut price-support rate over five years was tabled (killed) by a 59–36 vote.

The Senate passed HR 2854 by voice vote March 12, after substituting the text of S 1541. HR 2854 then went to conference.

Conference, Final Action

Negotiators, buoyed by the similarity of the House and Senate bills, hoped to quickly wrap up the conference. But they still faced several thorny differences.

The first hurdle for conferees was that the Senate bill contained about a half-dozen titles more than the House, including nutrition, credit, rural development, research and promotion. House negotiators agreed to accept the additional Senate titles, as well as the $300 million Fund for Rural America.

The conferees went along with the Senate decision to reauthorize the politically sensitive food stamp program but only for two years, not the seven years called for in the Senate bill. Other nutrition programs were extended for seven years.

After considerable wrangling, negotiators agreed to phase out price supports for butter, powdered milk and cheese over four years, after which a loan program would be established for those products. Milk marketing orders were to be consolidated, and the agriculture secretary was allowed to authorize the Northeast Interstate Dairy Compact. The Senate-passed bill had contained no dairy provisions.

In a big victory for Democrats, the conference bill retained permanent farm laws from 1938 and 1949, making it more likely that subsidies would continue after 2002.

The final bill created a commission to recommend future farm policy.

The Senate gave overwhelming backing to the final bill March 28, adopting the conference report (H Rept 104-494), 74–26, despite continuing opposition by Daschle and other midwestern Democrats. The House adopted the report in the session that began March 28 by a vote of 318–89, clearing the bill. HR 2854 was signed into law April 4.

MAJOR PROVISIONS

Following are major provisions of HR 2854, as enacted into law:

Direct Farm Payments

Within 45 days of the bill's enactment, the Agriculture Department was required to begin offering to sign seven-year "production flexibility contracts" with farmers of wheat, corn, cotton, rice, sorghum, barley and oats. To be eligible, farmers had to have participated in government programs in at least one of the previous five years, at least to the extent of registering their acreage with the Agriculture Department. Farmers had until Aug. 1, 1996, to enter into the contracts, which were to run from 1996 to 2002. They could enroll all their eligible acreage or just a percentage of it; they could subsequently reduce the amount of enrolled acreage.

Under the contracts, farmers were guaranteed fixed, declining government payments every year based on 85 percent of their base acreage and program yield, regardless of market conditions. Participating farmers had to adhere to erodible land and wetlands protection requirements, as well as certain planting restrictions. Farmers who violated contract conditions could be required to refund part of their payments received during the time of the violation and be barred from receiving future payments.

- **Eligibility.** Eligible farmers included landowners who assumed all or part of the risk of producing a crop and tenants with leases that expired on or after Sept. 30, 2002. Tenants with shorter leases could enter into the contracts, but they needed permission from their landowners if they chose to enroll less than 100 percent of the eligible cropland. Landlords and tenants could enter into the same contract. The contracts could be transferred if the farmland came under new owners or operators.

- **Payment Schedule.** The payments were due by Sept. 30 of each year. In fiscal 1996, farmers could receive one-half of their annual payment within 30 days of signing their contracts. In subsequent fiscal years, they could receive one-half of their payments on Dec. 15 or Jan. 15. Total annual fixed payments authorized by the bill were: $5.6 billion in fiscal 1996, $5.4 billion in fiscal 1997, $5.8 billion in fiscal 1998, $5.6 billion in fiscal 1999, $5.1 billion in fiscal 2000, $4.1 billion in fiscal 2001 and $4 billion in fiscal 2002.

Payments were to be apportioned on a per-bushel basis, depending on how much farmers of the various commodities had received in subsidies over the previous five years. The allocation among the former crop bases was (in rounded numbers): corn, 46.2 percent; wheat, 26.3 percent; upland cotton, 11.6 percent; rice, 8.5 percent; sorghum, 5.1 percent; barley, 2.2 percent; and oats, 0.2 percent. Rice producers were slated to get an additional $8.5 million annually from 1997 to 2002.

- **CCC Limitation.** The Agriculture Department was barred from using funds in the Commodity Credit Corporation (CCC)—which issued the direct payments and other assistance to farmers—for buying personal property. However, the department could spend up to $170 million in fiscal 1996 and $275 million annually in fiscal 1997–2002 for computer, telecommunications and other equipment. The CCC had to submit quarterly reports to Congress on all expenditures of more than $10,000.

Farm Payment Limitations

The bill retained the three-entity rule, which enabled farmers to double their subsidies by subdividing their operations. However, the per-person cap was reduced from $50,000 to $40,000, effectively reducing the per-farm limit from $100,000 to $80,000.

The per-person cap for marketing loan gains—a subsidy that primarily helped cotton and rice producers when world prices dropped below U.S. government loan rates—remained at $75,000. This payment also could be doubled, to $150,000, if the farmers subdivided their operations. This meant a per-farm limit, under the combination of subsidies, of $230,000.

Commodity Loans

- **Loan Rates.** Loan rates for wheat and feed grains were capped at 1995 levels: $2.58 per bushel of wheat and $1.89 per bushel of corn. As under prior law, the loans were set at 85 percent of the average of the previous five years, excluding the highest and the lowest, up to the level of the cap. The agriculture secretary, who formerly could reduce those basic loan rates by up to 20 percent under certain circumstances, could reduce those loans by no more than 10 percent.

Rice loans were fixed at $6.50 per hundredweight. Upland cotton loans could not be less than 50 cents per pound or more than 51.92 cents. The loan amount, as under former law, was based on either 85 percent of the previous five-year average, dropping the high and low years, or 90 percent of a 15-week average of the five lowest cotton-price quotes for northern Europe, whichever was lower. The loan rate for extra-long staple cotton was based on 85 percent of the previous five-year average, dropping the high and low years, and capped at 79.65 cents per pound. A provision in prior law allowing cotton farmers to extend their loans by eight months was ended, saving an estimated $77 million.

Soybean loan rates varied from $4.92 per bushel to $5.26 per bushel, depending on the previous five-year average excluding the high and low years. That was an increase compared with the existing rate, which was fixed at $4.92. Loan rates for several other oilseeds—sunflower seed, canola, rapeseed, safflower, mustard seed and flax seed—ranged from 87 cents to 93 cents per pound. The agriculture secretary was to set loan rates for other oilseeds.

The loans had to be repaid in nine months, except for cotton loans, which were for 10-month periods. The agriculture secretary was authorized to set the repayment rate for wheat, feed grains and oilseeds at the lesser of the loan rate plus interest, or the rate that the secretary determined would minimize forfeitures, accumulation of commodity stocks and cost to the government, as well as promote free and competitive markets. The repayment rate for cotton and rice was the lesser of the loan rate plus interest, or the prevailing world market price. The repayment rate for extra-long staple cotton was the loan rate plus interest.

Interest rates on new loans, which were computed monthly, were increased by 100 basis points, or 1 percent, producing an estimated $250 million in revenue. Marketing loans were continued; payments were linked to market conditions and not capped as they were under previous law. As a result, government outlays could increase if market prices dropped.

The agriculture secretary was authorized to make recourse loans to corn and grain sorghum producers whose crops contained more moisture than Agriculture Department standards for marketing loans. The loans were also available for seed cotton. (Under a recourse loan system, producers had to repay the government even if market prices dropped below the loan rate. In contrast, producers with nonrecourse loans had the option of forfeiting their products to the government.)

Planting Flexibility

All participating farmers were given broad flexibility on the base acreage used to determine subsidy levels. Unlike previous law, which required farmers to plant designated crops to receive subsidies, growers could continue to get fixed payments while planting program crops such as wheat and cotton, as well as soybeans and other oilseeds, mung beans, lentils, dry peas, and industrial and experimental crops. They could also use their base acreage for haying and grazing. However, they could not plant fruits, vegetables or potatoes on their base acreage, except in areas with a history of such crops, in which case the contract payment would be reduced by one acre for each contract acre on which fruits, vegetables or potatoes were planted.

Double-cropping, in which a second crop was planted with a contract crop of fruits, vegetables and potatoes in areas with a history of double-cropping, was allowed without penalty.

Subsidized farmers were given unlimited planting flexibility on their additional land—acreage that had never been enrolled in government programs.

Land-Idling Programs

• **Acreage Reduction.** Acreage reduction programs, which required subsidized farmers in certain years to idle land for economic reasons, were repealed. Also terminated were the so-called 0/85, 0/92, 50/85 and 50/92 programs, which paid farmers reduced subsidies for land that was idled or diverted to alternative crops. However, farmers with market transition contracts who idled their land would continue to get fixed payments without penalty.

Dairy Producers

• **Price Supports.** The new law ended government assessments on dairy producers.

Price supports for butter, cheese and powdered milk were to be phased out over four years. The declining price supports, based on a rate per hundredweight of milk, were set at: $10.35 during 1996; $10.20 in 1997; $10.05 in 1998; and $9.90 in 1999. The agriculture secretary had flexibility in allocating price supports between nonfat dry milk and butter to minimize government expenditures.

After the four-year phase-out, the government was to set up a recourse loan program for dairy producers. The loans would be based on a rate of $9.90 per hundredweight of milk.

• **Milk Marketing Orders.** The agriculture secretary was directed to consolidate the 33 milk marketing orders into no more than 10 to 14 orders within three years of enactment. The proposed consolidation had to be announced within two years, although the deadline could be extended if the agriculture secretary was enjoined by a court order from implementing the new system. If the agriculture secretary failed to implement the new

system within the time required, the department would be barred from collecting assessments from milk producers or handlers to administer the marketing orders.

California retained the authority to set its own standards for solids in fluid milk, as well as labeling requirements of those standards. The manufacturing, or make, allowance in California—a formula setting the amount of profit that a processor could make from a dairy product—was capped through Dec. 31, 1999, at $1.65 per hundredweight of milk for butter and nonfat dry milk, and $1.80 for cheese.

• **Dairy Export Programs.** The Fluid Milk Promotion Program, which promoted milk consumption, was reauthorized. The Dairy Export Incentive Program, which subsidized overseas sales of U.S. dairy products, was reauthorized at the full level allowable under World Trade Organization agreements. Dairy Export Incentive Program funds could be used for market development.

• **Northeast Interstate Dairy Compact.** The agriculture secretary could allow the six New England states to enter into a Northeast Interstate Dairy Compact, under which the states would temporarily increase the minimum price that processors paid fluid milk producers. Six other states—Delaware, Maryland, New Jersey, New York, Pennsylvania and Virginia—could enter the compact with congressional consent if they bordered a state already in the compact. The compact was to be dissolved upon the agriculture secretary's consolidation of milk marketing orders.

Sugar Growers

• **Loan Rates.** The sugar loan rate was frozen at 18 cents per pound of cane and 22.9 cents per pound of beet. Those rates were to be reduced if other major producing nations reduced their export and domestic subsidies beyond World Trade Organization commitments. As under previous law, the loans had to be repaid within nine months or by the end of the fiscal year, and supplemental loans would continue to be available in beet-producing regions.

• **Marketing Allotments.** The law repealed domestic marketing allotments on cane and beet processors, thereby allowing unlimited domestic production. However, the Agriculture Department would continue to restrict imports.

• **Import Levels.** Processors were barred from forfeiting their crops to the government during any fiscal year when import levels were set at 1.5 million short tons or less. In technical terms, this meant the traditional system of nonrecourse loans would convert to a system of recourse loans if import levels dropped, effectively doing away with government price supports during such periods.

If the quota was raised above 1.5 million short tons during the course of a fiscal year, the loans would automatically convert to a nonrecourse status. However, the opposite would not happen: Nonrecourse loans would not convert to recourse loans if the quota was reduced to 1.5 million short tons or less during a fiscal year.

Processors who forfeited sugar to the government during times of high imports would face a penalty of about 1 cent per pound, which would have the effect of reducing price supports by 1 cent.

• **No Net Cost.** As under prior law, the program had to be run at no net cost to the Agriculture Department, which meant the department generally had to continue to keep sugar prices above the loan rate.

• **Assessments.** Assessments on cane and beets were increased by 25 percent beginning in fiscal 1997, to 1.375 percent of the cane loan rate and 1.47425 percent of the beet loan rate, producing an estimated $51 million in additional money through fiscal 2002, according to the Congressional Budget Office.

Peanut Growers

• **Loan Rate.** The government loan rate was reduced from about $680 per ton to $610 per ton and frozen for seven years. The law eliminated a price-support provision, called a "cost escalator," that had increased the loan rate based on inflation.

Producers who declined to sell their peanuts to private handlers for two years in a row would be ineligible for the price supports in the next marketing year, if the written private offers were equal to or greater than the price supports.

• **Quotas.** The national poundage quota of 1.35 million short tons a year was terminated. Instead, the agriculture secretary was directed to set a quota each year based on projected "domestic edible" use.

In addition, undermarketing provisions, which allowed growers to take unused quotas and apply them in a future year, were eliminated. These quota provisions effectively eliminated taxpayer support of the price-support program, saving an estimated $412 million over seven years.

The agriculture secretary could continue to issue loans for peanuts in addition to the quota, based on various factors such as demand for peanut oil and peanut meal. The secretary could also allocate temporary quotas to producers who had seed peanuts in excess of their standard quota.

Beginning with the 1998 crop, public entities, such as city governments and schools, would be ineligible for the quotas. People who were not producers and who lived outside the state where the peanuts were grown also would be ineligible for the quotas. Valencia peanuts not produced in New Mexico were generally ineligible for the pools of that state, except those peanuts produced by Texas farmers who had previously entered the New Mexico pools.

Unlike under past law, growers could transfer, sell or lease their quotas across county lines within the same state under limited circumstances. However, not more than an aggregate of 40 percent of the total poundage quota within a county could be transferred outside a county. Counties with less than 100,000 pounds of quota could transfer, sell or lease that quota across county lines without restrictions.

• **Recovering Losses.** The law set priorities for recovering losses through area marketing associations, which were used by the Agriculture Department to administer and supervise price supports and promotions. The highest priority was to go to any loss resulting from a disaster-related transfer.

• **Disaster Transfers.** Disaster transfers, which permitted the transfer of additional peanuts to the quota loan pool under certain circumstances, were capped at 25 percent of the quota pounds. The transferred peanuts would receive 70 percent of the quota support rate.

• **Marketing Assessment.** The Agriculture Department was to continue to level a marketing assessment, set at 1.2 percent of the loan rate, for each of the 1997 to 2002 crops. Growers were to pay 54.2 percent of the assessment; purchasers were to pay 45.8 percent.

Other Price Supports

• **Honey.** Statutory authority for marketing loans to support honey prices was repealed. The program had been suspended in recent years because appropriations bills provided no funding for it.

• **Tobacco.** The tobacco price support program was continued without changes.

Cotton Exports

• **'Step 2.'** The "Step 2" program for cotton exports was capped at $701 million over seven years, for an estimated savings of $84 million. The formulas for determining payments did not change.

Crop Insurance and Related Provisions

• **Catastrophic Coverage.** The law ended the requirement that subsidized farmers buy catastrophic crop insurance. Producers instead could agree in writing to waive eligibility for future disaster payments. For fall-planted crops in 1996, however, the agriculture secretary had the option to require the purchase of catastrophic coverage. The provision was expected to save the government an estimated $153 million over seven years because of reduced liability.

The Agriculture Department, in consultation with private insurance companies, could continue to offer catastrophic crop insurance in states or regions that had an insufficient number of approved private insurance providers. In states that did have adequate private coverage, the department was to transfer its existing policies to approved private companies during the 1997 crop year for all sales, service and loss-adjustment functions.

• **Special Crop Insurance.** The Farm Service Agency was to continue operating a noninsured crop disaster assistance program for crops for which crop insurance was not available, such as ornamental nursery and Christmas tree crops, turfgrass and industrial crops. In addition, the program was expanded to include seed crops and aquaculture, including ornamental fish. The Noninsured Assistance Program was moved out of the Federal Crop Insurance Act; the Farm Service Agency would continue to administer it.

• **Price Fluctuation Protection.** The agriculture secretary was authorized to develop pilot programs to ascertain whether trading in the futures and options markets could be used by producers to reduce the risks of market price fluctuations. The agriculture secretary could conduct the program in as many as 100 counties, although no more than six could be in a single state. The secretary also could provide education about risk management strategies, including futures and options trading, and various insurance programs.

- **Office of Risk Management.** The Agriculture Department was directed to create an independent Office of Risk Management to oversee crop insurance and other risk management programs. The administrator of the office was also to serve as manager of the Federal Crop Insurance Corporation.

- **Pilot Revenue Insurance Program.** The Agriculture Department was directed to create a pilot revenue insurance program for the 1997–2000 crop years, to help protect producers of wheat, feed grains, soybeans or other crops from losses stemming from either low prices or poor harvests. The aim of the program was to help ensure producer income. The bill also established a two-year pilot program to insure crops damaged by natural disasters, such as insect infestation or disease.

Farm Program Eliminations

- **Emergency Feed Assistance and Farmer-Owned Reserve.** The law ended the emergency-feed assistance programs, which provided livestock feed to farmers in times of emergency, thereby saving $520 million. It saved an additional $81 million by ending the Farmer-Owned Reserve program, which paid farmers to store their crops when prices were low.

Future Farm Policy

- **Permanent Law.** The new law retained most permanent farm laws from 1938 and 1949. This meant that when the bill's provisions expired in 2002, Congress would have to take action or post–World War II price supports levels would go back into effect.

- **Policy Commission.** The law established a Commission on 21st Century Production Agriculture to make recommendations for future farm policy. Three of the 11 members on the commission were to be appointed by the president, and four each by the chairmen of the House and Senate Agriculture committees. At least three of the members were to be involved in production agriculture.

The commission was required to submit a preliminary report by June 1, 1998, and a final report by Jan. 1, 2001.

International Food Assistance

- **Food for Peace (PL 480).** The new law extended the authority for food aid agreements under the Food for Peace Program, also known as PL 480, through 2002.

Title I of PL 480, which authorized sales of U.S. agricultural commodities to developing countries on credit terms or for the local currency of the recipient nation, was to give greatest priority to countries with the potential to become commercial markets for U.S. products. Priority also was to be given to countries engaged in economic development efforts and those that had the most need for food.

For the first time, private entities, as well as developing countries, were eligible for low-interest loans to buy food under Title I. Loan recipients had 10 years to 30 years for repayment, depending upon their ability to repay, and could apply for an additional grace period of up to five years, compared with the seven-year grace period of past law.

To determine a developing country's market potential, the Agriculture Department could approve a marketing plan submitted by the country in conjunction with a U.S. agricultural trade organization. Such a trade organization had to promote the export of U.S. commodities but not stand to profit directly from the sales. The marketing plan had to provide for a means of measuring the project's success.

Title II of PL 480 authorized food donations for humanitarian purposes. The new law allowed private entities, such as voluntary organizations, cooperatives and intergovernmental organizations, to implement the distributions. An application for commodities could not be denied solely because the distribution would be in a country where the Agency for International Development did not have a presence.

Annual Agriculture Department funding was increased from $13.5 million to $28 million for administrative expenses, such as food transport and distribution, of private and nongovernmental organizations associated with emergency relief work.

Local currencies generated by the sale of commodities could be used in countries located in the same region as the distribution. In contrast, past law required that the local currencies be used only in the country of origin. The minimum amount of commodities that had to be sold for local currencies was 15 percent, instead of 10 percent as provided by past law.

The bill capped minimum annual tonnage levels at fiscal year 1995 levels. The annual levels were 2.025 million tons, of which 1.55 million were for nonemergency programs and 475,000 for emergency programs. The bill also required that at least 50 percent of the commodities bagged under Title II be done so within the United States.

Title III authorized multiyear, government-to-government food grants to underdeveloped countries to promote economic development and food security. The agriculture secretary could transfer up to 50 percent of the money earmarked for Title III of PL 480 into Title II in any fiscal year. The law did away with the previous requirement that Title III funds must be at least 40 percent of the combined funding for Title III and Title I. It allowed 10 percent of the local currencies generated by commodity sales to be used to support nongovernmental organizations.

- **Food for Progress.** Food for Progress, which provided commodities to countries that had tried to expand free enterprise in their agricultural commodities, was extended through 2002. Agricultural trade organizations and intergovernmental organizations were eligible to carry out such programs. The Commodity Credit Corporation could make sales on credit terms to countries other than those of the former Soviet Union.

- **Farmer-to-Farmer Program.** Funding for the Farmer-to-Farmer Program, which provided short-term technical assistance on a person-to-person basis, was increased from 0.2 percent to 0.4 percent of total PL 480 spending. Half of the funding was to be allocated to developing countries. Emerging markets were made eligible for the program. Local currencies generated by sales of other assistance programs could be used to support the Farmer-to-Farmer Program.

International Market Promotion

• **Export Enhancement.** Spending for the Export Enhancement Program, which subsidized overseas sales of U.S. products, was capped annually for a seven-year savings of $672 million. The annual caps were: $350 million in fiscal 1996, $250 million in fiscal 1997, $500 million in fiscal 1998, $550 million in fiscal 1999, $579 million in fiscal 2000, $478 million in fiscal 2001 and $478 million in fiscal 2002. Not more than $100 million annually could be spent for the sale of intermediate-value products, such as wheat flour or vegetable oil.

• **Market Promotion.** The Market Promotion Program, which helped promote U.S. agricultural products overseas, was renamed the "Market Access Program." Spending was capped annually at $90 million, a $20 million reduction compared with past levels. The funds were limited to small businesses, nonprofit trade associations and cooperatives; they could not be used to provide direct assistance to foreign, for-profit corporations to promote foreign-produced products.

• **Export Goals.** The Agriculture Department was required to develop an agricultural export promotion strategy with specific goals for the growth of U.S. exports, including high-value and value-added products. The strategy was supposed to increase agricultural exports each year at a greater rate than the increase in overall world agricultural trade.

The department also was to monitor how other nations implemented their commitments under the Uruguay Round Agreement on Agriculture under the General Agreement on Tariffs and Trade (GATT). If another country appeared to be limiting the opportunity for U.S. exports by failing to implement the agreement, the agriculture secretary was required to notify Congress and the U.S. trade representative.

The agriculture secretary also was required to monitor how other countries in the World Trade Organization implemented plant and animal sanitary measures. If any country failed to meet its commitments to such measures, the agriculture secretary had to notify Congress and the U.S. trade representative.

• **Foreign Market Development.** The Foreign Market Development Program, which helped develop overseas markets, was given statutory authority for the first time. The bill did not specify funding levels.

• **Lamb and Mutton Labeling.** The agriculture secretary was required to establish standards for the labeling of sheep products as "lamb" and "mutton." The standards were to be applied equally to domestic and imported products.

Export Credit Guarantees

As under past law, the Commodity Credit Corporation could guarantee loans obtained by eligible countries that purchased U.S. agricultural products from private U.S. sellers. Short-term credit guarantees under the GSM-102 program and intermediate-term guarantees under the GSM-103 program continued to be funded at a total of up to $5.5 billion annually. However, the Agriculture Department had flexibility to allocate money between the two programs.

The new law allowed credit guarantees for high-value products, such as snack foods, that had at least 90 percent U.S. content by weight, as opposed to the former requirement that the products be 100 percent U.S.-produced. A minimum amount of credit guarantees had to be available for processed and high-value products, unless that reduced bulk commodity sales under the programs. This minimum level was set at 25 percent of total credit guarantees in fiscal years 1996 and 1997, 30 percent in 1998 and 1999, and then 35 percent through 2002.

The law authorized a new, short-term supplier credit guarantee program, providing the agriculture secretary with authority to give credit guarantees to other nations for up to 180 days. The secretary was given more flexible criteria for determining countries' creditworthiness for GSM-103 intermediate-term credit guarantees.

The program was intended to provide emerging overseas markets with technical assistance and export credit guarantees. The Agriculture Department was directed to make available at least $1 billion of direct credit or credit guarantees from 1996 to 2002 to help countries take steps toward market-oriented economies.

Embargo Compensation

• **Unilateral Sanctions.** The Agriculture Department was required to compensate affected producers if the United States imposed a unilateral embargo on another country and no other nation with an agricultural economic interest joined the embargo within 90 days. Compensation could be in the form of payments to producers, or the funds could be used for export promotion or commodities for developing countries. Compensation could continue for three years or the duration of the embargo, whichever was shorter. The direct payments had to be equal to the Agriculture Department's estimate of the loss suffered by producers due to lower commodity prices resulting from the embargo. The funding for export promotion or food assistance would be set at 90 percent of the average annual value of U.S. exports to the embargoed country in the three years prior to the embargo. No compensation would be given in the event of a war.

Commodity Reserve

The new law established a Food Security Commodity Reserve to replace the former Food Security Wheat Reserve. The Agriculture Department was required to maintain up to 4 million metric tons of wheat, corn, sorghum and rice in the reserve. The department could release up to 500,000 metric tons in a fiscal year to help with overseas relief efforts. Congress could appropriate funds to replenish the reserve.

Farm Export Award

• **Edward R. Madigan Award.** The law established an award program in honor of Edward R. Madigan, former agriculture secretary during the Bush administration and a Republican representative from Illinois (1973–1991). The program aimed to identify and award efforts to expand markets for U.S. agriculture exports, through new product development and through innovative marketing techniques. A selection board was to recommend award recipients. The agriculture secretary was authorized to accept gifts from both public and private sources to carry out the program.

New Conservation Programs

• **Environmental Quality Incentives Program.** An Environmental Quality Incentives Program was established to provide technical assistance, cost-share payments (in which the government paid part of a project's cost), and incentive payments for farmers, especially those who faced serious threats to soil, water, grazing lands, wetlands and wildlife habitat. Eligible projects included manure management, irrigation, tillage methods and filter strips, as well as other conservation practices that reduced soil erosion, water runoff and other environmental problems. The projects had to provide maximum environmental benefits for the money. Government assistance was to be provided according to five- to 10-year contracts between farmers and the Agriculture Department.

Precedence went to farms in high-priority conservation areas and farms located in watersheds or other regions in which state or local governments also would provide assistance. The program was authorized at $130 million in fiscal year 1996 and $200 million each fiscal year thereafter until 2002; half those funds were earmarked for assistance to livestock producers.

The federal portion of cost-share payments was capped at 75 percent of the cost of the project, and such payments were not available to large confined livestock producers. The per-farmer amount of federal dollars was capped at $10,000 per year, or $50,000 for any multiyear contract, although the agriculture secretary had the authority to exceed the per-year cap, if necessary, to accomplish the project's goals.

• **Conservation Farm Option.** A pilot program, the Conservation Farm Option, was created for farmers who received market transition payments. To apply for the 10-year contracts, farmers had to submit a plan detailing conservation practices and also comply with highly erodible land and wetland conservation requirements. Funding for the program was authorized at $7.5 million in fiscal 1997, increasing to $62.5 million in fiscal 2002, for a total of $197.5 million over six years.

• **Private Grazing Resources.** A new voluntary technical and educational assistance program was created to preserve private grazing land resources. The program was designed to help ranchers and landowners preserve wildlife and fish habitat, protect water quality and manage weed problems. The agriculture secretary was authorized to establish two grazing management demonstration districts to promote sound grazing practices. The law authorized appropriations of $20 million in fiscal year 1996, $40 million in fiscal year 1997 and $60 million in each subsequent fiscal year.

• **Wildlife Habitat.** The law established a Wildlife Habitat Incentives Program to make cost-share payments to landowners to develop habitat for fish and wildlife, including threatened and endangered species. The program was authorized at $50 million over seven years.

• **Farmland Protection.** A new $35 million Farmland Protection Program authorized the agriculture secretary to buy easements or other interests on 170,000 to 340,000 acres of farmland that might otherwise be developed. The eligible farmland had to be subject to a pending offer by a state or local government seeking to protect it.

• **Frequently Flooded Cropland.** The agriculture secretary was authorized to pay farmers who received market transition payments to idle frequently flooded cropland. Payments were to equal at least 95 percent of the projected fixed payments. Participants had to comply with conservation requirements and agree to forgo future disaster payments. ❑

Farm Bill Implementation

The House by voice vote July 26, 1996, passed a bill (HR 3900) that sponsor Larry Combest, R-Texas, said was designed to address problems related to implementation of the seven-year farm bill (HR 2854—PL 104-127). However, the Senate did not act on the measure. *(Omnibus farm bill, p. 494)*

HR 3900 would have permitted farmers who received subsidies to plant a second crop of fruits and vegetables if an earlier crop failed. Combest said the planting of a second crop, called ghost acres, had been permitted in past years but that the Agriculture Department's interpretation of the new farm law would no longer permit the second planting. Combest's bill also called for the Agriculture Department to issue new rules for the Conservation Reserve Program, which paid farmers to idle environmentally sensitive land, so farmers would know how to properly plan the use of their land. ❑

Farm Credit

To make obtaining credit easier for farmers, Congress in 1996 cleared a bill easing regulatory requirements on the Farm Credit System, a system of borrower-owned financial institutions created to provide loans to the agricultural sector. The legislation (HR 2029—PL 104-105) also expanded the authority of the Federal Agricultural Mortgage Corporation, or Farmer Mac, a government-sponsored enterprise that had been losing money in recent years.

As signed into law by President Clinton on Feb. 10, 1996, HR 2029 allowed regulators to review lenders every 18 months, instead of yearly as required by existing law. Paperwork and administrative requirements would be reduced, and farm credit associations would have greater flexibility. HR 2029 also allowed the Farm Credit System Insurance Corporation to reduce insurance premiums and issue refunds to lending institutions at the discretion of the Farm Credit Administration, the regulatory agency charged with overseeing the Farm Credit System.

The final legislation also included provisions from another bill (HR 2130), giving Farmer Mac the authority for the first time to act as a pooler of loans. That meant Farmer Mac could purchase loans and issue securities based on those loans. Under existing law, Farmer Mac had been allowed to guarantee the securities used in pools of other institutions but not pool loans. Farmer Mac was given two years to increase its total core capital, or reserves, to an estimated $25 million, compared with its existing level of less than $12 million.

Farmer Mac had been authorized in 1987 (PL 100-233) to create a secondary market for agricultural real estate loans and certain rural housing loans, but it had lost money in part because of government restrictions and low commercial bank interest rates. It was hoped that the changes in HR 2029 would revitalize Farmer Mac and create more competition among loans, possibly reducing fixed-loan interest rates in rural areas by as much as 1 percent. *(1987 legislation, Congress and the Nation Vol. VII, p. 522)*

The House Agriculture Committee reported HR 2029 (H Rept 104-421) on Dec. 18, 1995, and HR 2130 (H Rept 104-446, Part I) on Jan. 4, 1996. The full House passed HR 2029 on Dec. 19, 1995, by voice vote.

The Senate passed HR 2029 by voice vote on Dec. 21, but only after adopting an amendment that greatly expanded the scope of the bill. The Senate amendment, sponsored by Rick Santorum, R-Pa., and others, added the Farmer Mac provisions from HR 2130 as well as proposals to boost farmland conservation efforts, such as education.

The House agreed to the Senate changes by voice vote Jan. 3, 1996—along with another amendment, requiring the bill to make one last trip to the Senate. The House amendment, among other things, deleted the Senate conservation proposals. The House adopted the amendment by voice vote and sent the bill back to the Senate, where it was cleared by voice vote Jan. 26. ❑

Poultry, Meat Regulations

Major battles were fought over proposed poultry and meat regulations in 1995, during consideration of the fiscal 1996 agriculture appropriations bill (HR 1976—PL 104-37).

The final bill included a Senate-added provision to block a proposed Agriculture Department rule to put "frozen" labels on poultry products chilled to less than 26 degrees. Southeastern poultry producers feared that the rule could put them at a competitive disadvantage when they shipped chilled products to the West Coast. California's senators, Democrats Barbara Boxer and Dianne Feinstein, led the charge against the provision, which had been added during Senate Appropriations Committee action, but an attempt to delete it from the bill on the Senate floor was rejected, 38–61, on Sept. 19, 1995. The provision survived an attempt in the House to send the bill back to the conference committee with instructions to remove the poultry provision. That motion was rejected, 158–264, on Oct. 12.

An earlier battle had been waged in the House over whether to put tough new meat inspection standards in place. Rep. James T. Walsh, R-N.Y., backed language in the bill to deny funding for the Agriculture Department to implement the standards on grounds that small meatpackers did not have a say in the regulations. He prevailed in the Appropriations Committee but then compromised in the face of strenuous protests from the Clinton administration and congressional liberals, who claimed it could lead to thousands of food poisoning deaths. Under the compromise, Agriculture Secretary Dan Glickman promised to consider industry comments on the proposed regulations. In return, Walsh removed his amendment, which would have required the

department to go through a lengthy review process and possibly would have delayed new standards for two years or more. A Walsh amendment allowing the regulations to be implemented was adopted, 427–0, on July 20. ❑

Commodity Futures

Congress in 1995 agreed to extend the authority of the Commodity Futures Trading Commission (CFTC) for five years through fiscal 2000. The bill (S 178—PL 104-9) was a simple reauthorization that made no changes to the commission and did not specify a dollar amount.

Created in 1974, the CFTC regulated the commodity futures markets, including the Chicago and Kansas City boards of trade. The agency's 600 employees did market surveillance and analysis, research, enforcement, audits and registration of futures firms.

The previous reauthorization, enacted in 1992, had lapsed in 1994. The 1992 law (PL 102-546), which had taken four years to develop and enact, had been delayed in part by a disagreement over the regulation of exotic financial instruments known as "hybrids" and "swaps." Hybrids combined the traits of more traditional financial instruments such as stocks or bonds, while swaps involved futures in debt obligations and currencies. PL 102-546 exempted these instruments from regulations applied to other futures products, pending creation of a more substantial regulatory framework. Lawmakers expected that a long-term regulatory solution would be enacted with the next reauthorization. S 178, however, contained no such changes in the law. *(1992 law, Congress and the Nation Vol. VIII, p. 551)*

S 178 was reported (S Rept 104-7) by the Senate Agriculture, Nutrition, and Forestry Committee on Feb. 3, 1995, and was passed by voice vote of the Senate Feb. 10. The House Agriculture Committee reported an identical bill April 6 (HR 618—H Rept 104-104). The full House that same day passed S 178 by voice vote, clearing it. The president signed it on April 21. ❑

Perishable Produce

Congress in 1995 cleared legislation (HR 1103—PL 104-48) requiring growers and shippers to pay more for a federal program that resolved disputes in fruit and vegetable trading.

The bill phased out over three years the fees paid by retailers and grocery wholesalers who bought fruits and vegetables. To offset the reduction, it increased licensing fees for growers and shippers from $400 to $550. The license fees paid for a $7.2 million Agriculture Department program that was created under the 1930 Perishable Commodities Act to settle disputes quickly and encourage fair trading. HR 1103 was a compromise between retailers and wholesalers, who wanted the act repealed, and growers, who insisted they needed the law to protect their produce.

HR 1103 was reported by the House Agriculture Committee July 26 (H Rept 104-207) and passed by voice vote of the full House July 28. The Senate passed HR 1103 by voice vote Nov. 7, and President Clinton signed it into law Nov. 15. ❑

CHAPTER 9

Health and Human Services

Health and Human Services

On the health and human services front, the years 1993–1996 will be remembered, in large part, for two high-profile fights that resulted in no legislation—President Clinton's failed effort in 1993–1994 to reshape the nation's health care system and the new Republican Congress's equally unsuccessful effort in 1995 to overhaul the huge federal Medicare and joint federal-state Medicaid programs.

But with the score for both Democrats and Republicans 0–1 for the first three years, in 1996 they decided to work together. The results were impressive—passage of the most sweeping welfare reform bill ever, as well as a health insurance reform bill that, while a shadow of the changes anticipated three years earlier, nevertheless represented the most significant health changes in a generation.

The divisive issue of abortion also continued to preoccupy Congress and the president. The 103rd Congress, with abortion-rights majorities in the House, Senate and White House for the first time in decades, managed to reverse several Reagan- and Bush-era policies. But it failed to pass the bill at the top of abortion-rights groups' wish list, the Freedom of Choice Act, which would have written the right to the procedure into federal law. Similarly, while the abortion-opposing 104th Congress managed to reinstitute many of the policies reversed by its predecessor, it could not manage to pass abortion opponents' top legislative priority, a measure to ban a specific procedure used late in pregnancy known to opponents as "partial-birth" abortion.

HEALTH CARE REFORM

The 103rd Congress began with members seemingly more than ready to pass what promised to be the most important piece of social legislation since the enactment of Social Security in the 1930s. The call for reform had reached a fever pitch, as the ranks of Americans lacking insurance topped the 40 million mark and the rapid increase of health care costs put increasing burdens on employers, not to mention government budgets from the smallest town up to the federal treasury. The political imperative had been evident at least since 1991, when in a special Senate election in Pennsylvania, the unknown Harris Wofford upset former Attorney General Richard Thornburgh after Wofford called for universal health insurance.

President Clinton failed to meet his own deadline of having a major health reform bill written within his first 100 days in office, but when the plan was unveiled in a September 1993 speech to a joint session of Congress, eventual enactment appeared inevitable. But it was not to be.

As more and more details emerged, more and more opponents began to emerge as well. And as more of the public began to wonder if the trade-offs involved in such a massive upheaval were worth it, Republicans began to wonder if they could benefit politically by denying Democrats any bill at all. In the end, Republicans just said no, and their reward at the polls in 1994 was control of both houses of Congress for the first time in 40 years.

In 1996, behind the leadership of Sens. Nancy Landon Kassebaum, R-Kan., and Edward M. Kennedy, D-Mass., chairman and ranking Democrat, respectively, on the Senate Labor and Human Resources Committee, Congress decided to enact the

REFERENCES

Discussion of health policy for the years 1945–1964 may be found in *Congress and the Nation Vol. I*, pp. 1122–1194; for the years 1965–1968, *Congress and the Nation Vol. II* pp. 665–707; for the years 1969–1972, *Congress and the Nation Vol. III*, pp. 551–580; for the years 1973–1976, *Congress and the Nation Vol. IV*, pp. 323–375; for the years 1977–1980, *Congress and the Nation Vol. V*, pp. 601–653; for the years 1981–1984, *Congress and the Nation Vol. VI*, pp. 521–556; for the years 1985–1988, *Congress and the Nation Vol. VII*, pp. 547–606; for the years 1989–1992, *Congress and the Nation Vol. VIII*, pp. 561–610.

Discussion of human services policy for the years 1945–1964 may be found in *Congress and the Nation Vol. I*, pp. 1225–1331; for the years 1965–1968, *Congress and the Nation Vol. II*, pp. 745–778; for the years 1969–1972, *Congress and the Nation Vol. III*, pp. 605–633; for the years 1973–1976, *Congress and the Nation Vol. IV*, pp. 403–432; for the years 1977–1980, *Congress and the Nation Vol. V*, pp. 679–712; for the years 1981–1984, *Congress and the Nation Vol. VI*, pp. 581–612; for the years 1985–1988, *Congress and the Nation Vol. VII*, p. 607–632; for the years 1989–1992, *Congress and the Nation Vol. VIII*, pp. 611–624.

Discussion of veterans' programs for the years 1945–1964 may be found in *Congress and the Nation Vol. I*, pp. 1335–1373; for the years 1965–1968, *Congress and the Nation Vol. II*, pp. 453–460; for the years 1969–1972, *Congress and the Nation Vol. III*, pp. 537–548; for the years 1973–1976, *Congress and the Nation Vol. IV*, pp. 158–181; for the years 1977–1980, *Congress and the Nation Vol. V*, pp. 177–191; for the years 1981–1984, *Congress and the Nation Vol. VI*, pp. 613–625; for the years 1985–1988, *Congress and the Nation Vol. VII*, p. 633–644; for the years 1989–1992, *Congress and the Nation Vol. VIII*, pp. 625–637.

Outlays for Income Security

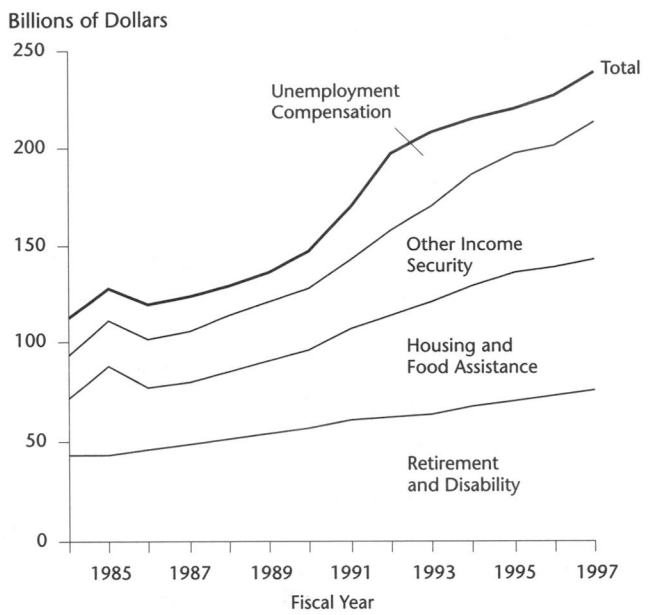

NOTE: Data for 1997 are estimated.

SOURCE: Office of Management and Budget, *Historical Tables, Budget of the United States Government: Fiscal Year 1998* (Washington, D.C.: U.S. Government Printing Office, 1997), Table 3.2.

pieces of health reform on which they did agree. Lost in the fight of two years earlier was the fact that there were significant areas of agreement, particularly on the issue of changing insurance rules to guarantee that people were not discriminated against simply because they got sick.

But the process by which the bipartisan bill emerged was anything but bipartisan. The measure reported unanimously from Kassebaum's committee languished for months, ultimately tied up in presidential politics as Majority Leader Bob Dole, R-Kan., tried to shore up support from conservatives. And in the House, Republicans added on to the bill some highly contentious provisions regarding medical malpractice and a free-market favorite called medical savings accounts. While both the House and Senate had passed their bills by April 1996, it took another three months to negotiate a bill on which House Republicans and Clinton could agree.

MEDICARE, MEDICAID

Eager to make a mark from the outset, the 104th Congress set out to simultaneously remake the Medicare program for the elderly, part of which was projected to go broke in 2002, and turn back the rapidly-growing Medicaid program for the poor to the states.

For Medicare, which by the end of 1996 served some 37 million elderly and disabled Americans, Republicans wanted a major new emphasis on managed care, which they hoped could ultimately save enough money to preserve the program for the massive baby boom generation that would begin to retire in the year 2010.

For Medicaid, which served an almost equal number of low-income women, children and elderly, Republicans in Congress proposed, as part of their overall emphasis on "devolution," to turn the program from an "entitlement" into a "block grant," and let states decide more about who and what to cover.

At the same time, though, Congress was moving to balance the budget, and expected the health programs to produce their share of the savings: $270 billion over five years from Medicare and $163 billion from Medicaid.

Apparently, they did not learn from Democrats' overestimation in 1993 of what could be accomplished in a single bill or a single session of Congress. Although they did something Democrats in the prior Congress could not—deliver a bill to the president's desk—Clinton's December 1995 veto left them as empty-handed as the Democrats were a year earlier.

And in the meantime, while Republicans had blasted Democrats relentlessly during the health reform fight about the potential effects of a "government takeover of health care," Democrats returned the favor in 1995, accusing Republicans of trying to scuttle, not save, Medicare and Medicaid.

ABORTION

The national debate over abortion continued during the four years from 1993 to 1996.

For the first two years, the pendulum swung very slightly toward those who supported continued legal access to the procedure. On only his second full day in office, President Clinton, the strongest proponent of abortion rights to occupy the White House since the landmark 1973 Supreme Court decision *Roe v. Wade* legalizing the procedure nationwide, by executive order overturned a handful of abortion restrictions imposed by Presidents Ronald Reagan and George Bush. Congress later that year relaxed several more restrictions imposed over that same period in various appropriations bills. For example, for the first time since 1981, the so-called Hyde amendment that barred federal abortion funding was revised to include exceptions for rape and incest.

But the achievements were disappointing to abortion-rights advocates, who had hoped for much more. Particularly disappointing was the failure to advance the "Freedom of Choice Act." Proponents of the legislation said it would have merely codified the *Roe* decision. But opponents said it would have gone considerably further, overturning many state restrictions, such as mandatory waiting periods or parental notification provisions, that the Supreme Court had ruled constitutional in subsequent decisions.

The 104th Congress, led and dominated by conservative abortion foes, came in determined to reverse course in 1995. And to some extent they did, forcing Clinton to swallow a reinstatement of many of the restrictions that were loosened by the 103rd Congress.

They also changed the terms of the abortion debate. Rather than arguing about whether women or lawmakers should decide abortion matters, abortion foes turned the spotlight to the procedure itself, specifically, to a rarely-used procedure performed late in pregnancy. Medically it was known as "dilation and extraction," or D&X. But in legislation to ban it, abortion opponents labeled it "partial-birth" abortion, and accused those of performing it to be committing near infanticide. Clinton vetoed the bill when it reached his desk in 1996, arguing that it needed to include an exception to preserve the health of the pregnant woman, not just her life. But it was clear by public opinion polls that abortion foes had found a potent issue, and while Congress fell just short of the votes needed for an override, lawmakers knew they had a bill that would live to fight another day.

OTHER HEALTH LEGISLATION

In 1996, the "managed-care backlash" reached Capitol Hill. With more and more Americans joining—or, in effect, being forced to join because their employers offer no alternative plan—"managed care" plans that restricted their choice of physicians and health care facilities, horror stories were beginning to emerge about patients who suffered or died as a result of having been denied care. Following the lead of more than half the states, Congress appended to an unrelated appropriations bill two provisions aimed at improving private health benefits, and considered a third.

One of the provisions that became law was aimed at ending so-called "drive-through" deliveries, the practice of many insurance companies of requiring new mothers and newborns to leave the hospital within 24 hours of birth. The second was a scaled-back version of legislation that originally called for "parity" between benefits offered for mental health and for physical ailments. The final language merely called for parity in annual and lifetime limits in coverage, but mental health advocates called it an important first step toward equal treatment. Several, albeit unsuccessful, attempts were made to ban "gag clauses" in managed-care contracts that prohibited doctors from telling patients about other doctors or treatments not covered by the plan.

The 104th Congress also failed in its effort to overhaul the Food and Drug Administration (FDA). As part of their theme of reducing federal regulation, Republicans took obvious aim at the agency that regulated products accounting for one of every four dollars spent in the U.S. economy. Critics had charged for years that the agency's slow approval process and overzealous enforcement was hindering both economic growth and preventing new and potentially life-saving products from reaching patients. But defenders of the agency charged that the FDA had been hindered by Congress itself, which had given it more and more assignments but not enough resources to get the job done. They argued that the proposed overhaul efforts, which included contracting out some of the FDA's approval work to private firms, presented the potential for dangerous conflicts of interest. They also pointed to the agency's exemplary record of having kept dangerous drugs and devices off the market.

WELFARE REFORM

When President Clinton vowed on the campaign trail in 1992 to "end welfare as we know it," he almost certainly had no idea that four years later he would sign a bill to end the federal

government's 61-year-old promise of cash aid to poor women and children.

Welfare was something of an afterthought for the 103rd Congress, which was preoccupied with the budget, health care reform and an omnibus crime bill. But when the Republicans took over in the next Congress, the legislative landscape changed altogether. While Clinton proposed some sweeping changes to the system—including a two-year time limit before welfare recipients would be required to go to work—Republicans' ideas were far more dramatic.

Clinton's time limits had a long list of exceptions, but Republicans were firm in their resolve—after five years, no more benefits, period. And, unlike Clinton, Republicans also wanted to cut off assistance to most noncitizens, including those in the country legally.

Republicans in 1995 pushed their proposal through Congress twice—first as part of a broad budget-balancing reconciliation bill and then as a stand-alone measure. Both times Clinton vetoed it, claiming it was too draconian and would hurt those it intended to help.

After the nation's governors were able to develop a bipartisan plan in 1996, Republicans decided to try a third time on welfare reform, originally packaging it with another attempt at turning the Medicaid health program back to the states. But when Clinton made it clear he would veto any bill with the Medicaid provisions attached, Republicans decided to send him a clean bill and make him choose whether to anger liberals who opposed ending welfare's entitlement status or break his own campaign vow. The dare worked—Clinton signed the bill—but even as he did, he promised to seek changes to lessen the impact on immigrants and others who might be hurt.

HEAD START

The 103rd Congress helped President Clinton keep another of his campaign promises—to broadly expand Head Start, the popular education, nutrition and social service program for low-income preschoolers. But the bill also continued an emphasis that had been growing for several Congresses toward ensuring that Head Start's quality was not compromised as its availability was increased.

Despite its popularity—and a 50 percent funding increase since 1989—by 1993 Head Start was reaching only about half of its eligible population. Still, some lawmakers, mostly Republicans, had been expressing concerns that the rapid expansion of the program was diminishing the quality of the experience. As a result, the authorization bill that cleared in 1994 continued a policy begun in 1990 of setting aside 25 percent of the increased funding for quality improvements.

VETERANS' AFFAIRS

Still smarting from criticism over lengthy delays in providing for the health needs of veterans exposed to the defoliant Agent Orange in Vietnam, the 103rd Congress moved quickly to ensure that veterans from the victorious Desert Shield and Desert Storm operations were better served. So when those who served in the 1990–1991 Persian Gulf conflict began to complain of a wide variety of unexplained symptoms, including nausea, hair loss, fatigue, rashes, and heart and respiratory problems, Congress did not hesitate to respond.

Despite the fact that doctors could not pinpoint the exact cause—candidates included exposure to oil fires in Kuwait, indigenous parasites, military vehicle paint and depleted uranium used to reinforce tank and artillery shells—Congress in 1994 approved legislation authorizing the Department of Veterans Affairs (VA) to pay disability benefits to those afflicted by what came to be called Persian Gulf syndrome. The bill was delayed for a time by a spat between VA Secretary Jesse Brown, who insisted he needed legislation to make the payments, and members of the Senate Veterans' Affairs Committee, who argued that Brown already had all the authority he needed.

The bill also authorized the VA to study the impact of Persian Gulf syndrome on the spouses and children of veterans who served in the war.

In 1996, Congress broke new ground on the veterans front, authorizing payments to children with the birth defect spina bifida who were born to veterans exposed to Agent Orange. Spina bifida occurred when a fetus's spine failed to form properly. The legislation, appended to the fiscal 1997 spending bill for the VA, represented the first time Congress agreed to pay veterans' benefits to children for harm they suffered as a result of their parents' military service.

The 104th Congress also cleared a major veterans health bill that sought to shift more services out of hospitals and into outpatient settings. While that shift had been evident—for reasons of cost as well as patient preference—in the rest of the health system, the VA was previously set up to discourage the use of outpatient care.

The 104th Congress failed, however, to accomplish a task begun in the 103rd Congress to make the VA's health care system more sensitive to the needs of women, who were expected to make up 11 percent of the veterans population by the year 2004. A bill that passed both the House and Senate in 1993 authorizing a series of new women's health services ultimately came to naught when conferees could not agree whether the offering of reproductive health care services might lead to the VA providing abortions.

Chronology of Action on Health

1993–1994

President Clinton's ambitious—and ultimately unsuccessful—effort to overhaul the nation's health system overshadowed all other health legislation in the 103rd Congress; indeed, it almost overshadowed all the other legislation considered in 1993 and 1994. The massive undertaking would have touched virtually every American, and its consideration did touch nearly every committee in Congress, down to those overseeing veterans and armed services. The failure of the effort—the House never even brought a bill to the floor—was credited by most analysts with helping the Republicans recapture Congress in the 1994 elections for the first time in a generation.

In fact, though, the 103rd Congress did take some significant steps in the health arena, from enacting a policy-setting authorization bill for the National Institutes for Health to making it a federal crime to block access to abortion clinics. The 103rd Congress also reversed a raft of abortion policies dating from the Ronald Reagan and George Bush presidencies, although most were reinstituted when the Republicans took over in 1995.

Health Care Reform

The health care overhaul that President Clinton had made the signature of his presidency was officially declared dead Sept. 26, 1994. Senate Majority Leader George Mitchell, D-Maine, who had passed up a chance to serve on the Supreme Court to see the massive health care bill through, made its demise official at a news conference that day.

The failure of the ambitious plan to restructure the nation's health care system was all but certain in late August when lawmakers left Washington for an abbreviated summer recess without either chamber having passed a health care reform bill. House and Senate leaders maintained that they could complete work on a scaled-down measure when they returned, but by then there was too little time and virtually no momentum left.

Democrats divided over Clinton's approach aimed at addressing the twin problems of spiraling health care costs and the 35 million to 38 million Americans who lacked health insurance. Most controversial were proposals that employers pay for most of their workers' health costs and that the government be given a hands-on role in the health care system. Republicans, for the most part, were united in opposition to the whole effort, which they regarded as relying too heavily on taxes and regulation.

Although big business initially pushed for reform, many of its leaders became convinced that Clinton's proposal would mean new taxes and more detailed prescriptions from the federal government about what kind of health insurance they could provide. Small-business groups worried that the costs would mean job losses, and they took that message to the public.

"Maybe it was too much to expect that in two years you could have changed so much of the health care system," reflected Sen. John D. Rockefeller IV, D-W.Va., one of the most stalwart supporters of Clinton's plan. "But we didn't know that when we started, and there wasn't any reason for us to know that."

In retrospect, however, it was possible to see at least three basic reasons why the process went awry.

First, Clinton's health care proposal, which sought to remake the entire system, suffered from being too sweeping and too difficult to explain to the public and to lawmakers. The very size of the bill made it vulnerable to criticism by special interests—notably the insurance industry, which used the bill's own language to lampoon the administration in television advertisements and to raise fears about the legislation.

Second, the congressional committee process broke down, particularly in the House, with multiple committees given jurisdiction and no committee achieving a bipartisan consensus that could serve as a basis for floor action.

Third, there was never any visible effort by the Clinton administration and the Senate leadership to produce a bipartisan measure until the final weeks of the session, when it was too late. Democratic leaders, unwilling to break with Clinton's goal of providing affordable health coverage to all Americans, never made a meaningful compromise offer to Republicans.

GOP leaders, for their part, had the luxury of being in the minority and, therefore, without any ultimate responsibility for the legislation. That freed them to criticize Clinton and the Democrats rather than attempting to craft viable alternatives.

CLINTON'S PLAN

Clinton had presented his health care plan—crafted under the direction of First Lady Hillary Rodham Clinton in a massive, secret and much-criticized task force process—on Sept. 22, 1993, in a nationally televised speech to Congress and the nation.

From early on, Clinton's drive to revamp the nation's health care system was likened to the New Deal policies of President Franklin D. Roosevelt. Its effect was projected to be at least as sweeping, and like Roosevelt's programs, its economic and social impact was expected to touch every American. But unlike the New Deal, the Clinton proposal—when it finally arrived—bore the marks of an era when even Democrats had become reluctant to support programs that carried high government costs. The plan always aimed to pay for itself without a broad-based tax—a sharp contrast to past Democratic social programs, such as Medicare and Social Security.

Its keystones were permanent health insurance coverage for all Americans, a requirement that employers pay at least 80 percent of the cost of a basic package of benefits for their employees, a proposal to put all Americans into new quasi-governmental health care alliances to increase their leverage with insurers and providers, and a cap on the annual increase in health insurance premium costs. It also included an increase of about 75 cents per pack in the federal tax on cigarettes, which cost it considerable support among lawmakers from tobacco-producing states.

Outlays for Health

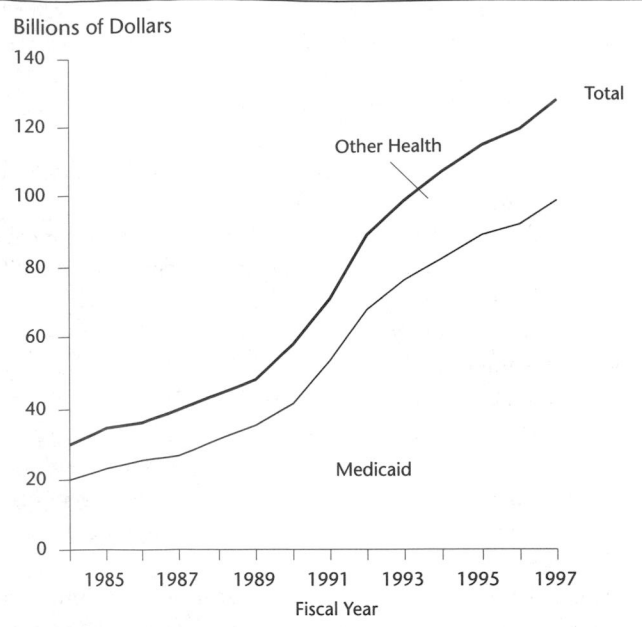

Billions of Dollars

NOTE: Data for 1997 are estimated.

SOURCE: Office of Management and Budget, *Historical Tables, Budget of the United States Government: Fiscal Year 1998* (Washington, D.C.: U.S. Government Printing Office, 1997), Tables 3.2 and 8.5.

The plan was sweeping, touching every problem area of the health care system, from workers' compensation to the shortage of primary care doctors. And while Clinton made clear he was prepared to negotiate changes to the proposal, he did maintain a singular bottom line: in his Jan. 25, 1994, State of the Union address, he vowed to veto any health care reform bill that did not guarantee permanent health care coverage, known as "universal coverage," to every American.

The initial reaction to the plan was almost uniformly positive—and the feeling of inevitability for the plan was buttressed by an unprecedented sweep of Capitol Hill hearing rooms by Hillary Clinton. In a single week, the first lady testified before the five key committees that would have jurisdiction over the plan: the House panels on Ways and Means, Energy and Commerce, and Education and Labor, and the Senate committees on Finance and on Labor and Human Resources.

Although Hillary Clinton was not the only first lady to testify before Congress, none had testified at such length or exhibited such depth of knowledge. She answered hundreds of questions about the plan over the course of the week, demonstrating not only a mastery of the details of the complicated proposal but also extensive knowledge of the lawmakers she was addressing as well. She filled her testimony with references to specific districts, hospitals and members' backgrounds.

But elsewhere, opposition was building. Soon after its unveiling, the proposal was met by an onslaught of negative ads and a barrage of news stories on the subject that left the public bewildered; polls showed public approval peaked with Clinton's speech and then steadily declined.

Conservative Republicans diagrammed the Clinton bill and came up with a mazelike picture that made the new system look like a bureaucratic nightmare. The Health Insurance Association of America—which had supported the idea of universal health coverage but opposed the prescriptive nature of the Clinton plan—launched what became know as its "Harry and Louise" ads, featuring a yuppie couple plowing through the Clinton Health Security Act, whose 1,342 pages rivaled the size of a dictionary. The couple pulled out technical-sounding provisions that, according to the ads, meant that Americans would pay more for less health care.

Lawmakers trying to sell the plan to constituents found they faced the uphill job of simultaneously explaining the new system and combating criticism of it. And there was no getting around the reality that the bill was immensely complex. Its simple goal was to provide affordable health insurance to all Americans by containing insurance prices and subsidizing care for those who could not afford insurance. But to achieve that end, the bill relied on an entirely new and hard-to-explain financing system.

Perhaps the final straw in terms of public understanding was the fact that Congress was writing its own complex bills at the same time that committees were working on the Clinton bill. As the Washington press corps scrambled to explain the flotilla of new approaches, the public just stopped reading.

Looking back, experts said it would have been better to start with something smaller that the public could understand. Americans rarely felt comfortable with broad changes made in one fell swoop, said Uwe Reinhardt, a professor of political economy at Princeton University and a noted health policy expert. "In most legislation, America is an incremental country, and, we have learned, health care too has to be done incrementally."

Health care also proved too difficult for the institution to digest. The committee system, designed to resolve both the policy and political problems of legislation, broke down entirely. Disarray in the committee process that would manifest itself most obviously in 1994, first surfaced in the fall of 1993, when House and Senate leaders declined to resolve the competition for jurisdiction over the bill by rival panels.

RIVAL JURISDICTIONS, PLANS

In the House, the leadership referred the bill to all three committees that had major jurisdictional claims: Ways and Means, Energy and Commerce, and Education and Labor. Secondary referrals went to seven committees, which were charged with working on specific sections covering issues such as health care for veterans and Native Americans, malpractice reform and insurance fraud.

In the Senate, the rules allowed only a single committee to have primary jurisdiction. Neither Finance Committee Chairman Daniel Patrick Moynihan, D-N.Y., nor Labor and Human Resources Committee Chairman Edward M. Kennedy, D-Mass., was willing to let the other have the prime position. Rather than choosing between them, the leadership left the bill on the calendar with plans to bring it directly to the floor in 1994. The Fi-

HEALTH LEADERSHIP

Donna E. Shalala, the first woman to head a Big Ten school as chancellor of the University of Wisconsin at Madison, won Senate voice vote approval Jan. 21, 1993, as President Clinton's secretary of health and human services (HHS). The Senate Finance Committee, which had jurisdiction over the nomination, approved Shalala by voice vote Jan. 19.

Shalala was a surprise pick to head HHS. She was mentioned as a possible secretary of the Department of Education because of her involvement in higher education, and as secretary of the Department of Housing and Urban Development because she served as an assistant secretary under President Jimmy Carter. Shalala had little experience in health policy but had been involved in children's programs as chairman of the board of the Children's Defense Fund, a children's advocacy group, succeeding Hillary Rodham Clinton in that post. *(Background, cabinet profiles, p. 1112)*

After two months of acrimony, the Senate on Sept. 7, 1993, approved by a vote of 65–34 the nomination of Dr. Joycelyn Elders to be the 16th Surgeon General of the United States. The Senate Labor and Human Resources Committee voted 13–4 to recommend her confirmation on July 30, but conservative opponents had used procedural maneuvers to delay a vote by the full Senate until after the annual summer recess.

A sharecropper's daughter who never saw a physician until she entered college, Elders served in the Army and later attended medical school on the GI bill. She became a pediatrician and later served as Health Director for the state of Arkansas under then-Gov. Bill Clinton. But her outspoken attitude on such matters as abortion and teenage sex got her labeled as a radical abortion rights proponent by foes who dubbed her the "condom queen." She was one of the most controversial nominees to survive the confirmation process. *(Controversial nominations, p. 1118)*

But Elders's views ultimately cost her the job of surgeon general. Clinton fired her on Dec. 9, 1994, after she made remarks on sex education with which the president disagreed.

Clinton had no better luck with his next nominee for surgeon general. The politics of abortion and the presidential race intertwined in 1995 to drag down the Feb. 2, 1995, nomination of Henry W. Foster Jr., a Nashville obstetrician/gynecologist, to succeed Elders.

Foster's nomination faced opposition from antiabortion activists, as well as from several senators who were vying for the GOP presidential nomination and seeking the support of the party's conservative wing. The Senate derailed the nomination by twice rejecting motions to block a threatened filibuster. The decisive vote came June 21, when the Senate, in a **key vote of 57–43 (R 11–43; D 46–0),** failed by three votes to cut off debate. There was no change in the second tally the next day. *(1995 key votes, p. 1025; controversial nominations, p. 1121)*

---

nance and Labor committees were left to draft rival bills that could be offered as floor amendments.

The legislative process was also complicated by the number of competing proposals from across the ideological spectrum—many of which enjoyed considerable, if still minority, support.

From liberal Democrats came a plan for a Canadian-style single-payer system, which would have had the government replace private insurance companies, collecting premiums and paying health care providers. The plan promised to cover everyone, control prices, impose massive new taxes and sharply cut health care profits. Rep. Jim McDermott, D-Wash., was its leading proponent.

From the other end of the ideological spectrum came Republican plans, including one by Sen. Phil Gramm of Texas, to minimize government involvement in health care and instead encourage consumers to put aside savings for their own health care expenses.

The two leading alternatives emerging from the center were sponsored by Rep. Jim Cooper, D-Tenn., and Sen. John Chafee, R-R.I. Neither bill included an employer mandate. Both aimed to reorganize the health care market, rather than control it through government regulation. The Cooper plan, backed in the Senate by John B. Breaux, D-La., got a boost Feb. 2, 1994, when the Business Roundtable, an influential group of 200 corporate leaders, endorsed it as "the best starting point for reform."

1994 COMMITTEE ACTION

Altogether, four committees—Ways and Means and Education and Labor in the House and Finance and Labor and Human Resources in the Senate—approved health care reform proposals, all of them different in various substantial ways from the original Clinton plan. The fifth committee with jurisdiction over the measure, House Energy and Commerce, never proceeded to markup, after Chairman John Dingell, D-Mich., found himself unable to produce a measure guaranteeing universal coverage—his and Clinton's bottom line—that would garner a majority of committee votes.

But in the end, none of the bills both met Clinton's requirement for universal coverage and had enough support to pass. As a result, on almost every key issue—from employer mandates to cost controls to the basic benefits package—the committee products were at best only building blocks for House and Senate Democratic leaders, who set out at midyear to craft their own bills. "Typically, the committee process clears out the underbrush on legislation. That didn't happen on health care," said Rep. David E. Skaggs, D-Colo.

House Education and Labor

The Education and Labor Committee on June 23, 1994, became the first House committee to approve its version of the health care bill (HR 3600). The liberal-leaning panel endorsed,

---

A HEALTH CARE CHRONOLOGY

1993

Jan. 25: President Clinton appointed Hillary Rodham Clinton to head a task force to draft a comprehensive overhaul of the nation's health care system. The goals: to provide universal coverage and cut rising health care costs.

March 3: Rep. Jim McDermott, D-Wash., introduced a bill (HR 1200) to set up a Canadian-style, single-payer system.

May: Task force was disbanded; the Clintons worked with cabinet members and top advisers to flesh out the plan.

Sept. 22: Clinton unveiled his long-awaited proposal in a nationally televised speech to a joint session of Congress. His bottom line: universal coverage.

Oct. 6: Reps. Jim Cooper, D-Tenn., and Fred Grandy, R-Iowa, introduced a bill (HR 3222) to increase coverage by reorganizing the health insurance market.

Nov. 20: Clinton's 1,342-page health care bill was introduced (HR 3600, S 1757). House leaders referred entire bill to three committees; two Senate panels competed to take the lead.

Nov. 22; Sen. John H. Chafee, R-R.I., introduced a bill (S 1770) requiring that all Americans have health insurance by 2005.

1994

Jan. 25: In his State of the Union address, Clinton vowed to veto any health bill that did not guarantee universal coverage.

June 9: Senate Labor and Human Resources became the first full committee to complete work, voting 11–6 along mainly partisan lines to approve a bill modeled on Clinton's plan.

June 23: House Education and Labor Committee voted 26–17 for an expanded version of Clinton's plan. To win the votes of the most liberal members, the committee also sent to the floor without recommendation a single-payer plan (HR 3960).

June 28: House Energy and Commerce Committee Chairman John D. Dingell, D-Mich., notified leadership that his panel, often seen as a bellwether of congressional opinion, could not agree on a health care bill.

June 30: House Ways and Means Committee approved a Clinton-style bill, 20–18. "No" votes included all 14 Republicans, joined by three conservative Democrats and one liberal.

July 2: Senate Finance Committee approved the only bipartisan measure to emerge from a committee; the vote was 12–8.

July 21: Democratic leaders told Clinton his bill would have to be scaled back.

July 29: Majority Leader Richard A. Gephardt, D-Mo., unveiled a House leadership bill.

Aug. 2: Majority Leader George J. Mitchell, D-Maine, released a Senate leadership bill.

Aug. 9: The Senate began floor debate on the Mitchell bill.

Aug. 19: A rump group of senators—led by Chafee and John B. Breaux, D-La., and known as the Mainstream Group—offered a bipartisan compromise.

Aug. 25: After a bitter debate on the crime bill, the Senate started its August recess without finishing a health care bill. The next day, Mitchell scrapped his bill, conceding that comprehensive health care reform would not come in 1994.

Sept. 26: Mitchell declared health care dead for the year, after a compromise bill that he negotiated with the Mainstream Group failed to attract enough votes.

26–17, an expanded version of Clinton's plan, filled with extra medical benefits and insurance premium subsidies.

The committee's 1,200-plus-page bill, which was formally reported July 22 (H Rept 103-601, Part II), represented more than three years of hearings and work. The full committee spent eight days working on the bill, acting on 87 amendments, 46 of which were adopted. The panel's Subcommittee on Labor-Management Relations had worked for five weeks on the bill, from April 21 through May 25.

As approved by the committee, the bill required employers to pay at least 80 percent of the health insurance premiums for their workers as a means to guarantee health coverage for all Americans. It included significant subsidies to help small businesses pay this cost, and it mandated a large, generous package of benefits that all health insurance policies would have to offer. It made Clinton's quasi-governmental health care alliances optional for states.

The committee also reported without recommendation on July 22 a single-payer plan (HR 3960—H Rept 103-618, Part I) that required the government to run the insurance system. Allowing the bill, which had the support of about 100 House Democrats, out of committee was the quid pro quo of the 15 single-payer supporters on the committee for their votes on the broader bill. But like health reform in general, the single-payer bill never made it to the House floor.

Republicans took the marathon effort very seriously. Attendance was high, and Republicans offered 49 amendments in full committee, many of which were not intended to embarrass Democrats or to make political points. The committee adopted 10 GOP amendments.

House Ways and Means

On June 30, the House Ways and Means Committee approved its health care reform bill by a narrow vote of 20–18, with all the panel's Republicans and four Democrats voting no. But it was considered something of an achievement that the panel managed to approve any bill at all, given the deep fissures among committee Democrats and the loss only a month earlier of veteran dealmaker and committee chairman Dan Rostenkowski, D-Ill.

The measure (HR 3600—H Rept 103-601, Part I), formally reported July 14, was shepherded through by Sam M. Gibbons, D-Fla., who became acting chairman May 31 when Rostenkowski was indicted on corruption charges and had to step aside as chairman. The concessions necessary to put together a majority in the committee left Gibbons with a patchwork plan that fully satisfied neither wing of his party. *(Rostenkowski case, p. 870)*

The committee's bill aimed to achieve universal coverage by 1998 by requiring most employers to pay at least 80 percent of the costs of health insurance for their workers. It called for the creation of a huge new government insurance program, known as Medicare Part C, to cover the poor, the uninsured and small-business employees. The bill sought to limit the rise in insurance premiums to the increase in the gross domestic product. It proposed to increase the cigarette tax from 24 cents to 69 cents a pack and to impose a 2 percent sales tax on insurance companies' premiums and on employers who self-insured their workers.

In order to get the bill through the committee, though, Gibbons had had to agree to a number of changes designed to win the support of panel Democrats worried about the interests of tobacco, small business and health insurers. To appease small business, Gibbons added to the bill an additional $20 billion in tax breaks for employers of low-wage workers. For the insurance industry, the bill delayed cost-controls on private insurance premiums and called for a commission to study the issue. And for tobacco farmers and companies, Gibbons reduced the tobacco tax increase from the 60 cents in the original bill to 45 cents per pack.

Senate Labor and Human Resources

On the other side of Capitol Hill, the Senate Labor and Human Resources Committee became the first panel in that chamber to act on health care overhaul, voting 11-6 on June 9 to approve a bill (S 1757) modeled on Clinton's. The committee proposed to provide health insurance for all Americans and require employers to pay the bulk of the costs. This was the very formula Republicans and many Democrats had dismissed as too bureaucratic and costly for U.S. business, leading critics to spurn the bill, sponsored by Chairman Edward M. Kennedy, D-Mass., and criticize the committee for failing to advance health reform. Indeed, most key decisions were ultimately made on largely party-line votes.

But S 1757 differed substantially from Clinton's plan, and every Democrat and Vermont Republican James M. Jeffords voted for it. That was hardly a bipartisan breakthrough—Jeffords was the lone Republican signed on to Clinton's bill—but the committee's product did incorporate critical compromises crafted with substantive GOP input.

The committee altered the Clinton plan in three key areas:
• While the committee retained Clinton's requirement that employers provide and pay for the bulk of workers' insurance costs, it included significant new exemptions and subsidies for business that employed 75 or fewer workers.
• The committee bill required states to establish at least one health insurance purchasing cooperative, or alliance, but it did not require participation, as Clinton's plan did, and it cut back on the federal regulatory structure that Clinton proposed.
• The panel approved a standard insurance benefits package for consumers that was more comprehensive than Clinton's. But it included a fail-safe mechanism to trim the package if it would cause unanticipated deficit spending.

For a time, a bipartisan group of panel moderates headed by Democrat Jeff Bingaman of New Mexico hoped to craft compromises that would increase Republican support on these issues. But while the committee accepted substantial changes proposed by Bingaman, they were not enough to win GOP support.

Republicans could not swallow any mandate on employers, they rejected requiring states to set up cooperatives and they argued that Congress should not be in the business of writing an insurance benefits package.

"This proposal has reached the end of its trail because it fails to offer a middle ground upon which the public or the majority in the Senate can stand," said ranking committee Republican Nancy Landon Kassebaum of Kansas, whose vote was considered essential to winning passage on the Senate floor.

S 1757 was never formally reported out of committee.

Senate Finance Committee

The Senate Finance Committee was the last of the major committees to complete work on the health care reform bill, approving its proposal (S 2351—S Rept 103-323) by a vote of 12-8 on July 2 and reporting it Aug. 2. Unlike the other committees, Finance produced a bill with bipartisan support. The measure, which relied far more heavily than the others on market forces, seemed certain to pull the Senate floor debate to the right of President Clinton and to reverberate in the House as well.

Chairman Daniel Patrick Moynihan, D-N.Y., appeared convinced from the outset that he would have to produce a bipartisan measure, a judgment dictated by the committee's makeup and politics: The panel had 11 Democrats, two of whom clearly would not support Clinton's bill, and nine Republicans.

Under pressure from the administration and a good portion of the committee Democrats, the panel considered briefly, and then abandoned, a Clinton-style bill with universal coverage and an employer mandate. Instead, the bill that was finally approved by the committee set a goal of covering 95 percent of Americans by 2002 through changing insurance market practices and providing subsidies to help low-income people buy insurance.

The subsidies were to be funded by $55 billion in Medicare cuts over five years, cuts in Medicaid and new taxes, including an increase in the cigarette tax to $1 a pack from 24 cents a pack. The bill also included a 1.75 percent tax on insurance premiums to support academic medical centers.

CLINTON PLAN HIGHLIGHTS

Clinton's health care overhaul bill, introduced Nov. 20, 1993 (HR 3600, S 1757), contained provisions to:

• **Universal Coverage.** Require all citizens to enroll in a health plan. Employers would pay at least about 80 percent of the average local cost of their employees' health plans; employees would pay the balance. The government would subsidize low-income individuals and families, as well as businesses with fewer than 75 employees.

All health plans would have to offer comprehensive benefits including mental health care, preventive dental care for children and some long-term care. Plans could not charge extra for particular benefits, nor could they limit the use of benefits. However, some benefits would be covered fully only with the consent of the plan.

• **Long-Term Care.** Create a federal entitlement program for states to pay for home health-care services for eligible individuals. The program would be financed predominantly by the federal government; states would pay a 5 percent to 22 percent match. The administration viewed this as a down payment toward full-fledged long-term care coverage. Eligibility was to be based not on income but on whether an individual met the federal criteria of needing help with at least three activities of daily living, such as eating, going to the bathroom and getting dressed. Nursing home care was not covered, but the grants would cover an extensive list of home health care services and adult day care.

• **Cost Sharing.** Limit health insurance premiums to 3.9 percent of an individual's income. Most consumers would choose among three payment formulas: a low-cost plan that was likely to provide care through a health maintenance organization (HMO) with a limited choice of doctors; a mid-price plan that offered care through a loose network of doctors with an option for consumers to go outside the network; and a high-cost plan that allowed consumers to choose their own doctors. Costs would vary by region and by family status, with the amount that each person paid pegged to employment status.

• **Employer and Employee Responsibilities.** Divide employers into three categories: small, defined as those with fewer than 75 employees; large, defined as those with more than 5,000 employees; and all others. Taxes, subsidies and other financial responsibilities would vary widely among these groups. Self-employed people would be treated as small businesses and would be eligible for the same subsidies on the employer share (80 percent) of the premium as other small businesses.

Employees would be responsible for about 20 percent of the cost. However, the portion of the premium paid by employees would vary depending on employment status (full-time, part-time, self-employed or retired), income and family status (single, married or married with children).

• **National Health Board.** Create a new federal entity, known as the National Health Board, to oversee the new system, setting quality standards and reviewing the benefits packages. It would act as a clearinghouse for information about the new system's problems and would approve state plans. Without National Health Board approval, no state could receive federal subsidies.

• **Other Federal Responsibilities.** Provide for the Department of Health and Human Services (HHS) and the Department of Labor to oversee the new system jointly. HHS would oversee alliance enrollment policies, premium and cost-sharing discounts and the alliances' overall financial management. HHS would set up a board, called the Advisory Council on Breakthrough Drugs, to review new drug prices. It would publish information about the reasonableness of prices and the cost-effectiveness of new products compared with existing treatments.

The Labor Department would enforce the sections of the bill that dealt with employer premium payments and the creation and operation of corporate alliances. It also would set up an insolvency fund to pay providers and ensure that enrollees continued to have care if a corporate alliance failed.

A new National Quality Management Council would develop national performance measures to be used in assessing every health plan in the country, and would collect and disseminate data on the plans. All health alliances would have to publish clear information for consumers on how local health-care plans were doing in terms of the national quality measures.

• **State Role.** Allow states to choose between a Canadian-style single-payer system or a managed-competition system. Once a state chose a system, state flexibility would be limited by federal rules and standards designed to ensure that despite state differences, residents had comparable choices.

States would have an ambiguous role: They would be responsible for making the new system work but would have little latitude to adjust the system's design. States would monitor the local health-care industry, enforce new laws and continue to finance health-care services for poor Americans. However, several state laws would be preempted.

• **Health Alliances.** Provide for quasi-governmental entities, to be set up by the states. These health alliances would coordinate the health care system for consumers in a region, replacing the role of insurance companies and employee benefits managers. A regional alliance could be set up as a private nonprofit corporation or as a state agency. Generally, a regional alliance's enrollees would primarily be full-time and part-time employees of businesses of fewer than 5,000 workers, the self-employed, and the working and nonworking poor, whose health care would be subsidized by the government. The alliance would be the fiscal heart of the new system, in many states handling hundreds of millions of dollars annually.

All states would permit "corporate alliances"—health care buying groups set up by companies with more than 5,000 employees, by unions or by the Rural Electric and Rural Telephone Cooperatives. The rationale would be to allow large multistate employers to avoid having to keep track of many different states' health insurance laws.

• **Health Plans.** Require most consumers to select a health plan rather than an individual doctor. The plan would be required to offer a package of guaranteed benefits, providing subscribers with access to a group of doctors (primary care physicians and specialists), hospitals, nonphysician care providers such as physical therapists, and outpatient clinics that offered services such as mental health treatment. Several plans probably would organize as HMOs or similar networks. Plans could be organized by health-care providers or by an insurance company. Plans could not turn down any subscriber for any reason, nor could they force anyone to pay a surcharge because of an illness or disability.

• **Public Health.** Redesign funding of the public health care system to create a block grant program for states. The grants could be used for collecting health data, environmental protection, violence reduction programs and public education about the hazards of tobacco, drugs and behavior that increased the risk of AIDS. The bill called for a total of $325 million for such grants in fiscal 1996, $450 million in fiscal 1997 and up to $750 million in 2000.

The bill also authorized $175 million in fiscal 1996 and $200 million from fiscal 1997 through 2000 for a separate HHS grant program to encourage disease prevention.

• **Medicare.** Retain the existing framework of Medicare, the government's health insurance program for the elderly. In the only major change to Medicare benefits, the bill would provide coverage for prescription drugs for Medicare beneficiaries for the first time.

The price of Medicare coverage would rise sharply for wealthier beneficiaries. The program's rate of growth would be sharply reduced, with most of the cuts borne by doctors and hospitals. The working elderly and their spouses would be required to buy health care through alliances rather than through Medicare.

• **Medicaid.** Subsume Medicaid, the federal-state health insurance program for the poor, into the new health alliance system. Medicaid patients would receive the same benefits package as other Americans. For patients who were receiving such services as transportation or translators, that would mean a reduction in benefits.

• **Malpractice, Fraud and Antitrust Law.** Require each health alliance to adopt an "alternative dispute resolution" system in an effort to avoid going to court over malpractice claims.

The bill also provided for a program to prevent health care fraud and abuse. And it proposed to repeal the McCarran-Ferguson Act of 1945, which effectively exempted the insurance industry from federal antitrust law.

• **Cost Controls.** Limit the annual rise in consumers' costs by controlling the percentage that premiums could rise. That would force health plans to limit payments and profits to doctors, hospitals and suppliers of medical equipment and pharmaceuticals. The bill also limited the amount the government could spend annually on subsidies for employers and individuals.

• **Tobacco Tax.** Raise the excise tax on cigarettes by 75 cents a pack, effective Oct. 1, 1994, bringing the federal tax on cigarettes to 99 cents. Taxes on other tobacco products would be subject to comparable increases.

• **Corporate Alliance Tax.** Require corporations of more than 5,000 employees that chose to provide health care through their own alliance to pay a tax equal to 1 percent of their total payroll.

The assessment would begin Jan. 1, 1996, and would help fund academic medical centers, which were being funded through Medicare.

• **Other Taxes.** Make a host of other changes in the tax code, including provisions to:

• Require wealthy taxpayers who enrolled in Medicare Part B, which subsidized physician care, to pay more on their individual income taxes.

The change would effectively raise Medicare Part B tax payments for these taxpayers from roughly 25 percent of the program's costs to about 75 percent. It would affect individuals with incomes of $90,000 or more (including adjusted gross income and tax-exempt interest income) and joint filers with incomes of $115,000 or more.

• Require all state and local government employees and their employers to pay the hospital insurance portion of the FICA (Social Security) tax, making them eligible for Medicare coverage.

• Impose a 1.5 percent assessment on premiums purchased through regional alliances to help underwrite academic medical centers and medical education.

• Require individuals to report benefits received under cafeteria plans as income for the purpose of calculating taxes owed. Beginning in 2003, employees would be taxed on supplemental health coverage paid by employers.

• Permit self-employed people to deduct the entire cost of insurance premiums paid to a health alliance for the benefits package.

• Require higher-income taxpayers who retired between the ages of 55 and 64 to repay subsidies provided for the employer share of their health insurance premiums. Repayment would be required for individual taxpayers with incomes over $90,000 and couples making above $115,000.

• Prevent employers from receiving a tax break for contributions to so-called retiree medical accounts, used for medical expenses as part of a pension plan.

• Exempt regional health alliances established under the bill from federal income tax.

• Permit individuals to claim a tax deduction on premiums for qualified long-term care insurance. In addition, taxpayers could exclude from their taxable income up to $150 a day for benefits paid through long-term care policies. The $150 cap would rise with inflation. Incapacitated people could claim a deduction for qualified long-term care expenses.

• Allow employers to claim a tax deduction on premiums paid on behalf of employees for long-term care coverage.

• Provide a tax credit of up to $7,500 to help defray the cost of certain services related to daily living purchased by the physically impaired.

• Provide a tax credit of up to $1,000 per month for up to 60 months for qualified physicians who practiced in areas with a shortage of doctors.

The bill did not require employers to buy insurance for their employees, though it provided for Congress to consider such a mandate if 95 percent of the people were not covered by 2002.

The Finance Committee bill contained no private-sector cost controls, relying instead on a new tax on expensive plans to hold down costs. The bill provided for two standard packages of benefits to be offered by all insurance plans—a comprehensive plan and a plan that would cover major illnesses, requiring consumers to pay for most other medical expenses.

For Clinton, the Finance Committee's movement was a mixed blessing. The bill differed substantially from his proposal. Yet senators and lobbyists on all sides said it was crucial for the committee to report out a bill with bipartisan support.

The bill's delayed appearance reflected the extreme difficulty the committee had in producing it. Some committee Democrats were unwilling to give up on Clinton's goals of universal coverage and government-run cost containment. Others wanted to work with Republicans on a compromise that would make gradual changes in the existing system and rely on market competition to cut spending.

Majority Leader George J. Mitchell, D-Maine, a member of the committee, hewed to Clinton's plan, as did committee members Tom Daschle, D-S.D., John D. Rockefeller IV, D-W.Va., and Donald W. Riegle Jr., D-Mich. All were leading proponents of the Clinton proposal, which their staffs helped prepare.

At the conservative end of the Democratic spectrum were John B. Breaux, La., David L. Boren, Okla., and Kent Conrad, N.D., who made up a core group that worked with moderate Republicans in an effort to shape an alternative bill. At the more liberal end were Max Baucus, D-Mont., David Pryor, D-Ark., and Bill Bradley, D-N.J. Chairman Moynihan, a maverick who often held neoconservative views on social issues, took a cautious approach, working for weeks to try to find a compromise.

In any other committee, the tensions might have generated less interest, but the Senate Finance Committee occupied a pivotal place in the health care debate. Many lawmakers, especially in the House, were counting on the panel to craft a grand compromise that could attract votes from both parties and pave the way for skittish members to vote for an overhaul bill. The committee's inability to move for many weeks had repercussions throughout Congress, slowing other committees and raising questions about whether any comprehensive bill could emerge in 1994.

House, Senate Armed Services

The House Armed Services Committee focused on how Medicare should reimburse the Defense Department for care provided to eligible military retirees and their families under Medicare. Armed Services approved its section of HR 3600 by voice vote July 26 after just 10 minutes of debate and reported the bill July 28 (H Rept 103-601, Part III). The Subcommittee on Military Forces and Personnel had approved the draft, 7–5, on July 20. The language approved by the panel included a provision to require Medicare to reimburse the Defense Department for health care provided to Medicare-eligible retirees or their dependents at military hospitals, a potential $1 billion annual bonus for the Defense Department.

The Senate Armed Services Committee took a somewhat different approach. On July 27, it approved provisions that would require Medicare to reimburse costs for military retirees and their dependents who chose a Defense Department health care plan through a new Pentagon health insurance system called Tricare. The Senate Committee did not require Medicare to pay for services rendered at military hospitals for retirees who did not belong to Tricare.

House Government Operations

On July 27, the House Government Operations Committee gave voice vote approval to legislation designed to beef up the prosecution of fraud and give added privacy protection to patients' medical records. The panel reported HR 3600 (H Rept 103-601, Part V) on Aug. 12.

The panel proposed to set up a fund, financed by fines and other financial penalties, that the attorney general could use to boost prosecutions.

It also proposed to designate all health care information that could be traced back to the patient as protected health care information. Unauthorized disclosure of such information could result in federal criminal penalties. The committee also proposed to classify people with access to these records as health information trustees, meaning they would be held liable for any unlawful disclosure.

House Judiciary

The House Judiciary Committee Aug. 2 by voice vote approved provisions that aimed to reduce malpractice costs, tighten antitrust rules to promote competition among health insurers and create a program to prevent fraud and abuse in the new health system. Under changes made by the panel, the use of "alternative dispute resolution" measures, such as mediation, would be voluntary rather than mandatory, as in Clinton's original proposal. Contingency fees would be capped at one third of any damage award, but lawyers could petition the court for an increase if the case was appealed. And with court approval, defendants could make periodic payments if damages in a malpractice suit exceeded $250,000.

On antitrust, the committee went even further than the administration's proposal to eliminate the antitrust exemption for insurers granted under the 1945 McCarran-Ferguson Act. While the Clinton plan would have eliminated the protections only for health insurers, the committee bill eliminated them for nearly all insurers. Under the proposal, insurers could still share some information, such as data on occupational accidents and illnesses qualifying for workers' compensation benefits. But the measure would have phased out the sharing of "trending" information, used to project costs and calculate rates.

House Natural Resources

At its markup July 20, the Natural Resources Committee endorsed Clinton's plan to create a new and improved Indian Health Service (IHS) to provide health care to the nation's 1.2

million Native Americans. The panel reported the bill (H Rept 103-601, Part VI) Oct. 6.

Under the provisions, which the panel approved by voice vote, the IHS would expand to eventually offer the same comprehensive set of benefits available to other U.S. citizens under Clinton's plan. Clinton's bill provided for the IHS to continue to offer Native Americans additional benefits such as adult dental care. The U.S. government was obligated to provide supplemental health benefits under treaties with Native American tribes.

Native Americans could choose private health plans, but the measure encouraged them to sign up with the IHS by making the coverage free to all Native Americans. Tribal governments and major employers on reservations also would have been exempt from health payments to the IHS. The measure included an authorization of $220 million in fiscal 1995 to improve IHS services and facilities and to continue supplemental health services. The amount for fiscal 1996 was $380 million; unspecified amounts were authorized thereafter.

Senate Indian Affairs

The Senate Indian Affairs Committee by a vote of 10-8 on June 30 approved provisions of S 1757 to expand and improve the IHS to serve as the primary health care provider for Native Americans. The IHS eventually would have offered the same comprehensive benefits guaranteed to all Americans under Clinton's plan.

At the markup, the panel adopted by voice vote the package of amendments developed by tribal leaders in conjunction with the Clinton administration and committee members.

House Post Office and Civil Service

The House Post Office and Civil Service Committee on July 28 approved provisions to allow millions of private-sector employees to join the health insurance plan that served Congress and other federal employees. The bill (HR 3600—H Rept 103-601, Part VII) was reported Oct. 7.

The committee bill, approved by voice vote, proposed to open the Federal Employees Health Benefits Program to the unemployed, the self-employed, and workers at firms with 100 or fewer employees. Clinton had proposed to eliminate the federal employees' insurance plan. "Members will be able to tell their constituents that they can receive the same health benefits that members of Congress receive," Chairman William L. Clay, D-Mo., said at the markup.

While opening up the plan had widespread appeal among private-sector workers, it was vehemently opposed by the powerful federal employee unions. They contended that adding so many people to the rolls would drive up the cost of insurance premiums for federal employees. To appease the unions, the bill proposed to keep federal workers and retirees already on the insurance plan in a separate pool for several years for purposes of calculating insurance premiums. The approach seemed to work. Robert M. Tobias, president of the National Treasury Employees Union, said July 29 that his union "supports what the chairman has done."

Moreover, nonfederal workers could join the program only after several insurance-industry changes had been put in place, including a ban on the practice of denying coverage to people with existing medical conditions.

House Veterans' Affairs

The House Veterans' Affairs Committee approved by voice vote July 21 and reported Aug. 2 provisions of HR 3600 (H Rept 103-601, Part IV) that would have allowed veterans and their families to choose between the Department of Veterans Affairs (VA) and other private medical providers. Under the proposal, which largely paralleled Clinton's bill, the VA would have maintained its independent status and competed with private providers for patients.

Before endorsing the legislation, though, the panel voted 14-20 to prevent abortion from being offered as a covered service in VA facilities or plans.

Senate Veterans' Affairs

Like its House counterpart, the Senate Veterans' Affairs Committee sought to integrate veterans health care services into whatever new medical system would ultimately be created under health care legislation. Meeting on July 14, the panel first approved a measure that largely mirrored Clinton's plan for the VA. The 8–4 vote was largely along party lines, with only Vermont Republican Jeffords joining the Democrats.

The committee then approved, 12–0, alternative proposals that would have allowed the VA to function under a variety of health care systems.

As in Clinton's proposal, the panel's principal bill, sponsored by Rockefeller, maintained the independence of the VA's medical system while forcing it to compete with private health care providers. The plan gave most veterans the option of purchasing health care services from the VA or from private medical providers. It also opened the door for spouses and children of veterans to purchase health services from the VA.

LEADERSHIP EFFORTS

For all their work, not one committee had managed to write a health care bill that the leadership was willing to bring to the floor. So Senate Majority Leader Mitchell, House Majority Leader Richard A. Gephardt, D-Mo., and others began to stitch together new legislation from pieces of Clinton's plan and from bills approved by various committees.

The first decisions that had to be made were what to do about the employer mandate and how universal to make "universal" coverage. These would set the parameters for other decisions, such as how to control costs and what changes to make in insurance practices. By July 21, Mitchell, Gephardt and House Speaker Thomas S. Foley, D-Wash., were ready to formally tell Clinton that they had to back off from the sweeping overhaul he had envisioned. At a late-night White House meeting, they told the president that the bills they were cobbling together for floor action would contain a long phase-in of the employer mandate and possibly exemptions for small businesses. Clinton, sensing that any chance for successful legislation was slipping away, accepted their judgment.

CLINTON HEALTH CARE OVERHAUL COMPARED WITH OTHER MAJOR PLANS

Plan	Coverage	Benefits	Alliances
CLINTON PLAN	Guaranteed health coverage for all Americans by 1998 by requiring employers to pay at least 80 percent of their employees' premiums as of Jan. 1 of that year.	Mandated a package of specific benefits covering routine doctor visits, hospitalization and emergency services, preventive care and limited coverage for mental illnesses and substance abuse; prescription drugs; rehabilitation services; hospice, home health and extended nursing care services; and lab and diagnostic services.	Required that states set up large consumer groups called "health alliances" to collect premiums, bargain with health plans and handle payments. All companies with 5,000 or fewer employees would have to buy coverage through an alliance.
SENATE LEADERSHIP PLAN	Aimed to cover 95 percent of Americans by 2000.	Required plans to provide a comprehensive package from preventive care to home health services and prescription drugs. The bill left the specific scope of coverage to be determined by a commission.	Allowed individuals and businesses of fewer than 500 workers to set up groups to purchase insurance. If no alliances were set up in a state, the federal government would have set one up through the Federal Employees Health Benefits Program.
DOLE PLAN	Aimed to give all Americans access to insurance, although a significant portion of the working poor would likely be uncovered. Provided subsidies to help the poorest, uninsured Americans afford insurance.	No standard package except for the very poor. A plan for families receiving subsidies would have had to include comprehensive coverage, preventive care, mental health and substance abuse services and take special account of the needs of children and other vulnerable populations.	Allowed but did not require businesses and individuals to form large pools to purchase insurance.
HOUSE LEADERSHIP PLAN	Aimed to cover all Americans by Jan. 1, 1999, by requiring businesses to help pay for workers' insurance and by setting up a new government insurance program called Medicare Part C.	Required all insurance plans to cover doctor visits, hospital care, limited skilled-nursing care, laboratory services, preventive care, family planning including abortion, and limited mental health and substance abuse coverage.	No requirement for alliances, though they could be formed by groups of businesses and consumers.
SINGLE PAYER PLAN	Guaranteed universal health coverage for all legal U.S. residents within one year of enactment. Replaced the insurance industry with a government-run plan that would have collected premiums and taxes and paid providers. Most of the program was to have been run at the state level.	Established a comprehensive benefits package with extensive preventive care benefits. Set up a national board to establish the complete package of benefits. There would have been copayments for long-term care, but no copayments or deductibles for acute or preventive care.	No alliances as there would have been no need to buy standard private insurance plans.

Financing

Required employers to pay at least 80 percent of the average health insurance plan in their areas for unmarried workers and an average of 55 percent of the family plan, but no more than 7.9 percent of payrolls for companies with fewer than 5,000 workers. Companies with 75 or fewer employees and average wages of $24,000 or less would be eligible for subsidies.

Taxes

Raised the 24-cents-a-pack cigarette tax by 75 cents, to 99 cents. Imposed a 1 percent payroll tax on companies with 5,000 or more workers that did not join health alliances. Allowed alliances to levy an additional 2.5 percent assessment to help pay their administrative costs.

Cost Controls

Limited the annual increase in the price of health insurance premiums after 2000 to the rate of inflation, adjusted for population and other socioeconomic factors. That was less than half the 10 percent-plus annual rate of growth in health care costs in recent years. Government costs would be controlled by a cap on spending for subsidies.

Relied primarily on a combination of cuts in Medicare, a retargeting of federal and state spending for Medicaid—the government's insurance program for the poor—and taxes to provide subsidies for low-income Americans. In addition, if mandated changes in insurance practices and other measures failed to boost coverage to 95 percent by 2000, employers might have to help pay for workers' insurance in some states.

Imposed an array of new taxes, most of them small. Among the large ones were a 1.75 percent tax on health plan premiums and an excise tax on gun ammunition. Raised premiums for high-income elderly people who received health care through the existing Medicare program.

Controlled private-sector costs primarily through a 25 percent tax on the amount that a high cost plan's premiums exceeded a target rate. Controlled public-sector costs by reducing the rate of increase in Medicare costs and capping the amount that could be spent annually on all government health care programs including Medicare and Medicaid. The cost controls on federal programs could have been suspended during a recession.

No requirement that employers or individuals buy insurance. Individuals and businesses with two to 50 workers could have bought into the Federal Employees Health Benefits Program.

No tax increases. The existing 25 percent deduction for self-employed people would have risen to 100 percent by 2000.

No provisions to control prices or costs.

Required employers to pay at least 80 percent of their employees' premiums, starting in 1997 for companies with more than 100 workers and in 1999 for smaller firms. Businesses with fewer than 100 employees could have enrolled in a private plan or in a new government insurance program called Medicare Part C. If an employer chose a private plan, its workers could have bought coverage through a version of the Federal Employees Health Benefits Program.

Increased the cigarette tax by 45 cents to 69 cents a pack and added a sales tax of 2 percent to all insurance premiums.

Controlled costs of the new Medicare Part C program by limiting the amounts that doctors, hospitals and other providers could be reimbursed for services to patients. Private sector cost controls were not to occur before 2000, when a commission was to determine whether health spending in each state exceeded a national growth target tied to the gross domestic product. If so, reimbursement limits similar to those used in Medicare were to be applied to providers in the state.

Required small employers (defined as fewer than 75 employees with an average salary of $24,000) to pay a 4 percent payroll tax. Larger employers would have paid an 8.4 percent payroll tax. Individuals would have paid 2.1 percent of their taxable income.

Raised the tax on cigarettes by $1.76 per pack to a total of $2, made proportional increases in other tobacco taxes and imposed a 50-cent excise tax on handguns and ammunition.

Established a federal budget for health care each year. Required each state to negotiate with health care providers and hospitals to ensure that it had met its budget each year. Bill sponsors also argued that eliminating the private insurance system would significantly cut administration costs.

Gephardt was the first to unveil a bill, presenting the House Democratic leadership's health care proposal at a July 29 Democratic Caucus session that some said at times took on the inspirational tone associated with Pentecostal tent meetings.

The bill relied heavily on the version put together by the Ways and Means Committee. It was designed to provide universal coverage by 1999, requiring all employers to pay at least 80 percent of their workers' insurance premiums. Instead of health care alliances, the bill adopted the Ways and Means plan to create a Medicare Part C, a new government health insurance program to serve the poor, the unemployed and those who worked part-time or in small businesses. Employees of small businesses could also join a version of the Federal Employees Health Benefits Plan.

Few of the proposed tax increases from Clinton's plan remained in the bill other than a cigarette tax increase of 45 cents a pack and a 2 percent sales tax on all insurance premiums.

Mitchell released his plan Aug. 2. Instead of aiming for universal coverage, he proposed to reach 95 percent coverage by 2000. In response to requests from conservative Democrats, he proposed to give market forces a chance to increase coverage before turning to government enforcement. The bill did not require any employers to contribute to employees' health care costs until 2002. Even if the employer mandate kicked in, firms would never be required to pay more than 50 percent of the cost of their workers' premiums; it would never affect businesses with fewer than 25 workers; and it would be enforced only in states that failed to achieve 95 percent coverage.

Mitchell's plan was a political high-wire act designed to push liberals as far to the center as possible without losing them and at the same time appeal to the party's conservatives. But if conservative Democrats still refused to go along, Mitchell could do little to modify the bill without losing liberals. Asked if he and other liberals would vote for a bill that boosted coverage more slowly, or bypassed an employer mandate altogether, Rockefeller, a leading proponent of the Clinton plan, said flatly: "No."

1994 SENATE FLOOR ACTION

As a wary House membership watched to see what would happen across the Capitol, the Senate began debate on the bill (S 2351) Aug. 9, with Mitchell insisting that he would keep senators in Washington as long as necessary—giving up part or all of their August recess—to complete action on health care. He brought his bill to the floor as a substitute amendment without the votes to pass it. His only consolation was that his opponents lacked the votes to hand him an outright defeat.

But Mitchell could not break the deadlock. Democrats were divided. Conservative Democrats, many of them Southerners, simply did not see great political gain in supporting the cause of extending insurance coverage to all Americans. The skittishness was heightened by the approach of the November elections, especially for the many members in marginal seats. And Republicans were virtually unanimous in their opposition.

Although the floor debate was historic because of the magnitude of the legislation, it often abandoned the ideological high ground as liberal Democrats and conservative Republicans engaged in rhetorical fistfights. Republicans accused Democrats of being big-government addicts. Democrats countered that Republicans were captives of business interests and willing to leave millions of people without insurance.

With tempers fraying, it was clear that Clinton's dream of overhauling the nation's health care system was all but dead. Still, unwilling to give up, a bipartisan rump group of some 20 moderate senators, led by Chafee and Breaux, worked daily in Chafee's Capitol hideaway trying to come up with an alternative that could win enough adherents to pass.

On Aug. 19, with the Senate frozen in partisan jockeying, this self-styled "Mainstream Group" announced its compromise plan. The focus was on slowing cost increases for health care and reducing the deficit by $100 billion over 10 years. While the group set a goal of universal coverage, their bill aimed to reach about 93 percent of Americans by 1999. "Health care reform must be achieved one step at a time," said Breaux.

The Chafee-Breaux plan did not require employers to pay for their workers' health care. Instead, it provided for a commission to review the extent of coverage; if coverage were not increased significantly by 2002, Congress would have to vote on the commission's recommendations. To limit cost increases, the plan relied primarily on required changes in insurance market practices and a controversial cap on the tax deductibility of health insurance costs. All insurance plans would have to offer a standard package of benefits, and no applicant could be denied coverage based on a preexisting condition.

The so-called tax cap had been left out of most of the other bills under consideration. Liberals feared it would force people with generous plans into ones with less choice and less coverage, while conservatives considered the cap a tax increase.

The plan proposed drastic cuts in Medicare and Medicaid, in part to cut the deficit and in part to provide health insurance subsidies to people with incomes of up to 200 percent of poverty. The bill also proposed to increase the tobacco tax from 24 cents to 69 cents per pack of cigarettes.

But in the end, what killed the health care bill was another Clinton priority—the omnibus crime bill (HR 3355). After an unexpected setback in the House, White House and Democratic leaders were forced to expend precious hours and energy getting that measure back on track. By the time the Senate approved the crime bill conference report on Aug. 25, it was too late to finish work on a health bill on which there was still no consensus. Leaders reluctantly sent members home for a delayed summer break while staff from the Mainstream group were detailed to see if an incremental bill could be salvaged from the legislative rubble. (Crime bill, p. 683)

THE END

When House members returned after Labor Day, it was clear that neither they nor their constituents had the stomach to keep the debate going. "Constituents aren't clamoring for [health care reform]. I think the whole country is exhausted by the debate, and there won't be as much retribution [for failing to act] as I thought," said Bill Richardson, D-N.M.

Republican leaders, meanwhile, saw no point in cooperating

even on an incremental bill. "Why should we be enthusiastic about helping Democrats pull their political fat out of the fire with our ideas?" said Dick Armey, R-Texas.

In the Senate, Mitchell negotiated through early September with the Mainstream Group, assembling a last-minute compromise bill. The revised bill was little changed from its original structure, but it made small accommodations to win the support of most Democrats, including such liberals as Kennedy and about eight to 10 Republicans. It still relied on a reorganized health insurance market rather than government mandates to reduce the numbers of Americans without insurance and to control the growth in health insurance costs. Health insurers and health maintenance organizations would be required to offer the same benefits to all customers so that people could comparison-shop, choosing their health insurance plans based on price and quality. Additionally, no insurer could refuse to cover someone because of a preexisting medical condition.

But when Mitchell, Chafee and others began counting votes, they could not find 60 senators willing to break a threatened GOP filibuster and bring the negotiated bill to the floor.

Bowing to the inevitable, Mitchell announced Sept. 26 that he would not continue his efforts to pass major health care legislation in 1994. At a news conference to acknowledge the close of the already moribund health debate, Mitchell blamed Republicans and special interests. "Even though Republicans are a minority in Congress, in the Senate they're a minority with a veto. They have the ability to block legislation, and they have chosen to do so," he said.

Moments later, Senate Republican leader Bob Dole of Kansas quickly blamed Democrats. "The bottom line is, the Democrats never had the votes for any reform plan," he said..   ❏

NIH Reauthorization

After years of contention centering on fetal tissue research, Congress in 1993 finally reauthorized selected programs at the National Institutes of Health (NIH), the nation's premier biomedical research establishment. President Clinton signed the three-year, $6.2 billion reauthorization measure (S 1—PL 103-43) into law on June 10, closing another chapter in the fight over abortion policy that had raged between Congress and his Republican predecessors, Presidents George Bush and Ronald Reagan. A year earlier, Bush had vetoed a similar measure because it would have lifted a 1988 Reagan administration ban on federal funding of research using fetal tissue from elective abortions. The House fell 14 votes short of the two-thirds majority needed to override that veto. *(Congress and the Nation Vol. VIII, p. 602)*

Clinton did not wait for Congress to reverse the Reagan-Bush policy. On Jan. 22, two days after his inauguration, he lifted the funding ban by executive order. Bush and other opponents had argued that fetal tissue research might encourage women to have abortions. But Clinton sided with biomedical researchers and others who said transplants of fetal tissue offered great hope in finding treatments or even cures for such diseases as diabetes, Parkinson's disease and Alzheimer's disease. S 1 codified Clinton's decision to permit federal funding

of fetal tissue research and included rules designed to prevent abuses.

BACKGROUND

Most of NIH—a sprawling complex of 17 institutes—was covered by a permanent authorization that required no renewal by Congress. But periodic reauthorizations were required for the National Cancer Institute and the National Heart, Lung and Blood Institute, the two largest, plus the National Institute on Aging. The measure was the first full-scale NIH reauthorization to make it through Congress since 1988, although a limited version had cleared in 1990. Annual appropriations bills had kept the affected institutes operating in the meantime.

Although the fetal tissue research fight took center stage in the bill's travails, the measure included several other major initiatives—some of them controversial. For example, the bill directed NIH to put a new emphasis on health research involving women and minorities. It required that in most cases women and members of racial and ethnic minority groups be included as subjects in NIH-funded research projects. It also codified in statute NIH's Office of Research on Women's Health, created in 1990 after women in Congress publicized the systematic way researchers had excluded women from research studies and downplayed diseases that primarily afflicted women.

The bill specifically authorized increased funding for research on ovarian and cervical cancer, osteoporosis, reproductive health, and particularly, breast cancer. The $325 million authorized in the bill for breast cancer research represented an increase of 160 percent from the fiscal 1993 appropriation. Indeed, over the preceding five years, total appropriations for breast cancer had grown 450 percent. No other cancer research received such increases.

The infusion of earmarked money gave pause even to some researchers who specialized in breast cancer, not to mention those who worked on other cancers and saw their funding levels remain relatively flat. Not only did scientists worry about politicians making decisions they thought should be left to them, but there was concern that breast cancer might not even be the most serious health problem afflicting women. More women died annually of lung cancer than breast cancer, for example, and while breast cancer mortality had remained steady for more than a decade, lung cancer mortality rates for women had risen 71.7 percent since 1973.

However, several observers noted that the coalition of groups lobbying for the increased breast cancer research funding had been extremely successful in making breast cancer funding a way for members of Congress—especially men—to show their commitment to women's health even if they opposed abortion rights.

The bill also codified NIH's Office of AIDS Research, and gave it significant new powers to control the flow of research funds within NIH on Acquired Immune Deficiency Syndrome (AIDS) and Human Immunodeficiency Virus (HIV), which caused AIDS.

But AIDS activists suffered a setback when Congress codified existing policy that HIV was a communicable disease and that infection with HIV could be grounds for excluding immigrants and travelers from entering the United States.

LEGISLATIVE ACTION

Freed from the politics of the abortion debate, the NIH bill (S 1) won 16–0 approval from the Senate Labor and Human Resources Committee on Jan. 26, 1993, with none of the Republican dissent that had stalled the measure in past years. The bill, formally reported (S Rept 103-2) the next day, codified Clinton's Jan. 22 action allowing fetal tissue research but also required the secretary of health and human services to set up safeguards governing the conduct of such research. For example, the purchase or sale of human fetal tissue was prohibited, along with the direct donation of such tissue.

S 1 made no attempt to eliminate or sanction a tissue bank that Bush had ordered created in May 1992. The bank was to continue collecting tissue samples from miscarriages and ectopic, or "tubal," pregnancies. But, in a departure from a compromise crafted after the 1992 veto, researchers no longer had to turn to the bank first as a source of fetal tissue. Scientists generally had found it difficult to obtain usable tissue from miscarriages because most miscarriages occurred outside sterile hospital settings. Although tissue from ectopic pregnancies was usable, such pregnancies were rare.

The Senate bill was very similar to the vetoed 1992 version. But it contained a new provision designed to improve the coordination of AIDS research activities among NIH institutes. The director of the Office of AIDS Research was given responsibility for overseeing all such agency research. The director also was to prepare a long-term plan to evaluate existing efforts toward a thorough AIDS research program. The director was to retain 25 percent of new research money for high-priority initiatives.

The Senate passed S 1 on Feb. 18 by a vote of 93–4. For Democratic sponsors, the price of passage was an amendment by Don Nickles, R-Okla., codifying rules that prevented immigrants from taking up U.S. residence if they carried HIV—an issue that would ultimately delay completion of the bill.

Although the fetal tissue question was basically settled, the bill did not escape abortion politics altogether. Jesse Helms, R-N.C., unsuccessfully sought to eliminate a provision to establish "ethics advisory boards" at NIH. The temporary boards were to be convened whenever the secretary of health and human services decided to withhold research funds based on ethical grounds, such as banning fetal tissue research. The advisory board could overrule such a decision by majority vote. Helms complained that yet another advisory panel would be unnecessary, could undermine the president's powers over agency decisions and most likely would be staffed by political appointees who would rubber-stamp a president's views. But bill sponsor Edward M. Kennedy, D-Mass., chairman of the Labor Committee, said that what Helms really wanted was to ensure that a future president who might oppose fetal tissue research would not be stymied by an ethics advisory board. Senators on Feb. 18 rejected Helms's amendment, 23–74.

Most of the Senate debate over the NIH bill involved the Nickles amendment to bar entry into the United States of HIV-infected immigrants. Within days of becoming president, Clinton had pledged to rescind the existing entry ban on people who had HIV, and administration officials in early February indicated that he was proceeding with plans to alter the policy. To preempt him, Nickles on Feb. 17 offered his amendment to keep the ban in place, saying it had prevented a potential influx of foreigners infected with HIV who might burden the health care system and put Americans at risk. His amendment the next day won overwhelming approval, 76–23, with all but one Republican and 22 Democrats voting for it. The vote came after senators defeated an alternative amendment by Kennedy, who sought to keep the ban in place for 90 days while the administration studied the cost and health implications of rescinding it. Kennedy's compromise fell, 42–56, when 19 Democrats joined 37 Republicans in voting against it.

The immigration debate took place against the grim backdrop of an ongoing hunger strike by some 260 HIV-infected Haitian refugees who had been cleared for political asylum hearings in the United States but were being held at the naval base at Guantanamo, Cuba, because they or their relatives tested positive for HIV. Senators on both sides of the debate invoked the image of those refugees and other Haitians who might enter if the ban were lifted. Opponents of the HIV immigration ban said existing law that allowed the government to keep out immigrants who were likely to become a "public charge" or to deport any who became dependent on state support within five years was sufficient to protect against a potential drain on public resources.

The vote on the amendment came just two weeks after Senate Democrats blocked a similar assault on Clinton's controversial plan to let homosexuals serve in the military. This time, however, Democrats appeared less willing to brave political fire, and the White House did not press them. Several Democratic senators said administration officials had not contacted them, generating no extra pressure to vote against Nickles's amendment. The Nickles amendment notwithstanding, the administration retained authority to grant various exemptions. In addition, Nickles's amendment specifically allowed the attorney general to grant waivers to those entering the country for medical treatment, tourism or other short-term visits.

HOUSE ACTION

The NIH reauthorization began moving through the House less than a week after it passed the Senate. On Feb. 24, the House Energy and Commerce Subcommittee on Health and the Environment voted 20–6 to approve HR 4, a bill reauthorizing NIH, increasing its funding, streamlining AIDS research and emphasizing research involving women and minorities.

As in the Senate, subcommittee members barely mentioned the once-divisive issue of fetal tissue transplants. Members sparred, however, over an amendment offered by subcommittee Chairman Henry A. Waxman, D-Calif., that authorized the Office of AIDS Research to distribute research dollars among NIH's institutes and write an overall AIDS research plan. Under existing law, each of the 21 NIH institutes, centers and divisions got its own AIDS research money, and no entity within NIH set

AIDS spending priorities. A substitute amendment, offered by ranking minority member Thomas J. Bliley Jr., R-Va., failed 12–13. It would have stripped the AIDS office of its power to distribute funds, leaving it with far less leverage over the institutes' research decisions. Bliley, with the backing of NIH institute directors, argued that the AIDS office would add bureaucracy and remove knowledgeable scientists from decisions about what research should be done.

Bliley also failed in an effort to attach a provision to the bill similar to the Nickles amendment in the Senate banning immigration by people infected with the AIDS virus.

Despite some partisan infighting over an effort to channel breast cancer study funds to New York, the House Energy and Commerce Committee on March 2 approved HR 4 by a vote of 34–10. Committee members offered several amendments to the bill, including one by Cliff Stearns, R-Fla., that was similar to Nickles' Senate amendment barring HIV-infected immigrants. However, Stearns's proposal was ruled nongermane to the NIH bill, which dealt primarily with biomedical research.

By voice vote, the committee approved a Waxman amendment that nullified the Bush administration's executive order requiring NIH to create fetal tissue banks to collect tissue from ectopic pregnancies and miscarriages instead of elective abortions. The effect of the amendment was to leave it up to NIH to decide whether to continue such tissue banks. In another action, the committee rejected, 17–27, an amendment by Bliley that would have required that only doctors, not other health professionals in an abortion clinic, inform women about fetal research regulations. The effect of this amendment would have been to slow the collection of fetal tissue.

HR 4 was reported (H Rept 103-28) on March 9 and the House passed the bill on March 11 by a vote of 283–131. The House then passed S 1 by voice vote, after substituting the provisions of its bill.

Much of the content of the measure was never discussed—even though the bill marked a turning point in NIH funding for women's health research and increased attention to AIDS research. Many of the specific authorizations for women's health and AIDS research, strongly supported by the Congressional Caucus for Women's Issues, drew criticism from some Republicans, who charged that the bill's Democratic authors were substituting their research opinions for those of scientists.

House leaders barred consideration of a floor amendment similar to the Senate amendment banning HIV-infected immigrants. But many members wanted to accept the Senate ban. The House on March 11 by 356–58 approved a nonbinding motion by Bliley to instruct House conferees on the bill to accept the Senate's provision.

By taking preemptive action to codify the HIV ban, the Republicans caught Democrats without a well-prepared response. The immediate reaction of most was to oppose a change that might allow more HIV-infected people into the country. And, as in the Senate, the administration did not appear prepared to expend political capital on the volatile issue. There was no evident White House lobbying before the Senate or House votes, and White House Press Secretary Dee Dee Myers said Clinton

was unlikely to push the issue over strong congressional objections.

The House March 11 approved, 250–161, an amendment by Bliley dealing with the donation of fetal tissue that had been modified substantially by Waxman. The modified amendment required that physicians certify that abortions in which fetal tissue was donated were performed in accordance with state law.

CONFERENCE, FINAL ACTION

House and Senate negotiators agreed on a conference report (H Rept 103-100) that included the ban on permanent immigration by foreigners infected with the AIDS virus. The issue of excluding HIV-infected foreigners had been the key sticking point in the conference. The administration did not fight to keep the HIV provision out of the conference report, although some conferees opposed it. Waxman and Kennedy sought at least to tone down the ban in conference. The final language banned permanent immigration by HIV-infected foreigners, including refugees, but left policy details to the attorney general. Under existing guidelines, the government generally did not test or restrict entry of short-term visitors.

The final bill also included the House provision—which was not in the Senate version—codifying Clinton's order lifting the Reagan-Bush ban on fetal tissue research. The conference report included rules designed to prevent abuses, such as banning the sale of fetal tissue.

The House on May 25 adopted the conference report on S 1 by a vote of 290–130. The Senate cleared the bill for the president by voice vote on May 28. Although some House members opposed the House-Senate conference report because it codified Clinton's fetal tissue research decision, the issue no longer had the potency to stymie the bill. It did, however, account for many of the "nay" votes on the conference report.

MAJOR PROVISIONS

As signed into law, S 1:

Ethics

• **Ethical Review Boards.** Permitted the secretary of health and human services (HHS), after public notice, to convene an ethics advisory board to examine the ethical implications of any NIH project. The board was to be made up of 14 to 20 people, none of whom could work for the federal government. Members were required to have expertise in biomedical and behavioral ethics and were to include at least one lawyer, one physician, one ethicist and one theologian. The board was to report within six months to the secretary, to the Senate Committee on Labor and Human Resources and to the House Committee on Energy and Commerce. The secretary could withhold funding for a project only if a majority of the board recommended doing so.

Fetal Tissue Research

• **Fetal Tissue Transplant Moratorium.** Stipulated that neither the secretary nor any executive branch official could prohibit research on the transplantation of fetal tissue. The secretary could withhold funds only in the case of a violation of fetal tissue research guidelines.

- **Research on Transplantation of Fetal Tissue.** Authorized funding for research on "the transplantation of fetal tissue for therapeutic purposes." Scientists hoped to learn more about Alzheimer's, Parkinson's and other diseases through research using transplanted fetal tissue. The tissue could be obtained from induced abortions, as well as from stillbirths and miscarriages.

- **Safeguards for Use of Fetal Tissue.** Required the woman providing the tissue to sign a statement declaring that she was donating fetal tissue for research, that she understood she could not designate the recipient of the tissue and that she was not aware of the recipient's identity. The physician performing the abortion was to certify that the woman gave her consent to have an abortion before she was asked about the fetal tissue donation. The physician also had to disclose any financial or other interest in the subsequent research as well as any known medical risks.

- **Prohibitions on the Use of Fetal Tissue.** Prohibited the sale or purchase of human fetal tissue from induced abortions and any donation intended for a specific person, including a relative of the donor. This was intended to prohibit a woman from getting pregnant in order to have an abortion and donate the tissue to a family member, for instance. Violators could be imprisoned for up to 10 years.

Women's Health Research

- **Inclusion of Women and Minorities in Clinical Research Funded by NIH.** Generally required that women and members of racial and ethnic minority groups be included as subjects in NIH-funded research projects. Exceptions were permitted if, for example, such inclusion would threaten the health of the research subjects. The bill stipulated that the cost of including women and minorities was not a permissible reason to exclude them from a research project. Women and minorities could be excluded if there were scientific reasons to assume the variables being studied did not affect women or minorities differently than white men.

The NIH director, in consultation with the director of the Office of Research on Women's Health and the Office of Research on Minority Health, was to create a program to recruit women and minorities as research subjects. Guidelines were to be published within 180 days of enactment.

- **Office of Research on Women's Health.** Authorized a women's health research office within the office of the NIH director. The office—which was created in 1990 but had never been formally authorized—was to ensure that women's health issues were identified and addressed in research activities.

- **Biennial Report.** Beginning Feb. 1, 1994, required that a report on the progress made in women's health research and treatment conducted or supported by the NIH be included in the NIH's biennial report to the president and Congress.

- **Data System and Clearinghouse on Research on Women's Health.** Required the creation of a single data system to collect and disseminate information regarding research on women's health conducted or supported by the NIH.

NIH-Wide Programs

- **Children's Vaccine Initiative.** Required the HHS secretary, in consultation with the director of the National Vaccine Program and the directors of other institutes and public and private programs, to develop affordable and improved vaccines. The vaccines were to provide long-lasting protection; require fewer contacts to deliver; not require refrigeration, needles or syringes; and protect against a large number of diseases. Authorized $20 million in fiscal 1994.

- **NIH Director Discretionary Fund.** Authorized $25 million in fiscal 1994 and unspecified sums for fiscal 1995 through fiscal 1996 for a fund that the NIH director could use for such purposes as research that did not fit clearly into the assignment of any existing institute or to respond to scientific emergencies and new issues.

- **Plan for Use of Animals in Research.** Required the NIH director to prepare a plan to study research methods that did not require the use of animals, methods that could reduce the number of animals needed in research and methods that reduced the amount of pain and distress for animals used in research.

- **Surveys of Sexual Behavior.** Stipulated that surveys of human sexual behavior to be funded by the NIH had to meet the same ethical and peer-review requirements as other research using human subjects, and that information to be obtained had to be expected to assist in reducing the incidence of sexually transmitted diseases, including AIDS, and in improving reproductive health or other health conditions.

- **Office of Alternative Medicine.** Established an Office of Alternative Medicine within NIH, responsible for the evaluation of alternative medical treatment including acupuncture, Oriental medicine, homeopathic medicine and physical manipulation therapies. The bill required the office director to establish an information clearinghouse to exchange information with the public about alternative medicine. The office had existed for several years but did not have statutory authority, which gave it more permanence.

- **Program of Research on Osteoporosis and Related Bone Disorders.** Authorized $40 million in fiscal 1994 and unspecified sums through fiscal 1996 for research on osteoporosis, Paget's disease and related bone disorders. These conditions afflicted about 27 million Americans.

- **Interagency Program for Trauma Research.** Required establishment of a comprehensive program to conduct and support research on all aspects of trauma, the leading cause of death and disability in children and young adults.

- **National Research Service Awards Program.** Authorized $400 million for the National Research Service Awards for fiscal 1994 and unspecified sums for fiscal 1995 and fiscal 1996. The program provided funds for individuals and institutions for the training of research scientists. The bill authorized grants for programs to recruit women, underrepresented minorities and people from disadvantaged backgrounds into biomedical or behavioral research.

- **Senior Biomedical Research Service.** Redesignated the Senior Biomedical Research Service as the Silvio Conte Senior Biomedical Research Service, honoring the late Massachusetts representative. Conte was the ranking Republican on the Appropriations subcommittee that oversaw NIH and an ardent backer of biomedical research funding. The provision also raised from 350 to 500 the number of researchers who could participate in the service at one time. The service allowed high-level researchers to be paid higher salaries than otherwise would be allowed under federal guidelines.

• **Loan Repayment Program.** Required establishment of a program to repay up to $20,000 per year in student loans for health professionals who agreed to conduct research at NIH on contraception and infertility, AIDS, or in a research area of demonstrated need.

A separate program established a similar, $20,000-per-year loan repayment program for minorities or people from underprivileged backgrounds who agreed to conduct clinical work at NIH.

National Foundation for Biomedical Research

• **Purpose.** Created a foundation to advance NIH collaboration with biomedical researchers in universities, industry and nonprofit organizations. The foundation could solicit and accept gifts, grants and other donations, and spend the money to support scientific research.

• **Supplementary Programs.** The foundation was to hire or recruit foreign scientists to do research in the United States and support scientists working on international projects. The foundation also was to support science education in elementary, secondary and postsecondary schools.

• **Authorization.** Authorized $200,000 for fiscal 1994 and 1995.

National Cancer Institute

• **Authorization.** Authorized $2.73 billion for fiscal 1994 and unspecified sums for fiscal 1995 and 1996.

• **Breast Cancer.** Authorized $225 million for research on the causes of and cures for breast cancer, and $100 million for prevention, detection and treatment in fiscal 1994, and unspecified sums for fiscal 1995 and 1996. This was the first time that the bill had earmarked an authorization for a particular cancer.

• **Female Reproductive System Cancers.** Authorized $75 million for research on the cause, detection and cure of ovarian and other reproductive system cancers in fiscal 1994 and unspecified sums for fiscal 1995 and 1996.

• **Prostate Cancer.** Authorized $72 million for research on the cause, prevention, detection and treatment of prostate cancer in fiscal 1994 and unspecified sums in fiscal 1995 and 1996.

National Heart, Lung and Blood Institute

• **Authorization.** Authorized $1.5 billion for fiscal 1994 and unspecified sums for fiscal 1995 and 1996.

National Institute on Aging

• **Authorization.** Authorized $500 million for fiscal 1994 and unspecified sums for fiscal 1995 and 1996, the institute's first separate authorization. The provision authorized research on the aging processes of women, with special concentration on the effects of menopause and the physiological and biological changes that accompany menopause.

National Institute on Allergy and Infectious Diseases

• **Chronic Fatigue Syndrome.** Authorized the development of centers to conduct basic and clinical research on the condition known as chronic fatigue syndrome.

National Institute on Child Health and Human Development

• **Research Centers on Contraception and Infertility.** Authorized $30 million in fiscal 1994 and unspecified sums in fiscal 1995 and 1996 to establish research centers to study improved methods of contraception and infertility treatment.

• **Child Health Research Centers.** Authorized existing child health research centers established by the National Institute on Child Health and Human Development. Most of the centers were at universities.

National Library of Medicine

• **Authorization.** Authorized $150 million for the National Library of Medicine, including grants to medical libraries and nonprofit biomedical publications for fiscal 1994, and unspecified sums for fiscal 1995 and 1996.

• **National Information Center on Health Services Research and Health-Care Technology.** Established a center for the collection, storage, analysis and dissemination of information on clinical practice guidelines, health-care technologies and health-services research.

AIDS and AIDS Research

• **Office of AIDS Research.** Created an Office of AIDS Research to oversee and evaluate all AIDS research within the NIH. The office's director was to be the primary federal official responsible for AIDS research and was to represent NIH at all executive branch task force and other committee meetings on AIDS research. This provision augmented the authority of the AIDS office, giving it more power to coordinate AIDS research activity.

• **AIDS Plan and Budget.** Required the office to write a plan setting priorities for AIDS research throughout the NIH by June 1994 and to revise the plan annually. The AIDS director was to submit a budget for carrying out the plan to the president as well as to the NIH director.

• **AIDS Emergency Discretionary Fund.** Authorized the creation of a $100 million fund each year from fiscal 1994 through fiscal 1996 for unanticipated research projects. The fund was designed to allow the AIDS office to respond to the rapid pace of AIDS research, augment funding for existing research or fund promising new projects.

• **Exclusion of Immigrants Infected with HIV.** Codified existing policy that AIDS was a public health threat and that infection with the HIV virus was a basis for excluding immigrants from entering the United States. The provision was aimed particularly at immigrants seeking permanent residence and refugees. The attorney general continued to have discretion to grant waivers from the HIV exclusion, particularly for short-term visits.

Other Agencies

• **National Institute for Nursing Research.** Redesignated the National Center for Nursing Research as the National Institute for Nursing Research, giving it additional prestige and potentially more clout in dealing with Congress. The nursing center thus became NIH's 17th institute.

• **National Center for Human Genome Research.** Authorized the National Center for Human Genome Research, which since 1989 had been coordinating and supporting efforts to map all human genes. The bill stipulated that at least 5 percent of available funding be reserved for projects to examine the ethical issues associated with the genome project. Official authorization as a center was its first step toward becoming an institute.

• **National Eye Institute.** Authorized research grants to one or more diabetes eye research institutions. Diabetes, which afflicted 14 million Americans, was the leading cause of new cases of blindness.

• **Division of Research Resources.** Redesignated the Division of Research Resources as the National Center for Research Resources. The agency oversaw the provision of equipment, laboratory animals and other supplies needed for research.

• **Research Facility Construction.** Authorized $150 million for fiscal 1993 and unspecified sums through fiscal 1996 for competitive matching grants to expand or renovate existing biomedical or behavioral research facilities or to construct new facilities. Up to $5 million was reserved for renovation of regional primate centers, where the most sophisticated animal research was done on AIDS and other diseases.

• **Toxicological Research and Testing.** Required the National Institute of Environmental Health Sciences to establish a program on the health effects of environmental agents, including selected chemicals. The program already existed but had not been authorized. The provision also required research on ways to reduce and eventually eliminate the use of animals in testing the toxicity of chemical agents such as pesticides.

• **Multiple Sclerosis Research.** Required the National Institute of Neurological Disorders and Stroke to conduct and support research on multiple sclerosis, including research on the effects of genetics and hormonal changes on the progress of the disease.

Scientific Integrity

• **Office of Scientific Integrity.** Authorized the Office of Scientific Integrity outside NIH and under the secretary of health and human services. The office, which already existed, was to monitor investigations carried out by universities and other recipients of NIH funding, as well as conduct independent investigations of potential scientific misconduct.

• **Whistleblower Protection.** Required regulations to protect those who reported or cooperated in investigations of scientific misconduct.

• **Financial Conflicts of Interest.** Required regulations establishing criteria to prevent scientists from having financial interests that might be in conflict or appear to be in conflict with their federal research or administrative responsibilities. The regulations were to guard against situations in which a researcher would have a bias in favor of obtaining a certain result or situations that could "be reasonably expected" to create such a bias.

Studies

• **Adolescent Study.** Authorized a study of adolescent health, and the behaviors and environments that promote or detract from good health in this age group.

• **Chronic Pain Conditions.** Authorized a study of chronic pain, including back injuries, and the effect of such cases on the cost of health care.

• **Life-Threatening Illnesses.** Authorized a study of the policies of insurance companies regarding coverage of clinical trial medications for terminally ill patients, including those with cancer or AIDS.

• **Malnutrition in the Elderly.** Authorized a three-year study of the nutritional status of the elderly and of efforts to provide the elderly with appropriate nutrition.

• **Breast Cancer Study.** Authorized a study of environmental causes and other potential risk factors contributing to breast cancer frequency in Nassau and Suffolk counties in Long Island, N.Y., and in two other counties in the Northeast with high mortality rates from the disease.

• **Cost of Care in Last Six Months of Life.** Authorized a study of the average health care expenditures incurred during the last six months of life.

• **Conditional Prohibition Against Funding for Project Aries.** Authorized the termination of funding for a study at the University of Washington that used telephone counseling to help gay men learn about safe sex, provided that another way could be found to accomplish the same results.

• **Biological Warfare.** Required the HHS secretary to report to Congress on "the appropriateness and impact" of giving NIH responsibility for research on the medical aspects of developing defenses for biological warfare. ❑

Medicare, Medicaid

In what the Clinton administration described as a "down payment" on health reform, the budget reconciliation bill that squeaked through Congress in 1993 included a raft of health-related changes, most notably provisions to trim nearly $63 billion over five years from Medicare and Medicaid, the two principal federally funded health programs.

Spiraling health costs made the two big health entitlements obvious targets for deficit cutting. And indeed, one of every four dollars of the $255 billion in spending cuts in the bill (HR 2264—PL 103-66) came from health accounts. But the bill also included provisions redirecting some of the nation's health-care dollars toward preventive and primary care and toward improving children's health—two major administration themes for health reform. Key among them was the creation of a new $1.5 billion entitlement to pay for immunizations to protect children against preventable diseases.

The deepest cuts in the bill were made in Medicare, the federal health insurance program for the elderly and disabled. Under the bill, Medicare was projected to grow by $55.8 billion less than it would have without the cuts. The bill also sought to slow the rising costs of Medicaid, the joint federal-state health plan for the poor, by $7.1 billion over five years. Unlike many of the previous deficit-reduction bills, the cuts this time were deep enough to be felt by Medicare beneficiaries as well as doctors, hospitals and other providers of care. The bill, for example, made it more difficult for the elderly to "spend down" their savings and qualify for long-term care services under Medicaid.

One far-reaching nonspending change clamped down hard on "self-referrals," when doctors sent patients to ancillary health facilities, such as imaging centers or clinical laboratories, in which the doctors had a financial interest. The 1989 budget bill (PL 101-239) banned Medicare and Medicaid payments for physician self-referrals to clinical laboratories in which the doctors had an interest. The 1993 bill continued that ban and extended the self-referral prohibitions to a variety of other services. *(1989 bill, Congress and the Nation Vol. VIII, p. 567)*

BACKGROUND

Health and Human Services Secretary Donna E. Shalala described the health cuts proposed in the plan as "the first down payment on health-care reform," designed to complement the more far-reaching changes that ultimately would be included in the president's health reform bill. Indeed, many of the proposals in the initial budget package were familiar ones, having been proposed in earlier years by Presidents Ronald Reagan and George Bush but never adopted by Congress.

The Clinton budget called for cuts of $1.9 billion in fiscal 1994 in Medicare payments to hospitals. Most of the proposed savings were to be achieved by cutting the annual increase in hospital reimbursements to one percentage point lower than the health-care inflation rate. Teaching hospitals were to be subjected to cuts both in their rates of reimbursement for the cost of training and in the salaries of residents and interns.

To replenish the dwindling Medicare hospital insurance fund, Clinton proposed using general fund revenues that he wanted to raise by subjecting 85 percent of the Social Security benefits of affluent retirees to the income tax, up from 50 percent. *(Social Security benefits tax, p. 661)*

The budget called for $742 million in fiscal 1994 savings in Medicare's Part B, which paid for physician and other outpatient services. Much of those savings were to be realized by lowering inflation increases for doctors, although primary care services were to be reimbursed at the full rate, reflecting the administration's desire to raise traditionally lower payments for such services. The budget also proposed reducing Medicare payments for clinical laboratory services.

HOUSE ACTION

The first committee action on the health elements of the Clinton budget was not what the president had in mind. On April 27, the House Ways and Means Subcommittee on Health ignored the administration's detailed proposals for making cuts in Medicare and substituted its own $50.6 billion, five-year package that would have simply frozen inflation adjustments for payments to doctors and hospitals. Subcommittee Chairman Pete Stark, D-Calif., said the package, approved by voice vote, was a "placeholder" for the Clinton health care reform plan, which was expected to make major changes to Medicare. "Why should we go through this twice?" asked Stark. The full committee approved the Health Subcommittee package in closed session May 6.

The House Energy and Commerce Committee, which shared partial jurisdiction over Medicare with Ways and Means and oversaw all of Medicaid, took a different approach. The panel's subcommittee on Health and the Environment approved a package of cuts by voice vote May 6. Many of the subcommittee's cuts differed from those the administration proposed. They included limiting inflation increases for physicians, although, like the administration, the subcommittee proposal preserved payments for primary care services. The panel also limited payments for anesthesia, clinical laboratory services and durable medical equipment.

For Medicaid, most of the bill's $8.9 billion in projected savings over five years were to be achieved by reducing payments to hospitals that treated large numbers of Medicaid patients and by eliminating a mandate that states provide personal care services to Medicaid beneficiaries. The change in the rules for reimbursing hospitals that treated a high number of low-income patients—known as disproportionate share hospitals—represented the committee's third attempt since 1989 to close loopholes in the law governing how states financed Medicaid. Previous provisions were attached to the 1990 reconciliation bill (PL 101-508) and a separate bill in 1991 (PL 102-234). *(1990 and 1991 action, Congress and the Nation Vol. VIII, pp. 578, 600)*

As it had in previous years, however, the subcommittee also added provisions costing about $744 million over five years, reducing the total net savings to $8.2 billion. That was still higher than the committee's deficit-reduction target for Medicaid of $7.8 billion.

The otherwise routine markup took a sudden controversial turn when Alex McMillan, R-N.C., offered an amendment to require wealthy Medicare beneficiaries to pay a larger portion of the premiums for the optional Part B coverage of physician and outpatient services. Under existing law, Medicare beneficiaries paid premiums equal to 25 percent of the program's cost, with the federal Treasury picking up the rest. McMillan's amendment, similar to a proposal first put forward by President Bush, would have reversed that for couples earning between $125,000 and $200,000 annually, requiring that they pay premiums equal to 75 percent of the program's per capita cost. The government subsidy would have been ended entirely for couples with annual incomes higher than $200,000.

Health and the Environment Subcommittee Chairman Henry A. Waxman, D-Calif., spoke against the amendment, but it drew support from some other panel Democrats. The subcommittee, however, rejected the amendment by voice vote, along with two other McMillan amendments that would have required beneficiaries to pay part of the costs of home health care and laboratory services.

The subcommittee bill also included the creation of a $1.8 billion entitlement program for childhood immunization.

The full Energy and Commerce Committee approved the package with few changes by voice vote May 11. One amendment, adopted 26–18, called for a one-year program to help states with large numbers of undocumented immigrants pay for their emergency health care, including the delivery of babies.

The panel also agreed by voice vote to soften slightly language making it more difficult for the elderly to transfer assets in an effort to qualify for Medicaid coverage of their long-term nursing home care. Advocates for the elderly had condemned the original measure as "draconian." The new language added a provision allowing states to waive the penalties for asset transfer if they would cause an undue hardship. Among the more controversial penalties was one requiring that elderly people pay the full cost of nursing home care until they had spent the same amount of money that they had transferred to a relative.

The House approved HR 2264 by a vote of 219–213 on May 27. *(Budget reconciliation bill, p. 44)*

SENATE ACTION

On the other side of the Capitol, the zeal for deficit reduction was far greater than in the House. Indeed, while the House-passed bill called for Medicare reductions of $50 billion over five years, the deficit-reduction package the Senate Finance Committee approved June 18 anticipated $67 billion in Medicare reductions. In addition, the Finance package, approved 11–9, transformed the House's $1.8 billion immunization entitlement into a money-saver.

To achieve the additional Medicare cuts, the committee further cut physician reimbursements to all but primary care doctors and hospital reimbursements for outpatient services. It also reduced payments to teaching hospitals for training interns and residents.

The Senate approved its version of the reconciliation bill by a vote of 50–49 on June 25, with Vice President Al Gore casting the tie-breaking vote. The leadership's negotiations with the conservative wing of the party had angered liberal Democrats, and a small but critical group that included Howard M. Metzenbaum of Ohio, Tom Harkin of Iowa, Barbara A. Mikulski of Maryland and Paul Wellstone of Minnesota threatened to vote against the bill because of the Finance Committee's additional Medicare cuts. The liberals wanted no more than $10 billion in added Medicare cuts; leaders insisted they needed something closer to $19 billion. But when the June 25 vote drew closer and the liberals dug in their heels, leaders agreed to lower the cuts by the full $9 billion, prompting Harkin and others to declare support for the package.

John D. Rockefeller IV, D-W.Va., chairman of the Finance Subcommittee that oversaw Medicare, offered a floor amendment to eliminate a series of specific Medicare reductions in a move tilted in part toward easing the burden of the cuts on in-ner-city and rural areas. The measure, which brought total Medicare cuts down to $58 billion, passed on a voice vote.

CONFERENCE, FINAL ACTION

The politics of the House-Senate conference on the reconciliation bill hinged on a new coalition among House liberals, progressives and the members of the Congressional Black Caucus, who worked together to ensure that no deal would go through without additional money for inner-city needs such as tuberculosis care and immunizations for poor children. At the crux of the deal was the Senate's insistence on deeper Medicare cuts to offset lower tax revenues. The House originally agreed to $48 billion in cuts; the Senate bill had $58 billion. Early on, conferees agreed on $54 billion. Then, negotiations pushed tax revenues down, and the Senate and the White House sought even more Medicare cuts. At that point, in concert with Waxman, the black caucus and liberals came up with a deal. "The condition for me to support the bill was that we had to get a lot of items back in, and we had to make sure the additional Medicare cuts didn't hurt beneficiaries," said Waxman. Among the items Waxman held out for were: $205 million for treatment of impoverished tuberculosis victims, an additional $293 million for Medicaid payments to Puerto Rico and other U.S. territories, and the $1.5 billion immunization program. The final bill reduced projected Medicare spending by an estimated $55.8 billion.

The final version of the immunization program, set to take effect in fiscal 1995, called for the federal government to purchase vaccines for an estimated 11 million children, including children on Medicaid, Native American children, and children with no insurance. Insured children whose coverage did not include immunizations would also be eligible to receive free shots at federally funded community health centers.

Although the program was expected to cost $1.5 billion, the net cost to the federal Treasury was estimated at only $585 million, because it would pay for shots that would otherwise have been underwritten by Medicaid.

Parliamentary problems caused several provisions to be dropped from the bill that would have increased access to vaccine services. Among them were a $250 million outreach program to lengthen clinic hours, creation of a vaccine registry for tracking a child's immunizations and a bonus program to reward states that improved their vaccination rates.

The House adopted the conference report on the bill (H Rept 103-213) by a **key vote of 218–216 (R 0–175; D 217–41; I 1–0)** on Aug. 5. The Senate approved the report and cleared the bill, 51–50, on Aug. 6; Gore again cast the tie-breaking vote. *(1993 key votes, p. 979)*

MAJOR PROVISIONS

As signed into law Aug. 10, the health-related provisions of HR 2264:

Medicare

• **Hospital Payments/Payment Updates.** Adjusted annual inflation increases for hospitals under Medicare's Prospective Payment System as follows:

• Urban hospitals in fiscal 1994 and 1995 would receive increases equal to the percentage increase in the "marketbasket" (a measure of goods and services purchased by hospitals) minus 2.5 percentage points. The fiscal 1994 marketbasket increase was 4.2 percent, so beginning Oct. 1, 1993, urban hospitals were to receive inflation increases of 1.7 percent.

• Rural hospitals, scheduled to receive increases of 5.7 percent in fiscal 1994 (marketbasket plus 1.5 percentage points), were to be subject to a 1 percentage point cut, for a total update of 4.7 percent. As under existing law, rural hospitals were to receive updates in fiscal 1995 sufficient to close the gap between the rates they received and the higher rates paid to urban facilities.

• Both urban and rural hospitals were to receive updates in fiscal 1996 that were equal to the marketbasket amount minus 2 percentage points. In fiscal 1997 the update would be marketbasket minus 0.5 percentage points, and in fiscal 1998 hospitals would receive the full marketbasket update.

• Specially designated sole community hospitals and Medicare-dependent small rural hospitals (which had been receiving specially augmented rates) were to receive updates of marketbasket minus 2.3 percent in fiscal 1994 and marketbasket minus 2.2 percent in fiscal 1995. Beginning in fiscal 1996, these hospitals were scheduled to receive the same rate of increase as other hospitals.

• Hospitals exempt from Medicare's Prospective Payment System (including children's hospitals, psychiatric hospitals, rehabilitation hospitals and cancer treatment centers) were to receive increases of the marketbasket percentage minus 1 percentage point for each of fiscal 1994 through 1997 and the full marketbasket update in fiscal 1998. No reduction was to be applied to hospitals whose operating costs exceeded a preset limit in fiscal 1990 by 10 percent or more.

• **Hospital Payments/Capital Costs.** Beginning in fiscal 1994, reduced by 7.4 percent payments to hospitals for capital-related costs (including depreciation, leases and rentals, interest and property taxes). The existing 10 percent reduction was set to expire at the end of fiscal 1995. Medicare capital payments were in the second year of a 10-year phase-in to be fully included in the Prospective Payment System.

• **Hospice Payments.** Increased payment rates for hospice services by the hospital marketbasket increase minus 2 percentage points in fiscal 1994, by marketbasket minus 1.5 percentage points in fiscal 1995 and 1996, by marketbasket minus 0.5 percentage points in fiscal 1997 and by the full marketbasket rate in fiscal 1998.

• **Skilled Nursing Facility Payments.** Delayed inflation updates for skilled nursing facilities until fiscal 1996. Beginning Oct. 1, 1993, special payments for "return on equity" for private nursing homes would be eliminated. (Similar payments for hospitals were phased out in the mid-1980s.) The bill also eliminated special payments for excess overhead costs for hospital-based facilities, beginning Oct. 1, 1993.

• **Medicare Hospital Payments/Regional Referral Centers.** Reinstated through Sept. 30, 1994, the 180 large rural hospitals that were designated as regional referral centers as of Sept. 30, 1992. Referral centers were paid at a higher rate than other rural hospitals. The provision also made the facilities eligible for back payments.

• **Medicare Hospital Payments/Small Rural Medicare-Dependent Hospitals.** Continued through fiscal 1994 special payments, on a phased-down basis, for certain small rural hospitals whose caseloads were at least 60 percent Medicare patients.

• **Medicare Hospital Payments/Regional Floor.** Extended through fiscal 1996 a special payment adjustment for hospitals in areas of the country with costs higher than the national average.

• **Part A Premium.** Reduced the premium charged to people 65 and older who did not qualify for Part A benefits but wanted to purchase Part A coverage. The premium was based on the actuarial value of Part A benefits ($221 monthly in 1993). It was to be reduced, on a phased-in basis, for people with credits for 30 or more quarters of taxes paid into the Social Security system and for surviving or divorced spouses of those people. The premium was to be reduced by 25 percent in calendar 1994, and by 45 percent in 1998 and thereafter.

Part B

• **Physician Fees: Payment Update.** Reduced the scheduled inflation adjustment in Medicare fees for physician services in fiscal 1994 and 1995. Under the Medicare fee schedule enacted in 1989, physician payments had to be adjusted each year for inflation and for the amount by which all physicians exceeded or failed to reach an aggregate target for the volume of services provided to Medicare beneficiaries. Because physicians remained far below the volume targets in 1992, under the formula 1994 fees for surgical services would have risen by 12.2 percent, while fees for all other services would have risen by 6.6 percent.

Instead, fee increases in 1994 were to be reduced by 3.6 percentage points for surgical services (resulting in an increase of 8.6 percent) and by 2.6 percentage points for all other services except primary care (resulting in an increase of the full 6.6 percent for primary care and 4 percent for all other services).

For 1995, increases for all services except primary care were to be reduced by 2.7 percentage points. Primary care services were to receive the full scheduled update.

• **Physician Fees: Primary Care, Anesthesia Services.** Beginning in fiscal 1994, put primary care in a separate category for the purpose of determining annual increases in physician fees; anesthesia services were put in the surgical services category.

• **Physician Fees: Practice Expenses.** Gradually reduced payments from 1994 to 1997 for the practice expense (overhead) component used to determine fees for individual physician services.

• **Physician Fees: Anesthesia Teams.** Gradually reduced payments to anesthesia care teams (a physician anesthesiologist supervising one or more certified registered nurse anesthetists) so that by 1998, payments to teams would not exceed those that would be made to an anesthesiologist practicing alone in the same locality.

• **Physician Fees: EKG Interpretations.** Repealed a provision of the 1990 reconciliation bill that prohibited separate payments for interpretation of routine electrocardiograms (EKGs) in conjunction with an office visit or consultation. The bill required the health and human services (HHS) secretary to establish fee schedule amounts for such interpretations.

• **Physician Fees: New Physicians.** Repealed provisions in the 1987 and 1990 reconciliation bills that reduced fees for physicians in their first four years of practice.

• **Payment for Allergy Antigens.** Beginning Jan. 1, 1995, provided that payment for antigens used in allergy treatment and related services be made under the Medicare physician fee schedule.

• **Outpatient Hospital Services.** Extended through fiscal 1998 the 10 percent reduction in Medicare payments for capital-related hospital outpatient costs. The reductions were set to expire at the end of fiscal 1995. Sole community hospitals and primary care hospitals remained exempt from the cuts. The bill also continued through fiscal 1998 the 5.8 percent reduction in operating costs payments for hospital outpatient services.

• **Ambulatory Surgical Centers.** Froze the level of fees paid to ambulatory surgical centers for fiscal 1994 and 1995.

• **Intraocular Lenses.** Beginning Jan. 1, 1994, reduced the $200 maximum payment for intraocular lenses used in cataract surgery to $150. The limit was to expire on Jan. 1, 1999.

• **Laboratory Services.** Froze most Medicare payments for laboratory fees for fiscal 1994 and 1995. Beginning in fiscal 1994, the maximum fee was to drop from 88 percent of the national median amount to 76 percent over three years.

• **Durable Medical Equipment.** Set national payment limits for durable medical equipment based on the median of local payment amounts, similar to the limits for laboratory services (see above). For fiscal 1994 and 1995, the bill froze payment levels for orthotics and prosthetics and enteral and parenteral supplies. Payments for transcutaneous electrical nerve stimulation (TENS) devices were reduced by an additional 30 percent.

• **Alzheimer's Demonstration Projects.** Reauthorized for one additional year demonstration projects to provide comprehensive services to Medicare beneficiaries with Alzheimer's disease.

• **Cancer Drugs.** Beginning Jan. 1, 1994, extended Medicare coverage to oral cancer drugs if they were the same chemical entity as anticancer drugs that were covered by Medicare when they were administered intravenously. (Generally, Medicare did not pay for drugs that could be self-administered.) The bill also extended Medicare coverage to off-label uses of anticancer drugs (uses other than those for which a drug originally was approved) in certain specific circumstances.

• **Municipal Health Service Demonstration Projects.** Extended through 1997 four municipal health service demonstration projects.

• **Native American Health Programs.** Extended Medicare coverage to certain programs and facilities operated by Native American tribes under the Indian Self-Determination Act.

• **Certified Nurse Midwife Services.** Clarified that Medicare coverage of certified nurse midwife services was not limited to services provided during pregnancy.

• **Outpatient Physical and Occupational Therapy.** Beginning Jan. 1, 1994, increased from $750 to $900 the annual limit on outpatient physical and occupational therapy services.

Parts A and B

• **Graduate Medical Education.** Froze for fiscal 1994 and 1995 the level of Medicare payments made to hospitals to offset the costs of training physicians who treated Medicare patients. Residents in obstetrics and gynecology were exempt from the freeze, as were those in primary care fields, including family medicine, general internal medicine, general pediatrics, preventive medicine, geriatric medicine and osteopathic general practice.

Beginning July 1, 1995, the period of eligibility for such "direct" medical education payments was redefined as the minimum number of years before a resident was eligible for board certification in his or her field of specialization.

• **Home Health Services.** From July 1, 1994, to July 1, 1996, eliminated the annual inflation adjustment for the maximum Medicare reimbursement for home health services. Beginning Oct. 1, 1993, special payments to hospital-based home health agencies were eliminated.

• **Medicare Secondary Payer Provisions.** Extended through Sept. 30, 1998, authority for Medicare officials to gain access to the records of the Social Security Administration and the Internal Revenue Service to identify Medicare beneficiaries with other sources of health insurance. By law, Medicare was supposed to be the "secondary payer" for many beneficiaries with other insurance, covering only those costs that were not covered by the primary insurer.

The bill also extended through Sept. 30, 1998, a provision making Medicare the secondary payer for disabled Medicare beneficiaries who were covered by employer health plans in businesses with more than 100 employees, as well as beneficiaries who qualified for Medicare as a result of end-stage renal disease.

• **Physician Referrals.** Extended a ban imposed in the 1989 reconciliation bill on physicians' referring patients to clinical laboratories in which they or their immediate family members had an ownership or investment interest. Beginning Dec. 31, 1994, such self-referrals also were to be banned for physical and occupational therapy services; radiology or other diagnostic services; radiation therapy services; durable medical equipment; parenteral and enteral nutrients, equipment and supplies; prosthetics, orthotics and prosthetic devices; home health services; outpatient prescription drugs; and inpatient and outpatient hospital services.

The bill revised and added a series of exceptions to the ban, including ones for services provided to rural residents in rural areas, those provided by group practices and those provided by or under the direct supervision of a physician or group of physicians. It also clarified circumstances in which ownership of investment securities constituted a relationship that triggered the referral ban, and it clarified permissible compensation arrangements and definitions of group practices.

• **Immunosuppressive Drugs.** Extended Medicare coverage of outpatient immunosuppressive drugs that were used to prevent rejection in organ-transplant patients. At the time, Medicare covered such drugs for one year following a transplant. Beginning Jan. 1, 1995, coverage was extended to 18 months; beginning Jan. 1, 1996, coverage would continue for 24 months; beginning Jan. 1, 1997, coverage would continue for 30 months; and beginning Jan. 1, 1998, and thereafter, coverage would continue for 36 months.

• **Erythropoietin Payments.** Beginning Jan. 1, 1994, reduced payments for Erythropoietin (an antianemia drug used by dialysis patients in Medicare's end-stage renal disease program) by $1 per 1,000 units. The bill also permitted dialysis patients to administer the drug themselves.

• **Social Health Maintenance Organization Demonstrations.** Continued for two additional years, through Dec. 31, 1997, authority for demonstration programs to offer Medicare beneficiaries integrated health and long-term care services on a prepaid basis.

• **Timing of Claims Payments.** Set new "floors" and "ceilings" for payment of Medicare claims by insurance companies that processed Medicare paperwork. Beginning Oct. 1, 1993, stipulated that "clean" claims (those properly submitted with all necessary information) submitted electronically could not be paid until the 14th day after receipt. (The federal government benefited because it could earn interest on the money in the interim.) Clean claims submitted on paper could not be paid until the 27th day after receipt. However, interest was to be paid to recipients for clean claims not paid within 30 days of receipt.

• **Part B Premium.** Extended through 1998 the requirement that the Medicare Part B premium be calculated to recoup 25 percent of the program's costs. The Treasury would continue to subsidize the remaining 75 percent. Without the change, after 1995 the Part B premium could not rise by more than the Social Security cost of living adjustment.

• **Medicare and Medicaid Coverage Data Bank.** Required the HHS secretary to establish a data bank to help identify and collect from private insurers appropriate reimbursement for services provided to Medicare and Medicaid beneficiaries. Beginning in 1994, employers were required to provide information regarding employee health insurance coverage.

Medicaid

• **Personal Care Services.** Repealed a mandate requiring states to provide personal care services for Medicaid beneficiaries outside the home and clarified that such services could be provided as a state option. (This corrected a drafting error in the 1990 reconciliation bill.)

• **Medicaid Prescription Drug Discount Program.** Permitted states to establish prescription drug formularies (restrictive lists of approved drugs that were to be covered by Medicaid) under certain circumstances. States were allowed to subject drugs to "prior authorization" before they were dispensed to Medicaid recipients—even in the first six months after they were approved by the Food and Drug Administration. Such drugs had been barred from inclusion in prior authorization programs during the first six months.

• **Optional Coverage of TB-related Services.** Beginning Jan.

1, 1994, allowed states to cover prescribed drugs, directly observed therapy and other services for low-income individuals infected with tuberculosis not otherwise eligible for Medicaid.

• **Emergency Services for Illegal Aliens.** Stipulated that services related to organ transplant procedures did not qualify as emergencies covered by Medicaid for illegal aliens.

• **Certified Nurse Midwife Services.** Beginning Oct. 1, 1993, clarified that Medicaid coverage of certified nurse midwife services was not limited to services provided during pregnancy.

• **Transfer of Assets to Facilitate Medicaid Eligibility.** Required a delay in granting eligibility for Medicaid nursing home coverage for institutionalized individuals (or their spouses) who disposed of assets for less than fair market value 36 months before the date they applied for benefits or the date they were institutionalized, whichever was later. Penalties could not be applied to transfers to spouses, to minor or disabled children, or to trusts solely for the benefit of disabled individuals under age 65.

• **Medicaid Estate Recoveries.** Required states to establish programs to recover the cost of long-term care services provided to Medicaid beneficiaries from their estates after their death. Recovery could be waived in cases in which "undue hardship" would result.

• **Disproportionate Share Hospitals.** Tightened conditions under which states could designate hospitals as serving a disproportionate share of low-income individuals (and hence qualifying for higher federal payments). A hospital could not be designated unless at least 1 percent of its inpatients were Medicaid beneficiaries. Special payments were limited to no more than the costs of providing inpatient and outpatient services to Medicaid and uninsured patients, less the amount the hospital received for those patients either from Medicaid or the patients themselves. The bill allowed a transition for high-volume public hospitals.

• **Third-Party Liability Laws.** Required states to enact laws that prohibited insurers, including group health plans under ERISA, from taking an individual's Medicaid eligibility or enrollment into account in enrolling them or paying claims. States also were required to enact laws making it possible to collect payments from group health plans and other private insurers of Medicaid beneficiaries.

• **Medical Child Support Laws.** Beginning April 1, 1994, required states to enact and implement laws to ensure that insurers and employers carried out court or administrative orders for medical child support.

• **Physician Referrals.** Beginning December 1994, applied to Medicaid the rules barring physicians from referring patients to facilities in which they had a financial interest (see Medicare, above).

• **State Medicaid Fraud Control.** Beginning Jan. 1, 1995, required states to operate "effective" Medicaid fraud control units that met requirements established by the HHS secretary, unless the state could demonstrate that operating such a unit would not be cost-effective and that the state could otherwise protect Medicaid beneficiaries from fraud and neglect.

• **Federal Medicaid Payments to U.S. Territories.** Beginning in fiscal 1994, increased the limit for federal matching payments to Medicaid programs in Puerto Rico, the Virgin Islands, Guam, the Northern Mariana Islands and American Samoa. Beginning in fiscal 1995, the new ceilings were to be adjusted for inflation.

Other Health Provisions

• **Permanent Extension of Vaccine Injury Compensation Trust Fund.** Made permanent the federal program to compensate families of children injured or killed by adverse reactions to vaccines to prevent childhood illnesses. The bill also made permanent the manufacturer's excise tax on certain vaccines that funded the compensation program. Both the tax and the program had expired as of Jan. 1, 1993, but the law provided that children affected after the expiration date would be eligible as if the coverage lapse had not occurred.

• **Immunization Entitlement.** Created a new program under Medicaid designed to guarantee availability of free childhood vaccines to all children eligible for Medicaid, all uninsured children, and all Native Americans. Children with health insurance but whose insurance did not cover the cost of vaccines could receive free vaccines at certain federally supported clinics, such as community health centers.

The program entitled each state to receive at no charge from the federal government a sufficient supply of vaccine to cover the designated class of children. The state in turn was required to make the vaccines available to all public and private healthcare providers who were willing to participate in the program and were authorized under state law to administer vaccines. Neither the state nor providers could charge patients for the vaccines, although providers could assess a limited fee for the actual administration.

The HHS secretary was ordered to negotiate with vaccine manufacturers for a bulk purchase price, which also was to be the price at which states could purchase additional amounts of vaccine for children not covered by the mandate.

The federal government also was to purchase an emergency stockpile of recommended vaccines as protection against unexpected shortages, such as manufacturing disruptions, or sudden needs, such as an epidemic.   ❑

Abortion

The abortion wars that had riven Congress and the country ever since the Supreme Court legalized the procedure nationwide in 1973 took a decided turn towards abortion-rights backers in the 103rd Congress, led by the first president on their side in more than a decade. Yet the steps taken were relatively limited, at least when measured against the agenda of abortion rights supporters. And many of them were reversed in the 104th Congress, when Republicans took control. *(1995–1996 action, p. 563)*

Congress did enact legislation to protect women seeking to enter abortion clinics, and it eliminated a host of restrictions that had been carried in various annual appropriations bills at the insistence of abortion opponents and Presidents Ronald Reagan and George Bush. President Clinton himself also reversed several policies imposed by his predecessors, including

ending enforcement of the so-called "gag rule" that prohibited abortion counseling and referrals at federally funded family planning clinics and lifting the ban on abortions in overseas military medical facilities if the woman paid for the procedure herself.

But Congress failed to even debate the so-called Freedom of Choice Act, which would have written the right to abortion into federal law. And it amended only slightly the government's primary abortion restriction, the "Hyde amendment"—named for sponsor Henry J. Hyde, R-Ill.—that barred federal funding of the procedure except to save the woman's life. Congress did enact new exceptions to the ban for women whose pregnancies were the result of rape or incest, but abortion rights backers had hoped for much more.

BACKGROUND

As in previous years, the abortion fight was a multifront war, with skirmishes on a wide variety of both spending and other bills. But while some of the controversies were old ones, 1993 was a watershed, with several issues put to rest, at least for the time being, and new ones popping up.

Clinton resolved many of the abortion-related fights of the previous four years on his second full day in office. In a series of executive orders issued Jan. 22, the new president, in addition to halting the gag rule and lifting the ban on abortions in military hospitals overseas, also:

• Rescinded a ban on funding research using tissue from aborted fetuses, thus freeing long-delayed legislation reauthorizing portions of the National Institutes of Health. Clinton signed the NIH bill, including codification of the end of the fetal tissue research ban, in June 1993. *(NIH reauthorization, p. 525)*

• Directed the Department of Health and Human Services to study whether to lift the "import alert" that prevented even small amounts of the abortion pill RU 486 from being brought into the country.

• Overturned the so-called Mexico City policy that since 1984 had banned U.S. aid to international organizations that performed or "actively promoted" abortions.

Abortion rights forces thought Clinton's Jan. 22 actions would be the first in a long list of accomplishments for the year. In the end, however, they proved to be the high-water mark.

Congress did loosen some of other abortion-related restrictions in addition to adding rape and incest exceptions to the Hyde language. The fiscal 1994 spending bills for the Treasury Department, Postal Service and general government and for the District of Columbia lifted bans on abortion coverage in health plans for federal employees and use of locally raised tax funds to pay for abortions for poor District women, respectively.

Despite the end of the controversy over the gag rule, the 103rd Congress failed to complete action on legislation to reauthorize the federal family planning program, Title X of the Public Health Service Act. The chief remaining obstacle was one that had helped prevent the formal renewal of the program since 1985—the question of whether parents should have to be notified before a teenager obtained an abortion.

Here are the major abortion-related controversies addressed by the 103rd Congress:

ABORTION CLINIC ACCESS

Congress in 1994 cleared legislation (S 636—PL 103-259) that made it a federal crime to use force, or the threat of force, to intimidate abortion clinic workers or women seeking abortions. Violators faced criminal penalties of jail time and fines. The bill also allowed affected individuals to sue for civil relief, such as compensatory damages or court injunctions to restrain block-aders. The same protections applied to pregnancy counseling centers run by anti-abortion groups and to places of worship. Clinton signed the bill, known as the Freedom of Access to Clinic Entrances Act (or FACE) May 26.

The legislation was prompted by a rash of violence at abortion clinics nationwide. During the congressional debate, the list of incidents grew to include the shootings of two abortion providers, one of whom died. Supporters argued that local laws were inadequate to address the problem and successfully framed the issue as a law-and-order question rather than an abortion vote, winning over some strong abortion opponents in both chambers despite complaints from anti-abortion groups that the law would impinge on the free speech rights of abortion foes.

The Supreme Court subsequently affirmed the power of government and the courts to place significant restrictions on anti-abortion protesters to ensure access to abortion clinics. The ruling came June 30, 1994, in *Madsen v. Women's Health Center, Inc. (Court decision, p. 791)*

Background

Both chambers had passed versions of the bill in the fall of 1993. In addition to the increase in violence outside abortion clinics, bill supporters were eager to act in the wake of a Jan. 13, 1993, Supreme Court ruling, *Bray v. Alexandria Women's Health Clinic*, which struck down one of the federal laws that had been used to bar protesters from harassing women seeking entrance to a clinic. *(Court decision, p. 790)*

The House approved its bill (HR 796) by voice vote Nov. 18, 1993, following a debate that had focused on the bill's constitutionality. HR 796 had been reported (H Rept 103-306) by the House Judiciary Committee Oct. 22.

The Senate Labor and Human Resources Committee had reported a bill (S 636—S Rept 103-117) on July 29, 1993. The full Senate passed it by a vote of 69–30 on Nov. 16, but not before making some changes that prevented a quick agreement with the House. One key Senate amendment extended the bill's reach to protect "any person lawfully exercising or seeking to exercise the First Amendment right of religious freedom at a place of worship." The amendment, offered by Orrin G. Hatch, R-Utah, had been adopted by voice vote. A second amendment distinguished between violent and nonviolent protest, providing lesser penalties for nonviolent actions. That amendment, proposed by bill sponsor and Labor Committee Chairman Edward M. Kennedy, D-Mass., had been adopted by a 56–40 vote Nov. 16.

What usually was a routine request to convene a conference with the Senate touched off a passionate debate in the House in 1994. As a prelude to going to conference, both chambers had to act on the same bill. Typically, one chamber simply called up the other's bill, inserted the text of its own version and passed it. In the House, such a procedure usually was handled by unanimous consent or under suspension of the rule. But on March 17, 1994, anti-abortion lawmakers—led by Christopher H. Smith, R-N.J.—insisted on using the process as a forum to air their opposition to the bill, forcing seven separate roll call votes. Along the way, opponents attempted to kill the bill by offering amendments to table it and to recommit it to the Judiciary Committee. In the last vote, the House agreed 398–2 to a nonbinding motion instructing its conferees to accept the Senate provisions extending the bill's protections to places of religious worship.

During the conference, Senator Kennedy offered a compromise proposal to preserve key features of the Senate bill while retaining the House version on several technical issues. The compromise included Senator Hatch's provision applying the rules in the bill to protesters at places of worship. Hatch cited several instances in which churchgoers had been harassed by protesters for various causes. House conferees agreed to the provision after clarifying that it would not create a new legal recourse for those praying while simultaneously demonstrating outside an abortion clinic.

House negotiators also accepted Kennedy's provision establishing lower maximum criminal penalties for nonviolent obstruction, such as lying down in front of a clinic door. Both bills provided for fines of up to $100,000 and up to one year in prison for a first offense, and up to $250,000 and three years in prison for a subsequent violation. But the Senate set lower penalties for nonviolent offenses: up to six months in jail and a $10,000 fine for a first offense, and up to 18 months and $25,000 for a subsequent one.

Conferees added so-called severability language specifying that if a part of the law was invalidated by the courts as unconstitutional, the rest would remain in effect.

The House adopted the conference report (H Rept 103-488) May 5 by a **241–174 (R 40–131; D 200–43; I 1–0) key vote,** but not until after nearly two more hours of emotional debate. The Senate cleared the bill May 12, by a **key vote of 69–30 (R 17–27; D 52–3)**. *(1994 key votes, p. 1003)*

FREEDOM OF CHOICE ACT

Abortion rights supporters thought the 103rd Congress would have an easy time writing a woman's right to abortion into federal law, particularly since Clinton had vowed during the presidential campaign to sign such a bill. But while both the House and Senate Judiciary committees approved bills (HR 25, S 25) in 1993, the legislation failed to reach the floor of either chamber. Congress balked at a number of the bill's possible effects, such as those prohibiting restrictions on third-trimester abortions, overturning several states' requirements that teenagers obtain the consent of one or both parents before having an abortion, and prohibiting requirements for a 24-hour waiting period before a woman could obtain an abortion. With the budget, health reform and the North American Free Trade Agreement occupying much of his time, Clinton proved unwilling to spend political capital on the divisive abortion issue. As a result, the bill was left to languish.

Backers, who had been pushing the proposal since 1989, insisted that the two-page bill merely codified the abortion protections of the landmark 1973 Supreme Court decision, *Roe v. Wade*. But opponents insisted that the bill would go much further, invalidating some restrictions the court had deemed permissible even under the *Roe* framework, such as state laws requiring parental notification or consent for a minor's abortion, or bans on using public funds for the procedure. *(1973 decision, Congress and the Nation Vol. IV, p. 635)*

As it had in 1990 and 1992, the House Judiciary Subcommittee on Civil and Constitutional Rights approved the Freedom of Choice Act. The panel approved the bill by voice vote on March 18. The subcommittee debated two amendments. One by bill opponent Henry J. Hyde, R-Ill., would have allowed only physicians and osteopaths to perform abortions. The 26-line version of the House bill did not specify the level of medical training required to perform an abortion, and abortion foes feared that states would make the abortion procedure more dangerous by authorizing so-called mid-level medical professionals, such as nurse-practitioners and physician assistants, to perform it. Hyde's amendment was defeated on a party-line vote of 3–5. *(1992 action, Congress and the Nation Vol. VIII, p. 599)*

By a vote of 5–2, the subcommittee did adopt an amendment offered by bill backers Patricia Schroeder, D-Colo., and Jerrold Nadler, D-N.Y., to strike from the measure language explicitly allowing states to require minors to involve a parent or other adult in their abortion decision. Nadler said he wanted to remove any suggestion that Congress condoned parental notice or consent laws. Abortion opponents also supported the amendment—but for a different reason. They saw removal of the language as making the bill more difficult to pass, since many politicians who supported abortion rights remained uncomfortable about excluding parents from an underage girl's abortion decision.

On May 19, the full House Judiciary Committee approved HR 25 by a vote of 20–15, after defeating several amendments offered by abortion opponents—many by one-vote margins. Many of the amendments offered at the markup by abortion foes were phrased to permit "constitutional" state restrictions, meaning they had to conform to the standard established by the Supreme Court in the 1992 decision *Planned Parenthood of Southeastern Pennsylvania v. Casey*. In that case, the Court allowed state restrictions as long as they did not impose an "undue burden" on the right to an abortion. Hyde, for example, offered an amendment to allow states to enact constitutional waiting periods. The amendment did not specify how long that period might be, on the theory that the then-permissible standard of 24 hours could be lengthened or reduced as a result of subsequent cases. The amendment failed on a 17–17 tie. *(1992 decision, Congress and the Nation Vol. VIII, p. 839)*

In action on other amendments, the committee:

• Defeated, 15–20, an amendment by Charles T. Canady, R-Fla., to permit states to ban abortion in the third trimester except to save the life of the woman.

• Adopted, 19–14, an amendment by bill sponsor Don Edwards, D-Calif., permitting states to enact parental notice or consent laws as long as such laws included a "bypass" feature allowing a minor to go to a judge or other state-appointed adult if she did not feel she could go to her own parents. The amendment restored the language struck during the subcommittee markup in March.

The Senate Labor and Human Resources Committee on March 24, 1993, approved S 25 a vote of 12–5—the identical margin by which the panel had approved the legislation a year earlier. But many of the dynamics had changed in the eight months since the panel had last considered the bill, not the least of which was the fact that Nancy Landon Kassebaum, R-Kan., an abortion rights backer, had replaced abortion opponent Orrin G. Hatch, R-Utah, as the committee's ranking minority member.

One dynamic that had not changed was the deep divisions between those on opposite sides of the issue. Members voted on no amendments at the markup, but several lawmakers said they voted for the bill only to move it to the floor, where they could get a full Senate vote on their amendments. Yet, in committee discussion, three factions emerged: those who would put very few limits on abortion rights; those who opposed abortion and wanted to place as many limits on it as possible; and those who sought a middle ground. Kassebaum said she represented the last group and announced that when the bill got to the floor she would propose a series of amendments to allow restrictions of the sort permitted by the Supreme Court in the *Casey* decision.

S 25 was reported (S Rept 103-42) on April 29, 1993, but went no further.

LABOR-HHS APPROPRIATION

As usual, the biggest abortion fight of the year occurred during consideration of the annual spending bill for the departments of Labor, Health and Human Services (HHS), Education and related agencies. Long the vortex around which Congress's abortion debate had swirled, the Labor-HHS appropriations bill since 1976 had carried language restricting federal spending for abortions for poor women in one way or another. The fiscal 1994 measure (HR 2518—PL 103-112) relaxed federal funding restrictions for the first time since 1977.

As signed into law by Clinton on Oct. 21, 1993, the bill still banned the use of most federal funds to pay for abortions for women on Medicaid, the joint federal-state health program for the poor. But it did permit abortion funding in cases of rape and incest, as well as when the life of the pregnant woman would be endangered if the fetus was carried to term. Since 1981, the bill had allowed federal abortion funding only in cases of life endangerment.

But in the topsy-turvy world of 1993 abortion politics, the relaxation of the restrictions was seen as a major loss for abortion rights backers, who only three years earlier had called it a major victory when they came close to getting the rape and incest exceptions reinstated. And the new language was a major win for abortion foes, who found themselves in the odd position of offering as an amendment language that until 1993 they had ardently opposed.

The reason could be summed up in a single word: expectations. Abortion rights advocates—already optimistic because of their new friends in the White House and the House—had their hopes boosted further in April, when Clinton sent Congress his annual budget request—minus the boilerplate language restricting federal funds for abortion that had been part of every budget request for the dozen years Republicans controlled the White House. But abortion rights backers turned out to have badly underestimated how difficult the funding issue would be—or how reluctant members would be, even legislators who supported abortion rights, to vote for the use of taxpayer dollars for the procedure when so many of their constituents considered abortion to be murder.

The first indications of congressional reluctance to lift the funding ban came during the House Appropriations Committee markup June 24. Although abortion rights backers preferred that the bill remain silent on the matter (thus eliminating the ban), two abortion amendments were offered. First, David R. Obey, D-Wis., offered an amendment that essentially would have allowed poor women to use Medicaid to pay for abortions in the first two trimesters of pregnancy. It lost, 18–27. Then William H. Natcher, chairman of both the full committee and the Labor-HHS Subcommittee, offered an amendment to prohibit federal funding of abortions except in cases of rape, incest or life endangerment. Natcher's amendment was adopted by a vote of 31–14. The bill was reported (H Rept 103-156) that same day.

The wake-up call for abortion rights backers came during House floor consideration of the Labor-HHS bill June 30. Initially, abortion rights supporters managed to strip the committee language on the grounds that it amounted to legislating on an appropriation. But, using a procedural twist based on a 1908 precedent, Hyde modified the restrictive language to make it acceptable. After an emotional debate that included unusually harsh words between Hyde and some women members of the House, members in a **key vote of 255–178 (R 157–16; D 98–161; I 0–1)** approved a slightly rewritten amendment to effectively ban abortion funding for poor women except to save the life of the pregnant woman or in cases of rape or incest. *(1993 key votes, p. 979)*

The vote mostly represented a strategic retreat by abortion foes, who offered language they had opposed in the past in order to prevent the ban from being lifted altogether. "Since 1989, what had been a pro-life majority had been eroding," said Hyde. "I didn't think the votes were there anymore for a straight ban on abortion funding."

But the votes also were not there for what Clinton sent to the House and what abortion rights lawmakers wanted: no restrictions on federal funding. For technical reasons having to do with the way the Medicaid statute was written, that policy would have amounted to a mandate that the federal government and the states pay for poor women's abortions in all cases, which would have overturned laws in at least 31 states.

In the Senate, traditionally more supportive of abortion rights, the Appropriations Committee agreed to leave the House-passed abortion restrictions out of the bill, approved Sept. 14 and reported (S Rept 103-143) Sept. 15. But in an embarrassing defeat for the Senate's five Democratic women, abortion rights supporters all, the Senate on Sept. 28 rejected, 40–59, the committee's recommendations. Instead, the Labor-HHS bill passed by the Senate 82–17 on Sept. 29 included the same abortion restrictions as the House version.

That settled the matter for the year, and, as it turned out, for the Congress. In 1994, the abortion language went unchallenged in the fiscal 1995 Labor-HHS bill (HR 4606—PL 103-333).

TREASURY-POSTAL SERVICE APPROPRIATION

For the first time since 1984, the annual spending bill for the Departments of the Treasury and the Postal Service (HR 2403—PL 103-123) enacted in 1993 did not include a provision barring health plans for federal workers from covering abortions. Previous language had prohibited the Office of Personnel Management, which oversaw the Federal Employee Health Benefits Program, from spending money to allow abortions as part of health coverage except in the case of life endangerment for a pregnant woman.

The initial impetus to drop the ban came from the new Treasury-Postal Appropriations Subcommittee chairman and abortion rights supporter, Steny H. Hoyer, D-Md. Subcommittee ranking Republican Jim Ross Lightfoot of Iowa sought to restore the language at the subcommittee markup May 26, but he failed on a voice vote.

For both political and parliamentary reasons, abortion foes opted not to fight to reinstate the language during full committee action or the House floor debate, choosing instead to focus their efforts on the higher-profile spending bill for the Labor and Health and Human Services departments. The House passed HR 2403 by a vote of 263–153 on June 22.

Abortion foes in the Senate tried to reinstate the ban, with some initial success. The Treasury-Postal Appropriations subcommittee July 20 approved an amendment by Christopher S. Bond, R-Mo., to restore the previous language. But at the full committee markup July 22, members voted 15–14 to strip the language. The vote, a procedural one, was engineered by abortion rights supporter Barbara A. Mikulski, D-Md.

Mikulski won a second procedural victory during Senate floor debate Aug. 3, when members voted 48–51 against allowing abortion opponent Don Nickles, R-Okla., to offer an amendment to reinstate the ban—voting, in effect, that the amendment amounted to inappropriate legislating on a spending bill. Nickles's amendment would have allowed female federal workers to receive abortions through their health plans but only if they paid a separate premium for the coverage.

Abortion was not an issue during conference action because neither the House nor the Senate bill had abortion provisions. But abortion opponents in the House, led by Congressional Pro-Life Caucus Chairman Christopher H. Smith, R-N.J., almost sank the bill when they quietly lobbied colleagues to oppose the conference report (H Rept 103-256). The report ultimately was adopted by a vote of 207–206. Abortion foes made no further attempts to reinstate the ban, and the Senate adopted the conference report by voice vote Oct. 26. Clinton signed the bill without the abortion ban Oct. 28.

The abortion issue was not debated at all during consideration of the fiscal 1995 Treasury-Postal bill (HR 4539—PL 103-329).

DISTRICT OF COLUMBIA APPROPRIATION

As with so many bills in 1993, the spending bill for the District of Columbia (HR 2492—PL 103-127) relaxed restrictions imposed in previous years. But the final version disappointed abortion rights backers and elated abortion foes by not going as far as both thought it might have.

As signed into law by Clinton Oct. 29, the measure allowed the city to use locally raised funds to pay for abortions for poor women through the joint federal-state Medicaid program, lifting a ban that had been in place since 1988. But it maintained restrictions on the use of federal funds appropriated in the bill.

Both the House and Senate had approved versions of the bill with no abortion restrictions, and a conference committee approved a final bill that was silent on the issue. Had that version become law, it would have been the first D.C. bill without abortion related-restrictions since 1979.

But in a debate dominated by abortion foes, the House rejected the conference report (H Rept 103-291) Oct. 20 by a vote of 206–224. Sent back to the drawing board, bill sponsors quickly produced a new version that permitted federal funds to be used for abortion only in cases of rape, incest or when the pregnancy endangered the life of the woman—tracking the language in the fiscal 1994 Labor-HHS bill (HR 2518). The new conference report (H Rept 103-303) was adopted relatively easily, 225–201, on Oct. 27. The Senate approved the new version by voice vote later that day.

The fiscal 1995 funding bill for the District of Columbia (HR 4649—PL 103-334) carried the previous year's abortion language.

FOREIGN OPERATIONS APPROPRIATION

Congress in 1993 ended an eight-year ban on aid to the United Nations Population Fund, when it included funding for the agency in the fiscal 1994 foreign operations appropriation bill (HR 2295—PL 103-87). But conditions were set on the aid because of the agency's involvement with China, where reportedly coercive population control practices were used to reach its one-child-per-family goal. (*U.N. Population Fund, box, p. 209*)

Since 1985, the annual foreign operations spending bill had explicitly barred funds from going to any organization that supported or participated in the "management of a program of coercive abortion or involuntary sterilization," which the Reagan and Bush administrations interpreted to include the U.N. Population Fund.

As passed by the House June 17, the fiscal 1994 spending bill provided $36.2 million for the population fund. But in order to spend the aid before March 1, 1994, it required the president to

certify that the U.N. agency had terminated its activities in China. The Senate version, passed Sept. 23, provided the full $50 million Clinton requested.

A House-Senate conference committee ultimately agreed to provide $40 million for the population fund, but it also required the administration to report to Congress on the agency's budget for its activities in China in 1994. Any amount above $10 million that the agency intended to spend in China was to be deducted from the U.S. contribution. President Clinton signed the bill Sept. 30.

FAMILY PLANNING

Although Clinton had taken the most contentious issue off the table by ending implementation of the "gag rule," Congress was still unable to complete work on legislation (HR 670) reauthorizing the federal family planning program, Title X of the Public Health Service Act. The House passed a bill in 1993; a companion Senate measure made it through committee that same year but did not reach the floor.

Various abortion-related controversies had kept the program running on stopgap funding since its last authorization expired in 1985. Congress did pass a reauthorization bill in 1992, but President George Bush vetoed it, primarily because it lifted the Reagan-era ban on abortion counseling and referrals in the program's 4,000 clinics. (*1992 action, Congress and the Nation Vol. VIII, p. 598*)

With the so-called gag rule lifted, the House Energy and Commerce Committee approved a two-year reauthorization of the program—including a 37 percent increase in funding—by voice vote Feb. 4, 1993, and reported it Feb. 16 (H Rept 103-14). In addition to reauthorizing the program, HR 670 codified referral practices that were in effect by administrative guidelines between 1981 and 1988, when the gag rule was formally promulgated. The language required that clinics counsel women with unintended pregnancies about all their options, including abortion. If, because of religious affiliation or moral beliefs, a clinic could not inform women of all their options, staff members would be required to refer them to a clinic that could offer them a complete list. An amendment to order Title X clinics that also offered abortion services to require teenagers to notify their parents before obtaining an abortion failed, 18–25.

The House on March 25 passed the family planning bill by a vote of 273–149. In a victory for the Clinton administration and sponsors of the Freedom of Choice Act, the House that same day rejected, 179–243, a motion to recommit the bill to committee with instructions to report it back with a restrictive federal parental notice requirement for those family planning clinics affiliated with nearby abortion facilities. The vote, however, seemed to turn less on the issue of parental involvement than on whether the federal government or the states should be the ones to determine how much involvement, if any, was appropriate. Many who rejected federal intervention said they were strong supporters of state parental notice or consent laws.

Much of the debate on the family planning bill consisted of a series of parliamentary maneuvers by Democrats that Republicans complained kept their amendments from reaching a vote.

For every Republican amendment allowed by the Rules Committee, the Democrats filed a second-degree amendment (an amendment to the amendment). Under House rules, those superseded the original versions, effectively precluding a vote on the GOP amendments.

That meant, for instance, that the House never voted on an amendment by Tom DeLay, R-Texas, that would have required that family planning counselors hold degrees in medicine, psychology or nursing. Instead, the House voted on DeLay's amendment as modified by HR 670 sponsor Henry A. Waxman, D-Calif. Waxman added to the list of approved counselors anyone approved by the secretary of the Department of Health and Human Services or anyone allowed to provide counseling under state law. The modified amendment was adopted, 408–16, on March 24.

The Senate Labor and Human Resources Committee approved the House bill, without change, by a vote of 15–2 on May 5. The panel reported the bill (S Rept 103-84) July 1. There was no further action.   ❑

Tobacco Industry Investigation

No legislation cleared Congress, but a subcommittee of the House Energy and Commerce Committee in 1994 conducted a high-profile investigation of the tobacco industry during which chief executives of seven U.S. tobacco companies testified under oath that they did not believe their products caused cancer or were addictive. The investigation was ended, however, after the 1994 elections elevated to the chairmanship of the Energy and Commerce Committee in the 104th Congress Rep. Thomas Bliley, Jr., R-Va., one of Congress's leading defenders of the tobacco industry.

The investigation, spearheaded by Rep. Henry A. Waxman, D-Calif., chairman of the panel's Subcommittee on Health and the Environment, focused on reports that cigarette makers were manipulating the levels of nicotine in their products. It began shortly after the Environmental Protection Agency (EPA) issued a report in January 1993 that blamed the lung-cancer deaths of 3,000 nonsmokers a year on environmental tobacco smoke, also known as secondhand smoke. This included both the mainstream smoke exhaled by smokers and the sidestream smoke emitted from the lit end of cigarettes, cigars and pipes.

Tobacco foes, including Waxman, used the EPA report as ammunition to argue for new smoking restrictions, and the House responded in late 1993 by passing a bill (HR 881) restricting smoking in most federal buildings to separately ventilated rooms. The Senate, however, never acted on it. (Federal smoking restrictions, p. 819)

In 1994, Waxman's subcommittee approved a still more sweeping measure, the Smoke-Free Environment Act (HR 3434), that would have restricted smoking in most buildings nationwide, but it, too, failed to advance further. That measure was approved by a vote of 14–11 on May 12.

Near the end of the session, the House on Oct. 3 did pass a bill (S 656) designed to improve the quality of indoor air by requiring the EPA to study indoor air pollution and develop vol-

untary guidelines aimed at reducing potential health hazards. But while the Senate had passed its own version of the measure Oct. 29, 1993, it did not have time to consider the House changes before the end of the Congress and the measure died. Bill sponsors Rep. Joseph P. Kennedy II, D-Mass., and Sen. George J. Mitchell, D-Maine, had tried for four years to get an indoor air quality bill through Congress, but without success. Critics complained the 1994 bill would lead to more regulations on businesses and duplicate extensive rules proposed by the Occupational Safety and Health Administration. (Indoor air bill, p. 431)

BACKGROUND

In February 1994, Food and Drug Administration (FDA) Commissioner David A. Kessler announced that his agency might consider regulating the nicotine in cigarettes as a drug because of evidence that tobacco manufacturers changed the levels of nicotine, a naturally occurring substance in tobacco, in an attempt to addict smokers.

Waxman began a series of subcommittee hearings soon after that revelation. Testifying before the panel March 25—the same day that the Labor Department proposed a sweeping ban on smoking in the workplace—Kessler outlined his case against the tobacco companies. He cited internal tobacco company memos and a series of cigarette patents that both described the effects of nicotine on the body and identified methods of manipulating the amount of nicotine smokers could get from a cigarette, such as adding nicotine to the paper, filter and other parts of the cigarette. Kessler said the evidence suggested that regulation might be necessary, but he warned Congress that if the FDA regulated the nicotine in cigarettes as a drug under existing law, it would have to ban cigarettes altogether. He asked lawmakers to intervene.

On April 14, the chief executives of the nation's seven largest tobacco companies made an unprecedented joint appearance before the panel, denying all of Kessler's allegations under oath. They also testified that they did not believe nicotine was addictive and that the level of nicotine in cigarettes had actually decreased in recent years. Waxman and other lawmakers pressed the tobacco executives for access to industry research on the nature of nicotine and requested that some former tobacco company employees be released from their agreements not to discuss such research. The executives reluctantly agreed.

Two weeks later, on April 28, two former scientists with Philip Morris, the largest U.S. tobacco manufacturer, said the company had quashed internal research in the 1980s that suggested the addictive nature of nicotine. A company spokesman denied the allegation.

The probe intensified again in mid-May when Waxman and Ron Wyden, D-Ore., a member of Waxman's subcommittee, along with several news organizations obtained internal documents of the Brown & Williamson Tobacco Corp. Lawyers for Brown & Williamson alleged that the documents were stolen by a former lawyer for the company and thus distributed illegally.

At the lawyers' request, a Kentucky judge issued subpoenas for the documents possessed by Waxman and Wyden. But U.S.

District Judge Harold H. Greene quashed the subpoenas June 6, ruling that they violated the clause of the Constitution that gave members of Congress broad protection for actions taken as part of congressional business. The federal court's decision paved the way for the Health Subcommittee to continue its investigation.

LEGISLATIVE EFFORTS

The hearings generated negative publicity for the tobacco industry, but Congress did not heed Kessler's advice to intervene. Antitobacco lawmakers did make one attempt at offering the guidance Kessler sought. Richard J. Durbin, D-Ill., asked the House Rules Committee for a waiver of the House rule prohibiting legislative language on a spending bill so that he could offer an amendment to the fiscal 1995 agriculture appropriations bill (HR 4554) directing the FDA to regulate tobacco products without banning them. The committee rejected that request June 15, and Durbin never offered the amendment, which contained some of the language of a broader bill (HR 2147) designed to regulate the manufacturing and marketing of tobacco products. HR 2147 was never considered elsewhere.

Waxman's bill to limit smoking in buildings regularly entered by 10 or more people to separately ventilated rooms similarly progressed no further after its subcommittee approval May 12. The bill would have required building managers to ban smoking if they chose not to designate such rooms. Tobacco state lawmakers, such as Bliley, said the legislation would infringe on the rights of smokers and intrude too deeply into people's private lives.

But opposition came from other fronts as well. The "hospitality industry"—restaurants, bars and hotels—argued that the restrictions would cost them the business of smokers, and Republicans objected because the bill would allow nonsmokers to file civil suits against building owners. In an attempt to assuage their concerns, Waxman agreed to narrow the bill's scope. The subcommittee adopted two amendments—one that exempted restaurants, bars, tobacco shops and prisons from the restrictions, and another that exempted private organizations, such as the Elks Lodge and the American Legion. Those changes won the key support of three Republicans on the subcommittee, and three Democrats who also had expressed reservations about the bill voted for it.

The Health Subcommittee's investigation waned as the session neared an end, and the Republican sweep of the November elections vaulted Bliley to the helm of the Energy and Commerce Committee (renamed the Commerce Committee) for the 104th Congress. Days after the election, Bliley announced that the investigation would end under his tenure, arguing, as he had during the hearings, that the probe was unnecessary.   □

Diet Supplement Rules

Manufacturers and consumers of vitamins, minerals and herbal remedies persuaded Congress in 1994 to limit the federal government's power to regulate dietary supplements. On the final day of the session, legislation cleared creating a commission to set labeling guidelines for vitamins and other supplements.

The Food and Drug Administration (FDA) was permitted to enforce existing regulations for up to four years while the commission completed its work. President Clinton signed the bill Oct. 25 (S 784—PL 103-417).

The bill seemed likely to result in looser rules for the health claims that dietary supplement manufacturers could make on product labels. But it also preserved the FDA's power to require and review evidence of product safety. And the FDA could halt sales of a supplement if it could show that the product posed a "significant or unreasonable risk" of illness or injury.

BACKGROUND

The legislation was the centerpiece of an intense national campaign by supplement manufacturers and advocates, who argued that without congressional action, the FDA would cut off access to alternative medical treatments. Health food stores had held petition drives and mail-in campaigns to target an FDA plan to prohibit manufacturers from making health claims unless they were backed up by "significant scientific agreement." That was the standard applied to foods under the 1990 Nutrition Labeling and Education Act (PL 101-535), which also required the FDA to develop labeling requirements for dietary supplements. The FDA began enforcing the new regulations for labeling supplements July 15, 1994. Opponents of the bill welcomed the new rules and said outrageous health claims and a lack of adequate safety standards for dietary supplements were reason enough for more regulation.

The initiative for the legislation came from Sen. Orrin G. Hatch, R-Utah, whose state was home to a number of supplement manufacturers and who was himself an avowed user of the products. As originally introduced by Hatch in 1993, the bill would have blocked the FDA's standards of "significant scientific agreement" to support health claims, instead allowing claims on labels unless the FDA determined through studies and the "totality of scientific evidence" that the claim was invalid. Senate Labor and Human Resources Committee Chairman Edward M. Kennedy, D-Mass., opposed the Hatch bill, and efforts to work out a compromise in 1993 failed. As a result, the committee put off action on the bill until 1994.

SENATE ACTION

The Senate Labor and Human Resources Committee approved a revised version of S 784 on May 11, 1994, by a vote of 12–5. The panel rejected, 5–12, a substitute proposed by Chairman Kennedy that would have given the FDA more regulatory powers than did Hatch's version. As approved by the committee, the bill barred the FDA from regulating dietary supplements as drugs or food additives by setting a broad statutory definition of supplements. This addressed manufacturers' complaints that the FDA too often tried to remove products from shelves by claiming that they were food additives or drugs subject to strict premarket approval and marketing rules. The legislation also required the FDA to prove that a supplement was unsafe, if used as directed, before pulling it from the shelves. Kennedy's version would have prohibited supplements if they presented a "reasonable possibility of harm."

In a significant concession to critics, Hatch's bill allowed the FDA to enforce the new regulations for two years while a new seven-member independent commission reviewed labeling of dietary supplements and determined what kind of rules were needed. All commissioners would have to have "expertise and experience in dietary supplements and in the manufacture, regulation, distribution and use of such supplements." The bill further stated that "no member of the commission shall be biased against dietary supplements."

The Senate passed the bill by voice vote Aug. 13 after accepting several modifications negotiated by Hatch and Tom Harkin, D-Iowa, in an effort to answer criticisms. For example, they tightened the definition of dietary supplements in response to concerns that the committee-passed language would have allowed many foreign prescription drugs to be sold in the United States without FDA approval. They also provided the FDA with emergency authority to act against dietary supplements that posed an imminent public health hazard.

The bill allowed health food stores and other establishments to display articles, pamphlets and books about supplements from sources other than the manufacturer, provided that the materials were not "false or misleading," did not promote a specific brand of diet supplement and were displayed in an area physically separate from the products. Health food stores often had sections that included pamphlets and booklets on herbal remedies, and supplement advocates were intent on protecting those publications.

HOUSE, FINAL ACTION

In the House, Hatch's bill ran into opposition from Henry A. Waxman, D-Calif., chairman of the Energy and Commerce Subcommittee on Health, and John D. Dingell, D-Mich., chairman of the full committee. Waxman and Dingell were anxious to preserve the FDA's power to regulate dietary supplements. In particular, they wanted supplement manufacturers to give the FDA data establishing a product's safety before it could be marketed, although under a lesser standard of scrutiny than that required for prescription drugs.

The final bill was hammered out in long negotiations between Hatch, Dingell and Waxman. The House then passed the compromise by voice vote Oct. 7. The Senate agreed to the House version of S 784, clearing the bill later the same day by voice vote.

MAJOR PROVISIONS

As signed into law, S 784:

• Extended to four years the time the FDA was allowed to enforce existing labeling regulations. During that time, a seven-member, independent commission was to decide what labeling regulations were needed, and the secretary of health and human services was to decide how to adjust the rules. Like the Senate version, the final bill required that commission members "have expertise and experience in dietary supplements and in the manufacture, regulation, distribution and use of such supplements."

• Allowed manufacturers leeway to explain a product's func-

tion on its label, with a disclaimer noting that the product did not promise to cure or treat disease.

• Allowed health food stores and other establishments to display articles on supplements from sources other than the manufacturers as long as the information was not "false or misleading."

• Allowed new supplements to be sold without prior FDA approval, but required manufacturers to submit evidence of a product's safety to the FDA 75 days before putting it on the market. If the FDA was not satisfied that the information was adequate to assure that the new product was safe, it could block the marketing.

• Allowed the FDA to halt sales of a supplement if it could show that a product caused a significant or unreasonable risk—a lower standard of proof than that required in the original Senate bill.

• Established an Office of Dietary Supplements within the National Institutes of Health and directed it to "promote scientific study of the benefits of dietary supplements in maintaining health and preventing chronic disease and other health-related conditions."

CDC Programs

Congress in 1993 approved legislation reauthorizing several programs at the Centers for Disease Control and Prevention (CDC), including $150 million in fiscal 1994 for early detection of women's reproductive and breast cancers. President Clinton signed the bill (HR 2202—PL 103-183) Dec. 14.

HR 2202 authorized $50 million for a program on domestic violence, $85 million for research on sexually transmitted diseases and $6 million to study regional trauma centers. The bill authorized $250 million in fiscal 1994 to fight tuberculosis—$200 million for grants to states for research, demonstration projects and training on the control and prevention of TB, and $50 million to the National Institute of Allergy and Infectious Diseases for research on the cause, diagnosis, prevention and treatment of the disease. HR 2202 also included provisions to allow the Department of Health and Human Services to issue temporary quality standards for mammography; final regulations were to be ready by Oct. 1, 1995. In addition to the specific amounts for fiscal 1994, the bill authorized "such sums as may be necessary" through fiscal 1998.

HOUSE ACTION

The final version incorporated a series of health bills—HR 2202, HR 2201, HR 2203 and HR 2205—that had been reported by the House Energy and Commerce Committee and passed by the House separately.

HR 2202 originally only reauthorized the program to provide grants to states to help pay for mammograms and pap smears for low-income women. As introduced it provided $100 million for the program; that amount was increased to $135 million by the full Energy and Commerce Committee, which reported the bill (H Rept 103-120) June 10, 1993. The House approved the bill, 365–2, on June 14.

HR 2201, reported (H Rept 103-119) June 10, authorized $50 million in fiscal 1994 for CDC grants for data collection and education programs on domestic violence. The House passed the bill, 305–61, on June 14.

HR 2203, which was reported (H Rept 103-131) June 15 and was passed by voice vote of the full House June 21, authorized $80 million in fiscal 1994 for block grants to states to develop and carry out "innovative" approaches to the prevention and control of sexually transmitted diseases.

HR 2205 authorized $45 million over three years for programs related to trauma care. The bill was reported (H Rept 103-122) June 10 and was passed June 14 by voice vote.

SENATE ACTION

The Senate Labor and Human Resources Committee gave voice vote approval July 30 to a bill (S 1318) that was an amalgam of several draft bills aimed at detecting and preventing a host of diseases. The panel reported the bill (S Rept 103-135) on Sept. 7.

On Nov. 2, the Senate passed HR 2202 by voice vote, after substituting the text of S 1318. The Senate-passed bill authorized $200 million in fiscal 1994 for the breast and cervical cancer detection grants, $132 million to prevent sexually transmitted diseases and $60 million for the CDC for research on violence and injuries. It authorized $226 million for the CDC's TB control programs; $46 million for the National Institute of Allergy and Infectious Diseases for research on the disease; $25 million for a grant program to renovate facilities devoted to the prevention and control of TB, and $5 million for a tuberculosis drug research program at the Food and Drug Administration. In addition to the amounts for fiscal 1994, the bill authorized unspecified sums through fiscal 1997.

In separate action, the Senate approved HR 2205 by voice vote June 29, after substituting the text of a Senate bill on trauma care (S 1113).

FINAL ACTION

Conferees on HR 2202 melded all the bills into a single measure. The House adopted the conference report (H Rept 103-397) on the bill Nov. 21 by a vote of 420–0. The Senate cleared it by voice vote the next day.   ❑

Disabilities Assistance

The 103rd Congress in 1994 cleared two bills reauthorizing programs to help those with disabilities lead more independent lives. One renewed a series of activities designed to provide education and training for those with developmental disabilities; the other reauthorized a program of federal grants to states to provide technology-related assistance for people with disabilities.

DEVELOPMENTAL DISABILITIES

With broad bipartisan support, Congress cleared legislation (S 1284—PL 103-230) to authorize $117 million in fiscal 1994 and unspecified sums in fiscal 1995 and 1996 for states and universities to assist the disabled. President Clinton signed the bill April 6, 1994.

The measure allocated money to four separate grant programs:

- **State Councils.** State developmental disabilities councils provided advice to state agencies that helped the disabled with job training, education, medical assistance, child welfare and other social service programs.
- **Advocacy Groups.** The legislation funded nonprofit agencies that published advocacy literature for the disabled and assisted in resolving complaints.
- **University Programs.** To help family members and professionals better understand the problems of the disabled, the bill funded university programs that ran early-intervention, aging and community support programs.
- **Discretionary Fund.** The legislation authorized a fund to be administered by the Department of Health and Human Services for special projects to promote independence, collect data, issue reports and assist state councils and university programs.

At the time, more than 3 million Americans suffered from mental or physical disabilities that affected their mobility, learning and ability to take care of themselves.

The Senate Labor and Human Resources Committee reported S 1284 (S Rept 103-120) on Aug. 3, 1993, and the full Senate passed it by voice vote Aug. 5. The House amended the Senate bill, substituting the text of its version (HR 3505) and passing the bill by voice vote Nov. 21. HR 3505 had been reported (H Rept 103-378) by the House Energy and Commerce Committee Nov. 18 and passed by voice vote of the House Nov. 21.

The House adopted the conference report (H Rept 103-442) by voice vote March 21, 1994. The Senate cleared the bill March 24, also by voice vote.

TECHNOLOGY GRANTS

Congress also in 1994 cleared a bill (HR 2339—PL 103-218) to reauthorize for five years federal grants to states to provide technology-related assistance for people with disabilities. The grants could be used for a variety of projects, from increasing public awareness to expanding training. The bill also aimed to help states establish low-interest consumer loan programs to aid the disabled in purchasing technology devices and services, such as automated wheelchairs. President Clinton signed it March 9, 1994.

The bill authorized $50 million in fiscal 1994 and unspecified sums through fiscal 1998 to support state efforts to develop technology for the disabled.

The House first passed the bill Aug. 2, 1993, by voice vote. It had been reported (H Rept 103-208) by the House Education and Labor Committee that same day. The Senate passed it Aug. 5, after substituting its own version (S 1283). S 1283 had been reported (S Rept 103-119) by the Senate Labor and Human Resources Committee Aug. 3 and passed by voice vote of the full Senate Aug. 5. The two chambers worked out a compromise on HR 2339, to which the House agreed by voice vote Feb. 8, 1994. The Senate cleared it by voice vote Feb. 11.   ❑

Human Drugs for Animals

Veterinarians, who had long routinely prescribed human drugs such as insulin for dogs and cats with diabetes, or penicillin to fight common respiratory infections in horses and cattle, finally gained legal authority to do so in 1994. Although the use of such drugs for animals had been common practice, it was illegal. The Food and Drug Administration (FDA) had approved those medications only for use in humans.

On Oct. 22, 1994, President Clinton signed into law a bill (S 340—PL 103-396) that gave veterinarians the authority to prescribe medication intended for use in other species. The Senate had passed the measure by voice vote Oct. 4, and the House cleared it by voice vote Oct. 7.

Veterinarians said they had long ignored drug use restrictions because the FDA had approved an insufficient number of drugs for all the diseases seen in different animal species. As a result, veterinarians commonly prescribed drugs approved for sheep, for example, to treat the same conditions in cows.

While the measure was strongly supported by veterinarians, the Food Animal Concerns Trust (FACT), a nonprofit organization based in Chicago that tracked misuse of veterinary drugs and monitored food-safety issues, strongly opposed the measure. FACT did not oppose broadening a veterinarian's powers to treat household pets, such as dogs and cats. But the group said there were risks in treating food-producing animals such as cattle, chickens, goats and swine with drugs that had not been specifically tested on and approved for them. Without studies to test the withdrawal times of medications in different animals, veterinarians had no way of knowing when a drug was out of an animal's system, the group said. Ingestion by humans of some drugs used on animals could cause a variety of allergic reactions as well as more serious conditions, such as cardiac arrest and pulmonary edema, doctors said.

To address those concerns, the new law did require the agency to establish regulations by October 1996 that set safe dosage levels, safe withdrawal times, methods for measuring drug residue in tissue, and enforcement procedures. ❑

Ephedrine Sales

President Clinton on Dec. 17, 1993, signed into law a measure (HR 3216—PL 103-200) expanding the Drug Enforcement Administration's (DEA) control over ephedrine, a common ingredient in over-the-counter allergy and other medications that was also increasingly being used in the manufacture of illegal substances.

The bill was aimed at curbing the spread of a new illegal stimulant called methcathinone, commonly known as CAT, of which ephedrine was a principal ingredient. CAT, which looked like but was more potent than crack cocaine, had become popular in the Upper Peninsula of Michigan and other areas of the Midwest.

Under the bill, companies that manufactured the pure form of ephedrine were required to register with the DEA and submit records of the drug's sales so that those who bought the drug could be tracked. The legislation also gave the attorney general power, on a case-by-case basis, to subject other legal chemicals to the sort of record-keeping requirements applicable to controlled substances.

The House Energy and Commerce Committee reported HR 3216 (H Rept 103-379, Part I) Nov. 18 and the full House passed it by voice vote Nov. 21. The Senate passed a similar bill (S 1767) by voice vote on Nov. 20, but agreed to the House version by voice vote Nov. 24, clearing the bill. ❑

Medicare Select

A last-minute deal in the House and Senate in 1994 preserved a supplemental health insurance program subscribed to by 400,000 older Americans, while also making technical corrections in programs such as Medicare and Aid to Families with Dependent Children, the nation's main welfare program. The House passed the bill by voice vote Oct. 7, and the Senate cleared it by voice vote Oct. 8. President Clinton signed it Oct. 31 (HR 5252—PL 103-432).

The bill made minor changes in Medicare, including some adjustments important to rural lawmakers. It loosened the rules under which rural hospitals could be reimbursed for serving Medicare patients. It also specified that psychologists as well as psychiatrists could be reimbursed for treating Medicare patients, of particular importance in rural areas, where there were few or no psychiatrists.

The supplemental health insurance program was extended for six months beyond Dec. 31, 1994. The program, known as Medicare Select, was an insurance option that allowed the elderly to subscribe to a less expensive "preferred provider organization" instead of the traditional fee-for-service option generally used by Medicare recipients.

The Medicare Select program was still experimental and was offered in 15 states. It applied to Medicare Part B, the section of Medicare that covered doctors' visits. The 104th Congress made Medicare Select permanent and extended its reach nationwide. *(1995 action, p. 567)*

The technical corrections had passed the House as part of the 1993 budget-reconciliation bill (HR 2264) but had been dropped in the Senate. ❑

U.S.-Mexico Border Health

President Clinton in 1994 signed legislation (S 1225—PL 103-400) to create a 26-member United States-Mexico Border Health Commission to assess health needs in border areas, coordinate public health efforts, educate residents about health problems and recommend ways that one country could reimburse the other for uncompensated care.

The bill had the support of the governors of the four U.S. states bordering on Mexico—Arizona, California, New Mexico and Texas—and of the six Mexican border states—Baja California, Chihuahua, Coahuila, Nuevo Leon, Sonora and Tamaulipas. Health problems along the border were among the most severe in the country, in part because several border communities had no public drinking water or sewer systems. Hepatitis and tuberculosis were among the prevalent diseases in those areas.

S 1225 was reported by the Senate Foreign Relations Committee Sept. 22, 1994, and passed by voice vote of the full Senate Sept. 30. The House Energy and Commerce Committee had reported a companion bill (HR 2305—H Rept 103-710, Part I) Aug. 19. An initial effort in the House to pass the Senate bill failed Oct. 4 when members gave it less than the two-thirds vote required to pass it under suspension of the rules. The vote was 246–169. The next day the House passed the bill by a vote of 308–103, clearing the bill. The president signed it Oct. 22.   ❏

Minority Health

Despite a two-year push, legislation (S 1569) to reauthorize minority health programs within the Department of Health and Human Services (HHS) died at the end of the Congress. Both chambers had passed versions of the bill, and conferees produced a House-Senate compromise, but Republicans blocked consideration of the conference report in the Senate.

The bill would have authorized $1.1 billion in fiscal 1995 for several programs, including the Office of Minority Health within HHS, scholarship and loan programs, health centers for migrant workers, health centers for the homeless and state rural health offices. The Office of Minority Health studied disease prevention and promoted research and health delivery for minorities.

First authorized in 1990, the programs sought to increase minority access to primary and preventive health care and to boost federal health scholarships for disadvantaged people, including poor whites.

Provisions of two other measures (S 1224 and S 725) had been added to the minority health bill. S 1224 was aimed at making interracial adoption easier; S 725 provided for studies on the effects of traumatic brain injuries.

LEGISLATIVE ACTION

The Senate passed S 1569 by voice vote March 26, 1994. The measure, reported (S Rept 103-200) Nov. 20, 1993, by the Labor and Human Resources Committee, authorized $20.5 million in fiscal 1994 and unspecified sums through 1998 for the Office of Minority Health.

The bill was amended to include S 1224, which prohibited adoption agencies that received federal funding from discriminating against people who wanted to adopt children of another race. The adoption bill stipulated that agencies could consider the race, color or national origin of prospective parents but could not use those characteristics as the only criteria in denying adoptions. The Senate Labor and Human Resources Committee had reported S 1224 on March 3, 1994.

The House Energy and Commerce Committee reported companion legislation (HR 3869—H Rept 103-501) on May 11, 1994. HR 3869 reauthorized the HHS minority health office at $21 million a year from fiscal 1995 through 1997. It also reauthorized federal programs that funded migrant health centers, health clinics in public housing developments and scholarships

for minority students hoping to enter the health professions. The bill included an authorization of $28 million in fiscal 1995, $30 million in fiscal 1996 and $32 million in fiscal 1997 for medical schools in areas with shortages of health care providers.

The panel added to the bill provisions to expand the study of traumatic brain injuries. Such injuries were the leading cause of death and disability for young people and the result most often of car accidents, sports injuries and falls. Similar provisions also passed both chambers as a separate bill (S 725) but debates over unrelated amendments added in both chambers killed the popular bill. S 725 had been reported (S Rept 103-243) by the Senate Labor and Human Resources Committee March 25, 1994, and passed by voice vote of the full Senate April 21. The House passed an amended version by voice vote Aug. 8. The Senate passed a clean version without the extraneous amendments Oct. 8, but the House adjourned without considering the revised bill.

The House passed HR 3869 by voice vote May 23. It then took up the Senate-passed version (S 1569) and inserted the provisions of its bill, passed the amended bill and requested a conference.

Among the issues House and Senate conferees resolved was how much of the $111 million in scholarship money for disadvantaged students to reserve for students who made a commitment to become primary-care physicians rather than specialists. Conferees agreed to channel 70 percent of the scholarship money to students who committed to primary care and 30 percent to students who did not commit to any field when they entered medical school.

The House adopted the conference report (H Rept 103-843) Oct. 7 by a vote of 394–5. But when the conference report reached the Senate, GOP leader Bob Dole of Kansas objected to it on behalf of several Republicans. Despite efforts by Orrin G. Hatch, R-Utah, who cosponsored the measure with Edward M. Kennedy, D-Mass., several Republicans refused to lift their holds, and the measure could not come up for a vote.   ❏

Organ Transplants

Both chambers passed a bill (HR 2659) aimed at increasing the number of organs available for transplant operations and expanding federal efforts to help states provide immunizations for children. Conferees were named, but the measure went no further.

As passed by voice vote of the House Oct. 5, 1993, HR 2659 would have authorized $20 million for organ and bone marrow transplants in fiscal 1994 and unspecified amounts in fiscal 1995 and 1996. It also included changes to the law aimed at better assuring that organs were provided to patients with the greatest medical need. HR 2659 had been reported (H Rept 103-272) by the House Energy and Commerce Committee Sept. 30.

Before passing HR 2659 on March 24, 1994, by voice vote, the Senate struck the House-passed language and substituted that of a Senate measure (S 1597) to reauthorize federal organ transplant programs through fiscal 1996, including an authorization of $8 million for fiscal 1994. The substitute amendment was approved by voice vote.

The Senate version directed the Department of Health and Human Services (HHS) to provide grants to organizations that procured organs for transplant. Procurement groups would be required to assess annually their success in acquiring organs. The bill also required procurement organizations to maintain one waiting list for all transplant candidates within their region for each type of organ. The Senate Labor and Human Resources Committee had reported S 1597 (S Rept 103-233) on March 7, 1994.

A second amendment to the measure inserted the provisions of a bill (S 732) to establish national immunization registries to allow doctors to track the immunization histories of individual children. The language authorized $152 million in fiscal 1994 to establish the registries. It also authorized $250 million in fiscal 1994 for states to expand immunization efforts, by extending the hours of clinics that administered immunizations and by educating the public on the importance of immunizing children. S 732 had been reported by the Senate Labor and Human Resources Committee Sept. 28, 1993, and passed by voice vote of the full Senate Nov. 4, 1993. ❑

Orphan Drugs

House and Senate committees in 1994 reported separate versions of legislation to reduce the length of time that drug companies had the exclusive right to market drugs developed for rare conditions—also known as orphan drugs. But the bills got no further and died at the end of the Congress.

Congress established protection for manufacturers of orphan drugs in 1983 (PL 97-414) to give them financial incentives to research medicines for rare diseases. The law recognized that drug sales for limited markets might be small, requiring a longer time for a company to recoup development costs. Companies that developed drugs to treat fewer than 200,000 patients were given tax advantages and could market the drugs exclusively for seven years. Competitors were effectively barred even from producing drugs that had the same effect. (1983 law, Congress and the Nation Vol. VI, p. 536)

Since then, some patients' rights groups had complained that drug companies, unchecked by competition, could charge excessive prices for the drugs. In addition, some drugs turned out to be useful for more people than expected, and manufacturers reaped huge profits. Efforts to revise the Orphan Drug Act in 1990 and 1992 were blocked by the Bush administration. (1990 and 1992 action, Congress and the Nation Vol. VIII, pp. 585, 603)

The Senate Labor and Human Resources Committee reported its version of the bill (S 1981—S Rept 103-366) on Sept. 14, 1994. S 1981 proposed to reduce drug companies' protected marketing rights for most orphan drugs from seven years to four years. The bill left the seven-year protection in place for drugs already on the market or in the approval process. Panel members rejected an amendment to set the exclusivity period at five years. Supporters of the amendment argued that without the longer protected period, companies would not bother to research new drugs for rare diseases. But others said that an association of biotechnology firms had endorsed the legislation.

The House Energy and Commerce Committee reported its bill (HR 4865—H Rept 103-746) on Sept. 26. The bill reduced the period of exclusivity to four years, but it allowed a three-year extension for drugs with "limited commercial potential," a phrase to be defined by regulators in the Department of Health and Human Services. The bill also provided for the withdrawal of exclusive marketing rights if the patient population for the treatment exceeded 200,000. The panel rejected an amendment to leave the seven-year exclusivity intact. ❑

Medical Device Fees

A bill to impose a user fee on manufacturers who sought Food and Drug Administration (FDA) approval for medical devices died at the end of the 103rd Congress. The House Energy and Commerce Committee reported the bill (HR 4864—H Rept 103-751) Sept. 26, 1994, but there was no further action.

The bill would have allowed the FDA to charge fees to manufacturers who sought the agency's approval to market new or modified medical devices. Manufacturers had complained for years that the agency took too long to test and approve new products. The FDA, which tested medical devices for safety and efficacy, said it needed the fees to hire more employees to do the testing. A similar scheme imposed for prescription drugs in 1992 had successfully speeded up the approval process for those products. (1992 action, Congress and the Nation Vol. VIII, p. 603)

The bill proposed to reduce the approval process to 90 days. The fees, which could be used to test only medical devices, would have ranged from $3,200 to $52,000, depending on the device and the level of testing required. The fees were expected to bring the FDA about $115 million through fiscal 1999. Companies would have been allowed to withhold 50 percent of the fee until an application was approved. ❑

1995–1996

On health care, the 104th Congress managed what the 103rd could not—it completed work on a significant health insurance reform bill—on a bipartisan basis. The measure, while a mere shadow of the plan proposed by President Clinton two years earlier, nevertheless represented the most substantial federal action on health insurance in a generation.

Only months earlier, Republicans experienced the same sort of searing disappointment on their top health priority—overhauling the massive Medicare and Medicaid programs—that Democrats experienced in 1994. By trying to reach too far too fast, Republicans ended up with the same thing Clinton and Democrats had in 1993–1994: no legislation at all.

Health Insurance Regulation

It was only a shadow of what he had campaigned for, but on Aug. 21, 1996, President Clinton got to do something he had dreamed about since the day he took office—sign a health insurance reform bill (HR 3103—PL 104-191) into law.

The legislation was miniature in scope compared with the president's famous but failed 1994 plan to overhaul the entire health care system, and it did little for the estimated 43 million Americans without insurance—the focus of Clinton's ill-fated proposal. Nevertheless, both Clinton and congressional Republicans claimed HR 3103 as a major achievement.

"This is a very important step," said Sen. Nancy Landon Kassebaum, chair of the Senate Labor and Human Resources Committee. "It gives people a sense of security." Kassebaum, who left the Senate at the end of the year, sponsored the initial proposal (S 1028) along with her panel's senior Democrat, Edward M. Kennedy of Massachusetts.

Kennedy, who had long advocated overhauling the health care system, said that while the bill fell short of proposing "health security for all citizens," it was a good interim step for millions of Americans who had medical conditions that could hamper their ability to get insurance.

Besides seeking to protect those who already had health coverage from losing it—a guarantee of health insurance "portability"—the measure also set up a pilot program for medical savings accounts, increased the deductibility of health insurance for the self-employed and provided tax breaks to increase the use of long-term care insurance. Medical savings accounts allowed individuals with high deductible health insurance plans to set up tax-deductible savings accounts for medical expenses.

A DIFFICULT JOURNEY

The measure got a quick start in the Senate Labor Committee in 1995, where it was approved by a unanimous vote in August, but the easy trip ended there. It then traveled a tortured path through Congress, enduring presidential campaign politics, partisan fighting and opposition from powerful interest groups.

It took months, for example, to bring the bill up on the Senate floor. The insurance industry, led by the Health Insurance Association of America, strenuously objected to portions of the bill because it sought to compel insurers who sold individual plans to sell to those leaving group policies. (The final agreement included such a provision, but gave insurers flexibility in deciding which policies to offer.)

Insurers argued that the people likely to buy individual policies, which were far more expensive than group plans subsidized by employers, would be those already in need of medical treatment and thus more expensive to insure.

After the 1994 failure, Clinton was eager to associate himself with the Kassebaum-Kennedy effort. The president backed the plan prominently in his State of the Union address Jan. 23, 1996, challenging Congress to pass it. "If our working families are going to succeed in the new economy," Clinton said to applause from both sides of the aisle, "they must be able to buy health insurance policies that they do not lose when they change jobs or when someone in their family gets sick."

That raised the bill's profile and put pressure on Republicans to act. In the House, GOP leaders swiftly put together a bill (HR 3103), after steering three bills through three committees and patching the pieces together into one measure that was at its core similar to the Senate bill. It passed the House on March 28, Senate Majority Leader Bob Dole, R-Kan., his party's presumed presidential nominee, forced his GOP colleagues to allow a Senate vote.

Kassebaum and Kennedy ushered a relatively clean version of HR 3103 through the Senate on April 23. They effectively blocked attachments, such as medical savings accounts, which they viewed as controversial enough to kill the bill.

There were several important differences between the House and Senate versions, which in the end made for difficult negotiations. The House bill, for example, included provisions allowing for medical savings accounts, a limit on monetary damages in medical malpractice lawsuits and a reduction in states' authority to regulate health insurance purchasing pools created by small businesses.

After battling for weeks, Kassebaum and the principal House sponsor, Ways and Means Committee Chairman Bill Archer, R-Texas, agreed to drop the provisions on insurance pooling and medical malpractice but to keep a scaled-down medical savings account demonstration.

Kassebaum's deal with Archer was not acceptable to Kennedy, however, and he blocked a formal House-Senate conference pending a more satisfactory compromise on the savings accounts. Kennedy and Archer finally agreed on a narrow pilot program that limited participants to roughly 750,000, and included only workers at companies of 50 or fewer employees, and the self-employed.

A provision on mental health coverage, added to the Senate bill but kept out of the House measure, also caused difficulties in final negotiations. Sponsored by Republican Sen. Pete V. Domenici of New Mexico, it would have required insurers to offer comparable coverage for mental and physical illnesses. Big business adamantly opposed the provision, arguing that it would raise health insurance costs so much that companies would either choose not to offer it or would be forced to scale back benefits. In the end, conferees dropped the provision—though Domenici succeeded later in the year in adding a scaled-back version to the fiscal 1997 appropriations bill for the departments of Veterans Affairs (VA) and Housing and Urban Development (HUD). *(Health care benefits, p. 565)*

LEGISLATIVE ACTION

The Senate Labor and Human Resources Committee approved S 1028 by a unanimous vote Aug. 2, 1995. The bill, formally reported (S Rept 104-156) Oct. 12, proposed to bar insurers from denying coverage for more than 12 months to people with diagnosed medical problems if they had been covered previously by a group plan. The committee bill also included a GOP amendment, adopted on a 9–7 party-line vote, urging the development of medical savings accounts as an option for coverage. Such accounts, which were loosely designed as individual retirement accounts to cover health care expenses, were popular among Republicans who wanted to encourage private-sector competition to lower health care costs.

S 1028 languished until early 1996 because of opposition from conservative senators who shared industry concerns over the group-to-individual portability provisions. Those senators put "holds" on the bill, thus blocking floor action.

Once Clinton endorsed the Senate bill in his 1996 State of the Union speech, the House scrambled to act on its own measure. Three House Committees—Commerce, Ways and Means, and Economic and Educational Opportunities—ultimately marked up bills in March 1996. While all three included the base provisions of the Senate measure, to ensure continued coverage for those with preexisting health conditions, the House measures went considerably further.

The Ways and Means bill (HR 3103), for example, included a significant tax package that would increase the deductibility of health insurance for the self-employed (then 30 percent), provide deductions for long-term care insurance and expenses, and allow widespread availability of tax-preferred medical savings accounts. It also included stiff new penalties for health fraud, allowed doctors to seek advisory opinions about whether business arrangements violated the federal anti-kickback statute, and capped noneconomic damages in malpractice suits at $250,000. HR 3103 was reported (H Rept 104-496, Part I) March 25.

The Commerce bill (HR 3070) was amended in committee to require insurers to cover minimum hospitals stays for mothers and newborns, a provision later enacted as part of the fiscal 1997 VA-HUD funding bill. HR 3070 was reported (H Rept 104-497, Part I) March 25. *(Health care benefits, p. 565)*

And the bill (HR 995) from the Economic and Educational Opportunities Committee included a controversial proposal that would have allowed small businesses to join together to "self-insure," thus bypassing state insurance regulations. The panel reported HR 995 (H Rept 104-498, Part I) also on March 25.

The three bills were combined by the House leadership, and the House passed HR 3103 by a largely party-line vote of 267–151 on March 28.

During debate, Democrats scolded Republicans for including controversial items, such as medical savings accounts and caps on medical malpractice liability, instead of backing a "clean" bill identical to the Senate's.

Much of the House debate focused on medical savings accounts. Republicans insisted that including them would not jeopardize enactment but would add value to what they called an otherwise minimalist bill. The House had included medical savings accounts in other legislation, principally the budget-reconciliation package vetoed in 1995, over strong opposition from Democrats.

Supporters said the accounts would provide a more economical way for people to buy health insurance and would therefore result in more individuals buying it. Opponents argued that the special accounts would be attractive only to wealthy, healthy people with enough disposable income to afford an insurance premium and still have enough to put into a medical savings account. They added that individuals who were sick would not benefit because their savings would not accrue: The money would be spent on medical bills.

Democrats also charged that Republicans included the accounts to please special interests, such as insurance companies

that sold the high-deductible plans and that made major contributions to GOP campaigns.

The Clinton administration opposed the accounts and several other House bill provisions. In a policy statement, the Office of Management and Budget (OMB) said the accounts "will provide a tax break for the healthiest and wealthiest individuals . . . and attract them out of the general health insurance market, potentially raising premiums for all other people."

The administration also objected to provisions aimed at creating more small-business insurance purchasing pools. Influential small-business groups, such as the National Federation of Independent Business, pushed hard for the provision. The administration and House Democrats said that by exempting the pools from state regulation, Congress was opening the door to fraud.

The Senate passed HR 3103, 100–0, on April 23, after substituting an amended version of S 1028. The unanimous vote masked the degree of controversy and political maneuvering associated with the bill.

Among other differences with the House bill, the Senate had adopted an amendment to S 1028, offered by Domenici and Paul Wellstone, D-Minn., to require health insurance plans to give serious mental illness the same coverage that they provided for physical ailments. The amendment, which would have been financed by tightening tax laws governing foreign trusts, was adopted by voice vote after an effort to table (kill) it failed, 30–68, on April 18.

Unlike the House, the Senate rejected medical savings accounts. The vote against including the accounts marked a defeat for Dole, who led the effort to insert them in the bill. In seeking to win approval for the accounts, Dole was going against the wishes of Kassebaum and Kennedy, who had built a broad coalition of support for the bill. The glue holding the coalition together was an agreement by all parties to actively oppose any controversial amendments.

The strategy held from the time of unanimous approval by Kassebaum's panel in 1995 until the day before the floor vote. On April 17, Dole announced that he would propose a broad amendment to the bill that included the controversial medical savings accounts. To tempt more senators to defy Kassebaum's no-amendment strategy, Dole offered an array of tax provisions in his amendment, including a widely popular proposal to increase the tax deductibility of health insurance costs for the self-employed. While the House bill would have raised the existing 30 percent deduction to 50 percent, Dole proposed to raise it to 80 percent.

Kassebaum and Kennedy succeeded in stripping the medical savings account provision from the Dole amendment in a dramatic floor vote. With Vice President Al Gore present to vote in the case of a tie, the Senate April 18, in a **key vote of 52–46 (R 5–46; D 47–0)**, agreed to excise the accounts from Dole's amendment. The Senate then voted 98–0 to accept the rest of Dole's amendment. *(1996 key votes, p. 1047)*

CONFERENCE, FINAL ACTION

Despite the overwhelming support for the measure, however, it nearly died. When Dole proposed a list of Senate conferees that would basically ensure the inclusion of medical savings accounts in the final bill—and a near certain presidential veto—Democrats blocked their appointment.

The sides feinted and jabbed for nearly three months, in the end resolving nearly everything except the medical savings account issue. Finally, the agreement for a four-year pilot project was worked out in a closed-door meeting between Kennedy and House Ways and Means Chairman Bill Archer, R-Texas. That cleared the way for the last bits of controversy—dropping the House malpractice provisions and the Senate mental health language—and the bill was a done deal.

Although the conference report received broad support in the House and Senate, a few senators were livid about the removal of the mental health provisions. Domenici let loose his frustration on the Senate floor July 31. "I would like to say publicly to the business community in the United States, in particular the large companies . . .shame, shame on you," he said.

And just when it appeared that Congress would easily approve the conference report, it stalled because of a provision added at the last minute to renew American Home Products' patent of a single drug, Lodine, that otherwise could be sold in a less expensive generic form by other manufacturers.

Pete Stark, D-Calif., one of only two House members to vote against the conference report, said during floor consideration that the provision was "an outrageous special interest handout that was inserted quietly in the hopes that no one would notice." But he was powerless to make any changes to the measure. The House adopted the conference report (H Rept 104-736) by a vote of 421–2 on Aug. 1.

In the Senate, it was a different story. Wellstone threatened to hold up the bill unless the drug patent provision was excised. He ultimately persuaded Senate Majority Leader Trent Lott, R-Miss., to allow it to be stricken. Both chambers passed by voice vote Aug. 2 a resolution (H Con Res 208) that excised it from the bill before it went to Clinton.

The Senate agreed to the conference report, 98–0, on Aug. 2, clearing the bill.

MAJOR PROVISIONS

As signed into law, HR 3103:

Group Insurance

The following provisions applied to group insurance plans, generally those purchased through and subsidized by an employer. The law:

- **Nondiscrimination.** Prohibited insurers and employers from establishing rules of insurance eligibility that discriminated against workers based on their health status or medical history. All workers eligible for a particular health plan had to be offered enrollment—at the same price—regardless of their health status.

- **Limits on Exclusions for Preexisting Medical Conditions.** Limited to 12 months the period in which an insurer could refuse or limit coverage to a new enrollee because of a health-related condition that was treated or diagnosed in the six months before enrollment. A medical condition that was not treated or diagnosed in that six-month period could not be used to exclude an enrollee or limit coverage. By allowing a limited waiting period instead of requiring immediate coverage, the provision aimed to prevent workers from purchasing insurance after they got sick.

However, newborns and adopted children covered within 30 days of arrival, as well as pregnancies, were exempt from the 12-month waiting period.

- **Group Insurance Portability.** Generally guaranteed that workers who had health insurance at a previous job would be eligible for coverage promptly at their next job as long as the new company provided insurance.

In conjunction with the limit on exclusions for preexisting medical conditions, this provision aimed to end so-called joblock. Previously, many insured workers who were ill or had sick dependents were afraid to change jobs for fear of being denied coverage or having to wait for it at their new job. The law required insurers to reduce the 12-month waiting period by the period of continuous coverage before enrollment. (Continuous coverage meant coverage without a lapse of more than 62 days.)

For example, if a worker with a medical condition had insurance for the previous seven months at his prior job, coverage at his new job could be denied or limited for only five months.

The new law did not restrict employers from denying coverage to new employees during a routine waiting period for benefits, often three months for health insurance. But the employee was to be considered continuously covered during the waiting period. Therefore, an employer-instituted waiting period could not be used by an insurer to declare an employee to have had a break in coverage, subjecting the employee to a 12-month insurer-mandated waiting period.

- **Special Enrollment.** Required that employees (and their dependents) who had previously declined coverage because they had other coverage be allowed to enroll within 30 days of losing the other coverage. An employee, for example, might initially opt not to enroll in the company health plan because of coverage under a spouse's plan. If the spouse was laid off and lost coverage, the employee could enroll in the company health plan within 30 days.

- **Guaranteed Availability.** Generally required insurers that sold policies to small employers (businesses with two to 50 employees) in a state to offer group health plans to all small employers in that state. There were some exceptions.

For example, an insurer could refuse to offer coverage to additional companies if it demonstrated that it did not have the financial reserves needed to underwrite more coverage. In that case, the insurer would be barred from selling more policies to any company for at least 180 days. Also, an insurer could limit the policy offered to a small company to employees of that company who lived, worked or resided in the service area for the plan.

- **Guaranteed Renewability.** Required insurers to renew most policies, with exceptions for fraud and nonpayment of premiums.

Also, an insurer could, with 180 days' notice, terminate coverage for all group plans in a given state. An insurer who did so would be barred from selling group plans in that state for five years.

• **State Flexibility.** Provided that the federal law did not preempt any state law with broader requirements. For example, a state law that required certain insurers to offer group plans to all companies with more than 50 employees—going beyond the two to 50 employees under the new law—would not be affected.

Individual Insurance

The following provisions applied to individual insurance policies, those generally purchased by an individual, not through an employer.

• **Guaranteed Availability.** Generally prohibited insurers who sold individual policies from denying coverage to eligible workers leaving a group insurance plan. The law prohibited insurers from imposing exclusions for preexisting medical conditions. The law allowed some flexibility to insurers in meeting the requirement to offer insurance; it also exempted from this requirement insurers in states that had another acceptable mechanism for guaranteeing that workers who left group plans could get individual coverage.

The law aimed to prohibit insurers from "cherry-picking," or covering only low-risk, healthy individuals. Cherry-picking often allowed an insurer to collect premiums without paying out substantial claims. In such cases, those most in need of health coverage—people who were ill and had no access to group insurance—often went without insurance.

The provision also aimed to prevent people from signing up for individual policies only when they were sick and needed health care. It made guaranteed coverage available only to those who had invested in health insurance for a substantial period.

Under the law, insurers were required to sell only to individuals who: 1) had had 18 months of continuous coverage, the most recent of which was in a group plan; 2) were not eligible for group health coverage; and 3) had exhausted available COBRA or other continuation coverage. COBRA, the Consolidated Omnibus Budget Reconciliation Act of 1985 (PL 99-272), required continued health care coverage for people at companies of 20 or more who quit or lost their job. Generally, under COBRA, employees who became ineligible for permanent coverage because they quit or were laid off could continue coverage for up to 18 months.

Under the new law, insurers were not required to offer individual policies to people coming from group plans if the secretary of health and human services (HHS) certified that the insurer's state insurance system provided a guarantee of coverage through other means. For example, the secretary would certify states that offered state-subsidized affordable insurance plans, often called state risk pools, or had an "open enrollment" insurer, typically a Blue Cross/Blue Shield plan. Blue Cross/Blue Shield received special tax consideration in exchange for generally accepting all enrollees.

Insurers required to offer individual policies had some flexibility in deciding what coverage to offer. They could offer their whole menu of policies, or they could limit the offering to two policies—one with a high deductible, one with a low deductible—that met two requirements: They had to be available to and marketed to all workers, not just those leaving group plans; and they had to either have the insurers' largest or second largest premium volume, or be representative of other plans offered by the insurer. These requirements were intended to ensure that the policies were viable policies, not just instruments for satisfying the requirement.

• **Guaranteed Renewability.** Required insurers to renew most policies, with exceptions for fraud and nonpayment of premiums. An insurer could discontinue a certain type of coverage if the insurer gave 90 days' notice, offered each policyholder the option to purchase any other type of individual coverage offered, and did not discontinue the coverage based on the health of enrollees or expected enrollees. An insurer could also discontinue all types of individual policies in a state, but only with 180 days' notice. Such an insurer would be barred from selling individual policies in that state for five years.

Medical Savings Accounts

• **Setting Up Plans.** Allowed individuals with high-deductible insurance plans—often called catastrophic plans—to set up medical savings accounts using tax-deductible contributions. Individuals could deduct employer contributions to the accounts from their taxable income as well. The accounts were to be used to pay for medical expenses; employees could save what they did not spend.

The accounts were to be available to a limited population of roughly 750,000 people for four years beginning Jan. 1, 1997. After the trial period, Congress was to vote on whether to expand eligibility to everyone.

The trial population included workers at companies with 50 or fewer employees, self-employed workers and the uninsured (who would have to buy catastrophic plans).

During the trial, the number of active policies held by small business and self-employed workers was to be tallied periodically to prevent a breach of the 750,000 cap. At set times during each year of the trial, the Internal Revenue Service was to count the number of active policies and determine if the rate of enrollment was high enough to breach the cap that year. If so, enrollment would be shut off except for employees of companies that had already established programs. At the beginning of the following year, another assessment would be made to decide whether to open enrollment again.

An unlimited number of the uninsured could enroll each year and would not be counted toward the cap, but only until self-employed and small business employees reached the cap. At that point, enrollment of the uninsured also would cease.

Those who established savings accounts could keep them and continue to contribute to them indefinitely, even if Congress decided after the trial not to lift the cap or expand eligibility. Also, companies that established medical savings account programs could offer them to employees, even new hires, indefinitely. The cap only prevented new programs.

• **Catastrophic Plans.** Restricted catastrophic health insurance plans offered in conjunction with medical savings accounts in several ways.

Deductibles could be no lower than $1,500 and no higher than $2,250 for individuals, and no lower than $3,000 and no higher than $4,500 for family policies. Out-of-pocket expenses—including the deductible—could not exceed $3,000 for individuals or $5,500 for families.

The minimum deductible was set to ensure that medical savings accounts were offered only with catastrophic health plans. The maximum deductible and out-of-pocket limit were set so that medical savings accounts would be sold with health plans that provided adequate coverage.

Also, to prevent the accounts from being used as tax shelters instead of medical expenses, annual contributions were limited to 65 percent of the deductible for individuals and 75 percent for a family policy.

• **Withdrawals.** Allowed individuals to draw money from the account, without a tax penalty, to cover medical expenses. Withdrawals made for other purposes would be taxable and subject to an early withdrawal penalty of 15 percent. After age 65, or if the individual became disabled, withdrawals for other purposes would be taxed as income, without the 15 percent penalty. If the account holder died and the surviving spouse was the account's beneficiary, the account would become the spouse's and receive the same preferential tax treatment. If the account was passed to another beneficiary, it would cease to be a medical savings account and would have to be included in the beneficiary's gross taxable income.

Taxes

• **Health Insurance Deductibility.** Increased the percent of health insurance premiums that the self-employed could deduct from their taxes. Previously, individuals could deduct 30 percent. The new law increased that to: 40 percent in 1997; 45 percent in 1998 through 2002; 50 percent in 2003; 60 percent in 2004; 70 percent in 2005; and 80 percent in 2006 and thereafter.

• **Long-term Care Insurance.** Excluded from an employee's income any contribution made by an employer to a long-term care health plan for an employee, the spouse and dependents. Previous law was not explicit in its tax treatment of long-term care insurance contracts or services. The new law clarified that for tax purposes, long-term care insurance was to be treated the same as accident and health insurance.

Benefits received under such plans—up to $175 per day, or $63,875 annually—were not taxable. That cap was to be indexed to the medical care cost component of the consumer price index.

Long-term care services were defined as necessary diagnostic, preventive, therapeutic and rehabilitative services, and personal care services such as feeding, bathing and dressing for a chronically ill person. A chronically ill person was one who had been certified in the previous 12 months to be unable to perform regular daily activities, such as bathing and eating, for at least 90 days.

Under the law, expenses for long-term care services not covered by insurance were tax-deductible after a person's medical expenses reached 7.5 percent of adjusted gross income.

Employee premiums were similarly deductible, but limited based on age. For example, they were deductible up to $200 per year for those under 40 years old, and up to $2,500 for those over 70.

The self-employed could deduct long-term care insurance premiums in the same manner they deducted health-care insurance premiums: 40 percent in 1997; 45 percent in 1998 through 2002; 50 percent in 2003; 60 percent in 2004; 70 percent in 2005; and 80 percent in 2006 and thereafter.

• **Accelerated Death Benefits.** Allowed chronically or terminally ill individuals to collect life insurance policy benefits before death without a tax penalty. Typically, the benefits would be collected early by selling all or part of an individual's life insurance policy to a third party called a "viatical settlement provider." The proceeds from that sale would not be taxed.

• **IRAs.** Allowed penalty-free withdrawals from Individual Retirement Accounts (IRAs) for medical expenses that exceeded 7.5 percent of a person's adjusted gross income. Generally, withdrawals from IRAs were assessed a 10 percent penalty until age 59 and a half.

Also, people who had been receiving federal or state unemployment compensation for at least 12 weeks could make penalty-free withdrawals to pay health insurance premiums—regardless of the 7.5 percent requirement. People who were reemployed for 60 days would lose that special exception for premiums.

• **Taxes on Expatriates.** Required taxpayers who gave up their U.S. citizenship to avoid paying taxes to continue to pay taxes for 10 years after expatriation on the income from their U.S. holdings. The provision applied to expatriates who earned at least $100,000 in each of the preceding five years or who had net holdings of more than $500,000. Also covered were people whose long-term residency was terminated.

• **Interest Deduction on Life Insurance.** Eliminated over five years the ability of corporations to deduct the interest on loans that they secured by taking out life insurance policies on their workers. Previously, some companies could deduct millions of dollars in interest by buying life insurance policies for their workers, then taking out loans against the policies and deducting the interest from the loans. These policies were owned by the companies, not the workers.

• **Foreign Tax Credit.** Eliminated a targeted tax provision enacted in 1986 to benefit the Ford Motor Credit Co. The provision allowed the company to be treated as a financial institution for purposes of computing its foreign tax credit—a credit that U.S. multinational corporations received to offset the taxes they paid to other countries. Financial institutions were allowed more advantageous interest deductions than other companies in computing their foreign tax credit.

Fraud and Abuse

The following provisions toughened existing laws, stiffened penalties and/or created laws to combat health care fraud, particularly in Medicare and Medicaid. Other provisions created exceptions to existing fraud statutes. The law:

• **Fraud and Abuse Control.** Established a joint program under the attorney general and the HHS secretary to coordinate federal, state and local law enforcement efforts against fraud in federal and private health care programs. Previously, HHS and the Department of Justice did not coordinate their efforts to investigate and prosecute health care fraud. The provision also set up a special account—funded by the collection of fines, forfeitures and damages from the coordinated antifraud effort—to help pay for the program.

• **Expanded Criminal Penalties.** Extended certain criminal penalties for Medicare and Medicaid fraud, prosecutable by the Justice Department, to similar violations in other federal health care programs. Under previous law, fraud in health programs outside Medicare and Medicaid was considered a civil violation, under the jurisdiction of the HHS inspector general.

• **Advisory Opinions and Safe Harbors.** Required the HHS secretary to issue legally binding "advisory opinions" on the legality of prospective business practices proposed by health care providers in Medicare and Medicaid programs. Previously, the department's guidance was generally not legally binding in court. The provision also expanded the list of "safe harbors," or exceptions that could be made to allow business practices that were otherwise prohibited.

Federal law, for example, generally prohibited health care providers from offering financial incentives to Medicare and Medicaid participants to use their services. But a doctor might offer a free baby car seat if a patient made all her prenatal appointments. While such a practice would probably mean the doctor would receive more federal reimbursement because of increased visits prompted by the baby seat offer—and therefore could be considered a kickback—the secretary might make an exception for such a practice because it would increase prenatal care.

This provision expanded the list of exceptions and required the department to issue advisory opinions on other potential exceptions.

• **Mandatory Exclusions.** Required the HHS secretary to exclude from federal programs for five years any health care provider convicted of a felony related to health care fraud or controlled substances. Previously, the exclusion was optional.

• **Additional Antikickback Exceptions.** Allowed managed-care plans to use incentives to draw Medicare and Medicaid patients to use their services if there was "substantial financial risk" for the health plan. In other words, if the incentive offered could potentially cost more than it brought in in federal reimbursements, it would generally be acceptable. For example, a health plan could waive copayments to attract more patients. Such a practice could cost the health plan more than it would gain from the additional federal reimbursements brought in by more patients.

• **Medicaid Eligibility Fraud.** Made it a crime for an individual to knowingly give away assets, usually to relatives or friends, in order to qualify for Medicaid. Individuals expecting to move to nursing homes, for example, sometimes gave away assets to meet Medicaid eligibility requirements, instead of spending those assets to pay for nursing home care until they had so little that they qualified for Medicaid.

• **Fraud Database.** Established a national health care fraud data collection program, administered by the HHS secretary, to report final adverse actions against health care providers, suppliers and practitioners. For example, if a doctor violated a Medicaid law, the violation and penalty would be filed in the data base. Program coordinators would disclose the information to federal and state agencies and health plans, while aiming to protect patients' privacy.

• **Civil Penalties.** Increased to $10,000 from $2,000 the penalty for health care fraud per violation.

The new law added two practices to the list of those subject to civil monetary penalties. One, commonly called "upcoding," was the practice of seeking a higher reimbursement than was allowed for a service by submitting it as another service that earned higher reimbursement. The other was submitting a claim for a service the provider knew was not medically necessary.

• **Intent to Commit Fraud.** Redefined the level of intent associated with fraud violations punishable by civil penalties. The new law said individuals had to know that they engaged in the prohibited activity and that they acted in "reckless disregard or deliberate ignorance" of the law. The previous standard was merely knowing the activity occurred but not necessarily consciously skirting the regulations.

• **Criminal Violations and Enforcement.** Made several fraudulent health care activities that were previously prosecuted through federal mail and wire fraud statutes and other laws specifically prosecutable as federal health care crimes. The aim was to make these activities easier to prosecute. The new categories were embezzling, making false statements, obstructing justice and money laundering.

The attorney general received new authority to seek court injunctions to stop health care fraud and to issue summonses for documents and other materials. These law enforcement tools were available previously, but through statutes that were not specifically for health care fraud. Upon conviction, a court could order forfeiture of property derived from a federal health care offense.

Other Provisions

• **Administrative Simplification.** Required the HHS secretary to adopt standards of uniformity and privacy for electronic transmission of health information by public and private health plans and health care providers. Electronic transmission of information was not required. Generally, the types of information covered by the new standards included health claims, premium payments, injury reports and enrollment information. The law required the secretary to encourage uniformity by developing a set of codes for health data, such as the coding used in the Medicare and Medicaid programs, to describe different medical services.

Privacy protection provisions aimed to restrict the disclosure of medical information on individuals by limiting access and the type of information available.

• **Medical Volunteers.** Generally protected certain health care volunteers from legal liability. The provision aimed to encourage health professionals to provide free medical services to the poor. Under the law, to be protected, the volunteer had to provide the services for free, provide them at a free clinic or other authorized facility, and advise the patient of the provider's limited liability.

- **Health Care Study.** Required the secretaries of HHS and the Department of Labor to study the availability of affordable health coverage, patient choice and access to health care. The studies were to be completed by Jan. 1, 2000. ❑

Medicare

Much as President Clinton had overreached by trying to accomplish too much too fast with his health reform plan in the 103rd Congress, Republicans in the 104th suffered the same fate with their proposals to overhaul the massive federal Medicare program for the elderly and disabled. In both cases Congress produced no legislation at the end of the day, and in both cases the failure had important political ramifications in the November elections: In 1994 Democrats' failure helped bring Republicans to power in Congress, while in 1996 Republican missteps on Medicare helped reelect Clinton president.

Republicans in the 104th Congress could claim an achievement that Democrats in the 103rd could not—they did manage to get a bill passed by both houses and to the president's desk, and in 1995, their first year in power. The Medicare changes, part of the massive balanced budget bill (HR 2491), would have reduced spending on the program by an estimated $270 billion over seven years. But Clinton vetoed the measure, singling out the Medicare and Medicaid portions as making "extreme cuts and other unacceptable changes." *(Budget reconciliation bill, p. 68; Medicaid, p. 559)*

BACKGROUND

Restructuring Medicare was a centerpiece of Republican plans to balance the budget by 2002. To reach their savings goal, Republicans proposed to reduce payment rates to doctors and hospitals, and make better-off seniors pay more for the optional Part B insurance that covered doctor and other outpatient care. The plan also counted on beneficiaries to choose managed care or other insurance options that would cost the government less, although the traditional fee-for-service program would still be available. If the required savings did not materialize, the fee-for-service portion of the program would be further squeezed by a complex "fail-safe" mechanism that would automatically cut payments to doctors, hospitals and other providers.

The proposal prompted sharp partisan rhetoric from the outset. Democrats accused Republicans of "balancing the budget on the backs of the elderly" and noted that the size of the Medicare cuts were not so coincidentally the same as the amount of the proposed tax cuts.

Republicans, meanwhile, noting that Medicare's own trustees had warned that the program's dwindling Hospital Insurance Trust Fund—Part A of the Medicare program which covered hospital insurance for seniors and was the "entitlement" portion—was likely to run out of money in the year 2002, retorted that Democrats would allow Medicare to go broke.

Republicans knew that tackling Medicare put them on risky political ground. The sheer size of the proposed cuts was unprecedented; the biggest previous reduction in projected Medicare spending was $56 billion over five years, enacted as part of the 1993 budget reconciliation bill (PL 103-66). *(Story, p. 44)*

Moreover, Medicare had been held largely sacrosanct by senior citizens and their families and by Congress, which had been controlled by Democrats during most of the program's history. Health care experts said the reductions would substantially affect the access, eligibility and out-of-pocket expenses of Medicare beneficiaries, and they were expected to result in more people moving into lower-cost managed-care plans that restricted access to doctors and medical technology.

But Republicans also knew they had no choice but to address the Medicare issue. Created in 1965 to provide the elderly with basic hospital insurance, Medicare accounted for about 11 percent of all federal spending. In fiscal 1996, it was expected to cover more than 36 million people at a cost of $178 billion. Medicare was the fourth-largest federal expenditure after Social Security, defense and interest on the debt. Having put those three items off-limits for budget cuts, the spotlight was on Medicare from the outset.

GOP PLAN

The House approved a target of $282 billion in Medicare cuts as part of the budget resolution (H Con Res 67) passed May 18, 1995. The Senate version, passed May 25, called for $256 billion in savings. House and Senate conferees spent much of the next month trying to resolve their differences, finally agreeing to seek $270 billion in Medicare reductions. The House adopted the plan June 29 on a vote of 239–194, followed by Senate passage, 54–46, later the same day. *(Budget resolution, p. 65)*

Having gotten agreement on the numbers, Republican leaders took their time crafting the actual proposal. House Speaker Newt Gingrich, R-Ga., handpicked an eight-member group that worked out of his conference room for more than four months, sometimes meeting daily, to write the Medicare bill. Determined not to make the same mistake as Clinton, who had left his massive health care reform bill exposed for months in 1994 while opponents hammered it, Republicans made a point of keeping the details to themselves until September.

Democrats tried to turn the tactic around, calling for public hearings on the details. "What is most outrageous is that the Republicans now say they will only share the details of their plan 14 days before it's supposed to be rubber-stamped by the House," House Minority Leader Richard A. Gephardt, D-Mo., said in June. "These cuts will devastate seniors for decades, but they want to ram them through Congress with almost no time for debate and discussion."

Democrats honed their message over the summer, finding a unity that had been largely missing up until then as they struggled to adjust to their new role as the minority party in Congress. Republicans, they repeated, were seeking deep cuts in spending on health care for the elderly to finance a tax cut for the rich and other GOP priorities. They criticized the $270 billion as excessive, noting that the April trustees' report of impending bankruptcy said $89 billion would shore up the Part A hospital insurance trust fund.

Republicans just as vehemently protested the Democratic attacks, saying the popular program had to be restructured to remain viable. "The Democrats have fabricated the Medicare-tax cut connection because it is useful politically," said Senate Majority Leader Bob Dole, R-Kan.

Meanwhile, though, Republicans had done a highly effective job neutralizing opposition from many of the interests that would be most affected by the cuts (a word Republicans steadfastly refused to use—they called the changes "reductions in growth").

Even the redoubtable American Association of Retired Persons (AARP) held its fire in the early going. AARP was concerned about the size of the proposed GOP cuts and the timetable but applauded several key elements of the plan. Crucial to AARP's agenda was ensuring that seniors paid only incrementally more for the optional Part B insurance that helped pay doctor bills and that they not face additional out-of-pocket payments for services such as lab tests or home health care. (AARP eventually began running ads against the Republican rewrite because of their concerns about the size of the cuts.)

For managed-care companies, there was the hope of getting access to a vast new pool of insured patients. While many of those patients were older and less healthy than most nonelderly subscribers, managed-care companies gambled that government premiums for healthy patients would offset the additional costs of those with expensive illnesses.

A key to winning the support of hospitals and doctors was a decision to allow "provider-sponsored networks" to contract with Medicare and compete for patients alongside managed-care companies and insurers. These networks, organized by doctors and hospitals, were similar to managed-care plans but had somewhat different financial structures. It was this provision, along with guarantees of payment increases—even if small—that helped seal the support of the American Medical Association (AMA) later in the debate.

There were other benefits for hospitals and doctors as well. For instance, Republicans proposed to relax antitrust rules, and also included strict medical malpractice provisions making it harder to sue doctors and hospitals, and they proposed tight limits on damages for pain and suffering and punitive damages.

Despite the sweeteners, hospitals, doctors and insurers worried about some aspects of the plan. High on the list was the proposed fail-safe mechanism that would automatically cut payments to providers. According to Robert D. Reischauer, a senior fellow at the Brookings Institution and a former director of the Congressional Budget Office (CBO), the mechanism would work, but there would be tremendous political pressure both on the administration and Congress not to implement it because it would hit the health system so hard.

House Republicans outlined their Medicare overhaul Sept. 14, pointedly stressing that they would hit their $270 billion target without directly nicking beneficiaries. They released details of their plan Sept. 29.

Under the plan, seniors would be shielded from increased deductibles or copayments, although premiums for the optional Part B supplementary insurance would be kept at higher levels than Congress intended when it set them several years earlier. Congress had for years been renewing a temporary provision setting premiums to cover 25 percent of the Part B program's costs (the remainder was subsidized from the federal Treasury). But when the program's costs grew more slowly than was anticipated, the dollar amount included by Congress in its 1990 budget reconciliation bill, instead of covering 25 percent of costs, actually covered 31.5 percent of the program. The GOP plan proposed to keep the percentage at 31.5 percent, which set off an angry debate between Democrats, who charged that the move represented a significant premium increase (which it did, since by law the premium was scheduled to revert back to 25 percent), and Republicans, who charged they were just continuing a current policy (also technically correct).

Under the plan, seniors could stay in the traditional Medicare program, but they were encouraged to choose alternative health care plans that Republicans said would offer better coverage while yielding substantial savings to the government.

In a move that outraged Democrats, Republicans set a hearing schedule that limited debate on the Medicare proposal to a single day. To protest the one-day hearing, House Democrats on Sept. 22 staged a rain-drenched hearing of their own outside the Capitol, setting up a table and chairs on the lawn and calling witnesses such as Labor Secretary Robert B. Reich to testify.

HOUSE COMMITTEE ACTION

It took the House Ways and Means Committee three days and nearly 36 hours, but the panel finished its work on a Medicare bill (HR 2425) Oct. 11, leading Chairman Bill Archer, R-Texas, to proclaim that the committee had "saved Medicare" for current and future beneficiaries. The committee approved the plan on a party-line, 22–14, vote. HR 2425 was formally reported Oct. 16 (H Rept 104-276, Part I).

Tempers had flared repeatedly, as members debated more than three dozen amendments. Democrats were particularly harsh about an endorsement of the plan from the AMA, which came in the middle of the markup on Oct. 10. The AMA support was sealed with assurances from Gingrich that doctors would not see payments below 1995 levels and that increases—even slight ones—would continue.

"They have decided to reward their rich friends and stick it to the women and sick people," said Pete Stark, D-Calif., contending that the "unethical, despicable, underhanded" deal was worth billions to the doctors and was a bribe from the Speaker.

Bill Thomas, R-Calif., chairman of the Ways and Means Health Subcommittee and a key architect of the House plan, called the accusations "absolutely false," saying: "Unless you have one shred of evidence to prove it, you owe every one of us that you have slandered an abject apology." He later said he expected the AMA's concerns to result in a "technical" correction of less than $400 million over seven years.

HIGHLIGHTS OF 1995 MEDICARE PLAN

Medicare provisions agreed upon by congressional Republicans were included in the budget reconciliation bill (HR 2491—H Rept 104-350), which was vetoed Dec. 6, 1995. The bill included provisions that would have:

Impact on Beneficiaries

• **Beneficiary Plans.** Allowed Medicare beneficiaries to remain in the existing fee-for-service program. But beneficiaries would have had new options, including joining health maintenance organizations (HMOs) or similar managed-care providers, buying a high-deductible insurance policy combined with a medical savings account, using a network of providers organized under new rules, or joining union or association health plans. Republicans estimated that the gradual migration of beneficiaries to these new options would save much more than the $26 billion projected by the Congressional Budget Office.

• **Medical Savings Accounts.** Established medical savings accounts, similar to individual retirement accounts, which individuals could have used for health care in conjunction with a high-deductible insurance plan to protect against major medical costs.

Medicare would have contributed a defined amount of money, adjusted for factors such as age and regional costs, toward the insurance, with leftover money placed in the savings account. If not used to pay deductibles or other health care costs, money in the account could have been rolled over for future years. If withdrawn, it would have been subject to tax penalties. The provisions were stricken from the original Senate bill on a procedural ruling. They were rewritten to avoid another procedural challenge.

• **Provider-Sponsored Organizations.** Allowed doctors and hospitals to form their own organizations by granting them some relief from solvency standards required of such potential competitors as HMOs. Like HMOs, the provider organizations would have been required to be licensed by the states. However, they could have applied to the secretary of health and human services (HHS) for a waiver of the state licensing. Antitrust provisions were struck from the conference report on procedural grounds.

• **Health Plan Premiums.** Allowed some plans to require a premium for Medicare's basic benefit package. If a beneficiary remained in the traditional program or a program licensed with Medicare, those providers would not have been allowed to charge for the basics. But some plans would not have been subject to the restrictions, if the cost of the benefits exceeded the capped federal Medicare contribution to the plan, meaning that beneficiaries could have had to pay part of the premiums.

• **'Balance Billing.'** Lifted some existing provisions that prevented Medicare providers from charging more than 15 percent more than Medicare-approved costs—a practice called "balance billing." Under the conference agreement, extra billing would have been permitted in private, non-Medicare fee-for-service plans (not the traditional Medicare fee-for-service program) or whenever a beneficiary in an HMO used services outside of their designated provider network.

• **Beneficiaries and Part B.** Kept monthly premiums for Part B at 31.5 percent of program costs for seven years. The general Treasury would have continued to fund the rest of the program's costs.

The wealthiest beneficiaries would have had to pay the entire cost of their Part B coverage. The Part B subsidy would have begun to phase out for individuals making $60,000 annually and couples making $90,000, with the costs gradually increasing until the subsidy ended at $110,000 for singles and $150,000 for couples.

Conferees rejected the Senate's plan to raise the Part B deductible from $100 under existing law to $150 in 1996, as well as a proposal that would have indexed an increase to inflation.

• **Low-Income Medicare Beneficiaries.** Repealed the existing "entitlement" under which state Medicaid programs paid the Medicare Part B premiums, deductibles and coinsurance for qualified low-income beneficiaries. States would have been required to set aside a pool of money—90 percent of a three-year average amount—for the premiums only.

Provider Changes

• **Hospital Reductions.** Used a variety of reductions in price indexes and readjusted the other scales by which payments to hospitals were determined, in order to alter inpatient and outpatient hospital payments, reduce the amount spent on capital costs of hospitals and nursing homes, and recalculate other payment formulas.

The House Commerce Committee approved a slightly different version of the bill Oct. 11, after a two-day markup. The 27–22 party-line vote came just hours after the Ways and Means vote. The Commerce Committee shared authority with Ways and Means over Part B and provisions that overlapped parts A and B. The Commerce panel reported HR 2425 (H Rept 104-276, Part II) on Oct. 16.

Commerce Committee Chairman Thomas J. Bliley, Jr., R-Va., had tried to begin work Oct. 2. But panel Democrats, angry at the committee's refusal to hold hearings on Medicare legislation, provoked a series of roll-call votes on relatively routine procedural matters and then walked out. "The Democratic members of this committee see no reason to participate further in this charade, which will rob seniors of their health care," said ranking Democrat John D. Dingell of Michigan, who led his troops out. Unruffled, Bliley continued with opening statements. But once he noticed that his Republicans were wandering off, opening the way for potential Democratic mischief, he abruptly halted the markup.

When the markup resumed, substance mixed with political theater. With a C-SPAN camera in the room, both Democratic and Republican members sometimes addressed their remarks to "those who are watching." At one point, a group of senior citizen activists protesting the plan disrupted the markup and were

• **Disproportionate Share Hospitals.** Reduced the extra payments to hospitals that served a high percentage of indigent patients by 5 percent in 1996 and 1997, by 7.5 percent in 1998 and 1999, and by 5 percent again in 2000. They would have remained at the 30 percent reduction in 2001 and 2002.

• **Medicare-Dependent Hospitals.** Continued a special funding arrangement for Medicare-dependent hospitals, facilities that served a high percentage of Medicare patients, through fiscal 2000.

• **Doctor Services.** Replaced the existing fee structure, which relied on multiple factors to determine reimbursement levels to doctors, to one with a single payment factor to try to ensure that no physician would see his or her payments decline during the seven-year period.

• **Hospice Payments.** Limited inflation adjustments for hospice payments from 1996 to 2002.

• **Skilled Nursing Facilities.** Required a negotiated fee structure by fiscal 1998, instead of the existing method of paying the facilities on a "reasonable cost" basis, which was more open-ended.

• **Home Health Services.** Established a prospective payment system beginning in fiscal 1997 to replace the existing system under which home health services were paid for reasonable costs. The HHS secretary would have been required to establish national average per-visit rates for each of the home health service disciplines covered under Medicare and update the payments annually according to a formula based on the costs of goods and services used by home health providers.

• **Durable Medical Equipment.** Froze the inflation updates for durable medical equipment, such as wheelchairs and hospital beds, for the seven-year period. Under existing law, Medicare paid on a fee schedule that was subject to a floor and ceiling and updated for inflation. Payments for prosthetics and orthotics would have been limited to 1 percent increases through 2002. Payments for oxygen would have been reduced by 20 percent in 1996, slightly reduced after that until hitting a 30 percent reduction in 2002.

Other Provisions

• **'Fail-Safe.'** Adopted the House's "fail-safe" budget mechanism, under which payments to providers would have been reduced automatically beginning in 1998 in the traditional Medicare program if budget targets were not met. The projected savings was $36 billion. There was no limit on the amounts that could be trimmed if budget targets were not met.

• **Medical Education.** Significantly changed the way graduate medical education was funded. Conferees accepted a House provision to establish a trust fund that would get its money from the general Treasury through annual appropriations (reaching $13.5 billion at the end of seven years) and transfers from the Medicare system. Hospitals would have continued to be paid for the direct costs (salaries, lodging) and the indirect costs (extra tests, extra staff) of training physicians. The Medicare funding to be funneled into the trust fund would have been reduced from existing levels by lowering the payment formula.

The conferees approved a provision to limit funding available for students beyond their initial residency training period, but they rejected a proposal to gradually eliminate funding for foreign medical students.

• **Fraud and Abuse.** Reduced sanctions for voluntary disclosure of fraud and abuse, protected "whistle-blowers," increased the civil monetary penalties for offenses, and added federal criminal sanctions for health fraud and abuse.

• **Physician Self-Referral.** Permitted doctors to refer certain kinds of services to an entity such as a laboratory with which they had a compensation arrangement. A ban on such referrals still would have applied to such facilities as clinical labs, parenteral and enteral services, and radiology services.

The conference agreement struck a provision that would have exempted a clinical laboratory in a doctor's office from some of the requirements included in the 1988 amendments (PL 100-578) to the 1967 Clinical Laboratory Improvement Act that gave the federal government strong regulatory oversight over virtually all laboratories.

• **'Lockbox.'** Established a "lockbox" for the savings generated from keeping beneficiaries' Part B premiums at 31.5 percent. The savings would have been transferred from the general Treasury, where Part B premiums were deposited, into the Part A Hospital Insurance Trust Fund, which was the "entitlement" part of Medicare that covered hospital costs.

arrested by Capitol police at the behest of Bliley. They were released later without being charged.

HOUSE FLOOR ACTION

In an effort to prove the Medicare reductions were not being made to pay for tax cuts, House leaders had split off the Medicare sections into a separate bill. With only six members leaving the Republican fold, the House on Oct. 19 passed HR 2425, the separate Medicare bill, in a **key vote of 231–201 (R 227–6; D 4–194; I 0–1).** The provisions then were forwarded to the Budget Committee to be included in the broader budget-reconciliation package (HR 2491). *(1995 key votes, p. 1025)*

Ignoring a fresh veto threat from Clinton and loud Democratic denunciations, Gingrich had worked behind the scenes to fine-tune the measure in order to minimize criticism from insiders and outsiders. When the floor speeches stilled, it was clear that his efforts to mollify provider groups, seniors' organizations and worried Republicans had made passage possible. The Speaker worked to appease rural Republicans concerned about payments to doctors and other health care providers until just hours before the bill appeared on the floor and continued closed-door meetings with members as the debate continued.

Clinton sharply criticized the bill, saying it would "eviscerate" the federal program that provided health insurance for the elderly. "My message to the Republicans is simple: I hope you will think again," he said at a news conference as the House debated the legislation Oct. 19. "I will not let you destroy Medicare, and I will veto this bill."

The key to House passage turned out to be a payment formula for managed care in rural areas. The changes largely quieted a group of Republican lawmakers, led by Greg Ganske of Iowa, Gil Gutknecht of Minnesota, Barbara Cubin of Wyoming and Wes Cooley of Oregon, who said they had the support of enough Republicans to defeat the bill if they were unsatisfied.

Under existing law, managed-care providers in a given county received 95 percent of the amount average fee-for-service patients in the county cost Medicare, a method that resulted in widely varied rates between rural counties and urban counties and between counties where the use of various services differed.

While the GOP bill sought to begin the process of closing the gap between payments in high- and low-paid areas, the bill did not go far enough for the Ganske-led Republicans, who were worried that payments would still not be high enough to encourage managed care to set up in their areas.

Before the bill got to the House Rules Committee, the leadership adjusted the payment to assure a minimum $250 monthly payment per patient to managed-care providers by tinkering slightly with the percentage increases allowed for all the areas. But Ganske and the others were still unhappy. The leadership then agreed to go further, establishing a floor of $300 in 1996 and $320 in 1997, about the amount that the rural lawmakers said would be necessary to encourage HMOs and similar providers into their areas. That settled the issue, and provided the margin of passage for the bill.

SENATE ACTION

In the Senate, Finance Committee Republicans outlined their proposals for Medicare and other elements of the budget-reconciliation package Sept. 22. In general, the Medicare plan tracked the House provisions, except that it proposed to hit beneficiaries slightly harder, offer seniors more incentive to opt out of the traditional Medicare program and gradually raise the Medicare eligibility age from 65 to 67.

Under the Senate bill, for example, wealthier beneficiaries would have had to pay the entire cost of Part B coverage, as in the House bill. The Finance plan would have begun to phase out the "subsidy" for individuals making $75,000 annually and for couples making $100,000. The government contribution would have ended at the $100,000 mark for individuals and $150,000 for couples. An amendment adopted during the markup, however, reduced those thresholds, so that the subsidy would begin to phase out for individuals making $50,000 and couples earning $75,000; the subsidy would be eliminated for individuals with incomes above $100,000 and couples with incomes over $150,000.

Finance continued the markup of its portion of the budget-reconciliation bill (HR 2491) for a week, finally approving the Medicare provisions by a vote of 11–9 on Sept. 30.

The Senate passed HR 2491 Oct. 28 by a mostly party-line key vote of 52–47 (R 52–1; D 0–46), after a marathon debate in which Medicare played a significant part. Only Republican William S. Cohen of Maine crossed party lines to oppose passage. The Medicare provisions emerged relatively unscathed. *(1995 key votes, p. 1025)*

Democrats' arguments against the GOP budget cuts got a boost when Republican leaders Dole and Gingrich gave speeches to interest groups Oct. 24 disparaging the Medicare system. Dole told the American Conservative Union, "I was there fighting the fight, voting against Medicare—1 of 12—because we knew it wouldn't work in 1965."

Gingrich, in a speech to Blue Cross/Blue Shield on the same day, said he expected the Health Care Financing Administration, which ran Medicare, to "wither on the vine" because the existing fee-for-service Medicare system would disappear. "We don't get rid of it in round one because we don't think that's politically smart, and we don't think that's the right way to go through a transition. But we believe it's going to wither on the vine because we think people are going to leave it [fee-for-service Medicare] voluntarily," Gingrich said.

Democrats blew up the quotes and pasted them on poster boards that they carried to the Senate floor to dramatize their assertion that the GOP's true goal was to get rid of the Medicare program altogether. Within 72 hours, the Democratic National Committee was running television ads featuring clips of the speeches. Democrats had little success revising the bill's provisions during floor debate, but they did succeed in striking numerous items—many of them favorites of conservative Republicans. Their weapon was the so-called Byrd rule—named for its author, Sen. Robert C. Byrd, D-W.Va.—which barred "extraneous" matter from reconciliation bills.

Democrats used the rule to knock out two key Medicare provisions: those to allow medical savings accounts and to increase the eligibility age for Medicare recipients from 65 to 67 years. They also eliminated the Senate version of the House fail-safe provision; not as tightly drawn as the House proposal, it did not produce savings, according to CBO.

CONFERENCE, FINAL ACTION

After nearly two weeks of off and on negotiations, conferees filed the conference report on the broad budget-reconciliation bill Nov. 17. Republicans had gone back and forth for days over the Medicare details, which were among the most politically potent issues in the budget debate. Clinton repeated his veto threats even as the negotiations proceeded behind closed doors, in a Republicans-only forum.

Conferees spent a good deal of time on such issues as the treatment of beneficiaries, medical savings accounts, payments to providers and malpractice.

For beneficiaries, conferees decided to keep the deductible for Part B at $100, rejecting the Senate proposal to raise the amount to $150 in 1996 and $10 more annually thereafter until 2002.

Conferees included the GOP plans for medical savings accounts as another option for beneficiaries, overcoming procedural hurdles in the Senate. Under the agreement, Medicare would contribute a certain amount of money, adjusted for factors such as age and regional costs, toward a beneficiary's purchase of high-deductible catastrophic health insurance. Leftover money would be placed in the accounts, which could be used toward the deductible for catastrophic coverage or other health care costs. Beneficiaries also could roll the money over for future health expenses or withdraw some of it, subject to tax penalties.

Proponents said the accounts would drive down medical costs by giving seniors a financial incentive to get the most for their health care dollars. Critics warned that they would entice healthy seniors out of Medicare, making the program's per-person costs skyrocket.

Conferees agreed to guarantee MedicarePlus providers a $300 monthly per-person minimum for 1996, a $350 level for 1997 and a guaranteed annual increase of at least 2 percent thereafter.

Perhaps the biggest single piece of the original plan that did not survive the conference was the House proposal—favored by many doctors—to limit malpractice "pain and suffering" awards to $250,000. Faced with potential procedural challenges and a less-than-enthusiastic Senate, conferees agreed to drop the provision.

The House adopted the conference report (H Rept 104-350) Nov. 17, 237–189, largely along party lines. The Senate a few hours later agreed, 52–47, to a motion to approve the report, after knocking two provisions out on procedural grounds. Because of the Senate revisions, the report had to go back to the House, which agreed to the changes and cleared the bill, 235–192, on Nov. 20. Clinton vetoed HR 2491 on Dec. 6. ❏

Medicaid

While they were successful in turning the nation's major cash-assistance program back to the states in the form of block grants, Republicans in 1996 were forced to retreat from their plan to do the same for Medicaid, the joint federal-state health program for the poor.

With the strong support of GOP governors, Republicans in Congress tried twice to end Medicaid's status as an entitlement and turn it into a block grant program, once in 1995 and again in 1996. In 1995, President Clinton vetoed the Medicaid plan as part of the omnibus balanced budget bill (HR 2491). No override was attempted. In 1996, lawmakers tried again, this time making Medicaid reform an element of the broader welfare reform bill (HR 3734). But Clinton vowed to veto that bill, too, if the Medicaid provisions were included, and Republicans backed down. (Budget reconciliation bill, p. 68; welfare reform, p. 578)

BACKGROUND

Created in 1965 to help states pay the medical bills of poor people, Medicaid had grown quickly and somewhat unexpectedly into a multibillion-dollar program that shored up a key part of the nation's so-called safety net for the neediest citizens. Coverage originally was largely restricted to welfare populations—chiefly single-parent families, the elderly, blind and disabled. No upper limit on federal spending was included.

But since the mid-1980s, as the number of uninsured had risen, Congress had acted repeatedly to break the links between Medicaid and cash assistance programs, thus providing Medicaid health coverage to a larger share of the low-income population, including more pregnant women, children and the elderly. By 1996, Medicaid covered some 37 million Americans, one out of every seven in the population, and as many as were eligible for Medicare.

But while the expansions kept the proportion of uninsured Americans from growing even higher, it came at a significant cost, particularly for the states, which on average paid about 45 percent of the program's costs, with the federal government picking up the rest. Not only were caseloads rising, Medicaid also suffered like the rest of the nation's health care system from rapidly rising prices for medical services and supplies. In 1994, Medicaid accounted for 19.4 percent of state spending, nearly double the 10.2 percent of 1987.

Republican governors insisted that they could make the program more cost-efficient if they didn't have to follow so many prescriptive rules from Washington. At the same time, GOP lawmakers in Washington saw Medicaid as a good place to cut the budget in an effort to bring it in balance by the year 2002, as they had pledged to voters in the 1994 elections. As part of their fiscal 1996 budget resolution passed in May 1995 (H Con Res 67), House Republicans called for $187 billion in Medicaid reductions over seven years; Senate Republicans sought $175 billion. Conferees on H Con Res 67 settled on $182 billion over seven years.

It was not only the question of how much control Washington should have over what would remain billions of dollars in federal tax dollars that made the task a difficult one. Another tricky issue was designing a formula for distributing Medicaid funds among the states. It was a crucial question that would determine how much each state would get from the federal government and how much of its own money it would have to use to cover needy populations.

Eastern and Rust Belt states with declining populations competed with high-growth Western and Sun Belt states. States that had tried to control Medicaid spending looked for some assurances that their efforts would not result in a lower baseline for future dollars. Also concerned about the allocation of federal dollars were states that had gotten permission from the federal government to experiment with ways to manage their Medicaid populations and had increased their spending based on the expectation of future federal guarantees.

The concerns of beneficiary groups were another factor in the debate. For example, advocates for pregnant women and children worried that those populations would suffer the brunt of the cutbacks to protect more politically active groups that represented the elderly and the disabled.

Indeed, in the end Republicans underestimated the political potency of a program that guaranteed not only health care to poor mothers and children but also to many formerly middle-income elderly who had become impoverished by nursing home costs. While Medicaid did not become the proverbial "third rail of politics," in the manner of Social Security or Medicare, it did prove to have a more substantial base of support than Republicans had anticipated.

1995 LEGISLATIVE ACTION

House Republicans released details of their new "Medi-Grant" plan Sept. 19, 1995, one day before the House Commerce Committee had scheduled hearings on the proposal. They said it would replace more than 1,100 pages of federal regulations with a more streamlined, state-controlled approach. "Medicaid is broken, and it's time to fix it," said Thomas J. Bliley, Jr., R-Va., chairman of the Commerce panel.

The Republican plan ended Medicaid's 30-year status as an "entitlement" that guaranteed coverage for anyone who met specified eligibility criteria. Instead, states would have been required to continue to cover certain populations (such as pregnant women and children with incomes up to the poverty line) but would have been allowed to decide how rich a benefits package to offer. In addition, states would have been freed from many other federal mandates, such as a series of staffing and inspection requirements enacted in 1987 as part of that year's budget reconciliation bill (PL 100-203) in an effort to improve the quality of nursing home care. *(1987 law, Congress and the Nation Vol. VII, p. 591)*

Democrats were nearly as vocal in their opposition to the repeal of the nursing home rules—the result of several years of legislative effort—as they were about the proposed repeal of the overall entitlement. "The reason for these rules was that patients were tied in their beds and drugged in unsafe facilities without adequate professional staffing," said John D. Dingell of Michigan, ranking Democrat on the Commerce Committee and one of the authors of the nursing home law.

The Republican proposal also dropped an existing requirement that states protect the spouse of a nursing home resident from becoming impoverished by nursing home costs. Under federal law, a nursing home resident was required to "spend down" his or her assets before qualifying for Medicaid coverage for nursing home costs, which on average reached more than $30,000 annually, but spouses were permitted to keep minimum levels of income and assets. Republicans said a number of states had statutes that protected the spouse. Democrats countered that the absence of federal protections would return many spouses to the days when they could lose their homes and all their assets to nursing home costs.

The proposed funding formula, drawn up with the participation of GOP governors, would have guaranteed all states a 7.24 percent increase in fiscal 1996, and promise all states at least a 2 percent increase annually thereafter. Republicans noted that reports from state Medicaid programs to the Health Care Financing Administration, which administered the existing federal-state program, estimated that Medicaid would grow 4.3 percent in fiscal 1995. The Congressional Budget Office (CBO) had projected an increase of about 10 percent.

House Republicans took their proposal directly to the Commerce Committee with only one hearing and no subcommittee meetings. At the end a three-day markup, the committee voted, 27–18, on Sept. 22 to approve the MediGrant legislation. During the markup, Republicans presented an almost unbroken wall of solidarity to thwart numerous Democratic efforts to restore individual guarantees on such issues as nursing home costs and standards, and eligibility guidelines. Only on the formula for dividing federal money among the states did the Republican march falter even slightly.

The MediGrant proposals were rolled into the huge budget reconciliation bill (HR 2491) for floor action. The House passed the bill, in a **key vote of 227–203 (R 223–10; D 4–192; I 0–1),** on Oct. 26, after a week of intense, last-minute deal-making. To shore up support, Speaker Newt Gingrich, R-Ga., added about $12 billion in Medicaid funds to help assuage concerns about funding cuts and the distribution of funds among the states. The revisions were included in a leadership substitute for the reconciliation bill that was approved as part of the rule governing debate. *(1995 key votes, p. 1025)*

Overall, the bill was projected to reduce federal Medicaid spending by $182 billion over seven years, about a 20 percent cut. But with passage in doubt, Gingrich scrambled and found about $5.8 billion for Northeastern states that had been hard hit by the funding changes, about $2.5 billion for high-growth states, and about $156 million for Oregon and $196 million for Tennessee, which had gotten recent federal waivers to overhaul and expand their Medicaid programs. To distribute the additional funds, the formula was revised to guarantee all states an increase of at least 3.5 percent in fiscal 1997, 3.0 percent in fiscal 1998, 2.5 percent in fiscal 1999 and 2.0 percent in each subsequent year.

The leadership also added about $3 billion for a fund to reimburse 12 states for the costs for treating illegal immigrants in emergency rooms.

The Senate Finance Committee approved proposed Medicaid changes Sept. 26 as part of its contribution to the omnibus reconciliation bill. The committee approved the package of provisions in the early hours of Sept. 30, by a party-line vote of 11–9.

The provisions largely tracked the House bill, proposing to give the states most of the power to decide who would be covered, end most federal restrictions on nursing homes and require states to spend their own money to qualify for federal funds.

However, the committee used a different calculation to determine how much federal money states would get. That allowed the panel to divide the money differently, at least in part to address the concerns of committee members.

Far more than in the House, Republicans had to deal with dissension within their own ranks. Throughout the week-long markup, they faced pressure from John H. Chafee, R-R.I., who teamed with the committee Democrats to try to amend the proposal. Moderate and conservative Republicans were worried about the proposed end of federal oversight on nursing homes. And a number of Republicans complained about the prospect of reducing entitlement spending at the same time they were proposing tax cuts.

Democrats were divided on Medicaid as well, with conservatives willing to cap the federal contribution but guarantee eligi-

HIGHLIGHTS OF 1995 MEDICAID PLAN

Following are key Medicaid proposals contained in the budget reconciliation bill (HR 2491—H Rept 104-350) vetoed by President Clinton on Dec. 6, 1995. The bill included provisions that would have:

• **Spending Levels.** Reduced federal spending on Medicaid by $163.4 billion from projected levels over seven years, a decline from the $182 billion reduction called for in the budget resolution and from the $170 billion level approved in both chambers on the original reconciliation bill. States could have chosen the higher of the House or Senate funding level. Federal spending was to total $791 billion over the seven years, an average annual increase of 5.2 percent, taking the program's federal cost from $97.1 billion in 1996 to $127.4 billion in 2002.

• **Block Grants.** Repealed most federal eligibility and coverage criteria that states were required to meet in order to get federal money. In effect, the bill proposed to replace the existing "entitlement," under which federal and state governments had to cover anyone who met eligibility requirements, with a fixed amount of money. In return, state governments were to get broad flexibility to determine whom to cover and how.

Before qualifying for any federal matching funds, states would have been required to design a plan that explained eligibility requirements, benefit packages and administrative guidelines. The bill required that states put up some of their own money and that they use the federal money for health care, but it gave them discretion to determine how much to pay doctors, hospitals and other health care providers.

Conferees on the bill proposed to delete the existing "Boren amendment"—named for former senator David L. Boren (D-Okla., 1979-94)—which required states to pay hospitals and nursing facilities rates that were "reasonable and adequate" to cover costs.

• **Formula.** Distributed the federal pool of dollars on a "needs based" formula, as measured by the number of poor residents in a state, the severity of the state's caseload and a state health care cost index. Every state was to be guaranteed minimum growth rates: at least 3.5 percent in 1997, 3 percent in 1998, 2.5 percent in fiscal 1999 and 2 percent in each subsequent year. The maximum growth rate was 9 percent in 1997 and 5.33 percent in later years. However, the 10 states with the lowest spending per person in poverty, which included Texas, Virginia, Florida and California, would be allowed to grow at a maximum of 7 percent in the later years.

The final bill gave states two options for determining how much money they would be required to spend in order to qualify for federal funds. The first was a formula, based on per capita income, with a maximum state contribution of 40 percent. The second was a new formula that took into account a state's total taxable resources to determine its ability to pay.

• **Beneficiary Spending.** Required states to continue the entitlement for health care coverage for poor pregnant women and children under age 13, with poor defined as 100 percent of the poverty level. However, the states would have determined what benefits to provide. States would have been required to spend a specified percentage (85 percent of a three-year average spent on mandatory benefits) on nursing home residents, senior citizens and the disabled, as defined by the state.

For low-income senior citizens, the bill proposed that states be required to help pay Medicare Part B premiums, which covered doctor visits and outpatient care. The payment was to be a minimum of 90 percent of a three-year average of state spending. Under existing law, states had to cover Part B copayments and deductibles as well.

The bill also required that states set aside a percentage of their funding for community health centers and rural health clinics, with the amount determined by the states' average payments to the centers.

• **Nursing Homes.** Retained most of the federal provisions governing nursing home standards, enacted in 1987 (PL 100-203) in response to reports of lax state standards and patient abuse. States were charged with enforcing the federal standards, with some federal oversight. Conferees dropped a provision added on the Senate floor that would have allowed states to substitute their own state standards for the federal rules.

Conferees agreed to retain provisions in existing law to prevent a spouse from becoming impoverished by the costs of nursing home care. The House originally had proposed leaving this up to the states.

• **Limits on Lawsuits.** Prohibited applicants, beneficiaries, providers or health plans from suing states over compliance with federal provisions. However, individuals could have registered a complaint against the state with the secretary of health and human services.

• **Childhood Immunizations.** Required states to cover childhood immunizations under a schedule to be determined by the states.

• **Abortion/Family Planning.** Restricted federal funding for abortions for poor women to cases of rape, incest or when the woman's life was in danger. States would have been required to provide prepregnancy family planning services and supplies.

• **Illegal Immigrants.** Created a $3.5 billion fund to help the 15 states with the largest populations of illegal immigrants pay for emergency treatment for those immigrants.

• **New Hampshire and Louisiana.** Required New Hampshire and Louisiana, which at one time relied heavily on federal payments to hospitals to boost their overall Medicaid spending without raising their state contribution, to gradually increase their state funding in order to receive their federal share.

bility and coverage, while more liberal members resisted any major change.

Just as Gingrich had done in the House, Majority Leader Bob Dole, R-Kan., spent much of the week before the Senate voted on the budget reconciliation bill shoring up support among members concerned about the Medicaid changes. The Senate passed the bill by a key vote of 52 47 (R 52 1; D 0 46) in the early moments of Oct. 28. *(1995 key votes, p. 1025)*

Senate moderates used their clout to increase Medicaid funding for poor people's health care and to reinstate federal nursing home standards. For much of the week, six moderate Republicans negotiated both individually and as a group with Dole to modify the bill. Several threatened to vote against it unless they got some of the changes they wanted. The group included Chafee, Olympia J. Snowe and William S. Cohen of Maine, Nancy Landon Kassebaum of Kansas, James M. Jeffords of Vermont and Ben Nighthorse Campbell of Colorado. Also supporting their efforts were Republicans Arlen Specter of Pennsylvania and Mark O. Hatfield of Oregon.

In the end, moderates won a $10 billion restoration of funds to help states offset cuts to a Medicaid program that aided hospitals that served a "disproportionate share" of low-income and uninsured patients. But the Senate rejected several Democratic amendments that would have further modified the funding cuts or retained Medicaid's entitlement status.

During final negotiations on the bill, conducted behind closed-doors between top Republican leaders and their aides and some of the GOP governors, conferees agreed to reduce the seven-year savings target to $163.4 billion, almost $20 billion less than the $182 billion called for in the original budget resolution and about $7 billion less than the amount the House and Senate agreed to in initial floor action. The additional money was needed to establish a funding formula that could pass both the House and Senate. The final compromise included two sets of numbers, allowing states to choose the calculation that would provide them with the most money.

To win critical moderate votes, conferees included language requiring that states provide some coverage for pregnant women and for children under age 13. However, they agreed to allow the states to define their own coverage for the disabled. Governors had protested against a Senate provision, modified by Chafee on the floor, to require coverage of the disabled, as defined by Congress.

Conferees also agreed to keep the 1987 nursing home standards, but some moderates continued to complain that enforcement had been weakened so as to render them meaningless.

The House adopted the conference report Nov. 17 by a vote of 237–189. The Senate later that same day agreed, 52–47, to a motion to approve the report after knocking out two provisions on procedural grounds. The House accepted the Senate changes and cleared the bill, 235–192, on Nov. 20. Clinton vetoed the measure on Dec. 6.

1996 LEGISLATIVE ACTION

For a while in 1996, before election-year warfare dominated the legislative agenda, there was some hope that bipartisan negotiations between Democratic and Republican governors—who had voted overwhelmingly at their February meeting to combine welfare and Medicaid overhauls—would produce a compromise that congressional Democrats and Republicans could translate into a viable Medicaid bill.

But when the bipartisan group of governors could not agree on a plan, Republican governors and members of Congress developed their own proposal. The Republican initiative (HR 3507, S 1795), released May 22, proposed Medicaid savings of $72 billion, considerably less than the $163 billion in cuts proposed the year before in the budget reconciliation bill (HR 2491).

Like the previous year's bill, the proposal would have ended Medicaid's entitlement status. But, unlike that bill, it would have required states to continue to cover certain populations, including those receiving Aid to Families with Dependent Children; pregnant women and children under age 6 whose family income fell below 133 percent of the poverty level; children ages 6 through 12 with family incomes at or below the poverty level; children receiving foster care and adoption assistance; disabled individuals who met certain income and financial resource standards; and elderly people who qualified for Supplemental Security Income (SSI) benefits.

States would have had to offer Medicaid beneficiaries a minimum package of benefits, but, in a fundamental change from existing law, the proposal would let states, instead of the federal government, determine the "amount, scope, and duration" of treatment.

Democratic governors and lawmakers disassociated themselves from the plan, saying it would not protect the poor. On May 29, leading Democratic governors sent a letter to Senate Finance Committee Chairman William V. Roth, Jr., R-Del., saying the plan was not faithful to the bipartisan outline: "Your Medicaid proposal is far from the NGA [National Governors' Association] agreement and appears to be more like the proposal vetoed by the president last year," they said.

Despite the threat of a veto hanging over the bill (HR 3507), the House Commerce Committee marched through a lengthy markup June 13, approving plans to overhaul Medicaid, 26–14, largely along party lines. Democrats spent much of the 10-hour markup maintaining that the GOP plan would give insufficient protection to the poor. They offered numerous amendments, almost all of which were defeated largely along party lines, to restore the federal entitlement status to many aspects of the program. The panel approved several GOP amendments, including one to phase in Medicaid coverage of adolescents ages 13 to 18, as under existing law.

The Senate Finance Committee approved its own bill (S 1795) to simultaneously overhaul the welfare and Medicaid systems June 26. The party-line vote of 11–9 dashed any remaining hope that the GOP proposal to link the two issues could gain bipartisan support.

Senate Finance Chairman Roth amended the bill before the markup to deflect some criticism that it was too harsh on the poor. He expanded the pool of individuals that states would have to cover to include children ages 13 to 18, as the House Commerce Committee had. And he added language giving states less authority to define the amount, duration and scope of benefits.

But even Max Baucus of Montana, the most reliable Democratic supporter of GOP welfare efforts, said he opposed linking the welfare changes to Medicaid provisions. He joined other

Democrats in welcoming Clinton's expected veto of the legislation, saying that Republicans would not provide enough money to help states run their Medicaid programs.

The Finance Committee considered a dozen amendments, most of them related to Medicaid and most offered by Democrats. The Democratic amendments were defeated on party-line votes or close to it, with Chafee the only Republican willing to cross party lines.

Meanwhile, Republicans on both sides of Capitol Hill were beginning to rethink their earlier strategy of linking welfare and Medicaid reforms. Originally, they had not wanted to send Clinton a free-standing welfare bill that he might sign and hail as a major accomplishment in an election year.

But by early summer, a growing number of Republican lawmakers, especially junior House members, became increasingly anxious about their own reelection prospects and more willing to share credit with Clinton on welfare in order to tout it as an accomplishment of their own.

If Clinton signed the bill, said House Ways and Means Committee member John Ensign, R-Nev., after the leaders relented, "It's good for the country, and we think his left will be very, very upset with him right before the convention."

Another factor was that the Republican governors most involved in the legislative effort told GOP congressional leaders in a July 9 telephone conversation that they were unhappy with changes in the Medicaid portion of the combined bill approved by the Senate Finance Committee on June 26.

The House effectively eliminated the Medicaid reform provisions July 18 when it adopted the rule for floor consideration of the welfare bill (HR 3734). The same day, the Senate agreed by voice vote to an amendment by Trent Lott, R-Miss., the new Senate majority leader, that deleted the Medicaid provisions from the Senate version of the welfare reform bill (S 1956). ❑

Abortion

Antiabortion activists scored some successes in the 104th Congress. Legislation criminalizing a controversial late-term abortion procedure passed both chambers but ultimately fell to a presidential veto. Through amendments to appropriations bills, abortion opponents succeeded in reinstating some of the restrictions lifted by the previous Congress, though not as many as they had hoped for. *(1993–1994 action, p. 536)*

LATE-TERM ABORTIONS

Congress cleared a bill (HR 1833) in 1996 to outlaw a type of abortion performed late in pregnancy. But proponents failed to override a presidential veto, and the bill did not become law.

The bill would have made it a federal crime, punishable by fines and up to two years in prison, for a doctor to perform the late-term abortion—known in the bill as a "partial-birth" abortion—unless it was deemed necessary to save the woman's life. The procedure was defined in the legislation as an abortion in which the doctor "partially vaginally delivers a living fetus before killing the fetus and completing the delivery." The bill also included a civil course of action for the woman's parents and the prospective father to sue the doctor for damages if the woman was a minor.

President Clinton vetoed the bill April 10, 1996, having vowed repeatedly to do so unless the exemption was broadened to include not only the life but also the health of the woman.

Bill supporters countered that the health exception was too broad and would defeat the bill's purpose. "The president and other proponents of partial-birth abortion know that adding an exception for health of the mother to HR 1833 is unnecessary and would gut the bill, allowing partial-birth abortion on demand," said sponsor Charles T. Canady, R-Fla.

Passage of the bill marked the first time either chamber had voted to criminalize an abortion procedure, and it reflected the newfound strength of abortion opponents resulting from the Republican takeover in the 104th Congress.

Proponents of the legislation, including Rep. Christopher H. Smith, R-N.J., denounced the veto, saying Clinton was the sole reason such abortions would continue to be performed. However, abortion foes also said they had scored a victory by drawing attention to the details of abortion.

Most of the legislative action on the bill took place in 1995. The House Judiciary Committee approved HR 1833 July 18 on a 20–12 party-line vote and formally reported it Sept. 27 (H Rept 104-267). After a highly charged debate, the House passed the bill Nov. 1 by a **key vote of 288–139 (R 215–15; D 73–123; I 0–1)**. *(1995 key votes, p. 1025)*

Senate supporters tried to bypass committee consideration and take the House-passed bill directly to the floor, but Democrats succeeded in forcing hearings in the Judiciary Committee first. When HR 1833 did reach the floor, the Senate passed a revised version on Dec. 7 by a **key vote of 54–44 (R 45–8; D 9–36)**, well short of the two-thirds that would be needed for a veto override.

The bill's fate in the Senate had rested largely on an amendments offered by Majority Leader Bob Dole, R-Kan., and Barbara Boxer, D-Calif. The Senate on Dec. 7 adopted the Dole amendment, 98–0, proposing a specific exception to the bill's prohibition when the life of the woman was endangered by a physical disorder, illness or injury, and no other medical procedure would suffice. But the Senate that same day rejected, 47–51, an attempt by Boxer to expand the exception to shield doctors who acted to preserve "the life or health" of the woman.

The Senate also limited prosecutions under the measure to actual physicians, defined as "any individual authorized to practice medicine or any individual who directly performs a partial-birth abortion." And members altered the bill to permit the prospective father to sue the doctor for damages only if he was married to the woman at the time of the abortion.

The House on March 27, 1996, acceded to the main provisions added by the Senate, clearing the bill for the president's signature. The **key vote was 286–129 (R 214–15; D 72–113; I 0–1)**. *(1996 key votes, p. 1047)*

As promised, Clinton vetoed the bill April 10. Surrounded by women who had undergone the procedure—and insisted that it saved not only their lives but also their future ability to bear children—Clinton argued that the procedure was sometimes essential for women whose health would be endangered by continuing the pregnancy.

Republicans waited until September, close to the end of the session and the fall elections, to attempt an override. Although they knew they lacked the needed two-thirds majority in the Senate, sponsors of the measure wanted to have the vote as close to the elections as possible, knowing that public opinion polls showed an overwhelming majority in support of the measure.

The House voted 285–137 on Sept. 19 to override the veto. The Senate acted Sept. 26, and, in a **key vote of 57–41 (R 45–6; D 12–35)**, fell nine votes short. Three senators—Patrick J. Leahy, D-Vt., Sam Nunn, D-Ga., and Arlen Specter, R-Pa.—voted for the override after voting against the measure when the Senate passed it in 1995. *(1996 key votes, p. 1047)*

Trent Lott, R-Miss., who had become majority leader when Bob Dole, R-Kan., resigned from the Senate, voted for the override, but he switched before the vote closed to preserve his right to call for another vote before Congress adjourned. He did not do so, however.

Even in defeat, though, bill supporters said the congressional debate had accomplished something they had long desired: a public examination of what constituted an abortion, or at least one kind of fairly rare abortion. "The two decades of coverup are over," said Smith.

Opponents, too, saw a broader agenda behind the bill. After passage, Jane Johnson, interim president of the Planned Parenthood Federation of America, said, "Not only does this vote place women's lives in jeopardy, it is the first step in a strategy to ban all abortions, procedure by procedure."

OTHER ABORTION ACTION

The 104th Congress in 1995 moved quickly to reinstate many of the abortion restrictions that were loosened by its predecessor. But just as the 103rd Congress, with an abortion-rights majority in both houses and the White House, failed to achieve the hopes of ardent abortion-rights backers, the first Congress controlled by the more antiabortion Republicans failed to achieve many of the goals espoused by foes of the procedure in the 1994 campaigns.

Some of the lack of progress was purposeful. Speaker Newt Gingrich, R-Ga., managed to steer the House away from the divisive abortion issue, as well as the similarly explosive issue of school prayer, lest it shatter the party's consensus over its "Contract with America" issues. But the fact also remained that despite a firm majority in the House who opposed abortion, the Senate remained more narrowly divided, with a large bloc of moderate Republicans who favored abortion rights spelling the difference.

Still, House abortion foes, bottled up for the first months of the new Congress, refused to be silenced throughout the appropriations season, and ultimately snarled a third of the must-pass spending bills with policy riders restricting abortion.

Because proabortion forces had greater clout in the Senate, many of the provisions adopted by the House were moderated in conference, leaving the antiabortion groups arguing that they had not won as much as they should have.

The following action occurred on appropriations bills:

Labor-HHS

The Senate was unable to bring the fiscal 1996 spending bill for the departments of Labor, Health and Human Services (HHS) and Education (HR 2127) to the floor for consideration in 1995, in part because of the stringent abortion restrictions contained in the House-passed version of the bill. The House bill proposed to allow states to decide whether to fund through Medicaid abortions for low-income women in cases of rape or incest. The Senate bill proposed to retain existing law, which mandated that states pay for abortions under those circumstances. The House bill also proposed to allow medical schools to receive federal funding even if they did not require students to receive abortion training, and it would have banned federal funding for research on human embryos outside the womb. The Senate bill contained no similar provisions.

In the end, the Senate never did consider the measure separately, and funding for the departments was packaged into an omnibus measure enacted more than halfway through the fiscal year it covered. In negotiations with the Senate, the House relented on the Medicaid abortion issue, essentially continuing the policy hammered out in the 1993 fight over the fiscal 1994 measure. The embryo funding ban and the abortion training provisions were enacted as part of the omnibus spending bill (HR 3019—PL 104-134), signed by President Clinton on April 26, 1996. *(1993 action, p. 538)*

Advocates on both sides of the issue held their fire during the abbreviated appropriations process for the fiscal 1997 bills, and that measure (HR 3610—PL 104-208), also folded into an omnibus bill, continued the abortion policies of the previous year.

Foreign Operations

Conferees on the fiscal 1996 foreign operations spending bill (HR 1868) spent much of the year deadlocked over House language prohibiting aid to family planning groups that performed abortions overseas and barring aid for the United Nations Population Fund unless it shut down its operations in China. *(U.N. Population Fund, box, p. 209)*

House conferees insisted on the language; Senate conferees were equally adamant that it be removed. A compromise measure signed by President Clinton on Feb. 12, 1996 (PL 104-107), dropped the House-passed reinstatement of the "Mexico City" policy that restricted funding of groups that supported abortion. But in exchange, abortion foes were able to cut by 35 percent funding for the international family planning program, and, in the absence of an authorization bill, to allow it only to be released by a set percentage per month over a 15-month period. *(1996 aid appropriations, p. 231)*

The scenario replayed itself in the fiscal 1997 bill (HR 3540), with the House having voted to cut aid to international family planning groups by an additional 50 percent if they performed or advocated for abortions, and the Senate and the White House wanting to continue full support. A complicated last-minute compromise included in the fiscal 1997 omnibus spending bill (HR 3610—PL 104-208) allowed the money to be appropriated

they relented. The House agreed to the conference report Sept. 24 by a vote of 388–25; the Senate cleared HR 3666 by voice vote Sept. 25. ❑

Medicare Select

Congress in 1995 cleared legislation (HR 483—PL 104-18) to expand a program that encouraged senior citizens to join managed-care health groups. The new law extended the 15-state pilot program, known as Medicare Select, to all states.

Despite initial reservations, President Clinton signed the bill on July 7, 1995. The White House had expressed concerns about changing Medicare Select into a permanent nationwide program before the Department of Health and Human Services (HHS) had finished reviewing the pilot. But the administration said it was satisfied with the final version of the bill, which included a provision for the program to be reexamined.

As signed into law, the bill extended Medicare Select to all 50 states until June 30, 1998, during which time HHS was to conduct its study. The program would then become permanent in 1998, unless the HHS secretary determined that it cost the government money, did not save beneficiaries money or did not provide quality health care.

Since 1991, seniors and other qualified Medicare recipients in the 15-state experiment had been able to buy discounted Medigap policies through health maintenance organizations (HMOs) and other managed-care providers as long as they agreed to use the doctors and locations in the plan's network. Medigap policies covered the difference between what Medicare paid and what health care cost.

Most of the Medicare Select programs offered beneficiaries premiums at a rate that was 5 percent to 10 percent lower than other supplemental Medicare insurance policies. As of 1995, about 450,000 of Medicare's 37 million beneficiaries had bought such policies.

The experimental Medicare Select program had been authorized in 1990 (PL 101-508) and extended for six months in 1994 (HR 5252—PL 103-432). *(1990 law, Congress and the Nation Vol. VIII, p. 582; 1994 law, p. 545)*

The Ways and Means Committee approved its bill to expand the program by a vote of 31–2 on March 8, 1995, and reported it March 15 (H Rept 104-79, Part I). The House Commerce Committee, which shared jurisdiction over Medicare's Part B, approved it by voice vote April 3 and reported it April 6 (H Rept 104-79, Part II).

The Rules Committee resolved the differences between the two versions of the bill April 5 before sending HR 483 to the House floor. Under the compromise, the program was to be extended through June 30, 2000; HHS would have until 1998 to review the program. Medicare Select was to become permanent after the five-year grace period, unless HHS found evidence of problems.

The House passed the bill April 6 by a vote of 408–14, after rejecting, 175–246, an amendment by Henry A. Waxman, D-Calif., that included provisions to bar increases in Medicare Select premiums solely on the basis of age, and to require

Medicare Select insurers to offer a traditional fee-for-service program to patients dissatisfied with Medicare Select.

The Senate passed a substitute version of HR 483 by voice vote May 17. That measure proposed to expand Medicare Select to all 50 states and extend it at first to Dec. 31, 1996, and then, if it met criteria outlined by HHS, permanently.

After House and Senate conferees resolved the minor differences between the two versions, the Senate adopted the conference report (H Rept 104-157) by voice vote June 26 and the House cleared the measure, 350–68, June 30. ❑

NIH Reauthorization

With no abortion-related fight over fetal tissue research to bog things down, the Senate in 1996 easily passed legislation (S 1897) to reauthorize expiring programs at the National Institutes of Health (NIH), but the House did not act.

NIH bills for most of the previous decade had been hampered by an emotional fight over whether the federal government should fund research using tissue from aborted fetuses. Congress in 1993 agreed to let the research proceed under certain conditions, as part of an NIH reauthorization measure (S 1—PL 103-43). *(1993 action, p. 525)*

The 1996 Senate bill, passed by voice vote Sept. 26, would have reauthorized six of NIH's 17 institutes, including the two largest—the National Cancer Institute and the National Heart, Lung and Blood Institute—for one year. (The remaining portions of NIH were permanently authorized.) S 1897 aimed to give NIH flexibility in spending federal money. It also would have created a new institute by elevating the National Center for Genome Research, which studied the human genetic map, to become the National Human Genome Research Institute.

Although the reauthorization stalled, Congress agreed as part of the fiscal 1997 omnibus appropriations bill (HR 3610—PL 104-208) to increase NIH funding by $820 million, bringing its total to $12.7 billion.

Medical research was one of the few areas in which congressional Republicans advocated spending more, rather than less, federal money. That penchant was underscored when the Senate Labor and Human Resources Committee approved S 1897 by a 16–0 vote on July 17. The bill was reported (S Rept 104-364) on Sept. 9.

To improve efficiency, the bill proposed to eliminate duplicative advisory boards, committees and requirements for annual reports, and to increase to $100,000 from $50,000 the amount that an institute could grant to researchers without approval by a special advisory council. The bill also proposed to enhance medical training and education of researchers by increasing to $35,000 from $20,000 the maximum level of educational loans that the federal government would repay for qualified NIH researchers.

Democrats accepted the idea of giving NIH more autonomy, but ranking Democrat Edward M. Kennedy of Massachusetts reminded the panel that Congress had had to pressure NIH to create the Office of Research on Women's Health in 1990 to correct what many saw as a disproportionately low level of effort in that area. "We have seen at times when the NIH needed encouragement," he said.   ❑

AIDS Program

Congress in 1996 cleared a five-year reauthorization of the federal government's key AIDS treatment program, the Ryan White CARE Act, which provided grants to cities and states to treat and support patients with AIDS (Acquired Immune Deficiency Syndrome) and HIV (Human Immunodeficiency Virus). President Clinton signed the bill (S 641—PL 104-146) on May 20.

The law was named for an Indiana youth who had been barred from school after he contracted the AIDS-causing HIV through a blood transfusion. Ryan White died in 1990, as the law (PL 101-381) was first being passed. *(1990 law, Congress and the Nation Vol. VIII, p. 588)*

Despite easy passage in each chamber in 1995, the bill had stalled in conference because of a dispute over mandatory testing of pregnant women and newborns for HIV. Since the law was last reauthorized, scientists had found that treating HIV-positive pregnant women with anti-AIDS drugs could prevent the virus from being passed on to the baby. Senate conferees favored counseling and voluntary testing of pregnant women. For women who tested positive for HIV, the Senate bill favored voluntary treatment with AZT, a drug that had been successful in reducing HIV transmission to newborns. House conferees wanted to require HIV testing of newborns if their mothers opted against testing.

The negotiators agreed to let Senate bill sponsor Nancy Landon Kassebaum, R-Kan., meet with two Republican lawmakers who were doctors, Sen. Bill Frist of Tennessee and Rep. Tom Coburn of Oklahoma, to work out a plan.   Under the compromise they reached, the states would share $10 million to promote voluntary counseling, testing and treatment for pregnant women. However, mandatory testing of newborns would be triggered if adequate progress was not made in preventing transmission to them.

Some AIDS groups blasted the compromise as unworkable and foolish. "States will put valuable resources into mandatory testing instead of putting resources into expanded access to voluntary counseling, testing and care," said Aimee Berenson of the AIDS Action Council, which represented more than 1,400 AIDS service organizations. The council said that of the 4.5 million live births each year, only 7,000 were to HIV-infected women. Of those, only 2,000 babies were infected by transmission.

The Senate had passed S 641 on July 27, 1995, by a vote of 97–3. S 641 had been reported (S Rept 104-25) by the Senate Labor and Human Resources Committee April 3.

On Sept. 18, 1995, the House passed by voice votes its version of the bill (HR 1872) and then S 641 after substituting the text of its bill. HR 1872 had been reported (H Rept 104-245) by the House Commerce Committee Sept. 14.

The House adopted the conference report on S 641 (H Rept 104-545) on May 1, 1996, by a vote of 402–4. The Senate agreed to the report by voice vote the following day, clearing the bill. ❑

FDA Overhaul

Despite bipartisan support for efforts to speed up product approval processes at the Food and Drug Administration, efforts to overhaul the agency sputtered and died at the end of the Congress in 1996 as negotiators failed to agree on the scope of the changes needed.

In the Senate, Labor and Human Resources Committee Chair Nancy Landon Kassebaum, R-Kan., succeeded in moving a bill (S 1477) through her panel in March with bipartisan backing. Kassebaum's bill was aimed at forcing the FDA to accelerate the review process for products it regulated, including pharmaceuticals, medical devices and food products. The bill, however, failed to reach the Senate floor.

House members introduced three bills to overhaul the FDA—focusing separately on pharmaceuticals (HR 3199), medical devices (HR 3201) and food products (HR 3200). Republicans had enough committee votes to move the bills but chose to negotiate with Democrats and the Clinton administration before pushing them through. Those negotiations, however, failed to produce a consensus, and none of the bills ever proceeded to markup.

BACKGROUND

The battle at its essence pitted patients and companies regulated by the FDA against consumer and some medical groups.

Republican deregulators in both chambers said Congress and the FDA had gone too far, that the process was interminable, and that patients were being made to suffer for FDA's foot-dragging. The FDA was required by statute to act within 180 days on applications to market most new drugs and devices. But that deadline was so rarely met that it had become almost irrelevant. In 1992, for example, the average approval time for a new drug was 19 months.

Critics said the FDA had moved beyond its role as consumer protector and instead acted as an abusive regulator that denied the public valuable, sometimes life-saving, products.

But opponents of the bill, led by the committee's ranking Democrat, Edward M. Kennedy of Massachusetts, warned that forcing the FDA to speed up its review of food and drug products would threaten public safety by putting potentially dangerous products on the market. They noted that while it took the FDA longer to approve products than many other nations' regulatory agencies, fewer products allowed on the market were found to be dangerous in the United States than in other nations.

In fact, the FDA—with a little help from Congress—had been cutting down on its approval times throughout the 1990s. A General Accounting Office study commissioned by Kassebaum found that review times declined 42 percent between 1987 and 1992. The FDA credited voluntary administrative changes for the decline.

In 1992, the prescription drug user fee law (PL 102-571) helped to speed up approvals still more by providing the agency funds that by law had to be used to hire more workers to review new drug applications. That law, backed by the pharmaceutical industry, also established new performance standards for reviewing applications. The FDA was ordered to review increasingly higher percentages of new drug applications within one year, double the statutory time limit. *(1992 law, Congress and the Nation Vol. VIII, p. 603)*

According to FDA Commissioner David A. Kessler, the agency was exceeding the law's requirements. In 1994, the 1992 law called for FDA to review 55 percent of pending applications within one year; the agency actually completed work on 96 percent of applications. The agency also had cut the backlog of pending applications for medical devices, which included products ranging from tongue depressors to pacemakers.

Industry representatives said the changes cited by Kessler were welcome but inadequate. "The fact of the matter is they are way short of their statutory requirement for approvals," said Jeffrey J. Kimbell, executive director of the Medical Device Manufacturers Association.

LEGISLATIVE ACTION

The Senate Labor and Human Resources Committee approved the Kassebaum proposal on March 28, 1996. The 12–4 vote gave a bipartisan boost to S 1477, which won the support of all panel Republicans as well as Democrats Christopher J. Dodd of Connecticut, Tom Harkin of Iowa and Barbara A. Mikulski of Maryland. The bill was reported (S Rept 104-284) on June 20.

Under S 1477, the FDA would have been required by July 1, 1998, to meet the existing statutory requirement to review new applications for many products within 180 days. If the agency did not meet this goal, it would have had to contract the review process out to the private sector. The FDA also would have been allowed to accept one well-controlled clinical trial to demonstrate a drug's safety and effectiveness, down from two. The bill also proposed to make it easier for seriously ill patients to get experimental products by easing restrictions on their distribution.

During the markup, the committee by an 11–4 vote approved an amendment by Daniel R. Coats, R-Ind., to allow private, FDA-accredited companies to review the safety of new medical devices. Some panel Democrats and the Clinton administration worried that allowing companies to hire and pay reviewers could lead to a conflict of interest.

At Kassebaum's suggestion, the committee also approved by voice vote an amendment to strike provisions in the bill that would have allowed manufacturers to market FDA-approved products for "off-label" uses—alternative uses that had not been approved by the agency. Under existing law, doctors could prescribe drugs and devices for uses other than those approved by the FDA, but manufacturers could not market them for such uses. Kassebaum said she and others would try to rewrite the provisions before the bill came to the Senate floor, to assuage some panel members' concerns that allowing off-label use could pose a danger to consumers.

By a vote of 9–7, the panel also adopted an amendment, offered by Coats, to limit the FDA commissioner to one five-year term in an effort, as Coats put it, to "depoliticize the office." Under the proposal, which was to take effect only after incumbent Commissioner Kessler left office, the president could not remove the commissioner except in cases involving dereliction of duty or malfeasance.

The panel also rejected several amendments, including one by Kennedy that would have eliminated provisions requiring the FDA to contract its work out to private companies if it could not approve product applications within 180 days. Under Kennedy's proposal, if the agency missed the 180-day deadline, it would have had to submit a plan to Congress outlining a way to meet the target. The amendment was rejected 7–9. ❑

Saccharin Warnings

Congress in 1996 cleared legislation repealing a federal requirement that retailers display warnings about the potential health effects of saccharin. President Clinton signed it into law April 1 (HR 1787—PL 104-124).

Bill supporters argued that saccharin warnings had become redundant because product labels already had warnings, and that the repeal would save retailers—and ultimately consumers—money spent to comply with the law. Warning signs were originally required in 1977 to give manufacturers of products containing saccharin time to place notices on the packages.

The House had passed the bill by voice vote Dec. 12, 1995. The House Commerce Committee had reported it (H Rept 104-386) Dec. 6. The Senate passed HR 1787 by voice vote March 19, 1996, clearing the bill. ❑

Drug Patent Rules

The Senate Judiciary Committee in 1996 approved a plan to allow certain generic drugmakers to make and sell their products before the patent ran out on the brand-name version of the drug. The bill (S 1277—S Rept 104-394) was reported Oct. 1, 1996, but went no further.

S 1277 addressed what critics called a loophole in a 1994 law implementing a revised General Agreement on Tariffs and Trade (GATT). That law (PL 103-465) extended the life of a patent from 17 years to 20 years. Manufacturers of generic products could not go to market until a patent expired.

GATT phased in the patent extension to accommodate generic manufacturers who had already invested in products whose patents were about to expire under the old laws. But the pharmaceutical industry was not included in the phase-in.

The bill, amended by panel Chairman Orrin G. Hatch, R-Utah, would have allowed the makers of generic drugs to market them if they could prove in court or administratively that they had made "substantial investments" to produce the drug before GATT changed the patent laws. Hank Brown, R-Colo., who wrote the original bill that Hatch amended, complained that the Hatch plan would tie up generic manufacturers in court until the patents ran out. ❑

Chronology of Action on Human Services

1993–1994

The 103rd Congress did not keep President Clinton's 1992 campaign vow to "end welfare as we know it," but it did produce some significant changes to existing human service programs. Action included continuing the efforts that began in the late 1980s to improve and expand the popular Head Start program for low-income preschoolers.

Welfare Reform

President Clinton's goal to "end welfare as we know it"—an important element of his 1992 presidential campaign—was postponed during the 103rd Congress, taking a back seat to health care, a crime bill and trade legislation. Clinton unveiled his welfare reform proposal (S 2224, HR 4605) June 14, 1994, and several committees held hearings, but no committee acted or voted on the bill. Welfare reform did clear the 104th Congress. *(1995–1996 action, p. 578)*

The long-advertised centerpiece of Clinton's plan was the requirement that recipients find work within two years of accepting welfare benefits. Those who could not find a job were to be placed in federally subsidized jobs. Because most welfare recipients had little education or job experience, the federal government would ease their transition into the workforce by spending more on job training and child care.

"We propose to offer people on welfare a simple contract," Clinton said in a speech at Kansas City, Mo. "We will help you get the skills you need, but after two years, anyone who can go to work must go to work—in the private sector if possible, in a subsidized job if necessary."

Clinton was forced to phase in his proposal—applying it only to people born after 1971—because it cost too much to include all welfare recipients immediately, and he had said in April 1994 that he would not suggest new taxes to pay for it. He also decided not to follow the lead of House Republicans and some moderate Democrats to cut off most welfare benefits to immigrants, although he did suggest new restrictions.

The administration outlined an array of financing plans worth $9.3 billion over five years to pay for the changes, including some restrictions in aid to immigrants, small cuts in some entitlement programs and fees diverted from unrelated programs.

1993 DOWNPAYMENT

Minor pieces of welfare reform were actually enacted in the 1993 budget reconciliation bill (HR 2264—PL 103-66). For example, that measure included an expansion of the earned-income tax credit (EITC), which helped low-income families with children offset the cost of income and payroll taxes. Families whose EITC exceeded their income tax bill received a check from the government. The bill raised the maximum credit to $3,554 for families with two or more children and to $2,050 for families with one child. *(Budget reconciliation bill, p. 44)*

The bill also set stricter federal guidelines for establishing paternity of children born out of wedlock—a crucial prerequisite to obtaining a court order for child support payments. *(Child support enforcement, p. 576)*

CONGRESSIONAL REACTION

Reaction in Congress to Clinton's 1994 proposal was decidedly mixed. Liberals balked at the two-year limit and objected to allowing states to limit benefit increases when welfare recipients had more children. But the strongest fire came from Republicans, who denounced the plan for encompassing only part of the caseload, providing too much flexibility in the time limits, doing too little to discourage illegitimate births, and continuing to give some welfare assistance to immigrants.

Clinton had been pressured to present his welfare bill by moderate Democrats who were eager to bring a plan before the voters in the fall and by Republicans who taunted him for neglecting his campaign pledge.

In the absence of an administration proposal, a number of welfare bills had been introduced in Congress.

House Minority Leader Robert H. Michel, R-Ill., introduced a bill cosponsored by most House Republicans calling for stiff penalties on recipients who refused to work, denying Aid to Families with Dependent Children (AFDC) to most noncitizens and cutting food and nutrition programs.

A group of moderate Democrats, led by Rep. Dave McCurdy of Oklahoma, offered a modified version of Clinton's plan that still cut deeply into aid to noncitizens. The toughest plan was introduced by Sen. Lauch Faircloth, R-N.C., and Rep. James M. Talent, R-Mo., who wanted to deny all AFDC and food stamp benefits to unwed mothers under age 21 and to their children. By contrast, a bill introduced by Rep. Robert T. Matsui, D-Calif., disdained time limits while increasing federal aid for educating and training welfare recipients.

By year's end, Republicans were vowing in their "Contract with America"—their 1994 campaign platform—to dismantle the federal welfare system. *(Contract with America, box, p. 885)*

CLINTON PLAN

Clinton's plan to revamp welfare included the following major elements:

Time Limits

Clinton proposed that recipients who were capable of working be limited to two years of government cash assistance throughout their lifetime.

Exemptions would be provided to those who were seriously ill or caring for a disabled or seriously ill child. As they entered the welfare system, recipients would receive a 12-month deferral from the time limits for their first child. They would receive a 12-week deferral for another child.

States could extend the time limit for individuals enrolled in an education or training program and for those who were learning-disabled, illiterate or who faced other "serious obstacles to employment." Extensions also would be given to those who were not given access to the services specified by the state in a written agreement with the applicant. These extensions could not amount to more than 10 percent of the eligible caseload.

Work and Training

All welfare recipients born after 1971 would be required to search for a job during their first 12 weeks on the welfare rolls. Those who could not find a job would be required either to attend school or to undergo job training. Those who could not find jobs within two years would be placed in federally subsidized positions. The requirement was expected to apply to about one-third of the welfare caseload in 1997 and two-thirds of all welfare recipients by 2004.

Training was to be provided mainly through expanding the Job Opportunities and Basic Skills (JOBS) program created by the 1988 overhaul (PL 100-485) of federal welfare programs. JOBS gave states funds for education, training and work for AFDC recipients. Clinton proposed raising the federal contribution to JOBS from $1 billion in fiscal 1994 to $1.5 billion in fiscal 1996 and increasing the federal matching rate to the states. *(1988 law, Congress and the Nation Vol. VII, p. 616)*

In all, the plan envisioned spending an additional $2.8 billion over five years for more education, training and job placement assistance for recipients.

States were also required to create WORK programs that made paid work assignments available to recipients who were unable to find private sector jobs within two years. States were to provide child care, transportation and other services to help individuals participate in the program.

WORK participants generally were to be paid the minimum wage. Participants who did not work the determined number of hours would have their wages reduced correspondingly. An individual's WORK assignment could last up to 12 months. Recipients then would be required to search for an unsubsidized job, followed, if necessary, by another WORK assignment.

The plan set aside $1.2 billion over five years for WORK slots. By fiscal 2000, the administration estimated, 394,000 people would be in subsidized jobs under the WORK program. Sanctions would be imposed on recipients who did not attend job training programs or refused to work.

Incentives, Child Care

The administration argued that forcing poor people off the welfare rolls required making work more financially rewarding.

Clinton's plan urged states to bolster the effect of the EITC by trying strategies such as paying the credit in installments throughout the year, rather than at year's end. The administration said Clinton's plan to overhaul the health care system would provide another incentive, ensuring that welfare recipients remained eligible for health coverage after they moved into the workforce.

The plan called for spending $2.7 billion over five years to pay for child care for those parents in the mandatory education and training programs, the WORK slots, and for one year after welfare recipients joined the workforce. It included another $1.5 billion to expand child care for working poor families.

Clinton also sought to allow welfare recipients to keep more of their income. Under existing law, AFDC recipients generally lost $1 of benefits for each $1 they earned by working. Clinton proposed disregarding at least $120 in earnings per month when calculating an individual's AFDC benefits. States also could let welfare parents keep more than the $50 in child support payments they were allowed to retain under existing law.

Illegitimacy, Child Support

Saying that illegitimate births made young women more likely to need welfare, Clinton proposed to lead a national campaign, orchestrated by a new nonprofit agency, against teen pregnancy. The plan envisioned a national information clearinghouse and grants to local programs to combat teen pregnancy, with a five-year cost of $300 million.

Every school-age parent or pregnant teenager who received or applied for welfare would be required to finish school or enroll in a JOBS program.

Parents who were minors would be required to live with a responsible adult, preferably a parent. Under existing law, states had the option of requiring these teenage mothers to reside in their parents' household. Under Clinton's plan, states also would have the option to limit benefit increases when all welfare recipients, including those born before 1972, had more children.

On the principle that parents should be the first source of support for their children, the administration proposed to spend $600 million over five years to improve enforcement of court orders for child support and related programs. Mothers who applied for AFDC would be required to cooperate to establish paternity. Once paternity information was given to the states, officials would have one year to establish paternity or risk losing a portion of their federal matching funds for AFDC benefits.

Eligibility Changes

The plan gave states the option of making it easier for two-parent families to be eligible for AFDC payments. Under existing law, AFDC eligibility for two-parent families was limited to those in which the principal wage earner was unemployed but had worked in six of the previous 13 calendar quarters. The administration said this penalized welfare recipients who wanted to get married. However, Republicans said that relaxing the laws would encourage married couples to apply for welfare and thereby expand the rolls significantly.

Financing

The administration proposed to offset the estimated $9.3 billion cost of the bill over five years, through the following changes in federal programs:

• **Aid to Noncitizens.** Restricting the eligibility of noncitizens for AFDC, Supplemental Security Income (SSI) and food stamps by requiring an immigrant's sponsor to be financially responsible for the immigrant for five years. Beginning in the sixth year, if the sponsor's income was above the national median family income, the immigrant would have to obtain citizenship before becoming eligible for the benefits. Estimated savings over five years: $3.7 billion.

• **Emergency Assistance.** Put a ceiling on each state's spending in the AFDC Emergency Assistance Program. States had wide latitude in using these funds, which were designed for short-term needs to help keep people off welfare. The administration estimated that without changes, the program would rise from $189 million in fiscal 1990 to almost $1 billion by fiscal 1999. Five-year savings: $1.6 billion.

• **Superfund Tax.** Extend through 1998 a broad-based corporate tax funding the superfund program to clean up hazardous wastes. The administration said that counting this as revenue for welfare would not affect the superfund. Five-year revenues: $1.6 billion.

• **Benefits to Alcoholics, Addicts.** Restrict benefits for people who were eligible for SSI benefits because of alcoholism or drug addiction. Five-year savings: approximately $800 million.

• **Farm Subsidies.** Limit agricultural subsidies for farmers with more than $100,000 in nonfarm income. Five-year savings: $500 million.

• **Meal Subsidies.** Restrict certain federal meal subsidies to family day-care homes. Five-year savings: $500 million.

• **Tax Credits.** Deny eligibility for the earned-income tax credit to nonresident immigrants. Five-year savings: $300 million.

• **Rail Safety.** Permanently extend railroad fees that were used to conduct safety inspections. Five-year revenues: $200 million.

• **Food Stamp Overpayments.** Bar states from keeping a portion of food stamp overpayments that they discovered by pursuing program violations. Five-year savings: $100 million. ❑

Head Start

President Clinton fulfilled one of his top campaign promises in 1994, signing into law a bill to both expand the reach and improve the quality of the popular Head Start preschool program. The bipartisan-backed bill (S 2000—PL 103-252) cleared Congress May 12 and Clinton signed it May 18.

The bill authorized the program through fiscal 1998 at unspecified sums. Clinton had requested $4 billion for Head Start in fiscal 1995, a $700 million increase over the fiscal 1994 appropriations and twice as much as appropriated three years before. Congress ultimately provided $3.5 billion as part of the fiscal 1995 appropriations bill for the departments of Labor, Health and Human Services and Education (HR 4606—PL 103-333).

The Head Start bill included a new program to serve families with infants and toddlers under age three. But the key to the bill's popularity in Congress was the fact that it focused not only on expanding Head Start but also on quality control. It sought to respond to widespread concerns that the quality of Head Start had suffered from rapid expansion, fostering mediocrity while the problems of childhood poverty deepened.

The legislation generally followed the January 1994 recommendations of an advisory panel appointed by Health and Human Services (HHS) Secretary Donna E. Shalala that called for new performance standards and quality controls.

BACKGROUND

Head Start, begun during President Lyndon B. Johnson's War on Poverty in 1965, had evolved into one of the federal government's most popular social service programs. The appeal arose largely from its emphasis on providing preventive services to low-income preschoolers and their families, and its record of success—short-term though it was—with participants.

Head Start provided preschoolers and their families with education, health care, nutrition and social services. The program served mostly three- and four-year-olds who were enrolled in part-day programs during the school year. Head Start funds were awarded to about 1,400 grant recipients that ran the programs in cities and counties. Most of the recipients were community action agencies and other nonprofit organizations that could, in turn, contract with local program operators.

Since 1965, nearly 14 million children from low-income families had participated in Head Start. By law, virtually all of them were from families whose incomes were below the federal poverty line. Still, the program served fewer than half the eligible children. Despite a 50 percent increase in enrollment since 1989, to nearly 714,000 in 1993, Head Start included only 53 percent of eligible four-year-olds and 21 percent of eligible three-year-olds.

When Clinton took office, a number of Republicans who had been supportive of Head Start began raising serious questions about its quality. Rep. Bill Goodling of Pennsylvania, ranking Republican on the House Education and Labor Committee, joined by Rep. Susan Molinari of New York and Sen. Nancy Landon Kassebaum, Kan., ranking Republican on the Senate Labor and Human Resources Committee, introduced bills (HR 1528, S 670) calling for tough new standards on how Head Start centers should operate.

Apparently sensing that questions about Head Start's quality could threaten bipartisan support for the program, HHS Secretary Shalala announced in March 1993 that the Clinton administration's goal of reaching every eligible Head Start child would be slowed down to deal with quality problems.

Shalala later appointed a 47-member bipartisan advisory committee that included Head Start representatives, congressional staff members and child experts, chaired by Mary Jo Bane, assistant secretary for the administration of children and families at HHS. The advisory committee laid the groundwork for legislative reauthorization by calling for improvements in staffing, local management, facilities and federal oversight, as well as continued expansion of services and enrollment.

LEGISLATIVE ACTION

The Senate Labor and Human Resources Committee approved its version of the Head Start reauthorization bill on April 13, 1994, by a vote of 17–0 and reported it April 19 (S 2000—S Rept 103-251). The Senate passed the bill April 21 by voice vote.

The House Education and Labor Committee approved by voice vote April 21 and reported April 26 a companion bill (HR

4250—H Rept 103-483, Part I). The full House by voice votes April 28 first passed HR 4250 and then approved S 2000 after substituting the text of HR 4250.

House and Senate conferees had to work out only minor differences in the two bills. They agreed to include a Senate provision allowing Head Start grantees to build new facilities when permitted to do so by HHS. Under existing law, grantees were allowed only to buy existing facilities. The House did not have a similar provision. Conferees struck Senate language that would have made Head Start children automatically eligible for subsidized school lunch and other nutrition programs.

The Senate agreed to the conference report (H Rept 103-497) May 11 by a vote of 98–1. The House followed suit May 12 by a vote of 393–20, clearing the bill for the president.

MAJOR PROVISIONS

As signed into law, S 2000:

• Reauthorized Head Start through fiscal 1998 at unspecified sums.

• Continued a policy begun in 1990 that set aside 25 percent of each year's increased spending for quality improvements.

• Required HHS to create a process for identifying poorly run programs and to develop a plan to help them improve. Program operators were required to show that the quality of their day care and social services met these new standards. Programs that fell short would lose their grants within one year.

• Created a program to serve children from birth to age three. The children and their families were to be provided with education, health care and social services to promote child development and parental self-sufficiency. The bill set aside 3 percent of Head Start funding in fiscal 1995 for this initiative. The set-aside was to increase to 5 percent by fiscal 1998.

In addition to Head Start funding, the bill also authorized several other programs, including:

• $525 million in fiscal 1995 for the Community Services Block Grants, which primarily funded local community action agencies serving the poor.

• $2 billion annually through fiscal 1999 for the Low Income Home Energy Assistance Program (LIHEAP), which helped low-income families pay heating and cooling bills and insulate their homes. The Clinton administration had recommended that LIHEAP's appropriation be cut from $1.5 billion in fiscal 1994 to $745 million in fiscal 1995. The administration argued that it was better to assist low-income households through more broadly targeted programs.

• $50 million in fiscal 1995 for a Community-Based Family Resource Program designed to prevent child abuse. ❑

Family Preservation

Congress in 1993 created a new "capped" entitlement program aimed at keeping troubled families together and giving early help to children at risk of being put into foster care. The initiative, approved as part of the 1993 budget reconciliation bill (HR 2264—PL 103-66), provided $930 million through fiscal 1998. The program sprang from concern that while states received considerable federal aid for programs to remove children from troubled homes and place them in foster care, there was relatively little federal assistance devoted to helping families overcome a crisis and stay together.

The program, which expanded the child welfare sections of the Social Security Act, provided the states with money to help keep families together. Such programs, which existed in more than 30 states, provided intense temporary counseling at home to troubled families. States were allowed to use the money for community services such as programs to improve parenting skills, temporary assistance to parents and other child guardians, activities to improve relationships between parents and children, information and referral services, and early developmental screening of children.

The "capped" entitlement made a set amount of money available to the states each year; the money was not subject to annual appropriations. (By contrast, unlimited entitlement programs provided whatever money was needed to cover all those eligible for benefits.) The law authorized $60 million for family preservation services in fiscal 1994, $150 million in 1995, $225 million in 1996, $240 million in 1997 and $255 million in 1998.

Congress cleared the bitterly partisan reconciliation bill on Aug. 6; President Clinton signed it on Aug. 10. (Budget reconciliation bill, p. 44)

BACKGROUND

There was widespread agreement in Congress that the existing child welfare law gave states an incentive to rely on the expensive and overburdened foster care system, rather than investing in preventive services. Under an existing, unlimited foster care entitlement, states were to receive about $2.6 billion from the federal government in fiscal 1993. By contrast, the federal government expected to pay only about $295 million in fiscal 1993 for child welfare services aimed at preventing children from needing foster care. The need for preventive services was clearly growing. According to child welfare advocates, child abuse and neglect cases had increased from 1.1 million in 1980 to 2.7 million in 1991.

The Bush administration and many GOP lawmakers had favored expanding services for abused and neglected children. But they balked at raising taxes for the purpose and objected to creating a new entitlement, preferring instead to reorient money within the foster care program. The House had passed a $7 billion overhaul of the child welfare system in 1992 that included a capped entitlement to help states pay for services designed to keep troubled families together; the program was to be paid for with a 10 percent surtax on millionaires. But the measure was incorporated into a larger tax bill that President George Bush vetoed. (1992 bill, Congress and the Nation Vol. VIII, p. 621)

Unlike his GOP predecessors, Clinton endorsed the idea of a capped entitlement for family support and preservation services.

LEGISLATIVE ACTION

The House Ways and Means Subcommittee on Human Resources approved the capped entitlement by voice vote April 27, authorizing $1.4 billion for the program over five years. The full Ways and Means Committee agreed May 11 to include the family preservation provisions in the reconciliation bill, and the House approved the overall bill, 219–213, on May 27.

John D. Rockefeller IV, D-W.Va., and Christopher S. Bond, R-Mo., introduced a family preservation bill (S 596) in the Senate early in the year, but the Senate did not include any family preservation provisions in its reconciliation bill. The $2.2 billion Rockefeller-Bond measure would have offered a more comprehensive overhaul of child welfare laws by creating three capped entitlements for family preservation and related programs. Some of the money would have been targeted for children in families beset by drug or alcohol abuse.

House and Senate conferees agreed to include the House-passed entitlement in the final reconciliation bill but scaled back the funding to $930 million over five years.   ❏

WIC, Child Nutrition

Congress in 1994 cleared legislation (S 1614—PL 103-448) reauthorizing several child nutrition programs, including the popular Special Supplemental Nutrition Program for Women, Infants and Children (WIC). The program, which was extended for four years at unspecified sums, provided food vouchers and nutrition education for low-income pregnant women and children up to age five. President Clinton signed the bill Nov. 2.

LEGISLATIVE ACTION

The House Education and Labor Committee approved HR 8, a bill to reauthorize the Child Nutrition Act at unspecified levels through fiscal 1998, by voice vote May 18 and reported it June 3 (H Rept 103-535, Part I). Members approved several amendments, including one to make Head Start participants automatically eligible for food programs beginning in fiscal 1996.

The committee also approved an amendment to permit some schools to drop whole milk from their menus if it accounted for less than 1 percent of the total milk consumed at the school in the previous year. The amendment initially was resisted by Steve Gunderson, R-Wis., whose dairy state long had supported the program's requirement that schools offer whole milk along with other varieties. Gunderson offered a substitute that would have allowed milk purchases to be based on a survey of students' preferences. He withdrew his amendment, saying afterward that he thought the proposed amendment would have little impact in most school districts.

In the only recorded vote, members voted 26–15 along party lines for an amendment to authorize $15 million annually through fiscal 1998 for a demonstration program for school breakfasts and lunches. All students could get free breakfast and lunch at a school where at least 30 percent of students qualified for free meals. Republicans objected that providing free school lunches for all students would be too costly.

On June 16, the House Agriculture Committee approved by voice vote a four-year reauthorization for the Commodity Distribution Program, which fell under its jurisdiction. The panel reported HR 8 (H Rept 103-535, Part II) on June 24.

The House passed the bill July 19 by a vote of 372–40.

The Senate Agriculture, Nutrition and Forestry Committee gave voice vote approval June 22 to a companion bill and reported it July 1 (S 1614—S Rept 103-300). The original bill mandated enough funding for WIC to provide benefits to every eligible family, but committee Chairman Patrick Leahy, D-Vt., dropped that language before the markup, citing lack of funds. The Senate passed the bill by voice vote Aug. 25.

Instead of sending the bill to a House-Senate conference, the House on Oct. 5 gave voice vote approval to a version of S 1614 that had been amended to reconcile differences between the two bills. The amendment had been agreed to beforehand by House and Senate lawmakers. The Senate cleared the bill for the president by voice vote Oct. 6.

MAJOR PROVISIONS

As signed into law, S 1614:

• Extended the Special Supplemental Nutrition Program for Women, Infants and Children for four years at unspecified sums.

• Increased the authorization for programs such as school breakfasts and lunches and meals for homeless children under age six by about $174 million over five years. And it required schools to meet the Dietary Guidelines for Americans by 1996 or, if they obtained a waiver, by 1998. But the bill also gave school lunch planners flexibility in meeting the guidelines, allowing them to continue using a food-based system that analyzed portions of meat, milk, bread, vegetables and fruit, rather than requiring them to switch to a nutrient-based system.

• Eliminated the existing requirement that schools offer whole milk, requiring instead that varieties of milk be offered based on a survey of the prior year's preference.

• Authorized $9 million to test the feasibility of schools serving all breakfast and lunches free and receiving a flat rate of reimbursement from the federal government.

• Permanently authorized a demonstration project that enabled some schools to receive cash or a commodity letter of credit instead of commodities for their lunch and breakfast programs.

• Reauthorized for four years the Summer Food Service Program, which provided food for children in low-income areas during the summer months when school was out of session. While more than 12 million low-income children received free or subsidized lunches every day during the school year, in 1992 only 1.9 million children ate a meal at a summer food service site.

• Gave permanent authorization to the homeless preschoolers' nutrition program, the breakfast start-up program and the nutrition education and training program. It made Head Start children automatically eligible to participate in the child- and adult-care food program.   ❏

Food Stamps

Several bills dealing with the nation's food stamp program were enacted in the 103rd Congress.

USE AT CONVENIENCE STORES

Convenience stores would be able to continue accepting food stamps under legislation (S 1926—PL 103-225) signed by President Clinton March 25, 1994. The action was prompted by an Agriculture Department survey that found that unless Congress acted, about half the 56,000 convenience stores authorized to accept food stamps would be disqualified because existing qualifications, based on the percentage of staple foods sold, had not kept up with changing retail practices or consumer buying habits.

If those stores no longer accepted food stamps, bill supporters said, poor residents of rural areas and inner-city neighborhoods lacking supermarkets would have trouble buying food.

S 1926 required a store to meet one of two conditions in order to accept food stamps. The first was that it continually offer staples from each of the four basic food groups, such as meat, bread, fruit and dairy products, and perishable foods in at least two of the groups. Alternatively, at least 50 percent of the outlet's total sales—not just food sales—had to consist of staples.

In addition, the bill modified some food stamp provisions related to Native American reservations contained in the 1990 farm bill (S 2830—PL 101-624) and set to take effect in 1994. One of those provisions required states to stagger monthly issuing dates of food stamps to Native American reservations. S 1926 allowed states to stagger the dates and required them to do so only if a tribe requested it. *(1990 farm bill, Congress and the Nation Vol. VIII, p. 537)*

The bill was based on a measure (HR 3436) the House had passed by voice vote Nov. 10, 1993. HR 3436 had been reported (H Rept 103-352) by the House Agriculture Committee that same day. S 1926 was passed by the Senate March 11, 1994, and was cleared by the House March 16, both by voice vote.

A short-term bill (S 1777—PL 103-205) had been signed into law, Dec. 17, 1993, allowing convenience stores to continue accepting food stamps while Congress completed work on the permanent measure.

PROGRAM EXPANSION

Congress expanded the food stamp program—primarily by allowing more families to qualify for benefits—as part of the massive 1993 budget reconciliation bill (HR 2264—PL 103-66). The changes were expected to cost $2.5 billion over five years.

The original House-passed measure would have provided considerably more money—$7.3 billion—and included an increase in benefit levels as well as changes in eligibility requirements. The Senate did not include the food stamp expansion in its version of the bill.

The final measure dropped a House provision that would have raised overall food stamp benefits by a maximum of $4 per month for a family of four. However, other changes included in the version that was signed into law by Clinton on Aug. 10, 1993, served to increase benefits, depending on one's circumstances. For example, a household could deduct more for housing costs in determining its income for food stamp purposes, and it no longer had to count money earned by family members who were still in high school. Deductions were also given for some child support payments and child care expenses. *(Budget reconciliation bill, p. 44)*

The food stamp provisions, known as the Mickey Leland Childhood Hunger Relief Act, were named for the first chairman of the House Select Committee on Hunger who died in a 1989 airplane crash during a hunger relief mission to Ethiopia.

EXPERIMENTAL PROGRAMS

The question of whether states should be allowed to experiment with administering the food stamp program touched off an emotional debate in 1994 during consideration of the fiscal 1995 Agriculture appropriations bill (HR 4554—PL 103-330).

Nine states had received federal waivers either to provide low-income food stamp recipients with cash instead of food stamps or to use the grants to subsidize jobs for the recipients. At the urging of Neal Smith, D-Iowa, the House included in the version it passed, 278–127, on June 17 a provision to prohibit any more such experiments. Smith said the cash-out concept could deprive children of enough nutritional food.

Smith's provision faced strong opposition from Sens. John McCain, R-Ariz., and Bob Kerrey, D-Neb., who successfully offered an amendment to strike the prohibition and let the federal government approve more cash-out experiments. Their amendment was adopted, 63–34, on July 19. The Senate passed the bill, 92–8, the next day.

The issue proved to be one of the more contentious items in conference. Conferees finally agreed, despite Kerry's objections, to limit such experiments to 25 locations nationwide. States typically applied for demonstrations in a small number of counties. The bill further limited experiments to no more than 3 percent of food stamp households nationwide. There were about 27 million food stamp participants in fiscal 1993.

The House adopted the conference report (H Rept 103-734) on Sept. 23 by a vote of 287–107 and the Senate cleared the bill by voice vote Sept. 27. It was signed into law Sept. 30. ❑

Child Support Enforcement

The 103rd Congress failed to enact comprehensive legislation to overhaul the nation's child support enforcement system, but it did clear separately several new requirements aimed at requiring absent parents—usually fathers—to pay more of the expenses of raising their children.

In 1993, the budget reconciliation bill (HR 2264—PL 103-66) included a number of provisions related to child support enforcement, which was traditionally a state-run activity operated under federal guidelines dating back to 1975. According to the 1990 census, about half of the fathers obligated to make child-support payments failed to do so. The delinquency rate often was cited as a primary reason why many single-parent households ended up on welfare rolls. *(Budget reconciliation bill, p. 44)*

The reconciliation bill required states to establish the paternity of 75 percent of children born out of wedlock who were receiving welfare or child-support enforcement services. States with paternity establishment rates between 50 percent and 75 percent had to increase their success by 3 percentage points per year; those with rates below 50 percent had to improve by at least 6 percentage points per year. States were also required to provide a simple civil procedure for voluntary acknowledgments of paternity, including a plan for obtaining such acknowledgments in the hospital just before or after the birth of a child. The reconciliation bill also contained a provision requiring states to force health insurers to provide coverage to a child born out of wedlock if the noncustodial parent was eligible for family coverage at a reasonable cost. The private insurance would be first recourse before the child could receive Medicaid coverage.

In 1994, the Congressional Caucus for Women's Issues backed a comprehensive bill (HR 4570), that included a number of enforcement mechanisms aimed at reducing the estimated $34 billion owed by deadbeat parents. The bill would have required hospitals to establish paternity at birth, would have required states to withhold driver's licenses from deadbeat parents, and would have modified the employee's federal tax withholding form (W-4) to include information about child-support payments for a new national child-support payment registry.

While many of the proposals mirrored those in the welfare overhaul plan that President Clinton unveiled June 14, the bill's sponsor, Rep. Patricia Schroeder, D-Colo., and other women members had hoped that even though Congress was not going to act on welfare reform in 1994, it would pass the child-support measure. The Clinton administration, however, argued against separating the provisions.

The comprehensive bill stalled in the House, though, after only two of seven panels with jurisdiction—the House Post Office and Civil Service Committee and an Armed Services subcommittee—acted on the measure.

With time running out late in the session, supporters of the comprehensive bill attempted to pass pieces of the package as separate bills or to attach them to other legislation. Four measures ultimately cleared in 1994; two other bills died.

The following child-support bills were enacted:

• **State Modification of Court Orders.** A bill (S 922—PL 103-383) signed into law Oct. 20, 1994, barred a state court from modifying a child-support order issued by another state's court unless the child and parent receiving the support payments had moved to the state where the modification was sought or had agreed to the change. The legislation started in the Senate Judiciary Committee, which reported it Aug. 25 (S Rept 103-361). The Senate passed the bill by voice vote Sept. 27 and the House cleared it by voice vote Oct. 5.

• **Small Business Loans.** Parents who failed to pay child support became ineligible for small-business loans under a bill (S 2060—PL 103-403) reauthorizing the Small Business Administration. The Senate Small Business Committee added the language to the bill Aug. 10, when it adopted by voice vote an amendment offered by Carol Moseley-Braun, D-Ill., for Frank R. Lautenberg, D-N.J. (*SBA reauthorization, p. 344*)

• **Bankruptcy.** Child support payments were designated as priority debts when an individual filed for bankruptcy under a bill (HR 5116—PL 103-394) overhauling the federal Bankruptcy Code. The bill made it more difficult for a divorced person who assumed the couple's marital debts in exchange for a reduction or elimination of alimony or child support to escape that obligation through bankruptcy, thereby saddling the other spouse with the debt. (*Bankruptcy overhaul, p. 347*)

• **Child Abuse Payments.** Congress cleared a separate bill (HR 3694—PL 103-358) that allowed the pensions of federal retirees found guilty of child abuse to be garnisheed for the purpose of paying court-ordered damages. (*Child abusers' federal pensions, p. 817*)

The House also passed two child-support bills in the closing days of the second session that did not see Senate action. They were:

• **Federal Employee Child Support.** By voice vote, the House Oct. 7, 1994, passed HR 5179, which required a federal agency that received a child-support garnishment order to withhold the required sums from a worker's pay and forward the money to the custodial parent within five days of the next payday. Agencies that did not act within 10 days of a payday could be fined $1,000 by the state requesting the child-support payments.

The bill also prohibited federal agencies from paying a variety of benefits to government workers who were in arrears on their child-support payments by more than three months or from hiring new employees who were similarly delinquent, and denied a U.S. passport to parents facing an outstanding arrest warrant for owing more than $10,000 in child support.

• **Armed Forces Child Support.** The House on Oct. 5, 1994, gave voice vote approval to legislation (HR 5140) aimed at making it easier to get court-ordered child support from active and retired members of the U.S. military. The House-passed measure required the secretary of defense to establish a centralized data bank containing the addresses of all military employees and to make that information available to the Federal Parent Locator Service. ❑

Holocaust Victims

Legislation (HR 1873—PL 103-286) signed by President Clinton Aug. 1, 1994, made more World War II Holocaust victims living in the United States eligible for federal aid programs such as food stamps and housing subsidies.

The bill, introduced by Rep. Henry A. Waxman, D-Calif., exempted from income calculations used to determine eligibility for federal programs reparation payments made by Germany and Austria to Holocaust survivors. An estimated 30,000 people in the U.S. received monthly payments of between $350 and $600, according to the Congressional Budget Office. Waxman's staff estimated that the bill would directly affect less than two-thirds of those recipients. Similar payments made by the U.S. government to Japanese Americans and others injured by U.S. policies were not counted as income for determining eligibility for federal aid programs.

The House passed HR 1873 by voice vote July 12, 1994, and the Senate cleared it July 19, also by voice vote. ❑

1995–1996

Having failed to gain a balanced budget bill in 1995, the Republican-led Congress changed its tactics in 1996 and was rewarded with a far-reaching welfare reform bill that President Clinton signed into law. The measure, while not as sweeping as many Republicans would have liked, nevertheless ended the federal guarantee of aid to poor women and children and turned most of the responsibility for their well-being back to the states.

Welfare Reform

The third time proved the charm as President Clinton in 1996 signed a landmark welfare reform bill that ended a 61-year-old entitlement to cash benefits for poor women and children. After vetoing two previous bills sent him by the GOP Congress in 1995 and 1996, Clinton on Aug. 22 signed the third effort (HR 3734—PL 104-193).

Under the new law, federal funds would be sent to the states in lump sums known as block grants, and states would have broad leeway over eligibility and benefits. It was the first time the federal government had transformed a major individual entitlement program into a block grant to the states. However, the law did impose some federal restrictions on the use of the funds. Among the most prominent: welfare recipients would be required to work within two years of receiving benefits and they would be limited to five years of aid.

The bill gained bipartisan approval in Congress, after Clinton announced he would sign it despite his objections to provisions cutting the food stamp program and denying various federal benefits to legal immigrants. These and related federal savings were expected to amount to $54.6 billion through fiscal 2002, according to the Congressional Budget Office (CBO).

The legislation's scope was narrower than many Republicans had once envisioned, but its provisions extended far beyond cash welfare programs. Besides the food stamp and immigration provisions, the act also made it harder for disabled children to qualify for federal aid, reorganized federal child-care-assistance programs and toughened enforcement of child-support orders.

But with Clinton having vetoed two earlier attempts at welfare overhaul—on Dec. 6, 1995, as part of the Republican deficit-reducing budget reconciliation bill (HR 2491), and then on Jan. 9, 1996, as a free-standing welfare bill (HR 4)—Republicans knew they had to compromise if they were to be able to take credit for what had been a centerpiece of their 104th Congress agenda.

Even scaled back, the bill still represented the most sweeping change in federal social policy since the inception of Medicare and Medicaid in 1965. The measure was expected to trim more than $23 billion from spending on food stamps, with other major savings derived from denying an array of federal benefits, including food stamps and Supplemental Security Income (SSI), to most legal immigrants.

The nation's poorest households, with incomes below half the federal poverty level, would lose an average of $650 a year in food stamp benefits, according to the Center on Budget and Policy Priorities, a liberal public research group. Half the poverty line was $6,250 for a family of three.

Still, the measure revamped fewer social policy programs than previous GOP welfare bills would have. Republicans had wanted to give states almost complete control over Medicaid, foster care and adoption programs, school meals and nutritional assistance for pregnant women and young children. They also wanted to give states the option to control their food stamp programs and to sharply reduce the number of people eligible for the earned-income tax credit, which served the working poor. In the end, the welfare overhaul did none of that.

When 1996 began, the outlook for the legislation was murky. In vetoing the two GOP plans, Clinton branded the measures as too harsh, more likely to hurt children than to help welfare recipients get jobs.

In his Jan. 23 State of the Union address, Clinton challenged Congress to send him a bipartisan welfare plan. But there was little enthusiasm for the idea until the nation's governors endorsed a plan Feb. 6 to overhaul welfare and Medicaid, the federal-state health insurance program for the poor.

GOP leaders began to warm to the notion of revamping welfare and Medicaid in a single bill, but Democrats quickly objected. Although Clinton had signaled his willingness to end the federal guarantee of welfare checks, he wanted to retain the Medicaid entitlement and was unwilling to transfer control of the program to the states as the GOP proposed. Clinton referred to the Medicaid provisions as a "poison pill" that would prompt him to veto the welfare legislation if the two matters were linked.

Senate Majority Leader Bob Dole, R-Kan., insisted that Republicans would move the welfare legislation only with the Medicaid changes. Clinton's veto threat seemed to matter little to Dole. As the likely GOP presidential nominee, he was eager to blast Clinton's vetoes and reluctant to send him a bill he might sign.

On May 22, Republican leaders unveiled a combined welfare-Medicaid bill. Although they narrowed and modified the scope of their original welfare proposal, the centerpiece remained unchanged: the federal government would end its guarantee of providing cash welfare to all eligible low-income mothers and children. Instead, federal funding would be sent to the states in block grants, giving states almost complete control over eligibility and benefits.

Because of the projected savings, Republicans designated the measure a budget reconciliation bill, which gave it protection from a filibuster in the Senate. Nevertheless, Clinton's opposition to the Medicaid provisions seemed certain to doom the effort.

But an increasing number of GOP lawmakers, especially in the House wanted to be part of historic changes in the nation's welfare laws and they were eager to claim that as an accomplishment for their reelection campaigns. They began urging the leadership to try to accommodate Clinton. And, they reasoned, if Clinton did veto the GOP welfare plan for the third time, he should not be allowed to cite his objections to the Medicaid provisions as an excuse.

Republicans moved the welfare and Medicaid legislation through House and Senate committees in June. But in July, a month after Dole had left the Senate to campaign full time for the presidency, GOP leaders bowed to internal pressure and dropped the Medicaid provisions. That permitted Democratic support for the welfare measure to grow, especially in the Senate. Both chambers passed versions of the welfare-only bill in July. A House-Senate conference committee then borrowed enough from the somewhat more moderate Senate bill to make Clinton and many congressional Democrats comfortable.

Clinton resisted a last-ditch appeal from liberals to reject the bill. After a dramatic meeting in the White House with top aides and some cabinet members July 31, Clinton announced that he would sign the bill despite misgivings about the food stamp savings and cuts in aid to legal immigrants.

With Clinton's announcement, approval in both chambers was assured. Democrats split on the measure, but Republicans supported it nearly unanimously.

BACKGROUND

Clinton had highlighted welfare reform as an issue in his 1992 presidential campaign, promising to "end welfare as we know it." Though the pledge was popular on the campaign trail, it was largely shunted aside in the first two years of his presidency while the White House concentrated on an ill-fated health care overhaul.

The administration did not present a detailed welfare proposal until June 14, 1994. Clinton's plan stressed getting people off welfare into jobs. "We will help you get the skills you need," said Clinton, "but after two years, anyone who can go to work must go to work—in the private sector if possible, in a subsidized job if necessary. But work is preferable to welfare. And it must be enforced." *(1993–1994 action, p. 571)*

But helping people move from welfare to jobs—with training, child-care help and other assistance—promised to cost the federal government more, not less, at least in the short run. And Republicans were looking at welfare reform as a way to save billions of dollars in federal spending.

1995 LEGISLATIVE ACTION

The upshot of the partisan skirmishes in 1995 was a compromise bill (HR 4) that proposed to end the nation's main welfare program—Aid to Families with Dependent Children (AFDC)— and to replace it with block grants to the states. Under the bill, states would have designed their own programs for providing cash benefits, child care and some services to low-income Americans, within certain federal limits. For example, recipients generally would not have been able to receive cash welfare for more than five years, and states could not have used federal funds to provide welfare checks for children born to welfare recipients, unless the state passed legislation to do so.

Beyond that, HR 4 included provisions to make it harder for drug addicts, alcoholics and disabled children to qualify for Supplemental Security Income (SSI), which provided cash to the low-income aged, blind and disabled. And it proposed to deny most social services to noncitizens.

House Action

The House-passed welfare bill had been the more sweeping of the two versions, proposing five block grants: for cash welfare; child protection programs, such as foster care and adoption assistance; child care; school lunch and breakfast programs; and the special nutrition program for pregnant women and young children. It also included controversial provisions to bar the use of federal funds to provide welfare checks to children born to unwed teenage mothers and to welfare recipients.

The House passed HR 4 on March 24, 1995, as part of its 100-day rush to fulfill its "Contract with America." But bipartisanship was in short supply—the **key vote was 234–199 (R 225–5; D 9–193; I 0–1).** *(1995 key votes, p. 1025)*

The legislation had begun in the House as three bills, marked up by three separate committees, which were later combined by the Rules Committee into HR 4.

Much of the legislation, including provisions on AFDC and child protection, went through the House Ways and Means Committee. Partisanship was the rule when the full committee approved its bill (HR 1157) by a near party-line vote of 22–11 on March 8. The panel formally reported the bill (H Rept 104-81, Part I) March 15.

House Republicans raised the stakes in their bid to upend the nation's welfare system Feb. 23 when the Economic and Educational Opportunities Committee voted to eliminate popular social services such as the national school lunch program and turn them over to the states. The committee approved its part of the welfare plan (HR 999) by a party-line 23–17 vote, over strenuous Democratic objections. The committee reported HR 999 (H Rept 104-75, Part I) on March 10.

The House Agriculture Committee gave its approval March 8 to a bitterly contested proposal to pare back the nation's food stamp program and require recipients to find work. The panel approved its bill (HR 1135) by a near party-line vote of 26–18. The bill was reported (H Rept 104-77) March 14.

House leaders and the Rules Committee basically combined the three committee-approved bills, although they did alter some provisions, particularly regarding benefits for noncitizens. The bill made legal immigrants eligible for more programs than the committee bills would have allowed, but it made qualifying for them contingent on the income of the immigrant's U.S. sponsor.

Some of the most fervent antiabortion House members nearly blocked the rule for floor debate on HR 4. They feared that provisions denying cash assistance to unwed teenage mothers and rewarding states for reducing out-of-wedlock births could prompt more abortions. Two amendments they sought were subsequently adopted, while two others were disallowed under the rule (H Res 119) that was adopted, 217–211, March 22.

If Republicans occasionally displayed unusual dissension in their ranks on the floor, Democrats showed unaccustomed unity. Although they were blocked by the rule from forcing floor votes on individual provisions, they nevertheless blasted the GOP bill throughout the debate. Two Democratic substitute proposals were rejected, including an alternative crafted by Nathan Deal of Georgia and other moderate-to-conservative Democrats that was less sweeping than HR 4 and would have retained entitlements for cash benefits, school lunches and other programs. The Deal amendment was defeated on March 23 on a largely party-line vote of 205–228.

Senate Action

The Senate had long been expected to be a moderating influence on the House's impulse toward a radical restructuring of the welfare system. The Senate did play that role, approving a narrower bill that would have created two block grants: for cash welfare assistance and child care.

But still the Senate generally accepted much of the broad framework of the House's bill. The centerpiece—turning AFDC into a block grant—was supported by the Senate Finance Committee. The panel approved a draft bill by a largely party-line vote of 12–8 on May 26. The bill covered fewer programs and contained fewer restrictions on the states regarding funding and eligibility than the House version had. HR 4 was reported (S Rept 104-96) by the Finance Committee June 9.

Another piece of the Senate's welfare plan fell into place May 26 when the Labor and Human Resources Committee gave strong bipartisan support—the vote was 16–0—to a bill (S 850) intended to help fund child care for low-income families. S 850 was reported (S Rept 104-94) June 8.

A third piece of the Senate's welfare puzzle was completed June 14 when the Agriculture, Nutrition and Forestry Committee endorsed a plan (S 904) to pare back spending on flood stamps and give states more control over the program. The bill was approved by a largely party-line vote of 11–7.

Widespread Republican dissension over aspects of the welfare overhaul bill forced Senate GOP leaders to delay floor action on the measure for several months. The most serious intraparty disputes were over the distribution of federal funds to states and the absence of provisions aimed at reducing out-of-wedlock births.

Senate Majority Leader Bob Dole, R-Kan., and his aides worked over the summer to rewrite portions of the Senate bill in hopes of appealing to both party moderates and conservatives. In a revised bill (S 1120) unveiled Aug. 4, Dole proposed to continue relying on historical spending patterns for distributing the bulk of federal funds. But he appeased senators from the South and West by setting aside additional money for states that had both high population growth rates and low welfare benefits. In an effort to appeal to conservatives, Dole agreed to give states the explicit option of denying welfare checks to unwed teenage mothers and for children born to welfare recipients.

The Senate debated its version of welfare reform for two weeks before passing it Sept. 19 on a **key vote of 87–12 (R 52–1; D 35–11).**

During floor action, two Democratic alternatives were rejected. But Democrats did join with moderate Republicans to modi-

fy the bill in ways that drew broad, if uneasy, bipartisan support and won praise from Clinton. Chipping away at conservatives' influence, the coalition added more federal money for child care, increased the amount states would have been required to spend on welfare, and rejected a key conservative proposal to replace the bill's optional provision with a mandatory ban on states' use of federal funds for welfare checks to unwed teenage mothers.

Presidential Vetoes

When HR 4 reached conference, the Democrats were largely ignored while Republicans struck a compromise between the House and Senate versions. GOP conferees decided to limit the block grants to cash welfare, child care and certain child protection programs. They also agreed to allow states to decide whether to deny checks to unwed teenage mothers and to children born to welfare recipients. The conference then stalled over the issue of whether states should gain control over the child nutrition programs by receiving their federal funding in block grants.

In the meantime, most of the provisions that conferees had agreed upon in HR 4 were included in the huge budget reconciliation package (HR 2491), which aimed to eliminate the federal deficit by 2002. The welfare provisions, expected to save $81.5 billion from projected spending over seven years, were a critical element of the GOP budget-balancing plan. The package, which cleared Nov. 20, 1995, also included a plan to revamp Medicaid, saving $163 billion over seven years. Clinton vetoed the reconciliation bill Dec. 6. *(Budget reconciliation bill, p. 68; Medicaid, p. 559)*

Conferees on HR 4, the stand-alone welfare bill, finally resolved their dispute, agreeing to allow up to seven states to receive their school lunch and breakfast funding in block grants. The House adopted the conference report (H Rept 104-430) by a 245–178 vote on Dec. 21 and the Senate cleared the bill, 52–47, the following day. The measure was expected to save $58 billion from projected spending over seven years.

But Clinton had made it clear he would veto the bill, and he did so Jan. 9, 1996, saying that while the existing welfare system was "broken and must be fixed," the Republican plan would do "too little to move people from welfare to work." He called on Congress to work with him to produce a bipartisan bill that was "tough on work and responsibility, but not tough on children and on parents who are responsible and who want to work."

GOVERNORS' INPUT

Much as they had in 1988, when a languishing welfare reform effort was jump-started by the nation's governors, led by then-Governor Clinton of Arkansas, in 1996 it was the governors again who revitalized the effort. Meeting in Washington on Feb. 6, the National Governors' Association did what Congress and the president had been unable to do in weeks of budget talks: they reached bipartisan agreement on controversial plans to overhaul welfare and Medicaid. *(1988 welfare legislation, Congress and the Nation Vol. VII, p. 616)*

The governors backed many key aspects of HR 4, including ending the entitlement to welfare. But they called for easing the bill's work requirements and many of its proposed restrictions on social services. For example, they wanted the states to decide whether to use federal money to provide welfare checks for children born to welfare recipients. They also asked for more federal child care money to help welfare recipients get and keep jobs.

But while many on Capitol Hill hailed the governors' achievement, many did not. Liberals decried ending the welfare entitlement, while conservatives complained about the loosening of some restrictions included in the vetoed bills. Still others pointed out that the governors' plan saved far less federal money than the congressional bills would have.

Among the opposition was the Clinton administration. Testifying before the Senate Finance Committee on Feb. 28, Health and Human Services Secretary Donna Shalala announced that the administration could not support the governors' proposal "in its present form."

1996 LEGISLATIVE PROPOSAL

The GOP combined welfare-Medicaid plan (HR 3507, S 1795), unveiled on May 22, 1996, retained the core Republican prescription for welfare—to impose new work requirements and time limits on welfare benefits, end its status as a federal entitlement, and allow states to make most decisions about how it was run while paying some of the tab with federal block grants.

Like HR 4, the new legislation generally required that recipients work within two years of receiving benefits and proposed to cut off their aid after five years. But states would be permitted to exempt up to 20 percent of their caseload from the five-year limit, up from 15 percent in the vetoed bill.

The new bill followed the governors' request to let states decide whether to deny cash assistance to additional children born to welfare recipients. Under HR 4, the states could only use federal funds to provide the aid if they passed legislation to do so.

The measure also included much of the additional child care and contingency funding that the governors requested. Republicans dropped a provision in HR 4 that would have provided less money for less severely disabled children who received SSI benefits. Also dropped were provisions to cap administration and training costs involved in foster care and adoption and to enable up to seven states to receive federal funding for their school meal programs in a block grant.

However, the revised welfare bill contained stricter requirements for states in moving welfare recipients into the workforce than the governors had asked for, including a narrower definition of what would count as "work." It also continued to include sharp reductions in social services for legal immigrants, a policy on which the governors took no position.

HOUSE COMMITTEES

The House Ways and Means Committee approved the welfare provisions under its jurisdiction on a 23–14 vote June 12, 1996. The measure (HR 3507) was supported by all of the Republicans and one Democrat—Gerald D. Kleczka of Wisconsin. The committee considered nearly 30 amendments, defeating most that would have made substantial changes to the bill.

Benjamin L. Cardin, D-Md., offered a substitute that contained a plan Clinton had forwarded to Congress in April. It proposed to retain welfare's entitlement status but place a five-year limit on the receipt of cash benefits. Those who lived in areas with more than 8 percent unemployment and those facing other hardships would be exempt from the limit. The amendment was defeated, 11-24, with all Republicans and three Democrats—Kleczka, L. F. Payne Jr., of Virginia and Pete Stark of California—voting against it.

The panel also considered a modified version of a bipartisan measure (HR 3266) introduced by Michael N. Castle, R-Del., and John Tanner, D-Tenn. The amendment sought to end welfare's entitlement status but authorize more overall funding to the states. It was defeated by voice vote.

Two other House committees worked on the welfare measure. The House Economic and Educational Opportunities Committee approved provisions under its jurisdiction—including welfare-to-work programs, child protection, child care and child nutrition programs—on June 12 by a vote of 23–11. The measure won the support of all the panel's Republicans, joined by five Democrats.

The committee's bill required adults receiving welfare benefits to begin working within two years, and required states to place at least 50 percent of their overall caseload in jobs by 2002. The bill combined seven child-care programs, including those for the working poor as well as for welfare recipients, into the Child Care and Development Block Grant, to be funded at $22 billion over seven years, and sought to combine 11 child protection programs into a single block grant.

Republicans did not include changes to the school lunch program. HR 4 had bogged down at one point in 1995 when House and Senate conferees could not agree on a controversial provision to permit some states to get their school lunch funds in a block grant.

Also working on the bill was the House Agriculture Committee, which gave voice vote approval June 13 to provisions affecting the food stamp program, after turning back Democratic amendments aimed at softening some of the GOP recommendations. The committee-approved draft proposed to scale back food stamp benefits by cutting individual allotments and requiring able-bodied recipients age 18 to 50 who did not have dependents to work. Allotments would be cut by ending all automatic annual increases, except for food benefits. Food benefits would still be linked to inflation, but individual allotments would be cut. The plan was projected to reduce federal spending on food stamps by about $23 billion over six years.

The food stamp provisions were nearly identical to those in HR 4. But unlike HR 4, the latest GOP plan dropped a proposed cap on food stamp spending. Chairman Pat Roberts, R-Kan., called that a concession to the Clinton administration and the governors.

SENATE COMMITTEES

In the Senate, two committees—Finance and Agriculture, Nutrition and Forestry—marked up portions of the welfare provisions.

The Senate Agriculture, Nutrition and Forestry Committee went first, voting 10–7 on June 19 to approve changes to nutrition programs, including food stamps, after agreeing unanimously to a Democratic substitute aimed at softening the proposed GOP cuts. Max Baucus of Montana was the only Democrat to vote with the GOP for final approval.

Like the House's recommendations, the measure proposed to scale back food stamp benefits by cutting individual allotments and requiring able-bodied recipients from age 18 to 50 who did not have dependents to work.

The Finance Committee voted 11–9 on June 26 to simultaneously overhaul the nation's welfare and Medicaid systems. The party-line vote dashed any prospects for bipartisan support of a combined bill.

Finance Committee Chairman William V. Roth Jr., R-Del., had made several modifications in the committee version of S 1795, including increasing the percentage of welfare recipients that states would be required to move into the workforce, up to at least 50 percent by 2002. Committee aides said that many of Roth's changes were similar to those made by House committees.

The panel defeated, by identical votes of 10–10, two amendments by John B. Breaux, D-La., to provide vouchers redeemable for goods and services to children of welfare recipients who exceeded the time limit on benefits. One amendment would have required vouchers to be provided in any state that imposed a time limit of less than five years and would have permitted them in other states. The other would have allowed states to provide the vouchers to those who exceeded the five-year time limit.

Also defeated was an amendment offered by Baucus to strip the Medicaid provisions from the bill. Six of the committee's nine Democrats voted against the amendment. Three of them—Moynihan, Bill Bradley of New Jersey and Carol Moseley-Braun of Illinois—had voted against the Senate version of HR 4 and indicated that they saw little hope for reaching a bipartisan agreement on welfare in 1996.

Three other Democrats—John D. Rockefeller IV of West Virginia, Bob Graham of Florida and David Pryor of Arkansas—were thought to be among the larger group of Senate Democrats eager to reach a consensus with the GOP. But Rockefeller said he saw little hope of agreeing on welfare with Republicans. He accused them of "pure, classic meanness" after they defeated the amendments to provide vouchers to children whose parents exceeded the time limit on benefits.

After insisting for months that they would not separate welfare and Medicaid, GOP leaders decided the week of July 8 to jettison the Medicaid provisions and move a welfare-only bill in both chambers. GOP leaders said they would still move the welfare measure as a reconciliation bill, giving it procedural protections that included immunity from a filibuster in the Senate.

The new GOP strategy forced Democrats to reassess their plans. Having dismissed the joint welfare-Medicaid bill out of hand, they now had to reevaluate it strictly on the policies and politics of welfare.

Some Democrats, led by Moynihan, rejected the whole premise of the GOP effort to end an individual's entitlement to welfare checks. Others had more specific concerns, such as denying social services to legal immigrants, restraining food stamp spending, or not providing enough federal and state money to ensure that welfare recipients could get jobs or that states could handle an economic recession.

Many Democrats wanted assurances that vouchers redeemable for goods and services would be available under certain circumstances to the children of welfare recipients who lost their eligibility for cash aid.

Meanwhile, the bill was rushed to the floor of both the House and Senate.

HOUSE FLOOR ACTION

The House acted first, passing the welfare-only bill (HR 3734) July 18 on a 256–170 vote. The bill had been reported (H Rept 104-651) by the House Budget Committee June 27.

Republican leaders left little to chance, permitting members to vote on only two amendments July 18. One was a successful GOP proposal to further restrict food stamp eligibility. The other was an unsuccessful Democratic substitute.

Republicans had made several changes to the bill since committee action, including adding Medicaid to the list of social services for which most legal immigrants—including those already residing in the United States—would be ineligible.

The food stamp amendment, sponsored by Bob Ney, R-Ohio, proposed to limit adults without dependents to three months of food stamps throughout their adult lives until age 50. Exceptions would be granted in those months in which recipients worked at least half the time or were in a workfare slot. The original bill would have allowed those food stamp recipients to receive the benefits for four months each year. It was approved by a vote of 239–184.

The Democratic substitute, which failed on a vote of 168–258, was actually the bipartisan Castle-Tanner bill (HR 3832, formerly HR 3266) that had been rejected by the Ways and Means Committee. Like the GOP bill, Castle-Tanner proposed to end the federal guarantee of welfare benefits, but it included several significant differences. It called for providing more federal funds to help states meet the work requirements and cope with economic downturns; at the same time, states would be required to spend more of their own money on welfare. States also would be required to provide vouchers to children whose parents exceeded the time limit if the limit was less than five years. All states could have provided vouchers after five years.

Supporters touted endorsement of the Castle-Tanner measure by Clinton, adding that their approach was more likely to help welfare recipients get jobs than the GOP plan and that it would protect children from their parents' mistakes. Tanner said the voucher provision was especially important because "holding a 3-year-old child to a standard of a 33-year-old parent is just wrong; it's not welfare reform." But an aggressive lobbying effort by House GOP leaders was successful—only nine Republicans ended up voting for the plan.

While Clinton kept everyone guessing about his view on the bill—in public he praised it even as his aides insisted on changes—it was the Senate's turn to consider the measure.

SENATE FLOOR ACTION

The Senate passed HR 3734 on July 23 by a vote of 74–24, after substituting the text of its own welfare bill (S 1956), which had been reported by the Senate Budget Committee July 16. The focus throughout the floor debate was on how many Democrats would support the bill. The final vote reflected their ambivalence: 23 Democrats voted for the bill and 23 opposed it, including Minority Leader Tom Daschle, D-S.D.

A core group of opponents, led by Moynihan, had decided in 1995 to work against any bill that would end the federal guarantee of a welfare check. Their ranks seemed to grow as more Democrats expressed concern about the proposed cuts in food stamps and aid to legal immigrants.

But other Democrats were eager to reach an accord with Republicans, and their resolve seemed to strengthen as the November elections neared. As occurred the previous September, Paul Wellstone of Minnesota was the only Democrat seeking reelection in 1996 who voted against the bill.

The Senate began its deliberations July 18, giving voice vote approval to a Trent Lott, R-Miss., amendment that removed the controversial Medicaid provisions. Senators then rejected the Democratic substitute to the bill, offered by Daschle, on a 46–53 party-line vote.

Democrats presented their alternative as being more stringent on work requirements for adult welfare recipients, while providing more of a safety net for children. They wanted to provide more money to states than the GOP bill, and they proposed requiring recipients to participate in community service programs after three months on welfare. Families would face a five-year limit on cash benefits, as under the GOP bill, but states would be required to offer noncash assistance to children after that.

Democrats focused much of their attention on the bill's impact on children, arguing that the GOP plan would have dire and unintended consequences. "No child asked to be here," Moynihan said. "Why then are we determined to punish them?"

Republicans argued as they had throughout the 104th Congress that no welfare system could be crueler to children than the existing one. "All of this concern here expressed for children has not panned out in reality as a cure for the problems of children," said Rick Santorum, R-Pa.

The bill became more palatable to Democrats and moderate Republicans with the approval July 23 of two key amendments—on Medicaid eligibility and food stamps.

The first amendment, by John H. Chafee, R-R.I., retained existing Medicaid eligibility requirements. Under existing law, cash welfare recipients were eligible for Medicaid. But because states would be able to create their own welfare eligibility requirements under the bill, Medicaid eligibility could have changed, too. The bill would have guaranteed Medicaid coverage only to pregnant women and to children under age 13. Chafee's amendment, approved by voice vote, extended Medicaid coverage in the bill to nonpregnant women and children ages 13–18, assuring that even if states changed their welfare eligibility, Medicaid requirements would remain unchanged. The

key action on Chafee's amendment had come earlier that day when the Senate rejected, 31–68, an attempt by Roth to limit Chafee's guarantees to welfare recipients who were receiving Medicaid at the time.

Democrats and moderate Republicans also teamed up behind an amendment by Kent Conrad, D-N.D., to strike bill language that would have allowed certain states to gain control over their food stamp program by receiving the federal money in a block grant. The amendment was approved 53–45.

As they had in 1995, Democrats also invoked the so-called Byrd rule to strike some sections of the bill. The rule, named after its author, Sen. Robert C. Byrd, D-W.Va., generally prohibited provisions in a reconciliation bill that were not germane to deficit reduction. The rule could only be waived by a 60-vote majority.

Among provisions dropped under the Byrd rule was the family cap, which would have prohibited the use of federal welfare funds for children born to welfare recipients unless authorized by separate state legislation. The language was the same as in the House bill and HR 4. An attempt by Budget Committee Chairman Pete V. Domenici, R-N.M., to waive the Byrd rule fell 42–57, far short of 60 votes needed.

But Democrats suffered setbacks, as well, including two separate votes July 23 rejecting an amendment by Wendell H. Ford, D-Ky., to allow federal welfare funds to be used for vouchers for families of welfare recipients who exceeded their five-year time limits. Republicans had argued throughout the debate that such vouchers would undermine the time limits. The Senate rejected the amendment by a 48–51 vote and then tabled (killed) a motion to reconsider by a 50–49 vote.

CONFERENCE, FINAL ACTION

Congressional negotiators began working to reconcile the House and Senate welfare bills July 25 on the assumption that Clinton would sign something similar to the version that had passed the Senate with bipartisan support.

But Clinton urged Republicans to moderate the legislation beyond the Senate's version, saying, "You can put wings on a pig, but you don't make it an eagle." He was particularly concerned about proposed cuts in food stamps and aid to legal immigrants. And he wanted to let states use federal welfare money to provide noncash benefits to children whose parents exceeded the time limit on benefits.

Senate Majority Leader Lott and House Speaker Newt Gingrich, R-Ga., however, declared themselves satisfied with their proposals. The GOP leaders vowed in a July 24 letter to Clinton that they would "not support any further changes that result in the passage of a weak welfare reform bill."

Clinton was under conflicting pressures from within Democratic ranks. Moderates urged him to sign a bill and fulfill his 1992 campaign promise. Liberals, arguing that the bill was fatally flawed, lined up for one last push against the legislation. On July 29, representatives of more than a dozen organizations, including civil rights, religious and low-income advocacy groups, urged Clinton to veto the bill.

The conference report (H Rept 104-725) was filed late during the night of July 30. Among the last changes was a decision to deny states the chance to take over their food stamp programs through block grants. Negotiators also modified provisions limiting food stamps for able-bodied, 18-to-50-year-olds without dependents who did not work.

After some dispute, they agreed to guarantee that Medicaid would remain available for anyone who met the existing welfare eligibility requirements. And they gave states the option to deny Medicaid to legal immigrants already in the United States.

They rebuffed Clinton's call to permit states to use federal welfare block grant money to give noncash benefits to children whose parents exceeded the five-year limit on benefits. But they allowed states to provide the vouchers from federal social services block grant funds.

For the first time, Republicans included Democrats in deliberations to reconcile the House and Senate versions of the welfare bill. But they left little doubt who was in charge. No Democrats were invited to a July 30 news conference called to reveal aspects of the conference agreement.

As details of the conference agreement emerged, more Democrats—eager to satisfy the public's yearning to change the welfare system, especially in an election year—found themselves drawn to it even as they acknowledged its shortcomings.

For days, Clinton seemed to be leaning toward signing the bill, but he did not make the decision until after a dramatic meeting with top advisers the morning of July 31. The meeting occurred as the House prepared for its final debate with many Democrats still uncertain how to vote. Attention shifted from the Capitol to the White House as members from both parties focused on Clinton's televised announcement. "Today, we have a historic opportunity to make welfare what it was meant to be: a second chance, not a way of life," Clinton said. "So, I will sign this bill—first and foremost because the current system is broken."

The endorsement quickly led to charges of betrayal from the left. Children's Defense Fund President Marian Wright Edelman, a prominent friend and supporter of Clinton's during the 1992 campaign, said Clinton's signature "makes a mockery of his pledge not to hurt children. It will leave a moral blot on his presidency and on our nation." Edelman's husband, Peter, a top adviser at HHS, quit his post in protest of the president's decision.

But Clinton's endorsement also made passage of the final bill a certainty. The House adopted the conference agreement in a **key vote of 328–101 (R 230–2; D 98–98; I 0–1)**, on July 31. The Senate cleared the legislation the next day, on a **key vote of 78–21 (R 53–0; D 25–21)**. *(1996 key votes, p. 1047)*

MAJOR PROVISIONS

Following are major provisions of HR 3734, as signed into law Aug. 22, 1996.

Welfare

The new law ended the federal guarantee of providing welfare checks to all eligible mothers and children. Instead, states were allowed to create their own welfare programs within certain federal restrictions, such as new work requirements and time limits on welfare benefits. Provisions of the bill:

State Plans

Created block grants for temporary assistance for needy families (TANF) to replace Title IV-A of the Social Security Act, which provided Aid to Families with Dependent Children (AFDC). Individuals and families were no longer entitled to benefits if they met the existing eligibility requirements.

Each state was required to file a plan with the secretary of health and human services (HHS) every two years that:

• Explained how it would serve all of the state's political subdivisions.

• Explained how it would require and ensure that parents and caretakers who received block grant assistance engaged in work activities within two months of receiving benefits.

• Established goals to prevent and reduce out-of-wedlock pregnancies.

• Explained whether the state intended to treat families moving into the state differently from other residents and how it would do that.

• Explained whether it intended to provide aid to noncitizens.

• Established criteria for delivering benefits and determining eligibility, and for providing fair and equitable treatment. The plan also had to explain how the state would provide an administrative appeals process for recipients.

• Required a parent or caretaker who was not engaged in work or exempt from work requirements and who had received assistance for more than two months to participate in community service. A state could opt out of this requirement if the governor sent a letter to the HHS secretary.

• Provided education and training on statutory rape, and expanded teenage pregnancy prevention programs to include men.

Each state also was required to certify that it would:

• Operate a child support enforcement program.

• Operate a foster care and adoption assistance program and ensure medical assistance for the children involved.

• Specify which state agencies would administer the welfare plan, and provide assurances that local governments and private sector organizations had been consulted on it.

• Provide Native Americans with equitable access to assistance.

• Establish standards to combat fraud and abuse.

• At state option, establish procedures to identify recipients with a history of domestic violence, and refer them to counseling and supportive services.

Funding

• **Federal Funds.** Authorized $16.4 billion annually from fiscal 1996 through fiscal 2001 for the new block grant to states. States were required to convert to block grants by July 1, 1997, and could choose to do so earlier.

Money was to be distributed to each state based on its federal funding for AFDC benefits and administration, emergency assistance, and the Job Opportunities and Basic Skills (JOBS) program in either fiscal 1995, fiscal 1994 or the average of fiscal 1992–1994, whichever was higher.

• **State Spending.** Required that to receive their full share of federal welfare funds in fiscal 1997–2001, states spend at least 75 percent of the state funds they spent in fiscal 1994 on AFDC benefits and administration, emergency assistance, JOBS, AFDC-related child care and at-risk child care. States that did not place the required percentage of welfare recipients into the workforce as stipulated by the legislation would be required to spend at least 80 percent of the funds spent in fiscal 1994. States would lose $1 in federal funding for each $1 they fell short of this requirement.

The following expenditures counted toward the requirement:

• State spending on programs created by the block grant for eligible families for cash and child care assistance; educational activities designed to increase self-sufficiency, job training and work (excluding most expenditures on public education); administrative costs (up to 15 percent of total qualified state expenditures); and any other funds used to accomplish the block grant's purposes. This also applied to state spending on block grant programs for those who lost their welfare eligibility because of the five-year time limit or the legislation's treatment of noncitizens.

• Spending on other state or local programs that benefited families who were eligible for the above activities if the amount spent exceeded the 1994 level.

• **Transferring Funds.** Allowed states to transfer up to 30 percent of funds paid under this block grant to the child care block grant or the social services block grant. However, states could not transfer more than 10 percent of the welfare block grant to the social services block grant. Also, money transferred into the social services block grant had to be spent on services to children and families whose incomes did not exceed 200 percent of the poverty level, as determined annually by the Office of Management and Budget.

• **Use of Funds.** Permitted states to use their welfare block grant funds "in any manner reasonably calculated to accomplish the purposes" of the program. That included activities authorized at the time of enactment under AFDC and the JOBS program, as well as those that helped low-income households with heating and cooling costs.

States could also opt to:

• Carry over funds to provide assistance in future years under the block grant.

• Pay or give vouchers to job placement services.

• Use an electronic benefits transfer (EBT) system for distributing welfare benefits.

• Fund individual development accounts established by recipients for postsecondary education expenses, first-home purchases and business capitalization.

• Provide newcomers from another state the same benefits the families would have received in their former state for up to 12 months.

• **Administrative Expenses.** Prohibited states from spending more than 15 percent of their welfare block grant on administration. Money for information technology and computerization needed to monitor the program was exempted from this cap.

• **Additional Federal Funds.** Authorized several additional sources of federal funds for the states. They were:

• **Out-of-Wedlock Births.** Financial incentives for states that demonstrated the largest decline in the proportion of out-of-wedlock births without increasing abortions. Between fiscal 1999 and 2002, the five states that best met this criterion were to receive $20 million each. If fewer than five states were eligible for this bonus, the grant would be $25 million each.

• **Supplemental Grant.** A supplemental grant, available between fiscal 1998 and 2001, for states with above-average population growth and below-average welfare benefits per recipient.

States that had particularly low welfare benefit payments in fiscal 1994 or particularly high population growth between April 1, 1990, and July 1, 1994, automatically qualified for the grant. Eligible states were to receive an additional 2.5 percent of the federal funds they received in fiscal 1994 for AFDC and related programs. The bill appropriated $800 million over four years for this fund. If that was insufficient, pro rata reductions were to be made to each qualifying state.

• **High Performance Grants.** A total of $1 billion in bonuses from fiscal 1999 to 2003 for states that were most successful in meeting the legislation's goals (such as moving welfare recipients into the workplace and reducing out-of-wedlock birth rates). The formula for measuring state performance and making the awards was to be developed by the HHS secretary after consulting with the National Governors' Association and the American Public Welfare Association.

• **Contingency Fund.** A total of $2 billion from fiscal 1997 to 2001 available to states with high unemployment or rapidly growing food stamp rolls. Eligible states had to continue to maintain 100 percent of their fiscal 1994 welfare expenditures. They also had to meet one of two criteria.

The first was to have an unemployment rate at least 6.5 percent in the most recent three-month period and at least 10 percent higher than the comparable quarter in either of the two preceding years.

The second was to have at least 10 percent more food stamp recipients in the most recent three-month period than the average number of recipients in the comparable quarter of fiscal 1994 or fiscal 1995 (whichever was lower). Adjustments in the calculation would be made to account for the legislation's impact on the food stamp caseload.

• **Loan Fund.** A $1.7 billion revolving loan fund available to states from fiscal 1997 through 2001. States could borrow up to 10 percent of their annual block grant, and they had to repay the loans, with interest, within three years. States that incurred penalties under the cash welfare block grant would be ineligible for a loan.

Work Requirements

Adults receiving benefits under the block grant were required to begin working within two years of receiving aid.

States could develop individual responsibility plans that set employment goals, the individual's obligations and the services the state would provide. States could reduce assistance to families that included an individual who did not comply with these plans.

- **Work Participation Rates.** Required states to have a certain percentage of their welfare caseload participating in work activities, starting at 25 percent in fiscal 1997 and rising to 50 percent in fiscal 2002.

A state's annual participation rate would be set at the average participation rate for each month in the fiscal year. The state's monthly participation rate would be the number of families receiving assistance that included an adult or minor head of household who was working, divided by the number of families receiving assistance (excluding those who had been subject to a recent penalty for refusing to work).

A state's required participation rate for a year would be reduced by the same percentage that it reduced its average monthly welfare caseload below fiscal year 1995 levels. However, those caseload reductions would not be considered if they were required by federal law—such as when recipients exceeded the five-year time limit on benefits—or resulted from changes in state eligibility criteria.

The work participation rates for the entire caseload were:

- Fiscal 1997: 25 percent.
- Fiscal 1998: 30 percent.
- Fiscal 1999: 35 percent.
- Fiscal 2000: 40 percent.
- Fiscal 2001: 45 percent.
- Fiscal 2002 and thereafter: 50 percent.

States also had to meet higher participation rates for two-parent families that received cash assistance, as follows:

- Fiscal 1996: 50 percent.
- Fiscal 1997–1998: 75 percent.
- Fiscal 1999 and thereafter: 90 percent.

- **State Options.** Allowed states to:

- Count those who received assistance under tribal family assistance in the work participation calculation.
- Count toward meeting the work requirement single parents with a child under age six, if the parent worked at least 20 hours per week.
- Exempt from the work requirement and the participation rates a parent of a child under age one. However, a parent could receive this exemption only for a total of 12 months, regardless of whether they were consecutive.

- **Work Activities.** Required that individuals engage in one or more of the following activities for a state to count them toward the work participation rate:

- Unsubsidized employment.
- Subsidized private sector employment.
- Subsidized public sector employment.
- Work experience if sufficient private sector employment was unavailable.

- On-the-job training.
- Job search and job readiness assistance for up to six weeks, no more than four weeks of which could be consecutive. Individuals in states with unemployment rates at least 50 percent above the national average could engage in these activities for up to 12 weeks.
- Community service programs.
- Vocational educational training, for up to one year. (No more than 20 percent of all families could count toward the work rate by participating in vocational education.)
- Jobs skills training directly related to employment.
- Education directly related to employment, for a recipient who lacked a high school diploma or equivalency and was under age 20.
- Satisfactory attendance at a secondary school, for a recipient who had not completed high school and was under age 20.
- Providing child care to another welfare recipient who was engaged in community service programs.

No more than 20 percent of all families could count toward the work rate by participating in vocational education, education directly related to employment, or secondary school.

- **Hours.** Required that to count toward the work participation rate, individuals work a minimum number of hours per week, as follows:

- Fiscal 1996–1998: 20 hours.
- Fiscal 1999: 25 hours.
- Fiscal 2000 and thereafter: 30 hours.

The primary wage earner in a two-parent family was required to work at least 35 hours per week to count toward the work participation rate.

Both parents in a two-parent family were required to engage in work activities if they also received federally funded child care. Exceptions would be granted in cases where one parent was disabled or caring for a severely disabled child.

- **Individual Penalties.** Required a state to reduce assistance to a family by at least the same pro rata percentage that an adult family member refused to work as required under the welfare block grant. Thus, someone who missed work 20 percent of the time would receive 20 percent less aid. A state could waive the penalty for good cause and other reasons established by the state.

A state also could terminate assistance to adults who refused to work, and end their Medicaid coverage—though Medicaid coverage would continue for their children.

A state could not penalize a single parent caring for a child under age six if the parent proved he or she failed to work because child care was unavailable.

- **State Penalties.** Reduced a state's block grant by 5 percent if it failed to meet the work requirements. Subsequent failures would result in an additional 2 percent reduction per year, reaching 7 percent the second year and 9 percent the third year, rising to a maximum deduction of 21 percent. However, the HHS secretary could reduce the penalty based on the degree of noncompliance, or if the state had a high unemployment rate or rapidly growing food stamp rolls as defined in criteria for the contingency fund.

Restrictions on Aid

- **Children.** Specified that only families with a minor child (who resided with a custodial parent or other adult relative) or a pregnant woman could receive assistance from the grant.
- **Time Limit.** Prohibited the use of block grant funds for adults who had received welfare for more than five years, although those who exceeded the time limit could still qualify for other federal, state and local funds. The time limit applied only to those who were the head of a household or the spouse of a household head. (Children could qualify later for five years of aid as parents, no matter how many years they got as children.)

The time limit also applied only to benefits received after the state accepted its welfare block grant.

States could exempt up to 20 percent of their caseload from the five-year time limit. They also could opt to impose a shorter time limit.

- **Paternity.** Reduced a family's benefits by at least 25 percent if parents did not cooperate in establishing paternity or in assisting a child support enforcement agency. States could choose to eliminate their benefit entirely. States also could exempt parents from these responsibilities for good cause.
- **Drug Abuse.** Denied welfare benefits and food stamps to individuals convicted of a felony offense for possessing, using or distributing an illegal drug. Family members or dependents of the individual would still be eligible for aid. Those penalized for drug abuse would still be eligible for emergency benefits, including emergency medical services. States could opt out of this prohibition if they passed legislation to do so.
- **Fraud.** Denied aid from the family assistance grant for 10 years to any person convicted of fraudulently misrepresenting his or her residence to obtain benefits in two or more states from the welfare grant, Medicaid, food stamps or Supplemental Security Income.
- **Unwed Teenagers.** Allowed unmarried parents under age 18 to qualify for block grant funds only if they attended high school or an alternative educational or training program and if they lived with a parent or in an adult-supervised setting.
- **State Options.** Gave states the option of choosing to:
  - Deny welfare assistance to children born to welfare recipients.
  - Deny welfare to all unwed parents under age 18.
  - Provide newcomers from another state the same benefits the families would have received from their former state for up to 12 months.

State Penalties

If a state's welfare block grant was reduced because of one of the following penalties, it would have to replace the penalized federal funds during the next fiscal year with state funds. The penalties were:

- Unauthorized use of block grant funds: repay amount used and, if the violation was intentional, repay an additional 5 percent of the state's quarterly block grant payments.

- Failure to submit a required report within one month of the end of each fiscal quarter: 4 percent of the annual block grant, to be rescinded if the state submitted the report before the end of the next fiscal quarter.
- Failure to satisfy minimum work participation rates: 5 percent of the block grant, plus an additional 2 percent each year for consecutive failures, up to a maximum of 21 percent.
- Failure to use an income and eligibility verification system: up to 2 percent of the annual block grant.
- Failure to enforce penalties sought by a child support agency: up to 5 percent of the block grant.
- Failure to repay a federal loan in a timely fashion: a reduction of the block grant by the amount of the outstanding loan, plus interest.
- Failure to maintain the proper percentage of state spending as required by the legislation: $1 reduction in the block grant for each $1 the state fell below the requirement for state spending.
- Failure of a state child support enforcement program to comply with federal law: for the first finding of noncompliance, a reduction of between 1 and 2 percent of a quarterly block grant payment; for the second consecutive finding of noncompliance, between 2 and 3 percent of the next quarterly payment; for the third or subsequent findings, between 3 and 5 percent.
- Failure to maintain 100 percent of state fiscal 1994 welfare expenditures when receiving money from the contingency fund: repay money received.
- Failure to provide benefits to single adult parents who had custody over their children but could not obtain child care for them, up to age six: up to 5 percent of the block grant.
- Failure to comply with the five-year time limit on benefits: 5 percent of the annual block grant.

Related Provisions

States also had to continue to provide Medicaid to those who would have been eligible for AFDC if that program were still in effect.

- **Federal Waivers.** Allowed states that previously received waivers of federal laws and regulations to conduct experimental welfare programs to continue those programs until the waivers expired.
- **Workforce Reduction.** Required HHS to reduce the number of positions within the department by 245 full-time equivalent positions—including 60 managerial positions—related to the conversion of several federal programs into the block grant.
- **Charitable and Religious Organizations.** Allowed states to provide family assistance services (as well as services under SSI, foster care, adoption assistance and independent living programs) by contracting with charitable, religious or private organizations.

Supplemental Security Income

The bill made it more difficult for disabled children to qualify for Supplemental Security Income (SSI), which provided cash assistance to the low-income aged, blind and disabled. The Congressional Budget Office estimated that about 315,000 children, or 22 percent, who would otherwise be receiving SSI in 2002 would lose their eligibility as a result of the legislation.

Provisions of the SSI section of the bill:

Disabled Children

- **Definition.** Denied SSI eligibility to a child under age 18 with an impairment of "comparable severity" to what would be considered a work disability in an adult.

The bill redefined a childhood disability to require that the child have a "medically determinable physical or mental impairment, which results in marked and severe functional limitations." As in prior law, this disability had to be expected to result in death or to last more than 12 months.

- **Assessments.** Eliminated an Individualized Functional Assessment (IFA) as a standard by which children could qualify for SSI. Under prior law, the Social Security Administration first determined whether a child was eligible for SSI by deciding whether he or she met or exceeded a "Listing of Impairments." A child who did not meet that test could still qualify for SSI through an easier-to-reach determination, known as an IFA, that analyzed whether a child's mental, physical and social functioning was substantially lower than children of the same age.

With elimination of the IFA as a standard, children could qualify for SSI only through the more stringent "Listing of Impairments." The legislation also eliminated references to "maladaptive behavior" when determining a child's personal and behavioral functioning.

- **Effective Date.** Gave the Social Security Administration one year after the law's enactment to decide whether children on SSI at the time of enactment met the new, more restrictive standard for determining SSI eligibility. Existing recipients would continue receiving SSI benefits until either July 1, 1997, or the date of redetermination, whichever was later.

- **Redeterminations.** Generally required the Social Security Administration to reevaluate the eligibility of each child who received SSI at least once every three years. Children whose medical condition was not expected to improve were generally exempted from a redetermination. At the time of the review, the child's parent or guardian had to present evidence showing that the child was receiving treatment that was medically necessary.

For children who qualified for SSI based on a low birthweight, reviews had to occur one year after birth.

Children who qualified for SSI had to have their eligibility redetermined using the criteria for an adult within one year after their 18th birthday.

The bill authorized an additional $150 million in fiscal 1997 and $100 million in 1998 to help the Social Security Administration conduct more continuing disability reviews and redeterminations. It also lifted the limits on discretionary spending to allow for the additional money.

- **Savings Account.** Required a child's parent or guardian to establish a separate savings account for any past-due SSI payments that exceeded six times the maximum monthly payment. The money could be used to cover specific expenses such as ed-

ucation or job skills training, special equipment or housing modifications and medical treatment.

- **Private Insurance.** Limited children who were hospitalized and whose medical costs were covered by private insurance to no more than the $30 monthly SSI benefit paid to children whose medical bills were covered by Medicaid.

Other SSI Provisions

- **Multistate Benefits.** Denied SSI benefits for 10 years to anyone convicted of fraudulently trying to get benefits from two or more states for several social service programs—including food stamps, welfare and SSI.

- **Fugitive Felons.** Denied eligibility for SSI to anyone fleeing to avoid prosecution, custody or confinement after being convicted of a felony or who violated probation or parole.

- **Prisoners.** Authorized financial incentives to state and local prisons and jails for reporting to the Social Security Administration inmates who fraudulently received SSI benefits. The correctional institution would receive $400 for each such prisoner who lost eligibility if the information was provided within 30 days of the inmate's arrival. The institution would receive $200 if the information was provided within 30 to 90 days.

- **Large Past-Due Payments.** Provided that an individual who was eligible for past-due SSI benefits in excess of 12 times the maximum monthly benefit payable to an eligible individual (at the time, $470) or couple ($705) would generally be paid in three installments at six-month intervals, rather than in a lump sum. The first and second installments could not exceed 12 times the maximum monthly payable benefit.

Child Support Enforcement

The bill put in place new procedures to establish paternity and enforce child support orders. Provisions of the bill:

Distribution of Payments

- Changed the way child support payments—and overdue payments known as arrearages—were disbursed to welfare recipients.

Under prior law, welfare recipients had to assign to the state the right to collect child support payments and any past-due payments on their behalf. The first $50 of monthly child support payments collected had to be given to the family as a "pass-through," without affecting the family's welfare eligibility or benefits. Next, the federal and state governments were reimbursed for their AFDC benefits paid to the family that month. If there was any money left, the family received it up to the amount of the existing month's child support. Any money beyond that paid arrearages, first to the state and federal governments, then to the family.

The legislation changed this structure in several ways:

- Beginning Oct. 1, 1997, child support received for arrearages that had accumulated after the family left welfare was to be paid to the family before the state could use that money to reimburse itself or the federal government.

- Beginning Oct. 1, 2000, child support received for arrearages that had accumulated before the family went on welfare was also to be paid to the family before the state could use the money to reimburse itself or the federal government. However, this provision was to be rescinded if Congress decided, based on an HHS study, that providing the money to the family first had not helped to keep people off welfare.

Exempted from both of these changes were child support arrearages collected by intercepting tax refunds.

The legislation gave states the option to "pass-through" the first $50 of any child support collected on behalf of a family on welfare, but no longer required it. If states chose this option, the federal government would still have to be paid its share of the child support.

Locating and Tracking Cases

• **State Registries.** Required states to create a central case registry to track the status of all child-support orders created or modified after Oct. 1, 1998. The registry would record basic information about both parents involved in a child support order, including their names, Social Security numbers, dates of birth and case identification numbers. Information was to be regularly updated and shared with other entities such as a federal case registry.

• **State Disbursement Units.** Required states to operate a centralized disbursement unit by Oct. 1, 1998. This entity would collect child support from employers who withheld an employee's child support obligations, noncustodial parents, and other states that were collecting money from a parent in their state. The unit would also distribute the money to custodial parents.

• **State Directory of New Hires.** Generally required states to establish a "new hire" registry by Oct. 1, 1997, to which employers would have to send the name, address and Social Security number of all new employees. States would compare information on new hires with the state and national registries of child support orders. The information also had to be used to establish paternity as well as to create, modify and enforce child support obligations. And it had to be shared with the state agency administering welfare, Medicaid, unemployment compensation, food stamps and SSI to verify individuals' income eligibility.

• **Income Withholding.** Required states to enact laws to ensure that child support orders issued or modified before Oct. 1, 1996, that were not otherwise subject to income withholding immediately became subject to income withholding if arrearages occurred.

• **Federal Parent Locator Service.** Expanded the Federal Parent Locator Service, which helped states and parents enforce support orders, to include a federal registry of child support orders and a national directory of new hires. Information in these two registries would be provided by states. It would be used to identify and locate parents subject to child support orders and to establish paternity. The legislation called for confidentiality in cases involving domestic violence or child abuse.

• **Social Security Numbers.** To assist in tracking child support orders, required that Social Security numbers be listed on applications for professional licenses, commercial driver's licenses, occupational licenses and marriage licenses. States also were required to list Social Security numbers in divorce decrees, child support orders, paternity determinations and death notices.

Uniform Procedures

• **State Laws.** Required states to adopt a model state law for handling interstate child support cases. The Uniform Interstate Family Support Act, developed in 1992 by the National Conference of Commissioners on State Uniform Laws, was designed to deal with desertion and nonsupport cases across state lines. It ensured that only one child support order from a court or agency would be in effect at any given time and helped eliminate jurisdictional disputes between states.

• **Interstate Cases.** Revised a federal law that restricted a state court's ability to modify a support order issued by another state unless the child and the custodial parent had moved there or had agreed to the modification. Among the revisions were those that clarified the definition of a child's home state and clarified the rules regarding which child support orders states had to honor when there was more than one order.

• **Forms.** Required the HHS secretary to issue standardized forms that states would have to use for income withholding, imposing liens and issuing administrative subpoenas in interstate cases.

• **Expedited Procedures.** Required states to adopt procedures giving the state child support agency the authority to enforce an order without having to first obtain an order from a court or other administrative entity.

States had to be able to: order genetic testing; issue subpoenas to obtain necessary information; require all entities in the state to provide information on employment, compensation and benefits of any employee or contractor; obtain access to a series of public and private records; change the name of the payee on the order or require income withholding when appropriate; intercept unemployment or workers' compensation, other state benefits, settlements, lottery winnings, assets held by financial institutions, and public and private retirement funds; gain access to public and private retirement funds to help pay past-due support; impose liens to force the sale of property, and automatically increase the monthly support due to include past-due payments.

Establishing Paternity

• **State Laws.** Amended existing laws to improve states' ability to establish paternity. Among the changes were requirements that:

• States permit paternity establishment at least until the child reached age 18.

• The child and other parties undergo genetic testing if a party involved in the case requested it and circumstances warranted it.

• Each state have procedures that allow men to voluntarily acknowledge paternity through a simple civil process and through hospitals.

• The HHS secretary issue regulations governing services whereby fathers could voluntarily acknowledge paternity.

States had to include the basic elements in their own such forms.

• Each state set up procedures under which a signed acknowledgment of paternity was considered a legal judgment after 60 days. Beyond that date, the paternity acknowledgment could be challenged only on the basis of fraud, duress or mistake of fact.

• Voluntary acknowledgments and adjudications of paternity be filed with the state registry of birth records and compared with the child support case registry.

• The Social Security numbers of both parents be used on voluntary acknowledgments of paternity.

• **Welfare Recipients.** Expanded existing requirements that individuals applying for welfare cooperate with the state in establishing paternity and child support orders. If the individual did not cooperate, states had to reduce the family's cash assistance benefit by at least 25 percent and could choose to eliminate it.

Administration

• **Funding.** Continued the practice of reimbursing state child support expenses so that the federal government paid 66 percent and states spent 34 percent. However, the HHS secretary was directed to revise the existing system of incentive payments in which states earned an additional 6 to 10 percent of federal matching aid, depending on the effectiveness of their child support enforcement.

• **Central Unit.** Required states to begin operating a centralized system to collect and disburse child support and to monitor and enforce child support collections by Oct. 1, 1998. States that processed payments through local courts could continue to do so until Sept. 30, 1999.

• **Technical Assistance.** Allowed the HHS secretary to set aside 1 percent of the federal share of child support collections obtained from families on welfare and use it to provide technical assistance to states.

• **Case Reviews.** Required states to review—and, where appropriate, adjust—child support orders at least once every three years or when either parent requested it. States could choose to review the orders on an individual basis, adjust them for inflation or use automated methods.

• **Health Care Coverage.** Required health insurance plans governed by the Employee Retirement Income Security Act (ERISA) to recognize child support orders issued by administrative agencies as well as by courts. The aim was to help custodial parents get their children covered by health plans provided by a noncustodial parent's employer.

The legislation also required that new employers of a noncustodial parent be notified by a state agency if the noncustodial parent was, as part of a support order, providing health care coverage of the child in the previous job. This notice would be used to enroll the child in the noncustodial parent's new health plan.

• **Visitation.** Authorized up to $10 million annually to help states provide access and visitation programs for noncustodial parents. Potential programs included mediation, counseling, education and visitation enforcement.

Enforcement

• **Federal Employees.** Clarified that federal employees were covered by federal child support laws. The bill also made a wider range of income sources subject to being used to satisfy child support obligations, including insurance benefits, retirement pay, survivor's benefits, veteran's benefits and workers' compensation.

• **Armed Forces.** Required the secretary of defense to keep an updated central record of addresses of military personnel, and to share the information with the Federal Parent Locator Service. The secretary of each military department was required to issue regulations to grant leave to military personnel so that they could attend hearings related to paternity establishment or child support orders.

• **Work Requirement.** Required states to adopt procedures giving them the authority to order (or request that a court order) an individual who owed past-due child support for a child on welfare to either pay the overdue support according to a plan approved by the court or child support agency or to participate in work activities.

• **Licenses.** Required states to adopt procedures giving them the authority to suspend driver's licenses, professional licenses, occupational licenses and recreational licenses of anyone who owed past due child support.

• **Passports.** Required the federal government to have procedures to deny, revoke or restrict the passport of anyone who owed more than $5,000 in past-due child support as of Oct. 1, 1997.

• **International Cases.** Allowed the secretary of state, after consulting with the HHS secretary, to enter into cooperative agreements with other countries to establish and enforce support orders.

• **Financial Institutions.** Required states to enter into agreements with financial institutions doing business in the state to have the institutions automatically search their files every three months to provide the name, address, Social Security number and other identifying information for each noncustodial parent who had an account at the institution and owed past-due child support.

• **Grandparents.** Gave states the option to enforce a child support order against the grandparents (the parents of the minor noncustodial parent) if the custodial parent was receiving assistance from the welfare block grant.

Native American Tribes. Allowed states and Native American tribes to enter into cooperative agreements regarding paternity establishment and child support orders.

Immigration

The bill imposed new restrictions on benefits for both legal and illegal immigrants, including provisions that:

Illegal Immigrants

• **Restrictions.** Restricted the federal benefits for which illegal immigrants and legal nonimmigrants, such as travelers and students, could qualify. The benefits specifically denied were those provided by a federal agency or by federal funds for:

- Any grant, contract, loan, professional license or commercial license.
- Any retirement, welfare, health, disability, food assistance or unemployment benefit.
- **Exceptions.** Allowed illegal immigrants and legal nonimmigrants to receive:
  - Emergency medical services under Medicaid. The conference report specifically denied coverage for prenatal or delivery care assistance that was not an emergency.
  - Short-term, noncash emergency disaster relief.
  - Immunizations and testing and treatment for the symptoms of communicable diseases.
  - Noncash programs identified by the attorney general that were delivered by community agencies—such as soup kitchens, counseling and short-term shelter—that were not conditioned on the individual's income or resources and were necessary for the protection of life or safety.
  - Certain housing benefits (for existing recipients only).
  - Licenses and benefits directly related to work for which a nonimmigrant had been authorized to enter the United States.
  - Certain Social Security retirement benefits protected by treaty or statute.
- **State and Local Programs.** Prohibited states from providing state or local benefits to most illegal immigrants, unless a state law was enacted after Aug. 22, 1996, the day HR 3734 was enacted, that explicitly made illegal immigrants eligible for the aid.

However, illegal immigrants were entitled to receive a school lunch and/or breakfast if they were eligible for a free public education under state or local law. A state could also opt to provide certain other benefits related to child nutrition and emergency food assistance.

Legal Immigrants

- **Current Immigrants.** Made most legal immigrants, including those already in the United States, ineligible for SSI and food stamps until they became citizens. Existing recipients had to have an eligibility review by August 1997.

Those exempted from this ban were:
  - Refugees, those granted asylum and immigrants whose deportation had been withheld. (Withholding of deportation was a form of relief in immigration law that was similar to asylum.) Immigrants in this category would be eligible for SSI and food stamps only for the first five years of residence in the United States—including any time they were here before the law was enacted.
  - Those who had worked in the United States for the equivalent of 10 years.
  - Veterans and those on active military duty, as well as their spouse and unmarried dependent children.
- **Future Immigrants.** Barred legal immigrants who arrived in the United States after Aug. 22, 1996, from receiving most low-income federal benefits for five years after arrival.

Individuals exempted from this ban were:
  - Refugees, those granted asylum and immigrants whose deportation had been withheld. Cuban and Haitian entrants could also be exempted.
  - Veterans and those on active military duty, as well as their spouse and unmarried children.

Programs exempted from this ban were:
  - Emergency medical services under Medicaid.
  - Short-term, noncash emergency disaster relief.
  - Child nutrition, including school lunches and the special supplemental nutrition program for Women, Infants and Children (WIC).
  - Immunization and testing and treatment of symptoms of communicable diseases.
  - Foster care and adoption assistance.
  - Noncash programs identified by the attorney general that were delivered by community agencies such as soup kitchens, counseling and short-term shelter that were not conditioned on the individual's income or resources and were necessary for the protection of life or safety.
  - Loans and grants for higher education.
  - Elementary and secondary education.
  - The Head Start program for preschool children.
  - Assistance from the Job Training Partnership Act.
- **State Options.** Allowed states to deny benefits from the welfare block grant, Medicaid and social services block grant to most legal immigrants—including those already in the United States. The exemptions were the same as those for SSI and food stamps. Future immigrants would first be subject to the five-year ban noted above.

Existing recipients had to continue receiving the benefits until Jan. 1, 1997.

States could generally determine the eligibility of legal immigrants, including those who were already in the United States, for benefits funded entirely by state or local money. Existing recipients remained eligible for the benefits until Jan. 1, 1997.

Exemptions were granted to refugees, those granted asylum and immigrants whose deportation had been withheld; those who had worked in the United States for the equivalent of 10 years; and veterans and those on active military duty, as well as their spouse and unmarried dependent children.

- **Sponsors.** Expanded the circumstances under which an immigrant's sponsor would be considered financially responsible for that individual. This generally affected those entering the United States sponsored by a member of their immediate family.

Previously when an immigrant applied for AFDC, food stamps or SSI, the sponsor's income and other resources were taken into account or "deemed" when determining the applicant's eligibility. The sponsor's finances were generally considered for three years after the immigrant arrived in the United States, and for five years for SSI. These terms still applied to legal immigrants who were already in the United States and receiving the aid.

Most legal immigrants who arrived in the United States after Aug. 22, 1996, would first be subject to the five-year ban noted above. After five years, the sponsor's finances would be considered for most federal programs to which the immigrant applied.

By February 1997, the new terms would also apply to immigrants who were already in the United States but who were not receiving the benefits when the bill was enacted.

The sponsor's financial responsibility would extend until the immigrant had worked in the United States for 10 years or had become an American citizen.

The affidavits of support would be legally enforceable against the sponsor by the sponsored immigrant as well as by federal, state and local agencies for up to 10 years after the immigrant last received benefits.

Programs exempted from deeming were the same as those exempted from the five-year ban on benefits to future legal immigrants.

• **Reporting and Verifying.** Required agencies that administered SSI, housing assistance or the welfare block grant to report quarterly to the Immigration and Naturalization Service the names and addresses of people they knew were unlawfully in the United States.

Within 18 months after enactment, the attorney general had to issue regulations requiring that anyone applying for federal benefits be in the United States legally. States administering federal benefits would have to comply with the verification system within 24 months after they were issued.

Child Protection

The legislation made modest changes to child protection programs, but generally retained their existing structure. Provisions of the bill:

• **Eligibility.** Continued the existing eligibility for child protection programs. Under existing law, children qualified for federal foster care and adoption assistance if they met AFDC eligibility requirements. The legislation retained those eligibility guidelines for foster care and adoption assistance even though AFDC was being eliminated.

• **Information Systems.** Extended the deadline for providing 75 percent federal funding for the Statewide Automated Child Welfare Information Systems from Oct. 1, 1996, to Oct. 1, 1997. The program helped states collect automated data on children in foster care and other child welfare services.

• **For-Profit Providers.** Permitted states to use federal foster care funds under Title IV-E of the Social Security Act to enable for-profit providers to care for children in foster care.

• **Preference to Relatives.** Required states to give preference to an adult relative when determining a child's placement, provided that the relative met all relevant state child protection standards.

Child Care

Most federal child care funding was to be provided to states through a revised block grant. The child care provisions of the bill:

Funding

• **Block Grant.** Folded several federal child care programs into the existing Child Care and Development Block Grant to the states. That block grant provided child care services for low-income families and activities to improve the quality and availability of child care.

The legislation ended the guarantee of federal matching funds to states without limits for families that participated in two of the child care programs to be consolidated. Those programs helped welfare recipients participate in work or training programs and helped them keep their jobs for a year after they left the welfare rolls. A third program to be consolidated, which provided child care for those at risk of needing welfare, had not been subject to a federal guarantee.

The effective date for the consolidated block grant was Oct. 1, 1996.

• **Mandatory Funding.** Set total mandatory or entitlement funding to the states for child care at $13.85 billion from fiscal 1997 through fiscal 2002. The money was to come from two accounts:

• States were to share a basic allocation of $1.2 billion per year. Each state would receive the amount of funds it received for child care for AFDC recipients, those making the transition from welfare and those at risk of needing welfare in fiscal 1994, fiscal 1995 or the average amount in fiscal 1992–1994, whichever was higher.

• Another $6.7 billion was to be available over six years in matching grants to qualified states. The amounts were $760 million in fiscal 1997, $860 million in fiscal 1998, $960 million in fiscal 1999, $1.16 billion in fiscal 2000, $1.36 billion in fiscal 2001 and $1.51 billion in fiscal 2002.

To qualify for these funds, states had to have spent all of their basic child care allocation. They also had to continue spending at least as much of their own funds on child care as they spent on AFDC-related child care in fiscal 1994 or fiscal 1995, whichever was higher.

Funds were to be distributed to states based on their proportion of children under age 13, with unused funds redistributed to other states.

• **Discretionary Funds.** Authorized $1 billion annually through fiscal 2001 in discretionary spending, based on the existing Child Care and Development Block Grant formula.

Use of Funds

• **Native American Tribes.** Required HHS to set aside between 1 percent and 2 percent of the child care funds annually for Native American tribes and organizations.

• **Targeted Population.** Required states to spend at least 70 percent of the mandatory funds to provide child care to help welfare recipients, those attempting to leave the welfare rolls and those at risk of needing welfare.

• **Quality.** Required at least 4 percent of the new consolidated block grant to be used for consumer education and improving the quality and availability of child care. The law previously required that 25 percent of state allotments from discretionary funds be reserved for improving quality, increasing the availability of early childhood development and expanding before- and after-school care.

• **Administrative Costs.** Allowed states to spend no more than 5 percent of the block grant on administrative costs.

- **Lead Agency.** Required states to designate a lead agency for the block grant, which could be a government or nongovernment entity.
- **Penalties.** Specified that states that did not comply with the legislation could be required to reimburse HHS for improperly spent funds. The HHS secretary could deduct from the administrative portion of the state allotment for the following fiscal year an amount equal to or less than the misspent funds. The legislation repealed a requirement that the secretary withhold further child care block grant payments to a state until noncompliance was corrected.

State Plan

States were required to certify that they had licensing requirements for child care services and describe how these requirements were enforced. They also were required to detail how they were meeting the specific child care needs of welfare recipients, those attempting to leave the welfare rolls and those at risk of needing welfare.

Child Nutrition

Provisions of the bill:

- **Summer Food Service and School Breakfasts.** Reduced federal subsidies for the Summer Food Service Program for Children.

The reimbursements, beginning with those that applied to the summer of 1997, were to be adjusted for inflation on Jan. 1, 1997, and each year thereafter. Assuming a 3 percent inflation adjustment in both the new and old reimbursement rates, the subsidy levels for 1997 would be an estimated $2.02 for each lunch or supper (down from a projected $2.23), $1.16 for each breakfast (down from $1.24) and 47 cents for each snack (down from 58 cents).

The legislation deleted funds set aside to help states initiate or expand the school breakfast and summer food service programs.

- **Child and Adult Care Food Program.** Reduced federal subsidies for meals and snacks served in family day-care homes in all but low-income neighborhoods. The existing rates generally would continue to apply to family day-care homes located in areas that met at least one of these criteria:
  - At least half of the children were in households that were below 185 percent of the poverty level.
  - At least half the elementary school students in the area qualified for free or reduced price school meals.
  - The day-care provider's income was below 185 percent of the poverty level.

The new subsidy structure for nonpoor homes was to begin on July 1, 1997, and be adjusted for inflation on that date and each year thereafter. Assuming a 3 percent inflation adjustment, the expected subsidies in nonpoor homes beginning July 1 were an estimated 97 cents for each lunch (down from a projected $1.62), 27 cents for each breakfast (down from 88 cents) and 13 cents for snacks (down from 48 cents).

The bill eliminated the option of reimbursing a child care center for serving a fourth meal or snack to children who were there for more than eight hours a day. Also eliminated were requirements that states expand the availability of the child and adult care food program, and that they provide training and technical assistance to help day care home sponsors increase participation in the program. Also, child care centers were no longer required to provide information about WIC.

- **Women, Infants and Children.** Repealed specific requirements that states show how they planned to serve women in prisons and juvenile detention facilities with WIC, which provided infant formula, milk and other basic foods to pregnant women, infants and young children. The legislation also deleted a requirement that the agriculture secretary promote WIC in specific ways.
- **Subsidy Rates.** Specified that federal subsidy rates be rounded down to the nearest cent—rather than quarter cent—when indexing for full-priced meals in the school breakfast and lunch programs, full-priced meals in child care centers and all subsidies to family day-care homes and summer food service providers.

Food Stamps

The food stamp program remained largely intact, though the bill made significant cuts in benefits and imposed a new work requirement for certain recipients. Provisions of the bill:

Benefits and Eligibility

- **Entitlement Status.** Continued to give benefits to anyone who met food stamp eligibility requirements, enabling the program to expand or contract with demand.
- **Individual Allotments.** Reduced individual allotments to 100 percent of the Agriculture Department's "Thrifty Food Plan," rather than 103 percent. The Thrifty Food Plan was intended to reflect the benefits needed to purchase food for minimal nutrition requirements.
- **Deductions.** Reduced benefits by changing various deductions that recipients could take from their income or assets when calculating eligibility and benefits. Among the changes:
  - The standard deduction—used for all food stamp applicants to help determine benefit levels—generally was kept at $134 per month. It had previously been indexed to inflation.
  - State and local energy assistance was to be considered as income when determining allotment levels (though federal energy assistance would continue to be excluded).
  - Earnings from students would be considered as part of the family's income once the person reached age 18 (instead of age 22, as had been the case).
  - The minimum monthly allotment of $10 in food stamp benefits for a one- or two-person household would no longer be indexed to inflation.
  - The threshold above which the fair market value of a vehicle was counted as an asset was set at $4,650 and frozen at that level. The vehicle allowance had been $4,600, and it was scheduled to increase to an estimated $5,150 on Oct. 1, 1996, and be adjusted for inflation after that.
  - The maximum shelter expense deduction generally was kept at $247 per month through Dec. 31, 1996, when it in-

creased to $250 per month. It was set at $275 per month in fiscal 1999 and 2000, and $300 per month in fiscal 2001 and thereafter. The limits on the deduction had been scheduled to expire on Jan. 1, 1997.

• All parents and children 21 years of age or younger living together were required to apply for food stamps as a single household. The legislation eliminated the exception that had allowed children who were married or had children of their own to apply as a separate household from their parents when living together.

Work Requirements

• **General Work Requirement.** Required able-bodied food stamp recipients between the ages of 18 and 50 who did not have dependents to work an average of at least 20 hours per week or participate in a state-approved work, training or workfare program. Otherwise, they could receive no more than three months of food stamps out of every three years, plus an additional three months if they reentered the program and then were laid off.

The agriculture secretary could waive this work requirement at the request of a state in an area where the unemployment rate was more than 10 percent or where there were not enough jobs to employ food stamp recipients.

The new work requirements did not apply to pregnant women and to those otherwise exempt from work registration requirements (such as those caring for incapacitated people).

• **Work and Training Programs.** Gradually increased federal funding for food stamp employment and training programs from $79 million in fiscal 1997 to $90 million in fiscal 2002. States also would get more leeway in running these work and training programs.

• **Waivers.** Permitted certain states to require parents of children as young as age 1 to work. A state could qualify if it had requested the option as a waiver from federal rules and had had the waiver denied as of Aug. 1, 1996. The age could be lowered to below age six for not more than three years. The law otherwise exempted parents of children up to age six from the food stamp work requirements.

State Flexibility

• **Waivers.** Gave broader authority to the agriculture secretary to waive federal food stamp requirements to encourage state experiments. State projects had to be consistent with the goal of providing food assistance to raise nutrition levels among low-income people. They also had to include an evaluation.

Permissible projects were those that improved administration, increased self-sufficiency of food stamp participants, tested innovative welfare overhaul plans or allowed more conformity with the rules of other social service programs.

However, if the secretary concluded that a project would reduce benefits by more than 20 percent for more than 5 percent of households in the project (excluding those whose benefits were reduced because they failed to comply with work or other conduct-related requirements), then the project:

• Could not include more than 15 percent of the state's food stamp population.

• Was limited to five years, unless an extension was approved.

The secretary could not approve a waiver that:

• Involved the payment of food stamp allotments in cash (unless the project was approved before enactment).

• Substantially transferred food stamp funds to services or benefits provided through another public assistance program.

• Used food stamp funds for anything but food, program administration or an employment or training program.

• Gave or increased housing expense deductions to households with either no out-of-pocket housing expenses or housing expenses that represented a low percentage of their income.

• Absolved the state from the responsibility of acting promptly on reported changes in income or household size.

• Was not limited to a specific time period.

• Waived a provision in a "simplified food stamp program," which states could set up for households in which all members received food stamps and cash assistance.

• **Waivers Prohibited.** Prohibited waivers from some provisions that were in effect before the legislation was enacted. These included:

• A general ban against providing benefits to people in institutions.

• The requirement to provide food stamp assistance to all who were eligible, as long as they met the program's rules.

• The income eligibility limit for households without elderly or disabled members.

• The rule that no parent or caretaker of a child under age six would be subject to work and training requirements (except as provided for above).

• The rule that employment or workfare programs be subject to the minimum wage.

• The requirement that food stamps not be considered income for other purposes.

• **Unified Rules.** Permitted states to create a "simplified food stamp program" for households in which all members were also receiving welfare cash assistance. States could establish a single set of benefit rules for food stamps, welfare checks and other programs.

States that chose this option would still have to follow certain food stamp rules, including calculating benefits by assuming 30 percent of household income was available for food purchases as determined under rules set by the state.

• **Cash-Out Options.** Allowed states to convert food stamp benefits to wage subsidies for employers who hired food stamp recipients. The recipients would then receive wages instead of food stamps. This option could not be used to displace nonsubsidized workers. Also, states that chose this option had to show how they were helping to move the recipients into unsubsidized jobs.

Also, certain states could choose to issue food stamps in cash to households that participated in the welfare block grant and in the food stamp program, if a member of the household had been working for at least three months and earned at least $350 a month in unsubsidized employment.

Penalties

• **Fraud.** Doubled the basic penalties for fraud and abuse. Those who intentionally violated food stamp program requirements the first time would be disqualified for one year instead of six months. The penalty for the second intentional violation—and first involving a controlled substance—was two years instead of one year.

• **Trafficking.** Permanently disqualified people convicted of trafficking in food stamp benefits of $500 or more from receiving food stamps. Also, property involved in or gained by food stamp trafficking had to be forfeited.

• **Work Requirements.** Disqualified for foods stamps individuals who refused to cooperate with a state in determining their job status or availability or who refused to work without good cause.

Those who violated the work requirements were to be disqualified for at least one month for the first violation and up to three months at state option. The second violation would draw a minimum disqualification of three months and a maximum of six months. For the third violation, individuals would be disqualified for six months—or permanently, if a state chose.

• **Violations of Other Programs.** Barred states from increasing food stamp benefits for a recipient who lost welfare benefits for failing to comply with the rules of welfare programs. States could reduce food stamp allotments by up to 25 percent for failure to comply with another low-income benefit program's rules. Stiffer penalties were possible for a recipient who violated rules regarding the welfare block grant.

• **Multiple Locations.** Disqualified individuals for food stamps for 10 years if a state agency (or federal or state court) concluded that they had fraudulently tried to receive food stamp benefits in more than one location at the same time.

• **Fleeing Felons.** Disqualified individuals for food stamps while they were fleeing to avoid prosecution, custody or confinement for a felony or attempted felony or violating a condition of probation or parole.

• **Businesses.** Increased the Agriculture Department's authority to penalize retailers and wholesalers considered likely to permit program violations—such as those who had been disqualified from WIC.

• **Child Support.** Permitted states to disqualify from the food stamps program:

• The custodial parents of children under age 18 who had an absent parent, unless the parent cooperated with the state child support agency to establish paternity and obtain support for the child. Cooperation was not required if the state found there was good cause.

• The noncustodial parents of children under 18 if they refused to cooperate with the state child support agency in establishing paternity and obtaining support for the child.

• Anyone who was delinquent in court-ordered child support payments, unless the court allowed a delay or the in-

dividual complied with a payment plan approved by the court or a state child support agency.

Other Food Stamp Provisions

• **Electronic Benefits.** Encouraged states to shift to an electronic benefit transfer system (EBT) and required them to do so by Oct. 1, 2002, unless they received a waiver from the agriculture secretary. Under EBT, food coupons were replaced by automatic teller machine cards.

Food stamp card holders would not be protected by the same federal regulation that protected credit card holders from losses stemming from stolen cards. The legislation directed that regulations regarding lost EBT benefits be similar to those regarding lost food stamp coupons.

• **Commodity Food Programs.** Consolidated The Emergency Food Assistance Program (TEFAP), which distributed commodities to operations providing emergency food, with similar programs for soup kitchens and food banks. The legislation set aside $100 million annually in food stamp funds from fiscal 1997 to 2002 to buy commodities for the revised TEFAP. Commodities were to be distributed to states based on the existing formula, which considered poverty and unemployment rates.

Miscellaneous Provisions

• **State Legislatures.** Clarified that federal aid for the family assistance and child care block grants was to be appropriated through state legislatures and not be controlled exclusively by governors.

• **Public Housing.** Disqualified for public housing or subsidized housing assistance anyone fleeing prosecution after being convicted of a felony. The prohibition also extended to those who violated probation or parole.

Also, anyone whose low-income assistance benefits were reduced because of an act of fraud could not receive additional public or subsidized housing aid to compensate for the penalty.

• **Teenage Pregnancies.** Required that by Jan. 1, 1997, the HHS secretary begin implementing a plan to prevent out-of-wedlock teenage pregnancies and assure that at least 25 percent of the nation's communities had programs in place to prevent teenage pregnancy.

• **Electronic Benefits.** Generally exempted those who received low-income assistance through automatic teller machine cards from the same federal regulation that protected credit card holders from losses stemming from stolen cards. The legislation specifically exempted from this protection any low-income assistance program created under state or local law or administered by a state or local government.

• **Social Services.** Reduced the social services block grant—which provided money to states for services such as child care—by 15 percent from the previously approved level of $2.8 billion annually. As a result, $2.4 billion annually would be set aside from fiscal 1997 through 2002. The $2.8 billion appropriation was to be reinstated in fiscal 2003 and thereafter.

The legislation explicitly permitted states to use social services block grant funds to provide noncash vouchers for children whose parents exceeded the five-year time limit on welfare benefits and for children born to welfare recipients.

• **Earned-Income Tax Credit.** Made modest changes to scale back the Earned-Income Tax Credit, which provided tax relief for low-income workers. The provisions generally aimed to tighten compliance with tax rules and make it harder for some people to qualify for the credit. The bill:

• Required use of a valid taxpayer identification number to allow the IRS to more closely track claimants' identity and income.

• Included additional categories of income, such as capital gains, to disqualify a taxpayer for the credit. It also lowered the threshold of disqualified income—which also included interest, dividends and rent—above which an individual could not qualify for the tax credit from $2,350 to $2,200, and indexed it for inflation.

• Excluded certain losses, such as net capital losses, that could be considered when determining whether a worker's adjusted gross income was low enough to qualify for the credit.

• **Abstinence Education.** Set aside $50 million annually from fiscal 1998 through 2002 to promote abstinence from sexual activity as one of the services provided under the Maternal and Child Health block grant. This block grant helped state and local health agencies provide services aimed at reducing infant mortality and improving the health of young children.   ❑

Chronology of Action on Veterans' Affairs

1993–1994

The 103rd Congress, hoping to avoid a repeat of the delays that occurred in providing help for veterans exposed to the defoliant Agent Orange during the Vietnam War, acted quickly to pass legislation to address the needs of those suffering from a wide array of symptoms that they said was linked to their service during the Persian Gulf War. Congress passed separate measures in 1993 and 1994 to ensure that those suffering from what came to be known as "Persian Gulf syndrome" would receive medical care and disability payments.

But Congress was less successful with another major initiative—expanding health care for the growing percentage of veterans who were women. An omnibus women veterans health bill was ultimately stripped of most of its key provisions after it became embroiled in an abortion debate.

Persian Gulf Illness

Mindful of criticism that Congress did not move fast enough to help Vietnam veterans exposed to the herbicide Agent Orange, Congress in 1994 cleared legislation (HR 5244—PL 103-446) authorizing the Department of Veterans Affairs (VA) to make disability payments to veterans whose conditions could have been linked to their service in the Persian Gulf War in 1991.

So-called Persian Gulf syndrome referred to a multitude of ailments reported by a growing number of military personnel who served in the Persian Gulf during the 1990–1991 confrontation with Iraq over its invasion of Kuwait. While no one was sure of causes or long-term effects, Gulf War veterans had experienced such symptoms as fatigue, nausea, hair loss, diarrhea, and heart and respiratory problems.

Preliminary investigations indicated that exposure to smoke from oil fires, desert parasites, vehicle paints and the depleted uranium used to reinforce tank and artillery shells all could have contributed to these ailments. Others suggested that the problem could be a condition known as "multiple chemical sensitivity," in which exposure to a variety of chemicals could cause illness.

Some reports suggested that U.S. and other soldiers might have been exposed to Iraqi chemical and biological weapons. A Department of Defense study released June 23, 1994, found no such evidence of exposure for U.S. soldiers.

HR 5244 gave the VA the authority to pay compensation to veterans who were at least 10 percent disabled and to study the impact of Persian Gulf syndrome on the spouses and children of veterans who had served in the war. The bill gave the secretary of veterans affairs the power to decide how long the agency would pay compensation and by what date the first symptoms would have to appear for a veteran to be eligible.

In 1993, Congress had cleared a bill (HR 2535—PL 103-210) that required the VA to give "priority" treatment to eligible Persian Gulf veterans—essentially guaranteeing that no patient legitimately seeking treatment could be turned away—until Dec. 1, 1994. The measure also reauthorized a number of unrelated VA programs that were about to expire, including priority treatment for veterans with conditions that could have been linked to exposure to Agent Orange and radiation (until June 30, 1994) and counseling for sexual trauma (until Dec. 31, 1994).

Although the VA and other government agencies were just beginning to study Persian Gulf syndrome, there was substantial political momentum in Congress to ensure that no potential victim was denied care in the meantime, given the regrets of many in Congress that it took more than a decade to guarantee priority treatment to those exposed to the defoliant Agent Orange. *(Agent Orange legislation, Congress and the Nation Vol. VI, pp. 615, 620)*

LEGISLATIVE ACTION

Veterans Administration Secretary Jesse Brown had insisted that he needed a congressional mandate to act because existing law prohibited him from compensating veterans disabled by undiagnosed conditions.

His position had strong support in the House, which approved HR 4386 by voice vote Aug. 8, 1994. The measure had been reported by the Veterans' Affairs Committee Aug. 4 (H Rept 103-669).

But some senators, led by Senate Veterans' Affairs Committee Chairman John D. Rockefeller IV, D-W.Va., argued that Brown already had the authority he needed to pay compensation. He said that the link between the illness and the time and place of military service was sufficient to warrant compensation. Rockefeller on July 27 introduced legislation (S 2330) to codify his contention that the VA already had authority it needed to pay compensation. But the dispute was not settled until late September, when Rockefeller and his allies relented to the House position. The Senate Veterans' Affairs Committee reported an amended version of Rockefeller's bill Sept. 28 (S Rept 103-386), which cleared the way for staff negotiations to resolve other outstanding issues.

A clean bill, HR 5244, was drafted to cover the results of negotiations between the House and Senate, and the House passed it by voice vote Oct. 7. The Senate followed suit the next day. President Clinton signed the bill Nov. 2.

Outlays for Veterans Benefits and Services

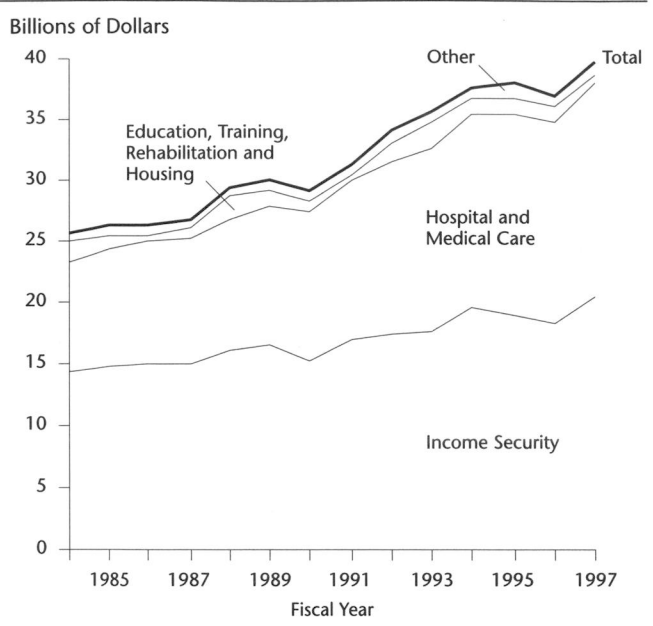

Billions of Dollars

NOTE: Data for 1997 are estimated.

SOURCE: Office of Management and Budget, *Historical Tables, Budget of the United States Government: Fiscal Year 1998* (Washington, D.C.: U.S. Government Printing Office, 1997), Table 3.2.

MAJOR PROVISIONS

As signed into law, HR 5244:

• Gave the VA the authority to pay compensation to veterans who were at least 10 percent disabled by so-called Persian Gulf syndrome. The secretary of veterans affairs was given the power to decide how long the agency would pay compensation and by what the date the first symptoms would have to appear for a veteran to be eligible.

• Authorized the VA to study the impact of Persian Gulf syndrome on the spouses and children of veterans who served in the 1991 war.

• Effectively exempted the Veterans Health Administration from all but 4,676 of the 21,000 job cuts that it otherwise would have had to make under Clinton's plan to "reinvent" the federal government. *(Story, p. 811)*

• Gradually raised the salaries of the 65 members of the Board of Veterans Appeals to match the pay received by administrative law judges. The provisions had been part a bill to aid homeless veterans, which the Senate Veterans' Affairs Committee had reported Sept. 27, 1994 (S 2325—S Rept 103-385). It also had been part of S 1927, which authorized a cost-of-living adjustment (COLA) for veterans benefits. *(COLA bill, p. 600)*

• Clarified that all veterans who participated in the atmospheric testing of a nuclear weapon by a foreign country were eligible to receive the same medical treatment and compensation from the VA that was offered to those who had been present at a nuclear test conducted by the United States. This provision had been included in a separate bill (S 1908—S Rept 103-280) to ease rules on lawsuits brought by veterans who claimed they had

been injured by exposure to radiation during military service. S 1908 had been passed by voice vote of the Senate Aug. 19, 1994.

• Granted eligibility for burial in a VA cemetery to veterans' spouses who died before the veteran. Eligibility was also given to spouses of deceased veterans who remarried. Previously, only spouses who survived the veteran and did not remarry could be buried in a veterans cemetery. The House had passed part of this provision as a separate bill (HR 3456—H Rept 103-350) by voice vote Nov. 16, 1993.

• Established a Center for Women Veterans to coordinate women's programs at the VA and to inform women about available services and benefits. Women were expected to make up 11 percent of the veterans population by 2004. The House had approved the provision in separate legislation (HR 3013—H Rept 103-538) it passed by voice vote June 13, 1994.

• Expanded eligibility for VA-guaranteed home loans, allowing veterans to obtain mortgages without a down payment. The provision waived a requirement that reservists discharged for service-connected injuries serve at least six years to qualify for a loan. Spouses of reservists killed on active duty also qualified for these loans. This language had been part of HR 4724 (H Rept 103-629), which the House passed by voice vote Aug. 1, 1994.

• Authorized the VA to establish up to eight facilities to provide comprehensive services to homeless veterans and to submit an annual report to Congress on services provided to homeless veterans.

• Expanded educational benefits by permanently reauthorizing a vocational flight training program available to all veterans. The language also increased, from $5 million to $6 million, the authorization for vocational counseling services that were contracted out by the VA. These provisions had been part of a separate bill (HR 4768—H Rept 103-631, Part I) passed by voice vote of the House Aug. 1, 1994.

• Required private companies with a federal contract valued at more than $10,000 to give hiring preference to any veteran who served in combat. The provision also required these contractors to inform veterans through local employment offices of job openings before announcing them to the general public.   ❏

Women's Health; VA Facilities

What began in 1993 as a legislative effort to expand medical services for women veterans ended in the last weeks of the 103rd Congress as little more than a routine construction authorization measure, after a fight over abortion led lawmakers to drop key women's health provisions. The bill (HR 3313—PL 103-452), which was signed into law on Nov. 2, 1994, authorized $379.3 million for construction of VA medical facilities. It also slightly expanded medical treatment for women at the Department of Veterans Affairs (VA).

Both chambers had passed bills that authorized an array of new services for the increasing number of women veterans, including pap smears, breast exams, mammography and treatment for osteoporosis, sexually transmitted diseases and conditions arising from menopause. The House had acted on its bill (HR 3313—H Rept 103-349) in 1993: the House Veterans' Affairs Committee reported it Nov. 10 and the full House passed it by voice vote Nov. 16. The Senate bill (S 1030—S Rept 103-136) was reported by the Senate Veterans' Affairs Committee Sept. 8, 1993, and the Senate passed it by voice vote May 25, 1994, and again on July 26.

The most significant difference between the House and Senate bills was language in S 1030 authorizing pre- and post-natal care and delivery services for women veterans. House sponsors argued that maternity services would be too costly. And, after months of negotiation, some members who opposed abortion remained concerned that the bill could be interpreted by the courts to allow a woman veteran to terminate her pregnancy at a VA facility. The impasse finally led negotiators to remove pregnancy services from the bill.

A similar fate befell language that would have allowed the VA to participate in up to five state health care reform plans, restructuring its health system in each state to fit the local plan. This provision had passed the House by voice vote as a separate bill (HR 4013—H Rept 103-477) on April 28, 1994; the Senate had passed HR 4103 by voice vote on June 8, after substituting its version of the bill (S 1974—S Rept 103-268). Bill supporters had planned to add this language to the women's health bill. Abortion foes said this, too, could open the door to VA-provided abortions and requested that a prohibition be included in the bill. Again negotiators refused, and the language was removed.

Senate Democratic staffers then stripped most of the other provisions in the bill even though no one had objected to them, with an eye toward reintroducing a comprehensive women's health bill early in 1995. They left in language authorizing the VA to provide counseling and treatment for sexual trauma and to require the VA, when possible, to include women and minorities in clinical research and testing.

In the interest of time and convenience, the House bill (HR 3313) containing the few remaining provisions on women's health agreed to by negotiators was then used as a legislative vehicle for language from the two noncontroversial construction authorization bills (HR 4425, S 2277).

The House construction bill, reported by the House Veterans' Affairs Committee on May 19, 1994 (H Rept 103-518), authorized $343.8 million in fiscal 1995 for nine major construction projects, roughly triple the $115 million requested by the administration. The House passed the bill May 23 by voice vote.

S 2277, reported by the Senate Veterans' Affairs Committee July 12 and passed by voice vote of the full Senate Aug. 19, included the same construction projects as the House-passed bill, with two exceptions. One was a $9.6 million outpatient clinic in Fort Myers, Fla., that was included in the House but not the Senate bill, and which was dropped from the final version. Left in the final package was $16.1 million for a research facility in Portland, Ore., that was in the Senate bill, but not the House bill.

The House passed an amended version of HR 3313 by voice vote Oct. 7 and the Senate cleared it the next day, also by voice vote.   ❏

Veterans Reemployment

Congress in 1994 cleared legislation that clarified and expanded reemployment rights for veterans after they returned from active duty. The bill, signed into law on Oct. 13 (HR 995—PL 103-353), was a response to longtime complaints from veterans that the 1940 Soldiers' and Sailors' Civil Relief Act, which governed reemployment, was confusing and difficult to interpret.

Originally reported by the House Veterans' Affairs Committee April 28, 1993 (H Rept 103-65, Part I), and passed by voice vote of the House May 4, the bill affirmed employer obligations to rehire any veteran who returned from military service within five years—up from four years in the 1940 act—of his or her last employment. Returning veterans were entitled to the same or a comparable job as well as any promotions that would have accrued had they not served in the military. The bill also instituted a new requirement that service personnel give reasonable notice to employers before leaving.

The Senate's slightly different bill (S 843—S Rept 103-158), reported by the Senate Veterans' Affairs Committee Oct. 18, 1993, and passed by voice vote of the full Senate on Nov. 2, also included language from an unrelated bill (S 1510) increasing from $184,000 to $203,000 the maximum amount that could be borrowed under the veterans' guaranteed home loan program. The language was added because larger loans generated larger loan fees to the government, offsetting the estimated $2 million cost of the reemployment program. The Senate added the provision to HR 995, before passing it by voice vote Nov. 8. The House accepted the home loan provision Sept. 13, 1994, passing an amended version of HR 995 by voice vote. The Senate cleared the bill by voice vote Sept. 28.   ❏

VA Health Staff Cutbacks

Congress in 1994 agreed to exempt most of the Veterans Health Administration (VHA) from staff cutbacks made elsewhere in the federal government under President Clinton's "reinventing government" program. As part of the plan, the VHA, which operated 171 hospitals and more than 350 outpatient clinics with a staff of 205,000, was to cut 21,000 positions over five years, beginning in 1995. But legislation that was originally a separate bill and ultimately folded into an omnibus veterans measure (HR 5244—PL 103-446) that authorized benefits for those suffering from illness related to the Persian Gulf War, exempted the VHA from all but 4,676 of those reductions. *(Persian Gulf illness, p. 597)*

House sponsors of the free-standing bill (HR 4013) argued that the personnel reductions conflicted with the new health care mission envisioned for the VA under Clinton's health care plan, which called on the VA to compete with private medical providers for patients. The House Veterans' Affairs Committee reported HR 4013 (H Rept 103-477) on April 14, 1994; the House passed it 282–118 on April 28.

But some House members, a majority of senators and the Clinton administration worried that if the VHA was exempted, then other parts of the government would have to take a bigger hit. The Senate stripped out the staff exemption before passing HR 4013 by voice vote June 8. The final compromise required the VHA to cut a total of 10,051 positions, but also allowed it to count as part of the personnel cuts federal employees whose salaries were not paid out of appropriated funds, including a group of 5,375 veteran canteen service workers who were paid from canteen income. ❑

Veterans COLAs

Congress in 1993 and 1994 cleared separate bills to set annual cost-of-living adjustments (COLAs) for disabled veterans and their survivors. Unlike veterans' pension benefits, payments to disabled veterans were not automatically indexed to inflation, requiring annual action by Congress and the president.

The 1993 bill (S 616—PL 103-140) set the increase to take effect Dec. 1, 1993, at 2.6 percent. The bill also set a flat $9 per month increase for spouses and dependent children of veterans who died as a result of service-related injuries. Under the pre-1992 system, they had received monthly payments that were higher than the $750 minimum set that year for all subsequent beneficiaries.

The Senate Veterans' Affairs Committee reported S 616 (S Rept 103-55) June 15, 1993; the full Senate approved the bill by voice vote July 14. The House Veterans' Affairs Committee reported its version (HR 3340—H Rept 103-312) Oct. 28; the House passed it by voice vote Nov. 2. The House then passed S 616 by voice vote, after inserting the provisions of HR 3340. The Senate went along with the House version, clearing the bill Nov. 4. President Clinton signed it on Nov. 11, Veterans Day.

The 1994 bill (S 1927—PL 103-418) set the COLA at 3 percent, effective Dec. 1 of that year. The Senate Veterans' Affairs Committee reported the measure (S Rept 103-254) April 26; the full Senate passed it by voice vote May 4. The House Veterans' Affairs Committee reported its own bill (HR 4088—H Rept 103-668) Aug. 4.

By voice votes Aug. 8, the full House first passed HR 4088 and then S 1927, after amending the Senate bill to include a raise for Veterans' Board of Appeals members. The Senate stripped the provision from the bill Oct. 6, to prevent it from blocking the COLA. The House accepted the change, clearing the measure by voice vote the next day. President Clinton signed it Oct. 25. ❑

Veterans Reconciliation

After lengthy negotiations, conferees on veterans issues reached agreement in 1993 on provisions that contributed $2.6 billion in revenue increases and tax cuts over five years to the 1993 budget reconciliation bill (HR 2264—PL 103-66).

The original House and Senate bills had both included a cut in pensions for veterans in Medicaid-approved nursing homes and an increase—from 1.25 percent to 2 percent—in the fee veterans paid for guaranteed home loans. These provisions were included in the final bill, which cleared Congress on Aug. 6 and was signed by President Clinton on Aug. 10. *(1993 budget reconciliation bill, p. 44)*

The final bill also froze the cost-of-living adjustment (COLA) on benefits in fiscal 1994 and held it to 50 percent in fiscal 1995, and halved the COLA on benefits to many spouses and dependent children of veterans who died of service-related injuries. Under the plan, only those beneficiaries who were receiving the minimum payment were given a full COLA. ❑

National Cemeteries

Recognizing the military's increased reliance on reservists due to the downsizing of the armed forces, Congress in 1994 cleared legislation that extended the right to be buried in national veterans cemeteries to people who served 20 years or more in the military reserves or the National Guard. President Clinton signed the bill (HR 821—PL 103-240) on May 4.

Previously, only active-duty military personnel and reservists who had been called up for active duty were eligible for burial in the cemeteries. The Department of Veterans Affairs, while not actively opposing the bill, had expressed concern that expanding eligibility would greatly increase cemetery maintenance costs. But supporters argued that the bill would result in no more than 800 additional burials a year. They also pointed to an estimate by the Congressional Budget Office that the annual cost of the bill would be less than $400,000.

The House had originally passed the bill by voice vote Aug. 2, 1993; it had been reported by the House Veterans' Affairs Committee July 29 (H Rept 103-197). The Senate passed it by voice vote Nov. 11, after expanding it to include spouses and dependent children, a provision that had been included in the version (S 1620) reported by the Senate Veterans' Affairs Committee Nov. 4.

The House added some technical changes to HR 821 on April 18, 1994, and sent it back to the Senate for final action. The Senate cleared the bill by voice vote April 20. ❑

Board of Veterans Appeals

Congress in 1994 cleared legislation (S 1904—PL 103-271) aimed at reducing the backlog of 40,000 claims pending before the Board of Veterans Appeals.

The bill attempted to speed up the claims process by reducing from three to one the number of board members needed to adjudicate a claim. The measure also allowed the panel to expand by removing the 65-member cap on the number of board members.

The Senate first passed S 1904 by voice vote on April 21; it had been reported by the Senate Veterans' Affairs Committee on April 14.

The House passed the bill with minor modifications by voice vote on June 13 and sent it back to the Senate, which agreed to the House version by voice vote June 15. President Clinton signed it on July 1.   ❑

Medal of Honor

Congress in 1993 cleared legislation (HR 3341—PL 103-161) to increase from $200 to $400 the monthly stipend to living veterans who had won the Medal of Honor, the highest U.S. military decoration, awarded by Congress for gallantry at the risk of life beyond the call of duty.

The bill had been reported by the House Veterans' Affairs Committee on Oct. 28 (H Rept 103-313). The House passed it by voice vote Nov. 2, and the Senate followed suit Nov. 17. President Clinton signed the bill Nov. 30.   ❑

Lockerbie Memorial

Congress in 1993 cleared legislation (S J Res 129—PL 103-158) that authorized a memorial in Arlington National Cemetery to the 270 victims of the 1988 terrorist bombing of an airliner over Lockerbie, Scotland.

The resolution was reported by the Senate Veterans' Affairs Committee on Nov. 4. It passed by voice vote in the Senate on Nov. 8 and in the House on Nov. 16. President Clinton signed the measure into law on Nov. 24.   ❑

1995–1996

The 104th Congress took only limited action on veterans' issues, with most of its attention focused on larger issues. But it did clear a significant veterans' health bill aimed at bringing to the massive VA health care system some of the efficiencies being realized elsewhere in the nation's health care system. The bill sought to reduce the emphasis on inpatient hospital care and focus efforts on outpatient treatment.

Lawmakers also addressed job rehabilitation issues for veterans, including overturning a 1995 court decision that could have opened the system to far more veterans than Congress ever intended.

Veterans' Health Care

Lawmakers in 1996 cleared legislation they hoped would allow the Department of Veterans' Affairs (VA) to move more veterans out of VA hospitals and into less expensive outpatient settings. President Clinton signed the veterans' health care bill (HR 3118—PL 104-262) into law on Oct. 9.

Veterans groups and the VA itself had long argued that existing VA health care rules too often required veterans to check into a VA hospital when a trip to an outpatient clinic would provide more appropriate and less expensive care. Previous attempts, however, had stalled over concerns that allowing the VA to treat more veterans as outpatients would prompt a flood of additional veterans seeking care and cost more than it would save. Under previous law, outpatient care was guaranteed only for severely disabled veterans with injuries connected to their military service and a few other categories of veterans.

But lawmakers solved the problem—after the Congressional Budget Office predicted that HR 3118 would provide coverage for a million additional veterans and cost $3 billion in fiscal 1997—by adding a spending cap to limit VA health care expenditures to near existing levels. The House accepted the cap—proposed by the Senate Veterans' Affairs Committee—which confined the VA's health care budget to $17.25 billion during fiscal 1997 and $17.9 billion for fiscal 1998. With the budget problem solved, the bill coasted to easy enactment.

The House Veterans' Affairs Committee reported HR 3118 (H Rept 104-690) July 18, 1996. The House passed the bill by a 416–0 vote on July 30. The Senate Veterans' Affairs Committee reported a similar bill (S 1359—S Rept 104-372) Sept. 26, after adding the two-year spending cap.

House and Senate negotiators ultimately agreed to use HR 3118 as a vehicle to move other veterans' bills passed by the House separately. The Senate passed the expanded bill by voice vote Sept. 28; the House cleared the measure, also by voice vote, later the same day.

MAJOR PROVISIONS

As signed into law, HR 3118:

• Eliminated statutory restrictions governing which categories of veterans were eligible for the full range of VA health care, including treatment in outpatient clinics, home care and other services as well as hospitalization. It gave the VA the authority to treat all veterans as it saw fit as long as it stayed within its budget. A spending cap was placed on the VA health care budget of $17.25 billion in fiscal 1997 and $17.9 billion in fiscal 1998. The bill required the VA to set up a priority system to decide which categories of veterans would receive care and in what order.

• Extended the VA's authority to provide treatment for Persian Gulf veterans through 1998, for veterans exposed to Agent Orange through 2002, and permanently for those exposed to radiation. All three authorizations were set to expire at the end of 1996, under legislation (HR 2353—PL 104-110) enacted Feb. 13, 1996. The provisions in HR 3118 were originally included in

HR 3643, which was reported by the House Veterans' Affairs Committee June 27, 1996 (H Rept 104-648) and passed by the House July 16 by voice vote.

• Gave the VA broad leeway to contract out medical services to the private sector. Originally part of a bill reported by the Senate Veterans' Affairs Committee Sept. 26, 1996 (S 1359—S Rept 104-372), the measure allowed the VA to contract out any medical services and administrative work as long as the outside arrangements did not lessen or lower the quality of services being provided by the VA at the time of enactment.

• Authorized $358.1 million in fiscal 1997 for renovations and expansions at VA medical facilities in 18 cities. The measure authorized an additional $12.2 million for the VA to lease space in six cities.

The House Veterans' Affairs Committee had reported a somewhat more generous construction authorization (HR 3376—H Rept 104-574) May 14, 1996, and the House passed it by voice vote June 4. The Senate Veterans' Affairs Committee approved its version of the construction bill July 24.   ❏

Agent Orange

Congress in 1996 instructed the Department of Veterans Affairs (VA) to pay health, vocational and cash benefits to certain disabled children of Vietnam veterans, as part of the fiscal 1997 funding bill for the VA, Housing and Urban Development (HUD) Department and independent agencies (HR 3666—PL 104-204).

Specifically, the bill authorized benefits for children born with spina bifida if one of their parents were exposed to the Agent Orange defoliant during the Vietnam War. A debilitating, incurable birth defect, spina bifida occurred when a fetus's spine failed to form properly. The National Academy of Sciences in March 1996 had reported that evidence suggested a link between spina bifida and Agent Orange.

The provision authorizing the payments had been added during Senate action on the bill, over the strong objections of Senate Appropriations VA-HUD Subcommittee Chairman Christopher S. Bond, R-Mo., and Senate Veterans' Affairs Committee Chairman Alan K. Simpson, R-Wyo. The amendment, proposed by Minority Leader Tom Daschle, D-S.D., was adopted by voice vote, after the Senate voted, 62–35, on Sept. 5, 1996, to declare it germane to the bill.

Critics said the provision would set a terrible precedent because Congress had never provided veterans' benefits to children for harm they suffered as a result of their parents' military service. Others questioned whether there was scientific proof of a link between the birth defect and Agent Orange.

Because of the continued opposition of Simpson, as well as House Veterans' Affairs Committee Chairman Bob Stump, R-Ariz., the conference report on HR 3666 (H Rept 104-812) included a compromise that authorized the benefits but delayed the effective date until Oct. 1, 1997, to give the Veterans' Affairs committees time to act on the issue.

HR 3666 cleared Sept. 25 and was signed into law by President Clinton the next day.   ❏

Job Rehabilitation Benefits

Congress in 1996 cleared an omnibus veterans benefits bill (S 1711—PL 104-275) making several changes to veterans benefits and training programs. President Clinton signed the bill on Oct. 9.

The bill's main provision overturned a 1995 Court of Veterans Appeals decision and reestablished that only disabled veterans whose employment handicap was directly related to a service-connected injury were eligible to receive VA job rehabilitation benefits. About 55,000 veterans received such benefits.

The bill started in the Senate as a measure to create a 12-member Commission on Service Members and Veterans Transition Assistance to study the effectiveness of veterans' readjustment programs. The Senate Veterans' Affairs Committee reported it Sept. 24, 1996, after adding nearly a dozen other measures (S Rept 104-371). One of the additions changed the official starting date of the Vietnam War from Aug. 5, 1964, to Feb. 28, 1961, the date of the first American casualty in Vietnam, thereby making up to 16,500 veterans who served in Southeast Asia between those dates eligible for benefits and recognition as Vietnam veterans. The full Senate passed the bill by voice vote Sept. 28, and the House cleared it by voice vote the same day.   ❏

Benefits Appeals Review

The House in 1996 passed a bill (HR 1483) that would have required the Department of Veterans' Affairs (VA) to review all appeals on benefits rulings from veterans alleging that the VA had made a "clear and unmistakable error." The Senate never acted on the measure, however.

Existing law allowed the VA's Board of Veterans' Appeals to review only those cases it found to have merit. Under the bill, the VA would have had to review all appeals claiming an obvious error, as long as the appeal was properly filed. While the measure was supported by veterans' groups, the VA strongly opposed it, claiming it would add to an already lengthy backlog of cases.

The House Veterans' Affairs Committee reported the bill (H Rept 104-571) May 10, 1996; the House passed it by voice vote May 21.   ❏

Job Preferences

The House in 1996 passed legislation (HR 3586) to make it easier for combat and disabled veterans to obtain and keep jobs with the federal government, but the measure died in the Senate.

The bill, reported by the House Government Reform and Oversight Committee July 12, 1996 (H Rept 104-675), and passed by voice vote of the full House July 30, would have expanded veterans preference to nonpolitical jobs in the legislative branch, the judicial branch, the White House and the General Accounting Office. It also would have bolstered the appeals options for veterans who believed they were unfairly denied preference and would have created extra protections for veterans when the government eliminated jobs.

Sponsors of the measure argued bolstering the preference was needed to protect veterans as the government continued to downsize its workforce. But opponents claimed that it would give veterans unfair advantages over other federal workers and would interfere with preference programs for different groups, such as women and minorities.

The existing job preference program, among other things, gave eligible veterans extra points on competitive civil service hiring exams and required agencies to keep veterans over equally qualified nonveterans when eliminating positions. The preference also gave veterans extra time to learn a new job if theirs was eliminated.   ❑

Veterans COLAs

Congress in 1995 and 1996 cleared separate bills to provide cost-of-living adjustments (COLAs) to some 2.5 million disabled veterans and survivors of veterans who died from service-connected injuries. The 1995 bill (HR 2394—PL 104-57), effective Dec. 1 of that year, provided for a 2.6 percent increase. The

1996 bill (HR 3458—PL 104-263) provided an increase of 2.9 percent.

The House Veterans' Affairs Committee reported HR 2394 (H Rept 104-273) on Oct. 6, 1995, and the full House passed it by voice vote Oct. 10. The Senate passed an amended version Nov. 9 and the House cleared it the next day, also by voice votes. President Clinton signed it into law Nov. 22.

The House Veterans' Affairs Committee reported HR 3458 (H Rept 104-647) on June 27, 1996, and the House passed it by voice vote July 16. The Senate passed an amended version Sept. 26 and the House cleared it Sept. 28, both by voice votes. Clinton signed it Oct. 9.   ❑

Veterans Reconciliation

The 1995 budget reconciliation bill (HR 2491), which Congress cleared Nov. 20, 1995, included proposed savings of $6.7 billion over seven years from veterans programs. However, President Clinton vetoed the bill Dec. 6. *(1995 budget reconciliation bill, p. 68)*   ❑

CHAPTER 10

Education Policy

Education Policy

"Education seems to be becoming a political target," said Education Secretary Richard W. Riley in 1995, after Republicans assumed the majority in the House and Senate. During the Democratic-controlled 103rd Congress in 1993–1994, President Clinton oversaw reauthorization of the Elementary and Secondary Education Act as well as enactment of the Goals 2000: Educate America Act, the National Service program, a new system of direct federal student loans and school-to-work transition legislation. Clinton's interest in education reached back to his tenure as governor of Arkansas, when, for example, he imposed controversial teacher competency testing as a means of improving education in the state.

The federal role in education traditionally was circumscribed by the issues of equity (lessening the disparities in educational spending between poor and rich districts) and access (ensuring the ability of poor, minority and disabled students to attain an education). Part of Clinton's legacy would be his efforts to expand the federal role from equity and access to educational quality. Furthermore, Clinton supported the idea of "human investment." He believed that, given the demands of the competitive global economy for a highly trained workforce, education was the key to opportunity. Better education meant better jobs.

After the GOP took control of the 104th Congress, increasingly loud cries emerged from conservatives of a federal takeover of education, polarizing the debate over policy. Even though the small federal share of total education funding had declined over time, from a high of 9.8 percent in the 1979–1980 school year to approximately 7 percent in the mid-1990s, Republicans argued that education was a state and local responsibility. They also said that the president's part should be largely confined to the bully pulpit—to advance education issues and talk up voluntary national standards and matters of educational organization, such as charter schools. While some conservatives proposed that the Department of Education's primary task be confined to research, other conservatives advocated dismantling of the federal department. House Republicans went so far as to link education with immigration policy, pushing to allow states to deny public schooling to children who were in the United States illegally. (*Immigration, p. 717*)

The battle lines were drawn, and the battlefield, in part, would prove to be the domain of education policy.

GOALS 2000

Goals 2000 was enacted as a bipartisan solution to improving student performance, with widespread support from educators, governors and business executives. With the 104th Congress, however, conservative opponents got the upper hand and dramatically changed the law's fortunes.

Clinton took part in the creation of Goals 2000, but the idea began with George Bush, who campaigned in 1988 on a pledge to serve as the "education president." Once in office, Bush started a national dialogue about the federal government's role in education. At a 1989 meeting in Charlottesville, Va., the president and the nation's governors developed national education goals.

Hardly anyone, including Bush, was enthusiastic about the ensuing legislation—the 1992 Neighborhood Schools Improvement Act, which would have provided block grants to states and schools, leaving specific reforms up to local educators. It died in the Senate following a dispute over school choice, Bush's proposal to allow federal funds to be used to help parents pay to send their children to private school.

Clinton was deeply involved in the 1989 education summit, embraced the idea of national standards as president, submitted his version of the legislation to Congress in 1993, and signed the Goals 2000 act into law in 1994. The measure provided a framework for what was expected of schools, teachers and students. It wrote into law eight national education goals—six proposed by Clinton from the summit, plus two added by the House. States that chose to participate were expected to work toward such goals as a 90 percent graduation rate, more parent involvement, and a set of national curriculum standards in English, math, science, civics and other subjects.

Although seen as a modest effort by many educators, Goals 2000 led to sometimes-vehement charges from conservatives in the 104th Congress of a creeping federal takeover of education. Under the guise of budget austerity and the desire to balance the budget, congressional Republicans sought to kill the program outright. Failing that, they ultimately rewrote parts of the law to minimize the federal role.

REFERENCES

Discussion of education policy for the years 1945–1964 may be found in *Congress and the Nation Vol. I,* pp. 1195–1215; for the years 1965–1968, *Congress and the Nation Vol. II,* pp. 709–733; for the years 1969–1972, *Congress and the Nation Vol. III,* pp. 581–604; for the years 1973–1976, *Congress and the Nation Vol. IV,* pp. 377–402; for the years 1977–1980, *Congress and the Nation Vol. V,* pp. 655–677; for the years 1981–1984, *Congress and the Nation Vol. VI,* pp. 555–580; for the years 1985–1988, *Congress and the Nation Vol. VII,* pp. 647–663; for the years 1989–1992, *Congress and the Nation Vol. VIII,* pp. 641–660.

Outlays for Education

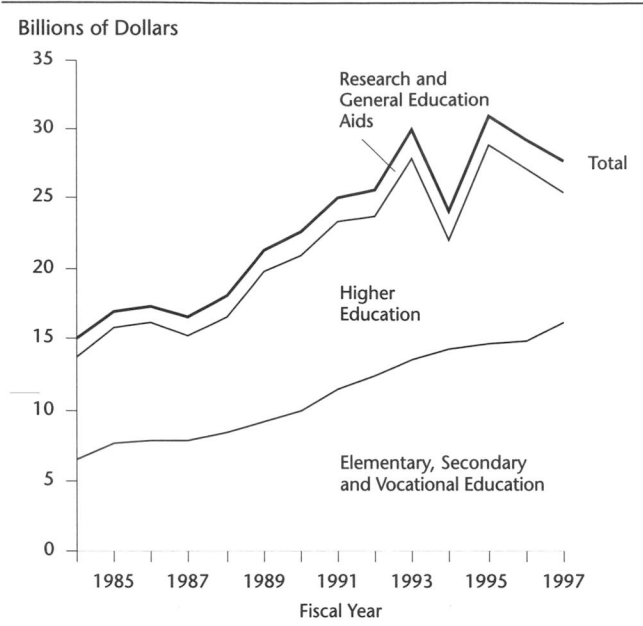

Billions of Dollars

Research and General Education Aids

Total

Higher Education

Elementary, Secondary and Vocational Education

Fiscal Year

NOTE: Data for 1997 are estimated.

SOURCE: Office of Management and Budget, *Historical Tables, Budget of the United States Government: Fiscal Year 1998* (Washington, D.C.: U.S. Government Printing Office, 1997), Table 3.2.

EDUCATION DEPARTMENT

Some Republicans in the 104th Congress were strong supporters of dismantling the Department of Education, which was established in 1979 and administered such programs as college student loans, aid for low-income elementary and secondary school students, and special education programs for the disabled. Although these members did not want to wipe out entirely all federal funding for education, closing down the department would have been a huge symbolic victory. The proposal to close the agency reflected the antigovernment sentiments of conservatives, their fear of federal dominance over education policy and their desire to hit hard in an area traditionally associated with liberal Democrats.

House Speaker Newt Gingrich, R-Ga., in February 1995 called for the elimination of the Education Department, charging that it had not "turned around education in any significant way." In May 1995, the House Education Task Force, a group of conservative House Republicans, unveiled the framework of legislation to abolish the department. The proposals, dubbed the Back to the Basics Education Reform Act, would establish two block grants for states—one for elementary and secondary education and one for higher education. College financial aid programs, such as Pell grants and guaranteed and direct student loans, would be moved to the Department of Health and Human Services. The Defense Department would absorb Impact Aid programs, which provided federal money to areas with high numbers of students whose parents were government employees. Native American education programs would be administered by the Interior Department. In addition, the proposals

called for the end of Goals 2000. Unspecified parts of other laws, including the Higher Education Act and the Elementary and Secondary Education Act, also would be repealed.

The Clinton administration and most congressional Democrats vigorously opposed GOP plans to eliminate the Education Department or to delegate some of its programs to other agencies. Education Secretary Riley, who characterized the proposals as "extreme and short-sighted," said such a step would hinder the ability of American students to get ahead in the global economy.

Despite the efforts of the House Republicans, no legislation to abolish the Education Department advanced in the 104th Congress.

1996 CAMPAIGN

Many Democrats, from the president on down, seized on education as a defining issue during the 1996 campaign in portraying Republicans as too extreme in their pursuit of federal spending cuts. Education usually was a low-level issue in presidential and congressional campaigns, rarely invoked as a matter on which the two parties sharply disagreed. But, for most of 1995 and 1996, Republicans tried to limit spending on most federal education programs and to undo many Clinton administration education initiatives. Democrats were sharply critical of the attempts and were buoyed by public opinion polls showing education topping the list of voters' concerns.

The public's edginess helped fuel a bipartisan push in the final days of the 104th Congress to spend more money on virtually every federal education program. And, as the general election approached, it prompted some Republicans to try to obscure their differences with Democrats on education issues, setting aside—at least for the moment—their argument that the federal role in education should be diminished.

Republicans acceded to Democrats' demands for more spending for several reasons. They hoped to blunt Clinton's rhetorical successes in playing up his support for education programs. They recognized that the desire for a college education—and the difficulty of getting one—had become an important middle-class issue. Between 1980 and 1994, tuition, room and board rose 45 percent at public schools, in constant dollars, and a staggering 71 percent at private schools. Furthermore, the overwhelmingly unpopular government shutdowns in 1995–1996 were triggered in part by Clinton's refusal to go along with the GOP's demands for deep cuts in education spending. Republicans did not want to be hammered on the campaign trail for cutting popular programs, and they did not want to take the blame for another politically damaging shutdown.

Meanwhile, Clinton continued to champion new education proposals. During the presidential campaign, he announced plans for "America Reads," which would aim to ensure that every child would be able to read by the end of the third grade; "Parents as First Teachers," which would provide grants to both national and regional organizations to help parents teach their children to read; and an expansion of the Head Start program. Clinton also put forth a program to offer after-school and summer tutoring for children in kindergarten through third grade.

Chronology of Action on Education

1993–1994

The 103rd Congress completed action on several major education initiatives. The Elementary and Secondary Education Act, which provided federal financial assistance for the nation's economically disadvantaged students, was reauthorized for five years. Eight national education goals, including improved high school graduation rates and schools free of drugs and violence, were established in the Goals 2000: Educate America Act. President Clinton realized one of his pet projects—the National Service program—in which young people would perform community services in exchange for financial assistance to pay for their higher education. A new system of direct federal student loans was created. And Congress cleared school-to-work transition legislation, encouraging local partnerships between schools and business to aid those secondary school students who did not go on to college.

Education Reauthorization

President Clinton on Oct. 20, 1994, signed a bill (HR 6—PL 103-382) to revise and expand federal programs for the nation's elementary and secondary schools. The measure authorized $12.7 billion in fiscal 1995 and unspecified sums through fiscal 1999.

The five-year authorization roughly followed the administration's proposals for overhauling the 1965 Elementary and Secondary Education Act (PL 89-10). However, lawmakers did not go along with a key administration plan to concentrate more money in the nation's poorest school districts at the expense of more affluent areas. After months of negotiations and counterproposals, members ultimately agreed to a compromise that left the existing formula largely intact, although it directed slightly more money to low-income children.

HR 6 shifted the focus of the Dwight D. Eisenhower program from broad grants to states to promote math and science education, to targeted grants for professional training for teachers, administrators and other school employees.

The final bill also included provisions dealing with the controversial issues of school prayer, sex education and guns in schools.

BACKGROUND

The 1965 education law was enacted as part of President Lyndon B. Johnson's War on Poverty. In addition to Title I grants for remedial education for disadvantaged children, the law provided for bilingual education, Drug Free Schools grants to prevent and treat alcohol and drug abuse, and the Eisenhower grants to improve the teaching of math and science. Most of the money under the act went to Title I programs. (Title I was renamed Chapter 1 in 1981 (PL 97-35). HR 6 changed the name back to Title I.) Authorized at $6.3 billion in fiscal 1994, Title I

provided five million students with extra help in reading, math and other subjects in which they had fallen behind. The funds went to schools to hire additional teachers, buy computers and pay for field trips, among other things. *(PL 89-10, Congress and the Nation Vol. II, p. 720; PL 97-35, Congress and the Nation Vol. VI, p. 559)*

The primary intent was to give extra help to poor children to bring them up to par with their classmates. A secondary goal was to help any educationally disadvantaged child who was doing poorly in class and on standardized tests, regardless of family income. But the political reality in 1994—as it had been in 1965—was that, to gain sufficient congressional support, Title I money had to flow to almost every school district in the country. While that made the program politically popular, criticism arose from education experts that it created a system of thinly spread general aid to schools without much regard to need.

In the early 1990s, more than half the students served were not poor, according to a study by the Rand Corp. in Santa Monica, Calif. Schools that received Title I money frequently used it for any child who was not doing well, not solely to help poor children. Under the existing formula, money was distributed based on census figures of the number of poor children per county, plus average state spending per pupil. On top of that, about 10 percent of the funding was aimed directly at high-poverty counties—those in which 15 percent or 6,500 children were poor—through concentration grants.

ADMINISTRATION PROPOSAL

The last time the Elementary and Secondary Education Act had been reauthorized was in 1988 (PL 100-297), and it was due to expire at the end of fiscal 1994. The Clinton administration presented a draft reauthorization proposal on Sept. 14, 1993, that included several changes aimed primarily at sending more Title I money to counties and school districts with the highest poverty rates. The administration proposed to increase the portion of funds devoted to concentration grants to 50 percent from 10 percent, shifting about $500 million from lower-poverty to higher-poverty counties. The wealthiest school districts would get no money. *(PL 100-297, Congress and the Nation Vol. VII, p. 655)*

In allocating the aid, the administration proposed to discount the first 2 percent of children in a school district who were poor. That meant that areas with low poverty levels would lose a substantial amount of money. However, the plan included a "hold-harmless" provision that would prevent an area from losing more than 15 percent of its money in a single year, despite changes in the formula or census figures.

The Clinton plan also included the following proposals:

• Require states that receive Title I money to develop performance and content standards describing what all children were expected to know and be able to do. The standards would be the same ones developed under the administration's Goals 2000 school reform measure (HR 1804) or they could be developed under the Title I program if the state was not participating in Goals 2000. *(Goals 2000, p. 620)*

• Replace existing multiple-choice basic skills tests for Title I students with a set of assessments designed to find out if children were meeting the state content standards. The administration wanted to eliminate multiple-choice testing in favor of more sophisticated assessments.

• Expand the number of schools providing Title I enrichment to the entire school instead of to a few pullouts from the classroom. The proposal would reduce the minimum poverty threshold, allowing schoolwide programs in 1995–1996 where 65 percent of a school's students met a poverty test, instead of 75 percent as under existing law. In later years, the threshold would be 50 percent. That would allow 12,000 more of the poorest schools to develop schoolwide programs, bringing the total to about 20,000 people.

• Prohibit schools from using Title I money to teach only low-level skills through repetitious drills. Instead, the administration wanted Title I programs to focus on more creative, higher-level concepts and skills.

• Require local school districts to give Title I money first to all schools where 75 percent of the students met a poverty test.

• Require districts to screen children for health and nutritional problems in elementary schools where at least 50 percent of the children met a poverty test. The administration also planned to ask the school districts to coordinate Title I programs with Head Start, school-to-work programs and health and social services.

• Require school districts to distribute Title I dollars to schools based on poverty, instead of the achievement of their schools. The proposed change reflected a concern that sending money to schools with the lowest achievement rates had created a disincentive for schools to raise their students' performance, because improvements could cause the schools to lose money.

HOUSE COMMITTEE ACTION

The House Education and Labor Committee reported HR 6 (H Rept 103-425) on Feb. 16, 1994.

Supporters of the committee-approved bill said it would make getting federal money easier for states—the federal government provided about 5.6 percent of local education budgets nationwide—and would give states and school districts much more spending leeway. For example, it would let more schools use money meant to help disadvantaged children for the benefit of all students. Schools also could create experimental charter schools. The Education Department could waive federal requirements in certain cases. The bill allowed consolidated applications for various grants and provided money to let schools coordinate grant programs. In return, the bill demanded more results, especially in connection with Title I money. Under the committee bill, states had to adopt challenging, high-quality curriculum content and performance standards for disadvantaged students and show progress toward achieving them. And the bill required states and school districts to take corrective action against districts and schools that failed to show enough progress—moves that could include putting the school system in receivership, turning certain schools over to private enterprises or authorizing students to transfer out.

Most Republicans voted against the bill to protest an amendment to require states seeking Title I money to adopt standards to ensure that educationally disadvantaged students got an "opportunity to learn" by assuring them high-quality learning materials, teachers, school buildings, libraries, laboratories and intangibles, such as gender equity policies. As with the bill's curriculum and performance standards, these standards had to be "as challenging and of the same high quality as they are for all children." Amendment sponsor Major R. Owens, D-N.Y., tried to appease Republicans by barring the Education Department from withholding funds from a state "on the basis of the specific content" of opportunity-to-learn standards—a curb on the department's power that did not apply to the other standards. However, Republicans called the proposal yet another unfunded mandate because the department could withhold funds by rejecting state plans, which were to include all the bill's required standards. The committee adopted the Owens amendment on a mostly partisan vote of 26–16.

A fight over how to allocate Title I money had raged for months. Internal Education Department documents detailing how Clinton's proposed formula would affect committee members' counties illustrated why it was so unpopular. About half the members could have suffered under the Clinton plan, with some losing up to 15 percent of their grants a year.

The Elementary, Secondary and Vocational Education Subcommittee had rejected the Clinton plan and approved instead an alternative drafted by Chairman Dale E. Kildee, D-Mich., and Tom Petri, R-Wis., that largely retained the existing allocation for most of the Title I money. Under their plan, $6.3 billion—the fiscal 1994 level—would be distributed under the old formula; the rest would be distributed under a new plan slightly more targeted to poor areas. Only the poorest districts stood to get significantly more money under the Kildee-Petri plan than they did under existing law—and they would benefit only if appropriations jumped significantly. Approved by a minority of Democrats allied with a near-solid bloc of Republicans, the plan left many committee liberals unhappy and angered the Democrats' traditional allies in the antipoverty lobby.

By full committee markup, Kildee and Petri devised a new formula that was somewhat more targeted toward poor areas than the subcommittee version. Administration officials, realizing that the liberal and urban-dominated subcommittee had been their best shot, came up with their own compromise. However, members coalesced around "Kildee-Petri II." Democrats persuaded Republicans whose districts would lose under the more targeted formula to go along with the revised plan by agreeing in return to support a GOP amendment to restore $435 million in Chapter 2 block grants, which had been dropped during subcommittee consideration. Republicans preferred the block grants, which allowed states and school districts to spend the money as they saw fit within broad guidelines, over the more tightly controlled categorical grants preferred by many Democrats. The committee approved the grant program by voice vote and the funding formula, 41–1.

In other action on amendments, the panel replaced a subcommittee amendment that would have required school districts receiving money under the legislation to expel for one year any student who brought a gun to school, with one requiring districts to adopt gun policies.

HOUSE FLOOR ACTION

The House March 24 passed HR 6, authorizing $12.7 billion, on a 289–128 vote. The House did not alter the compromise hammered out in committee for distributing up to $7.4 billion in Title I money to nearly every school district in the nation. No one offered Clinton's plan as an amendment on the floor. The only challenge to the committee's plan came when Puerto Rico Resident Commissioner Carlos Romero-Barceló, D/NPP, twice attempted to lift a cap that the bill imposed on Title I money for the commonwealth. His amendments were rejected, 70–358 on March 2 and 76–340 on March 3, after members were told that more for Puerto Rico meant less for their districts.

A George Miller, D-Calif., amendment requiring that teachers be certified by 1988 to teach in their assigned subject area, added in subcommittee, came under attack during floor debate on HR 6. Religious conservatives believed the language would require home-schooling parents to be certified by the government. Miller, of California, maintained that the provision was aimed at public school teachers only, to make sure they were qualified to teach their subjects. Democratic bill sponsors proposed to make a simple amendment asserting that nothing in the bill would affect home-schoolers. But Dick Armey, R-Texas, who defended the home-schoolers' cause, refused to go along. Education and Labor Chairman William D. Ford, D-Mich., and other Democrats then decided to kill the Miller amendment altogether and add language stating that the bill did not affect home-schoolers. Armey, still not satisfied, introduced a broader amendment stating that the bill did not "permit, allow, encourage or authorize any federal control over any aspect of any private, religious or home school." On Feb. 24, the House adopted the Democrats' amendment, 424–1, and then the Armey amendment, 374–53.

The bill's opportunity-to-learn standards were watered down in a bipartisan compromise and approved as part of a package of technical amendments adopted 422–1 on Feb. 24. The compromise narrowed the list of specific standards from seven to two, barred lawsuits over them, asserted that implementing them was strictly voluntary and limited the reporting requirements.

The House, 78–329 on March 3, rejected a Dana Rohrabacher, R-Calif., amendment to require school districts to determine the immigrant status of students and their parents. Rohrabacher said the data would help the federal government more accurately account for the money spent on illegal immigrants. Pat Roberts, R-Kan., offered a modification that would have reimbursed schools for the cost of carrying out the provision. It was rejected by voice vote. Another Rohrabacher amendment to prohibit any funds under the bill from being used to assist in the education of students whose parents were illegal immigrants was rejected by voice vote on March 22.

By voice vote, the House adopted a John A. Boehner, R-Ohio, amendment to allow school districts to use Title I funds for programs that allowed parents to choose which public school their

children would attend. Similar language had been rejected during committee consideration. Another Boehner amendment was rejected, 128–292 on March 3, which would have eliminated $10 million in transition programs for students moving from preschool to elementary school. Lawmakers adopted, by voice vote, a Steve Gunderson, R-Wis., amendment to establish a presidential awards program for outstanding schools.

The House, 353–70 on March 9, adopted an amendment, offered by Richard J. Durbin, D-Ill., to require that elementary and secondary school students be taught that tobacco was a dangerous substance, not unlike alcohol and drugs. Another Durbin amendment, adopted by voice vote, would have required all schools receiving federal funding to prohibit smoking, except in separately ventilated areas where children were not present. (Both Durbin amendments would be struck in conference, but the latter would survive as part of the Goals 2000 legislation.)

Bill Barrett, R-Neb., and Tim Roemer, D-Ind., offered an amendment to reserve 20 percent of a state's Drug Free Schools money for discretionary use by the governor. The amendment also required that 10 percent of a state's Title IV money be spent on Drug Abuse Resistance Education (DARE) programs. HR 6, as written, would have eliminated what historically had been a 30 percent set-aside for governors and target the money directly toward schools and local districts. Barrett contended that giving money to governors would provide greater flexibility. Opponents said the money could be used for unintended purposes if not adequately targeted. The amendment was adopted, 418–1 on March 9.

Mel Hancock, R-Mo., offered an amendment to prohibit school districts from using funds received under the act for programs that encouraged or supported homosexuality as a positive lifestyle. Jolene Unsoeld, D-Wash., offered an amendment to Hancock's language stating that school districts, not the federal government, would determine the acceptability of educational programs. The House March 24 adopted Unsoeld's modifying amendment, 224–194, before adopting the amended Hancock provision, 301–120.

John T. Doolittle, R-Calif., proposed all public elementary and secondary schools be required to teach abstinence as the only guarantee against sexually transmitted diseases and unintended pregnancies. Unsoeld proposed an amendment to Doolittle's language to encourage schools to include abstinence in sex education classes but to allow local officials control over the curriculum content. On March 22, Unsoeld's amendment was adopted, 262–166, and then Doolittle's amended language, 407–20.

Sam Johnson, R-Texas, offered an amendment to withdraw all federal funds from schools that denied students the right to constitutionally protected school prayer. Prayer in public schools had been prohibited as a regular devotional exercise since 1962, when the Supreme Court ruled that government-sponsored prayer was unconstitutional. Students could continue to pray voluntarily as long as prayer was not sponsored by local school officials. Exactly what type of school prayer was constitutionally protected remained unclear. Several Democrats objected to Johnson's amendment, arguing that it would divide schools and put school officials in the position of trying to make constitutional judgments. Pat Williams, D-Mont., proposed amending language to support voluntary school prayer but remove the threat of losing federal funds. The House March 21 rejected Williams's amendment, 171–239, before adopting Johnson's amendment, 345–64.

The House rejected, 173–245 on March 24, a substitute amendment by Minority Leader Robert H. Michel, R-Ill., to cut funding in the bill, cancel all new programs and eliminate the opportunity to learn standards, as well as the authorization of funds for family planning and abortion counseling.

SENATE COMMITTEE ACTION

The Senate Labor and Human Resources Committee reported a $12.7 billion companion measure (S 1513—S Rept 103-292) on June 24.

The committee approved a formula for allocating Title I money that had been crafted during subcommittee consideration by Labor and Human Resources Committee Chairman Edward M. Kennedy, D-Mass., and Education, Arts and Humanities Subcommittee Chairman Claiborne Pell, D-R.I. The formula was designed to aim money at needier students while ensuring that states did not lose large portions of their federal aid. Needy students were targeted more than under the House-passed version but less than in Clinton's plan. The Kennedy-Pell proposal did away with the concentration grants that went to counties with high poverty rates under existing law. Instead, all the money was to be distributed according to a formula that assigned various weights, or valuations, to students, depending on whether they lived in low-poverty areas or high-poverty areas. Grants still would be distributed using the number of poor children in a county as a factor, but the number could be derived either from the U.S. census or from the county, whichever yielded more money. Average state spending per pupil would continue to be a factor. The Kennedy-Pell formula also provided for bonuses for states that demonstrated high levels of "effort" and "equity" in educating students. Effort referred to willingness to pay taxes for education; equity, to attempts to equalize school spending between rich and poor areas.

While Kennedy-Pell targeted significant resources to poorer states, it also tended to reward certain wealthier areas represented by senators on the Labor panel. Meanwhile, California and Texas senators complained, saying Kennedy-Pell was inadequate to meet growing demands on their education systems caused largely by an influx of immigrants.

At the committee markup, Jeff Bingaman, D-N.M., who had unsuccessfully pushed the administration's plan during subcommittee consideration, offered a new proposal. This plan, he said, would achieve slightly more targeting than the Kennedy-Pell formula, but substantially less than Clinton's. A state-by-state breakdown of the Bingaman plan showed that certain states with high percentages of poor children—such as Alabama, Mississippi and Louisiana—would benefit. But the plan also benefited affluent states such as Connecticut, while taking money away from poorer states such as West Virginia and New Mexico. The Bingaman amendment was rejected on a voice vote.

The committee also rejected efforts to insert opportunity-to-learn standards in the Senate bill. Several senators argued that the standards amounted to an unfunded federal mandate that potentially could expose school districts to lawsuits from disgruntled parents. The panel instead adopted a weaker substitute encouraging states to help school districts develop the capacity to meet high standards, but not requiring them to do so.

The committee added language promoting the incorporation of computers and other advanced technologies into U.S. businesses. The amendment authorized federal grants to employers who wanted to involve workers in decisions regarding advanced technologies. Senate Labor and Human Resources also had approved the provision as a separate bill (S 1020). (*Workplace technology, p. 661*)

SENATE FLOOR ACTION

The Senate passed HR 6 by a vote of 94–6 on Aug. 2, after substituting the text of S 1513. The Senate-passed bill authorized $12.7 billion.

Senators, 46–54 on July 28, rejected an alternative funding formula proposed by Dale Bumpers, D-Ark. Under Bumpers's amendment, the nation's 10 poorest states would have received large increases in Title I funding. The increased targeting would have been achieved by replacing the effort and equity factors in the Kennedy-Pell plan with a formula to allot money at least in part based on per capita income in a county and income per school-age child.

Although Kennedy-Pell prevailed over the Bumpers's plan, the Senate, by voice vote Aug. 1, adopted an Orrin G. Hatch, R-Utah, amendment that would mean that 38 states stood to receive more money than under Kennedy-Pell. Hatch took exception to the equity factor in the committee formula, which provided bonuses to states that equalized spending, with a carefully crafted minimum and maximum bonus that any one state could receive. This tended to favor small and more affluent states with relatively high marks for equity. Hatch's amendment would remove the maximum and minimum constraints from the

Kennedy-Pell formula. To blunt the effect, Hatch's amendment phased in the change over three years. In fiscal 1995, no state was to have its allocation changed by more than 2 percent. That was to rise to 4 percent in fiscal 1996 and 6 percent in fiscal 1997. In fiscal 1998, the Hatch plan would take full effect.

Kennedy won voice vote approval Aug. 2 of an amendment to slightly alter the funding for Title I and school construction programs. The amendment contained a formula adjustment to guarantee minimum funding for the nation's least populous states: Alaska, Delaware, New Hampshire, Vermont and Wyoming. Under Kennedy's amendment, each of these states would get at least one-quarter of 1 percent of the total Title I allocation. The amendment also contained an adjustment to a $400 million federal construction grant program aimed at poorer school districts with physically deteriorating buildings. The program authorized grants to states that could demonstrate a need for renovation or construction of schools, libraries or other education facilities. The grants had been targeted primarily at urban areas such as Chicago and Detroit. The adjustment aimed to spread the money to rural areas as well. To qualify for grants, school districts had to have a child poverty rate of 15 percent or more.

The Senate adopted, 93–7 on July 27, an amendment by Labor committee ranking Republican Nancy Landon Kassebaum of Kansas to withhold federal money from any local school district found guilty of willfully violating a federal court order mandating a remedy to a violation of a student's constitutional right to prayer in public schools. The proposal was designed to appease conservative Republicans, while holding the support of moderates and liberal Democrats.

Kassebaum's amendment withstood a challenge from Jesse Helms, R-N.C., who called it "do-nothing language." Helms offered an amendment, rejected 47–53 on July 27, to cut off federal funds to districts that denied students their right to constitutionally protected prayer. The amendment did not explicitly state at what point a school district would lose its money or who would determine what type of prayer was protected. Helms argued that his amendment would not mandate school prayer but would encourage administrators to allow students to pray voluntarily.

By 91–9 on Aug. 2, the Senate adopted a Robert C. Smith, R-N.H., amendment to prohibit schools receiving money under the bill from using instructional materials or other resources to encourage or promote homosexuality. In a parliamentary move designed to protect Smith's proposal from substitute amendments, Helms offered a substitute containing essentially the same language. It was adopted 63–36 on Aug. 1. The House-passed bill had a similar provision. Kennedy and James M. Jeffords, R-Vt., won approval, 99–0 on Aug. 1, of an amendment to the Helms-Smith provision to prohibit the use of federal funds to encourage or promote any sexual activity, either homosexual or heterosexual.

The Senate adopted, 60–40 on July 28, an amendment by Slade Gorton, R-Wash., to allow local schools to set disciplinary policy for all students, including those with developmental disabilities, who brought weapons to school or demonstrated life-threatening behavior. Existing federal law prohibited the removal of disabled students from classrooms for more than 10 days, regardless of their actions. Under the Gorton amendment, local schools could place disabled students in an alternative educational setting for up to 90 days for violent or disruptive behavior. Subsequently, senators adopted, 100–0 on July 28, a Jeffords amendment that was similar to Gorton's but applied only to disabled students who brought weapons to school. Unarmed disabled students who threatened to bodily harm themselves or others were to be placed in alternative settings until it could be determined whether the violent behavior was related to their disability. If it was, they could return to the classroom.

Among other amendments adopted was one offered by John C. Danforth, R-Mo., to create 10 demonstration projects in school districts approved by the Education Department to allow experimentation with single-sex classes for low-income, educationally disadvantaged students. It was approved by a vote of 66–33 on Aug. 1.

The Senate rejected, 45–53 on July 27, an amendment cosponsored by Daniel R. Coats, R-Ind., and Minority Leader Bob Dole, R-Kan., that would have targeted $30 million for a school choice demonstration project to allow parents of low-income students in 20 violence-prone schools to use vouchers to move their children to safer schools.

CONFERENCE, FINAL ACTION

House and Senate conferees began negotiations Sept. 20 and settled their differences Sept. 27 after reaching an uneasy compromise on a funding formula for the Title I program. Arguments over the formula centered on economic winners and losers. House members maintained that their formula was superior because it spread the money widely. Senate formula supporters argued that their chamber did a better job of targeting limited federal resources to the educationally deprived. Conferees exchanged several formula proposals before striking a deal that ultimately directed slightly more money at low-income children than under existing law or under the House bill. But the compromise targeted poor children far less than the Senate or Clinton had proposed. Members included the Senate's controversial effort and equity bonuses as a separate program.

Conferees struck a compromise on opportunity-to-learn standards aimed at guaranteeing equal access to high-quality teachers, books and other educational resources. The final bill required states that did not already have such standards to develop strategies to ensure that all students were held to the same expectations and had equal educational opportunities. The original House-passed bill had included mandatory opportunity-to-learn standards. The Senate had had no such provision. Liberal House Democrats argued that the standards were needed to ensure equal access to a high-quality education. But Republicans and conservative Democrats in both chambers argued that such standards could expose school districts to lawsuits from dissatisfied parents, thereby placing the schools under financial strain.

Conferees agreed to retain Senate language requiring the Education Department to withhold federal funds from any school that was found by a court to have willfully violated a court order to allow constitutionally protected voluntary prayer. Kassebaum's language won out over the more stringent House-passed provision to cut off federal money if a school denied students the right to engage in voluntary prayer. The House had voted 369–55 on Sept. 20 to instruct its conferees to insist on the House provision, but such instructions were not binding.

The conference bill barred the use of federal funds to promote any heterosexual or homosexual activity, to distribute condoms at school or to develop or distribute obscene materials.

Conferees agreed to continue federal aid to school districts for migrant students for up to three years after they moved to another district. The House had proposed reducing the existing six-year provision to two years; the Senate, to four years.

The conference committee accepted Senate language stipulating that no programs under the bill could impose unfunded federal mandates on states and localities.

The bill required local school districts to adopt a policy of expelling for one year any student who brought a gun to school. Local school officials could modify the policy on a case-by-case basis.

Conferees rejected a Senate provision to allow 10 schools nationwide to experiment with single-gender classes for five years.

The House adopted the conference report on HR 6 (H Rept 103-761) by a vote of 262–132 on Sept. 30. A move by conservative Republicans to send the bill back to conference with instructions to insist on the House-passed school prayer language was rejected 184–215 on Sept. 30.

Helms, angry because conferees had dropped the stronger House school prayer provision, began a filibuster in the Senate on Oct. 3. Senators voted 75–24 on Oct. 5 to invoke cloture, thus limiting debate and proceeding to a vote on the conference report. Sixty votes had been needed to invoke cloture. The Senate adopted the conference report 77–20 on Oct. 5, completing congressional action.

MAJOR PROVISIONS

As enacted, the Elementary and Secondary Education Act reauthorization (HR 6—PL 103-382):

Title I—Educationally Disadvantaged Students

• **Grants Program.** Provided a $7.4 billion grants program to states to serve educationally disadvantaged children. The funding formula for state grants remained unchanged in fiscal 1995. Beginning in fiscal 1996, money up to Title I's fiscal 1995 appropriation of $6.6 billion would be sent to counties using the old formula. For amounts appropriated above that level, a targeted grant formula would take effect. Under targeted grants, students would be assigned weights, or valuations, depending on their level of poverty.

In fiscal 1996, no school district would receive less money than it did in fiscal 1995. This hold-harmless provision would drop to 85 percent of the previous year's grant for fiscal 1997 through fiscal 1999. The formula guaranteed that the five least populous states—Alaska, Delaware, New Hampshire, Vermont and Wyoming—would receive no less than one-quarter of 1 percent of annual Title I appropriations. The formula also called for the use of updated county census data beginning in fiscal 1997 and updated school district census data beginning in fiscal 1999.

• **Academic Standards.** Required state educational agencies that received Title I grants to develop state educational plans in cooperation with school district officials, teachers, school administrators, parents and other school personnel. Such plans were supposed to contain challenging content and student performance standards in subjects such as English, math and reading. States that already had such standards could be required to modify them to ensure that all children were held to the same high standards, regardless of their socioeconomic status. School districts also were required to submit similarly comprehensive plans to state educational agencies. Any state or local school district whose students failed to make progress in academic performance could be subject to corrective action. Such actions eventually could include withholding federal funds or authorizing the transfer of students to other schools.

• **Assessments.** Required that each state plan include a description of the standardized tests conducted annually in such subjects as math, reading and English. Tests administered to Title I students were to be the same as those given to other students, and the results of all tests were to be used as the primary means for measuring local school districts' performance in meeting state-mandated content and performance standards. School districts would be required to use state-approved tests.

• **Language Assessments.** Required state plans to identify all foreign languages spoken by students. If a state had students who spoke English as a second language and had no means to test such students' English language skills, the Education Department's Office of Bilingual Education and Minority Languages could provide the information necessary to develop appropriate tests.

• **Transitional Tests.** Allowed states that had no statewide tests to use temporary transitional tests for up to four years, with approval from the Education Department. During that time, those states had to make progress toward establishing permanent tests. If they did not, they could be forced to adopt tests and standards contained in other state plans previously approved by the Education Department.

• **Local Plans.** Required that any local school district receiving Title I funds have an approved educational plan on file with the state educational agency; districts were to consult with parents, teachers and other school employees in devising their plans. The plans had to detail the progress being made toward meeting state student performance standards and describe revisions to instructional programs undertaken to enable all children to meet such standards. The plans also were to describe strategies that local educational agencies would use to provide ongoing professional development, or training, for parents, teachers and other school employees.

• **Local Assistance.** Required local school districts to provide schools with the information and assistance needed to improve schools and to meet the state content and student performance standards.

• **Eligible School Attendance Areas.** Required local school districts to use Title I money only in areas where the percentage of poor children was equal to or greater than the percentage of poor children in the entire school district. In general, schools in which at least 35 percent of students came from low-income families were eligible for Title I money. However, in school districts where the amount of Title I money was insufficient to serve all eligible schools, districts were required to provide money first to schools with low-income populations of 75 percent or more. Money was to be provided to schools in rank order, from those with the highest poverty rates to those with the lowest.

• **Waiver for Desegregation Plans.** Authorized the Education Department to provide Title I money to schools in which at least 25 percent of the students were from low-income families if such schools were part of a state- or court-ordered desegregation plan. In noneligible areas where desegregation plans were in effect, schools could receive federal assistance if the percentage of students from low-income families was equal to or greater than ratios found in eligible schools in the district.

• **Schoolwide Programs.** Allowed schools, beginning in the 1995–1996 school year, to use Title I money for compensatory efforts for an entire school—instead of just for Title I children—if at least 60 percent of students in the school were from low-income families. In the 1996–1997 school year, the percentage was to decrease to 50 percent.

• **Alternative Schools.** Permitted Title I money to be sent to alternative public schools that served students who were failing or at risk of failing a state's performance standards. Such students could include those from low-income families, children with disabilities, migrants or students with limited proficiency in English.

• **School Choice.** Allowed school districts to use Title I money in combination with funds from other public or private sources to develop school choice plans for students eligible for Title I funds. Parents of such students were permitted to send their children to another public school within that system.

• **School Improvement.** Required school districts to identify schools in need of improvement if they had failed to make adequate progress as defined by the state's education plan for two consecutive school years. Such schools could be identified for mandatory school improvement activities such as professional training for teachers, administrators and other school employees. States would be required to support school improvement efforts. Such assistance could include establishing school support teams made up of teachers, educational experts and consultants, who periodically analyzed the performance of school districts and made recommendations.

• **Corrective Action.** Authorized school districts to take punitive actions against schools that failed to make adequate yearly progress. Such corrective actions could include withholding Title I money, revoking a school's authority to operate a schoolwide Title I program and allowing students to transfer to other public schools within the district.

State educational agencies would be required to review the progress of school districts annually and to disseminate results to teachers, other school employees, parents, students and the local community. States also would be required to provide technical assistance or other help needed by local districts to improve schools. Such assistance could include information and support teams of teachers that had been particularly successful in helping children make significant progress toward meeting the state's student performance standards.

• **Distinguished Schools.** Permitted states annually to designate distinguished schools that exceeded a state's definition of adequate yearly progress for three consecutive years. Such designations could include monetary awards to schools, which could be used for further improvements. School districts also could reward distinguished schools by granting them more authority to make decisions at the school level.

• **Distinguished Educators.** Required states to establish a corps of distinguished teachers and educational experts to help assist school districts in making school improvements.

• **Parental Involvement.** Required schools, in collaboration with parents, to develop written plans detailing the organized involvement of parents in the planning and review of school programs.

• **Professional Development.** Required school districts to provide teachers and other school professionals with opportunities to develop their skills. Special attention was to be given to activities such as elimination of gender and racial biases, integration of academic and vocational curricula, instruction about effective use of student tests and instruction in the use of technology.

• **Private School Participation.** Allowed educationally disadvantaged students who attended private elementary and secondary schools to receive secular, neutral and nonideological educational services, as consistent with existing law. For example, private school students could be given access to such services as educational radio and television programs, computer equipment and materials, and other technologies.

• **Fiscal Requirements.** Mandated that local school districts receiving Title I money use the funds to supplement—not replace—educational funding received from other sources.

• **Even Start.** Authorized $118 million in fiscal 1995 for the Even Start program, which aimed to promote literacy among adults and provide them with the skills necessary to become their children's first teachers. These services also would be made available to teenage parents.

• **Effort and Equity Grants.** Authorized $200 million in fiscal 1996 and unspecified sums in subsequent years for state grants based on states' performance in the areas of effort and equity. Effort referred to a state's willingness to pay taxes for the education of its children. Equity referred to a state's attempts to equalize education spending between richer and poorer areas.

• **Migrant Education.** Authorized $310 million in fiscal 1995 to help the children of migrant workers overcome educational disadvantages caused by their mobility. States and school districts would be allowed to develop customized programs to assist migrant children.

• **At-Risk Youths.** Authorized $40 million in fiscal 1995 for programs for juvenile delinquents and pregnant teens. Services would be provided at juvenile corrections facilities to help students make the transition back to school.

• **Implementation Manual.** Required the Education Department to prepare and distribute a program assistance manual aimed at helping state educational agencies, local school districts, parents and others to better understand how to implement Title I programs.

• **Prohibition on Federal Control.** Prohibited the federal government from exercising direct control or influence over the Title I activities of a state agency, school or local school district.

Title II—Dwight D. Eisenhower Professional Development Program

• **Eisenhower Professional Development Program.** Authorized $800 million in fiscal 1995 for professional development for teachers, administrators and other school employees. Special emphasis would be placed on improvement of teaching in the following core subjects: math, science, English, civics and government, foreign languages, arts, geography, history and economics. States would apply to the Education Department for the grants, and local school districts would apply to state agencies for money after submitting detailed training plans. If Title II appropriations fell below $250 million any year, all the money would be used for professional development in math and science.

• **National Teacher Training Project.** Organized national teacher training programs, particularly in core subjects and early childhood development, for those who taught kindergarten through college.

• **State Activities.** Authorized states to use grant money for such purposes as reforming teacher and administrator certification requirements, providing technical assistance to local school districts and developing teacher performance tests and peer review systems.

• **Local Improvement Plans.** Required school districts applying for Title II grants to submit plans to the state, including an assessment of training needs and specific descriptions of how teaching and learning in core academic subjects would be improved. The school district had to supply at least one-third of the cost of the training.

• **Higher Education Activities.** Encouraged state education agencies to develop partnerships and cooperative agreements with institutions of higher education to provide training opportunities to the state's teachers.

• **Training Demonstration Projects.** Authorized the Education Department to establish an unspecified number of demonstration projects across the country aimed at improving teachers' knowledge and performance. Projects would include teachers, administrators and other school employees.

Title III—Technology for Education

Title III authorized $350 million in fiscal 1995 and unspecified sums through fiscal 1999 for the nation's elementary and secondary schools to acquire advanced technology. Another $200 million was authorized to purchase technology for school libraries.

• **National Long-Range Plan.** Required the Education Department to publish by October 1995 a national long-range plan describing the effective use of technology in education.

• **Federal Leadership.** Authorized the Education Department to work with other federal agencies, such as the National Science Foundation, the Commerce Department and the U.S. National Commission on Libraries and Information Services, to provide technical assistance to state educational agencies or local school districts. The assistance would be provided through competitive grants or federal contracts to public or private for-profit or nonprofit organizations.

• **Funding Alternatives.** Required the Education Department to submit a study to Congress by October 1995 on the feasibility of providing a steady flow of public or private money to schools to acquire and maintain advanced educational technology.

• **Technology Grant Applications.** Required states seeking grants to outline long-term strategies for financing technology education and describe how the equipment they wanted to purchase would improve teaching and learning. The plans had to be approved by the Education Department. School districts also had to provide similar plans to states to receive grant money.

• **National Challenge Grants.** Authorized the Education Department, through competitive grants, to encourage local partnerships among school districts, institutions of higher education, businesses and software designers. Consortiums made up of such entities could receive five-year grants to provide technological education to students as well as training to teachers and other school employees.

• **Regional Technical Support.** Authorized $10 million in grants in fiscal 1995 to establish technical support groups known as regional educational technology consortiums. Such consortiums were to work with state educational agencies and local school districts to develop programs to improve teaching and learning through the use of advanced technology. The regional groups would be made up of state educational agencies, institutions of higher education and nonprofit organizations.

• **Educational Product Development.** Authorized $50 million in fiscal 1995 to develop educational hardware and software aimed at improving teaching and learning. Money would be directed toward groups made up of state educational agencies, local school districts, postsecondary institutions and public or private nonprofit organizations.

• **Star Schools Program.** Authorized $35 million in fiscal 1995 to improve teaching through the use of audio and video telecommunications services. The emphasis would be on student access to telecommunications services for instruction in such subjects as mathematics, science, foreign languages and vocational education. Students who could not read and those with limited proficiency in English also were targeted for assistance.

• **Ready-to-Learn Television.** Authorized $30 million in fiscal 1995 to develop educational television programs for preschool and elementary schoolchildren.

• **Telecommunications Math Demonstration Project.** Authorized $5 million in grants in fiscal 1995 to establish a national project aimed at improving math instruction through the use of telecommunications devices such as cable and broadcast television. Money would be awarded to nonprofit telecommunications firms or partnerships.

• **Math and Science Equipment.** Authorized $30 million in fiscal 1995 to purchase equipment and materials needed to improve teaching and learning in math and science.

• **School Libraries.** Authorized $200 million in fiscal 1995 to buy school library educational materials, including equipment and software.

Title IV—Safer Schools

Title IV authorized $655 million in fiscal 1995 for programs to prevent violence and the use of illegal drugs in and around the nation's schools. It reauthorized the Drug Free Schools and Communities Act of 1988 (PL 100-297).

• **Governors' Programs.** Gave governors a discretionary set-aside equal to 20 percent of their state's allotment under this section. Money could be used for drug and violence prevention and public awareness campaigns; drug prevention and intervention training for parents, law enforcement officers, social service providers and others who regularly interacted with students; and extracurricular student activities that promoted drug-free and nonviolent lifestyles. A mandatory minimum of 10 percent of a state's 20 percent set-aside had to be used to establish partnerships with local law enforcement officials for Drug Abuse Resistance Education (DARE) programs.

• **Local Drug and Violence Prevention.** Required local districts to develop programs to prevent students and school employees from engaging in violent acts or using illegal drugs, alcohol or tobacco.

• **Evaluation and Reporting.** Required the Education Department, in conjunction with the Department of Health and Human Services and other federal agencies, to evaluate the effect of prevention and intervention programs every two years. The Education Department was required to collect data and file a report to Congress by Jan. 1, 1998, on the frequency of violence in the nation's schools. States would be required to submit similar reports to the department, and local school districts to file such reports with the state.

• **Grants to Institutions of Higher Education.** Permitted the Education Department to contract with institutions of higher education to develop drug and violence prevention programs on campus.

• **Hate-Crime Prevention.** Authorized a grants program to local school districts and community-based organizations to assist areas directly affected by hate crimes—generally acts in which the defendant selected a victim on the basis of race, color, religion, national origin, ethnicity, gender, disability or sexual orientation.

Title V—Promoting Equity

• **Magnet Schools Assistance.** Authorized $120 million in fiscal 1995 for competitive grants to prevent minority students at magnet schools from becoming isolated from the rest of the student body. Magnet schools attempted to desegregate schools by offering special programs—in such subjects as the arts, computers and science—to attract Caucasian students to majority-African American schools or African American students to majority-Caucasian schools. Grant money would be used to expand existing magnet programs while also ensuring ethnic and gender diversity within them.

• **Equity for Women.** Authorized $5 million in fiscal 1995 in state grants to promote equity for women and girls and to combat discrimination against girls based on gender, race, ethnicity, limited English proficiency, disability or age. The money would be used for model programs.

• **School Dropout Prevention.** Authorized $50 million in state grants for programs to identify troubled students and to prevent them from dropping out of school. Such programs also would address the needs of dropouts, pregnant students and teenage parents.

Title VI—State Discretionary Grants

Title VI authorized $370 million in state grants for fiscal 1995 to be used by school districts at their discretion. The money could be used to reduce administrative burdens, provide services for private school students and encourage local flexibility and innovation. Local districts and schools would be allowed to use money to buy advanced technology, such as computer hardware and software, for educational purposes. Money also could be used to train teachers and other school officials in the effective use of advanced technology in education reform efforts.

Title VII—Bilingual Education

Title VII authorized $215 million in fiscal 1995 for bilingual education.

• **Education Grants.** Authorized grants to schools to establish bilingual educational programs. Money also could be used for innovative projects, such as family education, outreach to parents and training programs to encourage parents to become more involved in the education of their children.

• **Schoolwide Grants.** Permitted schools that served a majority of students with limited proficiency in English to use federal money to develop schoolwide bilingual education programs.

• **Systemwide Improvement Grants.** Allowed school districts to use federal money to develop bilingual education instruction programs.

• **National Clearinghouse.** Allowed the Education Department to establish a national clearinghouse for bilingual education to analyze the nation's bilingual programs.

• **Training Grants.** Provided unspecified amounts in grants for bilingual education teachers, school administrators and appropriate school employees to receive training at colleges, universities or other institutions that offered professional development courses in bilingual education.

• **Career Ladder Program.** Established a program aimed at improving the qualifications and skills of noncertified school employees such as teachers' aides who assisted in the education of bilingual students. Federal money could be used to provide such employees with training courses—offered by colleges, universities or the local school district—that would allow them to become teachers. The program also aimed to recruit and train secondary school students for careers in bilingual education.

• **Graduate Fellowships.** Authorized the Education Department to award bilingual education fellowships for graduate and postgraduate studies in such areas as teacher training, administration and research. Those receiving such fellowships would be required to work in bilingual education for a period equivalent to the length of the fellowship. Fellowship recipients had to repay the money if they did not complete the work requirement.

• **Foreign Language Assistance.** Authorized $35 million in fiscal 1995 for state grants to improve foreign language instruction.

• **Emergency Immigrant Education.** Authorized $100 million in fiscal 1995 to aid local school districts, such as those in Texas, California and other southwestern border states, that experienced large and unexpected student population increases because of immigration.

Title VIII—Impact Aid

Title VIII authorized $866 million in fiscal 1995 in assistance for local school districts financially affected by the presence of children whose parents were connected to large federal endeavors, such as military bases. The money would be used to educate children who lived on federal property, students whose parents worked on federal property, and local school districts that experienced sudden enrollment increases because of military realignments. Because many of the nation's public schools relied on property taxes as a primary source of education money, federal funds also could be used to aid school districts affected by the federal government's acquisition of taxable lands.

Title IX—Indian Education

Title IX authorized $114 million in fiscal 1995 for ongoing education programs for American Indians, native Alaskans and native Hawaiians.

Title X—Programs of National Significance

Title X authorized $422 million in fiscal 1995 for more than a dozen small state grant programs.

• **Fund for the Improvement of Education.** Authorized unspecified amounts in state grants for fiscal 1995 to promote education reforms or provide support for any nationally significant program. Money could be used to develop new curricula in math, English, science and social studies. It also could be used to train teachers, counselors and other school employees.

• **Elementary Counseling Demonstration.** Authorized the Education Department to award grants to school districts to expand guidance counseling services at schools.

• **Character Education Pilot Program.** Authorized the Education Department to award up to 10 grants annually to develop character education programs. The money would be awarded to partnerships of state educational agencies and local school districts. Character programs would focus on such issues as caring, respect, responsibility and trustworthiness. States and localities would consult with parents and teachers while developing such projects.

• **Scholar-Athlete Competition.** Authorized the Education Department to award grant money to a nonprofit organization to produce a scholar-athlete event in 1995 as a way to foster understanding and friendship among people of different backgrounds.

• **Small Learning Communities.** Authorized local school districts, with approval of the Education Department, to create small learning communities of students to improve teaching and learning opportunities.

• **National Student and Parent Mock Election.** Authorized unspecified sums in fiscal 1995 to establish voter participation and education programs for students and their parents, to be administered by nonprofit, nonpartisan organizations.

• **Gifted and Talented Children.** Authorized $10 million in fiscal 1995 for research programs on the education of gifted and talented children. This included demonstration projects and professional training for educators who taught gifted and talented students from economically disadvantaged backgrounds.

• **Public Charter Schools.** Authorized $15 million in fiscal 1995 in public charter school grants, which could be used to provide financial assistance for the design and establishment of such schools. Charter schools could be either public or private enterprises operating within public school systems. Often they were based on a contract between a school board and a private business seeking to run a certain school or group of schools. These schools often were released from most regulatory requirements and allowed to develop innovative teaching and learning techniques. Money also would be used to evaluate student achievement in such schools.

• **Arts in Education.** Authorized $45 million in grants in fiscal 1995 for arts education research, development of arts curricula and model arts education programs. Money also could be used to provide at-risk youths with cultural activities designed to develop an appreciation for the arts.

• **Book Distribution Program.** Authorized $10.3 million in fiscal 1995 to promote reading by supplying educationally disadvantaged students with inexpensive books.

• **Civic Education.** Authorized $15 million in fiscal 1995 to support programs that educated students about the Constitution, the Bill of Rights and the roles of civics, law and government in U.S. society.

• **Allen J. Ellender Fellowship Program.** Authorized $4.4 million in fiscal 1995 for fellowships through the Close-Up Foundation of Washington, D.C. The foundation was a nonpartisan, nonprofit organization that promoted knowledge about the federal government. Fellowships were to go to teachers and low-income students, recent immigrants, students of migrant parents and older Americans to improve teaching and learning about government issues.

• **De Lugo Territorial Education Improvement.** Reauthorized $3 million a year from fiscal 1994 through 1999 for education improvement grants to the Virgin Islands, Guam, American Samoa, the Northern Mariana Islands and Palau.

• **Twenty-First Century Community Learning Centers.** Authorized $20 million in fiscal 1995 to encourage collaboration between schools and other public and private nonprofit groups. Under these partnerships, schools could become local community centers for such activities as vocational and adult education, or school-to-work programs aimed at helping high school students who were not going to college to make a smooth transition to the workplace.

• **Urban and Rural Education Assistance.** Authorized $125 million in fiscal 1995 for state grants to assist poor urban and rural school districts. Money could be used for such purposes as tutoring, dropout prevention programs and teacher training. Another $25 million in grants to institutions of higher education was authorized in fiscal 1995 for the training and recruitment of teachers in rural school districts.

• **National Writing Project.** Reauthorized programs offered by the National Writing Project, a nonprofit organization that trained teachers to teach writing skills more effectively, at $4 million in fiscal 1995.

• **Longer School Year.** Authorized $90 million in fiscal 1995 for grants to promote flexibility in school scheduling and increase the amount of time students spent in academic programs.

• **Territorial Assistance.** Authorized $5 million a year from fiscal 1994 through 1999 for education assistance to the Virgin Islands.

Title XI—Coordinated Services

Title XI authorized unspecified sums to encourage local school districts to provide elementary and secondary school students and their families with better access to social, health and educational services. Such coordinated services could be provided in or near the school through a communitywide partnership with local public and private service agencies.

Title XII—School Facilities Improvement

Title XII authorized $200 million in state grants for fiscal 1995 for the repair, renovation and construction of public schools, libraries and other structures used for academic or vocational instruction. About 25 percent of U.S. schools were in serious physical decline. Grants would be based on such factors as a school district's financial capacity and its percentage of low-income children. Money would be competitively allocated to districts in six categories based on student population. The smallest category included districts with up to 25,000 students; the largest included those with more than 50,000.

Title XIII—Support and Assistance Programs

• **Comprehensive Regional Centers.** Authorized $70 million in fiscal 1995 to establish 15 regional educational centers to assist states and school districts that received federal money under the act. Staff members would be expected to have expertise in such areas as instruction, curriculum improvement, bilingual education and school reform.

• **National Network.** Authorized $25 million in fiscal 1995 to establish a national network of educational professionals to identify effective programs and disseminate information about them statewide or nationwide.

• **Eisenhower Regional Math and Science Consortia.** Authorized $23 million in fiscal 1995 to establish regional consortia

made up of public and private organizations to provide training to math and science teachers and to disseminate information about exemplary math and science instructional materials.

• **Technology-Based Assistance.** Authorized the Education Department to provide computer-based technical assistance to states and local school districts to support programs under the act. Such assistance could include legal and regulatory information and technical guidance for administrators.

Title XIV—General Provisions

• **School Prayer.** Required the Education Department to withhold federal money under the act from any school district found guilty of violating a federal court order to allow students to engage in constitutionally protected voluntary school prayer.

• **Discouraging Sexual Activity.** Prohibited the use of federal money received under the act to distribute materials or sex education programs that promoted or encouraged heterosexual or homosexual activity.

• **Prohibition on Federal Mandates.** Prohibited anything in the act from being construed to authorize the federal government to mandate, direct or control any aspect of state, school district or school activities.

• **Gun Possession.** Required any state receiving federal funds under the act to have a policy requiring that any student who brought a gun to school be expelled for at least one year. Local school district officials could modify the expulsion requirement on a case-by-case basis. School districts also had to refer such students to local law enforcement officials. Developmentally disabled children also were subject to expulsion for one year if they brought a gun to school. But if school officials established that the behavior of such students was related to their disability, the student could be placed in an alternative educational setting for up to 45 days, instead of being expelled.

• **Disclosure of Athletic Program Financial Data.** Required institutions of higher education that participated in intercollegiate athletics to submit annual reports to the Education Department disclosing expenses and revenues from men's and women's sports programs. The aim was to show whether inequities existed between men's and women's athletic programs.

• **Albert Einstein Distinguished Educator Fellowship.** Authorized $700,000 in fiscal 1995 to establish a national fellowship program within the Department of Energy for up to 12 elementary and secondary school math and science teachers to increase their knowledge and enhance their teaching skills.

• **Community-School Partnerships.** Authorized $10 million in fiscal 1995 grants to local community-based centers to provide educational support to students from low-income families. Money could be used for counseling, tutoring and scholarships for postsecondary education.

• **Workers Technology Skill Development.** Authorized unspecified grants in fiscal 1995 to local nonprofit organizations to improve workers' ability to incorporate advanced technologies into the workplace.

• **Multiethnic Adoptions.** Prohibited any organization that received federal assistance and was involved in adoption or foster care from discriminating on the basis of race, color or national origin. The purpose was to ease the process of adoptions across racial lines.   ❏

Goals 2000

Congress in 1994 cleared legislation (HR 1804—PL 103-227) that for the first time established national education goals for the country's schools. Under the Goals 2000: Educate America Act, states could apply for grants to improve their schools regardless of whether they participated in the goals programs.

Supporters said HR 1804 would provide a framework for what was expected of schools, teachers and students. The measure wrote into law a set of eight national education goals. The goals—six proposed by President Clinton and the last two added by Congress—prescribed that by the year 2000:

• All children would start school ready to learn.

• At least 90 percent of students would finish high school.

• Students would leave grades four, eight and twelve with demonstrated competence in English, math, science, foreign languages, civics and government, economics, arts, history and geography.

• The United States would be first in the world in math and science achievement.

• Every adult would be literate and possess the skills to compete in a global economy.

• Every school would be free of drugs and violence.

• Every school would promote involvement of parents in their children's education.

• Teachers would have access to programs for the continued improvement of their skills.

Most of the money in the bill—$400 million—would be competitively awarded in grants to states, which could use the funds at their discretion to reform their local education systems.

BACKGROUND

President George Bush had signaled his interest in education reform during the 1988 presidential race, promising to be "the education president" if elected. He started a national dialogue about what needed to be done to improve education and what role the federal government should play. In 1989 he convened a meeting in Charlottesville, Va., of the nation's governors in the first-ever summit meeting on education. However, bills aimed at improving public schools died in both the 101st and 102nd Congresses, after Bush and congressional Democrats failed to agree on the basic elements of the legislation. The most volatile issue was Bush's proposal to use federal funds to give parents more choice over whether to send their children to public or private schools. Disagreement also arose over national student testing, state and federal regulation of education, and the amount of federal money to spend on improving elementary and secondary education. (*Details, Congress and the Nation Vol. VIII, pp. 643, 657*)

Congressional Democrats had roundly denounced Bush during his tenure in the White House for not putting enough money into education. However, the estimated cost of Clinton's reform proposal was $420 million in fiscal 1994, well below Bush's second education proposal of $690 million and about the same as Bush's first education plan, which many Democrats then called "a Band-Aid." The Clinton plan, brought to Capitol Hill on April 22, 1993, by Education Secretary Richard W. Riley, included the six national education goals and called for the creation of three panels to work with the states:

• The National Education Goals Panel, which already existed but was to be written into law, to report on state and national progress toward achieving the national goals.

• The National Education Standards and Improvement Council to develop criteria for certifying content standards, opportunity-to-learn standards and state assessments. The Department of Education already had awarded grants to universities and other groups to develop content standards, which the states later could use as models. Opportunity-to-learn standards would prescribe what a school needed—such as competent teachers and up-to-date textbooks—to give children the opportunity to meet the goals and standards. All standards and testing were to be voluntary.

• A National Skills Standards Board to identify major occupations and develop standards and tests for people to show they were qualified to work in a particular field.

Many House Democrats were unhappy with the initial Clinton proposal because it did not emphasize the opportunity-to-learn standards. Democrats argued that testing children was unfair when no one knew whether the children were failing or the schools were failing the children. House Democrats also were concerned that provisions for testing children might turn into barriers for disadvantaged children. Republicans feared that opportunity-to-learn standards would become an onerous federal mandate, requiring school districts and states to spend billions of dollars to comply. They also argued that, if the plans were not effective, parents would sue school systems and states.

HOUSE ACTION

The House Education and Labor Committee reported HR 1804 (H Rept 103-168) on July 1, 1993. The bill had been approved on a party-line vote of 28–15, after weeks of partisan bickering over a subcommittee amendment requiring states, before they could get any federal money, to identify specific corrective action to be taken if a school or school system did not meet the states' standards. Republicans objected because the amendment, offered by Jack Reed, D-R.I., made the standards no longer voluntary. During full committee consideration, Reed agreed to tone down the language of his amendment.

Reed's modified amendment asked each state to describe how it would monitor its progress toward putting the state and local education plan in place and to describe the procedure it would use to ensure that schools and school districts met state opportunity-to-learn and content standards. Bill Goodling of Pennsylvania, ranking Republican on the committee, said the amendment created more unfunded mandates for state and local governments. He predicted that states would hesitate to apply for reform money knowing that they would be expected to try to meet opportunity-to-learn standards. The committee adopted the Reed amendment on another 28–15 party-line vote.

The House passed the HR 1804, 307–118, on Oct. 13. To win Republican support, Democrats agreed to accept Goodling language stating that nothing in the bill should be interpreted to give the federal government control over local prerogatives. Dale E. Kildee, D-Mich., chairman of the Elementary, Secondary and Vocational Education Subcommittee, said the bill still would ensure that opportunity-to-learn standards would help show whether a student was failing or a school was failing that student. The Goodling amendment was adopted, 420–0, on Oct. 13.

The most controversial floor amendment, by Dick Armey, R-Texas, would have provided $400 million for model schools, merit schools, school choice and decentralized management. It would have eliminated all commissions, standards and testing systems in the underlying bill. Armey said he offered the amendment "for the children of our country" who were forced to stay in public schools because their parents could not afford better private schools. He also argued that providing vouchers—or some means to pay for alternatives—would force public schools to improve to keep their students. Democrats maintained that the federal government should use its limited resources on public, not private, schools. The House rejected Armey's amendment 130–300 on Oct. 13. A similar amendment offered by Armey during committee markup also had been rejected.

Other amendments approved by the House included one by Dave McCurdy, D-Okla., adopted by voice vote, to add increased parental participation in schooling to the list of national education goals. Another goal, namely that all teachers should have access to good training programs, had been proposed by Tim Roemer, D-Ind., and added to the bill during subcommittee action.

SENATE ACTION

The Senate Labor and Human Resources Committee reported its version of the school reform legislation (S 1150—S Rept 103-85) on June 23, after resolving a dispute over a section of the bill aimed at creating a board to identify major trades and develop standards and tests for people to show they were qualified to work in a particular field. Some civil rights groups were concerned that businesses could use those standards to justify not hiring minorities. And some members questioned why a labor provision was in an education bill. The panel agreed to create a national skills standards board to be made up of representatives of business, organized labor and educational institutions in roughly equal strength. By a 10–7 party-line vote, the committee rejected a Nancy Landon Kassebaum, R-Kan., amendment calling for the board to be made up of 12 business representatives and eight others.

On Feb. 8, 1994, the Senate passed HR 1804, after substituting the text of S 1150, on a **key vote of 71–25 (R 17–25; D 54–0)**. The Senate-passed bill contained Clinton's six original goals. Like the House-passed measure, the Senate version required that states applying for Goals 2000 aid try to reach the national

goals. Each state plan was to include a way to create standards of content—what children should know in English, math and other subjects at certain grades, how to assess what students had learned and ideas for teacher training. The bill encouraged states to develop strategies, instead of standards, for providing all students with an opportunity to learn—a somewhat less prescriptive approach than that taken by the House. (1994 key votes, p. 1003)

During floor consideration on Feb. 3, the Senate adopted, 75–22, an amendment by Jesse Helms, R-N.C., to deny federal school funds to state or local agencies that barred constitutionally protected prayer in school. Senators subsequently approved amendments by Carl Levin, D-Mich., by voice vote, to ensure that no federal funds would be denied to a state or local agency because it had adopted a constitutionally permissible policy related to school prayer, and by John C. Danforth, R-Mo., 78–8 on Feb. 4, to express "the sense of the Senate" that schools be encouraged to offer a daily moment of silence. Also approved was an amendment by Christopher J. Dodd, by voice vote, to authorize grants of $75 million in fiscal 1994 and $100 million in fiscal 1995 to the school districts most troubled by crime and violence. (Provisions similar to those in the Dodd amendment also were passed by the House on Feb. 22, 1994, as a free-standing bill (HR 2455). That measure provided for a one-year, $50 million authorization.) (School safety, p. 629)

The Senate adopted an amendment by Labor and Human Resources Committee Chairman Edward M. Kennedy, D-Mass., 91–2 on Feb. 8, to encourage family participation in all federally funded contraceptive distribution programs, after it had rejected an amendment by Helms, 34–59 on Feb. 8, to prohibit the departments of Education and Health and Human Services (HHS) from promoting or distributing contraceptives—not only at schools—without parental consent.

The Senate also rejected amendments by Judd Gregg, R-N.H., 42–52 on Feb. 2, to strip the bill of references to opportunity-to-learn standards; by Daniel R. Coats, R-Ind., 41–52 on Feb. 8, to set aside $30 million for demonstration programs to allow some low-income children to attend private schools at public expense; and by Connie Mack, R-Fla., 32–61 on Feb. 8, to provide the money in the bill directly to local school boards without requiring them to address the Goals 2000 standards.

CONFERENCE

The most contentious issue dealt with by the conferees on HR 1804 was the opportunity-to-learn standards. Led by Major R. Owens, D-N.Y., and George Miller, D-Calif., House liberals insisted that the word "standards" be included in the bill's final language. Rep. Goodling raised strong objections, claiming federal government micromanagement and criticizing the imposition of unfunded mandates. William D. Ford, D-Mich., chairman of the House Education and Labor Committee, countered by saying that the bill would provide flexibility by allowing decisions to be made at the state and local levels. After several failed attempts to compromise, Sen. Paul Simon, D-Ill., suggested including the word "standards" but making clear that they would be voluntary for states; each state would establish its own standards. The alternative term "strategies," used in the Senate-passed bill, also was included. Goodling and Rep. Steve Gunderson, R-Wis., opposed Simon's compromise, arguing that school districts still would be open to lawsuits despite the softened language. However, the majority of conferees joined to adopt the compromise.

Sen. Arlen Specter, R-Pa., argued for a Senate amendment to allow public education agencies to use Goals 2000 money for privatization of local schools, in which companies contracted with local school districts to run public schools. House members insisted that all the planning and start-up costs be borne by the private firms, not school districts. The Senate conferees agreed, and the House conferees accepted the Senate provision.

An amendment to ban tobacco use from schools and "any place children might be present" ran into difficulty. Members ultimately agreed to include language banning smoking from places such as elementary and secondary school libraries, pediatric wings of hospitals, school gymnasiums and commercial day-care centers.

Conferees modified the language on school prayer that had been offered by Helms and approved by the Senate. Helms's provision would have withdrawn all federal education funds from any school that denied students a chance to engage in constitutionally protected school prayer. Conferees softened the language to prohibit schools merely from using federal money to deny students the right to pray voluntarily.

Conferees also authorized $50 million in fiscal 1994 for grants to local school systems to combat violence and enhance school safety.

When the conference report on HR 1804 (H Rept 103-446) came up in the House on March 22, Democrats believed the bipartisan bill would clear easily. However, Republicans were emboldened by a strong House vote the previous day in favor of adding Helms's school prayer language to HR 6, the elementary and secondary education reauthorization bill. John J. "Jimmy" Duncan Jr., R-Tenn., tried to send HR 1804 back to conference to rewrite the provision, but moderate Republicans as well as Democrats warned that it would essentially kill the bill. On March 23, Duncan's motion was rejected, 195–232, and the House adopted the conference report, 306–121.

Backed by many of his GOP colleagues, Helms employed arcane parliamentary procedures to delay final action in the Senate on HR 1804, until it was well after many senators had hoped to begin a scheduled two-week recess March 25. Senate Majority Leader George J. Mitchell, D-Maine, countered with several parliamentary tactics of his own to force a vote. Despite the absence of 15 senators, Mitchell persuaded the other 85 members to remain in town for a vote to invoke cloture (thus limiting debate), followed by a vote on the conference report, scheduled for Saturday, March 26. Shortly after midnight March 26, the Senate voted to invoke cloture, 62–23; 60 votes were required. The Senate then voted 63–22 to adopt the conference report, completing congressional action.

President Clinton signed HR 1804 (PL 103-227) on March 31, in time to use $105 million that had been appropriated in fiscal 1994 for the program in the annual funding bill (HR 2518—PL 103-112) for the departments of Labor, HHS and Education. Congress had specified that the money would be available only if the legislation were signed by April 1, 1994. The fiscal 1995 spending bill (HR 4606—PL 103-333) provided $403 million for Goals 2000. Clinton had requested $708 million.

PROVISIONS

As enacted, the Goals 2000: Educate America Act (HR 1804—PL 103-227):

• **National Goals.** Established eight national education goals for all students and schools:

(1) All children would start school ready to learn.

(2) At least 90 percent of students would finish high school.

(3) Students would leave grades four, eight and twelve with demonstrated competence in English, math, science, foreign languages, civics and government, economics, arts, history and geography.

(4) Teachers would have access to programs for the continued improvement of their skills.

(5) The United States would be first in the world in math and science achievement.

(6) Every adult would be literate and possess the skills to compete in a global economy.

(7) Every school would be free of drugs and violence.

(8) Every school would promote involvement of parents in their children's education.

• **Standards of Content.** Established a 19-member National Education Standards and Improvement Council to develop national curriculum content and student performance standards identifying what students should know and be able to do. The standards were voluntary.

Standards were to be created in such subjects as math, science, English, history, geography, foreign languages and the arts. The aim was to better prepare students for high-wage jobs in a competitive marketplace, increase opportunities for minorities and women, and improve national productivity.

States opting to participate in the Goals 2000 program had to adopt all or part of the national standards, or develop their own standards of equal or higher quality than those established by the national council. No school or local educational agency stood to lose any federal funding if it did not participate in the program.

• **Opportunity-to-Learn Standards.** Provided that the council also establish national opportunity-to-learn standards, outlining what schools needed to provide in order for students to meet the curriculum and performance standards. These standards, too, were voluntary.

In setting such standards, the council was to consider curriculum quality, materials and supplies, teacher qualifications, student assessment methods and physical surroundings.

States could either adopt the national standards or use them as a guide to set their own standards, which had to be at least as rigorous as the council standards.

• **Aid to States and Local Districts.** Authorized $400 million over five years beginning in fiscal 1994 to improve local schools. Money was to be distributed to states using the funding formula that was used at the time to calculate local education agencies' participation in Titles I and II of the Elementary and Secondary Education Act of 1965.

Under existing law, Title I funds were targeted toward educationally disadvantaged students, who tended to be poor. Based on census data, money under Title I was being distributed to about 90 percent of the nation's schools. Title II provided grants to increase local flexibility and encourage innovation.

States were required to apply to the secretary of education for grants by submitting a state improvement plan that detailed how education reforms would be carried out locally.

• **Oversight Boards.** Created an 18-member National Education Goals Panel to oversee and report on the nation's progress toward the eight goals. The panel was to include two presidential appointees, eight governors, four members of Congress and four state legislators.

The bill also created a National Skill Standards Board, made up of 28 representatives from business, labor, government and community organizations, to develop a national system of standards and testing to ensure that students had the skills necessary to compete in the workforce.

• **Safe Schools.** Authorized up to $3 million over two years for local educational agencies that had schools in urban and rural areas with high rates of violent crime. Local districts would determine how to spend the money to combat their problems. The law authorized $50 million in fiscal 1994.

• **Research Institutes.** Established five new research institutes within the Office of Educational Research and Improvement, which was authorized at $68 million in fiscal 1995. Modeled after the National Science Foundation, the five research arms were expected to support basic and applied research, apply research to schools and serve as a national data base on model programs.

They were the National Institutes on: Student Achievement, Curriculum and Assessment; Education of At-Risk Students; Educational Governance, Finance, Policy-Making and Management; Early Childhood Development and Education; and Postsecondary Education, Libraries, and Lifelong Education. ❑

National Service

President Clinton delivered on a campaign promise on Sept. 21, 1993, when he signed a bill (HR 2010—PL 103-82) establishing the National Service program. The program was designed to send young people from across the country into communities to serve others. In return, participants would receive limited financial assistance for their education.

BACKGROUND

In his inaugural address, Clinton called upon young Americans to give "a season of service." Friends of the president said that he believed national service could be the highlight of his administration—the equivalent of President John F. Kennedy's request to "ask not what your country can do for you; ask what you can do for your country." Unlike President George Bush's "points of light," which was based on volunteerism and was not an organized plan for serving the nation, what Clinton had in mind was rooted in the moderate Democratic Leadership Council's notion that Americans have to start giving before they can get. Advocates said a national service program would constitute a perfect model for linking responsibility and opportunity.

National service had its detractors, however. Doug Bandow, a senior fellow at the libertarian Cato Institute, said national service in exchange for student aid would not eliminate the entitlement mentality; instead, it would be reinforced. Some wondered whether the service performed by young people would be of much value. "We have to be careful these do not become make-work projects and the program becomes a laughingstock," said Richard F. Rosser, president of the National Association of Independent Colleges and Universities. Meanwhile, the AFL-CIO labor federation wanted assurances that the service performed not be something already provided. "There's no sense in supporting a program that hires the son but displaces the father," said Robert McGlotten, AFL-CIO director of legislation.

Clinton proposed providing education awards of $5,000 for a year of service in education, environment, human services or public safety. Under national service, people age 17 or older could perform community service before, during or after their postsecondary education. Local programs would offer stipends to participants, with the federal government providing an 85 percent match up to $7,400 a year. That amount was based on what volunteers for VISTA (Volunteers in Service to America), the domestic equivalent of the Peace Corps, received annually. The federal government also would provide up to 85 percent of the cost of health- and child-care benefits for participants. Nonprofit organizations, including institutions of higher education, local governments, school districts, states or federal agencies, would run the programs.

HOUSE ACTION

The House Education and Labor Committee reported HR 2010 (H Rept 103-155) on June 24, 1993. The committee bill included education awards of $5,000 a year to people age 17 or older who performed community service before, during or after their postsecondary education. The bill authorized $394 million in fiscal 1994 and unspecified sums for the following four years.

The House passed an amended version of HR 2010 on July 28 by a vote of 275–152. During floor action, Bill Goodling, R-Pa., ranking minority member of House Education and Labor, offered an amendment to scale back the national service initiative by limiting the education award to those who were financially needy. He said that, with a limited amount of money available for student aid, it was not right to give money to those who did not need help. But opponents said means-testing the awards would limit the program to a corps of poor young people, eliminating the advantage of common bond among diverse participants. Goodling directed his remarks to members who represented low-income, low-middle income and middle-income Americans. The money for national service, he said, was going to come from the pockets of low-income people who qualified for need-based student aid. Opponents reiterated that national service was not a student loan program. The House rejected Goodling's amendment 156–270 on July 21. His proposal also had been rejected during committee markup of the bill.

Susan Molinari, R-N.Y., offered an amendment to prevent Congress from funding national service until other student financial aid programs were funded at least at fiscal 1993 levels. The amendment was rejected 184–247 on July 21. The proposal had been rejected during committee consideration as well.

Bob Stump, R-Ariz., ranking minority member of the House Veterans Affairs Committee, initially offered an amendment to provide national service participants with education awards equal to 80 percent of the GI benefit, thus cutting the amount from $5,000 to $3,840 for each year of service. Stump said that the GI bill's education benefit was one of the military's most important recruiting tools, and unless it was substantially more than the benefit received for national service, the armed forces could have difficulty signing up recruits. The GI bill provided $4,800 per year for three years with a mandatory service commitment of three years. Service members had to put in $1,200 of their own money from military pay during their first year of service. The administration opposed the amendment, but Stump had the votes to win. As a result, Veterans Affairs Committee Chairman G. V. "Sonny" Montgomery, D-Miss., suggested compromising at 90 percent of the GI benefits, putting the education benefit at $4,725. Stump agreed, and the amendment was adopted by voice vote July 28.

During consideration of HR 2010, the House engaged in an emotional debate about illegal immigration and racism. Bill Baker, R-Calif., offered an amendment to require charities and other groups participating in the national service program to have a written policy stating that they provided no services to illegal aliens and would report illegal aliens to the Immigration and Naturalization Service. Otherwise, they would not qualify for federal funds. The amendment, which was modified to let illegal aliens obtain religious instruction and services, sparked an outcry among Democrats and minority lawmakers. The House July 28 adopted the perfecting amendment regarding religious services by a vote of 270–163, then rejected the Baker amendment 180–253.

SENATE ACTION

The Senate Labor and Human Resources Committee reported a companion measure (S 919—S Rept 103-70) on June 29. S 919 was similar to the version that had emerged from the House Education and Labor Committee, in that it provided for education awards of $5,000 a year to people who performed community service. Nancy Landon Kassebaum of Kansas, ranking Republican on Senate Labor and Human Resources, voiced her concern that the program, as advocated by the administration, was too big and that its price tag would be detrimental to other student financial aid. Kassebaum also worried that the education stipend would come at the expense of Pell grants, which helped low-income students pay for college.

The Senate passed HR 2010 on Aug. 3 by a **key vote of 58–41 (R 7–37; D 51–4).** *(1993 key votes, p. 979)*

During floor debate, the Senate, like the House, wrestled with setting priorities for scarce funds. Pete V. Domenici, R-

N.M., offered an amendment, similar to Molinari's in the House, to ensure funding of existing student aid programs before money was made available for national service. The Senate agreed to table (kill) his amendment, 55–44, on July 22.

Two Kassebaum amendments also were rejected. The first, defeated 38–59 on July 21, would have kept spending in fiscal 1994 at approximately $100 million, would have combined all existing service-type programs—including VISTA and the Peace Corps—into one program and would not have guaranteed the $5,000 post-service benefit to participants. A second attempt to limit spending and create a single consolidated program was rejected 42–57 on July 22. The Senate agreed to table (kill) a John McCain, R-Ariz., amendment, 56–42 on July 21, to make veterans eligible for national service education awards and a Larry E. Craig, R-Idaho, amendment, 64–35 on July 22, to deny family and medical leave benefits to national service participants. The Senate rejected, 46–53 on July 21, an amendment by Paul Coverdell, R-Ga., to delay funding national service until the portion of the deficit caused by fiscal 1993 emergency spending was eliminated.

Further action on HR 2010 was delayed, when a threatened GOP filibuster forced Democrats to pull the bill from floor consideration while they scrambled to get the 60 votes needed to invoke cloture, a parliamentary procedure to limit debate and bring the measure to a vote. The first cloture attempt failed, 59–41 on July 29. Democrats had the needed votes July 30, but Republicans allowed them to forgo the balloting and proceed to consideration of the last amendments to the bill.

A major point of contention among Republicans had been the program's cost. Aware of administration plans to jump from 25,000 participants to 150,000 participants in four years, they feared that the program would spiral out of control. To placate the Republicans, Edward M. Kennedy, D-Mass., chairman of the Senate Labor and Human Resources Committee, offered an amendment to restrict the spending to $1.5 billion over three years, with caps specified for each year. Republicans countered by saying they could live with a two-year authorization, not three-year, so they then could review the program. Administration officials said that was unacceptable because the program would take at least six months to get off the ground and participants would not know whether it would be reauthorized, allowing them to complete a two-year term. The Senate accepted Kennedy's proposal by unanimous consent July 30. An attempt by Arlen Specter, R-Pa., to require a reauthorization after two years failed, 41–52, on July 30.

CONFERENCE

The conferees had a relatively easy job of reconciling differences between the House- and Senate-passed versions of HR 2010. The House would have started the program at a faster rate, but conferees opted for the slower pace approved by the Senate: $300 million for the first year, $500 million for the second and $700 million for the third.

The House would have given one-third of the funds to the states based on population and one-third by competitive grants, with the remaining one-third going to federal agencies, national parks or national nonprofit groups to provide service opportunities. The Senate would give more money to the states automatically. Conferees adopted the House language after modifying it so that at least one-third of the money would go for competitive grants and whatever was left over would be used for federal agencies and national nonprofit groups.

The House adopted the conference report (H Rept 103-219) on a 275–152 vote Aug. 6. The Senate adopted it 57–40 on Sept. 8, clearing HR 2010.

PROVISIONS

As enacted, the national service bill (HR 2010—PL 103-82):

New Corporation

• Created a Corporation for National and Community Service to administer the program by combining two existing independent federal agencies, the Commission on National and Community Service and ACTION.

• Required the corporation to administer all programs authorized under the National and Community Service Act and Domestic Volunteer Service Act, including VISTA and the older Americans volunteer programs.

• Required each state to establish a commission on National Service to receive a federal grant. Commissions were to include 15 to 25 citizens or community service experts to be appointed by the governor on a bipartisan basis.

• Required state commissions to form plans for National Service and prepare applications to the corporation for funding. Commissions could not operate programs, though they could fund state agencies that did. Commissions were required to allocate at least 60 percent of funds to nonstate groups.

Participants

• Allowed people to serve before, during or after postsecondary education. Participants could be age 17 or older; they had to be high school graduates or agree to achieve general equivalency diplomas.

• Required that participants be chosen on a nondiscriminatory basis, without regard to political affiliation. Information about National Service was to be available through high schools, colleges and other placement offices. Recruiters were required to pay special attention to the needs of disadvantaged youths.

• Required that to earn an education award, a participant could serve one year of full-time service, two years of part-time service or three years of part-time service if the person were in school. A person could serve up to two terms and earn up to two education awards.

• Set education awards at $4,725 for one term of service. The awards had to be used within five years of completing a term of service.

• Set stipends at 85 percent of a minimum wage stipend equivalent to benefits received by VISTA volunteers. Programs could provide additional stipends up to twice this amount, with no federal match.

• Required that all participants without health insurance receive coverage, with federal funds paying up to 85 percent of the cost. Full-time participants were to receive child-care assistance if they needed it.

Funding

• Distributed the funds according to the House plan, giving one-third to the states based on population, a minimum of one-third to the states based on competition, and whatever was left up to one-third, to participating federal agencies and national not-for-profit organizations.

• Required that all participants receive education awards.

• Authorized the program for three years with funding set at $300 million in fiscal 1994, $500 million in fiscal 1995 and $700 million in fiscal 1996.

• Required programs to pay 15 percent of the stipend and health care benefits in cash, and 25 percent of other program costs receiving federal support. The 25 percent match could be in cash or in kind from any source other than programs funded under the national service act. ❑

Direct Student Loans

As part of the 1993 budget reconciliation bill (HR 2264—PL 103-66), Congress overhauled the nation's student loan program, creating a new system of direct federal loans that cut out the middleman role of banks, guarantee agencies and secondary markets that traditionally had supplied student loan funds. The legislation also gave students a choice of repayment options. *(Reconciliation, p. 44)*

BACKGROUND

Under the existing system, the federal government guaranteed student loans issued by private banks. If the student defaulted, a state guarantee agency reimbursed the bank, and eventually the federal government reimbursed the guarantee agency. While the student remained in school, the government paid the bank the interest on the loan, calculated at the 91-day Treasury bill rate plus 3.1 percent.

When students graduated, banks frequently sold their loans to secondary markets, such as the Student Loan Marketing Association, known as Sallie Mae. Sallie Mae then collected monthly payments from the students and sold loan-backed bonds on Wall Street.

The Bush administration briefly floated the idea of converting to direct federal loans as a way of eliminating the fees and subsidies that the government paid to the secondary markets. But by the time the House approved a direct loan plan in 1992 as part of a bill rewriting the Higher Education Act, the administration had rejected the idea, arguing that it would add to the debt and that the Education Department could not handle such a huge problem. With a veto threat hanging over the bill and a companion Senate measure that included no direct loan plan, proponents settled for creating a direct loan demonstration project. *(1992 action, Congress and the Nation Vol. VIII, p. 653)*

When Bill Clinton came into office, he called for turning the demonstration project into a comprehensive program that would replace guaranteed student loans by 1997. The Clinton administration estimated that the change would save $1.3 billion annually when it was fully phased in.

LEGISLATIVE ACTION

The House Education and Labor Committee agreed by voice vote on May 12, 1993, to scrap the existing guaranteed student loan program and replace it within four years with direct government loans. Direct loans were to constitute 4 percent of new loans in the 1994–1995 academic year, 25 percent in 1995–1996, 60 percent in 1996–1997 and 100 percent in 1997–1998. The change, projected to save $4.3 billion over five years, covered the bulk of the $5.8 billion in savings the committee had been instructed to achieve as part of the 1993 budget-reconciliation bill.

Proponents of direct loans said the savings from eliminating big subsidies to banks would go to reduce the interest rates that students paid on their loans. Committee Chairman William D. Ford, D-Mich., said interest rates could drop from 8 percent to as low as 3.65 percent with the new system and that the government eventually could save $2 billion a year after getting out of the loan business.

In general, GOP committee members opposed the switch to direct loans, arguing that it was untested and might not be properly administered by the Education Department. They also said that a direct loan system would add to the national debt because private banks would no longer be providing the capital to students and that many jobs would be lost.

The House approved the new direct loan program without change when it passed the reconciliation bill, 219–213, on May 27.

The Senate Labor and Human Resources Committee voted on June 10 to phase in the new system slowly—5 percent of new student loans for the 1994–1995 academic year, 30 percent the next year, 40 percent the following year and 50 percent in 1997–1998. The provisions were a compromise, mainly with Republicans who were reluctant to endorse a full-fledged direct loan system. To achieve the requisite reconciliation savings, the Senate plan also reduced the profits of lenders, secondary markets and guarantee agencies when they originated or transferred conventional student loans. The provisions imposed new fees on the private sector and increased its risk on defaulted loans.

The full Senate on June 25 passed, 50–49, the reconciliation bill, including the direct loan program provisions.

House and Senate conferees agreed to leave the existing guaranteed student loan system in place while partially phasing in the new direct loan program at a faster pace than the Senate had wanted. The change was expected to save $4.6 billion over five years.

Philosophically, the House and Senate positions were far apart. The Senate viewed its approach as setting up two systems to compete against each other and allow the market to decide which was more efficient. But the House feared that by cutting so deeply into the banks' profits, most of the small and medium-sized banks would pull out and many of the guarantee agencies would collapse. Members worried that that would eliminate access to loans for many students.

Another key difference between the House and Senate measures was the treatment of banks, guarantee agencies and secondary markets that ran the guaranteed student loan system. The House would have continued to subsidize the interest on the bank loans at the rate of the 91-day Treasury bill plus 3.1 percent while a student was attending school. The Senate would have cut that subsidy to the 91-day Treasury bill plus 2.5 percent to reap savings needed to make up for not moving completely to direct loans, which would have cut out the banks and their fees. Conferees agreed to the Senate plan.

PROVISIONS

As enacted, the 1993 budget-reconciliation bill (HR 2264—PL 103-66) included provisions establishing the direct student loan program and making changes in existing student loan programs. HR 2264:

• **Direct Student Loans.** Created a new Federal Direct Student Loan program that would gradually replace the existing Federal Family Education Loan program, which guaranteed student loans. Under the new program, students would apply to the federal government for loans through their schools, cutting out the middleman role of banks and guarantee agencies.

Direct loans were to be phased in on a schedule of 5 percent of new loan volume in academic year 1994–1995; 40 percent of new loan volume in academic year 1995–1996; 50 percent in academic years 1996–1997 and 1997–1998; and 60 percent in academic year 1998–1999.

Any school that wanted to participate in the direct loan program beginning in 1996–1997 could do so regardless of the fixed percentage. That meant that all schools potentially could participate in direct loans despite the 50 percent benchmark set by conferees.

• **Repayment Options.** Gave students several options for repaying both their direct and guaranteed loans, including a standard 10-year repayment schedule, graduated repayment, extended repayment and income-contingent repayment. Under graduated repayment, a student could pay back a small amount initially with payments increasing over the years. Under extended repayment, the time allowed to repay the loan was longer than usual.

• **Consolidation Loans.** Imposed a monthly fee on holders of consolidation loans—several loans that had been combined—equal to 1.05 percent of the outstanding loan principal. This applied only to new loans.

• **Consolidation of Programs.** Combined the Supplemental Loans for Students program and the unsubsidized Stafford Loan program—both guaranteed loan programs—so that students needed to apply for only one rather than two programs. The unsubsidized Stafford program was for students whose family incomes were too high to qualify for subsidized Stafford loans. It was created in the 1992 reauthorization of the Higher Education Act so that anyone who wanted a loan could get one.

• **Guarantee Agency.** Lowered the amount of money that guarantee agencies could keep from default collections from 30 percent to 27 percent on guaranteed loans.

• **Reduction in Borrower Interest Rates.** Lowered caps on interest rates for guaranteed student loans from 9 percent to 8.25 percent under both direct loans and guaranteed student loans. The interest rates paid by students was to be cut by 0.6 percent beginning in 1998.

• **Reduction in Loan Fees.** Reduced students' origination and insurance fees from a maximum of 8 percent to a maximum of 4 percent for all new direct and guaranteed loans.

• **Loan Fees from Lenders.** Imposed a user fee on lenders of 0.5 percent of their new guaranteed loan volume.

• **Fees from Sallie Mae.** Imposed a fee on the Student Loan Marketing Association (Sallie Mae), which bought loans and used them to back bonds it sold on Wall Street. The fee was 0.3 percent of Sallie Mae's outstanding loan volume, based only on new loans issued after the legislation went into effect.

• **Elimination of Tax-Exempt Floor.** Eliminated the 9.5 percent floor on yields on loans made with tax-exempt bonds.

• **Reinsurance Fees and Administrative Cost Allowance.** Eliminated the guarantee agency administrative cost allowance and reinsurance fees charged to the federal government. Defaulted loans were reimbursed to banks and guarantee agencies at varying rates, depending on such factors as when the bank requested reimbursement and whether the bank tried to collect on the loan. The bill reduced the federal reinsurance—or reimbursement—on guaranteed loans from 100–90–80 percent to 98–88–78 percent, except for lender-of-last-resort loans, loans made when there were no others available.

• **PLUS Loan Disbursements.** Required that PLUS loans (Parent Loans for Undergraduate Students) be disbursed in multiple payments rather than in single lump sums.

• **Supplemental Preclaims Assistance.** Changed the terms for government preclaims payments to collectors of defaulted guaranteed loans from $50 per claim to 1 percent of the total collection.

• **Cost Sharing by States.** Required states to cover a portion of the default costs of schools with default rates greater than 20 percent. States could decide to pass on all or some of the cost to the schools.   ❑

School-to-Work

Congress in 1994 cleared a school-to-work bill (HR 2884—PL 103-239) aimed at helping students who did not plan to attend college to move smoothly from high school into skilled jobs. The legislation was a priority for President Clinton, who promoted it as a way to raise education standards and improve the nation's competitiveness.

At that time, about 75 percent of all high school students did not receive college degrees, but few programs existed to help them obtain the skills and work experience needed for a career.

The new program, which was authorized at $300 million in fiscal 1995 and unspecified amounts through fiscal 1999, was to be administered jointly by the Education and Labor departments. It had the backing of business and labor groups and enjoyed bipartisan support in Congress.

Patterned after apprenticeship programs in Europe, HR 2884 sought to offer students on-site, work-based career training. By contrast, traditional vocational programs tended to focus on in-school learning that often had little relationship to the type of job the student eventually chose. The School-to-Work Opportunities program also included career planning and academic training—typically with a year or two at a postsecondary school. The bill authorized planning grants of up to $1 million a year for states to develop school-to-work programs and unspecified sums up to five years for states to implement them. After five years, states were to pay for their own programs.

BACKGROUND

The Clinton administration sent its school-to-work legislative proposal to Congress on Aug. 5, 1993. Secretary of Education Richard W. Riley and Secretary of Labor Robert B. Reich worked together to develop and promote the initiative.

The proposal called for $300 million in fiscal 1995 for federal grants to states to develop systems to help students who were not going to college to acquire work skills. School-to-work programs would vary from state to state, but each would have to provide learning about work with job training, paid work experience and workplace mentoring; learning at school with career counseling that could involve at least one year of postsecondary education and evaluations to identify students' academic strengths and weaknesses; and coordination among employers, schools and students, along with the training of teachers, mentors and counselors.

The administration plan included development grants for all states to create school-to-work systems; five-year implementation grants to states that had developed plans; waivers allowing other federal funds to be used with school-to-work programs; grants to localities that were ready to put a school-to-work program in place even if their state had not yet received an implementation plan; and direct grants to high-poverty areas.

LEGISLATIVE ACTION

The House Education and Labor Committee reported HR 2884 (H Rept 103-345) on Nov. 10, 1993, and the full House passed it by voice vote Nov. 15. The bill authorized $300 million for fiscal 1995 and unspecified sums through 2002. It required 10 percent of the appropriation in each fiscal year to go for programs in high-poverty areas. The House version also reauthorized through fiscal 1995 the job training for the homeless demonstration program created in 1990 under the reauthorization of the Stewart B. McKinney Homeless Assistance Act (PL 101-645). *(PL 101-645, Congress and the Nation Vol. VIII, p. 693)*

The Senate Labor and Human Resources Committee reported a companion measure (S 1361—S Rept 103-179) on Nov. 10. Like HR 2884, the Senate committee-approved bill authorized $300 million for fiscal 1995 and unspecified amounts through 2002. S 1361 would allow the secretaries of education and labor to reserve up to $30 million in fiscal 1995 for high-poverty areas.

By 62–31 on Feb. 8, 1994, the Senate passed HR 2884, after inserting the text of S 1361. During floor action, the Senate by voice vote approved amendments by Larry Pressler, R-S.D., to allow several congressional districts with low populations to form consortia to apply for grants; by Nancy Landon Kassebaum, R-Kan., to reduce the program's authorization from eight years to five years; by Don Nickles, R-Okla., to set the annual authorization for the program at $400 million in fiscal years 1996 and 1997, $330 million in fiscal 1998 and $220 million in fiscal 1999; and by Strom Thurmond, R-S.C., to give preference, in approving grants, to states that placed students in paying jobs. The Senate agreed, 50–43 on Feb. 8, to table (kill) a Slade Gorton, R-Wash., amendment to require administrators for the Summer Youth Employment and Training Program to give priority to placing students in private sector jobs. The program provided work for disadvantaged young people.

Few differences separated the House- and Senate-passed bills. One problem arose over whether states should be required to make sure that students in the program worked at paying jobs. Democrats argued that students would derive greater benefit from their experiences if they were paid. Republicans said such a mandate might make it economically impossible for some employers to participate in school-to-work programs. The final language provided for the secretaries of education and labor to give preference to applications from programs that included paid work.

Conferees also resolved differences over which state officials were to have authority over school-to-work programs. The House version gave the most power to chief state school officers; the Senate bill gave it to governors. Under the agreement, governors were required to submit their states' plans to the Education and Labor departments, which were given joint responsibility for the program. Other state officials, such as chief school officers, could submit dissenting views with the application.

The House adopted the conference report (H Rept 103-480) by a vote of 339–79 on April 20. The Senate adopted the conference report by voice vote April 21, completing congressional action. Clinton signed HR 2884 on May 4.

As part of the fiscal 1994 appropriations bill (HR 2518—PL 103-112) for the departments of Labor, Health and Human Services (HHS), and Education, Congress in 1993 had set aside $100 million under existing authority for a school-to-work program, if it were enacted. In 1994, Congress provided $250 million for the program in the fiscal 1995 spending bill for Labor, HHS and Education (HR 4606—PL 103-333).   ❑

Migrant Student Records

Congress in 1993 cleared legislation (HR 2683—PL 103-59) to extend the Migrant Student Record Transfer System until 1995. Lawmakers had planned to revise the transfer system as part of the Elementary and Secondary Education Act reauthorization (HR 6) but did not want the contract for the system to expire before a new one was ready. (HR 6, p. 609)

Bill Goodling of Pennsylvania, ranking Republican on the House Education and Labor Committee, said that before the system, which transferred migrant student records to their new schools, was created, "migrant students were often ignored, in-

appropriately placed below their grade level, and denied access to school because of the absence of health records." The House passed HR 2683 by voice vote July 26; the Senate followed suit July 28. President Clinton signed the bill on Aug. 2.   ❑

Math, Reading Tests

Congress in 1993 cleared legislation (S 801—PL 103-33) to allow the Department of Education to develop new tests in reading and math to be conducted in states across the country on a voluntary basis.

S 801 authorized the National Assessment of Educational Progress (NAEP), created in 1969 to measure the nation's progress in education, to administer tests in math to fourth-grade and eighth-grade students and in reading to fourth-graders. It also authorized the development of tests for twelfth-grade math and eighth- and twelfth-grade reading. The bill authorized unspecified sums to fund the project.

The Senate passed S 801 by voice vote April 21; the House on May 11. President Clinton signed the bill on May 25.   ❑

Student Loan Defaults

On April 28, 1994, President Clinton signed S 2004 (PL 103-235), which extended for four years a deadline for historically black colleges and tribally controlled Indian community colleges to reduce their student loan default rates. The bill allowed such schools to have a loan default rate of 25 percent or more until July 1, 1998.

Under the 1990 budget-reconciliation law (PL 101-508) and the 1992 Higher Education Act (PL 102-325), schools with high default rates generally lost the ability to participate in federal guaranteed student loan programs. However, existing law exempted historically black and tribally controlled Indian schools until July 1, 1994. Supporters of S 2004 said the deadline extension would give such schools more time to develop the institutional reforms to achieve long-term success in reducing high default rates. (PL 101-508, Congress and the Nation Vol. VIII, p. 649; PL 102-325, Congress and the Nation Vol. VIII, p. 653)

The Senate passed S 2004 by voice vote March 25, 1994. The House passed the bill, 283–136, on April 13, completing congressional action.   ❑

Historically Black Colleges

The House and Senate passed legislation (HR 2921) aimed at restoring and preserving significant buildings at the nation's historically black colleges and universities. The two chambers could not reconcile their differences over the bill, however, and it died upon adjournment.

As reported Nov. 20, 1993, by the House Natural Resources Committee, HR 2921 (H Rept 103-398) authorized a grant program to preserve and restore historic buildings at historically black colleges and universities at $20 million in fiscal year 1995 and no more than $15 million a year in fiscal 1996–1998. Five million dollars of the fiscal 1995 funds were earmarked for Fisk

University in Nashville, Tenn., and $10 million for the 11 structures at historically black colleges that had already been identified by the Interior Department as in need of the most help. The House passed HR 2921 by voice vote Nov. 23.

The Senate Energy and Natural Resources Committee reported its version of HR 2921 (S Rept 103-279) on May 25, 1994, and the Senate passed the bill by voice vote Aug. 10. The Senate bill authorized $65 million in matching grants over four years. The interior secretary was to make grants from the Historic Preservation Fund to restore and preserve buildings and architecture at qualifying institutions.

Senate Minority Leader Bob Dole, R-Kan., had sought $3.6 million over three years for Sterling College, a small liberal arts institution in Sterling, Kan., with a student enrollment that was 3 percent black. Dole said the college had historical significance because it admitted blacks at the turn of the century. Using a similar argument, Charles E. Grassley, R-Iowa, sought to add Simpson College in Indianola, Iowa, to the schools eligible for federal money. Most students at Simpson were Caucasian. In a compromise, senators adopted by voice vote an amendment, offered for Dole by Robert F. Bennett, R-Utah, to include Sterling and Simpson colleges in a separate section of HR 2921. That meant they would not compete directly against historically black colleges for money. The amendment authorized $3.6 million for Sterling and $1.5 million for Simpson.

Of the nation's 104 historically black colleges and universities, 46 had expressed interest in restoring their historic buildings. ❑

Educational Research Office

The House passed and the Senate Labor and Human Resources Committee reported legislation (HR 856) to reauthorize the Department of Education's Office of Educational Research and Improvement (OERI). The office gave grants to nonprofit organizations to study all aspects of education policy. The legislation sought to reorganize the office along the lines of the National Institutes of Health by creating five institutes or directorates to oversee different areas of research.

HR 856 was reported by the House Education and Labor Committee (H Rept 103-209) and was passed by voice vote of the House on Aug. 2, 1993. The four-year bill would have authorized $156 million in fiscal 1994 and $219 million in fiscal 1995.

The Senate Labor and Human Resources Committee reported a companion measure (S 286—S Rept 103-183) and HR 856 on Nov. 16. The Senate committee-approved measure was a six-year authorization, providing $217 million in fiscal 1994.

There was no further action on either bill, but the five new research institutes were authorized in the Goals 2000 school reform legislation (HR 1804). (Goals 2000, p. 620) ❑

School Safety

The Senate Labor and Human Resources Committee Nov. 10, 1993, reported (S 1125—S Rept 103-180) and the full House Feb. 22, 1994, by voice vote passed (HR 2455) legislation that sought to help local school districts make schools safer. At that time, approximately three million violent crimes and thefts were occurring at schools every year. Since 1985, almost one million youths a year between ages 12 and 19 had been victims of violent crime.

S 1125 authorized $75 million in fiscal 1994 and $100 million in fiscal 1995 to provide competitive grants to school districts most troubled by crime and violence. The grants, which could not exceed $3 million a year and could not last longer than two years, could be used several ways, including training school employees to deal with violence; setting up conflict resolution programs; providing alternative after-school programs as safe havens for students; educating students and parents about the dangers of guns and other weapons; and buying and installing metal detectors and hiring security guards.

HR 2455 would have authorized $50 million in fiscal 1994 for school districts to help end violence and crime in schools. School districts with high juvenile crime or homicide rates could apply for one-year grants of up to $3 million.

Congress subsequently folded the provisions of HR 2455 into the Goals 2000 school reform legislation (HR 1804). (Goals 2000, p. 620) ❑

School Technology

The Senate Labor and Human Resources Committee March 9, 1994, reported a bill (S 1040—S Rept 103-234) to authorize $352.5 million in fiscal 1995 to help equip the nation's classrooms with the latest technologies, such as interactive educational software and computer networks.

Before the Department of Education was created in 1979, the U.S. Office of Education played a lead role in fostering educational television and computing in schools. In 1981, Congress consolidated spending on such programs into the broader pool of the Chapter 2 block grant program to states. As a result, the direction provided by the federal government to help schools keep pace with technology was lost. The Education Department's Star Schools Program, an experiment in distance learning, was created in 1988 and by 1994 reached roughly 200,000 students. Apart from that, the federal role in coordinating school technology efforts had remained minimal.

S 1040 proposed to create a new Office of Educational Technology within the Education Department to oversee efforts to upgrade schools. The federal government was to grant states money using existing Education Department formulas that favored poorer school districts. Schools then would apply to the states for the funds, showing how they would use the money to improve their classroom communications technology. The grant program would be in addition to other federal efforts under way to help schools adapt to new technologies.

Although S 1040 saw no further congressional action, some of its provisions were incorporated in the Goals 2000 education bill (HR 1804) and the Elementary and Secondary Education Act reauthorization (HR 6). For example, HR 1804 provided for the creation of an Office of Educational Technology to carry out such goals as using technology to help ensure that all students could meet state performance standards. HR 6 included millions of dollars to help schools acquire advanced technology. (HR 1804, p. 620; HR 6, p. 609)

1995–1996

Education policy made only modest advances in 1995–1996. Lawmakers were unable to complete action on a reauthorization of the Individuals with Disabilities Education Act and a bill making changes in the federal direct student loan program. Members cleared legislation to disengage the federal government from involvement with the Student Loan Marketing Association (Sallie Mae) and the College Construction Loan Insurance Association (Connie Lee), to abolish the Goals 2000 standards review board and to ease requirements schools had to meet to show they were fulfilling nutritional guidelines for lunch and breakfast programs.

In related action, conferees on a federal job training bill (HR 1617) included a provision to repeal the 1994 school-to-work law (HR 2884—PL 103-239), which sought to help high school seniors ease into the workforce. HR 1617 died upon adjournment. (Job training, p. 669; school-to-work, p. 627)

IDEA Authorization

In 1996, reauthorization of the Individuals with Disabilities Education Act (IDEA) passed in the House (HR 3268) with bipartisan support, but intractable disputes killed a companion measure in the Senate (S 1578).

Both the House and Senate bills proposed to revamp the landmark 1975 law (PL 94-142) in many areas, including giving schools more flexibility to discipline unruly or violent disabled students. HR 3268 also contained a controversial proposal to change the program's funding formula. (PL 94-142, Congress and the Nation Vol. IV, p. 389)

The legislation's failure did not immediately impede the program's federal funding. Boosted in large measure by Republicans, the fiscal 1997 omnibus appropriations bill (HR 3610—PL 104-208) allocated $4 billion to IDEA, a $790.6 million increase from the year before.

BACKGROUND

IDEA was enacted to help states respond to federal and state court rulings that mandated a free public school education for all disabled children. Before that, about 1.75 million disabled children, usually the most severely handicapped, received no schooling, and many others were underserved. Subsequent IDEA reauthorizations created new programs for disabled infants and toddlers. (Reauthorizations, Congress and the Nation Vol. V, p. 658; Congress and the Nation Vol. VI, p. 567; Congress and the Nation Vol. VII, p. 652; and Congress and the Nation Vol. VIII, p. 647)

The 1975 act guaranteed the right of disabled children to a free education and assured that they would be placed in what ultimately was defined as "the least restrictive environment"—usually in schools and classrooms with students who were not disabled. The law required that each disabled child have an individualized education plan (IEP). Designed by the child's parents, teacher and school administrators, the IEP specified the child's performance levels, goals and any needed special services.

In 1996, the states were serving an estimated 5.4 million children with disabilities, most of them school age, with federal help under the disabilities act. Half the school-age children had learning disabilities, while the others had been diagnosed with physical, mental or emotional maladies. In all, these youngsters accounted for 10 percent of the nation's public school population.

IDEA was unusual for civil rights legislation in that it provided federal funds to carry out its mandates. While the federal funds covered a relatively small percentage of the cost of special education, they still made IDEA the second largest source of federal elementary and secondary aid. The basic grant program under the act was permanently authorized, but the special purpose funds needed periodic renewal.

SENATE ACTION

The Senate Labor and Human Resources Committee reported S 1578 (S Rept 104-275) on May 20, 1996.

Bill sponsor Bill Frist, R-Tenn., chairman of the Disability Policy Subcommittee, had offered a revised version of S 1578 that was approved in committee by voice vote. Frist's bill aimed to ease some of the law's paperwork and reporting requirements. It also required that states make mediation available to school authorities and parents who disagreed over a disabled student's education plan, instead of channeling them to a formal appeals process. And it sought to limit the amount of attorneys' fees that parents could collect in disputes with schools.

The most contentious element of the bill was a Frist amendment to give schools more flexibility to discipline disabled students. The amendment, put together with contributions from various education groups, appeared to narrow some of the differences between disciplinary policies for disabled students and those for other students. It provided that in extreme circumstances—when a weapon or drugs were involved—a disabled student could be expelled if the behavior was unrelated to the disability.

The committee rejected an amendment by Judd Gregg, R-N.H., to express a sense of the Senate that more federal money ought to be spent on IDEA before any new education programs were funded. Gregg said that the federal government contributed only 7 percent of the cost of educating disabled students, instead of the 40 percent to which Congress had committed itself. The committee also rejected an amendment by Nancy Landon Kassebaum, R-Kan., chairman of the Senate Labor and Human Resources Committee, to limit the expenses schools had to bear when providing services for disabled students that were not normally provided for other students.

Supporters tried unsuccessfully to move S 1578 to the floor immediately before the retirement of Majority Leader Bob Dole, R-Kan., a longtime program advocate who left the Senate to campaign full time for president. They tried again periodically until the final days before adjournment, but to no avail.

HOUSE ACTION

The House Economic and Educational Opportunities Committee reported HR 3268 (H Rept 104-614) on June 10, 1996. The committee version reflected input from a broad coalition of groups representing disabled children and the general education community. Controversy surrounded provisions to allow states to stop all educational services in extreme disciplinary cases and to impose a new funding formula.

Even though the committee removed references to "assault and battery" as a grounds for expulsion and added language providing federal definitions for "weapons" and "drugs," most of the interest groups objected to the notion of ending educational services to disabled students. Democrats agreed, arguing that it ran counter to the law's intent and would ultimately be more costly and problematic to society. Republicans countered that expulsion was appropriate in certain circumstances.

An attempt by Rep. Robert C. Scott, D-Va., to strike the provisions related to cessation of services to disabled students was rejected. The committee approved a George Miller, D-Calif., amendment to require that a hearing officer review every decision that a student's misconduct was unrelated to his or her disability in cases that could lead to cessation of services.

Traditionally, funds for the program were distributed to states based on the number of children identified as disabled. The House bill proposed instead to distribute the funds based mainly on each state's school-age population. A small adjustment would be made to reflect the number of children living in poverty in each state. Proponents said the new funding formula, which would be phased in over 10 years, would discourage states from identifying students as disabled as a way to qualify for more federal aid.

Assuming the amount of federal money remained unchanged after the 10-year transition period, the biggest losers would be Florida, Massachusetts and New Jersey. Big potential winners included California, Georgia, Louisiana and Michigan. The committee rejected an amendment offered by Robert E. Andrews, D-N.J., to retain the existing funding formula. Andrews argued that the bill would sever the link between the need for special education and the resources to provide it. He dismissed claims that states were gaming the system to gain more federal aid, noting that the federal government provided a relatively small proportion of special education money and that parents generally were not eager to have their children labeled as disabled. Rep. Marge Roukema, R-N.J., predicted that the new formula would set off "a war between the states." Rep. Randy "Duke" Cunningham, R-Calif., sponsor of HR 3268, said the new formula was simply an attempt to rationalize the way federal aid was distributed and to make it fairer.

The House passed HR 3268 by voice vote under suspension of the rules June 10. The committee version had been amended to assuage potential losers from the proposed new funding formula during the transition period. Under the revision, if a state stood to lose 10 percent or less of what it received in fiscal 1996, it would receive its full 1996 allotment. If a state was in line to lose more than 10 percent of its fiscal 1996 allotment, it would receive the formula amount plus 10 percent of its fiscal 1996 funding.

In the final days before adjournment, Frist made a pitch for a compromise that he hoped could substitute for a conference, but his effort failed.   ❑

Direct Student Loans

Congress in 1995 attempted to make changes in education aid programs, including scaling back a controversial direct student loan program under which the government bypassed banks and commercial lenders and sent aid for students directly to colleges, universities and postsecondary schools. However, the provisions were part of the deficit-reducing budget-reconciliation bill (HR 2491), which President Clinton vetoed Dec. 6. Clinton cited cuts in education programs, among other factors, in explaining his veto. *(Reconciliation, p. 68)*

The final reconciliation bill called for achieving about $5 billion in savings from education programs over seven years. Of that, $1.6 billion was to come from imposing a 10 percent ceiling on the direct loan program. Other savings were to come from severing the government's links to the Student Loan Marketing Association (Sallie Mae) and the College Construction Loan Insurance Association (Connie Lee) and from cutting federal subsidies to guaranty agencies. The final bill did not include House provisions that would have raised interest costs for students or parents. *(Sallie Mae, Connie Lee, p. 633)*

Companion legislation (HR 530, S 495) that sought to place a permanent 40 percent limit on direct student loans saw no congressional action.

BACKGROUND

Most student loans were guaranteed through the Federal Family Education Loan Program, a network of predominantly private sector banks and guaranty agencies created under the Higher Education Act of 1965 (PL 89-329). Under this system, the government paid interest subsidies to lenders who made, held, or collected loans and reimbursed guaranty agencies for administrative expenses and loans on which borrowers defaulted for any reason. *(PL 89-329, Congress and the Nation Vol. II, p. 716)*

The direct lending program began as a pilot program during the Bush administration under a 1992 bill that reauthorized the Higher Education Act (PL 102-325). When Clinton took office, supporters saw an opportunity to expand the program. The 1993 budget-reconciliation bill (HR 2264—PL 103-66) authorized an increase from the initial level of 5 percent of the student loan market to 60 percent by academic year 1998–1999. *(PL 102-325, Congress and the Nation Vol. VIII, p. 653; 1993 action, direct student loans, p. 625)*

The Congressional Budget Office estimated that overall the federal government would be responsible for $26.6 billion in direct and guaranteed loans in fiscal 1996. The government was expected to pay just over $2.4 billion in subsidies during that period to banks and guaranty agencies for both programs.

For Clinton and congressional Democrats, the appeal of the direct lending program was simple: cut out the banks and other middlemen to reduce bureaucracy and costs. They argued that the increased efficiencies that would result from expanding direct lending could save up to $1 billion in annual subsidies and fees and that the money could provide additional loans to millions of students. Moreover, Education Secretary Richard W. Riley argued that competition would spur innovation and improve services on new and existing loans for all colleges as the federal government and private banks competed for their business.

Republicans, however, did not agree that the government would do a more efficient job. Noting that the Education Department had little experience collecting money, House Republicans predicted that greater reliance on direct lending would lead to the loss of billions of dollars through waste and inefficiency. They contended that terminating the direct loan program would yield $1.5 billion through better collections, reduced waste and fewer federal bureaucracies. The rapid expansion of the program proposed by Clinton angered Republicans, many of whom had been willing to accept the program as a demonstration project or within the previous constraints.

HOUSE ACTION

The House Economic and Educational Opportunities Committee Sept. 28, 1995, approved its version of the education provisions of HR 2491, which aimed to produce $10.2 billion in deficit reduction from the college financial aid system over seven years.

The package contained provisions to eliminate the direct lending program, yielding $1.2 billion in savings, according to GOP committee staff members. It also terminated the interest-free grace period enjoyed by student borrowers during the first six months after graduation, for deficit reduction of $3.5 billion. In addition, the plan aimed to increase the maximum interest rates on loans to parents of dependent undergraduate students—called PLUS loans—from 9 percent to 11 percent. This change was estimated to yield $450 million. The provisions also were designed to reduce subsidies to lenders, loan holders and guaranty agencies, resulting in savings of about $5.1 billion. And they called for reducing the number of administrators at the Education Department responsible for overseeing banks and guaranty agencies and direct lending.

The House committee markup was characterized by ideological arguments and partisan bickering. Democrats charged that the changes proposed by the GOP would decrease loan availability and unnecessarily saddle former students with additional debt. Republicans countered that failure by Congress to balance the federal budget would have staggering long-term economic consequences.

SENATE ACTION

The Senate Labor and Human Resources Committee approved its education provisions in a markup that began Sept. 22 and continued Sept. 26. They aimed to achieve $10.9 billion in deficit reduction over seven years.

The package proposed to cap the direct loan program at 20 percent of total loan volume, generating nearly $1.5 billion in savings. It also proposed to eliminate the no-interest grace period for college graduates, though only for new borrowers, raising $2.7 billion. Postsecondary schools that participated in federal loan programs would be required to pay a new 0.85 percent fee based on the total number of students that received federally guaranteed loans at such institutions. The committee estimated that such participation fees would yield almost $2 billion. The Senate package called for privatizing Connie Lee, for $7 million in savings over seven years. In addition, the plan sought to raise $694 million by increasing the interest rate on PLUS loans from 9 percent to 10 percent.

Costs to lenders and holders of student loans would increase by almost $4 billion. For example, the amount paid to lenders by the government for defaulted loans would be decreased from 98 cents on the dollar to 95 cents. Fees paid to the government by lenders for each new student loan issued would increase from 0.5 percent to 1 percent. A new 0.05 percent annual fee on loan holders would be payable to the government for student loans made after Jan. 1, 1996.

Senate Labor and Human Resources rejected amendments by Daniel R. Coats, R-Ind., and Judd Gregg, R-N.H., to repeal the direct loan program, eliminate the grace period interest subsidy for recent college graduates and drop the 0.85 student loan participation fee on postsecondary institutions. It also rejected amendments by Edward M. Kennedy, D-Mass., to remove the proposed 0.85 percent participation fee on postsecondary schools, the 20 percent limit on the direct lending program, and the grace period interest-subsidy requirement and an amendment by Claiborne Pell, D-R.I., to drop the 0.85 percent participation fee.

When the reconciliation bill came to the Senate floor, lawmakers adopted 99–0 on Oct. 26 an amendment, sponsored by Labor and Human Resources Chairman Nancy Landon Kassebaum, R-Kan., that restored $5.9 billion in funding for education, eliminated the 0.85 percent fee for colleges and universities and the increase in interest rates on loans to parents of undergraduates, and retained the grace period for college student loans.

The Senate Oct. 26 also agreed, 51–48, to a Pete V. Domenici, R-N.M., motion to table (kill) a Kennedy amendment to restore $7 billion in student loan cuts by striking the bill's 0.85 percent fee imposed on universities based on their student loan volume, restoring the six-month postgraduation grace period on student loans, eliminating interest rate increases on PLUS loans and eliminating the 20 percent cap on direct lending. These changes would have been offset by striking the provisions to reduce the alternative minimum tax, which was used by some small businesses.

CONFERENCE

Conferees on the reconciliation bill dropped controversial House provisions that would have raised interest costs for parents or students. Instead, they agreed to impose a 10 percent ceiling on the federal direct loan program, splitting the difference between the Senate's 20 percent level and the House proposal to eliminate the program.   ❑

Sallie Mae, Connie Lee

Congress in 1996 severed federal ties to two government-sponsored enterprises—the Student Loan Marketing Association (Sallie Mae) and the College Construction Loan Insurance Association (Connie Lee). The changes were included in the fiscal 1997 appropriations bill for the departments of Labor, Health and Human Services, and Education (HR 3755), which in turn was folded into an omnibus appropriations bill (HR 3610—PL 104-208). *(Omnibus appropriations, p. 76)*

Sallie Mae, a private corporation, bought student loans from banks and other loan holders in the secondary market. Connie Lee, partly owned by the Education Department, insured bond financing for renovating and building higher education facilities.

HR 3610 gave Sallie Mae stockholders the right to vote to reorganize as a private company. If they did so, Sallie Mae could continue to purchase student loans through Sept. 30, 2007. The government-sponsored enterprise would dissolve a year later, and its charter would be repealed. If the stockholders voted against reorganization, Sallie Mae would have to conclude its business by July 1, 2013. The bill repealed the authorizing legislation for Connie Lee.

The House had passed the provisions as separate legislation (HR 1720) by voice vote under suspension of the rules Sept. 24, 1996. HR 1720 also would have abolished more than 50 higher education programs, including the State Postsecondary Review Program, a network of state-level organizations charged with reducing fraud by for-profit, proprietary postsecondary institutions. In addition, the measure would have prohibited the Department of Education from retroactively enforcing the so called 85/15 rule, which required for-profit trade schools to obtain at least 15 percent of their revenue from sources other than federally guaranteed student loans. The House Economic and Educational Opportunities Committee had reported HR 1720 (H Rept 104-153) on June 22, 1995.

The House had included provisions of HR 1720 in a bill (HR 1617) to overhaul job training programs, which it passed in 1995. However, HR 1617 died upon adjournment of the 104th Congress. In addition, the federal government's ties to Sallie Mae and Connie Lee would have been cut under the deficit-reducing fiscal 1996 budget reconciliation bill (HR 2491), but the president vetoed that measure Dec. 6, 1995. *(Job training, p. 669; budget reconciliation, p. 68)* ❑

School Lunch

Congress in 1996 cleared a bill (HR 2066) making it easier for schools to show they were meeting new federal nutritional guidelines for their lunch and breakfast programs. President Clinton signed the measure into law (PL 104-149) May 29.

HR 2066, sponsored by House Economic and Educational Opportunities Committee Chairman Bill Goodling, R-Pa., amended a 1994 law (PL 103-448) that required schools to meet new dietary guidelines by the 1996–1997 school year. A primary goal of the guidelines was to reduce schoolchildren's consumption of fat and saturated fats. *(1994 act, p. 575)*

Under the 1994 law, schools could choose to meet the nutrition requirements either through the existing system, which specified that certain types of food be on the menu, or through a new nutritional content analysis of food offered. But Goodling said existing U.S. Department of Agriculture (USDA) regulations would not give schools enough flexibility if they chose to meet the guidelines under the food-based menu plan. He said such schools would have to provide additional servings of low-fat foods, such as grains, fruits and vegetables—adding 10 cents to 17 cents to the cost of meals. Program administrators said they would not have the flexibility to meet guidelines by, for example, preparing food differently. The alternative, he said, was for schools to buy new computer hardware and get extensive training in nutritional analysis of their food.

As reported May 7, 1996, by the House Economic and Educational Opportunities Committee, HR 2066 (H Rept 104-561) specified that schools could use "any reasonable approach" to show compliance with the guidelines, and it clarified that they could use the food-based system in existence before enactment of the 1994 law as long as they met the dietary guidelines. USDA Undersecretary for Food, Nutrition, and Consumer Services Ellen Haas said the committee bill was a "misguided effort" that would erode the accountability necessary to ensure that schools met the requirements. The committee version was later amended to show that the reasonable approach had to be within guidelines established by USDA. The White House Office of Management and Budget then released a statement supporting the legislation.

The House passed HR 2066 on May 14 by voice vote under suspension of the rules. The Senate passed the measure by voice vote May 16. ❑

Goals 2000 Review Board

The House, by voice vote under suspension of the rules May 15, 1995, passed a bill (HR 1045) to eliminate a standards board under the 1994 Goals 2000 education reform law (HR 1804—PL 103-227); a companion bill (S 323) was not taken up in the Senate. However, Congress in 1996 acted in the omnibus fiscal 1996 appropriations bill (HR 3019—PL 104-134) that funded the Education Department and other agencies. *(Omnibus appropriations, p. 71)*

HR 1045 proposed to cancel the National Education Standards and Improvement Council, a presidentially appointed panel that was to review education standards submitted by states that participated in Goals 2000. Under Goals 2000, the federal government established eight national education goals, including the improvement of graduation rates and school safety. States could apply for grants under the law, regardless of whether they participated in the program. The law also required participating states to develop academic standards and submit them to the council. Even without the council, curriculum standards would be required for the states to receive grants. *(Goals 2000, p. 620)*

Conservatives said the council could usurp the authority of state and local governments. While some House Democrats supported the council, no one offered resistance to its elimination during consideration of HR 1045 in the House Economic and Educational Opportunities Committee or on the floor. Opportunities Committee Chairman Bill Goodling, R-Pa., chief sponsor of the bill, said eliminating the council might help stave off those who wanted to repeal the entire Goals program.

During committee markup, Rep. Lindsey Graham, R-S.C., offered an amendment to abolish Goals 2000. Rep. Tom Petri, R-Wis., moved that Graham's amendment was out of order because it was not germane to the bill, and it was set aside. Graham said that the law would have the effect of federalizing schools, historically a state and local responsibility.

HR 3019 repealed the council as well as the requirement that states develop any opportunity-to-learn standards or strategies. In addition, state reform plans developed under Goals 2000 no longer needed Education Department approval if states certified that they were pursuing a plan to meet the law's requirements. ❑

CHAPTER 11

Housing and Urban Aid

Housing and Urban Aid

When Henry G. Cisneros took the helm of the troubled Department of Housing and Urban Development (HUD) in 1993, his agenda for America's crumbling cities was expansive, ambitious and directly Democratic. The scourge of homelessness topped Cisneros's list, followed by the faded dream of urban renewal.

What a difference a couple of years and a change in control of Congress made. No major housing legislation passed the Republican-led 104th Congress, yet the ground beneath HUD shifted dramatically. Housing served as an example of how Republicans in Congress drove White House policy makers in directions they would not have gone otherwise.

COMPLAINTS ABOUT HUD

Even before the GOP became the majority party in Congress, few on Capitol Hill doubted that HUD needed to change. Nonpartisan and independent research groups, Democrats and Republicans all described it as a troubled agency, plagued by chronic mismanagement and a burgeoning budget.

HUD's mandate grew dramatically since it was created in 1965 to direct federal housing policies. It was charged with providing affordable housing for poor families, helping poor families pay their rent, providing mortgage insurance for low- and middle-income families, assisting the homeless, guaranteeing fair housing opportunities and providing funds for community development and other social services.

Critics of HUD said the agency was trying to do too much. The number of housing programs exploded—from 54 in 1980 to more than 200, according to a 1994 study by the National Academy of Public Administration, a group of scholars and government administrators who offered advice on public administration issues.

Critics also pointed to the nation's public housing developments as proof of HUD's ineptitude. Public housing programs, a federal-local effort, sought to provide affordable housing to poor families, the elderly and the disabled. In 1995, the country's 3,400 public housing authorities operated 13,200 developments, covering 1.25 million units serving about 3.4 million people. Most developments were in good shape, but many of the larger ones were not. The nation's public housing stock needed more than $20 billion in repairs and modernization, according to the General Accounting Office.

Another major complaint was that HUD consumed a growing part of the annual domestic discretionary budget. HUD's outlays—how much it spent in a given year—rose from $22.1 billion in fiscal 1992 to about $30 billion in fiscal 1995, a 35 percent increase, according to the Congressional Budget Office

(CBO). By contrast, outlays for all domestic discretionary programs rose 19.5 percent over the same period.

The HUD budget rose largely because of the soaring cost of assisted housing programs—rental assistance to low-income tenants. Assisted housing, one of HUD's primary responsibilities, helped roughly 4.7 million low-income households pay their rent through so-called Section 8 programs. These were divided into two types of subsidies: those tied to specific housing developments and those given directly to tenants in the form of vouchers and certificates.

The cost of rental assistance rose steadily since the mid-1970s as more households received assistance and the average cost of subsidies increased. Adjusted for inflation, outlays rose from $6.6 billion in 1977 to more than $22 billion in 1994, according to the CBO. Without changes, the cost of rental assistance was expected to mount by the year 2000 as long-term contracts were renewed. In the past, contracts were authorized for up to 40 years, and the money for the commitments was appropriated in the first year.

104TH CONGRESS

In the weeks following the 1994 elections, no agency faced more peril than HUD. Many Republicans began clamoring anew to eliminate the long-troubled department. They said the agency spent too much money while mismanaging its programs and failing in one of its primary missions: to provide adequate housing for poor people. Given the political situation, the Office of Management and Budget proposed serving up HUD as a sacrifice, and the White House almost went along.

Soon, however, the faction that wanted to kill the department outright—terminating many programs and spreading the

REFERENCES

Discussion of housing and urban aid action for the years 1945–1964 may be found in *Congress and the Nation Vol. I,* pp. 459–515; for the years 1965–1968, *Congress and the Nation Vol. II,* pp. 183–226; for the years 1969–1972, *Congress and the Nation Vol. III,* pp. 635–657; for the years 1973–1976, *Congress and the Nation Vol. IV,* pp. 471–502; for the years 1977–1980, *Congress and the Nation Vol. V,* pp. 429–448; for the years 1981–1984, *Congress and the Nation Vol. VI,* pp. 629–639; for the years 1985–1988, *Congress and the Nation Vol. VII,* pp. 667–684; for the years 1989–1992, *Congress and the Nation Vol. VIII,* pp. 663–700.

Outlays for Community and Regional Development

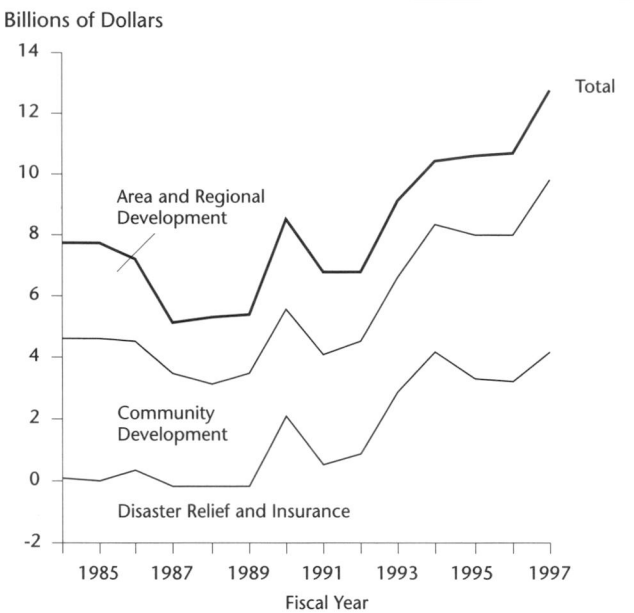

Billions of Dollars

Total

Area and Regional Development

Community Development

Disaster Relief and Insurance

Fiscal Year

NOTE: Data for 1997 are estimated.

SOURCE: Office of Management and Budget, *Historical Tables, Budget of the United States Government: Fiscal Year 1998* (Washington, D.C.: U.S. Government Printing Office, 1997), Table 3.2.

remaining responsibilities among other agencies—was overtaken by another bloc of lawmakers who favored a more moderate approach. This group wanted to fix HUD by shrinking it and delegating many of its functions to the states. This camp's efforts moved to the forefront when Senate and House budget leaders decided not to include the elimination of HUD in their 1996 budget resolution. They apparently decided that eliminating HUD to save money was easier said than done, in part because many federal housing programs have locked the government into long-term spending commitments.

Meanwhile, Rick A. Lazio, R-N.Y., chairman of the House Banking and Financial Services Subcommittee on Housing and Community Opportunity, and like-minded moderates developed proposals to remake HUD. Their efforts were driven by three major principles: cutting spending, transferring more authority to states and localities and redefining HUD's mission to make it an overseer instead of what they called an overzealous regulator of federal programs.

President Clinton and many Democrats agreed that HUD needed to be revamped, and, in a preemptive strike, Cisneros of-

fered a plan to consolidate 60 major HUD programs into three funds, saving up to $13 billion in outlays over five years. He aimed to increase competition for low-income tenants by giving federal public housing money directly to renters. Currently, public housing authorities received federal subsidies to maintain and operate housing developments. Under the new system, to be phased in over seven years, the subsidies would be converted into vouchers to be given directly to tenants. Public housing authorities would earn the operating funds formerly provided by the government by competing with the private market for renters.

While dismaying the public housing advocates who had heartily welcomed Cisneros's appointment, the administration's plan for HUD's consolidation and downsizing was generally greeted warmly on Capitol Hill. It was also very Republican, said House and Senate Republican staff members specializing in housing. For example, Cisneros's new "one-strike-and-you're-out" policy for drug abuse in public housing mirrored proposed GOP legislation.

CISNEROS UNSHACKLED

In some respects, the Republicans unshackled Cisneros to make bold moves a Democratic majority never would have allowed. Cisneros spent his first two years in office wrestling with Democrats over waiving the one-for-one rule, which said for every public housing unit destroyed, another would have to be built. That rule had tied the hands of Republican HUD secretaries for more than a decade.

By the end of 1996, HUD would tear down 23,000 public housing units, but how many would be replaced with new, low-rise units or housing vouchers neither HUD officials nor housing authorities could say. "Jack Kemp [Bush administration housing secretary] said, 'I don't want to be known as the secretary of demolition.' Henry Cisneros is doing things no Republican housing secretary could have gotten away with," a Senate Republican aide said.

At HUD, preservation and redesign were out; demolition, law enforcement and thrift were in. Cisneros in 1995 boasted that federal and local police made 6,826 arrests in public housing, seized 558 weapons and confiscated drugs worth nearly $3 million.

The agency's fiscal 1997 budget request called for merging more than 20 programs into three, the first phase of a plan to consolidate more than 60 programs, phase out 29 inactive programs, and shut down 37 others. That plan would reduce HUD employment from 11,650 employees to 10,447, with a goal of 7,500 by 2001.

Chronology of Action on Housing and Urban Aid

1993–1994

Enterprise Zones

In 1993, 13 years after the first enterprise zone legislation was introduced in Congress, provisions offering tax breaks and regulatory relief for economically distressed inner cities and rural towns were enacted, as part of a budget reconciliation measure (HR 2264—PL 103-66). *(Reconciliation, p. 44)*

BACKGROUND

Congress had debated enterprise zones annually since 1982, when Ronald Reagan was president. For several years, either the House or the Senate passed a variation of enterprise zone legislation, only to see the other chamber balk at the provisions.

Legislation finally was enacted in 1988 (PL 100-242) authorizing the Department of Housing and Urban Development (HUD) to designate 100 zones in which state and local governments would reduce taxes, fees and bureaucracy while they increased public services to encourage economic development. Two-thirds of the zones were in cities; one-third were in rural areas. But the law provided no federal tax breaks and little federal money—$1 million a year for administrative expenses. HUD developed regulations for the zones and accepted nearly 300 applications from areas seeking designation. However, Jack F. Kemp (R-N.Y., House 1971–1989), who served as HUD secretary from 1989 to 1993, believed that the law was flawed, especially because it lacked federal tax incentives. No federal enterprise zones were ever declared. *(1988 law, Congress and the Nation Vol. VII, p. 672)*

President George Bush in 1992 vetoed—for other reasons—two tax bills that included enterprise zone language. *(1992 action, Congress and the Nation Vol. VIII, p. 699)*

While the federal government debated the merits of zones in the 1980s, many states were putting them to a test. About 40 states authorized enterprise zones, and the 30 most active states named about 800. Typical incentives included loans and loan guarantees, reductions in sales and local property taxes for businesses that located in depressed areas and tax credits for hiring local employees. Proponents argued that new federal legislation was still necessary, mainly because a federal presence could lend more energy and influence. Federal tax breaks were in demand because federal taxes generally were higher than state and local taxes. Proponents also hoped that federal legislation would bring needed attention to depressed areas.

Originally, the state efforts were seen by some as a way to cut back the government's role in poor areas by reducing or eliminating taxes and regulations. But states and localities gradually became more involved in the zones, improving roads and sewers, enhancing social services, helping finance businesses and marketing the zone itself.

ADMINISTRATION PROPOSAL

President Clinton presented an enterprise zone plan May 4, 1993, that targeted poor neighborhoods with tax breaks and increased spending on social programs. The plan envisioned the competitive selection of 110 zones that would qualify for certain business tax incentives and federal money. Ten of these would be singled out as "empowerment zones," and many of the program's resources would be concentrated there. One hundred "enterprise communities" were to be eligible for smaller benefits. An enterprise board made up of cabinet secretaries from domestic agencies would coordinate the program.

Clinton's proposal called for $4.1 billion in new tax breaks over five years, including about $3 billion in tax breaks for employment and training wage credits in the 10 empowerment zones and $1 billion to fund other tax incentives.

Reaction to Clinton's proposal was not enthusiastic. Conservatives warned that it raised the specter of federal control over local activities and criticized the lack of incentives for capital formation, including a capital gains tax break for investment in the zones. Rep. Charles B. Rangel, D-N.Y., and others who represented low-income areas had hoped for a more potent plan to revitalize impoverished communities. Rangel played down the importance of increased tax incentives, maintaining that most businesses would not expand or relocate into depressed areas without improvements in infrastructure and social services. Rangel also said he would resist adding more zones unless more federal funds were available.

LEGISLATIVE ACTION

The House approved a $5.3 billion version of Clinton's enterprise zone proposal as part of HR 2264. As passed, the bill created 10 empowerment zones (six in urban areas, three in rural areas and one on a Native American reservation) and 100 enterprise communities (65 urban, 30 rural and five on Native American reservations) for fiscal 1994 and 1995. It also included a package of financial incentives for developing business in an enterprise area, for hiring zone residents and contributing to their retirement plans, for investing in depreciable property and for developing low-income housing. In addition, the bill stipulated that a board was to be established to coordinate the designation of zones.

The Senate did not include enterprise zone provisions in the reconciliation measure it passed.

The overarching task facing House and Senate conferees on the omnibus bill was to meet Senate demands for a much lower energy tax than the House had approved, while keeping the votes of liberals, particularly in the House, who insisted that enterprise zone provisions, as well as several other social spending programs, be retained. The Congressional Black Caucus, whose 38 House Democrats held a crucial bloc of votes, made clear that inclusion of enterprise zones was "nonnegotiable."

With hard lobbying by Rangel and others, the compromise bill included a scaled-back version of Clinton's proposal—$2.5 billion in tax incentives—plus a new social services block grant for the enterprise zones worth $1 billion over two years. The conference version of HR 2264 cut the number of zones by 10 percent and pared the incentives. The maximum credit for wages paid to zone employees went from $5,000 per employee in the House bill to $3,000 in the final bill. The write-off for investing in depreciable property went from $75,000 in the House bill to $37,500 in the first year. A provision expanding the targeted jobs tax credit to cover businesses outside the zone that hired zone residents was dropped, as were the retirement contribution credit and a provision allowing accelerated depreciation. Although the bill provided no capital gains tax targeted for enterprise zones, it included a nationwide capital gains tax deferment for stock in certain small businesses.

HR 2264 dropped the idea of creating an enterprise board. However, on Sept. 9, 1993, Clinton used existing authority to form the President's Community Enterprise Board. He instructed the board, headed by Vice President Al Gore and representing 17 federal agencies, to advise and assist him in coordinating federal policies in distressed areas.

• **Block Grant.** Created a new social services block grant worth $1 billion over two years. The urban zones would get $100 million each, the rural zones would get $40 million each, and the enterprise communities would get $2.95 million each.

• **Native American Reservations.** Provided certain tax incentives for Native American reservations, although no reservations were designated as enterprise zones. Businesses qualified for a shorter depreciation period for property used in connection with a trade or business on a Native American reservation. A 20 percent credit against income tax liability was provided to reservation employers for wages and health insurance costs paid to members of Native American tribes living on or near a reservation. The credit was available for the first $20,000 in wages or benefits paid to each qualified employee. ❏

Housing Reauthorization

The 103rd Congress was unable to clear a comprehensive, two-year reauthorization of federal housing programs. The House passed a reauthorization bill (HR 3838), but the Senate did not act on it. The Senate Banking, Housing and Urban Affairs Committee reported a companion measure (S 2281), but it never reached the floor. The House subsequently gave last-minute approval to a leaner bill (HR 5245), but the Senate did not consider it, either.

BACKGROUND

Created in 1937 by the U.S. Housing Act, public housing was a joint venture by federal and local governments to provide affordable housing to low-income families.

In the 1980s and early 1990s, federal housing policy became an ideological battleground between congressional Democrats who wanted the government to provide more low-income housing and Republicans who wanted to get government out of the housing business. Democrats concentrated on enacting legislation that tied the hands of federal bureaucrats who, under President Ronald Reagan, had been permitting housing author-

ities to tear down public housing without any plans for replacing it. But the restrictions pushed by the Democrats, coupled with a lack of funds, often meant that dilapidated projects were kept in place.

The political dynamics changed dramatically in 1994, with both parties embracing legislation to give state and local officials more control over housing initiatives. Democrats said they were willing to loosen federal requirements because they were no longer battling a Republican administration to preserve the programs. They also attributed some of the shortcomings of their previous efforts to a lack of funding. But implicit in the housing bill was a recognition that the quality of public housing had fallen short.

The Clinton administration opened the debate on federal housing programs April 20, 1994, when Housing and Urban Development (HUD) Secretary Henry G. Cisneros unveiled a series of initiatives to direct more money into assistance for the homeless, subsidized private housing and fair housing, while decreasing funds for public housing. Cisneros recommended cuts in public housing operating subsidies and modernization accounts; the HOME (Homeownership Made Easy) program, which provided matching grants to states and localities for affordable housing; and the Section 202 program, which provided grants to groups that developed housing for the elderly. Cisneros also proposed giving public housing authorities the flexibility to use modernization funds to demolish and replace blighted public housing.

LEGISLATIVE ACTION

The House Banking, Finance and Urban Affairs Committee on July 15, 1994, reported HR 3838 (H Rept 103-607), authorizing $31.2 billion in fiscal 1995 and $33.6 billion in fiscal 1996 for HUD and Farmers Home Administration (FmHA) programs. The bill relaxed the rent ceilings on working families who lived in public housing and gave local housing authorities more flexibility in using federal funds. It also merged the two forms of subsidized private housing under the Section 8 program, certificates and vouchers, into a single rental assistance program. The bill provided waivers to the so-called one-for-one replacement rule, in response to the situation in which many decrepit public housing buildings remained standing because authorities could not afford replacements or were unable to find locations for new units.

HR 3838 also consolidated several housing programs under the 1987 Stewart B. McKinney Homeless Assistance Act (PL 100-77) into a new grant program aimed at giving states, localities and nonprofit agencies more latitude in combating homelessness, beginning in fiscal 1996. The committee-approved bill authorized $635 million in fiscal 1995 for homeless grants under the existing system and $786.6 million in fiscal 1996 for the consolidated program. *(PL 100-77, Congress and the Nation Vol. VII, p. 677)*

The bill included provisions designed to boost Federal Housing Administration (FHA) activity, raising the amounts that could be insured under the FHA's single-family loan program. HR 3838 raised the FHA's basic limit on mortgages to $101,575 and the high-cost limit to $172,675. In addition, the bill permitted the FHA to form partnerships with state housing finance agencies to insure mortgages of up to $203,150 in high-cost areas, but it restricted the portion of the mortgage that FHA could insure in this arrangement to 35 percent of the principal. *(FHA loans, p. 644)*

Also included in the bill was a controversial provision preempting state and local laws and allowing housing authorities to obtain information about an applicant's or tenant's criminal convictions. Supporters of the language argued that law-abiding citizens in crime-ridden public housing buildings deserved more protection. Opponents said the amendment was too broad and objected to creating separate rules for low-income residents of public housing. To dampen the opposition, the committee voted to limit record searches to 10 years and provide penalties for unauthorized disclosure of the information. A provision to allow tenants to ban guns in their developments was rejected by the panel.

The House passed HR 3838 on July 22 by 345–36. The main controversy came over a Jay C. Kim, R-Calif., amendment to prohibit illegal immigrants from receiving aid under the McKinney Act for more than seven days. The proposal was part of an ongoing effort to restrict federal aid to illegal immigrants. Jose E. Serrano, D-N.Y., offered an amendment to block Kim's provision unless federal funds were provided to enable states, localities and other agencies to determine who would be entitled to aid. Marge Roukema, R-N.J., countered by amending Serrano's proposal to authorize whatever funds were necessary to carry out the provisions. Both the Serrano and Roukema proposals were adopted by voice vote. Roukema offered another amendment, approved 235–0 on a standing vote, that modified Kim's proposal so that it did not apply to any presidentially declared disaster, such as an earthquake. Kim's amended proposal was adopted 220–176 on July 22.

An amendment by Peter I. Blute, R-Mass., adopted by voice vote, generally prohibited nonelderly people with a history of drug or alcohol abuse from living in subsidized housing designated primarily for the elderly. In addition, nonelderly applicants for such housing were to be required to sign a statement that no one would live in the unit who "uses (or has a history of use of) alcohol" or drugs.

The Senate Banking, Housing and Urban Affairs Committee reported its version (S 2281—S Rept 103-307) on July 13. The committee bill authorized $28.1 billion for federal housing programs in fiscal 1995 and $39.1 billion in fiscal 1996. Like HR 3838, the bill consolidated several programs under the McKinney Act into a new grant program, and it merged the Section 8 certificate and voucher programs into a single rental assistance program. S 2281 raised the FHA's basic limit on mortgages from $67,500 to $77,500 and left unchanged the $151,725 limit in high-cost areas. However, the bill indexed the high-cost limit to annual percentage changes in the conforming loan limit for government-sponsored enterprises.

The only significant amendment considered by the Senate panel was a Republican proposal to require most public housing residents to perform public service tasks in and around their buildings for 10 hours a month; it was defeated on an 8–10 party-line vote. The Senate bill allowed local housing authorities to obtain a record of an applicant's or tenant's criminal convictions. Without discussion, however, language to ensure that tenants could ban guns in their developments was struck. Unlike HR 3838, the Senate measure permitted public housing authorities to finance the replacement of obsolete public housing developments.

Although widespread agreement existed among Democrats and Republicans (as well as between the two chambers) on the reauthorization legislation, Senate proponents were unable to schedule floor time to consider S 2281. Factors working against consideration of the bill included a threat to raise a number of contentious issues, including the FHA mortgage limits; a dispute involving the First Amendment rights of critics who opposed subsidized housing developments; the House amendment prohibiting nonelderly alcoholics and drug abusers in subsidized elderly housing; and a possible floor amendment requiring public housing residents to perform public service tasks.

When Congress seemed unlikely to enact a comprehensive reauthorization of federal housing programs, supporters offered a leaner bill. HR 5245 would have authorized the FmHA to issue loans to individuals, companies or Native American tribes to build or renovate rural rental housing. It also would have authorized HUD to extend certain low-income subsidized housing contracts with apartment owners. The House passed HR 5245 by voice vote Oct. 7. The bill died upon adjournment. ❑

HOUSING LEADERSHIP

By voice vote Jan. 21, 1993, the Senate confirmed Henry G. Cisneros as secretary of housing and urban development. Cisneros, a Hispanic, was mayor of San Antonio, Texas, from 1981 to 1989. As a mayor, Cisneros initiated extensive urban renewal programs, emphaszing economic development through innovative government-industry partnerships to revitalize urban areas. *(Background, cabinet profiles, p. 1113)*

Low-Income Housing

President Clinton on Oct. 27, 1993, signed into law a bill (HR 2517—PL 103-120) to help improve low-income housing.

HR 2517 authorized $200 million in fiscal 1994 for innovative programs to aid the homeless. It authorized $165 million for a demonstration project to help poor families move out of high-poverty areas. The bill also provided funding for low-income housing or renovation by combining federal housing subsidies with public and private pension funds. The measure set aside $100 million in Section 8 rental certificates for the demonstration program. The federally funded Section 8 program helped low-income tenants pay rent in privately owned buildings. HR 2517 limited the increase in fees paid to public housing authorities for administering the Section 8 certificate and voucher programs in fiscal 1994 to 3.5 percent above the rate paid in fiscal 1993. It also required that the fiscal 1994 fees not fall below the rate paid in fiscal 1993. Housing authorities were paid an administrative fee, which was a percentage of the fair market rents of units they administered. The legislation also reauthorized the National Commission on Manufactured Housing until Oct. 1, 1994, and increased the credit limit of Federal Housing Administration and Government National Mortgage Association mortgage-backed securities.

The House had passed three bills that subsequently were combined in one measure. Passed by voice vote June 29, HR 2517, the Homeless and Community Development Amendments Act, authorized $150 million in fiscal 1994 for innovative programs to aid the homeless. Also passed by voice vote June 29, HR 2531, the Housing Programs Extension Act, extended the authorization of the National Commission on Manufactured Housing as well as a reciprocity agreement between the Department of Housing and Urban Development (HUD) and the Department of Veterans Affairs related to approval of housing subdivisions. Passed 309–106 on Aug. 2, HR 2668 allowed low-income housing to be built or renovated by combining federal housing subsidies with public and private pension funds. The legislation was consistent with HUD Secretary Henry G. Cisneros's intention to get more impact from federal funds by using them to leverage resources from localities, nonprofit organizations and the private sector. Cisneros said that low-income renters would use up to 3,000 project-based certificates in housing projects constructed or rehabilitated by the pension funds. The pension funds would provide $350 million to $550 million in housing for the program.

The Senate passed HR 2517 by voice vote Sept. 23. The Senate version authorized $200 million in fiscal 1994 for innovative programs to aid the homeless. The Senate agreed with the House in increasing from $52.1 million to $165 million the authorization for the demonstration project. The Senate added a provision to limit the increase in fees paid to public housing authorities for administering the Section 8 certificate and voucher programs in fiscal 1994 to 3.5 percent above the rate paid in fiscal 1993. The legislation also required that the 1994 fees not fall below the rate paid in 1993.

The Senate-passed bill contained provisions similar to HR 2531, reauthorizing the National Commission on Manufactured Housing. It also included language similar to that in HR 2668, combining federal subsidies with public and private pension funds to provide funding for low-income housing. The bill set aside $100 million in Section 8 rental certificates for the demonstration program.

The House accepted the Senate changes by voice vote Oct. 6, completing congressional action.   ❑

FHA Foreclosures

Congress in 1994 cleared legislation (S 1299) giving the Department of Housing and Urban Development (HUD) greater flexibility in disposing of apartment buildings that had fallen into government possession through foreclosure. HUD had inherited the buildings when private developers defaulted on mortgages that had been insured by the Federal Housing Administration (FHA) as part of a program to expand the supply of rental housing for low- and moderate-income families.

To ensure that low-income housing stock was preserved and even enlarged, existing law required HUD to provide costly federal housing subsidies when it sold the properties. But HUD had received much less from Congress than it needed to offer those subsidies. As a result, the department had been unable to sell many of the properties, and its inventory was growing rapidly.

S 1299 grandfathered all tenants who had been receiving subsidies when the owner of the building defaulted, but HUD was no longer required to provide subsidies to tenants who had not previously received them. To protect low-income families in units that were not receiving federal subsidies, the bill stipulated that rents could be frozen for two years as a condition of the building sale.

The bill permitted the use of federal housing subsidies to help build replacement units. It also encouraged states and localities to make more use of the HOME (Homeownership Made Easy) Investment Partnerships Act, a block grant for housing needs. S 1299 removed a restriction that had made the program available only to first-time home buyers. It reduced from 30 percent to 25 percent the amount that states and localities had to contribute to new housing construction activities under the HOME program. The bill also extended the use of low-interest loan guarantee program designed to help communities spur economic development.

The Senate Banking, Housing and Urban Affairs Committee reported S 1299 (S Rept 103-174) on Nov. 9, 1993. Before passing the measure by voice vote Nov. 19, the Senate adopted an amendment offered by Donald W. Riegle Jr., D-Mich., and Paul S. Sarbanes, D-Md., giving states more flexibility to determine how much energy assistance to give residents of federally assisted housing. The amendment also allowed state and local governments to provide environmental reviews on behalf of their public housing authorities in certain circumstances. And it authorized $25 million in minority community development activities.

The House Banking, Finance and Urban Affairs Committee Nov. 10 included property disposition language in HR 3400, the government streamlining bill that resulted from Vice President Al Gore's "reinventing government" plan. In 1994, the House took up a modified version of the provisions in a new bill (HR 4067), which it passed 413–9 on March 22. The House then passed S 1299, by voice vote March 22, with the language of HR 4067. The House-passed version did not contain several provisions unrelated to the disposal of FHA buildings, including rent reforms for public housing and a crime prevention initiative.

The Senate agreed to the House changes by voice vote March 25, completing congressional action. President Clinton signed S 1299 (PL 103-233) on April 11. (*Reinventing government,* p. 811)   ❑

Flood Insurance

Congress acted to shore up the National Flood Insurance Program, which was in debt because of scant participation and repeated losses by a small number of homeowners. Flood insurance provisions were enacted in 1994 as part of unrelated legislation (HR 3474—PL 103-325) aimed at encouraging community development banks. *(Community development banks, p. 116)*

Part of the push to reform the program stemmed from the record floods that devastated the Midwest in 1993. Although all owners of homes in a flood plain were legally required to buy flood insurance, many allowed their policies—underwritten by the federal flood insurance fund—to lapse. As a result, only about 10 percent of those affected had flood insurance. Most residents whose homes were destroyed by the rains and rivers had to rely on federal disaster aid to help rebuild.

The federal program was established in 1968, largely because private insurers found providing flood insurance too risky. Although the fund was set up to be self-sustaining, shortfalls had risen since the beginning; in each case, the Treasury had made good on all claims. The program suffered from two major problems: Many homeowners did not regularly buy flood insurance policies, and those who did tended to live in the most flood-prone areas.

As enacted, HR 3474 required that mortgage lenders place in escrow flood insurance premium payments for people living in flood-prone areas. It also authorized lenders to purchase flood insurance for borrowers who refused to do so as required by law. The bill established a mitigation fund, financed by the flood insurance program, to help protect communities and homeowners against flood risks. The Federal Emergency Management Agency (FEMA) also was directed to study the problem as it pertained to coastal and river areas.

LEGISLATIVE ACTION

The House Banking, Finance and Urban Affairs Committee reported its version of the legislation (HR 3191—H Rept 103-414) on Jan. 26, 1994. The House passed HR 3191 on a 335–60 vote May 3. Before the floor debate, Joseph P. Kennedy II, D-Mass., stripped out the bill's most controversial provision—language that would have eliminated federally subsidized flood insurance for buildings located on land that eroded easily. The compromise mollified coastal lawmakers, who argued that the insurance cutoff would hurt economic development in their areas. But the new version prompted criticism from members who maintained that subsidizing insurance in those regions encouraged people to build in unwise locations.

A similar bill (S 1405) stalled in 1993 in the Senate Banking, Housing and Urban Affairs Committee. Several sections of the bill drew opposition from senators representing states with extensive coastal development in flood-prone areas, especially New York, Texas and Florida. Under S 1405, the cost of federal flood insurance to those areas was to increase by about 10 percent a year until the premiums matched the actuarial calculations of the real flood risk. New construction or significant renovations to existing property were not eligible for the insurance.

The increases were to kick in as soon as FEMA completed a map of the erosion zones.

On March 17, 1994, the Senate adopted by voice vote a John Kerry, D-Mass., amendment attaching most of the provisions of S 1405 to HR 3474, the community development bank bill. The Senate passed HR 3474 by voice vote the same day. The House had passed the bank bill by voice vote on Nov. 21, 1993.

The House version of the flood insurance measure was considered somewhat tougher than the Senate's. Among other things, it contained a surcharge on policy buyers to create the mitigation fund; the Senate authorized $45 million in spending from the insurance program for mitigation efforts through fiscal 1996. Senate sponsors removed House language that would have eliminated flood insurance in areas in which a major flood or major erosion was expected every 30 or 60 years.

Conferees on HR 3474 agreed to incorporate the flood insurance reform in that legislation after working out differences between the House and Senate versions. The House adopted the conference report on HR 3474 (H Rept 103-652) by 410–12 on Aug. 4, 1994. The Senate adopted the conference report by voice vote Aug. 9, completing congressional action.

PROVISIONS

As signed into law on Sept. 23, 1994, the flood insurance provisions of HR 3474:

- **Compliance.** Ensured that homeowners who should have flood insurance, as required under existing law, obtained and maintained it. The bill required lenders and companies that serviced mortgages to escrow flood insurance premiums if they maintained an escrow account for the loan for any other purpose. Mortgage lenders (and government-sponsored enterprises such as the Federal National Mortgage Association, or Fannie Mae) were made responsible for compliance with mandatory flood insurance purchase requirements.

Federally regulated lending institutions, including banks, savings and loans, and credit unions, were barred from making or refinancing loans on any structure located in a special flood hazard area unless flood insurance was purchased and maintained for the term of the loan. An exception was made for loans of less than $5,000 with repayment terms of one year or less.

Lenders who demonstrated a "pattern or practice" of noncompliance with flood insurance purchase or notification requirements could be fined by federal regulators up to $350 per loan, to a maximum of $100,000.

Fannie Mae and the Federal Home Loan Mortgage Corporation (Freddie Mac)—government-sponsored enterprises that purchased mortgages—were required to put in place procedures to ensure that any loan they purchased that was required to have flood insurance was indeed covered by a policy.

- **Force Placement.** Required lenders and loan servicers to force-place insurance if borrowers who were required by law to purchase it had not done so. If a lender determined that flood insurance had to be purchased, it was required to notify the borrower, who had 45 days to purchase it. If the borrower failed to buy insurance within that time, the lender would have to buy the insurance on the borrower's behalf.

- **Notice Requirements.** Required lenders to notify borrowers when property being financed was located in a flood hazard area; such notices had to include the fact that borrowers were required to purchase flood insurance, either through the federal program or through private insurers.
- **Community Rating System.** Codified an existing Community Rating System Program administered by FEMA. The rating system program provided incentives, through reduced insurance premiums, to communities that voluntarily adopted and enforced measures to reduce flood risks that exceeded FEMA standards.
- **Flood Risk Mitigation.** Established a new National Flood Mitigation Fund, financed by premiums paid to the National Flood Insurance Fund, to provide grants to state and local governments for projects and other programs designed to reduce potential flood damage. All projects had to be technically feasible, cost-beneficial and approved by FEMA. Such projects could include minor mitigation efforts such as flood-proofing sewers but not major projects such as dikes, levees and seawalls. Total grants from the mitigation fund were capped at $15 million in fiscal 1995 and $20 million thereafter.
- **Task Forces.** Established two task forces. The Flood Insurance Interagency Task Force was to recommend standardized procedures to improve enforcement of flood insurance requirements, as well as ways for federal agencies and the secondary market in mortgage loans to improve compliance. The task force on the Natural and Beneficial Functions of the Floodplain was to study the natural functions of flood plains that reduced flood losses and make recommendations on how to further reduce flood losses through the protection of flood plains.
- **Flood Maps.** Required FEMA to review every five years, and update if necessary, federal maps of flood plains and flood-risk areas. Any changes to federal flood maps (including additions and removals of flood hazard designations that affected flood insurance requirements) had to be published in the Federal Register or some other comparable publication. New flood maps and a compilation of flood map changes were to be made available to bank regulators, state and local governments and the public. The bill established a Technical Mapping Environmental Council of federal, state and private mapping experts to advise FEMA on ways to improve flood mapping and provide an evaluation of FEMA mapping efforts.
- **Erosion Hazards Study.** Directed FEMA to hire an independent entity to conduct a study on the effect of erosion, particularly of coastlines, on the federal flood insurance program. Critics of the flood insurance program said that in effect it subsidized the building of homes and other structures on coastal lands that eroded easily or on lake shores and flood plains that were subject to repeated flooding. Claims in such cases far exceeded the premiums paid on the policies.

The study was to determine how much in flood insurance claims was attributable to erosion, as well as the economic impact of denying flood insurance in such communities or making it available at market rates. FEMA also was to study the economic effects of increasing premiums on coastal buildings that were built prior to the imposition of more stringent building standards in 1975. Insurance claims on such structures exceeded premium income by $668 million over 1978–1992.

- **Effective Date of Policies.** Established that new contracts for flood insurance would not become effective for 30 days after purchase. This provision came in response to reports that some victims of the 1993 floods in the Midwest bought flood insurance only when flooding was imminent. An exemption was provided when a homeowner was financing or refinancing a loan or if coverage was purchased within one year of a remapping or map revision.
- **Agricultural Structures.** Exempted agricultural structures that were substantially damaged by flood from the law's building requirements under the act if they were assessed market (actuarial) rates and were no longer eligible for federal disaster assistance.
- **Prohibited Assistance.** Established that any building that was supposed to have flood insurance and received federal disaster assistance after a flood would not be eligible to receive disaster assistance a second time. ❑

Energy Assistance

On Dec. 14, 1993, President Clinton signed a bill (HR 3321—PL 103-185) to provide states with more flexibility in determining how much energy assistance to give residents of federally assisted housing.

The Low Income Home Energy Assistance Program (LIHEAP) provided federal grants to states to help low-income people pay their heating and cooling bills and to weatherize their homes. Some federally assisted housing programs—which included public housing and federally subsidized private housing—also provided allowances to individuals to help pay their energy bills.

The House passed HR 3321 by voice vote Nov. 15, 1993. The Senate followed suit Nov. 22, completing congressional action. ❑

FHA Loans

During consideration of the fiscal 1995 appropriations bill for the Department of Veterans Affairs, the Department of Housing and Urban Development, and independent agencies (HR 4624—PL 103-327), a dispute arose in 1994 over how active the Federal Housing Administration (FHA) ought to be in the single-family home loan market. FHA loans also were at issue during debate on a comprehensive housing reauthorization bill (HR 3838), which did not clear. *(Housing reauthorization, p. 640)*

FHA's single-family loan guarantee program was designed to encourage lenders to make loans to first-time buyers and others who did not have the money for a conventional down payment. It did so by insuring the private sector lenders against the risk of mortgage default. Under existing law, the basic limit for FHA guarantees was $67,500, increasing to $151,725 in high-cost areas.

The Clinton administration recommended that the FHA be allowed to insure higher-priced mortgages to more realistically reflect home prices and to stimulate more home ownership. Because the program was designed to be self-supporting, proponents of higher limits said that insuring the more lucrative mortgages on the high end would enable the fund to serve more low-end buyers. Opponents said that substantially higher limits would alter the FHA's mission by serving more middle- and upper-middle-income home buyers.

The conference committee on HR 4624 (H Rept 103-715) agreed Aug. 18, 1994, to make only a small boost in the federal home loan program. House conferees acceded to Senate demands to raise the basic cap from $67,500 to $77,197 and the cap in high-cost areas from $151,725 to $152,363. Both limits were to be indexed in future years to change in the conforming loan limit for government-sponsored enterprises. The House had wanted to raise the ceiling as high as $172,675. But senators warned that if the House did not back down, Senate opponents could filibuster the bill.   ❑

HOPE, HOME Funding

In 1993–1994, the Homeownership and Opportunity for People Everywhere (HOPE) program began being phased out, while the HOME (Homeownership Made Easy) Investment Partnerships program managed to hang on. Both housing programs were established by a 1990 law (PL 101-625). *(1990 law, Congress and the Nation Vol. VIII, p. 665)*

HOPE, a favorite of the Bush administration to help low-income families buy public housing, had fallen far short of its goal. Tenants expressed little interest in buying their units, and Democrats viewed the program as a badly designed Republican strategy. Although some of the housing units under consideration were well located and in relatively good condition, most were poorly located. Critics wondered whether tenants could afford to pay the operating costs of their purchased units, and they were concerned about losing public housing stock while waiting lists grew.

In the fiscal 1994 appropriations bill for the Department of Veterans Affairs (VA), the Department of Housing and Urban Development (HUD), and independent agencies (HR 2491—PL 103-124), Congress followed President Clinton's budget request and allocated a mere $109 million for HOPE. The measure also rescinded $250 million in fiscal 1992 and fiscal 1993 funds for the HOPE program. HOPE grants would be provided only to recipients whose plans were under way. In the fiscal 1994 emergency supplemental appropriations bill (HR 3759—PL 103-211), Congress rescinded $66 million in funds unspent at the end of fiscal 1993 for HOPE, as requested by the administration. The fiscal 1995 VA-HUD bill (HR 4624—PL 103-327) provided $50 million for HOPE.

Although the Democratic initiative HOME also had gotten off to a slow start, Congress and the Clinton administration continued to support it. HOME was supposed to function like a block grant for housing, with states and localities deciding how they wanted to use the money for low- and moderate-income housing needs. Only a small percentage of the funds allocated for HOME had been spent by mid-1993, however. Local author-

ities said they had shied away from using the program because of its complexity. HUD Secretary Henry G. Cisneros promised to encourage use of HOME funds by simplifying rules, allowing localities wider flexibility, improving public information about the program and providing more technical assistance.

As enacted, HR 2491 provided $1.3 billion for HOME in fiscal 1994, less than President Clinton requested but an increase over the fiscal 1993 appropriation. In his fiscal 1995 budget, Clinton proposed a reduction in budget authority for HOME, to $1.1 billion. However, HR 4624 earmarked $1.4 billion for HOME in fiscal 1995.   ❑

Homeless Assistance

The Senate passed two bills reauthorizing homeless programs. Neither became law.

S 1523 was reported by the Senate Labor and Human Resources Committee on Nov. 19, 1993, and passed by voice vote of the full Senate the next day. S 1523 reauthorized homeless programs concerning primary health services for children, community demonstration projects, education, job training, emergency community services and family support centers under the Stewart B. McKinney Homeless Assistance Act (PL 100-77). The measure would have put the programs on the same time frame for authorization as other federal programs for the homeless. *(PL 100-77, Congress and the Nation Vol. VII, p. 677)*

S 2218 was reported by the Senate Governmental Affairs Committee on Aug. 5, 1994, and passed by voice vote of the Senate on Aug. 10. S 2218 reauthorized, at $187.6 million in each of fiscal years 1995 and 1996, a program created under the McKinney Act to provide emergency food and shelter to the homeless. The House tried to extend the program as part of comprehensive housing reauthorization legislation (HR 3838), but that measure never made it to the Senate floor. The fiscal 1995 appropriations bill for the Department of Veterans Affairs, the Department of Housing and Urban Development (HUD), and independent agencies (HR 4624—PL 103-327) kept the program running through fiscal 1995. President Clinton had requested that the program, which was administered by the Federal Emergency Management Agency (FEMA), be transferred to HUD, but HR 4624 kept it in FEMA. *(Housing reauthorization, p. 640)*   ❑

1995–1996

Public Housing

The House and Senate were unable to resolve key differences over a bill (S 1260) to overhaul the nation's public housing system, and the legislation died upon adjournment of the 104th Congress.

The bill sought to transfer federal money and authority to the local housing agencies that directly administered public housing and subsidized housing programs. Both the Senate-

and House-passed versions would have consolidated federal funding for those programs into block grants and removed many federal restrictions and requirements on local authorities. Supporters said the changes would make the system less bureaucratic and more cost effective.

However, Senate negotiators refused to accept some of the more sweeping House proposals, including repeal of the U.S. Housing Act of 1937—the foundation of public housing programs—and elimination of the so-called Brooke Amendment, which generally required that public housing tenants pay no more than 30 percent of their income for rent, regardless of their income. The amendment was named for Sen. Edward W. Brooke (R-Mass., 1967–1979).

BACKGROUND

For a dozen years, federal housing policy had been an ideological battleground between congressional Democrats who wanted the government to provide more low-income housing and Republicans who wanted to get government out of the housing business. Democrats concentrated on enacting legislation that tied the hands of federal bureaucrats, who, under President Ronald Reagan, had permitted housing authorities to tear down public housing without any plans for replacing it. But the restrictions, coupled with a lack of funds, often meant that dilapidated housing projects were kept in place.

The political dynamics changed dramatically in 1994, when Democrats, with encouragement from the Clinton administration, joined Republicans in embracing legislation to give state and local officials more control over housing programs. The House passed a housing reauthorization bill (HR 3838) that sought to give local authorities more say over how to spend money to aid the homeless and more flexibility when selling or demolishing public housing units. The Senate Banking Committee reported a similar bill (S 2281), but it died in the crush of end-of-session business. *(Housing reauthorization, p. 640)*

The GOP takeover of Congress in 1995 pushed congressional thinking even further. Many Republicans wanted to abolish the Department of Housing and Urban Development (HUD). They held it up as a poster child of what they believed was wrong with the federal government: massive amounts of federal dollars being spent on a failed system. Bills to abolish HUD (S 1145, HR 2198) were introduced by Sen. Lauch Faircloth, R-N.C., and Rep. Sam Brownback, R-Kan., but the measures never got off the ground.

HUD Secretary Henry G. Cisneros moved quickly to propose radical changes at the department. Cisneros calculated that to withstand the massive cuts that he expected in federal funding, housing policy would have to become more flexible, allowing more to be accomplished with less money. As he anticipated, HUD appropriations dropped from $25.5 billion in fiscal 1995 to $19.1 billion in fiscal 1996.

But key GOP committee chairmen proved more moderate than those looking to extinguish HUD. A partnership developed among Cisneros, Rick A. Lazio, R-N.Y., chairman of the House Banking and Financial Services Subcommittee on Housing and Community Opportunity, Connie Mack, R-Fla., chairman of the Senate Banking, Housing, and Urban Affairs Subcommittee on Housing Opportunity and Community Development, and other key Republicans, such as Christopher S. Bond, R-Mo., chairman of the Senate Appropriations VA-HUD Subcommittee. Most of what Cisneros proposed to change at HUD—mainly, devolving power from HUD to local housing authorities and consolidating numerous and scattered federal housing programs—was consistent with the House and Senate versions of S 1260.

SENATE ACTION

The Senate Banking Committee reported S 1260 (S Rept 104-195) on Dec. 20, 1995. The committee adopted a Faircloth amendment to prohibit HUD from funding the construction of additional public housing units. The agency could still finance new units to replace existing and obsolete public housing. Another Faircloth amendment, to eliminate HUD in three years, was rejected.

The full Senate passed the measure by voice vote Jan. 10, 1996. The only amendment, offered by Mack, was adopted by voice vote. It increased the authority of local housing agencies to verify the legal residency status of applicants for public and subsidized housing, and it increased to 50 percent—from 40 percent in the reported bill—the amount of housing that would have to be reserved for tenants with incomes of less than 30 percent of the area's median income.

As passed by the Senate, S 1260 would:

• Convert HUD low-income housing programs into two block grants to local authorities, one for operating expenses and the other for construction. Local housing authorities, working with tenants and local government officials, would be required to draw up plans describing proposed policies and spending priorities. If approved by HUD, the plans were to serve as guidelines for allocating grant money.

• Repeal the so-called one-for-one replacement rule, thereby allowing local housing authorities to raze uninhabitable or substandard housing. Under the rule, vacant or dilapidated buildings often were left standing because housing authorities lacked the funds to build replacement units.

• Require HUD to crack down on "troubled" local housing authorities, taking over or appointing receivers for local authorities that failed to improve their performance.

• Repeal the federal preferences, or criteria, that local authorities had to use in deciding who would receive housing assistance, thus allowing local authorities to select tenants based on their own standards.

• Make it easier for local housing authorities to evict residents for drug-related crimes and require authorities to screen out applicants with drug or alcohol problems.

• Give local housing authorities greater leeway to set tenant rent levels but maintain safeguards against massive rent increases.

• Consolidate the Section 8 certificate and voucher rent subsidy programs into a single voucher program and require that the value of such vouchers be based on more realistic local market conditions.

HOUSE ACTION

The House Banking Committee reported a companion measure (HR 2406—H Rept 104-461) on Feb. 1, 1996. A supplemental report was filed April 25 (H Rept 104-461, Part II). The committee adopted amendments that would:

• Lower the minimum amount a housing authority could charge in rent from $30 to $25 per month per family and to exempt the elderly and disabled from an existing prohibition on owning pets in public housing.

• Require that HUD study the concentration of housing assistance recipients in Chicago and Cook County and, within 90 days of bill enactment, report to Congress on ways to disperse those tenants. The amendment, written by Jerry Weller, R-Ill., had been modified from the original, which proposed to bar Chicago public housing tenants from using vouchers to move to adjacent suburbs in southern Cook County. Democrats argued that Weller's original language was an attempt to keep the poor and minorities out of largely Caucasian areas.

• Phase in any rent increase of more than 30 percent over three years.

• Reserve 25 percent of public housing for tenants with incomes lower than 30 percent of median area income.

• Retain a HUD program that provided funds to local authorities to demolish, replace or restore uninhabitable public housing projects.

The House on May 9 passed HR 2406 by a vote of 315–107, then passed S 1260 with the provisions of HR 2406 by voice vote. Like the Senate-passed bill, the House version would create two block grants—one for operating expenses, one for capital expenses—for public housing authorities that met certain standards of service. The measure also would give local authorities control over a consolidated Section 8 rental assistance program and would expand eligibility to families with higher incomes. Unlike the Senate measure, the House bill called for local housing authorities to be made accountable to a new Housing Foundation and Accreditation Board, which would certify whether local authorities were professionally managed and operated and, therefore, eligible to receive federal block grant funding. The House version also called for repealing the 1937 Housing Act and eliminating restrictions that limited the rents of public housing tenants to 30 percent of income.

The Democrats' principle objection to the bill, shared by the Clinton administration, was the proposed repeal of the Brooke Amendment. Opponents of the amendment argued that tying rent to income discouraged tenants from working, because when their income rose, so did their rent. Barney Frank, D-Mass., proposed retaining the amendment, but with a change that he said would avoid the work disincentive. Under his plan, the Brooke language would act as a rent ceiling, not as both a ceiling and floor as in existing law. Rents would be limited to 30 percent of income, but would not have to rise in conjunction with income. The House May 9 rejected the Frank amendment, 196–222. The House adopted by voice vote a Lazio amendment providing for exceptions—giving rent-ceiling protection to the very poor and to those elderly and disabled tenants who were already living in public housing. Also adopted by voice vote was an amendment by Maurice D. Hinchey, D-N.Y., and Joseph P. Kennedy, D-Mass., to extend the 30 percent of income rent ceiling protection to any veterans or elderly or disabled residents, who moved into public housing in the future.

Both congressional Republicans and HUD had proposed opening up public housing to people with somewhat higher incomes to integrate working families into the communities to serve as role models. However, congressional Democrats and HUD said the House bill would go too far. During the floor debate, Kennedy negotiated a compromise that reserved a greater share of public and assisted housing for the very poor. The amendment was adopted by voice vote. The House also accepted Democrat-supported changes to cap minimum rents at $50 for public and assisted housing tenants. The original bill would have required all tenants to pay at least $25 per month and would have given housing authorities the right to set minimum rents even higher. Nydia M. Velázquez, D-N.Y., offered an amendment to cap minimum rents at $25 per month but lost on a 126–297 vote May 9.

The House on May 9 adopted, 375–48, an amendment by Carolyn B. Maloney, D-N.Y., to give senior citizens in public housing the right to own household pets. The original bill would have allowed housing authorities to set guidelines, including prohibition, for pet ownership. Existing law allowed pets only in developments designated as senior housing. Maloney's amendment allowed housing authorities to set rules regarding pets but precluded them from prohibiting the elderly from owning pets, regardless of where they lived.

The House also adopted by voice vote amendments that would:

• Prohibit housing assistance to persons convicted of possessing illegal drugs with an intent to sell.

• Allow the use of housing vouchers to rent mobile or manufactured housing, or to rent property on which such houses were situated.

• Establish a private sector "consensus committee" to work with HUD in developing federal safety and other standards for manufactured housing.

• Modify the federal government's Indian housing programs by converting them into a block grant and by providing tribes with greater flexibility in using such funds.

The House rejected, 106–318, an amendment by Richard J. Durbin, D-Ill., to establish criminal penalties for the possession or discharge of firearms in public housing developments.   ❑

Housing Reauthorization

President Clinton on March 28, 1996, signed into law a fiscal 1996 reauthorization bill (S 1494—PL 104-120) that covered a number of programs designed to increase home ownership and housing development. S 1494 also modified some existing housing programs, created new programs, and enhanced the ability of local housing authorities to screen out troublesome tenants and to designate certain housing for the elderly only.

SENATE ACTION

The Senate passed S 1494, which was sponsored by Senate Banking, Housing, and Urban Affairs Committee Chairman Alfonse M. D'Amato, R-N.Y., by voice vote Jan. 24, 1996. The bill would authorize funding for the following programs through Sept. 30:

• Expiring Section 8 low-income rental assistance contracts, to be renewed for one year at existing levels.

• The Community Development Block Grant home ownership program, which allowed cities to use grant funds to help pay low-income family mortgages.

• The Farmers Home Administration's Section 515 rural multifamily housing loan program.

• The Home Equity Conversion Mortgage program, which allowed elderly homeowners to use home equity loans for living expenses.

• The Federal Housing Administration (FHA) Multifamily Housing Risk-Sharing insurance program.

To garner House support for the bill, the Senate by voice vote adopted an amendment offered by Majority Whip Trent Lott, R-Miss., to:

• Authorize $50 million for Habitat for Humanity and other self-help housing groups to support the construction of houses for low-income families. The House had passed a bill (HR 1691) with similar language in 1995. (Homeless grants, p. 649)

• Allow public housing authorities to exclude and evict from public housing tenants with drug and alcohol problems. The House had passed similar legislation (HR 117) in 1995, and the Senate accepted the language as part of a housing overhaul bill (S 1260). (Public housing protection, p. 649; public housing overhaul, p. 645)

• Authorize $10 million for the National Cities in Schools Community Development program, which encouraged private investment in schools.

HOUSE ACTION

The House passed a revised version of S 1494 by voice vote under suspension of the rules Feb. 27. The House-passed bill was a substitute offered by Rick A. Lazio, R-N.Y., chairman of the House Banking Subcommittee on Housing and Community Opportunity, that had been negotiated as a compromise with Senate Banking Committee members.

Like the Senate-passed bill, the House version included fiscal 1996 reauthorization for Section 515 rural multifamily housing loans, certain Community Development Block Grant home ownership activities, the FHA's home equity conversion program for the elderly, the FHA's multifamily housing risk-sharing insurance program, $10 million for the National Cities in Schools program, and authority for the Department of Housing and Urban Development to renew expiring Section 8 rental contracts.

However, the revised bill modified the Senate version to:

• Allow local housing authorities to exclude and evict people having drug or alcohol problems from either public housing or privately owned federally subsidized housing. The Senate ver-

sion would have applied only to public housing. The House also added provisions to streamline the authority of local housing agencies to designate public housing projects for the elderly only, the disabled, or mixtures of the two. In addition, the House bill increased by 20,000 the number of "reverse mortgages" the FHA could insure.

• Drop most of the Section 8 contract renewals for subsidized housing, which had been authorized as part of a stopgap spending bill enacted after the Senate passed S 1494. The House substitute applied only to project-based Section 8 moderate rehabilitation contracts.

• Authorize $40 million for Habitat for Humanity and other similar self-help housing groups for land acquisition and infrastructure improvements associated with the construction of homes for low-income families, $10 million less than in the Senate bill. Like the Senate bill, however, $25 million of the total was earmarked for Habitat for Humanity.

• Authorize $10 million for the National Community Development Initiative, which helped nonprofit organizations that aided the poor.

• Create a new program under which the Agriculture Department could guarantee loans for the construction of rural multifamily rental housing. Funding had been included in the fiscal 1996 Agriculture appropriations bill (HR 1976).

• Increase from $3.5 billion to $4.5 billion the limit on loan guarantees under the Community Development Block Grant loan guarantee program.

• Extend the existing loan guarantee limit of the Government National Mortgage Association (Ginnie Mae).

The Senate March 12 agreed to the House changes, completing congressional action. ❑

Seniors-Only Complexes

On Dec. 28, 1995, President Clinton signed legislation (HR 660—PL 104-76) to protect "seniors-only" housing complexes from discrimination lawsuits.

The Fair Housing Act, as amended in 1988 (PL 100-430), generally prohibited housing discrimination against families with children. But it allowed an exception for senior citizen complexes, which it defined as housing intended for people aged 55 or older that provided "significant facilities and services" to meet the needs of older residents. However, precisely which housing qualified for the exemption had never been clear, and the confusion led to lawsuits and bad feelings in some communities. The issue was of particular concern to retirement communities in California and Florida. (1988 fair housing law, Congress and the Nation Vol. VII, p. 681)

To simplify and clarify the rules, HR 660—sponsored by Rep. E. Clay Shaw Jr., R-Fla.—eliminated the "facilities and services" requirement and instead defined a senior housing complex as one in which 80 percent of the units were occupied by at least one person who was 55 or older. It provided a "good faith" exemption from legal liability for anyone, including a private homeowner, who believed a complex qualified for the senior exemption and told that to a potential buyer or tenant.

The Justice Department said the change would go too far, opening the door to the very discrimination that PL 100-430 sought to prevent. The Department of Housing and Urban Development said it had drafted new regulations to clear up any confusion.

The House Judiciary Committee reported HR 660 (H Rept 104-91) on May 28, 1995. During committee markup, ranking Democrat John Conyers Jr. of Michigan took issue with a provision aimed at protecting real estate agents and others from personal liability in housing discrimination suits if they acted on a "good faith" belief that the housing in question qualified for the exemption. Conyers said the language would invite abuses of the antibias statute by allowing violators to offer an after-the-fact excuse of ignorance. His amendment to strike the language was defeated. However, lawmakers subsequently approved an amendment by Barney Frank, D-Mass., to scale back the "good faith" legal protection for real estate agents.

The House passed HR 660 April 6 by a 424–5 vote.

The Senate Judiciary Subcommittee on the Constitution, Federalism and Property Rights adopted an amendment to HR 660 by Paul Simon, D-Ill., specifying that senior citizens housing that qualified for the exemption must have at least 80 percent of its units occupied by one or more people aged 55 or older, not simply a goal of 80 percent. The full Judiciary Committee, which reported the bill (S Rept 104-172) Nov. 9, approved an amendment by Jon Kyl, R-Ariz., further specifying who could be sued for violating the terms of the law. Under the amended bill, real estate agents and others would not be personally liable in a housing discrimination suit if the housing complex had formally stated that it qualified for the exemption and the individual had no knowledge to the contrary.

The Senate passed the bill 94–3 Dec. 6. The House agreed to the Senate changes Dec. 18, completing congressional action.

HR 660 was originally part of a Social Security bill (HR 8) under the House GOP's Contract with America; much of that measure was folded into tax legislation (HR 1215). ❏

Public Housing Protection

The House Oct. 24, 1995, passed 415–0 a bill (HR 117) aimed at protecting elderly public housing residents from alcoholics and drug abusers. The Senate did not take up the measure.

Under existing law, housing authorities could set aside certain projects for the elderly and single people with mental or physical disabilities, allowing them to live apart from low-income families. But the definition of "disabled" included former drug and alcohol abusers who had been known to disturb their elderly neighbors.

Congress had addressed the issue in a 1992 public housing law (PL 102-550) when it permitted the creation of housing for the elderly only. But drug and alcohol abusers could still qualify for the housing if there were long-standing vacancies. (1992 law, Congress and the Nation Vol. VIII, p. 694)

HR 117, sponsored by Rep. Peter I. Blute, R-Mass., would allow the eviction of disabled tenants who were using illegal drugs or whose use of alcohol led housing authorities to believe they posed a threat to other tenants' health or safety. The measure also would extend a program that allowed older homeowners to use their homes to qualify for equity loans, or "reverse mortgages," that did not have to be paid off until the owners sold the home, moved or died. Such loans would allow retirees to gain access to cash without becoming burdened by monthly loan payments. Under the program, the Federal Housing Administration was to insure the loans. The provision, originally introduced separately as HR 1934 by Rick A. Lazio, R-N.Y., would reauthorize the program—which expired Oct. 1, 1995—through Sept. 30, 2002.

The House passed HR 117 as part of "corrections day," when time was set aside to consider legislation aimed at revising or eliminating laws or regulations that House leaders considered unwise. ('Corrections day,' p. 894)

The House Banking and Financial Services Committee had reported HR 117 (H Rept 104-281) on Oct. 18, 1995. During committee consideration, a dispute broke out over how much power public housing directors should have to exclude former drug abusers and alcoholics. Rep. Maxine Waters, D-Calif., offered, and then withdrew in face of substantial opposition, an amendment to bar directors from considering past substance abuse by a potential tenant if the individual had enrolled in a rehabilitation program or had made other efforts to treat the addiction. The committee instead approved a compromise amendment by Floyd H. Flake, D-N.Y., to allow administrators to consider efforts by drug and alcohol uses to rehabilitate themselves. The committee also adopted a Bob Ney, R-Ohio, amendment to streamline procedures for setting aside public housing developments solely for the elderly. ❏

Homeless Grants

The House Oct. 30, 1995, by voice vote under suspension of the rules passed a bill (HR 1691) to authorize housing grants to groups that helped the homeless and the poor. A companion measure (S 1387) languished in a Senate Banking, Housing, and Urban Affairs subcommittee.

HR 1691, sponsored by House Banking Subcommittee on Housing and Community Opportunity Chairman Rick A. Lazio, R-N.Y., would authorize $50 million in previously appropriated but unused funds for grants to organizations such as Habitat for Humanity, a nonprofit group based in Americus, Ga., that helped poor people build their own homes. Under the legislation, Habitat for Humanity would get half the money. Lazio said the bill was an example of how government "can provide a service without a big bureaucracy or huge federal subsidies." Rep. Henry B. Gonzalez of Texas, ranking Democrat on the House Banking and Financial Services Committee, disagreed, calling the measure "a pitiful small gesture" in light of GOP budget cuts in housing programs, but a worthy one nonetheless.

HR 1691 also included authorization for a program that provided loans for construction of rental properties for low- and moderate-income families in rural areas. The fiscal 1996 Agriculture appropriations bill (HR 1976—PL 104-37) provided $150 million for such loans in fiscal 1996, subject to authorization.   ❏

Housing Reconciliation

As part of the deficit-reducing budget reconciliation bill (HR 2491), Congress in 1995 agreed to save $4.1 billion over seven years through largely noncontroversial changes in two housing programs. However, the proposals fell, when President Clinton vetoed the bill Dec. 6. *(Reconciliation, p. 68)*

The housing provisions would have achieved $1.8 billion in savings by overhauling a Federal Housing Administration (FHA) foreclosure relief program. Under existing law, homeowners who were late with their mortgage payments could receive federal help to prevent foreclosure for up to three years. Under HR 2491, federal housing authorities would get greater flexibility to work with lenders and borrowers to prevent mortgage defaults. In exchange for a partial payment from the government on a federally insured mortgage in default, lenders would agree to modify the terms of loans so that borrowers could pay and foreclosure could be avoided.

Another $2.3 billion in savings were to be achieved through changes in the Section 8 subsidized private housing program. Under the program, low-income tenants paid a certain percentage of their income in rent, and the government made up the difference. HR 2491 proposed to reduce, by 1 percentage point, rent increases that the government was projected to pay to property owners for units in which no tenant turnover had occurred. Another provision proposed to limit annual rent increases for higher cost apartments, with landlords receiving increases based on cost increases instead of on market conditions.

The House Banking and Financial Services Committee Sept. 19 approved $1.9 billion in housing-related savings. The figure was later recalculated by the Congressional Budget Office (CBO), rising to $3.2 billion. The jump came from a proposal to eliminate the FHA foreclosure relief program. The action had been estimated to produce at least $400 million in savings, but CBO raised the estimate to $1.7 billion. The committee included the Section 8 subsidy reduction, for an estimated $1.3 billion in savings. The panel also proposed to generate $170 million in

revenue by selling multifamily housing projects that were in default and to save $31 million by terminating the Resolution Trust Corporation (RTC) and Federal Deposit Insurance Corporation (FDIC) affordable housing programs, which subsidized sales of properties seized from failed banks and thrifts to moderate-income purchasers.

The committee also approved a controversial plan to merge the banking and thrift industries and provide a cash infusion to shore up the severely undercapitalized deposit insurance fund for thrifts. *(Deposit insurance funds, p. 131)*

The bill was revised on the House floor to overhaul the FHA's foreclosure relief program instead of eliminating it. The new plan was to allow the agency to continue to pay mortgage claims for 12 months. During that time, lenders would be required to modify the terms of loans so that borrowers could make the payments. Estimated savings for the new program were considerably higher—$2.9 billion—because analysts presumed that federal housing officials would work with lenders to obtain concessions on all defaulted loans, not just those in the foreclosure relief program, thereby minimizing the potential costs.

The Senate Banking, Housing and Urban Affairs Committee Sept. 20 approved a reconciliation package that included about $1.7 billion in housing-related savings—later reestimated at $1.2 billion—from fiscal 1996 through fiscal 2002. The bill included the reduction in rental subsidies under the Section 8 housing programs. The Senate panel also proposed to curb rent increases for apartments that rented at or above prevailing market rates to reflect actual increases in operating costs instead of inflation elsewhere in the housing market.

House and Senate conferees on the housing section of HR 2491 accepted the modified House plan to overhaul the FHA foreclosure relief program. However, only loans originated after Oct. 1, 1995, were to be covered, for $1.8 billion in savings. The conferees agreed that projected savings from older mortgages, about $1.1 billion, would be used on the appropriations bill for the departments of Veterans Affairs and Housing and Urban Development (HR 2099). Conferees included the $2.3 billion in savings from changes in the Section 8 housing program. They deleted House provisions to scrap the affordable housing programs run by the RTC and FDIC and to change rural housing programs.   ❏

CHAPTER 12

Labor and Pension Policy

Labor and Pension Policy

By the time President Clinton was sworn into office in early 1993, the United States had already recovered from the 1990–1991 recession and was enjoying steady economic growth. These increases in the gross domestic product continued throughout the president's first term, averaging more than 2 percent per year. At the same time, inflation and interest rates remained at an all-time low.

The employment picture also was positive during most of Clinton's first term. While American corporate giants continued to announce thousands of layoffs—so common during the corporate downsizing trend of the 1980s and early 1990s—the unemployment rate as a whole dropped dramatically as the decade wore on. From its high of 7.5 percent in 1992, unemployment fell by more than two percentage points over the next four years. By the end of 1996, the jobless rate stood at 5.4 percent.

But, despite this rosy economic news, polls showed that Americans continued to feel insecure and uneasy about their future. One reason for this lingering pessimism was that wage growth, in real terms, was essentially flat during Clinton's first term.

In addition, union membership continued to fall during this period, reflecting, among other things, a further decline in the number of high-paying, blue-collar jobs. In 1992, 15.8 percent of all wage and salary workers were union members. By 1995, that figure had dropped to 14.9 percent.

LABOR LEGISLATION

After 12 years of Republican presidents, organized labor had high hopes for Bill Clinton. These hopes were buoyed almost immediately when the new president made the enactment of family and medical leave his first legislative priority. This measure, which required medium and large businesses to give workers up to 12 weeks of unpaid leave to care for a newborn or ill family member, had twice been vetoed by President George Bush. Clinton and his fellow Democrats in Congress pushed the bill through in record time, enacting it in February 1993, less than one month after the new president had been sworn in.

The following month, Clinton, along with Democratic congressional leaders, moved quickly to extend a temporary program that provided emergency federal benefits to the long-term unemployed, many of whom had exhausted their 26 weeks of state-paid basic benefits without finding jobs. When this extension expired later that year, the president helped push through Congress additional benefits to those still out of work.

But Clinton also disappointed his labor supporters, most notably by pressing for ratification of the North American Free Trade Agreement (NAFTA). Another letdown for labor came with the president's refusal to give more than lukewarm support for legislation prohibiting employers from permanently replacing striking workers. The measure died in the Senate during the summer of 1994 after failing to attract the support of a small group of moderate Republicans and Democrats, some of whom might have been swayed if the president had lobbied.

With the GOP victory in the congressional elections of 1994, hopes for labor's legislative agenda seemed dashed. In addition, unions soon found themselves fighting a rear guard action in Congress, as new GOP leaders set about scaling back laws that they said unfairly burdened businesses and taxpayers. Consequently, bills that would have rewritten the Occupational Safety and Health Act (OSHA), repealed the Davis-Bacon prevailing wage law and instituted labor-management teams were all pursued vigorously in 1995 and 1996, especially by House Republicans. While many of these measures advanced in Congress, none became law due to concerted opposition on the part of the White House and congressional Democrats.

In addition, prolabor forces actually scored a major victory in the summer of 1996, when Democrats and moderate Republicans successfully pressured GOP congressional leaders to allow Congress to pass an increase in the minimum wage, from $4.25 an hour to $5.15 by 1997.

Republican leaders had always argued that an increase in the minimum wage would jeopardize hundreds of thousands of low-wage jobs. But polls showed that the idea was popular with a substantial majority of the American people. With an election approaching and pressure by congressional Democrats mounting, GOP leaders were forced to give in to their rank-and-file,

REFERENCES

Discussion of labor and pension policy for the years 1945–1964 may be found in *Congress and the Nation Vol. I*, pp. 565–657, 1220–1272, 1289–1320; for the years 1965–1968, *Congress and the Nation Vol. II*, pp. 601–622, 734–743, 745–778; for the years 1969–1972, *Congress and the Nation Vol. III*, pp. 605–621, 703–742; for the years 1973–1976, *Congress and the Nation Vol. IV*, pp. 403–432, 681–713; for the years 1977–1980, *Congress and the Nation Vol. V*, pp. 231–251, 399–425; for the years 1981–1984, *Congress and the Nation Vol. VI*, pp. 643–672; for the years 1985–1988, *Congress and the Nation Vol. VII*, pp. 687–709; for the years 1989–1992, *Congress and the Nation Vol. VIII*, pp. 703–738.

Outlays for Social Security and Medicare

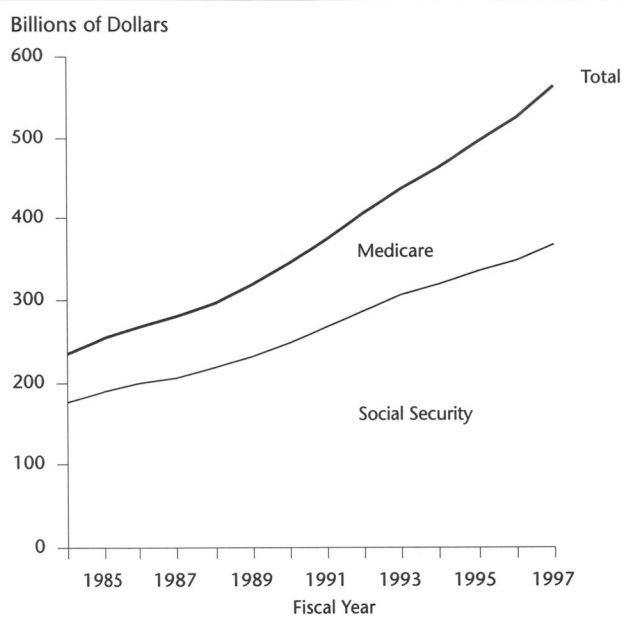

Billions of Dollars

NOTE: Data for 1997 are estimated.

SOURCE: Office of Management and Budget, *Historical Tables, Budget of the United States Government: Fiscal Year 1998* (Washington, D.C.: U.S. Government Printing Office, 1997), Table 3.2.

many of whom supported the increase and were demanding a vote on the issue.

PENSION POLICY

Various aspects of the Social Security program—taxes, benefits, the administering agency itself—appeared on Congress's agenda.

The Democratic-controlled 103rd Congress raised the portion of Social Security benefits subject to taxes for some higher-income retirees. The Republican-controlled 104th Congress failed in its attempts to repeal that tax but did manage to push through an increase in the level of earnings Social Security recipients were allowed before they started losing benefits.

After a series of embarrassing revelations that some of Clinton's high-level nominees had failed to pay Social Security taxes for their domestic workers, Congress in 1994 moved to update the often-disregarded law governing what soon was tagged as the "nanny tax."

Highlighting the significance of the Social Security program, Congress in 1994 voted to make the Social Security Administration an independent agency. The largest agency in the Health and Human Services Department and the ninth largest in the federal government, the Social Security Administration disbursed about $300 billion annually in benefits to retired and disabled workers and their dependents and survivors. The aim of the legislation was to heighten the agency's visibility and isolate it somewhat from the political party that controlled the White House.

During the 103rd Congress, a number of changes were made to the nation's laws governing private pensions as well. The most important of these alterations was the enactment, at the end of 1994, of legislation that tightened federal requirements on businesses that underfunded their pension plans.

In the 1980s, a host of companies, especially in Rustbelt industries such as steel and autos, had not made adequate contributions to their pension funds. As a result, the estimated pension fund shortfall doubled from $27 billion in 1987 to $53 billion in 1992, according to the Pension Benefit Guaranty Corporation (PBGC), the federal agency that guaranteed pension payments. The new law made a number of changes, including giving the PBGC the authority to collect more money from companies with underfunded pensions.

An additional, though narrow, victory for pensioners also came in 1994, when Congress cleared a measure that gave greater legal redress to 84,000 retirees and employees whose pension benefits were threatened by the insolvency of the Executive Life Insurance Company.

But another priority for pension advocates, restricting the right of a state to tax the pension benefits of its former residents, was not enacted, despite strong support for the idea in Congress. The measure passed the House in 1994 but was blocked in the Senate.

Chronology of Action on Labor and Pension Policy

1993–1994

The 103rd Congress began in a burst of hope for those in the labor movement. Democrats controlled the executive and legislative branches of government for the first time in 12 years, and organized labor's agenda would finally be taken seriously.

Indeed, the first session began with a bang for union supporters and others as the newly elected President Clinton fulfilled a key campaign promise and helped Democrats push through Congress a historic family and medical leave bill. The measure required medium and large employers to grant workers up to 12 weeks of unpaid leave to care for a newborn or sick relative.

Clinton and congressional Democrats also succeeded twice in 1993 in extending temporary federal benefits for the long-term unemployed. The following year, Congress enacted language tightening federal requirements for companies that underfunded their pension plans.

But the 103rd Congress also held disappointments for the labor moment. One priority, the enactment of legislation prohibiting employers from permanently replacing striking workers, was given only lukewarm support by the Clinton administration. The measure died in the Senate during the summer of 1994 after failing to attract the support of a small group of moderates.

Other important issues for labor, including bills aimed at strengthening workplace safety laws and improving benefits for miners and rail workers also died at the end of the Congress.

In the area of pension policy, Congress approved several changes in Social Security tax law and voted to make the Social Security Administration an independent agency.

Family Leave Act

President Clinton won his first legislative victory Feb. 4, 1993, when Congress cleared family and medical leave legislation (HR 1—PL 103-3). The Family and Medical Leave Act required businesses with 50 or more employees to grant unpaid leave of up to 12 weeks to all but their top employees for the birth or adoption of a child or the illness of a close family member. The bill was the Democrats' first priority in the new session, and Clinton and his allies in Congress heralded its passage as the end of gridlock on Capitol Hill after 12 years of divided government. Clinton signed the bill in a Rose Garden ceremony Feb. 5.

But the new era of Democratic control in the White House and Congress had not meant an effortless ride for the measure. GOP senators held up the bill for three days as they tried to gut it and use it as a vehicle for an unrelated goal: getting a floor vote on an amendment to ban homosexuals in the military. In addition, probusiness groups fought hard to kill the measure, arguing that it would hurt U.S. competitiveness and cost jobs.

BACKGROUND

Congressional Democrats had been pushing family-leave legislation for years but had been stymied, mainly by the Republican White House. The first bill was introduced in 1985; some early versions would have applied to companies with as few as 15 employees and to employees who had worked only three months. Republicans killed a 1988 version with a Senate filibuster. In 1990 and 1992, supporters mustered majorities for family-leave legislation in both chambers. But, on each occasion, the bill was vetoed by President George Bush, who said he opposed putting another government mandate on business. Both vetoes were sustained in the House. *(Parental leave, Congress and the Nation Vol. VIII, pp. 710, 730)*

But with the election of a Democratic president, the dynamics suddenly changed. Clinton had made family leave one of his lead campaign issues and had promised to sign a bill quickly. When the 103rd Congress convened, family and medical leave was at the top of the new administration's agenda.

Still, the opposition was not silent. During the debate, business organizations such as the U.S. Chamber of Commerce and the National Federation of Independent Business vigorously fought the bill, arguing that the government had no right to impose mandates that might increase business costs. In addition, they feared that Congress would revisit the issue in a year or two and require them to give their workers paid leave, a charge denied by Democratic leaders.

LEGISLATIVE ACTION

The House Education and Labor Committee reported HR 1 (H Rept 103-8, Part I) on Feb. 2. Before the panel approved the bill by a vote of 29–13 on Jan. 27, Democrats fought off more than a dozen GOP amendments designed to mitigate what Republicans said would be the measure's negative impact on the business community.

The panel did adopt one amendment that revised a Labor Department rule so that employers would be allowed to give salaried employees unpaid leave for part of a day without losing their exemption from paying overtime under the Fair Labor Standards Act.

The House Post Office and Civil Service Committee—which had jurisdiction over a section of the measure that guaranteed leave for federal civil service and postal workers—also reported the bill on Feb. 2 (H Rept 103-8, Part II), having approved it by voice vote on Jan. 27.

The bill quickly moved to the House floor, where it was passed on Feb. 3 by a **key vote of 265–163 (R 40–134; D 224–29; I 1–0).** *(1993 key votes, p. 979)*

During floor debate Feb. 3, bill opponents uniformly stressed that they supported family leave policies but argued that such arrangements were a private matter between worker and employer. The ranking Republican on the Education and Labor Committee, Bill Goodling, R-Pa., proposed an amendment that would have allowed employers to offer their workers a "cafeteria" plan of benefits that included family and medical leave. Under the amendment, workers could have chosen which benefits they wanted. The House rejected the language, 187–244.

The House did adopt, 223–209, another amendment offered by Goodling that would have allowed a worker to take part of a day's leave only upon agreement with the employer. The employer's consent would not be required when the leave was medically necessary.

In the Senate, an identical bill (S 5—S Rept 103-3) was reported by the Labor and Human Resources Committee on Jan. 27. That panel had approved the measure 13–4 with little debate the previous day.

Floor action on the bill was prolonged for several days when Republicans tried to use it as a vehicle for imposing a congressional ban on gays in the military to counter the president's attempt to partially lift the prohibition. GOP efforts failed when the Senate Feb. 4 voted 62–37 to table, or kill, an amendment offered by Minority Leader Bob Dole, R-Kan., that would have required Clinton to get congressional approval before lifting the ban by executive order. Instead, members approved by voice vote a nonbinding amendment offered by Majority Leader George J. Mitchell, D-Maine, calling on the Pentagon and Congress to review existing policy regarding homosexuals in the military. (Gays in the military, p. 284)

When the debate did focus on the bill, opponents of the measure, arguing that it would impose too great a burden on businesses, offered a slew of unfriendly amendments. Dole proposed one that would have allowed employers to ignore the law until the federal government paid all costs or certified that the law would not cost them any money. It was tabled (killed), 67–31, on Feb. 4.

The Senate voted 63–36 on Feb. 3 to table an amendment by Nancy Landon Kassebaum, R-Kan., that would have allowed workers to choose family and medical leave as part of a menu of benefits offered by an employer. The language was identical to that offered unsuccessfully by Goodling in the House. In other action, the Senate—unlike the House—tabled, 59–39, on Feb. 4 a Hank Brown, R-Colo., amendment to restrict the availability of partial-day leave.

The Senate then passed HR 1 by a vote of 71–27 on Feb. 4, after inserting the text of S 5 into the House bill.

Hours after the Senate passed HR 1, the measure was cleared for the president when the House voted 247–152 to adopt a rule that included automatic agreement with the Senate version. As a result, the bill included the nonbinding language on homosexuals in the military and excluded Goodling's amendment, which would have limited partial-day leave.

MAJOR PROVISIONS

As signed into law, HR 1:

• **Unpaid Leave.** Required employers to allow employees to take up to 12 weeks of unpaid leave during any 12-month period because of the birth of a child; the adoption of a child or the placement of a foster child; the serious illness of a child, spouse or parent; or the employee's own serious health condition.

• **Eligibility.** Covered people who had worked for the employer for at least 12 months and for at least 1,250 hours during that period.

• **Exclusions.** Excluded employees who worked for a business with fewer than 50 employees within a 75-mile radius.

• **Intermittent Leave.** Allowed employers to require workers who took intermittent leave for planned medical treatment to transfer temporarily to an available alternative position for which the worker was qualified, provided the position had equivalent pay and benefits and better accommodated the worker's schedule.

• **Accrual of Leave.** Allowed workers who received paid leave for fewer than 12 weeks to take the additional weeks of leave up to the 12 weeks but without pay.

• **Substitutions.** Allowed workers to substitute any accrued paid vacation leave, personal leave or family leave for any part of the unpaid 12-week leave. Or, employers could require the employee to substitute paid leave for the unpaid portion. In other words, if a company already granted six weeks of paid leave, it had to grant six weeks of unpaid leave to reach the 12 weeks. The company did not have to offer 12 weeks' unpaid leave after paid leave was used up.

• **Employer Notice.** Required employees to provide their employers with 30 days' notice when the leave was foreseeable, such as for the expected birth or adoption of a child.

• **Married Employees.** Limited the aggregate number of weeks of leave to 12 when both spouses were employed by the same employer.

• **Certification.** Allowed employers to require that a request for leave be supported by a health care provider's certification of the medical condition of the employee's child, spouse or parent, including the date on which the serious health condition began; the probable duration of the condition and other appropriate medical facts; a statement that the employee was needed to care for the child, spouse or parent, and an estimate of the amount of time that the employee was needed.

If the employee was ill, the certification was required to include a statement that the employee was unable to perform his or her job. When the certification was for intermittent leave for planned medical treatment, it was supposed to include the dates and duration of the treatment.

- **Second Opinion.** Allowed the employer to require, at its expense, that the employee obtain the opinion of a second health care provider when certifying the need for a leave of absence.
- **Third Opinion.** Allowed the employer to require, in cases in which the second opinion differed from the first, that the employee obtain a third opinion from a health care provider at the expense of the employer. The law required that the opinion of the third health care provider be the final opinion, binding upon the employer and the employee.
- **Equivalent Position.** Required that employers restore any employee who had taken leave to the position held by the employee when the leave began or restore the employee to an equivalent position with equivalent employment benefits, pay and other conditions.
- **Benefits.** Prohibited a leave of absence from causing the loss of any employment benefit accrued before the leave began.
- **Periodic Reports.** Allowed the employer to require employees on leave to report periodically on their status and intention to return to work.
- **Top Employees.** Allowed employers to deny leave to the highest-paid 10 percent of workers if such denial was necessary to prevent substantial and grievous economic injury to the business.
- **Health Care.** Required the employer to maintain health care benefits for employees on leave.
- **Congressional Employees.** Applied to employees of the House and Senate.
- **Effective Date.** Was to go into effect six months after signed into law. ❑

Unemployment Benefits

Congress acted twice in 1993 to extend a temporary program that provided emergency federal benefits to the long-term unemployed. The Clinton administration sought these extensions because tens of thousands of people were exhausting their 26 weeks of state-paid basic benefits without finding jobs. The federally financed emergency program, which had been in place in various forms since November 1991, allowed the long-term unemployed to receive additional cash assistance.

The first extension (HR 920—PL 103-6), which expired Oct. 2, provided an extra 20 to 26 weeks of emergency benefits to an estimated 1.5 million workers who had exhausted their state unemployment compensation. The second extension (HR 3167—PL 103-152) gave unemployed workers who had used up their 26 weeks of basic benefits an additional seven or 13 weeks and was good through Feb. 5, 1994.

Congress had extended emergency federal unemployment compensation three times in the previous two years. The most recent extension, enacted in July 1992, was to expire March 6, 1993. In both 1991 and 1992, congressional Democrats had tried to designate the money as emergency spending, which under budget rules did not have to be offset by other spending cuts

or tax increases and was instead added to the deficit. But, faced with veto threats from President George Bush, they backed down and found ways to offset the costs, mainly by increasing revenues. *(Congress and the Nation Vol. VIII, p. 721)*

FIRST ROUND: HR 920

With the expiration date for the previous extension looming, Congress cleared a bill (HR 920) on March 4 extending the period for new claims for federal emergency benefits from March 7 through Oct. 2, 1993. Clinton signed the bill the same day.

Although no new claims could be processed after Oct. 2, unemployed workers who had started collecting benefits would continue to receive them until they had gotten the full 20 or 26 weeks of federal benefits, or until Jan. 15, 1994. The extension was expected to cost $3.3 billion in fiscal 1993 and $2.4 billion in fiscal 1994, all of it designated as emergency spending that would be added to the deficit. Congress appropriated $4 billion for the extension in a separate supplemental spending bill.

Legislative action began in the House Ways and Means Committee, which reported HR 920 (H Rept 103-17) on Feb. 23. During markup, the panel rejected a number of amendments from Republicans who said the cost should be offset by cuts in federal spending.

The House passed the bill Feb. 24 by a vote of 254–161. Members considered the measure under a restrictive rule that barred amendments, but Republicans still were able to draw attention to the cost of the bill. Bill Archer of Texas, ranking Republican on the Ways and Means Committee, offered a motion to recommit the bill with the intent of requiring that the cost be offset. The motion was defeated 186–229, but it enjoyed unanimous GOP support.

On Feb. 25, the Senate Finance Committee reported a companion measure (S 382).

The full Senate passed HR 920 on March 3 by a vote of 66–33, after substituting the text of S 382.

Like their colleagues in the House, Senate Republicans argued unsuccessfully that the cost of the bill should be offset. "If this program is worthwhile—and it is—we should pay for it," said Bob Packwood of Oregon. Packwood offered an amendment that would have cut administrative services for the executive branch by 0.5 percent across the board. Packwood said that would save $3.3 billion, enough to cover the fiscal 1993 cost of the bill. The Senate tabled, or killed, Packwood's amendment on a straight party-line vote, 57–43.

Hank Brown, R-Colo., then offered an amendment to help pay for the bill by eliminating cost-of-living adjustments (COLAs) for federal employees and members of Congress. But Senate Majority Leader George J. Mitchell, D-Maine, preempted Brown's proposal by offering language to drop the COLA only for members of Congress. The Senate agreed to Mitchell's amendment by voice vote before voting 58–41 to kill Brown's amendment.

The measure then returned to the House, which approved the bill in a pair of votes March 4. First, members agreed to the bulk of the bill, 247–156. They then accepted the Senate's COLA freeze, 403–0.

Clinton asked Congress to appropriate funds to pay for the bill as part of his ill-fated $16.3 billion economic stimulus package. By the time that bill (HR 1335—PL 103-24) was enacted, the only surviving element was $4 billion for the emergency unemployment benefits. *(Economic stimulus package, p. 57)*

SECOND ROUND: HR 3167

The emergency benefits enacted in March 1993 expired Oct. 2 with Democrats still locked in a battle over how to pay for yet another extension. The dispute had delayed action on the new extension for several weeks as the administration scrambled to come up with a way to offset the cost of the bill. House Ways and Means Committee Chairman Dan Rostenkowski, D-Ill., had made it clear from the outset that he would not mark up another emergency benefits bill without a financing mechanism.

The bill (HR 3167), which did not clear until Nov. 23, 1993, extended the emergency program for four months. Unemployed workers who had exhausted their 26 weeks of basic benefits and who lived in a state with at least 9 percent total unemployment qualified for 13 weeks of emergency benefits. Those living in states with less than 9 percent total unemployment were eligible for seven weeks. The program was made retroactive to Oct. 2, when the previous program expired. Workers could qualify for benefits through Feb. 5, 1994.

To pay the $1.1 billion cost of the new program, the bill required each state agency that administered an unemployment insurance program to profile all new applicants for basic unemployment benefits. The idea was to identify people most likely to remain unemployed for long periods and provide them with job search assistance in hopes of getting them off the unemployment rolls sooner. The Congressional Budget Office estimated that the profiling system would save $764 million over five years.

The bill also changed the Supplemental Security Income (SSI) program by limiting the eligibility of recent legal immigrants to receive SSI benefits, which went to poor people who also were aged, blind or disabled.

House Action

The Ways and Means Committee reported the $1.1 billion four-month extension Sept. 29 (H Rept 103-268). The measure, as approved by the panel, included an administration proposal to finance part of the cost of the four-month extension by requiring states to identify those most likely to remain jobless for a long time and give them job search assistance. The legislation also included a provision aimed at saving $331 million by temporarily changing, from three to five years, the amount of time a legal immigrant must reside in the United States before qualifying for SSI payments.

The bill had been scheduled for floor action Sept. 30, two days before the existing program was set to expire. But it was abruptly pulled from the calendar when the Congressional Hispanic Caucus objected to the provision delaying new immigrants' eligibility for SSI payments.

When neither Rostenkowski nor the Hispanic Caucus would compromise on the issue, Speaker Thomas S. Foley, D-Wash.,

decided to send the bill to the floor under a "self-executing rule" (H Res 273—H Rept 103-287) that automatically dropped the SSI provision and scaled back the unemployment program by five weeks so it would end New Year's Day. But when the measure came to the floor Oct. 14, the House defeated the rule by a vote of 149–274.

Republicans generally opposed rules that limited their ability to offer amendments; in this case they also wanted to keep the SSI provision in the bill. Many Democrats opposed the rule because they did not want the unemployment program to expire at the end of the holiday season when Congress would be in recess.

After the first rule was rejected, the House dropped the self-executing procedure and adopted a new rule the morning of Oct. 15 that left the SSI provision in the bill. The House then passed the emergency unemployment bill that same day by a vote of 302–95.

Senate Action

While the bill did not see committee action in the Senate, it was almost two weeks before HR 3167 was taken up on the floor. Many members said they had not heard many complaints from constituents about being unable to get unemployment benefits.

Don Nickles, R-Okla., raised a parliamentary objection to the bill, pointing out that the program's cost was to be incurred over four months, while the offsetting revenues would take five years to accrue. Budget rules required offsets in the same year as the expenditures. Daniel Patrick Moynihan, D-N.Y., moved to waive the budget rules, which required 60 votes. He failed on the first try Oct. 26 by a vote of 59–38. But the following day, Moynihan managed to drum up a few more votes and the motion passed, 61–39.

On the same day, the Senate adopted, 52–43, an amendment by Brown that would have prohibited people with taxable incomes above $120,000 in 1992 from receiving the federal benefits. The restriction did not apply to the basic system of state unemployment benefits.

The Senate also debated a series of unrelated amendments on such issues as a retroactive tax increase, the space station, superconducting super collider and social security. Most of the amendments were not adopted. Phil Gramm, R-Texas, however, was successful with his amendment to reduce the number of federal employees by 252,000 over five years, as proposed by the Clinton administration in its so-called reinventing government plan. The administration had wanted to make the cuts without having Congress write them into law, but the Senate agreed to the amendment, 82–14, on Oct. 28.

Later that day, HR 3167 was finally put to a vote. It passed, 76–20.

Conference, Final Action

The final stage in the bill's legislative journey began Nov. 4, when House and Senate conferees immediately killed the two Senate amendments that had been added by Brown and Gramm, even though the House had voted 275–146 earlier that day to instruct conferees to accept Gramm's amendment. Democratic leaders in both chambers did not want to give Clinton's reinventing government proposal the force of law, arguing that it would lead to wholesale firings rather than well-thought-out reductions.

Angry at being ignored, the House refused Nov. 9 to take up the conference report (H Rept 103-333), voting 226–202 to send it back to conference with instructions to restore the Gramm amendment.

The conference report then went to the Senate, where Gramm refused the entreaties of Majority Leader Mitchell and tried to recommit it to conference with instructions to restore his amendment. Gramm said the potential savings of $21.8 billion were the impetus for holding out. But senators eager to adjourn before the Thanksgiving holiday were not willing to cooperate, and Gramm's motion was rejected, 36–63, on Nov. 20. The Senate then adopted the conference report, 79–20.

The next day, Rostenkowski and Moynihan filed a new conference report (H Rept 103-404). It was identical to the first report, despite House support for Gramm's amendment. With the Senate already having approved the conference report, the House was blocked procedurally from trying again to recommit the bill. Forced to vote the popular measure up or down, the House adopted the conference report, 320–105, on Nov. 23. It was the last recorded House vote of the year. President Clinton signed the bill into law the following day. ❑

Striker Replacement

Legislation (HR 5) to prohibit companies from permanently replacing striking workers easily passed the House in 1993. But, much to the chagrin of organized labor, the presence of a prounion Democrat in the White House was not enough to push a companion bill (S 55) through the Senate during the 103rd Congress. Despite their best efforts, Senate Democrats simply lacked the 60 votes needed to invoke cloture, limit debate and proceed to a vote on the striker replacement bill.

BACKGROUND

Banning the permanent replacement of striking workers was a top priority for the AFL-CIO and its 14 million union members, who largely supported Bill Clinton's candidacy during the 1992 presidential election campaign. Although he had not expressed much enthusiasm for a striker replacement bill during the campaign, Clinton did promise labor leaders that if Congress passed the measure, he would sign it.

Employers already were barred from hiring permanent replacement workers in strikes involving unfair labor practices, such as an employer's refusal to bargain in good faith. But that prohibition did not apply to replacing workers who went on strike for economic reasons, such as higher pay or other benefits. HR 5 and S 55 would have eliminated that distinction. At issue was the balance of power between unions and employers as they negotiated contracts and weighed the possibility of a strike.

Labor groups and their allies said that businesses upset this balance during the late 1970s and 1980s, exploiting the sup-

posed loophole in existing law to replace some striking workers and to intimidate others into accepting inadequate contracts. They argued that the striker replacement bill would restore a healthier balance of power and make the right to strike a meaningful, rather than illusory, option for workers. They said that, in turn, could strengthen labor-management relations and productivity.

But Republicans and many business groups argued that the unions already held substantial leverage in contract negotiations. In their view, the striker bill would hand too many cards to labor, encouraging more strikes and ultimately costing jobs.

LEGISLATIVE ACTION

The House Education and Labor Committee reported HR 5 (H Rept 103-116, Part I) on May 27, 1993, having approving it earlier by a 28–15 party-line vote. The House Energy and Commerce Committee and House Public Works and Transportation Committee reported the bill on June 8 (H Rept 103-116, Parts II and III).

On June 15, the bill was taken up on the floor and passed, 239–190. During debate that day, members rejected two amendments, including one by Chet Edwards, D-Texas, that would have exempted nonunion workers—thereby allowing employers to permanently replace workers who struck to create a union shop. The House voted it down, 94–339.

Tom Ridge, R-Pa., offered a substitute amendment that would have prohibited employers from hiring permanent replacements for 10 weeks, starting when the employer hired temporary workers. Democrats argued that employers would drag out strikes until the 10 weeks expired and then permanently replace their workers. The amendment was rejected, 58–373.

Many Republicans voted against the two amendments in the hope that the bill would be "as bad as possible" when it arrived in the Senate, giving opponents of the measure no reason to reconsider their position.

In the Senate, a companion measure (S 55—S Rept 103-110) was reported July 27 by the Labor and Human Resources Committee. The panel had approved it by a party-line vote of 10–7.

The credible threat of a Republican filibuster kept proponents of the measure from bringing it to the Senate floor for more than a year after committee approval. Finally, in the summer of 1994, supporters of the measure, led by its sponsor Howard M. Metzenbaum, D-Ohio, received a commitment from Senate Majority Leader George Mitchell, D-Maine, to allow a number of cloture votes on S 55 in mid-July.

In the weeks approaching the votes, Metzenbaum and others made a concerted effort to broker a compromise with some moderate Democrats and Republicans who opposed the legislation as written but favored additional protections for striking workers. A number of changes were discussed including one proposal to apply the new law only to large employers. But these negotiations never produced an agreement that could bring in the 60 votes needed to limit debate and allow a final vote on the bill. As a result, the first cloture vote on the measure, held on July 12, was 53–47—seven votes short. A second vote the next day produced a similar result: 53–46.

Striker replacement legislation had suffered the same fate in the previous Congress. (*Congress and the Nation Vol. VIII, p. 733*)   ❏

OSHA Overhaul

Legislation aimed at substantially overhauling the law governing workplace safety was reported by the House Education and Labor Committee on Oct. 3, 1994 (HR 1280—H Rept 103-825, Part I). But the bill, which was opposed by Republicans and some moderate-to-conservative Democrats, was never taken up on the House floor.

The cornerstone of HR 1280 was a requirement that employers with 11 or more workers use recommendations from the Occupational Safety and Health Administration (OSHA)—the federal agency that set safety standards in the workplace—to establish a written health and safety plan to reduce hazardous working conditions. The committee-approved bill also would have required OSHA to investigate potential safety violations within 24 hours of an accident in which unsafe conditions might have been a cause. In addition, the measure would have extended the safety standards under the 1970 Occupational Safety and Health Act (PL 91-596)—which applied to private sector and federal workers—to the employees of state and local governments. (*Congress and the Nation Vol. III, p. 713*)

Democratic supporters of the measure maintained that an overhaul of the act was long overdue. They pointed to National Safety Council statistics showing 8,500 people were killed in work-related accidents in 1992. But Republicans countered that the bill would lead to excessive regulation, hampering businesses and slowing economic growth.

The Education and Labor Committee had approved HR 1280 on March 10 by a largely party-line vote of 26–17. During markup, the panel amended the bill to require that OSHA standards be applied to congressional offices and to create an Office of Construction Safety, Health and Education within the Labor Department.

Similar legislation had been reported by the House panel in 1992. (*Congress and the Nation Vol. VIII, p. 734*)   ❏

Black Lung

The House, May 19, 1994, passed, 252–166, legislation (HR 2108) aimed at making it easier for coal miners suffering from black lung disease to receive federally mandated disability benefits. The bill was never taken up in the Senate.

The measure had been reported by the House Education and Labor Committee on May 12 (H Rept 103-507).

Under the Coal Mine Health and Safety Act of 1969 (PL 91-173), miners suffering from the disease, which is similar to emphysema, were entitled to payments from coal companies. In cases where there was a dispute, the burden of proof was on workers to establish that they had contracted black lung disease while working in a coal mine. In addition, each side could present an unlimited amount of evidence supporting its case.

Proponents for victims of the disease argued that the law's

dispute resolution system was unfair to miners because companies had much greater resources for building a case. (*1969 act, Congress and the Nation Vol. III, p. 707*)

The measure would have amended the act to prohibit companies from presenting more than one medical exam as evidence at a claims hearing.

During the May 19 floor debate, Harris W. Fawell, R-Ill., offered an amendment that would have eliminated the medical evidence provision from the bill. Fawell argued that procedurally stacking the deck against mining companies was not only unfair but unconstitutional. His amendment was defeated, 181–238.

A similar bill passed the House in 1992. (*Congress and the Nation Vol. VIII, p. 734*)   ❏

Railroad Workers

The House on Aug. 16, 1994, passed by voice vote a bill (HR 4868) that would have modified benefits under the railroad workers unemployment insurance system.

The measure would have reduced from two weeks to seven days the time a temporarily disabled or displaced rail worker had to wait before receiving unemployment benefits. It also would have increased the maximum daily amount that could be paid to rail workers receiving benefits from $36 to $40. The limit on extended benefits was to be reduced from 130 days to 65 days.

Supporters of the measure—which included both rail management and labor organizations—said that it would bring the railroad unemployment system in line with the unemployment system in most states.

The House Energy and Commerce Committee reported the bill (H Rept 103-693) on Aug. 10.   ❏

Davis-Bacon Revision

The House Education and Labor Committee on Oct. 7, 1994, reported revisions to a depression-era labor law that set standards for wages on federal contracts. The bill (HR 1231—H Rept 103-856), which had won the panel's approval by a party-line vote of 28–14, advanced no further in the 103rd Congress.

HR 1231 would have raised from $2,000 to $100,000 the threshold for contracts covered under the 1931 Davis-Bacon Act. Davis-Bacon required contractors on federally funded construction projects to pay the prevailing local wage, usually a union rate. The statute was intended to prevent big construction companies from hiring low-wage, itinerant workers and underbidding local companies for coveted government contracts during the Depression.

GOP opponents said that the Davis-Bacon Act was a relic of another era when there were hardly any federal labor standards, such as a minimum wage, and worker exploitation was common. Now, they said, it simply drove up the cost of public works projects because the prevailing local wage rate was usually a union rate that was higher than nonunion private sector pay rates.

But Democratic supporters of the bill argued that the act was still necessary. Raising the contract value threshold, they said, would update the law so that small contractors would not be troubled by paperwork and other requirements attendant with the law.

The committee rejected several GOP amendments, including one that would have raised the threshold to $1 million.

Republican attempts in the 104th Congress to repeal the Davis-Bacon Act were thwarted by Democratic opposition. *(1995 action, p. 660)*   ❑

Mandatory Retirement Age

The House Nov. 8, 1993, passed a bill (HR 2722) that would have allowed state and local public safety agencies to consider age in their hiring and retirement policies. The bill, which passed by voice vote, was not taken up by the Senate.

HR 2722 would have permanently exempted state and local public safety agencies from the Age Discrimination in Employment Act, as amended in 1986 (PL 99-592), and allowed a mandatory retirement age as low as 55. But the exemption would have applied only in public safety jobs that required physical ability. The bill also would have permitted elected judges who reached the state age of compulsory retirement to complete their terms. *(1986 amendments, Congress and the Nation Vol. VII, p. 690)*

The House Education and Labor Committee reported the bill (H Rept 103-314) on Nov. 1. During markup, the committee amended the bill to authorize $5 million over the following four years to develop guidelines for performance testing of public safety officers in lieu of setting a mandatory retirement age.   ❑

Workplace Technology

The Senate Labor and Human Resources Committee in 1994 approved two measures aimed at promoting the use of technology in schools and businesses.

The school measure (S 1040—S Rept 103-234), which was reported March 9, would have authorized $352.5 million in fiscal 1995 to help upgrade the nation's classrooms with new technologies such as computer networks. *(School technology, p. 629)*

The other bill (S 1020—S Rept 103-401), reported Oct. 5, would have authorized the Labor Department to award grants, at unspecified sums, to labor unions, educational institutions and other nonprofit groups to aid in the development of advanced workplace technologies.

While neither measure advanced to the Senate floor, the grant scheme of S 1020 was largely included in the elementary and secondary school reauthorization bill (HR 6—PL 103-382). *(HR 6, p. 609)*   ❑

Social Security Benefits Tax

Congress in 1993 went along with President Clinton's plan to increase the level of Social Security benefits subject to taxes for some higher-income retirees. The change was included in the 1993 Omnibus Budget-Reconciliation Act (HR 2264—PL 103-66).

The legislation raised the portion of Social Security benefits subject to taxation from the existing 50 percent to 85 percent for individuals making more than $34,000 a year and couples making more than $44,000 a year, beginning in 1994.

The new income threshold for the tax was higher than Clinton had proposed and either chamber had approved. Under Clinton's plan, the increase would have come for couples earning more than $32,000 and individuals more than $25,000. The House bill had agreed with those levels, but the Senate version had raised the threshold to $40,000 for couples and $32,000 for individuals.

Conferees initially agreed with the Senate-passed levels but finally settled on the higher levels in order to win the support of holdout Dennis DeConcini, D-Ariz. During floor action June 24, the Senate had rejected, 48–50, a DeConcini amendment to increase the income threshold. Earlier that day the Senate had voted 51–46 to table (kill) a Trent Lott, R-Miss., amendment to eliminate the tax increase on benefits. *(1993 budget reconciliation, p. 44)*   ❑

Domestic Worker Tax

Congress in 1994 cleared a bill (HR 4278—PL 103-387) updating an often-disregarded law requiring that Social Security taxes be paid for domestic workers. The law, which had not been changed since 1950, had required employers to pay Social Security and Medicare taxes for housekeepers, baby-sitters, gardeners and other domestic workers if they paid them more than $50 in a calendar quarter. The tax requirement, which also involved the filing of quarterly tax forms, was unknown to many household employers and widely ignored by others.

Failure to pay the so-called nanny tax had derailed Clinton's first nominee for attorney general, Zoë Baird, and embarrassed a number of other candidates for top government posts.

Lawmakers in both chambers agreed that the $50 wage threshold was outdated and virtually invited noncompliance, but they had difficulty agreeing on a new figure. The final compromise required employers to pay the tax on domestic workers who were paid more than $1,000 in a year.

LEGISLATIVE ACTION

In 1993, the House tried to raise the threshold to $1,800 annually as part of the broad-based budget reconciliation bill (HR 2264). But the Social Security provision was dropped in conference after Senate Finance Committee Chairman Daniel Patrick Moynihan, D-N.Y., balked at the House-passed threshold, which he regarded as too high, and warned that a little-known Senate rule barred consideration of a reconciliation bill that changed Social Security.

Clinton administration officials never proposed a plan of their own, though they indicated support for a threshold of up to $1,000.

The Senate Finance Committee on April 19, 1994, reported a bill (S 1231—S Rept 103-252) to raise the threshold to $620 annually for 1994. (That was the same as the amount an employee needed to earn in 1994 to get one quarter of Social Security benefits.) In future years, the threshold was to be indexed to the average national wage increase. S 1231 provided for employers to pay Social Security taxes along with their annual income tax returns instead of paying quarterly. It also exempted Social Security taxes on wages paid to workers under age 18.

S 1231 was largely symbolic because it contained revenue-raising provisions and therefore, under the Constitution, had to originate in the House. However, Moynihan, sponsor of the bill, wanted to show House leaders that senators were willing to move on the domestic worker problem without adding miscellaneous tax provisions.

The House Ways and Means Committee on May 4 reported its version (HR 4278—H Rept 103-491) calling for increasing the earnings limit to $1,200 in 1994 and $1,250 in 1995, and indexing it in future years to the national average wage increase. The measure, sponsored by Andrew Jacobs Jr., D-Ind., chairman of the Ways and Means Subcommittee on Social Security, provided for employers to pay Social Security taxes for domestic workers through estimated tax payments or increasing tax withholding from their own wages.

The House passed the Ways and Means bill without debate on May 12. The vote was 420–0.

The Senate took up the House-passed measure May 25, amended it to set the earnings threshold at $620 a year in 1994 and approved it by voice vote, setting the stage for a House-Senate conference.

Final passage was delayed over the summer while Moynihan and other key lawmakers turned their attention to health care reform. As a noncontroversial tax measure—a rarity in Congress—the bill also was considered a potential vehicle to carry other legislation. In the end, however, it attracted no riders.

Congress completed work on the measure at the end of the session, after Moynihan and Jacobs had agreed to set the threshold at $1,000 a year, to be indexed in future years to the national average wage increase. "We have decriminalized baby sitting," Moynihan declared Oct. 5 as a House-Senate conference approved the compromise (H Rept 103-842).

The House adopted the conference report Oct. 6 by a vote of 423–0; the Senate cleared it by voice vote the same day. President Clinton signed the bill into law Oct. 22.

PROVISIONS

As signed into law, HR 4278:

• Required employers to pay Social Security and Medicare taxes on domestic workers who were paid more than $1,000 a year. The bill indexed the threshold in future years to the national average wage increase and allowed the level to rise in $100 increments.

• Sought to simplify the paperwork involved in paying the taxes. Beginning with tax year 1995, employers would be allowed to settle their tax obligations for domestic workers on their annual federal income tax returns rather than in quarterly filings.

• Generally exempted domestic workers younger than 18 from Social Security taxes, unless their principal occupation was

household employment. That excluded occasional baby-sitters or gardeners but not full-time workers.

• To help make up for any loss in federal revenue from increasing the tax threshold, the bill broadened the existing prohibition of Social Security benefits to incarcerated felons. Because the definition of a felony varied by state, the bill extended the prohibition so that it applied to anyone convicted of an offense punishable by imprisonment of more than one year. In addition, the prohibition applied to criminal cases in which the defendant was found not guilty by reason of insanity and confined to an institution by court order. (*Social Security for prisoners, p. 675*)

• Responding to concerns by the Social Security Board of Trustees that the disability fund could be depleted by 1995, the bill reallocated 0.34 percent of both the employer and employee Social Security payroll tax from the Old Age and Survivors Insurance Trust Fund to the disability fund.   ❑

Social Security Administration

Congress in 1994 agreed to make the Social Security Administration an independent agency. The legislation (HR 4277—PL 103-296) called for Social Security to separate from the Department of Health and Human Services (HHS) by March 31, 1995. The move had long been sought by Senate Finance Committee Chairman Daniel Patrick Moynihan, D-N.Y., and Andrew Jacobs Jr., D-Ind., chairman of the House Ways and Means Subcommittee on Social Security.

The Social Security Administration Independence Act also became a vehicle for clamping down on drug addicts and alcoholics who received federal payments. A General Accounting Office (GAO) study had found that the federal government paid $1.4 billion in fiscal 1993 to 250,000 drug addicts and alcoholics under the SSI and disability insurance programs. Of that group, only the 79,000 SSI recipients were subject to some monitoring of how they used their payments. The Social Security Administration verified that only 10 percent of SSI recipients were in treatment.

BACKGROUND

Begun in 1935 during the Great Depression, Social Security initially was administered by a Social Security Board as an independent agency. In 1946, the Social Security Administration replaced the board. It continued as an independent agency until 1953, when it was included in the newly created Department of Health, Education and Welfare, which subsequently became HHS.

The Social Security Administration was the largest agency in HHS and the ninth largest in the federal government, with 65,000 employees and 1,300 field offices. In fiscal 1993, the agency made $298.1 billion in net benefits payments and spent $6.4 billion on administrative and other expenses. It ran the Old Age, Survivors and Disability Insurance program (OASDI) and SSI.

The Old Age and Survivors Insurance program provided monthly cash benefits to retired workers and their dependents and to survivors of insured workers. The Disability Insurance program, added in 1956, provided monthly cash benefits for disabled workers and their dependents. SSI benefits went to poor elderly, blind and otherwise disabled individuals.

Moynihan had argued for years that the Social Security Administration should be made independent as a way to heighten its visibility and isolate it somewhat from the political party that controlled the White House. But bills that would have granted the agency independence died in the Senate after passing the House in 1986, 1989 and 1992. *(1989 and 1992 action, Congress and the Nation Vol. VIII, pp. 737, 718; 1986 action, Congress and the Nation Vol. VII, p. 693)*

The Reagan and Bush administrations had maintained that Social Security was best left under the purview of HHS. Like her predecessors, Clinton's HHS secretary, Donna E. Shalala, also argued against granting the agency independence, saying that its presence within the department made it easier to coordinate services and gave it cabinet-level leadership.

LEGISLATIVE ACTION

Moynihan stepped up his effort in 1993, after assuming the chairmanship of the Finance Committee. His committee reported a bill to create an independent agency (S 1560—S Rept 103-221) on Nov. 19, 1993. It was the third time in five years that the panel had approved such a bill.

The Senate passed S 1560 by voice vote March 2, 1994. Moynihan was able to pick up some support from Republicans, who no longer had a GOP White House position to defend, without losing Democratic backing. The Senate agreed by voice vote to an amendment by William S. Cohen, R-Maine, to stop unsupervised payments to drug addicts and alcoholics.

After rejecting Republican-led efforts to sharply restrict access to SSI payments, the House Ways and Means Committee on May 12 reported its version of the bill (HR 4277—H Rept 103-506). In contrast to the Senate bill, which sought to put the independent Social Security agency under the direction of a single commissioner, advised by a seven-member board, the House bill put it under a three-person board appointed by the president. The board, in turn, was to appoint an executive director to manage Social Security's daily affairs. The board's term was six years.

The bill included a series of amendments restricting payments to those who received SSI or Social Security disability insurance payments because of a drug or alcohol addiction. The committee adopted an amendment to limit addicts' benefits to 36 months, despite Clinton administration objections to terminating benefits to anyone undergoing required treatment for addiction.

Republicans sought to tighten the restrictions further with amendments to stop paying SSI cash benefits to children under age 18 and to eliminate SSI benefits to most noncitizens. Several of the committee's Democrats, while opposing the amendments, indicated that they shared a desire to further restrict SSI eligibility.

Members expressed concern about reports that some children were being encouraged by their parents or others to act violently or otherwise misbehave in school to qualify as mentally

---

SOCIAL SECURITY LEADERSHIP

The Senate confirmed Shirley Sears Chater as the new head of the Social Security Administration by voice vote on Oct. 7, 1993. Chater had served as president of Texas Woman's University and as chairman of the Texas governor's Health Policy Task Force.

President Clinton announced Aug. 3 that he intended to nominate Chater to the post, but he delayed formally sending her name to the Senate. Administration officials said routine FBI background checks slowed the nomination. Chater had failed to pay Social Security taxes for part-time baby-sitters from 1969 to 1975. She paid the taxes earlier in 1993, however. The issue of nonpayment of Social Security taxes had derailed Clinton's first nominee for attorney general, Zoë Baird. *(Controversial nominations, p. 1117)*

The top Social Security post had been vacant since Oct. 1, 1992, when Gwendolyn S. King resigned. With 65,000 workers and 1,300 regional offices, the agency ran the federal government's largest domestic program and was expected to disburse nearly $300 billion in retirement, survivors' and disability benefits in 1993. The lengthy delay in filling the post prompted frequent criticism from Daniel Patrick Moynihan, D-N.Y., chairman of the Senate Finance Committee, which oversaw the Social Security system. "It's disgraceful," Moynihan said during a Sept. 14 hearing. "It indicates a lack of concern."

---

or emotionally disabled, winning eligibility for SSI benefits. Since a 1990 Supreme Court decision that made it easier for children to qualify for SSI, the number of children who received SSI payments had more than doubled, to 770,000. The committee added language requiring that all disabled children who received SSI benefits be reviewed by Social Security examiners before their 19th birthday. However, the committee rejected an amendment that would have replaced the SSI cash benefit for children under age 18 with a voucher that could be used for medical expenses not covered by their state's Medicaid program.

The committee rejected an amendment to eliminate SSI benefits to most noncitizens. The amendment would have exempted refugees and certain permanent residents over age 75.

The panel approved an amendment to require translators to certify under oath the accuracy of their translations. The requirement was a response to reports that translators were helping immigrants fake mental illness in order to get on the rolls. The amendment authorized civil penalties against translators, physicians and SSI recipients who fraudulently tried to enroll ineligible recipients. And it made SSI fraud a felony rather than a misdemeanor.

The House considered the bill under expedited procedures May 17 and passed it by a vote of 413–0. On May 23, the Senate approved HR 4277 by voice vote after substituting the text of S 1560. The bill then went to conference.

The Senate adopted the conference report on the bill (H Rept 103-670) Aug. 5 by voice vote. The House cleared the bill Aug. 11 by a vote of 431–0.

MAJOR PROVISIONS

As signed into law Aug. 15, 1994, HR 4277:

• Made the Social Security Administration an independent agency by March 31, 1995.

• Provided for the new agency to be governed by a commissioner and deputy commissioner appointed to six-year terms, subject to Senate confirmation. They were to be advised by a seven-member board: three members appointed by the president and two each by the House Speaker and Senate president pro tempore.

• Restricted benefits paid to alcoholics and drug addicts under the Supplemental Security Income (SSI) and Social Security disability programs to three years. Recipients of disability payments whose alcoholism or drug use contributed to their disability were to be required to receive their benefits through an intermediary who would be responsible for managing their finances. They also were to be required to participate in a substance abuse treatment program. These rules already applied to the SSI program.

In determining who should monitor disability beneficiaries whose disability was affected by alcoholism or drug use, the bill gave preference to nonprofit community-based organizations. Such organizations could receive up to 10 percent of a recipient's benefits—up to $50 a month, instead of $25 a month under previous law—to provide oversight.

For drug addicts and alcoholics receiving disability payments, the 36-month time limit was to exclude months where treatment was not available. For those receiving SSI, the time limit was to run regardless of whether treatment was available. In any case, recipients would continue to be eligible for Medicare or Medicaid after their disability benefits expired.

Additional sanctions were to apply to beneficiaries who did not comply with their treatment programs. For example, those who failed to comply with treatment for 12 successive months would be dropped from the SSI or disability rolls.

• Required all disabled children who received SSI benefits to be reviewed by Social Security examiners by their 19th birthday.

• Required translators to certify the accuracy of their translation of applications for benefits and to disclose the nature of their relationship to the applicant. Authorized civil penalties against those who fraudulently tried to enroll ineligible recipients and made SSI fraud a felony.

• Increased the penalties against misusing the names and symbols of the Social Security Administration, Health Care Financing Administration and the Treasury Department. The provision also eliminated the annual $100,000 cap on civil monetary penalties.

• Excluded from Federal Insurance Contributions Act (FICA) taxes the pay of election workers who made less than $1,000 annually. The previous threshold was $100.

• Required the GAO to assess the Social Security Administration's use of voice mail and other technologies to increase public telephone access to local offices, and to report to Congress by Jan. 31, 1996.   ❑

Underfunded Pensions

Congress tightened federal requirements on businesses that underfunded their pension plans. The provisions cleared Dec. 1, 1994, as part of implementing legislation for the General Agreement on Tariffs and Trade (GATT). President Clinton signed the GATT bill (HR 5110—PL 103-465) on Dec. 8. *(GATT, p. 161)*

Under the 1974 Employee Retirement Income Security Act (ERISA), which governed employee benefit plans, employers were supposed to set aside enough money to meet future pension commitments. While most private pensions were fully funded, some companies—particularly in the steel and auto industries—had failed to contribute all the money needed to pay future retiree benefits. As a result, estimated pension fund shortfall doubled from $27 billion in 1987 to $53 billion in 1992, according to Pension Benefit Guaranty Corporation (PBGC).

The PBGC, a federal nonprofit corporation, guaranteed private single employer pensions up to a maximum of $30,682 per worker, per year. To cover the cost of these guarantees, the PBGC collected from employers an annual fee of $19 per year for each worker whose pension was guaranteed. Companies with underfunded plans could be required to pay up to $53 per year, per worker, depending on the degree of deficit.

The pension provisions in HR 5110 gradually raised the $53 cap on employer premiums, phasing it out entirely after three years. This was intended to allow the PBGC to collect more from employers who were more likely to default on future benefits payments.

The language also required companies to maintain enough money in their pension accounts to pay at least three years' worth of benefits. Any new benefits given to workers had to be fully paid for within five to 14 years. Companies with underfunded pensions were required to notify workers of the pension plan's status.

In addition, employers were required to use uniform mortality and interest rate tables when determining future liability. PBGC officials said that many companies used high interest rate and mortality tables, allowing them to underestimate the cost of providing workers with benefits and thus pay less into the plan.

The language had begun as a separate bill (HR 3396—H Rept 103-632, Parts I and II), reported by the House Ways and Means Committee on July 29, 1994, and by the House Education and Labor Committee on Aug. 26.

Action on HR 3396 stopped after the provisions were incorporated into the GATT bill. The pension provisions were added to help offset the $12 billion in tariff income that was expected to be lost over the first five years of the GATT accord. By reducing the federal liability for pension failures, HR 3396 was expected to save an estimated $1 billion over the same five fiscal years.   ❑

Executive Life Benefits

Congress in 1994 cleared legislation (S 1312—PL 103-401) aimed at helping 84,000 retirees and employees whose pension benefits were threatened as a result of the insolvency of the Executive Life Insurance Company. The measure, which passed the Senate by voice vote Oct. 28, 1993, gave those retirees and workers greater latitude in seeking redress from their employers. The House cleared the bill, also by voice vote, Oct. 3, 1994. It was signed into law Oct. 22.

During the 1980s, many employers terminated their pension plans and replaced them with cheaper annuities offered by Executive Life and other insurance companies. Under this agreement, employers paid these companies to assume responsibility for paying retirees their pension benefits.

According to supporters of the bill, employers purchased these annuities to free up cash set aside in pension funds for other uses. But this arrangement added some risk for workers because, unlike standard company pensions, annuity payments were not guaranteed by the federal government under the 1974 Employee Retirement Income Security Act (ERISA—PL 93-406). Thus, when Executive Life became insolvent in 1991, retirees saw their pension payments from the company reduced for a year.

Executive Life beneficiaries suffered another blow in 1993 when the Supreme Court ruled on June 1 in *Mertens v. Hewitt Associates* that retirees could not sue their former employers for lost pension benefits, even if those companies violated ERISA.

Bill sponsor Sen. Howard M. Metzenbaum, D-Ohio, said that future pension benefits of retirees covered by Executive Life annuities were still in danger of being reduced or eliminated. In addition, he claimed, many employers purchased Executive Life annuities with the knowledge that the company was not on sound financial footing and were hence in violation of their fiduciary duty to their workers and retirees. S 1312 clarified that beneficiaries could receive monetary damages from those employers who bought Executive Life annuities in violation of this duty. ❏

Pension Benefit Taxes

The House Oct. 3, 1994, passed by voice vote a bill (HR 546) that would have restricted a state's right to tax the pension benefits of former residents. But attempts to push the bill through the Senate in the final days of the 103rd Congress stalled after Sen. Malcolm Wallop, R-Wyo., put a hold on the bill, arguing that it did not go far enough in relieving the burden of "double taxation" on senior citizens. Wallop said that Congress should prohibit all state taxation of nonresident income.

The debate over double taxation centered around the 10 states, including California and New York, that imposed some sort of "source tax" on the pension benefits of former long-term residents. These 10 jurisdictions argued that their taxation of former residents was justified since they had deferred taxing pension and other retirement benefits while the individuals resided in state. Because that money was never taxed, these states said, they had a right to collect once the workers retired and began drawing their pensions—regardless of where they lived.

Retirees, on the other hand, said that it was unjust for a state to tax the income of nonresidents who could not vote in that state or benefit from any of the services financed by their taxes.

The bill, which had been reported by the House Judiciary Committee on Oct. 3 (H Rept 103-776), would have barred states from taxing nonresidents whose annual pension payments totaled $30,000 or less. Any pension income in excess of $30,000 would have remained taxable. ❏

ERISA Preemption

The House in 1993 passed legislation (HR 1036) to give states more latitude in regulating certain employee benefits. But the bill stalled in the Senate over Republican concerns that it would hurt businesses and unfairly favor union workers.

Lawmakers did clear, as part of unrelated legislation, provisions clarifying that federal law did not preempt certain state health insurance regulations.

ERISA BILL

Pension plans and other worker benefits were governed by the 1974 Employee Retirement Income Security Act (ERISA—PL 93-406). The act sought to eliminate contradictory federal and state regulations by spelling out that federal law preempted state laws. *(1974 law, Congress and the Nation Vol. IV, p. 690)*

But supporters of HR 1036 said that recent federal appeals court decisions had broadened the scope of ERISA's preemption clause beyond the intent of Congress, interfering with the legitimate regulatory rights of states.

HR 1036 sought to bar the preemption of state law under ERISA in three particular areas:

• **Prevailing Wages.** In 1994, 31 states had laws that required employers to pay workers the prevailing local wage, in money and benefits, for work on state contracts. But some state courts had struck down these laws as a violation of the ERISA preemption clause.

• **Apprenticeship Programs.** All 50 states had passed laws establishing minimum standards for apprenticeship or other job training programs. But some of these laws were overturned because of the preemption clause. Bill supporters said Congress intended ERISA to govern only disclosure and reporting requirements for apprenticeship programs, not training standards.

• **Liens for Unpaid Pensions.** Some states allowed workers to acquire liens on the properties of those employers who had not fully paid into pension plans that were administered by more than one company. Two state court decisions struck down these laws, again on ERISA preemption grounds.

HR 1036 was reported by the House Education and Labor Committee (H Rept 103-253) Sept. 22, 1993, and was passed by the full House Nov. 9 by a vote of 276–150. The Senate Labor and Human Resources Committee, having approved the bill on a 10–7 party-line vote, reported it July 1, 1994 (S Rept 103-299). There was no further action.

The House had approved a similar bill in 1992, but the Senate had not taken up the legislation because of a veto threat. *(1992 bill, Congress and the Nation Vol. VIII, p. 737)*

HEALTH INSURANCE REGULATION

Congress included in the massive 1993 budget reconciliation act (HR 2264—PL 103-66) several provisions ensuring that ERISA did not preempt certain state laws regarding health insurance. *(1993 budget reconciliation bill, p. 44)*

One provision amended federal pension law to clarify that ERISA did not preempt states from seeking reimbursements from private insurers in cases in which a claim had been unnecessarily paid by Medicaid, the government health insurance program for the poor. Another provision in HR 2264 clarified that ERISA did not preempt state authority to force noncustodial parents to provide health insurance to their children. ❑

Airline Pensions

Congress in 1993 cleared legislation (S 400—PL 103-7) designed to guarantee retirees of troubled airlines their pension benefits and to preserve a Continental Airlines plan to reorganize in the wake of financial woes.

Continental had been liable for almost $694 million in pension funds when it filed for Chapter 11 protection in 1990. In an effort to resolve the liability claims, it gave 15 aircraft to the Pension Benefit Guaranty Corporation (PBGC), the federal agency established to help retirees obtain pensions promised by companies that no longer could deliver them because of financial troubles. When Continental agreed to lease the planes back from the PBGG, concerns were raised that the agreement would diminish special protections that the bankruptcy law gave equipment leasing companies and discourage similar financial arrangements that might be beneficial to airlines.

S 400 clarified that PBGC was the lessor in the agreement and therefore could foreclose on the planes if Continental went bankrupt. The measure, which applied generally to all airline bankruptcy cases, was passed by voice votes of the Senate March 11, 1993, and the House March 16 and was signed into law March 17. ❑

1995–1996

The sweeping GOP victory in the congressional elections of 1994 left prolabor advocates with a sense of impending dread. For starters, the Democrats, the traditional allies of labor, were now in the minority on Capitol Hill and in a state of disarray. In addition, the new Republican leadership, especially in the House, was committed to rolling back laws it considered overly burdensome to business, including a host of rules that unions said were essential to protecting American workers.

But the fears of prolabor advocates proved unfounded. Time and again, the GOP failed in its attempts to rewrite a variety of labor laws, ranging from the Occupational Safety and Health Act (OSHA) to the Davis-Bacon rules on prevailing wages in government contracting.

In addition, in 1996, the White House and congressional Democrats managed to forge an alliance with moderate Republicans to push through a 90-cents-an-hour increase in the minimum wage, over the objections of GOP leaders in the House and Senate.

Senior citizen groups won an important victory, when Congress approved an increase in the Social Security earnings test, which limited the amount older workers could earn before their benefits were curtailed.

Minimum Wage

President Clinton on Aug. 20, 1996, signed into law a bill (HR 3448—PL 104-188) that raised the federal minimum wage, putting an exclamation point at the end of the Democrats' greatest triumph of the 104th Congress. The minimum wage officially increased Oct. 1, 1996, from $4.25 an hour to $4.75. The law set it to go up again Sept. 1, 1997, to $5.15.

It was the first increase in the mandatory minimum wage since 1991 and the first legislation on the issue since 1989. The change came as the value of the minimum wage was nearing a 40-year low in inflation-adjusted dollars.

That it happened on the watch of a Republican Congress was remarkable. Republican leaders had always contended that an increase would destroy hundreds of thousands of low-wage jobs. But Democrats put on the pressure, tying up the Senate in knots for weeks by trying to attach a minimum wage increase to nearly every bill that came to the floor. They also launched an effective public relations campaign that painted GOP minimum wage opponents as unfair to the working poor and generous to wealthy business interests.

In the end, the defection of about two dozen Republican moderates in the House weakened the leadership's resolve to keep the issue off the floor and made a vote inevitable. Once legislation did come to the floor, it passed easily.

In an effort to save face and appease business interests that were clamoring for a tax cut in the 104th Congress, House lawmakers attached the minimum wage increase to a scaled-back version of a set of business tax cuts that were originally part of the GOP "Contract with America."

BACKGROUND

Congress first established a nationwide uniform minimum wage—25 cents an hour—in the Fair Labor Standards Act of 1938 (PL 75-718). Since then, it had been raised periodically.

The last battle over the wage had taken place in 1989, when President George Bush and the Democratic-controlled Congress had agreed to increase it from $3.35 an hour to $4.25, over two years. One issue that had almost derailed that bill (PL 101-157) was Bush's push for a lower "training wage" aimed at encouraging employers to hire new workers. Despite intense opposition from Democrats, who argued that businesses would use the lower wage as a loophole to keep paying all workers $3.35 per hour, a compromise was struck allowing the lower wage for teenagers and temporary workers. *(Minimum wage, Congress and the Nation Vol. VIII, p. 705)*

On Feb. 3, 1995, President Clinton proposed increasing the wage to $5.15 over two years. While the idea of raising the minimum wage enjoyed high levels of popular support, it was ignored by many key Republicans in Congress, such as House Majority Leader Dick Armey, R-Texas, who said it would lead to massive layoffs. Consequently, Clinton's idea was soon forgotten.

But the issue resurfaced in early 1996, when Patrick J. Buchanan's campaign for the GOP presidential nomination gained momentum by highlighting a sense of insecurity among American workers at a time of widespread corporate downsizing, soaring executive compensation and the pursuit of ever-higher profit margins. After Buchanan stormed to a first-place finish in the Feb. 20 New Hampshire primary, economic issues took center stage.

INITIAL MANEUVERING

The Democrats had the simplest response: raise the minimum wage. Their first attempt to do so occurred in the Senate on March 26, when Massachusetts Democrats Edward M. Kennedy and John Kerry surprised their Republican colleagues by offering amendments to a controversial federal parks bill (HR 1296) that would have raised the minimum wage to $5.15 per hour over the next two years. *(Parks bill, p. 461)*

After two days of debate, nervous GOP leaders, led by presidential candidate and Majority Leader Bob Dole, R-Kan., pulled the parks bill from the floor. Several weeks later, on April 16, Republicans pulled an immigration bill (S 1664) from the floor after Democrats maneuvered to amend it with a minimum-wage increase. Kennedy vowed to keep attaching the amendment to every piece of legislation that came to the floor. *(Immigration bill, p. 717)*

Senate Democratic maneuvering and the GOP retreat made it clear that a campaign-focused Dole was not going to lead a frontal charge to defeat the increase, and that many of his colleagues in the Senate were nervous about voting against it. And while Armey and other GOP leaders, such as Majority Whip Tom DeLay, R-Texas, attempted to rally their troops in the House against a minimum wage boost, many rank-and-file Republicans were pondering whether their loyalty to the leadership would cost them their seats in the approaching election.

The first crack in House GOP unity was exposed April 17 when a group of 20 Republican moderates, many of them from urban areas in the Northeast, introduced a bill to raise the minimum wage by $1. When House Speaker Newt Gingrich, R-Ga., met the same day with the Republican Conference behind closed doors and asked for a show of hands from those supporting a wage increase, many more than expected shot up.

Gingrich, Armey and other GOP leaders made one more attempt to head off a minimum wage vote by promising, on April 24, to bring to the floor a package of measures designed to raise wages by bolstering the economy through tax cuts, tort reform and other measures. But Christopher Shays, R-Conn., one of 20 House cosponsors of the GOP minimum wage bill, said that Republican moderates would join with Democrats to press for a vote.

Shays's threat was very real. At another GOP closed-door show of hands on May 1, as many as 70 House Republicans said they would vote for a wage increase. With Democrats nearly united in favor, an increase would pass easily.

In the Senate, there was equal Republican disarray, though it was not quite as public. On April 25, Dole offered to allow a vote in June as part of a broad labor package, including some proposals opposed by Democrats. Kennedy dismissed the offer on the Senate floor, telling Dole he wanted a clean vote or no vote.

By the first week of May, Republican leaders in both chambers conceded that they were going to have to move a minimum-wage hike to the floor. While Democrats clamored for a clean bill, GOP strategy was to pair it with legislation that was distasteful to Democrats but not anathema to them: a repeal (at least temporarily) of the 4.3-cents-per-gallon gasoline tax that had been a key element of Clinton's 1993 deficit-reduction package. *(1993 deficit reduction, p. 87)*

Complaining that Dole and the Republicans were blocking their minimum-wage increase, Democratic leaders ordered a filibuster and ground the Senate to a halt. A series of votes to invoke cloture failed.

On May 8, Clinton called for a political truce, pledging to go along with rolling back the gas tax, in view of rising gasoline prices. In return, he said, Republicans would have to agree to hold a vote, no strings attached, on raising the minimum wage. At first, Dole indicated that he might accept the president's offer. But eventually, the majority leader rejected the idea of separate votes.

Meanwhile, in the House, Republican leaders supported the gas tax rollback but did not link it to the minimum wage increase. Instead, they wanted it paired with legislation that would more directly placate key GOP constituencies: a proposal to reform both welfare and the Medicaid health care system for the poor. But that strategy threatened to provoke a veto from Clinton and moderates objected that it would jeopardize the minimum wage increase. On May 9, Armey withdrew the plan.

HOUSE ACTION

The eventual vehicle for the wage increase (HR 3448) emerged May 14 from the House Ways and Means Committee. It was a package of $7 billion in tax breaks for small businesses that included more generous write-offs for equipment purchases and a loosening of tax rules for family-owned and other small businesses. The measure had bipartisan support.

Meanwhile, House Republican leaders were eyeing another bill (HR 1227) as a minimum wage vehicle. HR 1227 amended a 1947 labor law to allow employees to commute in company cars without being paid for commuting time. The bill, which addressed a federal court ruling in Indiana that all time spent commuting in company vehicles had to be counted as hours worked, had been reported by the House Economic and Educational Opportunities Committee on May 20 (H Rept 104-585). Once on the floor, according to the GOP plan, HR 1227 was to be amended with the minimum wage increase and the small-business tax provisions.

The first step was a vote on a rule that provided for floor consideration of both the tax package (HR 3448) and the employee commuting bill (HR 1227), with an amendment to add the minimum wage increase. The rule stipulated that upon passage of both bills, the two measures would be combined into a single bill and sent to the Senate.

It was supposed to be a fairly straightforward series of floor votes, but the plan became a bit more complicated when Rules Committee Chairman Gerald B. H. Solomon, R-N.Y., decided to allow a package of amendments to HR 1227 to further insulate small businesses from the burden of a higher minimum wage.

The package, sponsored by Bill Goodling, R-Pa., chairman of the Economic and Educational Opportunities Committee, included four steps. Three were merely distasteful to Democrats: protecting employers such as restaurant owners from paying the higher wage to workers who relied on tips; freezing overtime requirements for computer professionals; and establishing a training, or "opportunity," wage of $4.25 an hour for youths during their first months on a job.

But the fourth provision—a proposal to exempt small businesses from the minimum wage and overtime requirements—was a lightning rod for criticism. Had it passed, an unlikely coalition of liberal Democrats opposing the exemption and conservative Republicans opposing the wage increase could have killed the bill. Performing a delicate high-wire act to balance the needs of GOP moderates with those of anti–minimum wage conservatives, Solomon broke the exemption provision out of the package for a separate vote.

Even so, Democrats and a few conservative Republicans came close to killing the rule (H Res 440). The vote, taken May 22, was 219–211.

The next step was passage May 22 of the Republicans' package of business tax breaks. HR 3448 was endorsed by a lopsided vote of 414–10.

Then came consideration of HR 1227, with a relatively cleancut vote on the merits of the minimum wage increase. Although its outcome was hardly in doubt, debate on a Frank Riggs, R-Calif., amendment to add the minimum wage provisions was passionate. Conservative Republicans painted the increase as a politically motivated job killer that would hurt the low-wage workers it was ostensibly meant to help. Supporters said it was a simple matter of fairness. The buying power of the minimum wage was at nearly a 40-year low, advocates said, and raising it to $5.15 would get it to the inflation-adjusted value of 1989.

The Riggs amendment was adopted easily on May 23 by a **key vote of 266–162 (R 77–156; D 188–6; I 1–0).** *(1996 key votes, p. 1047)*

The House then easily adopted, 239–188, Goodling's first amendment package, consisting of the provisions on tipped employees, computer professionals and a subminimum wage.

But Goodling's proposal to exempt small businesses from the minimum wage requirement drew a huge fight. The proposal would have exempted firms with annual sales below $500,000 from any requirements to pay the minimum wage or, equally important, to pay time-and-a-half for overtime work. Goodling and House GOP leaders maintained that this would merely reinstate a provision enacted by a Democratic Congress in 1989 but nullified by subsequent administrative interpretations.

But Democrats denounced the proposal, saying it was a "poison pill" to kill the minimum wage increase. Labor Secretary Robert Reich branded it "a dramatic leap backward from current law effectively exempting virtually all new employees of two-thirds of all firms."

In the end, Democrats won the day, defeating the proposal by a vote of 196–229.

Once Goodling's amendment was defeated on May 23, the final vote to pass HR 1227 came easily. The tally was 281–144, with 93 Republicans voting with 187 Democrats in support of the measure. Under the rule for floor consideration, the measure was then automatically combined with HR 3448 and sent to the Senate under that bill number.

SENATE ACTION

The measure stalled in the Senate for weeks after House passage, delayed first by Dole's reluctance to take up the issue and then by the vacuum leading up to Dole's resignation June 11 to devote full-time attention to his campaign. Some movement had occurred on June 12, when the Senate Finance Committee reported the small-business tax cut provisions in HR 3448. But the whens, wheres and hows of voting on the wage increase remained unresolved.

Dole's replacement as majority leader, Trent Lott, R-Miss., and the newly elected majority whip, Don Nickles, R-Okla., both opposed the wage increase. But after weeks of intense negotiations, Senate leaders from both parties reached an agreement June 25 to bring the measure to a vote July 8. Under the arrangement, Lott and Senate Minority Leader Tom Daschle, D-S.D., would together offer an amendment to broaden the tax breaks approved by the Senate Finance Committee. The Senate would take up an amendment offered by Kennedy to shorten the length of time for the "training wage" from 90 to 30 days and strike the tip-earners' exemption. Another amendment would be offered by Christopher S. Bond, R-Mo., to exempt employees of companies grossing less than $500,000 a year from the wage raise; extend the training wage from 90 days to 180 days and lift age restrictions; and delay implementation of the first 50-cent increase from July 1, 1996, to Jan. 1, 1997, and the second increase to Jan. 1, 1998.

On July 9, the Senate voted, 74–24, for the 90-cents-an-hour wage increase, 74–24. It was attached to HR 3448, as it was in the House, and was virtually identical, although there were differences in the tax provisions.

Earlier that day, the critical vote had come, as it had in the House, on whether to reduce the number of workers affected by the wage increase. Proponents of Bond's amendment were not helped by a June 28 letter from Clinton to Daschle, saying he would veto the bill if it contained Bond's language. Not surprisingly, the amendment was rejected by a **key vote of 46–52 (R 46–5; D 0–47).** *(1996 key votes, p. 1047)*

In both chambers, the winning margins were provided by northeastern Republicans, who tended to be sensitive to the concerns of organized labor, and by Republicans from states on the Pacific Coast, who traditionally supported minimum wage increases.

Kennedy's subsequent amendment to shorten the length of time that younger workers could be paid a training wage and extend the wage increase to waiters and workers who received tips was also defeated, by the same margin: 46–52.

The differences between the House and Senate versions of the bills concerned the tax provisions. The Senate version, which offered as much tax relief to big business as to small business, was estimated to cost $13 billion over eight years, almost double the House version's cost of about $7 billion.

FINAL ACTION

The House-Senate conference was relatively quick and devoid of the acrimony that had pervaded the issue earlier. The chief conferees, House Ways and Means Chairman Bill Archer, R-Texas, and Senate Finance Committee Chairman William V. Roth Jr., R-Del., agreed to use the legislation as a vehicle for several pieces of unfinished tax and trade legislation, including a bill that gave a $5,000 tax credit to offset the cost of adoption, which was part of the House GOP's "Contract with America." Also added to the bill was a popular project of Roth's, an expansion of Individual Retirement Accounts so that nonworking spouses could save up to $2,000 a year.

The tax breaks in the final bill—originally targeted for small businesses, but expanded to cover large ones such as Hewlett-Packard Co., Johnson & Johnson, Microsoft Corp. and Domino's Pizza Inc.—were estimated to cost $10.1 billion over five years.

The minimum wage provisions were identical in both bills and did not change except to fix the effective date of the first increase at Oct. 1, 1996, with the second increase to take effect Sept. 1, 1997.

The House approved the conference report (H Rept 104-737) on Aug. 2 by a vote of 354–72. The Senate cleared the bill hours later, 76–22.

MAJOR PROVISIONS

As signed into law, the labor-related provisions of HR 3448:

• **Wage Increase.** Required employers, as of Oct. 1, 1996, to pay a minimum wage of $4.75 an hour, up from $4.25 an hour. Beginning Sept. 1, 1997, the minimum wage would rise to $5.15 an hour.

• **Subminimum Training Wage.** Allowed employers to pay $4.25 an hour to newly hired workers under the age of 20 for the first 90 calendar days of employment. Under the provision, employers were forbidden to replace an employee earning the full minimum wage or more with a new worker receiving the training wage. An employer found guilty of doing so would face fines and penalties levied by the Labor Department.

• **Computer Professionals Exemption.** Exempted computer systems analysts, computer programmers, software engineers and other computer professionals from the effect of the minimum wage increase. Previous federal regulations said computer professionals who earned less than six-and-a-half times the minimum wage—$27.63 an hour, or $57,470 a year—had to be paid overtime for work over 40 hours a week. Under those rules, a minimum wage of $5.15 an hour would raise the cutoff to

$33.48 an hour, or $69,628 a year. The exemption froze the cutoff at $27.63 an hour.

• **Tip Credit Exemption.** Exempted employees making a substantial amount of their income from tips from an automatic pay raise tied to the minimum wage increase. Previous law allowed an employer to pay tipped employees 50 percent of the minimum wage—$2.13 under the $4.25 per hour minimum wage—with the understanding that tips would raise hourly wages above the mandatory minimum. If tips fell short of the minimum wage, employers had to make up the difference.

The provision froze the mandatory wage for tipped workers at $2.13 an hour, with the stipulation that an employer must make up the difference if tips did not bring an employee's hourly pay to the higher minimum wage.

• **Employee Commuting.** Amended the Portal-to-Portal Act (PL 80-49), a 1947 labor law, to clarify that workers commuting to and from work in a company-owned vehicle did not have to be paid for the driving time. The law stipulated that any agreement between an employer, an employee or a union to use company cars for commuting had to be voluntary. The commuting provision went into effect immediately after HR 3448 was signed into law Aug. 20. ❑

Job Training Overhaul

Despite early optimism on both sides of aisle, efforts to enact legislation (HR 1617) that would have overhauled federal job training programs fell apart in 1996 due to partisan bickering.

Democrats and Republicans generally agreed that the nation's job training system was too expensive and largely ineffective. Consequently, in the fall of 1995 both chambers passed measures aimed at consolidating and changing federal training programs for unemployed and economically disadvantaged adults, youths who had dropped out of school or were at risk of doing so, and workers who had been permanently laid off from their jobs.

But a full legislative plate in 1995 prevented staff from meeting to work out differences in the House- and Senate-passed measures until February 1996. The delay gave time to conservative groups—who feared the bill would lead to greater government meddling in business—and labor unions—who believed that the GOP would use the consolidation as an excuse to cut funding for training programs—to rupture the bipartisan coalition that had successfully passed the measure the year before. And even though conferees did approve a report (H Rept 104-707) on July 17, it never reached the floor of either chamber for a final vote.

BACKGROUND

Under existing law, the federal government operated more than 150 vocational education and job training programs that were administered by 14 agencies. Critics in both parties derided the system as a poorly run bureaucracy that wasted taxpayer money by failing to provide adequate training or by preparing people for jobs that did not exist. Many members said there was insufficient accountability and considerable overlap in the programs, which aimed to help the nation's two million disadvantaged and dislocated workers find jobs.

Democrats called for consolidating some programs and replacing others with a voucher system. Republicans favored a more radical approach that included turning many of the initiatives over to the states.

The Clinton administration generally supported the idea behind the House and Senate bills but was concerned the legislation would be used to drastically cut funding for job training.

HOUSE ACTION

The House Economic and Educational Opportunities Committee reported HR 1617 on June 22, 1995 (H Rept 104-152). The bill would have consolidated more than 100 programs into four block grants that would have received about $5 billion in fiscal 1997.

The four block grants outlined in the bill were designed to:

• Help noncollege-bound secondary and postsecondary students make the transition from school to the workplace.

• Train workers who lost their jobs and economically disadvantaged adults in need of basic education and employment skills.

• Provide vocational training for workers with special needs.

• Provide adult and family literacy training. This grant was to consolidate about two dozen initiatives, including public library funding and literacy programs for prisoners and homeless adults.

The House Sept. 19 took up and passed the measure by a comfortable margin, 345–79. This overwhelming show of support occurred only after one of the four block grants contained in the committee-approved version had been removed. That change came at the behest of Democrats, who were unhappy with the block grant that would have provided vocational training for workers with physical and mental impairments. In particular, Democrats opposed language that would have required people with special needs to seek services at the same places as able-bodied workers. An amendment offered by Gene Green, D-Texas, and Jay Dickey, R-Ark., that removed the vocational rehabilitation provisions from the bill, was adopted, 231–192.

Overall, the bill would have authorized almost $2.2 billion for training and educating adults, such as the chronically unemployed and those permanently laid off from their jobs. Another $2.3 billion was to have been provided for youths, including those in school and those who were "at risk" of dropping out or already had done so. Adult education, family literacy and library funding were to total $390 million.

SENATE ACTION

On July 24, the Senate Labor and Human Resources Committee reported a very different job-training overhaul bill (S 143—S Rept 104-118).

The committee bill would have repealed several education and training initiatives, such as the Trade Adjustment Assistance program, and consolidated about 80 federal job training and vocational education programs into a single block grant to states. Beginning in 1998, programs, such as Job Corps and School-to-Work, that were administered by the federal government would have been taken over by the states.

A sizable portion of the funds authorized under the bill, $1.5 billion, would have been used for state Job Corps programs. The remaining money, $6.5 billion, was to be distributed to the states according to a funding formula. This formula would have required states to use 25 percent of the money for workforce development, such as developing a network of one-stop career centers where workers could learn about education and training services and employment opportunities.

An additional 25 percent of the money received by states was to be dedicated to workforce education initiatives, such as vocational training and adult literacy programs.

The remaining 50 percent of the funds could be used to establish "flex accounts," which would allow states to direct money to education and training programs as needed.

The Senate passed HR 1617 on a 95–2 vote Oct. 11, after substituting the text of S 143.

In floor debate, the most controversial section of the bill proved to be the proposal to repeal the Trade Adjustment Assistance program, which helped workers permanently laid off from their jobs as a direct result of U.S. trade policies. Without the program, which was strongly supported by Democrats, those workers would have had to compete with others seeking training services.

On a 52–45 vote Oct. 10, members adopted an amendment by Daniel Patrick Moynihan, D-N.Y., to maintain the program at existing funding levels. Slightly more than $119 million had been appropriated for it in fiscal 1995.

On the next day, the Senate moved to retain another popular program, the Job Corps, in its existing form, by approving, 57–40, an Arlen Specter, R-Pa., amendment to continue operating the corps as a federal program.

Members also adopted, 54–43, a John Ashcroft, R-Mo., amendment aimed at requiring people applying to or participating in federally funded training or education programs to undergo random drug tests. The amendment was designed to allow testing if there was reasonable suspicion that an applicant or participant was using drugs.

CONFERENCE ACTION

The conference bill proposed to consolidate about 100 programs into a single block grant for state and local governments. The formula for block grant expenditures came close to the administration's request.

But the conference report did not have the support of a single Democratic conferee. The bill snubbed Democratic concerns by repealing Clinton's 1994 school-to-work law (HR 2884—PL 103-239) and failing to earmark $1.3 billion for dislocated workers. Education Secretary Richard W. Riley and Labor Secretary Robert B. Reich immediately recommended a presidential veto. (School-to-work law, p. 627)

The conference report was never taken up by either chamber.

OSHA Overhaul

Committees in both chambers attempted to revamp the Occupational Safety and Health Administration (OSHA) in 1996, but neither effort reached the floor before the 104th Congress adjourned.

Created in 1970 under the Occupational Safety and Health Act (PL 91-596), OSHA set and enforced rules for private-sector workplace safety and health. The agency inspected work sites and levied penalties against companies that violated safety regulations.

In the Senate, the Labor and Human Resources Committee on June 28, 1996, reported a bill (S 1423—S Rept 104-308) that would have allowed employers to create their own safety plans and hire outside inspectors to approve them. Companies that opted for this approach would have been exempted from regular OSHA inspections and subjected to reduced penalties if a violation occurred. It also would have repealed the requirement that OSHA make inspections whenever an employee filed a complaint. Penalties for minor violations, such as incorrect paperwork, would in many cases have been eliminated.

Bill sponsor Judd Gregg, R-N.H., said the measure would free OSHA from making unnecessary inspections and enforcing unimportant regulations, allowing the agency to focus on companies that were exposing their workers to physical hazards. But panel Democrats, united against the measure, argued that it would strip OSHA of needed authority.

The committee did approve one significant and surprising amendment: language, offered by Paul Simon, D-Ill., that would have applied national safety and health laws to federal, state and local governments. A 1995 law (PL 104-1) had applied the act to Congress but not to the rest of the federal government or its state counterparts.

Even though Gregg opposed Simon's amendment, it was approved 9–7 after two Republicans, James M. Jeffords of Vermont and Spencer Abraham of Michigan, broke ranks and voted with the panel's seven Democrats.

But the negotiations in committee was all for naught. In the end, Senate supporters were unable to get time for the bill on the packed floor calendar. Even if it had been taken up, it faced a possible Democratic filibuster and a promised presidential veto.

In the House, the Economic and Educational Opportunities Subcommittee on Workforce Protections approved a different set of changes (HR 3234) on April 17. But fierce Democratic opposition and a veto threat put the measure on a slow track and it never advanced to full committee.

The House bill would have applied cost-benefit analysis to new regulations issued by OSHA. In addition, the secretary of labor would have had the right to waive any fines against businesses of 250 or fewer employees if a minor safety violation was corrected quickly, or if the money for the fine was used to fix the problem. Also, the measure would have prohibited OSHA inspectors from issuing citations for paperwork violations unless an employer had "willfully or repeatedly violated" a regulation or if the violation had exposed a worker to a safety hazard.

During the markup, bill opponents argued that easing enforcement burdens on businesses with 250 workers or fewer would effectively exempt 99 percent of all work places from mandatory safety inspections and greatly endanger U.S. workers. But Republicans countered that the bill would allow OSHA to focus on businesses that had serious safety violations. ❑

Compensatory Time

Over strong objections from organized labor and from many Democrats, the House on July 30, 1996, passed a bill (HR 2391) that would have allowed nonunion employees to choose compensatory time off instead of overtime pay. However, the bill went no further. In the other chamber, where the minority had more clout, Democratic objections had blocked an attempt by Senate Majority Leader Trent Lott, R-Miss., to bring a comp time bill up for consideration July 26.

Democrats were concerned that the bill did not offer sufficient protection to ensure that employers would not coerce workers into accepting compensatory time instead of time-and-a-half pay for work beyond 40 hours a week. Republicans said the bill would let workers, not employers, determine whether to accept time or pay.

Under the 1938 Fair Labor Standards Act (PL 75-718), employers were required to compensate most work beyond a 40-hour work week at a rate of one-and-a-half times a worker's hourly wage. Employees who were considered professionals were exempt from federal wage-and-hour laws.

HR 2391 would have amended the 1938 act to permit employees to take up to 240 hours of compensatory time off a year instead of overtime pay. Banked comp time would have been cashed out at the end of each year. As with overtime pay, an hour of work performed beyond the 40-hour work week would have been compensated at time-and-a-half.

The House Economic and Educational Opportunities Committee approved the bill on a party-line vote of 20–16. In an effort to assuage Democratic opponents of the measure, the panel approved a substitute amendment that explicitly prohibited direct or indirect intimidation, threats or coercion to sway employees toward or against choosing compensatory time. In addition, workers who chose compensatory time would have been allowed to change their minds at any time and receive cash, based on their highest wage levels. The bill was reported July 11 (H Rept 104-670).

But the changes did not satisfy Democrats, most of whom voted against the bill when it passed the House, 225–195, on July 30. ❑

Mandatory Retirement Age

The House March 28, 1995, passed a bill (HR 849) that would have allowed states and localities to impose maximum hiring and mandatory retirement ages for police and firefighters. There was no action in the Senate.

The House bill, approved by voice vote under a suspension of the rules, would have amended the Age Discrimination in Employment Act of 1967 (PL 99-592) by exempting public safety workers permanently from the law, which protected workers 40 and older from age discrimination. Agencies would have been permitted to set maximum entry ages for recruits, and states and localities could have incorporated the rules into their overall personnel policies for public safety officers.

Congress had exempted firefighters and police officers from the age discrimination law in 1986, primarily because of the physically and mentally demanding nature of their work, but the exemption had expired in 1993. *(1986 amendments, Congress and the Nation Vol. VII, p. 690)*

The bill, approved by the House Economic and Educational Opportunities Committee on March 15 but never formally reported, was opposed by the American Association of Retired Persons, which contended that it could force the retirement of workers who still could perform their duties.

Earlier attempts to permanently exempt public safety workers from the age discrimination law had been unsuccessful. A House-passed extension (HR 2722) in late 1993 stalled in the Senate. *(1993 action, p. 661)*   ❑

Davis-Bacon Repeal

Republican efforts in 1995 to move bills (S 141, HR 500) that would have repealed the Davis-Bacon Act of 1931 stalled due to fierce opposition from Democrats in both chambers.

Davis-Bacon, a depression-era law aimed at protecting local laborers from being underbid by out-of-town workers, required federal contractors to pay their employees "local prevailing wages," often union rates. It applied to federal construction projects valued at $2,000 or more.

Republicans argued that Davis-Bacon's prevailing wage provision artificially inflated construction costs and imposed an unnecessary burden on taxpayers. But opponents of the repeal, including most Democrats and President Clinton, argued that the GOP-backed bills would depress laborers' earnings without resulting in significant savings for states and localities. They pushed for reform, not repeal, as they had in the 103rd Congress. *(1994 action, p. 660)*

The bill that progressed the furthest was S 141, which was approved by the Senate Labor and Human Resources Committee on a 9–7 party-line vote March 29, 1995, and reported out of committee May 12 (S Rept 104-80).

In the House, the Economic and Educational Opportunities Subcommittee on Workforce Protections approved HR 500 on March 2. On the same day, the panel approved a bill (HR 246) to repeal the Service Contract Act of 1965, which required locally prevailing-wage rates and fringe benefits for service workers, such as janitors and travel agents, who had federal contracts of $2,500 or more. Similar to Davis-Bacon, the act was designed to ensure that small contractors and low-skilled workers received fair wages for participating in federal contracts.

Following the subcommittee markup, House Republican leaders began playing down the importance of repealing Davis-Bacon, and the bills were not marked up by the full committee. Instead, there was one last attempt Sept. 28 to rescind the laws.

The Opportunities Committee voted, 23–14, to include provisions to repeal Davis-Bacon and the Service Contract Act as part of the budget reconciliation bill being prepared by the Budget Committee. The provisions were dropped from HR 2491 before it reached the House floor, however. *(Budget reconciliation bill, p. 68)*   ❑

Farmworker Protection

Legislation (HR 1715—PL 104-49) that barred injured migrant farmworkers from recovering monetary damages in addition to their workers' compensation benefits was signed into law by President Clinton Nov. 15, 1995.

The bill overturned a 1990 Supreme Court decision, *Adams Fruit Co. Inc. v. Barrett*, that allowed injured workers to sue their employer for monetary damages under the Migrant and Seasonal Agricultural Worker Protection Act, in addition to collecting workers' compensation benefits for the same injuries. Under HR 1715, employers still could be sued for punitive damages of up to $10,000 per victim if they were found in violation of certain safety standards such as transporting workers in unsafe vehicles. In instances of multiparty class action suits, such damages were capped at $500,000 total. *(1990 case, Congress and the Nation Vol. VIII, p. 848)*

The House Economic and Educational Opportunities Committee approved the bill June 22, despite near unanimous opposition by panel Democrats, who argued that it would leave migrant workers unprotected against possible abuse. But Republicans countered that the current law was unfair to farm owners.

Following the markup—and a series of negotiations involving members' staffs and representatives of agricultural employer and farmworker organizations—Republicans, led by committee chair and bill sponsor Bill Goodling, R-Pa., agreed to add several safeguards for farmworkers. The changes included new provisions that encouraged employers to provide safe transportation for farmworkers; required that farmworkers be notified of their rights under state workers' compensation laws; and increased statutory damages for egregious violations of the law from $500 to $10,000.

With these additions the bill won bipartisan support and House passage by voice vote Oct. 17, 1995. The Senate quickly followed suit, clearing the bill Oct. 31.   ❑

Striker Replacement

Republicans in 1995 tried, but failed, to push through Congress legislation to nullify an executive order by President Clinton barring companies with federal contracts of more than $100,000 from permanently replacing striking employees. But the issue was rendered moot after the U.S. Court of Appeals for the District of Columbia Circuit on Feb. 2, 1996, struck down Clinton's order, saying that the president had exceeded his authority because the policy amounted to a rewrite of federal labor law.

Clinton issued the directive March 8, 1995, on behalf of organized labor, which had tried unsuccessfully in the 103rd Congress to win enactment of legislation to prohibit private companies from replacing striking workers. The directive took effect immediately. Contractors found in violation were subject to having their contract canceled or being declared ineligible for new ones. *(1993–1994 action, p. 659)*

Republicans, furious over the executive order, called it an attempt to circumvent the will of Congress and appeared determined to pass legislation to undo it.

In the Senate, Nancy Landon Kassebaum, R-Kan., chair of the Labor and Human Resources Committee, immediately offered an amendment to a supplemental defense appropriations bill (HR 889). The amendment would have prohibited the Labor Department from using money appropriated in fiscal 1995 to administer or enforce the order. This led to a Democratic filibuster of the bill. On March 15, the Senate voted 58–39, two votes shy of the 60 needed, to end the filibuster, forcing Kassebaum to withdraw the amendment. *(Supplemental defense appropriations, p. 304)*

A provision aimed at overturning Clinton's directive also was attached to a fiscal 1996 funding bill for the departments of Labor, Health and Human Services (HHS) and Education (HR 2127), during Senate Appropriations Committee action. Senate Democrats blocked Republican attempts to bring up the bill on the Senate floor in 1995. *(Labor-HHS bill, p. 564)*

In the House, a bill (HR 1176—H Rept 104-163) that would have nullified the order was reported June 27, 1995, from the Economic and Educational Opportunities Committee on a party-line vote of 22–16. However, the measure stalled after committee action, due to fierce Democratic opposition. ❏

Labor-Management Teams

A bill (HR 743) that would have eased regulations on labor-management teams in the workplace cleared Congress July 18, 1996, but fell victim to a presidential veto.

Known as the Teamwork for Employees and Management (TEAM) Act, the bill (HR 743) would have modified the 1935 National Labor Relations Act to make clear that U.S. businesses could establish worker-management groups to address such issues as productivity, quality control and safety. The extra latitude was to be available only to companies whose workers were not represented by a union.

The National Labor Relations Act outlawed some employer-appointed groups on the grounds that they could be used to thwart unionization and unfairly control workers.

The bill's supporters argued that employer-employee labor-management teams were a modern cooperative management technique, needed for companies to compete in the international marketplace.

But some Democrats and labor unions said that it was an invitation for employers to set up sham unions. With these objections in mind, the Labor Department indicated that it would urge the president to veto the bill.

The measure began its legislative journey on June 22, 1995, when it was approved by the House Economic and Educational Opportunities Committee on a 22–19 party-line vote. The committee bill, which was formally reported Sept. 18 (H Rept 104-248), stated explicitly that employers in unionized companies would have a legal obligation to continue bargaining collectively with legitimate worker representatives after workplace teams were established.

The House passed the bill Sept. 27 by a vote of 221–202, after rejecting three attempts by Democrats to constrain the makeup and scope of the employer-employee groups.

In the Senate, action on the TEAM bill did not begin until 1996. On April 17, the Labor and Human Resources Committee approved, 9–7 along party lines, a version of the bill (S 295) that was almost identical to the House-passed measure. S 295 was reported May 1 (S Rept 104-259).

The full Senate passed HR 743 on July 10 on a largely party-line vote of 53–46, after substituting the text of S 295. During floor consideration, the Senate adopted, 61–38, a Nancy Landon Kassebaum, R-Kan., substitute amendment to make the Senate version conform with the House-passed bill. The Kassebaum amendment made three principal changes. It clarified that the teams could discuss "health and safety." It underscored that only companies in which workers were not represented by unions would be protected under the bill from unfair labor practice charges. And it made clear that workers as well as management could raise issues for team discussion.

The House agreed to these changes, clearing HR 743 by voice vote July 18. But Clinton vetoed the bill July 30, saying that it would "undermine the system of collective bargaining that has served this country so well for many decades."

Republicans did not attempt an override, knowing that House and Senate votes for the bill had been well under the two-thirds majority needed to enact it over the president's veto. ❏

Teen Labor Law

Congress in 1996 cleared legislation (HR 1114—PL 104-174) to amend the 1938 Fair Labor Standards Act (PL 75-718) to permit 16- and 17-year-olds working at businesses such as grocery stores to load paper balers and compactors.

HR 1114 allowed the teenage workers to load paper into machines that met the approval of the American National Standards Institute, a private organization that rated the safety of such equipment. Workers under 18 still could not operate or unload paper balers or compactors.

Supporters said the bill was needed to remove obsolete restrictions on U.S. businesses. They pointed out that balers and compactors had gone through significant safety design improvements over the last 20 years.

The bill had been reported Oct. 17, 1995, by the House Economic and Educational Opportunities Committee (H Rept 104-278) and passed by voice vote of the House Oct. 24. The Senate passed the bill by voice vote July 16, 1996, after amending it to, among other things, require reports to the secretary of labor of all significant injuries to minors caused by these machines during the two years following enactment. The House agreed to the Senate version by voice vote July 25, clearing the bill for the president's signature Aug. 6. ❏

Right-to-Work Bill

The Senate in 1996 rejected a bill (S 1788) that would have prevented unions from requiring workers at unionized companies to pay dues or other union fees. Dues would have been voluntary.

The national right-to-work bill died in a filibuster July 10, 1996, when senators voted 31–68 against a GOP effort to invoke cloture—29 votes short of the 60 votes needed to cut off debate. In killing the bill, 21 Republicans joined all 47 Democrats.

Supporters of S 1788 argued that the measure would have allowed American workplaces to become more competitive and that "compulsory unionism" violated individual liberty. But Democrats, led by Labor Secretary Robert B. Reich, called the bill an assault on organized labor and denounced it for giving benefits to workers who did not pay dues.   ❑

Social Security Earnings Limit

Congress in 1996 agreed to an increase in the Social Security earnings limit, a change long sought by senior citizen groups. The provision was included in legislation raising the federal debt limit (HR 3136—PL 104-121).

Previously, Social Security recipients ages 65 to 69 could earn up to $11,520 without losing any of their benefits, but, if they went above that threshold, they lost one dollar in benefits for every three dollars they earned. The new law increased the earnings threshold to $30,000 over seven years. *(Debt-limit increase, p. 76)*

The bill raised the maximum earnings threshold to $12,500 in 1996. It would then go up $1,000 a year until it hit $15,500 in 1999, after which it would jump to $17,000 in 2000, $25,000 in 2001 and $30,000 in 2002. The Social Security Administration said the increase would benefit 800,000 people when it was fully phased in.

The increase was expected to cost $7 billion over seven years. It was offset by eliminating Social Security disability benefits to alcoholics and drug addicts and by eliminating Social Security payments to stepchildren unless they were dependent on their stepparents.

The tradeoff drew criticism from some who argued that it effectively transferred money from needy people to those who were less needy, the working elderly. While the increase would help some elderly households that were barely making ends meet, it also would benefit those who had substantial unearned income from investments in stocks and bonds or from pensions (neither of which were counted for purposes of determining the earnings limit) and who still worked.

But supporters of the change said the existing limit was unfair to recipients with limited pension income and to those who went to work late in life.

BACKGROUND

The earnings test was begun in the New Deal to discourage seniors from working at a time when there was a glut of younger people seeking employment.

For years, a small group of members had proposed repealing the earnings test, but their legislation never advanced. The Democratic majority said the costs to the Treasury would be too high and maintained that ending the test would mostly benefit the wealthy.

The alternative, raising the limit on penalty-free earnings, had been advocated by the American Association of Retired Persons for more than 10 years. In 1992, President George Bush supported raising the limit by $1,000 a year for five years, but the proposal died when Congress could not agree on a way to pay for it. *(Congress and the Nation Vol. VIII, p. 736)*

LEGISLATIVE ACTION

The "Contract with America," the 1994 campaign manifesto of House GOP candidates, called for the earnings limit to increase to $30,000 in five years. It also proposed repeal of a 1993 tax increase on Social Security benefits for wealthier recipients. *(1993 tax, p. 89)*

The two proposals were included in a Republican package of tax and spending cuts reported by the House Ways and Means Committee March 21, 1995 (HR 1215—H Rept 104-84). The House approved the GOP tax bill April 5 by a vote of 246–188, but it went no further. *(GOP tax plan, p. 98)*

The earnings limit language and the 1993 tax repeal were incorporated into the House version of the 1995 budget reconciliation package (HR 2491), but both were dropped in conference. *(Budget reconciliation bill, p. 68)*

The Senate on Oct. 26, 1995, voted, 99–0, for a John McCain, R-Ariz., amendment to its version of the reconciliation bill (S 1357) expressing the sense of the Senate that the earnings limit should be raised without harming the solvency of the Social Security trust funds or budget-balancing efforts. The same day, the House suspended debate on the reconciliation package long enough to pass, 414–5, a concurrent resolution (H Con Res 109) expressing the sense of Congress that legislation raising the earnings limit should be passed by year's end.

Both chambers then considered stand-alone bills devoted specifically to increasing the earnings test. The House passed its version (HR 2684), but a Senate bill (S 1470) never reached the floor. HR 2684 was reported by the House Ways and Means Committee Dec. 4, 1995 (H Rept 104-379) and was passed by the full House the next day, 411–4. S 1470 was reported Dec. 15. Senate floor action on an earlier version (S 1372) had been blocked on a point of order.

In 1996, the Social Security earnings limit increase was added to HR 3136 as one of several sweeteners aimed at making it easier for members to pass the painful but critical bill raising the federal debt limit. The provision received little attention during floor debate, even from Democrats, who were focusing instead on an unsuccessful effort to force a vote on increasing the minimum wage.

The House passed HR 3136 on March 28 by a **key vote of 328–91 (R 201–30; D 127–60; I 0–1).** The Senate approved it hours later by voice vote. President Clinton signed it into law March 29. *(Debt-limit increase, p. 76; 1996 key votes, p. 1047)*   ❑

Social Security for Prisoners

The House passed a bill (HR 4039) by voice vote Sept. 17, 1996, to eliminate Social Security benefits for prisoners. At the time, prisoners incarcerated for less than a year could receive benefits. *(1994 action, p. 662)*

The measure originally had been included in the welfare overhaul bill (HR 3734) but had been dropped in the Senate on procedural grounds. But HR 4039's proposal to provide financial incentives to states and localities for reporting to the Social Security Administration the names of prisoners fraudulently receiving benefits was included in the final welfare bill. *(Welfare bill, p. 578)*

HR 4039 had been reported by the House Ways and Means Committee Sept. 16 (H Rept 104-786). The bill did not advance beyond House passage. ❏

Pension Fund Investments

The House in 1995 passed a bill (HR 1594) that would have prohibited the Labor Department from advising the nation's private pension fund managers to make investments based on social criteria. However, the issue advanced no further.

HR 1594 was aimed at barring the federal government from coercing participation in so-called economically targeted investments selected because of their social benefits as well as their potential earning capabilities. Such ventures often included investments in low-income housing, infrastructure improvement projects or economic development projects.

The largely GOP supporters of the measure contended that socially targeted investments tended to lose money and frequently posed threats to the financial stability and earning potential of pension plans. Fund managers, they said, should base investment decisions primarily on the return to investors.

Democrats countered that the bill was an attack on the policies of President Clinton that could deny many communities funds for economic development.

The measure was approved by the House Economic and Educational Opportunities Committee by a largely party-line vote of 23–15 on July 20 and was reported Sept. 1 (H Rept 104-238). The House passed the bill Sept. 12 by a vote of 239–179. ❏

CHAPTER 13

Law and Justice

Law and Law Enforcement

During President Clinton's first term in office, Democrats and Republicans waged a four-year bidding war to show who could be more tough on crime. The result was an unprecedented federal foray into local law enforcement and criminal justice.

Lawmakers would have gone even further in the name of protecting U.S. citizens against terrorist attacks, both foreign and domestic. But an odd alliance of conservative Republicans and liberal Democrats successfully opposed measures that would have given federal agents and prosecutors more power to eavesdrop on and search suspected terrorists.

The terrorism bill highlighted a division in the Republican ranks between law-and-order conservatives and those with libertarian leanings, most often expressed as a virulent opposition to any form of gun control. Such divisions were largely obscured while Democrats held the majority, but they rose to the surface after Republicans took control of both chambers of Congress in 1995.

The shift to Republican control also changed the agenda of the House and Senate Judiciary committees, elevating such social issues as immigration, affirmative action and school prayer. Still, partisan differences and divisions in the GOP ranks blocked some of the most sweeping proposals from becoming law or, in some cases, even coming up for a vote.

A LONG-DELAYED CRIME BILL

Traditionally, Congress had left state and local authorities to define, investigate, prosecute and punish most crimes. The federal government's role increased, however, as law and order rose in potency as a political issue. Legislation to combat crime became a staple during the Reagan and Bush administrations, although a fundamental split between Republican and Democratic philosophies generally prevented Congress from enacting more than modest, incremental changes in law. Some of the most aggressive efforts were made in the name of combating drugs, a problem whose interstate and international dimensions justified federal intervention.

During the Bush administration, leading congressional Democrats sought to improve their party's image on law and order issues by passing a major anticrime bill—one that reinstated and expanded the federal death penalty, built more prisons, sped executions and cracked down on handgun violence. The Democratic proposals did not go far enough on several key issues to satisfy Republicans, however, causing the legislation to stall. The disputes centered on how sharply to limit appeals by convicted criminals, how much leeway to give prosecutors with evidence obtained from improper searches, whether to impose new controls on gun purchases, and how much prison time to mandate for convicts.

Bill Clinton raised the political heat on his fellow Democrats in the 1992 campaign, pledging a new form of federal intervention in local crime fighting. Picking up on a theme from the stalled Democratic crime bills, Clinton championed a strategy called community policing, which sought to reduce crime by giving police officers a more visible presence in troubled neighborhoods. But Clinton proposed to go one step further, urging Congress to provide the money for 100,000 additional officers.

The proposal was part of Clinton's effort to position himself as a "New Democrat," a stance that sprinkled conservative positions on crime, welfare and selected other high-profile issues with a traditional Democratic belief in federal activism. His election shifted the playing field on crime legislation in the 103rd Congress to the right of congressional Democrats, particularly House Democrats, but still to the left of President George Bush.

Clinton's goals on crime were largely shared by the two congressional point men on crime legislation, the Democratic chairmen of the House and Senate Judiciary committees: Rep. Jack Brooks of Texas and Sen. Joseph R. Biden Jr. of Delaware. Brooks and Biden used as their starting point the stalled crime bill from 1992, a measure that had broad Democratic support.

Republicans, meanwhile, renewed their push for a more punitive bill that gave prosecutors more power and convicted criminals less chance to appeal. They sought more death penalties, longer sentences, greater federal jurisdiction and more prisons. The unstated message was that crime was a Republican issue, and Republicans were going to continue to label Democratic proposals "soft on crime."

REFERENCES

Discussion of law enforcement policy for the years 1945–1964 may be found in *Congress and the Nation Vol. I*, pp. 1671–1676; for the years 1965–1968, *Congress and the Nation Vol. II*, pp. 309–334; for the years 1969–1972, *Congress and the Nation Vol. III*, pp. 255–286; for the years 1973–1976, *Congress and the Nation Vol. IV*, pp. 559–618; for the years 1977–1980, *Congress and the Nation Vol. V*, pp. 715–753; for the years 1981–1984, *Congress and the Nation Vol. VII*, pp. 713–784; for the years 1989–1992, *Congress and the Nation Vol. VIII*, pp. 741–799.

Outlays for Law Enforcement

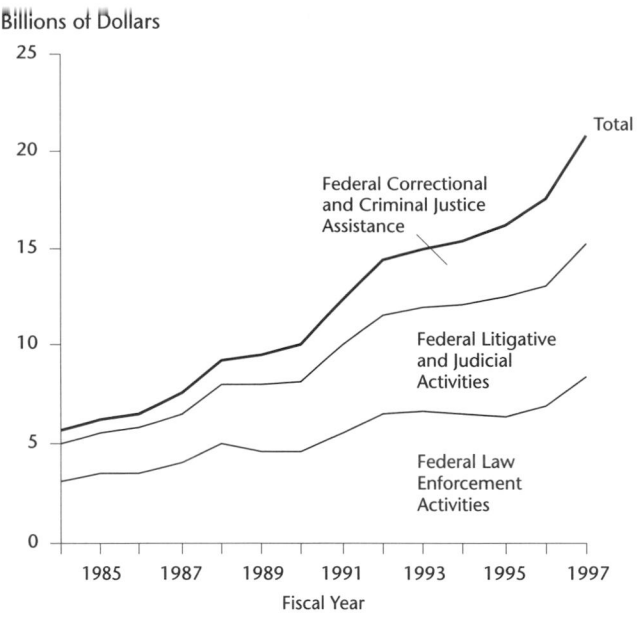

Billions of Dollars

NOTE: Data for 1997 are estimated.

SOURCE: Office of Management and Budget, *Historical Tables, Budget of the United States Government: Fiscal Year 1998* (Washington, D.C.: U.S. Government Printing Office, 1997), Table 3.2.

Reflecting the differences between the House and Senate, Brooks and Biden took different approaches to moving the legislation through their chambers. Biden sought to make peace with Republicans, agreeing to a number of GOP proposals that toughened the bill. The compromise was made easier by the infusion of cash—a huge pot of federal dollars that Senate Appropriations Committee Chairman Robert C. Byrd, D-W.Va., steered to anticrime measures. Byrd's accounting maneuver provided billions of dollars more for crime-fighting than Biden had originally proposed, and much of the money went to GOP priorities. Members from both parties also shared an interest in expanding federal jurisdiction, particularly over gun and gang offenses that traditionally had been left to state courts.

Brooks, by contrast, did not need Republican votes to move a crime bill through the House. The minority party in the House had so little power to stop legislation, Brooks merely had to keep the Democratic ranks in order. Those ranks were split, however, because liberals balked at the more punitive provisions of the draft measure. With a Democrat in the White House, they argued, Congress should try to do more than just ratchet up the penalties.

In particular, liberals wanted to tap more of the anticrime dollars for social programs addressing the root causes of crime, such as urban decay and drug addiction. Byrd's move had opened a spigot of dollars that liberals wanted to spend on preventing crime, not just on warehousing criminals. They also wanted to give minorities on death row a better chance to overturn their sentences as racially discriminatory—something the

Supreme Court had made increasingly difficult in recent decisions on death row appeals.

With support from Brooks and the House Democratic leadership, liberals prevailed in both of those areas as the bill moved through the House. They also succeeded in passing the strongest gun control measures in three decades: a mandatory waiting period for handgun purchases, which was enacted as a separate bill, and a ban on certain types of assault weapons, which was incorporated into the crime bill. Like the Senate bill, though, the House version proposed to stiffen punishments and to boost the power of federal courts by bringing far more crimes under their jurisdiction.

In conference, Democratic negotiators produced a middle-of-the-road document that seemed to meet the political objectives of the "New Democrats." However, they largely excluded Republicans from the deliberations and settled on a compromise that was far less punitive and more prevention-oriented than the GOP had advocated. At the same time, they dropped the House proposal on racially discriminatory death sentences, alienating some liberal Democrats, while including the proposed ban on assault weapons, alienating some conservatives in their party.

Thus, the seeds of defeat were planted as the conference report headed to the House floor. Republicans were nearly unanimous in their opposition, and Democrats were sharply divided. The House struck a fatal procedural blow to the conference report in August 1994, forcing Brooks and Biden back into negotiations—this time with moderate Republicans. Although the bill cleared 10 days later with only modest changes, the defeat left Democrats with a black eye and tarnished what should have been a triumph for Clinton and his allies.

Inclusion of the assault-weapons ban in the final version of the bill was a major defeat for the influential National Rifle Association (NRA), whose formidable grassroots lobbying techniques had blocked many previous gun control proposals. Just as bitter for the NRA was the enactment of the waiting period law, better known as the "Brady bill." The group exacted a measure of revenge in the 1994 elections, however, when it helped Republicans win control of both chambers.

THE DEBATE CONTINUES

When Republicans assumed the majority in 1995, they quickly set about reversing much of the newly enacted crime legislation. Just as Brooks had done to them in 1994, House Republicans used their majority power to ram a series of crime bills through the chamber over Democratic objections. These measures aimed to shift the crime law's priorities from prevention and community policing to prisons and punishment.

The Senate Democrats' filibuster power meant that Republicans in that chamber could not repeat their House colleagues' successes. Nevertheless, Republicans found ways to steer into law many of the provisions of the House-passed bills. These included the most punitive of the proposals—measures to build more prisons, speed the execution of condemned prisoners, hasten the deportation of immigrant criminals and prod states to lengthen the amount of time convicts spent behind bars. These provisions were appended to measures that Democrats supported, circumventing a filibuster or a veto.

The GOP fell short, though, on proposals that did not have widespread public support. Republicans had tried to end the 1994 crime law's grants for "cops on the beat" on federalism grounds, arguing that local governments should not be told how to fight crime. But police associations—a formidable political force—strongly supported the grants, and Clinton would not budge. House Republicans also passed a bill to repeal the ban on assault weapons, responding to the insistent appeals of the NRA. Polls showed that the public was solidly behind the ban, however, and the Senate never took up the measure.

Although Republicans took issue with much of the 1994 law, they had no qualms about the provisions extending the reach of the federal courts. In fact, they pushed numerous bills through the 104th Congress to expand the jurisdiction of the courts or federal agencies even further. These included measures cracking down on sex offenders, drug dealers, violent juveniles, arsonists (particularly those who burned churches), counterfeiters, computer hackers, stalkers and war criminals.

Meanwhile, Clinton was focusing on a new target for law enforcement: terrorists. The bombings at the World Trade Center in 1993 and an Oklahoma City federal building in 1995 had made the nation feel newly vulnerable to what once seemed a purely foreign menace. Taking another page out of the GOP playbook, Clinton and his Democratic allies pressed to give federal agents more power and money to combat terrorism. These included some distinctly un-Democratic proposals to permit more wiretaps, create deportation courts with the power to conceal evidence from the defendant, and allow prosecutors to use surveillance evidence that had been obtained improperly.

Just as the 1994 crime bill brought Democratic fissures to the fore, the antiterrorism legislation in 1995 and 1996 exposed deep divisions in the Republican ranks on crime. While many GOP leaders joined Clinton in supporting tough antiterrorism measures, conservatives (particularly House conservatives) did not. They sided with civil libertarians in objecting to the proposed increases in federal investigatory and prosecutorial power.

The conservatives' stance reflected the libertarian elements of the GOP, particularly in the West. This faction was deeply disturbed by two bloody incidents involving the Bureau of Alcohol, Tobacco and Firearms (ATF): an August 1992 shoot-out in the mountains of Ruby Ridge, Idaho, and the disastrous siege of the Branch Davidian compound in Waco, Texas, in early 1993. At Ruby Ridge, a federal marshal, a woman and her 14-year-old son were killed as agents tried to arrest the woman's husband, a former Green Beret named Randy Weaver who was wanted in connection with weapons charges. In Waco, the ATF launched an assault on the Davidian compound in an attempt to seize a cache of weapons, resulting in 10 deaths and a standoff that lasted 51 days. When federal agents ended their siege by pumping in smoke bombs, the Davidians set their compound on fire, immolating leader David Koresh and 85 followers.

Congressional panels held hearings in 1994 and 1995 to probe the federal government's actions in Waco, giving Republi-

cans a forum to blast the Clinton administration's handling of the Davidians. In a similar vein, a Senate Judiciary subcommittee held a series of hearings in the 104th Congress on the Ruby Ridge incident, allowing Republicans again to question whether federal agents had gone out of control.

These hearings provided the backdrop for the debate over terrorism. The administration sought to expand the power of agents and prosecutors not only for cases involving foreign terrorists, such as the World Trade Center bombing, but also when disaffected Americans were suspected, as in the Oklahoma City case. For example, Clinton wanted to require chemical tracers to be put not only in plastic explosives, the bomb ingredient of choice for foreign terrorists, but also in powder-based explosives, a key ingredient in domestic ammunition. To conservative Republicans, putting tracers in powder-based explosives amounted to gun control, and it was not acceptable.

The debate pitted House Judiciary Committee Chairman Henry J. Hyde, R-Ill., an influential conservative who sided with Clinton on the terrorism legislation, against freshman Rep. Bob Barr, R-Ga., a former federal prosecutor and a leader among dissidents at both ends of the political spectrum. Barr largely prevailed, as Congress ultimately enacted a stripped-down version of the bill.

The final version focused on foreign terrorists, aiming to speed their deportation, deny them entry into the United States and bar fund-raising on their behalf. Lawmakers also mandated studies on some of the proposals that conservatives would not support, such as putting tracers in black powder, and gave federal agencies hundreds of millions of dollars to beef up their defenses against terrorists. They did not, however, grant any significant new powers to federal agents on the trail of terrorists.

IMMIGRATION

Legislation on immigration was as divisive as anticrime bills, but the lines were not drawn so neatly along party or ideological lines. Instead, the differences were more regional, with lawmakers from border states, ports, rural areas, high-technology regions and immigrant-rich districts taking different tacks.

The 103rd Congress moved cautiously on the issue, shying away from proposals to overhaul the rules for refugees seeking asylum—a growing problem for states like Florida. In the 104th Congress, however, the House and Senate Judiciary committees moved aggressively to tighten the cap on all legal immigrants and attack illegal immigration.

The legislation reflected pressure from border-state lawmakers whose states were being pinched financially by their growing immigrant populations. The bills also tapped into a vein of populist sentiment, fed by Republican presidential candidate Pat Robertson, that native-born Americans were being hurt by the influx of Mexicans, Latin Americans and Asians.

There was little dispute among lawmakers about cracking down on illegal immigration, although Republicans and Democrats parted company over how much benefit of the doubt to give refugees seeking asylum. Lawmakers from both parties also were united in their lack of enthusiasm for a new employee-verification system to stop employers from hiring illegal immigrants, even though advocates of such a system said it was critical to discouraging illegal border crossings.

Congress was far less unified on the question of limiting legal immigration. Although the limits were embraced by some leading conservatives and liberals, they were opposed by a wide array of business and ethnic groups who argued that immigration was good for the American economy. Most of those provisions were blocked well short of passage; the main exceptions were GOP proposals to limit the public benefits paid to legal immigrants. Clinton forced Republicans to drop such proposals from the illegal immigration legislation that cleared in September 1996, but another set of restrictions was signed into law in August 1996 as part of a welfare-overhaul bill.

OTHER SOCIAL ISSUES

The House and Senate Judiciary committees took up few controversial social issues during the 103rd Congress. By contrast, the Republicans who led those committees in the 104th Congress put a number of such issues on the agenda. Outside of the immigration bill, however, their efforts were largely unavailing, mainly because of the lack of consensus among Republican members.

While the social conservatives in the party were eager to legislate in such arenas as school prayer, the moderates in the party argued that those efforts would drive away voters. Their differences paralleled the differences between the rural South, where many of the social conservatives were based, and the urban Northeast, the home of many GOP moderates.

A good example was affirmative action, long criticized by conservatives as counterproductive and discriminatory. The Supreme Court opened the door for Congress to end most federal affirmative-action programs in 1995 when it ruled in *Adarand Constructors v. Peña* that such programs were potentially unconstitutional. Conservatives offered proposals in the House and Senate to bar federal agencies from using race- or gender-based preferences, but moderates were cool to the idea. The legislation lost steam as the 1996 elections approached and Republicans worried about alienating important blocs of voters.

Conservatives had no trouble attracting the moderates' support for one of their proposals, however: a measure aimed at discouraging same-sex marriages. The bill, which emerged after Hawaii grew close to permitting such unions, proposed to let states not recognize same-sex marriages even if they had been performed in a state that allowed them. Clinton and many congressional Democrats also supported the measure, and it sped into law with little opposition.

Chronology of Action on Law Enforcement

1993–1994

With Democrats controlling the White House and both chambers of Congress, Democratic lawmakers achieved a number of long-frustrated objectives in the 103rd Congress. At the top of the list was enactment of a major anticrime bill that reestablished the federal death penalty, increased federal aid for local law enforcement and prison construction, and banned a range of "assault weapons" popular with criminals. To win support from liberal lawmakers, the measure also included billions of dollars in grants for social programs aimed at preventing crime.

Congress also cleared a bill mandating a five-day waiting period for handgun purchases, a proposal that had been stymied since 1988. And the independent counsel statute, which authorized the courts to appoint independent prosecutors to investigate allegations against top government officials, was renewed after a battle that stretched back to the 102nd Congress.

Resisting pressure from some border-state lawmakers, Congress did not approve legislation to cut back on the number of legal immigrants and the benefits they received. Instead, it adopted only modest, scattered revisions to federal immigration law.

Similarly, Congress did not approve the most sweeping of the proposals to change copyright law and ease the patenting of unique manufacturing processes. Instead, it enacted a pair of modest trademark measures that raised application fees and provided more protection for plant breeders.

Two Clinton nominees to the federal appeals court drew stiff Republican opposition in 1994, but both were confirmed. One of former President Jimmy Carter's appointees to the federal bench, Robert F. Collins, came under congressional scrutiny after his conviction on bribery charges was upheld on appeal, but Collins stepped down before impeachment proceedings could get under way.

Crime Bill

Culminating a six-year effort by congressional Democrats to improve their image as crime-fighters, Congress cleared a massive anticrime bill in 1994 aimed at putting more cops on the streets, imprisoning and executing more criminals, and preventing more crime through social programs.

The legislation (HR 3355—PL 103-322) took federal intervention in local crime to an unprecedented level, authorizing $30.2 billion in spending over six years. Most of the spending, however, was on grants to state and local governments, which were to continue to bear the major responsibility for fighting crime. These included grants to hire police officers, build prisons and provide recreation programs in inner cities.

The measure triggered a fierce struggle that lasted most of the 1994 session, pitting conservatives who wanted stiffer punishment for criminals against liberals who wanted to emphasize crime prevention. The final package contained elements of both approaches, including capital punishment for dozens of new federal crimes, mandatory life imprisonment for three-time violent offenders, and special drug courts to steer nonviolent drug offenders into treatment programs instead of jail.

The bill also banned 19 types of semiautomatic assault weapons, the first time in many years that Congress had prohibited the manufacture and possession of a type of gun. Fiercely resisted by gun rights lawmakers in both parties, the ban was a key demand of President Clinton and urban lawmakers.

One innovation in the bill was an anticrime trust fund, the brainchild of Senate Appropriations Committee Chairman Robert C. Byrd, D-W.Va. An accounting device, the trust fund was credited with the money that the government was expected to save over six years through personnel cuts. The balance in the fund could be spent only on anticrime programs.

Republicans argued that the bill put too much emphasis on wasteful prevention programs and not enough on punishing convicts. The GOP pushed in vain to funnel more money into prisons, speed executions and give prosecutors the ability to use some evidence that had been obtained improperly. Republicans almost killed the bill in the House, joining with disaffected Democrats to block consideration of the first conference report on HR 3355. But when the bill's Democratic sponsors agreed to trim spending on prevention programs and prison construction, moderate GOP lawmakers who favored gun control threw their support behind the second conference agreement, allowing HR 3355 to be enacted.

The bill was so unpopular among conservative Republicans, particularly rural and western ones, it became a campaign issue in the 1994 election and a target of repeated GOP attacks in the 104th Congress. Republicans succeeded in toughening punishment and deemphasizing prevention, but they were not able to lift the ban on assault weapons. *(1995–1996 action, p. 733)*

The biggest disappointment for liberal House Democrats was the demise of the Racial Justice Act, a provision in the House bill that would have allowed death row inmates to use sentencing statistics to challenge a death sentence as racially discriminatory. With Senate Republicans firmly opposed, conferees dropped the provision to avoid an insurmountable filibuster.

KEY ELEMENTS

The final version of the bill dealt with most of the hotly disputed crime policies that Congress had been struggling with since 1989. Among other issues, the measure:

• **Death Penalty.** Authorized the death penalty for dozens of existing or new federal crimes, such as murdering a federal law enforcement official or causing the death of a hostage. The law also laid out new procedures for imposing the death penalty, calling for a two-phase trial that would determine the defendant's guilt or innocence before considering the level of punishment. Previous federal law had authorized the death penalty for a number of crimes, such as assassinating a president, but a 1972 Supreme Court ruling (*Furman v. Georgia*) precluded executions because court procedures did not protect defendants' rights. *(1972 case summary, Congress and the Nation Vol. III, p. 511)*

Liberals argued against the federal death penalty on moral and practical grounds, citing examples of death row inmates who were found to be innocent. Their amendments to substitute life imprisonment without parole for the death penalty, however, were easily defeated.

Republicans went the other direction, attempting to make drug kingpins subject to capital punishment even when they could not be tied directly to a murder. Their proposal was adopted in the House but dropped in conference.

• **Trust Fund.** Established a $30.2 billion trust fund from fiscal 1995 through fiscal 2000 to pay for programs authorized in the bill, drawing on the expected savings from the elimination of more than 250,000 federal positions. The money could be spent only on crime programs; otherwise, it had to be used to reduce the federal deficit.

The federal personnel cuts had been mandated earlier in 1994 as part of a bill (HR 3345—PL 103-226) authorizing federal agencies to offer buyouts to selected employees. Byrd proposed the trust fund idea largely to block a move by Republicans and conservative Democrats to shrink federal spending by an amount equal to the projected savings from the personnel cuts. *(Employee buyouts, p. 814)*

Politically, the beauty of the trust fund was that it allowed lawmakers to multiply the amount of money authorized for anticrime programs without increasing federal spending. Indeed, the bill tripled in size after the trust fund was devised. Considerable doubts remained, however, that the personnel cuts would produce as much savings as the administration said they would. Even if the trust fund collected the full amount projected, skeptics doubted that appropriators would allow all $30.2 billion to be spent.

Indeed, many budget analysts said that any savings from the personnel cuts already had been spent, in effect, to shave spending enough to meet the freeze Congress imposed on discretionary appropriations. The trust fund would only siphon money out of available funds for other noncrime priorities, they said.

Procedurally, the trust fund worked much the same way the budget fire walls worked from 1991 to 1993. The existing cap on appropriations, dictated by the 1990 deficit reduction bill, was to be reduced (by some $2.4 billion for fiscal 1995) and that amount transferred into the anticrime category.

• **Community Policing.** Authorized $8.8 billion over six years to help communities hire 100,000 new police officers, fulfilling a campaign pledge that Clinton had made in 1992.

Lawmakers on both sides of the aisle supported the idea of sending more police into neighborhoods—on foot, horse, bicycle or other means—where they would be more visible and could develop closer ties to the community. But Republicans argued that the money was not nearly enough to hire 100,000 officers.

• **Prisons.** Authorized $7.9 billion in state construction grants for prisons and boot camps. Of that money, 50 percent was to be distributed to states that adopted "truth-in-sentenc-ing" laws requiring repeat violent offenders to serve at least 85 percent of their sentences. In addition to the construction grants, $1.8 billion was to go toward reimbursing states for the costs of incarcerating illegal immigrants who committed crimes.

This provision reflected the top Republican priority in the legislation: putting more criminals behind bars for longer periods of time. They had to overcome opposition from many House Democrats, however, who disliked the truth-in-sentencing provisions for the same reason that they opposed mandatory minimum sentences: the requirements were too rigid. State and local officials of both parties also had complained that truth-in-sentencing requirements amounted to a vast unfunded mandate.

• **Prevention Programs.** Authorized $6.9 billion for programs aimed at preventing crime, including $1.6 billion in "local partnership" grants to needy communities for crime reduction measures; $810 million to promote the educational and social development of disadvantaged children; $625.5 million for model, comprehensive anticrime efforts in areas long plagued by crime; $382.5 million to provide more substance abuse treatment for state and federal inmates; $377 million for local job, sports, fellowship and safety programs; $270 million for grants to promote community development in low-income areas; and $45.5 million for programs to deter youths from joining gangs.

Also included was $1 billion for drug courts, which sought to rehabilitate first-time or nonviolent drug offenders with intensive treatment and supervision rather than incarceration, and $1.6 billion for the Violence Against Women Act, a package of new federal penalties and grant programs designed to reduce crimes against women. Among other features, the Violence Against Women Act made a crime motivated by gender a federal civil rights violation.

Republicans derided many of the prevention efforts as "pork barrel" programs that would have little effect on crime. The local partnership program, they said, was nothing more than a retread of revenue sharing, which the federal government abandoned in the 1970s. But to top Democrats, the money was critical to winning votes for the overall crime package from liberals who opposed the bill's punishment provisions.

• **Assault Weapons.** Banned for 10 years the manufacture, sale or possession of 19 specific semiautomatic weapons, as well as copycat models and guns with two or more characteristics associated with assault weapons, such as flash suppressors. The measure exempted more than 670 specific semiautomatic weapons, focusing instead on guns designed to produce a rapid spray of bullets—weapons that were efficient at killing humans but of little use to sportsmen. Gun owners were allowed to keep guns that they owned legally at the time. The measure also banned ammunition-feeding devices that held more than 10 rounds.

Federal records indicated that assault weapons accounted for a small percentage of the nation's guns and were responsible for only about 1 percent of homicides. At the same time, they showed up in a disproportionate number of crimes, lending some credence to claims that they were the preferred weapons of criminals.

LAW LEADERSHIP

Controversy and scandal dogged many of President Clinton's choices for top spots in the Justice Department and related posts. His first nominee for attorney general—Zoë Baird, a corporate lawyer—was forced to withdraw after news circulated that she had hired two illegal immigrants as household help and failed to pay Social Security taxes for them. A top candidate after Baird, U.S. District Court Judge Kimba M. Wood, withdrew because she, too, had employed an illegal immigrant as a baby-sitter.

The president's third choice was Janet Reno, who had spent 15 years as the top prosecutor in crime-ridden Dade County, Florida. The Senate confirmed Reno 98–0 on March 11. Although praised by some for her independence, Reno was criticized for the department's assault on the heavily armed Branch Davidian cult compound in Waco, Texas, a fiasco that ended in the nationally televised immolation of 85 cult members.

Clinton also had trouble with other high-profile spots in the Justice Department. He withdrew his first nominee for head of the department's civil rights division, Lani Guinier, in June 1993 after conservatives accused her of holding dangerously radical views on minority rights. A former Justice Department attorney, Guinier was a law professor at the University of Pennsylvania whose writings on voting rights and redistricting alarmed conservatives.

Clinton's next choice, Washington lawyer John Payton, withdrew after getting tepid reviews from the Congressional Black Caucus. Finally, on March 22, 1994, the Senate confirmed by voice vote Clinton's third choice: Deval L. Patrick, a Boston attorney and former lawyer for the NAACP Legal Defense Fund.

Webster L. Hubbell, Clinton's pick for associate attorney general and a close friend of the president, won confirmation by voice vote May 28, 1993, despite some early controversy. But Hubbell resigned abruptly the following March after prosecutors targeted him for billing irregularities back at his law firm in Little Rock. He eventually was sentenced to 21 months in prison.

One of the few Clinton appointees who sailed through the confirmation process was Louis J. Freeh, Clinton's choice to head the Federal Bureau of Investigation. Freeh, a federal judge and former FBI agent, was confirmed by the Senate Aug. 6 by voice vote with no debate.

Freeh's supervision of the FBI later drew criticism from lawmakers, however, as did his attempt to promote an FBI official connected with the fatal shoot-out at Ruby Ridge, Idaho.

President Clinton's first director of the Office of National Drug Control Policy, or "drug czar," was Lee P. Brown, a veteran police official. Confirmed June 16, 1993, Brown became a lightning rod for GOP criticism of the Clinton administration's antidrug efforts and its cutbacks in the drug czar's office. The administration's approach to the war on drugs was so lax, Republicans argued, drug use among teenagers rose in 1993 and 1994 after 11 years of steady decline.

In January 1996, Clinton moved to toughen his image on drugs by nominating Gen. Barry McCaffrey, the former top officer of the U.S. military's Southern Command, as the new drug czar. A highly decorated war veteran, McCaffrey was confirmed by the Senate Feb. 29, 1996, by voice vote.

Supporters of the ban made their case with gory accounts of gun-related deaths. They also stressed support for the ban among such law enforcement groups as the National Association of Police Organizations and the Fraternal Order of Police.

Opponents argued that the ban was ineffectual, and that it would serve as the first step toward more sweeping prohibitions on gun ownership. A better approach, they argued, was to stiffen the penalties for criminals who used guns. In a nod to these critics, the final version of the bill increased the penalties for interstate gun trafficking and for gun use by violent felons and serious drug offenders. It also made a federal crime out of interstate gun theft, theft from a gun dealer or manufacturer, gun smuggling by drug traffickers and unlicensed gun importing, among other acts already prohibited by state laws.

• **Three Strikes.** Mandated life imprisonment for federal defendants convicted of a third violent felony, a policy known as "three strikes and you're out." The rule was waived for some elderly convicts, and its application was restricted on tribal lands.

Republicans and Democrats in the House clashed over what offenses should constitute a strike. Republicans wanted to count all serious drug offenses, but Democrats wanted to count serious drug offenses only as the first or second strike. Although Republicans prevailed on the House floor, the conference report allowed serious drug offenses to count as the first or second strike only.

• **Safety Valve.** Allowed federal judges to waive the existing mandatory minimum sentences for certain first-time, nonviolent drug offenders who exhibited good behavior while in prison.

• **Juveniles.** Allowed juveniles 13 and older to be tried as adults in the federal court system for certain violent crimes and crimes involving a gun. Previous law had set the minimum age for adult trials at 15.

The Senate had sought to mandate that juveniles be tried as adults in federal court if they were accused of serious violent offenses, such as murder and drive-by shooting. The House proposed to retain the previous rules, which gave prosecutors and judges the discretion to treat juveniles as adults, and the conferees agreed. The conferees retained a Senate proposal that juveniles' serious violent crimes be recorded on their permanent FBI records.

Reducing the cut-off age for adult trials drew protests from liberal House Democrats, such as Craig Washington of Texas, who argued that "certifying 13-year-olds as adults is an oxymoron." But proponents of the change said that some juveniles had committed such heinous crimes that they were no longer truly children.

• **Hate Crimes.** Mandated higher penalties for crimes motivated by the victim's race, color, religion, national origin, ethnicity, gender, disability or sexual orientation. The U.S. Sentencing Commission was instructed to raise penalties for such "hate crimes" generally by one-third.

The provision was backed by a number of religious, ethnic, homosexual and law enforcement groups. The House had passed legislation in 1992 to increase the penalties for hate crimes, but the Senate did not act on it.

On Sept. 21, 1993, the House passed by voice vote a similar bill against hate crimes (HR 1152) that the Judiciary Committee had reported earlier in the day (H Rept 103-244). The only dissent voiced in committee and on the floor came from liberal Democrats, who questioned the constitutionality of the measure as well as the courts' ability to discern a criminal's motivation. Under the legislation, the jury (or the judge at a nonjury trial) would have to determine beyond a reasonable doubt that the offense was a hate crime before the additional penalty could be imposed.

On Nov. 4, the Senate voted 95–4 to add an identical hate crimes proposal (S 1522) to its version of the omnibus crime bill. In conference, negotiators added crimes against the disabled to the list of possible hate crimes.

• **DNA Analysis.** Authorized a total of $40 million in grants from fiscal 1996 through fiscal 2000 to help states develop and use genetic tests. The FBI also was authorized to assemble an index of convicted criminals' DNA records, DNA samples from crime scenes and DNA samples from unidentified bodies. The law authorized $25 million over five years to fund the DNA index, as well as fund training and quality assurance programs at the FBI.

The provision was drawn from a bill (HR 829—H Rept 103-45) that the House Judiciary Committee had reported March 29, 1993. The House passed the bill the same day, but the Senate did not consider it. As enacted, it restricted access to DNA records, allowing only law enforcement officials and, where relevant, criminal defendants to view them.

• **Byrne Grants.** Added $1 billion over six years to an existing federal grant program, the Edward Byrne Memorial State and Local Enforcement Assistance Program, to help fund collaborative antidrug and anticrime programs. The measure also expanded the list of programs eligible for Byrne funding, adding efforts to prosecute drunken drivers and violent juveniles, deter gang violence and improve DNA analyses.

The House Judiciary Committee had reported a bill (HR 1385—H Rept 103-245) on Sept. 21, 1993, to allow Byrne grants to be used to prosecute drunken drivers, and the House passed the measure the same day by voice vote. Those provisions later were incorporated into the omnibus crime bill.

• **Drug Czar.** Gave the director of the Office of National Drug Control Policy, better known as the federal "drug czar," more power over the money appropriated for antidrug efforts. The law also ordered the director to make an annual assessment of the previous year's national drug control strategy, the availability of drugs and drug treatment and the level of drug use. The office was reauthorized through fiscal 1997.

The provision was drawn from a bill (HR 1926) that the House Government Operations Committee had approved by voice vote Nov. 19, 1993, and the House had passed by voice vote Nov. 21. The conferees on the crime bill did not include a proposal from HR 1926 to include the drug czar on the National Security Council, however.

BACKGROUND

Crime bills were a biannual exercise for Congress in the 1980s, with a major crackdown on violent offenders or drugs being proposed every Congress and a somewhat milder law being enacted—usually just before the elections. These efforts responded to public concern about crime, but they also had great political appeal. Democrats were eager to show that they were not "soft" on crime, an accusation that Republicans had levied since Richard Nixon seized the law-and-order mantle in the 1968 presidential campaign.

After Congress enacted a measure in 1989 to combat international drug trafficking (PL 101-231), Democratic leaders set about fashioning a tough anticrime package to help their party reclaim the crime issue from Republicans. Their proposal included reimposing the death penalty for 30 federal crimes, limiting the appeals of death row inmates and banning certain types of assault weapons. The House and Senate each passed versions of the legislation in 1990, but they were unable to resolve their differences over the most contentious provisions. The conferees ultimately scrapped the disputed provisions, and Congress cleared a stripped-down bill. The main provisions of the law (PL 101-647) raised the penalties for financial fraud and illegal steroid sales, increased support for drug enforcement agents and promoted alternatives to incarceration for state convicts. *(Congress and the Nation Vol. VIII, p. 764)*

Democrats tried again in the 102nd Congress, encountering the same problems. While Republicans pressed for tougher punishments, more prosecutorial power and less gun control, many Democrats protested the expansion in the death penalty, the limits on appeals and other proposed crackdowns. After Democrats overrode most GOP concerns in conference, Senate Republicans waged a filibuster that kept the Senate from voting on the conference report. The legislation never reached President George Bush's desk, rendering moot Bush's pledge to veto it.

Action on a new crime bill began in August 1993, when top congressional Republicans proposed an anticrime package. President Clinton outlined the core elements of a Democratic anticrime bill the following week, echoing some of the GOP proposals but putting less emphasis on prison construction and harsh sentences. Clinton asked for money to help hire 100,000 new police officers, new federal death penalties and an overhaul of the federal appeals process for death row inmates. He also endorsed a ban on assault weapons and backed the so-called Brady bill, which proposed a waiting period for handgun purchases. *(Brady bill, p. 703)*

House Judiciary Committee Chairman Jack Brooks, D-Texas, and Senate Judiciary Committee Chairman Joseph R. Biden Jr., D-Del., introduced bills in September including most of Clinton's proposals and some new ones. Like Clinton's plan, their bills were largely drawn from the 1992 conference agreement. By sticking to the contours of that bill, they hoped to win speedy congressional approval. As it turned out, more than 11 months were to pass before the final package cleared the Senate.

SENATE ACTION

Biden took a modified, $9.6 billion anticrime package (S 1607) directly to the Senate floor on Nov. 3, 1993, bypassing the Senate Judiciary Committee. The initial floor debate recalled past partisan showdowns over crime and law enforcement: Republicans demanded more prisons and tougher sentences to stop what they called a "revolving door" of criminal justice, while many Democrats stressed the need for new approaches to reduce crime, including drug treatment for inmates and alternative prisons. Reflecting the GOP priorities, the top Republican on the Judiciary Committee, Orrin G. Hatch of Utah, offered an amendment to add $6 billion to the bill for prison construction and promote "truth in sentencing" laws.

Meanwhile, Biden, Hatch and others were negotiating intensely behind the scenes. The talks produced a breakthrough Nov. 4—a bipartisan plan that combined the Democratic and Republican spending priorities and more than doubled the bill's price tag.

Byrd supplied a crucial element of the deal by devising the trust fund that made it possible to pay for the expensive compromise. Under Byrd's proposal, $22.3 billion of the expected five-year savings from the personnel cuts was to be deposited into the novel and somewhat controversial trust fund, making it impossible for appropriators to use the savings for other discretionary domestic programs. That money allowed lawmakers to pay for the entire Biden bill, a substantial portion of Hatch's prison initiative, and more. Senators voted 94–4 on Nov. 4 for the bipartisan amendment, sponsored by Byrd with the backing of Majority Leader George J. Mitchell, D-Maine, and Minority Leader Bob Dole, R-Kan.

Included in Byrd's amendment was an additional $3.7 billion for community policing programs, bringing the total to $8.9 billion for 100,000 "cops on the beat." Also included was an additional $3 billion for regional federal prisons, $1 billion more to help states build boot camps and other minimum-security facilities and $1.8 billion to combat violence against women. The amendment allowed states to send violent prisoners to the new regional prisons only if they adopted "truth in sentencing" laws.

After the amendment was approved, Hatch said senators might be close to forging a crime bill that both parties could support. But he warned that many Republicans could withdraw their support if Democrats attached gun control proposals, such as an assault weapons ban, to the bill. Two other issues also threatened to scuttle the bipartisan support for the bill. One was a proposal by Edward M. Kennedy, D-Mass., to make it a federal crime to bar access to abortion clinics. The second was an effort by Arlen Specter, R-Pa., to limit habeas corpus petitions, which prison inmates used to appeal their convictions to federal court.

Under a compromise engineered by Mitchell, senators agreed to take up the clinic access bill (S 636) and Specter's pro-

posal to overhaul habeas corpus petitions (S 1657) as separate bills. Biden agreed to drop his own habeas corpus proposal from the overall crime bill. On Nov. 16, the Senate passed the clinic access bill, 69–30. The next day, senators voted 65–34 to table, or kill, Specter's habeas corpus bill. *(Clinic access, p. 537)*

Biden had not included the ban on assault weapons in his crime package, sensitive to the division in his party over gun control. But Democrats closed ranks behind a proposal by Sen. Dianne Feinstein, D-Calif., Dennis DeConcini, D-Ariz., and Howard M. Metzenbaum, D-Ohio, to ban the manufacture, sale or possession of 19 specific weapons, "copycat" weapons and large ammunition clips. After narrowly defeating a motion to table, or kill, the underlying amendment, the Senate approved Feinstein's proposal Nov. 17 on a **key vote of 56–43 (R 10–34; D 46–9)**. Gun control opponents considered filibustering the bill over the amendment but gave up, apparently in hope of gutting or narrowing it in conference with the House, which had rejected an assault weapons ban in 1991. *(1993 key votes, p. 979)*

Senators also took another tack against gun violence, approving tougher mandatory sentences for federal crimes involving firearms. They also approved a proposal by Alfonse M. D'Amato, R-N.Y., to give federal courts jurisdiction over crimes involving a gun that had crossed state lines. Biden warned that the D'Amato proposal would flood the federal courts with tens of thousands of handgun crimes, but senators adopted it, 58–42, on Nov. 9.

The gun penalties were added the day after the Senate adopted a "three strikes" proposal by Trent Lott, R-Miss. His amendment, approved 91–1, required life imprisonment for criminals convicted of a third felony that had a maximum penalty of more than five years.

Senators approved a slew of other amendments during the two-and-a-half-week, tougher-than-thou bidding war over the bill. These included proposals to:

• Require criminal records to be maintained on juveniles convicted in adult courts on charges of murder, attempted murder, armed robbery or similar crimes. The Senate adopted the amendment 64–23 on Nov. 5.

• Make criminal gang activities a federal offense with mandatory minimum sentences. The amendment was adopted 60–38 on Nov. 9.

• Make all forms of carjacking a federal offense and authorize the death penalty for carjackings that result in death. It was adopted 65–34 on Nov. 9.

• Make juvenile possession of a handgun or ammunition a federal offense, except for juveniles who had parental permission to use guns for ranching, farming, hunting or target practice or who defended themselves against an intruder in their home. The amendment also made selling, delivering or giving handguns or ammunition to a juvenile a federal offense. The amendment was adopted 100–0 on Nov. 9.

• Provide up to $100 million a year through fiscal 1998 for state and local governments to hire more prosecutors, public defenders and judges. The amendment was approved Nov. 16 by voice vote.

- Extend the death penalty to so-called drug kingpins—the leaders of criminal enterprises that dealt in large amounts of illegal drugs. The amendment was adopted Nov. 17, 74–25.

- Limit the power of federal courts to impose population caps in prison crowding cases, bar class-action lawsuits in such cases, and retroactively apply the new limits to existing court-ordered caps. The amendment was adopted by voice vote Nov. 17 after the Senate rejected a move to kill the proposal, 31–68.

- Authorize the federal government to take custody of criminal aliens or to pay states for housing them. The amendment was approved by voice vote Nov. 16.

- Make prisoners ineligible for federal Pell grants for higher education. The amendment was adopted by voice vote Nov. 16.

Among the proposals rejected were an amendment by Sen. Paul Simon, D-Ill., to bar capital punishment for offenders less than 18 years old, which was tabled Nov. 8, 52–41; an amendment by Carl Levin, D-Mich., to substitute life in prison without parole for all of the death penalties in the bill, which was rejected Nov. 17, 25–75; and an amendment by Robert C. Smith, R-N.H., to reduce grants to states that did not adopt tougher sentencing laws, which was defeated Nov. 17, 26–73.

The Senate agreed on Nov. 19 to substitute the amended text of S 1607 for HR 3355, a House-passed bill to authorize $3.5 billion over six years for cops on the beat. It then passed HR 3355 on an overwhelming, 95–4 vote.

HOUSE ACTION

Brooks's initial hurdle was the House Judiciary Committee, which was dominated by liberal Democrats. The liberals introduced a bill (HR 3315) that emphasized crime prevention and criminal rehabilitation. It also proposed numerous gun control initiatives and sought to reinstate some of the protections for death row inmates that the Supreme Court had eliminated. Republicans on the committee, meanwhile, were backing an alternative anticrime package (HR 2872) that proposed to pay for anticrime programs with across-the-board cuts in federal administrative expenses.

Brooks decided to break the more popular and digestible pieces out of his omnibus bill and move them as separate bills. When Republicans tried in the Judiciary Committee to append some of their death penalty proposals and, at one point, the entire GOP crime bill, Brooks blocked them by ruling their amendments out of order. Eleven of the smaller bills went on to win House approval in 1993, and three were enacted into law, including the Brady bill. Thirteen other bills, tackling some of the more controversial issues, advanced through the committee in 1994 and were combined on the House floor into an omnibus package comparable to the Senate bill.

The following bills, which the Judiciary Committee reported on Nov. 3, 1993, passed the House in 1993:

- **Community Policing.** Passed by voice vote Nov. 3, HR 3355 (H Rept 103-324) proposed to authorize $3.5 billion over six years to help states and localities hire about 50,000 additional police officers.

- **Drug Treatment for Prisoners.** HR 3354 (H Rept 103-323) authorized $300 million over three years to help states pro-

vide drug treatment to inmates. It passed Nov. 3, 394–32. A related bill (HR 3350—H Rept 103-320) requiring drug treatment for federal inmates also passed on Nov. 3, 373–54.

- **Juvenile Gangs and Drug Trafficking.** HR 3353 (H Rept 103-322) authorized $200 million over two years to help states fight juvenile gangs and drug trafficking. The House passed the bill, 413–12, Nov. 3.

- **Alternative Sentencing.** HR 3351 (H Rept 103-321) proposed up to $200 million in grants to states to help develop alternative sentencing plans for certain youthful offenders age 22 or younger. An example of an alternative to prison was boot camps. The House first took up the bill Nov. 3 under suspension of the rules, voting 235–192—less than the two-thirds majority needed to pass it under those procedures. Republicans objected to grants for alternative punishments when, they said, the government was not doing more to support traditional incarceration. The House subsequently passed the bill, 336–82, on Nov. 19.

The following bills, reported by the Judiciary Committee on Nov. 20, passed the House the same day:

- **Crimes against Women.** HR 1133 (H Rept 103-395) included provisions prodding states to toughen laws against domestic violence, providing grants to prosecute and prevent crimes such as rape, and making interstate stalking and domestic violence federal crimes. The House passed the bill, 421–0.

- **Youth Handgun Ban.** HR 3098 (H Rept 103-389) prohibiting the sale or transfer of handguns and ammunition to minors. The bill, which passed by a vote of 422–0, included some exceptions, such as allowing minors to use guns under limited circumstances with proper parental supervision.

- **Crimes Against Minors.** HR 324 (H Rept 103-392) required people convicted of sexually assaulting a minor or similar crimes to notify police of their addresses for 10 years following their release from prison or their parole. Passed by voice vote, the bill included penalties for states that did not create registries for such criminals within three years.

Over the winter recess, lawmakers watched the crime issue climb in importance in public opinion polls and heard an earful from constituents about their fear of crime. Republicans and Democrats alike returned to Washington in 1994 declaring crime legislation a top priority for the year.

The House Judiciary Committee went back to work on crime legislation in March, approving 13 bills during a lengthy and sometimes heated mark-up on March 16 and 17. Brooks combined the measures with bills that the House had passed in 1993, creating an omnibus package (HR 4092) that he took to the House floor on April 14.

The following measures were included in HR 4092:

- **Prison Construction.** HR 3968, reported on March 25 (H Rept 103-462), proposed $3 billion in grants over five years to help states build new prisons or expand existing ones. The bill encouraged states to impose severe sentences on violent offenders, but it was not as demanding as the truth-in-sentencing proposal backed by Republicans and included in the Senate crime bill.

Republicans tried in committee to increase the money for prisons to $10 billion and add the truth-in-sentencing requirement, among other incentives for stiffer state penalties. Taking a page from the Republicans, however, Democrats argued that it would be arrogant and inappropriate to dictate sentencing policy for the states. The amendment was defeated, 13–22.

• **Death Row Appeals.** HR 4018, reported on March 25 (H Rept 103-470), proposed to overhaul the rules for habeas corpus petitions by death row inmates who had exhausted the state appeals process. It would have limited most prisoners to a single habeas corpus petition that had to be filed within one year of exhausting state appeals.

The bill also would have required states to provide competent lawyers for indigent defendants, and it would have reversed several Supreme Court rulings that made it difficult for prisoners to appeal their sentences on the basis of new evidence or new rules of law.

Lawmakers from both parties wanted to overhaul the habeas corpus rules, but for much different reasons. Republicans insisted that prisoners made a mockery of the death penalty by delaying its imposition with years of legal appeals. Democratic liberals argued that the Supreme Court had unduly tightened the opportunities for such appeals, increasing the risk that innocent prisoners would be executed.

The sponsor of HR 4018, Democrat Don Edwards of California, said his measure addressed both concerns. Committee Republicans complained, however, that the bill would prolong rather than shorten the lengthy appeals process. Henry J. Hyde, R-Ill., offered a substitute that he said would truly expedite the process, but the committee rejected it by voice vote.

• **Death Row Appeals Based on Race.** Known as the Racial Justice Act, HR 4017 proposed to let convicts use sentencing statistics to challenge a death sentence as racially discriminatory. The Judiciary Committee reported the bill on March 24 (H Rept 103-458).

Democrats pointed to figures indicating that prosecutors were far more likely to seek the death penalty when defendants were black and the victims were white. Republicans strongly criticized the bill, however, saying it could allow death sentences to be reversed on the basis of statistics without any evidence that race was a factor in those particular cases.

The two sides had clashed before, with Republicans emerging as the winner each time. Liberals and civil rights groups had been seeking the change in law since 1987, when Supreme Court ruled in *McCleskey v. Kemp* that statistical evidence of a racial disparity in sentencing was not enough to prove that a death penalty was unconstitutional. They tried to attach similar provisions to crime bills in 1990 and 1991, but their proposals were rejected in both chambers. *(1990 action, Congress and the Nation Vol. VIII, p. 767; 1991 action, Congress and the Nation Vol. VIII, p. 787)*

• **Death Penalty Procedures.** HR 4035, reported on March 25 (H Rept 103-467), proposed guidelines for determining whether an adult defendant should receive the death penalty. It also would have required the government to notify a defendant when it planned to seek the death penalty.

• **Crime Prevention.** HR 4033, reported March 24 (H Rept 103-459, Part I), proposed a $6.9 billion package of 10 preven-

tion programs, including community crime prevention, midnight sports programs and drug courts.

Republicans did not attempt to amend the bill, but they did complain about it. "It's becoming a license to raid the Treasury for anything and everything if you say it is for stopping crime," said Steven H. Schiff, R-N.M.

• **Three Strikes.** HR 3981, reported March 25 (H Rept 103-463), would have mandated life in prison for anyone convicted of a serious violent felony in federal court after having at least two prior convictions for such offenses. The bill, backed by the White House, defined "strikes" far more narrowly than did the Senate bill, excluding nonviolent drug crimes and some offenses involving substantial amounts of drugs.

The Judiciary Committee had agreed, 20–14, to permit the release of criminals sentenced under the three-strikes rule if they were at least 70 years old and had spent at least 30 years behind bars. The change addressed one of the criticisms of the three-strikes rule: that it would force the government to warehouse geriatric prisoners who were unlikely to commit more crimes.

The committee also voted to restrict the bill's application on tribal lands. Mike Synar, D-Okla., said the change was needed because Native Americans made up more than half the defendants prosecuted under federal law.

• **Safety Valve.** HR 3979, reported on March 24 (H Rept 103-460), proposed to reduce the mandatory minimum federal sentences for nonviolent drug offenders from five years to two years. It also proposed to let judges waive these mandatory minimums retroactively for offenders with little or no prior record.

• **Death Penalty.** HR 4032, reported on March 25 (H Rept 103-466), would have authorized federal courts to impose the death penalty for dozens of crimes, including first-degree murder, kidnapping, hostage-taking, drive-by shootings and carjackings resulting in death. Although some of the offenses had already been capital crimes under federal law, others had been left to state jurisdiction.

In committee, Republicans narrowly succeeded in amending the bill to make high-level drug traffickers eligible for the death penalty regardless of whether they had been tied to a murder. Bill McCollum, R-Fla., argued that anyone high up in the drug trade must have been indirectly responsible for at least one death and thus deserved to risk capital punishment. While some Democrats argued that the proposal violated the Constitution's guarantee against cruel and unusual punishment, several others joined the united Republicans to approve the amendment, 18–17.

• **Juvenile Criminals.** HR 4031, reported on March 25 (H Rept 103-465) proposed to allow, but not mandate, that individuals 13 and older be tried as adults in federal court for crimes such as murder, assault, robbery and rape.

• **Crime Victims.** HR 4030, reported on March 25 (H Rept 103-464, Part I), would have permitted victims of crime and sexual abuse to present information or make a statement at the defendant's sentencing. The bill also proposed to revise the formula for the allocation of money in the federal crime victims' fund, established in 1984. The fund compensated victims and helped them get counseling.

• **Insurance Fraud.** HR 665, reported on March 25 (H Rept 103-468), proposed to make defrauding an insurance company a federal crime, permitting federal prosecution for filing false statements with, embezzling from, or deceiving an insurance company.

• **Violence against Children.** HR 1120, reported on March 25 (H Rept 103-461), sought to strengthen federal penalties against people convicted of assaulting children 16 and younger. Penalties under the bill included a fine or imprisonment up to five years.

• **Sexual Abuse of Children.** HR 3993, reported on March 25 (H Rept 103-469) proposed to crack down on international trafficking in child pornography and called on states to pass tough laws against child pornography.

Brooks also included in the omnibus crime package a draft "Police Corps" bill to provide education grants to college students in exchange for four years of service with a state or local law enforcement agency. The proposed grants were capped at $30,000 per person, and each graduating class was limited to 20,000 participants.

Significantly, Brooks did not include a ban on assault weapons in his version of the omnibus bill. Instead, he insisted that it remain separate, leaving the battle between gun rights and gun control advocates to be fought after the House finished work on the crime bill.

House Debate

Republicans and Democrats had split repeatedly in the Judiciary Committee, and the partisan discord sharpened in the House Rules Committee. Although the final rule proposed by Democratic leaders would have allowed numerous GOP amendments, Republicans complained that several of their key initiatives were being blocked.

Rather than accommodating the Republicans, House leaders moved to shore up support for the bill among Democratic liberals, particularly the Congressional Black Caucus. For example, House Speaker Thomas S. Foley, D-Wash., promised to back the caucus' effort to keep the controversial Racial Justice Act in the bill. The efforts paid off, as only six Democrats voted against the rule on April 13. It passed, 244–176, without a single Republican vote.

One of the amendments that Republicans were not allowed to offer would have weakened the "exclusionary rule," making it easier for prosecutors to use evidence that had been obtained illegally. After debate began April 14, Republicans tried a parliamentary maneuver usually reserved for last-ditch efforts to kill a bill, saying they were trying to open the door for the exclusionary rule amendment. Brooks accused the Republicans of trying to stall or kill the crime package, and the GOP motion was rejected, 170–257.

Republicans tried the tactic three more times over the course of the debate, failing each time.

Much of the debate over the bill revolved around imposing and implementing the death penalty. On April 14, the House rejected three Democratic amendments designed to eliminate the death penalty for all or some crimes in the bill. The first, by Mike Kopetski of Oregon, would have replaced the death penalties throughout the bill with life imprisonment without parole. It was defeated 111–314. The second, by Melvin Watt of North Carolina, would have eliminated the death penalty for drug kingpins not directly responsible for a murder. It failed, 108–316. The third, by Robert C. Scott of Virginia, would have eliminated the death penalty for murders committed during carjackings, drive-by shootings and federal drug and gun crimes. It was defeated by voice vote.

Opponents of the death penalty lost again that day when the House took up the legal procedures for imposing capital punishment. George W. Gekas, R-Pa., argued that the proposed procedures would make it too hard to impose the death penalty. He offered an amendment to adjust them by, among other things, eliminating a requirement that juries be told they were never required to impose the death penalty. Despite warnings that the changes could open the federal death penalty to constitutional challenge, the amendment was adopted, 226–198.

On April 19, Republicans succeeded in excising the proposed changes in habeas corpus appeals. Although the disputed section included some restrictions on death row appeals that Republicans had been seeking for years, opponents argued that the overall effect would have been to increase appeals and delay executions. The vote to drop the provisions was 270–159.

The next day, the House took up the Racial Justice Act provision, a top priority for liberal Democrats and critical sticking point for Republicans. Bill McCollum, R-Fla., offered an amendment to replace the provision with language barring racial discrimination in sentencing, the same amendment he had offered successfully on the 1991 crime bill.

Delegate Eleanor Holmes Norton, D-D.C., defended the Racial Justice Act, arguing, "There is no check on the prosecutor today. He chooses blacks for death." Supporters of the provision also stressed that it would merely allow statistical evidence to be considered, and that courts generally would not overturn death sentences on statistics alone.

Gary A. Franks of Connecticut, the House's only black Republican, sided with McCollum. "Yes, there are a disproportionate number of minorities in our prison system. . . . [but] establishing quotas for the death penalty is not the answer," he said. "We do not correct social problems by constantly defining [the] remedy in terms of black and white."

The House rejected the McCollum amendment, 212–217, but the tally was even closer than it appeared: the "nays" included five House delegates who were not permitted under House rules to affect the outcome of a vote. If their votes had been excluded, the measure would have failed on a tie. And the tie resulted largely because Foley, who rarely voted as Speaker, voted "nay."

The razor-thin margin encouraged McCollum to try again on April 21, proposing to send the bill back to the Rules Committee with instructions to replace the racial justice language with his own. The House defeated the motion, 192–235.

As the debate wound down, lawmakers approved a number of amendments toughening the bill. For example, members voted 303–126 on April 19 to count all serious federal drug offenses toward the "three strikes" limit; 417–12 on April 20 to authorize

6,000 new agents and staff for the Border Patrol over five years; and 312–116 on April 20 to bar Pell grants to inmates in state and federal prisons.

As in the Senate, Democrats were able to win over some Republicans by pouring money into prison construction. Republicans had complained that the bill authorized more than $7 billion for social programs aimed at preventing crime while stinting on constructing prisons to lock up proven criminals. They pressed their point April 19, when the House took up several amendments to give states more than the $3 billion proposed for prison construction.

McCollum proposed to replace the $3 billion with $10 billion over five years for states that adopted "truth in sentencing" laws. The House narrowly rejected the proposal, voting 215–206 to reinstate the $3 billion. The House also agreed, however, to authorize $10.5 billion more over five years for state prison construction, with 25 percent of the money reserved for the states that had the strictest sentencing policies. That amendment, offered by conservative Democrat Jim Chapman of Texas, was approved, 377–50.

The Chapman amendment, along with an earlier amendment by Brooks that authorized $1.5 billion in additional spending, raised the bill's price tag close to $28 billion. The expanded measure won the support of 65 Republicans on April 21, passing the House by a vote of 285–141. The House then substituted its package for the text of the Senate-passed bill (HR 3355) and passed the amended bill by voice vote.

The House-passed measure was generally more liberal than the $22.3 billion Senate bill—less punitive and more generous toward prevention programs—and many Republicans complained that it was too soft on criminals. "This bill satisfies the academics and the sociologists, but God help you if you work the midnight shift and have to walk home," said Hyde.

Assault Weapons

Advocates of a ban on assault weapons started moving their proposal (HR 4296) shortly after the House finished work on the omnibus bill. Their bill was virtually identical to the ban included in the Senate-passed crime package.

The House Judiciary Committee approved the bill on a near party-line, 20–15 vote April 28. In one of the few amendments adopted, the committee softened the penalties against gun owners who failed to file the necessary paperwork when transferring an assault weapon that had been "grandfathered" under the bill. The committee reported the bill four days later (H Rept 103-489).

Brooks, who supported gun owners' rights, had little chance of stopping the bill in his committee, given its track record in favor of gun control. Instead, he hoped the House would defeat HR 4296, giving him the leverage to strip the ban from the omnibus crime bill in conference. Recent history was on his side; the House had voted 247–177 in 1991 to remove a similar ban from a previous anticrime package. (*Congress and the Nation Vol. VIII, p. 788*)

This time, however, the framework of the debate had changed, and a vote to ban assault weapons was seen as a vote to fight crime. "At a time when there is a very real and palpable fear of violent crime in this country, when law enforcement officials are outgunned by the offenders . . . we must do something significant to protect our families," said Michael A. Andrews, D-Texas, who switched from his 1991 stance to support the ban.

Polls had long indicated that gun control advocates had a majority of the public on their side. But in the past they could not compete with the intense political pressure generated by gun rights advocates and their leading lobbyist, the National Rifle Association (NRA). Even in 1994, lawmakers said, these opponents held the upper hand in campaign contributions and organized phone calls to members.

But this time, lawmakers faced an equally potent political force on the issue of crime. Just as public anger over violence drove lawmakers to approve record amounts for prison construction and other crime control programs, it pushed many toward a weapons ban that voters and police said could reduce violent killings.

Lawmakers also encountered an energetic and high-profile lobbying campaign by Clinton and his Cabinet. Clinton helped keep the issue on the nightly news in the days leading up to the vote and called dozens of members seeking their support. Treasury Secretary Lloyd Bentsen, a former Democratic senator from Texas, even went to Capitol Hill to hold last-minute meetings with undecided members in a room off the House floor.

On May 5, in a stunning turnaround, the House narrowly passed the bill, **on a key vote of 216–214 (R 38–137; D 177–77; I 1–0).** Supporters prevailed on the strength of votes from freshmen—who favored the ban by a 64 to 51 margin—and from the 30 veteran members who voted "yea" after having opposed the ban in 1991. (*1994 key votes, p. 1003*)

In the closing moments of the tense House floor vote, Andrew Jacobs Jr., D-Ind., reversed his recorded vote and cast a pivotal—perhaps deciding—"yea." Jacobs said he did not think it made sense to outlaw some semiautomatics and not others as the bill proposed to do. But he said he could not pass up the chance to do away with the large ammunition clips that allowed a criminal to fire many shots without reloading.

As expected, geography was a good indicator of members' votes. Lawmakers from urban areas and the Northeast corridor generally supported the ban, while those from rural areas and southern and western districts typically opposed it.

All told, 33 members switched their stances from 1991: 30 went from opposing to supporting the ban, and three went the other direction. Of the 30, eight were retiring from politics and four were seeking a statewide office. Four of the 30 had received contributions from the NRA in the 1993–1994 election cycle, as did one of the three who switched from support to opposition.

CONFERENCE AND FINAL ACTION

House and Senate conferees had held a single, ceremonial meeting June 16 before bogging down as Democrats struggled to resolve internal party conflicts, primarily on the death penalty. That logjam broke in mid-July, when the administration and Democratic leaders decided to split with liberals and the black caucus and drop the Racial Justice Act from the bill.

By that time, Brooks and Biden had narrowed many of the differences between the two bills and had compiled a draft compromise on all but the most contentious issues. The formal conference began in earnest the morning of July 26 and ended about 48 hours later, including a 16-hour marathon session that ran into the early hours of July 28.

House and Senate Republican negotiators initially complained that they had had little advance consultation on the emerging bill and that Brooks was trying to rush it through the conference. They proceeded to offer numerous amendments during the negotiating sessions, several of them aimed at securing more money for prison construction and greatly reducing the $7.6 billion in the bill for crime-prevention programs.

Hatch attacked many of those prevention programs as new versions of abandoned federal programs, such as revenue sharing, and said they had no place in an anticrime bill. But Democrats defeated efforts to cut such funds, which they said represented an equally if not more promising route toward crime reduction than increased incarceration.

Republicans got their way on the Racial Justice Act after Senate Republicans threatened to filibuster if the provision remained in the bill. Although the House Democratic conferees tried to keep the measure alive, they were blocked by Senate Democrats, who argued that the provision would kill the bill.

On the gun control front, Brooks scored a victory for gun rights advocates when he attached provisions to exempt pawnshops from the 1993 Brady law (HR 1025—PL 103-159). The exemption, which Metzenbaum and other gun control advocates tried in vain to block, allowed pawnbrokers to forgo background checks on customers trying to reclaim their own handguns.

Brooks also won inclusion of a Senate provision designed to protect hunters from protesters. Those concessions by gun control advocates helped clear the way for conferees to retain the ban on assault weapons in the final bill. After failing to delete the ban in behind-the-scenes negotiations, Brooks offered a motion to remove the ban during the conference. It was defeated by the House conferees, 4–6, with Hyde voting with five Democratic conferees to retain the ban.

The conference agreement also strengthened the rules for federal firearms dealers, prohibited most sales or transfers of handguns to minors and blocked people subject to a court restraining order from obtaining a gun.

Another key area of dispute was how much to spend on prison construction and what terms to attach to prison building grants. Republicans wanted to authorize about $13 billion for prison construction and require qualifying states to adopt stringent truth-in-sentencing laws. Most Democrats supported substantially less prison construction money and greater flexibility for states. The conferees eventually agreed to provide $8.7 billion for state prisons and boot camps, with half the money targeted to states with truth-in-sentencing laws. An additional $1.8 billion was authorized to help states incarcerate illegal immigrants who had been convicted of felonies.

One of Biden's top priorities in the bill was a Senate-passed provision to create a new federal civil rights violation for crimes motivated by gender. The measure allowed victims of such crimes to sue for damages or other relief. Advocates said it was an important, practical and symbolic step because many state justice systems did not take attacks on women seriously.

The House bill did not include the provision, and it came under attack as an unwarranted and unwieldy burden to the federal courts. Nevertheless, House Democrats deferred to Biden and agreed to keep the provision in the conference report.

The House conferees held the upper hand on a number of other issues. Over Republican objections, conferees dropped some of the "get-tough" Senate measures altogether, such as imposing mandatory minimum sentences for gang activity and making a federal crime out of any offense involving the interstate transportation of a gun. In other areas, such as trying certain juveniles as adults or mandating life imprisonment for a third violent crime, conferees adopted the less stringent versions favored by the House and the administration.

By the time the conferees had finished their work on July 28, the spending authorized by the bill had ballooned to $33 billion over six years, with $30.2 billion coming out of the trust fund—up from $22.3 billion over five years in the Senate bill. Clinton and top congressional Democrats hailed the result as a promising blend of crime-fighting strategies and a political breakthrough after years of partisan gridlock. Republicans, however, attacked Democrats for weighing down the bill with billions of dollars for social programs they said had little to do with crime fighting. "This is not a Christmas tree, this is the whole Emerald City of Oz," said Hyde, a House negotiator.

Rule Rejected

With Republicans steaming about Brooks's handling of the conference, Democratic leaders had to muster an unusual degree of party unity behind the conference report (H Rept 103-694) in order to win its approval. Instead, they were jarred by defections among liberals who opposed the bill's death penalty provisions and conservatives who opposed the ban on assault weapons.

In a stunning defeat for the Democratic leadership, the House rejected the proposed rule for debating the conference report Aug. 11 on a **key vote of 210–225 (R 11–167; D 198–58; I 1–0).** Most of the Democrats opposing the rule were southern gun rights advocates, but 10 were members of the Congressional Black Caucus who were angered by the deletion of the Racial Justice Act. *(1994 key votes, p. 1003)*

Democrats blamed tenacious opposition by the NRA and by Republicans intent on denying Clinton a political victory on the crime issue. Republicans, however, said the bill was brought down by its contents—too few measures to toughen punishment, too much social spending "pork"—and an arrogant House leadership that tried to force the final product on GOP members.

Indeed, Brooks had made full use of the powers of the majority in trying to push the conference report through the House. He waited until the last minute to file the text of the massive bill, delivering the hefty document to the House desk at 7 p.m. on Aug. 10—almost two weeks after the conferees had wrapped up their work. One hour later, the Rules Committee convened and approved the procedures for floor consideration on a 6–4, party-line vote.

The White House also had launched a major push, with Chief of Staff Leon E. Panetta and other administration officials patrolling the Hill to lobby undecided lawmakers. Democratic whips set up a command post in a room off the chamber with an open telephone line for Clinton to speak to wavering lawmakers. Still, the efforts were unavailing.

Immediately after the vote on the rule, Dole and House Minority Whip Newt Gingrich, R-Ga., faxed Clinton aboard *Air Force One*, offering to help rework the bill to win GOP votes. Republicans wanted to add more death penalties, mandatory sentences and prison construction money while cutting back on crime prevention activities. Many also opposed the weapons ban.

House Democratic leaders initially sought to win over enough of the dissident Democrats to salvage the conference report. Privately, Foley and other top Democrats floated plans to modify the assault weapons ban, shift it into a separate bill or drop it altogether. It eventually became clear, however, that there was no middle ground on the issue between the gun rights Democrats, who would not support any version of the ban, and Clinton, who insisted that the ban stay in the bill.

In the face of that impasse, House leaders turned toward cutting a deal with Republicans. GOP support had remained a moving target throughout the week after the vote, with Republicans split into factions with varied demands. Gingrich and the four key Republican crime bill conferees on Aug. 18 called for major changes in the bill, including dropping $5.5 billion in spending and inserting GOP-backed sentencing measures opposed by many Democrats. A cadre of moderate, pro-gun control Republicans sought their own deal with Democrats, seeking limited spending cuts and selected policy changes. This GOP group, whose leaders included Michael N. Castle of Delaware, Susan Molinari of New York and Scott L. Klug of Wisconsin, helped the White House and top congressional Democrats forge a package of amendments designed to secure the votes of Republican moderates.

Second Conference

On Aug. 19, House leaders sent the bill back to conference. A weekend of marathon negotiations produced agreement on a $30.2 billion bill that was approved by conferees shortly after 3 a.m. on Sunday, Aug. 21 (H Rept 103-711).

The revised bill cost $3.3 billion less than the original conference report, bringing the measure into line with the size of the trust fund. Most of the cuts—$2 billion—came from the prevention programs that Clinton and Democrats had favored. Negotiators shrank their funding from $8.9 billion to $6.9 billion by eliminating $900 million in job training for youths and trimming other programs by 10 percent. They also cut funding for the Violence Against Women Act from $1.8 billion to $1.6 billion, cut drug court funding from $1.3 billion to $1 billion and reduced prison construction grants from $8.7 billion to $7.9 billion.

Clinton succeeded in keeping the controversial ban on 19 assault weapons, although conferees made modest adjustments to it. The measure banned ammunition-feeding devices that held more than 10 rounds, but House negotiators struck a ban on any combination of parts that could be assembled into such a feeding device. Negotiators also changed a provision requiring a defendant charged with possession of a banned ammunition clip to prove that the clip was purchased before the ban was enacted. Instead, the prosecutor was required to show that a clip was purchased after the ban.

In an unusual Sunday session later that day, the House approved a rule for debating the second conference report, 239–189, with 42 Republicans voting "yea" and 55 Democrats voting "nay." A GOP motion to send the measure back to conference with instructions to drop the weapons ban, cut prevention money, add money for prisons and police and remove some of the new death penalty measures was defeated by a similar margin, 197–232. The House then adopted the second conference report on a **key vote of 235–195 (R 46–131; D 188–64; I 1–0)**. *(1994 key votes, p. 1003)*

Senate Maneuvers

The spirit of limited bipartisanship that had prevailed in the House on Aug. 21 evaporated as soon as the conference report reached the Senate. Minority Leader Dole rallied his troops against the legislation, arguing that it contained too much pork barrel spending on social programs and too few tough sentencing provisions. "We swallowed a little pork last fall," he said Aug. 23. "We can't swallow the whole hog."

Democrats saw things differently. Many felt that the GOP, at the behest of the NRA, was trying to hold up the bill to remove the weapons ban. Indeed, the NRA lobbied intensely during the week, and some Republicans felt strongly about dropping the gun ban. But GOP leaders insisted that other issues were fueling their fight. Indeed, Dole did not seek to drop the ban during the later stages of negotiations.

On Aug. 22, Dole threatened to subject the bill to a budgetary point of order, a procedural move to block legislation on the grounds that it violated Senate budget rules. Republicans said the crime bill broke the rules because its funding mechanism—the crime trust fund—had not been reviewed by the Senate Budget Committee. Sixty votes were needed to waive a point of order; 41 were needed to sustain it.

If the point of order had been sustained, the conference report would have been invalidated. Under that scenario, the Senate would have been forced to choose between passing the House version of HR 3355, which contained no weapons ban, and starting a new round of amendments and negotiations with the House.

On Aug. 23, Dole produced a letter with 40 GOP signatures, not including his own, threatening to support the point of order unless the administration and Democratic leaders agreed to negotiate changes in the bill. All but three Republicans—Arlen Specter, Pa., James M. Jeffords, Vt., and William V. Roth Jr., Del.—signed the letter. With the expected support of Democrat Richard C. Shelby, Ala., who opposed the crime bill, Dole seemed to have 42 votes—more than enough to back up his threat. However, three of the GOP signatories—John C. Danforth of Missouri, Nancy Landon Kassebaum of Kansas and John H. Chafee of Rhode Island—wanted a crime bill and signed the letter only to give Dole a chance to negotiate a deal with Mitchell.

The letter led to several offers and counteroffers between Dole and Mitchell. Dole sought the chance to vote on a series of GOP amendments to the bill, including a $5 billion cut in prevention programs and the addition of mandatory minimum sentences for drug and gun crimes. Mitchell refused, offering only to place the GOP proposals into a separate bill.

On Aug. 25, Mitchell offered to have the Senate vote on a $5 billion cut in prevention programs as part of a separate resolution making "technical" changes to the conference report. The proposal did not satisfy Dole, and the two sides agreed to battle over the second conference report on the Senate floor. Mitchell's offer was good enough, however, to give the moderate Republicans an excuse to split from their leader. When Dole raised his point of order later that day, Chafee, Kassebaum and Danforth defected. The Senate waived the point of order on a **key vote of 61–39 (R 6–38; D 55–1),** with Specter, Jeffords and Roth also joining the Democratic side and Shelby siding with Republicans. *(1994 key votes, p. 1003)*

After losing on the point of order, Dole demanded a cloture vote to allow those senators who vehemently opposed the weapons ban to speak and, in essence, vote on the issue once more before the conference report was adopted. After cloture was invoked by a vote of 61–38, the Senate approved the conference report by the same margin, clearing the measure for Clinton. He signed it Sept. 13.

MAJOR PROVISIONS

The enacted version of HR 3355 contained provisions to:

Police

• **Community Policing.** Authorize $8.8 billion over six years to help communities hire thousands of new police officers. The administration estimated that the money would help hire 100,000 new police officers, but some critics said it would provide substantially fewer new officers. The authorization included $1.3 billion in fiscal 1995, $1.9 billion in fiscal 1996, $1.95 billion in fiscal 1997, $1.7 billion in fiscal 1998, $1.7 billion in fiscal 1999 and $268 million in fiscal 2000.

The money was for a Justice Department grant program to promote community policing, a style of law enforcement that emphasized closer community-police relations. Communities were required to provide matching funds of at least 25 percent, with a preference for those that could pay more. Whenever the Justice Department approved multiyear grants, the federal share was supposed to decline each year. The attorney general had discretion to waive all or part of the match for needy communities.

A portion of the grant money—up to 15 percent—could be used for training or equipment to enhance community policing programs. The bulk of the money—at least 85 percent—had to be used to put more officers on the street, primarily through hiring or rehiring. However, some money could go for non-salary expenditures—such as overtime pay or computers—that had the effect of putting more officers on the street. That pool of money was limited to 20 percent in fiscal 1995 and 1996 and to 10 percent thereafter. The federal share of officer salaries was capped at $75,000 per officer.

The law included a formula guaranteeing that each state that applied for the community policing grants would receive at least one-half of 1 percent of that year's funds. It also reserved half the grants for communities with more than 150,000 people, half for those with smaller populations. Communities with more than 150,000 residents were required to apply directly to the Justice Department for the grants, while smaller communities were to apply through their state governments.

• **Police Corps.** Create a police corps program, administered by the Justice Department, to grant college or graduate scholarships for students who agreed to serve as state or local police officers for at least four years. Scholarships for each participant were capped at $10,000 per calendar year, and a total of $30,000. Participants who did not honor their commitments to serve as police officers had to repay the scholarships plus 10 percent interest. Lawmakers intended to authorize $20 million a year from fiscal years 1996 through 2000 for the program, but because of a printing or transcription error, the law specified only $20,000 a year.

The law also authorized $100 million in educational scholarships for police officers with at least two years' experience, as well as summer or part-time jobs for students interested in law enforcement careers. The federal money could provide no more than 60 percent of costs for scholarships and student jobs. The grant program was authorized at $20 million a year from fiscal 1996 through fiscal 2000, with 80 percent going for officer scholarships.

• **Police Recruiting.** Authorize $24 million a year from fiscal 1995 through fiscal 2000 for grants to help recruit and train police officers from minority neighborhoods and other areas that were underrepresented on the police force.

• **Family Support.** Authorize $25 million over five years for grants to help state and local law enforcement agencies develop "family friendly" policies for their officers. This could include offering family counseling, 24-hour child-care services and stress-reduction programs. Law enforcement agencies were supposed to match the federal funds with money or services from other sources.

• **Police Conduct.** Allow the U.S. attorney general to sue for civil relief to prohibit law enforcement officials or government authorities from engaging in a pattern of behavior that denied the civil rights of individuals. The measure required the attorney general to collect annual data on the use of excessive force by law enforcement officers.

Prisons

• **State Aid.** Authorize $7.9 billion in grants for states or multistate compacts to build new prison cells or alternative incarceration facilities, such as boot camps, to free up prison beds for violent offenders.

Half the money was for a general prison grant program designed to prod states into developing comprehensive prison management plans and helping pay for new cells. Within this pool of money, 85 percent was to be distributed to states on a formula basis designed to guarantee a minimum amount—one quarter of 1 percent—for every state, including small states. Above the minimum, money was to be allocated in proportion to the state's violent crime rate, a figure that roughly tracked population. The attorney general could award the remaining 15 percent on a discretionary basis for states with the greatest need or the ability to best utilize the money.

The other half of the overall grant money was to be awarded to states with the toughest sentencing laws, an incentive for states to adopt laws to keep prisoners in jail longer. States had to implement specific truth-in-sentencing measures, such as requiring that violent criminals serve at least 85 percent of their sentences. If states did not qualify or apply for all the money in this category, it could be transferred into the more general prison grant fund.

The grants were not supposed to constitute more than 75 percent of the total cost of a prison project. Overall, the law authorized: $175 million in fiscal 1995, $750 million in fiscal 1996, $1 billion in fiscal 1997, $1.9 billion in fiscal 1998, $2 billion in fiscal 1999 and $2.07 billion in fiscal 2000.

- **Young Offenders.** Authorize $150 million in grants to help states and localities develop alternatives to traditional incarceration for young offenders. Eligible programs included alternative sanctions, restitution or community service programs, and correctional options such as weekend incarceration and electronic monitoring.

Each participating state was guaranteed at least two-fifths of 1 percent of the grant money, with the remaining money to be distributed in proportion to the states' percentage of young offenders. The states in turn were required to distribute that money to local governments in proportion to their share of the state's corrections costs. The grants were limited to 75 percent of program costs.

- **Alien Incarceration.** Authorize $1.8 billion to help states pay for incarcerating illegal immigrants convicted of felonies. The law directed the attorney general, after receiving a written request from the affected state, to take custody of such criminal aliens—giving priority to incarcerating aggravated felons—or to compensate the state for imprisoning them. The legislation authorized $130 million in fiscal 1995, $300 million in fiscal 1996, $330 million in fiscal 1997, $350 million each in fiscal 1998 and 1999 and $340 million in fiscal 2000.

The first one-third of the money was reserved for seven states with high populations of illegal immigrants: Arizona, California, Florida, Illinois, New Jersey, New York and Texas. All 50 states could apply for the remaining money.

The provisions were initially subject to available appropriations, but the law made the payments mandatory as of October 2004.

- **Scholarships.** Prohibit federal college scholarships—known as Pell grants—from being given to federal or state prison inmates.

- **Tuberculosis.** Authorize $5 million to help develop and implement programs to prevent and treat tuberculosis in federal, state and local prisons.

- **Crowding.** Restrict the ability of federal courts to rule that prison crowding violated the Constitution's prohibition on cruel and unusual punishment by requiring that the prisoner bringing the suit prove that he or she personally was unfairly harmed by the conditions. The law specified that when federal courts did order remedies for prison overcrowding, they had to extend no further than necessary to correct the conditions for the plaintiff bringing the suit. The provisions also allowed states to seek to modify a consent decree or court order related to unfair prison conditions every two years.

- **Prisoner Suits.** Make it more difficult for prisoners to sue for civil rights violations by doubling the length of time, from 90 days to 180 days, during which they were blocked from filing suit and had to first exhaust administrative remedies.

- **Job Training.** Establish, within the Department of Justice, an office to promote job training and placement for prisoners and ex-offenders. The office would help coordinate such job training and placement within the federal government and provide technical assistance for comparable state and local efforts.

- **Military Bases.** Require, within 180 days of enactment, a joint Defense and Justice Department study examining the suitability of creating federal prison facilities at military bases slated to be closed.

- **Post-release Drug Testing.** Require drug testing for certain federal prisoners who were released on probation or parole. These prisoners had to agree to stay drug-free and would be subject to at least three drug tests, the first within 15 days of their release. A positive result could be grounds for reimprisonment.

- **Release Notification.** Require federal prison officials to notify local law enforcement officials when a prisoner convicted of a federal violent crime or drug trafficking offense was released into the community.

Prevention

- **Model Intensive Grants.** Authorize $625.5 million in fiscal 1996 through 2000 to funnel intensive prevention services to up to 15 poor, high-crime areas.

Communities that applied for grants had to present a comprehensive plan to combat factors that could foster crime—such as inadequate public facilities, poor lighting, unemployment or lack of drug treatment facilities.

The U.S. attorney general had discretion over how to award the grants, but the law directed that the resources be spread among different geographic areas, including rural as well as urban communities. It directed that priority be given to innovative programs and to finance a variety of approaches.

- **Local Partnership Act.** Authorize $1.6 billion in fiscal 1996 through 2000 for direct aid to poor communities. The aid was to be distributed according to a formula that took into account a community's relative poverty and unemployment rates, plus local tax rates—which would reward those that were doing more "self help" through local taxation. The aid was intended for education, substance abuse treatment or jobs programs related to crime prevention. Programs were supposed to be similar to federal efforts such as Head Start and the Job Training Partnership Act. The Department of Housing and Urban Development would distribute the grants.

The law set out fiscal guidelines for local grant expenditures and generally required that at least 10 percent of the contracts go to small businesses run by women or disadvantaged groups, and to colleges that were historically black or whose student bodies were at least 20 percent Hispanic or Native American. Local governments had to hold at least one public hearing on how they planned to spend the money.

• **Ounce of Prevention.** Create an "Ounce of Prevention" council to coordinate prevention programs authorized by the law and to help improve crime prevention policy and assistance to localities.

Nine top administration officials were to sit on the council—the heads of the departments of Justice, Education, Health and Human Services, Housing and Urban Development, Labor, Agriculture, Treasury and Interior as well as the head of the Office of National Drug Control Policy.

The law also authorized $90 million in fiscal 1995 through 2000 for "Ounce of Prevention" grants for after-school and summer youth programs (such as tutoring or recreation), employment skills and job placement, and substance abuse and prevention programs including outreach to troubled families.

The grants were not to make up more than 75 percent of program costs. The fiscal 1995 authorization to establish the council was $1.5 million, with the grant programs expected to begin in fiscal 1996.

• **School Programs.** Support children through several school programs, including:

• **In-school.** Grants for school-based programs to provide academic and other support to youth at risk of becoming involved in crime or drugs. The law authorized $243 million for these grants in fiscal 1995 through 2000, to be administered by the Department of Education and aimed at poor and high-crime neighborhoods.

• **After-school.** Grants of up to $567 million in fiscal 1995 through 2000 to help community organizations run after-school, weekend and summer programs for youth, including tutoring, crafts and athletics. This was to be a formula grant program to be run by the Department of Health and Human Services. The federal share of these programs would be capped at 75 percent in fiscal 1995 and decline to 60 percent or less in fiscal 1998 and later. The money could not be used for religious activities.

• **Youth Academies.** Grants of $36 million in fiscal 1996 through 2000 to public agencies and nonprofit organizations to help dropouts and other "at risk" youth, ages 11 through 19, improve their academic or job skills and enhance their self-esteem.

• **Economic Partnerships.** Seek to stimulate business and job opportunities for the unemployed and for low-income people. The law authorized the secretary of Health and Human Services to extend credit to community development corporations,

up to $2 million per agency, to help them provide loans for local economic development. These development corporations generally were required to produce local funds equal to or greater than the amount requested from the federal government. The law also authorized annual grants of up to $75,000 per agency to improve management skills within these community agencies and to help them operate or expand.

The program was authorized at $270 million in fiscal 1996 through 1999. Sixty percent of that money was earmarked for creating enhanced loan capability and 40 percent for grants to strengthen the development corporations.

• **Urban Parks.** Provide grants to create or expand recreation facilities in urban and high-crime neighborhoods. The law authorized $4.5 million for these grants in fiscal 1996 through 2000.

• **Family Unity.** Encourage experimental programs that placed certain nonviolent offenders in community corrections facilities where they could continue to live with their children, who would move in. The law authorized $19.8 million in fiscal 1996 through 2000 for such demonstration projects. Of that money, 90 percent was for state grants and 10 percent for use by federal prison officials.

• **Gang Resistance.** Expand an existing program to deter juveniles from joining gangs. The law authorized $45.5 million in fiscal 1995 through 2000 for the Gang Resistance Education and Training (GREAT) program, to fund at least 50 new projects.

• **Block Grant.** Establish a block grant program to help localities prevent crime, most of it for programs to steer young people away from crime. The law directed the attorney general to distribute grants to local governments under a formula that roughly tracked the violent crime rate but also guaranteed some funds for all states. The law authorized $377 million for the grants in fiscal 1996 through 2000, which could be used for one or more of the following:

• **Jobs Programs.** Programs aimed at steering youth and young adults, ages 16 through 25, to permanent employment.

• **Sports Programs.** Midnight sports leagues that provided night-time sports opportunities for youth, in conjunction with mandatory job counseling and education classes; other supervised sports programs outside of school, including Olympic Youth Development Centers to be run in coordination with the United States Olympic Committee.

• **Boys Clubs and Girls Clubs.** Grants to establish such clubs in public housing.

• **Visitation Centers.** Supervised visitation centers where a parent with a history of child abuse or domestic violence could visit a child.

• **Youth Violence.** Programs to prevent gang and drug involvement and create youth anticrime councils that would give teenagers a mechanism to work with school and community officials to combat youth violence.

• **Partnership with Kids.** Partnership programs between police agencies and child and family service organizations, such as round-the-clock consultation services for children who were crime victims, officer training in child psychology and training for children in how to resolve conflicts.

- **Seniors.** Programs to improve law enforcement and other surveillance in specific areas to create "safety corridors" for the elderly. In particular, the law sought to promote programs based on the "triad" model, involving alliances among local sheriffs, police chiefs and senior citizens' organizations.
- **Police Housing.** Free or subsidized housing for police officers to encourage them to live in high-crime areas.
- **Family Outreach Teams.** Teams with experience in youth, parent and school issues to train local volunteers in counseling and mentoring activities.

Violence Against Women

- **Federal Crimes.** Create federal penalties for interstate stalking or domestic abuse. The provision applied to cases in which the abuser crossed a state line to harass or injure his or her victim, or forced the victim to cross state lines under duress, and went on to physically harm the victim in the course of a violent crime. Offenders were subject to up to five years in prison for violating the law. Prison terms could run to 10 years, 20 years or life if the offender used a dangerous weapon, caused serious physical harm or killed the victim.

The law strengthened existing federal penalties for repeat sexual offenders and required restitution to victims in federal sex offense cases. It called for pretrial detention in federal sex offense or child pornography felonies and allowed evidence of prior sex offenses to be used in some subsequent trials regarding federal sex crimes.

The law set new rules of evidence specifying that a victim's past sexual behavior generally was not admissible in federal civil or criminal cases regarding sexual misconduct.

- **HIV Testing.** Allow rape victims to demand that their alleged assailants be tested for HIV, the virus that caused AIDS. A federal judge could order the testing after determining that the alleged conduct created a risk of HIV transmission. The results would be disclosed to the defendant, the victim and, at the court's discretion, the victim's parents or guardian. The victim would be allowed to share the results only with a doctor, family members, a counselor or any sexual partners since the alleged attack.
- **Civil Rights.** Create a civil rights violation for violent crimes motivated by gender, allowing victims of such crimes to sue for damages or court-ordered injunctions. The law applied to violent crimes that were generally classified as felonies provided that the victim could demonstrate, with a preponderance of evidence, that the crime was motivated by gender bias. A victim could bring a suit under this provision regardless of whether the underlying violent act was prosecuted as a criminal case. These civil rights claims could be brought in either state or federal court. The law specified that it did not give federal courts jurisdiction over state legal matters such as divorce settlements or child custody cases.
- **Grants.** Authorize $1.6 billion over six years for programs to fight violence against women.

Of that money, $800 million was authorized in fiscal 1995 through 2000 for state, tribal and local programs to improve law enforcement and victim services for crimes against women. The grants were to be administered by the Justice Department and distributed according to a formula reserving 4 percent for Native American tribes, guaranteeing at least $500,000 to each state, and distributing the rest according to state population. States and tribes were required to use at least 25 percent of the grant money for each of the following types of programs: prosecution, law enforcement and victim services.

To qualify for the grants, these governments had to pay for the medical exams of rape victims and, within two years, stop requiring victims of domestic violence to pay the court costs for filing criminal charges. Grants were limited to 75 percent of program costs.

Other grant programs included $325 million in fiscal 1996 through 2000 for battered women's shelters and $205 million for rape prevention and education programs conducted by rape crisis centers and other nonprofit agencies. The law authorized smaller grant programs to pay for training and other programs to help courts better handle domestic violence and other crimes against women, programs to help homeless or runaway youths who had been sexually abused, programs to help prosecute child abuse cases, safety improvements in parks and on public transportation, and enforcement of domestic violence and child abuse laws in rural areas.

- **Arrest Policies.** Seek to encourage states to adopt mandatory arrest policies for domestic abuse or violation of a protection order. The law authorized $120 million in grants from fiscal 1996 through 1998 to help implement such policies. To qualify, states had to show that their policies encouraged or required arrests for domestic violence and did not penalize victims—by forcing them, for instance, to bear the costs of filing criminal charges against their abusers. Grantees would have up to two years to meet the requirements.
- **Hotline.** Establish a toll-free national hotline on family violence, with funding authorized at $1 million in fiscal 1995 and $400,000 per year in fiscal 1996 through 2000.
- **Immigrant Women.** Allow battered immigrant spouses or children to petition for legal residency and obtain a work permit. The provision sought to address cases in which immigrants had to stay with an abuser or risk deportation. It set various conditions on who qualified for permission to stay in the United States.

Drug Treatment and Control

- **Prisoners.** Lay out a schedule for all federal inmates addicted to drugs to have access to drug treatment: 50 percent by the end of fiscal 1995, 75 percent by the end of fiscal 1996 and the rest by the end of fiscal 1997. The bill authorized $113 million for this treatment. It authorized the Bureau of Prisons to release nonviolent offenders up to one year early once they had successfully completed a drug treatment program.

The law also authorized $270 million for grants to help provide drug treatment for inmates in state prisons. The federal share of such programs was limited to 75 percent. To qualify for grants, states had to agree to conduct ongoing drug tests of program participants as long as they were in state custody. Each participating state would receive at least two-fifths of 1 percent of the grant money, with the rest allocated in proportion to the number of state prisoners per state.

• **Drug Courts.** Authorize $1 billion over six years for grant programs to promote so-called drug courts, aimed at rehabilitating nonviolent drug offenders. Typically, a drug court program offered offenders intensive probation, including drug testing, treatment and job training, in place of conventional incarceration. Anyone who violated the program's terms faced alternative punishment such as community service, electronic monitoring or boot camp. If these did not work, the offender eventually could face traditional incarceration.

The law specified that those convicted of violent offenses, including carrying a gun during a crime, could not participate in these programs. The Justice Department was directed to suspend support for a drug court program if this condition was being violated.

The federal share of drug court programs funded under this provision was capped at 75 percent. Annual appropriations were authorized as follows: $100 million in fiscal 1995, $150 million each in fiscal 1996 and 1997 and $200 million annually in fiscal 1998, 1999 and 2000.

• **Drug Sentencing.** Direct the U.S. Sentencing Commission to stiffen sentencing guidelines for manufacturing or dealing in areas designated as drug-free zones, usually near schools or playgrounds. The sentencing commission also was instructed to amend its guidelines to enhance sentencing for those possessing, smuggling or distributing illegal narcotics in federal prison. Prisoners convicted of such crimes would not be eligible for parole.

• **Recidivism.** Broaden the legal definition of a "prior felony drug offense" to include any drug offense punishable by more than one year in prison. Defendants with prior drug felonies could draw stiffer sentences for subsequent crimes.

• **Advertising.** Make illegal the placement of any written advertisement in a newspaper, magazine or other publication seeking to sell or offering to buy an illegal narcotic. This prohibition did not apply to ads that advocated a position concerning drugs, as long as they did not seek to facilitate or propose a transaction.

• **Emergency Areas.** Allow the president to designate Violent Crime and Drug Emergency Areas in any place with particularly high levels of violence and drug abuse. The president could direct federal agencies to help state and local law enforcement in these areas with manpower, funds and technical and advisory assistance.

• **Drug Control Strategy.** Codify an executive order requiring the director of the Office of National Drug Control Policy to submit budget directives on July 1 to those agencies involved in drug policy. Agencies were to comply with these instructions, which would address funding priorities.

The director also was to include an evaluation of federal drug control efforts for the previous year in each annual Drug Control Strategy, submitted every Feb. 1. This was to include: an assessment of drug availability, the levels of drug use and availability of drug treatment.

The office was to receive no more than $100 million each year from the Department of Justice's Special Forfeiture Fund, which contained forfeited assets seized by the department from convicted criminals.

The office was reauthorized until Sept. 30, 1997.

Death Penalty Offenses

• **Capital Crimes.** Authorize the death penalty for several dozen federal crimes, including treason, genocide and causing a death through a train wreck or mailing explosives. Most, but not all, of the death penalty offenses involved a direct killing. An exception was certain major drug felonies committed by a drug "kingpin." The bill also authorized the federal death penalty for gun murders committed during a federal drug felony or violent felony.

The law effectively reactivated the death penalty for more than a dozen capital crimes already on the books, including assassination of the president or other top government official, espionage and kidnapping resulting in death. These potential death penalties had been unenforceable since 1972, when the U.S. Supreme Court ruled that there were not sufficient safeguards against arbitrariness in capital punishment litigation. The new anticrime law sought to correct that legal defect by establishing new procedures for federal death penalty prosecutions, such as laying out aggravating and mitigating factors to be considered when determining if the death penalty should be invoked.

The legislation also extended the federal death penalty to dozens of new and existing federal crimes—including lethal drive-by shootings, a retaliatory murder of an informant or witness, and civil rights murders.

• **Procedures.** Require under the new procedures that federal prosecutors notify the court and the defendant a reasonable time before the start of a trial if they planned to seek the death penalty. The law required a two-phase trial, the first to determine guilt and, if there was a conviction, a second to determine whether the death penalty was warranted. Both were to be jury trials unless the defendant requested that a judge determine one or both. The government was required to provide two lawyers for poor defendants, instead of one as required in previous law. Any death penalty sentence was subject to review by a U.S. Court of Appeals and the Supreme Court. The federal government was barred from imposing the death penalty on those under 18 at the time of the crime, or those who were mentally retarded or lacked the mental capacity "to understand the death penalty and why it was imposed on that person." Women could not be executed while they were pregnant.

Jurors had to be told that they should not consider the race, color, religion, national origin or sex of the defendant or victim in determining the proper sentence, and they had to certify that they acted without such bias.

The federal death penalty generally would not apply on tribal lands, which typically were subject to federal jurisdiction, if the location of the crime was the only reason that it fell under federal jurisdiction.

Mandatory Sentences, Other Penalties

• **Three Strikes.** Require life imprisonment for someone convicted of a third violent felony, known as the "three strikes and you're out" provision. A "strike" consisted of a serious state or federal violent felony conviction, generally defined as those with a potential sentence of 10 years or more. The first two felonies could be state offenses, while the last had to be a federal violent felony charge. A serious drug offense could constitute one of the first two "strikes," but not the third. At least two of the three felony convictions had to stem from different incidents.

The law included a discretionary release clause for those prisoners sentenced to life under this provision who were at least 70 years old and had served at least 30 years.

The three-strike provisions did not apply to crimes on Native American lands unless the tribe chose to have them apply.

• **Safety Valve.** Allow a relaxation of existing mandatory minimum sentences for first-time nonviolent drug offenders in select circumstances. Judges were given authority to relax these mandatory sentences after determining that the defendant met certain criteria, among them that the defendant had provided all the information he or she had regarding the crime to law enforcement authorities. The law directed the U.S. Sentencing Commission to reexamine and potentially to adjust the corresponding sentencing guidelines for such offenses, but it also said the commission should retain a minimum penalty of at least two years.

This provision applied to sentences issued 10 days after the law's enactment, and onward.

• **Hate Crimes.** Direct the U.S. Sentencing Commission to increase sentences for so-called hate crimes—crimes in which the defendant selected a victim on the basis of race, color, religion, national origin, ethnicity, gender, disability or sexual orientation. The provision generally increased sentences by about one-third.

Guns

• **Assault Weapons.** Ban the manufacture, sale or possession of certain semiautomatic guns known as assault weapons. Guns affected by the ban included a list of about 19 specific guns, copycat models of those guns or semiautomatic weapons with at least two features associated with assault weapons. Such features, which were specified in the law, included a bayonet mount or grenade launcher, or folding or telescoping stock.

The law specifically exempted about 670 semiautomatic guns that gun control advocates said were used for sporting purposes, as well as guns possessed lawfully before enactment of the ban.

It also banned large-capacity feeding devices that held more than 10 rounds of ammunition. In prosecutions, the burden was to rest with the government to prove that such clips were purchased after the law's enactment. The law required serial numbers for any large capacity ammunition clips manufactured after enactment, presumably for use by law enforcement officials or others still allowed to possess them.

Violators of the weapons ban could be punished with a fine of up to $5,000, a five-year sentence or both. The restrictions expired after 10 years.

The military and police still could use the banned weapons and feeding devices. The law required the attorney general to complete, within two years of enactment, a study of the impact of the ban on drug trafficking and violent crime.

• **Youth Gun Ban.** Ban the sale or transfer of a handgun or handgun ammunition to a juvenile without parental consent, and generally prohibit juveniles from possessing a handgun or handgun ammunition except under specific circumstances, such as for ranching work, target practice, hunting or the military. Some of those exceptions required the juvenile to have prior written consent from a parent or guardian.

Violators, juvenile or otherwise, generally were subject to a maximum of one year in jail. But an adult who sold or transferred a handgun or ammunition to a minor knowing that the minor planned to use it in a violent crime could be imprisoned for up to 10 years.

• **Domestic Violence.** Prohibit the possession of a firearm by someone subject to a restraining order to prevent him or her from harassing, stalking or interfering with a spouse or intimate partner or that person's child. The court order had to find that the person was a credible threat to the intimate partner or child, and specifically prohibit the use or threat of force against them. Those who knowingly sold, transferred or obtained a gun in violation of the law were subject to up to 10 years in prison.

• **Firearms Licenses.** Strengthen federal requirements for obtaining a firearms dealer license, including mandating that applicants submit their photographs and fingerprints and certify that they would be in full compliance with state and local laws. Federal officials had 60 days, instead of 45, to act on applications and also had to notify local law enforcement officials about the application for a dealer license.

Firearms dealers were required to report the theft or loss of a gun within two days and to respond to federal tracing requests within 24 hours. Federal authorities had the right to inspect dealers whenever a gun used during a crime was traced back to them; under prior law, federal officials were limited to one inspection per year without a warrant.

• **Penalties.** Increase penalties for a number of federal gun crimes, including using a semiautomatic weapon in a federal violent or drug trafficking crime, interstate gun trafficking and making a false statement when purchasing a gun from a federally licensed dealer. The law also made it a penalty to smuggle guns into the country for use in a violent crime or drug trafficking.

• **Hunting Rights.** Make it a federal crime to physically interfere with a lawful hunt on federal land and provide for court injunctions to block potential interference. Violators were subject to civil penalties of up to $10,000.

• **Pawnbrokers.** Exempt pawnbrokers and their customers from the five-day waiting period required under the Brady bill (PL 103-159) when a customer was redeeming his or her own handgun. The waiting period was to allow for background checks on prospective purchasers.

Terrorism

• **Penalties** Make it a federal offense to provide material support, such as weapons or lodging, to a terrorist. The offense was punishable by fines and up to 10 years in jail.

The statute extended the legal deadlines for prosecuting certain types of terrorist-related crimes, and directed the U.S. Sentencing Commission to stiffen the recommended punishment for felonies intended to promote terrorism. It sought to extend the reach of U.S. criminal law to cover offenses committed by or against Americans on a ship scheduled to enter or depart from a U.S. port.

• **Informants.** Authorize the U.S. attorney general to admit a limited number of foreigners to the United States if they could provide information about criminal organizations or terrorist activities. These foreigners had to report regularly to the Justice Department and generally could not stay longer than three years.

Immigration

• **Border Patrol.** Authorize $1.2 billion, almost all of it in fiscal 1995 through 1998, to strengthen operations of the Immigration and Naturalization Service.

The money included $675 million in fiscal 1995–1998 to improve border enforcement, including adding 4,000 Border Patrol agents and purchasing up-to-date equipment for border agents, as well as strengthening inspection and deportation programs for those who illegally overstayed their visas.

• **Criminal Aliens.** Expedite deportation of nonpermanent resident aliens convicted of an aggravated felony, eliminating the existing requirement for an administrative deportation hearing. Judicial review of such deportation orders was to be available, but under several restrictions.

The law authorized $160 million in fiscal 1995–1998 to expand a program under which federal officials began deportation hearings before criminal aliens finished serving their sentences, allowing for prompt deportation upon release.

It also created a criminal alien tracking center, authorized at $18.4 million in fiscal 1996–2000, to help identify and locate aliens who were eligible for deportation because of their criminal records.

• **Asylum Claims.** Authorize $338 million in fiscal 1995–1998 to speed the processing of asylum claims and the deportation of those whose claims were denied. The money was to be used to hire more asylum officers and judges to hear these cases, which were seriously backlogged. The law generally authorized the U.S. attorney general to institute expedited procedures to hear asylum claims and deport unsuccessful applicants. It specified that asylum applicants were not eligible for work papers except with special Justice Department authorization.

• **Penalties.** Increase penalties for smuggling undocumented immigrants into the United States to up to 10 years in prison (and possible fines) for each smuggled alien. Alien smuggling that resulted in a death could bring life imprisonment or the death penalty.

The law also stiffened existing criminal penalties for immigration document fraud, including use of fraudulent work papers. It increased penalties for those who failed to obey a deportation order, or those with criminal records who tried to reenter the country illegally after deportation.

Youth Violence

• **Adult Trials.** Allow for juveniles 13 or older to be tried as adults for certain serious violent crimes and crimes involving a gun. Both the prosecutor and the presiding judge had to opt for an adult trial in these circumstances. However, the law specified that juveniles should not be incarcerated in adult prisons. It authorized sentencing adjustments, including supervised release, for defendants who showed a commitment to avoid further crimes. The provision did not apply on Native American tribal lands unless a tribe opted to implement it.

The law also authorized the federal government to help states develop systems to prosecute more 16- and 17-year-olds as adults for certain violent crimes.

• **Gangs.** Stiffen the sentences for certain federal crimes if they were committed by a repeat offender who was part of a gang. The law added up to 10 years to the sentence for certain federal drug and violent felonies.

Prosecutors were required to show that the defendant had ties to criminal gang activity but did not have to show any connection between those gang ties and the underlying offense.

• **Community Prosecutors.** Authorize $50 million over five years for a grant program to help local prosecutors, working with police, school officials and others, to identify and prosecute young violent offenders.

Crimes Against Children

• **Child Pornography.** Bar production of child pornography for import into the United States, with fines and up to 10 years in prison for the first offense and up to 20 years for a subsequent conviction. The law added this offense to the list of so-called predicate crimes that could trigger a prosecution under the Racketeer Influenced and Corrupt Organizations (RICO) Act.

The law made it a federal crime to travel overseas to have sex with a minor, even if doing so was legal in the overseas country.

It also clarified congressional intent in the 1984 child pornography law (PL 98-292), specifying that illicit child pornography included the lascivious display of genitals, either nude or covered.

• **Penalties.** Increase penalties for using children younger than 18 to distribute drugs at or near a drug-free zone, such as a school, playground or public swimming pool.

The law also strengthened federal criminal penalties against those who assaulted children 16 or younger, and directed the U.S. Sentencing Commission to stiffen recommended penalties for those who solicited a minor to commit a crime. It established a federal task force to work cooperatively with the National Center for Missing and Exploited Children and to better employ federal resources to help find such children.

Law Enforcement

• **Federal Agencies.** Authorize more than $1 billion in fiscal 1995 through 2000 in additional funds to help federal law enforcement agencies handle the increased workload expected to result from the law's enactment. The allocations were as follows: $199 million for the Justice Department; $550 million for law enforcement agencies within the Treasury Department; $245 million for the FBI; $150 million for the Drug Enforcement Administration; and $50 million for U.S. attorneys, the regional federal prosecutors nationwide.

• **Rural Crime.** Authorize $245 million from fiscal 1996 through 2000 to enforce antidrug laws in rural areas, including $5 million for special training programs for rural law enforcement officers. The law also authorized the attorney general to set up interagency task forces to combat drug trafficking in rural areas and increased the penalties for drug trafficking within 1,000 feet of a truck stop or highway rest area.

• **DNA Analysis.** Authorize measures to improve DNA analysis to solve crimes, including a total of $40 million from fiscal 1996 through 2000 in grants to states to develop and use genetic tests. The law directed the FBI to establish minimum state and federal standards regarding the quality of such tests and confidentiality of results. The law authorized $25 million to improve DNA analysis programs within the FBI.

• **Training and Automation.** Authorize $130 million in fiscal 1996 through 2000 in federal assistance to state, local and tribal criminal justice agencies to improve their training and technological capabilities. Most of the money, $100 million, was for grants for improved computer capabilities and features such as automated fingerprint identification. The rest could go toward training programs, pilot programs for gathering and analyzing information to solve violent serial crimes, and upgrading training facilities at the FBI's center in Quantico, Va.

• **Criminal Records.** Authorize $150 million in fiscal 1995 through 2000 to help states upgrade their criminal records to facilitate background checks for handgun purchasers, as required under the Brady law, and for child-care providers.

• **Criminal Registry.** Direct the attorney general to create guidelines for state registries of criminals convicted of certain crimes against children, such as kidnapping or sexual misconduct. Such criminals were required to register their addresses with state police officials for 10 years after their release from prison.

The registry program also applied to those convicted of a sexually violent offense. "Sexually violent predators"—those convicted of a violent sexual offense who a court determined had mental conditions that made them likely to commit such acts—were required to remain registered for life or until a court determined they were no longer likely to make a similar attack.

Law enforcement officials were authorized to release information from the registries to the public if it was considered necessary for public safety. States were supposed to create the registries within three years, with a possible two-year good-faith extension. Those that did not establish such registries would lose 10 percent of their federal crime-fighting funds available under the so-called Byrne program.

• **Byrne Grants.** Expand an existing grant program, known as Byrne grants, that helped fund collaborative anticrime and antidrug programs by state and local law enforcement agencies. The law authorized $1 billion from the crime trust fund for these grants in fiscal 1995 through 2000. It also expanded the list of eligible programs to include efforts aimed at improving DNA analysis, deterring gang violence, prosecuting drunken driving

offenses and prosecuting juveniles as adults for certain violent crimes.

• **Federal Judiciary.** Authorize $200 million from fiscal 1996 through 2000 to help pay for increased demands on the federal judiciary resulting from the law, including supervised release, pretrial and probation services.

• **State Courts and Prosecutors.** Authorize $150 million from fiscal 1996 through 2000 to help state courts, prosecutors and public defenders handle increased workloads resulting from the law's provisions.

Victims' Rights

• **Sentencing Hearing.** Expand the right, in federal court, of victims of violent crimes and sexual abuse to be heard at the defendant's sentencing hearing. This right could be exercised by a parent or legal guardian if the victim was younger than 18 or by one or more family members if the victim had died. Existing law gave victims the right to be heard, known as the right of allocution, only in cases where capital punishment was an option.

• **Crime Victims' Fund.** Mandate that the next $10 million deposited in the Crime Victims' Assistance Fund be made available for grants to states for crime victims' assistance. The fund was established in 1984 to compensate crime victims with money collected from federal offenders. Money on top of the $10 million was to be divided equally between grants for victims' assistance and grants for victims' compensation, with a small portion going for police training and technical assistance.

Protecting the Elderly

• **Alzheimer's Program.** Authorize $2.7 million from fiscal 1996 through 1998 to create a Missing Alzheimer's Disease Alert Program to locate missing people with Alzheimer's and related diseases.

• **Crimes Against the Elderly.** Direct the U.S. Sentencing Commission to review sentencing guidelines for violent crimes against the elderly to determine whether they were tough enough to deter these offenses.

• **Telemarketing Fraud.** Allow an additional five-year sentence for anyone convicted of telemarketing fraud. The provision allowed an additional 10-year sentence if the defendant victimized 10 or more people older than 55 or targeted people over 55.

Courts were required to order convicted defendants to pay full restitution to victims. The court was not allowed to consider the defendant's economic circumstances when determining the amount of restitution, but it could consider such circumstances when determining the manner and schedule in which restitution would be paid. The amount paid to a victim would offset any damages subsequently awarded in a civil trial. Payment of restitution was a condition for an offender's parole or supervised release.

• **Sentencing.** Direct the U.S. Sentencing Commission to review sentencing guidelines to ensure that sentences for fraud offenses against those older than 55 were stiff enough.

• **Rewards.** Allow the U.S. attorney general to pay up to $10,000 for information leading to a possible prosecution for fraud against the elderly. Informers were not eligible for this payment if they knowingly participated in the offense; had been employed by a federal, state or local government agency; gave information already publicly disclosed; or if the award would in some way benefit the person being investigated.

- **Authorization.** Authorize $20 million from fiscal 1996 through 2000 for the Department of Justice and the FBI to hire additional staff to investigate and prosecute telemarketing fraud cases and to coordinate with state agencies to prevent telemarketing fraud against senior citizens.

- **Information Network.** Require the U.S. attorney general to establish a toll-free hotline to provide general information on telemarketing fraud and to gather information related to violations.

Summit and Commission

- **Presidential summit.** Request that the president convene a national summit on violence and then establish a Commission on Crime Prevention and Control.

- **Commission on Prevention.** Authorize $1 million in fiscal 1996 to establish a 28-member Commission on Crime Prevention and Control. The commission was to develop a comprehensive proposal to prevent crime and violence that included: finding ways for federal, state and local law enforcement agencies to better coordinate their efforts; researching the economic and social factors that led to crime; determining the most efficient use of criminal justice resources such as scarce prison beds; examining the causes of drug use; determining the causes and best solutions for crime in schools and violence against women; and examining the impact of crime on minority groups. The commission was to report its findings to Congress and the president within two years.

Crime Trust Fund

Create a $30.2 billion trust fund to pay for anticrime programs authorized in the bill, drawing on the expected savings from an administration proposal to eliminate more than 250,000 federal jobs. Those workforce reductions were approved by Congress in the Federal Workforce Restructuring Act (HR 3345—PL 103-226). *(Federal buyouts, p. 814)*

The trust fund provision acted as a sort of budgetary fire wall, establishing a special budget account for the anticrime programs that was distinct from the general pot of money available for domestic programs. The arrangement effectively protected these crime-related authorizations from the usual competition for discretionary funds, while simultaneously shrinking the pot of money for which other domestic programs had to compete.

The law directed that the $30.2 billion be placed in the special budget account in yearly increments: $2.4 billion in fiscal 1995, $4.3 billion in fiscal 1996, $5 billion in fiscal 1997, $5.5 billion in fiscal 1998, $6.5 billion in fiscal 1999 and $6.5 billion in fiscal 2000.

The law limited outlays—the actual dollars spent in a given fiscal year as opposed to the amount obligated that year in the form of an appropriation—from the trust fund as follows: $703 million in fiscal 1995, $2.3 billion in fiscal 1996, $3.9 billion in fiscal 1997, $4.9 billion in fiscal 1998, $5.6 billion in fiscal 1999 and $6.2 billion in fiscal 2000. It called for sequestration—automatic across-the-board cuts—within the trust fund if spending for programs within the fund exceeded the specified limits. The law also set corresponding reductions in overall discretionary spending caps for those years.

The money was set aside for anticrime programs, but appropriators still had to approve the spending as part of the annual appropriations process. Unspent trust fund money could not be spent on other programs; it had to go for deficit reduction. Appropriators also had authority to shift up to 10 percent of a program's authorized funding to other anticrime programs in the law, as long as both programs were within the same one of these three categories: federal law enforcement, state and local law enforcement, and crime prevention.

Other Provisions

- **Motor Vehicle Records.** Generally ban state motor vehicle departments from disclosing personal information about license holders except to those with a legitimate business interest. The law did not affect access to these records by law enforcement and other government agencies, the courts, insurance agencies and other specific groups. The law established criminal fines for those who knowingly disclosed or obtained this information except as permitted. And it allowed victims of such abuses to sue for civil damages. The provisions were to take effect three years after the law's enactment.

- **Motor Vehicle Theft.** Give the Justice Department six months to establish a voluntary car theft prevention program. Under the program, car owners could agree to use a decal indicating how they used their car—for instance, only for daytime commuting. The police would be authorized to stop the car if it was being used in a manner inconsistent with the decal, on the presumption that it had been stolen. The law authorized $5 million in fiscal 1996 through 1998 to establish the program.

The law also made it a federal crime to alter or remove motor vehicle identification numbers or the new decals. Offenders were subject to fines and up to five years in jail.

- **Penalties.** Stiffen federal penalties for federal crimes such as assault, manslaughter, civil rights violations, conspiracy to commit murder-for-hire, and drug trafficking near public housing. The law significantly increased federal penalties for arson and extended the statute of limitations for prosecuting such crimes. It also set federal penalties for receiving the proceeds of a kidnapping or extortion, under certain circumstances, or property stolen from the U.S. mail.

- **Insurance Fraud.** Establish federal penalties for insurance fraud. The statute made it a federal offense to defraud an insurance company that did interstate business, such as by knowingly filing a false statement with an insurance regulator or by embezzling money from a company. Offenders faced criminal penalties including fines and jail terms of up to 15 years.

The law prohibited anyone convicted of a federal crime involving dishonesty, such as insurance fraud, from working in the insurance business except with the written consent of an insurance regulator. And it authorized the U.S. attorney general to impose civil fines of up to $50,000 for the insurance fraud violations.

• **Financial Institutions.** Authorize the Secret Service, through December 2004, to conduct investigations and make arrests in connection with fraud against financial institutions. The law banned those convicted of fraud and similar crimes from working in a federally insured credit union for at least 10 years.

• **Computer Crimes.** Establish federal penalties for sending a computer transmission that caused damage or loss of access to another computer that was involved in interstate commerce. Intentional violations were subject to up to five years in jail and fines up to $250,000. Victims of such crimes also could sue for civil damages if the crime was intentional. The law authorized lesser penalties for damage from reckless transmissions.

• **Bail Reporting.** Require federal and state court clerks to notify federal law enforcement officials if they received a cash bail payment of more than $10,000 for people charged with certain offenses. The provision applied to crimes such as drug offenses, racketeering or money laundering. The clerks had to provide the names and addresses of the accused and anyone posting the bail, and the amount received.

• **Cocaine Study.** Require the U.S. Sentencing Commission to prepare a study by the end of December 1994 on the penalties for the possession or distribution of different forms of cocaine and any recommendations for changes in these penalties. The provision was aimed at addressing the criticism that existing federal penalties, which were stiffer for crack cocaine than for a comparable amount of powder cocaine, discriminated against minorities. Most of those sentenced in federal court on crack cocaine offenses were minorities.

• **Drunken Driving.** Add a year to the prison sentence otherwise given to someone convicted of drunken driving if a child under 18 was in the car and the offense was committed on federal property. The sentence could be increased up to five years if the child was seriously injured, and up to 10 years if the child was killed.

• **Wiretaps.** Make it a federal crime to disclose the results of an authorized wiretap with the intention of disrupting a criminal investigation.

• **Art Theft.** Make it a federal crime to steal an important artwork or cultural object from a museum, or knowingly receive such a stolen good. The law applied to objects that were at least 100 years old and worth more than $5,000, or those worth at least $100,000. Offenders could be fined and imprisoned for up to 10 years.

• **Travelers.** Authorize the federal government to help state officials investigate violent crimes that appeared aimed at travelers.

• **Domestic Violence.** Require that individuals convicted of domestic violence crimes in federal courts participate in a rehabilitation program as a condition of probation or supervised release.

• **Care Providers.** Expand an existing law (PL 103-209), which encouraged states to do background checks on child-care providers, to also cover those who provided care to the elderly and disabled. The law also set an $18 cap on the amount states could charge for background checks on volunteers.

• **Lottery Tickets.** Expand an existing ban on interstate sale of lottery tickets to close a loophole that had allowed ticket brokers in other states to make such sales.

• **Made in America.** Codify existing penalties, established by the Federal Trade Commission, for fraudulent use of "Made in America" or "Made in U.S.A." labels on products.

• **Residency Requirement.** Relax an existing residency requirement for assistant U.S. attorneys, allowing them to live within 25 miles of the jurisdiction in which they worked. Previously these prosecutors generally were required to live in their jurisdiction.

• **Prison Capacity.** Require the Justice Department to furnish annual reports on the impact of the preceding year's legislation on federal prison capacity and costs. Any legislation proposed by the executive or judicial branch that could alter the federal prison population had to include a prison impact assessment, and the Justice Department was instructed to prepare assessments for other legislation at the request of Congress. ❑

Brady Bill

For the first time in 25 years, Congress in 1993 cleared legislation restricting the sale of guns to law-abiding citizens. The measure (HR 1025—PL 103-159), better known as the Brady bill, required a waiting period of five business days for the purchase of all handguns, giving police time to check the prospective buyer's criminal record and giving hot tempers time to cool.

Gun control advocates, led by former White House press secretary James S. Brady and his wife, Sarah, lobbied more than seven years for a mandatory waiting period. Their efforts were stymied in previous congresses by gun rights groups, led by the powerful National Rifle Association (NRA). In 1993, however, the gun control lobby was aided by growing public support for the measure and a new ally in the White House, Bill Clinton.

Although many on both sides characterized the bill as a modest measure, it triggered an intense and emotional struggle. Members aligned with the NRA viewed the bill as the first step toward more pervasive gun control laws, ones that would deter such legitimate pursuits as hunting, target shooting or home defense. They were partially correct; Congress enacted a tougher law the following year to ban the manufacture and possession of semiautomatic "assault weapons," although lawmakers exempted guns that had already been purchased as well as hundreds of models used by sportsmen. Supporters of the Brady bill also pushed for a more restrictive ban on handgun sales in 1994, but that measure (S 1882) never made it out of committee. (*Crime bill, p. 683*)

The faction aligned with the Bradys argued that the bill would prevent thousands of homicides and suicides by keeping handguns away from two particularly dangerous classes of buyers: felons and people in the midst of a crisis. Supporters of the bill acknowledged that it would not be as effective in keeping guns out of the hands of criminals as a nationwide system of instant background checks. Such a system was not expected to be available for several years, however, and advocates argued that the bill would help prevent gun crimes in the interim.

The final version of the bill lifted the waiting period five years after enactment on the assumption that an instant-background-check system would be in place by then. To help states computerize their criminal records—the main hurdle in establishing a national system—the bill authorized $200 million annually in grants. It also required that police be notified of any multiple-gun purchase and raised licensing fees for gun dealers.

BACKGROUND

Congress had last enacted a major gun control law in 1968, a year marked by race riots and the assassinations of the Rev. Dr. Martin Luther King Jr. and Sen. Robert F. Kennedy, D-N.Y. The Gun Control Act of 1968 barred mail-order and interstate shipments of firearms and ammunition. It also established detailed licensing procedures for those who manufactured, imported, sold or collected guns and ammunition.

The 1968 law was a thorn in the side of many gun owners and dealers, who argued that it put too many restrictions on their activities and subjected them to harassment by overzealous federal authorities. Congress responded to a number of those complaints in 1986, clearing legislation (PL 99-308) to lift the interstate ban on the sale of rifles and shotguns, allow gun owners to transport their weapons across state lines, and allow more gun sales to be made without a license. *(1986 law, Congress and the Nation Vol. VII, p. 734)*

Shortly thereafter, gun control advocates began pushing for a mandatory waiting period on handgun sales. In the forefront were James Brady, who was permanently disabled in 1981 by the pistol-wielding gunman who attempted to kill President Ronald Reagan, and Sarah Brady, the head of Handgun Control Inc. They attempted to attach the waiting period to the antidrug bill enacted in 1988 (PL 100-690) but were defeated on the House floor.

The House Judiciary Committee endorsed a freestanding Brady bill in 1990. The measure stalled short of the House floor, however, in part because of opposition from House Speaker Thomas S. Foley, D-Wash. In 1991, both chambers passed versions of a crime bill that included a five-day handgun waiting period, but the proposal died when the conference report languished in the Senate. Democratic supporters tried to bring up the Brady bill as separate legislation late in 1992, but they were blocked by Republicans. *(Background, Congress and the Nation Vol. VIII, p. 765)*

LEGISLATIVE ACTION

Clinton had included the Brady bill in the anticrime package he proposed in August 1993. Responding to the president's initiative, House Judiciary Committee Chairman Jack Brooks, a Democrat from Texas who was no fan of gun control, included the waiting period in the omnibus anticrime bill (HR 3131) he introduced the following month.

Brooks's proposal called for police to use the five-day waiting period to check whether the would-be purchaser was prohibited by federal or state law from buying a handgun. It also would have phased out the federal waiting period once a viable, nationwide instant background check system was in place to block sales to felons or other unqualified buyers, and it would have authorized $100 million a year to help states set up such a system. State and local waiting periods longer than five days would not have been affected.

Late in October, Brooks agreed to let the Brady bill move separately from the rest of the anticrime package, which was caught in a crossfire of opposition from liberal Democrats and conservative Republicans. The Judiciary Committee, divided largely along party lines, approved the Brady bill (HR 1025) on Nov. 4, 23–12, after narrowly rejecting numerous amendments from bill opponents. These included proposals to require an instant-check system in lieu of a waiting period, set a date for phasing out the waiting period, eliminate state and local waiting periods once the instant-check system was operating, and require a written explanation from the police when purchases were denied. The committee reported the bill Nov. 10 (H Rept 103-344).

With both sides lobbying House members fiercely, opponents of the bill were able to reverse two of their Judiciary Committee defeats on the House floor Nov. 10. The House approved an amendment by George W. Gekas, R-Pa., phasing out the waiting period after five years, 236–198, and an amendment by Jim Ramstad, R-Wis., requiring police to give a reason within 20 days for denying a handgun purchase, 431–2.

On the other hand, the House rejected an amendment by Bill McCollum, R-Fla., to end state and local waiting periods once the instant-check system was in place, 175–257. Although McCollum said that his amendment would have applied only to waiting periods, critics, including Attorney General Janet Reno, argued that the amendment would have eliminated other state limits on handgun purchases as well, such as Virginia's limit of one gun purchase per month.

The House went on to pass the modified version of the bill on a **key vote of 238–189 (R 54–119; D 184–69; I 0–1).** *(1993 key votes, p. 979)*

In the Senate, a similar version of the Brady bill (S 414) went directly to the floor on Nov. 19 after Majority Leader George J. Mitchell, D-Maine, drafted a compromise version with Minority Leader Bob Dole, R-Kan. The compromise proposed to end the waiting period as soon as 24 months after enactment if the instant-check system were in place, and no later than five years after enactment. It also would have preempted state and local waiting periods once the instant-check system was operating. Mitchell tried on the Senate floor to eliminate the five-year sunset, but his amendment was rejected, 43–56. He succeeded in removing the preemption provision, however, 54–45.

Gun rights advocates then threatened to filibuster the bill, demanding that the preemption be reinstated. Supporters failed on two motions Nov. 19 to stop a filibuster, falling three votes shy of the 60 needed to limit debate. The news media pronounced the bill dead for the year the next morning, and many observers thought that it was. But Assistant Minority Leader Alan K. Simpson, R-Wyo., said a handful of Republicans, unhappy with the outcome, wanted a straight vote on the matter before recessing for the year. That discontent sent Dole back to the negotiating table, where he had to settle for a version only superficially different from the one Republicans had filibustered the night before.

The change was a four-year sunset for the waiting period, with the attorney general getting the authority to extend it one more year if necessary. After modifying the bill, the Senate passed it easily on Nov. 20 by a **key vote of 63–36 (R 16–28; D 47–8).** *(1993 key votes, p. 979)*

House and Senate negotiators quickly agreed on a conference report, keeping the House-passed five-year time limit with no provision for an earlier sunset. Negotiators also agreed to drop several Senate-passed firearms provisions unrelated to the core of the bill. One would have expanded the definition of antique firearms, which were exempt from regular gun restrictions, to incorporate thousands of functioning World War I era rifles. Conferees also dropped a provision allowing face-to-face gun sales between dealers from different states. The report (H Rept 103-412) was filed Nov. 22.

With lawmakers eager to recess for the year, the House conducted only a perfunctory debate before adopting the conference report Nov. 23, 238–187. That left Mitchell, Dole and a handful of senators in town to approve the report by voice vote, craft an alternative, or declare an impasse. A flurry of action ensued, punctuated by frequent news conferences as each side sought to blame the other for killing a popular bill. Dole ultimately agreed to let the Brady bill become law in exchange for a promise that the Senate would revisit the issue shortly after reconvening the next year. In particular, the deal required the Senate to take up a Dole proposal in January to end the waiting period after four years, replace the waiting period with the instant-check system as soon as 24 months after enactment, and require states to submit mental health records for the national registry.

The Senate then adopted the conference report by voice vote Nov. 24, clearing HR 1025. Clinton signed the measure Nov. 30, and the waiting period went into effect March 1, 1994.

"BRADY 2"

Dole announced early in 1994 that he was reformulating his proposal to modify the Brady bill, releasing Mitchell from his November pledge. The year ended without Dole seeking any Senate action on S 1785.

Meanwhile, gun control advocates turned their attention to a new bill (S 1882), dubbed "Brady 2." The measure would have allowed people to buy a handgun only if they held a valid state handgun license, which they could obtain by passing a background check and a firearms safety course. Even with a license, retail buyers could purchase no more than one handgun per month. The measure also sought to tighten regulation and screening of gun dealers, require sales of used guns to be registered with state police, and require gun manufacturers to install safety devices on handguns to prevent small children from accidentally discharging them.

At a Senate Judiciary subcommittee hearing on the bill March 23, sponsor Howard M. Metzenbaum, D-Ohio, argued that stricter controls were needed to reduce the flow of handguns and to stop the "epidemic" of violence resulting from a plentiful supply of firearms. But Orrin G. Hatch, R-Utah, argued that the bill would do little to reduce violent crime. "Criminals generally obtain firearms in the black market or from other criminals—not gun shops and licensed dealers," he said.

The subcommittee took no further action on the bill. Rep. Charles E. Schumer, D-N.Y., chairman of the House Judiciary Subcommittee on Crime and Criminal Justice, introduced a companion bill (HR 3932), but that measure made no progress.

One element of Brady 2 did become law, however, as part of the omnibus anticrime bill (HR 3355—PL 103-322): the ban on certain types of assault weapons. *(Crime bill, p. 683)*   ❑

Independent Counsels

Congress cleared legislation (S 24—PL 103-270) in 1994 to renew the independent counsel law for five years, opening the door for a court-appointed prosecutor to investigate the Whitewater scandal.

Originally enacted in 1978 (PL 95-521), the law set up a process for conducting independent investigations into allegations against top government officials. It lapsed at the end of 1992, however, amid a partisan squabble over independent counsel Lawrence E. Walsh's investigation of the Iran-contra affair. *(1978 law, Congress and the Nation Vol. V, p. 829)*

The 1994 bill addressed some of the critics' concerns, adding several controls on the expenses and conduct of independent counsels. Although the measure did not go nearly as far as the GOP sought, the Republicans' opposition faded as their interest grew in probing Whitewater, a wide-ranging controversy surrounding President Clinton investment in a failed Arkansas land-development project. It passed both the Senate and the House with significant bipartisan support.

BACKGROUND

The Watergate scandal was the impetus for the original independent counsel law. Previously, all investigations of top federal officials were conducted by the Justice Department, which meant they were under the indirect control of the president. In October 1973, President Richard Nixon took advantage of this feature to force the firing of Archibald Cox, the special prosecutor that the Justice Department had appointed to investigate Watergate. *(Watergate, Congress and the Nation Vol. IV, p. 931)*

The conflict of interest made clear by this episode inspired Congress in 1978 to establish a new system for investigating allegations against the president, members of the Cabinet and other top federal officials. Under the independent counsel law, the U.S. attorney general was required to conduct a "threshold inquiry" when it received allegations against a top federal official to determine if the allegations involved a specific violation of the law and if their source was credible. If those two criteria were met, the attorney general had 90 days to conduct a preliminary investigation. If this investigation found that further probing or prosecution was warranted, the attorney general was required to ask a three-judge panel to appoint a special prosecutor from outside the federal government to take over the case.

The law required the attorney general to conduct a threshold inquiry if a majority of the Republicans or Democrats on the House or Senate Judiciary Committee sent a letter requesting a special prosecutor. The law also allowed, but did not require, the attorney general to seek a special prosecutor to handle investigations into members of Congress or any other individual who might pose a conflict of interest for the Justice Department. And it authorized the attorney general to fire a special prosecutor, subject to review by the three-judge panel, for good cause or for health reasons.

Congress reauthorized the law in 1982 (PL 97-409), changing "special prosecutor" to "independent counsel." The law was reauthorized again in 1987 (PL 100-191) with President Ronald Reagan's grudging support in the wake of the Iran-contra scandal. By 1992, however, Republicans were so angry at the length, cost and handling of Walsh's investigation that they blocked bills in the House and Senate to extend the law. *(1987 law, Congress and the Nation Vol. VII, p. 773; Iran-contra affair, Congress and the Nation Vol. VII, p. 253; 1992 action, Congress and the Nation Vol. VIII, p. 795)*

Particularly irksome to Republicans were the indictments Walsh obtained in 1992 against former defense secretary Caspar W. Weinberger, whom Walsh accused of withholding information from Congress. Shortly before leaving office, President George Bush pardoned Weinberger and five other former officials who were indicted or convicted in connection with Iran-contra. *(Iran-contra pardons, Congress and the Nation Vol. VIII, p. 284)*

Walsh's six-year investigation was wrapped up in August 1993, costing an estimated $37 million. His parting shot—a report to the three-judge panel—infuriated a number of Republicans, including Senate Minority Leader Bob Dole, R-Kan. Dole said that the allegations in the report amounted to an attempt by Walsh to smear some of the people whom he had not sought to indict.

Democrats, meanwhile, were steadfast in their support for the independent counsel law. Breaking with his two predecessors, President Clinton urged Congress to reauthorize the law, as did Attorney General Janet Reno.

Late in 1993, as questions mounted about Whitewater and related topics, pressure built for an independent probe. Clinton and other Democrats eventually joined Republicans in calling for an investigation. Unable to seek a court-appointed independent counsel because the law had lapsed, Reno announced on Jan. 20, 1994, that she was appointing former U.S. Attorney Robert B. Fiske Jr. to be a special counsel for Whitewater.

LEGISLATIVE ACTION

As legislation to renew the independent counsel law moved through the House and Senate in the 103rd Congress, Republicans repeatedly sought to place more controls on the counsel's spending and to limit the length of a probe. Although sponsors of the legislation had proposed audits and new guidelines to control the cost of investigations, many Republicans argued that

more strictures were needed. Democrats argued that the Republicans' proposed restrictions would impair the counsel's independence, and only a handful of the proposals were adopted.

The GOP also sought to require that allegations against members of Congress be investigated by an independent counsel; under previous law, the attorney general was allowed to handle such inquiries within the Justice Department. Several Republicans cited real or perceived conflicts when the Justice Department investigated members of Congress, particularly high-ranking lawmakers of the same political party. Democrats successfully resisted the GOP push, arguing that there was no evidence of attorneys general being reluctant to prosecute lawmakers. Instead, they proposed to clarify that the attorney general, at his or her discretion, could request an independent counsel to investigate a member of Congress.

The two chambers took up similar bills, with the Senate approving its version (S 24) on Nov. 18, 1993, and the House approving its proposal (HR 811) on Feb. 10, 1994. The Senate bill, which the Governmental Affairs Committee had reported July 20, 1993 (S Rept 103-101), drew opposition on the floor from Dole, who argued that there was no need for independent counsels. Dole succeeded in adding amendments to require the three-judge panel to review the counsel's appointment periodically and to bar the counsel's final report from including allegations against people whom the counsel had not sought to indict.

By a vote of 67–31, however, the Senate tabled, or killed, an amendment by John McCain, R-Ariz., to require independent counsels for allegations against members of Congress. Senators also rejected, 68–29, a substitute proposal by Thad Cochran, R-Miss., that would have allowed the president to appoint a special counsel within the Justice Department to handle cases that posed a conflict of interest. The Senate then voted, 76–21, to pass the bill.

The House Judiciary Committee had approved HR 811 on March 24, 1993, on a party-line, 21–14 vote after it rejected a series of Republican amendments. It reported the bill Aug. 6, 1993 (H Rept 103-224), but the full House did not take up the measure until the following February.

The bill triggered a long, heated and partisan debate, touching on the Iran-contra investigation, the House Post Office scandal and the unfolding Whitewater controversy. In a replay of the action in the Judiciary Committee, Democrats blunted Republican attempts to bring Congress more fully under the independent counsel law and to place more controls on the counsels' tenure and budget.

George W. Gekas, R-Pa., first proposed to require that investigations into members of Congress be handled by independent counsels. His amendment was gutted, however, when the House adopted a substitute amendment by John Bryant, D-Texas, that restated the bill's original language regarding members of Congress. The vote on the Bryant amendment was 230–188.

The House then rejected, 181–238, a comprehensive alternative by Henry J. Hyde, R-Ill., that would have required independent counsels for lawmakers and tightened the oversight of independent counsels. The House ultimately passed S 24 by voice vote Feb. 10 after inserting the text of HR 811, which it had approved by a vote of 356–56.

House and Senate conferees approved a final version of S 24 on a 4–3, party-line vote May 17, reflecting the partisan split that remained over the bill. One of the sources of friction between the parties was a provision added in conference to let Fiske stay on as an independent counsel if the three-judge panel concurred. Under the previous independent counsel law, Fiske could not have become the independent counsel because, as Reno's appointee, he was a federal employee.

Republicans argued that the provision would somehow make it possible for Clinton and other subjects of the Whitewater investigation to recoup their legal costs from the taxpayers. Under the terms of the previous law and the conference report, subjects of an independent counsel investigation who were not indicted could petition the three-judge panel for reimbursement of their attorney's fees. The issue became moot in August when the three-judge panel appointed Kenneth W. Starr, a Republican who served as U.S. Solicitor General during the Bush administration, as independent counsel instead of Fiske.

The conferees filed their report May 19 (H Rept 103-511). The Senate agreed to the report by voice vote six days later, and the House adopted the report on June 21, 317–105, clearing the bill.

MAJOR PROVISIONS

As signed into law June 30, S 24 included provisions to:

• **Threshold Inquiry.** Lengthen the time the attorney general had to conduct the initial, threshold inquiry from 15 days to 30 days.

• **Attorney General Recusal.** Clarify that attorneys general had to recuse themselves from any actions under the independent counsel law if they were directly implicated in the case. The conference agreement also retained general provisions from the 1987 law governing recusal, which directed the attorney general to delegate proceedings under the law to the next-ranking Justice Department official if the attorney general had a current or recent financial or personal relationship with the subject of the allegation.

• **Congressional Coverage.** Explicitly allowed the attorney general to seek an independent counsel to investigate a member of Congress if it would be in the public interest to do so.

Under the 1987 law, the attorney general could use the independent counsel process for any person, including a member of Congress, if the attorney general felt it would create a personal, financial or political conflict of interest to conduct the investigation through regular Justice Department channels. The conference report retained that discretionary coverage provision for the general public, but made it both easier and more explicit for members of Congress by substituting the simpler "public interest" standard for the "conflict of interest" finding in their case. That change enabled the attorney general to address perceived as well as actual conflicts in investigating members of Congress.

• **Post-employment Coverage.** Require that officials covered under the law remain subject to its provisions for one year after leaving office. The 1987 law provided coverage for up to three years in some cases.

• **Independent Counsel Reports.** Require an independent counsel to file a final and comprehensive report on the investigation, but eliminate a provision in the 1987 law requiring counsels to explain their reasons for not indicting a person under scrutiny. The bill also included a new requirement that independent counsels report annually to Congress on the progress of their investigation or prosecution.

• **Justice Department.** Clarify that independent counsels could request help from the Justice Department, such as a staff member with particular expertise, and that the Justice Department was generally expected to provide such assistance. The bill required that independent counsels follow Justice Department prosecution policies except in cases when doing so would undermine the purpose of the independent counsel law.

• **Expenses.** Include new restrictions on expenses such as salaries, office space and travel costs. The bill required an independent counsel to adhere to Justice Department spending policies except in cases when doing so would undermine the purpose of the independent investigation.

The bill mandated that an independent counsel assign an employee to certify that expenditures were reasonable and generally within specified Justice Department guidelines. Staff members were not permitted to be paid more than comparable employees in the U.S. attorney's office for the District of Columbia were paid.

• **Audits.** Increase financial oversight of independent counsel investigations by the General Accounting Office (GAO). The GAO was required to review independent counsel expenses at midyear, conduct a full audit at year's end and a final audit when the investigation was closed.

• **Attorneys' Fees.** Tighten a provision allowing subjects of an independent counsel investigation to petition the three-judge panel for repayment of their attorneys' fees if they were not indicted. The bill required the panel to ask both the independent counsel and the Justice Department for comments on the merits of the request.

• **Reappointment.** Require the three-judge panel to review an independent counsel's activities two years after appointment to determine if the investigation should be terminated. If the panel allowed the investigation to continue, it had to conduct another review in two years, and annually thereafter. The 1987 law authorized the special court to terminate an investigation if the work was finished or almost finished, without any deadlines for review.

• **Transitions.** Allow special prosecutor Robert B. Fiske Jr. to continue investigating the failed Whitewater Development Co. if that case became an independent counsel investigation under the reauthorized law.

The conference agreement also included transition provisions for two independent counsel investigations that began before the law lapsed but had not finished: one into improprieties at the Department of Housing and Urban Development and another concerning leaks of President Clinton's passport records during the 1992 campaign. For example, the bill specified that the new cost controls on certain travel expenses would apply to existing investigations after one year.

• **White House Staff.** Require the White House to file a semiannual report identifying the names and salaries of people employed or detailed to the White House, except for disclosures that would run counter to national security or foreign policy interests.   ❑

FBI Access to Phone Records

Congress cleared a bill in 1993 to make it easier for the Federal Bureau of Investigation to identify suspected spies and terrorists through their phone bills.

The legislation (HR 175—PL 103-142) required phone companies to give the FBI the names and addresses of people who had used their phones to call a suspected international terrorist or foreign spy. The FBI was not required to obtain a subpoena or court order; instead, top FBI officials would merely have to certify in a "national security letter" that there was enough evidence to support their request for the records.

The measure amended the Electronic Communications Privacy Act of 1986, which required law enforcement agents to obtain a subpoena, search warrant or court order in order to see phone records without the subscriber's knowledge. Congress had previously made an exception only for suspected terrorists and spies, allowing the FBI to obtain their records by issuing a national security letter.

The FBI wanted easier access to more phone records, arguing that the previous law shielded the activities of new converts to the cause of terrorism or espionage. For example, the FBI cited the case of an unidentified federal employee who had called a foreign embassy and offered sensitive information about U.S. spying capabilities. Although the government knew about the conversation, investigators could not obtain a court order for the phone records that would have identified the employee. As a consequence, the FBI said, the government could not stop sensitive information from being lost.

The House Judiciary Committee reported the bill March 29, 1993 (H Rept 103-46), and the House passed it the same day, 376–6. The Senate cleared the bill by voice vote Nov. 4, and President Clinton signed it Nov. 17.   ❑

Kidnapping by Parents

Congress gave speedy approval late in 1993 to a bill barring a parent from abducting children not in his or her sole custody and taking them out of the United States. The measure (HR 3378—PL 103-173) authorized the federal government to seek extradition of the parent to the United States for prosecution.

The House Judiciary Committee reported the bill on Nov. 20 (H Rept 103-390), and the House and Senate both passed it by voice vote that day. President Clinton signed the measure Dec. 2.

Although parental kidnapping was outlawed by all 50 states, it had not been a federal crime prior to the enactment of HR 3378. As a consequence, the parents who lost access to their chil-

dren had little power to pursue the abductors overseas. HR 3378 not only increased the likelihood of extradition, but it also provided fines and prison terms of up to three years for parental kidnappers.

The State Department reported that hundreds of children were removed each year from the United States by parents who did not have legal custody. The number of cases had risen from 320 in 1987 to 515 in 1992.

Enactment of HR 3378 culminated a four-year effort by Rep. George W. Gekas, R-Pa., who had introduced his first proposal on parental kidnapping in the 101st Congress. Provisions similar to HR 3378 were included in an omnibus crime bill that passed the House in 1991, but the measure was blocked by a Senate filibuster the following year.   ❑

Child-Care Background Checks

In an attempt to weed child abusers out of the day-care industry, Congress cleared legislation late in 1993 to promote a national system of criminal background checks for child-care providers.

The measure (HR 1237—PL 103-209) required states to report child-abuse arrests and convictions to the Federal Bureau of Investigation's data base of criminal records. It also encouraged states to mandate that child-care providers undergo background checks through the FBI data base.

The House Judiciary Committee reported the bill on Nov. 20 (H Rept 103-393), and the House and Senate approved the measure by voice vote that day. President Clinton signed the bill Dec. 8.

According to the committee, a leading force behind the legislation was Oprah Winfrey, the talk-show host and child advocate. Winfrey argued that federal action was needed to prevent children from coming into contact with convicted child abusers at day-care centers.   ❑

Arson Research, Prevention

Lawmakers agreed in 1994 to authorize a new arson-prevention effort, albeit only for two years.

The legislation (HR 1727—PL 103-254), which cleared in May, authorized $2 million in fiscal 1996 for arson investigation programs at federal and regional training sites. It also authorized $4.25 million annually in fiscal 1995 and 1996 to support arson research, prevention and control in up to 10 states or groups of states.

The House Science, Space, and Technology Committee reported the bill on July 13, 1993 (H Rept 103-172), and the House passed the bill by voice vote July 26. The Senate approved a similar version of the bill by voice vote Nov. 22, 1993, after substituting in the text of S 798, which the Commerce, Science, and Transportation Committee had reported that day (S Rept 103-204).

The House amended the bill again on April 26, 1994, and the Senate cleared that version on May 6. President Clinton signed the bill on May 19.   ❑

Armored Car Guards

Responding to complaints about red tape from armored car guards, Congress cleared a bill in 1993 to make some guards' gun permits valid when they crossed state lines.

The measure (HR 1189—PL 103-55) eliminated the need for guards to obtain gun permits in every state they passed through on the job, provided that their home states met certain standards. Permits issued by those states would be considered valid wherever the guard was on duty. To qualify, a state would have to check the guard's arrest record annually and certify that he or she underwent gun safety training every year.

The House Energy and Commerce Committee reported the bill April 22, 1993 (H Rept 103-62), and the House passed it by voice vote May 18. The Senate Commerce Committee passed the bill by voice vote June 30 after inserting the text of a similar measure (S 608—S Rept 103-67) that the Senate Commerce, Science, and Transportation Committee had reported on June 24. The House cleared the Senate version by voice vote July 13, and President Clinton signed it on July 28.

Fewer states met the bill's standards than the sponsors had anticipated, prompting the House to pass another bill on the issue in 1996. The Senate did not act on the measure, however. *(1996 action, p. 755)* ❑

Civil Rights

The 103rd Congress saw limited action on the civil rights front, as lawmakers twice attempted to overturn a law or Supreme Court ruling related to civil liberties. Congress cleared a bill to give religious practices more protection against state and local strictures, but legislation to apply the 1991 Civil Rights Act to workers at a major salmon cannery in Alaska stalled short of the House and Senate floors. Congress also reauthorized for two years a federal panel that advised lawmakers and the administration on civil rights issues.

RELIGIOUS FREEDOM

Overcoming an abortion-related standoff, Congress agreed in 1993 to reverse a controversial Supreme Court ruling that had made it easier for the government to interfere with religious practices.

The 1990 ruling (*Employment Division v. Smith*) held that state laws could limit religious freedoms indirectly if the laws served a valid state purpose. The 1993 legislation (HR 1308—PL 103-141) allowed state and federal laws to infringe on religious practices only if the laws served a compelling governmental interest and interfered as little as possible with religious freedom—the standard that had been in effect prior to the *Smith* ruling.

Supporters of HR 1308 said that since the *Smith* ruling, the courts had upheld dozens of laws restricting religious freedom. Noting the support from such diverse groups as Baptist churches and the American Civil Liberties Union, Sen. Edward M. Kennedy, D-Mass., said, "These organizations don't agree on much, but they do agree on the need to pass [the bill]."

Opponents argued that the measure would have unintended and undesirable consequences. In particular, they suggested that prisons would be forced to accommodate a myriad of dietary and other demands from inmates in the name of religious freedom. Answering some of the complaints, the Senate modified the bill to clarify that the government had to justify only those laws or actions that placed a substantial burden on the free exercise of religion.

The *Smith* case involved two Native Americans who were fired from their jobs at a drug rehabilitation clinic for using peyote, an illegal hallucinogenic drug, during a religious ceremony. Because they were fired for breaking the law, they were denied unemployment benefits, prompting them to sue. The Supreme Court rejected the lawsuit, ruling that the state did not have to meet the "compelling interest" test when defending a law that infringed on religious freedom indirectly.

Opponents of the ruling quickly introduced legislation to overturn it, but their proposals were stymied by antiabortion forces in the 101st and 102nd congresses. The National Right to Life Committee argued that the bills would have enabled women to circumvent state restrictions on abortions by claiming they had religious reasons for terminating their pregnancies.

Sponsors of HR 1308 overcame that hurdle with a provision ensuring that the bill could not be used to challenge state restrictions on abortion. Antiabortion lawmakers had tried to insert similar provisions in the previous bills, to no avail.

The House Judiciary Committee reported HR 1308 on May 11, 1993 (H Rept 103-88), and the House passed the bill by voice vote later that day. The Senate amended and passed the bill on Oct. 27, 97–3, after substituting in the text of a similar bill (S 578—S Rept 103-111) that the Judiciary Committee had reported on July 27.

The House cleared the Senate version of the bill Nov. 3, and President Clinton signed the measure on Nov. 16.

WARDS COVE

Democrats on the Senate Labor and Human Resources Committee sought in 1994 to undo one of the compromises behind the Civil Rights Act of 1991 (PL 102-166), but their efforts were fruitless.

At issue was whether the 1991 law would apply to an estimated 2,000 minority workers at the Wards Cove Packing Co. salmon canneries in Alaska. The workers argued that they had been shunted into low-paying, unskilled jobs, while white workers were given most of the higher-paying skilled positions.

The workers' initial lawsuit had led the Supreme Court to rule in 1989 that statistical evidence alone was not enough to prove racial discrimination in the workplace. Reversing a 1971 decision, the court held in *Wards Cove Packing Co. v. Atonio* that employees had to prove that the imbalance in hiring or promotion stemmed from specific discriminatory practices that were not a matter of business necessity.

The 1991 law put the burden back on businesses, not their employees, to prove that a discriminatory practice was a matter of business necessity. As part of the final negotiations over the legislation, however, the Wards Cove workers' lawsuit was specifically exempted from the new law. The exemption, which outraged numerous Democrats, was made to satisfy Alaska's two Republican senators. *(Congress and the Nation Vol. VIII, p. 780)*

On Sept. 14, 1994, a divided Labor and Human Resources Committee approved a bill (S 1037) to extend the 1991 law to the Wards Cove workers' claim. The party-line vote was 10–7. The committee did not report the bill to the full Senate, however, and the measure advanced no further.

The House Judiciary Subcommittee on Civil and Constitutional Rights approved a related bill (HR 1172) by voice vote March 17, 1993, but the full Judiciary Committee did not take up the measure.

CIVIL RIGHTS COMMISSION

With unusual ease, Congress reauthorized the U.S. Civil Rights Commission for two years in 1994, although it authorized only one year of funding.

Established in 1957, the commission researched and advised the president and Congress on civil rights issues, such as employment and housing discrimination. It had no enforcement power, so it exerted influence mainly through its reports and recommendations.

The commission's reputation was tarred in the 1980s, when its Republican and Democratic appointees were so sharply divided that the commission did little to fulfill its mission. Congress considered eliminating the panel in 1989, but decided instead to keep it alive on a short leash. Lawmakers hammered out a new compromise in 1991, reauthorizing the commission for three years and boosting its authorized funding level to $7.2 million in fiscal 1992. *(Congress and the Nation Vol. VIII, pp. 762 and 785)*

The reauthorization bill in 1994, by contrast, moved swiftly and with little debate. The Senate Judiciary Committee reported a three-year reauthorization bill (S 2372) on Sept. 28, 1994, and the Senate approved it by voice vote two days later. On Oct. 3, the House substituted in the text a similar bill (HR 4999—H Rept 103-775) that the House Judiciary Committee had reported earlier in the day, then passed the amended bill by voice vote. The House version of S 2372 proposed to reauthorize the commission only for fiscal 1995, at a funding level of $9.5 million.

The Senate amended the bill one last time on Oct. 6, extending the reauthorization through the end of fiscal 1996 but not authorizing any funding for that year. The Senate passed the bill by voice vote that day, the House cleared it on Oct. 7, and President Clinton signed it on Oct. 25 (PL 103-419).

The budget called for in the authorization bill was higher than the appropriators already had awarded the commission for fiscal 1995: $9 million. Even that amount, however, was a significant increase over fiscal 1994, when the commission received $7.8 million. ❑

Civil Law

Efforts to change civil and administrative procedures largely fell flat in the 103rd Congress. Among the few measures that cleared were bills to continue an experimental program that encouraged out-of-court settlements and to promote international collaboration on antitrust investigations.

LAWSUIT ARBITRATION

Congress twice agreed to continue experimenting with arbitration as a way to reduce the backlog of federal lawsuits, but two bills to expand the experiment fell short of passage.

Begun in 1989, the experiment with pretrial arbitration was limited to 20 of the nation's 94 federal court districts. On Nov. 24, 1993, 15 days after the authorization for the experiment expired, the Senate cleared a bill (S 1732—PL 103-192) to extend the program through the end of 1994. The House had amended and passed the bill by voice vote the day before, and the Senate had passed an earlier version by voice vote Nov. 20. President Clinton signed the measure Dec. 14.

On Oct. 7, 1994, the House cleared a bill (S 2407—PL 103-420) by voice vote to continue the arbitration program in 20 districts for three additional years. S 2407 also reauthorized the Judicial Automation Fund, which helped the federal courts use computers and related products and services. The bill, which had passed the Senate by voice vote Aug. 18, was signed into law Oct. 25.

Members of the House Judiciary Committee twice sought to expand the arbitration program to every district while also letting federal judges require nonbinding, pretrial arbitration in many civil cases. The committee reported their first proposal (HR 1102—H Rept 103-284) on Oct. 12, 1993, and the House passed it by voice vote later that day. Senate Judiciary Committee Chairman Howell Heflin, D-Ala., kept the bill from moving in the Senate, however, citing a request from the Judicial Conference of the United States for more study.

A second effort (HR 4357) was considered by the House Judiciary Committee on Sept. 29, 1994, but not approved.

CIVIL PROCEDURE

The House tried in 1993 to block two new rules for federal lawsuits, but the Senate declined to go along.

The disputed rules were part of a package of changes proposed early in 1993 by the Judicial Conference of the United States. One required all parties in a lawsuit to disclose automatically any evidence relevant to the specific allegations made in a lawsuit, rather than waiting for the information to be requested during the pretrial "discovery" process. Supporters said the change would save time and money, but critics argued that the requirement was vague and contrary to established legal principles.

The other change waived the requirement that depositions be recorded by a stenographer, allowing tape recordings and other alternatives to be used without a court order.

The House Judiciary Committee reported a bill to block the two disputed changes (HR 2814—H Rept 103-319) on Nov. 3, and the House passed the bill by voice vote the same day. The Senate did not act on the measure, however, allowing the proposed changes to take effect without amendment.

Under the 1934 Rules Enabling Act, any rule changes proposed by the Judicial Conference automatically went into effect seven months after Congress was notified unless legislation was enacted to block them. The Supreme Court had notified Congress of the Judicial Conference's proposed rule changes on April 22, 1993, giving lawmakers until Dec. 1 to intervene.

ADMINISTRATIVE LAW JUDGES

The Senate approved a bill (S 486) in 1993 to make administrative law judges more independent, but the measure did not advance in the House.

Administrative law judges helped to resolve disputes over the way federal agencies applied their regulations and policies. Under existing law, each administrative law judge worked for a single federal agency, which funded the judge's office and determined the cases to be decided. That system, critics said, put pressure on the judges to rule in favor of their agencies.

S 486 proposed to create an independent corps of administrative law judges to resolve complaints against all the agencies. As in existing law, however, the head of each agency would have retained the power to overrule an administrative judge's decision.

The Senate Judiciary Committee reported the bill Oct. 4, 1993 (S Rept 103-154), and the Senate passed the measure by voice vote Nov. 19. The House Judiciary Committee did not act on the bill or on its House counterpart, HR 2586.

ANTITRUST EVIDENCE

Congress opened the door in 1994 to more international antitrust investigations when it cleared legislation granting new powers to the Justice Department and the Federal Trade Commission.

The bill (HR 4781—PL 103-438) allowed the two agencies to negotiate agreements with their foreign counterparts for sharing evidence on antitrust cases. Previous law had barred the agencies from exchanging such information with other countries.

Assistant Attorney General Anne K. Bingaman told a House panel that the measure was needed to help obtain evidence abroad, particularly when foreign cartels were the target. The House Judiciary Committee reported the bill on Oct. 3, 1994 (H Rept 103-772), and the House passed it the same day by voice vote. The Senate cleared the measure by voice vote Oct. 8, and President Clinton signed it Nov. 2.

TORTURE LAWSUITS

Legislation to allow lawsuits in U.S. courts against foreign governments that torture, murder or abduct U.S. citizens died in the Senate after being significantly narrowed by the House.

The House Judiciary Committee reported a broad version of the proposal (HR 934—H Rept 103-702) on Aug. 16, 1994, and the Senate Judiciary Subcommittee on Courts and Administrative Practice approved a competing bill (S 825) on Sept. 22.

The Clinton administration weighed in against the proposals, arguing that they might open U.S. citizens to suits in foreign courts for less serious offenses. After amending HR 934 to allow lawsuits only against the German government and only for Holocaust-related violence, the House passed HR 934 by voice vote on Oct. 7. The Senate, however, did not act on either bill.

A similar measure foundered in the 102nd Congress after the Justice and State departments warned of retaliation by foreign governments. Instead, Congress cleared a bill in 1992 (PL 102-256) allowing lawsuits against former foreign officials living in the United States who had committed torture or murder. (Congress and the Nation Vol. VIII, p. 797)

INSLAW CLAIM

A House panel approved legislation in 1994 to let INSLAW Inc., a federal contractor, pursue its long-standing claim against the Justice Department. The measure advanced no further, however.

In 1982, the Justice Department had awarded INSLAW a three-year, $10 million contract to implement case-management software at its offices in the 94 judicial districts. After the department revoked the contract, INSLAW accused Justice of stealing the software.

A special counsel appointed by Attorney General William P. Barr in 1991 found no wrongdoing by the department, but Democrats on the House Judiciary Committee were not satisfied. They urged Barr in vain to seek a court-appointed independent counsel and ordered their own investigation, which found INSLAW's claims to be credible. (Congress and the Nation Vol. VIII, p. 792)

Divided along party lines, the Judiciary Committee reported a bill (HR 4862—H Rept 103-852) on Oct. 7, 1994, to let INSLAW present its case to the U.S. Court of Claims. It proposed to waive the statute of limitations, which otherwise would have blocked INSLAW's claim, and to bar the court from awarding punitive damages against the Justice Department.

The House did not take up the bill, and no similar measure was considered by the Senate. ❑

Legal Services Corporation

Supporters of the Legal Services Corporation, a federal agency that subsidized lawyers for the poor, failed again in the 103rd Congress to reauthorize the agency. Congress kept the corporation alive, however, through increasing annual appropriations.

The corporation gave grants to state and local legal-aid agencies, which supplied lawyers for low-income people in eviction, child custody, and other civil cases. It was a frequent target for criticism by Republicans, who argued that federally subsidized attorneys should be barred from such politically charged arenas as abortion and redistricting. Democrats were willing to support some restrictions, but not to the extent sought by the GOP. This partisan split helped to block every attempt by Congress to reauthorize the agency since 1980. (1992 action, Congress and the Nation Vol. VIII, p. 795)

On May 26, 1994, the House Judiciary Subcommittee on Administrative Law and Governmental Relations approved a draft bill by voice vote to reauthorize the Legal Services Corporation for five years. The bill, later introduced as HR 4508, would have set strict new accounting requirements for groups that received the agency's grants. It also would have eased some of the restrictions on lobbying and other controversial activities by subsidized lawyers.

The measure was not taken up by the full Judiciary Committee.

Despite the lack of authorization, Congress continued to provide money for the corporation in the annual appropriations bills for the departments of Commerce, Justice and State. The agency received $400 million in fiscal 1994, up from $357.3 million in fiscal 1993, and $415 million in fiscal 1995. ❑

Immigration

The 103rd Congress resisted the mounting pressure from border states to stem the flow of immigrants, approving only a modest package of revisions to the immigration and naturalization laws (HR 783—PL 103-416). A smattering of border-tightening provisions were included in the omnibus anticrime bill (HR 3355—PL 103-322), but an assortment of other restrictions on immigration stalled short of the House and Senate floors.

Congress would return to the immigration issue in 1995 and 1996, stepping up efforts to block illegal entries into the country. *(1995–1996 action, p. 717)*

HR 783 began as an effort to help resident aliens who were elderly or disabled become citizens. Existing law required resident aliens to pass a history and government exam before becoming citizens. The bill, which the House Judiciary Committee reported Nov. 20, 1993 (H Rept 103-387), proposed to let the U.S. attorney general waive the test for resident aliens older than 65 who had lived in the United States for 20 years, as well as those whose disabilities made it impossible for them to pass the test. The measure also proposed to make it easier for U.S. citizens to confer citizenship upon their children born in foreign lands.

The House passed the bill by voice vote Nov. 20. The Senate amended and passed the bill by voice vote the same day, attaching the text of a bill (S 1197) that the Senate had passed by voice vote July 1. S 1197 proposed a list of technical corrections to immigration law.

HR 783 idled for 10 months before the House expanded and passed it again by voice vote on Sept. 20, 1994. In addition to the earlier elements of the bill, the new version proposed a two-year extension for a popular program that allowed short-term visitors from 22 countries to enter the United States without visas. The program promoted tourism and business travel to and from countries that, in return, waived visas for short-term visitors from the United States. It was due to expire on Sept. 30, 1994, although the administration had extended it for 30 days in the hope that Congress would reauthorize it.

The amended bill also proposed a probationary visa waiver program for countries that were close to meeting the standards set for the existing waiver program. In addition, it proposed to reauthorize for three years a federal program that supported the resettlement of refugees who had been admitted into the United States.

The Senate expanded the bill further on Oct. 7, adding provisions to allow more aliens convicted of serious crimes to be de-

ported under expedited procedures. The bill passed by voice vote, and the House cleared it the same day. President Clinton signed it Oct. 25.

The deportation language expanded on provisions in the omnibus anticrime bill that allowed judges to order the deportation of certain criminal aliens at their sentencing hearings, rather than requiring a separate deportation proceeding. The measure also sped the deportation of immigrants whose asylum petitions had been denied, authorized the hiring of 4,000 new Border Patrol agents, increased the penalties for smuggling illegal immigrants and forging documents, and authorized $1.8 billion in grants over six years to help states incarcerate criminal aliens. *(Crime bill, p. 683)*

ASYLUM, OTHER ISSUES

House and Senate committees considered bills to address the burgeoning backlog of asylum cases, but no legislation reached the floor of either chamber.

By 1993, the Immigration and Nationalization Service (INS) was reporting a growing backlog of more than 300,000 applications for asylum from foreigners staying in the United States. Only a fraction of the applicants were detained; most were released, often with work authorizations, pending their asylum hearings some months in the future. If they did not return for the hearings, the INS was ill equipped to track them.

The House Judiciary Subcommittee on International Law, Immigration and Refugees approved a bill (HR 2602) by voice vote Oct. 20, 1993, to tighten the rules for asylum proceedings. The measure proposed to set up preinspection posts at several overseas airports, allow more asylum applicants to be denied at U.S. airports, and bar applications for asylum from foreigners who had been in the United States for more than 30 days.

Six days later, subcommittee chairman Romano L. Mazzoli, D-Ky., introduced a new version of the bill (HR 3363) that called for a larger increase in INS asylum officers and made it more difficult for foreigners awaiting asylum hearings to obtain work permits. Although the bill drew praise from Republicans, it was opposed by the Clinton administration and refugee advocacy groups, and neither HR 3363 nor HR 2602 advanced further. Still, the omnibus crime bill included one of the disputed elements of HR 3363: a provision denying work permits to foreigners awaiting asylum hearings unless the attorney general approved.

On Aug. 11, 1994, the Senate Judiciary Committee approved a bill (S 1333) by voice vote to make it easier for INS officers to exclude asylum-seeking aliens with improper documents. That bill did not advance either.

The Clinton administration helped to undercut the push for asylum legislation by moving to streamline the application reviews. Congress's final word on the issue was a nonbinding passage in the omnibus crime bill expressing the Senate's desire to keep aliens without proper documentation from entering the United States and to process applications for asylum faster.

House Republicans tried to add several immigration-related amendments to appropriations measures and other bills in 1994, to no avail. These included proposals to bar illegal immigrants from benefiting from federal programs, require school districts to determine the immigration status of students and parents, and eliminate Supplemental Security Income benefits for most noncitizens. The House did approve one such proposal: an amendment by Jay C. Kim, R-Calif., to put a seven-day limit on emergency food and shelter for homeless illegal immigrants. Adopted July 22 by a vote of 220–176, the proposal sank when the underlying housing reauthorization bill (HR 3838) stalled. ❑

Patent and Copyright Law

The 103rd Congress enacted a pair of routine measures related to intellectual property rights, raising the fees for trademark applications and affording more protection to specialty plants. More significant proposals fell short of passage, including efforts to revamp copyright registrations, ease the patenting of unique manufacturing processes and promote international protection of trademarks.

PATENT OFFICE REAUTHORIZATION

Congress raised the trademark application fee by one-sixth in 1993 to cover the increased costs of the federal Patent and Trademark Office. When some lawmakers tried to shield the patent office from personnel cuts the following year, however, their efforts were blocked unexpectedly on the House floor.

The fee increase was included in a bill (HR 2632—PL 103-179) reauthorizing the patent office for fiscal 1994. The measure, which raised the fee from $210 to $245, authorized $103 million for the office, but Congress provided only $88.3 million in the fiscal 1994 appropriations bill for the Departments of Commerce, Justice and State and related agencies (HR 2519—PL 103-121).

The House Judiciary Committee reported the reauthorization legislation on Oct. 12, 1993 (H Rept 103-285), and the House passed the bill by voice vote later that day. The Senate amended and passed the bill by voice vote Nov. 11, and the House amended it again and passed it by voice vote Nov. 19. The Senate cleared the bill the next day, and President Clinton signed it Dec. 3.

The measure included a provision allowing interim patent extensions for products undergoing regulatory review before hitting the market. It also included provisions from a Senate-passed bill (S 409) to extend three American Legion design patents for 14 years. It did not, however, include a provision of the Senate bill that would have extended the patent of olestra, a synthetic substitute for fat, through 1997.

The Senate Judiciary Committee had reported S 409 on June 23 (S Rept 103-64), after dropping a controversial provision renewing a design patent for the United Daughters of the Confederacy. The Senate passed the legislation by voice vote on July 14, but House did not act on it. *(Confederate insignia, see box this page)*

On Sept. 29, 1994, the House Judiciary Committee approved by voice vote a bill (HR 4608) to authorize $107 million for the Patent and Trademark Office in fiscal 1995. The committee

---

CONFEDERATE INSIGNIA

After an emotional filibuster by the Senate's lone African American member, lawmakers reversed course in 1993 and rejected a design patent for the emblem of the United Daughters of the Confederacy.

The group, which sponsored educational programs on the Confederacy and did charitable works, had regularly won patent extensions from Congress. But Sen. Carol Moseley-Braun, D-Ill., objected to a proposed extension in 1993, noting that the emblem featured the Confederate flag. "The issue is whether or not Americans such as myself . . . will have to suffer the indignity of being reminded time and time again that, at one point in this country's history, we were human chattel," Moseley-Braun said during the Senate debate.

The tussle over the emblem had two rounds. The proposed extension was included in a larger patent bill (S 409), but the Senate Judiciary Committee agreed May 6 to drop the extension at Moseley-Braun's request. The vote was 12–3.

In July, when the Senate took up a bill (S 919) to authorize President Clinton's National Service Initiative, Sen. Jesse Helms, R-N.C., proposed an amendment to extend the United Daughters of the Confederacy's patent. Helms and Sen. Strom Thurmond, R-S.C., argued that the patent should be extended because the group's mission was education, not discrimination.

Moseley-Braun attempted to kill the amendment on July 22 with a tabling motion, but the Senate rejected the motion, 48–52. She then vowed to filibuster "until this room freezes over," renewing the debate and eventually turning the tide. Later that day the Senate voted 76–24 to reconsider the tabling motion. It then agreed, 75–25, to table the amendment. Two Democrats, Sam Nunn of Georgia and Robert C. Byrd of West Virginia, joined 23 Republicans in voting not to kill the extension. *(National service, p. 623)*

---

dropped one disputed provision: a proposal to let the office spend all the money it collected in fees, rather than limiting it to the portion appropriated by Congress. But it left intact a provision exempting the patent office from the government-wide personnel cuts that Congress had approved earlier in the year (HR 3345—PL 103-226). The committee reported the bill on Oct. 3 (H Rept 103-777). *(Employee buyouts, p. 814)*

The Clinton administration opposed the exemption for the patent office, and its opposition contributed to the bill's surprising defeat on the House floor. The measure seemed well on its way to passage on Oct. 3 when lawmakers began switching their votes in droves from "yea" to "nay." All told, 178 House members from both parties switched their votes, and the bill was defeated, 146–251.

Congress had already agreed to provide $83 million for the patent office, down $5.3 million from fiscal 1994, as part of the fiscal 1995 Commerce, Justice and State appropriations bill (HR 4603—PL 103-317).

COPYRIGHT ROYALTY TRIBUNAL

Congress tried to cut the cost of the copyright process in 1993, eliminating the federal tribunal that mediated disputes between the owners and users of copyrighted material.

The legislation (HR 2840—PL 103-198) terminated the Copyright Royalty Tribunal, an independent agency of the legislative branch with a $1 million annual budget. The bill replaced the tribunal with ad hoc arbitration panels that were to be appointed by the librarian of Congress. These panels would mediate disagreements between the companies using copyrights and music publishers, television studios and other copyright holders.

Panelists were required to be members of professional arbitration associations with experience in resolving disputes. Unlike earlier versions of the bill, the final legislation did not give parties to the dispute any role in choosing the panelists.

In addition to mediating disputes, the tribunal distributed the royalties collected from cable operators, jukebox owners, satellite TV companies and other users of copyrighted material. Congress had attempted to cut the tribunal's costs in 1992, clearing legislation (PL 101-319) to shrink the panel from five members to three. (Congress and the Nation Vol. VIII, p. 773)

The bill required copyright royalties to cover the entire cost of administering the dispute-resolution program. Previously, about 15 percent of the tribunal's budget had been paid by federal taxpayers.

The House Judiciary Committee reported the bill Oct. 12, 1993 (H Rept 103-286), and the House passed the measure by voice vote later that day. The Senate amended and passed the bill on Nov. 20, and the House cleared the Senate version on Nov. 23. President Clinton signed the bill Dec. 17.

COPYRIGHT REGISTRATION

A House-passed bill to overhaul the registration of copyrights made no progress in the Senate in the 104th Congress.

Under existing law, works were considered to be copyrighted as soon as they were completed, although the owners were expected to register their copyrights by depositing three copies of the works with the Library of Congress. If someone infringed on the copyright, the owner could sue even if the copyright had not been registered. However, only the owners of registered copyrights could collect up to $20,000 in statutory damages for an infringement.

The House bill would have simplified the paperwork for registering copyrights, allowed owners of unregistered copyrights to collect the statutory damages and allowed the courts to waive all damages for unknowing copyright infringements. To ensure that the Library of Congress continued to receive copyrighted material, the measure also would have required the producer of a published work to deposit two copies at the library or pay the library's cost of obtaining the work.

The bill responded to complaints from photographers and software producers, among others, that the existing registration requirement was time-consuming and expensive. The House Judiciary Committee reported the bill on Nov. 20, 1993 (HR

897—H Rept 103-388), and the House passed it by voice vote the same day. The Senate Judiciary Committee did not act on the measure.

The following year, the House included provisions of HR 897 in a measure to make it easier for companies to obtain patents on unique manufacturing processes (HR 4307). That bill also stalled in a dispute with the Senate, however. (Biotechnology patents, below)

The original version of HR 897 would have eliminated the Copyright Royalty Tribunal, an independent federal panel that resolved disputes between the owners and users of copyrighted material. Those provisions were split off into a separate bill, which cleared Congress on Nov. 23, 1993. (Copyright royalties, this page)

BIOTECHNOLOGY PATENTS

Late in the 1994 session, the House and Senate passed competing versions of a bill (HR 4307) to help biotechnology firms win patents for their operations. The two chambers were unable to resolve their differences over the scope of the bill, however, before Congress adjourned.

The House version of the bill, which the House Judiciary Committee reported on Sept. 20 (H Rept 103-728), would have made it easier for biotechnology, pharmaceutical and chemical companies to win patents for the special processes that they used to make their products. It also contained a copyright overhaul proposal that the House had passed as a freestanding bill (HR 897) in 1993. The House passed HR 4307 by voice vote Sept. 20. (Copyright procedures, this page)

Before passing the bill by voice vote on Oct. 6, the Senate narrowed the bill to apply only to the processes used by biotechnology companies. The amendment by Sen. Dennis DeConcini, D-Ariz., responded to concerns voiced by the chemical industry. The Senate also dropped the provisions dealing with copyrights.

The legislation advanced no further in 1994. The following year, Congress easily cleared a measure similar to the Senate-passed bill. (1995 action, p. 756)

Companies with process patents could bar their competitors from manufacturing or importing products made in the same way. Such patents were the sole protection available to many biotechnology companies because their products—uncommon but naturally occurring substances—could not be patented, even though some of the intermediate materials were unique and novel. Without process patents, these companies could spend heavily to develop manufacturing techniques only to have them pirated by competitors.

Conflicting court rulings, however, had led the U.S. Patent and Trademark Office to set inconsistent criteria for process patents. This inconsistency made U.S. companies vulnerable to foreign competitors, who could take advantage of U.S. innovations without incurring the expense of developing them, bill supporters said.

PLANT PATENTS

The intellectual property rights of plant breeders expanded slightly in 1994 as Congress cleared a bill (S 1406—PL 103-349)

to implement an international agreement on the protection of new plant varieties.

The measure brought the Plant Variety Protection Act of 1970 (PL 91-577) into agreement with the 1991 Convention of the International Union for the Protection of New Varieties of Plants. Among other modest changes, the bill extended the period of patent-like protection for new plant varieties to 20 years, a two-year increase.

The only dispute over the legislation occurred in the House Agriculture Committee, which debated its own version of the bill (HR 2927) on Aug. 3, 1994. The 1991 convention barred farmers from selling seeds for protected varieties without the breeder's authorization, contrary to long-standing U.S. practice. Rep. Larry Combest, R-Texas, sought to let farmers continue selling one another a portion of their leftover seeds without compensating the plant breeder, arguing that it was a customary way to stretch farm incomes and help out neighbors in distress. Opponents of the amendment argued that it would discourage breeders from making the investment needed to develop new varieties, and the amendment failed to pass, 10–10.

The committee reported the bill (H Rept 103-699) on Aug. 12, 1994, and the House passed it by voice vote the same day. The House then substituted HR 2927 for the text of S 1406 and passed that bill by voice vote.

The Senate, which had passed the earlier version of S 1406 by voice vote May 25, cleared the House version of S 1406 by voice vote on Sept. 21. President Clinton signed it Oct. 6.

MADRID PROTOCOL

The House approved legislation in 1994 to enhance trademark protection for U.S. entities engaged in international commerce, but the Senate quashed the bill (HR 2129) after the White House called it premature.

The measure, which the House Judiciary Committee reported on Oct. 3 (H Rept 103-780), would have implemented the 1989 Madrid Protocol, an international agreement on the protection of trademarks. The Madrid agreement aimed to simplify the process of filing for trademark protection around the globe. The bill also would have made it easier for entities to merge their U.S. trademarks with international trademarks.

The House passed the bill, 387–3, on Oct. 3. The White House did not want to ratify the Madrid Protocol at that stage, however, because it was still wrangling with the European Union over voting rights in the World International Intellectual Property Organization, the body that was to register trademarks internationally. Reflecting the administration's stance, the Senate Judiciary Committee did not take up the measure.

PATENT CHALLENGES

The Senate passed a bill (S 2341) late in the 1994 session to give third parties a greater role when a patent was challenged. The House did not take up the measure, however.

The bill would have broadened the scope of the federal patent office's reexamination proceedings, which were used in lieu of litigation to settle patent disputes. It would have given people who were not patent owners more power to initiate reex-

amination proceedings and to appeal reexamination decisions. The Senate Judiciary Committee reported the bill on Sept. 28, and the Senate passed it by voice vote Oct. 4.

PRIOR USERS

Companies whose manufacturing processes became the subject of another company's patent would have been aided by a bill (S 2272) that the Senate passed near the end of the 1994 session. The House adjourned without taking action on the bill, however.

The measure would have allowed prior users of a patented process to continue using at least a portion of the process in certain cases, provided that they were using or preparing to use the process commercially in the United States when the patent application was filed. The Senate Judiciary Committee reported the bill on Sept. 28 (S Rept 103-405), and the Senate passed the bill by voice vote Oct. 8.   ❑

White House Travel Office

Republicans on the House Judiciary Committee tried to launch an inquiry in 1993 into the controversy surrounding the White House travel office, but Democrats blocked the probe.

Seven employees of the travel office, which made travel arrangements for reporters covering the White House, were fired May 19 for alleged mismanagement and possible financial wrongdoing. The employees later were cleared of any improprieties.

Republicans accused the White House of cronyism, saying the new administration fired the employees in order to help a longtime friend and a distant relative of President Clinton. They also accused the administration of politicizing the FBI and the IRS, which the White House had called in to investigate the travel office's procedures.

White House Chief of Staff Thomas F. McLarty III issued a report July 2 acknowledging that the dismissals were mishandled. Five of the seven fired employees were given new jobs in the government, and four of the aides involved in the dismissals were reprimanded. McClarty's actions did not satisfy many congressional Republicans, however, who wanted to look more deeply into the affair.

Rep. Henry J. Hyde, R-Ill., offered a resolution (H Res 198) to request a host of documents from the White House concerning nearly all aspects of the firings. When the Judiciary Committee took up the resolution July 14, Bill McCollum, R-Fla., proposed an amendment to request even more documents and expand the probe to cover first lady Hillary Rodham Clinton's role. The amendment was rejected on a party-line, 14–21 vote. The committee then voted 20–15 to recommend that the House defeat the resolution, with only one Democrat—Romano L. Mazzoli of Kentucky—joining the panel's Republicans in opposition.

The committee reported the resolution with an adverse recommendation on July 20 (H Rept 103-183), and the resolution saw no further action. After Republicans took control of Congress in 1995, however, the travel office affair came under scrutiny by the House Government Reform and Oversight Commit-

tee, and Congress cleared legislation to reimburse the fired employees for their legal expenses. (Travel office, p. 849)   ❑

Barkett Nomination

Accused by Republicans of being soft on crime, Rosemary Barkett nevertheless won confirmation from the Senate in 1994 as a federal judge on the 11th U.S. Circuit Court of Appeals, based in Atlanta.

Barkett, 54, had been serving as the first female chief justice of the Florida Supreme Court when President Clinton nominated her in 1993 for the federal appellate bench. Activists on both sides mounted a lengthy campaign for or against her nomination, releasing competing analyses of her record and responding to the other side's criticisms.

Sen. Orrin G. Hatch of Utah, the top Republican on the Senate Judiciary Committee, said that conservatives were particularly troubled by Barkett's record on capital punishment, which struck them as hostile to the death penalty. Republicans also accused Barkett of being a judicial activist who pursued a liberal agenda.

Barkett defended her record at a Judiciary Committee hearing on Feb. 3, 1994, saying she was simply following legal precedents on when to apply capital punishment. As for judicial activism, she said she was adhering to Florida law, not a political philosophy, when she invalidated several acts by the Florida legislature.

In her defense, Judiciary Committee Chairman Joseph R. Biden Jr., D-Del., said Barkett met the qualifications for the job and that she maintained an even judicial temperament on the bench. Barkett also won the endorsement of Florida's conservative Republican senator, Connie Mack, who said he respected her judgment and integrity even though he disagreed with some of her decisions. The American Bar Association's review panel rated her "well-qualified" for the appeals court.

The Judiciary Committee voted 11–7 on March 17, 1994, in favor of her nomination, with only one Republican in support. Opponents did not have the numbers to mount a successful filibuster on the Senate floor, so they agreed to let the Senate vote on the nomination after a daylong debate April 14.

The Senate confirmed the nomination, 61–37.

A 1970 graduate of the University of Florida Law School, Barkett had practiced law for a West Palm Beach firm before then-Gov. Bob Graham appointed her a state trial judge. She later was appointed to a state appeals court and, in 1985, the Florida Supreme Court. Her views on the death penalty prompted a fierce debate in 1992, when she ran to retain her seat on the Supreme Court, but voters kept her on the bench with about 61 percent of the vote.   ❑

Sarokin Nomination

A divided Senate agreed to elevate U.S. District Judge H. Lee Sarokin to the 3rd U.S. Circuit Court of Appeals in 1994, despite Republican accusations that Sarokin was a renegade judicial activist too sympathetic to accused criminals.

Of President Clinton's 19 nominees to federal appeals courts during the 103rd Congress, only Sarokin and Rosemary Barkett triggered a significant controversy. None of the nominees were rejected. (Barkett nomination, this page)

Republicans criticized Sarokin mainly on two fronts: crime and tobacco litigation. On crime, Republicans focused on several cases that they said showed Sarokin's excessive concern for criminals and insufficient concern for victims, including one in which Sarokin ordered a new trial for a man convicted of killing a police officer. "Judge Sarokin is the poster boy for soft-on-crime judges," said Trent Lott, R-Miss.

On tobacco, Sarokin drew criticism for his handling of Cipollone v. Liggett Group, the first federal-court case to make extensive use of internal tobacco company documents. Sarokin's rulings, although not all unfavorable to the tobacco companies, contained remarks so critical of the industry that the 3rd Circuit removed him from the case in 1992 to preserve the court's appearance of neutrality.

Judiciary Committee Chairman Joseph R. Biden Jr., D-Del., and Sen. Bill Bradley, D-N.J., led supporters in Sarokin's defense on the Senate floor, arguing that his controversial rulings turned on principled interpretations of complicated legal issues rather than on ideology. Seeking to counter claims that Sarokin was a renegade, Bradley noted that Sarokin had issued more than 2,000 rulings and had been reversed on only a small fraction of them.

At his confirmation hearing on Aug. 3, Sarokin had tried to assuage Republican concerns about judicial activism. When Sen. Strom Thurmond, R-S.C., asked Sarokin several times if he would follow Supreme Court precedent in all cases, Sarokin responded that he had no problem doing so.

The Judiciary Committee gave its support to Sarokin's nomination on Aug. 11, 12–5, and the Senate confirmed him on Oct. 4, 63–35.   ❑

Collins Impeachment

With the House set to begin impeachment proceedings against him, U.S. District Judge Robert F. Collins of Louisiana resigned from the federal bench in 1993.

Collins was convicted in September 1991 of taking a $100,000 bribe from a drug smuggler, drawing a prison sentence of almost seven years. His conviction was upheld by the Fifth U.S. Circuit Court of Appeals, and the Supreme Court declined to consider his case in April 1993.

Federal judges lost their posts only if they resigned or were impeached by Congress. Collins refused to resign in the aftermath of his conviction, meaning that he continued to draw his judicial salary in prison.

On June 22, 1993, the Judicial Conference of the United States recommended that Congress consider impeaching Collins. Two days later, House Judiciary Committee Chairman Jack Brooks, D-Texas, introduced a resolution to impeach Collins and announced that "an investigation will begin forthwith." Collins later resigned, rendering the resolution moot.   ❑

1995–1996

The House and Senate Judiciary committees spent much of their time in the 104th Congress working on the same issue that occupied them for much of the previous session: crime. Instead of assembling a host of smaller bills into a single, massive package, however, they generally went after their goals piecemeal. The strategy was largely successful, as Congress cleared legislation to limit death row appeals, prod states to toughen their sentencing laws, track and notify communities about paroled sex offenders, stiffen penalties for child pornography and certain illegal drugs, and clamp down on counterfeit goods and the theft of valuable data, among other objectives.

The largest of the crime-related measures enacted was one to combat illegal immigration. The measure was narrowed significantly en route to enactment, yet it still contained many of the get-tough provisions that Republicans sought on deportation, exclusion, document fraud, and public benefits for illegal immigrants.

On the other hand, conservative Republicans were stymied when they tried to boost penalties for juvenile criminals and repeal the ban on assault weapons. They also had limited success shifting money from crime prevention to prison construction, a change in priorities that President Clinton resisted. Similarly, Clinton's initiatives to guard Americans against terrorist attack were largely blocked by conservative House Republicans.

One wrinkle added by the GOP majority was a new attentiveness to social issues, such as affirmative action, school prayer and flag burning. Still, the issues were so contentious that Congress enacted little legislation. The main exception was a new law allowing states not to recognize same-sex marriages performed outside their borders.

Congress granted biotechnology companies and recording artists new protection for their intellectual property, culminating several years of debate and negotiations. A major effort to adapt copyright law to Information Age technologies, however, barely got off the ground.

Immigration

Like a tree moving from forest to sawmill to lathe, legislation to tighten federal immigration laws gradually shed a host of disputed provisions en route to becoming law in October 1996.

The leaders of the House and Senate Judiciary subcommittees on immigration launched their efforts in 1995 with far-reaching bills to crack down on illegal border crossings, reduce legal immigration and deny federal benefits to many nonnative residents. By the time the legislation emerged at the end of the 1996 session, almost all of the original provisions affecting legal immigrants had been removed, as had most of the provisions dealing with benefits for illegal immigrants.

The deletions were made in part to placate business groups and their GOP allies in Congress, in part to accommodate the Clinton administration. Indeed, President Clinton took full advantage of his end-of-session leverage to force changes in a measure that had broad bipartisan support.

The White House's stance almost spelled doom for the measure as House Republicans resisted some of the changes the president demanded. After intense last-minute negotiations, however, a modified version of the legislation was included in the omnibus appropriations bill for fiscal 1997 (HR 3610—PL 104-208). *(Omnibus spending bill, p. 76)*

Although Clinton forced the bill's sponsors to drop most of the provisions restricting benefits to legal immigrants, his victory was hardly complete. He had already signed into law a welfare-overhaul bill (HR 3734—PL 104-193) that barred most federal welfare benefits for legal immigrants until they became citizens or, in the case of new immigrants, for their first five years in America. *(Welfare reform, p. 578)*

There had been little disagreement over many items in the immigration bill, particularly the ones that stepped up enforcement at the nation's borders. The measure's main purpose was to thin the ranks of illegal immigrants, whose number was growing by an estimated 300,000 each year.

The final version of the bill authorized an additional 5,000 border guards and 1,200 Immigration and Naturalization Service investigative agents around the country. It also authorized $12 million for the second and third tiers of a 14-mile fence along the California-Mexico border, and stiffened penalties for those who smuggled illegal immigrants into the United States.

Its toughest provisions were in the area of exclusion and deportation. People arriving with borrowed or falsified documents were to be detained at the border and denied asylum unless they could show a "credible fear" of persecution back home. For immigrants in the United States illegally, the measure sped deportation by compressing the process into a single proceeding.

The weakest element of the bill, some critics said, was its approach to illegal immigrants in the workplace, even though most illegal immigrants came into the United States in search of jobs. Early in the debate, protests from business groups and civil libertarians led sponsors to drop proposals for a nationwide system to verify the immigration status of job applicants. Instead, the final version of the bill authorized three voluntary, experimental programs in a limited number of states to help employers avoid hiring illegal immigrants.

"The sad truth is the Congress failed to address any major problem," said Daniel A. Stein, director of the Federation for American Immigration Reform, a group advocating more restrictive immigration policies. "In the whole area of document verification, the bill is just very weak in these critical structural areas."

BACKGROUND

Congress had last tackled illegal immigration in the 1986 Immigration Reform and Control Act (PL 99-603), which instituted penalties for employers who knowingly hired immigrants who were not authorized to work. The law also gave amnesty to millions of foreigners who were living in the United States illegally. Four years later, Congress cleared legislation (PL 101-649) placing a cap on the total number of legal immigrants: about

700,000 each year for three years, then 675,000 annually after that, although additional visas were available for special categories of immigrants. *(1986 law, Congress and the Nation Vol. VII, p. 717; 1990 law, Congress and the Nation Vol. VIII, p. 752)*

The 1990 measure aimed to boost the number of visas for Europeans and for skilled workers without decreasing the number of visas for Latin American and Asian immigrants who had close relatives in the United States. Its cap on immigration, however, was porous; it placed no limit on the number of people admitted who were the spouses or unmarried children of U.S. citizens and permanent residents, or on the number of refugees fleeing persecution. For that reason, the number of new permanent residents rose more than 800,000 each year even as the cap dropped to 675,000.

The number of illegal immigrants also grew in the 1990s, rising to an estimated four million by 1996. As a consequence of these twin increases, border and port states were increasingly burdened by the cost of educating, treating and otherwise supporting immigrants.

While the 103rd Congress backed away from the most ambitious proposals to block the entry of refugees, the political pressure mounted for tightening the borders. In November 1994, voters in California approved a hotly disputed ballot initiative to deny more public services to illegal immigrants, a measure backed strongly by Republican Gov. Pete Wilson. *(1993–1994 action, p. 712)*

The Republican takeover of Congress gave control of the House and Senate Judiciary subcommittees on immigration to two longtime advocates of curbs on both legal and illegal entries: Rep. Lamar Smith, R-Texas, and Sen. Alan K. Simpson, R-Wyo. They were backed by Republicans and some Democrats from border states who complained that immigrants were putting too great a strain on public services, as well as those who argued that immigrants were creating a Balkanized community by failing to learn English and assimilate.

Simpson in particular warned that Congress needed to put new restrictions on legal immigration to avoid an even greater influx in coming years. His argument was buttressed by new projections from the Immigration and Naturalization Service (INS) of a surge in legal immigration in the late 1990s, as citizens naturalized under the 1986 Immigration Act petitioned to admit their relatives.

Smith and Simpson did not speak for the entire GOP, however; many Republicans were sensitive to the needs of corporations and farmers who relied on immigrant labor and who resisted any increase in regulation on hiring. Other Republicans worried about alienating ethnic voting blocs, such as Cuban Americans, that otherwise would favor conservative candidates.

Democrats also were torn between conflicting constituencies. Some liberals sought to restrict immigration in order to preserve entry-level jobs for native born Americans. Others, however, had large concentrations of Mexican Americans and other ethnic groups who wanted to keep the borders open for family reunification.

Moreover, it was not clear that immigrants posed an economic threat. Although some economists said that immigrants overtaxed public services while making it harder for the native born to find jobs, others argued that immigrants were an economic windfall or even a necessity. One influential former economics professor—House Majority Leader Dick Armey, R-Texas—insisted that legal immigration had been an economic boon and that there was no need for cutbacks.

Immigration Commission

In June 1995, a bipartisan commission headed by former Rep. Barbara Jordan, D-Texas, called for new curbs on legal immigration (Jordan died the following January). The commission's report recommended that the cap on legal immigration be pared eventually to 550,000, including 50,000 refugees and 100,000 slots for immigrants with needed job skills. The rest should be reserved for the parents, spouses and minor children of U.S. citizens or permanent U.S. residents, the commission said.

The biggest losers under the proposal would have been unskilled workers and the siblings and adult children of U.S. citizens and permanent residents, who would no longer have been given preference for admission.

The commission also proposed to require businesses to pay immigrants with work-related visas 5 percent more than the prevailing wage, eliminating the incentive to bring foreign labor into the United States to cut costs. Businesses also should be charged a fee to help fund training programs for U.S. workers, the commission said, and a national verification system established to help prevent illegal immigrants with false documents from obtaining jobs.

President Clinton endorsed the commission's report, raising expectations that the 104th Congress would address both legal and illegal immigration. A number of ethnic organizations and minority lawmakers attacked the report, however, saying the changes it advocated would harm their constituencies.

The issue took another turn early in 1996, when Republican presidential candidate Patrick J. Buchanan campaigned on an "America First" platform that called for a crackdown on illegal border crossings and a moratorium on legal immigration. Buchanan's strong performance in the early GOP primaries seemed to increase the pressure on Congress to act.

HOUSE ACTION

Smith and Simpson both introduced sweeping bills in 1995 to curb legal as well as illegal immigration. The provisions on legal immigration were gradually ground out of the legislation, however, in the face of determined opposition by the business community—particularly high-technology businesses.

The House Judiciary Committee acted first, approving Smith's bill (HR 2202, formerly HR 1915) on Oct. 24, 1995, after five weeks of markups that added dozens of amendments but made no major changes. The markup sessions often split along party lines, as the committee approved 56 of the 65 amendments offered by Republicans but only 26 of 81 sponsored by Democrats. The committee reported the bill (H Rept 104-469, Part I) on March 4, 1996.

The House Government Reform and Oversight Committee and the House Agriculture Committee then took up portions of the bill under their jurisdiction, reporting their proposed revisions on March 7 and 8, respectively (H Rept 104-469, Parts II, III and IV). The House passed the bill on March 21, 333–87, after three days of debate and several significant alterations.

The main points of debate over HR 2202 were on the following issues:

Legal Immigration

The House Judiciary Committee's version of HR 2202 proposed to lower the annual cap on visas for new permanent residents to roughly 535,000. Of that total, 330,000 slots would be for immediate relatives of legal U.S. residents, down from about 500,000; 135,000 for foreigners with needed job skills, down from 140,000; and 70,000 for refugees seeking asylum. The preference given to siblings and adult children of U.S. residents would have been eliminated. The bill also would have provided about 150,000 visas annually for five years to illegal immigrants made eligible for amnesty by the 1986 law.

The provisions first came under attack in the Judiciary Committee. Democrats sought to raise the number of visas for immediate relatives and reduce them for foreign entrepreneurs, while Republicans sought to provide more visas for refugees and to ease the qualifications for skilled-worker visas. Democrats also sought to cap the percent of an employer's jobs that could be filled by temporary foreign workers and to require employers to pledge not to replace U.S. workers with temporary foreign help.

The panel resisted the most significant changes, including an amendment by Howard Berman, D-Calif., to strike all the proposed provisions on legal immigration. However, members agreed to preserve the special category of visas for immigrants from Europe and other areas underrepresented among the applicants for family reunification visas. Smith had proposed to eliminate the 55,000 "diversity" visas, as had the Jordan commission, but the committee agreed to retain the program at half its previous size, 18–11.

On the House floor March 21, Berman and two influential GOP freshmen, Dick Chrysler of Michigan and Sam Brownback of Kansas, launched a new attack on all the proposed restrictions on legal immigration. Their amendment to remove the curbs on legal immigration, which was backed by the Clinton administration, was approved, 238–183, with about one-third of the Republican caucus joining all but 25 House Democrats in support.

The day before, the House had agreed by voice vote to remove the proposed cap on visas for refugees fleeing persecution. That amendment was sponsored by conservative Republican Christopher H. Smith of New Jersey.

Left in the bill were provisions altering the temporary visa program for workers with special skills, also known as H-1B workers. Under the bill, companies that fired U.S. workers and then hired temporary foreign workers would have to pay them at least 10 percent more than the U.S. workers had received. However, companies that filled a relatively small percentage of their positions with H-1B workers would be exempted from many of the federal regulations governing such workers.

Benefits for Legal Immigrants

Responding to complaints from border-state officials, the Judiciary Committee's version of the bill proposed to deny public assistance and other benefits to permanent residents who were not U.S. citizens.

The federal government already had the power to deport an illegal immigrant who had become a "public charge," but that provision was ill-defined and rarely enforced. HR 2202 proposed to allow illegal immigrants to be deported if they received state or federal welfare benefits for 12 or more months within their first seven years in the United States.

The bill also would have required the person who sponsored the immigrant's visa application to assume greater financial responsibility for the immigrant for a longer period. Sponsors would have been required to show that they could support themselves and the sponsored immigrants at no less than twice the federal poverty level.

In the Judiciary Committee, Democrats tried in vain to exempt refugees and successful applicants for asylum from the benefits restriction. They made no attempt to remove the restriction on the House floor, however.

Benefits for Illegal Immigrants

The Judiciary Committee's version of the bill proposed to bar illegal immigrants from receiving any federal benefit except emergency medical care, immunizations, short-term disaster aid and nutrition services. Over Democratic objections, the committee adopted an amendment by Elton Gallegly, R-Calif., to bar children who were citizens from receiving Food Stamps, Medicaid or welfare benefits through parents who were illegal immigrants. The same prohibition was proposed if the parents were legal immigrants who had lived less than seven years in the United States. The vote on Oct. 24 was 16–11.

On the House floor March 20, Democrat Nydia M. Velázquez of New York tried to strike the Gallegly provision. The House refused, 151–269.

Gallegly then offered a more controversial amendment, proposing to let states deny public education to illegal immigrants. The Supreme Court had blocked states from taking such action without congressional approval, ruling that immigration was a matter of federal policy.

The amendment drew strong support from the House GOP leadership, who said that states should not have to pay for a failed federal policy on illegal immigration. "Come to America for opportunity. Do not come to America to live off the law-abiding American taxpayer," House Speaker Newt Gingrich, R-Ga., said in an impassioned floor speech.

Opponents said the amendment was short-sighted and inhumane. "Why would we want a population of children in this country not in school?" asked John Bryant, D-Texas. "What would they be doing if they were not in school?" Nevertheless, the House adopted the amendment on a **key vote of 257–163 (R 213–20; D 44–142; I 0–1)**. *(1996 key votes, p. 1047)*

A third Gallegly provision authorized hospitals to seek reimbursement from the federal government for the emergency care they provided to illegal immigrants. Republican Ed Bryant of

Tennessee tried in committee and on the House floor to require any hospital that sought reimbursement to identify the adult illegal immigrants it treated, but opponents argued that the proposals would threaten public health by deterring illegal immigrants from seeking treatment. The House rejected the amendment March 20, 170–250.

Worker Verification

Although the 1986 law made it a crime for employers to hire illegal immigrants knowingly, it was often flouted by the easy availability of false immigration documents and spotty federal enforcement.

The original version of HR 2202 would have mandated a nationwide toll-free phone line by October 1999 that employers would use to verify that job applicants were eligible to work in the United States. The system was to use existing data to determine, among other things, whether the applicant's name matched the Social Security number provided and whether a foreign applicant had been authorized by the INS to work.

However, the Judiciary Committee agreed to limit the mandate to a five-year experiment in five of the states with the largest populations of illegal immigrants. Only businesses with four or more workers were to be required to participate.

The program was scaled back after the committee narrowly rejected an amendment by Steve Chabot, R-Ohio, to strip the entire verification proposal from the bill. Chabot and other conservative Republicans argued that the system was a costly intrusion on an employer's hiring prerogatives, while liberal Democrats said it could lead to more discrimination against workers who appeared foreign. Still, the amendment was rejected, 15–17, as four Democrats joined 13 Republicans in defending the verification system.

Before taking the bill to the House floor, Smith changed the proposed system to make employer participation voluntary, not mandatory. Still, Chabot proposed an amendment March 20 to delete the pilot programs. The House rejected the amendment, 159–260, then defeated an amendment by Gallegly to require employers to participate, 86–331.

Taking a different tack, Bill McCollum, R-Fla., proposed to require Social Security cards to be more resistant to counterfeiting. Critics said that the proposal amounted to mandating a federal identification card, and the amendment was rejected, 191–221.

Seasonal Work Visas

The Agriculture Committee sought one major change in the bill to assure farmers a steady supply of seasonal workers. The amendment, sponsored by Richard W. Pombo, R-Calif., would have made it easier for employers to obtain temporary visas for unskilled workers. Instead of waiting for the Labor Department to certify a shortage of U.S. workers, as in the existing system, employers under Pombo's proposal could have qualified for temporary visas by filing statements attesting to the need and agreeing to abide by certain conditions, such as paying the prevailing wage, providing housing and giving U.S. workers preference for the jobs.

The change was projected to open the door for hundreds of thousands of temporary workers, compared to the 10,000 to 20,000 brought in under the existing program.

The Agriculture Committee approved the amendment, 26–14, at its March 5 markup of the immigration bill. The provision was not included in the version of HR 2202 that went to the House floor, however, so Pombo offered a modified amendment during the debate on March 21. The amendment proposed a three-year experiment with the new guest-worker program.

Without the new program, Pombo warned, farmers might be caught in a labor shortage that prevented crops from being harvested and drove up food costs. Critics, however, argued that the program would only boost illegal immigration because many of the guest workers would stay in the United States after their visas expired. The House rejected the Pombo amendment, 180–242.

Border Security

One of the least contentious elements of the bill was a proposal to authorize the Border Patrol to hire an additional 1,000 officers each year for five years, more than doubling the force. To enhance enforcement, the bill proposed to give more power for law enforcement agencies to investigate and prosecute crimes associated with illegal immigration, along with stiffer penalties.

The bill also would have authorized $12 million for a 14-mile-long triple-layer fence along the border south of San Diego, running from the Pacific Ocean east. That section of the border, one of the heaviest crossing points for illegal immigrants, had a single-layer fence. Democrat Melvin Watt of North Carolina tried to eliminate the mandate for the triple fence at the Judiciary Committee markup, arguing that it could become a deadly trap for Border Patrol agents, but the committee rejected his amendment, 11–17.

Deportation and Exclusion

The bill proposed to make it easier to deport foreigners who entered or stayed illegally. Immigrants who remained illegally in the United States for one year or more were to be barred from immigrating legally for 10 years. Democrats tried repeatedly in the Judiciary Committee to remove the 10-year ban, but they were successful only in providing some exceptions.

The bill also proposed special deportation courts for foreign terrorists where prosecutors would be authorized to present wiretap evidence without revealing it to the defendants. Watt tried to strike the wiretapping provision in the Judiciary Committee, but he was defeated, 10–16.

Asylum

As passed by the House, the bill would have required any foreigner seeking asylum in the United States to apply for refugee status within 30 days of arriving. Under existing law, immigrants could apply for asylum at any point after arriving, although they had to demonstrate a credible fear of persecution in their home countries. The bill also proposed an immediate screening system to enable asylum-seeking foreigners to be turned away at the border if they arrived without proper documents.

The INS faced a growing backlog of asylum applications, and critics said that the process was frequently abused by foreigners seeking to remain in the United States after their visas expired. Lawmakers had considered proposals to overhaul the asylum process in the 103rd Congress, but those efforts made little headway. *(1993–1994 action, p. 712)*

SENATE ACTION

Simpson initially split his proposals for legal and illegal immigration into two bills, moving them separately through the Senate Judiciary Subcommittee on Immigration in 1995.

The illegal immigration bill (S 269), which the subcommittee approved June 14, proposed to authorize hundreds of new Border Patrol agents, bar most state and federal benefits to illegal immigrants, limit the federal benefits that legal immigrants could collect during their first five to 10 years in the United States, place an annual cap on refugees granted permanent residency, streamline deportation of criminal aliens and immigrants who arrived without documents, and crack down on illegal immigrant smuggling and document fraud. It also would have established a system for employers to verify the immigration status of job applicants, starting with pilot projects but graduating to a mandatory national system within eight years.

The legal immigration bill (S 1394), which the subcommittee approved on Nov. 29, proposed to lower the annual cap on immigration to 540,000, with only 90,000 slots for workers with special skills. It also proposed to require employers who hired permanent foreign workers to pay a fee of $10,000 or 10 percent of the worker's first-year compensation, whichever was greater, to help finance education and training programs for displaced U.S. workers. And it would have required employers who replaced a U.S. worker with a temporary foreign worker to pay the new employee 10 percent more than the previous worker's wage.

On Feb. 29, 1996, the full Judiciary Committee took up draft legislation that combined S 269 and S 1394. Simpson made a number of concessions aimed at keeping the legal immigration provisions in the bill, hoping to mollify the business groups that were the proposal's most influential adversaries. For example, he agreed to drop the fee on businesses that hired permanent foreign workers and lift the ceiling on visas for workers with special skills. He also agreed to limit the verification system to pilot programs after the committee rejected, 9–9, an amendment to eliminate the system.

His efforts were unavailing, however. On March 14, the committee voted, 12–6, to split the draft into two measures, one dealing with legal immigration and the other dealing with illegal immigration. The amendment, offered by freshman Republican Spencer Abraham of Michigan, was supported by a majority of the panel's members from each party.

The measure dealing with illegal immigration (later introduced as S 1664) was approved 13–4 on March 21, reported on April 10 (S Rept 104-249), and taken up by the full Senate April 15. On May 2, the Senate inserted the amended text of S 1664 into HR 2202 and passed the House bill, 97–3.

The bill dealing with legal immigration (later introduced as S 1665) was approved 13–4 on March 28 and reported on April 10 (S Rept 104-250), but the Senate never acted on it.

Legal Immigration

The Judiciary Committee weakened Simpson's proposed limits on legal immigration, then the full Senate rebuffed his efforts to add the limits to the illegal immigration bill.

During the March 28 markup of the legal immigration bill, the Judiciary Committee adopted, 11–4, an amendment by Abraham and Edward M. Kennedy, D-Mass., to set a loose cap on the number of visas for close relatives of U.S. residents at 425,000 over 10 years. That level was about 65,000 less than under existing law but 125,000 more than Simpson proposed. The amendment also proposed to reduce, rather than eliminate, the preference given to relatives other than minor children, spouses and parents, and it proposed to retain half of the 55,000 "diversity" visas instead of ending them. An amendment by Republican Jon Kyl of Arizona, adopted 8–6, stripped the provision requiring employers to pay temporary foreign workers a premium if they replaced U.S. workers.

On the Senate floor four weeks later, Simpson tried to attach a cap on legal immigration to S 1664. Simpson proposed to cap family reunification visas at 480,000 per year for five years, giving the highest priority to immediate relatives of U.S. citizens, followed by the spouses and minor children of permanent U.S. residents. The cap and the shift in preferences would have all but denied visas to siblings and adult children of permanent residents.

Simpson said his goal was to give first preference to the relatives most likely to live in the same household as their sponsors. He also said his amendment would eliminate the cruel anomalies of the existing system, which occasionally caused spouses or children of permanent residents to wait for visas while more distant relatives of citizens were admitted.

Although polls showed strong public support for limiting legal immigration, some senators argued that the Simpson amendment would go too far in preventing family reunification. Some of the most impassioned speeches against the proposal came from Republicans who praised the contributions of immigrants. The critics prevailed, and the amendment was soundly defeated April 25, 20–80. A similar amendment by Dianne Feinstein, D-Calif., was later killed on a tabling motion, 76–26.

Benefits for Legal Immigrants

Although it dealt primarily with illegal immigrants, S 1664 proposed to make it harder for many legal residents to qualify for federal, state or local benefit programs.

Under existing law, immigrants did not qualify for food stamps or welfare benefits during their first three years in America, or Supplemental Security Income (SSI) benefits during their first five years, unless their income and their sponsors' income together fell below the federal standard. S 1664 proposed to impose that eligibility test (called "deeming") on new immigrants for 10 years, covering all benefit programs that aided low-income residents. For immigrants already living in the United States, the eligibility test would remain in place for five years.

Kennedy tried to strip the provision in committee, but his amendment was defeated, 7–8. The panel did agree, 11–5, to a Feinstein amendment ending the 10-year requirement for sponsored aliens as soon as they became citizens.

Kennedy and other Democrats tried again on the Senate floor to remove or weaken the restrictions, with little success. For example, an amendment by Bob Graham, D-Fla., to limit the restrictions to 16 specific federal welfare and housing programs was defeated, 36–63, after Simpson noted that it would leave out Medicaid, job training, legal services and other costly assistance programs.

Paul Simon, D-Ill., took aim at a provision of the bill allowing immigrants to be deported if they received public assistance for 12 or more months in their first five years in America. Complaining that the provision was too broad, Simon proposed to count only the months that an immigrant benefited from a major welfare program. The amendment was rejected, 36–63.

Benefits for Illegal Immigrants

Similar to the House-passed bill, S 1664 proposed to make illegal immigrants ineligible for most federal, state and local benefit programs. Emergency medical care and some nutrition programs were not covered by the prohibition.

Adopting an amendment by Kyl, the committee proposed to require federal reimbursement for hospitals that treated illegal immigrants. The amendment also proposed reimbursement for local governments whose emergency ambulance services ferried illegal immigrants injured while crossing the border.

Worker Verification

Similar to the House bill, S 1664 proposed to authorize pilot projects for verifying an employee's eligibility to work. These projects came under attack on the Senate floor by Abraham, who argued that the verification system would impose unfair burdens on employers and job applicants, and Democrat Russ Feingold of Wisconsin, who said it would intrude on a vast number of workers' privacy in order to identify the small percentage who were employed illegally.

Their amendment would have eliminated the pilot projects and a proposal for new federal standards to deter counterfeiting of birth certificates and driver's licenses. Simpson defended the standards, saying that fraudulent birth certificates were the "breeder document" for other false papers used by illegal immigrants to obtain jobs or benefits.

The amendment was killed on a tabling motion May 1, 54–46.

The Judiciary Committee had deleted several other proposals by Simpson aimed at stopping illegal immigrants from working. These included provisions to raise the penalties for hiring illegal immigrants and allow INS agents to conduct warrantless searches for illegal agricultural workers in open fields.

Congress had banned warrantless searches of open fields in 1986, requiring the INS to obtain the property owner's permission in advance or come up with a warrant. Simpson tried on the Senate floor to restore the provision allowing warrantless searches, saying that farmers who hired illegal immigrants should not receive such unique protection. Other Republicans called Simpson's proposal an affront to private property rights, while Democrats warned that it could increase harassment of foreign-looking workers. The amendment was defeated, 20–79, on April 24.

Border Security

The bill proposed to authorize the Border Patrol to hire 1,000 additional agents annually for four years, yielding a total of 1,000 fewer agents than the House proposed. The Judiciary Committee appended a Kyl amendment authorizing $12 million for a 14-mile, three-layer fence south of San Diego, as in the House bill. Responding to concerns about the cost, safety and effectiveness of the fence, however, the Senate approved a Feinstein amendment by voice vote on May 1 that gave the Border Patrol discretion on how to spend the $12 million.

Deportation and Exclusion

The bill proposed to streamline the process for deporting foreigners who were in the United States illegally. It also proposed fines for foreigners who did not leave the country before their visas expired.

The Judiciary Committee added several Abraham amendments that sought to ease the deportation of illegal immigrants convicted of serious criminal offenses, such as murder, robbery or drug trafficking. One amendment, adopted 12–5, allowed the deportation of noncitizens sentenced to at least one year in prison, not five years as required under existing law. Another, adopted 13–4, called for prisons to continue holding illegal immigrants after they completed their sentences so that they would remain in custody pending their deportation proceedings. A third, adopted 12–6, proposed to end the right of criminal aliens to appeal a deportation order to federal court.

Asylum

As in the House bill, the Judiciary Committee's version of S 1664 proposed to make it easier to turn away foreigners seeking asylum who arrived without proper documentation. It called for the INS to conduct a quick screening at the arrival point to determine whether the person had a credible fear of persecution. If the answer was no, the bill proposed, the foreigner could be deported without a full hearing before an immigration judge.

Similar language was included in a counterterrorism bill that Congress had cleared in April (S 735—PL 104-132). But Patrick J. Leahy, D-Vt., challenged the provision, arguing that victims of persecution typically had to rely on fake papers to escape from their home countries. Leahy proposed to take the broad summary exclusion bill out of S 1664 and the counterterrorism law, replacing it with a process that could be used only if the United States was overwhelmed by a sudden influx of asylum seekers.

Simpson objected, saying that illegal immigrants were tying up the asylum system with frivolous claims. But the Senate backed Leahy on May 1, 51–49.

Simpson also lost on the issue of Cuban refugees. The Judiciary Committee's version of S 1664 would have repealed a 1966 law granting permanent resident status to any Cuban who stayed in the United States for a year, even those who had remained in the United States illegally after their tourist visas expired (PL 89-732). Graham argued that Fidel Castro's continued rule meant that the law had not outlived its usefulness. He proposed to keep the law in place until Cuba had a democratically elected government, and the Senate agreed, 62–37.

CONFERENCE AND FINAL ACTION

Republican negotiators spent much of the summer privately debating what to do about the Gallegly amendment on public education for illegal immigrants. Including the amendment in the conference report on HR 2202 would virtually guarantee a veto, as Clinton had pledged not to sign the bill unless the amendment were dropped.

One faction, led by Republican presidential nominee and erstwhile Senate Majority Leader Bob Dole, R-Kan., argued that the Gallegly amendment should remain in the bill. This group's goal was to force Clinton to kill the popular measure, handing the GOP a campaign issue in such key states as California, Texas, New Jersey and Illinois.

A second faction, which included Simpson and Smith, wanted to drop the Gallegly amendment and save the bill. Resisting the ministrations of the Dole campaign, Simpson and Smith held firm in opposition to the amendment as the negotiations dragged on into September. Their side gained strength among Republicans as the election approached and Dole faded in the polls, making the idea of sacrificing the bill for the sake of presidential politics less appealing.

Some Democrats, meanwhile, pressed the White House to join them in opposing other elements of the bill, such as the limits on benefits for legal immigrants and the quick deportation of asylum seekers who did not have the necessary papers. Still, the only complaint voiced by Clinton about the bill was the Gallegly provision.

With time running out in the session, House and Senate negotiators finally signed off on a conference report (H Rept 104-828) Sept. 24. It was signed by all the Republican conferees but only one of the Democrats, Feinstein.

The final product included items that were in neither the House nor the Senate bill. For example, conferees added a provision making it harder for the government to sue employers who used immigration laws to discriminate against individuals. The new language, crafted to supersede a provision of the 1986 immigration law, required the government to show that an employer intended to discriminate against individuals. The 1986 law had allowed lawsuits based on the employer's actions alone.

Conversely, conferees omitted some provisions that were in both bills, including proposals to authorize funds for additional Labor Department inspectors to police suspected sweatshops. The House bill would have funded 150 new inspectors; the Senate version had called for 350.

Most of the Democratic conferees looked to Clinton to stop a bill they abhorred. "This is bad legislation as well as bad procedure," said Simon, alluding to Democrats' exclusion from the negotiations.

The House adopted the conference report on Sept. 25, 305–123, but that did not stop the administration from raising new objections. White House lobbyist John Hilley told Republicans Sept. 26 that Clinton wanted the immigration bill wrapped into the omnibus spending bill and stripped of several disputed provisions.

Top-level GOP negotiators signaled a willingness the next day to accept the White House's central demand—that they drop the last remaining provisions on legal immigration, which proposed to restrict public benefits to legal immigrants and set income requirements for their sponsors. But many House Republicans adamantly opposed that strategy; some said they could accept striking some but not all of the proposals. The new White House demands were too much for Simpson, who took to the floor to speak his mind.

"The White House and Democrat allies have moved the goal posts. . . . I think they moved the end zones, the stadium and, as far as I know, the campus," Simpson said.

By later that evening, however, it was becoming increasingly clear that Republicans had little choice if they wanted to get out of town and hit the campaign trail. Kennedy could not stop the House-passed conference report single-handedly, but he could tie it up for days. Meanwhile, if no deal was reached with the White House by Oct. 1 on an omnibus spending bill, Republicans feared they would take most of the blame.

At a meeting in his office early in the morning on Sept. 28, Gingrich struck a deal with Hilley. He read through a list of what was to be dropped or modified to satisfy the White House. He also agreed to fold the immigration provisions into the omnibus spending bill that the House was scheduled to vote on later that day. Simpson and Smith, the two principal advocates of standing up to the White House, arrived at the meeting as it was winding down, too late to stop the deal.

Dropped from the bill were provisions that would have denied most benefits to legal immigrants and created an income test for their sponsors. These included proposals to raise the required income level for sponsors, make it harder for legal immigrants to qualify for welfare and other public benefits, and allow deportation of legal immigrants who collected public assistance for 12 months.

The administration did not get everything it wanted. Left in the bill was the provision making it harder for the government to sue employers who used the immigration laws to discriminate against workers, as well as a House-backed proposal to deport speedily or exclude illegal immigrants with fake or borrowed documents.

In a gesture more symbolic than substantive, the House rolled Gallegly's amendment on public schooling of illegal immigrants into a separate bill (HR 4134) and passed it, 254–175, on Sept. 25. The Senate did not act on it before adjourning.

The House adopted the conference report on the omnibus spending bill (H Rept 104-863), which included the final immigration language, on Sept. 28, 370–37. The Senate adopted the report on Sept. 30 by voice vote, clearing the bill. Clinton signed it later that day.

MAJOR PROVISIONS

As enacted, the immigration section of the omnibus spending bill included provisions to:

Border Controls

• **Border Agents.** Authorize funding to increase the number of Border Patrol agents by 1,000 per year through fiscal 2001, doubling the total force from 5,000 to 10,000. The bill also authorized funds to increase the number of clerical workers and other support personnel at the border by 300 per year through fiscal 2001.

The bill ordered the Immigration and Naturalization Service (INS) to relocate as many agents as possible to border areas with the largest numbers of illegal immigrants, and to coordinate relocation plans with local law enforcement agencies. The INS was required to report to Congress on these activities within six months of enactment.

• **Other INS Employees.** Authorize funding for 900 additional INS agents to investigate and prosecute cases of smuggling, harboring or employing illegal immigrants. The bill also authorized funding for 300 new agents to investigate people who overstayed their visas.

• **Border Fence.** Authorize $12 million for the second and third tiers of a triple fence along a 14-mile strip at the U.S.-Mexico border south of San Diego, and for roads surrounding the fence. The project was to be exempt from the strictures of the 1973 Endangered Species Act and the 1969 National Environmental Policy Act if either would prevent expeditious construction. (This obviated the need for an environmental impact study or any mitigation programs such as creating open spaces to compensate for land taken over by the fence.) The bill allowed the attorney general to acquire land through condemnation for the fence.

• **Border Crossing Cards.** Require the INS to develop alien identification cards that included a biometric identifier, such as a fingerprint, that could be read by machine. A fingerprint was the only commonly used biometric identifier in use at the time, but future cards were expected to take advantage of such devices as retina scanners.

• **Fleeing through Checkpoints.** Create a penalty of up to five years in prison for fleeing through an INS checkpoint. Those convicted were made eligible for deportation.

• **Entry-Exit System.** Order the attorney general, within two years of enactment, to create a data base of information gathered from the documents people filled out as they legally entered and left the country. The data base was to allow the INS to match entry and exit records to identify people who overstayed their visas.

• **Preinspection.** Require the INS to establish "preinspection" stations at five of the 10 foreign airports that were departure points for the largest number of inadmissible immigrants. The stations were to screen people who did not have proper documents.

• **State Federal Cooperation.** Allow the INS to enter into agreements with state and local governments for help in investigating, arresting, detaining and transporting illegal immigrants.

Document Fraud and Illegal Immigrant Smuggling

• **Wiretaps.** Grant wiretap authority to the criminal division of the Justice Department for investigating cases of immigration document fraud.

• **Penalties for Illegal Immigrant Smuggling.** Create felonies for illegal immigrant smuggling of up to 10 years in prison for the first and second offenses, and 15 years for subsequent offenses. The measure created a crime punishable by up to five years in prison for employers who knowingly hired 10 people or more who were smuggled into the United States.

• **Prosecutors.** Create 25 positions for assistant United States attorneys to prosecute cases of illegal immigrant smuggling and document fraud.

• **Undercover Operations.** Grant broad authority for the INS to conduct undercover operations to track organized illegal immigration rings. Under the provision, the INS could establish or acquire companies, deposit funds in bank accounts without regard to federal regulations, and use profits from front companies to offset expenses.

• **Document Fraud.** Increase the penalty for document fraud from five years in prison to 10 or 15 years in most cases. If the fraud involved facilitating a drug trafficking crime, the new penalty was 20 years in prison; if it involved terrorism, the penalty was 25 years.

• **Assisting in Document Fraud.** Create a civil penalty for helping someone make a false application for public benefits such as food stamps. The bill also created a criminal penalty for doing so and "knowingly and willfully" failing to disclose it. This offense was punishable by up to 15 years.

• **False Attestation of Citizenship.** Create a criminal penalty of up to five years in prison for falsely claiming U.S. citizenship.

• **Illegal Voting.** Create a criminal penalty of up to one year in prison for unlawfully voting in a federal election.

• **Seizure of Assets.** Allow courts, in imposing sentences against violators of immigration statutes, to seize vehicles, boats, airplanes and real estate if they were used in the commission of a crime or paid for from the proceeds of a crime.

• **Involuntary Servitude.** Increase the penalty from five years in prison to 10 years for employers who kept workers in a state of involuntary servitude. Some illegal immigrant smuggling rings had brought immigrants to employers in the United States who kept them under prison-like conditions and paid them little, if anything.

• **Subpoenas and Evidence.** Allow INS agents to subpoena witnesses and allow videotaped testimony at deportation proceedings.

Detention and Deportation

• **Readmission of Deported Illegal Immigrants.** Bar any deported illegal immigrant from reentering the United States for five years. The moratorium rose to 10 years if the illegal immigrant left while deportation proceedings were in progress or attempted to reenter the country unlawfully. Repeat offenders were barred for 20 years, as were people convicted of aggravated felonies.

- **Status of Illegal Immigrants.** Deny legal status to anyone who had resided in the United States unlawfully for at least 180 days. Under the bill, people in the United States unlawfully for 180 days to one year could not gain legal status for three years. People in the country illegally for a year or more could not become legal for 10 years. These time limits did not count for minors, nor for people with a pending application for asylum. Battered women and children also were exempt, as were people granted protection under the family unity provision of the 1990 immigration act (PL 101-649). That provision allowed spouses and minor children of people granted amnesty under the 1986 immigration act (PL 99-603) to stay in the United States, even if they entered illegally, while their applications for legal status were pending.

- **Inadmissibility of Arriving Aliens.** Allow people who arrived in the United States without legitimate documentation to be detained and deported without a hearing unless they could demonstrate a credible fear of persecution back home. An asylum officer was to screen each case. An officer who decided there was no credible fear could deport the applicant. The applicant could request a review by an immigration judge within seven days, during which time the applicant had to remain in detention. The review could take place by telephone or teleconference.

- **Detention of Certain Illegal Immigrants.** Require most illegal immigrants convicted of crimes to be detained after their prison terms were completed. The attorney general could release certain illegal immigrants from detention centers if there was insufficient space. The attorney general could release illegal immigrants who did not pose a security risk or a risk of fleeing, or who came from countries that would not take them back.

- **Deportation Proceeding.** Streamline deportation of illegal immigrants by replacing multiple proceedings with one. A deportation hearing could be conducted by teleconference or, with the consent of the alien, by telephone. Only 10 days' notice was required before a hearing.

The deportation could be canceled in some cases, for example, if the deportee was a long-standing resident and was of "good moral character"; or if the deportation would cause unusual hardship to a spouse, parent or child who was a U.S. citizen or permanent legal resident.

- **Departure.** Require illegal immigrants to be removed from the United States within 90 days of a deportation order. Detention during that period was mandatory. Violent criminal aliens would have to complete their prison term before being deported. Some nonviolent criminal aliens could be deported before completing their term.

- **Deportation Appeals.** Limit judicial review of deportation orders. The bill created criminal penalties for failing to depart after a deportation order had been given. The State Department could discontinue all visas for countries that declined to take back their deported nationals.

- **Criminal Alien Tracking.** Authorize $5 million for a criminal alien tracking center. This section also required that a crim-

inal alien data base authorized in the 1994 crime law (PL 103-322) be used to assist local governments in identifying criminals who might be deportable. *(1994 crime law, p. 683)*

- **Prisoner Transfer Treaties.** Advise the president to negotiate bilateral prisoner transfer treaties to allow criminals to serve their terms in their home countries. The secretary of state and attorney general were required to present a report to Congress by April 1, 1997, on the potential for such treaties.

- **Vaccinations.** Make a potential immigrant who did not have proof of proper vaccinations inadmissible to the United States.

- **Stalking.** Add stalking, domestic violence and child abuse to the list of crimes that made someone deportable.

- **"Benedict Arnold" Language.** Permanently bar from entry into the United States anyone who renounced his or her citizenship to avoid taxes.

- **Delegation of Authority.** Allow the attorney general to authorize local law enforcement officials to perform the duties of an immigration officer in the event of a mass influx of immigrants.

- **Judicial Deportation.** Broaden the authority of judges to issue deportation orders. They would be allowed to order someone deported as part of probation or a plea agreement.

- **Military Bases.** Create a pilot program on the use of closed military bases as INS detention centers.

Employee Verification

- **Employment Verification Programs.** Order the attorney general to create three pilot programs—a basic pilot program, a Citizen Attestation Program, and a Machine-Readable Document Pilot Program—to test the effectiveness of workplace verification systems.

Participation in the programs was voluntary for employers. The attorney general was to choose the states where each program would be tested, though in some cases employers in nonselected states could participate. All federal departments and agencies within the chosen states were required to participate in the program.

- **Basic Pilot Program.** Allow participating employers to contact the INS, presumably by telephone, fax or e-mail, to check the immigration status of a job applicant. The INS was directed to maintain a data base of names, Social Security numbers and other information to be used in verifying applicants' eligibility to work. The INS was required to respond tentatively to employer queries within three days. If the tentative response was that the applicant was not legal, the INS would have 10 days to confirm that determination. The program was to be tested in five of the seven states with the largest number of illegal immigrants.

- **Citizen Attestation Program.** Create a program similar to the basic program that would allow applicants to bypass the check if they attested that they were U.S. citizens. The penalty for false claims of citizenship (up to five years in prison) was presumed sufficient to prevent widespread abuse.

- **Machine-Readable Document Program.** Allow employers to scan a card into a machine, which would verify the owner's Social Security number with the INS data base. The machine would be put in place in states selected by the attorney general in which driver's licenses or other state documents included Social Security numbers that could be read by machine.

- **Nondiscrimination.** Make it harder for the government to sue employers who used immigration laws to discriminate against certain workers, job applicants or other individuals. The government was required to show that an employer acted "for the purpose, or with the intent, of discriminating against" the individual. This intent standard was higher than the previous standard, which allowed prosecution based on actions, such as demanding an extraordinary amount of documentation.

Public Benefits

- **Public Charges.** Allow any consular agent to deny an immigration visa to anyone on the basis that the person was likely to become a public charge.
- **Income Requirement.** Require sponsors of legal immigrants to earn at least 25 percent more than the federal poverty level—$15,569 a year for a family of four in 1996—and to sign an affidavit that they would be financially responsible for the people they sponsored.
- **Driver's License Pilot Programs.** Allow states to create pilot programs to explore the feasibility of denying driver's licenses to illegal immigrants. The attorney general was to report to Congress on these programs after three years.
- **Social Security.** Clarify that Social Security benefits were not to be paid to illegal immigrants. The 1996 welfare law (PL 104-193) included a similar provision.
- **Student Aid.** Order the General Accounting Office (GAO) to study the use of student aid by illegal immigrants. The report was to be submitted to Congress within one year of enactment.
- **Welfare.** Require the GAO to report to Congress within 180 days on the unlawful use of means-tested benefits—such as food stamps and cash welfare—by illegal immigrants.
- **Battered Women and Children.** Amend the 1996 welfare law to permit certain illegal immigrants who were victims of domestic violence to qualify for public benefits. To qualify, the immigrant had to be living in the same household as the person responsible for the battery. There also had to be a connection between the domestic violence and the need for benefits.
- **Nonprofit Organizations.** Amend the welfare law so that nonprofit charitable organizations were no longer required to verify the immigration status of applicants to determine their eligibility for benefits.
- **Food Stamps.** Allow legal immigrants who were receiving food stamps, and who would lose them under provisions of the new welfare law, to continue receiving them until at least April 1, 1997, but no longer than Aug. 22, 1997, when the process of certifying people for food stamps was to be completed.
- **Falsely Applying for Benefits.** Allow judges to double the monetary penalty and triple the term of imprisonment for anyone who forged or counterfeited any United States seal to make a false application for public benefits.
- **Reimbursement for Medical Care.** Authorize states and localities to be reimbursed for the emergency medical care of illegal immigrants, if the care was not already reimbursed through existing federal programs. The amount was subject to appropriations.

- **Assisted Housing.** Require the secretary of Housing and Urban Development (HUD) to deny subsidized housing benefits to families in which all members were illegal immigrants. If families were split between legal and illegal immigrants, HUD could adjust the size of the benefit to match the percentage of family members who were in the United States legally.

Other Provisions

- **Forced Population Control.** Stipulate that anyone who had been forced to undergo sterilization or an abortion, or who had been persecuted for failure to do so, could be eligible for asylum or refugee status. Only 1,000 people per year could be admitted to the United States under this program.
- **Parole.** Limit the ability of the INS to use parole of detainees to facilitate mass immigration. The most recent example of this was in 1994 when the INS allowed 20,000 Cubans into the United States through the use of a visa lottery and the parole of detainees at Guantanamo Bay and within the United States. When the government did use parole to facilitate immigration, the parolees would count toward caps on legal immigration.
- **Asylum.** Require that asylum applications from people already in the United States be filed no later than one year after entry. In most cases asylum interviews would have to take place within 45 days of application. A ruling had to be made within 180 days, and an appeal had to be filed within 30 days of the ruling.

Under the provision, asylum could be denied for many reasons, including the applicant's ability to settle in a third country, a previous, unsuccessful application for asylum, and a failure to apply for asylum within one year of arriving in the country. Also, asylum could be rescinded if circumstances changed, such as if a new government came to power in the home country of the person granted asylum.

- **Public Education.** Deny visas to immigrants whose intention was to attend a public elementary or secondary school for more than one year.
- **Visas.** Clarify that any short-term visa was void as soon as a person stayed longer than its term, and require that a new visa be issued in the home country of the applicant. Previously, anyone could obtain visas in nearby countries such as Canada and Mexico.
- **Buddhist Monks.** Allow the State Department unlimited authority to determine the procedures and locations for processing immigrant visa applications.

The provision allowed the State Department to require Vietnamese monks and nuns of the An Quang Buddhist sect in Thailand to return to Vietnam to apply for visas for the United States. The D.C. Circuit Court of Appeals ruled in 1995, in *LAVAS v. Department of State* that such a requirement by the State Department amounted to discrimination based on nationality. The Supreme Court heard the case Oct. 15, 1996, and was expected to rule in 1997 on whether such a practice constituted discrimination.

- **Genital Mutilation.** Create a crime punishable by five years in prison for performing female genital mutilation on someone 18 years of age or older.
- **Mail-order Brides.** Require "international matchmaking" organizations to disseminate to their clients information about U.S. immigration laws. The fine for failure to do so was $20,000. The attorney general was to produce a report to Congress on the mail-order bride business within a year of enactment.
- **Temporary Agriculture Workers.** Require the INS to issue a report by the end of 1996 on whether the United States could expect an adequate number of temporary agriculture workers in the future.
- **State-issued Documents.** Set national standards for state-issued birth certificates, driver's licenses and other identification cards. The Department of Transportation was to set standards for licenses and IDs. The agency for birth certificates was unspecified. Licenses and IDs would either have to contain Social Security numbers, or the state issuing them would have to keep these numbers on file and verify their accuracy with the Social Security Administration.

The standards, which were intended to make the documents more tamper-resistant, were to be issued within one year. States were required to comply by Oct. 1, 2000. The standards applied to birth certificates issued after the compliance date and to licenses and IDs issued, renewed or replaced after that date.

- **Tamper-proof Social Security Cards.** Require the Social Security Administration to develop a prototype tamper-proof Social Security card. ❑

Terrorism

A surge in suspected terrorist bombings led President Clinton to press the 104th Congress for new tools to combat terrorism. House GOP conservatives balked at giving federal agents more power, however, forcing Congress to scale back one antiterrorism bill (S 735—PL 104-132) and abandon another (HR 3953).

Republicans won several important concessions before allowing S 735 to clear in April 1996. They inserted a major piece of the House GOP's anticrime agenda: a bill to limit federal-court appeals by state and federal inmates. Bitterly opposed by liberal Democrats, the restriction on such "habeas corpus" petitions were aimed at speeding the execution of prisoners on death row. *(House crime package, p. 733)*

The measure also included provisions to speed the deportation of criminal aliens and suspected terrorists, block the entry of refugees without proper documentation, put a financial squeeze on foreign groups identified as terrorist organizations, outlaw financial transactions with terrorist states and allow lawsuits in U.S. courts against foreign nations where terrorist acts were committed against U.S. citizens.

Significantly, the bill provided few of the new investigatory and prosecutorial powers sought by the administration. The missing elements reflected the mistrust among many House Republicans for federal law enforcement agencies, particularly the Bureau of Alcohol, Tobacco and Firearms.

Clinton continued to press for enhanced wiretapping authority and related powers, to no avail. In a reversal from their roles in previous debates, congressional Democrats generally were the ones calling for tougher enforcement measures, while Republicans were the ones defending civil liberties and the rights of the accused.

Lawmakers were more responsive to Clinton's request to beef up security at U.S. airports and military installations, the most frequent targets of terrorists. Congress included $1.1 billion for antiterrorism initiatives in the fiscal 1997 omnibus spending bill (HR 3610—PL 104-208) that cleared in the last week of the session.

BACKGROUND

The legislative drive against terrorism began early in 1995 as a response to the 1993 bombing of the World Trade Center in New York. In their wide-ranging anticrime bill (S 3), Senate Majority Leader Bob Dole, R-Kan., and Senate Judiciary Committee Chairman Orrin G. Hatch, R-Utah, proposed in January to create special courts and secret proceedings to deport suspected foreign terrorists from the United States; raise federal penalties for terrorism-related crimes; give federal and state prosecutors jurisdiction over more terrorist incidents outside the United States; authorize wiretaps of suspected foreign terrorists and their accomplices; and make it a federal crime to willfully violate federal aviation security regulations.

The next month, Clinton offered a broader antiterrorism package. Among other provisions, his bill proposed to make terrorism a federal crime; allow investigators to obtain court orders for "roving wiretaps" on any telephone used by a suspect, rather than limiting surveillance to specified phone lines; speed the deportation of illegal immigrants linked to terrorists; allow the government to designate certain foreign organizations as terrorist groups, with prohibitions on entry into and fund-raising in the United States; and require chemical "taggants" in plastic explosives to help investigators track the source of detonated bombs.

The administration's wish list expanded after the Alfred P. Murrah Federal Building in Oklahoma City was decimated by a bomb on April 19, 1995, killing more than 165 people. Although international terrorists were the initial focus of speculation, police soon charged the bombing to a U.S. citizen with antigovernment views. The incident led the administration and senators to bolster the proposals on foreign terrorist activity and add new ones addressing domestic threats.

Shortly after the bombing, Clinton revised his package to propose an additional $1.25 billion in programs, many of them aimed at the domestic front. These included hiring 1,000 more federal agents to track terrorist threats and prosecute offenders; giving the FBI greater access to credit reports, telephone bills, hotel receipts and other consumer records; allow wiretap evidence to be used in court even if it had been obtained improperly, provided that the agents had been acting in good faith; allow the armed forces to assist on investigations involving chemical weapons, nerve agents and other weapons of mass destruction; require taggants in all explosives; and mandate at least 10 years in prison for anyone convicted of knowingly transferring a firearm or explosive for use in a violent crime or drug trafficking.

Dole and Hatch also pumped up their antiterrorism initiative. Their revised proposal, introduced as a freestanding bill (S 735) on April 27, drew heavily on Clinton's plan, including the proposals to ease deportation of suspected foreign terrorists, increase the FBI's access to consumer records and hire more investigators. In addition, however, they proposed to limit habeas corpus appeals by death row inmates in state prisons and ban foreign aid to countries that assisted the nations sponsoring international terrorism.

The competing proposals on terrorism both sought to shift the balance between personal liberties and public safety in favor of public safety. Soon after the bills were unveiled, civil libertarians and lawmakers at both ends of the political spectrum started voicing misgivings about such a shift. Others, however, suggested that the Oklahoma bombing signaled that it was time to reconsider the traditional balance. "Without order in our society," said Sen. Joseph I. Lieberman, D-Conn., "there is no liberty."

ROUND ONE

In an unusual display of bipartisanship, the Senate approved a modified version of S 735 on June 7, 91–8. The bill proposed to authorize $2.1 billion over five years for antiterrorism programs, with the money coming out of the Violent Crime Trust Fund that Congress created in the 1994 crime bill (PL 103-322). *(Crime bill, p. 683)*

The main questions during the two-week debate were whether to add more of Clinton's proposals and whether to delete the habeas corpus restrictions. Democrats offered a series of amendments to toughen the bill with Clinton initiatives, and many were adopted. These included an amendment authorizing roving wiretaps, adopted 77–19, and one allowing the military to aid the investigation of certain cases involving chemical or biological weapons, adopted by voice vote. A Lieberman amendment to allow federal agents to conduct emergency wiretaps for 48 hours without a court order, however, was killed on a tabling motion, 52–28.

Dole and Hatch had included a proposal to require taggants in plastic explosives, in conformance with a recent international treaty. Clinton sought to require taggants in more common explosives, but gun rights advocates fiercely resisted any effort to mandate taggants in black powder or smokeless powder, which were prime ingredients in ammunition.

Still, Dianne Feinstein, a California Democrat who had emerged as one of the Senate's leading players on gun control issues, convinced the Senate June 5 to require taggants in explosives other than the powders used in small arms ammunition. Her amendment was adopted, 90–0.

On the issue of habeas petitions, the bill included a set of restrictions similar to those in a free-standing bill (HR 729) that the House had passed in February. The Senate bill proposed to let most inmates file only one habeas corpus petition after exhausting their state-court appeals. Death row inmates were to have six months to file their petition, if they were in states that guaranteed prisoners access to competent lawyers, and other inmates were to have one year. The bill proposed to allow a second petition to a federal appeals court when inmates presented clear and convincing evidence of innocence. It also called for federal judges to let stand the state-court rulings on constitutional questions and other issues raised by the inmate unless the decisions were unreasonable.

Although most Democrats wanted to restrict habeas corpus petitions, many were concerned that the Dole-Hatch proposal went too far and would speed the execution of inmates who had been wrongfully convicted. They tried to remove the provision requiring federal judges to defer to state courts, limit the restrictions to federal inmates and allow second petitions from inmates who could show probable innocence, but Republicans defeated each amendment.

House Slowdown

Less than three weeks later, the House Judiciary Committee approved a similar antiterrorism bill (HR 1710—H Rept 104-383) by Chairman Henry J. Hyde, R-Ill., on a bipartisan, 23–12 vote. The measure hewed more closely to Clinton's proposal than the Senate bill did, and it was conspicuously silent on habeas corpus petitions.

The bill proposed a number of new powers for investigators and prosecutors, including the ability to authorize roving wiretaps, make emergency wiretaps without a court order, and use wiretap evidence in court that had been obtained improperly but in good faith. It also would have authorized the military to assist investigations into the use of chemical, biological or other weapons of mass destruction; allowed the administration to designate groups as terrorist organizations and bar their members from entering or raising money in the United States; and sped the expulsion of foreigners linked to terrorist groups.

The committee rejected amendments by Democrat Charles E. Schumer of New York to force explosives manufacturers to use taggants and to authorize a ban on armor-piercing "cop killer" bullets. It agreed, however, to amendments by Democrat Zoe Lofgren of California to drop a provision allowing the government access to credit records without a court order and to allow medical and religious materials to be donated to foreign terrorist organizations.

The momentum behind the bill quickly vanished. Conservative Republicans prevailed on the GOP leadership to keep the bill off the floor, arguing that it was an overreaction that would intrude too much on civil liberties.

Their complaints were echoed by an unusual coalition of conservative and liberal groups. Its members ranged from the liberal American Civil Liberties Union to the conservative National Rifle Association (NRA) and the libertarian Cato Institute.

To address the GOP concerns, Hyde negotiated two new versions of the bill with conservative freshman Bob Barr, R-Ga. Hyde agreed to abandon some key proposals, including those to increase wiretapping authority, allow military involvement in terrorism investigations and impose a surcharge on federal civil penalties to help telephone companies make their networks more conducive to wiretapping. He also added several GOP anticrime initiatives, including the limit on habeas corpus petitions from HR 729.

The new bills (HR 2703, HR 2768) were introduced in early December, and GOP leaders planned to take the revised terrorism legislation to the floor in the week of Dec. 18. They had to postpone that debate until 1996, however, when preliminary vote counts showed that close to 100 Republicans were opposed or undecided.

The setback was testimony to the strong distrust of federal law enforcement that had surfaced in Congress in 1995. "I think people are just psychologically against giving more resources to law enforcement," Hyde said.

Democratic supporters of the bill accused the GOP leadership of caving in to the NRA. Schumer, a key Democratic proponent of the bill, said the gun rights lobby and its allies were unwilling to let the terrorism bill go forward unless members were also guaranteed an opportunity to repeal the assault-weapons ban that Congress had included in the 1994 crime bill. Although the leadership and an NRA lobbyist denied any link between the two measures, the House later took up a bill to repeal the assault-weapons ban the week after it debated HR 2703. *(Assault weapons bill, p. 736)*

The terrorism bill finally reached the House floor on March 13, 1996. Although he had helped write HR 2703, Barr again sought major changes that would make the measure more acceptable to conservatives. He offered an amendment to remove several administration-backed provisions of the bill, including ones allowing the administration to designate groups as terrorist organizations; establishing special courts and procedures to speed the deportation of suspected foreign terrorists; allowing some improperly obtained wiretap evidence to be used in court; making it easier to prosecute those who provided guns later used in a violent crime; and requiring a government study of taggants in black and smokeless powder.

Barr argued that law enforcement officials did not need new powers because they already had ample authority to achieve many of the bill's aims. He was supported by numerous Republicans and some Democrats who argued that the public's mistrust of the federal government exceeded its fear of terrorism. GOP leaders also backed the Barr amendment, as did the NRA and other gun rights groups.

Hyde and other opponents of the amendment argued that it would gut the bill. Noting that Barr had negotiated the compromise that Barr was trying to rewrite, Hyde said, "We bent over backwards to accommodate the distinguished gentleman [Barr]. . . . Evidently, we didn't bend far enough."

The House adopted the Barr amendment on a **key vote of 246–171 (R 178–54; D 67–117; I 1–0)**. *(1996 key votes, p. 1047)*

The next day, the House defeated two attempts to delete the proposed restrictions on habeas petitions. The first, a Democratic proposal that also would have restored weaker versions of some of the provisions deleted by the Barr amendment, was rejected, 129 294. The second, a bipartisan amendment that addressed only the habeas petitions, was defeated on a **key vote of 135–283 (R 12–218; D 122–65; I 1–0)**. *(1996 key votes, p. 1047)*

The House passed the bill on March 14, 229–191. The bill drew opposition from 58 Republicans, most of them conservative freshmen who objected even to the diminished enforcement provisions.

Many of the 132 Democrats who opposed the bill, by contrast, did so because of the limits on habeas petitions. The House then inserted the text of HR 2703 into S 735 and passed the latter by voice vote.

Conference

House and Senate negotiators on S 735 were faced with the delicate task of making the bill tough enough to satisfy Clinton and the Senate without alienating House conservatives like Barr. They agreed to a conference report April 15 that congressional Democrats considered too weak but did not have the votes to change.

The conferees restored a modified version of a top administration priority: allowing the secretary of state to designate certain foreign groups as terrorist, enabling the government to deny visas to members of the group, bar fund-raising in the United States, and freeze their U.S. assets. They also restored an administration-backed provision establishing special courts and procedures to speed the deportation of criminal aliens. They did not agree to any expansion on federal wiretapping authority, however, in light of the opposition of House conservatives. Nor did they propose to mandate or even study the inclusion of taggants in smokeless or black powder.

Over Democratic objections, the conferees retained the limits on habeas petitions. They also included a provision allowing refugees seeking asylum from persecution abroad to be turned away at the U.S. border if they lacked proper documents. Proponents of the change said the asylum system was rife with abuse, but critics called it an unjust clampdown on valid refugees.

To help boost House GOP support, the conferees included provisions from two other House-passed anticrime bills: one (based on HR 668) to ease the deportation of criminal aliens and raising penalties for immigrant smuggling, and a second (based on HR 665) requiring federal judges to order restitution for people injured or financially harmed by federal criminals. Previous law had made restitution an option, not a requirement. *(House crime package, p. 733)*

The conferees filed their report on S 735 on April 15 (H Rept 104-518). The Senate adopted the report, 91–8, two days later, after Republicans defeated a series of Democratic motions to restore provisions sought by the administration.

The Senate also fought one more time over the proposed restrictions on habeas petitions. Daniel Patrick Moynihan, D-N.Y., argued that forcing federal judges to defer to state court rulings would undermine the Supreme Court's authority and possibly violate due process. He tried to send the bill back to conference with instructions to remove the restrictions, but the Senate killed his motion by tabling it, 64–35.

The House approved the report on April 18, 293–133, clearing the bill for White House approval. President Clinton signed it April 24.

ROUND TWO

Three new incidents of suspected terrorism in 1996—a truck-bomb attack on a U.S. military barracks in Saudi Arabia June 25, the fiery crash of TWA Flight 800 on July 17, and a pipe-bomb explosion at the Olympic Games in Atlanta July 27—spurred the administration to renew its push for the counterterrorism tools dropped from S 735. Again, the effort was blocked on most fronts by House conservatives.

Topping Clinton's list of priorities were expanded wiretapping authority, including emergency and roving wiretaps, and a mandate for taggants in gunpowder. The administration also sought money for phone companies to make their networks more conducive to wiretaps and more power to use the Racketeering Influenced and Corrupt Organizations (RICO) Act to prosecute people involved in terrorist acts.

On July 31, a bipartisan task force of congressional leaders and administration officials struck a tentative deal on a new antiterrorism package. The package included most of the administration's priorities, but House Republicans balked at the proposed expansion in wiretapping authority. They offered a compromise that would have made the federal government liable if any of its agents gathered evidence improperly, even if the evidence was not divulged. Negotiators for the White House declined the offer, saying it would stifle virtually all federal investigations.

The House eventually went forward with a comparatively narrow measure aimed mainly at improving bomb-detection and other security measures at airports. The bill, which passed 389–22 on Aug. 2, included only a handful of the lesser items sought by the administration. It would not have expanded wiretapping authority, and it called for studying taggants in gunpowder in lieu of mandating their use.

The Senate did not act on the bill. A number of its airport-security provisions, however, were included in the final version of a bill to reauthorize the Federal Aviation Administration (HR 3539—PL 104-264). *(FAA reauthorization, p. 359)*

The only victory for Clinton came on the fiscal 1997 defense authorization bill (HR 3230—PL 104-201). At the insistence of the Senate, the conference report on the bill (H Rept 104-724) included a provision allowing military forces, under certain circumstances, to help investigate terrorist attacks in the United States that employed chemical, biological or other weapons of mass destruction. *(Defense authorization, p. 306)*

ROUND THREE

While Congress was stingy in granting the administration new powers, it was far more generous in providing money to battle terrorism. The willingness to spend money on terrorism-related projects was first displayed in May 1995, when Clinton asked Congress for $142 million in emergency funding to respond to the Oklahoma blast, including money for enhanced counterterrorism activities. House and Senate appropriators quickly proposed an even larger sum—$250.5 million, including $34.2 million for a new Justice Department antiterrorism fund—in a bill to provide disaster relief and cancel previously approved projects. The final version of the bill (HR 1944—PL 104-19) cleared the Senate July 21 and was signed into law July 27.

For counterterrorism efforts in fiscal 1997, Clinton originally requested roughly $220 million as part of the bill for the departments of Commerce, Justice and State (HR 3814). The House approved $147 million, but after the Olympic bombing, Senate appropriators proposed to raise the number to nearly $300 million.

The administration came back on Sept. 9 with a new request: $1.1 billion for more FBI agents, heightened security at airports and greater protection for federal facilities, among other antiterrorism projects. Appropriators grumbled at the eleventh-hour demand, but they acknowledged that it was politically irresistible. The only question was how to pay for it.

The appropriators eventually sprinkled $1.1 billion into the fiscal 1997 omnibus spending bill (HR 3610) for antiterrorism projects at more than a dozen departments and agencies. The biggest slice—$353 million—went to the Defense Department. Part of the money was to be used by the Pentagon to examine each overseas installation for its vulnerability to terrorist attack. About a third of the sum was set aside to relocate troops, install fences and expand intelligence-gathering techniques in the Persian Gulf.

The departments of Commerce, Justice and State and the federal judiciary received the next biggest slice, $314 million. About half was slated for the FBI to double its complement of specialists in terrorism cases, add agents in selected global hot spots and update computerized identification systems. The rest was for improving safety at American diplomatic missions, hiring more prosecutors and improving building security, among other purposes.

The Department of Transportation received $237 million, almost all of it going to the Federal Aviation Administration to buy bomb-detection devices, profile passengers, screen cargo and improve airline safety. The Bureau of Alcohol, Tobacco and Firearms (ATF) received $80.6 million, largely to enhance its investigations, and the Customs Service collected $58 million to screen passengers.

The remaining $103 million was distributed among the federal departments, agencies and museums mainly to improve security at their facilities.

All of the antiterrorism funding was designated "emergency" appropriations, not subject to the annual spending caps. Still, appropriators paid for the increase largely by trimming other programs and by using unspent Defense Department funds from fiscal 1996.

The omnibus bill also addressed two issues left over from S 735.

First, it required the National Academy of Sciences to study the use of taggants in smokeless and black powder. In particular, the academy was asked to determine whether such additives would substantially assist law enforcement without imposing excessive costs, risking safety or harming the environment. Second, it provided $60 million to start paying the telephone companies to make their networks more conducive to wiretapping by law enforcement agents, as Congress had ordered in 1994 (PL 103-414). *(1994 law, p. 354)*

The House approved the conference report on HR 3610 (H Rept 104-863) on Sept. 28, 370–37. The Senate cleared the measure by voice vote Sept. 30, and Clinton signed it later that day.

MAJOR PROVISIONS

As enacted, S 735 contained provisions to:

Habeas Corpus

• **Overall.** Restrict significantly the opportunity for state and federal prisoners to challenge the constitutionality of their convictions in federal court by filing habeas corpus petitions.

• **Deadlines.** Require state prisoners seeking federal review to file petitions within one year of exhausting state appeals. The filing deadline in death penalty cases was set at six months, providing that the state supplied a competent lawyer for death penalty appeals. Federal courts also faced deadlines to act on these death row appeals.

• **Deference.** Direct federal judges to defer to the rulings of state judges on constitutional and other issues, unless the rulings were "unreasonable."

• **Second Review.** Require inmates seeking a second round of federal review to petition a panel of federal appellate judges, rather than taking a petition to any federal district court judge. To grant a second round of review, those judges would have to find that there was new evidence showing "clear and convincing" proof of the defendant's innocence, or that the claim was based on a new rule of law established by the U.S. Supreme Court and applied retroactively. Their decision could not be appealed.

Crime Victims

• **Victim Restitution.** Expand restitution requirements to encompass most federal offenses, although judges were given some discretion to waive restitution in certain cases, such as when it would be too difficult and time-consuming to determine what restitution should be made.

The restitution could include replacing stolen or damaged property, paying for medical or psychological bills related to the crime, or reimbursement for lost income. Payment of such restitution orders would be a factor in the granting of probation.

• **Victims of Terrorism.** Authorize grants to states to help residents who were the victims of terrorism or mass violence. The provision required that when certain federal criminal trials were moved out of state, the government provide closed-circuit television coverage of the case to affected victims. This provision was aimed at the Oklahoma City bombing trial, which was moved to Denver.

• **Limits on Payments.** Make general changes to the federal Crime Victims Fund, specifying that no payments were to be made to crime victims who had not paid outstanding fines or penalties stemming from their own criminal convictions. This provision was not to take effect, however, until an effective tracking system existed to identify who was delinquent on such debts.

Terrorist Groups and Nations

• **Designation.** Allow the secretary of state, in consultation with the attorney general and Treasury secretary, to designate certain foreign groups as terrorist. These designations would be subject to classified congressional review and, once final, to limited judicial review. The designation would lapse after two years, but could be extended for an additional two years.

Fund-raising. Block groups designated as terrorist from fund-raising in the United States. The Treasury secretary was authorized to freeze the U.S. assets of such groups once the administration notified Congress of the proposed designation.

• **Material Support.** Expand existing federal laws against providing material support to terrorists, in part by specifying that such support included virtually any kind of money, lodging, equipment or assets except medicine or religious materials.

• **Terrorist States.** Ban U.S. aid to countries that provided aid or military equipment to terrorist states, unless the president certified that such aid was in the national interest. The law prohibited U.S. citizens or companies to engage in financial transactions with terrorist states.

• **Lawsuits.** Authorize U.S. citizens to sue foreign nations in federal court for terrorist acts committed against U.S. citizens abroad. This provision applied to nations that the administration designated as state sponsors of terrorism under the terms of the 1979 Export Administration Act. Such nations could be held liable for monetary damages if they committed or ordered terrorist acts against U.S. citizens or permanent U.S. residents that resulted in personal injury or death. U.S. federal courts were given jurisdiction over acts outside the foreign state, or within a country whose government refused to negotiate over the claim for damages.

Exclusion and Deportation

• **Exclusion.** Allow the federal government to deny visas to foreigners who belonged to groups designated as terrorist.

• **Deportation Court.** Establish a special deportation court for illegal immigrants suspected of terrorism. The law created unique rules for the deportation court, allowing government lawyers to shield sensitive evidence from suspects. However, the rules required the government to give the illegal immigrants a summary of any classified information used against them.

• **Summary Exclusion.** Establish a process making it easier to turn away or deport foreigners who arrived without proper documents. Such foreigners could be removed without further hearing or review unless they claimed to be fleeing persecution and requested asylum. Those cases were to be referred to an asylum officer for immediate screening. A foreigner who demonstrated a "credible fear of persecution" would be allowed to file an asylum claim and remain in the United States pending a full hearing. These provisions were to apply to foreigners arriving at the border, or to those who were already in the United States but were found to have entered illegally.

• **Alien Criminals.** Streamline the deportation process for illegal immigrants convicted of crimes, restricting the right of noncitizens to appeal their deportation orders. The bill permitted nonviolent offenders to be deported before they served their entire sentence. It also authorized state and local law enforcement officials to detain illegal immigrants who were previously deported for committing crimes until they could be placed in federal custody.

- **Illegal Immigrant Smuggling.** Enhance law enforcement powers to catch and prosecute people who commit immigration crimes. The bill authorized wiretaps to investigate certain immigration offenses and made illegal immigrant smuggling subject to prosecution under the Racketeer Influenced and Corrupt Organizations (RICO) law.

Counterterrorism Funds

- **Authorization.** Authorize about $1 billion over four years to help federal law enforcement officials fight terrorism. The FBI was to receive the largest share, $468 million. The money was to be used to create a special counterterrorism and counterintelligence fund, and to help construct and operate a special FBI academy and laboratory.

Other authorizations included: an additional $100 million in Byrne anticrime grants to help local law enforcement officials develop plans and training programs to combat terrorism; $172 million to support the Drug Enforcement Administration; $90 million for Treasury Department counterterrorism measures, including enhanced presidential security; $41 million for the Justice Department to hire additional assistant U.S. attorneys and provide increased security at federal office buildings; and $41 million to help the federal judiciary keep up with the increased caseload expected to stem from the law.

Congress was authorized to take some or all of the money from a special anticrime trust fund created in the 1994 crime law (PL 103-322). *(1994 crime bill, p. 683)*

New Offenses and Penalties

- **General.** Broaden federal jurisdiction over terrorist-related activity and enhance penalties for crimes linked to terrorism.
- **International Terrorism.** Make it a federal crime to participate in international terrorism activities within the United States. The law applied to those who killed, kidnapped or seriously injured someone in the United States, or who put someone seriously at risk through property damage. The offense also had to involve conduct outside U.S. borders. The death penalty was authorized for such crimes if a death occurred.
- **Arson, Explosives.** Increase penalties for explosive offenses and arson, and make it a crime to transfer explosive materials "knowing or having reasonable cause to believe" they would be used in a violent crime or drug offense. The law extended the statute of limitations for arson offenses from five years to seven years.
- **Bomb-Making Information.** Require the U.S. attorney general to conduct a six-month study on the availability of bomb-manufacturing information in the print, electronic and film media. The study also was to examine whether this information was being used by terrorists. The attorney general was to consider the First Amendment protections for disseminating such information, as well as the need for additional regulation.

- **Federal Employees.** Make it a federal crime to target federal employees because of or in the course of their official duties.

Other Provisions

- **Law Enforcement Study.** Create a commission, with members appointed by Congress and the chief justice of the United States, to evaluate the conduct and effectiveness of federal law enforcement agencies. The law also directed the Justice Department to publish statistics, going back to 1990, on crimes and threats against federal, state and local government workers because of their official duties.
- **Tagging of Explosives.** Require the marking of plastic explosives for easier detection by law enforcement officials. The provisions, which carried out an international agreement made in Montreal in 1991, required such markers in all plastic explosives manufactured in, imported into or exported from the United States.

The law also ordered the Treasury Department to study whether tracing agents should be added to other explosive materials. If warranted by the study's findings, the Treasury secretary could draft regulations to require such taggants. Those rules were to take effect nine months after they were proposed unless Congress voted against such a mandate. Black and smokeless powder were excluded from the study.

The Treasury Department was instructed to examine whether some of the common chemicals used to make explosives could be made inert. The department's study also was to examine the state licensing requirements for various components, such as detonators and dynamite, used in explosives work.

- **Wiretapping Study.** Require, within three months of enactment, a study of laws on wiretapping and phone surveillance methods. The study was to make recommendations for the appropriate use of surveillance methods in monitoring terrorist or other criminal groups.
- **Armor Piercing Bullets.** Require the government to conduct a study of the threat to law enforcement officers from various types of guns and ammunition. The study was to determine whether existing types of body armor were sufficient to protect officers from bullets on the market.
- **Nuclear, Biological and Chemical Weapons.** Expand federal prohibitions against trafficking in nuclear materials, primarily by adding restrictions on trading in nuclear by-products and materials that were below weapons-grade strength.

The law also broadened federal jurisdiction over biological weapons, expanding federal prohibitions to include attempts to acquire or conspiracies involving such weapons. And it imposed new controls on potentially deadly human pathogens. The secretary of Health and Human Services was to issue a list of biological materials that could pose a serious threat to public safety, and was to regulate the proper transfers of such materials.

The statute criminalized the use of chemical weapons within the United States or against U.S. citizens abroad. And it called for a presidential task force to study whether the government should set up a special center to train law enforcement officials in how to respond to emergencies involving chemical or biological weapons.

- **Airline Security.** Require that foreign airlines using U.S. airports employ the same security measures required of U.S. carriers.
- **Voter Registration Cards.** Specify that voter registration cards did not count as proof of U.S. citizenship. ❑

House Crime Package

As part of their "Contract with America," House Republicans launched a major effort in 1995 to reshape the federal government's crime-fighting priorities. The effort produced mixed results: all but one of the contract bills sank in the Senate without a vote, but significant portions were enacted as part of larger bills.

The GOP sought to reverse many of the crime-fighting dictates set by Congress in 1994, when it was controlled by Democrats. The massive anticrime bill enacted that year (PL 104-322) placed too much emphasis on crime-preventing social programs, Republicans complained, and not enough on crime-deterring punishment and incarceration. *(1994 crime bill, p. 683)*

The House Republicans' effort began with an anticrime package (HR 3) designed to fulfill the promise of their contract. The package was split into six bills, which the GOP leadership rushed through committee and the floor in the first seven weeks of 1995. The Senate took up only one: HR 665, a bill to mandate restitution for victims of federal crimes, which the Senate amended and sent back to the House late in 1995.

Senate Republicans had their own anticrime package (S 3), which was similar to HR 3. Its proposals included shifting funds for crime prevention programs to prison construction and law enforcement, restricting death row appeals, allowing prosecutors to use evidence obtained in illegal searches and imposing mandatory penalties for using a gun in certain violent crimes.

Although there was bipartisan support for some features of S 3, such as its antiterrorism provisions and its restrictions on death row appeals, Democrats objected to many of the changes it sought to make in the 1994 law. Sen. Joseph R. Biden Jr. of Delaware, the top Democrat on the Judiciary Committee, asked at a hearing on S 3, "Where is the logic of dismantling this crime bill other than to say it has the name Clinton on it and therefore it is bad?"

Because of the power wielded by Senate Democrats, Republicans were left trying to decide whether to take their chances with a single, controversial omnibus bill or a number of less hotly disputed pieces, each subject to a potentially ruinous filibuster. They chose the latter course, inserting pieces of the House package into a variety of bills. Provisions of the restitution bill and two other House-passed crime measures were added to an antiterrorism bill (S 735—PL 104-132) that Congress cleared in April 1996.

A fourth House-passed proposal (HR 667), a bill to steer more money for prison construction to states that enacted tougher sentencing laws, was included in an omnibus spending bill for fiscal 1996 (HR 3019—PL 104-134). So were portions of the most hotly disputed piece of the House crime package, a bill (HR 728) to replace many of the crime-prevention programs authorized in 1994 with a smaller block grant.

The remaining piece of the House package—HR 666, a bill to let federal prosecutors use evidence obtained without a valid search warrant under certain circumstances—never resurfaced after passing the House. Clinton had sought to give federal prosecutors more limited powers to use wiretapping evidence obtained without a proper warrant, and the House Judiciary Committee included such a provision in an antiterrorism bill (HR 1710) in June 1995. But opposition from conservative House Republicans killed that proposal.

COMMUNITY POLICING

The most controversial of the six House bills was HR 728, which proposed a single, $10 billion block grant to replace several of the grant programs that were central to the 1994 law. In particular, the bill proposed to end the grants to help communities hire more police officers ($8.8 billion over six years), fund social programs to prevent crime ($4 billion over five years) and establish special courts to steer nonviolent drug offenders into rehabilitation ($1 billion over six years). The bill would have provided a list of suggested uses for the new block grant, but communities would largely have been left to spend their money as they saw fit.

The bill triggered an intense fight over community policing, the "cops on the beat" program that Clinton had championed during the 1992 campaign. Republican critics argued that the program would hire far fewer officers than promised and make little discernible impact on crime. And while some communities might need more police officers, they said, others had a more urgent need for police equipment, improved lighting in public places, or other crime fighting priorities.

Clinton and many congressional Democrats argued that hiring new officers was an expensive commitment that many communities were unlikely to make without some assistance. This was particularly true for community policing, a labor-intensive strategy that put police officers on regular beats where they could get to know the community and help prevent crime as well as apprehend criminals.

Republicans also argued that much of the spending in the 1994 law was "pork barrel" that had little to do with preventing crime. Democrats countered that the GOP block grants would invite waste or disappear into local budgets, as had been the case with the discredited Law Enforcement Assistance Administration block grants in the 1970s.

The Judiciary Committee had approved the bill Feb. 2 on a largely party-line, 21–13 vote, after defeating Democratic amendments to preserve the grants for community policing and specific crime-prevention programs. The committee reported the bill on Feb. 8 (H Rept 104-24).

On the House floor Feb. 14, Democrats pointed out that the community policing grants had already led more than 8,000 communities to hire about 17,000 officers—a pace that would yield 100,000 new officers over six years. Republicans maintained that the 100,000 plateau would never be reached, however, and they rejected an amendment by Charles E. Schumer,

D-N.Y., to preserve $7.5 billion for community policing, 196–235. An amendment by John Conyers Jr., D-Mich., to dedicate $5 billion of the block grants to prevention programs had been rejected by voice vote the previous day.

Responding to some Democratic criticisms about accountability, lawmakers added a requirement, proposed by Republican Bill Martini of New Jersey, that localities put up a 10 percent match to receive the crime-fighting grants. The revised bill passed, 238–192, with only 18 Democrats in support and only nine Republicans in opposition.

After the bill drew a veto threat, the House Appropriations Committee worked its provisions into the fiscal 1996 spending bill for the departments of Commerce, Justice and State (HR 2076), which the committee reported July 19 (H Rept 104-196). The spending bill proposed to provide a $2 billion block grant for anticrime programs in lieu of the community policing and crime-prevention programs.

On the House floor July 25, Rep. Alan B. Mollohan, D-W.Va., tried to remove the block grant money and restore funding for the police and prevention programs. His amendment was defeated, 184–232. The House passed the bill the next day, 272–151.

The Senate Appropriations Committee reported a new version of HR 2076 on Sept. 12 (S Rept 104-139) that called for a $1.7 billion block grant with more restrictions than the House had proposed. On the Senate floor Sept. 29, however, Republicans agreed by voice vote to abandon the block-grant approach and restore the grants for community policing, drug courts and a variety of prevention programs. The bill passed by voice vote later that day.

In conference, Republican appropriators negotiated a final version of the bill largely without consulting Democrats and without heeding Clinton's veto threats. The conference report (H Rept 104-378), filed Dec. 1, included $1.9 billion for a single law enforcement block grant, similar to the House proposal.

On the House floor Dec. 6, Democrats tried to send the bill back to conference with instructions to restore the grants for cops on the beat. Their motion was rejected, 190–231, and the conference report approved, 256–166. The Senate adopted the report the next day, 50–48, clearing the bill.

As expected, Clinton vetoed the bill Dec. 19, citing the cuts to the cops on the beat program and other administration priorities. The House failed to override the veto on Jan. 3, voting 240–159—far short of the needed two-thirds majority.

After months of difficult negotiations, the GOP appropriators and the administration struck a compromise. The omnibus spending bill for fiscal 1996 (HR 3019) included $1.4 billion in grants for community police and $503 million for a block grant modeled after HR 728. Of the $503 million, the Justice Department could reserve $18 million for drug courts. No money was provided, however, for most of the other prevention-oriented programs in the 1994 crime law.

The House approved the conference report on HR 3019 (H Rept 104-537) on April 25, 399–25, and the Senate followed suit later that day, 88–11, clearing the bill. Clinton signed it April 26.

The appropriators made no attempt to eliminate the com-

munity policing grants in fiscal 1997, although they provided substantially less than Clinton requested. The omnibus spending bill for fiscal 1997 (HR 3610—PL 104-208) included $1.4 billion for the community policing program—Clinton had requested just under $2 billion—and $523 million for local law enforcement block grants, as per HR 728. An additional $30 million was provided for drug courts, but no funds were appropriated for most of the prevention-oriented social programs in the 1994 law.

PRISONS

In addition to eliminating the dedicated funding for community policing and crime-prevention programs, Republicans sought to spend more of the anticrime trust fund on prison construction. In particular, they wanted to build more prisons in states that required convicts to serve at least 85 percent of their sentences before being released, a policy they dubbed "truth-in-sentencing."

To Republicans, there were few crime-prevention strategies more effective than putting violent criminals behind bars. The truth-in-sentencing concept was opposed most strongly by liberal Democrats, who argued that the states, not the federal government, should dictate incarceration policy for criminals convicted in state courts.

The debate was a replay of the one in the 103rd Congress, when Democrats agreed to include some truth-in-sentencing provisions in the 1994 crime bill but did not go as far as many Republicans wanted. The prisons piece of the House crime package (HR 667) proposed to dedicate $10.5 billion out of the anticrime trust fund for prison construction and operation, almost 33 percent more than the $7.9 billion authorized in the 1994 law. Half of the $10.5 billion was to be reserved for states that adopted truth-in-sentencing policies, with the remainder going to states that stiffened their sentencing policies to a lesser degree.

Democrats argued that only a fraction of the states—three in early 1995—could readily meet the truth-in-sentencing standard. Republicans countered that if the federal government was going to help states with prison expenses, it was critical that states move toward tougher sentences.

The bill also proposed to restrict inmates' ability to sue over their living conditions and limit the scope of court-ordered settlements in such lawsuits. The provisions, based on a bill sponsored by Charles T. Canady, R-Fla., tried to ensure that federal judges no longer placed caps on prison populations that forced the early release of some convicts.

The House Judiciary Committee approved the bill, 23–11, on Feb. 1, 1995, after rejecting Democratic amendments to drop the sentencing requirements and the prison-crowding provision. The committee reported the bill Feb. 6 (HR 667—H Rept 104-21).

The House passed the bill Feb. 10, 265–156, after rejecting an amendment by Schumer to drop the sentencing mandate, 179–251.

The Senate did not take up HR 667, but the Senate Appropriations Committee incorporated much of the bill into its version of HR 2076, the fiscal 1996 Commerce, Justice, and State appropriations bill. These provisions remained in the final version of HR 2076, which would have directed $405 million to the prison grants, $500 million to helping states incarcerate immigrant criminals, and $12.5 million to other specialized prison programs.

Although Clinton vetoed HR 2076, the omnibus spending bill for fiscal 1996 (HR 3019) included the same dollar amounts for prisons, along a modified set of truth-in-sentencing provisions from HR 667. The omnibus bill authorized $10.3 billion over five years to help states build or expand (but not operate) prisons. After subtracting the amounts for incarcerating criminal aliens and other specialized programs, the remainder was to be split evenly between states that adopted truth-in-sentencing policies and states that took lesser steps to toughen their sentences.

The omnibus bill also limited inmates' ability to sue for improved conditions and barred federal courts from forcing inmates to be released early because of crowded prisons.

HABEAS CORPUS

Republicans had long sought to speed the execution of convicted killers by limiting their ability to file successive appeals. The main tool used to challenge a death sentence was a writ of habeas corpus, a petition asking the federal court to examine the constitutionality of an inmate's conviction or sentence. Such petitions were filed after prisoners had exhausted their state-court appeals.

One of the pieces of the House GOP crime package (HR 729) proposed to place strict new limits on habeas petitions. As reported by the House Judiciary Committee on Feb. 8, 1995 (H Rept 104-23), the bill would have given state prisoners one year and federal prisoners two years to file their petitions. In states that provided competent counsels at the appeal stage of death penalty cases, prisoners would have been required to file a petition within six months.

Only one petition per inmate would have been permitted unless the Supreme Court provided a new constitutional remedy or the inmate provided "clear and convincing" evidence of innocence that could not have been uncovered earlier. Courts would have been required to meet stringent deadlines for ruling on habeas petitions.

The bill also would have required federal juries to impose the death penalty in cases where the aggravating circumstances outweighed mitigating considerations, rather than giving them the option of life imprisonment or a lesser sentence.

Conservatives contended that criminals had been able to make a mockery of the death penalty by dragging out their execution dates for years with appeals. But liberal Democrats had fought restrictions on habeas corpus, arguing that the federal appeals process offered a critical safeguard against wrongful executions and that the Supreme Court already had done more than enough to restrict such appeals.

Other Democrats and the Clinton administration supported some overhaul of the habeas process, but they wanted to tie new restrictions to guarantees that criminal defendants would get competent lawyers at their initial trial. At its markup on Feb. 1, 1995, the House Judiciary Committee rejected, 14 19, an amendment by Charles E. Schumer, D-N.Y., to require that states provide adequate lawyers at trial. One week later, the full House rejected, 149–282, a Schumer amendment that would have mandated a more extensive federal review of death penalty convictions when defendants were not provided competent attorneys at trial.

During floor debate, members also added a requirement that federal judges in habeas cases defer to the legal judgments of state courts except in cases where those decisions were "arbitrary or unreasonable." The amended bill passed on Feb. 8, 297–132.

Senate Republicans inserted similar provisions into the antiterrorism bill (S 735), which the Senate passed in June 1995. Despite protests from liberal Democrats, the restrictions remained in the final version of S 735, which the Senate passed on April 17, 1996, and the House cleared the next day. (Terrorism, p. 727)

Departing from the text of HR 729, the final version of S 735 set a one-year deadline for federal inmates to file habeas petitions. Also, it did not include the mandate for capital punishment in certain federal cases.

DEPORTATION

One of the few pieces of the House package that drew bipartisan support was a bill (HR 668) to crack down on the smuggling of foreigners into the United States and facilitate the deportation of immigrants convicted of serious crimes.

The 1994 crime bill had sped the deportation of violent alien felons by eliminating the need for administrative hearings, allowing the presiding judge to decide on deportation at the conclusion of the alien's trial. HR 668 proposed to expand the list of crimes that would trigger deportation, further restrict appeals, allow illegal immigrants convicted of nonviolent felonies to be deported before completing their sentence, and give prosecutors more tools to combat the smuggling of immigrants into the United States.

The main dispute over the bill was caused by an amendment by Howard L. Berman, D-Calif., that the House Judiciary Committee adopted, 20–14, on Jan. 27. The amendment would have required the federal government to start reimbursing states in fiscal year 1995 for the cost of incarcerating illegal immigrants who committed crimes. The 1994 crime law authorized $130 million to $350 million in annual grants to help states imprison illegal immigrants, but did not require Congress to appropriate any money for the states until fiscal year 2004. Meanwhile, the states' estimated annual expense was $650 million.

The committee approved the bill, 22–8, on Jan. 31, 1995, and reported it Feb. 6 (H Rept 104-22). Before the bill reached the House floor, however, top Republicans split over the Berman amendment. While some Republicans opposed creating what amounted to an entitlement program for border states, House Speaker Newt Gingrich, R-Ga., and other Sunbelt lawmakers argued that states should not bear the costs of weaknesses in federal border control.

After a behind-the-scenes scramble, sponsor Bill McCollum, R-Fla., proposed a compromise: in addition to the money authorized in the 1994 crime bill, states with undocumented criminal aliens to incarcerate would get first crack at the prison construction money appropriated each year by Congress. Although no money was guaranteed to be appropriated, Berman and his supporters agreed to the McCollum language in lieu of Berman's amendment. The McCollum amendment was approved by voice vote, and the House passed the bill, 380–20, on Feb. 10.

The Senate did not take up HR 668. Instead, in June 1995 it passed an antiterrorism bill (S 735) that included provisions limiting the ability of criminal aliens to challenge deportation orders and expanding the list of crimes that made an illegal immigrant subject to expedited deportation. The House amended and passed the bill the following March, which included a slightly modified version of HR 668.

The final version of the antiterrorism bill retained the central features of HR 668, minus the language on grants to states for incarcerating criminal aliens. The omnibus spending bill for fiscal 1996 (HR 3019) provided $500 million for such grants, and the omnibus spending bill for fiscal 1997 (HR 3610) provided $610 million. *(Provisions of antiterrorism bill, p. 731)*

RESTITUTION

A fifth piece of the House package was a bill (HR 665) that would have compelled federal judges to order convicted criminals to reimburse the people they injured or financially harmed. The bill also called for drug dealers with no identifiable victims to pay into a community restitution fund. Under previous law, judges were required to order restitution only in some domestic violence cases, with the reimbursement limited to the victim of the crime.

The bill had strong bipartisan support, and it moved easily through the House. The Judiciary Committee reported HR 665 on Feb. 2 (H Rept 104-16), and the House passed it unanimously on Feb. 7, 413–0.

Still, the bill drew numerous objections from civil liberties and criminal defense groups. One complaint was that restitution would be required regardless of the criminal's ability to pay, and nonpayment would be grounds for revoking probation. Taken together, they said, these provisions could send poorer people back to jail for nonpayment and create a modern-day debtors' prison. But sponsors said judges could take financial circumstances into account when setting or adjusting a payment schedule.

The Senate Judiciary Committee approved a modified version of the bill Nov. 16, 15–1, proposing to give judges more latitude than the House version would have provided. The committee's version, which was reported Dec. 6 (S Rept 104-179), would have made restitution mandatory unless the number of victims made such payments impractical or it would be too difficult to set an amount or monitor payment.

The Senate passed the amended bill by voice vote Dec. 22. Rather than taking up HR 665 again, the House included similar provisions in the antiterrorism bill (S 735) that it passed in March 1996. These provisions were retained in modified form in the conference report on the antiterrorism bill. *(Provisions of the antiterrorism bill, p. 731)*

EXCLUSIONARY RULE

Lawmakers from both parties had tried for several years to weaken the exclusionary rule, a legal doctrine that barred prosecutors from using evidence in violation of the Fourth Amendment guarantees against unreasonable search and seizure. HR 666 proposed to codify the Supreme Court's 1984 ruling in *United States v. Leon*, which created a "good faith" exception for evidence obtained with a search warrant later found to be invalid. The bill would have extended the exception to evidence obtained without a warrant, provided that the police had good reason to believe that the search was legal.

Republican supporters argued that society was punished unfairly when technical blunders by police let criminals go unpunished. But Democratic critics argued that the bill would remove the incentive for police officers to obtain proper warrants, possibly leading to unfair searches of innocent citizens.

The Judiciary Committee approved the bill, 19–14, on Jan. 27, 1995, after spurning a Democratic amendment not to provide a good-faith exception for warrantless searches, 13–21. The committee reported the bill Feb. 2 (H Rept 104-17).

During the House debate Feb. 7, lawmakers easily rejected Democratic amendments to limit the exception to evidence already admissible under *Leon* and to replace most of the bill with the words of the Fourth Amendment. On Feb. 8, however, the House adopted an amendment by voice vote specifying that the bill should not be interpreted as trying to override the Fourth Amendment. Members also adopted Democratic amendments to bar prosecutors from using the good-faith exception to rescue evidence seized improperly by the Bureau of Alcohol, Tobacco and Firearms and the Internal Revenue Service. They rejected another Democratic amendment, however, that would have applied the same rule to evidence seized improperly by the Immigration and Naturalization Service.

The House then passed the bill, 289–142. The Senate took no action on the measure.   ❑

Gun Control

Although many Republicans had pledged during their 1994 campaigns to overturn the newly enacted ban on assault weapons, Congress did no such thing in 1995 and 1996. Instead, it enacted more gun control, barring individuals convicted of domestic-violence misdemeanors from owning firearms.

ASSAULT WEAPONS

In an effort to pacify the National Rifle Association (NRA) and other gun rights groups, the House voted in 1996 to overturn the ban on assault weapons that Congress had included in the 1994 anticrime law. The measure (HR 125) went nowhere in the Senate, however, and it may have done more harm than good to the gun rights cause. Democrats in numerous districts made a campaign issue out of the bill, and at least one Republican was defeated as a direct consequence of his vote.

At issue was a hotly contested provision in the 1994 law (PL 103-322) banning the manufacture, sale or possession of 19 assault weapons, as well as copycat models and semiautomatic guns with two or more characteristics associated with assault weapons. Championed by police groups and lawmakers from urban districts, the ban drew fierce but fruitless protests from southern and western lawmakers who opposed all forms of gun control. *(1994 action, p. 691)*

The 1994 elections tilted the balance in the House in favor of gun rights advocates, sweeping into office numerous Republican freshmen who had campaigned against the assault-weapons ban. Of the 34 Democratic incumbents who lost their seats, 29 had voted for the crime bill and its ban on assault weapons. The freshmen Republicans remained close to the NRA, collecting almost $230,000 from the group's political action committee in 1995 alone.

Despite promises from GOP leaders in both chambers, however, the ban did not come up for a vote in 1995. A major factor in the delay was the April 1995 bombing of the Alfred P. Murrah Federal Building in Oklahoma City, which raised public concern about armed extremist groups and terrorists.

Indeed, the House GOP leadership seemed determined to act on legislation to combat terrorism before taking up the assault-weapons issue. The counterterrorism bill (HR 2703) was being resisted, however, by many of the same conservative Republicans who were demanding action on the assault-weapons ban. They objected in part to a provision that would have made it easier to prosecute people linked to gun traffickers. *(Terrorism, p. 727)*

The House finally passed the counterterrorism legislation in March 1996, minus the provision on gun trafficking. Eight days later, the GOP leadership brought to the House floor one of the several proposals to repeal the assault-weapons ban: a bill (HR 125) by conservative Democrat Jim Chapman of Texas. The measure had been plucked from the House Judiciary Committee without the benefit of hearings or mark-up sessions.

Some Republicans had tried to keep the bill off the floor, arguing that members had nothing to gain from voting on a bill that had no chance of becoming law. Senate Majority Leader Bob Dole, R-Kan., had said that the bill probably could not pass the Senate, where it was sure to encounter a filibuster. And even if the measure cleared Congress, President Clinton had vowed to veto it. "The president will look like a leader, and Congress will look like we succumbed to a special interest," said Christopher Shays, R-Conn., who opposed the bill.

HR 125 proposed to replace the assault-weapon ban with a more aggressive federal effort against armed criminals. In particular, it would have imposed mandatory prison terms of five to 30 years without parole for people who used guns or explosives while committing a federal crime. It also would have required prosecutors in each federal court district to set up task forces targeted at armed, violent criminals.

The debate on March 22 was often contentious, with members occasionally drawing on personal traumas and anxieties. Supporters of HR 125 said the ban was ineffective in controlling crime, while opponents accused the House GOP leadership of pandering to the NRA. The supporters prevailed, 239–173, with 183 Republicans and 56 Democrats voting "yea" and 42 Republicans, 130 Democrats and one Independent voting "nay."

The bill sank without a trace in the Senate, but the House vote sent ripples through the November elections. One freshman Republican who voted for the repeal, Dan Frisa of Long Island, N.Y., was handily defeated by Democrat Carolyn McCarthy, a converted Republican who would not have run had it not been for that vote. McCarthy's husband had been killed and her son critically wounded on a commuter train in 1993 by a psychopath armed with a semiautomatic pistol and a bag filled with ammunition.

The issue also played heavily in Democrat Ellen Tauscher's defeat of second-term Republican Bill Baker in California. Numerous other Democratic candidates cited the issue as well in trying to make the case that their opponents were extremists.

DOMESTIC VIOLENCE

Instead of attempting to repeal the ban on assault weapons, the Senate took up a proposal by Sen. Frank R. Lautenberg, D-N.J., to broaden the existing ban on felons buying or possessing firearms. Lautenberg's bill (S 1632) proposed to apply the ban to people convicted of any form of domestic violence, even misdemeanor offenses. The ban also would have applied to people under indictment for crimes of domestic violence.

Supporters, which included the Children's Defense Fund, the National Urban League and the National Organization of Women, said the bill was necessary and appropriate because many domestic violence cases were plea-bargained down from felonies to misdemeanors. Opponents, including the NRA, argued that the proposal was too broad.

The bill did not advance in the Senate Judiciary Committee, so Lautenberg tried to attach its provisions to a popular House bill (HR 2980) that targeted stalkers. After holding Lautenberg off for several months, the bill's main Senate sponsor, Republican Kay Bailey Hutchison of Texas, agreed to attach a modified version of the proposal to the bill.

The compromise proposed to extend the ban only to those who had been convicted of domestic-violence crimes, not people who were awaiting trial. The ban also would not have applied to people convicted of domestic-violence crimes who had neither been represented by an attorney nor "knowingly and intelligently" waived their right to counsel.

The modified measure passed the Senate by voice vote July 25, but the House took no action on it. Instead, the antistalking provisions were enacted as part of the fiscal 1997 defense authorization bill (HR 3230—PL 104-201). *(Stalking, p. 743)*

Lautenberg found another vehicle for his proposal, attaching it Sept. 12 to the fiscal 1997 appropriations bill (HR 3756) for the Treasury Department, Postal Service and general government agencies. The vote was 97–2. The bill quickly stalled in a partisan squabble, however, leaving the programs to be funded through the year-end omnibus spending bill (HR 3610—PL 104-208).

Top Democratic and White House negotiators insisted that the Lautenberg provision be included in the omnibus bill. They prevailed in late September with one further compromise: the ban would not apply to people who had been unwittingly denied a trial by jury, and it would not apply to those whose convictions had been expunged or set aside.

The House agreed to the conference report on the omnibus bill Sept. 28, 370–37, and the Senate approved it by voice vote Sept. 30, clearing the bill. President Clinton signed the measure later that day.   ❑

Sex-Related Crimes

The 104th Congress cleared four bills aimed at preventing or increasing penalties for child sexual abuse, violent sex crimes and child pornography.

COMMUNITY NOTIFICATION

Expanding on a provision in the 1994 crime bill (PL 103-322), Congress ordered state and local officials in 1996 to notify communities when someone moved in who had been convicted of a violent sex crime or child sexual abuse. The 1994 law required such offenders to register their current address with local police for at least 10 years after their release from incarceration, but it did not require the police to make this information public.

The community notification bill (HR 2137—PL 104-145) was dubbed "Megan's Law" after Megan Kanka, a 7-year-old New Jersey girl who was raped and murdered in 1994. Police charged the crime to a nearby resident who, unbeknownst to his neighbors, had twice been convicted of child molestation.

The bill allowed states to set up their own standards for notifying communities, although it required "relevant information" about the release and whereabouts of convicted sex offenders to be made public. States that failed to establish the required registration systems by September 1997 faced a cutback in their federal grants.

The House Judiciary Committee reported the bill on May 6, 1996 (H Rept 104-555), and the House passed it the next day, 418–0. The only criticism voiced in the Judiciary Committee came from Democrats Melvin Watt of North Carolina and Robert C. Scott of Virginia, who argued that convicts had paid their debt to society once they completed their prison terms.

The Senate passed the bill by voice vote on May 9, and President Clinton signed it on May 17.

INTERSTATE TRACKING

Closing a potential loophole left by the enactment of "Megan's Law," Congress and President Clinton both took steps in 1996 to track convicted sexual offenders as they moved their residences across state lines.

In June, Clinton issued an administrative order requiring the FBI to keep a national database of sexual offenders registered on state lists. Congress quickly followed suit, clearing a bill (S 1675—PL 104-236) in September requiring the FBI to record the addresses, fingerprints and photographs of all violent sex offenders, child molesters and sexual predators who had been released from prison.

The legislation aimed to provide a backstop in case an offender moved to a state that had yet to establish a satisfactory registration program. Offenders were required to register with their states, which were to forward copies of the information to the FBI. Offenders in states whose registration program did not meet federal standards were required to register directly with the FBI.

Also, the bill required offenders who moved across state lines to provide their new address, fingerprints and photograph to the state in which they settled and to the FBI. Sexually violent predators were ordered to verify their addresses with the FBI every 90 days, while other sex offenders were required to verify their addresses when requested by the FBI.

The registration requirement ended for some offenders 10 years after they were released from prison. Those convicted of more serious crimes, however, were required to register their addresses with the FBI for as long as they lived. The bill set a maximum penalty of 10 years in prison and a $100,000 fine for failing more than once to register an address.

The bill also required the FBI to keep state and local officials informed about the arrival of offenders so that they could alert the community.

The Senate passed S 1675 by voice vote on July 25, 1996. The House passed a similar proposal (HR 3456), 423–1, on Sept. 26, then cleared the Senate bill by voice vote. Clinton signed S 1675 on Oct. 3.

CHILD SEXUAL EXPLOITATION

Enacting one of the proposals from the House Republican "Contract with America," Congress cleared legislation in 1995 to lengthen the prison terms for those convicted of sexually exploiting children.

The bill (HR 1240—PL 104-71) directed the U.S. Sentencing Commission to increase the presumptive prison terms for making or selling child pornography and for transporting a child across state lines to engage in criminal sexual activity. The minimum recommended sentences were to be raised by at least six to 12 months, with an additional six months or more behind bars for those who used a computer to advertise or distribute their pornographic works. The commission set the guidelines that federal judges followed when meting out punishments.

A tougher version of the proposal was introduced by House Republicans as part of HR 11, the families plank of the GOP Contract. HR 11 proposed mandatory minimum prison terms for child pornographers, and it would have made certain sales or broadcasts of obscene material a violation of the 1970 Racketeer Influenced and Corrupt Organizations (RICO) law (PL 91-452).

Republicans split HR 11 into several pieces, with the sexual exploitation provisions being introduced as HR 1240. To sidestep opposition from some Democrats, sponsor Bill McCollum, R-Fla., dropped the mandatory minimum sentences in favor of stiffer sentencing guidelines, leaving judges some latitude when imposing prison terms. The House Judiciary Committee reported the bill (H Rept 104-90) on March 28, 1995, after it rejected a Democratic proposal to drop the RICO language. Echoing a frequent Republican criticism of the RICO law, Barney Frank,

D-Mass., argued that Congress had broadened RICO too far beyond its original mission of combating organized crime. McCollum countered that most obscenity crimes already were covered by RICO, so it made sense to add the two proposed by HR 1240.

Nevertheless, McCollum agreed to delete the RICO provision before the House acted on the bill, speeding its approval. The House passed the bill, 417–0, on April 4, and the Senate passed it by voice vote two days later after making a minor technical change. The House cleared the bill by voice vote Dec. 12, and President Clinton signed it Dec. 23.

CHILD PORNOGRAPHY

Congress toughened the penalties for producing child pornography and sexually exploiting children a second time as part of the fiscal 1997 omnibus appropriations bill (HR 3610—PL 104-208). The measure outlawed the use of computers to produce pictures that appeared to show children engaged in sexually explicit conduct, even if no minors had actually been involved.

The legislation began as a freestanding bill (S 1237) that the Senate reported on July 30, 1996 (S Rept 104-358). In addition to classifying computer-generated pictures as child pornography, S 1237 proposed to make it a federal crime, "aggravated sexual abuse of a minor," to cross state lines with the intention of having sex with anyone less than 12 years old or anyone less than 16 years old who was four or more years younger than the accused. The same prohibition was proposed for actions on federal property and in federal prisons.

The bill included a number of mandatory-minimum prison terms: two to five years for offenses related to child pornography, 10 to 30 years for the sexual exploitation of minors, and life in prison for aggravated sexual abuse of a minor if the defendant had been convicted once before of a similar crime. The bill also authorized capital punishment if a child sexual exploitation resulted in a death.

Sen. Paul Simon, D-Ill., blocked the Senate from taking up S 1237 in late September because he objected to the mandatory-minimum terms. The sponsors of S 1237 were able to include virtually identical provisions in the conference report on the year-end spending bill, however, with the support of top Democrats and the White House.

The House adopted the conference report on HR 3610 (H Rept 104-208) on Sept. 28, 370–37, and the Senate adopted it by voice vote Sept. 30, clearing the bill. President Clinton signed it later that day. ❑

Illegal Drugs

The 104th Congress toughened penalties for the possession or manufacture of two drugs rising in popularity among young adults—methamphetamine and flunitrazepam—while blocking a bid to reduce penalties for crack cocaine. The House also passed a bill to stop prison officials from giving inmates time off for completing a drug treatment program, but the measure floundered in the Senate.

SENTENCING GUIDELINES

Rejecting the advice of the U.S. Sentencing Commission, Congress voted in 1995 not to reduce the penalties for crack cocaine offenses or for money laundering.

The bill to block the commission's recommendations (S 1254—PL 104-38) triggered a racially charged debate in the House, as black lawmakers argued that the disparity between sentences for crack offenses and powder cocaine offenses favored white defendants. The bill's Republican sponsors said the disparity reflected the greater danger posed by crack, not the difference in clientele.

The commission—a bipartisan panel of legal experts formed in 1984—set guidelines for federal judges to follow when sentencing convicted criminals. Revised each year, the guidelines took effect automatically unless Congress countermanded them by Nov. 1 of that year. Before 1995, Congress had never rejected the commission's proposals.

S 1254 rejected two of the commission's 27 recommended changes. The first would have set the presumptive sentence for laundering more than $100,000 at 21 to 27 months, down from 37 to 46 months. Money laundering, a crime often associated with the drug trade, involved transactions designed to conceal the source of the funds.

The second recommendation challenged by S 1254 would have lightened the sentences for crack cocaine to eliminate the disparity between the penalties for crack and for powder cocaine. The existing guidelines imposed stiff minimum sentences for defendants caught with as little as five grams of crack: five years for possessing, 10 years for trafficking. Defendants had to possess or sell at least 500 grams of powder cocaine to qualify for comparable minimum sentences.

The Senate passed S 1254 by voice vote after adopting an amendment by Edward M. Kennedy, D-Mass., which directed the commission to make new recommendations for narrowing the disparity between the sentences for crack and powder cocaine.

The House Judiciary Committee reported a similar bill (HR 2259—H Rept 104-272) on Sept. 29, 1995, after rejecting a series of Democratic amendments to preserve the commission's recommended changes.

On the House floor Oct. 18, John Conyers Jr., D-Mich., tried again to preserve the commission's recommendation on crack. "Crack cocaine happens to be used by poor people, mostly black people, because it's cheap," said Melvin Watt, D-N.C. "Powder cocaine happens to be used by wealthy white people."

Sponsor Bill McCollum countered that crack was more addictive, more likely to be used by juveniles and more likely to be associated with violence. The House rejected the Conyers amendment, 98–316. It also rejected, 149–266, an amendment by Watt to require the commission to report back to Congress on the crack guidelines by March 1, 1996.

The House passed HR 2259, 332–83, after substituting in the text of S 1254. It then cleared S 1254 by voice vote. President Clinton signed the measure Oct. 30.

METHAMPHETAMINE

Congress cleared a bill late in the 1996 session to crack down on the production of methamphetamine, although the measure did not contain the mandatory minimum penalties favored by House Republicans.

The measure (S 1965—PL 104-237) responded to reports that methamphetamine use had become widespread. An illegal stimulant also known as "speed" or "crank," methamphetamine was having the same devastating effects in some communities that cocaine caused in the 1980s, supporters of the bill said.

The bill imposed more restrictions on the chemicals, laboratory equipment and supplies used to produce methamphetamine. It also allowed law enforcement agencies to regulate certain over-the-counter medications, including some cold and allergy remedies, that contained chemicals that could be used to manufacture methamphetamine.

Passed by the Senate on Sept. 17, the legislation set longer maximum prison terms for certain offenses involving methamphetamine and other controlled substances. It also called on the U.S. Sentencing Commission, which set the sentencing guidelines observed by federal judges, to toughen the penalties for manufacturing, importing, exporting and trafficking of methamphetamine.

The House passed a competing version of the bill (HR 3852) on Sept. 26 that would have imposed mandatory-minimum prison terms for possessing or trafficking in methamphetamine equal to the ones for crack cocaine. A number of Democrats in the Senate firmly opposed mandatory-minimum sentences, however, so the prospects for HR 3852 in the Senate seemed dim. Confronted with that hurdle, the House cleared S 1965 by voice vote Sept. 28, and President Clinton signed it Oct. 3.

DATE-RAPE DRUGS

Congress cleared a bill on the last day of the session making it a federal crime to drug someone to reduce his or her resistance to assault. Although the prohibition applied to any drug, the measure (HR 4137—PL 104-305) focused on flunitrazepam, a powerful and illegal sedative that was appearing with increasing frequency in cases of date rape.

Also known by the trade name Rohypnol and the nicknames "roofies" or "roachies," flunitrazepam was used by rapists to relax their victims to the point of virtual incapacitation and, in many cases, memory loss. It was inexpensive, colorless, odorless and tasteless. Although illegal to manufacture in the United States, it was used in more than 60 countries as a common remedy for insomnia and anxiety.

The bill set prison terms of up to 20 years and fines as high as $2 million for those convicted of slipping a controlled substance surreptitiously to an individual with intent to commit a violent crime. It also imposed stiffer penalties for the possession, distribution or manufacture of flunitrazepam.

As was the case with methamphetamines, the House and Senate parted company on the issue of mandatory minimum sentences. The original version of the bill, which the House passed Sept. 26 by a vote of 421–1, proposed to set mandatory-minimum prison terms. The provision was dropped in the Senate, which passed a revised version of the bill by voice vote Oct. 3.

The House also proposed to change the classification of flunitrazepam from a "Schedule IV" drug to a "Schedule I" drug, imposing far more stringent handling requirements and declaring that there were no medicinal uses. Although some senators had tried to make a similar change, many Republicans argued that it would be a mistake to attach such a stigma to a drug used in so many countries. The provision was dropped from the Senate version of the bill.

The House cleared the Senate version on Oct. 4 by voice vote, and President Clinton signed the bill Oct. 13.

EARLY RELEASE

Looking to change the incentives for drug-addicted convicts, the House passed a bill (HR 2650) in 1996 to eliminate the promise of early release for federal prisoners who completed a drug-treatment program. The Senate did not act on the measure, however.

Under existing law, federal prisoners could be released before the end of their court-imposed sentence only if they gained credit for good behavior. The law allowed prison officials to reward inmates who completed a drug-treatment program by giving them up to one year's time off their sentences.

HR 2650 would have barred such rewards, although it would have retained other incentives for entering treatment programs, such as preferred housing and job assignments. Instead, it would have required drug-addicted prisoners to complete a treatment program before they could earn any credits for good behavior. It also would have limited participation in treatment programs to inmates who were within two years of completing their sentences.

The House Judiciary Committee reported the bill on May 31, 1996 (H Rept 104-602), and the House passed it by voice vote June 4.   ❑

Juvenile Crime

A House GOP proposal to crack down on crime by juveniles foundered in the House Judiciary Committee in 1996 in the face of unrelenting opposition from Democrats.

The bill (HR 3565) would have toughened the federal government's response to juvenile crime and encouraged state and local governments to follow suit. Among other things, it proposed to let federal prosecutors order juveniles as young as 13 to be tried as adults and face adult penalties in cases involving a violent crime on federal property or Indian lands. It also would have mandated prison terms for anyone tried as an adult who possessed a gun while committing a violent federal crime or federal drug trafficking offense.

Approximately 400 juveniles were tried each year for federal crimes, including murder, rape, armed robbery and drug trafficking. The number of federal and state crimes by juveniles was expected to surge, however, as the population of teenagers grew in the coming decade.

Critics of the juvenile justice system, which was run largely by local juvenile courts, said it was not prepared for the increase in cases. Republicans also contended that the punishments meted out against juvenile offenders were too light, particularly given the increase in violent crime and drug use by juveniles.

Bill sponsor Bill McCollum, R-Fla., said violent juvenile offenders "should be thrown in jail, the key should be thrown away, and there should be very little or no effort to rehabilitate them."

Democrats argued that the GOP wanted to lock up poor children, most likely blacks and other minorities, many of whom could have been reached with prevention or rehabilitation programs. They also said that the rise in juvenile crime was overblown, pointing to a new study showing that the increase was largely confined to six of the country's largest states and four major cities.

When the Judiciary Committee began marking up HR 3565 on July 16, Democrats tied the panel up with a volley of amendments to the title and the nonbinding "findings" section at the beginning of the bill. The committee slogged through amendments for three more days, rejecting most Democratic proposals and adopting a handful of Republican ones, usually on party-line votes or voice votes. Finally, on Aug. 2, the panel aborted the markup.

The rejected Democratic amendments included proposals to allow juveniles to appeal a prosecutor's decision to try them as adults; give judges more control over whether juveniles were tried as adults; require youth development specialists at federal courts to guide delinquent juveniles and aid their families in order to discourage crime; and change the bill's title from the Violent Youth Crime Act to the Violent Youth Crime Creation Act.

JUVENILE JUSTICE PROGRAMS

HR 3565 also would have replaced the Justice Department's Office of Juvenile Justice and Delinquency Prevention with two grant programs for states: one to operate juvenile justice programs, and the other to reward states and cities that set tougher penalties for juvenile crimes. This section of the bill was under the jurisdiction of the House Economic and Educational Opportunities Committee, which took no action on it.

Instead, the committee reported a bill (HR 3876—H Rept 104-783) on Sept. 12, 1996, to reauthorize federal juvenile justice programs through fiscal year 2000. The bill would have made numerous changes to the programs, such as repealing provisions adopted in 1988 that made it more difficult for juvenile offenders to be detained with adults. It also would have created a grant program to reward states that tried allegedly violent juveniles as adults and released juvenile records to law enforcement agencies, courts and schools.

The House never voted on HR 3876, largely because of the demise of the larger juvenile crime bill.

The Senate Judiciary Committee took a less punitive tack, reporting a bill (S 1952—S Rept 104-369) on Aug. 1 to authorize several new research and grant programs to prevent crime by youths. These included a $70 million federal research effort and a $70 million grant program for state drug treatment programs and other prevention-related activities.

The full Senate did not act on the bill. ❑

Church Burnings

Responding to a wave of arsons at predominantly black churches in the South, Congress gave federal prosecutors more power in 1996 to intervene when arson or vandalism struck a house of worship.

The bill (HR 3525—PL 104-155) made it a federal crime to damage religious property if the offense affected interstate commerce or was motivated by racism. Under previous law, federal prosecutors could intervene only if the perpetrator crossed state lines, the damage was greater than $10,000 or the crime was motivated by religious bias.

The measure authorized the federal government to help nonprofit groups rebuild churches by providing loans or loan guarantees, and it made those injured eligible for compensation under the 1984 Victims of Crime Act (PL 98-473). It also doubled the maximum prison term for church burnings from 10 years to 20 years and extended the time limit for indictments from five years to seven years from the date of the crime.

Supporters of the bill noted that fire had damaged or destroyed 30 churches at predominantly black congregations in the South in less than 18 months. Although no lawmaker voted against it, some critics suggested that the bill might extend the Justice Department's jurisdiction to unconstitutional lengths.

The measure also inspired some partisan sniping as it raced through Congress. Some Republicans said President Clinton reacted too slowly to the problem, and they criticized a visit he made to a bombing site in South Carolina as crass politicking. Democrats suggested that Republicans' attacks on affirmative action programs had contributed to a climate of racial intolerance.

The House Judiciary Committee reported an early version of HR 3525, cosponsored by conservative Republican Henry J. Hyde of Illinois and liberal Democrat John Conyers Jr. of Michigan, on June 17, 1996 (H Rept 104-621). At the committee markup June 11, Bob Barr, R-Ga., questioned the bill's constitutionality, noting the Supreme Court's ruling in April 1995 on the limits of Congress' authority. In that case, *United States v. Lopez*, the court found that Congress had improperly usurped state powers by creating gun-free zones around public schools. Hyde disagreed, saying the Justice Department was confident that the bill would pass constitutional muster.

The House passed HR 3525 on June 18, 422–0. Eight days later, the Senate passed a broader version of the bill, 98–0, based on a measure (S 1890) cosponsored by conservative Republican Lauch Faircloth of North Carolina and liberal Democrat Edward M. Kennedy of Massachusetts. In addition to the House-passed provisions, the Senate bill proposed to authorize more loans and loan guarantees by the Department of Housing and Urban Development, more agents at the Bureau of Alcohol, Tobacco and Firearms to assist state investigators, and more counselors at the Justice Department to help communities deal with the aftermath of church fires.

The House cleared the revised version the next day by voice vote, and Clinton signed it on July 3.   ❑

Counterfeit Goods

Congress cracked down on counterfeit merchandise in 1996, clearing a bill to increase penalties and toughen enforcement at the borders. The measure (S 1136—PL 104-153) made trafficking in counterfeit goods a violation of the Racketeer Influenced and Corrupt Organizations Act (RICO). Enacted as part of the Organized Crime Control Act of 1970 (PL 91-452), the RICO law carried stiffer fines and longer prison terms than existing laws against counterfeiting.

The bill also allowed customs agents to seize and destroy pirated goods at the border rather than just denying them entry, and it authorized law enforcement agencies to seize airplanes, boats and vehicles used to transport counterfeit items.

Pirated software, pharmaceuticals, baby formula and other copyrighted or trademarked goods cost the U.S. economy about $200 billion annually, supporters of the bill estimated. According to House sponsor Robert W. Goodlatte, R-Va., counterfeiting involved "international crime syndicates, multibillion-dollar operations, highly sophisticated equipment, and terrorists."

The Senate Judiciary Committee reported S 1136 on Nov. 28, 1995 (S Rept 104-177), and the Senate passed the bill by voice vote Dec. 13. The House amended and passed the bill by voice vote June 4, 1996, after inserting the text of a similar measure (HR 2511) that the Judiciary Committee had reported on May 6 (H Rept 104-556). The Senate cleared the House version of the bill by voice vote June 14, and President Clinton signed it July 2.   ❑

Trade Secrets

Congress made it a federal crime in 1996 to steal trade secrets, setting higher penalties for thieves employed by foreign entities than those working for U.S. companies.

The legislation (HR 3723—PL 104-294) enabled the Justice Department to target industrial espionage, a crime previously subject only to state law enforcement. It outlawed the theft, copying or other unauthorized use of business plans, formulas, prototypes and other valuable information if the owner of the information had taken reasonable steps to keep it secret.

The measure set maximum penalties of 15 years in prison and a $500,000 fine for individuals who stole trade secrets for foreign entities, 10 years in prison and an unspecified fine for individuals who stole secrets for U.S. concerns. Organizations faced fines of up to $10 million if they stole secrets for foreign entities, $5 million if they stole for Americans.

The law did not protect U.S. companies overseas. It applied only to crimes on U.S. soil and crimes committed by U.S. citizens abroad.

The measure moved swiftly and easily through both chambers, with the most vocal protest coming at the House Judiciary Committee from John Conyers Jr., D-Mich. Conyers argued that the federal government was asserting jurisdiction over too many crimes.

The Senate Judiciary Committee moved first, reporting an industrial espionage bill (S 1556—S Rept 104-359) on July 30, 1996. The House Judiciary Committee reported HR 3723 (H Rept 104-788) on Sept. 16, 1996, proposing stiffer penalties. The House passed HR 3723 the next day by an overwhelming margin, 399–3.

The Senate passed an amended version of HR 3723 by voice vote Sept. 18, substituting in the text of S 1556. Included were provisions mandating a federal study on the use of computer "encryption" technology to conceal criminal behavior; authorizing $100 million in grants over five years to establish 1,000 new Boys and Girls Clubs in public housing projects and other distressed areas; and giving the federal government custody of people found not guilty by reason of insanity in Washington, D.C., courts.

After informal negotiations between the two chambers, the House passed another version of HR 3723 by voice vote Sept. 28. The new version struck a compromise between the House and Senate proposals for fines and imprisonment. It retained the three unrelated provisions added by the Senate and tacked on two more titles. One, based on a Senate-passed bill (S 982), set penalties for hackers who broke into computer files. The other, based on a House-passed bill (HR 2538), made numerous technical changes to federal criminal law. *(Computer hackers, this page)*   ❑

Computer Hackers

Faced with an increase in computer hacking, Congress agreed in 1996 to extend federal protection to more computer systems and stiffen the penalties for those who stole information or caused damage.

The measure, enacted as part of a bill to protect trade secrets (HR 3723—PL 104-294), made it a federal crime to damage or steal data from any computer system used in interstate or foreign commerce or communications, not just those used by banks and credit bureaus. It also expanded the definition of damage to cover physical injuries and threats to public health or safety.

First-time offenses would be treated as misdemeanors if the information was worth no more than $5,000, the theft did not threaten national security, and the data was not stolen for commercial purposes or personal financial gain. Otherwise, the offenses were classified as federal felonies.

Other provisions of the bill barred government employees from prying into confidential government data bases and barred computer viruses from being introduced into any government or bank network.

The Senate Judiciary Committee incorporated a similar set of provisions into a House-passed bill raising the penalties for federal prison escapes (HR 1533), which it reported on June 13, 1996. When that measure stalled, the committee reported the provisions as a freestanding bill (S 982—S Rept 104-357) on Aug. 2, 1996, and the Senate passed it on Sept. 18. With time running down in the session, the House incorporated S 982 into the trade secrets bill, which it passed on Sept. 28 and the Senate cleared on Oct. 2. *(Trade secrets, p. 742)*

Stalking

Expanding on existing state laws and the 1994 crime bill, the 104th Congress made it a federal crime to stalk someone across state lines or on federally controlled property, such as a military base. The measure was attached to the fiscal 1997 defense authorization bill (HR 3230—PL 104-201) after a House-passed stalking bill (HR 2980) became entangled in a dispute over gun control.

The 1994 anticrime law (PL 103-322) had made stalking by a spouse or former spouse a federal crime in some instances, but it did not apply to other stalkers. State laws and restraining orders, meanwhile, generally did not apply once the victim crossed state lines.

HR 2980 proposed to cover anyone who followed another person across state lines or on federally controlled property with the intention of harming or harassing that person. It also proposed to make restraining orders issued in one state valid in all states.

The House Judiciary Committee reported the bill on May 6, 1996 (H Rept 104-557), and the House passed it the next day by voice vote. The Senate Judiciary Committee reported the bill May 23 without amendment, but Sen. Frank Lautenberg, D-N.J., would not let the bill clear the Senate. On Lautenberg's insistence, the Senate added a modified version of S 1632, a bill barring people convicted of domestic-violence crimes from owning handguns, to HR 2980 before passing it by voice vote July 25.

Prodded by Sen. Kay Bailey Hutchison, R-Texas, House-Senate negotiators on the defense authorization bill included the antistalking language from HR 2980 in their conference report, which was filed July 30 (H Rept 104-724). The House adopted the report Aug. 1, 285–132, and the Senate followed suit on Sept. 10, 73–26, clearing the bill. President Clinton signed it Sept. 23. *(Defense authorization, p. 309)*

Rape by Carjackers

Eliminating an unforeseen loophole in the 1994 crime bill (PL 103-322), Congress cleared legislation (HR 3676—PL 104-217) in 1996 to ensure that carjackers would face greater federal penalties if they committed sexual assault while stealing vehicles.

Congress had made carjacking a federal crime in 1992 (PL 102-519), and lawmakers stiffened the penalty in 1994 for carjackers who caused "serious bodily injury" to their victims. In May 1996, however, the 1st Circuit Court of Appeals ruled that rape did not meet the crime bill's definition of "serious bodily injury." *(1992 act, Congress and the Nation Vol. VIII, p. 790; 1994 crime law, p. 683)*

HR 3676 defined sexual assault as an act causing serious bodily injury. The House Judiciary Committee reported the bill Sept. 16 (H Rept 104 787), and the House passed it by voice vote the next day. The Senate cleared the bill by voice vote Sept. 18, and President Clinton signed it Oct. 1.

Stolen Cars

Congress tried again in 1996 to create a federal index of stolen cars, hoping to prevent states from issuing new titles for stolen vehicles.

The bill (HR 2803—PL 104-152) required the Justice Department to establish a data base on stolen vehicles that states could check when they received applications for titles. The existing system for checking records was so ineffective, supporters of the bill said, states were issuing about 140,000 titles each year to vehicles that had been stolen in another state.

In the 1992 Anti-Car Theft Act (PL 102-519), Congress had ordered the Transportation Department to develop a data base for stolen vehicles by Jan. 31, 1996. The department failed to meet its deadline, however, prompting the swift passage of HR 2803. *(1992 act, Congress and the Nation Vol. VIII, p. 790)*

In addition to shifting responsibility for the data base to the Justice Department, the bill authorized larger grants to states for work related to the national data base, and it shielded state recordkeepers against lawsuits if they made mistakes without malicious intent.

The House Judiciary Committee reported the bill June 12, 1996 (H Rept 104-618), and the House passed it by voice vote June 18. The Senate passed it by voice vote two days later, and President Clinton signed it July 2.

Jury Tampering

Taking aim at gang members who tried to rig the outcome of criminal trials, Congress increased the penalties in 1996 for those who tampered with federal juries and witnesses.

The bill (HR 3120—PL 104-214) defined tampering as the use or threatened use of physical force. It allowed a judge to impose the higher of two penalties for someone convicted of tampering: 10 years in prison, which was the previous maximum penalty for tampering, or the sentence imposed on the defendant whose jury or witnesses had been tampered with. The latter penalty did not apply to death penalty cases, however.

The measure drew protests from some liberal Democrats in the House Judiciary Committee, who argued that it went overboard. Still, the committee rejected Democratic proposals to apply the increased penalties more narrowly.

The committee reported the bill May 1, 1996 (H Rept 104-549), and the House passed it by voice vote May 7. The Senate cleared the bill Sept. 19, and President Clinton signed it Oct. 1.

Lying to Congress

Reacting to an unexpected Supreme Court ruling, Congress cleared a bill in 1996 to restore the prohibition against lying to Congress or the judiciary. The measure (HR 3166—PL 104-292) carved out a broad exception, however, for testimony about legislative proposals and other lobbying activities.

The impetus for the bill was the Supreme Court's May 1995 ruling in *Hubbard v. United States.* Reversing a decision that the justices had made 40 years earlier, *Hubbard* held that a 1934 stricture against lying to a department or agency of the United States applied only to the executive branch, not to Congress or the judiciary. The law had been used to obtain more than 2,000 convictions in the previous five years and had played a major role in the Iran-contra prosecutions before that. *(Hubbard case, p. 774; Iran-contra cases, Congress and the Nation Vol. VIII, p. 287)*

HR 3166 made it a federal crime to lie to or conceal information from any of the three branches of the federal government, under certain circumstances. The new law did not cover statements made in court proceedings, and it applied to Congress only on administrative matters, such as financial disclosure forms, and authorized investigations. Thus, statements made in the context of a legislative debate were not covered. Republican Rep. Bill McCollum of Florida, who proposed this exception in the House Judiciary Committee, said the bill might otherwise have a chilling effect on vigorous lobbying and political debate within Congress.

The committee reported the bill on July 16, 1996 (H Rept 104-680) and the House passed it the next day, 417–6. The Senate passed the bill by voice vote July 25 after substituting in the text of a bill (S 1734) that the Senate Judiciary Committee had approved on July 22. The Senate bill also included provisions to make more executive branch officials subject to Senate subpoenas and to let Congress compel witnesses at ancillary proceedings to testify under a grant of immunity.

The House passed the bill again, 424–0, on Sept. 26 after clarifying that the strictures against lying to Congress applied only to administrative and certain investigatory matters. The Senate cleared the bill the next day, and President Clinton signed it Oct. 11.   ❑

War Criminals

Congress approved two measures in 1996 to prosecute alleged war criminals and encourage the release of government information about them.

The first (HR 3680—PL 104-192) made war crimes a violation of federal law wherever they occurred if they were committed by or against U.S. military personnel, citizens or permanent residents. The law set a maximum punishment of life imprisonment or, for war crimes that cost lives, the death penalty. The definition of what constituted a war crime was taken from the 1949 Geneva Conventions.

Congress had ratified the conventions in 1955, but it never adopted legislation to implement them because top federal officials believed that existing criminal laws were sufficient. Supporters of HR 3680 argued that court decisions limiting the jurisdiction of military tribunals, among other developments, had made it possible for war criminals to escape prosecution in the United States.

The House Judiciary Committee reported HR 3680 on July 24, 1996 (H Rept 104-698), and the House passed it by voice vote five days later. The Senate cleared the bill by voice vote Aug. 2, and President Clinton signed it Aug. 21.

The second measure (HR 1281—PL 104-309) encouraged but did not require the federal government to make public its records regarding alleged Nazi war criminals.

The original version of the bill would have barred the government from denying a Freedom of Information Act (FOIA) request for information about Nazi war criminals unless releasing the information would expose an intelligence agent or confidential informant. The intent, said sponsor Carolyn B. Maloney, D-N.Y., was to end the Central Intelligence Agency's practice of routinely denying all FOIA requests regarding alleged Nazi war criminals.

The House Government Reform and Oversight Committee reported a slightly modified bill on Sept. 24, 1996 (H Rept 104-819, Part I). By that time, however, objections from the CIA had effectively blocked the bill, so Maloney offered a new version that simply urged the government to make its records public. The House passed that version by voice vote Sept. 24, the Senate cleared it by voice vote Oct. 3, and President Clinton signed it Oct. 19.   ❑

Crimes Against Children and the Elderly

A bill to raise the penalties for federal crimes against children and the elderly stalled in the Senate after the House added provisions aimed at rapists and child molesters who crossed state lines.

The bill (HR 2974) was one of two failed efforts to force the U.S. Sentencing Commission to increase penalties for crimes against the elderly. The other measure addressed telemarketing fraud. The commission set the guidelines that federal judges followed when imposing sentences. *(Telemarketing fraud, p. 745)*

Opponents of the bill argued that Congress should not interfere with the commission's ability to set guidelines. After all, said Rep. Melvin Watt, D-N.C., Congress created the commission to help lawmakers "resist temptations to beat ourselves on the chest and proclaim as politicians how tough we are on crime." Proponents said the bill was needed because the commission had not heeded Congress' call in the 1994 crime bill (PL 103-322) to toughen penalties for crimes against the elderly.

The original version of the HR 2974 would have required the commission to boost by 50 percent the penalties for crimes against children 11 and under and adults 65 and older. Before reporting the bill on May 1, 1996 (H Rept 104-548), the House Judiciary Committee broadened it to cover children as old as 14, as well as any person with physical or mental disabilities.

On the House floor May 7, lawmakers voted 411–4 for an amendment by Louise M. Slaughter, D-N.Y., to make serious sexual assault a federal crime if the defendant had a previous rape conviction and had crossed state lines before or after the assault. Rapists convicted in federal court were to face a maximum penalty of life imprisonment. Republican Bill McCollum of Florida, chairman of the Judiciary Subcommittee on Crime, said the amendment was probably unconstitutional but too politically potent to oppose.

A second amendment, offered by Democrat Martin Frost of Texas, proposed to require life imprisonment without parole for twice-convicted child molesters who crossed state lines with the intention of molesting a child. The amendment was adopted by voice vote.

The House passed the amended bill that day, 414–4, but the Senate Judiciary Committee took no action on it. ❏

Mandatory Sentences

Near the end of the 1996 session, the Senate passed a watered-down proposal (S 1612) to mandate prison terms for possessing a gun while committing certain federal offenses. The House did not take up the bill, however.

Existing law mandated a prison term of at least five years for someone who "uses or carries" a firearm while committing a violent federal crime or federal drug-trafficking offense. In December 1995, the Supreme Court ruled in *Bailey v. United States* that simply possessing a firearm did not meet the definition of using or carrying.

On Oct. 3, the Senate passed S 1612 by voice vote after adopting an amendment by Senate Majority Leader Trent Lott, R-Miss. The Lott amendment would have overturned the *Bailey* ruling by replacing "uses and carries" with "possesses." It also would have recommended, but not required, higher sentences if the firearm was discharged.

As introduced by Sen. Jesse Helms, R-N.C., S 1612 would have mandated 10 years in prison for possessing a gun while committing a violent federal crime or drug-trafficking offense, and 20 years if the gun were discharged. ❏

DNA Testing

The House proposed in 1995 to speed the pace of federal aid for DNA testing programs, but the bill (HR 2418) went nowhere in the Senate.

As part of the 1994 crime bill (PL 103-322), Congress had authorized $40 million in grants over five years to help states develop systems to track crime suspects through DNA identification. HR 2418, which the House Judiciary Committee reported Dec. 11 (H Rept 104-393), proposed to provide more of the money in the early years of the program and less in later years.

Sponsor Bill McCollum, R-Fla., said the change would help states with the high cost of starting a DNA tracking system. The House passed the bill, 407–5, on Dec. 12, 1995, but the Senate Judiciary Committee did not act on it.

Congress ultimately appropriated $1 million in fiscal 1996 and $3 million in fiscal 1997 for state DNA systems, as authorized by the crime bill. ❏

Telemarketing Fraud

The House passed a bill (HR 1499) late in the 1996 session to stiffen the penalties for telemarketing fraud, but the Senate did not take up the measure.

The bill would have required the U.S. Sentencing Commis-

sion to increase by an average of 11 months the presumptive prison sentences for those convicted of using telemarketing to commit a crime. The presumptive penalty for telemarketers who defrauded the elderly would have been raised by an average of 25 months.

The measure followed up on the 1994 crime bill (PL 103–322), which raised the maximum penalty for telemarketing-related crimes. The crime bill instructed the commission to increase the presumptive sentence, if necessary, for telemarketing fraud against the elderly, and the commission had decided that no increase was needed. *(1994 action, p. 350)*

The House passed HR 1499 by voice vote Sept. 25, 1996. ❏

Jail Break Penalties

Legislation to stiffen the penalty for escaping from federal prison passed the House in 1995 but died in the Senate.

The bill (HR 1533) would have set a maximum penalty of 10 years in prison—twice the previous maximum—for convicts who escaped. The House Judiciary Committee reported the bill Dec. 11 (H Rept 104-392) and the House passed it the next day by voice vote.

The Senate Judiciary Committee reported an amended version on June 13, 1996, adding language targeting violent sexual predators and computer crimes. It also proposed to let federal and state agencies collect fees to pay for fingerprinting and checking the backgrounds of volunteers who worked with children. The modified bill stalled, although the provisions on sexual predators and computer crimes were enacted as parts of other bills. *(Sexual offenders, p. 738; computer crime, 742)* ❏

Civil Law

House Republicans proposed bills in the 104th Congress to alter some of the ground rules for federal lawsuits and administrative appeals, renewing a number of the battles fought in the 103rd Congress. All of the measures were blocked well short of enactment. Similarly, a proposal by Senate Republicans to split the western federal appeals circuit in two was gutted on the Senate floor and ignored by the House.

LEGAL CHALLENGES TO REFERENDUMS

The House passed a bill in 1995 to give state ballot initiatives more protection against legal challenges, but the Senate never took up the measure.

The bill (HR 1170) would have allowed only a three-judge panel, not a single federal district judge, to block implementation of referendum. The bill grew out of the fight over Proposition 187, a referendum that California voters adopted in 1994 to deny most public services to illegal immigrants. A district court judge had issued a temporary restraining order to keep the new law from taking effect while opponents challenged its constitutionality in court.

The bill's sponsor, Rep. Sonny Bono, R-Calif., argued that it was too easy for opponents of a referendum to block the will of the voters. If a three-judge panel were required to review challenges, Bono said, opponents of a referendum would no longer be able to shop for a judge sympathetic to their cause. Democrats on the House Judiciary Committee countered that referendums should not be given more protection than laws adopted by state legislatures, which could be blocked by a single district judge.

The Judiciary Committee reported the bill July 11, 1995 (H Rept 104-179) after adopting an amendment specifying that the measure would not be retroactive. As a result, it would not have affected Proposition 187.

On the House floor Sept. 28, members rejected an amendment by Patricia Schroeder, D-Colo., to limit the bill to the areas most susceptible to "judge shopping." The vote was 177–248. Lawmakers also rejected by voice vote an amendment by Melvin Watt, D-N.C., to limit the bill to California. The House then passed the measure, 266–159.

The Senate Judiciary Committee took no action on the bill.

9TH CIRCUIT COURT

Republican efforts to remove a number of western states from the 9th U.S. Circuit Court of Appeals ran aground in 1996.

The 9th Circuit was by far the largest of the nation's 12 appeals courts, covering nine western states and two U.S. territories in the Pacific Ocean. Two Senate western Republicans, Slade Gorton of Washington and Conrad Burns of Montana, proposed a bill (S 956) to shift their states and Alaska, Idaho and Oregon from the 9th Circuit to a new 12th Circuit.

Several western Republicans argued that the 9th Circuit was overburdened, forcing members of the panel to cut back on the number of opinions they wrote. Opponents of the bill, however, accused sponsors of trying to remove their states from the reach of California appeals-court judges, whom they considered too liberal.

The Senate Judiciary Committee approved S 956 by voice vote Dec. 7, 1995, after amending it to add Arizona and Nevada to the list of states in the new 12th District. The change would have left only California, Hawaii, Guam and the Northern Mariana Islands in the 9th Circuit. The committee reported the bill on Dec. 7 (S Rept 104-197).

On the Senate floor March 20, members approved a substitute by Dianne Feinstein, D-Calif., that called for studying the entire federal appeals court system instead of splitting the 9th Circuit. Adopted by voice vote, the amendment would have created a Commission on Structural Alternatives for the Federal Courts of Appeals with a $500,000 budget to conduct the study. The Judiciary Committee had narrowly rejected a similar amendment, 8–9, at the Dec. 7 markup.

The Senate approved the revised bill by voice vote, but the House took no action on it.

LAWSUIT ARBITRATION

Members of the House Judiciary Committee tried again in 1995 to promote out-of-court settlements of federal lawsuits, but they could not get their bill (HR 1443) out of committee.

The bill would have expanded an experimental program in lawsuit arbitration to all district courts. The program, which was first authorized in 1988 (PL 100-352), was limited to 20 of the 94 federal districts. The bill also would have made pretrial arbitration mandatory for claims worth $150,000 or less, optional for larger claims.

The House Judiciary Subcommittee on Courts and Intellectual Property approved the bill by voice vote May 16, 1995, but the full Judiciary Committee never took up the measure. A similar proposal passed the House in 1993 and died in the Senate. *(1993 action, p. 710)*

ADMINISTRATIVE LAW JUDGES

Picking up where the Senate left off in 1993, the House Judiciary Subcommittee on Commercial and Administrative Law approved a bill (HR 1802) in 1995 designed to make administrative law judges more independent. The full House Judiciary Committee never took up the measure, however.

The bill would have moved the judges, who were employed by the federal agencies, into an independent corps headed by a presidential appointee. The judges would have been assigned to subject areas that matched their experience at the agencies.

Supporters of the change said that the existing system led judges to favor the agencies that employed them. Opponents, however, contended that the existing system worked well and should not be disrupted.

The subcommittee approved the bill, 6–3, on Sept. 14, 1993, and the measure progressed no farther. The Senate passed similar legislation in 1993, only to have it die in the House. *(1993 action, p. 711)*

STENOGRAPHIC RECORDING

The House Judiciary Committee took aim again in 1995 at a federal court rule allowing audio or video recordings of depositions, to no avail. The committee reported a bill (HR 1445—H Rept 104-228) on Aug. 2, 1995, to reinstate a requirement that depositions be recorded by a stenographer, reversing a rule change made in 1993 by the Judicial Conference of the United States. The House took no action on the measure, however.

The House had passed a similar bill in 1993, but it died in the Senate. Sponsor Carlos J. Moorhead, R-Calif., said the measure was needed because tape recordings were not reliable, as demonstrated by the failed recording of a hearing for one of the suspects in the 1995 bombing of a federal building in Oklahoma City. ❏

Same-Sex Marriage

Three gay couples in Hawaii who sought to be legally married triggered a legal and political firestorm in 1996, leading Congress to clear a bill restricting same-sex marriages.

The bill (HR 3396—PL 104-199) was a major victory for social conservatives, a key Republican constituency. Yet most Democratic lawmakers and President Clinton also supported the measure, despite the opposition of some gay rights organizations—a small but vocal Democratic constituency.

The bill declared that states did not have to recognize any same-sex marriages sanctioned by other states, and it defined marriage for the purpose of federal agencies as the legal union between a man and a woman. The latter provision was intended to bar homosexual couples from filing joint tax returns or obtaining the spousal benefits provided by federal programs, such as Social Security.

A competing bill (S 2056) by Senate Democrats to bar employers from discriminating against gays was defeated shortly after the Senate cleared HR 3396. Thus, the marriage measure reached the president's desk without even a token nod to its opponents. *(Box, p. 748)*

Clinton signed the bill without comment or public ceremony in the early morning hours of Saturday, Sept. 21—a move that reflected his ambivalence about the measure. Although Clinton parted company with gay organizations early in the debate on HR 3396, he had openly courted their support during his first campaign and had backed their effort in 1993 to allow avowed homosexuals in the armed forces—a stance that proved politically costly. *(Gays in the military, p. 284)*

The roots of the measure had been planted more than five years before the bill started to move through the House Judiciary Committee. The three couples—one pair of men, two pairs of women—filed suit in Hawaii state court after being denied marriage licenses by the Hawaii Department of Health.

Although similar lawsuits had been filed to no avail, this case tried to take advantage of provisions in the Hawaii Constitution that explicitly protected privacy and barred discrimination on the basis of gender. The tack proved fruitful: in 1993, the Hawaii Supreme Court sent the case back to a lower court for reconsideration, indicating that the equal protection language in the Hawaii Constitution may well entitle the couples to marry.

Although the law at issue covered only one state, the implications of the ruling were national. Under the "full faith and credit" clause of the U.S. Constitution, states were obliged to honor the legal proceedings of other states, including marriages.

Some observers argued that states could refuse to acknowledge gay marriages sanctioned outside their borders. The prevailing opinion in Washington, however, was that a marriage deemed valid in Hawaii would have to have been recognized as valid in the 49 other states.

The same clause of the U.S. Constitution also allowed Congress to regulate aspects of the states' reciprocal legal arrangements, although it was not clear how far that power went. With that in mind, two Republicans with close ties to social conservatives—Rep. Bob Barr of Georgia and Sen. Don Nickles of Oklahoma—introduced similar bills in May 1996 to allow states not to recognize same-sex marriages.

Supporters of the legislation, dubbed the "Defense of Marriage Act," said action was needed to combat what they described as a radical effort to broaden the traditional concept of marriage. Said Rep. Charles T. Canady, R-Fla., "What is at stake in this controversy? Nothing less than our collective moral understanding. . . . of the essential nature of the family."

Proponents also contended that legalizing gay marriage would send children a message that homosexuality was appropriate, pushing them away from traditional heterosexual relationships. One supporter, Republican Bob Inglis of South Car-

olina, even suggested that loosening the definition of marriage might ultimately lead to the legalization of polygamy.

Opponents called the legislation premature, given that no state had yet legalized gay marriage, and said it was a potentially unconstitutional intrusion on state autonomy. Several constitutional scholars argued that HR 3396 would punch a hole in a part of the Constitution that was crucial to the functioning of a federal system of government. "A good deal of the entire federal system could be undone," University of Chicago law professor Cass Sustein told a Senate panel in July.

In response to the supporters' arguments on morality, bill opponents accused sponsors of intolerance and compared the resistance to gay marriage to past civil rights abuses. They also argued that the bill was calculated to drive an election-year wedge between moderate and liberal Democrats.

LEGISLATIVE ACTION

The House Judiciary Committee approved the Barr bill (HR 3396) on June 12, 20–10, with two Democrats joining all 18 Republicans at the markup in support. The debate featured an unusually personal appeal by openly gay Democrat Barney Frank of Massachusetts, who lived with a male partner. Noting that he bore the same federal responsibilities and burdens as heterosexuals, Frank said, "I ask only that the law allow me the same benefits."

The committee rejected amendments by Frank to strike the proposed federal definition of marriage and to require the federal government to recognize any gay marriages sanctioned by state law or referendum. It also rejected two amendments by Patricia Schroeder, D-Colo.: one to change the bill's federal definition of marriage to cover only monogamous unions, and another to deny spousal benefits to the new partners of divorced men and women unless they had made fair financial arrangements for their original families.

The committee reported the bill on July 9 (H Rept 104-664), and the House took it up two days later. Lawmakers clashed angrily for two days over the timing, necessity and constitutionality of the bill, with some proponents of HR 3396 denouncing homosexuality and some opponents calling it an exercise in politically motivated intolerance.

Frank again tried to eliminate the proposed federal definition of marriage, but the House rejected the amendment by voice vote. His proposal to require federal recognition of same-sex marriages in states where they were validated by law or court order was defeated, 103–311.

The House passed the measure July 12 by a wide margin, 342–67.

Senate leaders took HR 3396 directly to the floor in September, but lawmakers threatened to sink it under a wave of controversial amendments. The bill was salvaged, however, by a compromise that called for consecutive votes on the marriage bill and S 2056, the job discrimination bill.

Opposition to the Defense of Marriage Act in the Senate was led by liberal Democratic Sen. Edward M. Kennedy of Massachusetts. "I regard this bill as a mean-spirited form of Republican legislative gay-bashing cynically calculated to try to inflame

EMPLOYMENT DISCRIMINATION

Immediately after clearing the so-called Defense of Marriage Act, the Senate narrowly defeated a bill (S 2056) to end employment discrimination against gays. Proponents of the bill were encouraged even in defeat, saying it was the first time either chamber had voted on legislation designed to enhance the rights of homosexuals.

The bill would have amended the 1964 Civil Rights Act (PL 88–352) to outlaw employment discrimination on the basis of sexual orientation. The prohibition would not have applied to the military, businesses with fewer than 15 employees and non-profit religious organizations. It also would have barred quotas and preferential treatment designed to help homosexuals acquire or retain jobs.

Nondiscrimination legislation for homosexuals had been around the Capitol since 1975, when Rep. Bella S. Abzug, D-N.Y., first introduced such a bill. But gay rights legislation did not get a hearing until the 103rd Congress, when the Senate Labor and Human Resources Committee gave the issue some attention.

The committee's chairman at the time was Sen. Edward M. Kennedy, D-Mass., who later sponsored S 2056. In exchange for letting the same-sex marriage bill (HR 3396) proceed quickly to a Senate vote, Kennedy extracted a promise from Senate GOP leaders that the Senate vote on S 2056 as the next order of business. *(Same-sex marriage, p. 746)*

Opponents of the discrimination bill said it would cause a flood of claims by gays. To prove that they were not hostile to gay employees, companies would have to identify the sexual preference of their workers—a serious breach of privacy, said Orrin G. Hatch, R-Utah. Conservatives also contended that the bill would compel people with heartfelt beliefs on the immorality of homosexuality to hire gays.

The Senate defeated the bill Sept. 10 on a **key vote of 49–50 (R 8–45; D 41–5)**. *(1996 key votes, p. 1047)* One probable supporter, Democrat David Pryor of Arkansas, was absent, sparing Vice President Gore from having to cast a tie-breaking vote. Gore had been expected to vote for the bill. Even if the Senate had passed the bill, however, the House had not been expected to act on it before adjourning.

the public eight weeks before the Nov. 5 election," Kennedy said.

Majority Leader Trent Lott, R-Miss., defended the bill and its proponents, saying, "This is not prejudiced legislation. . . . It is a preemptive measure to make sure that a handful of judges in a single state cannot impose a radical social agenda upon the entire nation."

On September 10, only 13 senators, all Democrats, joined Kennedy in opposing the bill. The Senate cleared the measure, 85–14.

Three months later, the state court in Hawaii handling the three couples' lawsuit ruled in favor of gay marriages. Circuit Judge Kevin Chang found that the state had not shown a compelling reason to discriminate against gay unions. State officials appealed to the Hawaii Supreme Court, and the ruling was put temporarily on hold.

The prospect of gay marriages being validated in Hawaii had not gone unnoticed in other state capitals. By December 1995, 16 state legislatures had enacted laws declaring that gay marriages would not be considered valid in their states. ❑

Other Social Issues

Despite the influx of conservative Republicans in the House, the 104th Congress did little to answer the long-standing GOP concerns about affirmative action, school prayer and family privacy. Republicans did manage to order a federal study on the effects of legalized gambling, however. Congress also cleared a bill aimed at easing the adoption of foreign children in single-parent families.

AFFIRMATIVE ACTION

Three Republican proposals to curtail federal affirmative action programs died in House and Senate committees in 1996, stalled by intraparty divisions and the GOP leadership's nervousness about the November elections.

Although their sweeping proposals fell flat, Republicans did manage to knock out a little-used racial preference program in 1995: a tax break that encouraged sales of radio and television stations to minority-owned businesses. The tax break had been awarded less than 20 times a year, on average, since its inception in 1978.

The federal government had been promoting affirmative action since the mid-1960s, when President Lyndon B. Johnson ordered federal contractors to adopt affirmative action plans. President Richard M. Nixon later expanded that directive to require "set asides"—minimum levels of minority participation in federal projects. Congress, meanwhile, established employment nondiscrimination standards in the 1964 Civil Rights Act (PL 88–352) that prodded private employers to hire and promote minorities in order to avoid lawsuits.

The Reagan administration was the first one to challenge federal affirmative action policies. The administration weakened enforcement of some programs, but Congress insisted that the requirements on federal contractors be maintained. Congressional Democrats pushed successfully in 1991 for new protections against job discrimination, clearing a compromise civil rights bill (PL 102–166) over objections that it would encourage racial quotas in the workplace. *(1991 law, Congress and the Nation Vol. VIII, p. 780)*

Race- and gender-based policies came under increasing fire in the 1990s, with critics mounting successful challenges in the courts, at the ballot box and in state legislatures. When Republicans took control of Congress in 1995, both sides in the debate over affirmative action expected the GOP majority to come out swinging.

Indeed, Congress moved swiftly in 1995 to eliminate one preference program: a Federal Communications Commission (FCC) policy that allowed the seller of a broadcast station or cable TV system to defer taxes on the profits if the buyer was a company at least partially owned by a minority. The repeal was motivated more by financial necessity, however, than by opposition to racial preferences.

Republicans sought to repeal the FCC program to help cover the cost of a bill (HR 831) to renew the tax deduction for self-employed workers' health insurance premiums. Supporters of the preference program were in a tough spot—they could either find another way to raise money for the health insurance tax break, or they could try to kill the bill. In the end, the bipartisan support for HR 831 overwhelmed the efforts to preserve the FCC preferences. The Senate cleared HR 831 by voice vote April 3, 1995, and President Clinton signed it April 11 (PL 104-7). *(Health insurance deduction, p. 102)*

A far more significant blow to affirmative action was struck in June 1995, when the U.S. Supreme Court held in *Adarand Constructors v. Peña* that federal preferences for minorities were subject to the same constitutional prohibitions that barred governments from discriminating against minorities. The 5–4 decision did not strike down any federal affirmative action programs, it just made them more vulnerable to challenge in court. *(Case summary, p. 791)*

President Clinton responded first to the decision, announcing on July 19, 1995, that a five-month review of federal affirmative action programs had found some problems but also an overriding need. "We should have a simple slogan: Mend it, but don't end it," Clinton said.

The next day, one of Clinton's prospective opponents, Republican Sen. Phil Gramm of Texas, launched what he called an all-out effort to prohibit set-asides for minority or women-owned businesses in federal contract awards. He said he would offer an amendment to each of the 13 annual appropriations bills that would bar such preferences.

Gramm's crusade did not endure, however. After senators twice rejected his proposals by large margins—on the annual spending bills for the Legislative Branch (HR 2492) and the departments of Commerce, Justice and State (HR 2076)—he stopped offering them.

On July 27, 1995, Senate Majority Leader Bob Dole, the Kansas Republican who would become the GOP nominee for president in 1996, and Rep. Charles T. Canady, the Florida Republican who chaired the House Judiciary Subcommittee on the Constitution, introduced bills in the Senate (S 1085) and House (HR 2128) to stop the federal government from discriminating or giving preferences on the basis of race, gender or national origin.

The bills also proposed to bar the government from requiring or encouraging the recipients of federal dollars to grant such preferences. They would not have prohibited federal officials from encouraging women and minorities to apply for jobs, contracts or programs, as long as no quotas were imposed.

Federal contracts with historically black colleges and Indian tribes would have been exempt from the bills' prohibitions. The legislation also would have preserved a section of the 1964 Civil Rights Act that allowed women or men to be excluded from occupations if gender was considered a bona fide occupational qualification, if privacy was paramount, or if national security or military issues were at stake.

The bills would not have affected state or local affirmative action programs or voluntary preferences adopted by private businesses and universities.

Opponents of affirmative action argued that preference programs benefited only a few, privileged minorities or women rather than helping the truly disadvantaged. They also contended that the programs discriminated against more qualified white men, stigmatized the recipients of the preferences and exacerbated the racial and gender divisions already present in society.

Defenders of the programs said that affirmative action forced employers to scrutinize the biases that worked against whole classes of applicants and employees. All parties ultimately benefited, they said, when workplaces became more diverse and objective factors replaced the "old-boy network" in personnel decisions.

Early in 1996, GOP leaders and conservatives who wanted to repeal affirmative action policies were confident that they had the votes to pass the Dole/Canady proposal. They also believed that the issue would help topple President Clinton.

Canady's subcommittee took up HR 2128 on March 7, approving it on a party-line, 8–5 vote.

At the markup, Canady said the bill would remove the "sprawling regime of hundreds of federal programs that treat citizens differently based on skin color and sex." Democrats countered that the bill was damaging to women and minorities and unnecessary, given that the *Adarand* decision had already clarified the acceptable boundaries of affirmative action policies.

The subcommittee defeated a series of amendments by Democrats aimed at deterring reverse discrimination lawsuits and allowing some use of numerical goals. On Canady's suggestion, however, the panel agreed to remove a provision barring the federal government from entering consent decrees that provided racial or gender-based preferences.

House Republican leaders decided to put off further action on the affirmative action bill until later in the year—partly to move the debate closer to the November elections, partly to buy time for conservatives to shore up support among GOP moderates. The political tides turned and moderate Republicans gained influence, however, causing the legislation to founder.

Canady offered to amend HR 2128, limiting it to a repeal of racial and gender-based preferences in federal contracting. Still, his bill made no further progress.

Clinton, meanwhile, took steps to limit federal preferences, preempting some of the Republicans' moves.

For example, the day before Canady's subcommittee marked up HR 2128, Clinton announced that he soon would issue rules limiting racial preferences in government contracting to instances where there was proof of prior discrimination. The ensuing executive order suspended for three years all programs that reserved contracts for minority- and women-owned companies.

The Senate never attempted to move Dole's bill, remaining silent on the issue after Labor and Human Resources Committee Chairwoman Nancy Landon Kassebaum, R-Kan., announced in April that she was "struggling" with the measure.

Late in the session, the House GOP leadership shifted its focus to a much narrower measure (HR 3994) introduced in August by House Small Business Committee Chairwoman Jan Meyers, R-Kan. It would have repealed a Small Business Administration (SBA) program known as Section 8(a), which reserved small government contracts for minority-owned businesses.

Under the 8(a) program, federal agencies used the SBA to find certified, socially or economically disadvantaged businesses to fulfill contracts worth less than $3 million. Opponents of the program said it discouraged competition and resulted in the government paying inflated fees to contractors. They also argued that more than one-half of certified businesses consistently were overlooked for contracts, leaving the rest to reap all the benefits of the program.

HR 3994 went no further than a hearing in the Small Business Committee in September. By that time, House members were anxious to adjourn, and Republicans were skittish about offending women voters—the main beneficiaries of affirmative action policies, according to some studies.

SCHOOL PRAYER

Religious conservatives renewed their push for prayer in public schools in 1995, but their efforts made no discernible progress despite a sympathetic GOP leadership.

The effort divided Republicans and their conservative Christian allies into two camps, each headed by a conservative House member. Unable to find a compromise and seeing little that might prevail on the House floor, the House GOP leadership let the issue die without a vote in the 104th Congress.

One group, led by House Judiciary Committee Chairman Henry J. Hyde of Illinois, backed a wide-ranging constitutional amendment (H J Res 121) that would have prohibited federal and state governments from denying people equal access to benefits or otherwise discriminating against them because of their religious beliefs or practices. The amendment would have overturned the court rulings that had caused public schools and agencies to place unequal restrictions on religious and secular activities.

The other group, led by Rep. Ernest Istook of Oklahoma, backed a constitutional amendment that gave more explicit support to voluntary prayer in public schools. Istook's proposal (H J Res 127) would have declared that the Constitution neither prohibited student-sponsored prayer in public schools nor barred "acknowledgment of the religious heritage, beliefs or traditions of the people." It also would have forbidden the federal and state governments to compose official prayers, compel people to pray or discriminate against religious expression or belief.

Hoping to find middle ground among Republicans, House Majority Leader Dick Armey, R-Texas, introduced another constitutional amendment (H J Res 184) similar to Hyde's proposal. The House Judiciary Subcommittee on the Constitution planned to take up H J Res 184 in mid-1996, but members could not settle their differences and the markup never took place.

Even if the two factions had struck a compromise, the resolution had virtually no chance of garnering a two-thirds majority in the House or Senate. Democrats in both chambers were almost unanimously opposed to such a proposal, and many Republicans also were ambivalent or wary of alienating moderates in their party. Conservative Christian groups pressed the GOP leadership to put members on record before the 1996 elections, but the leadership did not comply.

Advocates of a school-prayer amendment argued that it was needed because religion had been incrementally squeezed out of public life as the government's influence increased. Opponents countered that the law already protected religious expressions, and an amendment would only advance the interests of religious majorities.

The First Amendment of the Constitution barred Congress from prohibiting the free exercise of religion, but it also forbade Congress to adopt any laws establishing a religion. The latter clause eventually was interpreted by the Supreme Court to bar any government-sanctioned expressions of religion, ending the common practice of compulsory prayers and Bible readings in school classrooms.

Two key Supreme Court rulings came in 1962 *(Engel v. Vitale)* and 1963 *(Abington School District v. Schempp)*, when the justices prohibited government-sponsored religious exercises in public schools even if they were voluntary. Rulings in the 1980s and 1990s barred the public schools from requiring a moment of silent prayer and from offering prayers at graduation ceremonies.

Conservative lawmakers tried repeatedly after the *Abington* decision to amend the Constitution to permit voluntary prayer in the public schools, but their efforts were unavailing. In 1995, the influential Christian Coalition, a grassroots lobbying organization for conservative Christians, set its sights on a broader amendment that would permit voluntary prayer in any public place.

The amendment topped the coalition's legislative wish list for the 104th Congress, dubbed the "Contract with the American Family." The coalition released its contract in May 1995, just after the House finished work on the GOP's "Contract with America"—an effort that the Christian Right had supported despite the lack of attention to social issues. The implicit but unmistakable message from the coalition's May announcement was, "Our turn."

The Christian Right appeared to have a friend in House Speaker Newt Gingrich, R-Ga., who had pledged repeatedly that religious freedom would be a top priority for the House. Gingrich and other top House leaders praised the "Contract with the American Family," with Gingrich saying in a televised interview, "We have to bring God and the concept of a creator back more into the public square than it has been in recent years." But Gingrich also said he was not convinced a constitutional amendment was required, and he explored the feasibility of a statute that could withstand a court challenge.

The coalition's announcement also rallied opponents of school-prayer legislation. A number of mainstream religious organizations joined forces with advocacy groups such as the

American Civil Liberties Union and the liberal People for the American Way in a new Coalition to Preserve Religious Liberty, which held a news conference the same day as the Christian Coalition to underscore its opposition.

The chairman of the Coalition to Preserve Religious Liberty, a Baptist minister from the District of Columbia, conceded that religious expression was sometimes stifled in school settings through unwitting ignorance or neglect. But he said the answer was educating the public about what was permissible, not amending the Bill of Rights.

The only formal legislative activity on the school-prayer issue was a series of hearings in mid-1995 by the House Judiciary Subcommittee on the Constitution. At least four constitutional amendments to allow voluntary school prayer were introduced in the Senate in 1995, but the Senate Judiciary Committee took no action on any of them.

GAMBLING COMMISSION

Concerned about the impact of legalized gambling on America, Congress created a nine-member commission in 1996 to study the issue.

The legislation (HR 497—PL 104-169) gave the commission two years to submit a report detailing the economic impact of gambling on an area's businesses and families. The commission also was instructed to examine Native American gambling, gambling on the Internet and the relationship between gambling and crime.

Sponsored by conservative Republican Frank R. Wolf of Virginia in the House and liberal Democrat Paul Simon of Illinois in the Senate, the legislation came in response to a nationwide surge in legalized gambling. Forty-eight states permitted some form of gambling in 1996, up from two states in 1976.

Backers of the legislation said that the rapid growth had brought problems to communities, including a rise in crime and gambling addiction.

Opponents of the bill countered that state governments, not federal lawmakers, were responsible for regulating gaming. The commission would only intrude on an industry that already was more heavily regulated than most, critics of the bill said.

The industry formed a lobbying organization and sharply increased its donations to federal candidates in an apparent effort to sway the debate over the bill. In the end, Congress approved a commission with less power than Wolf had wanted but more than the industry would have liked.

Although there was broad support for the proposed study, lawmakers struggled over the scope, duration and powers of the commission. Several allies of the industry also expressed concern that the commission would be biased against gambling.

The House Judiciary Committee reported an amended version of the bill on Dec. 21, 1995 (H Rept 104-440, Part I), proposing a two-year study instead of the three-year inquiry envisioned by Wolf. The amended version called on the president and congressional leaders to consult with each other to ensure a balance on the commission among the various viewpoints.

The bill, which the House approved March 5, also would have given the commission broad subpoena powers, including the authority to call witnesses and request documents. Congress did not give most advisory commissions subpoena power, and the gambling industry vigorously opposed the proposal. Advocates of the commission, however, saw the subpoena power as critical to its success.

Simon's bill (S 704) proposed no subpoena powers. It also would have limited the commission to studying the social and economic impact of gambling and alternative sources of revenue.

The Senate Governmental Affairs Committee reported an amended version of S 704 on June 20 that moved closer to the House bill. As reported, the bill proposed to let the commission subpoena documents and, if necessary, witnesses to explain the documents. It also expanded the scope of the study to include the relationship between gambling and crime, as well as the impact of gambling and related advertising on families, businesses and society.

On the Senate floor July 17, the Senate amended S 704 again to require the commission to keep confidential the information it gathered and not to reveal the identity of its sources. It then inserted the text of S 704 into HR 497 and passed the House bill by voice vote.

Wolf criticized the Senate for not giving the commission enough power, but he decided not to push for changes. The House cleared the Senate version of HR 497 on July 22, and President Clinton signed it on Aug. 3.

FAMILY PRIVACY

Addressing a concern voiced by social conservatives, the House passed a bill (HR 1271) early in 1995 to shield children from intrusive questions on surveys by federally funded programs. The measure stalled before it reached the Senate floor, however.

The bill began as part of the Family Reinforcement Act (HR 11), one of the House GOP's "Contract with America" proposals. It would have required parental consent before a minor could be asked to provide information on any of seven topics: religious beliefs, sex, psychological problems, illegal or antisocial behavior, family relationships, parental political beliefs or privileged relationships, such as those with lawyers, doctors or the clergy.

The requirement would not have applied to criminal or immigration investigations, inquiries made to protect the health or welfare of a minor, customs or tax inquiries, or welfare applications.

The House Government Reform and Oversight Committee reported the bill March 29 (H Rept 104-94), and the House passed it April 4, 418–7. The House added one amendment to toughen the measure, requiring the parental consent to be in writing. The amendment, approved 379–46, also allowed parents to sue for an unlimited amount of compensatory damages if their children were surveyed without the required consent.

The bill ran into trouble in the Senate Governmental Affairs Committee the following April, as Democrats argued that it would make research on important social issues virtually impossible. At the markup April 18, John Glenn, D-Ohio, offered a substitute that would have required advance written notice of surveys and allowed parents to object in writing, but the amendment was rejected on a party-line, 6–8 vote. The committee then voted along party lines to approve the bill, 7–5.

The panel reported the bill on Aug. 2 (S Rept 104-351), but the Senate did not act on it.

ENGLISH ONLY

A bill to require all official federal business to be conducted in English passed the House in 1996 but advanced no further.

The measure (HR 123) would have declared English the official language of the federal government, permitting federal agencies to use other languages only in limited circumstances. The exceptions included protecting public health and safety, providing for national security and protecting the rights of criminal defendants and crime victims.

The bill also would have repealed the portion of the Voting Rights Act of 1965 (PL 89-110) that required states with significant concentrations of non-English-speaking voters to supply bilingual ballots. The House Judiciary Committee had reported a similar proposal as a separate bill (HR 351—H Rept 104-728) on July 31, 1996, but that measure received no further attention.

The bill would not have affected federal aid for bilingual education, nor would it have required federal employees to speak English on the job. Instead, it applied mainly to reports and documents used by the government, such as tax forms.

The push for the bill was led by Randy "Duke" Cunningham, a Republican whose southern California district was not far from the Mexican border. Cunningham called English a unifying force that was key to success in America, and said the bill would persuade non-English-speaking residents to learn the language.

Another Republican supporter, John Linder of Georgia, argued that well-meaning programs intended to help non-English-speaking immigrants had actually held them back. "The problem is not that the government has done too little, but that the government is doing too much," he said.

Numerous Democrats decried the effort as election-year "immigrant bashing," saying the bill would do nothing to help people learn English. Instead, critics said, it would simply prevent many residents from understanding their government. Besides, they said, virtually all government business was already conducted in English.

The House Economic and Educational Opportunities Committee narrowly approved the bill, 19–17, on July 24, 1996, after a lengthy and highly partisan debate. The panel rejected Democratic proposals to allow the continuation of services in languages other than English or to permit official business in another language if it would be more efficient. It agreed by voice vote, however, to exempt the decennial census from the bill on the grounds that requiring English could heighten the challenge of counting minorities.

The committee reported the bill on July 30 (H Rept 104-723). The Judiciary Committee had approved HR 351 two weeks earlier, 17–12, with only Republican Steven H. Schiff of New Mexico crossing party lines to vote "nay."

As amended in 1992 (PL 102-344), the Voting Rights Act required bilingual voter registration materials and ballots to be provided in any jurisdiction where at least 5 percent of the population or 10,000 residents did not speak English. Democrats argued that ending the requirement would disenfranchise people based on their national origin, but Republicans said that the bilingual requirement discouraged non-English-speaking citizens from learning the language. (1992 voting act amendments, Congress and the Nation Vol. VIII, p. 793)

The House passed the broader English-only bill on Aug. 1, 259–169. The Senate did not take up the legislation.

FOREIGN ADOPTION

Congress cleared a bill (S 457—PL 104-51) in 1995 amending federal adoption law to help U.S. citizens adopt children from foreign countries.

The measure addressed a problem caused by a shift in terminology overseas. Under existing law, U.S. citizens could adopt foreign children if they were orphans or if they were "illegitimate" and the mother agreed to the adoption. But many countries no longer referred to children as "illegitimate," labeling them "born out of wedlock" instead. The federal Immigration and Naturalization Service (INS) held that such children did not qualify for adoption unless both parents approved.

Bill sponsor Paul Simon, D-Ill., said that the INS' interpretation derailed the adoption of hundreds of foreign children whose absentee fathers could not be tracked down for approval. His bill substituted "born out of wedlock" for "illegitimate" in U.S. immigration law, enabling such children to be adopted with only their mother's approval.

The Senate Judiciary Committee reported the bill June 22, and the Senate passed it by voice vote July 17. The House cleared the bill by voice vote Oct. 30, and President Clinton signed it Nov. 15.   ❑

Legal Services Corporation

Conservatives were unable to terminate the Legal Services Corporation (LSC) in the 104th Congress, but they succeeded in slashing its budget and reining in its activities.

The embattled corporation subsidized lawyers who represented the poor in civil matters, such as disputes over rent and alimony. The House Judiciary Committee approved legislation (HR 2277) in 1995 to replace the LSC with a restrictive block grant program to the states, but a division in the GOP ranks kept the bill off the House floor. The Senate Labor and Human Resources Committee endorsed a bill (S 1221) the following year that would have placed similar restrictions on the lawyers funded by the corporation, but that measure stalled in the face of opposition from Senate Democrats and the White House.

The appropriators picked up where the authorizing committees left off, cutting the corporation's funding by 30 percent and barring federally subsidized lawyers from participating in a host of activities. The prohibitions, which were included in spending bills for fiscal 1996 and 1997, included filing class-action lawsuits, lobbying and working on abortion cases.

The funding cuts led to the closure of 100 neighborhood "legal aid" clinics. Still, some conservatives had hoped to end all federal support for legal aid lawyers, and Congress did not go nearly that far.

BACKGROUND

Congress created the LSC in 1974 (PL 93-355) to give legal aid programs a steady source of funding, shielding them from the political pressure they might face if they were financed solely by state and local governments. It quickly ran into political pressure from Congress, however, as conservatives objected to some of the work done by legal aid lawyers.

In particular, conservatives wanted the subsidized lawyers to stay away from hot-button social issues, such as abortion rights and labor law. They argued that tax dollars were being used to advance a liberal political agenda, rather than simply aiding the poor with such bread-and-butter cases as evictions and job discrimination. Other critics contended that some federally funded attorneys, especially in rural areas, devoted themselves to harassing farmers and small-business owners under the guise of protecting the rights of workers.

Supporters of the LSC argued that the agency helped provide essential legal services to thousands of lower-income Americans every year. The complaints about legal aid lawyers stemmed from a few isolated incidents, not a fundamental flaw in the system, they said.

Congress reauthorized the corporation in 1977 for three years, but no subsequent reauthorization bill was able to navigate the roiling political waters. President Ronald Reagan tried in vain to abolish the corporation, then used recess appointments to stack the LSC's 11-member board with sharp critics of the corporation. The board adopted limits on lobbying and class-action lawsuits by legal aid lawyers that congressional Democrats tried but failed to remove.

Hoping to quiet the controversy, President Bush appointed a new board of directors during the 101st Congress. Still, Bush and Congress split over whether legal aid lawyers should be permitted to work on abortion and redistricting issues, scuttling efforts to reauthorize the corporation. *(Background, Congress and the Nation Vol. VIII, pp. 773, 795)*

Supporters of the corporation tried again in 1994 to reauthorize the LSC and ease some of the restrictions on lobbying and other disputed activities by legal aid lawyers. The bill never made it out of the House Judiciary Committee, however. Meanwhile, the appropriators steadily increased the corporation's funding. *(1994 action, p. 711)*

By the end of 1995, the corporation was funding 323 legal aid programs that represented about 5 million people in 1.6 million cases. At least 40 percent of the corporation's funding came from sources outside the federal government.

LEGISLATIVE ACTION

On Sept. 13, 1995, a sharply divided House Judiciary Committee approved a bill (HR 2277) to replace the LSC with a dwindling federal block grant and impose stringent new restrictions on the lawyers who received the money. In the course of the two-day markup, however, the committee adopted an amendment from a leading critic of the LSC that would prove fatal to the bill.

As reported on Sept. 21 (H Rept 104-255), the bill proposed a list of cases that federally subsidized lawyers would be permitted to take, including landlord-tenant disputes, debt collection, government benefit denials, insurance claims, and child support or custody actions. It also would have barred legal aid lawyers from lobbying, filing class-action suits, or working on abortion or redistricting cases, even if they did not use federal funds. Existing rules allowed such activities if they were not subsidized by federal taxpayers. Finally, the bill would have prohibited legal aid lawyers from representing certain types of clients, including prison inmates and immigrants who were not permanent U.S. residents.

The committee rejected numerous Democratic amendments to ease the proposed strictures, although it accepted Republican proposals to allow legal aid lawyers to work on consumer fraud, divorce and separation cases. More significantly, it approved two Republican amendments to raise and extend the block grants.

The original version of HR 2277 proposed to authorize $278 million in block grants for legal aid programs in fiscal 1996 and $141 million in fiscal 1997. By a 14–13 vote, the committee adopted an amendment by Michael Patrick Flanagan, R-Ill., to raise the fiscal 1997 grants to $250 million. Then, by a vote of 18–13, the committee adopted an amendment by Bill McCollum, R-Fla., to authorize $175 million in grants in fiscal 1998 and $100 million in fiscal 1999.

The McCollum amendment outraged a group of conservative Republicans, led by Charles H. Taylor of North Carolina, who wanted the subsidies ended after two years. They blocked efforts by bill sponsor George Gekas, R-Pa., to bring the bill to the House floor, effectively killing the measure.

The House bill's problems led Republican Sen. Nancy Landon Kassebaum of Kansas, chairwoman of the Senate Labor and Human Resources Committee, to put her reauthorization bill for the corporation on hold. That bill (S 1221) proposed to keep the corporation going with reduced funding for five years, but with restrictions on cases similar to those in the House bill.

The committee finally approved the bill, 10–3, on June 26, 1996. Kassebaum did not report it to the full Senate until Sept. 30, shortly before Congress adjourned (S Rept 104-392). No further action was taken on the bill.

Appropriations

In contrast to Gekas and Kassebaum's struggles, the appropriators were able to start cutting the corporation's budget early in 1995. One of the first bills cleared by the 104th Congress, a supplemental spending measure in April for the Defense Department (HR 889—PL 104-6), canceled $15 million from the $415 million that the previous Congress had appropriated for the corporation in fiscal 1995.

In July 1995, the House Appropriations Committee proposed to cut the corporation's fiscal 1996 funding to $278 million as part of a spending bill (HR 2076) for the departments of

Commerce, Justice and State and related agencies. The House passed HR 2076 on July 26, 272–151.

The original Senate draft of the bill proposed to eliminate the LSC and all federal support for legal aid programs, but the Senate Appropriations Committee amended it Sept. 7 to propose a $210 million block grant program. The Senate amended the bill again on Sept. 29, proposing to retain the corporation and provide $340 million. The Senate then passed the amended bill by voice vote.

The final version of HR 2076, which cleared the Senate Dec. 7, knocked the corporation's funding back down to $278 million. Although President Clinton vetoed the bill, Congress subsequently cleared an omnibus spending bill for fiscal 1996 (HR 3019—PL 104-134) in April 1996 that kept the funding for the LSC at $278 million.

In addition, the bill barred legal-aid lawyers from using funds from any source to work on redistricting, lobby any branch of government, participate in a class-action lawsuit, represent a foreigner not legally in the United States, conduct training programs for political or labor activists, take part in abortion-related lawsuits, advocate changes in welfare policy, generate cases through unsolicited legal advice or seek reimbursement for legal fees. It also required the corporation to distribute its grants to the lowest bidders, as HR 2277 proposed, ending the preference given to previously funded legal aid programs.

Three months later, House appropriators proposed to cut the corporation's funding to $141 million as part of the Commerce, Justice and State bill for fiscal 1997 (HR 3814). Not satisfied, conservative Republicans sought to delete all funding for the corporation by invoking a House rule against funding programs that had not been authorized. The House GOP leaders sided with the appropriators, however, and they blocked the conservatives' gambit. Then, on July 23, members voted 247–179 to change the corporation's proposed funding to $250 million. Fifty-six Republicans joined 190 Democrats and Independent Bernard Sanders of Vermont in supporting the higher level.

The Senate appropriators also proposed $250 million for the corporation, but their version of HR 3814 did not reach the Senate floor. Instead, funding for the Commerce, Justice and State programs were rolled into an omnibus spending bill for fiscal 1997 (HR 3610—PL 104-208).

House, Senate and White House negotiators on HR 3610 battled intensely over funding for the corporation before settling on a slight increase, to $283 million. Still, the measure continued the restrictions on legal aid lawyers that Congress had imposed in the fiscal 1996 bill. The Senate cleared HR 3610 on Sept. 30.   ❑

Independent Counsels

Trying to address a long-standing Republican complaint, the House Judiciary Subcommittee on Crime approved a bill (HR 3239) in 1996 to curb spending by independent counsels. The measure raised concerns among members from both parties, however, and it advanced no further.

The bill revisited a battle that Republicans had lost in 1994, when Congress had renewed the independent counsel law (PL 103-270). The GOP had pushed in vain for more controls on spending by the counsels, who were appointed by a special three-judge panel to investigate allegations against top federal officials. *(1994 action, p. 705)*

HR 3239 proposed to require the counsels to report quarterly to Congress on their expenses, and it would have made any investigation lasting more than two years subject to congressional appropriations. Under existing law, the counsels were essentially given a blank check by the Justice Department, and their investigations often cost millions of dollars.

The bill also would have prohibited independent counsels from performing legal work on issues not directly related to the case they were investigating. Democrats had accused the special counsel investigating the Whitewater scandal, Kenneth W. Starr, of a conflict of interests because he handled controversial, politically charged cases while directing the Whitewater probe. The bill would not have applied to Starr or any other counsel who had already been appointed, however.

The subcommittee approved the bill by voice vote Sept. 19. Still, Republicans and Democrats on the panel said they were not happy with the conflict-of-interest provision, among other items. The full Judiciary Committee never took up the measure.   ❑

Flag Desecration

A proposed constitutional amendment aimed at protecting the U.S. flag was endorsed by the House in 1995 but narrowly rejected by the Senate. It was the third time in six years that Congress had voted not to send such an amendment to the states for ratification.

The critical opposition to the amendment (H J Res 79, S J Res 31) came from Democrats and a handful of Republicans who were uncomfortable with the notion of amending the Bill of Rights. They were not swayed by the polls showing strong public support for the amendment, nor by threats from activists to make the vote a campaign issue in 1996.

Advocates of the amendment—mainly Republicans, but also some conservative Democrats—argued that the flag, as the ultimate national symbol, deserved special protection. Opponents—mainly Democrats, but also some libertarian Republicans—responded that the First Amendment would be undermined if it did not protect unpopular forms of expression. Besides, they said, flag burning was hardly sweeping the nation, with only three confirmed incidents in 1994.

The roots of the proposed amendment were planted during the 1984 Republican National Convention in Dallas, when a protester doused a U.S. flag in kerosene and set it alight at Dallas City Hall. The protester was convicted of violating a Texas law against desecrating a venerated object, but the Supreme Court ruled in June 1989 *(Texas v. Johnson)* that all such state and federal laws violated the First Amendment right of free expression. *(Case summary, Congress and the Nation Vol. VIII, p. 836.)*

Congress quickly passed a law in 1989 against deliberately burning, mutilating or defiling a U.S. flag (PL 101-131). A proposed constitutional amendment to ban flag desecration, on the other hand, fell 15 votes short of the necessary two-thirds majority in the Senate that October. *(1989 action, Congress and the Nation Vol. VIII, p. 761)*

Less than a year after handing down its *Johnson* decision, the Supreme Court declared in *United States v. Eichman* that the 1989 law was an unconstitutional abridgment of the right to free speech. The ruling made it clear that if the government wanted to outlaw flag burning, it would have trouble doing so without amending the Constitution.

Prodded by President George Bush, lawmakers again considered a constitutional amendment that would have allowed Congress and the states to ban the physical desecration of the flag. Still, the amendment fell far short in both chambers of the necessary two-thirds majority. *(1990 action, Congress and the Nation Vol. VIII, p. 762; Eichman case summary, Congress and the Nation Vol. VIII, p. 836)*

To propose a constitutional amendment, Congress had to approve a joint resolution by a two-thirds vote in each chamber. The amendment then had to be ratified by legislatures in three-fourths of the states. A flag-burning amendment seemed certain to be ratified because 49 state legislatures had passed measures urging Congress to propose such an amendment.

LEGISLATIVE ACTION

The House Judiciary Committee started the legislative debate in 1995 by reporting a resolution (H J Res 79—H Rept 104-151) on June 22 that proposed to add one paragraph to the Constitution: "The Congress and the States shall have power to prohibit the physical desecration of the flag of the United States."

The committee had approved the amendment on June 7 on a party-line, 18–12 vote. The debate mainly turned on the type of activity that would be subject to a ban, as Democrats questioned what constituted a flag and what would be considered desecration.

Only one amendment was offered, a proposal by Jack Reed, D-R.I., to limit any ban to burning, trampling or rending a flag. The amendment was rejected, 6–22, with six Democrats joining 16 Republicans in opposition.

On the House floor June 28, opponents again raised repeated questions about how to define flag and desecration. The House easily rejected a Democratic motion to limit the ban to burning, trampling, soiling or rending, 63–369. It then approved the resolution, 312–120, 22 more than a two-thirds majority. The margin was boosted by three Republicans and 13 Democrats who switched from opposing the amendment in 1990 to supporting it in 1995.

The following month, the Senate Judiciary Committee approved an identical resolution (S J Res 31), 12–6, after members agreed to save their amendments for the Senate floor. The committee reported the resolution on Sept. 27 (S Rept 104-148).

On the Senate floor in December, members adopted an amendment by Judiciary Committee Chairman Orrin G. Hatch, R-Utah, giving Congress the sole authority to bar flag desecration. Approved by voice vote, the amendment was aimed at avoiding 50 different state flag-protection laws.

Two other amendments were rejected by wide margins. By a vote of 5–93, the Senate defeated a proposal by the Judiciary Committee's top-ranking Democrat, Joseph R. Biden Jr. of Delaware, to allow only burning, mutilating or trampling a flag to be banned. And by a vote of 28–71, lawmakers rejected an amendment by Mitch McConnell, R-Ky., to drop the constitutional amendment in favor of a statutory ban on some instances of flag desecration.

As the final vote approached on Dec. 12, 60 senators had committed to supporting the amendment and three more were expected to vote for it. Thirty other senators—26 Democrats and four Republicans—had announced their opposition, as had President Clinton.

That left the outcome in the hands of three Democrats—Bill Bradley of New Jersey, Barbara A. Mikulski of Maryland and Joseph I. Lieberman of Connecticut—who remained publicly undecided throughout the debate.

All three voted "nay," and the resolution failed on a **key vote of 63–36 (R 49–4; D 14–32),** three votes shy of a two-thirds majority. (At the time, the seat vacated by Bob Packwood, R-Ore., remained empty.) *(1995 key votes, p. 1025)*

Mikulski said she wanted Congress to try passing another statute to ban flag desecration instead of changing the Constitution. Amendments should be used to expand democracy, not constrict it, she said.

Bradley called flag burners "ungrateful lowlifes," but said, "The question now is whether protecting the flag merits amending the Bill of Rights." In his view, it did not.

Supporters of the amendment vowed to keep fighting after the 1996 elections. "This amendment is not going to go away," Hatch said minutes after the final vote. "We will debate it in the next Congress." ❑

Armored Car Guards

Trying again to help armored car guards avoid red tape, the House passed a bill (HR 3431) in 1996 to make more guards' gun permits valid when they crossed state lines. The Senate did not act on the measure, however. *(1993 action, p. 709)*

Congress had cleared legislation in 1993 (PL 103 55) to make a guard's gun permit valid throughout the United States, provided that the state issuing the permit required annual training and criminal background checks. The goal was to eliminate the need for guards to obtain gun permits from each state they traversed. By 1996, however, only five states' permits were meeting the standard for national reciprocity.

On June 17, 1996, the House Commerce Committee reported HR 3431 (H Rept 104-623), which would have eased the requirements of the 1993 law. The requirements for annual training and background checks would have been dropped for guards renewing their permits, giving states more freedom to set training requirements and check criminal records.

The House passed the bill by voice vote July 9, but it progressed no further. A similar Senate bill (S 2003) never made it out of the Senate Commerce, Science, and Transportation Committee. ❑

Patents and Copyrights

Completing work left over from previous sessions, lawmakers cleared bills in 1995 to clarify the criteria for biotechnology patents and provide limited copyright protection for the performers of recorded works. The 104th Congress also cleared a pair of modest bills to protect famous trademarks from being usurped and aid small businesses whose patents were trampled by the federal government.

Less successful was an effort to provide U.S. authors and artists the same degree of copyright protection as their European counterparts received. Also falling by the wayside was a proposal to protect intellectual property rights against digital piracy, which could not overcome the conflicting interests of copyright holders, computer networks and the computer industry.

BIOTECHNOLOGY PATENTS

Congress cleared legislation in 1995 to help biotechnology firms patent their manufacturing processes, eliminating the confusion caused by conflicting court rulings.

The measure (S 1111—PL 104-41) declared that a biotechnology process was automatically patentable if it resulted in or made use of a patentable product. Although biotechnology firms generally produced naturally occurring substances that could not be patented, they did so through the use of unique "host cells" that were patentable.

The legislation effectively exempted biotechnology firms from a 1985 decision by the U.S. Court of Appeals for the Federal Circuit, *In Re Durden*. Under *Durden*, a manufacturing process was not automatically patentable just because it made a new and nonobvious product out of novel and nonobvious materials.

Similar legislation had been passed by the House and Senate in different forms in 1994, but the two chambers were unable to reconcile their differences prior to adjourning. *(1994 action, p. 714)*

The Senate Judiciary Committee reported S 1111 on Sept. 18, 1995, and the Senate passed it by voice vote Sept. 28. The House Judiciary Committee had reported an identical bill July 11, 1995 (HR 587—H Rept 104-178), and the House passed that bill by voice vote Oct. 17. The House cleared S 1111 by voice vote the same day, and President Clinton signed it Nov. 1.

DIGITAL TRANSMISSION COPYRIGHTS

Resolving a long-standing dispute among songwriters, musicians, broadcasters and record companies, Congress agreed in 1995 to provide limited copyright protection for performers whose recordings were transmitted digitally.

The legislation (S 227—PL 104-39) gave copyright protection to audio recordings transmitted in digital format through interactive services, such as a computer network, or subscription services, such as a new satellite-delivered radio format called Digital Audio Radio. These interactive services were required to pay the performers and their record companies a royalty for each transmission, with the amount set through negotiations.

Under previous law, only songwriters and their publishing houses were protected by copyrights. Singer Frank Sinatra, for example, received no royalties when radio stations played his compact disks; instead, the stations paid royalties to the people who wrote the songs Sinatra sang, or to the music publishers who owned the songwriters' copyrights. Sinatra and his record company made their money off the sale of his tapes and CDs. And because radio broadcasts promoted the sales of tapes and CDs, the record companies encouraged radio stations to play their products despite the absence of royalties.

Unlike conventional radio broadcasts, however, digital transmissions were seen as a threat to tape and CD sales because they allowed perfect copies to be made of the works being transmitted. Although songwriters did not stand to lose income, performers and their record labels did.

The idea of performance copyrights was resisted by broadcasters, who argued that the new royalties would be too expensive, and by music publishers, who contended that the royalties would come at the expense of songwriters. The record companies struck a compromise with the broadcasters, exempting radio and television stations from the requirement to pay performance royalties even after they shift to digital formats. And Congress tried to mollify the music publishers by declaring that songwriters' royalties should not be diminished by the legislation.

The bill required no royalty payments by companies supplying background music and businesses playing background music on their premises. Featured performers were guaranteed 45 percent of the royalties for the digital transmission of their works, while other musicians and vocalists were guaranteed a total of 5 percent.

The Senate Judiciary Committee reported the bill on Aug. 4, 1995 (S Rept 104-128), and the Senate passed it by voice vote Aug. 8. The House Judiciary Committee reported a similar bill (HR 1506—H Rept 104-274) on Oct. 11, and the House passed that measure by voice vote Oct. 17. The House cleared the Senate bill by voice vote the same day, and President Clinton signed the measure on Nov. 1.

TRADEMARK DILUTION

Congress gave speedy approval in 1995 to a bill restricting the use of famous trademarks for unrelated products.

The measure (HR 1295—PL 104-98) made it a violation of federal copyright law to dilute trademarks—to erode their distinctive association with a particular product. For example, the law barred a company from selling "Pepsi" jeans or "Nike" batteries.

Trademark dilution had already been outlawed by state legislatures in half the states. Supporters of HR 1295 said the bill would create a uniform national standard and help efforts to promote trademark protection around the globe.

The House Judiciary Committee reported the bill Nov. 30, 1995 (H Rept 104-374), after amending it to clarify that news coverage would not be restricted. The House passed the bill by voice vote Dec. 12, the Senate cleared it by voice vote Dec. 29, and President Clinton signed it Jan. 16, 1996.

SMALL BUSINESS PATENTS

Congress cleared legislation in 1996 to aid small businesses and inventors whose patents were violated by the federal government.

The bill (HR 632—PL 104-308) allowed businesses with less than 500 employees, nonprofit organizations and freelance inventors who successfully sued the government for patent infringement to collect their legal fees and court costs. Under previous law, parties could sue the government for the damages they sustained but not for the cost of bringing the lawsuit.

The House Judiciary Committee reported the bill Nov. 30, 1995 (H Rept 104-373), and the House approved it by voice vote Dec. 12. The Senate passed the bill by voice vote Oct. 3, 1996, with an amendment denying legal fees in cases less than 10 years old if the government's position was substantially justified. The House cleared the Senate version of the bill the next day, and President Clinton signed it Oct. 19.

COPYRIGHT TERMS

The Senate Judiciary Committee approved a bill (S 483) in May 1996 to lengthen the terms of copyrights by 20 years, but the measure advanced no further.

The purpose behind the bill was to keep the United States on par with the European Union. As of July 1995, the copyrights for works published in European countries were extended to 70 years after the author's death. In the United States, copyrights expired 50 years after the author's death.

S 483 would have extended copyrights for artists, authors, songwriters and other individuals to 70 years. Corporate copyrights on commissioned works would have been extended to 95 years from the time the work was completed.

The main debate in the committee concerned a proposal by Sens. Hank Brown, R-Colo., and Strom Thurmond, R-S.C., to reduce the royalties that religious radio stations and small to midsized restaurants and bars paid for airing copyrighted material. Their amendment was blocked on a tabling motion, 12–6, and the bill was approved, 15–3.

Although the Judiciary Committee reported the bill on July 10, 1996 (S Rept 104-315), the Senate never acted on it. Among the problems for the bill were the dispute over royalties and a push by library associations for greater freedom to disseminate copyrighted material during the proposed 20-year extension period.

The House Judiciary Subcommittee on Courts and Intellectual Property had held a hearing in July 1995 on a similar bill (HR 989), but that proposal did not advance, either.

DIGITAL COPYRIGHT PROTECTION

Legislation to adapt federal copyright law to the Internet and other computer networks failed to emerge from the House Judiciary Committee in 1996 as copyright holders were unable to settle their differences with the computer industry.

The bill (HR 2441) aimed to enhance copyright protection for authors, publishers, movie studios, software developers and others whose intellectual property could easily be copied and redistributed in digital form via computer networks. A central, unresolved question was whom to hold liable for an unauthorized distribution: the person who made the copy, the computer software and hardware companies that facilitated the copying or the "online" service that provided access to the digital network? Copyright holders wanted to mandate that online services block the distribution of pirated works, but no agreement could be negotiated on that front.

A second troublesome issue was a provision in the bill to ban devices that were designed to circumvent copyright protection systems. Computer manufacturers argued that the provision was so broad, it could be interpreted to ban computers.

After months of negotiations failed to bear fruit, the House Judiciary Subcommittee on Courts and Intellectual Property abandoned efforts to mark up HR 2441 in mid-June 1996. "It was like nailing Jell-O to the wall," said Rep. Robert W. Goodlatte, R-Va. "The problem is that there were just too many contingencies to build the necessary support to pass the underlying legislation."

The Senate Judiciary Committee held a hearing on a companion bill (S 1284) May 7, 1996, but took no further action.

DRUG PATENTS

The Senate Judiciary Committee approved a bill (S 1277) in 1996 to allow some generic drugs to be manufactured before the patents expired on their name-brand counterparts, but the full Senate never took up the measure.

The bill applied to generic drugs adversely affected by the new General Agreement on Tariffs and Trade (GATT), which Congress implemented in 1994 (PL 103-465). The pact extended the life of pharmaceutical patents to 20 years, up from 17 under previous law. S 1277 would have allowed generic-drug manufacturers to market their products despite the extended patents if they had made substantial investments to produce the drug before the new GATT was implemented.

The original version of the bill would have allowed a generic drug to be marketed if the manufacturer could prove simply that its request to offer the drug had been approved before June 8, 1995. But the Judiciary Committee amended the bill at its markup on May 2, 1996, to require proof of a substantial investment, such as a new manufacturing plant. Bill sponsor Hank Brown, R-Colo., argued that the amendment by Chairman Orrin G. Hatch, R-Utah, would tie up generic-drug manufacturers in court until the extended patents ran out, but Hatch prevailed, 10–7.

The committee reported the bill on Oct. 1, 1996 (S Rept 104-394). No further action was taken on it. ❑

Dennis Nomination

The Senate in 1995 grudgingly confirmed the nomination of Louisiana Supreme Court Judge James L. Dennis to the 5th U.S. Circuit Court of Appeals, based in New Orleans. Dennis was the only judicial nominee to trigger a fight on the Senate floor in the 104th Congress, in part because no circuit-court nominations were brought up for a vote in 1996.

Opposition to Dennis was led by Mississippi's two Republican senators, Thad Cochran and Trent Lott. Cochran urged the Senate on Sept. 28 to send Dennis' nomination back to the Senate Judiciary Committee for more investigation, faulting Dennis for not recusing himself from a case in which he might have had a personal interest. In that case, Dennis and five of the other six state Supreme Court judges had held that a New Orleans newspaper could not view state legislators' records about special scholarships at Tulane University. Dennis had a potential conflict of interests because his son had once received such a scholarship, Cochran contended.

Dennis was backed by leaders of the Judiciary Committee, which had endorsed his nomination by voice vote on July 20, and by Louisiana's two Democratic senators. Joseph R. Biden Jr. of Delaware, the top Democrat on the Judiciary Committee, said the committee had looked into the Tulane case and found no reason for Dennis to recuse himself. Judiciary Committee Chairman Orrin G. Hatch, R-Utah, suggested that Cochran and Lott's main objection was that the nomination had not gone to someone from their state.

The Senate defeated Cochran's motion to send the nomination back to committee, 46–54, with eight Republicans joining all 46 Democrats in opposition. The Senate then confirmed the nomination by voice vote.   ❏

Fletcher Nomination

The following year, Republicans and Democrats on the Senate Judiciary Committee tangled over the nomination of William A. Fletcher to the 9th Circuit Court of Appeals, based in San Francisco. A law professor at the University of California at Berkeley, Fletcher was widely regarded as having strong credentials. However, some Republicans argued that his appointment would violate an obscure federal antinepotism law, given that his mother also was also on the 28-member 9th Circuit panel.

Democrats argued that the law, first enacted in 1887 and revised in 1911, was intended only to prevent judges from hiring their relatives as court staff, not to stop two members of the same family from serving as judges. Some viewed the nepotism argument as an attempt by conservatives to force the retirement of Fletcher's mother, Betty B. Fletcher, who was regarded as one of the most liberal judges on a liberal circuit.

Hatch agreed to let Fletcher's nomination move forward after Betty Fletcher offered to shift to senior status—a form of judicial semiretirement—once her son was confirmed. After a one-week delay sought by other Republicans on the panel, the committee voted 12–6 to send Fletcher's nomination to the floor for confirmation. Hatch and three other Republicans supported the nomination, along with all eight of the committee's Democrats.

By that time, however, Senate Majority Leader Bob Dole of Kansas, the presumed GOP nominee for president, had started making a campaign issue of President Clinton's appointees to the bench. Dole accused Clinton of appointing liberal judges and warned that another four years of Clinton nominees could dangerously tilt the composition of the federal bench. Clinton responded by noting that Dole had supported virtually all of the administration's judicial nominees when they came up for a vote in the Senate.

Fletcher's nomination languished on the Senate calendar for the rest of the year, one of four appellate and three district-court nominees to be endorsed by the Judiciary Committee but not confirmed by the Senate. The Senate confirmed 17 district-court nominees in 1996, but no appeals-court nominees received a vote.   ❏

Stack Nomination

One other disputed nominee, Charles Stack, withdrew from consideration in May 1996 as the Judiciary Committee was about to debate his nomination. A Florida lawyer, Stack was nominated to the 11th U.S. Circuit Court of Appeals, which covered Alabama, Florida and Georgia. Some Republicans had questioned Stack's qualifications and suggested that he was rewarded for his work as a Democratic fund-raiser, not for any distinguished legal service.

By the end of 1996, 30 of Clinton's 105 judicial nominees in the 104th Congress had failed to win confirmation. The Senate did not reject any of the 30 by vote; instead, they were stymied before they reached the Senate floor.   ❏

The Supreme Court

The Supreme Court continued to steer a mostly conservative course during President Bill Clinton's first term, despite his appointment of two moderately liberal justices, Ruth Bader Ginsburg and Stephen G. Breyer. The Court's conservative majority flexed its muscles by moving to restrict use of racial preferences, limit the federal government's power vis-à-vis the states and ease the rules on government aid to religion. The Court also continued to back law enforcement in important criminal law decisions and to take a narrow view of individual rights in most areas except for free speech.

Those decisions epitomized the judicial philosophy of Chief Justice William H. Rehnquist, who began his eleventh term as chief in October 1996. Rehnquist led a fairly reliable conservative majority that included four other Republican-appointed justices: Sandra Day O'Connor, Antonin Scalia and Anthony M. Kennedy, all appointed by President Ronald Reagan, and Clarence Thomas, who was named by President George Bush.

Ginsburg and Breyer, the first Democratic-appointed justices since Lyndon B. Johnson's presidency, joined a liberal-leaning bloc that also included two GOP appointees: John Paul Stevens, named by President Gerald R. Ford, and David H. Souter, a Bush appointee. The bloc occasionally mustered a majority in closely divided cases, usually by winning over either O'Connor or Kennedy, who held centrist views on some issues.

In naming Ginsburg and Breyer, Clinton opted for veteran federal appellate judges with excellent reputations for legal craftsmanship and judicious decision making. Both won Senate confirmation easily with bipartisan support. *(Ginsburg, Breyer confirmations, box, p. 760)*

The Court's decisions on race, religion and federalism were marked departures from rulings of earlier eras that had looked with favor on affirmative action, set up barriers to government aid to religion and imposed few obstacles to congressional or presidential expansion of federal powers. The decisions cheered most conservatives, but provoked criticism from many liberals, who accused the conservative justices of judicial activism despite their professed support for judicial restraint.

Liberal advocacy groups could count a few victories, however. In one important sex discrimination case, the Court appeared to make it more difficult for governments to defend laws that treat men and women differently. In another, it threw out a state ballot measure prohibiting enactment of laws to ban discrimination against homosexuals. The Court also struck down state ballot measures attempting to impose term limits on members of Congress. And, although the justices steered clear of any major substantive rulings on abortion, they ruled that courts could impose some limits on antiabortion protests if necessary to ensure women and medical staff access to clinics where abortions are performed.

Statistically, the Court was far from active. The justices continued to produce fewer signed decisions even as the total caseload reached a new peak. The Court issued only 75 signed opinions in its 1995–1996 term, the lowest number since the 65 signed opinions in the 1953–1954 term. The number had fallen each year since Rehnquist became chief justice at the start of the 1986–1987 term. Meanwhile, the number of cases on the Court's docket rose to 8,100 in the 1994–1995 term, the highest ever. The figure dropped to 7,565 cases in the 1995–1996 term.

CIVIL RIGHTS

The Court repeatedly injected itself into the wrenching national debate over how far to go in using racial considerations to remedy past discrimination and equalize opportunities for African Americans, Hispanics and other minority groups. In a number of closely divided rulings, the Court limited efforts to create majority-minority congressional districts to help elect more blacks and Hispanics to Congress. It also adopted a stricter test against the use of racial preferences in awarding government contracts. In addition, the Court sent lower federal court judges a strong signal to move more quickly to get out of school desegregation cases and restore schools to local control.

The dispute over racial redistricting stemmed from efforts by civil rights groups, minority lawmakers and the federal government after the 1990 census to use the federal Voting Rights Act to force states to create more congressional districts with majority African American or Hispanic populations. These so-called majority-minority districts helped elect a record number

---

REFERENCES

Discussion of the Supreme Court for the years 1945–1964 may be found in *Congress and the Nation Vol. I*, pp. 1441–1454; for the years 1965–1968, *Congress and the Nation Vol. II*, pp. 335–340; for the years 1969–1972, *Congress and the Nation Vol. III*, pp. 289–327; for the years 1973–1976, *Congress and the Nation Vol. IV*, pp. 619–659; for the years 1977–1980, *Congress and the Nation Vol. V*, pp. 755–791; for the years 1981–1984, *Congress and the Nation Vol. VI*, pp. 711–768; for the years 1985–1968 *Congress and the Nation Vol. VII*, pp. 785–840; for the years 1989–1992, *Congress and the Nation Vol. VIII*, pp. 801–851.

GINSBURG, BREYER CONFIRMED TO HIGH COURT

President Clinton's two Supreme Court nominees, Ruth Bader Ginsburg and Stephen G. Breyer, won easy Senate confirmation in 1993 and 1994, respectively, despite close questioning by senators about their judicial views. Both Ginsburg and Breyer ducked many of the specific questions put to them by members of the Senate Judiciary Committee, but in some of their less guarded comments, the nominees indicated liberal views on issues such as abortion, civil rights and women's rights.

Although she refused to say whether she would vote to uphold capital punishment, Ginsburg presented herself as a judicial moderate and promised not to write her personal views into law. "I don't confuse my own predilections with what is the law," Ginsburg said. Breyer explicitly said he accepted the Court's decisions upholding the constitutionality of capital punishment as "settled law."

The two appointments left the Court's general ideological division largely unchanged. Ginsburg replaced Justice Byron R. White, a Democrat appointed by President Kennedy in 1962. Breyer succeeded Justice Harry A. Blackmun, a Republican named by President Nixon in 1970. White had sided with liberals on many issues despite his conservative stands on abortion rights and criminal law; Blackmun had evolved into the Court's most liberal member by his retirement.

Ginsburg first came to national prominence as the architect of a legal strategy in the 1970s that led to the Supreme Court's first rulings setting constitutional limits on sex discrimination in the law. She had served on the federal appeals court for the District of Columbia since 1980. White House aides said President Clinton picked her after being especially impressed with her account of having overcome the discrimination against women in the legal profession and then working to open opportunities for women as a legal advocate.

The nomination won bipartisan approval on Capitol Hill and produced a sense of relief on the Senate Judiciary Committee. The committee had gone through two bruising Supreme Court confirmation fights in the previous six years—the unsuccessful nomination of Robert Bork and Clarence Thomas's narrow approval in the face of accusations of sexual harassment of a former employee.

Ginsburg presented herself as an advocate of judicial restraint. "My approach is neither liberal or conservative," she told the committee in her opening statement. But she later said that courts have a role in forcing social change when groups are "shut out of the political process." And she gave a clear indication that she would regard as legally suspect any law that treated men and women differently.

The committee approved the nomination, 18–0. Ginsburg went on to win confirmation by a **key vote of 96–3 (R 41–3, D 55–0)**

the three conservative Republicans who cast the only dissenting votes said they feared Ginsburg would be a judicial activist. *(1993 key votes, p. 979)*

Breyer, a leading contender for the previous vacancy, won Clinton's nod for the Court when Blackmun announced his retirement. A former Senate Judiciary Committee staff director, Breyer had served on the federal appeals court in Boston since 1980. In both positions, he had gained a reputation as a pragmatist and a consensus-builder on complex issues such as airline deregulation, trucking deregulation and federal sentencing guidelines.

As with Ginsburg, Breyer won bipartisan praise on Capitol Hill. But his confirmation hit a snag when critics raised conflict-of-interest questions based on Breyer's hearing several insurance-related cases while he had funds invested in Lloyd's of London, the famous British insurance syndicate. Breyer sought to preempt the issue in his opening statement before the Judiciary Committee. After tracing a life devoted to law and public service, Breyer declared, "There is nothing more important to me than my integrity and my reputation for impartiality." He had reviewed the cases, Breyer told the committee, and was convinced there was no conflict of interest in his having sat on them. But to eliminate any questions, he said he would divest himself of all holdings in insurance companies.

On substantive issues, Breyer avoided most specifics, but told the senators that he accepted the Court's rulings upholding the death penalty as well as its abortion rights precedents. He also gave qualified support to affirmative action, stressing the need to fulfill the "basic promise of fairness" in the post–Civil War Fourteenth Amendment.

The Judiciary Committee gave Breyer a unanimous recommendation, 18–0. Sen. Richard Lugar, R-Ind., opposed the nomination, saying in a floor speech that Breyer had shown "extraordinarily bad judgment" in the insurance investment. Breyer won confirmation, 87–9. Lugar and eight other Republicans voted no, but most of the dissenters were more concerned with Breyer's legal views than the ethics issue, observers said.

The new justices made the Court more diverse in terms of the backgrounds of its members. Ginsburg is the second female justice. She was also the first Jew to serve on the Court since Abe Fortas resigned in 1969. With Breyer's appointment the Court had two Jewish justices for the second time in history. Justice Thomas's reconversion to Roman Catholicism in 1996 brought the number of Catholics on the Court to three, including Antonin Scalia and Anthony Kennedy. For the first time in its history, the Court did not have a Protestant majority.

of minorities to Congress in 1992. But many of the districts were highly irregular in shape. White voters in some states challenged the maps, contending that the deliberate use of race in drawing district lines violated their rights to equal protection under the Fourteenth Amendment.

The Court in 1993 allowed a challenge to a North Carolina

district with an especially bizarre shape. The newly drawn district wound 160 miles through the center of the state in order to link black neighborhoods in four of the state's metropolitan areas. Writing for a 5–4 majority, O'Connor said that a district with a highly irregular shape that could be understood only as an effort to segregate voters by race could be challenged under the Equal Protection Clause and could be allowed only if the state could meet the so-called strict scrutiny test. Under that test, a racial classification can be upheld only if it is narrowly tailored to serve a compelling government interest.

The Court's four other conservatives—Chief Justice Rehnquist and Justices Scalia, Kennedy and Thomas—joined in the decision. Four justices dissented: Byron R. White, Harry A. Blackmun, Stevens and Souter. White, in his final opinion as a justice, argued that it was "unrealistic" to try to eliminate considerations of race from the redistricting process and contended that white voters had suffered no legal injury. He pointed out that whites constituted 79 percent of the state's population and comprised majorities in 10 of the 12 congressional districts.

The ruling returned the North Carolina case to the lower court to determine whether the redistricting plan met the strict scrutiny test. As the case continued, challenges to racially drawn redistricting plans were proceeding in other states, including Georgia and Texas. The Supreme Court used those cases over the next few years to refine its position on racial redistricting.

In its next ruling, the Court in 1995 struck down a Georgia plan that had created three majority-black districts, including one that stretched from the Atlanta suburbs across half the state to the coastal cities of Augusta and Savannah. The conservative justices again prevailed in a 5–4 vote, but the Court laid down a slightly different rule. Writing for the majority, Kennedy said that redistricting plans were subject to challenge if race was "the predominant factor motivating the legislature's decision to place a significant number of voters within or without a particular district." Ginsburg and Breyer joined Stevens and Souter in dissenting.

A year later, the Court applied that test to strike down racially drawn districts in two states: North Carolina and Texas. In the North Carolina case, the Court rejected a lower court's finding that the racial redistricting was justified to remedy past discrimination or to comply with the Voting Rights Act. In the Texas case, the Court invalidated three irregularly shaped districts: majority black districts in the Dallas and Houston areas and a majority Latino district in Houston. The ruling rejected arguments by the state, the federal government and civil rights groups that the irregular shapes resulted in part from efforts to protect the districts of incumbent lawmakers.

The votes in both cases were again 5–4. In a dissenting opinion, Stevens criticized what he called the Court's "unnecessary intrusion" into states' ability to provide "long-excluded groups the opportunity to participate more effectively in the political process."

Civil rights groups harshly criticized the redistricting rulings. One civil rights leader said they could "resegregate our political institutions." President Clinton also criticized the decisions, calling them "a setback in the struggle to ensure that all Americans participate fully in the political process." But conservative lawmakers and interest groups generally praised them, saying they moved the country toward the goal of a "color-blind society." The effects of the rulings were also subject to debate. In 1996 the black lawmakers representing previous majority-minority districts in Georgia and North Carolina won reelection from the newly redrawn, majority-white districts.

The Court's ruling on minority preferences in government contracting came in 1995. The case arose when a white contractor challenged the federal policy that gave minority businesses an advantage in bidding for federally funded highway projects. By a 5–4 vote, the Court ruled that federal race-based programs were subject to the strict scrutiny test that it had applied, in a 1989 ruling, to state and local minority preference programs. The decision overturned a 1990 ruling that had allowed the federal government to adopt racial preferences under a less stringent test: the so-called intermediate scrutiny standard, which only required proof of an "important" governmental objective.

The majority justices disagreed about the likely effects of the ruling. O'Connor said that some minority preferences could survive the strict scrutiny test. In a separate concurrence, however, Scalia wrote, "Government can never have a 'compelling interest' in discriminating on the basis of race in order to 'make up for' past racial discrimination in the opposite direction." For their part, the four dissenters said the program should have been upheld. But Ginsburg said the decision still allowed Congress some authority to create programs "to counteract discrimination's lingering effects."

The Court's pronouncement on school desegregation came in a challenge to a federal judge's order requiring the predominantly black Kansas City school system to adopt a number of changes to try to attract white students from adjacent suburban districts. The plan required a 30 percent teacher salary increase and construction of new "magnet" schools with expensive facilities and equipment. In a 5–4 decision, the Court in 1995 ruled that the judge had gone beyond his authority to eliminate the "vestiges" of segregation. Observers saw the ruling as a clear indication to judges in similar cases that they should wrap up their oversight of desegregation plans and return school systems to control of local boards.

The Court's rulings in other major civil rights cases were less divided and more favorable for liberal advocacy groups. For example, in an important sex discrimination case, the Court in 1995 ordered the all-male Virginia Military Institute to admit women or give up its state funding. Writing for the Court in the 7–1 decision, Ginsburg said the refusal to admit women amounted to an equal protection violation. To uphold different treatment of men and women, Ginsburg said, a government must show "an exceedingly persuasive justification" and could not rely on "an overbroad generalization . . . about the way that most women (or men) are." Ginsburg said she was applying the Court's previous rulings on sex discrimination, but Chief Justice Rehnquist in a separate concurrence said her opinion actually made the test more stringent than it had been in prior decisions.

In another sex discrimination case, the Court in 1994 ruled that lawyers cannot exclude people from juries solely because of their sex. The 6–3 decision extended a line of cases dating from 1986 that had barred lawyers from excluding potential jurors on the basis of race.

The Court also gave gay rights advocates an important victory with a decision that overturned a Colorado ballot measure

THE COURT OF 1997

The members of the U.S. Supreme Court in 1997 were:
• Chief Justice William H. Rehnquist, born in 1924, appointed to the Court by President Nixon in 1971; promoted to chief justice by President Reagan in 1986.
• Justice John Paul Stevens, born in 1920, appointed by President Ford in 1975.
• Justice Sandra Day O'Connor, born in 1930, appointed by President Reagan in 1981.
• Justice Antonin Scalia, born in 1936, appointed by President Reagan in 1986.
• Justice Anthony M. Kennedy, born in 1936, appointed by President Reagan in 1987.
• Justice David H. Souter, born in 1939, appointed by President Bush in 1990.
• Justice Clarence Thomas, born in 1948, appointed by President Bush in 1991.
• Justice Ruth Bader Ginsburg, born in 1933, appointed by President Clinton in 1993.
• Justice Stephen G. Breyer, born in 1938, appointed by President Clinton in 1994.

barring the state or local governments from enacting any measures to prohibit discrimination on the basis of sexual orientation except by a state constitutional amendment. By a 6–3 vote, the Court held the measure violated the Equal Protection Clause because it had no "rational relationship" to legitimate state interests. Writing for the majority, Kennedy said the initiative imposed a "special disability" on homosexuals "not to further a proper legislative end but to make them unequal to everyone else."

The gay rights groups' victory was limited, however. The decision made no mention of the Court's controversial 1986 decision upholding, by a 5–4 vote, enforcement of state antisodomy laws against homosexuals. And in fall 1996, the Court refused to take up a challenge by gay rights groups to the military's policy permitting discharge of openly homosexual service members.

FEDERALISM

The Court unsettled expectations about federal powers in a pair of 5–4 rulings that cited states' rights in striking down two congressional statutes. But it also disappointed states' rights advocates as well as congressional critics by striking down state-enacted term limits for members of Congress.

The first of the pro-states' rights rulings invalidated a popular 1990 law that made it a federal crime to possess a gun near a school. Writing for the conservative majority in the 1995 decision, Chief Justice Rehnquist said the statute went beyond Congress's power to regulate interstate commerce. Upholding the law, he said, would amount to giving Congress "a general police power of the sort retained by the States." Dissenting justices said

the decision would thwart Congress's power to deal with criminal behavior that threatened either economic or social harm.

A year later, the Court struck down a somewhat obscure provision of a 1988 law that allowed Native American tribes to sue states in federal court in disputes over gambling on Indian reservations. In another opinion written by Rehnquist, the Court said the provision violated the Eleventh Amendment, which generally prohibits private citizens from suing states in federal court.

The ruling on the gun law in particular cheered conservatives, who viewed it as reinforcing the anti-Washington sentiment that helped Republicans capture control of both houses of Congress in the 1994 midterm elections. "It's absolutely consistent with the mood of the country that wants to get Washington off our backs," said Roger Pilon, a constitutional law expert at the Cato Institute. But some constitutional law experts said the decision was unlikely to have broad impact. "There's much less here than meets the eye," noted Laurence Tribe, a well-known liberal law professor at Harvard Law School.

The end-of-term ruling came a month after conservatives had suffered a narrow but bitter defeat on another key issue: congressional term limits. Since 1990, 23 states had enacted provisions to set fixed tenure limits for members of Congress elected from their states. Supporters pushed term limits as a way to make Congress more accountable and to increase electoral competition. Opponents said the measures would reduce popular choice, deprive Congress of valuable experience and shift power from Capitol Hill to the president. But they had no success in opposing the state ballot measures, most of which were approved by substantial margins.

Despite their success at the ballot box, term limit proponents suffered a potentially fatal setback at the Supreme Court. In a 5–4 decision, the Court said neither the states nor Congress itself could limit the numbers of terms for members of Congress except by passing a constitutional amendment. "Allowing individual States to adopt their own qualifications for congressional service would be inconsistent with the Framers' vision of a uniform National Legislature representing the people of the United States," Justice Stevens wrote for the majority in the May 1995 decision.

Justice Kennedy, who deserted the conservative bloc to provide the critical fifth vote for striking down the term limit measures, said they amounted to "state interference" with the relation between citizens and their legislative representatives. But Justice Thomas, writing for the four dissenters, said, "Nothing in the Constitution deprives the people of each State of the power to prescribe eligibility requirements for the candidates who seek to represent them in Congress."

Term limit supporters said they would continue to pursue their goal through a constitutional amendment, even though they had failed to win the needed two-thirds majority when several term limit proposals came to the House floor earlier in the year. For his part, former House Speaker Tom Foley, a Washington Democrat who lost his bid for reelection in 1994 in part because of his opposition to term limits, told reporters, "My belief is that term limits is dead."

CHURCH AND STATE

Religious groups won several victories in efforts to relax the rules requiring separation of church and state.

In two rulings, the Court eased restrictions on allowing government aid under neutral programs to flow to religious individuals and groups. In 1993 the Court held that the government could pay for a sign-language interpreter to help a deaf student at a church-affiliated school. Two years later, it ruled that a state university could not deny funding to a student-published religious magazine solely because of its content. Dissenters in the two 5–4 rulings said the use of public funds in both cases violated the constitutional prohibition against establishment of religion.

In two other rulings, the Court said religious groups had a free speech right to use public buildings or grounds that were open to other groups for meetings or displays. The decisions, in 1993 and 1995 respectively, allowed an evangelical group in New York to use a public school to show religious-oriented films and permitted the Ku Klux Klan to erect a Christian cross on the grounds of the Ohio state capitol.

Advocates of government accommodation of religious groups suffered one defeat, but the effect of the ruling was expected to be limited because of the unusual fact-setting and the division among the justices. The dispute involved the New York legislature's decision to create a special school district for a village inhabited exclusively by members of the Satmar Hasidim, a small orthodox Jewish sect. By a 6–3 vote, the Court ruled the law an improper establishment of religion. But there was no majority opinion. "The case had the look of special treatment," said Douglas Kmiec, a constitutional law professor who advocated greater accommodation of religion. "I don't think it stands for much."

In one other church-state conflict, the Court struck down a Florida city's ban on ritual animal sacrifices because the ordinance interfered with the practices of an Afro-Cuban religion. The Court said the city of Hialeah, Florida, had improperly targeted followers of the Santeria religion when it passed the ordinance, which was enacted in the wake of a public controversy following the establishment of a Santerian church in the city.

FREE SPEECH

The Court backed free speech claims in a number of cases, sometimes by narrow margins but sometimes in unanimous or near-unanimous decisions.

Key parts of a recent federal law aimed at restricting the availability of sexually explicit programming on cable television were struck down in 1996. The Court nullified two provisions that required cable operators to put sexual material on a separate channel and allowed them to censor such programming on public-access channels. But it upheld a third provision that allowed cable operators to block indecent material on commercially leased channels.

In an earlier cable television ruling, the Court in 1994 ordered a new lower court hearing in a challenge to a federal law

U.S. Supreme Court Caseload

	1992–1993	1993–1994	1994–1995	1995–1996
Number of cases on docket	7,245	7,786	8,100	7,565
Cases decided summarily	109	64	66	117
Cases argued and decided	120	105	97	93
Cases disposed of by signed opinions	111	93	91	87
Number of signed opinions	107	84	82	75

NOTE: In earlier edition of *Congress and the Nation*, the number of signed opinions figures actually reflected the total number of cases disposed of by signed opinions. In some instance, the Supreme Court joins together several related cases and disposes of them in a single opinion. The number of signed opinions therefore differs from the number of cases disposed of by signed opinions.

SOURCE: U.S. Supreme Court

requiring cable operators to carry the signals of local broadcast stations. Cable operators were encouraged by the decision, but the Court, ruling on the case a second time in 1997, decided to uphold the statute.

The justices in 1996 ruled that political parties may make unlimited independent expenditures in support of congressional candidates. But the 7–2 decision stopped short of invalidating all federal campaign contribution limits on parties.

The Court broadened commercial speech rights in a pair of unanimous decisions. It struck down a federal law that barred brewers from listing the alcohol content of beer on labels and a Rhode Island statute that prohibited liquor stores from advertising prices. But by a 5–4 vote, the Court upheld a Florida legal ethics rule that restricted direct mail solicitation by attorneys of accident victims or their families.

In other cases, the Court struck down a federal law prohibiting government workers from accepting honoraria for speeches or publications and unanimously invalidated a local ordinance prohibiting anonymous campaign literature. It also gave government contractors protections against loss of business for airing political views or refusing to make political contributions.

The justices rejected a free speech claim brought by anti-abortion protesters seeking to undo a lower court injunction limiting demonstrations at a Florida abortion clinic. By a 6–3 vote, the Court in 1994 held that judges can establish "buffer zones" preventing protesters from setting up blockades or preventing access to clinics. The decision was written by Rehnquist, who had been a consistent opponent of abortion rights and had voted as recently as 1992 to overturn the *Roe v. Wade* abortion decision.

CRIMINAL LAW

The Court continued to back police and prosecutors in most criminal law decisions, but it moved to control the use of forfeitures in criminal cases and to limit police power to conduct "no-knock" searches.

In the forfeiture ruling, the Court in 1993 unanimously held that the Eighth Amendment's prohibition against excessive fines limits the government's power to seize property from criminals or suspects. The ruling required a new hearing for a South Dakota man whose mobile home and $4,700 in cash were seized after he was convicted of selling two grams of cocaine to an undercover agent. Three years later, however, the Court backed forfeitures in two closely watched decisions. In one, the Court held that the Double Jeopardy Clause did not prevent the government from instituting a criminal prosecution and a civil forfeiture against an individual for the same offense. In the other ruling, the Court said the government can seize property even if the owner had no knowledge someone else was using it for criminal activity.

In the no-knock search case, the Court in 1995 said police officers should ordinarily knock and announce their identity before entering a home with a search warrant unless they have reasonable fear of physical danger or destruction of evidence. Justice Thomas based the unanimous decision on English and American common law at the time of the adoption of the Fourth Amendment. In several other decisions, however, the Court gave police more leeway in conducting searches. In 1996 the Court unanimously ruled that officers may temporarily detain a motorist on a traffic violation even if they are primarily interested in some other law enforcement purpose, such as looking for drugs.

The Court turned back most challenges in death penalty cases, but it somewhat eased the burden on inmates seeking to attack a conviction on grounds of actual innocence rather than constitutional violations. The justices also ruled that federal judges must appoint a lawyer for a death row inmate who requests help in drawing up a federal habeas corpus petition. But in 1996 it set a stricter test for prisoners to meet to show they have been improperly denied access to the courts.

OTHER ISSUES

Business groups and landowners won significant victories in their long campaigns to limit punitive damage awards and to expand property owners' protections against government regulation. In a separate area, the Court gave local school authorities the power to require drug testing for all athletes.

Civil Suits

The Court in 1994 held that states must permit judicial review of the amount of punitive damage awards by juries in civil suits. Two years later, the Court reinforced the message by overturning as "grossly excessive" a $2 million punitive damage award in an Alabama case. Without laying down specific guidelines, the justices warned against using punitive damages to impose "economic sanctions" against large corporations.

Property Rights

By a 5–4 vote, the Court in 1994 limited the power of local governments to force landowners to permit public use of their property in return for approval for development or construction on the site. Municipalities must show "a rough proportionality," the Court held, between conditions imposed on a permit and any claimed harm to the public from the development.

Drug Testing

The Court in 1994 upheld, on a 6–3 vote, an Oregon school district's policy requiring athletes to submit to random drug testing even if there was no basis for suspecting the individual of drug use. Scalia said the policy was "reasonable and hence constitutional" because it served the "important" purpose of deterring drug use while resulting in only "negligible" intrusion on personal privacy.

Supreme Court Decisions

October 1992–July 1996

Business Law

ANTITRUST

Spectrum Sports, Inc. v. McQuillan DBA Sorboturf Enterprises (506 U.S. 447), decided by a 9–0 vote, Jan. 25, 1993; White wrote the opinion.

A defendant in an antitrust suit cannot be found liable for attempted monopolization unless evidence proves a dangerous probability that it would monopolize a relevant market and a specific intent to monopolize.

Professional Real Estate Investors, Inc. v. Columbia Pictures Industries, Inc. (508 U.S. 49), decided by a 9–0 vote, May 3, 1993; Thomas wrote the opinion.

The Court virtually precluded the use of antitrust laws as a defensive tactic in legal disputes between business competitors. A defendant who claims a lawsuit brought by a competitor amounted to a violation of the antitrust law must first show that the litigation was "objectively baseless," the Court held. Then it must also show that the lawsuit was intended as "an attempt to interfere directly" with its business relationships through use of the judicial process.

Brooke Group Ltd. v. Brown & Williamson Tobacco Corp. (509 U.S. 209), decided by a 6–3 vote, June 21, 1993; Kennedy wrote the opinion; Stevens, White and Blackmun dissented.

The Court rejected a major antitrust case growing out of a cigarette industry price war in the mid-1980s. The divided ruling made it harder for a business to prevail in an antitrust suit claiming injury from a competitor's below-cost or predatory pricing scheme.

AVIATION LAW

Northwest Airlines, Inc. v. County of Kent, Michigan (510 U.S. 355), decided by a 7–1 vote, Jan. 24, 1994; Ginsburg wrote the opinion; Thomas dissented; Blackmun did not participate.

The Court rejected an airline industry challenge to fees imposed by local airports, but fortified the power of the federal Department of Transportation to regulate the charges. The ruling shifted the focus of a growing, high-stakes controversy between airlines and local airports from federal courts to the Transportation Department. The department promised after the decision to take a more active role in airport fee disputes.

American Airlines, Inc. v. Wollens (513 U.S. 219), decided by a 6–2 vote, Jan. 18, 1995; Ginsburg wrote the opinion; O'Connor and Thomas dissented; Scalia did not participate.

Airline passengers can bring breach-of-contract suits in state courts to enforce provisions of airlines' frequent-flyer programs.

BANKING

United States National Bank of Oregon v. Independent Insurance Agents of America, Inc. (508 U.S. 439), decided by a 9–0 vote, June 7, 1993; Souter wrote the opinion.

The Court reinstated a 1916 federal law that federal bank regulators used to permit national banks to sell insurance from their branches in small towns on a nationwide basis. The unanimous decision reversed a ruling by the U.S. Circuit Court of Appeals for the District of Columbia that Congress had, inadvertently, repealed the 1916 law two years later. The Supreme Court said that the apparent repeal resulted from a punctuation error and that the law "remains in force."

NationsBank of North Carolina, N.A. v. Variable Annuity Life Insurance Co. (513 U.S. 251), decided by a 9–0 vote, Jan. 18, 1995; Ginsburg wrote the opinion.

The Court upheld the power of national banks to sell annuities, rejecting efforts by the insurance industry to stifle competition in the growing market for long-term investment instruments.

Bank One Chicago, N.A. v. Midwest Bank & Trust Co. (516 U.S. 264), decided by a 9–0 vote, Jan. 17, 1996; Ginsburg wrote the opinion.

Federal courts have jurisdiction over damage suits filed by one bank against another bank over dishonored checks.

Barnett Bank of Marion County, N.A. v. Nelson, Florida Insurance Commissioner (517 U.S. 25), decided by a 9–0 vote, March 26, 1996; Breyer wrote the opinion.

National banks may sell insurance from small-town branches despite state laws to the contrary. The ruling was based on a 1916 federal law codified as section 92 of the Banking Code, which authorizes any national bank in a town with a population under 5,000 to "act as the agent for any fire, life, or other insurance company."

Smiley v. Citibank (South Dakota), N.A. (517 U.S. 735), decided by a 9–0 vote, June 3, 1996; Scalia wrote the opinion.

National banks may impose late payment charges and other fees according to the law of their home state even if the charges violate laws in the customer's state.

BANKRUPTCY

Pioneer Investment Services Co. v. Brunswick Associates Limited Partnership (507 U.S. 380), decided by a 5–4 vote, March 24, 1993; White wrote the opinion; O'Connor, Scalia, Souter and Thomas dissented.

A creditor may be allowed to file a late claim in a bankruptcy action if the delay was due to an attorney's inadvertent failure to meet the deadline. The decision eased the interpretation of a bankruptcy rule permitting a tardy claim if the delay was "the result of excusable neglect." Several federal appeals courts had held that the rule could be applied only if the delay was due to circumstances beyond the creditor's control.

Nobelman v. American Savings Bank (508 U.S. 324), decided by a 9–0 vote, June 1, 1993; Thomas wrote the opinion.

Homeowners given bankruptcy court approval for creditor repayment plans under Chapter 13 cannot reduce the outstanding mortgage balance to the value of the home. The decision protected mortgage lenders' contractual rights in cases where declining property values left their loans "undersecured"—that is, secured by property worth less than the balance due. Some federal appeals courts had ruled that homeowners in such cases could "strip down" the mortgage to the home's market value.

Rake v. Wade, Trustee (508 U.S. 464), decided by a 9–0 vote, June 7, 1993; Thomas wrote the opinion.

Individuals who are granted bankruptcy court approval for plans to repay their creditors over time must pay interest on delinquent home mortgage payments. Mortgage holders are entitled to interest even if the mortgage contract does not require interest payments. Two separate provisions of the bankruptcy code entitle creditors to interest if their claim is "oversecured"—that is, if the value of the property securing the claim is greater than the amount owed.

BFP v. Resolution Trust Corporation, as receiver of Imperial Federal Savings and Loan Association (511 U.S. 531), decided by a 5–4 vote, May 23, 1994; Scalia wrote the opinion; Souter, Blackmun, Stevens and Ginsburg dissented.

The Court limited the ability of debtors in bankruptcy to nullify a foreclosure sale of real property they owned before seeking court protection from creditors. Debtors cannot use a bankruptcy code provision to undo a foreclosure sale even if the price paid is less than the property's market value.

Celotex Corp. v. Edwards (514 U.S. 300), decided by a 7–2 vote, April 19, 1995; Rehnquist wrote the opinion; Stevens and Ginsburg dissented.

The Court made it more difficult for people to collect money they have won in lawsuits from companies that later seek bankruptcy law protection from creditors. The decision, significant though highly technical, said the bankruptcy injunction had to be obeyed.

Citizens Bank of Maryland v. Strumpf (516 U.S. 16), decided by a 9–0 vote, Oct. 31, 1995; Scalia wrote the opinion.

Banks or other creditors may temporarily withhold payment of money owed to a debtor in bankruptcy without violating the automatic stay provisions of federal bankruptcy law.

Field v. Mans (516 U.S. 59), decided by a 7–2 vote, Nov. 28, 1995; Souter wrote the opinion; Breyer and Scalia dissented.

The Court relaxed the legal standard for creditors to collect money owed them by individuals in bankruptcy who have been guilty of false pretenses in connection with the debt. The decision construed a provision of the bankruptcy code that a debt cannot be discharged in bankruptcy if it results from "false pretenses, a false representation, or actual fraud."

Things Remembered, Inc. v. Petrarca (516 U.S. 124), decided by a 9–0 vote, Dec. 5, 1995; Thomas wrote the opinion.

The Court limited appellate review of lower court decisions on whether individual lawsuits should be heard in state courts or as part of federal bankruptcy proceedings. The unanimous decision held that federal appeals courts cannot review a lower court's decision to return to a state court a dispute originally filed in the state court and then "removed" to federal bankruptcy proceedings.

United States v. Noland (517 U.S. 535), decided by a 9–0 vote, May 13, 1996; Souter wrote the opinion.

The bankruptcy code provision giving Internal Revenue Service claims priority over claims by other creditors cannot be altered by federal courts on general grounds of equity.

United States v. Reorganized CF&I Fabricators of Utah, Inc. (518 U.S. 213), decided by 9–0 and 8–1 votes, June 20, 1996; Souter wrote the opinion; Thomas dissented in part.

A bankruptcy court was wrong to give low priority to the federal government's claim against a Utah company for an unpaid penalty for failing to make required contributions to employee pension plans. The Court also rejected the government's argument that the penalty was entitled to high priority as an excise tax.

COPYRIGHT

Fogerty v. Fantasy, Inc. (510 U.S. 517), decided by a 9–0 vote, March 1, 1994; Rehnquist wrote the opinion.

The Court made it easier for a successful defendant in a copyright infringement suit to be awarded attorney's fees, ruling that plaintiffs and defendants are to be treated alike under the Copyright Act provision permitting judges to award attorney's fees to the prevailing party in an infringement suit.

Campbell, a/k/a Skyywalker v. Acuff-Rose Music, Inc. (510 U.S. 569), decided by a 9–0 vote, March 7, 1994; Souter wrote the opinion.

A parody of a copyrighted work may be legally protected even if it copies a substantial part of the original and is produced for commercial purposes.

Lotus Development Corp. v. Borland International, Inc. (516 U.S. 233), decided by a 4–4 vote, Jan. 16, 1996; *per curiam* (unsigned) opinion; Stevens did not participate.

The Court deadlocked and let stand a ruling by the federal appeals court in Boston in a closely watched case testing the extent of federal copyright protection for computer software. The justices divided on a bid by Lotus Development Corp. to reinstate a $100 million-plus damage suit against a competitor for using the command menu of its popular spreadsheet in rival products. Although computer programs may be copyrighted, the appeals court had ruled that a command menu—the words displayed on a computer screen to operate a program—cannot be copyrighted.

INSURANCE

United States Department of the Treasury v. Fabe, Superintendent of Insurance of Ohio (508 U.S. 491), decided by a 5–4 vote, June 11, 1993; Blackmun wrote the opinion; Kennedy, Scalia, Souter and Thomas dissented.

States can adopt laws to give policyholders of insolvent insurance companies priority over the federal government in settling claims in liquidation proceedings.

Hartford Fire Insurance Co. v. California (509 U.S. 764), decided by votes of 9–0 and 5–4, June 28, 1993; Souter wrote the main opinion; Scalia wrote for a five-justice majority on one issue; Scalia, O'Connor, Kennedy and Thomas dissented in part.

The Court cleared the way for the trial of a major antitrust suit by 19 states against four big U.S. insurance companies and London-based "reinsurance" companies, including the famous Lloyds of London. The Court held that the U.S. insurers did not forfeit their immunity from antitrust law by dealing with foreign reinsurers. All nine justices also agreed that an illegal boycott could still be the basis of a suit.

John Hancock Mutual Life Insurance Co. v. Harris Trust & Savings Bank, as Trustee of Sperry Master Retirement Trust No. 2 (510 U.S. 86), decided by a 6–3 vote, Dec. 13, 1993; Ginsburg wrote the opinion; Thomas, O'Connor and Kennedy dissented.

The Court required insurance companies to comply with the federal Employee Retirement Income Security Act (ERISA) in managing a common type of retirement account bought by employee pension plans.

MARITIME LAW

American Dredging Co. v. Miller (510 U.S. 443), decided by a 7–2 vote, Feb. 23, 1994; Scalia wrote the opinion; Kennedy and Thomas dissented.

A state may block ship owners and operators from using a standard legal doctrine to try to move seaman injury suits to another jurisdiction if the state is not the most "convenient" place for the case to be tried.

McDermott, Inc. v. AmClyde (511 U.S. 202), decided by a 9–0 vote, April 20, 1994; Stevens wrote the opinion.

Losing defendants in a maritime lawsuit must pay their proportionate share of damages instead of getting a reduction for any settlements paid by other defendants. The Court adopted the pro-plaintiff "proportionate share" rule for federal courts to follow in maritime suits: defendants who go to trial may not try to recover any amounts paid from the settling defendants.

Boca Grande Club, Inc. v. Florida Power & Light Co., Inc. (511 U.S. 222), decided by a 9–0 vote, April 20, 1994; Stevens wrote the opinion.

Losing defendants in maritime lawsuits are not entitled to seek a contribution from defendants that settle claims before

trial. The one-paragraph decision followed the Court's ruling in a related case, *McDermott, Inc. v. AmClyde*.

Howlett v. Birkdale Shipping Co., S.A. (512 U.S. 92), decided by a 9–0 vote, June 13, 1994; Kennedy wrote the opinion.

Ship owners can be held liable for injuries to longshoremen only if the vessel's crew knew of a latent safety hazard or were negligent in failing to learn of the danger.

Jerome B. Grubart, Inc. v. Great Lakes Dredge & Dock Co. (513 U.S. 527), decided by a 7–0 vote, Feb. 22, 1995; Souter wrote the opinion; Stevens and Breyer did not participate.

Federal courts have maritime law jurisdiction over suits arising from the Great Chicago Flood of 1992, a costly disaster caused by damage to a freight tunnel under the Chicago River. The city of Chicago and owners of flooded downtown buildings charged that the Great Lakes Dredge & Dock Co. damaged the tunnel while using a crane on a barge to repair piers. Under maritime law, the company's liability would be limited to the value of the "vessel"—the barge—involved in the accident. The ruling returned the case to lower federal courts for further proceedings.

City of Milwaukee v. Cement Division, National Gypsum Co. (515 U.S. 189), decided by an 8–0 vote, June 12, 1995; Stevens wrote the opinion; Breyer did not participate.

Prejudgment interest should be awarded in an admiralty collision case even if there is a dispute over who is to blame and both sides are ultimately determined to be at fault.

Vimar Seguros y Reaseguros, S.A. v. M/V Sky Reefer (515 U.S. 528), decided by a 7–1 vote, June 19, 1995; Kennedy wrote the opinion; Stevens dissented; Breyer did not participate.

The Court upheld the enforceability of foreign arbitration clauses in maritime contracts, rejecting arguments that they lessen ship owners' liability in violation of a federal law aimed at protecting shippers. The decision effectively overruled a widely followed 1967 ruling by the federal appeals court in New York that foreign forum selection clauses were invalid under the Carriage of Goods by Sea Act.

Yamaha Motor Corporation, U.S.A. v. Calhoun (516 U.S. 199), decided by a 9–0 vote, Jan. 9, 1996; Ginsburg wrote the opinion.

State remedies, not federal law, apply in fatal maritime accidents unless the victim is a seaman, longshore worker or someone engaged in a maritime trade.

Exxon Co., U.S.A. v. Sofec, Inc. (517 U.S. 830), decided by a 9–0 vote, June 10, 1996; Thomas wrote the opinion.

The owner of an oil tanker that sank because of navigation errors by the vessel's captain was held completely responsible for the loss despite negligence by the operators of a mooring facility to which the tanker had been tied. The ruling resolved the issue of how to apply two doctrines from tort law—proximate cause and comparative fault—in a maritime accident. In any damages action, a defendant may be held liable only if its negligent conduct is the "proximate cause" of an injury. Under the comparative fault doctrine, however, damages can be apportioned among several defendants—or between the plaintiff and any defendants—if each of them was guilty of negligence that proximately caused the injury.

PATENTS

Cardinal Chemical Co. v. Morton International, Inc. (508 U.S. 83), decided by a 9–0 vote, May 17, 1993; Stevens wrote the opinion.

The federal court that hears appeals in patent cases was directed to discontinue its practice of automatically refusing to rule on the validity of a patent if it first rejects a claim that the patent has been infringed.

Asgrow Seed Co. v. Winterboer dba DeeBees (513 U.S. 179), decided by an 8–1 vote, Jan. 18, 1995; Scalia wrote the opinion; Stevens dissented.

Seed companies won a victory in their effort to use a federal law giving patent-like protection to the development of new seeds against farmers engaged in unauthorized sale of the seeds. The ruling had limited significance because Congress in 1994 amended the law to eliminate farmers' right to resell novel seed varieties for use as seed.

Markman v. Westview Instruments, Inc. (517 U.S. 370), decided by a 9–0 vote, April 23, 1996; Souter wrote the opinion.

Judges, not juries, have exclusive responsibility for construing the terms of a patent claim—the part of a patent that defines the scope of the patent holder's rights. The ruling was seen as a setback for patent holders because juries may take a broader view of a patent's meaning than do judges. Under the ruling, juries still have responsibility for deciding whether an infringement has occurred, but experts said that in many cases the construction of the patent claim will be the decisive issue.

SECURITIES LAW

Musick, Peeler & Garrett v. Employers Insurance of Wausau (508 U.S. 286), decided by a 6–3 vote, June 1, 1993; Kennedy wrote the opinion; Thomas, Blackmun and O'Connor dissented.

Defendants in federal securities fraud cases may seek to force parties not named in the suits to pay part of the damages if they have joint responsibility for the securities law violations. The 1934 Securities Act did not explicitly authorize private antifraud suits, but the Supreme Court in 1975 upheld a so-called implied right of action under the Securities and Exchange Commission's Rule 10b-5. In this case, the Court said that it would also imply a "right of contribution" in Rule 10b-5 suits to avoid unfairness to defendants required to pay damages.

Central Bank of Denver, N.A. v. First Interstate Bank of Denver, N.A. (511 U.S. 164), decided by a 5–4 vote, April 19, 1994; Kennedy wrote the opinion; Stevens, Blackmun, Souter and Ginsburg dissented.

The Court sharply limited the ability of defrauded investors to recover losses from accountants, lawyers or other professionals for indirectly aiding a securities fraud. The Court held that private plaintiffs may not maintain an action for aiding-and-abetting a violation of the broad antifraud section 10(b) of the federal Securities Exchange Act of 1934 or its companion regulation, Rule 10b-5.

Morgan Stanley & Co., Inc. v. Pacific Mutual Life Insurance Co. (511 U.S. 658), judgment affirmed by an equally divided Court, May 23, 1994; *per curiam* (unsigned) opinion; O'Connor did not participate.

The Court failed on a tie vote to decide the constitutionality of a law reinstating some federal securities suits dismissed after the Court changed the time limit for bringing such cases. The issue arose from the Court's 1991 ruling in *Lampf v. Gilbertson,* which established a three-year statute of limitations for federal securities fraud suits. Congress responded by passing a law to block application of the new deadline to pending suits and to permit reinstatement of suits already dismissed because of the ruling.

One federal appeals court ruled that the provision permitting suits to be revived was an unconstitutional violation of the doctrine of separation of powers. But the Fifth U.S. Circuit Court of Appeals upheld the law, allowing an insurance company to revive a securities fraud suit against three investment banking firms and an accounting firm.

The Court's vote had the effect of upholding the appeals court ruling. Two weeks later the Court agreed to review in the coming term another case posing the same issue (*Plaut v. Spendthrift Farm, Inc.*).

Gustafson v. Alloyd Co., Inc. (513 U.S. 561), decided by a 5–4 vote, Feb. 28, 1995; Kennedy wrote the opinion; Thomas, Scalia, Ginsburg and Breyer dissented.

A powerful securities law remedy for investors who have been misled about the value of stock applies only to initial public offerings, not to the purchase of stock in subsequent "secondary" trading. The closely divided decision narrowed the scope of a securities law provision—section 12(2) of the Securities Act of 1933—that allows investors to rescind a stock sale if they were given misleading information "by means of a prospectus or oral communication." The Court ruled that the section applies only to initial stock offerings and that a "prospectus" refers only to the formal financial disclosure required for an initial public offering, not to the more informal exchange of information in a private stock sale.

Plaut v. Spendthrift Farm, Inc. (514 U.S. 211), decided by a 7–2 vote, April 18, 1995; Scalia wrote the opinion; Stevens and Ginsburg dissented.

The Court struck down, on separation-of-powers grounds, a law passed by Congress reinstating a group of securities fraud suits that had been dismissed because of an earlier ruling by the Court. The decision nullified Congress's effort to resolve an issue created by the Court's June 1991 decision in *Lampf v. Gilbertson,* which shortened the time for bringing federal securities fraud suits. The law, signed in Dec. 1991, provided that the new statute of limitations would not apply to pending cases and that cases dismissed because of the ruling could be reinstated.

The Court said Congress "exceeded its authority" by requiring federal courts to "reopen final judgments entered before [the law's] enactment."

TAXATION

Commissioner of Internal Revenue v. Soliman (506 U.S. 168), decided by an 8–1 vote, Jan. 12, 1993; Kennedy wrote the opinion; Stevens dissented.

The Court made it harder for a self-employed taxpayer to claim a deduction for home office expenses by tightening the rules for determining whether the home office is the taxpayer's "principal place of business." Generally, the Court said, taxpayers must spend most of their time or do the most important part of their business at home in order to qualify for the deduction.

Bufferd v. Commissioner of Internal Revenue (506 U.S. 523), decided by a 9–0 vote, Jan. 25, 1993; White wrote the opinion.

The time for the Internal Revenue Service (IRS) to challenge tax benefits of shareholders of certain types of small businesses runs from the date of the shareholder's tax return instead of the date of the business's return.

Shareholders of so-called Subchapter S corporations may claim a portion of the corporation's losses or deductions on their individual tax returns. The shareholder in this case claimed a loss deduction based on the corporation's tax return for the prior year. When the IRS challenged the deduction, the taxpayer argued the agency had failed to act within three years of the corporation's return. The Court, however, ruled unanimously that the filing date of the shareholder's return was the relevant date.

United States v. Hill (506 U.S. 546), decided by a 9–0 vote, Jan. 25, 1993; Souter wrote the opinion.

The Court limited a tax break used by investors in exploration for oil, gas, coal or other minerals. The decision prevented taxpayers from using the cost of tools and equipment to increase the income sheltered under the percentage depletion allowance. This controversial tax provision was intended to take account of the "depletion" of mineral deposits as they are extracted, but it can be calculated to allow tax deductions in excess of the taxpayer's actual investment.

The Court held that the cost of tangible items such as tools and equipment could not be included in the taxpayer's investment—his "adjusted basis"—in the mineral deposit. Instead, those costs can be deducted only according to normal, less generous depreciation rules.

United States by and through Internal Revenue Service v. McDermott (507 U.S. 448), decided by a 6–3 vote, March 24, 1993; Scalia wrote the opinion; Thomas, Stevens and O'Connor dissented.

The Court gave the IRS preference in seeking to collect unpaid taxes from people who also owe money to private creditors. The case involved how to determine the priority of creditors' competing "liens" on property owned by the debtor. The Court held that a federal tax lien filed before a delinquent taxpayer acquires real property must generally be given priority over a private creditor's lien in the same property. The Court said that under federal law, a federal tax lien is dated from the filing of the lien, while the creditor's lien cannot attach until after the debtor acquires the property.

Newark Morning Ledger Co., as Successor to The Herald Company v. United States (507 U.S. 546), decided by a 5–4 vote, April 20, 1993; Blackmun wrote the opinion; Souter, Rehnquist, White and Scalia dissented.

A business taxpayer is entitled to take a depreciation deduction for the value of a customer list if it can show that the customers' continued patronage has a value that diminishes over time. The closely divided ruling—a multibillion-dollar victory for businesses—rejected the argument by the IRS that customer lists are part of a company's "goodwill."

United States v. Irvine (511 U.S. 224), decided by an 8–0 vote, April 20, 1994; Souter wrote the opinion; Blackmun did not participate.

The government can collect gift tax on a taxpayer's delayed decision to give up interest in a trust even if the trust was created before the gift tax was passed. The ruling allowed the Internal Revenue Service to collect $10 million in taxes, interest and penalties from the children of a Minnesota woman who, in 1979, disclaimed her right to a trust established by her grandfather in 1917. Under terms of the trust, the money was divided among her five children.

An IRS regulation, which the Court upheld in 1982, allows a taxpayer to avoid the gift tax in such a situation only if he or she disclaims the interest "within a reasonable time." The children contended that the 1932 gift tax did not apply to a trust created earlier. The Court said the gift tax applied to the decision to give up the money, not to the creation of the trust.

United States v. Carlton (512 U.S. 26), decided by a 9–0 vote, June 13, 1994; Blackmun wrote the opinion.

Congress has broad discretion to enact retroactive tax changes if the revisions are rationally related to a legitimate purpose and extend to a "modest" period before enactment. The ruling upheld a law passed by Congress in 1987 to close an estate tax loophole adopted one year earlier.

United States v. Williams (514 U.S. 527), decided by a 6–3 vote, April 25, 1995; Ginsburg wrote the opinion; Rehnquist, Kennedy and Thomas dissented.

The Court created a limited exception to the general rule against allowing tax refund suits by someone other than the person who was assessed the tax.

Commissioner of Internal Revenue v. Schleier (515 U.S. 323), decided by a 6–3 vote, June 14, 1995; Stevens wrote the opinion; O'Connor, Souter and Thomas dissented.

Any money recovered for back pay or damages in a federal age discrimination suit is subject to federal income taxation. The Court ruled that an Internal Revenue Service regulation exempts damage awards only if they are based on a "tort or tort type" suits, such as an automobile accident case.

Commissioner of Internal Revenue v. Lundy (516 U.S. 235), decided by a 7–2 vote, Jan. 17, 1996; O'Connor wrote the opinion; Thomas and Stevens dissented.

The Court set a two-year time limit for a taxpayer who fails to file a return and then later seeks a refund in Tax Court. In a densely statutory ruling, the Court ruled that the correct "lookback" period for a taxpayer who failed to file a return was two years.

United States v. International Business Machines Corp. (517 U.S. 843), decided by a 6–2 vote, June 10, 1996; Thomas wrote the opinion; Kennedy and Ginsburg dissented; Stevens did not participate.

A federal tax on insurance premiums paid to foreign insurers for shipment of exported goods violates the Constitution's ban on taxing exports. Congress passed the tax provision in 1942 to eliminate the advantage foreign insurers have from not being subject to federal income tax.

TRADEMARKS

Qualitex Co. v. Jacobson Products Co., Inc. (514 U.S. 159), decided by a 9–0 vote, March 28, 1995; Breyer wrote the opinion.

A color can be registered as a trademark under federal law and provide the basis for a trademark infringement claim. The Court said the broadly worded federal trademark law—the Lanham Act—permits "the registration of a trademark that consists, purely and simply, of a color" and noted that the U.S. Patent and Trademark Office had previously permitted the registration of a particular shape (the Coca-Cola bottle), a particular sound (the NBC chimes) and a particular odor (a scented thread).

Courts and Procedure

ABSTENTION

Quackenbush, California Insurance Commissioner v. Allstate Insurance Co. (517 U.S. 706), decided by a 9–0 vote, June 3, 1996; O'Connor wrote the opinion.

The abstention doctrine, which permits federal courts to refrain from deciding certain cases to avoid conflict with state judiciaries, cannot be invoked to dismiss a suit for damages.

APPEALS

Swint v. Chambers County Commission (514 U.S. 35), decided by a 9–0 vote, March 1, 1995; Ginsburg wrote the opinion.

The Court cleared the way for trial of a civil rights suit against an Alabama county and the county sheriff after ruling that a federal appeals court had no power to grant the county's plea for favorable ruling without trial.

Behrens v. Pelletier (516 U.S. 299), decided by a 7–2 vote, Feb. 21, 1996; Scalia wrote the opinion; Breyer and Stevens dissented.

A government official named as a defendant in a federal civil rights suit may be allowed two pretrial appeals on a claim that he is entitled to qualified immunity from the suit.

ARBITRATION

Allied-Bruce Terminix Cos., Inc. v. Dobson (513 U.S. 265), decided by a 7–2 vote, Jan. 18, 1995; Breyer wrote the opinion; Thomas and Scalia dissented.

States must enforce mandatory arbitration clauses in consumer contracts for any transactions that involve interstate commerce. The Federal Arbitration Act, passed in 1925, provides that courts must enforce arbitration agreements in any "contract evidencing a transaction involving commerce." The Court held that the act applies even if the parties to a contract "did not contemplate" a transaction in interstate commerce.

Mastrobuono v. Shearson Lehman Hutton, Inc. (514 U.S. 52), decided by an 8–1 vote, March 6, 1995; Stevens wrote the opinion; Thomas dissented.

The Court reinstated a punitive damage award imposed by an arbitrator against a securities brokerage firm, saying the firm's contract with customers did not clearly bar punitive damages in arbitration.

First Options of Chicago, Inc. v. Kaplan (514 U.S. 938), decided by a 9–0 vote, May 22, 1995; Breyer wrote the opinion.

Courts can independently determine whether a dispute is subject to arbitration unless the parties have clearly agreed that the issue of arbitrability is itself to be decided by arbitration.

Doctor's Associates, Inc. v. Casarotto (517 U.S. 681), decided by an 8–1 vote, May 20, 1996; Ginsburg wrote the opinion; Thomas dissented.

The Court struck down on federal preemption grounds a Montana law requiring that contractual arbitration clauses be printed in underlined capital letters and appear on a contract's first page.

ATTORNEYS

Heintz v. Jenkins (514 U.S. 291), decided by a 9–0 vote, April 18, 1995; Breyer wrote the opinion.

Attorneys who regularly engage in consumer debt-collection litigation are subject to the federal Fair Debt Collection Practices Act. The ruling rejected an argument by an Indiana lawyer that the law, aimed at controlling abusive debt-collection practices, does not apply to attorneys' handling of court cases. The Court said lawyers regularly engaged in debt-collection litigation met the act's definition of a debt collector and noted that a broad exemption for lawyers included in the original law in 1977 had been repealed and not replaced in 1986.

CONTEMPT OF COURT

United Mine Workers v. Bagwell (512 U.S. 821), decided by a 9–0 vote, June 30, 1994; Blackmun wrote the opinion.

The Court threw out a $52 million contempt of court fine imposed on the United Mine Workers union for violating an injunction aimed at preventing violence in a 1989 coal strike, ruling the penalty was too serious to be imposed without a jury trial.

DECLARATORY JUDGMENTS

Wilton v. Seven Falls Co. (515 U.S. 277), decided by an 8–0 vote, June 12, 1995; O'Connor wrote the opinion; Breyer did not participate.

Federal courts have broad discretion to hold up proceedings in a declaratory judgment action while a state court considers the same issues in a parallel case. The Court reinforced a 1942 precedent that courts may hold off ruling in a declaratory judgment action to await a state court decision on the issue.

EVIDENCE

Daubert v. Merrell Dow Pharmaceuticals, Inc. (509 U.S. 579), decided by votes of 9–0 and 7–2, June 28, 1993; Blackmun wrote the opinion; Rehnquist and Stevens dissented in part.

The Court held that the liberal Federal Rules of Evidence governed the use of scientific testimony in federal courts, but told federal judges they should act as "gatekeepers" to make sure such evidence is "not only relevant, but reliable." The ruling scrapped a 70-year-old case, *Frye v. United States* (1923), that required "general acceptance" of a scientific method or theory before it could be used in trials.

FEDERAL COURTS

Church of Scientology of California v. United States (506 U.S. 9), decided by a 9–0 vote, Nov. 16, 1992; Stevens wrote the opinion.

A taxpayer may go to court to challenge the Internal Revenue Service's efforts to obtain confidential records, even if the records have already been turned over to the IRS.

The IRS obtained under court order tape recordings of conversations between Church of Scientology officials and their attorneys. The church claimed the conversations were privileged, but the tapes were turned over while the issue was being appealed. A federal appeals court dismissed the church's case as moot because the tapes had already been turned over. The Court disagreed, saying that a court could still grant the church some legal relief. Even though the government had already received the tapes, a court could order the IRS to destroy or return any copies.

Keene Corp. v. United States (508 U.S. 200), decided by an 8–1 vote, May 24, 1993; Souter wrote the opinion; Stevens dissented.

The Court upheld the dismissal of claims filed by a manufacturer of asbestos products against the United States in the Court of Federal Claims because the company had filed similar claims in federal district courts. In a significant but highly technical ruling, the Court declined to create an exception to a federal law that bars the Court of Federal Claims from exercising jurisdiction over a claim if the plaintiff has a similar suit "pending in any other court."

O'Melveny & Myers v. Federal Deposit Insurance Corporation, as receiver for American Diversified Savings Bank (512 U.S. 79), decided by a 9–0 vote, June 13, 1994; Scalia wrote the opinion.

State law, not federal law, governs professional negligence suits brought by the Federal Deposit Insurance Corporation (FDIC) as receiver for a failed savings and loan association.

INDIGENTS

Rowland, Former Director, California Department of Corrections v. California Men's Colony, Unit II Men's Advisory Council (506 U.S. 194), decided by a 5–4 vote, Jan. 12, 1993; Souter wrote the opinion; Thomas, Blackmun, Stevens and Kennedy dissented.

Only individuals—not groups, associations or corporations—qualify as "persons" who may be entitled to bring a federal court suit without paying filing fees and other court costs. A group of California inmates challenging a decision to discontinue free tobacco for prisoners tried to bring their suit under a federal law that spares poor litigants the need to prepay fees, costs or appeal bonds.

JUDGMENTS

U.S. Bancorp Mortgage Co. v. Bonner Mall Partnership (513 U.S. 18), decided by a 9–0 vote, Nov. 8, 1994; Scalia wrote the opinion.

Lower courts cannot routinely vacate—or wipe out—rulings in civil cases if the parties reach a settlement while the case is on appeal. The decision stemmed from the common practice, called "vacatur," whereby defendants agree to settle a civil case after an unfavorable ruling in exchange for an agreement from the plaintiffs to have the court vacate the decision. Supporters said the practice encouraged settlements. Critics said it allowed insurance companies and other deep-pocket defendants to skew the development of the law by erasing unfavorable precedents.

Peacock v. Thomas (516 U.S. 349), decided by an 8–1 vote, Feb. 21, 1996; Thomas wrote the opinion; Stevens dissented.

Federal courts have no jurisdiction over a suit to enforce a judgment won by a litigant in one case against an individual or corporation that is not otherwise liable for the judgment.

JUDICIAL DISQUALIFICATION

Liteky v. United States (510 U.S. 540), decided by 9–0 and 5–4 votes, March 7, 1994; Scalia wrote the opinion; Kennedy, Blackmun, Stevens and Souter concurred in the judgment but disagreed with the ruling on the legal issue.

Federal judges generally cannot be disqualified from a case for bias on the basis of their comments or conduct in the courtroom. The ruling upheld the refusal by a federal judge in Georgia to step aside from the 1991 trial of three peace activists for a protest at a military base. The defendants claimed the judge made prejudicial remarks during the proceedings and during an earlier trial of one of the defendants for similar charges in 1983.

JURY SELECTION

J. E. B. v. Alabama ex rel. T. B. (511 U.S. 127), decided by a 6–3 vote, April 19, 1994; Blackmun wrote the opinion; Scalia, Rehnquist and Thomas dissented.

Lawyers may not exclude people from serving on juries solely because of their sex. The Equal Protection Clause prohibits discrimination in jury selection based on gender. The ruling extended the reasoning of a line of cases beginning in 1986 that had barred lawyers from excluding potential jurors on account of race.

JURY TRIALS

Gasperini v. Center for Humanities, Inc. (518 U.S.___), decided by 6–3 and 5–4 votes, June 24, 1996; Ginsburg wrote the opinion; Stevens disagreed with the result but agreed with the legal holding; Scalia, Rehnquist and Thomas dissented.

Federal courts hearing damage suits in diversity-of-citizenship cases may apply state law permitting judges to reduce jury awards without violating the Seventh Amendment's protections for jury trials in federal courts.

PRIVILEGES

Jaffee v. Redmond (518 U.S. 1), decided by a 7–2 vote, June 13, 1996; Stevens wrote the opinion; Scalia and Rehnquist dissented.

Federal courts cannot force psychotherapists or other mental health professionals to disclose patients' statements or records as evidence in judicial proceedings. The Court held that federal courts ordinarily must recognize a psychotherapist privilege. The privilege was needed because compelled disclosure of psychotherapy sessions "may impede development of the confidential relationship necessary for successful treatment," but the privilege "must give way" if disclosure was required to prevent harm to the patient or to others.

SETTLEMENTS

Kokkonen v. Guardian Life Insurance Co. of America (511 U.S. 375), decided by a 9–0 vote, May 16, 1994; Scalia wrote the opinion.

A federal court cannot enforce the terms of an agreement settling a suit unless the agreement specifically provides for court enforcement.

Digital Equipment Corp. v. Desktop Direct, Inc. (511 U.S. 863), decided by a 9–0 vote, June 6, 1994; Souter wrote the opinion.

A party to a civil suit is not entitled to an immediate appeal of a judge's refusal to enforce a settlement agreement that would preclude trial of the case. The ruling came in a trademark infringement suit filed by a small computer company, Desktop Direct, against the giant Digital Equipment Corp. A judge set aside a settlement in the case after Desktop alleged misrepresentation and fraud. Digital then tried to appeal the ruling, claiming that it had a contractual right to avoid trial of the case.

Matsushita Electric Industrial Co., Ltd. v. Epstein (516 U.S. 367), decided by 9–0 and 6–3 votes, Feb. 27, 1996; Thomas wrote the opinion; Ginsburg, Stevens and Souter dissented in part.

Federal courts must recognize a state court's approval of a settlement even if the agreement releases claims that are within the exclusive jurisdiction of federal courts.

STATUTES OF LIMITATIONS

Reynoldsville Casket Co. v. Hyde (514 U.S. 749), decided by a 9–0 vote, May 15, 1995; Breyer wrote the opinion.

An Ohio woman, who had been injured in a traffic accident involving a truck owned by an out-of-state firm, failed to get around an earlier ruling by the Court that invalidated a state law that gave Ohio plaintiffs unlimited time to file suit against out-of-state residents.

Criminal Law and Procedure

ACQUITTALS

Carlisle v. United States (517 U.S. 416), decided by a 7–2 vote, April 29, 1996; Scalia wrote the opinion; Stevens and Kennedy dissented.

A federal judge cannot consider a defendant's postverdict motion for acquittal filed after the seven-day time limit established by the Federal Rules of Criminal Procedure.

APPEALS

Ortega-Rodriguez v. United States (507 U.S. 234), decided by a 5–4 vote, March 8, 1993; Stevens wrote the opinion; Rehnquist, White, O'Connor and Thomas dissented.

The Court struck down a federal appeals court rule prescribing automatic dismissal of an appeal by a defendant who becomes a fugitive while awaiting sentencing but is recaptured before filing an appeal. Since 1876 the Court had recognized that an appellate court may dismiss an appeal by a defendant who is at large while the appeal is pending. In 1975 the Court also upheld a Texas law mandating dismissal of a fugitive's appeal. In this case, however, the Court said that the automatic fugitive appeal dismissal rule adopted by the Eleventh U.S. Circuit Court of Appeals went too far.

ARREST

Powell v. Nevada (511 U.S. 79), decided by a 7–2 vote, March 30, 1994; Ginsburg wrote the opinion; Thomas and Rehnquist dissented.

DUE PROCESS, EQUAL PROTECTION

. . . Nor shall any state deprive any person of life, liberty, or property, without due process of law; nor deny to any person within its jurisdiction the equal protection of the laws.

14th Amendment, U.S. Constitution

A Nevada man won a second appeal of his conviction in a child abuse-murder case because the state's supreme court failed to apply a decision requiring suspects to be brought before a magistrate within 48 hours of their arrest. The Court left open the possibility, however, that the state justices could affirm the defendant's conviction and death sentence after a second appeal.

CAPITAL PUNISHMENT

Richmond v. Lewis, Director, Arizona Department of Corrections (506 U.S. 40), decided by an 8–1 vote, Dec. 1, 1992; O'Connor wrote the opinion; Scalia dissented.

An Arizona murderer twice sentenced to death won a reprieve because a lower court judge used an unconstitutionally vague sentencing factor and the state's supreme court failed to correct the error.

Herrera v. Collins, Director, Texas Department of Criminal Justice, Institutional Division (506 U.S. 390), decided by a 6–3 vote, Jan. 25, 1993; Rehnquist wrote the opinion; Blackmun, Stevens and Souter dissented.

A death row inmate ordinarily is not entitled to federal habeas corpus relief based solely on a claim that he is actually innocent. The inmate must also have an independent claim of constitutional error in his state court trial or other proceedings. Dissenting justices argued that a death row inmate should be granted a federal habeas hearing if he can show that he is "probably innocent."

Delo, Superintendent, Potosi Correctional Center v. Lashley (507 U.S. 272), decided by a 7–2 vote, March 8, 1993; *per curiam* (unsigned) opinion; Stevens and Blackmun dissented.

A capital defendant that wants the jury to consider a lack of prior criminal history as a mitigating factor must present evidence to show no previous arrests or offenses. The Court summarily reversed a federal appeals court's decision that the prosecution had the burden to show the defendant's prior criminal record to block use of the instruction.

Arave, Warden v. Creech (507 U.S. 463), decided by a 7–2 vote, March 30, 1993; O'Connor wrote the opinion; Blackmun and Stevens dissented.

The Court upheld a provision of Idaho's capital punishment statute allowing the death penalty for murderers who show "utter disregard for human life." The justices, overturning a federal appeals court decision that the law was too vague, said that the Idaho Supreme Court had adequately narrowed the aggravating circumstance to refer to a "cold-blooded, pitiless slayer." The provision satisfied a second rule that a capital sentencing scheme must "genuinely narrow the class of defendants eligible for the death penalty." The case was remanded for resentencing on other issues.

Johnson v. Texas (509 U.S. 350), decided by a 5–4 vote, June 24, 1993; Kennedy wrote the opinion; O'Connor, Blackmun, Stevens and Souter dissented.

Texas's former capital punishment law adequately allowed juries to consider a defendant's youth as a mitigating factor in deciding whether to impose the death penalty. The law provided the death penalty in first-degree murder cases if a jury found the murder was committed deliberately and the defendant would probably commit violent crimes in the future.

Schiro v. Farley, Superintendent, Indiana State Prison (510 U.S. 222), decided by a 7–2 vote, Jan. 19, 1994; O'Connor wrote the opinion; Stevens and Blackmun dissented.

A judge may impose a death sentence for intentional murder even if a jury fails to return a verdict for that offense. The ruling upheld a death sentence imposed on Thomas Schiro after he was convicted of raping and killing an Indiana woman in 1981. The jury convicted Schiro of one capital count—murder while committing a rape—but did not specify a verdict on two other capital counts, including intentional murder.

Although the jury unanimously recommended against imposition of capital punishment, the judge imposed the death penalty after finding that Schiro had "committed the murder by intentionally killing the victim."

Romano v. Oklahoma (512 U.S. 1), decided by a 5–4 vote, June 13, 1994; Rehnquist wrote the opinion; Ginsburg, Blackmun, Stevens and Souter dissented.

A defendant sentenced to death is not entitled to a new penalty hearing if the jury was told the defendant had already been sentenced to death in a prior case.

Simmons v. South Carolina (512 U.S. 154), decided by a 7–2 vote, June 17, 1994; Blackmun wrote a plurality opinion for four justices; O'Connor wrote a concurring opinion for three justices; Scalia and Thomas dissented.

Jurors in a capital case must be told about the possibility of sentencing a defendant to life in prison without parole if the prosecution uses the defendant's dangerousness as an argument for the death penalty.

McFarland v. Scott, Director, Texas Department of Criminal Justice, Institutional Division (512 U.S. 849), decided by 6–3 and 5–4 votes, June 30, 1994; Blackmun wrote the opinion; O'Connor dissented in part; Thomas, Rehnquist and Scalia dissented.

Federal judges must appoint a lawyer for a death row inmate who requests assistance in drawing up a habeas corpus petition and can stay the inmate's execution until the petition is filed. The closely divided ruling interpreted a provision of the Anti-Drug Abuse Act of 1988 that created a right to counsel for capital defendants in federal habeas corpus proceedings.

Tuilaepa v. California (512 U.S. 967), decided by an 8–1 vote, June 30, 1994; Kennedy wrote the opinion; Blackmun dissented.

The Court rejected pleas by two California death row inmates to strike down as unconstitutionally vague three factors listed in state law for juries to consider in deciding whether to impose the death penalty. Among 19 factors in all, the state's capital murder law instructed jurors to consider "the circumstances of the crime," "the presence or absence of criminal activity [involving] the use or attempted use of force or violence . . . ," and the age of the defendant.

Harris v. Alabama (513 U.S. 504), decided by an 8–1 vote, Feb. 22, 1995; O'Connor wrote the opinion; Stevens dissented.

States may give judges the power to sentence a capital defendant to death even if the jury votes not to impose the death penalty.

Tuggle v. Netherland, Warden (516 U.S. 10), decided by a 9–0 vote, Oct. 30, 1995; *per curiam* (unsigned) opinion.

A Virginia death row inmate was allowed to challenge his death sentence because the state's supreme court failed to correct the effects of a constitutional error in his capital sentencing hearing. The inmate was convicted of murder and then sentenced to death after prosecutors introduced evidence to show two "aggravating factors"—"vileness" and "future dangerousness." The evidence of dangerousness was later ruled inadmissible because the defendant had not been provided a court-appointed psychiatrist.

Loving v. United States (517 U.S. 748), decided by a 9–0 vote, June 3, 1996; Kennedy wrote the opinion.

The Court upheld the military death penalty, rejecting a separation-of-powers challenge to a 1984 presidential directive revising the system to cure constitutional defects.

COMPETENCY

Cooper v. Oklahoma (517 U.S. 348), decided by a 9–0 vote, April 16, 1996; Stevens wrote the opinion.

A defendant seeking to prove that he is incompetent to stand trial cannot be required to make that showing by the heightened standard of "clear and convincing evidence." The ruling affected laws in four states: Connecticut, Oklahoma, Pennsylvania and Rhode Island. All other states and the federal courts used a "preponderance of the evidence" standard on competency questions in criminal cases.

CRIMINAL OFFENSES

Ratzlaf v. United States (510 U.S. 135), decided by a 5–4 vote, Jan. 11, 1994; Ginsburg wrote the opinion; Blackmun, Rehnquist, O'Connor and Thomas dissented.

The Court made it harder for the government to prosecute individuals who keep their cash transactions with banks under $10,000 in order to avoid federal currency reporting requirements. The ruling weakened the 1986 Money Laundering Act, which Congress passed to help the government detect proceeds from drug trafficking, gambling or other lucrative criminal activities.

Posters 'N' Things, Ltd. v. United States (511 U.S. 513), decided by a 9–0 vote, May 23, 1994; Blackmun wrote the opinion.

The Court somewhat eased the government's burden of proof under a federal law prohibiting the sale of "drug paraphernalia" by ruling that a defendant may be convicted under the law for selling merchandise generally used with illegal drugs. The justices rejected arguments by the owner of a "head shop" that the government had to prove she specifically knew that a particular customer intended to use the items with drugs.

Staples v. United States (511 U.S. 600), decided by a 7–2 vote, May 23, 1994; Thomas wrote the opinion; Stevens and Blackmun dissented.

The Court tightened somewhat the government's burden of proof under the federal law prohibiting possession of unregistered machine guns. The ruling overturned the conviction of a man for owning an unregistered semiautomatic rifle that had been modified to fire automatically. The government argued the weapon fell under the National Firearms Act's definition of a machine gun. The defendant said he had not known that the rifle had been modified.

United States v. Shabani (513 U.S. 10), decided by a 9–0 vote, Nov. 1, 1994; O'Connor wrote the opinion.

A defendant can be convicted under the federal drug conspiracy statute even if the government fails to prove any "overt act" he committed to carry out the conspiracy.

United States v. X-Citement Video, Inc. (513 U.S. 64), decided by a 7–2 vote, Nov. 29, 1994; Rehnquist wrote the opinion; Scalia and Thomas dissented.

The Court saved the 1977 federal child pornography statute, which makes it a criminal offense to "knowingly" transport or ship in interstate commerce "any visual depiction" if the production "involves the use of a minor engaging in sexually explicit conduct," from constitutional attack by construing the law to require prosecutors to prove the defendant knew that minors were depicted in the material.

United States v. Lopez (514 U.S. 549), decided by a 5–4 vote, April 26, 1995; Rehnquist wrote the opinion; Breyer, Stevens, Souter and Ginsburg dissented.

The Court overturned a popular federal criminal law banning possession of a firearm in or near a school on grounds it went beyond Congress's power to regulate interstate commerce. The decision invalidated the 1990 Gun-Free School Zones Act, which made it a federal crime to possess a firearm within 1,000 feet of a school. The Court said the law exceeded Congress's power under the Constitution's Commerce Clause.

United States v. Robertson (514 U.S. 669), decided by a 9–0 vote, May 1, 1995; *per curiam* (unsigned) opinion.

The Court reinstated the federal racketeering conviction of a former prosecutor-turned-narcotics-trafficker for using proceeds of drug transactions to operate an Alaska gold mine.

Hubbard v. United States (514 U.S. 695), decided by a 6–3 vote, May 15, 1995; Stevens wrote the opinion; Rehnquist, O'Connor and Souter dissented.

Overturning a 40-year-old precedent, the Court held that the federal law against making false statements to a "department or agency" of the government does not apply to statements made to a federal court.

United States v. Aguilar (515 U.S. 593), decided by votes of 8–1 and 6–3, June 21, 1995; Rehnquist wrote the opinion; Stevens dissented in part; Scalia, Kennedy and Thomas dissented in part.

The Court reinstated the conviction of a federal judge for disclosing a court-ordered wiretap but agreed with a federal appeals court in striking down his conviction for obstruction of justice.

Bailey v. United States (516 U.S. 137), decided by a 9–0 vote, Dec. 6, 1995; O'Connor wrote the opinion.

A defendant cannot be convicted under a federal law providing at least five years' imprisonment for "using" a firearm in connection with a drug offense unless he actively employed the weapon during the crime. The decision narrowed the interpretation of a 1988 law that federal prosecutors used to win longer sentences in drug cases.

Rutledge v. United States (517 U.S. 292), decided by a 9–0 vote, March 27, 1996; Stevens wrote the opinion.

A defendant convicted of conducting a "continuing criminal enterprise" cannot also be convicted of a criminal conspiracy for the same activities.

Montana v. Egelhoff (518 U.S. 37), decided by a 5–4 vote, June 13, 1996; Scalia wrote the plurality opinion; O'Connor, Stevens, Souter and Breyer dissented.

States may prohibit juries from considering a defendant's intoxication when deciding whether the defendant had the required mental state to be convicted of a crime.

CRIMINAL PROCEDURE

Crosby v. United States (506 U.S. 255), decided by a 9–0 vote, Jan. 13, 1993; Blackmun wrote the opinion.

A court cannot try a defendant in his absence if the defendant is not present at the beginning of the trial. The ruling limited the use of a federal rule of criminal procedure that permits a trial to proceed in the defendant's absence if he "is voluntarily absent after the trial has commenced." On the basis of that rule, a federal district court had conducted a trial in a complex mail fraud case even though one of the defendants had absconded and was not present for the start of the trial.

Zafiro v. United States (506 U.S. 534), decided by a 9–0 vote, Jan. 25, 1993; O'Connor wrote the opinion.

Codefendants are not entitled to separate trials under federal rules of criminal procedure merely because they plan to present "mutually antagonistic" defenses.

Fex v. Michigan (507 U.S. 43), decided by a 7–2 vote, Feb. 23, 1993; Scalia wrote the opinion; Blackmun and Stevens dissented.

The 180-day limit for bringing a prisoner to trial on a charge lodged by another state begins when prosecutors receive the prisoner's request to dispose of the charge, not when the prisoner makes the request. The ruling backed states and the federal government in interpreting a provision of the Interstate Agreement on Detainers that gives prisoners the right to demand resolution of charges pending against them in another state.

Godinez, Warden v. Moran (509 U.S. 389), decided by a 7–2 vote, June 24, 1993; Thomas wrote the opinion; Blackmun and Stevens dissented.

A defendant who is found mentally competent to stand trial is not entitled to a stricter evaluation of his mental competence to plead guilty or waive the right to counsel. The Court refused to tighten the standard it adopted in 1960, which requires a defendant be able to understand the charges against him and to consult with a lawyer to be found competent to stand trial.

DISCRIMINATION

United States v. Armstrong (517 U.S. 456), decided by an 8–1 vote, May 13, 1996; Rehnquist wrote the opinion; Stevens dissented.

A defendant cannot use pretrial discovery procedures to support a race-based claim of selective prosecution without first presenting some evidence that the government failed in similar cases to prosecute persons of a different race.

DOUBLE JEOPARDY

United States v. Dixon and Foster (509 U.S. 688), decided by votes of 5–4 and 6–3, June 28, 1993; Scalia wrote the opinion; White, Blackmun, Stevens and Souter dissented on the main legal issue; Rehnquist, Blackmun, O'Connor and Thomas dissented from the result in *Dixon;* White, Stevens and Souter dissented from the result in *Foster.*

The Court eased the constitutional bar against double jeopardy by overturning an earlier ruling, *Grady v. Corbin* (1990), which had broadened the double jeopardy provision to bar multiple prosecutions when the two offenses involved the same conduct. The Court held that multiple prosecutions are permitted if the two offenses contain different elements.

Montana Department of Revenue v. Kurth Ranch (511 U.S. 767), decided by a 5–4 vote, June 6, 1994; Stevens wrote the opinion; Rehnquist, O'Connor, Scalia and Thomas dissented.

DOUBLE JEOPARDY, SELF-INCRIMINATION

. . . Nor shall any person be subject for the same offense to be twice put in jeopardy of life or limb nor shall be compelled in any criminal case to be a witness against himself, nor be deprived of life, liberty, or property, without due process of law. . . .

Fifth Amendment, U.S. Constitution

The Court struck down a stiff state tax on illegal drugs, saying the measure was punitive and violated the constitutional prohibition against multiple punishments. The ruling invalidated a 1987 Montana law that set a tax of $100 per ounce on marijuana and similarly high levies on other illegal drugs.

Witte v. United States (515 U.S. 389), decided by an 8–1 vote, June 14, 1995; O'Connor wrote the opinion; Stevens dissented.

Double jeopardy principles do not prevent the government from prosecuting a defendant for conduct that was previously used to increase the defendant's sentence for a separate conviction.

The Court softened the impact of the decision, however, by ruling that the sentence for a second conviction in such cases ordinarily should run concurrently with the remainder of the term for the first offense.

EVIDENCE

Williamson v. United States (512 U.S. 594), decided by 9–0 and 6–3 votes, June 27, 1994; O'Connor wrote the opinion; Kennedy, Rehnquist and Thomas concurred in the judgment but disagreed with the ruling on the legal issue.

The Court limited prosecutors' ability to introduce out-of-court statements made by an accomplice who does not testify in person at the defendant's trial.

Tome v. United States (513 U.S. 150), decided by a 5–4 vote, Jan. 10, 1995; Kennedy wrote the opinion; Breyer, Rehnquist, O'Connor and Thomas dissented.

The Court strictly construed an evidentiary rule limiting the introduction of out-of-court statements made by a witness to try to support the credibility of her in-court testimony.

United States v. Mezzanatto (513 U.S. 196), decided by a 7–2 vote, Jan. 18, 1995; Thomas wrote the opinion; Souter and Stevens dissented.

The Court cleared the way for federal prosecutors to enforce agreements permitting them to use statements made by a defendant during plea bargaining to cross-examine the defendant at trial.

The Federal Rules of Evidence and Federal Rules of Criminal Procedure both provide that, with limited exceptions, a defendant's statements during plea negotiations cannot be used against the defendant later.

But the Court upheld a growing practice among federal prosecutors to have defendants waive that right as a condition of entering into plea discussions.

Wood, Superintendent, Washington State Penitentiary v. Bartholomew (516 U.S. 1), decided Oct. 10, 1995, by a 5–4 vote; *per curiam* (unsigned) opinion; Stevens, Souter, Ginsburg and Breyer dissented.

Prosecutors need not disclose to a defendant unfavorable results of a polygraph examination given to a prosecution witness if the information will not help find evidence that would be admissible at trial.

FORFEITURE

Republic National Bank of Miami v. United States (506 U.S. 80), decided by a 9–0 vote, Dec. 14, 1992; Blackmun and Rehnquist wrote opinions.

A federal appeals court can rule on the government's seizure of a house under the drug forfeiture law even if the house has been sold and the proceeds deposited to the federal Treasury. The ruling reinstated an appeal by a Miami bank, which had contested the forfeiture under the "innocent owner" defense. The lower court had rejected the bank's argument, and the government sold the house while the appeal was pending.

United States v. A Parcel of Land, Buildings, Appurtenances and Improvements, known as 92 Buena Vista Avenue, Rumson, New Jersey (507 U.S. 111), decided by a 6–3 vote, Feb. 24, 1993; Stevens wrote the main opinion; Kennedy, Rehnquist and White dissented.

The government cannot seize property bought with drug money after it has been given to or purchased by someone who can show he or she had no knowledge of the source of the funds. The decision said the "innocent owner" defense included in a 1978 drug forfeiture law was not limited to "bona fide purchasers" but could also be used by someone who was given property. The Court also rejected the government's argument that it could claim ownership of property from the time it was purchased with proceeds of illegal transactions.

Alexander v. United States (509 U.S. 544), decided by a 5–4 vote, June 28, 1993; Rehnquist wrote the opinion; Kennedy, Blackmun, Stevens and Souter dissented.

The seizure of a chain of adult bookstores and destruction of their entire inventory under the forfeiture provisions of the federal the Racketeer Influenced and Corrupt Organizations Act did not violate the First Amendment. The Court remanded the case to a federal appeals court, however, to reconsider the owner's claim that the forfeiture violated the Eighth Amendment's prohibitions against "excessive fines."

Austin v. United States (509 U.S. 602), decided by a 9–0 vote, June 28, 1993; Blackmun wrote the opinion.

The Eighth Amendment's prohibition against excessive fines limits the government's power in civil forfeiture proceedings to seize the property of criminals or suspects. The Court's decision—along with its ruling the same day in *Alexander v. United States*—marked the first broad constitutional limit on the government's increasing use of forfeiture in drug trafficking, racketeering, money-laundering and other offenses.

United States v. James Daniel Good Real Property (510 U.S. 43), decided by a 5–4 vote, Dec. 13, 1993; Kennedy wrote the opinion; Rehnquist, O'Connor, Scalia and Thomas dissented.

The Court made it harder for law enforcement officers to use strengthened forfeiture laws to seize property from drug traffickers or other suspected criminals. The Court ruled that a property owner is ordinarily entitled to notice and a hearing before the government can seize real estate through civil forfeiture. The ruling came less than six months after the Court's decision in *Austin v. United States,* holding that the Eighth Amendment's Cruel and Unusual Punishment Clause limits the government's power to seize property in forfeiture proceedings.

Libretti v. United States (516 U.S. 29), decided by an 8–1 vote, Nov. 7, 1995; O'Connor wrote the opinion; Stevens dissented.

A federal judge is not required to determine the factual basis for a property forfeiture agreed to by a defendant as part of a guilty plea.

Bennis v. Michigan (516 U.S. 442), decided by a 5–4 vote, March 4, 1996; Rehnquist wrote the opinion; Stevens, Kennedy, Souter and Breyer dissented.

The government can seize property even if the owner had no knowledge that someone else was using it for criminal activity. The decision rejected a Michigan woman's claim that her constitutional rights were violated by the forfeiture of a car she co-owned with her husband after his arrest for having sex with a prostitute in the car. She argued that the Fourteenth Amendment's Due Process Clause required the government to recognize an "innocent owner defense."

Degen v. United States (517 U.S. 820), decided by a 9–0 vote, June 10, 1996; Kennedy wrote the opinion.

A federal court cannot bar a fugitive criminal defendant from presenting, through an attorney, a defense in a related civil forfeiture proceeding.

United States v. Ursery (518 U.S. 267), decided by an 8–1 vote, June 24, 1996; Rehnquist wrote the opinion; Stevens dissented in part.

The government can both prosecute an individual and seek to seize his or her property by a civil forfeiture proceeding without violating the Constitution's Double Jeopardy Clause. The ruling backed the government in overturning two federal appeals court decisions that the combined prosecution and forfeiture actions violated the constitutional ban against successive punishments.

HABEAS CORPUS

Dobbs v. Zant, Warden (506 U.S. 357), decided by a 7–2 vote, Jan. 19, 1993; *per curiam* (unsigned) opinion; Rehnquist and White dissented.

A death row inmate in Georgia was allowed a second chance to invalidate his sentence on grounds of ineffective assistance of counsel after belatedly obtaining a transcript of his lawyer's closing argument. The Court ruled that a federal appeals court was wrong to refuse to reopen the inmate's federal habeas corpus petition.

Graham v. Collins, Director, Texas Department of Criminal Justice, Institutional Division (506 U.S. 461), decided by a 5–4 vote, Jan. 25, 1993; White wrote the opinion; Souter, Blackmun, Stevens and O'Connor dissented.

The Court turned aside a Texas death row inmate's argument that the state's former capital punishment law improperly limited a jury's role in considering evidence favorable to defendants. The Court rejected the inmate's federal habeas corpus petition on the ground that he was asking for a new rule of constitutional law.

Brecht v. Abrahamson, Superintendent, Dodge Correctional Institution (507 U.S. 619), decided by a 5–4 vote, April 21, 1993; Rehnquist wrote the opinion; White, Blackmun, O'Connor and Souter dissented.

Improper use at trial of a defendant's silence after being given *Miranda* warnings is not grounds for federal habeas corpus relief unless the evidence had a substantial effect on the verdict. The Court announced a relaxed rule for reviewing trial-related errors in habeas corpus cases. Previously, the Court had required that errors be proved harmless beyond a reasonable doubt. Under the new standard, habeas corpus relief is available only if an error had "substantial and injurious effect or influence in determining the jury's verdict."

Withrow v. Williams (507 U.S. 680), decided by a 5–4 vote, April 21, 1993; Souter wrote the opinion; O'Connor, Rehnquist, Scalia and Thomas dissented.

Federal courts in habeas corpus cases may throw out state court convictions when police fail to advise a suspect of his *Miranda* rights before interrogating him. The decision ordered a new trial for a defendant in a double murder case who had confessed without having been advised of his right to remain silent.

Gilmore v. Taylor (508 U.S. 333), decided by a 7–2 vote, June 7, 1993; Rehnquist wrote the opinion; Blackmun and Stevens dissented.

The Court refused to grant federal habeas relief based on a decision finding a constitutional defect in part of the standard jury instructions used in Illinois murder cases.

Caspari, Superintendent, Missouri Eastern Correctional Center v. Bohlen (510 U.S. 383), decided by an 8–1 vote, Feb. 23, 1994; O'Connor wrote the opinion; Stevens dissented.

The Court denied habeas corpus relief to a Missouri inmate who claimed the Double Jeopardy Clause prevented prosecutors from having a second chance to enhance his sentence under the state's persistent offender statute. Without deciding the merits of the inmate's claim, the Court held he was not entitled to rely on a "new rule" of law to win habeas corpus relief.

Schlup v. Delo, Superintendent, Potosi Correctional Center (513 U.S. 298), decided by a 5–4 vote, Jan. 23, 1995; Stevens wrote the opinion; Rehnquist, Scalia, Kennedy and Thomas dissented.

The Court made it somewhat easier for a state death row inmate who claims to be innocent to win a federal court hearing on alleged constitutional errors at his trial. The decision relaxed the standard for permitting a death row inmate to avoid the normal rule against consideration of successive habeas corpus petitions in federal courts. The Court held that an inmate is entitled to a hearing on his claim if he shows that a constitutional violation "probably resulted" in the conviction of one who is actually innocent.

Duncan, Warden v. Henry (513 U.S. 364), decided by an 8–1 vote, Jan. 23, 1995; *per curiam* (unsigned) opinion; Stevens dissented.

The Court tightened the requirements for prison inmates to raise constitutional issues in state courts before using the same claims to challenge convictions through federal habeas corpus proceedings.

O'Neal v. McAninch, Warden (513 U.S. 432), decided by a 6–3 vote, Feb. 21, 1995; Breyer wrote the opinion; Thomas, Rehnquist and Scalia dissented.

A federal judge should grant a state prison inmate's habeas corpus petition if the prisoner proves a constitutional error at trial and the judge is in doubt whether the error might have affected the outcome.

The decision reversed a ruling by the Sixth U.S. Circuit Court of Appeals requiring that inmates challenging their state court convictions had the burden of showing prejudice from a constitutional violation at trial. The Court in 1993 ruled that an error should be considered harmless unless it had a substantial effect on the trial but left unresolved whether the state or the inmate had the burden of proof on the question.

Goeke, Superintendent, Renz Correctional Center v. Branch (514 U.S. 115), decided by a 9–0 vote, March 20, 1995; *per curiam* (unsigned) opinion.

The Court summarily wiped out a federal appeals court ruling that would have limited the power of state courts to dismiss appeals by defendants who become fugitives while their appeals are pending.

The Court said the appeals court ruling amounted to a new rule of law that could not be retroactively applied in a habeas corpus case. The Court acknowledged that it had adopted a similar limit on the power of courts to dismiss appeals by fugitive defendants in 1993 but said that ruling applied only in federal, not state, courts.

Kyles v. Whitley, Warden (514 U.S. 419), decided by a 5–4 vote, April 19, 1995; Souter wrote the opinion; Scalia, Rehnquist, Kennedy and Thomas dissented.

The Court ordered a new trial for a Louisiana death row inmate because the prosecution failed to disclose material evidence it found that might have produced a different result at trial.

Garlotte v. Fordice, Governor of Mississippi (515 U.S. 65), decided by a 7–2 vote, May 30, 1995; Ginsburg wrote the opinion; Thomas and Rehnquist dissented.

A state prison inmate serving consecutive sentences for separate offenses can use federal habeas corpus law to challenge a conviction even if he has completed the sentence for that offense.

Thompson v. Keohane, Warden (516 U.S. 99), decided by a 7–2 vote, Nov. 29, 1995; Ginsburg wrote the opinion; Thomas and Rehnquist dissented.

The Court somewhat strengthened the ability of prison inmates to challenge their convictions by attacking state court rulings permitting the use of statements made during police interrogation. The Court held that federal judges must make an independent determination whether an inmate was "in custody" during questioning. Police need not give the so-called *Miranda* warnings to a suspect who is not in custody.

Lonchar v. Thomas, Warden (517 U.S. 314), decided by 9–0 and 5–4 votes, April 1, 1996; Breyer wrote the opinion; Rehnquist, Scalia, Kennedy and Thomas concurred in the result, but disagreed with one of the legal holdings.

A federal appeals court was wrong to dismiss on "general equitable grounds" a state death row inmate's first federal habeas corpus petition filed on the day of his scheduled execution.

Calderon, Warden v. Moore (518 U.S. 149), decided by a 9–0 vote, June 17, 1996; *per curiam* (unsigned) opinion.

The Court summarily rebuked a federal appeals court for dismissing a state's appeal of a habeas corpus ruling granting a new trial to a death row inmate. The Court said the Ninth U.S. Circuit Court of Appeals was wrong to dismiss the state's appeal as moot once the state had scheduled the inmate's retrial. ". . . [A] decision in the State's favor would release it from the burden of the new trial itself," the Court said.

Gray v. Netherland, Warden (518 U.S. 152), decided by a 5–4 vote, June 20, 1996; Rehnquist wrote the opinion; Ginsburg, Stevens, Souter and Breyer dissented.

The Court blocked a new trial for a Virginia death row inmate by throwing out a lower court decision that prosecutors surprised him by using evidence at his sentencing hearing linking him to another murder. But the Court left open the possibility that the inmate could win a new trial by showing that prosecutors deliberately misled him.

Felker v. Turpin, Warden (518 U.S.___), decided by a 9–0 vote, June 28, 1996; Rehnquist wrote the opinion.

The Court upheld part of a new law aimed at limiting death row inmates' ability to challenge their convictions and sentences in federal court, but said inmates can still bring pleas directly to the Court itself. The decision rejected a challenge to a provision of the Antiterrorism and Effective Death Penalty Act of 1996, which required inmates to obtain permission from a federal appeals court before filing a second habeas corpus petition.

INSANITY

Shannon v. United States (512 U.S. 573), decided by a 7–2 vote, June 24, 1994; Thomas wrote the opinion; Stevens and Blackmun dissented.

Federal judges are not required to tell jurors that a defendant found not guilty by reason of insanity may be committed to a mental hospital after a further hearing.

INTERROGATION

Stansbury v. California (511 U.S. 318), decided by a 9–0 vote, April 26, 1994; *per curiam* (unsigned) opinion.

A California man convicted of the rape-murder of a young girl was given a second chance to win a new trial because police failed to give him *Miranda* warnings at the start of interrogation. The Court said the California Supreme Court applied the wrong standard in upholding use of a statement the defendant gave to police while being questioned about the 1982 slaying. The California court had ruled that no *Miranda* warnings were required because police initially considered the defendant to be a witness, not a suspect. But the Court said that objective circumstances, not a police officer's subjective belief, determine whether an individual is in custody and must be given *Miranda* warnings. The ruling returned the case to the California court for a decision under that standard.

United States v. Alvarez-Sanchez (511 U.S. 350), decided by a 9–0 vote, May 2, 1994; Thomas wrote the opinion.

A suspect who confesses to a federal crime while in state custody cannot use a federal law governing the time of the initial hearing before a magistrate to block the use of the confession. A federal law provides that a confession is not inadmissible because of delay in bringing a suspect before a magistrate if the hearing takes place within six hours of the arrest.

Davis v. United States (512 U.S. 452), decided by 9–0 and 5–4 votes, June 24, 1994; O'Connor wrote the opinion; Souter, Blackmun, Stevens and Ginsburg concurred in the judgment but disagreed with the legal ruling.

Police do not need to stop questioning a suspect who makes an ambiguous statement about wanting an attorney or try to clarify the suspect's wishes about having legal help.

JURIES

United States v. Olano (507 U.S. 725), decided by a 6–3 vote, April 26, 1993; O'Connor wrote the opinion; Stevens, White and Blackmun dissented.

A federal appeals court may not reverse a criminal conviction on its own because a trial judge wrongly allowed alternate jurors to be present during jury deliberations.

Sullivan v. Louisiana (508 U.S. 275), decided by a 9–0 vote, June 1, 1993; Scalia wrote the opinion.

A criminal conviction must be thrown out if a jury is not properly instructed on the need for proof beyond a reasonable doubt before returning a guilty verdict. The Court said that an improper instruction on the reasonable doubt standard can never be deemed a harmless error that does not require reversal.

Victor v. Nebraska (511 U.S. 1), decided by 9–0 and 7–2 votes, March 22, 1994; O'Connor wrote the opinion; Blackmun and Souter dissented in part.

The Court criticized but refused to prohibit jury instructions used in many states to define the prosecution's burden to prove a criminal defendant guilty beyond a reasonable doubt.

United States v. Gaudin (515 U.S. 506), decided by a 9–0 vote, June 19, 1995; Scalia wrote the opinion.

A trial judge violated the jury trial rights of a defendant charged under the federal false statement statute—section 1001 of Title 18—by refusing to allow jurors to decide whether the statements were "material" as required for a conviction.

JURY SELECTION

Purkett, Superintendent, Farmington Corrections Center v. Elem (514 U.S. 765), decided by a 7–2 vote, May 15, 1995; *per curiam* (unsigned) opinion; Stevens and Breyer dissented.

The Court eased the burden on prosecutors to refute charges of improperly using peremptory challenges to exclude potential jurors because of their race. The justification must be race-neutral but not necessarily rational, the Court said.

JURY TRIALS

Lewis v. United States (518 U.S.___), decided by 7–2 and 5–4 votes, June 24, 1996; O'Connor wrote the opinion; Kennedy and Breyer concurred in the judgment but disagreed with the legal holding; Stevens and Ginsburg dissented.

A defendant has no right to a trial by jury for an offense punishable by six months' imprisonment or less even if he faces multiple counts that could carry a longer cumulative sentence.

PAROLE

California Department of Corrections v. Morales (514 U.S. 499), decided by a 7–2 vote, April 25, 1995; Thomas wrote the opinion; Stevens and Souter dissented.

States may retroactively reduce the frequency of parole hearings for convicted murderers without violating the Constitution's Ex Post Facto Clause.

PRELIMINARY HEARINGS

El Vocero de Puerto Rico v. Puerto Rico (506 U.S. 147), decided by a 9–0 vote, May 17, 1993; *per curiam* (unsigned) opinion.

Puerto Rico's law providing for closed preliminary hearings unless the defendant requests an open hearing was held unconstitutional. In a brief opinion issued without hearing argument, the Court said the law conflicted with its 1982 ruling that generally required preliminary hearings be open.

PRISONS AND JAILS

Helling v. McKinney (509 U.S. 25), decided by a 7–2 vote, June 18, 1993; White wrote the opinion; Thomas and Scalia dissented.

The Court opened the door to prison inmate suits claiming that involuntary exposure to second-hand tobacco smoke poses an unreasonable risk to health in violation of the Eighth Amendment's ban on cruel and unusual punishment. The ruling, however, laid out a number of conditions an inmate must meet to prevail in a suit over so-called environmental tobacco smoke. The decision returned to lower federal courts a suit

SEARCH AND SEIZURE

The right of the people to be secure in their persons, houses, papers and effects, against unreasonable searches and seizures, shall not be violated, and no warrants shall issue, but upon probable cause, supported by oath or affirmation and particularly describing the place to be searched, and the persons or things to be seized.

Fourth Amendment, U.S. Constitution

brought by a Nevada state prisoner whose cellmate smoked five packs of cigarettes a day.

Farmer v. Brennan, Warden (511 U.S. 825), decided by a 9–0 vote, June 6, 1994; Souter wrote the opinion.

Prison officials may be held liable for injuries to an inmate only if they know the prisoner faces a substantial risk of harm and fail to take reasonable measures to prevent it. The ruling set a strict standard for prisoners to meet in civil rights suits brought under the Court's 1991 decision *Wilson v. Seiter.* That ruling allowed prison authorities to be held liable for "deliberate indifference" to an inmate's health or safety.

Sandin, Unit Team Manager, Halawa Correctional Facility v. Conner (515 U.S. 472), decided by a 5–4 vote, June 19, 1995; Rehnquist wrote the opinion; Breyer, Stevens, Souter and Ginsburg dissented.

Inmates must show that they are being subjected to unusual and significant hardship in order to bring a due process challenge to their treatment by prison management. The decision raised the standard for a common type of inmate suit by repudiating a line of Court decisions since 1979.

Lewis, Director, Arizona Department of Corrections v. Casey (518 U.S.___), decided by 8–1 and 5–4 votes, June 24, 1996; Scalia wrote the opinion; Souter, Ginsburg and Breyer dissented in part; Stevens dissented.

The Court overturned a federal judge's order requiring Arizona to expand its prison law libraries and made it harder for inmates in future cases to show they have been unconstitutionally denied access to the courts. The ruling narrowed the Court's 1977 decision, *Bounds v. Smith,* that had required corrections systems to provide inmates access to law libraries and "persons trained in the law."

RIGHT TO COUNSEL

Lockhart, Director, Arkansas Department of Correction v. Fretwell (506 U.S. 364), decided by a 7–2 vote, Jan. 25, 1993; Rehnquist wrote the opinion; Stevens and Blackmun dissented.

A death row inmate lost a bid for a new trial based on his attorney's failure to raise an objection at trial under a court decision on the books at the time but later overturned. The Court

rejected the inmate's argument that the lawyer's "deficient performance" amounted to ineffective assistance of counsel in violation of the Sixth Amendment and said the inmate had not suffered any "prejudice" as defined in earlier cases dealing with the effective assistance of counsel.

SEARCH AND SEIZURE

United States v. Padilla (508 U.S. 83), decided by a 9–0 vote, May 3, 1993; *per curiam* opinion.

Criminal co-conspirators have no legal right to contest police searches of one another's cars, homes or other possessions. A co-conspirator must prove an individual property or privacy right to block a police search, the Court said.

Minnesota v. Dickerson (508 U.S. 366), decided by a 6–3 vote, June 7, 1993; White wrote the opinion; Rehnquist, Blackmun and Thomas dissented in part.

Police may seize drugs or other contraband from a suspect if they can feel the material during a limited "stop-and-frisk" search for weapons. The Court adopted a "plain feel" exception to the general rule requiring police to have either a warrant or probable cause to believe a crime has been committed before searching a suspect.

Arizona v. Evans (514 U.S. 1), decided by a 7–2 vote, March 1, 1995; Rehnquist wrote the opinion; Ginsburg and Stevens dissented.

The Court refused to bar the use of evidence obtained from a defendant after he was arrested on the basis of an erroneous computer warrant. But it limited the ruling to mistakes made by court employees, not law enforcement officials.

Wilson v. Arkansas (514 U.S. 927), decided by a 9–0 vote, May 22, 1995; Thomas wrote the opinion.

Police should ordinarily knock and announce their identity before entering a home with a search warrant. But an unannounced entry may be reasonable if police fear physical violence or destruction of evidence.

Ornelas v. United States (517 U.S. 690), decided by an 8–1 vote, May 28, 1996; Rehnquist wrote the opinion; Scalia dissented.

Appellate courts should conduct an independent review of lower court decisions on whether police have adequate grounds to make an investigatory stop or warrantless search.

Whren v. United States (517 U.S. 806), decided by a 9–0 vote, June 10, 1996; Scalia wrote the opinion.

Police may temporarily detain a motorist if they have probable cause to believe a traffic violation has occurred even if they are primarily interested in some other law enforcement purpose, such as looking for drugs.

Pennsylvania v. Labron (518 U.S.___), decided by a 7–2 vote, July 1, 1996; *per curiam* (unsigned) opinion; Ginsburg and Stevens dissented.

The Court summarily overturned two rulings by the Pennsylvania Supreme Court that limited police power to conduct warrantless searches of an automobile after arresting the driver or passengers.

SENTENCING

Parke, Warden v. Raley (506 U.S. 20), decided by a 9–0 vote, Dec. 1, 1992; O'Connor wrote the opinion.

A state may count convictions based on guilty pleas to increase a repeat offender's sentence even if there is no transcript of the earlier proceedings.

United States v. Dunnigan (507 U.S. 87), decided by a 9–0 vote, Feb. 23, 1993; Kennedy wrote the opinion.

A federal sentencing guideline that permits a judge to give a stiffer sentence to a defendant who lies on the witness stand does not violate the defendant's right to testify. The guidelines provide for increasing a defendant's sentence if the defendant "willfully impeded or obstructed, or attempted to impede or obstruct the administration of justice during the investigation or prosecution" of the case.

Stinson v. United States (508 U.S. 36), decided by a 9–0 vote, May 3, 1993; Kennedy wrote the opinion.

The Court strengthened the power of the U.S. Sentencing Commission by ruling that federal courts generally must follow the commentary as well as the main provisions of the commission's guidelines manual.

Deal v. United States (508 U.S. 129), decided by a 6–3 vote, May 17, 1993; Scalia wrote the opinion; Stevens, Blackmun and O'Connor dissented.

A federal law providing a mandatory 20-year sentence for a "second or subsequent conviction" of a crime committed with the use of a firearm can be applied to a defendant convicted of multiple counts in a single trial.

Smith v. United States (508 U.S. 233), decided by a 6–3 vote, June 1, 1993; O'Connor wrote the opinion; Scalia, Stevens and Souter dissented.

A defendant who offered to swap a machine gun for drugs was properly sentenced under a provision imposing a mandatory 30-year sentence for using a firearm during a drug-related crime.

Wisconsin v. Mitchell (508 U.S. 476), decided by a 9–0 vote, June 11, 1993; Rehnquist wrote the opinion.

States may impose increased penalties on criminals who select their victims on the basis of race, religion, ethnic origin or other protected status. The Court held that so-called hate crime penalty enhancement laws do not violate the First Amendment's guarantee of freedom of speech.

United States v. Granderson (511 U.S. 39), decided by a 7–2 vote, March 22, 1994; Ginsburg wrote the opinion; Scalia and

Kennedy concurred in the judgment; Rehnquist and Thomas dissented.

The Court eased the impact of a law requiring a prison term for any defendant found in possession of drugs while on probation. The drug possession provision—part of the 1988 Anti-Drug Act—requires a judge to revoke a defendant's probation and "sentence the defendant to not less than one-third of the original sentence." Some federal appeals courts interpreted the law to mean a prison term equal to one-third of the length of the probation. Others read it to require imprisonment for one-third of the possible sentence for the defendant's crime. The Court ruled for a minimum sentence of one-third of the maximum term that the defendant could have received originally.

Beecham v. United States (511 U.S. 368), decided by a 9–0 vote, May 16, 1994; O'Connor wrote the opinion.

A state's decision to restore the civil rights of a convicted felon does not wipe out a prior federal conviction for purposes of the federal law prohibiting possession of firearms by felons.

Custis v. United States (511 U.S. 485), decided by a 6–3 vote, May 23, 1994; Rehnquist wrote the opinion; Souter, Blackmun and Stevens dissented.

The Court sharply limited defendants' ability to challenge the constitutionality of prior conviction used to impose stiffer prison sentences under a federal law on armed "career criminals." The Court ruled that a defendant being sentenced under provisions of the Armed Career Criminal Act of 1984 cannot, with one exception, contest the validity of earlier state court convictions used to lengthen the defendant's new prison term. The only exception, the Court said, is in cases where the defendant had been denied the right to counsel.

Nichols v. United States (511 U.S. 738), decided by a 6–3 vote, June 6, 1994; Rehnquist wrote the opinion; Blackmun, Stevens and Ginsburg dissented.

Judges can use a defendant's prior misdemeanor conviction to lengthen a new prison sentence even if the defendant had no lawyer in the earlier case. The ruling overturned a splintered decision in a 1980 case, *Baldasar v. Illinois,* in which the Court held that the Sixth Amendment's right to counsel prevented the use of an uncounseled misdemeanor conviction to convert a later misdemeanor into a felony.

Reno, Attorney General v. Koray (515 U.S. 39), decided by an 8–1 vote, June 5, 1995; Rehnquist wrote the opinion; Stevens dissented.

Federal prisoners are not entitled to credit for time served in private community treatment centers or halfway houses prior to sentencing. The Court held that time spent in a private treatment center or halfway house does not amount to "official detention" for purposes of federal sentencing law.

Neal v. United States (516 U.S. 284), decided by a 9–0 vote, Jan. 22, 1996; Kennedy wrote the opinion.

Reaffirming a five-year-old precedent, the Court said sentences for defendants in LSD cases must be based on the weight of the material carrying the drug, not the weight of the drug itself. The ruling effectively nullified a 1993 guideline by the U.S. Sentencing Commission. LSD is ordinarily diffused in blotter paper before distribution. The guideline directed judges to use a per-dose estimate of the weight of the drug in setting sentences in LSD cases, instead of the total weight of the blotter paper.

Koon v. United States (518 U.S. 81), decided by 9–0, 8–1 and 6–3 votes, June 13, 1996; Kennedy wrote the opinion; Stevens dissented in part on one issue; Souter, Ginsburg and Breyer dissented in part on another issue.

Federal courts of appeals should defer to a lower court judge's decisions to depart from Sentencing Guidelines except in cases of abuse of judicial discretion or legal error.

Melendez v. United States (518 U.S. 120), decided by a 7–2 vote, June 17, 1996; Thomas wrote the opinion; Breyer and O'Connor dissented in part.

A federal defendant cannot be given a sentence below the statutory minimum in exchange for cooperating with the government unless the prosecution explicitly asks the judge to do so. The ruling upheld a strict interpretation of procedures under the U.S. Sentencing Guidelines for reducing sentences for defendants who provide "substantial assistance" in the investigation or prosecution of other offenders.

SPEEDY TRIAL

Reed v. Farley, Superintendent, Indiana State Prison (512 U.S. 339), decided by a 5–4 vote, June 20, 1994; Ginsburg wrote a plurality opinion; Blackmun, Stevens, Kennedy and Souter dissented.

The Court barred federal habeas corpus relief to an Indiana prison inmate who was brought to trial after the deadline set by an interstate agreement for handling prisoners from other states. The ruling involved a provision in the Interstate Agreement on Detainers that required an inmate transferred from one state for prosecution in another state to be brought to trial within 120 days. The compact provides for dismissal of the charge if the deadline is not met.

MISCELLANEOUS CRIMINAL CASE

Negonsott v. Samuels, Warden (507 U.S. 99), decided by a 9–0 vote, Feb. 24, 1993; Rehnquist wrote the opinion.

Kansas state courts have jurisdiction, under a federal law—the Kansas Act of 1940—to prosecute violations of state criminal law committed by or against Native Americans on reservations.

Election Law

CAMPAIGN FINANCE

Colorado Republican Federal Campaign Committee v. Federal Election Commission (518 U.S.___), decided by a 7–2 vote, June 26, 1996; Breyer wrote a plurality opinion; Stevens and Ginsburg dissented.

The Court held that political parties may make unlimited independent expenditures in support of congressional candidates, but it stopped short of invalidating all federal campaign contribution limits for parties.

FEDERAL ELECTION COMMISSION

Federal Election Commission v. NRA Political Victory Fund (513 U.S. 88), decided by a 7–1 vote, Dec. 6, 1994; Rehnquist wrote the opinion; Stevens dissented; Ginsburg did not participate in the case.

The Federal Election Commission (FEC) has no independent statutory authority to represent itself in cases before the Supreme Court. The procedural ruling turned aside the FEC's effort to overturn a federal appeals court decision that it had been illegally constituted for many years because two congressional representatives served as nonvoting members. Without reaching the separation of powers issue, the Court said that the law establishing the FEC gives it no authority to pursue cases beyond the appeals court level.

REAPPORTIONMENT AND REDISTRICTING

Growe, Secretary of State of Minnesota v. Emison (507 U.S. 25), decided by a 9–0 vote, Feb. 23, 1993; Scalia wrote the opinion.

Federal courts generally should defer to state courts if both are hearing legal challenges to state redistricting plans. The decision threw out a federal court ruling that had blocked a legislative redistricting plan devised by a state court and instead adopted its own plan.

Voinovich, Governor of Ohio v. Quilter, Speaker Pro Tempore of Ohio House of Representatives (507 U.S. 146), decided by a 9–0 vote, March 2, 1993; O'Connor wrote the opinion.

The federal Voting Rights Act does not prevent states from deliberately creating legislative districts dominated by minority voters unless the plan dilutes the minority bloc's voting strength. The decision overturned a lower court's ruling that blocked an Ohio legislative redistricting plan. The Court also reversed a finding that the plan violated the Fifteenth Amendment, saying there was no evidence of intentional discrimination against blacks. The case was remanded for further hearings on whether the population disparities between legislative districts under the plan violated the Fourteenth Amendment.

Shaw v. Reno, Attorney General (509 U.S. 630), decided by a 5–4 vote, June 28, 1993; O'Connor wrote the opinion; White, Blackmun, Stevens and Souter dissented.

White voters can use the Equal Protection Clause to challenge a congressional redistricting plan creating a highly irregular district that can be understood only as an effort to separate voters by race. Federal courts can order the district redrawn if the plan lacks sufficient justification. The Court's decision opened the door to new legal contests over "majority-minority" districts for congressional or state legislative seats. The ruling reinstated a challenge by white voters in North Carolina to the state's new Twelfth Congressional District. The serpentine 160-mile-long district was drawn to include a majority black population and elected a black representative to Congress in 1992.

Johnson, Speaker of the Florida House of Representatives v. De Grandy (512 U.S. 997), decided by a 7–2 vote, June 30, 1994; Souter wrote the opinion; Thomas and Scalia dissented.

The federal Voting Rights Act does not require legislative districting plans to maximize the number of districts in which minority groups are in the majority. Instead, the Court ruled, state legislatures usually can satisfy the Voting Rights Act if minority voters form "effective voting majorities in a number of districts roughly proportional to the minority voters' respective shares in the voting-age population."

United States v. Hays (515 U.S. 737), decided by a 9–0 vote, June 29, 1995; O'Connor wrote the opinion.

The Court sidestepped a decision on a racial redistricting plan for congressional seats in Louisiana on grounds that the voters contesting the plan did not live in the district being challenged. The Court held that the voters lacked standing to challenge the plan.

Miller v. Johnson (515 U.S. 900), decided by a 5–4 vote, June 29, 1995; Kennedy wrote the opinion; Ginsburg, Stevens, Souter and Breyer dissented.

The use of race as "the predominant factor" in drawing voting district lines is presumptively unconstitutional. The ruling required the state of Georgia to revise a plan that created three congressional districts with majority black populations.

Shaw v. Hunt, Governor of North Carolina (517 U.S. 899), decided by a 5–4 vote, June 13, 1996; Rehnquist wrote the opinion; Stevens, Souter, Ginsburg and Breyer dissented.

The Court struck down a majority-black congressional district in North Carolina, saying the plan was racially motivated and failed to serve a "compelling state interest" needed to justify race-based districting. The ruling—the Court's second in the case—overturned a three-judge district court's decision to uphold the bizarrely shaped district that tied together predominantly black areas in several noncontiguous metropolitan areas.

In its first ruling (*Shaw v. Reno, Attorney General*, 1993), the Court held that racial redistricting plans are subject to challenge under the Equal Protection Clause. The Court then remanded the case, brought by white voters who lived in the newly drawn Twelfth Congressional District, for further consideration by the three-judge court.

On remand, the three-judge court agreed the plan classified voters by race, but said it was justified by the state's interest in eradicating past discrimination and in complying with the federal Voting Rights Act. Reversing that decision, the Court held that race was the predominant motive in drawing the district and found none of the justifications sufficient to satisfy the "strict scrutiny" applied to racial classifications.

Bush, Governor of Texas v. Vera (517 U.S. 952), decided by a 5–4 vote, June 13, 1996; O'Connor wrote the plurality opinion; Stevens, Souter, Ginsburg and Breyer dissented.

The Court struck down three majority-minority congressional districts in Texas, saying the district lines were primarily motivated by race and not justified by legitimate state interests. But a majority of the justices said states can deliberately create majority-minority districts in some circumstances.

TERM LIMITS

U.S. Term Limits, Inc. v. Thornton (514 U.S. 779), decided by a 5–4 vote, May 22, 1995; Stevens wrote the opinion; Thomas, Rehnquist, O'Connor and Scalia dissented.

Neither Congress nor the states can directly limit the number of terms for members of Congress or try to accomplish the same goal by handicapping incumbents' access to the ballot. The Court held that congressional term limit measures adopted in nearly half the states were unconstitutional because they attempted to impose qualifications for serving in Congress beyond those listed in the Constitution.

VOTING RIGHTS

Holder v. Hall (512 U.S. 874), decided by a 5–4 vote, June 30, 1994; Kennedy wrote a plurality opinion; Blackmun, Stevens, Souter and Ginsburg dissented.

The size of a governing body—in this case a single county commissioner with executive and legislative authority—is not subject to challenge under the federal Voting Rights Act. The decision barred a statutory challenge to the unusual governmental structure used in rural Bleckley County, Georgia. Blacks, who made up about 20 percent of the county's population, claimed the single-member commission violated the Voting Rights Act by "diluting" their opportunity to elect blacks to office. The Court rejected the claim by saying there was "no objective and workable standard" to use in deciding how many members the county commission should have.

Morse v. Republican Party of Virginia (517 U.S. 186), decided by a 5–4 vote, March 27, 1996; Stevens wrote the main opinion; Thomas, Rehnquist, Scalia and Kennedy dissented.

The Voting Rights Act's requirement for some states to obtain prior Justice Department approval of changes in voting procedures applies to convention rules adopted by major political parties that may limit the ability of voters to participate. The ruling backed a suit brought by three University of Virginia law students challenging a registration fee imposed by the state Republican Party to participate in the convention that selected its 1994 nominee for the U.S. Senate. The students said the fee—$35 or $45—violated the Voting Rights Act provision, Section 5, requiring Virginia and a handful of other states to obtain "preclearance" of "any voting qualification or prerequisite" established after the law took effect.

Environmental Law

ENDANGERED SPECIES ACT

Babbitt, Secretary of the Interior v. Sweet Home Chapter of Communities for a Great Oregon (515 U.S. 687), decided by a 6–3 vote, June 29, 1995; Stevens wrote the opinion; Scalia, Rehnquist and Thomas dissented.

The Endangered Species Act gives the federal government authority to regulate the use of private land in order to protect habitat for rare wildlife species.

HAZARDOUS WASTE

City of Chicago v. Environmental Defense Fund (511 U.S. 328), decided by a 7–2 vote, May 2, 1994; Scalia wrote the opinion; Stevens and O'Connor dissented.

Federal law does not exempt the ash produced by municipal incinerators from the costly regulations that govern disposal of hazardous waste. The decision literally interpreted a 1984 amendment to the federal Resource Conservation and Recovery Act, which gives the Environmental Protection Agency (EPA) broad powers to regulate generation, transportation, storage and disposal of hazardous waste. Municipalities contended that incinerators, which burn trash and produce energy in the process, were exempt from the regulations under the 1984 amendment and an earlier EPA regulation.

Key Tronic Corp. v. United States (511 U.S. 809), decided by a 6–3 vote, June 6, 1994; Stevens wrote the opinion; Scalia, Blackmun and Thomas dissented.

Private parties cannot recover attorneys' fees for legal proceedings under the federal Superfund law to force others to share the costs of cleaning up toxic waste sites. The ruling settled a conflict between lower federal courts over how to interpret provisions of the Comprehensive Environmental Response, Compensation and Liability Act, first passed in 1980 and amended in 1986. The law seeks to spread the cost of toxic waste cleanups by permitting one party—typically, the property owner—to sue polluters for "any . . . necessary costs of response" incurred in cleaning up the site. The Court ruled the law does not authorize recovery of legal fees related to litigation or negotiation over cleanup liability.

SOLID WASTE

Oregon Waste Systems, Inc. v. Department of Environmental Quality (511 U.S. 93), decided by a 7–2 vote, April 4, 1994; Thomas wrote the opinion; Rehnquist and Blackmun dissented.

A surcharge imposed by the state of Oregon for disposing of out-of-state solid waste was struck down as an unconstitutional discrimination against interstate commerce.

C & A Carbone, Inc. v. Town of Clarkstown (511 U.S. 383), decided by a 6–3 vote, May 16, 1994; Kennedy wrote the opinion; Souter, Rehnquist and Blackmun dissented.

The Court barred local governments from passing laws requiring all trash generated within their borders to be processed at a designated waste-treatment facility.

TOXIC WASTE

Meghrig v. KFC Western, Inc. (516 U.S. 479), decided by a 9–0 vote, March 19, 1996; O'Connor wrote the opinion.

Owners of contaminated property cannot use the 1976 federal Resource and Conservation Recovery Act to recover toxic waste cleanup costs from the previous owners of the property. The Court said the citizen suit provisions in the law did not authorize a private cause of action to recover past costs for cleaning up toxic wastes. The ruling did not affect legal remedies under other federal or state laws.

WATER

PUD No. 1 of Jefferson County v. Washington Department of Ecology (511 U.S. 700), decided by a 7–2 vote, May 31, 1994; O'Connor wrote the opinion; Thomas and Scalia dissented.

States can set stricter environmental standards, including minimum water flow requirements, for hydroelectric projects than those imposed by federal law. The decision upheld efforts by Washington State to limit the diversion of water by a planned dam on a river in the Olympic National Forest in order to protect fish habitats.

Federal Government

CENSUS

Wisconsin v. City of New York (517 U.S. 1), decided by a 9–0 vote, March 20, 1996; Rehnquist wrote the opinion.

The federal government has no constitutional duty to correct an acknowledged undercounting in the census of African Americans and other minority groups in the nation's cities. The decision rejected an effort by New York, several other cities, and some civil rights organizations to reverse the decision in 1991 by the Bush administration's secretary of commerce, Robert Mosbacher, not to make a statistical adjustment in the actual population count. The Census Bureau had acknowledged that minorities are undercounted and had recommended using a statistical estimation method to adjust the figures.

FEDERAL EMPLOYEES

Gutierrez de Martinez v. Lamagno (515 U.S. 417), decided by a 5–4 vote, June 14, 1995; Ginsburg wrote the opinion; Souter, Rehnquist, Scalia and Thomas dissented.

Federal courts can review a Justice Department determination that a federal employee named in a civil suit was acting within the scope of employment and should be dismissed from the suit. The ruling resolved an issue involving a 1988 law called the Westfall Act that, as the Court explained, only rarely affects a plaintiff's chances of recovery. Under the law, once a federal employee is dismissed from a suit, the United States is substituted as a defendant, and the case can proceed under the Federal Tort Claims Act.

FEDERAL REGULATION

Reiter v. Cooper, Trustee for Carolina Motor Express, Inc. (507 U.S. 258), decided by an 8–1 vote, March 8, 1993; Scalia wrote the opinion; Blackmun dissented.

A shipper may seek to recover money paid under an "unreasonable rate" charged by a motor carrier through a counterclaim in a legal action initiated by the carrier. The shipper does not have to present the "unreasonable rate" claim first to the Interstate Commerce Commission, but a federal court may refer the issue to the agency after balancing the equities in an individual case.

CSX Transportation, Inc. v. Easterwood (507 U.S. 658), decided by a 7–2 vote, April 21, 1993; White wrote the opinion; Thomas and Souter dissented in part.

Federal railroad safety regulations preempt a state law wrongful death action based on a claim that a railroad train was traveling at excessive speed. But the regulations do not preempt a claim based on the alleged absence of proper warning devices at a street crossing.

Cisneros, Secretary of Housing and Urban Development v. Alpine Ridge Group (508 U.S. 10), decided by a 9–0 vote, May 3, 1993; White wrote the opinion.

The federal government may use market studies to limit annual adjustments in rental subsidies paid to developers of low-income housing.

Federal Communications Commission v. Beach Communications, Inc. (508 U.S. 307), decided by a 9–0 vote, June 1, 1993; Thomas wrote the opinion.

The Court upheld a provision of the 1984 Cable Communications Policy Act that exempted some "private cable systems" serving big apartment buildings from local franchising requirements.

Good Samaritan Hospital v. Shalala, Secretary of Health and Human Services (508 U.S. 402), decided by a 6–3 vote, June 7, 1993; White wrote the opinion; Souter, Stevens and Scalia dissented.

The federal government does not have to reimburse hospitals or other health care providers under the Medicare program for costs beyond the "reasonable costs" set by the Department of Health and Human Services. The decision involved a section of the Medicare law requiring that the government "provide for the making of suitable retroactive cost adjustments" for health care providers.

Darby v. Cisneros, Secretary of Housing and Urban Development (509 U.S. 137), decided by a 9–0 vote, June 21, 1993; Blackmun wrote the opinion.

A party challenging a federal agency's action in court under the Administrative Procedure Act does not have to exhaust administrative remedies unless a separate law or agency rule specifically imposes such a requirement.

Security Services, Inc. v. Kmart Corp. (511 U.S. 222), decided by a 7–2 vote, May 16, 1994; Souter wrote the opinion; Thomas and Ginsburg dissented.

The Court limited the ability of bankrupt motor carriers to use defective rate filings with the Interstate Commerce Commission to collect higher-than-agreed charges from shippers. The decision narrowed an earlier ruling—*Maislin Industries, U.S., Inc. v. Primary Steel* (1990)—that allowed a bankrupt motor carrier to collect its "filed rate" from shippers even if they negotiated a lower rate.

MCI Telecommunications Corp. v. American Telephone & Telegraph Co. (512 U.S. 218), decided by a 5–3 vote, June 17, 1994; Scalia wrote the opinion; Stevens, Blackmun and Souter dissented; O'Connor did not participate.

The Federal Communications Commission (FCC) exceeded its statutory authority in exempting AT&T's long-distance competitors from filing tariffs of rates and services. The ruling overturned the "permissive detariffing" policies that the FCC began adopting in the early 1980s to enhance competition in long-distance telephone service. The FCC said rate-filing requirements hindered the ability of MCI Telecommunications Corp. and other new long-distance carriers to compete with AT&T. But the agency kept the requirements in place for AT&T. The Court agreed with AT&T that the detariffing policies went beyond the FCC's authority under the Communications Act of 1934 to "modify" rate-filing requirements.

Thomas Jefferson University dba Thomas Jefferson Hospital v. Shalala, Secretary of Health and Human Services (512 U.S. 504), decided by a 5–4 vote, June 24, 1994; Kennedy wrote the opinion; Thomas, Stevens, O'Connor and Ginsburg dissented.

Teaching hospitals are not entitled to reimbursement from Medicare for the administrative costs of training medical interns and residents. The ruling upheld the interpretation by the Department of Health and Human Services (HHS) of a regulation regarding reimbursement of university-affiliated hospitals for treating elderly patients under the federal Medicare program.

Interstate Commerce Commission v. Transcon Lines (513 U.S. 138), decided by a 9–0 vote, Jan. 10, 1995; Kennedy wrote the opinion.

Motor carriers can be blocked from collecting normal charges from shippers under previous rate regulations if they failed to comply with federal credit-disclosure regulations.

Anderson, Director, California Department of Social Services v. Green (513 U.S. 557), decided by a 9–0 vote, Feb. 22, 1995; *per curiam* (unsigned) opinion.

The Court dismissed a case testing the constitutionality of a California law limiting welfare benefits for new arrivals to the state.

Shalala, Secretary of Health and Human Services v. Guernsey Memorial Hospital (514 U.S. 87), decided by a 5–4 vote, March 6,

1995; Kennedy wrote the opinion; O'Connor, Scalia, Souter and Thomas dissented.

The secretary of Health and Human Services does not have to follow general accounting principles in determining reimbursements under the Medicare program for hospitals or other health care providers.

The ruling upheld a decision to stretch out reimbursement to a hospital for an accounting loss of $672,000 resulting from a refinancing of bonds. The hospital argued standard accounting rules—so-called Generally Accepted Accounting Principles or GAAP—called for the loss to be recognized in the year of the financing. The department cited informal guidelines in ruling that the loss should be amortized over the life of the original bonds.

Anderson, Director, California Department of Social Services v. Edwards (514 U.S. 143), decided by a 9–0 vote, March 22, 1995; Thomas wrote the opinion.

States can count all children living in a home as a single family unit, whether or not they are siblings, in setting payments under the Aid to Families With Dependent Children (AFDC) program. The decision reinstated a California rule adopted in 1991 that treated a household with nonsibling children as a single "assistance unit." The effect was to lower the benefits per child just as they would be scaled back for a household consisting only of sibling children.

Shalala, Secretary of Health and Human Services v. Whitecotton (514 U.S. 268), decided by a 9–0 vote, April 18, 1995; Souter wrote the opinion.

A person claiming compensation under the federal law for vaccine-related injuries must show that the first symptoms of the injury occurred after the vaccination. The ruling strictly construed burden-of-proof provisions of the National Childhood Vaccine Injury Act, which Congress passed to simplify compensation for vaccine-related injuries. The act permits compensation without proof of causation if a child or infant suffers any of a number of specified conditions after receiving a vaccination and "the first symptom" of the condition was manifested after the vaccination.

Freightliner Corp. v. Myrick (514 U.S. 280), decided by a 9–0 vote, April 18, 1995; Thomas wrote the opinion.

Two truck manufacturers failed in their effort to bar product liability suits in state courts because of a suspended federal safety standard. But the ruling included a passage that could help similar federal preemption claims in other product liability suits.

New York State Conference of Blue Cross & Blue Shield Plans v. Travelers Insurance Co. (514 U.S. 645), decided by a 9–0 vote, April 26, 1995; Souter wrote the opinion.

States may require health insurers and health maintenance organizations to pay surcharges to hospitals to cover the costs of uninsured patients without violating the federal law regulating employee health benefit plans.

Medtronic, Inc. v. Lohr (518 U.S.   ), decided by 9–0 and 5–4 votes, June 26, 1996; Stevens wrote the main opinion; O'Connor, Rehnquist, Scalia and Thomas dissented in part.

The federal law regulating medical devices does not completely bar consumers from suing manufacturers in state courts, but the ruling left uncertain whether the act preempts some state law claims. The act, passed to strengthen federal regulation of medical devices, bars states from enforcing "any requirement" relating to safety or effectiveness "different from, or in addition to" federal requirements.

FREEDOM OF INFORMATION

United States Department of Justice v. Landano (508 U.S. 165), decided by a 9–0 vote, May 24, 1993; O'Connor wrote the opinion.

The FBI may not rely on a blanket presumption that all sources providing information in connection with criminal investigations are confidential to protect the information from disclosure under the Freedom of Information Act.

United States Department of Defense v. Federal Labor Relations Authority (510 U.S. 487), decided by a 9–0 vote, Feb. 23, 1994; Thomas wrote the opinion.

Federal agencies may not disclose workers' home addresses to public employee unions. The Court said that the federal Privacy Act prohibits agencies from providing the workers' addresses unless required to do so by other federal law. The Court said that disclosure was not required by the federal employee labor-management relations law or by the Freedom of Information Act, which itself contains privacy exemptions.

GOVERNMENT CONTRACTS

Hercules, Inc. v. United States (516 U.S. 417), decided by a 6–2 vote, March 4, 1996; Rehnquist wrote the opinion; Breyer and O'Connor dissented; Stevens did not participate.

Two chemical companies—Hercules, Inc., and Thompson Co.—failed to force the government to pay the costs of litigation brought by Vietnam veterans relating to liability for manufacturing the defoliant Agent Orange used during the Vietnam War. The two companies then sued the government in U.S. Claims Court to recover the money, along with $9 million in legal fees and expenses. They contended the government made an implied promise to indemnify them when it required them to manufacture the defoliant under the Defense Production Act. The Court rejected the argument, ruling that the act does not guarantee indemnification.

United States v. Winstar Corp. (518 U.S.___), decided by a 7–2 vote, July 1, 1996; Souter wrote the plurality opinion; Rehnquist and Ginsburg dissented.

The government may be held liable for billions of dollars of breach of contract damages for tightening accounting rules for savings and loan institutions that took over failing thrifts at the government's behest. The ruling upheld decisions by two lower federal courts sustaining breach of contract claims filed by three thrift institutions that agreed to so-called supervisory mergers as part of the S&L bailout during the 1980s. To induce healthy thrifts to take over failing S&Ls, the Federal Savings and Loan Insurance Corporation allowed them to count "supervisory goodwill" as an asset. But in 1989, Congress passed a law prohibiting the accounting gimmick, forcing many thrifts that had agreed to the mergers into financial difficulty or liquidation. Some 100 thrifts filed breach of contract claims against the government, which raised as defenses two legal rules—the unmistakability doctrine and the public or general acts doctrine—that limit government liability in contract cases.

The Court agreed the government was liable for damages in the three cases brought before it. The decision returned the three cases to lower courts to determine damages.

GOVERNMENT CORPORATIONS

Lebron v. National Railroad Passenger Corporation (Amtrak) (513 U.S. 347), decided by an 8–1 vote, Feb. 21, 1995; Scalia wrote the opinion; O'Connor dissented.

Amtrak, the government-created rail passenger corporation, is to be treated as a government agency for purposes of the First Amendment. The ruling allowed artist Michael Lebron to pursue a free speech claim against Amtrak for refusing to permit him to display a political advertisement on a giant billboard in Pennsylvania Station in New York City. The decision returned the case to lower federal courts to determine whether Amtrak's policy of refusing all political advertising violated the First Amendment.

IMPEACHMENT

Nixon v. United States (506 U.S. 244), decided by a 9–0 vote, Jan. 13, 1993; Rehnquist wrote the opinion.

A Senate rule permitting evidence in impeachment proceedings to be heard by a fact-finding committee instead of the full Senate cannot be challenged in federal court. The decision upheld a procedural shortcut that the Senate had used in removing three federal judges since 1986.

MILITARY

Conroy v. Aniskoff (507 U.S. 511), decided by a 9–0 vote, March 31, 1993; Stevens wrote the opinion.

A member of the armed services does not have to show prejudice or hardship to take advantage of a federal law that delays forfeiture proceedings for failure to pay real estate property taxes during a period of military service. The 1940 Soldiers' and Sailors' Civil Relief Act provides that the period of military service "shall not be included in computing any period . . . provided by any law for the redemption of real property sold or forfeited to enforce any obligation, tax, or assessment." The Court said the provision was "unambiguous, unequivocal and unlimited" and rejected a ruling by Maine state courts that a member of the armed forces must first demonstrate some hardship or prejudice resulting from military service.

Weiss v. United States (510 U.S. 163), decided by a 9–0 vote, Jan. 19, 1994; Rehnquist wrote the opinion.

The Court rejected a constitutional challenge to the method of appointing military judges. It refused to require that officers be given a separate presidential appointment before serving as military judges or that military judges be given a fixed term of office.

Dalton, Secretary of the Navy v. Specter (511 U.S. 462), decided by a 9–0 vote, May 23, 1994; Rehnquist wrote the opinion.

Courts cannot review decisions to close defense bases under a 1990 law aimed at making it easier to close unneeded military and naval facilities. The Court held that the Defense Base Closure and Realignment Act of 1990 bars judicial review. Under the law a special commission recommended bases for closure and submitted its recommendations to the president, who had to accept or reject the package as a whole. If the president agreed, Congress could disapprove, but again only by rejecting the whole package.

Ryder v. United States (515 U.S. 177), decided by a 9–0 vote, June 12, 1995; Rehnquist wrote the opinion.

The Court refused to let the military justice system get around a ruling that appellate panels in a handful of cases had been illegally constituted.

NATIVE AMERICANS

Lincoln, Acting Director, Indian Health Service v. Vigil (508 U.S. 182), decided by a 9–0 vote, May 24, 1993; Souter wrote the opinion.

The Court rejected a challenge to a decision by the Indian Health Service to terminate a program providing services to handicapped children in the Southwest and use the funds to establish a nationwide treatment program. The program, in operation from 1979 to 1985, had been funded from a general appropriations measure. The Court said that the allocation of funds from a lump-sum appropriation was protected from judicial review because it was "traditionally regarded as committed to agency discretion."

South Dakota v. Bourland (508 U.S. 679), decided by a 7–2 vote, June 14, 1993; Thomas wrote the opinion; Blackmun and Souter dissented.

The Cheyenne River Sioux Tribe has no power to regulate hunting or fishing by non-Native Americans on lands and waters located along the Oahe Dam and Reservoir in north-central South Dakota.

Hagen v. Utah (510 U.S. 399), decided by a 7–2 vote, Feb. 23, 1994; O'Connor wrote the opinion; Blackmun and Souter dissented.

The Court upheld Utah state court jurisdiction over an area that had been located in the Uintah Indian Reservation but was opened to non-Native Americans in 1902. The ruling permitted Utah courts to try a Native American arrested on drug charges in the area.

VETERANS

Brown, Secretary of Veterans Affairs v. Gardner (513 U.S. 115), decided by a 9–0 vote, Dec. 12, 1994; Souter wrote the opinion.

RELIGION, SPEECH AND PRESS

Congress shall make no law respecting an establishment of religion, or prohibiting the free exercise thereof; or abridging the freedom of speech, or of the press; or the right of the people peaceably to assemble, and to petition the Government for a redress of grievances.

First Amendment, U.S. Constitution

Veterans may recover damages for injuries received during medical treatment at facilities of the Department of Veterans Affairs without proving that the injury was caused by medical negligence. The Court ruled that a 60-year-old regulation requiring proof of fault went beyond the 1924 statute authorizing compensation for veterans' medical injuries.

MISCELLANEOUS FEDERAL CASE

United States v. Texas (507 U.S. 529), decided by an 8–1 vote, April 5, 1993; Rehnquist wrote the opinion; Stevens dissented.

States may be required, under federal common law, to pay prejudgment interest—interest calculated from some date prior to a court judgment—on debts owed to the federal government.

First Amendment

CABLE TELEVISION

Turner Broadcasting System, Inc. v. Federal Communications Commission (512 U.S. 622), decided by a 5–4 vote, June 27, 1994; Kennedy wrote the opinion; O'Connor, Scalia, Thomas and Ginsburg dissented in part.

The Court extended to cable television First Amendment protections comparable to those enjoyed by print media, but it left unresolved a constitutional challenge to the 1992 law requiring cable systems to carry local broadcast stations.

CHURCH AND STATE

Lamb's Chapel v. Center Moriches Union Free School District (508 U.S. 385), decided by a 9–0 vote, June 7, 1993; White wrote the opinion.

A school district policy that permits the use of school buildings after hours by community groups but bars similar use by religious groups violates the First Amendment's Freedom of Speech Clause.

Church of the Lukumi Babalu Aye, Inc. v. City of Hialeah (508 U.S. 520), decided by a 9–0 vote, June 11, 1993; Kennedy wrote the opinion.

The Court struck down a Florida city's ban on ritual animal sacrifices, saying that the ordinances unconstitutionally interfered with the practices of an Afro-Cuban religion. The Court said that the city of Hialeah, Florida, had improperly targeted followers of the Santeria religion in 1987 when it adopted four ordinances prohibiting ritual sacrifice of animals. The justices agreed that the ordinances infringed on the Santerians' freedom to exercise religion under the First Amendment.

Zobrest v. Catalina Foothills School District (509 U.S. 1), decided by a 5–4 vote, June 18, 1993; Rehnquist wrote the opinion; Blackmun, Stevens, O'Connor and Souter dissented.

The government can pay for a sign-language interpreter to accompany a deaf student in a parochial school without violating the separation of church and state. The decision reversed lower court rulings that found the practice would violate the First Amendment's Establishment Clause.

Board of Education of Kiryas Joel Village School District v. Grumet (512 U.S. 687), decided by a 6–3 vote, June 27, 1994; Souter wrote the opinion; Scalia, Rehnquist and Thomas dissented.

A New York law creating a special school district to serve disabled children of a Hasidic sect was struck down as an unconstitutional establishment of religion.

Capitol Square Review and Advisory Board v. Pinette (515 U.S. 753), decided by a 7–2 vote, June 29, 1995; Scalia wrote the main opinion; Stevens and Ginsburg dissented.

A private group can place a religious display on government property traditionally used as a public forum if there is no appearance of government endorsement of the religious message.

Rosenberger v. Rector and Visitors of University of Virginia (515 U.S. 819), decided by a 5–4 vote, June 29, 1995; Kennedy wrote the opinion; Souter, Stevens, Ginsburg and Breyer dissented.

A state university that funds student publications from a mandatory student activity fee cannot deny funding to a religious magazine solely because of its religious content.

COMMERCIAL SPEECH

City of Cincinnati v. Discovery Network, Inc. (507 U.S. 410), decided by a 6–3 vote, March 24, 1993; Stevens wrote the opinion; Rehnquist, White and Thomas dissented.

The Court struck down a Cincinnati ordinance that prohibited the use of newsracks on public property to distribute "commercial handbills" but permitted sidewalk vending machines for newspapers.

Edenfield v. Fane (507 U.S. 761), decided by an 8–1 vote, April 26, 1993; Kennedy wrote the opinion; O'Connor dissented.

A state may not prohibit accountants from personally soliciting new clients. The decision struck down a rule by the Florida Board of Accountancy that prohibited certified public accountants from engaging in "direct, in-person, uninvited solicitation" to obtain new clients. Three other states—Louisiana, Minnesota and Texas—had similar rules.

United States v. Edge Broadcasting Co. (509 U.S. 418), decided by a 7–2 vote, June 25, 1993; White wrote the opinion; Stevens and Blackmun dissented.

The Court upheld a federal law that banned the broadcast of lottery advertising by radio and television stations licensed to a state that prohibits lotteries but permitted such advertising on stations in states where lotteries are legal.

Ibanez v. Florida Department of Business and Professional Regulation, Board of Accountancy (512 U.S. 136), decided by 9–0 and 7–2 votes, June 13, 1994; Ginsburg wrote the opinion; O'-Connor and Rehnquist dissented in part.

States may not prohibit lawyers from truthfully advertising themselves as certified public accountants or certified financial planners.

Rubin, Secretary of the Treasury v. Coors Brewing Co. (514 U.S. 476), decided by a 9–0 vote, April 19, 1995; Thomas wrote the opinion.

The Court struck down a 1935 law that prohibited brewers from listing the alcohol content of their products on labels, saying the measure violated the First Amendment protections for commercial speech. Two lower federal courts had struck down the law in a challenge brought by the Colorado-based Coors Brewing Co. The government defended the law by claiming that it prevented brewers from engaging in so-called "strength wars"—competing for customers on the basis of a higher alcohol content.

Florida Bar v. Went For It, Inc. (515 U.S. 618), decided by a 5–4 vote, June 21, 1995; O'Connor wrote the opinion; Kennedy, Stevens, Souter and Ginsburg dissented.

States may temporarily ban lawyers from direct mail solicitation of accident victims or their families in order to protect the victims' privacy and enhance the public image of the legal profession. The ruling reversed the Court's trend of striking down regulation of lawyer advertising and other forms of commercial speech.

44 Liquormart, Inc. v. Rhode Island (517 U.S. 484), decided by a 9–0 vote, May 13, 1996; Stevens wrote the main opinion.

The Court struck down a state law banning liquor price advertising in a fractured ruling that nevertheless suggested a substantially stiffened test for upholding laws or regulations affecting commercial speech.

The ruling stemmed from a challenge by two liquor retailers to a 1956 Rhode Island law that prohibited liquor stores from making any reference to prices in their advertising and barred newspapers or other media from publishing any such advertisements. A federal district court judge struck the law down, but the First U.S. Circuit Court of Appeals upheld it on grounds that it promoted the state's interest in temperance. Alternatively, the court held that the Twenty-first Amendment, which repealed prohibition, gave the states authority to regulate liquor advertising without regard to First Amendment protections for commercial speech. The justices unanimously agreed that the Rhode Island law violated the First Amendment and was not protected from invalidation by the Twenty-first Amendment.

FREEDOM OF SPEECH

Waters v. Churchill (511 U.S. 661), decided by a vote of 7–2, May 31, 1994; O'Connor wrote a plurality opinion; Stevens and Blackmun dissented.

A splintered Court gave public employees limited procedural rights against being fired for things they say. The ruling prohibits a government employer from discharging a worker for something the worker said unless it has a "reasonable belief" that the comments were either disruptive or unrelated to matters of "public concern." The decision did not spell out procedures for employers to use, but three of the justices complained of what they called the "proposed right to an investigation before dismissal for speech."

City of Ladue v. Gilleo (512 U.S. 43), decided by a 9–0 vote, June 13, 1994; Stevens wrote the opinion.

Cities may not completely prohibit residents from displaying signs on their property. The ruling struck down a St. Louis suburb's ordinance aimed at minimizing "visual clutter" by prohibiting most signs on residential property.

United States v. National Treasury Employees Union (513 U.S. 454), decided by 6–3 and 5–4 votes, Feb. 22, 1995; Stevens wrote the opinion; O'Connor dissented in part; Rehnquist, Scalia and Thomas dissented.

The Court struck down on free speech grounds a federal law banning most federal civil servants from being paid for outside speeches, articles or appearances. Extending a ban on so-called honoraria for its members, Congress in 1991 barred payments to executive branch employees for outside speeches and writings even if they had no connection to the employee's official duties.

Two federal courts struck the law down as a violation of the First Amendment. The Court agreed and said that the government had failed to show any "evidence of misconduct related to honoraria in the vast rank and file of federal employees."

McIntyre v. Ohio Elections Commission (514 U.S. 334), decided by a 7–2 vote, April 19, 1995; Stevens wrote the opinion; Scalia and Rehnquist dissented.

The First Amendment protects an individual's right to distribute anonymous campaign literature. The ruling overturned an Ohio law that required campaign literature to include the name and address of the author or a campaign official.

Hurley v. Irish-American Gay, Lesbian and Bisexual Group of Boston (515 U.S. 557), decided by a 9–0 vote, June 19, 1995; Souter wrote the opinion.

The Court overturned rulings by Massachusetts courts requiring the private organizers of the St. Patrick's Day parade in Boston to allow a group of Irish-American homosexuals to march in the event. Massachusetts courts ruled that the South Boston Allied War Veterans Council violated the state's antidiscrimination law by refusing to allow the Irish-American Gay, Lesbian and Bisexual Group to march as a unit in the parade.

Board of County Commissioners, Wabaunsee County, Kansas v. Umbehr (518 U.S.___), decided by a 7–2 vote, June 28, 1996; O'Connor wrote the opinion; Scalia and Thomas dissented.

A government contractor cannot be terminated for exercising freedom of speech on a matter of public interest unless the government demonstrates some legitimate interests that outweigh the contractor's First Amendment rights.

O'Hare Truck Service, Inc. v. City of Northlake (518 U.S.___), decided by a 7–2 vote, June 28, 1996; Kennedy wrote the opinion; Scalia and Thomas dissented.

A government contractor cannot be terminated for refusing to make political contributions. The ruling backed a free speech claim by the operator of a Chicago area towing service who said he was removed from a list of companies used by the city of Northlake after refusing to contribute to the mayor's reelection campaign. The Court said independent contractors and service providers are protected against retaliatory action for exercising political rights.

TELECOMMUNICATIONS

United States v. Chesapeake and Potomac Telephone Company of Virginia (516 U.S. 415), decided by a 9–0 vote, Feb. 27, 1996; *per curiam* (unsigned) opinion.

The Court sidestepped a ruling on the government's power to limit telephone companies from providing cable television service after Congress passed a law lifting the restriction.

Denver Area Educational Telecommunications Consortium, Inc. v. Federal Communications Commission (518 U.S.___), decided by 7–2, 6–3 and 5–4 votes, June 28, 1996; Breyer wrote the main opinion; Kennedy and Ginsburg dissented from one part of the decision; Thomas, Rehnquist and Scalia dissented from two parts of the decision, joined by O'Connor on one part.

The Court struck down provisions of the Cable Television Consumer Protection and Competition Act of 1992 that required cable system operators to put sexually explicit programming on a restricted-access channel and permitted them to censor such programming on public access channels. But the justices upheld another provision of the law allowing cable operators to block indecent material on commercially leased channels.

Immigration Law

AMNESTY

Reno, Attorney General v. Catholic Social Services, Inc. (509 U.S. 43), decided by a 6–3 vote, June 18, 1993; Souter wrote the opinion; Stevens, White and Blackmun dissented.

The Court threw out the bulk of two lawsuits challenging regulations that had restricted access to the government's amnesty program for undocumented aliens. The ruling had the effect of overturning lower court decisions extending the congressional deadline for aliens to apply for the amnesty.

IMMIGRATION PROCEDURE

Reno, Attorney General v. Flores (507 U.S. 292), decided by a 7–2 vote, March 23, 1993; Scalia wrote the opinion; Stevens and Blackmun dissented.

The Court upheld an Immigration and Naturalization Service (INS) policy of detaining alien juveniles while awaiting deportation hearings unless they can be released to a parent, close relative or legal guardian. The ruling overturned lower court decisions striking down the INS policy of refusing to release the juveniles to other responsible adults or a social service agency.

Sale, Acting Commissioner, Immigration and Naturalization Service v. Haitian Centers Council, Inc. (509 U.S. 155), decided by an 8–1 vote, June 21, 1993; Stevens wrote the opinion; Blackmun dissented.

The president has the power to order the Coast Guard to intercept undocumented aliens on the high seas and return them to their home country without conducting hearings to determine whether they are refugees who qualify for asylum. The decision upheld a policy adopted by the Bush administration and defended by the Clinton administration of stopping Haitians seeking to sail to the United States and summarily returning them to Haiti.

Stone v. Immigration and Naturalization Service (514 U.S. 386), decided by a 6–3 vote, April 19, 1995; Kennedy wrote the opinion; Breyer, O'Connor and Souter dissented.

Filing a motion for reconsideration of a deportation order issued by the Board of Immigration Appeals does not extend the 90-day time limit for seeking review of the order by a federal court of appeals. The highly technical decision endorsed a stand taken by the Immigration and Naturalization Service to reduce an alien's opportunities to use review procedures to delay deportation.

Individual Rights

ABORTION

Bray v. Alexandria Women's Health Clinic (506 U.S. 263), decided by votes of 6–3 and 5–4, Jan. 13, 1993; Scalia wrote the opinion; Souter dissented in part; Stevens, Blackmun and O'Connor dissented.

A Reconstruction-era civil rights law that prohibits conspiracies to deprive any person or class of equal protection of the laws cannot be used to prevent blockades of abortion clinics by antiabortion demonstrators. The Court held that the blockades did not involve "invidious discrimination" against women by reason of their sex.

National Organization for Women, Inc. v. Scheidler (512 U.S. 249), decided by a 9–0 vote, Jan. 24, 1994; Rehnquist wrote the opinion.

Abortion clinics can bring a civil damage suit under the federal antiracketeering law for violent protests or demonstrations even if the protesters have no economic motive for their actions. The decision reinstated a closely watched suit by two abortion clinics against a coalition of antiabortion groups called the Pro-Life Action Network. The clinics claimed the protesters were using force and violence to try to close them down and asked for damages under the Racketeer Influenced and Corrupt Organizations Act, commonly called RICO.

Madsen v. Women's Health Center, Inc. (512 U.S. 753), decided by a 6–3 vote, June 30, 1994; Rehnquist wrote the opinion; Scalia, Kennedy and Thomas dissented.

Judges can establish "buffer zones" preventing antiabortion protesters from getting too close to clinics where abortions are performed, but they cannot restrict "more speech than necessary" to protect access to clinics or other government interests. The ruling upheld a 36-foot buffer zone around most of the clinic and a broad noise ban during hours when abortions were performed. The Court struck down three other restrictions: a ban on use of signs visible from within the clinic, a 300-foot "no approach" zone limiting demonstrators from trying to speak with staff or patients or offering them literature, and a 300-foot buffer zone around homes of clinic doctors and staff.

Dalton, Director, Arkansas Department of Human Services v. Little Rock Family Planning Services (516 U.S. 474), decided by a 9–0 vote, March 18, 1996; *per curiam* (unsigned) opinion.

The Court rejected an effort by the state of Arkansas to enforce a state constitutional amendment prohibiting Medicaid-funded abortions in cases of rape or incest. The ruling stemmed from a conflict between a 1989 voter-approved measure and federal abortion funding provisions, which allowed payment for terminating pregnancies resulting from rape or incest.

A group of physicians and clinics providing abortion services challenged the amendment on grounds it was preempted by the federal law. A federal district court judge agreed and issued an injunction striking down the amendment "in its entirety." In a brief, unsigned ruling, the Court said it was "accepting (without deciding)" the lower court's ruling on the preemption issue, but the Court narrowed the injunction, saying the state might apply the broader abortion-funding ban in fully state-financed programs.

Leavitt, Governor of Utah v. Jane L. (518 U.S. 137), decided by a 5–4 vote, June 17, 1996; *per curiam* (unsigned) opinion; Stevens, Souter, Ginsburg and Breyer dissented.

The Court cleared the way for the possible reinstatement of part of Utah's 1991 antiabortion statute, ruling that a federal appeals court misconstrued state law in striking down the entire act.

AFFIRMATIVE ACTION

Northeastern Florida Chapter of the Associated General Contractors of America v. City of Jacksonville, Florida (508 U.S. 656), decided by a 7–2 vote, June 14, 1993; Thomas wrote the opinion; O'Connor and Blackmun dissented.

A nonminority contractor may challenge a minority set-aside ordinance without demonstrating that it would have been awarded a contract but for the law.

Adarand Constructors, Inc. v. Peña, Secretary of Transportation (515 U.S. 200), decided by a 5–4 vote, June 12, 1995; O'-Connor wrote the opinion; Stevens, Souter, Ginsburg and Breyer dissented.

In a sharp setback for advocates of affirmative action, the Court raised the standard for reviewing racial classifications in federal programs to the same high level applied to state and local programs six years earlier. The Court held that federal minority contracting provisions or other affirmative action policies are subject to "strict scrutiny" in court and can be upheld only if they serve a compelling government interest and are narrowly tailored to achieve that goal. The decision returned to lower courts a challenge by a white contractor in Colorado to a Department of Transportation program that gave contractors a financial incentive to award subcontracts to minority-owned concerns.

AGE DISCRIMINATION

Hazen Paper Co. v. Biggins (507 U.S. 604), decided by a 9–0 vote, April 20, 1993; O'Connor wrote the opinion.

The Court limited the use of the Age Discrimination in Employment Act in cases that allege interference with employees' pension rights, but the Court also eased the requirements for plaintiffs to prove a "willful" violation of the act to recover double damages in an age discrimination suit. The Court held that an employer's decision to dismiss an employee to deprive him of his pension rights does not necessarily amount to age discrimination. However, that dismissal might violate a separate federal law, the Employee Retirement Income Security Act.

O'Connor v. Consolidated Coin Caterers Corp. (517 U.S. 308), decided by a 9–0 vote, April 1, 1996; Scalia wrote the opinion.

A plaintiff can win an age discrimination suit without proving he was replaced by someone under 40 years old, the threshold age for coverage under the federal Age Discrimination in Employment Act.

ATTORNEYS' FEES

Farrar and Smith, Co-Administrators of Estate of Joseph D. Farrar v. Hobby (506 U.S. 103), decided by a 5–4 vote, Dec. 14, 1992; Thomas wrote the opinion; White, Blackmun, Stevens and Souter dissented.

A plaintiff in a federal civil rights suit who wins only nominal damages and no other significant legal relief is ordinarily not entitled to an award of attorneys' fees. The decision threw out a $280,000 award for attorneys' fees for a plaintiff who won a nominal $1 damage award in a malicious prosecution suit.

Shalala, Secretary of Health and Human Services v. Schaefer (509 U.S. 292), decided by 7–2 and 9–0 votes, June 24, 1993; Scalia wrote the opinion; Stevens and Blackmun concurred in the judgment.

The Court set an earlier deadline for Social Security claimants to apply for attorneys' fees in suits challenging administrative decisions to deny benefits.

DAMAGE SUITS

Soldal v. Cook County, Illinois (506 U.S. 56), decided by a 9–0 vote, Dec. 8, 1992; White wrote the opinion.

A federal civil rights plaintiff may use the Fourth Amendment to recover damages for violation of his property rights even if his privacy or liberty was not harmed.

Leatherman v. Tarrant County Narcotics Intelligence and Coordination Unit (507 U.S. 163), decided by a 9–0 vote, March 3, 1993; Rehnquist wrote the opinion.

Plaintiffs in federal civil rights suits against local governments do not have to provide more detail in their complaints than plaintiffs in other types of suits. In a brief opinion, the Supreme Court said the federal rules did not permit a more stringent standard for suits against local governments. The decision returned for trial two suits brought by homeowners who claimed that poorly trained police officers had violated their rights in drug raids.

Antoine v. Byers & Anderson, Inc. (508 U.S. 429), decided by a 9–0 vote, June 7, 1993; Stevens wrote the opinion.

A court reporter is not absolutely immune from damages liability for failing to produce a transcript of a federal criminal trial.

The Court said that court reporters do not exercise the kind of discretionary judgment that is protected by the doctrine of judicial immunity. The decision remanded a suit brought by a defendant whose appeal had been delayed for four years because of a court reporter's failure to produce a transcript.

Buckley v. Fitzsimmons (509 U.S. 259), decided by 9–0 and 5–4 votes, June 24, 1993; Stevens wrote the opinion; Kennedy, Rehnquist, White and Souter dissented in part.

Prosecutors do not enjoy absolute immunity from damage suits for conducting investigative actions normally performed by police officers or for making statements to the news media. The decision reinstated a federal civil rights suit by a defendant in a publicized murder case who charged state prosecutors in Illinois with fabricating evidence and making false statements against him. Charges against the man were dropped after a jury failed to reach a verdict in the case.

Albright v. Oliver (510 U.S. 266), decided by a 7–2 vote, Jan. 24, 1994; Rehnquist wrote a plurality opinion; Blackmun and Stevens dissented.

Someone who has been falsely accused of a crime and arrested cannot use the Fourteenth Amendment's guarantee of due process of law to bring a federal civil rights suit against the officials responsible for the baseless prosecution.

Federal Deposit Insurance Corporation v. Meyer (510 U.S. 471), decided by a 9–0 vote, Feb. 23, 1994; Thomas wrote the opinion.

Federal agencies cannot be sued for money damages for violating an individual's constitutional rights.

Elder v. Holloway (510 U.S. 510), decided by a 9–0 vote, Feb. 23, 1994; Ginsburg wrote the opinion.

Appellate courts should consider all relevant case law, not just cases cited by opposing lawyers, in reviewing a lower court decision on the defense of qualified immunity in federal civil rights suits.

Heck v. Humphrey (512 U.S. 477), decided by 9–0 and 5–4 votes, June 24, 1994; Scalia wrote the opinion; Souter, Blackmun, Stevens and Ginsburg concurred in the judgment but disagreed with the legal ruling.

A defendant in a state criminal prosecution ordinarily cannot bring a federal civil rights suit for damages if the suit challenges the legality of the conviction or sentence.

Johnson v. Jones (515 U.S. 304), decided by a 9–0 vote, June 12, 1995; Breyer wrote the opinion.

Public officials cannot appeal a pretrial ruling that rejects the factual basis for raising a qualified immunity defense in a damage suit charging them with violating an individual's constitutional rights.

Kimberlin v. Quinlan (515 U.S. 321), decided by a 9–0 vote, June 12, 1995; *per curiam* (unsigned) opinion.

The Court revived a damage suit by a former federal prison inmate who claimed officials improperly prevented him from airing allegations that he once sold marijuana to former vice president Dan Quayle. The unsigned decision ordered a lower court to reexamine the suit in the light of a decision in an unrelated case released the same day, *Johnson v. Jones*.

DISABILITY RIGHTS

Florence County School District Four v. Carter (510 U.S. 7), decided by a 9–0 vote, Nov. 9, 1993; O'Connor wrote the opinion.

The Court made it easier for parents of students with disabilities to obtain reimbursement for private school tuition costs if public school districts do not provide an appropriate education as required by federal law.

City of Edmonds v. Oxford House, Inc. (514 U.S. 725), decided by a 6–3 vote, May 15, 1995; Ginsburg wrote the opinion; Thomas, Scalia and Kennedy dissented.

Municipalities cannot use single-family zoning laws to completely exclude group homes for disabled persons, including recovering alcoholics and drug addicts.

Lane v. Peña, Secretary of Transportation (518 U.S. 187), decided by a 7–2 vote, June 20, 1996; O'Connor wrote the opinion; Stevens and Breyer dissented.

The federal government does not have to pay money damages for violating the law that prohibits discrimination against disabled persons in programs run by federal agencies.

DRUG TESTING

Vernonia School District No. 47J v. Acton (515 U.S. 646), decided by a 6–3 vote, June 26, 1995; Scalia wrote the opinion; O'Connor, Stevens and Souter dissented.

Public schools can require an athlete to submit to random drug testing even if there is no basis for suspecting the individual of using drugs. The ruling rejected a federal constitutional challenge to a drug-testing policy that was adopted in 1989 by a school system that required urinalyses for all school athletes at any grade level at the beginning of the season and permitted random testing of 10 percent of a school's athletes each week thereafter.

GAY RIGHTS

Romer, Governor of Colorado v. Evans (517 U.S. 620), decided by a 6–3 vote, May 20, 1996; Kennedy wrote the opinion; Scalia, Rehnquist and Thomas dissented.

A Colorado constitutional amendment that prohibited enactment of any state or local law to prevent discrimination against homosexuals was struck down as a violation of equal protection. The ruling, a major victory for gay rights' groups, struck down an initiative approved by Colorado voters as Amendment 2 in 1992. The amendment repealed existing anti-gay discrimination laws and prohibited enactment of any such laws in the future.

JOB DISCRIMINATION

St. Mary's Honor Center v. Hicks (509 U.S. 502), decided by a 5–4 vote, June 25, 1993; Scalia wrote the opinion; Souter, White, Blackmun and Stevens dissented.

A plaintiff in a job discrimination suit is not automatically entitled to a judgment when a judge or jury rejects the employer's nondiscriminatory explanations for an adverse employment action. Instead, the Court held, the plaintiff must prove a discriminatory motive for the action.

Landgraf v. USI Film Products (511 U.S. 244), decided by an 8–1 vote, April 26, 1994; Stevens wrote the opinion; Blackmun dissented.

Provisions of a 1991 civil rights act giving plaintiffs the right to jury trials and compensatory and punitive damages in job discrimination suits do not apply to cases pending when the law was passed. The ruling—and a companion decision announced the same day, *Rivers v. Roadway Express, Inc.*—rejected civil rights plaintiffs' efforts to win retroactive application of liberal provisions contained in the 1991 law. Congress passed the law in part to overturn a series of Supreme Court rulings in 1989 that had narrowed plaintiffs' remedies in employment discrimination cases.

The 1991 law did not explicitly say whether Congress intended it to have retroactive effect. President George Bush had vetoed an earlier version that included a retroactivity provision.

Rivers v. Roadway Express, Inc. (511 U.S. 298), decided by an 8–1 vote, April 26, 1994; Stevens wrote the opinion; Blackmun dissented.

Provisions of a 1991 civil rights act allowing employees to sue in federal court for racial harassment in the workplace do not apply to cases pending when the law took effect. The justices rejected arguments that the provisions should be applied retroactively because Congress intended to overturn the Court's 1989 decision rejecting racial harassment suits.

McKennon v. Nashville Banner Publishing Co. (513 U.S. 352), decided by a 9–0 vote, Jan. 23, 1995; Kennedy wrote the opinion.

An employee in a job discrimination suit does not lose her right to any relief if the employer discovers evidence of wrongdoing that would have justified her dismissal if known earlier.

MENTAL HEALTH

Heller, Secretary, Kentucky Cabinet for Human Resources v. Doe (509 U.S. 312), decided by a 5–4 vote, June 24, 1993; Kennedy wrote the opinion; Souter, Blackmun, Stevens and O'Connor dissented.

A state law that makes it easier to involuntarily commit the mentally retarded than to commit the mentally ill does not violate the Equal Protection or Due Process clauses of the Fourteenth Amendment.

SCHOOL DESEGREGATION

Missouri v. Jenkins (515 U.S. 70), decided by a 5–4 vote, June 12, 1995; Rehnquist wrote the opinion; Souter, Stevens, Ginsburg and Breyer dissented.

The federal judge overseeing the Kansas City school desegregation case exceeded his authority by ordering salary increases and creation of magnet schools to attract white students from neighboring districts. The Court held that the orders went beyond federal courts' power to remedy the "vestiges" of previous legal segregation.

SEX DISCRIMINATION

United States v. Virginia (518 U.S.___), decided by a 7–1 vote, June 26, 1996; Ginsburg wrote the opinion; Scalia dissented; Thomas did not participate.

The Court ordered the all-male Virginia Military Institute to admit women or lose public funding. The decision also appeared to tighten the Court's standards for reviewing laws that treat men and women differently.

SEXUAL HARASSMENT

Harris v. Forklift Systems, Inc. (512 U.S. 17), decided by a 9–0 vote, Nov. 9, 1993; O'Connor wrote the opinion.

An employee claiming job discrimination on the basis of sexual harassment must prove the existence of a "hostile" or "abusive" work environment but does not need to show that he or she suffered serious psychological injury as a result.

International Law

Saudi Arabia v. Nelson (507 U.S. 349), decided by votes of 8–1 and 6–3, March 23, 1993; Souter wrote the opinion; Kennedy and Blackmun dissented in part; Stevens dissented.

Americans who are mistreated by foreign law enforcement officials while working abroad generally cannot sue the foreign government in United States courts.

Labor Law

ANTITRUST EXEMPTION

Brown v. Pro Football, Inc., dba Washington Redskins (518 U.S. 231), decided by an 8–1 vote, June 20, 1996; Breyer wrote the opinion; Stevens dissented.

A group of employers that has reached an impasse in joint labor negotiations can unilaterally adopt the terms of its last offer without violating federal antitrust laws. The ruling stemmed from a dispute between the National Football League owners and the Players Association, but applied to other industries where joint employers' groups bargain with unions representing workers.

LABOR-MANAGEMENT RELATIONS

National Labor Relations Board v. Town & Country Electric, Inc. (516 U.S. 85), decided by a 9–0 vote, Nov. 28, 1995; Breyer wrote the opinion.

Federal labor law protects workers from antiunion discrimination even if a union is paying the worker to help organize the company. The ruling protected the tactic—called "salting"—of placing union members with nonunion companies to try to organize the company's employees from within.

Holly Farms Corp. v. National Labor Relations Board (517 U.S. 392), decided by 9–0 and 5–4 votes, April 23, 1996; Ginsburg wrote the opinion; O'Connor, Rehnquist, Scalia and Thomas dissented in part.

The Court extended federal labor law protection to "chicken-catcher" crews, rejecting a major poultry processor's claim that the workers were agricultural laborers exempt from the federal statute.

Auciello Iron Works, Inc. v. National Labor Relations Board (517 U.S. 781), decided by a 9–0 vote, June 3, 1996; Souter wrote the opinion.

An employer cannot disavow a collective bargaining agreement based on doubts about a union's majority status that the employer held prior to formation of the contract.

LABOR RELATIONS

Building and Construction Trades of the Metropolitan District v. Associated Builders and Contractors of Massachusetts/Rhode Island, Inc. (507 U.S. 218), decided by a 9–0 vote, March 8, 1993; Blackmun wrote the opinion.

Federal labor law does not prevent an independent state authority from entering into a labor agreement requiring employees on construction projects to be union members. The National Labor Relations Act generally preempts state regulation of labor relations. The act also specifically authorizes employers in the construction industry to enter into so-called prehire collective bargaining agreements that require all employees to join the designated union within seven days of being hired.

National Labor Relations Board v. Health Care & Retirement Corporation of America (511 U.S. 571), decided by a 5–4 vote, May 23, 1994; Kennedy wrote the opinion; Ginsburg, Blackmun, Stevens and Souter dissented.

The Court made it more difficult for nurses with supervisory responsibilities to organize collectively or enjoy other protections of federal labor law.

LAYOFFS AND PLANT CLOSINGS

North Star Steel Co. v. Thomas (515 U.S. 29), decided by a 9–0 vote, May 30, 1995; Souter wrote the opinion.

State law determines the time period for employees to sue their employer for violating a federal law requiring at least 60 days' advance notice before a plant closing or mass layoff. The ruling interpreting the 1988 Worker Adjustment and Retraining Notice Act backed labor unions' argument for a longer statute of limitations than would have been provided under federal law. The Court said state law generally determines the time period for bringing suits in cases where Congress fails to specify one unless the state statute of limitations would frustrate the enforcement of the federal law.

MINE SAFETY

Thunder Basin Coal Co. v. Reich (510 U.S. 200), decided by a 9–0 vote, Jan. 19, 1994; Blackmun wrote the opinion.

Mining companies cannot go to federal court to challenge implementation of mine safety regulations in advance of an agency action to enforce the rules. The decision prevented operators of a nonunionized coal mine in Wyoming from blocking a requirement that union representatives be allowed to participate in mine safety inspections.

PENSIONS AND BENEFITS

The District of Columbia v. The Greater Washington Board of Trade (506 U.S. 125), decided by an 8–1 vote, Dec. 14, 1992; Thomas wrote the opinion; Stevens dissented.

Federal law prevents states from requiring employers to provide disabled workers the same health insurance they offer to other employees. In a victory for business groups, the Court held that such a requirement is preempted by the federal Employee Retirement Income Security Act, which regulates employee pension and benefits plans.

Commissioner of Internal Revenue v. Keystone Consolidated Industries, Inc. (508 U.S. 152), decided by an 8–1 vote, May 24, 1993; Blackmun wrote the opinion; Stevens dissented.

Employers cannot satisfy their funding obligations under the federal pension protection law by contributing real estate instead of money to employee pension plans. The Court held that a section of the Employee Retirement Income Security Act of 1974 prohibited contributions of real estate to so-called defined-benefit pension plans even if the property is not subject to a mortgage or similar lien.

Mertens v. Hewitt Associates (508 U.S. 248), decided by a 5–4 vote, June 1, 1993; Scalia wrote the opinion; White, Rehnquist, Stevens and O'Connor dissented.

The federal pension protection law does not permit workers to obtain monetary damages from outside advisers for mismanagement. The Court's majority interpreted a provision of the Employee Retirement Income Security Act that permits suits against outside advisers for "appropriate equitable relief" to authorize injunctions or other court orders but not compensatory or punitive damages.

Local 144 Nursing Home Pension Fund v. Demisay (508 U.S. 581), decided by a 9–0 vote, June 14, 1993; Scalia wrote the opinion.

Federal courts have no general power to require union pension and welfare funds to be administered according to federal labor law.

Concrete Pipe & Products of California, Inc. v. Construction Laborers Pension Trust for Southern California (508 U.S. 602), decided by a 9–0 vote, June 14, 1993; Souter wrote the opinion.

The Court again upheld a federal law requiring employers who withdraw from an industrywide pension plan to pay their share of the plan's obligations before pulling out. The decision rejected a due process challenge to provisions of the law making it difficult for employers to contest the determination of their "withdrawal liability." The Court had twice before, in 1984 and 1986, rejected broader challenges to the law, the Multiemployer Pension Plan Amendments Act.

Milwaukee Brewery Workers' Pension Plan v. Jos. Schlitz Brewing Co. (513 U.S. 414), decided by a 9–0 vote, Feb. 21, 1995; Breyer wrote the opinion.

The Court slightly eased a company's cost of withdrawing from an underfunded industry pension plan by reducing the interest on the contributions required under federal law. The decision agreed with business groups' interpretation of a provision of the Multiemployer Pension Plan Amendments Act, a 1980 law aimed at shoring up financially troubled industrywide pension plans. The law imposes a withdrawal charge, to be paid in annual installments with interest, on companies that pull out of multiemployer plans.

Curtiss-Wright Corp. v. Schoonejongen (514 U.S. 73), decided by a 9–0 vote, March 6, 1995; O'Connor wrote the opinion.

The Court eased the legal requirements for companies to amend employee health benefit plans. The Court held that a standard provision reserving a company's right "to amend or modify" an employee health plan satisfies a provision of the Employee Retirement Income Security Act that requires plans to specify the "procedure" for changes.

Varity Corp. v. Howe (516 U.S. 489), decided by a 6–3 vote, March 19, 1996; Breyer wrote the opinion; Thomas, O'Connor and Scalia dissented.

Workers may bring individual suits against employers under the federal Employee Retirement Income Security Act for intentionally misleading them about employee health or pension benefits.

Lockheed Corp. v. Spink (517 U.S. 882), decided by 9–0 and 7–2 votes, June 10, 1996; Thomas wrote the opinion; Breyer and Souter dissented in part.

Employers can require workers to give up any employment-related legal claims in order to receive increased pension benefits under an early buyout plan.

PLANT CLOSINGS

United Food and Commercial Workers Union Local 751 v. Brown Group, Inc., dba Brown Shoe Co. (517 U.S. 544), decided by a 9–0 vote, May 13, 1996; Souter wrote the opinion.

Labor unions can sue on behalf of their members to enforce a federal law that requires employers to give advance notice of plant closings and provides backpay damages for violations of the act. The Court said that the Worker Adjustment and Retraining and Notification Act explicitly gives unions the right to sue on behalf of their members and that Congress had power to authorize suits by unions despite a court-made doctrine limiting the ability of associations to sue on behalf of members.

PUBLIC EMPLOYEES

Moreau v. Klevenhagen, Sheriff of Harris County, Texas (508 U.S. 22), decided by a 9–0 vote, May 3, 1993; Stevens wrote the opinion.

State and local governments that do not permit collective bargaining by public employees may unilaterally adopt overtime policies giving employees compensatory time off instead of premium pay.

RAILROAD EMPLOYEES

Brotherhood of Locomotive Engineers v. Atchison, Topeka & Santa Fe Railroad Co. (516 U.S. 152), decided by a 9–0 vote, Jan. 8, 1996; Kennedy wrote the opinion.

Railroad crews are not counted as on duty while waiting for "deadhead transportation" back to a terminal or rest station after having completed their shifts.

Norfolk & Western Railway Co. v. Hiles (516 U.S. 400), decided by a 9–0 vote, Feb. 27, 1996; Thomas wrote the opinion.

The Court slightly limited a railroad's liability for injuries to an employee resulting from problems in the operation of the automatic coupling mechanism required on railroad cars since 1893 by the federal Safety Appliance Act.

REMEDIES

ABF Freight System, Inc. v. National Labor Relations Board (510 U.S. 317), decided by a 9–0 vote, Jan. 24, 1994; Stevens wrote the opinion.

The Court upheld a decision by the National Labor Relations Board to order back pay and reinstatement to an employee fired for union activities, even though the worker lied under oath about the events prior to his dismissal.

Livadas v. Bradshaw, California Labor Commissioner (512 U.S. 107), decided by a 9–0 vote, June 13, 1994; Souter wrote the opinion.

The Court struck down a state policy of refusing to enforce a state wage law in complaints brought by union workers covered by collective bargaining agreements.

Hawaiian Airlines, Inc. v. Norris (512 U.S. 246), decided by a 9–0 vote, June 20, 1994; Blackmun wrote the opinion.

The federal labor law covering railway and airline industry workers does not prevent employees from filing wrongful discharge suits in state courts.

Consolidated Rail Corporation v. Gottshall (512 U.S. 532), decided by a 6–3 vote, June 24, 1994; Thomas wrote the opinion; Ginsburg, Blackmun and Stevens dissented.

Railroads are liable to employees for negligent infliction of emotional distress only if the employee sustains a physical impact or is placed in immediate risk of physical impact as a result of the negligence. The ruling adopted a restrictive "zone of danger" test for suits under the Federal Employers' Liability Act, a 1908 law protecting railroad workers injured on the job.

SEAMAN SUITS

Henderson v. United States (517 U.S. 654), decided by a 6–3 vote, May 20, 1996; Ginsburg wrote the opinion; Thomas, Rehnquist and O'Connor dissented.

The Court loosened the time period for a merchant mariner injured aboard a vessel owned by the United States to have the complaint served on the attorney general or local U.S. attorney. The ruling resolved a conflict between a provision of the 1920 Suits in Admiralty Act, requiring service of process "forthwith," and recent revisions of the Federal Rules of Civil Procedure, setting a 120-day time period that judges have broad discretion to extend. The Court held that the general rule on service of process "supersedes" the provision in the 1920 law.

WORKERS' COMPENSATION

Bath Iron Works Corp. v. Director, Office of Workers' Compensation Programs (506 U.S. 153), decided by a 9–0 vote, Jan. 12, 1993; Stevens wrote the opinion.

The Court interpreted a federal workers' compensation law covering shipbuilders and ship repairers to allow more generous benefits for some workers who are injured on the job but file for benefits only after retiring.

Director, Office of Workers' Compensation Programs, Department of Labor v. Greenwich Collieries (512 U.S. 267), decided by a 6–3 vote, June 20, 1994; O'Connor wrote the opinion; Souter, Blackmun and Stevens dissented.

The Court struck down a Labor Department rule that made it easier for injured workers to recover benefits under federal laws protecting longshore workers and coal miners.

Director, Office of Workers' Compensation Programs, Department of Labor v. Newport News Shipbuilding & Dry Dock Co. (514 U.S. 122), decided by a 9–0 vote, March 21, 1995; Scalia wrote the opinion.

The Court barred the Labor Department office responsible for two federal workers' compensation programs from appealing decisions by the agency's benefits review board on claims brought by longshore workers.

Metropolitan Stevedore Co. v. Rambo (515 U.S. 291), decided by an 8–1 vote, June 12, 1995; Kennedy wrote the opinion; Stevens dissented.

Federal disability benefits to injured longshore workers can be modified when there is a change in the employee's wage-earning capacity even without a change in the employee's physical condition.

Chandris, Inc. v. Latsis (515 U.S. 347), decided by 9–0 and 6–3 votes, June 14, 1995; O'Connor wrote the opinion; Stevens, Thomas and Breyer concurred in the result but dissented from the legal ruling.

A maritime worker must have a substantial connection to a ship in navigation to qualify as a "seaman" under the federal law allowing damage suits for on-the-job injuries. The ruling was aimed at clarifying the dividing line between two categories of maritime workers: seamen and longshore workers. A 1920 law called the Jones Act allows a seaman to file a damage suit for job-related injuries. The Longshore and Harbor Workers' Compensation Act limits longshore workers to scheduled payments under an administrative workers' compensation system.

Property Law

Dolan v. City of Tigard (512 U.S. 687), decided by a 5–4 vote, June 24, 1994; Rehnquist wrote the opinion; Stevens, Blackmun, Souter and Ginsburg dissented.

The Court limited the power of local governments to force landowners to permit public use of their property in return for approval of development or construction on the site. The Court held that municipalities have the burden of showing a connection and a "rough proportionality" between conditions imposed on a development permit and any claimed harm to the public from the development.

States

BORDER DISPUTES

Mississippi v. Louisiana (506 U.S. 73), decided by a 9–0 vote, Dec. 14, 1992; Rehnquist wrote the opinion.

A federal statute that gives the Supreme Court "original and exclusive jurisdiction of all controversies" between two or more states prevents lower federal courts from determining a state boundary dispute as part of a lawsuit between private parties over property lines.

Louisiana v. Mississippi (516 U.S. 22), decided by a 9–0 vote, Oct. 31, 1995; Kennedy wrote the opinion.

The Court sided with Mississippi in a border dispute involving 2,000 acres of land that had gradually shifted from an island in the Mississippi River to adjoin the river's western bank in Louisiana.

The Court unanimously upheld findings by the special master it appointed to hear the case and ruled that the disputed land should be awarded to Mississippi. The land had moved as the river shifted to the east. The Court explained that a boundary established around an island remains fixed even if the river's main channel shifts to the other side.

COMMERCE CLAUSE

West Lynn Creamery, Inc. v. Healy (512 U.S. 186, decided by a 7–2 vote, June 17, 1994; Stevens wrote the opinion; Rehnquist and Blackmun dissented.

The Court struck down a Massachusetts dairy farmer subsidy scheme on grounds that it discriminated against out-of-state milk producers.

IMMUNITY

Puerto Rico Aqueduct and Sewer Authority v. Metcalf & Eddy, Inc. (506 U.S. 139), decided by an 8–1 vote, Jan. 12, 1993; White wrote the opinion; Stevens dissented.

States or state agencies may take an immediate appeal of a ruling that rejects their claim of immunity from federal court suit under the Eleventh Amendment. The Court's decision allowed states to take advantage of the "collateral order doctrine," which permits an immediate appeal of some pretrial rulings. Most pretrial rulings cannot be appealed until after trial.

Hess v. Port Authority Trans-Hudson Corporation (513 U.S. 30), decided by a 5–4 vote, Nov. 14, 1994; Ginsburg wrote the opinion; O'Connor, Rehnquist, Scalia and Thomas dissented.

The Court somewhat narrowed the constitutional protection for interstate agencies from being sued in federal court. The decision cleared the way for two federal court suits on behalf of injured workers of a bistate railway, the Port Authority Trans-Hudson Corporation (PATH). The workers brought the suit under the Federal Employers' Liability Act, a 1907 law providing federal court jurisdiction over railway workers' suits. But PATH, a subsidiary of the Port Authority of New York and New Jersey, said the federal court suit was barred by the Eleventh Amendment, which gives state governments immunity from federal court suits. Resolving the conflict, the Court ruled that the railway was not entitled to protection from federal court suit because it was financially independent from its parent states, New Jersey and New York.

Seminole Tribe of Florida v. Florida (517 U.S. 44), decided by a 5–4 vote, March 27, 1996; Rehnquist wrote the opinion; Souter, Stevens, Ginsburg and Breyer dissented.

A federal law authorizing Native American tribes to sue states to force negotiations over gaming on Native American reservations violates the Eleventh Amendment's restriction on suits against states in federal courts. The decision—a major ruling on states' rights and federal court jurisdiction—struck down parts of the Indian Gaming Regulatory Act, passed by Congress in 1988, which required states to negotiate "in good faith" with Native American tribes over gaming issues and gave tribes the right to sue in federal court to enforce the requirement.

TAXATION

Itel Containers International Corp. v. Huddleston, Commissioner of Revenue of Tennessee (507 U.S. 60), decided by an 8–1 vote, Feb. 23, 1993; Kennedy wrote the opinion; Blackmun dissented.

States may impose sales taxes on a domestic company's leasing of cargo containers used in international shipping.

United States v. California (507 U.S. 746), decided by a 9–0 vote, April 26, 1993; O'Connor wrote the opinion.

The federal government was blocked from recovering state sales taxes that it said the state had wrongfully assessed against a federal contractor.

Oklahoma Tax Commission v. Sac and Fox Nation (508 U.S. 114), decided by a 9–0 vote, May 17, 1993; O'Connor wrote the opinion.

The Court strengthened the rule against state taxation of Native American tribal members by extending the exemption to Native Americans living in Indian communities but outside formal reservations. The unanimous Court held that without explicit congressional authority, a state may not tax tribal members who live and work in "Indian country." The Court said that Congress had defined Indian country to include formal or informal reservations, allotted lands and dependent Indian communities.

Harper v. Virginia Department of Taxation (509 U.S. 86), decided by a 7–2 vote, June 18, 1993; Thomas wrote the opinion; O'Connor and Rehnquist dissented.

The Court required retroactive application of a four-year-old decision entitling federal retirees to tax relief from states that had denied them a tax benefit granted to state and local government pensioners. The immediate effect of the ruling was to force Virginia and 15 other states to consider refunds or other relief totaling hundreds of millions of dollars for federal retirees who had been taxed on their pension benefits. The Court also used the case to announce a broad new rule that its decisions normally be given full retroactive effect in any kind of civil case.

Department of Revenue of Oregon v. ACF Industries, Inc. (510 U.S. 332), decided by an 8–1 vote, Jan. 24, 1994; Kennedy wrote the opinion; Stevens dissented.

The Court rejected a railroad industry challenge to state property tax systems that do not give railroads the same tax exemptions accorded to other businesses.

Associated Industries of Missouri v. Lohman, Director of Revenue of Missouri (511 U.S. 641), decided by a 9–0 vote, May 23, 1994; Thomas wrote the opinion.

States may not impose higher taxes on goods bought from outside the state than on in-state purchases even if the difference is small and due to local-option sales taxes.

Department of Taxation and Finance of New York v. Milhelm Attea & Bros., Inc. (512 U.S. 61), decided by a 9–0 vote, June 13, 1994; Stevens wrote the opinion.

The Court upheld New York State regulations aimed at preventing evasion of millions of dollars in taxes in the sale of untaxed cigarettes to non-Native Americans at stores on Native American reservations.

Barclays Bank PLC v. Franchise Tax Board of California (512 U.S. 298), decided by 9–0 and 7–2 votes, June 20, 1994; Ginsburg wrote the opinion; O'Connor and Thomas dissented in part.

States can tax multinational corporations on the basis of their worldwide income instead of on their earnings within a state unless Congress acts to prevent the practice. The ruling rejected pleas by international business groups, Britain and other U.S. trading partners to bar the so-called "worldwide combined reporting" accounting method for taxing multinational firms. They claimed the system—used in California until 1988 and in some form in six other states—subjected multinationals to double taxation.

Reich v. Collins, Revenue Commissioner of Georgia (513 U.S. 106), decided by a 9–0 vote, Dec. 6, 1994; O'Connor wrote the opinion.

The Court overturned efforts by the state of Georgia to avoid paying refunds to federal retirees for state income taxes paid under a scheme that had been struck down in earlier Court decisions. The Court said that the state had, in effect, changed the rules for obtaining refunds in the midst of the dispute.

Nebraska Dept. of Revenue v. Loewenstein (513 U.S. 123), decided by a 9–0 vote, Dec. 12, 1994; Thomas wrote the opinion.

States may tax income from mutual funds that invest in federal securities through so-called repurchase agreements, or "repos." The ruling resolved the tax status of a financial instrument in which an investor transfers federal securities to a mutual fund and agrees to "repurchase" it later at a premium.

Oklahoma Tax Commission v. Jefferson Lines, Inc. (514 U.S. 175), decided by a 7–2 vote, April 3, 1995; Souter wrote the opinion; Breyer and O'Connor dissented.

A state may impose a sales tax on the sale of bus tickets for interstate travel without dividing the proceeds with other states.

Oklahoma Tax Commission v. Chickasaw Nation (515 U.S. 450), decided by 9–0 and 5–4 votes, June 14, 1995; Ginsburg wrote the opinion; Breyer, Stevens, O'Connor and Souter dissented in part.

The Court barred Oklahoma from enforcing a gasoline excise tax on retail outlets owned by members of the Chickasaw tribe and operated on tribal lands, but it allowed the state to collect income taxes from tribal members who are employed by the tribe but live outside the Chickasaw reservation.

National Private Truck Council, Inc. v. Oklahoma Tax Commission (515 U.S. 582), decided by a 9–0 vote, June 19, 1995; Thomas wrote the opinion.

A taxpayer cannot use section 1983 of Title 42, a federal civil rights law, in state tax cases to block enforcement of a state levy or seek attorneys' fees as long as the state provides other procedures for contesting a tax.

Fulton Corp. v. Faulkner, Secretary of Revenue of North Carolina (516 U.S. 325), decided by a 9–0 vote, Feb. 21, 1996; Souter wrote the opinion.

A state may not tax stock owned by state residents in out-of-state corporations while exempting in-state corporate stock from the levy. The unanimous decision ruled North Carolina's so-called intangibles tax was unconstitutional because it discriminated against interstate commerce.

Richards v. Jefferson County, Alabama (517 U.S. 793), decided by a 9–0 vote, June 10, 1996; Stevens wrote the opinion.

Alabama courts improperly dismissed a federal law challenge to a county occupation tax brought by taxpayers who had not been parties to a previous unsuccessful state lawsuit against the levy.

WATER RIGHTS

Nebraska v. Wyoming (507 U.S. 584), decided by a 9–0 vote, April 20, 1993; O'Connor wrote the opinion.

The Court upheld a special master's recommendations resolving parts of a water rights dispute among Nebraska, Wyoming and the federal government involving the North Platte River and its tributaries. The dispute involved a 1945 Supreme Court decree that had allotted 75 percent of the North Platte's flow to Nebraska during the irrigation season and 25 percent to Wyoming. The Court backed Nebraska and the federal Bureau of Reclamation in diverting and storing water in irrigation reservoirs in western Nebraska. It also allowed Nebraska to proceed with a challenge to a new reservoir on the tributary Deer Creek.

United States v. Idaho ex rel. Director, Idaho Department of Water Resources (508 U.S. 1), decided by a 9–0 vote, May 3, 1993; Rehnquist wrote the opinion.

The federal government cannot be required to pay a filing fee when a state joins it as a defendant in a state court proceeding to adjudicate water rights.

Kansas v. Colorado (514 U.S. 673), decided by a 9–0 vote, May 15, 1995; Rehnquist wrote the opinion.

Colorado violated an interstate compact with Kansas on dividing the waters of the Arkansas River by allowing well-pumping to increase above the amount set when the agreement was reached in 1949. The ruling returned the case to the Court-appointed special master for further proceedings.

Nebraska v. Wyoming (515 U.S. 1), decided by an 8–1 vote, May 30, 1995; Souter wrote the opinion; Thomas dissented in part.

The Court allowed both Nebraska and Wyoming to add new claims to a long-running dispute over water rights for the North Platte River. The Court in 1945 issued a decree dividing the water among Colorado, Nebraska and Wyoming. Nebraska returned to the Court in 1986 claiming that Wyoming was taking more than its share of water under the decree. The Court settled some of the issues in a ruling in 1993. Both states then sought to raise new issues. Most notably, Nebraska sought to add a claim that Wyoming's violations of the decree were harming wildlife in the state, while Wyoming contended that the United States was reducing its water allocations by improper management of federal reservoirs in the state. The Court said the special master appointed to hear the case had acted properly in allowing most of the new claims.

MISCELLANEOUS STATE CASE

Delaware v. New York (507 U.S. 490), decided by a 6–3 vote, March 30, 1993; Thomas wrote the opinion; White, Blackmun and Stevens dissented.

Delaware won a lucrative victory in a dispute with New York over which state could claim hundreds of millions of dollars in unclaimed stock dividends. The Court ruled that dividends that cannot be traced to individual owners can be claimed by the state where the bank or brokerage firm holding the money is incorporated.

Torts

FEDERAL TORT CLAIMS ACT

Smith v. United States (507 U.S. 197), decided by an 8–1 vote, March 8, 1993; Rehnquist wrote the opinion; Stevens dissented.

The Federal Tort Claims Act (FTCA) does not authorize lawsuits against the United States government for negligent actions or omissions occurring in Antarctica. The decision barred a wrongful death action by the widow of a man who died in a fall in Antarctica, where he had been working for a construction company on contract to the federal National Science Foundation. The FTCA waives the federal government's sovereign immunity for certain tort claims, but it does not apply to "[a]ny claim arising in a foreign country." The Court held that Antarctica comes within that exception even though it has no recognized government.

McNeil v. United States (508 U.S. 106), decided by a 9–0 vote, May 17, 1993; Stevens wrote the opinion.

The Court refused to create an exception to the Federal Tort Claims Act's requirement that an individual exhaust administrative remedies before instituting a claim.

PUNITIVE DAMAGES

TXO Production Corp. v. Alliance Resources Corp. (509 U.S. 443), decided by a 6–3 vote, June 25, 1993; Stevens wrote the main opinion; O'Connor, White and Souter dissented.

In a blow to business groups and other critics of the civil justice system, the Court refused for the fifth time in recent years to set strict guidelines for juries to follow in awarding punitive damages.

Honda Motor Co., Ltd. v. Oberg (512 U.S. 415), decided by a 7–2 vote, June 24, 1994; Stevens wrote the opinion; Ginsburg and Rehnquist dissented.

States must permit judicial review of the amount of punitive damage awards by juries in civil suits. The ruling struck down a provision of Oregon's constitution that prohibited courts from reviewing the amount of punitive damages awarded by juries unless there was "no evidence" to support the verdict. No other state had a similar restriction.

BMW of North America, Inc. v. Gore (517 U.S. 559), decided by a 5–4 vote, May 20, 1996; Stevens wrote the opinion; Scalia, Rehnquist, Ginsburg and Thomas dissented.

The Court overturned as "grossly excessive" a $2 million punitive damage award to an Alabama man for an automobile manufacturer's failure to disclose a refinished paint job on a car he purchased as new. The Court ruled that the award "exceeds the constitutional limit" under the Due Process Clause. The decision, an important victory for critics of punitive damage awards, left it to the Alabama Supreme Court to determine whether to reconsider the amount of punitive damages itself or to order a new trial.

RACKETEERING

Reves v. Ernst & Young (507 U.S. 170), decided by a 7–2 vote, March 3, 1993; Blackmun wrote the opinion; Souter and White dissented.

The federal antiracketeering law can be used only against persons who participate in the operation or management of an illegal enterprise. It cannot be wielded against outside advisers such as accountants or lawyers who do not have a part in directing the enterprise's affairs.

The ruling marked the first time the Court had narrowed the controversial Racketeer Influenced and Corrupt Organizations Act, which provides stiff civil and criminal penalties for conducting unlawful activities through businesses or other organizations.

WARSAW CONVENTION

Zicherman v. Korean Air Lines Co. (516 U.S. 217), decided by a 9–0 vote, Jan. 16, 1996; Scalia wrote the opinion.

Relatives of passengers killed in an airplane crash over international waters cannot recover damages for loss of companionship. The Court ruled that the Warsaw Convention left it up to each country to apply its own law in determining what damages can be recovered and that the crash was covered by the federal Death on the High Seas Act, which expressly limits damage awards to pecuniary losses.

CHAPTER 14

General Government

General Government

Government efficiency and cost containment were key themes in general government legislation considered in 1993–1996.

'REINVENTING GOVERNMENT,' FEDERAL WORKERS

Vice President Al Gore was the chief architect of an ambitious executive branch plan to "reinvent government" by making it more efficient and more effective. The recommendations of the National Performance Review were released with much fanfare in September 1993. While Congress did not clear a comprehensive "reinventing government" bill, the Clinton administration succeeded in pushing through piece by piece a number of its proposals that sought to streamline government operations.

As part of the "reinventing government" initiative, legislation cleared that simplified the procedures used by federal agencies to make purchases; cut the federal workforce and provided cash incentives for bureaucrats to retire early; improved financial management and reduced personnel costs in the executive branch; permitted federal workers to use sick leave to care for ailing family members; and trimmed federal paperwork requirements for individuals, educational institutions, and state and local governments.

Congress cleared several other bills that directly affected federal workers. After almost 20 years of trying, Congress revamped the 1939 Hatch Act, easing restrictions on federal workers' political activities. For the first time, White House and many presidential appointees were put under the protection of federal civil rights and labor laws. And federal employees were permitted to use other employees' leave time to deal with personal or family medical emergencies; incentives were provided to federal employees to find ways to commute to and from work besides driving alone; protections were expanded for federal whistleblowers—those who reported fraud, waste, abuse and criminal activity in the workplace; and the pensions of federal retirees found guilty of child abuse were allowed to be garnished for the purpose of paying court-ordered damages.

REGULATORY OVERHAUL

Congressional Republicans in 1995 launched a multi-pronged attack on federal regulatory powers, attempting to lighten the burden on certain key industries while making it harder to impose new limits on businesses and property owners. However, the grand proposals failed to become law. Republicans instead in 1996 managed, with bipartisan support, to clear as part of a bill to raise the limit on the federal debt two small pieces of the regulatory overhaul package—one giving Congress 60 days to review and challenge any major new rule before it took effect, the other giving small businesses more power to demand special regulatory treatment.

Originally, the central effort was a package of House bills to protect the rights of property owners and change the way federal agencies developed regulations. These pieces were augmented by bills, for example, to halt temporarily any new rulemaking and to reexamine the need for existing regulations. The property rights bill emphasized that regulations had costs as well as benefits and sought to impose those costs on the taxpayers instead of individual landowners. Other legislation would limit the regulatory agencies' horizons, focusing them on the greatest hazards and the least costly responses.

The proposals illustrated the difference between Democratic and Republican views on what role the government should play. To Democrats, federal agencies helped protect an unsuspecting public against a world of hidden perils; liberals in particular had been pushing for tougher, more comprehensive rules. Many Republicans and some conservative Democrats, meanwhile, saw the agencies as overreaching and ineffective, incapable of distinguishing between real dangers and fanciful ones. They seemed to see the public more as the victim of regulation than the beneficiary.

The debate recalled the battles in the 1980s and early 1990s over the White House's intervention in regulatory proposals. This time, however, the roles were reversed, with Congress interceding on the behalf of business and the White House objecting.

REFERENCES

Discussion of general government action for the years 1945–1964 may be found in *Congress and the Nation Vol. I*, pp. 1455–1516; for the years 1965–1968, *Congress and the Nation Vol. II*, pp. 655–660; for the years 1969–1972, *Congress and the Nation Vol. III*, pp. 435–468; for the years 1973–1976, *Congress and the Nation Vol. IV*, pp. 795–826; for the years 1977–1980, *Congress and the Nation Vol. V*, pp. 817–870; for the years 1981–84, *Congress and the Nation Vol. VI*, pp. 771–793; for the years 1985–1988, *Congress and the Nation Vol. VII*, pp. 843–867; for the years 1989–1992, *Congress and the Nation Vol. VIII*, pp. 855–909.

Outlays for Science, Space and General Government

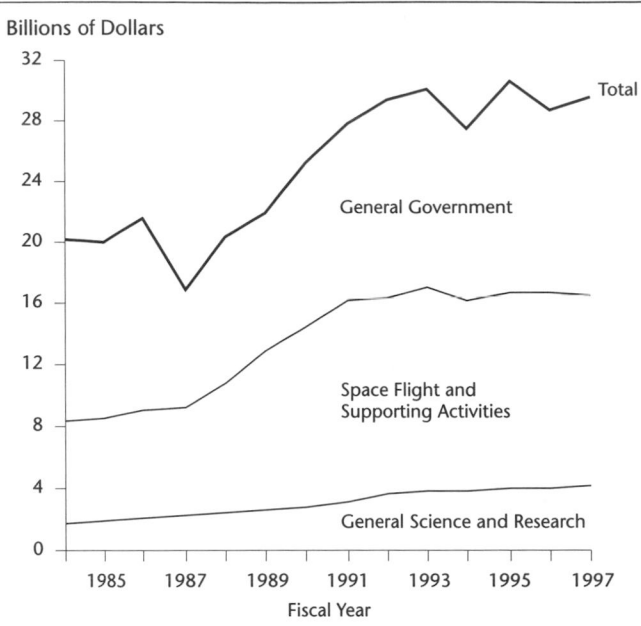

Billions of Dollars

NOTE: Data for 1997 are estimated.

SOURCE: Office of Management and Budget, *Historical Tables, Budget of the United States Government: Fiscal Year 1998* (Washington, D.C.: U.S. Government Printing Office, 1997), Table 3.2.

OTHER MAJOR BILLS

Three other major bills falling under the purview of general government legislation were cleared by Congress: "motor voter" registration, unfunded mandates and lobbying disclosure.

The "motor voter" bill, which allowed voters to register to vote by mail and when applying for a driver's license, became law in large part because Bill Clinton became president. George Bush had vetoed a similar measure in 1992, and the Senate sustained the veto. Republicans generally opposed the legislation because they believed it invited voter fraud and would be expensive for states to implement. Candidate Clinton was vocal in his support for "motor voter," and he signed it into law within months of taking office.

Clinton, a former governor, also endorsed legislation to bar Congress from imposing mandates on state and local governments without providing the funds to pay for them. Congressional efforts to enact unfunded mandates legislation stalled in 1994. It became a priority in 1995, however, as part of the GOP's "Contract with America." Liberal opposition to the measure centered on fears that it would result in weakened public health, civil rights and environmental laws.

In an unanticipated turn, the 103rd Congress was unable to complete action on a lobby disclosure reform bill. Although both chambers originally had passed the legislation by overwhelming margins, opposition swelled among Republicans and lobbyists when it emerged from conference. Supporters accused members of blocking the bill because they disliked provisions in the legislation imposing a strict ban on gifts. The 104th Congress separated the lobby registration requirements and the gift ban into different bills and thus succeeded in clearing a lobby disclosure measure.

SCIENCE PROGRAMS

Deficit-reduction concerns were evident in lawmakers' decisions regarding the federal government's big-science projects.

Members in 1993 killed the superconducting supercollider, which was intended to reveal the basic nature of matter and energy. Billions of dollars had been spent on the project, under construction since 1990. The supercollider had the misfortune to be of undistinguished scientific merit, a low priority for the Clinton administration, and in production during a time of strong budget-cutting sentiment.

Despite attempts to withdraw its funding, the National Aeronautics and Space Administration's space station managed to survive—with its size and scope reduced. The project's redesign, strong endorsement from the Clinton administration, and foreign policy implications through international agreements contributed to the strengthening of its support.

DISTRICT OF COLUMBIA

Congress in 1995 established a financial review board to work with the beleaguered District of Columbia, which suffered ongoing economic problems. The board had the authority to reorganize city government and to cut spending. Imposition of the board represented the biggest change to the District government since home rule was enacted in 1973.

In other notable District-related action, the House in 1993 voted on legislation that would grant statehood to the District and thus allow it voting representation in the House and Senate. It was the first time either chamber had taken such a vote. However, the bill was rejected.

NATIVE AMERICAN LEGISLATION

The 103rd and 104th Congresses also cleared numerous bills affecting Native American affairs, many of which were aimed at giving tribes more autonomy. Legislation was enacted that provided resources to tribal court systems, sought to have tribes create programs to manage farmlands and ranches, made implementation of federal environmental laws on Native American lands easier, settled a land dispute between the Catawba tribe and South Carolina landowners, allowed tribes to handle their own trust funds, provided that the federal government stop distinguishing between "historic" and "created" tribes, protected Native Americans' religious use of the drug peyote, encouraged cleanup of suspected toxic waste dumps on Native American reservations, aimed to curtail child abuse on reservations, ratified an agreement regarding a territorial dispute between the Hopi and Navajo tribes, and repealed a prohibition against some federal employees and their spouses making business deals with Native Americans.

Chronology of Action on General Government

1993–1994

Hatch Act Revisions

After trying for nearly two decades, Congress in 1993 cleared legislation (HR 20—PL 103-94) to revise and simplify the 1939 Hatch Act, which restricted political activities by federal and postal employees.

HR 20 barred federal employees from engaging in political activity while on duty, including wearing a campaign button on the job. While off duty, federal employees could hold office in a political party, participate in campaigns and political rallies, publicly endorse candidates and raise political funds from within their agency's political action committee. They were prohibited, however, from running for partisan elective offices or soliciting contributions from the general public. The new law was expected to affect nearly three million federal employees. Existing Hatch Act restrictions were maintained for certain high-level employees and sensitive agencies.

BACKGROUND

The legislation, named for Sen. Carl A. Hatch, D-N.M. (1933–1949), originally was written to shield elections from spoilers who pressed workers to contribute to campaigns in exchange for federal job protections. Hatch called for restricting the activities of federal workers after a Senate panel found that political appointees in the Works Progress Administration had coerced employees into contributing to political campaigns to protect their jobs. At the time, less than 32 percent of the 950,000-member federal workforce were career public servants; the rest were political appointees.

For years, proponents of revising the Hatch Act had argued that it denied federal workers the right to political expression that was guaranteed to other citizens, that it was outdated because the federal workforce was comprised mostly of career professionals and that the jumble of rules and restrictions was confusing and contradictory. Under the original law, federal employees could not actively participate in partisan campaigns, although no restrictions were placed on participation in nonpartisan elections, such as those for local school boards or town councils. While federal employees were allowed to contribute money to candidates, they could not stuff envelopes or work on a get-out-the-vote effort for a particular candidate or party. However, federal employees were allowed to sport buttons during work and have bumper stickers on their cars.

Opponents argued that revising the Hatch Act would politicize the federal workforce and pointed out that the Supreme Court had twice upheld the constitutionality of the law, in 1947 and in 1972.

Efforts to revise the law had been blocked repeatedly by Republican presidents. Gerald R. Ford vetoed a bill in 1976.

Ronald Reagan prevented a measure from reaching his desk in 1988 by threatening a veto. George Bush vetoed an attempt to revise the Hatch Act in 1990 and used a veto threat to prevent any action in the 102nd Congress. *(Details, Congress and the Nation Vol. IV, pp. 815, 822; Congress and the Nation Vol. VII, p. 857; Congress and the Nation Vol. VIII, pp. 859, 886)*

LEGISLATIVE ACTION

The House Post Office and Civil Service Committee reported HR 20 (H Rept 103-16) on Feb. 22, 1993. The bill stumbled off the fast track two days later, when the House failed to muster the two-thirds vote needed to push HR 20 through under suspension of the rules, an expedited procedure that barred amendments. The 275–142 tally was three votes shy.

On March 3, under normal procedures, the House passed HR 20 with bipartisan support on a 333–86 vote. The bill allowed federal and Postal Service employees to participate in a full range of political activities on their own time, while disallowing on-the-job political activity. It permitted employees to solicit political contributions but prohibited job-related requests, including seeking money from fellow workers on the job. It barred federal employees from using official influence or information for partisan political purposes. And it prohibited them from wearing political campaign buttons while in government buildings and on duty.

The House by voice vote approved two Republican-sponsored amendments. One, by Nancy L. Johnson of Connecticut, tightened a provision that allowed federal workers to run for any political office; the amendment permitted them to run only for local offices such as town council. The other, by Fred Upton of Michigan, maintained existing restrictions on the political activities of Federal Election Commission workers.

The Senate Governmental Affairs Committee reported a more restrictive version of the bill (S 185—S Rept 103-57) on June 16. Unlike the House measure, S 185 did not allow federal employees to run for local partisan elective office, and it prohibited federal workers from soliciting the general public for political contributions. It did provide for unionized federal workers to solicit nonsubordinate union members for political contributions for that group's political action committee. The committee included an amendment incorporating the language from a bill (S 253) that would allow wage garnishment—court-ordered payments for a legal debt taken from an employee's wages—for all federal employees. Wage garnishment laws had applied only to private sector and postal employees. The panel also approved an amendment, offered by Governmental Affairs Chairman John Glenn, D-Ohio, to prohibit the use of recommendations from political officeholders in hiring or promoting civil service employees. A number of amendments by ranking Republican William V. Roth Jr. of Delaware were rejected by voice vote. One would have exempted certain employees from the legislation, including those at the Internal Revenue Service (IRS), the Justice Department and the Central Intelligence Agency. Roth also tried unsuccessfully to exempt employees such as supervisors and administrative law judges and to retain the president's right to issue an executive order limiting political activity by federal workers.

Roth had some success on the Senate floor. Senators adopted, 92–4 on July 14, a Roth amendment to express the sense of the Senate that federal employees could not solicit political contributions from the general public or run for a local partisan public office, two provisions allowed under HR 20. Anticipating a tough conference fight, Roth said he wanted to ensure that the Senate sent a message that it strongly opposed the House-approved provisions.

Another Roth amendment, adopted 88–7 on July 14, clarified that an employee would be dismissed for a first violation of the Hatch Act unless the Merit Systems Protection Board unanimously voted instead to suspend the employee's pay for 30 days. On July 20, the Senate adopted by voice vote a Roth amendment to maintain existing Hatch Act restrictions on employees of the Justice Department's criminal division. The amendment was accepted after a motion to table (kill) it was rejected, 43–56.

A motion to table a Roth amendment to give federal employees a referendum on whether they wanted to be covered under the existing Hatch Act or under S 185 was agreed to, 62–34 on July 14. On July 20, a motion to table another Roth amendment, to maintain restrictions on IRS examiners and auditors, was agreed to, 51–48. Senators also agreed, 58–41, to table an amendment offered by Nancy Landon Kassebaum, R-Kan., to bar federal employees from soliciting political funds. The Senate adopted by voice vote an unrelated amendment offered by John McCain, R-Ariz., expressing the sense of the Senate that further U.S. aid to Nicaragua should be halted pending an investigation into the involvement of the Sandinista National Liberation Front in international terrorist activities.

After substituting the text of S 185, the Senate July 20 passed HR 20 by 68–31. In a move that avoided a contentious conference, the House accepted the Senate changes, 339–85 on Sept. 21, completing congressional action.

PROVISIONS

As signed into law on Oct. 6, HR 20 (PL 103-94):

• **Policy.** Stated that federal employees should be encouraged to exercise, fully and freely and without fear of reprisal, their right to participate or to refrain from participating in the political process.

• **Federal Employees.** Defined employees covered under the bill to be any individual, other than the president or vice president or General Accounting Office workers, employed or holding office in an executive agency or in a competitive civil service position that was not in an executive agency.

• **Postal Workers.** Covered United States Postal Service and Postal Rate Commission workers.

• **Other Workers.** Covered employees of the District of Columbia government other than the mayor, city council members and the recorder of deeds. Excluded members of the armed forces. Military personnel fell under separate Defense Department rules governing the political activities of the military.

• **Partisan Political Office.** Defined a partisan political office as one for which a candidate was nominated or elected as representing a party that received electoral votes in the last presidential election. The definition did not include any office or position within a political party or affiliated organization.

• **Political Contribution.** Defined a political contribution as a gift or contribution made for any political purpose.

• **Off-Duty Political Activities.** Allowed federal employees to manage political campaigns or take an active role in political parties and groups, including seeking and holding positions in local and national political parties; stuffing envelopes, organizing and participating in phone banks and participating in voter registration drives; carrying posters at a political rally, distributing campaign material and soliciting votes off the job; organizing and participating in political meetings; publicly endorsing candidates; and soliciting contributions for the political action committee of a federal employees' organization from other members of that employees' organization who did not work under the person soliciting funds.

Federal employees had been prohibited from any kind of solicitation of funds. Under the new law, employees could solicit or receive political contributions only from an employee who was a member of the same agency's political action committee. However, federal employees were barred from soliciting funds from a member of the political action committee when the targeted employee was a subordinate worker.

• **Off-Duty Limits.** Prohibited federal employees, on or off the job, from running for partisan political office; using official authority to interfere with or affect the result of an election; and soliciting or discouraging the political activity of any person with business pending before the employee's office. Such business included an application for any compensation, grant, contract, ruling, license, permit or certificate. Federal employees also were barred from soliciting or discouraging political activity by any person who was the subject of an ongoing audit, investigation or enforcement action.

• **Exceptions for Sensitive Posts.** Kept in place the original Hatch Act restrictions, forbidding active participation in political management or political campaigns for certain federal employees in sensitive positions. Such employees included those at the Federal Election Commission; Federal Bureau of Investigation; Secret Service; Central Intelligence Agency; National Security Council; National Security Agency; Defense Intelligence Agency; Merit Systems Protection Board; Office of Special Counsel; Office of Criminal Investigations of the Internal Revenue Service; Office of Investigative Programs of the U.S. Customs Service; Office of Law Enforcement of the Bureau of Alcohol, Tobacco and Firearms; and Criminal Division of the Justice Department. Also included were administrative law judges, career Senior Executive Service employees and Contract Appeal Board members.

• **On-Duty Political Activity.** Barred federal employees from engaging in political activity while on duty, in any room or building used by government employees for official business. Such activities also were barred when a government employee was wearing a uniform or official insignia identifying his or her office or position or using any U.S. government vehicle. The law prohibited a federal employee from wearing a campaign button on the job, a form of political expression that had been permitted under the old Hatch Act.

• **Exceptions.** Made exceptions for employees whose duties continued outside usual hours and away from the usual post, and whose jobs were paid for by an appropriation for the Executive Office of the President or were subject to presidential appointment and Senate confirmation, and involved determination of U.S. foreign policy.

• **Areas with Many Federal Workers.** Permitted the Office of Personnel Management to write rules making exceptions for the local political involvement of federal employees who lived in certain areas such as Maryland, Virginia, the District of Columbia or where the majority of voters were federal employees.

• **Coercion.** Made it illegal for any person to intimidate, threaten, command or coerce any federal employee to engage in or not engage in a political activity. The law made it illegal to threaten federal workers to vote or not vote for any particular candidate, to make or not make a political contribution for any candidate or to work or not work for a particular candidate.

• **Violations.** Allowed employees who violated the law to be fired. Any person who intimidated, threatened or coerced a federal employee to participate in political activity also could face fines of up to $5,000 or up to three years in jail.

• **Other Penalties.** Stated that a minimum penalty of 30 days' suspension without pay could be imposed if the Merit Systems Protection Board, a quasi-judicial agency that safeguarded the civil service against political partisanship and other unfair practices, found by a unanimous vote that a violation did not warrant firing.

• **Prohibited Recommendations.** Specified that a federal manager making a personnel decision such as a hiring, promotion or transfer had to make that decision without regard for any recommendations by a member of Congress or congressional employee, state elected official or official of a political party; or any recommendations made on the basis of the party affiliation of the prospective employee. Those politically affiliated individuals could not make such recommendations, and agencies or employees could not solicit or accept such recommendations. The head of each agency had to ensure that employees and applicants were aware of these restrictions.

• **Permitted Recommendations.** Allowed an agency or manager to solicit and accept recommendations regarding a prospective federal employee only if the recommendation was furnished by a former employer and addressed only the work performance and ability or security standards of the job candidate.

• **Garnisheeing Wages.** Allowed creditors to garnishee wages of federal employees through the same legal process that they followed with a private citizen. Garnisheeing wages, a legal remedy for taking a part of the regular pay of an employee, had been used by creditors to recoup debts from a financially delinquent private individual. Previously, federal employees had been exempted from having wages garnisheed.

It limited the percentage of wages that could be garnisheed to 25 percent or the amount by which the disposable earnings for the week exceeded 30 times the federal minimum wage, whichever was less. It required that child support and alimony judgments against a federal employee be given precedence over other legal garnishment orders.

• **Nicaragua.** Stated that it was the sense of the Senate that no further aid should go to Nicaragua until an investigation took place of the potential involvement of the Sandinista National Liberation Front in any terrorist activities that threatened U.S. security or the political stability and economic prosperity of the Western Hemisphere. The nonbinding resolution stated that an explosion in Managua, Nicaragua, on May 23, 1993, exposed a cache of weapons and 310 passports from 21 countries including the United States. It also said that documents in the possession of those apprehended in connection with the Feb. 26, 1993, bombing of the World Trade Center in New York had been traced to Nicaragua. The provision questioned the ability of the Nicaraguan government to stop the export of terrorism by the Sandinista National Liberation Front.   ❏

'Motor Voter'

President Clinton on May 20, 1993, signed "motor voter" legislation (HR 2—PL 103-31) requiring states to provide all eligible citizens the opportunity to register to vote when they applied for or renewed a driver's license. It also required states to allow mail-in registration and to provide registration forms at certain agencies that supplied public assistance, such as welfare checks or help for the disabled. The costs were to be borne by the states. Backers estimated that the changes, which were to take effect in 1995, would add 50 million citizens to the voting rolls.

BACKGROUND

Virtually every politician and political scholar subscribed to the tenet that a legislative body was made more representative and more wholly democratic when voter participation was highest. However, according to the Federal Election Commission, only about 50 percent of those eligible to vote in the United States typically went to the polls on election day. That figure had remained largely unchanged since World War II, even though the voting age population had been steadily increasing.

Efforts to increase registration nationwide had met with partisan politics. Republicans had been effective for a number of years in blocking enhanced registration bills, which they warned would lead to a new wave of voter fraud, cost too much for states to implement and fail to have any ultimate effect on turnout. They also objected to proposed requirements that states make voter registration forms available at welfare offices, arguing that Democrats were trying to register inner-city residents who tended to vote Democratic. Democrats roundly denied the charge.

Efforts to increase voter registration had begun in a handful of states by the mid-1980s, with state legislatures ordering motor vehicle departments to provide voter registration forms. By 1992, 27 states had some type of motor voter practices in place. But state programs varied in their degree of sophistication and in their effect on turnout.

Lawmakers debated motor voter legislation at length in the 101st and 102nd Congresses. In 1990, the House passed a motor voter bill, only to see it die in the Senate after Republicans blocked floor consideration. In 1991, Senate Republicans again

CENSUS COUNT

A federal judge in New York on April 13, 1993, let stand the Census Bureau's 1990 census, thus ordering no adjustment to correct its undercount of racial minorities. The head count is used as the official basis for apportioning House seats, drawing congressional district lines and distributing federal funds.

In 1991 the Census Bureau estimated the net undercount at 5.3 million people. Census officials, including Director Barbara E. Bryant, recommended adjustment. But Commerce Secretary Robert A. Mosbacher in July 1991 reversed the recommendation. Mosbacher's decision was protested by big cities, big states, many minority group leaders and most congressional Democrats. *(Background, Congress and the Nation Vol. VIII, p. 1145)*

Judge Joseph M. McLaughlin, with the 2nd U.S. Circuit Court of Appeals, said Mosbacher probably erred when he refused to adjust the count. But he said no evidence existed that Mosbacher's decision to use the count was "arbitrary and capricious." As a result, he said, it could not be overturned.

---

held off a floor vote, as supporters were unable to muster the 60 votes necessary to break off debate and take up a motor voter measure. In 1992, Senate sponsors were able for the first time to round up enough votes to limit debate and pass a motor voter bill. The House agreed to the Senate bill and sent it to the White House. But President George Bush vetoed the measure, saying it amounted to an "open invitation to fraud and corruption." The Senate subsequently sustained the veto. *(1990 action, Congress and the Nation Vol. VIII, p. 871; 1991–1992 action, Congress and the Nation Vol. VIII, p. 893)*

During the 1992 presidential campaign, Bill Clinton said he would have signed the bill.

LEGISLATIVE ACTION

The House Administration Committee reported HR 2 (H Rept 103-9) on Feb. 2, 1993. The bill was nearly identical to the one Bush had vetoed in 1992. It required states to make registration forms available not only at motor vehicle departments but also at numerous state offices, including unemployment compensation offices, welfare offices and agencies that served the disabled. HR 2 elevated voter fraud to a federal offense punishable by as much as five years in prison. It allowed, but did not require, states to use information from change-of-address forms filed with the U.S. Postal Service to update voter lists. The committee rejected a series of GOP amendments, including ones that would have placed a cap on how long a registered voter who failed to vote could be kept on an active list, made the bill voluntary until money was provided to states to pay for implementation and removed mandates for mail-in registration.

On the floor, the House rejected, 166–253 on Feb. 4, a Bill Thomas, R-Calif., motion to send HR 2 back to committee with instructions to include language to delay implementation of the bill until state election officials notified the Justice Department

that "sufficient procedures" were in place to prevent noncitizens from voting. Republicans argued that noncitizens applying for drivers licenses might automatically be put on the voter rolls unless more checks were installed. Democrats said the states already had procedures to prevent such illegal registration and charged that the GOP language was an attempt to gut the bill by allowing states to avoid implementing motor voter systems. The House passed HR 2, 259–160, on Feb. 4.

The Senate Rules Committee reported a nearly identical companion bill (S 460—S Rept 103-6) Feb. 25.

Republican opponents, led by Mitch McConnell, R-Ky., used parliamentary tactics and extensive floor debate to slow the bill's advance and win substantial changes in the measure. Republicans began their delaying tactics March 5, when McConnell, with considerable help from Minority Leader Bob Dole, R-Kan., rounded up the votes needed to prevent the Senate from taking up the bill for consideration. With low attendance on a Friday morning, senators voted 52–36 on a motion to cut off debate and proceed to the bill; supporters needed 60 votes to prevail. However, a second cloture motion was agreed to March 9 by a vote of 62–38. Once the Senate turned to the bill, Republican opponents continued efforts to thwart it.

After a long debate, the Senate voted 45–52 on March 10 to reject an amendment, offered by John McCain, R-Ariz., to give the president line-item veto authority, which would enable him to veto individual provisions of appropriations bills. The Senate agreed 55–42 on March 11 to table (kill) another McCain amendment, to bar an agency from registering to vote citizens who received direct financial aid from the agency (except for people with disabilities). McCain and other GOP senators argued that welfare recipients might feel pressured into registering to vote when they picked up their checks. Democrats said the amendment was a veiled attempt to prevent poor people from voting. The Senate March 11 also agreed, 53–43, to a motion to table (kill) an amendment by Don Nickles, R-Okla., to require Congress to provide funds to pay for implementation of the measure. On March 16, the Senate adopted, 99–0, a package of amendments offered by Wendell H. Ford, D-Ky., that included provisions requiring states to make available voter registration forms at military recruitment centers and requiring driver's license applicants to fill out a separate form for registering to vote. The original language provided that a driver's license application would have automatically registered those eligible to vote unless the applicant checked a box declining registration. Ford's amendment was intended to answer concerns of the GOP and to shore up support for passage of the bill.

Final passage came hours after Democratic and Republican leaders agreed to a compromise that removed provisions to require states to make available registration forms at public assistance agencies. The compromise said states "may" provide registration forms at such offices instead of requiring them to do so. The Senate passed HR 2, after substituting the text of S 460, by 62–37 on March 17.

The largest outstanding difference between the House and Senate versions was the Senate's decision to drop the requirement that voter registration be provided at public assistance agencies. Conferees on HR 2 agreed to accept the House language but added new language requiring public agencies to make it clear to beneficiaries that registering to vote was optional and that not registering would not affect the amount of assistance they received. House conferees agreed to drop the requirement that registration forms be made available at unemployment offices. And the conference committee dropped Senate language crafted by Alan K. Simpson, R-Wyo., to allow states to require a registrant to produce documentation of citizenship upon request by election officials. Opponents of the Simpson language said it would lead to discrimination against people who appeared foreign or who had foreign-sounding names.

The House May 5 rejected, 170–253, a GOP motion to send the bill back to conference and require the inclusion of Simpson's language. The House then adopted the conference report (H Rept 103-66) on May 5 by a vote of 259–164. After agreeing, 63–37, to a motion to invoke cloture, the Senate on May 11 voted 62–36 to adopt the conference report, clearing HR 2.   ❑

Lobbying Disclosure

Legislation (S 349) to revamp lobbying disclosure requirements and tighten gift rules for members of Congress passed both chambers but died at the close of the 103rd Congress, the victim of election-year pressures and disintegrating support from members. Defeat of the bill killed the last remaining item on the Democratic list of political reforms backed by President Clinton.

The blocking of the measure was striking because both chambers originally had approved the provisions by overwhelming margins. But the apparent support for the legislation masked a deep ambivalence among many members of Congress about toughening gift rules and among lobbyists and organizations whose activities would be scrutinized far more closely under the proposed rules.

Republicans, whose filibuster in the Senate blocked action on the bill's conference report, argued that it contained provisions that could require grassroots lobbying organizations to disclose information about their contributors that would deter citizen involvement in politics. Bill sponsors accused the Republicans of ginning up objections to kill the measure in order to deny the Democrats and President Clinton a victory. They also said some members of both parties joined the effort to preserve their ability to accept gifts from lobbyists. Republicans responded that they had raised objections about the bill earlier but had been ignored. (Gift rules, p. 919)

BACKGROUND

Congress had considered lobbying disclosure proposals since the late 1800s. Passage of the Foreign Agents Registration Act of 1938 and the Federal Regulation of Lobbyists Act of 1946 did little to put the issue to rest; both laws long had been considered ineffective. The Justice Department in 1983 called the 1946 law unenforceable, and registration came to be viewed as voluntary by lobbyists.

President Harry S. Truman appointed a commission to reform lobbying laws in 1948. Nothing happened. Likewise, efforts in the 1950s failed. Lobbying bills passed in 1976 and 1978, but Congress failed to agree on how much disclosure to require of whom—mainly whether to require disclosure of registrants' grassroots activities and of lobbying groups' big contributors. In 1989, in response to an influence-peddling scandal at the Department of Housing and Urban Development, Congress enacted a set of lobbying disclosure requirements (PL 101-121) for certain recipients of federal grants, contracts or loans. But the Senate Governmental Affairs Committee found little meaningful information provided by the 1989 law and decided to try again in 1992. The bill the panel reported that year never got to the Senate floor. (1976 action, Congress and the Nation Vol. IV, p. 840; 1978 action, Congress and the Nation Vol. V, p. 910; 1989 action, Congress and the Nation Vol. VIII, p. 862; 1992 action, Congress and the Nation Vol. VIII, p. 887)

President Clinton helped put the issue of lobbying reform on the front burner early in his administration by railing against the influence of lobbyists. When he began selling his painful package of tax increases and spending cuts to the American people with a televised speech Feb. 15, 1993, he called "high-priced lobbyists" the "defenders of decline" and predicted that they would be out in full force to defeat his proposals minutes after they were made public. His package included a special dig at lobbyists: It eliminated the business income tax deduction for lobbying expenses. That provision was later enacted as part of the budget-reconciliation bill (HR 2264). In a speech to Congress on Feb. 17, he called on lawmakers to "deal with the undue influence of special interests" by expanding lobby registration and disclosure requirements. (Reconciliation, p. 44)

LEGISLATIVE ACTION

The Senate passed its lobbying disclosure bill (S 349) by a vote of 95–2 on May 6, 1993. S 349 had been reported (S Rept 103-37) by the Senate Governmental Affairs Committee on April 1.

In general, the Senate-passed bill required registration by anyone who received or spent money to contact members, their nonclerical staff or a wide array of senior executive branch officials in connection with bills, regulations, policies or programs. Organizations with in-house lobbyists were to register for their employees, as were lobbying firms, though with separate registration for each client.

More specifically, registration was to be required for those whose incomes or expenses were more than $5,000 per half-year for all clients they lobbied for or more than $1,000 for any single client in half a year. Registrants were required to disclose the names of their employee-lobbyists and their clients, connections to foreign entities, whether their lobbyists had served in the previous two years in key government positions, and the issues on which they lobbied. Organizations with in-house operations were required to disclose the cost of their lobbying activities, while outside lobbyists had to disclose their lobbying income. A single office within the Justice Department, the Office of Lobbying Registration and Public Disclosure, was to be established to administer and enforce the new law. Lobbyists could be fined up to $10,000 for minor violations of the law and up to $200,000 for major violations, including failure to register and extensive or repeated violations.

The bill also included language limiting the gifts and other financial benefits that lobbyists and their clients could give to members and congressional staff. S 349 sponsors Carl Levin, D-Mich., and William S. Cohen, R-Maine, had vigorously resisted efforts to attach gift rules to their narrowly crafted lobby disclosure bill. Levin said he did not want the bill to become an all-purpose vehicle for reform, arguing that past efforts to strengthen lobbying registration had been sunk by such extraneous amendments. But, under pressure from public interest groups and editorial writers, the Senate on May 5 had adopted by voice vote an amendment requiring lobbyists to disclose any gifts worth more than $20—including meals, trips and entertainment—given to a member of Congress or a staff member. *(Details on gift rules, p. 919)*

House leaders had hoped to bring lobby legislation to the floor in late October 1993. But action was delayed until 1994, after Democratic freshmen took up the gift rules cause, demanding stricter gift limits than senior members from both parties said were necessary. A bipartisan task force came up with a compromise on the gift issue which the House Judiciary Subcommittee on Administrative Law and Government Relations, chaired by John Bryant, D-Texas, incorporated in its lobbying disclosure bill (HR 823) but it was too late for further action in the 1993 session.

By the time the House was ready to take up the legislation in the next session, the compromise on the gift limits had begun to fall apart. But, after surviving a key procedural test, a revised version of S 349 sailed to passage March 24, 1994, on a 315–110 vote. With the gift provisions drawing heated objections, the lobbying provisions—substantially the same as in the Senate-passed version of the bill—never generated much controversy. The bill required anyone paid to lobby members of Congress, their staffs or senior executive branch officials to register at a new independent agency. Registration was to be required of entities whose lobbying income or expenses exceeded $2,500 in a six-month reporting period.

The Senate reentered the fray in May 1994, passing a free-standing measure to toughen gift rules (S 1935). The next step was for House and Senate negotiators, lead by Levin and Bryant, to craft a compromise bill, working from the two chambers' lobbying bills plus the Senate gift ban measure.

With the gift ban again the most difficult issue, the rewrite of lobbying disclosure requirements was considered almost routine. Conferees came to agreement on S 349 on Sept. 26. Nearly anyone spending money or being paid to lobby Congress or the executive branch would be required to register with a new federal agency and report on how much they made, what issues they followed and how they spent their money. Firms or people who spent less than 10 percent of their time lobbying or who made less than $2,500 lobbying in a six-month period would be exempt.

The conference agreement appeared headed for easy approval until Republicans began raising objections about the bill's effect on grassroots lobbying. Minority Whip Newt Gingrich, R-Ga., caught Democratic leaders off guard, when he led a last-minute effort to block S 349 from the House floor. Gingrich and several other GOP members contended that the bill would infringe on the rights of religious groups to lobby Congress by forcing them to disclose grassroots efforts. Their target was language that called for disclosure of the name, address and place of business of "any person or entity other than the client" who paid for someone to lobby on his behalf. Conferees had included the provision, which was in the House-passed version of the bill, in an effort to get at the increasingly common tactic of Washington lobbyists urging constituents to call lawmakers on particular issues.

The bill, Gingrich claimed, "threatens the American people's rights to be active citizens." He charged that the administration would fill the directorship of the new Office of Lobbying Registration and Public Disclosure with a "secular, antireligious liberal" who, he said, could use registration information to squelch religious viewpoints. The Christian Coalition, a conservative group that lobbied on social issues, released a statement saying the bill amounted to a "gag rule" on religious organizations.

The vote was on whether to adopt the rule (H Res 550) accompanying the conference report on S 349 (H Rept 103-750)—in effect, a vote on whether to bring the bill up for a final vote. Sponsors knew that few members would have the temerity to vote down the lobbying bill, and risk being tagged as antireform, on the final vote. So the rule vote was the opponents' last chance to stop the bill in the House. Although the focus was on the lobbying provisions, many members had mixed feelings about toughening gift rules. By leaving the vote open for several minutes while they twisted arms and persuaded several pliable Democrats to switch their vote, Democratic leaders were able to get the rule adopted on Sept. 29, by a **key vote of 216–205 (R 5–170; D 210–35; I 1–0)**. The House then adopted the conference report, 306–112. *(1994 key votes, p. 1003)*

After its near-death experience in the House, the conference report was easy pickings for opponents in the Senate. The Senate failed to cut off a Republican-led filibuster Oct. 6, when a motion to invoke cloture (thus limiting debate) was rejected on a **key vote of 52–46 (R 7–36; D 45–10)**. Because the bill would change Senate rules, a two-thirds vote of those present and voting was required to invoke cloture. The next day, a second cloture vote failed 55–42. Opposition grew rapidly among Republicans in the days before the cloture votes as outside groups, many of which would have been forced to disclose their lobbying activities for the first time, began to voice objections about the bill's scope. In particular, they said it could require grassroots lobbying organizations to disclose information about their contributors that would chill citizen involvement in politics. Sens. Levin and Cohen disputed that interpretation in an Oct. 6 letter to Minority Leader Robert Dole, R-Kan. The provision was intended to prevent organizations from avoiding the disclosure requirements by having someone else pay a lobbyist's expenses, they said. Despite such protestations, opposition intensified.

Senate Majority Leader George J. Mitchell, D-Maine, made a last-ditch effort Oct. 7 to save the bill by trying to bring up a resolution to excise entirely the disputed provisions on grassroots lobbying. But that required unanimous consent, and several Republicans objected, saying they had not had time to study the issue. S 349 died upon adjournment.

'Reinventing Government'

President Clinton and Vice President Al Gore on Sept. 7, 1993, unveiled a proposal that they claimed would save $108 billion over five years while making government work better. The report—entitled *From Red Tape to Results: Creating a Government That Works Better and Costs Less,* which became widely known as the "reinventing government" plan—outlined four broad purposes: making government services more responsive to the public; cutting red tape; giving rank-and-file government employees more flexibility and responsibility; and making programs more efficient. Most of the recommendations would take years to carry out; about half could be achieved by presidential order.

BACKGROUND

The administration's plan grew out of a six-month National Performance Review launched by Gore in March 1993. While some of the resulting report—the twelfth plan in a century to streamline the government—recycled old ideas, the proposal's premise was new. It was drawn largely from the 1992 corporate self-help book *Reinventing Government* by David Osborne and Ted Gaebler. Past efforts at reform, such as the Grace Commission of 1982–1984, focused on less government, a central tenet of Republican ideology. Gore's plan hewed to the conservative Democratic doctrine of making government more entrepreneurial, lean and responsive to customers' needs. *(Grace Commission, Congress and the Nation Vol. VI, p. 791)*

The report's main theory was that the federal government's management style had long been abandoned by even the most rigid private companies. The government remained a large, top-down bureaucracy that fostered loyalty only to bloated chains of command and adherence to procedure. The information-age economy, in which products changed and data flowed at lightning speed, required a decentralized government with power and accountability distributed among the lower echelons of the federal workforce, the report said. Gore's plan aimed to adopt corporate management techniques such as rewarding performance and innovation instead of fealty to rules.

Clinton and Gore launched a campaign to sell the reinvention by heading for town halls and talk shows. The vice president appeared on *Late Show with David Letterman* to dramatize wasteful tests required for government-issued products. By pitching a new "customer service contract" with American taxpayers, the administration hoped to create a populist movement to propel Capitol Hill to accept numerous government changes that had been shelved several times before. Clinton and Gore sought allies in the freshman congressional class, which was voted into office in 1992 on a tide of voter anger against government. The White House rallied Republicans who viewed Gore's promise of "better government" as at least close to their call for

"less government." Within their own ranks, Clinton and Gore hoped to win over vulnerable veteran Democrats pressured by voters eager to realize 1992 independent presidential candidate Ross Perot's call for better government.

With release of the report came the first round of executive orders to carry out the reinventing government plan. The initial orders set "customer service" standards for agencies that dealt directly with taxpayers. For example, the Internal Revenue Service promised to return tax refunds within 40 days, or 14 days if the return was filed electronically and 21 days if the refund was deposited into the taxpayer's bank account electronically. Clinton ordered federal agencies to eliminate half their internal regulations within three years.

On Oct. 1, he signed an executive order that created a layer of bureaucracy—the National Partnership Council—which the report said was to smooth relations between management and labor in the federal workforce. Because rank-and-file workers were promised a larger voice in management issues, the three largest federal employee unions supported the reinventing government plan.

LEGISLATIVE ACTION

On Nov. 22, 1993, by 429–1, the House passed a large chunk of the reinventing government plan in a $37 billion, five-year package of spending cuts (HR 3400). Most of the savings included in HR 3400, $32.5 billion, were to be achieved by reducing the federal workforce by 252,000 over five years. Other savings included trimming the number of field offices at the Department of Agriculture and the Department of Housing and Urban Development, canceling the Energy Department's advanced liquid metal reactor program and farming out executive branch printing duties to private companies. House action came on the bill after members thwarted an effort to enact more drastic deficit reduction. HR 3400 was formally reported from 10 House committees on Nov. 15: Science, Space and Technology (H Rept 103-366, Part I); Veterans' Affairs (Part II); Post Office and Civil Service (Part III); Public Works and Transportation (Part IV); Natural Resources (Part V); House Administration (Part VI); Merchant Marine and Fisheries (Part VII); Judiciary (Part VIII); Agriculture (Part IX); and Banking, Finance and Urban Affairs (Part X). *(Rescissions, p. 59)*

On March 24, 1994, the Senate Governmental Affairs Committee approved those sections of HR 3400 that dealt with improving financial management and cutting personnel costs. When no other Senate panel with jurisdiction over HR 3400 took action, Governmental Affairs reported its provisions in a scaled-down bill (S 2170—S Rept 103-281) on June 9. The Senate passed S 2170 by voice vote Sept. 28, and the House followed suit Oct. 4. Clinton signed the measure into law (PL 103-356) on Oct. 13.

The central feature of S 2170 was a requirement that 24 federal agencies submit audited financial statements every year, beginning in March 1997. Under existing law, 10 agencies were preparing such statements on a pilot basis. The bill also limited automatic cost-of-living raises for members of Congress and other top federal officials to the amount given rank-and-file federal workers. It allowed the Office of Management and Budget to recommend consolidation or elimination of any other report that federal agencies made to Congress.

Various other elements of the reinventing government plan were addressed in a piecemeal approach through numerous bills, including those to allow federal agencies to offer cash buyouts to workers who voluntarily resigned, to streamline federal purchasing procedures, to establish performance standards for federal agencies, to reorganize the Agriculture Department, to rework the federal aid programs for elementary and secondary schools, to modernize the customs service, and to end the subsidies for wool, mohair and honey producers. *(Cash buyouts, p. 814; federal procurement, p. 812; performance standards, p. 814; Agriculture reorganization, p. 481; elementary and secondary schools, p. 609; subsidies, p. 489)* ❑

Federal Procurement

Congress in 1994 cleared legislation (S 1587—PL 103-355) to streamline federal purchasing, with the aim of speeding the acquisition process and saving the government money. The bill was a key element in the Clinton administration's "reinventing government" initiative spearheaded by Vice President Al Gore. *('Reinventing government,' p. 811)*

S 1587 encouraged federal agencies to buy more goods off the shelf in routine commercial transactions, instead of conducting elaborate negotiations to secure items designed to meet unique government specifications. It also exempted commercial purchases and the purchase of most goods and services costing less than $100,000 from many of the complex procedural requirements that typically delayed and boosted the price of federal purchases. Some of those rules had been designed to head off waste, fraud and abuse; others were intended to promote social policies, such as the development of small and minority-owned businesses.

BACKGROUND

The drive to streamline government purchasing got rolling in earnest in 1990, when Congress included in the annual defense authorization bill (PL 101-510) a provision requiring the Pentagon to set up a blue-ribbon panel to recommend changes in existing procurement laws. Named for the section of the legislation that established it, the Section 800 panel issued an 1,800-page report in January 1993 that recommended amending or repealing nearly 300 laws. The report called for greater reliance on commercial products and simplified contracting methods for small and commercial purchases.

Those themes were echoed in the report issued in September 1993 by Gore's reinventing government task force.

In addition to the high visibility that President Clinton and Vice President Gore gave the issue, Defense Secretary William J. Perry, whose agency accounted for three-quarters of the federal government's $200 billion annual procurement budget, made procurement streamlining one of his top priorities. He maintained that a revamped purchasing system would give the Pentagon easier access to cutting-edge technology being developed in the marketplace. And he warned that projected defense budgets would not cover the significant increases in weapons procurement slated to begin in fiscal 1997 unless the department used more businesslike acquisition methods and financial management systems to stretch its purchasing dollars.

In a related move, Perry signed a potentially far-reaching order on June 29, 1994, intended to slash the number of purchases for which the Defense Department required the supplier to meet highly detailed and unique specifications ("mil-specs") regulating not only how an item performed but also how it was manufactured. Perry predicted that the shift would save billions of dollars annually. And, as with the streamlined procurement rules, he argued that eliminating the unique military specifications would allow the Pentagon to do business with a broader range of high-tech companies. Many such companies were loath to deal with federal purchasing rules they deemed too rigid, too complicated and too expensive. Perry conceded that unique specifications made sense when Pentagon-sponsored research was the cutting edge of technology. "But in the fields of technology most important to the Defense Department today—semiconductors, computers, software, telecommunications—the technical leadership is in industry," he said.

LEGISLATIVE ACTION

The Senate Governmental Affairs Committee reported S 1587 (S Rept 103-258) on May 11, 1994; the Senate Armed Services Committee reported it (S Rept 103-259) the next day. The full Senate passed the bill by voice vote June 8, after adopting several amendments, none of which significantly altered the bill.

The House Government Operations Committee had approved a companion measure (HR 2238) in July 1993 but did not formally report it (H Rept 103-545, Part I) until June 13, 1994. The House Armed Services Committee reported the bill (H Rept 103-545, Part II) June 17. On June 27, the House first passed HR 2238 by voice vote, and then, after substituting the text of HR 2238, passed S 1587 by voice vote.

In most of their key provisions, the Senate and House versions were similar. The bills authorized the use of greatly simplified procedures and waived many procurement-related laws for any contract valued at less than $100,000. Under existing law, purchases for less than $25,000 were simplified, though to a lesser degree than the pending legislation allowed. The bills also authorized simplified contracting procedures for any contract for the purchase of commercial products and expanded the definition of "commercial" items to include novel products that were not widely sold but were intended for the commercial marketplace.

Unlike the Senate bill, HR 2238 allowed the higher $100,000 ceiling for simplified purchases only for agencies that participated in a new publicly accessible computer network through which federal contracts would be advertised and awarded. Clinton already had ordered all federal purchasing agencies to participate in such a computer network. Nearly 250 Pentagon offices, which accounted for 80 percent of small defense purchases, were slated to be on-line within two years.

S 1587 included provisions extending the streamlining process by waiving, in some cases, procurement laws intended to steer more federal contracts toward small and minority-owned businesses. Similar provisions had been dropped from HR 2238 at the insistence of the House Small Business Committee, which had not formally considered the bill.

The Senate adopted the conference report on S 1587 (H Rept 103-712) by voice vote Aug. 23. The House adopted the conference report, 425–0, on Sept. 20. The conferees on S 1587 had reached a compromise that raised the threshold for the use of simplified procedures on federal contracts to $50,000—$100,000 if the agency used a computerized network to solicit and receive the contract.

Conferees left intact the existing requirement that most companies receiving $500,000 or more as federal contractors or subcontractors prepare subcontracting plans setting percentage goals for the amount of work the company intended to farm out to small and minority-owned businesses. The requirement for such plans "flowed down" to subcontractors that were not themselves small businesses. Clinton administration officials had called for a change in the law, arguing that many commercial companies refused to do business with the federal government rather than have their established business relationships disrupted in order to meet the goals of a subcontracting plan. The Senate version would have exempted from the requirement companies that were subcontractors providing commercial items to a federally funded contractor. But that effort was vehemently opposed by lobbyists for some small and minority business groups. In their report, the conferees observed that existing law allowed a commercial firm to meet the requirement for a subcontracting plan by filing one plan to cover all of its operations for a year, instead of filing a separate plan for each federal contract. They implied that such an umbrella plan gave commercial firms sufficient flexibility to avoid disrupting their established supplier relationships.

MAJOR PROVISIONS

As signed into law on Oct. 13, S 1587:

Small and 'Micro' Purchases

• Exempted an agency, once plugged into a publicly accessible Federal Acquisition Computer Network (FACNET) over which contract bids could be solicited and received electronically, from the existing requirement that any bid solicitation for a contract of more than $25,000 be delayed until 15 days after the agency had published notice of the impending solicitation in the *Commerce Business Daily*.

• Increased from $25,000 to $50,000 the value below which contracts could be awarded by so-called simplified procedures, which involved less administrative work. The threshold for these simplified procedures was raised to $100,000 for any agency that plugged into FACNET.

The limit would revert to $50,000 after five years unless, by then, the agency had implemented an expanded version of FACNET that allowed a broader range of transactions to be conducted electronically.

• Gave agencies greater leeway to make "micro" purchases that cost less than $2,500. Instead of filling out forms, for example, an office manager could send someone to the nearest discount store for office supplies.

Commercial Items

• Expanded the definition of what constituted a commercial item that could be bought under liberalized procedures. Existing law defined commercial items as products that were sold to the public in substantial quantities at established catalog or market prices. The definition was expanded to include items that had evolved from existing commercial items because of advances in technology; items that had been modified in relatively minor ways to meet government requirements; and services that were sold competitively, in the commercial marketplace, at established catalog prices for specific tasks.

• Applied federal procurement laws, in the case of commercial purchases, only to prime contractors—not to their subcontractors, the subcontractors' subcontractors and so forth.

• Strengthened the exemption of all purchases of commercial items from the requirement that contractors provide federal officials with meticulously detailed cost or pricing data and that they certify the data to be "current, accurate and complete."

• Permanently increased to $500,000 the level above which the data requirement applied to contracts for all federal agencies.

Small Business, Minority Issues

• Reserved contracts worth more than $2,500 but less than $100,000 for small businesses, provided that at least two qualified companies bid on the job. Under existing law, this "small business reserve" applied only to contracts worth less than $25,000.

• Set a nonbinding goal for civilian agencies of awarding to minority-owned companies contracts worth 5 percent of the total value of contracts and subcontracts awarded. To achieve that goal, agencies could use several techniques, such as restricting competition for some contracts to minority-owned firms or awarding a contract to such a company provided that its price was no more than 10 percent higher than the lowest bid. In effect, this provision extended the Defense Department's Section 1207 program to other agencies.

• Established a nonbinding goal for all agencies of awarding 5 percent of the total value of contracts and subcontracts to companies owned by women. The provision did not authorize the kind of set-asides and price differentials authorized for minority-owned companies.

Contract Award Protests

• Stipulated that bidders had to be notified of the result of a competition within three days of a contract award. Unsuccessful bidders could request a briefing on the selection within three days of the notification. The briefing, to take place within five days of the request, would report, among other things, the purchasing agent's evaluation of significant weaknesses in that contractor's bid. However, the briefing would not include a point-by-point comparison of that contractor's bid with any other bid. The goal was to reduce the number of protests that were filed by contractors simply to force the government to disclose information about the basis on which the winning firm was selected.

• Authorized the government to pay the fees of consultants and expert witnesses engaged by companies that filed contract award protests. Fees were limited to no more than $150 an hour, but that limit did not apply to consultants or experts retained by small businesses.

Other Provisions

• Authorized several procurements to be managed on an experimental basis as pilot programs to test acquisition management changes beyond the scope of those authorized by the bill.

• Stipulated that the Pentagon's director of operational testing had the right to communicate directly with the secretary of defense, without securing the approval of any other official.   ❑

Performance Standards

As part of the administration plan to "reinvent government," President Clinton on Aug. 3, 1993, signed into law a bill (S 20—PL 103-62) requiring federal agencies to develop performance standards and to use them to measure and account for progress on specific programs by March 31, 2000. (*'Reinventing government,' p. 811*)

S 20 required that by Sept. 30, 1997, each agency that spent more than $20 million annually had to submit to the Office of Management and Budget (OMB) a five-year plan setting out its strategic goals. Agencies had to update the plan at least every three years. Beginning with fiscal 1999, OMB was required to submit a governmentwide performance plan with the annual budget.

Each agency in turn was required to submit to OMB an annual performance plan covering all the programs in its budget, with indicators for measuring success or failure. Beginning March 31, 2000, agency heads were required to submit to the president and Congress annual reports on actual performance for the previous year. S 20 provided for OMB to start the process by selecting 10 agencies to carry out pilot performance review projects in fiscal 1994–1996.

Federal employees opposed to the bill argued that it would require agencies to revamp their budgeting systems and would result in unnecessary and time-consuming paperwork. Supporters said the measure, which allowed managers to waive some administrative requirements with approval of OMB and the Office of Personnel Management, gave federal managers and other employees more autonomy, along with recognition for making programs successful.

The Senate Governmental Affairs Committee reported S 20 (S Rept 103-58) on June 16, 1993. The Senate passed the measure by voice vote June 23. The House Government Operations Committee on May 25 reported its version (HR 826—H Rept 103-106, Part I), which was essentially identical to S 20. The House passed HR 826 by voice vote the same day. The House

passed S 20 by voice vote on July 15, completing congressional action.   ❑

Federal Employee Buyouts

President Clinton on March 30, 1994, signed legislation (HR 3345—PL 103-226) that allowed federal agencies to offer cash buyouts of up to $25,000 to workers who voluntarily resigned. A key component of Vice President Al Gore's plan for "reinventing government," the buyouts were designed to help agencies prune excess layers of middle management through voluntary retirements instead of layoffs. (*'Reinventing government,' p. 811*)

HR 3345 required the federal government to cut 252,000 positions over six years. Agencies were ordered to reduce their personnel on a one-for-one basis for every buyout offer that was accepted. An employee who accepted the voluntary retirement and was rehired by the federal government within five years had to repay the full amount of the buyout.

BACKGROUND

According to Gore's September 1993 report, the average federal agency had one manager for every seven workers, compared with one for every 25 or more in many well-managed private companies. The report recommended that the equivalent of 252,000 full-time workers be trimmed from the federal workforce by fiscal 1999, a 12 percent cut. The goal was a federal workforce of roughly 1.9 million, the smallest since President Lyndon B. Johnson inaugurated the Great Society social welfare programs in the 1960s.

Trying to achieve such a goal through layoffs posed a number of problems. Senior employees whose positions were eliminated could collect paychecks for a lengthy severance period if they chose to leave the government: one week's salary for each of their first 10 years' experience, two weeks' salary for each year after that and an additional 10 percent if they were over age 40. For a well-entrenched employee, that translated into nearly a full year's pay. They also could choose to stay, even if their jobs were terminated. Under the "bump rule," an employee whose position was eliminated could claim the spot of a less senior worker and continue to collect his or her previous salary. The less senior worker could either bump another worker further down the ladder or be laid off.

A better approach, said federal officials, was for the one used by private industry: offering cash incentives for middle management to resign or retire early. A dispute arose over whether buyouts would be cheaper than layoffs, at least in the short run. The Office of Personnel Management (OPM) said that the average buyout would cost $6,200 less per position than the average layoff. The Congressional Budget Office (CBO), in a 1993 report, estimated that buyouts would be more expensive in the short term, although they would save almost as much money in the long term. Unlike OPM, the budget office assumed that buyouts would be taken not only by employees whose positions were slated to be cut but also by employees who would have to be replaced. CBO also factored in the increase in pension costs caused by employees who would retire immediately after taking the buyout. The long-term savings, according to CBO, would be great no matter what approach was taken—$951,000 per job eliminated through layoffs; $898,000 to $950,000 per job eliminated through buyouts.

The higher short-term pension costs were a problem under the "pay-as-you-go" rules of the 1990 budget law (PL 101-508), which were intended to stop Congress from running up the deficit. Under those rules, any bill that increased the cost of an entitlement program, such as federal pensions, had to pay for that increase through tax increases or cuts in other entitlements. The savings expected from reducing the workforce could not be used because they were savings from discretionary accounts, which were governed by separate budget rules. *("Pay-as-you-go" rules, Congress and the Nation Vol. VIII, p. 56)*

LEGISLATIVE ACTION

The House Post Office and Civil Service Committee reported HR 3345 (H Rept 103-386) on Nov. 19, 1993. The Senate Governmental Affairs Committee reported a companion version (S 1535—S Rept 103-223) on Feb. 4, 1994.

Both bills authorized temporary separation incentive payments up to $25,000 for federal employees who voluntarily retired or resigned; both allowed agencies to train employees for different positions in their own or other federal agencies.

The House bill required federal workers who took the buyout to repay the full amount if they were rehired by the federal government with two years; the Senate committee extended that to five years. Both bills required agencies to deposit into the federal pension fund an amount equal to 9 percent of the final pay of an employee who took early retirement. The chief difference was a Senate provision requiring that 252,000 positions be eliminated by 1999.

The House passed HR 3345 on a 391–17 vote on Feb. 10. Earlier the same day, members adopted, 409–1, a Timothy J. Penny, D-Minn., amendment to codify the workforce reduction target of 252,000 jobs by fiscal 1999 and to extend the restrictions on rehiring federal workers who took the buyout from two to five years. The House overcame the pay-as-you-go problem by adopting a rule for floor debate Feb. 10 that effectively waived the budget act, a move made possible by the strong bipartisan support for HR 3345 in that chamber. However, leaders of the Senate Governmental Affairs Committee—Chairman John Glenn, D-Ohio, and ranking Republican William V. Roth Jr., Del.—balked at trying a similar tactic, which would have required the approval of 60 senators. A proposal to attach the contents of HR 3345 to an emergency disaster aid appropriations bill (HR 3759)—and thereby classify the short-term costs of the buyout as emergency spending, exempt from the pay-as-you-go rule—also was rejected. *(Supplemental appropriations, p. 62)*

By voice vote Feb. 11, the Senate passed its version of HR 3345, which contained a number of changes added by Roth. The most contentious was a pair of provisions that required the transfer of $22.3 billion over five years—the estimated savings from reducing the federal workforce—into an anticrime trust fund and reduced existing limits on discretionary spending by the same amount. To cover the increase in pension costs that

would result from the buyout, Roth required that agencies pay into the federal pension fund an amount equal to 17 percent of the salary of each employee taking the buyout. The payment was in addition to the 9 percent going to the Treasury for each retiree.

William L. Clay, D-Mo., House Post Office and Civil Service chairman and sponsor of HR 3345, objected so strongly to the Senate-passed version of the bill that he declined to call for a conference. In particular, he objected to the anticrime trust fund, which he said would trade the jobs of thousands of federal employees for less than half that number of police officers. He also criticized Roth's proposal to charge federal agencies for the increase in pension costs associated with the buyouts. OPM Director James B. King said that change would make it too expensive for agencies to offer the buyouts to all except the highest-paid civil servants in fiscal 1994. Roth argued that some way had to be found to pay for the increase in pension costs. The White House Office of Management and Budget responded that no such provision was necessary because the cut in payroll would more than offset the increase in pension costs.

On March 8, the House agreed by voice vote to accept a number of minor provisions added by the Senate. The revised bill did not provide for the anticrime trust fund, however. Clay's compromise was to have the agencies pay the pension an amount equal to 9 percent of the salaries of employees who took early retirement immediately after accepting a buyout in fiscal 1994 and 1995. For fiscal 1995 through 1998, agencies would also have to pay the pension fund $80 for every active employee participating in the pension plan.

Buyout proponents in the Senate hoped to take the new version quickly to conference, an approach that Roth and Glenn advocated. But Phil Gramm, R-Texas, blocked that move, demanding that the Senate first restore the anticrime trust fund. The Senate adopted the Gramm amendment, offered March 11 on a separate bill on competitiveness (S 4), by 90–2. Later the same day, the House agreed to go to conference and agreed 231–150 to a nonbinding motion to instruct its conferees to accept the Senate trust fund provision. *(Competitiveness, p. 342)*

Despite the votes in both chambers, the conferees dropped the trust fund from the bill. Three House chairmen—Clay; Jack Brooks, D-Texas, of Judiciary; and John Conyers Jr., D-Mich., of Government Operations—dug in their heels against adding the trust fund to the buyout bill. Roth said he would accept a compromise offered by Rep. John T. Myers, R-Ind., that would drop the trust fund but keep the $22 billion cut in discretionary spending. But conferees rejected that proposal by voice vote. In other action, conferees added to the bill a provision sought by Mississippi's two Republican senators, Trent Lott and Thad Cochran, authorizing separation payments of $5,000 each to up to 200 workers who were displaced as a result of the termination of the Mississippi-based Advanced Solid Rocket Motor project. *(National Aeronautics and Space Administration authorization, p. 827)*

The House adopted the conference report (H Rept 103-435) by voice vote March 23. Brooks pledged on the House floor to support an anticrime trust fund in negotiations with the Senate over an anticrime bill. That pledge helped Clay defeat another motion to send HR 3345 back to conference with nonbinding instructions to restore the trust fund. The motion was rejected March 23 by 166–261. Brooks's statement was not enough to satisfy Gramm, however. Gramm sent a letter to House members warning that he would filibuster the conference report if it came to the Senate without the trust fund, and he kept his word. The fate of the bill then came down to its supporters' ability to garner the 60 votes needed to end Gramm's filibuster. They fell short on their first attempt March 24 by a vote of 58–41. The Senate immediately held a second vote, and the motion to invoke cloture (thus limiting debate) was agreed to 63–36. The Senate adopted the conference report 99–1 on March 24, completing congressional action.   ❑

Federal Pay and Benefits

Congress froze pay for federal civilian employees in fiscal 1994 and trimmed federal benefits. However, congressional appropriators preserved a scheduled locality-based pay increase and provided funds for a pay raise for military personnel.

In February 1993, President Clinton called on Congress to save money by eliminating a scheduled 2.2 percent pay increase for federal workers in fiscal 1994, limiting increases in 1995–1997 to 1 percent below the rise in the cost of living and postponing a locality-based pay raise scheduled to begin in 1994. Enacted in 1990, locality pay was an effort to close the gap between federal and nonfederal white collar pay levels by giving pay increases to federal employees in high-wage areas of the country. The program was supposed to be phased in over nine years. Clinton also proposed ending the lump-sum retirement option, under which retiring federal workers could choose to get a lump-sum refund of their retirement contributions in exchange for a permanently reduced annuity.

• **Reconciliation.** The 1993 budget-reconciliation bill (HR 2264—PL 103-66) contained a number of federal pay and benefits provisions.

The House Post Office and Civil Service Committee, which had jurisdiction over the U.S. Postal Service and federal civil service, was instructed to come up with $10.6 billion in savings

from direct spending programs over five years. The panel proposed to achieve most of that—$8.8 billion—by ending the lump-sum retirement option effective Jan. 1, 1994. The committee suggested delaying the cost-of-living adjustments (COLAs) for civilian federal retirees in fiscal 1994–1996 for three months—from Dec. 1 to March 1—saving $788 million. Limitations were placed on fees for physician and outpatient care for the 220,000 retirees 65 and older who did not participate in the optional portion of Medicare (Medicare Part B) but who were covered by the Federal Employees' Health Benefits Program, the nation's largest health insurance program. The panel repealed the 2.2 percent raise for federal and Foreign Service employees in 1994, extended the freeze to other pay systems in the executive branch and reduced by 1 percent the federal pay adjustments scheduled to take effect in 1995, 1996 and 1997. The panel approved an amendment allowing locality pay adjustments to begin in July 1994. The locality pay increase, which would partially offset the effect of Clinton's freeze in regular pay, would be funded by cutting, though attrition, the number of civilian employees in the executive branch by 150,000 over five years. Beginning in 1995, annual pay adjustments would be delayed from January until July. The amendment also capped the amount of leave that Senior Executive Service employees could build up and ended bonus awards to employees through fiscal 1998.

The Senate Governmental Affairs Committee approved $10.7 billion in spending cuts over five years. Retiree COLAs would be delayed three months in fiscal 1994–1996, and the lump-sum retirement option would be repealed. The panel added a requirement that the District of Columbia on Oct. 1, 1993, begin to pay the employer share of Federal Employee Health Benefit premiums for district retirees. The committee also required a permanent reduction in a federal retiree's annuities if the retiree married after retirement and opted for survivor coverage, and it required that the Postal Service make payments for COLAs and health benefits for its past retirees. Senate Governmental Affairs did not authorize a one-year pay freeze.

Conferees on HR 2264 agreed to the COLA delay, the lump-sum benefit repeal, the limit on physician's fees, the requirement that the Postal Service make payments for COLAs and health benefits for its past retirees, and the permanent reduction in federal annuities for a retiree who later married and opted for survivor coverage. Conferees dropped provisions limiting accumulated leave for senior executives, prohibiting cash bonuses in fiscal 1994–1998, reducing the government's total number of civilian employees by 150,000 over five years and requiring that the District of Columbia begin paying the employer share of Federal Employee Health Benefit premiums for its retirees. *(Bonus restrictions, p. 817)*

In related action, the House Armed Services Committee voted to freeze pay for active-duty military in fiscal 1994 and maintain pay increases at 1 percent below inflation for fiscal 1995–1998, saving an estimated $11.6 billion over five years. The committee also adopted language to provide a full COLA on a delayed schedule; instead of taking effect Jan. 1, the payments were to be made May 1 in 1994 and Aug. 1 in 1995–1998. The delay saved an estimated $2.36 billion over five years. The

Senate Armed Services Committee agreed to delay payment of the retiree COLA to Oct. 1 in fiscal 1994–1997 and to Sept. 1 in fiscal 1998. The committee did not approve a pay freeze. Conferees dropped the president's plan to freeze military pay in fiscal 1994 and scale it back in the following four years. A delay was agreed to in the annual COLA for military retirees to April 1 in fiscal 1994 and to Oct. 1 in fiscal 1995–1998.

The House Foreign Affairs and Senate Foreign Relations committees recommended delaying COLAs for retired Foreign Service officers. The Senate committee also recommended eliminating the lump-sum retirement option for participants in the Foreign Service retirement system who retired after September 1995 (except individuals who were critically ill). Reconciliation conferees agreed to both the COLA delay and the repeal of the lump-sum retirement option for foreign service employees.

• **Treasury, Postal Service Appropriations.** Included in the fiscal 1994 appropriations bill for the Treasury, Postal Service and general government (HR 2403—PL 103-123) was locality pay increases for about 60 percent of federal white-collar workers. Under existing law, a maximum of $1.8 billion could be spent on the program in its first year. Because there was not enough money was in HR 2403 both to start the locality pay program and to provide the 2.2 percent pay raise in 1994, conferees on the bill decided to eliminate the general pay raise.

• **Defense Appropriations.** Active-duty military personnel, members of the National Guard and reserve personnel got their 2.2 percent pay raise as part of the fiscal 1994 defense appropriations bill (HR 3116—PL 103-139). The measure provided $1.05 billion for the raise.

• **Commerce, Justice Appropriations.** The fiscal 1994 appropriations bill for the departments of Commerce, Justice, State and the Judiciary (HR 2519—PL 103-121) did not include a pay raise for Foreign Service employees. ❏

Bonus Restrictions

The Senate passed a bill (S 1070) by voice vote Nov. 24, 1993, to ban bonuses to noncareer political appointees from June 1 of a presidential election year to Jan. 20 of the following year. It also prohibited career appointees who made more than $108,200 from receiving bonuses at any time.

S 1070 sprang from a controversy that arose in late 1992, as the Bush administration prepared to leave office. The Office of Personnel Management found that the number of bonuses awarded to political appointees and other highly paid federal workers during the November to January transition period rose to 133 from just 49 in the same period in 1991.

The Senate Governmental Affairs Committee had reported S 1070 on Nov. 19. ❏

Honoraria Ban

The House Judiciary Subcommittee on Administrative Law on Nov. 18, 1993, by voice vote approved a bill (HR 1095) to allow all federal employees in the executive, legislative and judicial branches making less than $108,000 annually to accept honoraria—writing or speaking fees. Federal workers still could not accept honoraria related to their official duties or payments in excess of $2,000, in an effort to prevent influence peddling and conflicts of interest. The measure stalled in the face of opposition in the Senate and the Clinton administration.

Congress barred House members and all government employees except those working for the Senate from accepting honoraria as part of the Ethics Reform Act of 1989 (PL 101-194), which also sharply increased House members' salaries. The Senate followed suit two years later, when senators voted themselves a pay raise and barred honoraria in that chamber (PL 102-90). *(1989 law, Congress and the Nation Vol. VIII, pp. 858, 920; 1991 action, Congress and the Nation Vol. VIII, p. 970)*

Congress's main aim was to stop its own members from accepting speaking fees from special interest groups, but the law swept all employees in the government's three branches under the honoraria ban. Lower-level executive branch employees protested that they could not accept speaking and writing fees even if their subjects or honoraria sources had no connection with their jobs. The employees sued in federal court and won at the U.S. District Court level March 19, 1992. The U.S. Court of Appeals for the District of Columbia Circuit upheld that decision March 30, 1993, on a 2–1 vote, declaring the ban an overly broad restriction on free speech. Supporters of HR 1095 had hoped that the ruling would increase pressure on members to enact the measure. *(1992 action, Congress and the Nation Vol. VIII, p. 886)* ❏

Child Abusers' Federal Pensions

Congress in 1994 cleared a bill (HR 3694—PL 103-358) to allow the pensions of federal retirees found guilty of child abuse to be garnisheed for the purpose of paying court-ordered damages.

Bill supporters noted that convicted child abusers often avoided payment by liquidating their assets and relocating. If the abuser was a federal retiree, the federal government protected that worker's pension by refusing to pay court-ordered damage awards. Advocates for child abuse victims said court-awarded damages often were levied against retired workers because victims frequently waited until reaching adulthood before taking action against parents or relatives who abused them.

Garnisheeing, a legal remedy for taking part of the regular pay or pension of an employee, was typically used by creditors to recoup debts from a financially delinquent individual. Until 1993, however, federal workers were protected by law from having their wages or pensions garnisheed. The exemption for federal workers ended when Congress revised the 1939 Hatch Act, the law regulating the political activity of government employees. Included in the 1993 rewrite (PL 103-94) were provisions allowing creditors to garnishee wages of federal employees through the same legal process that they followed with private citizens. Child support and alimony judgments also were required to be given precedence over other legal garnishment orders. HR 3694 added court-ordered damages for child abuse to the list of debts for which federal pensions could be garnisheed. *(Hatch Act revisions, p. 805)*

Federal workers also were included under a separate bill (HR 4570) aimed at strengthening the nation's child support enforcement system, but that measure died upon adjournment of the 103rd Congress. *(Child support enforcement, p. 576)*

HR 3694 was reported by the House Post Office and Civil Service Committee (H Rept 103-721) on Sept. 19, 1994, and passed by voice vote of the full House that same day. The Senate passed the measure by voice vote Sept. 30, completing congressional action. President Clinton signed HR 3694 into law on Oct. 14. ❑

Flexible Leave

Congress in 1993 cleared legislation (S 1130—PL 103-103) extending programs that allowed federal employees to either donate annual leave to a pooled leave bank or transfer it directly to coworkers who were facing personal or family medical emergencies. *(Related action, federal worker sick leave, this page)*

The bill made permanent a five-year experimental program that was due to expire in October 1993. More than 23,000 employees facing unpaid absences from work received donations of leave time in 1991 and 1992, according to an Office of Personnel Management report. Delegate Eleanor Holmes Norton, D-D.C., said S 1130 should save money because higher paid employees typically donated to lower paid employees while the government paid for time at the salary rate of the lower paid employees. The bill also limited to five days the accrual of more annual or sick leave while on extended leave for a medical emergency.

The Senate Governmental Affairs Committee reported S 1130 on June 30, 1993. The Senate passed the bill by voice vote July 14. The House Post Office and Civil Service Committee reported it (H Rept 103-246) on Sept. 21, and the full House passed an amended version by voice vote the same day. The Senate agreed to the House amendment Sept. 23, completing congressional action. President Clinton signed the bill on Oct. 8. ❑

Federal Worker Sick Leave

President Clinton on Oct. 22, 1994, signed into law a measure (HR 4361—PL 103-388) granting federal workers the right to use sick leave to care for family members who were ill or to attend to the death of a relative. *(Related action, flexible leave, this page)*

HR 4361 also allowed federal workers to transfer annual leave to family members who worked for the federal government. It authorized the changes for a three-year trial period and required the Office of Personnel Management (OPM) to report to Congress on the results at least six months before the trial period ended. Under existing law, federal employees earned 13 days of sick leave a year, but they were allowed to use the time only for their own illness, not to care for a sick relative.

Vice President Al Gore's 1993 National Performance Review, a sweeping proposal to make the federal government more efficient, noted that employers in both the private and public sectors permitted their workers to use sick leave to care for family members and recommended that the same benefits be extended

to federal workers. In response, OPM in May 1994 proposed regulations permitting federal workers to use up to five days of sick leave per year to care for sick family members or to attend the funerals of relatives. OPM set the limit at five days based on findings that federal employees typically used only eight of their 13 days of sick leave earned per year. HR 4361 did not include any restrictions on the number of sick days that could be used. *('Reinventing government,' p. 811)*

Since 1988 (PL 100-566), government workers could donate annual leave to federal workers who faced unpaid absences caused by medical emergencies. HR 4361 changed the program to allow family members to share annual leave as they saw fit, provided that a worker's leave balance did not exceed 30 days. A 1992 survey by the General Accounting Office found that about 30 percent of all federal employees had family members who also worked for the government. *(1988 law, Congress and the Nation Vol. VII, p. 858)*

The House Post Office and Civil Service Committee reported HR 4361 (H Rept 103-722) on Sept. 19, 1994. The House passed the bill by voice vote the same day. The Senate passed an amended version, by voice vote, Oct. 7. The House agreed to the Senate changes Oct. 8, completing congressional action. ❑

Federal Workplace Safety

The House Post Office and Civil Service Committee Oct. 7, 1994, reported a bill (HR 115—H Rept 103-858) to improve workplace health and safety at federal and postal facilities. HR 115 required federal agencies to enforce Occupational Safety and Health Administration (OSHA) standards, extending to federal and postal employees the same protections against unsafe and unhealthy working conditions that applied to private sector workers.

The bill contained language requiring that federal managers personally pay penalties if they willfully violated safety standards. The measure required the establishment of health and safety committees at all federal facilities with 11 or more employees, as well as at postal facilities. These committees, including worker and management representatives, were to be charged with investigating, documenting and correcting on-site safety and health hazards. HR 115 also required OSHA to set governmentwide ergonomic standards. Ergonomics is the study of the effect of certain types of work, such as repetitive motion, on physical well-being. ❑

Federal Commuters

Congress in 1993 cleared a bill (HR 3318—PL 103-172) aimed at encouraging federal workers to commute via mass transit, bicycles and other alternatives to driving alone.

HR 3318 authorized federal agencies, courts and Congress to establish programs that would provide transit passes, bicycle facilities or other, nonmonetary incentives to those who avoided driving. Unlike existing law, these programs did not have to be offered in conjunction with state or local transit agencies—a requirement that deterred some agencies.

The House Post Office and Civil Service Committee reported the bill (H Rept 103-356, Part I) on Nov. 10, 1993. The House passed the measure by voice vote Nov. 15; the Senate followed suit Nov. 20, completing congressional action. President Clinton signed HR 3318 on Dec. 2. ❑

Federal Smoking Restrictions

The House, by voice vote Nov. 15, 1993, passed a bill (HR 881) restricting smoking in most federal buildings to separately ventilated rooms. The measure would have effectively banned smoking in all federal buildings—with the exception of military installations and Department of Veterans Affairs (VA) health care facilities—because of the cost of creating smoking areas.

Antismoking advocates had sought federal restrictions on smoking for years without much success. Their biggest victory came in 1989, when Congress voted to permanently ban smoking on all but a handful of domestic airline flights. The ban was enacted as part of the fiscal 1990 transportation spending bill (PL 101-164). Tobacco opponents suffered a setback in 1992, when lawmakers overturned a VA directive banning smoking in VA hospitals as part of a bill to improve medical care for veterans (PL 102-585). *(Smoking on airlines, Congress and the Nation Vol. VIII, p. 419; smoking in VA hospitals, Congress and the Nation Vol. VIII, p. 635)*

An Environmental Protection Agency (EPA) report, released in January 1993, changed the political climate. The report blamed the lung cancer deaths of 3,000 nonsmokers a year on environmental tobacco smoke, and it linked the smoke to numerous other health problems. Environmental tobacco smoke, also known as secondhand smoke, included both the mainstream smoke exhaled by smokers and the sidestream smoke emitted from cigarettes, cigars and pipes. Supporters said smoking restrictions legislation was necessary because the EPA report could make the federal government liable for the poor health of workers exposed to secondhand smoke. The report prompted some federal agency chiefs to unilaterally ban smoking in buildings under their jurisdiction. Opponents said the legislation would infringe on the rights of smokers.

Lawmakers who wanted a ban on smoking in federal buildings first opted for a back-door approach. Illinois Democrat Richard J. Durbin, chairman of the House Appropriations Agriculture Subcommittee, successfully added language to the fiscal 1994 agriculture spending bill (HR 2493—PL 103-111) that banned smoking in offices of the Women, Infants and Children nutrition program. However, conferees on the fiscal 1994 Treasury-Postal Service appropriations bill (HR 2403—PL 103-123) dropped Senate language to restrict smoking in most federal buildings to separately ventilated areas.

HR 881 sponsor James A. Traficant Jr., D-Ohio, initially sought to ban smoking in all federal buildings, with no exceptions. He lowered his sights when opposition to an all-out ban threatened to kill the initiative before it got off the ground. Traficant and his allies crafted a compromise that exempted military installations and VA hospitals from the legislation and allowed

separately ventilated areas. Tobacco-state lawmakers tried unsuccessfully to further weaken the bill.

The Public Works and Transportation Committee reported HR 881 (H Rept 103-298, Part I) on Oct. 15. The committee rejected a Tim Valentine, D-N.C., substitute amendment to require federal agency heads to set aside special smoking areas, including zones within cafeterias and other dining facilities, instead of making such areas optional. On the House floor, Valentine made one last appeal for a compromise that would require designated smoking areas, but to no avail.

The Senate did not consider HR 881 or a companion measure (S 262). ❑

Mansfield Fellowship

The Senate Governmental Affairs Committee June 9, 1993, rejected, 4–5, a bill (S 587) to establish a Mike Mansfield Fellowship Program that would award two-year grants to federal workers to study the Japanese language and political and economic systems. Democratic panel members argued against starting a new program at a time when others had to be cut.

Mike Mansfield (D-Mont., House 1943–1953; Senate 1953–1977) had served as Senate majority leader and as ambassador to Japan under presidents Jimmy Carter, Ronald Reagan and George Bush. ❑

Displaced FBI Workers

Congress in 1994 agreed to give Federal Bureau of Investigation (FBI) workers who were unwilling to relocate to a new fingerprint center in West Virginia help finding jobs elsewhere in the federal government. The House by voice vote Aug. 16, 1994, had passed a separate bill (HR 4884), but House and Senate negotiators subsequently inserted the provisions into the final version of the fiscal 1995 appropriations bill for the departments of Commerce, Justice and State. President Clinton signed the legislation (HR 4603—PL 103-317) into law on Aug. 26.

In 1990, Senate Appropriations Committee Chairman Robert C. Byrd, D-W.Va., inserted language in supplemental appropriations legislation (PL 101-302) that provided $185 million for a state-of-the-art fingerprint center, with the understanding that it would be located in Byrd's home state. Delegate Eleanor Holmes Norton, D-D.C., with the cosponsorship of many District-area lawmakers, introduced HR 4884 in the 103rd Congress in response to the FBI plans to relocate the Criminal Justice Information Services Division, which was responsible for maintaining the agency's fingerprint files, from Washington to Clarksburg, W.Va., by 1999.

According to the FBI, nearly half of the division's 2,600 employees did not wish to move. Many were African Americans who cited the low number of minorities in West Virginia as one of their concerns. Despite FBI promises to find other jobs for these employees, budget cuts and hiring freezes had limited the number of openings. The workers could not easily transfer to new jobs elsewhere in the federal government, because FBI employees were "excepted service" personnel, not part of the regular competitive civil service. In 1992, the FBI and Justice Department sought a waiver of competitive status to allow the fingerprint employees to seek jobs at Justice, where their experience would have been most valuable. But the Office of Personnel Management said it lacked authority to grant such a waiver.

The House Civil Service and Post Office Committee adopted an amendment to HR 4884 to provide the competitive status only to permanent employees at the fingerprint center and offer it for up to two years after their separation from the FBI. The original bill would have included temporary employees and would have been in effect until Sept. 30, 1999.   ❑

Ethics Office Reauthorization

Legislation to reauthorize the Office of Government Ethics stalled at the end of the 103rd Congress. Authorization for the agency—which oversaw financial disclosure, conflict of interest and employee conduct matters for the executive branch—ran out Sept. 30, 1994.

The Senate Governmental Affairs Committee on July 15, 1994, reported S 1413 (S Rept 103-315), which provided an eight-year reauthorization at unspecified amounts. The bill included several technical changes to the office's authorizing statute, the Ethics in Government Act of 1978 (PL 95-521). The Senate passed S 1413 by voice vote Oct. 6. (1978 law, Congress and the Nation Vol. V, p. 824)

The House Post Office and Civil Service Committee Oct. 3 reported an eight-year authorization (HR 2289—H Rept 103-785, Part I). It instructed appropriators to provide up to $14 million a year to the ethics office. The House Judiciary Committee Oct. 7 reported a version (H Rept 103-785, Part II) that authorized appropriations of $8.1 million in fiscal 1995, $8.4 million in fiscal 1996, $8.8 million in fiscal 1997, $9.1 million in fiscal 1998 and $9.5 million in fiscal 1999. The panel limited the authorization to five years to give Congress more oversight of the office.   ❑

Federal Worker Discrimination Claims

One Senate committee in 1993 and two House committees in 1994 reported legislation (S 404, HR 2721) to overhaul the procedures for handling federal workers' discrimination complaints. But there was no further action.

Under the existing system, federal employees who believed they had been discriminated against on the basis of race, color, religion, gender, national origin, disability or age filed their complaint within their agency. The agency then carried out the investigation. Critics said the system was too complex and guaranteed a conflict of interest.

As reported on Oct. 27, 1993, by the Senate Governmental Affairs Committee (S Rept 103-167), S 404 required that all complaints be dealt with by the Equal Employment Opportunity Commission (EEOC), an independent agency. Federal departments and agencies were to shift resources and personnel to the EEOC so that the commission could meet its new responsibilities. To ensure that no decision was rushed, S 404 extended,

from 30 to 180 days, the time an employee had to file a complaint. The Congressional Budget Office said the bill would save the government about $25 million annually.

The House Education and Labor Committee reported HR 2721 (H Rept 103-599, Part I) on July 13, 1994. The bill transferred responsibility for processing discrimination claims from the employee's agency to the EEOC. It also would cover employees of the House of Representatives.

The House Post Office and Civil Service Committee reported its version of HR 2721 (H Rept 103-599, Part II) on Aug. 19. The bill offered federal employees several options for getting their complaints handled, including a review by the EEOC. It also permitted a federal employee to take a workplace discrimination case to court if the issue was not resolved promptly.

Similar legislation to revamp the federal complaint process had died in the 102nd Congress. (Congress and the Nation Vol. VIII, p. 888)   ❑

Whistleblower Protection

On Oct. 29, 1994, President Clinton signed into law a bill (HR 2970—PL 103-424) expanding existing protections for federal employees who blew the whistle on fraud, waste, abuse or criminal activity in the workplace and reauthorizing the Office of Special Counsel through fiscal 1997.

HR 2970 extended whistleblower protections to employees in the Department of Veterans Affairs, the Federal Deposit Insurance Corporation (FDIC) and the Resolution Trust Corporation (RTC). The bill provided that FDIC and RTC employees who had separate whistleblower protection as a result of the savings and loan bailout legislation (S 714—PL 103-204) had to choose to follow those procedures or the ones in HR 2970. The bill attempted to strengthen the accountability of agency leaders in protecting whistleblowers. It expanded the list of personnel practices that could not be used as retaliation to include requiring psychiatric testing and denying or revoking a security clearance. (Savings and loan bailout, p. 122)

Established in 1979, the Office of Special Counsel was an independent agency within the executive branch charged with investigating allegations by federal employees that they had been demoted, reassigned or otherwise wrongly treated as a result of racial discrimination, as a form of political coercion or as a reprisal for exposing corruption or other violations in the workplace. HR 2970 tightened limits on the information the Office of Special Counsel could disclose on an employee's case. During House floor debate, bill sponsor Frank McCloskey, D-Ind., said that 59 percent of complainants had reported to the General Accounting Office that the special counsel undercut their rights by leaking information about their cases to their employers.

The House Post Office and Civil Service Committee reported HR 2970 (H Rept 103-769) on Sept. 30, 1994. In its report, the committee stressed the importance of protecting whistleblowers if the administration's goal of "reinventing government" to make it more efficient was to bear fruit. The report also was highly critical of the special counsel's office, stating that "contrary to its rhetoric, the [Office's] empirical track record is one of hostility to its stated mission as the rule, rather than the exception. Despite 400 to 500 cases yearly and the most sympathetic legal standards in history, the Office still has not litigated a single case to restore a whistleblower's job since the [Whistleblower Protection] Act's 1989 passage [PL 101-12], or indeed since 1979." *(1989 law, Congress and the Nation Vol. VIII, p. 862)*

The House passed HR 2970 by voice vote on Oct. 3. The Senate followed suit on Oct. 7, after eliminating House language expanding the legal alternatives open to aggrieved federal employees. The House-passed bill had included the option in certain cases of initiating a civil action in the appropriate U.S. district court. The House accepted the Senate changes by voice vote the same day, completing congressional action.   ❏

Postal Service Inspector General

On June 27, 1994, the House Post Office and Civil Service Committee formally reported and the full House by voice vote passed HR 4400 (H Rept 103-561, Part I), which would have established an inspector general at the U.S. Postal Service to carry out independent audits and review postal programs and operations.

At that time, the inspector general function was being performed by the chief postal inspector, who reported to the Postal Service's board of governors—a panel of nine presidential appointees responsible for hiring and firing the postmaster general. The independent inspector general provided for in HR 4400 was to be appointed by the president and confirmed by the Senate. The bill also would have expanded the role of the board of governors, requiring it to appoint the upper management of the Postal Service.

HR 4400 would have prevented the Postal Service from paying confidential informants in drug investigations unless they involved the mail. This provision stemmed from a botched sting operation at the Cleveland Post Office. Convicted felons were hired to go undercover in the post office and report back on drug users. Police said the felons used the drugs themselves and fingered innocent employees.   ❏

Paperwork Reduction

The Senate by voice vote Oct. 6, 1994, passed a bill (S 560) to amend the Paperwork Reduction Act of 1980 (PL 96-511) to require each agency to review its paperwork requirements to ensure that the least possible burden was imposed on the public. S 560, which was reported (S Rept 103-392) from the Senate Governmental Affairs Committee Sept. 30, also aimed to enhance the opportunity for public comment during the agency review process.

S 560 sought to improve the government's collection, management and dissemination of information, its use of new information technology and its computer security practices. The main purpose of the 1980 law was to reduce the paperwork burden that the federal government imposed on businesses and individuals. The act established a special unit within the Office of Management and Budget (OMB) to review requests for infor-

mation by federal agencies to determine whether the information was necessary, could not be found elsewhere and was being collected efficiently. During the Reagan and Bush administrations, OMB's Office of Information and Regulatory Affairs (OIRA) used its power under the law to gain increasing control over both the form and the content of regulations issued by federal agencies. Critics charged that OIRA was misusing its authority to review regulations, delaying proposed rules that the White House disagreed with and changing others behind the scenes without giving the public a chance to comment. As passed by the Senate, S 560 authorized $8 million annually for OIRA and maintained the existing law's goal of reducing the paperwork burden by 5 percent each year.

One of the bill's most controversial provisions would have overturned the 1990 Supreme Court decision in *Dole v. United Steelworkers of America,* which had been hailed by unions and consumer groups and denounced by business interests. The Court said that the paperwork law allowed OMB to review requests for data intended for government use but did not extend to regulations intended to force businesses to generate information for a third party, such as the public or their employees. S 560 would have included such third-party disclosures in the definition of "collection of information," making them subject to OMB's paperwork review. *(1990 decision, Congress and the Nation Vol. VIII, pp. 832, 868)*

In related action, the Senate Governmental Affairs Committee Sept. 26, 1994, reported S 2156 (S Rept 103-375), which would have eliminated 196 reports that federal agencies were required to submit to Congress and would have modified 68 others.

FREEDOM OF INFORMATION ACT

The Senate in 1994 passed a measure (S 1782) to extend the 1966 Freedom of Information Act (FOIA) to many government records compiled and stored on computers.

The bill, reported by the Senate Judiciary Committee Aug. 22, 1994 (S Rept 103-365) and passed by a voice vote of the full Senate Aug. 25, proposed to require federal agencies to publish in the Federal Register an index of all information retrievable or stored in electronic form. Public records, such as agency regulations, were to be made accessible by computer telecommunications.

The House did not take up the bill and S 1782 died at the end of the 103rd Congress. *(1996 action, p. 849)*   ❏

Unfunded Mandates

Action stalled on legislation aimed at making it harder for Congress to mandate requirements, so-called unfunded mandates, on state and local governments without providing them with adequate funding. *(104th Congress action, p. 837)*

Keenly aware of the political potency of the issue, the Clinton administration took steps to rein in unfunded mandates. President Clinton issued two executive orders in September and October 1993, one calling for federal agencies to consult with state and local government officials when feasible before making regulations, and the other directing federal agencies to avoid whenever possible regulations that involved unfunded mandates. The president also pledged to work with Congress to draft some form of mandate relief legislation.

Federal regulations enacted between 1983 and 1990 imposed from $8.9 billion to $12.7 billion in costs on states and localities, according to the Advisory Commission on Intergovernmental Relations. Such mandates included anything from setting standards for clean drinking water to providing access to public buildings for disabled people. The call to stem these federal edicts had galvanized influential state and local government groups, such as the U.S. Conference of Mayors.

However, many public interest groups feared that any legislation designed to address the issue would undermine laws meant to protect health, safety and civil rights. Some environmentalists complained that the campaign was a smoke screen for an attack on environmental laws.

SENATE ACTION

The Senate Governmental Affairs Committee Aug. 10, 1994, reported S 993 (S Rept 103-330), a compromise bill drafted by panel Chairman John Glenn, D-Ohio, and freshman Dirk Kempthorne, R-Idaho. Kempthorne—a former mayor of Boise, Idaho—had originally introduced an aggressive bill to block all unfunded initiatives, but he agreed to work on a compromise with Glenn and the administration. Under the Glenn-Kempthorne substitute, any congressional committee reporting an authorization bill that mandated a federal program had to request a Congressional Budget Office (CBO) cost estimate. CBO was to provide a detailed report on any legislation that would impose net costs on local governments of more than $50 million. To clear the way for floor consideration, CBO would have to certify that a mandate would not impose costs of more than $50 million, or the committee would have to authorize additional assistance to affected local governments. Otherwise, the bill would be subject to a point of order allowing senators to block floor consideration. Under the bill, authorizations governing emergency disaster assistance, civil rights, fraud prevention, national security and international treaties were exempt. The bill would not apply to annual appropriations.

Over Glenn's objections, the committee adopted an amendment to require that CBO also analyze the cost of new unfunded mandates of more than $200 million on the private sector. To fund the CBO studies, S 993 authorized $6 million per year for the budget office in fiscal 1995–1998.

The Senate voted 88–0 on Oct. 6 on a motion to proceed to consideration of S 993. However, immediately after the vote, the bill was overcome by add-ons. It became an all-too-inviting vehicle for unrelated, end-of-session amendments, including one by Paul Simon, D-Ill., to establish a National African American Museum within the Smithsonian Institution and one by Phil Gramm, R-Texas, to repeal a 1993 tax increase on Social Security benefits. S 993 subsequently was set aside, and it died upon adjournment. (*African American museum, p. 825; 1993 tax, p. 87*)

HOUSE ACTION

The House Government Operations Subcommittee on Human Resources and Intergovernmental Relations on Aug. 11, 1994, approved HR 4771, a companion to the Glenn-Kempthorne measure. HR 4771 required CBO to review any legislation authorizing an unfunded mandate and to provide a detailed analysis of bills imposing costs of more than $50 million. The bill provided for a point of order against legislation unless CBO certified that it did not reach the $50 million threshold, or unless the committee authorized funding to cover the cost of the mandate. Some members complained that the point of order requirement, modeled after the provisions in S 993, would be ineffective in the House, where the Rules Committee routinely waived points of order. But attempts to strengthen HR 4771's enforcement measures to reflect House procedures were rejected.

The full House Government Operations Committee approved a revised unfunded mandates bill (HR 5128) on Oct. 5. At the behest of GOP members, the committee strengthened the bill's point of order provisions to reduce the Rules Committee's ability to override them.

HR 5128 had the backing of the so-called Big Seven, seven state and local government associations that had actively opposed unfunded mandates. But the revisions were rejected by committee members Gary A. Condit, D-Calif., as too weak and by Henry A. Waxman, D-Calif., as too strong. An attempt by Condit to replace the language in HR 5128 with the text of a more far-reaching bill (HR 140), which would have barred Congress from imposing mandates without providing funding, was rejected. Waxman's amendments suffered the same fate. Waxman said HR 5128 would chip away at necessary health and safety protections while creating "a bewildering number of procedural roadblocks, the full implications of which no one understands." He took particular exception to a provision requiring federal agencies to seek the input of state and local governments before establishing regulatory requirements. But the panel rejected a Waxman amendment aimed at preventing state and local governments from receiving preferential treatment over private enterprise. Also rejected was another Waxman amendment to require that the benefits of federal mandates, such as reduced health care costs, be taken into account when totaling the aggregate cost of an unfunded mandate.

After the markup, Waxman claimed his right to hold the bill for three days to file dissenting views to the committee report, effectively freezing the bill and preventing the House from taking further action as it neared adjournment.   ❑

Federal Land Payments

Congress in 1994 cleared legislation (S 455—PL 103-397) authorizing an increase in payments to local governments on lands that were under federal control. These "payments in lieu of taxes" were intended to compensate local governments for amounts they would have received in property tax revenue if the lands in their jurisdictions had not been under federal control.

S 455 adjusted the existing formula to increase the payments gradually over five years to about $227 million in 1999, raising the rate from 75 cents to $1.65 per acre of federal land. Payments in subsequent years were to be indexed to inflation. Congress had appropriated $109 million in fiscal 1994. S 455 also raised the limitation on payments to local governments from $50 times the population to $110 times the population.

Western lawmakers argued that the payment formula had not been changed since it was established in 1976 and that dollar amounts had not kept up with inflation. The Clinton administration supported payments to the states but did not back S 455 because the increase in discretionary spending meant cuts in other programs.

The Senate Energy and Natural Resources Committee reported S 455 (S Rept 103-231) on Feb. 25, 1994. The Senate passed the bill, 78–20, on April 13. The House Natural Resources Committee reported S 455 (H Rept 103-838) on Oct. 5. During floor action, the House on Oct. 7 rejected, 160–262, an amendment offered by Natural Resources Committee Chairman George Miller, D-Calif., that would have authorized a temporary two-year increase in payments, while the General Accounting Office studied the issue. Miller argued that the measure was a "massive, uncapped increase" that would cost $484 million in new spending over four years for a program whose soundness was questionable. The House that same day also rejected, 195–223, a Bruce F. Vento, D-Minn., amendment to eliminate the provisions that tied future increases to the rate of inflation. The House passed S 455 by voice vote Oct. 7, completing congressional action. President Clinton signed the bill (PL 103-397) on Oct. 22.

Guam Land Return

Congress in 1994 cleared a bill (HR 2144—PL 103-339) to return land to Guam.

The U.S. federal government owned one-third of the land on Guam, much of it condemned by military tribunals in the 1940s before the island had its own government. The land consisted of 3,219 acres scattered around U.S. Navy and Air Force installations on the island. Guam officials said many residents thought that they were merely leasing their land to the U.S. military, and they resented the failure to return it. Congress had debated but not approved a variety of proposals since 1975 to return the property, despite the Defense Department's declaration 15 years earlier that it did not need the land. Under federal law, any federal land deemed to be excess was put up for sale to the highest bidder. Guam officials opposed that procedure, because it would have allowed investors to outbid the original owners for the land.

Delegate Robert A. Underwood, D-Guam, sponsor of HR 2144, proposed that the land be turned over without charge to the Guam government on the condition that it be reserved for "public benefit use," such as schools, hospitals, housing or economic development. The House Natural Resources Committee reported HR 2144 (H Rept 103-391, Part I) on Nov. 20, 1993. The House passed the measure by voice vote Jan. 26, 1994. The

House added requirements that the land be offered first to other federal agencies, then appraised. Congress then would have 180 days to review the appraisals and a land-use plan submitted by Guam. No structures tall enough to interfere with air navigation could be built within six nautical miles of an airport. The House also amended the bill to require Guam to grant the National Park Service administrative control over the undeveloped lands it owned within the War in the Pacific National Historical Park. The provision barred any use of those lands that was not compatible with the park.

The Senate Energy and Natural Resources Committee reported HR 2144 (S Rept 103-293) on June 24. The Senate passed the bill by voice vote Sept. 21, completing congressional action. President Clinton signed the bill Oct. 6.

D.C. Statehood

For the first time, House members in 1993 debated on the floor whether the District of Columbia should become a state. However, the statehood measure (HR 51) was rejected. HR 51 would have created an enclave of government buildings and monuments to remain under the control of the federal government; the remaining areas of the city were to become the fifty-first state, New Columbia, represented by two senators and one representative.

A bill to make the District a state died in the 102nd Congress without full House action. Statehood supporters had been unwilling to take up House floor time to debate the issue, knowing that they could not override a threatened veto by President George Bush. (Congress and the Nation Vol. VIII, p. 896)

Statehood supporters contended that District residents deserved statehood because they were being taxed but did not have equal representation in Congress. District residents voted for one delegate to represent their interests in the House; they had no representation in the Senate. The District's population of more than half a million people was larger than that in the states of Alaska, Vermont or Wyoming. (Delegate voting privileges, p. 881)

Republicans generally opposed D.C. statehood. For one thing, the District's residents traditionally voted Democratic. Moreover, many Republicans, and some Democrats, questioned whether granting the area statehood would be constitutional given that the founders had designated it the nation's capital area. Article I, Section 8, Clause 17 of the U.S. Constitution said Congress had the power "to exercise exclusive legislation in all cases whatsoever, over such District (not exceeding 10 miles square) as may, by cession of particular states, and the acceptance of Congress, become the Seat of Government of the United States." The Bush administration argued that a constitutional amendment was required before Congress could give back control over the lands ceded to it by Maryland and Virginia more than 200 years earlier. The Clinton administration supported the statehood effort.

The House District of Columbia Committee reported HR 51 (H Rept 103-371) on Nov. 17, 1993. The full House rejected the bill on Nov. 21 by 153–277. Statehood supporters had hoped to win at least 120 "yea" votes in the House to ensure that they would make a respectable showing. When the vote reached 150, supporters packed in the gallery broke into applause and those on the House floor embraced. In deciding to go for a floor vote, bill sponsor Delegate Eleanor Holmes Norton, D-D.C., said the vote would give statehood supporters a baseline and a working list of members whom they needed to bring into the fold. Norton took the long view on the effort, citing the more than 40 years it took for Alaska and Hawaii to become states. Norton praised the White House lobbying effort, saying President Clinton had called 15 members at her request. Clinton also wrote Norton a letter stating his strong support for statehood and urging House members to vote for HR 51.

All House members of the Congressional Black Caucus voted for the bill, as did most of the House Democratic leadership, including Speaker Thomas S. Foley, D-Wash., who rarely voted. However, most lawmakers representing jurisdictions neighboring the District opposed statehood because it would allow the District to enact a "commuter tax" on suburban residents who worked in the city.   ❏

JFK Commission

President Clinton on Oct. 6, 1994, signed into law a bill (HR 4569—PL 103-345) to extend the authorization of a five-member commission appointed to review and release to the public information related to the assassination of President John F. Kennedy (JFK). The review board was authorized to continue work until Sept. 30, 1996, with an optional one-year extension if it had not completed its work by then.

The controversy over who killed Kennedy had raged since the Warren Commission in 1964 investigated the Nov. 22, 1963, assassination and found that Lee Harvey Oswald acted alone in killing the president. Five years later a special House committee finished its investigation of the assassination, with the majority of panel members concluding that the president "was probably assassinated as a result of a conspiracy." Congress decided to create the special five-member commission in 1992 (PL 102-526) in the wake of Oliver Stone's movie *JFK,* which renewed interest in whether a conspiracy surrounded Kennedy's death. The panel was given the authority to make public hundreds of thousands of pages of secret government documents, testimony and evidence related to Kennedy's death. *(PL 102-526, Congress and the Nation Vol. VIII, p. 892)*

The House passed HR 4569 by voice vote July 12, 1994. The Senate Governmental Affairs Committee reported the measure Aug. 2. The Senate passed an amended version by voice vote Aug. 10. The House agreed to the Senate changes Sept. 27, clearing the bill.   ❏

King Holiday

Legislation (HR 1933—PL 103-304) to extend federal funding for the Martin Luther King Jr. Federal Holiday Commission for five years was signed into law Aug. 23, 1994.

Authorization for the commission, which was established in 1984 to promote a national holiday in observance of the slain civil rights leader, expired April 20, 1994. Congress had been appropriating $300,000 annually for the commission, which was privately financed before 1990. HR 1933 authorized a total of $2 million over five years, gradually increasing annual authorizations to $500,000. It also directed the commission to promote community service activities in memory of King.

The House Post Office and Civil Service Committee reported HR 1933 (H Rept 103-418, Part I) on Feb. 3, 1994. The House passed the measure by voice vote March 15. The Senate Judiciary Committee reported it May 5. On the floor May 24, the Senate rejected, 28–70, a Jesse Helms, R-N.C., amendment to block federal funding for the commission. Helms argued that, with a civil rights holiday observed in all 50 states, the commission had served its purpose. He said that the Martin Luther King Center for Non-Violent Social Change raised $20 million to $30 million per year and that such private funds should be used for the advancement of King's teachings. But bill supporters, led by Carol Moseley-Braun, D-Ill., the Senate's lone African American, and Harris Wofford, D-Pa., said that, under the legislation, the commission would gain new responsibility to promote community service and other volunteer programs related to King's teachings. The Senate passed HR 1933, 94–4, on May 24. On Aug. 10, the House agreed to technical changes in the Senate-passed version, clearing the bill.   ❏

NEA, NEH Reauthorization

Congress failed to complete action on a two-year reauthorization for the National Endowment for the Arts (NEA), the National Endowment for the Humanities (NEH) and the Institute of Museum Services. The legislation (HR 2351, S 1218) made no policy changes on the controversial issues of what was art and what was obscenity.

The House Education and Labor Committee reported HR 2351 (H Rept 103-186) on July 21, 1993. The full House passed the bill, 304–119, on Oct. 14.

During floor debate Oct. 14, the House rejected a Philip M. Crane, R-Ill., amendment, 103–326, to abolish the arts endowment; a Robert K. Dornan, R-Calif., amendment, 151–281, to cut the fiscal 1994 authorization for all three agencies by 40 percent; and a Randy "Duke" Cunningham, R-Calif., motion, 210–214, to send the bill back to committee with instructions to reiterate an existing ban on NEA grants to illegal immigrants.

The House adopted by voice vote an amendment offered by Steve Gunderson, R-Wis., and Louise M. Slaughter, D-N.Y., to freeze a state's NEA allocation at the previous year's level if the state's current year arts spending was less than the average amount it had spent annually during the three most recent years. Gunderson's attempts to press the issue of state arts spending during committee consideration of HR 2351 had been unsuccessful. Although previous reauthorization legislation had forbidden states from using increases in federal money in place of state money, Gunderson said that was exactly what had been happening. He said that, in fiscal 1991, 24 states or territories reduced arts funding from the previous year's level by an average of 16 percent. At the same time, NEA basic grants to states increased almost 22 percent, from $21.5 million to $26.2 million. In fiscal 1992, according to Gunderson, 36 states and territories cut arts funding from the fiscal 1991 level.

The Senate Labor and Human Resources Committee reported a companion version (S 1218—S Rept 103-182) on Nov. 12. It was identical to the House-passed measure. ❏

Air and Space Museum Annex

Legislation (HR 847—PL 103-57) authorizing an extension of the Smithsonian Institution's National Air and Space Museum at Dulles International Airport in Virginia was signed into law Aug. 2, 1993.

HR 847 authorized $8 million in fiscal 1994 for the planning and design of the annex, which would serve as an additional site to store and display aeronautical and space flight equipment. Some said the equipment was at risk of deterioration at the Garber Facility in Suitland, Md., where it was being stored. Past attempts to enact legislation were stymied by a dispute over whether the Smithsonian should be required to subject the project to competitive bidding instead of assigning it to the Dulles location.

The House passed HR 847 by voice vote June 29, 1993. The Senate followed suit July 22, completing congressional action. ❏

African American Museum

The House passed and a Senate committee reported legislation (HR 877) authorizing the establishment of a National African American Museum—devoted to the history, art and culture of African Americans—as part of the Smithsonian Institution.

The museum, which African American lawmakers and others had advocated for years, would be housed in the Smithsonian's Arts and Industries Building in Washington, D.C., and modeled on the National Museum of the American Indian. HR 877 would have authorized $5 million for fiscal 1994.

The House Public Works and Transportation Committee reported HR 877 on June 18, 1993, and the House Administration Committee reported the bill on June 28 (H Rept 103-140, Parts I and II). The House passed HR 877 by voice vote June 29.

The Senate Rules and Administration Committee removed specific fiscal years and funding levels, after members expressed concern that private funds being sought by the Smithsonian would not be enough to cover the new museum.

The committee reported HR 877 (S Rept 103-284) on June 16, 1994.

There was no further action. ❏

Space Station

The nation's premier big-science project, the space station, survived attempts in 1993 and 1994 to dismantle it.

BACKGROUND

The space station was conceived in 1984 (PL 98-361) as an $8 billion orbiting manned laboratory in which astronauts would live and conduct experiments for prolonged periods. By the time Bill Clinton took office in 1993, $8.5 billion had been spent on the uncompleted project and it was expected to cost $30 billion to $40 billion by the year 2000. Other countries had promised to contribute $8 million. *(PL 98-361, Congress and the Nation Vol. VI, p. 789)*

Critics derided the space station as a boondoggle with little or no scientific value; defenders called it critical for the future of manned space research and stressed its importance for local jobs.

President Clinton called on the National Aeronautics and Space Administration (NASA) to redesign the space station; by various counts, it was the fifth or sixth redesign since the project's inception. In early March 1993, NASA Administrator Daniel S. Goldin announced that a team of as many as 35 officials from NASA and participating foreign space agencies would completely redesign the space station. After a 90-day cram session, NASA officials presented an independent blue-ribbon panel with three design options. Clinton reviewed the team's work and then announced June 17 that he had chosen a variation of the middle-priced option—a modular design that amounted to a smaller version of the previous *Freedom* blueprints. New components could be added to the station over time, culminating in 2001 with the capability of sustaining five astronauts for up to 30 days in space. The crew would perform research on life sciences, advanced materials and microgravity. The space station was renamed *Alpha*.

Clinton also brought the Russians into the process. On Sept. 2, Vice President Al Gore and Russian Prime Minister Victor S. Chernomyrdin signed an agreement that called for a joint effort to design and construct *Alpha* as an international space station. In November, Clinton met with key space station backers and won their support for Russian involvement in exchange for his commitment to more actively promote the project.

LEGISLATIVE ACTION

The space station had weathered almost annual challenges to its existence since 1987. *(Congress and the Nation Vol. VII, p. 861; Congress and the Nation Vol. VIII, pp. 877, 899)*

1993 Action

During floor action on a NASA authorization bill (HR 2200), the House June 23, 1993, voted 215–216 to reject an amendment, offered by Tim Roemer, D-Ind., and Dick Zimmer, R-N.J., to kill the space station. Similar amendments had been rejected earlier during committee consideration of the bill. The floor vote was not quite as close as it looked: the "yea" tally included four delegates who, under new House rules, were allowed to cast votes only so long as doing so did not determine the outcome. Still, the vote was the closest the project had ever come to cancellation. During the debate, proponents touted the space station's potential for spurring medical advances, materials research and retaining a U.S. presence in manned space exploration. Critics said it held little potential for curing cancer or other diseases and said the project's main purpose was as a "pork-barrel" jobs program primarily of benefit to Texas, Florida, California and Alabama. (NASA authorization, p. 827)

During markup of the fiscal 1994 funding bill for the Department of Veterans Affairs (VA), Department of Housing and Urban Development (HUD), and related agencies (HR 2491), the House VA-HUD Appropriations Subcommittee approved $1.9 billion for the space station. Clinton had proposed spending $2.1 billion a year on the program for fiscal 1994 through 1998. The full committee added $250 million to the subcommittee recommendation, bringing the total to what Clinton had requested. The full House June 28 rejected, 196–220, an amendment, offered by Roemer and Zimmer to HR 2491, to terminate the space station program.

As approved by the Senate VA-HUD Appropriations Subcommittee and by the full Appropriations Committee, HR 2491 provided $1.9 billion for space station development. That was comparable to the House-approved amount because, at the administration's request, the Senate shifted $154 million in certain space-related costs to other NASA program areas. The Senate committee bill barred NASA from spending more than $1 billion of the space station's appropriation before Jan. 31, 1994, enabling Congress to assess the final design plan before agreeing to release the balance.

Appropriators also were wary of the agreement with the Russians. The Senate spending bill prohibited any space station appropriation from being used to pay Russia. The legislation did set aside $50 million to expand joint activities with the Russian *Mir* space station and another $50 million for space science activities with the Russians.

The space station dominated most of the Senate floor debate on HR 2491. Dale Bumpers, D-Ark., Jim Sasser, D-Tenn., and John W. Warner, R-Va., offered an amendment to kill the program and apply the savings to reducing the budget deficit. A motion to table (kill) their amendment was agreed to 59–40 on Sept. 21. The Senate also tabled, 55–39 on Sept. 21, a Warner amendment to require further congressional approval before NASA could spend more than $1 billion in fiscal 1994 funds for the space station.

As cleared, HR 2491 (PL 103-124) provided $1.9 billion for the manned orbiting space laboratory.

1994 Action

During consideration of a NASA authorization measure (HR 4489) in 1994, the House Science, Space and Technology Committee rejected a Roemer amendment to cancel funding for the space station but adopted another Roemer amendment to limit annual funding for the project to $2.1 billion. As passed by the House, HR 4489 made a joint space station venture between the United States and Russia conditional on certification that a minimal Russian troop presence was evident in the Baltic nations. It required the president to certify each year, for the joint venture to continue, that actions by Russia "do not violate the sovereignty" of any former Soviet republic. The bill also required an accounting of the $112 million in fiscal 1995 and any future U.S. funds sent to Russia for space station development.

The Senate Commerce, Science and Transportation Committee removed from HR 4489 the House language that conditioned the joint venture on annual certification that Russia was not violating the sovereignty of any former Soviet republic. (NASA authorization, p. 827)

During consideration of the fiscal 1995 veterans and housing funding bill (HR 4624), the House VA-HUD Appropriations Subcommittee approved $2.1 billion for the space station. On the House floor, members June 29 rejected a Roemer amendment to kill the space station on a **key vote of 155–278 (R 40–136; D 114–142; I 1–0)**. Clinton, Gore and NASA Administrator Goldin personally lobbied members to support the station. They argued that the 1993 agreement with Russia to cooperate on the project—and international agreements with other countries—were essential to the administration's foreign policy goals and that the project's redesign would keep costs under control. (1994 key votes, p. 1003)

The Senate Aug. 3 rejected, 36–64, a Bumpers amendment to the VA-HUD bill to terminate the space station.

As cleared, HR 4624 (PL 103-327) provided $2.1 billion for the space station. ❑

Superconducting Supercollider

In a stunning upset for the scientific community, the superconducting supercollider was killed in 1993.

Under construction in Waxahachie, Texas, since 1990, the superconducting supercollider was intended to allow scientists to smash atomic particles into each other in a 54-mile underground tunnel at nearly the speed of light in the hope of discovering the smallest particle of matter. Advocates, who had been pushing the project since 1984, argued that it was crucial to keep the United States at the forefront of high-energy physics. But critics, noting the slow pace of construction and cost overruns, called it, at best, a scientific luxury and, at worst, a "pork-barrel" boondoggle for Texas and for Louisiana, where high-powered magnets were being built. Congress had poured a total of $1.6 billion into the project, but instead of symbolizing extraordinary technological advance, it became a symbol of profligate spending. The cost of the supercollider, which had started out at $4.4 billion in 1987, in 1993 was estimated at $11 billion by completion.

In 1992, the House voted to kill the project, but the Senate restored funding and persuaded the House to continue the program. In 1993, however, the atom smasher fell victim to strong budget-cutting sentiment in the House and to lukewarm support from President Clinton, who, unlike avowed Texan George Bush, did not visibly lobby to save the project. (1992 action, Congress and the Nation Vol. VIII, p. 901)

The House Energy and Water Development Appropriations Subcommittee unanimously supported funding for the superconducting supercollider in the annual energy and water spending bill (HR 2445), approving $620 million in fiscal 1994, $20 million less than the administration sought. The House Appropriations Committee concurred in the subcommittee's funding level for the supercollider. The full House, however, on June 24 voted 280–150 to adopt an amendment, offered by Jim Slattery, D-Kan., and Sherwood Boehlert, R-N.Y., to kill the project. During floor debate on HR 2445, Slattery, Boehlert and others reiterated the cost overruns and delays in the program, the failure of foreign governments to participate as promised and the need for frugality amid budget deficits. The opponents were given fresh ammunition the day before the vote in the form of news accounts of an internal Energy Department draft document alleging that $216 million in subcontractor expenses were unnecessary or excessive. Project managers denied the allegations. Supercollider advocates argued that nothing less than the United States' preeminence in basic research was at stake and said the project annually represented only a minute fraction of the total U.S. research budget.

The Senate Appropriations Committee provided $640 million for the supercollider in fiscal 1994. The full Senate granted a temporary reprieve to the project, voting 57–42 on Sept. 30 to table (kill) a Dale Bumpers, D-Ark., amendment to terminate the supercollider. The conferees on HR 2445 subsequently preserved the program. Slattery and Boehlert Oct. 19 rallied the House to overcome seemingly insurmountable institutional and political obstacles to again kill the project. The House Oct. 19 first blocked adoption of the conference report (H Rept 103-292) with supercollider funding in it, by rejecting in a **key vote of 159–264 (R 61–111; D 98–152; I 0–1)**, a pivotal procedural motion. The House then agreed 282–143 to send the bill back to conference with specific instructions to terminate the project. The House Oct. 26 also adopted, 227–190, an amendment to the second conference report (H Rept 103-305) that called on the energy secretary to submit a plan by July 1, 1994, to terminate the supercollider project, while maximizing the funds already invested. As signed into law, HR 2445 (PL 103-126) provided $640 million to terminate the program. *(1993 key votes, p. 979)* ❏

NASA Authorization

The 103rd Congress was unable to clear a National Aeronautics and Space Administration (NASA) authorization bill. The agency was funded through annual appropriations legislation for veterans and housing programs and related agencies. Efforts to terminate the space station were thwarted. *(Space station, p. 825)*

1993 ACTION

The House Science, Space and Technology Committee reported its fiscal 1994–1995 NASA authorization bill (HR 2200—H Rept 103-123) on June 10, 1993. The bill included a Tim Roemer, D-Ind., amendment discontinuing the Advanced Solid Rocket Motor (ASRM), a project aimed at creating a rocket motor for the space shuttle program that could carry heavier payloads into space more efficiently. The program had come under attack for being unnecessary and too costly. The Roemer amendment provided $150 million for fiscal 1994 and $35 mil-

lion for fiscal 1995 to cover the cost of terminating the program and transferring the production of the space shuttle and other solid rocket motor nozzles, as well as the refurbishment of redesigned solid rocket motor cases, to a new production site located near Yellow Creek, Miss.

The House, by voice vote July 29, passed HR 2200, authorizing up to $14.8 billion for fiscal 1994 and $15.6 billion for fiscal 1995. During floor action on the bill, the House on June 23 turned back an attempt to kill the space station by a 215–216 vote. That same day the House adopted, 411–11, a Ralph M. Hall, D-Texas, amendment to limit the fiscal 1994 authorization to no more than 3.1 percent above the amount authorized in fiscal 1993, reducing the total in the bill by $264 million.

Adopted 276–139 on July 23 was an F. James Sensenbrenner Jr., R-Wis., amendment to cancel $35 million in fiscal 1995 for completing work on the solid rocket facility in Mississippi and $25 million slated for relocation of the facility from Utah to Mississippi. Sensenbrenner argued that the physical plant was no longer needed because HR 2200 already canceled the ASRM program, the reason for building the facility.

House Science Committee Chairman George E. Brown Jr., D-Calif., said that the new plant, which was 90 percent complete, should be used to build more traditional solid rocket motors that propelled the space shuttle. The contractor that built the motors, Thiokol Corp., wanted to shift its solid rocket motor facilities—and roughly 1,000 jobs—from Utah to the Mississippi plant.

On a 319–109 vote July 29, the House adopted an amendment offered by C. Christopher Cox, R-Calif., and Barney Frank, D-Mass., to allow NASA to buy helium from private sources. The space agency had been required to purchase its helium, an inert gas used for spacecraft and space missions, from a government reserve established for national security reasons in the 1920s, when it was believed that natural sources of helium were rapidly depleting. The gas since had been found to be naturally abundant. By 1993, 90 percent of the helium in the United States was produced by private industry and sold at prices lower than NASA paid for helium from the stockpile. *(Helium sales, p. 436)*

The Senate did not act on NASA authorization legislation in 1993.

The fiscal 1993 appropriations bill for the Department of Veterans Affairs, Department of Housing and Urban Development, and related agencies (HR 2491—PL 103-124) provided $14.6 billion for NASA, including $100 million to terminate the ASRM project.

1994 ACTION

The House Science, Space and Technology Committee on Aug. 3 reported a two-year NASA authorization bill (HR 4489—H Rept 103-654) that would enable the agency to launch eight space shuttle flights a year and fund the Mars surveyor program, a robotic probe to map the surface of the planet. The bill, which would have authorized $14.1 billion in fiscal 1995 and $14.3 billion in fiscal 1996, proposed to trim NASA's budget by $450 million in fiscal 1995. Some of the savings were to be achieved by eliminating planned shuttle upgrades and trimming the Mission to Planet Earth program.

The House passed HR 4489 by voice vote Aug. 8, after adopting a Brown amendment that stripped the bill of any specific funding levels or spending authority for NASA. Because funding was being provided for in the fiscal 1995 appropriations bill for veterans and housing (HR 4624), Brown wanted HR 4489 to focus on policy directives. The revised bill's broad policy guidelines included encouraging partnerships between NASA and private companies for technology development and promoting better accountability in the often criticized space agency. HR 4489 required NASA to consider cost savings in the space shuttle program; allowed the transportation secretary to license commercial satellite operations to ensure that reentry plans were safe; gave NASA and the Commerce Department, instead of the Defense Department, broader authority over launching a new satellite under the Land Remote Sensing Policy Act of 1992 (Landsat).

The Senate Commerce, Science and Transportation Committee reported HR 4489 Sept. 28. The committee incorporated into the bill the provisions of a separate bill (S 1881) setting criteria for awarding NASA technology development grants. S 1881, which included language granting authority to license commercial reentry spacecraft and prohibiting the launch of outer space advertisements, had been reported (S Rept 103-362) from Senate Commerce on Sept. 7 and passed by the full Senate on a voice vote Oct. 6. The House did not act on S 1881.

The Senate passed HR 4489 by voice vote Oct. 5. The measure saw no further congressional action.

The fiscal 1995 spending bill for Veterans Affairs, Housing and Urban Development, and related agencies (HR 4624—PL 103-327) provided $14.4 billion for NASA.   ❑

NASA Buyouts

Both the House and Senate in 1993 passed a bill (HR 2876) giving the National Aeronautics and Space Administration (NASA) authority to offer buyouts of up to $25,000 to employees to achieve personnel reductions associated with the space station *Freedom* redesign. *(Space station, p. 825)*

NASA officials said HR 2876 promised to help the agency avoid imposing agencywide furloughs or permanent staff cuts. Gen. Spence M. Armstrong, NASA's associate administrator for human resources, gave the agency an Oct. 1 deadline to eliminate 1,100 of the 1,300 full-time positions allocated for the space station in the fiscal 1994 budget.

The House passed HR 2876 by voice vote Aug. 6, 1993. The Senate passed the bill by voice vote Nov. 22, after amending it to include a stipulation by Governmental Affairs Committee Chairman John Glenn, D-Ohio, that the incentive money "should be subject to the availability of appropriations" for that purpose. If, by Sept. 30, 1994, not enough civil service employees had retired or resigned, NASA was required to implement furloughs to achieve reductions in personnel.

There was no further action.   ❑

NSF Funding

The House passed and two Senate committees reported legislation (HR 3254, S 2344) to reauthorize the National Science Foundation (NSF). Differences could not be reconciled by the end of the 103rd Congress, however.

The NSF was an independent agency that supported basic and applied research and education programs in more than 2,000 colleges, universities and nonprofit organizations. A key feature of both bills was an increase in spending for construction of academic research facilities. The Clinton administration sought $55 million for that purpose in fiscal 1995. HR 3254 nearly tripled that request, authorizing $150 million in fiscal 1995. S 2344 increased it further, to $300 million.

House bill sponsors hoped to dissuade appropriators from steering money toward specific hometown academic institutions for research facilities, a practice known as earmarking, which critics said unfairly bypassed the merit-based peer review process followed by the NSF. HR 3254 would have barred the NSF from awarding facilities improvement grants to academic institutions that received earmarked construction money from appropriators. However, some lawmakers defended earmarks as necessary to address a grant system that favored larger, more prestigious universities.

The House Science, Space and Technology Committee on April 13, 1994, reported HR 3254 (H Rept 103-475), authorizing $3.2 billion for the NSF in fiscal 1995 and $3.4 billion in fiscal 1996. On the floor, the House May 4 adopted, 227–197, a Sherwood Boehlert, R-N.Y., amendment that trimmed the authorization to $3.15 billion for fiscal 1995 and $3.23 billion for fiscal 1996. The House then passed HR 3254 May 4 on a 396–22 vote.

The Senate Labor and Human Resources Committee reported S 2344 (S Rept 103-328) on Aug. 9. The Senate Commerce, Science and Transportation Committee reported the measure Sept. 28. S 2344 authorized $3.5 billion in fiscal 1995, increasing gradually to $5.1 billion in fiscal 1999. The bill did not include a provision barring future facilities grants to academic institutions that had received construction money under an earmark.

Congress had last authorized the NSF in 1988 for fiscal years 1989 through 1993. Congress appropriated $3 billion for the agency in fiscal 1994 and about $3.4 billion in fiscal 1995. *(1988 action, Congress and the Nation Vol. VII, p. 860)*   ❑

Science and Technology Policy

The House Science, Space and Technology Committee April 12, 1994, reported a bill (HR 3476—H Rept 103-473) aimed at addressing an issue that had long confounded science advocates: how to set federal priorities for the vast complex of federally backed research, particularly in a tight, post–cold war budget climate. Similar, but pared down, provisions were included in the Senate version of a competitiveness bill (S 4) that did not clear Congress. *(Competitiveness programs, p. 342)*

HR 3476 would have given the White House Office of Science and Technology Policy a more direct role in formulating the government's research and development spending priorities. The science office would have been required to work with the Office of Management and Budget to review the budget proposals of each agency and to issue budget guidance to federal agencies to ensure that public policy spurred the nation's science and technology effects. In addition, the White House science and budget offices were to prepare an annual report to Congress setting specific priorities for science and technology programs, including a consolidated national research and development budget proposal.

The bill also provided for creation of a National Science and Technology Council to replace the Federal Coordinating Council for Science, Engineering and Technology, which had been criticized as ineffective. The new council, recommended in Vice President Al Gore's 1993 National Performance Review, was to parallel the National Economic Council and the National Security Council to ensure that the president's science priorities were reflected in the budget and other federal priorities. The council was to consist of the director of the White House science office, cabinet secretaries and directors of the National Aeronautics and Space Administration, National Science Foundation, National Institutes of Health and other federal agencies. (*'Reinventing government,' p. 811*) ❏

High-Tech Library of Congress

Congress in 1993 failed to fund most of the Library of Congress's "information age" budget or authorize the library to provide cost-recovering information services. Citing harsh budget realities, appropriators cut the library's forward-looking science and technology programs and special projects from the fiscal 1994 legislative branch appropriations bill (HR 2348—PL 103-69). The library ended up with $250.8 million, $2 million less than the previous year. Authorizers also were unable to push through a bill (S 345) to expand the library's authority to charge for services for the first time since 1902.

Librarian of Congress James H. Billington requested an increase of nearly $30 million in funding for the main library and several related programs, including the Congressional Research Service and the Books for the Blind Program. Testifying before the Senate Legislative Branch Appropriations Subcommittee Feb. 25, 1993, Billington offered a vision of what the world's largest library might be in the 21st century. His seven-year plan included overcoming a backlog of 32 million uncatalogued materials, securing and translating vast collections into digital format, and introducing computerized document searches and deliveries to Congress, the private sector, and the scientific and technical research community. To help pay for the modernization, he proposed that the library offer specialized fee-based services. That stirred controversy, with appropriators responding that the library was established to help Congress, not provide noncongressional customers with high-tech information services. Many on the panel said the library was moving too hastily into the electronic age.

Appropriators warned that the technology was costly and said they could not support new ventures into automation when they were cut-

ting agency budgets across the board. They said they would need to determine how to make the technology available to the general public before they could commit funding for pilot projects such as American Memory—a history project that brought original cartoons, photographs, audio recordings, manuscripts and full motion video to hundreds of children in its two years of testing. Some librarians feared that a national library focused on electronically based resources could exclude the hundreds of local libraries that had no equipment to receive information from fiber-optic networks. They also worried that all the attention on electronic information services would diminish investments in traditional services such as cataloging, reference and interlibrary loans. Publishers of print and information services feared that a more service-oriented, technological library could snuff out their document search businesses.

For several years running, the library had suffered mandated reductions in service and heightened criticism of it management—all of which made big funding increases harder to justify. Furthermore, in August 1993, U.S. District Judge Norma Holloway Johnson ruled that the library had illegally discriminated against its black administrative and professional employees. And severe security problems had forced the library to close its stacks to scholars in 1992.

The Senate Rules and Administration Committee on May 26, 1993, reported S 345 (S Rept 103-50), which would have allowed the library to offer and charge for costly, technologically advanced services that appropriations or philanthropy could not support. The library would have had to recover costs for 11 types of specialized research services frequently requested, such as detailed legal analysis and document delivery. Recovered fees were to be deposited in a revolving U.S. Treasury fund. S 345 divided library information products and services into three categories—core, national and specialized—and preserved free access to core services.

In early June, House appropriators in need of savings eliminated American Memory's budget along with two other information age initiatives. Senate appropriators did the same. However, on July 23, Harry Reid, D-Nev., and Mark O. Hatfield, R-Ore., got the full Senate to approve by voice vote an amendment to HR 2348 to restore the last $1 million for American Memory for completion of the project's report. Conferees on HR 2348 (H Rept 103-210) warned the library not to "extend its role in the creation or assembly of educational materials" beyond its core services; staff from American Memory and special projects could be used in arrearage, automation or human resources core programs.

On Nov. 18, the Bell Atlantic Corp. announced it would distribute American Memory as part of its northern Virginia technology test. The library supplied the digitized primary source material from its collection, and Bell Atlantic provided the system for delivering the material to home computers. Bell Atlantic also announced plans for marketing the collection to the general public in 1994.

Bell Atlantic was one of 18 corporations, including GTE, Microsoft Corp., IBM and Simon & Schuster, that had donated money, software and equipment to the library's National Demonstration Laboratory, a multimedia demonstration center that contained much of the technology needed to create a library capable of allowing worldwide remote access. America Online, which made library exhibits part of a free introductory offer to its commercial network, paid the costs of setting up "Revelations from the Russian Archives" online to entertain current subscribers and entice new ones to hook up. The arrangement enabled the library to be the first such institution to make electronic versions of its exhibits. ❑

Federal Emergency Management Agency

S 1697, to shift the focus of the Federal Emergency Management Agency (FEMA) from the cold war scenario of nuclear attack-related disasters to better reflect its primary function of providing relief after natural disasters, was reported from the Senate Governmental Affairs Committee Oct. 5, 1994 (S Rept 103-400).

The bill required both the president and FEMA to submit plans for providing federal assistance and establishing chains of command. Those plans were to specify federal duties in case of emergency and the relationship between the federal government and state, local and private agencies. The bill also stipulated how FEMA should be reorganized, including relocating certain regional offices to high-risk areas. It included provisions to create a targeted grant program to allow state and local governments to better prepare for emergencies. The measure authorized $200 million per year through fiscal 1998 for the grant program. ❑

Federal Disaster Insurance

The House Public Works and Transportation Committee Oct. 7, 1994, reported legislation (HR 2873—H Rept 103-848, Part I) aimed at reducing the huge bills for disaster relief that were regularly paid by the federal government. The Senate Commerce, Science and Transportation Committee held hearings in 1993 on its version (S 1350), but the measure went no further.

In four out of the five years from 1990 to 1994, natural disasters had caused at least four times as many losses as the federal government had budgeted for in its main emergency account. As a result, Congress cleared eight spending bills to provide an additional $23.6 billion for disaster relief. HR 2873 and S 1350 would have established a federal disaster insurance program under the Robert T. Stafford Disaster Relief and Emergency Assistance Act (PL 100-707), the main federal law governing disaster relief. *(PL 100-707, Congress and the Nation Vol. VII, p. 494)*

The legislation provided financial incentives to encourage insurance companies to include broad-ranging disaster insurance in their homeowners' policies. Premiums were to be based on long-range prospects for earthquakes, tidal waves, volcanic eruptions, hurricanes, tornadoes and other natural disasters in each locale. By collecting premiums from all property owners and spreading the risk, insurance companies could cut the price of earthquake coverage drastically and still amass a sufficient pool of reserves, according to bill supporters. Existing earthquake coverage was so expensive that only about 25 percent of the property owners in earthquake-prone areas had it. To help

the insurance industry afford the risk of covering disasters, the legislation provided for a backup pool of money funded over time by the industry itself. Private companies already provided such a backup, called reinsurance, but recent disasters had raised its costs and threatened its availability. As a consequence, some leading insurance companies had dropped or cut back their coverage. To help cover the cost of disasters, the legislation also included incentives for the states to adopt and enforce better building codes. ❑

Earthquake Preparedness

President Clinton Oct. 19, 1994, signed into law a bill (HR 3485—PL 103-374) to extend federal earthquake research and preparedness programs for two years.

HR 3485 would have reauthorized the National Earthquake Hazards Reduction Program at $103.2 million in fiscal 1995 and $106.3 million in fiscal 1996. Four agencies, including the Federal Emergency Management Agency, would have been required to conduct an assessment of the nation's earthquake monitoring facilities and report their findings to Congress within nine months. According to the U.S. Geological Survey, 39 states were at significant risk of a damaging earthquake.

On Nov. 15, 1993, the House Science, Space and Technology Committee reported and the full House by voice vote passed HR 3485 (H Rept 103-360, Part I), which provided a three-year authorization. The Senate Commerce, Science and Transportation Committee reported a two-year version of the bill (S Rept 103-354) on Aug. 22, 1994, and the full Senate passed it by voice vote Sept. 30. The House by voice vote agreed to the Senate change Oct. 5, completing congressional action. ❑

Native American Land Claims

Congress in 1993 cleared legislation (HR 2399—PL 103-116) resolving a 153-year-old land dispute between the Catawba tribe and 62,000 South Carolina landowners.

The dispute stemmed from an 1840 treaty under which the state of South Carolina purchased 144,000 acres from the Catawbas. The tribe called the sale invalid because Congress never ratified it. The Catawbas had tried in court since 1980 to regain the land and threatened to sue the private landowners. Early in 1993, a settlement was reached. Congressional approval and the president's signature were required to ratify the agreement.

In exchange for giving up its land claim, the tribe would receive $50 million over five years. The federal government would contribute $32 million; the remaining $18 million would be raised from state, local and private sources. HR 2399 earmarked $7.5 million to be spread among 1,400 members of the Catawba tribe.

The agreement restored the Catawbas' status as a federally recognized Native American tribe, making members eligible for additional federal assistance. In 1959, Congress had stripped the Catawbas of their official status as part of a federal effort to assimilate Native Americans into mainstream society.

On Sept. 27, 1993, the House Natural Resources Committee reported (H Rept 103-257, Part I) and the full House by voice vote passed HR 2399. The Senate Indian Affairs Committee had reported its version (S 1156—S Rept 103-124) on Aug. 5 and the full Senate by voice vote had passed it the next day. The Senate passed an amended HR 2399 by voice vote Oct. 5. The House Oct. 12 agreed to the Senate changes, completing congressional action. President Clinton signed the bill Oct. 27.   ❑

Tribal Courts

President Clinton Dec. 3, 1993, signed into law a bill (HR 1268—PL 103-176) funneling technical and financial resources to tribal court systems. HR 1268 authorized $58 million annually through fiscal 2000, more than four times the amount provided in fiscal 1993. Most of the funding was to be used to create an Office of Tribal Justice Support within the Bureau of Indian Affairs (BIA); it would replace the bureau's Branch of Judicial Services.

Many Native American tribes, recognized as quasi-independent nations, operated judicial systems outside the jurisdiction of U.S. courts. Under federal law, Native American tribes were accorded authority over any tribal governance that was not specifically given to Congress. A 1968 civil rights law (PL 90-284) ensured that Native American tribes had the right to exercise legal jurisdiction over their affairs. Traditionally, however, the tribal courts were underfunded. Legislative efforts to shore up the courts were hung up in 1992 over Senate provisions that would have given tribal judicial conferences some say in the administration of Native American justice programs. *(1968 law, Congress and the Nation Vol. II, p. 385; 1992 action, Congress and the Nation Vol. VIII, p. 906)*

On Aug. 2, 1993, the House Natural Resources Committee reported (H Rept 103-205) and the full House by voice vote passed HR 1268. The Senate passed an amended HR 1268 by voice vote Aug. 6. The House and Senate versions differed over granting tribal judicial conferences control over certain aspects of the programs. Conferees subsequently agreed that conferences could contract with the BIA to employ judges and judicial staff; develop standards of conduct; train personnel; construct law libraries; and develop innovative projects for victims services, alternative dispute resolution and child abuse. On Nov. 19, the House adopted the conference report on HR 1268 (H Rept 103-383) by voice vote. The Senate followed suit the next day, clearing the measure.   ❑

Native American Farmlands

Congress in 1993 cleared legislation (HR 1425—PL 103-177) encouraging tribes to develop their own programs, tailored to the specific needs of their reservations, to manage Native American farmlands and ranches. The Senate had passed a similar measure during the 102nd Congress. *(1992 action, Congress and the Nation Vol. VIII, p. 907)*

On Nov. 16, the House Natural Resources Committee reported (H Rept 103-367) and the full House passed by voice

vote HR 1425. The Senate Indian Affairs Committee reported the bill (S Rept 103-186) on Nov. 18. The Senate passed HR 1425 by voice vote Nov. 20, completing congressional action. President Clinton signed the bill on Dec. 3.   ❑

Native American Dams

By voice vote July 20, 1993, the Senate passed S 442, which directed the interior secretary to fix and maintain dams on Native American lands, including 53 dams that were considered dangerous. Proponents of the measure said the Bureau of Indian Affairs had not complied with a 1980 dam safety program.

The Senate Indian Affairs Committee had reported S 442 (S Rept 103-86) on July 13. The House took no action on the bill. ❑

Native American Environmental Laws

President Clinton on Nov. 24, 1993, signed into law a bill (S 654—PL 103-155) aimed at simplifying the implementation of federal environmental laws on Native American lands.

S 654 extended the authorization for the 1992 Indian Environmental General Assistance Program Act, at $15 million per year, through fiscal 2003. The act allowed the Environmental Protection Agency (EPA) to provide omnibus grants to Native American tribes to administer environmental laws, thereby reducing paperwork and federal spending. Without the program, EPA would have to issue separate grants for each federal environmental statute.

The Senate Indian Affairs Committee reported the bill (S Rept 103-87) on July 13. The Senate passed it by voice vote July 20. The House passed an amended version by voice vote Nov. 8. The Senate accepted the House changes by voice vote Nov. 11, clearing the bill.   ❑

Native American Waste Dumps

Signed into law Oct. 22, 1994, S 720 (PL 103-399) sought to clean up potentially toxic waste dumps on Native American reservations. There were approximately 600 potentially hazardous dumps on Native American lands that could pose health risks to livestock and people. Improperly secured dumps could lead to contamination of groundwater. As of late 1994, only two of the 600 dumps met Environmental Protection Agency regulations governing the disposal of solid waste.

S 720 required the Indian Health Service (IHS) to locate and inventory all of the open dumps and to rank them according to the risk they posed. The IHS then would assist tribes in cleaning up or closing down the dangerous landfills. The IHS also would be required to report to Congress annually on the status and cost of the cleanup effort.

The Senate Indian Affairs Committee reported S 720 (S Rept 103-253) on April 25, 1994. The Senate passed the bill by voice vote May 12. The House Natural Resources Committee reported it (H Rept 103-783) on Oct. 3. The House passed an amended version by voice vote Oct. 5. The Senate accepted the House changes Oct. 8, completing congressional action.   ❑

Native American Trading Ban

The Senate by voice vote Nov. 20, 1993, passed legislation (S 1501) to repeal the 1834 Trading with Indians Act, which prohibited federal employees from engaging in trade with Native Americans.

The 1834 law was designed to prevent federal employees from taking advantage of Native Americans. But bill supporters said it placed impractical restrictions on federal employees, such as barring some federal employees from selling a car to a Native American.

S 1501 had been reported (S Rept 103-190) from the Senate Indian Affairs Committee on Nov. 18.   ❑

Tribal Independence

In its continuing effort to restore the independence of Native American nations, Congress in 1994 cleared legislation (HR 4842—PL 103-413) to streamline and expand programs that granted tribes greater autonomy and authority over federal programs designed for their benefit. President Clinton signed the bill on Oct. 25.

Under treaties dating back to the 1700s, the federal government had recognized Native American tribes as sovereign nations within the United States. In the treaties, the government pledged to provide public services, such as education and health care, to the tribes in exchange for land, other resources and peace. Despite the tribes' independent status, however, the federal government kept a tight grip on the management of public services until 1974, when the Indian Self-Determination and Education Assistance Act (PL 93-638) was enacted. The law permitted tribes to take over, through self-determination contracts, the administration of individual federal programs that otherwise would have been managed by the Interior Department's Bureau of Indian Affairs (BIA) or by the Indian Health Service in the Department of Health and Human Services. In practice, however, tribes were held back in their attempts to take over federal programs by a large federal bureaucracy and excessive regulations. (1974 law, Congress and the Nation Vol. IV, p. 810)

In 1988, Congress amended the act (PL 100-472) to create a demonstration project within the BIA that allowed 20 tribes to take over the administration of certain federal programs for their tribes. Congress in 1991 (PL 102-184) authorized funding for an additional 10 tribes to participate in the demonstration project. (1991 action, Congress and the Nation Vol. VIII, p. 906)

In 1993, the Senate approved legislation (S 1618) to create a permanent tribal self-governance program and allow up to 20 new tribes to join the program every year. The Senate Indian Affairs Committee had reported S 1618 (S Rept 103-205) on Nov. 22 and the full Senate passed it by voice vote Nov. 24. The House did not consider S 1618 but took up similar legislation (HR 3508) in 1994.

HR 4842, the bill ultimately enacted, combined two initiatives. The first—the contents of the original HR 4842—provided for a model contract that tribes could use to cut through red tape, and it limited the paperwork demands on tribes and ex-

empted many contracts from federal procurement rules. The second—language included in HR 3508—expanded and made permanent the demonstration program under which tribes could take over whole blocks of federal programs. HR 3508 permitted up to 20 new tribes to join the self-governance program every year. Under the program, tribes had greater flexibility over how to spend federal funds and could redesign programs to meet unique demands found on their reservations. Indian Health Service programs would remain a temporary part of the self-governance program while Congress studied their inclusion on a permanent basis.

The House Natural Resources Committee reported HR 3508 (H Rept 103-653) on Aug. 3, 1994. The House passed the bill by voice vote Aug. 16. After amending HR 4842 to include the language of HR 3508, the House Oct. 7 passed HR 4842 by voice vote. The Senate followed suit later the same day, completing congressional action.   ❑

'Historic' Tribes

President Clinton signed into law May 31, 1994, legislation (S 1654—PL 103-263) that prohibited the federal government from making a distinction between "historic" Native American tribes—which included almost all tribes—and "created" tribes. The Bureau of Indian Affairs considered roughly 20 tribes to be "created" because they could not sufficiently document their tribal history. Historic tribes enjoyed greater autonomy, including the right to levy taxes and handle law enforcement on Native American lands.

The Senate Indian Affairs Committee had reported S 1654 (S Rept 103-191) on Nov. 19, 1993. The Senate passed the bill by voice vote Nov. 24. On April 19, 1994, the House Natural Resources Committee reported (H Rept 103-479, Part I) and the full House, by a vote of 414–2, passed S 1654. The Senate agreed to the House changes with amendments May 19. The House then agreed to the Senate changes May 23, clearing the bill.   ❑

Tribal Recognition

On a 337–54 vote, the House Oct. 3, 1994, passed HR 4462, to improve the process of granting formal recognition to Native American tribes. The House Natural Resources Committee had reported the bill (H Rept 103-782) earlier that day. The Senate did not act on the measure.

Federally recognized tribes were eligible for government services and other benefits. HR 4462 would have created an independent Commission on Indian Recognition to determine whether specific Native American groups should be recognized as tribes.

LUMBEE TRIBE

The House, by a vote of 228–184 on Oct. 28, 1993, passed legislation (HR 334) making the Lumbee tribe of Cheraw Indians in eastern North Carolina eligible for federal social services.

HR 334 amended a 1956 law that recognized the Lumbees as an Native American tribe but prohibited its members from receiving federal funds through the Bureau of Indian Affairs (BIA) and the Indian Health Service. The 1956 law also forbade the Lumbee tribe from seeking formal recognition, and thus federal benefits, through the process administered by the BIA. The Lumbee tribe first sought federal recognition in 1890, but it was routinely denied for economic and political reasons.

Republicans opposed HR 334 because of its cost—$80 million to $100 million a year, according to the Congressional Budget Office—and precedent. If the bill were enacted, said Rep. Craig Thomas, R-Wyo., other tribes would be encouraged to seek recognition legislatively instead of administratively. On the House floor, Thomas offered an amendment to set up a process for the Lumbees to apply for recognition through the Interior Department, instead of extending federal recognition to the tribe through legislation. The House Oct. 28 rejected the amendment 178–238.

The House Natural Resources Committee had reported the measure (H Rept 103-290) on Oct. 14.

MENOMINEE TRIBE

By voice vote Aug. 6, 1993, the Senate passed a bill (S 1335) to allow the Menominee tribe of Wisconsin to sue the federal government for damages resulting from elimination of the tribe's federal recognition from 1954 to 1973. Tribes with federal recognition were eligible for federal benefits. ❑

Native American Trust Funds

On Oct. 25, 1994, President Clinton signed into law a bill (HR 4833—PL 103-412) that allowed tribes to directly manage their trust funds and to receive periodic statements on accounts that remained with the Interior Department. HR 4833 established a special trustee within the department to draft and execute a comprehensive plan to clean up and manage the trust funds.

The bill also created a nine-member advisory board made up of tribal and individual account holder representatives, plus people with experience in investment management, to assist the trustee; required the interior secretary to give all individual and tribal account holders a quarterly financial statement; required that funds held in trust for individual Native Americans be invested in interest-bearing Treasury notes and bonds, just as tribal funds were; and authorized Native American tribes to withdraw their accounts from the trust funds and take over the management of those accounts, once they had won approval from the secretary and the special trustee.

For 150 years, the Interior Department had been entrusted with money that resulted from agreements between the federal government and tribes over land use, mineral rights and other claims. Members of Congress and tribal leaders had long criticized the department for its management of the Native American funds, which amounted to $2.1 billion.

On Oct. 3, 1994, the House Natural Resources Committee reported (H Rept 103-778) and the full House, 353–39, passed

HR 4833. The Senate passed the bill by voice vote Oct. 7, completing congressional action. ❑

Native American Child Protection

The Senate, by voice vote Oct. 6, 1994, passed a bill (S 2075) designed to beef up a 1990 law (PL 101-630) to prevent child abuse on Native American reservations.

The 1990 law had authorized new federal programs to treat Native American victims of child abuse and to increase the reporting of abuse cases. Congress acted in response to reports that several teachers employed by the Bureau of Indian Affairs had sexually abused Native American students. The law also had aimed to ensure that workers dealing with Native American children had no criminal record. (1990 law, Congress and the Nation Vol. VIII, p. 883)

However, the two agencies charged with putting the programs in place—the Bureau of Indian Affairs and the Indian Health Service—were unclear about their roles. S 2075 would have transferred more authority to the health service. The bill also provided funds to investigate employees working with children and to combat family violence.

The Senate Indian Affairs Committee had reported S 2075 (S Rept 103-394) on Oct. 3. ❑

Indian Health Service Director

The Senate, by voice vote Sept. 21, 1994, passed a bill (S 2067) to elevate the director of the Indian Health Service to an assistant secretary of Native American health. The purpose was to give the director more clout within the Department of Health and Human Services.

The Senate Indian Affairs Committee reported S 2067 (S Rept 103-327) on Aug. 8, 1994. ❑

Peyote Use

Congress in 1994 cleared legislation (HR 4230—PL 103-344) to protect the right of Native Americans to use peyote as a religious sacrament.

Since 1966, Native Americans had been exempt from laws banning the use of peyote, a hallucinogenic drug made from spineless cacti found in the Southwest. However, tribal leaders feared that the regulatory exemption did not protect their free exercise of religion under the First Amendment. Their fears were based, in part, on a 1990 Supreme Court ruling, Employment Division, Department of Human Resources of Oregon v. Smith. The ruling declared that the sacramental use of peyote was not necessarily protected under the Constitution, unless individual states provided exemptions. At the time, 28 states had such laws on the books. (1990 ruling, Congress and the Nation Vol. VIII, p. 835)

HR 4230 gave the regulatory exemption for peyote use the force of law. It also prohibited states from discriminating against Native Americans who used the drug. HR 4230 was a narrower version of legislation protecting native religions (S 2269). (Native American religious freedom, p. 834)

The House Natural Resources Committee reported HR 4230 (H Rept 103-675) on Aug. 5, 1994. The House passed the bill by voice vote Aug. 8. The Senate followed suit Sept. 27. President Clinton signed the measure Oct. 6.   ❏

Native American Religious Freedom

The Senate Indian Affairs Committee on Oct. 8, 1994, reported legislation (S 2269—S Rept 103-411) containing broad protections for native religions.

For years, Native American tribes demanded federal protections for certain sacred sites so they could worship and gather sacred plants undisturbed. Protection of these areas was a top priority for tribal leaders, who viewed the fight as a struggle to preserve their culture and heritage. But the lands were located off reservations, and loggers, developers, tourists and four-wheel vehicle enthusiasts also wanted to use them.

To protect the lands, S 2269 would have required the federal government to prove a "compelling interest" before it could disturb a sacred Native American site. That standard would have increased the burden on the federal government to show that it needed to take actions that would interfere with Native Americans' religious practices. The bill included provisions aimed at establishing ways to facilitate negotiations between tribes and federal land managers to permit multiple use of federal lands.

S 2269 also would have protected Native Americans' right to use peyote, an otherwise illegal hallucinogen, in religious ceremonies. Separate legislation (HR 4230) protecting that right was enacted in 1994. *(Peyote use, p. 833)*

Other provisions of S 2269 permitted Native American prisoners to practice their religions, wear traditional headgear and have access to their religious practitioners. The bill also eased restrictions for Native Americans in obtaining protected eagle feathers and plants from the Fish and Wildlife Service for use in religious ceremonies.   ❏

1995–1996

Lobbying Disclosure

Less than a year after objections from Senate Republicans buried legislation that would have imposed new disclosure requirements on lobbyists, Congress in 1995 cleared a similar bill (S 1060). President Clinton signed the measure (PL 104-65) on Dec. 19. *(Earlier action, p. 809)*

S 1060 was designed to close loopholes in the 1946 lobbying law that had enabled most lobbyists to avoid registering. Under the bill, any lobbyist who received at least $5,000 in a six-month period from a single client was required to register with the clerk of the House and the secretary of the Senate. Lobbyists had to list the congressional chambers and federal agencies they contacted, the issues they lobbied on, and how much money was spent. The reporting requirement also applied to organizations that used their own employees to lobby and spent at least $20,000 in a six-month period on that effort.

Republican leaders resisted taking up the legislation, and it cleared only because of determined rank-and-file pressure from members of both parties. Early in 1995, Republicans beat back Democratic attempts in both chambers to attach lobbying reform and a gift ban to a bill (S 2) applying workplace laws to Congress as well as to new House rules. *(Gift restrictions, p. 919; workplace compliance, p. 882; House rules, p. 864)*

SENATE ACTION

Majority Leader Bob Dole, R-Kan., reached agreement with Democrats led by Minority Leader Tom Daschle of South Dakota, Paul Wellstone of Minnesota and Carl Levin of Michigan to take up a lobbying disclosure bill and a gift ban proposal no later than July 28. The two sides agreed to create a bipartisan commission of senators to try to craft a bill. If their efforts failed, the Senate would consider legislation (S 101) sponsored by Levin and William S. Cohen, R-Maine, with separate votes on lobbying disclosure and gift restrictions. S 101 tracked the unsuccessful 1994 measure, although it dropped the controversial provisions on grassroots groups.

The Senate passed a compromise lobbying disclosure bill (S 1060) by a **key vote of 98–0 (R 53–0; D 45–0)** on July 25. The compromise dropped a proposal from the 1994 bill to create an independent agency to regulate lobbyists. It also specifically exempted grassroots lobbying, such as letter writing and telephone campaigns, from its provisions. The compromise was offered as a substitute on the floor and adopted, 98–0, on July 24. *(1995 key votes, p. 1025)*

S 1060 applied to individuals who spent at least 20 percent of their time lobbying members of Congress, their staffs or top executive branch officials. Lobbyists who received at least $5,000 in a six-month period from a single client would have to register with the clerk of the House and secretary of the Senate. In addition, organizations that used their employees to lobby had to register if they spent at least $20,000 in any six-month period on such activities. The bill required semiannual reports from lobbyists, and it required that they disclose much more information than in the past. They were required to report the chamber and federal agencies that they approached, the subjects they discussed with officials, and the amount of money spent on the effort. S 1060 required the clerk of the House and the secretary of the Senate to turn over any potential violations of the bill to the Justice Department, which would decide whether to prosecute. Those found guilty would face up to $50,000 in civil penalties.

The Senate adopted an amendment by Alan K. Simpson, R-Wyo., as modified by Larry E. Craig, R-Idaho, 59–37, to prevent 501(c)(4) nonprofit organizations that lobbied Congress from receiving federal funds; and one by Frank R. Lautenberg, D-N.J., 72–26, to express the sense of the Senate that the tax deduction for lobbying expenses, which had been eliminated in 1993, should not be restored. *(1993 action, p. 809)*

On voice votes, the Senate also adopted amendments by John McCain, to repeal the Ramspeck Act, which allowed former congressional or judicial employees to obtain civil service jobs without having to take the competitive exam; by Hank Brown, R-Colo., to expand senators' financial disclosure statements by adding several more categories to describe the value of assets and liabilities; and by Dole, to prohibit former U.S. trade representatives or deputies from representing or advising foreign governments, political parties or businesses. In addition, no one who had represented a foreign government in a trade dispute with the United States would be eligible to serve as trade representative or deputy.

HOUSE ACTION

Faced with a revolt by his own members and a near-unanimous Democratic Caucus, Majority Leader Dick Armey, R-Texas, announced Oct. 27 that a House vote on lobby registration legislation would proceed. House GOP leaders had wanted to postpone consideration of both the lobby registration and the gift ban rules changes until 1996 or later. However, after the Senate acted, pressure intensified for Armey and other Republican leaders to bring up the lobby bill. Christopher Shays, R-Conn., even threatened to retire if the lobbying and gift ban bills were not considered. Democrats used the delay to brand Republicans as antireform—a position not popular with the public and the interest groups devoted to good government.

Armey's announcement was designed to help GOP leaders regain control over the issue of institutional change and to help Republicans, especially freshmen, carry through on their pledge to shake up business-as-usual in Congress. Just two days before the announcement, a group of House freshmen had teamed with lobby disclosure and gift ban proponents and forced the leadership to postpone a vote on the legislative branch spending bill (HR 2492) after they threatened to support Democratic efforts to attach the lobby registration and the gift ban measures to the bill. House Speaker Newt Gingrich, R-Ga., then pulled the appropriations bill from the schedule.

The key word in House action on the lobby bill (HR 2564) became "no amendments." If the House passed the measure in the exact form as the Senate, the bill would avoid a potentially deadly conference and instead would head straight to Clinton, who promised to sign it. But the House Rules Committee approved an open rule for the bill, giving the members who had proposed amendments a free shot. Shays, Charles T. Canady, R-Fla., Barney Frank, D-Mass., and other supporters urged their colleagues to oppose any and all amendments. The good-government groups that had fought for the new lobby requirements also helped fend off amendments.

Victory was ensured more than 12 hours before the final vote on HR 2564, when the House on Nov. 28 rejected on a **key vote of 190–238 (R 176–56; D 14–181; I 0–1)** a House Government Reform and Oversight Committee Chairman William F. Clinger, R-Pa., amendment to prohibit federal agencies from using public funds to provide information to outside groups in the hope that they would galvanize their members to support or oppose congressional proposals. Adoption would have opened the door to other changes and a likely veto by Clinton. The defeat was a signal to others with pending amendments, and most withdrew them. Among the amendments withdrawn were four

controversial proposals by Ernest Jim Istook Jr., R-Okla., and David M. McIntosh, R-Ind., to restrict the ability of certain organizations that received federal grants to lobby Congress.

The House did vote on—and reject—other amendments to prohibit lobbyists from giving gifts to lawmakers; to impose a lifetime ban on the secretary of commerce and the commissioner of the International Trade Commission from representing foreign entities; and to require lobbyists to list the dates, amounts and recipients of speaking fees paid to journalists.

The House Judiciary Committee reported HR 2564 (H Rept 104-339, Part I) on Nov. 14, 1995. On Nov. 29, the House passed the bill, 421–0, then passed S 1060 by voice vote.

Before S 1060 reached the president's desk, some Senate Republicans launched an unsuccessful attempt to change a provision they said would prevent some nonprofit organizations from lobbying, or even contacting, the federal government. The Blue Cross/Blue Shield Association and other groups that contracted with the federal government to perform services complained that a provision added by Simpson to limit the lobbying of large, tax-exempt nonprofit groups would inadvertently hamper their contacts with the federal government. Blue Cross/Blue Shield handled Medicare claims and insured many federal workers.

MAJOR PROVISIONS

As cleared, S 1060:

Definitions

Defined a lobbyist as someone who was employed or retained by a client, made more than one contact on behalf of that client and spent at least 20 percent of his or her time during a six-month period providing that service to the client.

A lobbying firm was defined as an entity that had at least one person who was hired to represent someone other than his or her employer. The term also applied to self-employed individuals who represented other people or entities.

A lobbying contract was defined as a communication, either oral or written, on behalf of a client to a covered executive or legislative branch official regarding legislation, rules, regulations, grants, loans, permits, programs or the nomination of anyone subject to Senate confirmation.

Exceptions

Carved out several exceptions for contracts with federal officials, including testimony before congressional committees, responses to notices in the *Federal Register,* public petitions to agency actions, speeches to the public, and meetings (including those to check on the status of an action) that did not involve trying to influence executive or legislative branch officials. Contacts initiated by public officials were exempt. Tax-exempt religious organizations, such as churches, also were exempt.

When to File

Required lobbyists to register with the secretary of the Senate and the clerk of the House within 45 days of the first contact, or within 45 days of being hired, whichever came first.

Organizations with one lobbyist or more could file a single registration form for each client, even if that client was represented by several lobbyists. A lobbyist who made more than one contact for the same client needed to file only one form detailing all of those contacts.

Lobbyists or firms that expected to receive no more than $5,000 in a six-month period did not have to register, nor did an organization's in-house lobbyist who expected to spend less than $20,000 in a six-month period.

The dollar amounts were to be adjusted for inflation on Jan. 1, 1997, and every four years thereafter.

What to File

Required that the registration include the following information:

• The name, address, principal place of business and business phone number for the registrant and a general description of the registrant's business or activities.

• The name, address and principal place of business for the client and a general description of the client's business or activities.

• The name, address, principal place of business and amount of money spent by anyone, other than the client, who contributed more than $10,000 in a six-month period to the lobbying activities of the registrant and played a major role in planning, supervising or controlling such activities.

• Foreign entities that owned at least 20 percent of a client or a firm that contributed to a client's lobbying efforts, was affiliated with a client or an organization that contributed to the client's efforts, or played a major role in planning, financing or supervising the lobbying effort were required to disclose the extent of their ownership and the amount they contributed, if above $10,000, to the lobbying activities of the registrant.

• A list of the general issue areas that the registrant expected to lobby on and specific issues, to the extent possible, that were likely to be addressed.

• The name of each lobbyist and whether the lobbyist had previously served as an executive or legislative branch official covered under the law within two years of becoming a lobbyist.

Terminating Registration

Enabled registrants who no longer represented a particular client to end the registration by notifying the clerk of the House and the secretary of the Senate.

Semiannual Reports

Required all registrants to file reports twice a year, one covering the period Jan. 1 to June 30 and the other covering the period July 1 to Dec. 31. The reports had to be filed within 45 days after the end of the period.

The reports had to contain:

• The name of the registrant, name of the client and any changes to the initial registration.

• For each general issue area, a list of specific issues, including, to the extent possible, bill numbers and references to specific executive branch actions; a list of the chambers of Congress and the executive branch agencies contacted; the names of the lobbyists; and a description of any foreign entity's interest in a particular issue. The lobbyist was not required to disclose the names of the lawmakers, staff members or committees contacted.

• For lobbying firms, a "good-faith estimate" of the amount of money paid by the client or any person on behalf of the client.

• For registrants conducting their own lobbying, a "good-faith estimate" of the total expenses incurred.

Nonprofit charitable, educational and other tax-exempt groups incorporated under section 501(c)(3) of the Internal Revenue Code that already reported their lobbying expenditures to the Internal Revenue Service (IRS) were allowed to file a copy of their IRS Form 990 with the secretary of the Senate and the clerk of the House instead of making a separate estimate for their lobbying registration forms.

Disclosure and Enforcement

Required the secretary of the Senate and the clerk of the House to develop standards and procedures for complying with the registration requirements; to review and verify the information; and to develop a system to make available to the public a list of all registered lobbyists, firms and clients, and the registrations and filings. The secretary and clerk also were instructed to compile and summarize the information every six months "in a clear and complete manner."

If asked, lobbyists who contacted executive and legislative branch officials were required to state whether they were registered under the act, identify their clients, and whether the client was a foreign organization.

The clerk of the House or the secretary of the Senate was required to notify registrants in writing if they failed to comply with the act. If the registrant did not respond within 60 days, the clerk or secretary was to notify the U.S. attorney for the District of Columbia.

Registrants who failed to correct a defective filing within 60 days after being notified, or failed to comply with other provisions of the act, faced a civil fine of up to $5,000.

Constitutional Rights

Stated that the lobbying act would not interfere with "the right to petition the government for the redress of grievances, the right to express a personal opinion, or the right of association protected by the First Amendment to the Constitution."

Foreign Agents

Amended the Foreign Agents Registration Act of 1938 by striking several references to "the dissemination of political propaganda." The act initially was passed to disclose the activities of Nazi supporters.

The bill also eliminated a registration exemption for lobbyists who worked on behalf of a U.S. subsidiary of a foreign-owned company.

Changes in Other Laws

Repealed the 1946 lobbying law and 1989 amendments to housing law concerning lobbying disclosure.

Byrd Amendment

Made the so-called Byrd amendment conform to the language in the new bill. In 1989, Sen. Robert C. Byrd, D-W.Va., pushed through an amendment to the Interior appropriations bill (PL 101-121) preventing recipients of at least $100,000 in federal grants, loans or contracts from using those funds to lobby for those grants, loans or contracts.

Estimated Expenses

Allowed businesses and nonprofit organizations to estimate their lobbying expenses under the same rules they used when filing with the IRS, thus saving the groups from having to keep two sets of books.

The comptroller general was asked to study the differences between the IRS rules and the definition of "lobbying activities" in this act.

Ramspeck Act

Repealed the 1940 law that allowed former congressional or judicial employees to obtain civil service jobs without having to take a competitive examination. The Office of Personnel Management was instructed to develop regulations that took into account the experience of noncivil service employees in considering appointments for competitive jobs, including any legislative or judicial experience, but the new rules could not grant any preferences to former employees of the two other branches of government.

Some Republicans had objected when Democratic congressional staff members who faced the loss of their jobs when the GOP captured the House and Senate as a result of the 1994 elections used the Ramspeck Act to obtain civil service jobs in the executive branch.

This provision was to take effect two years after the bill was enacted.

Nonprofit Restrictions

Prohibited nonprofit social welfare and employee organizations incorporated under section 501(c)(4) of the Internal Revenue Code from receiving any federal grants, awards, contracts or loans if they engaged in lobbying activities.

The provision was aimed at groups, such as the American Association of Retired Persons, which lobbied Congress on Social Security and Medicare, among other issue.

Financial Disclosure

Added new categories to the annual financial disclosure reports filed by senators and certain staff members. Instead of a category of more than $1 million, the forms henceforth were to include the following categories for income: greater than $1 million but not more than $5 million; and greater than $5 million.

The forms were to include the following categories for assets and liabilities: greater than $1 million but not more than $5 million; greater than $5 million but not more than $25 million; greater than $25 million but not more than $50 million; and greater than $50 million.

Trade Representative

Prohibited anyone who had represented or assisted a foreign entity in any trade negotiation from serving as U.S. trade representative or deputy U.S. trade representative.   ❏

Unfunded Mandates

On March 22, 1995, President Clinton signed into law S 1 (PL 104-4), a bill to curb unfunded federal mandates—those requirements that Congress or federal agencies imposed on state and local governments without providing the money to pay for them. The legislation was part of the GOP's "Contract with America," but the final version was not as wide-ranging as the original Republican proposal. Efforts to curb federal mandates had gained broad bipartisan support in Congress in 1994 but failed to win approval in either chamber. *(Contract with America, box, p. 885; earlier action, p. 821)*

S 1 was backed by bipartisan organizations of local and state officials, as well as by Republicans and many conservative Democrats in Congress. Supporters said the legislation was needed because Congress had imposed dozens of new, expensive mandates on state and local governments in recent years, taking money away from local priorities. Liberal legislators, however, worried that the bill was a backdoor attempt to weaken many of the nation's long-standing public health, civil rights and environmental laws.

An informal analysis by the Advisory Commission on Intergovernmental Relations, an independent government agency, predicted that the bill would have its greatest impact on environmental legislation and a minimal impact on many other mandates such as the Americans with Disabilities Act. The analysis concluded that two-thirds of major mandates could be exempt under the new law.

Overall, the law amended Title IV of the Congressional Budget and Impoundment Control Act of 1974 (PL 93-344) by creating a new section on unfunded mandates. It specified that any bill that would impose unfunded mandates of more than $50 million on state and local governments would be subject to a point of order in either chamber. The procedural hurdle could be scaled back and the mandate imposed only if a majority of members voted to override the point of order. *(1974 law, Congress and the Nation Vol. IV, p. 71)*

Authorizing committees in both chambers were required to include information about mandates in their legislative reports. The law required the Congressional Budget Office (CBO) to estimate the costs of all new mandates of $50 million or more a year on state or local governments and requirements of $100 million or more a year on private businesses.

Federal agencies were required to conduct cost-benefit analyses of many new regulations and consult with affected state and local government officials before imposing rules containing mandates. The Advisory Commission on Intergovernmental Relations would report on ways to pare back existing mandates.

The provisions regarding the cost-benefit analysis took effect when the bill was signed into law; other provisions, such as the procedural hurdles to restrict Congress from imposing new mandates, would take effect at the beginning of 1996.

SENATE ACTION

Partisan bickering surfaced early during Senate Governmental Affairs Committee and Senate Budget Committee consideration of S 1, with Democrats denouncing a GOP decision not to issue committee reports detailing the provisions, history and cost of the legislation. The heads of the two committees— William V. Roth Jr., R-Del., and Pete V. Domenici, R-N.M., respectively—responded that, at the request of the GOP leadership, the panels would issue no bill report so as not to delay floor action. Republicans on Governmental Affairs rejected a motion by David Pryor, D-Ark., to issue a report, and the Budget Committee voted to report the bill without a written report. However, Governmental Affairs (S Rept 104-1) and Budget (S Rept 104-2) subsequently reported S 1 on Jan. 9, 1995.

Democrats on Governmental Affairs raised questions about the bill's procedural implications. The committee rejected an amendment by ranking Democrat John Glenn of Ohio to exempt floor amendments from being subject to a point of order under the bill. The panel then rejected three amendments offered by Carl Levin, D-Mich., to allow CBO to declare it impossible to provide an accurate estimate of the costs of a bill; to allow Congress to pass, without any new procedural restriction, bills governing state and local government employment practices; and to make the law expire, or "sunset," in 1998. The Budget Committee rejected three amendments offered by Barbara Boxer, D-Calif., to set a 1998 expiration date; to sunset the legislation in 2000; and to sunset it in 2002.

The Senate passed S 1 by 86–10 on Jan. 27.

In a dramatic effort to reestablish his party as a force to be reckoned with, Robert C. Byrd, D-W.Va., rallied Senate Democrats on Jan. 19 to reject a motion to limit debate on the bill. Byrd complained that the Republicans were trying to railroad the mandates bill through. The 54–44 vote fell six votes short of the 60 needed to invoke cloture. Byrd said the vote transcended the mandates bill and went to the heart of whether the sometimes demoralized Democrats would stand firm against Republican tactics. His display of parliamentary might triggered five successful tabling votes on Jan. 19 to clear the way for debate on amendments. Senate leaders reached a unanimous consent agreement late the same day to limit debate to 62 amendments.

The Senate Jan. 19 adopted, 99–0, a Levin amendment to permit CBO to report that it could not accurately estimate the costs of a piece of legislation, thereby allowing the legislation to be exempt from the additional procedural hurdle. The change met some objections of Democrats who worried that the bill would tie Congress in procedural knots. Levin, Glenn and others warned that CBO could not accurately estimate the costs of each amendment on about 87,000 state and local governments across the country, especially if the bill covered several years.

But senators rejected attempts to assuage another Democratic concern—that the bill would give state and local governments an advantage over private companies. The Senate agreed,

53–44 on Jan. 19, to a Dirk Kempthorne, R-Idaho, motion to table (kill) a Joseph I. Lieberman, D-Conn., amendment to allow points of order only against amendments that applied to the public sector, eliminating them for amendments that would place private businesses at a disadvantage with their public competitors. The Senate also agreed, 73–25 on Jan. 19, to a William S. Cohen, R-Maine, motion to table (kill) a Bumpers amendment to allow state and local governments to tax property sold by out-of-state companies to state residents.

A Levin amendment to exempt from the bill's reach legislation regarding age discrimination was adopted 96–0 on Jan. 19. The bill also exempted laws that governed civil rights, matters of national defense, international treaties, emergency assistance and compliance with federal accounting procedures. Senators agreed 55–42 on Jan. 19 to a Kempthorne motion to table (kill) a Paul Wellstone, D-Minn., amendment to require committee reports to examine the effects of the unfunded mandates bill on hungry and homeless children. Republicans also succeeded in killing a number of Democratic amendments to provide exceptions for federal mandates dealing with additional health and welfare issues.

The Senate adopted, 99–0 on Jan. 25, a Charles E. Grassley, R-Iowa, nonbinding resolution calling for federal agencies to evaluate the costs, using CBO estimates, of planned regulations as they were being drafted. A Kempthorne resolution expressing the sense of the Senate that implementing legislation to balance the budget should not cut Social Security was adopted 83–16 on Jan. 26.

Byrd won approval, 100–0 on Jan. 26, for a "clarifying" amendment to require that federal agencies report back to authorizing committees when appropriators provided insufficient money to comply with a mandate. Congress would then have to act under expedited procedures either to pare back the mandate or produce more revenue to pay for it—potentially giving appropriators a role in rescuing or cutting underfunded programs. If Congress did not act within 60 days, the mandate would be eliminated. The Senate Jan. 26 adopted 93–6 a Bob Graham, D-Fla., amendment to provide a budget point of order against a bill, resolution, or amendment that would reduce or eliminate funding for programs that were the constitutional responsibility of the federal government.

HOUSE ACTION

Partisan haggling dictated House Government Reform and Oversight Committee consideration of the House version of the unfunded mandates legislation (HR 5). Before Committee Chairman William F. Clinger, R-Pa., could introduce the bill, Democrats denounced his effort to "steamroll" the measure by not holding a hearing first. Republicans defeated three Democratic proposals for committee rules changes, including a proposal by Cardiss Collins, D-Ill., to require the panel to hold at least one hearing before a markup.

Democrats strongly criticized Clinger's decision to allow bill sponsor Rob Portman, R-Ohio, who was not a member of the committee, to make a statement during markup. They said that having a member testify before the committee amounted to a hearing and that they should be allowed to call their own witnesses.

Democrats offered eight amendments to provide exceptions in the legislation for certain health and safety laws, which were defeated. Also defeated was a Henry A. Waxman, D-Calif., amendment to exempt the provisions of the bill from review by the courts. The panel adopted an amendment by Paul E. Kanjorski, D-Pa., to exempt the Social Security system from the provisions of the bill.

The House Rules Committee, which shared jurisdiction over HR 5, rejected an amendment by ranking Democrat Joe Moakley of Massachusetts to make the bill effective upon enactment, instead of on Oct. 1, 1995. The amendment would have made legislation enacted as part of the GOP Contract with America subject to the unfunded mandates law. The committee adopted a David Dreier, R-Calif., amendment to set up an elaborate procedure for deciding what would be defined as an unfunded mandate.

HR 5 was reported from House Rules (H Rept 104-1, Part I) and House Government Reform (H Rept 104-1, Part II) on Jan. 13, 1995.

House floor action on HR 5 proceeded under an open rule—H Res 38, adopted 350–71 on Jan. 19—that allowed virtually unlimited amendments. The rule set the stage for gridlock, but Republicans, who had fought closed rules when they were in the minority, were loath to use one with the mandates bill. Democrats offered a slew of amendments to exempt a number of laws from the bill, including those protecting the environment, fair labor practices, public health, children and welfare recipients. All were defeated. One of the few Democratic amendments adopted (by voice vote) was a Chaka Fattah, D-Pa., amendment to require the federal government to investigate the role of unfunded state mandates on local governments and the private sector.

Continued accusations of obstructionism by the Republicans and festering resentment of the Democrats that the legislation was brought to the floor with minimal committee consideration culminated on Jan. 24 in hissing and booing on the floor by both sides. Speaker Newt Gingrich, R-Ga., responded by pulling the bill in favor of another GOP priority, the balanced budget resolution.

The House returned to HR 5 on Jan. 27. More Democratic amendments were offered and defeated. The few Democratic amendments to pass included one by Collin C. Peterson, D-Minn., to require CBO to estimate the cost of any legislation that would impose an unfunded mandate of $50 million or more on private business; one by James P. Moran, D-Va., to direct federal agencies to adopt the most cost-effective regulations that were reasonable to carry out a mandate; and one by Jimmy Hayes, D-La., amendment to require federal agencies to prepare cost-benefit analyses of regulations that might cause the loss of 10,000 or more jobs.

Republican amendments passed included one by Deborah Pryce, R-Ohio, to require the White House Office of Management and Budget to report to Congress annually on agency compliance with the bill; one by Wayne Allard, R-Colo., to require a federal agency to cite a specific statute before imposing an unfunded mandate; and one by Portman to require congressional committees to analyze the degree to which federal mandates could affect competition between the private and public sectors.

After eight days of sometimes rancorous debate, the House passed HR 5 on Feb. 1 by a 360–74 vote, then passed S 1 with the text of HR 5 by voice vote.

FINAL ACTION

Despite the similarities between the Senate- and House-passed versions of the legislation, conferees had to resolve three key differences: the threshold for reviewing private sector mandates, procedures for handling underfunded mandates and whether to allow judicial review.

Conferees agreed to require CBO to estimate the cost of any legislation that would impose an unfunded mandate of $100 million or more on private business. The House bill had a $50 million threshold; the Senate measure, $200 million.

The House accepted the Byrd amendment requiring Congress to use expedited procedures if it was notified during a fiscal year that a mandate was underfunded. The provision provoked debate over such issues as how the expedited procedures would be implemented, whether Congress would have to cut short a recess to vote on a mandate and whether congressional report language would be needed routinely to instruct agencies about how to handle potential underfunding. The provision was of particular concern in the House, where expedited procedures were traditionally handled by the Rules Committee, instead of by the authorizers designated by the amendment. Byrd characterized his effort as a balance-of power issue, enabling Congress, and not the executive branch, to make the final determination regarding underfunded mandates.

The biggest sticking point among the conferees was a House provision exposing federal agencies to lawsuits if they approved new regulations imposing unfunded mandates without doing cost-benefit analyses or considering input from state and local officials, as required by the bill. The Senate version barred such challenges. House conferees insisted that judicial review was needed to ensure that federal agencies complied with the law. A concern was raised, however, that unlimited judicial review would allow private companies to delay the enactment of federal regulations for years. Conferees agreed to allow courts to consider only whether agencies conducted a cost-benefit analysis, not whether the analysis was done well. The compromise clarified that agencies would not have to do such analyses under certain emergency situations. It also waived the requirement if the law on which the new regulation was based specifically stated that a cost-benefit analysis was unnecessary.

The Senate adopted the conference report on S 1 (H Rept 104-76) on March 15 by 91–9. The House followed suit, 394–28 the next day, completing congressional action.

MAJOR PROVISIONS

As cleared, S 1:

• Required any authorizing committee that approved a bill or joint resolution containing a federal mandate to draw attention to the mandate in its report. The report had to describe the direct costs of the mandate on state, local and tribal governments, as well as on private companies, and explain whether the committee created a new mechanism to fund the mandate or whether other, existing sources of federal funding were identified that would help pay for the mandate.

If the committee intended for an intergovernmental mandate to be partly or entirely unfunded, it had to explain why any of the costs should be borne at the state or local level.

The authorizing committee was required to submit the bill to the Congressional Budget Office (CBO) for an estimate of a mandate's costs.

• Required CBO to estimate the impact of any mandate on state, local or tribal governments that would cost $50 million or more in the fiscal year that it took effect, or in any of the subsequent four fiscal years. If the cost of the mandate was estimated to fall short of the $50 million threshold, CBO had to explain why the mandate would be so inexpensive.

• Required CBO to estimate the impact of any mandate that would cost private companies $100 million or more in the fiscal year that it took effect, or in any of the subsequent four fiscal years. An estimate of any increased authorizations in the bill that would help pay for the mandate was to be included as well as an explanation if the mandate was estimated to cost less than $100 million.

• Allowed any chairman or ranking member to request that CBO look at the effect of a mandate on the productivity, economic growth, full employment and international competitiveness of private businesses. CBO could also be asked to compare its cost estimates with those of the federal agency overseeing the mandate.

• Required federal agencies to determine whether sufficient funds were available to carry out mandates under their jurisdiction. If the funds were insufficient, the appropriate congressional authorizing committees were to be notified within 30 days of the beginning of the fiscal year.

The agency could then submit a reestimate, based on consultations with state, local and tribal governments or submit recommendations for implementing a less costly mandate or making the mandate ineffective for the fiscal year.

Congress would have 30 days to consider the recommendations under expedited procedures. If Congress took no action within 60 days, the mandate would be abolished.

• Required federal agencies, before issuing rules that would impose an intergovernmental mandate on private businesses costing more than $100 million yearly, to prepare a cost-benefit analysis of the mandate. The analysis had to consider both quantitative and qualitative factors, including the mandate's effect on health, safety and the natural environment and the amount of federal money available to help implement the mandate. ❑

Paperwork Reduction

Congress in 1995 cleared legislation (S 244) designed to reduce the burden of federal paperwork on individuals, educational institutions, and state and local governments. The bill was expected to cut the cost to government of collecting, maintaining and disseminating the information from the required paperwork.

S 244 set a governmentwide paperwork reduction goal of 10 percent in each of the first two years of the law and 5 percent from fiscal 1998 through fiscal 2001. It provided a six-year reauthorization for the office responsible for implementing the law—the Office of Information and Regulatory Affairs (OIRA) at the White House's Office of Management and Budget (OMB).

The bill also specified that all paperwork requirements, including those for a third party, were subject to OIRA review. It thus overturned a 1990 Supreme Court decision that had been hailed by unions and consumer groups but denounced by business organizations. The Court, in *Dole v. United Steelworkers of America,* said the existing paperwork law allowed OIRA to review internal government requests for data intended for government use but did not extend to regulations intended to force businesses to generate information for a third party, such as the public or their employees. *(1990 decision, Congress and the Nation Vol. VIII, pp. 832, 868)*

Trimming federal paperwork requirements was a goal of both the administration's "reinventing government" initiative and the House Republican's Contract with America. *('Reinventing government,' p. 811; Contract with America, box, p. 885)*

BACKGROUND

S 244 was the culmination of a six-year effort to strengthen the Paperwork Reduction Act of 1980 (PL 96-511). The law had been reauthorized in 1986 but had been allowed to lapse in 1989. The 1980 act established OIRA to review requests by federal agencies for information to determine whether the information was necessary, could be found elsewhere, and was being collected efficiently. *(1980 law, Congress and the Nation Vol. V, p. 849; 1986 action, Congress and the Nation Vol. VII, p. 849)*

During the Reagan and Bush administrations, OIRA used this authority to gain increasing control over both the form and content of federal regulations. Critics charged that OIRA was abusing the law to delay and alter proposed rules that the White House opposed.

One reason for the ease of passage in 1995 was the overall political climate that made reducing government regulations a popular cause. Also, both the House and Senate versions of the bill were virtually identical to a measure (S 560) that the Senate had passed in 1994. *(1994 action, p. 821)*

HOUSE ACTION

The House Government Reform and Oversight Committee reported its version of the paperwork bill (HR 830—H Rept 104-37) on Feb. 15, 1995. As introduced, HR 830 would reduce information collection by 5 percent a year and permanently reauthorize OIRA. The committee adopted a Jon D. Fox, R-Pa., amendment to double the annual goal for paperwork reduction to 10 percent. The committee dropped controversial language to limit federal government control of public information, particularly if it was trying to compete with private businesses that added "value" to public information. The committee rejected a Cardiss Collins, D-Ill., amendment to delete the provision that made all paperwork requirements—including those of a third party—subject to OIRA review and a Carolyn B. Maloney, D-N.Y., amendment to require the legislation to expire after five years.

The House passed HR 830 by 418–0 on Feb. 22. The House adopted by voice vote amendments to make it a priority for OIRA to reduce the paperwork burden for companies of 50 employees or fewer, give private citizens the right to challenge in court paperwork regulations that had not been cleared by OMB, and require recordkeeping rules to indicate how long the information had to be held. Members rejected amendments by Collins, 170–254 on Feb. 22, to delete the provision overturning the ruling on OIRA's regulatory oversight authority and by Maloney, 156–265, to limit OIRA's reauthorization to five years.

SENATE ACTION

The Senate Governmental Affairs Committee reported its version of the legislation (S 244—S Rept 104-8) on Feb. 14, 1995. The committee-approved bill set a governmentwide paperwork reduction goal of 5 percent a year and made it easier for private individuals to request a review of a federal rule that required paperwork. The measure overturned the 1990 Supreme Court decision by including third-party disclosures in the definition of "collection of information," subjecting such disclosures to OMB's paperwork review. The bill provided a five-year, $8 million per year reauthorization of OIRA.

The Senate passed S 244 by 99–0 on March 7. The Senate adopted by voice vote a John McCain, R-Ariz., amendment to end after five years most of the annual or semiannual reports that Congress required of federal agencies. Exceptions would be made for reports triggered by events, such as an assessment on weapons sales or implementation of the War Powers Act. The Senate also adopted by voice vote an amendment to eliminate more than 200 reporting requirements that congressional committees imposed on federal agencies. An amendment by Paul Wellstone, D-Minn., stating the sense of Congress that it should not enact any legislation that would increase the number of hungry or homeless children, was tabled (killed) 51–47 on March 7.

Before the legislation got to the floor, the Senate disposed of one potential roadblock when Paul Coverdell, R-Ga., agreed to a weakened version of an amendment that would have made it voluntary for businesses to provide quarterly financial reports to the Census Bureau. Under existing law, the reports were mandatory for approximately 9,600 companies chosen each year. The information was used to calculate the gross domestic product (GDP) and other key economic indicators that tracked the nation's financial well-being. The Commerce Department, in a Feb. 13 memorandum to the Governmental Affairs Committee, stressed the importance of mandatory compliance in completing the quarterly financial reports. Coverdell agreed to language calling for a demonstration program, to expire Sept. 30, 1998, within the Census Bureau to reduce the paperwork burden associated with the quarterly reports. The Senate adopted the amendment by voice vote.

FINAL ACTION

The House passed an amended S 244 by voice vote March 10, 1995.

Conferees dropped Senate language targeting reports and reporting requirements that Congress asked of federal agencies. House conferees said they did not have sufficient time to review the list of reports that would be eliminated.

The Senate adopted the conference report on S 244 (H Rept 104-99) by voice vote April 6. The House concurred the same day, 423–0. President Clinton signed the bill (PL 104-13) on May 22.

MAJOR PROVISIONS

As cleared, S 244:

• **Office of Information and Regulatory Affairs.** Reauthorized the Office of Information and Regulatory Affairs (OIRA) in the White House's Office of Management and Budget (OMB).

• **Assignment of Tasks and Deadlines.** Required the OMB director to set a governmentwide paperwork reduction goal of at least 10 percent a year in fiscal 1996 and fiscal 1997, and 5 percent a year from fiscal 1998 to fiscal 2001. OIRA was to work with each government department and independent regulatory agency to reduce paperwork. In addition, OIRA was to work with certain agencies on pilot projects aimed at easing the federal requirements.

• **Federal Agencies.** Made the head of each department responsible for complying with the paperwork reduction goal. A department head could appoint a senior official to implement the policy; the defense secretary or secretary of a military service also could designate an individual to handle the task. Those individuals were required to establish an independent process in the department or agency to determine whether proposed paperwork requirements should be adopted. The purpose of the review was to evaluate the need for the information, describe the way the material would be collected, and provide an estimate of the time and financial resources an individual, small business, state or local government, or educational institution would have to expand to fulfill the requirement.

• **Public Information Collection Activities.** Barred an agency from imposing paperwork requirements unless it had conducted a review, published a notice in the *Federal Register,* evaluated the public comments it received, and submitted information to the director of OMB.

• **Review of Information Requests.** Required the OMB director to decide whether the paperwork requirements of a department or agency were necessary. Before making a decision, the director was authorized to give the department an opportunity to make its case, either at a hearing or in writing. If the director determined that the requirements were unnecessary, the agency would be barred from instituting the paperwork requests.

• **Central Collection Agency.** Permitted the director of OMB to designate a central collection agency to get information for two or more departments.

• **Agency Cooperation.** Allowed the OMB director to order a department to make information obtained by paperwork requirements available to another department. All laws relating to unlawful disclosure of information applied to the employees of the department receiving the information, as well as the workers at the department that initially received the information.

• **Tracking Information.** Directed the OMB director to create a department-based electronic Government Information Locator Service. Consistent with the bill's goal of helping departments and the public find and share information, the service was to maintain data on what information each department possessed. This did not apply to the files of the Central Intelligence Agency.

• **Public Protections.** Shielded an individual from penalties for failing to comply if a paperwork requirement did not carry a valid control number assigned by the OMB director or if the department failed to inform the individual about the valid control number.

• **Reporting Requirements.** Directed the OMB director to inform Congress of governmentwide efforts to reduce the paperwork burden and submit annual reports to the president of the Senate and the House Speaker. The reports were to include a description of the steps taken by departments to lessen the paperwork burden, as well as to list violators, additional paperwork requirements, departments that failed to reduce the paperwork burden, and any improvements in the quality of statistical information, public access to data, and overall performance of government programs. Information for the reports was to come from department reports and was not supposed to increase the paperwork burden on those outside the federal government.

• **Consultations.** Allowed any individual to ask the OMB director to review the paperwork requirements imposed by a federal department to determine if the request was valid. If the director determined that the inquiry was legitimate and not frivolous, the director was required to notify the individual within 60 days, unless the director notified the individual of an extension. The director also could take action to change the requirement.

• **Authorization.** Authorized appropriations of $8 million for each of the fiscal years from 1996 to 2001 for OIRA.

• **Census Bureau Financial Reporting Program.** Barred the commerce secretary from selecting a business to participate in its survey of quarterly financial reports for the Census Bureau if the company had assets of less than $50 million, took part in a prior survey in the preceding 10 years and was chosen for the survey after Sept. 30, 1990. The prohibition also applied to companies with assets of more than $50 million and less than $100 million that took part in the survey in the preceding two years and that were selected after Sept. 30, 1995. The bill required the establishment of a toll-free hotline to help companies that were participating in the survey.

• **Effective Date.** Made the provisions effective Oct. 1, 1995.◻

Regulatory Overhaul

Republicans were able to realize little of their broad deregulatory agenda in the 104th Congress. The most sweeping proposals were sidelined. And, with the exception of key provisions of a measure (S 942) strengthening the ability of small businesses to challenge federal regulations in court that were included in must-past legislation (HR 3136—PL 104-121) raising the federal debt limit, efforts to enact narrower deregulation bills failed. *(Debt limit, p. 76)*

BACKGROUND

Republicans took over the House in 1995 eager to carry out promises made in the Contract with America to sharply reign in federal safety, health and environmental regulations and dramatically increase protection for property owners. To that end, HR 9 was introduced, which called for federal agencies to conduct highly detailed assessments of the risks that new regulations ought to address and laid out a specific process for analyzing the costs and benefits of such rules. It also proposed to boost private property rights by greatly expanding the traditional scope of the Fifth Amendment, which required "just compensation" to landowners for government "takings" of private property. In addition, it called for agencies to reduce the paperwork burdens they placed on businesses and individuals.

The House package subsequently was split into four pieces—risk assessment (HR 1022), cost-benefit analysis (HR 926), property rights (HR 925) and paperwork reduction (HR 830)—to expedite the legislative process. Each was passed separately, then reassembled into a new version of HR 9. The House passed HR 9 (H Rept 104-33, Parts I and II) by a **key vote of 277–141 (R 219–8; D 58–132; I 0–1)** on March 3, 1995. However, the legislation stalled in the Senate. *(1995 key votes, p. 1025)*

The exception was the paperwork reduction bill (S 244—PL 104-13), which cleared in 1995. *(Paperwork reduction, p. 840)*

Other failed attempts to restrict regulations included bills regarding local government waivers (HR 2086, S 88), retroactive review (HR 994) and federal rulemaking powers (S 343, S 291, S 333). Legislation (HR 450, S 219) providing for a moratorium on implementing new regulations while Congress worked on the broad overhaul measure also stalled. *(Regulatory moratorium, p. 847)*

FLEXIBILITY FOR SMALL BUSINESSES

The Senate Small Business Committee reported S 942 (no written report) on March 6, 1996. The centerpiece of the bill, sponsored by Christopher S. Bond, R-Mo., was a proposal to allow small businesses to take federal agencies to court if they did not comply with the relevant provisions of the 1980 Regulatory Flexibility Act (PL 96-354). Under that act, agencies were required to minimize the impact of any proposed rule on small businesses if a substantial number of them would be affected. However, it did not allow small businesses to challenge agency actions under the act in court. *(1980 law, Congress and the Nation Vol. V, p. 850)*

The committee-approved S 942 also included the following provisions:

• Required federal agencies to simplify forms and publish a "plain English" guide to help small businesses comply with federal regulations.

• Directed federal agencies to waive fines for first-time violations by small businesses if the violations were corrected within a certain period.

• Created an ombudsman within the Small Business Administration to solicit information from businesses about enforcement practices.

The Senate passed S 942 by 100–0 on March 19, after adopting by voice vote a Don Nickles, R-Okla., and Harry Reid, R-Nev., amendment to allow Congress to review all proposed rules to determine whether they should take effect. Under the amendment, Congress could postpone for 45 days the implementation of any rule considered "major," usually defined as having an economic impact of more than $100 million, while lawmakers reviewed whether to approve the rule.

The Clinton administration voiced muted praise for the Senate-passed bill but indicated that it had concerns about language to allow small businesses to recoup attorneys' fees in some lawsuits.

The House was prepared for floor consideration of a revised version of HR 994, fashioned by Judiciary Committee Chairman Henry J. Hyde, R-Ill., to allow small businesses to go to court to enforce the 1980 regulatory act. The proposals had already passed the House in 1995 in HR 926. Hyde's bill also directed agencies to conduct an "administrative review" of their rules and determine whether to continue, modify, consolidate or terminate them. No required sunsetting of relations was specified, as in HR 926. However, GOP leaders pulled HR 994 from the schedule at the last minute because of internal divisions over the language providing retroactive review of existing regulations.

The Clinton administration and many Democrats took aim at the agency review provisions, arguing that they would tie up federal agencies and undermine environmental protection and enforcement of health and safety rules. House Republicans were divided: Many were skittish about being tagged as enemies of environmental protection, while many conservatives wanted to make HR 994 more stringent.

Republicans subsequently agreed to add key provisions of S 942 to HR 3136, raising the debt limit. As cleared, HR 3136:

• Permitted business owners to recover attorneys' fees and related costs in civil and administrative actions between businesses and federal agencies.

• Allowed small businesses to file lawsuits to compel federal agencies to comply with the Regulatory Flexibility Act.

• Required the Environmental Protection Agency and the Occupational Safety and Health Administration, as part of their rulemaking processes, to collect advice and recommendations from small businesses to improve their analyses of the impact of proposed regulations.

• Required the appointment of a Small Business and Agriculture Regulatory Enforcement Ombudsman to work with each agency with regulatory authority to ensure that small businesses had a way to comment on regulatory enforcement.

PROPERTY RIGHTS

In 1995, the House passed property rights legislation (HR 925) and a Senate committee reported a companion bill (S 605),

but both measures died upon adjournment of the 104th Congress.

The House Judiciary Committee reported HR 925 (H Rept 104-46) on Feb. 23, 1995. Sponsored by Charles T. Canady, R-Fla., the bill called for compensation when federal action reduced the fair market value of a property by at least 10 percent or when the federal government occupied the property. Exceptions were provided for federal actions to prevent an identifiable hazard to public health or safety and to prevent imminent damage to other property. Owners who were denied a particular use of their property could not seek compensation if that use was prohibited or considered a nuisance under state law, independent of any federal action. Owners would have 180 days to seek compensation after receiving notice of an agency's action. Agencies would be allowed to negotiate with owners to establish the amount of compensation, but owners could demand binding arbitration or file suit if no agreement was reached within 180 days. HR 925 also provided that agencies pay compensation out of their annual appropriations. Landowners receiving compensation would have to refund the money if they violated the limits that the agency placed on the property.

The most significant change adopted by the committee was a proposal by Lamar Smith, R-Texas, to require compensation in more cases. While Canady's original language would have required compensation whenever a federal action reduced property values by one-third or more, Smith's amendment lowered the threshold to a 10 percent reduction in value. The committee rejected eight Democratic attempts to limit the bill's reach, including proposals to reduce the compensation paid for federally subsidized farmland; bar compensation to owners who acquired property that they knew or should have known would be limited by an agency action; reduce the compensation for lost uses that had imposed costs on other parties; bar compensation for actions stemming from previously enacted laws; and bar compensation for actions reasonably related to federal laws that were constitutional.

Before passing HR 925 by 277–148 on March 3, the House acted on several amendments to the bill. It adopted, 301–129 on March 2, a W. J. "Billy" Tauzin, D-La., amendment to limit the bill's reach to actions taken under the Endangered Species Act, the wetlands provisions of the clean water law and the 1985 farm bill, and certain laws pertaining to water rights in the West. Tauzin's amendment also required that the government offer to buy all of an affected property when an agency action under those laws caused the property to lose 50 percent or more of its value.

The House also adopted, by voice vote on March 3, a Canady amendment to require a 10 percent reduction only in the value of the portion of the property affected by federal action. The original bill would have required a property to lose at least 10 percent of its entire value before compensation would be mandated.

The House March 2 rejected, 210–211, a Porter J. Goss, R-Fla., amendment to raise the threshold in the Canady amendment to 30 percent. However, on March 3, the House adopted a Goss amendment, 338–83, to set the threshold at 20 percent.

The House rejected, 173–252 on March 3, a Norman Y. Mineta, D-Calif., amendment to increase the threshold to 20 percent for the value of the entire property.

The Senate Judiciary Committee reported S 605 (S Rept 104-239) on Dec. 22, 1995. Under S 605, which was sponsored by Dole, the government would be required to compensate an owner if the property value was diminished by 33 percent or more, the property was taken for public use, or the owner was deprived of substantially all of its economic benefit. The burden of proof would be on property owners to establish their loss and on the government to establish that its action substantially advanced the government's purpose. No payment would be required for property that was determined to be a nuisance. S 605 applied to all federal regulations that affected property rights. It required that agencies submit analyses of any potential taking of private property before issuing regulations, with limited exceptions. Rules that required takings without compensation would be prohibited.

Dole was unable to bring S 605 to the floor before he resigned from the Senate in June 1996. The vote count in the Senate was strongly in doubt, and President Clinton had said he would veto the bill. As a result, little chance existed that the measure would have become law, let alone overcome an expected Democratic-led filibuster.

Hatch introduced a revised version (S 1954) in July, but it also never came to the floor. Hatch proposed to narrow the definition of property and increase the threshold for compensation from a 33 percent loss of property value to a 50 percent loss.

RISK ASSESSMENT

The House passed HR 1022, by 286–141 on Feb. 28, 1995, to require risk analysis for any major new rule, defined as any regulation that was likely to result in an annual increase in economic costs of more than $25 million. This cutoff was low enough to cover nearly all federal regulations, given their national scope.

The legislation prescribed a long list of data and variables that a federal agency would have to take into account in performing a risk analysis on a proposed regulation. The agency would have to:

• Present detailed scientific data evaluating the health risk caused by a substance or activity.

• Document research, if available, that showed a low potential risk as well as that which showed a high risk.

• Compare the risk in question with similar risks and those encountered in everyday life, such as car accidents and lightning strikes.

• Prepare an analysis of risks that could be caused by a substance or activity that could be substituted for the item to be regulated.

In a second step, agencies would be required to prove that the benefits of a regulation justified and were reasonably related to its economic costs. They also would have to show that the rule would be the most cost-effective alternative for accomplishing the agency's goal. A separate, cost-benefit analysis bill (HR 926)

fleshed out those requirements for regulations with a projected impact of $50 million or more.

As a third step, "major" health, safety and environmental regulations with an annual economic impact of $100 million or more would be subject to critique by peer review panels. Individuals with a financial interest in a regulation would be allowed to participate on the peer review panel, as long as their interests were disclosed.

Regulations that made it through this process could be challenged further, as HR 1022 provided an expanded right to judicial review for those affected by the rules. Under existing law, interested parties could sue the government on grounds that the final rule was in error. Under the bill, those parties also could sue on grounds that an agency did not follow one or more of the new risk assessment and cost-benefit procedures.

Affected parties also would be able to petition an agency to review a previously adopted regulation, provided the request was based on substantial new information that suggested the regulation should be altered. Exemptions would be reserved for those rules dealing with narrowly defined emergency situations, activities involving military readiness, product labelings required by law, and approval of state programs and plans by federal agencies.

HR 1022 also contained a controversial "supermandate" that could effectively override health- or technology-based standards written into existing health, safety and environmental laws. Any new regulation under those laws would have to undergo the cost-benefit analyses required by the legislation. If those tests identified a less costly alternative to that in the proposed regulations, the least-cost method would prevail, regardless of the requirements of the existing law.

Opponents failed in six attempts to modify the bill on the floor. The House rejected amendments by George E. Brown Jr., D-Calif., 174–246 on Feb. 27, to lay out more generic risk-assessment and cost-benefit requirements; Brown, 157–263 on Feb. 28, to exempt more regulations; Tim Roemer, D-Ind., 192–231 on Feb. 28, to alter the judicial review provisions; Sherwood Boehlert, R-N.Y., 181–238 on Feb. 28, to eliminate the "supermandate" provision; Edward J. Markey, D-Mass., 177–247 on Feb. 28, to bar what he called "Gucci-clad lobbyists" from serving on a peer review panel to examine a major proposed regulation; and Joe L. Barton, R-Texas, 206–220 on Feb. 28, to let parties petition federal agencies to review and revoke existing regulations.

The House Commerce Committee and the House Science Committee had approved the risk-assessment portion of HR 9, which subsequently was introduced as HR 1022.

COST-BENEFIT ANALYSIS

The House by 415–15 on March 1, 1995, passed HR 926, requiring that federal agencies follow an elaborate analysis and reporting process before adopting any major new rule. The bill, sponsored by George W. Gekas, R-Pa., defined a major rule as one likely to have an annual effect on the economy of at least $50 million, cause a major increase in consumer costs, or have a significant adverse effect on competition. The House Judiciary Committee had reported HR 926 (H Rept 104-48) on Feb. 23.

As part of the "impact analysis" mandated by the bill, agencies would have to describe the potential costs and benefits of the proposed rule and explore alternative approaches, including nonregulatory ones. No major rule could be adopted without the written approval of the director of the White House Office of Management and Budget (OMB), although the impact analysis would be waived for certain rulemakings done under a deadline or in emergencies. The process outlined in HR 926 expanded on the risk-assessment requirement in HR 1022.

Under HR 926, small businesses would be able to seek relief from new federal regulations in federal court if an agency decided not to give them special treatment. Under the 1980 Regulatory Flexibility Act, agencies were required to minimize the impact of any proposed rule on small businesses if they found that it would significantly affect a substantial number of them. The bill would allow a small business to sue agencies to enforce the requirements of the 1980 law. The suit would have to be filed within 180 days of a rule being adopted. The bill also included protections for private sector "whistleblowers" who reported wrongdoing by federal regulators.

The House had adopted only a few, minor amendments to HR 926, including those by Thomas W. Ewing, R-Ill., 420–5 on March 1, to give small businesses one year to challenge certain agency decisions in court, instead of six months; Gekas, by voice vote, to exempt regulations dealing with taxes; James A. Traficant Jr., D-Ohio, by voice vote, to exempt regulations imposing sanctions on countries for certain illegal trade activities against the United States; and John Conyers Jr., D-Mich., 406–23 on March 1, to require all contracts with an agency regarding a rulemaking to be recorded and described to the public.

Four Democratic attempts to narrow the bill's scope were defeated. Three, rejected by voice vote, were offered by Melvin Watt of North Carolina to exempt banking regulations, limit appeals by small business and give the U.S. District Court for the District of Columbia exclusive jurisdiction over appeals. The fourth, by Jack Reed of Rhode Island, would define a major rule as one having an economic impact of at least $100 million annually, not $50 million. It was rejected 159–266 on March 1.

The House Small Business Committee on Feb. 23, 1995, reported HR 937 (H Rept 104-49, Part I) to provide greater regulatory flexibility for small businesses. The bill was similar to the small business provisions of HR 926. Sponsored by Small Business Chairman Jan Meyers, R-Kan., HR 937 would amend the 1980 Regulatory Flexibility Act to allow small businesses to bring suit to enforce the law. Federal agencies would be required to work more closely with the chief counsel of the Small Business Administration (SBA) in crafting regulations to minimize the impact on small businesses. Regulations involving the safety and soundness of financial institutions were exempt from the requirement that the SBA's chief counsel do a preliminary review.

FEDERAL RULEMAKING

On the broad issue of limiting federal rulemaking powers, the Senate considered two competing bills—one (S 343) by Majority Leader Bob Dole, R-Kan., that sought to place major restraints on the bureaucracy and a less sweeping measure (S 291) by William V. Roth Jr., R-Del.

The bills had much in common. Each proposed unprecedented steps to force agencies to justify the need for a regulation and to choose the most cost-effective regulatory option. Each required that in many instances federal agencies show that the benefits of proposed regulations justified their costs to society. Both would subject many rules to risk assessment to prove that health, safety or environmental risks were serious enough to justify government action. And both required that federal agencies set a schedule for review of all existing regulations and specified that such reviews be completed within 10 years of the enactment of a regulatory overhaul law.

However, the more moderate S 291 reflected concerns of some Republicans and many Democrats that S 343 would go too far and affect too many regulations. Among the major differences:

• Roth's bill applied only to regulations expected to have a gross annual economic effect of $100 million or more; the Dole bill had a threshold of $50 million.

• S 291 covered 11 federal agencies; S 343 applied to all agencies.

• The cost-benefit and risk assessment requirements of S 291 were not meant to supersede health and environmental technology requirements in existing law; S 343 arguably contained such an overriding "supermandate," as did the House-passed HR 1022.

• The Roth bill provided for courts to review the substance of a rule, as under existing law, but not the agency's rulemaking procedure. The Dole bill would allow lawsuits over procedures as well as substance.

• Under S 343, individuals would be able to petition a federal agency for a cost-benefit analysis that could revoke or force changes in an existing rule. If an agency denied such a petition, under the Dole bill the affected parties could not challenge that decision in court. S 291 did not contain such a provision.

To ensure that Dole's bill did not gain priority over his, Roth took the unusual step of having the Senate Governmental Affairs Committee approve his bill twice. The committee first voted on an amended version of S 291, then stripped out the original text of S 343, replaced it with the text of S 291, and then approved the revised S 343. A Roth substitute amendment to S 291 included two provisions from Dole's bill, giving Congress 45 days after a final regulation was issued to block it by passing a joint resolution disapproving it and allowing citizens to sue agencies for failing to consider the interests of small businesses in developing regulations, as required by the 1980 Regulatory Flexibility Act.

S 343 was less approved than propelled from the Senate Judiciary Committee by its chairman, Orrin G. Hatch, R-Utah. Infuriated at what he saw as Democrats' breach of an agreement to finish the markup, Hatch used his prerogative as chairman to cut off debate and order the bill reported. The committee had rejected two amendments, by Joseph R. Biden Jr., D-Del., to eliminate the provision allowing petitions for the repeal or modification of existing regulations and by Edward M.

Kennedy, D-Mass., to exempt the Occupational Safety and Health Administration from certain requirements of the bill.

The Senate Governmental Affairs Committee on May 25, 1995, reported S 291 (S Rept 104-88). S 343 was jointly reported (S Rept 104-89) from Senate Governmental Affairs and Senate Judiciary on May 26, 1995.

When the regulatory overhaul legislation reached the Senate floor in late June, Dole had united most Republicans behind a revised version of S 343. He had struck a deal stipulating that existing statutory requirements would not be superseded by the bill; affected parties would have to challenge the substance of final rule, not just the rulemaking procedures; and Congress would have 60 days to block new rules, not 45. The compromise also won the support of Roth.

On the floor, opponents succeeded in scaling back the bill significantly. The Senate adopted, 53–45 on July 11, a J. Bennett Johnston, D-La., amendment to waive the bill's requirements for agency actions with less than $100 million in annual economic impact, up from $50 million. The doubling of the threshold sharply reduced the number of regulations that would have to clear the procedural hurdles required by the bill.

Three more Johnston amendments—to provide a blanket exemption for regulations, including meat inspection rules, that were proposed before April 1, 1995; to exempt waste cleanups and other environmental management activities; and to allow agencies up to a year to complete the bill's risk assessment and cost-benefit analysis requirements for those health and safety regulations that were put into effect on an emergency basis, as opposed to the 180-day deadline in the bill— were adopted easily.

In response to Democratic claims that major health and safety regulations would be delayed or deterred by the legislation, Dole offered an amendment to specify that rules to address food-safety threats were included in the bill's exemption for emergency regulations. The Senate adopted it 99–0 on July 11.

The Senate also adopted by voice votes amendments to require federal agencies and OMB to keep public records of agency regulations under review by OMB and of any communication by agency or OMB officials concerning those regulations; to exempt regulations protecting children from poisoning from the risk assessment and cost-benefit analysis requirements of the bill; to extend expiration dates on permits for grazing on National Forest System lands; and to amend the Federal Food, Drug, and Cosmetic Act to require the issuance of regulations concerning contaminants in bottled drinking water.

Several attempts to narrow the scope of the bill were rejected. These include amendments to exempt regulations dealing with contamination of drinking water supplies by cryptosporidium and other water-borne microbes; to exempt occupational and mine safety and health regulations; and to eliminate provisions that would make it harder to include substances on the Toxic Release Inventory, a list of chemicals whose release into the environment had to be publicly reported by businesses.

Some amendments put further restrictions on federal regulatory powers. The Senate adopted, 60–36, a Sam Nunn, D-Ga.,

amendment to require federal agencies to meet the bill's procedural requirements, even for regulations that fell below the dollar threshold, if those rules would have a significant economic impact on a substantial number of small businesses. An amendment by Spencer Abraham, R-Mich., to require federal agencies to review existing regulations at the request of the SBA to determine if those regulations imposed undue burdens on small businesses was adopted, 96–0 on July 10.

By voice votes, the Senate also adopted amendments to strengthen the bill's requirements that 11 federal department and agencies scientifically compare the risks that they sought to regulate, draw up priority lists based on their comparative risk analyses, and apply those priorities to their annual budget decisions; to strengthen provisions of the 1980 Equal Access to Justice Act that permitted individuals and small businesses to recover costs for successful legal actions against federal agencies; and to bar penalties for violations after an agency reinterpreted a regulation, if the regulated entity had made a good-faith effort to comply with earlier interpretations.

The bill's supporters tried to curb debate for the first time on July 17 but fell short of the required 60 votes. The vote was 48–46. Glenn, John H. Chafee, R-R.I., and Carl Levin, D-Mich., on July 18 offered a substitute amendment with more moderate provisions. The substitute would require cost-benefit analysis and risk assessments for many new regulations, but it would give agency officials much greater latitude in carrying out the cost-benefit tests, limit judicial review of agency procedures, and not allow individuals to petition agencies for regulatory review. The substitute was rejected 48–52. The Senate July 18 then rejected a second motion to limit debate, 53–47. As the debate neared its conclusion, Dole was caught between Democrats and moderate Republicans who favored a limited regulatory overhaul and GOP conservatives who wanted a far-reaching bill. Managers of S 343 informed Chafee that they would accede on several issues that had drawn fire from Republican moderates. Chafee announced the deal on the floor, to the surprise of uninformed Democrats. The agreement won the support of the Republicans who had voted against one or both of the motions to invoke cloture, but it did not bring enough Democrats into Dole's fold to end the filibuster. The Senate July 20 for the third time failed to curb debate, on a **key vote of 58–40 (R 54–0; D 4–40).** Dole then declared the bill dead. *(1995 key votes, p. 1025)*

In related action, the Senate Energy and Natural Resources Committee May 25, 1995, reported its proposal for regulatory overhaul (S 333—S Rept 104-87). The bill, cosponsored by Committee Chairman Frank H. Murkowski, R-Alaska, and Johnston, covered all major federal rules connected with health, safety or environmental risks. "Major" was defined as having an annual economic impact of at least $75 million.

S 333 required that agencies prepare a risk assessment and cost-benefit analysis for major new rules. The same procedures had to be followed for environmental management activities, such as toxic waste cleanups, that cost $25 million or more. The bill prescribed a set of principles that agencies had to observe when conducting risk assessments, including maximizing public participation and the use of peer review. Before a rule was issued, the head of the agency had to certify that the rule or action was likely to reduce risks significantly, that no less costly alternative was equally effective, and that the rule or action was likely to improve human health or the environment enough to justify its cost. No risk assessment would be required for emergency situations; actions related to the introduction of a product; the issuance of a permit; the registration of pesticides or hazardous chemicals; or actions related to product labels.

Under S 333, agencies had to bring existing risk assessments into conformance with the bill's principles, following instructions issued by the president within 18 months. Agencies had to appoint advisory committees of outside experts to help in their review of risk assessments and accept petitions from the public for review of previous assessments. Like the Roth bill (S 291), S 333 did not provide for individuals to challenge an agency's procedures in court except as part of a suit challenging the substance of a final rule. It did, however, propose that individuals be allowed to sue if their petition for review of an existing risk assessment was denied, contrary to the recommendation of the agency's advisory committee. Also like S 291, the cost-benefit analysis and risk assessment requirements of S 333 would not supersede health and environmental technology requirements in existing law.

RETROACTIVE REVIEW

The House Government Reform and Oversight Committee on Oct. 19, 1995, reported HR 994 (H Rept 104-284, Part I), requiring a review of existing federal regulations. The House Judiciary Committee reported the measure (H Rept 104-284, Part II) on Nov. 7, 1995. The bill saw no further legislative action. Similar provisions were included in a regulatory relief bill (S 343).

HR 994, which was sponsored by Jim Chapman, D-Texas, and John L. Mica, R-Fla., provided that federal agencies review significant existing regulations in four to seven years. If a regulation was determined to be obsolete, unnecessary, duplicative, excessively costly or in conflict with an underlying statute, it would have to be modified, consolidated or terminated. Regulations not reviewed within the seven-year deadline would automatically be terminated. Regulations determined by agencies to be the most burdensome to businesses or individuals would be reviewed first. Businesses and individuals could petition the agencies to review nonsignificant regulations that had an adverse impact on them. Among the regulations that would have to be reviewed were those with an annual economic impact of $100 million or more. New regulations would have to be reviewed within three years of their issuance.

The Government Reform Committee adopted amendments by Paul E. Kanjorski, D-Pa., to terminate the bill's provisions in 10 years, and Louise M. Slaughter, D-N.Y., to raise the threshold from $50 million to $100 million. The Judiciary Committee adopted a Conyers amendment to require agencies to keep a written record of all contact with private citizens during the review—a move aimed at curtailing the influence of lobbyists and others over the process. The committee rejected a Zoe Lofgren,

D-Calif., amendment to exempt regulations that, if allowed to expire, could result in death or serious injury.

LOCAL GOVERNMENT WAIVERS

Bills (HR 2086, S 88) to give eligible local governments and private nonprofit groups more flexibility to spend federal money were reported from committee but went no further.

Under the legislation, dubbed the Local Empowerment and Flexibility Act, local governments and nonprofit groups would be allowed to consolidate disparate federal grants into more flexible spending plans. The recipients, who administered housing, economic development and social service programs, also could seek waivers from the federal Community Empowerment Board from regulations that would hinder implementation of their plans. The board, impaneled under the 1993 budget reconciliation law (PL 103-66), could approve plans and waivers that did not "diminish civil rights, labor, environmental or financial services standards" or "threaten public health and safety." The 19-member board consisted of cabinet members and other administration officials. *(Reconciliation, p. 44)*

Supporters said the legislation would reduce red tape and permit state and local governments to tailor programs to meet their needs. Opponents, including labor unions, argued that it would allow local agencies to subvert labor, environmental, and safety laws under the pretext of increased efficiency. The Clinton administration came out against the legislation, saying it would not safeguard critical laws and regulations.

The House Government Reform and Oversight Committee reported HR 2086 (H Rept 104-847) on Sept. 26, 1996. The bill, sponsored by Christopher Shays, R-Conn., would allow local governments and organizations to pool two or more of the 271 federal grants they might receive into one package and draft a "flexibility plan" to govern how the pooled funds could be spent. Edolphus Towns, D-N.Y., offered an amendment to prohibit the waiver of any federal law, though waivers of regulations would still be allowed. Constance A. Morella, R-Md., further amended the Towns proposal to allow waivers of laws that dealt with procedural or administrative changes. The committee adopted Morella's amendment, then adopted Towns's proposal as amended. The committee also adopted a Bernard Sanders, I-Vt., amendment to require legislative or regulatory waivers to be posted in local newspapers and subjected to public hearings.

The Senate Governmental Affairs Committee reported S 88 (S Rept 104-331) on July 23, 1996. The committee tabled (killed) two amendments by Carl Levin, D-Mich., to prohibit waivers of certain federal requirements relating to health, public safety and the environment and to prevent the commingling of federal funds. ❑

Regulatory Moratorium

House Republicans in 1995 unsuccessfully pushed for a moratorium on implementing most new federal regulations while Congress worked on a broad overhaul of the regulatory process. *(Regulatory overhaul, p. 842)*

HOUSE ACTION

HR 450, sponsored by Majority Whip Tom DeLay, R-Texas, was reported from the House Government Reform and Oversight Committee on Feb. 16, 1995 (H Rept 104-39, Part I). The committee rejected a Louise M. Slaughter, D-N.Y., and Cardiss Collins, D-Ill., amendment to exempt from the moratorium Food and Drug Administration rules aimed at strengthening meat and poultry inspections. The committee also rejected six more Democratic amendments, including a proposal to exempt rules related to drinking water and mines. The committee did agree to end the moratorium no later than Dec. 31, 1995.

The House passed HR 450 on Feb. 24 by 276–146. The bill provided for a moratorium freeze through the end of 1995 on most regulations issued after Nov. 20, 1994. The moratorium was to end earlier if Congress enacted laws requiring regulations to undergo a cost-benefit analysis and risk assessment. The president could lift the moratorium for certain actions, including ones related to "imminent threats" to health or safety, law enforcement, regulatory relief, national security and trade agreements.

President Clinton issued an implied threat to veto HR 450 and related bills, accusing supporters of a backdoor effort to undo health, safety and environmental regulations that they had long opposed. DeLay responded by charging Clinton with engaging in scare tactics.

The House defeated, 177–249, a proposal by Slaughter to exempt regulations dealing with meat and poultry inspections, the cryptosporidium parasite in public water supply, and importation of food in lead cans. Cryptosporidium was blamed for the deaths of more than 100 people in Milwaukee in 1993.

The House also rejected, 181–242, a Collins amendment to exempt such "common sense" regulations as those regarding the personal use of campaign funds, processing of immigrant asylum requests, improvements to Department of Housing and Urban Development programs, compensation to Persian Gulf War veterans, the development of a database that identified child molesters, and the rules governing hunting season for migratory birds.

The House, however, adopted amendments to exempt rules related to hunting and other recreational or subsistence activities; to exempt several specific regulations to benefit U.S. industry, including rules related to international trade agreements, textile imports, customs modernization, auctions and licenses of radio frequencies and trade sanctions against China; to extend the moratorium until Dec. 31, 1996, for new listings and designations under the Endangered Species Act; and to extend the moratorium until June 30, 1996, for any regulation affecting a business with 100 or fewer employees.

SENATE ACTION

The Senate Governmental Affairs Committee reported its version (S 219—S Rept 104-15) on March 16, 1995.

Under the original bill, federal agencies would be barred from proposing or issuing most regulations until Jan. 1, 1996, or whenever a comprehensive regulatory overhaul bill was enacted.

S 219 included retroactive provisions to prohibit agencies from carrying out most regulations proposed or issued since Nov. 9, 1994, the day after the elections that gave Republicans control of Congress. An exemption was provided for regulations dealing with imminent threats to human health or safety or other emergencies.

The committee narrowed the bill to address Democratic criticisms. Substitute language was proposed by Chairman William V. Roth Jr., R-Del., and drafted by the bill's author, Don Nickles, R-Okla. The substitute would freeze only those regulations that were projected to have an annual impact on the economy of $100 million or more. Neither the original Senate bill nor HR 450 had such a monetary threshold. The Roth substitute also would bar lawsuits aimed at blocking presidential actions to implement regulations exempted by the bill. Such judicial review would be allowed under the House bill.

The committee expanded the moratorium by adopting a Ted Stevens, R-Alaska, amendment to bar federal agencies from restricting recreational, commercial or subsistence uses of public lands. Stevens wanted to prevent the government from limiting such things as western grazing rights and access to timber in Alaska's Tongass National Forest on what he called dubious environmental grounds. Democratic opponents argued that the amendment was too broad and would prevent the government from regulating virtually any activity in national parks or other public lands.

The issue of which regulations would be exempt from the moratorium spurred the sharpest partisan fight of the markup. The battle focused on the meaning of "imminent" threat. Democrats said "imminent" implied that only regulations to halt an immediate danger would be exempt. They said the bill thus would freeze federal efforts to develop long-term plans to prevent such unpredictable but potentially deadly dangers as contamination of meat and drinking water. Republicans countered that "imminent" was used to prevent the health and safety exclusion from becoming a loophole, not to prevent common-sense regulatory actions by the president. The committee rejected amendments by Carl Levin, D-Mich., to drop "imminent" from the health and safety exemption and by John Glenn, D-Ohio, to exempt regulations dealing with improved meat and poultry inspection procedures and testing for microbes in public water supplies. The panel adopted a Glenn amendment to waive the freeze for rules dealing with airplane and commuter airline safety and restrictions on lead in paint, soil, and drinking water.

The Senate passed S 219, 100–0 on March 29, after abandoning the moratorium in favor of a congressional review period. Nickles was convinced that the measure would not survive the opposition of Democrats and moderate Republicans. As a result, he turned to a proposal in a separate regulatory overhaul bill (S 343), giving Congress the chance to veto a regulation before it took effect. On March 24, Nickles unveiled a substitute version of S 219, which bore little resemblance to either the original or the House-passed measure. Cosponsored by Harry Reid, D-Nev., the substitute would suspend implementation of significant new regulations—those with an expected economic impact of $100 million or more a year—for 45 days after they were issued. Congress could block a significant regulation by passing a joint resolution of disapproval, provided that the resolution was not vetoed or the veto was not sustained. Less significant regulations would go into effect upon issuance, but Congress could also revoke them, using the same 45-day process. The substitute contained a "look-back" provision that would allow Congress 45 days from the date of enactment to review any significant regulation issued since Nov. 20, 1994.

The Senate action gave new life to the concept of the "legislative veto," which had been dormant for more than a decade. It also appeared to avoid constitutional obstacles that had undercut earlier procedures. *(Legislative veto, Congress and the Nation Vol. VI, p. 833)*

The House on May 17 passed S 219 by voice vote, after inserting the text of HR 450. The moratorium legislation died upon adjournment. ❑

Freedom of Information

To modernize the federal government's response to information requests, Congress in 1996 cleared legislation (HR 3802) requiring federal agencies to make their records available electronically. President Clinton signed HR 3802 (PL 104-231) on Oct. 2. The Senate passed a similar bill in 1994, but it died in the House. *(1994 action, p. 821)*

HR 3802 clarified that computer-generated federal records were subject to the Freedom of Information Act (FOIA), the law that required government agencies to release most types of documents upon formal request from the public. The measure also was designed to improve the government's response time on FOIA requests. Some agencies had backlogs of months or even years. HR 3802 required agencies to report annually on the number of pending requests and how long it would take to fulfill them. The bill clarified that federal records were subject to disclosure unless their release would affect national security, criminal investigations, trade secrets or individual privacy.

The original Senate bill (S 1090) differed from the House-passed version most notably in that it had a section defining an electronic record. Critics said the definition was too sweeping and might include such things as e-mail, extensive databases, informal notes kept on a computer hard drive, and software programs developed by a federal agency. HR 3802 as cleared did not define exactly what a document was. As was the case with the original FOIA, it left this question to agencies and, if necessary, the courts to decide.

S 1090, sponsored by Patrick J. Leahy, D-Vt., was reported from the Senate Judiciary Committee (S Rept 104-272) on May 15, 1996. The bill contained the following provisions:

• Clarified that agency records kept on computer were public records.

• Required agencies to make reasonable efforts to provide their information in the form requested, including through e-mail or the Internet. Agencies would be required to publish regulations, opinions and policy statements electronically and provide online indexes of their major information systems. They would have to indicate where and to what extent electronic documents had been edited.

• Improved agencies' response time to FOIA requests. The bill would extend from 10 days to 20 days agencies' deadlines for responding to requests, under the theory that they would meet that deadline more often and would able to reduce their backlogs. If agencies maintained consistently good turnaround times, they would be able to keep half the request-related fees they collected. Agencies would be authorized to create a dual-track response system, one for routine requests and the other for more complex cases.

The House Government Reform and Oversight Committee reported HR 3802 (H Rept 104-795) on Sept. 17. The bill stipulated that computerized documents were subject to the same FOIA requirements as printed documents. It called for agencies to make a reasonable attempt to provide documents in the requested printed or electronic format. And it proposed to codify the common practice of treating requests on different timetables depending on how complicated they were and how compelling was the public's interest. Unlike S 1090, HR 3802 did not attempt to define exactly what a document was. The committee adopted a Carolyn B. Maloney, D-N.Y., amendment to require agencies to prepare annual reports on the number of pending information requests and the amount of time required to meet those requests.

The House passed HR 3802 by 402–0 under suspension of the rules Sept. 17. The Senate passed S 1090 by voice vote the same day. On Sept. 18, senators said they made a clerical error in passing S 1090 instead of the House version. The Senate then passed HR 3802 by voice vote, completing congressional action. ❑

White House Employees

Congress in 1996 cleared legislation (HR 3452) that would allow White House and many presidential appointees to receive protection under federal civil rights and labor laws. President Clinton signed the bill (PL 104-331) on Oct. 26.

HR 3452 applied 11 civil rights, labor, and employment laws to most presidential appointees except those who were confirmed by the Senate, appointed by advisory committees, or part of the military. The bill protected White House employees and the specified presidential appointees from discrimination based upon race, color, religion, sex, national origin, age or disability. It also granted them protection under the Family and Medical Leave Act of 1993, which allowed employees to take unpaid time off to care for family members or for medical emergencies. *(Family leave, p. 655)*

Other laws covered in HR 3452 included the Occupational Health and Safety Act, the Americans with Disabilities Act, and the Fair Labor Standards Act. In addition, the White House would be subject to all future employment laws unless employees were specifically exempted.

The bill was fashioned after the Congressional Accountability Act of 1995 (S 2—PL 104-1), which made Congress subject to the 11 federal laws. *(PL 104-1, p. 890)*

FEDERAL DOWNSIZING

Responding to the Republican drive to slash federal spending, President Clinton on March 27, 1995, unveiled a plan aimed at streamlining the federal government and saving taxpayers $13.1 billion over five years. Clinton presented the proposal as part of the administration's overall call for "reinventing government." He billed the plan as a more humane option of government restructuring, compared with GOP efforts to cut popular aid programs. *('Reinventing government,' p. 811)*

Among the administration's proposed cuts were:

• Changing contract operations at the National Aeronautics and Space Administration (NASA) and restructuring the agency, saving $8 billion and eliminating 2,000 jobs in five years.

• Closing outdated Interior Department offices, including the territories' bureau, and allowing offshore oil and gas royalties to be acquired through buyouts, cutting 2,000 jobs and saving about $3.8 billion.

• Eliminating subsidies that the Small Business Administration (SBA) paid on loans and imposing fees on lenders and borrowers, saving $1.2 billion and cutting 500 government jobs.

• Transferring some Federal Emergency Management Agency (FEMA) functions to states so they could more quickly declare disaster areas, saving approximately $100 million and eliminating 305 jobs.

A number of these proposals appeared in other legislation in an altered form during the year. For example, the appropriations bill for Veterans Affairs, Housing and Urban Development, and independent agencies (HR 2099) proposed to cut funding for NASA and required some restructuring of the agency. Also, S 895 (PL 104-36) largely allowed the outlines of Clinton's plan to change the SBA loan program. The bill lowered the federal guarantee rate for the loans, which meant that Congress would have to appropriate less to cover loan defaults for an increased number of loans. *(SBA loan guarantees, p. 383)*

The House Government Reform and Oversight Committee reported HR 3452 (H Rept 104-820, Part I) on Sept. 24, 1996. The committee adopted an amendment by Charles Bass, R-N.H., to require that an Office of the Inspector General be established in the White House. The committee-approved bill also would tighten financial management at the White House by requiring the president to appoint a chief financial officer for the executive office of the president. The House passed HR 3452 by 410–5 under suspension of the rules on Sept. 24.

The administration said that it supported the spirit of the bill and had already put many of its requirements in place but that it could not support the bill unless lawmakers struck the inspector general provision, which it said raised "serious constitutional concerns on separation of powers grounds."

Following negotiations, GOP leaders agreed to drop the inspector general and chief financial officer provisions. The Senate passed the revised bill by voice vote Oct. 3. The House accepted the changes the next day, completing congressional action. ❏

Federal Personnel

The House Sept. 27, 1996, by voice vote passed a bill (HR 3841) aimed at softening the blow to federal workers who lost their jobs as a result of downsizing.

HR 3841 would allow federal workers to keep health benefits for 18 months with the federal share being paid and to continue participating in the government life insurance program if they paid both the employer and employee contributions. It also provided for retraining, and it included provisions to ease the rules for establishing demonstration projects for innovative personnel policies.

The House by voice vote agreed to drop controversial language to allow federal agencies to place greater weight on performance when determining which workers to keep during force reductions. Bill sponsor John L. Mica, R-Fla., described the provision as "the cornerstone" of efforts to reward employees for good performance. But the provision drew strong objections, including opposition from African Americans concerned that it could open the way for racial discrimination.

The bill approved by the House Government Reform and Oversight Civil Service Subcommittee included provisions to make it easier for workers with outstanding performance records to keep their jobs during layoffs, as well as to provide greater assistance to employees leaving their jobs. The subcommittee version also would expand the options available to federal employees under their tax-deferred retirement plans. Similar provisions subsequently were enacted as part of the fiscal 1997 omnibus appropriations bill (HR 3610—PL 104-208). The panel deleted a section of the bill aimed at streamlining the process for appeals on workplace issues. *(Appropriations, p. 76)*

The full committee reported HR 3841 (H Rept 104-831) on Sept. 24, 1996. The committee adopted a Constance A. Morella, R-Md., amendment to ensure that, when an agency had multiple performance-evaluation systems, the Office of Personnel Management would assure equitable treatment.

HR 3841 initially failed to pass, 224–201, under suspension of the rules, falling short of the two-thirds majority requirement. The next day, the controversial performance review provision was removed, and the bill passed. ❏

Federal Procurement

The House, 423–0 on Sept. 14, 1995, passed a bill (HR 1670) that sought to further streamline the federal procurement system and give government contracting officers more flexibility to determine which contractors and bids to consider. The Senate did not act on the legislation. Portions of the bill were included in the Defense authorization bill (HR 1530), which President Clinton vetoed Dec. 28, 1995. *(Defense authorization, p. 294)*

HR 1670 would make it easier for the government to purchase commercial items, reduce the amount of paperwork required of federal contractors, and set new bidding standards designed to ensure "maximum practicable" competition for federal contracts. Existing law stipulated "full and open competition" in which federal officials were required to accept bids from all companies that met certain qualifications. Backers of HR 1670 said the existing standard gave all sources a right to bid on a contract, whether or not they had "a realistic" chance to supply the goods and services specified.

The bill also would create a single, consolidated U.S. Board of Contract Appeals to resolve contracting disputes and protests about bid awards. The new board would replace existing agency boards of appeals and the General Accounting Office bid protest section.

The House Government Reform and Oversight Committee reported HR 1670 (H Rept 104-222, Part I) on Aug. 1, 1995. Two other committees—Small Business and National Security—also held hearings on the measure. Government Reform Chairman William F. Clinger, R-Pa., the bill's chief sponsor, said cost outlays for federal procurement were 20 percent higher than necessary because of the extensive requirements imposed on federal purchasing officials and government contractors. He described numerous mandates that he said left "little room for the exercise of business judgment, initiative and creativity." But some Democrats objected, saying the requirement for maximum practicable competition would knock smaller businesses out of the running for government contracts.

On the House floor, members Sept. 13 rejected, 182–239, a Cardiss Collins, D-Ill., amendment to strike the language proposing a new bidding standard and instead allow agencies to make preliminary assessments to determine whether bids had a chance of winning approval. Also rejected, 164–259 on Sept. 14, was an amendment by Carolyn B. Maloney, D-N.Y., to retain a tax on weapons purchases by foreign governments. Under existing law, a tax was levied on such sales if the U.S. government had spent significant amounts of money to develop the weapons. The Defense Department was allowed to waive that tax to help secure a sale. Language in HR 1670 would repeal the tax on all weapons sales; Maloney's amendment would have stripped that provision from the bill. But Clinger successfully argued that the repeal would allow the United States to be more competitive in the world market because other countries did not levy similar taxes.

HR 1670 was a follow-up to the 1994 Federal Acquisition Streamlining Act (S 1587—PL 103-355). *(1994 act, p. 812)* ❑

Space Station

Efforts to kill the space station—the last of the big-science projects—failed in 1995, in part because of a strong lobbying campaign by House Republicans who viewed the project as a symbol of America's leadership in space exploration. And the space station-related contracts that were spread throughout the nation did not hurt the cause. *(1993–1994 action, p. 812)*

The House passed a seven year authorization bill (HR 1601) that covered the entire amount required to complete the development and construction of the space station, as well as to begin operations. However, the Senate passed a simple one-year authorization (S 1048), and the differences were not reconciled.

VA-HUD Appropriations. During floor debate on the appropriations bill (HR 2099) for the departments of Veterans Affairs (VA) and Housing and Urban Development (HUD), the House rejected a David R. Obey, D-Wis., amendment, on July 27, 1995, by 126–299, to terminate the station and assign the money to science, housing, and other programs. The next day, the House rejected a Tim Roemer, D-Ind., amendment, 132–287, to kill the station and use the money for deficit reduction.

In the Senate, a Dale Bumpers, D-Ark., amendment to terminate the space station was rejected 35–64 on Sept. 26.

As cleared by Congress, HR 2099 included $2.1 billion for the space station in fiscal 1996, the full amount requested by President Clinton. The bill, however, was vetoed on other grounds.

The House by voice vote Sept. 28, 1995, passed HR 1601, to authorize $13.1 billion through 2002 for the orbiting laboratory—with an annual cap of $2.1 billion. The bill had been reported from the House Science Committee (H Rept 104-210) on July 28. The committee rejected a Roemer amendment to cancel the project and a Sheila Jackson-Lee, D-Texas, amendment to make the authorization contingent on an appropriation equal to the Clinton budget or a certification by the National Aeronautics and Space Administration (NASA) administrator that a "balanced space and aeronautics program has been maintained."

The Senate agreed to authorize the space station, but only for fiscal 1996. The proposal was part of a larger NASA authorization bill (S 1048) that passed by voice vote Oct. 19. S 1048 earmarked $2.1 billion for the space station. The bill had been reported (S Rept 104-155) from the Senate Commerce, Science, and Transportation Committee on Oct. 11. ❑

Omnibus Science Authorization

In a departure from past practice, the House twice in the 104th Congress passed legislation authorizing an array of federal civilian science programs. The bills (HR 2405, HR 3322) were designed to refocus science research, emphasizing basic science and paring back or terminating research that the legislation's supporters said could be better performed by the private sector. The Senate offered no comparable legislation but did consider narrower bills (S 1048, S 1839) providing one-year authorizations for the National Aeronautics and Space Administration (NASA).

Both chambers had passed versions of a NASA authorization bill in 1994, but they were unable to settle their differences before the end of the 103rd Congress. *(1994 action, p. 827)*

HR 2405

The House on Oct. 12, 1995, by 248–161, passed an omnibus science authorization bill (HR 2405). The $21.9 billion measure covered civilian science-related programs at seven agencies; the research programs traditionally had been authorized on an agency-by-agency basis. Bringing the various science programs under a single authorization bill was a major victory for House Science Committee Chairman Robert S. Walker, R-Pa., who had long argued that Congress should set overall priorities for federal science activities and restrict certain categories of scientific research. Walker wanted to move the government out of the business of applied science.

HR 2405 contained $2 billion less than the $24 billion that was appropriated for the combined research activities in fiscal 1995. Most of the agencies were slated for a one-year authorization. Nearly half the funding—$11.5 billion—was for NASA, including $1 billion for Mission to Planet Earth, a climate-study program favored by the Clinton administration. The NASA authorization had been considered separately by the House Science Committee, which reported an $11.5 billion bill (HR 2043—H Rept 104-233) on Aug. 4. The total did not include funding for the space station, which was handled in another bill (HR 1601). *(Space station, p. 851)*

HR 2405 would terminate research programs for alternative energy sources including solar and hydropower, as well as some research on developing a new generation of nuclear reactors. Many of those cuts were strongly opposed by Democrats. President Clinton vowed to veto the bill "because of unacceptably deep reductions in, and termination of, federal investments in science and technology."

Before passing HR 2405, the House Oct. 12 rejected an amendment by the ranking Democrat on the Science Committee George E. Brown Jr. of California, to increase the authorization by $3.2 billion to $25.1 billion. The House also rejected a number of amendments, including ones that sought to cut the number of personnel at all nondefense laboratories; to privatize all of the Energy Department laboratories other than the Los Alamos, Sandia and Lawrence Livermore national laboratories; to strike a prohibition on funding research on indoor air pollution; and to eliminate a prohibition in the bill on funding the EPA's Environmental Technology Initiative, which was aimed at providing the private sector with resources and information to help develop technologies for the protection of the environment.

HR 3322

The House by voice vote May 30, 1996, passed HR 3322, authorizing $19.7 billion for civilian science programs administered by NASA, EPA, the National Science Foundation, the U.S. Fire Administration, the National Oceanic and Atmospheric Administration (NOAA), the National Institute of Standards and Technology (NIST), the Federal Aviation Administration and the National Earthquake Hazards Reduction Program.

House Science Committee consideration of HR 3322 was best remembered as an exhibition of the partisan hostilities that had been brewing on the committee since the Republicans took over control of Congress in 1995. Committee Democrats, led by ranking member Brown, complained that they were frozen out of the process of writing the bill, which they claimed was rushed through the committee. They accused Committee Chairman Walker of running the panel with a heavy hand. Walker justified the committee's quick work on the legislation on the grounds that it had to reach the House floor in a timely fashion to have any effect on the fiscal 1997 appropriations process.

The $19.7 billion committee-approved bill, reported (H Rept 104-550, Part I) on May 1, 1996, was 6 percent below President Clinton's request. Furthermore, two programs favored by the president were targeted for funding cuts. Republicans contended that public-private technology partnerships, most of which were coordinated by the NIST, amounted to misguided "industrial policy" in which the government tried to choose winners and losers among new technologies. They also said Mission to Planet Earth could be conducted at a much lower cost.

On party-line votes, the committee rejected nearly a dozen Democratic amendments aimed at preserving funding for various projects. One would have removed the authorization cap on funding for NOAA; another would have restored funding for research on global warming. Democratic fiscal hawks also lost in their efforts to cut a controversial project that was a high priority for Walker and other advocates of manned space travel: the space station. The committee rejected two Roemer amendments—one to eliminate all funding for the space station and another symbolic one to cut $100 million from the space station's annual budget of $2.1 billion. The panel adopted a Joe L. Burton, R-Texas, amendment to change the name of the National Science Foundation to the National Science and Engineering Foundation.

A sense existed that the full House was just going through the motions as it acted on HR 3322. Clinton had threatened to veto the measure, mainly because it would provide less money than he wanted for his administration's public-private technology research partnerships and for Mission to Planet Earth. The Senate continued to show no interest in the bill. And the measure was being bypassed by the appropriations process.

Strong partisan overtones marked floor debate on HR 3322, as in committee. Brown accused Republicans of trying to pile up cuts in science to make room for "tax cuts for the wealthy." Lloyd Doggett, D-Texas, said the only science coming out of the Science Committee was "political science." Republicans countered by accusing the Democrats of being obstructionists and failing to understand the importance of spending cuts.

Supporters managed to salvage one public-private partnership. The House by voice vote adopted a Constance A. Morella, R-Md., amendment to provide $90 million for the Commerce Department's Manufacturing Extension Partnership, which provided money for private researchers to develop technologies to make U.S. companies more competitive in world markets.

SENATE ACTION

The Senate passed S 1048 by voice vote Oct. 19, 1995. S 1048 would authorize NASA at $13.8 billion in fiscal 1996, including $2.1 billion for the space station and $1.4 billion for Mission to Planet Earth. The Senate Commerce, Science, and Transportation Committee had reported S 1048 (S Rept 104-155) on Oct. 11. Commerce Committee Chairman Larry Pressler, R-S.D., a strong defender of Mission to Planet Earth, told colleagues that the bill contained provisions aimed at discouraging NASA from altering the climate-study program. The core of the project was a series of earth-observing satellites, due to be launched in 1998, that would study how the oceans and atmosphere interacted.

The Senate Commerce, Science, and Transportation Committee reported S 1839 (S Rept 104-327) on July 22, 1996. The bill would authorize $13.7 billion for NASA in fiscal 1997. The House recommended a slightly lower amount—$13.5 billion—in its broader omnibus science bill (HR 3322). Senate Commerce debate on S 1839 was perfunctory. No attempts were made to go after the space station or any other major NASA project. The committee considered and adopted only one amendment, by John D. Rockefeller IV, D-W.Va., to require NASA to provide Congress by July 1997 with an outline of educational programs based on the agency's space exploration programs, including the space station.

APPROPRIATIONS

The fiscal 1996 spending bill for Veterans Affairs (VA), Housing and Urban Development (HUD), and related agencies (HR 2099) provided $13.8 billion for NASA, but Clinton vetoed the measure Dec. 18, 1995. A subsequent fiscal 1996 omnibus appropriations bill (HR 3019—PL 104-134) earmarked $13.9 billion for NASA. The fiscal 1997 VA-HUD appropriations bill (HR 3666—PL 104-204) provided $13.7 billion for NASA. ❏

Science Privatization

On Sept. 17, 1996, the House Government Reform and Oversight Committee formally reported and the full House by voice vote under suspension of the rules passed a bill (HR 3936—H Rept 104-801, Part I) to promote commercial development of outer space and move the National Aeronautics and Space Administration (NASA) toward transferring some of its core functions to the private sector. The Senate never acted on the measure.

HR 3936—sponsored by House Science Committee Chairman Robert S. Walker, R-Pa., and supported by the committee's ranking Democrat, George E. Brown Jr. of California—would facilitate efforts by private companies to launch satellites, conduct experiments in space and bring the experiments and the launch vehicles back to Earth. It would require the Transportation Department to draw up regulations for licensing reentries from orbit and authorize government insurance for such reentries. If the transportation secretary did not formulate these regulations, states would be authorized to do so for launches within their boundaries. However, the secretary would have to certify that such launches would not jeopardize public health, safety or property or endanger national security or the nation's foreign policy.

The bill also would:

• Require NASA to study the potential role for the private sector in such federal programs as the space station; the Global Positioning System, a network of satellites and ground stations that could pinpoint the location of an individual or item on Earth; and the Mission to Planet Earth, another network of satellites for collecting data on the Earth's atmosphere and environment.

• Require NASA to purchase space-derived science information from the private sector to the maximum extent possible.

• Require the federal government to use private launch services when sending payloads into space, with several exceptions.

The bill also would make it easier for the Defense Department to use such private services, a practice that was already common at NASA.

• Allow excess ballistic missiles to be converted to use as space transportation vehicles. ❏

NEA, NEH Reauthorization

House and Senate committees in 1995 reported legislation (HR 1557, S 856) to scale back the National Endowment for the Arts (NEA) and the National Endowment for the Humanities (NEH). The organizations, which distributed federal grant money to states and communities for cultural projects, had been under fire from conservatives who said the government should not be sponsoring artists and who disapproved of many of the specific arts projects that received funding.

HR 1557, reported from House Economic and Educational Opportunities (H Rept 104-170) on June 29, 1995, would place funding for both endowments on a "glide path" to termination by fiscal 1999. Funding for the NEA would be authorized at a maximum of $97.5 million in fiscal 1996, $58.5 million in 1997, and $46.8 million in fiscal 1998, with termination by 1999. The NEH would be authorized at $137.9 million in fiscal 1996, $110.3 million in 1997, and $88.3 million in 1998. Supporters said that the three years would give the NEA and NEH time to line up alternative funding. The bill also provided funding for a third endowment, the Institute of Museum Services. It would get $28.7 million a year during the same period and would not be eliminated.

Eighteen members of both parties voted "present" on the bill to protest the speed with which it moved through the committee. Several members contended that under normal circumstances the bill would have been the subject of numerous hearings over several months. Instead, no hearings or subcommittee markups took place. Bill Goodling, R-Pa., House Economic Committee chairman and chief sponsor of HR 1557, said he understood the members' frustration, but he described the bill as an effort to stave off attempts by House deficit hawks to eliminate funding for the endowments immediately.

The committee rejected a Pat Williams, D-Mont., substitute to extend the endowments for two years and establish their authorization levels at "such sums as necessary." Also rejected was a Sam Johnson, R-Texas, amendment to repeal federal involvement in the NEA and NEH immediately.

The Senate Labor and Human Resources Committee reported S 856 (S Rept 104-135) on Aug. 30, 1995. The bill—the text of which was offered as a substitute by chief sponsor James M. Jeffords, R-Vt.—would reauthorize the endowments, at reduced levels, through fiscal 2000. The NEA would be authorized at $153.9 million in fiscal 1996; the NEH, at $160.1 million.

S 856 also sought to tighten controls over how federal money could be used. For example, greater authority would be given to the National Foundation on the Arts and the Humanities, which would oversee the activities of both endowments and the Institute of Museum and Library Services. The foundation would be responsible for developing a comprehensive national policy for federal support of cultural projects. Moreover, money was to be distributed to state and local cultural organizations by block grants under the bill. With the exception of individual fellowship grants for literature, specific categories for cultural endeavors such as choreography, jazz and design would no longer be offered.

The Senate committee also adopted an amendment by Christopher J. Dodd, D-Conn., to allow the endowments to use $150,000 of their appropriated funds in fiscal 1996 to study the feasibility of creating an independent and permanent national endowment that would not be threatened periodically by politics. The Senate rejected several Republican amendments to phase out funding for the endowments over several years.

The fiscal 1996 Interior appropriations bill (HR 1977) provided $99.5 million for NEA and $110 million for NEH. However, HR 1977 was vetoed by President Clinton. Fiscal 1996 funding for the two endowments, at the same level as in HR 1977, was included in an omnibus supplemental appropriations measure (HR 3019—PL 104-134). Members held steady in fiscal 1997, providing $99.5 million for NEA and $110 million for NEH in HR 3610 (PL 104-208). *(1993–1994 action, p. 824)*   ❑

Puerto Rico Status

Two House committees in 1996 reported legislation (HR 3024) to help Puerto Rico achieve full self-government. HR 3024 would create a congressionally recognized framework for Puerto Rican citizens to express how they wished to attain self-government—the first such framework since Puerto Ricans became U.S. citizens in 1917.

Currently, residents of Puerto Rico were subject to most federal laws and courts and to the military draft but were ineligible to vote in presidential elections. Puerto Ricans elected one nonvoting representative to Congress.

The House Resources Committee reported HR 3024 (H Rept 104-713, Part I) on July 26, 1996. The bill, sponsored by Don Young, R-Alaska, outlined a three-stage process for Puerto Rican self-government. The first stage was a referendum in Puerto Rico, to be held by the end of 1998. Voters would choose between the existing commonwealth status and a path leading to either independence or statehood. If voters chose independence or statehood, they would be asked in another question in the same referendum to indicate which of the two paths they preferred. If voters chose the status quo, a referendum would be taken every four years until a majority decision was reached on the island's status. The second stage was a 10-year transition period to draft and carry out the referendum's outcome. The third was implementation.

Ranking Democrat on House Resources George Miller of California offered, then withdrew, an amendment to give Puerto Ricans in the first part of the ballot three distinct choices: the status quo, statehood or independence. He argued that the proposed process "unfairly skews" the statehood and independence options. Another Miller amendment, to require that the results of the 1998 referendum be immediately binding instead of allowing a 10-year transition period to carry out the referendum

decision, was rejected by the committee. The panel adopted an Elton Gallegly, R-Calif., amendment to allow Puerto Ricans to maintain their U.S. citizenship if voters opted for independence. No one born after the vote for independence would be eligible for U.S. citizenship, however.

The House Rules Committee reported the bill (H Rept 104-713, Part II) on Sept. 18, 1996. The panel had jurisdiction over a section of the legislation that laid out the procedures under which Congress would respond to the results of a referendum, whenever it was held. Panel members amended the section to give the Resources Committee 120 calendar days, instead of 180 days, to report a bill responding to the results. If the Resources panel failed to meet that deadline, any member of the House could call up the bill on the floor.

In a 1993 plebiscite, 48.4 percent of the island's voters favored an enhanced commonwealth; 46.2 percent opted for statehood; and 4.4 percent chose independence.   ❑

D.C. Issues

The 104th Congress considered a number of issues relating to the District of Columbia.

FINANCIAL REVIEW BOARD

Congress in 1995 cleared legislation (HR 1345) creating a powerful, five member board—officially titled the District of Columbia Financial Responsibility and Management Assistance Authority—to work with the city and the administration to bring the city's finances under control and to borrow money to pay city workers and suppliers as well as provide basic municipal services.

HR 1345 sought to return the District to self-sufficiency without ongoing federal supervision. It was modeled in part on temporary financial controls imposed on such cities as New York, Cleveland and Philadelphia. Lawmakers said they did not want the board to oversee day-to-day city management. However, the board was given broad power to reorganize city government, slash programs and reject union contracts over the following several years if city officials did not cut spending. Board members were to be appointed by the president.

The board was given authority to review all contracts and approve the city's borrowing. It also had authority to confirm the mayor's nominations for a chief financial officer, who would carry out programs and procedures for budgetary control, and an inspector general, who would manage an annual audit of the city's finances.

Once the city had produced four consecutive balanced budgets and earned adequate access to the credit markets, the board would only monitor city actions. It would suspend all its activities once the city had repaid any money it might have borrowed with the review board's help.

The provisions were the most sweeping changes to the District government since the 1973 Home Rule Act (PL 93-198), which gave the District partial self-government. They represented a middle ground between some city advocates who favored a cash bailout with few strings attached and some conservatives who preferred to revoke home rule altogether. *(Home rule, Congress and the Nation Vol. IV, p. 797)*

The House Government Reform and Oversight Committee reported HR 1345 (H Rept 104-96) on March 30, 1995. The House passed the bill by voice vote under suspension of the rules April 3. The Senate passed the measure by voice vote April 6, after adopting an amendment by William S. Cohen, R-Maine, James M. Jeffords, R-Vt., and William V. Roth Jr., R-Del., to expand the list of who would be eligible to serve on the board. The Senate language required members of the new review board to either maintain "a primary residence" or have "a primary place of business" in the District. The bill originally required all board members to be District taxpayers. The change made District business owners or partners who lived in the suburbs eligible to serve on the board. The amendment also clarified that the board would be exempt from District government procurement and hiring rules. And it barred both the board and the District mayor and City Council from imposing changes on the District court system. The House accepted the changes April 7, completing congressional action. President Clinton signed the bill (PL 104-8) on April 17, 1995.

HIGHWAY FUNDS

Congress in 1995 cleared legislation (HR 2017) that allowed the District to spend about $170 million in federal highway money without immediately contributing local matching funds. The president signed the measure (PL 104-21) on Aug. 4.

HR 2017, sponsored by Del. Eleanor Holmes Norton, D-D.C., deferred the District's matching contribution requirements for fiscal 1995 and fiscal 1996, giving the financially strapped city until September 1998 to make its final matching payments for 1996 federal highway funds. To ensure the repayment and prevent the city from falling into arrears again, the bill required the District to establish a dedicated highway fund by Dec. 31, 1995. Local gas taxes and other motor vehicle taxes had to be deposited into the fund in amounts sufficient to repay the deferred amounts for 1995 and 1996 and to meet annual matching highway payments in the future. Previously, gas taxes collected by the District had gone into the general fund.

Under the 1991 surface transportation law (PL 102-240), states, territories, and the District received money each year from the Highway Trust Fund but could not spend much of it unless they put up $1 for every $4 in federal aid. The District government's share in fiscal 1995 was $87 million; $82 million remained unspent because the District was unable to contribute $16 million in matching funds. The city would have lost the $82 million if Congress had not intervened by Aug. 1. *(1991 law, Congress and the Nation Vol. VIII, p. 437)*

The House Transportation and Infrastructure Committee reported HR 2017 (H Rept 104-217, Part I) on July 31, 1995. The same day, the House and Senate passed the bill by voice votes, completing congressional action.

The Senate had passed an earlier version of the legislation (S 1023) by voice vote July 20. S 1023 would have allowed the District to spend all its highway aid in fiscal 1995 and 1996, with the local match due by Sept. 30, 1996. If the District could not pro-

duce the matching money by then, its fiscal 1997 aid would have been cut by that amount. Unlike HR 2017, S 1023 did not require the District to place gasoline taxes and highway user fees in a separate highway fund. The Senate Environment and Public Works Committee had reported S 1023 (S Rept 104-111) on July 12.

The Clinton administration originally had proposed to let the District government use all its federal highway aid without requiring any local contribution. House appropriators had included that proposal in an early version of a bill (HR 1944—PL 104-19) to rescind previously approved spending, but the language subsequently was removed. *(Rescissions bill, p. 73)*

APPROPRIATIONS BILLS

Members' attempted inclusion of social mandates in the annual appropriations bill for the District of Columbia had become commonplace.

In 1995, the fiscal 1996 bill (HR 2546) stalled over a controversial school voucher program for the District. The House added an amendment by Steven Gunderson, R-Wis., to set up a federally and privately financed fund to award poor children as much as $3,000 to attend the private or public school of their choice. The Senate refused to accept the provision, deadlocking the conference at year's end. In January 1996, House and Senate negotiators settled on a compromise. The basic framework of the House voucher language would be retained, although Senate D.C. Appropriations Subcommittee Chairman James M. Jeffords, R-Vt., managed to weaken it by making it contingent on D.C. City Council approval. The conference agreement would give the parents of some low-income children up to $3,000 apiece to attend the private or public school of their choice. A nonprofit corporation would run the program, decide who got the vouchers and solicit funds from private industry.

The bill would authorize about $5 million for the voucher program and nearly $10 million to repair dilapidated school buildings, create a charter school system and expand the city's Even Start program for elementary school students and their parents. It called for the creation of three new boards to oversee, respectively, the entire city school system, school curricula and the voucher program. In addition to $712 million for the federal payment and pension fund contribution, the conferees agreed to appropriate $14.9 million for the education overhaul provisions.

The White House objected to language in HR 2546 to bar the D.C. government from using federal or local funds for abortion, except in cases of rape, incest or danger to the woman's life. The bill also retained a prohibition on federal or local funding of the D.C. domestic partnership act, which allowed city employees to buy health insurance coverage for their partners, including homosexual partners. A new provision would bar unmarried couples from adopting children, unless one of the partners was the child's biological parent.

The House accepted the conference agreement, but the voucher language remained a sore point for critics in both parties. Senate Democratic opponents then stopped the bill with a filibuster threat. As a result, House leaders gave in, agreeing to drop the school voucher provision, in exchange for removal of $10 million earmarked for education overhaul. HR 2546 subsequently was folded into the fiscal 1996 omnibus appropriations bill (HR 3019—PL 104-134).

The fiscal 1997 bill (HR 3845—PL 104-194), cleared in 1996, barred the District from spending either federal or local funds to provide abortions, except in cases of rape, incest or a threat to the life of the mother. It also barred the District from spending government funds to implement its Domestic Partner Act, a local ordinance that gave unmarried partners of city workers access to the same benefits spouses received. Members did not attempt to include school voucher language.

WOODROW WILSON MEMORIAL BRIDGE

A 1995 bill (S 440—PL 104-59) designating routes for the new National Highway System, among other things, authorized the federal government to pay the entire cost of a replacement for the Woodrow Wilson Memorial Bridge over the Potomac River at the southern tip of Washington, D.C. S 440 authorized $97.5 million to design the new bridge and make interim repairs to the existing span. The project was championed by Republican Senator John W. Warner, many of whose constituents in northern Virginia relied on the bridge. *(National Highway System, p. 363)*

TAXES

Lawmakers in 1996 from the left and right embraced the idea of helping the financially floundering District by giving its residents some tax relief. Members were concerned about the exodus from D.C. by middle- and upper-income residents, among its other problems. Del. Eleanor Holmes Norton, D-D.C., said Washington had lost more residents between 1990 and 1995 than in all of the 1980s, thus undermining its tax base and support for schools and other public institutions.

Norton offered a bill (HR 3244) to reduce the federal income tax rate for D.C. residents to 15 percent, effectively giving more than half the city's residents a tax cut of 50 percent or more. The bill also would eliminate taxes on capital gains from the sale of property in the District. The House Government Reform and Oversight Committee's D.C. Subcommittee held hearings on HR 3244, but it went no further.   ❑

Navajo-Hopi Land Dispute

President Clinton signed into law June 21, 1995, a bill (S 349—PL 104-15) to extend a program that relocated Native Americans caught in the middle of a territorial dispute between the Navajo and Hopi tribes. Congress in 1996 cleared legislation (S 1973—PL 104-301) aimed at ending the federal government's involvement in the land dispute.

The Navajo and Hopi tribes had been fighting over territory in the southwestern United States for more than a century. Congress attempted to resolve the dispute in 1974 with a law (PL 93-531) that partitioned the lands between the two tribes and created the Navajo-Hopi Relocation Housing Program, which offered new housing to resettle families on the wrong side of the boundaries. Under the 1974 law, the federal government had spent more than $350 million to relocate families, exceeding original cost estimates by 900 percent. *(1974 law, Congress and the Nation Vol. IV, p. 809)*

RELOCATION

S 349, sponsored by Senate Indian Affairs Committee Chairman John McCain, R-Ariz., authorized $30 million a year for the relocation program through fiscal 1997. Supporters hoped the measure would be the last one needed to complete the relocation effort.

Senate Indian Affairs reported S 349 (S Rept 104-29) on April 6, 1995. The Senate passed the bill by voice vote April 26. The House followed suit June 8, clearing the measure.

LAND DISPUTE

S 1973, also sponsored by McCain, ratified an agreement between the Hopi tribe and the federal government that settled four claims by the Hopis against the United States for damages. In exchange, the federal government agreed to pay $50.2 million to the Hopi tribe for issuing 75-year leases to Navajo families who wished to continue living on the Hopi land. Navajo families that left would be given a set time to apply for federal relocation benefits.

Under the agreement, the Hope tribe would use the money to buy rural, agricultural land and range land in northern Arizona. The land would be held in trust, or reserved for Hopi use, by the interior secretary. But none of the land would be placed in trust until at least 85 percent of eligible Navajo families either relocated or signed a lease agreement to stay on the land.

The Senate Indian Affairs Committee reported S 1973 (S Rept 104-363) on Sept. 9, 1996. The Senate passed the bill by voice vote Sept. 26, after amending it to define the Hopi tribe's water rights for the new trust lands. The House passed the measure by voice vote Sept. 28, clearing it. President Clinton signed the bill Oct. 11.   ❑

Native American Trading Ban

Congress in 1996 cleared a bill (HR 3215) to repeal an 1834 law that prohibited certain federal employees and their spouses from making any business deals with Native Americans. President Clinton signed HR 3215 (PL 104-178) on Aug. 6.

The 162-year-old Trading with the Indians Act was originally enacted to protect Native Americans from unscrupulous Native American agents and other federal employees who used their positions to make private business deals that exploited Native Americans. HR 3215 primarily affected employees of the Bureau of Indian Affairs and the Indian Health Service, whose spouses had been prohibited from working on reservations or conducting business with Native Americans. Bill supporters said any legitimate conflicts of interest could be regulated under the Standards of Ethical Conduct for Government employees.

HR 3215, sponsored by J. D. Hayworth, R-Ariz., was reported from House Judiciary (H Rept 104-681) on June 17, 1996. The House passed the bill by voice vote under suspension of the rules July 29. The Senate passed HR 3215, also by voice vote, on July 31, completing congressional action. The Senate Indian Affairs Committee had approved identical legislation (S 199) on June 24, which it reported (S Rept 104-349) on Aug. 1.   ❑

Native American Child Protection

Congress in 1995 cleared legislation (S 441) authorizing $43 million a year through fiscal 1997 to extend the 1990 Indian child protection act (PL 101-630), a law to fight child abuse on Native American reservations. President Clinton signed the measure (PL 104-16) on June 21. *(1990 law, Congress and the Nation Vol. VIII, p. 883)*

The 1990 law authorized funds to treat abuse victims and set up safeguards to ensure that workers dealing with Native American children did not have criminal records. But, as of 1995, the Bureau of Indian Affairs (BIA) had yet to issue regulations implementing the act. The 1990 law also called for the creation of 12 family service centers to develop policies and provide treatment for child abuse and family violence in Native American tribes. The BIA had not created the centers, although some bureau regional offices had assigned existing employees to tasks dealing with child abuse. S 441 authorized $3 million a year to create the centers.

Senate Indian Affairs reported the bill (S Rept 104-53) on April 18, 1995. Committee Chairman John McCain, R-Ariz., sponsored the measure. The Senate passed S 441 by voice vote April 26; the House, June 8, completing congressional action.   ❑

Native American Adoption

The Senate passed (S 1962) and a House committee reported (HR 3828) legislation in 1996 to expedite the legal process for adopting Native American children.

Both measures sought to amend the Indian Child Welfare Act of 1978 (PL 95-608) by setting strict deadlines throughout the adoption process to assure all parties, including the child's tribe, a chance to participate. For example, time periods would be set for notifying a Native American tribe that a Native American child was up for adoption, for the tribe to intervene, and for the biological parents to withdraw consent for the adoption. The legislation aimed to create some certainty in the adoption process; in a handful of cases, tribes had attempted to intervene after children were placed with adoptive families.

Senate sponsor and Indian Affairs Committee Chairman John McCain, R-Ariz., said S 1962 embodied a consensus reached by the National Congress of American Indians. That agreement assured Native American tribes that they would receive prompt notice when a Native American child was involved in an adoption, a key demand of tribal leaders. Also included was "hammer language" that would impose penalties on lawyers or other private parties for lying or hiding the fact that a child was a Native American. Adoptive parents and adoption lawyers received assurances that, if a tribe waived its rights to intervene or failed to register its objection within the established time frame, it could no longer interfere in an adoption.

S 1962 also encouraged open adoptions, in which a child would live with adoptive parents but be in regular contact with the birth parents. When such visitations were approved by all parties, they would be enforceable by law.

Senate Indian Affairs reported S 1962 (S Rept 104-335) on July 26, 1996. The Senate passed the bill by voice vote Sept. 26, with an amendment to clarify that criminal penalties in the measure would apply to anyone who "knowingly and willingly" lied to the court about a child's Native American background.

The House Resources Committee reported HR 3828 (H Rept 104-808) on Sept. 19.   ❑

BIA Overhaul

The Senate Indian Affairs Committee Jan. 26, 1996, reported legislation (S 814—S Rept 104-227) to allow Native American tribes greater say in the way the Bureau of Indian Affairs (BIA) was run. S 814 would shift authority from the bureau's central office in Washington, D.C., to agency and area offices, which had the most contact with tribes. There were 12 area offices, most in major urban areas, and about 90 agency offices on or near reservations.

Bill sponsor and Committee Chairman John McCain, R-Ariz., said the legislation followed recommendations of a task force of tribal, bureau and Interior Department representatives who reported in 1994 that too much bureau power was concentrated at the top and that Native American tribes had been kept out of the budget process. BIA was created in 1824 as a link between Native American tribes and the federal government. Over the years, more than 1,000 studies concluded that it should be overhauled.

S 814 would open the way for substantial structural changes at the bureau, but it did not dictate what the changes should be, relying instead on Native American tribes to play a central role in determining what type of federal presence they wanted.

Under a substitute amendment offered by McCain and adopted by the committee, the Interior Department would have 150 days to conclude negotiations with tribes about how to revamp bureau offices and reorder funding priorities. A majority of the tribes would have to approve the reorganization plans, which would be implemented within eight months of the bill's enactment. Tribes could renegotiate the plans each year.   ❑

Native American Gaming

The Senate Indian Affairs Committee March 14, 1996, reported a bill (S 487—S Rept 104-241) to increase federal oversight of the burgeoning gaming industry run by Native Americans on tribal lands. A House companion measure (HR 1512), which would give state governments more power to regulate and limit Native American gaming, stalled.

S 487, sponsored by Committee Chairman John McCain, R-Ariz., would establish a powerful three-member Federal Indian Gaming Regulatory Commission charged with regulating an industry that generated $2.6 billion annually, according to government estimates.

The bill would authorize $5 million a year for the commission from fiscal 1997 through fiscal 1999. The commission would develop operating standards for Native American gaming nationwide. The new body would be authorized to impose fines of up to $50,000 a day for violations of such standards and would have the power to shut down gaming operations when necessary.

The panel would replace the National Gaming Commission, created by Congress in 1988 (PL 100-497), which had limited jurisdiction over gaming activities on tribal lands. *(1988 law, Congress and the Nation Vol. VII, p. 864)*

The committee adopted two amendments by Harry Reid, R-Nev., to increase the size of a federal advisory board to the commission to eight members from seven and to require that, when developing federal standards for gaming, the commission consider such factors as the sovereign rights of Native American tribes to regulate their own affairs.

Supporters of Native American gaming said the gambling operations were necessary as a means to raise money because of recent cuts in federal programs for Native Americans.

Native American gaming operations, including slot machines and casino gambling, generally operated under an agreement—known as a compact—between the state government and the tribe. But compacts had been increasingly difficult to reach in some states, particularly where gambling was illegal. Governors and state attorneys general had been reluctant to carve out exceptions for Native American tribes while fending off complaints from those who either opposed gambling or wanted to establish their own operations.

Numerous disputes between states and tribes had sparked interest in increased federal oversight. Under HR 487, a tribe would negotiate directly with the secretary of the interior—instead of with the state—after it took a state to court for failing to negotiate in good faith. States would retain the right to ban certain high-stakes gambling on tribal lands within state boundaries, and the federal government would have no authority to override state law to permit gambling in states where such activities were illegal. Primarily for that reason, Native American tribal leaders said they were unlikely to support the bill.   ❑

Native American Information Center

The Senate Indian Affairs Committee Dec. 12, 1995, approved a bill (S 1159) to establish an information clearinghouse for legislators shaping federal Native American policy. Sponsored by Daniel K. Inouye, D-Hawaii, S 1159 would create an American Indian Policy Information Center, authorized at unspecified sums through 2000. The center would be located at George Washington University in Washington, D.C., for two years, then other accredited colleges or universities could apply to house it.

Inouye said the facility was necessary because federal decisionmakers and Native American tribes had little access to policy-related information on the nation's Native American population and tribal governments. The center was to create an electronic database of Native American-related information.   ❑

Tribal Recognition

The House Resources Subcommittee on Native American and Insular Affairs June 19, 1996, approved a bill (HR 2591) to establish an administrative procedure for the federal government to recognize Native American tribes. A companion bill (S 479), sponsored by Senate Indian Affairs Committee Chairman John McCain, R-Ariz., saw no legislative action.

Federal recognition of a tribe established a formal government-to-government relationship and made tribal members eligible for federal benefits, including social services, economic development and job training. About 450 tribes were federally recognized, and 150 could have sought such a status. Under existing law, jurisdiction over tribal recognition was shared by the executive and legislative branches. The process took about 12 to 14 years on average to complete.

HR 2591, sponsored by Del. Eni F. H. Faleomavaega, D-Am. Samoa, would give the executive branch exclusive jurisdiction by creating a Commission on Indian Recognition, with three full-time members nominated by the president and confirmed by the Senate. The independent commission would hear and decide petitions for recognition. Under existing law, the Interior Department managed such requests..   ❑

CHAPTER 15

Inside Congress

Inside Congress

"Reform" was the watchword in Congress in 1993–1996. When the 103rd Congress officially opened with its record number of women and minorities, talk of change filled the air. The large freshman class was intent on making its mark; incumbents promised that they had heard the voters' message and were going to improve the operations of both chambers. But actual reforms proved harder to come by. Partisan politics still prevailed despite claims by both sides that gridlock would be broken. And one respected commentator noted freshman members were neither reformers nor innovators but "dutiful Democrats and regular Republicans."

Along with pledges of reform were promises—and hopes—that Congress could burnish images, especially in the wake of the uproar in 1991–1992 over shoddy practices in the House bank and inquiries into operations of the House Post Office. Instead, each chamber found itself enmeshed in difficult ethics cases. For example, the Senate was faced with an inquiry into sexual misconduct allegations against Bob Packwood, R-Ore., which turned into an uncomfortable airing of privacy issues over Packwood's personal diaries. And in the House, Dan Rostenkowski, D-Ill., the influential chairman of the Ways and Means Committee, was fighting off allegations relating to questionable dealings at the House Post Office. By the end of 1994, despite enormous amounts of time and effort, none of the changes that congressional Democrats and President Clinton wanted to make in the way Congress operated had become law.

The Democrats suffered stunning losses at the poll on election day in November 1994. As a result, for the first time in 40 years, the Republicans became the majority in both chambers of Congress.

REPUBLICAN MAJORITY

Rep. Newt Gingrich, R-Ga., widely regarded as the mastermind of the GOP's 1994 upset victory, moved quickly to consolidate power at the beginning of the 104th Congress like no Speaker since Republican Joseph "Uncle Joe" Cannon of Illinois early in the twentieth century. In part, Gingrich capitalized on two previous decades of incremental change that had gradually centralized control in the Speaker's office. Bolstered by wide support in the Republican Conference, Gingrich effectively named the new House committee chairmen, although the power to appoint chairmen technically belonged to the Republican Committee on Committees. In a dramatic break with tradition, Gingrich also appointed several freshmen to subcommittee chairmanships, and he gave freshmen seats on the major committees—Appropriations, Commerce, Budget, Ways and Means, and Rules. The moves cemented the already strong loyalty that the younger members felt for Gingrich.

On the first day of the 104th Congress, the House worked overtime to change the way it did business. The effort to modify House rules was in keeping with a pledge that Republicans made in the "Contract with America" they unveiled in the 1994 election campaign. The House approved a series of GOP proposals—usually with broad bipartisan support—that gave the House majority leadership more power, made it easier to cut spending but harder to raise taxes, and increased public scrutiny of House actions.

The most significant provisions ended funding for three House committees and 28 legislative caucuses; cut the committee staff by one-third; limited members to three consecutive terms as committee or subcommittee chairs or four consecutive terms as Speaker; barred committees from meeting in private, with limited exceptions; required committees to allow radio and television coverage; and required committee members to be present to establish a quorum or to vote. The House also eliminated a procedural barrier to amendments that proposed to bar spending on a specific program—a technique used to block the administration from carrying out a disputed policy. An additional rule required a three-fifths majority to pass any legislation containing an income tax increase. The House and Senate quickly passed another major reform, a bill requiring Congress to comply with the same workplace laws that other employers had to obey.

The Senate experienced many of the same pressures to change as the House, but it handled them in its own, more deliberate, fashion. For example, the Senate in 1995 voted to cut

REFERENCES

Discussion of congressional affairs for the years 1945–1964 may be found in *Congress and the Nation Vol. I*, pp. 1407–1431; for the years 1965–1968, *Congress and the Nation Vol. II*, pp. 893–924; for the years 1969–1972, *Congress and the Nation Vol. III*, pp. 353–433; for the years 1973–1976, *Congress and the Nation Vol. IV*, pp. 743–794; for the years 1977–1980, *Congress and the Nation Vol. V*, pp. 873–953; for the years 1981–1984, *Congress and the Nation Vol. VI*, pp. 797–840; for the years 1985–1988, *Congress and the Nation Vol VII*. pp. 871–910; for the years 1989–1992, *Congress and the Nation Vol. VIII*, pp. 913–988.

committee budgets, which resulted in staff reduction of almost 250 positions, but it was more reluctant than the House to purge the institution of entire committees or other panels on which senators relied.

Subsequently, in both chambers, the Republican leadership's interest in institutional self-examination began to wane. The rank and file, however, had other ideas. Reform-minded Republicans joined Democrats to force votes on proposals to clamp down on gifts to lawmakers and increase disclosure by lobbyists. Both measures passed by wide margins. But campaign finance reform stalled, and a hotly disputed proposal to amend the Constitution to limit congressional terms also went nowhere.

CONGRESSIONAL ETHICS

Furthermore, Congress's image on the ethics front continued to suffer. In the high-profile case of Sen. Packwood, the Senate Ethics Committee in September 1995 called for his expulsion. Packwood resigned rather than force the Senate to air openly the charges against him, which included sexual harassment and tampering with evidence. In addition, House Speaker Gingrich was dogged by numerous allegations of misconduct. After two years of denials, Gingrich acknowledged Dec. 21, 1996, that he failed to obtain proper legal advice when he used tax-exempt money for purposes that appeared to be political. He also admitted that he twice gave "inaccurate, incomplete, and unreliable" information to the ethics committee, but said he did so inadvertently.

The GOP leaders conducted an intense public and private campaign to reassure rank-and-file members that the violations were technical and not serious enough to warrant Gingrich's removal as Speaker. The effort paid off when Gingrich won a second term in the top House leadership post, the first Republican to do so in almost 68 years. In January 1997, the House voted to reprimand Gingrich—the first such punishment meted out to a sitting Speaker—and to impose a fine for partial reimbursement of the cost of the investigation to the ethics committee. While Gingrich was able to retain his post, support among the party faithful for the once high-flying Speaker was badly shaken.

Chronology of Action on Congress: Members and Procedures

1993–1994

Ethical and legal problems dogged a number of members of the 103rd Congress. In one of the most high-profile cases, an indictment was handed down against Rep. Dan Rostenkowski, D-Ill., for his involvement in the House Post Office scandal. Rostenkowski subsequently was forced to relinquish the chairmanship of the House Ways and Means Committee, which he had held since 1981, and lost his bid for reelection in 1994. Also garnering considerable media attention was Sen. Bob Packwood, R-Ore., who faced charges of sexual harassment brought by two dozen women. Heightening interest in Packwood's predicament was the revelation of the existence of diaries covering the senator's entire tenure in Congress.

A congressional reform effort came to naught in 1993–1994. A joint committee formed to study how Congress operated offered recommendations for changes, but partisan differences kept them from being implemented. Support also fell short for legislation requiring that labor laws governing companies in the private sector also be applied to Congress and its agencies. However, the House did adopt a rule to subject the chamber to workplace compliance requirements.

The House also allowed its delegates to vote on the floor in the Committee of the Whole, albeit with the proviso that their votes would not count if they affected the outcome of an issue.

Organization

While leadership changes were minimal in the 103rd Congress, the new faces on the GOP side increasingly reflected its ideological conservatism and confrontational style.

Democrats in the House instituted rules changes with the purpose, they maintained, of streamlining the legislative process and enhancing leadership power to direct it. To Republicans, the new rules were a transparent effort to bind and gag them.

SENATE

Senate Democrats and Republicans kept their leadership teams virtually intact.

Majority Leadership

No top leadership races were contested on the Democratic side. Reelected in a closed-door caucus Nov. 10, 1992, were George J. Mitchell, Maine, as majority leader; Wendell H. Ford, Ky., as majority whip; and David Pryor, Ark., as secretary of the Democratic Conference. Robert C. Byrd, W.Va., continued to serve as president pro tempore.

Minority Leadership

On the Republican side, Bob Dole of Kansas was reelected by acclamation. Alan K. Simpson, Wyo., was returned as minority whip, beating a long-shot challenge by Slade Gorton, Wash.,

25–14. Republican Conference Chairman Thad Cochran, Miss., was reelected without opposition. Conservative Trent Lott, Miss., won the single open race, replacing the defeated Bob Kasten, Wis., as secretary of the Republican Conference. Lott's main opponent, the more moderate Christopher S. Bond, Mo., got 14 votes, while five voted for Frank H. Murkowski, Alaska.

Committees

When Lloyd Bentsen of Texas left the chairmanship of Senate Finance to become Treasury secretary, Daniel Patrick Moynihan, N.Y., succeeded him with no opposition. Max Baucus, Mont., assumed the chairmanship of Environment and Public Works, which Moynihan vacated to become Finance chairman. With his eight-year term on the Intelligence Committee expiring, David L. Boren, Okla., stepped down as chairman; he was succeeded by Dennis DeConcini, Ariz. John D. Rockefeller IV, W.Va., took over as chairman of Veterans' Affairs from Alan Cranston, Calif., who had retired. Richard H. Bryan, Nev., succeeded Terry Sanford, N.C., as chairman of the Ethics Committee. Sanford had been defeated for reelection to the Senate.

Nancy Landon Kassebaum, Kan., replaced Orrin G. Hatch, Utah, as ranking Republican on the Labor and Human Resources Committee. Hatch succeeded Strom Thurmond, S.C., as top GOP member of the Judiciary Committee. Thurmond, in turn, became ranking Republican on Armed Services, succeeding John W. Warner, Va., who became vice chairman of Intelligence. Warner succeeded Murkowski on Intelligence; Murkowski then replaced Arlen Specter, Pa., as the ranking member on Veterans' Affairs. Alfonse M. D'Amato, N.Y., took over the ranking GOP slot on Banking and Urban Affairs; Jake Garn, Utah, had retired from Congress. On the Rules Committee, Larry Pressler, S.D., succeeded Bob Kasten, Wis., as ranking Republican. Kasten had been defeated for reelection to the Senate. Mitch McConnell, Ky., assumed the vice chairmanship of the Ethics Committee; Warren B. Rudman, N.H., had retired from Congress.

HOUSE

A bigger shake-up in top committee posts took place than in House majority and minority leadership positions. The Democrats and Republicans also adopted a number of rules changes.

Majority Leadership

The full House on Jan. 5, 1993, reelected Thomas S. Foley, Wash., as Speaker on a straight party-line vote of 255–174. He was challenged by Robert H. Michel, R-Ill., the minority leader since 1981. *(Foley's 1994 electoral defeat, box, p. 864)*

At their organizing caucus Dec. 7–10, 1992, House Democrats unanimously renamed Richard A. Gephardt, Mo., as majority leader; David E. Bonior, Mich., as majority whip; and Steny H. Hoyer, Md., as chairman of the Democratic Caucus. Vic Fazio, Calif., also continued as chairman of the Democratic Congressional Campaign Committee.

Minority Leadership

When the House GOP Conference met Dec. 7–9, 1992, Minority Leader Michel and Minority Whip Newt Gingrich, Ga.,

SPEAKER FOLEY'S ELECTORAL DEFEAT

The rout that swept the Democrats out of power Nov. 8, 1994, took with it a string of prominent lawmakers—chief among them Thomas S. Foley, D-Wash., the first House Speaker to be defeated since 1862.

Foley got 49.5 percent of the vote to his challenger's 50.5 percent. No single misstep toppled him. Instead, his Republican rival, George Nethercutt, a Spokane lawyer and former Spokane County GOP chairman, was able to paint Foley's long career as the profile of an entrenched and worn politician. He pounced on Foley for challenging the constitutionality of a term limit initiative approved by Washington state voters in 1992. While Foley maintained that he wanted only to preserve the integrity of the House, Nethercutt made much of the image: career politician locked in a litigious relationship with his constituents. The National Rifle Association, Foley's longtime ally, also trained its sights on the Speaker for supporting a ban on military-style assault weapons. *(Term limits, Congress and the Nation Vol. VIII, p. 963)*

Foley was elected to Congress in 1964. His steady climb to the pinnacle of his party came without the kind of vaunting ambition usually associated with such success. In 1974, he chaired the Democratic Study Group, which was the strategy and research arm of liberal and moderate Democrats. The next year, he became House Agriculture Committee chairman in unusual circumstances. His predecessor, the elderly and conservative W. R. Poage, D-Texas, was targeted for removal by the large bloc of reform-minded "Watergate baby" Democrats. Ever the institutionalist, Foley backed Poage; but, when he was unseated, the insurgents promoted Foley over several more senior members.

Foley continued to rise within Democratic ranks, becoming chairman of the caucus in 1977. After the 1980 election, the majority whip's job opened up. Speaker Thomas P. "Tip" O'Neill Jr., D-Mass., facing an adversarial relationship with newly elected President Ronald Reagan, was looking for someone with parliamentary skills. Rep. Dan Rostenkowski, D-Ill., was first in line, but when he decided to take over the House Ways and Means Committee instead, Foley was selected. When O'Neill announced his plan to retire at the end of the 99th Congress, Foley did not seem to be guaranteed the majority leader's spot, but no challenger emerged. The same dynamic was apparent when, in 1989, Foley rose without opposition to succeed Jim Wright, D-Texas, as Speaker.

Foley's characteristic graciousness, rooted in reverence for the House, thwarted him as he struggled to balance his dual role as the institutional leader of the House against his partisan position as congressional torchbearer of his party. For example, in the 102nd Congress, as the scandal involving members' overdrafts at the House bank unraveled, Foley's measured response looked to panicked colleagues like indecision. Members blamed him for failing to anticipate the outrage of the electorate. Foley reacted by pushing reforms of House procedures and asserted himself more directly to project a Democratic legislative agenda. Moreover, he politicked for his own job, lining up the support of key chairmen and campaigning in behalf of members, senior and junior alike. Bill Clinton's election further invigorated Foley and strengthened his support. His colleagues had often bristled at his laidback style and tendency to seek conciliation during George Bush's presidency. At the outset of the Clinton administration, Foley succeeded in pushing the president's politically hazardous economic program to passage in the House. However, throughout the early months of 1993, many Democrats, including some who had chastised him as unwilling to lead, chafed at being pushed and shoved.

Foley's defeat at the polls marked only the third time that a sitting Speaker had been denied reelection, according to the House historian, Raymond W. Smock. William Pennington, R-N.J., lost in 1860; Galusha A. Grow, R-Pa., in 1862.

---

were unchallenged in their bids for reelection to the leadership. *(Michel's retirement, box, p. 866)*

The most hotly contested race was for the No. 3 job on the minority leadership ladder: chairman of the Republican Conference. Jerry Lewis, Calif., was unseated, 88–84, by Dick Armey, Texas. The more conservative and confrontational Armey had accused the more moderate and easy-going Lewis of being too accommodating to the Democrats.

Promoted to the leadership unopposed were Henry J. Hyde, Ill., as chairman of the Republican Policy Committee and Bill Paxon, N.Y., as chairman of the National Republican Congressional Committee. Hyde and Paxon succeeded Mickey Edwards, Okla., and Guy Vander Jagt, Mich., respectively, both of whom had suffered primary defeats.

Rules

The House Jan. 5, 1993, adopted a far-reaching package of rules changes (H Res 5) on a largely party-line vote of 221–199. Republicans were most vocally opposed to a change giving the four delegates and the resident commissioner—all Democrats—the power to vote on the floor when the House met in the Committee of the Whole. *(Delegate voting privileges, p. 881)*

The eight major committees plus the Government Operations and House Administration panels were limited to six subcommittees, reduced from eight; the remaining committees could have five. The Appropriations and the Ways and Means committees were exempt from the limit. Protests by the Congressional Black Caucus and several African ambassadors persuaded House leaders to support a waiver of the rule for the Foreign Affairs Committee. The committee was allowed a seventh subcommittee, ensuring the survival of a separate panel devoted to Africa. Members could be assigned to no more than five subcommittees—including select committees and task forces, except for the Select Intelligence Committee.

Committees would be allowed to meet while the House or the Committee of the Whole was in session. Previously, the "five-minute rule" prevented committees from meeting, without permission of the House, while amendments were being debated on the floor. Democrats claimed the five-minute rule made scheduling committee meeting and routine floor action difficult; Republicans argued that the new rule would discourage floor participation and permit chairmen to abuse the system.

Committee chairmen were allowed to declare the quorum needed to draft legislation once a majority of members were in attendance for some part of the session. Previously, a bill could be ruled out of order once it reached the House floor if a quorum had not been present at the same time during committee action.

The Speaker was given the power to remove any House conferee from a House-Senate conference or add members. Democrats said the purpose was to prevent gridlock, but Republicans protested that the Speaker was being given too much power.

The Speaker also was allowed to delay for two legislative days debate on privileged motions dealing with the rights of the House collectively and the integrity of its proceedings. Previously, privileged motions took precedence over other floor action. Left unaffected were the privileged motions offered by majority and minority leaders and those regarding an individual member's rights, which would continue to receive immediate attention.

Once a principal method of voting, "teller votes"—in which members filed past stations where the number for and against a question was counted—were abolished on the ground that they wasted time.

The House Democratic Caucus on Dec. 9, 1992, voted 174–35 to set strict limits on special orders, the time reserved at the end of the day for members to speak on any subject. Under the proposed rules change, the speeches could not go on for more than three hours or after 9 p.m., whichever came first. Democrats hoped to save money and to curb what they saw as GOP use of the House floor for political issues instead of legislation. Republicans viewed the speeches, which were broadcast nationwide on the Cable Satellite Public Affairs Network (C-SPAN), as a rare and essential chance for the minority party to be heard. At Speaker Foley's behest, the caucus subsequently reversed its position. It also retreated from a proposed rules change to limit each party to 10 one-minute speeches at the beginning of the day. One-minutes, as they were known, would go on as long as party leaders permitted.

The House Sept. 28, 1993, voted 384–40 to adopt a resolution (H Res 134) to make public the signatures on discharge petitions, which bring measures that were bottled up in committee to the floor. The action overturned a 61-year-old precedent under which signatures were kept secret until a majority (218 members) had signed a petition. James M. Inhofe, R-Okla., led the effort, with the strong support of the *Wall Street Journal* editorial page, independent presidential candidate Ross Perot and conservative radio talk show hosts across the country. Inhofe and Republicans said the secrecy allowed the Democratic leadership to more easily pressure members to withhold signatures for bills it opposed, such as term limits, the line-item veto and the balanced budget amendment. House leaders argued that the change could permit bills to come to the floor without proper committee consideration. They also warned that ending the se-

crecy could result in members feeling pressured to sign discharge petitions, thereby increasing the influence of interest groups and thwarting the House's deliberative pace. Nevertheless, the tide toward openness could not be stemmed, so the leadership backed off formal opposition to the proposal.

During a closed-door session June 9, 1993, the House Democratic Caucus decided not to take any action against 11 subcommittee chairmen who had voted against President Clinton's economic package. Before the critical May 27 House vote was taken on the reconciliation bill (HR 2264), freshman Leslie L. Byrne of Virginia circulated a petition calling for the caucus to remove any committee or subcommittee chairman who opposed the Clinton package, in the name of party discipline. Within hours, she had collected 81 signatures, more than enough to demand a vote on whether to remove a chairman. Two chief deputy whips and eight committee chairmen signed the petition. *(Reconciliation, p. 44)*

The House on Oct. 7, 1994, voted overwhelmingly, 348–3, to approve a resolution (H Res 578) that amended House rules to make the House subject to the labor laws it enacted. The House took the action because stronger legislation (HR 4822) had stalled in the Senate. *(Workplace compliance, p. 882)*

The House Republican Conference voted 82–44 on Dec. 8, 1992, to approve a proposal prohibiting anyone in the caucus from holding any committee's top post (chairman or ranking member) for more than six consecutive years. The decision represented a fundamental shift for Republicans, who even more than Democrats usually gave their top committee posts to each panel's most senior member. The proposal had strong backing from the GOP freshman class, many of whom supported congressional term limits in their campaigns and promised to voluntarily retire from Congress after a set number of terms. Opposition came mostly from senior members who feared they would lose their committee leadership slots six years hence.

In other action, the conference agreed to prohibit most committees' ranking Republicans from serving as top GOP members of any subcommittee starting in 1995, thus empowering junior members at the expense of senior members; to give the freshman class a spot in the leadership; to require that whenever the Republicans were granted a preferential motion—to instruct conferees to adopt a certain position in negotiations with the Senate, for example—the leadership had to choose the proposal that best reflected the views of the GOP caucus and leaders; and to give the leadership more sway over top Republican committee members by requiring them to work closely with the leadership in drafting written plans for dealing with key issues.

House Republicans Aug. 4, 1993, approved a rule requiring committee and party leaders who were indicted to relinquish their posts. But the new policy did not apply to pending cases, thus exempting Joseph M. McDade, Pa., the ranking Republican on the Appropriations Committee. He had been indicted in 1992 on charges of taking favors, bribes and illegal gratuities. The Democratic Caucus already had a similar rule in effect. Under both parties' rules, indicted committee and subcommittee leaders had to step aside in favor of the next ranking member if indicted for a felony punishable by two years or more in prison.

MICHEL'S RETIREMENT

Upon his retirement at the end of the 103rd Congress, House Minority Leader Robert H. Michel, R-Ill., had the unfortunate distinction of having served in the House minority longer than any other member in history. Michel's departure from the party hierarchy also marked the ascendancy of a confrontational brand of Republicanism, making his consensus-oriented style seem like an anachronism.

Michel began his career on Capitol Hill as a congressional staffer, serving as administrative assistant to Rep. Harold Velde (R-Ill., 1949–1957), the chairman of the House Un-American Activities Committee from 1953 to 1955. Succeeding the retiring Velde, Michel was elected in 1956, the year Dwight D. Eisenhower won his second term as president and two years after Republicans lost their majority in the House.

In his second term, Michel became a member of the Appropriations Committee, where he served for a quarter century. Michel said his committee work taught him the importance of detail and the art of collaborative politics. He was chairman of the House Republican's campaign committee in the post-Watergate election of 1974, which produced 75 Democratic freshmen. Michel's GOP colleagues did not hold the election results against him, however; they elected him minority whip.

In 1980, during organization for the 97th Congress, the more junior and conservative elements of the House GOP rebelled against Minority Leader John J. Rhodes of Arizona. Michel was elevated to minority leader, beating Guy Vander Jagt of Michigan by 103–87. Michel's first two years as party leader were almost certainly his most exciting. Ronald Reagan's administration depended on his sense of strategy and timing in moving its budget and tax cuts through the Democratic House. Michel's ties to GOP moderates and Democratic conservatives helped marshal the needed votes.

However, a cadre of feistier conservatives—centering on the class of 1978, which included Rep. Newt Gingrich, R-Ga.—was growing. They focused more on drawing clear lines between parties than on finding common ground in legislation. This school of thought gained more and more adherents among the Republicans elected in the 1980s. They began a stampede from the back benches to the leadership in 1989, when Gingrich was elected minority whip. Every Congress after that, more conservative activists joined Gingrich in the leadership. Michel became increasingly isolated, although he was too respected to be pushed from office. But Gingrich did talk to colleagues about his aim of becoming leader—leaving the clear impression that he would run for the top GOP spot in the 104th Congress whether Michel retired or not.

When he announced his retirement on Oct. 4, 1994, Michel said he saw "a big generational gap between my style of leadership and my sense of values and my whole thinking processes" and those of the younger, more confrontational leaders. Without naming names, he decried members bent on "trashing the institution," as well as those who chose confrontation before compromise.

If the charges were dropped or reduced or if the member was acquitted, the member would resume the committee leadership post. If the member was convicted or censured by the House, caucus members would choose a permanent replacement. *(McDade, p. 875)*

Committees

The Democrats' Steering and Policy Committee stripped the ailing Jamie L. Whitten, Miss., of his Appropriations Committee chairman title, and the appropriations panel—voting 7–29—took away his chairmanship of the Agriculture Subcommittee. William H. Natcher, Ky., had assumed day-to-day running of the full committee during the 102nd Congress after Whitten suffered a stroke. Steering and Policy on Dec. 8, 1992, gave Natcher the title as well as the job of chairman of House Appropriations. The next day Richard J. Durbin, Ill., won the subcommittee chairmanship, with 35 votes for him and one abstention. *(Congressional milestones, box, p. 868)*

At the beginning of the 103rd Congress, Lee H. Hamilton, Ind., stepped up to the chairmanship from the second slot on Foreign Affairs to succeed retiring Dante B. Fascell, Fla. Norman Y. Mineta, Calif., became chairman of Public Works and Transportation as a result of the retirements of incumbent chairman Robert A. Roe, N.J., and the more senior committee member Glenn M. Anderson, Calif.

President Clinton opened two additional House committee chairmanships when he named Leon E. Panetta, Calif., as director of the Office of Management and Budget and Les Aspin, Wis., as defense secretary. Martin Olav Sabo, Minn., and John M. Spratt Jr., S.C., vied for the top spot on the House Budget Committee, which had been headed by Panetta. On Jan. 6, 1993, behind closed doors, Democrats chose Sabo, by 149–112. Despite the stark philosophical differences between the two, observers said Sabo's win was more the result of the well-liked representative's networking and preemptive campaigning than a measure of House Democrats' political temperature. Ronald V. Dellums, Calif., was unopposed to succeed Aspin as head of Armed Services. Despite his left-wing principles, Dellums' political savvy and procedural fair play smoothed over any skepticism about his ability to handle the job. Dellums was officially named chairman on Jan. 27, 1993, after a 198–10 vote of the Democratic Caucus.

Speaker Foley created another vacancy when he decided not to reappoint Dave McCurdy, Okla., as chairman of the Intelligence Committee. McCurdy said he was told he was being replaced mainly because he had been a committee member for nine years, far longer than the usual six-year term. But McCurdy had been known to rub the leadership and other colleagues the wrong way with his aggressiveness and ambition. He also had floated his own name as a possible challenger to Foley as Speaker. Foley named Dan Glickman, Kan., as Intelligence chairman on Jan. 11, 1993.

The Veterans' Affairs chairmanship, held by G. V. "Sonny" Montgomery, Miss., was seriously challenged by Lane Evans, Ill. Montgomery, who was very conservative and rarely supported the Democratic leadership, maintained the top spot by a four-vote margin.

Jim McDermott, Wash., was named chairman of the House Committee on Standards of Official Conduct on Feb. 4, 1993. He replaced Louis Stokes, Ohio, who had agreed to chair the committee for only the 102nd Congress.

Natcher, like Whitten before him, suffered from declining health. The House Democratic Caucus, on March 23, 1994, elected David R. Obey of Wisconsin over Neal Smith of Iowa, 152–106, as acting chairman of House Appropriations. Obey assumed permanent status when Natcher died less than a week later, on March 29.

The House's other most powerful chairmanship also turned over in 1994, when Sam M. Gibbons, Fla., assumed the gavel of the Ways and Means Committee on May 31 after Dan Rostenkowski, Ill., chairman since 1981, was indicted on criminal charges. Gibbons, who led the committee Democrats in seniority, became acting chairman under Democratic Caucus rules that required a chairman to step aside temporarily while under indictment. *(Rostenkowski, p. 870)*

Thirteen Republicans moved up as the 103rd Congress convened to become ranking minority members on full committees: John R. Kasich, Ohio, took over the ranking spot on the House Budget Committee; Pat Roberts, Kan., on Agriculture; Floyd Spence, S.C., on Armed Services; Jim Leach, Iowa, on Banking, Finance and Urban Affairs; Carlos J. Moorhead, Calif., on Energy and Commerce; Benjamin A. Gilman, N.Y., on Foreign Affairs; William F. Clinger Jr., Pa., on Government Operations; Jack Fields, Texas, on Merchant Marine and Fisheries; John T. Myers, Ind., on Post Office and Civil Service; Bud Shuster, Pa., on Public Works and Transportation; Larry Combest, Texas, on Select Intelligence; Jan Meyers, Kan., on Small Business; and Fred Grandy, Iowa, on Standards of Official Conduct.

In other committee-related action, four House select committees—which had the power to study issues but not to approve legislation—ceased to exist as of April 1, 1993. They were: Aging; Narcotics Abuse and Control; Children, Youth and Families; and Hunger. A fifth select committee, Intelligence, survived because it had a permanent authorization as well as authority to report legislation. The others had to be reviewed at the start of each Congress. Members from both sides of the aisle argued that the select committees had outlived their usefulness and were a waste of money. Another panel, the Joint Committee on the Organization of Congress, went out of existence at the end of 1993. *(Congressional reform, p. 878)* ❑

House Post Office

Repercussions continued to be felt in 1993–1994 from the scandal involving the House Post Office, which erupted in 1991. Most notably, the Justice Department investigation led to a 17-count indictment against Rep. Dan Rostenkowski, D-Ill., the powerful chairman of the House Ways and Means Committee. *(1995–1996 action, p. 906)*

BACKGROUND

The House Post Office ran its postal operations under contract with the U.S. Postal Service; it was headed by a postmaster who was an elected House official. In mid-1991, Jay B. Stephens, U.S. attorney for the District of Columbia, began looking into accusations that stamp clerks had been stealing funds from the House Post Office and dealing drugs there. Several post office employees eventually pleaded guilty to various charges. Investigations—including one by the House Administration Committee in 1992—depicted a sloppily run operation where cash and stamps were treated casually and where workers were beholden to political sponsors, not to professional managers. Its status as a House office was ended and its operations turned over to the Postal Service in 1992. *(Congress and the Nation Vol. VIII, p. 939)*

The first word of the possible involvement of House members came in May 1992, when the House learned that the grand jury probing the House Post Office had subpoenaed records of Reps. Rostenkowski, Joe Kolter, D-Pa., and Austin J. Murphy, D-Pa. A post office supervisor, James C. Smith, reportedly had told the grand jury that he helped members get thousands of dollars in cash through false transactions disguised as stamp purchases. Public records showed that Rostenkowski, Kolter and Murphy all had large amounts of stamp purchases for the six-and-a-quarter-year period under review by the grand jury: Rostenkowski, $29,672 in purchases; Kolter, $17,374; and Murphy, $9,244. Because members could send virtually all public business for free using the franking privilege, they seemed to have little need for stamps.

The Justice Department in March ordered the replacement of all U.S. attorneys who were holdovers from Republican administrations, including the District of Columbia's Stephens. Stephens protested publicly that the administration's move could disrupt the inquiry, although he did not directly accuse the administration of deliberately doing so. Administration officials insisted that their desire to install a Democratic cadre of prosecutors had nothing to do with the probe of Rostenkowski. Stephens was replaced in April by the temporary appointment of J. Ramsey Johnson. Eric Holder Jr. subsequently was chosen by President Clinton and sworn in Oct. 8.

WEAVER, ROTA GUILTY PLEAS

Gerald W. Weaver III, administrative assistant to Kolter from 1983 to 1987, pleaded guilty March 31, 1993, to three felonies related to the post office scandal and agreed to cooperate with investigators. Weaver admitted obstructing justice, distributing cocaine and conspiring to distribute more than 50 grams of cocaine. Prosecutors said Weaver bought $2,800 worth of cocaine from a postal clerk, financing the deal by cashing checks at the post office. In a failed attempt to mislead the grand jury, they said, Weaver had a former business associate concoct a letter stating that Weaver had been reimbursed for buying a similar amount of postage. Prosecutors also said that Weaver sold cocaine to lobbyists and congressional aides.

CONGRESSIONAL MILESTONES

Both Jamie L. Whitten, D-Miss., and his successor as chairman of the House Appropriations Committee, William H. Natcher, D-Ky., occupied special places in the annals of congressional service.

Whitten announced April 5, 1994, that he would not run for re-election in 1994 after 53 years in Congress, the longest service in the history of the House. Elected in a 1941 special election, Whitten began his career the month before the Japanese attack on Pearl Harbor and was on the House floor the day President Franklin D. Roosevelt gave the "Day of Infamy" speech that sent the nation into World War II. As a product of the era in which the House was dominated by conservative Democratic committee chairmen from the Solid South, Whitten adapted to changing times. In 1954, he denounced the Supreme Court's decision in *Brown v. Board of Education*, and in 1956, he signed the Southern Manifesto defending segregation. But as Whitten rose in the House, he followed the majority of his party in supporting civil rights legislation and social programs such as food stamps.

He won a seat on Appropriations in 1943 and became chairman of its Agriculture Subcommittee in 1949. He became the unsurpassed master of federal farm programs and was known as the "permanent secretary of agriculture." When the growing ranks of environmentalist liberals plotted to oust him from the agriculture chair in 1975, he kept his post by agreeing to give up power over environmental and consumer issues. As chairman of the full committee from 1979 to 1992, Whitten tried to keep the spirit of the New Deal alive. Soon after he set the record for House service on Jan. 6, 1992, he was hospitalized, reportedly after a stroke. In mid-1992, he al-

lowed Natcher to run Appropriations as acting chairman but refused to give up his title until forced to in late 1992. Although Whitten ended his career with little formal power, he left Congress after having channeled billions of dollars in federal aid to his poor, rural district in northern Mississippi. His most spectacular legacy was the Tennessee-Tombigbee Waterway, a huge public works project two decades in the making that cut through his district to create a new link to the Gulf of Mexico.

At the time of his death on March 29, 1994, Natcher was best known for a record without precedent: he had voted at every opportunity—18,401 roll calls—until illness brought him down. Natcher's struggle to maintain that record created the sort of fuss in his final days that he always abhorred. But he and the House went to extraordinary lengths to keep his string alive. On March 1, 1994, the House canceled its votes to enable Natcher to stay in the hospital for medical treatment. On March 2, he was brought to the Capitol by ambulance and wheeled into the House chamber four times on a gurney to vote. His last vote was cast just before 8 p.m. on a resolution relating to an ethics investigation of the House Post Office scandal. Natcher was unable to return on March 3, missing four votes.

Natcher had cast his first legislative vote Jan. 21, 1954, to approve the building of the Air Force Academy in Colorado. He had won office Aug. 1, 1953, in a special election, but Congress adjourned before he could be sworn in. For years, acknowledging the burden he had imposed on himself, Natcher warned other members not to try to follow in his footsteps.

More stunning to official Washington was the guilty plea entered July 19 by Robert V. Rota, the former House postmaster. Rota pleaded guilty to three misdemeanors—one count of conspiracy to embezzle and two of aiding and abetting members who he called Congressman A and Congressman B "in willfully and knowingly embezzling" U.S. funds. Prosecutors said no evidence existed that Rota pocketed any money for himself. Documents related to Rota's plea bargain detailed certain stamp purchases as fake. The alleged sham purchases made by Congressman A matched precisely with stamp purchases attributed in public House records to Rostenkowski; Congressman B's purchases matched those of Kolter.

The scheme, according to the court papers and Rota's account, worked as follows: Congressman A or Congressman B would present Rota with a signed expense voucher requesting from $600 to $2,300 worth of stamps, certifying "that they are for use in or by my office in the discharge of my duties." Sometimes the member would not have a voucher, and Rota would ask a subordinate—such as Joanna G. O'Rourke—to type one from a stack of blanks kept at the post office. O'Rourke, the former post office chief of staff, agreed to a plea bargain in 1992 in return for cooperation with prosecutors.

Rota would then take the voucher to his supervisor of ac-

counts—either Mary C. Bowman, who held that job until May 1987, or James Smith, who held it from May 1989 until mid-1992. Bowman or Smith would take the voucher from Rota and in return give him either cash or stamps. (The two-year hiatus—from May 1987 to May 1989—occurred when Paul Tomme held the accounts supervisor position. Rota said "that he could not trust the new employee [Tomme] to carry out the scheme.") If it was cash, Rota "then would and did deliver the cash to the members who had signed the vouchers," prosecutors said. If Rota came back with stamps, the member would return them later to Rota, who would redeem them for cash for the member, again through the supervisor of accounts.

Rota told the prosecutors that he had been supplying members of Congress with cash in exchange for vouchers, stamps, and campaign and political action committee checks since shortly after he became postmaster in 1972. At that time, members were allowed to "cash out" certain unused office expense accounts to supplement their incomes. The House did not specifically allow or prohibit redeeming stamps for cash, and some members took advantage of the ambiguity. Reforms implemented in 1977–1978 were supposed to end all cash-outs. As early as 1980, federal prosecutors caught wind of a cash-for-vouchers scam and asked Rota and Bowman about it. Rota admitted that he and Bowman lied to prosecutors on May 5, 1980, when they denied giving members cash. After the successful cover-up, Rota said he continued funneling money to several members, through April 1991.

On July 24, Rostenkowski held a news conference to deny that he had done anything wrong, to promise to push his legislative agenda and to announce that he had hired one of Washington's most aggressive defense lawyers, Robert S. Bennett.

1992 HOUSE ADMINISTRATION STUDY

Republicans took to the floor July 22, 1993, and demanded full disclosure of the records of the House Administration Committee task force that in 1992 had examined the House bank scandal and issued two reports, one by the GOP members and one by Democrats. Republicans suggested that the documents contained damaging information about Democrats.

Speaker Thomas S. Foley, D-Wash., initially said he would support releasing the transcripts after giving the Justice Department 10 days to review whether any of the materials would endanger its probe. However, he backed off after U.S. Attorney Johnson said in a letter that releasing anything "could have a significant adverse effect on the ongoing criminal investigation." Republicans pressed for release of the information anyway, with Minority Leader Robert H. Michel, R-Ill., introducing a resolution (H Res 222) ordering the immediate public disclosure of all the transcripts.

Democratic leaders used Johnson's letter to rally their troops around an alternative resolution (H Res 223) barring the release at least until the U.S. attorney dropped his objection. The House July 22 adopted the Democratic resolution by a mostly party-line vote of 244–183 and then agreed to a motion to table (kill) Michel's alternative 242–186.

ETHICS COMMITTEE INVESTIGATION

Some House Republicans, over the objections of their party's leaders on the House Committee on Standards of Official Conduct, began agitating for an immediate ethics investigation of Rota's allegations. H Res 238, with 17 cosponsors, was introduced by Rep. Ernest Jim Istook Jr., R-Okla., on Aug. 4, 1993. The committee had agreed to a Justice Department request that it delay an ethics inquiry until the local U.S. attorney's office finished its criminal probe. As a resolution dealing with the rights and integrity of the whole House, Istook's measure could be called up on the floor with two days' notice. Istook said he would demand a vote on the resolution after the House returned from a break Sept. 8, but he had not done so by the end of the session.

On Oct. 20, House Administration Committee leaders called for an ethics inquiry of the House Finance Office after employees told them that the office violated its rules in overseeing Rostenkowski's payroll. The move came after House employees discovered they could not locate Rostenkowski payroll records that had been subpoenaed. U.S. Attorney Holder decided not to seek an indictment before the grand jury's term expired Oct. 29.

Istook announced on Feb. 11, 1994, that he intended to call up H Res 238 on Feb. 23. Majority Leader Richard A. Gephardt, D-Mo., drafted an alternative that would give the go-ahead to an ethics committee inquiry only if the Justice Department did not object. On Feb. 23, Holder sent a letter to House leaders urging them to postpone an investigation. The same day, Istook agreed to put off action on the resolution for at least a week so that leaders could try to reach a compromise. They could not, and on March 2, the House voted 238–186 to table (kill) the Istook resolution. The action came after the House adopted, by a largely party-line vote of 241–184, a resolution (H Res 375) offered by Gephardt directing the committee to continue to consult with the U.S. attorney and to proceed with its own investigation only when it determined that "a committee inquiry would no longer interfere with the criminal investigation."

REPAYMENTS, PLEA NEGOTIATIONS

In early 1994, Rostenkowski issued three reimbursement checks to the Treasury totaling $82,095, acknowledging that taxpayer funds might have been used improperly to purchase items at the House office supply store for his own use. In a statement issued Feb. 10, Rostenkowski said he decided to repay the House "for all sums arguably due" after he reviewed several years' worth of purchases to see if they comported with House expense account rules, which he asserted were ambiguous, flexible and ever-changing. Over the weekend of Feb. 12–13, Rostenkowski's lawyer Bennett released copies of correspondence between Rostenkowski and House Administration Committee Chairman Charlie Rose, D-N.C., explaining the repayments. Rostenkowski said that many of the items—including clocks, china, books, luggage and furniture—had been used for official purposes but that he could not find records to prove it. Some items, he said, were used as gifts to officials, and he said he was not aware that this violated House Administration Committee rules.

After Rostenkowski's reimbursement was disclosed, Democratic and Republican leaders agreed to have their staffs look into what role, if any, House officers and employees played in arranging the repayment. Leadership aides met during the week of Feb. 14 with Bennett, who told them that Rostenkowski had consulted only with House Administration Committee staff. Republicans, who had complained about the pace of the investigation since the Clinton administration took over the case, raised questions about the repayment. Minority Whip Newt Gingrich, R-Ga., demanded more information. House Administration Committee Chairman Rose refused to make his aides available to Gingrich's staff, but he said he would meet with Gingrich personally to answer his concerns, such as why he did not advise Rostenkowski to pay the House instead of the Treasury and why House leaders were not informed.

With rumors of plea negotiations and an impending indictment circulating around Washington, Rostenkowski on May 30 issued a statement declaring that he would fight to the end: "Federal prosecutors threaten to indict me if I fail to plead guilty to a series of crimes I did not commit. I will not make any deals with them. I did not commit any crimes." Rostenkowski said that, if he were indicted, he would relinquish his Ways and Means chairmanship but remain active in committee deliberations. House Democratic Caucus rules stipulated that a committee chairman accused or convicted of a felony punishable by two years' imprisonment or more must step down until the charges were dropped or reduced or the member was acquitted.

ROSTENKOWSKI INDICTMENT

On May 31, Holder announced in Washington, D.C., at a news conference carried live on the Cable News Network (CNN) and Chicago television that Rostenkowski had been indicted on 17 criminal charges. Though long anticipated, the indictment stunned Rostenkowski supporters and critics alike, for it accused him more directly and in more detail than expected. If convicted on all charges, Rostenkowski was likely to face up to six years in prison under sentencing guidelines that included enhanced penalties for crimes involving obstruction of justice. Rostenkowski reportedly had turned down a deal that would have given him about six months in jail and a $150,000 fine (minus the $82,095 repayment and the value of cars that would have been repossessed). As part of the deal, prosecutors would have stopped pursuing cases against his aides.

According to figures cited in the indictment, Rostenkowski misused $668,000 in public funds and $56,267 in campaign funds, for a total of $724,267. Rostenkowski's alleged crimes and the evidence against him could be divided into four areas:

• **Ghost Employees.** The government said Rostenkowski padded his payroll with so-called ghost employees, people who did little or no official work. Most allegedly were paid public funds for personal, business or campaign services provided to Rostenkowski and his family. Rostenkowski allegedly maintained close personal control over his payroll and instructed House finance officials not to disclose information about it to his aides. He placed some individuals on his payroll at irregular intervals, the government said, and he arranged to have the same payroll counselor oversee his account for more than a decade, in violation of a two-year rotation policy. Several of the alleged ghost employees were required to return their pay to Rostenkowski's Chicago district office manager, who supposedly paid them "substantially smaller" sums as they performed services for Rostenkowski.

The indictment listed 14 people paid a total of $529,200 over varying periods of time between July 1971 and July 1992 as doing little or no official work. Cited only by number, the employees were identified on June 1 by the *Chicago Sun-Times*. All but a few of the 14 said they did official work for their pay, sometimes at home.

The government faced possible statute-of-limitations challenges because the payments involved in nine of the charges were more than five years old, and four more involved at least some payments over the five-year limit.

• **Stationery Store Purchases.** Rostenkowski was accused of spending about $42,200 in taxpayer funds for items at the House stationery store that he or his family gave away as gifts or kept for personal use. These included items for which the representative had reimbursed the government in early 1994.

• **Stamps for Cash.** The indictment alleged that Rostenkowski pocketed at least $49,300 in cash from the House Post Office through sham transactions made to look like stamp pur-

chases. Rostenkowski allegedly worked the scheme with Rota, the postmaster. Rostenkowski supposedly got cash in three ways: First, from 1978 to 1987, he traded stamps he previously procured with House expense vouchers for cash; the indictment detailed seven such transactions worth $11,500. Second, in 1989–1990, he traded stamps or stamp vouchers for cash; the indictment said $9,800 was taken in this period. Third, in 1989–1990, he cashed $28,000 in checks from his campaign and political action committee (America's Leaders Fund) and reported them as postage purchases on Federal Election Commission reports.

The indictment alleged previously unknown details about the stamp scam: Rota supposedly gave Rostenkowski a computer-generated list so he could compare his annual stamp purchases with those of other members. Rostenkowski supposedly promised Rota that he would pay Rota's legal bills, on the day after Rota resigned in March 1992. "Rostenkowski then instructed Rota, 'Remember—I always got my stamps,'" the indictment said. Rota, it added, then falsely denied knowing of the scheme to congressional investigators.

Investigators had determined from voucher numbers and typewriter analysis that some of the vouchers suspected of being phony came from a supply kept in the post office, not from Rostenkowski's office supply.

• **Family Vehicles.** Rostenkowski obtained personal ownership and clear title to a series of seven vehicles for himself and his family from Wil-Shore Motor Sales in suburban Chicago by paying the dealership $73,500 in House funds and $28,267 in campaign funds—a total of $101,767. The only personal payment made by Rostenkowski and his family on a Wil-Shore debt of more than $100,000 was $5,294 from a daughter, the government said. The indictment said Rostenkowski had an account at Wil-Shore that allowed him to take lien-free title to cars without down payment, promissory notes or interest.

The House funds came in the form of seventy monthly payments of $1,050 each made on "fraudulent lease agreements" filed with the House Finance Office. The leases were supposedly for "mobile district offices," but the government said the vans became Rostenkowski's personal property and "were seldom if ever used for official purposes." He also allegedly used $1,800 in taxpayer funds to garage one of his vans for 18 months in a three-year period.

AFTERMATH OF INDICTMENT

In the aftermath of the indictment, Rostenkowski parted company with Bennett on June 2, replacing him soon afterward with an experienced trial lawyer, Dan K. Webb.

House Republicans again pressed for release of thousands of documents from the House Administration Committee's 1992 probe. After U.S. Attorney Holder said June 9 that he no longer objected, the Democrats backed a GOP release resolution (H Res 450), and it was adopted 399–2. The House released 3,293 pages of secret transcripts on July 7. As expected, they contained no major revelations but provided details backing up the investigation's finding that the mismanaged mail operation's top officials were bent on pleasing certain members by doing special favors that sometimes had little to do with official mail delivery. Among the new details were statements from mailroom workers that top postal officials were especially eager to please Rostenkowski, dispatching workers to help answer his office phones and stamp his name on calendars to be mailed to constituents.

On June 30, Rep. Christopher Shays, R-Conn., filed an ethics complaint against Rostenkowski based on the indictment. Pressured by Republicans to at least open a preliminary inquiry, an ethics panel delegation met with Holder on Aug. 11 to see if anything could be investigated without interfering with the prosecutors. The answer was no. The House ethics committee on Aug. 17 voted again to defer investigating Rostenkowski.

Rostenkowski pleaded not guilty to graft charges on June 10. Taking an aggressive tack, Rostenkowski's lawyers on Aug. 5 went to court asking to have the entire indictment against him dismissed on separation-of-powers grounds. Rostenkowski's lawyers argued in court papers that the charges violated constitutional provisions giving Congress the power to make and enforce its own rules and shielding members from prosecutions based on legislative acts. They also said House rules on office budgets and campaign funds were so vague and gave members so much discretion that the case was "ill-suited for judicial resolution." In papers filed Sept. 2, lawyers working for Holder argued that Rostenkowski was claiming, "in effect, that the Constitution places the whole question of whether he systematically looted the public treasury beyond the reach of the criminal law." Prosecutors also said the indictment was far removed from the legislative process—speeches, committee deliberations and the like. "His argument . . . is really a pitch for virtually absolute legislative immunity for any acts, even administrative ones, that are at all connected to his official (not legislative) duties," they said.

U.S. District Judge Norma Holloway Johnson Oct. 14 rejected Rostenkowski's arguments. Rostenkowski's attorneys filed an appeal with the U.S. Court of Appeals for the District of Columbia Circuit on Oct. 25. The case was still pending at the end of 1994.

Rostenkowski lost his reelection bid on Nov. 8 to Michael Patrick Flanagan, a Republican.

KOLTER INDICTMENT

Former representative Kolter was indicted Oct. 18, 1994, on five counts stemming from the House Post Office investigation. He was accused of billing $33,000 worth of personal purchases at the House stationery store to official accounts and converting $11,000 worth of postage stamps to cash for his own use. The indictment stated that Kolter instructed Rota to convert vouchers and stamps into cash over a six-year period. Kolter pleaded not guilty on Oct. 28. He served in the House from 1983 to 1993 and was defeated in a primary in 1992.   ❑

Ethics Probes

Besides Rep. Dan Rostenkowski, D-Ill., and former representative Joe Kolter, D-Pa., who were caught up in the House Post Office scandal, a number of members from both the House and Senate faced ethical misconduct and criminal charges during 1993–1994. (*House Post Office, p. 867*)

SEN. BOB PACKWOOD

The Senate Ethics Committee continued its probe in 1993–1994 of sexual harassment charges leveled against Sen. Bob Packwood, R-Ore., with no resolution. (*1995–1996 action, p. 896*)

Days before the Nov. 3, 1992, general election, the *Washington Post* confronted Packwood about allegations of sexual misconduct. Packwood denied the charges and asked the paper for time to gather information to discredit the women. The Post thus delayed running the story. On election day, Packwood beat his Democratic challenger, Rep. Les AuCoin, 52.1 percent to 46.5 percent. The Post on Nov. 22, 1992, detailed the first of many allegations concerning Packwood's behavior toward women since joining the Senate in 1969. Packwood subsequently apologized for any misconduct and said he was dealing with a potential alcohol problem. The ethics panel began its investigation into the allegations on Dec. 1. Packwood in January 1993 signaled that he would present an aggressive defense, a shift from the apologetic stance he had adopted earlier. (*Congress and the Nation Vol. VIII, p. 943*)

Five groups of Oregon citizens, about 250 in all, claimed in petitions to the Senate that Packwood defrauded voters before his narrow reelection victory by denying that he had made unwanted advances to numerous women and by allegedly trying to discredit and intimidate his accusers to prevent a story about his behavior from appearing before the election. Packwood's lawyers denied that he defrauded the voters and argued that, in any event, the Senate did not have the authority to deny him a seat because he received the most votes and was therefore the rightful winner. On Jan. 5, 1993, Packwood was sworn in "without prejudice," meaning the Senate could later decide he was not properly elected and exclude him by majority vote, instead of the two-thirds required by the Constitution to expel a member. The Senate Rules Committee voted unanimously Jan. 28 to begin considering the Packwood petitions. The panel was faced with the question of whether the Senate could or should exclude someone who lied about "personal, historical facts" to win a seat. At a May 10 public hearing, several members of the committee were clearly troubled by suggestions that it should. Without debate or dissent, the Rules Committee May 20 dismissed the petitions. Senators said afterward that even investigating the charges would set a bad precedent that would lead to numerous challenges over campaign rhetoric.

The Senate Ethics Committee in February said it would focus on three types of allegations against Packwood: sexual misconduct, attempts to intimidate accusers and misuse of Senate staff in such attempts. The panel said that it would prohibit questions about witnesses' sexual pasts and it rejected calls for the appointment of an outside counsel to handle the case. Allegations of sexual misconduct against Packwood mounted when the Post reported Feb. 7 that 13 more women said he made unwanted advances toward them. The Post's initial story cited accusations by 10 women, plus one who said Packwood told her sexual jokes, for a total of 24 women claiming impropriety between 1969 and 1990.

The probe proceeded quietly through the spring and summer. The committee planned to finish its preliminary inquiry by the end of October, but, as that deadline approached, a dispute over diaries kept by Packwood stalled the investigation. The panel twice in the previous 10 months had asked the senator for all documents relevant to its sexual misconduct inquiry, but he never turned over anything from his diaries, running 8,200 pages and covering his entire time in the Senate. On Oct. 5 and 6, committee aides began deposing Packwood, who referred to the diaries to bolster his version of certain events. Asked about them, he explained that he dictated his recollections each morning and then had them transcribed by his secretary. Once the committee members learned that the diaries contained relevant information, they halted the deposition and demanded to review them. After lengthy negotiations, Packwood and his lawyers agreed to provide them, except for references to legal, medical or private family matters. Ethics Committee Chairman Richard H. Bryan, D-Nev., said the committee staff warned Packwood's lawyers that the panel would pursue any other misconduct found in the diaries.

Packwood's lawyers masked the privileged passages with redacting tape and then watched committee aides read each page. The aides plowed through 5,000 pages covering 1969–1988, but the agreement collapsed as the staff began reviewing more recent years. When the dispute first surfaced publicly on Oct. 21, no mention was made by either side that the committee staff had found evidence of potential wrongdoing unrelated to sexual misconduct in the later diaries. What was reported was that after staff perused entries from 1989 and 1990, Packwood refused to produce copies of certain entries that the committee said it "determined are directly relevant to the current preliminary inquiry" but that Packwood's lawyer said were "wholly unrelated to the sexual misconduct/intimidation issues." Packwood also refused to provide more diaries unless he was allowed to mask additional information. The committee insisted on access to the diaries as provided by the original agreement. It decided that an independent hearing examiner should review the masked entries to ensure that only those covered by the original three exemptions were hidden. Packwood refused.

Packwood's lawyer offered a compromise Oct. 20, asking the committee to allow him to mask what he called "collateral issues" unrelated to sexual misconduct. He said the committee could seek those entries after its sexual misconduct inquiry was finished "in connection with any separate investigation it decides to initiate." The committee refused and on Oct. 20 voted to subpoena the 1989-to-present diaries. Under the subpoena, the diaries were to be turned over to an independent examiner, former solicitor general Kenneth W. Starr, who would make sure that only matters covered by the three original exemptions had been masked. The subpoena was delivered to Packwood on Oct. 21, but he told the committee that he "simply cannot agree at this to point to comply forthwith." That day, the committee voted unanimously to ask the Senate to go to court to enforce the subpoena. Chairman Bryan introduced a resolution (S Res 153)

to that effect. If the Senate prevailed in such a civil proceeding and Packwood continued defying the subpoena, a judge could find him in contempt and jail or fine him to induce compliance.

In an Oct. 22 statement, Packwood's lawyer said the disputed entries included information about another senator's affair with an aide; an affair between a Democratic congressional leader and a Senate staff member; consensual personal relationships with nonstaff having nothing to do with sexual misconduct by Packwood; fund-raising activities; Packwood's divorce; and lobbyists' visits to Packwood's office that had nothing to do with sexual activity. Packwood, on the Senate floor Oct. 25, denied that his lawyer's statement was an implicit threat. "This was not so-called gray mail," he said. "The secrets in that diary are safe with me."

A Nov. 1–2 floor debate on subpoenaing the diaries focused on issues of fairness, privacy and precedent as the Senate discussed how far its in-house investigators could go in probing allegations against one of its own. During the debate, Bryan and Packwood revealed that the entries that caused the dispute raised questions about whether Packwood had exchanged official favors for job offers for his estranged wife from lobbyists and other associates while he was in divorce court trying to minimize his alimony payments.

On Nov. 2, Arlen Specter, R-Pa., and John C. Danforth, R-Mo., offered an amendment based on Packwood's proposal to turn over "every scintilla of information" related to the sexual misconduct charges and the jobs matter. Under the amendment, Packwood would turn over the diaries to Starr, who would cull them for all relevant entries. The Ethics Committee rejected the idea, arguing that Starr would be required to ignore any other misdeeds noted in the diaries and that Starr would not always know what was relevant. Specter subsequently withdrew the amendment in favor of a more vague proposal, sponsored by GOP whip Alan K. Simpson of Wyoming. The Senate rejected the Simpson amendment on a **key vote of 23–77 (R 22–22; D 1–55)**. The Senate then adopted S Res 153, 94–6, to go to court. *(1993 key votes, p. 979)*

On Nov. 19, Packwood was reported to be considering resigning. If he resigned, the Ethics Committee's case and subpoena would become moot because the panel had jurisdiction over only sitting members. But Packwood decided against resignation after the Justice Department served him with a subpoena for the documents to block him from destroying them. On Nov. 22, the Ethics Committee went to court to enforce its subpoena. The case was assigned to U.S. District Judge Thomas Penfield Jackson. In court papers arguing against the Ethics Committee's subpoena, Packwood on Dec. 8 invoked the Fifth Amendment for the first time.

The Ethics Committee on Nov. 22 first questioned Cathy Wagner Cormack, who began transcribing the diaries from Packwood's daily recorded recollections after she became his secretary in 1969 and continued doing so after she left his full-time employ in the early 1980s. The committee wanted to determine whether Packwood had violated campaign finance laws or Senate rules barring the use of campaign funds for personal use. The panel also hoped to rebut Packwood's claim that the diaries were personal and therefore protected by his privacy rights by showing that the senator paid Cormack with Senate and campaign funds that could not be converted to personal use. Court records showed that she was paid $4,393 in Senate funds in 1982–1983 and $38,666 in campaign funds in 1984–1993 for typing the diaries.

In her initial deposition, Cormack said she never talked to Packwood about the substance of the diaries. But she corrected herself in an affidavit Dec. 10. She said Packwood had retrieved some of his tapes after the Ethics Committee investigation began. Later, she said she noticed that he might have revised some of the tapes. "Subsequently, he confirmed that he had," she swore. On Dec. 14, the Ethics Committee filed an urgent request asking Judge Jackson to seize the diaries for safekeeping while the case was litigated. Cormack provided details of her disclosure to the committee on Dec. 15. Following a Dec. 16 court hearing, Jackson issued an order seizing the diaries—all tapes and transcripts, copies and originals. The developments prompted Nancy Landon Kassebaum, Kan., on Dec. 16 to become the first Republican senator to publicly urge Packwood to resign. Democrats Robert C. Byrd of West Virginia, Daniel K. Inouye of Hawaii and Barbara Boxer of California previously made similar comments.

On Jan. 24, 1994, Judge Jackson upheld the Ethics Committee's subpoena. In his ruling, Jackson rejected Packwood's three main legal arguments—that the subpoena was overly broad and that it violated his privacy and self-incrimination rights under the Fourth and Fifth Amendments. Jackson declared that the subpoena was not too broad: "This court . . . has no authority to restrict the scope of the Ethics Committee's investigation." He said the panel had broad powers similar to a grand jury's. He called Packwood's contention that the committee could demand only entries relevant to its probe "manifestly inpracticable" in that it would give the probe's subject the power to decide what evidence could be used. Jackson also ruled that Packwood's privacy rights under the Fourth Amendment's ban on "unreasonable searches and seizures" were outweighed by the committee's need to examine the documents as part of its constitutional duty to police the Senate. He said the committee had met the standard of "reasonableness," citing its plan to allow Packwood to mask certain private entries. Furthermore, Jackson said Packwood's lawyer relied on an outdated Supreme Court case, the 108-year-old *Boyd v. United States,* to argue that the Fifth Amendment's bar against compelled self-incrimination covered private papers.

Packwood appealed the decision and sought a stay of the order to turn over the diaries until the case could be heard. Arguing against a stay, lawyers for the Ethics Committee said that Packwood was unlikely to succeed on the merits of his case and that the committee would be hampered by further delay. On Feb. 18, a three-judge panel of the U.S. Court of Appeals for the District of Columbia Circuit ruled against Packwood. On Feb. 25, Packwood took his request for a stay to the U.S. Supreme Court. Chief Justice William H. Rehnquist rejected Packwood's request on March 2.

Packwood dropped his challenge to the subpoena on March 14. The process agreed upon by both sides provided for the taped diaries and typed manuscripts to be reviewed by Starr. FBI experts would copy the diaries in a way that protected the originals for possible testing later to see if Packwood tried to obstruct the Ethics Committee's inquiry. The FBI would be barred from reading the transcripts or listening to the tapes to avoid aiding the Justice Department's separate criminal probe of Packwood. Starr would provide copies of the diaries to Packwood, who could mask medical and family matters. Starr would then review Packwood's work and give him 24 hours' notice before handing the papers over to the Ethics Committee.

The Ethics Committee resumed its investigation in May. Signaling a formal expansion of the probe, the panel began issuing subpoenas for documents and testimony concerning the suspicions that Packwood improperly solicited job offers for his estranged wife. Ethics lawyers questioned Georgie Packwood on July 21. The Ethics Committee did not complete its investigation in 1994. The committee staff spent much of the remainder of the year reviewing Packwood's diaries.

SEN. DAVE DURENBERGER

A federal grand jury in Washington, D.C., reindicted Sen. Dave Durenberger, R-Minn., on Feb. 25, 1994, on charges that he fraudulently billed the Senate for his use of a Minnesota condominium he secretly owned. The two felony charges—one count of conspiring to make $3,825 in false claims to the Senate for stays in his condominium and one count of making the false claims—were identical to indictments handed down on April 2, 1993, and dismissed on Dec. 3. The charges against Durenberger carried penalties of up to 10 years in prison and a $500,000 fine.

Federal prosecutors had been investigating the condo arrangement since 1990, when the Senate denounced Durenberger for a larger set of condo reimbursements and for other financial transactions found to be "clearly and unequivocally unethical." Prosecutors declined to pursue the broader case against Durenberger that was outlined in the Senate Ethics Committee investigation. The committee had found that, from 1983 to 1989, Durenberger had billed the Senate $40,055 for lodging in the condominium—"essentially his personal residence in Minneapolis." Durenberger in early 1990 repaid $11,005 and at the time of his denouncement was ordered to pay back the rest plus interest. *(Ethics probe, Congress and the Nation Vol. VIII, p. 921)*

The indictment focused on several months in 1987 after a partnership Durenberger had formed in 1983 to collect condo reimbursements dissolved and the senator sought ways to continue collecting reimbursements. It said that Durenberger and two friends—Michael C. Mahoney, a Minnesota attorney, and Paul P. Overgaard, Durenberger's 1978 campaign manager—"did devise and carry out a scheme by which the cost of defendant Durenberger's condominium would continue to be paid by the Senate." They allegedly "hid defendant Durenberger's ownership interest in the condominium" by making it appear he was renting his condominium from Overgaard's company, ISC, although the company did not own the property at the time. When the company did later buy the condo, the indictment said, Overgaard agreed that the senator could eventually buy it back at the same price—"effectively allowing him to 'park' the property with ISC," the Justice Department said in a statement. The indictment quoted a "totally confidential" 1989 letter to Durenberger from Overgaard in which he expressed fear that he would be accused of "participating in a sham transaction by which you collect per diem from the Senate for a residence you actually own. That is certainly a conclusion that could be reached as things stand now."

U.S. District Judge Warren K. Urbom threw out the first set of indictments in 1993 on grounds that Justice Department lawyers had violated a constitutional provision barring prosecutions of members of Congress based on what they said during official speeches and debates. Urbom acted after finding that 11 pages from the Senate Ethics Committee's report and the report of its special counsel had been presented to the grand jury— material that Urbom said was inadmissible under the Constitution's provision that members "shall not be questioned" outside Congress "for any Speech or Debate in either House."

The first case included indictments against Mahoney and Overgaard. Those indictments were dismissed at the Justice Department's request Dec. 29, 1993. The two were not reindicted with Durenberger in 1994.

Durenberger pleaded not guilty on March 10, 1994. He again asked to have the case thrown out on separation of powers grounds, but U.S. District Judge Stanley S. Harris refused July 8. Durenberger appealed to the U.S. Court of Appeals for the District of Columbia Circuit. *(1995 action, p. 907)*

In other action, a Minnesota judge on Aug. 24, 1993, dismissed a civil suit filed against Durenberger in 1992 by a Minnesota woman who accused him of raping her and fathering her child in 1963 when he served as her divorce attorney. Durenberger had denied the charges repeatedly and on Aug. 3 said that blood tests by two independent Minnesota laboratories showed that he was not the father.

SEN. KAY BAILEY HUTCHISON

Sen. Kay Bailey Hutchison, R-Texas, was exonerated Feb. 11, 1994, of criminal ethics charges—five counts of misusing Texas state workers and equipment for personal and political gain while she was state treasurer and tampering with state records relating to the case. Judge John Onion Jr. ordered a directed verdict of not guilty before a single piece of evidence was presented. Onion, who had moved the trial to Fort Worth from Austin, told the jury to find Hutchison not guilty after prosecutors indicated they were not prepared to go forward. The abrupt conclusion came shortly after Onion refused to indicate whether he would allow the prosecutors to submit as evidence phone and computer records that were gathered in a raid of Hutchison's office five days after she won a special election in June 1993 to the U.S. Senate.

Hutchison was first indicted Sept. 27, 1993, on five felony charges of misconduct. The indictments were thrown out Oct. 26 because one of the grand jurors had an outstanding warrant for his arrest relating to a years-old misdemeanor charge and thus was not qualified to sit on the grand jury. On Dec. 8, a grand jury reindicted Hutchison on four felony counts and one misdemeanor similar to the original counts. Four of the new in-

dictments were dismissed Dec. 29 for being too vague. Prosecutors were given time to redraw the indictments, which they subsequently did. The charges were reinstated, and Hutchison pleaded not guilty on Jan. 7, 1994.

The case did not go to the Senate Ethics Committee because it involved actions taken before Hutchison was a senator.

SEN. ORRIN G. HATCH

The Senate Ethics Committee announced Nov. 20, 1993, that it had ended a seven-month probe of Sen. Orrin G. Hatch, R-Utah, with a unanimous finding that Hatch had acted neither illegally nor unethically in his dealings with the scandal-ridden Bank of Credit and Commerce International (BCCI). The bank was closed in 1991 in a global crackdown after investigators of various governments uncovered widespread fraud involving billions of dollars and many other crimes, including bribes to leaders around the world, arms trafficking, income tax evasion, smuggling and illegal bank acquisitions. Contacts between Hatch, one of his aides and key insiders of BCCI had been the subject of numerous news reports since 1991. Hatch called for an ethics investigation in August 1992 after denying wrongdoing. The Ethics Committee announced April 7, 1993, that it had opened a "preliminary inquiry" into the matter.

SEN. DANIEL K. INOUYE

The Senate Ethics Committee announced April 7, 1993, that it had decided against pursuing sexual misconduct allegations against Sen. Daniel K. Inouye, D-Hawaii, because no alleged victim would cooperate in the investigation. The charges against Inouye surfaced during his 1992 campaign for election to a sixth term. *(Background, Congress and the Nation Vol. VIII, p. 944)*

SEN. CHARLES S. ROBB

Ending a 19-month investigation, a federal grand jury in Virginia voted Jan. 12, 1993, not to indict that state's Democratic senator, Charles S. Robb, on charges of conspiracy and obstruction of justice. The case involved an alleged scheme to disclose an illegally recorded cellular phone conversation that Robb aides perceived as damaging to Virginia's Democratic governor, L. Douglas Wilder, a longtime Robb rival. *(Background, Congress and the Nation Vol. VIII, p. 944)*

SEN. EDWARD M. KENNEDY

On Oct. 13, 1994, the Senate Ethics Committee announced that it had decided unanimously in June not to open a formal investigation into allegations that Sen. Edward M. Kennedy, D-Mass., had harassed a female staff member and used illegal drugs. The suggestions had been made by former Kennedy aide Richard E. Burke in his controversial 1992 book *The Senator: My Ten Years with Ted Kennedy.*

The committee routinely looked into published allegations of wrongdoing by members but rarely made a public announcement unless it found grounds for the charge. The statement in the Kennedy case came after a conservative media watchdog group, Accuracy in Media, quoted Burke as saying the committee had received sworn statements alleging harassment from women who had worked for Kennedy. In its announcement, the committee said it never received such statements and went on to not only denounce the charges but also criticize Burke, saying it found "no basis for his allegations nor anyone who could substantiate those allegations."

REP. HAROLD E. FORD

Ending three days of deliberations after a five-week trial in federal court in Memphis, a jury of 11 whites and one black on April 9, 1993, found Tennessee's first black representative, Democrat Harold E. Ford, not guilty of one count of conspiracy, three counts of bank fraud and 14 counts of mail fraud. The jury also acquitted two codefendants. Earlier in the week, U.S. District Judge Jerome Turner had thrown out one mail fraud count against Ford and 11 counts against the other two.

Since he was indicted in 1987, Ford had accused prosecutors of pursuing a racist vendetta because he was a politically successful black. He was repeatedly reelected by healthy margins despite the charges. He initially was tried in Memphis in 1990, but that case ended in a hung jury, which reportedly split along racial lines. The second trial had been slated to be held in Jackson instead of Memphis to avoid what the first trial judge, who was black, had perceived as pressure on black jurors to acquit Ford. (Jackson was less than 20 percent black, while Memphis was about 40 percent black.) The controversy that ensued dragged the Clinton administration into an imbroglio involving allegations of racism and political favoritism. The Justice Department ultimately backed Ford's motion to select another jury from Memphis.

The final acquittal allowed Ford to resume the chairmanship of the House Ways and Means Subcommittee on Human Resources. Under Democratic Caucus rules, he had to give up that post when he was indicted. *(Earlier action, Congress and the Nation Vol. VIII, p. 927)*

Ford's legal troubles stemmed from the 1983 failure of a system of Tennessee banks controlled by two politically connected brothers, Jacob F. and C. H. Butcher Jr. The two brothers pleaded guilty to crimes connected to the failures and served multiyear prison terms. On trial in 1993 were Ford and two Butcher bank insiders. The three were accused of conspiring with the Butchers to defraud several Butcher banks by obtaining bogus loans to finance Ford's "extravagant and lavish lifestyle" while Ford "would use his political influence as a United States congressman to further the political and business goals" of the Butchers. The loans totaled more than $1 million, but the exact amount was unclear because some loans were used to pay off others. After the banks failed, Ford settled the largest debt, $350,000, for $25,000. Ford insisted that the loans were legitimate business transactions related to his family funeral home. He admitted using some of the money to pay off personal debts because he said the funeral home owed him the money. Ford said he was only a friend of the Butchers.

REP. JOSEPH M. MCDADE

In a 2–1 decision, a three-judge panel of the U.S. Circuit Court of Appeals in Philadelphia on June 15, 1994, refused to dismiss a corruption indictment against Rep. Joseph M. McDade, R-Pa. McDade appealed to the Supreme Court, but on March 6, 1995, the Court turned down his appeal without comment, thus clearing the way for a trial. *(1995–1996 action, p. 865)*

McDade, who had steadfastly denied wrongdoing, was indicted on May 5, 1992, on racketeering, conspiracy and illegal gratuity charges. On Jan. 11, 1993, McDade asked a federal judge to dismiss the indictment, maintaining, in part, that the charges violated the limited immunity afforded members of Congress in the Constitution's Speech or Debate Clause, which said, "for any Speech or Debate in either House," members "shall not be questioned in any other Place." McDade also asked that any trial be moved from Philadelphia to a locale in or near his district in northeast Pennsylvania. U.S. District Judge Robert S. Gawthrop III, on May 6, refused to throw out the indictments and declined McDade's request to move the trial. McDade then appealed that decision to the U.S. Circuit Court of Appeals. *(Background, Congress and the Nation Vol. VIII, p. 944)*

Unlike most pretrial motions, a judge's decision on speech or debate claims could be appealed by either side all the way to the Supreme Court before the case went to trial.

Meanwhile, the House Republican Conference on May 4, 1993, adopted a rule requiring that GOP committee chairmen or ranking members step aside if indicted on felony charges. Because the rule did not apply to pending cases, McDade, ranking Republican on the House Administration Committee, was exempt. *(House rules changes, p. 865)*

REP. WALTER R. TUCKER III

Rep. Walter R. Tucker III, D-Calif., was indicted on Aug. 11, 1994, on federal charges of soliciting and accepting bribes while serving as mayor of Compton, Calif., and of failing to report the funds on his federal income tax returns. The 10-count indictment alleged that Tucker received $30,000 in bribes in 1991 and 1992 from a company that wanted to build a trash incineration plant. Tucker allegedly later demanded $250,000 more from the company. Tucker pleaded not guilty Aug. 22.

The FBI spearheaded the two-year investigation of Compton officials. News reports said meetings were videotaped in which Tucker appeared to take money from an undercover agent in exchange for putting items on the city council agenda.

If convicted under any of the eight extortion charges, Tucker would face a prison term of up to 20 years and a $250,000 fine. The income tax charges both carried maximum penalties of three years in prison and a $100,000 fine. *(1995 action, p. 907)*

REP. MEL REYNOLDS

A Cook County, Ill., grand jury on Aug. 19, 1994, indicted Rep. Mel Reynolds, D-Ill., on three counts of child pornography, one count of solicitation of child pornography, one count of criminal sexual assault, eight counts of aggravated criminal sexual abuse of a child, five counts of obstructing justice and one count of communicating with a witness with intent to deter the witness from testifying truthfully before the grand jury.

The charges stemmed from an alleged sexual relationship Reynolds had with a campaign worker from June 1992, when she was 16 years old, to September 1993. Prosecutors alleged that Reynolds, in June 1994, requested that the victim obtain "lewd photographs of another girl who was age fifteen." The age of consent in Illinois was 17. The indictment also alleged that Reynolds "induced the victim to provide false information to police and leave the state" and that he gave false information to authorities.

Reynolds denied ever engaging in sexual relations with the young woman. He pleaded not guilty on Sept. 12.

On Oct. 3, a Cook County grand jury indicted Reynolds on another charge. State prosecutors charged that Reynolds harassed a witness, saying that he had told his accuser that she could be jailed for her actions. *(1995 action, p. 902)*

REP. CHARLIE ROSE

Rep. Charlie Rose, D-N.C., settled a five-year-old lawsuit on Oct. 27, 1994, by paying a $12,500 civil fine to the Justice Department. Rose had been accused of failing to disclose loans from 1979 to 1985 totaling more than $100,000. Some of the money was improperly taken from his campaign committee, according to the House Committee on Standards of Official Conduct, which rebuked him in 1988 for making false financial statements. The Justice Department had sought fines of $30,000, as allowed under the 1978 Ethics in Government Act (PL 95-521). *(Background, Congress and the Nation Vol. VIII, p. 946; Congress and the Nation Vol. VII, p. 886)*

Rose had gone to court to block the government's suit, filed in May 1989, on constitutional grounds, but a panel of the U.S. Court of Appeals for the District of Columbia Circuit on July 12, 1994, unanimously rejected arguments by Rose and House lawyers that the civil suit violated the Constitution's separation of powers doctrine because the Justice Department relied on Rose's statements to the House ethics committee and because that panel already had investigated and rebuked him for the same false statements. One month later, Rose asked his attorney to try to negotiate a deal with the Justice Department to settle the lawsuit.

HOUSE SPEAKER THOMAS S. FOLEY

House Speaker Thomas S. Foley, D-Wash., announced July 26, 1993, that he would no longer allow a friend to give him access to low-risk stock deals. Foley also said he would pay Peter de Roetth an advice fee of 1 percent of assets, which de Roetth had waived because Foley's account was small.

The Speaker's investments stirred controversy after the Capitol Hill newspaper *Roll Call* disclosed them June 28. De Roetth had invested Foley's money in 42 initial public offerings of stock since 1989, earning him more than $100,000 when 40 of them sold for quick profits. Considered almost sure winners, so-called IPOs generally were available only to big-money investors, a category that did not include Foley. Foley's dealings with de Roetth were first disclosed in the *Washington Post* in 1988, when his profits were much smaller.

REP. NEWT GINGRICH

The House Committee on Standards of Official Conduct announced Nov. 29, 1994, that it did not have enough information to decide whether House Republican Whip Newt Gingrich, Ga., violated House rules in soliciting tax-deductible contributions for a college course he taught. The matter was carried over into the 104th Congress. Gingrich became Speaker of the House in 1995. *(104th Congress action, p. 898)*

The original complaint against Gingrich was filed Sept. 7, 1994, by his opponent in the November election, former representative Ben Jones (D-Ga., 1989–1993). It contended that Gingrich improperly used funds donated to a political action committee, GOPAC, which he had headed since 1986, to support a college course that he taught—"Renewing American Civilization." Jones suggested that the course was a partisan political exercise that, under tax law, should have been kept free of partisan influence. A primary focus of GOPAC was to facilitate the election of state and local Republicans to office by offering education and training programs to candidates.

Gingrich decided to teach the class in 1993, and Kennesaw State College in Georgia expressed an interest in hosting it. The college's tax-exempt foundation was to be the recipient of contributions to pay for the course. Jeffrey A. Eisenach, a longtime Gingrich associate, left his position as executive director of GOPAC to run the course. However, he maintained close ties to the political action committee. His consulting firm, Washington Policy Group, took on GOPAC as a client at the same time he was raising money through tax-deductible contributions to fund Gingrich's course.

In the fall of 1993, when controversy arose over the class, the Georgia Board of Regents voted to stop elected officials from teaching courses at state colleges. Gingrich then moved the course to private Reinhardt College, and it was made available to other groups and some GOP organizations by satellite and on video. Its financing was taken over by the Progress and Freedom Foundation, incorporated in April 1993 as a tax-exempt corporation and headed by Eisenach.

Jones asked the House ethics committee whether the Progress and Freedom Foundation had tilted too far toward the Republicans. Federal law required such foundations to be nonpartisan, and some groups had lost their tax-exempt status for training political operatives of just one party. According to the *Atlanta Journal-Constitution,* Gingrich had stated that he hoped his course would help mold debate in the 1996 presidential campaign and help recruit 200,000 grassroots workers nationwide. Of the $1.5 million spent by the foundation between April 1993 and December 1994, 43 percent, or $632,115, went for the college course and a weekly call-in show, "Progress Report," that Gingrich hosted on National Empowerment Television, a cable network. Jones maintained that the majority of donors were merely looking for a way to contribute to Gingrich in excess of federal campaign limits. Jones also said that Gingrich improperly used his Washington office for the project by involving two of his congressional press secretaries and using government equipment and stationery.

In December 1994, two weeks before he was to be sworn in as Speaker, Gingrich signed a deal with the publishing company HarperCollins to write one book and edit another. He was to receive an advance of $4.5 million. Immediately, the deal was attacked by Democrats, as well as some Republicans, who believed Gingrich was cashing in on his office. Gingrich subsequently agreed to forgo the advance, taking instead $1 plus royalties—15 percent for each hardcover book sold and 10 percent for each paperback and audiocassette sold. The controversy subsided until the *New York Daily News* on Jan. 12, 1995, reported that, while negotiations for the book deal were under way, Gingrich met with media mogul Rupert Murdoch, who owned Harper-Collins and the Fox Broadcasting Co. and who spent $135,881 to lobby Congress in 1994 in favor of deregulating the broadcasting industry. Gingrich said he was unaware that Murdoch owned the publishing company; both men said the book deal never came up during their meeting. Jones amended his complaint in January 1995 to include the controversial book deal.

REP. MARTIN FROST

The House Committee on Standards of Official Conduct announced Nov. 29, 1994, that it had dismissed a complaint brought by Dallas County GOP Chairman Robert Driegert over congressional redistricting work for the 1992 elections done by the staff of Martin Frost, D-Texas. The committee wrote in a letter to Frost: "The committee accepts your statement that you were unaware of the prohibition on utilizing official funds for activities relating to redistricting and is of the opinion that you could have reasonably relied on House approvals for related activities in forming your belief that the expenditures were properly made."

Frost said he would reimburse the Treasury for any money spent on redistricting.

FORMER MEMBERS

Nicholas Mavroules

Former representative Nicholas Mavroules (D-Mass., 1979–1993) pleaded guilty April 15, 1993, to 15 offenses that included accepting illegal gratuities and failing to report all his income. Prosecutors dropped two racketeering charges against him. On June 29, Mavroules was sentenced to 15 months in prison with three years of probation after his prison term and a $15,000 fine. He reported to prison on Aug. 1. (*Background, Congress and the Nation Vol. VIII, p. 945*)

Albert G. Bustamante

A federal jury in San Antonio, Texas, on July 21, 1993, convicted former representative Albert G. Bustamante (D-Texas, 1985–1993) of racketeering and accepting an illegal gift. The jury found that he had accepted a $35,000 bribe in 1986 from a food service company in exchange for influencing the Air Force to renew a contract with the company. He also was found guilty of accepting a no-risk loan during a failed bid to buy a San Antonio TV station. Bustamante was found not guilty on eight other charges, which included allegations that he had accepted money from a real estate company and his wife's law firm. His wife, Rebecca, was found not guilty of aiding and abetting the former member. Bustamante was sentenced on Oct. 1 to three-and-a-half years in prison and was told to pay $55,100 in fines and court costs.

Lawrence J. Smith

On Aug. 2, 1993, a U.S. District judge in Miami sentenced former representative Lawrence J. Smith (D-Fla., 1983–1993) to three months in jail with two years' probation on charges of tax evasion and lying to the Federal Election Commission. Smith pleaded guilty to the charges in May 1993. They included a scheme in which Smith funneled $10,000 from his campaign fund to his personal use. He reported to prison on Oct. 4.

Carl C. Perkins Jr.

Former representative Carl C. Perkins Jr. (D-Ky., 1985–1993) pleaded guilty Dec. 20, 1994, to three federal felony charges stemming from overdrafts at the House bank, false reports filed with the Federal Election Commission and omissions on his 1990 financial disclosure statement. On March 13, 1995, he was sentenced to 21 months in prison as well as ordered to serve three years' probation, to perform 250 hours of community service and to complete any alcohol treatment program required by his probation officer.

Carroll Hubbard Jr.

On April 5, 1994, former representative Carroll Hubbard Jr. (D-Ky., 1975–1993) pleaded guilty to charges that he misused congressional employees, violated federal election laws and obstructed justice. On Nov. 9, he was sentenced to three years in prison for three felony convictions and ordered to pay $153,000 in restitution. Hubbard's wife, Carol Brown Hubbard, pleaded guilty to a misdemeanor charge in connection with the case and was put on probation. ❑

House Bank

Fallout from the 1991 House bank scandal continued to be felt during the 103rd Congress.

FINAL GAO REPORT

The General Accounting Office (GAO) April 28, 1993, issued a final audit of the since-closed House bank showing that some members continued to write checks on their accounts with insufficient funds after the matter had become a full-blown scandal. A 1991 GAO audit had first generated controversy about the House bank, disclosing that members routinely overdrew their accounts without penalty. (*Background, Congress and the Nation Vol. VIII, p. 929*)

The 1993 audit covered the 18 months before the bank was closed at the end of 1991. It found no losses related to the bank's closing, but it criticized bank employees for the way they implemented the Sept. 25, 1991, order by Speaker Thomas S. Foley, D-Wash., that henceforth, without exception, "checks with insufficient funds to cover them will be returned at the close of business on the day they are received." The GAO found 97 insufficient-funds checks were presented to the bank after that day. Only one was returned, and that was done at the request of the member who wrote it. Of the 96 that were not returned, 69 worth a total of $36,313 were dated after Sept. 25, 1991. All were honored because the members covered them with new deposits after receiving a call from the bank informing them the checks would be returned the next morning if not made good.

House leaders of both parties argued that the bank employees' actions were "consistent with both the Speaker's statement . . . and regular banking practices."

RUSS SENTENCING

Former House sergeant-at-arms Jack Russ became the first person to be prosecuted for passing bad checks at the House bank. Part of Russ's duty as sergeant-at-arms was overseeing the bank.

Under a plea bargain, Russ on Oct. 6, 1993, acknowledged in federal court that he had embezzled public funds by knowingly cashing 17 bad checks worth $75,300 at the bank in 1989; that he defrauded investors and lenders out of $445,000 in a business deal; and that he omitted from his 1989 financial disclosure $221,125 owed to business associates and the House bank. U.S. District Judge Stanley S. Harris on Dec. 17 gave Russ the lightest sentence available under federal sentencing guidelines: two years in prison. He also ordered Russ to pay $445,000 in restitution and to perform 250 hours of community service.

HOUSE INSPECTOR GENERAL

House leaders on Oct. 27, 1993, named John W. Lainhart IV, an assistant inspector general for the Transportation Department, as the first House inspector general. The position was created in April 1992, in the midst of controversy over the House bank. (*Congress and the Nation Vol. VIII, p. 947*)

House rules specified that the House inspector general would conduct periodic financial audits of the office of the director of nonlegislative and financial services (which had been created at the same time as the inspector general post), the clerk, the sergeant-at-arms and the doorkeeper; inform them of his findings and suggestions; notify the Speaker and party leaders of "any financial irregularity" discovered; and give them all audit reports produced. The House inspector general was "subject to the policy direction and oversight of the Committee on House Administration." ❏

Congressional Reform

Despite repeated vows by Democratic leaders to make the 103rd a "reform Congress," efforts to improve Congress's image by revamping the way it did business ran aground, the victim of partisan bickering and opposition from senior members who stood to lose power.

BACKGROUND

The Joint Committee on the Organization of Congress was established in 1992 with equal numbers of members from each party and each chamber. The official mandate stated that the committee would begin work after the 1992 election and be dissolved by Dec. 31, 1993. (*Background, Congress and the Nation Vol. VIII, p. 948*)

The Senate members named to the special panel were David L. Boren, D-Okla.; Harry Reid, D-Nev.; Jim Sasser, D-Tenn.;

Wendell H. Ford, D-Ky.; Paul S. Sarbanes, D-Md.; David Pryor, D-Ark.; Pete V. Domenici, R-N.M.; Nancy Landon Kassebaum, R-Kan.; Trent Lott, R-Miss.; Ted Stevens, R-Alaska; William S. Cohen, R-Maine; and Richard G. Lugar, R-Ind.

The House members were Lee H. Hamilton, D-Ind.; David R. Obey, D-Wis.; Al Swift, D-Wash.; John M. Spratt Jr., D-S.C.; Sam Gejdenson, D-Conn.; Eleanor Holmes Norton, D-D.C.; Bill Gradison, R-Ohio; Robert S. Walker, R-Pa.; Gerald B. H. Solomon, R-N.Y.; David Dreier, R-Calif.; Bill Emerson, R-Mo.; and Wayne Allard, R-Colo.

Boren and Domenici were chairman and vice chairman, respectively, of the Senate contingent; Hamilton and Gradison, of the House contingent. Gradison resigned from the House on Jan. 31, 1993; his place heading House Republicans was filled by Dreier. Jennifer Dunn, R-Wash., was chosen to fill the vacancy on the panel.

Hearings

Between Jan. 26 and July 1, 1993, the committee heard from 243 witnesses during about 114 hours of testimony over 36 days. The top five congressional leaders (the Speaker and the House and Senate majority and minority leaders) testified at the first public hearing held by the panel—a first in congressional annals. They warned of the political and constitutional obstacles to overhauling Congress. House Speaker Thomas S. Foley, D-Wash., said, "There are limits to what organization and institutional reform can do. Fundamentally this will and must remain an institution where there is political dissent, debate and disagreement, and there is nothing that can or should distract us from the character of the institution." Moreover, familiar patterns quickly emerged on the panel. Democrats cited a need for streamlined legislative management that would let the majority achieve its objectives; Republicans, a need for fairness that would protect minority rights.

Senate Minority Leader George J. Mitchell, D-Maine, on Jan. 26 outlined a plan to streamline Senate procedures. Mitchell said he had no intention of denying senators the right to fully debate or filibuster an issue, but he said he was fed up with "unlimited delay and obstruction." He proposed seven specific changes (S Res 25-32 and 37) that he said would allow the Senate to operate in a "more orderly and efficient manner." The proposals would have limited debate to two hours on a motion to proceed; required a three-fifths vote of the Senate to overturn a ruling of the chair once cloture had been invoked; allowed committee-reported amendments and amendments to the committee amendment to automatically be considered germane after cloture was invoked; counted time consumed by quorum calls during cloture against the senator who suggested the absence of a quorum; allowed the Senate to go to conference with the House after passage of a single motion to proceed; dispensed with the reading of a conference report; and provided for a motion to require that amendments be ruled germane.

Senate Republicans argued that Mitchell's proposals would fundamentally undermine their rights. They "dilute the ability of the minority to function," said Minority Whip Alan K. Simpson, R-Wyo. Minority Leader Bob Dole, R-Kan., emphasized that the rights of any minority coalition were at stake. In defense, Mitchell cited statistics showing that the number of cloture votes to end filibusters had mushroomed over the previous quarter century, and he complained that filibusters were threatened for "reasons as trivial as a senator's travel schedule."

Senate President Pro Tempore Robert C. Byrd, D-W.Va., on Feb. 2 had a nearly three-hour dialogue with the panel on the history, traditions and rationale of the Senate rules. Byrd cautioned the committee against getting caught up in an "obsession with process," which he said put more emphasis on the rules under which legislation was considered than on the quality of debate about it. Like other Democrats, Byrd complained that debate in the Senate was not as thoughtful or thorough as it should be. But unlike Mitchell, Byrd did not locate the problem in Senate rules but in the membership. He told the committee that senators needed to become less concerned with appearing on television and raising campaign funds and more concerned with studying the issues of the day. "Senate debate is dying as a legislative art," he said.

On Feb. 14, the panel got a litany of recommendations from 14 House Democrats and 27 Republicans who responded in person to the committee's call for testimony. Another half-dozen members submitted written statements. Several freshmen recommended term limits for committee chairmen. A bipartisan group told the panel that Congress should no longer exempt itself from laws that other Americans had to abide by.

The panel invited businessman and 1992 independent presidential candidate Ross Perot to make suggestions on overhauling congressional procedures and improving the public image and understanding of Congress. But after an hour, hearing exhortations reminiscent of Perot's self-financed presidential campaign, several members on March 2 grew weary of his tone and lack of specifics. "You've now given us forty-five minutes of sound bites and five minutes of material," said Sen. Reid, who went on to advise Perot to "start checking your facts a little more and stop listening to the applause as much." When Perot was asked what the panel's top priority should be, he said, "Standing out all alone is ethics and integrity." In response, Rep. Hamilton said, "Do you believe that most of us here are crooks? . . . are dishonest? . . . are untrustworthy?" Perot changed course and praised the panel's members and mission. He said they each deserved a "medal of courage" for joining the committee.

In back-to-back appearances before the joint committee on April 1, leaders of the House Democratic and Republican freshman classes offered contrasting prescriptions for reform. Without public dissent, the 47 Republicans united behind their 19-point package, which included limiting members' terms, eliminating the Appropriations Committee, lowering franking funds, requiring a three-fifths vote for any tax increase and ending proxy voting on committees. The 63 Democrats had a harder time reaching consensus. The first two items on their agenda were legislative proposals backed by the leadership: campaign finance and lobby disclosure. The class endorsed the standard Democratic fare of voluntary spending limits, but it ducked the issue of how to generate the public funds needed to entice candidates to participate in the system. The freshman Democrats dropped most controversial elements, including a line-item veto. The most contentious points left in the package were recommendations that members hold only one committee or subcommittee chair and that the legislative branch appropriations be reduced 25 percent over five years. Two items aimed squarely at the GOP were that motions to adjourn be considered out of order unless the House had been in session at least five hours (and no member could make more than one such motion a day) and that daily votes to approve the *Journal*, a formal record of previous proceedings, be abolished.

Survey

Twenty-two of the 24 members of the joint committee attended an overnight retreat in Annapolis, Md., on June 27–28 to begin reviewing the hundreds of proposals. The committee's leaders on June 28 released the results of a survey it had sent to all 535 members of the House and Senate in May. The leaders said the results were a reliable barometer, although only 145 members answered the 80 or so questions. The results were as follows:

• Nearly 90 percent of the respondents agreed that "major improvements are needed in the way Congress conducts its legislative business."

• The respondents' top five priorities for reorganizing Congress were the committee structure, the budget process, floor procedures, ethics and public understanding of Congress.

• Respondents overwhelmingly supported reducing the number of subcommittees, limiting members' committee assignments and establishing parallel House/Senate committee jurisdictions.

• Lukewarm support was found for allowing outsiders a role in the process for dealing with members' ethics transgressions.

• A large majority favored a two-year budget cycle instead of the existing one-year cycle, and 77 percent favored sunsetting entitlement programs after 10 years. About 74 percent favored eliminating one step from the existing three-step budget process (budget resolution, authorization and appropriation); of those, 43 percent thought the appropriations process should be eliminated.

• While 68 percent of the House respondents said too many limits were placed on floor amendments and debate, House Republicans accounted for much of that sentiment—with 98 percent agreeing, compared with 40 percent for House Democrats. In the Senate, 33 percent said too few limits were imposed on floor debate, with Democrats more apt to favor greater limits.

• Half the respondents thought that Congress was overstaffed, with Republicans much more likely to think so than Democrats. Relatively few said members' personal staffs should be cut. More popular was cutting the staffs of committees and congressional support agencies.

SENATE AND HOUSE PROPOSALS

Although the joint committee planned to draft its report in September or October, lack of consensus caused delays. Tensions between the Senate and House ran high, and the two chambers ended up reporting separate recommendations in November. Their proposals, however, had much in common.

Senate

Boren and Domenici on Nov. 4 moved ahead with a separate Senate proposal, which called for limiting committee and subcommittee assignments, limiting the number of subcommittees, killing joint committees, abolishing any committee that shrank to less than half its existing size as a result of limiting members' assignments, instituting a two-year budget cycle and multiyear authorizations, banning the use of proxies in committee if they made a difference in the outcome and cutting congressional staff by about 12 percent. The Senate proposal also included provisions to reduce filibusters. Under the plan, a motion to consider a bill no longer could be filibustered. After cloture was invoked, it would take a three-fifths vote to overturn a ruling of the chair, and quorum-call time would count against the member who called for it.

The senators on the joint committee unanimously adopted the recommendations with few changes on Nov. 10. They agreed to defer action on ethics recommendations because a separate task force, headed by Senate Ethics Chairman Richard R. Bryan, D-Nev., was studying the matter. Boren and Domenici had proposed using former senators and other outsiders to conduct some Senate ethics investigations. They also suggested splitting the ethics process so that one set of senators investigated allegations and another adjudicated charges. The senators on the panel also deferred action on ending congressional exemptions from laws because that subject, too, was being considered by a task force, headed by Sen. Reid. *(Workplace compliance, p. 882)*

House

Following weeks of delay, Rep. Hamilton on Nov. 16 released recommendations for the House on his own. They called for bringing outsiders into the ethics process, streamlining the committee system and simplifying the budget process. Consideration of the proposal spanned five days, and 36 amendments were debated in angry and occasionally personal terms. The House delegation completed its markup on a sour and partisan note Nov. 22, on an 8–4 vote. A majority of Republicans were opposed, but Dreier and Emerson reluctantly voted for the proposals, saying they hoped that the GOP could make major changes on the House floor.

Republicans complained that Hamilton backed away from one of the most important items on the joint committee's agenda: restructuring full committees. Hamilton himself expressed disappointment, but he said that, after meeting with committee chairmen and the leadership, he did not believe a bill that included committee restructuring could pass.

As adopted, the House proposals would have limited committee and subcommittee assignments and called for the Rules Committee to consider abolishing any committee whose size was reduced by more than half because of these new limits. Another provision would have allowed private citizens to participate in the initial investigations in ethics cases. Also under the plan, budget resolutions and appropriations bills were to cover

two years and reports on legislation were to include a list of any earmarks directing funds to particular projects. The plan would have established a new office to propose regulations to bring congressional employees under protections of federal workplace laws and to handle complaint investigations.

The final recommendations also included a Republican amendment to guarantee the minority the right to offer a motion to recommit with instructions immediately before the House voted on final passage. The House Rules Committee frequently, but not always, gave Republicans such opportunities to get an up-or-down vote on their version of legislation. To Republicans, it was simply a matter of fairness, and they reacted with fury when Obey and Hamilton suggested that House Democrats were unlikely to consider any extension of minority rights until the Senate limited filibusters. However, the amendment subsequently was adopted Nov. 21 by 10–2.

But many other GOP amendments were rejected, including proposals to ban proxy voting in committee, restructure the committee system, make it harder for the majority party to bring bills to the floor under fast-track procedures, give Republicans more committee staff and make other changes that would strengthen the minority party.

LEGISLATIVE ACTION

While academics criticized the Senate and House proposals for offering little to streamline committee jurisdictions, reduce committee assignments or smooth floor procedures, the joint committee's suggestions proved too controversial for members of Congress. With little public pressure in evidence, most of the proposals never got to the floor of either chamber to test their popularity.

Senate

On July 1, 1994, the Senate Rules Committee reported a bill (S 1824—S Rept 103-297) to institute a two-year congressional budget process and to take steps toward applying health and safety laws to Congress. The committee had adopted a Byrd amendment, removing appropriations from the two-year plan. Byrd said that budgeting was an imprecise art, beginning more than a year in advance; a two-year spending cycle would require many more revisions. Also, he said, agencies should have to justify their expenditures each year. S 1824 also contained provisions to end Congress's exemptions from worker protection laws, but it required the General Accounting Office to study the impact of bringing Congress under such laws before changes could be made.

On June 16, the Rules Committee approved S Res 227, reducing the number of seats on most standing committees and specifying that senators could not serve concurrently on the Finance and Appropriations committees or the Foreign Relations and Armed Services committees.

The Rules Committee, also on June 16, approved S Res 228, streamlining Senate floor procedures. Under the resolution, adding unrelated riders to appropriations bills would have been made more difficult, and amendments that changed legislative language instead of funding would have been declared out of order. To overturn a parliamentary ruling that an amendment was not germane would have required 60 votes. Under existing procedures, only a majority was needed. S Res 228 also would have blocked members from filibustering motions to proceed to consideration of a bill. Supporters of the provision said the minority would retain the right to filibuster the bills when the Senate was considering them. Opponents countered that the ability to block floor consideration was one of the few ways the minority could influence the floor agenda. The committee removed language in the resolution that would have charged to individual members' time limits any time spent in quorum calls once cloture had been invoked. Byrd argued that many quorums were called for legitimate reasons and that individual members should not have their remaining debate time shortened.

Anticipating that the recommendations would not make it to the floor, Boren and Domenici offered the full package of joint committee proposals to streamline committee and legislative procedures as an amendment to the fiscal 1995 District of Columbia appropriations bill (HR 4649). But at the urging of Byrd, the Senate refused to waive Senate budget rules and make the Boren-Domenici amendment in order. The Sept. 29 vote was 58–41; 60 votes were needed to waive budget rules.

House

The House Rules Committee considered its version of the joint committee recommendations (HR 3801) but did not reach a final agreement on the bill.

At the first markup session on Aug. 4, Rules Committee Chairman Joe Moakley, D-Mass., offered a new draft of HR 3801 with several changes, the most prominent of which dropped a plan for a two-year appropriations cycle. When members resumed the markup session Sept. 21, the panel voted on only one amendment before recessing. The committee adopted an amendment to delete the requirement for a two-year budget cycle. There was no further action.   ❑

Professional Administrator

Despite assurances from Speaker Thomas S. Foley, D-Wash., that he had full operating authority, the House's first professional administrator, Leonard P. Wishart III, abruptly resigned effective Jan. 21, 1994. The position, formally known as director of nonlegislative and financial services, was created by the House in April 1992, during the controversy surrounding overdrafts at the House bank and embezzlement at the House Post Office. *(Congress and the Nation Vol. VIII, p. 947)*

Wishart supervised a budget of more than $14 million and more than 600 employees. He had several run-ins with the House Administration Committee, which provided policy direction and oversight of the professional administrator. The legislation creating Wishart's job included a list of tasks that he was to be in charge of, but House Administration Chairman Charlie Rose, D-N.C., argued that it implicitly gave his panel the power to alter the list and was not binding on the current Congress. Wishart was not allowed to assume control over several opera-

tions within the clerk's office, including the photography office and the telephone system, as well as the chamber's computer system, which had 254 employees.

Rose had argued that the computer system was a legislative function that needed to remain under the direct control of members. The House Administration Oversight Subcommittee split along party lines on the issue, with Republicans supporting Wishart. In a letter to Republican leaders in November 1993, lead committee Republican Bill Thomas, Calif., complained, "The transfers [to Wishart] have appeared to bog down as they have gotten closer to Chairman Rose's power base." An aide denied that Rose was trying to protect his power.

Wishart was temporarily replaced by Randall Medlock, his deputy. *(House rules changes, p. 887)*   ❑

Delegate Voting Privileges

At the start of the 103rd Congress, the House amended its rules to give the resident commissioner from Puerto Rico and the delegates from American Samoa, the District of Columbia, Guam and the Virgin Islands the right to vote on the floor when the House was considering bills for amendment in the Committee of the Whole, a parliamentary framework that expedited action. Delegates already could vote in committee. However, the new rule stipulated that, if the delegates' votes made the difference between winning and losing, an automatic revote would take place in which they would not participate. This proviso was added to fend off charges that delegate voting was unconstitutional and to assuage Republicans whose 10-vote gain in the 1992 elections would be halved by giving voting privileges to the five, who were all Democrats. *(Background, Congress and the Nation Vol. VIII, p. 948)*

But Republicans were not assuaged. House Minority Leader Robert H. Michel, R-Ill., a dozen GOP members and three citizens filed suit Jan. 7, 1993, challenging the new voting procedure. At a Feb. 9 hearing, they offered three main arguments: (1) The Committee of the Whole was not a committee, as the Democrats claimed. It was, they argued, tantamount to the full House and should be governed by the Constitution's provisions detailing House powers. (2) A vote in the Committee of the Whole effectively franchised citizens of the territories and the District of Columbia at the expense of state citizens and their representatives, whose voting power was diminished by the greater vote totals. (3) Delegates were granted committee voting privileges by law, not House rule, and the House could not expand those powers without statutory authority granted by the full Congress and the president.

U.S. District Judge Harold H. Greene said in *Michel v. Anderson* on March 8 that the rule was constitutional because of the provision for automatic revotes. Michel and several other Republicans appealed the decision. On Jan. 25, 1994, the U.S. Court of Appeals for the District of Columbia Circuit reaffirmed Judge Greene's ruling. However, Judge Laurence H. Silberman, writing for the unanimous three-judge panel, said the House had come "perilously close" to violating the Constitution in instituting the procedure. It would be "blatantly unconstitutional" to allow anyone who is not a full member of the House the right to a real vote, Silberman wrote.

Of the 404 times that delegates were eligible to vote during the 103rd Congress, only three times—all in 1994—did their votes prove decisive, thus triggering an automatic revote:

• On March 27, an amendment to a proposed balanced-budget constitutional amendment (H J Res 103), which would have made raising taxes difficult, was rejected 213–215. All the delegates voted "nay"; on the revote, the amendment was adopted 211–204.

• On June 23, an amendment to protect fiscal 1995 appropriations for the National Endowment for the Arts (HR 4602) was adopted 218–214. Four delegates voted "yea" and one did not vote; on the revote, the amendment was rejected 210–216.

• On June 24, amendment to the fiscal 1995 Commerce, Justice, State appropriations bill (HR 4603), which would have eliminated a program to create a global network of schoolchildren collecting environmental data, was rejected 190–192. Three delegates voted "nay" and two did not vote; on the revote, the amendment was rejected on a 184–184 tie vote.

The five delegates had lower participation rates than regular representatives. In 1993, the delegates voted 79 percent of the time on the 189 votes for which they were eligible, compared with 96 percent for the full House. In 1994, the delegates voted in 81 percent of the 215 opportunities, compared with 95 percent for the full House.

As soon as the delegates cast their first votes in 1993, the Republicans, in protest, began a parliamentary counterattack by taking advantage of a House rule that allowed members to demand a new vote on any amendment adopted in the Committee of the Whole. On those votes, taken by the full House, the delegates could not vote. No vote was automatically retaken in 1993, because the delegates' votes never determined the outcome of a vote. But revotes demanded by Republicans were common, and they contributed to an extraordinary number of House roll calls. In 1993, the House took 597 votes (excluding quorum calls), 26 percent more than in 1992 and the highest number of recorded votes since 1979. Sixty-nine were revotes or separate votes on amendments that had been adopted in the Committee of the Whole. The GOP retreated from the strategy in 1994, demanding only one such revote that year. *(House rules changes, p. 887)* ❑

Workplace Compliance

The House passed and a Senate committee reported legislation (HR 4822) that would have subjected Congress to the same labor laws that governed private sector companies. When Republicans blocked floor action on HR 4822 in the Senate, the House proceeded to change its rules to make the House subject to the compliance requirements. *(1995–1996 action, p. 890)*

BACKGROUND

For decades, Congress exempted itself from certain laws, primarily those that would affect congressional staff, citing the Constitution's separation of powers doctrine. Leaders of both parties argued that neither executive branch agencies nor the courts should be able to interfere with internal operations of the legislative branch. They also worried that members could get dragged into lawsuits designed to create political embarrassment.

In recent years, Congress established alternative mechanisms for enforcing the laws that did not involve the courts or the executive branch. The House set up the Office of Fair Employment Practices in 1989 to counsel staff, mediate conflicts and render decisions on formal complaints regarding discrimination, harassment and overtime. The Senate had its own Office of Fair Employment Practices, created in 1991, with limited judicial review of internal decisions. However, according to a survey released Sept. 17, 1993, conducted for the Joint Committee on the Organization of Congress, about 40 percent of House workers and 30 percent of Senate workers surveyed said concerns about confidentiality and notification made them unlikely to file complaints through these offices.

The Senate, traditionally jealous of its prerogatives, set up a bipartisan task force in the fiscal 1993 legislative branch appropriations bill (PL 102-392) to examine the issue of congressional workplace compliance and report to the joint committee. The task force, headed by Sen. Harry Reid, D-Nev., sent its recommendations to Majority Leader George J. Mitchell, D-Maine, the week of Dec. 6, 1993, but they were not made public. However, in an Aug. 13, 1993, letter to Mitchell, Reid said the task force had unanimously voted that the Senate should keep the system for assuring compliance and handling grievances within the Senate instead of using extra-congressional enforcement boards. On the House side, members, largely for political reasons, were more willing to move aggressively to address the situation. Speaker Thomas S. Foley, D-Wash., sent a letter in August 1993 to the joint committee, saying, "I believe now is the time to develop a workable mechanism to apply and enforce those laws in Congress." *(Congressional reform, p. 878)*

LEGISLATIVE ACTION

The House passed HR 4822 by a vote of 427–4 on Aug. 10, 1994. The bill had been reported Aug. 2 from the House Rules and House Administration committees (H Rept 103-650, Parts I and II)

HR 4822 would have brought Congress under the coverage of a host of labor and worker protection laws: the Fair Labor Standards Act of 1938 (PL 75-718), which had been amended in 1989 to extend some provisions to the House (PL 101-157); Americans with Disabilities Act of 1990 (PL 101-336); Civil Service Reform Act of 1978 (PL 95-454); Occupational Safety and Health Act of 1970 (PL 91-596); Civil Rights Act of 1964 (PL 88-352); Age Discrimination in Employment Act of 1967 (PL 90-202); Family and Medical Leave Act of 1993 (PL 103-3); Employee Polygraph Protection Act of 1988 (PL 100-347); and Worker Adjustment and Retraining Notification Act of 1988 (PL 100-379).

HR 4822 also would have established an Office of Compliance to issue regulations and enforce the workplace laws for both chambers. The office would have been overseen by a board of eight directors evenly divided between House and Senate appointees. The office would have determined whether nonsalaried congressional employees were eligible for overtime or should be compensated with time off for hours worked over 40 in a week.

The bill would have provided a four-part process for filing grievances on alleged violations of the law. The steps were counseling, mediation, formal administrative hearing and, if either an employee or a member was dissatisfied with the results, judicial review of the situation.

The House Administration Committee struck language to apply the Freedom of Information Act to Congress. The panel also approved an amendment to clarify that the institution, not individual members, would be held liable for violations of the labor laws.

During the floor debate, the House adopted, 374–57, a Leslie L. Byrne, D-Va., amendment to require that any "standard benefits package" approved as part of a health care bill apply to members of Congress. By voice vote, members adopted amendments to prohibit the personal use by members or staff of frequent flier travel awards that accrued from official travel, to require the Office of Compliance to report annually on the demographics of congressional employees, to require that meetings of the board of the compliance office be open to the public and to allow former members and staff to be on the board of the compliance office but bar former members from serving as executive director. The bill already prohibited lobbyists from serving on the board. The House rejected, 216–220, an amendment offered by Eric D. Fingerhut, D-Ohio, that would have barred not only former members and lobbyists but also former congressional employees from serving as executive director. Members also rejected amendments to require congressional employees to complete an administrative review of complaints before filing a lawsuit in federal court and to decrease the time for congressional compliance with certain labor laws from one year to six months after enactment.

The Senate Governmental Affairs Committee reported an amended HR 4822 (S Rept 103-397) on Oct. 3. The committee amended the bill to allow congressional employees to take claims to a federal appeals court after a counseling process but before they had completed internal administrative processes. Despite having wide, bipartisan support in the Senate, the bill never got to the floor. Trent Lott, R-Miss., on Oct. 6 blocked a move to take up the bill, saying he was doing so for another, unidentified member of his party.

HOUSE RULES CHANGE

With the bill snagged in the Senate, the House on Oct. 7 voted 348–3 to approve a resolution (H Res 578) that amended House rules to make the House subject to the labor laws it enacted.

The rules change was designed to let members tell constituents they had done what they could to address a common voter complaint: that Congress imposed laws on others that it was not willing to live by. It also allowed freshmen to say they delivered on a key "reform" even though more sweeping proposals to alter Congress's operations ran aground.

Using the rules approach, however, effectively nullified the section of HR 4822 that would have allowed any of the roughly 40,000 congressional employees to take employment grievances straight to federal court. The resolution provided only an internal administrative review and mediation process, the results of which could be appealed to the directors of a compliance board for a final decision.

Legislative Branch Staff

The fiscal 1994 legislative branch appropriations bill (HR 2348—PL 103-69) directed that all legislative branch agencies with more than 100 employees cut their staffs by 4 percent by the end of fiscal 1995—at least 2.5 percent by the end of fiscal 1994. The measure also stipulated that 10 percent of the positions had to be higher-pay jobs. The cuts were intended to mirror the executive branch reductions ordered by President Clinton in 1993 as part of his plan to "reinvent government." ('Reinventing government,' p. 811)

The base for calculating the cuts was the number of employees on staff on Sept. 30, 1992, unless the House and Senate Appropriations Committees approved a later date (up to Sept. 30, 1993) for a particular agency. In June 1993, House Appropriations estimated that the provision would reduce the Sept. 30, 1992, employment level of the covered entities by 920 in fiscal 1994—from 37,087 to 36,167—for a total savings of more than $50 million.

HR 2348 allowed the General Accounting Office, the Government Printing Office and the Library of Congress to offer early retirement options to their employees in an attempt to cut their staffs. The library reported on Oct. 14, 1993, that 149 staffers took advantage of the option on the first day it was offered, accepting up to $25,000 each.

The House Administration Committee on March 9, 1994, acted unilaterally to cut 319 full-time positions. The House's restaurant operations would be turned over to a private contractor, taking 180 jobs off the legislative branch payroll. The committee also counted as eliminated the 86 staff positions lost from the four select committees that were abolished in early 1993. Furthermore, the director of nonlegislative and financial services, also known as the professional administrator, was directed to cut another 53 positions from his own staff or the staffs of the clerk and the sergeant-at-arms.

Senior House Administration Committee Republicans Bill Thomas, Calif., and Pat Roberts, Kan., protested that they had not been consulted. But the plan was approved 12–7 along party lines. "This kind of sacrifice is sort of a gimmick," said Roberts. He said he thought members who had voted to reduce the size of the legislative branch would be surprised to learn that they did not need to cut any staff positions. The committee action did not need the approval of the full House.

'Ghost Voting'

House Speaker Thomas S. Foley, D-Wash., and Minority Leader Robert H. Michel, R-Ill., announced May 18, 1994, that no basis existed for an investigation into "ghost voting" by members.

Foley and Michel acknowledged looking into rumors that one member might have used the voting cards of other members to record votes for them on the House's electronic voting system—a violation of House rules. Richard W. Pombo, R-Calif., said in a May 18 statement that in February he saw several voting cards in the possession of one member and reported it to Michel. He did not allege that he saw a member use the voting cards. On May 17, Michel obtained electronic voting records for two days, one each in February and March, according to a GOP aide. The next morning, Chief Deputy Whip Robert S. Walker, R-Pa., alluded to ghost voting in a floor speech. A few hours later, Foley and Michel stated that no evidence existed of any voting irregularities.

Foley on May 19 said that many members had multiple voting cards because they had been issued replacements for cards that had been temporarily misplaced. Sometimes, he said, members took several cards to the floor to figure out which one had been activated for voting.

In 1987, Austin J. Murphy, D-Pa., was reprimanded for several instances of misconduct, including allowing someone else to vote for him. *(Congress and the Nation Vol. VII, p. 885)* ❏

1995–1996

The 1994 elections brought a changed landscape—Republican majorities in both the House and Senate. As a result of legislation enacted in 1995, members of Congress for the first time were subject to the same workplace laws as other employers. Efforts to place restrictions on the lobbying activities of former members stalled in the 104th Congress. But a measure consolidating several House accounts was signed into law. The House acted on a number of internal matters: a so-called "Corrections Day" calendar was set up to abolish federal regulations, the mail and printing operations were privatized and new rules were established regarding members' use of their computer Web sites.

The ethics case of Bob Packwood, R-Ore., was resolved in 1995 with his resignation from the Senate. Many other members were investigated for alleged wrongdoing, most notably House Speaker Newt Gingrich, R-Ga.

Organization

The historic transfer of power from the Democrats to the Republicans at the beginning of the 104th Congress was quickly translated into not only a switch in the leadership of the House and Senate but also changes in how each chamber conducted its business. Reform-minded House GOP members, in particular, instituted numerous rules changes.

SENATE

The conservative bent of the Republican majority resulted in a slight shakeup in the leadership. The Democrats, meanwhile, had to choose a new leader.

Majority Leadership

Senate Republicans chose their leadership for the 104th Congress in a closed caucus Dec. 2, 1994. Robert Dole, Kan., was unopposed as the new majority leader, a post he held in 1985–1986.

By a vote of 27–26, Trent Lott of Mississippi won the job of majority whip, edging out Alan K. Simpson of Wyoming, who had held the second highest Republican leadership position for a decade. Lott's victory was a milestone for the strongly partisan conservative wing of the party, and a signal of its desire for a bolder style in pushing the party's agenda. The narrowness of the vote was emblematic of the divide between moderate Republicans and the GOP right.

Thad Cochran, Miss., retained his post as chairman of the Republican Conference. Connie Mack of Florida became Republican Conference secretary, and Strom Thurmond, S.C., was named president pro tempore.

Dole resigned from the Senate on June 11, 1996, to devote his full attention to running for president. Lott was elected majority leader June 12, defeating Cochran by a lopsided, secret ballot vote of 44–8. Don Nickles of Oklahoma was chosen to succeed Lott as majority whip.

Minority Leadership

Senate Democrats faced a scramble because their leader, George J. Mitchell of Maine, had retired at the end of the 103rd Congress, and a leading contender to succeed him—Jim Sasser of Tennessee—had been defeated in the November 1994 elections.

In a secret ballot Dec. 2, 1994, Senate Democrats by 24–23 chose Tom Daschle, S.D., as minority leader, over Christopher J. Dodd, Conn. Initially, the vote was deadlocked 23–23. The tie was broken when the lone proxy vote, cast by Ben Nighthorse Campbell of Colorado, went to Daschle.

For the two other elected party posts, the caucus reelected Wendell H. Ford of Kentucky as minority whip, and Barbara A. Mikulski of Maryland ran unopposed to replace David Pryor, Ark., as conference secretary.

Committees

With the GOP takeover of the Senate, all committee and ranking member seats were occupied anew. Committee chairmen at the beginning of the 104th Congress were: Agriculture, Nutrition, and Forestry, Richard G. Lugar, Ind.; Appropriations, Mark O. Hatfield, Ore.; Armed Services, Strom Thurmond, S.C.; Banking, Housing, and Urban Affairs, Alfonse M. D'Amato, N.Y.; Budget, Pete V. Domenici, N.M.; Commerce, Science, and Transportation, Larry Pressler, S.D.; Energy and Natural Resources, Frank H. Murkowski, Alaska; Environment and Public Works, John H. Chafee, R.I.; Finance, Bob Packwood, Ore.; Foreign Relations, Jesse Helms, N.C.; Governmental Affairs, William V. Roth Jr., Del.; Indian Affairs, John McCain, Ariz.; Judiciary, Orrin G. Hatch, Utah; Labor and Human Resources, Nancy Landon Kassebaum, Kan.; Rules and Administration, Ted Stevens, Alaska; Select Ethics, Mitch McConnell, Ky.; Select Intelligence, Arlen Specter, Pa.; Small Business, Christopher S.

CONTRACT WITH AMERICA

On Sept. 27, 1994, six weeks before the Nov. 8 election, approximately 350 House Republican members and candidates unveiled a 10-point campaign manifesto—they called it their "Contract with America." The event, staged on the Capitol lawn and spearheaded by Minority Whip Newt Gingrich, R-Ga., was aimed at creating a high-profile national platform from which Republicans could attack the Democratic Congress and present their own priorities. When the GOP won a major victory in 1994, the contract became the agenda for House Republicans' first 100 days in office in the 104th Congress. GOP leaders promised only that the House would vote on the proposals, not that all would pass or be enacted.

Following are the 10 subject areas covered by the contract, as well as the changes in internal House procedures discussed in the contract's preface.

• **Preface: Congressional Process.** Require that Congress end its exemptions from 11 workplace laws (S 2—PL 104-1); and revise House rules to cut committees and their staff, impose term limits on committee chairmen, end proxy voting, require three-fifths majority votes for tax increases (H Res 6). *(Workplace compliance, p. 890; House rules, p. 887)*

• **Balanced Budget Amendment, Line-Item Veto.** Send to the states a constitutional amendment requiring a balanced budget (H J Res 1); and give the president enhanced rescissions power to cancel (line-item veto) any appropriation or targeted tax break (S 4—PL 104-130). *(Balanced budget amendment, p. 80; enhanced rescissions, p. 78)*

• **Crime.** Require restitution to victims; modify the exclusionary rule; increase grants for prison construction; speed deportation of criminal immigrants; create block grants to give communities flexibility in using anticrime funds; and limit death row appeals (S 735—PL 104-132 and HR 3610—PL 104-208 each covered some elements). *(House crime package, p. 733; terrorism, p. 727)*

• **Welfare.** Cap spending on cash welfare; impose a lifetime five-year limit on welfare benefits; deny benefits to unwed mothers under age 18; give states new flexibility, including the option to receive federal welfare payments as a block grant (HR 2491 and HR 4 were vetoed; HR 3734—PL 104-193 went further than the contract in some respects and made some requirements optional to states). *(Welfare reform, p. 578)*

• **Families and Children.** Require parental consent for children participating in surveys (HR 1271); provide tax benefits for adoptions (HR 3448—PL 104-188) and home care for the elderly (HR 2491 was vetoed); increase penalties for sex crimes against children (HR 1240—PL 104-71); and strengthen enforcement of child support orders (HR 3734—PL 104-193). *(Family privacy, p. 751; business tax breaks, p. 100; budget reconciliation, p. 68; sex-related crimes, p. 738; welfare reform, p. 578)*

• **Middle-Class Tax Cut.** Add $500-per-child tax credit; ease "marriage penalty" for filers of joint tax returns; and expand individual retirement account savings plans (HR 3448—PL 104-188 covered some elements; HR 2491, covering other elements, was vetoed). *(Business tax breaks, p. 100; budget reconciliation, p. 68)*

• **National Security.** Prohibit use of U.S. troops in U.N. missions under foreign command (HR 3019—PL 104-134; HR 3610—PL 104-208); prohibit defense cuts to finance social programs; develop a missile defense system for U.S. territory; and cut funding for U.N. peacekeeping missions (HR 7, HR 3308). *('GOP Contract' proposals, p. 315; U.N. command of U.S. troops, p. 318; antimissile defenses, p. 316; U.N. peacekeeping missions, p. 236)*

• **Social Security.** Repeal the 1993 increase in Social Security benefits subject to income tax; permit senior citizens to earn up to $30,000 a year without losing benefits; and give tax incentives for buying long-term care insurance (HR 3136—PL 104-121 and HR 3103—PL 104-191 covered some elements; HR 2491, covering other elements, was vetoed). *(Social Security earnings limit, p. 674; health insurance regulation, p. 547; budget reconciliation, p. 68)*

• **Capital Gains and Regulations.** Cut capital gains taxes; allow for accelerated depreciation of business assets; increase first-year deductions for small businesses (HR 3448—PL 104-188 covered some elements; HR 2491 was vetoed); reduced unfunded mandates (S 1—PL 104-4); reduce federal paperwork (S 244—PL 104-13); and require federal agencies to assess risks, use cost-benefit analysis, reduce paperwork, and reimburse property owners for reductions in value as a result of regulations (HR 9, S 291, S 333, S 343, S 605). *(Business tax breaks, p. 100; budget reconciliation, p. 68; unfunded mandates, p. 837; paperwork reduction, p. 840; regulatory overhaul, p. 842)*

• **Civil Law and Product Liability.** Establish national product liability law with limits on punitive damages (HR 956 was vetoed); make it harder for investors to sue companies (HR 1058—PL 104-67); and apply "loser pays" rule to certain federal cases (HR 988). *(Product liability, p. 376; securities fraud lawsuits, p. 142)*

Bond, Mo.; Special Aging, William S. Cohen, Maine; and Veterans' Affairs, Alan K. Simpson, Wyo.

Packwood Sept. 7, 1995, resigned his chairmanship of Finance upon the announcement of his impending resignation from the Senate in the face of almost certain expulsion on charges of sexual harassment and other misconduct. He was succeeded as chairman by Roth. Roth was succeeded as chairman of Governmental Affairs by Stevens, who was succeeded as chairman of Rules and Administration by John W. Warner, Va.

The Democratic ranking members on Senate committees were: Agriculture, Nutrition, and Forestry, Patrick J. Leahy, Vt.; Appropriations, Robert C. Byrd, W.Va.; Armed Services, Sam Nunn, Ga.; Banking, Housing, and Urban Affairs, Paul. S. Sarbanes, Md.; Budget, Jim Exon, Neb.; Commerce, Science, and Transportation, Ernest F. Hollings, S.C.; Energy and Natural Resources, J. Bennett Johnston, La.; Environment and Public Works, Max Baucus, Mont.; Finance, Daniel Patrick Moynihan, N.Y.; Foreign Relations, Claiborne Pell, R.I.; Governmental Affairs, John Glenn, Ohio; Indian Affairs, Daniel K. Inouye, Hawaii; Judiciary, Joseph R. Biden Jr., Del.; Labor and Human

HATFIELD CHALLENGE

One hallmark of the GOP success in Congress was its solidarity. As a result, Senate Republicans were in an uproar after Appropriations Committee Chairman Mark O. Hatfield, R-Ore., March 2, 1995, voted against the balanced budget amendment (H J Res 1), the lone GOP "nay" for a high-profile measure that lost by one vote. *(Balanced-budget amendment, p. 80)*

Alfonse M. D'Amato, R-N.Y., the chairman of the National Republican Senatorial Committee, suggested the day after the vote that the party might withhold funds from Hatfield's reelection campaign in 1996 as punishment. Majority Whip Trent Lott, R-Miss., publicly criticized Hatfield for his vote, saying a committee chairman had a responsibility to adhere to the party position. Majority Leader Bob Dole, R-Kan., revealed on CBS-TV's *Face the Nation* that Hatfield had offered to resign before the vote, a proposal Dole rejected.

A full-scale rebellion subsequently began brewing to unseat Hatfield. The leaders of the revolt, Rick Santorum of Pennsylvania and Connie Mack of Florida, declared that the GOP conference should vote on whether Hatfield should keep his chairmanship. The two senators argued that the balanced budget amendment was the centerpiece of the Republican agenda and that Hatfield, as the Appropriations Committee chairman, had to support it. Hatfield was defiant in the face of the challenge, rejecting calls to step down and standing by what he called a vote of conscience.

The issue was taken up March 8 in a senators-only conference meeting. Before the session, Mack said he would not seek a vote if it was clear he did not have enough support; no vote occurred.

Stripping a chairmanship from a member was a rare event in the Senate. Furthermore, a single vote had never cost a senator a chairmanship.

Resources, Edward M. Kennedy, Mass.; Rules and Administration, Wendell H. Ford, Ky.; Select Ethics, Richard H. Bryan, Nev. (vice chairman); Select Intelligence, Bob Kerrey, Neb. (vice chairman); Small Business, Dale Bumpers, Ark.; Special Aging, David Pryor, Ark.; and Veterans' Affairs, John D. Rockefeller IV, W.Va.

Bryan left Select Ethics in January 1996. Byron L. Dorgan, N.D., was named the new vice chairman.

Rules

Senate Republicans voted July 19, 1995, on a package of rules changes intended to make senior members more beholden to the party. Dole had formed a task force in March to consider changes after a "nay" vote by Appropriations Committee Chairman Hatfield helped defeat the balanced budget amendment. *(Hatfield challenge, box, this page)*

Senate Republicans imposed a six-year term limit on committee chairmanships beginning in 1997. The new rule would apply even if the Republicans were in the minority. A member who had served six years as chairman could continue another

six years as ranking minority member. The conference also voted to require rotation every six years in all leadership positions except the top jobs of GOP leader and president pro tempore.

Republicans voted to require a chairman, beginning in 1997, to step aside if indicted for a felony until the case was resolved. If convicted, the member would lose his slot. Effective immediately, the conference dropped a requirement that a member vacate a chairmanship if indicted on a misdemeanor "relating to conduct of official Senate business." Members said they feared politically inspired charges that would force chairmen to step down.

The conference adopted a rule preventing a member who left a committee and then returned from reclaiming his position on the seniority ladder.

Republicans voted to adopt a formal legislative agenda at the start of each Congress, with positions on issues determined by a three-fourths vote of the GOP senators. Badly outnumbered by conservatives, moderates in the party tried to defeat the rule, complaining about ideological litmus tests, but it passed overwhelmingly.

Republicans rejected a task force proposal to give the authority to nominate committee chairmen to the party leader, subject to ratification by the conference in secret balloting. The existing rule, under which chairmen were nominated by their committee members and later ratified by the conference, was retained. Republicans did impose a requirement that the committee vote on the chairman by secret ballot, giving junior members the opportunity to put forward another candidate without fear of retribution.

None of the party rule changes applied to Democrats.

The Senate in 1995 also adopted gift restrictions. *(Gift restrictions, p. 922)*

HOUSE

New leaders abounded in the House—on both sides of the aisle. And a Republican became Speaker for the first time in 40 years.

Majority Leadership

House Republicans opened their party caucus Dec. 5, 1994, with a spirited endorsement of Newt Gingrich of Georgia as Speaker and the election of Dick Armey of Texas as majority leader. The GOP used elections to settle six lower leadership races, balancing the Southern tilt at the top with geographic diversity below and including two women.

Tom DeLay, Texas, won the most heated contest, a three-way race for majority whip. With a reputation as an able fund-raiser, he amassed 119 votes on the first secret ballot by aggressively courting incumbents and incoming freshmen. Robert S. Walker of Pennsylvania, who had Gingrich's vote but not an official endorsement, came in second with 80 votes, and Bill McCollum of Florida finished third with 28.

John A. Boehner, Ohio, defeated Duncan Hunter, Calif., for the post of conference chairman in what was seen as a victory for the party's newer members. The vote was 122–102. C. Christopher Cox, Calif., was elected Policy Committee chairman over Jim Kolbe of Arizona, 148–77. Although he was considered less combative than his colleagues, Cox said he endorsed the confrontational style espoused by Gingrich. In an uncontested race, the conference reelected Bill Paxon, N.Y., as chairman of the National Republican Congressional Committee.

Perhaps the biggest surprise during the GOP's organizational meetings was the election of two women, Susan Molinari of New York and Barbara F. Vucanovich of Nevada, to leadership posts. It was the first time that two women from the same party had been in the leadership together. By 124–100, Molinari beat Cliff Stearns, Fla., for the post of Republican Conference vice chair, despite attempts by antiabortion groups to defeat her. Vucanovich defeated Tim Hutchinson, Ark., for the conference secretary job, 138–90.

Minority Leadership

House Democrats gathered Nov. 30, 1994, and elected veteran leaders with liberal records. Richard A. Gephardt of Missouri, majority leader since 1989, was elected as minority leader, 150–58, over Charlie Rose of North Carolina. (Thomas S. Foley of Washington, who had served as Speaker since 1989, was defeated in the November 1994 elections.) David E. Bonior of Michigan was elected minority whip, defeating Charles W. Stenholm of Texas. The vote was 145–60. The resounding rejection of Southern conservatives Rose and Stenholm raised concerns that unhappy conservative Democrats might bolt and join the Republican ranks.

Vic Fazio, Calif., triumphed for the caucus chairmanship, 149–57, over Kweisi Mfume, Md. Barbara B. Kennelly of Connecticut edged out Louise M. Slaughter of New York, 93–90, as vice chair of the caucus.

Committees

The Republican Conference Dec. 7, 1994, ratified a slate of new committee chairmen proposed by Gingrich, with no one offering a challenge. Gingrich passed over the senior Republicans on three crucial committees—Appropriations, Commerce and Judiciary—to anoint more vigorous and assertive conservatives as chairmen.

Robert L. Livingston, La., was picked to head Appropriations. The panel's ranking Republican, Joseph M. McDade, Pa., was under federal indictment on corruption charges and was ordered to step aside until the case against him was resolved. (Although McDade was acquitted in 1996, Gingrich refused to accept Livingston's resignation to make way for McDade; Gingrich preferred Livingston's more conservative bent.) Carlos J. Moorhead, Calif., was passed over for chairman at both Commerce and Judiciary. Gingrich tapped the more aggressive Thomas J. Bliley Jr., of Virginia for Commerce and the widely respected Henry J. Hyde of Illinois for Judiciary.

Gingrich elevated two moderates—Benjamin A. Gilman, N.Y., to chair International Relations and Bill Goodling, Pa., to chair Economic and Educational Opportunities. Gerald B. H. Solomon, N.Y., was chosen Rules Committee chairman, even though he had challenged Gingrich in 1993 for the top GOP leadership position upon the retirement of Minority Leader Robert H. Michel, Ill.

The other House committee chairmanships were assigned as follows: Agriculture, Pat Roberts, Kan.; Banking and Financial Services, Jim Leach, Iowa; Budget, John R. Kasich, Ohio; Government Reform and Oversight, William F. Clinger, Pa.; House Oversight, Bill Thomas, Calif.; National Security, Floyd D. Spence, S.C.; Resources, Don Young, Alaska; Science, Robert S. Walker, Pa.; Select Intelligence, Larry Combest, Texas; Small Business, Jan Meyers, Kan.; Standards of Official Conduct, Nancy L. Johnson, Conn.; Transportation and Infrastructure, Bud Shuster, Pa.; Veterans' Affairs, Bob Stump, Ariz.; and Ways and Means, Bill Archer, Texas.

House Democrats Dec. 13–15, 1994, fell back on the venerable rule of seniority to make their committee assignments. The picks for ranking minority members were almost a mirror image of the Democrats who chaired the panels during the 103rd Congress. But Gephardt did replace Rose, who challenged him for the leadership post, as top Democrat on the Oversight Committee.

The ranking Democrats on House committees were: Agriculture, E. "Kiki" de la Garza, Texas; Appropriations, David R. Obey, Wis.; Banking and Financial Services, Henry B. Gonzalez, Texas; Budget, Martin Olav Sabo, Minn.; Commerce, John D. Dingell, Mich.; Economic and Educational Opportunities, William L. Clay, Mo.; Government Reform and Oversight, Cardiss Collins, Ill.; House Oversight, Vic Fazio, Calif.; International Relations, Lee H. Hamilton, Ind.; Judiciary, John Conyers Jr., Mich.; National Security, Ronald V. Dellums, Calif.; Resources, George Miller, Calif.; Rules, Joe Moakley, Mass.; Science, George E. Brown Jr., Calif.; Select Intelligence, Norm Dicks, Wash.; Small Business, John J. LaFalce, N.Y.; Standards of Official Conduct, Jim McDermott, Wash.; Transportation and Infrastructure, Norman Y. Mineta, Calif.; Veterans' Affairs, G. V. "Sonny" Montgomery, Miss.; and Ways and Means, Sam M. Gibbons, Fla.

Mineta, who resigned from Congress Oct. 10, 1995, was succeeded as ranking member on Transportation and Infrastructure by James L. Oberstar, Minn.

Rules

With a string of lopsided votes, the Republican majority on Jan. 4, 1995, put in place a package of House rules changes (H Res 6). The changes reflected promises made in the GOP "Contract with America" to act on the first day of the new Congress to reform the way the House conducted its business. Under H Res 6:

- **Committees Eliminated.** Three committees were abolished: District of Columbia, Merchant Marine and Fisheries, and Post Office and Civil Service. Several other committees were renamed.
- **Committee Jurisdictions.** The jurisdiction of the Post Office and Civil Service Committee and the District of Columbia Committee was transferred to the Government Reform and Oversight Committee. Matters handled by the Merchant Marine and Fisheries Committee were split among three other committees. Several issues formerly handled by the Energy and Commerce Committee were parceled out to other committees.

- **Committee Staff Cuts.** The total number of committee staff was cut by one-third compared with the levels in the 103rd Congress.

- **Subcommittee Limits.** With three exceptions, no committee was allowed more than five subcommittees. The exceptions were Appropriations (13), Government Reform and Oversight (seven) and Transportation and Infrastructure (six).

- **Subcommittee Staff.** Staff hiring was to be controlled by committee chairmen. Subcommittee chairmen and ranking minority members no longer had authority to hire one staffer each.

- **Assignments.** Members could serve on no more than two standing committees and four subcommittees, except for chairmen and ranking members, who could serve ex officio on all subcommittees. Exceptions to the membership limit had to be approved by party caucuses and the House.

- **Proxy Voting.** The rules prohibited the practice of allowing a chairman or other designee to cast an absent member's vote in committee. Several committees had long had such a ban.

- **Published Votes.** Committees were required to publish the names of members voting for or against all bills and amendments.

- **Rolling Quorums.** Chairmen could no longer hold open a vote in committee indefinitely, allowing members to show up at their convenience to vote.

- **Open Meetings.** Committees and subcommittees were barred from closing their meetings to the public, except when an open meeting would endanger national security, compromise sensitive law enforcement information, or possibly degrade, defame or incriminate any person. Closing a meeting under those exceptions would require a majority vote of the committee. Immediate past rules allowed a committee to vote to close its meetings without specifying the circumstances.

- **Broadcast Coverage.** Committees were required to allow radio and television broadcasts, as well as still photography, of all open meetings.

- **Budget Estimates.** Bills that increased spending on existing programs had to contain a cost estimate that showed the existing cost of the programs. The rule formalized a practice common in most committees.

- **Multiple Referrals.** The Speaker could no longer send a bill to more than one committee simultaneously for consideration. The Speaker was allowed to send a bill to a second committee after the first was finished acting, or he could refer parts of a bill to separate committees.

- **Term Limits.** The Speaker could serve no more than four consecutive two-year terms. Chairmen of committees and subcommittees could hold their positions for no more than three consecutive terms, beginning with the 104th Congress. Members could serve on the Budget Committee for four terms during any six Congresses. Previously, members were limited to three terms in any five Congresses. For the Select Intelligence Committee, members could serve up to four terms in any six successive Congresses. The chairman and ranking minority member could serve in one additional Congress if they began their terms in the preceding Congress. Previously, members were limited to three terms.

- **Supermajority for Tax Increases.** A three-fifths majority of members voting was required to pass any bill, amendment or conference report containing an increase in income tax rates.

- **Retroactive Tax Increases.** No retroactive tax increases that took effect before the date of enactment of the bill that required them were allowed.

- **Delegate Voting.** Delegates from the District of Columbia, Guam, the Virgin Islands and American Samoa, and the resident commissioner of Puerto Rico could no longer vote in or preside over the Committee of the Whole, which the House entered into when it was amending a bill on the floor. The Democrats had permitted delegates to vote under such circumstances. Delegates could continue to vote in committees. (*Delegate voting privileges, p. 881*)

- **Verbatim *Congressional Record*.** Members could no longer delete or change remarks made on the floor in the *Congressional Record* except for technical or grammatical corrections. Remarks inserted through unanimous consent to revise and extend a speech would appear in the *Record* in a different typeface.

- **Roll Call Votes.** Automatic roll call votes were required on bills and conference reports that made appropriations and raised taxes. The annual budget resolution and its conference report would have a mandatory roll call as well.

- **Appropriations Amendments.** Members were guaranteed the right to offer limitation amendments, which specified that no funds be spent for a particular purpose, without having to defeat a motion to end amendments—unless the majority leader offered that motion.

- **Motions to Recommit.** The minority leader or his designee was guaranteed the right to offer a motion to recommit with instructions on a bill under consideration in the House. Such a motion enabled the minority to propose changes, and the vote was on sending the bill back to committee to make those revisions.

- **Commemoratives.** Commemorative legislation—often passed as the behest of interest groups—could not be introduced or considered.

- **Administrative Offices.** The Office of the Doorkeeper was abolished, its function transferred to the sergeant at arms. A new position of chief administrative officer (CAO) was created, replacing the director of nonlegislative services. The CAO was to be nominated by the Speaker and elected by the full House.

- **House Audit.** The House inspector general was instructed to complete an audit of the financial records of the House while it was under the control of the Democrats. He could contract with a private accounting firm to perform the audit, if necessary. (*House audit, box, p. 889*)

- **Legislative Service Organization.** Funding for legislative service organizations, the 28 caucuses in the House that received office space and budgets to operate in the House, was abolished.

The House Dec. 22, 1995, voted 259–128 to bar members from accepting advances for books and to require that book contracts be cleared by the ethics committee (H Res 299). The resolution took effect Jan. 1, 1996.

The House in 1995 also imposed a broad ban on most gifts from outside interests. (*Gift restrictions, p. 922*) ❑

HOUSE AUDIT

The accounting firm of Price Waterhouse on July 18, 1995, delivered to House Republican leaders the first-ever outside audit of the chamber's books. The focus was on the 15-month period between Sept. 30, 1993, and Jan. 1, 1995, but auditors were allowed to go back before September 1993 to pursue problems. The audit cost $3.2 million.

Under the existing system, House members submitted vouchers for office, travel and other official expenses, which were then paid by the House Finance Office. The principal source of information about House spending was an annual report by the House clerk, which typically listed more than 90,000 disbursements ranging from a few dollars for newspaper subscriptions to tens of thousands of dollars for staff salaries. The General Accounting Office regularly audited House operations and, in recent years, had generally been positive about its financial state, although the agency did raise questions about its accounting system.

In its report, Price Waterhouse declined to give an opinion on the state of House finances, saying the problems were so severe and the accounting practices so antiquated that they could not be certain the numbers were reliable. The audit showed that the House accounts were partly kept in written ledgers with numbers frequently crossed out, that staff members were accidentally overpaid tens of thousands of dollars, that waste in paying for goods and services was rampant, that the House computer system was vulnerable to hackers, and that the House spent $5 million in designing a computerized financial system that proved inadequate. Price Waterhouse auditors found an additional $4.3 million in waste and unneeded spending.

Without naming names, the audit turned up 2,200 instances of possible double payments to members, staff and credit card companies for travel expenses during late 1993 and 1994. The overpayments may have totaled as much as $450,000. Records also showed that five unnamed House members overspent their office allowances. In one case, the overspending reached $11,000. Members were personally liable for such overspending. Some members also may have violated House rules by failing to report credit card debts exceeding $10,000 on their financial disclosure forms, the audit reported.

The auditors concluded that many of the violations resulted from poor accounting practices or lax enforcement that sometimes allowed members to overspend inadvertently or with the approval of House administrators. While expenditures were supposed to follow rules in the *Congressional Handbook*, the audit found that the rules were frequently waived, for example, to allow members to buy higher-priced office equipment not approved for House use or to grant staff retroactive pay increases.

Among the auditors' recommendations for overhauling the operation were to:

• Institute an accounting system called the accrual method that would enable administrators to track more easily when goods and services were ordered, received and paid for. The goal was to force members and their staff to budget for the full cost of the goods and services they used.

Under an accrual system, revenues and expenses were allocated over a fiscal year, amortized to give a more accurate picture of an institution's financial health at any given time. In contrast, Congress then was using cash-based accounting, which, like a family checkbook, calculated only money received or spent.

• Add controls on franked mail to prevent members from overspending appropriated amounts.

• Centralize authority for buying goods and services in the Office of Procurement and Purchasing and require open bidding for contracts.

• Redesign staff payroll practices to prevent overpaying salaries and benefits.

• Require members to abide by the office allowances for staff salaries, office expenses and mail costs, and combine those three accounts to allow members to spend their allowances as they chose. Such a consolidation was enacted in 1996 (HR 2739—PL 104-186). *(Members' accounts, p. 894)*

The House by 414-0 on July 18, 1995, voted for a resolution (H Res 192) to give House Inspector General John W. Lainhart IV until Nov. 30, 1995, to investigate whether violators should be forced to reimburse the House and whether allegations of wrongdoing should be referred to the House Committee on Standards of Official Conduct. On Nov. 30, Lainhart told the House Oversight Committee that he had found no pattern of fraud in House accounting practices but asked for, and received, an extension so he could continue to gather information.

Lainhart in July 1996 reported on the results of a follow-up to the Price Waterhouse audit, saying the House system for financial recordkeeping and accounting still had problems. He reiterated the recommendation that the House switch to the accrual method of accounting, saying his follow-up audit showed that "a systematic infrastructure is not fully in place to efficiently and effectively meet the House's financial management requirements."

Lainhart said four members had exceeded their spending allowances in 1995 and would have to reimburse House accounts from their personal expenses. He further said that:

• The House Office of Finance needed to provide members and committees with more accurate and timely information so they could better manage their own budgets.

• The Finance Office should hire more experienced staff, because it had become dependent on outside contractors to implement accounting changes and piled up "significant backlogs" in processing vouchers.

• The office needed to improve its monitoring of member expenses against allowances to avoid overspending.

• The House needed to identify the requirements for a permanent financial system, "which accurately and timely records obligations and commitments" so the chamber could know its liabilities at any given time.

Workplace Compliance

The first bill enacted during the Republican-led 104th Congress was S 2 (PL 104-1), which extended 11 federal labor and antidiscrimination laws to Congress and its related offices. The measure, which replaced a haphazard mix of internal protections, applied to about 34,000 congressional employees.

In a change that had met resistance over the years from senior members, S 2 allowed congressional employees to take claims to federal court after an initial mediation and counseling stage. Some members opposed allowing workers to drag them into court, particularly during the heat of an election campaign. But backers of the bill said that, without the option of using an independent court to seek redress, congressional employees would be denied the same rights given to private sector employees. The bill explicitly allowed members to discriminate in their hiring based on party affiliation or "political compatibility." The legislation also specified that the House and Senate ethics committees retained the power to discipline members, officers and employees for violating rules on nondiscrimination in employment.

BACKGROUND

Congress for decades had exempted itself from numerous workplace laws, often claiming that it was required to do so by the separation of powers doctrine and to protect members from politically inspired retaliation by disgruntled employees. But the exemptions ultimately became the target of reformers both inside and outside the institution, who attacked the practice as an arrogant failure by Congress to live under the laws it passed.

S 2 avoided a problem with separation of powers, which prevented the executive branch from administering laws that applied to the legislative branch, by setting up an Office of Compliance outside the executive branch to oversee congressional adherence to workplace laws. The new office was charged with issuing regulations to apply laws to the legislative branch and with setting up a system to handle complaints from employees.

A similar bill to require Congress to observe health and safety rules, set up a separate office to oversee compliance, and allow employees to sue in court had attracted bipartisan support in the 103rd Congress, but it got bogged down at the end of the session when an unidentified GOP senator blocked floor action on it. Ted Stevens, R-Alaska, later said he had asked for the bill to be stopped because he was in the hospital at the time and wanted a chance to review it. *(103rd Congress action, p. 882)*

HOUSE ACTION

The House passed its version of the Congressional Accountability Act (HR 1) by 429–0 in the session that began Jan. 4, 1995, and went well into the morning of Jan. 5. The bill applied 10 major laws to Congress and included language that was not in the new workplace compliance rules adopted by the House at the end of the second session of the 103rd Congress. In particular, HR 1 gave congressional employees the right to sue Congress in federal court for failure to abide by the laws and to recover damages. The rules changes had provided no outside legal recourse for congressional employees. In addition, HR 1 applied to employees of the Library of Congress, the General Accounting Office and other congressional agencies that were not covered under the 1994 rules changes. The bill required that, if a court mandated that a member of Congress pay damages, those fees were to be paid for by Congress out of taxpayer funds. *(Rules changes, p. 887)*

Barney Frank, D-Mass., opposed the rushed procedure under which the bill was considered, which he said denied members the opportunity to improve the legislation. Frank also bristled at the Republican leaders claiming credit for the measure. He reminded the House that the 1994 bill had passed the House with the support of the Democratic leadership but had died in the Senate because of objections from Republicans. Other lawmakers pointed out that HR 1 did not put Congress under the Freedom of Information Act (FOIA), which provided a mechanism for the public to seek government documents. The bill did call for a study to explore applying FOIA to Congress.

SENATE ACTION

The Senate version of the workplace compliance legislation (S 2) was largely similar to the House-passed HR 1 and to the measure that the House had passed in 1994. However, it did contain some changes that had been worked out in consultation with House sponsors. S 2:

• Added one law—the Veterans Re-employment Act of 1994, which sought to ensure swift reemployment of returning veterans—to the list of statutes that would apply to Congress.

• Provided for separate offices within the new Office of Compliance to administer the laws in each chamber. The House bill had proposed a unified office responsible for both chambers.

• Proposed to amend the various statutes to apply them to Congress, instead of leaving it to the Office of Compliance to draft regulations, as HR 1 did. Backers of the Senate bill said courts could interpret the regulations written by the compliance office differently from the precise language of the laws already on the books.

The Senate rejected a series of amendments that Democrats claimed were central to the theme of congressional accountability. Republicans said they supported many of the amendments but did not want to have them weigh down the underlying bill.

On the floor, the Senate:

• Tabled (killed), 52–39 on Jan. 5, a Carl Levin, D-Mich., and Paul Wellstone, D-Minn., amendment to institute a strict prohibition against members of Congress receiving substantive gifts from anyone except members of their family and close friends.

• Tabled, 64–35 on Jan. 10, a John Kerry, D-Mass., amendment to ban the personal use of campaign funds.

• Tabled, 79–20 on Jan. 10, a Patrick J. Leahy, D-Vt., amendment to bar congressional employers from requesting that employees or applicants fill out a questionnaire stating their political leanings.

• Tabled, 61–38 on Jan. 11, a Frank R. Lautenberg, D-N.J., amendment to cut members' salaries if budget law required across-the-board cuts in other programs.

• Tabled, 55–44 on Jan. 10, a Wellstone amendment to urge the Senate to consider by May 31, 1995, legislation to incorporate a strict ban on members receiving gifts.

• Tabled, 56–43 on Jan. 10, a Wellstone amendment to urge Congress not to enact any legislation that might raise the number of homeless and hungry children.

• Adopted, by voice vote on Jan. 10, a Wendell H. Ford, D-Ky., amendment to codify an existing rule that barred senators and staff from taking any frequent flier miles accrued from official travel for their own use. The Senate had agreed by a 55–44 vote earlier that day to a Republican motion that removed the House from the amendment on the grounds that it was improper for one chamber to dictate the other's internal operations. No ban on the use of frequent flier miles was imposed in the House.

The Senate passed S 2 by a vote of 98–1 on Jan. 11. Robert C. Byrd, D-W.Va., cast the sole vote against the measure, arguing that it would let the executive and judicial branches interfere with the legislative branch. Bill supporters rejected his argument, saying the new Office of Compliance would act as a buffer against any intrusion from the other branches of government. But Byrd said he was also troubled by the amount of authority the bill would vest with the compliance office, which was charged with enforcing laws and handling complaints.

Richard H. Bryan, D-Nev., eased passage of the bill by agreeing not to offer a contentious amendment to lower the rate at which members accrued pension benefits. The Bryan amendment proposed to bring the congressional pension rates for members and staff into parity with the pension rates of executive branch workers. Congressional employees accrued pensions at the rate of 2.5 percent of salary per year of service; the amendment proposed to lower that to between 1.5 percent and 2 percent, based on years of service, or the same rates applied to civil service pensions.

The Senate also passed an amended version of HR 1 by voice vote Jan. 12.

FINAL ACTION, MAJOR PROVISIONS

The House passed S 2, without change, by a vote of 390–0 on Jan. 17. President Clinton signed the bill into law on Jan. 23.

Following are the major provisions of S 2, as cleared:

Laws Applied to Congress

The law amended 11 statutes to apply specifically to Congress. They were the:

• **Civil Rights Act of 1964**—which prohibited discrimination in employment on the basis of race, color, religion, sex or nationality (PL 88-352). *(Civil rights act, Congress and the Nation Vol. I, p. 1635)*

• **Occupational Safety and Health Act of 1970 (OSHA)**—which set safety regulations for workplaces (PL 91-596). *(OSHA, Congress and the Nation Vol. III, p. 713)*

• **Age Discrimination in Employment Act of 1967**—which prohibited workplace discrimination against people age 40 and older (PL 90-202). *(Age discrimination, Congress and the Nation Vol. II, p. 620)*

• **Rehabilitation Act of 1973**—a law that provided federal aid for a variety of programs for disabled workers and for the training of personnel to work with the disabled (PL 93-112). *(1973 act, Congress and the Nation Vol. IV, p. 687)*

• **Americans with Disabilities Act of 1990**—which prohibited workplace discrimination against people with disabilities (PL 101-336). *(Americans with disabilities, Congress and the Nation Vol. VIII, p. 743)*

• **Family and Medical Leave Act of 1993**—a law that set criteria for unpaid parental and medical leave for employees seeking to spend time with children or ailing family members (PL 103-3). *(Family and medical leave, p. 655)*

• **Fair Labor Standards Act of 1938**—a statute dealing with minimum wage and mandatory overtime or compensation for employees who worked more than 40 hours per week, as updated in 1989 (PL 101-157). (The minimum wage was increased again in 1996.) *(1989 increase, Congress and the Nation Vol. VIII, p. 705; 1996 increase, p. 666)*

• **Employee Polygraph Protection Act of 1988**—a law restricting the use of polygraph tests of employees by employers (PL 100-347). The use of legal lie detector tests by the Capitol Police would not be affected by application of this law. *(Polygraph protection, Congress and the Nation Vol. VII, p. 700)*

• **Worker Adjustment and Retraining Notification Act of 1988**—a law requiring a 60-day advance notice of a plant closing or large layoffs of permanent workers (PL 100-379). *(1988 law, Congress and the Nation Vol. VII, p. 704)*

• **Veterans Re-employment Act of 1994**—which required employers to rehire at the same or similar position returning veterans who left their jobs after being called into military service (PL 103-353). *(Veterans reemployment, p. 599)*

• **Labor-Management Dispute Procedures**—a part of the U.S. Code (Chapter 71 of Title V) that established procedures for resolving federal labor-management disputes.

Offices Covered

Congressional officers covered by the bill included:

• Each office of the House and Senate, including each office of a member and each committee.

• Each joint committee.

• The Office of Technology Assessment.

• The Capitol Police.

• The Congressional Budget Office.

• The office of the architect of the Capitol.

• Senate and House restaurants and gift shops.

• The Botanic Garden.

• Office of the attending physician.

• The Capitol Guide Service.

• The Office of Compliance.

The Administrative Conference of the United States was charged with conducting a study on applying the law to related offices, including the General Accounting Office, the Government Printing Office and the Library of Congress. The report was to be submitted to Congress no later than two years after enactment, or Jan. 23, 1997. The law would be extended to these offices one year after the study was submitted.

Office of Compliance

- **New Office.** The law created a bicameral, independent Office of Compliance to be set up in the legislative branch to enforce the labor and antidiscrimination statutes in various offices, to act on complaints filed by employees and to provide counseling.

Executive branch regulatory agencies were not empowered by the bill to enforce laws on Congress.

- **Board of Directors.** The Compliance Office was to have a five-member board of directors appointed jointly by the Speaker of the House, the majority leader of the Senate, and the House and Senate minority leaders. To be considered, board members had to have had direct experience in the application of rights and protections under the law. Former members of Congress or registered lobbyists could not be candidates. Terms for board members were staggered at three years and five years; board members would choose their chairman.

- **Executive Director.** The board was directed to hire an executive director of the office to act as the chief operating officer in charge of daily operations. The first executive director had a seven-year term. Future directors were limited to a five-year term. The executive director was to hire hearing officers and other staff.

- **Other Officers.** The board was required to name two deputy executive directors, one for the House and one for the Senate, who would maintain records and regulations for their respective chambers. The board was also charged with approving a general counsel to represent the Compliance Office in any judicial proceedings and act as an adviser to compliance officers and the board. The bill required the executive director and the deputy executive directors and counsel to be hired without regard to their political affiliation.

- **Education Programs.** Initially, the Compliance Office was to carry out a broad education program, including a series of seminars, for members of Congress and other employers in the legislative branch and provide instruction about application of the laws. Detailed information about coverage of the laws was to be distributed to congressional offices and also to all congressional employees. Similar seminars were to be held periodically for the benefit of employees.

- **Regulations.** The board's initial priority was to adopt and issue three separate bodies of regulations on implementing the laws: one for Senate offices and employees, one for House offices and employees, and one for all other covered employees. After a 30-day comment period, the board could adopt the proposed regulations, which were to be published in the *Congressional Record*.

In developing regulations, the board and directors of the office were required to consult with the Labor Department, the Federal Labor Relations Authority, the Office of Personnel Management and the Administrative Conference of the United States.

Any interested party could petition the board to issue, amend or repeal a regulation.

The House and Senate were to adopt implementing regulations forwarded by the board either by concurrent resolution or joint resolution.

- **Authorization.** The legislation authorized such sums as necessary on an ongoing basis each fiscal year for the operations of the Compliance Office, with the appropriations to be split between the two chambers.

- **Oversight.** Except with respect to individual cases and proceedings, the Compliance Office was subject to ongoing oversight by the Senate Committee on Rules and Administration, the Senate Committee on Governmental Affairs and the House Committee on House Oversight.

- **Unions.** The board was authorized to determine the rights of various sets of employees to unionize. Employees could not unionize if they worked in offices where the board determined that unionization could pose a conflict of interest or could affect the legislative operations and responsibilities of Congress.

Employees working in members' offices, committee offices and leadership offices were not allowed to unionize, nor were workers in offices such as the secretary of the Senate, the House clerk and the parliamentarian. And unionization was not allowed for employees at the Congressional Budget Office, the Office of Technology Assessment or the Office of Compliance.

Backers of the bill generally expected workers in the Botanic Garden, the Capitol Police, the office of the architect, and the House and Senate restaurants to be able to unionize. But unionized workers were barred from going on strike.

- **Date.** The office was to open one year after enactment, or by Jan. 23, 1996, and be ready for receipt of complaints and request by employees for counseling.

Complaint Procedures

- **Process.** Employees of the House and Senate with grievances covered by the law were required to go through a formal complaint, mediation and hearing process conducted by the Compliance Office.

- **Counseling.** The first step for an employee wanting to initiate a proceeding was to request private counseling by the Compliance Office no later than 180 days after the date of the alleged violation. The office, upon receipt of a complaint or a request for counseling, had to provide the aggrieved employee with all relevant information with respect to employee rights and protections.

The counseling period was 30 days unless the employee and the Compliance Office agreed to reduce it. Employees were to be notified in writing when the counseling phase ended.

All counseling was to be strictly confidential, except when the Compliance Office and the covered employee agreed to notify the employing office of the allegations.

- **Mediation.** At the end of the counseling phase, but no later than 15 days afterward, an aggrieved employee who wanted to proceed had to file a request for mediation with the office.

Typically, the mediation process would involve communications between the Compliance Office, the employee, members of the employing office and other individuals involved in the case. Under direction of the Compliance Office, the parties had to consider recommendations for resolving the dispute offered by experienced adjudicators and arbitrators assigned by the Compliance Office in each particular case.

The mediation process also involved meetings with the parties and with the Compliance Office, either separately or jointly.

The mediation period was limited to 30 days and could be extended only with a joint request of the covered employee and the employing office.

• **Formal Decision.** No later than 90 days and no sooner than 30 days after the end of the mediation process, an employee who was unsatisfied with the mediation efforts and wished to continue the process could choose between two options: filing a formal complaint with the Compliance Office to request hearings and a decision by a hearing officer, or abandoning the internal review process and filing a civil lawsuit in the United States District Court where the employee worked or in the District of Columbia District Court.

• **Civil Suit.** A civil lawsuit could include a jury trial, if demanded by the employee plaintiff. The defendant in the case of a civil trial would be the employing office where the alleged violation occurred.

• **Hearings.** If the complaint was filed with the Compliance Office instead of with the court, the executive director of the Compliance Office would have to appoint an independent hearing officer to consider the complaint and render a decision.

The hearing officer could dismiss claims determined to be frivolous. Hearing officers were to be selected on a rotational or random basis from a list developed by the Compliance Office that included members of the bar of a state or the District of Columbia, as well as retired judges.

Hearings—to be conducted in closed session and on the record by the hearing officer—were to commence no later than 60 days after the formal complaint was filed.

A hearing officer could issue subpoenas for the attendance of witnesses and for the production of documents. The board was to review objections to subpoenas, and a federal court could be called on to enforce the subpoena if it were disregarded.

The hearing officer in charge of a given case was required to issue a written decision on the matter no later than 90 days after the conclusion of the hearings. If the decision was not appealed to the board, the decision was final.

• **Appeals.** Parties not satisfied with the decision by the hearing officer were permitted to file a petition for review by the Compliance Office board no later than 30 days after the hearing officer's decision was rendered.

After an appeal was made to the board, the parties involved or referred to in the complaint would have an opportunity to communicate concerns to the board through written statements and, at the discretion of the board, through oral testimony.

The board was then required to issue a decision affirming or reversing the hearing officer's decision. It could also order further hearings to explore areas of the complaint that it determined were not adequately explored by the hearing officer.

The board was required to make final decisions public if they were in favor of the employee who initiated the proceeding or if they reversed decisions by a hearing officer who decided in favor of the employee. The board could also make public any other decisions at its discretion.

• **Appeals Court.** An aggrieved party not satisfied with the final board decision could appeal it to the United States Court of Appeals for the Federal Circuit. At the appeals level, there would be no jury trial.

The appeals court had exclusive jurisdiction to affirm, set aside or suspend in whole or in part decisions rendered by the board. A final appeal could be made to the U.S. Supreme Court.

Awards for Damages

Except for violations of OSHA, funds for damage awards were to be appropriated from the Treasury.

Fines for OSHA violations could be paid only from appropriations made to the employing offices in question. The bill authorized such sums as necessary for fines and awards.

• **Members' Liability.** Members of Congress were not to be held personally liable for damage awards.

• **Punitive Damages.** The bill prohibited punitive damage awards in court cases.

Miscellaneous

• **Political Considerations.** The bill specified that members of Congress could consider the party affiliation, residence or the "political compatibility" of employees and applicants in making employment decisions without violating antidiscrimination statutes.

• **Disciplinary Actions.** The Senate Select Committee on Ethics and the House Committee on Standards of Official Conduct retained full power to discipline members, officers and employees for violating rules on nondiscrimination in employment.

• **Judicial Branch.** The bill ordered the Judicial Conference of the United States to deliver a report to Congress no later than Dec. 31, 1996, on the application of the labor and antidiscrimination laws to the judicial branch of government. The report was to include recommendations for legislation to apply the laws to the judicial branch in the same manner as the legislative branch.

• **Frequent Flier Miles.** Travel awards that senators, officers or employees of the Senate earned through official travel accrued to the office for which the travel was performed and could not be used for personal trips. The bill codified an existing ban that had been imposed by Senate rules. The measure did not affect the use of such awards in the House, where there was no internal ban. ❑

Lobbying Restrictions

The House Judiciary Subcommittee on the Constitution gave voice vote approval May 30, 1996, to a bill (HR 3434) to restrict lobbying by former members of Congress and their staffs, as well as former executive branch officials. However, HR 3434 died upon adjournment. In separate action, the Senate by voice vote July 30, 1996, adopted an amendment to the fiscal 1997 legislative branch appropriations bill (HR 3754) to toughen lobbying restrictions for former members of Congress and top staff aides. But the amendment was subsequently dropped.

LOBBYISTS' HOUSE ACCESS

House Republicans announced May 24, 1995, that lobbyists no longer would be given special access to the inner sanctums of the House.

Rep. Jim Nussle, R-Iowa, said the special visitor's badge known as a building access card would be eliminated June 1, 1995. For years, lobbyists used the identification cards to wander House offices, halls, lobbies and other restricted areas where the public was not allowed. The badge also provided lobbyists with access to congressional buildings after hours.

Under the new policy, lobbyists needed a visitor's pass to gain access to areas usually off-limits or closed for the day. Such day passes were granted only at the request of a member of Congress or senior staff member.

Some lobbyists suggested that the new policy could breed favoritism, with large organizations that made hefty campaign contributions getting special attention. The policy did not affect former members of Congress, who had privileged access to the House floor and other areas.

In a separate move May 24, the House Oversight Committee voted to end the informal practice of granting parking spaces to lobbyists and to open to the public more than 850 parking spaces predominantly used by House staff members.

HR 3434 would have required former executive branch officials, former members of Congress and former congressional staff to wait a decade before lobbying in behalf of foreign political parties or governments. Those wanting to represent foreign corporations, associations or individuals would have had to wait five years. However, foreign companies that opened U.S. subsidiaries would not have been subject to the same rules. Under existing law, former members had to wait one year before lobbying for foreign governments, political parties or corporations. HR 3434 would have prohibited lobbying by all former members, staff and executive branch officials convicted of felonies related to their service in government. They would not have been allowed to register as lobbyists, as required by the 1995 lobbying disclosure law (S 1060—PL 104-65) and, therefore, could not have contacted lawmakers directly. *(1995 law, p. 834)*

The Senate amendment, offered by Russell D. Feingold, D-Wis., on behalf of John McCain, R-Ariz., would have increased from one year to five the length of time top congressional aides (defined as those earning more than $100,200) would have had to wait after leaving before they could have lobbied Congress. It proposed to double to two years the time former members would have had to wait before lobbying Congress. ❑

Members' Accounts

Legislation (HR 2739—PL 104-186) that consolidated three official House allowances into a single account was signed into law Aug. 20, 1996.

The single account, called the Members' Representational Allowance (MRA), was intended to give House members more flexibility. The MRA merged the office accounts that covered the payment of staff, the costs of franked mail to constituents and the reimbursement of personal expenses such as travel.

HR 2739 also made more than a dozen other administrative changes to House rules. It allowed the Capitol Police to issue citations and release prisoners from custody, and it transferred responsibility for House audits from the General Accounting Office to the inspector general.

The House Oversight Committee reported HR 2739 (H Rept 104-482) on March 14, 1996, and the full House passed it by voice vote March 19. The Senate Governmental Affairs Committee, which reported the measure June 19, stripped a provision that would have allowed the House to offer its employees a variety of health benefits, known as a "cafeteria plan." Sen. John Glenn of Ohio, the ranking Democrat on the committee, said that offering only House employees expanded benefits was unfair, especially when they would cost taxpayers $500,000 a year. The Senate passed the bill by voice vote June 28. The House accepted the Senate changes by voice vote Aug. 2, completing congressional action.

In related action, the House on March 15, 1995, by 421–6, approved a measure (H Res 107—H Rept 104-74) overhauling the chamber's bookkeeping system to make it easier to determine how much each committee spent by consolidating into a single account the various sources that committees previously had used to support their operations. Because H Res 107 concerned the House's internal affairs, the vote was the final action on the measure. ❑

'Corrections Day'

The Republican-led House on June 20, 1995, adopted by a 271–146 vote a new floor procedure (H Res 168) to expedite the repeal of federal rules and regulations that members of Congress deemed excessive, obsolete or "dumb." The so-called Corrections Day calendar was the brainchild of Speaker Newt Gingrich, R-Ga.

Bills on the calendar could be called up on the second and fourth Tuesday of each month. They were subject to one hour of debate, without amendment, and required a three-fifths majority for passage. The procedure applied only to the House.

The House Rules Committee had reported H Res 168 (H Rept 104-144) on June 16. The resolution abolished the consent calendar, a floor schedule established in 1909 that allowed non-controversial legislation, once cleared by official objectors from both parties, to receive quick floor action. Such unanimity had been hard to come by in recent years, and the schedule had not been used since the 101st Congress.

Under the new procedure, a measure had to be listed on the Corrections Day calendar for at least three legislative days before it could be considered on the floor. While the Speaker would be charged with deciding which bills went on the calendar, only bills reported favorably from committee would be eligible. Bills on the calendar would be subject to one hour of debate equally divided between the chairman and ranking member of the committee of jurisdiction. Only amendments recommended by the reporting committee or those offered by the committee chairman would be permitted. In a concession to Democrats, Republicans included a provision to allow for a vote on whether to recommit individual corrections bills to committee.

The Rules Committee rejected a Democratic attempt to raise the threshold for passage of such bills from a three-fifths to a two-thirds vote. Republicans also rejected a Democratic proposal that the House minority leader be given a veto over proposed correction bills before they were placed on the calendar. Republicans said the request would "undermine" their leadership; instead, Republicans amended the bill to require "consultation" with the minority leader.

A 12-member bipartisan panel was appointed to coordinate the correction bills process. The task force would monitor the committee progress of correction bills and screen and advise GOP leaders on legislation placed on the corrections schedule. The informal panel would advise the Speaker throughout the process, but he would remain the final arbitrator of legislation considered under the new procedure. ❑

House Mail, Printing

As part of its overhaul of House administration operations, the House Oversight Committee voted June 14, 1995, to privatize House mail and printing operations and to cut service staff in the House. The unnumbered resolutions approved by the committee did not require action by the House and went into effect immediately.

The Oversight Committee voted to terminate by Dec. 31, 1995, no-bid contracts with two private printers who received office space in a Capitol office building. The committee also voted to close the Folding Office, which prepared and processed mass mailing to congressional districts. The moves left members to make their own arrangements with outside printers. The committee authorized the House chief administrative officer to seek bids from companies for a contract to take over internal pickup and delivery of mail to House congressional offices.

The committee also cut staff in the television office and reduced staff in the photography office to save salary costs during slow periods. Members used the television studio for appearances on local news shows and for taping talk shows for broadcast in their districts. Members would have to pay the full cost of such services out of their office funds, instead of the subsidized prices they had paid in the past. Office funds were increased to partially cover the cost of these services. The fiscal 1996 appropriations bill for the legislative branch (HR 2492—PL 104-53) eliminated subsidies long provided to members for television and photographic services in the Capitol.

Web Site Rules

The House Oversight Committee on July 31, 1996, by voice vote adopted regulations governing members' use of their official World Wide Web sites on the Internet. The rules provided that members could not offer political or campaign information on Web pages created with public funds. The rules also precluded such sites from carrying advertisements, business promotions or links to partisan political organizations. Members were barred from posting personal information not related to their official business on public Web pages, although they could post a personal biography. The House rules were to go into effect on Sept. 1, 1996.

Vic Fazio of California, ranking Democrat on the House Oversight Committee, took exception to a clause that prevented the minority from having committee home pages that were independent of the GOP-controlled pages. But Oversight Committee Chairman Bill Thomas, R-Calif., said the rule simply paralleled the tradition of allowing the minority space at the end of a committee report, but not a separate report. During consideration of the fiscal 1997 legislative branch appropriations bill (HR 3754), Fazio used a procedural motion, rejected 191–230 on July 10, 1996, to try to reduce spending on computer information services and to make implementation of the new Web site rule harder for Republicans.

The Senate Rules and Administration Committee adopted a similar set of regulations, but Patrick J. Leahy, D-Vt., and 39 other senators sent the committee a letter in September 1996 protesting that the policy's ban on promotional material could be seen as prohibiting all links to Web sites in members' home states. Rules Committee Chairman John W. Warner, R-Va., subsequently reassured the group that no blanket ban was imposed on such links, and the committee said enforcement of the policy would largely be left up to individual members. ❑

TECHNOLOGY OFFICE

Congress in 1995 voted to abolish the Office of Technology Assessment (OTA), which had been created nearly a quarter century before to advise Congress on scientific and technical issues. The fiscal 1996 legislative branch appropriations bill (HR 2492—PL 104-53) included $3.6 million to shut down the office, instead of the $22 million requested by the Clinton administration for OTA.

Republicans said the office had lost sight of its original mission, expanding into areas such as health care, and was no longer defensible in a year of budget cuts. Democratic supporters argued that OTA's evaluations had saved taxpayers' money, but their attempts to fund OTA's operations failed during action on an earlier version of the bill (HR 1854).

HR 1854 was vetoed by President Clinton because Congress had not completed action on most of the other appropriations bills. Clinton said that Congress should not take care of its own business before paying for other parts of the government. Congress subsequently cleared HR 2492, an identical bill.

OTA had been created by Congress in 1972 (PL 92-484) and had gone into operation in 1974. (OTA, Congress and the Nation Vol. III, p. 381).

Senate Operations

A task force studying the operations of the full Senate released its recommendations Jan. 23, 1995. They were drawn largely from the work of the 1992–1993 Joint Committee on the Organization of Congress. The proposals needed approval by the Senate to take effect. *(Congressional reform, p. 878)*

Senate Majority Leader Bob Dole, R-Kan., appointed the task force in December 1994. It was headed by Connie Mack, R-Fla., and Pete V. Domenici, R-N.M., and composed of Republicans senators. The task force called for:

• Barring major committees except Appropriations from having more than five subcommittees in the 104th Congress and four subcommittees in the 105th Congress. Those were less stringent limits than the three-subcommittee ceiling proposed by the Joint Committee.

• Barring senators from sitting on more than two major and one minor committee, although waivers still would be granted for the 104th Congress.

• Abolishing any committee that, as a result of the new assignment limitations, dropped to less than 50 percent of the membership it had in the 102nd Congress.

• Abolishing Congress's four joint committees: on printing, the library, taxation, and the Joint Economic Committee.

• Allowing proxy voting in committee only if it did not affect the outcome of a vote. The House in 1995 abolished proxy voting altogether.

• Establishing a two-year cycle for appropriations and budgets.

• Curbing one opportunity for senators to filibuster by setting a two-hour limit on debate on motions to bring up legislation.

Ethics Probes

The ethics investigations of House Speaker Newt Gingrich, R-Ga., and Senate Finance Committee Chairman Bob Packwood, R-Ore., threw their respective chambers into turmoil for a time. Despite the bright spotlight on the Gingrich and Packwood cases, the ethics committees in 1995–1996 also were kept busy with alleged transgressions by numerous other members.

SEN. BOB PACKWOOD

Senate Finance Committee Chairman Bob Packwood, R-Ore., announced Sept. 7, 1995, that he would resign his seat instead of face almost certain expulsion on charges of sexual harassment and other personal misconduct. Packwood agreed to leave the Senate by Oct. 1 and to relinquish his chairmanship immediately. *(Earlier action, p. 871)*

The Senate Ethics Committee held some 50 closed-door meetings and engaged in a legal fight over subpoenas that went all the way to the Supreme Court. The panel assembled a startling 10,145-page dossier, some of it in Packwood's own words, showing that the senator had made unwanted sexual advances to at least 17 women, tampered with evidence, and abused his office by pressuring lobbyists to find his estranged wife a job.

The stakes in the investigation increased dramatically when the Republicans took control of the Senate in 1995 and Packwood became chairman of the powerful Finance Committee, a post that made him a chief architect of the tax and welfare proposals that were at the heart of the GOP agenda. The senator's pivotal role fueled speculation that, while the new GOP majority would handle the case carefully, the Ethics Committee would never vote to expel him. The six-member Ethics Committee consisted of three Republicans and three Democrats.

On March 22 and 23, 1995, the committee met unannounced to review a staff report on the accusations against Packwood. On May 16, the panel unanimously passed a resolution stating that it had gathered "substantial credible evidence" that Packwood had engaged in sexual misconduct at least 18 times with 17 women, sought job offers for his estranged wife from lobbyists and business people with matters before his committee, and obstructed the ethics probe by altering his diaries.

The announcement pushed the 30-month investigation into its final, trial-like phase. Exercising his right at that point to meet with the committee, Packwood offered a detailed defense against the allegations in private sessions June 27–29. During the meetings, Packwood had one bit of good news: The Justice Department said it had closed its investigation and had decided not to prosecute him on the allegations that he had arranged for lobbyists to offer jobs to his wife in exchange for official acts.

The next decision for the committee was whether to hold public hearings. Packwood had the right to seek such hearings, but on July 5, his attorney told the committee he would not do so. That left the decision up to the committee, setting off a divisive and partisan debate.

Barbara A. Mikulski, D-Md., the only woman on the committee, had called for public hearings. The panel faced similar calls from women's groups and from conservative Christian organizations, groups that usually were on opposite sides. But there was also considerable pressure inside the Senate to keep the case out of the public's view. Most often cited were fears that public hearings would damage the institution.

On July 10, five female senators—Barbara Boxer, D-Calif.; Dianne Feinstein, D-Calif.; Carol Moseley-Braun, D-Ill.; Patty Murray, D-Wash.; and Olympia J. Snowe, R-Maine—sent a letter to Ethics Committee Chairman Mitch McConnell, R-Ky., and Committee Vice Chairman Richard H. Bryan, D-Nev., requesting public hearings. Bryan sent a written response July 11 in which he publicly endorsed open hearings. Bryan's statement drew a sharp rebuke from McConnell, who had sought to keep the committee's deliberations secret.

Boxer quickly upped the ante, threatening to introduce a resolution calling for public hearings unless the committee agreed by July 21 to hold them. Under Senate rules, Boxer could seek to attach such a resolution to virtually any piece of legislation, forcing a potentially embarrassing floor vote.

During a closed-door Ethics Committee meeting, McConnell was said to have warned that the Republicans would offer companion amendments calling for public hearings on pending allegation against Senate Minority Leader Tom Daschle, D-S.D., and on the role of Edward M. Kennedy, D-Mass., in the 1969 drowning at Chappaquiddick, Mass. *(Daschle, p. 900)*

The dispute spilled onto the Senate floor July 21. Boxer, whose deadline for committee action had come and gone, vowed to introduce a resolution calling for public hearings at the earliest opportunity. McConnell responded by suspending the committee deliberations.

Boxer did not introduce a resolution, and on July 31, the committee met and voted, 3–3, along party lines not to conduct public hearings. On a 6–0 vote, the panel agreed to make its voluminous files of depositions, transcripts of testimony and other evidence public.

On Aug. 2, Boxer brought her motion for public hearings to the Senate floor. After a heated and emotional debate, it was defeated on a **key vote of 48–52 (R 3–51; D 45–1)**. The proposal was offered as an amendment to the fiscal 1996 Defense Department authorization bill (S 1026). It would have changed Senate rules to require that the Ethics Committee hold public hearings in all cases in which the panel found "substantial credible evidence" of wrongdoing, including the Packwood case, and had begun investigating the charges. Under the amendment, the committee could decide not to hold hearings by a majority vote. *(1995 key votes, p. 1025)*

McConnell immediately offered his own amendment, a nonbinding resolution expressing the sense of the Senate that the ethics panel in the Packwood case should follow its normal procedures without interference from the full Senate and should not hold public hearings in the case. The Senate adopted the amendment, 62–38, on Aug. 2.

All eight women senators spoke during the debate. Six of them, including Republican Snowe, argued that a failure to hold hearings would signal that the Senate was still unwilling to consider sexual misconduct a serious charge. Nancy Landon Kassebaum of Kansas joined fellow Republican Kay Bailey Hutchison of Texas in opposing public hearings.

Bryan reiterated that the Ethics Committee had held public hearings in all four previous cases that had reached the final, or investigative, stage, as had the Packwood case. McConnell countered that the full Senate had never interfered with an Ethics Committee investigation before the panel made its final recommendation and now was not the time to start. He said the committee voted against public hearings because it had all the evidence it needed and hearings would add months to the investigation. McConnell said that ordering the Ethics Committee to hold public hearings at a certain stage would allow partisan politics to be interjected.

With the Senate vote cast, the Ethics Committee was poised to issue a final verdict. Possible sanctions ranged from a censure by the full Senate to expulsion and included recommending that the Senate Republican Conference strip Packwood of his Senate Finance Committee chairmanship.

Then, on Aug. 3, the committee abruptly adjourned its closed-door deliberations, announcing it needed to give its staff time to investigate two additional allegations of sexual misconduct, one involving a former summer intern who accused the senator of making an unwanted sexual advance when she was 17 years old. The complaint was the first involving a minor, and senators said they considered it the most serious because of her age.

The woman had not filed a formal complaint with the Ethics Committee until July 20. She gave her account to the *Washington Post* under an agreement of anonymity. Members of the Ethics Committee had not been formally told of the new charge until Aug. 3.

Packwood screamed foul. He said his lawyers had been assured that the investigation was complete, the case closed. On the *Larry King Live* television program Aug. 9, Packwood said he had no intention of resigning and renewed his opposition to public hearings in the case. Two days later, he issued a statement naming the former summer intern, whose identity had been kept confidential, and challenged her account. Six days later, one of his attorneys released four depositions purporting to contradict some of the testimony given to the Ethics Committee.

Then, on Aug. 25, Packwood reversed his long-held position and declared that he wanted the chance to defend himself in public hearings. McConnell said the committee would take up Packwood's request after the Senate returned in September from its recess. But Packwood's tactics angered senators, and his support among Republicans began to erode.

On Sept. 6, the Ethics Committee resumed its deliberations. In less than two hours, the committee decided to drop its investigation of the two additional charges and vote on the extensive evidence already gathered. By a unanimous vote, the committee adopted a resolution calling for Packwood's expulsion. The committee found Packwood guilty of all the charges it had levied against him in May. While the resolution excluded the two additional sexual misconduct allegations, it said they were "serious and highly credible."

The expulsion resolution was the first approved by the committee since 1981, when the panel voted to expel Harrison A. Williams Jr., R-N.J., who had been convicted in the Abscam scandal. *(Williams, Congress and the Nation Vol. VI, p. 802)*

The 10 volumes of evidence accumulated by the Ethics Committee and released Sept. 7 contained details as mundane as dinner plans and as lurid as a tryst with a staffer on an office rug. The counsel's report, also issued by the committee, stated that the evidence taken collectively revealed to the committee a clear pattern that reflected "an abuse of his United States Senate office by Sen. Packwood, and . . . this conduct is of such a nature as to bring discredit upon the Senate."

The committee report stated that "these incidents, taken collectively, reflect a pattern of abuse by Sen. Packwood of his position of power over women who were in a subordinate position. . . . These women were not on an equal footing with Sen. Packwood, and he took advantage of that disparity to visit upon them uninvited and unwelcome sexual advances, some of which constituted serious assaultive behavior." The report said that "regardless of his state of sobriety at the time of any given incident, Sen. Packwood is responsible for his actions."

The resolution calling for Packwood's expulsion stated that, sometime between December 1992 and November 1993, Packwood "intentionally altered diary materials that he knew or should have known the committee had sought or would likely seek" as part of its preliminary inquiry, which began Dec. 1, 1992. Sections of the diary flagged by the committee ranged from questions about possible campaign violations to sexual misconduct beyond the scope of the charges by Packwood's accusers.

In an entry dated March 6, 1992, Packwood detailed a promise by an unnamed senator to raise $100,000 for party building. The committee found that the passage "raises questions about the possible violation of campaign finance laws" and that Packwood "substituted in its place . . . an innocuous passage discussing campaign funding." The incident, which it was later learned involved Sen. Phil Gramm, R-Texas, was the subject of a separate Ethics investigation. *(Gramm, p. 900)*

A March 27, 1993, excerpt detailed a breakfast meeting with Oregon home builders. "The Oregon home builders all said they were mad," wrote Packwood. ". . I said the home builders could make it up with me with a contribution of $10,000 for my legal defense trust fund." A revised version of the diary marked "altered" by Packwood omitted any mention of soliciting the contribution.

The committee also found that Packwood "solicited or otherwise encouraged offers of financial assistance from five persons who had a particular interest in legislation or issues that Sen. Packwood could influence." In particular, the panel said, Packwood sought to drum up employment for his wife to reduce his alimony payment. In a Jan. 24, 1990, diary entry, Packwood wrote that he wanted to secure his wife "at least $20,000 in offers." He added, "I'm scating [sic] on thin ice here."

In a Nov. 3, 1989, entry, Packwood asked Steve Saunders, an old friend and a registered foreign agent for the Mitsubishi Electric Corp., for a job for his estranged wife: "I said, 'I wonder if you can put Georgie on retainer.' He says, 'How much.' I said, '7,500 a year.' he said, 'Consider it done.' "

Packwood said he did not recall the events and was drunk at the time. He also denied any wrongdoing. But the committee came to a different conclusion: "Senate Ethics Counsel finds that Sen. Packwood did in fact solicit or otherwise encourage an offer of personal financial assistance from Mr. Saunders, an individual representing a client with a particularized interest in matters that the Senator could influence."

Packwood's first response to release of the evidence was to continue his public relations blitz, stepping up his attack on the committee, a move that further diminished his political support in the Senate. He went from one TV studio to another, taking his case to the American people and declaring that he would not resign. Meanwhile, on Capitol Hill, senator after senator called upon Packwood to resign. With the tide turning against him, Packwood ultimately resigned. However, he maintained to the end that he was guilty of no more than "overeager kissing."

The Justice Department's Public Integrity Section notified Packwood in a one-sentence letter to Packwood's lawyer dated July 18, 1996, that it was closing its investigation into whether he altered his diaries to obstruct a Senate investigation of charges of sexual and official misconduct.

SPEAKER NEWT GINGRICH

In a negotiated settlement with the House Committee on Standards of Official Conduct (ethics committee), Speaker Newt Gingrich, R-Ga., on Dec. 21, 1996, admitted that he had brought discredit to the House by giving the committee false information. And while he admitted no violation of federal law, he acknowledged that he had failed to receive proper legal advice when he used a network of tax-exempt foundations to raise money for a televised workshop in 1990 and a televised college course he taught from 1993 to 1995.

The House on Jan. 21, 1997, voted 395–28 to accept the committee's recommendation to reprimand Gingrich and to impose a $300,000 penalty to reimburse costs related to sorting out the misleading information he gave the committee. The action was the first time in history that the House voted to reprimand a sitting Speaker.

The ethics case stemmed from a wide-ranging complaint filed against Gingrich on Sept. 12, 1994, by his Democratic challenger that year, former representative Ben Jones (1989–1993). Jones accused Gingrich of misusing the college course, called "Renewing American Civilization," for political gain. Jones also alleged that a $4.5 million book publishing contract that Gingrich entered into with media magnet Rupert Murdoch was improper because Murdoch had considerable business interests in pending telecommunications legislation. In addition, Jones said Gingrich had intervened with federal regulators on behalf of political contributors and that he had improperly used longtime political adviser Joe Gaylord to help run his congressional office. *(Earlier action, p. 876)*

In 1995, the ethics committee held 50 meetings on those allegations and other complaints filed by Democrats against Gingrich. At the end of the year, the committee unanimously found that the Speaker had violated House rules in three cases, but it took no action to sanction him. The committee found that Gingrich violated rules governing the proper use of the House floor by touting his college course and by promoting a GOPAC seminar in floor speeches. (GOPAC was the political action committee Gingrich had used to build support for the GOP takeover of Congress.) In the third instance, the committee said that he improperly allowed Gaylord to interview candidates for jobs in the Speaker's office. The ethics committee did not find that Gingrich's book deal broke the rules, but members sharply criticized the arrangement for creating "the impression of exploiting one's office for personal gain."

The committee was unable to resolve the question of whether Gingrich improperly used tax-exempt foundations for political gain, but it ceded to Democrats' demands to appoint a special counsel to examine the issue. On Dec. 22, 1995, the panel hired James M. Cole, a former prosecutor with the Justice Department's public integrity unit and a partner in the Washington office of the St. Louis-based law firm Bryan Cave. Cole also had been chief of staff for the Justice Department's special counsel in the House bank scandal of the early 1990s.

Democrats called on the committee to give Cole authority to follow whatever leads he found in investigating the foundations—especially if information led him to GOPAC, which Democrats believed to be the highly secretive financial engine of Gingrich's rise to power. But Republicans on the ethics committee succeeded in keeping the investigation focused on the issue of tax-exempt foundations and their possible role in Gingrich's political activities in the first half of the 1990s. Cole's instructions from the ethics committee were to examine two tax-exempt foundations—the Kennesaw State College Foundation Inc. and the Progress and Freedom Foundation—which were used as repositories for contributions Gingrich and his associates raised to fund the course.

While the Kennesaw college foundation had no previous affiliation with Gingrich, it contracted with one of his close advisers, Jeff Eisenach, to raise money for the course. Gingrich taught the course at the publicly run Kennesaw State College in Georgia in 1993, but it was moved the following year to the small, private Reinhardt College in Georgia after faculty members and administrators at Kennesaw concluded it was too political and barred Gingrich from teaching there. When the course moved, the opportunity to raise money through the college's foundation was lost. Gingrich needed money for the high costs of televising the course. Its 1993 budget was $290,000 for advertising, for production of a video-tape copy of the course and for satellite broadcast of 20 hours of Gingrich lectures. Responsibility for raising money for the course was transferred to the Progress and Freedom Foundation, a new, tax-exempt think tank set up by Eisenach.

Gingrich stopped teaching the course in 1995 because, he said, he was too busy with his job as Speaker.

Cole's investigation began in earnest in 1996. Cole delved into a number of unresolved questions: What was Gingrich's intent in teaching the course? Did the involvement of former GOPAC operatives, including Eisenach, in the fundraising give the lecture series a political taint? Who, if anyone, benefited? Did Gingrich's aggressive fundraising techniques somehow violate House rules?

Gingrich's critics maintained that the course was fundamentally political. It was beamed via satellite to other campuses but also to many GOP or GOP-leaning groups. Even if Gingrich did not openly advocate defeat of congressional Democrats, they said, his aim was to spread his views and create a cadre of activists dedicated to helping him take control of Congress. They seized on evidence of close involvement in the course by staff members associated with GOPAC, whose objective was to elect Republicans. Gingrich had headed the political action committee from 1986 to May 1995.

Gingrich said that the course complied with federal tax law and insisted that it was educational in purpose. He also said on several occasions that GOPAC had no formal involvement in the course.

Minority Whip David E. Bonior of Michigan and four other Democrats filed another complaint against Gingrich on Feb. 1, 1996, expanding on the earlier complaint filed by Jones. The new complaint alleged that, from 1989 to 1991, Gingrich improperly commingled money from tax-free foundations, political action committees, his personal campaign committee and

his official resources and staff. The complaint alleged that Gingrich:

• Used the Abraham Lincoln Opportunity Foundation, run by then GOPAC chairman Howard "Bo" Callaway, to fund three televised workshops promoting Gingrich's ideas and aimed at recruiting conservative activists in the early 1990s. The organization had been founded by Callaway years earlier to help inner city youth.

• Wrote to federal agencies asking for help for several GOPAC contributors, including executives of Southdown Inc., a Houston-based cement producer.

• Used GOPAC to help his 1990 reelection effort.

The complaint was based on roughly 8,000 pages of documents obtained from the Federal Election Commission (FEC). The FEC had released documents related to GOPAC in the course of a lawsuit in which it alleged that the political action committee was improperly involved in federal races at a time when it claimed to be engaged only in local and state races. A federal judge on Feb. 29, 1996, threw out the government lawsuit against GOPAC, ruling that the group did not illegally involve itself in federal elections in 1989 and 1990 and so did not have to register during that time as a federal political action committee or disclose its donors.

The ethics committee in a March 29, 1996, letter told the Speaker that he had failed to comply with House rules by allowing Donald Jones, a part-owner of two telecommunications companies, to volunteer in his office. House rules allowed members to use volunteers as long as they participated under a program designed to be educational. For the fourth time, the committee chose not to sanction the Speaker.

The ethics committee's protracted investigation, its reluctance to sanction Gingrich for rules violations, and the enmity many Democrats felt toward Gingrich because of the role he played in the 1989 resignation of Democratic Speaker Jim Wright of Texas fueled bitter partisan feuding in the House and led to a breakdown of the ethics process. Democrats accused committee Republicans of dragging their feet to protect Gingrich; Republicans accused Democrats of an election-year vendetta against the Speaker. Gingrich told reporters that he believed Democrats were out to "destroy" him. *(Wright resignation, Congress and the Nation Vol. VIII, p. 917)*

The House June 27, 1996, voted 229–170 to table (kill) a Harry A. Johnston, D-Fla., privileged resolution (H Res 468) to require the ethics committee to forward the Democrats' complaints to Cole. Also killed, on tabling motions, were similar Johnston-sponsored resolutions to require the committee to report to the House on its investigation of Gingrich.

The committee members Aug. 12 received a preliminary report summarizing Cole's findings, but the contents were not released publicly while the four-member investigatory subcommittee in charge of the case deliberated. Democrats demanded public release of the report and all supporting documents, and they accused Republicans of deliberately delaying release of the Cole report. Republicans, meanwhile, complained about interference by the Internal Revenue Service, which had begun investigating Gingrich's use of the foundations.

Despite the unprecedented infighting among its members, the committee Sept. 26 agreed with a recommendation from Cole to expand the probe into some new areas while keeping it mostly contained within the original parameters set by the committee. The most explosive new issue was the charge that Gingrich might have been untruthful in his testimony about the role of politics in his college course. Cole raised the issue of whether the Speaker had provided the committee with "accurate, reliable and complete information concerning the course" and its relationship to GOPAC. Another serious new path for the investigation was a look into the use of the Abraham Lincoln Opportunity Foundation to finance the workshops.

The committee Sept. 28 dismissed two charges involving GOPAC and favors Gingrich was alleged to have done for big donors. The first was an allegation that Gingrich intervened with Environmental Protection Agency Administrator William Reilly in 1990 for a GOPAC donor who had complained that asbestos regulation was hurting his business. The second was a charge that Gingrich intervened with the Commerce Department in 1989 in behalf of Southdown Inc., which had asked for government help in stopping the influx of cheap Mexican cement into the U.S. market.

Although the committee's actions in September were a mixed blessing for Gingrich—with some charges dismissed and others expanded—the Speaker was spared the worst possible outcome. Republican feared that a highly damaging finding of guilt before the Nov. 5 election could return control of the House to the Democrats. The committee's actions in effect delayed a final verdict until after the election.

House Republicans were jarred by Gingrich's sudden admission on Dec. 21 of guilt after two years of proclaiming his innocence. His support among the GOP was heavily damaged, and talk was heard of finding an alternative candidate for Speaker in the 105th Congress. However, Gingrich was reelected Speaker on Jan. 7, 1997.

SEN. TOM DASCHLE

The Senate Ethics Committee on Nov. 30, 1995, dismissed allegations that Senate Minority Leader Tom Daschle, D-S.D., improperly intervened with federal regulators to help a friend's air charter company.

A complaint against Daschle was filed Feb. 8, 1995, by David A. Keene, chairman of the American Conservative Union, seeking an investigation into Daschle's dealings with federal airline regulators in behalf of B&L Aviation of Rapid City, S.D. A second request for an investigation came from the widows of three Indian Health Service doctors killed when one of B&L's planes crashed Feb. 24, 1994.

Daschle came under scrutiny because in 1992 he began efforts to get federal regulators to consolidate aviation inspections under the Federal Aviation Administration (FAA). Other federal agencies had been involved in safety inspections because the charters ferried government officials into less-than-hospitable areas, such as back-country wilderness.

While B&L's planes passed FAA inspections, the U.S. Forest Service found a number of violations during its safety reviews,

and the charter company consequently was banned in the winter of 1994 from flying Forest Service employees. The plane that crashed had passed both FAA and Forest Service inspections. The National Transportation Safety Board blamed the crash on pilot error and bad weather.

"Contacts and actions by Sen. Daschle and his staff were routine and proper constituent services," the committee said.

In September, the Transportation Department's inspector general cleared Daschle's wife, Linda, an FAA deputy administrator, of intervening in the case, and reported that no evidence existed that documents were destroyed.

Daschle offered a detailed report Feb. 17, 1995, chronicling his involvement with B&L and his attempts to consolidate airplane inspections.

SEN. ALFONSE M. D'AMATO

The Senate Ethics Committee on Sept. 18, 1996, cleared Alfonse M. D'Amato, R-N.Y., of wrongdoing for any special treatment he might have received from a New York brokerage firm that earned him a lucrative, one-day stock profit. The Congressional Accountability Project, a group affiliated with consumer advocate Ralph Nader, filed the ethics complaint June 11, asking the committee to look into D'Amato's stock dealing with Stratton Oakmont, a firm based in Lake Success, N.Y.

A Securities and Exchange Commission (SEC) report prepared by an independent consultant found that Stratton Oakmont in a 1993 transaction gave D'Amato "atypical" treatment that yielded the senator a $37,125 profit in one day. A judge released the report June 5. At the time of D'Amato's one-day profit, the SEC was investigating Stratton Oakmont and D'Amato was the top Republican on the Senate Banking Committee.

The firm allowed D'Amato to purchase shares in an initial public offering of a computer company, enabling him to post the large profit. D'Amato was allowed to open an account with the brokerage, even though he did not meet the company's financial criteria, and then to buy more shares of the company than other investors with similarly valued accounts.

Stratton executives contributed $12,000 to D'Amato's 1992 reelection campaign, though he later returned most of the money after the SEC first filed charges against the firm. D'Amato disclosed the one-day profit on his 1994 financial disclosure forms. The SEC report did not say that D'Amato violated any laws. After the disclosure, D'Amato placed his retirement savings in a blind trust.

SEN. PHIL GRAMM

The Senate Ethics Committee in 1995 decided not to investigate whether Phil Gramm, R-Texas, attempted to violate federal campaign laws in helping Oregon Republican Sen. Bob Packwood's 1992 reelection effort.

At issue was whether Gramm, then chairman of the National Republican Senatorial Committee, intended to spend $100,000 for Packwood in excess of federal spending limits. The issue arose from Packwood's diaries, which were released by the panel Sept. 7, 1995. (Packwood, p. 896)

Packwood's March 6, 1992, entry detailed a promise by an

unnamed senator, later identified as Gramm, to raise $100,000 for party building activities that instead would go for Packwood's reelection. "What was said in that room would be enough to convict us all of something," Packwood wrote. "He [Sen. X] says, now, of course you know there can't be any legal connection between this money and Sen. Packwood, but we know that it will be used for his benefit."

Gramm said the discussion was about so-called soft money, which was used for party building and get-out-the-vote drives and was not subject to the same limits as contributions to federal candidates. "Sen. Packwood's diary entry reflects an obvious misunderstanding of the election law," Gramm wrote to the committee Sept. 7.

SEN. LAUCH FAIRCLOTH

North Carolina Republican Sen. Lauch Faircloth's multimillion-dollar investment in hog farming did not conflict with his responsibilities on Capitol Hill, the Senate Ethics Committee said Feb. 22, 1995.

Faircloth, a major hog farmer in North Carolina, had requested the ruling following a series of articles in the *Charlotte Observer* in late 1994 questioning his financial and political ties. Senate Rule 37 said senators could not push for legislation that would benefit themselves or their families, or "the financial interests of a limited class to which such individuals belong." The Ethics Committee said the hog industry affected so many people that Faircloth's actions did not violate the rule.

SENS. ORRIN G. HATCH, SLADE GORTON

The Senate Ethics Committee dismissed separate complaints alleging that Sens. Orrin G. Hatch, R-Utah, and Slade Gorton, R-Wash., allowed lobbyists to have improper influence in the bill drafting process in 1995.

Congress Watch, a watchdog group associated with Ralph Nader, asked the Ethics Committee to investigate whether Hatch and Gorton had violated rules against accepting in-kind contributions. The complaints were based on news accounts that Gorton had sought drafting help from the Endangered Species Reform Coalition and that Hatch's Judiciary Committee staff had permitted utility lobbyists to brief committee aides on provisions in a regulatory reform bill (S 343) then pending in the committee.

In June 13 letters to Congress Watch, Ethics Committee Chief Counsel Victor M. Baird concluded that Senate rules did not prohibit lobbyists from "voluntarily providing to a senator or his or her staff research, memoranda, legislative language, or draft report language." Baird added that such exchanges "are common and acceptable."

REP. DICK ARMEY

The House Committee on Standards of Official Conduct on June 13, 1995, cited Majority Leader Dick Armey, R-Texas, for improperly writing a letter on a facsimile of House stationery that was mailed by an outside group, but the committee said it would take no action.

Armey's letter was mailed April 12, 1995, to business leaders

by the Capital Research Center, a conservative advocacy group that had criticized corporate executives for contributing to liberal advocacy groups. On May 31, consumer advocate Ralph Nader and Gary Ruskin, director of Nader's Congressional Accountability Project, asked the ethics committee to investigate the use of official House letterhead for something other than official House business. On June 2, Armey wrote the committee that he regretted the "unintentional" mistake.

REP. RICHARD A. GEPHARDT

The House ethics committee Sept. 28, 1996, dismissed an ethics complaint filed against Minority Leader Richard A. Gephardt, D-Mo., but the panel upbraided him for failing to properly disclose income from a vacation property. The complaint, filed Feb. 1 by Jennifer Dunn, R-Wash., had been widely viewed as a retaliatory strike against Democrats for their aggressive use of the ethics process against Speaker Newt Gingrich, R-Ga.

At issue in the Gephardt complaint was property in Duck, N.C., that Gephardt traded in 1991 for a piece of beachfront land in nearby Corolla. By trading instead of selling the Duck home, Gephardt was able to avoid capital gains taxes. Such tax-free exchanges were permitted for investment properties only. But Dunn noted that Gephardt listed the Duck property as a "vacation home" and did not disclose any rental income from the property on his financial disclosure form in 1991.

In a response to the charges, Gephardt lawyer Robert F. Bauer on Feb. 8, 1996, denied that Gephardt had violated either House reporting requirements or tax laws. In 1991, the property "was not held for the production of income, and was, therefore, not reported as investment property" on Gephardt's financial disclosure form, Bauer said. But tax laws permitted Gephardt to make the tax-free exchange, he added. The property had been rented in previous years, according to Gephardt's disclosure statements.

Gephardt did not disclose the exchange in his 1991 report, Dunn said. In 1992, the ethics committee questioned Gephardt about the discrepancy. Gephardt said he did not think the exchange of the home needed "to be disclosed if it was not used for rental purposes." At that time, he informed the committee of the exchange.

In 1992, the Gephardts received permanent financing for the Corolla property, on which they and another couple with equal interests in the property built a large home. The complaint alleged that Gephardt told a mortgage company in applying for a loan that he planned to use the new home as personal vacation property. But Gephardt subsequently listed rental income coming from the property in his financial disclosure statements.

Dunn alleged that Gephardt either "made a false statement on a bank loan document" or filed an inaccurate disclosure statement. Bauer said that the bank "was completely aware that the . . . property was acquired and the house it was financing would be constructed for rental purposes. The loan documents do not prohibit the owners from renting."

Dunn's complaint also alleged that Gephardt failed to report two loans totaling $60,000 on his disclosure form. Bauer said

that Gephardt had reported one of the loans and was not required to report the other. Dunn also asked the committee to
investigate whether Gephardt fundraising events on North Carolina's Outer Banks may have generated personal benefit for
Gephardt.

On Sept. 27, the day before the committee dropped the complaint, Gephardt filed an amended financial disclosure form listing rental income of $25,000 to $50,000 on the property for
1992. In a terse letter to Gephardt, the panel said that it expected
him to be "more diligent in the future and adhere strictly to the
requirements to file timely and accurate financial disclosure
statements."

REP. DAVID E. BONIOR

The House ethics committee refused to pursue a series of
complaints lodged against House Democratic Whip David E.
Bonior of Michigan by the conservative Landmark Legal Foundation.

In 1995 and 1996, the foundation sought to have the ethics
committee investigate whether Bonior broke House rules in
writing his 1984 book *The Vietnam Veteran: A History of Neglect*;
whether his employment of his wife violated nepotism rules;
and whether he misused his public office to wage a political war
against House Speaker Newt Gingrich, R-Ga.

On May 8, 1996, the ethics committee announced it had
found no substance to the nepotism charge. Bonior said his wife
worked in his office for four years before they were married in
1991.

On May 9, the committee rejected the Landmark complaint
about Bonior's book because House rules prohibited the investigation of an incident that took place more than three Congresses (six years) before the complaint was filed, unless it could be
shown that it was directly related to a more recent incident under investigation.

The committee returned the set of complaints questioning
Bonior's battle against Gingrich to Landmark. The committee
said the foundation did not have the standing to file the complaint, and no members were willing to file it on the organization's behalf.

REP. JOSEPH M. MCDADE

A jury on Aug. 1, 1996, found Rep. Joseph M. McDade not
guilty of peddling influence as ranking Republican on the
House Defense Appropriations Subcommittee. The government had accused McDade of accepting $100,000 in illegal
gifts, favors and bribes from defense contractors in return for
helping them get federal contracts. The verdict came eight
years after the FBI launched its investigation into the case.
(Earlier action, p. 875)

McDade's 1992 indictment had been upheld in 1994 by the
Third U.S. Circuit Court of Appeals. The Supreme Court decided March 6, 1995, not to hear a constitutional challenge to the
McDade indictment. The issues brought to the Supreme Court
focused not on the merits of the case but on whether the Justice
Department, under the Constitution, could indict McDade at
all. In asking the Court to hear the case, McDade's lawyers con-

tended that the Constitution prohibited officials of the other
branches of government from interfering with Congress's legislative duties. The Justice Department argued in response that
the constitutional provisions could be cited by McDade as part
of his defense at trial but did not prevent an indictment. Upholding a lower court ruling, an appeals court in the spring of
1996 rejected McDade's argument that the charges should be
thrown out because prosecutors were applying criminal penalties to House rules, thus clearing the way for McDade to stand
trial.

The facts in the McDade case were not in question during
the trial. What was in question was McDade's intent. The prosecution called his intent criminal. They charged him with violating the 1970 Racketeer Influenced and Corrupt Organizations
(RICO) act, saying he ran his office like a criminal enterprise. In
a seven-week trial, federal prosecutors in Philadelphia attempted to prove that McDade extorted items—ranging from a golf
jacket to a $7,500 Georgetown University Law School scholar-
ship for his son—from five defense firms and a lobbyist between
1983 and 1988. In return, they charged, McDade helped the
businesses get $68 million in federal contracts. *(RICO, Congress
and the Nation Vol. III, p. 272)*

The verdict was important because lawmakers and lobbyists
saw the trial of McDade, who ranked atop the House Republicans' seniority list, as a referendum on the ethical conduct of
members. Washington watched the trial closely because the
items McDade was accused of taking were not much different
from what many lawmakers had accepted before the House
clamped down on gifts in 1995. Even more troublesome to lawmakers was the fact that McDade had reported many, if not
most, of the gifts and contributions on his financial disclosure
forms.

Although by seniority McDade was in line for the chairmanship of the House Appropriations Committee, Speaker Newt
Gingrich, R-Ga., retained Robert L. Livingston, R-La., in the
post after McDade's acquittal. Livingston had offered his resignation from the chairmanship to make way for McDade, but
Gingrich refused to accept it. (House GOP rules forbid an indicted member to hold a top committee slot.) Livingston was
seen as more of a true believer in the Republican "revolution."

REP. MEL REYNOLDS

Rep. Mel Reynolds, D-Ill., resigned from the House Oct. 1,
1995, following his Aug. 22 conviction in Illinois on charges of
sexual misconduct, witness tampering and child pornography.

He was convicted of having sex with a former campaign
worker when she was 16 and 17 years old and trying to sabotage
an investigation of the allegations. He was indicted in 1994.
(Earlier action, p. 875)

Cook County Judge Fred Suria Sept. 28, 1995, sentenced
Reynolds to four years in prison, the mandatory minimum, for
criminal sexual assault, and a concurrent four-year term for soliciting child pornography. Suria added a year for obstruction of
justice.

The House ethics committee Aug. 23, 1995, announced that
it had launched a preliminary investigation of Reynolds. The

committee had voted to begin the inquiry, the first step in a formal investigation, on June 28, but put off an announcement until after Reynolds's trial in Chicago.

Before the trial began, prosecutors dropped four of the seven sexual abuse counts against Reynolds, leaving 12 criminal charges.

The prosecution's key witness, former Reynolds campaign worker Beverly Heard, at first balked at testifying against him. Heard was the woman with whom Reynolds allegedly had sex when she was underage. She had tried to recant her allegations in January. She was held in contempt of court July 26 for her refusal to testify; after 13 nights in jail, she took the witness stand Aug. 7 and 8 to testify about several sexual incidents and about Reynolds asking her to get him lewd photographs of a 15-year-old girl. Prosecutors also produced tapes of telephone conversations between Heard and Reynolds.

In his defense, Reynolds testified that he only had "phone sex" with Heard. He said Heard had made up the accusations to extort money from him.

The obstruction of justice charges involved preparing false affidavits for Heard and another woman involved in the case, Karren Lawson. The indictment charged that Reynolds tried to get Heard and Lawson to sign false affidavits saying they were coerced into approving the taping of phone calls with Reynolds.

REP. CHARLES WILSON

The Federal Election Commission (FEC) in 1995 levied a $90,000 fine against Rep. Charles Wilson, D-Texas. The penalty—the largest FEC fine ever against a congressional candidate—came after charges that Wilson had broken federal election law 15 times and might have violated the 1978 Ethics in Government Act (PL 95-521) and House financial disclosure rules. (1978 law, Congress and the Nation Vol. V, p. 824)

Wilson paid the fine, which the FEC disclosed Sept. 6, 1995, but his attorney insisted that the accusations were untrue. Wilson said he paid the fine to avoid further legal complications.

The FEC alleged that Wilson borrowed $26,500 from his campaign committee in 1988–1990 without disclosing the loans or repayments. Wilson spent the money, according to the FEC, for personal expenses, including hotel and travel costs and a $2,051 catering bill.

On Dec. 8, 1995, the House Committee on Standards of Official Conduct rebuked Wilson for borrowing from his campaign committee, saying he should have known that he was not allowed to do so. It then closed its books on the case.

In 1992, Wilson admitted that he funded his reelection campaign in part with bad checks from the House bank, where he had 81 overdrafts. (House bank, Congress and the Nation Vol. VIII, p. 929)

REP. GERALD D. KLECZKA

Rep. Gerald D. Kleczka, D-Wis., was arrested May 13, 1995, on drunken driving charges in Alexandria, Va., a suburb of Washington. He subsequently entered an alcohol abuse treatment center. In a statement released by his office May 14, Kleczka asked for his constituents' forgiveness.

Kleczka had pleaded guilty to driving while intoxicated in Fairfax County, Va., in 1987 and was sentenced to 30 days in jail. That punishment was lifted after he completed an alcohol awareness course. Kleczka was also charged with public drunkenness, again in Fairfax County, in 1990.

REP. ENID GREENE WALDHOLTZ

Utah Rep. Enid Greene Waldholtz, a rising star of the GOP, saw her congressional career collapse as a federal grand jury in 1995 began investigating possible bank fraud schemes by her estranged husband, Joseph P. Waldholtz, to fund her 1994 campaign. Investigators in 1996 concluded that no proof was found that she was part of her husband's crimes and did not charge her in the case. The freshman representative was divorced in 1996 and dropped her husband's name.

Joseph Waldholtz pleaded guilty on June 5, 1996, to three felony counts, including bank fraud, and one misdemeanor. He was sentenced Nov. 7 to 37 months in prison. Under the terms of the plea agreement, the U.S. attorney's office agreed to take no further action against him on a 27-count bank fraud indictment handed down on May 2 over an alleged check-kiting scheme. Waldholtz agreed to repay $14,910 that he gained in the bank fraud. He admitted providing Greene with false information used to complete her 1993 taxes. He pleaded guilty to making a false statement to the Federal Election Commission (FEC). He also admitted failing to report a campaign contribution to the FEC.

Greene spent a record $1.8 million to unseat incumbent Democrat Karen Shepherd in 1994. At a tearful Dec. 11, 1995, news conference, she admitted that the money came principally not from her and her husband's funds—as she had said at the time—but from her father. But she said her husband, a GOP political operative who she said handled virtually all financial transactions, had tricked her father and herself. Federal campaign law limited donations from individuals other than the candidate to $1,000 per election. (Primary, run-off, general and special elections each counted as a separate election with a separate $1,000 limit.)

Greene said that, at first, she thought the money for her campaign was coming out of $5 million her husband had promised her as a wedding present. When that money proved unavailable, he arranged to get money from her father in a series of payments in 1994, usually without her knowledge, she said. She said her husband promised to transfer a Pennsylvania property to her father in return for the money, but that was fraudulent.

Greene acknowledged filing a false financial disclosure statement with the House Committee on Standards of Official Conduct but said that she did so unknowingly because of her husband's deceptions. House rules prohibited members from knowingly filing false disclosure statements. She prepared amended returns.

Her lawyers also acknowledged that she had made mistakes in her campaign disclosure forms filed with the FEC not only in 1994 but also in 1992, when she ran unsuccessfully for Congress. Waldholtz served as campaign treasurer during the last month of her 1992 campaign.

In a statement issued Nov. 15, 1995, Greene alleged that her husband had used the credit card of an aide in her Washington office to charge $45,000 in unspecified "personal expenses." Greene testified before a federal grand jury Dec. 14. Greene's former campaign manager had resigned after sending her memos detailing discrepancies on FEC documents prepared by her husband.

Greene did not run for reelection in 1996.

REP. BARBARA-ROSE COLLINS

The House Committee on Standards of Official Conduct announced plans Dec. 5, 1995, to launch a formal investigation into alleged financial misconduct by Rep. Barbara-Rose Collins, D-Mich. The probe looked into alleged "misuse of official, campaign and scholarship fund resources" by Collins and members of her district office in Detroit.

Among the dealings under investigation were reports that, in 1994, Collins wrote a check for several thousand dollars to one of her aides that was drawn on a scholarship fund intended to assist low-income students. The staff member then allegedly cashed the check and gave the money to Collins. The committee also looked into a 1994 incident in which Collins allegedly paid members of her family more than $20,000 in campaign money, while she ran unopposed in the Democratic primary. Other news reports said that scholarship money earmarked for needy high school students was awarded to the son of a former staff member and that Collins made questionable purchases with the campaign money.

In addition, the Justice Department conducted a separate investigation into allegations that she broke federal campaign finance and other laws. In a report made public May 31, 1996, the Federal Election Commission reported to the House ethics committee that it had found "reason to believe" that Collins violated campaign contribution limits during her 1990 campaign by taking and misrepresenting two loans totaling $75,000 that other individuals guaranteed.

The House ethics committee on Jan. 2, 1997, issued a scathing report regarding Collins. The committee found that Collins allowed improper campaign activities by her congressional staff, that she used official funds for campaign and personal purposes, that she misused funds intended for a scholarship program, and that she gave huge, temporary raises to some members of her staff to give them enough money to accompany her on a trip to Africa.

REP. THOMAS J. BLILEY JR.

In June 1995, Rep. Thomas J. Bliley Jr., R-Va., announced that he was putting his extensive stock holdings into a blind trust to quell questions about conflicts between his investments and his role as chairman of the powerful House Commerce Committee. The move followed news reports that, before and since becoming chairman, Bliley had taken actions and political positions helpful to companies in his portfolio.

Bliley held stocks worth between $385,000 and $1.1 million, according to his 1994 financial disclosure forms. He had owned most of the stocks for many years and rarely bought or sold

shares. But he had intervened several times with federal regulators in behalf of companies in which he held stock and took legislative action that could have benefited some of his holdings.

In April Bliley had turned his investments over to an independent investor, an arrangement that allowed Bliley to remain informed about the contents of his portfolio and to communicate with the broker. The blind trust announced in June would shield him from knowledge of what his holdings were.

REP. WES COOLEY

Rep. Wes Cooley, R-Ore., was indicted Dec. 10, 1996, on charges he lied about his military record when he supplied biographical information for Oregon's voter education pamphlets. The indictment alleged that Cooley falsely claimed in 1994 primary and general election pamphlets that he had been a member of the Army Special Forces in Korea. Cooley was found guilty March 18, 1997, and sentenced to two years' probation and ordered to perform community service and to pay fines and expenses.

The pamphlets were published by the state and distributed to voters to provide information about candidates. Supplying false information was a felony.

Cooley said that records that would support his claims had been destroyed in a fire. Press records said Cooley never left the United States during the war and that he did not even finish his training at Fort Bragg, N.C., until Aug. 19, 1953, almost a month after the war ended.

Another Marion County, Ore., grand jury was investigating whether Cooley and his wife, Rosemary, illegally accepted veterans' benefits by hiding their marriage from the government. Rosemary Cooley, the widow of a Marine, was entitled to compensation provided she did not remarry or cohabitate with a man.

Cooley canceled his 1996 reelection campaign under pressure from Republican leaders.

REP. JAY C. KIM

California Republican Rep. Jay C. Kim's campaign treasurer, Seokuk Ma, was indicted Dec. 17, 1996, on charges of knowingly receiving illegal campaign contributions from eight corporations, as well as attempting to intimidate a witness into lying to a federal grand jury.

Five South Korea-based companies had pleaded guilty to giving illegal contributions to Kim and had been fined an aggregate of $1.6 million.

A continuing federal probe was prompted by reports in the Los Angeles Times that Kim's firm, JayKim Engineers Inc., improperly contributed about $485,000 to his first campaign in 1992. Corporate contributions to federal campaigns were illegal, even if the corporation was owned by the candidate. Ma's indictment, however, grew out of a Kim fund-raiser held in 1994.

A Kim attorney said repeatedly that Kim considered himself a target of the investigation, although he consistently denied any wrongdoing and had not been charged.

Kim returned at least $17,000 in illegal campaign contributions to the Treasury. Jane Chong, a former Kim office manager and campaign treasurer, alleged in interviews with the FBI in April 1996 that Kim and his wife destroyed evidence and knowingly accepted illegal contributions. Kim called Chong's allegations "totally unsubstantiated."

REP. JIM MCDERMOTT

The House Committee on Standards of Official Conduct on July 24, 1996, dismissed an ethics complaint against its senior Democrat, Jim McDermott of Washington. Peter T. King, R-N.Y., filed the three-count complaint July 17 and called for the appointment of an outside counsel to probe the conduct of McDermott in the ethics investigation of Speaker Newt Gingrich, R-Ga.

The first two counts called on the panel to investigate whether McDermott knew that Stephen J. Jost, a McDermott fund-raiser, drew up a complaint against Gingrich that was pending before the committee. The complaint filed by Gingrich's 1994 election opponent, former representative Ben Jones, D-Ga. (1989–1993), alleged that Gingrich had improperly used funds donated to GOPAC, a political action committee he then headed, for a college course he taught. That issue had been turned over to an outside counsel in December 1995. *(Gingrich, p. 898)*

In another count, King charged that McDermott violated committee rules when he spoke with reporters July 27, 1995, about another case involving Gingrich's stewardship of GOPAC.

King filed the complaint less than a day after McDermott gave a late night floor speech July 16, 1996, criticizing the ethics committee for failing to act swiftly on the additional ethics complaints against Gingrich involving GOPAC. McDermott called on the committee to report on the status of its probe to the full House in closed session. McDermott declared that ending the 104th Congress with the issues unresolved would be "totally unacceptable."

In its ruling, the ethics committee said that King had not sufficiently substantiated his conflict of interest allegation. The panel also admonished all its members to avoid public statements "concerning the work of the ethics committee that could be viewed as inconsistent with the letter or the spirit of our very restrictive rules."

REP. DAVID M. MCINTOSH

The House ethics committee the week of March 23, 1996, dismissed two complaints against David M. McIntosh, R-Ind., clearing him of violating House rules when he distributed documents created by his staff using an advocacy group's letterhead. But the committee admonished McIntosh privately against doing it again.

The committee's handling of the case provoked controversy because the panel did not publicly release its letter to McIntosh, letting him announce the dismissal of the case in a news release that made only passing reference to the committee's criticism.

Democratic Reps. Louise M. Slaughter of New York and Luis V. Gutierrez of Illinois filed the complaint against McIntosh on behalf of the Alliance for Justice, a coalition of civil rights and advocacy groups, and Public Citizen, a consumer advocacy group, for using public funds to create a phony poster and letters. The complaint grew from hearings held in 1995 by the Government Reform and Oversight Subcommittee on National Economic Growth, Natural Resources, and Regulatory Affairs, which McIntosh chaired, on the lobbying activities of organizations that received federal grants. During the hearing, McIntosh displayed a poster and distributed press releases produced by his staff on Alliance for Justice letterhead, which claimed to show the value of federal grants that the alliance's member organizations had received. The documents included no disclaimers, and the groups complained that they were incorrect. McIntosh, who also displayed the poster on the House floor, said his staff had mistakenly failed to include a disclaimer.

REP. BUD SHUSTER

An ethics complaint against House Transportation and Infrastructure Committee Chairman Bud Shuster, R-Pa., died at the end of the 104th Congress because the ethics committee had not reached a conclusion.

The Congressional Accountability Project, a Ralph Nader group, filed the complaint Sept. 5, 1996, asking the ethics committee to investigate whether Shuster violated illegal gratuities law as a result of his relationship with ex-staffer Ann Eppard. Because no member of Congress was willing to file the complaint, the group was allowed under House rules to do so.

The group cited a Feb. 8, 1996, story in the Capitol Hill newspaper *Roll Call* that detailed Shuster's close business and personal ties to Eppard, a transportation industry lobbyist and a former top staffer to Shuster. Eppard was Shuster's key fund-raiser and a political adviser, for which she was paid $3,000 a month from his campaign. The newspaper reported that Shuster repeatedly spent the night at Eppard's Virginia home. Both Shuster and Eppard said they were longtime family friends.

The ethics committee did issue a letter to Shuster regarding his ties with Eppard, but the letter itself was unclear as to whether he broke the rules or whether he was exempt because of his lengthy friendship with Eppard.

The Congressional Accountability Project also called on the Justice Department to investigate the situation.

REP. GERALD B. H. SOLOMON

The House ethics committee on May 9, 1996, dismissed a complaint against Rules Committee Chairman Gerald B. H. Solomon, R-N.Y., but warned him to be more careful in the language he used on official letterhead.

Democratic New York State Assemblyman Richard L. Brodsky alleged that Solomon had threatened to take political reprisals against him if he did not cease a state investigation of a controversial environmental cleanup deal. Brodsky chaired the Assembly Environment Conservation Committee. He was disturbed that the state Department of Environmental Conservation proposed settling a major environmental violation by General Electric (GE) by asking the company to spend $200,000 to erect a boat launch. State environmental officials said that GE, a major employer in Solomon's congressional district, had illegally dumped hazardous materials into the soil and allowed a hazardous wastes fire at its site near Albany for nearly a year.

Solomon—who received $4,000 in campaign contributions from GE's political action committee in 1995 and $6,400 when he ran for reelection in 1994, according to Federal Election Commission records—took exception to Brodsky's queries into the GE matter. "New York state has had enough of media-hungry liberals looking for political gain at the expense of business and jobs for New Yorkers," Solomon wrote to Brodsky on Feb. 1 on official congressional letterhead. "As chairman of the Rules Committee," he wrote, "I could easily retaliate by involving myself in the activities of your Assembly district."

In dismissing Brodsky's complaint, the ethics committee issued Solomon a written warning to "avoid even the appearance of impropriety and be judicious in the language used on official letterhead." The committee said "a reader of your letter to Mr. Brodsky could form the impression that you did intend to retaliate against him in some way." But the committee said Solomon's statement that he did not intend to retaliate against Brodsky was persuasive.

FORMER MEMBERS

Dan Rostenkowski

Former Democratic representative Dan Rostenkowski of Illinois (1959–1995) pleaded guilty to corruption charges April 9, 1996. On July 22, he began serving a 17-month prison term for mail fraud.

Rostenkowski pleaded guilty to two counts of felony mail fraud stemming from his misuse of public funds to purchase gifts and to pay employees who did little or no official work. Federal prosecutors dropped 11 other corruption charges in a plea agreement worked out with Rostenkowski. The action grew out of the investigation into the House Post Office and the chamber's patronage and expense allowance system. *(House Post Office, p. 867)*

Standing with his hands in his pockets before U.S. District Judge Norma Holloway Johnson in Washington, D.C., Rostenkowski softly conceded that he had put employees on his payroll to "perform personal and political services." Johnson said he "shamelessly abused" his position and that the charges he pleaded guilty to did not "reflect the breadth of your criminality." Outside the courtroom, Rostenkowski was defiant, claiming that he had been singled out for prosecution for practices that were common in Congress.

In addition to prison time, Johnson levied a fine of $100,000, much of which Rostenkowski had already paid by reimbursing the Treasury for $82,000 in gifts purchased with congressional funds. In the plea agreement, Rostenkowski admitted sending payroll checks through the mail to his Chicago district office on Aug. 28, 1990, to pay employees who the ex-lawmaker acknowledged performed "personal or political service." He also admitted sending a check to Lenox China on Jan. 14, 1992, to pay for gifts for friends and political associates.

In the original 17-count indictment, Rostenkowski was charged with embezzling hundreds of thousands of dollars in public funds and using tens of thousands of dollars in campaign funds for personal purposes between mid-1971 and late 1992. Four of the counts against Rostenkowski—those that charged him with lying to Congress—were thrown out by Judge Johnson in March 1996, in response to a 1995 Supreme Court decision in *Hubbard v. United States* that said a law that had been widely used to prosecute individuals for lying to Congress applied only to untruthful statements made to executive branch officials. *(Court ruling, p. 774)*

A unanimous three-judge federal appeals court panel July 18, 1995, had refused to dismiss any charges against Rostenkowski. Judge Johnson on Nov. 14, 1995, had turned down a request by Rostenkowski's attorneys to shift the case to Chicago, Rostenkowski's hometown.

Joe Kolter

At a federal court in Washington on July 31, 1996, former representative Joe Kolter, D-Pa. (1983–1993), was sentenced to six months in prison, fined $20,000, and ordered to pay $9,300 in restitution for his role in the House Post Office scandal. Kolter had pleaded guilty May 7 to one count of conspiring to steal thousands of dollars in taxpayers' money by converting government-purchased stamps at the House Post Office into cash. *(House Post Office, p. 867)*

Kolter argued that his age and medical problems warranted nonprison confinement, but U.S. District Judge Norma Holloway Johnson said, "We have to do what is legally right as opposed to what is emotionally right." In April, Judge Johnson had dropped two of five original embezzlement counts against Kolter, citing a Supreme Court decision that covered lying to Congress, and narrowed a third count to conspiracy, to which Kolter pleaded guilty. As part of the plea agreement, prosecutors dropped the remaining charges against Kolter, who also was accused of bilking taxpayers of $33,000 worth of china, timepieces, pens and gold necklaces from the House stationery store. Kolter admitted to conspiring with House postmaster Robert V. Rota to steal $9,300 in cash after converting stamps and stamp vouchers into cash. When Kolter was originally indicted in October 1994, prosecutors said that he had converted $11,000 worth of stamps to cash.

Kolter used two procedures to get stamps from the House Post Office, one legitimate and the other illegal, according to documents filed with the court as part of the Kolter plea. Prosecutors found that Kolter's legitimate vouchers for postage stamps were typically in small dollar amounts, ranging from $10 to $50 and were prepared by a staff member. The fake vouchers were in large amounts, usually $1,000 or $2,000 and were prepared inside the House Post Office and signed by Kolter. Documents also said that Kolter and Rota took steps to conceal the scheme. For example, the two used blank House office vouchers, instead of those issued to Kolter's office, when preparing the fake vouchers, to hide the transactions from Kolter's staff. Rota also kept a list that ranked members by the volume of their stamp purchases. The list allowed the two to gauge how Kolter's stamp purchases stood in relation to others in particular years.

Dave Durenberger

Avoiding a trial on felony charges, former senator Dave Durenberger, R-Minn. (1978–1995), pleaded guilty Aug. 22, 1995, to five misdemeanor charges of hiding his ownership of a Minneapolis condominium to collect reimbursement for lodging when he traveled home.

Durenberger was indicted in 1994 on charges that he received thousands of dollars in reimbursement from April to August 1987. The guilty plea covered 10 specific days, for which he claimed a total of $425 in reimbursement. On Nov. 29, 1995, U.S. District Court Judge Stanley Harris fined Durenberger $1,000 and placed him on a year's probation. (Earlier action, p. 873)

Carl Perkins

Former representative Carl Perkins, D-Ky. (1985–1993), was sentenced March 13, 1995, to 21 months in prison for writing bad checks, filing false financial disclosure statements, and lying on his campaign finance reports. Perkins was also sentenced to probation for three years, given 250 hours of community service and ordered to complete an alcohol treatment program.

The case against Perkins, who pleaded guilty to the charges in December 1994, stemmed from the Justice Department's investigation of the House bank.

Walter E. Fauntroy

Former delegate Walter E. Fauntroy, D-D.C. (1971–1991), pleaded guilty March 24, 1995, to a felony charge stemming from the House bank investigation. Fauntroy admitted falsely reporting a $23,887 donation to a church on his financial disclosure form for 1988.

The charge later was reduced to a misdemeanor, after the Supreme Court on May 15 ruled that the law that Fauntroy had been prosecuted under did not cover lying to Congress. He was instead charged with a misdemeanor under District of Columbia law. On Aug. 9, he was sentenced to two years probation, fined $1,000, and sentenced to 300 hours of community service. The original charge carried a maximum penalty of five years in prison and a $250,000 fine.

According to a Justice Department release, Fauntroy listed the donation to the New Bethel Baptist Church of Washington, where he was pastor, in an attempt to skirt requirements that at the time limited members' outside income to 30 percent of their congressional salary. Fauntroy said he gave a check to the church in December 1988, but with instructions that it not be cashed until he could sell two properties to raise the funds to cover it. The check cleared on June 12, 1989, a month after he had reported the gift on his 1988 financial disclosure form.

The March 22 indictment alleged that Fauntroy also failed to disclose a $24,200 loan he received from Dominion Bank in 1988.

Donald E. "Buz" Lukens

Former representative Donald E. "Buz" Lukens, R-Ohio (1967–1971, 1987–1990), faced a new trial after a federal jury in October 1995 deadlocked on two conspiracy and bribery charges brought against the Ohio Republican. The same jury acquitted Lukens of three lesser bribery charges.

The mistrial involved whether Lukens accepted $27,500 from the Cambridge Technical Institute, an Ohio trade school, in exchange for political favors. At a retrial, Lukens was convicted March 15, 1996, of bribery.

In 1989, a jury convicted Lukens of having paid for sex with a minor. He lost his May 1990 primary and resigned Oct. 24, 1990, after it was alleged that he had made an improper advance toward a Capitol elevator operator. (1989 action, Congress and the Nation Vol. VIII, p. 925)

Walter R. Tucker III

Former representative Walter R. Tucker III, D-Calif. (1993–1995), was sentenced on April 17, 1996, to 27 months in federal prison. Tucker was found guilty in U.S. District Court on Dec. 8, 1995, on seven counts of extortion and two counts of tax evasion. He resigned his seat on Dec. 15, 1995, preempting preliminary moves by F. James Sensenbrenner Jr., R-Wis., to hold a vote to expel him.

The conviction stemmed from a 1994 indictment charging Tucker with taking $30,000 in payments from a company that wanted to build a trash incineration plant in Compton, Calif., while he was mayor. He also was accused of demanding another $250,000 from the firm. Tucker was charged with failing to report the $30,000 on his federal income tax returns. On June 1, 1995, a federal grand jury handed up additional indictments, charging Tucker with taking a $5,000 bribe from a firm that collected garbage in Compton and with taking an additional $2,500 to help extend the company's municipal contract.

Tucker maintained that he was set up by government prosecutors.

Mary Rose Oakar

Former representative Mary Rose Oakar, D-Ohio (1977–1993), was indicted Feb. 22, 1995, on seven felony counts. She was charged with lying to the FBI about asking the House bank to stop payment on three checks, writing a $16,000 check even though she knew not enough money was in the account to cover it, trying to evade campaign finance law, and failing to report a $50,000 loan on her 1991 financial disclosure form.

The indictment said Oakar's nephew and former campaign aide, Joseph DeMio, and an unnamed person called people and asked permission to use their names as donors on Federal Election Commission (FEC) campaign disclosure reports. In addition, a $28,000 loan was converted into $1,000 campaign contributions, the indictment said. DeMio was charged with making false statements to the FEC.

On March 21, 1996, U.S. District Judge Harold Greene threw out two of seven counts against Oakar. One of the accounts dismissed by Greene alleged that Oakar had lied to Congress by filing false financial statements. The Supreme Court in 1995 had ruled that the prohibition against lying did not apply to statements made to Congress.

The second charge thrown out by Greene alleged that Oakar

had committed a crime by writing a $16,000 overdraft check at the House bank. Greene said no House rule prohibited overdrafts. He said the courts could not create a crime, because that would tread on Congress's rulemaking power.

Oakar pleaded guilty Sept. 30, 1997, to a misdemeanor conspiracy charge and a misdemeanor campaign finance violation. She admitted shifting $16,000 in campaign contributions from her House bank account to her campaign using fake names to evade individual contribution limits and giving false information to the FEC. Under a plea agreement with the Justice Department, Oakar was likely to receive probation and a $32,000 fine. ❏

Chronology of Action on Congress: Election Issues

1993–1994

The 103rd Congress added to the long line of unsuccessful attempts to enact campaign finance reform legislation. Democrats' inability to iron out their internal differences as well as steadfast Republican opposition to public funding of congressional campaigns and GOP use of the filibuster contributed to the legislation's death.

The Federal Election Commission issued regulations regarding spending campaign funds on personal needs.

Campaign Finance

Legislation (S 3) to limit spending on congressional campaigns and provide candidates with partial public funding died at the end of the 103rd Congress, the victim of a GOP-led filibuster. Failure to enact the bill was a major defeat for President Clinton and Democratic congressional leaders. *(104th Congress action, p. 914)*

Democrats, however, had set the stage for defeat by waiting until the eleventh hour to come up with a compromise version. Indeed, the long history of the legislation was rich with evidence that many Democrats in both chambers shared GOP objections to establishing a system that would provide congressional candidates with federal subsidies. Other Democrats, particularly in the House, were deeply, if privately, opposed to an overhaul of the financing system that had protected their seats and majority status for years. In the end, it was the inability of Democrats to iron out their internal differences that delayed the 1993–1994 bill so long that it became vulnerable to procedural snags. Some supporters of the legislation blamed President Clinton, who had campaigned on the issue but brought little pressure to bear on it in 1994.

BACKGROUND

The debate over campaign finance had been revisited regularly since 1986 but without much progress on the fundamental issues that divided the parties.

Although House and Senate Democrats had different perspectives on the role of political action committees (PACs) and a handful of other related issues, on the major campaign finance issues broad agreement existed within the party. Most Democrats advocated partial public funding of candidates who promised to abide by spending limits, which they said would allow challengers to spend on a level equal to incumbents. Under the 1976 Supreme Court decision in *Buckley v. Valeo*, spending limits had to be voluntary. The Court said that public financing was a legitimate carrot to encourage compliance with those voluntary limits—a concept some Democrats supported anyway, calling public funding "clean money."

Most Republicans strenuously opposed taxpayer financing of congressional campaigns, which they likened to welfare for

politicians. Many Republicans also argued that spending limits locked in incumbent advantages. They said challengers needed the option to outspend incumbents to make themselves equally visible to voters. *(1976 decision, Congress and the Nation Vol. IV, pp. 639, 995)*

In 1987–1988, debate over these issues threw the Senate into a virtually unprecedented procedural fit. Consideration of a bill that included spending limits and federal funding stretched over nine months and forced a record eight cloture votes in an effort to break a Republican filibuster. A 53-hour, 24-minute session and a senator placed under arrest and physically carried to the floor highlighted the proceedings. In the end, the Senate failed to overcome partisan divisions, and the measure succumbed to the process. *(Congress and the Nation Vol. VII, p. 894)*

Over the next several years, with a Republican in the White House pledging to veto any campaign finance reform bill cleared by the Democratic Congress, neither party showed much interest in restaging the drama. Instead, when an ethics scandal broke—such as the Keating Five affair in the early 1990s, in which five senators were accused of accepting favors from a savings and loan magnate—campaign finance legislation was trotted out as a symbol of reform. The two chambers reached agreement on a bill in 1992 after the House came under siege over the House bank scandal. That measure merely stapled a plan House Democrats had crafted to an entirely different plan Senate Democrats had sanctioned. Both plans, however, included spending limits and public financing. As promised, President George Bush vetoed the legislation. *(Keating Five, Congress and the Nation Vol. VIII, p. 975; 1992 bill, Congress and the Nation Vol. VIII, p. 959; House bank scandal, Congress and the Nation Vol. VIII, p. 929)*

During the 1992 campaign, many Democratic challengers and those running in open seats decried the veto and the existing campaign finance system with its escalating spending and interest group money. Though redistricting and a record number of retirements made 1992 unusual, expenditures on congressional campaigns shot up 52 percent. Democratic presidential nominee Bill Clinton also vowed to overhaul the system. The 103rd Congress opened with high expectations for enactment of a new law.

ADMINISTRATION PROPOSAL

After months of work and countless hours of backroom negotiations, Clinton and Democratic congressional leaders gathered on the White House lawn May 7, 1993, to present their proposal to rewrite campaign finance laws. Their labors produced a plan that was much like the one Bush vetoed.

Based on projections made by the Congressional Budget Office (CBO) in 1992, the White House estimated that public funding of congressional campaigns would cost about $150 million for the first election cycle. But that estimate was based on lower spending limits. Most outside groups set the price closer to $200 million. Clinton expected to finance the bill by increasing the taxpayer checkoff for federal elections from $1 to $5 and by ending the tax exemption for lobbying expenses. The administration said that the higher checkoff would raise $150 million a year and that the change in tax law would add $978 million in new revenue over five years. The budget reconciliation bill (HR 2264) raised the checkoff to $3. (*Reconciliation, p. 44*)

The Clinton plan included the following elements:

• **Spending Limits.** General election spending limits in the Senate would range from $1.2 million to $5.5 million, depending on state population. These levels were to rise with inflation after the 1996 election. The spending limit for the House was set at $600,000, but it was to be indexed for inflation from 1992 forward to 1996. At the existing 3 percent inflation rate, the spending ceiling was expected to exceed $675,000.

The spending limits would increase if a candidate faced an opponent who exceeded the cap, was the target of a substantial independent expenditure (money spent by an independent group) or (for House members only) won a competitive primary. Some expenses did not count, such as limited spending for fund raising (House) and legal and accounting work to comply with the law (both houses).

• **Benefits.** Communications vouchers—to be used for media advertising, printing costs and postage—would be provided to candidates who complied with the spending limits. Senate candidates would get vouchers equal to 25 percent of their spending limits. Broadcasters would be obliged to sell Senate candidates discounted advertising time. House candidates would receive vouchers worth up to 33 percent of the limit.

• **PAC Contributions.** For presidential candidates, a limit of $1,000 would be set on contributions from any one PAC. The limit for Senate candidates was $2,500 for a primary, plus another $2,500 for a general election. House candidates could get up to $5,000 for each election. A complying candidate's aggregate contributions from PACs could not total more than 33 percent of the House spending limit; 20 percent of the Senate limit.

• **Contributions from Lobbyists.** A ban would be imposed on contributions to a member of Congress from anyone who had lobbied that member or an aide in the previous year. Those who lobbied executive branch officials could not give to the president's campaign for a year, although they could give to party committees. The proposal assumed enactment of new lobbying legislation.

• **Small Donors.** Complying candidates would be required to get a portion of their funds from small donations. To get full public benefits, House candidates would have to raise at least one-third of the spending limit in contributions smaller than $200. Senate candidates would have to raise 20 percent of the limit in contributions less than $250.

• **Bundling.** When an organization or individual raised money for a candidate, usually from associates, group members or employees, and then forwarded the checks together to the candidate, or otherwise made known their common bond, the practice was known as "bundling." Democrats could not reach full agreement on this issue. Clinton and Senate leaders recommended prohibiting bundling by all lobbyists, PACs, unions and corporations. House Democrats wanted to exempt PACs that did not lobby Congress to bundle contributions—a provision designed to help EMILY's List, a donor network that gathered contributions for Democratic women candidates who backed abortion rights.

• **Soft Money.** So-called "soft money" was essentially unregulated money raised outside federal limits. Parties could raise unlimited amounts of soft money from unions, corporations, trade associations and individuals for state and local party activities. Although this money could not by law be used for federal candidates, when it was channeled into such grassroots activities as voter registration, education and voter turnout drives, party candidates at all levels benefited.

Clinton's plan aimed at prohibiting state and national parties from spending soft money to influence federal elections. At the same time, the total an individual could give in a two-year election cycle would be increased to $60,000, from the existing limit of $50,000. The plan provided for three competing pots of money. Keeping within the overall contributions limit, an individual could donate up to $25,000 per year to federal candidates, $20,000 to national party committees and $20,000 to new state party grassroots funds. State parties could use the grassroots funds to finance generic media and coordinated campaigns, which under existing law could be partially funded with soft money. Each presidential nominee would get an estimated $11 million for such activities—equal to 2 cents for each voting-age person.

The parties still could raise money that exceeded federal contribution limits if the money was transferred directly to state parties and used for state campaigns and administrative costs. Contributions for party building funds, which supported construction and purchase of office space, also were exempt.

SENATE ACTION

Without waiting for Clinton to unveil his plan, the Senate Rules and Administration Committee on April 28, 1993, reported a bill (S 3—S Rept 103-41) that was identical to the 1992 measure vetoed by Bush.

When Republicans complained that the legislation was being rushed to the floor without hearings, the Rules and Administration Committee held a three-and-a-half-hour hearing May 19. Though no amendments were approved, Democratic leaders short-circuited a GOP plan to attack provisions allowing PAC contributions by including a PAC ban in their bill. With that exception, the bill mirrored the Clinton plan.

Senate floor action on S 3 began on May 21, and the early debate was so lethargic that on May 28, immediately before recessing for Memorial Day, a visibly frustrated Majority Leader George J. Mitchell, D-Maine, threatened to end his policy of trying to schedule votes and debates at times convenient to senators. The dull pace masked growing apprehension within the Democratic Party over the provisions to provide public funding to candidates. The lead Republican critic, Mitch McConnell of Kentucky, offered an amendment to dedicate the revenue from ending the tax break for lobbying expenses to deficit reduction. Democrats hoped to use the money to pay for public funding of campaigns, and so Democratic floor manager David L. Boren of Oklahoma offered an amendment to allow the money to be used to "eliminate special interests" in campaigns as well as for deficit reduction. In turn, McConnell offered a motion to table (kill) the Boren amendment. The motion was rejected by a close 48–50 vote on May 26; five Democrats voted for the motion. The Boren amendment and the McConnell amendment as modified by the Boren amendment subsequently were adopted by voice votes. An amendment by John Kerry, D-Mass., which would have set public financing of congressional campaigns at 90 percent of the general election spending limits for candidates who raised 10 percent of the limits in contributions of less than $250, was rejected 35–60 on May 27. An Ernest F. Hollings, D-S.C., amendment expressing the sense of the Senate in favor of a constitutional amendment permitting mandatory spending limits was adopted 52–43 on May 27, 15 votes short of the two-thirds majority needed in both chambers to approve a constitutional amendment.

The Senate by voice vote accepted an amendment by John H. Chafee, R-R.I., to prohibit out-of-state fund raising during the first four years of a senator's term. The Senate also approved, 85–12 on May 26, a Larry Pressler, R-S.D., amendment to ban PACs in House and Senate campaigns. If the PAC ban were found unconstitutional, then PAC contributions would be limited to $1,000 in any federal election, and an aggregate cap for PAC contributions would be set at 20 percent of the spending limit for both chambers. The Pressler amendment made negotiating with Senate Republicans easier for Democrats, but it guaranteed a conference showdown with House Democrats.

Democrats maintained that the 1994 election cycle already was under way and no law could take effect until the following election. Republicans and editorial writers accused Democrats of delay. John McCain, R-Ariz., offered an amendment to move the effective date of the legislation to 1994 (without addressing money candidates had raised in 1993) from 1996, as provided in the bill. Democrats tried to adopt it by voice vote, but Minority Leader Bob Dole, R-Kan., demanded a recorded vote. The amendment was adopted 85–7 on June 8.

For the first three weeks of the debate, Democrats held fast to public financing, repeatedly complaining of a "Republican filibuster." To underscore the point, Democrats forced two cloture votes, knowing full well that both would be rejected. The first went down June 10 on a 53–41 vote; the second June 15 on a 52–45 vote. To invoke cloture (and thus limit debate) required 60 votes. In neither instance did a single Republican cross the line. By the second cloture vote, it became apparent that many Democratic senators would not vote to hit taxpayers with an estimated $200 million tab for public funding. Bargaining with the GOP to curb federal benefits thus became essential not only to win Republican votes but also to keep the Democrats on board.

The final deal to strike public funding but retain spending limits was worked out among Mitchell, Boren, Jim Exon, D-Neb., and a group of five "swing" Republicans—Chafee, McCain, Dave Durenberger of Minnesota, William S. Cohen of Maine and James M. Jeffords of Vermont. It was a complicated merger of two plans: one by Exon to forgo public funding until a candidate complying with spending limits was confronted with an opponent breaking them; and another by Durenberger

to impose a receipts tax on campaigns that did not agree to spending limits. Lifting an existing tax exemption for campaigns, the amendment set the tax for campaigns at the highest corporate tax rate unless the candidate agreed to comply with spending limits. (The top corporate rate was 34 percent. It went to 35 percent as part of the budget reconciliation bill.) The revenue would go into a fund to provide federal communication vouchers worth up to 100 percent of the spending limit for any complying candidate who faced an opponent who exceeded the limit. If that money was insufficient, the fund could be supplemented with money from the Treasury, which sponsors said could be counted as money raised by ending the deduction for lobbying expenses. (The deduction was ended as part of the reconciliation bill.)

Before voting on the Exon-Durenberger deal, the Senate voted 53–44 on June 16 to table (kill) an amendment, offered by McConnell and Richard C. Shelby, D-Ala., to strip from the bill all public funding and spending limits. Winning support among traditional Democrats for the Exon-Durenberger amendment, which many said sounded a death knell for public funding, was difficult. Building on a perception that a stalemate would look bad for Congress and Clinton, Mitchell made direct personal appeals to many reluctant senators. He portrayed the vote as essential to passage of the bill, and his case got a big boost when Common Cause endorsed the Exon-Durenberger amendment. While the citizens group's backing was critical, it infuriated many who saw public funds early in a campaign as essential to leveling the playing field for challengers. The remaining benefits for complying candidates—a mailing discount for two letters per voter, a 50 percent broadcast discount and backup funds in the event of an independent campaign or a big-spending opponent—appeared a pittance to some, particularly because they did not come until after a primary.

The Exon-Durenberger amendment was adopted 52–47 on June 16. If the protracted debate over public funding stretched Democratic alliances, it splintered the Republicans. Led by McConnell, GOP stalwarts argued vociferously that spending limits locked in the advantages of incumbency for Democrats. They also said tight new restrictions on party spending would undermine the Republicans' ability to defend themselves against unregulated, unlimited spending by labor unions in behalf of Democrats. On an ideological plane, many Republicans regarded any public funding of congressional campaigns as a misuse of taxpayer dollars. Even some of those who worked toward a compromise said the relatively small amount of public money left in the bill was a problem.

In the Democrats' third attempt, a cloture motion was agreed to 62–37 on June 16. The Democratic leaders ensured that the five swing Republicans got enough of what they asked for to box them into voting "yea" on cloture. At the last minute, Mitchell agreed to allow voice vote approval of a Cohen amendment to strip language designed to strengthen the Federal Election Commission. That final deal paved the way to halt debate and proceed to a vote on the bill. S 3 was passed by the Senate on June 17 on a **key vote of 60–38 (R 7–35; D 53–3)**. *(1993 key votes, p. 979)*

HOUSE ACTION

Five months later, on Nov. 17, the House Administration Committee reported its campaign finance reform bill (HR 3—H Rept 103-375, Part I). HR 3 was similar to the vetoed 1992 legislation—limiting spending, providing up to one-third of the money in federally funded communications vouchers and restricting candidates to raising no more than one-third of their money from PACs.

However, HR 3 differed from the 1992 version and the Clinton plan in a few key areas, notably new exemptions that could raise the spending limit from $600,000 to nearly $1 million for many campaigns by the time it took effect for the 1996 elections. The committee-approved bill also would have allowed members to run their own PACs—so-called leadership PACs—and carry over war chests from one election to the next. The 1992 bill forbade both practices. HR 3 would have allowed federal candidates to raise soft money to aid state candidates, a practice barred in the 1992 measure. Neither the 1992 nor the 1993 bill included a way to pay for federal benefits, one that would cover the cost of the vouchers without tapping general revenues. Clinton's proposal to tax lobbying expenses already had been included in the budget reconciliation bill. An alternative plan was dropped after the Ways and Means Committee refused to sanction a revenue-raising provision that it did not originate.

GOP attempts during markup to amend the bill were defeated.

The House on Nov. 22 passed HR 3 by 255–175, then passed S 3, with the language of HR 3, by voice vote. The legislation came within a whisker of not even making it to the House floor.

Mike Synar, D-Okla., had announced Nov. 19 that he had the votes to block consideration of the bill. He said members on both sides of the aisle would reject a rule that prohibited amendments or alternatives other than the one put forward by the Republican leadership—alternatives such as his own. Long a backer of public financing, Synar abandoned that position, saying it lacked the votes to pass. Together with a group of Republicans, he advocated lower PAC and individual contribution limits in lieu of a spending cap. Public interest groups, including Common Cause, attacked his effort as a subterfuge for killing a campaign finance overhaul. Editorials in the *Washington Post* and the *New York Times* echoed those objections on Nov. 20, when the Rules Committee was set to meet.

The Rules Committee sat through more than three hours of testimony and, as expected, rejected all 35 proposed amendments—all but six from Republicans—as well as three substitute measures. On a partisan 7–3 vote, the panel approved a rule (H Res 319) allowing only a vote on the Democratic plan and another on a GOP plan. After vigorous lobbying by the Democratic leadership and the White House, the House adopted the rule on a **key vote of 220–207 (R 3–168; D 216–39; I 1–0)** on Nov. 21.

Before final passage of HR 3 the next day, the House rejected, 173–263, the GOP alternative, which would have banned PACs. The Republican plan also would have required candidates to raise a majority of their funds in their districts. Republicans said this would level the playing field for challengers and enhance voter confidence in the system. Democrats argued that confining fund raising would put those from poor districts and those lacking access to affluent voters at a disadvantage.

Republicans attacked the House-passed version for lacking a funding mechanism and suggested that Democrats would soon be picking taxpayer's pockets to foot the bill. CBO estimated that the benefits in the House bill would cost $93 million, and the total election cycle cost was put at $181 million.

COMPROMISE REACHED

Democratic House leaders put off appointing conferees on S 3 while they tried to negotiate a compromise package outside the confines of a normal conference. They chose this tactic because, once conferees were appointed, the conference committee would have to be able to file a report within 20 days or Republicans could begin offering embarrassing motions to instruct the negotiators on a variety of issues.

By spring of 1994, agreement reportedly had been reached on the use of soft money and independent expenditures. Differences on these issues had been minor. The biggest obstacles to full joint agreement remained public funding and PACs. Getting the necessary number of Senate votes for any system that included significant public funding appeared impossible. And Senate Republicans had dug in to support the elimination of PACs, while House Democrats depended heavily on PAC funding.

The logjam over PACs was finally broken Sept. 29, when House and Senate Democratic leaders unveiled a plan they hoped a conference committee would rubber stamp. The compromise included provisions to:

• **Voluntary Spending Limits.** Set state-by-state limits for Senate campaigns for the 1996 elections ranging from $1.2 million to $5.5 million for general elections, with lower limits for primaries. Set a uniform limit for House candidates of approximately $675,000 (once inflation was factored in) for 1996. Limits would rise for candidates who won a primary with a margin of less than 20 percent and for those forced into runoff elections.

• **Benefits.** Offer Senate candidates a 50 percent discount for television broadcast time as an inducement to comply with spending limits. Complying House candidates could receive vouchers for advertising and postage costs up to one-third of the spending limit and funds to counter opponents who exceeded the spending limits. Candidates for either chamber could receive funds to respond to independent expenditure campaigns.

• **PACs.** Limit the amount political action committees could give to federal candidates to $6,000 per election cycle, down from the existing limit of $10,000. A maximum of $5,000 could be given for a primary. Total PAC contributions could amount to no more than one-third of the spending limit for House candidates; 20 percent for Senate candidates.

• **Leadership PACs.** Bar members, starting in 1997, from having their own PACs as a way of making contributions to other candidates.

- **Bundling.** Bar individuals and committees connected with corporations, trade associations and labor unions from collecting and forwarding individual donations to federal candidates. EMILY's List could continue.
- **Personal Use.** Prohibit present and former candidates from spending campaign funds for any use that conferred a personal benefit.
- **Soft Money.** Prohibit national or state parties from raising funds outside federal restrictions, with some exceptions.
- **Individual Contributions.** Increase the amount an individual could contribute to candidates, political parties and PACs to $60,000 per two-year election cycle from the existing cap of $25,000 per year.
- **Franked Mail.** Prohibit senators and House members who became candidates for the Senate from sending mass mail using the franking privilege in the year of the election.
- **Minors.** Bar dependents below voting age from making contributions to federal candidates.
- **Financing.** Raise revenue from a variety of sources to finance the program, estimated by CBO to cost $168 million over five years. The agreement would allow taxpayers to add $5 ($10 for those filing jointly) to their annual federal income tax bills; require PACs to pay a 5 percent fee on annual receipts; require candidates who rejected spending limits and public funding to pay a 35 percent tax on spending in excess of the expenditure limit; require candidates' committees to pay a 35 percent tax on investment income instead of the existing 15 percent; require that lobbyists pay a new annual registration fee of $500; increase registration fees for foreign agents; and eliminate the tax deduction available to lobbyists and businesses for meals and entertainment expenses that involved officeholders or federal employees.

GOP FILIBUSTER

With the Oct. 7 target date for adjournment fast approaching, Republicans found a new weapon to derail the compromise agreement: a filibuster against the procedural steps that usually were a routine part of convening a conference. On Sept. 22, the Senate agreed 96–2 to a motion to invoke cloture on the first step—a motion to disagree with the House's amendments to the bill. Republicans then insisted on using up all the time available for debate on the motion itself, talking straight through the night and through most of Sept. 23 before the Senate voted 93–0 to disagree with the House. Republicans then mounted a filibuster against the next procedural hurdle, a motion to go to conference, and advised that they had enough further procedural moves to bring the Senate to a halt for weeks. Mitchell was outraged, calling the effort "total obstructionism" that was unprecedented in the history of the Senate.

The effort stalled there. Two votes to invoke cloture on the motion to request a conference fell well short of the 60 votes required. On Sept. 27, the first motion was rejected 57–43. The coup de grace came Sept. 30 when six Democrats joined Republicans in the **key vote of 52–46 (R 2–40; D 50–6).** Speaker Foley called the GOP maneuverings "the worst case of obstruction by filibuster by any party that I've ever seen in my 30 years in Con-

gress." Republicans seemed unfazed by allegations that they were causing gridlock. "I make no apologies for killing this turkey of a bill," said McConnell. *(1994 key votes, p. 1003)*

FEC COMPOSITION

The Supreme Court, in a 7–1 decision handed down Dec. 6, 1994, rejected an appeal brought by the Federal Election Commission (FEC) against a 1993 court ruling concerning its composition. In that decision by the D.C. Circuit Court of Appeals, the lower court ruled that the commission had violated the constitutional separation of powers by including two nonvoting congressional staff members in its deliberations. The FEC voted to exclude the two members but asked the Supreme Court to rule that past FEC decisions were still valid. The Court accepted the case, *FEC v. the National Rifle Association Political Victory Fund,* on June 20, 1994. *(Court case, p. 782)*

The Court rejected the appeal on technical grounds, ruling that the agency lacked authority to appeal the matter to the Supreme Court. Chief Justice William H. Rehnquist, writing for the majority, said the law establishing the FEC gave only the solicitor general the authority for such appeals. The decision left the 1993 ruling in place and left a legal cloud hanging over similar court challenges of FEC actions. The Court did not speak to the merits of the constitutional challenge.

Campaign Finance Spending Regulations

The Federal Election Commission (FEC) on Dec. 1, 1994, adopted regulations to stop congressional candidates from spending campaign dollars on personal needs. Congress barred the conversion of campaign funds to personal use in 1979, but the FEC had never issued regulations defining "personal use." The House and Senate had adopted their own rules for incumbents, allowing the use of campaign money for any "political expense" by House members or "officially connected expense" by senators. *(1979 action, Congress and the Nation Vol. V, p. 951)*

BACKGROUND

The writing of the regulations was a yearlong process. The FEC held six hours of hearings on Jan. 12, 1994, on draft regulations that had been published Aug. 30, 1993. The hearings followed on news stories such as a *Los Angeles Times* report that Sen. Daniel K. Inouye, D-Hawaii, used campaign contributions to buy meals totaling $545 at a hotel in Jakarta, Indonesia, or a story in the *Wall Street Journal* noting that Rep. Curt Weldon, R-Pa., bought a $5,100 vintage fire truck with campaign funds. Reps. Michael A. Andrews, D-Texas, and Duncan Hunter, R-Calif., paid their House gym dues with campaign money, according to various news accounts.

In the August 1993 draft regulations, the commission proposed prohibiting the use of campaign money for any expense "that would exist irrespective of the candidate's campaign or responsibilities as a federal officeholder." During the public hearings in January 1994, interest groups and private lawyers found fault with the proposed standard. Even FEC chairman Trevor Potter suggested that any general standard would be insufficient. "It's very easy to come up with a political explanation for almost any expense," Potter said.

A revised draft of the regulations went to commissioners May 5. It barred campaigns from paying a salary to candidates. The regulations continued to leave much to the candidates' discretion but included a litany of specific expenses that would be illegal. The FEC held another hearing May 19 and ordered its staff to prepare a new draft. In the July 27 draft, the commission proposed transferring much of the responsibility for determining what constituted personal use to the House and Senate ethics committees. But after critics such as Common Cause President Fred Wertheimer and Elizabeth Hedlund of the Center for Responsive Politics protested that this would let abuses continue, the FEC changed its proposal for its Aug. 11 meeting, keeping such determinations for itself.

NEW REGULATIONS

The regulations approved Dec. 1 provided the same standard for incumbents and challengers alike. Candidates would be barred from dipping into their campaign coffers to pay bills that would have existed whether or not they had run for office. The regulations listed specific personal expenses that could not be funded by a campaign. The list included household food, rent, mortgage payments, utility bills and supplies; funeral expenses; clothing, other than campaign handouts such as T-shirts and caps; tuition payments; tickets to entertainment events that were not part of a specific campaign or officeholder activity; and membership dues, tips and fees at clubs, recreation centers and other nonpolitical organizations, unless they were part of a fund-raising event at the club or center. The new regulations would go into effect in early 1995.

The new regulations applied to presidential candidates as well, although those campaigns already were covered by separate laws and regulations regarding the use of public funding.

Absent from the new regulations was a ban on candidates' use of campaign funds to pay themselves a salary. Such a provision would have affected only challengers, as members of Congress already were prohibited by law from drawing any salary beyond their congressional pay. The commission's lawyers had proposed the salary ban, saying it was needed to prevent challengers from circumventing the law against using campaign contributions for personal needs. But FEC Chairman Potter, a Republican appointee, said salaries should be allowed, to enable people who were not wealthy to run for Congress.

The six-member commission deadlocked on the proposed ban, with three Democrats voting for it and three Republicans voting against it. Because four votes were required to adopt any proposed regulation, the ban was dropped from the new rules. Potter then proposed letting candidates use campaign funds to pay themselves salaries no greater than the ones they received before entering the race. That proposal also fell, 3–3, with Republicans supporting it and Democrats opposing. With no clear regulatory guidance, challengers who paid themselves salaries were unlikely to be stopped by the FEC, although they could wind up in court.

1995–1996

A considerable amount of talk was heard about campaign finance reform and congressional term limits. However, Congress failed to enact legislation on either issue.

Lawmakers did complete action on a bill to make filing campaign finance reports easier.

Campaign Finance

Both the Senate and House failed to pass campaign finance overhaul legislation in the 104th Congress. A bipartisan effort (S 1219) was stopped by a filibuster in the Senate; a GOP bill (HR 3820) and a Democratic substitute were defeated in floor votes in the House. Furthermore, the Supreme Court dealt a blow to the existing campaign finance law, ruling in 1996 that federal spending limits on state and national party organizations did not apply as long as the parties spent money independently of a candidate's campaign. *(Party spending limits, box, p. 915)*

Campaign finance legislation had stalled in the 103rd Congress, but hopes for reform were raised on June 11, 1995, when, at a New Hampshire forum, President Clinton and House Speaker Newt Gingrich, R-Ga., shook hands on an agreement to create a commission to explore changes in the campaign finance system. The administration subsequently issued a statement outlining how the commission should be structured, and Gingrich responded several months later with his proposal. Both advocated modeling such a panel on the base-closing commission that had been able to sidestep parochial interests in Congress in deciding which military bases should be shut down. In June 1996, Senate Majority Leader Bob Dole, R-Kan., offered a plan to create a bipartisan commission on campaign practices. But advocates of campaign finance reform rejected the idea as a prescription for yet more delay. *(103rd Congress action, p. 909)*

SENATE ACTION

S 1219 was sponsored by John McCain, R-Ariz., Fred Thompson, R-Tenn., and Russell D. Feingold, D-Wis. The major provisions of the bipartisan bill would have:

• **Spending Limits and Benefits.** Set voluntary spending limits on primary and general Senate elections based on the voting-age population of a state. A Senate candidate in California, for example, would have been able to spend about $8 million, while an individual seeking office in Wyoming could have spent close to $1.5 million.

In return, a candidate would have received 30 minutes of free, prime-time air time from television stations within the state or an adjacent state, reduced broadcast rates calculated at 50 percent of the lowest amount a station charged, and discounted postage rates. Taxpayers would have paid for the mail discounts; broadcasters would have been required to provide the free television time.

A candidate whose opponent rejected the limits would have been allowed to accept larger contributions from individuals, as much as $2,000 per election, up from the $1,000 limit. Candidates who faced a wealthy opponent who spent more than $250,000 of his or her own funds campaigning would also have been able to accept up to $2,000 from individuals.

A candidate would have had to raise 60 percent of his or her campaign funds from individuals in his or her home state.

• **Reduction of Special Interest Influence.** Allowed only individuals to contribute to candidates and only a candidate's official election committee to solicit funds. The bill proposed to ban contributions from political action committees (PACs), traditionally used by special interest groups to raise funds for and funnel contributions to candidates.

The goal was to level the political playing field by eliminating the advantages that incumbents typically had against challengers in fundraising. A 1995 Federal Election Commission report showed that incumbents received $59 million in PAC money in a nonelection year, while challengers collected just $3 million.

If the U.S. Supreme Court ruled such a ban on PAC contributions unconstitutional, the bill would have allowed a PAC to contribute to a candidate but would have required the committees to adhere to the same contribution limits imposed on individuals.

• **Soft Money.** Banned soft money, the unlimited funds that national political parties raised from corporations, unions and other sources to spend on party-building activities.

Republicans raised $121 million in soft money over a 21-month period beginning in January 1995, an increase of 166 percent from the previous presidential election cycle. Democrats collected $102 million in soft money, a jump of 232 percent from 1991 to 1992.

Soft money spending by state committees on voter registration or get-out-the-vote activities that might influence a federal election could have been made only from funds that were subject to federal limits and prohibitions.

• **Contribution Limits.** Prohibited contributions from being "bundled," a method that allowed an individual to collect several contributions and give them as a group to a candidate. All bundled contributions would have been considered the individual contributions of the intermediary and would have been subject to limits on individual contributions. Under existing law, bundled contributions were counted separately.

• **Reporting Requirements.** Lowered the threshold for reporting contributions and expenditures from the existing $200 to $50.

• **Severability** Required that if any provisions of the legislation were ruled unconstitutional, the other provisions would remain in effect.

The Senate failed June 25, 1996, on a **54–46 (R 8–45; D 46–1) key vote,** to limit debate on S 1219, falling six votes short of the 60 votes needed to invoke cloture. Leading the filibuster was Mitch McConnell, who had played the same role in 1994.

PARTY SPENDING LIMITS

The Supreme Court in a June 26, 1996, ruling threw out restrictions on expenditures by political parties that were made independent of a candidate's campaign. The Court issued its decision in *Colorado Republican Federal Campaign Committee v. Federal Election Commission* by a 7–2 vote. *(Court ruling, p. 782)*

Campaign finance rules enacted in 1974 (PL 93-443) limited the amount political parties could spend on congressional campaigns to 2 cents multiplied by the voting-age population of a state for Senate elections and about $30,000 for House races. The Supreme Court, however, said that parties could spend unlimited amounts on such things as advertising, as long as they did not coordinate those expenditures with a particular candidate's campaign. The court ruling continued to limit spending on party-led efforts that were coordinated with a candidate. *(1974 law, Congress and the Nation Vol. IV, p. 991)*

The decision meant that national political parties could run unlimited ads for favored candidates, a tool previously denied them. That was in addition to the unregulated funds that state and national party committees already spent on advertising that enhanced a particular campaign but did not specifically urge votes for or against a candidate. In a 1976 ruling, *Buckley v. Valeo,* the high court struck down limits on independent expenditures. *(1976 ruling, Congress and the Nation Vol. IV, pp. 639, 995)*

In the 1996 case, the Supreme Court was acting on an appeal by the Colorado Republican Party of a June 23, 1995, decision by the 10th U.S. Circuit Court of Appeals. The appellate court had upheld in its entirety the campaign finance law imposing strict spending limits on parties' national and state committees. At issue was a $15,000 campaign ad broadcast by the Colorado GOP in April 1986 against Rep. Timothy Wirth, a Democrat seeking his party's nomination to the Senate. Under federal law, a state party could either spend money itself to help a federal candidate or assign the right to the federal party, as the Colorado GOP did to the National Republican Senatorial Committee. When the Colorado GOP ran the ads, the Federal Election Commission argued that, by assigning its spending level to the national party, the state party had sacrificed its right to spend money on its own.

Bill opponent Trent Lott, R-Miss., who had succeeded Dole as majority leader following his resignation from the Senate, subsequently withdrew the measure and indicated that it was dead for the year. Lott pressured several GOP senators to vote against cloture, making it clear to a number of committee chairmen that, if they wanted leadership support, they should vote "no." *(1996 key votes, p. 1047)*

The bill's prospects also were hurt by a last-minute campaign by the National Right to Life Committee and the Christian Coalition. The organizations contended that the legislation's definition and limits on express advocacy threatened their voting guides and education activities. In hopes of assuaging these concerns, McCain, Thompson and Feingold included a provision exempting guides that were "limited to providing information about votes by elected officials on legislative matters" from restrictions on independent expenditures. But the effort failed.

The Clinton administration publicly supported S 1219.

HOUSE ACTION

In November 1995, House Republican leaders tapped Peter Hoekstra, R-Mich., to head a task force to look at internal reforms, including revamping the campaign finance system. In February 1996, he presented Gingrich with a "middle of the road" alternative. The draft legislation did not propose to bar PAC contributions in federal campaigns or eliminate soft money. Instead, Hoekstra proposed to restrict PAC contributions to somewhere between $1,000 and $2,500 per election, compared with an existing limit of $5,000. The draft also called for requiring candidates to raise the majority of their contributions in their home states.

The House Government Reform and Oversight Committee on July 16, 1996, reported its campaign finance bill (HR 3760—H Rept 104-677). The measure included provisions that would have:

• Required House candidates to raise more than 50 percent of their total campaign funds from within their congressional district.

• Equalized contributions from individuals and PACs. The bill proposed to increase the maximum individual contribution to a candidate from $1,000 to $2,500 for the primary and the general election, indexed to inflation. The maximum PAC contribution would drop from $5,000 to $2,500 for each election.

• Increased the total amount a person could have given each year to all candidates, political party committees and PACs from $25,000 to $72,500, indexed to inflation. The limit on individual contributions to political party committees would have increased from $20,000 for national parties and $5,000 for state parties to $58,000 for each organization.

• Banned leadership committees, which were used by congressional leaders to curry favor with rank-and-file members, and eliminated joint fundraising committees, which were typically set up when two or more candidates wanted to raise money at a single large event.

• Allowed candidates to exceed contribution limits when facing a wealthy self-funded opponent. If an opponent spent $150,000 or less of personal funds, a political party could have matched that amount to help a candidate be competitive. If an opponent spent more than $150,000, a candidate could have accepted contributions that exceeded federal limits until he or she matched the level of personal funds used by the opponent. However, a majority of the contributions still had to come from within the district.

Democrats said HR 3760 only would have exacerbated problems in the existing system. For example, they said that it would have raised individual contribution limits, while doing nothing to address the problem of soft money. Committee Republicans defeated a Democratic substitute to ban soft money and set voluntary spending limits of $600,000 per two-year cycle on House candidates in return for deep discounts on broadcast advertising and postage rates. The committee also rejected four Democratic amendments to better define and increase disclosure requirements for independent expenditures—money spent by corporations, labor unions or nonprofit organizations in attempts to influence the outcome of elections.

Republican leaders planned to bring a clean version of campaign finance legislation (HR 3820) to the floor for a vote in mid-July as the centerpiece of what they had dubbed "Reform Week." The idea was to feature GOP efforts to overhaul campaign finance and boost congressional accountability. However, HR 3820 quickly ran into trouble.

The bill was savaged by newspaper editorials, public interest groups and an organization whose opinion weighed heavily with lawmakers—Ross Perot's United We Stand America. Opponents said that, under the bill, the nation's wealthiest could have contributed more than $3 million a year to candidates and political parties. Some Republicans complained that the measure only reinforced the image of the GOP as a party of the wealthy. Alienating another faction of the Republican conference was a leadership decision to attach to the campaign finance bill a section from a bill called the "Worker Right to Know Act" (HR 3580) that would have required labor unions to get signed agreements from workers before using their dues for political contributions. At least two dozen Republicans saw the union provisions as antilabor and opposed their inclusion.

Meanwhile, in a move described by the parliamentarian's office as unprecedented, the House Rules Committee July 17 reported a rule (H Res 481—H Rept 104-685) to govern floor debate on HR 3820 without recommendation and without a recorded vote. The Rules action signaled to House Republicans that they were free to vote against the rule without fear of retribution. The rule granted time only to the leadership bill and to a Democratic alternative, with no opportunity for a vote on a bipartisan bill (HR 2566) that was similar to S 1219. The rule automatically revised HR 3820 to answer some of the objections to it.

The House on July 25 adopted the rule by 270–140; rejected the Democratic alternative, offered by Vic Fazio of California in the form of a substitute amendment, by a vote of 177–243; then defeated HR 3820 by a 162–259 vote. As modified by the rule, HR 3820 would have:

• Kept the cap on individual contributions at $1,000 but allowed them to increase with inflation.

• Increased the aggregate amount an individual could give to a variety of sources, including candidates, PACs and political parties, from $25,000 a year to $50,000.

• Lifted the caps on contributions from individuals, PACs and parties when a candidate faced a wealthy opponent spending at least $150,000 in personal funds on the campaign. The candidate could have raised money up to the amount in personal funds spent by his opponent.   ❑

Campaign Finance Reports

Legislation (HR 2527—PL 104-79) to expedite the process by which congressional candidates filed their campaign finance reports with the Federal Election Commission (FEC) was signed into law on Dec. 28, 1995.

HR 2527 amended the Federal Election Campaign Act of 1971 (PL 92-225) to allow the FEC to receive electronic campaign finance reports after Dec. 31, 1996. It also required candidates for House seats, both incumbents and challengers, to file their campaign finance reports directly with the FEC. The decision of whether to file by paper or electronically was left to the candidate. The FEC was required to provide at least one means by which to verify the report other than by signature. States having access to the FEC's computer system did not have to file duplicate reports with the commission. *(1971 act, Congress and the Nation Vol. III, p. 397)*

Under the existing system, all House candidates were required to file campaign reports with the clerk of the House; Senate candidates filed on paper with the secretary of the Senate. The paper reports were then forwarded to the FEC. The clerk of the House estimated that the change would save about $500,000 a year.

PL 92-225 required all candidates for federal office to file financial statements with the FEC, but it barred the agency from receiving electronic statements. Most of the FEC's campaign records were filed on paper and some were handwritten, making disclosure forms difficult for campaigns to submit and for readers to understand.

The House passed HR 2527 by voice vote Nov. 13, 1995. The Senate Rules and Administration Committee reported the measure on Dec. 14. The Senate passed the bill by voice vote Dec. 20, completing congressional action.

Democrats supported HR 2527 but expressed concern that the FEC receive additional funding to implement it. Bill Thomas, R-Calif., sponsor of HR 2527, earlier in 1995 had tried to advance the modernization effort at the FEC as part of a bill (HR 1372) to authorize $27.6 million for the agency in fiscal 1996. The bill directed the FEC to speed up implementation of an electronic filing system for candidates' financial records and earmarked $1.5 million for that use. The House Oversight Committee approved HR 1372 on April 4, but the bill went no further. The committee rejected an amendment to increase the authorization to $29.2 million, the amount requested by the Clinton administration. Congress subsequently appropriated $26.5 million for the FEC as part of the fiscal 1996 Treasury-Postal Service spending bill (HR 2020—PL 104-52). The measure provided $1.5 million for internal automated data processing systems and required that, before using the money, the agency provide the Appropriations committees with a systems requirements analysis on the development of such a system.

The House Oversight Committee approved a $26.5 million authorization bill (HR 3461) for the FEC in fiscal 1997, with a minimum of $1.5 million to be spent on computer modernization to comply with PL 104-79's provision allowing electronic filing of candidate's reports. The committee rejected an amendment to increase the FEC's authorization to $29.4 million, as recommended by the administration. HR 3461 saw no further action and died upon adjournment. Lawmakers appropriated $28.2 million for the agency for fiscal 1997 as part of the omnibus appropriations bill (3610—PL 104-208). ❑

Term Limits

The House in 1995 and the Senate in 1996 failed to pass a constitutional amendment (H J Res 73, S J Res 21) to limit the terms of members of Congress.

The term limits movement had burst onto the national scene in the early 1990s. Within five years, backers of term limits had won ballot initiatives or laws in at least 23 states. But the departure of scores of senior lawmakers through retirement and electoral defeat tempered the movement. In 1995, the Supreme Court ruled in *U.S. Term Limits Inc. v. Thornton* and *Bryant v. Hill* that states could not impose limits on congressional terms, which gave term limits supporters only one path: a constitutional amendment. To be adopted, a constitutional amendment had to pass both chambers with a two-thirds majority and then be ratified by three-fourths (38) of the states. *(Term limits box, box, p. 9; Court ruling, p. 783)*

Term limit supporters argued that mandatory retirement after 12 years was necessary to bring new people and viewpoints into Congress, to diminish the emphasis on getting reelected, and to help control federal spending, which supporters said was fueled by career politicians too close to interest groups seeking federal largess. Opponents countered that term limits would strip Congress of experienced legislators, diminish the political power of less-populated states that were often helped by the seniority of their members, and merely speed up, not solve, the problem of lawmakers getting too friendly with special interests. Depriving the electorate of the right to vote for an incumbent would be undemocratic, opponents said.

HOUSE ACTION

In a sign of trouble to come in the House, the Judiciary Committee agreed Feb. 28, 1995, to send its version of the term limits constitutional amendment (H J Res 2) to the floor without recommendation. The measure was formally reported (H Rept 104-67) on March 6.

The original bill provided a lifetime ban after 12 years of service, but the committee adopted an amendment to apply the limit only to consecutive service. Under the amended bill, a member could serve 12 years, sit out an election and then return. The committee rejected a Democratic amendment to apply the 12-year limit retroactively. Panel Democrats also forced a vote on a controversial amendment to preempt any state term limit laws, an issue Republicans were not eager to address. The committee first adopted an amendment to give states the option of capping term limits at a level below that mandated by the constitutional amendment. But then the panel adopted an amendment to nullify that language and make sure the constitutional amendment would preempt state laws. The Judiciary Committee also rejected three alternate constitutional amendments.

The House Rules Committee abandoned the controversial H J Res 2 and instead sent to the floor a "clean" resolution (H J Res

73), which proposed a 12-year lifetime limit on members of each chamber.

H J Res 73 was defeated March 29 by a **227–204 (R 189–40; D 38–163; I 0–1) key vote,** falling 61 votes short of a two-thirds majority (288 in this case). Republicans claimed partial victory, however, for having brought a term limit proposal to the floor for the first time, and they were quick to blame Democrats for its defeat.

The bulk of the GOP defectors were those with the most to lose: 30 of the 40 Republicans who voted against the measure chaired a committee or subcommittee. The vote on H J Res 73 was the first outright defeat on a plank of the House Republicans' "Contract with America." *(1995 key votes, p. 1065; Contract with America, box, p. 885)*

The full House also rejected on March 29 three alternative term limit amendments:

• By 135–297, a Pete Peterson, D-Fla., and John D. Dingell, D-Mich., proposal to apply the 12-year cap retroactively and allow states to impose shorter limits.

• By 114–316, a Bob Inglis, R-S.C., amendment to limit House terms to six years while leaving the Senate term limit at 12 years.

• By 164–265, a Van Hilleary, R-Tenn., substitute to allow states to set lower caps.

SENATE ACTION

The Senate Judiciary Committee reported S J Res 21 (S Rept 104-158) on Sept. 29, 1995. The joint resolution would have limited senators to two six-year terms and House members to six two-year terms. S J Res 21 originally called for limits of 12 years in the Senate and six years in the House. But the Judiciary Subcommittee on the Constitution, Federalism, and Property Rights adopted an amendment to change the limit for representatives to 12 years. The full Judiciary Committee rejected a Democratic move to make the provisions retroactive.

S J Res 21 stalled on the Senate floor April 23, 1996. A vote to shut off debate on the measure failed 58–42, two short of the 60 votes needed. All 53 Senate Republicans voted for cloture, even though some opposed limiting congressional terms, leaving Democrats alone in blocking the Senate from moving to an up-or-down vote on the term limits amendment. The GOP strategy exposed how politicized the term limits debate was: Majority Leader Bob Dole, R-Kan., the presumed GOP presidential nominee, brought the measure up partly to demonstrate his commitment to the House's Contract with America. Other Senate supporters wanted a vote they could use against term limit opponents in the fall campaigns. Shortly after the vote, Dole pulled the bill from the floor, shelving the issue for the 104th Congress. ❑

Chronology of Action on Congress: Pay and Benefits

1993–1994

Disagreement over strict new rules governing the ability of lawmakers and congressional staffers to accept gifts helped derail a lobby disclosure bill.

Partly in response to the mood of austerity in the country and in Congress, and partly as a result of politics, members denied themselves a pay raise for two consecutive years.

Gift Rules

Legislation (S 349) to revamp lobbying disclosure requirements and tighten gift rules for members of Congress passed both chambers but died at the end of the 103rd Congress.

Controversy over the new gift rules had delayed the bill for months. By the time a conference agreement was reached in late September 1994, the bill was vulnerable to end-of-session ploys. Republicans raised objections to the bill's lobbying disclosure provisions—an area that had been largely noncontroversial up to that point—and managed to block final action on the bill in the Senate. (*Lobbying disclosure, p. 834*)

Sponsors of the bill attributed the defeat both to election year politics and to an unwillingness on the part of some members of both parties to give up their ability to accept gifts from lobbyists. The proposed changes in gift rules would have prohibited lobbyists from giving members and congressional staff almost anything except campaign contributions. Rules on gifts from nonlobbyists would have been less restrictive.

1993 SENATE ACTION

Under the lash of public outrage over members' perquisites, the Senate passed S 349 on May 6, 1993, by the overwhelming vote of 95–2. The bill had been reported by the Senate Governmental Affairs Committee (S Rept 103-37) on April 1.

The committee bill, sponsored by Carl Levin, D-Mich., chairman of the Governmental Affairs Subcommittee on Oversight of Government Management, had not included new gift rules for members. Levin and bill cosponsor William S. Cohen, R-Maine, had vigorously resisted the idea that their narrowly crafted bill should be expanded to require lobbyists to disclose gifts to members of Congress and their staffs. Time and again, Levin said that he did not want the bill to become an all-purpose vehicle for reform, arguing that past efforts to strengthen lobbying registration had been sunk by such extraneous amendments. But under pressure from public interest groups and editorial writers, the bill was amended to include new gift regulations.

Rules governing gifts had last been tightened in 1989 as part of legislation that also raised members' pay. But in 1991, Congress angered public interest groups by easing the rules. Under those revisions, members could accept unlimited gifts worth $100 or less from anyone, but they could not accept more than $250 worth of $100-plus gifts a year from anyone other than relatives without permission from their ethics committee. Reimbursements for travel related to speaking engagements, fact-finding trips, charity golf tournaments and similar events, as well as meals and drinks, did not count as gifts. On annual financial statements, members were required to disclose only a limited amount of information about their trips and nothing about meals unrelated to travel or gifts worth less than $250. (*Congress and the Nation Vol. VIII, pp. 920, 970*)

Paul Wellstone, D-Minn., offered an amendment to S 349 requiring lobbyists to disclose any gifts worth more than $20—including meals, trips, entertainment and fund-raising help—given to a member of Congress or a staff member. Levin and Cohen criticized the mechanics of the amendment, saying it was inconsistent with Senate rules, shifted the burden of disclosure from members of Congress to lobbyists and fell short of their goal of eliminating such gifts. The Senate was in abeyance for hours on May 5 as opponents of the Wellstone amendment tested the waters for a vote on it and tried to persuade Wellstone to drop the matter. When it became clear that Wellstone would not budge and few were willing to vote against the amendment, Levin proposed a few minor changes to it.

The Levin changes provided exemptions for gifts from family members and for gifts that were returned, as well as for attendance at large receptions that were not for the benefit of particular members. All other meals, gifts, entertainment or other financial benefits to a member or staffer worth more than $20 each or an aggregate of $50 annually were to be reported by the lobbyist on a member-by-member or staffer-by-staffer basis. Both Levin's alterations and Wellstone's amendment were adopted by voice vote on May 5.

Before final passage of S 349 on May 6, the Senate adopted, 98–1, a nonbinding amendment, offered by Frank R. Lautenberg, D-N.J., requiring that gifts to members from lobbyists be further restricted. The amendment said Congress should pass a gift rule "substantially similar" to the executive branch's. The executive and the legislative branch each based its gifts rules on the same 1989 law (PL 101-194), but the executive branch drafted more stringent standards. Executive branch employees could not accept gifts worth more than $20 per occasion or totaling more than $50 per source a year from anyone interested in their agency's work unless the giver was clearly motivated by family relationship or personal friendship.

Lautenberg subsequently introduced a separate gift bill (S 885), banning lawmakers and staff from accepting gifts of $20 or more each, or $50 in the aggregate, from a single source.

1993 HOUSE ACTION

The Senate's action on gifts prompted freshman House Democrats to take up the cause, making gift restrictions a priority issue on their reform agenda. Led by Eric D. Fingerhut of Ohio and Karen Shepherd of Utah, they pressed the leadership to attach the language in the Wellstone amendment and Lautenberg's bill to the House version of the lobbying reform bill (HR 823). House Speaker Thomas S. Foley, D-Wash., endorsed greater disclosure and indicated that the $20 limit on gifts would be acceptable if an exemption were made for meals—an exemption the freshmen were not prepared to embrace.

John Bryant, D-Texas, sponsor of HR 823 and chairman of the House Judiciary Subcommittee on Administrative Law and Governmental Relations, scheduled markup on the legislation for Oct. 21. Bryant planned to use the bill to limit the financial favors (including meals) that lobbyists could give members to $20 (and no more than $50 a year) and to restrict lobbyist-funded trips. Foley told reporters Oct. 14 that the House was "tending toward" Bryant's approach.

But some members of both parties protested, including Minority Leader Robert H. Michel, R-Ill. "To bar someone from having dinner with somebody—jeepers, creepers—or going to a ballgame, or a show. To think our vote is going to be contingent on somebody taking us to dinner just ticks me off," Michel said. The markup was postponed, and leaders subsequently appointed a bipartisan task force to study the issue.

The sweeping agreement reached by the task force was approved Nov. 22 by the Judiciary Administrative Law Subcommittee as part of HR 823. The provisions banned lobbyists and clients from giving members and congressional staffers financial benefits of any kind—gifts, travel, entertainment, meals, loans. But the proposal also contained a lengthy list of exceptions. Gifts motivated by "personal friendship" were exempt, provided that a history of reciprocity existed and that the cost of the gift was paid personally by the lobbyist and not deducted as a business expense. So were items such as baseball caps and T-shirts of "little intrinsic value," potentially costlier books and videos, home-state products of minimal value used for promotional purposes and modest types of food such as coffee and doughnuts. Though lobbyists could not, clients, corporate employees and union representatives could use their expense accounts to pay for meals and entertainment for staffers and bring along their lobbyists. If they revealed the cost in twice-yearly disclosure reports, lobbyists or clients could throw big parties in behalf of members, such as the lavish fetes that were staples at political conventions. They also could pay, subject to disclosure, for "a conference, retreat or similar event" for groups of members, such as the soirees congressional party caucuses attended. Also exempt from the ban but subject to disclosure were speaking fees donated to charities on members' behalf and contributions to members' legal defense funds. Travel reimbursements for speaking engagements and fact-finding trips still were allowed, subject to more detailed disclosure rules. Entertainment on such trips was banned, unless in a "group setting in which all other attendees are invited." Members could continue to accept free trips to charity events, such as the corporate-backed golf tournaments various members frequented, or political events, also subject to more disclosure. The rules exempted meals and attendance fees at charitable or political events.

1994 HOUSE ACTION

Although opposition to the gift ban came from both sides of the aisle, the House floor debate in 1994 was strictly partisan, an atmosphere fueled by intense maneuvering over the details of the gift ban and over which party would get credit. "Do you

folks want to join us in making it against the law for a lobbyist to buy a free meal for a member of Congress or not?" Bryant demanded, looking at Republicans.

On March 23, Democratic leaders tried to get consent to bring S 349 up the following day under suspension of the rules, a procedure that required a two-thirds vote for passage instead of a simple majority. Republicans objected, however, complaining that the legislation had not been considered by the full Judiciary Committee and that the procedure, usually reserved for noncontroversial measures, prohibited amendments and allowed each side only 20 minutes for debate. That objection required the House to approve a rule for floor debate that allowed the bill to be considered under suspension of the rules.

Democrats said they were faced with a choice between a good, though imperfect, bill or none at all. Virtually every Democrat who spoke in support of the bill cited a need to assuage public concern about the influence of special interests on Congress. Republicans argued strenuously against the process that denied them a chance to amend the legislation. They also argued that full disclosure of gifts, meals and travel payments by lobbyists was preferable to a complex set of rules to restrict activities that Democrats and Republicans agreed were not improper. But public perception was the order of the day. The rule was adopted on a 221–202 vote on March 24. The House then passed S 349 by a vote of 315–110. The House-passed bill included several minor amendments to the version approved by Bryant's Judiciary subcommittee in 1993.

1994 SENATE ACTION

The Senate then reentered the fray, passing a free-standing measure (S 1935) to ban most gifts instead of requiring only disclosure of gifts as the Senate version of S 349 had.

S 1935 sponsors Wellstone and Lautenberg pressured the Senate to act on the gift issue so that the Senate's position would be clear when the lobbying disclosure bill went to conference. Crafted with the help of Common Cause, their proposal was based on the House bill but sought to remove or tighten some of the exceptions.

Levin objected to several aspects of the Lautenberg-Wellstone approach. He proposed to rewrite Senate and House gift rules, dictating what members could not accept and what they had to disclose, leaving enforcement in the hands of the two ethics committees. The House bill and the Lautenberg-Wellstone proposal, by contrast, sought to supplement existing rules with a new law laying out what lobbyists and their clients could not give and what they had to disclose, giving the executive branch an enforcement role.

Levin offered a substitute to S 1935, which was reported by the Senate Governmental Affairs Committee (S Rept 103-255) on April 26. It barred members and staff from accepting just about anything from lobbyists unless they were verifiable friends or family. Most gifts from anyone else would have to be worth less than $20. Members still could accept invitations to some events and free trips, but only if they were related to official duties and did not include free recreational activities. Trip costs would have to be disclosed in detail. Gone would be the free meals that lobbyists bought for members and their staff—a practice pervasive enough that local restaurateurs petitioned senators to relax the bill's meal restrictions lest their livelihoods be threatened. Meals from others would be subject to the gift limits unless provided by a nonlobbyist in a member's home state in which case higher limits (to be established later in each chamber) would apply.

Levin said he wanted to avoid a floor vote and go straight to conference using his version as the Senate's position on gifts, but Lautenberg and Wellstone, as well as cosponsor Russell Feingold, D-Wis., said they were not sure they wanted to relinquish their rights to a floor debate. The three senators were particularly worried about the provision in Levin's version allowing meals and entertainment in a member's home state from anyone but lobbyists, within higher limits to be set later. They also said they were not sure allowing gifts from friends to be unlimited in value was wise. And they wanted to make sure the issue was addressed to their satisfaction in conference and not knocked out of the bill on procedural grounds.

The Senate passed S 1935 by 95–4 on May 11. During floor debate May 5, a more lenient alternative, in the form of an amendment sponsored by Ethics Committee Vice Chairman Mitch McConnell, R-Ky., and J. Bennett Johnston, D-La., was rejected 39–59. The McConnell-Johnston proposal would have allowed virtually unlimited free meals and unlimited gifts worth less than $75, down from the $100 threshold under existing rules. Johnston and his allies argued that the Levin bill was insulting because it implied that members could be bought for the price of a dinner. At one point, Johnston complained that he would not be able to go to a charity opera ball. Wellstone responded, "You can go to any opera you want to. You pay for it, just like regular people pay for it when they go to the opera. It's that simple." After defeating the alternative, senators voted 90–3 on May 5 to adopt a Dale Bumpers, D-Ark., amendment to strip the $20 exemption for gifts from nonlobbyists from Levin's version of the bill. Frank H. Murkowski, R-Alaska, offered an amendment to allow free travel and lodging expenses for members who participated in charity events. Many members regularly attended corporate-backed golf and tennis tournaments or ski trips that raised money for needy causes by charging lobbyists and others fees to play with notable politicians and other renowned individuals. Murkowski's amendment was rejected 37–58 on May 5.

A package of uncontested amendments also was adopted May 5. Included was the language stipulating that meals and entertainment provided by nonlobbyists in members' home states would be subject to separate limits to be established later for each chamber. Also exempt would be free attendance at certain widely attended events where an official was speaking or "performing a ceremonial function appropriate to his or her official position." Members and staff could not accept "entertainment collateral to the event." All gifts from relatives and friends were to be exempt, although the Ethics Committee would be required to approve a friend's gift worth more than $250. Either chamber's ethics committee could waive the gift ban "in an unusual case." Gift giving from friends would have to be clearly motivated not by an official's position but by friendship (taking into account the history of the relationship and whether gifts have been exchanged in the past). Nor could such gifts be used as the basis for a tax deduction or for a business reimbursement request.

CONFERENCE

The two chambers' versions of the lobbying bill (S 349) plus the Senate gift ban measure (S 1935) went to conference together. The Senate's near-total ban on gifts was not popular in the House. Bryant worried about antagonizing a bloc of members who only grudgingly accepted more lenient restrictions and could kill the legislation by joining forces with members who opposed the ban. In the Senate, a determined group of gift-limit supporters said they would fight any bill not deemed restrictive enough. After months without progress, Democratic leaders from both chambers began trying to prod things along in late July, meeting with Bryant and Levin. Speaker Foley told reporters Aug. 2 that the House would be willing to move toward the stricter Senate bill as long as there was "some give on both sides."

Bryant and Levin unveiled their compromise proposal on Sept. 22. As approved by conferees Sept. 26, S 349 (H Rept 103-750) prohibited lobbyists from giving members and staff almost anything except campaign contributions, tickets to fund-raisers and other political events, and modest food items. Gifts from nonlobbyists would be subject to somewhat less restrictive limits. Allowed from nonlobbyists would be food and refreshments worth less than $20, meals and entertainment worth more if they took place in the member's home state and contributions to legal defense funds. Private interests still could subsidize travel for speaking engagements, fact-finding trips and other events related to official duties. Substantially recreational trips, including the popular charity golf tournaments and the like, would be banned. So would entertainment collateral to the trip's main purpose. Gifts based on certain personal and family relationships were exempt from the rules.

The gift provisions were based largely on the stricter Senate bill. Bryant and Levin adopted some more stringent provisions from the House bill, including an enforcement mechanism that gave the executive branch a role. Under the Senate version, only the ethics committees would have had enforcement power. Under the compromise, the new Office of Lobbying Registration and Public Disclosure would be responsible for investigating lobbyists alleged to have given improper gifts, while the ethics committees would investigate members alleged to have accepted them. Lobbyists found to have violated any provision of the law would face fines of up to $200,000.

Bryant and Levin dropped more stringent Senate proposals in only a few cases, including provisions that would have barred members from taking a family member on free trips and would have stopped private groups from subsidizing issue retreats for congressional groups. Also dropped was a controversial provision from the House version that could have made it more difficult for prosecutors to charge members with taking illegal gratuities, a criminal offense akin to bribery.

Public interest groups and members who supported a strict gift ban were giddy over the provisions, which they said exceeded their most optimistic expectations. "It's a major achievement in the fight to end the practice of special interests paying for the lifestyles of members of Congress," said Fred Wertheimer, president of Common Cause. Their enthusiasm was short-lived, however, as S 349 ran into trouble over its lobbying disclosure requirements, specifically as pertaining to grassroots efforts. The bill died in the Senate, after supporters failed to cut off a Republican-led filibuster. *(Lobbying disclosure, p. 809)*   ❑

Congressional Pay

For two consecutive years, Congress denied itself a pay raise, keeping the salary for all members (except leaders, who earned more) at $133,600.

Majority Leader George J. Mitchell, D-Maine, and House Speaker Thomas S. Foley, D-Wash., announced on Feb. 24, 1993, that lawmakers would forgo a cost-of-living adjustment (COLA) they were scheduled to receive in 1994. President Clinton had proposed scrapping a 1994 COLA for federal workers, and the Democratic leaders said Congress should follow suit. Members of Congress had received a 3.2 percent COLA on Jan. 1, 1993, that raised their salaries to $133,600. *(Federal workers' COLA, p. 816)*

In 1994, an increase in pay was blocked not by congressional leaders but by Rep. Jim Ross Lightfoot, R-Iowa. Steny H. Hoyer, D-Md., who chaired the House Treasury, Postal Service and General Government Appropriations Subcommittee and whose district in the Washington, D.C., suburbs housed many federal workers, wrote a provision into the fiscal 1995 Treasury-U.S. Postal Service appropriations bill (HR 4539) giving federal employees an average raise of 1 percent higher than recommended in the president's budget. Accompanying the provision for federal workers was low-profile language to block the congressional COLA. Hoyer said he added the language to insulate his federal pay raise from attacks that it would trigger a higher COLA for Congress. However, after Clinton agreed in August to embrace Hoyer's higher pay increase, the provision no longer was needed, and House and Senate conferees made plans to drop it, along with the language to block the congressional pay raise.

Lightfoot had written to House leaders in July to inform them that he would seek to block the congressional COLA. When Hoyer and others, with support from House leaders from both parties, produced a tentative version of the Treasury-Postal Service conference agreement that preserved the COLA, Lightfoot vowed Sept. 19 that he would make a motion to instruct the House conferees to drop the pay raise. The next day, the conferees met and reluctantly killed the raise themselves. Democrats said Lightfoot grabbed the issue for political gain, while Republicans blamed Hoyer for creating the issue in the first place.

In related action, a three-judge panel of the U.S. Court of Appeals for the District of Columbia on July 29, 1994, rejected a constitutional challenge to the congressional pay raise instituted in January 1993. Rep. John A. Boehner, R-Ohio, 27 other mem-

bers and more than 100 congressional candidates filed suit in October 1992 to block the 7.2 percent COLA for members of Congress and other high government officials, provided for in the 1989 congressional pay law (PL 101-194). The plaintiffs argued that the COLA violated the Twenty-Seventh Amendment to the Constitution, drafted by James Madison in 1789 and ratified in 1992, which stated: "No law varying the compensation for the services of the Senators and Representatives shall take effect, until an election of Representatives shall have intervened." U.S. District Judge Stanley Sporkin dismissed the case Dec. 16, 1992, but Boehner appealed. The appeals panel upheld Sporkin's decision, ruling that the annual raises specified by the 1989 law did not go into effect until after the 1990 election and the seating of a new Congress and were therefore constitutional. *(1989 law, Congress and the Nation Vol. VIII, p. 965; Madison amendment, Congress and the Nation Vol. VIII, p. 972)*   ❑

1995–1996

Gift giving to members was reined in by new guidelines established in both chambers. Lawmakers also decided to forgo cost-of-living pay increases in 1995 and 1996.

Congress did not complete action on legislation to keep members convicted of felonies from receiving pension benefits.

Gift Rules

The Senate and House in 1995 adopted new rules that placed restrictions on gifts that lawmakers could accept. The changes were in the form of separate Senate and House resolutions (S Res 158, H Res 250) that applied only to the chamber that passed them and did not have the force of law.

1995 SENATE ACTION

The Senate leadership agreed in June 1995 to consider gift ban provisions as well as new lobbying restrictions, after Democrats said they would not raise the issues during debate on a high-priority overhaul of telecommunications law (S 652). *(Telecommunications overhaul, p. 387)*

A task force of nine Democrats and six Republicans was set up to devise a compromise that incorporated parts of a lobbying and gift ban bill (S 101), introduced by William S. Cohen, R-Maine, and Carl Levin, D-Mich., and proposals from Senate Republicans who had successfully filibustered the gift ban and lobby overhaul effort in 1994. If no alternative had been agreed to by the end of July, the Senate was to vote on the Cohen-Levin gift provisions. The Cohen-Levin bill included provisions to ban most gifts from lobbyists and prohibit charity trips—when lawmakers and lobbyists golfed and skied together to raise money for charities. It also stipulated tough new lobbying restrictions, which were to be considered separately. *(1994 action, p. 919; lobbying disclosure, p. 809)*

Mitch McConnell, R-Ky., introduced a GOP alternative (S Res 126), under which members would be allowed to accept gifts worth less than $100 from lobbyists and participate in charitable events as long as they were publicly disclosed.

When the Senate began floor debate July 24, the task force had not reached agreement on gift restrictions. As a result, the Senate took up the gift provisions from the Cohen-Levin bill, which had been introduced as S 1061. Meanwhile, the negotiations continued. On July 28, the Senate by voice vote adopted a bipartisan compromise offered by John McCain, R-Ariz., as a substitute amendment. The victory did not come without a fight, however.

McCain's original language would have allowed senators to accept meals and gifts worth no more than $20, with no more than $50 from any one source. But the Senate adopted, 54–46 on July 28, an amendment by Majority Whip Trent Lott, R-Miss., to raise the limit to $50 and allow up to $100 in gifts from any one source. Lott's amendment also exempted gifts under $50 from counting toward the $100 total. In response, Paul Wellstone, D-Minn., offered a further amendment to require all gifts of $10 or more to count toward the $100 annual cap. Because most senators wanted to avoid potential political trouble from voting against strong ethics requirements, Lott accepted Wellstone's amendment, which was adopted by voice vote.

In other action, the Senate:

• Rejected, on a **39–60 (R 30–23; D 9–37) key vote** on July 28, a Frank H. Murkowski, R-Alaska, amendment to allow lobbyists or other special interests to continue to pay for senators to attend golf and ski trips that raised money for charity. *(1995 key votes, p. 1025)*

• Adopted, 75–23 on July 28, a Robert C. Bryd, D-W.Va., amendment expressing the sense of the Senate that the judicial branch should review its regulations on gifts and travel.

• Adopted, by voice vote, a Hank Brown, R-Colo., amendment to require a more detailed estimate on senators' annual financial disclosure forms of assets and liabilities valued at more than $1 million.

The Senate adopted a modified version of the bipartisan compromise July 28 by a vote of 98–0. The final vote, on S Res 158, changed Senate rules and required no further action before taking effect. The Senate Ethics Committee was charged with enforcing the new rules and determining penalties on a case-by-case basis.

Following are the major provisions of S Res 158, as adopted:

• **Gifts.** A $50 limit was placed on the value of gifts, including meals and entertainment, that senators and their staff could accept. The resolution placed a $100 annual limit on gifts from any one source, with no gift permitted to exceed $50 in value. The resolution did not, however, cap the cumulative total of gifts that any single senator or Senate staff member could accept in a year.

Senators and their staffs could accept unlimited gifts from family members and close personal friends, although they had to get Ethics Committee approval for such gifts valued at more than $250.

Gifts to the spouses and dependents of senators or their staff were subject to the same restrictions if the senator or staff member had reason to believe the gifts were given in connection with his or her official position.

• **Charity Outings and Events.** Senators were barred from accepting free travel to events that were substantially recreational. The provision applied to the so-called charity trips where senators and lobbyists golfed and skied together to raise money for charities.

• **Trips.** Senators and their staff could continue to accept free travel for meetings, speaking engagements and fact-finding tours that were in connection with their official duties. The trips were capped at seven days for international travel, exclusive of travel time, and three days for domestic trips. Spouses were permitted on such trips if they were "appropriate to assist in the representation of the Senate."

• **Legal Defense Funds.** Lobbyists could not contribute to a senator's or staff member's legal defense fund. Previous rules had permitted such contributions, up to $10,000 per person, if they were disclosed.

• **Charitable Contributions.** Lobbyists were barred from contributing to charities maintained or controlled by a senator or a Senate staffer.

However, lobbyists could continue to make contributions of up to $2,000 to any charity designated by a member in lieu of paying a speaking fee to a senator or Senate staffer.

• **Exceptions and Clarifications.** Senators and their staff could continue to accept: campaign contributions from lobbyists; contributions to a legal defense fund from those who were not registered lobbyists; gifts from other senators and staffers; anything of value resulting from an outside business not connected with official business; pensions and benefits; informational materials, such as books and videotapes; honorary degrees, including travel to ceremonies; items of little intrinsic value, such as plaques and trophies; inheritances; or any gift for which the Senate Ethics Committee provided a waiver.

1995 HOUSE ACTION

House GOP leaders initially resisted bringing the gift restrictions and the lobby bill to the floor, claiming that the agenda was already overflowing and that they had fulfilled their promise to change the way Congress operated by passing workplace compliance legislation (S 2). However, the clamor for action grew after the Senate adopted S Res 158 and reached a crescendo Oct. 25, when House Republican leaders were forced to pull the fiscal 1996 legislative branch appropriations bill (HR 2492) from floor consideration after it became apparent that enough GOP freshmen and other Republican advocates of new gift and lobby rules would join with the Democrats to attach the Senate versions to the spending measure. *(Workplace compliance, p. 890)*

Gift ban supporters urged that the House simply pass the same rules the Senate had adopted. They were concerned that any effort to alter the provisions could start a process that would result in a resolution so weak that proponents would have to vote against it. House opposition to the gift rules was arrayed in three camps: Those who considered the rules so vague as to invite inadvertent violations; those who wanted to use the gift resolution to address other reform issues, such as campaign finance; and those who wanted to preserve lobbyist-funded golf, tennis and ski trips that helped raise money for charities.

Among the opponents was Dan Burton, R-Ind., who called for discarding the Senate's approach and merely requiring more disclosure. House Rules Committee Chairman Gerald B. H. Solomon, R-N.Y., offered a deal: During floor consideration, Burton could offer a substitute amendment to the House version (H Res 250) of the Senate gift rules, and the House would vote first on that proposal. However, House Speaker Newt Gingrich, R-Ga., took another tack. Agreeing that rules along the lines of the Senate's gift restrictions were too complicated and would invite unknowing violations, he pushed for all-or-nothing—a complete gift ban or no bill. His amendment would be voted on last, thus making it politically difficult for members to reject it if the Burton substitute was rejected. At the same time, it could encourage members to support Burton, given that the alternative was no gifts at all.

The rule that shaped the gift ban debate was carefully crafted. Members first rejected, on a **key vote of 154–276 (R 108–125; D 46–150; I 0–1)** on Nov. 16, the Burton amendment, which would have allowed members to receive up to $250 a year from a single source, with all gifts valued at $50 or more counting toward the cumulative annual total. It would have required disclosure of all gifts worth $50 or more and would have allowed most charity golf and tennis tournaments to continue to pay the way for members. Gingrich then offered his proposal for a complete ban, which was adopted 422–8 on Nov. 16. Under the rule, Gingrich was able to offer his amendment only because the House had defeated the Burton amendment. And only if members had rejected the Gingrich ban could they vote on the underlying provisions of H Res 250, which was virtually identical to the new Senate-passed gift rules. No such vote took place, however, because Gingrich's complete ban was adopted.

Before the House voted on Gingrich's amendment, John Bryant, D-Texas, tried to use a unanimous consent agreement to amend Gingrich's proposal to allow members to accept ceremonial caps and T-shirts as well as promotional products from their home states. Gingrich had inadvertently deleted those exceptions in his amendment. Jim Nussle, R-Iowa, objected to Bryant's actions, however, and the House passed the complete ban. Subsequently, on Nov. 30, the House by voice vote approved an amendment to House rules that made an exception for those items.

The House on Nov. 16 by 422–6 adopted H Res 250, the strongest prohibition against gifts in its history. The measure required no further action and went into effect Jan. 1, 1996. As adopted, H Res 250 included the following major provisions:

- **Gifts.** House members could no longer accept any gifts, except those from close personal friends or family. That meant no fruit baskets, no turkeys at Thanksgiving, no dinners or lunches, no tickets to sports events.

Members could still accept unlimited gifts from family and friends, but such gifts valued at more than $250 required a waiver from the House Committee on Standards of Official Conduct.

- **Widely Attended Events.** Members could attend conventions, charity events and similar occasions with their expenses picked up by the sponsor, so long as the event was connected with a member's official duties. For example, a member could accept a free ticket to a baseball game if he or she was scheduled to throw out the first ball. A member could attend the local Chamber of Commerce or charity dinner, as long as the group and not a lobbyist was picking up the tab. Members could take their spouse or another individual to widely attended events when the sponsoring organization, and not a lobbyist, was paying their way. Members could not solicit such trips.

- **Charity Outings.** The resolution eliminated the practice of members taking lobbyist-paid trips to participate in golf, skiing and tennis tournaments to raise money for charity. The sponsor of such an event could waive the entrance fee for members, but not provide any travel expenses, such as transportation, food and lodging.

- **Trips.** Members could continue accepting all-expense paid trips for fact-finding purposes or associated with a members' official duties, such as flying to a private group's convention to speak about Congress. Lobbyist and foreign agents, though, were specifically prohibited from paying a member's travel expenses for such trips. International trips were limited to seven days, excluding travel time, and domestic trips were capped at four days. Members could bring along a spouse or family member.

1996 LEGISLATIVE ACTION

The House and Senate ethics committees in 1996 were flooded with requests to clarify the new rules for accepting gifts from lobbyists. Instead of trying to respond to all the individual queries, both panels issued new guidelines.

Clubs and Charity Events

The House ethics committee July 8, 1996, issued a new directive that prohibited members and their staffs from accepting honorary memberships in organizations that waived initiation and periodic fees. The guidelines, which were binding and did not require further legislative action, allowed members to accept free memberships in Rotary and other private clubs under some circumstances.

Under the initial interpretation of the gift rule, the value of a gift membership in a private club was determined by the extent to which an individual lawmaker or aide used it. But the difficulty in determining the exact value of gift memberships under the "use" standard quickly became clear. The new guidelines replaced that standard with a blanket prohibition on honorary memberships "if acceptance entails the waiver of initiation fees and/or periodic fees."

The directive also tightened restrictions on members and their staffs accepting free attendance to golf tournaments and other charity events. The new interpretation allowed legislators and staff members to accept free attendance to such events only if the primary purpose of the event was to raise funds for an organization eligible to receive tax-deductible contributions. Such invitations had to come from an event sponsor and not be solicited.

The rule allowed members and staff to accept offers of local transportation by a sponsor but prohibited them from accepting reimbursement for housing and other transportation costs to a charity event. Members could accept items of nominal value given to all participants in a group setting at a charity event. Members could accept all items given to other participants if they paid the entrance fee. Members also could accept a "skill" prize, such as for the lowest score in a golf tournament, and any door prize worth more than $250, provided they listed such prizes on their annual financial disclosure statements.

Party Conventions

Regarding activities permissible at the national political conventions, the House ethics committee—instead of issuing an exemption to the gift rule—released a letter of clarification March 29, 1996, that permitted members to attend most of the receptions, parties and meals that were customary at the conventions. The committee concluded that convention festivities were covered by an exemption in the rules that allowed participation in "widely attended" events—those with at least 25 "noncongressional" participants. Also, the organizer of the event had to issue the invitation. Events sponsored by local and state governments and the political parties also were permitted.

House members and staff were allowed to accept meals, lodging, transportation and tickets to sporting, theatrical and other entertainment events, as long as they came from one of the two major political parties, a campaign fundraising committee, or a local or state party organization. Members could accept the gifts and handouts that convention delegates got as long as they were items given to everybody, not just lawmakers. But members could not accept gifts from lobbyists, the letter said.

The Senate Ethics Committee issued guidelines similar to those in the House. Senators attending the conventions could accept free food, lodging, entertainment, gifts and transportation if they were provided by local, state or federal governments or the host city's official committee, according to a letter issued by the ethics panel dated April 30, 1996.

Senators could accept invitations to privately financed functions that were "widely attended events," defined as gatherings of at least 25 people from outside of Congress. The committee also allowed attendance at receptions and the acceptance of T-shirts and items of "little intrinsic value." ❑

Congressional Pay

In both 1995 and 1996, Congress refused to accept an annual cost-of-living adjustment (COLA) pay raise that was instituted in 1989 to insulate members from the political consequences of voting for an increase in their own salaries. Most members made $133,600 a year; the leadership was paid more. Members had gotten their last pay raise in January 1993. *(1989 action, Congress and the Nation Vol. VIII, p. 965; 1993 action, p. 922)*

In 1995, a provision blocking an automatic COLA was included in the fiscal 1996 Treasury-Postal Service appropriations

bill (HR 2020—PL 104-52). The language was added on the Senate floor Aug. 5 as an amendment by Fred Thompson, R-Tenn. It generated no controversy and was adopted by voice vote. A pay freeze was included in the Senate version of the fiscal 1996 budget resolution (S Con Res 13), but that required implementing legislation to take effect.

In 1996, the House accepted a provision in the fiscal 1997 Treasury-Postal Service appropriations bill (HR 3756) to block the automatic increase to members of Congress, federal judges, the vice president, cabinet officers and members of the senior executive service. The amendment, offered by Jack Metcalf, R-Wash., was adopted 352–67 on July 16. The increase was worth about $3,000 per member. The Senate, by voice vote Sept. 11, adopted an amendment by Jesse Helms, R-N.C., to block the increase. However, Helms's amendment would have allowed federal judges to get the COLA. In the end, the House language prevailed. The rejection of the COLA became final on Sept. 30, as part of the omnibus fiscal 1997 appropriations bill (HR 3610—PL 104-208) that became law that day. ❑

Pension Restrictions

By 391–32, the House Sept. 26, 1996, passed a bill (HR 4011) to deny congressional retirement benefits to members convicted of felonies, beginning in the 105th Congress. The Senate never took up companion legislation (S 1794).

HR 4011, the Congressional Pension Forfeiture Act, was a Republican-crafted response to the conviction of former representative Dan Rostenkowski, D-Ill., the once-powerful chairman of the House Ways and Means Committee, on charges of mail fraud. Rostenkowski continued receiving a congressional pension of nearly $100,000 while serving a 17-month jail sentence. *(Rostenkowski ethics probe, p. 869)*

S 1794 would have applied to the executive, judicial and legislative branches as well.

The Justice Department criticized the legislation, saying that it would complicate efforts to work out plea bargains in public corruption cases.

The House Oversight Committee adopted an amendment to HR 4011 to allow a member convicted of a felony to receive all funds from the Thrift Savings Account, including member and government contributions as well as interest payments. After a lump sum payment, the convicted member no longer would have been allowed to participate in the plan. The Thrift Savings Account was the government equivalent of an individual 401(k) fund. The government contributed to the account based on 5 percent of a lawmaker's salary. Under the original bill, a member would have lost any interest or government contributions to the account if convicted.

The committee also adopted an amendment stating that the criminal offenses that would result in denying a former member pension benefits had to be abuses of public office. ❑

## CHAPTER 16

The Clinton Presidency

The Clinton Presidency

The persona of Bill Clinton and the events of his first term as president proved dichotomous. Teachers, friends, relatives and others recognized the leadership potential in Clinton when he was just a boy. Predictions abounded that someday he would be president. Ambition, intelligence and charm propelled him to the governorship of Arkansas at the tender age of 32. When Clinton in 1993 took the oath of office as the nation's forty-second president, he became the third youngest person to enter the White House, the first person elected president from the "baby boom" generation born after World War II and the first president who was a Rhodes scholar. His success in politics could be attributed in part to his ability to communicate a sense of empathy and compassion. Even his critics marveled at Clinton's personal magnetism that allowed him to connect with people in short order. His friends saw him as a dedicated problem-solver with the best intentions.

However, the enthusiasm exhibited for Clinton by some was counterbalanced by the suspicion of him by others. Detractors saw Clinton as severely flawed, with ambition and untrustworthiness superseding principles and truthfulness. The invective aimed at Clinton reached fever pitch while he was in the White House. For example, House Speaker Newt Gingrich, R-Ga., called the president "the biggest liar in the history of the office." Peggy Noonan, speechwriter for presidents Ronald Reagan and George Bush, referred to Clinton as "the Great Conniver" in a *Time* magazine article.

Pundits and other political observers deemed Clinton's first term as two presidencies in one. In his first two years, Clinton struggled to master his office. His presidency resembled that of fellow southerner Jimmy Carter, who had to wrangle with an entrenched Democratic Congress. Democrats controlled both chambers in the 103rd Congress, and their fractiousness interacted with the unity of the Republican opposition to frustrate major elements of Clinton's agenda, from his economic stimulus package to his massive health care reform proposal. That era of the Clinton presidency ended with the widespread voter rejection of the Democrats in the 1994 elections, which resulted in the GOP takeover of both the Senate and the House, and the frequent pronouncement that Clinton would be a one-term president.

At the beginning of the second phase of his presidency, Clinton found himself constrained by the Republican congressional majorities. Then, he reprised the role of Democratic president Harry S. Truman and used the Republican Congress as a foil for his political comeback. He proved far more popular with the voting public as he positioned himself as a centrist defender of the national interest against conservative Republican overreach.

Clinton began to practice the politics of "triangulation," distancing himself not only from the strident conservatism of the Republican Congress but also from the liberal tenets of congressional Democrats. As the 1996 elections approached, both Clinton and the Republicans in Congress saw the benefits of cooperation to be able to claim legislative successes. Clinton subsequently became the first Democrat since Franklin D. Roosevelt in 1936 to win reelection to a second term

Candidacy

On Oct. 3, 1991, in Little Rock, Ark., Clinton announced his candidacy for the Democratic presidential nomination. Clinton called for a "new covenant" between Americans and their government. "It's the government's responsibility to create more opportunity for everybody," he said, "and our responsibility to make the most of it." He proposed tax breaks for the middle class, a revamped welfare system that would give money only to those who could not find work and a "domestic GI Bill" providing college loans that could be repaid through several years' work as a teacher, as a police officer or through other forms of community service. He said, "I want to reinvent government to make it more efficient and effective. I would spend our tax dollars with discipline."

Clinton was the only candidate in the Democratic field to support President George Bush's use of force in the Persian Gulf. Also, as the governor of a death penalty state, Clinton oversaw executions in Arkansas. Democratic presidential candidates as well as the Democratic Party traditionally opposed capital punishment. Despite these seeming conservative views, Clinton could tack to the left on many issues without appearing awkward. He supported abortion rights, courted African Americans throughout his political career—for example, he testified before Congress in 1991 in behalf of statehood for the District of Columbia—and expended considerable effort to improve educational standards in Arkansas.

From the beginning of his campaign, Clinton sought to position himself thematically to do battle with Bush for the votes of moderate and conservative swing voters. At the same time, he could not be unpalatable to liberals, who dominated the Democratic primaries. Clinton was able to devise a well-honed, coherent campaign message aimed at the "forgotten middle class" that he effectively conveyed in an articulate manner. Most important, perhaps, was that the boyishly good-looking politician with the charming personality who could raise funds and garner big-name endorsements had the air of "electability."

BILL CLINTON: SCHOLAR, TEACHER AND POLITICIAN

William Jefferson Blythe IV was born in Hope, Ark., on Aug. 19, 1946, three months after his father was killed in an automobile accident. He spent his first couple of years living with his maternal grandparents in Hope, while his mother, Virginia, trained as a nurse-anesthetist in New Orleans. When he was four, his mother married Roger Clinton, a car dealer. Three years later, the family moved to Hot Springs, Ark.

When he was fifteen, William Blythe legally became William Jefferson Clinton. He had been known as a boy as Bill Clinton or Billy Clinton, but he later said he had taken his stepfather's name in a show of family solidarity. Virginia and Roger Clinton had a volatile relationship, frequently separating, then getting back together. They had a son—Roger Clinton Jr.—when Bill Clinton was ten years old. Clinton Sr. was an alcoholic who turned mean and violent when drunk. During one altercation, Clinton confronted his stepfather about his behavior. As a result, the overt violence within the family stopped, but Clinton Sr. did not stop drinking.

From an early age, Clinton demonstrated a love of learning and reading. He was highly verbal and was seemingly interested in everything. He showed an early aptitude for music and was said to have a good tenor voice. He studied the saxophone, which he would play into adulthood, and formed a jazz combo in high school with two classmates. He was elected president of the junior class but lost the race for senior class secretary. At seventeen, he was elected a delegate to Boys Nation, which proved a seminal event in his life. Clinton went to Washington, D.C., with Boys Nation in July 1963 and got the opportunity to shake hands with President John F. Kennedy at the White House. The event happened to be taped, and Clinton would use the footage of himself and Kennedy in his 1992 presidential campaign. Before the trip to Washington, Clinton considered a future as a minister, musician or teacher; after the trip, he was determined to enter politics.

In 1964, Clinton enrolled in Georgetown University, the only college to which he had applied. At Georgetown, he was elected president of his freshman and sophomore classes. Because he needed money to help pay for school, he worked throughout his undergraduate years. During one summer, he became involved in the gubernatorial campaign of Frank Holt in Arkansas. Although Holt would lose, the contact proved fruitful for Clinton because he got to know Holt's nephew, Arkansas Supreme Court Justice Jack Holt. Jack Holt wrote a recommendation for Clinton, which was instrumental in his obtaining a job in the Washington office of Sen. William J. Fulbright, D-Ark.

Every weekend for six weeks in 1967, Clinton drove from Washington to Durham, N.C., where his stepfather was being treated for cancer. The two men were able to forge a reconciliation before Clinton Sr. died. Years later, when Clinton would enter the national arena as a presidential contender, armchair and professional psychologists would point to Clinton's contentious childhood as the source of his desire to be liked, to bring people together and to please everyone.

Clinton graduated from Georgetown in 1968, with a major in international government studies. Although he said he did not think he had a chance of getting one, Clinton applied for and won a Rhodes scholarship. Clinton studied at Oxford University for two years—from 1968 to 1970—but did not complete a degree program.

Clinton passed up a third year at Oxford to enter Yale University Law School in 1971. Although he was on scholarship, he took on numerous part-time jobs, including teaching at a community college, working for a Hartford city councilman and investigating cases for a New Haven lawyer. At Yale, Clinton met his future wife, Hillary Rodham. In 1972, Clinton and Hillary worked for the George McGovern presidential campaign in Texas.

Despite Clinton's ambitions, he did not exhibit a desire for accolades for the sake of accolades. For example, while in law school, he was actively pursued to join the *Yale Law Review,* an honor in and of itself as well as a known stepping stone to a U.S. Supreme Court clerkship and then a lucrative position with a New York law firm. Clinton, however, was not interested and did not take up the offer. He was intent on returning to Arkansas and saw no value in being on law review. Furthermore, he never was motivated by personal wealth or material success.

In 1973, Clinton graduated from Yale and became a law professor at the University of Arkansas at Fayetteville. Meanwhile, Hillary Rodham headed to Washington, D.C., to work for the House Judiciary Committee investigating the Watergate scandal. When President Richard Nixon resigned in 1974, Hillary joined Clinton at the University of Arkansas, also teaching law. That same year, Clinton entered big-league politics when he challenged GOP representative John Paul Hammerschmidt in the heavily Republican Third District of Arkansas. Although Clinton lost the election, he came closer to beating the popular incumbent than any other candidate before or since. He also gained widespread, positive attention with his enthusiasm and charisma. On Oct. 11, 1975, Bill Clinton and Hillary Rodham were married.

Clinton's candidacy came under serious threat of being derailed in early 1992. In January, the supermarket tabloid *Star* published allegations that Clinton had had an affair with Gennifer Flowers, an Arkansas state government employee and former singer and TV reporter, from 1977 to 1989. She was paid by *Star* to take the story public. Fueling the allegations was the questions of character that sunk the presidential candidacy of former senator Gary Hart of Colorado in 1987 under similar charges. Clinton and his wife subsequently appeared on the CBS

Program *60 Minutes* to discuss their marriage. Without offering any details, Clinton said, "I have acknowledged wrongdoing. I have acknowledged causing pain in my marriage." Despite the intense negative media coverage of the story, polls taken at the time indicated continued support for Clinton. A poll published in *USA Today* found only 10 percent of respondents saying they were less likely to vote for Clinton because of Flowers's story. And an ABC News poll that asked whether the news media should drop the investigation found 81 percent saying yes.

Clinton won his first statewide election in 1976, for Arkansas attorney general. During his tenure, he worked to keep the big utility interests in the state from raising rates and endorsed an expanded work-release program to reduce prison overcrowding. In 1978, Clinton was elected governor, the youngest in the nation.

1980 proved memorable to Clinton for two reasons. First, he became a father with the birth of his daughter, Chelsea. Second, he was drummed out of the governorship in an embarrassing defeat. On the second point, Clinton was hampered by a series of problems. One of them, an election-year increase in automobile license fees, was largely of his making. But the Democratic administration of Jimmy Carter hurt him by housing Cuban refugees at Fort Chaffee in Arkansas and refusing to move them. Some voters saw this as a demonstration of Clinton's lack of influence in Washington. To boot, many voters saw him as arrogant and ambitious. The result was the election of Frank D. White, a Republican savings and loan executive.

A more contrite Clinton ran in 1982, saying that he had heard the message voters sent him in 1980 and promised not to "lead without listening." He survived a Democratic primary runoff and, with Arkansas badly hurt by the recession, easily beat White. Clinton would hold the governorship until the end of 1992, shortly before being inaugurated president.

As governor, Clinton became closely associated with the issue of education reform. He pushed several tax hikes to increase funding for education, including raises in teachers salaries. Considerably more controversial was his proposal to require teachers to pass competency tests. The Arkansas Education Association, which had been a strong Clinton supporter, was vehemently opposed to the tests and worked to block them. In the end, however, teacher testing became law in Arkansas.

Clinton also found himself at odds with a traditional Democratic base of support—organized labor. Many of the differences involved taxes. Labor accused the governor of raising the state's "regressive" sales tax to fund his programs while approving numerous tax loopholes that benefited well-connected special interests. Clinton's defenders maintained that he relied on the sales tax because it was the easiest of all state taxes to change. An amendment added to the state constitution in the 1930s required three-fourths of the state legislature to approve any increase in a tax that was in existence at that time. Because the sales tax was instituted later, the legislature could raise it by a simple majority. That reasoning, however, did little to assuage Arkansas labor.

A personal and professional crisis arose in 1984 for Clinton when he learned from the Arkansas state police that his half-brother was using as well as trafficking in cocaine. Clinton kept the information to himself while the investigation was completed. Roger Clinton subsequently was arrested, plead guilty and spent more than a year in federal prison. Bill Clinton would enter a period of self-examination to understand the dynamics of the alcoholic family in which he was raised.

Clinton considered vying for the 1988 Democratic presidential nomination. He bowed out in July 1987, however, relating that "my heart says no." He indicated that he did not want to expose his seven-year-old daughter to the rigors of a national campaign. Although his image as a rising star in politics remained, Clinton flubbed his first live appearance before a large national audience when he delivered a 35-minute nominating speech for Michael S. Dukakis at the 1988 Democratic convention. He went on for so long that the delegates became visibly bored and restless. Clinton became the butt of jokes but redeemed himself with a self-deprecating appearance on *The Tonight Show with Johnny Carson.* He also played saxophone on the program with the band.

In 1990, Clinton seemed unsure whether he wanted to stay on as governor. Many Arkansas voters seemed to be equally unsure, and Clinton won with less than 60 percent of the vote in both the primary and the general election. Along the way, he promised that he would serve a full four-year term if reelected. After deciding to run for president, he visited diners across the state to tell voters why he felt it necessary to renege on his pledge.

Meanwhile, Clinton remained highly regarded by his peers in governors' mansions across the country. He played an active role in the National Governors' Association (NGA) in the late 1980s—including serving a term as chairman in 1986–1987—showing a knack for quickly recognizing cutting-edge social issues. He helped craft NGA initiatives on welfare reform, then education and child care, and finally Medicaid and health care. In addition, in 1990–1991, he was chairman of the Democratic Leadership Council (DLC), which had been created to position the Democratic Party more in the mainstream of American politics, away from old-style New Deal liberalism and toward a centrist philosophy that was less beholden to special interests. The council emphasized progrowth, prodefense and anticrime themes. And, Clinton was ranked as the nation's most effective governor in a *Newsweek* magazine poll of governors taken in June 1991.

In February, the *Wall Street Journal* suggested that Clinton calculatingly evaded the draft during the Vietnam War, which coincided with the time he was in college. It alleged that he signed up for the Reserve Officers' Training Corps (ROTC) to get a deferment, then dropped out when he found out that he got a high number in the draft lottery. Clinton had said he was eligible for the draft but was not called. Like many people in the 1960s, Clinton received a student deferment for his undergraduate years. He went to Oxford without a deferment, however.

While in England, he got a notice of induction, but the reporting date had passed. He subsequently contacted the draft board, which granted him a deferment for the remainder of the school year. Not expecting to get a deferment for his second year at Oxford, Clinton decided to attend the University of Arkansas Law School and join the ROTC. His reasoning was that, because he would be receiving military training through ROTC, he most likely would receive deferments while he was in law school. However, he ultimately decided to go back to Oxford for a second year. By quitting the ROTC, he became eligible for the draft lottery. He received a high number and was not drafted.

Clinton also repeatedly said he had "attended" antiwar protests but did not participate in them. However, a 1969 letter to the head of the ROTC at the University of Arkansas surfaced in 1992 that belied that assertion. Clinton wrote that he had "written and spoken and marched against the war" and that he went "to England to organize the Americans . . . for demonstrations." In the same letter, Clinton wrote: "The decision not to be a resister and the related subsequent decisions were the most difficult of my life. I decided to accept the draft in spite of my beliefs for one reason: to maintain my political viability within the system. For years I have worked to prepare myself for a political life characterized by both practical political ability and concern for rapid social progress. It is a life I still feel compelled to lead." Clinton's critics pointed in derision to his blatant ambition and characterized his actions as duplicitous and his explanations as doublespeak.

Clinton also did not help himself on the issue of marijuana. During the 1990 gubernatorial campaign when asked about marijuana use, Clinton, speaking more like a lawyer than a candidate, said that he "never violated the drug laws of the state as an adult in Arkansas." Then, in 1991, when asked if he ever used any illegal drug as a college student, Clinton said no. However, in a 1992 interview, he admitted experimenting with marijuana while in England. He said, "I didn't like it. I didn't inhale and never tried it again." The "didn't inhale" line elicited ridicule for years after, largely because many people simply did not believe him.

In March, the *Washington Post* reported on the Arkansas state business handled by the Rose Law Firm, where Hillary Clinton was a partner. The *Post* stopped short of making any accusations of impropriety by the Clintons. However, presidential contender Jerry Brown, in a debate among the Democratic candidates, characterized the practice as "corruption."

Meanwhile, the *New York Times* reported that the Clintons had been business partners with James B. McDougal, who ran a failed savings and loan that was regulated by the state and was represented by the Rose Law Firm. McDougal and his wife were partners with the Clintons in Whitewater, a failed real estate deal.

Despite all of the so-called waffling and the questions of character that arose during the campaign, Clinton was elected in 1992 with 43 percent of the popular vote in a three-way race, defeating President George Bush (38 percent) and independent candidate Ross Perot (19 percent).

Presidential Nominations

Upon his election as president, Clinton stated that he sought to choose his closest advisers based on their ability to work together as well as to complement each other. He reiterated that he wanted to be surrounded by people who represented a variety of views. And, in specific reference to the cabinet, Clinton said his goal was to appoint a diverse group of people who "look like America."

With his first announced appointments—his economic team—Clinton called upon highly respected Washington, D.C., and Wall Street insiders, whose selection sent a message of political steadfastness and a new administration's desire to work closely with Congress. Follow-up choices to head the departments of Labor and Health and Human Services (HHS) also showed an incoming president intent on surrounding himself with top officials who would be credible spokespersons and able navigators for his legislative agenda.

Possibly the most significant signal sent by Clinton's first choices was that his primary concern was practical politics: getting his program enacted. Sen. Lloyd Bentsen, D-Texas, and Rep. Leon E. Panetta, D-Calif., named to head the Treasury Department and the Office of Management and Budget (OMB), respectively, were two highly regarded members of Congress who would be called upon to sell Clinton's ideas to their former colleagues. Bentsen was expected to use his vast experience with the tax code and the federal budget to shape Clinton's economic plan and to convince the financial markets of its validity. The good-humored Panetta, one of Congress's most persistent deficit hawks, gained considerable credibility by becoming an expert in the technical details of budgeting while serving as a member and subsequently chairman of the House Budget Committee. Panetta's deputy at OMB was Alice M. Rivlin, a Brookings Institution economist who had earned her bona fides on Capitol Hill as the first director of the Congressional Budget Office in the late 1970s and early 1980s. Robert E. Rubin, cochairman of Goldman Sachs Corp., was tapped to head the newly created National Economic Council (NEC), coordinating economic policy decisions among departments and agencies and advising the president. Rubin reportedly had played the honest broker among competing economic camps during the presidential campaign and following the general election.

Clinton's first economic appointments indicated that he was much more concerned about the nation's long-term economic health than about the residual short-term effects of the latest recession. And, by picking individuals who, for the most part, represented mainstream thinking, Clinton reinforced his own moderate economic outlook. But he also made clear that he planned to be his own chief economic adviser and to tap disparate points of view.

The president-elect selected Harvard University's Kennedy School of Government lecturer Robert B. Reich as labor secretary and University of Wisconsin at Madison chancellor Donna E. Shalala as HHS secretary. While both worked outside Washington, they were no novices to federal policy. Reich, a longtime friend of Clinton's since their days as Rhodes scholars at Oxford University, was a former director of policy planning at the Federal Trade Commission under President Jimmy Carter and an assistant solicitor general in the Justice Department during the Ford administration. Shalala was an assistant secretary of housing and urban development under Carter.

In the next round of initial appointments, Clinton added to the diversity of his cabinet by naming the first minority group members. They touted a wide range of political experience. Ronald H. Brown, chairman of the Democratic National Committee as well as a partner in the Washington law firm of Patton, Boggs & Blow, was nominated commerce secretary. Disabled American Veterans executive director Jesse Brown was tapped for veterans affairs secretary. Secretary-designate of the Department of Housing and Urban Development (HUD) Henry G. Cisneros had made a national name for himself as mayor of San Antonio, Texas. The two Browns were African Americans; Cisneros, Hispanic American.

Clinton wrapped up his initial top-level selections the day before Christmas 1992. He picked Aetna Life & Casualty Co. vice president and legal counsel Zoë Baird to be the first female attorney general; Rep. Les Aspin to be defense secretary; former deputy secretary of state Warren M. Christopher to be secretary of state; League of Conservation Voters president and former Arizona governor Bruce Babbitt to be interior secretary; Rep. Mike Espy to be the first African American agriculture secretary; former Denver, Colo., mayor Federico F. Peña to be the first Hispanic transportation secretary; Northern States Power Company executive vice president Hazel R. O'Leary to be the first African American female energy secretary; former South Carolina governor Richard W. Riley as education secretary; and Georgetown University professor and Center for National Policy president Madeleine K. Albright to be U.N. ambassador, a post Clinton would accord cabinet-level status.

The desire for appointees who reflected the diversity that Clinton sought put him under pressure from groups that wished to be represented. Women's groups, in particular, expressed concern that his early appointments seemed to be dominated by Caucasian males. Interest groups also appeared to have had an impact on final choices. For example, Babbitt, who was chosen as interior secretary, was strongly favored by environmental groups.

Despite speculation that Republicans would seek retribution for the failed nominations of Robert Bork for associate justice of the Supreme Court during the Reagan administration and John Tower for defense secretary during the Bush administration, the Senate gave quick approval to Clinton's cabinet, with the exception of Baird. Overall, the Democratic-controlled Senate confirmed the Democratic president's nominees at the same pace that a Republican-controlled Senate dispatched Republican President Ronald Reagan's nominees in 1981. Clinton's nominations moved slightly faster than those of President George Bush in 1989, when Democrats were reviewing GOP picks.

Baird's nomination as attorney general was withdrawn after it ran aground over the controversy created by her illegal hiring of two undocumented immigrants as household workers and her failure to pay proper taxes on their behalf. Further stirrings resulted when federal district judge Kimba M. Wood removed her name from consideration for the Justice Department post because her baby-sitter had been an illegal immigrant. Some women's groups were furious to see Baird and Wood knocked out of consideration on an issue that had not hampered male nominees. The attorney general slot finally was filled by veteran Florida prosecutor Janet Reno. She became the first woman to hold the position. Single with no children, Reno had never hired an illegal immigrant.

The nomination of litigator and professor Lani Guinier as assistant attorney general in charge of the civil rights division met with fierce attacks from conservatives, who accused her of holding dangerously radical views on minority rights. Clinton withdrew the nomination, noting that he, too, had difficulty with some of her ideas. He admitted that he had not read her legal writings before selecting her. Unlike Baird, who went down without real protest from political interest groups, Guinier had the active support of prominent groups such as the Congressional Black Caucus, which expressed anger and disappointment over Clinton's actions. Some quarters accused the president of weak leadership as a result of the episode.

Also kicking up dust was Clinton's nomination of Roberta Achtenberg, a homosexual rights activist, as assistant secretary for fair housing and equal opportunity at HUD. However, Achtenberg was confirmed, thus becoming the first avowed lesbian to hold such a high federal office.

The Clinton administration experienced relatively little turnover among its highest ranks during the first term. And many who did leave their posts did so for other positions in the administration.

Aspin, although well liked on Capitol Hill, had been faulted for his lack of administrative skills and bogged down in controversies ranging from gays in the military to peacekeeping in Somalia. The national debate over how to lift the military's ban on homosexuals was a major detraction for the fledgling administration during the first half of 1993, and the disastrous raid in Somalia in October 1993 in which 18 U.S. soldiers were killed incited public and congressional anger over the direction of White House foreign policy. Aspin resigned as defense secretary in early 1994. Clinton's choice of retired admiral Bobby Ray Inman to head the Pentagon imploded in an odd manner, when Inman abruptly withdrew his nomination, contending that a partisan attack was being planned against him. Deputy Defense Secretary William J. Perry subsequently was quickly confirmed to succeed Aspin.

In mid-1994, Panetta left OMB to become White House chief of staff, replacing Thomas F. "Mack" McLarty III. Rivlin was elevated to OMB director.

At the end of 1994, Treasury Secretary Bentsen returned to private life, amidst high praise for his public service. Espy's resignation as agriculture secretary was prompted by an investigation into allegations that he improperly accepted gifts. And Surgeon General Joycelyn Elders was fired after making remarks about sex education with which Clinton disagreed. In 1995, NEC head Rubin succeeded Bentsen as Treasury secretary. Rep. Dan Glickman won easy approval to follow Espy at Agriculture. Clinton's choice to succeed Elders was not so lucky, however. The nomination of Henry W. Foster Jr., an obstetrician and gynecologist, became ensnared in the politics of abortion and the 1996 presidential race. While Foster clearly had enough support to win the simple majority needed in the Senate for confirmation, he did not have 60 votes—the number required to block a threatened filibuster—and his nomination effectively was defeated.

In 1996, Ron Brown was killed when the jet he was in crashed in Croatia during a trade development trip. U.S. Trade

VICE PRESIDENT AL GORE: TRUSTED PARTNER OF THE PRESIDENT

Bill Clinton's choice of Al Gore—another young, southern moderate—to be his running mate in 1992 was something of a surprise, given the historical penchant for presidential candidates to seek ideological or geographic balance in their vice-presidential pick. Clinton said he saw Gore as a complement to himself, bringing to the mix experience that Clinton lacked; for example, service in the military and in Congress. While the office of the vice presidency has been a paper tiger, Clinton allowed Gore to make the position his own and assert himself in ways no other second-in-command had. Partly as a result, Gore emerged as a leading contender for the Democratic presidential nomination in 2000.

Background

Albert Arnold Gore Jr. was born March 31, 1948, in Washington, D.C. His father—Albert Sr.—served more than 30 years in Congress (D-Tenn., House 1939–1944, 1945–1953; Senate 1953–1971).

Albert Jr. attended Washington's St. Albans prep school, where he was an honors student and football team captain. Gore spent his summers on the family farm in Carthage, Tenn., an hour's drive east of Nashville. He graduated from Harvard University in 1969 with a degree in government. As an undergraduate, he developed an interest in writing. The Vietnam War, which Gore opposed, intervened in his career plans, however. He got a low draft number and, after considering all his options, he decided to enlist.

Gore married Mary Elizabeth "Tipper" Aitcheson, then reported for Army training. His tour in Vietnam lasted six months. He served as a reporter in an engineering unit and never witnessed a casualty. He did a considerable amount of writing while in the Army, and some of his stories ran in the *Nashville Tennessean*. The newspaper hired him as a reporter after he left the Army in 1971. During the time he was working for the *Tennessean*, Gore studied religion and law at Vanderbilt University.

Gore and his wife had four children: three girls (Karenna, Kristin and Sarah) and a boy (Albert III).

Service in Congress

In 1976, Gore entered politics, vying for the seat created by the retirement of Democrat Joe Evins, who had represented Carthage's congressional district since Albert Sr. had moved on to the Senate. Gore's campaign themes had a populist bent. He called for higher taxation of the rich, tighter strip mine laws and cuts in defense spending. Gore would win four House general elections—serving from 1977 to 1985—with never less than 79 percent of the vote. He made frequent trips home and talked with constituents at open meetings.

As a member of the House, Gore quickly developed a reputation for conducting investigative and well-publicized hearings. His efforts, for example, resulted in legislation cracking down on the sale of worthless insurance to senior citizens and requiring that infant formula sold in the United States meet certain nutrition and safety standards. A common thread to Gore's investigative work was a populist belief that an unwary public needed federal help in dealing with the business community and that corporate offenders should pay when something went wrong. He actively promoted public awareness of congressional action, as indicated by his leadership in the fight to televise House floor proceedings. Gore also showed a particular interest in scientific matters, biotechnology and computer development.

Gore further distinguished himself when he took on the issue of nuclear disarmament. Inspired, he said, by children's concerns about a possible nuclear war, he immersed himself on the subject in the single-minded, disciplined way that became his trademark. Beginning in 1980, he spent eight hours a week for thirteen months studying the issue and being briefed by experts. He emerged with a plan for both the United States and the Soviet Union to remove multiple weapons, an idea that immediately caught Soviet attention.

In the early 1980s, MX critics in the House appeared close to thwarting President Ronald Reagan's plan to deploy 100 MX missiles in existing silos. Gore feared that such congressional action would allow Reagan to brand the Democrats as soft on defense and would result in a withdrawal of arms negotiations with the Soviets. Gore and a few other Democrats supported limited MX production in return for a promise from the administration of flexibility at strategic arms talks. Gore pursued the issue while in the Senate. (He was elected in 1984 with 61 percent of the vote to the seat vacated by Republican Howard H. Baker Jr. Gore won reelection in 1990 with 68 percent of the vote.) Gore worked with a small group of Democrats on an agreement with the Reagan administration holding MX deployment to 50 missiles.

Presidential Run

Long viewed as groomed for national office, Gore entered the 1988 presidential race after getting support from numerous well-funded donors. He staked his claim as a moderate on such defense and policy issues as his support for the 1983 invasion of Grenada, nonmilitary aid to the Nicaragua contras and flight-testing ballistic missiles. Most of his efforts and gains were made in the South. He did not fare as well in other areas of the country, however. He was accused of pandering to dairy farmers in Wisconsin and Jewish voters in New York. He drew only 10 percent of the vote in New York and

Representative Mickey Kantor succeeded Brown as commerce secretary. Also in 1996, Rivlin was confirmed as vice chairman of the Federal Reserve Board. Her job as OMB director was filled by Franklin D. Raines, who was serving as Fannie Mae vice chairman. Alan Greenspan, meanwhile, was confirmed as Fed chairman, for a third consecutive term.

Clinton got the opportunity to fill two Supreme Court vacancies. In 1993, the president named Ruth Bader Ginsburg to fill the slot created by the retirement of Justice Byron R. White. Ginsburg was expected to carry on White's centrist tradition, but with a somewhat more liberal tilt. Her voting bore out the predictions. An active interrogator, Ginsburg generally took liberal positions on women's rights, civil rights, church-state and First Amendment issues but had a more mixed record in other

suspended his campaign after getting drawn into a nasty spat between New York City Mayor Edward I. Koch—who had endorsed him—and the civil rights activist Rev. Jesse Jackson.

Speculation arose that a 1992 presidential race was in the offing when Gore broke with his party and voted to authorize use of military force against Iraq in January 1991. However, in August 1991, Gore announced he would not run, citing family concerns after his son was seriously injured in an automobile accident. A factor in Gore's decision also may have been the perceived strength and popularity of President George Bush following the Persian Gulf War.

Gore wrote *Earth in the Balance: Ecology and the Human Spirit*, which was published in 1992 and reached the *New York Times* bestseller list. He led the Senate delegation to the United Nations Earth Summit held in Rio de Janeiro, Brazil, in 1992.

Vice President

President Jimmy Carter was credited with first treating his vice president—Walter F. Mondale—as a trusted partner in his presidency. George Bush, as Reagan's vice president, and Dan Quayle, as Bush's, also were given specific areas of responsibility. However, some argued that Gore played a more central role at the White House, not only in policy discussions and administration responsibilities but also in the critical sector of media politics. Clinton and Gore forged a close working as well as personal relationship. Gore was viewed as the quintessential team player but was not shy about offering advice or criticism, even if it meant challenging Clinton.

Early on, Gore scored some well-publicized albeit unglamorous points for the administration with the National Performance Review, which he headed. The review was followed by the "reinventing government" initiative, a proposal aimed at saving taxpayers' money and making government more efficient. The effort helped blunt criticism of Democrats as the party of bureaucratic bloat.

As vice president, Gore asserted himself in the areas of computer development and environmental protection. He encouraged widespread use of the Internet, called for computers in all classrooms and helped influence the telecommunications overhaul legislation. In 1995, he unveiled a seven-year plan to restore south Florida's ecosystem, an area that includes Everglades National Park. He also was credited with persuading Secretary of State Warren M. Christopher to include environmental issues as a top priority in U.S. diplomatic affairs.

Gore debated Ross Perot on national television at the height of the struggle over the North America Free Trade Agreement (NAFTA). His impressive performance helped turn around the politics of the issue. Gore engaged in more traditional lobbying of members of Congress on a wide range of issues, including the space station, health care reform, Mexico loan guarantees and deployment of U.S. troops as part of a North Atlantic Treaty Organization (NATO)-led force to police a peace agreement in Bosnia. He also spoke out about Republican efforts to repeal the ban on assault weapons and about the (unsuccessful) nomination of Dr. Henry W. Foster Jr. as surgeon general. Gore visited flood areas in the Midwest during the summer of 1993, and he put forth a proposal to create a global network of schoolchildren to collect data about their environment. In the wake of the July 1996 crash of TWA Flight 800 off the coast of East Moriches, N.Y., Gore was assigned to head a commission on aviation safety, airline security and the pace of modernization of the air traffic control system.

Critics said that Gore was not without missteps. During consideration of the 1993 omnibus budget reconciliation bill, Gore pushed an unpopular proposal to boost energy (Btu) taxes to help reduce the deficit. The Btu tax provisions subsequently were removed from the package. By some accounts, Gore also was among those urging Clinton to permit gays to serve openly in the military. The issue ignited a firestorm on Capitol Hill that raged during the early months of the administration.

Filling in a weak spot in his résumé—lack of experience in international affairs—Gore became cochair with Russian Prime Minister Viktor Chernomyrdin of a commission, established in 1993 as a space, energy and technology group, aimed at creating more opportunities for dialogue between the two nations while helping to reform and open the Russian economy. Over the next three years, the commission's scope expanded significantly, becoming a venue for discussion of public and private economic development projects as well as a back channel for diplomatic messages on such issues as the war in Bosnia and the military conflict in Chechnya.

The other, often unspoken contribution Gore made to the Clinton administration was his clean personal image. While scandals and tribulations afflicted the Clinton White House, Gore managed to stay close to the first family without being besmirched—although it remained to be seen whether revelations of irregularities in 1996 Democratic campaign fund-raising would damage his reputation. Gore's image as a family man was bolstered during the 1980s by the efforts of his wife to protect children by urging recording companies to place warning labels on popular music that contained suggestive and explicit lyrics. As vice president, Gore was critical of television violence and was the chief architect of the V-chip, which would allow parents to block television programs with violent content.

areas, including criminal law. The message in Clinton's choice was perceived to be his interest in moderation and consensus instead of dramatic ideological change. Liberals praised her experience in advocating women's rights; conservatives praised her record of judicial restraint. Ginsburg joined Sandra Day O'Connor as the second woman appointed to the Court. She also became the first Jewish justice on the Court since 1969.

As with the Ginsburg nominee, Clinton, when required to replace the retiring Justice Harry A. Blackmun, settled on a highly regarded federal judge with centrist inclinations and the promise of an easy Senate confirmation—Stephen G. Breyer. Clinton repeatedly had indicated that he wanted to put a politician on the Court, which was dominated by former judges. However, one favorite, Senate Majority Leader George J.

Mitchell, D-Maine, took himself out of the running, and another, Interior Secretary Babbitt, was expected to face stiff opposition. As a judge and then chief judge on the First U.S. Circuit Court of Appeals, Breyer was relatively liberal on most civil and individual rights issues but more conservative on criminal rights and business law. While Breyer had amassed an impressive record as a legal scholar and was roundly praised for his professional accomplishments, he was considered somewhat aloof and did not obviously possess the "big heart" that Clinton had spoken of seeking in a nominee. During Breyer's first two terms on the Court, he compiled a moderately liberal record. He dissented from several conservative rulings on race and religion and wrote the dissenting opinion in a decision that struck down a federal law prohibiting the possession of firearms near schools. However, Breyer displayed a conservative bent on criminal law issues, such as when he sided with the majority in permitting random drug testing of high school athletes. Breyer joined Ginsburg as the Court's second Jewish justice. The Court last had two sitting Jewish members in the 1930s.

After Clinton won reelection in 1996, several members of the cabinet and other top aides announced their intention to leave public service. Guiding Clinton in his new selections was a desire to govern from the "vital center" and "to have a government that can unify the country." He said that he would cast a wide net in looking for replacements and that he believed the American people wanted Democrats, Republicans and Independents to work together

The Economy

The 1992 Clinton presidential campaign was guided by the fateful phrase "It's the economy, stupid." Feelings of economic anxiety among the electorate helped usher Clinton into office. A widespread perception existed that George Bush was not doing enough to address Americans' fear and discontent over what they saw as their worsening personal financial situation. When Bush left office, the projected annual deficit was more than $290 billion, the accumulated national debt was about $4 trillion, the unemployment rate hovered around 8 percent, and the annual trade deficit was more than $100 billion.

In his 1996 State of the Union address, Clinton said that the U.S. "economy is the healthiest it has been in three decades." Economists and administration officials attributed a significant portion of Clinton's economic policy success to actions he took during his first year in office. Inheriting a federal budget deficit larger than anticipated, Clinton decided to abandon his campaign promise for middle-class tax cuts. Instead, he pushed through Congress, with no GOP support, a deficit reduction package that included higher tax rates that fell mostly on the rich as well as significant spending cuts. Wall Street, in response, came to believe that Clinton intended to bring the federal budget under control, thus paving the way for the lower interest rates, the falling unemployment rate and the booming stock market that played out over the next few years.

Clinton both deviated from and stood as a stark defender of traditionally Democratic positions regarding economic policy.

For example, with the support of congressional Republicans, he pursued free trade agreements and signed on to the notion of a balanced federal budget. Meanwhile, he won political points for tempering the conservative onslaught by vowing to protect Social Security and Medicare and by endorsing an increase in the minimum wage.

Not all the economic news reported during Clinton's first term was good. The income gap between the richest and the poorest Americans widened; wages and family incomes were stagnant; the trade deficit increased; and the rate of national economic growth was modest at best. Furthermore, changes—real or threatened—brought, for example, by corporate downsizing, the global economy, technological advances and stock market volatility bred insecurity. However, to Clinton's benefit, according to public opinion polls, most people did not hold him responsible for the anxiety of the times and most believed that the overall U.S. economy was healthy.

Legislative Action

Clinton's legislative accomplishments and defeats proved a curious study in partisan politics and coalition building.

When Democrat Clinton assumed office after 12 years of GOP occupation of the White House, the Democratic-majority Congress quickly cleared a number of bills—including "motor voter" registration and medical and family leave—that had broad Democratic agreement and that had been blocked by Republican presidents. The ease with which these measures were enacted belied Clinton's experience with Congress otherwise. Clinton would find that he could not always depend on complete Democratic loyalty in enacting his legislative agenda and that Republican intransigence was often steadfast.

Clinton's 1993 effort to redraw the nation's tax and spending policies played out in three pieces of legislation: the budget resolution, a so-called stimulus package provided for in a supplemental appropriations measure and a reconciliation bill. Congress in early April completed action on the budget resolution, which largely embraced Clinton's proposed tax increases (higher tax rates on upper-income taxpayers and a broad-based tax on virtually all forms of energy), spending cuts on a wide range of programs, and "investment" spending in areas such as education, children's nutrition, and health programs. Not one Republican in either chamber voted for the budget resolution in committee or on the floor. Republicans said the plan contained too many tax provisions and not enough spending cuts.

Later in April, Clinton suffered his first major legislative setback. Senate Republicans succeeded in killing the stimulus package. In the House, the Democratic leadership settled on a tough partisan strategy that virtually shut Republicans out of the process, thus enabling the legislation to pass. In the Senate, however, the rules were more generous to the minority party, which allowed Republicans to get deleted from the bill almost all of Clinton's provisions. The major objection was that the new appropriations would be considered emergency spending not subject to budget caps, meaning the deficit would be driven upward.

Following that embarrassment, Clinton began to play a higher-profile role in lobbying Congress on matters that were a priority for him. He came out a big winner in August, with passage of the budget reconciliation measure. That measure, embodying a clear break from GOP fiscal policies, raised taxes on gasoline and other transportation fuels and on upper-income individuals, cut the defense budget and increased funds for some social and antipoverty programs. Like with the budget resolution, Republicans refused to have any part of the reconciliation bill; it did not get a single GOP vote in either chamber. With Democratic leaders watching whip counts closely and Clinton waging an intense and personal campaign to woo individual members—arguing, cajoling, trading and doing almost anything within reason to get his way—the president managed to overcome defections from conservatives in his party and get the reconciliation measure passed by the narrowest of margins.

Clinton used similar tactics to obtain approval in November 1993 of the North American Free Trade Agreement (NAFTA), which had been negotiated by Bush. His victory on NAFTA was considered his most extraordinary legislative success of the year, because it came in the face of unusually strong opposition within his party as well as from organized labor, a bulwark of support for the Democratic Party. To build Democratic support, Clinton argued that NAFTA was an important leg of his plan to create more high-wage, high-skill jobs. To help ensure a strong GOP vote for the pact, he depended on high-ranking Republicans who usually were his adversaries. The administration unabashedly cut deals to resolve some lawmakers' problems with the agreement, and outside Congress, Clinton waged a high-profile public relations campaign. By the end of the year, he had become so renowned for importuning members that he was being likened to President Lyndon B. Johnson, who had legendary powers of persuasion in his early White House years. Some saw Clinton's reliance on shifting coalitions as a sign of political agility—and a necessary skill in a political world where party discipline was weak.

The accolades subsided in 1994, however, because of the administration's mishandling of health care reform. Clinton and his congressional allies, not expecting much, if any, Republican support for the plan, decided early on to forgo a bipartisan, less confrontational approach to health care reform. The strategy of depending on Democratic votes alone to pass the legislation proved unworkable, however. Despite months of negotiations by leaders of both chambers, Democrats could not agree among themselves about the contents of a bill. Clinton had proposed hybrid legislation that would use the market to contain health care costs, but Democratic centrists saw too much government involvement and found the measure too complicated to explain to the public.

The inglorious demise of Clinton's health care initiative had far wider effects than were immediately realized. It crowded out other priorities, leaving unfinished at session's end bills dealing with campaign finance, lobbying disclosure, telecommunications and the "superfund." More damaging to the administration, Republicans emerged from the debate more convinced than ever that they could profit politically by obstructing Clinton's agenda and, on the evidence of the health care reform proposal, by branding the president a liberal, which in recent years had become a dirty word.

1994 did not pass without legislative wins for Clinton, but even some of his most notable successes were overshadowed by rancorous partisanship on Capitol Hill. For example, the crime bill finally emerged after a long struggle between conservatives, who wanted stiffer sentencing and ridiculed prevention programs, and liberals, who railed against what they saw as a failed policy of overzealous incarceration and advocated more prevention programs. Some suggested that Republican opposition stemmed in part from a desire to deny Clinton a political victory on the crime issue, which had been a GOP stronghold. The bill also was temporarily derailed in the House when 58 Democrats joined forces with most Republicans to defeat the rule for floor consideration of the measure. The administration subsequently was forced to make concessions on the legislation.

Even the implementing legislation for the General Agreement on Tariffs and Trade (GATT), a business-oriented deal engineered by Clinton's two Republican predecessors that should have been an easy win, got caught up in the grinder. The primary foes of GATT were Democrats who saw U.S. free trade policy as detrimental to the country's industrial jobs base. Meanwhile, Republicans who advocated free trade, as did their constituency in the U.S. business community, lined up in support. Congress had to return for a brief lame duck session to approve the measure, giving Clinton a crucial victory only after the 1994 elections.

Partisan politics entered a new dimension in 1995, when Republicans took control of both houses of Congress and of the legislative agenda. As a general strategy, Clinton sought to set limits on how far Congress wanted to go in redirecting his policies, and he tried to reshape GOP agenda. For example, he supported welfare reform, but not if it slighted work incentives. He wanted spending cuts, but not in certain education programs. And he endorsed regulatory reform, but not if it loosened environmental controls. By the summer, however, Clinton made the veto threat his weapon of choice for trying to influence the Republican Congress. He and other administration officials threatened vetoes against a slew of major bills, including the GOP welfare reform measure, a spending cut and disaster aid package, a House rewrite of the clean water law, a bill to slash and reorganize foreign aid programs, and the budget-reconciliation measure. Clinton faced only a moderate risk that his vetoes would be reversed, because the Republican majorities in both houses were slim and Democratic crossover was not significant. Clinton embraced the veto strategy as Republicans blanched at the idea of watering down their agenda to get Clinton's signature. More ideologically driven members favored confrontation with Clinton instead of the accommodation preached by Democrats and a few GOP colleagues.

The Republican strategy to go head-to-head with Clinton culminated with two government shutdowns. Republicans underestimated Clinton's willingness to fight. Instead of waiting to bargain over their huge reconciliation measure, they tried to win major White House budget concessions in exchange for

HILLARY RODHAM CLINTON: A CONTROVERSIAL FIRST LADY

By the end of her first four years in the White House, Hillary Rodham Clinton, wife of President Bill Clinton, had become arguably the most controversial first lady in U.S. history. She was a representative of changes in the status of women that many had a hard time understanding and supporting. Nevertheless, she piqued interest if only because she served as her husband's closest adviser and confidant throughout their relationship.

Background

Hillary Rodham was born October 26, 1947, to an independent businessowner and a homemaker. She was raised in Park Ridge, Ill.—an upper-middle-class, conservative community located north of Chicago—with her two younger brothers.

Her political philosophy evolved during her time at Wellesley College, which coincided with significant developments in society at large in the areas of civil rights and women's rights. By 1968, the former Goldwater Girl was helping campaign for Democrat Eugene McCarthy for president. In her senior year, Hillary was chosen, as student representative, to speak at commencement. Before her prepared remarks, she offered a soft, ad-libbed rebuke to Sen. Edward Brooke, R-Mass., whose keynote speech she thought to be clichéd and uninsightful. Hillary gained national recognition when *Life* magazine published an article about college graduations that included excerpts of her remarks as well as a photograph of her.

Hillary's interest in children crystallized during her time at Yale University Law School. Upon graduation, Hillary became a staff attorney for the Children's Defense Fund and a member of its board of directors. Then, she was hired by the House Judiciary Committee, which was preparing impeachment proceedings against President Richard Nixon. Her job centered on transcribing tapes. When Nixon resigned, she joined Bill Clinton, whom she had met at Yale, at the University of Arkansas at Fayetteville as an assistant professor of law, teaching criminal law, civil procedure and a seminar in children's rights. She and Clinton were married in 1975.

Hillary became part of the Rose Law Firm, in Little Rock, in 1977, while Clinton was serving as state attorney general. She primarily took cases in the area of intellectual property—copyright, trademarks and licensing. President Jimmy Carter named her to the board of the Legal Services Corporation, and she served from 1978 to 1981. Meanwhile, she was named a full partner at the Rose Law Firm in 1979 and gave birth to a daughter (Chelsea) in 1980.

Upon her marriage to Bill Clinton, Hillary kept her name for use in her personal as well as professional life. When Clinton was elected governor, some Arkansans speculated that Hillary's retention of her maiden name indicated that something was wrong with the relationship between her and her husband and that she was too independent and domineering. In what some saw as a response to Arkansans' desire for a more traditional first lady, she began going under the name Hillary Rodham Clinton when her husband sought to regain the governorship in 1982.

In other ways, however, Hillary was not traditional. In an unprecedented move, she was named by her husband, who had made education reform a top priority during his tenure as governor, to chair the newly created Education Standards Committee. The committee was charged with recommending minimum requirements for Arkansas schools, regarding, for example, class size and length of the school year. She also spoke publicly in support of the controversial proposal to require that Arkansas teachers be tested for competency.

In 1987, Hillary was elected chair of the board of directors of the Children's Defense Fund as well as of the New World Foundation. She was named among the "One Hundred Most Influential Lawyers in America" by the *National Law Journal* in 1988 and 1991.

1992 Campaign

Hillary Clinton sported an image as a modern, strong-minded career woman who played a crucial role in her husband's political rise. She was instrumental in rescuing her husband's 1992 presidential campaign, which was in deep trouble when tabloids published accounts of Bill Clinton's alleged affairs. The Clintons appeared on the CBS television program *60 Minutes* and acknowledged problems with their marriage, but they said they had worked them out. Hillary defended her husband by saying, "I honor what he's been through and what we've been through together, and, you know if that's not enough for people, then, heck, don't vote for him."

As the campaign went on, however, her characteristic bluntness helped lay the groundwork for critics to attack her. She found herself on the defensive when Democratic presidential contender Jerry Brown charged that the Rose Law Firm had benefited because of her marriage to the state's governor. "I suppose I could have stayed home and baked cookies and had teas. But what I decided to do was pursue my profession, which I entered before my husband was in public life," she shot back in response. The comment would follow her throughout the campaign and beyond.

First Lady

As first lady, Hillary Clinton was often compared with Eleanor Roosevelt, wife of President Franklin D. Roosevelt, whose independent activism on issues was inspiring to some and shocking to others. Bill Clinton reinforced the perception that his wife was an important player in policy matters by appointing her to head his efforts to overhaul the nation's health care system. She made an impressive showing in presenting the administration's reform proposal in testi-

agreeing to reopen the government temporarily. As a result, what Republicans had hoped the public would view as a great debate about redefining the role of the federal government instead was seen as a silly, schoolyard brawl over whether to keep the government operating while the two sides negotiated over the budget. The Republicans lost control of the debate and their message just as the White House and the passive congressional Democrats found new self-assurance and grew more confident

mony to Congress. However, she was criticized for crafting the plan in private and was accused by Republicans of wanting to socialize health care. The plan also inflamed passions among groups with interests at stake. For example, she was burned in effigy in Kentucky because the plan called for increased federal taxes on cigarettes. Much of the blame for the death of health care reform was laid at the first lady's feet.

Health care reform was not the only matter that put Hillary in the spotlight. For example, seven employees of the White House travel office were fired for alleged mismanagement and possible financial wrongdoing. The White House issued a report saying that the first lady was kept informed of the investigation into the reported problems in the office. However, a General Accounting Office report portrayed her as having a more active role, urging that the staffers be replaced. Hillary maintained to the House Government Reform and Oversight Committee that she played "no decision-making role" in the firings.

In July 1993, Deputy White House Counsel Vincent W. Foster Jr. was found dead of an apparently self-inflicted gunshot wound to the head. Some questioned whether he committed suicide, but several subsequent investigations confirmed that he did take his own life. Foster had been a long-time friend of Hillary Clinton's and a partner at the Rose Law Firm. Republicans unsuccessfully sought to show that Hillary was instrumental in limiting access to Foster's office to hamper the investigation into Foster's death and to remove embarrassing documents dealing with Whitewater, the failed Arkansas land development venture in which the Clintons had invested. Allegations also arose that Hillary had a hand in delaying the release of a torn-up note written by Foster and found after his death. However, no evidence existed to back up those assertions.

Whitewater became the focus of both congressional hearings and an independent counsel investigation. In April 1994, Hillary denied having any knowledge of any money flowing into the Whitewater venture from a failed Arkansas thrift owned by the Clintons' partner in the land investment, James B. McDougal. The Rose Law Firm had done legal work on behalf of the thrift, Madison Guaranty Savings and Loan. Independent counsel Kenneth W. Starr interviewed Hillary in April 1995 to gather information about Whitewater to be presented to a grand jury. In January 1996, Hillary testified before a federal grand jury in Washington, D.C., about Rose Law Firm legal records that were mysteriously found two years after they had been subpoenaed. The appearance was the first time in U.S. history that a first lady testified under oath before a grand jury.

The Senate Special Whitewater Committee report by the Republican majority excoriated Hillary, portraying her as the chief culprit in White House attempts to impede investigations into Whitewater,

the dissolution of Madison Guaranty and Foster's death. The Republicans contended that the first lady's actions fit a pattern of "concealing, controlling and even destroying damaging information." However, they stopped short of charging her with any criminal behavior. Senate Democrats, in their minority report, however, found no evidence of unethical or unlawful conduct by the first lady and were dismayed by the GOP attacks on her.

News of Hillary's experience in trading in commodities futures between October 1978 and March 1980 kicked up a storm in early 1994. Her initial investment of about $1,000 yielded earnings of about $100,000. Hillary's detractors lost no time speculating that she had benefited from insider trading information. Some of her defenders, however, said that her profits were similar to those of others who were in the cattle futures market at the time she was.

From 1995 to 1996, Hillary adopted a less visible role in the administration, although she was still one of her husband's most important informal advisers. She continued to make public appearances mainly to address issues involving women and children. After much talk about the appropriateness of her attendance at the Fourth World Conference on Women, held in Beijing, China, in September 1995, Hillary went to the meeting and spoke out about the abuses of women that occurred in China and other parts of the world, including sterilization and forced abortions. Her outspokenness won her praise from some quarters and silenced critics for the time being.

In 1996, reports—which stemmed from Bob Woodward's book *The Choice*—emerged that the first lady had consulted a New Age spiritual adviser. Also revealed was that she engaged in imagined conversations with Eleanor Roosevelt, among others. Hillary laughed off the revelations and said she simply had met with a variety of thinkers to get their views on American life.

In *It Takes a Village*, published in 1995, Hillary summed up her ideas about children's issues. The title invoked an African saying that expresses the idea that a child is raised by a community of people. However innocuous that notion may be, the book became a target of criticism at the 1996 Republican national convention. GOP presidential nominee Bob Dole said, "I am here to tell you it does not take a village to raise a child. It takes a family to raise a child."

Hillary had a chance to respond to Dole's oblique attack when she gave her speech two weeks later at the Democratic convention. She said parenting had taught her "that to raise a happy, healthy and hopeful child, it takes a family." But she then listed other crucial influences on a child's life, including teachers and clergy, before adding, "Yes, it takes a village, and it takes a president" who supports communitarian values such as those propounded by her husband.

about attacking GOP priorities. Clinton came to be seen as a check on the draconian policy proposals of the Republican-led Congress, raising his stock with the public.

Chastised via public opinion polls about their questionable

tactics and mindful of the looming 1996 elections, Republicans in Congress recognized the value of getting something done. Clinton consequently could claim victory on issues ranging from economics to social policy. Congress enacted a spate of bills he supported, including measures to revamp the welfare system, raise the minimum wage and guarantee health insurance for workers who leave their jobs. The president also wrung major concessions from the GOP on appropriations, winning additional funding for domestic programs that Republicans had initially refused to spend.

Nevertheless, Clinton continued to face constraints in dealing with a Congress controlled by the opposing party. Republicans clearly set the agenda and could justifiably claim that the ideological battle was waged on their turf. Clinton largely appropriated the GOP agenda, then tried to get as much of what he wanted that he could. For example, he was able to soften the provisions of the welfare reform measure and, with its enactment, fulfill his public vow to "end welfare as we know it." However, its central point—ending the six-decade federal guarantee of cash assistance to poor mothers and children—was anathema to many Democrats

Foreign Policy

Clinton, in a July 8, 1996, interview with the *New York Times,* outlined his three foreign policy objectives: (1) completing "the unfinished business of leaving the cold war behind"; (2) "dealing with the new security threats, ethnic hatreds and other kinds of internal blood-baths"; and (3) "building a new structure of opportunity and peace through trade investment and commerce."

The administration's pursuit of the first goal was evident in its policies regarding, for example, Russia and China. During his first term in office, Clinton requested, and Congress approved, billions of dollars for the former Soviet republics to encourage democratic and economic reforms and to help dismantle the Soviet nuclear arsenal. Clinton and Congress also continued to support Russian president Boris N. Yeltsin—despite his dissolution of the conservative-dominated Russian legislature and his ordering of an assault on the parliament building to oust the hard-liners—as democracy's best hope in Russia. The Friendship Act was enacted in 1993, which removed from the law books requirements for the registration of communist front organizations in the United States. Furthermore, as a result of a two-day summit in 1994, Clinton and Yeltsin agreed to accelerate the timetable provided for by the Strategic Arms Reduction Treaty (START II) for deactivating nuclear warheads. And Clinton announced that funds would be provided to underwrite trade and investment programs for Russia at the Commerce Department and the Overseas Private Investment Corporation and to pay for anticrime programs and support the establishment of new legal systems in Russia. The administration also certified that Russia was in compliance with the Jackson-Vanik amendment to the 1974 Trade Act, which was a step toward fully normalizing trade relations between Russia and the United States.

In a controversial move, Clinton granted most-favored-nation (MFN) trade status to China. As a candidate in 1992, Clinton talked tough about China, advocating confrontation with China's leaders over issues such as human rights. After assuming the presidency, however, Clinton found that his perspective changed and he began to pursue a policy of engagement. As he explained to the *New York Times,* "I concluded that if we were to revoke MFN we might cause serious short-term damage to them economically, but that they would not change their human rights policy—if anything, they would become more repressive—and that we would risk creating a new, I hesitate to say, cold war, but a very long-term fissure with a country that I think we still have some chance of influencing in a very positive way, to be a constructive partner in the 21st century." Looming behind these policy decisions was the possibility that China would emerge as the rival to America's status as the lone world superpower.

Regarding the second goal, Clinton waded into seemingly intractable situations in, for example, Somalia, Haiti and Bosnia, and he emerged with a mixed bag of successes and failures. Despite allegations that he governed by public opinion polls, Clinton took risky actions that clearly did not have the support of most Americans at the time and that were vehemently and publicly criticized by members of Congress.

Various clans took up arms to determine control of the east African nation of Somalia after the 22-year regime of strongman Mohammed Siad Barre collapsed in 1991. The following year, the U.N. Security Council endorsed an international airlift of food and medical supplies, and President Bush announced that the United States would send 28,000 troops to Somalia to join a U.N. peacekeeping force to distribute food. The peacekeepers came under attack in 1993 from the forces of Gen. Mohammed Farah Aidid, a local warlord whose faction controlled much of the Somalia capital city of Mogadishu. In response, the U.N. expanded what had been a humanitarian mission to include tracking down Aidid. The result of a series of subsequent attacks was numerous U.N. soldiers, U.S. Army Rangers and Somali civilians dead and wounded.

Clinton administration officials acknowledged that, having turned over the operation to the U.N., they failed to appreciate the ramifications of the changed mission, which directly involved U.S. troops in Somalia's domestic infighting. Clinton announced that most U.S. forces would be withdrawn from Somalia by March 31, 1994. In May Clinton issued a policy directive that the president would no longer relinquish command authority over U.S. forces participating in any U.N. peacekeeping mission, and that the administration would thoroughly review any new missions—to determine whether clearly defined goals and a clear "exit strategy" existed to conclude the operation. Despite this change in executive policy, critics—especially Republican leaders in Congress—continued to point to the Somalia fiasco to argue for restricting U.S. involvement in future U.N. peacekeeping missions.

During his first two years in office, Clinton struggled to end totalitarian rule in Haiti. Jean-Bertrand Aristide, democratically elected president of Haiti in 1990, was ousted by a military coup in 1991. In 1993, the United States was instrumental in getting the U.N. to impose an oil, arms and financial embargo against Haiti to pressure the military regime to step down. In response, the coup leaders agreed to permit Aristide's return by Oct. 30, 1993. However, as the deadline approached, armed Haitians

THE CLINTON PRESIDENCY 941

chased off U.S. and Canadian military engineers who were to aid in rebuilding efforts in keeping with the agreement. Clinton subsequently ordered the deployment of Navy ships to the waters off Haiti to enforce the embargo. Tensions ratcheted upward in 1994. The U.N. announced an almost complete economic embargo against Haiti; the Clinton administration imposed additional restrictions, including limits on financial transactions and a ban on commercial air service between Haiti and the United States. Haiti's military leaders ordered the expulsion of about 100 international human rights monitors from the island. By the fall, the administration had plans to invade Haiti. Although most members of Congress opposed an invasion, they did nothing to block it. Still, by ignoring demands that he seek congressional authorization before moving against the military regime in Haiti, Clinton took a gamble. Ultimately, the use of force was averted by an agreement forged by a high-level delegation dispatched by Clinton—which consisted of former president Jimmy Carter, former Joint Chiefs of Staff chairman Colin L. Powell Jr. and Senate Armed Services Committee Chairman Sam Nunn, D-Ga.—and Haitian military leaders. The coup leaders were able to leave the country safely, with their financial assets, in exchange for giving up power. Aristide subsequently resumed the presidency, and the embargo and other sanctions were dropped.

Following the end of the cold war, Yugoslavia broke into feuding republics riven by ancient ethnic rivalries. What remained of Yugoslavia was controlled by the Serbs, who fought for dominance and territory with the neighboring Croatians and the Bosnia-Herzegovina's Muslims. Although brutality and aggression emanated from all sides, the general consensus was that the Muslims were the outgunned victims. Debate among Clinton administration officials and members of Congress centered on three issues—whether airstrikes would work to deter Serbian aggression, whether the United States should act unilaterally to lift an international arms embargo that prevented Bosnian Muslims from adequately defending themselves, and whether U.S. ground forces should join United Nations peacekeepers in the former Yugoslavia. For years, however, no one on either side of Pennsylvania Avenue had an adequate answer to the Bosnia question or even a politically palatable solution.

In 1993, the administration initiated humanitarian airdrops to Bosnia; failed to persuade European allies on proposals to sell arms to Bosnia and conduct airstrikes on Serbian positions; and committed U.S. air power to defend allied peacekeeping forces that were assigned to protect six newly created Muslim enclaves. The administration received hard-won praise in 1994 for arranging talks aimed at establishing a Muslim-Croat union. While the White House authorized limited airstrikes against Serbian positions, which were largely unsuccessful in deterring further aggression by the Serbs, by year's end it acquiesced in the more conciliatory approach favored by the Europeans. Also, the United States stopped helping North Atlantic Treaty Organization (NATO) countries enforce the arms embargo, but it continued to observe the U.N.-mandated restriction and sold no arms to the Bosnian Muslims. In the spring of 1995, after Serb forces overran U.N.-designated "safe areas," Clinton said the United

States should be prepared to join its NATO allies to strengthen the U.N. peacekeeping forces. In the summer, U.S. and other NATO aircraft launched an assault on Serb military targets in response to the heavy shelling the Serbs had administered on Sarajevo, the capital of Bosnia-Herzegovina. The bombing attacks were suspended when Serb leaders agreed to enter into negotiations for a cease-fire. In a dramatic turn of events, U.S.-brokered talks among the warring Yugoslav factions produced a peace agreement. Despite widespread public and congressional opposition, Clinton agreed to deploy U.S. ground troops to enforce the agreement. By 1996, 20,000 U.S. troops were committed to the peacekeeping mission, with no resulting combat casualties. U.S. and NATO forces achieved their primary goals of pacifying the country and separating the warring parties. However, civil reconstruction and political unification lagged badly, necessitating the continued deployment of NATO troops.

Clinton's efforts toward his third stated goal, linking peace with trade, could be seen, for example, in his push for NAFTA and GATT, his extension of MFN to China and his lifting by executive order of the 18-year trade embargo against Vietnam. His actions meant, for NAFTA, alienating organized labor, a Democratic stronghold; for MFN to China, retreating from his campaign position; and for Vietnam, risking a public outcry over the sensitive POW-MIA issue. On the subject of commerce, Clinton told the *New York Times*, "I think it's been wrongly positioned as are you choosing money over values. It seems to me that if America is in the center of these emerging networks, it dramatically increases our leverage to work with people for peace, for human rights and for stability in the world."

Relationship with Congress

Clinton's success with Congress, as measured by Congressional Quarterly's annual presidential support study, went from near-record highs to a record low to a record rebound. The numbers both revealed and masked aspects of the president's changing relationship with Congress from 1993 to 1996.

In conducting the presidential support study, CQ reporters and editors examined each roll call vote to determine if the president took a position on it. The success rate is the percentage of times the House and Senate voted to support the president's position. The CQ study has several limitations and should be regarded as only one of several tools for measuring a president's effectiveness. One limitation is that the study does not include voice votes, even though some important issues are decided without a recorded vote, particularly in the Senate. In addition, the study does not include presidential positions that never reached the floor. For example, a controversial nomination that is withdrawn and never is voted on does not count against the president. Such an event, however, clearly would have an impact on the chief executive's overall effectiveness in Congress. The study also tends to conceal those instances in which the president settles for less than he sought. While he supports the final version of a bill, his willingness to compromise throughout the legislative process is not reflected in the support score. Furthermore, the CQ study gives equal standing to all floor votes, regardless of their significance. So, a vote on which the president has invested considerable political capital and a vote on a routine authorization are weighed the same.

Clinton's 1992 election gave the Democrats control of both the executive and legislative branches for the first time in a dozen years. As Clinton took office, the Democratic leadership in Congress seemed intent on establishing an image of competence at governing. By far the most significant factor in Clinton's high success rate in 1993—86.4 percent of the 191 roll calls votes on which he declared a position—was that he was working with a Congress controlled by his party. However, Democratic loyalty was not the sole reason for the victories. Clinton showed a willingness and considerable ability to work with Congress. In addition, legislation that Democrats in Congress favored and that had been blocked or diluted by vetoes or veto threats by Republican administrations moved swiftly through the process once Clinton was sworn in. The president gained points on his success rate simply by expressing support for those bills. Clinton's 1993 tally ranked him near the top for presidents in their first year in office. In 1953, Republican Dwight D. Eisenhower had an 89 percent success rate, and in 1964, Democrat Lyndon B. Johnson's success rate was 88 percent.

1994 proved a paradox for Clinton: He won a remarkable 86.4 percent of the 140 roll call votes on which he took a position, but by most accounts he had a mediocre legislative year and a disastrous political year. Congress backed him a very high percentage of the time, but it did not vote on a large chunk of his agenda. Health care reform became the focus of the administration's efforts, but health care legislation never made it to the floor of either chamber. Other priorities were shoved aside. Democratic leaders in Congress also mistakenly advised Clinton that they could deliver his legislative agenda without the help of Republicans; many legislative victories from the year before came with no GOP support at all. However, the Democratic troops proved less loyal in 1994 than in 1993, while, for the most part, Republicans remained steadfastly opposed to the administration. Clinton's support score made him unmatched as a second-year president since Lyndon Johnson, who in 1965 racked up a 93 percent record.

In a record-setting year of reversal on Capitol Hill, Clinton in 1995 had a success rate in Congress of 36.2 percent of the 235 roll call votes on which he took a position, the lowest score since CQ began its study in 1953. The drastic drop from 1993 and 1994 reflected the energy and unity of the new Republican majority in Congress. Votes were more frequent and more partisan than in any previous session studied by CQ. The Republican leadership's agenda, including the "Contract with America," eclipsed Clinton's legislative plans. Although the president supported some GOP initiatives, he opposed far more of them. The strategy of filibuster, cloture and veto threats led to major elements of the Republican agenda either dead, vetoed or in trouble. Some argued that this was evidence that Clinton had a very good year with Congress, notwithstanding his low success rate on votes. Furthermore, Clinton's standoff with Congress seemed to raise his stock with the public, according to poll results.

Clinton's fortunes changed dramatically in 1996. The "Comeback Kid" set a record with a turnabout in the legislative arena. His success score was 55.1 percent, based on 138 roll call votes, which was the largest one-year jump since CQ began measuring presidential support. Clinton was able to reemerge as a legislative force in 1996 for several reasons. First, the House Republicans who stormed into Washington under a banner of revolutionary change following the 1994 elections came to recognize the benefits of compromise and incremental change. Second, Clinton tacked to the right on a number of issues in a determined bid to seize the political center. Third, the 1996 elections exerted powerful pressures on the president and members of both parties in Congress to produce legislative accomplishments. As a result, votes were far less partisan and more legislation moved through the process. The Republicans also hurt themselves badly by betting that by shutting down much of the federal government they could force Clinton to accept their plan to balance the budget. The public disliked their tactics, and the president emerged from the showdown in a far stronger position.

Scandals

The Clinton administration was plagued by so-called scandals and alleged ethical lapses. The character issue surrounding Clinton that was raised during the 1992 campaign laid the groundwork for the suspicion with which various incidents relating to the administration and to the president were met. Perhaps more important, beginning with the 104th Congress, attack politics permeated Republican-controlled investigatory and oversight committees. The GOP aggressively used the ethics process as a political bludgeon. While some administration officials were forced to resign and other individuals were convicted of wrongdoing as a result of their activities, Clinton was readily reelected and saw his approval rating rise as time went on.

The issues under investigation included the Clintons' personal financial involvement in a failed Arkansas land deal, the firing of White House travel office employees, the request for FBI background files on former Republican administration officials, a pending sexual harassment suit and 1996 campaign financing.

WHITEWATER

Throughout Clinton's first term, questions persisted about a 1978 investment Bill and Hillary Clinton made in an Arkansas real estate venture as well as their involvement with a rogue Arkansas thrift operator, James McDougal. The real estate venture was the Whitewater Development Co., which was formed by McDougal and his wife, Susan, with the Clintons. McDougal was to run the business. A 1992 report commissioned by the Clintons said the couple had invested $68,900, a 50 percent stake, and had lost almost all the money. Among the issues in contention were whether the Clintons took an appropriate tax loss on their investment, whether McDougal got preferential treatment for his thrift—Madison Guaranty Savings and Loan—from regulators because of his relationship with the

Clintons, and whether any money was improperly diverted from the thrift into Clinton's 1984 gubernatorial campaign. Madison Guaranty was regulated by Arkansas officials appointed by then-Gov. Clinton. Hillary Clinton, as an attorney at the Rose Law Firm, represented the thrift before state regulators. Also under investigation was Capital Management Services, an investment firm that made loans guaranteed by the Small Business Administration. The firm was owned by David Hale, a Clinton supporter who said Clinton asked him to make a $300,000 loan from Capital Management to Susan McDougal. More than $100,000 of the loan ended up in Whitewater accounts. The Clintons denied any wrongdoing.

Further complicating the Whitewater controversy was the July 1993 suicide of deputy White House counsel Vincent W. Foster Jr. A Clinton friend and adviser as well as former partner in the Rose Law Firm, Foster had had some Whitewater dealings in the Clintons' behalf. And, some insisted that Foster had not committed suicide but had been murdered and his body secretly moved to the spot where U.S. Park Police discovered it.

Attorney General Janet Reno on Jan. 20, 1994, appointed Robert B. Fiske Jr., a Wall Street lawyer who had served as a U.S. attorney, as special counsel to investigate Whitewater. On June 30, 1994, Fiske announced that no evidence existed to warrant charging any White House or Treasury Department official with obstructing the Resolution Trust Corporation (RTC) investigation of Madison, and no evidence of foul play was found in Foster's death. With reauthorization of the independent counsel law (PL 103-270), a federal three-judge panel on Aug. 5, 1994, named former U.S. solicitor general Kenneth W. Starr as independent counsel for Whitewater.

In 1994 the Democratic-led Congress also held hearings on the growing Whitewater controversy, focusing on whether the White House attempted to influence the federal investigation. Although the hearings proved embarrassing for the administration, no evidence was produced to indicate criminal wrongdoing. After the Republicans won control of Congress as a result of the 1994 elections, the Senate established a special Whitewater committee to reopen the congressional inquiry. The committee examined the Clintons' land investments in Arkansas, their connection to Madison Guaranty and Foster's suicide. *(Congressional hearings, box, p. 944)*

In 1996, Starr secured indictments against James B. McDougal, the owner of Madison Guaranty and a partner in Whitewater, and others associated with the thrift. An Arkansas jury acquitted two Arkansas bankers who were accused of illegally funneling bank funds into Clinton's 1990 gubernatorial campaign. A second jury convicted McDougal; his wife, Susan; and Democratic Arkansas Gov. Jim Guy Tucker on bank fraud charges.

WHITE HOUSE TRAVEL OFFICE AND FBI FILES

Seven employees of the travel office, which made travel arrangements for the White House press corps, were fired in 1993 for alleged financial mismanagement. Republicans suggested that the shake-up was precipitated by people close to the president who were looking to benefit financially. A White House report acknowledged that the dismissals were mishandled due to bad judgment. Five of the seven fired employees were reinstated in different positions, and four aides involved in the dismissal were reprimanded. *(Congressional hearings, box, p. 944)*

The White House personnel security office in 1993 and 1994 obtained hundreds of FBI files on federal employees of past GOP administrations. The White House insisted that it was an error; Clinton called it an "honest bureaucratic snafu." Both the House and Senate held hearings to determine how the Clinton administration came to have the files and what was done with them. The hearings sparked bitter division between Democrats, who said Republicans were exploiting for political purposes a serious but innocent bureaucratic blunder, and Republicans, who contended that Clinton's team may have been engaging in a dirty-tricks campaign to dig up sensitive information on former GOP officials. *(Congressional hearings, box, p. 944)*

CABINET OFFICERS

Three Clinton administration cabinet officers became the subject of independent counsel investigations. Agriculture Secretary Mike Espy was alleged to have improperly accepted gifts from businesses regulated by the Agriculture Department. He resigned at the end of 1994.

Several facets of Commerce Secretary Ronald Brown's financial dealings came under question, including a $500,000 profit from a business deal in which he did not invest his own money, an alleged $700,000 bribe Brown agreed to accept to help lift the U.S. ban on trade with Vietnam and claims that he filed misleading financial disclosure forms. Brown strongly denied any wrongdoing. With Brown's 1996 death in a plane crash, the probe was closed.

During the background check before being confirmed in his post, HUD Secretary Cisneros underreported to the FBI how much he had paid to his former mistress after his affair with her ended in the late 1980s. The false statements to the government could be considered criminal if they were "material," or capable of altering the outcome of a decision. Cisneros resigned as HUD secretary at the beginning of Clinton's second term.

A fourth member of the Clinton cabinet also came under fire—Energy Secretary Hazel O'Leary. Republicans in Congress initiated hearings on her allegedly extravagant foreign trade missions. A 1996 Energy Department inspector general report said poor planning and bad management accounted for the high expenses, but it did not single out any individual for blame. Republicans, who pressed for her resignation, also questioned O'Leary about her hiring of a media tracking service to rate reporters. She left the administration in early 1997.

PAULA JONES

Former Arkansas state employee Paula Jones filed a lawsuit in 1994 charging that she had been sexually harassed by Clinton when he was governor of Arkansas. Jones claimed that Clinton had sent a state trooper to invite her to Clinton's hotel room, where he asked her for sex. Clinton denied the charge. In December 1994, a federal court granted a stay in the Jones matter,

WHITEWATER, TRAVEL OFFICE, FBI FILES BROUGHT ON CONGRESSIONAL INQUIRIES

Congress held hearings on Clinton administration scandals regarding Whitewater, the White House travel office and FBI background files.

Whitewater

"Whitewater" became shorthand for investigations into the failed Arkansas land deal in which the Clintons had invested in the 1980s; the dissolution of Madison Guaranty Savings and Loan, an Arkansas thrift at the center of Whitewater; and the suicide of Deputy White House Counsel Vincent W. Foster Jr., who had handled legal work for the Clintons related to Whitewater.

Beginning the week of July 25, 1994, the House and Senate Banking committees held separate hearings on the narrow "Washington" sliver of the controversy, exploring potentially improper contacts between White House staff aides and bank regulators. Although no evidence was produced to indicate that any Clinton administration official tried to derail the probe by the regulators, the hearings uncovered details of a number of improper contacts, evasive testimony before Congress by administration officials and a widespread Whitewater political damage control effort within the White House. Two top Treasury officials resigned as a result of the hearings: Deputy Treasury Secretary Roger C. Altman, who had been acting head of the Resolution Trust Corporation, which conducted the original investigation into the Whitewater-Madison link, and White House counsel Bernard Nussbaum, who participated in briefings with Altman and advised the Clintons on Whitewater.

In the final report issued Jan. 3, 1995, Senate Banking Committee Democrats said no laws or ethical standards were breached as a result of the contacts between White House aides and Treasury officials. The Democrats detailed many conflicts and inconsistencies in the testimony of administration officials but did not say whose testimony they believed to be more accurate. Republicans launched a stinging assault on administration officials and their lack of candor.

In the Republican-led 104th Congress, the Senate voted May 17, 1995, to set up the Special Committee on Whitewater, adopting S Res 120 by 96–3. The resolution provided $950,000 for the staff and for other expenses and gave the committee subpoena power and the authority to grant immunity to witnesses. Chairing the panel was Sen. Alfonse M. D'Amato, R-N.Y.

The Senate opened July 18, 1995, with questions about what went on in Foster's office between the time his body was discovered until U.S. Park Police and FBI agents were given supervised access to the office. The panel also examined phone calls between Hillary Rodham Clinton, first lady chief of staff Margaret Williams, and attorney friend Susan Thomases shortly after Foster's death; the transfer of Foster's files from Williams to one of the Clintons' personal lawyers; and disclosures that Treasury officials made to the White House.

Averting a court showdown, the White House Dec. 22, 1995, turned over notes taken by White House Associate Counsel William Kennedy III during a Nov. 5, 1993, meeting in which administration aides had discussed Whitewater. The White House had refused to release the notes, contending that they were protected by attorney-client privilege. On Dec. 20, the Senate voted 51–45 to refer the matter to a federal court. The Senate 45–51 rejected a substitute offered by Paul Sarbanes, D-Md., to direct the Whitewater Committee to exhaustively explore ways of getting Kennedy's notes without going to court.

On April 17, 1996, members adopted S Res 246, calling for a continuation of hearings until June 14 and authorizing an additional $450,000. The committee's initial authorization expired Feb. 29.

On June 11, 1996, committee Democrats blocked GOP efforts to give former Arkansas banker and municipal judge David L. Hale special immunity to testify before the panel. Hale had directly linked Clinton to misdeeds regarding Whitewater, accusations Clinton had denied under oath.

In their final report issued June 18, 1996, committee Republicans portrayed a fledgling Clinton administration that feared the legal and political fallout from investigations into Whitewater and that used the power of the executive branch to undermine the probes. Crossing the line of propriety, the report said, senior administration officials obtained confidential information about the RTC inquiry into Madison. The Republicans said the White House's misuse of power was clearly evident in the hours and days following Foster's suicide. White House officials mishandled documents in Foster's office and thwarted law enforcement authorities in their investigation of Foster's death, the report said. The GOP report alleged that Mrs. Clinton in 1988 ordered the destruction of records related to her representation of Madison Guaranty at the same time federal regulators were investigating the savings and loan. But the Republicans stopped short of charging her with criminal behavior. In their questioning of Mrs. Clinton's actions, Republicans also pointed out the discovery in August 1995 of missing billing records from the Rose Law Firm, where Mrs. Clinton worked, in the White House private quarters. The Republicans contended that she likely placed the records in the White House book room.

The Democrats on the Senate Special Whitewater Committee issued a dissenting report, which drew sharply different conclusions. They said Clinton did not misuse his office as either president or governor of Arkansas. The Democrats expressed surprise at the Republican "venom" directed toward Mrs. Clinton. The Democrats concluded that the White House did not interfere with ongoing investigations into Whitewater and related matters by the Resolution Trust Corporation and other agencies. The evidence presented to the committee showed no unethical or unlawful conduct by any

accepting the White House contention that the president should not be subject to civil suits while in office. That ruling was appealed, and the U.S. Supreme Court decided in May 1997 that a sitting president was not excused from facing lawsuits over issues unrelated to his official duties.

CAMPAIGN FINANCE

In August 1996, an Arkansas jury acquitted two bankers of felony charges that they illegally used bank funds to reimburse political donations to Clinton's 1990 gubernatorial campaign.

White House official in the days after Foster's suicide, Democrats said. As for the billing records, Democrats pointed out that the documents supported Mrs. Clinton's claim that she did minor work for Madison Guaranty during the time she was with the Rose Law Firm.

Before the House Banking Committee in August 1996, RTC investigator L. Jean Lewis testified that administration officials repeatedly tried to obstruct her inquiry into Madison. Lewis said that substantial evidence existed of wrongdoing at Madison and that the Clintons should have known that the thrift was probably covering Whitewater losses. Democrats on the committee pointed out that the Bush administration's Justice Department did not pursue the investigation because Lewis had provided insufficient proof of criminal activity.

White House Travel Office

Seven White House travel office employees were fired on May 19, 1993, amid allegations of mismanagement and possible financial wrongdoing. In a report issued July 2, 1993, White House chief of staff Thomas F. McLarty III acknowledged that poor judgment led to the firings. Five fired employees were offered new jobs, and Congress provided $150,000 in the fiscal 1994 transportation appropriations bill (PL 103-122) to cover their legal expenses.

Office director Billy Dale was indicted on charges of embezzling $68,000 from the travel office; he was acquitted in November 1995. Dale admitted moving more than $50,000 to his personal checking account from office funds, but he said the money went back into arranging accommodations for reporters traveling with the president, the office's main function. He was the only one of the seven to be indicted.

The House Judiciary Committee on July 20, 1993, adversely reported H Res 198 (H Rept 103-183), to force a congressional inquiry into allegations of misconduct at the travel office. However, when the GOP assumed the majority in the 104th Congress, the House Government Reform and Oversight Committee opened an investigation.

In the committee report issued Sept. 18, 1996, Republicans said the president and first lady fired the employees so they could hire their own supporters and then falsely accused the employees of corruption. It said the White House "politicized" the FBI and the Internal Revenue Service by inappropriately bringing them into the White House travel office investigation to create the impression that the administration was concerned about possible criminal activity. The report also said that the White House obstructed the review of documents belonging to deputy counsel Foster after his suicide, in part because of concerns about the travel office matter.

Democrats said the Clintons legally could fire the employees for running an office with questionable financial practices and they accused Republicans of using smear tactics.

Committee Chairman William F. Clinger, R-Pa., had threatened to force a House vote on a resolution lodging contempt of Congress charges against White House counsel Jack Quinn after Clinton invoked executive privilege in refusing to give additional files on the case to the committee. Clinger then expanded his request to included documents relating to another matter—the White House's possession of FBI background files on hundreds of Republicans. An agreement was reached that allowed members of Congress and their staffs access to documents relating to probes of the travel office and the FBI files.

Congress in 1996 appropriated $500,000 to reimburse the travel office employees for legal costs incurred defending themselves. The bulk of the money, provided for in the fiscal 1997 omnibus appropriations bill (PL 104-208), was earmarked for Dale. Sens. Harry Reid, D-Nev., and Carl Levin, D-Mich., said reimbursing Dale would reverse years of precedent in which Congress had declined to reimburse indicted persons. A Reid and Levin amendment to permit the reimbursement only if the U.S. Court of Claims determined that the compensation was legal and equitable was rejected 46–52 on Sept. 12.

FBI Files

The House and Senate in 1996 inquired into reports that the White House in 1993 and 1994 had improperly collected hundreds of FBI files on Reagan and Bush administration officials.

The House Government Reform and Oversight Committee held a hearing on the matter June 26. White House personnel security director Craig Livingstone, who had directed the file search, told the committee he was resigning. Livingstone acknowledged that some of the files contained financial reports from the Internal Revenue Service, but he denied that any information was used for nefarious reasons. He said the list of people needing backgrounds checks that was provided by the Secret Service was out of date. However, Secret Service official Richard Miller had told the Senate Judiciary Committee that his agency would not have provided such a list without a specific request. House committee Republicans also pressured Livingstone to disclose who hired him.

Anthony B. Marceca, a former civilian Army employee who was detailed to Livingstone's office, told the House committee that he had obtained the files as part of a project to update the list of those needing White House security clearance.

Livingstone replayed much of the testimony before the Senate Judiciary Committee June 28. Marceca refused to appear, invoking his Fifth Amendment protection against self-incrimination. The Judiciary Committee voted July 16 to subpoena Marceca and also commanded him to turn over relevant documents regarding the unauthorized gathering of FBI files. Marceca appeared in a closed-door session July 18 but again invoked the Fifth Amendment and did not produce any documents.

Senior Clinton aide Bruce R. Lindsey had been named as an unindicted coconspirator in the case. Clinton testified by videotape as a witness for the defense.

In the closing days of the 1996 presidential campaign, a rash of news stories emerged about foreign contributions—in partic-

ular, from Asian interests—to the Democratic National Committee (DNC). Before the election, the Democrats returned contributions that they could not determine the source of and that they found came from the parent company in a foreign nation instead of its U.S. subsidiary. (Federal election law allows American subsidiaries of foreign companies to contribute to political campaigns if the money was earned in the United States.)

After the election, more disturbing details emerged about the Democrats' fund-raising efforts. Republicans seized the issue and initiated congressional inquiries in 1997. At the heart of the probes by the House Government Reform and Oversight Committee and the Senate Governmental Affairs Committee were questions about whom Democrats were willing to associate with and accept money from to finance Clinton's reelection campaign. Issues to be examined included:

• White House "coffees" with the president, overnight stays and attendance at other White House events. The White House hosted more than 100 coffees between the 1994 and 1996 elections and invited nearly 1,000 guests to spend the night at the White House during Clinton's first term, many in the Lincoln Bedroom. Republican critics questioned whether participation in these activities were offered in exchange for political donations. And, while these events may have been legal, Republicans hoped to paint a picture of an administration too willing to push the bounds of propriety in a quest for campaign cash. Democrats pointed out that previous Republican administrations had hosted similar fund-raising events on White House grounds.

• Illegal campaign contributions from foreigners. The FBI investigated whether the Chinese government attempted to influence the 1996 elections and U.S. policy with illegal contributions. Republicans criticized Clinton and the DNC for relying on fund-raisers with connections to China, even after the FBI warned two midlevel National Security Council aides and six members of Congress of the alleged plan to influence congressional races. Chinese officials denied the allegations, and Clinton said neither he nor his senior aides were told of the FBI briefing.

• Vice President Al Gore's fund-raising efforts. Critics suggested that fund-raising calls Gore made from the White House using a DNC credit card violated a federal statute that prohibited political fund-raising on federal property. In a March 1997 news conference, Gore insisted he had done nothing wrong and that there was "no controlling legal authority that says that any of these activities violated any law."

• Donation accepted on White House grounds. Margaret Williams, the first lady's chief of staff, accepted a campaign donation at the White House. The check was for the DNC, and Williams forwarded it to party headquarters. Federal employees were legally prohibited from accepting or soliciting contributions while on government property. Williams explained that she had acted out of politeness, and White House lawyers insisted that she had not violated any law on political solicitations on government property.

• Computerized database of White House visitors. Republicans wanted to know if White House aides improperly granted access to the computerized database of White House visitors to Democratic campaign workers for fund-raising purposes. The computerized database, which was maintained at taxpayer expense, contained the names, addresses and other identifying information of about 230,000 people who visited the White House

for reasons ranging from official visits to Christmas parties.

• Former associate attorney general Webster L. Hubbell's income. Hubbell, who went to prison for overbilling clients at the Rose Law Firm, reportedly received more than $400,000 in income from businesses controlled by the Riadys, the family that owned the Indonesia-based conglomerate the Lippo Group; other Clinton associates; and Democratic donors since he left the Justice Department in 1994. Of particular interest was $100,000 that Hubbell reportedly received from one of James T. Riady's Hong Kong companies following a June 1994 meeting that Riady attended at the White House. Republicans in Congress and independent counsel Starr questioned whether the payment was made to discourage Hubbell from cooperating with Whitewater investigators. Hubbell denied the suggested link. The Justice Department and Congress investigated whether the Chinese government tried to funnel donations and payments through Lippo subsidiaries to influence U.S. elections. Republicans also charged that contributions that could be tied to the Riadys influenced U.S. policy toward Indonesia. The Clinton administration denied the charge.

Reno in April 1997 rejected a request from Senate Judiciary Committee Chairman Orrin G. Hatch of Utah and nine other Republicans on the committee for an independent counsel to deal with questions about 1996 Democratic fund-raising on federal property and whether foreign countries curried favor with campaign donations. She said the allegations did not meet the standard for appointment of an independent counsel

Reelection

Clinton assumed the presidency in 1993 with big plans for an activist government. But his reach exceeded his grasp. His first two years were fraught with failures and missteps, which were capped by the demise of the administration's health care reform proposal. After the 1994 elections, when Republicans won a majority in both houses of Congress for the first time in 40 years, Clinton was asked to defend his "relevance." The pundits and the prognosticators who foresaw his electoral defeat in 1996 were wrong, however. Clinton won reelection in a three-way race with 49.2 percent of the popular vote, 379 electoral votes, and 31 states and the District of Columbia. That Clinton was able to recover from the devastating blow of the Democrats' loss of Congress and to score a landslide electoral college triumph was a testament to his political skills as well as his tenacity.

While media attention focused on the GOP-led 104th Congress, House Speaker Newt Gingrich and the "Contract with America" in early 1995, Clinton started aggressively building up his campaign war chest. Then, in an unprecedented move in June 1995, 17 months before the presidential election, Clinton television advertisements began running across the country. The purpose of the ad campaign was to reshape the perception voters had of Clinton, to educate the electorate as to what he had done as president and to delineate policy proposals he supported. For example, the first set of ads sought to counter the president's liberal image by focusing on Clinton's record in the area of crime. Unlike traditional Democrats, Clinton supported the death penalty and stiff sentencing laws. He also had endorsed the Brady bill as well as the ban on assault weapons. By touting his record on crime, the ads effectively took the issue off the table as a point of contention with Republicans. A set of subsequent ads sought to brand the GOP as the enemy of Medicare and to cast Clinton as its defender and protector. The ad campaign, which was directed by political strategist Dick Morris, was concentrated in key swing states such as California, Florida, Ohio and Pennsylvania. The TV spots were kept from major media markets such as New York City, Los Angeles and the District of Columbia so that the press, which was concentrated in those areas, would not bring attention to them. The strategy worked.

Morris, in his 1997 book *Behind the Oval Office: Winning the Presidency in the Nineties,* stressed the importance, he believed, of the 1996 State of the Union address, in which Clinton articulated his "values" agenda. Morris wrote: "He tapped into a conclusion many people have reached in their personal lives: that the impediment to a better life is not primarily one's economic performance but communal problems—the quality of life for everyone. Such problems as too little time for family life, crime, environmental damage, the high cost of college, ubiquitous TV violence, the drug subculture and teen smoking, can be addressed only if we band together as a community." The idea was to couple values with economics and to stress the importance of families as well as personal responsibility. Clinton, for example, proposed expanding tax deductions for college tuition, installing V-chips in TV sets to allow parents to screen out violence and sexually explicit programs, preserving his Goals 2000 education initiative and expanding the earned income tax credit for working families. Clinton also said that government's responsibility to its citizens' economic future "begins with balancing the budget in a way that is fair to all Americans." And he declared that the era of big government was over. Generally speaking, Clinton appropriated traditional conservative themes, moved to the political middle and made a more direct appeal to the middle class.

In running for reelection in 1996, Clinton was able to exploit several unique assets. Upbeat reviews of the economy enabled him to stress optimism in the same way the "Morning in America" theme so effectively played in President Reagan's 1984 reelection bid. Clinton also muted differences with Republicans on volatile "wedge" issues such as crime and welfare reform by taking nontraditionally Democratic positions. And the absence of primary opposition early in 1996 freed Clinton to move to the political center while running ads in targeted states, tying Republican challenger Bob Dole to controversial and highly unpopular House Speaker Gingrich at a time when Dole was financially exhausted by his primary competition and unable to respond effectively.

Despite an economy that was humming and a world that was largely at peace, Clinton slumped at the end of the 1996 campaign. His 8 percentage point margin of victory over Dole was less than half the lead he enjoyed in a number of public opinion surveys just a week or two before the election. The cascade of stories about Democratic fund-raising improprieties took a toll, as did pointed attacks by Dole and Reform Party candidate Ross Perot on the series of scandals that reflected on the character of the president, the first lady and administration officials. Perot, for example, called Clinton the "all-time, world-record, grand-prize winner for corrupt campaign funding." Clinton's failure to reach the 50 percent threshold in the popular vote also was attributed, in part, to his decision to campaign for congressional candidates as the election approached—and his victory seemed assured—instead of making appearances solely on his own behalf to drive up his numbers. Many Democrats complained, however, that Clinton, who fared well as a counterweight to the Republican-controlled Congress, had turned his attention to congressional races too late in the campaign.

In geographical breadth, Clinton's reelection victory was strikingly similar to his first presidential victory in 1992. He swept the entire Northeast, most of the Midwest, all of the Pacific Coast states, and chunks of the Mountain West and the South. Of the nation's nine largest states, Clinton won eight (losing only Texas). Nationwide exit polling revealed the extent of Clinton's appeal. He won a majority of votes in every age group, running best among young voters. He ran ahead of Dole among all education categories, except college graduates. And he won a number of key voting blocs, such as Catholics and self-described moderates. The demographic advantage for Clinton most often mentioned during the campaign was the strong support he received from women voters. While Dole ran virtually even with Clinton among men, the incumbent ran roughly 16 percentage points ahead among women, the largest margin ever. Clinton was even with Dole among whites but enjoyed a big edge among minority voters. Clinton also won most major urban areas, took many of the nation's most populous suburban jurisdictions, and made deep inroads in rural America. Dole bested Clinton among upper-income voters; he won a plurality of the 1992 Perot voters who abandoned the third-party candidate in 1996; and he largely maintained the Republican base.

Despite Clinton's reelection, no one suggested it was the dawn of a new Democratic presidential era. Even Clinton was shy about claiming a mandate, especially given that he did not receive a majority of the popular vote and Republicans maintained control of both chambers of Congress. Both parties seemed aware that neither would have the upper hand. In the minds of most voters, Gingrich and the Republicans had gone too far in the 104th Congress. Voters were wary of GOP plans to radically reduce the size of government and to cut federal programs to provide tax breaks for the wealthy. Americans seemed to prefer small, doable proposals to grandiose schemes, evolutionary change to revolutionary convulsions. As a result, as Clinton took the oath of office for a second term, his agenda was chock-full of minimalist initiatives that would require the expenditure of little in the way of money or political capital.

Appendix

Glossary of Congressional Terms

AA—*(See Administrative Assistant.)*

Absence of a Quorum—Absence of the required number of members to conduct business in a house or a committee. When a quorum call or roll-call vote in a house establishes that a quorum is not present, no debate or other business is permitted except a motion to adjourn or motions to request or compel the attendance of absent members, if necessary by arresting them.

Absolute Majority—A vote requiring approval by a majority of all members of a house rather than a majority of members present and voting. Also referred to as constitutional majority.

Account—Organizational units used in the federal budget primarily for recording spending and revenue transactions.

Act—(1) A bill passed in identical form by both houses of Congress and signed into law by the president or enacted over his veto. A bill also becomes an act without the president's signature if he does not return it to Congress within 10 days (Sundays excepted) and if Congress has not adjourned within that period. (2) Also, the technical term for a bill passed by at least one house and engrossed.

Adjourn—A formal motion to end a day's session or meeting of a house or a committee. A motion to adjourn usually has no conditions attached to it, but it may specify the day or time for reconvening or make reconvening subject to the call of the chamber's presiding officer or the committee's chairman.

Adjourn for More Than Three Days—Under Article I, Section 5 of the Constitution, neither house may adjourn for more than three days without the approval of the other. The necessary approval is given in a concurrent resolution and agreed to by both houses, which may permit one or both to take such an adjournment.

Adjournment Sine Die—Final adjournment of an annual or two-year session of Congress; literally, adjournment without a day. The two houses must agree to a privileged concurrent resolution for such an adjournment. A sine die adjournment precludes Congress from meeting again until the next constitutionally fixed date of a session (January 3 of the following year) unless Congress determines otherwise by law or the president calls it into special session. Article II, Section 3 of the Constitution authorizes the president to adjourn both houses until such time as he thinks proper when the two houses cannot agree to a time of adjournment, but no president has ever exercised this authority.

Adjournment to a Day (and Time) Certain—An adjournment that fixes the next date and time of meeting for one or both houses. It does not end an annual session of Congress.

Administration Bill—A bill drafted in the executive office of the president or in an executive department or agency to implement part of the president's program. An administration bill is introduced in Congress by a member who supports it or as a courtesy to the administration.

Administrative Assistant (AA)—The title usually given to a member's chief aide, political advisor, and head of office staff. The administrative assistant often represents the member at meetings with visitors or officials when the member is unable (or unwilling) to attend.

Adoption—The usual parliamentary term for approval of a conference report. It is also commonly applied to amendments.

Advice and Consent—The Senate's constitutional role in consenting to or rejecting the president's nominations to executive branch and judicial offices and the treaties he submits. Confirmation of nominees requires a simple majority vote of the full Senate. Treaties must be approved by a two-thirds majority of senators present and voting.

Aisle—The center aisle of each chamber. When facing the presiding officer, Republicans usually sit to the right of the aisle, Democrats to the left. When a member speaks of "my side of the aisle" or "this side," he means his party.

Amendment—A formal proposal to alter the text of a bill, resolution, amendment, motion, treaty, or some other text. Technically, it is a motion. An amendment may strike out (eliminate) part of a text, insert new text, or strike out and insert—that is, replace all or part of the text with new text. The texts of amendments considered on the floor are printed in full in the *Congressional Record*.

Amendment in the Nature of a Substitute—Usually, an amendment to replace the entire text of a measure. It strikes out everything after the enacting clause and inserts a version that may be somewhat, substantially, or entirely different. When a committee adopts extensive amendments to a measure, it often incorporates them into such an amendment. Occasionally, the term is applied to an amendment that replaces a major portion of a measure's text.

Annual Authorization—Legislation that authorizes appropriations for a single fiscal year and usually for a specific amount. Under the rules of the authorization-appropriation process, an annually authorized agency or program must be reauthorized each year if it is to receive appropriations for that year. Sometimes Congress fails to enact the reauthorization but nevertheless provides appropriations to continue the program, circumventing the rules by one means or another.

Appeal—A member's formal challenge of a ruling or decision by the presiding officer. On appeal, a house or a committee may overturn the ruling by majority vote. The right of appeal ensures the body against arbitrary control by the chair. Appeals are rarely made in the House and are even more rarely successful. Rulings are more frequently appealed in the Senate and occasionally overturned, in part because its presiding officer is not the majority party's leader, as in the House.

Apportionment—The action, after each decennial census, of allocating the number of members in the House of Representatives to each state. By law, the total number of House members (not counting delegates and a resident commissioner) is fixed at 435. The number allotted to each state is based approximately on its proportion of the nation's total population. Since the Constitution guarantees each state one representative no matter how small its population, exact proportional distribution is virtually impossible. The mathematical formula currently used to determine the apportionment is called the Method of Equal Proportions. *(See Method of Equal Proportions.)*

Appropriated Entitlement—An entitlement program, such as veterans' pensions, that is funded through annual appropriations rather than by a permanent appropriation. Because such an entitlement law requires the government to provide eligible recipients the benefits to which they are entitled, whatever the cost, Congress must appropriate the necessary funds.

Appropriation—(1) Legislative language that permits a federal agency to incur obligations and make payments from the Treasury for specified purposes, usually during a specified period of time. (2) The specific amount of money made available by such language. The Constitution prohibits payments from the Treasury except "in Consequence of Appropriations made by Law." With some exceptions, the rules of both houses forbid consideration of appropriations for purposes that are unauthorized in law or of appropriation amounts larger than those authorized in law. The House of Representatives claims the exclusive right to originate appropriation bills—a claim the Senate denies in theory but accepts in practice.

At-Large—Elected by and representing an entire state instead of a district within a state. The term usually refers to a representative rather than to a senator. *(See Apportionment, Congressional District, Redistricting.)*

August Adjournment—A congressional adjournment during the month of August in odd-numbered years, required by the Legislative Reorganization Act of 1970. The law instructs the two houses to adjourn for a period of at least 30 days before the second day after Labor Day, unless Congress provides otherwise or if, on July 31, a state of war exists by congressional declaration.

Authorization—(1) A statutory provision that establishes or continues a federal agency, activity or program for a fixed or indefinite period of time. It may also establish policies and restrictions and deal with organizational and administrative matters. (2) A statutory provision that authorizes appropriations for an agency, activity, or program. The appropriations may be authorized for one year, several years, or an indefinite period of time, and the authorization may be for a specific amount of money or an indefinite amount ("such sums as may be necessary"). Authorizations of specific amounts are construed as ceilings on the amounts that subsequently may be appropriated in an appropriation bill, but not as minimums; either house may appropriate lesser amounts or nothing at all.

Authorization-Appropriation Process—The two-stage procedural system that the rules of each house require for establishing and funding federal agencies and programs: first, enactment of authorizing legislation that creates or continues an agency or program; second, enactment of appropriations legislation that provides funds for the authorized agency or program.

Automatic Roll Call—Under a House rule, the automatic ordering of the yeas and nays when a quorum is not present on a voice or division vote and a member objects to the vote on that ground. It is not permitted in the Committee of the Whole.

Backdoor Spending Authority—Authority to incur obligations that evades the normal congressional appropriations process because it is provided in legislation other than appropriation acts. The most common forms are borrowing authority, contract authority, and entitlement authority.

Balanced Budget Amendment—A proposal for a constitutional amendment mandating that federal expenditures not exceed federal revenues in any fiscal year.

Baseline—A projection of the levels of federal spending, revenues, and the resulting budgetary surpluses or deficits for the upcoming and subsequent fiscal years, taking into account laws enacted to date and assuming no new policy decisions. It provides a benchmark for measuring the budgetary effects of proposed changes in federal revenues or spending, assuming certain economic conditions.

Bicameral—Consisting of two houses or chambers. Congress is a bicameral legislature whose two houses have an equal role in enacting legislation. In most other national bicameral legislatures, one house is significantly more powerful than the other.

Bill—The term for the chief vehicle Congress uses for enacting laws. Bills that originate in the House of Representatives are designated as H.R., those in the Senate as S., followed by a number assigned in the order in which they are introduced during a two-year Congress. A bill becomes a law if passed in identical language by both houses and signed by the president, or passed over his veto, or if the president fails to sign it within 10 days after he has received it while Congress is in session.

Bills and Resolutions Introduced—Members formally present measures to their respective houses by delivering them to a clerk in the chamber when their house is in session. Both houses permit any number of members to join in introducing a bill or resolution. The first member listed on the measure is the sponsor; the other members listed are its cosponsors.

Bills and Resolutions Referred—After a bill or resolution is introduced, it is normally sent to one or more committees that have jurisdiction over its subject, as defined by House and Senate rules and precedents. A Senate measure is usually referred to the committee with jurisdiction over the predominant subject of its text, but it may be sent to two or more committees by unanimous consent or on a motion offered jointly by the majority and minority leaders. In the House, a rule requires the Speaker to refer a measure to the committee that has primary jurisdiction. The Speaker is also authorized to refer measures sequentially to additional committees.

Bipartisan Committee—A committee with an equal number of members from each political party. The House Committee on Standards of Official Conduct and the Senate Select Committee on Ethics are the only bipartisan, permanent full committees.

Borrowing Authority—Statutory authority permitting a federal agency, such as the Export-Import Bank, to borrow money from the public or the Treasury to finance its operations. It is a form of backdoor spending. To bring such spending under the control of the congressional appropriation process, the Congressional Budget Act requires that new borrowing authority shall be effective only to the extent and in such amounts as are provided in appropriations acts.

Budget—A detailed statement of actual or anticipated revenues and expenditures during an accounting period. For the national government, the period is the federal fiscal year (October 1–September 30). The budget usually refers to the president's budget submission to Congress early each calendar year. The president's budget estimates federal government income and spending for the upcoming fiscal year and contains detailed recommendations for appropriation, revenue, and other legislation. Congress is not required to accept or even vote directly on the president's proposals, and it often revises the president's budget extensively. *(See Fiscal Year.)*

Budget Act—Common name for the Congressional Budget and Impoundment Control Act of 1974, which established the basic procedures of the current congressional budget process; created the House and Senate budget committees; and enacted procedures for reconciliation, deferrals, and rescissions. *(See Budget Process, Deferral, Impoundment, Reconciliation, Rescission. See Also Gramm-Rudman-Hollings Act of 1985.)*

Budget and Accounting Act of 1921—The law that, for the first time, authorized the president to submit to Congress an annual budget for the entire federal government. Prior to the act, most federal agencies sent their budget requests to the appropriate congressional committees without review by the president.

Budget Authority—Generally, the amount of money that may be spent or obligated by a government agency or for a government program or activity. Technically, it is statutory authority to enter into obligations that normally result in outlays. The main forms of budget authority are appropriations, borrowing authority, and contract authority. It also includes authority to obligate and expend the proceeds of offsetting receipts and collections. Congress may make budget authority available for only one year, several years, or an indefinite period, and it may specify definite or indefinite amounts.

Budget Process—(1) In Congress, the procedural system it uses (a) to approve an annual concurrent resolution on the budget that sets goals for aggregate and functional categories of federal expenditures, revenues, and the surplus or deficit for an upcoming fiscal year; and (b) to implement those goals in spending, revenue, and, if necessary, reconciliation and debt-limit legislation. (2) In the executive branch, the process of formulating the president's annual budget, submitting it to Congress, defending it before congressional committees, implementing subsequent budget-related legislation, impounding or sequestering expenditures as permitted by law, auditing and evaluating programs, and compiling final budget data. The Budget and Accounting Act of 1921 and the Congressional Budget and Impoundment Control Act of 1974 established the basic elements of the current budget process. Major revisions were enacted in the Gramm-Rudman-Hollings Act of 1985 and the Budget Enforcement Act of 1990.

Budget Resolution—A concurrent resolution in which Congress establishes or revises its version of the federal budget's broad financial features for the upcoming fiscal year and several additional fiscal years. Like other concurrent resolutions, it does not have the force of law, but it provides the framework within which Congress subsequently considers revenue, spending, and other budget-implementing legislation. The framework consists of two basic elements: (1) aggregate budget amounts (total revenues, new budget authority, out-

lays, loan obligations and loan guarantee commitments, deficit or surplus, and debt limit); and (2) subdivisions of the relevant aggregate amounts among the functional categories of the budget. Although the budget resolution does not allocate funds to specific programs or accounts, the budget committees' reports accompanying the resolution often discuss the major program assumptions underlying its functional amounts. Unlike those amounts, however, the assumptions are not binding on Congress.

By Request—A designation indicating that a member has introduced a measure on behalf of the president, an executive agency, or a private individual or organization. Members often introduce such measures as a courtesy because neither the president nor any person other than a member of Congress can do so. The term, which appears next to the sponsor's name, implies that the member who introduced the measure does not necessarily endorse it. A House rule dealing with by-request introductions dates from 1888, but the practice goes back to the earliest history of Congress.

Calendar—A list of measures or other matters (most of them favorably reported by committees) that are eligible for floor consideration. The House has five calendars; the Senate has two. A place on a calendar does not guarantee consideration. Each house decides which measures and matters it will take up, when, and in what order, in accordance with its rules and practices.

Calendar Wednesday—A House procedure that on Wednesdays permits its committees to bring up for floor consideration nonprivileged measures they have reported The procedure is so cumbersome and susceptible to dilatory tactics, however, that committees rarely use it.

Call Up—To bring a measure or report to the floor for immediate consideration.

Casework—Assistance to constituents who seek assistance in dealing with federal and local government agencies. Constituent service is a high priority in most members' offices.

Casting Vote—The vice president's vote while presiding over the Senate. It may be cast only to break a tie vote, but the vice president is not required to vote.

Caucus—(1) A common term for the official organization of each party in each house. (2) The official title of the organization of House Democrats. House and Senate Republicans and Senate Democrats call their organizations "conferences." (3) A term for an informal group of members who share legislative interests, such as the Black Caucus, Hispanic Caucus, and Children's Caucus.

Censure—The strongest formal condemnation of a member for misconduct short of expulsion. A house usually adopts a resolution of censure to express its condemnation, after which the presiding officer reads its rebuke aloud to the member in the presence of his colleagues.

Chairman—The presiding officer of a committee, a subcommittee, or a task force. At meetings, the chairman preserves order, enforces the rules, recognizes members to speak or offer motions, and puts questions to a vote. The chairman of a committee or subcommittee usually appoints its staff and sets its agenda, subject to the panel's veto.

Chamber—The Capitol room in which a house of Congress normally holds its sessions. The chamber of the House of Representatives, officially called the Hall of the House, is considerably larger than that of the Senate because it must accommodate 435 representatives, four delegates, and one resident commissioner. Unlike the Senate chamber, members have no desks or assigned seats. In both chambers, the floor slopes downward to the well in front of the presiding officer's raised desk. A chamber is often referred to as "the floor," as when members are said to be on or going to the floor. Those expressions usually imply that the member's house is in session.

Christmas Tree Bill—Jargon for a bill adorned with amendments, many of them unrelated to the bill's subject, that provide benefits for interest groups, specific states, congressional districts, companies, and individuals.

Classes of Senators—A class consists of the 33 or 34 senators elected to a six-year term in the same general election. Since the terms of approximately one-third of the senators expire every two years, there are three classes.

Clean Bill—After a House committee extensively amends a bill, it often assembles its amendments and what is left of the bill into a new measure that one or more of its members introduces as a "clean bill." The revised measure is assigned a new number.

Clerk of the House—An officer of the House of Representatives responsible principally for administrative support of the legislative process in the House. The clerk is invariably the candidate of the majority party.

Clerk-Hire—The personal staff to which a member is entitled. The House sets a maximum number of staff and a monetary allowance for each member. The Senate does not have a maximum staff level, but does set a monetary allowance for each member.

Cloakrooms—Two rooms with access to the rear of each chamber's floor, one for each party's members, where members may confer privately, sit quietly, or have a snack. The presiding officer sometimes urges members who are conversing too loudly on the floor to retire to their cloakrooms.

Closed Rule—A special rule reported from the House Rules Committee that prohibits amendments to a measure or that only permits amendments offered by the reporting committee.

Cloture—A Senate procedure that limits further consideration of a pending proposal to 30 hours in order to end a filibuster. Sixteen senators must first sign and submit a cloture motion to the presiding officer. One hour after the Senate meets on the second calendar day thereafter, the chair puts the motion to a yea-and-nay vote following a live quorum call. If three-fifths of all senators (60 if there are no vacancies) vote for the motion, the Senate must take final action on the cloture proposal by the end of the 30 hours of consideration and may consider no other business until it takes that action. Cloture on a proposal to amend the Senate's standing rules requires approval by two-thirds of the senators present and voting.

Code of Official Conduct—A House rule that bans certain actions by House members, officers, and employees; requires them to conduct themselves in ways that "reflect creditably" on the House; and orders them to adhere to the spirit and the letter of House rules and those of its committees. The code's provisions govern the receipt of outside compensation, gifts, and honoraria and the use of campaign funds; prohibit members from using their clerk-hire allowance to pay anyone who does not perform duties commensurate with that pay; forbid discrimination in members' hiring or treatment of employees on the grounds of race, color, religion, sex, handicap, age, or national origin; order members convicted of a crime who might be punished by imprisonment of two or more years not to participate in committee business or vote on the floor until exonerated or reelected; and restrict employees' contact with federal agencies on matters in which they have a significant financial interest. The Senate's rules contain some similar prohibitions.

College of Cardinals—A popular term for the subcommittee chairmen of the appropriations committees, reflecting their influence over appropriation measures. The chairmen of the full appropriations committees are sometimes referred to as popes.

Comity—The practice of maintaining mutual courtesy and civility between the two houses in their dealings with each other and in members' speeches on the floor. Although the practice is largely governed by long-established customs, a House rule explicitly cautions its members not to characterize any Senate action or inaction, refer to individual senators except under certain circumstances, or quote from Senate proceedings except to make legislative history on a measure. The Senate has no rule on the subject, but references to the House have been held out of order on several occasions. Generally, the houses do not interfere with each other's appropriations, although minor conflicts sometimes occur. A refusal to receive a message from the other house has also been held to violate the practice of comity.

Committee—A panel of members elected or appointed to perform some service or function for its parent body. Congress has four types of committees: standing; special or select; joint; and, in the House, a Committee of the Whole.

Committees conduct investigations, make studies, issue reports and recommendations, and, in the case of standing committees, review and prepare measures on their assigned subjects for action by their respective houses. Most committees divide their work among several subcommittees. With rare exceptions, the majority party in a house holds a majority of the seats on its committees, and their chairmen are also from that party.

Committee Jurisdiction—The legislative subjects and other functions assigned to a committee by rule, precedent, resolution, or statute. A committee's title usually indicates the general scope of its jurisdiction but often fails to mention other significant subjects assigned to it.

Committee of the Whole—Common name of the Committee of the Whole House on the State of the Union, a committee consisting of all members of the House of Representatives. Measures from the union calendar must be considered in the Committee of the Whole before the House officially completes action on them; the committee often considers other major bills as well. A quorum of the committee is 100, and it meets in the House chamber under a chairman appointed by the Speaker. Procedures in the Committee of the Whole expedite consideration of legislation because of its smaller quorum requirement, its ban on certain motions, and its five-minute rule for debate on amendments. Those procedures usually permit more members to offer amendments and participate in the debate on a measure than is normally possible. The Senate no longer uses a Committee of the Whole.

Committee Ratios—The ratios of majority to minority party members on committees. By custom, the ratios of most committees reflect party strength in their respective houses as closely as possible.

Committee Report on a Measure—A document submitted by a committee to report a measure to its parent chamber. Customarily, the report explains the measure's purpose, describes provisions and any amendments recommended by the committee, and presents arguments for its approval.

Committee Veto—A procedure that requires an executive department or agency to submit certain proposed policies, programs, or action to designated committees for review before implementing them. Before 1983, when the Supreme Court declared that a legislative veto is unconstitutional, these provisions permitted committees to veto the proposals. They no longer do so, and the term is now something of a misnomer. Nevertheless, agencies usually take the pragmatic approach of trying to reach a consensus with the committees before carrying out their proposals, especially when an appropriations committee is involved.

Concurrent Resolution—A resolution that requires approval by both houses but is not sent to the president for his signature and therefore cannot have the force of law. Concurrent resolutions deal with the prerogatives or internal affairs of Congress as a whole. Designated H. Con. Res. in the House and S. Con. Res. in the Senate, they are numbered consecutively in each house in their order of introduction during a two-year Congress.

Conferees—A common title for managers, the members from each house appointed to a conference committee. The Senate usually authorizes its presiding officer to appoint its conferees. The Speaker appoints House conferees and, under a rule adopted in 1993, can remove conferees "at any time after an original appointment" and also appoint additional conferees at any time. Conferees are expected to support the positions of their houses despite their personal views, but in practice this is not always the case. The party ratios of conferees generally reflect the ratios in their houses.

Each house may appoint as many conferees as it pleases. House conferees often outnumber their Senate colleagues; however, each house has only one vote in a conference, so the size of its delegation is immaterial.

Conference—(1) A formal meeting or series of meetings between members representing each house to reconcile House and Senate differences on a measure (occasionally several measures). Since one house cannot require the other to agree to its proposals, the conference usually reaches agreement by compromise. When a conference completes action on a measure, or as much action as appears possible, it sends its recommendations to both houses in the form of a conference report, accompanied by an explanatory statement. (2) The official title of the organization of all Democrats or Republicans in the Senate and of all Republicans in the House of Representatives. *(See Party, Caucus.)*

Conference Committee—A temporary joint committee formed for the purpose of resolving differences between the houses on a measure or, occasionally, several measures. Voting in a conference committee is not by individuals, but by house as determined by a ma-

jority vote of each houses' conferees respectively. Both houses require that conference committees open their meetings to the public, although closed meetings can be held under certain circumstances. Otherwise, there are no congressional rules governing the organization of, or procedure in, a conference committee.

Conference Report—A document submitted to both houses that contains a conference committee's agreements for resolving differences on a measure. It must be signed by a majority of the conferees from each house separately and must be accompanied by an explanatory statement. Both houses prohibit amendments to a conference report and require it to be accepted or rejected in its entirety.

Congress—(1) The national legislature of the United States, consisting of the House of Representatives and the Senate. (2) The national legislature in office during a two-year period. Congresses are numbered sequentially; thus, the 1st Congress of 1789–1791 and the 102d Congress of 1991–1993. Before 1935, the two-year period began on the first Monday in December of odd-numbered years. Since then it has extended from January of an odd-numbered year through noon on January 3 of the next odd-numbered year. A Congress usually holds two annual sessions, but some have had three sessions and the 67th Congress had four. When a Congress expires, measures die if they have not yet been enacted.

Congressional Accountability Act of 1995 (CAA)—An act applying 11 labor, workplace, and civil rights laws to the legislative branch and establishing procedures and remedies for legislative branch employees with grievances in violation of these laws. The following laws are covered by the CAA: the Fair Labor Standards Act of 1938; Title VII of the Civil Rights Act of 1964; Americans with Disabilities Act of 1990; Age Discrimination in Employment Act of 1967; Family and Medical Leave Act of 1993; Occupational Safety and Health Act of 1970; Chapter 71 of Title 5, *U.S. Code* (relating to federal service labor-management relations); Employee Polygraph Protection Act of 1988; Worker Adjustment and Retraining Notification Act; Rehabilitation Act of 1973; and Chapter 43 of Title 38, *U.S. Code* (relating to veterans' employment and reemployment).

Congressional Budget Office (CBO)—A congressional support agency created by the Congressional Budget and Impoundment Control Act of 1974 to provide nonpartisan budgetary information and analysis to Congress and its committees. Under the original version of the Gramm-Rudman-Hollings Act, CBO played an equal role with the Office of Management and Budget in calculating sequestration data. After the Supreme Court struck down a related part of that act as unconstitutional in 1986, CBO's role was limited to providing advisory sequestration reports.

Congressional Directory—The official who's who of Congress, usually published during the first session of a two-year Congress.

Congressional District—The geographical area represented by a single member of the House of Representatives. For states with only one representative, the entire state is a congressional district. As of 1998, seven states had only one representative each: Alaska, Delaware, Montana, North Dakota, South Dakota, Vermont and Wyoming.

Congressional Record—The daily, printed, and substantially verbatim account of proceedings in both the House and Senate chambers. Extraneous materials submitted by members appear in a section titled "Extensions of Remarks." A "Daily Digest" appendix contains highlights of the day's floor and committee action plus a list of committee meetings and their agendas for the next day's session.

Although the official reporters of each house take down every word spoken during the proceedings, members are permitted to edit and "revise and extend" their remarks before they are printed. In the Senate section, all speeches, articles, and other material submitted by senators but not actually spoken or read on the floor are set off by large black dots, called bullets. However, bullets do not appear when a senator reads part of a speech and inserts the rest. In the House section, undelivered speeches and materials are printed in a distinctive typeface. The term "permanent *Record*" refers to the bound volumes of the daily *Records* of an entire session of Congress.

Congressional Research Service (CRS)—Established in 1917, a department of the Library of Congress whose staff provide nonpartisan, objective analysis and information on virtually any subject to committees, members, and staff of Congress. Originally the Legislative Reference Service, it is the oldest congressional support agency.

Congressional Terms of Office—A term normally begins on January 3 of the year following a general election and runs two years for representatives and six years for senators. A representative chosen in a special election to fill a vacancy is sworn in for the remainder of his predecessor's term. An individual appointed to fill a Senate vacancy usually serves until the next general election or until the end of the predecessor's term, whichever comes first. Some states, however, require their governors to call a special election to fill a Senate vacancy shortly after an appointment has been made.

Consent Calendar—Before being abolished in 1995, a house calendar, and the procedures associated with it, used to expedite passage of noncontroversial legislation.

Contempt of Congress—Willful obstruction of the proper functions of Congress. Most frequently, it is a refusal to obey a subpoena to appear and testify before a committee or to produce documents demanded by it. Such obstruction is a misdemeanor, and persons cited for contempt are subject to prosecution in federal courts. A house cites an individual for contempt by agreeing to a privileged resolution to that effect reported by a committee. The presiding officer then refers the matter to a U.S. attorney for prosecution.

Continuing Body—A characterization of the Senate on the theory that it continues from Congress to Congress and has existed continuously since it first convened in 1789. The rationale for the theory is that under the system of staggered six-year terms for senators, the terms of only about one-third of them expire after each Congress and, therefore, a quorum of the Senate is always in office. Consequently, under this theory, the Senate, unlike the House, does not have to adopt its rules at the beginning of each Congress because those rules continue from one Congress to the next. This makes it extremely difficult for the Senate to change its rules against the opposition of a determined minority because those rules require a two-thirds vote of the senators present and voting to invoke cloture on a proposed rules change.

Continuing Resolution (CR)—A joint resolution that provides funds to continue the operation of federal agencies and programs at the beginning of a new fiscal year if their annual appropriation bills have not yet been enacted; also called continuing appropriations.

Contract Authority—Statutory authority permitting an agency to enter into contracts or incur other obligations even though it has not received an appropriation to pay for them. Congress must eventually fund them because the government is legally liable for such payments. The Congressional Budget Act of 1974 requires that new contract authority may not be used unless provided for in advance by an appropriation act, but it permits a few exceptions.

Controllable Expenditures—Federal spending that is permitted but not mandated by existing authorization law and therefore may be adjusted by congressional action in appropriation bills. *(See Appropriation.)*

Correcting Recorded Votes—The rules of both houses prohibit members from changing their votes after a vote result has been announced. Nevertheless, the Senate permits its members to withdraw or change their votes, by unanimous consent, immediately after the announcement. In rare instances, senators have been granted unanimous consent to change their votes several days or weeks after the announcement.

Votes tallied by the electronic voting system in the House may not be changed. But when a vote actually given is not recorded during an oral call of the roll, a member may demand a correction as a matter of right. On all other alleged errors in a recorded vote, the Speaker determines whether the circumstances justify a change. Occasionally, members merely announce that they were incorrectly recorded; announcements can occur hours, days, or even months after the vote and appear in the *Congressional Record*.

Cosponsor—A member who has joined one or more other members to sponsor a measure.

Credit Authority—Authority granted to an agency to incur direct loan obligations or to make loan guarantee commitments. The Congressional Budget Act of 1974 bans congressional consideration of credit authority legislation unless the extent of that authority is made subject to provisions in appropriation acts.

C-SPAN—Cable-Satellite Public Affairs Network, which provides live, gavel-to-gavel coverage of Senate floor proceedings on one cable television channel and coverage of House floor proceedings on another channel. C-SPAN also televises important committee hearings in both houses. Each house also transmits its televised proceedings directly to congressional offices.

Current Services Estimates—Executive branch estimates of the anticipated costs of federal programs and operations for the next and future fiscal years at existing levels of service and assuming no new initiatives or changes in existing law. The president submits these estimates to Congress with his annual budget and includes an explanation of the underlying economic and policy assumptions on which they are based, such as anticipated rates of inflation, real economic growth, and unemployment, plus program caseloads and pay increases.

Custody of the Papers—Possession of an engrossed measure and certain related basic documents that the two houses produce as they try to resolve their differences over the measure.

Dance of the Swans and the Ducks—A whimsical description of the gestures some members use in connection with a request for a recorded vote, especially in the House. When a member wants his colleagues to stand in support of the request, he moves his hands and arms in a gentle upward motion resembling the beginning flight of a graceful swan. When he wants his colleagues to remain seated in order to avoid such a vote, he moves his hands and arms in a vigorous downward motion resembling a diving duck.

Dean—Within a state's delegation in the House of Representatives, the member with the longest continuous service.

Debate—In congressional parlance, speeches delivered during consideration of a measure, motion, or other matter, as distinguished from speeches in other parliamentary situations, such as one-minute and special order speeches when no business is pending. Virtually all debate in the House of Representatives is under some kind of time limitation. Most debate in the Senate is unlimited; that is, a senator, once recognized, may speak for as long as he chooses, unless the Senate invokes cloture.

Debt Limit—The maximum amount of outstanding federal public debt permitted by law. The limit (or ceiling) covers virtually all debt incurred by the government except agency debt. Each congressional budget resolution sets forth the new debt limit that may be required under its provisions.

Deferral—An impoundment of funds for a specific period of time that may not extend beyond the fiscal year in which it is proposed. Under the Impoundment Control Act of 1974, the president must notify Congress that he is deferring the spending or obligation of funds provided by law for a project or activity. Congress can disapprove the deferral by legislation.

Deficit—The amount by which the government's outlays exceed its budget receipts for a given fiscal year. Both the president's budget and the annual congressional budget resolution provide estimates of the deficit or surplus for the upcoming and several future fiscal years.

Degrees of Amendment—Designations that indicate the relationships of amendments to the text of a measure and to each other. In general, an amendment offered directly to the text of a measure is an amendment in the first degree, and an amendment to that amendment is an amendment in the second degree. Both houses normally prohibit amendments in the third degree—that is, an amendment to an amendment to an amendment.

Delegate—A nonvoting member of the House of Representatives elected to a two-year term from the District of Columbia, the territory of Guam, the territory of the Virgin Islands, or the territory of American Samoa. By law, delegates may not vote in the full House, but they may participate in debate, offer motions (except to reconsider), and serve and vote on standing and select committees. On their committees, delegates possess the same powers and privileges as other members, and the Speaker may appoint them to appropriate conference committees and select committees.

Denounce—A formal action that condemns a member for misbehavior; considered by some experts to be equivalent to censure. (See Censure.)

Dilatory Tactics—Procedural actions intended to delay or prevent action by a house or a committee. They include, among others, offering numerous motions, demanding quorum calls and recorded votes at every opportunity, making numerous points of order and parliamentary inquiries, and speaking as long as the applicable rules permit. The Senates rules permit a battery of dilatory tactics, especially lengthy speeches, except under cloture. In the House, possible dilatory tactics are more limited. Speeches are always subject to time limits and debate-ending motions. Moreover, a House rule instructs the Speaker not to entertain dilatory motions and lets the Speaker decide whether a motion is dilatory. However, the Speaker may not override the constitutional right of a member to demand the yeas and nays, and in practice usually waits for a point of order before exercising that authority. (See Cloture.)

Discharge a Committee—Remove a measure from a committee to which it has been referred in order to make it available for floor consideration. Noncontroversial measures are often discharged by unanimous consent. However, because congressional committees have no obligation to report measures referred to them, each house has procedures to extract controversial measures from recalcitrant committees. Six discharge procedures are available in the House of Representatives. The Senate uses a motion to discharge, which is usually converted into a discharge resolution.

Division Vote—A vote in which the chair first counts those in favor of a proposition and then those opposed to it, with no record made of how each member votes. In the Senate, the chair may count raised hands or ask senators to stand, whereas the House requires members to stand; hence, often called a standing vote. Committees in both houses ordinarily use a show of hands. A division usually occurs after a voice vote and may be demanded by any member or ordered by the chair if there is any doubt about the outcome of the voice vote. The demand for a division can also come before a voice vote. In the Senate, the demand must come before the result of a voice vote is announced. It may be made after a voice vote announcement in the House, but only if no intervening business has transpired and only if the member was standing and seeking recognition at the time of the announcement. A demand for the yeas and nays or, in the House, for a recorded vote, takes precedence over a division vote.

Doorkeeper of the House—A former officer of the House of Representatives who was responsible for enforcing the rules prohibiting unauthorized persons from entering the chamber when the House is in session. The doorkeeper was usually the candidate of the majority party. In 1995, the office was abolished and its functions transferred to the sergeant at arms.

Effective Dates—Provisions of an act that specify when the entire act or individual provisions in it become effective as law. Most acts become effective on the date of enactment, but it is sometimes necessary or prudent to delay the effective dates of some provisions.

Electronic Voting—Since 1973 the House has used an electronic voting system to record the yeas and nays and to conduct recorded votes. Members vote by inserting their voting cards in one of the boxes at several locations in the chamber. They are given at least 15 minutes to vote. When several votes occur immediately after each other, the Speaker may reduce the voting time to five minutes on the second and subsequent votes. The Speaker may allow additional time on each vote, but he may also close a vote at any time after the minimum time has expired. Members can change their votes at any time before the Speaker announces the result. The House also uses the electronic system for quorum calls. While a vote is in progress, a large panel above the Speaker's desk displays how each member has voted. Smaller panels on either side of the chamber display running totals of the votes and the time remaining. The Senate does not have electronic voting.

Enacting Clause—The opening language of each bill, beginning "Be it enacted by the Senate and House of Representatives of the United States of America in Congress assembled..." This language gives legal force to measures approved by Congress and signed by the president or enacted over his veto. A successful motion to strike it from a bill kills the entire measure.

Engrossed Bill—The official copy of a bill or joint resolution as passed by one chamber, including the text as amended by floor action, and certified by the clerk of the House or the secretary of the Senate (as appropriate). Amendments by one house to a measure or amendments of the other also are engrossed. House engrossed documents are printed on blue paper; the Senate's are printed on white paper.

Enrolled Bill—The final official copy of a bill or joint resolution passed in identical form by both houses. An enrolled bill is printed on parchment. After it is certified by the chief officer of the house in which it originated and signed by the House Speaker and the Senate president pro tempore, the measure is sent to the president for his signature.

Entitlement Program—A federal program under which individuals, businesses, or units of government that meet the requirements or qualifications established by law are entitled to receive certain payments if they seek such payments. Major examples include Social Security, Medicare, Medicaid, unemployment insurance, and military and federal civilian pensions. Congress cannot control their expenditures by refusing to appropriate the sums necessary to fund them because the government is legally obligated to pay eligible recipients the amounts to which the law entitles them.

Ethics Rules—Several rules or standing orders in each house that mandate certain standards of conduct for members and congressional employees in finance, employment, franking, and other areas. The Senate Permanent Select Committee on Ethics and the House Committee on Standards of Official Conduct investigate alleged violations of conduct and recommend appropriate actions to their respective houses.

Exclusive Committee—(1) Under the rules of the House Democratic Caucus, a standing committee whose Democratic members usually cannot serve on any other standing committee. As of 1997 the Appropriations, Commerce (beginning in the 105th Congress), Ways and Means, and Rules committees were designated as exclusive committees. (2) Under the rules of the two party conferences in the Senate, a standing committee whose members may not simultaneously serve on any other exclusive committee.

Executive Calendar—The Senates calendar for committee reports on its executive business, namely treaties and nominations. The calendar numbers indicate the order in which items were referred to the calendar but have no bearing on when or if the Senate will consider them. The Senate, by motion or unanimous consent, resolves itself into executive session to consider them

Executive Document—A document, usually a treaty, sent by the president to the Senate for approval. It is referred to a committee in

the same manner as other measures. Executive documents are designated as Executive A, 102d Congress, 1st Session, Executive B, and so on.

Executive Order—A unilateral proclamation by the president that has a policy-making or legislative impact. Members of Congress have challenged some executive orders on the grounds that they usurped the authority of the legislative branch. Although the Supreme Court has ruled that a particular order exceeded the president's authority, it has upheld others as falling within the presidents general constitutional powers.

Executive Privilege—The assertion that presidents have the right to withhold certain information from Congress. Presidents have based their claim on: (1) the constitutional separation of powers; (2) the need for secrecy in military and diplomatic affairs; (3) the need to protect individuals from unfavorable publicity; (4) the need to safeguard the confidential exchange of ideas in the executive branch; and (5) the need to protect individuals who provide confidential advice to the president.

Expulsion—A member's removal from office by a two-thirds vote of his house; the super majority is required by the Constitution. It is the most severe and most rarely used sanction a house can invoke against a member. Although the Constitution provides no explicit grounds for expulsion, the courts have ruled that it may be applied only for misconduct during a member's term of office, not for conduct before the member's election. Generally, neither house will consider expulsion of a member convicted of a crime until the judicial processes have been exhausted. At that stage, members sometimes resign rather than face expulsion. In 1977 the House adopted a rule urging members convicted of certain crimes to voluntarily abstain from voting or participating in other legislative business.

Federal Debt—The total amount of monies borrowed and not yet repaid by the federal government. Federal debt consists of public debt and agency debt. Public debt is the portion of the federal debt borrowed by the Treasury or the Federal Financing Bank directly from the public or from another federal fund or account. For example, the Treasury regularly borrows money from the Social Security trust fund. Public debt accounts for about 99 percent of the federal debt. Agency debt refers to the debt incurred by federal agencies like the Export-Import Bank, but excluding the Treasury and the Federal Financing Bank, which are authorized by law to borrow funds from the public or from another government fund or account.

Filibuster—The use of obstructive and time-consuming parliamentary tactics by one member or a minority of members to delay, modify, or defeat proposed legislation or rules changes. Filibusters are also sometimes used to delay urgently needed measures in order to force the body to accept other legislation. The Senate's rules permitting unlimited debate and the extraordinary majority it requires to impose cloture make filibustering particularly effective in that chamber. Under the stricter rules of the House, filibusters in that body are short-lived and therefore ineffective and rarely attempted

Fiscal Year—The federal government's annual accounting period. It begins October 1 and ends on the following September 30. A fiscal year is designated by the calendar year in which it ends and is often referred to as FY. Thus, fiscal year 1996 began October 1, 1995, ended September 30, 1996, and is called FY96. In theory, Congress is supposed to complete action on all budgetary measures applying to a fiscal year before that year begins. It rarely does so.

Five-Minute Rule—In its most common usage, a House rule that limits debate on an amendment offered in Committee of the Whole to five minutes for its sponsor and five minutes for an opponent. In practice, the committee routinely permits longer debate by two devices: the offering of pro forma amendments, each debatable for five minutes, and unanimous consent for a member to speak longer than five minutes. Also a House rule that limits a committee member to five minutes when questioning a witness at a hearing until each member has had an opportunity to question that witness.

Floor—The ground level of the House or Senate chamber where members sit and the houses conduct their business. When members are attending a meeting of their house, they are said to be on the floor. Floor action refers to the procedural actions taken during floor consideration, such as deciding on motions, taking up measures, amending them, and voting.

Floor Manager—A majority party member responsible for guiding a measure through its floor consideration in a house and for devising the political and procedural strategies that might be required to get it passed. The presiding officer gives the floor manager priority recognition to debate, offer amendments, oppose amendments, and make crucial procedural motions.

Frank—Informally, a member's legal right to send official mail postage-free under his or her signature; often called the franking privilege. Technically, it is the autographic or facsimile signature used on envelopes instead of stamps that permits members and certain congressional officers to send their official mail free of charge. The franking privilege has been authorized by law since the first Congress, except for a few months in 1873. Congress reimburses the U.S. Postal Service for the franked mail it handles.

Function or Functional Category—A broad category of national need and spending of budgetary significance. A category provides an accounting method for allocating and keeping track of budgetary resources and expenditures for that function because it includes all budget accounts related to the function's subject or purpose such as agriculture, administration of justice, commerce and housing and energy. Functions do not necessarily correspond with appropriations acts or with the budgets of individual agencies.

Gag Rule—A pejorative term for any type of special rule reported by the House Rules Committee that proposes to prohibit amendments to a measure or only permits amendments offered by the reporting committee.

Galleries—The balconies overlooking each chamber from which the public, news media, staff, and others may observe floor proceedings.

General Accounting Office (GAO)—A congressional support agency, often referred to as the investigative arm of Congress. It evaluates and audits federal agencies and programs in the United States and abroad on its own initiative or at the request of congressional committees or members.

General Appropriation Bill—A term applied to each of the 13 annual bills that provide funds for most federal agencies and pro-

grams and also to the supplemental appropriation bills that contain appropriations for more than one agency or program.

General Pair—A voting pair between two absent members that does not indicate their positions on the question. They may agree or disagree.

Germane—Basically, on the same subject as the matter under consideration. A House rule requires that all amendments be germane. In the Senate, only amendments proposed to general appropriation bills and budget resolutions or under cloture must be germane. Germaneness rules can be evaded by suspension of the rules in both houses, by unanimous consent agreements in the Senate, and by special rules from the Rules Committee in the House.

Gerrymandering—The manipulation of legislative district boundaries to benefit a particular party, politician, or minority group. The term originated in 1812 when the Massachusetts legislature redrew the lines of state legislative districts to favor the party of Gov. Elbridge Gerry, and some critics said one district looked like a salamander. *(See also Congressional District, Redistricting.)*

Gramm-Rudman-Hollings Act of 1985—Common name for the Balanced Budget and Emergency Deficit Control Act of 1985, which established new budget procedures intended to balance the federal budget by fiscal year 1991—a goal subsequently extended to 1993. The act's chief sponsors were Senators Phil Gramm (R-Texas), Warren Rudman (R-N.H.), and Ernest Hollings (D-S.C.).

Grandfather Clause—A provision in a measure, law, or rule that exempts an individual, entity, or a defined category of individuals or entities from complying with a new policy or restriction. For example, a bill that would raise taxes on persons who reach the age of 65 after a certain date inherently grandfathers out those who are 65 before that date. Similarly, a Senate rule limiting senators to two major committee assignments also grandfathers some senators who were sitting on a third major committee prior to a specified date.

Grants-in-Aid—Payments by the federal government to state and local governments to help provide for assistance programs or public services.

Hearing—Committee or subcommittee meetings to receive testimony on proposed legislation, during investigations, or for oversight purposes. Relatively few bills are important enough to justify formal hearings. Witnesses often include experts, government officials, spokespersons for interested groups, officials of the General Accounting Office, and members of Congress. Also, the printed transcripts of hearings.

Hold—A senator's request that his or her party leaders delay floor consideration of certain legislation or presidential nomination. The majority leader usually honors a hold for a reasonable period of time, especially if its purpose is to assure the senator that the matter will not be called up during his or her absence or to give the senator time to gather necessary information.

Hold (or Have) the Floor—A member's right to speak without interruption, unless he violates a rule, after recognition by the presiding officer. At the member's discretion, he or she may yield to another member for a question in the Senate or for a question or statement in the House, but may reclaim the floor at any time.

Hold-Harmless Clause—In legislation providing a new formula for allocating federal funds, a clause to ensure that recipients of that funds do not receive less in a future year than they did in the current year if the new formula would result in a reduction for them. Similar to a grandfather clause, it has been used most frequently to soften the impact of sudden reductions in federal grants. *(See Grandfather Clause.)*

Hopper—A box on the clerk's desk in the House chamber into which members deposit bills and resolutions to introduce them. In House jargon, to drop a bill in the hopper is to introduce it.

Hour Rule—A House rule that permits members, when recognized, to hold the floor in debate for no more than one hour each. The majority party member customarily yields one-half the time to a minority member. Although the hour rule applies to general debate in Committee of the Whole as well as in the House, special rules routinely vary the length of time for such debate and its control to fit the circumstances of particular measures.

House as in Committee of the Whole—A hybrid combination of procedures from the general rules of the House and from the rules of the Committee of the Whole, sometimes used to expedite consideration of a measure on the floor.

House Calendar—The calendar reserved for all public bills and resolutions that do not raise revenue or directly or indirectly appropriate money or property when they are favorably reported by House committees.

House Manual—A commonly used title for the handbook of the rules of the House of Representatives, published in each Congress. Its official title is *Constitution, Jefferson's Manual, and Rules of the House of Representatives.*

House of Representatives—The house of Congress in which states are represented roughly in proportion to their populations, but every state is guaranteed at least one representative. By law, the number of voting representatives is fixed at 435. Four delegates and one resident commissioner also serve in the House; they may vote in their committees and in Committee of the Whole but not in the House sitting as the House. Although the House and Senate have equal legislative power, the Constitution gives the House sole authority to originate revenue measures. The House also claims the right to originate appropriation measures, a claim the Senate disputes in theory but concedes in practice. The House has the sole power to impeach, and it elects the president when no candidate has received a majority of the electoral votes. It is sometimes referred to as the lower body.

Immunity—(1) Members' constitutional protection from lawsuits and arrest in connection with their legislative duties. They may not be tried for libel or slander for anything they say on the floor of a house or in committee. Nor may they be arrested while attending sessions of their houses or when traveling to or from sessions of Congress, except when charged with treason, a felony, or a breach of the peace. (2) In the case of a witness before a committee, a grant of protection from prosecution based on that person's testimony to the committee. It is used to compel witnesses to testify who would otherwise refuse to do so on the constitutional ground of possible self-incrimination. Under such a grant, none of a witness's testimony may be used against him or her in a court proceeding except in a prosecu-

tion for perjury or for giving a false statement to Congress. *(See also Contempt of Congress.)*

Impeachment—The first step to remove the president, vice president, or other federal civil officers from office and to disqualify them from any future federal office "of honor, Trust or Profit." An impeachment is a formal charge of treason, bribery, or "other high Crimes and Misdemeanors." The House has the sole power of impeachment and the Senate the sole power of trying the charges and convicting. The House impeaches by a simple majority vote; conviction requires a two-thirds vote of all senators present.

Impoundment—An executive branch action or inaction that delays or withholds the expenditure or obligation of budget authority provided by law. The Impoundment Control Act of 1974 classifies impoundments as either deferrals or rescissions, requires the president to notify Congress about all such actions, and gives Congress authority to approve or reject them. The Constitution is unclear on whether a president may refuse to spend appropriated money, but Congress usually expects the president to spend at least enough to achieve the purposes for which the money was provided whether or not he agrees with those purposes.

Instruct Conferees—A formal action by a house urging its conferees to uphold a particular position on a measure in conference. The instruction may be to insist on certain provisions in the measure as passed by that house or to accept a provision in the version passed by the other house. Conferees are not bound by instructions, and a conference report is not subject to a point of order on the ground that instructions were violated.

Investigative Power—The authority of Congress and its committees to pursue investigations, upheld by the Supreme Court but limited to matters related to, and in furtherance of, a legitimate task of the Congress. Standing committees in both houses are permanently authorized to investigate matters within their jurisdictions. Major investigations are sometimes conducted by temporary select, special, or joint committees established by resolutions for that purpose.

Some rules of the House provide certain safeguards for witnesses and others during investigative hearings. These permit counsel to accompany witnesses, require that each witness receive a copy of the committee's rules, and order the committee to go into closed session if it believes the testimony to be heard might defame, degrade, or incriminate any person. The committee may subsequently decide to hear such testimony in open session. The Senate has no rules of this kind.

Item Veto—A procedure (sometimes called a line-item veto), available in 1997 for the first time, permitting a president to cancel amounts of new discretionary appropriations (budget authority), as well as new items of direct spending (entitlements) and certain limited tax benefits, unless Congress disapproves by law within a limited period of time. After the president signs a bill, he may act within five calendar days to propose the cancellation of one or more such items; a cancellation becomes permanent unless, within 30 days, Congress passes a joint resolution to disapprove it. The president may veto such a joint resolution; in that case, it requires a two-thirds vote in both houses to override the president's veto of the joint resolution disapproving his action. The authority to cancel amounts of new discretionary appropriations applies only to amounts specifically identified in the law or one of the accompanying standing or conference committee reports. The authority for this procedure expires at the end of 2004 unless Congress extends it by law.

Joint Committee—A committee composed of members selected from each house. The functions of most joint committees involve investigation, research, or oversight of agencies closely related to Congress. Permanent joint committees, created by statute, are sometimes called standing joint committees. Once quite numerous, only four joint committees remained as of 1997: Joint Economic, Joint Taxation, Joint Library, and Joint Printing. None has authority to report legislation.

Joint Resolution—A legislative measure that Congress uses for purposes other than general legislation. Like a bill, it has the force of law when passed by both houses and either approved by the president or passed over the president's veto. Unlike a bill, a joint resolution enacted into law is not called an act; it retains its original title.

Most often, joint resolutions deal with such relatively limited matters as the correction of errors in existing law, continuing appropriations, a single appropriation, or the establishment of permanent joint committees. Unlike bills, however, joint resolutions also are used to propose constitutional amendments; these do not require the president's signature and become effective only when ratified by three-fourths of the states. The House designates joint resolutions as H.J. Res., the Senate as S.J. Res. Each house numbers its joint resolutions consecutively in the order of introduction during a two-year Congress.

Joint Session—Informally, any combined meeting of the Senate and the House. Technically, a joint session is a combined meeting to count the electoral votes for president and vice president or to hear a presidential address, such as the State of the Union message; any other formal combined gathering of both houses is called a joint meeting.

Joint Sponsorship—Two or more members sponsoring the same measure.

Journal—The official record of House or Senate actions, including every motion offered, every vote cast, amendments agreed to, quorum calls, and so forth. Unlike the *Congressional Record,* it does not provide reports of speeches, debates, statements, and the like. The Constitution requires each house to maintain a *Journal* and to publish it periodically.

Junket—A member's trip at government expense, especially abroad, ostensibly on official business but, it is often alleged, for pleasure.

King of the Mountain (or Hill Rule)—*(See Queen of the Hill Rule.)*

LA—*(See Legislative Assistant.)*

Lame Duck—Jargon for a member who has not been reelected, or did not seek reelection, and is serving the balance of his or her term. Lame Duck Session: A session of a Congress held after the election for the succeeding Congress, so-called after the lame duck members still serving.

Law—An act of Congress that has been signed by the president, passed over the president's veto, or allowed to become law without the president's signature.

Legislation—(1) A synonym for legislative measures: bills and joint resolutions. (2) Provisions in such measures or in substantive amendments offered to them. (3) In some contexts, provisions that change existing substantive or authorizing law, rather than provisions that make appropriations.

Legislation on an Appropriation Bill—A common reference to provisions changing existing law that appear in, or are offered as amendments to, a general appropriation bill. A House rule prohibits the inclusion of such provisions in general appropriation bills unless they retrench expenditures. An analogous Senate rule permits points of order against amendments to a general appropriation bill that propose general legislation.

Legislative Assistant (LA)—A member's staff person responsible for monitoring and preparing legislation on particular subjects and for advising the member on them; commonly referred to as an LA.

Legislative Day—The day that begins when a house meets after an adjournment and ends when it next adjourns. Because the House of Representatives normally adjourns at the end of a daily session, its legislative and calendar days usually coincide. The Senate, however, frequently recesses at the end of a daily session, and its legislative day may extend over several calendar days, weeks, or months. Among other uses, this technicality permits the Senate to save time by circumventing its morning hour, a procedure required at the beginning of every legislative day.

Legislative History—(1) A chronological list of actions taken on a measure during its progress through the legislative process. (2) The official documents relating to a measure, the entries in the *Journals* of the two houses on that measure, and the *Congressional Record* text of its consideration in both houses. The documents include all committee reports and the conference report and joint explanatory statement, if any. Courts and affected federal agencies study a measure's legislative history for congressional intent about its purpose and interpretation.

Legislative Process—(1) Narrowly, the stages in the enactment of a law from introduction to final disposition. An introduced measure that becomes law typically travels through reference to committee; committee and subcommittee consideration; report to the chamber; floor consideration; amendment; passage; engrossment; messaging to the other house; similar steps in that house, including floor amendment of the measure; return of the measure to the first house; consideration of amendments between the houses or a conference to resolve their differences; approval of the conference report by both houses; enrollment; approval by the president or override of the president's veto; and deposit with the Archivist of the United States. (2) Broadly, the political, lobbying, and other factors that affect or influence the process of enacting laws.

Legislative Veto—A procedure, declared unconstitutional in 1983, that allowed Congress or one of its houses to nullify certain actions of the president, executive branch agencies, or independent agencies. Sometimes called congressional vetoes or congressional disapprovals. Following the Supreme Court's 1983 decision, Congress amended several legislative veto statutes to require enactment of joint resolutions, which are subject to presidential veto, for nullifying executive branch actions.

Line Item—Generally, an amount in an appropriation measure. It can refer to a single appropriation account or to separate amounts within the account. In the congressional budget process, the term usually refers to assumptions about the funding of particular programs or accounts that underlie the broad functional amounts in a budget resolution. These assumptions are discussed in the reports accompanying each resolution and are not binding.

Line-Item Veto—*(See Item Veto.)*

Live Pair—A voluntary and informal agreement between two members on opposite sides of an issue under which the member who is present for a recorded vote withholds or withdraws his or her vote because the other member is absent.

Loan Guarantee—A statutory commitment by the federal government to pay part or all of a loan's principal and interest to a lender or the holder of a security in case the borrower defaults.

Lobby—To try to persuade members of Congress to propose, pass, modify, or defeat proposed legislation or to change or repeal existing laws. A lobbyist attempts to promote his or her own preferences or those of a group, organization, or industry. Originally the term referred to persons frequenting the lobbies or corridors of legislative chambers in order to speak to lawmakers. In a general sense, lobbying includes not only direct contact with members but also indirect attempts to influence them, such as writing to them or persuading others to write or visit them, attempting to mold public opinion toward a desired legislative goal by various means, and contributing or arranging for contributions to members' election campaigns. The right to lobby stems from the First Amendment to the Constitution, which bans laws that abridge the right of the people to petition the government for a redress of grievances.

Logrolling—Jargon for a legislative tactic or bargaining strategy in which members try to build support for their legislation by promising to support legislation desired by other members or by accepting amendments they hope will induce their colleagues to vote for their bill.

Mace—The symbol of the office of the House sergeant at arms. Under the direction of the Speaker, the sergeant at arms is responsible for preserving order on the House floor by holding up the mace in front of an unruly member, or by carrying the mace up and down the aisles to quell boisterous behavior. When the House is in session, the mace sits on a pedestal at the Speaker's right; when the House is in Committee of the Whole, it is moved to a lower pedestal. The mace is 46 inches high and consists of 13 ebony rods bound in silver and topped by a silver globe with a silver eagle, wings outstretched, perched on it.

Majority Leader—The majority party's chief floor spokesman, elected by that party's caucus—sometimes called floor leader. In the Senate, the majority leader also develops the party's political and procedural strategy, usually in collaboration with other party officials and committee chairmen. He negotiates the Senate's agenda and committee ratios with the minority leader and usually calls up measures for floor action. The chamber traditionally concedes to the majority leader the right to determine the days on which it will meet and the hours at which it will convene and adjourn. In the House, the majority leader is the Speaker's deputy and heir apparent. He helps plan the floor agenda and the party's legislative strategy and often speaks for the party leadership in debate.

Managers—(1) The official title of members appointed to a conference committee, commonly called conferees. The ranking majority and minority managers for each house also manage floor consideration of the committee's conference report. (2) The members who manage the initial floor consideration of a measure. (3) The official title of House members appointed to present impeachment articles to the Senate and to act as prosecutors on behalf of the House during the Senate trial of the impeached person.

Mandatory Appropriations—Amounts that Congress must appropriate annually because it has no discretion over them unless it first amends existing substantive law. Certain entitlement programs, for example, require annual appropriations.

Markup—A meeting or series of meetings by a committee or subcommittee during which members mark up a measure by offering, debating, and voting on amendments to it.

Members' Allowances—Official expenses that are paid for or for which members are reimbursed by their houses. Among these are the costs of office space in congressional buildings and in their home states or districts; office equipment and supplies; postage-free mailings (the franking privilege); a set number of trips to and from home states or districts, as well as travel elsewhere on official business; telephone and other telecommunications services; and staff salaries.

Method of Equal Proportions—The mathematical formula used since 1950 to determine how the 435 seats in the House of Representatives should be distributed among the 50 states in the apportionment following each decennial census. It minimizes as much as possible the proportional difference between the average district population in any two states. Because the Constitution guarantees each state at least one representative, 50 seats are automatically apportioned. The formula calculates priority numbers for each state, assigns the first of the 385 remaining seats to the state with the highest priority number, the second to the state with the next highest number, and so on until all seats are distributed. *(See Apportionment.)*

Midterm Election—The general election for members of Congress that occurs in November of the second year in a presidential term.

Minority Leader—The minority party's leader and chief floor spokesman, elected by the party caucus; sometimes called minority floor leader. With the assistance of other party officials and the ranking minority members of committees, the minority leader devises the party's political and procedural strategy.

Minority Staff—Employees who assist the minority party members of a committee. Most committees hire separate majority and minority party staffs, but they also may hire nonpartisan staff.

Morning Business—In the Senate, routine business transacted at the beginning of the morning hour at the demand of any senator.

Morning Hour—A two-hour period at the beginning of a new legislative day during which the Senate is supposed to conduct routine business, call the calendar on Mondays, and deal with other matters described in a Senate rule. In practice, it often does not occur because the Senate frequently recesses, rather than adjourns, at the end of a daily session and therefore the rule does not apply when it next meets.

Motion—A formal proposal for a procedural action, such as to consider, to amend, to lay on the table, to reconsider, to recess, or to adjourn. It has been estimated that at least 85 motions are possible under various circumstances in the House of Representatives, somewhat fewer in the Senate. Not all motions are created equal; some are privileged or preferential and enjoy priority over others. And some motions are debatable, amendable or divisible, while others are not.

Multiyear Appropriation—An appropriation that remains available for spending or obligation for more than one fiscal year; the exact period of time is specified in the act making the appropriation.

Multiyear Authorization—(1) Legislation that authorizes the existence or continuation of an agency, program, or activity for more than one fiscal year. (2) Legislation that authorizes appropriations for an agency, program, or activity for more than one fiscal year.

Nomination—A proposed presidential appointment to a federal office submitted to the Senate for confirmation. Approval is by majority vote. The Constitution explicitly requires confirmation for ambassadors, consuls, public ministers (department heads), and Supreme Court justices. By law, other federal judges, all military promotions of officers, and many high-level civilian officials must be confirmed.

Oath of Office—Upon taking office, members of Congress must swear or affirm that they will "support and defend the Constitution . . . against all enemies, foreign and domestic," that they will "bear true faith and allegiance" to the Constitution, that they take the obligation "freely, without any mental reservation or purpose of evasion," and that they will "well and faithfully discharge the duties" of their office. The oath is required by the Constitution; the wording is prescribed by a statute. All House members must take the oath at the beginning of each new Congress.

Omnibus Bill—A measure that combines the provisions of several disparate subjects into a single and often lengthy bill.

Open Rule—A special rule from the House Rules Committee that permits members to offer as many floor amendments as they wish as long as the amendments are germane and do not violate other House rules.

Order of Business (House)—The sequence of events during the meeting of the House on a new legislative day prescribed by a House rule; also called the general order of business. The sequence consists of (1) the chaplain's prayer; (2) approval of the *Journal;* (3) pledge of allegiance; (4) correction of the reference of public bills; (5) disposal of business on the Speaker's table; (6) unfinished business; (7) the morning hour call of committees and consideration of their bills (largely obsolete); (8) motions to go into Committee of the Whole; and (9) orders of the day (also obsolete). In practice, on days specified in the rules, the items of business that follow approval of the *Journal* are supplanted in part by the special order of business (for example, the corrections, discharge, or private calendars or motions to suspend the rules) and on any day by other privileged business (for example, general appropriation bills and special rules) or measures made in order by special rules. By this combination of an order of business with privileged interruptions, the House gives precedence to certain categories of important legislation, brings to the floor other major legislation from its calendars in any order it chooses, and provides expeditious processing for minor and noncontroversial measures.

Order of Business (Senate)—The sequence of events at the beginning of a new legislative day prescribed by Senate rules. The sequence consists of (1) the chaplain's prayer; (2) *Journal* reading and correction; (3) morning business in the morning hour; (4) call of the calendar during the morning hour; and (5) unfinished business.

Original Jurisdiction—The authority of certain committees to originate a measure and report it to the chamber. For example, general appropriation bills reported by the House Appropriations Committee are original bills, and special rules reported by the House Rules Committee are original resolutions.

Other Body—A commonly used reference to a house by a member of the other house. Congressional comity discourages members from directly naming the other house during debate.

Outlays—Amounts of government spending. They consist of payments, usually by check or in cash, to liquidate obligations incurred in prior fiscal years as well as in the current year, including the net lending of funds under budget authority. In federal budget accounting, net outlays are calculated by subtracting the amounts of refunds and various kinds of reimbursements to the government from actual spending.

Override a Veto—Congressional enactment of a measure over the president's veto. A veto override requires a recorded two-thirds vote of those voting in each house, a quorum being present. Because the president must return the vetoed measure to its house of origin, that house votes first, but neither house is required to attempt an override, whether immediately or at all. If an override attempt fails in the house of origin, the veto stands and the measure dies.

Oversight—Congressional review of the way in which federal agencies implement laws to ensure that they are carrying out the intent of Congress and to inquire into the efficiency of the implementation and the effectiveness of the law. The Legislative Reorganization Act of 1946 defined oversight as the function of exercising continuous watchfulness over the execution of the laws by the executive branch.

Pairing—A procedure that permits two or three members to enter into voluntary arrangements that offset their votes so that one or more of the members can be absent without changing the result. The names of paired members and their positions on the vote (except on general pairs) appear in the *Congressional Record.* Members can be paired on one vote or on a series of votes.

Parliamentarian—The official advisor to the presiding officer in each house on questions of procedure. The parliamentarian and his assistants also answer procedural questions from members and congressional staff, refer measures to committees on behalf of the presiding officer, and maintain compilations of the precedents. The House parliamentarian revises the House Manual at the beginning of every Congress and usually reviews special rules before the Rules Committee reports them to the House. Either a parliamentarian or an assistant is always present and near the podium during sessions of each house

Party Caucus—Generic term for each party's official organization in each house. Only House Democrats officially call their organization a caucus. House and Senate Republicans and Senate Democrats call their organizations conferences. The party caucuses elect their leaders, approve committee assignments and chairmanships (or ranking minority members, if the party is in the minority), establish party committees and study groups, and discuss party and legislative policies. On rare occasions, they have stripped members of committee seniority or expelled them from the caucus for party disloyalty.

Permanent Appropriation—An appropriation that remains continuously available, without current action or renewal by Congress, under the terms of a previously enacted authorization or appropriation law. One such appropriation provides for payment of interest on the public debt and another the salaries of members of Congress.

Permanent Authorization—An authorization without a time limit. It usually does not specify any limit on the funds that may be appropriated for the agency, program, or activity that it authorizes, leaving such amounts to the discretion of the appropriations committees and the two houses.

Pocket Veto—The indirect veto of a bill as a result of the president withholding approval of it until after Congress has adjourned sine die. A bill the president does not sign, but does not formally veto while Congress is in session, automatically becomes a law 10 days (excluding Sundays) after it is received. But if Congress adjourns its annual session during that 10-day period, the measure dies even if the president does not formally veto it.

Point of Order—A parliamentary term used in committee and on the floor to object to an alleged violation of a rule and to demand that the chair enforce the rule. The point of order immediately halts the proceedings until the chair decides whether the contention is valid.

Pork or Pork Barrel Legislation—Pejorative terms for federal appropriations, bills, or policies that provide funds to benefit a legislator's district or state, with the implication that the legislator presses for enactment of such benefits to ingratiate himself or herself with constituents rather than on the basis of an impartial, objective assessment of need or merit.

The terms are often applied to such benefits as new parks, post offices, dams, canals, bridges, roads, water projects, sewage treatment plants, and public works of any kind, as well as demonstration projects, research grants, and relocation of government facilities. Funds released by the president for various kinds of benefits or government contracts approved by him allegedly for political purposes are also sometimes referred to as pork.

Postcloture Filibuster—A filibuster conducted after the Senate invokes cloture. It employs an array of procedural tactics rather than lengthy speeches to delay final action. The Senate curtailed the postcloture filibuster's effectiveness by closing a variety of loopholes in the cloture rule in 1979 and 1986.

Power of the Purse—A reference to the constitutional power Congress has over legislation to raise revenue and appropriate monies from the Treasury. Article I, Section 8 states that Congress

"shall have Power To lay and collect Taxes, Duties, Imposts and Excises, [and] to pay the Debts." Section 9 declares "No Money shall be drawn from the Treasury, but in Consequence of Appropriations made by Law."

Preamble—Introductory language describing the reasons for and intent of a measure, sometimes called a whereas clause. It occasionally appears in joint, concurrent, and simple resolutions but rarely in bills.

Precedent—A previous ruling on a parliamentary matter or a long-standing practice or custom of a house. Precedents serve to control arbitrary rulings and serve as the common law of a house.

President of the Senate—The vice president of the United States in his constitutional role as presiding officer of the Senate. The Constitution permits the vice president to cast a vote in the Senate only to break a tie, but he is not required to do so.

President Pro Tempore—Under the Constitution, an officer elected by the Senate to preside over it during the absence of the vice president of the United States. Often referred to as the "pro tem," he is usually the majority party senator with the longest continuous service in the chamber and also, by virtue of his seniority, a committee chairman. When attending to committee and other duties, the president pro tempore appoints other senators to preside.

Presiding Officer—In a formal meeting, the individual authorized to maintain order and decorum, recognize members to speak or offer motions, and apply and interpret the chamber's rules, precedents, and practices. The Speaker of the House and the president of the Senate are the chief presiding officers in their respective houses.

Previous Question—A nondebatable motion which, when agreed to by majority vote, usually cuts off further debate, prevents the offering of additional amendments, and brings the pending matter to an immediate vote. It is a major debate-limiting device in the House; it is not permitted in Committee of the Whole or in the Senate.

Private Bill—A bill that applies to one or more specified persons, corporations, institutions, or other entities, usually to grant relief when no other legal remedy is available to them. Many private bills deal with claims against the federal government, immigration and naturalization cases, and land titles.

Private Calendar—Commonly used title for a calendar in the House reserved for private bills and resolutions favorably reported by committees. The private calendar is officially called the Calendar of the Committee of the Whole House.

Private Law—A private bill enacted into law. Private laws are numbered in the same fashion as public laws.

Privilege—An attribute of a motion, measure, report, question, or proposition that gives it priority status for consideration. Privileged motions and motions to bring up privileged questions are not debatable.

Privilege of the Floor—In addition to the members of a house, certain individuals are admitted to its floor while it is in session. The rules of the two houses differ somewhat, but both extend the privilege to the president and vice president, Supreme Court justices, cabinet members, state governors, former members of that house, members of the other house, certain officers and officials of Congress, certain staff of that house in the discharge of official duties, and the chamber's former parliamentarians. They also allow access to a limited number of committee and members' staff when their presence is necessary.

Pro Forma Amendment—In the House, an amendment that ostensibly proposes to change a measure or another amendment by moving "to strike the last word" or "to strike the requisite number of words." A member offers it not to make any actual change in the measure or amendment but only to obtain time for debate.

Pro Tem—A common reference to the president pro tempore of the Senate or, occasionally, to a Speaker pro tempore. *(See President Pro Tempore, Speaker Pro Tempore.)*

Proxy Voting—The practice of permitting a member to cast the vote of an absent colleague in addition to his own vote. Proxy voting is prohibited on the floors of the House and Senate, but the Senate permits its committees to authorize proxy voting, and most do. In 1995, House rules were changed to prohibit proxy voting in committee.

Public Bill—A bill dealing with general legislative matters having national applicability or applying to the federal government or to a class of persons, groups, or organizations.

Public Debt—Federal government debt incurred by the Treasury or the Federal Financing Bank by the sale of securities to the public or borrowings from a federal fund or account.

Public Law—A public bill or joint resolution enacted into law. It is cited by the letters P.L. followed by a hyphenated number. The digits before the hyphen indicate the number of the Congress in which it was enacted; the digits after the hyphen indicate its position in the numerical sequence of public measures that became law during that Congress. For example, the Budget Enforcement Act of 1990 became P.L. 101-508 because it was the 508th measure in that sequence for the 101st Congress. *(See also Private Law.)*

Queen of the Hill Rule—A special rule from the House Rules Committee that permits votes on a series of amendments, especially complete substitutes for a measure, in a specified order, but directs that the amendment receiving the greatest number of votes shall be the winning one. This kind of rule permits the House to vote directly on a variety of alternatives to a measure. In doing so, it sets aside the precedent that once an amendment has been adopted, no further amendments may be offered to the text it has amended. Under an earlier practice, the Rules Committee reported "king of the hill" rules under which there also could be votes on a series of amendments, again in a specified order. If more than one of the amendments was adopted under this kind of rule, it was the last amendment to receive a majority vote that was considered as having been finally adopted, whether or not it had received the greatest number of votes.

Quorum—The minimum number of members required to be present for the transaction of business. Under the Constitution, a quorum in each house is a majority of its members: 218 in the House and 51 in the Senate when there are no vacancies. By House rule, a quorum in Committee of the Whole is 100. In practice, both houses

usually assume a quorum is present even if it is not, unless a member makes a point of no quorum in the House or suggests the absence of a quorum in the Senate. Consequently, each house transacts much of its business, and even passes bills, when only a few members are present.

For House and Senate committees, chamber rules allow a minimum quorum of one-third of a committee's members to conduct most types of business.

Quorum Call—A procedure for determining whether a quorum is present in a chamber. In the Senate, a clerk calls the roll (roster) of senators. The House usually employs its electronic voting system.

Ramseyer Rule—A House rule that requires a committees report on a bill or joint resolution to show the changes the measure, and any committee amendments to it, would make in existing law.

Rank or Ranking—A member's position on the list of his party's members on a committee or subcommittee. When first assigned to a committee, a member is usually placed at the bottom of the list, then moves up as those above leave the committee. On subcommittees, however, a members rank may not have anything to do with the length of his service on it.

Ranking Member—(1) Most often a reference to the minority member with the highest ranking on a committee or subcommittee. (2) A reference to the majority member next in rank to the chairman or to the highest ranking majority member present at a committee or subcommittee meeting.

Ratification—(1) The president's formal act of promulgating a treaty after the Senate has approved it. The resolution of ratification agreed to by the Senate is the procedural vehicle by which the Senate gives its consent to ratification. (2) A state legislature's act in approving a proposed constitutional amendment. Such an amendment becomes effective when ratified by three-fourths of the states.

Reapportionment—*(See Apportionment.)*

Recess—(1) A temporary interruption or suspension of a meeting of a chamber or committee. Unlike an adjournment, a recess does not end a legislative day. Because the Senate often recesses from one calendar day to another, its legislative day may extend over several calendar days, weeks, or even months. (2) A period of adjournment for more than three days to a day certain, especially over a holiday or in August during odd-numbered years.

Recess Appointment—A presidential appointment to a vacant federal position made after the Senate has adjourned sine die or has adjourned or recessed for more than 30 days. If the president submits the recess appointee's nomination during the next session of the Senate, that individual can continue to serve until the end of the session even though the Senate might have rejected the nomination. When appointed to a vacancy that existed 30 days before the end of the last Senate session, a recess appointee is not paid until confirmed.

Recommit—To send a measure back to the committee that reported it; sometimes called a straight motion to recommit to distinguish it from a motion to recommit with instructions. A successful motion to recommit kills the measure unless it is accompanied by instructions.

Recommit a Conference Report—To return a conference report to the conference committee for renegotiation if some or all of its agreements. A motion to recommit may be offered with or without instructions.

Recommit with Instructions—To send a measure back to a committee with instructions to take some action on it. Invariably in the House and often in the Senate, when the motion recommits to a standing committee, the instructions require the committee to report the measure "forthwith" with specified amendments.

Reconciliation—A procedure for changing existing revenue and spending laws to bring total federal revenues and spending within the limits established in a budget resolution. Congress has applied reconciliation chiefly to revenues and mandatory spending programs, especially entitlements. Discretionary spending is controlled through annual appropriation bills.

Recorded Vote—(1) Generally, any vote in which members are recorded by name for or against a measure; also called a record vote or roll-call vote. The only recorded vote in the Senate is a vote by the yeas and nays and is commonly called a roll-call vote. (2) Technically, a recorded vote is one demanded in the House of Representatives and supported by at least one-fifth of a quorum (44 members) in the House sitting as the House or at least 25 members in Committee of the Whole.

Recorded Vote by Clerks—A voting procedure in the House where members pass through the appropriate "aye" or "no" aisle in the chamber and cast their votes by depositing a signed green (yea) or red (no) card in a ballot box. These votes are tabulated by clerks and reported to the chair. The electronic voting system is much more convenient and has largely supplanted this procedure. *(See Committee of the Whole, Recorded Vote, Teller Vote.)*

Redistricting—The redrawing of congressional district boundaries within a state after a decennial census. Redistricting may be required to equalize district populations or to accommodate an increase or decrease in the number of a state's House seats that might have resulted from the decennial apportionment. The state governments determine the district lines. *(See Apportionment, Congressional District, Gerrymandering.)*

Referral—The assignment of a measure to committee for consideration. Under a House rule, the Speaker can refuse to refer a measure he believes is "of an obscene or insulting character."

Report—(1) As a verb, a committee is said to report when it submits a measure or other document to its parent chamber. (2) A clerk is said to report when he or she reads a measure's title or text or the text of an amendment to the body at the direction of the chair. (3) As a noun, a committee document that accompanies a reported measure. It describes the measure, the committee's views on it, its costs, and the changes it proposes to make in existing law; it also includes certain impact statements. (4) A committee document submitted to its parent chamber that describes the results of an investigation or other study or provides information it is required to provide by rule or law.

Representative—An elected and duly sworn member of the House of Representatives who is entitled to vote in the chamber. The Constitution requires that a representative be at least 25 years old, a citizen of the United States for at least seven years, and an inhabitant of the state from which he or she is elected. Customarily, the member resides in the district he or she represents. Representatives are elected in even-numbered years to two-year terms that begin the following January.

Reprimand—A formal condemnation of a member for misbehavior, considered a milder reproof than censure. The House of Representatives first used it in 1976. The Senate has not used the term. *(See also Censure, Code of Official Conduct, Denounce, Ethics Rules, Expulsion, Seniority Loss.)*

Rescission—A provision of law that repeals previously enacted budget authority in whole or in part. Under the Impoundment Control Act of 1974, the president can impound such funds by sending a message to Congress requesting one or more rescissions and the reasons for doing so. If Congress does not pass a rescission bill for the programs requested by the president within 45 days of continuous session after receiving the message, the president must make the funds available for obligation and expenditure. If the president does not, the comptroller general of the United States is authorized to bring suit to compel the release of those funds. A rescission bill may rescind all, part, or none of an amount proposed by the president, and may rescind funds the president has not impounded.

Reserving the Right to Object—A member's declaration that at some indefinite future time he or she may object to a unanimous consent request. It is an attempt to circumvent the requirement that a member may prevent such an action only by objecting immediately after it is proposed.

Resident Commissioner from Puerto Rico—A nonvoting member of the House of Representatives, elected to a four-year term. The resident commissioner has the same status and privileges as delegates. Like the delegates, the resident commissioner may not vote in the House or Committee of the Whole.

Resolution—(1) A simple resolution; that is, a nonlegislative measure effective only in the house in which it is proposed and not requiring concurrence by the other chamber or approval by the president. Simple resolutions are designated H. Res. in the House and S. Res. in the Senate. Simple resolutions express nonbinding opinions on policies or issues or deal with the internal affairs or prerogatives of a house. (2) Any type of resolution: simple, concurrent, or joint. *(See Concurrent Resolution, Joint Resolution.)*

Resolution of Inquiry—A resolution usually simple rather than concurrent calling on the president or the head of an executive agency to provide specific information or papers to one or both houses.

Resolution of Ratification—The Senate vehicle for agreeing to a treaty. The constitutionally mandated vote of two-thirds of the senators present and voting applies to the adoption of this resolution. However, it may also contain amendments, reservations, declarations, or understandings that the Senate had previously added to it by majority vote.

Revenue Legislation—Measures that levy new taxes or tariffs or change existing ones. Under Article I, Section 7, Clause 1 of the Constitution, the House of Representatives originates federal revenue measures, but the Senate can propose amendments to them. The

House Ways and Means Committee and the Senate Finance Committee have jurisdiction over such measures, with a few minor exceptions.

Revise and Extend One's Remarks—A unanimous consent request to publish in the *Congressional Record* a statement a member did not deliver on the floor, a longer statement than the one made on the floor, or miscellaneous extraneous material.

Revolving Fund—A trust fund or account whose income remains available to finance its continuing operations without any fiscal year limitation.

Rider—Congressional slang for an amendment unrelated or extraneous to the subject matter of the measure to which it is attached. Riders often contain proposals that are less likely to become law on their own merits as separate bills, either because of opposition in the committee of jurisdiction, resistance in the other house, or the probability of a presidential veto. Riders are more common in the Senate.

Roll Call—A call of the roll to determine whether a quorum is present, to establish a quorum, or to vote on a question. Usually, the House uses its electronic voting system for a roll call. The Senate does not have an electronic voting system; its roll is always called by a clerk.

Rule—(1) A permanent regulation that a house adopts to govern its conduct of business, its procedures, its internal organization, behavior of its members, regulation of its facilities, duties of an officer, or some other subject it chooses to govern in that form. (2) In the House, a privileged simple resolution reported by the Rules Committee that provides methods and conditions for floor consideration of a measure or, rarely, several measures.

Second-Degree Amendment—An amendment to an amendment in the first degree. It is usually a perfecting amendment.

Secretary of the Senate—The chief administrative and budgetary officer of the Senate. The secretary manages a wide range of functions that support the operation of the Senate as an organization as well as those functions necessary to its legislative process, including record-keeping, document management, certifications, housekeeping services, administration of oaths, and lobbyist registrations.

Section—A subdivision of a bill or statute. By law, a section must be numbered and, as nearly as possible, contain "a single proposition of enactment."

Select or Special Committee—A committee established by a resolution in either house for a special purpose and, usually, for a limited time. Most select and special committees are assigned specific investigations or studies, but are not authorized to report measures to their chambers.

Senate—The house of Congress in which each state is represented by two senators; each senator has one vote. Article V of the Constitution declares that "No State, without its Consent, shall be deprived of its equal Suffrage in the Senate." The Constitution also gives the Senate equal legislative power with the House of Representatives. Although the Senate is prohibited from originating revenue measures, and as a matter of practice it does not originate appropriation measures, it can amend both. Only the Senate can give or withhold con-

sent to treaties and nominations from the president. It also acts as a court to try impeachments by the House and elects the vice president when no candidate receives a majority of the electoral votes. It is often referred to as "the upper body," but not by members of the House.

Senate Manual—The handbook of the Senate's standing rules and orders and the laws and other regulations that apply to the Senate, usually published once each Congress.

Senator—A duly sworn elected or appointed member of the Senate. The Constitution requires that a senator be at least 30 years old, a citizen of the United States for at least nine years, and an inhabitant of the state from which he or she is elected. Senators are usually elected in even-numbered years to six-year terms that begin the following January. When a vacancy occurs before the end of a term, the state governor can appoint a replacement to fill the position until a successor is chosen at the state's next general election or, if specified under state law, the next feasible date for such an election, to serve the remainder of the term. Until the Seventeenth Amendment was ratified in 1913, senators were chosen by their state legislatures.

Senatorial Courtesy—The Senate's practice of declining to confirm a presidential nominee for an office in the state of a senator of the president's party unless that senator approves.

Seniority—The priority, precedence, or status given members according to the length of their continuous service in a house or on a committee.

Seniority Loss—A type of punishment that reduces a member's seniority on his or her committees, including the loss of chairmanships. Party caucuses in both houses have occasionally imposed such punishment on their members, for example, for publicly supporting candidates of the other party.

Seniority Rule—The customary practice, rather than a rule, of assigning the chairmanship of a committee to the majority party member who has served on the committee for the longest continuous period of time.

Seniority System—A collection of long-standing customary practices under which members with longer continuous service than their colleagues in their house or on their committees receive various kinds of preferential treatment. Although some of the practices are no longer as rigidly observed as in the past, they still pervade the organization and procedures of Congress.

Sequestration—A procedure for canceling budgetary resources—that is, money available for obligation or spending—to enforce budget limitations established in law. Sequestered funds are no longer available for obligation or expenditure.

Sergeant at Arms—The officer in each house responsible for maintaining order, security, and decorum in its wing of the Capitol, including the chamber and its galleries. Although elected by their respective houses, both sergeants at arms are invariably the candidates of the majority party.

Session—(1) The annual series of meetings of a Congress. Under the Constitution, Congress must assemble at least once a year at noon on January 3 unless it appoints a different day by law. (2) The meeting of Congress or of one house convened by the president under his constitutional authority, called a special session. (3) A house is said to be in session during the period of a day when it is meeting.

Severability (or Separability) Clause—Language stating that if any particular provisions of a measure are declared invalid by the courts, the remaining provisions shall remain in effect.

Slip Law—The first official publication of a measure that has become law. It is published separately in unbound, single-sheet form or pamphlet form. A slip law usually is available two or three days after the date of the law's enactment.

Speaker—The presiding officer of the House of Representatives and the leader of its majority party. The Speaker is selected by the majority party and formally elected by the House at the beginning of each Congress. Although the Constitution does not require the Speaker to be a member of the House, in fact, all Speakers have been members.

Speaker Pro Tempore—A member of the House who is designated as the temporary presiding officer by the Speaker or elected by the House to that position during the Speaker's absence.

Speaker's Vote—The Speaker is not required to vote, and his name is not called on a roll-call vote unless he so requests. Usually, the Speaker votes either to create a tie vote, and thereby defeat a proposal, or to break a tie in favor of a proposal. Occasionally, the Speaker also votes to emphasize the importance of a matter or his special interest in it.

Special Session—A session of Congress convened by the president, under his constitutional authority, after Congress has adjourned sine die at the end of a regular session. (*See Adjournment Sine Die, Session.*)

Spending Authority—The technical term for backdoor spending. The Congressional Budget Act of 1974 defines it as borrowing authority, contract authority, and entitlement authority for which appropriation acts do not provide budget authority in advance. Under the Budget Act, legislation that provides new spending authority may not be considered unless it provides that the authority shall be effective only to the extent or in such amounts as provided in an appropriation act.

Sponsor—The principal proponent and introducer of a measure or an amendment.

Staff Director—The most frequently used title for the head of staff of a committee or subcommittee. On some committees, that person is called chief of staff, clerk, chief clerk, chief counsel, general counsel, or executive director. The head of a committee's minority staff is usually called minority staff director.

Standing Committee—A permanent committee established by a House or Senate standing rule or standing order. The rule also describes the subject areas on which the committee may report bills and resolutions and conduct oversight. Most introduced measures must be referred to one or more standing committees according to their jurisdictions.

Standing Order—A continuing regulation or directive that has the force and effect of a rule, but is not incorporated into the standing rules. The Senate's numerous standing orders, like its standing rules, continue from Congress to Congress unless changed or the order states otherwise. The House uses relatively few standing orders, and those it adopts expire at the end of a session of Congress.

Standing Rules—The rules of the Senate that continue from one Congress to the next and the rules of the House of Representatives that it adopts at the beginning of each new Congress.

Standing Vote—An alternative and informal term for a division vote, during which members in favor of a proposal and then members opposed stand and are counted by the chair.

Star Print—A reprint of a bill, resolution, amendment, or committee report correcting technical or substantive errors in a previous printing; so called because of the small black star that appears on the front page or cover.

State of the Union Message—A presidential message to Congress under the constitutional directive that he shall "from time to time give to the Congress Information of the State of the Union, and recommend to their Consideration such Measures as he shall judge necessary and expedient." Customarily, the president sends an annual State of the Union message to Congress, usually late in January.

Statutes at Large—A chronological arrangement of the laws enacted in each session of Congress. Though indexed, the laws are not arranged by subject matter nor is there an indication of how they affect or change previously enacted laws. The volumes are numbered by Congress, and the laws are cited by their volume and page number. The Gramm-Rudman-Hollings Act, for example, appears as 99 Stat. 1037.

Straw Vote Prohibition—Under a House precedent, a member who has the floor during debate may not conduct a straw vote or otherwise ask for a show of support for a proposition. Only the chair may put a question to a vote.

Strike from the *Record*—Expunge objectionable remarks from the *Congressional Record,* after a member's words have been taken down on a point of order.

Subcommittee—A panel of committee members assigned a portion of the committee's jurisdiction or other functions. On legislative committees, subcommittees hold hearings, mark up legislation, and report measures to their full committee for further action; they cannot report directly to the chamber. A subcommittee's party composition usually reflects the ratio on its parent committee.

Subpoena Power—The authority granted to committees by the rules of their respective houses to issue legal orders requiring individuals to appear and testify, or to produce documents pertinent to the committee's functions, or both. Persons who do not comply with subpoenas can be cited for contempt of Congress and prosecuted.

Subsidy—Generally, a payment or benefit made by the federal government for which no current repayment is required. Subsidy payments may be designed to support the conduct of an economic enterprise or activity, such as ship operations, or to support certain market prices, as in the case of farm subsidies.

Sunset Legislation—A term sometimes applied to laws authorizing the existence of agencies or programs that expire annually or at the end of some other specified period of time. One of the purposes of setting specific expiration dates for agencies and programs is to encourage the committees with jurisdiction over them to determine whether they should be continued or terminated.

Sunshine Rules—Rules requiring open committee hearings and business meetings, including markup sessions, in both houses, and also open conference committee meetings. However, all may be closed under certain circumstances and using certain procedures required by the rules.

Super Majority—A term sometimes used for a vote on a matter that requires approval by more than a simple majority of those members present and voting; also referred to as extraordinary majority.

Supplemental Appropriation Bill—A measure providing appropriations for use in the current fiscal year, in addition to those already provided in annual general appropriation bills. Supplemental appropriations are often for unforeseen emergencies.

Suspension of the Rules (House)—An expeditious procedure for passing relatively noncontroversial or emergency measures by a two-thirds vote of those members voting, a quorum being present.

Suspension of the Rules (Senate)—A procedure to set aside one or more of the Senate's rules; it is used infrequently, and then most often to suspend the rule banning legislative amendments to appropriation bills.

Task Force—A title sometimes given to a panel of members assigned to a special project, study, or investigation. Ordinarily, these groups do not have authority to report measures to their respective houses.

Tax Expenditure—Loosely, a tax exemption or advantage, sometimes called an incentive or loophole; technically, a loss of governmental tax revenue attributable to some provision of federal tax laws that allows a special exclusion, exemption, or deduction from gross income or that provides a special credit, preferential tax rate, or deferral of tax liability.

Televised Proceedings—Television and radio coverage of the floor proceedings of the House of Representatives have been available since 1979 and of the Senate since 1986. They are broadcast over a coaxial cable system to all congressional offices and to some congressional agencies on channels reserved for that purpose. Coverage is also available free of charge to commercial and public television and radio broadcasters. The Cable-Satellite Public Affairs Network (C-SPAN) carries gavel-to-gavel coverage of both houses.

Teller Vote—A voting procedure, formerly used in the House, in which members cast their votes by passing through the center aisle to be counted, but not recorded by name, by a member from each party appointed by the chair. The House deleted the procedure from its rules in 1993, but during floor discussion of the deletion a leading member stated that a teller vote would still be available in the event of a breakdown of the electronic voting system.

Third-Degree Amendment—An amendment to a second-degree amendment. Both houses prohibit such amendments.

Third Reading—A required reading to a chamber of a bill or joint resolution by title only before the vote on passage. In modern practice, it has merely become a pro forma step.

Tie Vote—When the votes for and against a proposition are equal, it loses. The president of the Senate may cast a vote only to break a tie. Because the Speaker is invariably a member of the House, he is entitled to vote but usually does not. He may choose to do so to break, or create, a tie vote.

Title—(1) A major subdivision of a bill or act, designated by a roman numeral and usually containing legislative provisions on the same general subject. Titles are sometimes divided into subtitles as well as sections. (2) The official name of a bill or act, also called a caption or long title. (3) Some bills also have short titles that appear in the sentence immediately following the enacting clause. (4) Popular titles are the unofficial names given to some bills or acts by common usage. For example, the Balanced Budget and Emergency Deficit Control Act of 1985 (short title) is almost invariably referred to as Gramm-Rudman (popular title). In other cases, significant legislation is popularly referred to by its title number (see definition (1) above). For example, the federal legislation that requires equality of funding for women's and men's sports in educational institutions that receive federal funds is popularly called Title IX.

Track System—An occasional Senate practice that expedites legislation by dividing a day's session into two or more specific time periods, commonly called tracks, each reserved for consideration of a different measure.

Transfer Payment—A federal government payment to which individuals or organizations are entitled under law and for which no goods or services are required in return. Payments include welfare and Social Security benefits, unemployment insurance, government pensions, and veterans benefits.

Treaty—A formal document containing an agreement between two or more sovereign nations. The Constitution authorizes the president to make treaties, but he must submit them to the Senate for its approval by a two-thirds vote of the senators present. Under the Senate's rules, that vote actually occurs on a resolution of ratification. Although the Constitution does not give the House a direct role in approving treaties, that body has sometimes insisted that a revenue treaty is an invasion of its prerogatives. In any case, the House may significantly affect the application of a treaty by its equal role in enacting legislation to implement the treaty.

Trust Funds—Special accounts in the Treasury that receive earmarked taxes or other kinds of revenue collections, such as user fees, and from which payments are made for special purposes or to recipients who meet the requirements of the trust funds as established by law. Of the more than 150 federal government trust funds, several finance major entitlement programs, such as Social Security, Medicare, and retired federal employees pensions. Others fund infrastructure construction and improvements, such as highways and airports.

Unanimous Consent—Without an objection by any member. A unanimous consent request asks permission, explicitly or implicitly, to set aside one or more rules. Both houses and their committees frequently use such requests to expedite their proceedings.

Uncontrollable Expenditures—A frequently used term for federal expenditures that are mandatory under existing law and therefore cannot be controlled by the president or Congress without a change in the existing law. Uncontrollable expenditures include spending required under entitlement programs and also fixed costs, such as interest on the public debt and outlays to pay for prior-year obligations. In recent years, uncontrollables have accounted for approximately three-quarters of federal spending in each fiscal year.

Unfunded Mandate—Generally, any provision in federal law or regulation that imposes a duty or obligation on a state or local government or private sector entity without providing the necessary funds to comply. The Unfunded Mandates Reform Act of 1995 amended the Congressional Budget Act of 1974 to provide a mechanism for the control of new unfunded mandates.

Union Calendar—A calendar of the House of Representatives for bills and resolutions favorably reported by committees that raise revenue or directly or indirectly appropriate money or property. In addition to appropriation bills, measures that authorize expenditures are also placed on this calendar. The calendars full title is the Calendar of the Committee of the Whole House on the State of the Union.

Upper Body—A common reference to the Senate, but not used by members of the House.

U.S. Code—Popular title for the *United States Code: Containing the General and Permanent Laws of the United States in Force on. . . .* It is a consolidation and partial codification of the general and permanent laws of the United States arranged by subject under 50 titles. The first six titles deal with general or political subjects, the other 44 with subjects ranging from agriculture to war, alphabetically arranged. A supplement is published after each session of Congress, and the entire code is revised every six years.

User Fee—A fee charged to users of goods or services provided by the federal government. When Congress levies or authorizes such fees, it determines whether the revenues should go into the general collections of the Treasury or be available for expenditure by the agency that provides the goods or services.

Veto—The president's disapproval of a legislative measure passed by Congress. He returns the measure to the house in which it originated without his signature but with a veto message stating his objections to it. When Congress is in session, the president must veto a bill within 10 days, excluding Sundays, after he has received it; otherwise it becomes law without his signature. The 10-day clock begins to run at midnight following his receipt of the bill. *(See also Committee Veto, Item Veto, Override a Veto, Pocket Veto.)*

Voice Vote—A method of voting in which members who favor a question answer aye in chorus, after which those opposed answer no in chorus, and the chair decides which position prevails.

Voting—Members vote in three ways on the floor: (1) by shouting "aye" or "no" on voice votes; (2) by standing for or against on division votes; and (3) on recorded votes (including the yeas and nays), by answering "aye" or "no" when their names are called or, in the House, by recording their votes through the electronic voting system.

War Powers Act of 1973—An act that requires the president "in every possible instance" to consult Congress before he commits U.S. forces to ongoing or imminent hostilities. If he commits them to a combat situation without congressional consultation, he must notify Congress within 48 hours. Unless Congress declares war or otherwise authorizes the operation to continue, the forces must be withdrawn within 60 or 90 days, depending on certain conditions.

Well—The sunken, level, open space between members' seats and the podium at the front of each chamber. House members usually address their chamber from their party's lectern in the well on its side of the aisle. Senators usually speak at their assigned desks.

Whip—The majority or minority party member in each house who acts as assistant leader, helps plan and marshal support for party strategies, encourages party discipline, and advises his leader on how his colleagues intend to vote on the floor. In the Senate, the Republican whip's official title is assistant leader.

Yeas and Nays—A vote in which members usually respond "aye" or "no" (despite the official title of the vote) on a question when their names are called in alphabetical order. The Constitution requires the yeas and nays when a demand for it is supported by one-fifth of the members present, and it also requires an automatic yea-and-nay vote on overriding a veto. Senate precedents require the support of at least one-fifth of a quorum, a minimum of 11 members with the present membership of 100.

Zone Whip—A member responsible for whip duties concerning his or her party colleagues from specific geographical areas.

The Legislative Process in Brief

Note: Parliamentary terms used below are defined in the glossary.

INTRODUCTION OF BILLS

A House member (including the resident commissioner of Puerto Rico and non-voting delegates of the District of Columbia, Guam, the Virgin Islands and American Samoa) may introduce any one of several types of bills and resolutions by handing it to the clerk of the House or placing it in a box called the hopper. A senator first gains recognition of the presiding officer to announce the introduction of a bill. If objection is offered by any senator, the introduction of the bill is postponed until the following day.

As the next step in either the House or Senate, the bill is numbered, referred to the appropriate committee, labeled with the sponsor's name and sent to the Government Printing Office so that copies can be made for subsequent study and action. Senate bills may be jointly sponsored and carry several senators' names. Until 1978, the House limited the number of members who could cosponsor any one bill; the ceiling was eliminated at the beginning of the 96th Congress. A bill written in the executive branch and proposed as an administration measure usually is introduced by the chairman of the congressional committee that has jurisdiction.

Bills—Prefixed with HR in the House, S in the Senate, followed by a number. Used as the form for most legislation, whether general or special, public or private.

Joint Resolutions—Designated H J Res or S J Res. Subject to the same procedure as bills, with the exception of a joint resolution proposing an amendment to the Constitution. The latter must be approved by two-thirds of both houses and is thereupon sent directly to the administrator of general services for submission to the states for ratification instead of being presented to the president for his approval.

Concurrent Resolutions—Designated H Con Res or S Con Res. Used for matters affecting the operations of both houses. These resolutions do not become law.

Resolutions—Designated H Res or S Res. Used for a matter concerning the operation of either house alone and adopted only by the chamber in which it originates.

COMMITTEE ACTION

With few exceptions, bills are referred to the appropriate standing committees. The job of referral formally is the responsibility of the Speaker of the House and the presiding officer of the Senate, but this task usually is carried out on their behalf by the parliamentarians of the House and Senate. Precedent, statute and the jurisdictional mandates of the committees as set forth in the rules of the House and Senate determine which committees receive what kinds of bills. An exception is the referral of private bills, which are sent to whatever committee is designated by their sponsors. Bills are technically considered "read for the first time" when referred to House committees.

When a bill reaches a committee it is placed on the committee's calendar. At that time the bill comes under the sharpest congressional focus. Its chances for passage are quickly determined—and the great majority of bills falls by the legislative roadside. Failure of a committee to act on a bill is equivalent to killing it; the measure can be withdrawn from the committee's purview only by a discharge petition signed by a majority of the House membership on House bills, or by adoption of a special resolution in the Senate. Discharge attempts rarely succeed.

The first committee action taken on a bill usually is a request for comment on it by interested agencies of the government. The committee chairman may assign the bill to a subcommittee for study and hearings, or it may be considered by the full committee. Hearings may be public, closed (executive session) or both. A subcommittee, after considering a bill, reports to the full committee its recommendations for action and any proposed amendments.

The full committee then votes on its recommendation to the House or Senate. This procedure is called "ordering a bill reported." Occasionally a committee may order a bill reported unfavorably; most of the time a report, submitted by the chairman of the committee to the House or Senate, calls for favorable action on the measure since the committee can effectively "kill" a bill by simply failing to take any action.

After the bill is reported, the committee chairman instructs the staff to prepare a written report. The report describes the purposes and scope of the bill, explains the committee revisions, notes proposed changes in existing law and, usually, includes the views of the executive branch agencies consulted. Often committee members opposing a measure issue dissenting minority statements that are included in the report.

Usually, the committee "marks up" or proposes amendments to the bill. If they are substantial and the measure is complicated, the committee may order a "clean bill" introduced, which will embody the proposed amendments. The original bill then is put aside and the clean bill, with a new number, is reported to the floor.

The chamber must approve, alter or reject the committee amendments before the bill itself can be put to a vote.

FLOOR ACTION

After a bill is reported back to the house where it originated, it is placed on the calendar.

There are five legislative calendars in the House, issued in one cumulative calendar titled *Calendars of the United States House of Representatives and History of Legislation.* The House calendars are:

The Union Calendar to which are referred bills raising revenues, general appropriations bills and any measures directly or indirectly appropriating money or property. It is the Calendar of the Committee of the Whole House on the State of the Union.

The House Calendar to which are referred bills of public character not raising revenue or appropriating money.

The Corrections Calendar to which are referred bills to repeal rules and regulations deemed excessive or unnecessary when the Corrections Calendar is called the second and fourth Tuesday of each month. (Instituted in the 104th Congress to replace the seldom-used Consent Calendar.) A three-fifths majority is required for passage.

The Private Calendar to which are referred bills for relief in the nature of claims against the United States or private immigration bills that are passed without debate when the Private Calendar is called the first and third Tuesdays of each month.

The Discharge Calendar to which are referred motions to discharge committees when the necessary signatures are signed to a discharge petition.

There is only one legislative calendar in the Senate and one "executive calendar" for treaties and nominations submitted to the Senate. When the Senate Calendar is called, each senator is limited to five minutes' debate on each bill.

Debate

A bill is brought to debate by varying procedures. If a routine measure, it may await the call of the calendar. If it is urgent or important, it can be taken up in the Senate either by unanimous consent or by a majority vote. The majority leader, in consultation with the minority leader and others, schedules the bills that will be taken up for debate.

In the House, precedence is granted if a special rule is obtained from the Rules Committee. A request for a special rule usually is made by the chairman of the committee that favorably reported the bill, supported by the bill's sponsor and other committee members. The request, considered by the Rules Committee in the same fashion that other committees consider legislative measures, is in the form of a resolution providing for immediate consideration of the bill. The Rules Committee reports the resolution to the House where it is debated and voted on in the same fashion as regular bills. If the Rules Committee fails to report a rule requested by a committee, there are several ways to bring the bill to the House floor—under suspension of the rules, on Calendar Wednesday or by a discharge motion.

The resolutions providing special rules are important because they specify how long the bill may be debated and whether it may be amended from the floor. If floor amendments are banned, the bill is considered under a "closed rule," which permits only members of the committee that first reported the measure to the House to alter its language, subject to chamber acceptance.

When a bill is debated under an "open rule," amendments may be offered from the floor. Committee amendments always are taken up first but may be changed, as may all amendments up to the second degree; that is, an amendment to an amendment to an amendment is not in order.

Duration of debate in the House depends on whether the bill is under discussion by the House proper or before the House when it is sitting as the Committee of the Whole House on the State of the Union. In the former, the amount of time for debate either is determined by special rule or is allocated with an hour for each member if the measure is under consideration without a rule. In the Committee of the Whole the amount of time agreed on for general debate is equally divided between proponents and opponents. At the end of general discussion, the bill is read section by section for amendment. Debate on an amendment is limited to five minutes for each side; this is called the "five-minute rule." In practice, amendments regularly are debated more than ten minutes, with members gaining the floor by offering pro forma amendments or obtaining unanimous consent to speak longer than five minutes.

Senate debate usually is unlimited. It can be halted only by unanimous consent or by "cloture," which requires a three-fifths majority of the entire Senate except for proposed changes in the Senate rules. The latter requires a two-thirds vote.

The House considers almost all important bills within a parliamentary framework known as the Committee of the Whole. It is not a committee as the word usually is understood; it is the full House meeting under another name for the purpose of speeding action on legislation. Technically, the House sits as the Committee of the Whole when it considers any tax measure or bill dealing with public appropriations. It also can resolve itself into the Committee of the Whole if a member moves to do so and the motion is carried. The Speaker appoints a member to serve as the chairman. The rules of the House permit the Committee of the Whole to meet when a quorum of 100 members is present on the floor and to amend and act on bills, within certain time limitations. When the Committee of the Whole has acted, it "rises," the Speaker returns as the presiding officer of the House and the member appointed chairman of the Committee of the Whole reports the action of the committee and its recommendations. The Committee of the Whole cannot pass a bill; instead it reports the measure to the full House with whatever changes it has approved. The full House then may pass or reject the bill—or, on occasion, recommit the bill to committee. Amendments adopted in the Committee of the Whole may be put to a second vote in the full House.

Votes

Voting on bills may occur repeatedly before they are finally approved or rejected. The House votes on the rule for the bill and on various amendments to the bill. Voting on amendments often is a more illuminating test of a bill's support than is the final tally. Sometimes members approve final passage of bills after vigorously supporting amendments that, if adopted, would have scuttled the legislation.

The Senate has three different methods of voting: an untabulated voice vote, a standing vote (called a division) and a recorded roll call to which members answer "yea" or "nay" when their names are called. The House also employs voice and standing votes, but since January 1973 yeas and nays have been recorded by an electronic voting device, eliminating the need for time-consuming roll calls.

Another method of voting, used in the House only, is the teller vote. Traditionally, members filed up the center aisle past counters; only vote totals were announced. Since 1971, one-fifth of a quorum can demand that the votes of individual members be recorded, thereby forcing them to take a public position on amendments to key bills. Electronic voting now is commonly used for this purpose.

After amendments to a bill have been voted upon, a vote may be taken on a motion to recommit the bill to committee. If carried, this vote removes the bill from the chamber's calendar and is usually a death blow to the bill. If the motion is unsuccessful, the bill then is "read for the third time." An actual reading usually is dispensed with. Until 1965, an opponent of a bill could delay this move by objecting and asking for a full reading of an engrossed (certified in final form) copy of the bill. After the "third reading," the vote on final passage is taken.

The final vote may be followed by a motion to reconsider, and this motion may be followed by a move to lay the motion on the table. Usually, those voting for the bill's passage vote for the tabling motion, thus safeguarding the final passage action. With that, the bill has been formally passed by the chamber. While a motion to reconsider a Senate vote is pending on a bill, the measure cannot be sent to the House.

ACTION IN SECOND CHAMBER

After a bill is passed it is sent to the other chamber. This body may then take one of several steps. It may pass the bill as is—accepting the other chamber's language. It may send the bill to committee for scrutiny or alteration, or reject the entire bill, advising the other house of its actions. Or it simply may ignore the bill submitted while it continues work on its own version of the proposed legislation. Frequently, one chamber may approve a version of a bill that is greatly at variance with the version already passed by the other house, and then substitute its contents for the language of the other, retaining only the latter's bill number.

A provision of the Legislative Reorganization Act of 1970 permits a separate House vote on any non-germane amendment added by the

How a Bill Becomes Law

This graphic shows the most typical way in which proposed legislation is enacted into law. There are more complicated, as well as simpler, routes, and most bills never become law. The process is illustrated with two hypothetical bills, House bill No. 1 (HR 1) and

Senate bill No. 2 (S 2). Bills must be passed by both houses in identical form before they can be sent to the president. The path of HR 1 is traced by a black line, that of S 2 by a gray line. In practice, most bills begin as similar proposals in both houses.

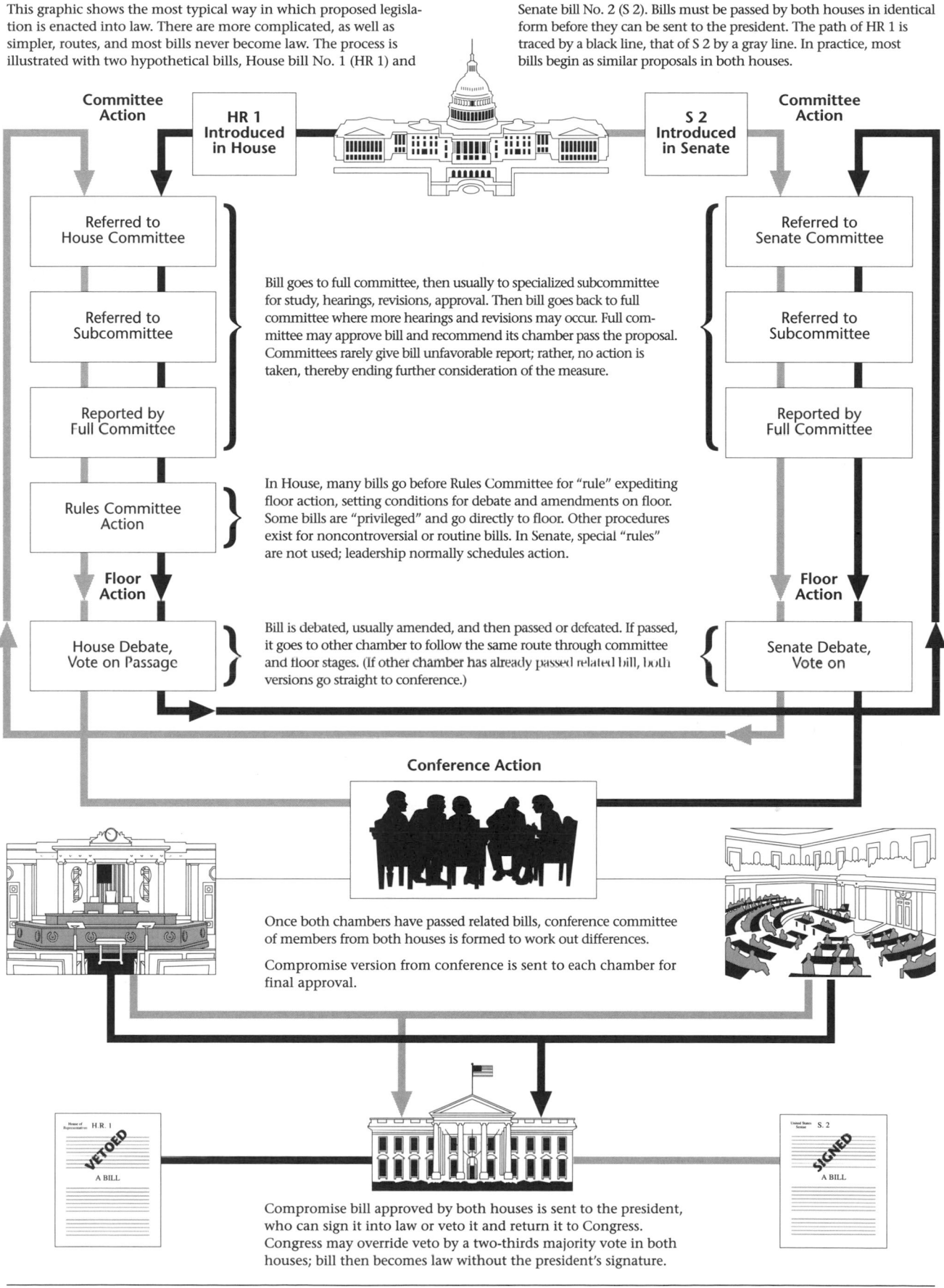

Committee Action

HR 1 Introduced in House

S 2 Introduced in Senate

Committee Action

Referred to House Committee

Referred to Subcommittee

Reported by Full Committee

Referred to Senate Committee

Referred to Subcommittee

Reported by Full Committee

Bill goes to full committee, then usually to specialized subcommittee for study, hearings, revisions, approval. Then bill goes back to full committee where more hearings and revisions may occur. Full committee may approve bill and recommend its chamber pass the proposal. Committees rarely give bill unfavorable report; rather, no action is taken, thereby ending further consideration of the measure.

Rules Committee Action

In House, many bills go before Rules Committee for "rule" expediting floor action, setting conditions for debate and amendments on floor. Some bills are "privileged" and go directly to floor. Other procedures exist for noncontroversial or routine bills. In Senate, special "rules" are not used; leadership normally schedules action.

Floor Action

House Debate, Vote on Passage

Bill is debated, usually amended, and then passed or defeated. If passed, it goes to other chamber to follow the same route through committee and floor stages. (If other chamber has already passed related bill, both versions go straight to conference.)

Floor Action

Senate Debate, Vote on

Conference Action

Once both chambers have passed related bills, conference committee of members from both houses is formed to work out differences.

Compromise version from conference is sent to each chamber for final approval.

H.R. 1 VETOED A BILL

S. 2 SIGNED A BILL

Compromise bill approved by both houses is sent to the president, who can sign it into law or veto it and return it to Congress. Congress may override veto by a two-thirds majority vote in both houses; bill then becomes law without the president's signature.

Examples of Legislative Documents

Senate to a House-passed bill and requires a majority vote to retain the amendment. Previously the House was forced to act on the bill as a whole; the only way to defeat the non-germane amendment was to reject the entire bill.

Often the second chamber makes only minor changes. If these are readily agreed to by the other house, the bill then is routed to the president. However, if the opposite chamber significantly alters the bill submitted to it, the measure usually is "sent to conference." The chamber that has possession of the "papers" (engrossed bill, engrossed amendments, messages of transmittal) requests a conference and the other chamber must agree to it. If the second chamber does not agree, the bill dies.

CONFERENCE ACTION

A conference works out conflicting House and Senate versions of a legislative bill. The conferees usually are senior members appointed by the presiding officers of the two houses, from the committees that managed the bills. Under this arrangement the conferees of one house have the duty of trying to maintain their chamber's position in the face of amending actions by the conferees (also referred to as "managers") of the other house.

The number of conferees from each chamber may vary, the range usually being from three to nine members in each group, depending upon the length or complexity of the bill involved. There may be five representatives and three senators on the conference committee, or the reverse. But a majority vote controls the action of each group so that a large representation does not give one chamber a voting advantage over the other chamber's conferees.

Theoretically, conferees are not allowed to write new legislation in reconciling the two versions before them, but this curb sometimes is bypassed. Many bills have been put into acceptable compromise form only after new language was provided by the conferees. The 1970 Reorganization Act attempted to tighten restrictions on conferees by forbidding them to introduce any language on a topic that neither chamber sent to conference or to modify any topic beyond the scope of the different House and Senate versions.

Frequently the ironing out of difficulties takes days or even weeks. Conferences on involved appropriations bills sometimes are particularly drawn out.

As a conference proceeds, conferees reconcile differences between the versions, but generally they grant concessions only insofar as they remain sure that the chamber they represent will accept the compromises. Occasionally, uncertainty over how either house will react, or the positive refusal of a chamber to back down on a disputed amendment, results in an impasse, and the bills die in conference even though each was approved by its sponsoring chamber.

Conferees sometimes go back to their respective chambers for fur-

ther instructions, when they report certain portions in disagreement. Then the chamber concerned can either "recede and concur" in the amendment of the other house or "insist on its amendment."

When the conferees have reached agreement, they prepare a conference report embodying their recommendations (compromises). The report, in document form, must be submitted to each house.

The conference report must be approved by each house. Consequently, approval of the report is approval of the compromise bill. In the order of voting on conference reports, the chamber that asked for a conference yields to the other chamber the opportunity to vote first.

FINAL ACTION

After a bill has been passed by both the House and Senate in identical form, all of the original papers are sent to the enrolling clerk of the chamber in which the bill originated. He then prepares an enrolled bill, which is printed on parchment paper.

When this bill has been certified as correct by the secretary of the Senate or the clerk of the House, depending on which chamber originated the bill, it is signed first (no matter whether it originated in the Senate or House) by the Speaker of the House and then by the president of the Senate. It is next sent to the White House to await action.

If the president approves the bill, he signs it, dates it and usually writes the word "approved" on the document. If he does not sign it within 10 days (Sundays excepted) and Congress is in session, the bill becomes law without his signature.

However, should Congress adjourn before the 10 days expire, and the president has failed to sign the measure, it does not become law. This procedure is called the pocket veto.

A president vetoes a bill by refusing to sign it and, before the 10-day period expires, returning it to Congress with a message stating his reasons. The message is sent to the chamber that originated the bill. If no action is taken on the message, the bill dies. Congress, however, can attempt to override the president's veto and enact the bill, "the objections of the president to the contrary notwithstanding." Overriding a veto requires a two-thirds vote of those present, who must number a quorum and vote by roll call.

Debate can precede this vote, with motions permitted to lay the message on the table, postpone action on it or refer it to committee. If the president's veto is overridden by a two-thirds vote in both houses, the bill becomes law. Otherwise it is dead.

When bills are passed finally and signed, or passed over a veto, they are given law numbers in numerical order as they become law. There are two series of numbers, one for public and one for private laws, starting at the number "1" for each two-year term of Congress. They are then identified by law number and by Congress—for example, Private Law 21, 97th Congress; Public Law 250, 97th Congress (or PL 97-250).

Key Votes

Congressional Quarterly each year selects a series of key votes on major issues. An issue is judged by the extent it represents one or more of the following:

- A matter of major controversy.
- A test of presidential or political power.
- A decision of potentially great impact on the nation and lives of Americans.

For each series of related votes on an issue only one key vote is usually chosen. This vote is the roll call in the House or Senate that in the opinion of Congressional Quarterly was the most important in determining the outcome.

Senate

1. BUDGET RESOLUTION

The Senate vote on President Clinton's fiscal 1994 budget blueprint in March exemplified two themes that would reappear again and again in the battle over tax and spending issues in 1993. First, Democrats evinced deep unease about voting for many of Clinton's economic proposals, particularly the tax increases that formed the core of his plan to reduce the deficit. Second, at crucial moments, Democrats put aside their fears and backed Clinton, saving his plan from imminent defeat.

The Senate version of the budget resolution (H Con Res 64) embodied a slightly modified version of Clinton's $1.5 trillion budget. Because the budget resolution set in motion the so-called reconciliation process, in which various committees drafted contributions to a bill putting tax increases and spending cuts into law, it provided the initial test of the Senate's willingness to follow the president's economic plan.

The budget resolution passed the Senate on March 25 on an almost strictly party-line vote of 54–45: R 0–43; D 54–2 (ND 41–0, SD 13–2).

The only two Democrats to vote against it were Bob Krueger of Texas, who was defeated in a special election May 1, and Richard C. Shelby of Alabama, who opposed Clinton's economic plan at every stage.

Throughout the six-day floor debate on the budget resolution, Democrats appeared sorely tempted to abandon key elements of Clinton's plan. Republicans crafted amendment after amendment to put them on the spot. But the Democrats stuck together and voted down amendments that, for example, would have stripped out a tax increase imposed on better-off Social Security beneficiaries, would have knocked out Clinton's proposed spending and tax increases and would have restored money that Clinton wanted to cut from defense.

The resolution did reflect an important shift in fiscal policy. It laid out a goal of cutting the deficit by more than $500 billion over five years, somewhat more than had been suggested by Clinton. It proposed net new taxes of $295 billion and net spending cuts of slightly more than $200 billion. All these figures would be adjusted as the budget moved through Congress, but the basic thrust of the plan would remain intact.

Keeping nervous Democrats in line required enormous lobbying pressure from Democratic leaders and from the president himself. Clinton and the leadership were able to succeed partly by appealing to lawmakers to give the president's program a chance. But many Democrats also knew that the specific tax and spending decisions would be made later in the year on the budget-reconciliation bill (HR 2264).

The vote on the budget resolution overstated the level of support among Democrats for the specifics of Clinton's program. Later in the summer, many of the same Democrats who voted for the budget gave the administration fits and forced revisions to key elements of the program. In particular, a proposed energy tax based on the heat content of fuels was dropped, and additional spending cuts were substituted for it.

Throughout the debate on the budget resolution, Republicans remained on the outside. Every GOP effort to make a substantive change in the blueprint was voted down. Not a single Republican voted for the Clinton plan, nor would any for the rest of the year.

2. ECONOMIC STIMULUS

Senate Republicans in April killed President Clinton's first piece of fiscal legislation—an economic stimulus package—refusing to accept a multibillion-dollar increase in the deficit in exchange for several hundred thousand temporary jobs.

The bill's Democratic sponsors had the 50 votes needed to pass the bill but not the 60 needed to limit debate. The fourth and final attempt to end a GOP filibuster came April 21, after Clinton had agreed to cut 25 percent from the bill's spending in the hope of attracting a few Republican votes. The motion to invoke cloture failed, however, by a vote of 56–43: R 0–42; D 56–1 (ND 42–0, SD 14–1).

Billed as one of the three cornerstones of Clinton's economic program, the stimulus package took the form of a $16.3 billion supplemental appropriations bill for fiscal 1993 (HR 1335). It was a blend of diverse elements: public works projects to create jobs and spur economic development, summer jobs for youths and unskilled laborers, social programs for the poor and high-technology purchases for the federal government.

The White House had pushed the bill through the House without changes and tried to do the same in the Senate. The first hurdle it encountered was a trio of dissident Democrats—David L. Boren of Oklahoma, John B. Breaux of Louisiana and Richard H. Bryan of Nevada. Saying that the public wanted spending cuts, not increases, the trio wanted to postpone much of the spending in the bill until after Congress adopted a deficit-cutting budget-reconciliation bill.

When the stimulus package reached the Senate floor March 25, its manager, Senate Appropriations Committee Chairman Robert C. Byrd, D-W.Va., set up a parliamentary obstacle course to stop the dissident Democrats. He offered two slightly different versions of Clinton's entire stimulus package as substitute amendments, setting up an "amendment tree" that could wipe out any other amendments adopted by the Senate. The tactic bought time for Byrd, allowing the White House to negotiate a compromise with Boren, Breaux and Bryan. It also provoked an angry response from Republicans, even after Byrd dismantled his amendment tree.

After failing in several attempts to cut the bill, Republicans released a letter March 31 announcing their willingness to filibuster unless changes were made in HR 1335. The Democrats clamped down further, taking control of the Senate floor and allowing no amendments to be offered. Senate Majority Leader George J. Mitchell, D-Maine, threatened to delay the two-week Senate recess that was scheduled to begin April 5 until the stimulus package passed. But Republicans held their ground, voting as a bloc against motions to limit debate on April 2, April 3 and April 5. With Democrat Richard C. Shelby of Alabama joining the Republicans, the bill's sponsors fell at least five votes short of cloture each time.

The Senate then recessed for two weeks, and Clinton signaled his willingness to compromise. His proposed 25 percent cut, however, did not meet the basic Republican demand: any spending beyond the $4 billion for extended unemployment benefits had to be offset with cuts in other programs. Although a handful of Republican moderates said they were interested in compromising, none voted for cloture April 21.

Mitchell offered to trim the bill to $12.9 billion in appropriations and trust-fund spending, with $5 billion in offsetting cuts. Minority Leader Bob Dole, R-Kan., rejected that proposal, and Mitchell refused Dole's counteroffer of a $6.55 billion package with $2.55 billion in offsetting cuts.

By voice vote, the Senate then agreed to strip the bill down to one provision—a $4 billion emergency appropriation for extended unemployment benefits. The truncated measure quickly passed, and Clinton signed it into law April 23 (PL 103–24). *(House key vote 3)*

3. CAMPAIGN FINANCE

For three years in a row—from 1990 through 1992—the Senate approved campaign finance legislation that would have provided substantial public funding to candidates who agreed to comply with spending limits. But in 1993 Democrats could not break a Republican-led filibuster until they stripped out all public funding.

While concern over the deficit was a key factor, another was the occupant of the White House. Republicans had not tried to filibuster those previous bills because they knew that then-president George Bush would veto them. President Clinton, on the other hand, had promised to sign a bill.

Democrats had long argued that the way to reform the campaign finance system was to limit spending, which they said would keep incumbents from winning on the strength of their fundraising advantages. The only way limits could be imposed within the confines of the Supreme Court's 1976 decision in *Buckley v. Valeo* was to make them voluntary and encourage compliance by offering partial public financing.

Republicans, on the other hand, objected to spending caps, which they said would prevent challengers from being as visible as incumbents. They also objected to asking taxpayers to foot even part of the bill for congressional campaigns.

After two cloture votes failed on largely party lines to end the 1993 filibuster, Democrats agreed to a demand by five key Republicans that public funding be eliminated and replaced with a new 34 percent tax on contributions to candidates who rejected spending limits.

The tax amendment, offered by Sen. Dave Durenberger, R-Minn., passed on a 52–47 vote June 16, with 47 Democrats in support. Though many said the tax would not pass constitutional muster—they argued that it was a tax on speech—the absence of public funding paved the way for a 62–37 vote to shut off debate hours later.

The bill as passed by the Senate set spending limits ranging from $8.25 million for a candidate in California to $2 million for those in small states. It banned political action committee contributions, prohibited groups that lobbied Congress from bundling individual contributions to a candidate and restricted the use of money raised outside federal guidelines in federal elections.

With the exception that it lacked public funding, the bill essentially modeled a plan endorsed by Clinton on May 7. The Senate passed the bill on June 17 by a vote of 60–38: R 7–35; D 53–3 (ND 42–0; SD 11–3). *(House key vote 15)*

4. BUDGET-RECONCILIATION

It was the closest Senate vote in six years, and President Clinton came perilously close to seeing his entire economic plan go down to defeat at the hands of rebellious Democrats. But in the end, he won passage of the budget-reconciliation bill (HR 2264—PL 103–66) that was designed to put a reworked version of his plan into law.

The bill passed only with the intervention of Vice President Al

Gore, who cast the tie-breaking vote shortly after 3 a.m. June 25. The vote was 50–49: R 0–43; D 49–6 (ND 38–3, SD 11–3).

Clinton's heavy reliance on tax increases to reduce the deficit was initially the cause of the division among Senate Democrats. Conservative Democrats, many of them from energy producing states, balked at his proposal for an energy tax, based on the heat content of fuels. They wanted more emphasis on spending cuts, and when the bill came over from the House, some were determined to kill the energy tax, even if it meant bringing down the entire package. *(House key vote 6)*

The leading Democratic opponent was David L. Boren of Oklahoma, who had initially praised the Clinton plan but later became a vocal critic. In the weeks leading up to the Senate vote, Clinton had to rewrite key elements of his plan. But every attempt to produce a formula satisfactory to the conservatives caused problems with other party factions.

Deeper spending cuts drew protests from liberal senators, who wanted to defend programs for the poor and elderly. Pro-business moderates were upset that costly business tax breaks were to be scaled back to pay for a smaller energy tax.

Each group was able to exercise a sort of veto power over the deal because of Clinton's strategy to rely entirely on Democratic votes to pass his program. It was a strategy born partly of necessity, partly of choice. Republican leaders worked hard to keep their rank and file unified in opposition to Clinton's plan. The White House had almost no opportunity to seek a bipartisan coalition in support of its economic program.

At the same time, the White House and Senate Democratic leaders made little effort to attract moderate Republicans, some of whom said they would have supported tax increases if the administration had been willing to make a more serious attempt at cutting spending in entitlement programs, such as Social Security and Medicare.

The upshot was that Clinton's plan had to rise or fall with the Democrats alone. Democrats escaped this quagmire with a laboriously crafted compromise that junked Clinton's energy tax and replaced it with an increase in federal excise taxes on gasoline and other transportation fuels. Liberals had to accept deeper cuts in Medicare, but they managed to limit the damage. And the moderates won a commitment from Clinton to fight for business tax breaks when the final version of the bill was written in conference with the House.

When the bargaining was over, the broad outlines of Clinton's package looked roughly the same. But many key details had been changed. Even then, when the bill went to the floor, there was plenty of doubt whether Democrats could energize their majority, put aside their worries about voting for tax increases and pass their president's plan.

When the roll was called, the Democrats lost six of their own, two of whom were up for reelection in 1994: Richard H. Bryan of Nevada and Frank R. Lautenberg of New Jersey. A third opponent, Dennis DeConcini of Arizona, later announced that he would not run for reelection the next year. Three Southern conservatives—J. Bennett Johnston of Louisiana, Sam Nunn of Georgia and Richard C. Shelby of Alabama—also voted no. Every Republican was opposed.

Two senators were absent: Patty Murray, D-Wash., and Arlen Specter, R-Pa. With 49 votes for the plan and 49 against, Gore had to break the tie.

Although the victory had Pyrrhic overtones, Clinton had accomplished something that had looked nearly impossible in the weeks before the vote. He had kept a recognizable version of his plan alive when it seemed headed for certain death in the Senate. And he set up a party-defining showdown for the Democrats later in the summer, when House and Senate leaders would sit down to write the final version of the bill. The conference agreement on HR 2264 ultimately was adopted by a 51–50 vote that reprised the June test, including Gore's tie-breaker.

5. NATIONAL SERVICE

President Clinton must never have believed it would be so difficult to enact his plan to create a National Service corps for young people to earn financial credit toward their postsecondary education in return for their contribution of community service. At stops across the country during the 1992 presidential campaign, he received more applause for mentioning National Service than for almost any other initiative.

But the feel-good program of the campaign turned into a gridlocked program in the Senate. It went through a series of revisions, compromises and delays before the Senate ultimately passed the National Service bill (HR 2010) on Aug. 3 by 58–41: R 7–37; D 51–4 (ND 38–3, SD 13–1).

Passage came only after a threatened Republican filibuster knocked the bill off the floor the week before, when Democrats scrambled—but failed—to come up with 60 votes to invoke cloture, stop Republican delaying tactics and bring the measure to a vote. Democrats had united in their attempts to stop the filibuster, but they failed by one vote July 29 to muster the necessary 60-vote majority. Four Democrats later voted against final passage: Robert C. Byrd of West Virginia, Ernest F. Hollings of South Carolina and Jim Exon and Bob Kerrey of Nebraska.

Democratic sponsors broke the impasse by scaling back the measure to a three-year program with specified cost ceilings each year. That lured enough Republican support that a second cloture vote proved unnecessary. The cost ceilings of $300 million in fiscal 1994, $500 million in fiscal 1995 and $700 million in fiscal 1996 were projected to reduce the maximum number of service workers to about 100,000 from an earlier estimate of 150,000. Nonetheless, Clinton proclaimed victory despite enactment of a bobtailed version of his campaign promise.

Once over the initial Senate hurdle, a conference compromise was quickly worked out that had no trouble winning adoption in the House or Senate, though final action in the Senate was delayed by the August congressional recess.

As enacted, the National Service program was designed to give awards of as much as $4,725 a year for no more than two years to individuals age 17 or older who performed community service before, during, or after their postsecondary education. Local programs were to offer stipends to participants of as much as $7,400 a year, with the federal government providing 85 percent of the stipend. The federal government was to provide up to 85 percent of the cost of health-care and child-care benefits.

Nonprofit organizations, including institutions of higher education, local governments, school districts and state or federal agencies, were to run the individual programs. Young people would work in such positions as nurses' aides in hospitals or helpers in police departments, or in environmental jobs in national parks.

6. SUPREME COURT NOMINATION

The announced retirement of Supreme Court Justice Byron R. White in March gave the Democrats their first opportunity in 26 years to fill a Supreme Court vacancy. However, President Clinton's choice of U.S. Court of Appeals Judge Ruth Bader Ginsburg did not reflect a desire to begin reshaping a court that had been molded by Republican presidents. Instead, Clinton chose a noncontroversial and well-respected centrist, acceptable to most parts of the political spectrum.

Concerned about the public perception that his presidency was drifting toward the left, Clinton made it clear from the outset that he was inclined to pick a centrist judge. He was still smarting from his recent withdrawal of Justice Department nominees Zoë Baird and Lani Guinier. Baird, nominated for attorney general, withdrew following disclosures that she had hired two illegal immigrants as domestic workers and failed to pay Social Security taxes on them. Guinier, nominated to head Justice's civil rights division, ran into ideological problems, particularly regarding writings on such issues as voting rights that suggested to many that she was too far to the left.

The president's choice of Ginsburg came only after he conducted a long and very public search, eventually passing over two touted finalists—Interior Secretary Bruce Babbitt and U.S. Appeals Court Judge Stephen G. Breyer.

Ginsburg, only the second woman to be nominated to the high court, seemed an ideal candidate. Considered a liberal on civil rights issues and somewhat conservative on criminal and business law, she was generally perceived as a political moderate. In addition, Ginsburg had impressive professional credentials and a solid reputation for personal integrity. A potential snag—her criticism of the landmark 1973 Supreme Court decision in *Roe v. Wade,* which legalized abortion nationwide—dissipated as a threat to her nomination after she publicly reiterated her support for abortion rights.

After four days of low-key testimony before the Senate Judiciary Committee in late July, the Senate confirmed Ginsburg on Aug. 3, 96–3: R 41–3; D 55–0 (ND 41–0, SD 14–0).

The Senate's overwhelming support for Clinton's choice reflected not only Ginsburg's qualities as a candidate but also the president's decision to consult with key senators during the selection process. This was a break with the recent past, when Republican presidents and the Democratic-controlled Senate often squared off over high court nominations. Ginsburg's confirmation proceeded at a relatively fast pace, with the Senate vote coming a little more than seven weeks after her nomination—roughly half the time it took to confirm Clarence Thomas in 1991. Still, the process was not as speedy as it once was. White, for example, nominated by President John F. Kennedy in 1962, was confirmed within 12 days.

7. GAYS IN THE MILITARY

President Clinton's image and his relations with Congress during the first months of his administration were colored by a dispute over his campaign promise to eliminate the military's ban on homosexuals.

The first major party presidential nominee to openly seek gay support, Clinton had pledged months before he secured the Democratic nomination that he would lift the long-standing ban on gay and lesbian service members. Though Clinton repeated the promise several times during the campaign, it never became a focal point of the Democratic message, and George Bush's campaign did little to highlight it.

The issue leapt into prominence almost immediately after the election, in part because it was one of the few controversial campaign pledges that Clinton did not either recant or turn over to a committee for study. The issue also rekindled the campaign debate over whether Clinton's avoidance of the draft during the Vietnam War demonstrated a fundamental antipathy toward the U.S. military.

The vast majority of senior military personnel, including Gen. Colin L. Powell Jr., chairman of the Joint Chiefs of Staff, vehemently opposed Clinton's pledge. Clinton's military critics, who maintained that abolition of the gay ban would undermine cohesion within combat units, were supported by many conservative members of Congress, particularly Senate Armed Services Committee Chairman Sam Nunn, D-Ga.

After an uproar that lasted for months and under the threat of being reversed by Congress, Clinton backed down and ordered only minor changes in the ban. The new policy banned homosexual conduct, and its definition of "conduct" included a service member's private disclosure to a friend of his or her homosexual orientation.

However, under the new policy, recruits no longer would be asked if they were gay. Moreover, investigations of suspected homosexuals could be initiated only by a senior officer acting on the basis of credible information.

The Senate Armed Services Committee declined to let the issue rest, adding language to the defense authorization bill that sealed the military's gay ban into law. In addition, the committee included in the bill strongly worded findings that homosexuality posed "an unacceptable risk" to morale, order and discipline in the armed forces. These findings were intended to buttress the new policy against anticipated court challenges.

In a key vote during debate on the fiscal 1994 defense authorization bill (S 1298), opponents of the gay ban attempted on Sept. 9 to remove from the bill all language on the issue and to explicitly cede the subject to the president. But that amendment, by Barbara Boxer, D-Calif., was rejected 33–63: R 3–38; D 30–25 (ND 29–12; SD 1–13). *(House key vote 8)*

8. STRATEGIC DEFENSE

The Clinton administration renamed the Strategic Defense Initiative (SDI), endorsed a less ambitious focus for the antimissile defense program and dramatically reduced its projected funding. But the rechristened Ballistic Missile Defense program was not scaled back enough for the Senate. For the second year in a row, the Senate demonstrated its willingness to cut more money from the budget for antimissile defenses than was requested by the Pentagon or recommended by the Senate Armed Services Committee.

The Senate's action in 1993 reduced funding for the Ballistic Missile Defense program to $2.8 billion, significantly less than the average annual budget of $3.6 billion that Defense Secretary Les Aspin had outlined for the Clinton administration's approach to antimissile defense. President Clinton had eliminated the budget increases that President George Bush had planned for the program, requesting $3.8 billion—including $121 million for procurement—instead of the $6.3 billion that Bush had projected for fiscal 1994.

Clinton also reshaped the antimissile work along lines mandated by Congress in 1991, placing more emphasis on early deployment of ground-based defenses against attacks by a small number of intercontinental-range ballistic missiles or shorter-range "theater" missiles. It was a far less ambitious approach than that of President Ronald Reagan, who founded SDI in 1983 with a vision of rendering nuclear missiles "impotent and obsolete." The program's original goal was to deploy a shield of antimissile defenses that could make the United States impregnable to an all-out attack by the Soviet Union.

In drafting the fiscal 1994 defense authorization bill (HR 2401), the Armed Services Committee shifted part of the antimissile defense request—$253 million sought for the Brilliant Eyes missile detection satellite—to another account, then approved $3.2 billion for the remaining projects.

In a key vote on the defense authorization bill, the Senate on Sept. 9 approved an amendment by Jim Sasser, D-Tenn., to cut the Ballistic Missile Defense program to $2.8 billion, not including the separate funding for Brilliant Eyes. The amendment was adopted 50–48: R 6–36; D 44–12 (ND 36–6; SD 8–6).

Advocates of the cut argued that the antimissile program was still spending too much on "global" defenses that were relics of the Cold War nuclear competition with Moscow. Arguing the case on fiscal grounds, Sasser, chairman of the Budget Committee, said the biggest threat to U.S. national security was no longer ballistic missiles but a federal budget deficit that "threatens the very survival of our nation."

Opposing the cut, Howell Heflin, D-Ala., argued that even though the Soviet Union was gone, "we are still without any means of defending against attacks from hostile and possibly irrational Third World leaders."

Two staunch backers of the antimissile program, Republicans Malcolm Wallop, Wyo., and Frank H. Murkowski, Alaska, did not vote.

The Senate's action essentially settled the funding issue because the version of the bill crafted by the House Armed Services Committee and passed by the House authorized roughly the same amount.

In 1992, Senate Armed Services recommended $4.3 billion for the program for fiscal 1993. But the Senate on a procedural vote in effect endorsed an amendment by Sasser and Dale Bumpers, D-Ark., that would have cut the program by an additional $1 billion. Action on the defense bill was stalled for weeks of negotiations. Eventually, the Senate compromised on $3.8 billion for SDI in fiscal 1993, the level that Clinton requested for fiscal 1994.

9. GRAZING FEES

Working against an unyielding phalanx of Western senators, the Clinton administration tried and failed in 1993 to initiate a plan to more than double grazing fees and impose tough environmental standards on publicly held rangeland. It was a major setback for President Clinton and his Interior secretary, Bruce Babbitt, who kicked off the year proposing to overhaul all public lands policies.

Members of Congress had tried since 1976 to force Western ranchers to pay market prices for leasing federal lands, most of which were in the West. The existing grazing fee rate, based on a formula established by a 1985 executive order by then-president Ronald Reagan, was $1.86 per "animal unit month"—enough forage to feed one cow and calf, five sheep or one horse for a month. That was about one-fifth the amount charged on private lands, although ranchers contended that it did not account for the costs of fences, stock ponds and other amenities that those who used commercial rangeland did not have to pay.

Another concern was the damage done by grazing. On many public lands, lush rangeland had turned to stubble and once-verdant areas near streams were nearly gone.

Nevertheless, Western senators fiercely opposed Clinton's proposals on grazing. At stake were the livelihoods of 27,000 ranchers—a fraction of the nation's ranchers but a politically potent force on an issue that had all the makings of a broader showdown on Western land policies for timber, mining and agriculture.

Malcolm Wallop of Wyoming, the ranking Republican on the Energy and Natural Resources Committee, set the tone early by pushing an amendment to Clinton's budget that would have cut out nearly all the proposed increases. While the amendment was killed, 59–40, on March 23 on a tabling motion by Budget Committee Chairman Jim Sasser, D-Tenn., Western opponents to overhauling public land policy made it clear that they would fight any attempt to impose new burdens on ranchers, miners and farmers.

A week later, Environment and Public Works Committee Chairman Max Baucus, D-Mont., led a small band of Western senators to lobby Clinton to reverse his budget proposals. To their surprise and to the chagrin of environmentalists, Clinton decided to back off on all the fee increases.

For the most part, the move left the proponents of overhauling public land policy looking to Congress to update such laws as the 1872 Mining Law. Still, on grazing, Babbitt had the administrative authority to increase fees without congressional approval.

Babbitt took a step in that direction Aug. 9, saying he would gradually raise grazing fees over three years to $4.28 per animal unit month. But Babbitt angered Western lawmakers and the cattle industry by also proposing an overhaul of rangeland management policies by tying the duration of a grazing permit to a rancher's environmental stewardship record.

On Sept. 14, during Senate debate on the fiscal 1994 appropriations bill for the Interior Department (HR 2520), Western senators argued that Babbitt's proposals were too sweeping to be implemented by executive order. Led by Pete V. Domenici, R-N.M., and Harry Reid, D-Nev., the Western senators pushed through an amendment to prohibit Babbitt from implementing the grazing package during fiscal 1994. All but three senators from Western, Rocky Mountain or Plains states voted in favor of the one-year moratorium. Even some Easterners who supported grazing fee increases voted with Domenici and Reid, who prevailed 59–40: R 38–5; D 21–35 (ND 14–28, SD 7–7).

The vote demonstrated the unique balance of power in the Senate and the unusual voting allegiances it created. A contentious battle over the entire Interior spending bill ensued. Reid immediately began working on a compromise and crafted an amendment that would only increase grazing fees moderately while codifying some of Babbitt's land management proposals.

House negotiators easily approved Reid's amendment in conference committee, while Senate conferees split on a party-line vote. The full House on Oct. 20 affirmed the compromise, 317–106, but it got no further. Using the Senate's unlimited debate rules, 40 Republicans and 5 Democrats from Western, Rocky Mountain and Plains states kept the Interior bill in a procedural stranglehold for three weeks.

During that time, Democratic sponsors of the grazing fee increase failed three times to cut off the filibuster, so Reid finally agreed on Nov. 9 to withdraw his compromise. In exchange, Domenici dropped the one-year moratorium, ended the filibuster and cleared the way for final passage of the fiscal 1994 Interior spending bill.

Both sides claimed victory. Babbitt retained the power to impose grazing fee increases but acknowledged that, as a result of the Senate's intransigence, he would proceed with extra deliberation and consultation with Western interests before doing so.

10. EX-SOVIET AID

Patrick J. Leahy, D-Vt., said it was "a real roll of the dice" to bring the fiscal 1994 foreign operations appropriations bill to the Senate floor while Russia was teetering on the brink of political collapse.

The Senate began consideration of the measure (HR 2295)—which included $2.5 billion in aid for Russia and its neighbors—on Sept. 22, just one day after Russian president Boris N. Yeltsin had thrown his nation into turmoil by disbanding Parliament.

With Yeltsin locked in a test of wills with his hard-line political rivals, Leahy feared that senators would be reluctant to vote for the massive aid package.

The gamble paid off. The Senate overwhelmingly backed the legislation, handing President Clinton a foreign policy triumph. Clinton had urged the Senate to send a signal of support to the Russian leader.

In a key vote Sept. 23, the Senate approved the foreign operations bill, 88–10: R 36–7; D 52–3 (ND 40–2, SD 12–1).

Leahy, who chaired the Appropriations Subcommittee on Foreign Operations, really had no choice but to press for quick Senate action. The bill's unusual funding formula had created a tight timetable. Of the $2.5 billion in aid for the former Soviet Union, $1.6 billion was in the form of a supplemental appropriation for fiscal 1993.

That money—drawn from unexpended balances of defense and foreign aid funds—would have become unavailable on Sept. 30, the last day of the fiscal year.

Lawmakers ended up acting in time to fully fund the administration's request. Congress cleared the foreign operations bill Sept. 30, and Clinton signed it into law the same day.

Surprisingly, Russia's political chaos was barely mentioned during the Senate debate. The Senate adopted a host of conditions that reflected concerns over various policies being pursued by Moscow, but none were regarded as "killer" amendments that would have prevented disbursement of the aid.

Senators seemed generally content to follow Clinton's lead in backing Yeltsin. After the vote, Leahy told reporters that the Senate's virtual silence on the issue should be read as support for the administration's policy. After all, he said, any senator could have held up the bill.

No one was more pleased by the outcome than Strobe Talbott, the ambassador-at-large for the former Soviet Union. Talbott had been criticized by Leahy and other senators for not adequately consulting with Congress on the massive aid program for the former Soviet republics.

"It's a big victory for American foreign policy," Talbott said after the vote. "It would have been the worst possible signal to in any way pull back."

The administration and Congress remained committed to Yeltsin as a crisis in Moscow reached a bloody climax less than a week later. The standoff ended Oct. 4 as troops loyal to the Russian president launched a military assault on the Russian Parliament building, which had been occupied for two weeks by Yeltsin's opponents. *(House key vote 4)*

11. ABORTION

From the beginning, Sen. Barbara A. Mikulski, D-Md., had insisted that she had the votes to lift the long-running ban on using federal dollars to pay for most abortions for poor women.

The House had been unable to kill the Hyde amendment, named after sponsor Henry J. Hyde, R-Ill. Instead, the House voted to relax slightly the restrictions on Medicaid, the federal-state health insurance program for the poor, allowing it to pay for abortions only in cases of rape and incest, as well as when the woman's life was in danger, a long-standing exception.

When the revised Hyde language came to the Senate as part of a spending bill (HR 2518) for the departments of Labor, Health and Human Services, and Education, Mikulski persuaded the Senate Appropriations Committee to strike it. The committee's action would have allowed poor women to receive abortions under most circumstances—paid for by Medicaid.

Mikulski and the four other female Democratic senators—all abortion rights supporters—believed they could maintain that position on the floor. The Senate had always been more liberal than the House when it came to abortions paid for by Medicaid. For the previous decade, the House had usually voted to restrict Medicaid from paying for abortions except when the life of the woman was in danger. In the Senate, members had usually voted to allow Medicaid to pay for abortions in cases of rape and incest as well. But in conference, the House had always prevailed.

In 1993, female lawmakers in the Senate wanted to move beyond their usual position and drop all restrictions without any compromise. They worried that if they offered a compromise and lost, it would hurt attempts to insure abortion in President Clinton's universal health-care plan.

Mikulski's calculation proved way off the mark. On Sept. 28, when abortion opponents forced a vote on the Appropriations Committee proposal to strike the Hyde language from the House-passed bill, the Senate voted it down, 40–59: R 6–38; D 34–21 (ND 31–11, SD 3–10).

In the end, 21 Democrats sided with 38 Republicans to defeat the amendment. While some of those Democrats supported a woman's right to an abortion, they would not go so far as to allow taxpayers' funds to be used to pay for the procedure.

The vote meant that the House language would stay in the bill, prohibiting Medicaid from paying for abortions except in cases of rape and incest and when the life of the woman was in danger. The vote also was a key test of clout for the five Democratic female senators, working together as a bloc. The large majority against federal funding suggested that future proposals—particularly on a health insurance reform bill affecting all women—would run into similar obstacles in the Senate.

Abortion rights supporters fared better on another abortion-related bill to make it a federal crime to intimidate by force or threat of force a woman seeking to obtain an abortion, or abortion clinic workers. The Senate passed that bill (S 636—S Rept 103–117) on Nov. 16 by 69–30. But just as in the House, the clinic access debate turned more on the issue of free speech versus fear of terrorism, rather than on the fundamental question of abortion.

In the end, both House and Senate were willing to go only so far to protect and ensure access to abortion services. (*House key vote 5*)

12. SOMALIA/PEACEKEEPING

Amid a growing controversy over the U.S. role in international peacekeeping missions, the Senate voted Oct. 15 to effectively cut off funding for participation by U.S. forces in the United Nations' Somalia operation after March 31, 1994. President Clinton already had agreed to that deadline, but only in the face of a growing threat that Congress might insist on an even earlier U.S. pullout.

In February, when the mission still retained broad congressional support, the Senate by voice vote adopted S J Res 45, authorizing the initial phase of the humanitarian mission that had been launched in December 1992 by President George Bush. Most of the 20,000 U.S. troops initially deployed were withdrawn from Somalia by May 4, when the military mission was handed over to a multilateral U.N. force.

Congressional approval for the U.S. commitment began to wane as troops loyal to Somali warlord Gen. Mohammed Farah Aidid began a relatively low-level but deadly campaign of harassment against U.S. and other U.N. forces in the Somali capital of Mogadishu.

On Sept. 9, the Senate adopted 90–7 a nonbinding amendment by Appropriations Committee Chairman Robert C. Byrd, D-W.Va.—attached to the defense authorization bill (HR 2401, formerly S 1298)—urging Clinton to report to Congress by Oct. 15 on the objectives of the Somalia operation and to seek congressional approval if he wanted to continue the deployment beyond Nov. 15.

The issue boiled over after 18 U.S. soldiers were killed Oct. 3 in a bloody battle with Aidid's forces as they tried to arrest several leaders of Aidid's clan. When the Appropriations panel marked up the de-

fense appropriations bill (HR 3116) the following day, Byrd announced that he would force a Senate vote on an amendment to the bill intended to force an end to U.S. participation in the Somalia operation early in 1994.

Majority Leader George J. Mitchell, D-Maine, Armed Services Committee Chairman Sam Nunn, D-Ga., and other Senate leaders negotiated with Byrd and with the White House to work out a compromise Somalia amendment, which the Senate added to the defense appropriations bill Oct. 15.

The compromise measure endorsed Clinton's March 31 pullout date but cut off most U.S. funds after that. In a key vote Oct. 15, the Senate approved the compromise amendment, offered by Byrd, 76–23: R 24–20; D 52–3 (ND 38–3; SD 14–0).

Aside from writing into law Clinton's acquiescence in congressional demands for a firm end point to the Somalia deployment, the Byrd amendment also was significant on several other levels. It highlighted the opposition of many Republicans to such multinational peacekeeping ventures, and it marked the first time since the Vietnam War that either chamber had voted to cut off funds for an ongoing overseas military operation.

Before the Byrd amendment was adopted, the Senate first quashed an effort to mandate an earlier withdrawal date, voting 61–38 to table (kill) an amendment by John McCain, R-Ariz., to require a "prompt" withdrawal of U.S. forces.

A week after the Somalia showdown, Clinton survived another confrontation with GOP critics, as the Senate defeated, 33–65, an amendment that would have required congressional approval before the president placed U.S. forces under foreign command.

But deep dissatisfaction with Clinton's peacekeeping policies was underscored by passage of nonbinding resolutions urging the administration to come to Congress before dispatching troops on such missions, including to Haiti and Bosnia. (*House key vote 11*)

13. ETHICS ENFORCEMENT

The Constitution gave each chamber of Congress the power to "punish its members for disorderly behavior." After more than 200 years, however, the House and Senate could not shake the public perception that misbehavior was rampant on Capitol Hill, but punishment was not.

When ABC News asked a sample of Americans in August about allegations that Ways and Means Committee Chairman Dan Rostenkowski, D-Ill., had embezzled cash from the House Post Office, 68 percent said that sort of activity represented "business as usual in Congress."

It was in this atmosphere of public distrust that the Senate confronted sexual harassment allegations against Bob Packwood, R-Ore., first revealed in the *Washington Post* in November 1992.

Reconstituted with all new members in 1993, the Senate Ethics Committee toughened its image under its most prosecutorial-minded chairman in years, Richard H. Bryan, D-Nev. Within two weeks of being named, the panel barred questions about the Packwood accusers' sexual histories after hints that he might raise them in his defense, and it expanded its inquiry to include allegations that he tried to intimidate his accusers. Though accusers feared that the committee would limit its probe to the 11 women named by the *Washington Post*, it mailed letters to every woman who had ever worked for Packwood.

After interviewing 150 witnesses, the committee in October prepared to wrap up the first phase of its inquiry so it could decide whether to hold public hearings. Its final task involved taking a deposition from Packwood.

During his testimony, Packwood referred to his personal diaries. Despite concerns about the personal nature of such documents, the committee demanded to see them. It was the clearest signal yet of a tough new era. Packwood initially allowed the panel to review them and copy relevant passages. But he balked when committee aides requested passages raising questions about whether he traded official favors for job offers to his estranged wife when he was in divorce court trying to minimize his alimony. The committee subpoenaed the diaries and asked the Senate to go to court to enforce the demand. Embodied in a resolution (S Res 153), the request sparked a wrenching fight unlike any the Senate had seen in years.

Packwood accused the committee of prying into the sexual lives of other lawmakers. Bryan accused Packwood of possible criminal acts. Members begged the two sides to compromise to avoid what one called "a floor debacle"—to no avail.

For 15 hours on Nov. 1–2, with a majority of senators present most of the time, the Senate debated fine legal points and big constitutional issues. Bryan coolly stated the case against Packwood, who responded with insulted anger. Ethics members from both parties accused Packwood and his lawyers of bad faith. Freshman Democratic women insisted that the Senate take a hard line against sexual harassment by backing the committee.

Packwood's few public defenders—Republicans Alan K. Simpson, Wyo., Arlen Specter, Pa., and John C. Danforth, Mo.—protested that his privacy rights were being trampled. The precedent, they said, would haunt all senators forever.

For all the debate's complex facets, however, the mindset of the Senate was best framed by Ethics Committee Vice Chairman Mitch McConnell, R-Ky. "A lot of people—in the media, in the public— think that we can't handle the job of disciplining our fellow members and guarding the integrity of this institution," he said. "The question before us today is really whether we are up to the job."

It was clear from the start that Packwood's only hope was to limit the scope of the subpoena. On the second day, he offered to turn over all entries related to the sexual charges and to the job offers; an independent examiner would make sure he turned over everything required.

The committee refused the offer. Bryan said it would have required the examiner to ignore any other misdeeds that might be in the diaries. Nor would the examiner know for sure what was relevant. He insisted that the precedent set by the sweeping subpoena was limited because Packwood had introduced the diaries into the proceeding, and then let the committee peruse them and find other possible misdeeds that required further study.

On Nov. 2, Simpson offered the pivotal amendment—to limit the subpoena to "relevant" entries. He argued that the discovery process in civil proceedings was limited to relevant evidence. The Ethics Committee countered that its proceeding was more akin to that of a grand jury, which had broad subpoena powers.

In the end, the Senate decided that it could not risk the appearance that it treated its own more leniently than the government treated other citizens. The vote against Simpson's amendment, and the rebuke of Packwood, was overwhelming—23–77: R 22–22; D 1–55 (ND 1–41, SD 0–14). The Senate then approved the resolution to enforce the subpoena by 94–6.

14. CRIME BILL/ASSAULT WEAPONS

The annual Senate showdown over crime took an unusual turn in 1993 when key Republicans and Democrats struck a deal: Instead of fighting over whose approach to crime-fighting was more worthy, they stitched together a bill in early November that included enough money to make both sides happy. The result was a $22.3 billion measure (HR 3355) that included Republican prison proposals and Democratic rehabilitation efforts, as well as funds that both parties wanted for 100,000 new police officers.

The two sides agreed that they could not agree on how to limit death penalty appeals, so they dealt with that Republican issue separately, quietly killing it for the year and probably for the 103rd Congress. They also dealt separately with the Democrats' so-called Brady bill (HR 1025—PL 103–159), a five-day waiting period for handguns, which made it to the president's desk.

Only one thing stood in the way of the crime bill's final passage: the insistence of gun-control advocates, most of them Democrats, on a semiautomatic assault weapons ban. Though a narrow Senate majority had favored such a move since 1990, gun-control opponents might have been willing to filibuster the crime bill to death had it included a ban.

Gun-control advocates decided to risk it. Backed by the Clinton administration, Dianne Feinstein, D-Calif., crafted a compromise that was stricter than one successfully offered by Dennis DeConcini, D-Ariz., in 1990 and less strict than one advocated by the chamber's biggest antigun exponent, Howard M. Metzenbaum, D-Ohio. Feinstein's proposal banned the manufacture, sale and possession of 19 specific weapons, as well as so-called copycats and most ten-bullet-plus feeders. It explicitly exempted 650 named sporting and hunting guns and existing semiautomatic assault weapons.

"It really comes down to a question of blood or guts—the blood of innocent people or the Senate of the United States having the guts to do what we should do when we take that oath to protect the welfare of our citizens," Feinstein said, as she and other advocates recounted the horror of recent random attacks with assault weapons.

Opponents reiterated their arguments—that toughening and enforcing existing criminal laws was the better solution; that relatively few crimes involved assault weapons; that knives and blunt objects killed more people than rifles; and that gun bans gave criminals an edge over law-abiding citizens seeking to protect themselves.

Their most compelling argument did not involve the amendment's merits. "This particular amendment could cause us to lose this bill," said Orrin G. Hatch, R-Utah. Added Phil Gramm, R-Texas, "The fragile alliance we put together could be torn apart."

The threats proved empty after the Senate rejected a motion to kill the amendment on Nov. 9 by a 49–51 vote (with Ben Nighthorse Campbell, D-Colo., switching his 1991 House position to vote for the amendment at the last minute). It became clear that a filibuster would not materialize the next day, when the two parties late on Nov. 10 struck a deal to allow the amendment and the bill to come to a final vote. In the end, five Republicans who had voted to table Feinstein's amendment switched sides to vote for it, and the amendment carried on Nov. 17 by a comfortable margin, 56–43: R 10–34; D 46–9 (ND 38–3, SD 8–6).

Whether the gun ban would survive into law was very much in doubt. The House, by 247–177, had voted against a ban in 1991. DeConcini said he would not be surprised if the same thing happened again. He had good reason to say so: The National Rifle Association (NRA) was quite influential in the House. The Senate bill contained many get-tough provisions that liberals abhorred; faced with a chance to scrap them, the Democrats might just be willing to dump the assault weapons ban.

Then again, the Senate vote—cast in the throes of a tenuous compromise on the rest of the crime bill—demonstrated anew the mood in that chamber for gun control. Combined with the Brady bill vote to impose a waiting period on handgun purchases, the Senate once again put the NRA forces on the defensive.

15. HANDGUN CONTROL

It took seven years of debate and a harrowing final week of political maneuvering, but the so-called Brady bill (HR 1025—PL 103–159) finally became law as Congress adjourned for the year. Public pressure for the well-known handgun waiting-period measure was instrumental in breaking an eleventh-hour legislative logjam and passing the first major gun control legislation since 1968.

The bottleneck was in the Senate. The House had passed its version of the bill Nov. 10. Senate Republicans led a filibuster against the bill, which imposed a five-day waiting period for handgun purchases and led to a nationwide system of instant checks of criminal records to make sure guns were not sold to felons or other unqualified buyers. The bill was named after former White House press secretary James S. Brady, who was wounded during the 1981 assassination attempt on President Ronald Reagan.

Advocates said the measure would save lives by keeping guns away from some potential killers. But critics complained that it would simply inconvenience law-abiding gun owners while doing little or nothing to fight crime, and many on both sides described the bill as a modest measure that at best would make only a small dent in fighting crime.

Throughout the week of Nov. 15, Senate Minority Leader Bob Dole, R-Kan., had negotiated with Majority Leader George J. Mitchell, D-Maine, and Senate Judiciary Committee Chairman Joseph R. Biden Jr., D-Del., over how to proceed with the legislation. They eventually settled on a compromise version of the bill, to be voted on if supporters could muster the 60 votes for cloture needed to limit debate.

When they failed on two cloture votes on Nov. 19, many observers declared the bill dead for the year. But the legislation had a huge following. Brady's wife, Sarah, expressed frustration at the prospect of letting the bill die for the year, as did President Clinton. So did the public. That unsettled some Republicans who had voted against cloture but did not want to be blamed for killing the bill.

Their concerns sent Dole back into negotiations. He emerged with a version that was only superficially different from the legislation Republicans had filibustered the night before. Instead of ending the waiting period after five years, the new compromise called for a four-year sunset and gave the attorney general the authority to extend it into a fifth year.

That version carried the Senate on Nov. 20, when more Republicans agreed to abandon the filibuster. The bill passed by 63–36: R 16–28; D 47–8 (ND 38–3, SD 9–5).

Republicans who voted against cloture but for final passage were Christopher S. Bond, Mo.; Daniel R. Coats, Ind.; William S. Cohen, Maine; Kay Bailey Hutchison, Texas; Richard G. Lugar, Ind.; Bob Packwood, Ore.; and Strom Thurmond, S.C. Meanwhile, Democrat Patrick J. Leahy of Vermont voted for cloture then voted against the bill.

More intrigue followed. During a raucous House-Senate negotiating session Nov. 22, Biden showed little interest in fighting for many aspects of the Senate version. Conferees essentially took the House bill intact. But while the House readily agreed to the conference version shortly after midnight, Dole balked in the Senate, accusing Democrats of abandoning the Senate's position.

A tense period ensued, with Mitchell threatening to reconvene the Senate after Thanksgiving to consider cloture votes. But Republicans did not want to be blamed for bucking public opinion by thwarting the bill. Opponents agreed to let the bill go through the Senate by voice vote Nov. 24 on the condition that Congress consider revising the law in 1994. *(House key vote 12)*

16. NAFTA IMPLEMENTATION

When the Senate on Nov. 20 passed the bill (HR 3450) implementing the North American Free Trade Agreement (NAFTA), the controversial trade deal had cleared its last hurdle and a wrenching national debate about trade policy had come to an end.

The outcome in the Senate was never in doubt, and the debate never reached the intensity it did in the House. That was because Republicans, who overwhelmingly supported the agreement, were proportionately more numerous in the Senate. Also, the body as a whole was less susceptible to the localized pressures for protection against foreign competition that nearly sank the trade deal in the House. *(House key vote 13)*

The Senate vote was significant, nonetheless. It suggested that Clinton's victory on NAFTA in the House, achieved as it was through furious deal-cutting and bare-knuckles lobbying, was not an isolated event, owed exclusively to the persuasive powers of the president. The White House expended virtually no effort or time rounding up votes in the Senate. Yet NAFTA passed in that chamber by a comfortable margin, 61–38: R 34–10; D 27–28 (ND 18–23, SD 9–5).

The Senate vote exhibited the same divisions that made NAFTA such a tough sell in the House. Clinton once again owed his victory more to opposition Republicans than to members of his own party; Southern Democrats, as in the House, were key, however.

Senate NAFTA opponents included an unusual mix of liberals and conservatives. Many were from states that had suffered severe manufacturing job losses or had industries that expected fiercer competition as trade barriers with Mexico were removed. Conservatives opposed the agreement because they said it would create a multinational bureaucracy that would undermine U.S. sovereignty.

More representative of the sentiment in the Senate was that expressed by Democrats Edward M. Kennedy of Massachusetts and Tom Harkin of Iowa. Both had close ties to organized labor but voted for the agreement because, they said, Mexico offered their states expanded export opportunities.

House

1. FAMILY AND MEDICAL LEAVE

In the end, it seemed almost too easy. Sixteen days after Bill Clinton was sworn into office as president, he signed into law the Family and Medical Leave Act. Congress's quick action belied the eight years and repeated rounds of negotiations that it took for the measure to be enacted.

In signing the 1993 version of the bill (HR 1—PL 103–3) during a Feb. 5 Rose Garden ceremony, Clinton granted most workers the right to unpaid leave of up to 12 weeks for the birth or adoption of a child or for the illness of a close family member.

It was Clinton's election, not a change in Congress, that allowed the measure to become law. Family leave was one of Clinton's top campaign issues. Vice President Al Gore spoke frequently during the campaign of how fortunate he was to be able to take time off from work in 1989 when his young son lay critically injured in the hospital after being hit by a car.

President George Bush had vetoed bills similar to HR 1 in 1990 and 1992, saying he refused to place another government mandate on business.

Bush's opposition notwithstanding, family leave bills had attracted bipartisan support in previous years. Republican Rep. Marge

Roukema of New Jersey became a sponsor in 1990 after businesses with fewer than 50 employees were exempted. A bipartisan compromise in the Senate at the start of the 102nd Congress—brokered by Christopher J. Dodd, D-Conn., and Christopher S. Bond, R-Mo.—exempted key employees and made other changes. That change attracted the support of conservatives, such as Daniel R. Coats, R-Ind., who signed on to what they called a profamily bill.

Despite the new compromises, only the Senate was able to muster the two-thirds majority needed to override Bush's 1992 veto. Though a strong majority of the House was in favor, supporters fell short of the votes needed to override the veto.

With Clinton in the White House, that impediment was removed: There would be no veto and a simple majority would suffice. The House passed HR 1 on Feb. 3 by 265–163: R 40–134; D 224–29 (ND 162–8, SD 62–21); I 1–0.

The Senate amended the measure the next day and passed it 71–27; the House then immediately cleared the Senate-passed version, 247–152.

2. BUDGET RESOLUTION

The House provided the first big legislative test for Bill Clinton's presidency when it considered the fiscal 1994 budget on March 18.

The Democratic majority gave the president a key victory and at the same time took full advantage of its opportunity to put an end to 12 years of Republican economic policy. The fiscal 1994 budget resolution (H Con Res 64) was adopted on a largely party-line vote of 243–183: R 0–172; D 242–11 (ND 164–6, SD 78–5); I 1–0.

The budget blueprint called for nearly $500 billion in net deficit reduction over five years, almost evenly divided between spending cuts and tax increases. It closely followed Clinton's budget request, though it included $63 billion in spending cuts beyond what the president had proposed.

The victory margin was comfortable in part because the vote was tied to others the same day on a second element of Clinton's economic package—a bill (HR 1335) to target spending increases as an aid to the nation's struggling economy. Nervous Democrats had insisted that it was politically important to adopt the budget before the stimulus bill, to give credence to their claim that they were cutting spending first.

The budget resolution represented an important shift in fiscal policy. Its heavy reliance on tax increases, aimed primarily at upper-income taxpayers, and more than $140 billion in spending increases for favored domestic programs differentiated Clinton's budget from those offered by Republican presidents George Bush and Ronald Reagan.

Its adoption was critical for several reasons. Though few of the recommendations built into the budget resolution were binding, it was the adoption of the resolution that forced Congress to consider a budget-reconciliation bill that actually cut spending and raised taxes to meet the deficit-reduction goals the resolution laid out. (Senate key vote 1)

Moreover, though debate on the budget was partly symbolic, giving lawmakers a chance to inject broad themes into the multifaceted budget process, in 1993 that aspect took on added importance because the first Democrat in more than a decade had just taken office as president.

Conservative Democrats, although not thrilled by the tax-heavy deficit-reduction plan, won modest concessions in the Budget Committee strengthening their support for it on the floor. House leaders added the $63 billion in further spending reductions to mollify lawmakers who claimed Clinton's plan did not go far enough.

The support of conservatives solidified, Democrats used the floor debate to outmuscle and outvote the Republicans, who were limited to just two amendments to the plan, neither of which had a chance of adoption. A detailed package of spending cuts to replace Clinton's tax increases failed on a 135–295 vote. A second GOP amendment containing some tax increases was rejected even more soundly.

Republicans would remain outside the budget debate for the rest of the year. But the Democrats would not have an easy time deciding among themselves how to carry out the broad recommendations of the budget resolution. They would spend the rest of the summer—and countless hours of negotiations—finishing the job.

3. ECONOMIC STIMULUS

One of President Clinton's few early triumphs in Congress came shortly after midnight March 19, when the House approved his economic stimulus package by a vote of 235–190. The victory was sealed two hours earlier, though, when the House cast a key vote, approving a rule barring hostile amendments by a vote of 240–185: R 0–172; D 239–13 (ND 165–4, SD 74–9); I 1–0.

Billed as one of the three cornerstones of Clinton's economic program, the stimulus package took the form of a $16.3 billion supplemental appropriations bill for fiscal 1993 (HR 1335). It was a blend of diverse elements: public works projects to create jobs and spur economic development, summer jobs for youths and unskilled laborers, social programs for the poor and high-technology purchases for the federal government.

Republicans opposed the bill en masse, as they did Clinton's budget. Their main complaint was that all $16.3 billion would be treated as emergency spending—a designation that translated into a multi-billion-dollar increase in the deficit. Many Democrats had qualms about the spending, too. To address some of the complaints, the White House and the House leadership accelerated the fiscal 1994 budget resolution so lawmakers could vote on future spending cuts before voting on current spending increases.

The change in timing was not enough to satisfy conservative House Democrats. Led by Texan Charles W. Stenholm, they asked the administration to pare the stimulus package back to the elements that would create jobs quickly. When the administration declined, Stenholm readied an amendment that would have required spending cuts to offset at least $11 billion of the bill's proposed outlays.

Republicans also prepared amendments to cut proposals that they ridiculed as "pork barrel" or frivolous spending. This included the proposed increases in spending on Community Development Block Grants, summer jobs for youths, a federal fish-mapping program and energy-efficiency grants to industry.

Concerned that these amendments could attract a winning coalition of Republicans and dissident Democrats, the House Democratic leadership proposed a rule for floor debate allowing only one amendment to HR 1335. That amendment, which would make unspecified cuts in the bill, would be offered by House Appropriations Committee Chairman William H. Natcher, D-Ky., only if needed to shore up Democratic support for the bill.

As conservative Democrats worked to defeat the rule, they were undercut by their own success in trimming the fiscal 1994 budget resolution. Moderate and liberal Democrats argued that the full stimulus package was needed to boost the economy before Congress started clamping down on the deficit in 1994. They also noted that Democrats in the Senate were likely to cut HR 1335, and they wanted the House to go into conference with the largest possible bill.

Clinton intervened personally with House Democrats in meetings and telephone calls, urging them to vote for the rule even if they opposed the bill. In the final tally, only Stenholm and 12 other Democrats joined the united Republican bloc in voting against the rule. *(Senate key vote 2)*

4. EX-SOVIET AID

The House put aside deep philosophical and political differences over President Clinton's domestic agenda to approve his request for $2.5 billion in aid for the former republics of the Soviet Union.

In a striking display of bipartisanship, top congressional leaders were nearly unanimous in their support of the aid package. President George Bush's aid request for the former Soviet republics also had received bipartisan backing, but its price tag did not approach Clinton's huge proposal.

The only challenge to the aid package came from a disparate alliance that included some conservatives and a handful of members of the Congressional Black Caucus. The conservatives were critical of various Russian policies, while some in the black caucus opposed funding a massive foreign aid initiative when domestic programs were facing budget reductions.

Except for those defections, this was one instance when the House stood solidly behind its leadership. Before passing the fiscal 1994 foreign operations bill (HR 2295), the House on June 17 easily defeated an amendment to cut $1.6 billion from the aid package for Russia and its neighbors. In a key vote, the House rejected the amendment, offered by Sonny Callahan, R-Ala., 140–289: R 93–79; D 46–210 (ND 30–143, SD 16–67); I 1–0.

The key to the victory was the strong backing provided by leading Republicans. Minority Whip Newt Gingrich, Ga., and other members of the GOP signed on to the administration's rationale that the aid package would serve U.S. security interests.

Majority Leader Richard A. Gephardt, D-Mo., had worked to buttress support for the request by arranging for a delegation of senior members of both parties to visit Russia and Ukraine in April. Agricultural businesses and other commercial interests lobbied for the request, saying much of the aid would be funneled through U.S. companies.

The administration also avoided seeking the aid as an emergency supplemental appropriation. Such a request would have drawn the ire of House budget-cutters as well as lawmakers who favored more domestic spending.

Instead, the administration and its congressional allies came up with a formula that tapped $1.6 billion from unexpended balances of defense and foreign aid from fiscal 1993. While that funding was sought in the form of a supplemental appropriation—which Callahan targeted with his amendment—it lacked the baggage of an emergency, off-budget request.

The remaining $900 million came from the regular foreign operations appropriation for fiscal 1994. Appropriations Foreign Operations Subcommittee Chairman David R. Obey, D-Wis., proposed reductions of nearly $1.4 billion from the administration's $14.4 billion foreign operations request, making it easier for many members to tolerate sending aid abroad.

After disposing of Callahan's amendment, the House approved the foreign aid measure, 309–111. *(Senate key vote 10)*

5. ABORTION

Abortion rights supporters were expecting big things to happen during President Clinton's first year in office. No longer would they have to worry about the president vetoing bills that expanded access to abortion, as George Bush had done consistently for four years. Despite some marginal gains in 1993, it was not nearly as easy as abortion rights forces had hoped. On the most significant legislative front, the gain for abortion rights advocates was so slight it could hardly be called a win.

Once again, the main venue for the abortion debate was the appropriations bill that paid for programs under the departments of Labor, Health and Human Services, and Education. That was because members had to decide whether Medicaid, the joint federal-state health insurance program, would pay for abortions for poor women. Since 1981, Congress had placed strict restrictions on federal abortion funding, permitting exceptions only to save the life of the woman. That provision was known as the Hyde amendment, after its original sponsor, Henry J. Hyde, R-Ill.

The 1992 elections suggested that the mood of the nation might be different in 1993. With 24 more women and 16 more African-American members in the House, abortion rights supporters believed they had to votes to kill the Hyde restriction and open the door to full abortion access for poor women.

But any thought that Democratic control of the White House would lead to congressional consensus on the abortion issue vanished June 30, when the Labor-HHS bill (HR 2518) came to the floor. As reported by the Appropriations Committee, the bill prohibited funding of abortions except in cases of rape, incest or life endangerment. This language represented a slight loosening of the original Hyde amendment by adding the exceptions for rape and incest.

During an increasingly bitter floor debate, abortion rights lawmakers tried to use the Democratic majority's parliamentary advantage to fend off abortion opponents' amendments. The floor swarmed with members attempting to follow the parliamentary guerrilla war, as Democrats corralled newcomers and handed out sheets explaining how to vote on procedural motions.

At the beginning of the debate, it appeared as if abortion rights supporters would prevail when they succeeded in having the committee's restrictive language struck from the bill on a point of order that it constituted legislating on a spending bill. House rules prohibited policy language in appropriations bills.

That left Hyde with the challenge of finding a way to get the committee language back into the bill. He ultimately trumped a potential point of order through careful rewording.

Hyde then struggled for permission to present the revised amendment. Abortion rights lawmakers used procedural maneuvers to block him from speaking. But Hyde finally succeeded with the help of Appropriations Committee Chairman William H. Natcher, D-Ky., an abortion opponent, who worked out a deal with the House leadership.

Natcher offered a procedural motion to report the bill back to the full House, a move that would have prohibited additional amendments placing limits on the use of funds. But the House rejected that motion, 190–244, thus opening the door for Hyde to offer his amendment.

The House then adopted Hyde's new language, 255–178: R 157–16; D 98–161 (ND 54–120, SD 44–41); I 0–1.

The vote was a pivotal test of the strength of abortion rights supporters and showed it to be wanting. It may also have foreshadowed the upcoming debate over Clinton's health plan (S 1757, HR 3600) and whether it would ensure access to abortions. If federal dollars were involved in a universal health plan—as they were in Medicaid—antiabortion activists would try to keep the plan from including abortions.

The House made a bigger change in abortion law on the appropriations bill that paid for the Treasury, Postal Service and General Government spending (HR 2403—PL 103–123). The bill lifted a decade long ban on allowing women who were federal workers to receive abortions through their taxpayer-subsidized health-care plans. But antiabortion lawmakers almost toppled the bill when the conference report was brought to the House floor Sept. 29. Working quietly, they lobbied members to vote against the measure. The measure barely prevailed, 207–206.

Abortion rights forces also found some success when the House and Senate passed a bill (HR 796—H Rept 103–306) to make it a federal crime to intimidate by force or threat of force a woman seeking to obtain an abortion, or abortion clinic workers. But the clinic-access debate turned more on questions of terrorist activities versus freedom of speech and assembly than it did on abortion rights. A number of abortion opponents supported the clinic access bill.

Over the course of the year, then, the debate over the Hyde amendment overshadowed any other gains that abortion rights supporters made in Congress. The vote demonstrated that, despite election-year gains of abortion rights supporters, there was still a large, bipartisan majority in the House that was wary of using taxpayer funds to pay for abortions. *(Senate key vote 11)*

6. BUDGET-RECONCILIATION

At the end of a long, torturous summer of negotiations over President Clinton's budget, the House was confronted with one final, climactic vote in which neither of the choices had much appeal for many lawmakers. It was the vote on the conference report for the budget-reconciliation bill (HR 2264)—the final version of Clinton's economic plan.

Wavering members were faced, on one hand, with the knowledge that rejecting the measure would cripple Clinton early in his presidency and throw the budget process into turmoil. But, hard as the bill was to swallow, most lawmakers found at least something to like in the budget deal—a tax and spending package that was estimated to reduce the deficit by almost $500 billion over the next five years.

A no vote would have killed the whole thing. But a yes vote evoked at least as many terrors. The final deal was the product of intense negotiations between the House and Senate, and many lawmakers found the terms inadequate—either the deal relied too heavily on taxes and not enough on spending cuts, or it was not generous enough in granting tax breaks for the poor and businesses.

Many members had come to Washington pledging to put an end to gridlock, but to vote yes on a controversial and possibly flawed measure merely to break a partisan stalemate struck many as foolish politics and bad policy.

No member felt the cross-pressures more intensely than freshman Democrat Marjorie Margolies-Mezvinsky of Pennsylvania. She had pledged during her campaign and even the day before the vote that she would vote against a bill that increased taxes. But Democratic leaders extracted a private promise from her to support the deficit-reduction package if her vote proved necessary to pass it.

In the end, Margolies-Mezvinsky's vote was necessary, and she voted yes. Her vote was among the last cast during the Aug. 5 roll call in the House, and it gave Clinton a razor-thin victory, 218–216: R 0–175; D 217–41 (ND 155–18, SD 62–23); I 1–0.

Twenty-four hours later, the Senate adopted the conference report, also with only one vote to spare, and that a tie-breaker supplied by Vice President Al Gore.

Again, not a single Republican voted with Clinton. It was the first time in postwar congressional history and possibly the first time ever that the majority party had passed major legislation with absolutely no support from the opposition.

The narrow House margin was something of a surprise. When the

original version of the bill came before the House, it passed by the comparatively comfortable margin of 219–213. But it had returned in somewhat different form, owing to changes demanded in conference by the Senate. Conservative Democrats were particularly upset that the final bill was missing an "entitlement review" provision that would have set targets for spending on entitlement programs, such as Social Security and Medicare.

House leaders and the administration went into overdrive, cutting deals and making commitments to get the necessary votes. For example, Clinton issued an executive order setting up a complex process that would in effect bind the White House and the House to some action if entitlement spending exceeded projections.

Clinton went to Capitol Hill to lobby Democrats, and he and top White House officials were everywhere, working uncommitted or wavering members for votes right up until the roll call began.

When the vote was over and the conference report was adopted, Clinton claimed that he had succeeded in reorienting the nation's fiscal policy. Clinton asserted that his administration was setting the stage for lower long-term interest rates, economic growth and a healthier economy sometime in the future. The nervous Democrats who voted with him could only hope that he was right. *(Senate key vote 4)*

7. THRIFT BAILOUT FINANCING

Rounding up the requisite votes to pass bills to salvage failed savings and loan institutions had never been an easy task for House leaders. In 1993 action on an unpopular bill (HR 1340) to finance the bailout's final round proved to be no exception. But unlike 1992, Congress ultimately met the challenge.

The key House vote to pass the bailout measure came in September, nearly a year and a half after Congress allowed the bulk of an earlier $25 billion appropriation for the Resolution Trust Corporation (RTC), the thrift salvage agency, to revert to the Treasury. The resulting delay left the cleanup essentially without money and cost taxpayers more than $1 billion as the RTC was forced to operate failed thrifts at a loss rather than move quickly to pay off depositors or transfer those deposits to other institutions.

The House had last faced the issue in April 1992, when a standoff between Democrats and Republicans stopped an effort to replenish the RTC's coffers. House Democratic leaders had agreed with the Bush administration that the RTC should be financed on a bipartisan basis—that majorities of both parties would be required to pass the financing bill. So when Republicans abandoned the 1992 effort, Democrats also jumped ship. The bailout languished without cash for 20 months, until the measure cleared on Nov. 23.

House members had always viewed voting for the bailout as politically risky, even though the taxpayer-provided money was used to make good on the federal government's deposit-insurance guarantee. Some saw a vote for the bailout as carrying the taint of the savings and loan debacle of the 1980s. Members criticized the RTC for not always getting the best deal possible for taxpayers when selling the acquired assets of failed thrifts, for failing to give enough contracts to minority-owned businesses and law firms and for freezing out some smaller investors who wanted to purchase real estate and thrift franchises.

The election of Democrat Bill Clinton as president added a new twist: It put the responsibility for passing the financing bill squarely on Democrats, many of whom had never voted to replenish the bailout when it was being pushed by the Treasury Department under Republican president George Bush. Moreover, the mood of the sizable freshman class on this issue was unknown.

Members ignored the administration's request for a "clean" $45 billion bill free of congressional mandates on agency operations. It likewise became obvious that the full financing request—$28 billion for the RTC and $17 billion to capitalize the thrift industry's new deposit insurance fund—would be pared significantly. As reported by the House Banking Committee in May, the bill included an $18.3 billion appropriation to be obtained by lifting the April 1, 1992, date on which the previous RTC appropriation reverted to the Treasury.

The bill was ready for floor action by early summer, and Democratic whip counts appeared favorable, but House leaders were skittish about bringing up the measure, having seen prior RTC bills rejected by wide margins.

Democratic leaders pressed top Banking Committee members to accommodate Republican concerns about provisions directing agency contracts to women- and minority-owned businesses and authorizing future appropriations for the new Savings Association Insurance Fund. Even so, those compromises barely picked up any GOP votes. The House on Sept. 14 narrowly passed HR 1340, 214–208: R 24–148; D 190–59 (ND 131–34, SD 59–25); I 0–1.

At one point during the roll call, the bill was behind by 20 votes, but Democratic vote counts proved accurate and the measure squeaked by. Once over that hurdle, the road to final action was less arduous, though it took until the last day of the session.

After passing HR 1340, the House took up a companion Senate bill (S 714), amended it to include the text of HR 1340 and passed it by voice vote. The Senate had passed S 714 on May 13 by a bipartisan 61–35 vote. The Senate adopted the conference report on S 714 by 54–45 on Nov. 20, and the House cleared the measure in the early hours of Nov. 23 by a healthier 235–191 margin.

8. GAYS IN THE MILITARY

Before passing the defense authorization bill (HR 2401), the House weighed in on the explosive issue of homosexuals in the military, a debate that had been centered primarily in the Senate for much of the year.

By the time the House took up the issue, President Clinton had abandoned his campaign pledge to lift the military's ban on homosexuals, settling for an easing of its application to gay service members who remained chaste and discreet about their orientation.

When the House Armed Services Committee drafted its version of the annual defense authorization bill late in July, it adopted without change language that had been written into the Senate version of the bill a few days earlier by Democrat Sam Nunn of Georgia, chairman of the Armed Services Committee.

That provision wrote into law the essentials of the military's previous regulations banning homosexual conduct by service members, a ban broad enough to cover a soldier's private disclosure to a friend of his or her homosexual orientation.

While many members of the House panel argued for an even more restrictive approach, Military Forces and Personal Subcommittee Chairman Ike Skelton, D-Mo., and a majority of others accepted the Senate language, partly in the hope of putting an end to the emotionally charged debate that had drowned out most other defense issues during the first several months of the Clinton presidency.

On the House floor, opponents of the gay ban offered an amendment to the defense authorization bill. Like an amendment by California Democrat Barbara Boxer that was defeated in the Senate, the amendment would have stripped from the defense bill the language reasserting the military ban and would have explicitly left the issue to the president.

In a key vote Sept. 28, the House rejected the amendment, by Martin T. Meehan, D-Mass., 169–264: R 11–163; D 157–101 (ND 131–43; SD 26–58); I 1–0.

Before that vote, the House also defeated, 144–291, a conservative amendment that would have toughened the ban by renewing the policy—which Clinton had ended—of questioning new recruits about their sexual orientation. The House later adopted, 301–134, an amendment reaffirming the gay ban language in the bill.

The congressional language took a harder line than the position Clinton finally arrived at in July.

Clinton's stated policy asserted that "homosexual orientation is not a bar to military service" in the absence of conduct. But the Nunn-Skelton language rejected that view, declaring instead that the presence of openly homosexual members in a military unit "would create an unacceptable risk to the high standards of morale, good order and discipline and unit cohesion that are the essence of military capability."

The congressional provision left to the secretary of defense the decision of whether to resume asking recruits about their sexual orientation, thus leaving intact the administration's decision in January to suspend that practice. It was silent on two other facets of administration policy: Clinton's insistence that Pentagon investigators evenhandedly pursue any alleged violation of military law, which prohibited both homosexual and heterosexual sodomy; and his effort to curb dragnet-style hunts intended to discover service members who were secretly homosexual. *(Senate key vote 7)*

9. ENDANGERED SPECIES/PROPERTY RIGHTS

For the previous 20 years, Congress had regularly embraced the environmental movement by passing laws to clean the air and water, to force polluters to clean up toxic waste sites and to preserve the nation's wilderness and endangered species.

In 1993 landowners began to push the pendulum back in the other direction. A critical House vote helped spawn a political force that was likely to reemerge during coming debates over the reauthorization of the 1973 Endangered Species Act (PL 93–205) and the overhaul of wetlands policy in the 1972 Federal Pollution Control Act (PL 92–500), known as the clean water law.

Landowners contended that enforcement of such environmental laws had driven down the market value of their private property and, in some cases, rendered their property useless for farming or development. A key test of that idea came Oct. 6, when the House considered a bill (HR 1845) to authorize a new survey of the nation's plants and animals, known as the National Biological Survey.

The National Biological Survey was the brainchild of Interior Secretary Bruce Babbitt, who billed it as a way to avoid legal conflicts arising from implementation of the endangered species law. Conservatives said the survey would lead to more regulations and to decisions over wetlands that would favor environmentalists instead of farmers.

To counter Babbitt's initiative, Charles H. Taylor, R-N.C., offered an amendment to the bill to require that the government obtain written permission from a landowner before entering private property to conduct the survey. It also required the government to disclose its findings to the landowner. Before passing the bill, House members overwhelmingly agreed to include Taylor's amendment, 309–115: R 171–3; D 138–111 (ND 72–95, SD 66–16); I 0–1.

The House vote was particularly significant because it was usually the more conservative Senate that sided with landowners. In 1991 the Senate adopted by voice vote an amendment by then-senator Steve Symms, R-Idaho, that would have required the government to compensate landowners who could not use their property because of federal regulations.

The Fifth Amendment to the U.S. Constitution required the government to provide "just compensation" when it took away private property for public use—to build a highway, for example. The Supreme Court also had embraced the concept that regulations themselves can effectively cause the government to take away private property.

A driving force behind adoption of Taylor's amendment was conservative Democrats such as Reps. W. J. "Billy" Tauzin of Louisiana and Gary A. Condit of California, who represented a Central Valley farming district that was embroiled in a dispute over protecting the California smelt fish.

The vote on Taylor's amendment dampened the hopes of many environmentalists that Congress would be able to reauthorize the Endangered Species Act in the 103rd Congress. Tauzin was gathering support for a reauthorization bill (HR 1490) that he said would strike a balance between species conservation and financial impact on property owners. But environmentalists contended that Tauzin was trying to gut the law, which had helped bring species such as the bald eagle back from the brink of extinction.

"We won round one of a zillion rounds," said Charles S. Cushman, executive director of the Battleground, Washington-based American Land Rights Association, an advocacy group for the rights of private property owners.

Environmental lobbyists were bracing for a long fight on similar issues. "We will see property rights amendments on everything," said Betsy Loyless, political director of the League of Conservation Voters. "The environmental community needs to focus on this."

10. SUPERCONDUCTING SUPERCOLLIDER

Like a group of big-game hunters searching for a prize trophy in the name of deficit reduction, House lawmakers emerged in 1993 with a big kill: The $11 billion superconducting supercollider.

The coup de grace for the giant atom smasher, an Energy Department project that sought to isolate the smallest atomic particles that are the building blocks of matter, followed a previous House vote to terminate the Energy Department project June 24 as part of the energy and water development spending bill (HR 2445) for fiscal 1994.

But that was essentially a reprise of House votes in previous years. On those occasions, the Senate would subsequently restore funding for the supercollider, and the House, with members fearful of losing other pet projects in the energy-water bill, would ultimately cave in to the Senate position.

The key 1993 vote on the project's future was cast Oct. 19, when the energy-water bill came back from a House-Senate conference, and House members were forced to choose between killing the supercollider or appeasing powerful appropriations conferees, who once again had restored the project to full funding.

But the actual vote was not so simple as "yea" or "nay." The two main opponents of the project, Jim Slattery, D-Kan., and Sherwood Boehlert, R-N.Y., had to battle arcane House rules that favored appropriators and made the choice for House members difficult to follow, at best. Their task was to convince lawmakers that a complex parliamentary maneuver amounted to a vote to reaffirm the House's desire to kill the supercollider.

Before members voted on the final adoption of a conference report, House rules allowed the minority to offer one motion—and only one motion—to recommit the conference report to committee for further deliberation. Slattery and Boehlert were not allowed to offer that motion, however. House rules and customs gave the nod to John T. Myers, R-Ind., the ranking minority leader of the subcommittee that wrote the bill.

Myers, a supporter of the supercollider, offered a motion to recommit that had no instructions. If it prevailed, the final version of the spending bill would bounce back to the House with supercollider funding intact. The only vote then would be up or down on the entire spending bill.

The only way for Slattery and Boehlert to pick the procedural lock was to call for a vote on the "previous question"—a step that asked the House to shut off debate on Myers' recommital motion and vote on it. In this case, Slattery and Boehlert wanted House members to defeat the previous question so they could amend Myers' motion with new instructions to terminate the supercollider.

Slattery and Boehlert handed out pink slips naming those who voted against the supercollider June 24 and urged them to vote "nay" on the previous question. Despite the pleas of appropriators and active support for the project from the Clinton administration, the "nays" prevailed, 159–264: R 61–111; D 98–152 (ND 47–121, SD 51–31); I 0–1.

Only 18 House members switched their votes from June 24 to defend the supercollider project. In a rare show of class solidarity, 81 of the 113 voting House freshmen stood with opponents of the supercollider.

The House then voted on the motion to recommit as amended by Slattery to kill the supercollider. At that point, supercollider opponents pulled out green leaflets that told the same lawmakers to vote "yea." They prevailed again, by a vote of 282–143.

After the vote, Senate Energy and Water Appropriations Subcommittee Chairman J. Bennett Johnston, D-La., decided to give up the fight to save the supercollider. He complained that House lawmakers had been carried away by an "emotional tide" for spending cuts that took as its victim one of the premier U.S. science projects.

In the end, the death of the supercollider served only as a symbolic nod to fiscal austerity. The project still received $640 million in the fiscal 1994 energy and water appropriations bill (HR 2445). Lawmakers instead put those funds toward the costs of shutting down the project, already 20 percent complete in Waxahachie, Texas.

11. SOMALIA

Even after promising to withdraw U.S. forces from Somalia, the Clinton administration had trouble disengaging from the political skirmishing that persisted on Capitol Hill.

The administration escaped an embarrassing setback when the House endorsed the March 31 pullout date that President Clinton had previously accepted under strong Senate pressure. Yet the confusing, contradictory House actions of Nov. 9 underscored congressional opposition to an operation that, as of that date, had cost the lives of 35 U.S. troops.

Divided along party lines, lawmakers narrowly backed Clinton's timetable. The key vote came on an amendment to a nonbinding resolution (H Con Res 170), which the House approved 226–201: R 2–170; D 224–30 (ND 150–21, SD 74–9); I 0–1.

Just an hour earlier, the House had voted 224–203 to call on the president to withdraw U.S. forces by Jan. 31. But under the "king of the hill" procedures that the Rules Committee set for debate, the vote was superseded by the adoption of the latter amendment.

The zigzagging votes had purely symbolic significance. The House had already signaled its support for a Senate-passed provision in the fiscal 1994 defense appropriations bill that put the force of law behind the March 31 date.

But a defeat would have reinforced the perception that the administration's foreign policy lacked public and congressional support. The timing was critical because the administration was about to face a tougher vote—with much higher stakes—on the North American Free Trade Agreement.

The administration strongly opposed the amendment backing the Jan. 31 pullout date that was offered by Benjamin A. Gilman, N.Y., the ranking Republican on the Foreign Affairs Committee. House Democratic leaders delayed the debate for several hours to allow the administration to lobby wavering members.

Despite those efforts, 55 Democrats bucked the administration in backing Gilman's amendment. All but three of the 171 Republicans voting backed the proposal.

It was clear that many of the Democrats—and even some Republicans—viewed Gilman's amendment as a low-cost opportunity to blast the administration's policy. The king-of-the-hill procedure afforded lawmakers the chance to reverse that vote by supporting the amendment by Lee H. Hamilton, D-Ind., chairman of the Foreign Affairs Committee, endorsing the March 31 deadline.

After losing in the initial skirmishing, Democrats hauled out the heavy artillery in support of Hamilton's amendment. House Speaker Thomas S. Foley, D-Wash., delivered an impassioned plea not to undercut the president's plan for an "orderly withdrawal" from Somalia.

"It would be a tragic moment for American resolve, American principle and the American position around the world," Foley said. "Do not do this to the president of the United States. We should not do this to any president, Republican or Democrat."

Republicans, who had complained for weeks that Democratic leaders had denied them a debate on Somalia, argued vehemently in favor of a quick withdrawal. "Helping the authors of our failed policy in Somalia save face is not worth the life of one American soldier," Gilman said.

While the GOP remained solid in opposing the superseding amendment, 24 Democrats who backed the Jan. 31 deadline turned around and supported Clinton's pullout date as well, providing the margin of victory. The group included such senior lawmakers as Charles E. Schumer of New York and G. V. "Sonny" Montgomery of Mississippi.

But the debate highlighted position shifts by members of both parties. Gilman had forced quick action on the issue by invoking a provision of the 1973 War Powers Resolution, which most Republicans believed was unconstitutional. *(Senate key vote 12)*

12. HANDGUN CONTROL

Few members of Congress embraced the so-called Brady bill as an anticrime panacea, but advocates hoped the bill (HR 1025) to establish a five-day waiting period for handgun purchases would send a signal to constituents weary of crime that Congress was willing to take on gun violence and the lobbying clout of the powerful National Rifle Association (NRA).

In fact, House passage of the measure Nov. 10 opened the way for the first major federal gun control legislation since 1968. The bill was first introduced in 1987, six years after an assassination attempt on then-president Ronald Reagan permanently disabled his press secretary (and the bill's namesake), James S. Brady. The House had passed a crime bill including Brady provisions in 1991, but that bill never became law.

But in 1993, a self-standing Brady bill passed on a 238–189 vote: R 54–119; D 184–69 (ND 138–31, SD 46–38).

The bill required would-be gun purchasers to wait five business days before purchasing a handgun, allowing local law enforcement officials to conduct a personal background check on them. The measure aimed to prevent the sale of handguns to convicted felons and other unqualified buyers, as well as to people making the purchase

while they were angry. It also authorized $200 million per year toward creating an instant background checking system.

The bill had experienced almost annual setbacks in its battle for passage, despite a steady increase of gun violence nationwide, the support of the nation's law enforcement officers and a persistent personal campaign by Brady and his wife, Sarah. Detractors argued that the bill would fail to reduce crime while imposing unfair restrictions on people who wanted to buy guns legally. Criminals, they said, would purchase guns on the black market, while state and local authorities spent time and money trying to institute a gun purchase tracking system.

The biggest obstacle to passage was the NRA's enormous political clout. "It's a lobby that could put 15,000 letters in your district overnight," bill advocate William J. Hughes, D-N.J., once said.

Brady argued that he had endured far more than lawmakers were likely to suffer at the hands of the NRA, but politicians were reluctant to lend their support. It took four years from the bill's introduction before Reagan endorsed it. President George Bush had threatened to veto crime legislation that contained it.

President Clinton, however, backed Brady.

Lawmakers on both sides went into the House floor debate knowing there were almost certainly enough votes to pass some version of the bill—but which version was unclear. Neither side knew who would prevail on a series of Republican amendments that were endorsed by Judiciary Committee Chairman Jack Brooks, D-Texas, a Brady bill opponent.

One successful amendment, by George W. Gekas, R-Pa., mandated the end of the five-day waiting period five years after enactment. Republican Bill McCollum of Florida was unsuccessful in offering an amendment that would have preempted state waiting periods once the instant-check system was in place. Clinton signed the bill Nov. 30, saying that "Americans are finally fed up with violence that cuts down another citizen with gunfire every 10 minutes." *(Senate key vote 15)*

13. NAFTA IMPLEMENTATION

When the House passed implementing legislation for the North American Free Trade Agreement (NAFTA) on Nov. 17, it brought to an end one of the most emotional, divisive and momentous national debates in many years. Despite overwhelming opposition from within his own party, President Clinton pushed hard to win congressional approval for the agreement and snatched a victory from near defeat. In the process, he charted a course for U.S. trade policy.

Never before had the United States been part of a trade agreement based on removing virtually all economic walls that guarded the nation from a country as poor and as different as Mexico. Bringing Mexico into a free-trade alliance along with Canada created a huge North American free trade zone with 358 million consumers and a $6.5 trillion market. Broadening that alliance to include other countries in Central and South America was widely viewed as the next step.

Even more important, the vote in favor of NAFTA reaffirmed the position of the United States as the world's leading champion of an open trading system, and it boosted continuing U.S. efforts to dismantle trade barriers worldwide.

But the debate and vote—especially in the House—also exposed deep anxiety about the pervasive job loss that had wracked the U.S. economy in preceding years. Organized labor and other NAFTA opponents charged that the agreement invited companies to relocate to Mexico and put U.S. workers out of their jobs. That charge struck a chord with many members, particularly Midwestern Democrats groping for a response to the upheaval in the industrial sector.

Opposition to the agreement scrambled conventional political alliances. Former independent presidential candidate Ross Perot joined with conservative Republican Pat Buchanan and liberal crusader Ralph Nader in opposing the agreement. Some environmental groups attacked the agreement, and some endorsed it. Farmers in the Midwest were avidly for it, but growers in Florida, California and elsewhere feared an increase in imports of Mexican fruits and vegetables.

NAFTA was one of the most explosive issues awaiting Clinton when he took office. He had endorsed the trade pact during the campaign but had finessed his position by insisting that "side agreements" with Mexico were needed to ensure enforcement of labor and environmental laws there. Clinton got the side deals, but they did nothing to mollify labor. Clinton could not remove the wedge that NAFTA drove through the Democratic Party.

Clinton proceeded to seek congressional approval for NAFTA anyway. Beginning his lobbying effort in early September, he turned to Republicans for the first time during his administration, asking them to provide the majority of the votes needed to pass the bill implementing NAFTA (HR 3450). After some initial reluctance to back a Democratic president, House Republicans responded to his appeal, urged on by their leadership.

In the dramatic House showdown, Republicans and Southern Democrats provided the victory margin. The measure passed 234–200: R 132–43; D 102–156 (ND 49–124, SD 53–32); I 0–1.

Passage in the Senate followed three days later and was not in doubt. (Senate key vote 16)

Though the victory demonstrated Clinton's ability to move beyond a traditional Democratic coalition on issues he considered important, it remained to be seen whether his success at putting together a centrist coalition would lead him to test similar bipartisan tactics in the future.

But Clinton's forceful defense of free trade, at the expense of alienating a major constituency within his party, added credibility to his claim to be a new type of Democrat.

Even more important, the House vote symbolized a new era in U.S.-Mexico relations, which for years had been characterized by suspicion on both sides of the border, particularly in Mexico. Most economists predicted that reducing or eliminating trade and other barriers with Mexico would have only slight benefits for the massive U.S. economy over the following several years. But it could help raise the anemic Mexican standard of living, providing a huge future market for U.S. goods.

14. MINING ROYALTIES

Members had tried since 1987 to revamp the 1872 Mining Law, one of the last remaining "homesteading" measures enacted to entice development of the West. But as with other natural resource and public lands issues, western senators had long managed to outmuscle their House colleagues on mining disputes, so the 121-year-old law remained in a virtual stalemate.

The House in 1993 gave a big boost to supporters of an overhaul by passing a tough mining bill (HR 322) on Nov. 18. The lopsided vote was expected to give the House much leverage in negotiations with the Senate, which had passed a much leaner version by voice vote on May 25.

House passage came on a 316–108 vote: R 70–102; D 245–6 (ND 166–3, SD 79–3); I 1–0.

The 1872 Mining Law required no royalties to be collected from miners who extracted valuable ores from federal lands. It also allowed miners to buy, or "patent," claims on federal lands for as little as $2.50

an acre. The law required limited repair of abandoned hard-rock mines.

Under the House-passed bill, sponsored by Nick J. Rahall II, D-W.Va., miners would be required to pay an 8 percent royalty on hard-rock minerals but would be allowed to deduct the costs of transportation. The bill would eliminate patenting and require miners to pay an annual lease fee of $100 on existing claims and $200 a year for new claims. The bill also would impose tough federal standards for the repair of federal land and require miners to be more environmentally sensitive.

The House passed HR 322 despite strong objections from Republicans that the measure would lead to a loss of jobs in states where the mining of gold, silver, copper and other hard-rock minerals was a dominant industry.

Only six Democrats voted against the measure, while nine Republicans from western, Rocky Mountain or Plains states voted for the measure, including New Mexico's Steven H. Schiff and Joe Skeen, who hailed from a state with large copper mines.

The Senate's alternative bill (S 775), crafted by Larry E. Craig, R-Idaho, imposed a 2 percent royalty but would have allowed most exploration, mining and development costs to be deducted. Patenting still would be allowed, although miners would be required to purchase federal land at fair market prices. The bill balked at establishing new federal reclamation standards, choosing instead to allow state laws to govern the repair of damaged public lands.

The House vote on mining overhaul was especially important because of the unusual "ticket to conference" strategy adopted by the Senate. At the behest of Energy and Natural Resources Committee Chairman J. Bennett Johnston, D-La., the Senate quickly moved Craig's bill through committee and the floor with no amendments and little debate. The Senate's leading mining reform advocate, Dale Bumpers, D-Ark., agreed to hold his fire until the House-Senate negotiations.

The Senate's western coalition, usually in agreement on public lands issues, was expected to split on mining reform. Because the final bill was likely to be written in conference, the strength of the House vote gave House negotiators added leverage against divided Senate conferees.

George Miller, D-Calif., chairman of the House Natural Resources Committee, Rahall and Energy and Mineral Resources Subcommittee Chairman Richard H. Lehman, D-Calif., crafted HR 322 so it would leave no doubt about the House's position on mining while still appeasing House Democrats from states containing most of the nation's hard-rock minerals.

"The House was not ambivalent on this issue," said Philip M. Hocker, president of the conservationist Mineral Policy Center. "The House does not want an ambivalent conference."

15. CAMPAIGN FINANCE

For most of 1993, House Democratic leaders resisted action on legislation to overhaul the campaign finance system. But in the waning days of the first session of the 103rd Congress, under pressure from the freshman class and editorial writers, they reversed course and used their clout to wrest a bill from defeat at the hands of an unusual bipartisan coalition.

Early in the year, House leaders delayed completion of a joint administration-congressional Democratic plan by demanding that the existing $5,000 limit on political action committee (PAC) contributions be maintained for House candidates. Then—after the plan was presented May 7 and the Senate passed its version June 17—House leaders delayed further, saying they did not have the votes to pass a bill because of opposition to provisions calling for partial federal funding of campaigns.

For years, Democrats had struggled with the Supreme Court mandate that spending limits must be voluntary and accompanied by direct federal subsidies to candidates. Most Democrats supported restrictions on spending, but many resisted providing public benefits. With concern about the deficit high, the funding question became particularly salient.

Nearly all Republicans opposed any federal funding of congressional campaigns, and many objected to spending limits. Alone, they could do little to block a Democratic bill, but this time they were joined by an odd assortment of Democrats—some who resisted federal funding; some who said the spending and PAC limits were too high; and yet others who resisted change in the system that elected them. For months, Democratic leaders made little effort to unite their party on the issue.

By early fall, however, they were under pressure from first-term members who said voters would not tolerate inaction. Although October—once dubbed "reform month"—came and went without public action, Democratic leaders did begin serious private negotiations to reach a consensus within the House Democratic Caucus.

They cobbled together a funding mechanism that met with preliminary caucus approval. It relied heavily on voluntary taxpayer contributions and a new PAC registration fee. But when the Ways and Means Committee balked at waiving its right to review tax legislation, it was dropped from the plan, and an unfunded bill was readied for floor action.

In that way, the 1993 bill was identical to a plan Congress approved in 1992 that was vetoed by President George Bush. The two bills were also similar in that both included spending limits with up to one-third coming in federal money; both also capped PAC and large individual contributions at one-third of a candidate's total funds.

The 1993 spending limits, however, were potentially far higher than those in the 1992 bill. The new plan also permitted leadership PACs and allowed candidates to roll over substantial war chests from one election to the next, practices restricted in the earlier bill.

Once the bill was formally presented, the coalition that had stymied action began to lose steam. Naysayers were more adamant behind closed doors than in public; many Democrats who had voted for or endorsed the 1992 bill when it was certain to be vetoed were reluctant to vote no now.

The loose coalition had one last card to play: the vote on the rule bringing the bill to the floor. From the Republican bloc to the scattered Democrats, all had amendments they wanted to support, but the rule forbade them.

To overcome their campaign to defeat the rule, Democratic leaders—even Speaker Thomas S. Foley, D-Wash.—worked the House floor for hours during an unusual Sunday session. The vote was delayed repeatedly as party whips counted and recounted their votes. Late in the day, Nov. 21, the House narrowly approved the rule, 220–207: R 3–168; D 216–39 (ND 156–15, SD 60–24); I 1–0.

Passage of the bill the next day was anticlimactic. Many members who were willing to vote against the rule were unwilling to vote against the package. *(Senate key vote 3)*

16. 'REINVENTING GOVERNMENT'/SPENDING CUTS

When President Clinton eked out enough votes to pass his five-year deficit-reduction plan in August, the hard-fought victory came with a price: To win the votes of recalcitrant fiscal conservatives who

thought the package of budget savings and tax increases did not cut enough, Clinton had to promise they would get another chance to glean more savings before the year's end.

Clinton kept that promise and gave lawmakers another vote on spending cuts, in the form of a package of rescissions from just-passed appropriations for fiscal 1994, plus selected cost-saving proposals from Vice President Al Gore's "reinventing government" initiative. But when that package (HR 3400) came to the floor Nov. 22, it opened the door for a bipartisan group of aggressive "deficit hawks" to offer their own deficit-reduction package, forcing the administration once again to scramble for votes to protect the president's five-year budget plan.

The showdown vote came on an amendment by Timothy J. Penny, D-Minn., and John R. Kasich, R-Ohio, who wanted to cut the budget by $90 billion over five years. It was Penny who had extracted the promise from Clinton and House Democratic leaders for a chance to offer a major deficit-cutting plan.

The original Clinton proposal was a relatively modest package of about $11.5 billion in savings. When the Congressional Budget Office later declared that the package would save only $305 million, the White House beefed up its plan by adding language already proposed by the administration to trim the federal work force by 252,000 employees over five years, bringing total savings to $37.1 billion in outlays.

By contrast, a large bulk of Penny-Kasich savings—$34.2 billion—would have come from cuts in the Medicare program, the health-care subsidy for the elderly and disabled. Clinton was planning his own revisions to the Medicare system to help pay for his proposed overhaul of the health-care system, while the Penny-Kasich amendment would have steered Medicare savings only toward reducing the deficit.

The other feature of the Penny-Kasich bid that made the White House and Democratic leaders nervous was its mandate to lower ceilings on annual appropriations below levels ordered in the August deficit-reduction plan. Under that law, discretionary spending was capped for five years at fiscal 1993 levels. The Penny-Kasich amendment would have reduced those limits by another $43 billion through fiscal 1998.

"We have just begun to look for places to reduce the deficit," conceded Majority Leader Richard A. Gephardt, D-Mo., in a floor speech that paid homage to the spirit, if not the content, of the Penny-Kasich amendment. "But if we act on this amendment tonight, we act prematurely, because we not only cut, we take the caps down further."

Defense Appropriations Subcommittee Chairman John P. Murtha, D-Pa., helped lead the charge against the amendment on grounds that the lower spending limits would endanger defense spending, because budget rules no longer put up protective "fire walls" to insulate defense from spending cuts.

Other chairmen of appropriations subcommittees launched their own lobbying assaults. One tactic criticized by lawmakers was a form letter by Energy and Water Appropriations Subcommittee Chairman Tom Bevill, D-Ala., and ranking Republican John T. Myers of Indiana threatening that specific water projects in members' districts might be at risk should the Penny-Kasich amendment pass.

Before the vote, Clinton called wavering lawmakers and recruited Cabinet secretaries and first lady Hillary Rodham Clinton to urge freshmen to vote against it. Clinton prevailed again as the House rejected Penny-Kasich, 213–219: R 156–18; D 57–200 (ND 33–139, SD 24–61); I 0–1.

The vote was not only a late-session affirmation of Clinton's continued ability to thwart attempts by fiscal conservatives for more drastic deficit reduction; it also showed that he could still count on the votes of labor-oriented liberal Democrats just days after the fractious vote on the North American Free Trade Agreement (NAFTA).

In contrast to the NAFTA vote of Nov. 17, Clinton enjoyed help from labor groups, which considered the cuts too draconian: 125 Democrats came back to Clinton on the Penny-Kasich amendment after opposing him on the free trade agreement vote. Lobbyists for the AFL-CIO and other unions were lined up outside the House, calling on lawmakers to kill the amendment, though some continued to speak bitterly about Clinton's treatment of labor during the NAFTA debate.

1. H Con Res 64. Fiscal 1994 Budget Resolution/Adoption. Adoption of the concurrent resolution to set binding budget levels for the fiscal year ending Sept. 30, 1994: budget authority, $1.505 trillion; outlays, $1.498 trillion; revenues, $1.251 trillion; deficit, $247.5 billion. Adopted 54–45: R 0–43; D 54–2 (ND 41–0, SD 13–2), March 25, 1993. A "yea" was a vote in support of the president's position.

2. HR 1335. Fiscal 1993 Supplemental Appropriations/Cloture. Motion to invoke cloture (thus limiting debate) on the bill to provide $12.2 billion in new budget authority and $3.1 billion in trust fund spending to implement the administration's compromise stimulus package to help in the economic recovery. The funds would be designated as emergency spending, making them exempt from discretionary spending caps. Motion rejected 56–43: R 0–42; D 56–1 (ND 42–0, SD 14–1), April 21, 1993. Three-fifths of the total Senate (60) is required to invoke cloture. A "yea" was a vote in support of the president's position.

3. S 3. Campaign Finance/Passage. Passage of the bill to encourage federal candidates to abide by voluntary spending limits by providing benefits such as reduced broadcast and mailing rates. Candidates who reject spending limits would be subject to a new federal tax on campaigns equal to the highest corporate rate, now 34 percent. Passed 60–38: R 7–35; D 53–3 (ND 42–0, SD 11–3), June 17, 1993. A "yea" was a vote in support of the president's position.

4. HR 2264. Fiscal 1994 Budget-Reconciliation/Passage. Passage of the bill to raise taxes by $243 billion, cut spending by $256 billion and reduce the deficit by $499 billion over five years by tracking President Clinton's economic proposals. Passed 50–49: R 0–43; D 49–6 (ND 38–3, SD 11–3), with Vice President Al Gore casting a "yea" vote, June 25, 1993 (in the session that began and the *Congressional Record* dated June 24). A "yea" was a vote in support of the president's position.

5. HR 2010. National Service/Passage. Passage of the bill to authorize $300 million in fiscal 1994, $500 million in fiscal 1995 and $700 million in fiscal 1996 for the National Service program, which would provide people age 17 or older with $4,725 a year for up to two years in education awards in return for work in community service programs. Passed 58–41: R 7–37; D 51–4 (ND 38–3, SD 13–1), Aug. 3, 1993. A "yea" was a vote in support of the president's position.

6. Ginsburg Confirmation. Confirmation of Ruth Bader Ginsburg as an associate justice of the Supreme Court of the United States, replacing retired Associate Justice Byron R. White. Confirmed 96–3: R 41–3; D 55–0 (ND 41–0, SD 14–0), Aug. 3, 1993. A "yea" was a vote in support of the president's position.

7. S 1298. Fiscal 1994 Defense Authorization/Gay Ban. Boxer, D-Calif., amendment to strike language in the bill regarding homosexuals in the military and to express the sense of Congress that the policy regarding the subject should be determined by the president. Rejected 33–63: R 3–38; D 30–25 (ND 29–12, SD 1–13), Sept. 9, 1993.

8. S 1298. Fiscal 1994 Defense Authorization/Strategic Weapons. Sasser, D-Tenn., amendment to cut the Ballistic Missile Defense program from $3.4 billion to $3 billion. Adopted 50–48: R 6–36; D 44–12 (ND 36–6, SD 8–6), Sept. 9, 1993. A "nay" was a vote in support of the president's position.

9. HR 252. Fiscal 1994 Interior Appropriation/Grazing Fees. Domenici, R-N.M., amendment to prohibit the administration for one year from using funds in the bill to implement higher grazing fees and other public land-management reforms. Adopted 59–40: R 38–5; D 21–35 (ND 14–28, SD 7–7), Sept. 14, 1993. A "nay" was a vote in support of the president's position.

10. HR 2295. Fiscal 1994 Foreign Aid Appropriations/Passage. Passage of the bill to provide $12,526,854,047 in new budget authority for foreign assistance and related programs in fiscal 1994. The bill includes the $2.5 billion requested by the administration for the former Soviet Union. The administration requested $14,425,993,066. Passed 88–10: R 36–7; D 52–3 (ND 40–2, SD 12–1), Sept. 23, 1993. A "yea" was a vote in support of the president's position.

11. HR 2518. Fiscal 1994 Labor, HHS, Education Appropriations/Abortion. Committee amendment to strike the Hyde amendment provisions included in the House bill that prohibit federal funds from covering abortions except in cases of rape, incest or when the life of the woman is endangered. Rejected 40–59: R 6–38; D 34–21 (ND 31–11, SD 3–10), Sept. 28, 1993. A "yea" was a vote in support of the president's position.

12. HR 3116. Fiscal 1994 Defense Appropriations/Somalia Policy. Byrd, D-W.Va., amendment to prohibit funding of U.S. military operations in Somalia after March 31, 1994, unless the president requests and Congress authorizes an extension. The amendment would also limit the U.S. mission to protecting U.S. personnel and bases, sustaining relief supplies and giving logistical and security aid to U.N. forces, and would require that U.S. forces in Somalia be under the command and control of U.S. commanders. Adopted 76–23: R 24–20; D 52–3 (ND 38–3, SD 14–0), Oct. 15, 1993 (in the session that began and the *Congressional Record* dated Oct. 14).

13. S Res 153. Packwood Diaries/Relevancy Requirement. Simpson, R-Wyo., amendment to add that all materials requested in the Ethics Committee subpoena of the diaries of Sen. Bob Packwood, R-Ore., be relevant. Rejected 23–77: R 22–22; D 1–55 (ND 1–41, SD 0–14), Nov. 2, 1993.

14. S 1607. Omnibus Crime/Assault Weapons Ban. Feinstein, D-Calif., amendment to ban the manufacture, sale and future possession of 19 semiautomatic weapons and copycat guns. Adopted 56–43: R 10–34; D 46–9 (ND 38–3, SD 8–6), Nov. 17, 1993. A "yea" was a vote in support of the president's position.

15. HR 1025. Brady Bill/Passage. Passage of the bill to require a five-business-day waiting period before an individual could purchase a handgun, to allow local officials to conduct a background check. A compromise provided that the waiting period would expire four years after enactment unless the attorney general extended the waiting period for a fifth year. Passed 63–36: R 16–28; D 47–8 (ND 38–3, SD 9–5), Nov. 20, 1993. A "yea" was a vote in support of the president's position.

16. HR 3450. NAFTA Implementation/Passage. Passage of the bill to approve the North American Free Trade Agreement and make the necessary changes to U.S. statutory law to implement the trade agreement. Passed 61–38: R 34–10; D 27–28 (ND 18–23, SD 9–5), Nov. 20, 1993. A "yea" was a vote in support of the president's position.

---

[a] Bob Krueger, D-Texas, was appointed Jan. 5, replacing Lloyd Bentsen. He was sworn in Jan. 20 and was eligible to vote on key votes 1–2. Kay Bailey Hutchison, R-Texas, defeated Krueger in a June 5 special election and was sworn in June 14. She was eligible to vote on key votes 3–16.

KEY				
		Democrats	*Republicans*	
Y	Voted for ("yea")		–	Announced against
N	Voted against ("nay")		P	Voted "present"
+	Announced for		C	Voted "present" to avoid possible conflict of interest
#	Paired for		?	Did not vote or otherwise make a position known
X	Paired against			

ND Northern Democrats
SD Southern Democrats
Southern states – Ala., Ark., Fla., Ga., Ky., La., Miss., N.C., Okla., S.C., Tenn., Texas, Va.

Senate Key Votes	1	2	3	4	5	6	7	8	9	10	11	12	13	14	15	16
ALABAMA																
Heflin	Y	Y	N	Y	Y	Y	N	N	Y	Y	N	Y	N	N	N	N
Shelby	N	N	N	N	Y	Y	N	N	Y	Y	N	Y	N	N	N	N
ALASKA																
Murkowski	N	N	N	N	N	Y	-	?	Y	Y	N	N	Y	N	N	Y
Stevens	N	N	N	N	Y	Y	N	N	Y	Y	Y	Y	N	N	N	N
ARIZONA																
DeConcini	Y	Y	Y	N	Y	Y	Y	Y	Y	Y	N	Y	N	Y	Y	Y
McCain	N	N	Y	N	N	Y	N	N	Y	Y	N	N	N	N	N	Y
ARKANSAS																
Bumpers	Y	Y	Y	Y	Y	Y	N	Y	N	Y	Y	Y	N	Y	Y	Y
Pryor	Y	Y	Y	Y	Y	Y	N	Y	N	Y	?	Y	N	Y	Y	Y
CALIFORNIA																
Boxer	Y	Y	Y	Y	Y	Y	Y	Y	N	Y	Y	Y	N	Y	Y	N
Feinstein	Y	Y	Y	Y	Y	Y	Y	Y	Y	Y	Y	+	N	Y	Y	N
COLORADO																
Campbell	Y	Y	Y	Y	Y	Y	Y	Y	Y	Y	Y	Y	N	Y	N	N
Brown	N	N	N	N	N	Y	N	N	Y	Y	N	N	Y	Y	N	Y
CONNECTICUT																
Dodd	Y	Y	Y	Y	Y	Y	Y	Y	N	Y	Y	Y	N	Y	Y	Y
Lieberman	Y	Y	Y	Y	Y	Y	Y	N	N	Y	Y	Y	N	Y	Y	Y
DELAWARE																
Biden	Y	Y	Y	Y	Y	Y	Y	Y	N	Y	N	Y	N	Y	Y	Y
Roth	N	N	N	N	N	Y	N	N	N	N	N	N	N	Y	Y	Y
FLORIDA																
Graham	Y	Y	Y	Y	Y	Y	N	N	N	Y	N	Y	N	Y	Y	Y
Mack	N	N	N	N	N	Y	N	N	Y	Y	N	N	N	N	N	Y
GEORGIA																
Nunn	Y	Y	Y	N	Y	Y	N	N	N	Y	N	Y	N	Y	Y	Y
Coverdell	N	N	N	N	N	Y	N	N	Y	Y	N	Y	N	N	N	Y
HAWAII																
Akaka	Y	Y	Y	Y	Y	Y	Y	Y	N	Y	Y	Y	N	Y	Y	N
Inouye	?	Y	Y	Y	Y	Y	Y	N	N	Y	Y	Y	N	Y	Y	N
IDAHO																
Craig	N	N	N	N	N	Y	N	N	Y	N	N	N	Y	N	N	N
Kempthorne	N	N	N	N	N	Y	N	N	Y	N	N	N	Y	N	N	N
ILLINOIS																
Moseley-Braun	Y	Y	Y	Y	Y	Y	Y	Y	N	Y	Y	Y	N	Y	Y	Y
Simon	Y	Y	Y	Y	Y	Y	Y	Y	N	Y	Y	Y	N	Y	Y	Y
INDIANA																
Coats	N	N	N	N	N	Y	N	N	Y	Y	N	N	N	N	Y	Y
Lugar	N	N	N	N	N	Y	N	N	Y	Y	N	Y	N	Y	Y	Y
IOWA																
Harkin	Y	Y	Y	Y	Y	Y	Y	Y	N	Y	Y	Y	N	Y	Y	Y
Grassley	N	N	N	N	N	Y	N	Y	N	Y	N	N	N	N	N	Y
KANSAS																
Dole	N	N	N	N	Y	Y	N	N	Y	Y	Y	N	Y	Y	N	Y
Kassebaum	N	N	Y	N	N	Y	N	Y	Y	Y	N	Y	N	Y	Y	Y
KENTUCKY																
Ford	Y	Y	Y	Y	Y	Y	N	Y	N	Y	Y	Y	N	Y	Y	N
McConnell	N	N	N	N	N	Y	N	N	Y	Y	N	Y	N	N	N	Y
LOUISIANA																
Breaux	Y	Y	Y	Y	Y	Y	N	Y	Y	?	N	Y	N	N	N	Y
Johnston	Y	Y	Y	N	Y	Y	N	Y	N	Y	N	Y	N	N	N	Y
MAINE																
Mitchell	Y	Y	Y	Y	Y	Y	N	Y	N	Y	Y	Y	N	Y	Y	Y
Cohen	N	N	N	N	N	Y	N	N	N	Y	Y	Y	N	Y	Y	N
MARYLAND																
Mikulski	Y	Y	Y	Y	Y	Y	Y	Y	N	Y	Y	Y	N	Y	Y	N
Sarbanes	Y	Y	Y	Y	Y	Y	Y	Y	N	Y	Y	Y	N	Y	Y	N
MASSACHUSETTS																
Kennedy	Y	Y	Y	Y	Y	Y	Y	Y	N	Y	Y	Y	N	Y	Y	Y
Kerry	Y	Y	Y	Y	Y	Y	Y	Y	N	Y	Y	Y	N	Y	Y	Y
MICHIGAN																
Levin	Y	Y	Y	Y	Y	Y	Y	Y	N	Y	Y	Y	N	Y	Y	N
Riegle	Y	Y	Y	Y	+	+	Y	Y	N	Y	Y	Y	N	Y	Y	N
MINNESOTA																
Wellstone	Y	Y	Y	Y	Y	Y	Y	Y	N	Y	Y	Y	N	Y	Y	N
Durenberger	N	N	Y	N	Y	Y	Y	N	Y	Y	N	Y	Y	N	Y	Y
MISSISSIPPI																
Cochran	N	N	N	N	N	Y	N	N	Y	Y	N	Y	N	N	N	Y
Lott	N	N	N	N	N	Y	N	N	Y	Y	N	Y	N	N	N	Y
MISSOURI																
Bond	N	N	N	N	N	Y	N	N	Y	Y	Y	Y	N	Y	Y	Y
Danforth	N	N	N	N	N	Y	N	N	Y	Y	N	Y	Y	Y	Y	Y
MONTANA																
Baucus	Y	Y	Y	Y	Y	Y	N	Y	Y	Y	Y	N	Y	N	Y	Y
Burns	N	N	N	N	N	Y	N	N	Y	Y	N	Y	N	N	N	N
NEBRASKA																
Exon	Y	Y	Y	N	Y	N	N	N	Y	N	Y	N	Y	N	Y	N
Kerrey	Y	Y	Y	N	Y	Y	Y	Y	Y	Y	Y	N	Y	N	Y	Y
NEVADA																
Bryan	Y	Y	Y	N	Y	Y	N	N	N	Y	N	Y	N	N	N	N
Reid	Y	Y	Y	Y	Y	Y	N	Y	Y	Y	N	Y	N	N	Y	N
NEW HAMPSHIRE																
Gregg	N	N	N	N	N	Y	N	N	Y	Y	N	N	N	N	N	Y
Smith	N	N	N	N	N	N	N	N	Y	N	N	N	N	N	N	N
NEW JERSEY																
Bradley	Y	Y	Y	Y	Y	Y	Y	Y	N	Y	Y	N	Y	Y	Y	Y
Lautenberg	Y	Y	Y	N	Y	Y	Y	Y	N	Y	Y	Y	N	Y	Y	N
NEW MEXICO																
Bingaman	Y	Y	Y	Y	Y	Y	Y	N	Y	Y	N	Y	Y	N	Y	Y
Domenici	N	N	N	N	N	Y	N	N	Y	Y	N	Y	Y	N	N	Y
NEW YORK																
Moynihan	Y	Y	Y	Y	Y	Y	Y	Y	Y	Y	N	Y	N	Y	Y	Y
D'Amato	N	N	N	N	N	Y	Y	Y	N	Y	Y	N	N	Y	N	N
NORTH CAROLINA																
Faircloth	N	N	N	N	Y	N	N	N	Y	N	N	Y	N	N	N	N
Helms	N	N	N	N	N	N	N	N	Y	N	N	Y	N	N	N	N
NORTH DAKOTA																
Conrad	Y	Y	Y	Y	Y	Y	N	Y	Y	Y	N	Y	N	Y	Y	N
Dorgan	Y	Y	Y	Y	Y	Y	N	Y	Y	Y	N	Y	N	?	?	?
OHIO																
Glenn	Y	Y	Y	Y	Y	Y	?	Y	N	Y	Y	Y	N	Y	Y	N
Metzenbaum	Y	Y	Y	Y	Y	Y	Y	Y	N	Y	Y	Y	N	Y	Y	N
OKLAHOMA																
Boren	Y	Y	Y	Y	Y	Y	N	N	Y	Y	N	Y	N	Y	Y	Y
Nickles	N	N	N	N	N	N	N	N	Y	Y	N	N	N	N	N	Y
OREGON																
Hatfield	N	N	N	N	N	Y	N	N	Y	Y	N	Y	Y	Y	Y	Y
Packwood	N	N	N	N	N	Y	N	N	Y	Y	Y	Y	Y	Y	Y	Y
PENNSYLVANIA																
Wofford	Y	Y	Y	Y	Y	Y	N	Y	N	Y	N	Y	N	Y	Y	N
Specter	N	N	?	?	Y	Y	N	N	N	Y	Y	Y	Y	N	N	Y
RHODE ISLAND																
Pell	Y	Y	Y	Y	Y	Y	Y	Y	N	Y	Y	N	Y	N	Y	Y
Chafee	N	N	Y	N	Y	Y	Y	Y	N	Y	Y	Y	N	Y	Y	Y
SOUTH CAROLINA																
Hollings	Y	Y	N	Y	N	Y	N	N	Y	N	Y	N	N	N	N	N
Thurmond	N	N	N	N	Y	N	N	N	Y	Y	N	Y	N	Y	N	N
SOUTH DAKOTA																
Daschle	Y	Y	Y	Y	Y	Y	N	Y	N	Y	Y	N	Y	N	Y	Y
Pressler	N	N	N	N	Y	N	N	N	Y	Y	N	N	N	Y	N	N
TENNESSEE																
Mathews	Y	Y	Y	Y	Y	Y	N	Y	N	Y	N	Y	N	Y	Y	Y
Sasser	Y	Y	Y	Y	Y	Y	N	Y	N	Y	N	Y	N	N	Y	N
TEXAS																
Gramm	N	N	N	N	Y	N	N	?	Y	Y	N	N	Y	N	N	Y
Krueger/*Hutchison*[a]	Y	Y	N	N	Y	Y	-	N	Y	Y	N	Y	N	N	Y	Y
UTAH																
Bennett	N	N	N	N	N	Y	N	N	Y	Y	N	Y	N	N	N	Y
Hatch	N	N	N	N	N	Y	N	N	Y	Y	N	Y	N	N	N	Y
VERMONT																
Leahy	Y	Y	Y	Y	Y	Y	Y	Y	N	Y	Y	Y	N	Y	Y	Y
Jeffords	N	N	Y	N	Y	Y	Y	Y	N	Y	Y	Y	N	Y	Y	Y
VIRGINIA																
Robb	Y	Y	Y	Y	Y	Y	Y	N	N	Y	Y	Y	N	Y	Y	Y
Warner	N	N	N	N	N	Y	N	N	Y	Y	N	Y	N	N	Y	Y
WASHINGTON																
Murray	Y	Y	Y	+	Y	Y	Y	Y	N	Y	Y	Y	N	Y	Y	N
Gorton	N	N	N	N	N	Y	N	N	Y	Y	N	N	N	N	N	Y
WEST VIRGINIA																
Byrd	Y	Y	Y	Y	N	Y	N	Y	N	N	N	Y	N	Y	Y	N
Rockefeller	Y	Y	Y	Y	Y	Y	N	Y	N	Y	N	Y	N	Y	Y	N
WISCONSIN																
Feingold	Y	Y	Y	Y	Y	Y	Y	N	Y	Y	N	N	Y	N	N	N
Kohl	Y	Y	Y	Y	Y	Y	N	Y	N	Y	N	Y	N	N	Y	N
WYOMING																
Simpson	N	-	-	N	N	Y	N	N	Y	+	N	Y	Y	N	N	Y
Wallop	N	N	N	N	N	Y	-	-	Y	N	N	N	Y	N	N	Y

1. HR 1. Family and Medical Leave/Passage. Passage of the bill to require employers of more than 50 employees to provide 12 weeks of unpaid leave for an illness or to care for a new child or sick family member. Passed 265–163: R 40–134; D 224–29 (ND 162–8, SD 62–21); I 1–0, Feb. 3, 1993. A "yea" was a vote in support of the president's position.

2. H Con Res 64. Fiscal 1994 Budget Resolution/Adoption. Adoption of the concurrent resolution to set binding budget levels for the fiscal year ending Sept. 30, 1994: budget authority, $1.506 trillion; outlays, $1.495 trillion; revenues, $1.242 trillion; deficit, $253.5 billion. Adopted 243–183: R 0–172; D 242–11 (ND 164–6, SD 78–5); I 1–0, March 18, 1993. A "yea" was a vote in support of the president's position.

3. HR 1335. Fiscal 1993 Supplemental Appropriations/Rule. Adoption of the rule (H Res 132) to waive points of order against and provide for House floor consideration of the bill to provide $16.3 billion in new budget authority and approve $3.4 billion in trust fund spending to implement the administration's stimulus package to help the economy recover. The funds would be designated as emergency spending, making them exempt from discretionary spending caps. Adopted 240–185: R 0–172; D 239–13 (ND 165–4, SD 74–9); I 1–0, March 18, 1993. A "yea" was a vote in support of the president's position.

4. HR 2295. Fiscal 1994 Foreign Operations Appropriations/Aid to Russia. Callahan, R-Ala., amendment to cut the $1.6 billion fiscal 1993 supplemental appropriation for aid to Russia. Rejected in the Committee of the Whole 140–289: R 93–79; D 46–210 (ND 30–143, SD 16–67); I 1–0, June 17, 1993. A "nay" was a vote in support of the president's position.

5. HR 2518. Fiscal 1994 Labor, HHS, Education Appropriations/Abortion Prohibition. Hyde, R-Ill., amendment to prohibit funds in the bill from being spent for an abortion except when it is made known that it is a case of rape, incest or necessity to save the woman's life. Adopted in the Committee of the Whole 255–178: R 157–16; D 98–161 (ND 54–120, SD 44–41); I 0–1, June 30, 1993.

6. HR 2264. 1993 Budget-Reconciliation/Adoption. Adoption of the conference report to reduce the deficit by an estimated $496 billion over five years through almost $241 billion in additional taxes and $255 billion in spending cuts by closely tracking President Clinton's economic proposals. Of the cuts in the bill, $102 billion would come through a freeze of discretionary spending at fiscal 1993 levels through fiscal 1998. Adopted 218–216: R 0–175; D 217–41 (ND 155–18, SD 62–23); I 1–0, Aug. 5, 1933. A "yea" was a vote in support of the president's position.

7. HR 1340. Resolution Trust Corporation/Passage. Passage of the bill to provide $18.3 billion to resolve failed savings and loan institutions, authorize funds for the new Savings Association Insurance Fund for fiscal 1994–1998, direct new management reforms, expand the Resolution Trust Corporation's affordable housing program and impose new requirements for contracting with businesses owned by minorities and women. Passed 214–208: R 24–148; D 190–59 (ND 131–34, SD 59–25); I 0–1, Sept. 14, 1993. A "yea" was a vote in support of the president's position.

8. HR 2401. Fiscal 1994 Defense Authorization/Gay Ban. Meehan, D-Mass., amendment to strike the provisions codifying a ban on homosexuals in the military and express the sense of Congress that the issue should be determined by the president and his advisers. Rejected in the Committee of the Whole 169–264: R 11–163; D 157–101 (ND 131–43, SD 26–58); I 1–0, Sept. 28, 1993.

9. HR 1845. National Biological Survey/Non-Federal Property. Taylor, R-N.C., amendment to require the National Biological Survey to obtain written consent before going on nonfederal lands and to require reports describing the survey's activities on nonfederal lands. Adopted in the Committee of the Whole 309–115: R 171–3; D 138–111 (ND 72–95, SD 66–16); I 0–1, Oct. 6, 1993.

10. HR 2445. Fiscal 1994 Energy and Water Appropriations/Previous Question. Motion to order the previous question (thus ending debate and the possibility of amendment) on the Myers, R-Ind., motion to recommit to conference the conference report to provide $22,215,382,000 for energy and water development for fiscal 1994. Motion rejected 159–264: R 61–111; D 98–152

(ND 47–121, SD 51–31); I 0–1, Oct. 19, 1993. A "yea" was a vote in support of the president's position.

11. H Con Res 170. Somalia Troop Removal/March 31 Deadline. Hamilton, D-Ind., substitute amendment to change the deadline for the removal of U.S. troops from Somalia back to March 31, 1994, from the Jan. 31, 1994, date substituted by the Gilman, R-N.Y., amendment. Adopted 226–201: R 2–170; D 224–30 (ND 150–21, SD 74–9); I 0–1, Nov. 9, 1993. A "yea" was a vote in support of the president's position.

12. HR 1025. Brady Bill/Passage. Passage of the bill to require a five-business-day waiting period before an individual could purchase a handgun, to allow local officials to conduct a background check. Passed 238–189: R 54–119; D 184–69 (ND 138–31, SD 46–38); I 0–1, Nov. 10, 1993. A "yea" was a vote in support of the president's position.

13. HR 3450. NAFTA Implementation/Passage. Passage of the bill to approve the North American Free Trade Agreement and make the necessary changes to U.S. statutory law to implement it. Passed 234–200: R 132–43; D 102–156 (ND 49–124, SD 53–32); I 0–1, Nov. 17, 1993. A "yea" was a vote in support of the president's position.

14. HR 322. 1872 Mining Law Overhaul/Passage. Passage of the bill to require hard-rock mining companies to pay an 8 percent royalty on ores extracted from federal lands, with the money going toward cleanup of abandoned mines, and to require increased environmental regulation of such mining operations. Passed 316–108: R 70–102; D 245–6 (ND 166–3, SD 79–3); I 1–0, Nov. 18, 1993. A "yea" was a vote in support of the president's position.

15. HR 3. Campaign Finance/Rule. Adoption of the rule (H Res 319) to provide for House floor consideration of the bill to give House candidates up to $200,000 in federal benefits if they agree to voluntary spending limits of $600,000. The sums would be indexed for inflation from 1992 forward. Adopted 220–207: R 3–168; D 216–39 (ND 156–15, SD 60–24); I 1–0, Nov. 21, 1993. A "yea" was a vote in support of the president's position.

16. HR 3400. Fiscal 1994 Spending Cuts and Government Restructuring/Penny-Kasich Amendment. Penny, D-Minn., amendment to cut federal spending by $90 billion over five years through various proposals, including $34 billion in Medicare cuts, $52 billion in discretionary spending cuts and $4 billion in other entitlement cuts and user fee increases. Rejected in the Committee of the Whole 213–219: R 156–18; D 57–200 (ND 33–139, SD 24–61); I 0–1, Nov. 22, 1993. A "nay" was a vote in support of the president's position.

---

[a] Sam Farr, D-Calif., won a runoff election June 8 to fill the seat vacated by Leon Panetta. He was sworn in June 16 and was eligible to vote on key votes 4–16.

KEY

Democrats — *Republicans* — **Independent**

Y Voted for ("yea")
N Voted against ("nay")
\+ Announced for
\# Paired for
X Paired against
– Announced against
P Voted "present"
C Voted "present" to avoid possible conflict of interest
? Did not vote or otherwise make a position known

ND Northern Democrats
SD Southern Democrats
Southern states – Ala., Ark., Fla., Ga., Ky., La., Miss., N.C., Okla., S.C., Tenn., Texas, Va.

House Key Votes	1	2	3	4	5	6	7	8	9	10	11	12	13	14	15	16
ALABAMA																
1 *Callahan*	N	N	N	Y	Y	N	N	N	Y	Y	N	N	Y	N	N	Y
2 *Everett*	N	N	N	Y	Y	N	N	N	Y	Y	N	N	N	N	N	Y
3 Browder	N	Y	Y	N	Y	N	N	N	Y	Y	Y	N	N	Y	Y	Y
4 Bevill	Y	Y	Y	N	Y	Y	N	N	Y	Y	Y	N	N	Y	Y	N
5 Cramer	Y	Y	Y	N	Y	Y	N	N	Y	Y	Y	N	N	Y	Y	N
6 *Bachus*	N	N	N	N	Y	N	N	N	Y	Y	N	N	Y	N	N	Y
7 Hilliard	Y	Y	Y	Y	N	Y	N	Y	Y	Y	Y	N	N	Y	Y	N
ALASKA																
AL *Young*	Y	N	N	?	Y	N	Y	N	Y	Y	N	N	N	N	N	Y
ARIZONA																
1 Coppersmith	Y	Y	Y	N	N	N	Y	Y	N	N	Y	Y	Y	Y	Y	Y
2 Pastor	Y	Y	Y	N	N	Y	Y	Y	N	Y	Y	Y	Y	Y	Y	N
3 *Stump*	N	N	N	Y	Y	N	N	N	Y	Y	N	N	Y	N	N	Y
4 *Kyl*	N	N	N	Y	Y	N	N	N	Y	N	N	N	Y	N	?	Y
5 *Kolbe*	N	N	N	N	Y	N	N	N	Y	Y	N	N	Y	N	N	Y
6 English	Y	Y	Y	N	N	Y	Y	Y	N	N	Y	Y	Y	Y	Y	N
ARKANSAS																
1 Lambert	Y	Y	N	N	N	Y	N	N	Y	N	Y	N	Y	Y	Y	Y
2 Thornton	Y	Y	Y	N	Y	N	Y	N	Y	Y	Y	N	Y	Y	Y	N
3 *Hutchinson*	N	N	N	Y	Y	N	N	N	Y	N	N	N	Y	N	N	Y
4 *Dickey*	N	N	N	N	Y	N	N	N	Y	N	Y	N	Y	Y	N	Y
CALIFORNIA																
1 Hamburg	Y	Y	Y	N	N	Y	Y	Y	N	N	Y	Y	N	Y	Y	N
2 *Herger*	N	N	N	Y	Y	N	N	N	Y	N	N	N	Y	N	N	Y
3 Fazio	Y	Y	Y	N	N	Y	Y	Y	Y	Y	Y	Y	Y	Y	Y	N
4 *Doolittle*	N	N	N	Y	Y	N	N	N	Y	N	N	N	N	N	N	Y
5 Matsui	Y	Y	Y	N	N	Y	Y	Y	N	Y	Y	Y	Y	Y	Y	N
6 Woolsey	Y	Y	Y	N	N	Y	Y	Y	N	N	Y	Y	N	Y	Y	N
7 Miller	Y	Y	Y	N	N	Y	?	Y	N	N	Y	Y	N	Y	Y	N
8 Pelosi	Y	Y	Y	-	N	Y	Y	Y	N	N	Y	Y	Y	Y	Y	N
9 Dellums	Y	Y	Y	N	N	Y	Y	Y	N	N	Y	Y	N	Y	Y	N
10 *Baker*	N	N	N	Y	Y	N	N	N	Y	N	N	Y	Y	N	N	Y
11 *Pombo*	N	N	N	Y	Y	N	N	N	Y	N	N	N	N	N	N	Y
12 Lantos	Y	Y	Y	N	N	Y	Y	Y	Y	N	Y	Y	N	Y	Y	N
13 Stark	Y	Y	Y	N	N	Y	Y	Y	N	N	Y	Y	N	Y	Y	N
14 Eshoo	Y	Y	Y	N	N	Y	Y	Y	N	N	Y	Y	Y	Y	Y	N
15 Mineta	Y	Y	Y	N	N	Y	Y	Y	N	Y	Y	Y	Y	Y	Y	N
16 Edwards	Y	Y	Y	N	N	Y	Y	Y	N	?	Y	Y	N	Y	Y	N
17 Farr[a]				N	N	Y	Y	Y	N	N	Y	Y	Y	Y	Y	N
18 Condit	Y	Y	Y	Y	Y	N	N	Y	Y	N	Y	Y	N	Y	Y	Y
19 Lehman	Y	Y	Y	N	N	N	?	N	Y	N	Y	Y	Y	Y	Y	N
20 Dooley	Y	Y	Y	N	N	N	Y	Y	Y	Y	Y	Y	Y	Y	Y	Y
21 *Thomas*	N	N	N	N	Y	N	N	N	Y	Y	N	Y	Y	N	N	Y
22 *Huffington*	Y	N	N	Y	Y	N	?	Y	Y	N	N	Y	Y	Y	N	Y
23 *Gallegly*	N	N	N	Y	Y	N	N	N	Y	Y	N	Y	N	Y	N	Y
24 Beilenson	Y	Y	Y	N	N	Y	Y	Y	N	N	Y	Y	Y	Y	Y	N
25 *McKeon*	N	N	N	Y	Y	N	N	N	Y	N	N	N	Y	N	N	Y
26 Berman	Y	Y	Y	N	N	Y	Y	Y	N	N	Y	Y	Y	Y	Y	N
27 *Moorhead*	N	N	N	Y	Y	N	N	N	Y	Y	N	N	Y	Y	N	Y
28 *Dreier*	N	N	N	N	Y	N	N	N	Y	Y	N	N	Y	N	N	Y
29 Waxman	Y	Y	Y	N	N	Y	Y	Y	N	N	Y	Y	N	Y	Y	N
30 Becerra	Y	Y	Y	Y	N	Y	Y	Y	N	N	Y	Y	Y	Y	Y	N
31 Martinez	Y	Y	Y	N	N	Y	Y	Y	Y	N	Y	N	N	?	Y	N
32 Dixon	Y	Y	Y	N	N	Y	Y	Y	N	Y	Y	Y	N	Y	Y	N
33 Roybal-Allard	Y	Y	Y	N	N	Y	Y	Y	N	N	Y	Y	Y	Y	Y	N
34 Torres	Y	Y	Y	N	N	Y	Y	Y	N	Y	Y	Y	Y	Y	Y	N
35 Waters	Y	Y	Y	Y	N	Y	Y	Y	N	N	Y	Y	N	Y	Y	N
36 Harman	Y	Y	Y	N	N	Y	Y	Y	N	N	Y	Y	N	Y	Y	Y
37 Tucker	Y	Y	Y	Y	N	Y	Y	Y	N	N	Y	Y	N	Y	Y	N
38 *Horn*	Y	N	N	N	N	N	N	Y	Y	Y	N	Y	Y	Y	N	N
39 *Royce*	N	N	N	Y	Y	N	N	N	Y	N	N	N	N	N	N	Y
40 *Lewis*	N	N	N	N	Y	N	N	N	Y	Y	N	N	Y	N	N	Y
41 *Kim*	N	N	N	Y	Y	N	N	N	Y	N	N	N	Y	N	N	Y
42 Brown	Y	Y	Y	N	N	Y	?	Y	N	Y	Y	Y	Y	Y	Y	N
43 *Calvert*	N	N	N	N	Y	N	N	N	Y	N	N	N	Y	N	N	Y
44 *McCandless*	N	N	N	N	Y	N	N	N	Y	Y	N	?	Y	N	N	Y
45 *Rohrabacher*	N	N	N	Y	Y	N	N	N	Y	N	N	N	Y	N	N	Y
46 *Dornan*	N	N	N	Y	Y	N	N	N	Y	Y	N	N	Y	N	N	Y
47 *Cox*	N	N	N	Y	Y	N	N	N	Y	Y	N	N	Y	N	N	Y
48 *Packard*	N	N	N	Y	Y	N	N	N	Y	Y	N	N	Y	N	N	Y
49 Schenk	Y	Y	Y	N	N	Y	Y	Y	Y	N	Y	Y	N	Y	Y	Y
50 Filner	Y	Y	Y	N	N	Y	N	Y	N	N	Y	Y	N	Y	Y	N
51 *Cunningham*	N	N	N	Y	Y	N	N	N	Y	N	N	N	Y	Y	N	Y
52 *Hunter*	N	N	N	Y	Y	N	?	N	Y	N	?	N	N	N	N	Y
COLORADO																
1 Schroeder	Y	Y	Y	N	N	Y	N	Y	Y	N	?	Y	Y	Y	N	N
2 Skaggs	Y	Y	Y	N	N	Y	Y	Y	N	N	Y	Y	Y	N	Y	N
3 *McInnis*	N	N	N	Y	Y	N	N	N	Y	N	N	N	Y	N	N	Y
4 *Allard*	N	N	N	Y	Y	N	N	N	Y	N	N	N	Y	N	N	Y
5 *Hefley*	N	N	N	Y	Y	N	N	N	Y	N	N	N	Y	N	N	Y
6 *Schaefer*	N	N	N	Y	Y	N	N	N	Y	N	N	N	Y	N	N	Y
CONNECTICUT																
1 Kennelly	Y	Y	Y	N	N	Y	Y	Y	N	N	Y	Y	N	Y	Y	N
2 Gejdenson	Y	Y	Y	N	N	Y	Y	Y	N	N	Y	Y	N	Y	Y	N
3 DeLauro	Y	Y	Y	N	N	Y	N	Y	N	N	Y	Y	N	Y	Y	N
4 *Shays*	Y	N	N	Y	N	N	Y	Y	N	N	N	Y	Y	Y	N	Y
5 *Franks*	N	N	N	Y	N	N	N	N	Y	Y	N	N	Y	Y	N	Y
6 *Johnson*	Y	N	N	N	N	N	Y	Y	Y	Y	N	Y	Y	Y	N	Y
DELAWARE																
AL *Castle*	Y	N	N	N	Y	N	N	N	Y	N	N	Y	Y	Y	N	Y
FLORIDA																
1 Hutto	N	Y	Y	Y	Y	N	N	N	Y	N	Y	Y	Y	Y	N	N
2 Peterson	Y	Y	Y	N	Y	Y	Y	N	Y	Y	Y	N	N	Y	Y	N
3 Brown	Y	Y	Y	N	N	Y	Y	N	Y	Y	Y	Y	N	Y	Y	N
4 *Fowler*	N	N	N	Y	Y	N	Y	N	Y	N	N	Y	Y	Y	N	Y
5 Thurman	Y	Y	Y	Y	Y	Y	Y	N	Y	N	Y	N	N	Y	Y	N
6 *Stearns*	N	N	N	Y	Y	N	N	N	Y	N	N	Y	N	Y	N	Y
7 *Mica*	N	N	N	Y	Y	N	N	N	Y	Y	N	N	N	N	N	Y
8 *McCollum*	N	N	N	N	Y	N	N	N	Y	Y	N	N	Y	N	N	Y
9 *Bilirakis*	N	N	N	Y	Y	N	N	N	Y	N	N	Y	N	Y	N	Y
10 *Young*	Y	N	N	Y	Y	N	N	N	Y	N	N	Y	Y	Y	N	Y
11 Gibbons	Y	Y	Y	N	Y	Y	Y	Y	N	Y	Y	Y	Y	Y	Y	N
12 *Canady*	N	N	N	Y	Y	N	N	N	Y	N	N	N	N	Y	N	Y
13 *Miller*	N	N	N	Y	Y	N	N	N	Y	N	N	N	Y	Y	N	Y
14 *Goss*	N	N	N	Y	Y	N	N	N	Y	N	N	Y	Y	Y	N	Y
15 Bacchus	Y	Y	Y	N	N	Y	Y	Y	N	Y	Y	Y	Y	Y	Y	Y
16 *Lewis*	N	N	N	Y	Y	N	N	N	Y	N	?	N	Y	Y	N	Y
17 Meek	Y	Y	Y	N	N	Y	Y	Y	N	Y	Y	Y	Y	Y	Y	N
18 *Ros-Lehtinen*	Y	N	N	Y	Y	N	N	N	Y	N	N	Y	N	Y	N	N
19 Johnston	Y	Y	Y	N	N	Y	Y	Y	N	N	Y	Y	Y	Y	Y	N
20 Deutsch	Y	Y	Y	N	N	Y	Y	Y	N	N	Y	Y	N	Y	Y	N
21 *Diaz-Balart*	Y	N	N	Y	Y	N	N	N	Y	Y	N	Y	N	Y	N	N
22 *Shaw*	N	N	N	N	Y	N	N	N	Y	N	N	Y	Y	Y	N	Y
23 Hastings	Y	Y	Y	N	N	Y	Y	Y	N	Y	Y	Y	Y	Y	Y	N
GEORGIA																
1 *Kingston*	N	N	N	Y	Y	N	N	N	Y	N	N	N	N	N	N	Y
2 Bishop	Y	Y	Y	N	N	Y	Y	N	Y	Y	Y	N	N	Y	Y	N
3 *Collins*	N	N	N	Y	Y	N	N	N	Y	N	N	N	N	N	N	Y
4 *Linder*	N	N	N	N	Y	N	N	N	Y	N	N	N	Y	N	N	Y
5 Lewis	Y	Y	Y	N	N	Y	N	Y	N	N	Y	Y	N	Y	Y	N
6 *Gingrich*	N	N	N	N	Y	N	N	N	Y	Y	N	N	Y	Y	N	Y
7 Darden	N	Y	Y	N	Y	Y	N	N	Y	Y	Y	Y	Y	Y	Y	N
8 Rowland	N	Y	Y	N	Y	N	Y	N	Y	N	Y	Y	Y	Y	N	Y
9 Deal	N	Y	N	N	Y	N	N	N	Y	N	N	-	Y	Y	N	Y
10 Johnson	N	Y	Y	N	N	Y	N	N	Y	N	Y	N	Y	Y	Y	Y
11 McKinney	Y	Y	Y	N	N	Y	Y	Y	Y	N	Y	Y	N	Y	Y	N
HAWAII																
1 Abercrombie	Y	Y	Y	N	N	Y	Y	Y	N	N	Y	Y	N	Y	Y	N
2 Mink	Y	Y	Y	N	N	Y	Y	Y	N	N	Y	Y	N	Y	Y	N
IDAHO																
1 LaRocco	N	Y	Y	Y	N	Y	Y	Y	N	Y	Y	N	N	Y	Y	Y
2 *Crapo*	N	N	N	Y	Y	N	N	N	Y	Y	N	N	N	N	N	Y
ILLINOIS																
1 Rush	Y	Y	Y	N	N	Y	Y	Y	N	N	Y	Y	N	Y	Y	N
2 Reynolds	Y	Y	Y	Y	N	Y	Y	Y	N	Y	Y	Y	Y	Y	Y	N
3 Lipinski	Y	N	Y	N	Y	N	?	N	Y	N	Y	Y	N	Y	Y	N
4 Gutierrez	Y	Y	Y	Y	N	Y	Y	Y	N	N	Y	Y	N	Y	Y	N
5 Rostenkowski	Y	Y	Y	N	Y	Y	Y	Y	N	N	Y	Y	Y	Y	N	N
6 *Hyde*	Y	N	N	N	Y	N	C	N	Y	N	N	Y	Y	Y	N	Y
7 Collins	Y	Y	Y	Y	N	Y	Y	Y	N	N	Y	Y	N	Y	Y	N
8 *Crane*	N	N	N	Y	Y	N	N	N	Y	N	N	N	Y	N	N	Y
9 Yates	Y	Y	Y	N	N	Y	Y	Y	?	Y	Y	Y	N	Y	Y	N
10 *Porter*	N	N	N	N	Y	N	Y	N	Y	N	N	Y	Y	Y	N	Y
11 Sangmeister	Y	Y	Y	N	Y	Y	Y	N	Y	N	Y	Y	N	Y	N	N
12 Costello	Y	Y	Y	N	Y	Y	N	N	Y	N	N	N	N	Y	Y	N
13 *Fawell*	N	N	N	N	Y	N	Y	N	Y	N	N	Y	Y	Y	N	Y
14 *Hastert*	N	N	N	Y	Y	N	N	N	Y	N	N	N	Y	Y	N	Y
15 *Ewing*	N	N	N	Y	Y	N	N	N	Y	N	N	N	Y	N	N	Y
16 *Manzullo*	N	N	N	Y	Y	N	N	N	Y	N	N	N	Y	N	N	Y

KEY

	Democrats	*Republicans*	Independent
Y	Voted for ("yea")	–	Announced against
N	Voted against ("nay")	P	Voted "present"
+	Announced for	C	Voted "present" to avoid possible conflict of interest
#	Paired for	?	Did not vote or otherwise make a position known
X	Paired against		

ND Northern Democrats
SD Southern Democrats
Southern states – Ala., Ark., Fla., Ga., Ky., La., Miss., N.C., Okla., S.C., Tenn., Texas, Va.

House Key Votes	1	2	3	4	5	6	7	8	9	10	11	12	13	14	15	16
17 Evans	Y	Y	Y	N	N	Y	N	Y	N	N	N	Y	N	Y	Y	N
18 *Michel*	N	N	N	N	Y	N	Y	N	Y	Y	N	N	Y	N	N	Y
19 Poshard	Y	Y	Y	Y	Y	Y	N	N	N	N	N	N	N	N	N	Y
20 Durbin	Y	Y	Y	N	Y	Y	Y	Y	Y	N	Y	N	Y	Y	Y	N
INDIANA																
1 Visclosky	Y	Y	Y	N	N	Y	N	Y	N	N	Y	Y	N	Y	Y	N
2 Sharp	Y	Y	Y	N	Y	Y	N	Y	Y	N	Y	Y	N	Y	Y	Y
3 Roemer	Y	Y	Y	Y	Y	Y	N	Y	Y	Y	Y	Y	N	Y	Y	Y
4 Long	Y	N	Y	N	Y	N	N	N	Y	N	Y	Y	N	Y	Y	Y
5 *Buyer*	N	N	N	Y	Y	N	N	N	Y	Y	N	N	Y	N	N	Y
6 *Burton*	N	N	N	Y	N	N	N	Y	?	N	N	N	N	N	N	Y
7 *Myers*	N	?	?	N	Y	N	N	N	Y	Y	N	N	N	N	N	N
8 McCloskey	Y	Y	Y	N	Y	Y	Y	Y	?	Y	Y	Y	N	Y	Y	N
9 Hamilton	N	Y	N	N	Y	Y	N	Y	N	Y	Y	Y	Y	Y	Y	Y
10 Jacobs	Y	N	Y	Y	?	Y	Y	N	Y	N	N	Y	N	Y	N	N
IOWA																
1 *Leach*	Y	N	N	N	Y	N	Y	Y	Y	N	N	Y	Y	Y	N	Y
2 *Nussle*	N	N	N	N	Y	N	N	N	Y	N	N	N	Y	N	N	Y
3 *Lightfoot*	N	N	N	N	Y	N	Y	N	Y	Y	N	N	Y	N	N	N
4 Smith	Y	Y	Y	N	N	Y	Y	Y	Y	Y	Y	Y	N	Y	Y	N
5 *Grandy*	N	N	N	N	Y	N	Y	Y	Y	N	N	N	Y	Y	N	Y
KANSAS																
1 *Roberts*	N	N	N	Y	N	N	N	N	Y	N	Y	N	N	Y	N	N
2 Slattery	N	Y	N	N	Y	N	N	N	Y	N	Y	Y	N	Y	Y	Y
3 *Meyers*	N	N	N	N	N	N	N	N	Y	N	N	Y	Y	N	Y	Y
4 Glickman	N	Y	Y	N	Y	Y	Y	N	Y	N	Y	Y	Y	Y	Y	N
KENTUCKY																
1 Barlow	Y	Y	Y	N	N	Y	N	Y	N	Y	Y	Y	N	Y	Y	Y
2 Natcher	Y	Y	Y	N	Y	Y	Y	N	Y	Y	Y	Y	N	Y	Y	Y
3 Mazzoli	Y	Y	Y	N	Y	Y	N	N	Y	Y	N	Y	Y	N	Y	Y
4 *Bunning*	N	N	N	Y	Y	N	N	N	Y	N	N	N	N	N	?	Y
5 *Rogers*	N	N	N	Y	Y	N	N	N	Y	N	N	N	N	N	N	Y
6 Baesler	Y	Y	N	N	Y	N	Y	N	Y	Y	Y	Y	Y	Y	Y	Y
LOUISIANA																
1 *Livingston*	N	N	N	N	Y	N	N	N	Y	Y	N	N	N	N	N	Y
2 Jefferson	Y	Y	Y	N	N	Y	Y	Y	N	Y	Y	Y	Y	Y	Y	N
3 Tauzin	N	Y	N	Y	Y	N	N	N	Y	N	N	N	N	N	N	Y
4 Fields	Y	Y	Y	N	Y	Y	Y	Y	N	Y	Y	Y	N	Y	Y	N
5 *McCrery*	N	N	N	N	Y	N	N	N	Y	N	Y	N	N	N	N	Y
6 *Baker*	N	N	N	Y	N	N	N	N	Y	N	N	N	N	N	N	Y
7 Hayes	N	Y	Y	N	Y	N	Y	N	Y	Y	?	N	Y	N	N	Y
MAINE																
1 Andrews	Y	Y	Y	N	N	Y	Y	Y	N	N	Y	Y	N	Y	Y	N
2 *Snowe*	Y	N	N	Y	N	N	N	N	N	N	N	N	N	Y	N	Y
MARYLAND																
1 *Gilchrest*	N	N	N	Y	N	Y	N	N	N	N	Y	N	Y	?	N	Y
2 *Bentley*	N	N	N	N	Y	N	N	N	Y	Y	N	N	N	N	N	Y
3 Cardin	Y	Y	Y	N	N	Y	Y	Y	N	N	Y	Y	Y	Y	Y	N
4 Wynn	Y	Y	Y	N	Y	Y	Y	Y	N	N	Y	Y	N	Y	Y	N
5 Hoyer	Y	Y	Y	N	Y	Y	Y	Y	Y	Y	Y	Y	Y	Y	Y	Y
6 *Bartlett*	N	N	N	Y	N	Y	N	N	N	Y	Y	N	N	N	N	Y
7 Mfume	Y	Y	Y	N	Y	Y	Y	Y	N	N	Y	Y	N	Y	Y	N
8 *Morella*	Y	N	N	N	N	N	Y	N	N	N	Y	N	Y	Y	Y	N
MASSACHUSETTS																
1 Olver	Y	Y	Y	N	N	Y	Y	Y	N	N	N	Y	N	Y	Y	N
2 Neal	Y	Y	Y	N	Y	Y	Y	Y	N	N	Y	Y	N	Y	Y	N
3 *Blute*	Y	N	N	Y	Y	N	N	N	Y	Y	N	N	Y	N	N	Y
4 Frank	Y	Y	Y	N	N	Y	Y	Y	N	N	Y	Y	N	Y	Y	N
5 Meehan	Y	Y	Y	N	Y	Y	Y	Y	N	N	Y	Y	N	Y	Y	N
6 *Torkildsen*	N	N	N	N	Y	N	N	N	Y	N	N	N	Y	N	N	Y
7 Markey	Y	Y	Y	N	N	Y	Y	Y	N	N	Y	Y	N	Y	Y	N
8 Kennedy	Y	Y	Y	N	Y	Y	Y	Y	N	N	Y	Y	N	Y	Y	N
9 Moakley	Y	Y	Y	N	?	Y	Y	Y	N	?	?	#	N	Y	Y	N
10 Studds	Y	Y	Y	N	N	Y	Y	Y	N	N	Y	Y	N	Y	Y	N
MICHIGAN																
1 Stupak	Y	Y	Y	N	Y	N	Y	N	Y	N	N	N	N	N	Y	N
2 *Hoekstra*	N	N	N	N	Y	N	N	N	N	N	N	Y	N	N	N	Y

House Key Votes	1	2	3	4	5	6	7	8	9	10	11	12	13	14	15	16
3 *Henry* [b]	?	?	?	?	?											
4 *Camp*	N	N	N	Y	Y	N	N	N	Y	N	N	N	Y	N	N	Y
5 Barcia	Y	Y	Y	Y	Y	N	N	N	Y	N	N	N	N	N	N	Y
6 *Upton*	N	N	N	N	Y	N	N	N	Y	N	N	Y	Y	Y	N	Y
7 *Smith*	N	N	N	N	Y	N	N	N	Y	?	N	Y	N	N	N	Y
8 Carr	N	Y	Y	N	N	Y	N	Y	Y	N	Y	N	N	Y	N	N
9 Kildee	Y	Y	Y	N	Y	N	Y	N	Y	N	N	Y	N	Y	Y	N
10 Bonior	Y	Y	Y	N	Y	Y	Y	Y	N	Y	Y	Y	N	Y	Y	N
11 *Knollenberg*	N	N	N	N	Y	N	N	N	N	N	N	N	N	N	N	Y
12 Levin	Y	Y	Y	N	N	Y	Y	Y	N	Y	N	Y	N	Y	Y	N
13 Ford	Y	Y	Y	N	N	Y	Y	Y	N	N	Y	Y	N	Y	?	N
14 Conyers	Y	Y	Y	Y	N	Y	?	?	?	N	Y	Y	N	Y	Y	N
15 Collins	Y	Y	Y	Y	N	Y	Y	Y	N	N	Y	Y	N	Y	Y	N
16 Dingell	Y	Y	Y	N	N	Y	Y	N	N	N	Y	N	N	Y	Y	N
MINNESOTA																
1 Penny	N	Y	Y	N	Y	Y	N	Y	Y	N	Y	N	Y	Y	Y	Y
2 Minge	Y	Y	Y	N	+	N	Y	Y	Y	N	Y	N	Y	N	Y	Y
3 *Ramstad*	Y	N	N	Y	Y	N	N	N	Y	N	N	N	Y	N	N	Y
4 Vento	Y	Y	Y	N	N	Y	Y	Y	N	N	Y	Y	N	Y	Y	N
5 Sabo	Y	Y	Y	N	N	Y	Y	Y	N	N	Y	N	N	Y	Y	N
6 *Grams*	N	N	N	Y	Y	N	N	N	Y	Y	N	N	N	N	N	Y
7 Peterson	Y	Y	Y	N	N	Y	N	N	N	Y	N	N	N	Y	N	Y
8 Oberstar	Y	Y	Y	N	Y	Y	Y	Y	Y	N	Y	N	Y	Y	Y	N
MISSISSIPPI																
1 Whitten	Y	Y	Y	N	N	Y	N	Y	N	Y	N	Y	Y	Y	Y	N
2 Espy/Thompson [c]			Y	N	Y	N	Y	Y	Y	Y	N	Y	N	Y	Y	N
3 Montgomery	N	Y	N	N	Y	N	Y	N	Y	Y	Y	N	Y	Y	Y	N
4 Parker	N	Y	N	N	Y	N	Y	N	Y	N	Y	N	Y	Y	Y	N
5 Taylor	Y	N	N	N	Y	N	N	Y	N	N	N	N	N	N	Y	Y
MISSOURI																
1 Clay	Y	Y	Y	Y	N	Y	Y	Y	N	Y	Y	Y	N	Y	Y	N
2 *Talent*	N	N	N	N	Y	N	N	N	Y	N	N	N	N	N	N	Y
3 Gephardt	Y	Y	Y	N	Y	Y	Y	Y	N	Y	Y	Y	N	Y	Y	N
4 Skelton	N	Y	Y	N	Y	N	N	Y	N	Y	N	N	N	Y	N	Y
5 Wheat	Y	Y	Y	N	N	Y	Y	Y	N	N	Y	Y	N	Y	Y	N
6 Danner	Y	Y	Y	Y	N	Y	N	Y	N	Y	N	N	N	Y	N	Y
7 *Hancock*	N	N	N	N	Y	N	N	N	Y	N	N	N	N	N	N	Y
8 *Emerson*	N	N	N	N	Y	N	N	N	Y	N	N	N	N	N	N	Y
9 Volkmer	Y	Y	Y	Y	Y	Y	N	Y	N	Y	Y	N	Y	N	Y	N
MONTANA																
AL Williams	Y	Y	?	N	N	Y	N	N	Y	N	Y	N	N	Y	Y	N
NEBRASKA																
1 *Bereuter*	N	N	N	N	Y	N	N	N	Y	N	N	N	N	N	N	Y
2 Hoagland	Y	Y	Y	N	Y	Y	Y	N	Y	N	Y	N	Y	Y	Y	Y
3 *Barrett*	N	N	N	N	Y	N	N	N	Y	N	N	N	N	N	N	Y
NEVADA																
1 Bilbray	Y	Y	Y	N	Y	Y	Y	N	Y	N	N	N	N	Y	Y	N
2 *Vucanovich*	N	N	N	Y	Y	N	N	N	Y	Y	N	N	N	N	N	Y
NEW HAMPSHIRE																
1 *Zeliff*	N	N	N	Y	Y	N	N	N	Y	N	N	N	N	N	N	Y
2 Swett	Y	Y	Y	?	Y	N	Y	Y	Y	N	Y	Y	N	Y	Y	Y
NEW JERSEY																
1 Andrews	Y	N	Y	N	N	N	N	N	Y	N	Y	N	Y	N	N	Y
2 Hughes	Y	Y	N	N	Y	N	N	N	Y	N	Y	Y	N	Y	Y	N
3 *Saxton*	N	N	N	N	Y	N	N	N	Y	N	N	N	Y	N	N	Y
4 *Smith*	Y	N	N	N	N	N	N	N	Y	N	N	N	Y	N	N	Y
5 *Roukema*	Y	Y	N	N	N	N	Y	N	N	N	Y	N	Y	Y	N	N
6 Pallone	Y	Y	Y	N	Y	N	Y	N	Y	N	Y	Y	N	Y	Y	N
7 *Franks*	Y	Y	Y	N	N	N	N	N	Y	N	N	N	Y	N	N	N
8 Klein	Y	Y	Y	N	N	N	Y	N	Y	N	Y	Y	N	Y	Y	N
9 Torricelli	Y	Y	Y	N	Y	N	Y	?	Y	Y	Y	Y	N	Y	Y	N
10 Payne	Y	Y	Y	N	Y	Y	Y	N	Y	N	Y	Y	N	Y	Y	N
11 *Gallo*	N	N	N	N	Y	N	N	N	Y	N	Y	Y	Y	Y	Y	N
12 *Zimmer*	Y	N	N	N	N	N	N	N	N	Y	N	Y	Y	Y	Y	N
13 Menendez	Y	Y	Y	N	N	Y	N	Y	N	Y	Y	N	N	Y	Y	N
NEW MEXICO																
1 *Schiff*	N	N	N	N	N	N	N	Y	?	N	Y	Y	Y	N	Y	
2 *Skeen*	N	N	N	N	+	N	N	N	Y	Y	N	N	Y	Y	N	N
3 Richardson	Y	Y	Y	N	N	Y	Y	Y	N	Y	Y	N	Y	Y	Y	N
NEW YORK																
1 Hochbrueckner	Y	Y	Y	N	N	Y	Y	Y	N	N	Y	Y	N	Y	Y	N
2 *Lazio*	Y	N	N	N	Y	N	Y	N	Y	N	N	N	Y	N	N	Y
3 *King*	N	N	N	N	Y	N	N	N	Y	N	Y	Y	N	Y	N	Y
4 *Levy*	N	N	N	N	Y	N	N	N	Y	N	N	N	N	N	N	Y
5 Ackerman	Y	Y	Y	N	N	Y	N	Y	N	?	Y	Y	N	Y	Y	N
6 Flake	Y	Y	Y	Y	N	Y	Y	Y	N	?	N	Y	N	Y	Y	N
7 Manton	Y	Y	Y	N	?	Y	Y	Y	N	N	Y	Y	N	Y	Y	N
8 Nadler	Y	Y	Y	N	N	Y	Y	Y	N	N	Y	Y	N	Y	Y	N
9 Schumer	Y	Y	Y	N	N	Y	Y	Y	N	N	Y	Y	N	Y	Y	N
10 Towns	Y	Y	Y	N	N	Y	?	Y	N	N	Y	Y	N	Y	Y	N
11 Owens	Y	Y	Y	N	N	Y	N	?	N	Y	Y	Y	N	Y	Y	N

House Key Votes	1	2	3	4	5	6	7	8	9	10	11	12	13	14	15	16
12 Velazquez	Y	Y	Y	Y	N	Y	Y	Y	N	N	Y	Y	N	Y	Y	N
13 *Molinari*	Y	N	N	N	N	N	N	N	Y	N	N	Y	Y	N	N	Y
14 Maloney	Y	Y	Y	N	N	Y	Y	Y	N	N	Y	Y	N	Y	Y	N
15 Rangel	Y	Y	Y	Y	N	Y	Y	Y	N	N	Y	Y	N	Y	Y	N
16 Serrano	Y	Y	Y	N	N	Y	Y	Y	N	N	Y	Y	N	Y	Y	N
17 Engel	Y	Y	Y	N	N	Y	N	Y	N	-	Y	Y	N	Y	Y	N
18 Lowey	Y	Y	Y	N	N	Y	N	Y	N	Y	Y	Y	Y	Y	Y	N
19 *Fish*	Y	N	N	N	Y	N	N	N	Y	N	N	Y	Y	Y	N	Y
20 *Gilman*	Y	N	N	N	N	N	N	Y	Y	N	N	Y	N	Y	N	N
21 McNulty	Y	Y	Y	N	Y	Y	N	N	Y	Y	N	Y	N	Y	Y	N
22 *Solomon*	Y	N	N	Y	Y	N	N	N	Y	N	N	N	N	N	N	Y
23 *Boehlert*	Y	N	N	N	N	N	Y	Y	Y	N	N	Y	Y	Y	Y	N
24 *McHugh*	Y	N	N	Y	N	N	N	N	Y	N	N	N	N	N	N	Y
25 *Walsh*	Y	N	N	Y	Y	N	N	N	Y	N	N	Y	N	N	N	Y
26 Hinchey	Y	Y	Y	N	N	Y	Y	Y	N	N	Y	Y	N	Y	Y	N
27 *Paxon*	N	N	N	N	Y	N	N	N	Y	N	N	N	Y	N	N	Y
28 Slaughter	Y	Y	Y	N	N	Y	N	Y	Y	N	N	Y	N	Y	Y	N
29 LaFalce	Y	Y	Y	N	Y	Y	Y	N	N	N	Y	Y	N	Y	Y	N
30 *Quinn*	Y	N	N	Y	Y	N	N	N	Y	N	N	Y	N	N	N	Y
31 *Houghton*	N	N	N	N	Y	N	Y	N	Y	N	Y	N	Y	N	N	Y
NORTH CAROLINA																
1 Clayton	Y	Y	Y	N	N	Y	Y	Y	N	N	Y	Y	N	Y	Y	N
2 Valentine	N	Y	Y	Y	Y	Y	Y	N	Y	N	Y	Y	Y	Y	N	N
3 Lancaster	N	Y	N	Y	Y	Y	Y	N	Y	N	Y	Y	N	Y	N	Y
4 Price	Y	Y	Y	N	N	Y	Y	N	Y	N	Y	Y	Y	Y	Y	N
5Neal	Y	Y	Y	N	Y	Y	Y	N	Y	N	Y	Y	Y	Y	Y	N
6 *Coble*	N	N	N	Y	Y	N	N	N	Y	N	N	N	Y	N	N	Y
7 Rose	Y	Y	Y	N	N	Y	Y	?	Y	Y	Y	Y	Y	?	Y	N
8 Hefner	Y	Y	Y	N	Y	Y	N	N	Y	N	Y	Y	Y	Y	Y	N
9 *McMillan*	N	N	N	N	?	N	Y	N	Y	N	N	Y	Y	Y	N	Y
10 *Ballenger*	N	N	N	N	Y	N	N	N	Y	N	N	N	Y	N	N	Y
11 *Taylor*	N	N	N	Y	Y	N	N	N	Y	Y	N	N	N	N	N	Y
12 Watt	Y	Y	Y	N	N	Y	Y	Y	N	N	Y	Y	N	Y	Y	N
NORTH DAKOTA																
AL Pomeroy	Y	Y	Y	N	Y	Y	N	N	+	N	Y	N	N	Y	Y	Y
OHIO																
1 Mann	Y	Y	Y	N	Y	N	Y	N	N	N	Y	Y	Y	Y	Y	Y
2 *Gradison/Portman*[d]				Y	Y	N	N	N	Y	N	N	N	Y	Y	N	Y
3 Hall	Y	Y	Y	N	Y	Y	Y	N	Y	N	Y	Y	N	Y	?	?
4 *Oxley*	N	N	N	N	Y	N	N	N	?	Y	N	Y	Y	N	N	Y
5 *Gillmor*	Y	N	N	N	Y	N	N	N	Y	N	N	N	Y	N	N	Y
6 Strickland	Y	Y	Y	N	N	Y	Y	Y	Y	N	Y	N	N	Y	Y	N
7 *Hobson*	N	N	N	N	Y	N	N	N	Y	N	N	N	Y	Y	N	Y
8 *Boehner*	N	N	N	N	Y	N	N	N	Y	Y	N	N	Y	N	N	Y
9 Kaptur	Y	Y	Y	N	Y	Y	N	N	Y	N	Y	Y	N	Y	N	Y
10 *Hoke*	Y	N	N	Y	Y	N	N	N	Y	N	N	N	N	N	N	Y
11 Stokes	Y	Y	Y	N	N	Y	Y	Y	N	Y	Y	Y	N	Y	Y	N
12 *Kasich*	N	N	N	N	Y	N	N	N	Y	N	N	N	Y	N	N	Y
13 Brown	Y	Y	Y	N	Y	Y	Y	Y	Y	N	N	Y	N	Y	Y	N
14 Sawyer	Y	Y	Y	N	N	Y	Y	Y	Y	N	Y	Y	Y	Y	Y	N
15 *Pryce*	N	N	N	N	Y	N	N	N	Y	N	N	N	Y	Y	N	Y
16 *Regula*	Y	N	N	Y	Y	N	N	N	Y	N	N	Y	N	Y	N	Y
17 Traficant	Y	N	Y	Y	N	N	N	N	Y	Y	N	Y	N	Y	N	N
18 Applegate	Y	Y	Y	Y	Y	Y	N	Y	Y	N	N	Y	N	Y	Y	N
19 Fingerhut	Y	Y	Y	N	N	Y	Y	Y	Y	N	N	Y	N	Y	Y	Y
OKLAHOMA																
1 *Inhofe*	N	N	N	Y	Y	N	N	N	Y	N	N	N	N	N	N	Y
2 Synar	Y	Y	Y	N	N	Y	N	Y	N	N	Y	Y	Y	Y	N	N
3 Brewster	N	Y	Y	Y	Y	N	N	N	Y	N	Y	N	Y	Y	N	N
4 McCurdy	Y	Y	Y	N	N	N	Y	N	?	?	Y	Y	Y	Y	N	Y
5 *Istook*	N	N	N	N	Y	N	N	N	Y	N	N	N	Y	N	N	Y
6 English	Y	Y	Y	Y	Y	N	N	N	Y	N	Y	N	Y	Y	N	N
OREGON																
1 Furse	Y	Y	Y	N	N	Y	Y	Y	N	Y	Y	Y	N	Y	Y	N
2 *Smith*	N	N	N	N	Y	N	N	N	Y	N	N	N	Y	N	N	Y
3 Wyden	Y	Y	Y	N	N	Y	Y	Y	Y	N	N	Y	Y	Y	Y	N
4 DeFazio	Y	Y	Y	Y	N	Y	N	Y	Y	N	N	Y	N	Y	Y	N
5 Kopetski	Y	Y	Y	N	N	Y	Y	Y	Y	Y	Y	-	Y	Y	N	N
PENNSYLVANIA																
1 Foglietta	Y	Y	Y	N	N	Y	Y	Y	N	Y	Y	Y	N	Y	Y	N
2 Blackwell	Y	Y	Y	Y	N	Y	Y	Y	N	Y	Y	Y	N	Y	Y	N
3 Borski	Y	Y	Y	N	Y	Y	?	N	?	Y	Y	Y	N	Y	Y	N
4 Klink	Y	Y	Y	N	Y	Y	Y	N	Y	Y	Y	N	N	?	Y	Y
5 *Clinger*	N	N	N	N	Y	N	N	N	Y	N	N	N	Y	?	?	?
6 Holden	Y	Y	Y	N	Y	Y	N	N	Y	N	Y	N	N	Y	Y	Y
7 *Weldon*	Y	N	N	N	Y	N	N	N	Y	N	N	Y	N	Y	N	Y
8 *Greenwood*	N	N	N	N	N	N	N	N	Y	N	N	Y	Y	Y	N	Y
9 *Shuster*	N	N	N	Y	Y	N	N	N	Y	N	N	?	N	Y	N	Y
10 *McDade*	Y	N	N	?	Y	N	Y	?	Y	Y	N	Y	Y	Y	N	N
11 Kanjorski	Y	Y	Y	N	Y	Y	Y	N	Y	N	Y	N	N	Y	Y	N
12 Murtha	Y	Y	Y	N	Y	Y	Y	N	Y	Y	Y	N	N	Y	Y	N
13 Margolies-Mezv.	Y	N	Y	N	N	Y	Y	Y	Y	N	Y	Y	N	Y	Y	Y

House Key Votes	1	2	3	4	5	6	7	8	9	10	11	12	13	14	15	16
14 Coyne	Y	Y	Y	N	N	Y	Y	Y	N	Y	Y	Y	N	Y	Y	N
15 McHale	Y	Y	Y	N	Y	Y	Y	N	Y	Y	N	Y	N	Y	Y	Y
16 *Walker*	N	N	N	N	Y	N	N	N	Y	N	N	N	Y	N	N	Y
17 *Gekas*	N	N	N	Y	Y	N	N	N	Y	N	N	N	Y	N	N	Y
18 *Santorum*	N	N	N	Y	Y	N	N	N	Y	Y	N	N	N	N	N	Y
19 *Goodling*	N	N	N	N	Y	N	N	N	Y	N	N	Y	Y	N	N	Y
20 Murphy	Y	Y	N	Y	Y	Y	Y	N	N	?	Y	X	N	Y	N	Y
21 *Ridge*	N	N	N	N	Y	N	N	N	Y	N	N	N	Y	?	N	Y
RHODE ISLAND																
1 *Machtley*	Y	N	N	Y	N	N	N	N	Y	N	N	Y	Y	Y	N	N
2 Reed	Y	Y	Y	N	N	Y	Y	Y	N	N	Y	Y	N	Y	Y	N
SOUTH CAROLINA																
1 *Ravenel*	Y	N	N	N	Y	N	N	N	Y	N	N	N	N	Y	N	Y
2 *Spence*	N	N	N	Y	Y	N	N	N	Y	Y	N	N	N	Y	N	Y
3 Derrick	Y	Y	Y	N	N	Y	Y	N	?	Y	N	Y	N	Y	Y	N
4 *Inglis*	N	N	N	Y	Y	N	N	N	Y	N	N	N	N	N	N	Y
5 Spratt	Y	Y	Y	N	Y	Y	Y	N	Y	N	Y	Y	Y	Y	Y	N
6 Clyburn	Y	Y	Y	Y	N	Y	Y	Y	Y	Y	Y	Y	N	Y	Y	N
SOUTH DAKOTA																
AL Johnson	Y	Y	Y	N	Y	Y	Y	N	Y	N	N	Y	N	Y	Y	N
TENNESSEE																
1 *Quillen*	N	?	?	Y	Y	N	N	N	Y	Y	N	N	Y	N	N	N
2 *Duncan*	N	N	N	Y	Y	N	N	N	Y	N	N	N	Y	Y	N	Y
3 Lloyd	Y	Y	Y	N	Y	N	N	N	Y	Y	Y	Y	Y	Y	N	N
4 Cooper	Y	Y	Y	N	Y	Y	N	N	Y	Y	N	Y	Y	Y	Y	Y
5 Clement	Y	Y	Y	N	Y	N	N	N	Y	N	Y	Y	Y	Y	Y	N
6 Gordon	Y	Y	Y	N	Y	Y	?	N	Y	Y	Y	Y	Y	Y	Y	Y
7 *Sundquist*	N	N	N	Y	Y	N	N	N	Y	N	N	N	Y	N	?	Y
8 Tanner	Y	Y	Y	N	Y	Y	N	N	Y	N	Y	N	Y	Y	N	Y
9 Ford	?	?	?	Y	N	Y	Y	Y	N	?	Y	Y	Y	Y	Y	N
TEXAS																
1 Chapman	Y	Y	Y	Y	Y	N	N	N	Y	Y	Y	Y	Y	?	N	N
2 Wilson	Y	Y	Y	N	N	Y	Y	N	Y	Y	?	N	N	?	Y	N
3 *Johnson, Sam*	N	N	N	Y	Y	N	N	N	Y	Y	N	N	Y	N	N	Y
4 Hall	N	N	N	Y	Y	N	Y	N	Y	Y	N	N	N	Y	Y	Y
5 Bryant	Y	Y	Y	N	N	Y	Y	Y	Y	?	Y	Y	Y	Y	Y	N
6 *Barton*	N	N	N	N	Y	N	N	N	Y	Y	N	N	Y	N	N	Y
7 *Archer*	N	N	N	Y	Y	N	N	N	Y	N	N	N	Y	N	N	Y
8 *Fields*	N	N	N	+	Y	N	N	N	Y	Y	N	N	Y	N	N	Y
9 Brooks	Y	Y	Y	N	N	Y	Y	N	Y	Y	Y	N	N	Y	Y	N
10 Pickle	Y	Y	Y	?	N	Y	Y	Y	Y	Y	Y	Y	Y	Y	Y	N
11 Edwards	Y	Y	Y	N	Y	N	Y	N	Y	Y	Y	N	Y	Y	Y	Y
12 Geren	N	N	Y	N	Y	N	Y	N	Y	Y	Y	N	Y	Y	N	Y
13 Sarpalius	N	Y	Y	Y	Y	Y	Y	N	Y	Y	Y	N	Y	Y	Y	N
14 Laughlin	N	Y	Y	N	Y	N	Y	N	Y	Y	Y	N	Y	Y	Y	Y
15 de la Garza	Y	Y	Y	?	Y	Y	Y	N	?	Y	Y	N	Y	Y	Y	N
16 Coleman	Y	Y	Y	N	N	Y	Y	N	Y	Y	Y	N	Y	Y	Y	N
17 Stenholm	N	Y	N	N	Y	N	Y	N	Y	Y	Y	N	Y	N	N	Y
18 Washington	Y	Y	Y	N	N	Y	Y	Y	N	N	Y	Y	N	Y	?	N
19 *Combest*	N	N	N	Y	Y	N	N	N	Y	Y	N	N	Y	N	N	N
20 Gonzalez	Y	Y	Y	N	N	Y	Y	Y	N	Y	Y	Y	N	Y	Y	N
21 *Smith*	Y	N	N	Y	Y	N	N	N	Y	Y	N	N	Y	N	N	Y
22 *DeLay*	N	N	N	Y	Y	N	N	N	Y	Y	N	N	Y	N	N	Y
23 *Bonilla*	N	N	N	Y	Y	N	N	N	Y	Y	N	N	Y	N	N	Y
24 Frost	Y	Y	Y	N	N	Y	Y	N	Y	Y	Y	Y	Y	Y	N	N
25 Andrews	Y	Y	Y	N	N	Y	N	N	Y	Y	Y	Y	Y	Y	N	Y
26 *Armey*	N	N	N	N	Y	N	N	N	Y	Y	N	N	Y	N	N	Y
27 Ortiz	Y	Y	Y	N	Y	Y	Y	N	Y	Y	Y	N	Y	Y	Y	N
28 Tejeda	Y	Y	Y	N	Y	Y	Y	N	Y	Y	Y	N	Y	Y	Y	N
29 Green	Y	Y	Y	Y	N	Y	Y	Y	Y	Y	N	N	N	Y	Y	N
30 Johnson, E.B.	Y	Y	Y	N	N	Y	Y	Y	Y	Y	Y	Y	Y	Y	Y	N
UTAH																
1 *Hansen*	N	N	N	Y	Y	N	N	N	Y	Y	N	N	Y	N	N	Y
2 Shepherd	Y	Y	Y	N	N	Y	Y	Y	N	N	Y	Y	Y	Y	Y	N
3 Orton	N	Y	Y	N	Y	N	Y	N	Y	N	Y	N	N	N	Y	Y
VERMONT																
AL **Sanders**	Y	Y	Y	Y	N	Y	N	Y	N	N	N	N	N	Y	Y	N
VIRGINIA																
1 *Bateman*	N	N	N	N	Y	N	N	N	Y	Y	N	Y	Y	N	N	Y
2 Pickett	N	N	Y	N	N	N	Y	N	Y	Y	Y	N	Y	Y	N	N
3 Scott	Y	Y	Y	N	N	Y	Y	Y	Y	Y	Y	Y	N	Y	Y	N
4 Sisisky	N	N	Y	N	N	Y	Y	N	Y	N	Y	N	N	Y	N	N

[b] Paul B. Henry, R-Mich., died July 31. He was eligible to vote on key votes 1–5.

[c] Mike Espy, D-Miss., resigned Jan. 22. Bennie Thompson, D-Miss., won a special election April 13 and was sworn in April 20. He was eligible tote on key votes 4–16.

[d] Bill Gradison, R-Ohio, resigned Jan. 31. Rob Portman, R-Ohio, won a special election May 4 and was sworn in May 5. He was eligible to vote on key votes 4–16.

KEY

	Democrats	*Republicans*	**Independent**	
Y	Voted for ("yea")		–	Announced against
N	Voted against ("nay")		P	Voted "present"
+	Announced for		C	Voted "present" to avoid possible conflict of interest
#	Paired for			
X	Paired against		?	Did not vote or otherwise make a position known

ND Northern Democrats
SD Southern Democrats
Southern states – Ala., Ark., Fla., Ga., Ky., La., Miss., N.C., Okla., S.C., Tenn., Texas, Va.

House Key Votes	1	2	3	4	5	6	7	8	9	10	11	12	13	14	15	16
5 Payne	N	Y	Y	N	N	Y	Y	N	Y	Y	Y	N	Y	Y	Y	Y
6 *Goodlatte*	N	N	N	N	Y	N	N	N	Y	N	N	Y	N	N	N	Y
7 *Bliley*	N	N	N	N	Y	N	N	N	Y	N	N	Y	N	N	N	Y
8 Moran	Y	Y	Y	N	N	Y	Y	Y	N	Y	Y	Y	Y	Y	Y	N
9 Boucher	Y	Y	Y	N	N	Y	Y	N	Y	Y	Y	N	N	Y	N	N
10 *Wolf*	N	N	N	N	Y	N	N	N	Y	N	N	Y	Y	Y	N	Y
11 Byrne	Y	Y	Y	N	N	Y	Y	Y	Y	N	N	Y	N	Y	Y	N
WASHINGTON																
1 Cantwell	Y	Y	Y	N	N	Y	Y	Y	Y	N	Y	Y	Y	Y	Y	Y
2 Swift	Y	Y	Y	N	N	Y	Y	Y	Y	Y	Y	Y	Y	Y	Y	N
3 Unsoeld	Y	Y	Y	?	N	Y	Y	Y	N	N	Y	N	N	Y	Y	N
4 Inslee	Y	Y	Y	Y	N	N	Y	Y	Y	N	Y	N	Y	Y	Y	Y
5 Foley [e]				N	Y					Y			Y		Y	N
6 Dicks	Y	Y	Y	N	N	Y	Y	Y	Y	Y	Y	Y	Y	?	Y	N
7 McDermott	Y	Y	Y	N	N	Y	Y	Y	N	Y	Y	Y	Y	Y	Y	N
8 *Dunn*	N	N	N	N	Y	N	N	N	Y	Y	N	N	Y	N	N	Y
9 Kreidler	Y	Y	Y	N	N	Y	Y	Y	N	Y	Y	Y	Y	Y	Y	N

House Key Votes	1	2	3	4	5	6	7	8	9	10	11	12	13	14	15	16
WEST VIRGINIA																
1 Mollohan	Y	Y	Y	N	N	Y	Y	Y	N	Y	Y	N	N	Y	Y	N
2 Wise	Y	Y	Y	N	N	Y	Y	N	Y	Y	Y	N	N	Y	Y	N
3 Rahall	Y	Y	Y	Y	Y	Y	N	N	N	Y	Y	N	N	Y	Y	N
WISCONSIN																
1 Aspen/Barca [f]				N	Y	Y	N	Y	Y	N	Y	Y	N	Y	Y	Y
2 *Klug*	Y	N	N	N	Y	N	N	N	Y	N	N	Y	Y	Y	N	Y
3 *Gunderson*	N	N	N	N	Y	N	N	N	Y	N	N	N	Y	Y	N	Y
4 Kleczka	Y	Y	Y	N	Y	Y	Y	Y	Y	N	N	Y	N	Y	Y	N
5 Barrett	Y	Y	Y	N	N	Y	Y	Y	Y	N	Y	Y	N	Y	Y	Y
6 *Petri*	Y	N	N	Y	N	Y	N	Y	N	?	N	Y	Y	Y	Y	Y
7 Obey	Y	Y	Y	N	Y	Y	Y	Y	Y	N	Y	N	N	Y	Y	N
8 *Roth*	N	N	N	Y	N	Y	N	N	Y	N	N	N	Y	Y	N	N
9 *Sensenbrenner*	N	N	N	N	Y	N	N	N	Y	N	N	N	Y	Y	N	Y
WYOMING																
AL *Thomas*	Y	N	N	Y	Y	N	N	N	Y	N	N	N	Y	N	N	Y
DELEGATES																
de Lugo, V.I.	D	D	D	N	N	D	D	Y	N	D	D	D	D	D	D	?
Faleomavaega, Am.S.	D	D	D	N	N	D	D	Y	?	D	D	D	D	D	D	?
Norton, D.C.	D	D	D	N	N	D	D	Y	N	D	D	D	D	D	D	?
Romero-B., P.R.	D	D	D	?	N	D	D	N	?	D	D	D	D	D	D	?
Underwood, Guam	D	D	D	N	Y	D	D	?	N	D	D	D	D	D	D	?

[e] Thomas S. Foley, D-Wash., as Speaker of the House, voted at his discretion.

[f] Les Aspin, D-Wis., resigned Jan. 20. Peter W. Barca, D-Wis., won a May 4 special election and was sworn in June 8. He was eligible to vote on key votes 4–16.

Senate

1. VIETNAM TRADE EMBARGO

For nearly two decades, the U.S. trade embargo against Vietnam served as an enduring reminder of the decade-long Vietnam War. But the Senate opened a new chapter in relations between the United States and Vietnam on Jan. 27 when it voted overwhelmingly in favor of lifting the trade ban against Hanoi.

Over the strong objections of some veterans groups and their congressional allies, the Senate voted to adopt an amendment to the biennial State Department authorization bill (S 1281) calling on President Clinton to scrap the long-standing economic embargo. The amendment had significant bipartisan support; it was adopted 62–38: R 20–24; D 42–14 (ND 31–11; SD 11–3).

While the amendment was nonbinding, the vote proved to be one of the most important foreign policy votes of the year. Just one week after the Senate adopted the amendment, Clinton ordered an end to the 19-year-old trade embargo.

The president did not need Congress's go-ahead to lift the Vietnam sanctions. He could have accomplished that with the stroke of a pen. Clinton, who avoided the draft during the Vietnam War, clearly was uncomfortable with the prospect of acting without the cover of a congressional vote. Equally important was the involvement of a pair of senators who served with distinction in Vietnam, John McCain, R-Ariz., and John Kerry, D-Mass. They led the movement to end the embargo.

For years, the trade embargo had been linked to painful questions surrounding the fate of more than 2,000 American servicemen listed as missing in action (MIA) from the war. Many veterans groups argued that the embargo provided the United States with its only effective leverage in its talks with Hanoi over the MIAs.

McCain and Kerry argued that ending the embargo would actually spur Vietnam to greater cooperation. "This is not a reward to Vietnam," Kerry said. "It's not a question of taking away leverage, but of giving leverage to us."

Sen. Robert C. Smith, R-N.H., another Vietnam veteran who had devoted much of his career to investigating the fate of MIAs, led opposition to the amendment. Smith charged that lifting the embargo would be the equivalent of "getting down on your knees and hoping and praying that the Vietnamese will give us all this information."

But after nearly 20 years of a U.S. policy designed to isolate Vietnam economically, most senators wanted to put trade relations on more normal footing. In addition some U.S. oil companies and other business interests, which had been frozen out of a potentially lucrative market, conducted an effective lobbying campaign against the trade ban.

2. "GOALS 2000"

In 1989 President George Bush, concerned about poor schools and the potential inability of U.S. workers to compete in a global economy, convened a two-day summit in Virginia with the nation's governors to produce an education reform plan. They reached an unprecedented agreement to set national performance goals by 1990.

In 1991 Bush proposed "America 2000" legislation to establish voluntary national testing, create nontraditional schools and send limited federal aid to states and localities to fund model programs. The measure also included a controversial "school choice" voucher program that would have sent public funds to some private schools. Democrats fought school choice, and in the end, neither Democrats nor Republicans could muster much enthusiasm for the measure, which died in the Senate in a Republican filibuster.

The political dynamic changed in 1993 after Bill Clinton was elected president. Democrats renewed the education reform debate, hoping to capitalize on control of the White House and both chambers of Congress for the first time since 1980.

The Clinton administration introduced a $420 million "Goals 2000" bill (HR 1804—PL 103–227), using the Bush proposal as a basis. But Clinton removed the school choice provisions and added national standards and goals. These standards, although voluntary, opened the door for federal involvement in public schools and set markers that many local school districts would have difficulty ignoring. School districts seeking grants were required to strive for the national goals; they were given the flexibility to either adopt national content and performance standards, or to develop their own standards to reach the goals. The House easily passed the measure in 1993.

The bill included such goals as improving high school graduation rates and making schools safer. It also included controversial "opportunity to learn" standards prescribing what a school needed—such as competent teachers and up-to-date textbooks—to give children the opportunity to meet the goals and standards.

Liberal Democrats argued such standards were necessary to ensure that all students had access to high quality educational programs. Conservatives said they could leave school districts open to lawsuits from parents displeased about their child's school.

In the end a majority of members decided that the opportunity to learn standards were acceptable because they were voluntary and states would be able to develop them locally.

With major sticking points such as school choice and opportunity to learn out of the way, Senate Democrats and moderate Republicans found common ground on the school reform measure. Before passing the bill Feb. 8, senators waded through a series of amendments, including an unsuccessful last-ditch effort by conservatives to include a school choice demonstration project. The Senate subsequently passed the bill, 71–25: R 17–25; D 54–0 (ND 41–0, SD 13–0).

After House-Senate conferees ironed out their differences, the House adopted the conference report March 23 and the Senate cleared the bill March 26.

3. BUDGET DEFICIT

Using an earthquake relief bill for Southern California as their vehicle, a bipartisan group of senators moved early in the 1994 session to test Congress's will to cut the budget deficit more deeply than it had in 1993.

The bill (HR 3759—PL 103–211) combined $10 billion in emergency spending on disaster relief and military missions with $1 billion in routine supplemental appropriations and $3.26 billion in rescissions. On Feb. 9 the bipartisan group—led by Bob Kerrey, D-

Neb., and Hank Brown, R-Colo.—offered an amendment to slash spending by $94 billion over five years.

Their proposal was killed on a key tabling motion by Appropriations Committee Chairman Robert C. Byrd, D-W.Va. The vote was 65–31: R 23–19; D 42–12 (ND 31–9, SD 11–3).

The defeat foreshadowed the difficulties that deficit hawks would have all year. Unlike in 1993, Congress rejected all the major spending cuts proposed in 1994.

The Kerrey-Brown amendment also epitomized the changed politics of disaster relief. After years of routinely handing out millions to communities hit by natural disasters, Congress could not help victims of the devastating California earthquake without at least a nod in the direction of offsetting spending cuts.

The first sign of this political shift had come the previous year, when Republicans and conservative Democrats in the House temporarily derailed an emergency flood-relief bill (HR 2667—PL 103–75) to protest its impact on the deficit. The bill passed only after the Democratic leadership promised to create a task force examining how Congress responds to disasters.

Kerrey, Brown and four colleagues began work on their plan for spending cuts in November 1993. Their original target had been HR 3400, a bill containing numerous elements from Vice President Al Gore's "reinventing government" plan. That bill passed the House at the end of the 1993 session but never made it to the Senate floor.

When the bipartisan group offered its amendment on the disaster-relief bill, it attracted 11 cosponsors. The amendment's main elements were cuts in spending on Medicare of $30.5 billion over five years through higher charges on selected participants; reductions of 252,000 in the federal work force, saving $26.7 billion; and limits on government administrative expenses, saving $21 billion.

Other provisions of the amendment would have stopped the government from buying any more buildings, saving $2 billion; denied unemployment benefits to those who left the military voluntarily, saving $1.2 billion; limited cost of living increases for retired government employees, saving $1.2 billion; and cut the salaries of congressmen and senior government executives, saving $297 million.

Byrd cast the savings as largely fictitious. Any Medicare savings would be consumed by health care reform, he said, and the personnel savings would be channeled to crime fighting programs. The Clinton administration, meanwhile, already had placed a lower limit on government expenses than the Kerrey-Brown amendment would have imposed.

Byrd's hand was strengthened by the Senate Appropriations Committee, which increased the amount of rescissions to $3.41 billion from the House-passed level of $2.56 billion. This amount was enough to offset not only the routine supplemental spending proposals, but also the additional defense spending and some of the disaster aid.

The Senate went on to clear the $11 billion package by voice vote Feb. 11.

4. BALANCED-BUDGET AMENDMENT

It took a furious lobbying effort by the administration and key Senate leaders, but in the end their efforts secured enough votes to defeat a constitutional amendment requiring a balanced budget (S J Res 41).

With Democratic opponents uncertain of their ability to muster the 34 votes needed to kill the proposed amendment outright, Senate leaders put forward a less stringent alternative in a successful effort to siphon enough votes away from a bipartisan effort led by Sens. Paul Simon, D-Ill., and Orrin G. Hatch, R-Utah.

The original measure would have banned deficit spending unless three-fifths of the full House and Senate approved it. A separate three-fifths vote would have been required to raise the limit on the total public debt, and a majority vote would have been needed to raise taxes.

In the end the tactics of amendment opponents paid off, and supporters fell four votes shy of the two-thirds required as the Senate rejected the amendment March 1 by a 63–37 vote: R 41–3; D 22–34 (ND 12–30, SD 10–4).

After the painful debate in 1993 over the budget, congressional leaders and the administration wanted 1994 to be relatively calm on the budget front as the health care overhaul debate took precedence. Adoption of the amendment could have pressured Congress to deliberate over painful spending cuts in politically sensitive areas.

But after failing to win approval in either the House or Senate in 1992 and falling even to get the proposal to the floor of either chamber in 1993, advocates won a pledge from Senate Majority Leader George J. Mitchell, D-Maine, to bring it to a vote early in 1994.

Supporters of the amendment hoped that election year pressure would be enough to reverse earlier defeats. In 1986 the amendment fell just one vote short.

The lobbying in the weeks leading up to the vote was intense. Mitchell and Appropriations Committee Chairman Robert C. Byrd, D-W.Va., led the opponents' charge. Only five of the 15 Democrats who served under Byrd on the committee defied the chairman and voted for the amendment.

President Clinton also weighed in, saying that a provision in the Simon-Hatch amendment that would have required a three-fifths majority to approve an increase in the national debt limit provided too much power to a minority and amounted to "a recipe for total paralysis."

But supporters countered that Congress repeatedly had demonstrated that it lacked the political courage to make the painful budget cuts or politically risky tax increases to balance the budget and that a constitutional requirement was the only way to make it happen.

Many of the opponents of the amendment said the 1993 deficit-reduction bill had brought the deficit under sufficient control and that further cuts might undermine the economy.

At the same time, concern over Social Security played into the hands of opponents. The American Association of Retired Persons conducted an all-out drive against the amendment, saying it eventually would lead to cuts in Social Security.

Only three Republicans, Nancy Landon Kassebaum, Kan., Mark O. Hatfield, Ore., and Ted Stevens, Alaska, voted against the amendment. Twenty-two Democrats voted for it; 34 were opposed. Ten Republicans voted against the amendment in 1986.

Twenty-two senators voted for the milder alternative, offered by Harry Reid, D-Nev.; but seven of them, having gone on record as supporting Reid's effort, then voted against the tougher version.

Supporters of the amendment said Reid's alternative was critical in providing political cover for opponents. Reid's version contained several provisions that would have made it more likely that Congress could continue to run a deficit, and it would have protected Social Security by keeping surplus Social Security receipts off-limits to deficit cutters. *(House key vote 3)*

5. ABORTION CLINIC ACCESS

Legislation designed to safeguard access to abortion clinics found a receptive audience in the Senate, which traditionally had been more supportive of abortion rights than the House. But even in the Senate, supporters had to frame the issue narrowly—as a law-and-order matter rather than as a question of abortion rights—to gain passage. The bill's advocates fended off criticism that the legislation (S 636—PL 103–259) would infringe on the free speech rights of abortion opponents, but in the end, they had to make some concessions.

The quest for legislation was prodded by a January 1993 Supreme Court decision barring clinic operators from using a 19th century civil rights law to obtain relief from blockaders. Advocates also pointed to a rash of violence at abortion clinics nationwide, including shootings, arson and massive blockades. They won support for the legislation from the new Democratic president, Bill Clinton, and from Attorney General Janet Reno, who gave the measure the administration's official endorsement at a hearing before the Senate Labor and Human Resources Committee on May 12, 1993.

The legislation made it a federal crime to intimidate abortion clinic workers or women seeking abortions, by force or threat of force. Violators faced criminal penalties of jail time and fines. The law also allowed affected individuals to sue for civil remedies, such as compensatory damages or court injunctions to restrain blockaders. *(House key vote 6)*

Most Democratic senators and some Republicans supported the measure, condemning the violent behavior of radical antiabortion activists. But others thought the legislation would impinge on the free speech rights of protesters and sought to further narrow the bill's scope.

These objections led the Senate to make some changes that ultimately prevented a quick agreement with the House in 1993. One provision, suggested by Orrin G. Hatch, R-Utah, extended the bill's protections to places of worship. Another, offered by Labor Committee Chairman Edward M. Kennedy, D-Mass., set lower maximum criminal penalties for nonviolent obstruction, such as lying down in front of a clinic door. House and Senate negotiators adopted these provisions when they reached a final accord April 26.

Still, Senate opponents, unconvinced by assurances that the bill was modeled on civil rights laws to discourage violent conduct, warned that the legislation would have a chilling effect on those seeking to oppose abortion through nonviolent means. "To inflict harsher punishment on one group is discrimination against a particular political viewpoint," said Don Nickles, R-Okla., during Senate consideration of the conference report.

But supporters argued that local trespassing laws were inadequate and that national resources were needed to combat a national effort to disrupt clinic operations. They again concentrated on the law-and-order aspect of the bill. "We're reacting to violence, not words," said Barbara Boxer, D-Calif. The final vote on May 12 to adopt the conference report, clearing the bill, was 69–30: R 17–27; D 52–3 (ND 41–1, SD 11–2).

6. BUDGET RESOLUTION

Although it took weeks of bickering to reach an agreement, the Senate's final approval of the conference report on the 1995 budget resolution largely endorsed President Clinton's request that Congress take a year off from deep budget cuts, frustrating those lawmakers who had hoped to make additional reductions.

On May 12 a largely Democratic majority approved the conference report of the 1995 budget resolution (H Con Res 218) 53–46: R 2–42; D 51–4 (ND 39–3, SD 12–1).

The vote and debate were striking primarily for their low profile in contrast to the previous year's budget vote, which was Clinton's first major legislative victory, setting the course for some $433 billion in deficit reduction over five years.

The fiscal 1995 budget resolution, an internal congressional document that did not need to be signed by the president, required just $13 billion in additional spending cuts over five years, all of it from appropriations outlays. That differed from the previous year's resolution, which was accompanied by controversial reconciliation instructions that required tax increases and spending cuts in both appropriated and entitlement programs in order to meet specific deficit reduction targets.

The conference report to H Con Res 218 highlighted the intense frustration of Appropriations Committee members, who felt that their domestic spending budgets already were tight. The opposition to additional spending cuts came from a new coalition of liberals and conservatives who opposed deeper budget cuts—liberals because they did not want to make deeper cuts in social programs and conservatives because they wanted to avoid further cuts in defense spending.

When the budget resolution was under consideration in the Senate, deficit hawks succeeded in cutting the appropriations budget by an additional $26.1 billion over five years. But they ran into trouble in conference, when, in a reversal of his previous stance, Senate Budget Committee ranking Republican Pete V. Domenici, N.M., surprised his colleagues by opposing the cuts because he was worried that they would fall mainly on defense spending.

His turnaround put him on the same side as Clinton and Democratic leaders, who eschewed the cuts because of the potential impact on defense and other programs. The House budget did not contain the additional $26.1 billion in cuts. After a tortuous debate, conferees agreed to limit cuts to $13 billion. *(House key vote 4)*

The extra cuts were phased in gradually, with just $500 million taking effect in 1995. That accelerated to an additional $5.4 billion in 1996 and the balance of $7.1 billion in 1997–1999.

7. SAFE DRINKING WATER

A key Senate vote to require the Environmental Protection Agency (EPA) to study the costs and benefits of new, major regulations underscored the Clinton administration's difficulty in trying to appease states that felt burdened by costly federal mandates without jeopardizing public health and safety. Known as risk assessment, the issue was a major element of a larger and potent backlash against federal regulations that became a recurrent theme during environmental debates in the 103rd Congress.

The backlash eventually would derail key elements of President Clinton's ambitious environmental agenda, including an overhaul of the 1974 Safe Drinking Water Act and an ongoing effort to make the EPA the fifteenth Cabinet-level department.

The key vote came May 18 on an amendment by J. Bennett Johnston, D-La., to a bill (S 2019) designed to make the Safe Drinking Water Act more flexible for states, local governments and small water system operators.

A conservative Democrat, Johnston said he was concerned that federal environmental regulations were sometimes based on public opinion rather than on scientific facts. A commonly cited example was the rush to evacuate Times Beach, Mo., in the 1980s because of the presence of dioxin, believed to cause cancer.

The Johnston amendment was considered one of the stumbling blocks for the drinking water bill, which eventually passed the Senate and House but died at the end of the legislative session.

The Senate passed the cost-benefit amendment 90–8: R 41–3; D 49–5 (ND 36–5, SD 13–0). But the overwhelming margin belied the behind-the-scenes struggle of Johnston, Senate Environment and Public Works Committee Chairman Max Baucus, D-Mont., and the White House Office of Management and Budget (OMB).

Under existing law, the EPA conducted some cost-benefit studies for regulations, but not on a widespread basis.

A chief concern of Baucus's and such environmental groups as the Natural Resources Defense Council was that an amendment requiring more studies would lead to "paralysis by analysis." They also argued that the results of these studies could be used to weaken existing health or safety rules if it was determined that the regulation actually posed little benefit for its costs.

Johnston sparked this politically explosive debate in 1993 with a much broader but little-noticed amendment to a bill to elevate the EPA to Cabinet-level status (S 171). That earlier amendment would have required cost-benefit studies of all federal agencies. It also would have required these studies to include comparisons to health risks more commonly understood by people, such as being hit by a car or struck by lightning.

Eventually, the negotiators were able to persuade Johnston to limit the amendment on the drinking water bill to new EPA regulations that would have had an economic impact of $100 million or more. He also agreed to restrict any risk studies to six comparisons: three regulated by the EPA or other federal agencies and three not regulated by the federal government.

Sally Katzen, who oversaw regulatory affairs for OMB, said the compromise would affect about 20 to 25 EPA regulations—a fraction of the 600 to 900 reviewed annually by the EPA. The compromise was able to sway such environmentally minded Democrats as Baucus, Senate Majority Leader George J. Mitchell, D-Maine, and Daniel Patrick Moynihan, D-N.Y., Moynihan had long argued that the EPA should prioritize regulations.

But the deal did little to satisfy the concerns of eight senators, most of whom were close allies of the environmental movement, including John H. Chafee, R-R.I. It also eventually became a sticking point with the House.

8. PRODUCT LIABILITY

After 17 years of lobbying and deal-making, advocates of limiting product liability thought that 1994 would be the year they finally pushed a bill through Congress. Instead, trial lawyers and consumer groups who opposed the effort demonstrated how adept they were at turning supporters into opponents.

The fate of the bill (S 687) was decided June 29. That day, the Senate rejected a motion to limit debate, falling three votes short of the 60 necessary to end the opponents' filibuster. The motion to invoke cloture failed 57–41: R 38–6; D 19–35 (ND 13–27, SD 6–8).

Senate Majority Leader George J. Mitchell, D-Maine, pulled the bill off the floor, and its supporters vowed to try again in 1995.

Business groups and insurance companies had been trying to limit product liability suits since the mid-1970s, arguing that the suits stifled innovation and forced companies to devote significant resources to combating plaintiffs, many of whom had dubious claims. But their allies in Congress had never been able to bring any legislation to the House or Senate floors.

Their primary goal had been to set tough new standards for awarding punitive damages—which were designed to punish a defendant for particularly gross and malicious negligence. Among the most important provisions in S 687 was language that would have required plaintiffs in personal injury cases to present "clear and convincing" evidence that their injuries stemmed from a defendant's flagrant disregard for safety. Also included was language that would have ended joint liability for noneconomic damages. With joint liability, one defendant was responsible for paying the share of a damage award owed by other defendants if they were unable to pay.

To broaden the bill's appeal, a bipartisan group of sponsors, led by John D. Rockefeller IV, D-W.Va., added provisions aimed at benefiting victims of faulty products. For instance, they included language that would have extended the traditional two-year statute of limitations in cases where the nature or cause of an injury had not been discovered. They also removed the proposed penalties for victims who rejected out-of-court settlements, while proposing less protection from punitive damages for the manufacturers of drugs and medical devices.

The changes seemed to bring a number of lawmakers into the supporters' camp. A narrower bill to protect light-plane manufacturers from liability lawsuits (S 1458—PL 103–298) easily passed the Senate on March 16, further encouraging Rockefeller's allies. As S 687 neared the floor, Rockefeller said he was confident he had the 60 votes needed to overcome the expected filibuster.

Opponents of the measure, meanwhile, made an emotional pitch that focused on people maimed by faulty medicines and medical devices. They said the bill, which would have banned punitive damages against companies whose products had been approved by the Food and Drug Administration or the Federal Aviation Administration, would remove incentives for greedy corporations to act responsibly and not hurt people with their products.

The opponents' Senate allies also threatened to bring up a number of amendments designed to force their colleagues to vote on tough, unrelated issues such as gun control and smoking.

Rockefeller fell six votes short of breaking the filibuster June 28. In order to attract more support, he and cosponsor Slade Gorton, R-Wash., promised to remove the section prohibiting punitive damages against companies with federally approved products. These changes brought three more Democrats and two Republicans into the supporters' column. But the following day, supporters could only muster 57 votes, still three short of the needed 60. This was due to two defections among the supporters—Larry Pressler, R-S.D., and Donald W. Riegle Jr., D-Mich.—and the absence of Dennis DeConcini, D-Ariz., a bill supporter who missed the vote.

9. HAITI

As President Clinton moved inexorably toward ordering a military invasion of Haiti, the Senate rejected several Republican-led proposals to halt an intervention. But the defeat of those amendments hardly represented a sweeping endorsement of military action to oust Haiti's ruling dictators. Rather, it demonstrated the Senate's traditional reluctance to tie the president's hands on crucial national security issues.

Sen. Judd Gregg, R-N.H., tried to tap into the anti-invasion mood June 29 by offering an amendment to the fiscal 1995 foreign operations appropriations bill (HR 4426) that would have barred U.S. military intervention in Haiti unless the president first sought congressional approval or determined that intervention was necessary to protect U.S. citizens or security interests.

The Senate rejected the amendment 34–65, with Democrats voting unanimously against it. Republicans supported the amendment 34–10, but some critics of an invasion were uneasy with an imposition of restraints on a president's ability to commit troops abroad.

Gregg and other Republicans insisted that Clinton had an obligation to come to Congress before committing thousands of troops to an operation that was widely viewed as risky. Jesse Helms, R-N.C., bluntly warned the president against intervening in Haiti.

"Surely they have not gone out of their minds entirely down there on Pennsylvania Avenue, because if the president does, in fact, do that, I suspect it will be a decision he will long regret," Helms said.

But Democrats countered that the Republicans were trying to embarrass the president for partisan reasons.

Some conservatives, such as John McCain, R-Ariz., were concerned that the amendment would set a dangerous precedent. "I cannot support any resolution which prospectively limits the powers of the president as commander in chief," he said.

In the House, Clinton avoided a rebuke when members defeated an amendment harshly criticizing the deployment in Haiti. The House adopted a milder substitute requiring reports from the president on the operation. *(House key vote 15)*

Congress's ambivalence over policy toward Haiti continued well after Clinton launched the military occupation of the Caribbean island nation Sept. 19. But as the mission proceeded with virtually no U.S. casualties, lawmakers adjourned without imposing significant restrictions.

10. BOSNIA ARMS EMBARGO

For more than two years, Congress had been torn by the question of whether the United States should level the military balance in the Bosnian war by providing weapons to the outgunned Muslims.

Those deep divisions were on display July 1 when the Senate cast a key vote on an amendment that would have forced President Clinton to cease complying with the international arms embargo against the former Yugoslavia and begin arming the Muslims. The House had approved similar language June 9. *(House key vote 7)*

The Senate was split down the middle as it rejected the proposal on a 50–50 tie. The vote came on an amendment offered by Senate Minority Leader Bob Dole, R-Kan., and Joseph I. Lieberman, D-Conn. to the fiscal 1995 defense authorization bill (S 2182). Republicans supported the amendment 37–7, while Democrats opposed it 13–43 (ND 11–31; SD 2–12). The Senate's action proved crucial in the back-and-forth congressional battle over the embargo.

In June the House had approved an amendment for a mandatory end to the embargo, but House and Senate negotiators on the defense authorization bill rejected that provision. The conference committee eventually agreed on a compromise that cut off U.S. funding for enforcement of the embargo Nov. 15.

Senate proponents of the Dole-Lieberman amendment argued that the embargo favored the heavily armed Serbs, who were widely seen as the aggressors in the Bosnian conflict, by preserving their military advantage over the Muslims.

But Clinton and his top aides weighed in with a strong lobbying campaign against the amendment. The president said taking unilateral action to break the U.N.-mandated arms ban would encourage other nations to violate international sanctions that the United States supports, such as the trade sanctions against Iraq. The president's personal touch may have been decisive. Several Democrats hailed the effectiveness of the president's lobbying effort.

Democrats by and large supported an alternative nonbinding amendment, offered by Armed Services Committee Chairman Sam Nunn, D-Ga., which urged the president to seek a peaceful solution to the Bosnian conflict. That proposal was approved 52–48 on July 1.

11. ETHANOL USE

A federal rule promoting the use of ethanol in reformulated gasoline engulfed the Senate in such a conflagration that it took Vice President Al Gore's tie-breaking vote to beat back a drive to kill the regulation. The vote came on an amendment to the fiscal 1995 appropriations bill for the departments of Veterans Affairs and Housing and Urban Development (HR 4624).

The vote posed a classic conflict between two industry titans—agriculture and oil—each vying for a lucrative share of the domestic energy market. The skirmish breached party lines, and instead broke along regional ones. Each side boasted powerful Senate backers: Farm-state senators who favored ethanol, a derivative of agricultural products such as corn, lined up against oil-state senators who favored methanol, a derivative of natural gas.

The issue stemmed from the 1990 rewrite of the Clean Air Act. The law required nine cities with poor air quality to begin in 1995 selling gasoline reformulated to increase its oxygen content, thereby decreasing its carbon monoxide pollution. The act had left it up to the marketplace to determine how to reformulate the gasoline.

The Environmental Protection Agency (EPA), however, proposed a rule in December 1993 requiring that at least 30 percent of the gasoline sold in certain markets contain a "renewable" oxygenate. The rule effectively required one-tenth of all gasoline sold in the United States to contain ethanol or its derivative. The EPA had concluded that the use of ethanol would cut dependence on foreign oil and lower vehicle emissions that could cause global warming.

Agriculture groups such as the National Corn Growers Association hailed the decision and rallied corn-state senators to their side. But with billions of dollars of the U.S. gasoline market at stake, the oil industry decried the rule as a political ploy by the Clinton administration to win favor in the farm belt. Oil industry lobbyists solicited the help of senators with ties to their industry.

Enter Senate Energy and Natural Resources Chairman J. Bennett Johnston, a Democrat from oil-rich Louisiana. Johnston spearheaded the charge against the regulation in committee, proposing an amendment to the VA-HUD bill to block its implementation. After fellow Democrats Bob Kerrey of Nebraska and Tom Harkin of Iowa, both corn-state senators, objected, Johnston allowed the amendment to be withdrawn at a full Appropriations Committee markup July 14.

Johnston did not give up, though. He returned to the fray Aug. 3 as the full Senate considered the VA-HUD appropriations bill. He cosponsored another amendment with Democrat Bill Bradley, whose state of New Jersey was home to many oil refineries, to deny EPA funding to carry out the rule. Johnston assailed the administration's position as "a gigantic flimflam to the American public."

Midwestern farm-state senators mounted an impressive counterattack, saying the rule would create jobs and help clean the air. They were backed by powerful agriculture companies, most notably the Archer-Daniels-Midland Corp.

The vote broke down so strongly along regional lines that senators from just eight states split their votes, with those from the other 42 states voting the same way. Northeastern and Gulf Coast senators with petroleum interests supported Johnston's move, while senators from the nation's heartland opposed it unanimously. The division was so close that Gore had to cast his third deciding vote in the Senate since becoming vice president, killing the Johnston amendment on a tabling motion 51–50; R 19–25; D 31–25 (ND 26–16, SD 5–9).

12. CRIME BILL

Given the crime bill's tortured six-year journey through Congress, it was not surprising that the last crucial votes clearing the measure Aug. 25 came after four days of partisan maneuvering and acrimonious debate.

The action came on the heels of a GOP triumph in the House, where Republican leaders forced Democrats to trim more than $3 billion from the measure before agreeing Aug. 21 to support adoption of the conference report. *(House key votes 12, 13)*

The omnibus bill (HR 3355—PL 103–322) represented an un-precedented federal venture into crime fighting designed to appeal to liberals, conservatives and voters fed up with crime. It included billions of dollars to hire more police officers, build more prisons and support crime-prevention programs. It also created dozens of new federal capital crimes and banned 19 types of semiautomatic assault weapons.

Surprised and emboldened by the success of their upstart House counterparts, Minority Leader Bob Dole, R-Kan., and Senate Judiciary Committee ranking Republican Orrin G. Hatch, Utah, complained that their concerns had not been considered seriously during House negotiations on the bill. Dole threatened to use Senate procedure to stall the $30.2 billion measure unless Democrats agreed to vote on several amendments to further cut spending on prevention programs and stiffen sentencing provisions.

But Democrats were in no mood to compromise. President Clinton insisted on the weapons ban, and Majority Leader George J. Mitchell, D-Maine, argued that House Democrats already had addressed GOP concerns. Other Senate Democrats accused Republicans of trying to deny Clinton a legislative victory before the November elections. "This has an awful lot to do with presidential politics," said David Pryor, D-Ark.

For the four days after the House adopted the conference report, both sides scrambled for votes to deal with a Republican plan to raise a point of order that would have blocked the bill on the grounds that it violated budget rules. Republicans said the bill's funding mechanism—a crime trust fund—had not been reviewed by the Senate Budget Committee. The GOP needed 41 votes to sustain the point of order.

The vote to waive the budget rules determined the crime bill's fate. If the point of order had been sustained, the conference report would have been invalidated and the Senate would have been forced to take up the original House-passed bill because that was the vehicle that conferees worked from. The bill, which contained no assault weapons ban, would have been open for amendment. The legislative process effectively would have reverted to a much earlier stage, which most lawmakers agreed would have killed the crime bill for the year.

Dole and Mitchell met several times in an effort to hammer out an agreement. Dole wanted up or down votes on 10 amendments, including provisions to impose mandatory minimum sentences for drug and gun offenses and to cut $5 billion in crime prevention programs. Mitchell offered to allow one vote on an amendment to cut spending on crime prevention. This amendment, which almost certainly would have been rejected, would have saved Senate Democrats from having to vote against tougher new sentences. GOP leaders rejected the offer.

With no deal in sight, the measure's fate hung with a handful of Republican moderates torn between party loyalty and their inclination to support the bill. Mitchell had support from 55 of 56 Democrats. He needed five Republicans to cross party lines to waive the budget point of order.

Dole had received 40 Republican signatures, not including his own, on a letter demanding changes in the bill. But GOP solidarity was never strong. Several of the 40 Republicans who signed the letter did so only to let Dole use it as a negotiating tool. When Mitchell offered to allow a vote on the spending-cut amendment, three moderate Republican letter-signers—John C. Danforth, Mo.; Nancy Landon Kassebaum, Kan.; and John H. Chafee, R.I.—decided that Mitchell had made a good faith effort and joined bill supporters.

In the end the point of order was defeated 61–39: R 6–38; D 55–1 (ND 42–0, SD 13–1), with support from six Republicans: Kassebaum;

Danforth; Chafee; Arlen Specter, Pa.; James M. Jeffords, Vt.; and William V. Roth Jr., Del.

Later that day, Democrats invoked cloture, 61–38, leading to final adoption of the conference report, 61–38. William S. Cohen, R-Maine, who had voted to sustain the point of order, voted for final passage. Russell D. Feingold, D-Wis., who had supported Mitchell on the point of order, voted against the bill, saying he opposed its death penalty provisions. Malcolm Wallop, R-Wyo., who had voted to sustain the point of order, missed the final vote.

13. CAMPAIGN FINANCE

Reformers fighting to change the way congressional campaigns were financed thought they saw the light at the end of the tunnel after seven years.

Efforts to change campaign finance laws in 1987 and 1989 died at the hands of a Senate Republican filibuster. A bill finally made it through the Senate in 1992, only to be vetoed by President George Bush. But the new occupant of the White House, Bill Clinton, had pledged to sign a bill. And when the Senate passed an overhaul bill (S 3) on June 17, 1993, and the House followed suit on Nov. 22 of that same year, the long battle appeared to be ending.

It was not to be. Clinton turned his attention to other issues. Democrats in the House and Senate were badly divided. Democratic leaders spent almost 10 months trying to find a compromise. When they were ready to stitch one together at the last minute, it could not attract GOP votes and became one of several bills filibustered to death by Senate Republicans in the closing days of the regular session.

Actually, the bill itself never got to the floor of the Senate in 1994. The GOP waged its war over an ordinarily routine motion to request a conference with the House on the legislation. Republican senators forced several cloture votes on procedural motions, each requiring 60 votes, and the Democrats never had a chance against a near-unanimous GOP. On the fourth such vote, on Sept. 30, only two Republicans joined with the Democratic majority to shut off debate, while six Democrats defected to the other side. That left campaign finance supporters eight votes short, 52–46: R 2–40; D 50–6 (ND 40–2, SD 10–4). Senate Majority Leader George J. Mitchell, D-Maine, said it was the first-ever cloture vote on a motion to go to conference.

Following the vote, Democratic congressional leaders proclaimed the campaign finance effort dead. "The worst case of obstruction by filibuster by any party that I've ever seen in my 30 years in Congress," declared House Speaker Thomas S. Foley, D-Wash.

But the Democrats paved the way for the bill's defeat by taking so long to come up with a final bill. Most Republicans said the Democratic plan would hurt their party, and a small group of Senate Republicans who had voted for that chamber's bill had warned in 1993 that they would not support a bill that did not meet criteria such as tight limits on political action committees (PACs) and a single system for both chambers' campaigns.

Nevertheless, the House and Senate remained deadlocked until September 1994, largely because House Democrats would not hear of PAC limits. Finally, as Congress prepared to adjourn for the fall elections, Foley agreed to restrict PAC contributions to $6,000 per election cycle instead of the existing $10,000 limit. Mitchell signed off on the compromise. But that was not enough for Senate Republicans, particularly since the bill would have set up separate rules for House and Senate campaigns. Republicans seized on the time crunch to prevent a conference from convening, and that scuttled the campaign finance effort for the fourth consecutive Congress.

14. LOBBYING

The Democrats were seeing bill after bill on their agenda blocked when the Senate turned to consideration of the conference report on the lobbying disclosure and gift ban bill (S 349) in the last days of the regular session. They did not expect the same fate to befall the lobbying bill, but they were not prepared for an onslaught of opposition that stripped the already tenuous support for the bill.

The measure never even came to a final vote in the Senate. It died Oct. 6 when the Senate failed to limit debate on the measure, permitting a GOP-led filibuster to continue. The cloture motion failed 52–46 (R 7–36; D 45–10: ND 38–4, SD 7–6), and Democratic leaders pulled the bill the next day after a last-ditch effort yielded only three additional votes for cloture, which required a two-thirds vote because it would change Senate rules.

Defeat of the cloture motion ended an extraordinary odyssey for the bill. Efforts to stiffen lobbying disclosure laws had gone on for decades; restrictions on gifts to members were tagged to the bill in the Senate in 1993. Initially passed overwhelmingly by both chambers, the lobbying disclosure and gift bans were stalled for months in 1994 while House-Senate negotiators tried to work out a final bill.

The conference agreement was completed in late September, and it seemed headed for easy passage until it ran into problems in the House and was turned back in the Senate. (House key vote 14)

Opposition to the bill emerged in the days before the vote as trade organizations and lobbying groups, many of which would have had to disclose their contributors for the first time, voiced objections about the bill's scope.

Expanding on a theme first heard in the House, Republicans seized on language that called for disclosure of the name, address and place of business of "any person or entity" who provided contributions to fund a lobbying campaign. They said that provision could be used to require grass-roots lobbying organizations to disclose information about their contributors that could chill citizen involvement in politics.

Groups as diverse as the American Civil Liberties Union and the National Right to Life Committee came out against the bill. "They know that under this legislation, their members' names will be reported," said Sen. Don Nickles, R-Okla.

In a blistering floor speech before the vote, Senate Majority Leader George J. Mitchell, D-Maine, called that assertion "a fictional objection" that senators were using "to change their position." Backing up Mitchell's assertion, several grass-roots organizations, including Public Citizen, Common Cause and United We Stand America, endorsed the bill, saying it would not infringe on their members' activities.

The chief Senate sponsor, Carl Levin, D-Mich., said that the sudden opposition to the bill was part of a GOP strategy "to stop us from doing anything significant in the way of reform, trying to persuade the public that Congress can't reform itself."

15. CALIFORNIA DESERT

After eight years of trying to protect a huge swath of California's fragile desert from developers, the Senate was faced with a crucial vote that carried serious implications for which political party would control the upper chamber after the 1994 elections.

It also paved the way for passage of the only environmental bill in 1994. The vote came Oct. 8 on a motion to shut off debate on the conference report to a bill (S 21—PL 103–433) that kept about 7.5 million acres of California desert away from developers and designated it as wilderness. It passed, 68–23: R 14–23; D 54–0 (ND 41–0, SD 13–0).

Republicans, led by Malcolm Wallop of Wyoming, argued that the bill would block access to the desert and that the federal government could not afford the bill's centerpiece of creating two national parks and a hunting preserve.

But the debate over substance was overshadowed by political maneuverings.

Bill sponsor Dianne Feinstein, D-Calif., who was facing a tough reelection challenge from GOP Rep. Michael Huffington, portrayed the issue as though her political future was at stake. With Republicans poised to wrest control of the Senate from the Democrats, members of both political parties agreed that the outcome of the California election could be a decisive factor in determining which political party would be in power.

A last-minute deal between Senate Majority Leader George J. Mitchell, D-Maine, and Minority Leader Bob Dole, R-Kan., meant that the vote to invoke cloture would come on a Saturday morning—about 10 hours after the House had closed up shop for the regular legislative year.

The Senate had passed the bill in April by a decisive 69–29 margin, breaking an eight-year deadlock by California Republicans on the measure. But Mitchell and Feinstein could afford to lose only nine votes to still have the necessary 60 votes to shut off debate.

Mitchell, for instance, arranged for a private plane to carry back one Democratic senator from the campaign trail and cajoled others to change their schedules.

"He made sure the fat lady never got to sing," said Barbara Boxer, D-Calif.

Feinstein persuaded colleagues such as William V. Roth Jr., R-Del.; Frank R. Lautenberg, D-N.J.; and James Sasser, D-Tenn., to suspend for a few hours their own reelection campaigning and come back to Washington for the vote. Joseph I. Lieberman, D-Conn., an Orthodox Jew, spent Friday night in a hotel near Capitol Hill so that he could observe the religious practice of not driving on Saturday, the Sabbath.

Republicans, meanwhile, furiously lobbied their own with the notion of denying Feinstein a victory and damaging her reelection bid.

Sources said a GOP caucus meeting Oct. 8 during the final hour of debate was tense with the idea that control of the Senate was hanging in the balance. But in the end, it was the balky garage door of Carol Moseley-Braun, D-Ill., that nearly thwarted the Democrats. With the voting clock ticking away and Feinstein just one vote short of the required 60, Moseley-Braun came running onto the Senate floor to cast an "aye" vote for her clearly worried friend.

Moseley-Braun's vote provided political cover for several Republicans, such as Pete V. Domenici of New Mexico and Nancy Landon Kassebaum of Kansas, who were holding back as the votes were being tallied.

Fourteen Republicans eventually voted for the bill, many of them either with moderate views on the environment or mindful of the Senate tradition of not opposing conservation measures pertaining to only one state that have the support of both senators from that state. (House key vote 10)

16. GATT

Following a 20-hour debate, the Senate on Dec. 1 gave overwhelming approval to a bill (HR 5110—PL 103–465) to implement the Uruguay Round pact strengthening the General Agreement on Tariffs and Trade (GATT). The United States signed the agreement April 15.

The House had passed the GATT bill 288–146 on Nov. 29. At the heart of the GATT debate was a sharp philosophical difference on U.S.

trade policy. The Clinton administration insisted that the continued reduction of trade barriers would greatly benefit U.S. businesses, spurring billions of dollars in economic growth and thousands of new jobs. But opponents, led by Sen. Ernest F. Hollings, D-S.C., insisted that free-trade policies had over the years left U.S. industries vulnerable to foreign competition, destroying millions of jobs.

Congress had a long-standing pattern of supporting the free-trade viewpoint. That gave supporters of HR 5110 confidence to predict passage before the planned early October congressional adjournment.

However, it took the administration and lawmakers several months to fine-tune the GATT implementing bill, providing Hollings with an opportunity to delay action.

The bill was submitted Sept. 27 under fast-track rules for trade legislation, which allowed each chamber only an up-or-down vote on the bill without amendments. But the rules also allowed every committee chairman with jurisdiction to take up to 45 days to review the bill. Hollings, chairman of the Commerce Committee, demanded this prerogative, forcing the Democratic Senate leadership to delay the debate and vote until a two-day postelection session that began Nov. 30.

Hollings held eight Commerce Committee hearings to lay out his case against U.S. free-trade policy. He also raised other arguments against the agreement, including the claim that the new World Trade Organization (WTO)—created under the deal to arbitrate and strictly enforce multilateral trade agreements—would impinge on U.S. legal sovereignty.

Hollings brought his critique to the Senate floor, leading the opposition during the lame-duck debate. He was parried by the GATT bill's managers, Finance Committee Chairman Daniel Patrick Moynihan, D-N.Y., and ranking Republican Bob Packwood of Oregon.

The supporters argued that the agreement would be a boon to U.S. exporters who had been hindered by other countries' trade barriers in such areas as agriculture, services and intellectual property. They rebutted the sovereignty issue, noting that the bill would require express congressional action to change any law even if the WTO had found it in violation of U.S. trade commitments.

With the numbers running against them on the merits of the bill, the opponents hung their hopes on blocking a procedural motion that required 60 votes to pass.

The Senate's pay-as-you-go budget rules required that new legislation fully offset any federal spending increases or revenue reductions over the first 10 years after enactment, an obligation that the GATT bill fell about $30 billion short of meeting.

Contending that U.S. voters had made a strong call for fiscal responsibility when they elected Republican majorities in the House and Senate on Nov. 8, the GATT opponents rallied around a point of order raised by Sen. Robert C. Byrd, D-W.Va., that HR 5110 violated the Senate budget rules. GATT supporters trumped that claim by arguing that increased economic activity spurred by the new trade deal ultimately would result in increased revenues to the federal Treasury.

A motion by Moynihan to waive the budget rules carried, 68–32: R 31–15; D 37–17 (ND 29–13, SD 8–4). The Senate then immediately voted to clear the implementing bill itself by a vote of 76–24. *(House key vote 16)*

agenda in 1994. The issue would later form the basis for an antiregulatory proposal in the Republicans' "Contract with America."

At issue was whether the proposed Department of Environmental Protection should be required to study the costs and benefits of regulations before implementing new rules. These types of studies were just a small part of a scientific process, known as risk assessment, that tried to estimate the type and magnitude of risks to human health posed by the exposure to chemical substances.

The Rules Committee did not allow first-term Florida Reps. John L. Mica, R, and Karen L. Thurman, D, to offer an amendment requiring cost-benefit studies to a bill (HR 3425) to elevate the Environmental Protection Agency (EPA) to Cabinet status. That made the rule for floor debate the key vote.

At stake was more than Clinton's promise to quickly give the EPA a formal seat at the Cabinet table.

Environmentalists contended that the Mica-Thurman amendment would have paralyzed the federal government through costly studies, whose results could then be used to weaken existing health and safety laws.

But Mica and Thurman, with the help of the GOP leadership, argued that environmental regulations had become a financial burden on states and local governments. They said some regulations also provided little health benefit. The goal of the amendment, Mica and Thurman said, was to provide some common-sense and sound scientific reasoning to environmental rule-making.

Vice President Al Gore heavily lobbied the large Democratic freshman class to vote for the rule (H Res 312), which banned all amendments except those pertaining to the structure of the proposed Department of Environmental Protection. Gore, a key environmental ally, and other supporters of the bill argued that it was the wrong measure through which to try to broadly rewrite environmental policy. The rule was rejected 191–227: R 5–167; D 185–60 (ND 140–28; SD 45–32); I 1–0. It was one of the rare occasions in the 103rd Congress in which a rule was defeated.

Only five Republicans—Christopher Shays of Connecticut, Constance A. Morella of Maryland, John Edward Porter of Illinois and New York members Sherwood Boehlert and Benjamin A. Gilman—voted to adopt the rule. All five members had voting records that favored environmental policies.

Gore's tactic of targeting freshmen also proved futile. Sixty-four freshmen, many of whom campaigned on a plank of less government and a new way of doing federal business, voted to reject the procedural motion.

The vote was seen as a sign that the House favored cost-benefit studies and less government regulation. With no rule, the EPA Cabinet bill was never brought up again on the House floor, and Clinton was unable to fulfill his promise for speedy action on the measure.

The subject of risk assessment also would scuttle an attempt to make the Safe Drinking Water Act more flexible for states, local governments and small water system operators and bog down an effort to reorganize the Agriculture Department. *(Senate key vote 7)*

House Republicans promised a vote on an antiregulatory proposal, which included a cost-benefit provision similar to the Mica-Thurman amendment, as part of their "Contract with America" in the first 100 days of the 104th Congress.

House

1. EPA CABINET

A House vote Feb. 2 on a routine procedural motion sparked a politically explosive backlash against federal regulations that also proved disastrous to elements of President Clinton's environmental

2. DEFENSE SPENDING

Early in the year, the House beat back an effort by liberals to make relatively minor cuts in defense spending to pay for new social programs, demonstrating that Congress would not tolerate raids on defense beyond reductions contained in President Clinton's budget.

In his fiscal 1995 budget Clinton requested $263.7 billion to fund national defense programs. He said in his State of the Union address that his request "draws the line against further defense cuts. . . . We must not cut defense further."

Nevertheless, liberal activists in Congress believed that Clinton would not fight hard to fend off cuts in the defense request. That assumption was driven, in part, by the fact that cuts in the defense budget were virtually the only source from which Congress could squeeze funds to pay for new domestic initiatives. The liberals made their move on the budget resolution (H Con Res 218), with an amendment sponsored by Rep. Barney Frank, D-Mass. to reduce defense budget authority in fiscal 1995 by $2.4 billion.

However, Clinton, his top aides and the House Democratic leadership lobbied vigorously against the Frank amendment. It was defeated March 10 by a vote of 105–313: R 12–160; D 92–153 (ND 82–85, SD 10–68); I 1–0.

After that, no other effort to significantly reduce the defense budget request came close to adoption in either the House or the Senate.

During the 1992 presidential campaign, Clinton had vowed to cut $60 billion from the $1.4 trillion that President George Bush projected in total defense budgets for fiscal 1994–1997. But the defense program Clinton unveiled early in 1993 cut Bush's projected total by $123 billion—more than twice the promised amount.

Administration officials insisted that changing economic circumstances accounted for the deeper cut and that Clinton's program would meet his goal of paying for a modernized and combat-ready force large enough to win two simultaneous regional wars. But Republican defense specialists and some centrist Democrats warned that Clinton's budgets were shortchanging the "two-war" force.

The funding squeeze was exacerbated when Congress rejected out of hand Clinton's plan to restrain the annual cost of living raises for military personnel. The fiscal 1994 defense authorization and appropriations bills included a 2.2 percent military pay raise, rather than the freeze that Clinton proposed.

To cover the future costs of only the fiscal 1994 congressionally mandated military raise, the administration agreed to boost Clinton's multiyear defense funding plan by $11.4 billion. Clinton's request for fiscal 1995 included $2.4 billion of that pay-raise add-on, the amount the liberals targeted for elimination with the Frank amendment.

3. BALANCED-BUDGET AMENDMENT

With the Senate having rejected the proposal only two weeks before, members of the House could have taken a free ride and cast a politically popular vote to adopt a proposed constitutional amendment to require a balanced federal budget.

House Democratic leaders opposed to the balanced budget amendment worked the issue hard, and after they used subtle but effective procedural tactics and demanded discipline from the large class of Democratic freshmen, the proposed amendment fell 12 votes short of the two-thirds majority required to pass.

The measure (H J Res 103) came to the floor only after chief sponsor Charles W. Stenholm, D-Texas, gathered more than the necessary 218 signatures from colleagues on a so-called discharge petition to force a floor vote without committee action.

The fact that Stenholm was able to get the signatures in a single afternoon attested to the frustration many lawmakers felt over the inability of Congress to reduce the deficit. The constitutional amendment was a popular refuge for members to prove they were deficit hawks while not having to vote for the specific spending cuts or taxes needed to make a balanced budget a reality.

Stenholm's amendment was identical to the version previously rejected by the Senate. It would have required a balanced budget by fiscal 2001 or the second year after ratification by the states, whichever came later. A three-fifths vote would have been required to approve deficit spending. (Senate key vote 4)

Having won the right to get a vote on his proposal, Stenholm faced a difficult battle as House leaders opposed to the measure structured debate on several alternatives to siphon sufficient votes to derail Stenholm's version. The measure ultimately failed March 17, 271–153: R 171–1; D 99–151 (ND 47–122, SD 59–29); I 0–1. It needed 283 "yeas" to pass.

During the debate, the House considered four alternative balanced-budget amendments. A significantly less stringent version, drafted by Bob Wise, D-W. Va., with the blessing of Democratic leaders, was soundly defeated on a 111–318 vote. Sixty-four Democrats who voted for Wise's alternative did not vote for Stenholm's.

Another alternative, pushed by Reps. Joe L. Barton, R-Texas, and W. J. "Billy" Tauzin, D-La., was more stringent. Their version—which paralleled one outlined later in the House GOP's "Contract with America"—would have required Congress to muster a three-fifths supermajority for any tax increase.

Needing only a simple majority for preliminary approval, the Barton-Tauzin version was adopted 211–204. But Stenholm's version was sent on for final consideration—and eventual defeat—after it was adopted later by voice vote.

The constitutional amendment had returned to the House floor two years after the House defeated a similar measure on a 280–153 vote, after a late lobbying blitz by organized labor and senior citizens.

Seniors, led by the American Association of Retired Persons (AARP), again pulled out all stops, blasting the proposal for threatening Social Security. Phones in the Capitol started ringing off the hook after the AARP sent out a huge overnight mailing to its members asking them to lobby against the amendment. Wise's version, which would have protected Social Security, gave members political cover, allowing them to vote in favor of the politically popular constitutional limitation while not alienating seniors.

In light of the preceding action by the Senate, Democratic leaders urged rank-and-file members, especially freshmen, to avoid the temptation to consider support of the Stenholm version a free vote. To go on record supporting Stenholm would have given the proposal a better chance of passing in the future. In the end the critical voting bloc of 64 Democratic freshmen stayed with the leadership by a 2–1 ratio; only 20 Democratic freshmen voted for the Stenholm amendment, and 43 were opposed.

4. BUDGET RESOLUTION

In contrast to the battle Congress went through in 1993, the budget resolution debate was almost a nonevent, in large part because President Clinton asked that Congress hold the line on further spending cuts. The request came as a relief to the Democratic Congress, which already had a full agenda wrestling with the mammoth task of trying to reshape the nation's health care system.

Still, it took a barrage of last-minute lobbying by the administration to turn the tide April 14 when deficit hawks demanded a vote on a motion to instruct conferees (H Con Res 218) to increase the budget cuts in the fiscal 1995 budget resolution. Offered by Rep. John R. Kasich, R-Ohio, it was rejected on a largely party line vote of 202–216: R 159–6; D 43–209 (ND 29–141, SD 14–68); I 0–1. (Senate key vote 6)

The motion would have required conferees to accept the Senate's proposal to cut an additional $26.1 billion in appropriations outlays over five years. The cuts would have gone beyond the $433 billion already in the five-year package Congress passed in 1993, which Clinton and Democratic leaders said provided sufficient deficit reduction for the next few years.

The main argument that administration officials advanced against the Senate proposal was that it could result in cuts in defense which, Clinton said during his State of the Union speech, should not be cut any further. The administration made its case with the help of the Joint Chiefs of Staff, who led the lobbying effort against the motion saying the cuts posed a serious threat to defense and had to be stopped.

Kasich and Democratic budget cutters who joined him in support of the reductions rejected that argument, pointing out that the Senate's proposed cuts represented the only chance lawmakers would have to pursue serious deficit reduction. They said the administration's contention that the cuts were a threat to defense was a scare tactic.

The House and Senate Appropriations committees had the authority to allocate the cuts in any way they saw fit when they divided up the discretionary budget among the 13 appropriations subcommittees—something they did once the budget resolution set their overall spending limit. The House's pattern had been to allocate about half the cuts to defense because defense made up half the budget's discretionary spending.

The effort to make deeper cuts and its rejection was a familiar theme for House deficit hawks, who had tried before to promote spending cuts. In 1993 Kasich tried unsuccessfully to make an additional $90 billion in cuts in the budget resolution beyond the $433 billion already in it.

5. ASSAULT WEAPONS BAN

Gun control advocates won their second major victory in less than a year when Congress, in late August 1994, passed a ban on certain semiautomatic assault weapons as part of its omnibus anticrime bill (HR 3355—PL 103–322). The pivotal vote came in the House, which approved the gun ban 216–214 on May 5. The Senate already had approved a similar proposal in 1993 as part of its sweeping crime bill, and the House action made it all but certain that the gun control measure would become law.

Gun control groups knew their fortunes had changed when President Clinton took office in 1993. Clinton was the first president in recent years to actively support gun control. By the end of the year, gun control supporters had passed the Brady bill (HR 1025—PL 103–159), a nationwide waiting period and background check for handgun purchasers.

Prospects for the assault weapons ban (HR 4296), however, were considered far slimmer. When the House voted on the issue in 1991, lawmakers defeated the ban by 70 votes. The National Rifle Association (NRA) had been a powerful lobby in the House, and Rep. Jack Brooks, D-Texas, chairman of the Judiciary Committee, which oversaw crime legislation, had long fought off gun control proposals. Even when the Senate passed the assault weapons ban in November 1993 as part of its crime bill, many observers predicted it would die in the House.

Gun control advocates had new leverage: With crime at the top of voter concerns, lawmakers were eager to embrace anything seen as a tool for fighting violence. Moreover, many law enforcement groups lobbied for the ban and helped transform the issue from a "gun control" cause into a "tough on crime" issue.

The proposed ban explicitly outlawed 19 assault-style weapons, as well as copycat models and other semiautomatic guns with two or more features identified with assault weapons. It also banned large-capacity ammunition clips. But the proposal specifically exempted more than 650 guns that presumably were used by hunters and other sportsmen, as well as any gun legally owned at the time of the law's passage.

Gun control advocates and law enforcement groups pushed for the ban, saying assault weapons were the preferred weapons of criminals and were designed to kill humans rather than for sporting use. The NRA and its allies said the guns were no more lethal than other semiautomatic firearms and that banning them would do nothing to stop criminals from killing.

As the floor vote approached, both sides mounted furious publicity and lobbying campaigns. The Clinton administration added its weight to the battle, with the president and several Cabinet members making phone calls to undecided lawmakers leading up to the vote May 5.

House members began an emotional floor debate on the legislation with the outcome too close to call. Marge Roukema, R-N.J., a leading Republican supporter of the ban, invoked images of the gruesome carnage caused by the weapons. "Today our cities are war zones and our hospital emergency rooms are MASH units," she said. Other supporters cited polls showing strong popular support for the ban.

But opponents ridiculed the ban as ineffective and perhaps unconstitutional. They said the guns to be banned under the legislation were no more powerful than hundreds of others that would be exempt—just uglier.

Once the roll call began, the two sides stayed closely matched. In the final minutes the tally hovered at 213–214, giving opponents the edge. But Rep. Andrew Jacobs Jr., D-Ind., shocked his colleagues by reversing his vote—drawing cheers from the bill's supporters as the vote total flipped to 214–213 in favor of passage. Three holdouts divided 2–1 in casting the final votes, bringing the final tally to 216–214: R 38–137; D 177–77 (ND 137–34, SD 40–43); I 1–0.

The vote was a stunning setback for the NRA and its allies. They went on to fight the ban during House-Senate negotiations on the final crime bill. But with both chambers on record in favor of the ban, the stage was set for final passage. It was approved as part of the crime bill conference report in late August and signed into law by Clinton in September. *(Senate key vote 12)*

6. ABORTION CLINIC ACCESS

Abortion rights supporters expected to make big gains in the 103rd Congress—even in the recalcitrant House—with the arrival of President Clinton, who supported their cause. But abortion remained a deeply controversial and complicated issue, and most initiatives to secure abortion rights stalled. The only significant legislation that emerged was one focused on safeguarding access to abortion clinics (S 636—PL 103–259), and even that had to overcome persistent opposition in both chambers.

The bill's advocates were prodded by a January 1993 Supreme Court decision blocking clinic operators from using a 19th century civil rights law to obtain injunctions and other relief against blockaders. A rash of violence at abortion clinics nationwide, including shootings, arson and massive blockades, further fueled the quest for a federal solution. Supporters framed the measure not as a vote on abortion rights but as a law-and-order issue.

Even so, abortion rights advocates were on the defensive from the time the House first considered the legislation in 1993. Many members—including several who opposed legal abortion—condemned the behavior of radical antiabortion activists, but they also expressed concern about approving a bill that might limit the First Amendment right to freedom of expression. From subcommittee action to House approval Nov. 18, 1993, the bill's opponents tried to limit its scope and leave the issue in the hands of local authorities.

The legislation made it a federal crime to intimidate abortion clinic workers or women seeking abortions, by force or threat of force. Violators faced criminal penalties of jail time and fines. The law also allowed affected individuals to sue for civil remedies, such as compensatory damages or court injunctions to restrain blockaders. *(Senate key vote 5)*

During House floor debate, much of the criticism centered on questions about the measure's constitutionality. Opponents charged that it singled out one point of view for censure. But the bill ultimately gained the support of several members who were ambivalent or even opposed to abortion rights but were disturbed enough by the violence to support legislation focused on that aspect of the problem.

Both chambers had passed similar measures in 1993, and a conference committee met in 1994 to work out minor differences. Even getting to a conference took some doing, however, given the emotional nature of the issue. Opponents, led by Christopher H. Smith, R-N.J., forced a series of procedural votes March 17, using them to pound away at the bill.

After conferees ironed out their differences, the House on May 5 considered adopting the conference report, setting off another wave of emotional debate. F. James Sensenbrenner Jr., R-Wis., objected to a provision to allow plaintiffs but not defendants in clinic cases to recoup legal fees, and he tried to return the bill to conference. When that failed, opponents complained that the measure was too broad and its penalties excessive. "We're just looking for the punishment to be in sync with the crime," Smith said.

Supporters noted the increased violence at abortion clinics and maintained that local trespassing laws were insufficient or unenforced. "The right to choose is meaningless without the access to choose," said Carolyn B. Maloney, D-N.Y. The vote to approve the conference report was 241–174: R 40–131; D 200–43 (ND 139–26, SD 61–17); I 1–0.

7. BOSNIA ARMS EMBARGO

For two years, lawmakers had expressed increasing frustration with the inability of successive administrations to halt Serbian aggression in Bosnia. But they always stopped short of actually trying to dictate policy toward the former Yugoslavian republic.

That changed June 9, when the House voted overwhelmingly to require President Clinton to end compliance with the international arms embargo against the Bosnian Muslims. The House approved the measure, which was an amendment to the fiscal 1995 defense authorization bill, 244–178: R 127–45; D 117–132 (ND 84–87, SD 33–45); I 0–1. The Senate rejected a similar proposal July 1 on a 50–50 tie and approved a nonbinding amendment urging the president to look for a peaceful solution to the Bosnian conflict. *(Senate key vote 10)*

Debate on the amendment highlighted the sharply conflicting views among House members over how to end the brutal conflict.

Supporters of the amendment argued that the U.N. arms embargo, which was imposed on all the former Yugoslavia republics in 1991, had worked to the disadvantage of Bosnia's Muslim-led government forces. The Serbs, widely viewed as the aggressors in the conflict, had inherited heavy weaponry from the Yugoslavian army. The Muslims were relatively lightly armed.

House Democratic Whip David E. Bonior, D-Mich., cast the issue in stark terms. "If we don't lift this embargo and at least let the people of Bosnia defend themselves," he said, "then the blood of Bosnia isn't just on the hands of the Serbs—it's on all of us."

Foreign Affairs Committee Chairman Lee H. Hamilton, D-Ind., argued that the amendment would eliminate chances for a peaceful resolution of the conflict. "If we lift this embargo, we are going to intensify the war, and by intensifying the war, that is another way of saying we are going to be killing a lot more people," he said.

The Clinton administration also worked to defeat the amendment, as senior officials warned lawmakers that ending the embargo would undermine the fragile multilateral peace negotiations.

The administration labored under a tactical disadvantage. The vote on the amendment originally was scheduled to coincide with the president's trip to Europe. The White House, concerned that Clinton might be dealt a high-profile setback as he met with allied leaders, successfully won a delay of the vote.

In return, administration officials promised not to personally lobby lawmakers on the embargo issue. In the end the administration lost many of its Democratic allies, including Bonior and Democratic Caucus Chairman Steny H. Hoyer of Maryland.

8. TELECOMMUNICATIONS

Thanks largely to the work of two powerhouse committee chairmen, the House on June 28 overwhelmingly approved a major and contentious bill to rewrite the nation's 60-year-old communications law. The victory proved hollow, however, when lingering disagreements within the telecommunications industry scuttled the legislation in the Senate.

Still, the House vote on the bill (HR 3626) demonstrated that it was possible to unite trust-busting Democrats and deregulatory Republicans in support of a move toward unfettered competition in telecommunications products and services. The tally was 423–5: R 173–1; D 249–4 (ND 168–3, SD 81–1); I 1–0.

The bill would have superseded the 1982 court order that limited the regional Bell telephone monopolies mainly to the local telephone market and AT&T mainly to long distance and equipment manufacturing. Instead of having a federal judge decide when to remove those restrictions, the bill would have put the issue in the hands of the Federal Communications Commission, the Justice Department and state regulators.

The Bells were eager to lift those restrictions, and they had a key ally in Energy and Commerce Committee Chairman John D. Dingell, D-Mich. But another House titan, Judiciary Committee Chairman Jack Brooks, D-Texas, argued for maintaining tough limits on what the Bells could do as long as they dominated the local phone markets.

Through a series of compromises, Dingell and Brooks came up with a proposal for lifting the restrictions that had the unanimous support of their committees and the endorsement of almost every segment of the telecommunications industry. They whisked their bill to the House floor under a fast-track, no-amendment procedure usually reserved for minor bills—a stunning achievement for such a complex piece of legislation on a topic involving diverse, competing interests.

A companion bill by Reps. Edward J. Markey, D-Mass., and Jack Fields, R-Texas, that would have enabled competition in the local telephone and cable-television markets (HR 3636) passed the same day by a similar margin, 423–4. The House then folded HR 3636 into HR 3626. So broad was the support for the two bills that both Minority Whip Newt Gingrich, R-Ga., and Majority Whip David E. Bonior, D-Mich., took the floor to urge "yes" votes. The easy passage of the Brooks-Dingell bill disguised a major weakness in its legislative foundation, however: The $60 billion long-distance industry did not support it. Rather than trying to fight it out in the House, the long-distance carriers focused their attention on the Senate, where leaders of the Senate Commerce Committee had introduced a companion bill (S 1822) far more favorable to their interests.

Thus, an important legislative battle was postponed until the Senate Commerce Committee tried to move S 1822 in July. Even though the leaders of the committee were able to broker a deal between the Bells and the long-distance carriers over the Bells' entry into the long-distance market, they could not unite the telecommunications industry behind the legislation. After several senators threatened end-of-session filibusters, Commerce Committee Chairman Ernest F. Hollings, D-S.C., pulled the plug on the bill.

9. SPACE STATION

The year dawned ominously for NASA's space station. Congress had demonstrated in 1993 that big-science projects were not immune to budget-cutting fervor when it killed the superconducting super collider. The House served notice that the space station could be the next to go when members came within one vote of ending its authorization and within 24 votes of axing its fiscal 1994 appropriation.

Then, in the spring, two key lawmakers said they were noncommittal about continuing the project in fiscal 1995. House Science Committee Chairman George E. Brown Jr., D-Calif., was concerned that the space station would siphon funds from other National Aeronautics and Space Administration science programs. House VA-HUD Appropriations Subcommittee Chairman Louis Stokes, D-Ohio, warned that the space station might suffer if there was a shortage of money in the VA-HUD appropriations bill, which funded the departments of Veterans Affairs (VA), Housing and Urban Development (HUD) and independent agencies such as NASA.

By June, Brown and Stokes had decided to support spending $2.1 billion in fiscal 1995 for the station, intended to be an orbiting space laboratory for research in biotechnology, chemistry and physics. After a closed-door subcommittee markup June 9, Stokes said he endorsed the project "because the president wanted it and felt that it was a vital part of his foreign policy."

Nevertheless, the space station's future was uncertain—as it had been for several years when it was the most controversial element of the VA-HUD spending bill. The federal government already had spent more than $11 billion on the space station, once known as Freedom, which it had envisioned in 1984 as an $8 billion project. The renamed Alpha project, a scaled-back version of the original, now carried a total price tag of about $30 billion.

Leading the anti-station fight again were Tim Roemer, D-Ind., and Dick Zimmer, R-N.J. On June 29 they offered an amendment to the VA-HUD bill (HR 4624—PL 103-327) to bar using money to continue the project and redistributing the $2.1 billion to other NASA programs.

Opponents blasted the project for being too expensive, unfocused in its mission, dependent on unreliable agreements with Russia and too reliant on job creation for its political support. "It's time for the Congress to do what it should have done years ago—cut our losses . . . and put an end to this budgetary black hole in space," Zimmer said.

Momentum had shifted in favor of funding the space station. The project's redesign, strong support from the Clinton administration and foreign policy implications through international agreements with Russia and other countries helped strengthen its support. "The 216–215 vote last year woke up a sleeping giant," Roemer said of the lobbying blitz that preceded the 1994 vote. Roemer's amendment was defeated 155–278: R 40–136; D 114–142 (ND 101–72, SD 13–70); I 1–0.

Afterward, Brown said one reason he had waffled earlier in the year was to prod the station's supporters to step up their efforts. Vice

President Al Gore—who along with President Clinton and NASA administrator Daniel S. Goldin had personally lobbied members to support the project—expressed hope that the outcome would end the annual funding battle. "The strength of the House vote signals the end of doubt about America's commitment to space exploration," Gore said in a statement.

The Senate, traditionally a stronger supporter of the project, on Aug. 3 rejected an amendment to kill the space station, 36–64.

10. CALIFORNIA DESERT

The political muscle of environmentalists in the House proved to be no match for gun control opponents in a key vote July 12 on whether to permit hunting in an ecologically sensitive part of California's desert.

Due largely to the support of the bipartisan Congressional Sportsmen's Caucus, one of the largest membership-driven organizations on Capitol Hill, the gun control opponents won by a vote of 239–183: R 146–26; D 92–157 (ND 39–131, SD 53–26); I 1–0.

The strength of the vote later persuaded Sen. Dianne Feinstein, D-Calif., and House Natural Resources Committee Chairman George Miller, D-Calif., to compromise on a crucial provision of a bill (S 21—PL 103–433) aimed at keeping a huge swath of California desert out of the hands of developers. (Senate key vote 15)

The vote came on an amendment by Larry LaRocco, D-Idaho, to designate the East Mojave Scenic Area as a national preserve instead of the more coveted national park status preferred by Feinstein, Miller, the Clinton administration and a host of environmental groups.

"Preserve" was a label rarely used by the National Park Service that allowed hunting, fishing and trapping to continue on protected federal land.

The House easily approved a similar amendment in 1991. But environmentalists considered the California desert protection bill one of their legislative priorities for 1993–1994 and pressured lawmakers to give maximum protection to the land.

The LaRocco amendment eventually became a crucial element in the floor strategy of Rep. Jerry Lewis and four other California Republicans to try to weaken the desert bill before it moved to a House-Senate conference committee. Lewis signed on as the amendment's chief cosponsor.

LaRocco, a member of the sportsmen's caucus, initially lost to Miller when the Natural Resources Committee voted 17–25 on May 4 to reject the amendment. But LaRocco lobbied hard among the caucus's 182 House members and was supported on the floor by such groups as the National Rifle Association and the Safari Club.

Although the sportsmen's caucus took no formal position on gun control, its members generally opposed such legislation. The caucus worked to preserve the interests of hunters, fishermen and people who shot for sport. A comparison of the votes for LaRocco's hunting amendment and the assault weapons ban in the 1994 crime bill showed that only 11 of the caucus's 182 House members voted against both measures.

Several senior committee Democrats—LaRocco, Nick J. Rahall II of West Virginia, Austin J. Murphy of Pennsylvania and Pat Williams of Montana—voted for the hunting amendment. Miller downplayed the vote, saying Democrats were voting the wishes of their districts.

11. BUDGET PROCESS

Deficit hawks generally pointed to entitlements such as Social Security, Medicare and food stamps, which made up roughly half the federal budget, as the place to look for serious deficit reduction.

When a bill (HR 4604) to rein in entitlement spending came to the floor in July, there was more agreement on what not to cut than on anything else. The bill would have set limits on entitlement spending and required spending cuts or tax increases or both if the entitlement caps were breached.

In a vote that stood as testament that Social Security remained the untouchable "third rail" of American politics, the House overwhelmingly rejected a substitute plan put forward by Charles W. Stenholm, D-Texas, that would have kept Social Security on the chopping block along with entitlements such as Medicare, Medicaid, unemployment insurance and others.

Stenholm's plan would have forced real cuts. It would have set entitlement caps from 1996 through 2000 low enough to force as much as $150 billion in cuts from projected entitlement spending. His proposal would have capped entitlements at fiscal 1995 levels, with adjustments for the Consumer Price Index and demographic changes. If the Office of Management and Budget determined that the limits would be breached, the president would have had to propose legislation to close the gap or raise the caps. If Congress failed to agree on how to meet the targets, sequestration procedures would have kicked in.

With Social Security making up 44 percent of all entitlements, members were loath to vote with Stenholm, especially since the underlying bill gave them a more politically palatable alternative. Stenholm's entitlement cutting plan was overwhelmingly defeated July 21, 37–392: R 9–165; D 28–226 (ND 15–157, SD 13–69); I 0–1.

Instead, the House passed, 316–107, a plan that would have required the White House to set the entitlement targets. The final bill was virtually identical to the plan passed by the House (but not the Senate) during the 1993 debate over President Clinton's five-year deficit-reduction package and later implemented by executive order.

With entitlement spending remaining below the targets set in 1993, neither the existing rules nor the House passed bill would have caused cuts in the near future. Along the way, the House rejected, 194–233, an alternative offered by John R. Kasich, R-Ohio, that would have required Congress and the White House each year to set caps on individual entitlement programs except Social Security.

The action on entitlements came amid a growing sense that spiraling growth in such programs needed to be addressed if Congress was going to seriously attempt to cut the deficit. The 1993 budget deal put a major squeeze on money available to appropriators for discretionary spending but largely left entitlements alone.

While the lopsidedness of the vote on Stenholm's amendment was attributable in part to the fact that members had politically palatable alternatives to vote for, the fact that it attracted so few votes highlighted one enduring truth: Congress might want to attack the deficit by curbing growth in entitlement spending, but not if it meant cutting Social Security, the biggest entitlement of them all.

12. CRIME BILL/RULE

President Clinton and House Democratic leaders suffered one of their most embarrassing moments of the 103rd Congress on Aug. 11, when lawmakers blocked action on a major anticrime bill. Democratic leaders had pulled out all the stops to pass a procedural motion allowing the crime bill (HR 3355) to come to the House floor.

Nearly 60 Democrats joined with almost all Republicans to defeat the rule (H Res 517). The vote highlighted divisions within the Democratic Caucus and severely imperiled passage of one of the president's key legislative priorities.

Democrats had struggled from the beginning to write a crime bill that could win House approval. When the House passed its version of

the crime bill in April, they thought they had succeeded. That bill cost about $28 billion. It included dozens of new death penalties and other criminal punishments, as well as billions of dollars for police hiring, prison construction and social programs designed to prevent crime. It was a balance that satisfied a majority of Democrats and some Republicans, and the bill passed by a comfortable 285–141 margin.

The final, $33 billion crime bill that emerged from House-Senate negotiations generally followed the House bill with a notable exception—it added a ban on certain semiautomatic assault-style weapons. House lawmakers had approved a ban as separate legislation (HR 4296) in May, but without the votes of some of the lawmakers who had supported the crime bill. *(House key vote 5)*

That presented House leaders with a difficult equation as they rounded up votes to bring the conference report to the floor. While numerous Republicans were expected to vote for the bill on final passage, GOP lawmakers routinely voted against proposed rules for floor debate because they saw such rules as a tool used by Democrats to suppress Republican views. Democratic leaders usually could count on solid party support for such votes.

In this case, however, a large group of Democrats who opposed gun control insisted they could not cast a vote that would facilitate bringing the assault weapons ban to the House floor. Several members of the Congressional Black Caucus also withheld their support because of objections to the death penalty provisions in the measure.

Clinton and the House leadership mounted a furious campaign to round up the necessary 218 votes. With little movement among the gun-rights Democrats, these leaders pinned their hopes on a group of Republican lawmakers who had voted for the House crime bill and also supported the assault weapons ban. These Republicans also felt pressure from their own party leadership, which insisted that GOP lawmakers hold together on the procedural vote.

Republican leaders made procedural complaints about the crime legislation, saying Democratic leaders had ridden roughshod over GOP attempts to amend or influence the bill. They attacked the substance of the final product as weak on punishment and fiscally bloated, particularly with respect to crime prevention programs.

Democrats defended the final bill as worthy and essential, and many charged that Republicans were simply trying to deny Clinton and his party a legislative success on an issue of great concern to voters. In the test of party allegiances, the Republicans prevailed. All but 11 GOP lawmakers voted against the rule while 58 Democrats broke with their party leadership on the issue. Most of those Democratic votes came from opponents of the gun ban, but 10 were from black lawmakers upset about the death penalty language and the decision to omit a provision aimed at combating alleged racial bias in death penalty sentencing.

The final vote was 210–225: R 11–167; D 198–58 (ND 148–25, SD 50–33); I 1–0. In the aftermath, Republicans were jubilant about their show of power. Democratic leaders, badly shaken, began scrambling for ways to salvage the crime bill, which eventually cleared in late August (PL 103–322). *(Senate key vote 12, House key vote 13)*

13. CRIME BILL/CONFERENCE

Public distress over violent crime proved stronger than congressional infighting Aug. 21, when House lawmakers overcame bitter disagreements to adopt the conference report on a massive, $30.2 billion anticrime bill (HR 3355). Just 10 days earlier, House Republicans and renegade Democrats had blocked action on the legislation. That vote was a stunning setback for President Clinton and the Democratic leadership, and it set up the possibility of lawmakers heading home empty-handed on an issue that many voters had identified as their top concern. (*House key vote 12*)

Ultimately, that scenario was too threatening to numerous lawmakers in both parties. After a week of frantic and wearying negotiations, Democratic leaders agreed to revise the final bill to attract additional Republican votes. The new version trimmed $3.3 billion from the original bill and adjusted certain policy provisions.

When the crime measure emerged from House-Senate negotiations in late July, most lawmakers and political analysts considered it unstoppable. Lawmakers in both parties were eager to take action on the issue of violent crime, and Democratic leaders appeared to have crafted an acceptable compromise: The final legislation included billions for prison construction sought by conservatives, social programs advocated by liberals and police hiring supported by almost everyone. To make sure the programs actually received promised funding, the legislation included a novel trust fund designed to devote the expected savings from federal layoffs to the anticrime programs.

Even so, the measure foundered on two highly contentious issues: gun control and the death penalty. Almost 60 House Democrats opposed to either the assault weapons ban or the death penalty provisions in the bill joined forces with all but 11 Republicans to keep the legislation from the House floor Aug. 11. As the legislation lay wounded, lawmakers became more vocal about other complaints—some long-standing, some newly articulated. Republicans had complained that the bill was larded with wasteful social programs that they said would do little to reduce crime, while stinting on some of the penalties advocated by GOP lawmakers. They pressed these and other complaints in the days following the Aug. 11 vote.

Democratic leaders defended the bill and complained that Republicans were simply seeking to deny Clinton and his party an important legislative success. Still, they had little choice but to negotiate. Although some House Democratic leaders advocated dropping the assault weapons ban to pick up support from Democrats opposed to gun control, Clinton insisted that the ban remain in the bill. That left key Democrats struggling to craft a package of modifications that could attract moderate Republican votes without jeopardizing any existing support within their own party.

Some Republicans also had ample incentive to find a solution. Several dozen GOP lawmakers had supported the crime bill and assault weapons ban in earlier House votes and did not want to be seen as killing the legislation. Some Republican leaders also were skittish about appearing obstructionist on an issue of such concern to voters.

After several days of tense, marathon negotiations, Democrats came up with a package that could pick up the needed extra votes from pro-gun control Republicans: cut $3.3 billion, most of it from crime prevention programs, and adjust certain penalties—agreeing, for example, to track convicted sex offenders after they were released from prison. House and Senate conferees convened shortly after 3 a.m. on Aug. 21 to adopt the changes. The new conference report went to the House floor later that day, where lawmakers voted 239–189 to take up the legislation. Forty-two Republicans were among those supporting the parliamentary motion. Shortly thereafter, the House approved the conference report, 235–195: R 46–131; D 188–64 (ND 141–31, SD 47–33); I 1–0.

Although the legislation went on to face last-minute difficulties in the Senate, the House vote was a major victory for its supporters and one that renewed momentum toward final passage. It was a flawed but vital victory for Clinton and his party as they headed into the fall elections, particularly with the Democrats' goal of health care reform all but abandoned for the year. (*Senate key vote 12*)

The vote also represented a watershed in Congress' crime fighting efforts, the legislation (PL 103–322) marked an unprecedented federal commitment on the issue of violent crime, which had been primarily a state and local responsibility, and some lawmakers predicted that Congress would find the responsibility hard to abandon in the future.

14. LOBBYING

Considered a certainty earlier in the year, passage of a bill (S 349) to overhaul lobbying disclosure requirements and ban lobbyist gifts to members was nearly derailed in the House on a procedural vote Sept. 29. But House Democratic leaders saved the measure—a key element of their agenda of political reform—by leaving the vote open for several minutes while they twisted arms and persuaded several pliable Democrats to switch their votes.

The closeness of the vote, however, presaged the bill's death at the hands of the Senate a week later. (*Senate key vote 14*)

The vote was on whether to adopt the rule (H Res 550) accompanying the conference report on the lobbying disclosure bill—in effect, a vote on whether to bring the bill up for a final vote. Sponsors knew that few members would have the temerity to vote down the lobbying bill, and risk being tagged as antireform, on the final vote. So the rule vote was the opponents' last chance to stop the bill in the House.

Ninety-three members who eventually voted for the bill tried to kill it by voting against the rule. Finally, the rule was approved 216–205 (R 5–170; D 210–35: ND 156–13, SD 54–22, I 1–0). Shortly afterward the conference report itself was approved 306–112.

The vote was close for several reasons. House Republican leaders, emboldened by their success at frustrating President Clinton and the Democrats on many fronts, tried to kill the bill on the procedural vote, even though many of them had voted for it when the House passed its first version of the bill 315–110 on March 24.

Some lawmakers from both parties privately disliked a provision in the bill that barred members from accepting most meals, gifts and entertainment from lobbyists. But the public debate centered on last-minute objections raised by GOP Whip Newt Gingrich of Georgia. He contended that the disclosure requirement on grass-roots organizations would force them to disclose contributors to grassroots efforts. He predicted that the Clinton administration would fill the directorship of the new office handling lobby registrations with a "secular, antireligious liberal" who could use his powers to squelch religious viewpoints.

The bill's House sponsor, John Bryant, D-Texas, countered that the bill would specifically exempt religious groups from disclosure requirements unless they hired lobbyists to conduct the campaign. Gingrich's arguments failed in the House, but they bore fruit in the Senate.

Democratic leaders not only had to contend with Republicans who wanted to deny them a legislative victory and with Democrats wanting to preserve privileges, they also had to woo normally loyal allies in the Congressional Black Caucus. Several members of the caucus decided to vote against the rule merely to remind Democratic leaders not to take their votes for granted. Caucus Chairman Kweisi Mfume, D-Md., switched his vote from no to yes in the waning moments of the vote. That helped save the bill from going down.

15. HAITI

Almost as soon as President Clinton dispatched thousands of troops to Haiti on Sept. 19, some lawmakers began discussing plans to bring them home. By the time the House took up a resolution (H J

Res 16) providing limited authorization for the deployment of troops until March 1, 1995, however, any momentum for setting a hard and fast deadline was gone. The administration, with the strong backing of senior military officers, had convinced Congress that setting a date certain for withdrawal could endanger American forces.

Republicans, who had been itching for an opportunity to debate Haiti policy, were determined to voice their objections. Minority Leader Robert H. Michel, R-Ill., and Benjamin A. Gilman, R-N.Y., offered a GOP alternative that blasted Clinton for dispatching troops to Haiti in the first place.

The amendment called for a pullout of U.S. forces from the Caribbean island "as soon as possible in a manner consistent with the safety of those forces." It provided expedited procedures for a vote to shut down the mission after the 104th Congress convened in January.

During the hours of debate on the amendment, Republicans went to the well to warn their colleagues that the administration was on the way toward becoming trapped in a "quagmire" in Haiti.

While the proposal would not have placed any binding restraints on the administration, it clearly had the potential to embarrass Clinton. Democrats, overcoming their own uneasiness with the operation, rallied behind the president. The Michel-Gilman amendment was rejected 205–225 in a vote that divided largely along partisan lines: R 173 1; D 32–223 (ND 21–153, SD 11–70); I 0–1.

After the House defeated the Michel-Gilman amendment, it adopted a far milder substitute that did little more than require detailed reports from the president on the Haiti operation. It chided the president for failing to seek congressional assent before dispatching U.S. forces, but it included no withdrawal deadline. *(Senate key vote 9)*

The vote on that amendment, which was offered by an unlikely alliance of pro-Pentagon lawmakers and liberal members of the Congressional Black Caucus, was 258–167.

16. GATT

Acting in a rare lame-duck session, the House on Nov. 29 and the Senate on Dec. 1 gave President Clinton a big legislative victory by passing the bill (HR 5110—PL 103–465) to implement the Uruguay Round pact strengthening the General Agreement on Tariffs and Trade (GATT).

The GATT victory reaffirmed trade policy as the strong suit of Clinton's agenda in the 103rd Congress. It came almost exactly one year after the enactment of the North American Free Trade Agreement (NAFTA) linking the United States, Canada and Mexico.

However, the GATT victory came nearly a month too late to give the election-year political boost that Clinton had hoped the bill could provide for himself and his beleaguered fellow Democrats, who lost control of both chambers of Congress with the Nov. 8 elections.

The trade pact sharply reduced tariffs and trade barriers around the world and brought such key industries as intellectual property, agriculture and services under worldwide trade disciplines.

The administration promised it would result in billions of dollars in economic growth and thousands of new jobs for the United States.

The same coalition of organized labor, environmentalists, political populists and "America First" conservatives who spearheaded the emotional fight against NAFTA tried again on GATT. They failed to arouse much interest. But the administration and congressional GATT supporters took several months to fine-tune the implementing bill, giving opponents an opportunity to delay action.

The president finally submitted the bill to Congress on Sept. 27, under rules that gave each committee chairman with jurisdiction up to 45 days to review the bill. Sen. Ernest F. Hollings, D-S.C., who insisted that free-trade policies had damaged the U.S. economy, demanded his 45 days, forcing the Senate leadership to schedule a two-day lame-duck session beginning Nov. 30.

Clinton asked for the House to press on and approve the bill before its October adjournment. Many members of both parties expressed anxiety about taking a stand on the complex legislation before the election, and Minority Whip Newt Gingrich, R-Ga., warned that he could not promise sufficient Republican votes to guarantee passage of the bill.

The Democratic House leadership therefore delayed consideration of the legislation until the one-day session Nov. 29. The House returned on that date for a debate that was tepid compared with the previous one on NAFTA. Even the opponents recognized that supporters had more than enough votes to pass HR 5110 and reserved their stronger efforts for the Senate, where the bill first had to clear a key procedural hurdle.

Voting under fast-track procedures for trade legislation, which allowed only for an up-or-down vote with no amendments, the House passed the GATT bill 288–146: R 121–56; D 167–89 (ND 107–66, SD 60–23); I 0–1. GATT supporters hailed the outcome as a sign that Clinton would find room for bipartisan cooperation with the incoming Republican majority. *(Senate key vote 16)*

1. S 1281. Fiscal 1994–1995 State Department Authorization/Relations with Vietnam. Kerry, D-Mass., amendment to express the sense of the Senate that in order to expand and maintain Vietnamese cooperation in resolving POW/MIA cases, the president should lift the U.S. trade embargo against Vietnam. Adopted 62–38: R 20–24; D 42–14 (ND 31–11, SD 11–3), Jan. 27, 1994.

2. HR 1804. Goals 2000: Educate America/Passage. Passage of the bill to authorize $422 million for competitive grants for schools seeking to improve their performance, write into law six national education goals and establish tests and standards for elementary and secondary students. Passed 71–25: R 17–25; D 54–0 (ND 41–0, SD 13–0), Feb. 8, 1994. (Before passage the Senate struck all after the enacting clause and inserted the text of S 1150 as amended.) A "yea" was a vote in support of the president's position.

3. HR 3759. Fiscal 1994 Disaster Supplemental Appropriations/Rescissions. Byrd, D-W.Va., motion to table (kill) the Kerrey, D-Neb., amendment to rescind $94 billion over five years from 54 programs. Motion agreed to 65–31: R 23–19; D 42–12 (ND 31–9, SD 11–3), Feb. 9, 1994. (The motion also killed a Hatfield, R-Ore., amendment to the Kerrey amendment, with $18.6 billion in defense rescissions.) A "yea" was a vote in support of the president's position.

4. S J Res 41. Balanced-Budget Amendment/Passage. Passage of the joint resolution to propose a constitutional amendment to require a balanced budget by 2001 or the second fiscal year after ratification by three-fourths of the states, whichever is later. Congress could waive the balanced-budget requirement if three-fifths of the House and Senate approved deficit spending, or by a simple majority when a declaration of war was in effect or when there was a threat to national security. The amendment would prohibit the courts from ordering tax increases or spending cuts unless specifically authorized by Congress. Rejected 63–37: R 41–3; D 22–34 (ND 12–30, SD 10–4), March 1, 1994. A two-thirds majority vote (67 in this case) is required to pass a joint resolution proposing an amendment to the Constitution. A "nay" was a vote in support of the president's position.

5. S 636. Abortion Clinic Access/Conference Report. Adoption of the conference report to establish federal criminal and civil penalties for people who use force, the threat of force or physical obstruction to block access to abortion clinics. Adopted (thus cleared for the president) 69–30: R 17–27; D 52–3 (ND 41–1, SD 11–2), May 12, 1994. A "yea" was a vote in support of the president's position.

6. H Con Res 218. Fiscal 1995 Budget Resolution/Conference Report. Adoption of the conference report to set budget levels for the fiscal year ending Sept. 30, 1995: budget authority, $1.541 trillion; outlays, $1.514 trillion; revenues, $1.338 trillion; and a deficit of $175.4 billion. The resolution calls for an additional $13 billion in cuts over five years below the spending caps established last year. Adopted (thus cleared) 53–46: R 2–42; D 51–4 (ND 39–3, SD 12–1), May 12, 1994.

7. S 2019. Safe Drinking Water Act Reauthorization/Risk Assessment. Johnston, D-La., amendment to require an analysis of risk, costs and benefits for regulations issued by the Environmental Protection Agency to enforce the bill that would have an impact of $100 million or more. Adopted 90–8: R 41–3; D 49–5 (ND 36–5, SD 13–0), May 18, 1994.

8. S 687. Product Liability Reform/Cloture. Motion to invoke cloture (thus limiting debate) on the bill to set standards for awarding punitive damages, encourage out-of-court settlements, bar product liability claims against most product sellers, set time limits for such lawsuits, end joint liability for noneconomic damages and hold injured parties responsible for their use of alcohol or drugs. Motion rejected 57–41: R 38–6; D 19–35 (ND 13–27, SD 6–8), June 29, 1994. Three-fifths of the total Senate (60) is required to invoke cloture.

9. HR 4426. Fiscal 1995 Foreign Operations Appropriations/Congressional Approval for Action in Haiti. Gregg, R-N.H., amendment to prohibit military action in Haiti unless the operations are authorized in advance by Congress or the action is necessary to protect U.S. citizens or national security interests. A "nay" was a vote in support of the president's position. Rejected 34–65: R 34–10; D 0–55 (ND 0–41, SD 0–14), June 29, 1994.

10. S 2182. Fiscal 1995 Defense Authorization/Unilateral Termination. Dole, R-Kan., amendment to require the president to terminate the U.S. arms embargo of Bosnia-Herzegovina upon receipt from that government of a request for assistance in its right of self-defense. Rejected 50–50: R 37–7; D 13–43 (ND 11–31, SD 2–12), July 1, 1994. A "nay" was a vote in support of the president's position.

11. HR 4624. Fiscal 1995 VA-HUD Appropriations/Ethanol Mandate. Mikulski, D-Md., motion to table (kill) the Johnston, D-La., amendment to prohibit the Environmental Protection Agency from implementing its renewable oxygenates rule for reformulated gasoline, which would require a minimum of 15 percent and eventually 30 percent of the oxygenates used in reformulated gasoline to come from renewable sources, such as ethanol. The amendment also would have cut NASA's procurement budget by $39.3 million. Motion agreed to 51–50: R 19–25; D 31–25 (ND 26–16, SD 5–9), Aug. 3, 1994, with Vice President Gore casting a "yea" vote, Aug. 3, 1994. A "yea" was a vote in support of the president's position.

12. HR 3355. Omnibus Crime Bill/Budget Act Waiver. Mitchell, D-Maine, motion to waive the budget act with respect to the Domenici, R-N.M., point of order against the crime conference report for violating Section 306 of the 1974 Congressional Budget Act and encroaching on the Budget Committee's jurisdiction by establishing a trust fund not considered by the committee. The conference report would authorize $30.2 billion over six years and require that all spending authorized by the bill come from a crime trust fund realized from eliminating 270,000 federal jobs. The bill would authorize $6.9 billion for crime prevention programs, $8.8 billion for community policing programs and the hiring of 100,000 new police officers, and a $7.9 billion grant program to build state and local prisons. The bill also would ban 19 specific assault weapons, expand the death penalty to dozens of new federal crimes, mandate life imprisonment without parole for three-time violent felons, provide for community notification of violent sex offenders, and allow prior sex offenses to be admitted in federal trials. Motion agreed to 61–39: R 6–38; D 55–1 (ND 42–0, SD 13–1), Aug. 25, 1994. A three-fifths majority vote (60) of the total Senate is required to waive the budget act. (Subsequently, the point of order fell.) A "yea" was a vote in support of the president's position.

13. S 3. Campaign Finance/Cloture. Motion to invoke cloture (thus limiting debate) on the motion to request a conference with the House on the bill to establish a system for voluntary spending caps on congressional campaigns. Motion rejected 52–46: R 2–40; D 50–6 (ND 40–2, SD 10–4), Sept. 30, 1994. Three-fifths of the total Senate (60) is required to invoke cloture. A "yea" was a vote in support of the president's position.

14. S 349. Lobbying Disclosure/Cloture. Motion to invoke cloture (thus limiting debate) on the conference report to expand the disclosure of lobbying activities and impose new restrictions on gifts to members of Congress and their staffs. Motion rejected 52–46: R 7–36; D 45–10 (ND 38–4, SD 7–6), Oct. 6, 1994. Because the bill would change Senate rules, two-thirds of those present and voting (66 in this case) is required to invoke cloture.

15. S 21. California Desert Protection/Cloture. Motion to invoke cloture (thus limiting debate) on the conference report to designate about 7.5 million acres of California desert as wilderness and to establish the Death Valley and Joshua Tree national parks and the Mojave National Preserve. Motion agreed to 68–23: R 14–23; D 54–0 (ND 41–0, SD 13–0), Oct. 8, 1994. Three-fifths of the total Senate (60) is required to invoke cloture. A "yea" was a vote in support of the president's position.

16. HR 5110. General Agreement on Tariffs and Trade/Budget Waiver. Moynihan, D-N.Y., motion to waive the budget act with respect to the Byrd, D-W.Va., point of order against the bill to implement the General Agreement on Tariffs and Trade (GATT) for violating the budget act. The bill would make statutory changes to implement the new world trade agreement negotiated under the Uruguay Round of GATT. Motion agreed to 68–32: R 31–15; D 37–17 (ND 29–13, SD 8–4), Dec. 1, 1994. A three-fifths majority vote (60) of the total Senate is required to waive the budget act. (Subsequently, the budget act was waived and the point of order fell.) A "yea" was a vote in support of the president's position.

---

[a] Richard C. Shelby, Ala., switched to the Republican Party on Nov. 9, 1994. He voted as a Republican on key vote 16.

[b] David L. Boren, D-Okla., resigned Nov. 15, 1994. He voted on all key votes through vote 15. James M. Inhofe, R-Okla., was sworn in on Nov. 17, 1994, replacing Boren. He voted on key vote 16.

KEY			
		Democrats	*Republicans*
Y	Voted for ("yea")		– Announced against
N	Voted against ("nay")		P Voted "present"
+	Announced for		C Voted "present" to avoid possible conflict of interest
#	Paired for		? Did not vote or otherwise
X	Paired against		make a position known

ND Northern Democrats
SD Southern Democrats
Southern states – Ala., Ark., Fla., Ga., Ky., La., Miss., N.C., Okla., S.C., Tenn., Texas, Va

Senate Key Votes	1	2	3	4	5	6	7	8	9	10	11	12	13	14	15	16
ALABAMA																
Heflin	N	Y	Y	Y	Y	Y	Y	N	N	N	N	Y	N	N	Y	N
Shelby[a]	N	Y	Y	Y	?	?	?	N	N	Y	N	N	N	N	Y	N
ALASKA																
Murkowski	Y	N	N	Y	N	N	Y	Y	Y	Y	N	N	N	?		N
Stevens	Y	Y	Y	N	Y	N	Y	Y	Y	Y	N	N	N	?	?	N
ARIZONA																
DeConcini	N	Y	N	Y	Y	Y	Y	#	N	Y	Y	Y	Y	Y	Y	Y
McCain	Y	N	N	Y	N	N	Y	Y	N	Y	N	N	N	N	N	Y
ARKANSAS																
Bumpers	Y	Y	Y	N	Y	Y	Y	N	N	N	Y	Y	Y	Y	Y	N
Pryor	Y	Y	Y	N	Y	Y	Y	Y	N	N	Y	Y	Y	Y	Y	Y
CALIFORNIA																
Boxer	Y	Y	Y	N	Y	Y	N	N	N	Y	N	Y	Y	Y	Y	Y
Feinstein	Y	Y	Y	Y	Y	Y	Y	N	N	N	N	Y	Y	Y	Y	Y
COLORADO																
Campbell	N	Y	Y	Y	Y	Y	Y	N	N	N	Y	Y	N	N	Y	N
Brown	N	N	N	Y	Y	N	Y	Y	Y	Y	N	N	N	Y	N	N
CONNECTICUT																
Dodd	Y	Y	Y	N	Y	Y	Y	N	N	N	Y	Y	Y	Y	Y	Y
Lieberman	Y	Y	N	Y	Y	Y	Y	Y	N	N	Y	N	Y	Y	Y	Y
DELAWARE																
Biden	Y	Y	Y	N	Y	Y	Y	N	N	N	Y	Y	Y	Y	Y	Y
Roth	N	Y	Y	Y	Y	N	N	N	Y	Y	N	Y	N	Y	Y	Y
FLORIDA																
Graham	Y	Y	N	Y	Y	Y	Y	N	N	N	N	Y	Y	Y	Y	Y
Mack	N	N	N	Y	N	N	Y	Y	N	Y	N	N	N	N	N	Y
GEORGIA																
Nunn	Y	Y	Y	Y	Y	N	Y	Y	N	N	Y	Y	Y	N	Y	Y
Coverdell	N	N	N	Y	N	N	Y	Y	Y	Y	N	N	N	N	N	Y
HAWAII																
Akaka	Y	Y	Y	N	Y	Y	Y	N	N	N	Y	Y	Y	Y	Y	Y
Inouye	Y	Y	Y	N	Y	Y	Y	N	N	N	Y	Y	Y	Y	Y	N
IDAHO																
Craig	N	N	N	Y	N	N	Y	Y	Y	Y	N	N	N	N	N	N
Kempthorne	N	N	N	Y	N	N	Y	Y	Y	Y	Y	N	N	N	N	N
ILLINOIS																
Moseley-Braun	N	+	Y	Y	Y	Y	Y	N	N	N	Y	Y	Y	Y	Y	Y
Simon	Y	Y	N	Y	Y	Y	Y	N	N	N	Y	Y	Y	Y	Y	Y
INDIANA																
Coats	N	N	Y	Y	N	N	Y	Y	Y	Y	N	N	N	N	N	Y
Lugar	N	N	Y	Y	N	N	Y	Y	Y	Y	N	N	N	N	N	Y
IOWA																
Harkin	Y	Y	Y	N	Y	Y	Y	N	N	N	Y	Y	Y	Y	Y	N
Grassley	N	N	N	Y	N	N	Y	Y	Y	Y	Y	N	N	N	N	Y
KANSAS																
Dole	N	N	Y	Y	N	N	Y	Y	Y	Y	Y	N	N	N	N	N
Kassebaum	Y	Y	N	N	Y	N	Y	Y	N	Y	Y	N	N	N	Y	N
KENTUCKY																
Ford	Y	Y	Y	N	Y	Y	Y	N	N	N	Y	Y	Y	Y	Y	N
McConnell	Y	N	Y	Y	Y	N	Y	Y	Y	Y	Y	N	N	N	?	Y
LOUISIANA																
Breaux	Y	Y	Y	N	Y	N	Y	N	N	N	N	Y	Y	N	Y	Y
Johnston	Y	?	Y	N	N	Y	N	N	N	N	N	Y	N	Y	Y	Y
MAINE																
Mitchell	Y	Y	Y	N	Y	Y	Y	N	N	N	N	Y	Y	Y	Y	Y
Cohen	Y	Y	N	Y	Y	Y	Y	N	N	Y	N	N	N	Y	Y	Y
MARYLAND																
Mikulski	Y	Y	+	N	Y	Y	Y	Y	N	N	N	Y	Y	Y	Y	Y
Sarbanes	Y	Y	Y	N	Y	Y	Y	N	N	N	Y	Y	Y	Y	Y	Y
MASSACHUSETTS																
Kennedy	Y	Y	Y	N	Y	Y	Y	N	N	N	N	Y	Y	Y	Y	Y
Kerry	Y	Y	Y	N	Y	N	Y	N	N	N	N	Y	Y	Y	Y	Y
MICHIGAN																
Levin	Y	Y	Y	N	Y	Y	Y	N	N	N	Y	Y	Y	Y	Y	Y
Riegle	N	Y	Y	N	Y	Y	?	N	N	N	Y	Y	Y	Y	Y	Y
MINNESOTA																
Wellstone	N	Y	Y	N	Y	Y	N	N	N	N	Y	Y	Y	Y	Y	N
Durenberger	N	Y	N	Y	Y	N	Y	N	Y	N	Y	N	N	N	Y	Y
MISSISSIPPI																
Cochran	Y	Y	Y	Y	N	Y	N	Y	Y	Y	Y	N	N	N	N	Y
Lott	N	N	Y	Y	N	N	Y	Y	Y	Y	N	N	N	N	N	Y
MISSOURI																
Bond	Y	Y	Y	Y	Y	N	Y	Y	Y	Y	Y	N	N	N	?	Y
Danforth	Y	Y	N	Y	Y	Y	N	Y	N	N	Y	Y	N	N	N	Y
MONTANA																
Baucus	Y	Y	N	N	Y	Y	Y	N	N	N	Y	Y	Y	Y	Y	N
Burns	N	N	Y	Y	N	N	Y	Y	N	N	Y	N	N	N	?	N
NEBRASKA																
Exon	Y	Y	N	N	Y	N	Y	Y	N	N	Y	Y	Y	Y	Y	N
Kerrey	Y	Y	N	N	Y	Y	Y	N	N	N	Y	Y	N	Y	Y	Y
NEVADA																
Bryan	Y	Y	Y	Y	Y	Y	N	N	?	N	Y	Y	Y	Y	Y	N
Reid	Y	Y	Y	N	Y	Y	Y	N	N	N	Y	Y	Y	Y	Y	N
NEW HAMPSHIRE																
Gregg	N	N	Y	N	N	Y	Y	Y	N	N	N	N	N	N	Y	Y
Smith	N	N	Y	N	N	Y	Y	Y	N	N	N	N	N	N	Y	Y
NEW JERSEY																
Bradley	Y	Y	?	N	Y	N	Y	N	N	N	Y	N	Y	Y	Y	?
Lautenberg	N	Y	N	N	Y	N	Y	N	N	Y	N	Y	Y	Y	Y	Y
NEW MEXICO																
Bingaman	Y	Y	Y	Y	Y	Y	N	N	N	N	Y	Y	N	Y	N	Y
Domenici	N	Y	Y	Y	Y	N	Y	Y	Y	Y	N	N	N	N	N	Y
NEW YORK																
Moynihan	Y	Y	Y	N	Y	Y	Y	N	N	N	Y	Y	Y	Y	Y	Y
D'Amato	N	N	Y	Y	N	N	Y	N	Y	N	N	N	N	N	N	Y
NORTH CAROLINA																
Faircloth	N	N	N	Y	N	N	Y	Y	Y	Y	N	N	N	N	N	N
Helms	N	N	Y	Y	N	N	Y	Y	Y	Y	Y	N	N	N	-	N
NORTH DAKOTA																
Conrad	N	Y	Y	N	Y	Y	Y	Y	N	N	Y	Y	Y	N	Y	Y
Dorgan	N	Y	Y	Y	Y	Y	Y	Y	N	N	Y	Y	Y	Y	Y	N
OHIO																
Glenn	Y	Y	Y	N	Y	Y	Y	N	N	N	Y	Y	Y	Y	Y	Y
Metzenbaum	Y	Y	Y	N	Y	Y	N	X	N	N	Y	Y	Y	Y	Y	N
OKLAHOMA																
Boren/Inhofe[b]	Y	Y	N	Y	Y	Y	Y	N	N	N	Y	Y	Y	Y	Y	N
Nickles	Y	N	N	Y	N	N	Y	Y	Y	Y	N	N	?	N	N	Y
OREGON																
Hatfield	Y	Y	Y	N	Y	Y	Y	Y	N	Y	N	N	N	Y	Y	Y
Packwood	Y	Y	N	Y	Y	N	Y	Y	Y	Y	Y	N	N	N	?	Y
PENNSYLVANIA																
Wofford	N	Y	Y	Y	Y	Y	Y	N	N	N	Y	Y	Y	Y	Y	Y
Specter	N	Y	N	Y	Y	N	Y	Y	Y	Y	N	Y	N	Y	Y	Y
RHODE ISLAND																
Pell	Y	Y	Y	N	Y	Y	Y	N	N	N	N	Y	Y	Y	Y	Y
Chafee	Y	Y	N	Y	Y	N	Y	N	N	N	Y	Y	Y	Y	Y	Y
SOUTH CAROLINA																
Hollings	Y	Y	Y	Y	Y	Y	Y	N	N	N	Y	Y	Y	N	?	N
Thurmond	N	Y	Y	Y	N	N	Y	Y	Y	Y	Y	N	N	N	N	N
SOUTH DAKOTA																
Daschle	Y	Y	Y	Y	Y	Y	Y	Y	N	N	Y	Y	Y	Y	Y	Y
Pressler	Y	N	Y	Y	N	N	Y	N	Y	Y	Y	N	N	N	N	N
TENNESSEE																
Mathews	Y	Y	Y	N	Y	Y	Y	Y	N	N	Y	Y	Y	Y	Y	N
Sasser	N	Y	Y	Y	Y	Y	Y	N	N	N	Y	Y	?	Y	Y	Y
TEXAS																
Gramm	N	-	?	Y	N	Y	Y	N	Y	N	N	N	N	N	N	Y
Hutchison	N	?	?	Y	Y	N	Y	Y	Y	Y	N	N	N	N	N	Y
UTAH																
Bennett	Y	N	Y	Y	N	N	Y	Y	Y	Y	N	N	?	N	N	Y
Hatch	N	N	N	Y	N	N	Y	Y	Y	Y	N	N	N	N	N	Y
VERMONT																
Leahy	Y	Y	Y	N	Y	Y	Y	N	N	N	Y	Y	Y	Y	Y	N
Jeffords	Y	Y	Y	Y	Y	Y	N	Y	N	N	Y	Y	Y	Y	Y	N
VIRGINIA																
Robb	Y	Y	N	Y	Y	Y	Y	N	N	N	Y	N	Y	Y	Y	Y
Warner	Y	N	Y	Y	N	N	Y	Y	N	N	N	N	N	N	Y	Y
WASHINGTON																
Murray	Y	Y	Y	N	Y	Y	Y	N	N	N	Y	Y	Y	Y	Y	Y
Gorton	Y	Y	Y	Y	Y	N	Y	Y	Y	Y	Y	N	N	N	N	Y
WEST VIRGINIA																
Byrd	N	Y	Y	N	Y	Y	Y	N	N	N	Y	Y	N	Y	N	Y
Rockefeller	Y	Y	Y	N	Y	Y	Y	N	N	N	Y	Y	Y	Y	Y	Y
WISCONSIN																
Feingold	N	Y	N	N	Y	Y	N	N	N	N	Y	Y	Y	Y	Y	N
Kohl	Y	Y	Y	N	Y	Y	Y	N	N	N	Y	Y	Y	Y	Y	Y
WYOMING																
Simpson	Y	Y	N	Y	Y	N	Y	N	Y	N	N	N	N	N	N	Y
Wallop	Y	N	Y	Y	N	N	Y	Y	Y	Y	N	N	N	N	N	N

1. HR 3425. Department of Environmental Protection/Rule. Adoption of the rule (H Res 312) to provide for House floor consideration of the bill to elevate the Environmental Protection Agency to cabinet-level status. Rejected 191–227: R 5–167; D 185–60 (ND 140–28, SD 45–32); I 1–0, Feb. 2, 1994.

2. H Con Res 218. Fiscal 1995 Budget Resolution/Defense Cuts. Frank, D-Mass., substitute amendment to reduce the $263.3 billion in defense budget authority in the resolution by $2.4 billion. Rejected in the Committee of the Whole 105–313: R 12–160; D 92–153 (ND 82–85, SD 10–68); I 1–0, March 10, 1994. A "nay" was a vote in support of the president's position.

3. H J Res 103. Balanced-Budget Constitutional Amendment/Passage. Passage of the joint resolution to propose a constitutional amendment to require a balanced budget by 2001 or the second fiscal year after ratification by three-fourths of the states, whichever is later. Congress could waive the balanced-budget requirement if three-fifths of the House and Senate approve, or when a declaration of war was in effect or when there was a declared military threat to national security. Rejected 271–153: R 172–1; D 99–151 (ND 47–122, SD 52–29); I 0–1, March 17, 1994. A two-thirds majority vote of those present and voting (283 in this case) is required to pass a joint resolution proposing an amendment to the Constitution. A "nay" was a vote in support of the president's position.

4. H Con Res 218. Fiscal 1995 Budget Resolution/Instruct Conferees. Kasich, R-Ohio, motion to instruct the House conferees to agree to the Senate amendment to provide an additional $26.1 billion in deficit reduction over the next five years and to protect defense spending from further cuts. Motion rejected 202–216: R 159–6; D 43–209 (ND 29–141, SD 14–68); I 0–1, April 14, 1994. A "nay" was a vote in support of the president's position.

5. HR 4296. Assault Weapons Ban/Passage. Passage of the bill to ban the manufacture and possession of 19 types of semiautomatic weapons and high-capacity ammunition clips but exempt existing guns and about 670 guns that are deemed to have a legitimate sporting purpose. Passed 216–214: R 38–137; D 177–77 (ND 137–34, SD 40–43); I 1–0, May 5, 1994. A "yea" was a vote in support of the president's position.

6. S 636. Abortion Clinic Access/Conference Report. Adoption of the conference report to establish federal criminal and civil penalties for persons who use force, the threat of force or physical obstruction to block access to abortion clinics. Adopted 241–174: R 40–131; D 200–43 (ND 139–26, SD 61–17); I 1–0, May 5, 1994. A "yea" was a vote in support of the president's position.

7. HR 4301. Fiscal 1995 Defense Authorization/Bosnia Arms Embargo Unilateral Termination. McCloskey, D-Ind., amendment to require the president to terminate unilaterally the arms embargo of Bosnia-Herzegovina upon receipt from that government of a request for assistance in its right of self-defense, authorizing the president to provide up to $200 million in defense articles and services. Adopted in the Committee of the Whole 244–178: R 127–45; D 117–132 (ND 84–87, SD 33–45); I 0–1, June 9, 1994. A "nay" was a vote in support of the president's position.

8. HR 3626. Revising Restrictions on the Regional Bell Companies/Passage. Brooks, D-Texas, motion to suspend the rules and pass the bill to set conditions for the regional Bell telephone companies to enter the long-distance, telecommunications manufacturing, alarm service and electronic publishing markets. Motion agreed to 423–5: R 173–1; D 249–4 (ND 168–3, SD 81–1); I 1–0, June 28, 1994. A two-thirds majority of those present and voting (286 in this case) is required for passage under suspension of the rules. A "yea" was a vote in support of the president's position.

9. HR 4624. Fiscal 1995 VA, HUD Appropriations/Space Station. Roemer, D-Ind., amendment to terminate the space station and reallocate the $2.1 billion to other NASA programs. Rejected in the Committee of the Whole 155–278: R 40–136; D 114–142 (ND 101–72, SD 13–70); I 1–0, June 29, 1994. A "nay" was a vote in support of the president's position.

10. HR 518. California Desert Protection/Hunting Exception. LaRocco, D-Idaho, en bloc amendment to designate the East Mojave Scenic Area a national preserve rather than a national park, thus permitting hunting, fishing and trapping to continue in the area. Adopted in the Committee of the Whole 239–183: R 146–26; D 92–157 (ND 39–131, SD 53–26); I 1–0, July 12, 1994.

11. HR 4604. Entitlement Spending Control/Stenholm Substitute. Stenholm, D-Texas, substitute amendment to set caps on all entitlement spending (including Social Security) for fiscal 1996–2000 that would result in some $150 billion in cuts below current projections; require automatic cuts in all programs (including Social Security) if Congress failed to pass reconciliation legislation to prevent spending from exceeding the caps; and prohibit the use of tax increases or cuts in discretionary spending to offset excess entitlement spending. Rejected in the Committee of the Whole 37–392: R 9–165; D 28–226 (ND 15–157, SD 13–69); I 0–1, July 21, 1994.

12. HR 3355. Omnibus Crime Bill/Rule. Adoption of the rule (H Res 517) to waive points of order against and provide for House floor consideration of the $33 billion crime conference report to help hire 100,000 new police officers through an $8.8 billion community policing program, build state and local prisons through an $8.7 billion state grant program, provide $7.6 billion for crime prevention programs such as after-school sports leagues and job training programs, create a crime trust fund directing $30.2 billion over six years to combat crime, ban 19 specific assault weapons and expand the death penalty to dozens of federal crimes. Rejected 210–225: R 11–167; D 198–58 (ND 148–25, SD 50–33); I 1–0, Aug. 11, 1994. A "yea" was a vote in support of the president's position.

13. HR 3355. Omnibus Crime Bill/Conference Report. Adoption of the conference report to authorize $30.2 billion over six years and to require that all spending authorized by the bill come from a six-year, $30.2 billion crime trust fund realized from eliminating 270,000 federal jobs. The bill would authorize $6.9 billion for crime prevention programs, such as after-school sports leagues and job training programs, $8.8 billion for community policing programs and the hiring of 100,000 new police officers, and a $7.9 billion grant program to build state and local prisons. The bill also would ban 19 specific assault weapons, expand the death penalty to dozens of new federal crimes, mandate life imprisonment without parole for three-time violent felons, provide for community notification of violent sex offenders, allow prior sex offenses to be admitted in federal trials and require HIV testing when requested in federal rape trials. Adopted (thus sent to the Senate) 235–195: R 46–131; D 188–64 (ND 141–31, SD 47–33); I 1–0, Aug. 21, 1994. A "yea" was a vote in support of the president's position.

14. S 349. Lobbying Disclosure/Rule. Adoption of the rule (H Res 550) to provide for House floor consideration of the conference report to expand the disclosure of lobbying activities and impose new restrictions on gifts to members of Congress and their staffs. Adopted 216–205: R 5–170; D 210–35 (ND 156–13, SD 54–22); I 1–0, Sept. 29, 1994.

15. H J Res 416. U.S. Troops in Haiti/Immediate Withdrawal. Gilman, R-N.Y., substitute amendment to express the sense of Congress that the president should not have ordered U.S. troops to occupy Haiti and that the president should immediately commence "the safe and orderly withdrawal" of all U.S. forces from Haiti. The substitute also would provide for consideration of a joint resolution to be introduced Jan. 3, 1995, that if enacted would prohibit the continued use of U.S. troops in Haiti within 30 days. Rejected in the Committee of the Whole 205–225: R 173–1; D 32–223 (ND 21–153, SD 11–70); I 0–1, Oct. 6, 1994. A "nay" was a vote in support of the president's position.

16. HR 5110. General Agreement on Tariffs and Trade/Passage. Passage of the bill to make statutory changes to implement the new world trade agreement negotiated under the Uruguay Round of the General Agreement on Tariffs and Trade (GATT). The agreement would reduce tariffs and trade barriers, ensure stricter enforcement of world trade rules through the newly established World Trade Organization, and expand GATT rules to cover such economic sectors as agriculture, services and intellectual property. The bill also would accelerate tax payment schedules, change eligibility standards for certain federal programs, and make other changes to offset lost revenues from tariff reductions in order to comply with pay-as-you-go budget rules. Passed 288–146: R 121–56; D 167–89 (ND 107–66, SD 60–23); I 0–1, Nov. 29, 1994. A "yea" was a vote in support of the president's position.

KEY

Democrats — *Republicans* — **Independent**

- Y Voted for ("yea")
- N Voted against ("nay")
- \+ Announced for
- # Paired for
- X Paired against
- – Announced against
- P Voted "present"
- C Voted "present" to avoid possible conflict of interest
- ? Did not vote or otherwise make a position known

ND Northern Democrats
SD Southern Democrats
Southern states – Ala., Ark., Fla., Ga., Ky., La., Miss., N.C., Okla., S.C., Tenn., Texas, Va.

House Key Votes	1	2	3	4	5	6	7	8	9	10	11	12	13	14	15	16
ALABAMA																
1 *Callahan*	N	N	Y	Y	N	N	Y	Y	N	Y	N	N	?	N	Y	Y
2 *Everett*	N	N	Y	Y	N	N	Y	Y	N	Y	N	N	N	N	Y	N
3 Browder	N	N	Y	Y	N	N	N	Y	N	Y	Y	N	Y	Y	N	N
4 Bevill	Y	N	Y	N	N	?	N	Y	N	Y	N	Y	N	Y	N	Y
5 Cramer	N	N	Y	N	N	Y	N	Y	N	Y	N	Y	Y	Y	N	N
6 *Bachus*	N	N	Y	Y	N	N	N	Y	N	Y	N	N	N	N	Y	N
7 Hilliard	Y	N	N	N	N	Y	N	?	N	Y	N	N	N	Y	N	N
ALASKA																
AL *Young*	N	N	Y	Y	N	N	Y	Y	N	Y	N	N	N	N	Y	N
ARIZONA																
1 Coppersmith	Y	N	Y	Y	Y	Y	Y	Y	Y	N	N	Y	Y	Y	Y	Y
2 Pastor	Y	N	N	N	Y	Y	Y	Y	N	N	N	Y	Y	Y	N	Y
3 *Stump*	N	N	Y	Y	N	N	Y	Y	N	Y	N	N	N	N	Y	N
4 *Kyl*	N	N	Y	Y	N	N	Y	Y	N	Y	N	N	Y	N	Y	Y
5 *Kolbe*	N	N	Y	Y	N	Y	Y	Y	Y	Y	N	N	Y	N	Y	Y
6 English	Y	Y	Y	Y	Y	Y	Y	Y	Y	N	N	Y	Y	Y	N	Y
ARKANSAS																
1 Lambert	Y	Y	Y	Y	Y	Y	Y	Y	Y	Y	Y	Y	Y	Y	Y	Y
2 Thornton	Y	N	N	N	N	Y	N	Y	N	Y	N	Y	Y	Y	N	Y
3 *Hutchinson*	N	N	Y	Y	N	N	Y	Y	Y	Y	N	N	N	N	Y	N
4 *Dickey*	N	N	Y	Y	N	N	Y	Y	N	Y	N	N	N	N	N	N
CALIFORNIA																
1 Hamburg	Y	Y	N	N	Y	Y	N	Y	Y	N	N	Y	Y	Y	N	N
2 *Herger*	N	N	Y	Y	N	?	N	Y	Y	?	N	N	N	N	Y	Y
3 Fazio	Y	N	N	N	Y	Y	Y	Y	N	N	N	Y	Y	Y	N	Y
4 *Doolittle*	N	N	Y	?	N	X	Y	Y	N	Y	N	N	N	N	Y	N
5 Matsui	Y	N	N	N	Y	Y	N	Y	N	N	N	Y	Y	Y	N	Y
6 Woolsey	Y	Y	N	N	Y	Y	N	Y	Y	N	N	Y	Y	Y	N	N
7 Miller	Y	?	N	N	Y	Y	N	Y	Y	N	N	Y	Y	Y	N	N
8 Pelosi	Y	?	N	N	Y	Y	N	Y	Y	N	N	Y	Y	Y	N	Y
9 Dellums	Y	Y	N	N	Y	Y	N	Y	Y	N	N	Y	N	Y	N	N
10 *Baker*	N	N	Y	Y	N	N	N	Y	N	Y	N	N	N	N	Y	Y
11 *Pombo*	N	N	Y	Y	N	N	Y	?	N	Y	N	N	N	N	Y	N
12 Lantos	Y	N	Y	N	Y	Y	Y	Y	N	N	N	Y	Y	Y	N	N
13 Stark	Y	Y	N	N	Y	#	N	Y	Y	N	N	Y	Y	Y	N	N
14 Eshoo	Y	Y	N	N	Y	Y	N	Y	N	N	N	Y	Y	Y	N	Y
15 Mineta	Y	N	N	N	Y	Y	N	Y	N	N	N	Y	Y	Y	N	Y
16 Edwards	Y	?	N	N	Y	Y	N	Y	N	N	N	Y	Y	Y	N	N
17 Farr	Y	Y	?	N	Y	Y	N	Y	N	N	N	Y	Y	Y	N	Y
18 Condit	N	N	Y	Y	Y	Y	N	Y	Y	Y	N	Y	Y	N	Y	N
19 Lehman	X	N	N	Y	Y	Y	N	Y	Y	N	N	Y	Y	N	N	Y
20 Dooley	N	?	Y	Y	Y	Y	Y	Y	N	N	Y	Y	Y	N	N	Y
21 *Thomas*	N	N	Y	?	N	Y	Y	Y	N	Y	?	N	N	N	Y	Y
22 *Huffington*	N	N	Y	Y	Y	Y	?	Y	N	?	?	N	Y	N	?	Y
23 *Gallegly*	N	N	Y	Y	N	N	Y	Y	N	Y	N	N	Y	N	Y	N
24 Beilenson	Y	Y	N	N	Y	Y	Y	Y	N	N	N	Y	Y	Y	N	Y
25 *McKeon*	N	N	Y	Y	N	N	Y	Y	N	Y	N	N	N	N	Y	Y
26 Berman	Y	Y	N	N	Y	Y	Y	Y	N	N	N	Y	Y	Y	N	Y
27 *Moorhead*	N	N	Y	Y	N	N	Y	Y	N	Y	N	N	N	N	Y	N
28 *Dreier*	N	N	Y	Y	N	N	Y	Y	N	Y	N	N	N	N	Y	Y
29 Waxman	Y	Y	N	N	Y	Y	N	Y	Y	N	N	Y	Y	Y	N	N
30 Becerra	Y	Y	N	N	Y	Y	Y	Y	N	N	N	Y	Y	Y	N	Y
31 Martinez	Y	N	Y	N	Y	Y	Y	Y	N	Y	N	Y	Y	Y	N	Y
32 Dixon	Y	N	N	N	Y	Y	N	Y	N	N	N	Y	Y	Y	N	Y
33 Roybal-Allard	Y	Y	N	N	Y	Y	N	Y	N	N	N	Y	Y	Y	N	Y
34 Torres	Y	N	N	N	Y	Y	N	Y	N	N	N	Y	Y	Y	N	Y
35 Waters	Y	Y	N	N	Y	Y	Y	Y	N	N	N	N	N	Y	N	Y
36 Harman	N	N	Y	N	Y	Y	N	Y	N	N	N	Y	Y	Y	Y	Y
37 Tucker	Y	N	N	N	Y	N	X	Y	N	N	?	Y	?	Y	?	N
38 *Horn*	N	N	Y	Y	Y	Y	Y	Y	N	N	N	N	Y	N	Y	Y
39 *Royce*	N	N	Y	Y	N	N	?	Y	N	Y	N	N	N	N	Y	N
40 *Lewis*	N	?	Y	#	N	N	Y	Y	N	Y	N	N	N	N	Y	Y
41 *Kim*	N	N	Y	Y	N	N	Y	Y	N	Y	N	N	N	N	Y	Y
42 Brown	Y	N	N	N	Y	Y	N	Y	N	?	N	Y	Y	Y	N	Y
43 *Calvert*	N	N	Y	Y	N	N	Y	Y	N	Y	N	N	N	N	Y	Y
44 *McCandless*	N	N	Y	Y	N	Y	Y	Y	N	Y	N	N	N	N	Y	Y
45 *Rohrabacher*	N	N	Y	Y	N	N	Y	Y	N	Y	N	N	N	N	Y	N
46 *Dornan*	X	N	Y	Y	N	N	Y	?	N	Y	N	N	N	N	Y	N
47 *Cox*	N	N	Y	Y	N	N	Y	Y	N	Y	N	N	N	N	Y	Y
48 *Packard*	N	N	Y	Y	N	N	Y	Y	N	Y	N	N	N	N	Y	Y
49 Schenk	Y	N	Y	Y	Y	Y	Y	Y	Y	N	N	Y	Y	Y	Y	Y
50 Filner	Y	Y	N	N	Y	Y	N	Y	N	N	N	Y	Y	Y	Y	Y
51 *Cunningham*	N	N	Y	Y	N	Y	N	Y	N	Y	N	N	N	N	Y	Y
52 *Hunter*	N	N	Y	Y	N	N	Y	Y	N	Y	N	N	N	N	Y	N
COLORADO																
1 Schroeder	Y	Y	N	N	Y	Y	N	Y	Y	N	N	Y	Y	Y	N	Y
2 Skaggs	Y	N	N	N	Y	Y	N	Y	Y	N	Y	Y	Y	Y	N	Y
3 *McInnis*	N	N	Y	Y	N	Y	Y	Y	N	Y	N	N	N	N	Y	N
4 *Allard*	N	N	Y	Y	N	N	Y	Y	N	Y	N	N	N	N	Y	Y
5 *Hefley*	N	N	Y	Y	N	N	N	Y	N	Y	N	N	N	N	Y	N
6 *Schaefer*	N	N	Y	Y	N	N	Y	Y	Y	Y	Y	N	N	N	Y	N
CONNECTICUT																
1 Kennelly	Y	N	N	N	Y	Y	Y	Y	N	N	N	Y	Y	Y	N	Y
2 Gejdenson	Y	N	N	N	Y	Y	N	Y	N	N	N	Y	Y	Y	N	Y
3 DeLauro	Y	N	N	N	Y	Y	Y	Y	N	N	N	Y	Y	Y	N	Y
4 *Shays*	Y	Y	Y	Y	Y	Y	Y	Y	Y	N	Y	Y	Y	N	Y	Y
5 *Franks*	N	N	Y	?	N	Y	Y	Y	N	N	N	N	Y	Y	Y	Y
6 *Johnson*	N	N	Y	Y	Y	Y	N	Y	N	Y	Y	Y	Y	N	Y	Y
DELAWARE																
AL *Castle*	N	N	Y	Y	Y	Y	Y	Y	N	Y	N	N	Y	N	Y	Y
FLORIDA																
1 Hutto	N	N	Y	N	N	N	N	Y	N	Y	Y	Y	N	?	N	Y
2 Peterson	N	N	Y	N	N	Y	N	Y	N	Y	N	N	N	Y	N	Y
3 Brown	Y	N	N	N	Y	Y	N	Y	N	N	N	Y	Y	N	N	Y
4 *Fowler*	N	N	Y	Y	N	Y	N	Y	N	Y	N	N	N	N	Y	Y
5 Thurman	N	N	N	N	N	Y	Y	Y	N	Y	N	N	N	Y	N	N
6 *Stearns*	N	N	Y	Y	N	N	Y	Y	N	Y	N	N	N	N	Y	N
7 *Mica*	N	N	Y	Y	N	N	Y	Y	N	Y	N	N	N	N	Y	N
8 *McCollum*	N	N	Y	Y	N	X	N	Y	N	Y	N	N	N	N	Y	Y
9 *Bilirakis*	N	N	Y	N	N	N	N	Y	N	Y	N	N	N	N	Y	N
10 *Young*	N	N	Y	N	Y	N	Y	Y	N	Y	N	N	N	N	Y	Y
11 Gibbons	Y	N	N	N	Y	Y	N	Y	N	N	N	Y	Y	Y	N	Y
12 *Canady*	N	N	Y	Y	N	N	N	Y	N	Y	N	N	Y	Y	Y	Y
13 *Miller*	N	N	Y	Y	Y	N	Y	Y	N	Y	N	N	N	N	Y	Y
14 *Goss*	N	N	Y	N	N	N	Y	Y	N	N	N	N	N	N	Y	Y
15 Bacchus	Y	N	Y	N	Y	Y	N	Y	N	N	Y	Y	Y	Y	N	Y
16 *Lewis*	X	N	Y	Y	N	N	Y	Y	N	Y	N	N	N	N	Y	Y
17 Meek	?	N	N	N	Y	Y	N	Y	N	N	N	Y	Y	N	N	Y
18 *Ros-Lehtinen*	N	N	Y	Y	Y	N	Y	Y	N	N	?	N	Y	N	Y	N
19 Johnston	Y	Y	Y	N	Y	Y	N	Y	N	N	N	Y	Y	Y	N	Y
20 Deutsch	Y	N	Y	N	Y	Y	N	Y	N	N	N	Y	Y	Y	N	Y
21 *Diaz-Balart*	N	N	Y	Y	N	N	Y	Y	N	Y	N	N	Y	N	Y	N
22 *Shaw*	N	N	Y	Y	Y	N	Y	Y	N	Y	N	N	Y	N	Y	Y
23 Hastings	?	?	?	N	Y	Y	Y	Y	N	N	N	Y	Y	Y	N	N
GEORGIA																
1 *Kingston*	N	N	Y	Y	N	N	Y	Y	N	Y	N	N	N	N	Y	N
2 Bishop	N	N	Y	N	Y	Y	N	Y	N	Y	N	Y	Y	Y	N	Y
3 *Collins*	N	N	Y	Y	N	N	Y	Y	Y	Y	N	N	N	N	Y	N
4 *Linder*	N	N	Y	Y	N	N	Y	Y	N	Y	N	N	N	N	Y	Y
5 Lewis	Y	Y	N	N	Y	Y	Y	Y	N	N	N	N	N	Y	N	N
6 *Gingrich*	N	N	Y	Y	N	N	Y	Y	N	Y	N	N	N	N	Y	Y
7 Darden	N	N	Y	N	N	Y	N	Y	N	Y	N	Y	Y	Y	N	Y
8 Rowland	N	N	Y	N	N	Y	N	Y	N	Y	N	Y	-	N	N	Y
9 Deal	N	N	Y	Y	N	N	N	Y	N	Y	Y	N	N	N	N	N
10 Johnson	N	N	Y	Y	Y	Y	N	Y	Y	Y	Y	Y	Y	Y	N	Y
11 McKinney	Y	Y	N	N	Y	Y	N	Y	Y	N	N	Y	Y	Y	N	N
HAWAII																
1 Abercrombie	Y	Y	N	N	N	Y	Y	N	N	Y	Y	Y	Y	Y	N	Y
2 Mink	Y	Y	N	N	Y	Y	Y	Y	Y	N	N	Y	Y	Y	N	N
IDAHO																
1 LaRocco	N	N	Y	Y	N	Y	N	Y	N	Y	Y	N	N	Y	N	Y
2 *Crapo*	N	N	Y	Y	N	N	Y	Y	N	Y	N	N	N	N	Y	N
ILLINOIS																
1 Rush	Y	Y	N	N	Y	Y	Y	Y	Y	N	N	Y	Y	Y	N	N
2 Reynolds	?	?	N	N	Y	Y	N	Y	N	N	N	Y	Y	Y	N	Y
3 Lipinski	Y	N	Y	N	Y	N	Y	Y	Y	Y	N	Y	Y	Y	Y	N
4 Gutierrez	Y	?	N	N	Y	Y	Y	Y	Y	N	N	Y	Y	Y	N	N
5 Rostenkowski	Y	N	N	N	Y	Y	N	Y	N	N	N	Y	Y	N	N	Y
6 *Hyde*	N	N	Y	Y	Y	N	Y	Y	N	Y	N	N	N	N	Y	Y
7 Collins	Y	?	N	N	Y	Y	N	Y	Y	N	N	Y	Y	N	N	N
8 *Crane*	N	?	Y	Y	N	N	N	Y	N	Y	N	N	N	N	Y	Y
9 Yates	Y	Y	N	N	Y	Y	Y	N	Y	N	N	Y	Y	Y	N	Y
10 *Porter*	Y	N	Y	Y	Y	Y	Y	Y	Y	N	N	N	Y	N	Y	Y
11 Sangmeister	Y	Y	Y	N	Y	Y	N	Y	Y	Y	Y	Y	Y	Y	N	Y
12 Costello	Y	N	Y	N	N	N	Y	Y	Y	Y	N	N	Y	Y	N	N
13 *Fawell*	N	N	Y	Y	Y	Y	Y	Y	Y	N	N	N	N	N	Y	Y
14 *Hastert*	N	N	Y	Y	N	N	N	Y	Y	Y	N	N	N	N	Y	Y
15 *Ewing*	N	N	Y	Y	N	N	Y	Y	N	Y	N	N	N	N	Y	Y
16 *Manzullo*	N	N	Y	Y	N	N	N	Y	Y	Y	N	N	N	N	Y	Y

KEY

Democrats	*Republicans*	**Independent**

Y	Voted for ("yea")	–	Announced against
N	Voted against ("nay")	P	Voted "present"
+	Announced for	C	Voted "present" to avoid possible conflict of interest
#	Paired for	?	Did not vote or otherwise make a position known
X	Paired against		

ND Northern Democrats
SD Southern Democrats
Southern states – Ala., Ark., Fla., Ga., Ky., La., Miss., N.C., Okla., S.C., Tenn.,

House Key Votes	1	2	3	4	5	6	7	8	9	10	11	12	13	14	15	16
17 Evans	Y	Y	N	N	Y	Y	N	Y	Y	N	N	Y	Y	Y	N	N
18 *Michel*	N	N	#	Y	Y	N	N	Y	N	Y	N	N	N	N	Y	Y
19 Poshard	N	Y	Y	Y	N	N	Y	Y	Y	N	N	Y	Y	N	Y	Y
20 Durbin	Y	Y	N	N	Y	Y	N	Y	Y	N	N	Y	Y	Y	N	Y
INDIANA																
1 Visclosky	Y	N	N	N	Y	Y	N	Y	Y	Y	Y	Y	Y	Y	N	Y
2 Sharp	N	N	Y	N	Y	Y	Y	Y	N	Y	Y	Y	Y	Y	N	Y
3 Roemer	N	N	Y	Y	Y	Y	N	Y	Y	Y	Y	Y	Y	Y	N	Y
4 Long	Y	N	Y	N	-	#	Y	Y	Y	N	Y	Y	Y	Y	N	Y
5 *Buyer*	N	N	Y	Y	N	N	N	Y	N	Y	N	N	N	N	N	Y
6 *Burton*	N	N	Y	Y	N	Y	Y	Y	N	Y	N	N	N	N	Y	N
7 *Myers*	N	N	Y	Y	Y	N	N	Y	N	Y	N	Y	N	N	Y	N
8 McCloskey	Y	N	Y	N	N	Y	Y	Y	N	Y	Y	Y	Y	Y	N	Y
9 Hamilton	N	N	N	Y	N	Y	N	Y	Y	N	Y	N	Y	Y	N	Y
10 Jacobs	Y	Y	Y	N	N	Y	N	Y	Y	N	N	Y	Y	Y	N	Y
IOWA																
1 *Leach*	N	Y	Y	Y	Y	Y	Y	Y	Y	Y	N	N	Y	N	Y	Y
2 *Nussle*	N	Y	Y	Y	N	N	N	Y	Y	Y	N	N	N	N	Y	Y
3 *Lightfoot*	N	N	Y	Y	N	Y	N	Y	Y	Y	N	N	N	N	Y	Y
4 Smith	N	N	N	N	N	Y	N	Y	N	Y	N	N	Y	Y	Y	Y
5 *Grandy*	N	N	#	?	N	N	?	Y	?	Y	Y	Y	Y	N	Y	Y
KANSAS																
1 *Roberts*	N	N	Y	Y	N	N	Y	N	Y	N	N	N	N	N	Y	Y
2 Slattery	N	N	N	N	Y	Y	Y	Y	N	?	N	Y	Y	?	?	Y
3 *Meyers*	N	N	Y	Y	Y	Y	Y	Y	N	Y	N	N	Y	Y	Y	Y
4 Glickman	N	N	Y	N	Y	Y	Y	Y	N	N	N	Y	Y	Y	N	N
KENTUCKY																
1 Barlow	Y	N	N	N	N	N	-	Y	Y	Y	N	Y	N	Y	N	N
2 Natcher/*Lewis*[a]	Y	?	?				Y	Y	N	Y	N	N	N	N	Y	N
3 Mazzoli	Y	N	Y	N	Y	N	N	Y	N	Y	N	Y	Y	Y	N	Y
4 *Bunning*	N	N	Y	Y	N	N	Y	N	Y	N	N	N	N	N	N	Y
5 *Rogers*	N	N	Y	Y	?	X	Y	Y	N	Y	N	N	N	N	Y	N
6 Baesler	N	N	Y	Y	N	Y	N	Y	N	Y	N	Y	Y	Y	N	Y
LOUISIANA																
1 *Livingston*	N	N	Y	Y	N	Y	Y	Y	N	Y	N	N	N	N	N	Y
2 Jefferson	Y	N	N	N	Y	Y	?	Y	N	N	N	Y	Y	Y	N	Y
3 Tauzin	N	N	Y	Y	N	N	?	Y	Y	Y	N	N	N	N	N	Y
4 Fields	Y	Y	N	N	Y	Y	Y	Y	N	N	N	N	N	?	N	N
5 *McCrery*	N	N	Y	N	Y	N	N	Y	N	Y	N	N	N	?	Y	Y
6 *Baker*	N	N	Y	Y	N	Y	N	Y	N	Y	N	N	N	N	N	Y
7 Hayes	N	N	Y	Y	N	N	Y	N	Y	N	N	N	?	N	N	N
MAINE																
1 Andrews	Y	Y	N	N	Y	Y	N	Y	Y	N	N	Y	Y	Y	N	N
2 *Snowe*	N	N	Y	Y	N	Y	Y	Y	Y	Y	N	N	Y	Y	Y	N
MARYLAND																
1 *Gilchrest*	N	N	Y	Y	Y	N	Y	Y	N	Y	N	N	N	Y	N	Y
2 *Bentley*	N	N	Y	Y	N	N	N	Y	N	Y	N	N	N	N	Y	N
3 Cardin	Y	Y	N	N	Y	Y	Y	Y	N	N	Y	Y	Y	Y	N	Y
4 Wynn	Y	Y	N	N	Y	Y	Y	Y	N	N	N	Y	Y	Y	N	Y
5 Hoyer	Y	N	Y	N	Y	Y	Y	Y	N	N	Y	Y	Y	Y	N	Y
6 *Bartlett*	N	N	Y	Y	N	Y	N	Y	N	Y	N	N	N	N	Y	Y
7 Mfume	Y	Y	N	N	Y	Y	Y	Y	N	N	N	Y	Y	Y	-	N
8 *Morella*	Y	Y	Y	N	Y	Y	?	Y	N	N	N	Y	Y	Y	Y	Y
MASSACHUSETTS																
1 Olver	Y	Y	N	N	Y	Y	Y	Y	N	N	N	Y	Y	Y	N	Y
2 Neal	Y	Y	N	N	Y	Y	Y	Y	N	N	N	Y	Y	Y	N	Y
3 *Blute*	N	N	Y	Y	Y	N	Y	Y	N	Y	Y	Y	Y	Y	N	N
4 Frank	Y	Y	N	N	Y	Y	Y	Y	N	N	N	Y	Y	Y	Y	N
5 Meehan	Y	Y	Y	Y	Y	Y	Y	Y	N	N	Y	Y	Y	Y	Y	Y
6 *Torkildsen*	N	N	Y	Y	N	Y	N	Y	N	Y	N	N	N	N	Y	Y
7 Markey	Y	Y	N	N	Y	Y	Y	Y	N	N	N	Y	Y	Y	N	Y
8 Kennedy	Y	Y	N	N	Y	Y	Y	Y	N	N	N	Y	Y	Y	N	Y
9 Moakley	Y	Y	N	N	Y	Y	Y	Y	N	N	N	Y	Y	Y	N	Y
10 Studds	Y	Y	N	N	Y	Y	N	Y	N	N	N	Y	Y	Y	N	Y
MICHIGAN																
1 Stupak	N	N	N	N	N	N	N	N	Y	N	N	N	N	N	N	N
2 *Hoekstra*	N	N	Y	Y	N	N	Y	Y	Y	Y	N	N	N	N	Y	Y

House Key Votes	1	2	3	4	5	6	7	8	9	10	11	12	13	14	15	16
3 *Ehlers*	N	N	?	Y	N	N	N	Y	?	Y	N	N	N	N	?	?
4 *Camp*	N	N	Y	Y	N	N	Y	Y	Y	Y	N	N	N	N	Y	Y
5 Barcia	Y	N	Y	N	N	N	Y	N	Y	Y	N	N	N	N	N	Y
6 *Upton*	N	Y	Y	Y	N	Y	Y	Y	N	Y	N	N	N	Y	N	Y
7 *Smith*	N	N	Y	N	N	N	Y	Y	Y	Y	N	N	N	N	N	Y
8 Carr	Y	N	N	Y	Y	Y	Y	N	?	?	Y	Y	Y	Y	Y	Y
9 Kildee	Y	Y	N	N	Y	N	N	Y	Y	N	N	Y	Y	Y	Y	N
10 Bonior	Y	Y	N	N	Y	Y	Y	Y	N	N	N	Y	Y	Y	N	N
11 *Knollenberg*	N	N	Y	Y	N	N	Y	Y	Y	Y	N	N	N	N	N	Y
12 Levin	Y	N	N	N	Y	Y	Y	Y	N	N	Y	Y	Y	Y	N	Y
13 Ford	Y	Y	N	N	Y	Y	Y	?	Y	?	Y	Y	Y	Y	N	N
14 Conyers	Y	Y	N	N	Y	Y	Y	Y	N	N	N	Y	Y	N	Y	Y
15 Collins	Y	Y	N	N	Y	Y	#	Y	Y	N	N	Y	Y	Y	N	Y
16 Dingell	Y	N	N	N	N	Y	Y	Y	N	N	N	Y	Y	Y	N	Y
MINNESOTA																
1 Penny	N	Y	Y	Y	Y	N	N	Y	N	Y	N	Y	N	Y	N	Y
2 Minge	N	Y	Y	Y	N	Y	Y	Y	Y	Y	Y	Y	Y	Y	N	Y
3 *Ramstad*	N	N	Y	Y	N	Y	Y	Y	N	Y	N	N	N	N	Y	Y
4 Vento	Y	Y	N	N	Y	Y	Y	Y	N	N	N	Y	Y	Y	N	Y
5 Sabo	Y	N	N	N	Y	Y	Y	Y	N	N	N	Y	Y	Y	N	N
6 *Grams*	N	N	Y	N	Y	N	N	Y	N	Y	N	N	N	N	N	Y
7 Peterson	N	Y	Y	Y	N	Y	Y	Y	Y	Y	N	N	N	N	N	Y
8 Oberstar	Y	Y	N	N	N	Y	Y	N	N	Y	N	Y	Y	N	Y	N
MISSISSIPPI																
1 Whitten	N	N	Y	N	N	N	?	Y	N	?	Y	Y	Y	Y	?	Y
2 Thompson	Y	N	N	N	Y	Y	Y	Y	N	N	N	Y	Y	?	N	N
3 Montgomery	N	N	Y	N	N	N	Y	N	Y	Y	Y	Y	Y	Y	Y	N
4 Parker	N	N	Y	N	N	Y	Y	Y	N	Y	N	N	N	Y	Y	Y
5 Taylor	N	N	N	N	N	N	Y	N	Y	Y	N	N	N	N	Y	N
MISSOURI																
1 Clay	Y	N	N	N	Y	Y	N	Y	Y	N	N	N	N	N	N	N
2 *Talent*	N	N	Y	Y	N	Y	N	Y	N	Y	N	N	N	Y	N	Y
3 Gephardt	Y	N	N	N	Y	Y	N	Y	Y	N	N	N	Y	N	Y	N
4 Skelton	N	N	Y	N	N	N	N	Y	N	Y	N	N	N	N	Y	N
5 Wheat	Y	N	N	N	Y	Y	Y	Y	Y	?	N	Y	Y	?	N	Y
6 Danner	N	Y	Y	N	N	Y	Y	Y	N	N	N	N	N	Y	Y	N
7 *Hancock*	N	N	Y	Y	N	Y	N	Y	N	Y	N	N	N	N	Y	N
8 *Emerson*	N	N	Y	Y	N	N	Y	Y	Y	Y	N	N	N	N	Y	N
9 Volkmer	Y	N	Y	N	N	N	Y	N	N	Y	N	N	N	N	Y	N
MONTANA																
AL Williams	N	N	N	N	Y	N	Y	Y	Y	N	N	N	N	N	N	N
NEBRASKA																
1 *Bereuter*	N	N	Y	Y	Y	Y	Y	Y	Y	Y	N	N	N	N	N	Y
2 Hoagland	Y	N	Y	Y	Y	N	Y	Y	N	Y	N	N	Y	Y	N	Y
3 *Barrett*	N	N	Y	Y	N	N	Y	N	Y	N	N	N	N	N	P	Y
NEVADA																
1 Bilbray	N	N	Y	N	N	Y	Y	Y	N	N	N	Y	Y	Y	N	N
2 *Vucanovich*	N	N	Y	Y	N	N	N	Y	N	N	N	N	N	N	Y	Y
NEW HAMPSHIRE																
1 *Zeliff*	N	N	Y	N	Y	N	Y	Y	N	N	N	N	N	N	N	Y
2 Swett	Y	N	Y	Y	Y	#	Y	Y	Y	N	N	Y	Y	N	Y	N
NEW JERSEY																
1 Andrews	Y	?	Y	Y	Y	Y	Y	Y	N	N	Y	Y	Y	Y	Y	N
2 Hughes	Y	N	N	N	Y	Y	N	Y	Y	N	N	Y	Y	Y	N	Y
3 *Saxton*	N	N	Y	Y	Y	Y	N	Y	N	Y	N	N	Y	Y	N	Y
4 *Smith*	N	N	Y	Y	Y	N	Y	Y	N	Y	N	N	Y	Y	N	Y
5 *Roukema*	N	Y	Y	+	Y	Y	N	Y	N	Y	N	N	Y	Y	N	Y
6 Pallone	Y	N	Y	Y	Y	Y	Y	Y	N	N	N	Y	Y	Y	N	N
7 *Franks*	N	N	Y	Y	Y	Y	Y	Y	N	Y	N	N	Y	Y	N	Y
8 Klein	Y	Y	N	N	Y	Y	Y	Y	N	N	Y	Y	Y	Y	N	Y
9 Torricelli	Y	?	Y	N	Y	Y	Y	Y	N	N	Y	Y	Y	Y	N	Y
10 Payne	Y	Y	-	N	Y	Y	Y	Y	N	N	N	Y	Y	N	Y	N
11 *Gallo*[b]	N	?	?	?	N	Y	Y	Y	N	?	?	N	N	?	?	
12 *Zimmer*	N	Y	Y	Y	Y	Y	Y	N	Y	N	N	N	Y	N	Y	Y
13 Menendez	Y	N	N	N	Y	Y	Y	Y	N	N	N	Y	Y	Y	N	Y
NEW MEXICO																
1 *Schiff*	N	N	Y	Y	N	Y	Y	Y	N	Y	N	N	N	N	Y	N
2 *Skeen*	N	N	Y	Y	N	Y	N	Y	N	N	Y	N	N	N	Y	N
3 Richardson	Y	N	Y	N	?	N	Y	N	Y	N	N	N	N	Y	N	Y
NEW YORK																
1 Hochbrueckner	Y	N	N	N	Y	Y	N	Y	Y	N	N	N	N	Y	N	N
2 *Lazio*	N	N	Y	Y	Y	Y	Y	Y	N	Y	N	N	N	Y	N	Y
3 *King*	N	N	Y	N	Y	Y	N	Y	N	Y	N	N	N	Y	N	Y
4 *Levy*	N	N	Y	Y	Y	N	Y	Y	N	Y	N	N	N	Y	N	Y
5 Ackerman	Y	Y	N	N	Y	Y	Y	Y	N	N	N	Y	Y	Y	N	Y
6 Flake	Y	Y	N	N	Y	Y	N	+	N	?	N	Y	Y	Y	N	Y
7 Manton	Y	N	?	N	N	Y	N	Y	N	N	N	Y	Y	Y	N	Y
8 Nadler	Y	Y	N	N	Y	Y	Y	Y	N	N	N	Y	Y	Y	N	Y
9 Schumer	Y	Y	N	N	Y	Y	Y	Y	N	N	N	Y	Y	Y	N	Y
10 Towns	Y	Y	N	N	Y	Y	?	Y	N	N	N	Y	Y	Y	N	N
11 Owens	Y	Y	N	N	Y	Y	Y	Y	N	N	N	Y	Y	Y	N	N

House Key Votes	1	2	3	4	5	6	7	8	9	10	11	12	13	14	15	16
12 Velazquez	Y	Y	N	N	Y	Y	N	Y	Y	N	N	Y	Y	Y	N	N
13 *Molinari*	N	N	Y	Y	Y	Y	Y	Y	N	Y	N	N	Y	N	Y	Y
14 Maloney	Y	Y	N	N	Y	Y	Y	Y	Y	N	N	Y	Y	Y	N	Y
15 Rangel	Y	Y	N	N	Y	Y	N	Y	?	N	N	N	N	Y	N	N
16 Serrano	Y	Y	N	N	Y	?	Y	Y	Y	N	N	Y	Y	Y	N	Y
17 Engel	Y	Y	N	N	Y	Y	Y	Y	N	N	N	Y	Y	Y	N	N
18 Lowey	Y	N	N	N	Y	Y	Y	Y	Y	N	N	Y	Y	Y	N	Y
19 *Fish*	N	N	Y	?	N	?	Y	Y	N	N	N	N	N	N	Y	Y
20 *Gilman*	Y	N	N	N	N	Y	Y	Y	N	N	N	N	N	N	Y	Y
21 McNulty	Y	N	Y	N	Y	N	Y	Y	Y	Y	N	Y	Y	?	Y	Y
22 *Solomon*	N	N	Y	Y	N	N	Y	Y	Y	Y	N	N	N	N	Y	N
23 *Boehlert*	Y	N	Y	N	Y	Y	Y	Y	N	N	N	Y	Y	N	Y	Y
24 *McHugh*	N	N	Y	Y	N	Y	Y	Y	Y	Y	N	N	N	N	Y	N
25 *Walsh*	N	N	Y	Y	N	N	Y	Y	N	Y	N	N	Y	N	Y	Y
26 Hinchey	Y	Y	N	N	N	Y	N	Y	N	N	N	Y	Y	Y	N	N
27 *Paxon*	N	N	Y	Y	N	N	Y	Y	Y	Y	N	N	N	N	Y	Y
28 Slaughter	Y	Y	N	N	Y	Y	Y	Y	Y	N	N	Y	Y	Y	N	Y
29 LaFalce	Y	Y	N	N	Y	N	Y	Y	Y	N	N	Y	Y	Y	N	Y
30 *Quinn*	N	N	Y	Y	Y	N	Y	Y	N	Y	N	Y	Y	N	Y	N
31 *Houghton*	N	N	Y	Y	Y	Y	N	Y	N	Y	N	Y	Y	N	Y	Y
NORTH CAROLINA																
1 Clayton	Y	Y	N	N	Y	Y	Y	Y	N	N	N	Y	Y	Y	N	Y
2 Valentine	Y	N	Y	N	Y	Y	N	Y	N	N	Y	Y	?	N	N	Y
3 Lancaster	N	N	Y	N	N	Y	Y	Y	Y	Y	N	N	Y	Y	N	Y
4 Price	Y	N	N	N	Y	?	Y	Y	N	N	N	Y	Y	Y	N	Y
5 Neal	Y	N	Y	N	Y	?	Y	Y	Y	Y	N	Y	Y	Y	N	Y
6 *Coble*	N	N	Y	Y	N	N	Y	Y	N	Y	N	N	N	N	Y	N
7 Rose	Y	N	N	N	N	Y	N	Y	N	N	N	Y	Y	N	N	N
8 Hefner	Y	N	Y	N	N	Y	N	Y	N	Y	N	Y	Y	Y	N	N
9 *McMillan*	N	?	Y	Y	N	Y	Y	Y	N	Y	Y	N	N	N	Y	Y
10 *Ballenger*	N	N	Y	Y	N	N	Y	Y	N	Y	N	N	N	N	Y	Y
11 *Taylor*	N	N	Y	Y	N	N	Y	Y	N	Y	N	N	N	N	Y	N
12 Watt	Y	Y	N	N	Y	Y	N	Y	N	N	N	N	N	Y	N	N
NORTH DAKOTA																
AL Pomeroy	N	N	N	Y	Y	Y	N	Y	Y	Y	N	Y	Y	Y	Y	Y
OHIO																
1 Mann	Y	N	Y	Y	Y	Y	N	Y	Y	N	N	Y	Y	Y	N	Y
2 *Portman*	N	N	Y	Y	N	N	+	Y	Y	Y	N	N	N	N	Y	Y
3 Hall	Y	N	N	N	Y	N	Y	Y	N	N	N	Y	Y	Y	N	Y
4 *Oxley*	N	N	Y	Y	N	N	Y	Y	N	Y	N	N	N	N	Y	Y
5 *Gillmor*	N	N	Y	Y	N	N	Y	Y	N	N	N	N	N	N	Y	Y
6 Strickland	N	N	N	N	N	Y	N	Y	Y	Y	N	N	N	Y	N	N
7 *Hobson*	N	N	Y	Y	N	N	Y	Y	N	N	N	N	Y	N	Y	Y
8 *Boehner*	N	N	Y	Y	N	N	Y	Y	N	Y	N	N	N	N	Y	Y
9 Kaptur	Y	N	N	?	Y	N	Y	Y	Y	N	N	Y	Y	Y	N	N
10 *Hoke*	N	Y	Y	Y	N	N	Y	?	N	Y	N	N	N	N	Y	Y
11 Stokes	Y	Y	N	N	Y	Y	N	Y	N	N	N	N	N	Y	N	N
12 *Kasich*	N	N	Y	Y	Y	N	Y	Y	Y	Y	N	N	Y	N	Y	Y
13 Brown	Y	Y	Y	Y	Y	Y	Y	Y	Y	N	N	Y	Y	Y	N	N
14 Sawyer	Y	N	N	N	Y	Y	Y	Y	N	Y	N	Y	Y	Y	N	Y
15 *Pryce*	N	N	Y	Y	Y	Y	Y	Y	N	Y	N	N	Y	N	Y	Y
16 *Regula*	N	N	Y	Y	N	N	Y	Y	N	Y	N	N	N	N	Y	Y
17 Traficant	Y	N	N	N	Y	Y	Y	Y	N	Y	N	Y	Y	N	Y	N
18 Applegate	N	N	N	N	Y	N	N	Y	N	Y	N	Y	Y	?	?	N
19 Fingerhut	N	N	Y	Y	Y	Y	Y	Y	N	N	N	Y	Y	Y	N	Y
OKLAHOMA																
1 *Inhofe/Largent*[c]	N	N	Y	Y	N	N	Y	Y	N	Y	N	N	N	N	Y	N
2 Synar	Y	Y	N	N	Y	Y	N	Y	Y	N	N	Y	N	Y	N	Y
3 Brewster	N	N	Y	Y	N	Y	N	Y	N	Y	N	N	N	N	N	Y
4 McCurdy	N	N	Y	N	Y	Y	Y	Y	N	?	N	N	Y	?	Y	Y
5 *Istook*	N	N	Y	Y	N	N	Y	Y	Y	?	N	N	N	N	Y	N
6 English/*Lucas*[d]							Y	Y	N	Y	N	N	N	N	Y	N
OREGON																
1 Furse	Y	Y	N	N	Y	Y	N	Y	Y	N	N	Y	Y	Y	N	Y
2 *Smith*	?	N	Y	Y	N	N	N	Y	N	Y	N	N	N	N	Y	Y
3 Wyden	Y	Y	N	N	Y	Y	N	Y	Y	N	N	Y	Y	Y	N	Y
4 DeFazio	Y	Y	Y	Y	N	Y	N	Y	Y	?	N	N	N	Y	N	N
5 Kopetski	Y	?	N	N	N	Y	+	Y	N	Y	N	Y	N	Y	N	Y
PENNSYLVANIA																
1 Foglietta	Y	Y	N	N	Y	?	?	Y	Y	N	N	Y	Y	Y	N	Y
2 Blackwell	Y	Y	N	?	Y	?	N	Y	Y	N	N	Y	Y	Y	N	Y
3 Borski	#	N	N	N	Y	N	N	Y	N	N	N	Y	Y	Y	N	Y
4 Klink	N	N	N	N	N	N	Y	Y	Y	N	N	N	N	Y	N	N
5 *Clinger*	N	N	Y	Y	N	N	N	Y	N	Y	N	N	N	N	Y	Y
6 Holden	Y	N	N	N	N	N	Y	N	Y	Y	N	N	Y	N	Y	N
7 *Weldon*	N	N	Y	Y	N	N	Y	Y	N	N	N	N	Y	N	Y	Y
8 *Greenwood*	N	N	Y	Y	Y	Y	Y	Y	N	Y	N	N	Y	N	Y	Y
9 *Shuster*	N	N	Y	Y	N	N	N	Y	Y	Y	N	N	N	N	Y	Y
10 *McDade*	N	N	Y	Y	Y	N	N	Y	N	?	N	N	N	?	Y	Y
11 Kanjorski	Y	N	N	N	N	N	N	Y	Y	Y	N	Y	N	Y	N	N
12 Murtha	Y	N	N	N	N	N	N	Y	N	Y	N	Y	N	N	N	Y
13 Margolies-Mezv.	Y	Y	N	Y	Y	Y	Y	Y	Y	N	Y	Y	Y	Y	Y	Y
14 Coyne	Y	Y	N	N	Y	Y	Y	Y	Y	N	N	Y	Y	Y	N	Y
15 McHale	Y	N	Y	Y	Y	Y	Y	Y	N	N	Y	Y	Y	Y	N	Y
16 *Walker*	N	N	Y	Y	N	N	Y	Y	N	Y	N	N	N	N	Y	Y
17 *Gekas*	N	N	Y	Y	N	N	Y	Y	N	Y	N	N	N	N	Y	Y
18 *Santorum*	N	N	Y	Y	N	N	Y	Y	N	Y	N	N	N	N	Y	Y
19 *Goodling*	N	N	Y	Y	N	N	N	Y	Y	Y	N	N	N	N	Y	Y
20 Murphy	N	N	N	?	N	N	N	Y	N	Y	N	Y	N	Y	N	N
21 *Ridge*	?	N	Y	?	Y	Y	Y	?	N	?	N	N	Y	Y	Y	Y
RHODE ISLAND																
1 *Machtley*	N	N	Y	Y	Y	Y	Y	Y	?	Y	N	N	Y	N	Y	Y
2 Reed	Y	N	N	N	Y	Y	N	Y	Y	N	N	Y	Y	Y	N	Y
SOUTH CAROLINA																
1 *Ravenel*	N	N	Y	Y	N	N	Y	Y	Y	N	N	N	N	N	Y	N
2 *Spence*	N	N	Y	Y	N	N	N	Y	N	Y	N	N	N	N	Y	N
3 Derrick	Y	N	Y	N	Y	Y	N	Y	Y	N	N	Y	Y	Y	N	Y
4 *Inglis*	N	N	Y	Y	N	N	N	Y	Y	Y	Y	N	N	N	Y	N
5 Spratt	Y	N	Y	N	Y	Y	Y	Y	Y	Y	N	Y	Y	Y	N	N
6 Clyburn	Y	N	N	N	Y	Y	Y	Y	N	Y	N	Y	Y	Y	N	Y
SOUTH DAKOTA																
AL Johnson	N	Y	Y	N	N	Y	N	Y	Y	Y	N	Y	Y	Y	Y	Y
TENNESSEE																
1 *Quillen*	N	N	Y	?	N	N	Y	Y	N	Y	N	N	N	N	Y	Y
2 *Duncan*	N	Y	Y	Y	N	N	N	Y	Y	Y	N	N	N	N	Y	N
3 Lloyd	N	N	Y	N	Y	Y	N	Y	N	Y	Y	Y	Y	?	N	Y
4 Cooper	Y	N	Y	Y	N	Y	N	Y	N	Y	N	N	N	Y	N	Y
5 Clement	Y	N	Y	Y	N	?	N	Y	N	N	N	Y	Y	N	N	Y
6 Gordon	Y	Y	Y	Y	N	Y	N	Y	Y	Y	N	Y	Y	Y	N	Y
7 *Sundquist*	N	N	Y	Y	N	N	?	Y	N	Y	N	N	N	N	?	Y
8 Tanner	N	N	Y	N	N	Y	Y	Y	N	Y	N	N	N	N	N	Y
9 Ford	?	?	N	N	Y	Y	Y	Y	N	Y	N	Y	Y	Y	N	Y
TEXAS																
1 Chapman	?	N	Y	N	N	Y	N	Y	N	Y	N	N	Y	N	N	N
2 Wilson	?	N	Y	N	N	Y	Y	Y	N	Y	N	N	N	N	N	Y
3 *Johnson, Sam*	N	N	Y	Y	N	N	N	Y	N	Y	N	N	N	N	Y	N
4 Hall	N	N	Y	Y	N	N	N	Y	N	Y	N	N	N	N	Y	N
5 Bryant	Y	Y	Y	N	Y	Y	Y	Y	N	N	N	Y	Y	Y	N	Y
6 *Barton*	N	N	Y	?	N	N	Y	Y	N	Y	Y	N	N	N	Y	Y
7 *Archer*	N	N	Y	Y	N	N	N	Y	N	Y	N	N	N	N	Y	Y
8 *Fields*	N	N	Y	Y	N	N	N	Y	N	Y	N	N	N	N	Y	Y
9 Brooks	Y	?	N	N	N	Y	N	Y	N	Y	N	Y	Y	Y	N	Y
10 Pickle	Y	N	Y	N	Y	Y	Y	Y	N	Y	Y	Y	Y	Y	N	Y
11 Edwards	N	N	Y	N	Y	Y	N	Y	N	Y	N	Y	Y	Y	N	Y
12 Geren	N	N	Y	N	N	Y	Y	Y	N	Y	Y	N	N	N	Y	Y
13 Sarpalius	N	N	Y	N	N	N	N	Y	N	Y	N	N	N	N	Y	Y
14 Laughlin	Y	N	Y	N	N	?	Y	Y	N	?	N	N	N	N	N	Y
15 de la Garza	?	N	Y	N	N	N	Y	Y	N	Y	N	N	N	Y	N	Y
16 Coleman	Y	N	N	N	Y	Y	Y	Y	N	Y	N	Y	Y	Y	N	Y
17 Stenholm	N	N	Y	Y	N	N	Y	Y	N	Y	Y	N	N	N	Y	Y
18 Washington	Y	?	N	X	Y	Y	?	Y	N	?	?	N	?	?	?	Y
19 *Combest*	N	N	Y	Y	N	N	N	Y	N	Y	N	N	N	N	Y	N
20 Gonzalez	Y	N	N	N	Y	Y	N	N	N	N	N	Y	Y	Y	N	N
21 *Smith*	N	N	Y	Y	N	N	Y	Y	N	Y	N	N	N	N	Y	Y
22 *DeLay*	N	N	Y	Y	N	N	N	Y	N	Y	N	N	N	N	Y	Y
23 *Bonilla*	N	N	Y	Y	N	N	Y	Y	N	Y	N	N	N	N	Y	Y
24 Frost	Y	N	Y	N	N	Y	Y	Y	N	Y	N	Y	Y	Y	N	Y
25 Andrews	#	?	Y	Y	Y	Y	N	Y	N	Y	N	Y	Y	Y	N	Y
26 *Armey*	N	N	Y	Y	N	N	N	Y	N	Y	N	N	N	N	Y	Y
27 Ortiz	N	N	Y	N	N	N	Y	Y	N	Y	N	N	N	Y	N	Y
28 Tejeda	N	N	N	N	N	N	Y	Y	N	Y	N	N	N	Y	N	Y
29 Green	Y	N	X	N	N	Y	N	Y	N	Y	N	Y	Y	Y	N	Y
30 Johnson, E.B.	Y	N	N	N	Y	Y	Y	Y	N	N	N	Y	Y	Y	N	Y
UTAH																
1 *Hansen*	N	N	Y	Y	N	N	Y	Y	N	Y	Y	N	N	N	Y	Y
2 Shepherd	#	Y	Y	N	Y	Y	N	Y	Y	N	N	Y	Y	Y	N	Y
3 Orton	N	N	Y	Y	N	Y	N	Y	Y	Y	Y	N	N	N	N	Y

[a] William H. Natcher, D-Ky., died March 29. The last vote for which he was eligible was key vote 3. Ron Lewis, R-Ky., was sworn in May 26, 1994. The first key vote for which he was eligible was key vote 7.

[b] Dean A. Gallo, R-N.J., died Nov. 6, 1994. Key vote 15 was the last vote for which he was eligible.

[c] Rep. James M. Inhofe, R-Okla., resigned Nov. 15, 1994, to replace Sen. David L. Boren, D-Okla. The last vote for which Inhofe was eligible was key vote 15. Steve Largent, R-Okla., was sworn in Nov. 29, 1994, to replace Inhofe. The first vote for which he was eligible was key vote 16.

[d] Glenn English, D-Okla., resigned effective Jan. 7, 1994. Frank D. Lucas, R-Okla., was sworn in May 17, 1994. The first vote for which he was eligible was key vote 7.

KEY

	Democrats	*Republicans*	**Independent**

Y	Voted for ("yea")	–	Announced against
N	Voted against ("nay")	P	Voted "present"
+	Announced for	C	Voted "present" to avoid possible conflict of interest
#	Paired for	?	Did not vote or otherwise make a position known
X	Paired against		

ND   Northern Democrats
SD   Southern Democrats
Southern states – Ala., Ark., Fla., Ga., Ky., La., Miss., N.C., Okla., S.C., Tenn., Texas, Va.

House Key Votes	1	2	3	4	5	6	7	8	9	10	11	12	13	14	15	16
VERMONT																
AL **Sanders**	Y	Y	N	N	Y	Y	N	Y	Y	Y	N	Y	Y	Y	N	N
VIRGINIA																
1 *Bateman*	N	N	Y	Y	Y	N	N	Y	N	Y	Y	N	N	N	Y	Y
2 Pickett	N	N	N	N	N	Y	Y	Y	N	Y	N	N	N	N	N	Y
3 Scott	Y	N	N	N	Y	Y	N	Y	N	N	N	N	N	N	N	Y
4 Sisisky	N	N	Y	N	N	Y	N	Y	N	Y	N	N	N	N	N	N
5 Payne	N	N	Y	Y	N	Y	N	Y	Y	Y	N	N	N	N	N	N
6 *Goodlatte*	N	N	Y	Y	N	N	Y	Y	Y	Y	N	N	N	N	Y	Y
7 *Bliley*	N	N	Y	Y	N	Y	N	Y	N	Y	N	N	N	N	Y	Y
8 Moran	N	N	Y	N	Y	Y	Y	Y	N	N	N	Y	Y	Y	N	Y
9 Boucher	Y	N	N	N	N	Y	Y	Y	N	Y	N	N	N	N	Y	Y
10 *Wolf*	N	N	Y	Y	N	N	Y	Y	N	Y	N	N	N	N	Y	N
11 Byrne	Y	N	N	N	Y	Y	Y	Y	N	N	N	Y	Y	Y	N	Y
WASHINGTON																
1 Cantwell	Y	N	N	Y	Y	Y	N	Y	N	N	N	Y	Y	Y	N	Y
2 Swift	Y	N	N	N	Y	Y	Y	Y	N	Y	N	Y	Y	Y	N	Y
3 *Unsoeld*	Y	Y	N	N	Y	Y	N	Y	N	N	N	N	N	Y	N	N
4 Inslee	Y	Y	Y	Y	Y	Y	N	Y	Y	Y	N	Y	Y	Y	N	Y
5 Foley [e]			N							Y	Y	Y	N	Y		
6 Dicks	Y	N	N	N	Y	Y	N	Y	N	Y	N	Y	Y	Y	N	Y
7 McDermott	Y	Y	N	N	Y	Y	Y	Y	N	N	N	Y	Y	Y	N	Y
8 *Dunn*	N	N	Y	Y	N	Y	Y	Y	N	Y	N	N	N	N	Y	Y
9 Kreidler	Y	N	N	N	Y	Y	N	Y	N	N	N	Y	Y	Y	N	Y
WEST VIRGINIA																
1 Mollohan	Y	N	N	N	N	N	Y	Y	N	Y	N	N	N	Y	N	N
2 Wise	Y	N	N	N	N	Y	N	Y	N	Y	N	N	N	Y	N	N
3 Rahall	Y	Y	N	N	N	N	Y	Y	N	Y	N	N	N	Y	N	N
WISCONSIN																
1 Barca	N	Y	N	Y	N	Y	N	Y	Y	N	Y	Y	Y	Y	Y	N
2 *Klug*	N	Y	Y	Y	Y	Y	Y	Y	N	Y	N	N	Y	N	Y	N
3 *Gunderson*	N	N	Y	Y	N	N	Y	Y	N	N	N	N	N	N	Y	N
4 Kleczka	Y	Y	N	N	N	Y	N	Y	Y	N	Y	Y	Y	Y	N	Y
5 Barrett	Y	Y	N	N	N	Y	N	Y	Y	N	Y	Y	Y	Y	N	Y
6 *Petri*	N	Y	Y	Y	N	N	N	N	N	Y	N	N	N	N	Y	N
7 Obey	Y	N	N	N	Y	Y	N	Y	?	N	Y	Y	Y	Y	N	N
8 *Roth*	N	N	Y	Y	N	N	N	Y	N	Y	N	N	N	N	Y	N
9 *Sensenbrenner*	N	Y	Y	Y	N	N	Y	Y	N	Y	N	N	N	N	Y	N
WYOMING																
AL *Thomas*	N	N	Y	Y	N	N	Y	Y	Y	N	Y	N	N	N	N	Y
DELEGATES																
de Lugo, V.I.	D	Y	D	D	D	Y	D	Y	N	N	D	D	D	N	D	
Faleomavaega, Am.S.	D	N	D	D	D	?	D	?	N	?	D	D	D	N	D	
Norton, D.C.	D	Y	D	D	D	N	D	Y	N	N	D	D	D	N	D	
Romero-B., P.R.	D	N	D	D	D	Y	D	?	N	N	D	D	D	N	D	
Underwood, Guam	D	N	D	D	D	N	D	Y	N	?	D	D	D	N	D	

[e] Rep. Thomas S. Foley, D-Wash., as Speaker of the House, voted at his discretion.

Senate

1. BALANCED-BUDGET AMENDMENT

Six Democrats who voted in 1994 in favor of a constitutional amendment to require a balanced federal budget switched their votes less than a year later to sink a virtually identical measure.

Senate floor debate on the proposed constitutional amendment (H J Res 1) consumed the month of February. The House had already passed the measure, and Senate passage would have sent it to the states for ratification.

But the rhetoric was overshadowed by an ever-shifting vote count and a dramatic conclusion when Republicans fell one tantalizing vote short of the 67 (two-thirds majority) needed for passage. After Majority Leader Bob Dole, R-Kan., changed his vote to "no" to preserve his ability under Senate rules to call for a revote later, the measure failed 65–35: R 51–2; D 14–33 (ND 9–28, SD 5–5). *(House key vote 1)*

Throughout the Senate debate, it was clear that the outcome would be close. A similar amendment had received 63 votes in 1994. The 1994 Republican landslide, while installing eight new GOP senators in seats previously held by Democrats, ended up providing a net gain of only four votes, since the other four GOP newcomers replaced pro-amendment Democrats. If all remaining senators had voted the way they previously had, the balanced-budget amendment would have passed with the bare minimum of 67 votes.

Amending the Constitution to require that expected spending equal expected revenues had long been the top priority for deficit hawks who argued that, barring such a requirement, Congress and the president would not be able to muster the courage to balance the budget. Opinion polls showed overwhelming support for the amendment, though its popularity slipped once poll respondents were reminded that cuts in popular programs might be required.

When the debate started Jan. 30, it appeared an uphill task for opponents. Two of the three Republicans who opposed the amendment in 1994 (Ted Stevens of Alaska and Nancy Landon Kassebaum of Kansas) soon signaled that they would come on board, leaving Appropriations Committee Chairman Mark O. Hatfield of Oregon as the only Republican in opposition.

But several Democrats who voted for the amendment in 1994 quickly shifted into the undecided column. And some, including Dianne Feinstein of California and Ernest F. Hollings of South Carolina, declared that they would vote against the amendment unless it was broadened to protect Social Security. "We have some senators who have voted for it in the past, thinking it was a free vote, who are now shooting with real bullets," said Dole.

Still, these Democratic defections seemed to be offset by the conversions of three former Democratic opponents—Joseph R. Biden Jr. of Delaware, Tom Harkin of Iowa and Max Baucus of Montana—each of whom faced reelection in 1996.

As the debate wound to a close, the focus turned to a handful of Democrats, including Sam Nunn of Georgia, and Byron Dorgan and Kent Conrad, both of North Dakota. Dorgan and Nunn had voted for the amendment in 1994; Conrad had voted against it. If two of the three voted "yes," the amendment would pass.

After a delay that alarmed the amendment's floor managers, Nunn again supported the amendment but only after winning a belated change to block federal courts from enforcing its provisions.

Meanwhile, it became clear that Dorgan and Conrad—top lieutenants to Minority Leader Tom Daschle, D-S.D., who had himself earlier switched to oppose the amendment—were tilting against. They cited concerns over Social Security.

Others pointed to their close relationship with Daschle and suggested the endgame was being carefully choreographed to ease political damage for Democrats while ensuring the amendment—which was opposed by President Clinton—went down to defeat.

In the end, it came down to Conrad, whom Republicans tried to coax over during last-minute negotiations on the floor over Social Security. But the talks, while dramatic, proved fruitless, and the amendment went down to defeat.

The loss represented a bitter defeat for Dole and his fellow Senate Republicans and served as a potent reminder that most of the House GOP's "Contract with America" would have a tough time in the Senate.

2. LINE-ITEM VETO

By an unexpectedly large margin and with surprising speed, the Senate on March 23 passed a bill to give the president the functional equivalent of a line-item veto. The bill passed 69–29: R 50–2; D 19–27 (ND 13–23, SD 6–4).

The measure proposed to dramatically shift power over spending decisions from Congress to the executive branch.

For Republicans, especially Majority Leader Bob Dole, R-Kan., passage of the bill (S 4) represented a much-needed opportunity to prove that the Senate was not a graveyard for the House GOP's "Contract with America." Promise of a line-item veto was a key plank in the contract. But to get the bill to the floor required Dole to dramatically rework the measure after serious rifts between supporters of competing bills threatened to shatter Republican unity and produce what one GOP aide called "Republican-on-Republican violence."

In the end, the Senate opted for an approach under which appropriations bills or other measures containing special interest tax breaks or new entitlement spending would be broken apart into hundreds of new bills. These "separately enrolled" bills would each then be subject to a presidential veto.

By going for the separate enrollment idea, Dole headed off a confrontation between conservatives backing an "enhanced rescissions" measure (HR 2) that had passed the House and a smaller bloc of GOP moderates lined up behind a less stringent "expedited rescissions" bill (S 14) that proposed to shift far less power to the White House. The split had threatened to sink the entire effort.

Ironically, the separate enrollment idea had its strongest backing from a handful of Democrats such as Ernest F. Hollings of South Carolina, Joseph P. Biden Jr. of Delaware and Bill Bradley of New Jersey.

Contributing to the speedy passage of the bill in 1995 was the defeat of the balanced-budget constitutional amendment only three weeks earlier at the hands of Senate Democrats. That made it much more difficult for Democrats to oppose the line-item veto bill or even to slow it down. It sped through the Senate in four days, which seemed like warp speed after the protracted balanced-budget amendment battle.

Also helping Republicans was a statement by Clinton urging the Senate "to pass the strongest possible line-item veto and to make it effective immediately."

Throughout the Senate debate, the bill drew heaps of scorn from opponents, who derided the separate enrollment idea as unworkable. Even supporters admitted the bill was less than perfect. But any opposition was swamped by widespread sentiment that something needed to be done to change the existing process, which allowed Congress to bury questionable spending items in appropriations bills that the president had little option but to sign.

The bill did not make it to Clinton's desk, however. House and Senate Republicans made only halting efforts to reconcile the huge differences between their versions, clearly hesitant to give such sweeping new powers to a Democratic president.

3. PRODUCT LIABILITY

Efforts to curb product liability damage awards had spanned more than a decade. In 1995 the Republican-controlled Congress gave proponents their best chance ever to break a Senate logjam.

In March the House passed a broad product liability bill (HR 956) that included limits on medical malpractice and frivolous lawsuits as part of the Republicans' "Contract with America." Attention then turned to the Senate, where Majority Leader Bob Dole, R-Kan., backed efforts to pass a bill that tracked the House proposal. Dole was under pressure to move legislation to shore up his support among conservatives as he sought the GOP presidential nomination.

But Dole was bested by Sen. John D. Rockefeller IV of West Virginia, the chief Democratic sponsor of a much more narrowly drawn bill. Throughout Senate floor debate, Rockefeller warned that a broad bill could not command the 60 votes needed to end a certain filibuster. His prediction rang true after two back-to-back cloture votes May 4 failed to cut off debate. The second motion to cut off debate was rejected 47–52: R 45–9; D 2–43 (ND 2–33, SD 0–10).

The setback forced Dole and his allies to regroup and back a narrow version of HR 956 that passed on a 61–37 vote May 10. Dropped from the final version were protections against liability for doctors and sanctions to limit frivolous lawsuits.

In the days leading up to the defeat of the cloture motions, the Senate had taken a series of votes to broaden the bill, narrowly approving amendments to extend new protections to doctors, small and large businesses, and charitable organizations, as well as to manufacturers of faulty products.

Proponents of the broad Senate bill argued that expanding the legislation could build grass-roots support beyond the relatively small coalition of manufacturers who were covered by the narrow bill. (The House had taken a similar tack with great success, overcoming initial unease that the strategy would undermine prospects for passage.)

In the end, the Senate's retreat made reaching a compromise with the House more difficult. Even Senate advocates of a broad bill conceded that a final bill could not be much different than the Senate-passed version. At year's end, House and Senate conferees on HR 956 had failed to broker their differences.

4. TELECOMMUNICATIONS OVERHAUL

In 1994 Congress's effort to rewrite the 60-year-old federal telecommunications law foundered in the Senate. In 1995 the Senate overcame its own internal divisions on telecommunications issues with such a convincing margin as to give the legislation early momentum and limit President Clinton's veto options.

Several things had changed since the 103rd Congress. The Senate membership had become decidedly more Republican and more inclined to reduce regulation. And S 652, the 1995 bill, was drafted in a fashion much more favorable to the regional Bell operators, who were instrumental in the defeat of the Senate bill in late 1994.

S 652 sought to rewrite decades of telecommunications laws considered out of date with rapidly evolving digital telecommunications technology. Its principal provisions included removing the barriers that separated local and long-distance telephone companies since the breakup of AT&T in 1982.

From the outset, the main political fight was between interests allied with regional Bell companies and those allied with the long-distance carriers. The vote to pass S 652 was a resounding demonstration of the clout wielded by the Bells.

It also represented an early, and controversial, entry by Congress into the business of regulating objectionable content on the Internet and private on-line computer services. The bill included an amendment by Sen. Jim Exon, D-Neb., to ban the on-line dissemination of indecent material. Once S 652 passed, there was little doubt the House would have to address that issue as well.

The margin of the June 15 Senate vote on passage was impressive, especially given that the previous year's efforts went nowhere. The vote was 81–18: R 51–2; D 30–16 (ND 23–13, SD 7–3).

That strong showing undermined Clinton's position early. He complained about some of the bill's provisions, but refrained from issuing a veto threat until later, just before the House bill passed by a narrower, but still veto-proof margin. (*House key vote 9*)

The Senate vote had an effect on internal Democratic politics as well. Throughout the year, Ernest F. Hollings of South Carolina counseled White House officials to restrain from being too vigorous in its opposition. The big vote allowed him to argue that he—and not the White House—should assume the role of chief Democratic negotiator as the bill moved into a House-Senate conference.

5. HIGHWAY SPEED LIMITS

S 440 was supposed to be a minor highway bill designating the routes of a new National Highway System that had been created in 1991. But when it was drafted to include the repeal of all federal speed limits, it quickly became a vehicle for states' rights and deregulation. With much of the GOP agenda blocked by interchamber divisions or presidential veto, the speed limit issue stood out as one of the few successful bids to give power held by the federal government back to the states.

On many issues, the Senate had been more cautious than the House about devolving federal power. But on speed limits, the Senate embraced the concept enthusiastically—in part because rural states, where federally mandated speed limits were unpopular, held proportionately greater power.

The speed limit provision was included from the outset in S 440 and remained unchallenged during consideration in the Environment and Public Works Committee in early May. But Frank R. Lautenberg, D-N.J., former chairman of the committee and a prime advocate of highway safety programs, vowed to kill it on the floor.

Instead, it was Lautenberg's amendment to strike the provision that was killed June 20, in the form of a tabling motion offered by Don Nickles, R-Okla. The vote to table was 65–35: R 50–4; D 15–31 (ND 10–26, SD 5–5). The bill itself passed by voice vote two days later.

Repealing federal speed limits had long been a goal of Western states with long stretches of empty highways. Before the enactment of the 55 mph limit in 1974 (amended in 1987 to allow a 65 mph limit on rural portions of interstate highways), states had set their own limits. With the passage of S 440, speed limits once again went up. Montana, for instance, returned to its pre-1974 policy of having no specific limits for cars at all on some highways during daylight hours.

Speed limits were first intended to reduce oil consumption on the heels of the Arab oil embargo. But by the time S 440 came up for debate, the world had been awash in oil for more than a decade. The debate was framed as a safety issue by Lautenberg and as a states' rights issue by Republican and Western lawmakers. The states' rights side won handily.

A similar provision was included in the House version of the National Highway System bill (HR 2274) passed Sept. 20, and a move to strike it was handily rejected 112–313. Despite the reluctance of committee leaders in both chambers to take steps that could be interpreted as weakening highway safety laws, the provision was included in the conference report on S 440 that cleared Nov. 18. President Clinton vigorously denounced the repealing of speed limits, but the strength of the Senate vote and the need to release highway money to the states led his advisers to conclude that he might not be able to sustain a veto. He signed the bill into law Nov. 28.

6. FOSTER NOMINATION

Antiabortion activists got an early indication of the impact of the 1994 elections when the Senate derailed the nomination of President Clinton's choice to become surgeon general. Although abortion was one catalyst in the fight over the nomination of Nashville obstetrician and gynecologist Henry W. Foster Jr., the politics of the 1996 presidential contest could not be discounted in the outcome.

Almost as soon as Clinton nominated Foster to replace Joycelyn Elders (who had become controversial for her stands on sex education as well as abortion), antiabortion activists raised questions about the number of abortions Foster had performed and suggested that even one could be enough to disqualify him for the position as the nation's top health spokesman.

Foster and the White House stumbled initially after the nomination was announced in February. White House officials announced that Foster had performed only one abortion; Foster then said he had done about a dozen. A further check indicated that Foster was the physician of record for 39 abortions.

The confusion opened the door to further attacks on Foster's credibility, including his knowledge about an infamous syphilis study in Tuskegee, Ala., before it was disclosed in 1972. In that study, infected black men were left untreated so federal officials could study the disease. Foster was also questioned about the success of his highly touted program to discourage inner-city teen pregnancy.

Further muddying the waters were the maneuvers of two Republican presidential hopefuls—Sens. Bob Dole of Kansas and Phil Gramm of Texas. Dole, the majority leader and considered the GOP front-runner, and Gramm, one of Dole's most serious challengers, both were looking for support from the party's conservative antiabortion activists, considered key to winning certain Republican primaries and caucuses. While Gramm threatened to filibuster, Dole countered that he might not bring the nomination to the floor.

Meanwhile, Clinton, another player in the presidential sweepstakes, stood by his nominee throughout the grueling five-month process, amid accusations that he was trying to shore up his support among abortion-rights advocates by selecting Foster in the first place.

Foster's strong performance at a hearing of the Labor and Human Resources Committee, which ultimately recommended that he be confirmed, left Dole with little choice but to move forward with the nomination. Easing his no-vote suggestion, Dole met with Foster and then agreed to bring up the nomination for a vote.

But the controversy would not end. In a move that stole some of Gramm's thunder, Dole scheduled a cloture vote to see if there would be the 60 votes necessary to cut off Gramm's threatened filibuster. The move also prevented a straight up-or-down vote on Foster's nomination, which would have required only 51 votes for confirmation. Eventually two cloture votes were held a day apart, but the decisive vote turned out to be the first on June 21, which failed by three votes to cut off debate 57–43: R: 11–43; D: 46–0 (ND 36–0, SD 10–0). That ended Foster's chances; there was no change in the tally when the Senate failed again June 22 to invoke cloture.

7. REGULATORY OVERHAUL

Senate Majority Leader Bob Dole, R-Kan., made passage of an overhaul of federal regulations a top priority for 1995. To this end, he sponsored S 343, a tough bill that would have required cost-benefit analyses and risk assessment for many new regulations.

The attack on federal regulations as burdensome and costly resonated with the party's conservative constituencies and, in particular, with small-business owners. Passage of S 343 was viewed as a test of Dole's ability to deliver. But Dole was forced to shelve the measure July 20 after an unyielding bloc of Democratic opponents narrowly rejected his motion to cut off their filibuster of the bill. The vote was 58–40: R 54–0; D 4–40 (ND 0–34, SD 4–6). It was Dole's third unsuccessful cloture effort the week of July 17 on a bill that had tied up the Senate floor for nearly two weeks.

During the debate, Dole made several concessions to opponents, but he continued to insist that the Senate pass a tough measure that would require extensive cost-benefit and risk analysis for major regulations, expand opportunities for regulated parties to sue federal agencies over their adherence to administrative procedures and allow individuals to petition agencies to modify or revoke regulations.

On July 18, when the Senate voted on a comprehensive and less restrictive substitute amendment, it became clear that support for Dole's approach was not overwhelming. The thinly bipartisan alternative, offered by John Glenn, D-Ohio, and John H. Chafee, R-R.I., was narrowly rejected 48–52. Unlike S 343, the Glenn-Chafee substitute would have given agency officials much greater latitude in carrying out cost-benefit tests, limited judicial review of agency procedures and disallowed individuals to petition agencies for regulatory review.

By the final cloture vote, the battle drawn-out had been distilled to rhetorical shorthand: Are Senate Democrats defending the status quo and thwarting legislation to stem costly overregulation, or are they protecting the American people by preventing Republicans from tying federal agencies in procedural knots and allowing special interests to gut health, safety and environmental protections?

8. LOBBY REGISTRATION

Having successfully staged a filibuster to kill legislation in the 103rd Congress to strengthen reporting requirements for lobbyists, some Senate Republicans were not eager to see the issue return. But once the matter came to a vote July 25, the Senate unanimously passed a bill (S 1060) to impose significant new reporting requirements. The vote was 98–0: R 53–0, D 45–0 (ND 36–0, SD 9–0).

The vote was critical because bipartisan Senate support for the bill, sponsored by William S. Cohen, R-Maine, and Carl Levin, D-Mich., brought political pressure on House Republicans to bring an identical lobby registration measure to the floor of that chamber. House Majority Leader Dick Armey, R-Texas, had said June 21 that he would not schedule a vote on lobby legislation until the Senate acted. Once House Republican leaders scheduled a vote, the House cleared the measure for President Clinton's signature. *(House key vote 17)*

Still, the unanimous Senate vote belied the uncertainty that surrounded the bill up until it passed. First, bill supporters had a hard time getting Senate Majority Leader Bob Dole, R-Kan., to agree to bring the bill to the floor. In June Levin and Paul Wellstone, D-Minn., threatened to try to attach the measure to the big telecommunications deregulation bill (S 652), a priority of the GOP leadership. It was only then that Dole said he would set aside time in July for the lobby bill.

With the Republican takeover the previous fall fueling demands to change the way Congress operated, GOP leaders found themselves with a Hobson's choice of enacting tough lobby legislation or passing no bill at all. Inaction, though, carried steep political risks from a public demanding an end to business as usual.

Mindful of that, Mitch McConnell, R-Ky., led the GOP efforts to come up with a bipartisan lobbying bill that would attract wide support. Dole and Minority Leader Tom Daschle, D-S.D., appointed a bipartisan task force in late June to try to develop such a compromise. McConnell and Levin, both members of the task force, announced a breakthrough July 24, the same day debate began on the original bill, which had lacked broad bipartisan support.

The Senate adopted the McConnell-Levin substitute by a 98–0 vote July 24 and with that vote all but assured final passage a day later.

9. BOSNIA TROOP DEPLOYMENT

After four years of televised atrocities and horrific stories of "ethnic cleansing," most senators knew that no bill or law could stop the war in Bosnia. But they also had come to the realization that the status quo was no longer tenable. With that sense of grim resignation, the Senate on July 26 voted overwhelmingly to unilaterally break the U.N. embargo that had barred arms shipments to Bosnia's beleaguered Muslims. It was a bipartisan demand for a change in U.S. policy toward the Balkans, even though that change risked a wider war and a deeper American military role in the conflict. But frustration with the largely diplomatic approach pursued by the Clinton administration and U.S. allies outweighed the risks.

The die had been cast well before the vote. Having all but conceded defeat, the White House focused its lobbying efforts on keeping the vote below the two-thirds margin needed to override a threatened presidential veto.

The administration did not even achieve that modest objective. The Senate passed the lift-the-embargo bill (S 21), sponsored by Majority Leader Bob Dole, R-Kan., and Connecticut Democrat Joseph I. Lieberman, by a vote of 69–29: R 48–5; D 21–24 (ND 19–17, SD 2–7).

The Senate action set the stage for a momentous foreign policy clash between President Clinton and Congress. Less than a week later, on Aug. 1, the House easily passed the measure, 298–128, sending the legislation to the president. Again, the margin was sufficient to override a veto.

The bill crafted by Dole and Lieberman included no direct military aid for the outgunned Bosnian Muslims, widely perceived to be the victims of Serb aggression. It merely ordered the president to break the arms embargo imposed on all of the former Yugoslavia in 1991. In order to produce a strong vote, Dole included waivers and conditions enabling the president to delay that action for months.

Clinton, as promised, vetoed the legislation Aug. 11, calling it "the wrong step at the wrong time." The president contended that ending the arms ban would shred allied unity, force the withdrawal of U.N. forces from Bosnia and ultimately drag the United States into the conflict.

The votes in Congress, combined with a series of unrelated events on the ground in Bosnia, already were pushing the administration into a far more aggressive policy. Most significantly, the United States and its allies responded in a meaningful fashion to an act of Serb aggression. After an Aug. 28 Serb mortar attack on the Bosnian capital of Sarajevo, scores of U.S. and other NATO aircraft began pounding Serb positions. That changed the course of the war and Western diplomacy in the Balkans. Clinton signaled that the United States, after years of deferring to its allies in a failed policy of negotiations and pinprick air strikes, was finally prepared to lead.

The administration's new assertiveness also reduced the temperature in the congressional debate over ending the embargo. Dole was still intent on arming the Bosnians, but he indicated he would postpone a showdown on overriding Clinton's veto to give the new policy time to work.

Dole also maintained that the air strikes were necessitated, at least in part, by Congress's uncompromising stance. "The West knew what would happen if it didn't respond to the latest Serb atrocity," he said Aug. 30. "Congress would override President Clinton's veto of the legislation lifting the U.S. embargo on Bosnia."

The votes on overriding the veto never took place, as a new, U.S.-led diplomatic offensive produced a peace agreement among Bosnia's bitter enemies. Clinton received the grudging support of Congress, as he deployed 20,000 U.S. troops to help enforce that accord.

10. GIFT BAN

Against a backdrop of widespread discontent with Congress, the Senate prepared in July to limit the gifts and trips that senators and their aides could accept from special interests. The real question, though, came down to how strict those limits should be.

Sens. John McCain, R-Ariz., William S. Cohen, R-Maine, and Carl Levin, D-Mich., were in one camp. They proposed a package of changes to Senate internal rules (S Res 158) that required senators to turn down any gift or meal valued at more than $50. Senators and their aides also would be limited to no more than an aggregate total value of $100 in gifts from any one source in a year. In a central provision, the proposal called for banning senators and their aides from accepting lobbyist-financed recreational trips to golf, ski and tennis resorts to raise money for charities.

Frank H. Murkowski was in another camp. The Alaska Republican believed McCain's proposal went too far and threatened to stifle fund-raising for good causes. Murkowski offered an amendment that would have allowed senators to continue to accept free recreational trips for charitable events. "I think we have a clear choice," Murkowski said. "Do we want to establish the same lodging and transportation rules for charitable fund-raisers as we have for political fund-raising, or do we want to make it harder, harder to raise money for worthy charities?"

Paul Wellstone, D-Minn., was solidly in McCain's camp. "It does not serve any of us as individual senators well when lobbyists pay for senators and their spouses or their family to go on weekend golf, tennis, skiing or fishing trips," he said. "It is inappropriate. We ought not to be taking these gifts. People in the country do not think it is right."

In a critical test of politics as usual, the Senate rejected the Murkowski amendment July 28. The vote was 39–60: R 30–23, D 9–37 (ND 2–34, SD 7–3).

The vote showed that there was a clear majority in the Senate for toughening gift rules. It also revealed support for ending lavish, lobbyist-paid recreational trips. Further, it sent a message to voters that the Senate was trying to change the way institutional Washington operated. The trips had become a point of particular public ire.

The fact that a majority of senators rejected Murkowski's proposal in favor of tough gift rules helped Wellstone push through by voice vote an even tougher amendment that called for counting all gifts and meals of $10 or more toward the $100 aggregate limit.

Murkowski's defeat also cleared the way for the Senate later the same day to adopt the final rules change package by a vote of 98–0. The new gift restrictions applied only to the Senate and went into effect Jan. 1. The unanimous vote reflected what Senate leaders had always known: Once the measure was on the floor, senators found it politically impossible to oppose tough gift restrictions. For this reason, there was considerable resistance initially to bringing up any gift rule proposals that had not first been vetted behind closed doors by all sides.

In late 1994 Senate Republicans had staged a filibuster and killed similar provisions. A year later Wellstone and Levin forced the gift restrictions to the floor by threatening to attach the provisions along with those relating to new lobby registration requirements to a telecommunications deregulation bill (S 652), a legislative priority for the GOP leadership.

The Senate action put pressure on the House GOP leadership to take up the issue as well. In fact, the House went even further than the Senate and voted to ban virtually all gifts, except those from family and friends. *(House key vote 14)*

11. PACKWOOD HEARINGS

The nearly three-year-old sexual misconduct case against Sen. Bob Packwood, chairman of the powerful Finance Committee, eventually brought down a pivotal figure in the Republican drive to cut taxes and reduce federal spending. The case also threatened the reputation of the institution that the Oregon Republican had called home for almost 27 years.

Stung by public revulsion to the televised hearings of sexual misconduct charges leveled in 1991 by Anita F. Hill against then-Supreme Court nominee Clarence Thomas, most senators shuddered at the idea of dragging the institution through another spectacle.

Majority Leader Bob Dole, R-Kan., was trying to build a presidential campaign on the strength of his work in the Senate, and one thing he did not need in mid-1995 was a parade of witnesses testifying against a key ally.

It was one of the four Democratic women elected to the Senate in 1992 in the wake of voter outrage over the Thomas-Hill hearings who forced the critical issue of public hearings on Packwood to the Senate floor. The effort by Barbara Boxer of California opened old wounds and caused the Ethics Committee to bring its inquiry of Packwood to an abrupt halt for 10 days.

Throughout July, a virtually unanimous Republican Party—including all three GOP members of the Ethics Committee—stood by their embattled colleague. On July 11, six days after Packwood declined to ask the committee to hold public hearings on his case, Boxer announced that she would try to force a floor vote to urge public hearings.

Boxer's announcement put senators in an uncomfortable position. The choice: avert public hearings on sexual misconduct allegations and avoid a lengthy and steamy public spectacle; or confront political pressure from female members of Congress, women's organizations and even some conservative Christian groups—all of which had called for public hearings.

Boxer's vow prompted Ethics Committee Chairman Mitch McConnell, R-Ky., to threaten to hold public hearings on ethical allegations leveled against Democratic senators. McConnell then abruptly called off the committee's deliberations on Packwood from July 21–31. When the committee met again at the end of July, it voted

along party lines, 3–3, against holding public hearings in the Packwood case. It was the first time the ethics panel decided not to hold public hearings in a case that had reached the final stage of committee deliberations.

True to her word, Boxer on Aug. 2 then offered her amendment calling for public hearings to the defense authorization bill (S 1026). After a lengthy debate, in which the three Republican members of the Ethics Committee spoke against the amendment and the three Democratic members backed the measure, the Senate voted down Boxer's amendment, 48–52: R 3–51; D 45–1 (ND 35–1, SD 10–0). Only William S. Cohen, R-Maine; Olympia J. Snowe, R-Maine; Arlen Specter, R-Pa.; and Daniel Patrick Moynihan, D-N.Y., crossed party lines. Packwood raised eyebrows when he voted against the amendment rather than abstain.

The controversy behind them, members of the committee resumed their deliberations on the Packwood case the next day. Those talks were again put on hold after the committee announced that they would investigate two new allegations of sexual misconduct against Packwood, one involving a minor.

Packwood lashed out at the committee for reopening the case and announced that he would fight back. On Aug. 25 Packwood both stunned and angered his allies in the Senate by reversing his position and calling for public hearings.

On Sept. 6, without ever taking public testimony, the committee unanimously voted to expel Packwood on charges of sexual misconduct, abuse of office and obstruction of justice. A day later, after meeting with two close allies, Dole and Sen. John McCain, R-Ariz., Packwood announced his resignation on the floor of the Senate.

12. DEFENSE SPENDING

The two types of raptors in the Senate's Republican aviary—deficit hawks whose top priority was slicing the federal budget and defense hawks intent on reversing a decade of inflation-adjusted decline in Pentagon spending—more or less split the difference to hammer out a defense appropriations bill for fiscal 1996. So, although the Senate was consumed in brutal fights over how deeply to cut nearly every other discretionary program in the federal budget, it approved a $7 billion addition to Clinton's defense request without much of a fight and by nearly a two-thirds majority.

Two senior Republicans on the Armed Services Committee, Arizona's John McCain and Virginia's John W. Warner, opened the bidding in this curiously low-profile defense budget debate by calling for a fiscal 1996 budget that would provide the same purchasing power as the budget Congress had approved for fiscal 1995—in other words, provide the Pentagon with enough of an increase to cover the cost of inflation. This would have required adding $12 billion to $15 billion to Clinton's $258 billion request. That proposal ran afoul of other Republicans determined to reduce all federal spending.

Senate Democrats were split three ways. Most liberals preferred a smaller defense budget than Clinton requested. Others, mostly from the political center, supported a boost in Clinton's budget, though favoring a smaller increase than McCain had proposed. Yet others had a strong stake in any bill that funded programs that were vital to constituents' jobs.

The basic issue of how much to spend for defense was settled by the Congressional Budget Resolution (H Con Res 67), which presumed an increase of $7 billion. Although there was no evidence of broad support for such an increase, the entire issue of defense spending had little resonance with the public. Perhaps for that reason, Democratic heavyweights never mounted a serious effort to challenge the $7 billion increase.

Money for military construction and for nuclear weapons programs conducted by the Energy Department was contained in separate legislation. The clearest test of Senate support for higher defense spending was passage of the defense appropriations bill (S 1087), which covered all Pentagon programs other than construction.

The Senate passed the bill, which included $6.4 billion more than the administration requested, by a vote of 62–35: R 48–4; D 14–31 (ND 7–28, SD 7–3).

13. WELFARE OVERHAUL

The Senate's passage of the welfare overhaul bill (HR 4) stood in stark contrast to the outcome in the House. While debate in the House was swift and raucous, leaving conservatives firmly in command, the Senate acted deliberately and in a more muted atmosphere, giving moderates from both parties the edge. The final product provided a road map for a bipartisan overhaul that was ultimately disdained.

Republican Senators, like House Republicans, agreed to make block grants their principal instrument of change. The aim was to give states broad authority to run their own welfare programs, with lump sum federal payments to help offset costs. (House key vote 3)

But Senate Republicans disagreed among themselves on many specifics. Majority Leader Bob Dole, R-Kan., tried to bring both sides together by postponing the Senate's August recess and getting members to focus on his own overhaul plan (S 1120), which revised legislation that had been approved by several committees.

However, many Republicans were reluctant to embrace Dole's bill. Conservatives sought more restrictions on social services and more block grants to the states. Moderates wanted assurances that states would maintain their existing welfare funding and guarantees that welfare recipients who were required to work would have access to child care. With no easy resolution in sight, Dole pulled the bill off the floor after a day and a half of opening speeches.

When Dole's bill, offered as an amendment to HR 4, returned to the floor after Labor Day, the most influential senators turned out to be a small group of moderate Republicans who occasionally formed a powerful coalition with the chamber's 46 Democrats. They reshaped the bill more to their liking, through negotiations with the leadership and victories on a few hotly contested amendments. Their efforts bolstered the bill's spending for child care and increased how much states would have to contribute to their welfare programs. They also blunted conservative attempts to impose more restrictions on welfare assistance.

The split between moderate and conservative Republicans crystallized over whether to prohibit federal welfare assistance payments to children born to welfare recipients. The House bill had included this so-called family cap, and Dole added it to the Senate version when pressed to do so by conservatives. But moderates insisted that each state should decide whether to deny checks in those instances. They found overwhelming support for their position in the Senate, which voted 66–34 on Sept. 13 in favor of an amendment by Pete V. Domenici, R-N.M., to strike the provision.

President Clinton, who had been at odds with House Republicans over their version of the bill, praised the Senate measure. It passed 87–12 on Sept. 19, with a strong, if fragile, majority from both parties: R 52–1; D 35–11 (ND 25–11, SD 10–0).

Not everyone rejoiced. Liberals warned that the bill would destroy the social safety net, and they objected to ending the 60-year-old guarantee of providing welfare checks to eligible low-income mothers and children. Conservatives grumbled that the Senate version did not do enough to try to stem out-of-wedlock births.

Both sides looked ahead warily to the House-Senate conference. When the conference produced a compromise that included some important elements of the House version, Democratic support largely vanished, and Clinton vetoed it.

14. BUDGET RECONCILIATION

For several months after the watershed November 1994 elections, the newly Republican Senate seemed much less inclined than the feisty new House GOP majority to find a way to reconcile the Republicans' campaign pledges to cut taxes and balance the budget while leaving more than half of federal spending (Social Security, defense, interest on the debt) off the table.

Led by men who had witnessed the failures of the Reagan fiscal revolution of the 1980s, the Senate adopted a go-slow approach. Senate Majority Leader Bob Dole, R-Kan., and Budget Committee Chairman Pete V. Domenici, R-N.M., both evinced much less interest in deep tax cuts than their House counterparts, and Domenici called early in 1995 for just a "down payment" on a balanced budget.

But once the House charged ahead, the Senate had little choice but to follow. Domenici developed a seven-year plan to balance the budget by 2002, and he reluctantly made room for $170 billion in tax cuts—roughly half the House's $353 billion—that would kick in only after the Congressional Budget Office had certified that the detailed spending cuts in the budget-reconciliation bill would actually balance the budget.

The Senate budget targeted for overhaul many of the same politically volatile programs the House went after. It proposed ending entitlement status for Medicaid and welfare, introducing more market forces into Medicare and slashing away at scores of long-standing domestic spending programs.

The Senate handily adopted both its own fiscal 1996 budget resolution (S Con Res 13) May 25 and a compromise House-Senate version (H Con Res 67) on June 29. In that June compromise, the House came a little more than halfway toward the Senate on tax cuts, reducing the figure to $245 billion. But the budget still called for spending cuts tougher than a small but powerful group of Senate GOP moderates wanted.

Heading into the key showdown over the budget reconciliation bill (HR 2491), which translated the budget resolution into actual spending cuts, leaders worked hard to find ways to keep the moderates on board. In the end, it took two floor amendments to keep a swing group of six GOP moderates behind the reconciliation bill.

One rider added nearly $6 billion for education programs, mostly in the form of subsidies for college loans. The other added back some $12 billion for Medicare and Medicaid. Centrist Republicans, whom Democrats had hoped might blow up the reconciliation bill, instead voted for it in a big showdown Oct. 28, as the Senate passed the measure, 52–47: R 52–1; D 0–46 (ND 0–36, SD 0–10).

Said moderate Republican John H. Chafee of Rhode Island, "You've got to remember one driving force that is pushing this: We've got to get these deficits under control. So we've been able to swallow a lot of things to achieve that goal."

15. LATE-TERM ABORTIONS

Following the House lead, the Senate in late 1995 stepped deeper into antiabortion territory and passed a bill to ban a certain type of late-term abortion. The bill proposed to make it a federal crime, punishable by fines and imprisonment, to perform a controversial type of late-term abortion that sponsors called a "partial birth abortion." The term appeared to apply to a procedure in which the doctor partially extracted the fetus from the womb and might collapse the head before completing the abortion. Abortion foes said the procedure was needlessly brutal, while many abortion rights advocates said it was a rare but potentially important option for doctors handling certain problem pregnancies.

The Senate was closely divided on abortion and had often served to brake antiabortion initiatives generated in the House. After the House on Nov. 1 passed a bill (HR 1833) to ban certain abortions, it appeared that pattern might be repeated. Senators first voted to delay action on the bill and then appeared poised to blunt its impact significantly.

Ultimately, however, senators on Dec. 7 adopted a version of the bill substantially similar to the House measure. As in the House, it marked the first time the Senate had voted to outlaw a type of abortion. The vote was 54–44: R 45–8; D 9–36 (ND 5–30, SD 4–6). *(House key vote 12)*

Yet senators acted knowing that the bill would probably not become law. President Clinton had promised to veto the legislation as written, and there was little prospect of gathering the votes needed for an override.

Abortion rights advocates had only limited hopes of defeating the bill outright. Instead, when senators took up the legislation the week of Dec. 4, the key fight was over whether to allow the disputed abortion procedure if the doctor believed it was necessary to safeguard the life or health of the woman.

Many senators were prepared to support an exemption to protect the life of the pregnant woman. The House bill already provided some legal protection from prosecution in cases in which the woman's life was at risk. Majority Leader Bob Dole, R-Kan., offered an amendment to strengthen that language, and it was adopted 98–0 on Dec. 7.

Sen. Barbara Boxer, D-Calif., tried to go further, offering an amendment to extend that exemption to cases affecting the woman's health as well as her life. Abortion rights advocates said that broader exemption was necessary to make the bill constitutional and, according to administration statements, to win Clinton's signature. Despite those admonishments, Boxer's amendment failed, 47–51.

Abortion opponents had insisted the Boxer proposal would all but destroy the bill. Senators went on to narrowly endorse the overall bill, which went no further in 1995.

16. FLAG DESECRATION

The debate over protecting the U.S. flag had raged since 1990, when the Supreme Court struck down a 1989 federal law banning mistreatment of the flag, saying it violated First Amendment rights to free expression. With newly empowered Republicans controlling Congress in 1995, the House easily passed a bill in June seeking a constitutional amendment to allow the government to pass laws banning physical desecration of the flag. Proponents and opponents knew that the measure's fate would be decided in the Senate.

Supporters of the bill (S J Res 31) seemed to have the momentum on their side going into the vote. The House version (H J Res 79) passed by a vote of 312–120, a comfortable 24 votes more than the two-thirds needed to send a constitutional amendment to the states for ratification. Moreover, polls indicated that about 80 percent of Americans supported an amendment to protect the flag, and 49 state legislatures had passed resolutions calling on Congress to pass the amendment.

In the Senate, supporters struggled to come up with the two-thirds majority. Throughout the year, the number of firm supporters hovered around 60, well below the number needed if all senators voted. The Senate measure proposed a constitutional amendment allowing Congress to pass laws banning flag desecration. The House version also would have allowed states to enact such laws.

Proponents argued that the flag, as the ultimate symbol of the United States, deserved special protection. Opponents said the price of liberty included protecting forms of expression that many people found offensive.

Proponents jockeyed for support in the weeks before the Dec. 12 vote. In the end, they could not win over the last three fence-sitting Democrats—Bill Bradley of New Jersey, Barbara A. Mikulski of Maryland and Joseph I. Lieberman of Connecticut—who ultimately decided that they were more uncomfortable amending the Constitution than tolerating flag burners.

Bradley called flag burners "lowlifes" but said, "The question now is whether protecting the flag merits amending the Bill of Rights." The bill failed to get the necessary majority, falling on a vote of 63–36: R 49–4; D 14–32 (ND 7–29, SD 7–3).

17. SHAREHOLDER LAWSUITS

Personal pleas from President Clinton failed to sway a single Democrat supporting a controversial securities litigation bill (HR 1058) to sustain his veto of the measure. Instead, following the House's similar action, the Senate on Dec. 22 quickly overrode Clinton's veto by a vote of 68–30: R 48–4; D 20–26 (ND 17–19, SD 3–7). It was the only one of Clinton's 11 vetoes in 1995 that the GOP-dominated 104th Congress was able to reverse. *(House key vote 18)*

The brief override battle was unusual in that it pitted Clinton against Christopher J. Dodd, D-Conn., a loyal supporter of the president and titular head of the Democratic Party. Dodd, who played a prominent role in lining up veto-proof margins on two prior floor votes on the bill, prevailed easily.

The bill, which became law with the Senate's vote, was intended to make it more difficult for investors to win securities fraud lawsuits against corporations that issue erroneous predictions of company performance, against securities firms that underwrote and sold stock issues and against accountants who audited corporate books.

Clinton's veto came unexpectedly and literally at the 11th hour of Dec. 19, the last day he had to act on the bill. By the time the House overrode the veto the next afternoon, Dodd had already started lining up commitments from most of the 20 Democrats who had previously voted for it. When Clinton started lobbying in earnest that night and the following day, he hit a brick wall. "I told the president that when I give my word, I keep it," said Jim Exon, D-Neb., who gave a commitment to Dodd before receiving a late-night call from Clinton.

Most senators, aides and lobbyists closely following the bill agreed that if the administration had objections to the conference report, they should have been raised when the Senate debated the measure earlier in the month. Instead, the administration was silent; the president had not yet focused on the issue, and a split existed among his top advisers over whether he should sign the bill.

By the time the veto came, members already had voted twice on the measure—first on the bill itself, then on the conference report. Both had earlier passed by veto-proof margins. Having twice gone on record, members had little incentive to change their votes on the arcane but intensely lobbied bill.

It did not help the president's cause that his principal objection was to a fairly technical legal nuance that required plaintiffs to provide a greater level of proof in the early stages of a lawsuit. The administration had not raised the issue previously, adding to a sense of exasperation among members supporting the bill.

Dodd had repeatedly expressed confidence that Clinton would sign the bill. He met with Clinton on Dec. 18, the night before the president's decision was due, and emerged from the White House believing Clinton would probably sign it.

House

1. BALANCED-BUDGET AMENDMENT

The historic House vote in favor of amending the Constitution to require a balanced federal budget gave House Republicans their first significant victory in 1995. Even though the constitutional amendment died in the Senate a month later, the debate set the stage for the House and Senate to craft and pass their own seven-year plans to balance the budget.

The House passed the amendment (H J Res 1) on Jan. 26, by a vote of 300–132: R 228–2; D 72–129 (ND 34–105, SD 38–24); I 0–1. *(Senate key vote 1)*

Although public opinion—and an overwhelming majority of the House—appeared strongly in favor of the idea, House leaders had to perform a political high-wire act to assemble the two-thirds majority required to send a constitutional amendment to the states for ratification. Passage ultimately required an impressive display of Republican discipline as well as support from a minority of moderate-to-conservative Democrats.

What gave the Republican leadership difficulty was the decision to try to pass a version of the amendment that included a provision requiring three-fifths majorities in each chamber to pass future tax increases. This "tax limitation" provision had been included in the House GOP's "Contract with America." But the controversy over its inclusion threatened to scuttle the amendment because it was supported by only about half the approximately 60 Democrats whose votes were needed. Opponents said it would be a guarantee of future gridlock and would give too much power to a minority in Congress.

The task facing House leaders was to construct a floor procedure that would maximize votes for the contract bill, but also pave the way for passage of an alternative offered by Charles W. Stenholm, D-Texas, and Dan Schaefer, R-Colo. The Stenholm-Schaefer amendment required a balanced-budget by 2002 or two years after ratification, whichever came later. A three-fifths majority would be required to approve budgets that projected deficit spending, but there was no similar requirement for tax increases.

Deficit hawks from both parties had rallied around that version of the amendment for years, and even supporters of the stricter resolution acknowledged that it was the only one with a chance to garner the necessary two-thirds majority.

House leaders decided to let the House take preliminary votes on both the contract version, sponsored by Joe L. Barton, R-Texas, and Stenholm's version. Whichever measure received the most votes would be presented for a final vote.

A small but potentially pivotal group of conservatives was unhappy with the approach and complained that GOP leaders were not doing enough to fight for passage of the contract version. When the leadership began to send signals in the weeks before the vote that the freshmen would eventually have to vote for the weaker Stenholm alternative, it touched off a mini-revolt among GOP freshmen, some of whom threatened to vote against Stenholm on final passage. Had they followed through, they could have sunk the bill.

The House voted first on Barton's version, which received only 253 votes, well short of the two-thirds that would be required for passage. After a variety of other Democratic alternatives were rejected, Stenholm's version received 293 votes and was awarded a final vote.

"We all saw clearly at the end of this day we had to have a balanced-budget amendment," said House Majority Leader Dick Armey, R-Texas. By that time, the GOP whip organization had brought the reluctant freshmen into line.

2. REGULATORY OVERHAUL

Overhauling federal regulations and extending new rights to property owners were top priorities for House Republicans, who devoted a plank in their "Contract with America" to the issues.

During the week of Feb. 27, the House easily passed three landmark bills, all derived from the contract, to make it more difficult for federal agencies to issue health, safety and environmental rules.

The push was stoked by a coalition of Republicans and some conservative Democrats itching to overhaul what they view as a burdensome and heavy-handed federal bureaucracy.

Bills that passed with wide margins of support were a risk-assessment measure (HR 1022) that outlined a procedure for highly detailed scientific and economic analyses, a cost-benefit bill (HR 926), and a bill (HR 925) to make it easier for private property owners to be compensated for government limits on the use of their land.

In the end, the House merged the three bills into HR 9, along with a paperwork reduction bill (HR 830) that had passed Feb. 22. On March 3, the House passed HR 9, the original contract vehicle for the regulatory measures, by a vote of 277–141; R 219–8; D 58–132 (ND 23–110, SD 35–22); I 0–1. However, the Senate was stymied in its effort to move a companion bill (S 343). *(Senate key vote 7)*

In pursuing such a far-reaching agenda, House Republican leaders gambled. While they contended that the 1994 elections gave them a broad mandate to shrink the federal government, the changes in the regulatory process drew criticism that they were trying to undercut popular laws that protected health and the environment. Opponents of the measure portrayed the effort as a backdoor attempt, promoted by corporate interests, to block enforcement of health, safety and environmental laws that protected average Americans.

Supporters of the bureaucracy-bridling legislation, however, argued that unnecessary federal regulations imposed a $500 billion burden on the economy. They illustrated their position with numerous "horror story" anecdotes about poorly designed, overly expensive rules and excessive enforcement. They said federal agencies freely imposed new rules without producing sufficient scientific evidence that such rules were necessary to prevent significant hazards to human health and the environment.

3. WELFARE OVERHAUL

House Republicans gained passage of a critical element of their "Contract with America" when the House voted March 24 to overhaul 60 years of federally controlled welfare and related social service programs. But the vote was so partisan and so bitterly contested that it became clear that the bill (HR 4) would have to be modified before the Senate would pass it. *(Senate key vote 13)*

The legislation had evolved from the contract version through alterations by House leaders and in committee, with conservatives holding the upper hand throughout.

The bill that reached the floor proposed to give states unprecedented authority over cash welfare, child protection programs such as foster care and adoption assistance, child care, school meals, and special nutrition assistance for pregnant women and their young children. It also proposed to deny cash benefits to certain low-income alcoholics, drug addicts and disabled children, as well as a wide array of social services to legal immigrants.

Perhaps most significantly, the legislation proposed to eliminate the 60–year-old guarantee of providing welfare checks to low-income mothers and their children. Instead, states would generally be permitted to determine eligibility.

Republicans hailed the legislation as historic, enabling states to experiment freely with their welfare programs and allowing welfare recipients to wrest themselves from government dependency.

But the bill won few converts. Democrats bitterly accused Republicans of proposing harsh cuts in antipoverty aid to finance tax breaks for the wealthy. President Clinton, who had proposed a less sweeping welfare overhaul plan in 1994, denounced the bill as "weak on work and tough on children."

Republican leaders also faced dissent from within their own party. They were confident that the bill would pass, but they nonetheless spent a few weeks leading up to the vote trying to assuage concerns of party moderates. In one concession, they added provisions designed to improve child-support enforcement.

The leadership ultimately faced a stronger revolt on the floor from the House's most fervent antiabortion members, who worried that denying cash to unwed teenage mothers could encourage more abortions. These members also said that rewarding states for reducing out-of-wedlock births could prompt more abortions.

The rule for floor debate denied votes on most substantive amendments, including two of the four amendments sought by the antiabortion critics. The rule was adopted, 217–211, largely along party lines.

Many Democrats, who were incensed that they had virtually no role in writing the bill, objected to having relatively few opportunities to amend it on the floor. They claimed that the measure would not provide enough resources, especially child care, to help welfare recipients get jobs. They were especially critical of plans to eliminate the popular school lunch program. Republicans responded that they were simply letting states control school lunch programs while limiting federal assistance.

In the end, relatively few Republicans dissented from the party line. Most of those who were critical of parts of the bill still voted for it as an improvement over the status quo that would be further modified in the Senate. The vote for passage was 234–199: R 225–5; D 9–193 (ND 3–135, SD 6–58); I 0–1.

4. TERM LIMITS

The one item in the House GOP's "Contract with America" that most affected the lives of members of Congress was defeated in the House. A proposed constitutional amendment limiting the number of years lawmakers could serve did not come close to attracting the necessary two-thirds majority for passage. It was the only one of the 10 planks of the House GOP's contract to fail in the House.

The House could not muster the necessary two-thirds majority for a bill (H J Res 73) that would have sent to the states for ratification a constitutional amendment imposing a 12-year term limit on members of each chamber. The vote on March 29 was 227–204: R 189–40; D 38–163 (ND 22–117, SD 16–46); I 0–1. That was 61 votes short of the 288 votes needed for House passage. Three other alternative versions considered on the same day failed even to attract simple majorities.

Although House Republicans blamed Democrats for the failure of the term limits measure, the GOP had ample problems of its own. The Republican conference was fractured over the issue, with newly elected members who supported term limits at odds with veteran lawmakers who opposed them.

Members of the leadership, including Majority Whip Tom DeLay of Texas, also opposed the amendment. DeLay said he could not in good faith line up votes for the proposal so he turned that duty over to his chief deputy, Dennis Hastert of Illinois. Party discipline, which led to a string of victories on other contract items, was nowhere to be seen on term limits.

During Judiciary Committee consideration of the measure, seven-term Rep. George W. Gekas, R-Pa., won adoption of an amendment to apply the 12-year limit only to consecutive terms, on a 21–13 vote. The change would have meant that members could sit out a term after hitting the limit and then run again. Term-limit backers said the change "emasculated" the effect of adopting term limits. But six Republicans joined committee Democrats in voting for the Gekas amendment.

The committee then sent the term limits measure to the floor without recommendation, on a 21–14 vote.

Faced with potentially humiliating defeat on the floor in mid-March, House Majority Leader Dick Armey, R-Texas, delayed action until the end of the month. He vowed that the leadership, which had shown little enthusiasm for the proposal despite its inclusion in the contract, would aggressively try to whip up support for it.

Armey's strategy was aimed not so much at winning sufficient votes for passage, which was considered a long shot, but at soothing Republican divisions and mollifying term limit fans outside Congress. Many key Republican constituencies supported the amendment, including the Christian Coalition, the National Federation of Independent Business, United We Stand America, the National Taxpayers Union and the American Conservative Union.

On the day of the vote, Judiciary Committee Chairman Henry J. Hyde, R-Ill., won a standing ovation for a speech condemning the idea. He noted that many amendment supporters would not go so far as to call for term limits to apply retroactively. "I am reminded of the famous prayer of St. Augustine, who said, 'Dear God, make me pure, but not now.' "

5. TAX CUTS

Hailed by Speaker Newt Gingrich, R-Ga., as the "crowning jewel" of the House GOP's "Contract with America," a bill (HR 1215) to reduce taxes by $189 billion over five years sailed easily through the House on April 5. All but a handful of Republicans voted for it, and 27 Democrats crossed party lines to join the bill's supporters. On final passage, the vote was 246–188: R 219–11; D 27–176 (ND 9–130, SD 18–46); I 0–1.

The approval of the tax cut bill raised the price tag for zeroing out the deficit and handed Democrats fodder for one of their most piercing attacks against future Republican efforts to balance the federal budget. Democrats charged that the GOP was cutting programs for the elderly and poor in order to pay for a tax cut for the rich.

Republicans viewed tax relief as a political key to winning support for budget efforts. The tax cut bill was to be folded later into the budget-balancing reconciliation bill (HR 2491), providing a sweetener that would help win support for the bitter medicine of spending cuts.

The tax relief package was carefully constructed to help a wide array of interest groups: families, investors, Wall Street and Main Street. It included a $500-per-child tax credit for people earning adjusted gross incomes of up to $200,000 a year, the elimination of the alternative minimum tax paid by corporations, a reduction in the effective capital gains tax rate for individuals from 28 percent to 19.8 percent and the creation of a new form of individual retirement accounts. The lost revenue was to be offset by $100 billion in cuts from unspecified domestic discretionary spending programs, by increasing federal employees' pension contributions and by freezing reimbursement rates in certain Medicare programs.

There was little discussion on the House floor of the bill's long-term costs because the House did not request estimates of the seven-year and 10-year costs of the bill. When estimates were later done by the Treasury Department, the numbers showed that the $189 billion price tag over five years would balloon into a cost of more than $600 billion over 10 years as the tax cuts took hold.

In retrospect, the vote looked like an easy win, but the House leadership was anxious in the days leading up to it. Three groups of GOP rank-and-file members raised objections to the bill. One was a group of deficit hawks worried that the tax cut would undermine efforts to balance the budget. The second was a handful of members who had large numbers of federal employees in their districts and who objected to the increased pension fund contributions. A third group of more than 100 members—led by freshman GOP member Greg Ganske, R-Iowa—wanted at least a vote on reducing to $95,000 a year the family income eligibility for the per-child tax credit.

The concerns of deficit hawks were assuaged by the addition of a clause guaranteeing that the tax cuts would not be enacted until a budget-reconciliation bill had put the deficit on a path to zero. The large group of members militating for a lower threshold on the per-child tax credit melted away under pressure from the leadership. The only group that remained opposed to the bill were members with large numbers of federal employees in their districts.

Two efforts by Democrats to reduce the size of the tax cut and require specific spending cuts to pay for the tax reductions were rejected overwhelmingly. Indeed, a substitute tax cut bill offered by Minority Leader Richard A. Gephardt, D-Mo., which would have cut taxes by $31.6 billion over five years, won just 119 votes, with Democrats who wanted a large tax cut joining Republicans in opposing the Gephardt alternative and some liberal Democrats voting against it because they opposed all tax cuts when Congress was aiming to reduce the deficit.

6. CLEAN WATER ACT REWRITE

During the first 100 days of the 104th Congress, House Republicans easily pushed through legislation to overhaul health, safety and, most importantly, environmental regulations. So when the House took up a major rewrite of the clean water act (HR 961), the leadership did not anticipate significant opposition. Indeed, the bill easily passed May 16.

Supporters, led by Transportation and Infrastructure Committee Chairman Bud Shuster, R-Pa., said the bill would maintain the goal of cleaning up the nation's waterways. They said it would reverse what they called excessive federal regulations that had caused undue hardship for industry, states and local governments. The vote to pass the bill was 240–185: R 195–34; D 45–150 (ND 19–114, SD 26–36); I 0–1.

After the House vote, it became increasingly clear that passage of the measure had helped expose a weakness for the Republican Party that rippled through the appropriations and budget processes and was likely to continue into the 1996 election year. During the debate, opponents hammered away at the clean water bill, calling it a sweetheart deal for polluters. Many Republicans who voted for the bill had to contend with angry environmentalists in their home districts afterward. That reaction helped soften further GOP antiregulatory efforts and, according to moderates such as Sherwood Boehlert, R-N.Y., laid the foundation for future victories on other environmental issues.

A typical carryover effect was an amendment adopted, 212–206, on July 28 that dropped a provision in the spending bill for the departments of Veterans Affairs and Housing and Urban Development (HR 2099). That provision would have prevented the Environmental Protection Agency from enforcing some environmental laws, including sections of the Clean Water Act and the Clean Air Act. *(House key vote 8)*

7. ABM TREATY COMPLIANCE

House Republicans backed up their commitment to early deployment of antimissile defenses—the most concrete element of their defense program—by rejecting legislation that would have required the GOP's missile defense effort to comply with the 1972 treaty limiting antiballistic missile (ABM) defenses.

Republicans were generally united in complaining that President Clinton's defense budget request was too anemic. They insisted that the Pentagon's hardware accounts, funding research and procurement, were particularly in need of additional dollars. But when it came to parceling out the added money, the party was all over the lot, with prominent Republican defense mavens locked in vehement debates over the B-2 bomber, the navy's next class of nuclear-powered submarines and other weapons systems.

The only really controversial weapons issue on which the GOP fell into line was on a commitment to quickly deploy an ABM system that would protect U.S. territory. Contending that Libya, North Korea and other hostile Third World states might acquire ballistic missiles armed with nuclear, chemical or biological warheads, Republicans pressed not only for accelerating the deployment of national antimissile defenses, but also for a commitment to deploy as soon as possible a defense that could block a relatively small number of warheads.

Virtually all Democrats—including some centrists who supported developing a missile defense option that might be exercised at some later date—contended that a decision to begin deploying such defenses would be premature. At best, they warned, it would lock the Pentagon into existing technologies that might shortly be overtaken. Much worse, they argued, any defense that could cover all 50 states against even a handful of missiles would have to violate the ABM Treaty, which allowed only a single U.S. missile defense site.

The Clinton administration likewise opposed any provisions that might trespass on the ABM Treaty. Because of tactical miscues, the House Republicans fumbled their missile defense initiative in HR 7, the bill embodying defense-related provisions of the "Contract with America."

GOP defense specialists allowed Democrats to drape the proposed program in the flamboyant rhetoric—and hefty price tag—of President Ronald Reagan's far more elaborate Strategic Defense Initiative, which critics had derided as "star wars." So, by a vote of 218–212, the House agreed to drop from HR 7 a provision that would have declared an antimissile defense for U.S. territory to be a national goal.

However, by the time Republicans brought the fiscal 1996 defense authorization bill (HR 1530) to the House floor, they had regained their footing. When the House turned to the missile defense issue on June 14, it rejected nearly along party lines an amendment that would have deleted $628 million of the $763 million the bill would add to Clinton's $3 billion missile defense request.

The House divided along nearly the same lines on a key amendment offered by John M. Spratt Jr., D-S.C., which stipulated that none of the bill's provisions would violate the ABM Treaty. The amendment was rejected 185–242: R 7–221; D 177–21 (ND 126–10; SD 51–11); I 1–0. The missile defense language was ultimately dropped in conference with the Senate.

8. ENVIRONMENTAL REGULATIONS

Moderate Republicans bucked their party's leadership and handed the environmental movement an important victory July 28 by voting to strike legislative language in an appropriations bill that would have limited the regulatory authority of the Environmental Protection Agency (EPA). Although the House reversed its vote three days later, environmentalists eventually prevailed, and nearly all the language died.

The votes occurred on the fiscal 1996 appropriations bill (HR 2099) for Veterans Affairs (VA), Housing and Urban Development (HUD) and independent agencies. The EPA, slated for a 32 percent spending cut, was the hardest hit among the major agencies funded by the measure.

A series of 17 legislative riders concerning the EPA, not the proposed spending cut, drew the most controversy. These provisions sought to restrict the EPA's ability to regulate, among other things, emissions from industrial facilities and from oil and gas refineries, raw sewage overflows, arsenic and radon in drinking water and traces of cancer-causing substances in processed foods.

The riders were pushed by conservatives who believed that the EPA had been overzealously enforcing regulations and discouraging business development. These conservatives were emboldened after the House voted May 16 for a bill (HR 961) to relax many regulations in the clean water act. *(House key vote 6)*

Several authorizing committee chairmen supported the provisions in the VA-HUD bill, saying they would reinforce some changes that the House had already approved in other environment-related bills. But moderate Republicans, led by Sherwood Boehlert of New York, joined with many Democrats in describing these provisions as breaks for polluters. During a two-hour floor debate, they warned of an environmental disaster if Congress prevented the EPA from enforcing key regulations. They also said that such sweeping policy changes should be debated by authorizing committees after a series of public hearings, rather than being added to an appropriations bill.

There was little expectation that the environmentalists would prevail. But they did, 212–206: R 51–175; D 160–31 (ND 122–10, SD 38–21); I 1–0. The Republicans who broke party ranks to vote to strike the riders were mostly from Northeastern and Great Lakes states and from Florida. They more than canceled out the opposing votes of 31 Democrats, many of whom were conservatives from the South and Midwest.

John A. Boehner of Ohio, chairman of the Republican Conference, attributed the moderates' successful uprising less to policy considerations than to "a bursting out of a lot of frustration." But Boehlert, who cosponsored with Louis Stokes, D-Ohio, the amendment to strike the riders, said Republicans had started to come under fire for moving to weaken environmental regulations.

Regardless, the moderates' unexpected victory left GOP leaders scrambling for a new strategy. When angry conservatives threatened to vote against the entire appropriations bill, Republican leaders abruptly moved to postpone further consideration of the bill.

The leadership called for another vote when the House reconvened July 31 and barely prevailed when the amendment to strike fell on a tie vote, 210–210. That kept the legislative provisions in the bill.

The Senate generally disdained the House-passed EPA riders in its version of the bill. When the House formally voted Nov. 2 to convene a conference committee, members approved nonbinding instructions urging conferees to drop the riders. In the end, six Senate EPA riders, one of which was in the House bill, were retained in the version of the VA-HUD bill that President Clinton vetoed Dec. 18.

9. TELECOMMUNICATIONS OVERHAUL

When the House passed its landmark telecommunications overhaul bill, it did not do so with as strong a showing as did the Senate.

But it demonstrated that both chambers could pass a bill with a veto-proof margin.

The House vote Aug. 4 was all the more significant because it came just days after President Clinton issued a veto threat. Clinton's threats were enough to give him a one-vote majority of Democrats, but that was not nearly enough to stop the avalanche of support for the sweeping measure. HR 1555 passed 305–117: R 208–18; D 97–98 (ND 52–84; SD 45–14); I 0–1. *(Senate key vote 4)*

If the vote represented a setback for Clinton, it was an advance for bipartisanship. In a year when virtually all other major issues were settled on largely party-line votes, this was perhaps the exception that proved the rule. Not until HR 1555 reached conference committee did partisan rhetoric and posturing begin.

Both the House and Senate bills aimed to rewrite existing telecommunications laws, in large part by removing the barriers that separated local and long-distance telephone companies. The House bill, however, went further in curtailing regulation than the Senate's. It required less from the regional Bell companies hoping to enter the long-distance business, and it did not include the Senate's extensive language requiring telecommunications providers to offer their services in remote areas.

The House vote represented a resounding defeat for long-distance companies, which were considerably happier with the version of the bill approved by the House Commerce Committee May 25. House Speaker Newt Gingrich, R-Ga., had reworked the bill to the advantage of the regional Bells and put his changes in the form of a manager's amendment agreed to before final passage.

The measure was stalled in conference at year's end, with House Republicans arguing that the House-Senate compromise did not reduce regulations enough.

10. MEDICARE REVISIONS

Months of behind-the-scenes work paid off for the Republican leadership in October when the House voted to make the biggest changes in the Medicare program since its inception in 1965.

As part of their plan to balance the budget in seven years, Republican leaders knew they would have to address the huge and growing costs of Medicare, the federal health insurance program for the elderly, which had been held sacrosanct for years by the Democratic majority. Buoyed by an April report from Medicare's trustees that, without action, the program faced bankruptcy, Republicans saw their chance.

Responding to Democratic charges that they were trying to use the reduced spending in Medicare to offset the cost of a promised multibillion-dollar tax cut, Republicans separated their Medicare overhaul plan—at least initially—from the broad deficit-reduction package. A separate Medicare bill (HR 2425) went to the floor before its provisions were rolled into the broader package (HR 2491).

The Medicare plan, carefully crafted by Speaker Newt Gingrich, R-Ga., and a select GOP health care team working in consultation with key lobbying groups, called for cuts of $270 billion from projected spending over seven years. The savings were to come mostly from limiting payments to doctors, hospitals and other providers; the proposals also urged seniors to choose care options besides the traditional fee-for-service structure and froze the payment of the optional Part B health insurance at 31.5 percent of the program's costs rather than permitting a scheduled drop in payments.

Unaccustomed to having their hands tied on the 30-year-old program, Democrats howled about their lack of input in the process and in the final bill, which was presented only a few days before the Ways and Means Committee began its markup. They contended that the Republican changes would force many seniors into low-quality managed care options and that the cuts would cripple providers' abilities to care for their patients.

After a swift markup resulting in party-line approval of the Republican plan, the measure moved to the floor. Democrats, by this time well aware that they did not have the votes to stop the Republican march, continued to snipe at the plan, hoping it would collapse under public scrutiny or a promised presidential veto.

Gingrich and company, however, had appeased many of the critics with an amendment worked out shortly before the critical vote Oct. 19. Most of the interest groups got enough—or were relieved that they were not hit harder—to keep their guns holstered. Still, the Speaker had to work furiously right up until the final vote to mollify Republicans with specific complaints about portions of the bill.

After all the shouting ended, the Republican leadership lost only six members—four from New Jersey and one from Massachusetts—who were concerned about hospital payments, and one Iowan who was concerned about rural payment formulas. The losses, however, were almost offset by the defection of four conservative Southern Democrats, who voted with the Republican majority. The vote was 231–201: R 227–6; D 4–194 (ND 0–137, SD 4–57); I 0–1.

11. BUDGET RECONCILIATION

Conventional wisdom said Republicans could never make good on their seemingly contradictory campaign promises to cut taxes and balance the budget, while leaving most federal spending (Social Security, defense, interest on the debt) off the table.

President Ronald Reagan had fumbled the same set of pledges, carrying through on taxes and defense but utterly failing to balance the budget during his eight years in office in the 1980s.

So when the House easily adopted a budget resolution (H Con Res 67) in May (and a House-Senate compromise budget in June) that made good on those promises, skeptics scoffed that that was the easy part. They predicted Republicans would choke when it came to approving the real thing: a budget-balancing reconciliation bill that filled in the budget resolution's broad outlines with detailed spending cuts.

Just two years earlier, President Clinton had breezed through the then-Democratic House with a controversial deficit-reducing budget resolution, only to encounter what one House Democrat called a "near-death experience" when the follow-up reconciliation bill was nearly defeated on a 219–213 vote.

But with the huge new class of fiscally radical GOP freshmen leading the way and House Republican leaders enforcing much stricter party discipline than their Democratic predecessors, Republicans lost just 10 of their members on the showdown vote Oct. 26, handily passing the House's version of the reconciliation bill (HR 2491). The vote was 227–203: R 223–10; D 4–192 (ND 0–137, SD 4–55); I 0–1. *(Senate key vote 14)*

Although the size of the House vote and the seemingly inevitable momentum Republicans had developed earlier on the budget made it all look easy, it was not. GOP leaders faced brush-fire revolts from rank-and-file members, including moderates who objected to some of the more extreme cuts, farm-state members unhappy with agriculture provisions and numerous members from states that would lose funding under the new, block-grant Medicaid system.

House GOP leaders worked frantically during the final days before the vote to shore up support, bargaining with individual members and entire state delegations, giving ground in some areas and drawing the line in others. Leaders refused to strip a provision to open up wilderness in Alaska for oil and gas exploration, for example, but they added money back to the Medicaid program. In some cases

they told members to defer their concerns to the House-Senate conference that would produce the final bill.

In the end, leaders appealed to Republicans to swallow their objections on individual matters and take a broad view, arguing that the budget plan was the single most important thing the new Republican Congress would do all year. That had an impact. "There's a bigger picture out there, and that bigger picture is balancing the budget," said Saxby Chambliss, R-Ga.

Having cleared this hurdle, both the House and Senate went on to pass a compromise reconciliation bill in November. Clinton vetoed the measure, starting budget summit talks that sputtered inconclusively into the new year.

12. LATE-TERM ABORTION FIGHT

House lawmakers made a dramatic new assault on abortion rights in 1995, voting for the first time to criminalize a particular type of abortion procedure. The vote signaled the new-found strength of abortion opponents in Congress.

The fight came over a bill (HR 1833) to ban so-called partial birth abortions, a term critics used to describe a procedure for late-term abortions in which the doctor partially extracts the fetus from the womb and sometimes collapses the head before completing the abortion.

Critics characterized it as an unnecessarily brutal act that no one should tolerate. "You wouldn't treat an animal this way," Judiciary Committee Chairman Henry J. Hyde, R-Ill., one of the House's foremost abortion opponents, said during floor debate on the bill. Charles T. Canady, R-Fla., the bill's chief sponsor, said the procedure was perilously close to homicide.

Although the procedure accounted for a tiny fraction of the hundreds of thousands of abortions performed in the United States each year, both sides said the stakes surrounding the legislation were far higher—ultimately threatening the 1973 *Roe v. Wade* decision establishing a woman's right to abortion.

Given those claims, the vote might well have been fairly close. Yet when the bill came to the floor Nov. 1, lawmakers were moved more by the grisly depictions of the disputed procedure than by arguments of constitutional law or medical discretion. Members voted 2-to-1 in favor of the ban, 288–139: R 215–15; D 73–123 (ND 46–90, SD 27–33); I 0–1. House passage was by a far wider margin than a subsequent Senate vote to pass a similar version of the bill. *(Senate key vote 15)*

In the past, most congressional abortion battles had focused on money, for example, whether the federal government should finance abortions for poor women or family planning clinics that discussed abortion. Abortion opponents had continued to wage those battles and, on the strength of electoral gains in 1994, had made headway toward rolling back some of the victories that abortion rights advocates achieved under President Clinton and the majority Democratic 103rd Congress.

But in 1995 they also took the innovative and effective new tack of singling out a particularly controversial form of abortion and targeting it for criminalization. Their graphic accounts of the details proved more powerful than opponents' arguments that the ban would deter doctors from performing any type of late-term abortion, or would force women to carry fatally deformed fetuses to term.

As the bill came to the floor, even some abortion rights lawmakers were inclined to support it, or at least unwilling to oppose it publicly.

Critics wanted to clearly exempt from the ban those late-term abortions performed to safeguard the life or health of the woman. They said the controversial procedure was usually used because of complications involving severe fetal abnormalities or the woman's health. That dispute threatened to become the legislation's defining issue.

The sponsors stood their ground against such a change, insisting that a broader provision would effectively destroy the bill. The GOP leadership took the sponsors' side, bringing the bill to the floor under a rule that allowed no floor amendments. That irked some Republicans, 39 of whom voted against the rule. But they were more than offset by 47 Democrats, and the rule passed, 237–190.

Once the bill was on the floor, members were faced with an up or down judgment and voted overwhelmingly to ban the procedure.

13. DEFENSE SPENDING

Republican deficit hawks reined in the party's defense hawks when it came to deciding how much money to add to President Clinton's defense budget request. Even so, the Republican-led House and Senate added nearly $7 billion to Clinton's defense appropriations bill—making defense the only discretionary category to get more money for fiscal 1996 than Clinton requested, and more than Congress had appropriated for fiscal 1995.

In the weeks after the November 1994 election, the Republican Party's defense hawks came out swinging, warning that Clinton was starving the defense establishment at the same time he was burdening it with new peacekeeping missions around the globe. In particular, GOP defense specialists insisted that the Pentagon needed more money for weapons procurement—a portion of its budget that had declined more than 60 percent in inflation-adjusted terms since defense budgets topped out in 1985.

Even before the new Congress convened, Rep. Duncan Hunter, R-Calif., called for adding $24 billion to Clinton's projected defense request, raising it to the level projected by President George Bush. But domestic and budgetary issues loomed larger for most Republicans, whose top priorities were cutting both taxes and deficits.

Democrats, too, were split on defense spending. Wisconsin's David R. Obey, the senior Democrat on the Appropriations Committee, clearly spoke for a majority of his party's House members when he argued that Clinton's $258 billion defense request was excessive in light of the end of the Cold War. On the other hand, a significant number of centrist Democrats—most from Southern and border states—concurred in the GOP critique. Others supported a larger package because of its potential effect on defense-related jobs back home.

Defense Secretary William J. Perry insisted that Clinton's request was tight and that future defense budgets would have to increase to allow procurement spending to rise. In the main, however, House Democratic leaders backed Clinton's request.

For practical purposes, the size of the fiscal 1996 defense budget was settled by the congressional budget resolution. The House had proposed adding $10 billion to Clinton's request; the compromise resolution set the defense ceiling at $265 billion, $7 billion more than requested.

The most remarkable thing about that outcome was that, despite the wrenching battles over practically every other component of the budget, there was no concerted effort to eliminate the proposed increase to Clinton's defense request. Amendments to defense bills that would have reduced overall spending were debated in a largely perfunctory manner and then rejected. For 1995, at least, the potential alliance between liberal Democrats and GOP deficit hawks went unrealized.

While other appropriations bills provided funding for military construction and for defense-related projects of the Energy Department, the basic test of sentiment on the defense budget was the defense appropriations bill, which financed all Pentagon activities other than the construction of facilities. For this bill (HR 2126), Clinton requested $236.3 billion, but House-Senate conferees approved a final version that provided $243.3 billion.

Initially, the House rejected that conference report because antiabortion Republicans, unhappy with an abortion-related provision, joined Democrats to kill the measure. But after the contentious abortion provision was revised, the bill sailed through.

The key test of House sentiment on boosting the defense budget was this second vote on approving the defense appropriations conference report. It was adopted 270–158: R 195–37; D 75–120 (ND 35–102; SD 40–18); I 0–1.

14. GIFT BAN

It took a revolt by key Republican freshmen and a near-unanimous Democratic Caucus to persuade reluctant House Republican leaders to hold a floor vote on proposed new rules to restrict gifts to members (H Res 250).

Months earlier, the Senate had adopted tough new restrictions of its own (S Res 158), which barred senators and their aides from accepting all-expense-paid recreational trips and limiting to $50 the value of gifts and meals that senators and their aides could accept from lobbyists, with a maximum of $100 from any one source. (Senate key vote 10)

Gift ban supporters in the House wanted to pass the same rules as the Senate, fearing that any attempt to revise the provisions would weaken the restrictions. Opponents included Dan Burton, R-Ind., who wanted to avoid the Senate approach and merely require more disclosure of the source of gifts. Burton and his fellow Conservative Action Team members said that rules such as those approved by the Senate would stifle worthy fundraising efforts for charity causes, lead to an avalanche of inadvertent violations, and set off a flood of ethics complaints that could unfairly sully the reputations of House members.

At a closed-door meeting of all House Republicans on Nov. 8, Burton and his allies were so vociferous in their opposition that the GOP leadership agreed to allow them to offer a far weaker package of gift restrictions during floor debate. Under Burton's proposal, House members would retain their ability to attend most lobbyist-funded golf, tennis and ski trips to help raise money for charities and could continue accepting gifts of up to $250. Members would have to disclose gifts of $50 or more.

Under the deal, proposed by Rules Committee Chairman Gerald B. H. Solomon, R-N.Y., the House would vote first on Burton's amendment. If it failed, Speaker Newt Gingrich, R-Ga., who agreed that the Senate rules were too complicated, would propose a different solution: a complete ban on most gifts. Only if members rejected the complete ban would they vote on the underlying resolution, which reflected the Senate language.

The plan seemed to strengthen Burton's chances of prevailing. But a coalition of GOP freshmen, veteran House Republicans and House Democrats held firm. For the Republican freshmen, banning gifts was a key element of their election platform to change the way Congress operated. For veteran Republicans, in the majority for the first time in 40 years, as well as for the group of House Democratic proponents, banning gifts was something they had long sought.

On Nov. 16, the coalition defeated the Burton substitute by a vote of 154–276: R 108–125; D 46–150 (ND 21–116, SD 25–34); I 0–1. The House then went on to adopt Gingrich's amendment, 422–8. The new restrictions went into effect Jan. 1, 1996.

15. BOSNIA TROOP DEPLOYMENT

House Republicans paused in their budgetary battles with President Clinton to launch a furious assault against the administration's major foreign policy initiative: a plan to send U.S. forces to Bosnia to help enforce a peace accord.

For the Republicans, it mattered little that U.S.-brokered peace talks among Bosnia's warring parties, being held at the unlikely venue of Dayton, Ohio, were at a crucial stage. Or that Clinton's pledge of 20,000 U.S. troops to back a viable peace accord was a significant element in bringing the negotiations to the brink of success.

Instead, GOP lawmakers focused on the dangers lurking for U.S. soldiers in a region whose thirst for violence seemed insatiable. California Republican Dana Rohrabacher, a leading opponent of the deployment, asked: "Whose nutty idea is this to send American troops into a meat grinder in Bosnia?"

Colorado Republican Joel Hefley, urged on by the aggressive GOP freshman class and more senior conservatives like Rohrabacher, introduced legislation (HR 2606) to block Clinton's plan to deploy U.S. forces to Bosnia unless Congress approved funds for the deployment. The House on Nov. 17 easily passed Hefley's bill on a largely partisan vote of 243–171: R 214–12; D 28–159 (ND 19–110, SD 9–49); I 1–0.

The vote represented a sharp rebuke of the president's Bosnia policy and reflected deep public skepticism of the proposed peace mission. It also showed that the GOP freshmen and their allies, in contrast to many of their elders in both parties, were unafraid to challenge the president in his role as commander in chief.

But the practical significance of the House action was limited, because Senate GOP leaders had all but ruled out an early vote on Hefley's bill. That knowledge may have made it easier for House members to take a strong public stand against the unpopular operation. (Congress had previously voted to overturn the U.N. embargo on selling arms to the states of the former Yugoslavia, but none had been enacted into law.)

The administration was clearly concerned by the House vote, which came just as the Dayton talks appeared to be bearing fruit. "I can't believe the House would do this," State Department spokesman Nicholas Burns said.

Ultimately, however, the House Republicans failed in their quest to derail the Bosnia peacekeeping operation. The Dayton talks reached their climax Nov. 21, with a laboriously negotiated peace accord.

By the time Congress cast showdown votes on the deployment Dec. 13, momentum for cutting off funds for the mission had slowed. The first U.S. military units were already setting up shop in Bosnia, and the president was making headway with his argument that the nation's credibility would suffer inestimable damage if Congress scrapped the mission.

Those arguments carried the day in the Senate. Majority Leader Bob Dole, R-Kan., and Arizona Republican John McCain—both decorated veterans—led efforts to oppose a measure modeled on Hefley's bill. *(Senate key vote 9)*

House GOP opponents of military involvement in Bosnia would not go quietly. They fought on, even as many of their own leaders echoed the prevailing view of Senate Republicans that nothing could be done to stop the mission. A new proposal (HR 2770) aimed at denying funding for troops in Bosnia was rejected, but by the surprisingly narrow margin of 210–218.

16. CONTINUING APPROPRIATIONS

The government-closing "train wreck" that Republicans threatened from early in the year if they did not get their way on plans to cut taxes and balance the budget happened well ahead of schedule, before Congress had even cleared the Republican's huge, budget-balancing reconciliation bill. When temporary appropriations to keep the government open ran out at midnight Nov. 13 and President Clinton refused to agree to GOP terms for another extension, federal departments and agencies whose appropriations bills had not been enacted began to shut down.

The government had closed nine times previously, but never for more than three days. By Nov. 17, the shutdown had lasted four days, putting about 800,000 federal employees on involuntary furlough. The political stakes rose rapidly. By the weekend of Nov. 18–19, both the White House and Republicans were looking for a way out.

Republicans were determined to bring Clinton to the table to negotiate on balancing the budget in seven years, using numbers approved by the Congressional Budget Office (CBO). Clinton had moved a long way since the days when he said he would do no more deficit reduction than he had done in his big 1993 budget package. But the president was still insisting on a nine-year plan that used the somewhat more optimistic deficit projections developed by the White House's Office of Management and Budget (OMB). Those projections allowed the administration to claim it could balance the budget with shallower spending cuts than Republicans said were necessary. Republicans argued that the OMB numbers were phony, and both sides seemed immovable.

Public disgust was running high, however. Polls showed that voters blamed congressional Republicans roughly two-to-one over Clinton for the shutdown, but the episode was contributing to a generalized frustration with Washington that seemed likely to hurt both parties.

It was lawyerly writing that finally offered a temporary way out. With both sides exhibiting a little give, negotiators worked out a compromise that seemingly allowed each to claim victory. The government would reopen until Dec. 15 to give budget talks a chance to proceed. Clinton would agree to enact a budget-balancing deal by early January that would get the deficit to zero in seven years using CBO numbers and would also include tax cuts. Republicans would agree to protect Clinton's priorities in Medicare, Medicaid, education, the environment and other areas.

Triumphant Republicans bragged that Clinton had finally come to terms with them, promising to balance the budget in seven years with CBO scoring. But Democrats had written in some fine print that gave them reason to celebrate as well: The deal would be scored only after CBO had consulted with OMB and other budget experts, and the notion that any balanced-budget deal would protect Clinton's favorite programs gave him wide latitude to object to GOP proposals to cut spending deeper than he liked.

For the moment, however, this provided everyone a face-saving retreat from the shutdown. The Senate passed the continuing resolution (H J Res 122) by voice vote Nov. 19, taking up a measure it had passed earlier, substituting new language and sending it back to the House. The House cleared the bill for the president Nov. 20, agreeing to a motion to concur in the Senate amendment. The vote was 421–4: R 227–2; D 193–2 (ND 134–2, SD 59–0); I 1–0.

The measure ended the shutdown after six days and provided temporary appropriations for almost another month, giving programs no less than 75 percent of the money they had received in fiscal 1995 (which had ended Sept. 30).

It was to be a short-term reprieve from chaos. After a break for the Thanksgiving holiday, budget negotiators got down to work at the Capitol, but the talks went nowhere. With neither side inclined to give further ground, the government entered another partial shutdown Dec. 16 that lasted into January.

17. LOBBY REGISTRATION

A key test of whether the House would follow the Senate's lead and pass (thus clearing for the president) legislation imposing new reporting requirements on lobbyists came in the form of an amendment offered by William F. Clinger, R-Pa., chairman of the House Government Reform and Oversight Committee. Clinger sought to prevent federal agencies, controlled by appointees of Democratic President Clinton, from spending money to drum up grass-roots support or opposition to the GOP agenda in the House.

Clinger's amendment to the lobby registration bill (HR 2564) was backed by House GOP leaders and should have had little trouble in the Republican-controlled House. But, the lobby bill's supporters, many of them freshman Republicans, said it would sound a death knell for the lobby legislation and threaten a key election-year pledge many freshmen had made to voters to change the way Washington operated. GOP freshmen had joined with members of the Democratic minority to force the reluctant House Republican leadership to bring the lobby registration bill to the floor and were not eager to see the bill die after getting so far.

They feared that House adoption of Clinger's amendment would invite other changes in the Senate-passed bill. Any changes would have extended the bill's legislative journey, requiring it to be hashed out by a House-Senate conference committee and then to be sent back to the Senate floor, where its fate was far from certain. It was in the Senate that Republicans had staged a filibuster against the final version of a similar attempt to overhaul the lobbying laws in the 103rd Congress, killing the bill in 1994.

Another factor: Many of the proposed House changes, including the Clinger amendment, were expected to draw a veto threat from President Clinton, who was prepared to sign the Senate version of the bill.

Clinger's amendment was debated on Nov. 16 as members prepared to leave town for the Thanksgiving holiday. But the vote did not occur for another 12 days, at the request of bill sponsors, who wanted to ensure that lawmakers would not back the amendment hastily, without reflecting on the fact that any change could doom the underlying effort.

When the vote came, a coalition of GOP freshmen, Democrats and senior Republicans who had worked long to change the way Congress operated, provided enough votes to defeat the amendment, overcoming efforts by DeLay's whip organization to get the amendment adopted.

Bill supporters won their critical test vote Nov. 28 when lawmakers rejected the Clinger amendment. The vote was 190–238: R 176–56; D 14–181 (ND 5–131, SD 9–50); I 0–1.

The defeat of Clinger's amendment made it clear to those hoping to alter the bill that there was a firm majority against changes. Indeed, after the House rejected the amendment, two other proposed alterations were quashed, leading other lawmakers to withdraw amendments they had planned to offer.

The success in staving off amendments to the bill came despite a concerted effort by House Republican leaders to lay the bill open to as many amendments as possible. The lobby bill had few supporters among House leaders: Speaker Newt Gingrich, R-Ga., had helped whip up the opposition that encouraged Senate Republicans to fili-

buster the similar bill in the 103rd Congress, and Majority Leader Dick Armey, R-Texas, and Majority Whip Tom DeLay, R-Texas, also opposed the 1995 bill. In the end, Armey and DeLay both voted for final passage. *(Senate key vote 8)*

The next day, Nov. 29, the House passed, 421–0, a lobbying bill identical to the Senate version, clearing it for Clinton.

18. SHAREHOLDER LAWSUITS

A bipartisan House coalition supporting a measure to overhaul laws governing securities fraud lawsuits quickly overrode an unexpected and last-minute veto of the bill by President Clinton.

The Dec. 20 vote came barely 13 hours after Clinton sent the bill back to Congress. Clinton's veto was announced shortly before the midnight Dec. 19 deadline for him to act on the bill or watch it become law without his signature. It was the first successful override of a Clinton veto, but since it came on an arcane and highly technical bill that was vetoed on narrow grounds, most members did not appear to view it as a major blow to the president.

The bill (HR 1058) sought to make it more difficult for investors to win securities lawsuits against corporations that issued erroneous predictions of company performance, securities firms that underwrote and sold such stock issues and accounting firms that verified corporate books. Supporters said the existing system permitted class-action attorneys to extort settlements from innocent companies.

Driving the measure into law was a powerful business coalition, especially high-technology companies and accounting firms. Many Democrats from states with a considerable presence of high-tech firms, such as California, strongly supported the bill.

The veto genuinely stunned bill supporters, but it was the White House and bill opponents who were caught flat-footed the next morning. Opponents got only 15 minutes' warning before the brief debate on the override began, and the White House had barely any time to lobby members. The earlier House votes had carried by impressive veto-proof margins.

The veto was easily overridden, 319–100: R 230–0; D 89–99 (ND 56–76, SD 33–23); I 0–1. (The Senate subsequently followed suit, enacting the bill.) *(Senate key vote 17)*

Less than a handful of votes changed from the 320–102 previous vote to adopt the conference agreement on the bill.

Members on both sides of the question agreed that Clinton had fumbled. His veto came after members had twice before voted on the bill. The administration was silent during the debate on the conference report when its objections might have been more effective.

Clinton's main objection to the bill—on a provision to make it easier for defendants to get disputes thrown out of court before investors got a chance to prove their case—had not been raised by the White House during previous legislative rounds.

The mishandling of the issue by the White House appeared to make it easy for Democrats to vote against Clinton. In addition, the top Senate supporter of the bill, Democrat Christopher J. Dodd of Connecticut, came over to the House floor to rally support for the veto override. Dodd was the general chairman of the Democratic National Committee and normally a Clinton loyalist.

1. H J Res 1. Balanced-Budget Amendment/Passage. Passage of the joint resolution to propose a constitutional amendment to balance the budget by 2002 or two years after ratification by three-fourths of the states, whichever is later. Three-fifths of the entire House and Senate would be required to approve deficit spending or an increase in the public debt limit. A simple majority could waive the requirement in times of war or in the face of a serious military threat. The courts would be prohibited from raising taxes or cutting spending unless specifically authorized by Congress. Rejected 65–35: R 51–2; D 14–33 (ND 9–28, SD 5–5), March 2, 1995. A two-thirds majority vote of those present and voting—67 in this case—is required to pass a joint resolution proposing an amendment to the Constitution. A "nay" was a vote in support of the president's position.

2. S 4. Line-Item Veto/Passage. Passage of the bill to provide for the separate enrollment of each individual spending item in an appropriations bill, targeted tax breaks in a revenue bill, or new entitlement spending, thus allowing the president to veto each item and require Congress to muster a two-thirds vote of each House to override the veto. Passed 69–29: R 50–2; D 19–27 (ND 13–23, SD 6–4), March 23, 1995. A "yea" was a vote in support of the president's position.

3. HR 956. Product Liability Overhaul/Cloture. Motion to invoke cloture (thus limiting debate) on the Gorton, R-Wash., substitute amendment to cap punitive damages in product liability cases, medical malpractice cases, and all civil cases at the state and federal level at two times compensatory damages. Motion rejected 47–52: R 45–9; D 2–43 (ND 2–33, SD 0–10), May 4, 1995. Three-fifths of the entire Senate (60) is required to invoke cloture. A "nay" was a vote in support of the president's position.

4. S 652. Telecommunications/Passage. Passage of the bill to promote competition and deregulation in the broadcasting, cable and telephone industries by requiring local phone companies to open their networks to competitors, allowing those companies to offer cable service, permitting the regional Bell telephone companies to enter the long-distance and manufacturing markets under certain conditions, easing ownership and licensing restrictions on broadcasters and reducing price controls on cable companies. Passed 81–18: R 51–2; D 30–16 (ND 23–13, SD 7–3), June 15, 1995.

5. S 440. National Highway System/Speed Limits. Nickles, R-Okla., motion to table (kill) the Lautenberg, D-N.J., amendment to maintain the current requirements that states post a maximum speed limit of 55 mph in metropolitan areas and 65 mph in rural areas but repeal the federal sanctions on states that fail to report on the enforcement of speed limits. Motion agreed to 65–35: R 50–4; D 15–31 (ND 10–26, SD 5–5), June 20, 1995. A "nay" was a vote in support of the president's position.

6. Foster Nomination/Cloture. Motion to invoke cloture (thus limiting debate) on the confirmation of Dr. Henry W. Foster Jr. to be surgeon general. Motion rejected 57–43: R 11–43; D 46–0 (ND 36–0, SD 10–0), June 21, 1995. Three-fifths of the total Senate (60) is required to invoke cloture. A "yea" was a vote in support of the president's position.

7. S 343. Regulatory Overhaul/Cloture. Motion to invoke cloture (thus limiting debate) on the Dole, R-Kan., substitute amendment to require federal agencies to conduct risk-assessment and cost-benefit analyses on new regulations with an expected annual economic impact of $100 million or more. Motion rejected 58–40: R 54–0; D 4–40 (ND 0–34, SD 4–6), July 20, 1995. A three-fifths majority (60) of the total Senate is required to invoke cloture.

8. S 1060. Lobbying Disclosure/Passage. Passage of the bill to require lobbyists who are paid at least $5,000 over a six-month period or organizations with lobbying expenses of at least $20,000 over a six-month period to register with the Clerk of the House and the Secretary of the Senate within 45 days. The bill specifically exempts grass-roots lobbying activity. Passed 98–0: R 53–0; D 45–0 (ND 36–0, SD 9–0), July 25, 1995.

9. S 21. Bosnian Arms Embargo/Passage. Passage of the bill to require the president to end the participation of the United States in the international arms embargo on Bosnia after the 25,000-person United Nations Protection Force is withdrawn or 12 weeks after Bosnia requests such a withdrawal. Passed 69–29: R 48–5; D 21–24 (ND 19–17, SD 2–7), July 26, 1995. A "nay" was a vote in support of the president's position.

10. S 1061. Congressional Gift Ban/Travel, Lodging Exemption. Murkowski, R-Alaska, amendment to exclude travel, lodging and meals related to charity fundraising events from the ban on gifts. Rejected 39–60: R 30–23; D 9–37 (ND 2–34, SD 7–3), July 28, 1995.

11. S 1026. Fiscal 1996 Defense Authorization/Packwood Hearings. Boxer, D-Calif., amendment to require the Senate Ethics Committee to hold public hearings on the allegations of sexual misconduct against Sen. Bob Packwood, R-Ore., as well as in any future case where the committee finds substantial credible evidence of violations and has undertaken an investigation. The committee may waive this requirement by a recorded majority vote. Rejected 48–52: R 3–51; D 45–1 (ND 35–1, SD 10–0), Aug. 2, 1995.

12. S 1087. Fiscal 1996 Defense Appropriations/Passage. Passage of the bill to provide $242.7 billion in new budget authority for the Department of Defense in fiscal 1996. The bill would provide $2.3 billion less than the fiscal 1995 level of $245 billion and $6.4 billion more than the administration's request of $236.4 billion. Passed 62–35: R 48–4; D 14–31 (ND 7–28, SD 7–3), Sept. 5, 1995. A "nay" was a vote in support of the president's position.

13. HR 4. Welfare Overhaul/Passage. Passage of the bill to save about $65.8 billion over seven years; end the entitlement status of welfare programs; replace Aid to Families with Dependent Children with a block grant giving states wide flexibility to design their own programs; require welfare recipients to work after receiving benefits for two years and limit lifetime benefits to five years; allow states to deny cash assistance to unwed teenage mothers and for children born to welfare recipients; and for other purposes. Passed 87–12: R 52–1; D 35–11 (ND 25–11, SD 10–0), Sept. 19, 1995.

14. HR 2491. Fiscal 1996 Budget Reconciliation/Passage. Passage of the bill to cut spending by about $900 billion and taxes by $245 billion in order to balance the budget by 2002. The bill would reduce spending on Medicare by $270 billion, Medicaid by $182 billion, welfare by $65 billion, the earned-income tax credit by $43.2 billion, and agriculture programs by $13.6 billion. The bill allows oil drilling in the Arctic National Wildlife Refuge, scales back the capital gains tax, and expands Individual Retirement Accounts. Passed 52–47: R 52–1; D 0–46 (ND 0–36, SD 0–10), Oct. 28, 1995 (in the legislative day and the *Congressional Record* dated Oct. 27). Before passage, the Senate struck all after the enacting clause and inserted the text of S 1357 as amended. A "nay" was a vote in support of the president's position.

15. HR 1833. Abortion Procedures/Passage. Passage of the bill to impose penalties on doctors who perform certain late-term abortions, in which the person performing the abortion partially delivers the fetus before completing the abortion. Passed 54–44: R 45–8; D 9–36 (ND 5–30, SD 4–6), Dec. 7, 1995. A "nay" was a vote in support of the president's position.

16. S J Res 31. Flag Desecration/Passage. Passage of the joint resolution to propose a constitutional amendment to grant Congress the power to prohibit the physical desecration of the U.S. flag. Rejected 63–36: R 49–4; D 14–32 (ND 7–29, SD 7–3), Dec. 12, 1995. A two-thirds majority vote of those present and voting, 66 in this case, is required to pass a joint resolution proposing an amendment to the Constitution. A "nay" was a vote in support of the president's position.

17. Shareholder Lawsuits/Veto Override. Passage, over President Clinton's Dec. 19 veto, of the bill to curb class-action securities lawsuits. The bill includes provisions to allow judges to sanction attorneys and plaintiffs who file frivolous lawsuits, give plaintiffs greater control over a lawsuit, modify the system for paying attorneys' fees, and establish a system of "proportionate liability" for defendants who do not knowingly engage in securities fraud. It would create a "safe harbor" for companies that make predictions of future performance that are accompanied by cautionary statements. Passed (thus enacted into law) 68–30: R 48–4; D 20–26 (ND 17–19, SD 3–7), Dec. 22, 1995. A two-thirds majority of those present and voting (66 in this case) of both houses is required to override a veto. A "nay" was a vote in support of the president's position.

[a]Ben Nighthorse Campbell, Colo., switched to the Republican Party on March 3, 1995. He voted as a Democrat on key vote 1 and as a Republican on key votes 2-17.

[b]Bob Packwood, R-Ore., resigned Oct. 1, 1995. He voted on key votes 1-13.

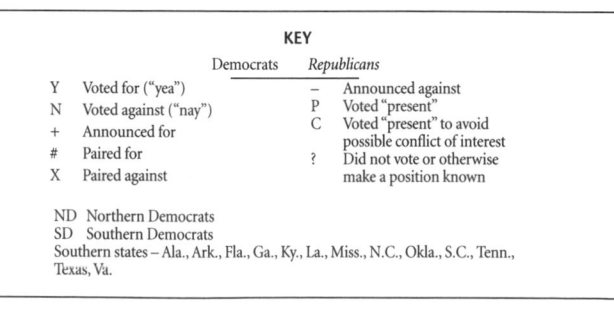

KEY			
		Democrats	*Republicans*
Y	Voted for ("yea")		– Announced against
N	Voted against ("nay")		P Voted "present"
+	Announced for		C Voted "present" to avoid possible conflict of interest
#	Paired for		? Did not vote or otherwise make a position known
X	Paired against		

ND Northern Democrats
SD Southern Democrats
Southern states – Ala., Ark., Fla., Ga., Ky., La., Miss., N.C., Okla., S.C., Tenn., Texas, Va.

Senate Key Votes	1	2	3	4	5	6	7	8	9	10	11	12	13	14	15	16	17
ALABAMA																	
Shelby	Y	Y	N	Y	Y	N	Y	Y	Y	N	N	Y	Y	Y	Y	Y	N
Heflin	Y	Y	N	Y	N	Y	Y	Y	N	Y	Y	Y	Y	N	Y	Y	N
ALASKA																	
Murkowski	Y	Y	Y	Y	Y	N	Y	Y	Y	Y	N	?	Y	Y	Y	Y	Y
Stevens	Y	?	Y	Y	Y	N	Y	Y	Y	?	N	Y	Y	Y	Y	Y	Y
ARIZONA																	
Kyl	Y	Y	Y	Y	Y	N	Y	Y	Y	N	N	Y	Y	Y	Y	Y	Y
McCain	Y	Y	Y	N	Y	N	Y	Y	Y	N	N	N	Y	Y	Y	Y	N
ARKANSAS																	
Bumpers	N	N	N	N	N	Y	N	Y	N	Y	Y	N	Y	N	N	N	N
Pryor	N	N	N	N	N	Y	N	Y	N	Y	Y	N	Y	N	N	N	N
CALIFORNIA																	
Boxer	N	N	N	N	N	Y	N	Y	Y	N	Y	N	Y	N	N	N	N
Feinstein	N	Y	N	Y	N	Y	N	Y	Y	N	Y	N	Y	N	N	Y	Y
COLORADO																	
Brown	Y	Y	Y	Y	Y	N	Y	Y	Y	N	N	N	Y	Y	Y	Y	Y
Campbell[a]	Y	Y	Y	Y	Y	Y	Y	Y	Y	Y	N	Y	Y	Y	N	Y	Y
CONNECTICUT																	
Dodd	N	N	N	Y	N	Y	N	Y	N	Y	Y	N	Y	N	N	N	Y
Lieberman	N	Y	Y	N	N	Y	N	Y	Y	N	Y	Y	Y	N	N	N	Y
DELAWARE																	
Roth	Y	Y	N	Y	Y	N	Y	Y	Y	Y	N	N	Y	Y	Y	Y	Y
Biden	Y	Y	N	Y	N	Y	N	Y	Y	N	Y	N	Y	N	Y	N	N
FLORIDA																	
Mack	Y	Y	Y	Y	Y	N	Y	Y	Y	Y	N	Y	Y	Y	Y	Y	Y
Graham	Y	Y	N	N	Y	Y	N	?	N	N	Y	N	Y	N	N	Y	N
GEORGIA																	
Coverdell	Y	Y	Y	Y	Y	N	Y	Y	Y	Y	N	Y	Y	Y	Y	Y	Y
Nunn	Y	N	N	Y	Y	Y	Y	Y	Y	Y	Y	Y	Y	N	N	Y	Y
HAWAII																	
Akaka	N	N	N	Y	Y	Y	N	Y	N	N	Y	?	N	N	N	N	N
Inouye	N	N	N	Y	Y	Y	X	Y	N	N	Y	Y	Y	N	N	N	N
IDAHO																	
Craig	Y	Y	Y	Y	Y	N	Y	Y	Y	N	N	Y	Y	Y	Y	Y	Y
Kempthorne	Y	Y	Y	Y	Y	N	Y	Y	Y	N	N	Y	Y	Y	Y	Y	Y
ILLINOIS																	
Moseley-Braun	Y	N	N	Y	N	Y	N	Y	Y	N	Y	N	N	N	N	N	Y
Simon	Y	N	N	N	N	Y	N	Y	Y	N	Y	N	N	N	N	N	N
INDIANA																	
Coats	Y	Y	Y	Y	Y	N	Y	Y	Y	Y	N	Y	Y	Y	Y	Y	Y
Lugar	Y	Y	Y	Y	Y	N	Y	Y	Y	N	N	Y	Y	Y	Y	Y	Y
IOWA																	
Grassley	Y	Y	Y	Y	Y	N	Y	Y	Y	N	N	Y	Y	Y	Y	Y	Y
Harkin	Y	Y	N	Y	N	Y	N	Y	Y	Y	N	Y	N	N	N	N	Y
KANSAS																	
Dole	N	Y	Y	Y	Y	N	Y	Y	Y	Y	N	Y	Y	Y	Y	Y	Y
Kassebaum	Y	Y	Y	Y	Y	Y	Y	Y	N	N	N	N	Y	Y	Y	N	Y
KENTUCKY																	
McConnell	Y	Y	Y	Y	Y	N	Y	Y	Y	Y	N	Y	Y	Y	Y	N	Y
Ford	N	Y	N	Y	N	Y	N	Y	N	N	Y	Y	Y	N	Y	Y	Y
LOUISIANA																	
Breaux	Y	Y	N	Y	Y	Y	Y	Y	N	Y	Y	Y	N	Y	N	Y	N
Johnston	N	N	N	Y	Y	Y	Y	Y	N	Y	Y	Y	Y	N	Y	Y	Y
MAINE																	
Cohen	Y	Y	N	Y	Y	Y	Y	Y	Y	N	Y	Y	Y	N	N	Y	N
Snowe	Y	Y	Y	Y	Y	Y	Y	Y	Y	N	Y	Y	Y	Y	N	Y	Y
MARYLAND																	
Mikulski	N	N	N	Y	N	Y	N	Y	N	N	Y	Y	Y	N	N	N	Y
Sarbanes	N	N	N	Y	N	Y	N	Y	N	N	N	N	N	N	N	N	Y
MASSACHUSETTS																	
Kennedy	N	Y	N	Y	N	Y	N	Y	N	N	N	N	N	N	N	N	Y
Kerry	N	Y	N	Y	Y	Y	N	Y	N	N	Y	N	Y	N	N	N	Y
MICHIGAN																	
Abraham	Y	Y	Y	Y	Y	N	Y	Y	Y	N	N	Y	Y	Y	Y	Y	Y
Levin	N	N	N	Y	N	Y	N	Y	Y	N	Y	N	Y	N	N	N	N
MINNESOTA																	
Grams	Y	Y	Y	Y	Y	N	Y	Y	Y	Y	N	Y	Y	Y	Y	Y	Y
Wellstone	N	Y	N	N	N	Y	N	Y	Y	N	Y	N	N	N	N	N	N
MISSISSIPPI																	
Cochran	Y	Y	N	Y	Y	N	Y	Y	Y	Y	N	Y	Y	Y	Y	Y	Y
Lott	Y	Y	Y	Y	Y	N	Y	Y	Y	Y	N	Y	Y	Y	Y	Y	Y
MISSOURI																	
Ashcroft	Y	Y	Y	Y	Y	N	Y	Y	Y	Y	N	Y	Y	Y	Y	Y	Y
Bond	Y	Y	Y	Y	Y	N	Y	Y	Y	Y	N	Y	Y	Y	Y	Y	C

Senate Key Votes	1	2	3	4	5	6	7	8	9	10	11	12	13	14	15	16	17
MONTANA																	
Burns	Y	Y	Y	Y	Y	N	Y	Y	N	Y	N	Y	Y	Y	Y	Y	Y
Baucus	Y	N	N	Y	Y	Y	N	Y	Y	N	Y	N	Y	N	N	Y	Y
NEBRASKA																	
Exon	Y	Y	Y	Y	N	Y	N	Y	N	N	Y	N	Y	N	Y	Y	Y
Kerrey	N	N	N	N	N	Y	N	Y	N	N	Y	N	N	N	N	N	N
NEVADA																	
Bryan	Y	N	N	Y	Y	Y	N	Y	Y	N	Y	N	Y	N	N	Y	N
Reid	N	N	N	N	Y	Y	N	Y	Y	N	Y	Y	Y	N	Y	Y	Y
NEW HAMPSHIRE																	
Gregg	Y	Y	Y	Y	Y	N	Y	Y	Y	N	Y	N	Y	Y	Y	Y	Y
Smith	Y	Y	Y	Y	Y	N	Y	Y	Y	Y	N	Y	Y	Y	Y	Y	Y
NEW JERSEY																	
Bradley	N	Y	N	Y	N	Y	N	Y	Y	N	Y	N	N	N	N	N	Y
Lautenberg	N	N	N	Y	N	Y	N	Y	Y	N	N	N	N	N	N	N	Y
NEW MEXICO																	
Domenici	Y	Y	Y	Y	Y	N	Y	Y	Y	Y	N	Y	Y	Y	Y	Y	Y
Bingaman	N	N	N	N	Y	Y	N	Y	N	N	Y	N	N	N	N	N	Y
NEW YORK																	
D'Amato	Y	Y	N	Y	Y	N	Y	Y	Y	Y	N	Y	Y	Y	Y	Y	Y
Moynihan	N	N	N	N	N	Y	N	Y	Y	N	N	Y	N	N	?	N	N
N. CAROLINA																	
Faircloth	Y	Y	Y	Y	Y	N	Y	Y	Y	N	N	Y	N	Y	Y	Y	Y
Helms	Y	Y	Y	Y	N	Y	Y	Y	Y	Y	N	+	Y	Y	Y	Y	Y
N. DAKOTA																	
Conrad	N	N	N	Y	N	Y	N	Y	Y	N	Y	N	Y	N	Y	N	N
Dorgan	N	Y	N	N	N	Y	N	Y	Y	N	Y	Y	Y	N	Y	N	N
OHIO																	
DeWine	Y	Y	Y	Y	N	N	Y	Y	Y	N	N	Y	Y	Y	Y	Y	Y
Glenn	N	N	N	Y	N	Y	N	Y	N	N	Y	N	Y	N	N	N	N
OKLAHOMA																	
Inhofe	Y	Y	Y	Y	Y	N	Y	Y	Y	Y	N	Y	Y	Y	Y	Y	Y
Nickles	Y	Y	Y	Y	Y	N	Y	Y	Y	Y	N	Y	Y	Y	Y	Y	Y
OREGON																	
Hatfield	N	N	Y	Y	N	N	Y	Y	N	N	N	N	+	Y	Y	Y	Y
Packwood[b]	Y	Y	N	N	Y	Y	Y	Y	Y	Y	N	Y	Y				
PENNSYLVANIA																	
Santorum	Y	Y	Y	Y	Y	N	Y	Y	Y	N	N	Y	Y	Y	Y	Y	Y
Specter	Y	Y	N	Y	Y	Y	Y	Y	Y	N	Y	Y	Y	Y	N	Y	N
RHODE ISLAND																	
Chafee	Y	Y	Y	Y	N	Y	Y	Y	Y	Y	N	Y	Y	Y	N	N	Y
Pell	N	N	+	Y	N	Y	#	Y	N	N	Y	N	Y	N	N	N	Y
S. CAROLINA																	
Thurmond	Y	Y	Y	Y	Y	N	Y	Y	Y	Y	N	Y	Y	Y	Y	Y	Y
Hollings	N	Y	N	Y	N	Y	N	Y	+	Y	Y	Y	Y	N	N	Y	N
S. DAKOTA																	
Pressler	Y	Y	Y	Y	Y	N	Y	Y	Y	Y	N	Y	Y	Y	Y	Y	Y
Daschle	N	Y	N	Y	N	Y	N	Y	N	N	Y	N	Y	N	N	N	N
TENNESSEE																	
Frist	Y	Y	Y	Y	Y	Y	Y	Y	Y	N	N	Y	Y	Y	Y	Y	Y
Thompson	Y	Y	N	Y	Y	N	Y	Y	Y	N	N	Y	Y	Y	Y	Y	Y
TEXAS																	
Gramm	Y	?	Y	Y	Y	N	Y	Y	Y	Y	N	Y	Y	Y	Y	Y	Y
Hutchison	Y	Y	Y	Y	Y	N	Y	Y	Y	Y	N	Y	Y	Y	Y	Y	Y
UTAH																	
Bennett	Y	Y	Y	Y	Y	N	Y	?	?	Y	N	Y	Y	Y	Y	N	Y
Hatch	Y	Y	Y	+	Y	N	Y	Y	Y	Y	N	Y	Y	Y	Y	Y	Y
VERMONT																	
Jeffords	Y	N	Y	Y	Y	Y	Y	Y	Y	Y	N	Y	Y	Y	Y	N	Y
Leahy	N	N	N	N	Y	Y	N	Y	N	N	Y	N	N	N	N	N	N
VIRGINIA																	
Warner	Y	Y	Y	Y	Y	N	Y	Y	Y	Y	N	Y	Y	Y	Y	Y	Y
Robb	Y	Y	N	Y	Y	Y	N	Y	Y	N	Y	Y	Y	N	N	N	Y
WASHINGTON																	
Gorton	Y	Y	Y	Y	Y	Y	Y	Y	Y	Y	N	Y	Y	Y	Y	Y	Y
Murray	N	N	N	Y	N	Y	N	Y	N	N	Y	Y	Y	N	N	N	Y
WEST VIRGINIA																	
Byrd	N	N	N	Y	N	Y	N	Y	N	N	Y	N	Y	N	N	Y	N
Rockefeller	N	N	N	Y	N	Y	N	Y	N	N	Y	N	Y	N	N	Y	Y
WISCONSIN																	
Feingold	N	Y	N	N	Y	Y	N	Y	Y	N	Y	N	Y	N	N	N	N
Kohl	Y	Y	N	Y	N	Y	N	Y	Y	N	Y	N	Y	N	N	N	Y
WYOMING																	
Simpson	Y	Y	Y	Y	Y	N	Y	Y	Y	N	Y	N	Y	Y	Y	Y	Y
Thomas	Y	Y	Y	Y	Y	N	Y	Y	Y	N	N	Y	Y	Y	Y	Y	Y

1. H J Res 1. Balanced-Budget Amendment/Passage. Passage of the joint resolution to propose a constitutional amendment to balance the budget by the year 2002 or two years after ratification by three-fourths of the states, whichever is later. Under the proposal three-fifths of the entire House and Senate would be required to approve deficit spending or an increase in the public debt limit. A simple majority could waive the requirement in times of war or in the face of a serious military threat. Passed 300–132: R 228–2; D 72–129 (ND 34–105, SD 38–24); I 0–1, Jan. 26, 1995. A two-thirds majority vote of those present and voting—288 in this case—is required to pass a joint resolution proposing an amendment to the Constitution. A "nay" was a vote in support of the president's position.

2. HR 9. Omnibus Regulatory Overhaul/Passage. Passage of the bill incorporating into one omnibus bill the text of four bills concerning the federal regulatory process: HR 830 (paperwork reduction), HR 925 (private property rights), HR 926 (regulatory overhaul) and HR 1022 (risk assessment). Passed 277–141: R 219–8; D 58–132 (ND 23–110, SD 35–22); I 0–1, March 3, 1995. A "nay" was a vote in support of the president's position.

3. HR 4. Welfare Overhaul/Passage. Passage of the bill to end the entitlement status of welfare programs by replacing dozens of social service programs with five predetermined block grants to states encompassing cash welfare, child welfare programs such as foster care, child care, school meals and nutrition programs for pregnant women and infants; to give states wide flexibility to design their own programs; to require welfare recipients to engage in work activities after receiving cash benefits for two years and limit benefits to five years; to deny cash benefits to unwed mothers under age 18 but provide them with vouchers for infant care; to deny most benefits to legal and illegal immigrants; to limit federal spending on the food stamp program; to reduce federal spending and eligibility for Supplemental Security Income; to require states to withhold driver's licenses, professional and occupational licenses, and recreational licenses of parents who fail to pay child support; and for other purposes. Passed 234–199: R 225–5; D 9–193 (ND 3–135, SD 6–58); I 0–1, March 24, 1995. A "nay" was a vote in support of the president's position.

4. H J Res 73. Term Limit Constitutional Amendment/Passage. Passage of the joint resolution to propose a constitutional amendment to impose a 12-year lifetime limit on congressional service in each chamber. Rejected 227–204: R 189–40; D 38–163 (ND 22–117, SD 16–46); I 0–1, March 29, 1995. A two-thirds majority vote of those present and voting (288 in this case) is required to pass a joint resolution proposing an amendment to the Constitution.

5. HR 1215. Tax and Spending Cuts/Passage. Passage of the bill to cut taxes by $189 billion over five years through a variety of proposals, including a $500-per-child tax credit for families earning up to $200,000 a year; the elimination of the corporate alternative minimum tax; a lowering of the capital gains tax rate from 28 percent to 19.8 percent; the easing of the "marriage penalty" in the tax code; the establishment of "back loaded" individual retirement accounts; and the repeal of the 1993 tax increase on Social Security benefits. The cost of the bill would be offset through various proposals, including cutting discretionary spending by $100 billion over five years; increasing federal employees' pension contribution; and freezing reimbursement rates in certain Medicare programs. Passed 246–188: R 219–11; D 27–176 (ND 9–130, SD 18–46); I 0–1, April 5, 1995. A "nay" was a vote in support of the president's position.

6. HR 961. Clean Water Act Revisions/Passage. Passage of the bill to authorize $2.3 billion a year for five years for state revolving loan funds that provide money for clean water projects under the Federal Water Pollution Control Act of 1972; ease or waive numerous federal water pollution control regulations and subject them to cost-benefit analysis; allow states to continue to rely on voluntary measures to deal with unmet water pollution problems; restrict the ability of federal agencies to declare wetlands off-limits to development; require the federal government to reimburse landowners if wetlands regulations cause a 20 percent decrease in land value; and for other purposes. Passed 240–185: R 195–34; D 45–150 (ND 19–114, SD 26–36); I 0–1, May 16, 1995. A "nay" was a vote in support of the president's position.

7. HR 1530. Fiscal 1996 Defense Authorization/1972 ABM Treaty Compliance. Spratt, D-S.C., amendment to stipulate that the bill's provisions calling for development and deployment of a national missile defense system do not violate the 1972 U.S.-Soviet Anti-Ballistic Missile (ABM) Treaty. Rejected 185–242: R 7–221; D 177–21 (ND 126–10, SD 51–11); I 1–0, June 14, 1995. A "yea" was a vote in support of the president's position.

8. HR 2099. Fiscal 1996 VA, HUD Appropriations/Environmental Enforcement. Stokes, D-Ohio, amendment to strike the bill's provisions prohibiting the Environmental Protection Agency from enforcing environmental laws, including sections of the clean water act and the Clean Air Act and the Delaney Clause of the Federal Food, Drug and Cosmetic Act regarding pesticides on food. Adopted 212–206: R 51–175; D 160–31 (ND 122–10, SD 38–21); I 1–0, July 28, 1995. A "yea" was a vote in support of the president's position.

9. HR 1555. Telecommunications/Passage. Passage of the bill to promote competition and deregulation in the broadcasting, cable, and telephone industries by requiring local phone companies to open their networks to competitors, allowing those companies to offer cable service, permitting the regional Bell Operating Companies to enter the long-distance and manufacturing markets under certain conditions, easing ownership and licensing requirements on broadcasters, and eliminating many of the price controls on cable companies. Passed 305–117: R 208–18; D 97–98 (ND 52–84, SD 45–14); I 0–1, Aug. 4, 1995. A "nay" was a vote in support of the president's position.

10. HR 2425. Medicare Revisions/Passage. Passage of the bill to cut $270 billion over seven years from Medicare, the federal health insurance program for the elderly. The bill would make all health care fraud federal crimes, limit increases in payments to hospitals and other providers to keep solvent the Medicare Part A trust fund until fiscal 2010, and freeze the Part B Medicare premium at 31.5 percent of program costs. Passed 231–201: R 227–6; D 4–194 (ND 0–137, SD 4–57); I 0–1, Oct. 19, 1995. A "nay" was a vote in support of the president's position.

11. HR 2491. 1995 Budget-Reconciliation/Passage. Passage of the bill to cut spending by about $900 billion and taxes by $245 billion over the next seven years in order to provide for a balanced budget by fiscal 2002. Over seven years the bill would reduce spending on Medicare by $270 billion, Medicaid by $170 billion, welfare programs by $102 billion, the earned-income tax credit by $23.2 billion, agriculture programs by $13.4 billion, student loans by $10.2 billion and federal employee retirement programs by $9.9 billion. The bill abolishes the Commerce Department; allows oil drilling in the Arctic National Wildlife Refuge in Alaska; and increases the debt limit from $4.9 trillion to $5.5 trillion. Passed 227–203: R 223–10; D 4–192 (ND 0–137, SD 4–55); I 0–1, Oct. 26, 1995. A "nay" was a vote in support of the president's position.

12. HR 1833. Abortion Procedures/Passage. Passage of the bill to ban partial birth abortions. Passed 288–139: R 215–15; D 73–123 (ND 46–90, SD 27–33); I 0–1, Nov. 1, 1995. A "nay" was a vote in support of the president's position.

13. HR 2126. Fiscal 1996 Defense Appropriations/Conference Report. Adoption of the conference report on the bill to provide $243,251,297,000 in new budget authority for the Department of Defense in fiscal 1996. The bill provides $1,698,226,000 more than the $241,553,071,000 provided in fiscal 1995 and $6,907,280,000 more than the $236,344,017,000 requested by the administration. Adopted (thus cleared for the president) 270–158: R 195–37; D 75–120 (ND 35–102, SD 40–18); I 0–1, Nov. 16, 1995. A "nay" was a vote in support of the president's position.

14. H Res 250. Gift Rules/Full Disclosure Alternative. Burton, R-Ind., amendment to require House members to fully disclose trips, meals, and gifts worth more than $50, with an annual limit of $250 from one source. The original resolution would ban gifts over $50 and prohibit lawmakers from accepting more than $100 in gifts from any one source annually. Gifts of $10 or more would count against the $100 limit. The amendment would also allow lawmakers to attend certain all-expenses-paid recreational events that raise money for charity. Rejected 154–276: R 108–125; D 46–150 (ND 21–116, SD 25–34); I 0–1, Nov. 16, 1995.

15. HR 2606. Bosnia Troop Deployment Prohibition/Passage. Passage of the bill to prohibit the use of federal money for the deployment of U.S. ground troops in Bosnia and Herzegovina as part of any peacekeeping operation unless specifically appropriated. Passed 243–171: R 214–12; D 28–159 (ND 19–110, SD 9–49); I 1–0, Nov. 17, 1995. A "nay" was a vote in support of the president's position.

16. H J Res 122. Fiscal 1996 Continuing Resolution/Senate Amendment. Livingston, R-La., motion to concur in the Senate amendments to the joint resolution to provide continuing appropriations through Dec. 15 for those fiscal 1996 spending bills not yet enacted. The resolution would set spending levels at the lowest level of the fiscal 1995 bill, the House-passed 1996 bill, or the Senate-passed 1996 bill. Programs could continue at a maximum of 75 percent of their 1995 spending levels, if either House has voted to cut them more deeply, unless such a reduction would require the furlough of federal employees. The joint resolution commits the president and Congress to enact a balanced budget by fiscal 2002 based on the most current assumptions of the Congressional Budget Office in consultation with the Office of Management and Budget and private economists. Motion agreed to (thus cleared for the president) 421–4: R 227–2; D 193–2 (ND 134–2, SD 59–0); I 1–0, Nov. 20, 1995. A "yea" was a vote in support of the president's position.

17. HR 2564. Lobby Restrictions/Federal Agency Lobbying. Clinger, R-Pa., amendment to prohibit federal agencies from using public funds on any activity intended to promote public support or opposition to any legislative proposal. Rejected 190–238: R 176–56; D 14–181 (ND 5–131, SD 9–50); I 0–1, Nov. 28, 1995.

18. HR 1058. Shareholder Lawsuits/Veto Override. Passage, over President Clinton's Dec. 19 veto, of the bill to curb class-action securities lawsuits. The bill includes provisions to allow judges to sanction attorneys and plaintiffs who file frivolous lawsuits, give plaintiffs greater control over a lawsuit, modify the system for paying attorneys' fees and establish a system of "proportionate liability" for defendants who do not knowingly engage in securities fraud. It would create a "safe harbor" for companies that make predictions of future performance that are accompanied by cautionary statements. Passed 319–100: R 230–0; D 89–99 (ND 56–76, SD 33–23); I 0–1, Dec. 20, 1995. A two-thirds majority of those present and voting (280 in this case) of both houses is required to override a veto. A "nay" was a vote in support of the president's position.

[a] Norman Y. Mineta, D-Calif., resigned Oct. 10, 1995. He was eligible to vote on key votes 1-9. Tom Campbell, R-Calif., was sworn in Dec. 15, 1995, replacing Mineta. Campbell was eligible to vote on key vote 18.

[b] Walter R. Tucker III, D-Calif., resigned Dec. 15, 1995. He was eligible to vote on key votes 1-17.

	KEY		
	Democrats	*Republicans*	Independent
Y	Voted for ("yea")	–	Announced against
N	Voted against ("nay")	P	Voted "present"
+	Announced for	C	Voted "present" to avoid possible conflict of interest
#	Paired for	?	Did not vote or otherwise make a position known
X	Paired against		

ND Northern Democrats
SD Southern Democrats
Southern states – Ala., Ark., Fla., Ga., Ky., La., Miss., N.C., Okla., S.C., Tenn., Texas, Va.

House Key Votes	1	2	3	4	5	6	7	8	9	10	11	12	13	14	15	16	17	18
ALABAMA																		
1 Callahan	Y	Y	Y	Y	Y	Y	N	N	Y	Y	Y	Y	Y	Y	N	Y	Y	Y
2 Everett	Y	Y	Y	Y	Y	Y	N	N	Y	Y	Y	Y	Y	Y	N	Y	Y	Y
3 Browder	Y	Y	N	Y	Y	Y	N	Y	N	N	N	Y	Y	N	Y	N	N	Y
4 Bevill	Y	Y	N	Y	Y	Y	Y	Y	N	N	Y	Y	Y	N	Y	N	N	Y
5 Cramer	Y	Y	N	Y	Y	Y	N	Y	N	N	N	Y	Y	N	Y	N	N	Y
6 Bachus	Y	Y	Y	Y	Y	Y	N	N	Y	Y	Y	Y	Y	Y	Y	Y	Y	Y
7 Hilliard	N	Y	N	N	N	Y	Y	Y	N	N	–	N	N	N	Y	N	N	N
ALASKA																		
AL *Young*	Y	Y	Y	Y	N	Y	N	N	?	Y	Y	Y	Y	Y	Y	Y	Y	?
ARIZONA																		
1 *Salmon*	Y	Y	Y	N	Y	Y	N	N	Y	Y	Y	Y	Y	N	Y	Y	Y	Y
2 Pastor	N	N	N	N	N	N	Y	Y	N	N	N	N	Y	N	N	Y	N	N
3 *Stump*	Y	Y	Y	Y	Y	Y	N	N	Y	Y	Y	Y	Y	Y	Y	Y	Y	Y
4 *Shadegg*	Y	Y	Y	N	Y	Y	N	N	Y	Y	Y	Y	Y	N	Y	Y	Y	Y
5 *Kolbe*	Y	Y	Y	Y	Y	Y	N	N	Y	Y	Y	Y	N	Y	N	Y	N	Y
6 *Hayworth*	Y	Y	Y	Y	Y	Y	N	N	Y	Y	Y	Y	Y	N	Y	Y	Y	Y
ARKANSAS																		
1 Lincoln	Y	Y	N	N	Y	Y	N	N	Y	N	N	N	N	N	N	Y	N	Y
2 Thornton	N	Y	N	N	Y	N	N	Y	N	N	N	Y	N	N	N	Y	N	Y
3 *Hutchinson*	Y	Y	Y	Y	Y	Y	N	N	Y	Y	Y	Y	Y	N	Y	Y	Y	Y
4 *Dickey*	Y	Y	Y	Y	Y	Y	N	N	Y	Y	Y	Y	Y	Y	Y	Y	Y	Y
CALIFORNIA																		
1 *Riggs*	Y	Y	Y	Y	Y	Y	N	N	Y	Y	Y	Y	Y	N	Y	Y	Y	Y
2 *Herger*	Y	Y	Y	Y	Y	Y	N	N	Y	Y	Y	Y	Y	Y	Y	Y	Y	Y
3 Fazio	N	Y	N	N	N	N	Y	Y	N	N	N	N	N	N	N	Y	N	Y
4 *Doolittle*	Y	Y	Y	Y	Y	Y	N	N	Y	Y	Y	Y	Y	Y	Y	Y	Y	Y
5 Matsui	N	N	N	N	N	N	Y	Y	N	N	N	N	N	N	N	Y	N	N
6 Woolsey	N	N	N	N	N	–	Y	Y	N	N	N	N	N	N	N	Y	N	N
7 Miller	N	?	N	N	N	N	Y	Y	N	N	N	N	N	N	N	Y	N	N
8 Pelosi	N	?	N	N	N	N	Y	Y	N	N	N	N	N	N	N	Y	N	Y
9 Dellums	N	N	N	N	N	N	Y	Y	N	N	N	N	N	N	N	Y	N	N
10 *Baker*	Y	Y	Y	Y	Y	Y	N	N	Y	Y	Y	Y	Y	Y	Y	Y	Y	Y
11 *Pombo*	Y	Y	Y	Y	Y	Y	N	N	Y	Y	Y	Y	Y	N	Y	Y	Y	Y
12 Lantos	N	N	N	N	N	N	Y	Y	N	N	N	N	N	N	N	Y	N	?
13 Stark	N	N	N	N	N	N	Y	Y	N	N	N	N	N	N	#	Y	N	N
14 Eshoo	N	N	N	N	N	N	Y	Y	N	N	N	N	N	N	N	Y	N	Y
15 Mineta/*Campbell*[a]	N	N	N	N	N	N	Y	Y	Y									Y
16 Lofgren	N	N	N	N	N	N	Y	Y	N	N	N	N	N	N	P	Y	N	Y
17 Farr	N	N	N	N	N	N	Y	Y	N	N	N	N	N	N	N	Y	N	Y
18 Condit	Y	Y	N	Y	Y	Y	N	N	Y	N	N	Y	N	N	Y	Y	Y	Y
19 *Radanovich*	Y	Y	Y	Y	Y	Y	N	N	Y	Y	Y	Y	Y	Y	Y	Y	Y	Y
20 Dooley	Y	Y	N	N	Y	Y	N	Y	N	N	N	Y	N	N	Y	N	N	?
21 *Thomas*	Y	Y	Y	Y	Y	Y	N	N	Y	Y	Y	Y	Y	Y	Y	Y	Y	Y
22 *Seastrand*	Y	Y	Y	Y	Y	Y	N	N	Y	Y	Y	Y	Y	N	Y	Y	Y	Y
23 *Gallegly*	Y	Y	Y	Y	Y	Y	N	N	Y	Y	Y	Y	Y	N	Y	Y	Y	Y
24 Beilenson	N	N	N	N	N	N	Y	Y	N	N	N	N	N	N	N	Y	N	N
25 *McKeon*	Y	Y	Y	Y	Y	Y	N	N	Y	Y	Y	Y	Y	N	Y	Y	Y	Y
26 Berman	N	N	N	N	N	?	Y	?	N	N	N	N	N	N	?	N	N	N
27 *Moorhead*	Y	Y	Y	Y	Y	Y	N	N	Y	Y	Y	Y	Y	Y	Y	Y	Y	Y
28 *Dreier*	Y	Y	Y	N	Y	Y	N	N	Y	Y	Y	Y	Y	N	Y	Y	Y	Y
29 Waxman	N	N	N	N	N	N	Y	Y	N	N	N	N	N	N	X	Y	N	N
30 Becerra	N	N	N	N	N	N	Y	Y	N	N	N	–	N	N	N	Y	N	N
31 Martinez	N	N	N	N	N	N	Y	Y	N	N	N	N	Y	N	Y	N	N	N
32 Dixon	N	N	N	N	N	N	Y	Y	N	N	N	Y	N	N	Y	Y	N	N
33 Roybal-Allard	N	N	N	N	N	N	Y	Y	N	N	N	N	N	N	N	Y	N	N
34 Torres	N	N	N	N	N	N	Y	Y	N	N	N	N	N	N	N	Y	N	N
35 Waters	N	N	N	N	N	–	Y	Y	N	N	N	N	N	N	N	Y	N	N
36 Harman	Y	Y	N	Y	N	N	Y	Y	N	N	N	Y	N	N	P	Y	N	Y
37 Tucker[b]	N	N	N	N	N	N	Y	Y	?	?	?	?	?	?	?	?	?	
38 *Horn*	Y	Y	Y	Y	Y	Y	N	Y	N	Y	Y	N	Y	N	Y	Y	Y	Y
39 *Royce*	Y	Y	Y	Y	Y	Y	N	N	Y	Y	Y	Y	Y	Y	Y	Y	Y	Y
40 *Lewis*	Y	Y	Y	N	Y	Y	N	N	Y	Y	Y	Y	Y	N	Y	N	Y	Y
41 *Kim*	Y	Y	Y	Y	Y	Y	N	N	Y	Y	Y	Y	Y	Y	Y	Y	Y	Y
42 Brown	N	?	–	N	N	N	Y	Y	N	N	N	N	N	N	N	Y	N	N
43 *Calvert*	Y	Y	Y	Y	Y	Y	N	N	Y	Y	Y	Y	Y	Y	Y	Y	N	Y
44 *Bono*	Y	Y	Y	Y	Y	Y	N	N	Y	Y	Y	Y	Y	Y	Y	Y	Y	Y
45 *Rohrabacher*	Y	Y	Y	Y	Y	Y	N	N	Y	Y	Y	Y	Y	N	Y	Y	Y	Y
46 *Dornan*	Y	#	Y	Y	Y	Y	N	N	Y	Y	Y	Y	Y	Y	Y	Y	Y	?
47 *Cox*	Y	Y	Y	Y	Y	Y	N	N	Y	Y	Y	Y	Y	Y	Y	Y	Y	Y
48 *Packard*	Y	Y	Y	Y	Y	Y	N	N	Y	Y	Y	Y	Y	Y	Y	Y	Y	Y
49 *Bilbray*	Y	Y	Y	Y	Y	Y	N	N	Y	Y	Y	Y	Y	N	Y	Y	N	Y
50 Filner	N	N	N	N	N	N	Y	#	N	N	N	N	N	N	N	Y	N	X
51 *Cunningham*	Y	Y	Y	Y	Y	Y	N	N	Y	Y	Y	Y	Y	Y	Y	Y	Y	Y
52 *Hunter*	Y	Y	Y	N	Y	Y	N	N	Y	Y	Y	Y	Y	Y	Y	Y	Y	Y
COLORADO																		
1 Schroeder	N	N	N	N	N	N	Y	Y	N	N	N	N	N	N	N	Y	N	N
2 Skaggs	N	N	N	N	N	N	Y	Y	N	N	N	N	N	N	N	Y	N	N
3 *McInnis*	Y	Y	Y	Y	Y	Y	N	N	Y	Y	Y	Y	Y	Y	Y	Y	Y	Y
4 *Allard*	Y	Y	Y	Y	Y	Y	N	N	Y	Y	Y	Y	Y	Y	Y	Y	Y	Y
5 *Hefley*	Y	Y	Y	N	Y	Y	N	N	Y	Y	Y	N	Y	Y	Y	N	Y	Y
6 *Schaefer*	Y	Y	Y	Y	Y	Y	N	N	Y	Y	Y	Y	Y	Y	Y	Y	Y	Y

KEY

	Democrats	*Republicans*	Independents

- Y Voted for ("yea")
- N Voted against ("nay")
- \+ Announced for
- \# Paired for
- X Paired against
- – Announced against
- P Voted "present"
- C Voted "present" to avoid possible conflict of interest
- ? Did not vote or otherwise make a position known

ND Northern Democrats
SD Southern Democrats
Southern states – Ala., Ark., Fla., Ga., Ky., La., Miss., N.C., Okla., S.C., Tenn., Texas, Va.

House Key Votes	1	2	3	4	5	6	7	8	9	10	11	12	13	14	15	16	17	18
CONNECTICUT																		
1 Kennelly	N	N	N	N	N	N	Y	Y	N	N	N	N	Y	N	N	Y	N	Y
2 Gejdenson	N	N	N	N	N	N	Y	Y	N	N	N	N	Y	N	N	Y	N	Y
3 DeLauro	N	N	N	N	N	N	Y	Y	N	N	N	N	Y	N	N	Y	N	Y
4 *Shays*	Y	N	Y	N	Y	N	Y	Y	N	Y	Y	N	N	N	Y	Y	N	Y
5 *Franks*	Y	Y	Y	Y	Y	Y	N	Y	Y	Y	Y	N	Y	N	Y	Y	Y	Y
6 *Johnson*	Y	?	Y	N	Y	N	N	Y	Y	Y	Y	N	Y	N	Y	Y	Y	Y
DELAWARE																		
AL *Castle*	Y	Y	Y	Y	Y	N	N	Y	Y	Y	Y	Y	Y	N	Y	Y	N	Y
FLORIDA																		
1 *Scarborough*	Y	Y	Y	Y	?	Y	N	Y	?	Y	N	Y	Y	Y	Y	Y	Y	Y
2 Peterson	Y	Y	N	Y	N	N	Y	Y	Y	N	N	N	Y	N	N	Y	N	Y
3 Brown	N	N	N	N	N	N	Y	Y	Y	N	N	N	N	Y	N	Y	N	N
4 *Fowler*	Y	Y	Y	Y	Y	Y	N	N	N	Y	Y	Y	Y	Y	Y	Y	?	Y
5 Thurman	N	Y	N	N	N	N	Y	Y	?	N	N	N	Y	N	N	Y	N	N
6 *Stearns*	Y	Y	Y	Y	Y	Y	N	N	Y	Y	Y	Y	Y	Y	Y	Y	Y	Y
7 *Mica*	Y	Y	Y	Y	Y	Y	N	N	Y	Y	Y	Y	Y	N	Y	Y	Y	Y
8 *McCollum*	Y	Y	Y	Y	Y	Y	N	N	Y	Y	Y	Y	Y	Y	Y	Y	N	Y
9 *Bilirakis*	Y	Y	Y	Y	Y	Y	N	N	Y	Y	Y	Y	Y	N	Y	Y	N	Y
10 *Young*	Y	Y	Y	Y	Y	Y	N	Y	Y	Y	Y	Y	Y	N	Y	Y	N	Y
11 Gibbons	Y	N	N	N	N	N	Y	Y	N	N	N	N	Y	N	N	Y	N	N
12 *Canady*	Y	Y	Y	Y	Y	Y	N	N	Y	Y	Y	Y	Y	N	Y	Y	N	Y
13 *Miller*	Y	Y	Y	Y	Y	Y	N	N	Y	Y	Y	Y	Y	N	Y	Y	N	Y
14 *Goss*	Y	Y	Y	Y	Y	N	N	Y	Y	Y	Y	Y	Y	N	Y	Y	N	Y
15 *Weldon*	Y	Y	Y	Y	Y	Y	N	N	Y	Y	Y	Y	Y	N	Y	Y	Y	Y
16 *Foley*	Y	Y	Y	Y	Y	Y	N	N	Y	Y	Y	Y	Y	N	Y	Y	N	Y
17 Meek	N	N	N	N	N	N	Y	Y	Y	N	N	N	Y	Y	N	Y	N	N
18 *Ros-Lehtinen*	Y	Y	N	Y	Y	N	N	Y	Y	Y	Y	Y	Y	Y	Y	Y	N	Y
19 Johnston	Y	?	N	N	N	N	Y	X	N	N	N	N	N	N	N	Y	N	N
20 Deutsch	Y	N	N	Y	N	N	Y	Y	?	N	N	N	N	N	N	Y	N	Y
21 *Diaz-Balart*	Y	Y	N	Y	Y	N	N	Y	Y	Y	Y	Y	Y	Y	Y	Y	N	Y
22 *Shaw*	Y	Y	Y	Y	Y	Y	N	Y	Y	Y	Y	Y	Y	N	Y	Y	N	Y
23 Hastings	N	N	N	N	N	N	Y	Y	Y	N	N	N	Y	Y	N	Y	N	N
GEORGIA																		
1 *Kingston*	Y	Y	Y	Y	Y	Y	N	N	Y	Y	Y	Y	Y	Y	Y	Y	Y	Y
2 Bishop	?	Y	N	N	N	Y	Y	Y	Y	N	N	N	Y	Y	N	Y	N	Y
3 *Collins*	Y	Y	Y	Y	Y	Y	N	N	Y	Y	Y	Y	Y	Y	Y	Y	Y	Y
4 *Linder*	Y	Y	Y	Y	Y	Y	N	N	Y	Y	Y	Y	Y	N	Y	Y	Y	Y
5 Lewis	N	N	N	N	N	N	Y	Y	Y	N	N	N	N	N	N	Y	N	N
6 *Gingrich*[c]	Y	Y	Y	Y	Y		N			Y	Y							Y
7 *Barr*	Y	Y	Y	Y	Y	Y	N	N	Y	Y	Y	Y	Y	Y	Y	Y	Y	Y
8 *Chambliss*	Y	Y	Y	Y	Y	Y	N	N	Y	Y	Y	Y	Y	Y	Y	Y	Y	Y
9 *Deal*[d]	Y	Y	N	Y	Y	Y	N	N	Y	Y	Y	Y	Y	N	Y	Y	N	Y
10 *Norwood*	Y	Y	Y	Y	Y	Y	N	?	Y	Y	Y	Y	Y	Y	Y	Y	Y	Y
11 McKinney	N	N	N	N	N	N	Y	?	Y	N	N	N	N	N	N	Y	N	N
HAWAII																		
1 Abercrombie	N	N	N	N	N	N	Y	Y	N	N	N	N	Y	Y	N	Y	N	-
2 Mink	N	N	N	N	N	N	Y	Y	N	N	N	N	Y	N	N	Y	N	N
IDAHO																		
1 *Chenoweth*	Y	Y	Y	Y	Y	Y	N	N	Y	Y	Y	Y	Y	N	Y	Y	Y	Y
2 *Crapo*	Y	Y	Y	Y	Y	Y	N	N	Y	Y	Y	Y	Y	Y	Y	Y	Y	Y
ILLINOIS																		
1 Rush	-	N	N	N	N	N	Y	Y	Y	N	N	N	N	N	N	Y	N	Y
2 Reynolds/Jackson[e]	N	N	N	N	?	N	Y	?	?									Y
3 Lipinski	Y	N	Y	N	Y	?	N	Y	N	N	N	Y	N	N	Y	Y	N	Y
4 Gutierrez	N	N	N	N	N	N	Y	Y	N	N	N	N	N	N	N	Y	N	N
5 *Flanagan*	Y	Y	Y	Y	Y	Y	N	N	Y	Y	Y	Y	Y	N	Y	Y	N	Y
6 *Hyde*	Y	Y	Y	N	Y	Y	N	N	Y	Y	Y	Y	Y	N	?	Y	N	Y
7 Collins	N	?	N	N	N	-	Y	Y	N	N	N	N	N	Y	?	Y	N	N
8 *Crane*	Y	Y	Y	Y	Y	Y	N	N	Y	Y	Y	Y	Y	Y	Y	Y	Y	?
9 Yates	N	N	N	N	N	N	?	Y	N	N	N	N	N	N	N	Y	N	N
10 *Porter*	Y	N	Y	N	N	N	Y	Y	Y	Y	Y	Y	Y	N	Y	Y	Y	Y
11 *Weller*	Y	Y	Y	Y	Y	Y	N	N	Y	Y	Y	Y	Y	N	Y	Y	Y	Y
12 Costello	Y	N	N	N	N	Y	Y	Y	N	N	N	Y	N	N	Y	Y	N	N
13 *Fawell*	Y	Y	Y	N	Y	Y	N	Y	N	Y	Y	Y	Y	N	Y	Y	N	Y
14 *Hastert*	Y	Y	Y	Y	Y	Y	N	N	Y	Y	Y	Y	Y	Y	Y	Y	Y	Y
15 *Ewing*	Y	Y	Y	Y	Y	Y	N	N	Y	Y	Y	Y	Y	Y	Y	Y	Y	Y
16 *Manzullo*	Y	Y	Y	Y	Y	Y	N	N	Y	Y	Y	Y	Y	N	Y	Y	Y	Y
17 Evans	N	N	N	N	N	N	Y	Y	N	N	N	N	N	N	Y	Y	N	N
18 *LaHood*	Y	Y	Y	Y	N	Y	N	N	Y	Y	N	Y	N	Y	Y	Y	N	Y
19 Poshard	Y	Y	N	Y	N	Y	Y	N	N	N	N	Y	N	N	Y	Y	N	N
20 Durbin	N	N	N	N	N	N	Y	Y	N	N	N	N	N	N	Y	Y	N	N
INDIANA																		
1 Visclosky	Y	N	N	N	N	N	Y	Y	N	N	N	N	Y	N	N	Y	N	Y
2 *McIntosh*	Y	Y	Y	Y	Y	Y	N	N	Y	Y	Y	Y	Y	Y	Y	Y	Y	Y
3 Roemer	Y	Y	N	N	N	N	Y	N	Y	N	N	Y	N	N	Y	Y	N	Y
4 *Souder*	N	Y	Y	Y	Y	Y	N	N	Y	Y	Y	Y	Y	N	Y	P	Y	Y
5 *Buyer*	Y	Y	Y	Y	Y	Y	N	N	Y	Y	Y	Y	Y	N	Y	Y	Y	Y
6 *Burton*	Y	Y	Y	Y	Y	Y	N	N	Y	Y	Y	Y	Y	Y	Y	Y	Y	Y
7 *Myers*	Y	?	Y	N	Y	Y	N	N	N	Y	Y	Y	Y	Y	Y	Y	Y	Y
8 *Hostettler*	N	Y	Y	N	Y	Y	N	N	Y	Y	Y	Y	Y	Y	Y	Y	Y	Y
9 Hamilton	Y	Y	N	N	N	Y	Y	Y	Y	N	N	Y	Y	N	N	Y	N	Y
10 Jacobs	Y	Y	N	Y	N	N	Y	Y	Y	N	N	Y	N	N	Y	Y	Y	N
IOWA																		
1 *Leach*	Y	Y	Y	Y	Y	Y	Y	Y	N	Y	Y	Y	Y	N	Y	Y	N	Y
2 *Nussle*	Y	Y	Y	Y	Y	Y	N	N	Y	Y	Y	Y	Y	N	Y	Y	Y	Y
3 *Lightfoot*	Y	Y	Y	Y	Y	Y	N	N	Y	N	Y	Y	Y	Y	Y	Y	Y	Y
4 *Ganske*	Y	Y	Y	Y	Y	Y	N	N	Y	Y	Y	Y	N	N	Y	Y	N	Y
5 *Latham*	Y	Y	Y	Y	Y	Y	N	N	Y	Y	Y	Y	Y	Y	Y	Y	Y	Y
KANSAS																		
1 *Roberts*	Y	Y	Y	N	Y	Y	N	N	Y	Y	Y	Y	Y	N	Y	Y	Y	Y
2 *Brownback*	Y	Y	Y	Y	Y	Y	N	N	Y	Y	Y	Y	Y	N	Y	Y	N	Y
3 *Meyers*	Y	Y	Y	Y	Y	N	N	#	N	Y	Y	N	Y	N	Y	Y	N	Y
4 *Tiahrt*	Y	Y	Y	Y	Y	Y	N	N	Y	Y	Y	Y	Y	N	Y	Y	Y	Y
KENTUCKY																		
1 *Whitfield*	Y	Y	Y	Y	Y	Y	N	N	Y	Y	Y	Y	Y	Y	Y	Y	Y	Y
2 *Lewis*	Y	Y	Y	Y	Y	Y	N	N	Y	Y	Y	Y	Y	Y	Y	Y	Y	Y
3 Ward	N	N	N	N	N	N	Y	Y	Y	N	N	N	Y	N	N	Y	N	Y
4 *Bunning*	Y	Y	Y	Y	Y	Y	N	N	N	Y	Y	Y	Y	Y	Y	Y	Y	Y
5 *Rogers*	Y	Y	Y	N	N	Y	N	N	Y	Y	Y	Y	Y	Y	Y	Y	Y	Y
6 Baesler	Y	Y	N	N	N	N	N	N	N	N	N	Y	Y	N	N	Y	N	Y
LOUISIANA																		
1 *Livingston*	Y	Y	Y	N	Y	Y	N	N	Y	Y	Y	Y	Y	Y	?	Y	Y	Y
2 Jefferson	N	N	N	N	N	N	Y	Y	Y	N	N	N	Y	Y	N	Y	N	Y
3 *Tauzin*[f]	Y	Y	Y	Y	Y	Y	N	N	Y	Y	Y	Y	Y	Y	Y	Y	Y	Y
4 Fields	-	N	N	N	N	N	Y	Y	N	N	N	?	?	?	?	Y	N	Y
5 *McCrery*	Y	Y	Y	Y	Y	Y	N	N	Y	Y	Y	Y	Y	Y	?	Y	Y	Y
6 *Baker*	Y	Y	Y	N	Y	Y	N	N	Y	Y	Y	Y	Y	Y	?	Y	N	Y
7 *Hayes*[g]	Y	?	Y	Y	Y	Y	N	N	Y	N	N	Y	?	Y	Y	Y	Y	Y
MAINE																		
1 *Longley*	Y	Y	Y	N	Y	Y	N	Y	Y	Y	Y	Y	Y	N	N	Y	Y	Y
2 Baldacci	N	N	N	Y	N	N	Y	Y	N	N	N	N	Y	N	N	Y	N	N
MARYLAND																		
1 *Gilchrest*	Y	N	Y	Y	Y	N	N	Y	Y	Y	Y	Y	Y	N	Y	Y	N	Y
2 *Ehrlich*	Y	Y	Y	N	Y	N	N	Y	Y	Y	Y	Y	Y	Y	Y	Y	Y	Y
3 Cardin	N	N	N	N	N	N	Y	Y	Y	N	N	N	N	N	N	Y	N	Y
4 Wynn	N	N	N	N	N	N	Y	Y	Y	N	N	N	N	N	N	Y	N	Y
5 Hoyer	Y	N	N	N	N	N	Y	Y	Y	N	N	N	Y	N	N	Y	N	Y
6 *Bartlett*	Y	Y	Y	Y	Y	Y	N	N	Y	Y	Y	Y	Y	N	Y	+	Y	Y
7 Mfume	N	N	N	N	N	N	Y	Y	N	N	N	N	N	Y	N	Y	N	N
8 *Morella*	Y	N	N	N	N	N	Y	Y	Y	Y	N	N	N	N	Y	Y	N	Y
MASSACHUSETTS																		
1 Olver	N	N	N	N	N	N	Y	Y	Y	N	N	N	N	N	N	Y	N	N
2 Neal	N	N	N	N	N	N	Y	Y	Y	N	N	Y	Y	N	N	Y	N	Y
3 *Blute*	Y	Y	Y	Y	N	Y	N	N	Y	Y	Y	Y	N	N	Y	Y	N	Y
4 Frank	N	N	N	N	N	Y	Y	Y	N	N	N	N	N	N	N	Y	N	Y
5 Meehan	Y	N	N	Y	N	N	Y	Y	Y	N	N	N	N	N	N	Y	N	Y
6 *Torkildsen*	Y	Y	N	Y	Y	Y	N	Y	Y	N	Y	N	Y	N	Y	Y	N	Y
7 Markey	N	N	N	N	N	N	Y	Y	N	N	N	N	N	N	N	Y	N	N
8 Kennedy	Y	N	N	N	N	N	Y	Y	N	N	N	N	N	N	N	Y	N	Y
9 Moakley	N	X	N	N	N	N	Y	?	?	N	N	Y	N	N	N	Y	N	N
10 Studds	N	N	N	N	N	N	Y	Y	N	N	N	N	N	N	N	Y	N	N
MICHIGAN																		
1 Stupak	N	Y	N	N	N	N	Y	Y	N	N	N	Y	N	N	N	Y	N	N
2 *Hoekstra*	Y	Y	Y	Y	Y	Y	N	N	Y	Y	Y	Y	N	N	Y	Y	N	Y
3 *Ehlers*	Y	Y	Y	Y	Y	N	N	Y	Y	Y	Y	Y	N	N	Y	Y	Y	Y
4 *Camp*	Y	Y	Y	Y	Y	Y	N	N	Y	Y	Y	Y	N	N	Y	Y	Y	Y
5 Barcia	Y	Y	N	Y	N	Y	N	N	N	N	N	Y	N	N	N	Y	N	Y
6 *Upton*	Y	Y	Y	Y	Y	Y	N	Y	Y	Y	Y	Y	N	N	Y	Y	Y	Y
7 *Smith*	Y	Y	Y	Y	Y	Y	N	N	Y	Y	Y	Y	Y	N	?	Y	Y	Y
8 *Chrysler*	Y	Y	Y	Y	Y	Y	N	N	Y	Y	Y	Y	Y	N	Y	Y	Y	Y
9 Kildee	N	N	N	N	N	N	Y	Y	N	N	N	Y	N	N	N	Y	N	N
10 Bonior	N	N	N	N	N	N	Y	Y	Y	N	N	Y	N	N	N	Y	N	N
11 *Knollenberg*	Y	Y	Y	Y	Y	Y	N	N	Y	Y	Y	Y	Y	N	Y	Y	Y	Y
12 Levin	N	N	N	N	N	N	Y	Y	N	N	N	N	N	N	N	Y	N	N
13 Rivers	N	N	N	N	N	N	Y	Y	N	N	N	N	N	N	N	Y	N	N
14 Conyers	N	N	N	N	N	N	Y	Y	N	N	N	N	N	N	N	Y	N	N
15 Collins	N	?	N	N	N	N	Y	?	N	N	N	N	N	Y	N	Y	N	N
16 Dingell	N	N	N	N	N	N	Y	Y	Y	N	N	Y	N	N	N	Y	N	N

House Key Votes	1	2	3	4	5	6	7	8	9	10	11	12	13	14	15	16	17	18
MINNESOTA																		
1 *Gutknecht*	Y	Y	Y	Y	Y	Y	N	N	Y	Y	Y	Y	N	N	Y	Y	Y	Y
2 Minge	Y	Y	N	Y	N	N	Y	N	N	N	N	Y	N	N	N	Y	N	Y
3 *Ramstad*	Y	Y	Y	Y	Y	N	N	Y	Y	Y	Y	Y	N	N	Y	Y	Y	Y
4 Vento	N	N	N	N	N	N	Y	Y	N	N	N	N	N	N	N	Y	N	Y
5 Sabo	N	N	N	N	N	N	Y	Y	N	N	N	N	N	N	N	Y	N	Y
6 Luther	Y	N	N	Y	N	N	Y	Y	N	N	N	N	N	N	N	Y	N	Y
7 Peterson	Y	Y	N	Y	N	Y	N	N	Y	N	N	Y	N	N	Y	Y	Y	?
8 Oberstar	N	N	N	N	N	N	Y	Y	N	N	N	Y	N	N	N	Y	N	N
MISSISSIPPI																		
1 *Wicker*	Y	Y	Y	N	Y	Y	N	N	Y	Y	Y	Y	Y	Y	Y	Y	Y	Y
2 Thompson	N	N	N	N	N	N	Y	Y	Y	N	N	N	Y	Y	N	Y	N	N
3 Montgomery	Y	?	Y	N	Y	Y	N	N	Y	Y	Y	Y	Y	Y	N	Y	N	Y
4 *Parker*[h]	Y	Y	N	N	Y	Y	N	N	Y	Y	Y	Y	Y	Y	N	Y	Y	Y
5 Taylor	Y	Y	N	N	N	N	N	Y	Y	N	N	Y	Y	N	Y	Y	Y	N
MISSOURI																		
1 Clay	N	N	N	N	N	N	Y	Y	Y	N	N	N	N	Y	N	Y	N	N
2 *Talent*	Y	Y	Y	Y	Y	Y	N	N	Y	Y	Y	Y	Y	N	Y	Y	Y	Y
3 Gephardt	N	N	N	N	N	?	Y	Y	Y	N	N	Y	Y	N	N	Y	N	N
4 Skelton	Y	Y	?	N	Y	Y	Y	X	N	N	N	Y	Y	N	N	Y	N	Y
5 McCarthy	Y	N	N	Y	N	N	Y	Y	N	N	N	N	N	N	N	Y	N	Y
6 Danner	Y	Y	N	Y	Y	Y	Y	N	Y	N	N	Y	N	Y	Y	Y	N	Y
7 *Hancock*	Y	Y	Y	Y	Y	Y	N	N	Y	Y	Y	Y	Y	Y	Y	Y	Y	Y
8 *Emerson*	Y	Y	Y	Y	Y	Y	N	N	Y	Y	Y	Y	Y	Y	Y	Y	Y	?
9 Volkmer	Y	Y	N	N	N	Y	Y	?	N	N	N	Y	N	Y	?	Y	?	N
MONTANA																		
AL Williams	N	N	N	N	N	N	Y	Y	?	N	N	N	N	Y	N	N	N	N
NEBRASKA																		
1 *Bereuter*	Y	Y	Y	Y	Y	Y	N	Y	N	Y	Y	Y	N	N	Y	Y	Y	Y
2 *Christensen*	Y	Y	Y	N	Y	Y	N	N	Y	Y	Y	Y	Y	N	Y	Y	Y	Y
3 *Barrett*	Y	Y	Y	Y	Y	Y	N	N	Y	Y	Y	Y	Y	N	Y	Y	Y	Y
NEVADA																		
1 *Ensign*	Y	Y	Y	Y	Y	Y	N	N	Y	Y	Y	Y	N	N	Y	Y	Y	Y
2 *Vucanovich*	Y	Y	Y	Y	Y	Y	N	N	Y	Y	Y	Y	Y	Y	Y	Y	Y	Y
NEW HAMPSHIRE																		
1 *Zeliff*	Y	Y	Y	Y	Y	Y	N	N	Y	Y	Y	Y	N	Y	Y	Y	Y	Y
2 *Bass*	Y	Y	Y	Y	Y	Y	N	Y	Y	Y	Y	Y	Y	N	Y	Y	Y	Y
NEW JERSEY																		
1 Andrews	Y	N	Y	N	Y	N	N	Y	?	N	N	N	Y	N	Y	Y	N	Y
2 *LoBiondo*	Y	Y	Y	Y	Y	N	N	Y	Y	N	N	Y	N	N	Y	Y	Y	Y
3 *Saxton*	Y	Y	Y	Y	Y	N	N	Y	Y	N	N	Y	Y	Y	Y	Y	N	Y
4 *Smith*	Y	Y	Y	N	Y	N	N	Y	Y	N	N	Y	Y	N	Y	Y	N	Y
5 *Roukema*	Y	N	Y	N	Y	N	Y	Y	Y	Y	Y	N	N	N	Y	Y	N	Y
6 Pallone	Y	N	N	N	Y	N	Y	Y	N	N	N	N	N	N	N	Y	N	Y
7 *Franks*	Y	Y	Y	Y	Y	Y	N	Y	N	Y	Y	Y	N	N	Y	Y	N	Y
8 *Martini*	Y	Y	Y	Y	Y	N	N	Y	Y	Y	Y	Y	N	N	Y	Y	N	Y
9 Torricelli	Y	N	N	N	Y	N	Y	Y	Y	N	N	N	N	N	N	Y	N	N
10 Payne	N	N	N	N	N	N	Y	Y	Y	N	N	N	N	Y	N	Y	N	N
11 *Frelinghuysen*	Y	Y	Y	Y	Y	N	N	N	N	Y	Y	N	Y	N	Y	Y	N	Y
12 *Zimmer*	Y	N	Y	Y	Y	N	N	Y	N	N	N	N	N	N	Y	Y	N	Y
13 Menendez	N	N	N	N	N	N	Y	Y	Y	N	N	N	N	N	N	Y	N	N
NEW MEXICO																		
1 *Schiff*	Y	Y	Y	Y	N	Y	N	Y	Y	Y	Y	Y	Y	N	Y	Y	N	Y
2 *Skeen*	Y	Y	Y	N	Y	Y	N	N	Y	Y	Y	Y	Y	Y	Y	Y	Y	Y
3 Richardson	Y	N	N	N	N	N	Y	Y	N	N	N	N	Y	N	N	Y	N	N
NEW YORK																		
1 *Forbes*	Y	Y	Y	Y	Y	N	N	Y	Y	Y	Y	Y	Y	N	Y	Y	Y	Y
2 *Lazio*	Y	Y	Y	Y	Y	N	N	Y	Y	Y	Y	Y	Y	N	Y	Y	Y	Y
3 *King*	Y	Y	Y	N	Y	Y	N	N	Y	Y	Y	Y	Y	Y	N	Y	N	Y
4 *Frisa*	Y	Y	Y	Y	Y	Y	N	N	Y	Y	Y	Y	Y	Y	Y	Y	Y	Y
5 Ackerman	N	N	N	N	N	N	Y	Y	Y	N	N	N	N	N	N	Y	N	Y
6 Flake	N	N	N	N	N	N	Y	Y	Y	N	N	Y	N	N	N	Y	N	Y
7 Manton	N	N	N	N	Y	N	Y	Y	Y	N	N	Y	Y	Y	Y	Y	N	Y
8 Nadler	N	N	N	N	N	N	Y	Y	N	N	N	N	N	N	N	Y	N	N
9 Schumer	N	N	N	N	N	N	Y	Y	Y	N	N	N	N	N	N	Y	N	Y
10 Towns	N	N	N	N	N	N	Y	Y	Y	N	N	N	N	Y	N	Y	N	Y
11 Owens	N	N	N	N	N	N	Y	Y	Y	N	N	N	N	Y	N	N	N	N
12 Velazquez	N	N	N	N	N	N	Y	Y	N	N	N	N	N	N	N	Y	N	N
13 *Molinari*	Y	Y	Y	N	Y	Y	N	N	Y	Y	Y	Y	Y	N	Y	Y	Y	Y
14 Maloney	N	N	N	N	N	N	Y	Y	N	N	N	N	N	N	N	Y	N	Y
15 Rangel	N	?	N	N	N	N	Y	Y	Y	N	N	N	N	Y	N	Y	N	N
16 Serrano	N	N	N	N	N	N	Y	Y	Y	N	N	N	N	N	N	Y	N	N
17 Engel	N	N	N	N	N	N	Y	Y	N	N	N	N	N	N	N	Y	N	N
18 Lowey	N	N	N	N	N	N	Y	Y	Y	N	N	N	N	N	N	Y	N	C
19 *Kelly*	Y	Y	Y	Y	Y	Y	N	Y	Y	Y	Y	N	Y	Y	Y	Y	Y	Y
20 *Gilman*	Y	Y	Y	N	Y	N	N	Y	Y	Y	Y	N	N	N	Y	Y	Y	Y
21 McNulty	Y	Y	N	Y	N	N	N	Y	N	N	N	Y	Y	N	Y	Y	Y	Y
22 *Solomon*	Y	Y	Y	Y	Y	Y	N	N	Y	Y	Y	Y	Y	N	Y	Y	Y	Y
23 *Boehlert*	Y	N	Y	N	Y	N	N	Y	Y	Y	N	N	Y	Y	Y	Y	N	Y
24 *McHugh*	Y	Y	Y	N	Y	Y	N	N	Y	Y	N	Y	+	Y	Y	Y	Y	Y
25 *Walsh*	Y	Y	Y	Y	Y	Y	N	N	Y	Y	Y	Y	Y	N	Y	Y	N	Y
26 Hinchey	N	N	N	N	N	N	Y	Y	N	N	N	N	N	N	N	Y	N	N
27 *Paxon*	Y	Y	Y	Y	Y	Y	N	N	Y	Y	Y	Y	Y	N	Y	Y	Y	Y
28 Slaughter	N	N	N	N	N	N	+	Y	N	N	N	N	N	N	N	Y	N	Y
29 LaFalce	N	N	N	N	N	N	+	Y	N	N	N	Y	N	Y	N	Y	N	Y
30 *Quinn*	Y	Y	Y	Y	Y	Y	N	Y	?	Y	Y	Y	Y	N	Y	Y	N	Y
31 *Houghton*	Y	Y	Y	Y	N	Y	N	Y	Y	Y	Y	P	Y	Y	N	Y	Y	Y
N. CAROLINA																		
1 Clayton	N	N	N	N	N	N	Y	Y	N	N	N	N	N	N	N	Y	N	N
2 *Funderburk*	Y	Y	Y	Y	Y	Y	N	N	Y	Y	Y	Y	Y	Y	Y	Y	Y	Y
3 *Jones*	Y	Y	Y	Y	Y	Y	N	N	Y	Y	Y	Y	Y	Y	Y	Y	Y	Y
4 *Heineman*	Y	Y	Y	Y	Y	Y	N	N	Y	Y	Y	Y	N	N	Y	Y	Y	Y
5 *Burr*	Y	Y	Y	Y	Y	Y	N	N	Y	Y	Y	Y	Y	Y	Y	Y	Y	Y
6 *Coble*	Y	Y	Y	Y	Y	Y	N	N	N	Y	Y	Y	N	N	Y	Y	Y	Y
7 Rose	Y	Y	Y	Y	Y	Y	Y	Y	N	N	N	Y	Y	Y	N	?	N	Y
8 Hefner	Y	Y	N	N	N	Y	Y	Y	Y	N	N	Y	Y	N	N	Y	?	N
9 *Myrick*	Y	Y	Y	Y	Y	Y	-	N	Y	Y	Y	Y	Y	N	Y	Y	Y	Y
10 *Ballenger*	Y	Y	Y	Y	Y	Y	N	N	Y	Y	Y	Y	Y	N	Y	Y	Y	Y
11 *Taylor*	Y	Y	Y	Y	Y	Y	N	N	Y	Y	Y	Y	Y	Y	Y	Y	Y	Y
12 Watt	N	N	N	N	N	N	Y	Y	Y	N	N	N	N	Y	N	Y	N	N
N. DAKOTA																		
AL Pomeroy	N	Y	N	?	N	N	Y	Y	N	N	N	Y	N	N	N	Y	N	N
OHIO																		
1 *Chabot*	Y	Y	Y	Y	Y	Y	N	N	Y	Y	Y	Y	N	N	Y	Y	Y	Y
2 *Portman*	Y	Y	Y	Y	Y	Y	N	N	Y	Y	Y	Y	N	N	N	Y	Y	Y
3 Hall	N	N	N	N	N	N	Y	?	Y	N	N	Y	Y	N	N	Y	N	N
4 *Oxley*	Y	Y	Y	N	Y	Y	N	N	Y	Y	Y	Y	Y	Y	Y	Y	Y	Y
5 *Gillmor*	Y	Y	Y	Y	Y	Y	N	Y	Y	Y	Y	Y	Y	Y	Y	Y	Y	Y
6 *Cremeans*	Y	Y	Y	Y	Y	Y	N	N	Y	Y	Y	Y	Y	N	Y	Y	Y	Y
7 *Hobson*	Y	Y	Y	Y	Y	Y	N	N	Y	Y	Y	Y	Y	N	Y	Y	Y	Y
8 *Boehner*	Y	Y	Y	Y	Y	Y	N	N	Y	Y	Y	Y	Y	Y	Y	Y	Y	Y
9 Kaptur	Y	N	N	N	N	N	Y	Y	N	N	N	Y	N	N	N	Y	N	N
10 *Hoke*	Y	Y	Y	Y	Y	Y	N	Y	Y	Y	Y	Y	N	N	Y	Y	N	Y
11 Stokes	N	N	N	N	N	N	Y	Y	N	N	N	N	N	N	N	Y	N	N
12 *Kasich*	Y	Y	Y	Y	Y	Y	N	N	Y	Y	Y	Y	Y	N	Y	Y	Y	Y
13 Brown	Y	N	N	Y	N	N	Y	Y	Y	N	N	N	N	N	N	Y	N	Y
14 Sawyer	N	N	N	N	N	N	Y	Y	Y	N	N	N	N	N	N	Y	N	Y
15 *Pryce*	Y	Y	Y	Y	Y	Y	N	N	Y	Y	Y	Y	Y	N	Y	Y	Y	+
16 *Regula*	Y	Y	Y	Y	Y	Y	N	Y	N	Y	Y	Y	Y	Y	Y	Y	Y	Y
17 Traficant	N	Y	Y	Y	Y	Y	N	N	Y	N	N	Y	Y	Y	Y	Y	Y	Y
18 *Ney*	Y	Y	Y	Y	Y	Y	N	N	Y	Y	Y	Y	Y	Y	Y	Y	Y	Y
19 *LaTourette*	Y	Y	Y	Y	Y	Y	N	Y	Y	Y	N	Y	Y	N	Y	Y	Y	Y
OKLAHOMA																		
1 *Largent*	Y	Y	Y	Y	Y	Y	N	X	Y	Y	Y	Y	N	N	?	Y	Y	Y
2 *Coburn*	Y	Y	Y	Y	Y	Y	N	N	Y	Y	Y	Y	Y	Y	Y	Y	Y	Y
3 Brewster	Y	Y	N	Y	Y	?	Y	N	Y	N	N	Y	Y	Y	?	Y	Y	Y
4 *Watts*	Y	Y	Y	Y	Y	Y	N	N	Y	Y	Y	Y	Y	Y	Y	Y	Y	+
5 *Istook*	Y	Y	Y	Y	Y	Y	N	X	Y	Y	Y	Y	Y	Y	Y	Y	Y	Y
6 *Lucas*	Y	Y	Y	Y	Y	Y	N	N	Y	Y	Y	Y	Y	Y	Y	Y	Y	Y
OREGON																		
1 Furse	N	N	N	Y	N	N	Y	Y	Y	N	N	N	N	N	N	Y	N	Y
2 *Cooley*	Y	Y	Y	Y	Y	Y	N	N	N	Y	Y	Y	N	Y	Y	N	Y	Y
3 Wyden	N	N	N	N	N	N	Y	Y	Y	N	N	N	N	N	Y	Y	N	Y
4 DeFazio	Y	N	N	N	N	N	Y	Y	N	N	N	N	N	N	Y	Y	N	N
5 *Bunn*	Y	Y	N	Y	Y	Y	N	N	N	Y	Y	Y	Y	Y	Y	Y	Y	Y
PENNSYLVANIA																		
1 Foglietta	N	N	N	N	N	N	Y	Y	N	N	N	Y	N	N	N	Y	N	N
2 Fattah	N	N	N	N	N	N	Y	Y	N	N	N	N	N	Y	?	Y	N	N
3 Borski	N	N	N	N	N	N	Y	Y	N	N	N	Y	N	N	N	Y	N	N
4 Klink	N	N	N	N	N	Y	Y	Y	N	N	N	Y	Y	Y	N	Y	N	N
5 *Clinger*	Y	Y	Y	Y	Y	Y	N	N	Y	Y	Y	Y	Y	Y	N	Y	Y	Y
6 Holden	N	Y	N	Y	N	Y	Y	Y	N	N	N	Y	Y	N	Y	Y	N	Y
7 *Weldon*	Y	Y	Y	Y	Y	N	N	Y	Y	Y	Y	?	Y	N	Y	Y	Y	Y
8 *Greenwood*	Y	N	Y	Y	Y	N	Y	Y	Y	Y	Y	N	Y	N	Y	Y	Y	Y
9 *Shuster*	Y	Y	Y	Y	Y	Y	N	N	Y	Y	Y	Y	Y	Y	Y	?	Y	Y
10 *McDade*	Y	Y	Y	N	Y	Y	N	N	Y	Y	Y	Y	Y	Y	Y	Y	Y	Y
11 Kanjorski	N	N	N	N	N	N	Y	Y	N	N	N	Y	N	N	N	Y	N	N

[c] Newt Gingrich, R-Ga., as Speaker of the House, voted at his discretion.

[d] Nathan Deal, Ga., switched to the Republican Party on April 10, 1995. He voted as a Democrat on key votes 1-5 and as a Republican on key votes 6-18.

[e] Mel Reynolds, D-Ill., resigned Oct. 1, 1995. He was eligible to vote on key votes 1-9. Jesse L. Jackson Jr., D-Ill., was sworn in Dec. 14, 1995, replacing Reynolds. Jackson was eligible to vote on key vote 18.

[f] W.J. "Billy" Tauzin, La., switched to the Republican Party on Aug. 6, 1995. He voted as a Democrat on key votes 1-9 and as a Republican on key votes 10-18.

[g] Jimmy Hayes, La., switched to the Republican Party on Dec. 1, 1995. He voted as a Democrat on key votes 1-17 and as a Republican on key vote 18.

[h] Mike Parker, Miss., switched to the Republican Party on Nov. 10, 1995. He voted as a Democrat on key votes 1-12 and as a Republican on key votes 13-18.

KEY

	Democrats	*Republicans*	Independent

Y	Voted for ("yea")	–	Announced against
N	Voted against ("nay")	P	Voted "present"
+	Announced for	C	Voted "present" to avoid possible conflict of interest
#	Paired for	?	Did not vote or otherwise make a position known
X	Paired against		

ND Northern Democrats
SD Southern Democrats
Southern states – Ala., Ark., Fla., Ga., Ky., La., Miss., N.C., Okla., S.C., Tenn., Texas, Va.

House Key Votes	1	2	3	4	5	6	7	8	9	10	11	12	13	14	15	16	17	18
12 Murtha	N	N	N	N	N	N	N	Y	N	N	N	Y	Y	Y	N	Y	N	Y
13 *Fox*	Y	Y	Y	Y	Y	N	N	Y	Y	Y	Y	Y	Y	N	Y	Y	Y	Y
14 Coyne	N	N	N	N	N	N	Y	Y	N	N	N	N	N	N	N	Y	N	N
15 McHale	Y	N	N	N	N	N	Y	N	Y	N	N	Y	N	N	Y	N	N	Y
16 *Walker*	Y	Y	Y	Y	Y	Y	N	N	Y	Y	Y	Y	Y	N	Y	Y	Y	Y
17 *Gekas*	Y	Y	Y	Y	Y	Y	N	Y	Y	Y	Y	Y	Y	N	Y	Y	Y	Y
18 Doyle	Y	Y	N	Y	N	Y	Y	Y	N	N	N	Y	N	N	N	N	N	Y
19 *Goodling*	Y	Y	Y	Y	Y	+	Y	N	Y	Y	Y	Y	Y	Y	Y	Y	Y	Y
20 Mascara	N	N	N	Y	N	Y	Y	Y	Y	N	N	N	Y	N	N	N	N	N
21 *English*	Y	Y	Y	Y	Y	N	Y	Y	Y	Y	Y	Y	Y	N	Y	Y	Y	Y
RHODE ISLAND																		
1 Kennedy	N	N	N	N	N	N	Y	Y	Y	N	N	Y	Y	N	N	Y	N	Y
2 Reed	N	N	N	N	N	N	Y	Y	Y	N	N	N	Y	N	N	Y	N	Y
S. CAROLINA																		
1 *Sanford*	Y	Y	Y	Y	Y	N	N	Y	Y	Y	Y	Y	Y	N	Y	Y	N	Y
2 *Spence*	Y	Y	Y	Y	Y	Y	N	N	Y	Y	Y	Y	Y	Y	Y	Y	Y	Y
3 *Graham*	Y	Y	Y	Y	Y	Y	N	N	Y	Y	Y	Y	Y	Y	Y	Y	N	Y
4 *Inglis*	Y	Y	Y	Y	Y	Y	N	N	Y	Y	Y	Y	Y	N	Y	Y	N	Y
5 Spratt	Y	Y	N	N	N	N	Y	Y	Y	Y	Y	N	Y	N	N	Y	N	Y
6 Clyburn	Y	N	N	N	N	N	Y	Y	Y	N	N	N	Y	N	Y	N	N	N
S. DAKOTA																		
AL Johnson	Y	Y	N	Y	N	Y	Y	Y	N	N	N	Y	N	N	Y	Y	N	N
TENNESSEE																		
1 *Quillen*	Y	Y	Y	N	Y	Y	N	N	?	Y	Y	Y	Y	Y	Y	Y	Y	Y
2 *Duncan*	Y	Y	Y	Y	Y	Y	N	N	N	Y	Y	Y	N	N	Y	Y	Y	Y
3 *Wamp*	Y	Y	Y	Y	Y	Y	N	N	Y	Y	Y	Y	Y	N	Y	Y	Y	Y
4 *Hilleary*	Y	Y	Y	Y	Y	Y	N	N	Y	Y	Y	Y	Y	N	Y	Y	Y	Y
5 Clement	Y	N	N	Y	Y	Y	Y	Y	Y	N	N	Y	N	Y	N	Y	N	Y
6 Gordon	Y	Y	N	Y	Y	Y	Y	Y	Y	N	N	Y	N	Y	N	N	N	Y
7 *Bryant*	Y	Y	Y	Y	Y	Y	N	N	Y	Y	Y	Y	Y	Y	Y	?	Y	Y
8 Tanner	Y	Y	N	Y	Y	Y	Y	?	Y	N	Y	Y	Y	Y	N	Y	Y	Y
9 Ford	Y	N	N	N	N	N	Y	N	Y	N	N	Y	N	N	N	N	N	N
TEXAS																		
1 Chapman	Y	Y	N	N	N	Y	N	N	Y	N	N	N	N	N	Y	Y	N	?
2 Wilson	Y	Y	N	Y	Y	Y	?	Y	Y	N	N	N	Y	N	Y	N	N	N
3 *Johnson, Sam*	Y	Y	Y	Y	Y	Y	N	N	Y	Y	Y	Y	Y	Y	Y	Y	Y	Y
4 Hall	Y	Y	Y	Y	Y	Y	N	N	Y	Y	Y	Y	Y	N	Y	Y	Y	Y
5 Bryant	Y	?	N	N	N	N	Y	N	Y	N	N	N	N	N	N	N	N	N
6 *Barton*	Y	Y	Y	N	Y	Y	N	N	Y	Y	Y	Y	Y	Y	Y	Y	Y	Y
7 *Archer*	Y	Y	Y	N	Y	Y	N	N	Y	Y	Y	Y	Y	N	Y	Y	Y	Y
8 *Fields*	Y	Y	Y	Y	Y	Y	?	N	Y	Y	Y	Y	Y	Y	Y	Y	Y	Y
9 *Stockman*	Y	Y	Y	P	Y	Y	?	N	Y	Y	Y	Y	Y	N	N	Y	N	Y
10 Doggett	N	N	N	N	N	N	Y	Y	Y	N	N	N	N	N	N	N	N	N
11 Edwards	Y	Y	N	N	N	Y	N	Y	Y	N	N	N	Y	N	N	Y	N	#
12 Geren	Y	Y	N	N	Y	Y	N	Y	Y	Y	Y	Y	Y	N	Y	N	N	Y
13 *Thornberry*	Y	Y	Y	Y	Y	Y	N	Y	Y	Y	Y	Y	Y	Y	Y	Y	Y	Y
14 *Laughlin* [i]	Y	?	N	N	Y	Y	Y	N	Y	Y	Y	Y	Y	Y	Y	Y	Y	Y
15 de la Garza	Y	Y	N	?	N	Y	Y	N	Y	N	N	Y	Y	N	Y	N	Y	?
16 Coleman	N	N	N	N	N	N	Y	Y	Y	N	N	N	Y	N	N	N	N	N
17 Stenholm	Y	Y	N	N	Y	Y	Y	N	Y	N	N	Y	Y	Y	N	Y	Y	Y

House Key Votes	1	2	3	4	5	6	7	8	9	10	11	12	13	14	15	16	17	18
18 Jackson-Lee	N	N	N	N	N	N	Y	Y	Y	N	N	N	N	N	N	Y	N	Y
19 *Combest*	Y	Y	Y	Y	Y	Y	N	N	Y	Y	Y	Y	Y	Y	Y	Y	Y	Y
20 Gonzalez	N	?	N	N	N	N	Y	N	Y	N	N	N	N	N	N	Y	N	N
21 *Smith*	Y	Y	Y	Y	Y	Y	N	N	Y	Y	Y	Y	Y	N	Y	Y	N	Y
22 *DeLay*	Y	Y	Y	N	Y	Y	N	N	Y	Y	Y	Y	Y	Y	Y	Y	Y	Y
23 *Bonilla*	Y	Y	Y	Y	Y	Y	N	N	Y	Y	Y	Y	Y	Y	Y	Y	Y	Y
24 Frost	Y	Y	N	?	N	N	Y	Y	Y	N	N	N	Y	N	N	Y	N	Y
25 Bentsen	N	Y	N	N	N	N	Y	Y	Y	N	N	N	N	N	N	Y	N	Y
26 *Armey*	Y	Y	Y	Y	Y	Y	N	N	Y	Y	Y	Y	Y	N	Y	Y	Y	Y
27 Ortiz	Y	Y	N	N	N	Y	Y	N	?	N	N	Y	Y	Y	N	N	N	Y
28 Tejeda	N	Y	N	N	N	Y	Y	N	Y	N	N	Y	Y	Y	N	Y	N	Y
29 Green	N	?	N	N	N	Y	Y	Y	Y	N	N	N	Y	N	N	Y	N	Y
30 Johnson, E.B.	N	N	N	N	N	N	Y	Y	Y	N	N	N	N	N	N	Y	N	N
UTAH																		
1 *Hansen*	Y	Y	Y	Y	Y	Y	N	N	Y	Y	Y	Y	Y	Y	Y	Y	Y	Y
2 *Waldholtz*	Y	Y	Y	Y	Y	Y	N	N	Y	Y	Y	Y	Y	N	Y	Y	Y	Y
3 Orton	Y	Y	N	Y	N	Y	Y	Y	Y	N	N	Y	N	N	N	N	N	Y
VERMONT																		
AL **Sanders**	N	N	N	N	N	N	Y	Y	N	N	N	N	N	N	N	Y	N	N
VIRGINIA																		
1 *Bateman*	Y	Y	Y	N	Y	Y	N	–	+	Y	Y	Y	Y	Y	Y	Y	N	Y
2 Pickett	N	Y	N	N	N	Y	Y	N	Y	N	N	N	Y	N	N	Y	N	Y
3 Scott	N	N	N	N	N	N	Y	Y	N	N	N	N	Y	N	N	N	N	N
4 Sisisky	Y	Y	N	N	N	N	Y	N	Y	N	?	Y	Y	Y	N	N	N	Y
5 Payne	Y	Y	N	N	N	Y	Y	N	Y	N	N	Y	N	N	N	Y	N	Y
6 *Goodlatte*	Y	Y	Y	Y	Y	Y	N	N	Y	Y	Y	Y	Y	N	Y	Y	N	Y
7 *Bliley*	Y	Y	Y	N	Y	Y	N	N	Y	Y	Y	Y	Y	Y	Y	Y	Y	Y
8 Moran	Y	Y	Y	N	Y	Y	N	N	Y	Y	N	N	Y	N	Y	N	N	Y
9 Boucher	N	N	N	N	N	N	Y	Y	Y	N	N	N	Y	N	N	N	N	Y
10 *Wolf*	Y	Y	Y	Y	Y	Y	N	N	Y	Y	Y	Y	Y	Y	Y	Y	N	Y
11 *Davis*	Y	Y	Y	N	N	N	Y	N	Y	Y	Y	Y	Y	N	N	Y	N	Y
WASHINGTON																		
1 *White*	Y	Y	Y	Y	Y	Y	N	N	Y	Y	Y	Y	Y	N	N	Y	Y	Y
2 *Metcalf*	Y	Y	Y	Y	Y	Y	N	N	Y	Y	Y	Y	Y	N	Y	Y	Y	Y
3 *Smith*	Y	Y	Y	Y	Y	Y	N	N	Y	Y	Y	Y	Y	N	Y	Y	Y	Y
4 *Hastings*	Y	Y	Y	Y	Y	Y	N	N	Y	Y	Y	Y	Y	Y	Y	Y	Y	Y
5 *Nethercutt*	Y	Y	Y	Y	Y	Y	N	N	Y	Y	Y	Y	Y	N	Y	Y	Y	Y
6 Dicks	N	N	N	N	N	N	Y	Y	Y	N	N	N	N	N	N	Y	N	N
7 McDermott	N	N	N	N	N	N	Y	Y	Y	N	N	N	N	N	–	Y	N	N
8 *Dunn*	Y	Y	Y	Y	Y	Y	N	N	Y	Y	Y	Y	Y	Y	Y	Y	Y	Y
9 *Tate*	Y	Y	Y	Y	Y	Y	N	N	Y	Y	Y	Y	Y	Y	Y	Y	Y	Y
WEST VIRGINIA																		
1 Mollohan	N	Y	N	N	N	N	Y	N	Y	N	N	N	Y	N	N	Y	N	N
2 Wise	N	N	N	N	N	N	Y	Y	Y	N	N	N	N	N	N	Y	N	N
3 Rahall	N	N	N	N	N	N	Y	N	Y	N	N	Y	N	N	N	Y	N	N
WISCONSIN																		
1 *Neumann*	Y	Y	Y	Y	Y	Y	N	N	Y	Y	Y	Y	Y	N	?	Y	Y	Y
2 *Klug*	Y	Y	Y	N	N	Y	Y	Y	Y	Y	Y	Y	Y	N	Y	Y	Y	Y
3 *Gunderson*	Y	Y	Y	Y	N	N	N	Y	Y	Y	Y	Y	Y	N	Y	Y	Y	Y
4 Kleczka	Y	N	N	N	–	+	Y	Y	Y	N	N	N	N	N	Y	N	N	Y
5 Barrett	N	N	N	N	N	N	Y	Y	Y	N	N	N	N	N	N	Y	N	Y
6 *Petri*	Y	Y	Y	N	Y	Y	N	N	Y	Y	Y	Y	Y	N	N	Y	N	Y
7 Obey	N	N	N	N	N	N	Y	Y	Y	N	N	N	N	N	N	Y	N	N
8 *Roth*	Y	Y	Y	N	Y	Y	N	N	Y	Y	Y	Y	Y	N	Y	Y	Y	Y
9 *Sensenbrenner*	Y	Y	Y	N	Y	Y	N	N	N	Y	Y	Y	Y	N	Y	Y	N	Y
WYOMING																		
AL *Cubin*	Y	Y	Y	Y	Y	Y	N	N	Y	Y	Y	Y	Y	Y	Y	Y	Y	Y

[i] Greg Laughlin, Texas, switched to the Republican Party on June 26, 1995. He voted as a Democrat on key votes 1-7 and as a Republican on key votes 8-18.

Senate

1. TELECOMMUNICATIONS

Like the House, the Senate adopted the conference report on a sweeping overhaul of the nation's telecommunications regulations (S 652) by an overwhelming margin. The Senate vote on Feb. 1 was 91–5; R 51–1; D 40–4 (ND 30–4, SD 10–0). *(House key vote 3)*

Yet the vote almost did not happen, as the Senate struggled to complete a years-long process of building the complicated legislation. The bill's purpose was to tear down regulatory barriers that separated global telecommunications into several discrete industries—long distance carriers, local telephone companies, cable and broadcast.

As 1996 began, the measure was stalled in conference, as it had been for five months, and its problems seemed to be growing, not shrinking.

A deal negotiated between the White House and key lawmakers in late December had been halted by restive House Republicans, who complained that GOP negotiators had given up too much on issues being pushed by Democrats, such as limits on foreign ownership of U.S. telecommunications companies and on the number of broadcast stations a single company could own.

Before those issues were resolved, Senate Majority Leader Bob Dole, R-Kan., clouded the picture further. Dole had long complained that television broadcasters were slated to receive free access to spectrum frequencies—allowing them to set up new channels worth billions of dollars. He noted that other telecommunication businesses, such as cellular phone and satellite television services, had to pay top dollar for their portions of the airwaves.

In January, Dole stepped up his opposition, insisting he would not allow a vote on the telecommunications conference report until the bill explicitly prohibited what he called a giveaway of electromagnetic spectrum to the television broadcasters. In doing so, however, Dole was going against clear majorities in both chambers that favored the free spectrum allocations.

It seemed briefly that the bill might face the same fate as a telecommunications overhaul bill that foundered at the end of the 103rd Congress. But that possibility acted as a wake-up call to the bickering parties, who decided they were too close to allow the bill to sink.

The House Republicans dropped their opposition to proceeding on the bill. Dole, whose focus had turned almost completely to his presidential campaign, said he would be happy to deal with the spectrum issue separately. (Hearings on the issue were held, but separate legislation never moved.)

Once it got the green light to come to the Senate floor, the telecommunications bill received almost universal praise. The opposition was limited to a few isolated pockets. John McCain, R-Ariz., for instance, argued that the bill did not go far enough in deregulating telecommunications. Paul Wellstone, D-Minn., believed it went too far. Democrats Patrick J. Leahy of Vermont, Paul Simon of Illinois and Russell D. Feingold of Wisconsin all expressed deep reservations about the constitutionality of the bill's provision restricting obscene material on computer on-line services, or "cyber-pornography."

President Clinton pulled out all the stops when he signed the bill into law (PL 104–104) on Feb. 8, holding a signing ceremony at the Library of Congress and using a high-tech pen to write his name.

2. FARM SUBSIDIES

The sweeping Republican proposal to overhaul federal farm subsidy programs received a major boost Feb. 7, when the Senate passed its version of the seven-year farm bill (S 1541) by a two-to-one ratio despite intense opposition from Midwestern Democrats.

The so-called Freedom to Farm bill was a top priority of many Republicans, who wanted to break the historic link between government subsidies and commodity prices. The measure aimed to move the nation's agricultural production toward the free market, giving farmers broad planting flexibility and setting up a system of fixed, declining subsidies that could be phased out after 2002.

The proposal was derided by many Democrats, including Minority Leader Tom Daschle of South Dakota. They said it would give farmers too much money in times of high market prices and too little when prices dropped, thereby unraveling the government's historic safety net for farmers.

In the days leading up to the Senate vote, Daschle appeared to have the edge. His Democratic allies successfully tied up the Senate with a filibuster. Frustrated Republicans tried to invoke cloture and cut off debate, but fell seven votes short Feb. 1.

Two key Republicans, Majority Leader Bob Dole of Kansas and Agriculture, Nutrition and Forestry Committee Chairman Richard G. Lugar of Indiana, appeared to concede defeat. Both men were seeking the GOP presidential nomination, and under pressure to hit the campaign trail, they quickly offered to let the Democrats dictate terms, as long as the resulting bill was passed by the evening of Feb. 1.

Eager Democrats began discussing a proposal to keep at least some of the traditional subsidies, while reauthorizing nutrition and conservation programs administered by the Agriculture Department. Yet, as the evening of Feb. 1 wore on, the Democrats fumbled away the initiative. Either because of unresolved technical issues, or because of a split in the caucus, they asked for a delay of several days.

Republicans accused Democrats of stalling. In the days that followed, GOP leaders withdrew their offer and focused instead on a divide-and-conquer strategy to lure Democrats from the Daschle camp.

They picked up several northeastern lawmakers by promising to back food stamps, conservation programs and dairy supports. They also enticed the two Louisiana Democrats, J. Bennett Johnston and John B. Breaux, with higher rice subsidies, and swayed Carol Moseley-Braun of Illinois with higher soybean loan rates.

Overwhelmed, Daschle dropped his filibuster and fell back instead on trying to amend the bill on the floor. In a last-ditch effort to blunt the GOP measure, Democratic leaders tried to rally their troops behind an amendment by Byron L. Dorgan, D-N.D., that would have required farmers to plant a government-subsidized crop in order to receive the fixed payments. But the amendment failed on a tie vote, 48–48.

With 20 Democrats abandoning Daschle to vote for the farm bill, the measure passed by a vote of 64–32: R 44–6; D 20–26 (ND 13–23, SD 7–3).

Although Daschle and other Midwestern Democrats continued to hammer away at the farm bill's provisions, they never again got a chance to make substantial changes in the legislation, which was signed into law April 4 (PL 104–127).

3. CUBA SANCTIONS

At the end of the first session, congressional opponents of the Cuban regime of Fidel Castro had grown bitter and frustrated. Facing a Senate filibuster, they had been forced to scale back a package of harsh economic sanctions (HR 927) aimed at punishing foreign companies that invested in Cuba. On Feb. 24, 1996, the bill received a tremendous boost from an unlikely source: That day, Cuban MiG fighters shot down a pair of U.S.-registered Cessna civilian aircraft, killing four Americans from an anti-Castro group.

After the incident, most opposition to the measure melted away. When House and Senate negotiators sat down to reconcile differing versions of the bill Feb. 28, they agreed to include a controversial section that had provoked the filibuster in 1995.

That provision permitted U.S. firms to file suit in U.S. District Court against foreign companies that acquired or otherwise "trafficked" in properties that had been confiscated by Castro's government and were claimed by a U.S. citizen.

On March 5, the Senate, which had blocked the sanctions bill just four months earlier, easily adopted the conference report. The vote was 74–22: R 47–4; D 27–18 (ND 19–17, SD 8–1). Token opposition came from a handful of moderates and liberals.

There was no real mystery behind the Senate's turnaround. Anger at Castro was running so high that President Clinton, who had opposed the bill in its earlier form, had little choice but to go along with the conference report. Although U.S. allies that traded with Cuba issued strong objections to the bill, there was a bipartisan desire to punish Castro.

"Farewell Fidel, that's the message of this bill," said Senate Foreign Relations Committee Chairman Jesse Helms, R-N.C., who sponsored the legislation along with Indiana Republican Rep. Dan Burton.

At the administration's behest, conferees on the bill agreed to allow the president to delay implementation of the "right of action" indefinitely. But otherwise, the final bill was stronger than either the House or the Senate versions. It barred executives from companies found to be trafficking in expropriated property claimed by U.S. citizens, along with their families, from entering the United States. The legislation also codified the 34-year-old U.S. trade embargo against Cuba, which meant that the president could not lift the trade ban without the approval of Congress.

Given the supercharged atmosphere for Cuban issues and Clinton's desire to court conservative Cuban-American voters in advance of November's election, a presidential veto was out of the question. The House adopted the conference report March 6. Clinton signed the measure into law (PL 104–114) on March 12.

4. PRODUCT LIABILITY

Senate adoption of the conference report on the product liability bill (HR 956) marked a striking, if short-lived, triumph for proponents of the sweeping legislation after years of failure.

For more than a decade, advocates of overhauling the nation's laws on faulty or dangerous products had pushed for new national limits on legal damages that could be awarded to consumers. Manufacturers said that costly litigation stifled innovation and prevented them from bringing to market safe products that would benefit consumers.

When Democrats controlled Congress, all such measures had been bottled up by Democratic House committee chairmen or had run into filibusters led by Ernest F. Hollings, D-S.C., and other opponents. In the 104th Congress, with the GOP in charge of both chambers and public awareness of the issue growing, proponents believed their time had come.

Their efforts were rewarded March 21, when the Senate adopted the conference report on the bill, which for the first time would have set a single national standard for faulty product lawsuits. The vote was 59–40: R 47–6; D 12–34 (ND 9–27, SD 3–7). The path had been cleared the day before, when the Senate voted, 60–40, to end a filibuster of the conference report.

On final passage, Republican Arlen Specter of Pennsylvania was the only senator who voted to end the filibuster but voted against adoption of the conference report. Democrat Bob Kerrey of Nebraska voted against ending the filibuster but did not vote on adoption.

The House easily cleared the bill March 29.

The proponents' victory was only temporary. President Clinton vetoed the bill May 2, saying it would go too far in restricting legal redress for damages caused by faulty products, and the House upheld the veto. *(House key vote 10)*

Trial lawyers and consumer groups said the bill would have barred the courthouse door to consumers with legitimate claims against manufacturers and would have taken away a deterrent to marketing faulty products.

5. LINE-ITEM VETO

A historic bill to give the president the equivalent of the line-item veto was among the most significant new laws produced by the 104th Congress—and among the few upon which hard-line deficit-cutting Republicans and President Clinton could wholeheartedly agree.

Yet when the Senate prepared to vote on the conference report on the line-item veto bill (S 4—PL 104–130) in March, senators were preoccupied by other, more immediate, concerns, chiefly a critical bill (HR 3136) to raise the federal government's borrowing authority.

As a result, the line-item veto measure became a pawn in a legislative chess match that seemed to drain the debate of much of its drama. That was extraordinary, considering that Congress was giving away a piece of its cherished power over the purse and handing Clinton enormous leverage in his dealings with Capitol Hill, should he choose to wield it.

Starting Jan. 1, 1997, the bill gave the president the power to automatically rescind individual items in spending bills, certain targeted tax breaks and new entitlement programs included in bills that he had signed into law. It would, in effect, take a two-thirds vote in both houses to reverse such a presidential "veto."

House leaders wanted to link the line-item measure to the essential but very unpopular bill to raise the debt ceiling as a way to build support for the latter measure among conservatives. But Senate leaders wanted to bring the conference report on the line-item veto to the floor on its own, both for procedural protection and because of the importance of the measure.

The solution was a complicated House rule that attached the line-item veto to the debt-limit bill until the Senate officially notified the House that it had adopted the line-item veto conference report. At that point, the line-item veto language was dropped from the debt-limit bill and automatically cleared for the president. *(House key vote 9)*

On March 27, the Senate adopted the line-item veto conference report on a vote of 69–31: R 50–3; D 19–28 (ND 16–21, SD 3–7). The debate was brief and devoid of suspense. The bill had considerable Democratic support and backing from Clinton, so it was clear that any potential filibuster by opponents such as Robert C. Byrd, D-W.Va., would have been easily quashed.

The maneuvering ended a difficult path into law for the bill, and the saga required some creative leadership from Majority Leader Bob Dole, R-Kan. The final version of the measure followed the "enhanced rescissions" framework favored by the House and by Senate supporters such as John McCain, R-Ariz.

When the Senate first acted on the measure in March 1995, that framework had been dropped because of opposition from key Republicans such as Pete V. Domenici of New Mexico and Ted Stevens of Alaska. Instead, the Senate originally passed a line-item veto bill that would have required each appropriations bill to be broken into hundreds or thousands of mini-bills that the president could veto—an unwieldy and probably unworkable procedure.

It took grudging acquiescence by Domenici and Stevens to adopt the House's approach, and that came only after it was beginning to prove embarrassing to Republicans in general—and presidential candidate Dole in particular—that GOP foot-dragging was holding up the bill, a key plank of the House Republicans' "Contract with America."

6. HEALTH INSURANCE

Congress cleared a health insurance bill (HR 3103—PL 104–191), after the Senate narrowly agreed to exclude controversial medical savings accounts from the legislation. Had the Senate vote gone the other way, the health bill likely would have died.

President Clinton had made the health insurance portability bill a high priority. By itself, the measure—which generally guaranteed that workers could maintain insurance coverage if they left or lost their jobs—had unanimous support. But Senate Majority Leader Bob Dole of Kansas and other Republicans wanted to add medical savings accounts, allowing individuals with high-deductible health plans to accrue tax-deductible savings to be used for medical expenses.

Dole introduced an amendment to add the accounts—as well as other provisions—to the underlying bill. With the tally expected to be close, Clinton dispatched Vice President Al Gore to the Senate to break a tie if necessary. Besides deciding the fate of the bill, the vote also tested the leadership skills of Dole, who by then was the presumed GOP presidential nominee.

The procedurally complicated vote came on the question of whether to strip the medical savings accounts from the Dole amendment to the underlying bill.

The bill's sponsors, Labor and Human Resources Committee Chairwoman Nancy Landon Kassebaum, R-Kan., and the panel's ranking Democrat, Edward M. Kennedy of Massachusetts, strongly opposed including the controversial accounts. Kassebaum feared they would kill the health bill, and Kennedy contended that such accounts would favor the healthy and wealthy at the expense of the poor and sick.

The Senate backed Clinton, Kassebaum and Kennedy, defying Dole. Senators voted April 18 to strip the medical savings accounts 52–46: R 5–46; D 47–0 (ND 37–0, SD 10–0).

Gore, sitting in the president's chair, allowed Dole to hold the vote open well past the standard 15 minutes while the majority leader worked to bring straying Republicans over to his side. Dole swayed William S. Cohen of Maine, who switched his vote, as well as Bill Frist of Tennessee, who withheld his vote until the end.

But Dole finally gave up, realizing that none of the five remaining Republicans who had voted to strip the savings accounts would switch to support him. The Dole amendment—which included an increase in the deductibility of health insurance for the self-employed and provisions to make long-term care insurance and expenses tax deductible—was then adopted by a vote of 98–0.

The vote was a clear defeat for Dole and a victory for Clinton. If the Senate had not voted to strip the special accounts from the Dole amendment, opponents appeared ready to mount a filibuster, possibly dooming the overall bill.

The final version of the legislation did include medical savings accounts, but only a small demonstration project. Dole, who resigned from the Senate to run for president full time before Congress cleared the bill, received little credit for the popular health insurance legislation.

7. BUDGET RESOLUTION

Although the Senate rejected a bipartisan budget plan proposed by a centrist coalition, the vote marked the coalition's strongest showing yet. The group fell four votes short of winning a majority for its budget proposal—which sought to eliminate the deficit in seven years without deep cuts in social programs. That was closer than even the coalition's leaders expected and amounted to more support than the group had ever received for its legislation.

The budget plan was offered May 23 as an alternative to the Republican budget resolution (S Con Res 57). The GOP plan aimed to produce a balanced budget in a shorter period—six years—but it relied on deeper cuts in social programs such as Medicare, the government's health insurance for the elderly, and Medicaid, the government's health plan for the poor and disabled.

The final vote on the coalition's plan was 46–53: R 22–30; D 24–23 (ND 18–19, SD 6–4). While the core of the centrist support came from liberal Republicans and conservative Democrats, the plan drew a surprising amount of support from GOP conservatives and backing from several Democrats generally considered liberals.

Among the more conservative Republicans who voted for the plan were Daniel R. Coats and Richard G. Lugar of Indiana, Lauch Faircloth of North Carolina, Thad Cochran of Mississippi, Mike DeWine of Ohio, Rick Santorum of Pennsylvania and Orrin G. Hatch of Utah. Among the more liberal Democrats who voted for it were Daniel K. Akaka and Daniel K. Inouye of Hawaii, Barbara Boxer of California, Patrick J. Leahy of Vermont, Patty Murray of Washington and Claiborne Pell of Rhode Island.

The bipartisan coalition decided that the key to getting support from both parties was to target at least some of the proposed spending cuts toward programs that benefited the wealthy and to provide the bulk of the tax cuts to middle-income taxpayers. To do that, they proposed to increase the amount the wealthy paid for Medicare and reduce the income-eligibility threshold for a $500-per-child tax credit that both parties were proposing.

The centrist plan would have reduced projected spending on Medicare by $154 billion, on Medicaid by $62 billion and on discretionary spending by $268 billion. It would have given a net tax cut of $105 billion.

Another essential element of the bipartisan budget was a controversial proposal to change the way the government used the Consumer Price Index to calculate annual cost of living adjustments in Social Security payments. The centrist budget would have saved $126 billion primarily by reducing the annual Social Security benefit increases and allowing tax brackets, indexed for inflation, to rise more slowly. The tax bracket change would have had the effect of pushing more taxpayers into higher brackets.

The centrists' budget resolution was the result of months of discussions by a core group of fewer than a dozen members led by John H. Chafee, R-R.I., and John B. Breaux, D-La. Once the proposal was complete, both recruited other senators to join the group but neither anticipated that they would get support from nearly half the Senate.

The strong showing for their budget resolution presaged the success the group would have later in 1996 in getting portions of its welfare overhaul proposal accepted as compromise language in place of GOP provisions.

8. BALANCED-BUDGET AMENDMENT

As one of his last acts before leaving the Senate to run full time for president, Majority Leader Bob Dole , R-Kan., held a revote on a constitutional amendment to require a balanced federal budget.

In sharp contrast to the initial debate—the outcome of which gave the Kansas Republican perhaps his greatest disappointment in the 104th Congress—the second time around had a perfunctory, going-through-the-motions feel.

In March 1995, with the amendment (H J Res 1) falling one vote short, Dole had switched his "aye" to "nay," so he could call for another vote. At the time, supporters had real hopes of finding the 67th vote they needed to win adoption of the amendment and send it to the states for ratification.

When Dole called the revote June 6, he lost ground. The Senate killed the amendment, 64–35: R 52–1; D 12–34 (ND 7–29, SD 5–5).

In 1995 Dole had assembled 66 votes. Since then, however, Rep. Ron Wyden, D-Ore., an opponent of the amendment, had succeeded GOP supporter Bob Packwood in the Senate. And supporter Jim Exon, D-Neb., had angrily announced he was switching his vote in response to Republican efforts to repeal the 4.3-cents-per-gallon gasoline tax increase enacted by Democrats in 1993.

In the weeks before the 1996 vote proponents such as Larry E. Craig, R-Idaho, reached out to Democrats, such as Wyden and Ernest F. Hollings of South Carolina, who said they could support the amendment if it were modified to exempt Social Security taxes and payments from deficit calculations. (The Democrats wanted a "firewall" blocking Social Security surpluses from being used, in effect, to finance general government operations.)

Republican negotiators offered to meet Democrats halfway and segregate Social Security from the rest of the budget beginning in 2006, instead of 2002, as Democrats sought. But that was not enough to bring Wyden and Hollings on board.

Republicans had hoped to get a political boost from the second defeat, but the issue came and went with little fanfare, in part because the Senate was tied up in knots over politically resonant issues such as whether to increase the minimum wage. During the presidential campaign, Dole tried to blame President Clinton for killing the amendment, but the issue had little impact.

9. CAMPAIGN FINANCE

Failure to cut off a Senate filibuster finished off a bill to overhaul campaign finance, reflecting the shared ambivalence of Congress and President Clinton toward rewriting Watergate-era laws in an election year.

Despite the nearly universal view that the existing system was out of control, the bipartisan campaign finance bill (S 1219), sponsored by John McCain, R-Ariz., and Russell D. Feingold, D-Wis., was doomed from the start. It languished for months in the Senate despite the sponsors' threats to attach it to other legislation. Finally in June, the new Senate majority leader, Republican Trent Lott of Mississippi, mollified the sponsors by allotting time for the Senate to consider the issue. Election-year pressures and a crowded legislative schedule made it obvious to senators before the vote that campaign finance reform would not happen in 1996. Clinton's eleventh-hour endorsement failed to sway a single senator.

Prospects for the bill grew worse as the National Right to Life Committee and the Christian Coalition lobbied for its defeat, contending that the bill's definition of advocacy and its proposed limits on the practice would threaten their voting guides and education activities. The final blow was administered by Lott, who opposed the bill and pressured GOP senators to do the same in a test of their loyalty.

On June 25, after three days of debate, the Senate rejected a motion to invoke cloture and thus limit debate on the bill, by a vote of 54–46: R 8–45; D 46–1 (ND 37–0, SD 9–1). Three-fifths of the total Senate (60) was required to invoke cloture.

After the vote, Lott immediately withdrew the bill from the Senate floor.

The new GOP majority in Congress had hoped to succeed where Democrats had failed, but the increased spoils for the victors had quickly dampened any enthusiasm for change.

The bill would have banned political action committees and provided incentives, such as free broadcast time and reduced postage rates, to candidates who complied with spending limits. It also would have banned "soft money," the unlimited funds that national political parties raise from corporations, unions and other sources to spend on party-building activities.

Leading the opposition to the bill was Sen. Mitch McConnell, R-Ky., who cast the legislation as an infringement on the constitutional right of free speech. He dismissed the notion that the bill would put challengers on a par with incumbents in the money chase created by political campaigns. "You cannot create a level playing field; it is impossible," McConnell said.

10. MINIMUM WAGE

By the time legislation (HR 3448) to raise the minimum wage reached the floor of the Senate, its passage should have been a cinch.

GOP leaders were eager to end four months of Democratic attacks and legislative guerrilla warfare that had tied the Senate in knots. The battle over the minimum wage had slowed work on fiscal 1997 spending bills to a crawl. The wage raise—bitter to conservative Republicans, who said it would reduce employment—had been sweetened considerably by a package of business tax cuts likely to be the only significant tax legislation to pass the 104th Congress.

Senate Democrats said that an increase in the wage, which had not been changed since 1991, was overdue; enough moderate Republicans, primarily from the Northeast, sided with the Democrats to ensure passage.

With all that going for it, the minimum wage increase—which the House had approved as part of HR 1227 on May 23—still faced a major hurdle when it reached the Senate floor July 9. Republicans planned to attach a conservative amendment that had been denounced by Democrats as a poison pill. *(House key vote 11)*

The amendment, by Christopher S. Bond, R-Mo., would have exempted businesses with less than $500,000 in annual sales from the wage increase. It also would have delayed the bill's effective date until Jan. 1, 1997, and allowed employers to pay all new employees a sub-minimum training wage of $4.25 an hour for the first six months, twice as long as the 90 days stipulated in the House version of the bill.

Edward M. Kennedy, D-Mass., made it clear that liberal Democrats would vote against any wage increase that included the Bond provisions. Their defections, coupled with "no" votes from conservative Republicans adamantly opposed to raising the minimum wage, would have ensured its defeat—and a resumption of Democratic warfare. President Clinton had also issued a veto threat.

Bond's amendment ultimately failed, 46–52: R 46–5; D 0–47 (ND 0–37, SD 0–10). The five Republicans who crossed the aisle to vote with a united Democratic front against the amendment were Ben Nighthorse Campbell of Colorado, Alfonse M. D'Amato of New York, Mark O. Hatfield of Oregon, Arlen Specter of Pennsylvania and James M. Jeffords of Vermont.

When a subsequent amendment by Kennedy failed by the same margin, the bill's passage was assured. Kennedy's amendment would have shortened by half the time that teenage workers could be paid a subminimum training wage and extended wage increases to waiters and other tip-earners. Had the amendment been adopted, it could have discouraged moderate Republicans from supporting final passage. The vote on final passage was 74–24.

The final version of the minimum wage legislation (PL 104–188) raised the hourly minimum wage to $4.75 on Oct. 1, 1996, and to $5.15 on Sept. 1, 1997.

11. NUCLEAR WASTE STORAGE

A Senate vote on July 31 to establish a temporary nuclear waste dump in the Nevada desert appeared to be a blow to the bill's most fervent opponents: the state's Democratic senators, Richard H. Bryan and Harry Reid. The passage of S 1936 came after a dogged three-month filibuster mounted by the Silver State's senators.

Bryan and Reid were able to claim victory in defeat. President Clinton was on their side, and the Senate vote to pass S 1936 was short of the two-thirds that supporters would need to override a threatened veto. That fact alone was enough to dissuade House Republican leaders from even taking up the bill for consideration during the session.

The Senate vote breakdown was 63–37: R 50–3; D 13–34 (ND 7–30, SD 6–4).

The bill was the latest chapter in Congress' effort to find a repository for the highly hazardous waste products that had been piling up in temporary holding areas at the nation's nuclear facilities. The measure would have instructed the Department of Energy to begin taking possession of some of the nation's spent nuclear reactor fuel within six months of enactment. Electric utilities would have begun shipping up to 60,000 metric tons of waste to a temporary dump at Nevada's Yucca Mountain site, 100 miles outside Las Vegas, before the end of the century.

Supporters—including utilities, other elements of the nuclear power industry and most congressional Republicans—said the legislation was vital if the federal government was to live up to a 1982 law requiring it to take responsibility for civilian nuclear waste by 1998.

But the nuclear waste threat was not enough. Along with 34 Democratic senators, three Republicans—John H. Chafee of Rhode Island, Ben Nighthorse Campbell of Colorado and Daniel R. Coats of Indiana—provided crucial votes to keep the waste out of Nevada.

Chafee's vote swung on the environmental issue. Environmental groups said the bill would set too low a safety standard for the Nevada waste site and expose the nation to potential disasters during transportation of nuclear waste. Coats' vote was more personal. He was trying to win passage of legislation to permit state and local governments to bar the dumping of garbage from other states. Under the circumstances, he could hardly vote to foist nuclear waste on Nevada.

Democratic unity was maintained in part because of presidential politics. Clinton—who was influenced on the issue by Nevada's Democratic governor, Bob Miller—said he opposed the bill because Yucca Mountain was the only location under consideration for a permanent nuclear-waste repository; the siting of a temporary storage facility there, he said, would compromise ongoing scientific studies of the site's long term suitability.

Clinton also wanted to win Nevada's four electoral college votes. A threatened veto of a bill considered public enemy No. 1 by Nevada residents could only help. Clinton went on to carry the state by a narrow margin.

Generally, Democrats who voted for the temporary dump—such as Carol Moseley-Braun and Paul Simon of Illinois, Carl Levin of Michigan, Patty Murray of Washington and Patrick J. Leahy of Vermont—had serious nuclear waste problems in their states. Many faced strong pressure from their home-state utilities. But the nuclear power industry failed to make the waste disposal issue resonate beyond those states in which it was most pressing.

12. WELFARE OVERHAUL

The Senate on Aug. 1 cleared a bill that replaced six decades of federal welfare policy with a new reliance on the states, ending the government's guarantee of providing welfare checks to all eligible low-income mothers and children. The lopsided vote came only after previous attempts to enact similar measures went down amid partisan disagreements.

President Clinton had announced the day before that he would sign the bill (HR 3734) despite his reservations, and the House easily adopted the conference report shortly thereafter. *(House key vote 14)*

The Senate, which had lurched to and from bipartisanship on the issue in the 104th Congress, concluded its action with Republicans unanimously favoring the legislation and Democrats split. The vote to adopt the conference report was 78–21: R 53–0; D 25–21 (ND 17–20, SD 8–1).

The Senate's bipartisan interest in enacting welfare legislation had been thwarted earlier in the session. After House Republicans passed a bitterly contested welfare bill (HR 4) in March 1995, a Senate coalition of moderate Republicans and Democrats trimmed some of the more radical elements from it, picking up significant Democratic support. But that support largely vanished when GOP conferees ignored Democrats while working out differences between the House and Senate versions.

As a result, Clinton twice vetoed GOP welfare plans—on Dec. 6, 1995, as part of the deficit-reducing budget reconciliation bill (HR 2491), then on Jan. 9, as a free-standing welfare bill (HR 4). He complained that the measures were too harsh, more likely to hurt children than to help welfare recipients get jobs.

Efforts to revive the legislation gained some support in February, when the National Governors' Association endorsed recommendations to overhaul both welfare and Medicaid, the federal-state health insurance program for the poor.

But Clinton was unwilling to end the entitlement for Medicaid, and Senate Majority Leader Bob Dole, R-Kan., insisted on keeping the Medicaid provisions in the bill.

When Dole left the Senate in June to campaign for the presidency full time, however, GOP leaders succumbed to pressure from their own ranks and dropped the Medicaid portion of the bill. Once again, a coalition of moderate Republicans and Democrats massaged the welfare bill a bit in the Senate. Their biggest victories were making sure that welfare recipients would remain eligible for Medicaid and ensuring that states could not gain control over their food stamp programs by choosing to receive their federal money in a block grant.

Even so, some Democratic opponents spoke in almost apocalyptic terms when describing the measure's potential impact on poor children. As the Senate vote began, about 10 protesters shouted, "Shame!

Shame!" and blew whistles from the visitors' gallery until they were removed by police.

Republicans placed less emphasis on the bill's savings—$54.6 billion through fiscal 2002, mainly from cutting food stamps and aid to legal immigrants—than on their revolutionary attempt to end welfare as an entitlement and push welfare recipients into the workforce.

13. GAY RIGHTS

The socially conservative 104th Congress cast a surprisingly close vote on a civil rights bill for homosexuals. On Sept. 10, the Senate narrowly defeated a bill (S 2056) that would have outlawed workplace discrimination based on sexual orientation. The vote likely would have gone the other way if David Pryor, D-Ark., had been in town. Pryor's vote for the bill would have allowed Vice President Al Gore to cast the tie-breaking vote in favor of it.

However, House leaders had shown no interest in the bill, and House rules did not give members of the minority party the leverage they had in the Senate to bring things to the floor.

Also, the vote was taken at the end of the Congress when it was clear the bill would go no further than the Senate. The chance for a vote had been offered as a quid pro quo for bringing another bill (HR 3396—PL 104-199), to the Senate floor. That bill, which restricted same-sex marriages, had overwhelming support and passed easily. Its opponents, led by Sen. Edward M. Kennedy, D-Mass., could not block the measure, but did get a chance for a separate vote on the workplace bill.

Nevertheless, the near-win in one chamber, particularly in a conservative Congress, was hailed by gay rights organizations as a significant victory. The vote was 49-50: R 8-45; D 41-5 (ND 35-2, SD 6-3).

The workplace vote, in conjunction with HR 3396, served several functions. It suggested that while lawmakers opposed sanctioning marriage—and all the rights and privileges that came with it—for gay couples, they were more divided on how civil rights issues should apply to gay individuals.

The vote gave gay rights groups something to cheer about in what for them was a clearly unfriendly Congress. It saved President Clinton from some of the heat he would have taken from gay Democrats for his support of the same-sex marriage bill. The workplace bill gave Clinton a gay rights bill to champion and provided an escape valve for gay rights groups that did not want to start a fight with Clinton.

14. ABORTION

By sustaining President Clinton's veto of legislation to ban so-called partial-birth abortions, the Senate blocked what would have been the first law barring a specific abortion procedure.

The Senate was the last barrier to enactment of the controversial legislation. Both chambers had passed the bill, and the House on Sept. 19 had overridden the president's April 10 veto. The Senate on Sept. 26 rejected the override attempt 57-41: R 45-6; D 12-35 (ND 7-30, SD 5-5) (House key vote 8)

Antiabortion lobbyists mounted an extensive nationwide campaign—using graphic descriptions—to pressure lawmakers to support the ban. They contended that the procedure was abhorrent, with some saying it amounted to killing babies. They used direct mail, advertising and church leaflets, and enlisted religious leaders, including key Roman Catholic clerics and other high-profile public figures.

Opponents of the ban called upon women who had had the procedure to explain why it was necessary, as Clinton had done when he vetoed the bill. They said it was relatively rare, and was used to pro- tect the life or health of the woman—sometimes to protect her ability to have a child later.

However, the vote lacked suspense because the initial Senate vote to pass the bill had not drawn enough support to override a threatened presidential veto. On Dec. 7, 1995, the Senate passed the legislation 54-44, many votes short of the two-thirds majority needed for an override.

The measure would have made it a federal crime for a doctor to perform a type of late-term abortion known in the legislation as a partial-birth abortion, except to save the woman's life. In vetoing the bill, Clinton said the exemption should have been broadened to allow the procedure to protect the woman's health, as well as her life. The bill defined the partial-birth procedure as taking place when a doctor partially "vaginally delivers a living fetus before killing the fetus and completing delivery."

Under the bill, doctors who performed these late-term abortions would have faced fines and up to two years in prison. Other provisions would have exempted the woman from criminal penalties and allowed the woman's parents and the prospective father to sue the doctor for damages if the woman was a minor.

Though the bill was not enacted, abortion opponents declared victory in the debate, satisfied that they had trained public attention on the discomfiting specifics of abortion and away from the more philosophical question of the right to have one.

In the past, congressional votes on abortion-related issues typically had involved a variation on the broader question of a woman's right to have one, as guaranteed by the Supreme Court in the landmark 1973 case, *Roe v. Wade*.

House

1. DEFENSE AUTHORIZATION

The Republicans' central challenge to President Clinton's defense program stalled on the first day of the 1996 session when the House sustained Clinton's veto of a bill that would have accelerated the deployment of a nationwide defense against ballistic missiles.

The $265 billion authorization bill (HR 1530) covered all defense-related programs for fiscal 1996, including $7 billion more for defense programs than Clinton requested. But in his veto message, Clinton singled out as particularly objectionable a provision that, he said, would put the country on a collision course with the 1972 treaty limiting the use of antiballistic missile (ABM) weapons.

The key provision would have required the deployment by 2003 of an ABM system that could protect all 50 states against attack by a small number of missiles.

The administration said that, to cover the western-most parts of Alaska and Hawaii, missile defenses likely would have to be deployed at several locations, thus violating the 1972 ABM Treaty, which permitted their deployment at only a single site. For that reason, administration officials warned, enactment of the disputed provisions might induce Russia to stop decommissioning thousands of nuclear warheads as required by the START I arms reduction treaty. Moreover, they said, the bill might induce Russia not to ratify the pending START II treaty, which required even deeper cuts in U.S. and Russian nuclear arsenals.

Republicans called the Clinton team's argument a red herring intended to cover up the administration's lack of enthusiasm for deploying antimissile defenses in any case. GOP missile-defense advocates pointed out that Army and Air Force agencies each had drawn up proposals intended to protect all 50 states with a treaty-compliant, single-site defense. As for the two START treaties, they pointed out that those pacts faced strong political opposition in Moscow for a variety of reasons that had nothing to do with the ABM Treaty.

Besides using the omnibus bill to boost defense funding above the amount Clinton requested, Senate and House Republicans had loaded it up with various other policy initiatives that were anathema to the president. But in the prolonged Senate-House conference on the bill, most of the contentious provisions other than the antimissile deployment requirement had dropped off.

Some Republican strategists contended that it would be hard for Democrats to vote against defending the country against rogue states, such as North Korea, which might acquire long-range missiles. But 139 House Democrats did join virtually all the Republicans in voting Jan. 3 to override the president's decision. However, the motion still fell short of the required two-thirds majority. The motion failed on a vote of 240–156: R 206–16; D 34–139 (ND 12–109; SD 22–30); I 0–1. With that number of members voting, 264 "ayes" would have been needed to override the veto.

2. GOVERNMENT SHUTDOWN

When lawmakers returned to Washington to begin the second session, nine Cabinet departments and dozens of agencies were shut down—their fiscal 1996 appropriations bills either vetoed by the president or unfinished by Congress. Republicans had vowed to continue the closure, which began Dec. 16, 1995, until President Clinton accepted their plans for balancing the budget in seven years. Until then, they said, there would be no temporary appropriations bill to put federal workers back on the job.

The tactic backfired. Clinton refused to back down, instead vetoing the budget reconciliation bill that contained much of the Republicans' agenda, along with several appropriations bills that he felt provided too little money or imposed unacceptable policy changes. While the public seemed disgusted with both sides, the GOP was getting the brunt of the blame for the mess in Washington.

Republicans were frustrated and angry. House GOP leaders insisted they would continue to play hardball. "If the president wants to end this shutdown," said House Majority Leader Dick Armey, R-Texas, "then he can get serious and come to agreement on a balanced budget."

But the House firebrands were quickly losing support. On Jan. 2 Senate Majority Leader Bob Dole, R-Kan., declared, "Enough is enough." Dole, at the time the leading contender for the Republican presidential nomination, pushed a government-reopening stopgap spending bill (HR 1643) through the Senate. On Jan. 3 more than 50 House Republicans voted in a closed-door meeting of the entire House GOP to consider a compromise.

On Jan. 5 Republican leaders threw in the towel. Facing down those who still wanted to hang tough, Gingrich told members to vote to put federal employees back to work and fund high-profile programs such as Meals on Wheels, child welfare and national parks. "If you don't like the way we're doing it, run for the leadership yourself," Gingrich said.

In the end, only 15 Republicans defied the Speaker as the motion to accept a modified version of the Senate bill passed overwhelmingly, 401–17: R 214–15; D 186–2 (ND 133–0, SD 53–2); I 1–0, Jan. 5, 1996.

Though the budget battle was not over, the bill was the first of a series of measures that kept the government open while the two sides slowly reached agreement on the rest of the fiscal 1996 appropriations bills. The broader GOP plan to balance the budget in seven years was ultimately abandoned.

3. TELECOMMUNICATIONS

The overwhelming margin by which the House adopted the conference report on the sweeping telecommunications bill (S 652—PL 104–104) belied how hard it had been to balance the high-stakes political and industry interests involved.

Proponents had contended for years that an overhaul was needed to bring U.S. law in line with technological advances, but efforts to make far-reaching changes had collapsed in previous Congresses.

The House and Senate had passed separate versions of an overhaul in 1995, and after months of negotiations, conferees had seemingly settled all of their differences. Vice President Al Gore and the chairmen and ranking members of the two Commerce committees announced Dec. 20 that they had a deal.

But the conference report did not go as far in deregulating telecommunications as many House Republicans wanted. They complained bitterly that Senate Commerce Committee Chairman Larry Pressler, R-S.D., had given away too much to the White House and his committee's ranking Democrat, Ernest F. Hollings of South Carolina.

At the end of 1995, House Republicans—led by Jack Fields of Texas, chairman of the Commerce Telecommunications Subcommittee—blocked the conference agreement. One of the group's members, Michael G. Oxley, R-Ohio, called the bill as "dead as Elvis."

Rumors of the telecommunications bill's demise turned out to be exaggerated. Gore and Hollings simply bided their time, as they pushed for greater consumer protections and a generally less deregulatory bill. As the issue persisted into the election year, the Republican group realized that further delay could threaten passage of the entire bill.

Once agreement was reached, final passage was assured. The House adopted the conference report on the bill Feb. 1 by a 414–16 vote: R 236–0; D 178–15 (ND 123–14, SD 55–1); I 0–1. The Senate cleared the bill the same day. (Senate key vote 1)

Fields roundly praised the measure, which was virtually identical to the one he and other Republicans had derided just a few weeks earlier. "I believe this means American companies will dominate the field of global telecommunications," he said of the bill.

The new law was designed to break down barriers between different types of telecommunications services. It aimed to create one giant telecommunications marketplace, for everything from phone services to movies-on-demand, from what had been segmented industries.

The bill mainly avoided the partisan gridlock that affected most important measures in the 104th Congress. It provided an early lesson to some House Republicans that they could get much of what they wanted if they let President Clinton share the credit. With telecommunications, both the GOP and Clinton got ample bragging rights to the first major bill enacted in the 104th Congress.

4. FARM SUBSIDIES

By passing the seven-year farm bill (HR 2854) on Feb. 29 by a wide margin, the House swept away the last remaining resistance to the Republican-led drive to move heavily subsidized U.S. agricultural production toward greater reliance on the free market. The Senate had easily passed a similar version of the bill (S 1541) early in the month. (Senate key vote 2)

The historic legislation was guided through the House by its author, Agriculture Committee Chairman Pat Roberts, R-Kan. Often called "Freedom to Farm," the measure aimed to do away with traditional federal farm subsidies, replacing them with a system of fixed, declining payments that could be phased out altogether after 2002. Instead of planting specified crops and idling land, farmers would have broad flexibility to plant for growing domestic and foreign markets.

Before the bill could pass, GOP leaders had to overcome powerful efforts to end sugar and peanut price-support programs, staged by a bipartisan coalition of Democrats from nonfarm districts and Republican fiscal hawks. Without the price supports, the broad coalition backing the farm bill might have unraveled, exposing the measure to possible defeat on the floor.

As a result, rural lawmakers focused their attention on blocking amendments to do away with the price supports, rather than the vote on the overall bill.

Leading the charge against the price supports were suburban lawmakers, who contended the programs inflated consumer prices and interfered with the free market. Backing their efforts was a broad coalition of user groups, such as candy and soft drink manufacturers, who wanted to lower the costs of the commodities.

Rural lawmakers fought back, contending that the underlying farm bill already scaled back the price-support programs. Further changes could devastate peanut and sugar growers, they warned. Roberts privately exhorted his colleagues to preserve the programs, lest some rural districts face economic devastation.

The showdown took place Feb. 28, as the House took up an amendment by Christopher Shays, R-Conn., and others to phase out the peanut program by 2002. In a dramatic vote that split along regional rather than party lines, the House defeated the amendment, 209–212.

The close vote appeared to portend trouble for the sugar program, which faced more organized opposition. But the well-heeled sugar lobby scored a big victory that day, as an amendment to phase out sugar price supports, sponsored by Dan Miller, R-Fla., and Charles E. Schumer, D-N.Y., was rejected, 208–217.

By more decisive margins, lawmakers rejected amendments that would have phased out all subsidy programs and eliminated a key cotton loan program. With such divisive issues out of the way, the House easily passed the overall measure the next day, 270–155: R 216–19; D 54–135 (ND 21–112, SD 33–23); I 0–1.

As farm organizations generally rallied behind the bill, lawmakers quickly wrapped up the conference and cleared the measure. President Clinton signed the farm bill into law (PL 104–127) on April 4, despite his concerns that the fixed payments would be insufficient to help farmers if market prices fell.

The sugar and peanut programs came under assault again during consideration of the fiscal 1997 agriculture appropriations bill (HR 3603—PL 104–180). But again they survived, as rural lawmakers reminded their colleagues that many of the arguments had already been aired during the farm bill debate.

5. ANTITERRORISM BILL

The House passed a long-stalled antiterrorism bill (HR 2703) on March 14, but only after stripping the measure of what its supporters saw as its most potent law enforcement tools—including provisions that would have expanded federal surveillance capabilities and eased restrictions on deporting noncitizens suspected of terrorism.

President Clinton had requested the bill in the wake of the April 19, 1995, bombing of the federal building in Oklahoma City, which killed 168 people. GOP leaders, eager to show their toughness against terrorism, used his proposal as a platform for their own measure, which included get-tough provisions such as limiting appeals by death-row prisoners. (House key vote 6)

When freshman Republican Bob Barr of Georgia garnered enough votes to prevail on an amendment that removed the committee-approved provisions to fight terrorism, it smacked of an insurgency against his party. The vote stood out because Barr formed an unusual alliance between a conservative group of Republicans and a predominantly liberal group of Democrats. The Republicans contended that federal agents had overstepped their bounds in a bloody battle with the Branch Davidian cult in Waco, Texas, and a standoff with an antigovernment group in Ruby Ridge, Idaho.

While some conservative Democrats agreed, most of the 67 Democrats who supported Barr were concerned about infringing upon civil liberties in other ways, including giving law enforcement officials enhanced wiretapping authority in terrorism cases.

The House approved the amendment on March 13 by a vote of 246–171: R 178–54; D 67–117 (ND 39–91, SD 28–26); I 1–0.

The next day the House passed the bill 229–191, sending it to a difficult conference with a broader Senate measure. Some of the provisions that Barr stripped from the bill were put back in at conference, but most of Barr's targets remained dead.

The vote on the Barr amendment showed how the freshman Republicans, when they decided to exercise their power, could throw a monkey wrench into the plans of even the most senior GOP leaders. Overall, the freshman class voted 72 to 14 in favor of the amendment, with Republicans making up the bulk of the majority, with 68 votes.

The amendment was an affront to Judiciary Committee Chairman Henry J. Hyde, R-Ill., and other Republicans who had spent months hammering out the bill's provisions with Barr and other conservative freshmen. When Barr introduced his amendment, Hyde said it would "eviscerate the bill." During the floor debate, Hyde dueled with Barr, saying the amendment was a "frail representation of what started out as a robust answer to the terrorist menace."

Barr won, however, by appealing to a majority of Republicans and Democrats who were worried about entrusting the government with more power. Among the provisions removed by Barr's amendment were proposals to allow the administration to designate certain foreign groups as terrorist and then deny their members entry visas and bar them from fund raising in the United States, allow authorities to use illegally obtained wiretap evidence in terrorism cases, expedite the deportation of aliens linked to terrorism and lower the standard of proof to prosecute those who provided the guns used in violent crimes.

Behind the scenes, the amendment had backing from the National Rifle Association and other gun-rights groups upset about making it easier to prosecute people linked to gun crimes. Barr's amendment also appealed to them by exempting black and smokeless powder from a proposed government study of explosives and by altering a proposed study on armor-piercing bullets.

6. DEATH-ROW APPEALS

Placing restrictions on death-row appeals was a Republican goal that had been debated since President Ronald Reagan's administration. Then, in the 104th Congress, a perfect vehicle for achieving that goal appeared: a bill to fight terrorism (HR 2703). With the memory of the bombing of the federal building in Oklahoma City on April 19, 1995, still fresh, the bill was a fast-moving piece of legislation that had a strong chance of passage in both chambers. (House key vote 5)

Although many Democrats argued that federal death-row appeals—known as habeas corpus petitions—had little to do with terrorism, the provision became the cornerstone of the terrorism bill.

Even a bipartisan amendment from Melvin Watt, D-N.C., and Helen Chenoweth, R-Idaho—opposites on the political spectrum—could not muster enough votes to remove the habeas corpus section.

The House rejected the Watt-Chenoweth amendment March 14, by a vote of 135–283: R 12–218; D 122–65 (ND 96–35, SD 26–30); I 1–0. Later the same day, members passed the terrorism bill, which GOP leaders advertised as the "The Effective Death Penalty and Public Safety Act of 1996," by a vote of 229–191.

In rejecting the Watt-Chenoweth amendment, the House was agreeing to impose the most severe limitations on the constitutional right to seek federal review of convictions since the Civil War. Habeas corpus was the only legal avenue for state inmates to obtain a federal review of their cases.

Ultimately enacted as S 735—PL 104–132, the new law set a deadline on when petitions could be filed by state prisoners—generally one year after exhausting all appeals in state court—and made it extremely difficult for prisoners to file more than one appeal. The limit for death-row inmates was even stricter. They were given six months to file an appeal assuming the state had provided a competent lawyer for their appeals.

Death-row inmates had used the appeals process to delay executions and, in some cases, win a new trial. "Sometimes the government makes mistakes," said Watt in an impassioned floor speech to gain support for his amendment. "We can't sacrifice our constitutional principles because we're angry at people for bombing," he said. Individual citizens, Watt said, ought to have the ability to petition the judicial branch to have government mistakes redressed.

Judiciary Committee Chairman Henry J. Hyde, R-Ill., and a majority of Republicans argued that changes were needed to stop prisoners from abusing the appeals system. "We seek closure and finality for the judgment that has been rendered and some compassion for the families of the victims who wait years and years," Hyde said.

The House had passed a free-standing bill to limit death-row appeals (HR 729—H Rept 104–23) on Feb. 8, 1995, by 297–132. The bill, sponsored by Bill McCollum, R-Fla., never made it to the Senate floor.

While some Democrats agreed that changes to the appeals process were needed, most said the changes were too restrictive and could send innocent people to their deaths.

7. IMMIGRATION

In 1996 Congress decided to take a stern—critics called it hostile—approach toward immigrants. The new welfare law (HR 3734—PL 104–193) restricted benefits to legal immigrants. The House version of the immigration bill (HR 2202) went further, including a provision aimed at allowing states to deny free public schooling to children of illegal immigrants.

While that language was removed during conference negotiations in the face of a threatened presidential veto and Senate filibuster, its adoption by the House underscored how far House Republicans were willing to go to get tough on illegal immigration.

Approval of the so-called Gallegly amendment on March 20 came after an emotional debate and heavy lobbying by the Republican leadership. The vote was 257–163: R 213–20; D 44–142 (ND 25–104, SD 19–38); I 0–1.

The benefits cuts in the welfare bill, equally controversial, did become law. They were embedded in the larger bill, and necessary to meet its budgetary target. The education issue, in contrast, was a straight up-or-down vote on something that did not affect the rest of the immigration measure. The rest of the bill focused on increasing border controls and otherwise stemming illegal immigration.

Proponents argued that the Gallegly amendment would help reduce the flow of illegal immigrant families into the United States. Its author, Elton Gallegly, R-Calif., was one of many members from the California delegation and among freshman Republicans who enthusiastically supported the proposal. California's Republican governor, Pete Wilson, made it a priority as well.

The amendment exposed fissures on the issue elsewhere in the GOP, however. Its detractors said it was unworkable and would lead to cities full of juveniles unprepared for the life ahead of them.

Both of Texas's Republican senators, Phil Gramm and Kay Bailey Hutchison, opposed it, as did the state's GOP governor, George W. Bush. Had the amendment survived the conference, as many as 10 Republican senators would have helped sustain a Democratic filibuster.

As the November presidential election approached, the Gallegly amendment became an overtly political issue. Republican presidential candidate Bob Dole sent his campaign director, Scott Reed, to Capitol Hill to argue that keeping the language was the most effective way to kill the overall bill. The Dole camp would have been happy to have the bill die and deny President Clinton another legislative victory.

A debate broke out among GOP lawmakers as to whether they wanted to pass a bill or have a good election issue. In the end, Republican supporters of the Gallegly language concluded they would rather have a bill than an issue, and the amendment was dropped in conference.

The provisions of the immigration bill were ultimately passed as part of the omnibus fiscal 1997 appropriations package (HR 3610—PL 104–208).

8. ABORTION

A House vote March 27 to pass a bill (HR 1833) banning certain late-term abortions marked the first time Congress had cleared legislation to outlaw a specific abortion procedure. Although the measure ultimately fell in the face of a presidential veto, abortion opponents arguably emerged victorious.

The bill represented a shift in the perennial abortion debate. Many previous votes had offered variations on the underlying question of whether women had the right to an abortion. The vote on HR 1833 reframed the question, forcing members to decide about a specific procedure rather than general abortion rights.

The House vote followed Senate passage of the same measure in 1995 and was the closest that abortion opponents had come to enacting a partial rollback of the landmark 1973 Supreme Court decision in *Roe v. Wade*, which guaranteed the right to have an abortion. Members voted to ban the so-called partial-birth abortion procedure, 286–129: R 214–15; D 72–113 (ND 47–83, SD 25–30); I 0–1.

The vote was also significant because the margin of support was unusually high—nine votes over what would be needed to override the president's promised veto. Indeed, the House voted Sept. 19 to override the veto, but the Senate sustained it Sept. 26. (*Senate key vote 14*)

The measure would have made it a federal crime for a physician to perform a type of late-term abortion known in the bill as a "partial-birth" abortion, unless the procedure was needed to save the woman's life. Clinton argued that the bill should have included an exemption to protect the woman's health, as well. The bill defined the partial-birth procedure as taking place when a doctor partially "vaginally delivers a living fetus before killing the fetus and completing delivery."

If enacted, doctors who performed these late-term abortions would have faced fines and up to two years in prison. The measure exempted the woman from criminal penalties and would have allowed the woman's parents and the prospective father to sue the doctor for damages if the woman was a minor.

Proponents of the ban argued that the procedure was inhumane, amounting to the extermination of "a defenseless little life," as Henry J. Hyde, R-Ill., described it. Opponents argued that the procedure was used only in extreme circumstances and that the legislation would "prevent women from getting the medical care they need," in the words of Nita M. Lowey, D-N.Y.

In making the partial-birth procedure their highest priority, abortion foes forced members to decide whether to protect the practice of a type of abortion much of the public found unacceptable. Although they could not prevail in the final Senate vote, even clearing a bill to undercut *Roe v. Wade* was a victory for them.

9. DEBT LIMIT

Republican congressional leaders pushed the government closer to default than at any other time in recent history. An increase in the cap on the Treasury's borrowing authority became a weapon in their battle with President Clinton over their plan to balance the budget in seven years.

The trouble with the debt limit started in 1995, when Republicans decided they would increase it only as part of their deficit-reducing, budget reconciliation bill (HR 2491). GOP leaders said they did not want to increase the debt unless they also guaranteed that the budget would be balanced. But the reconciliation bill was vetoed by Clinton, killing the debt-limit increase as well.

By that point, the government had all but exhausted the amount it could borrow under the existing $4.9 trillion statutory debt ceiling. Nonetheless, the Republicans dug in their heels and refused to raise the limit, forcing Treasury Secretary Robert E. Rubin to juggle accounts for nearly five months and rely on stopgap measures to pay the government's bills.

Rubin repeatedly warned that a default was imminent, that unless Congress raised the limit, the government would be unable to meet its obligations to foreign and domestic bond holders, Social Security recipients and creditors such as hospitals reimbursed through the Medicare system.

Only after heavy lobbying by Wall Street bankers fearful of default and a series of delicate negotiations between Rubin and the House GOP leadership did Congress agree to increase the debt limit. At first there was no consensus on how to craft a long-term debt-limit increase, and on March 7, Congress passed a temporary increase (HR 3021) that expired March 29.

Different factions argued about which measures should be added to the debt-limit bill to make it more palatable to Republicans. Among the suggestions were a version of the welfare system overhaul, spending cuts that would amount to a down payment on balancing the budget and legislation giving the president the equivalent of a budgetary line-item veto.

The separate line-item veto legislation was agreeable to a majority in both chambers, but the final version had gotten hung up in conference on details. The urgent need to pass the debt-limit increase, combined with the possibility of attaching the line-item veto to it, mobilized the Senate and House negotiators.

Spurred by Senate Majority Leader Bob Dole, R-Kan., they struck a deal on the line-item veto language. The final agreement allowed the House to attach the veto to the bill increasing the debt limit to $5.5 trillion, but then detach the veto provisions when the bill moved to the Senate. That allowed the Senate to vote on the line-item veto as a stand-alone piece of legislation. *(Senate key vote 5)*

Attaching the debt-limit increase to the veto in the House gave cover to conservatives who wanted to say they were voting to help balance the budget. On March 28 the debt-limit bill (HR 3136) passed 328–91: R 201–30; D 127–60 (ND 82–48, SD 45–12); I 0–1.

Two other "sweeteners" contributed to passage of the debt-limit increase: an increase in the Social Security earnings limit long sought by senior citizens, and a loosening of the rules that limited the ability of small businesses to go to court to challenge government regulations.

10. PRODUCT LIABILITY

Overhauling the nation's laws on faulty or dangerous products was a major goal of the House GOP's "Contract with America." Republicans and their business allies said costly litigation stifled innovation and discouraged businesses from developing products.

When the House cleared a product liability bill (HR 956) March 29 after months of fitful negotiations with the Senate, proponents faced a political showdown with President Clinton and lost: They were unable to override his veto. Clinton had been widely expected to veto the legislation, but he had hedged his public comments, suggesting some flexibility. Some of his closest supporters had predicted he could be persuaded to sign a bill.

In fact, Clinton's own veto message on May 2 suggested that he was hewing to a fine political line, stating his general support for product liability legislation but opposing HR 956 as too restrictive. He said that while he could have signed legislation "appropriately limited in scope," HR 956 would go too far in restricting legal redress for damage caused to consumers by faulty products.

The bill sought to rewrite the rules governing product liability lawsuits in state and federal courts and place limits on damage awards intended to punish negligent behavior.

The Republican leadership charged that the president's real reason for opposing the bill was loyalty to the nation's trial lawyers, who were major supporters of the Democrats. Trial lawyers and other opponents contended that the bill would bar lawsuits by consumers with legitimate claims against manufacturers.

Though it was clear in advance that the effort would fail, Republicans sought to override the president's veto on May 9 to press their political case. The veto was sustained 258–163: R 225–5; D 33–157 (ND 15–118, SD 18–39); I 0–1. A two-thirds majority of those present and voting (281 in this case) was required to override a veto.

Republicans vowed to push the issue in the presidential election race, but product liability hardly came up in the campaign.

11. MINIMUM WAGE

Democrats turned two months of political guerrilla warfare into their biggest triumph of the Republican 104th Congress on May 23, when an increase in the federal minimum wage sailed through the House. But the lopsided vote on an amendment to raise the mandatory minimum wage from $4.25 to $5.15 an hour belied a House more divided than that margin indicated. Support for raising the minimum wage was wide, but among Republicans it was not particularly strong.

Opponents, on the other hand, were resolute. The GOP leadership, knowing it did not have the votes to block a wage raise outright, had tried for months to avoid bringing the issue to the floor. The defection of about two dozen Republican moderates—many of whom had confronted intense pressure from organized labor in their districts—forced House leaders to go forward with a minimum wage vote. They also hoped to defuse a potent Democratic campaign issue.

GOP leaders chose a relatively noncontroversial vehicle for the wage raise, a bill (HR 1227), favored mainly by Republicans, clarifying that employees could commute to and from work in company cars without being compensated for their driving time. Unions and labor Democrats opposed the commuter bill, but GOP leaders figured correctly that the probusiness measure would not poison the process.

Frank Riggs, R-Calif., a moderate facing a tough reelection bid, was selected to amend the commuting bill with a provision to raise the hourly minimum wage to $4.75 on July 1 and to $5.15 a year later. Two controversial amendments by Bill Goodling, R-Pa., both designed to insulate some employers from the effects of the wage increase, would follow. Whatever passed that day would be married to a popular package of business tax breaks (HR 3448), then sent to the Senate. (Senate key vote 10)

The leadership carefully orchestrated the floor action to ensure that conservatives could vote for the tax cut—the most significant tax legislation of the 104th Congress—without having to throw in their lot for a minimum wage increase they found loathsome.

Riggs' amendment was the only pure vote on the minimum wage increase. The final vote was influenced by a Republican desire to see the attached tax package through to passage.

Debate over Riggs's wage raise was passionate. Conservative Republicans portrayed the increase as a politically motivated job killer that would hurt the low-wage workers it was ostensibly meant to help. Democrats and moderate Republicans said raising the minimum wage for the first time since 1991 was a simple matter of fairness. They pointed out that the buying power of the minimum wage had slipped to nearly a 40-year low in inflation-adjusted dollars. The Riggs amendment was adopted 266–162: R 77–156; D 188–6 (ND 136–0, SD 52–6); I 1–0.

Even that comfortable margin displayed an increasing resolve by GOP conservatives to take politically unpopular stands. If getting the wage raise to the floor was a testament to the power of labor unions and popular opinion, resolute Republican opposition reflected the remaining strength of a conservative tide.

In 1989, the previous time the House voted to raise the minimum wage, 135 Republicans joined 247 Democrats to pass a two-tiered, 90-cent increase, 382–37. This time, 37 Republicans who voted for a minimum wage increase in 1989 voted against an almost identical measure.

12. DEFENSE APPROPRIATIONS

The facade of unity behind which House Republicans had increased President Clinton's defense budget dropped away briefly June 13. The occasion was an amendment to the fiscal 1997 defense appropriations bill (HR 3610) that energized GOP deficit hawks who saw the Pentagon budget as a large part of the overall budget problem.

In the early weeks of 1995 House Republicans eager to cut the deficit and those anxious to boost defense spending had reached a rough compromise on how much to add to Clinton's Pentagon funding request. GOP deficit hawks and defense specialists agreed on a budget increase that was lower than the $15 billion to $25 billion rise the defense specialists had been pushing.

Under this plan, embodied in slightly modified form in the fiscal 1997 budget resolution (H Con Res 178), Congress would slightly increase Clinton's projected defense budgets for fiscal 1997–2002, which together would total $1.62 trillion. The Republican plan was to add several billion dollars annually to Clinton's projected requests for most of that period, then spend less on defense than Clinton planned in the last year.

Proponents of the spending increase insisted that the additional funding was needed because Clinton's budgets were starving the armed services at the same time that the president was burdening the military with new peacekeeping and humanitarian missions around the globe. In particular, they argued, the Pentagon needed more for weapons procurement, which had declined about 70 percent in inflation-adjusted terms since 1985, the peak year of the Reagan administration defense buildup.

Though they had signed on to the compromise, many Republican deficit cutters agreed with liberal Democrats that defense hard-liners had overstated the need for additional Pentagon spending. The deficit hawks also warned that if Republicans were lenient with the Defense Department, they would have a harder time cutting other parts of the federal bureaucracy.

The issue came to a head when GOP deficit hawk Christopher Shays of Connecticut joined with liberal Democrat Barney Frank of Massachusetts to sponsor an amendment that would have trimmed about $1.9 billion from the $245.2 billion defense funding bill. Had it been adopted, the amendment would have frozen the bill at the amount passed for fiscal 1996, which still would have been $8.7 billion more than Clinton requested for fiscal 1997.

Although the amendment was rejected, it won support from several dozen GOP deficit hawks, including Budget Committee Chairman John R. Kasich, R-Ohio. The vote was 194–219: R 60–161; D 133–58 (ND 113–23; SD 20–35); I 1–0.

13. PESTICIDES

For nearly two decades, lawmakers had run into one impasse after another over proposals to overhaul federal pesticide regulations. Potential compromises foundered in the face of deep divisions over health standards, with pesticide makers and users squaring off against environmentalists and consumer activists.

So it came as something of a shock when the House not only passed a sweeping pesticide bill (HR 1627) on July 23, but did so without any dissent. The vote was 417–0: R 229–0; D 187–0 (ND 132–0, SD 55–0); I 1–0.

"It's amazing to me," said Agriculture Committee Chairman Pat Roberts, R-Kan., who helped write the bill. "All the stars in the heavens were in the right places."

Nor were House members the only elected officials who liked the compromise measure, which established a uniform health standard for pesticide residues in both raw and processed foods. The Senate cleared the bill by voice vote July 24, and President Clinton signed it into law Aug. 3 (PL 104–170).

Much of the impetus that freed the pesticide legislation from deadlock came from the federal judiciary. Recent court rulings had interpreted pesticide regulations barring potentially cancer-causing agents so strictly that the Environmental Protection Agency had begun to cancel the use of some common agricultural chemicals. Farm-state members warned of crop losses and economic dislocation.

Election-year politics also contributed to the bill's sudden progress. After being branded as "anti-environment" for pursuing a deregulatory agenda early in the 104th Congress, GOP leaders were hungry for an environmental achievement. Lobbyists on all sides of the issue, tired of waging the same battle year after year, were ready to settle for a compromise.

Movement toward a consensus bill began in the House Agriculture Committee, which marked up less-controversial sections of HR 1627 on June 19. The legislation hit a snag in the Commerce Committee, with Republicans and Democrats divided over how to change the so-called Delaney Clause of the 1958 Federal Food, Drug and

Cosmetic Act. The Delaney Clause barred processed food from containing even minute amounts of cancer-causing chemicals.

Republicans, spurred by farmers and chemical companies, urged a more flexible approach that would allow processed foods, like raw foods, to contain small amounts of some carcinogens. But Democrats, voicing the concerns of environmentalists and public health advocates, insisted on retaining strict health standards.

Finding a solution fell to the leaders of the opposing camps on pesticide law: Commerce Committee Chairman Thomas J. Bliley Jr., R-Va., and veteran committee liberal Henry A. Waxman, D-Calif. The two had been bitter adversaries, but to the amazement of many, they emerged with a deal after about five days of closed-door meetings.

Their compromise allowed residues of cancer-causing chemicals in both raw and processed foods—a major victory for the agriculture industry. But those residues had to be in such small amounts as to pose no reasonable risk of harm, meaning that consumption of the food product would cause only about a one-in-a-million risk of cancer. In addition, the compromise contained strict standards to safeguard the health of infants and children.

Despite some grumbling, lobbyists on all sides signed off on the measure. In the eight days following the deal, the legislation swept through one subcommittee markup, two committee markups and the House and Senate floors, without a single dissenting vote.

14. WELFARE OVERHAUL

House approval of a sweeping welfare overhaul bill (HR 3734) brought an element of bipartisanship to an issue that had been contentious throughout the 104th Congress. The vote also topped a tumultuous day in which Democrats and Republicans alike waited eagerly to hear whether President Clinton would sign the bill.

It was a foregone conclusion that Republicans could pass practically any welfare bill they liked, as they had in 1995. The question was whether Clinton and a significant number of congressional Democrats would fall into line despite liberal opposition to the measure. They did, and the House adopted the conference report on July 31, 328–101: R 230–2; D 98–98 (ND 62–76, SD 36–22); I 0–1. The Senate cleared the bill the next day. *(Senate key vote 12)*

Clinton had twice vetoed GOP welfare plans—on Dec. 6, 1995, as part of the deficit-reducing budget reconciliation bill (HR 2491), then on Jan. 9, as a free-standing welfare bill (HR 4). He branded the measures as too harsh, more likely to hurt children than to help welfare recipients get jobs.

The push to revisit the legislation began Feb. 6 when the National Governors' Association endorsed recommendations to overhaul both welfare and Medicaid, the federal-state health insurance program for the poor. The centerpiece of the welfare provisions remained unchanged: The federal government would end its 61-year-old guarantee of providing welfare checks to all eligible low-income mothers and children. Federal funding would be sent to states in predetermined lump-sum payments known as block grants, giving states almost complete control over eligibility and benefits.

While Clinton seemed willing to end an individual's entitlement to welfare, he was unalterably opposed to ending the entitlement for Medicaid. On the other side, Senate Majority Leader Bob Dole, R-Kan., insisted the Medicaid provisions remain in the bill.

However, once Dole left the Senate in June to campaign for president full time, GOP leaders succumbed to pressure from their own ranks and dropped the Medicaid provisions. A growing number of Republicans wanted to give Clinton a clean shot at the welfare bill and were prepared to either share credit with him for having over-

hauled the system or blast him for defending an unpopular status quo.

For days, Clinton seemed to be leaning toward signing the bill, but he did not make a final decision until after a dramatic meeting with top advisers the morning of July 31. House Democrats used procedural maneuvers to stall action for a few hours that day, waiting for a signal from the White House and for details of the conference report that had been filed late the night before. Many Democrats wanted to make sure they were on the same side as the president. Like Clinton, they did not want to be seen as supporting the existing system but had concerns about the bill's potential effect on the poor.

Although Clinton's announcement that he would sign the bill made the subsequent debate anticlimactic, it also underscored the historic nature of the effort, which would directly affect millions of low-income people.

Many Democrats who opposed the legislation spoke fervently against it. Only two of the party's 34 black members, two of its 12 Hispanic members and nine of its 31 women voted for the conference report.

Democrats who supported the bill, some of whom were swayed by Clinton, typically explained that they were willing to take a chance with a new, untested approach. Among Republicans, many members said they were motivated by compassion to help the poor. They did not focus on the $54.6 billion in savings through fiscal 2002 that would come mainly from cutting food stamps and aid to legal immigrants. Only two Republicans opposed the measure—Reps. Lincoln Diaz-Balart and Ileana Ros-Lehtinen, both Cuban-Americans from South Florida, who objected to provisions cutting benefits for legal immigrants.

15. APPROPRIATIONS

For months it was a mystery: How would a Republican Congress bent on cutting domestic discretionary spending simultaneously satisfy President Clinton, who wanted more money for his favorite programs, and its own hard-core budget-cutters, who wanted less?

It had taken Republicans almost seven months past the Oct. 1, 1995, start of fiscal 1996 to work out their disputes with Clinton and finish all the spending bills. They would not have that luxury this time.

Leaders and most rank-and-file members were desperate to go home to campaign in what was shaping up to be a make-or-break election for the GOP Congress. To get out of Washington by the early October target adjournment date, they would have to finish all 13 appropriations bills (or pass a continuing resolution) by Oct. 1.

That gave the president huge leverage. By vetoing almost any bill he deemed too frugal, he could freeze Republicans in place while they worked to craft another one.

In the end, it was that burning desire to go home that persuaded most Republicans not to make a fight of it. Even many hard-line GOP deficit hawks looked the other way as leaders gave Clinton an additional $6.5 billion he had demanded as the price of his signature. Republican leaders even added money Clinton had not asked for, responding to rank-and-file concerns that GOP candidates were being hurt by accusations that they wanted to gut education and environmental programs.

The leaders insisted the extra spending was paid for by cuts elsewhere, but when the Congressional Budget Office got through scrubbing the numbers later, only about half turned out to have been legitimately offset.

In the final analysis, Republicans could rightly claim that they held appropriations sharply below the levels Democrats would have spent had they continued to control Congress in 1995–1996. But the Republicans had retreated from the ambitious goal they had set in early 1995, when they fixed a $487.4 billion limit for discretionary spending in fiscal 1997. The final number was about $503 billion.

The final appropriations vote came Sept. 28 on a package that wrapped up six bills embodying the final deal between Clinton and GOP leaders. Republican fiscal hawks had a stark choice: Stand on principle, vote no, kill the deal and hang around Washington hoping for a better one or swallow hard, vote yes, go home to campaign and come back to fight another day. Most opted to head home as the measure (HR 3610) passed easily, 370–37: R 202–24; D 167–13 (ND 113–11, SD 54–2); I 1–0.

1. S 652. Telecommunications Overhaul/Conference Report. Adoption of the conference report to promote competition and deregulation in the broadcasting, cable and telephone industries by requiring local phone companies to open their networks to competitors, allowing those companies to offer cable service, permitting the regional Bell operating companies to enter the long-distance and manufacturing markets, easing ownership requirements on broadcasters, and deregulating cable rates for small cable TV systems. The bill also would require most televisions sold in the United States to be equipped with a device that would allow parents to block TV shows rated inappropriate for children and would bar the dissemination of "indecent" material on the Internet and online computer services. Adopted (thus cleared for the president) 91–5: R 51–1; D 40–4 (ND 30–4, SD 10–0), Feb. 1, 1996. A "yea" was a vote in support of the president's position.

2. S 1541. Farm Bill/Passage. Passage of the bill to reauthorize for seven years, through 2002, all major federal farm programs, overhauling certain programs to give farmers a fixed, declining payment regardless of market conditions rather than traditional subsidies and to give farmers more flexibility in deciding what to plant. The bill reauthorizes the food stamp program for seven years and expands conservation and rural development programs. Passed 64–32: R 44–6; D 20–26 (ND 13–23, SD 7–3), Feb. 7, 1996.

3. HR 927. Cuba Sanctions/Conference Report. Adoption of the conference report on the bill to strengthen the trade embargo against Cuba, to discourage foreign investment in Cuba and to direct the president to prepare to support a transition to democracy in Cuba. The bill would allow U.S. nationals to bring lawsuits against entities that traffic in confiscated Cuban property; it would codify all existing Cuban economic sanctions dating back to 1962; it would deny entry into the United States to foreigners who traffic in confiscated Cuban property; and it would proportionally reduce U.S. foreign aid to countries that support Cuba. Adopted (thus sent to the House) 74–22: R 47–4; D 27–18 (ND 19–17, SD 8–1), March 5, 1996. A "yea" was a vote in support of the president's position.

4. HR 956. Product Liability/Conference Report. Adoption of the conference report to limit punitive damages in product liability cases to two times compensatory damages or $250,000, whichever is greater, with lower limits for small businesses. Under the bill, a plaintiff could bring a lawsuit up to two years after discovering both the cause and the injury itself. The bill would limit the time to file a suit to 15 years after the delivery of a product, but the limit would apply only to some types of products. The bill also would abolish joint and several liability for noneconomic damages. Adopted (thus sent to the House) 59–40: R 47–6; D 12–34 (ND 9–27, SD 3–7), March 21, 1996. A "nay" was a vote in support of the president's position.

5. S 4. Line-Item Veto/Conference Report. Adoption of the conference report to the bill to grant the president on or after Jan. 1, 1997, the authority to cancel individual spending items, limited tax breaks or new entitlement programs from larger bills already signed into law. The proposed cancellations would take effect unless both chambers pass a bill (itself subject to veto) to reverse them. The provisions of the bill would expire on Jan. 1, 2005. Adopted (thus sent to the House) 69–31: R 50–3; D 19–28 (ND 16–21, SD 3–7), March 27, 1996. A "yea" was a vote in support of the president's position.

6. S 1028. Health Insurance Revisions/Medical Savings Accounts. Kassebaum, R-Kan., amendment to strike the provisions in the Dole, R-Kan., amendment that establish medical savings accounts, which allow individuals to make tax deductible contributions to special accounts set up to pay medical expenses. Adopted 52–46: R 5–46; D 47–0 (ND 37–0, SD 10–0), April 18, 1996. A "yea" was a vote in support of the president's position.

7. S Con Res 57. Fiscal 1997 Budget Resolution/Centrist Coalition Alternative. Chafee, R-R.I., substitute amendment to save $679 billion over seven years and provide for a balanced budget by 2003. The substitute would reduce projected spending over seven years for Medicare by $154 billion, Medicaid by $62 billion, welfare by $58 billion and discretionary spending by $268 billion. The substitute includes a net $105 billion in tax cuts, would save $126 billion by adjusting the Consumer Price Index and would save $25 billion by eliminating certain tax preferences. Rejected 46–53: R 22–30; D 24–23 (ND 18–19, SD 6–4), May 23, 1996.

8. H J Res 1. Balanced-Budget Amendment/Passage. Passage of the joint resolution to propose a constitutional amendment to balance the budget by the year 2002 or two years after ratification by three-fourths of the states, whichever is later. Three-fifths of the entire House and Senate would be required to approve deficit spending or an increase in the public debt limit. A simple majority could waive the requirement in times of war or in the face of a serious military threat. The courts would be prohibited from raising taxes or

cutting spending unless specifically authorized by Congress. Rejected 64–35: R 52–1; D 12–34 (ND 7–29, SD 5–5), June 6, 1996. A two-thirds majority vote of those present and voting (66 in this case) is required to pass a joint resolution proposing an amendment to the Constitution. On June 4 the Senate had by voice vote agreed to reconsider a vote on March 2, 1995, by which the Senate had rejected passage of H J Res 1 by 65–35. A "nay" was a vote in support of the president's position.

9. S 1219. Campaign Finance Overhaul/Cloture. Motion to invoke cloture (thus limiting debate) on the bill to institute voluntary campaign spending limits with reduced broadcast and postal rates, to outlaw political action committees and to ban unlimited contributions to political parties (so-called soft money). Motion rejected 54–46: R 8–45; D 46–1 (ND 37–0, SD 9–1), June 25, 1996. Three-fifths of the total Senate (60) is required to invoke cloture.

10. HR 3448. Small Business Tax Package-Minimum Wage Increase/Wage Delay and Exemptions. Bond, R-Mo., amendment to delay by six months a 90–cent increase in the minimum wage, to exempt employees of businesses with annual gross sales under $500,000 from the minimum wage increase and to deny any new employees the minimum wage increase for the first six months of employment. Rejected 46–52: R 46–5; D 0–47 (ND 0–37, SD 0–10), July 9, 1996. A "nay" was a vote in support of the president's position.

11. S 1936. Nuclear Waste Storage/Passage. Passage of the bill to establish a temporary nuclear waste storage site at Yucca Mountain, 100 miles northwest of Las Vegas, Nev. Passed 63–37: R 50–3; D 13–34 (ND 7–30, SD 6–4), July 31, 1996. A "nay" was a vote in support of the president's position.

12. HR 3734. Budget Reconciliation-Welfare Overhaul/Conference Report. Adoption of the conference report on the bill to reduce spending over six years by about $54.1 billion, mostly by cutting aid to legal immigrants and scaling back food stamp and Supplemental Security Income (SSI) spending. The bill ends the federal guarantee of welfare benefits, gives states broad discretion over their own programs through block grants, generally requires welfare recipients to work within two years of receiving benefits and limits recipients to five years of welfare benefits. The bill also imposes tighter eligibility standards on low-income children seeking SSI benefits due to disability and denies most legal immigrants SSI and food stamp benefits. Adopted (thus cleared for the president) 78–21: R 53–0; D 25–21 (ND 17–20, SD 8–1), Aug. 1, 1996. A "yea" was a vote in support of the president's position.

13. S 2056. Sexual Orientation Nondiscrimination/Passage. Passage of the bill to prohibit job discrimination based on sexual orientation by extending the remedies of the 1964 Civil Rights Act to sexual orientation. Rejected 49–50: R 8–45; D 41–5 (ND 35–2, SD 6–3), Sept. 10, 1996. A "yea" was a vote in support of the president's position.

14. HR 1833. Abortion Procedure Ban/Veto Override. Passage, over President Clinton's April 10 veto, of the bill banning a late-term abortion procedure, where the physician partially delivers the fetus before completing the abortion. Anyone convicted of performing such an abortion would be subject to a fine and up to two years in prison. An exception would be granted when the procedure is necessary to save the life of the woman, provided no other medical procedure can be used. Rejected 57–41: R 45–6; D 12–35 (ND 7–30, SD 5–5), Sept. 26, 1996. A two-thirds majority of those present and voting (66 in this case) of both houses is required to override a veto. A "nay" was a vote in support of the president's position.

---

[a] Bob Dole, R-Kan., resigned June 11. He was eligible to vote on key votes 1–8. Sheila Frahm, R-Kan., was sworn in June 11, replacing Dole. She was eligible to vote on key votes 9–14.

[b] Ron Wyden, D-Ore., was sworn in Feb. 6, replacing Bob Packwood, R-Ore., who resigned Oct. 1, 1995. He was eligible to vote on key votes 2–14.

KEY			
		Democrats	*Republicans*
Y	Voted for ("yea")	–	Announced against
N	Voted against ("nay")	P	Voted "present"
+	Announced for	C	Voted "present" to avoid possible conflict of interest
#	Paired for	?	Did not vote or otherwise make a position known
X	Paired against		

ND Northern Democrats
SD Southern Democrats
Southern states – Ala., Ark., Fla., Ga., Ky., La., Miss., N.C., Okla., S.C., Tenn., Texas, Va.

Senate Key Votes	1	2	3	4	5	6	7	8	9	10	11	12	13	14
ALABAMA														
Shelby	Y	Y	Y	N	Y	N	N	Y	N	Y	Y	Y	N	Y
Heflin	Y	Y	Y	N	N	Y	N	Y	N	N	Y	Y	N	Y
ALASKA														
Murkowski	Y	Y	Y	Y	Y	N	N	Y	N	Y	Y	Y	N	Y
Stevens	Y	Y	Y	Y	Y	N	N	Y	N	Y	Y	Y	N	Y
ARIZONA														
Kyl	Y	Y	Y	Y	Y	N	N	Y	N	Y	Y	Y	N	Y
McCain	N	Y	Y	Y	Y	N	N	Y	Y	Y	Y	Y	N	Y
ARKANSAS														
Bumpers	Y	N	N	N	N	Y	N	N	Y	N	N	N	Y	N
Pryor	Y	N	Y	Y	N	Y	Y	N	Y	N	N	?	?	N
CALIFORNIA														
Boxer	Y	Y	N	N	N	Y	Y	N	Y	N	N	N	Y	N
Feinstein	Y	Y	Y	N	Y	Y	Y	N	Y	N	N	N	Y	N
COLORADO														
Brown	Y	Y	Y	Y	Y	N	Y	N	Y	Y	Y	Y	N	Y
Campbell	Y	Y	Y	Y	Y	?	Y	Y	N	N	N	Y	N	?
CONNECTICUT														
Dodd	?	N	N	Y	N	Y	N	N	Y	N	N	N	Y	N
Lieberman	Y	Y	Y	Y	Y	Y	Y	N	Y	N	N	Y	Y	N
DELAWARE														
Roth	Y	Y	?	N	Y	N	N	Y	N	Y	Y	Y	N	Y
Biden	Y	Y	Y	N	Y	Y	N	Y	Y	N	N	Y	Y	Y
FLORIDA														
Mack	Y	Y	Y	Y	Y	?	N	Y	N	Y	Y	Y	N	Y
Graham	Y	Y	Y	N	Y	Y	Y	Y	Y	N	Y	Y	Y	N
GEORGIA														
Coverdell	Y	Y	Y	Y	Y	N	N	Y	N	Y	Y	Y	N	Y
Nunn	Y	Y	?	Y	N	Y	Y	Y	Y	N	Y	Y	N	Y
HAWAII														
Akaka	Y	Y	N	N	N	Y	Y	N	Y	N	N	N	Y	N
Inouye	Y	Y	?	N	N	Y	Y	N	Y	N	N	N	Y	N
IDAHO														
Craig	Y	Y	Y	Y	Y	N	N	Y	N	Y	Y	Y	N	Y
Kempthorne	Y	Y	Y	Y	Y	N	N	Y	N	Y	Y	Y	N	Y
ILLINOIS														
Moseley-Braun	Y	Y	N	Y	N	Y	N	Y	Y	N	Y	N	Y	N
Simon	N	Y	N	Y	Y	Y	Y	Y	Y	N	Y	N	Y	N
INDIANA														
Coats	Y	Y	Y	Y	Y	N	Y	N	Y	N	Y	N	Y	Y
Lugar	Y	Y	?	Y	Y	N	Y	Y	N	Y	Y	Y	N	Y
IOWA														
Grassley	Y	Y	Y	Y	Y	N	N	Y	N	Y	Y	Y	N	Y
Harkin	Y	N	N	N	Y	Y	N	Y	Y	N	Y	Y	Y	N
KANSAS														
Dole/Frahm[a]	Y	Y	Y	Y	Y	N		Y	N	Y	Y	Y	N	Y
Kassebaum	Y	Y	Y	Y	Y	Y	Y	Y	Y	Y	Y	Y	N	N
KENTUCKY														
McConnell	Y	Y	Y	Y	Y	N	N	Y	N	Y	Y	Y	N	Y
Ford	Y	Y	Y	N	N	Y	N	N	Y	N	N	Y	N	Y
LOUISIANA														
Breaux	Y	Y	Y	N	Y	Y	Y	Y	Y	N	N	Y	Y	Y
Johnston	Y	Y	Y	Y	N	Y	Y	N	Y	N	Y	Y	Y	Y
MAINE														
Cohen	Y	N	Y	N	N	N	Y	Y	Y	+	Y	Y	Y	?
Snowe	Y	N	Y	Y	Y	N	Y	Y	Y	Y	Y	Y	Y	N
MARYLAND														
Mikulski	Y	N	Y	N	N	Y	N	N	Y	N	N	N	Y	N
Sarbanes	Y	N	Y	N	N	Y	N	N	Y	N	N	N	Y	N
MASSACHUSETTS														
Kennedy	Y	N	N	N	Y	Y	N	N	Y	N	N	N	Y	N
Kerry	Y	N	N	N	Y	Y	N	N	Y	N	N	Y	Y	N
MICHIGAN														
Abraham	Y	Y	Y	Y	Y	N	N	Y	N	Y	Y	Y	N	Y
Levin	Y	N	N	N	N	Y	Y	N	Y	N	Y	Y	Y	N
MINNESOTA														
Grams	Y	Y	Y	Y	Y	N	N	Y	N	Y	Y	Y	N	Y
Wellstone	N	N	N	N	Y	Y	N	N	Y	N	N	N	Y	N
MISSISSIPPI														
Cochran	Y	Y	Y	Y	Y	N	Y	Y	N	?	Y	Y	N	Y
Lott	Y	Y	Y	Y	Y	N	N	Y	N	Y	Y	Y	N	N
MISSOURI														
Ashcroft	Y	Y	Y	Y	Y	N	N	Y	N	Y	Y	Y	N	Y
Bond	Y	Y	N	Y	Y	Y	N	Y	N	Y	Y	Y	N	Y

Senate Key Votes	1	2	3	4	5	6	7	8	9	10	11	12	13	14
MONTANA														
Burns	Y	Y	Y	Y	Y	N	N	Y	N	Y	Y	Y	N	Y
Baucus	Y	Y	Y	N	N	Y	N	Y	Y	N	N	Y	Y	N
NEBRASKA														
Exon	Y	N	Y	Y	Y	N	N	N	Y	N	N	N	Y	Y
Kerrey	Y	N	N	?	N	Y	Y	N	Y	N	N	N	Y	N
NEVADA														
Bryan	Y	N	Y	N	N	Y	Y	Y	Y	N	N	Y	Y	N
Reid	Y	N	Y	N	N	Y	N	Y	Y	N	N	Y	Y	Y
NEW HAMPSHIRE														
Gregg	Y	N	Y	Y	Y	N	N	Y	N	Y	Y	Y	N	Y
Smith	Y	Y	Y	Y	Y	N	N	Y	N	Y	Y	Y	N	Y
NEW JERSEY														
Bradley	Y	?	Y	N	Y	Y	Y	N	Y	N	N	N	Y	N
Lautenberg	Y	N	Y	N	N	Y	N	N	Y	N	N	N	Y	N
NEW MEXICO														
Domenici	Y	?	Y	Y	Y	N	N	Y	N	Y	Y	Y	N	Y
Bingaman	Y	N	N	N	N	Y	Y	N	Y	N	N	N	Y	N
NEW YORK														
D'Amato	Y	Y	Y	N	Y	N	Y	N	Y	Y	Y	Y	Y	Y
Moynihan	Y	Y	N	N	N	Y	Y	N	Y	N	N	N	Y	Y
NORTH CAROLINA														
Faircloth	Y	Y	Y	Y	Y	N	Y	Y	N	Y	Y	Y	N	Y
Helms	Y	Y	Y	Y	Y	N	N	Y	N	Y	Y	Y	N	Y
NORTH DAKOTA														
Conrad	Y	N	Y	N	N	Y	N	N	Y	N	N	N	Y	Y
Dorgan	Y	N	Y	Y	Y	N	N	N	Y	N	N	Y	Y	Y
OHIO														
DeWine	Y	Y	Y	Y	Y	N	Y	Y	N	Y	Y	Y	N	Y
Glenn	Y	N	Y	Y	N	Y	N	N	Y	N	N	N	Y	N
OKLAHOMA														
Inhofe	Y	Y	Y	Y	Y	N	N	Y	N	Y	Y	Y	N	Y
Nickles	Y	Y	Y	Y	Y	N	N	Y	N	Y	Y	Y	N	Y
OREGON														
Hatfield	Y	?	N	N	Y	N	Y	N	N	Y	Y	Y	Y	Y
Wyden[b]		Y	Y	N	Y	Y	N	N	Y	N	N	Y	Y	N
PENNSYLVANIA														
Santorum	Y	N	Y	Y	Y	N	Y	Y	N	Y	Y	Y	N	Y
Specter	Y	Y	Y	N	Y	N	Y	Y	Y	N	Y	Y	Y	Y
RHODE ISLAND														
Chafee	Y	N	N	Y	Y	Y	Y	N	Y	N	Y	N	Y	N
Pell	Y	Y	N	Y	N	Y	Y	-	Y	N	N	N	Y	N
SOUTH CAROLINA														
Thurmond	Y	Y	Y	Y	Y	N	N	Y	N	Y	Y	Y	N	Y
Hollings	Y	N	Y	N	N	Y	N	N	Y	N	Y	Y	Y	N
SOUTH DAKOTA														
Pressler	Y	Y	Y	Y	Y	N	N	Y	N	Y	Y	Y	N	Y
Daschle	Y	N	Y	N	Y	N	N	N	Y	N	N	N	Y	N
TENNESSEE														
Frist	Y	Y	Y	Y	Y	N	Y	Y	N	Y	Y	Y	N	Y
Thompson	Y	Y	Y	Y	Y	N	N	Y	N	Y	Y	Y	N	Y
TEXAS														
Gramm	?	?	Y	Y	Y	N	N	Y	N	Y	Y	Y	N	Y
Hutchison	Y	Y	Y	Y	Y	N	N	Y	N	Y	Y	Y	N	Y
UTAH														
Bennett	Y	Y	Y	Y	Y	N	Y	Y	N	Y	Y	Y	N	Y
Hatch	Y	Y	Y	Y	Y	N	Y	Y	N	Y	Y	Y	N	Y
VERMONT														
Jeffords	Y	N	N	Y	N	N	Y	Y	Y	N	Y	Y	Y	N
Leahy	N	Y	N	N	N	Y	Y	N	Y	N	Y	N	Y	Y
VIRGINIA														
Warner	Y	Y	Y	Y	Y	N	N	Y	N	Y	Y	Y	N	Y
Robb	Y	Y	Y	N	Y	Y	Y	Y	Y	N	Y	Y	Y	N
WASHINGTON														
Gorton	Y	Y	Y	Y	Y	Y	Y	Y	N	Y	Y	Y	N	Y
Murray	Y	N	N	N	N	Y	Y	N	Y	N	N	N	Y	N
WEST VIRGINIA														
Byrd	Y	N	Y	N	N	Y	N	N	Y	N	N	N	Y	N
Rockefeller	?	N	Y	Y	N	Y	N	N	Y	N	N	N	Y	N
WISCONSIN														
Feingold	N	N	N	N	Y	Y	N	N	Y	N	N	Y	Y	N
Kohl	Y	N	Y	Y	Y	Y	Y	Y	Y	N	Y	Y	Y	N
WYOMING														
Simpson	Y	Y	Y	N	Y	N	Y	Y	Y	Y	Y	Y	N	Y
Thomas	Y	Y	Y	Y	Y	N	N	Y	N	Y	Y	Y	N	Y

1. HR 1530. Fiscal 1996 Defense Authorization/Veto Override. Passage, over President Clinton's Dec. 28 veto, of the bill to authorize $265.3 billion for fiscal 1996 for military activities of the Department of Defense, military construction and defense activities of the Department of Energy; and to prescribe personnel strengths for the armed forces. The bill authorizes $7.1 billion more than requested by the administration, and it would require the Pentagon to make plans to deploy a missile defense system by 2003. Rejected 240–156: R 206–16; D 34–139 (ND 12–109, SD 22–30); I 0–1, Jan. 3, 1996. A two-thirds majority of those present and voting (264 in this case) of both houses is required to override a veto. A "nay" was a vote in support of the president's position.

2. HR 1643. Fiscal 1996 Targeted Appropriations/Continue Funding. Livingston, R-La., motion that the House concur in the Senate amendment with an amendment to substitute language to provide appropriations for selected government functions and to enable federal employees to return to work until Jan. 26. Motion agreed to 401–17: R 214–15; D 186–2 (ND 133–0, SD 53–2); I 1–0, Jan. 5, 1996.

3. S 652. Telecommunications Overhaul/Conference Report. Adoption of the conference report on the bill to promote competition and deregulation in the broadcasting, cable and telephone industries by requiring local phone companies to open their networks to competitors, allowing those companies to offer cable service, permitting the regional Bell operating companies to enter the long-distance and manufacturing markets, easing ownership requirements on broadcasters and deregulating cable rates for small cable TV systems. The bill would require televisions sold in the United States to be equipped with a device that would allow parents to block TV shows rated as inappropriate for children and would bar the dissemination of "indecent" material on the Internet and on-line computer services. Adopted 414–16: R 236–0; D 178–15 (ND 123–14, SD 55–1); I 0–1, Feb. 1, 1996. A "yea" was a vote in support of the president's position.

4. HR 2854. Farm Bill/Passage. Passage of the bill to reauthorize through 2002 all major federal farm programs, replacing current price-support programs with a system of fixed annual payments to farmers that would decline over the next seven years. The bill gives farmers more flexibility in deciding what to plant, extends the sugar and peanut support programs with some modifications and phases out price supports for butter and dry milk. Passed 270–155: R 216–19; D 54–135 (ND 21–112, SD 33–23); I 0–1, Feb. 29, 1996.

5. HR 2703. Antiterrorism and Death Penalty Enforcement/Law Enforcement Authority. Barr, R-Ga., amendment to eliminate many of the bill's antiterrorism provisions that expand the authority of law enforcement officials, including the bill's authorization for the State Department and attorney general to label organizations as terrorist, and language allowing evidence gathered by wiretaps that violated constitutional protections to be admitted in court. The amendment also would strike provisions allowing aliens to be excluded or denied asylum in the United States, based on their membership in a suspected or known terrorist organization, and would delete provisions that impose mandatory penalties on a person who transfers a firearm and has reasonable cause to believe that the weapon will be used in violent crime activity. Adopted 246–171: R 178–54; D 67–117 (ND 39–91, SD 28–26); I 1–0, March 13, 1996. A "nay" was a vote in support of the president's position.

6. HR 2703. Antiterrorism and Death Penalty Enforcement/Habeas Corpus Appeals. Watt, D-N.C., amendment to strike the bill's habeas corpus provisions that place strict limits on the ability of state death-row and other prisoners to challenge in federal court the constitutionality of their sentence. Rejected 135–283: R 12–218; D 122–65 (ND 96–35, SD 26–30); I 1–0, March 14, 1996.

7. HR 2202. Immigration Restrictions/Public Education. Gallegly, R-Calif., amendment to give states the option to deny public education to illegal aliens. The amendment allows parents to challenge the state's decision by proving that they are citizens or lawfully present in the United States. Adopted 257–163: R 213–20; D 44–142 (ND 25–104, SD 19–38); I 0–1, March 20, 1996. A "nay" was a vote in support of the president's position.

8. HR 1833. Abortion Procedure Ban/Agreeing to the Senate Amendments. Canady, R-Fla., motion to agree to the Senate amendments to shift the burden of proof from the defendant to the prosecution to show beyond a reasonable doubt that the abortion procedure was not necessary to save the life of the woman, to clarify who can be held liable for performing the procedure and to allow a prospective father to sue for civil damages only if he was married to the woman at the time of the abortion. The bill would impose penalties in the case of certain late-term abortions, in which the person performing the abortion partially delivers the fetus before completing the abortion. An exception would be granted where the procedure was necessary to save the life of the woman. Motion agreed to (thus clearing the bill for the president) 286–129: R 214–15; D 72–113 (ND 47–83, SD 25–30); I 0–1, March 27, 1996. A "nay" was a vote in support of the president's position.

9. HR 3136. Debt Limit Extension/Passage. Passage of the bill to increase the federal debt limit from $4.9 trillion to $5.5 trillion, to allow Social Security beneficiaries to earn more outside income without losing their benefits, to expand the ability of small businesses to challenge government regulations in court and to give the president line-item veto authority beginning in 1997. Under the rule for the bill (H Res 391), because the Senate had previously adopted the conference report on the bill (S 4) giving the president line-item veto authority, the line-item veto provision was to be stripped from HR 3136 and the House was to be deemed to have adopted the conference report on S 4, thus clearing it for the president. Passed 328–91: R 201–30; D 127–60 (ND 82–48, SD 45–12); I 0–1, March 28, 1996. A "yea" was a vote in support of the president's position.

10. HR 956. Product Liability/Veto Override. Passage, over President Clinton's May 2 veto, of the bill to limit punitive damages in product liability cases to two times compensatory damages or $250,000, whichever is greater, with lower limits for small businesses. Under the bill, a plaintiff could bring a lawsuit up to two years after discovering both the cause and the injury itself. The bill would limit the time to file a suit to 15 years after the delivery of a product, but the limit would apply only to some types of products. The bill also would abolish joint and several liability for noneconomic damages. Rejected 258–163: R 225–5; D 33–157 (ND 15–118, SD 18–39); I 0–1, May 9, 1996. A two-thirds majority of those present and voting (281 in this case) of both houses is required to override a veto. A "nay" was a vote in support of the president's position.

11. HR 1227. Employee Commuting Act/Minimum Wage Increase. Riggs, R-Calif., amendment to increase the minimum wage by 90 cents per hour over two years, thereby raising the minimum wage from its current level of $4.25 per hour to $4.75 per hour on July 1, 1996, and to $5.15 per hour on July 1, 1997. Adopted 266–162: R 77–156; D 188–6 (ND 136–0, SD 52–6); I 1–0, May 23, 1996. A "yea" was a vote in support of the president's position.

12. HR 3610. Fiscal 1997 Defense Appropriations/Spending Freeze. Shays, R-Conn., amendment to reduce the bill's total appropriation to the amount provided by the fiscal 1996 Defense Appropriations Act, approximately $243 billion. Rejected 194–219: R 60–161; D 133–58 (ND 113–23, SD 20–35); I 1–0, June 13, 1996.

13. HR 1627. Pesticide Regulations/Passage. Roberts, R-Kan., motion to suspend the rules and pass the bill to repeal the Delaney Clause of the 1958 Federal Food, Drug and Cosmetic Act, which imposes a zero tolerance standard for cancer-causing pesticide residues on food. In its place, the bill would impose a single health-based standard for chemical residues on both raw and processed foods. Motion agreed to 417–0: R 229–0; D 187–0 (ND 132–0, SD 55–0); I 1–0, July 23, 1996. A two-thirds majority of those present and voting (278 in this case) is required for passage under suspension of the rules. A "yea" was a vote in support of the president's position.

14. HR 3734. Budget Reconciliation-Welfare Overhaul/Conference Report. Adoption of the conference report on the bill to reduce spending over six years by about $54.1 billion, mostly by cutting aid to legal immigrants and scaling back food stamp and Supplemental Security Income (SSI) spending. The bill would end the federal guarantee of welfare benefits, give states broad discretion over their own programs through block grants, generally require welfare recipients to work within two years of receiving benefits and limit recipients to five years of welfare benefits. The bill also would impose tighter eligibility standards on low-income children seeking SSI benefits due to disability and deny most legal immigrants SSI and food stamp benefits. Adopted (thus sent to the Senate) 328–101: R 230–2; D 98–98 (ND 62–76, SD 36–22); I 0–1, July 31, 1996. A "yea" was a vote in support of the president's position.

15. HR 3610. Fiscal 1997 Omnibus Appropriations/Conference Report. Adoption of the conference report on the bill to appropriate more than $600 billion in new budget authority, including $382.6 billion in discretionary spending, for those Cabinet departments and federal agencies whose fiscal 1997 appropriations bills were never enacted. The measure incorporates all of the six previously separate bills: Defense, Labor-HHS-Education, Interior, Treasury-Postal, Foreign Operations, and Commerce-Justice-State. The measure also includes a modified version of the conference report to restrict illegal immigration. Adopted (thus sent to the Senate) 370–37: R 202–24; D 167–13 (ND 113–11, SD 54–2); I 1–0, Sept. 28, 1996. A "yea" was a vote in support of the president's position.

[a] Juanita Millender-McDonald, D-Calif., was sworn in April 16, replacing Walter R. Tucker III, D-Calif., who resigned Dec 15, 1995. She was eligible to vote on key votes 10-15.

KEY		
Democrats	*Republicans*	Independent
Y Voted for ("yea")		− Announced against
N Voted against ("nay")	P	Voted "present"
+ Announced for	C	Voted "present" to avoid possible conflict of interest
# Paired for		
X Paired against	?	Did not vote or otherwise make a position known

ND Northern Democrats
SD Southern Democrats
Southern states – Ala., Ark., Fla., Ga., Ky., La., Miss., N.C., Okla., S.C., Tenn., Texas, Va.

House Key Votes	1	2	3	4	5	6	7	8	9	10	11	12	13	14	15
ALABAMA															
1 Callahan	?	Y	Y	Y	Y	N	Y	Y	Y	Y	N	N	Y	Y	Y
2 Everett	Y	Y	Y	Y	Y	N	Y	Y	Y	Y	N	N	Y	Y	Y
3 Browder	Y	Y	Y	Y	Y	N	Y	Y	Y	Y	N	Y	Y	Y	Y
4 Bevill	Y	Y	Y	Y	Y	N	Y	Y	Y	?	Y	?	Y	Y	Y
5 Cramer	Y	Y	Y	Y	Y	N	Y	Y	Y	Y	N	Y	Y	Y	Y
6 Bachus	Y	Y	Y	Y	Y	N	Y	Y	Y	Y	N	Y	Y	Y	Y
7 Hilliard	N	Y	N	Y	N	Y	N	N	N	N	Y	Y	Y	N	Y
ALASKA															
AL Young	Y	Y	Y	Y	Y	N	Y	Y	Y	Y	Y	N	Y	Y	Y
ARIZONA															
1 Salmon	Y	Y	Y	Y	Y	N	Y	Y	N	Y	N	N	Y	Y	N
2 Pastor	X	Y	Y	N	N	Y	N	N	Y	N	Y	Y	Y	N	Y
3 Stump	Y	Y	Y	Y	Y	N	Y	Y	N	Y	N	N	Y	Y	Y
4 Shadegg	Y	N	Y	Y	Y	N	Y	Y	N	Y	N	N	Y	Y	Y
5 Kolbe	Y	Y	Y	Y	Y	N	N	N	Y	N	Y	N	N	Y	Y
6 Hayworth	Y	Y	Y	Y	Y	N	Y	Y	N	Y	N	N	Y	Y	Y
ARKANSAS															
1 Lincoln	N	Y	Y	N	N	N	Y	Y	Y	Y	Y	?	?	Y	?
2 Thornton	N	Y	Y	N	N	N	Y	Y	Y	N	Y	?	Y	Y	Y
3 Hutchinson	?	Y	Y	Y	Y	N	Y	Y	Y	Y	N	Y	Y	Y	Y
4 Dickey	Y	N	Y	Y	Y	N	Y	Y	Y	+	N	N	Y	Y	Y
CALIFORNIA															
1 Riggs	Y	Y	Y	Y	Y	N	Y	Y	Y	Y	Y	Y	Y	Y	Y
2 Herger	Y	Y	Y	Y	Y	N	Y	Y	N	Y	N	N	Y	Y	Y
3 Fazio	?	?	Y	N	N	Y	N	N	Y	N	Y	Y	+	Y	Y
4 Doolittle	Y	Y	Y	Y	Y	N	Y	Y	N	Y	N	N	Y	Y	Y
5 Matsui	N	Y	Y	N	N	Y	N	N	N	N	Y	N	?	N	Y
6 Woolsey	N	Y	Y	N	N	Y	N	N	N	N	Y	Y	Y	N	Y
7 Miller	N	Y	Y	N	N	Y	N	N	N	N	Y	Y	Y	N	Y
8 Pelosi	?	Y	Y	N	N	Y	N	N	N	N	Y	Y	Y	N	Y
9 Dellums	N	Y	Y	N	N	Y	N	N	N	N	Y	Y	Y	N	?
10 Baker	Y	Y	Y	Y	Y	N	Y	Y	Y	N	Y	N	N	Y	Y
11 Pombo	Y	Y	Y	Y	Y	N	Y	Y	N	Y	N	N	Y	Y	Y
12 Lantos	N	Y	Y	N	N	Y	N	N	?	Y	?	Y	Y	Y	N
13 Stark	?	?	N	N	N	Y	?	N	N	N	Y	Y	Y	N	Y
14 Eshoo	N	Y	Y	N	N	Y	N	N	Y	N	Y	Y	Y	N	Y
15 Campbell	Y	Y	Y	Y	Y	Y	N	N	Y	N	Y	N	Y	Y	Y
16 Lofgren	N	Y	Y	N	N	Y	N	N	Y	N	Y	Y	Y	N	Y
17 Farr	N	Y	Y	N	N	Y	N	N	Y	N	Y	Y	Y	N	Y
18 Condit	N	Y	Y	Y	Y	N	Y	Y	N	Y	Y	Y	Y	Y	Y
19 Radanovich	Y	Y	Y	Y	Y	N	?	Y	Y	Y	N	N	Y	Y	Y
20 Dooley	N	Y	Y	N	N	N	N	N	Y	Y	Y	Y	Y	Y	Y
21 Thomas	Y	Y	Y	Y	Y	N	#	Y	Y	Y	N	N	Y	Y	Y
22 Seastrand	Y	Y	Y	Y	Y	N	Y	Y	Y	Y	N	N	Y	Y	Y
23 Gallegly	?	Y	Y	Y	Y	N	Y	Y	Y	Y	N	Y	Y	Y	Y
24 Beilenson	N	Y	Y	N	N	Y	N	N	N	N	Y	Y	Y	N	N
25 McKeon	Y	Y	Y	Y	Y	N	Y	Y	Y	Y	N	N	Y	Y	Y
26 Berman	?	Y	Y	N	N	Y	N	N	N	N	Y	Y	Y	N	#
27 Moorhead	Y	Y	Y	Y	N	N	Y	Y	Y	Y	N	N	Y	Y	Y
28 Dreier	Y	Y	Y	Y	Y	N	Y	Y	Y	Y	N	N	Y	Y	Y
29 Waxman	N	Y	Y	N	X	Y	N	N	N	N	Y	Y	Y	N	?
30 Becerra	N	Y	Y	N	N	Y	N	N	N	?	+	Y	Y	N	N
31 Martinez	N	Y	Y	N	?	Y	N	Y	N	N	N	Y	N	Y	N
32 Dixon	?	Y	Y	N	N	Y	N	N	Y	N	Y	?	Y	N	Y
33 Roybal-Allard	N	Y	Y	N	N	Y	N	N	N	N	Y	Y	Y	N	N
34 Torres	N	Y	Y	N	N	Y	N	N	Y	N	Y	Y	Y	Y	Y
35 Waters	N	Y	Y	N	Y	Y	−	N	N	N	Y	Y	Y	N	+
36 Harman	Y	Y	Y	N	Y	N	N	X	Y	Y	Y	N	Y	Y	Y
37 Millender-McDonald[a]										N	Y	Y	Y	N	Y
38 Horn	Y	Y	Y	Y	N	N	Y	N	Y	Y	+	N	Y	Y	Y
39 Royce	Y	Y	Y	Y	Y	N	Y	Y	Y	Y	N	N	Y	Y	Y
40 Lewis	Y	Y	Y	Y	Y	N	Y	Y	Y	Y	N	Y	?	Y	Y
41 Kim	Y	Y	Y	Y	Y	N	Y	Y	Y	Y	N	N	Y	Y	Y
42 Brown	N	Y	Y	N	N	Y	N	N	Y	N	Y	Y	Y	N	Y
43 Calvert	Y	Y	Y	Y	Y	Y	Y	Y	Y	Y	N	Y	Y	Y	Y
44 Bono	Y	Y	Y	Y	Y	N	Y	Y	Y	Y	N	N	Y	Y	Y
45 Rohrabacher	Y	Y	Y	Y	Y	N	Y	Y	Y	Y	N	Y	Y	Y	N
46 Dornan	Y	Y	Y	Y	Y	Y	Y	?	Y	Y	N	N	Y	Y	P
47 Cox	Y	Y	Y	Y	Y	N	Y	Y	Y	Y	N	N	Y	Y	N
48 Packard	Y	Y	Y	Y	Y	N	Y	Y	Y	Y	N	N	Y	Y	Y
49 Bilbray	Y	Y	Y	Y	Y	N	Y	Y	Y	Y	Y	?	Y	Y	Y
50 Filner	N	Y	+	N	N	Y	N	?	X	N	Y	Y	Y	N	?
51 Cunningham	Y	Y	Y	Y	Y	N	Y	Y	Y	Y	N	?	Y	Y	Y
52 Hunter	Y	Y	Y	Y	Y	N	Y	Y	Y	Y	N	N	Y	Y	Y
COLORADO															
1 Schroeder	N	Y	N	N	N	Y	N	N	N	?	Y	Y	Y	N	N
2 Skaggs	N	Y	Y	N	N	Y	N	N	N	N	Y	Y	Y	Y	Y
3 McInnis	N	Y	Y	Y	Y	N	Y	Y	Y	Y	N	Y	Y	Y	Y
4 Allard	Y	Y	Y	Y	Y	N	Y	Y	Y	Y	N	N	Y	Y	Y

KEY

	Democrats	Republicans	*Independent*		
Y	Voted for ("yea")		–	Announced against	
N	Voted against ("nay")		P	Voted "present"	
+	Announced for		C	Voted "present" to avoid possible conflict of interest	
#	Paired for		?	Did not vote or otherwise make a position known	
X	Paired against				

ND Northern Democrats
SD Southern Democrats
Southern states – Ala., Ark., Fla., Ga., Ky., La., Miss., N.C., Okla., S.C., Tenn., Texas, Va.

House Key Votes	1	2	3	4	5	6	7	8	9	10	11	12	13	14	15
5 *Hefley*	Y	Y	Y	Y	Y	N	Y	Y	Y	Y	N	N	Y	Y	N
6 *Schaefer*	Y	Y	Y	Y	Y	N	Y	Y	Y	Y	N	N	Y	Y	Y
CONNECTICUT															
1 Kennelly	Y	Y	Y	N	N	Y	N	N	Y	Y	N	Y	N	Y	Y
2 Gejdenson	N	Y	Y	N	N	Y	N	N	Y	N	N	Y	N	Y	Y
3 DeLauro	N	Y	Y	N	N	Y	N	N	Y	N	N	Y	N	N	Y
4 *Shays*	N	Y	Y	Y	N	N	Y	N	N	Y	Y	Y	Y	Y	Y
5 *Franks*	Y	Y	Y	Y	N	N	Y	Y	Y	Y	N	N	Y	Y	Y
6 *Johnson*	Y	Y	Y	Y	N	N	Y	N	Y	Y	N	Y	N	Y	Y
DELAWARE															
AL *Castle*	Y	Y	Y	Y	N	N	Y	Y	Y	Y	Y	Y	Y	Y	Y
FLORIDA															
1 *Scarborough*	Y	Y	Y	Y	Y	Y	Y	Y	N	Y	N	N	Y	Y	N
2 Peterson	N	Y	Y	Y	N	N	?	N	Y	N	Y	N	Y	Y	Y
3 Brown	?	Y	Y	Y	N	Y	N	N	Y	N	Y	N	Y	N	Y
4 Fowler	Y	Y	Y	Y	Y	N	Y	#	#	Y	N	N	Y	Y	+
5 Thurman	N	Y	Y	N	Y	Y	N	Y	Y	N	N	Y	Y	Y	Y
6 *Stearns*	Y	Y	Y	Y	Y	N	Y	Y	Y	Y	N	N	Y	Y	N
7 *Mica*	Y	Y	Y	Y	Y	N	Y	Y	Y	Y	N	N	Y	Y	Y
8 *McCollum*	?	Y	Y	Y	N	N	Y	Y	Y	Y	N	N	Y	Y	Y
9 *Bilirakis*	Y	Y	Y	Y	N	N	Y	Y	Y	Y	Y	N	Y	Y	Y
10 *Young*	Y	Y	Y	Y	Y	N	Y	Y	Y	Y	N	?	?	Y	Y
11 Gibbons	?	N	Y	N	N	Y	N	?	Y	N	Y	N	Y	N	Y
12 *Canady*	Y	Y	Y	Y	N	N	Y	Y	Y	Y	N	N	Y	Y	Y
13 Miller	Y	Y	Y	Y	N	N	Y	Y	Y	Y	N	Y	Y	Y	Y
14 *Goss*	Y	Y	Y	Y	N	N	Y	Y	Y	Y	N	N	Y	Y	Y
15 *Weldon*	Y	Y	Y	Y	N	Y	Y	Y	Y	Y	N	N	Y	Y	Y
16 Foley	Y	Y	Y	Y	N	Y	Y	Y	Y	Y	Y	Y	Y	Y	Y
17 Meek	?	Y	Y	N	N	Y	N	N	N	Y	N	Y	N	N	Y
18 *Ros-Lehtinen*	Y	Y	Y	Y	N	N	Y	Y	#	Y	Y	N	Y	Y	Y
19 Johnston	N	Y	Y	N	N	Y	?	N	N	Y	N	Y	Y	Y	Y
20 Deutsch	N	Y	Y	N	N	Y	N	N	Y	N	Y	N	Y	Y	Y
21 *Diaz-Balart*	Y	Y	Y	Y	N	N	Y	Y	Y	Y	N	Y	N	N	Y
22 *Shaw*	Y	Y	Y	Y	N	Y	Y	Y	Y	Y	N	Y	Y	Y	Y
23 Hastings	N	N	Y	?	N	Y	N	N	N	N	Y	N	Y	N	Y
GEORGIA															
1 *Kingston*	Y	Y	Y	Y	N	N	Y	N	Y	N	Y	N	Y	Y	Y
2 Bishop	Y	Y	Y	Y	Y	N	N	Y	N	Y	N	Y	N	Y	Y
3 *Collins*	Y	Y	Y	Y	N	N	Y	Y	Y	N	Y	N	N	Y	Y
4 *Linder*	Y	Y	Y	Y	N	N	Y	Y	Y	N	Y	N	N	Y	Y
5 Lewis	N	Y	Y	N	N	Y	N	N	Y	N	Y	N	Y	N	Y
6 *Gingrich*[b]	Y						Y			Y				Y	Y
7 *Barr*	Y	N	Y	Y	N	N	Y	N	Y	N	Y	N	Y	Y	Y
8 *Chambliss*	Y	Y	Y	Y	N	N	Y	Y	Y	N	Y	N	N	Y	Y
9 *Deal*	Y	Y	Y	Y	N	N	Y	Y	Y	Y	Y	Y	Y	Y	Y
10 *Norwood*	?	Y	Y	Y	N	N	Y	Y	Y	N	Y	N	N	Y	Y
11 McKinney	N	Y	Y	?	N	Y	N	N	N	N	Y	Y	Y	N	Y
HAWAII															
1 Abercrombie	#	Y	N	N	Y	Y	N	N	N	N	Y	N	Y	N	Y
2 Mink	N	Y	Y	Y	N	Y	N	N	N	N	Y	Y	Y	N	Y
IDAHO															
1 *Chenoweth*	Y	N	Y	Y	+	Y	Y	Y	N	Y	N	N	Y	Y	N
2 *Crapo*	Y	Y	Y	Y	Y	Y	Y	Y	N	Y	N	N	Y	Y	Y
ILLINOIS															
1 Rush	N	Y	Y	N	?	Y	?	N	Y	N	Y	Y	Y	N	Y
2 Jackson	N	Y	Y	N	N	Y	N	N	N	N	Y	Y	Y	N	Y
3 Lipinski	Y	Y	Y	Y	N	N	Y	N	Y	N	Y	N	Y	Y	?
4 Gutierrez	N	Y	Y	N	N	Y	N	N	Y	N	Y	Y	Y	N	Y
5 *Flanagan*	Y	Y	Y	Y	N	N	Y	N	Y	Y	N	Y	Y	Y	Y
6 *Hyde*	Y	Y	Y	Y	N	N	Y	Y	Y	Y	N	N	Y	Y	Y
7 Collins	N	Y	Y	?	?	?	?	?	X	N	Y	N	?	N	Y
8 *Crane*	Y	Y	Y	Y	N	N	Y	Y	Y	Y	N	N	Y	Y	Y
9 Yates	N	Y	N	N	N	Y	N	N	N	N	Y	N	Y	N	Y
10 *Porter*	Y	Y	Y	Y	N	N	+	Y	Y	Y	Y	Y	Y	Y	Y
11 *Weller*	Y	Y	Y	Y	N	N	Y	Y	Y	Y	Y	Y	Y	Y	Y

House Key Votes	1	2	3	4	5	6	7	8	9	10	11	12	13	14	15
12 *Costello*	Y	Y	Y	Y	N	N	Y	Y	Y	N	Y	N	Y	Y	Y
13 *Fawell*	Y	Y	Y	Y	N	N	Y	Y	Y	Y	N	Y	Y	Y	Y
14 *Hastert*	Y	Y	Y	Y	N	N	Y	Y	Y	Y	N	N	Y	Y	Y
15 *Ewing*	Y	Y	Y	Y	N	N	Y	Y	Y	Y	N	Y	Y	Y	Y
16 *Manzullo*	Y	Y	Y	Y	N	Y	Y	Y	Y	Y	N	N	Y	Y	Y
17 Evans	N	Y	N	N	Y	Y	N	N	N	N	Y	Y	Y	N	Y
18 *LaHood*	Y	Y	Y	Y	N	Y	Y	Y	Y	Y	Y	Y	Y	Y	Y
19 Poshard	Y	Y	Y	Y	N	Y	Y	N	N	Y	N	Y	Y	Y	Y
20 Durbin	?	Y	Y	Y	N	?	N	N	Y	N	Y	Y	Y	Y	?
INDIANA															
1 Visclosky	?	Y	Y	Y	N	Y	Y	N	Y	N	Y	N	Y	Y	Y
2 *McIntosh*	Y	Y	Y	Y	Y	Y	Y	Y	Y	Y	N	?	Y	Y	Y
3 Roemer	N	Y	Y	Y	Y	N	Y	N	Y	N	Y	N	Y	Y	Y
4 *Souder*	?	N	Y	Y	Y	Y	Y	Y	Y	Y	N	?	Y	Y	Y
5 *Buyer*	Y	Y	Y	Y	N	N	Y	Y	Y	Y	N	Y	N	Y	Y
6 *Burton*	Y	Y	Y	Y	N	N	Y	Y	Y	Y	N	N	Y	Y	Y
7 *Myers*	Y	?	Y	Y	Y	N	Y	Y	Y	Y	N	N	Y	Y	?
8 *Hostettler*	Y	N	Y	Y	Y	N	+	Y	Y	Y	N	N	Y	Y	Y
9 Hamilton	Y	Y	Y	Y	Y	N	Y	Y	Y	Y	N	Y	Y	Y	Y
10 Jacobs	N	Y	Y	N	Y	Y	Y	N	N	Y	Y	Y	Y	N	N
IOWA															
1 *Leach*	Y	Y	Y	Y	N	N	Y	N	Y	Y	Y	Y	Y	Y	Y
2 *Nussle*	Y	Y	Y	Y	N	N	Y	Y	Y	Y	N	N	Y	Y	Y
3 *Lightfoot*	#	+	Y	Y	Y	N	Y	Y	Y	Y	N	Y	Y	Y	Y
4 *Ganske*	N	N	Y	Y	N	N	Y	Y	Y	Y	Y	Y	Y	Y	Y
5 *Latham*	Y	Y	Y	Y	N	Y	Y	Y	Y	Y	N	Y	Y	Y	Y
KANSAS															
1 *Roberts*	Y	Y	Y	Y	N	Y	Y	Y	Y	?	Y	N	Y	Y	Y
2 *Brownback*	Y	Y	Y	Y	N	N	Y	Y	Y	Y	N	N	Y	Y	Y
3 *Meyers*	Y	Y	Y	Y	N	N	Y	N	Y	Y	N	N	Y	Y	Y
4 *Tiahrt*	Y	N	Y	Y	Y	N	Y	Y	Y	Y	N	Y	Y	Y	N
KENTUCKY															
1 *Whitfield*	Y	Y	Y	Y	N	Y	Y	Y	Y	Y	N	Y	Y	Y	Y
2 *Lewis*	Y	Y	Y	Y	N	N	Y	Y	Y	Y	N	N	Y	Y	Y
3 Ward	Y	Y	Y	N	N	N	-	Y	N	+	N	Y	Y	Y	Y
4 *Bunning*	Y	Y	Y	Y	N	N	Y	Y	Y	Y	N	N	Y	Y	Y
5 *Rogers*	Y	Y	Y	Y	N	Y	Y	Y	Y	Y	N	Y	Y	Y	Y
6 Baesler	Y	Y	Y	N	N	N	Y	N	Y	Y	Y	Y	Y	Y	Y
LOUISIANA															
1 *Livingston*	Y	Y	Y	N	N	N	Y	Y	Y	Y	N	N	Y	Y	Y
2 Jefferson	N	Y	Y	Y	Y	N	Y	N	N	Y	N	N	Y	N	Y
3 *Tauzin*	Y	Y	Y	Y	N	N	Y	Y	Y	Y	N	Y	Y	Y	Y
4 Fields	N	Y	Y	N	Y	N	N	?	N	Y	Y	Y	?	N	Y
5 *McCrery*	Y	Y	Y	Y	N	Y	Y	Y	Y	Y	N	N	Y	Y	Y
6 *Baker*	Y	Y	Y	Y	N	N	Y	Y	Y	Y	N	N	Y	Y	?
7 *Hayes*	Y	?	Y	Y	N	Y	Y	Y	Y	Y	?	Y	Y	Y	?
MAINE															
1 *Longley*	Y	Y	Y	Y	N	N	Y	N	Y	Y	Y	N	Y	Y	Y
2 Baldacci	N	Y	Y	N	Y	Y	N	N	Y	N	Y	Y	Y	Y	Y
MARYLAND															
1 *Gilchrest*	Y	Y	Y	Y	N	N	Y	Y	Y	Y	N	Y	Y	Y	Y
2 *Ehrlich*	Y	Y	Y	Y	N	N	Y	Y	Y	Y	N	N	Y	Y	Y
3 Cardin	N	Y	Y	N	N	Y	N	Y	N	Y	?	Y	Y	Y	?
4 Wynn	N	Y	Y	N	N	Y	N	N	Y	N	Y	N	Y	Y	Y
5 Hoyer	N	Y	Y	N	N	N	N	N	Y	N	Y	Y	Y	Y	Y
6 *Bartlett*	Y	Y	Y	Y	N	N	Y	Y	Y	Y	N	N	Y	Y	Y
7 Mfume/Cummings[c]	?	Y	Y							N	Y	Y	Y	N	Y
8 *Morella*	N	Y	Y	Y	N	N	N	N	Y	Y	Y	Y	Y	Y	Y
MASSACHUSETTS															
1 Olver	N	Y	Y	N	N	Y	N	N	N	N	Y	Y	Y	N	Y
2 Neal	N	Y	Y	N	N	N	N	N	Y	N	Y	Y	Y	Y	Y
3 *Blute*	N	Y	Y	N	N	Y	N	N	Y	Y	Y	Y	Y	Y	Y
4 Frank	N	Y	N	N	N	Y	N	N	N	N	Y	Y	Y	N	?
5 Meehan	N	Y	Y	N	N	Y	N	N	N	N	Y	Y	Y	Y	Y
6 *Torkildsen*	Y	Y	Y	N	N	Y	N	N	Y	Y	Y	Y	Y	Y	Y
7 Markey	N	Y	Y	N	N	Y	N	N	N	N	Y	Y	Y	Y	Y
8 Kennedy	N	Y	Y	N	N	Y	N	N	N	N	Y	Y	Y	N	Y
9 Moakley	N	Y	Y	N	?	?	?	N	N	N	Y	Y	Y	N	Y
10 Studds	?	?	Y	N	N	Y	N	N	N	N	Y	Y	Y	N	Y
MICHIGAN															
1 Stupak	N	Y	Y	N	N	Y	N	N	Y	N	Y	Y	Y	Y	Y
2 *Hoekstra*	Y	N	Y	Y	Y	N	Y	N	Y	N	Y	N	Y	Y	N
3 *Ehlers*	Y	Y	Y	Y	Y	N	Y	N	Y	Y	N	Y	Y	Y	Y
4 *Camp*	N	Y	Y	Y	N	N	Y	Y	Y	Y	N	Y	Y	Y	Y
5 Barcia	N	Y	Y	N	N	Y	N	N	Y	+	Y	Y	Y	Y	N
6 *Upton*	Y	Y	Y	Y	N	N	Y	N	Y	Y	N	Y	Y	Y	Y
7 *Smith*	Y	Y	Y	Y	N	N	Y	N	Y	Y	N	N	Y	Y	Y
8 *Chrysler*	Y	Y	Y	Y	N	N	Y	Y	Y	Y	N	N	Y	Y	Y
9 Kildee	N	Y	Y	N	N	Y	N	Y	N	N	Y	Y	Y	Y	Y
10 Bonior	N	Y	Y	N	N	Y	N	Y	Y	N	Y	Y	Y	N	Y

House Key Votes	1	2	3	4	5	6	7	8	9	10	11	12	13	14	15
11 *Knollenberg*	Y	Y	Y	Y	Y	N	Y	Y	Y	Y	N	N	Y	Y	Y
12 Levin	N	Y	Y	N	N	Y	N	N	Y	N	Y	Y	Y	Y	Y
13 Rivers	N	Y	Y	N	Y	Y	N	N	Y	N	Y	Y	Y	Y	Y
14 Conyers	N	Y	N	N	N	Y	N	N	N	N	Y	?	Y	N	?
15 Collins	N	Y	Y	N	N	Y	N	N	N	N	Y	Y	Y	N	?
16 Dingell	N	Y	Y	Y	Y	N	N	Y	N	Y	Y	Y	Y	Y	Y
MINNESOTA															
1 *Gutknecht*	N	Y	Y	Y	Y	N	Y	Y	Y	Y	N	N	Y	Y	Y
2 Minge	N	Y	Y	N	N	Y	N	Y	Y	Y	Y	Y	Y	Y	Y
3 *Ramstad*	N	Y	Y	Y	Y	N	Y	Y	Y	Y	Y	Y	Y	Y	Y
4 Vento	N	Y	Y	N	N	Y	N	N	Y	N	Y	Y	Y	Y	Y
5 Sabo	N	Y	Y	N	N	Y	N	N	Y	N	Y	Y	Y	N	Y
6 Luther	N	Y	Y	N	N	Y	N	N	Y	N	Y	Y	Y	Y	Y
7 Peterson	N	Y	N	N	Y	N	Y	N	Y	N	Y	Y	Y	Y	Y
8 Oberstar	N	Y	Y	N	Y	Y	N	Y	N	N	Y	Y	Y	N	Y
MISSISSIPPI															
1 *Wicker*	Y	Y	Y	Y	Y	N	Y	Y	Y	Y	N	N	Y	Y	Y
2 Thompson	N	Y	Y	Y	N	Y	N	N	N	N	Y	N	Y	N	Y
3 Montgomery	Y	Y	Y	Y	Y	N	Y	Y	Y	Y	Y	N	N	Y	Y
4 *Parker*	Y	Y	Y	Y	Y	N	Y	Y	Y	Y	Y	N	N	Y	Y
5 Taylor	Y	Y	Y	N	Y	N	Y	Y	Y	N	Y	Y	N	Y	Y
MISSOURI															
1 Clay	?	Y	Y	N	N	Y	N	N	N	N	Y	Y	Y	N	Y
2 *Talent*	Y	Y	Y	Y	Y	N	Y	Y	Y	Y	N	N	Y	Y	Y
3 Gephardt	N	Y	Y	N	N	Y	N	Y	N	Y	Y	Y	Y	N	Y
4 Skelton	Y	Y	Y	Y	Y	N	Y	Y	Y	N	Y	N	Y	Y	Y
5 McCarthy	N	Y	Y	N	N	Y	N	N	Y	N	Y	Y	Y	Y	Y
6 Danner	Y	Y	Y	Y	Y	N	Y	Y	Y	Y	Y	Y	Y	Y	Y
7 *Hancock*	Y	Y	Y	Y	Y	N	Y	Y	Y	Y	N	N	Y	Y	?
8 *Emerson*[d]	Y	Y	Y	Y	Y	N	Y	Y	Y	Y	N	N			
9 Volkmer	N	Y	N	N	Y	N	N	Y	Y	N	Y	Y	?	Y	Y
MONTANA															
AL *Williams*	N	Y	N	N	Y	Y	N	N	Y	N	Y	Y	Y	N	Y
NEBRASKA															
1 *Bereuter*	Y	Y	Y	Y	N	N	Y	Y	Y	Y	N	N	Y	Y	Y
2 *Christensen*	Y	Y	Y	Y	Y	N	Y	Y	Y	Y	N	N	Y	Y	Y
3 *Barrett*	Y	Y	Y	Y	N	N	Y	Y	Y	Y	N	N	Y	Y	Y
NEVADA															
1 *Ensign*	Y	Y	Y	Y	Y	N	Y	Y	Y	Y	N	N	Y	Y	Y
2 *Vucanovich*	Y	Y	Y	Y	Y	N	Y	Y	Y	Y	N	N	Y	Y	Y
NEW HAMPSHIRE															
1 *Zeliff*	Y	Y	Y	Y	Y	N	Y	Y	Y	Y	N	N	Y	Y	Y
2 *Bass*	Y	Y	Y	Y	Y	N	Y	Y	Y	Y	N	Y	Y	Y	Y
NEW JERSEY															
1 Andrews	N	Y	Y	N	N	N	N	Y	Y	N	Y	Y	Y	Y	Y
2 *LoBiondo*	N	Y	Y	N	Y	Y	N	Y	Y	Y	Y	Y	Y	Y	Y
3 *Saxton*	Y	Y	Y	N	Y	N	Y	Y	Y	Y	N	?	?	Y	Y
4 *Smith*	Y	Y	Y	Y	Y	N	Y	Y	Y	Y	N	Y	Y	Y	Y
5 *Roukema*	?	Y	Y	Y	N	N	Y	?	N	Y	Y	Y	Y	Y	Y
6 Pallone	N	Y	Y	N	N	N	N	N	Y	N	Y	Y	Y	Y	Y
7 *Franks*	N	Y	Y	N	N	?	Y	Y	Y	Y	Y	Y	Y	Y	Y
8 *Martini*	N	Y	Y	N	N	N	Y	Y	Y	N	Y	Y	Y	Y	Y
9 Torricelli	N	Y	Y	N	N	N	Y	?	?	?	Y	Y	?	Y	Y
10 Payne	N	Y	Y	N	N	Y	N	N	N	N	Y	Y	Y	N	Y
11 *Frelinghuysen*	Y	Y	Y	N	N	N	N	Y	Y	Y	N	N	Y	Y	Y
12 *Zimmer*	N	Y	Y	N	N	N	N	Y	N	Y	Y	Y	Y	Y	Y
13 Menendez	N	Y	Y	Y	N	?	N	N	Y	N	Y	Y	Y	N	X
NEW MEXICO															
1 *Schiff*	Y	Y	Y	Y	N	Y	N	Y	Y	Y	Y	Y	Y	Y	Y
2 *Skeen*	Y	Y	Y	Y	Y	N	Y	Y	Y	Y	N	N	Y	Y	Y
3 Richardson	N	Y	Y	N	Y	N	N	P	Y	N	Y	N	Y	Y	Y
NEW YORK															
1 *Forbes*	Y	Y	Y	Y	Y	N	Y	Y	N	Y	Y	N	Y	Y	Y
2 *Lazio*	Y	Y	Y	Y	N	N	Y	Y	Y	Y	Y	N	Y	Y	Y
3 *King*	Y	Y	Y	Y	Y	N	Y	Y	Y	N	Y	?	Y	Y	Y
4 *Frisa*	Y	Y	Y	Y	Y	N	Y	Y	Y	Y	N	N	Y	Y	Y
5 Ackerman	N	Y	Y	N	N	Y	N	N	Y	N	Y	?	Y	Y	Y
6 Flake	N	+	Y	N	N	Y	N	Y	N	Y	Y	Y	?	?	?
7 Manton	N	Y	Y	N	N	N	Y	N	Y	N	Y	Y	Y	Y	Y
8 Nadler	N	Y	N	N	N	Y	-	N	Y	N	Y	Y	Y	N	N
9 Schumer	N	Y	Y	N	N	N	N	Y	N	Y	Y	Y	Y	N	Y
10 Towns	N	Y	Y	N	N	Y	N	N	N	N	Y	Y	Y	N	Y
11 Owens	N	Y	Y	N	N	Y	N	N	N	N	Y	Y	Y	N	Y
12 Velazquez	N	Y	Y	N	N	Y	N	N	N	N	Y	Y	Y	N	Y
13 *Molinari*	Y	Y	Y	Y	Y	N	N	Y	Y	?	?	N	Y	Y	Y
14 Maloney	N	Y	Y	N	N	Y	N	N	Y	N	Y	Y	Y	N	Y
15 Rangel	N	Y	Y	N	N	Y	N	N	N	N	Y	Y	?	N	Y
16 Serrano	N	Y	Y	N	N	Y	N	N	N	N	Y	Y	Y	N	Y
17 Engel	N	Y	Y	N	N	Y	N	N	Y	-	Y	Y	Y	N	Y
18 Lowey	N	Y	Y	N	N	Y	N	N	N	Y	Y	Y	Y	Y	Y
19 Kelly	Y	Y	Y	Y	Y	N	Y	N	Y	Y	Y	Y	Y	Y	Y

House Key Votes	1	2	3	4	5	6	7	8	9	10	11	12	13	14	15
20 *Gilman*	Y	Y	Y	Y	N	N	N	N	Y	N	Y	N	Y	Y	Y
21 McNulty	Y	Y	Y	N	N	N	Y	?	Y	Y	Y	Y	Y	N	Y
22 *Solomon*	Y	Y	Y	Y	N	N	N	Y	Y	Y	Y	N	Y	Y	Y
23 *Boehlert*	Y	Y	Y	N	N	N	N	N	Y	Y	Y	Y	Y	Y	Y
24 *McHugh*	Y	Y	Y	Y	Y	N	Y	Y	Y	Y	Y	?	Y	Y	Y
25 *Walsh*	Y	Y	Y	Y	Y	N	Y	Y	Y	Y	Y	N	Y	Y	Y
26 Hinchey	N	Y	N	N	Y	Y	N	N	Y	N	Y	Y	Y	N	Y
27 *Paxon*	Y	Y	Y	Y	Y	N	Y	Y	?	N	N	Y	Y	Y	Y
28 Slaughter	N	Y	Y	N	N	N	Y	N	N	Y	Y	Y	Y	N	Y
29 LaFalce	N	Y	Y	N	N	Y	N	N	N	Y	Y	Y	Y	N	?
30 *Quinn*	Y	Y	Y	Y	N	N	N	Y	Y	Y	Y	?	Y	Y	Y
31 *Houghton*	Y	Y	Y	Y	N	N	N	Y	Y	Y	Y	N	Y	Y	Y
NORTH CAROLINA															
1 Clayton	N	Y	Y	N	N	Y	N	N	N	N	Y	Y	Y	N	Y
2 *Funderburk*	Y	Y	Y	Y	Y	N	Y	Y	Y	Y	N	N	Y	Y	Y
3 *Jones*	Y	Y	Y	Y	Y	N	Y	Y	Y	Y	N	N	Y	Y	Y
4 *Heineman*	Y	Y	Y	Y	N	N	Y	Y	Y	Y	Y	N	Y	Y	?
5 *Burr*	Y	Y	Y	Y	Y	N	Y	Y	Y	Y	N	N	Y	Y	N
6 *Coble*	Y	Y	Y	Y	Y	N	Y	Y	Y	Y	N	N	Y	Y	N
7 Rose	N	?	?	Y	N	Y	N	N	N	N	N	Y	Y	Y	Y
8 Hefner	N	Y	Y	Y	Y	N	Y	Y	Y	Y	Y	N	Y	Y	Y
9 *Myrick*	Y	Y	Y	Y	Y	N	Y	Y	Y	Y	N	N	Y	Y	Y
10 *Ballenger*	Y	Y	Y	Y	Y	N	Y	Y	Y	Y	N	N	Y	Y	Y
11 *Taylor*	Y	Y	Y	Y	Y	N	Y	Y	Y	Y	N	N	Y	Y	?
12 Watt	N	Y	Y	N	Y	Y	N	N	N	N	Y	Y	Y	N	Y
NORTH DAKOTA															
AL Pomeroy	N	Y	Y	N	Y	Y	N	Y	Y	N	Y	Y	Y	Y	Y
OHIO															
1 *Chabot*	N	N	Y	Y	Y	N	Y	Y	Y	Y	N	Y	Y	Y	N
2 *Portman*	Y	Y	Y	Y	Y	N	Y	Y	Y	Y	N	Y	Y	Y	Y
3 Hall	Y	Y	Y	N	N	Y	Y	Y	Y	Y	Y	N	Y	N	Y
4 *Oxley*	Y	Y	Y	Y	N	N	Y	Y	Y	Y	N	N	Y	Y	Y
5 *Gillmor*	Y	Y	Y	Y	Y	N	Y	Y	Y	Y	?	N	Y	Y	Y
6 *Cremeans*	Y	Y	Y	Y	Y	?	Y	Y	Y	Y	Y	N	Y	Y	Y
7 *Hobson*	Y	Y	Y	Y	Y	N	Y	Y	Y	Y	Y	N	Y	Y	Y
8 *Boehner*	Y	Y	Y	Y	Y	N	Y	Y	Y	Y	N	N	Y	Y	Y
9 Kaptur	N	Y	Y	Y	N	Y	N	Y	Y	Y	Y	Y	Y	Y	N
10 *Hoke*	#	Y	Y	N	Y	N	Y	Y	Y	Y	Y	Y	Y	Y	Y
11 Stokes	N	Y	Y	X	?	#	?	X	X	N	Y	Y	N	Y	Y
12 *Kasich*	Y	Y	Y	Y	Y	N	Y	Y	Y	Y	N	N	Y	Y	Y
13 Brown	?	Y	Y	N	N	Y	N	N	N	N	Y	Y	Y	N	Y
14 Sawyer	?	Y	Y	N	N	Y	N	N	Y	N	Y	N	Y	Y	Y
15 *Pryce*	Y	Y	Y	Y	Y	N	Y	Y	Y	Y	N	N	Y	Y	Y
16 Regula	Y	Y	Y	Y	Y	N	Y	Y	Y	Y	N	Y	Y	Y	Y
17 Traficant	Y	Y	Y	N	Y	N	Y	N	N	N	Y	Y	Y	N	Y
18 *Ney*	Y	Y	Y	Y	Y	N	Y	Y	Y	Y	N	Y	Y	Y	Y
19 *LaTourette*	+	Y	Y	Y	Y	N	Y	Y	Y	Y	Y	Y	Y	Y	Y
OKLAHOMA															
1 *Largent*	Y	N	Y	Y	Y	N	Y	Y	N	Y	N	N	Y	Y	N
2 *Coburn*	Y	Y	Y	Y	?	N	Y	N	Y	N	N	Y	Y	Y	N
3 Brewster	Y	Y	Y	Y	Y	N	Y	Y	Y	Y	N	N	Y	Y	Y
4 *Watts*	Y	Y	Y	Y	X	N	Y	Y	Y	Y	N	N	Y	Y	Y
5 *Istook*	Y	Y	Y	Y	Y	N	Y	Y	Y	Y	N	N	Y	N	N
6 Lucas	Y	Y	Y	Y	Y	N	Y	Y	Y	Y	N	N	Y	Y	Y
OREGON															
1 Furse	N	Y	Y	#	N	Y	N	N	Y	N	N	Y	Y	Y	Y
2 *Cooley*	Y	Y	Y	Y	Y	Y	Y	Y	N	Y	N	N	Y	Y	N
3 Wyden/Blumenauer[e]	?	?	Y									Y	Y	N	?
4 DeFazio	X	Y	N	N	N	Y	N	N	N	N	Y	Y	Y	Y	N
5 *Bunn*	Y	Y	Y	Y	Y	N	N	Y	N	Y	Y	Y	Y	Y	Y
PENNSYLVANIA															
1 Foglietta	-	Y	Y	N	N	Y	N	Y	N	Y	N	Y	Y	N	Y
2 Fattah	N	Y	Y	N	N	Y	N	N	N	N	Y	Y	?	N	Y
3 Borski	N	Y	Y	N	N	N	N	N	N	N	Y	Y	Y	Y	Y
4 Klink	N	Y	Y	N	Y	N	Y	N	?	Y	N	Y	N	Y	N
5 *Clinger*	Y	Y	Y	Y	Y	N	Y	Y	Y	Y	N	-	Y	Y	Y
6 Holden	N	Y	Y	N	Y	N	Y	Y	Y	Y	N	Y	Y	Y	Y
7 *Weldon*	Y	Y	Y	N	N	Y	?	?	?	Y	N	Y	Y	Y	Y
8 *Greenwood*	Y	Y	Y	Y	N	N	Y	N	Y	Y	Y	Y	Y	Y	Y

[b] Newt Gingrich, R-Ga., as Speaker of the House, voted at his discretion.

[c] Kweisi Mfume, D-Md., resigned Feb. 18. He was eligible to vote on key votes 1-3. Elijah E. Cummings, D-Md., was sworn in April 25, replacing Mfume. Cummings was eligible to vote on key votes 10-15.

[d] Bill Emerson, R-Mo., died June 22. He was eligible to vote on key votes 1-12.

[e] Ron Wyden, D-Ore., resigned from the House on Feb. 5 to take a seat in the Senate. He was eligible to vote on key votes 1-3. Earl Blumenauer, D-Ore., was sworn in May 30, replacing Wyden. Blumenauer was eligible to vote on key votes 12-15.

KEY

	Democrats	*Republicans*	**Independent**

- Y Voted for ("yea")
- N Voted against ("nay")
- + Announced for
- # Paired for
- X Paired against
- − Announced against
- P Voted "present"
- C Voted "present" to avoid possible conflict of interest
- ? Did not vote or otherwise make a position known

ND Northern Democrats
SD Southern Democrats
Southern states – Ala., Ark., Fla., Ga., Ky., La., Miss., N.C., Okla., S.C., Tenn., Texas, Va.

House Key Votes	1	2	3	4	5	6	7	8	9	10	11	12	13	14	15
9 *Shuster*	?	Y	Y	Y	Y	N	Y	Y	Y	Y	N	N	Y	Y	Y
10 *McDade*	Y	Y	Y	Y	Y	Y	Y	Y	Y	Y	Y	?	?	?	Y
11 Kanjorski	N	Y	Y	N	Y	N	Y	N	Y	N	Y	Y	Y	Y	N
12 Murtha	N	Y	Y	Y	Y	N	Y	N	Y	N	Y	N	Y	Y	Y
13 *Fox*	Y	Y	Y	Y	N	N	Y	Y	Y	Y	Y	Y	Y	Y	Y
14 Coyne	N	Y	Y	N	N	Y	N	N	Y	N	Y	Y	Y	N	Y
15 McHale	N	Y	Y	N	N	N	Y	Y	Y	N	Y	Y	Y	Y	Y
16 *Walker*	Y	Y	Y	Y	Y	N	Y	Y	Y	Y	N	N	Y	Y	Y
17 *Gekas*	Y	Y	Y	Y	Y	N	Y	Y	Y	Y	N	N	Y	Y	Y
18 Doyle	N	Y	Y	N	Y	N	Y	Y	Y	N	Y	Y	Y	Y	Y
19 *Goodling*	Y	Y	Y	Y	Y	N	Y	Y	Y	Y	N	Y	Y	Y	Y
20 Mascara	N	Y	Y	N	Y	N	Y	Y	Y	N	Y	Y	Y	Y	Y
21 *English*	Y	Y	Y	Y	Y	N	Y	Y	Y	Y	Y	?	Y	Y	Y
RHODE ISLAND															
1 Kennedy	Y	Y	Y	N	N	Y	N	Y	N	Y	N	Y	N	Y	N
2 Reed	N	Y	Y	N	N	Y	N	N	Y	Y	Y	N	Y	Y	Y
SOUTH CAROLINA															
1 *Sanford*	Y	N	Y	Y	Y	N	N	Y	N	Y	N	Y	Y	Y	N
2 *Spence*	Y	Y	Y	Y	Y	N	Y	Y	Y	Y	N	N	Y	Y	Y
3 *Graham*	Y	N	Y	Y	Y	N	Y	Y	Y	Y	N	N	Y	Y	Y
4 *Inglis*	Y	Y	Y	Y	Y	N	Y	Y	Y	Y	N	N	Y	Y	Y
5 Spratt	N	Y	Y	Y	Y	N	Y	Y	Y	Y	Y	Y	Y	Y	Y
6 Clyburn	N	Y	Y	Y	N	Y	N	N	N	Y	N	Y	Y	N	Y
SOUTH DAKOTA															
AL Johnson	N	Y	N	N	Y	N	Y	Y	Y	Y	Y	Y	Y	Y	Y
TENNESSEE															
1 *Quillen*	#	?	Y	Y	Y	N	Y	Y	Y	Y	N	N	Y	Y	?
2 *Duncan*	Y	Y	Y	Y	#	N	Y	Y	Y	Y	Y	Y	Y	Y	N
3 *Wamp*	Y	Y	Y	N	Y	N	Y	Y	Y	Y	N	Y	Y	Y	Y
4 *Hilleary*	Y	Y	Y	Y	Y	N	Y	Y	Y	Y	N	Y	Y	Y	Y
5 Clement	Y	Y	Y	N	Y	N	Y	Y	Y	Y	Y	N	Y	Y	Y
6 Gordon	N	Y	Y	Y	Y	N	Y	Y	Y	Y	Y	Y	Y	Y	Y
7 *Bryant*	Y	Y	Y	Y	Y	N	Y	Y	Y	Y	N	N	Y	Y	Y
8 Tanner	?	Y	Y	Y	Y	N	Y	Y	Y	?	Y	N	Y	Y	Y
9 Ford	N	Y	Y	N	N	Y	N	?	Y	N	Y	Y	?	?	Y
TEXAS															
1 Chapman	?	?	?	N	?	?	N	N	Y	N	Y	Y	Y	Y	Y
2 Wilson[f]	?	?	Y	Y	?	?	Y	N	Y	N	Y	N	?	Y	Y
3 *Johnson, Sam*	Y	Y	Y	Y	Y	N	Y	Y	Y	Y	N	N	Y	Y	Y
4 Hall	Y	Y	Y	Y	Y	N	Y	Y	Y	Y	N	Y	Y	Y	N
5 Bryant	?	?	?	N	?	Y	N	?	?	N	Y	Y	Y	Y	Y
6 *Barton*	Y	N	Y	Y	Y	Y	N	Y	N	Y	N	N	Y	Y	N
7 *Archer*	Y	Y	Y	Y	Y	?	Y	Y	Y	Y	N	N	Y	Y	Y
8 *Fields*	?	?	Y	Y	Y	N	Y	Y	Y	Y	N	N	Y	Y	Y
9 *Stockman*	?	?	Y	Y	Y	Y	Y	N	Y	N	Y	N	Y	Y	N
10 Doggett	N	Y	Y	N	N	Y	N	N	Y	N	Y	Y	Y	Y	Y
11 Edwards	Y	Y	Y	Y	Y	N	N	Y	Y	Y	Y	N	Y	Y	Y
12 Geren	Y	Y	Y	N	Y	N	Y	Y	Y	Y	N	Y	Y	Y	Y
13 *Thornberry*	Y	Y	Y	Y	Y	N	Y	Y	Y	Y	N	N	Y	Y	Y
14 *Laughlin*	Y	Y	Y	Y	?	N	Y	Y	Y	?	N	N	?	Y	Y

House Key Votes	1	2	3	4	5	6	7	8	9	10	11	12	13	14	15
15 de la Garza	Y	Y	Y	?	?	?	N	Y	Y	N	N	N	Y	Y	Y
16 Coleman	N	Y	Y	Y	Y	Y	N	N	N	Y	N	Y	N	N	N
17 Stenholm	Y	Y	Y	Y	Y	Y	N	Y	Y	N	N	Y	N	Y	Y
18 Jackson-Lee	N	Y	Y	N	N	Y	N	Y	N	Y	N	Y	N	N	Y
19 *Combest*	Y	Y	Y	Y	Y	N	Y	Y	Y	Y	N	N	Y	Y	Y
20 Gonzalez	N	Y	Y	N	N	Y	N	N	N	Y	N	Y	N	N	Y
21 *Smith*	Y	Y	Y	Y	Y	N	Y	Y	Y	Y	Y	N	Y	Y	Y
22 *DeLay*	Y	Y	Y	Y	Y	N	Y	Y	Y	Y	N	N	Y	Y	Y
23 *Bonilla*	Y	Y	Y	Y	Y	Y	Y	Y	Y	Y	N	N	Y	Y	Y
24 Frost	Y	Y	Y	Y	Y	N	Y	N	Y	Y	N	Y	N	Y	Y
25 Bentsen	N	Y	Y	N	Y	N	N	N	Y	Y	Y	Y	Y	Y	Y
26 *Armey*	Y	Y	Y	Y	Y	N	Y	Y	Y	Y	N	N	Y	Y	Y
27 Ortiz	Y	Y	Y	Y	Y	N	Y	Y	Y	Y	N	Y	N	Y	Y
28 Tejeda	Y	Y	Y	N	Y	N	Y	Y	Y	Y	N	Y	N	Y	Y
29 Green	N	Y	Y	N	Y	N	N	N	Y	Y	N	Y	Y	Y	?
30 Johnson, E.B.	N	Y	Y	N	N	Y	N	Y	N	Y	N	−	Y	N	Y
UTAH															
1 *Hansen*	Y	Y	Y	Y	Y	N	Y	Y	Y	Y	N	N	Y	Y	Y
2 *Greene*	Y	Y	Y	Y	Y	N	N	Y	Y	Y	N	N	Y	Y	Y
3 Orton	N	Y	Y	Y	Y	N	N	Y	Y	N	Y	Y	Y	Y	Y
VERMONT															
AL **Sanders**	N	Y	N	N	Y	Y	N	N	N	N	Y	Y	N	Y	Y
VIRGINIA															
1 *Bateman*	Y	Y	Y	Y	Y	N	Y	Y	Y	Y	N	N	Y	Y	Y
2 Pickett	Y	Y	Y	N	N	Y	N	Y	N	Y	N	Y	N	Y	Y
3 Scott	Y	Y	Y	Y	N	Y	N	N	Y	N	Y	N	Y	N	Y
4 Sisisky	Y	Y	Y	?	N	Y	N	Y	Y	Y	Y	Y	Y	Y	Y
5 Payne	Y	Y	Y	Y	N	Y	N	Y	Y	Y	N	Y	N	Y	Y
6 *Goodlatte*	Y	Y	Y	Y	Y	N	Y	Y	Y	Y	N	Y	Y	Y	Y
7 *Bliley*	Y	Y	Y	Y	N	Y	Y	Y	Y	Y	N	N	Y	Y	Y
8 Moran	N	Y	Y	N	N	N	Y	Y	Y	Y	N	Y	N	Y	Y
9 Boucher	N	Y	Y	Y	Y	Y	N	Y	Y	Y	N	Y	Y	Y	?
10 *Wolf*	Y	Y	Y	Y	N	N	Y	Y	Y	Y	N	N	Y	Y	Y
11 *Davis*	Y	Y	Y	Y	Y	N	Y	Y	Y	Y	N	?	Y	Y	Y
WASHINGTON															
1 *White*	Y	Y	Y	Y	Y	N	N	Y	N	Y	N	N	Y	Y	Y
2 *Metcalf*	Y	Y	Y	N	Y	Y	Y	Y	Y	Y	N	Y	Y	Y	Y
3 *Smith*	Y	N	Y	Y	Y	Y	?	#	Y	Y	Y	Y	Y	Y	Y
4 *Hastings*	Y	Y	Y	Y	Y	N	Y	Y	Y	Y	N	N	Y	Y	Y
5 *Nethercutt*	Y	Y	Y	Y	Y	N	Y	Y	Y	Y	N	N	Y	Y	Y
6 Dicks	N	Y	Y	N	N	Y	N	N	Y	N	Y	N	Y	Y	Y
7 McDermott	N	Y	Y	N	N	Y	N	N	N	N	Y	Y	N	N	Y
8 *Dunn*	Y	Y	Y	Y	N	N	Y	Y	Y	Y	N	N	Y	Y	Y
9 *Tate*	Y	Y	Y	Y	Y	N	Y	Y	Y	Y	N	N	Y	Y	Y
WEST VIRGINIA															
1 Mollohan	N	Y	Y	Y	Y	Y	N	Y	N	Y	N	Y	N	N	Y
2 Wise	N	Y	Y	N	Y	Y	N	N	Y	N	Y	Y	Y	Y	Y
3 Rahall	N	Y	Y	N	Y	Y	N	Y	N	N	Y	N	Y	N	Y
WISCONSIN															
1 *Neumann*	Y	Y	Y	N	Y	N	Y	Y	Y	Y	Y	Y	Y	Y	N
2 *Klug*	N	Y	Y	N	Y	N	Y	Y	Y	Y	N	Y	Y	Y	N
3 *Gunderson*	N	Y	Y	Y	N	N	Y	Y	Y	Y	Y	Y	Y	?	Y
4 Kleczka	N	Y	Y	N	Y	N	N	Y	Y	Y	N	Y	Y	Y	Y
5 Barrett	N	Y	Y	N	N	Y	N	Y	Y	Y	N	Y	Y	N	Y
6 *Petri*	Y	Y	Y	N	Y	N	Y	Y	Y	Y	N	Y	Y	Y	Y
7 Obey	N	Y	Y	N	Y	N	Y	N	Y	Y	N	Y	Y	Y	Y
8 *Roth*	Y	Y	Y	N	Y	N	Y	Y	Y	Y	N	Y	Y	Y	Y
9 *Sensenbrenner*	Y	Y	Y	N	Y	N	Y	Y	Y	Y	N	Y	Y	Y	N
WYOMING															
AL *Cubin*	Y	Y	Y	Y	Y	N	Y	Y	Y	Y	N	N	Y	Y	Y

[f] Charles Wilson, D-Texas, resigned Oct. 8. He was eligible to vote on all key votes.

Congress and Its Members

Senate Membership in the 103rd Congress

Lineup as of Jan. 5, 1993: Democrats 57, Republicans 43

Alabama
Howell Heflin (D)
Richard C. Shelby (D)[a]

Alaska
Ted Stevens (R)
Frank H. Murkowski (R)

Arizona
Dennis DeConcini (D)
John McCain (R)

Arkansas
Dale Bumpers (D)
David Pryor (D)

California
Dianne Feinstein (D)
Barbara Boxer (D)

Colorado
Hank Brown (R)
Ben Nighthorse Campbell (D)

Connecticut
Christopher J. Dodd (D)
Joseph I. Lieberman (D)

Delaware
William V. Roth Jr. (R)
Joseph R. Biden Jr. (D)

Florida
Bob Graham (D)
Connie Mack (R)

Georgia
Sam Nunn (D)
Paul Coverdell (R)

Hawaii
Daniel K. Inouye (D)
Daniel K. Akaka (D)

Idaho
Larry E. Craig (R)
Dirk Kempthorne (R)

Illinois
Paul Simon (D)
Carol Moseley-Braun (D)

Indiana
Richard G. Lugar (R)
Daniel R. Coats (R)

Iowa
Charles E. Grassley (R)
Tom Harkin (D)

Kansas
Bob Dole (R)
Nancy Landon Kassebaum (R)

Kentucky
Wendell H. Ford (D)
Mitch McConnell (R)

Louisiana
J. Bennett Johnston (D)
John B. Breaux (D)

Maine
William S. Cohen (R)
George J. Mitchell (D)

Maryland
Paul S. Sarbanes (D)
Barbara A. Mikulski (D)

Massachusetts
Edward M. Kennedy (D)
John Kerry (D)

Michigan
Donald W. Riegle Jr. (D)
Carl Levin (D)

Minnesota
Dave Durenberger (R)
Paul Wellstone (D)

Mississippi
Thad Cochran (R)
Trent Lott (R)

Missouri
John C. Danforth (R)
Christopher S. Bond (R)

Montana
Max Baucus (D)
Conrad Burns (R)

Nebraska
Jim Exon (D)
Bob Kerrey (D)

Nevada
Harry Reid (D)
Richard H. Bryan (D)

New Hampshire
Robert C. Smith (R)
Judd Gregg (R)

New Jersey
Bill Bradley (D)
Frank R. Lautenberg (D)

New Mexico
Pete V. Domenici (R)
Jeff Bingaman (D)

New York
Daniel Patrick Moynihan (D)
Alfonse M. D'Amato (R)

North Carolina
Jesse Helms (R)
Lauch Faircloth (R)

North Dakota
Kent Conrad (D)
Byron L. Dorgan (D)

Ohio
John Glenn (D)
Howard M. Metzenbaum (D)

Oklahoma
Don Nickles (R)
David L. Boren (D)
  (resigned Nov. 15, 1994)
James M. Inhofe (R)
  (sworn in Nov. 17, 1994)

Oregon
Mark O. Hatfield (R)
Bob Packwood (R)

Pennsylvania
Arlen Specter (R)
Harris Wofford (D)

Rhode Island
Claiborne Pell (D)
John H. Chafee (R)

South Carolina
Ernest F. Hollings (D)
Strom Thurmond (R)

South Dakota
Larry Pressler (R)
Tom Daschle (D)

Tennessee
Jim Sasser (D)
Harlan Mathews (D)[b]
  (resigned Dec. 1, 1994)
Fred Thompson (R)
  (sworn in Dec. 9, 1994)

Texas
Phil Gramm (R)
Lloyd Bentsen (D)
  (resigned Jan. 20, 1993)
Bob Krueger (D)[c]
  (sworn in Jan. 21, 1993; resigned June 5, 1993)
Kay Bailey Hutchinson (R)
  (sworn in June 14, 1993)

Utah
Orrin G. Hatch (R)
Robert F. Bennett (R)

Vermont
Patrick J. Leahy (D)
James M. Jeffords (R)

Virginia
John W. Warner (R)
Charles S. Robb (D)

Washington
Slade Gorton (R)
Patty Murray (D)

West Virginia
Robert C. Byrd (D)
John D. Rockefeller IV (D)

Wisconsin
Herb Kohl (D)
Russell D. Feingold (D)

Wyoming
Malcolm Wallop (R)
Alan K. Simpson (R)

---

[a] Richard C. Shelby switched to the Republican Party on Nov. 9, 1994.

[b] Appointed Jan. 5, 1993, to fill the seat vacated by Al Gore, who resigned Jan. 2, 1993 to become vice president; Mathews's term expired Dec. 1, 1994, when the Tennessee secretary of state certified the Nov. 8, 1994, election of Thompson.

[c] Krueger was appointed Jan. 5, 1993, to fill the seat vacated by Bentsen when he resigned to become Treasury secretary. The interim appointment was until the remainder of the term was filled by special election. Krueger was then defeated in a June 5, 1993, runoff election.

House Membership in the 103rd Congress

Lineup as of Jan. 5, 1993: Democrats 258, Republicans 176, Independent 1

Alabama
1. Sonny Callahan (R)
2. Terry Everett (R)
3. Glen Browder (D)
4. Tom Bevill (D)
5. Robert E. "Bud" Cramer (D)
6. Spencer Bachus (R)
7. Earl F. Hilliard (D)

Alaska
AL Don Young (R)

Arizona
1. Sam Coppersmith (D)
2. Ed Pastor (D)
3. Bob Stump (R)
4. Jon Kyl (R)
5. Jim Kolbe (R)
6. Karan English (D)

Arkansas
1. Blanche Lambert (D)
2. Ray Thornton (D)
3. Tim Hutchinson (R)
4. Jay Dickey (R)

California
1. Dan Hamburg (D)
2. Wally Herger (R)
3. Vic Fazio (D)
4. John T. Doolittle (R)
5. Robert T. Matsui (D)
6. Lynn Woolsey (D)
7. George Miller (D)
8. Nancy Pelosi (D)
9. Ronald V. Dellums (D)
10. Bill Baker (R)
11. Richard W. Pombo (R)
12. Tom Lantos (D)
13. Pete Stark (D)
14. Anna G. Eshoo (D)
15. Norman Y. Mineta (D)
16. Don Edwards (D)
17. Leon E. Panetta (D)
    (resigned Jan. 21, 1993)
    Sam Farr (D)
    (sworn in June 16, 1993)
18. Gary A. Condit (D)
19. Richard H. Lehman (D)
20. Cal Dooley (D)
21. Bill Thomas (R)
22. Michael Huffington (R)
23. Elton Gallegly (R)
24. Anthony C. Beilenson (D)
25. Howard P. "Buck" McKeon (R)
26. Howard L. Berman (D)
27. Carlos J. Moorhead (R)
28. David Dreier (R)
29. Henry A. Waxman (D)
30. Xavier Becerra (D)
31. Matthew G. Martinez (D)
32. Julian C. Dixon (D)
33. Lucille Roybal-Allard (D)
34. Esteban E. Torres (D)
35. Maxine Waters (D)
36. Jane Harman (D)
37. Walter R. Tucker III (D)
38. Steve Horn (R)
39. Ed Royce (R)
40. Jerry Lewis (R)
41. Jay C. Kim (R)

42. George E. Brown Jr. (D)
43. Ken Calvert (R)
44. Al McCandless (R)
45. Dana Rohrabacher (R)
46. Robert K. Dornan (R)
47. Christopher Cox (R)
48. Ron Packard (R)
49. Lynn Schenk (D)
50. Bob Filner (D)
51. Randy "Duke" Cunningham (R)
52. Duncan Hunter (R)

Colorado
1. Patricia Schroeder (D)
2. David E. Skaggs (D)
3. Scott McInnis (R)
4. Wayne Allard (R)
5. Joel Hefley (R)
6. Dan Schaefer (R)

Connecticut
1. Barbara B. Kennelly (D)
2. Sam Gejdenson (D)
3. Rosa DeLauro (D)
4. Christopher Shays (R)
5. Gary A. Franks (R)
6. Nancy L. Johnson (R)

Delaware
AL Michael N. Castle (R)

Florida
1. Earl Hutto (D)
2. Pete Peterson (D)
3. Corrine Brown (D)
4. Tillie Fowler (R)
5. Karen L. Thurman (D)
6. Cliff Stearns (R)
7. John L. Mica (R)
8. Bill McCollum (R)
9. Michael Bilirakis (R)
10. C. W. Bill Young (R)
11. Sam M. Gibbons (D)
12. Charles T. Canady (R)
13. Dan Miller (R)
14. Porter J. Goss (R)
15. Jim Bacchus (D)
16. Tom Lewis (R)
17. Carrie P. Meek (D)
18. Ileana Ros-Lehtinen (R)
19. Harry A. Johnston (D)
20. Peter Deutsch (D)
21. Lincoln Diaz-Balart (R)
22. E. Clay Shaw Jr. (R)
23. Alcee L. Hastings (D)

Georgia
1. Jack Kingston (R)
2. Sanford D. Bishop Jr. (D)
3. Mac Collins (R)
4. John Linder (R)
5. John Lewis (D)
6. Newt Gingrich (R)
7. George "Buddy" Darden (D)
8. J. Roy Rowland (D)
9. Nathan Deal (D)
10. Don Johnson (D)
11. Cynthia A. McKinney (D)

Hawaii
1. Neil Abercrombie (D)
2. Patsy T. Mink (D)

Idaho
1. Larry LaRocco (D)
2. Michael D. Crapo (R)

Illinois
1. Bobby L. Rush (D)
2. Mel Reynolds (D)
3. William O. Lipinski (D)
4. Luis V. Gutierrez (D)
5. Dan Rostenkowski (D)
6. Henry J. Hyde (R)
7. Cardiss Collins (D)
8. Philip M. Crane (R)
9. Sidney R. Yates (D)
10. John Edward Porter (R)
11. George E. Sangmeister (D)
12. Jerry F. Costello (D)
13. Harris W. Fawell (R)
14. Dennis Hastert (R)
15. Thomas W. Ewing (R)
16. Donald Manzullo (R)
17. Lane Evans (D)
18. Robert H. Michel (R)
19. Glenn Poshard (D)
20. Richard J. Durbin (D)

Indiana
1. Peter J. Visclosky (D)
2. Philip R. Sharp (D)
3. Tim Roemer (D)
4. Jill L. Long (D)
5. Steve Buyer (R)
6. Dan Burton (R)
7. John T. Myers (R)
8. Frank McCloskey (D)
9. Lee H. Hamilton (D)
10. Andrew Jacobs Jr. (D)

Iowa
1. Jim Leach (R)
2. Jim Nussle (R)
3. Jim Ross Lightfoot (R)
4. Neal Smith (D)
5. Fred Grandy (R)

Kansas
1. Pat Roberts (R)
2. Jim Slattery (D)
3. Jan Meyers (R)
4. Dan Glickman (D)

Kentucky
1. Tom Barlow (D)
2. William H. Natcher (D)
   (died March 29, 1994)
   Ron Lewis (R)
   (sworn in May 26, 1994)
3. Romano L. Mazzoli (D)
4. Jim Bunning (R)
5. Harold Rogers (R)
6. Scotty Baesler (D)

Louisiana
1. Robert L. Livingston (R)
2. William J. Jefferson (D)
3. W. J. "Billy" Tauzin (D)
4. Cleo Fields (D)

5. Jim McCrery (R)
6. Richard H. Baker (R)
7. Jimmy Hayes (D)

Maine
1. Thomas H. Andrews (D)
2. Olympia J. Snowe (R)

Maryland
1. Wayne T. Gilchrest (R)
2. Helen Delich Bentley (R)
3. Benjamin L. Cardin (D)
4. Albert R. Wynn (D)
5. Steny H. Hoyer (D)
6. Roscoe G. Bartlett (R)
7. Kweisi Mfume (D)
8. Constance A. Morella (R)

Massachusetts
1. John W. Olver (D)
2. Richard E. Neal (D)
3. Peter I. Blute (R)
4. Barney Frank (D)
5. Martin T. Meehan (D)
6. Peter G. Torkildsen (R)
7. Edward J. Markey (D)
8. Joseph P. Kennedy II (D)
9. Joe Moakley (D)
10. Gerry E. Studds (D)

Michigan
1. Bart Stupak (D)
2. Peter Hoekstra (R)
3. Paul B. Henry (R)
   (died June 22, 1993)
   Vernon J. Ehlers (R)
   (sworn in Jan. 1, 1994)
4. Dave Camp (R)
5. James A. Barcia (D)
6. Fred Upton (R)
7. Nick Smith (R)
8. Bob Carr (D)
9. Dale E. Kildee (D)
10. David E. Bonior (D)
11. Joe Knollenberg (R)
12. Sander M. Levin (D)
13. William D Ford (D)
14. John Conyers Jr. (D)
15. Barbara-Rose Collins (D)
16. John D. Dingell (D)

Minnesota
1. Timothy J. Penny (D)
2. David Minge (D)
3. Jim Ramstad (R)
4. Bruce F. Vento (D)
5. Martin Olav Sabo (D)
6. Rod Grams (R)
7. Collin C. Peterson (D)
8. James L. Oberstar (D)

Mississippi
1. Jamie L. Whitten (D)
2. Mike Espy (D)
   (resigned Jan. 22, 1993)
   Bennie Thompson (D)
   (sworn in April 20, 1993)
3. G. V. "Sonny" Montgomery (D)
4. Mike Parker (D)
5. Gene Taylor (D)

Missouri
1. William L. Clay (D)
2. James M. Talent (R)
3. Richard A. Gephardt (D)
4. Ike Skelton (D)
5. Alan Wheat (D)
6. Pat Danner (D)
7. Mel Hancock (R)
8. Bill Emerson (R)
9. Harold L. Volkmer (D)

Montana
AL   Pat Williams (D)

Nebraska
1. Doug Bereuter (R)
2. Peter Hoagland (D)
3. Bill Barrett (R)

Nevada
1. James Bilbray (D)
2. Barbara F. Vucanovich (R)

New Hampshire
1. Bill Zeliff (R)
2. Dick Swett (D)

New Jersey
1. Robert E. Andrews (D)
2. William J. Hughes (D)
3. H. James Saxton (R)
4. Christopher H. Smith (R)
5. Marge Roukema (R)
6. Frank Pallone Jr. (D)
7. Bob Franks (R)
8. Herb Klein (D)
9. Robert G. Torricelli (D)
10. Donald M. Payne (D)
11. Dean A. Gallo (R)
      (died June 22, 1996)
12. Dick Zimmer (R)
13. Robert Menendez (D)

New Mexico
1. Steven H. Schiff (R)
2. Joe Skeen (R)
3. Bill Richardson (D)

New York
1. George J. Hochbrueckner (D)
2. Rick A. Lazio (R)
3. Peter T. King (R)
4. David A. Levy (R)
5. Gary L. Ackerman (D)
6. Floyd H. Flake (D)
7. Thomas J. Manton (D)
8. Jerrold Nadler (D)
9. Charles E. Schumer (D)
10. Edolphus Towns (D)
11. Major R. Owens (D)
12. Nydia M. Velázquez (D)
13. Susan Molinari (R)
14. Carolyn B. Maloney (D)
15. Charles B. Rangel (D)
16. Jose E. Serrano (D)
17. Eliot L. Engel (D)
18. Nita M. Lowey (D)
19. Hamilton Fish Jr. (R)
20. Benjamin A. Gilman (R)
21. Michael R. McNulty (D)
22. Gerald B. H. Solomon (R)
23. Sherwood Boehlert (R)
24. John M. McHugh (R)
25. James T. Walsh (R)
26. Maurice D. Hinchey (D)
27. Bill Paxon (R)
28. Louise M. Slaughter (D)
29. John J. LaFalce (D)
30. Jack Quinn (R)
31. Amo Houghton (R)

North Carolina
1. Eva Clayton (D)
2. Tim Valentine (D)
3. H. Martin Lancaster (D)
4. David Price (D)
5. Stephen L. Neal (D)
6. Howard Coble (R)
7. Charlie Rose (D)
8. W. G. "Bill" Hefner (D)
9. Alex McMillan (R)
10. Cass Ballenger (R)
11. Charles H. Taylor (R)
12. Melvin Watt (D)

North Dakota
AL   Earl Pomeroy (D)

Ohio
1. David Mann (D)
2. Bill Gradison (R)
      (resigned Jan. 31, 1993)
      Rob Portman (R)
      (sworn in May 3, 1993)
3. Tony P. Hall (D)
4. Michael G. Oxley (R)
5. Paul E. Gillmor (R)
6. Ted Strickland (D)
7. David L. Hobson (R)
8. John A. Boehner (R)
9. Marcy Kaptur (D)
10. Martin R. Hoke (R)
11. Louis Stokes (D)
12. John R. Kasich (R)
13. Sherrod Brown (D)
14. Tom Sawyer (D)
15. Deborah Pryce (R)
16. Ralph Regula (R)
17. James A. Traficant Jr. (D)
18. Douglas Applegate (D)
19. Eric D. Fingerhut (D)

Oklahoma
1. James M. Inhofe (R)
      (resigned Nov. 15, 1994)
      Steve Largent (R)[a]
      (sworn in Nov. 29, 1994)
2. Mike Synar (R)
3. Bill Brewster (D)
4. Dave McCurdy (D)
5. Ernest Jim Istook Jr. (R)
6. Glenn English (R)
      (died Jan. 7, 1994)
      Frank D. Lucas (R)
      (sworn in May 17, 1994)

Oregon
1. Elizabeth Furse (D)
2. Bob Smith (R)
3. Ron Wyden (D)
4. Peter A. DeFazio (D)
5. Mike Kopetski (D)

Pennsylvania
1. Thomas M. Foglietta (D)
2. Lucien E. Blackwell (D)
3. Robert A. Borski (D)
4. Ron Klink (D)
5. William F. Clinger (R)
6. Tim Holden (D)
7. Curt Weldon (R)
8. James C. Greenwood (R)
9. Bud Shuster (R)
10. Joseph M. McDade (R)
11. Paul E. Kanjorski (D)
12. John P. Murtha (D)
13. Marjorie Margolies-
      Mezvinsky (D)
14. William J. Coyne (D)
15. Paul McHale (D)
16. Robert S. Walker (R)
17. George W. Gekas (R)
18. Rick Santorum (R)
19. Bill Goodling (R)
20. Austin J. Murphy (D)
21. Tom Ridge (R)

Rhode Island
1. Ronald K. Machtley (R)
2. Jack Reed (D)

South Carolina
1. Arthur Ravenel Jr. (R)
2. Floyd D. Spence (R)
3. Butler Derrick (R)
4. Bob Inglis (R)
5. John M. Spratt Jr. (D)
6. James E. Clyburn (D)

South Dakota
AL   Tim Johnson (D)

Tennessee
1. James H. Quillen (R)
2. John J. "Jimmy"
      Duncan Jr. (R)
3. Marilyn Lloyd (D)
4. Jim Cooper (D)
5. Bob Clement (D)
6. Bart Gordon (D)
7. Don Sundquist (R)
8. John Tanner (D)
9. Harold E. Ford (D)

Texas
1. Jim Chapman (D)
2. Charles Wilson (D)
3. Sam Johnson (R)
4. Ralph M. Hall (D)
5. John Bryant (D)
6. Joe L. Barton (R)
7. Bill Archer (R)
8. Jack Fields (R)
9. Jack Brooks (D)
10. J. J. Pickle (D)
11. Chet Edwards (D)
12. Pete Geren (D)
13. Bill Sarpalius (D)
14. Greg Laughlin (D)
15. E. "Kika" de la Garza (D)
16. Ronald D. Coleman (D)
17. Charles W. Stenholm (D)
18. Craig Washington (D)
19. Larry Combest (R)
20. Henry B. Gonzalez (D)
21. Lamar Smith (R)
22. Tom DeLay (R)
23. Henry Bonilla (R)
24. Martin Frost (D)
25. Michael A. Andrews (D)
26. Dick Armey (R)
27. Solomon P. Ortiz (D)
28. Frank Tejeda (D)
29. Gene Green (D)
30. Eddie Bernice Johnson (D)

Utah
1. James V. Hansen (R)
2. Karen Shepherd (D)
3. Bill Orton (D)

Vermont
AL   Bernard Sanders (I)

Virginia
1. Herbert H. Bateman (R)
2. Owen B. Pickett (D)
3. Robert C. Scott (D)
4. Norman Sisisky (D)
5. Lewis F. Payne Jr. (D)
6. Robert W. Goodlatte (R)
7. Thomas J. Bliley Jr. (R)
8. James P. Moran (D)
9. Rick Boucher (D)
10. Frank R. Wolf (R)
11. Leslie L. Byrne (D)

Washington
1. Maria Cantwell (D)
2. Al Smith (D)
3. Jolene Unsoeld (D)
4. Jay Inslee (D)
5. Thomas S. Foley (D)
6. Norm Dicks (D)
7. Jim McDermott (D)
8. Jennifer Dunn (R)
9. Mike Kreidler (D)

West Virginia
1. Alan B. Mollohan (D)
2. Bob Wise (D)
3. Nick J. Rahall II (D)

Wisconsin
1. Les Aspin (D)
      (resigned Jan. 20, 1993)
      Peter W. Barca (D)
      (sworn in June 8, 1993)
2. Scott L. Klug (R)
3. Steve Gunderson (R)
4. Gerald D. Kleczka (D)
5. Thomas M. Barrett (D)
6. Tom Petri (R)
7. David R. Obey (D)
8. Toby Roth (R)
9. F. James Sensenbrenner Jr. (R)

Wyoming
AL   Craig Thomas (R)

NOTE: Members of the 103rd Congress also included delegates Ron de Lugo, D-Virgin Islands; Eni F. H. Faleomavaega, D-American Samoa; Eleanor Holmes Norton, D-D.C.; Robert Underwood, D-Guam; and resident commissioner Carlos Romero-Barcelo, D-Puerto Rico.

[a] Largent was elected Nov. 8, 1994, to complete the remainder of Inhofe's term and to the 104th Congress.

103rd Congress

Member/Party	Died	Resigned	Switched parties	Successor/Party	Elected	Sworn in
Senate						
Lloyd Bentsen, D-Texas		1/20/93		Bob Krueger, D	1/5/93[a]	1/21/93
Bob Krueger, D-Texas		6/5/93[b]		Kay Bailey Hutchinson, R	6/5/93	6/14/93
Richard C. Shelby, D-Ala.			R, 11/9/94			
David L. Boren, D-Okla.		11/15/94		James M. Inhofe, R	11/8/94[c]	11/17/94
Harlan Mathews, D-Tenn.		12/1/94[d]		Fred Thompson, R	11/8/94	12/9/94
House						
Les Aspin, D-Wis.		1/20/93		Peter W. Barca, D	5/4/93	6/8/93
Leon E. Panetta, D-Calif.		1/21/93		Sam Farr, D	6/8/93	6/16/93
Mike Espy, D-Miss.		1/22/93		Bennie Thompson, D	4/13/93	4/20/93
Bill Gradison, R-Ohio		1/31/93		Rob Portman, R	5/4/93	5/5/93
Paul B. Henry, R-Mich.	7/31/93			Vernon J. Ehlers, R	12/7/93	1/25/94
Glenn English, D-Okla.		1/7/94		Frank D. Lucas, R	5/10/94	5/17/94
William H. Natcher, D-Ky.	3/29/94			Ron Lewis, R	5/24/94	5/26/94
Dean A. Gallo, R-N.J.	11/6/94					
James M. Inhofe, D-Okla.		11/15/94[c]		Steve Largent, R	11/8/94[e]	11/29/94

104th Congress

Member/Party	Died	Resigned	Switched parties	Successor/Party	Elected	Sworn in
Senate						
Ben Nighthorse Campbell, D-Colo.			R, 3/3/95			
Bob Packwood, D-Ore.		10/1/95		Ron Wyden, D	1/30/96[f]	2/6/96
Bob Dole, R-Kan.		6/11/96		Sheila Frahm, R	5/24/96[g]	6/11/96
Sheila Frahm, R-Kan.		11/27/96[g]		Sam Brownback, R	11/5/96[h]	11/27/96
House						
Nathan Deal, D-Ga.			R, 4/10/95			
Greg Laughlin, D-Texas			R, 6/26/95			
W.J. "Billy" Tauzin, D-La.			R, 8/6/95			
Mel Reynolds, D-Ill.		10/1/95		Jesse L. Jackson Jr., D	12/12/95	12/14/95
Norman Y. Mineta, D-Calif.		10/10/95		Tom Campbell, R	12/12/95	12/15/95
Mike Parker, D-Miss.			R, 11/10/95			
Jimmy Hayes, D-La.			R, 12/1/95			
Walter R. Tucker III, D-Calif.		12/15/95		Juanita Millender-McDonald, D	3/26/96	4/16/96
Ron Wyden, D-Ore.		2/5/96		Earl Blumenauer, D	5/21/96	5/30/96
Kweisi Mfume, D-Md.		2/18/96		Elijah E. Cummings, D	4/16/96	4/25/96
Bill Emerson, R-Mo.	6/22/96			Jo Ann Emerson, R	11/5/96[i]	
Charles Wilson, D-Texas		10/8/96				
Sam Brownback, R-Kan.		11/6/96		Jim Ryun, R	11/5/96	11/27/96

[a] Appointed Jan. 5, 1993, to fill the seat vacated by Bentsen; the interim appointment was until the remainder of the term was filled by special election.
[b] Lost a June 5, 1993, runoff election to Hutchinson.
[c] Elected Nov. 8, 1994, to complete the remainder of Boren's term.
[d] Appointed Jan. 5, 1993, to fill the seat vacated by Al Gore, who resigned Jan. 2, 1993; Mathews's term expired Dec. 1, 1994, when the Tennessee secretary of state certified the Nov. 8, 1994, election of Thompson.
[e] Elected Nov. 8, 1994, to complete the remainder of Inhofe's term and to the 104th Congress.
[f] Elected Jan. 30, 1996, in a special election to complete the remainder of Packwood's term.
[g] Appointed May 24, 1996, to the seat vacated by Dole; Frahm was defeated in the Republican primary Aug. 6, 1996.
[h] Elected Nov. 5, 1996, to complete the remainder of Dole's term.
[i] Elected Nov. 5, 1996, to complete the remainder of her husband's term and to the 105th Congress.

Senate Membership in the 104th Congress

Lineup as of Jan. 4, 1995: Republicans 53, Democrats 47

Alabama
Howell Heflin (D)
Richard C. Shelby (R)

Alaska
Ted Stevens (R)
Frank H. Murkowski (R)

Arizona
John McCain (R)
Jon Kyl (R)

Arkansas
Dale Bumpers (D)
David Pryor (D)

California
Dianne Feinstein (D)
Barbara Boxer (D)

Colorado
Hank Brown (R)
Ben Nighthorse Campbell (D)[a]

Connecticut
Christopher J. Dodd (D)
Joseph I. Lieberman (D)

Delaware
William V. Roth Jr. (R)
Joseph R. Biden Jr. (D)

Florida
Bob Graham (D)
Connie Mack (R)

Georgia
Sam Nunn (D)
Paul Coverdell (R)

Hawaii
Daniel K. Inouye (D)
Daniel K. Akaka (D)

Idaho
Larry E. Craig (R)
Dirk Kempthorne (R)

Illinois
Paul Simon (D)
Carol Moseley-Braun (D)

Indiana
Richard G. Lugar (R)
Daniel R. Coats (R)

Iowa
Charles E. Grassley (R)
Tom Harkin (D)

Kansas
Nancy Landon Kassebaum (R)
Bob Dole (R)
  (resigned June 11, 1996)
Sheila Frahm (R)[b]
  *(sworn in June 11, 1996;
    resigned Nov. 27, 1996)*
Sam Brownback (R)
  (sworn in Nov. 27, 1996)

Kentucky
Wendell H. Ford (D)
Mitch McConnell (R)

Louisiana
J. Bennett Johnston (D)
John B. Breaux (D)

Maine
William S. Cohen (R)
Olympia J. Snowe (R)

Maryland
Paul S. Sarbanes (D)
Barbara A. Mikulski (D)

Massachusetts
Edward M. Kennedy (D)
John Kerry (D)

Michigan
Carl Levin (D)
Spencer Abraham (R)

Minnesota
Paul Wellstone (D)
Rod Grams (R)

Mississippi
Thad Cochran (R)
Trent Lott (R)

Missouri
Christopher S. Bond (R)
John Ashcroft (R)

Montana
Max Baucus (D)
Conrad Burns (R)

Nebraska
Jim Exon (D)
Bob Kerrey (D)

Nevada
Harry Reid (D)
Richard H. Bryan (D)

New Hampshire
Robert C. Smith (R)
Judd Gregg (R)

New Jersey
Bill Bradley (D)
Frank R. Lautenberg (D)

New Mexico
Pete V. Domenici (R)
Jeff Bingaman (D)

New York
Daniel Patrick Moynihan (D)
Alfonse M. D'Amato (R)

North Carolina
Jesse Helms (R)
Lauch Faircloth (R)

North Dakota
Kent Conrad (D)
Byron L. Dorgan (D)

Ohio
John Glenn (D)
Mike DeWine (R)

Oklahoma
Don Nickles (R)
James M. Inhofe (R)

Oregon
Mark O. Hatfield (R)
Bob Packwood (R)
  (resigned Oct. 1, 1995)
Ron Wyden (D)
  (sworn in Feb. 6, 1996)

Pennsylvania
Arlen Specter (R)
Rick Santorum (R)

Rhode Island
Claiborne Pell (D)
John H. Chafee (R)

South Carolina
Strom Thurmond (R)
Ernest F. Hollings (D)

South Dakota
Larry Pressler (R)
Tom Daschle (D)

Tennessee
Fred Thompson (R)
Bill Frist (R)

Texas
Phil Gramm (R)
Kay Bailey Hutchison (R)

Utah
Orrin G. Hatch (R)
Robert F. Bennett (R)

Vermont
Patrick J. Leahy (D)
James M. Jeffords (R)

Virginia
John W. Warner (R)
Charles S. Robb (D)

Washington
Slade Gorton (R)
Patty Murray (D)

West Virginia
Robert C. Byrd (D)
John D. Rockefeller IV (D)

Wisconsin
Herb Kohl (D)
Russell D. Feingold (D)

Wyoming
Alan K. Simpson (R)
Craig Thomas (R)

[a] Campbell switched to the Republican Party on March 3, 1995.
[b] Frahm was appointed to the seat vacated by Dole when he resigned. Frahm was then defeated in the Republican primary in Kansas on Aug. 6, 1996. She resigned Nov. 27, 1996, to allow Brownback to be sworn in early.

House Membership in the 104th Congress

Lineup as of Jan. 4, 1995: Republicans 230, Democrats 204, Independent 1

Alabama
1. Sonny Callahan (R)
2. Terry Everett (R)
3. Glen Browder (D)
4. Tom Bevill (D)
5. Robert E. "Bud" Cramer (D)
6. Spencer Bachus (R)
7. Earl F. Hilliard (D)

Alaska
AL Don Young (R)

Arizona
1. Matt Salmon (R)
2. Ed Pastor (D)
3. Bob Stump (R)
4. John Shadegg (R)
5. Jim Kolbe (R)
6. J. D. Hayworth (R)

Arkansas
1. Blanche Lambert Lincoln (D)
2. Ray Thornton (D)
3. Tim Hutchinson (R)
4. Jay Dickey (R)

California
1. Frank Riggs (R)
2. Wally Herger (R)
3. Vic Fazio (D)
4. John T. Doolittle (R)
5. Robert T. Matsui (D)
6. Lynn Woolsey (D)
7. George Miller (D)
8. Nancy Pelosi (D)
9. Ronald V. Dellums (D)
10. Bill Baker (R)
11. Richard W. Pombo (R)
12. Tom Lantos (D)
13. Pete Stark (D)
14. Anna G. Eshoo (D)
15. Norman Y. Mineta (D)
      (resigned Oct. 10, 1995)
    Tom Campbell (R)
      (sworn in Dec. 15, 1995)
16. Zoe Lofgren (D)
17. Sam Farr (D)
18. Gary A. Condit (D)
19. George P. Radanovich (R)
20. Cal Dooley (D)
21. Bill Thomas (R)
22. Andrea Seastrand (R)
23. Elton Gallegly (R)
24. Anthony C. Beilenson (D)
25. Howard P. "Buck" McKeon (R)
26. Howard L. Berman (D)
27. Carlos J. Moorhead (R)
28. David Dreier (R)
29. Henry A. Waxman (D)
30. Xavier Becerra (D)
31. Matthew G. Martinez (D)
32. Julian C. Dixon (D)
33. Lucille Roybal-Allard (D)
34. Esteban E. Torres (D)
35. Maxine Waters (D)
36. Jane Harman (D)
37. Walter R. Tucker III (D)
      (resigned Dec. 15, 1995)
    Juanita Millender-
    McDonald (D)
      (sworn in April 16, 1996)

38. Steve Horn (R)
39. Ed Royce (R)
40. Jerry Lewis (R)
41. Jay C. Kim (R)
42. George E. Brown Jr. (D)
43. Ken Calvert (R)
44. Sonny Bono (R)
45. Dana Rohrabacher (R)
46. Robert K. Dornan (R)
47. Christopher Cox (R)
48. Ron Packard (R)
49. Brian P. Bilbray (R)
50. Bob Filner (D)
51. Randy "Duke"
      Cunningham (R)
52. Duncan Hunter (R)

Colorado
1. Patricia Schroeder (D)
2. David E. Skaggs (D)
3. Scott McInnis (R)
4. Wayne Allard (R)
5. Joel Hefley (R)
6. Dan Schaefer (R)

Connecticut
1. Barbara B. Kennelly (D)
2. Sam Gejdenson (D)
3. Rosa DeLauro (D)
4. Christopher Shays (R)
5. Gary A. Franks (R)
6. Nancy L. Johnson (R)

Delaware
AL Michael N. Castle (R)

Florida
1. Joe Scarborough (R)
2. Pete Peterson (D)
3. Corrine Brown (D)
4. Tillie Fowler (R)
5. Karen L. Thurman (D)
6. Cliff Stearns (R)
7. John L. Mica (R)
8. Bill McCollum (R)
9. Michael Bilirakis (R)
10. C. W. Bill Young (R)
11. Sam M. Gibbons (D)
12. Charles T. Canady (R)
13. Dan Miller (R)
14. Porter J. Goss (R)
15. Dave Weldon (R)
16. Mark Foley (R)
17. Carrie P. Meek (D)
18. Ileana Ros-Lehtinen (R)
19. Harry A. Johnston (D)
20. Peter Deutsch (D)
21. Lincoln Diaz-Balart (R)
22. E. Clay Shaw Jr. (R)
23. Alcee L. Hastings (D)

Georgia
1. Jack Kingston (R)
2. Sanford D. Bishop Jr. (D)
3. Mac Collins (R)
4. John Linder (R)
5. John Lewis (D)
6. Newt Gingrich (R)
7. Bob Barr (R)
8. Saxby Chambliss (R)
9. Nathan Deal (D)[a]

10. Charlie Norwood (R)
11. Cynthia A. McKinney (D)

Hawaii
1. Neil Abercrombie (D)
2. Patsy T. Mink (D)

Idaho
1. Helen Chenoweth (R)
2. Michael D. Crapo (R)

Illinois
1. Bobby L. Rush (D)
2. Mel Reynolds (D)
      (resigned Oct. 1, 1995)
    Jesse L. Jackson Jr.
      (sworn in Dec. 14, 1995)
3. William O. Lipinski (D)
4. Luis V. Gutierrez (D)
5. Michael Patrick Flanagan (R)
6. Henry J. Hyde (R)
7. Cardiss Collins (D)
8. Philip M. Crane (R)
9. Sidney R. Yates (D)
10. John Edward Porter (R)
11. Jerry Weller (R)
12. Jerry F. Costello (D)
13. Harris W. Fawell (R)
14. Dennis Hastert (R)
15. Thomas W. Ewing (R)
16. Donald Manzullo (R)
17. Lane Evans (D)
18. Ray LaHood (R)
19. Glenn Poshard (D)
20. Richard J. Durbin (D)

Indiana
1. Peter J. Visclosky (D)
2. David M. McIntosh (R)
3. Tim Roemer (D)
4. Mark E. Souder (R)
5. Steve Buyer (R)
6. Dan Burton (R)
7. John T. Myers (R)
8. John Hostettler (R)
9. Lee H. Hamilton (D)
10. Andrew Jacobs Jr. (D)

Iowa
1. Jim Leach (R)
2. Jim Nussle (R)
3. Jim Ross Lightfoot (R)
4. Greg Ganske (R)
5. Tom Latham (R)

Kansas
1. Pat Roberts (R)
2. Sam Brownback (R)
      (resigned Nov. 6, 1996)
    Jim Ryun
      (sworn in Nov. 27, 1996)
3. Jan Meyers (R)
4. Todd Tiahrt (R)

Kentucky
1. Edward Whitfield (R)
2. Ron Lewis (R)
3. Mike Ward (D)
4. Jim Bunning (R)
5. Harold Rogers (R)
6. Scotty Baesler (D)

Louisiana
1. Robert L. Livingston (R)
2. William J. Jefferson (D)
3. W. J. "Billy" Tauzin (D)[b]
4. Cleo Fields (D)
5. Jim McCrery (R)
6. Richard H. Baker (R)
7. Jimmy Hayes (D)[c]

Maine
1. James B. Longley Jr. (R)
2. John Baldacci (D)

Maryland
1. Wayne T. Gilchrest (R)
2. Robert L. Ehrlich Jr. (R)
3. Benjamin L. Cardin (D)
4. Albert R. Wynn (D)
5. Steny H. Hoyer (D)
6. Roscoe G. Bartlett (R)
7. Kweisi Mfume (D)
      (resigned Feb. 18, 1996)
    Elijah E. Cummings (D)
      (sworn in April 25, 1996)
8. Constance A. Morella (R)

Massachusetts
1. John W. Olver (D)
2. Richard E. Neal (D)
3. Peter I. Blute (R)
4. Barney Frank (D)
5. Martin T. Meehan (D)
6. Peter G. Torkildsen (R)
7. Edward J. Markey (D)
8. Joseph P. Kennedy II (D)
9. Joe Moakley (D)
10. Gerry E. Studds (D)

Michigan
1. Bart Stupak (D)
2. Peter Hoekstra (R)
3. Vernon J. Ehlers (R)
4. Dave Camp (R)
5. James A. Barcia (D)
6. Fred Upton (R)
7. Nick Smith (R)
8. Dick Chrysler (R)
9. Dale E. Kildee (D)
10. David E. Bonior (D)
11. Joe Knollenberg (R)
12. Sander M. Levin (D)
13. Lynn Rivers (D)
14. John Conyers Jr. (D)
15. Barbara-Rose Collins (D)
16. John D. Dingell (D)

Minnesota
1. Gil Gutknecht (R)
2. David Minge (D)
3. Jim Ramstad (R)
4. Bruce F. Vento (D)
5. Martin Olav Sabo (D)
6. William P. "Bill" Luther (D)
7. Collin C. Peterson (D)
8. James L. Oberstar (D)

Mississippi
1. Roger Wicker (R)
2. Bennie Thompson (D)
3. G. V. "Sonny"
      Montgomery (D)

4. Mike Parker (D)[d]
5. Gene Taylor (D)

Missouri
1. William L. Clay (D)
2. James M. Talent (R)
3. Richard A. Gephardt (D)
4. Ike Skelton (D)
5. Karen McCarthy (D)
6. Pat Danner (D)
7. Mel Hancock (R)
8. Bill Emerson (R)[e]
   (died June 22, 1996)
9. Harold L. Volkmer (D)

Montana
AL Pat Williams (D)

Nebraska
1. Doug Bereuter (R)
2. Jon Christensen (R)
3. Bill Barrett (R)

Nevada
1. John Ensign (R)
2. Barbara F. Vucanovich (R)

New Hampshire
1. Bill Zeliff (R)
2. Charles Bass (R)

New Jersey
1. Robert E. Andrews (D)
2. Frank A. LoBiondo (R)
3. H. James Saxton (R)
4. Christopher H. Smith (R)
5. Marge Roukema (R)
6. Frank Pallone Jr. (D)
7. Bob Franks (R)
8. Bill Martini (R)
9. Robert G. Torricelli (D)
10. Donald M. Payne (D)
11. Rodney Frelinghuysen (R)
12. Dick Zimmer (R)
13. Robert Menendez (D)

New Mexico
1. Steven H. Schiff (R)
2. Joe Skeen (R)
3. Bill Richardson (D)

New York
1. Michael P. Forbes (R)
2. Rick A. Lazio (R)
3. Peter T. King (R)
4. Daniel Frisa (R)
5. Gary L. Ackerman (D)
6. Floyd H. Flake (D)
7. Thomas J. Manton (D)
8. Jerrold Nadler (D)
9. Charles E. Schumer (D)
10. Edolphus Towns (D)
11. Major R. Owens (D)
12. Nydia M. Velázquez (D)
13. Susan Molinari (R)
14. Carolyn B. Maloney (D)
15. Charles B. Rangel (D)
16. Jose E. Serrano (D)
17. Eliot L. Engel (D)
18. Nita M. Lowey (D)
19. Sue W. Kelly (R)
20. Benjamin A. Gilman (R)
21. Michael R. McNulty (D)
22. Gerald B. H. Solomon (R)
23. Sherwood Boehlert (R)
24. John M. McHugh (R)
25. James T. Walsh (R)
26. Maurice D. Hinchey (D)
27. Bill Paxon (R)
28. Louise M. Slaughter (D)
29. John J. LaFalce (D)
30. Jack Quinn (R)
31. Amo Houghton (R)

North Carolina
1. Eva Clayton (D)
2. David Funderburk (R)
3. Walter B. Jones Jr. (R)
4. Fred Heineman (R)
5. Richard M. Burr (R)
6. Howard Coble (R)
7. Charlie Rose (D)
8. W. G. "Bill" Hefner (D)
9. Sue Myrick (R)
10. Cass Ballenger (R)
11. Charles H. Taylor (R)
12. Melvin Watt (D)

North Dakota
AL Earl Pomeroy (D)

Ohio
1. Steve Chabot (R)
2. Rob Portman (R)
3. Tony P. Hall (D)
4. Michael G. Oxley (R)
5. Paul E. Gillmor (R)
6. Frank A. Cremeans (R)
7. David L. Hobson (R)
8. John A. Boehner (R)
9. Marcy Kaptur (D)
10. Martin R. Hoke (R)
11. Louis Stokes (D)
12. John R. Kasich (R)
13. Sherrod Brown (D)
14. Tom Sawyer (D)
15. Deborah Pryce (R)
16. Ralph Regula (R)
17. James A. Traficant Jr. (D)
18. Bob Ney (R)
19. Steven C. LaTourette (R)

Oklahoma
1. Steve Largent (R)
2. Tom Coburn (R)
3. Bill Brewster (D)
4. J.C. Watts (R)
5. Ernest Jim Istook Jr. (R)
6. Frank D. Lucas (R)

Oregon
1. Elizabeth Furse (D)
2. Wes Cooley (R)
3. Ron Wyden (D)
   (resigned Feb. 5, 1996)
   Earl Blumenauer (D)
   (sworn in May 30, 1996)
4. Peter A. DeFazio (D)
5. Jim Bunn (R)

Pennsylvania
1. Thomas M. Foglietta (D)
2. Chaka Fattah (D)
3. Robert A. Borski (D)
4. Ron Klink (D)
5. William F. Clinger (R)
6. Tim Holden (D)
7. Curt Weldon (R)
8. James C. Greenwood (R)
9. Bud Shuster (R)
10. Joseph M. McDade (R)
11. Paul E. Kanjorski (D)
12. John P. Murtha (D)
13. Jon D. Fox (R)
14. William J. Coyne (D)
15. Paul McHale (D)
16. Robert S. Walker (R)
17. George W. Gekas (R)
18. Mike Doyle (D)
19. Bill Goodling (R)
20. Frank R. Mascara (D)
21. Phil English (R)

Rhode Island
1. Patrick J. Kennedy (D)
2. Jack Reed (D)

South Carolina
1. Mark Sanford (R)
2. Floyd D. Spence (R)
3. Lindsey Graham (R)
4. Bob Inglis (R)
5. John M. Spratt Jr. (D)
6. James E. Clyburn (D)

South Dakota
AL Tim Johnson (D)

Tennessee
1. James H. Quillen (R)
2. John J. "Jimmy" Duncan Jr. (R)
3. Zach Wamp (R)
4. Van Hilleary (R)
5. Bob Clement (D)
6. Bart Gordon (D)
7. Ed Bryant (R)
8. John Tanner (D)
9. Harold E. Ford (D)

Texas
1. Jim Chapman (D)
2. Charles Wilson (D)
   (resigned Oct. 8, 1996)
3. Sam Johnson (R)
4. Ralph M. Hall (D)
5. John Bryant (D)
6. Joe L. Barton (R)
7. Bill Archer (R)
8. Jack Fields (R)
9. Steve Stockman (R)
10. Lloyd Doggett (D)
11. Chet Edwards (D)
12. Pete Geren (D)
13. William M. "Mac" Thornberry (R)
14. Greg Laughlin (D)[f]
15. E. "Kika" de la Garza (D)
16. Ronald D. Coleman (D)
17. Charles W. Stenholm (D)
18. Sheila Jackson-Lee (D)
19. Larry Combest (R)
20. Henry B. Gonzalez (D)
21. Lamar Smith (R)
22. Tom DeLay (R)
23. Henry Bonilla (R)
24. Martin Frost (D)
25. Ken Bentsen (D)
26. Dick Armey (R)
27. Solomon P. Ortiz (D)
28. Frank Tejeda (D)
29. Gene Green (D)
30. Eddie Bernice Johnson (D)

Utah
1. James V. Hansen (R)
2. Enid Greene Waldholtz (R)
3. Bill Orton (D)

Vermont
AL Bernard Sanders (I)

Virginia
1. Herbert H. Bateman (R)
2. Owen B. Pickett (D)
3. Robert C. Scott (D)
4. Norman Sisisky (D)
5. L. F. Payne Jr. (D)
6. Robert W. Goodlatte (R)
7. Thomas J. Bliley Jr. (R)
8. James P. Moran (D)
9. Rick Boucher (D)
10. Frank R. Wolf (R)
11. Thomas M. Davis III (R)

Washington
1. Rick White (R)
2. Jack Metcalf (R)
3. Linda Smith (R)
4. Richard "Doc" Hastings (R)
5. George Nethercutt (R)
6. Norm Dicks (D)
7. Jim McDermott (D)
8. Jennifer Dunn (R)
9. Randy Tate (R)

West Virginia
1. Alan B. Mollohan (D)
2. Bob Wise (D)
3. Nick J. Rahall II (D)

Wisconsin
1. Mark W. Neumann (R)
2. Scott L. Klug (R)
3. Steve Gunderson (R)
4. Gerald D. Kleczka (D)
5. Thomas M. Barrett (D)
6. Tom Petri (R)
7. David R. Obey (D)
8. Toby Roth (R)
9. F. James Sensenbrenner Jr. (R)

Wyoming
AL Barbara Cubin (R)

NOTE: Members of the 104th Congress also included delegates Eni F. H. Faleomavaega, D-American Samoa; Victor O. Frazer, I-Virgin Islands; Eleanor Holmes Norton, D-D.C.; Robert Underwood, D-Guam; and resident commissioner Carlos Romero-Barcelo, D-Puerto Rico.

[a] Deal switched to the Republican Party on April 10, 1995.

[b] Tauzin switched to the Republican Party on Aug. 6, 1995.

[c] Hayes switched to the Republican Party on Dec. 1, 1995.

[d] Parker switched to the Republican Party on Nov. 10, 1995.

[e] Jo Ann Emerson was elected Nov. 5, 1996, to complete the remainder of her husband's term and to the 105th Congress.

[f] Laughlin switched to the Republican Party on June 26, 1995.

The names in this list include, alphabetically, all senators, representatives, resident commissioners and territorial delegates who served in the 103rd and 104th Congresses—from 1993 to 1996.

The material is organized as follows: name; relationship to other members and presidents and vice presidents; party, state (of service); date of birth; date of death (if applicable); congressional service; service as president, vice president, member of the Cabinet or Supreme Court, governor, Speaker of the House, president pro tempore of the Senate, majority leader, minority leader and chairman of the Democratic or Republican National Committee.

If the member changed parties during his or her congressional service, the party designation appearing after the member's name is that which applied at the end of such service and further breakdown is included after the dates of congressional service. Where the service date is left open, the member was still serving in the 105th Congress (as of January 1997).

Dates of service are inclusive, starting in year of service and ending when service ends. Under the Constitution, terms of service since 1934 have been from Jan. 3 to Jan. 3. In actual practice, members have been sworn in on other dates at the beginning of a Congress. The exact date is shown (where available) if a member began or ended his or her service in midterm.

The major sources for the following list were Congressional Quarterly's *Biographical Directory of the American Congress 1774–1996; Almanac; American Leaders 1789–1994: A Biographical Summary; Weekly Report*; and the Washington Alert on-line database.

In the list, D stands for Democrat; I, Independent; and R, Republican.

A

Abercrombie, Neil (D-Hawaii) June 26, 1938– ; House Sept. 23, 1986–1987, 1991– .

Abraham, Spencer (R-Mich.) June 12, 1952– ; Senate 1995– .

Ackerman, Gary L. (D-N.Y.) Nov. 19, 1942– ; House March 1, 1983– .

Akaka, Daniel K. (D-Hawaii) Sept. 11, 1924– ; House 1977–May 16, 1990; Senate May 16, 1990– .

Allard, Wayne (R-Colo.) Dec. 2, 1943– ; House 1991–1997; Senate 1997– .

Andrews, Michael A. (D-Texas) Feb. 7, 1944– ; House 1983– .

Andrews, Robert E. (D-N.J.) Aug. 4, 1957– ; House 1990– .

Andrews, Thomas H. (D-Maine) March 22, 1953– ; House 1991– .

Applegate, Douglas (D-Ohio) March 27, 1928– ; House 1977– .

Archer, Bill (R-Texas) March 22, 1928– ; House 1971– .

Armey, Dick (R-Texas) July 7, 1940– ; House 1985– ; House majority leader 1995– .

Ashcroft, John (R-Mo.) May 9, 1942– ; Senate 1995– .

Aspin, Les (D-Wis.) July 21, 1938–May 21, 1995; House 1971–Jan. 20, 1993; Secy. of Defense Jan. 22, 1993–Feb. 2, 1994.

B

Bacchus, Jim (D-Fla.) June 21, 1949– ; House 1991– .

Bachus, Spencer (R-Ala.) Dec. 28, 1947– ; House 1993– .

Baesler, Scotty (D-Ky.) July 9, 1941– ; House 1993– .

Baker, Bill (R-Calif.) June 14, 1940– ; House 1993–1997.

Baker, Richard H. (R-La.) May 22, 1948– ; House 1987– .

Baldacci, John (D-Maine) Jan. 30, 1955– ; House 1995– .

Ballenger, Cass (great-great grandson of Lewis Cass) (R-N.C.) Dec. 6, 1926– ; House 1986– .

Barca, Peter W. (D-Wis.) Aug. 7, 1955– ; House June 8, 1993–1995.

Barcia, James A. (D-Mich.) Feb. 25, 1952– ; House 1993– .

Barlow, Tom (D-Ky.) Aug. 7, 1940– ; House 1993–1995.

Barr, Bob (R-Ga.) Nov. 5, 1948– ; House 1995– .

Barrett, Bill (R-Neb.) Feb. 9, 1929– ; House 1991– .

Barrett, Thomas M. (D-Wis.) Dec. 8, 1953– ; House 1993– .

Bartlett, Roscoe G. (R-Md.) June 3, 1926– ; House 1993– .

Barton, Joe L. (R-Texas) Sept. 15, 1949– ; House 1985– .

Bass, Charles (son of Perkins Bass) (R-N.H.) Jan. 8, 1952– ; House 1995 .

Bateman, Herbert H. (R-Va.) Aug. 7, 1928– ; House 1983– .

Baucus, Max (D-Mont.) Dec. 11, 1941– ; House 1975–Dec. 14, 1978; Senate Dec. 15, 1978– .

Becerra, Xavier (D-Calif.) Jan. 26, 1958– ; House 1993– .

Beilenson, Anthony C. (D-Calif.) Oct. 26, 1932– ; House 1977–1997.

Bennett, Robert F. (R-Utah) Sept. 18, 1933– ; Senate 1993– .

Bentley, Helen Delich (R-Md.) Nov. 28, 1923– ; House 1985–1995.

Bentsen, Ken (nephew of Lloyd Bentsen) (D-Texas) June 3, 1959– ; House 1995– .

Bentsen, Lloyd (uncle of Ken Bentsen) (D-Texas) Feb. 11, 1921– ; Senate 1971–Jan. 20, 1993; Secy. of the Treasury Jan. 22, 1993–Dec. 22, 1994.

Bereuter, Doug (R-Neb.) Oct. 6, 1939– ; House 1979– .

Berman, Howard L. (D-Calif.) April 15, 1941– ; House 1983– .

Bevill, Tom (D-Ala.) March 27, 1921– ; House 1967–1997.

Biden, Joseph R. Jr. (D-Del.) Nov. 20, 1942– ; Senate 1973– .

Bilbray, Brian P. (nephew of James Bilbray) (R-Calif.) Jan. 28, 1951– ; House 1995– .

Bilbray, James (uncle of Brian P. Bilbray) (D-Nev.) May 19, 1938– ; House 1987–1995.

Bilirakis, Michael (R-Fla.) July 16, 1930– ; House 1983– .

Bingaman, Jeff (D-N.M.) Oct. 3, 1943– ; Senate 1983– .

Bishop, Sanford D. Jr. (D-Ga.) Feb. 4, 1947– ; House 1993– .

Blackwell, Lucien E. (D-Pa.) Aug. 1, 1931– ; House 1991–1995.

Bliley, Thomas J. Jr. (R-Va.) Jan. 28, 1932– ; House 1981– .

Blumenauer, Earl (D-Ore.) Aug. 16, 1949– ; House May 30, 1996– .

Blute, Peter I. (R-Mass.) Jan. 28, 1956– ; House 1993–1997.

Boehlert, Sherwood (R-N.Y.) Sept. 28, 1936– ; House 1983– .

Boehner, John A. (R-Ohio) Nov. 17, 1949– ; House 1991– .

Bond, Christopher S. (R-Mo.) March 6, 1939– ; Senate 1987– .

Bonilla, Henry (R-Texas) Jan. 2, 1954– ; House 1993– .

Bonior, David E. (D-Mich.) June 6, 1945– ; House 1977– .

Bono, Sonny (R-Calif.) Feb. 16, 1935– ; House 1995– .

Boren, David L. (son of Lyle H. Boren) (D-Okla.) April 21, 1941– ; Senate 1979–Nov. 15, 1994; Gov. 1975–1979.

Borski, Robert A. (D-Pa.) Oct. 20, 1948– ; House 1983– .

Boucher, Rick (D-Va.) Aug. 1, 1946– ; House 1983– .

Boxer, Barbara (D-Calif.) Nov. 11, 1940– ; House 1983–1993; Senate 1993– .

Bradley, Bill (D-N.J.) July 28, 1943– ; Senate 1979–1997.

Breaux, John B. (D-La.) March 1, 1944– ; House Sept. 30, 1972–1987; Senate 1987– .

Brewster, Bill (D-Okla.) Nov. 8, 1941– ; House 1991–1997.

Brooks, Jack (D-Texas) Dec. 18, 1922– ; House 1953–1995.

Browder, Glen (D-Ala.) Jan. 15, 1943– ; House April 18, 1989–1997.

Brown, Corrine (D-Fla.) Nov. 11, 1946– ; House 1993– .

Brown, George E. Jr. (D-Calif.) March 6, 1920– ; House 1963–1971, 1973– .

Brown, Hank (R-Colo.) Feb. 12, 1940– ; House 1981–1991; Senate 1991–1997.

Brown, Sherrod (D-Ohio) Nov. 9, 1952– ; House 1993–1997.

Brownback, Sam (R-Kan.) Sept. 12, 1956– ; House 1995–Nov. 6, 1996; Senate Nov. 27, 1996– .

Bryan, Richard H. (D-Nev.) July 16, 1937– ; Senate 1989– ; Gov. 1983–1989.

Bryant, Ed (R-Tenn.) Sept. 7, 1948– ; House 1995– .

Bryant, John (D-Texas) Feb. 22, 1947– ; House 1983–1997.

Bumpers, Dale (D-Ark.) Aug. 12, 1925– ; Senate 1975– .

Bunn, Jim (R-Ore.) Dec. 12, 1956– ; House 1995–1997.

Bunning, Jim (R-Ky.) Oct. 23, 1931– ; House 1987– .

Burns, Conrad (R-Mont.) Jan. 25, 1935– ; Senate 1989– .

Burr, Richard M. (R-N.C.) Nov. 30, 1955– ; House 1995– .

Burton, Dan (R-Ind.) June 21, 1938– ; House 1983– .

Buyer, Steve (R-Ind.) Nov. 26, 1958– ; House 1993– ; Gov. 1971–1975.

Byrd, Robert C. (D-W.Va.) Nov. 20, 1917– ; House 1953–1959; Senate 1959– ; Senate minority leader, 1981–1987; Senate majority leader 1977–1981, 1987–1989; Pres. pro tempore 1989–1995.

Byrne, Leslie L. (D-Va.) Oct. 27, 1946– ; House 1993–1995.

C

Callahan, Sonny (R-Ala.) Sept. 11, 1932– ; House 1985– .

Calvert, Ken (R-Calif.) June 8, 1953– ; House 1993– .

Camp, Dave (R-Mich.) July 9, 1953– ; House 1991– .

Campbell, Ben Nighthorse (R-Colo.) April 13, 1933– ; House 1987–1993; Senate 1993– (1987–March 3, 1995, Democrat).

Campbell, Tom (R-Calif.) Aug. 14, 1952– ; House 1989–1993; Dec. 15, 1995– .

Canady, Charles T. (R-Fla.) June 22, 1954– ; House 1993– .

Cantwell, Maria (D-Wash.) Oct. 13, 1958– ; House 1993–1995.

Cardin, Benjamin L. (D-Md.) Oct. 5, 1943– ; House 1987– .

Carr, Bob (D-Mich.) March 27, 1943– ; House 1975–1981, 1983–1995.

Castle, Michael N. (R-Del.) July 2, 1939– ; House 1993– .

Chabot, Steve (R-Ohio) Jan. 22, 1953– ; House 1995– .

Chafee, John H. (R-R.I.) Oct. 22, 1922– ; Senate 1976– ; Gov. 1963–1969.

Chambliss, Saxby (R-Ga.) Nov. 10, 1943– ; House 1995– .

Chapman, Jim (D-Texas) March 8, 1945– ; House 1985–1997.

Chenoweth, Helen (R-Idaho) Jan. 27, 1938– ; House 1995– .

Christensen, Jon (R-Neb.) Feb. 20, 1963– ; House 1995– .

Chrysler, Dick (R-Mich.) April 29, 1942– ; House 1995–1997.

Clay, William L. (D-Mo.) April 30, 1931– ; House 1969– .

Clayton, Eva (D-N.C.) Sept. 16, 1934– ; House Nov. 4, 1992– .

Clement, Bob (D-Tenn.) Sept. 23, 1943– ; House 1988– .

Clinger, William F. (R-Pa.) April 4, 1929– ; House 1979–1997.

Clyburn, James E. (D-S.C.) July 21, 1940– ; House 1993– .

Coats, Daniel R. (R-Ind.) May 16, 1943– ; House 1981–Jan. 1, 1989; Senate Jan. 3, 1989– .

Coble, Howard (R-N.C.) March 18, 1931– ; House 1985– .

Coburn, Tom (R-Okla.) March 14, 1948– ; House 1995– .

Cochran, Thad (R-Miss.) Dec. 7, 1937– ; House 1973–Dec. 26, 1978; Senate Dec. 27, 1978– .

Cohen, William S. (R-Maine) Aug. 28, 1940– ; House 1973–1979; Senate 1979–1997.

Coleman, Ronald D. (D-Texas) Nov. 29, 1941– ; House 1983–1997.

Collins, Barbara-Rose (D-Mich.) April 13, 1939– ; House 1991–1997.

Collins, Cardiss (widow of George Washington Collins) (D-Ill.) Sept. 24, 1931– ; House June 5, 1973–1997.

Collins, Mac (R-Ga.) Oct. 15, 1944– ; House 1993– .

Combest, Larry (R-Texas) March 20, 1945– ; House 1985– .

Condit, Gary A. (D-Calif.) April 21, 1948– ; House Sept. 20, 1989– .

Conrad, Kent (D-N.D.) March 12, 1948– ; Senate 1987–Dec. 14, 1992, Dec. 14, 1992– .

Conyers, John Jr. (D-Mich.) May 16, 1929– ; House 1965– .

Cooley, Wes (R-Ore.) March 28, 1932– ; House 1995–1997.

Cooper, Jim (D-Tenn.) June 19, 1954– ; House 1983– .

Coppersmith, Sam (D-Ariz.) May 22, 1955– ; House 1993– .

Costello, Jerry F. (D-Ill.) Sept. 25, 1949– ; House Aug. 11, 1988– .

Coverdell, Paul (R-Ga.) Jan. 20, 1939– ; Senate 1993– .

Cox, Christopher (R-Calif.) Oct. 16, 1952– ; House 1989– .

Coyne, William J. (D-Pa.) Aug. 24, 1936– ; House 1981– .

Craig, Larry E. (R-Idaho) July 20, 1945– ; House 1981–1991; Senate 1991– .

Cramer, Robert E. "Bud" (D-Ala.) Aug. 22, 1947– ; House 1991– .

Crane, Philip M. (brother of Daniel Bever Crane) (R-Ill.) Nov. 3, 1930– ; House 1969– .

Crapo, Michael D. (R-Idaho) May 20, 1951– ; House 1993– .

Cremeans, Frank A. (R-Ohio) April 5, 1943– ; House 1995–1997.

Cubin, Barbara (R-Wyo.) Nov. 30, 1946– ; House 1995– .

Cummings, Elijah E. (D-Md.) Jan. 18, 1951– ; House April 25, 1996– .

Cunningham, Randy "Duke" (R-Calif.) Dec. 8, 1941– ; House 1991 .

D

D'Amato, Alfonse M. (R-N.Y.) Aug. 1, 1937– ; Senate 1981– .

Danforth, John C. (R-Mo.) Sept. 5, 1936– ; Senate Dec. 27, 1976–1995.

Danner, Pat (D-Mo.) Jan. 13, 1934– ; House 1993– .

Darden, George "Buddy" (D-Ga.) Nov. 22, 1943– ; House Nov. 8, 1983–1995.

Daschle, Tom (D-S.D.) Dec. 9, 1947– ; House 1979–1987; Senate 1987– ; Senate minority leader 1995– .

Davis, Thomas M. III (R-Va.) Jan. 5, 1949– ; House 1995– .

de la Garza, E. "Kika" (D-Texas) Sept. 22, 1927– ; House 1965–1997.

de Lugo, Ron (D-V.I.) Aug. 2, 1930– ; House (Delegate) 1981–1995.

Deal, Nathan (R-Ga.) Aug. 25, 1942– ; House 1993– (1993–April 10, 1995, Democrat).

DeConcini, Dennis (D-Ariz.) May 8, 1937– ; Senate 1977–1995.

DeFazio, Peter A. (D-Ore.) May 27, 1947– ; House 1987– .

DeLauro, Rosa (D-Conn.) March 2, 1943– ; House 1991– .

DeLay, Tom (R-Texas) April 8, 1947– ; House 1985– .

Dellums, Ronald V. (D-Calif.) Nov. 24, 1935– ; House 1971– .

Derrick, Butler (D-S.C.) Sept. 30, 1936– ; House 1975– .

Deutsch, Peter (D-Fla.) April 1, 1957– ; House 1993– .

DeWine, Mike (R-Ohio) Jan. 5, 1947– ; House 1983–1991; Senate 1995– .

Diaz-Balart, Lincoln (R-Fla.) Aug. 13, 1954– ; House 1993– .

Dickey, Jay (R-Ark.) Dec. 14, 1939– ; House 1993– .

Dicks, Norm (D-Wash.) Dec. 16, 1940– ; House 1977– .

Dingell, John D. (son of John David Dingell) (D-Mich.) July 8, 1926– ; House Dec. 13, 1955– .

Dixon, Julian C. (D-Calif.) Aug. 8, 1934– ; House 1979– .

Dodd, Christopher J. (son of Thomas Joseph Dodd) (D-Conn.) May 27, 1944– ; House 1975–1981; Senate 1981– .

Doggett, Lloyd (D-Texas) Oct. 6, 1946– ; House 1995– .

Dole, Bob (R-Kan.) July 22, 1923– ; House 1961–1969; Senate 1969–June 11, 1996; Chrmn. Rep. Nat. Comm. 1971–1973; Senate majority leader 1985–1987, 1995–June 11, 1996; Senate minority leader 1987–1995.

Domenici, Pete V. (R-N.M.) May 7, 1932– ; Senate 1973– .

Dooley, Cal (D-Calif.) Jan. 11, 1954– ; House 1991– .

Doolittle, John T. (R-Calif.) Oct. 30, 1950– ; House 1991– .

Dorgan, Byron L. (D-N.D.) May 14, 1942– ; House 1981–Dec. 14, 1992; Senate Dec. 15, 1992– .

Dornan, Robert K. (R-Calif.) April 3, 1933– ; House 1977–1983, 1985–1997.

Doyle, Mike (D-Pa.) Aug. 5, 1953– ; House 1995– .

Dreier, David (R-Calif.) July 5, 1952– ; House 1981– .

Duncan, John J. "Jimmy" Jr. (son of John J. Duncan) (R-Tenn.) July 21, 1947– ; House 1988– .

Dunn, Jennifer (R-Wash.) July 29, 1941– ; House 1993– .

Durbin, Richard J. (D-Ill.) Nov. 21, 1944– ; House 1983–1997; Senate 1997– .

Durenberger, Dave (R-Minn.) Aug. 19, 1934– ; Senate Nov. 8, 1978–1995.

E

Edwards, Chet (D-Texas) Nov. 24, 1951– ; House 1991– .

Edwards, Don (D-Calif.) Jan. 6, 1915– ; House 1963– .

Ehlers, Vernon J. (R-Mich.) Feb. 6, 1934– ; House Jan. 25, 1994– .

Ehrlich, Robert Jr. (R-Md.) Nov. 25, 1957– ; House 1995– .

Emerson, Bill (husband of Jo Ann Emerson) (R-Mo.) Jan. 1, 1938–June 22, 1996; House 1981–June 22, 1996.

Emerson, Jo Ann (widow of Bill Emerson) (R-Mo.) Sept. 16, 1950– ; House 1997– .

Engel, Eliot L. (D-N.Y.) Feb. 18, 1947– ; House 1989– .

English, Glenn (D-Okla.) Nov. 30, 1940– ; House 1975–Jan. 7, 1994.

English, Karan (D-Ariz.) March 23, 1949– ; House 1993–1995.

English, Phil (R-Pa.) June 20, 1956– ; House 1995– .

Ensign, John (R-Nev.) March 25, 1958– ; House 1995– .

Eshoo, Anna G. (D-Calif.) Dec. 13, 1942– ; House 1993– .

Espy, Mike (D-Miss.) Nov. 30, 1953– ; House 1987–Jan. 22, 1993; Secy. of Agriculture Jan. 22, 1993–Dec. 31, 1994.

Evans, Lane (D-Ill.) Aug. 4, 1951– ; House 1983– .

Everett, Terry (R-Ala.) Feb. 15, 1937– ; House 1993– .

Ewing, Thomas W. (R-Ill.) Sept. 19, 1935– ; House July 10, 1991– .

Exon, Jim (D-Neb.) Aug. 9, 1921– ; Senate 1979–1997; Gov. 1971–1979 .

F

Faircloth, Lauch (R-N.C.) Jan. 14, 1928– ; Senate 1993– .

Faleomavaega, Eni F. H. (D-Am. Samoa) Aug. 15, 1943– ; House (Delegate) 1989– .

Farr, Sam (D-Calif.) July 4, 1941– ; House June 16, 1993– .

Fattah, Chaka (D-Pa.) Nov. 21, 1956– ; House 1995– .

Fawell, Harris W. (R-Ill.) March 25, 1929– ; House 1985– .

Fazio, Vic (D-Calif.) Oct. 11, 1942– ; House 1979– .

Feingold, Russell D. (D-Wis.) March 2, 1953– ; Senate 1993– .

Feinstein, Dianne (D-Calif.) June 22, 1933– ; Senate Nov. 10, 1992– .

Fields, Cleo (D-La.) Nov. 22, 1962– ; House 1993–1997.

Fields, Jack (R-Texas) Feb. 3, 1952– ; House 1981–1997.

Filner, Bob (D-Calif.) Sept. 4, 1942– ; House 1993– .

Fingerhut, Eric D. (D-Ohio) May 6, 1959– ; House 1993–1995.

Fish, Hamilton Jr. (son of Hamilton Fish born in 1888, grandson of Hamilton Fish born in 1849, great grandson of Hamilton Fish born in 1808) (R-N.Y.) June 3, 1926–July 23, 1996; House 1969–1995.

Flake, Floyd H. (D-N.Y.) Jan. 30, 1945– ; House 1987– .

Flanagan, Michael Patrick (R-Ill.) Nov. 9, 1962– ; House 1995–1997.

Foglietta, Thomas M. (D-Pa.) Dec. 3, 1928– ; House 1981– (1981–1982, Independent).

Foley, Mark (R-Fla.) Sept. 8, 1954– ; House 1995– .

Foley, Thomas S. (D-Wash.) March 6, 1929– ; House 1965–1995; House majority leader 1987–June 6, 1989; Speaker June 6, 1989–1995.

Forbes, Michael P. (R-N.Y.) July 16, 1952– ; House 1995– .

Ford, Harold E. (D-Tenn.) May 20, 1945– ; House 1975–1997.

Ford, Wendell H. (D-Ky.) Sept. 8, 1924– ; Senate Dec. 28, 1974– ; Gov. 1971–1974.

Ford, William D. (D-Mich.) Aug. 6, 1927– ; House 1965– .

Fowler, Tillie (R-Fla.) Dec. 23, 1942– ; House 1993– .

Fox, Jon D. (R-Pa.) April 22, 1947– ; House 1995– .

Frahm, Sheila (R-Kan.) March 22, 1945– ; Senate June 11, 1996–Nov. 27, 1996.

Frank, Barney (D-Mass.) March 31, 1940– ; House 1981– .

Franks, Bob (R-N.J.) Sept. 21, 1951– ; House 1993– .

Franks, Gary A. (R-Conn.) Feb. 9, 1953– ; House 1991–1997.

Frazer, Victor O. (I-Virgin Is.) May 24, 1943– ; House (Delegate) 1995– .

Frelinghuysen, Rodney (son of Peter Hood Ballentine Frelinghuysen) (R-N.J.) April 29, 1946– ; House 1995– .

Frisa, Daniel (R-N.Y.) April 27, 1955– ; House 1995–1997.

Frist, Bill (R-Tenn.) Feb. 22, 1952– ; Senate 1995– .

Frost, Martin (D-Texas) Jan. 1, 1942– ; House 1979– .

Funderburk, David (R-N.C.) April 28, 1944– ; House 1995–1997.

Furse, Elizabeth (D-Ore.) Oct. 13, 1936– ; House 1993– .

G

Gallegly, Elton (R-Calif.) March 7, 1944– ; House 1987– .

Gallo, Dean A. (R-N.J.) Nov. 23, 1935–Nov. 6, 1994; House 1985–Nov. 6, 1994.

Ganske, Greg (R-Iowa) March 31, 1949– ; House 1995– .

Gejdenson, Sam (D-Conn.) May 20, 1948– ; House 1981– .

Gekas, George W. (R-Pa.) April 14, 1930– ; House 1983– .

Gephardt, Richard A. (D-Mo.) Jan. 31, 1941– ; House 1977– ; House majority leader June 14, 1989–1995; House minority leader 1995– .

Geren, Pete (D-Texas) Jan. 29, 1952– ; House Sept. 20, 1989–1997.

Gibbons, Sam M. (D-Fla.) Jan. 20, 1920– ; House 1963–1997.

Gilchrest, Wayne T. (R-Md.) April 15, 1946– ; House 1991– .

Gillmor, Paul E. (R-Ohio) Feb. 1, 1939– ; House 1989– .

Gilman, Benjamin A. (R-N.Y.) Dec. 6, 1922– ; House 1973– .

Gingrich, Newt (R-Ga.) June 17, 1943– ; House 1979– ; Speaker 1995– .

Glenn, John (D-Ohio) July 18, 1921– ; Senate 1974– .

Glickman, Dan (D-Kan.) Nov. 24, 1944– ; House 1977–1995.

Gonzalez, Henry B. (D-Texas) May 3, 1916– ; House 1961– .

Goodlatte, Robert W. (R-Va.) Sept. 22, 1952– ; House 1993– .

Goodling, Bill (son of George Atlee Goodling) (R-Pa.) Dec. 5, 1927– ; House 1975– .

Gordon, Bart (D-Tenn.) Jan. 24, 1949– ; House 1985– .

Gorton, Slade (R-Wash.) Jan. 8, 1928– ; Senate 1989– .

Goss, Porter J. (R-Fla.) Nov. 26, 1938– ; House 1981–1987, 1989– .

Gradison, Bill (R-Ohio) Dec. 28, 1928– ; House 1975–Jan. 31, 1993.

Graham, Bob (D-Fla.) Nov. 9, 1936– ; Senate 1987– .

Graham, Lindsey (R-S.C.) July 9, 1955– ; House 1995– .

Gramm, Phil (R-Texas) July 8, 1942– ; House 1979–Jan. 5, 1983, Feb. 22, 1983–1985 (1979–Jan. 5, 1983, Democrat); Senate 1985– .

Grams, Rod (R-Minn.) Feb. 4, 1948– ; House 1993–1995; Senate 1995– .

Grandy, Fred (R-Iowa) June 29, 1948– ; House 1987–1995.

Grassley, Charles E. (R-Iowa) Sept. 17, 1933– ; House 1975–1981; Senate 1981– .

Green, Gene (D-Texas) Oct. 17, 1947– ; House 1993– .

Greenwood, James C. (R-Pa.) May 4, 1951– ; House 1993– .

Gregg, Judd (R-N.H.) Feb. 14, 1947– ; Senate 1993– .

Gunderson, Steve (R-Wis.) May 10, 1951– ; House 1981–1997.

Gutierrez, Luis V. (D-Ill.) Dec. 10, 1954– ; House 1993– .

Gutknecht, Gil (R-Minn.) March 20, 1951– ; House 1995– .

H

Hall, Ralph M. (D-Texas) May 3, 1923– ; House 1981– .

Hall, Tony P. (D-Ohio) Jan. 16, 1942– ; House 1979– .

Hamburg, Dan (D-Calif.) Oct. 6, 1948– ; House 1993–1995.

Hamilton, Lee H. (D-Ind.) April 20, 1931– ; House 1965– .

Hancock, Mel (R-Mo.) Sept. 14, 1929– ; House 1989–1997.

Hansen, James V. (R-Utah) Aug. 14, 1932– ; House 1981– .

Harkin, Tom (D-Iowa) Nov. 19, 1939– ; House 1975–1985; Senate 1985– .

Harman, Jane (D-Calif.) June 28, 1945– ; House 1993– .

Hastert, Dennis (R-Ill.) Jan. 2, 1942– ; House 1987– .

Hastings, Alcee L. (D-Fla.) Sept. 5, 1936– ; House 1993– .

Hastings, Richard "Doc" (R-Wash.) Feb. 7, 1941– ; House 1995– .

Hatch, Orrin G. (R-Utah) March 22, 1934– ; Senate 1977– .

Hatfield, Mark O. (R-Ore.) July 12, 1922– ; Senate 1967–1997; Gov. 1959–1967.

Hayes, Jimmy (R-La.) Dec. 21, 1946– ; House 1987–1997 (1987–Dec. 1, 1995, Democrat).

Hayworth, J. D. (R-Ariz.) July 12, 1958– ; House 1995– .

Hefley, Joel (R-Colo.) April 18, 1935– ; House 1987– .

Heflin, Howell (D-Ala.) June 19, 1921– ; Senate 1979–1997.

Hefner, W. G. "Bill" (D-N.C.) April 11, 1930– ; House 1975– .

Heineman, Fred (R-N.C.) Dec. 28, 1929– ; House 1995–1997.

Helms, Jesse (R-N.C.) Oct. 18, 1921– ; Senate 1973– .

Henry, Paul B. (R-Mich.) July 9, 1942–July 31, 1993; House 1985–July 31, 1993.

Herger, Wally (R-Calif.) May 20, 1945– ; House 1987– .

Hilleary, Van (R-Tenn.) June 20, 1959– ; House 1995– .

Hilliard, Earl F. (D-Ala.) April 9, 1942– ; House 1993– .

Hinchey, Maurice D. (D-N.Y.) Oct. 27, 1938– ; House 1993– .

Hoagland, Peter (D-Neb.) Nov. 17, 1941– ; House 1989–1995.

Hobson, David L. (R-Ohio) Oct. 17, 1936– ; House 1991– .

Hochbrueckner, George J. (D-N.Y.) Sept. 20, 1938– ; House 1987–1995.

Hoekstra, Peter (R-Mich.) Oct. 30, 1953– ; House 1993– .

Hoke, Martin R. (R-Ohio) May 18, 1952– ; House 1993–1997.

Holden, Tim (D-Pa.) March 5, 1957– ; House 1993– .

Hollings, Ernest F. (D-S.C.) Jan. 1, 1922– ; Senate Nov. 9, 1966– ; Gov. 1959–1963.

Horn, Steve (R-Calif.) May 31, 1931– ; House 1993– .

Hostettler, John (R-Ind.) July 19, 1961– ; House 1995– .

Houghton, Amo (grandson of Alanson Bigelow Houghton) (R-N.Y.) Aug. 7, 1926– ; House 1987– .

Hoyer, Steny H. (D-Md.) June 14, 1939– ; House June 3, 1981– .

Huffington, Michael (R-Calif.) Sept. 3, 1947– ; House 1993–1995.

Hughes, William J. (D-N.J.) Oct. 17, 1932– ; House 1975– .

Hunter, Duncan (R-Calif.) May 31, 1948– ; House 1981– .

Hutchinson, Tim (R-Ark.) Aug. 11, 1949– ; House 1993–1997; Senate 1997– .

Hutchison, Kay Bailey (R-Texas) July 22, 1943– ; Senate June 14, 1993– .

Hutto, Earl (D-Fla.) May 12, 1926– ; House 1979– .

Hyde, Henry J. (R-Ill.) April 18, 1924– ; House 1975– .

I

Inglis, Bob (R-S.C.) Oct. 11, 1959– ; House 1993– .

Inhofe, James M. (R-Okla.) Nov. 17, 1934– ; House 1987– Nov. 15, 1994; Senate Nov. 17, 1994– .

Inouye, Daniel K. (D-Hawaii) Sept. 7, 1924– ; House Aug. 21, 1959–1963; Senate 1963– .

Inslee, Jay (D-Wash.) Feb. 9, 1951– ; House 1993–1995.

Istook, Ernest (R-Okla.) Feb. 11, 1950– ; House 1993– .

J

Jackson, Jesse Jr. (D-Ill.) March 11, 1965– ; House Dec. 14, 1995– .

Jackson-Lee, Sheila (D-Texas) Jan. 12, 1950– ; House 1995– .

Jacobs, Andrew Jr. (son of Andrew Jacobs Sr., husband of Martha Elizabeth Keys) (D-Ind.) Feb. 24, 1932– ; House 1965–1973, 1975–1997.

Jefferson, William J. (D-La.) March 14, 1947– ; House 1991– .

Jeffords, James M. (R-Vt.) May 11, 1934– ; House 1975–1989; Senate 1989– .

Johnson, Don (D-Ga.) Jan. 30, 1948– ; House 1993–1995.

Johnson, Eddie Bernice (D-Texas) Dec. 3, 1935– ; House 1993– .

Johnson, Nancy L. (R-Conn.) Jan. 5, 1935– ; House 1983– .

Johnson, Sam (R-Texas) Oct. 11, 1930– ; House May 22, 1991– .

Johnson, Tim (D-S.D.) Dec. 28, 1946– ; House 1987–1997; Senate 1997– .

Johnston, Harry A. (D-Fla.) Dec. 2, 1931– ; House 1989–1997.

Johnston, J. Bennett (father-in-law of Tim Roemer) (D-La.) June 10, 1932– ; Senate Nov. 14, 1972–1997.

Jones, Walter B. Jr. (son of Walter Beaman Jones) (R-N.C.) Feb. 10, 1943– ; House 1995– .

K

Kanjorski, Paul E. (D-Pa.) April 2, 1937– ; House 1985– .

Kaptur, Marcy (D-Ohio) June 17, 1946– ; House 1983– .

Kasich, John R. (R-Ohio) May 13, 1952– ; House 1983– .

Kassebaum, Nancy Landon (R-Kan.) July 29, 1932– ; Senate Dec. 23, 1978–1997.

Kelly, Sue W. (R-N.Y.) Sept. 26, 1936– ; House 1995– .

Kempthorne, Dirk (R-Idaho) Oct. 29, 1951– ; Senate 1993– .

Kennedy, Edward M. (father of Patrick J. Kennedy, brother of John Fitzgerald Kennedy and Robert Francis Kennedy, grandson of John Francis Fitzgerald, uncle of Joseph P. Kennedy II)(D-Mass.) Feb. 22, 1932– ; Senate Nov. 7, 1962– .

Kennedy, Joseph P. II (son of Robert Francis Kennedy, nephew of Edward M. Kennedy and John Fitzgerald Kennedy, cousin of Patrick J. Kennedy, great grandson of John Francis Fitzgerald) (D-Mass.) Sept. 24, 1952– ; House 1987– .

Kennedy, Patrick J. (son of Edward M. Kennedy, nephew of John Fitzgerald Kennedy and Robert Francis Kennedy, cousin of Joseph P. Kennedy, great grandson of John Francis Fitzgerald) (D-R.I.) July 14, 1967– ; House 1995– .

Kennelly, Barbara B. (D-Conn.) July 10, 1936– ; House Jan. 25, 1982– .

Kerrey, Bob (D-Neb.) Aug. 27, 1943– ; Senate 1989– ; Gov. 1983–1989.

Kerry, John (D-Mass.) Dec. 11, 1943– ; Senate 1985– .

Kildee, Dale E. (D-Mich.) Sept. 16, 1929– ; House 1977– .

Kim, Jay C. (R-Calif.) March 27, 1939– ; House 1993– .

King, Peter T. (R-N.Y.) April 5, 1944– ; House 1993– .

Kingston, Jack (R-Ga.) April 24, 1955– ; House 1993– .

Kleczka, Gerald D. (D-Wis.) Nov. 26, 1943– ; House April 10, 1984– .

Klein, Herb (D-N.J.) June 24, 1930– ; House 1993–1995.

Klink, Ron (D-Pa.) Sept. 23, 1951– ; House 1993– .

Klug, Scott L. (R-Wis.) Jan. 16, 1953– ; House 1991– .

Knollenberg, Joe (R-Mich.) Nov. 28, 1933– ; House 1993– .

Kohl, Herb (D-Wis.) Feb. 7, 1935– ; Senate 1989– .

Kolbe, Jim (R-Ariz.) June 28, 1942– ; House 1985– .

Kopetski, Mike (D-Ore.) Oct. 27, 1949– ; House 1991–1995.

Kreidler, Mike (D-Wash.) Sept. 28, 1943– ; House 1993–1995.

Krueger, Bob (D-Texas) Sept. 19, 1935– ; Senate Jan. 21, 1993–June 14, 1993.

Kyl, Jon (son of John Henry Kyl) (R-Ariz.) April 25, 1942– ; House 1987–1995; Senate 1995– .

L

LaFalce, John J. (D-N.Y.) Oct. 6, 1939– ; House 1975– .

LaHood, Ray (R-Ill.) Dec. 6, 1945– ; House 1995– .

Lancaster, H. Martin (D-N.C.) March 24, 1943– ; House 1987–1995.

Lantos, Tom (father-in-law of Dick Swett) (D-Calif.) Feb. 1, 1928– ; House 1981– .

Largent, Steve (R-Okla.) Sept. 28, 1955– ; House Nov. 29, 1994– .

LaRocco, Larry (D-Idaho) Aug. 25, 1946– ; House 1991–1995.

Latham, Tom (R-Iowa) July 14, 1948– ; House 1995– .

LaTourette, Steven C. (R-Ohio) July 22, 1954– ; House 1995– .

Laughlin, Greg (R-Texas) Jan. 21, 1942– ; House 1989–1997 (1989–June 26, 1995, Democrat).

Lautenberg, Frank R. (D-N.J.) Jan. 23, 1924– ; Senate Dec. 27, 1982– .

Lazio, Rick A. (R-N.Y.) March 13, 1958– ; House 1993– .

Leach, Jim (R-Iowa) Oct. 15, 1942– ; House 1977– .

Leahy, Patrick J. (D-Vt.) March 31, 1940– ; Senate 1975– .

Lehman, Richard H. (D-Calif.) July 20, 1948– ; House 1983–1995.

Levin, Carl (brother of Sander M. Levin) (D-Mich.) June 28, 1934– ; Senate 1979– .

Levin, Sander M. (brother of Carl Levin) (D-Mich.) Sept. 6, 1931– ; House 1983– .

Levy, David A. (R-N.Y.) Dec. 18, 1953– ; House 1993–1995.

Lewis, Jerry (R-Calif.) Oct. 21, 1934– ; House 1979– .

Lewis, John (D-Ga.) Feb. 21, 1940– ; House 1987– .

Lewis, Ron (R-Ky.) Sept. 14, 1946– ; House May 26, 1994– .

Lewis, Tom (R-Fla.) Oct. 26, 1924– ; House 1983– .

Lieberman, Joseph I. (D-Conn.) Feb. 24, 1942– ; Senate 1989– .

Lightfoot, Jim Ross (R-Iowa) Sept. 27, 1938– ; House 1985–1997.

Lincoln, Blanche Lambert (D-Ark.) Sept. 30, 1960– ; House 1993–1997.

Linder, John (R-Ga.) Sept. 9, 1942– ; House 1993– .

Lipinski, William O. (D-Ill.) Dec. 22, 1937– ; House 1983– .

Livingston, Robert L. (R-La.) April 30, 1943– ; House Sept. 7, 1977– .

Lloyd, Marilyn (D-Tenn.) Jan. 3, 1929– ; House 1975–1995.

LoBiondo, Frank A. (R-N.J.) May 12, 1946– ; House 1995– .

Lofgren, Zoe (D-Calif.) Dec. 21, 1947– ; House 1995– .

Long, Jill L. (D-Ind.) July 15, 1952– ; House April 5, 1989–1995.

Longley, James B. Jr. (R-Maine) July 7, 1951– ; House 1995–1997.

Lott, Trent (R-Miss.) Oct. 9, 1941– ; House 1973–1989; Senate 1989– ; Senate majority leader June 12, 1996– .

Lowey, Nita M. (D-N.Y.) July 5, 1937– ; House 1989– .

Lucas, Frank D. (R-Okla.) Jan. 6, 1960– ; House May 17, 1994– .

Lugar, Richard G. (R-Ind.) April 4, 1932– ; Senate 1977– .

Luther, William P. "Bill" (D-Minn.) June 27, 1945– ; House 1995– .

M

Machtley, Ronald K. (R-R.I.) July 13, 1948– ; House 1989– .

Mack, Connie (R-Fla.) Oct. 29, 1940– ; House 1983–1989; Senate 1989– .

Maloney, Carolyn B. (D-N.Y.) Feb. 19, 1948– ; House 1993– .

Mann, David (D-Ohio) Sept. 25, 1939– ; House 1993–1995.

Manton, Thomas J. (D-N.Y.) Nov. 3, 1932– ; House 1985– .

Manzullo, Donald (R-Ill.) March 24, 1944– ; House 1993– .

Margolies-Mezvinsky, Marjorie (wife of Edward Maurice Mezvinsky) (D-Pa.) June 21, 1942– ; House 1993–1995.

Markey, Edward J. (D-Mass.) July 11, 1946– ; House Nov. 2, 1976– .

Martinez, Matthew G. (D-Calif.) Feb. 14, 1929– ; House July 15, 1982– .

Martini, Bill (R-N.J.) Feb. 10, 1947– ; House 1995–1997.

Mascara, Frank R. (D-Pa.) Jan. 19, 1930– ; House 1995– .

Mathews, Harlan (D-Tenn.) Jan. 17, 1927– ; Senate Jan. 5, 1993–Dec. 1, 1994.

Matsui, Robert T. (D-Calif.) Sept. 17, 1941– ; House 1979– .

Mazzoli, Romano L. (D-Ky.) Nov. 2, 1932– ; House 1971–1995.

McCain, John (R-Ariz.) Aug. 29, 1936– ; House 1983–1987; Senate 1987– .

McCandless, Al (R-Calif.) July 23, 1927– ; House 1983– .

McCarthy, Karen (D-Mo.) March 18, 1947– ; House 1995– .

McCloskey, Frank (D-Ind.) June 12, 1939– ; House 1983–1985; May 1, 1985–1995.

McCollum, Bill (R-Fla.) July 12, 1944– ; House 1981– .

McConnell, Mitch (R-Ky.) Feb. 20, 1942– ; Senate 1985– .

McCrery, Jim (R-La.) Sept. 18, 1949– ; House 1988– .

McCurdy, Dave (D-Okla.) March 30, 1950– ; House 1981– .

McDade, Joseph M. (R-Pa.) Sept. 29, 1931– ; House 1963– .

McDermott, Jim (D-Wash.) Dec. 28, 1936– ; House 1989– .

McHale, Paul (D-Pa.) July 26, 1950– ; House 1993– .

McHugh, John M. (R-N.Y.) Sept. 29, 1948– ; House 1993– .

McInnis, Scott (R-Colo.) May 9, 1953– ; House 1993– .

McIntosh, David M. (R-Ind.) June 8, 1958– ; House 1995– .

McKeon, Howard P. "Buck" (R-Calif.) Sept. 9, 1939– ; House 1993– .

McKinney, Cynthia A. (D-Ga.) March 17, 1955– ; House 1993– .

McMillan, Alex (R-N.C.) May 9, 1932– ; House 1985–1995.

McNulty, Michael R. (D-N.Y.) Sept. 16, 1947– ; House 1989– .

Meehan, Martin T. (D-Mass.) Dec. 30, 1956– ; House 1993– .

Meek, Carrie P. (D-Fla.) April 29, 1926– ; House 1993– .

Menendez, Robert (D-N.J.) Jan. 1, 1954– ; House 1993– .

Metcalf, Jack (R-Wash.) Nov. 30, 1927– ; House 1995–1997.

Metzenbaum, Howard M. (D-Ohio) June 4, 1917– ; Senate Jan. 4–Dec. 23, 1974, Dec. 29, 1976–1995.

Meyers, Jan (R-Kan.) July 20, 1928– ; House 1985–1997.

Mfume, Kweisi (D-Md.) Oct. 24, 1948– ; House 1987–Feb. 18, 1996.

Mica, John L. (R-Fla.) Jan. 27, 1943– ; House 1993– .

Michel, Robert H. (R-Ill.) March 2, 1923– ; House 1957–1995; House minority leader 1981–1995.

Mikulski, Barbara A. (D-Md.) July 20, 1936– ; House 1977–1987; Senate 1987– .

Millender-McDonald, Juanita (D-Calif.) Sept. 7, 1938– ; House April 16, 1996– .

Miller, Dan (R-Fla.) May 30, 1942– ; House 1993– .

Miller, George (D-Calif.) May 17, 1945– ; House 1975– .

Mineta, Norman Y. (D-Calif.) Nov. 12, 1931– ; House 1975–Oct. 10, 1995.

Minge, David (D-Minn.) March 19, 1942– ; House 1993– .

Mink, Patsy T. (D-Hawaii) Dec. 6, 1927– ; House 1965–1977, Sept. 27, 1990– .

Mitchell, George J. (D-Maine) Aug. 20, 1933– ; Senate May 17, 1980–1995; majority leader 1989–1995.

Moakley, Joe (D-Mass.) April 27, 1927– ; House 1973– (elected as an Independent Democrat; changed affiliation to Democrat Jan. 2, 1973).

Molinari, Susan (daughter of Guy V. Molinari, wife of Bill Paxon) (R-N.Y.) March 27, 1958– ; House March 27, 1990– .

Mollohan, Alan B. (son of Robert Homer Mollohan) (D-W.Va.) May 14, 1943– ; House 1983– .

Montgomery, G. V. "Sonny" (D-Miss.) Aug. 5, 1920– ; House 1967–1997.

Moorhead, Carlos J. (R-Calif.) May 6, 1922– ; House 1973–1997.

Moran, James P. (D-Va.) May 16, 1945– ; House 1991– .

Morella, Constance A. (R-Md.) Feb. 12, 1931– ; House 1987– .

Moseley-Braun, Carol (D-Ill.) Aug. 16, 1947– ; Senate 1993– .

Moynihan, Daniel Patrick (D-N.Y.) March 16, 1927– ; Senate 1977– .

Murkowski, Frank H. (R-Alaska) March 28, 1933– ; Senate 1981– .

Murphy, Austin J. (D-Pa.) June 17, 1927– ; House 1977– .

Murray, Patty (D-Wash.) Oct. 11, 1950– ; Senate 1993– .

Murtha, John P. (D-Pa.) June 17, 1932– ; House Feb. 5, 1974– .

Myers, John T. (R-Ind.) Feb. 8, 1927– ; House 1967–1997.

Myrick, Sue (R-N.C.) Aug. 1, 1941– ; House 1995– .

N

Nadler, Jerrold (D-N.Y.) June 13, 1947– ; House Nov. 4, 1992– .

Natcher, William H. (D-Ky.) Sept. 11, 1909–March 29, 1994; House 1953–March 29, 1994.

Neal, Richard E. (D-Mass.) Feb. 14, 1949– ; House 1989– .

Neal, Stephen L. (D-N.C.) Nov. 7, 1934– ; House 1975– .

Nethercutt, George (R-Wash.) Oct. 7, 1944– ; House 1995– .

Neumann, Mark W. (R-Wis.) Feb. 27, 1954– ; House 1995– .

Ney, Bob (R-Ohio) July 5, 1954– ; House 1995– .

Nickles, Don (R-Okla.) Dec. 6, 1948– ; Senate 1981– .

Norton, Eleanor Holmes (D-D.C.) June 13, 1937– ; House (Delegate) 1991– .

Norwood, Charlie (R-Ga.) July 27, 1941– ; House 1995– .

Nunn, Sam (D-Ga.) Sept. 8, 1938– ; Senate Nov. 8, 1972–1997.

Nussle, Jim (R-Iowa) June 27, 1960– ; House 1991– .

O

Oberstar, James L. (D-Minn.) Sept. 10, 1934– ; House 1975– .

Obey, David R. (D-Wis.) Oct. 3, 1938– ; House April 1, 1969– .

Olver, John W. (D-Mass.) Sept. 3, 1936– ; House June 18, 1991– .

Ortiz, Solomon P. (D-Texas) June 3, 1937– ; House 1983– .

Orton, Bill (D-Utah) Sept. 22, 1948– ; House 1991–1997.

Owens, Major R. (D-N.Y.) June 28, 1936– ; House 1983– .

Oxley, Michael G. (R-Ohio) Feb. 11, 1944– ; House June 25, 1981– .

P

Packard, Ron (R-Calif.) Jan. 19, 1931– ; House 1983– .

Packwood, Bob (R-Ore.) Sept. 11, 1932– ; Senate 1969–Oct. 1, 1995.

Pallone, Frank Jr. (D-N.J.) Oct. 30, 1951– ; House Nov. 8, 1988– .

Panetta, Leon E. (D-Calif.) June 28, 1938– ; House 1977–Jan. 21, 1993.

Parker, Mike (R-Miss.) Oct. 31, 1949– ; House 1989– (1993–Nov. 10, 1995, Democrat).

Pastor, Ed (D-Ariz.) June 28, 1943– ; House Oct. 3, 1991– .

Paxon, Bill (husband of Susan Molinari, son-in-law of Guy Molinari) (R-N.Y.) April 29, 1954– ; House 1989– .

Payne, Donald M. (D-N.J.) July 16, 1934– ; House 1989– .

Payne, Lewis F. Jr. (D-Va.) July 9, 1945– ; House June 21, 1988–1997.

Pell, Claiborne (son of Herbert Claiborne Pell Jr.) (D-R.I.) Nov. 22, 1918– ; Senate 1961–1997.

Pelosi, Nancy (daughter of Thomas D'Allesandro Jr.) (D-Calif.) March 26, 1940– ; House June 9, 1987– .

Penny, Timothy J. (D-Minn.) Nov. 19, 1951– ; House 1983–1995.

Peterson, Collin C. (D-Minn.) June 29, 1944– ; House 1991– .

Peterson, Pete (D-Fla.) June 26, 1935– ; House 1991–1997.

Petri, Tom (R-Wis.) May 28, 1940– ; House April 3, 1979– .

Pickett, Owen B. (D-Va.) Aug. 31, 1930– ; House 1987– .

Pickle, J. J. (D-Texas) Oct. 11, 1913– ; House Dec. 21, 1963–1995.

Pombo, Richard W. (R-Calif.) Jan. 8, 1961– ; House 1993– .

Pomeroy, Earl (D-N.D.) Sept. 2, 1952– ; House 1993– .

Porter, John Edward (R-Ill.) June 1, 1935– ; House Jan. 22, 1980– .

Portman, Rob (R-Ohio) Dec. 19, 1955– ; House May 5, 1993– .

Poshard, Glenn (D-Ill.) Oct. 30, 1945– ; House 1989– .

Pressler, Larry (R-S.D.) March 29, 1942– ; House 1975–1979; Senate 1979–1997.

Price, David (D-N.C.) Aug. 17, 1940– ; House 1987–1995, 1997– .

Pryce, Deborah (R-Ohio) July 29, 1951– ; House 1993– .

Pryor, David (D-Ark.) Aug. 29, 1934– ; House Nov. 8, 1966–1973; Senate 1979–1997; Gov. 1975–1979.

Q

Quillen, James H. (R-Tenn.) Jan. 11, 1916– ; House 1963–1997.

Quinn, Jack (R-N.Y.) April 13, 1951– ; House 1993– .

R

Radanovich, George P. (R-Calif.) June 20, 1955 ; House 1995– .

Rahall, Nick J. II (D-W.Va.) May 20, 1949– ; House 1977– .

Ramstad, Jim (R-Minn.) May 6, 1946– ; House 1991– .

Rangel, Charles B. (D-N.Y.) June 11, 1930– ; House 1971– .

Ravenel, Arthur Jr. (R-S.C.) March 29, 1927– ; House 1987– .

Reed, Jack (D-R.I.) Nov. 12, 1949– ; House 1991–1997; Senate 1997– .

Regula, Ralph (R-Ohio) Dec. 3, 1924– ; House 1973– .

Reid, Harry (D-Nev.) Dec. 2, 1939– ; House 1983–1987; Senate 1987– .

Reynolds, Mel (D-Ill.) Jan. 8, 1952– ; House 1993–Oct. 1, 1995.

Richardson, Bill (D-N.M.) Nov. 15, 1947– ; House 1983– .

Ridge, Tom (R-Pa.) Aug. 26, 1945– ; House 1983– .

Riegle, Donald W. Jr. (D-Mich.) Feb. 4, 1938– ; House 1967–Dec. 30, 1976 (1967–Feb. 27, 1973, Republican); Senate Dec. 30, 1976–1995.

Riggs, Frank (R-Calif.) Sept. 5, 1950– ; House 1995– .

Rivers, Lynn (D-Mich.) Dec. 19, 1956– ; House 1995– .

Robb, Charles S. (son-in-law of Lyndon Baines Johnson) (D-Va.) June 26, 1939– ; Senate 1989– ; Gov. 1982–1986.

Roberts, Pat (R-Kan.) April 20, 1936– ; House 1981–1997; Senate 1997– .

Rockefeller, John D. IV (nephew of Nelson Aldrich Rockefeller and great grandson of Nelson Aldrich) (D-W.Va.) June 18, 1937– ; Senate Jan. 15, 1985– ; Gov. 1977–1985.

Roemer, Tim (son-in-law of J. Bennett Johnston) (D-Ind.) Oct. 30, 1956– ; House 1991– .

Rogers, Harold (R-Ky.) Dec. 31, 1937– ; House 1981– .

Rohrabacher, Dana (R-Calif.) June 21, 1947– ; House 1989– .

Romero-Barceló, Carlos (D-P.R.) Sept. 4, 1932– ; House (Resident Commissioner) 1993– .

Rose, Charlie (D-N.C.) Aug. 10, 1939– ; House 1973–1997.

Ros-Lehtinen, Ileana (R-Fla.) July 15, 1952– ; House 1989– .

Rostenkowski, Dan (D-Ill.) Jan. 2, 1928– ; House 1959–1995.

Roth, Toby (R-Wis.) Oct. 10, 1938– ; House 1979–1997.

Roth, William V. Jr. (R-Del.) July 22, 1921– ; House 1967–Dec. 31, 1970; Senate Jan. 1, 1971– .

Roukema, Marge (R-N.J.) Sept. 19, 1929– ; House 1981– .

Rowland, J. Roy (D-Ga.) Feb. 3, 1926– ; House 1983– .

Roybal-Allard, Lucille (D-Calif.) June 12, 1941– ; House 1993– .

Royce, Ed (R-Calif.) Oct. 12, 1951– ; House 1993– .

Rush, Bobby L. (D-Ill.) Nov. 23, 1946– ; House 1993– .

Ryun, Jim (R-Kan.) April 29, 1947– ; House Nov. 27, 1996– .

S

Sabo, Martin Olav (D-Minn.) Feb. 28, 1938– ; House 1979– .

Salmon, Matt (R-Ariz.) Jan. 21, 1958– ; House 1995– .

Sanders, Bernard (I-Vt.) Sept. 8, 1941– ; House 1991– .

Sanford, Mark (R-S.C.) May 28, 1960– ; House 1995– .

Sangmeister, George E. (D-Ill.) Feb. 16, 1931– ; House 1989–1995.

Santorum, Rick (R-Pa.) May 10, 1958– ; House 1991–1995; Senate 1995– .

Sarbanes, Paul S. (D-Md.) Feb. 3, 1933– ; House 1971–1977; Senate 1977– .

Sarpalius, Bill (D-Texas) Jan. 10, 1948– ; House 1989–1995.

Sasser, Jim (D-Tenn.) Sept. 30, 1936– ; Senate 1977–1995.

Sawyer, Tom (D-Ohio) Aug. 15, 1945– ; House 1987– .

Saxton, H. James (R-N.J.) Jan. 22, 1943– ; House 1984– .

Scarborough, Joe (R-Fla.) April 9, 1963– ; House 1995– .

Schaefer, Dan (R-Colo.) Jan. 25, 1936– ; House April 7, 1983– .

Schenk, Lynn (D-Calif.) Jan. 5, 1945– ; House 1993–1995.

Schiff, Steven H. (R-N.M.) March 18, 1947– ; House 1989– .

Schroeder, Patricia (D-Colo.) July 30, 1940– ; House 1973–1977.

Schumer, Charles E. (D-N.Y.) Nov. 23, 1950– ; House 1981– .

Scott, Robert C. (D-Va.) April 30, 1947– ; House 1993– .

Seastrand, Andrea (R-Calif.) Aug. 5, 1941– ; House 1995–1997.

Sensenbrenner, F. James Jr. (R-Wis.) June 14, 1943– ; House 1979– .

Serrano, Jose E. (D-N.Y.) Oct. 24, 1943– ; House March 28, 1990– .

Shadegg, John (R-Ariz.) Oct. 22, 1949– ; House 1995– .

Sharp, Philip R. (D-Ind.) July 15, 1942– ; House 1975– .

Shaw, E. Clay Jr. (R-Fla.) April 19, 1939– ; House 1981– .

Shays, Christopher (R-Conn.) Oct. 18, 1945– ; House Sept. 9, 1987– .

Shelby, Richard C. (R-Ala.) May 6, 1934– ; House 1979–1987; Senate 1987– (1979–Nov. 19, 1994, Democrat).

Shepherd, Karen (D-Utah) July 5, 1940– ; House 1993–1995.

Shuster, Bud (R-Pa.) Jan. 23, 1932– ; House 1973– .

Simon, Paul (D-Ill.) Nov. 29, 1928– ; Senate 1985–1997.

Simpson, Alan K. (son of Milward Lee Simpson) (R-Wyo.) Sept. 2, 1931– ; Senate Jan. 1, 1979–1997.

Sisisky, Norman (D-Va.) June 9, 1927– ; House 1983– .

Skaggs, David E. (D-Colo.) Feb. 22, 1943– ; House 1987– .

Skeen, Joe (R-N.M.) June 30, 1927– ; House 1981– .

Skelton, Ike (D-Mo.) Dec. 20, 1931– ; House 1977– .

Slattery, Jim (D-Kan.) Aug. 4, 1948– ; House 1983– .

Slaughter, Louise M. (D-N.Y.) Aug. 14, 1929– ; House 1987– .

Smith, Bob (R-Ore.) June 16, 1931– ; House 1983–1995, 1997– .

Smith, Christopher H. (R-N.J.) March 4, 1953– ; House 1981– .

Smith, Lamar (R-Texas) Nov. 19, 1947– ; House 1987– .

Smith, Linda (R-Wash.) July 16, 1950– ; House 1995–1997.

Smith, Neal (D-Iowa) March 23, 1920– ; House 1959–1995.

Smith, Nick (R-Mich.) Nov. 5, 1934– ; House 1993– .

Smith, Robert C. (R-N.H.) March 30, 1941– ; House 1985–Dec. 7, 1990; Senate Dec. 7, 1990– .

Snowe, Olympia J. (wife of John R. McKernan Jr.) (R-Maine) Feb. 21, 1947– ; House 1979–1995; Senate 1995– .

Solomon, Gerald B. H. (R-N.Y.) Aug. 14, 1930– ; House 1979– .

Souder, Mark (R-Ind.) July 18, 1950– ; House 1995– .

Specter, Arlen (R-Pa.) Feb. 12, 1930– ; Senate 1981– .

Spence, Floyd D. (R-S.C.) April 9, 1928– ; House 1971– .

Spratt, John M. Jr. (D-S.C.) Nov. 1, 1942– ; House 1983– .

Stark, Pete (D-Calif.) Nov. 11, 1931– ; House 1973– .

Stearns, Cliff (R-Fla.) April 16, 1941– ; House 1989– .

Stenholm, Charles W. (D-Texas) Oct. 26, 1938– ; House 1979– .

Stevens, Ted (R-Alaska) Nov. 18, 1923– ; Senate Dec. 24, 1968– .

Stockman, Steve (R-Texas) Nov. 14, 1956– ; House 1995–1997.

Stokes, Louis (D-Ohio) Feb. 23, 1925– ; House 1969– .

Strickland, Ted (D-Ohio) Aug. 4, 1941– ; House 1993–1995, 1997– .

Studds, Gerry E. (D-Mass.) May 12, 1937– ; House 1973–1997.

Stump, Bob (R-Ariz.) April 4, 1927– ; House 1977– (1977–June 11, 1982, Democrat).

Stupak, Bart (D-Mich.) Feb. 29, 1952– ; House 1993– .

Sundquist, Don (R-Tenn.) March 15, 1936– ; House 1983–1995; Gov. 1995–.

Swett, Dick (son-in-law of Tom Lantos) (D-N.H.) May 1, 1957– ; House 1991–1995.

Swift, Al (D-Wash.) Sept. 12, 1935– ; House 1979–1995.

Synar, Mike (D-Okla.) Oct. 17, 1950–Jan. 9, 1996; House 1979–1995.

T

Talent, James M. (R-Mo.) Oct. 18, 1956– ; House 1993– .

Tanner, John (D-Tenn.) Sept. 22, 1944– ; House 1989– .

Tate, Randy (R-Wash.) Nov. 23, 1965– ; House 1995–1997.

Tauzin, W. J. "Billy" (R-La.) June 14, 1943– ; House May 17, 1980– (1980–Aug. 6, 1995, Democrat).

Taylor, Charles H. (R-N.C.) Jan. 23, 1941– ; House 1991– .

Taylor, Gene (D-Miss.) Sept. 17, 1953– ; House Oct. 24, 1989– .

Tejeda, Frank (D-Texas) Oct. 2, 1945–Jan. 30, 1997; House 1993–Jan. 30, 1997.

Thomas, Bill (R-Calif.) Dec. 6, 1941– ; House 1979– .

Thomas, Craig (R-Wyo.) Feb. 17, 1933– ; House May 2, 1989–1995; Senate 1995–.

Thompson, Bennie (D-Miss.) Jan. 28, 1948– ; House April 20, 1993– .

Thompson, Fred (R-Tenn.) Aug. 19, 1942– ; Senate Dec. 9, 1994– .

Thornberry, William M. "Mac" (R-Texas) July 15, 1958– ; House 1995– .

Thornton, Ray (D-Ark.) July 16, 1928– ; House 1973–1979, 1991–1997.

Thurman, Karen L. (D-Fla.) Jan. 12, 1951– ; House 1993– .

Thurmond, Strom (R-S.C.) Dec. 5, 1902– ; Senate Dec. 24, 1954–April 4, 1956, Nov. 1956– (1947–Sept. 16, 1964, Democrat); Pres. pro tempore 1981–1987, 1995–1997; Gov. 1947–1951.

Tiahrt, Todd (R-Kan.) June 15, 1951– ; House 1995– .

Torkildsen, Peter G. (R-Mass.) Jan. 28, 1958– ; House 1993–1997.

Torres, Esteban E. (D-Calif.) Jan. 27, 1930– ; House 1983– .

Torricelli, Robert G. (D-N.J.) Aug. 26, 1951– ; House 1983–1997; Senate 1997– .

Towns, Edolphus (D-N.Y.) July 21, 1934– ; House 1983– .

Traficant, James A. Jr. (D-Ohio) May 8, 1941– ; House 1985– .

Tucker, Walter R. III (D-Calif.) May 28, 1957– ; House 1993–Dec. 15, 1995.

U

Underwood, Robert A. (D-Guam) July 13, 1948– ; House (Delegate) 1993– .

Unsoeld, Jolene (D-Wash.) Dec. 3, 1931– ; House 1989–1995.

Upton, Fred (R-Mich.) April 23, 1953– ; House 1987– .

V

Valentine, Tim (D-N.C.) March 15, 1926– ; House 1983–1995.

Velázquez, Nydia M. (D-N.Y.) March 22, 1953– ; House 1993– .

Vento, Bruce F. (D-Minn.) Oct. 7, 1940– ; House 1977– .

Visclosky, Peter J. (D-Ind.) Aug. 13, 1949– ; House 1985– .

Volkmer, Harold L. (D-Mo.) April 4, 1931– ; House 1977–1997.

Vucanovich, Barbara F. (R-Nev.) June 22, 1921– ; House 1983–1997.

W

Waldholz, Enid Greene (R-Utah) Oct. 5, 1958– ; House 1995–1997.

Walker, Robert S. (R-Pa.) Dec. 23, 1942– ; House 1977–1997.

Wallop, Malcolm (R-Wyo.) Feb. 27, 1933– ; Senate 1977–1995.

Walsh, James T. (R-N.Y.) June 19, 1947– ; House 1989– .

Wamp, Zach (R-Tenn.) Oct. 28, 1957– ; House 1995– .

Ward, Mike (D-Ky.) Jan. 7, 1951– ; House 1995–1997.

Warner, John W. (R-Va.) Feb. 18, 1927– ; Senate Jan. 2, 1979– .

Washington, Craig (D-Texas) Oct. 12, 1941– ; House Dec. 9, 1989–1995.

Waters, Maxine (D-Calif.) Aug. 15, 1938– ; House 1991– .

Watt, Melvin (D-N.C.) Aug. 26, 1945– ; House 1993– .

Watts, J. C. (R-Okla.) Nov. 18, 1957– ; House 1995– .

Waxman, Henry A. (D-Calif.) Sept. 12, 1939– ; House 1975– .

Weldon, Curt (R-Pa.) July 22, 1947– ; House 1987– .

Weldon, Dave (R-Fla.) Aug. 31, 1953– ; House 1995– .

Weller, Jerry (R-Ill.) July 7, 1957– ; House 1995– .

Wellstone, Paul (D-Minn.) July 21, 1944– ; Senate 1991– .

Wheat, Alan (D-Mo.) Oct. 16, 1951– ; House 1983– .

White, Rick (R-Wash.) Nov. 6, 1953– ; House 1995– .

Whitfield, Edward (R-Ky.) May 25, 1943– ; House 1995– .

Whitten, Jamie L. (D-Miss.) April 18, 1910–Sept. 9, 1995; House Nov. 4, 1941–1995.

Wicker, Roger (R-Miss.) July 5, 1951– ; House 1995– .

Williams, Pat (D-Mont.) Oct. 30, 1937– ; House 1979–1997.

Wilson, Charles (D-Texas) June 1, 1933– ; House 1973–Oct. 8, 1996.

Wise, Bob (D-W.Va.) Jan. 6, 1948– ; House 1983– .

Wofford, Harris (D-Pa.) April 9, 1926– ; Senate May 9, 1991–1995.

Wolf, Frank R. (R-Va.) Jan. 30, 1939– ; House 1981– .

Woolsey, Lynn (D-Calif.) Nov. 3, 1937– ; House 1993– .

Wyden, Ron (D-Ore.) May 3, 1949– ; House 1981–Feb. 5, 1996; Senate Feb. 6, 1996– .

Wynn, Albert R. (D-Md.) Sept. 10, 1951– ; House 1993– .

Y

Yates, Sidney R. (D-Ill.) Aug. 27, 1909– ; House 1949–1963, 1965– .

Young, C. W. Bill (R-Fla.) Dec. 16, 1930– ; House 1971– .

Young, Don (R-Alaska) June 9, 1933– ; House March 6, 1973– .

Z

Zeliff, Bill (R-N.H.) June 12, 1936– ; House 1991–1997.

Zimmer, Dick (R-N.J.) Aug. 16, 1944– ; House 1991–1997.

Congressional Committees, 103rd and 104th Congresses

Following is a list of congressional committees and subcommittees as of the start of the 103rd and 104th Congresses. Committee jurisdictions, party ratios, committee chairmen and the dates of their service in that capacity, ranking minority members (in italics) and subcommittee chairmen are included. Political and joint committees also are listed.

In the 103rd Congress the Senate and House committee and subcommittee chairmen are Democrats and ranking minority members are Republicans; in the 104th Congress the Senate and House committee and subcommittee chairmen are Republicans and ranking minority members are Democrats.

Party ratios for House committees do not include delegates or the resident commissioner.

Senate Committees

AGRICULTURE, NUTRITION AND FORESTRY

Agriculture in general; animal industry and diseases; crop insurance and soil conservation; farm credit and farm security; food from fresh waters; food stamp programs; forestry in general; home economics; human nutrition; inspection of livestock, meat and agricultural products; pests and pesticides; plant industry, soils and agricultural engineering; rural development, rural electrification and watersheds; school nutrition programs.

D 10–R 8 (*103rd Congress*)

Patrick J. Leahy, Vt.
Richard G. Lugar, Ind.

Agricultural Credit—Kent Conrad, N.D.
Agricultural Research, Conservation, Forestry, and General Legislation—Tom Daschle, S.D.
Agricultural Production and Stabilization of Prices—David Pryor, Ark.
Domestic and Foreign Marketing and Product Promotion—David L. Boren, Okla.
Nutrition and Investigations—Tom Harkin, Iowa
Rural Development and Rural Electrification—Howell Heflin, Ala.

R 9–D 8 (*104th Congress, first session*)
R 10–D 8 (*104th Congress, second session*)

Richard G. Lugar, Ind.
Patrick J. Leahy, Vt.

Forestry, Conservation and Rural Revitalization—Larry E. Craig, Idaho
Marketing, Inspection and Product Promotion—Jesse Helms, N.C.
Production and Price Competitiveness—Thad Cochran, Miss.
Research, Nutrition and General Legislation—Mitch McConnell, Ky.

APPROPRIATIONS

Appropriation of revenue; rescission of appropriations; new spending authority under the Congressional Budget Act.

D 16–R 13 (*103rd Congress*)

Robert C. Byrd, W.Va.
Mark O. Hatfield, Ore.

Agriculture, Rural Development and Related Agencies—Dale Bumpers, Ark.
Commerce, Justice, State and Judiciary—Ernest F. Hollings, S.C.
Defense—Daniel K. Inouye, Hawaii
District of Columbia—Herb Kohl, Wis.
Energy and Water Development—J. Bennett Johnston, La.
Foreign Operations—Patrick J. Leahy, Vt.
Interior—Robert C. Byrd, W.Va.
Labor, Health and Human Services and Education—Tom Harkin, Iowa
Legislative Branch—Harry Reid, Nev.
Military Construction—Jim Sasser, Tenn.
Transportation—Frank Lautenberg, N.J.
Treasury, Postal Service and General Government—Dennis DeConcini, Ariz.
VA, HUD and Independent Agencies—Barbara Mikulski, Md.

R 15–D 13 (*104th Congress*)

Mark O. Hatfield, Ore., chairman
Robert C. Byrd, W.Va.

Agriculture, Rural Development and Related Agencies—Thad Cochran, Miss.
Commerce, Justice, State and Judiciary—Phil Gramm, Texas (104th Congress, first session); Judd Gregg, N.H. (104th Congress, second session)
Defense—Ted Stevens, Alaska
District of Columbia—James M. Jeffords, Vt.
Energy and Water Development—Pete V. Domenici, N.M.
Foreign Operations—Mitch McConnell, Ky.
Interior—Slade Gorton, Wash.
Labor, Health and Human Services and Education—Arlen Specter, Pa.
Legislative Branch—Connie Mack, Fla.
Military Construction—Conrad Burns, Mont.
Transportation—Mark O. Hatfield, Ore.
Treasury, Postal Service and General Government—Richard C. Shelby, Ala.
VA, HUD and Independent Agencies—Christopher S. Bond, Mo.

ARMED SERVICES

Defense and defense policy generally; aeronautical and space activities peculiar to or primarily associated with the development of weapons systems or military operations; maintenance and operation of the Panama Canal, including the Canal Zone; military research and development; national security aspects of nuclear energy; naval petroleum reserves (except Alaska); armed forces generally; Selective Service System; strategic and critical materials.

D 11–R 9 (*103rd Congress, first session*)
D 12–R 10 (*103rd Congress, second session*)

Sam Nunn, Ga.
Strom Thurmond, S.C.

Coalition Defense and Reinforcing Forces—Carl Levin, Mich.
Defense Technology, Acquisition and Industrial Base—Jeff Bingaman, N.M.
Force Requirements and Personnel—Richard C. Shelby, Ala.
Military Readiness and Defense Infrastructure—John Glenn, Ohio
Nuclear Deterrence, Arms Control and Defense Intelligence—Jim Exon, Neb.
Regional Defense and Contingency Forces—Edward M. Kennedy, Mass.

R 11–D 10 (*104th Congress*)

Strom Thurmond, S.C.
Sam Nunn, Ga.

Acquisition and Technology—Robert C. Smith, N.H.
Airland Forces—John W. Warner, Va.
Personnel—Daniel Coats, Ind.
Readiness—John McCain, Ariz.
Seapower—William S. Cohen, Maine
Strategic Forces—Trent Lott, Miss.

BANKING, HOUSING AND URBAN AFFAIRS

Banks, banking and financial institutions; price controls; deposit insurance; economic stabilization and growth; defense production; export and foreign trade promotion; export controls; federal monetary policy, including Federal Reserve System; financial aid to commerce and industry; issuance and redemption of notes; money and credit, including currency and coinage; nursing home construction; public and private housing, including veterans' housing; renegotiation of government contracts; urban development and mass transit; international economic policy.

R 9–D 7 (*103rd Congress*)

Donald W. Riegle Jr., Mich.
Alfonse M. D'Amato, N.Y.

Economic Stabilization and Rural Development—Richard C. Shelby, Ala.
Housing and Urban Affairs—Paul S. Sarbanes, Md.
International Finance and Monetary Policy—Jim Sasser, Tenn.
Securities—Christopher J. Dodd, Conn.

R 9–D 7 (*104th Congress*)

Alfonse M. D'Amato, N.Y.
Paul S. Sarbanes, Md.

Financial Institutions and Regulatory Relief—Richard C. Shelby, Ala.
Housing Opportunity and Community Development—Connie Mack, Fla.
HUD Oversight and Structure—Lauch Faircloth, N.C.
International Finance—Christopher S. Bond, Mo.
Securities—Phil Gramm, Texas

BUDGET

Federal budget generally; concurrent budget resolutions; Congressional Budget Office.

D 12–R 9 (*103rd Congress*)

Jim Sasser, Tenn.
Pete V. Domenici, N.M.

R 12–D 10 (*104th Congress*)

Pete V. Domenici, N.M.
Jim Exon, Neb.

No standing subcommittees.

COMMERCE, SCIENCE AND TRANSPORTATION

Interstate commerce and transportation generally, Coast Guard; coastal zone management; communications; highway safety; inland waterways, except construction; marine fisheries; Merchant Marine and navigation; nonmilitary aeronautical and space sciences; oceans, weather and atmospheric activities; interoceanic canals generally; regulation of consumer products and services; science, engineering and technology research, development and policy; sports; standards and measurement; transportation and commerce aspects of outer continental shelf lands.

D 11–R 9 (*103rd Congress*)

Ernest F. Hollings, S.C.
John C. Danforth, Mo.

Aviation—Wendell H. Ford, Ky.
Communications—Daniel K. Inouye, Hawaii
Consumer—Richard H. Bryan, Nev.
Foreign Commerce and Tourism—John Kerry, Mass.
Merchant Marine—John B. Breaux, La.
National Ocean Policy Study—Ernest F. Hollings, S.C.
Science, Technology and Space—John D. Rockefeller IV, W.Va.
Surface Transportation—Jim Exon, Neb.

R 10–D 9 (*104th Congress*)

Larry Pressler, S.D.
Ernest F. Hollings, S.C.

Aviation—John McCain, Ariz.
Communications—Bob Packwood, Ore. (resigned Oct. 1, 1995); Larry Pressler, S.D. (through 104th Congress)

Consumer Affairs, Foreign Commerce and Tourism—Slade Gorton, Wash.
Oceans and Fisheries—Ted Stevens, Alaska
Science, Technology and Space—Conrad Burns, Mont.
Surface Transportation and Merchant Marine—Trent Lott, Miss.

ENERGY AND NATURAL RESOURCES

Energy policy, regulation, conservation, research and development; coal; energy-related aspects of deep-water ports; hydroelectric power, irrigation and reclamation; mines, mining and minerals generally; national parks, recreation areas, wilderness areas, wild and scenic rivers, historic sites, military parks and battlefields; naval petroleum reserves in Alaska; nonmilitary development of nuclear energy; oil and gas production and distribution; public lands and forests; solar energy systems; territorial possessions of the United States.

D 11—R 9 *(103rd Congress)*

J. Bennett Johnston, La.
Malcolm Wallop, Wyo.

Energy Research and Development—Wendell H. Ford, Ky.
Mineral Resources Development and Production—Daniel K. Akaka, Hawaii
Public Lands, National Parks and Forests—Dale Bumpers, Ark.
Renewable Energy, Energy Efficiency and Competitiveness—Jeff Bingaman, N.M.
Water and Power Bill Bradley, N.J.

R 11—D 7 *(104th Congress, first session)*
R 11—D 9 *(104th Congress, second session)*

Frank H. Murkowski, Alaska
J. Bennett Johnston, La.

Energy Production and Regulation—Don Nickles, Okla.
Energy Research and Development—Pete V. Domenici, N.M.
Forests and Public Land Management—Larry E. Craig, Idaho
Oversight and Investigations (104th Congress, second session)—Craig Thomas, Idaho
Parks, Historic Preservation and Recreation—Craig Thomas, Wyo. (104th Congress, first session); Ben Nighthorse Campbell, Colo. (104th Congress, second session)

ENVIRONMENT AND PUBLIC WORKS

Environmental policy, research and development; air, water and noise pollution; construction and maintenance of highways; environmental aspects of outer continental shelf lands; environmental effects of toxic substances other than pesticides; fisheries and wildlife; flood control and improvements of rivers and harbors; non-military environmental regulation and control of nuclear energy; ocean dumping; public buildings and grounds; public works, bridges and dams; regional economic development; solid waste disposal and recycling; water resources.

D 10–R 7 *(103rd Congress)*

Max Baucus, Mont.
John H. Chafee, R.I.

Clean Air and Nuclear Regulation—Joseph I. Lieberman, Conn.
Clean Water, Fisheries and Wildlife—Bob Graham, Fla.
Superfund, Recycling and Solid Waste Management—Frank R. Lautenberg, N.J.
Toxic Substances, Research and Development—Harry Reid, Nev.
Water Resources, Transportation, Public Buildings and Economic Development—Daniel Patrick Moynihan, N.Y.

R 9–D 7 *(104th Congress)*

John H. Chafee, R.I.
Max Baucus, Mont.

Clean Air, Wetlands, Private Property and Nuclear Safety—Lauch Faircloth, N.C.
Drinking Water, Fisheries and Wildlife—Dirk Kempthorne, Idaho
Superfund, Waste Control and Risk Assessment—Robert C. Smith, N.H.
Transportation and Infrastructure—John W. Warner, Va.

FINANCE

Revenue measures generally; taxes; tariffs and import quotas; reciprocal trade agreements; customs; revenue sharing; federal debt limit; Social Security; health programs financed by taxes or trust funds.

D 11–R 9 *(103rd Congress)*

Daniel Patrick Moynihan, N.Y.
Bob Packwood, Ore.

Deficits, Debt Management and Long-Term Economic Growth—Bill Bradley, N.J.
Energy and Agricultural Taxation—Tom Daschle, S.D.
Health for Families and the Uninsured—Donald W. Riegle Jr., Mich.
International Trade—Max Baucus, Mont.
Medicare and Long-Term Care—John D. Rockefeller, W.Va.
Private Retirement Plans and Oversight of the Internal Revenue Service—David Pryor, Ark.
Social Security and Family Policy—John B. Breaux, La.
Taxation—David L. Boren, Okla.

R 11–D 9 *(104th Congress)*

Bob Packwood, Ore. (resigned chair Sept. 12, 1995)
William W. Roth, Del. (through 104th Congress)
Daniel Patrick Moynihan, N.Y.

International Trade—Charles E. Grassley, Iowa
Long-Term Growth, Debt and Deficit Reduction—Larry Pressler, S.D. (104th Congress, first session); Alfonse M. D'Amato, N.Y. (104th Congress, second session)

Medicaid and Health Care for Low-Income Families—John H. Chafee, R.I.

Medicare, Long-Term Care and Health Insurance—Bob Dole, Kan. (resigned June 11, 1996); John H. Chafee, R.I.(acting chairman through 104th Congress)

Social Security and Family Policy—Alan K. Simpson, Wyo.

Taxation and IRS Oversight—Orrin G. Hatch, Utah

FOREIGN RELATIONS

Relations of the United States with foreign nations generally; treaties; foreign economic, military, technical and humanitarian assistance; foreign loans; diplomatic service; International Red Cross; international aspects of nuclear energy; International Monetary Fund; intervention abroad and declarations of war; foreign trade; national security; oceans and international environmental and scientific affairs; protection of U.S. citizens abroad; United Nations; World Bank and other development assistance organizations.

D 11–R 8 (103rd Congress)

Claiborne Pell, R.I.

Jesse Helms, N.C.

African Affairs—Paul Simon, Ill.

East Asian and Pacific Affairs—Charles S. Robb, Va.

European Affairs—Joseph R. Biden Jr., Del.

International Economic Policy, Trade, Oceans and Environment—Paul S. Sarbanes, Md.

Near Eastern and South Asian Affairs—Daniel Patrick Moynihan, N.Y.

Terrorism, Narcotics and International Operations—John Kerry, Mass.

Western Hemisphere and Peace Corps Affairs—Christopher J. Dodd, Conn.

R 10–D 8 (104th Congress)

Jesse Helms, N.C.

Claiborne Pell, R.I.

African Affairs—Nancy Landon Kassebaum, Kan.

East Asian and Pacific Affairs—Craig Thomas, Wyo.

European Affairs—Richard G. Lugar, Ind.

International Economic Policy, Export and Trade Promotion—Fred Thompson, Tenn.

International Operations—Olympia Snowe, Maine

Near Eastern and South Asian Affairs—Hank Brown, Colo.

Western Hemisphere and Peace Corps Affairs—Paul Coverdell, Ga.

GOVERNMENTAL AFFAIRS

Archives of the United States; budget and accounting measures; census and statistics; federal civil service; congressional organization; intergovernmental relations; government information; District of Columbia; organization and management of nuclear export policy; executive branch organization and reorganization; Postal Service; efficiency, economy and effectiveness of government.

D 8–R 5 (103rd Congress)

John Glenn, Ohio

William V. Roth Jr., Del.

Federal Service, Post Office and Civil Service—David Pryor, Ark.

General Services, Federalism and the District of Columbia—Jim Sasser, Tenn.

Oversight of Government Management—Carl Levin, Mich.

Permanent Subcommittee on Investigations—Sam Nunn, Ga.

Regulation and Government Information—Joseph I. Lieberman, Conn.

R 8–D 7 (104th Congress)

William V. Roth Jr., Del. (104th Congress, first session)

Ted Stevens, Alaska (104th Congress, second session)

John Glenn, Ohio

Oversight of Government Management and the District of Columbia—William S. Cohen, Maine

Permanent Investigations—William V. Roth Jr., Del.

Post Office and Civil Service—Ted Stevens, Alaska

INDIAN AFFAIRS

Problems and opportunities of Native Americans, including Native American land management and trust responsibilities, education, health, special services, loan programs and claims against the United States.

D 10–R 8 (103rd Congress)

John McCain, Ariz.

Daniel K. Inouye, Hawaii

R 10–D 7 (104th Congress, first session)
R 9–D 7 (104th Congress, second session)

Daniel K. Inouye, Hawaii

John McCain, Ariz.

No standing subcommittees.

JUDICIARY

Civil and criminal judicial proceedings in general; penitentiaries; bankruptcy, mutiny, espionage and counterfeiting; civil liberties; constitutional amendments; apportionment of representatives; government information; immigration and naturalization; interstate compacts in general; claims against the United States; patents, copyrights and trademarks; monopolies and unlawful restraints of trade; holidays and celebrations.

D 10–R 8 (103rd Congress)

Joseph R. Biden Jr., Del.

Orrin G. Hatch, Utah

Antitrust, Monopolies and Business Rights—Howard Metzenbaum, Ohio

Constitution—Paul Simon, Ill.

Courts and Administrative Practice—Howell Heflin, Ala.
Immigration and Refugee Affairs—Edward M. Kennedy, Mass.
Juvenile Justice—Herb Kohl, Wis.
Patents, Copyrights and Trademarks—Dennis DeConcini, Ariz.
Technology and the Law—Patrick J. Leahy, Vt.

R 10–D 8 *(104th Congress)*

Orrin G. Hatch, Utah
Joseph R. Biden Jr., Del.

Administrative Oversight and the Courts—Charles E. Grassley, Iowa
Antitrust, Business Rights and Competition—Strom Thurmond, S.C.
Constitution, Federalism and Property Rights—Hank Brown, Colo.
Immigration—Alan K. Simpson, Wyo.
Terrorism, Technology and Government Information—Arlen Specter, Pa.
Youth Violence—Fred Thompson, Tenn.

LABOR AND HUMAN RESOURCES

Education, labor, health and public welfare in general; aging; arts and humanities; biomedical research and development; child labor; convict labor; domestic activities of the Red Cross; equal employment opportunity; handicapped people; labor standards and statistics; mediation and arbitration of labor disputes; occupational safety and health; private pensions; public health; railway labor and retirement; regulation of foreign laborers; student loans; wages and hours; agricultural colleges; Gallaudet University; Howard University; St. Elizabeth's Hospital in Washington, D.C.

D 10–R 7 *(103rd Congress)*

Edward M. Kennedy, Mass.
Nancy Landon Kassebaum, Kan.

Aging—Barbara Mikulski, Md.
Children, Family, Drugs and Alcoholism—Christopher J. Dodd, Conn.
Disability Policy—Tom Harkin, Iowa
Education, Arts and Humanities—Claiborne Pell, R.I.
Employment and Productivity—Paul Simon, Ill.
Labor—Howard Metzenbaum, Ohio

R 9–D 7 *(104th Congress)*

Nancy Landon Kassebaum, Kan.
Edward M. Kennedy, Mass.

Aging—Judd Gregg, N.H.
Children and Families—Daniel R. Coats, Ind.
Disability Policy—Bill Frist, Tenn.
Education, Arts and Humanities—James M. Jeffords, Vt.

RULES AND ADMINISTRATION

Senate administration in general; corrupt practices; qualifications

of senators; contested elections; federal elections in general; Government Printing Office; *Congressional Record;* meetings of Congress and attendance of members; presidential succession; the Capitol, congressional office buildings, the Library of Congress, the Smithsonian Institution and the Botanic Garden.

D 9–R 7 *(103rd Congress)*

Wendell H. Ford, Ky.
Ted Stevens, Alaska

R 9–D 7 *(104th Congress)*

Ted Stevens, Alaska (104th Congress, first session)
John Warner, Va. (104th Congress, second session)
Wendell H. Ford, Ky.

No standing subcommittees.

SELECT ETHICS

Studies and investigates standards and conduct of Senate members and employees and may recommend remedial action.

D 3–R 3 *(103rd Congress)*

Richard H. Bryan, Nev.
Mitch McConnell, Ky. (vice chairman)

R 3–D 3 *(104th Congress)*

Mitch McConnell, Ky.
Richard H. Bryan, Nev. (vice chairman, 104th Congress, first session)
Byron L. Dorgan, N.D. (vice chairman, 104th Congress, second session)

No standing subcommittees.

SELECT INTELLIGENCE

Legislative and budgetary authority over the Central Intelligence Agency, the Defense Intelligence Agency, the National Security Agency and intelligence activities of the Federal Bureau of Investigation and other components of the federal intelligence community.

D 9–R 8 *(103rd Congress)*

Dennis DeConcini, Ariz.
John W. Warner, Va. (vice chairman)

R 9–D 8 *(104th Congress)*

Arlen Specter, Pa.
Bob Kerrey, Neb. (vice chairman)

No standing subcommittees.

SMALL BUSINESS

Problems of small business; Small Business Administration.

D 12–R 9 *(103rd Congress, first session)*
D 12–R 10 *(103rd Congress, second session)*

Dale Bumpers, Ark.
Larry Pressler, S.D.

Competitiveness, Capital Formation and Economic Opportunity—Joseph I. Lieberman, Conn.
Export Expansion and Agricultural Development—Harris Wofford, Pa.
Government Contracting and Paperwork Reduction—Sam Nunn, Ga.
Innovation, Manufacturing and Technology—Carl Levin, Mich.
Rural Economy and Family Farming—Paul Wellstone, Minn.
Urban and Minority-Owned Business Development—John Kerry, Mass.

R 10–D 9 *(104th Congress)*

Christopher S. Bond, Mo.
Dale Bumpers, Ark.

No standing subcommittees.

SPECIAL AGING

Problems and opportunities of older people including health, income, employment, housing, and care and assistance. Reports findings and makes recommendations to the Senate, but cannot report legislation.

D 11–R 10 *(103rd Congress)*

David Pryor, Ark.
William S. Cohen, Maine

R 10–D 9 *(104th Congress)*

William S. Cohen, Maine
David Pryor, Ark.

No standing subcommittees.

VETERANS' AFFAIRS

Veterans' measures in general; compensation; life insurance issued by the government on account of service in the armed forces; national cemeteries; pensions; readjustment benefits; veterans' hospitals, medical care and treatment; vocational rehabilitation and education.

D 7–R 5 *(103rd Congress)*

John D. Rockefeller IV, W.Va.
Frank H. Murkowski, Alaska

R 8–D 4 *(104th Congress, first session)*
R 7–D 5 *(104th Congress, second session)*

Alan K. Simpson
John D. Rockefeller IV, W.Va.

No standing subcommittees.

POLITICAL COMMITTEES

Democratic Policy Committee (an arm of the Democratic Caucus that advises on legislative priorities)—George J. Mitchell, Maine, chairman (103rd Congress); Tom Daschle, S.D., chairman (104th Congress)

Democratic Senatorial Campaign Committee (campaign support committee for Democratic senatorial candidates)—Bob Graham, Fla., chairman (103rd Congress); Bob Kerrey, Neb., chairman (104th Congress)

Democratic Steering and Coordination Committee—104th Congress (makes Democratic committee assignments)—John Kerry, Mass., chairman

Democratic Steering Committee—103rd Congress (makes Democratic committee assignments)—Daniel K. Inouye, Hawaii, chairman

Democratic Technology and Communications Committee (seeks to improve communications with the public about the Democratic Party and its policies)—John D. Rockefeller IV, W.Va., chairman

Republican Committee on Committees (makes Republican committee assignments)—Conrad Burns, Mont., chairman (103rd Congress); Larry E. Craig, Idaho, chairman (104th Congress)

Republican Policy Committee (advises on party action and policy)—Don Nickles, Okla., chairman

National Republican Senatorial Committee (campaign support committee for Republican senatorial candidates)—Phil Gramm, Texas, chairman (103rd Congress); Alfonse M. D'Amato, N.Y., chairman (104th Congress)

House Committees

AGRICULTURE

Agriculture generally; forestry in general, and forest reserves other than those created from the public domain; adulteration of seeds, insect pests, and protection of birds and animals in forest reserves; agricultural and industrial chemistry; agricultural colleges and experiment stations; agricultural economics and research; agricultural education extension services; agricultural production and marketing and stabilization of prices of agricultural products, and commodities (not including distribution outside the United States); animal industry and diseases of animals; commodities exchanges; crop insurance and soil conservation; dairy industry; entomology and plant quarantine; extension of farm credit and farm security; inspection of livestock, poultry, meat products, seafood and seafood products; human nutrition and home economics; plant industry, soils and agricultural engineering; rural electrification; rural development; water conservation related to activities of the Department of Agriculture.

D 27–R 18 *(103rd Congress, first session)*
D 29–R 19 *(103rd Congress, second session)*

E. "Kika" de la Garza, Texas
Pat Roberts, Kan.

Department Operations and Nutrition—Charles W. Stenholm, Texas

Environment, Credit and Rural Development—Glenn English, Okla. (resigned Jan. 7, 1994); Tim Johnson, S.D. (through 103rd Congress)

Foreign Agriculture and Hunger—Timothy J. Penny, Minn.

General Farm Commodities—Tim Johnson, S.D. (103rd Congress, first session); Bill Sarpalius, Texas (103rd Congress, second session)

Livestock—Harold L. Volkmer, Mo.

Specialty Crops and Natural Resources—Charlie Rose, N.C.

R 27–D 22 *(104th Congress)*

Pat Roberts, Kan.
E. "Kika" de la Garza, Texas

Department Operations, Nutrition and Foreign Agriculture—Bill Emerson, Mo. (died June 22, 1996); Robert W. Goodlatte, Va. (through 104th Congress)

General Farm Commodities—Bill Barrett, Neb.

Livestock, Dairy and Poultry—Steve Gunderson, Wis.

Resource Conservation, Research and Forestry—Wayne Allard, Colo.

Risk Management and Specialty Crops—Thomas W. Ewing, Ill.

APPROPRIATIONS

Appropriation of the revenue for the support of the government; rescissions of appropriations contained in appropriation acts; transfers of unexpended balances; new spending authority under the Congressional Budget Act.

D 37–R 23 *(103rd Congress)*

William H. Natcher, Ky. (died March 29, 1994)
David R. Obey, Wis. (through 103rd Congress)
Joseph M. McDade, Pa.

Agriculture, Rural Development and Related Agencies—Richard J. Durbin, Ill.

Commerce, Justice, State and Judiciary—Neal Smith, Iowa

Defense—John P. Murtha, Pa.

District of Columbia—Julian C. Dixon, Calif.

Energy and Water Development—Tom Bevill, Ala.

Foreign Operations—David R. Obey, Wis.

Interior—Sidney R. Yates, Ill.

Labor, Health and Human Services, and Education—William H. Natcher, Ky. (died March 29, 1994); Neal Smith, Iowa (through 104th Congress)

Legislative Branch—Vic Fazio, Calif.

Military Construction—W. G. "Bill" Hefner, N.C.

Transportation—Bob Carr, Mich.

Treasury, Postal Service and General Government—Steny H. Hoyer, Md.

Veterans Affairs, Housing and Urban Development and Independent Agencies—Louis Stokes, Ohio

R 32–D 24 *(104th Congress, first session)*
R 33–D 25 *(104th Congress, second session)*

Robert L. Livingston, La.
David R. Obey, Wis.

Agriculture, Rural Development, FDA and Related Agencies—Joe Skeen, N.M.

Commerce, Justice, State and Judiciary—Harold Rogers, Ky.

District of Columbia—James T. Walsh, N.Y.

Energy and Water Development—John T. Myers, Ind.

Foreign Operations, Export Financing and Related Programs—Sonny Callahan, Ala.

Interior—Ralph Regula, Ohio

Labor, Health and Human Services, and Education—John Edward Porter, Ill.

Legislative Branch—Ron Packard, Calif.

Military Construction—Barbara F. Vucanovich, Nev.

National Security—C. W. Bill Young, Fla.

Transportation—Frank R. Wolf, Va.

Treasury, Postal Service and General Government—Robert L. Livingston, La.

Veterans Affairs, Housing and Urban Development and Independent Agencies—Jerry Lewis, Calif.

ARMED SERVICES[a]

Common defense generally; Department of Defense, including the Departments of the Army, Navy and Air Force; ammunition depots; forts; arsenals; army, navy, and air force reservations and establishments; conservation, development, and use of naval petroleum and oil shale reserves; pay, promotion, retirement, and other benefits and privileges of members of the armed forces; scientific research and development in support of the armed services; selective service; size and composition of the army, navy, and air force; soldiers' and sailors' homes; strategic and critical materials necessary for the common defense; and military applications of nuclear energy.

D 33–R 22–I 1 *(103rd Congress)*

Ronald V. Dellums, Calif.
Floyd D. Spence, S.C.

Military Acquisition—Ronald V. Dellums, Calif.

Military Forces and Personnel—Ike Skelton, Mo.

Military Installations and Facilities—Dave McCurdy, Okla.

Oversight and Investigations—Norman Sisisky, Va.

Readiness—Earl Hutto, Fla.

Research and Technology—Patricia Schroeder, Colo.

BANKING AND FINANCIAL SERVICES[b]

Banks and banking, including deposit insurance and federal monetary policy; bank capital markets activities generally; depository institution securities activities generally, including the activities of any affiliates, except for functional regulation under applicable securities laws not involving safety and soundness; economic stabilization, defense production, renegotiation, and control of the price of commodities, rents, and services; financial aid to commerce and industry (other than transportation); international finance; international financial and monetary organizations; money and credit, including currency and the issuance of notes and redemption thereof; gold and silver, including the coinage thereof; valuation and revaluation of the dollar; public and private housing; urban development.

R 27–D 22–I 1 (104th Congress, first session)
R 28–D 25–I 1 (104th Congress, second session)

Jim Leach, Iowa
Henry B. Gonzalez, Texas

Capital Markets, Securities and Government-Sponsored Enterprises—Richard H. Baker, La.
Domestic and International Monetary Policy—Michael N. Castle, Del.
Financial Institutions and Consumer Credit—Marge Roukema, N.J.
General Oversight and Investigations—Spencer Bachus, Ala.
Housing and Community Opportunity—Rick A. Lazio, N.Y.

BANKING, FINANCE AND URBAN AFFAIRS[c]

Banks and banking, including deposit insurance and federal monetary policy; money and credit; currency; issuance and redemption of notes; gold and silver; coinage; valuation and revaluation of the dollar; urban development; public and private housing; economic stabilization; defense production; renegotiation; price controls; international finance; financial aid to commerce and industry.

D 30–R 20–I 1 (103rd Congress)

Henry B. Gonzalez, Texas
Jim Leach, Iowa

Consumer Credit and Insurance—Joseph P. Kennedy II, Mass.
Economic Growth and Credit Formation—Paul E. Kanjorski, Pa.
Financial Institutions Supervision, Regulation and Deposit Insurance—Stephen L. Neal, N.C.
General Oversight, Investigations and the Resolution of Failed Financial Institutions—Floyd H. Flake, N.Y.
Housing and Community Development—Henry B. Gonzalez, Texas
International Development, Finance, Trade and Monetary Policy—Barney Frank, Mass.

BUDGET

Congressional budget process generally; concurrent budget resolutions; measures relating to special controls over the federal budget; Congressional Budget Office.

D 26–R 17 (103rd Congress)

Martin Olav Sabo, Minn.
John R. Kasich, Ohio

R 24–D 18 (104th Congress)

John R. Kasich, Ohio
Martin Olav Sabo, Minn.

No standing subcommittees.

COMMERCE[d]

Interstate and foreign commerce generally; biomedical research and development; consumer affairs and consumer protection; health and health facilities, except health care supported by payroll deductions; interstate energy compacts; measures relating to the exploration, production, storage, supply, marketing, pricing, and regulation of energy resources, including all fossil fuels, solar energy, and other unconventional or renewable energy resources; measures relating to the conservation of energy resources; measures relating to energy information generally; measures relating to (A) the generation and marketing of power (except by federally chartered or federal regional power marketing authorities), (B) the reliability and interstate transmission of, and ratemaking for, all power, and (C) the siting of generation facilities, except the installation of interconnections between government water power projects; measures relating to general management of the Department of Energy, and the management and all functions of the Federal Energy Regulatory Commission; national energy policy generally; public health and quarantine; regulation of the domestic nuclear energy industry, including regulation of research and development reactors and nuclear regulatory research; regulation of interstate and foreign communications; securities and exchanges; travel and tourism; nuclear and other energy, and nonmilitary nuclear energy and research and development including the disposal of nuclear waste.

R 25–D 21 (104th Congress, first session)
R 27–D 22 (104th Congress, second session)

Thomas J. Bliley Jr., Va.
John D. Dingell, Mich.

Commerce, Trade and Hazardous Materials—Michael G. Oxley, Ohio
Energy and Power—Dan Schaefer, Colo.
Health and Environment—Michael Bilirakis, Fla.
Oversight and Investigations—Joe L. Barton, Texas
Telecommunications and Finance—Jack Fields, Texas

DISTRICT OF COLUMBIA[e]

Municipal affairs of the District of Columbia.

D 7–R 4 (103rd Congress)

Pete Stark, Calif.
Thomas J. Bliley Jr., Va.

Fiscal Affairs and Health—Jim McDermott, Wash.
Government Operations and Metropolitan Affairs—Alan Wheat, Mo.
Judiciary and Education—Eleanor Holmes Norton, D.C.

ECONOMIC AND EDUCATIONAL OPPORTUNITIES[f]

Measures relating to education or labor generally; child labor; Columbia Institution for the Deaf, Dumb and Blind; Howard University; Freedmen's Hospital; convict labor and the entry of goods made by convicts into interstate commerce; food programs for children in schools; labor standards and statistics; mediation and arbitration of labor disputes; regulation or prevention of importation of foreign laborers under contract; U.S. Employees' Compensation Commission; vocational rehabilitation; wages and hours of labor; welfare of miners; work incentive programs.

R 24–D 19 (104th Congress)

Bill Goodling, Pa.
William L. Clay, Mo.

Early Childhood, Youth and Families—Randy "Duke" Cunningham, Calif.
Employer-Employee Relations—Harris W. Fawell, Ill.
Oversight and Investigations—Peter Hoekstra, Mich.
Postsecondary Education, Training and Life-Long Learning—Howard P. "Buck" McKeon
Workforce Protections—Cass Ballenger, N.C.

EDUCATION AND LABOR[g]

Education and labor generally; child labor; convict labor; labor standards and statistics; mediation and arbitration of labor disputes; regulation of foreign laborers; school food programs; vocational rehabilitation; wages and hours; welfare of miners; work services programs; Howard University; Columbia Institution for the Deaf, Dumb and Blind; Freedmen's Hospital.

D 24–R 15 (103rd Congress)

William D. Ford, Mich.
Bill Goodling, Pa.

Elementary, Secondary and Vocational Education—Dale E. Kildee, Mich.
Human Resources—Matthew G. Martinez, Calif.
Select Education and Civil Rights—Major R. Owens, N.Y.
Labor Standards, Occupational Health and Safety—Austin J. Murphy, Pa.
Labor-Management Relations—Pat Williams, Mont.
Postsecondary Education and Training—William D. Ford, Mich.

ENERGY AND COMMERCE[h]

Interstate and foreign commerce generally; national energy policy generally; exploration, production, storage, supply, marketing, pricing, and regulation of energy resources; nuclear energy; solar energy; energy conservation; generation and marketing of power; inland waterways; railroads and railway labor and retirement; communications generally; securities and exchanges; consumer affairs; travel and tourism; public health and quarantine; health-care facilities; biomedical research and development; Department of Energy; Federal Energy Regulatory Commission.

D 27–R 17 (103rd Congress)

John D. Dingell, Mich.
Carlos J. Moorhead, Calif.

Commerce, Consumer Protection and Competitiveness—Cardiss Collins, Ill.
Energy and Power—Philip R. Sharp, Ind.
Health and the Environment—Henry A. Waxman, Calif.
Oversight and Investigations—John D. Dingell, Mich.
Telecommunications and Finance—Edward J. Markey, Mass.
Transportation and Hazardous Materials—Al Swift, Wash.

FOREIGN AFFAIRS[i]

Relations of the United States with foreign nations generally; foreign loans; international conferences and congresses; intervention abroad and declarations of war; diplomatic service; foreign trade; neutrality; protection of Americans abroad; Red Cross; United Nations; international economic policy; export controls including nonproliferation of nuclear technology and hardware; international commodity agreements; trading with the enemy; international financial and monetary organizations; international education.

D 26–R 18 (103rd Congress)

Lee H. Hamilton, Ind.
Benjamin A. Gilman, N.Y.

Africa—Harry Johnston, Fla.
Asia and the Pacific—Gary L. Ackerman, N.Y.
Economic Policy, Trade and the Environment—Sam Gejdenson, Conn.
Europe and the Middle East—Lee H. Hamilton, Ind.
International Operations—Howard L. Berman, Calif.
International Security, International Organizations and Human Rights—Tom Lantos, Calif.
Western Hemisphere Affairs—Robert G. Torricelli, N.J.

GOVERNMENT OPERATIONS[j]

Budget and accounting measures, generally; overall economy and efficiency in government, including federal procurement; executive branch reorganization; general revenue sharing; intergovernmental relations; National Archives; off-budget treatment of federal agencies and programs.

D 25–R 16–I 1 (103rd Congress)

John Conyers Jr., Mich.
William F. Clinger, Pa.

Commerce, Consumer and Monetary Affairs—John M. Spratt Jr., S.C.
Employment, Housing and Aviation—Collin C. Peterson, Minn.
Environment, Energy and Natural Resources—Mike Synar, Okla.
Human Resources and Intergovernmental Relations—Edolphus Towns, N.Y.
Information, Justice, Transportation and Agriculture—Gary A. Condit, Calif.
Legislation and National Security—John Conyers, Calif.

GOVERNMENT REFORM AND OVERSIGHT[k]

Civil service, including intergovernmental personnel; the status of officers and employees of the United States, including their compensation, classification, and retirement; measures relating to the municipal affairs of the District of Columbia in general, other than appropriations; federal paperwork reduction; budget and accounting measures, generally; holidays and celebrations; overall economy, efficiency and management of government operations and activities, including federal procurement; National Archives; population and demography generally, including the census; Postal Service generally, including the transportation of mail; public information and records; relationship of the federal government to the states and municipalities generally; reorganizations in the executive branch of the government.

R 27–D 22–I 1 *(104th Congress, first session)*
R 28–D 23–I 1 *(104th Congress, second session)*

William F. Clinger, Pa.
Cardiss Collins, Ill.

Civil Service—John L. Mica, Fla.
District of Columbia—Thomas M. Davis III, Va.
Government Management, Information and Technology—Steve Horn, Calif.
Human Resources and Intergovernmental Relations—Christopher Shays, Conn.
National Economic Growth, Natural Resources and Regulatory Affairs—David M. McIntosh, Ind.
National Security, International Affairs and Criminal Justice—Bill Zeliff, N.H.
Postal Service—John M. McHugh, N.Y.

HOUSE ADMINISTRATION[l]

House administration generally; contested elections; federal elections generally; corrupt practices; qualifications of members of the House; *Congressional Record*; the House wing of the Capitol; Library of Congress; Smithsonian Institution; Botanic Garden.

D 12–R 7 *(103rd Congress)*

Charlie Rose, N.C.
Bill Thomas, Calif.

Accounts—Martin Frost, Texas
Administrative Oversight—Charlie Rose, N.C.
Elections—Al Swift, Wash.
Libraries and Memorials—William L. Clay, Mo.
Office Systems—Sam Gejdenson, Conn.
Personnel and Police—Thomas J. Manton, N.Y.

HOUSE OVERSIGHT[m]

Accounts of the House generally; assignment of office space for members and committees; disposition of useless executive papers; matters relating to the election of the president, vice president, or members of Congress; corrupt practices; contested elections; credentials and qualifications; federal elections generally; appropriations from accounts for committee salaries and expenses (except for the Committee on Appropriations), House Information Systems, and allowances and expenses of members, House officers and administrative offices of the House; auditing and settling of all such accounts; expenditure of such accounts; employment of persons by the House, including clerks for members and committees, and reporters of debates; Library of Congress and the House Library; statuary and pictures; acceptance or purchase of works of art for the Capitol; the Botanic Garden; management of the Library of Congress; purchase of books and manuscripts; Smithsonian Institution and the incorporation of similar institutions; Franking Commission; printing and correction of the *Congressional Record*; services to the House, including the House restaurant, parking facilities and administration of the House office buildings and of the House wing of the Capitol; travel of members of the House; raising, reporting and use of campaign contributions for candidates for office of representative in the House of Representatives, of delegate, and of resident commissioner to the United States from Puerto Rico; compensation, retirement and other benefits of the members, officers, and employees of the Congress.

R 7–D 5 *(104th Congress)*

Bill Thomas, Calif.
Vic Fazio, Calif.

No standing subcommittees.

INTERNATIONAL RELATIONS[n]

Relations of the United States with foreign nations generally; acquisition of land and buildings for embassies and legations in foreign countries; establishment of boundary lines between the United States and foreign nations; export controls, including nonproliferation of nuclear technology and nuclear hardware; foreign loans; international commodity agreements (other than those involving sugar), including all agreements for cooperation in the export of nuclear technology and nuclear hardware; international conferences and congresses; international education; intervention abroad and declarations of war; measures relating to the diplomatic service; measures to foster commercial intercourse with foreign nations and to safeguard American business interests abroad; measures relating to international economic policy; neutrality; protection of American citizens abroad and expatriation; American National Red Cross; trading with the enemy; U.N. organizations.

R 23–D 19 *(104th Congress, first session)*
R 24–D 20 *(104th Congress, second session)*

Benjamin A. Gilman, N.Y.
Lee H. Hamilton, Ind.

Africa—Ileana Ros-Lehtinen, Fla.
Asia and the Pacific—Doug Bereuter, Neb.
International Economic Policy and Trade—Tody Roth, Wis.
International Operations and Human Rights—Christopher H. Smith, N.J.
Western Hemisphere—Dan Burton, Ind.

JUDICIARY

The judiciary and judicial proceedings, civil and criminal; administrative practice and procedure; apportionment of representatives; bankruptcy, mutiny, espionage, and counterfeiting; civil liberties; constitutional amendments; federal courts and judges, and local courts in the territories and possessions; immigration and naturalization; interstate compacts, generally; measures relating to claims against the United States; meetings of Congress, attendance of members and their acceptance of incompatible offices; national penitentiaries; patents, the Patent Office, copyrights, and trademarks; presidential succession; protection of trade and commerce against unlawful restraints and monopolies; revision and codification of the Statutes of the United States; state and territorial boundaries; subversive activities affecting the internal security of the United States.

D 21–R 14 (103rd Congress)

Jack Brooks, Texas
Hamilton Fish Jr., N.Y.

Administrative Law and Governmental Relations—John Bryant, Texas
Civil and Constitutional Rights—Don Edwards, Calif.
Crime and Criminal Justice—Charles E. Schumer, N.Y.
Economic and Commercial Law—Jack Brooks, Texas
Intellectual Property and Judicial Administration—William J. Hughes, N.J.
International Law, Immigration and Refugees—Romano L. Mazzoli, Ky.

R 20–D 15 (104th Congress)

Henry J. Hyde, Ill.
John Conyers Jr., Mich.

Commercial and Administrative Law—George W. Gekas, Pa.
Constitution—Charles T. Canady, Fla.
Courts and Intellectual Property—Carlos J. Moorhead, Calif.
Crime—Bill McCollum, Fla.
Immigration and Claims—Lamar Smith, Texas

MERCHANT MARINE AND FISHERIES[o]

Merchant marine generally; oceanography and marine affairs, including coastal zone management; Coast Guard, fisheries and wildlife; regulation of common carriers by water and inspection of merchant marine vessels, lights and signals; lifesaving equipment and fire protection; navigation; Panama Canal, Canal Zone and interoceanic canals generally; registration and licensing of vessels and small boats; rules and international arrangements to prevent collisions at sea; international fishing agreements; Coast Guard and Merchant Marine academies and state maritime academies.

D 24–R 15 (103rd Congress)

George Miller, Calif.
Don Young, Alaska

Coast Guard and Navigation—W. J. "Billy" Tauzin, La.
Environment and Natural Resources—Gerry E. Studds, Mass.

Fisheries Management—Thomas J. Manton, N.Y.
Merchant Marine—William O. Lipinski, Ill.
Oceanography, Gulf of Mexico and the Outer Continental Shelf—Solomon P. Ortiz

NATIONAL SECURITY[p]

Common defense generally; Department of Defense generally, including the Departments of the Army, Navy, and Air Force generally; ammunition depots; forts; arsenals; army, navy and air force reservations and establishments; conservation, development and use of naval petroleum and oil shale reserves; interoceanic canals generally, including measures relating to the maintenance, operation, and administration of interoceanic canals; Merchant Marine Academy, and State Maritime Academies; military applications of nuclear energy; tactical intelligence and intelligence related activities of the Department of the Defense; national security aspects of merchant marine, including financial assistance for the construction and operation of vessels, the maintenance of the U.S. shipbuilding and ship repair industrial base, cabotage, cargo preference and merchant marine officers and seamen as these matters relate to the national security; pay, promotion, retirement, and other benefits and privileges of members of the armed forces; scientific research and development in support of the armed services; selective service; size and composition of the army, navy, Marine Corps, and air force; soldiers' and sailors' homes; strategic and critical materials necessary for the common defense.

R 30–D 25 (104th Congress)

Floyd D. Spence, S.C.
Ronald V. Dellums, Calif.

Military Installations—Joel Hefley, Colo.
Military Personnel—Robert K. Dornan, Calif.
Military Procurement—Duncan Hunter, Calif.
Military Readiness—Herbert H. Bateman, Va.
Military Research and Development—Curt Weldon, Pa.

NATURAL RESOURCES[q]

Public lands, parks and natural resources generally; Geological Survey; interstate water compacts; irrigation and reclamation; Native American affairs; minerals, mines and mining; petroleum conservation on public lands; regulation of domestic nuclear energy industry, including waste disposal; territorial affairs of the United States.

D 24–R 15 (103rd Congress)

George Miller, Calif.
Don Young, Alaska

Energy and Mineral Resources—Richard H. Lehman, Calif.
Insular and International Affairs—Ron de Lugo, Virgin Islands
National Parks, Forests and Public Lands—Bruce F. Vento, Minn.
Native American Affairs—Bill Richardson, N.M.
Oversight and Investigations—George Miller, Calif.

POST OFFICE AND CIVIL SERVICE[r]

Postal Service and federal civil service; census and the collection of statistics generally; Hatch Act; holidays and celebrations; commemorative bills and resolutions.

D 14–R 9 (103rd Congress)

William L. Clay, Mo.
John T. Myers, Ind.

Census, Statistics and Postal Personnel—Tom Sawyer, Ohio
Civil Service—Frank McCloskey, Ind.
Compensation and Employee Benefits—Eleanor Holmes Norton, D.C.
Oversight and Investigations—William L. Clay, Mo.
Postal Operations and Services—Barbara-Rose Collins, Mich.

PUBLIC WORKS AND TRANSPORTATION[s]

Flood control and improvement of rivers and harbors; construction and maintenance of roads; oil and other pollution of navigable waters; public buildings and grounds; public works for the benefit of navigation, including bridges and dams; water power; transportation, except railroads; Botanic Garden, Library of Congress; Smithsonian Institution.

D 37–R 24 (103rd Congress, first session)
D 38–R 25 (103rd Congress, second session)

Norman Y. Mineta, Calif.
Bud Shuster, Pa.

Aviation—James L. Oberstar, Minn.
Economic Development—Bob Wise, W.Va.
Investigations and Oversight—Robert A. Borski, Pa.
Public Buildings and Grounds—James A. Traficant Jr., Ohio
Surface Transportation—Nick J. Rahall II, W.Va.
Water Resources and Environment—Douglas Applegate, Ohio

RESOURCES[t]

Public lands generally, including entry, easements, and grazing; mining interests generally; fisheries and wildlife, including research, restoration, refuges, and conservation; forest reserves and national parks created from the public domain; forfeiture of land grants and alien ownership, including alien ownership of mineral lands; Geological Survey; international fishing agreements; interstate compacts relating to apportionment of waters for irrigation purposes; irrigation and reclamation, including water supply for reclamation projects, and easements of public lands for irrigation projects, and acquisition of private lands when necessary to complete irrigation projects; measures relating to the care and management of Native Americans, including the care and allotment of Native American lands and general and special measures relating to claims which are paid out of Native American funds; measures relating generally to the insular possessions of the United States, except those affecting the revenue and appropriations; military parks and battlefields, national cemeteries administered by the secretary of the Interior, parks within the District of Columbia, and the erection of monuments to the memory of indi-

viduals; mineral land laws, claims and entries; mineral resources of the public lands; mining schools and experimental stations; marine affairs (including coastal zone management), except for measures relating to oil and other pollution of navigable waters; oceanography; petroleum conservation on the public lands and conservation of the radium supply in the United States; preservation of prehistoric ruins and objects of interest on the public domain; relations of the United States with the Native Americans and the Native American tribes; Trans-Alaska Oil Pipeline (except rate-making).

R 25–D 20 (104th Congress, first session)
R 27–D 22 (104th Congress, second session)

Don Young, Alaska
George Miller, Calif.

Energy and Mineral Resources—Ken Calvert, Calif.
Fisheries, Wildlife and Oceans—H. James Saxton, N.J.
National Parks, Forests and Lands—James V. Hansen, Utah
Native American and Insular Affairs—Elton Gallegly, Calif.
Water and Power Resources—John T. Doolittle, Calif.

RULES

Rules and joint rules (other than rules or joint rules relating to the Code of Official Conduct), and order of business of the House; recesses and final adjournments of Congress; authorized to sit and act whether or not the House is in session.

D 9–R 4 (103rd Congress)

Joe Moakley, Mass.
Gerald B. H. Solomon, N.Y.

Legislative Process—Butler Derrick, S.C.
Rules of the House—Anthony C. Beilenson, Calif.

R 9–D 4 (104th Congress)

Gerald B. H. Solomon, N.Y.
Joe Moakley, Mass.

Legislative and Budget Process—Porter J. Goss, Fla.
Rules and Organization of the House—David Dreier, Calif.

SCIENCE[u]

All energy research, development, and demonstration, and projects therefor, and all federally owned or operated nonmilitary energy laboratories; astronautical research and development, including resources, personnel, equipment, and facilities; civil aviation research and development; environmental research and development; marine research; measures relating to the commercial application of energy technology; National Institute of Standards and Technology, standardization of weights and measures and the metric system; National Aeronautics and Space Administration; National Space Council; National Science Foundation; National Weather Service; outer space, including exploration and control thereof; science scholarships; scientific research, development, and demonstration, and related projects.

R 27– 23 (*104th Congress*)

Robert S. Walker, Pa.
George E. Brown Jr., Calif.

Basic Research—Steven H. Schiff, N.M.
Energy and Environment—Dana Rohrabacher, Calif.
Space and Aeronautics—F. James Sensenbrenner Jr., Wis.
Technology—Constance Morella, Md.

SCIENCE, SPACE AND TECHNOLOGY[v]

Astronautical research and development, including resources, personnel, equipment and facilities; National Institute of Standards and Technology, standardization of weights and measures and the metric system; National Aeronautics and Space Administration; National Aeronautics and Space Council; National Science Foundation; outer space, including exploration and control; science scholarships; scientific research, development, and demonstration; federally owned or operated nonmilitary energy laboratories; civil aviation research and development; environmental research and development; energy research, development and demonstration; National Weather Service.

D 33–R 22 (*103rd Congress*)

George E. Brown Jr., Calif.
Robert S. Walker, Pa.

Energy—Marilyn Lloyd, Tenn.
Investigations and Oversight—Jimmy Hayes, La.
Science—Rick Boucher, Va.
Space—Ralph M. Hall, Texas
Technology, Environment and Aviation—Tim Valentine, N.C.

SELECT INTELLIGENCE

Legislative and budgetary authority over the National Security Agency and the director of central intelligence, the Defense Intelligence Agency, the National Security Agency, intelligence activities of the Federal Bureau of Investigation and other components of the federal intelligence community.

D 12–R 7 (*103rd Congress*)

Dan Glickman, Kan.
Larry Combest, Texas

Legislation—Ronald D. Coleman, Texas
Oversight and Evaluation—Norm Dicks, Wash.
Program and Budget Authorization—Dan Glickman, Kan.

R 9–D 7 (*104th Congress*)

Larry Combest, Texas
Norm Dicks, Wash.

Human Intelligence, Analysis and Counterintelligence—Jerry Lewis, Calif.
Technical and Tactical Intelligence—Robert K. Dornan, Calif.

SMALL BUSINESS

Assistance to and protection of small business, including financial aid, regulatory flexibility, and paperwork reduction; participation of small business enterprises in federal procurement and government contracts.

D 27–D18 (*103rd Congress*)

John J. LaFalce, N.Y.
Jan Meyers, Kan.

Minority Enterprise, Finance and Urban Development—Kweisi Mfume, Md.
Procurement, Taxation and Tourism—James Bilbray, Nev.
Regulation, Business Opportunities and Technology—Ron Wyden, Ore.
Rural Enterprises, Exports and the Environment—Bill Sarpalius, Texas
SBA Legislation and the General Economy—John J. LaFalce, N.Y.

R 22–D 19 (*104th Congress, first session*)
R 23–D 20 (*104th Congress, second session*)

Jan Meyers, Kan.
John J. LaFalce, N.Y.

Government Programs—Peter G. Torkildsen, Mass.
Procurement, Exports and Business Opportunities—Donald Manzullo, Ill.
Regulation and Paperwork—James M. Talent, Mo.
Tax and Finance—Linda Smith, Wash.

STANDARDS OF OFFICIAL CONDUCT

Measures relating to the Code of Official Conduct.

D 7–R 7 (*103rd Congress*)

Jim McDermott, Wash.
Fred Grandy, Iowa

R 5–D 5 (*104th Congress*)

Nancy L. Johnson, Conn.
Jim McDermott, Wash.

No standing subcommittees.

TRANSPORTATION AND INFRASTRUCTURE[w]

Coast Guard; federal management of emergencies and natural disasters; flood control and improvement of waterways; inspection of merchant marine vessels; navigation and related laws; rules and international arrangements to prevent collisions at sea; measures, other than appropriations, that relate to construction, maintenance and safety of roads; buildings and grounds of the Botanic Gardens, the Library of Congress and the Smithsonian Institution and other government buildings within the District of Columbia; post offices, customhouses, Federal courthouses, and merchant marine, except for national security aspects of merchant marine; pollution of navigable waters, bridges and dams; related transportation regulatory agencies, transportation, including civil aviation, railroads, water transportation, infrastructure, labor, and railroad retirement and unemployment (except revenue measures); water power.

R 33–D 28 (104th Congress)

Bud Shuster, Pa.
Norman Y. Mineta, Calif. (resigned Oct. 10, 1995)
James L. Oberstar, Minn. (through 104th Congress)

Aviation—John J. "Jimmy" Duncan Jr., Tenn.
Coast Guard and Maritime Transportation—Howard Coble, N.C.
Public Buildings and Economic Development—Wayne T. Gilcrest, Md.
Surface Transportation—Tom Petri, Wis.
Railroads—Susan Molinari, N.Y.
Water Resources and Environment—Sherwood Boehlert, N.Y.

VETERANS' AFFAIRS

Veterans' measures generally; cemeteries of the United States in which veterans of any war or conflict are or may be buried, whether in the United States or abroad, except cemeteries administered by the secretary of the Interior; compensation, vocational rehabilitation, and education of veterans; life insurance issued by the government on account of service in the armed forces; pensions of all the wars of the United States, readjustment of servicemen to civil life; soldiers' and sailors' civil relief; veterans' hospitals, medical care and treatment of veterans.

D 21–R 14 (103rd Congress)

G. V. "Sonny" Montgomery, Miss.
Bob Stump, Ariz.

Compensation, Pension and Insurance—Jim Slattery, Kan.
Education, Training and Employment— G. V. "Sonny" Montgomery, Miss.
Hospitals and Health Care—J. Roy Rowland, Ga.
Housing and Memorial Affairs—George E. Sangmeister, Ill.
Oversight and Investigations—Lane Evans, Ill.

R 18–D 15 (104th Congress)

Bob Stump, Ariz.
G. V. "Sonny" Montgomery, Miss.

Compensation, Pension, Insurance and Memorial Affairs—Terry Everett, Ala.
Education, Training, Employment and Housing—Steve Buyer, Ind.
Hospitals and Health Care—Tim Hutchinson, Ark.

WAYS AND MEANS

Revenue measures generally; reciprocal trade agreements; customs, collection districts, and ports of entry and delivery; revenue measures relating to the insular possessions; bonded debt of the United States; deposit of public moneys; transportation of dutiable goods; tax-exempt foundations and charitable trusts; national Social Security, except (A) health care and facilities programs that are supported from general revenues as opposed to payroll deductions and (B) work incentive programs.

D 24–R 14 (103rd Congress)

Dan Rostenkowski, Ill.[x]
Sam Gibbons, Fla. (acting chairman through 103rd Congress)
Bill Archer, Texas

Health—Pete Stark, Calif.
Human Resources—Harold E. Ford, Tenn.[y]
Oversight—J. J. Pickle, Texas
Select Revenue Measures—Charles B. Rangel, N.Y.
Social Security—Andrew Jacobs Jr., Ind.
Trade—Sam M. Gibbons, Fla.

R 21–D 15 (104th Congress, first session)
R 23–D 16 (104th Congress, second session)

Bill Archer, Texas
Sam M. Gibbons, Fla.

Health—Bill Thomas, Calif.
Human Resources—E. Clay Shaw Jr., Fla.
Oversight—Nancy L. Johnson, Conn.
Social Security—Jim Bunning, Ky.
Trade—Philip M. Crane, Ill.

POLITICAL COMMITTEES

Democratic Congressional Campaign Committee (provides campaign support for Democratic House candidates)—Martin Frost, Texas
Democratic Policy Committee (studies and proposes legislation and makes public Democratic policy positions)—Richard A. Gephardt, Mo.
Democratic Steering Committee (makes Democratic committee assignments)—Richard A. Gephardt, Mo., cochairman; Steny H. Hoyer, Md., cochairman
National Republican Congressional Committee (provides campaign support for Republican House candidates)—Bill Paxon, N.Y., chairman; Jim Nussle, Iowa, vice chairman
Republican Policy Committee (advises on party action and policy)—Christopher Cox, Calif.
Republican Steering Committee (makes Republican committee assignments)—Newt Gingrich, Ga.

Joint Committees

Joint committees are set up to examine specific questions and are established by public law. Membership is drawn from both chambers and both parties. When a senator serves as chairman, the vice chairman usually is a representative, and vice versa. The chairmanship traditionally rotates from one chamber to the other at the beginning of each Congress (except for the Committee on Taxation chairmanship, which rotates at the start of each session).

ECONOMIC

Studies and investigates all recommendations in the president's annual *Economic Report to Congress*. Reports findings and recommendations to the House and Senate.

Rep. David R. Obey, D-Wis., chairman (1985–1987, 1993–1995)
Sen. Connie Mack, R-Fla., chairman (104th Congress)
Sen. Paul S. Sarbanes, D-Md., vice chairman (1989–1991, 1993–1995)
Rep. H. James Saxton, R-N.J., vice chairman (104th Congress)

No standing subcommittees.

LIBRARY

Management and expansion of the Library of Congress; receipt of gifts for the benefit of the library; development and maintenance of the Botanic Garden; placement of statues and other works of art in the Capitol.

Rep. Charlie Rose, D-N.C., chairman (103rd Congress)
Sen. Mark O. Hatfield, R-Ore., chairman (104th Congress)
Sen. Claiborne Pell, D-R.I., vice chairman (1989–1991, 1993–1995)
Rep. Bill Thomas, R-Calif., vice chairman (104th Congress)

No standing subcommittees.

ORGANIZATION OF CONGRESS

Make a full and complete study of the organization and operation of the Congress of the United States; and recommend improvements in such organization and operation with a view toward strengthening the effectiveness of the Congress, simplifying its operations, improving its relationships with and oversight of other branches of the United States government and improving the orderly consideration of legislation. The study shall include an examination of the organization and operation of each house of the Congress, and the structure of, and the relationships between, the various standing, special, and select committees of the Congress; the relationship between the two Houses of Congress; the relationship between the Congress and the executive branch of the government; the resources and working tools available to the legislative branch as compared to those available to the executive branch; and the responsibilities of the leadership, theirability to fulfill those responsibilities, and how that relates to the ability of the Senate and the House of Representatives to perform

their legislative functions. The committee shall report to the Senate and the House of Representatives the result of its study, together with its recommendations, not later than Dec. 31, 1993. All reports and findings of the Committee shall be referred to the appropriate committees of the Senate and the appropriate committees of the House of Representatives.

Sen. David L. Boren, D-Okla., cochairman (1993)
Rep. Lee H. Hamilton, D-Ind., cochairman (1993)

PRINTING

Probes inefficiency and waste in the printing, binding and distribution of federal government publications. Oversees arrangement and style of the *Congressional Record*.

Sen. Wendell H. Ford, D-Ky., chairman (1989–1991, 1993–1995)
Rep. Bill Thomas, R-Calif., chairman (104th Congress)
Rep. Charlie Rose, D-N.C., vice chairman (103rd Congress)
Sen Ted Stevens, R-Alaska, vice chairman (1995)
Sen. John W. Warner, R-Va., vice chairman (1996)

No standing subcommittees.

TAXATION

Operation, effects and administration of the federal system of internal revenue taxes; measures and methods for simplification of taxes.

Rep. Dan Rostenkowski, D-Ill., chairman (1981, 1983, 1985, 1987, 1989, 1991, 1993)
Sen. Daniel Patrick Moynihan, D-N.Y., chairman (1994)
Rep. Bill Archer, R-Texas, chairman (1995)
Sen. William V. Roth Jr., R-Del., chairman (1996)
Sen. Daniel Patrick Moynihan, D-N.Y., vice chairman (1993)
Rep. Dan Rostenkowski, D-Ill., vice chairman (1982, 1984, 1986, 1988, 1990, 1992, 1994²)
Sen. Bob Packwood, R-Ore., vice chairman (1995)
Rep. Bill Archer, R-Texas, vice chairman (1996)

No standing subcommittees.

ᵃ Reorganized as National Security in the 104th Congress.
ᵇ Reorganized from Banking, Finance and Urban Affairs in the 103rd Congress.
ᶜ Reorganized as Banking and Financial Services in the 104th Congress.
ᵈ Reorganized from Energy and Commerce in the 103rd Congress.
ᵉ Reorganized as a subcommittee of Government Reform and Oversight in the 104th Congress.
ᶠ Reorganized from Education and Labor in the 103rd Congress.
ᵍ Reorganized as Economic and Educational Opportunities in the 104th Congress.
ʰ Reorganized as Commerce in the 104th Congress.
ⁱ Reorganized as International Relations in the 104th Congress.
ʲ Reorganized as Government Reform and Oversight in the 104th Congress.
ᵏ Reorganized from Government Operations in the 103rd Congress.
ˡ Reorganized as House Oversight in the 104th Congress.

[m] Reorganized from House Administration in the 103rd Congress.

[n] Reorganized from Foreign Affairs in the 103rd Congress.

[o] Reorganized as a subcommittee of Transportation and Infrastructure in the 104th Congress.

[p] Reorganized from Armed Services in the 103rd Congress.

[q] Reorganized as Resources in the 104th Congress.

[r] Reorganized as a subcommittee of Government Reform and Oversight in the 104th Congress.

[s] Reorganized as Transportation and Infrastructure in the 104th Congress.

[t] Reorganized from Natural Resources in the 103rd Congress.

[u] Reorganized from Science, Space and Technology in the 103rd Congress.

[v] Reorganized as Science in the 104th Congress.

[w] Reorganized from Public Works and Transportation in the 103rd Congress.

[x] Rostenkowski was required to step down from the chairmanship upon being indicted May 31, 1994.

[y] Ford resumed the chairmanship April 9, 1993, when he was acquitted of charges that had forced him to relinquish the chairmanship April 24, 1987.

[z] Rostenkowski was required to step down upon being indicted May 31, 1994.

Postelection Sessions

Congress has held eight postelection sessions since 1945.

1948. The 1948 postelection session of the 80th Congress lasted only two hours. Both chambers swore in new members, approved several minor resolutions and received last-minute reports from committees.

In addition to final floor action, several committees resumed work. The most active was the House Un-American Activities Committee, which continued its investigation of alleged communist espionage in the federal government.

1950. After the 1950 elections, President Harry S. Truman sent a "must" agenda to the lame-duck session of the 81st Congress. The president's list included supplemental defense appropriations, an excess profits tax, aid to Yugoslavia, a three-month extension of federal rent controls and statehood for Hawaii and Alaska. During a marathon session that lasted until only a few hours before its successor took over, the 81st Congress acted on all of the president's legislative items except the statehood bills, which were blocked by a Senate filibuster.

1954. Only one chamber of the 83rd Congress convened after the 1954 elections. The Senate returned Nov. 8 to hold what has been called a "censure session," a continuing investigation into the conduct of Sen. Joseph R. McCarthy, R-Wis. (1947–1957). By a 67–22 roll call, the Senate Dec. 2 voted to "condemn" McCarthy for his behavior.

In other postelection floor action, the Senate passed a series of miscellaneous and administrative resolutions and swore in new members.

1970. President Richard Nixon criticized the lame-duck Congress as one that had "seemingly lost the capacity to decide and the will to act." Filibusters and intense controversy contributed to inaction on the president's request for trade legislation and welfare reform.

Congress nevertheless claimed some substantive results during the session, which ended Jan. 2, 1971. Several major appropriations bills were cleared for presidential signature. Congress also approved foreign aid to Cambodia, provided interim funding for the supersonic transport (SST) plane and repealed the Tonkin Gulf Resolution that had been used as a basis for American military involvement in Vietnam.

1974. In a session that ran from Nov. 18 to Dec. 20, 1974, the 93rd Congress cleared several important bills for presidential signature, including a mass transit bill, a Labor-Health, Education and Welfare appropriations bill and a foreign assistance package. A House-Senate conference committee reached agreement on a major strip-mining bill, but President Gerald R. Ford vetoed it.

Congress approved the nomination of Nelson A. Rockefeller as vice president. It also overrode presidential vetoes of two bills—one broadening the Freedom of Information Act, a second authorizing educational benefits for Korean War and Vietnam-era veterans.

1980. The lame-duck session of the 96th Congress was productive, at least until Dec. 5, the original adjournment date set by congressional leaders. By that date a budget had been approved, along with a budget reconciliation measure. Ten regular appropriations bills had cleared, though one subsequently was vetoed. Congress had approved two major environmental measures—an Alaskan lands bill and toxic waste "superfund" legislation—as well as a three-year extension of general revenue sharing.

After Dec. 5, however, the legislative pace slowed noticeably. Action on a continuing appropriations resolution for those departments and agencies whose regular funding had not been cleared was delayed, first by a filibuster on a fair housing bill and later by more than 100 "Christmas tree" amendments, including a $10,000-a-year pay raise for members. After the conference report failed in the Senate and twice was rewritten, the bill was shorn of virtually all its "ornaments" and finally cleared by both chambers on Dec. 16.

1982. Despite the reluctance of congressional leaders, President Ronald Reagan urged the convening of a postelection session at the end of the 97th Congress, principally to pass remaining appropriations bills.

Rising unemployment—and Democratic election gains in the House—made job creation efforts the focus of the lame-duck Congress, however. Overriding the objections of Republican conservatives, Congress passed Reagan-backed legislation raising the federal gasoline tax from 4 cents to 9 cents a gallon to pay for highway repairs and mass transit. Supporters said the legislation would help alleviate unemployment by creating 300,000 jobs.

Congress eventually cleared four additional appropriations bills, packaging the remaining six in a continuing appropriations resolution that also included a pay raise for House members. Conferees dropped funding for emergency jobs programs to avert a threatened veto of the resolution.

The lame-duck session also was highlighted by Congress' refusal to fund production and procurement of the first five MX intercontinental missiles. This was the first time in recent history that either house of Congress had denied a president's request to fund production of a strategic weapon.

1994. Congress reconvened to reconsider, and ultimately approve, the Uruguay Round pact strengthening the General Agreement on Tariffs and Trade (GATT). The bill had been submitted Sept. 27, 1994, by President Clinton under fast-track rules for trade legislation, which allowed each chamber only an up-or-down vote on the bill without amendments. But the rules also allowed every chairman with jurisdiction to take up to 45 days to review the bill. Sen. Ernest F. Hollings, D-S.C., demanded his 45 days, forcing the Senate leadership to schedule a two-day lame-duck session.

Clinton asked the House to approve the bill before the October adjournment, but the Democratic leadership delayed consideration. The House reconvened for a one-day session Nov. 29 and passed the GATT bill by a wide margin.

Following a 20-hour debate Nov. 30 and Dec. 1, the Senate gave overwhelming approval to the bill.

Recent Lame-Duck Sessions

Year	Congress	Dates
1948	80th	Dec. 31, 1948 (2-hour session)
1950	81st	Nov. 27, 1950—Jan. 2, 1951
1954	83rd	Nov. 8, 1954—Dec. 2, 1954
1970	91st	Nov. 16, 1970—Jan. 2, 1971 (Senate)
1974	93rd	Nov. 18, 1974—Dec. 20, 1974
1980	96th	Nov. 12, 1980—Dec. 16, 1980
1982	97th	Nov. 29, 1982—Dec. 23, 1982 (Senate)
		Nov. 29, 1982—Dec. 21, 1982 (House)
1994	103rd	Nov. 29, 1994 (House)
		Nov. 30, 1994—Dec. 1, 1994 (Senate)

Senate Cloture Votes, 1917–1996

The Senate's ultimate check on the filibuster is the provision for cloture, or limitation of debate, contained in Rule 22 of its Standing Rules. The original Rule 22 was adopted in 1917 following a furor over the "talking to death" of a proposal by President Woodrow Wilson for arming American merchant ships before the United States entered World War I. The new cloture rule required the votes of two-thirds of all the senators present and voting to invoke cloture. In 1949, during a parliamentary skirmish preceding scheduled consideration of a Fair Employment Practices Commission bill, the requirement was raised to two-thirds of the entire Senate membership.

A revision of the rule in 1959 provided for limitation of debate by a vote of two-thirds of the senators present and voting, two days after a cloture petition was submitted by 16 senators. If cloture was adopted by the Senate, further debate was limited to one hour for each senator on the bill itself and on all amendments affecting it. No new amendments could be offered except by unanimous consent. Amendments that were not germane to the pending business and dilatory motions were out of order. The rule applied both to regular legislation and to motions to change the Standing Rules.

Rule 22 was revised significantly in 1975 by lowering the vote needed for cloture to three-fifths of the Senate membership (60, if there were no vacancies). That revision applied to any matter except proposed rules changes, for which the old requirement of a two-thirds majority of senators present and voting still applied.

In a further revision of the rule, the Senate in 1979 limited postcloture delaying tactics by providing that once cloture was invoked, a final vote had to be taken after no more than 100 hours of debate. All time spent on quorum calls, roll-call votes and other parliamentary procedures was to be included in the 100-hour limit.

When the Senate decided to televise its floor proceedings in 1986, it further tightened up the time on postcloture debate. Rule 22 was revised to reduce to 30 hours, from 100, the time allowed for debate, procedural moves and roll-call votes after the Senate had invoked cloture to end a filibuster.

Following is a list of the 431 cloture votes taken between 1917, when Senate Rule 22 was adopted, and the end of 1996; 148 of the votes (in **bold type**) were successful.

Issue	Date	Vote	Yeas needed
Versailles Treaty	Nov. 15, 1919	78–16	63
Emergency tariff	Feb. 2, 1921	36–35	48
Tariff bill	July 7, 1922	45–35	54
World Court	Jan. 25, 1926	68–26	63
Migratory birds	June 1, 1926	46–33	53
Branch banking	Feb. 15, 1927	65–18	56
Disabled officers	Feb. 26, 1927	51–36	58
Colorado River	Feb. 26, 1927	32–59	61
D.C. buildings	Feb. 28, 1927	52–31	56
Prohibition Bureau	Feb. 28, 1927	55–27	55
Banking Act	Jan. 19, 1933	58–30	59
Anti-lynching	Jan. 27, 1938	37–51	59
Anti-lynching	Feb. 16, 1938	42–46	59
Anti-poll tax	Nov. 23, 1942	37–41	52
Anti-poll tax	May 15, 1944	36–44	54
Fair Employment Practices Commission	Feb. 9, 1946	48–36	56
British loan	May 7, 1946	41–41	55
Labor disputes	May 25, 1946	3–77	54
Anti-poll tax	July 31, 1946	39–33	48
Fair Employment	May 19, 1950	52–32	64
Fair Employment	July 12, 1950	55–33	64
Atomic Energy Act	July 26, 1954	44–42	64
Civil Rights Act	March 10, 1960	42–53	64
Amend Rule 22	Sept. 19, 1961	37–43	54
Literacy tests	May 9, 1962	43–53	64
Literacy tests	May 14, 1962	42–52	63
Comsat Act	Aug. 14, 1962	63–27	60
Amend Rule 22	Feb. 7, 1963	54–42	64
Civil Rights Act	June 10, 1964	71–29	67
Legislative reapportionment	Sept. 10, 1964	30–63	62
Voting Rights Act	May 25, 1965	70–30	67
Right-to-work repeal	Oct. 11, 1965	45–47	62
Right-to-work repeal	Feb. 8, 1966	51–48	66
Right-to-work repeal	Feb. 10, 1966	50–49	66
Civil Rights Act	Sept. 14, 1966	54–42	64
Civil Rights Act	Sept. 19, 1966	52–41	62
D.C. Home Rule	Oct. 10, 1966	41–37	52
Amend Rule 22	Jan. 24, 1967	53–46	66
Open Housing	Feb. 20, 1968	55–37	62
Open Housing	Feb. 26, 1968	56–36	62
Open Housing	March 1, 1968	59–35	63
Open Housing	March 4, 1968	65–32	65
Fortas Nomination	Oct. 1, 1968	45–43	59
Amend Rule 22	Jan. 16, 1969	51–47	66
Amend Rule 22	Jan. 28, 1969	50–42	62
Electoral College	Sept. 17, 1970	54–36	60
Electoral College	Sept. 29, 1970	53–34	58
Supersonic transport	Dec. 19, 1970	43–48	61
Supersonic transport	Dec. 22, 1970	42–44	58
Amend Rule 22	Feb. 18, 1971	48–37	57
Amend Rule 22	Feb. 23, 1971	50–36	58
Amend Rule 22	March 2, 1971	48–36	56
Amend Rule 22	March 9, 1971	55–39	63
Military Draft	June 23, 1971	65–27	62
Lockheed Loan	July 26, 1971	42–47	60
Lockheed Loan	July 28, 1971	59–39	66
Lockheed Loan	July 30, 1971	53–37	60
Military Draft	Sept. 21, 1971	61–30	61
Rehnquist nomination	Dec. 10, 1971	52–42	63
Equal Job Opportunity	Feb. 1, 1972	48–37	57
Equal Job Opportunity	Feb. 3, 1972	53–35	59
Equal Job Opportunity	Feb. 22, 1972	71–23	63
U.S.-Soviet Arms Pact	Sept. 14, 1972	76–15	61
Consumer Agency	Sept. 29, 1972	47–29	51
Consumer Agency	Oct. 3, 1972	55–32	58
Consumer Agency	Oct. 5, 1972	52–30	55
School Busing	Oct. 10, 1972	45–37	55
School Busing	Oct. 11, 1972	49–39	59
School Busing	Oct. 12, 1972	49–38	58
Voter Registration	April 30, 1973	56–31	58
Voter Registration	May 3, 1973	60–34	63
Voter Registration	May 9, 1973	67–32	66
Public Campaign Financing	Dec. 2, 1973	47–33	54
Public Campaign Financing	Dec. 3, 1973	49–39	59
Rhodesian Chrome Ore	Dec. 11, 1973	59–35	63
Rhodesian Chrome Ore	Dec. 13, 1973	62–33	64
Legal Services Program	Dec. 13, 1973	60–36	64
Legal Services Program	Dec. 14, 1973	56–29	57
Rhodesian Chrome Ore	Dec. 18, 1973	63–26	60
Legal Services Program	Jan. 30, 1974	68–29	65
Genocide Treaty	Feb. 5, 1974	55–36	61
Genocide Treaty	Feb. 6, 1974	55–38	62
Government Pay Raise	March 6, 1974	67–31	66
Public Campaign Financing	April 4, 1974	60–36	64
Public Campaign Financing	April 9, 1974	64–30	63
Public Debt Ceiling	June 19, 1974	50–43	62
Public Debt Ceiling	June 19, 1974	45–48	62
Public Debt Ceiling	June 26, 1974	48–50	66
Consumer Agency	July 30, 1974	56–42	66
Consumer Agency	Aug. 1, 1974	59–39	66
Consumer Agency	Aug. 20, 1974	59–35	63
Consumer Agency	Sept. 19, 1974	64–34	66
Export-Import Bank	Dec. 3, 1974	51–39	60
Export-Import Bank	Dec. 4, 1974	48–44	62

Issue	Date	Vote	Yeas needed	Issue	Date	Vote	Yeas needed
Trade Reform	Dec. 13, 1974	71–19	60	Debt Limit Increase	Sept. 13, 1982	45–35	60
Fiscal 1975 Supplemental Funds	Dec. 14, 1974	56–27	56	Debt Limit Increase	Sept. 15, 1982	50–44	60
Export-Import Bank	Dec. 14, 1974	49–35	56	Debt Limit Increase	Sept. 20, 1982	50–39	60
Export-Import Bank	Dec. 16, 1974	54–34	59	Debt Limit Increase	Sept. 21, 1982	53–47	60
Social Services Programs	Dec. 17, 1974	70–23	62	Debt Limit Increase	Sept. 22, 1982	54–46	60
Tax Law Changes	Dec. 17, 1974	67–25	62	Debt Limit Increase	Sept. 23, 1982	53–45	60
Rail Reorganization Act	Feb. 26, 1975	86–8	63	Antitrust Equal Enforcement Act	Dec. 2, 1982	38–58	60
Amend Rule 22	March 5, 1975	73–21	63	Antitrust Equal Enforcement Act	Dec. 2, 1982	44–51	60
Amend Rule 22	March 7, 1975	73–21	63	**Transportation Assistance Act**	Dec. 13, 1982	75–13	60
Tax Reduction	March 20, 1975	59–38	60	Transportation Assistance Act	Dec. 16, 1982	48–50	60
Tax Reduction	March 21, 1975	83–13	60	Transportation Assistance Act	Dec. 16, 1982	5–93	60
Agency for Consumer Advocacy	May 13, 1975	71–27	60	**Transportation Assistance Act**	Dec. 19, 1982	89–5	60
Senate Staffing	June 11, 1975	77–19	64	**Transportation Assistance Act**	Dec. 20, 1982	87–8	60
New Hampshire Senate Seat	June 24, 1975	57–39	60	**Transportation Assistance Act**	Dec. 23, 1982	81–5	60
New Hampshire Senate Seat	June 25, 1975	56–41	60	Emergency Jobs Appropriations/			
New Hampshire Senate Seat	June 26, 1975	54–40	60	Interest Withholding	March 16, 1983	50–48	60
New Hampshire Senate Seat	July 8, 1975	57–38	60	Emergency Jobs Appropriations/			
New Hampshire Senate Seat	July 9, 1975	57–38	60	Interest Withholding	March 16, 1983	59–39	60
New Hampshire Senate Seat	July 10, 1975	54–38	60	International Trade and Investment/			
Voting Rights Act	July 21, 1975	72–19	60	Interest Withholding	April 19, 1983	34–53	60
Voting Rights Act	July 23, 1975	76–20	60	International Trade and Investment/			
Oil Price Decontrol	July 30, 1975	54–38	60	Interest Withholding	April 19, 1983	39–59	60
Labor-HEW Appropriations	Sept. 23, 1975	46–48	60	Defense Authorizations, 1984	July 21, 1983	55–41	60
Labor-HEW Appropriations	Sept. 24, 1975	64–33	60	**Radio Broadcasting to Cuba**	Aug. 3, 1983	62–33	60
Common-Site Picketing	Nov. 11, 1975	66–30	60	**National Gas Policy Act**	Nov. 3, 1983	86–7	60
Common-Site Picketing	Nov. 14, 1975	58–31	60	**Capital Punishment**	Feb. 9, 1984	65–26	60
Common-Site Picketing	Nov. 18, 1975	62–37	60	**Hydroelectric Power Plants**	July 30, 1984	60–28	60
Rail Reorganization	Dec. 4, 1975	61–27	60	Wilkinson Nomination	July 31, 1984	57–39	60
New York City Aid	Dec. 5, 1975	70–27	60	Agriculture Appropriations, Fiscal 1985	Aug. 6, 1984	54–31	60
Rice Production Act	Feb. 3, 1976	70–19	60	**Agriculture Appropriations, Fiscal 1985**	Aug. 8, 1984	68–30	60
Antitrust Amendments	June 3, 1976	67–22	60	**Wilkinson Nomination**	Aug. 9, 1984	65–32	60
Antitrust Amendments	Aug. 31, 1976	63–27	60	**Financial Services Competitive**			
Civil Rights Attorneys' Fees	Sept. 23, 1976	63–26	60	**Equity Act**	Sept. 10, 1984	89–3	60
Draft Resisters Pardons	Jan. 24, 1977	53–43	60	**Financial Services Competitive**			
Campaign Financing	July 29, 1977	49–45	60	**Equity Act**	Sept. 13, 1984	92–6	60
Campaign Financing	Aug. 1, 1977	47–46	60	**Broadcasting of Senate Procedures**	Sept. 18, 1984	73–26	60
Campaign Financing	Aug. 2, 1977	52–46	60	Broadcasting of Senate Procedures	Sept. 21, 1984	37–44	60
Natural Gas Pricing	Sept. 26, 1977	77–17	60	**Surface Transportation and**			
Labor Law Revision	June 7, 1978	42–47	60	**Uniform Relocation Assistance Act**	Sept. 24, 1984	70–12	60
Labor Law Revision	June 8, 1978	49–41	60	**Continuing Appropriations**	Sept. 29, 1984	92–4	60
Labor Law Revision	June 13, 1978	54–43	60	**Anti-Apartheid**	July 10, 1985	88–8	60
Labor Law Revision	June 14, 1978	58–41	60	Line-item veto	July 18, 1985	57–42	60
Labor Law Revision	June 15, 1978	58 39	60	Line item veto	July 23, 1985	57 41	60
Labor Law Revision	June 22, 1978	53–45	60	Line-item veto	July 24, 1985	58–40	60
Revenue Act of 1978	Oct. 9, 1978	62–28	60	Anti-Apartheid	Sept. 9, 1985	53–34	60
Energy Taxes	Oct. 14, 1978	71–13	60	Anti-Apartheid	Sept. 11, 1985	57–41	60
Windfall Profits Tax	Dec. 12, 1979	53–46	60	Anti-Apartheid	Sept. 12, 1985	11–88	60
Windfall Profits Tax	Dec. 13, 1979	56–40	60	Debt Limit/Balanced Budget	Oct. 6, 1985	57–38	64
Windfall Profits Tax	Dec. 14, 1979	56–39	60	Debt Limit/Balanced Budget	Oct. 9, 1985[a]	53–39	62
Windfall Profits Tax	Dec. 17, 1979	84–14	60	**Conrail Sale**	Jan. 23, 1986	90–7	60
Lubbers Nomination	April 21, 1980	46–60	60	**Conrail Sale**	Jan. 30, 1986	70–27	60
Lubbers Nomination	April 22, 1980	62–34	60	**Fitzwater Nomination**	March 18, 1986	64–33	60
Rights of Institutionalized	April 28, 1980	44–39	60	Washington Airports Transfer	March 21, 1986	50–39	60
Rights of Institutionalized	April 29, 1980	56–34	60	**Washington Airports Transfer**	March 25, 1986	66–32	60
Rights of Institutionalized	April 30, 1980	53–35	60	Hobbs Act Amendments	April 16, 1986	44–54	60
Rights of Institutionalized	May 1, 1980	60–34	60	Defense Authorization, Fiscal 1987	Aug. 6, 1986	53–46	60
Bottlers' Antitrust Immunity	May 15, 1980	86–6	60	Military Construction Appropriations,			
Draft Registration Funding	June 10, 1980	62–32	60	Fiscal 1987 (Aid to Contras)	Aug. 13, 1986	59–40	60
Zimmerman Nomination	Aug. 1, 1980	51–35	60	**South Africa Sanctions**	Aug. 13, 1986	89–11	60
Zimmerman Nomination	Aug. 4, 1980	45–31	60	**Military Construction Appropriations,**			
Zimmerman Nomination	Aug. 5, 1980	63–31	60	**Fiscal 1987 (Aid to Contras)**	Aug. 13, 1986	62–37	60
Alaska Lands	Aug. 18, 1980	63–25	60	**Rehnquist Nomination**	Sept. 17, 1986	68–31	60
Vessel Tonnage/Strip Mining	Aug. 21, 1980	61–32	60	**Product Liability Reform**	Sept. 25, 1986	97–1	60
Fair Housing Amendments	Dec. 3, 1980	51–39	60	Omnibus Drug Bill	Oct. 15, 1986	58–38	60
Fair Housing Amendments	Dec. 4, 1980	62–32	60	**Immigration Reform**	Oct. 17, 1986	69–21	60
Fair Housing Amendments	Dec. 9, 1980	54–43	60	Contra Aid Moratorium	March 23, 1987	46–45	60
Breyer Nomination	Dec. 9, 1980	68–28	60	Contra Aid Moratorium	March 24, 1987	50–50	60
Justice Department Authorization	July 10, 1981	38–48	60	Contra Aid Moratorium	March 25, 1987	54–46	60
Justice Department Authorization	July 13, 1981	54–32	60	**Relief for the Homeless**	April 9, 1987	68–29	60
Justice Department Authorization	July 29, 1981	59–37	60	Defense Authorization, Fiscal 1988	May 15, 1987	52–36	60
Justice Department Authorization	Sept. 10, 1981	57–33	60	Defense Authorization, Fiscal 1988	May 19, 1987	58–41	60
Justice Department Authorization	Sept. 16, 1981	61–36	60	Defense Authorization, Fiscal 1988	May 20, 1987	59–39	60
Justice Department Authorization	Dec. 10, 1981	64–35	60	Campaign Finance	June 9, 1987	52–47	60
State, Justice, Commerce,				Campaign Finance	June 16, 1987	49–46	60
Judiciary Appropriations	Dec. 11, 1981	59–35	60	Campaign Finance	June 17, 1987	51–47	60
Justice Department Authorization	Feb. 9, 1982	63–33	60	Campaign Finance	June 18, 1987	50–47	60
Broadcast Senate Proceedings	April 20, 1982	47–51	60	Campaign Finance	June 19, 1987	45–43	60
Criminal Code Reform Act	April 27, 1982	45–46	60	Trade (Kuwaiti tanker reflagging)	July 9, 1987	57–42	60
Urgent Supplemental Appropriations,				Trade (Kuwaiti tanker reflagging)	July 14, 1987	53–40	60
Fiscal 1982	May 27, 1982	95–2	60	Trade (Kuwaiti tanker reflagging)	July 15, 1987	54–44	60
Voting Rights Act	June 15, 1982	86–8	60	**Wells Nomination**	Sept. 9, 1987	65–24	60
Debt Limit Increase	Sept. 9, 1982	41–47	60	Campaign Finance	Sept. 10, 1987	53–42	60

Issue	Date	Vote	Yeas needed
Campaign Finance	Sept. 15, 1987	51–44	60
Defense Authorization, Fiscal 1988 (Kuwaiti tanker escort)	Oct. 1, 1987	54–45	60
Defense Authorization, Fiscal 1988	Oct. 1, 1987	41–58	60
Verity Nomination	Oct. 13, 1987	85–8	60
War Powers Compliance	Oct. 20, 1987	67–28	60
Energy and Water Appropriations (Nuclear Waste Depository)	Nov. 10, 1987	87–0	60
Campaign Finance	Feb. 26, 1988	53–41	60
Polygraph Protection	March 3, 1988	77–19	60
Intelligence Oversight	March 15, 1988	73–18	60
Risk Notification	March 23, 1988	33–59	60
Risk Notification	March 24, 1988	2–93	60
Risk Notification	March 28, 1988	41–44	60
Risk Notification	March 29, 1988	42–52	60
Campaign Spending Limitations	April 21, 1988	52–42	60
Campaign Spending Limitations	April 22, 1988	53–37	60
Extension of Immigration Legalization Program	April 28, 1988	40–56	60
Death Penalty for Drug-Related Killings	June 9, 1988	70–26	60
Great Smoky Mountain Wilderness Act	June 20, 1988	49–35	60
Great Smoky Mountain Wilderness Act	June 21, 1988	54–42	60
Plant-Closing Notification	June 29, 1988	58–39	60
Plant-Closing Notification	July 6, 1988	88–5	60
Textile Import Quotas	Sept. 7, 1988	68–29	60
Minimum Wage Restoration	Sept. 22, 1988	53–43	60
Minimum Wage Restoration	Sept. 23, 1988	56–35	60
Parental and Medical Leave	Oct. 3, 1988	85–6	60
Parental and Medical Leave	Oct. 7, 1988	50–46	60
Defense Authorization, Fiscal 1990	Aug. 2, 1989	84–13	60
Airline Smoking Ban	Sept. 14, 1989	77–21	60
Eastern Airlines Strike Commission	Oct. 3, 1989	61–36	60
Nicaraguan Election Aid	Oct. 13, 1989	52–42	60
Nicaraguan Election Aid	Oct. 17, 1989	74–25	60
Eastern Airlines Strike Commission	Oct. 26, 1989	62–38	60
Capital Gains Tax Cut	Nov. 14, 1989	51–47	60
Capital Gains Tax Cut	Nov. 15, 1989	51–47	60
Government Pay-and-Ethics Package	Nov. 17, 1989	90–9	60
Armenian Genocide Day of Remembrance	Feb. 22, 1990	49–49	60
Armenian Genocide Day of Remembrance	Feb. 27, 1990	48–51	60
Hatch Act Revisions	May 1, 1990	70–28	60
AIDS Emergency Relief	May 15, 1990	95–3	60
Chemical Weapons Sanctions	May 17, 1990	87–4	60
Omnibus Crime Package	June 5, 1990	54–37	60
Omnibus Crime Package	June 7, 1990	57–37	60
Air Travel Rights for the Blind	June 12, 1990	56–44	60
Civil Rights Act of 1990	July 17, 1990	62–38	60
Fiscal 1991 Defense Authorization	Aug. 3, 1990	58–41	60
Motor Vehicle Fuel Efficiency Act	Sept. 14, 1990	68–28	60
Motor Vehicle Fuel Efficiency Act	Sept. 25, 1990	57–42	60
Title X Family Planning Amendments	Sept. 26, 1990	50–46	60
National Motor-Voter Registration	Sept. 26, 1990	55–42	60
Fiscal 1991 Foreign Operations Appropriations	Oct. 12, 1990	51–38	60
Vertical Price Fixing	May 7, 1991	61–37	60
Vertical Price Fixing	May 8, 1991	63–35	60
Crime Bill	June 28, 1991	41–58	60
Crime Bill	July 10, 1991	56–43	60
Crime Bill	July 10, 1991	71–27	60
National Motor-Voter Registration	July 18, 1991	57–41	60
Fiscal 1992 VA-HUD Appropriations	July 18, 1991	57–40	60
National Motor-Voter Registration	July 18, 1991	59–40	60
Foreign Aid Authorization	July 24, 1991	87–10	60
Foreign Aid Authorization	July 25, 1991	52–44	60
Foreign Aid Authorization	July 25, 1991	63–33	60
Extended Unemployment Benefits	July 29, 1991	96–1	60
Fiscal 1992 Defense Authorization	Aug. 2, 1991	58–40	60
Fiscal 1992 Interior Appropriations	Sept. 19, 1991	55–41	60
Federal Facility Compliance Act	Oct. 17, 1991	85–14	60
Civil Rights Act	Oct. 22, 1991	93–4	60
National Energy Policy	Nov. 1, 1991	50–44	60
Banking Reform	Nov. 13, 1991	76–19	60
Iranian Hostage Release Investigation	Nov. 22, 1991	51–43	60
Crime Conference Report	Nov. 27, 1991	49–38	60
School Improvement Bill	Jan. 21, 1992	93–0	60
National Energy Strategy	Feb. 4, 1992	90–5	60
Joint Ventures Antitrust	Feb. 25, 1992	98–0	60
Lumbee Tribe Recognition	Feb. 27, 1992	58–39	60
Corp. for Public Broadcasting	March 3, 1992	87–7	60
Crime Bill	March 19, 1992	54–43	60
Defense/Domestic Spending Walls	March 26, 1992	50–48	60
NIH Reauthorization/ Fetal Tissue Research	March 31, 1992	98–2	60
Motor-Voter Bill	May 7, 1992	61–38	60
Motor-Voter Bill	May 12, 1992	58–40	60
Drug Abuse Mental Health	June 9, 1992	84–9	60
Striker Replacement	June 11, 1992	55–41	60
Striker Replacement	June 16, 1992	57–42	60
Gov't Sponsored Enterprises/ Balanced Budget Amendment	June 30, 1992	56–39	60
Gov't Sponsored Enterprises/ Balanced Budget Amendment	July 1, 1992	56–39	60
National Energy Strategy	July 23, 1992	58–33	60
National Energy Strategy	July 28, 1992	93–3	60
Edward Carnes Nomination	Sept. 9, 1992	66–30	60
Product Liability	Sept. 10, 1992	57–39	60
Product Liability	Sept. 10, 1992	58–38	60
School Improvement Bill	Sept. 15, 1992	85–6	60
Labor/HHS/Education Appropriations	Sept. 16, 1992	56–38	60
START Treaty	Sept. 29, 1992	87–6	60
School Improvement Bill	Oct. 2, 1992	59–40	60
Crime Bill	Oct. 2, 1992	55–43	60
NIH Reauthorization/ Fetal Tissue Research	Oct. 2, 1992	85–12	60
National Energy Strategy	Oct. 8, 1992	84–8	60
Tax Bill	Oct. 8, 1992	80–10	60
Motor-Voter Bill	March 5, 1993	52–36	60
Motor-Voter Bill	March 9, 1993	62–38	60
Motor-Voter Bill	March 16, 1993	59–41	60
Stimulus Package	April 2, 1993	55–43	60
Stimulus Package	April 3, 1993	52–37	60
Stimulus Package	April 5, 1993	49–29	60
Stimulus Package	April 21, 1993	56–43	60
Motor-Voter Bill	May 11, 1993	63–37	60
Campaign Finance	June 10, 1993	53–41	60
Campaign Finance	June 15, 1993	52–45	60
Campaign Finance	June 16, 1993	62–37	60
National Service	July 29, 1993	59–41	60
Dellinger Confirmation	Oct. 7, 1993	59–39	60
Interior Appropriations	Oct. 21, 1993	53–41	60
Interior Appropriations	Oct. 26, 1993	51–45	60
Interior Appropriations	Oct. 28, 1993	54–44	60
State Department Nominations	Nov. 3, 1993	58–42	60
Brady Bill	Nov. 19, 1993	57–42	60
Napolitano Confirmation	Nov. 19, 1993	72–26	60
Brady Bill	Nov. 19, 1993	57–41	60
Competitiveness Bill	March 15, 1994	56–42	60
Federal Worker Retirement Buyout	March 24, 1994	58–41	60
Federal Worker Retirement Buyout	March 24, 1994	63–36	60
Education Goals 2000	March 26, 1994	62–23	60
Derek Shearer Nomination	May 24, 1994	63–35	60
Sam Brown Jr. Nomination	May 24, 1994	54–44	60
Sam Brown Jr. Nomination	May 25, 1994	56–42	60
Product Liability	June 28, 1994	54–44	60
Product Liability	June 29, 1994	57–41	60
Striker Replacement	July 12, 1994	53–47	60
Striker Replacement	July 13, 1994	53–46	60
Crime Bill	Aug. 25, 1994	61–38	60
Campaign Finance	Sept. 22, 1994	96–2	60
California Desert Protection	Sept. 23, 1994	73–20	60
Campaign Finance	Sept. 27, 1994	57–43	60
Campaign Finance	Sept. 30, 1994	52–46	60
Ricki Tigert Nomination	Oct. 3, 1994	63–32	60
H. Lee Sarokin Nomination	Oct. 4, 1994	85–12	60
Elementary and Secondary Education	Oct. 5, 1994	75–24	60
Lobbying Disclosure/Gift Ban	Oct. 6, 1994	52–46	66
Lobbying Disclosure/Gift Ban	Oct. 7, 1994	55–42	65
California Desert Protection	Oct. 8, 1994	68–23	60
Unfunded Mandates	Jan. 19, 1995	54–44	60
Balanced-Budget Amendment	Feb. 16, 1995	57–42	60
Defense Supplemental (Striker Replacement)	March 15, 1995	58–39	60
Health Insurance Tax Deduction	April 3, 1995	83–0	60
Supplemental Appropriations and Rescissions	April 6, 1995	56–44	60
Product Liability	May 4, 1995	46–53	60
Product Liability	May 4, 1995	47–52	60
Product Liability	May 8, 1995	43–49	60
Product Liability	May 9, 1995	60–38	60
Interstate Waste	May 12, 1995	50–47	60

Issue	Date	Vote	Yeas needed	Issue	Date	Vote	Yeas needed
Telecommunications	June 14, 1995	89–11	60	**Product Liability**	March 20, 1996	60–40	60
Foster nomination	June 21, 1995	57–43	60	Whitewater Committee Extension	March 20, 1996	53–47	60
Foster nomination	June 22, 1995	57–43	60	Whitewater Committee Extension	March 21, 1996	52–46	60
Regulatory Overhaul	July 17, 1995	48–46	60	Presidio Park Management	March 27, 1996	51–49	60
Regulatory Overhaul	July 18, 1995	53–47	60	Presidio Park Management	March 28, 1996	55–45	60
Regulatory Overhaul	July 20, 1995	58–40	60	Whitewater Committee Extension	April 16, 1996	51–46	60
State Department Authorization	Aug. 1, 1995	55–45	60	Term Limits Constitutional Amendment	April 23, 1996	58–42	60
State Department Authorization	Aug. 1, 1995	55–45	60	**Immigration Revision**	April 29, 1996	91–0	60
Cuba Sanctions	Oct. 12, 1995	56–37	60	**Immigration Revision**	May 2, 1996	100–0	60
Cuba Sanctions	Oct. 17, 1995	59–36	60	White House Travel Office Reimbursement	May 7, 1996	52–44	60
Cuba Sanctions	Oct. 18, 1995	98–0	60	White House Travel Office Reimbursement	May 8, 1996	53–45	60
Farm Bill	Feb. 1, 1996	53–45	60	White House Travel Office Reimbursement	May 9, 1996	52–44	60
Farm Bill	Feb. 6, 1996	59–34	60	White House Travel Office Reimbursement	May 14, 1996	54–43	60
District of Columbia Appropriations	Feb. 27, 1996	54–44	60	Missile Defense	June 4, 1996	53–46	60
District of Columbia Appropriations	Feb. 29, 1996	52–42	60	Campaign Finance Overhaul	June 25, 1996	54–46	60
District of Columbia Appropriations	March 5, 1996	53–43	60	Defense Authorization	June 26, 1996	52–46	60
District of Columbia Appropriations	March 12, 1996	56–44	60	Defense Authorization	June 28, 1996	53–43	60
Whitewater Committee Extension	March 12, 1996	53–47	60	Right-to-work legislation	July 10, 1996	31–68	60
Whitewater Committee Extension	March 13, 1996	53–47	60	**Nuclear Waste Storage**	July 16, 1996	65–34	60
Whitewater Committee Extension	March 14, 1996	51–46	60	**FAA Reauthorization**	Oct. 3, 1996	66–31	60

[a] Vote was taken after midnight in the session that began Oct. 8, 1985.

The Presidency

President Bill Clinton came into office with both houses of Congress under Democratic control. Few of his nominees to cabinet, sub-cabinet and other executive branch posts ran into serious opposition to their confirmation by the Senate. To accommodate the new president, confirmation hearings on most of the nominees were held before the Jan. 20, 1993, inauguration, and most had been confirmed by the day after Clinton was sworn in.

The one major exception was his selection of an attorney general. The first nominee for the post, corporate lawyer Zoë Baird, ran into strong public opposition and withdrew because she had hired illegal immigrants as domestic help and at that time had not paid Social Security or unemployment taxes on their wages. Clinton's apparent second choice, U.S. District Court Judge Kimba M. Wood, also withdrew her name from consideration because she had hired an illegal immigrant, although she had broken no laws. After the two false starts, Clinton selected Florida prosecutor Janet Reno to head the Justice Department; her nomination proceeded smoothly through the Senate.

Clinton had promised a cabinet that "looks like America." His initial cabinet appointees included four African Americans, two Hispanics and three women. His pledge to name a Republican to the cabinet went unfulfilled.

By the end of Clinton's first term, there had been turnovers in four cabinet departments: Treasury, defense, agriculture and commerce. Three resignations occurred in 1994, and Secretary of Commerce Ron Brown was killed in an airplane crash in 1996. Five of the original cabinet members remained at their posts at the start of the second Clinton administration. *(Clinton cabinet, box, p. 1111)*

Clinton named two associate justices to the U.S. Supreme Court: Ruth Bader Ginsburg in 1993 and Stephen G. Breyer in 1994. He also appointed 198 district and circuit court judges—about one-fourth of the federal bench. As he had with his cabinet, Clinton focused on building a federal judiciary that looked more like America. He was the first president whose appointments were not made up of a majority of white men. Of the 198 confirmed by the Senate, 105 were women or members of racial or ethnic minorities, or both. *(Supreme Court appointments, box, p. 760)*

With a new Republican majority in the House and Senate, the 104th Congress was more active, more partisan and more willing to defy a president than ever before in the post–World War II period. As part of its effort to shrink the federal government, the House attempted to abolish the Commerce Department. The attempt failed, but disputes became commonplace throughout the second half of Clinton's term. Sen. Jesse Helms, R-N.C., continued his long-standing practice of blocking action on various ambassadorial nominees because he either disagreed with their views or wanted to use the appointments as leverage in a policy dispute with the administration.

Below are profiles of cabinet members and others who served in key executive branch positions during the first Clinton administration, followed by brief accounts of major controversial nominations.

Cabinet, 1993–1996

AGRICULTURE

Former Democratic representative **Mike Espy** of Mississippi was confirmed by the Senate to be secretary of agriculture by voice vote Jan. 21, 1993. The Senate Agriculture Committee had approved the nomination by voice vote two days earlier.

Espy was the first African American and the first person from the Deep South to head the U.S. Department of Agriculture (USDA). During his tenure in the House (1987–1993), he had served on the Agriculture Committee and was an active member of the House Select Committee on Hunger.

Espy glided through a Jan. 14 Senate confirmation hearing, promising to make the restructuring of the Agriculture Department a top priority. Most of the panel's questions centered on the USDA downsizing, as well as upcoming international trade agreements and federal farm subsidies.

Some senators expressed concern that Espy would tilt agricultural policy toward the cotton and sugar cane farmers of the South at the expense of wheat and feed-grain farmers of the upper Midwestern states. But Espy assured them that he intended to be an agriculture secretary for the nation and that while crops differed from one region to another, the nation's agricultural interests overlapped. Increasing farm income, cutting regulation, opening world markets and reducing government overhead would help farmers nationwide and allay concerns of any regional bias, Espy said.

The only hint of controversy came when ranking Republican Richard G. Lugar of Indiana asked Espy about a Justice Department investigation into accounting irregularities in campaign finance reports that Espy had filed with the Federal Election Commission during his four congressional races. Espy said the problem stemmed from a misunderstanding about the reports and had been resolved to the Justice Department's satisfaction.

Espy resigned his position on Dec. 31, 1994, amid allegations of impropriety. *(Agriculture leadership, box, p. 483)*

The Senate on March 30, 1995, voted 94–0 to confirm the nomination of former Democratic representative **Dan Glickman** of Kansas (1977–1995) to succeed Espy as agriculture secretary. He was sworn in the same day.

At his confirmation hearing March 21 before the Senate Agriculture Committee, Glickman promised to be an "advocate" for agriculture and cautioned against trimming farm programs beyond the $1.5 billion in unspecified cuts over five years proposed by President Clinton. Senate Agriculture Chairman Richard G. Lugar, R-Ind., had called for $15 billion in cuts over five years.

Glickman, an 18-year veteran of the House Agriculture Committee who lost his bid for a 10th House term in November 1994, came before the committee with some high-profile bipartisan support. Lugar joined three fellow Republicans—Senate Majority Leader Bob Dole, Sen. Nancy Landon Kassebaum and House Agriculture Committee Chairman Pat Roberts, all from Kansas—in expressing their desire to see Glickman speedily confirmed.

Clinton nominated Glickman in December 1994, but the administration delayed formally sending the nomination to the Senate because of an extensive FBI background check that uncovered concerns about the use by Glickman's daughter of campaign credit cards. Glickman assured senators that the FBI probe uncovered no problems. He also said he had been exonerated in the 1991 House bank scandal for his 105 overdrafts; that he had paid the District of Columbia $1,050 in back parking fines; and that he had adequately reimbursed his campaign committee for his personal use of a credit card designated for his reelection effort.

The committee voted to send the nomination to the floor with a favorable recommendation March 23.

ATTORNEY GENERAL

Janet Reno, a veteran Florida prosecutor, was confirmed as attorney general, 98–0, on March 11, 1993, one day after the Senate Judiciary Committee had unanimously endorsed her. She was the first woman to serve in that position.

It took President Clinton three tries to find a nominee who could win Senate confirmation, but after he finally named Reno to head the Justice Department, she quickly became his most popular cabinet member. Judiciary Committee members, like Clinton, were eager to get an attorney general in place. Clinton's first selection, corporate attorney Zoë Baird, was forced to withdraw amid controversy over her hiring of two illegal immigrants as childcare and household help and her failure to pay Social Security taxes for them; a second leading candidate, federal Judge Kimba M. Wood, dropped out over a similar, albeit less severe, "nanny problem." *(Controversial nominations, p. 1117)*

Reno, who was single and had no children, disavowed any similar problem. "I've never hired an illegal alien. And I think I paid all my Social Security taxes," she remarked in a light moment after her nomination.

Reno, who had a strong reputation for integrity, for 15 years had been the state's attorney for crime-ridden Dade County, which included Miami. She managed an office of 900 workers and supervised thousands of criminal cases. She had garnered national attention as an innovator in the criminal justice field, and her appointment drew praise from many in Congress.

Most of the Senate Judiciary questioning focused on Reno's area of expertise: fighting crime. Reno repeatedly cited her philosophy of combining tough, certain punishment for criminals with opportunities for diversion or rehabilitation where appropriate.

Some conservatives had complained that Reno's inclinations ran more to social work than to fighting crime. Reno took issue with that assessment, saying she had been tough on hardened criminals and believed many should serve more time in jail than they did. But she also stressed the need for early intervention and education to wean children from a culture of violence.

During the hearings, Reno reiterated Clinton administration positions in support of a ban on assault weapons and a waiting period for handgun purchases. Reno said she personally opposed the death penalty, but she went out of her way to assure senators that her opposition had not deterred her from using the death penalty in Dade County, nor would it hamper her willingness to pursue it at the federal level.

COMMERCE

Ronald H. Brown was confirmed by the Senate as secretary of the Department of Commerce by voice vote on Jan. 21, 1993. The former Democratic National Committee chairman secured unanimous approval from the Senate Commerce Committee the same day, after earlier fending off questions about his past lobbying activities.

Brown, the man widely credited for keeping Democrats unified in the 1992 presidential election, gave three hours of testimony Jan. 6 before the Commerce Committee in which he promised to work in "close partnership" with industry to strengthen the economy and protect U.S. trade interests. The longtime partner in the prominent Washington law firm of Patton, Boggs & Blow vowed to obey strict ethics rules and refrain from dealing directly with former clients for

one year. (Brown resigned from partnership in the firm the day before his confirmation.)

Members of the Commerce Committee focused on his lobbying activities, which included representing the former Haitian dictator Jean-Claude "Baby Doc" Duvalier and U.S. subsidiaries of Japanese electronics firms. Committee Chairman Ernest F. Hollings, D-S.C., attempted to put to rest conflict of interest questions, saying he had examined Brown's record and was "satisfied that [he] acted properly."

The most intense grilling came from Mississippi Republican Trent Lott, who was tapped by the GOP to examine Clinton's nominees. Lott told Brown that the combination of his lobbying and fund raising for the Democratic Party "convey at least the appearance that your nomination is at odds" with the ethical standards set by Clinton.

Brown easily defused questions and presented himself as a formidable negotiator primed to advocate American business interests. He defended his work with the Duvalier regime by saying he was trying to persuade the Haitian government to bring about changes in labor laws and human rights in exchange for trade preferences from the United States. He said his work for Japanese electronics firms would help him in his new role as chief advocate for U.S. business interests.

Brown also called "totally false" news reports that he helped a Louisiana-based company called Chemfix Technologies Inc., on whose board of directors he served, secure a sludge-hauling contract with New York City in exchange for his influence in selecting New York as host of the 1992 Democratic National Convention. He said the city had always been the front-runner to host the convention.

Brown was killed April 3, 1996, when the U.S. military airplane he was traveling in crashed in Dubrovnik, Croatia.

Mickey Kantor, the U.S. trade representative since the start of the Clinton administration, was named April 12, 1996, to succeed Brown. In announcing his selection, President Clinton praised Kantor's work on the North American Free Trade Agreement, the General Agreement on Tariffs and Trade and about 200 other international trade deals. *(U.S. trade representative, p. 1117)*

Because Kantor's appointment as commerce secretary came during a congressional recess, Senate confirmation was not constitutionally required until the end of 1997. The Senate initially planned to go ahead with confirmation hearings, which would have given House Republicans eager to dismantle the Commerce Department an opportunity to press their case. GOP Reps. John L. Mica of Florida and Dick Chrysler of Michigan had vowed to lobby the Senate against Kantor's confirmation as commerce secretary and to block the confirmation of any successor to Kantor as U.S. trade representative.

Republican Larry Pressler of South Dakota, chairman of the Senate Commerce, Science and Transportation Committee, announced the week of June 17 that he had decided to forgo the hearings. Pressler said his decision had nothing to do with the issue of dismantling the Commerce Department. The committee was simply too busy, he said.

Kantor had served as the national chairman of the 1992 Clinton-Gore campaign and was a visible leader in the Clinton transition team. Prior to coming to Washington, Kantor had lobbied and practiced corporate law in Los Angeles.

DEFENSE

The nomination of **Les Aspin,** a Democratic representative from Wisconsin (1971–1993), to become secretary of defense was approved by the Senate Armed Services Committee on Jan. 20, 1993, just a few hours after President Clinton took the oath of office. The full Senate gave voice vote approval to the Aspin nomination the

CLINTON ADMINISTRATION CABINET

Following is a list of Cabinet officers who served in the Clinton administration from the time President Clinton took office on Jan. 20, 1993, through the end of his first administration. Where service date is left open, the Cabinet officer continued to serve in Clinton's second administration.

Dates given are for actual service in office, which may vary from dates of confirmation by the Senate. *(Presidents and their cabinets, 1933–1980, Congress and the Nation Vol. V. , p. 1111; Reagan cabinet, 1981–1989, Congress and the Nation Vol. VII, p. 1045; Bush cabinet, 1989–1993, Congress and the Nation Vol. VIII, p. 1171)*

Secretary of State
Warren M. Christopher—Jan. 22, 1993–Jan. 23, 1997

Secretary of the Treasury
Lloyd Bentsen—Jan. 22, 1993–Dec. 22, 1994
Robert E. Rubin—Jan. 10, 1995–

Secretary of Defense
Les Aspin[a]—Jan. 22, 1993–Feb. 2, 1994
William J. Perry—Feb. 3, 1994–Jan. 24, 1997

Attorney General
Janet Reno— March 12, 1993–

Secretary of the Interior
Bruce Babbitt—Jan. 22, 1993–

Secretary of Agriculture
Mike Espy—Jan. 22, 1993–Dec. 31, 1994
Dan Glickman—March 30, 1995–

Secretary of Commerce
Ronald H. Brown—Jan. 22, 1993–April 3, 1996
Mickey Kantor[b]—April 12, 1996–Jan. 29, 1997

Secretary of Labor
Robert B. Reich—Jan. 22, 1993–Jan. 12, 1997

Secretary of Health and Human Services
Donna E. Shalala—Jan. 22, 1993–

Secretary of Education
Richard W. Riley—Jan. 22, 1993–

Secretary of Housing and Urban Development
Henry G. Cisneros—Jan. 22, 1993–Jan. 29, 1997

Secretary of Transportation
Federico F. Peña—Jan. 22, 1993–Feb. 13, 1997

Secretary of Energy
Hazel R. O'Leary—Jan. 22, 1993–March 12, 1997

Secretary of Veteran Affairs
Jesse Brown—Jan. 22, 1993–

[a] Aspin was sworn in at a small ceremony at the House Armed Services Committee on Jan. 20 and again at a formal White House ceremony on Jan. 22.
[b] Kantor served as a recess appointment; Senate confirmation was not constitutionally required until the end of 1997.

same day, after Senate Armed Services Committee Chairman Sam Nunn, D-Ga., lavishly praised Aspin's mastery of defense-related issues.

To ensure a smooth transition at the Pentagon, Aspin was sworn in two hours later at a small ceremony at the House Armed Services Committee, which Aspin chaired from 1985 until he stepped down to head the Defense Department. He was sworn in again Jan. 22 with other confirmed cabinet and cabinet-level officers in a White House ceremony.

From a congressional vantage point on the sidelines of defense policy, Aspin had been instrumental in devising guiding principles for an active U.S. military in the post–cold war era. During his Jan. 7 confirmation hearing before the Senate Armed Services panel, he made clear his conviction that U.S. force could and should be used—even for limited objectives with uncertain outcomes. Aspin's penchant for the limited use of force was questioned by some conservative Republicans who worried that limited interventions might lead to Vietnam-like conflicts.

During his years in Congress, Aspin had become one of the most influential voices in public debate on U.S. defense policy. But he had

limited management experience, never having run anything larger than the House Armed Services Committee.

At the Pentagon, Aspin was criticized for his loose management style and frequently became bogged down in controversies that ranged from gays in the military to peacekeeping in Somalia. His troubled tenure ended with his resignation on Feb. 2, 1994. *(Aspin tenure, p. 259)*

William J. Perry was unanimously confirmed by the Senate on Feb. 3, 1994, to become President Clinton's second secretary of defense. After Aspin announced in late 1993 his impending resignation, Clinton first tapped retired admiral Bobby Ray Inman as his replacement, but Inman abruptly withdrew Jan. 18, 1994. *(Controversial nominations, p. 1119)*

The Senate's swift action on Perry—it confirmed him just 10 days after he was selected—and the 97–0 vote underscored the extraordinarily high regard that Democrats and Republicans alike had for Perry, a mathematician and defense technologist who had served as Aspin's deputy. Perry had also been the Pentagon's research and engineering chief during the Carter administration.

The high regard for Perry was demonstrated by the effusion of praise during the Senate Armed Services Committee's Feb. 2 hearing on the nomination. "One of the bright spots at the Department of Defense of this past year," ranking Republican Strom Thurmond, S.C., said of Perry. "I am confident he will not disappoint us."

Armed Services Chairman Sam Nunn, D-Ga., underscored his enthusiasm by departing from his practice of keeping confidential his advice to presidents. Nunn said that since the 1992 election, he had talked with Clinton three times to recommend potential defense secretaries: "Each time, I put Bill Perry's name at the top of the list."

During the three-hour Armed Services hearing Feb. 2, committee Republicans linked kudos for Perry with broadsides at Clinton. They accused the president of seeking budgets too small to fund his announced defense strategy and of taking too soft a line toward North Korea, which was widely believed to be developing nuclear weapons.

The committee approved Perry's nomination Feb. 3 by a vote of 22–0.

EDUCATION

Richard W. Riley was confirmed by voice vote Jan. 21, 1993, to be secretary of education. Two days earlier, the Senate Labor and Human Resources Committee had given voice vote approval to the nomination.

At his confirmation hearing, Riley reaffirmed his support for direct student loans and his opposition to private school choice. Democrats at the hearing could hardly contain their glee at the prospect of one of their own setting the country's education agenda after 12 years of Republican rule. "The nation's long nightmare in education nonsense is over," said Ernest F. Hollings, D-S.C. Even Republicans, though they disputed Hollings's "nightmare" scenario, seemed genuinely pleased with Riley's credentials and demeanor.

The only hint of tension in an otherwise cordial hearing came when several Republicans pressed the nominee on school choice—a plan long favored by conservatives to establish a voucher system giving some federal money to parents to help them pay private school tuition. Reiterating earlier statements, Riley unequivocally opposed private school choice, arguing that funneling public money to private schools would undermine the public education system.

Riley had served as governor of South Carolina from 1979 to 1987. During his tenure in the state house, he acquired a reputation as an innovative education reformer, leading a fight in 1984 to enact sweeping changes in the state's school system.

After retiring as governor, Riley joined the large South Carolina law firm of Nelson, Mullins, Riley & Scarborough as a full partner in 1987. The firm represented companies that disposed of nuclear and other hazardous wastes, leading some environmental groups to oppose the nominee as someone who had profited from representing polluters. But Riley effectively dismissed these charges, saying that he had built a strong environmental record during his years in the state house. In addition, he said that he had not been directly involved in any environmental litigation while at the firm.

ENERGY

Hazel R. O'Leary was confirmed as secretary of energy by voice vote of the Senate Jan. 21, 1993, after she had won approval in a Jan. 20 telephone poll of Senate Energy and Natural Resources Committee members.

During her confirmation hearing Jan. 19, O'Leary advocated some of the environmental community's top priorities without disparaging the coal, oil and nuclear industries. She appealed to both sides on such controversial issues as nuclear power, nuclear waste and offshore drilling. O'Leary also echoed President Clinton's environmentally oriented pledges on energy, calling several times for more energy conservation and cleaner sources of power. Yet she offered the committee members, who tended to favor the domestic energy industry, reason to support her with comments on the limits to conservation and the need for continued domestic energy production.

O'Leary had been executive vice president of Northern States Power Co., an electric and gas utility in Minnesota that serviced 1.7 million people in the Dakotas, Michigan, Minnesota and Wisconsin. The company generated much of its electricity from coal and nuclear reactors—the environmental community's least favorite sources of energy—but it also had invested heavily in wind power and energy conservation. O'Leary's prior experience in government included directing the Federal Energy Administration's Office of Consumer Affairs under President Gerald R. Ford and the Energy Department's Economic Regulatory Administration under President Jimmy Carter.

O'Leary pledged to shift the Energy Department's research budget toward research into renewable energy and antipollution technologies, as Clinton had promised during his presidential campaign. She also voiced support for reducing the money spent on nuclear weapons testing, speeding up decisions on natural gas pipelines and weeding out problems in the department's contracting and procurement.

HEALTH AND HUMAN SERVICES

Donna E. Shalala, the first woman to head a Big Ten school as chancellor of the University of Wisconsin at Madison, won voice vote approval from the Senate on Jan. 21, 1993, as secretary of health and human services (HHS). The Senate Finance Committee had approved Shalala by voice vote Jan. 19.

The Finance Committee hearing on the nomination was dominated by health care issues familiar from the 1992 presidential campaign. Shalala said the government had to ensure health coverage for the roughly 35 million Americans who had no health insurance and another 35 million with inadequate coverage.

Senators pressed Shalala about when Clinton's health care reform bill would arrive on Capitol Hill. Clinton previously had said he wanted to put together a plan during his first 100 days in office. Shalala said the president would not back away from his commitment to revamp the country's health care system, but that the new administration needed to take over the department and determine program costs before sending a bill to Congress.

Shalala also pledged to make the first four years of the Clinton administration the "years of the woman" in health care, with continued research to find cures and treatment for ovarian, cervical and breast cancers, and osteoporosis.

For children, she said the department would increase immunizations to combat polio, rubella, mumps and measles. She also called for a strengthened commitment to Head Start, the education and health program for low-income preschoolers.

Shalala said the department had to develop a more comprehensive, aggressive program to deal with AIDS, including education, treatment and research to find a vaccine and a cure.

Shalala was a surprise pick to head HHS. She was mentioned as a possible secretary of education because of her involvement in higher education, and as secretary of the Department of Housing and Urban Development because she served as an assistant secretary under President Jimmy Carter. Shalala had little experience in health policy but had been involved in children's programs as chairman of the board of the Children's Defense Fund, a children's advocacy group. She had succeeded Hillary Rodham Clinton in that post.

HOUSING AND URBAN DEVELOPMENT

Henry G. Cisneros, a Hispanic former mayor of San Antonio with extensive experience in urban renewal programs, was confirmed by voice vote of the Senate Jan. 21, 1993, as President Clinton's secretary of housing and urban development. His confirmation came one day after the Senate Banking, Housing and Urban Affairs Committee reported the nomination by a vote of 19–0.

During a Jan. 12 confirmation hearing, Cisneros received praise from both Democratic and Republican panel members, as well as a startling show of support from the outgoing head of the department. "If there is one man who was born to be HUD secretary, it is Henry Cisneros," former secretary Jack F. Kemp, a Republican, said at the start of the hearing.

Cisneros said HUD's mission under his leadership would be to restore "safety and prosperity" to communities and to "ensure a livable and steady supply of affordable housing."

About the only challenging questions for Cisneros came from freshman Lauch Faircloth, R-N.C., who suggested that HUD had too many programs for the homeless and that the deficit could be reduced if Cisneros proposed cuts in the department's budget. But Chairman Donald W. Riegle Jr., D-Mich., interrupted Faircloth, saying, "No agency in the 1980s was marched to the chopping block more than [HUD]."

While generally liberal on social issues, as mayor of San Antonio from 1981 to 1989, Cisneros placed an emphasis on economic development through innovative government and industry partnerships to revitalize urban areas. He was touted as a rising national star, mentioned as a potential senator or governor, and seriously considered as Walter F. Mondale's vice-presidential running mate in 1984.

However, he became tainted by a highly publicized extramarital affair with a campaign supporter. The affair and his son's medical problems contributed to Cisneros's decision not to seek reelection as mayor in 1989. He spent the next four years prior to becoming secretary of HUD running a financial consulting company, Cisneros Asset Management, as well as a health and benefit planning company and a communications firm. During Clinton's 1992 presidential campaign, Cisneros was instrumental in focusing on Hispanic voters.

INTERIOR

Bruce Babbitt was confirmed as secretary of the interior by voice vote Jan. 21, 1993, after the nominee had won a 20–0 endorsement from the Senate Energy and Natural Resources Committee.

In two days of hearings Jan. 19 and 21, the former Arizona governor and 1988 Democratic presidential contender emphasized that he was not a radical and would not toe the environmentalists' line as head of the Interior Department. Babbitt—a committed environmentalist but also a member of one of Arizona's oldest ranching families—noted that he grew up on a western cattle ranch, was trained as a geologist and a lawyer, and had represented ranchers, small towns, Native American tribes and environmental groups. He pointed to his ability as governor to bring opposing groups together on such controversial issues as groundwater protection and wildlife preservation.

Still, several senators made it clear to Babbitt that they were troubled by his barbed comments from 1991 to 1993 as president of the League of Conservation Voters, the self-described political arm of the environmental movement.

The interior secretary had responsibility for managing about 442 million acres of public land nationwide, which was open to competing interests—mining, grazing, logging, recreation and wilderness. Babbitt had been a persistent critic of the management of the Interior Department and had called for a new philosophy of public-land management that would downgrade the importance of traditional uses such as mining and ranching to give more weight to environmental and recreational needs.

Western Republicans tried with limited success to have Babbitt support such Western interests as low-cost grazing and mining on public lands, private-property rights, the multiple-use system of managing public lands and a more cautious administration of the Endangered Species Act. Babbitt said he would not back away from the Endangered Species Act but promised to listen to suggestions for improving it. On most other topics, Babbitt remained noncommittal.

LABOR

The Senate confirmed **Robert B. Reich** as secretary of labor by voice vote on Jan. 21, 1993. Two days earlier, the Senate Labor and Human Resources Committee reported the nomination also by voice vote.

During the committee's confirmation hearing Jan. 7, Reich reiterated President Clinton's desire to sign a family and medical leave bill, to require businesses to set aside 1.5 percent of their payrolls for job training and to sign a striker replacement bill to prohibit companies from permanently replacing striking workers.

In his prodigious writings on the economy, Reich (who was not an economist) had stressed job training, a top Clinton priority, and the need not just for more jobs but for higher-wage jobs. Businesses performed best, he argued, when they viewed their workers as their most "precious asset," involving them in decision-making about products and the workplace.

Labor groups hesitated little in backing Reich. The AFL-CIO expressed delight in having a labor secretary who was close to the president and intimately involved with economic planning. Reich had been a close friend of Clinton's since their days as Rhodes scholars, and he headed Clinton's economic policy-planning group during the presidential transition period.

Advocates for business stressed concern about Reich's desire for higher wages and more benefits, and small-business groups were worried about the possibility of payroll tax to fund job training.

Before being tapped to be labor secretary, Reich was a lecturer at Harvard University's Kennedy School of Government, a director of policy planning at the Federal Trade Commission under President Jimmy Carter and an assistant solicitor general in the Justice Department during the Ford administration.

STATE

The Senate approved the nomination of **Warren M. Christopher** to be secretary of state by voice vote on Jan. 20, 1993. The Senate Foreign Relations Committee easily approved his nomination, 19–0, on Jan. 19.

Christopher, who was deputy secretary of state in the Carter administration, had two grueling days of testimony Jan. 13 and 14 before the committee, after which aides to conservative Republican Sen. Jesse Helms, N.C., submitted more than 400 additional questions in writing.

During the hearings, Christopher seemed determined to erase the Democratic Party's long-standing image of ineptitude in national security matters and downplay his own reputation as an advocate of negotiation over confrontation. He told panel members the Clinton administration would not shrink from using force to buttress diplomacy.

At the same time, the Los Angeles corporate lawyer said there were limits to what the United States could achieve as the world's lone surviving superpower. "We cannot respond to every alarm," he said, assuring the American people that "we will not turn their blood and treasure into an open account for use by the rest of the world."

In Bosnia, Somalia and other countries torn by strife, Christopher said he would look to the United Nations and European allies to do more than they had so far. He blasted European nations for the "abysmal way" that they had responded to the Bosnian crisis, a situation that he said cried out for multilateral action.

TRANSPORTATION

Former Denver mayor **Federico F. Peña** won Senate voice vote approval Jan. 21, 1993, as secretary of transportation. Earlier the same day, the Senate Commerce and Transportation Committee approved the nomination by voice vote.

At a smooth two-hour confirmation hearing Jan. 7, Peña showed his political skills as he fielded questions from the Commerce panel, committing himself only to study concerns and seek compromises despite numerous attempts to pin him down on an array of transportation issues.

Committee members handled Peña with a light touch, asking no questions about his limited experience in transportation issues. Peña served as mayor of Denver from 1983 to 1991 and later was an investment adviser and lawyer in Denver. According to his financial disclosure forms, his two biggest legal clients were communications companies: Western Union and U.S. West, a regional Bell Telephone company.

As mayor, he helped assemble a series of major building projects to boost the economy at a time of regional recession. The largest of these, a $2.7 billion regional airport, gave Peña his introduction to the Transportation Department.

TREASURY

Lloyd Bentsen, a four-term Democratic senator from Texas, won Senate confirmation as Treasury secretary by voice vote Jan. 20, 1993. Bentsen's nomination had breezed through the Senate Finance Committee with unanimous support.

Until he was confirmed, Bentsen kept his Senate seat and remained the chairman of the Finance Committee, the same panel that reviewed his qualifications. Daniel Patrick Moynihan, D-N.Y., who was taking over as Finance chairman, held a roll call on Bentsen's nomination 20 minutes into the Jan. 12 hearing, before questioning had even begun. The committee approved the nomination by a 19–0 vote.

In his testimony before the Finance panel, Bentsen stressed that trimming the deficit topped President Clinton's list of priorities, although he noted that it was possible to "overdo it" by cutting the deficit too quickly—a course that he said could "put the economy back into a serious recession." He indicated that if unemployment remained high, a modest deficit-widening stimulus package might be necessary to promote job growth.

Bentsen refused to rule out tax increases on the middle class and made it clear that the administration expected to make cuts in entitlement spending. He floated a gasoline tax increase, higher estate taxes and cuts in Medicare as deficit-reduction options. Bentsen emphasized a point frequently made by Clinton, that efforts to limit federal spending for Medicare and Medicaid, the nation's fastest growing entitlements, would only be successful if accompanied by an overhaul of the nation's health care system.

Bentsen had served in the House from December 1948 to 1955 and in the Senate from 1971 to 1993. He had chaired the Senate Finance Committee since 1987. He was presidential candidate Michael S. Dukakis's vice-presidential running mate on the Democratic ticket in 1988.

Bentsen resigned his post as Treasury secretary on Dec. 22, 1994, and retired from public life at the age of 73.

Robert E. Rubin received unanimous approval, 99–0, from the Senate Jan. 10, 1995, to succeed Bentsen as Treasury secretary. He was sworn in the same day.

Rubin's ride through the confirmation process proved even smoother than anticipated. There was no floor debate, and hours earlier the Senate Finance Committee voted by voice to approve Rubin's nomination even before questioning was fully under way.

Majority Leader Bob Dole, R-Kan., set the tone for the hearing, saying President Clinton had "made an outstanding choice" in nominating Rubin to the post. "His self-effacing attitude toward getting things done has earned the respect of many of us on Capitol Hill," Dole said.

Throughout his confirmation hearing, Rubin emphasized the importance of deficit reduction.

Rubin joined the administration in 1993 as the first chairman of the National Economic Council, where he coordinated policy among several agencies, including the Treasury Department, and made recommendations to the president. Clinton created the NEC along the lines of the White House National Security Council in fulfillment of his campaign pledge to focus "like a laser beam" on the economy. The NEC position had not required Senate confirmation.

Prior to the NEC, Rubin had spent 26 years with the Wall Street investment bank Goldman, Sachs & Co., eventually becoming cochairman of the bank. He also was a major Democratic fund-raiser.

VETERANS AFFAIRS

Jesse Brown, a lobbyist for disabled veterans and a Purple Heart recipient who lost partial use of his right arm as a Marine in Vietnam, won Senate confirmation as secretary of veterans affairs (VA) by voice vote on Jan. 21, 1993. To expedite the confirmation process, the Senate Veterans' Affairs Committee agreed to allow floor consideration without a committee vote on the nomination.

During his Jan. 7 appearance before the veterans' panel, Brown said his background as a veterans' advocate gave him "an intimacy with veterans' issues that can only come from hard work, every day, year in, year out, in a single field." Brown had lobbied repeatedly for more funding for veterans as the executive director of the Disabled American Veterans (DAV) and spent more than half his life with the organization before being nominated.

Brown's 26-year affiliation with the DAV brought questions from Alan K. Simpson, R-Wyo., concerning a substantial pension provided to him by his former employer. Simpson, long a critic of veterans' advocacy groups, asked if the DAV pension—which Simpson said amounted to $41,000 per year or $960,000 if paid in one lump sum—would create the wrong perception.

Brown defended his association with the organization and argued that the pension was "not an unreasonable amount" for someone with his experience and years of service. He also disputed Simpson's figures, saying the lump sum would total $500,000 to $600,000. On his financial disclosure form, Brown checked off a box saying his pension was worth $500,000 to $1 million.

Brown promised to go directly to the president to press for funding increases if budget woes led to unfair cuts in veterans' programs. Brown spoke of broad goals for the VA such as increasing the department's efficiency while providing higher quality health care. He said that could be done in tandem with President Clinton's proposed overhaul of the nation's general health care system.

Other Key Positions

CENTRAL INTELLIGENCE AGENCY

R. James Woolsey was confirmed by the Senate Feb. 3, 1993, by voice vote to become director of central intelligence. The Senate Select Intelligence Committee approved his nomination earlier that day by a vote of 17–0.

During Woolsey's confirmation hearing Feb. 2, Intelligence Committee members applauded the former arms negotiator as someone who would advise them on how to balance the need for budget cuts in the wake of the cold war against emerging demands for intelligence on a range of issues, from obscure ethnic conflicts to economic and environmental threats.

Sounding more like committee Republicans than his fellow Democrats, Woolsey cautioned that "the number and complexity of very serious threats" to U.S. interests had grown, not shrunk, in recent years. "In many ways, today's threats are harder to observe and understand than the one that was once presented by the U.S.S.R.," he told the committee. "Yes, we have slain a large dragon. But we live in a jungle filled with a bewildering variety of poisonous snakes."

Woolsey came to the job with close ties to Capitol Hill. He served as general counsel to the Senate Armed Services Committee in the early 1970s and was an undersecretary of the navy during the Carter administration. He was an arms control negotiator for the Reagan administration and led the U.S. negotiating team for the Bush administration on a treaty to reduce arms and conventional forces in Europe.

Woolsey resigned his post on Jan. 9, 1995. Controversy had surrounded his response to the Aldrich H. Ames espionage case, and his relations with the White House and Capitol Hill had become increasingly strained. *(Ames espionage case, p. 219)*

John M. Deutch won Senate confirmation May 9, 1995, to succeed Woolsey as director of central intelligence. He was confirmed by a vote of 98–0 and sworn in the next day.

Deutch's path to the job was convoluted. In January 1995, Deutch, who then was serving as deputy defense secretary, had rejected President Clinton's initial entreaties to head the Central Intelligence Agency (CIA). But he relented when the White House's nominee, retired air force general Michael P. C. Carns, withdrew his name March 10. *(Controversial nominations, p. 1120)*

Deutch only agreed to take on the challenge of reviving an agency desperate for a focus in the post–cold war era when Clinton acceded to his demand that the CIA director be promoted to cabinet rank. That step troubled lawmakers, who feared that, as a member of the cabinet, the CIA director would succumb to policy making and fail to provide the unfettered information required of the spy chief.

Deutch repeatedly sought to reassure the Senate Select Committee on Intelligence during his confirmation hearing April 26 that he would draw a clear line between intelligence provider and policy maker.

Deutch, a chemist and former provost at the Massachusetts Institute of Technology, had been confirmed twice by the Senate since 1993, once to serve as the Pentagon's acquisitions chief and later to succeed Defense Secretary William J. Perry as deputy defense secretary.

COUNCIL OF ECONOMIC ADVISERS

Laura D'Andrea Tyson, President Clinton's choice to head the Council of Economic Advisers (CEA), won voice vote approval in the

---

CLINTON JUDICIAL APPOINTMENTS

During his first term, President Clinton appointed two Supreme Court justices and 198 federal district and circuit court judges. In making these appointments, Clinton appeared to be building a federal judiciary that, like his cabinet, looked more like America.

Clinton was the first president whose judicial appointments were not made up of a majority of white men. His Supreme Court appointments included one woman. *(Supreme Court appointments, box, p. 760)*

Of his lower court appointments—which constituted about one-fourth of all district and circuit court judges—105 were women or members of racial or ethnic minorities, or both. Almost a third of Clinton's judges were women. Nineteen percent were African American; 7 percent were Hispanic; and 2 percent were Asian American or Native American.

The diversity reflected the Democratic Party as a whole, which included more women and minorities than the GOP. It also moved the federal bench more to the left, because women and minorities tended to be more liberal than white men.

Still diversity rather than ideology appeared to be the key to Clinton's judges and the philosophy behind their selection. Like President George Bush and unlike President Ronald Reagan, Clinton did not make judicial selection a high-profile activity. He avoided sending provocative nominations to the Republican-controlled Senate in the 104th Congress.

According to political scientists who ranked judges on a liberal-to-conservative spectrum, Clinton's appointees generally came out in the middle, about equal to those of President Gerald R. Ford.

But to conservatives, judges like Ford's were not acceptable, given the country's shift to the right since the 1970s. Relative to the political landscape of the 1990s, they argued, Clinton's judges were ideological liberals or judicial activists determined to use their judgeships to impose their own agendas.

Senate on Feb. 4, 1993, one day after the Senate Banking, Housing and Urban Affairs Committee had approved her nomination by a vote of 18–0.

Tyson, an economist at the University of California at Berkeley, went before the Senate Banking Committee on Jan. 21 determined to counter critics who questioned her commitment to free markets and her credentials for the job.

Clinton's choice of Tyson, a microeconomist who had concentrated on trade and competitiveness issues, for a position usually filled by a macroeconomist had raised questions about the role of the CEA in the new administration. There were also doubts about how much influence Tyson would wield, because Clinton had created another entity for giving economic advice, the National Economic Council, headed by Robert E. Rubin.

Panel Democrats praised Tyson for being pragmatic on trade and economic issues. She had just published a book on high-technology trade and competitiveness, titled *Who's Bashing Whom*, which outlined an aggressive trade policy to assist U.S. companies hurt by trade barriers and subsidized foreign competition.

Tyson left the CEA job on Feb. 21, 1995, to succeed Rubin in the cabinet-level job of chairman of the National Economic Council. During her tenure at the CEA, she had won praise both inside and outside the administration as an energetic and articulate advocate of the administration's economic policies. Tyson's new job did not require Senate confirmation.

Joseph E. Stiglitz succeeded Tyson as chairman of the Council of Economic Advisers. A CEA member since 1993, Stiglitz's original appointment to the council had been reported by the Senate Banking Committee on July 22, 1993, and confirmed by voice vote of the full Senate July 26. His selection as CEA chairman did not require further Senate action.

Stiglitz was on leave from Stanford University, where he had been a professor of economics since 1988. He previously taught at Princeton, Yale and Oxford.

ENVIRONMENTAL PROTECTION AGENCY

Carol M. Browner was confirmed as administrator of the Environmental Protection Agency (EPA) by voice vote on Jan. 21, 1993, two days after she received the approval of the Senate Environment and Public Works Committee on a 15–0 vote.

Browner was a close ally of Vice President Al Gore, an ardent environmentalist, and worked as legislative director of his Senate office from 1989 to 1991. She spent two years as secretary of the Florida Department of Environmental Regulation before being named to the EPA position.

She promised a regulatory climate that would not be hostile to business but revealed few specifics about her plans for EPA. Repeating a refrain often sounded by Clinton and Gore during the 1992 presidential campaign, she said, "We can ease the regulatory burden on business without compromising the environment."

FEDERAL BUREAU OF INVESTIGATION

Louis J. Freeh was sworn in as the new director of the Federal Bureau of Investigation on Sept. 1, 1993, after sailing through the confirmation process. The Senate Judiciary Committee approved Freeh's nomination, 18–0, on Aug. 3 with no debate, and the full Senate approved the nomination Aug. 6 on a voice vote, again with no debate.

Democrats and Republicans alike had high praise for Freeh, who took on the 10-year post with accolades for his past work as an FBI agent, a federal prosecutor and a federal district judge in New York. Senators still were grumbling, however, about the circumstances surrounding the vacancy. Former director William S. Sessions was forced out amid allegations of ethical improprieties, but some lawmakers believed he deserved to keep his job.

At a confirmation hearing July 29, senators hailed Freeh as an ideal choice to revive the agency's faded image and to meet the challenges of terrorism and other national threats. They praised his abilities and his willingness to give up a lifetime post on the federal bench. President George Bush had appointed Freeh to a judgeship in 1991, after Freeh had spent 10 years as a prosecutor.

FEDERAL DEPOSIT INSURANCE CORPORATION

Ricki R. Tigert was confirmed 90–7 by the Senate Oct. 4, 1994, to head the Federal Deposit Insurance Corporation (FDIC). The Senate Banking Committee had approved the nomination, 16–1, on Feb. 10.

Lauch Faircloth, R-N.C., was the only senator to vote against Tigert's nomination in committee, citing her acquaintance with President Clinton. He said their relationship posed a potential conflict of interest, noting that the FDIC would be one agency investigating allegations of financial impropriety at the failed Arkansas-based Madison Guaranty Savings and Loan, which was related to the Whitewater controversy. Earlier, Tigert wrote to panel members and promised to recuse herself from any involvement in the FDIC's investigation of Madison. (*Whitewater, p. 942*)

After the easy committee approval, Republicans held up the nomination for months. Initially, they sought to pressure Democrats to hold hearings on Whitewater. Later, the delay was attributed to the questions about Tigert's close relationship with the Clintons. Ultimately, seven Republicans joined with Democrats on a 63–32 vote Oct. 3 to cut off a threatened GOP filibuster on the nomination.

The FDIC had been without a permanent chairman since William Taylor died in August 1992. Bankers had voiced concerns that the void at the top had created a big morale problem at the agency, which was the primary federal regulator for about 8,800 state-chartered banks.

Tigert, a Washington banking lawyer with experience at the Treasury Department and the Federal Reserve, was the first woman to head the FDIC.

FEDERAL RESERVE BOARD

Federal Reserve Board Chairman **Alan Greenspan** won a third four-year term in 1996. His nomination was endorsed by a 16–0 vote of the Senate Banking Committee on March 27, 1996, and confirmed by a 91–7 vote of the full Senate on June 20.

Greenspan had won Senate approval only after enduring criticism from a group of Democratic senators who wanted to change the Reserve Board's slow-growth policies. The Democrats' demand for time on the Senate floor to debate Greenspan's stewardship delayed his confirmation for nearly three months.

Greenspan was first nominated as chairman in 1987 by President Ronald Reagan. A lifelong Republican, he was nominated to a second term in 1992 by President George Bush and to a third term in 1996 by President Clinton, who heeded GOP demands that he be kept on. (*Congress and the Nation Vol. VII, p. 1049; Congress and the Nation Vol. VIII, p. 1176*)

Before coming to the Federal Reserve in 1987, Greenspan was a private consultant with the firm of Townsend-Greenspan and Co., which he founded in 1953. He had served as chairman of the Council of Economic Advisers during the Ford administration and as an adviser on economic matters to President Richard Nixon.

His third term as chairman was to extend through 2000; his 14-year term as a board member was to expire in 2006.

OFFICE OF MANAGEMENT AND BUDGET

Former California Democratic representative **Leon E. Panetta** was confirmed by the Senate by voice vote Jan. 21, 1993, to be director of the Office of Management and Budget (OMB). The Senate Governmental Affairs Committee had approved Panetta's nomination by voice vote on Jan. 13.

Panetta, who had served in the House from 1977 until 1993 and chaired the House Budget Committee since 1989, told the Governmental Affairs Committee Jan. 11 that deficit reduction would be the new administration's highest priority—ahead of a middle-class tax cut or a short-term economic stimulus package. Panetta also said that President Clinton's commitment to a long-term investment in education, infrastructure and the like was not incompatible with the goal of reducing the deficit.

Panetta promised that the Clinton team would deliver a "bold" deficit-reduction package, and he argued strongly that increased taxes of some kind would have to be part of the mix.

Panetta left OMB in July 1994 to become Clinton's chief of staff.

Alice M. Rivlin won confirmation by voice vote of the Senate Oct. 7, 1994, to become President Clinton's second budget director. She had been serving as acting director since Panetta's departure. The Senate Governmental Affairs Committee approved her nomination Sept. 30 by voice vote.

Rivlin had been deputy OMB director since 1993. Her nomination to that position had been confirmed by voice vote of the Senate Jan. 21, 1993. Prior to that she had been a senior fellow at the Brookings Institution and the first director of the Congressional Budget Office (CBO) when that agency was formed in 1975. She served as CBO director until 1983, when she became director of economic studies at Brookings. She was on leave from Brookings, teaching at Virginia's George Mason University, when she was tapped by Clinton to be OMB deputy director.

Along the way, Rivlin had earned a reputation as a fierce and outspoken deficit hawk. In *Reviving the American Dream,* a book published shortly before she was named to the administration, Rivlin called the deficit "the biggest single impediment to reviving the American economy" and recommended aggressive action to reduce it.

Rivlin left OMB in 1996 to take a position as a member and vice chairman of the board of directors of the Federal Reserve System in 1996. Her nomination to the Federal Reserve was confirmed June 20, 1996, by a vote of 57–41, after encountering significant opposition from Republicans who complained about her tactics during the failed balanced-budget negotiations.

Franklin D. Raines, vice chairman and a director of the Federal National Mortgage Association (Fannie Mae), was confirmed by voice vote of the Senate Sept. 6, 1996, to succeed Rivlin as OMB director. The Senate Governmental Affairs Committee had approved the nomination by voice vote July 25.

Raines's confirmation initially stalled when Rivlin's nomination was held up by Democrats who opposed the reappointment of Alan Greenspan to a new term as the Federal Reserve Board chairman. But then Raines ran into some opposition of his own.

Some influential Republicans who objected to Clinton's economic policies, which Raines had enthusiastically endorsed, threatened to oppose Raines. Governmental Affairs Chairman Ted Stevens, R-Alaska., said he feared Raines was "too political." But the opponents backed down in the face of end-of-session time pressures.

Raines became the first African American to serve as OMB director. It was Raines's second stint at OMB. In 1978–1979, under President Jimmy Carter, he served as the agency's associate director. He left OMB in 1979 to take a job at the Wall Street investment banking firm of Lazard Freres & Co. In 1991 he returned to Washington to work at Fannie Mae.

OFFICE OF U.S. TRADE REPRESENTATIVE

Mickey Kantor, a former Los Angeles lobbyist and Clinton campaign operative, was confirmed by the Senate by voice vote Jan. 21, 1993, as U.S. trade representative. Two days earlier the nominee had won unanimous approval from the Senate Finance Committee.

Kantor met little difficulty, despite criticism about his lack of experience in the international trade arena and the deep division that beset Democrats on trade issues. The major faultline, which came into sharp focus with the North American Free Trade Agreement (NAFTA) looming, was between old-time free-traders and those who wanted a more aggressive, protectionist posture. During the campaign, Clinton had identified himself as a free-trader. But during his Jan. 19 appearance before the Senate Finance Committee, Kantor acknowledged that the new administration had yet to make key strategic decisions regarding imminent trade issues.

Kantor's supporters said that his talents as a negotiator would more than compensate for his inexperience. They pointed out that previous trade representatives, including his widely lauded predecessor, Carla A. Hills, came to the job without much background in international trade.

Kantor was selected on April 12, 1996, to succeed Ronald H. Brown as commerce secretary. *(Commerce secretary, p. 1110)*

UNITED NATIONS

Madeleine K. Albright received voice vote approval from the Senate on Jan. 26, 1993, as the permanent representative to the United Nations. The Senate Foreign Relations Committee had unanimously approved the nomination the same day.

President Clinton boosted the prestige of Albright's post by according it cabinet-level status. Clinton also made Albright, who had served as an aide to national security adviser Zbigniew Brzezinski during the Carter administration, a member of the National Security Council (NSC).

During her confirmation hearing before the Foreign Relations panel Jan. 21, Albright told senators that the humanitarian tragedy in Bosnia-Herzegovina was "clearly the highest priority" for both the president and the NSC.

Albright also indicated that she would lobby Congress to pay nearly $300 million in arrearages owed to the United Nations—a sensitive issue in Congress in an era when appropriations labeled as foreign aid faced significant opposition.

Albright came to the United States in 1948. Her father, who was Czechoslovakia's ambassador to the United Nations, defected to the United States after communists seized power in their native land. Foreign Relations Committee Chairman Claiborne Pell, D-R.I., commented that Albright had come "full circle" in that she would soon represent her adopted country in the United Nations.

Controversial Nominations

1993

Zoë Baird. Clinton's first choice for attorney general was a surprise pick. Baird, a corporate attorney, was little known in Washington political circles and had no experience in law enforcement. She had taken few public positions on the key legal issues she was tapped to oversee, including civil rights and criminal justice.

Baird's only government experience had been during the Carter administration, when she spent two years in the Justice Department's Office of Legal Counsel. Her work came to the attention of White House Counsel Lloyd Cutler, and at his instigation she moved to the White House legal office as an associate counsel. After the White House changed hands in 1981, Baird went to the Washington firm of O'Melveny and Myers, where she worked with Clinton's nominee for secretary of state, Warren Christopher. In 1990 she became general counsel for Aetna Life & Casualty Co.

But what sank Baird's nomination was not her professional background but her personal life—in particular, her child-care arrangements. In July 1990, Baird and her husband illegally hired a Peruvian woman to take care of their son and employed the woman's husband to work as a driver. Neither had papers allowing them to work in the United States and, under a 1986 immigration law, it was unlawful to hire undocumented workers. In addition, Social Security and unemployment taxes were not paid on the couple's wages. According to Baird, a lawyer told them they could not pay those taxes until the couple had Social Security numbers. Baird and her husband did apply to sponsor the couple and to win them special certification to work legally.

Baird said a lawyer for the Clinton transition team explained that it was possible to pay the Social Security taxes, which she and her husband then did. And just days prior to her confirmation hearing before the Senate Judiciary Committee, Baird paid a $2,900 fine for violating immigration laws.

The issue erupted with a vengeance at the confirmation hearings Jan. 19 and 21, 1993, fueled by angry calls that flooded Senate switchboards. Baird apologized repeatedly during two long days of testimony, but that did not assuage a public that showed little sympathy for the child-care difficulties of a corporate attorney with a $500,000 annual salary.

Baird asked Clinton to withdraw her nomination late Jan. 21, the day after his inauguration. She said the controversy had damaged her ability to lead the Justice Department. Clinton did so, faulting himself and his transition team for not fully analyzing the significance of the issue before nominating Baird.

Clinton consulted repeatedly with Senate Judiciary Committee Chairman Joseph R. Biden Jr., D-Del., after Baird's withdrawal as he sought a new nominee. On Feb. 5, U.S. District Court Judge Kimba M. Wood was reported to be Clinton's top choice for the job of attorney general. But that afternoon Clinton said no decision had been made, and late that day Wood withdrew because a baby sitter she employed had been an illegal immigrant. Although at the time Wood hired the woman it was not illegal to employ an undocumented alien and Wood said she had paid all applicable Social Security and taxes, she had still concluded that "in the current political environment proceeding further . . . would be inappropriate."

Clinton's third and final choice for attorney general was Janet Reno. (Reno, p. 1110)

Joycelyn Elders. After two months of acrimonious opposition from conservatives, the Senate on Sept. 7, 1993, voted 65–34 to approve Elders, a black Arkansas pediatrician, as surgeon general of the United States. She was sworn in the next morning.

The Senate Labor and Human Resources Committee had recommended Elders's confirmation on July 30 by a vote of 13–4. All 10 Democrats on the committee voted in favor of Elders, along with three Republicans.

The Clinton administration wanted Elders confirmed before the month-long August recess, but a handful of Republicans successfully blocked the vote by refusing to grant unanimous consent to take up the matter. Before leaving for the recess, the Senate finally agreed to vote on the nomination Sept. 7.

When the full Senate did vote, 13 Republicans backed Clinton's choice. Some said they supported Elders because of her moving personal history or because of her ability to raise awareness about pressing issues such as teenage pregnancy. Four Democrats opposed Elders.

During her confirmation hearing July 23, Elders pledged to be "the voice and the vision for the poor and the powerless." She said, "I would like to make every child born in America a planned, wanted child."

A sharecropper's daughter who did not visit a physician until she entered college, Elders attended medical school on the GI Bill after serving in the army. She was health director for the state of Arkansas under then-Governor Clinton and in 1992 was selected as president of the Association of State and Territorial Health Officials. She had written extensively on children and the treatment of hormone-related illnesses.

Critics attacked Elders for her fiery rhetoric and firm views on politically charged issues such as abortion and teenage sex. They depicted her as a radical abortion rights proponent, labeled her the "condom queen" and recounted some of her most dramatic statements. Those included a suggestion that drug-addicted prostitutes use the birth control device Norplant, advice to teenage girls to carry condoms on dates, support for the use of marijuana for medicinal purposes and a remark that antiabortion activists should get over their "love affair with the fetus."

"She continues to make a lot of statements that I find intolerant, radical, clearly out of the mainstream and offensive to hundreds of Americans," said Oklahoma Republican Don Nickles, who led the attack on Elders. Nickles and others objected to Elders's characterization of the Catholic Church as a "celibate, male-dominated" institution.

The nomination had been delayed not only by conservative Republicans but also by the Labor Committee's need to reschedule hearings to allow the administration more time to clarify issues, including Elders's husband's failure to pay Social Security taxes for a nurse, Elders's role on the board of directors in the alleged mismanagement of the National Bank of Arkansas, and whether Elders exceeded state payroll limits as Arkansas health director.

Clinton fired Elders on Dec. 9, 1994, because of controversial remarks she made on sex education. Clinton's nominee to succeed Elders, Henry W. Foster Jr., provoked controversy as well and failed to win Senate approval. (Foster, p. 1121)

Lani Guinier. Guinier's nomination April 29, 1993, to become assistant attorney general and head the Justice Department's civil rights division immediately came under attack from conservatives, who accused her of holding dangerously radical views on minority rights. Even some moderate Democrats expressed doubts and urged Clinton not to send her before an uneasy Senate for confirmation. Guinier's allies turned up the heat on Clinton to stand by his nominee.

Guinier's civil rights experience included more than seven years at the National Association for the Advancement of Colored People's Legal Defense and Educational Fund. She also served as special assistant to Drew S. Days III when Days headed the civil rights division under President Jimmy Carter; Days had joined the Justice Department under Clinton as the solicitor general.

What got Guinier into trouble were academic writings that spoke to some of the most difficult and volatile issues of race and political power. Clinton said he had not read Guinier's legal writings prior to selecting her—and would not have nominated her if he had.

Some observers saw the criticisms as payback for the failed 1987 Supreme Court nomination of Judge Robert H. Bork, who sank in the Democrat-led Judiciary Committee in part because of his extensive and controversial academic writings. (Bork nomination, Congress and the Nation Vol. VII, p. 786)

Lobbying for and against the appointment intensified the week of May 31, culminating in a meeting between Guinier and Clinton. Clinton called an evening news conference June 3 to announce that he was withdrawing Guinier's name.

Clinton's decision spared senators a difficult vote, but it enraged members of the Congressional Black Caucus as well as leaders of civil rights and women's groups who had argued strenuously for letting Guinier proceed.

Roberta Achtenberg. After three days of impassioned floor debate, the Senate voted 58–31 on May 24, 1993, to confirm Achtenberg as assistant secretary for fair housing and equal opportunity at the Department of Housing and Urban Development. She was the first avowed lesbian appointed to such a high federal office. The Senate Banking, Housing, and Urban Affairs Committee had approved the nomination May 9 by a vote of 14–4; hearings were held on April 29.

Opponents, led by Sen. Jesse Helms, R-N.C., said Achtenberg was unqualified for the post and eager to impose her social agenda on the agency and extend fair housing laws to cover homosexuals as a class. Helms described Achtenberg as a "militant activist" who wanted society to accept as normal "a lifestyle that most of the world's religions consider immoral and which the average American voter instinctively finds repulsive." Helms denied that he was engaging in "gay-bashing" and said he was simply "standing up for America's traditional family values."

Many of the GOP attacks centered on Achtenberg's actions as a member of the San Francisco Board of Supervisors and as a local United Way board member in pressuring the Boy Scouts to reverse its policy of excluding homosexuals. She tried to remove city money from the Bank of America because it contributed to the Boy Scouts.

Achtenberg's defenders, mostly Democrats, suggested that the tenor of the debate was demeaning; that the nominee was unfairly characterized; and that she was being subjected to personal attacks, many of them related to her sexual orientation.

Five Democrats voted against the nomination, while 13 Republicans voted for it.

George T. Frampton Jr. President Clinton's nominee to head the Interior Department's fish, wildlife and national parks programs, won voice vote approval from the Senate June 30, 1993.

The Senate Energy and Natural Resources Committee had delayed voting on Frampton's nomination twice before finally approving him June 16 on a vote of 13–5. Frampton, who had served as president of the Wilderness Society from 1986 to 1993, had drawn criticism from western lawmakers, who considered him to be a blunt, outspoken environmentalist. Several senators said they were especially concerned about how he would administer the Endangered Species Act. But the immediate cause of the delay was a charge that the former assistant Watergate prosecutor had overstepped his authority as a consultant to the Interior Department while awaiting confirmation.

Senate Energy's first vote had been postponed when western senators objected, saying Frampton had violated a federal management policy that prohibited consultants from directing the activities of federal employees. The Office of Personnel Management (OPM) ruled June 7 that Frampton did not break the policy, arguing that he was carrying out orders from Interior Secretary Bruce Babbitt's chief of staff. A second scheduled vote was delayed until the week of June 14 because OPM's written explanation had not yet circulated among panel members.

When the committee finally voted, three western Republicans joined the panel's 10 Democrats to recommend the nomination. The Senate Environment Committee, which also had jurisdiction, had approved Frampton's nomination by voice vote May 25.

Walter E. Dellinger III. The Senate voted 65–34 on Oct. 13, 1993, to confirm the nomination of Dellinger, a Duke University constitutional law professor, to head the Justice Department's Office of Legal Counsel. The Senate Judiciary Committee had voted unanimously July 22 to send Dellinger's nomination to the floor.

North Carolina's two Republican senators, Jesse Helms and Lauch Faircloth, had initiated a filibuster against the nomination, criticizing Dellinger's liberal views and what they called an attempt to ram through his appointment despite Senate concerns. A 59–39 vote on Oct. 7 to cut off debate on the nomination fell one vote short of the 60 needed to invoke cloture. But Republicans subsequently relented and allowed the confirmation vote to take place.

Janet Ann Napolitano. Bitter memories of the 1991 fight over Supreme Court Justice Clarence Thomas complicated Napolitano's nomination to be U.S. attorney for Arizona. She came under fire for her role as a lawyer to Anita F. Hill, who accused Thomas of sexual harassment. In particular, Napolitano, citing attorney-client privilege, refused to answer questions about her involvement with one of Hill's supporting witnesses. (*Thomas nomination, Congress and the Nation Vol. VIII, p. 802*)

The Senate Judiciary Committee approved Napolitano's nomination 12–6 on Sept. 30, 1993, but Republicans blocked the nomination from coming to the floor. The Senate finally confirmed Napolitano on Nov. 19. The approval occurred by voice vote immediately after the Senate voted 72–26 on a cloture motion to end a Republican filibuster.

1994

Morton H. Halperin. A prolific defense analyst and a civil liberties activist who forcefully criticized U.S. covert operations in the 1970s and 1980s, Halperin had been tapped by Defense Secretary Les Aspin to fill a new job as assistant secretary of defense for democracy and peacekeeping.

But even before Clinton formally sent Halperin's name to the Senate Aug. 6, 1993, conservatives mounted a strenuous campaign to block the nomination. The critics contended that Halperin's public statements and writings revealed a dangerous aversion to the use of military force or covert operations to further U.S. interests abroad.

Neither the Senate Armed Services panel nor the full Senate acted on the nomination, which thus lapsed at the end of the first session of the 103rd Congress. The administration insisted Clinton would resubmit the nomination in 1994, but after Aspin, Halperin's sponsor, announced that he would step down as Pentagon chief early in 1994, Halperin asked that his name be withdrawn. In a Jan. 10 exchange of letters, Halperin wrote, "I believe that cabinet officers should have the freedom to select their subordinates." Clinton responded that he appreciated Halperin's "understanding of the circumstances involved in a new secretary of defense coming on board."

Halperin subsequently went to the National Security Council, where he was given the title of senior director for democracy. The White House job was not subject to Senate confirmation.

Bobby Ray Inman. Retired admiral Inman was nominated by President Clinton to become defense secretary Dec. 16, 1993, one day after Les Aspin announced that he would resign in early 1994. An intelligence specialist held in high regard across the political spectrum, Inman boasted a gilt-edged résumé that included significant experience as a manager of complex programs.

Although he was expected to win confirmation easily in the Senate, Inman abruptly withdrew his nomination on Jan. 18, 1994. In a news conference Inman blasted several newspaper columnists who had criticized him, calling them practitioners of a "new McCarthyism." He also contended that Senate Majority Leader Bob Dole, R-Kan., was planning a partisan attack on the nomination, perhaps in collusion with *New York Times* columnist William Safire. "I don't wish to subject myself to that on a daily basis as the cost of trying to produce change," Inman said.

Dole and Safire each dismissed as ridiculous Inman's allegation that they were conspiring against him, and Inman later retracted his charge.

Strobe Talbott. The Senate confirmed Talbott on Feb. 22, 1994, as deputy secretary of state, but not before leading Republicans sharpened their attacks on his past writings and his prospects for a future promotion to secretary of state. Dividing along partisan lines, the Senate voted 66–31 to confirm Talbott as the State Department's second-ranking official. Republicans cast all 31 nay votes, while 12 GOP senators joined with 54 Democrats to provide the margin of victory.

The Senate Foreign Relations Committee had voted 17–2 on Feb. 9 to confirm the Russia scholar and former journalist, who was serving at the time as ambassador-at-large to the former Soviet Union. Talbott had been expected to waltz into the deputy secretary's slot without significant opposition, but many Republicans attacked the former *Time* magazine columnist for some of his writings, including columns on the demise of the Soviet Union and the strategic importance of Israel to the United States.

With the nomination never in real doubt, few Democrats felt compelled to defend him. Some shared concerns with Republicans that Talbott's past writings on Israel had been unduly harsh. Those columns were the focal point of Talbott's confirmation hearing before the Foreign Relations Committee.

During his testimony to the committee Feb. 8, Talbott tried to defuse the controversy by affirming his unqualified support for Israel. Talbott told the committee that he no longer had any doubts about Israel's strategic value to the United States. "On that I have simply changed my opinion," he said. He also reminded senators that part of his role as a columnist was to stimulate debate.

Robert Pastor. Over the passionate objections of ranking Republican Jesse Helms of North Carolina, the Senate Foreign Relations Committee in 1994 approved the nomination of Robert Pastor to be U.S. ambassador to Panama. But, given the near certainty of a Helms filibuster on the floor, Senate Democratic leaders declined to bring up the nomination, killing it for the year.

The Foreign Relations Committee agreed to recommend Pastor's nomination Oct. 4 by a vote of 14–3. Earlier, on Sept. 29, Helms had effectively filibustered the nomination in committee and prevented the panel from voting. Helms spoke against the nomination for almost an hour and a half. Then he invoked a Senate rule that prohibited committees from meeting for more than two hours while the Senate was in session. The committee was forced to quit for that day without acting on Pastor's nomination.

Sam Brown. Conservative Senate Republicans blocked President Clinton's nomination of Sam Brown, who had once led nationwide protests against the Vietnam War, as ambassador to head the U.S. delegation to the Conference on Security and Cooperation in Europe (CSCE). Based in Vienna, the multilateral organization monitored arms control agreements and served as a forum for European security.

Brown had organized a national moratorium against the Vietnam War in 1969. After a debate that touched on old divisions over Vietnam and sharp criticism of Clinton's foreign policy, the Senate twice rejected Democratic attempts to break a GOP-led filibuster against Brown's nomination. The votes—54–44 on May 24 and 56–42 on May 25—fell short of the 60 votes needed to invoke cloture.

Brown eventually went to represent the United States at the CSCE but without ambassadorial rank.

Derek Shearer. The Senate handed Clinton a victory May 24, 1994, when it confirmed embattled nominee Shearer as ambassador to Finland. The Senate approved the nomination by a 67–31 vote, after first voting 63–35 to cut off debate on the nomination.

Conservative Republicans seized on the nomination to paint Clinton as outside the political mainstream. Sen. Phil Gramm, R-Texas, said that past writings by Shearer, a college professor and the brother-in-law of Deputy Secretary of State Strobe Talbott, showed him to be a "socialist."

Robert C. Smith, R-N.H., said, "The president continues to surround himself with the type of people he protested with in the golden years of the antiwar movement, and it is having a devastating effect on the quality and effectiveness of our national security policy."

Frank B. Kelso II. After a heated debate over the navy's treatment of women, the Senate voted 54–43 on April 19, 1994, to permit Admiral Kelso to retire with his full retirement pay.

As chief of naval operations since June 1990, Kelso had headed the navy during the rowdy 1991 convention of the Tailhook Association, where numerous women and a few men were sexually assaulted by naval officers. The navy investigation into the incident was widely criticized as incomplete and incompetent.

Clinton nominated Kelso to be placed on the retirement list as a four-star admiral with an annual pension of $84,340, a recommendation easily approved on a 20–2 vote by the Senate Armed Services Committee April 14.

But others thought Kelso should be held accountable for the navy's inadequate investigation and be retired at the two-star rank with an annual pension of $67,422 per year. They ultimately lost, but not before the seven women in the Senate pulled together across party lines to force a protracted, emotional and sometimes bitter six-hour floor debate over the navy's handling of its female work force, particularly in cases of sexual abuse and harassment.

Henry H. Mauz Jr. Despite concerns among female senators about his diligence in handling sexual harassment complaints, the Senate on Sept. 20 voted 92–6 to retire Admiral Mauz, commander of the Atlantic Fleet, at the rank of a four-star admiral. The higher rank was worth about $17,000 annually in additional retirement benefits.

The Senate's five Democratic women contended that he had not acted quickly enough to protect an officer against retributions after she successfully brought a sexual harassment complaint against a superior officer in 1992. Critics also noted an incident in which a petty officer complained that, after he had exposed a junket by Mauz to Bermuda that drew highly critical television coverage, the admiral had manipulated the navy's legal system to retaliate.

Senate Armed Services Committee Chairman Sam Nunn, D-Ga., whose panel had twice deferred action on the nomination to probe new allegations, insisted that inquiries by the navy and the Pentagon's inspector general had satisfied the committee that Mauz was innocent of any wrongdoing. The panel approved Mauz's nomination Aug. 12 by a 22–0 vote.

Buster C. Glosson. In the final hours before the Oct. 8, 1994, recess, the Senate confirmed the nomination of air force Lt. Gen. Glosson to retire at the lieutenant general rank. The nomination had been contested by Iowa Republican Charles E. Grassley, a frequent Pentagon critic.

Glosson, a former fighter pilot and Vietnam veteran who was the chief planner of the 1991 air war against Iraq, had been a rising star in the air force. But his career stalled in 1993, when the air force and Defense Department inspectors general concluded that Glosson had attempted to prejudice a promotion board against a more junior officer and subsequently lied about his actions. Glosson received a letter of admonishment from the air force, which in effect barred him from future advancement. He opted to resign.

Clinton nominated Glosson to retire as a lieutenant general, for an annual pension about $6,700 higher than the one he would have gotten if he retired at the lower rank of major general. Ultimately, a specially convened panel concluded that although Glosson broke the rules by trying to influence the promotion board, he did not deliberately lie.

The Senate Armed Services Committee approved the nomination, 14–7. The Senate confirmed it, 59–30.

1995

Michael P. C. Carns. Clinton on Feb. 8, 1994, tapped Carns, a retired air force general, to head the CIA.

Carns had served as staff director of the Joint Chiefs of Staff during the invasion of Panama and the Persian Gulf War. In May 1991 he became the air force's vice chief of staff, a post he held until he retired Sept. 1, 1994. Carns had been deputy chief of staff for operations and intelligence for the air force command center in the Pacific for one year—his only experience running an intelligence operation.

One month after his nomination, Carns was forced to step aside amid revelations that he had broken immigration laws when he brought a Philippine domestic to the United States. Carns acknowledged falsely telling immigration officials that he brought Elbino Runas to the United States to work for his family full time. Runas also worked outside the Carns home.

Henry W. Foster Jr. The Senate derailed the nomination of Dr. Henry W. Foster Jr., to be surgeon general in two votes June 21 and 22, 1995. By twice rejecting motions to block a threatened filibuster, the Senate denied Foster, a Nashville obstetrician and gynecologist, a direct vote and effectively killed his nomination. The Senate Labor and Human Resources Committee had voted 9–7 on May 26 to recommend that the full Senate confirm Foster's nomination.

President Clinton had nominated Foster on Feb. 2, 1995, to succeed Joycelyn Elders, who had been fired by the president in December 1994. Almost immediately, antiabortion activists raised questions about the number of abortions Foster had performed and suggested that even one could be enough to disqualify him for the position as the nation's top health spokesman.

Foster and the White House stumbled at first. White House officials announced that Foster had performed only one abortion. Foster then said he had done about a dozen. A further check indicated that Foster was the physician of record for 39 abortions. The confusion opened the door to further attacks on Foster's credibility.

The nomination also got caught up in politics, when Senate Majority Leader Bob Dole, R-Kan., and Sen. Phil Gramm, R-Texas, both of whom were vying for the GOP presidential nomination and were seeking support from their party's conservative antiabortion activists, threatened to block action.

Clinton stood by his nominee throughout the grueling five-month process, amid accusations that he was trying to shore up his support among abortion-rights advocates by selecting Foster in the first place.

Agreement was finally reached to allow the nomination to come to the Senate floor, but the attempts to cut off a threatened filibuster both failed by 57–43 votes. Sixty votes were needed to invoke cloture.

President Clinton vetoed a total of 17 bills (all public ones) during his first term in office. That was the lowest number of presidential vetoes during a full term since Woodrow Wilson vetoed 10 bills in his first term (1913–1917). It was also less than half that of Clinton's Republican predecessor, George Bush, who vetoed 44 bills (43 public, 1 private) in four years while facing a Democratic-controlled Congress. Bush's predecessor, Republican Ronald Reagan, vetoed 78 bills (70 public, 8 private) during his two terms. Reagan's predecessor, Democrat Jimmy Carter, vetoed 31 bills (29 public, 2 private) during his four-year tenure.

Clinton did not cast any vetoes during the 103rd Congress (1993–1994), when the Democrats controlled both chambers. That made him the first president since 1853 to go an entire Congress without vetoing a single bill. The last president to do so had been Millard Fillmore, during the 32nd Congress (1851–1853). The last year without a single veto had been 1979 under Carter; however, Carter did veto a bill in 1980 that Congress had passed in 1979. The last time a president did not veto any bill passed during a single year of Congress was President Richard M. Nixon in 1969.

Grover Cleveland issued the most vetoes in one term—414.

Franklin Roosevelt, who served as president for three full terms, vetoed the most measures—635. Seven presidents issued no vetoes.

Congress made seven override attempts on Clinton's vetoes; only one was successful. Veto overrides require a two-thirds majority vote of both houses. Only four presidents who vetoed more than ten bills never had a veto overridden. William McKinley Jr. (1897–1901) had the most vetoes without an override, 42. He was followed by Lyndon B. Johnson (1963–1969), with 30; John F. Kennedy (1961–1963), 21; and Andrew Jackson (1829–1937), 12.

The record for veto overrides—15—was held by Andrew Johnson. Harry S. Truman and Gerald Ford both had 12 vetoes overridden.

Clinton never used the pocket veto in his first term, making him the first president since Franklin Pierce (1853–1857) to serve an entire term without using the device. When Congress is in session, a bill becomes a law without the president's signature if he does not act upon it within ten days, excluding Sundays, from the time he receives it; if Congress adjourns within that ten-day period, the bill is killed, or pocket-vetoed, without the president's signature.

Following is the list of bills vetoed by Clinton during his first term, 1993–1996.

1995

1. HR 1158
(FY 1995 Recissions/Supplemental)
Vetoed: June 7, 1995
No override attempt
(Story, p. 73)

2. S 21
(Bosnia arms embargo)
Vetoed: Aug. 11, 1995
No override attempt
(Story, p. 225)

3. HR 1854
(FY 1996 Legislative branch
appropriations)
Vetoed: Oct. 3, 1995
No override attempt
(Story, p. 72)

4. HR 2586
(Temporarily increase public
debt limit)
Vetoed: Nov. 13, 1995
No override attempt
(Story, p. 77)

5. HJ Res 115
(FY 1996 Continuing appropriations)
Vetoed: Nov. 13, 1995
No override attempt
(Story, p. 72)

6. HR 2491
(FY 1996 Budget reconciliation)
Vetoed: Dec. 6, 1995
No override attempt
(Story, p. 70)

7. HR 1977
(FY 1996 Interior appropriations)
Vetoed: Dec. 18, 1995
House sustained Jan. 4, 1996:
239–177
(Story, p. 72)

8. HR 2099
(FY 1996 VA-HUD appropriations)
Vetoed: Dec. 18, 1995
No override attempt
(Story, p. 72)

9. HR 2076
(FY 1996 Commerce/Justice/State
appropriations)
Vetoed: Dec. 19, 1995
House sustained Jan. 3, 1996:
240–159
(Story, p. 72)

10. HR 1058
(Securities litigation)
Vetoed: Dec. 19, 1995
Veto overridden Dec. 22, 1995
House, 319–100, Dec. 20, 1995
Senate, 68–30, Dec. 22, 1995
(Story, p. 143)

11. HR 1530
(FY 1996 Defense authorization)
Vetoed: Dec. 28, 1995
House sustained Jan. 3, 1996:
240–156
(Story, p. 298)

1996

12. HR 4
(Welfare overhaul)
Vetoed: Jan. 9, 1996
No override attempt
(Story, p. 580)

13. HR 1833
(Partial-birth abortion ban)
Vetoed: April 10, 1996
House overrode Sept. 19, 1996:
285–137
Senate sustained Sept. 26, 1996: 57–41
(Story, p. 563)

14. HR 1561
(State Department authorization)
Vetoed: April 12, 1996
House sustained April 30, 1996:
234–188
(Story, p. 231)

15. HR 956
(Product liability lawsuits)
Vetoed: May 2, 1996
House sustained May 9, 1996: 258–163
(Story, p. 379)

16. HR 743
(Labor-management teams)
Vetoed: July 30, 1996
No override attempt
(Story, p. 673)

17. HR 2909
(Land acquisition in wildlife refuge)
Vetoed: Oct. 2, 1996
No override attempt
(Story, p. 465)

President Bush's Fiscal 1994 Budget Message

Following is the Congressional Record *text of President George Bush's fiscal 1994 budgetary statement, sent to Congress Jan. 6, 1993.*

To the Congress of the United States:

I am pleased to present the budgetary statement: *Budget Baseline, Historical Data, and Alternatives for the Future.*

The Budget Enforcement Act of 1990 (BEA) changed the date by which the President is required to transmit his budget from the first Monday after January 3rd to the first Monday in February. It also established January 21, 1993, as the date for the official presentation and determination of the BEA budget deficit adjustment. Accordingly, the full 1994 Budget must be submitted by the new Administration.

In order to provide a perspective from which to evaluate choices and actions, this document provides the following:

- a review of current policies and the implications of their extension into the future;
- near-term and long-term budget projections under alternative economic and technical assumptions;
- assessments of hidden liabilities with associated policy reforms, and assessments of high risk management areas with associated recommendations for systems improvement; and
- updated options and recommendations for spending control.

It is my hope that this will be useful to the Congress and the new Administration in the effort to produce both a responsible budget and strong economic growth.

GEORGE BUSH
January 6, 1993

Bill Clinton's Inaugural Address

Following is the Reuter transcript of President Bill Clinton's inaugural address, delivered on the West Front of the Capitol, Jan. 20, 1993.

My fellow citizens, today we celebrate the mystery of American renewal. This ceremony is held in the depth of winter, but by the words we speak and the faces we show the world, we force the spring, a spring reborn in the world's oldest democracy that brings forth the vision and courage to reinvent America. When our Founders boldly declared America's independence to the world and our purposes to the Almighty, they knew that America, to endure, would have to change; not change for change's sake but change to preserve America's ideals: life, liberty, the pursuit of happiness. Though we marched to the music of our time, our mission is timeless. Each generation of Americans must define what it means to be an American.

On behalf of our Nation, I salute my predecessor, President [George] Bush, for his half-century of service to America. And I thank the millions of men and women whose steadfastness and sacrifice triumphed over depression, fascism, and communism.

Today, a generation raised in the shadows of the cold war assumes new responsibilities in a world warmed by the sunshine of freedom but threatened still by ancient hatreds and new plagues. Raised in unrivaled prosperity, we inherit an economy that is still the world's strongest but is weakened by business failures, stagnant wages, increasing inequality, and deep divisions among our own people.

When George Washington first took the oath I have just sworn to uphold, news traveled slowly across the land by horseback and across the ocean by boat. Now, the sights and sounds of this ceremony are broadcast instantaneously to billions around the world. Communications and commerce are global. Investment is mobile. Technology is almost magical. And ambition for a better life is now universal.

We earn our livelihood in America today in peaceful competition with people all across the Earth. Profound and powerful forces are shaking and remaking our world. And the urgent question of our time is whether we can make change our friend and not our enemy. This new world has already enriched the lives of millions of Americans who are able to compete and win in it. But when most people are working harder for less; when others cannot work at all; when the cost of health care devastates families and threatens to bankrupt our enterprises, great and small; when the fear of crime robs law-abiding citizens of their freedom; and when millions of poor children cannot even imagine the lives we are calling them to lead, we have not made change our friend.

We know we have to face hard truths and take strong steps, but we have not done so; instead, we have drifted. And that drifting has eroded our resources, fractured our economy, and shaken our confidence. Though our challenges are fearsome, so are our strengths. Americans have ever been a restless, questing, hopeful people. And we must bring to our task today the vision and will of those who came before us. From our Revolution to the Civil War, to the Great Depression, to the civil rights movement, our people have always mustered the determination to construct from these crises the pillars of our history. Thomas Jefferson believed that to preserve the very foundations of our Nation, we would need dramatic change from time to time. Well, my fellow Americans, this is our time. Let us embrace it.

Our democracy must be not only the envy of the world but the engine of our own renewal. There is nothing wrong with America that cannot be cured by what is right with America. And so today we pledge an end to the era of deadlock and drift, and a new season of American renewal has begun.

To renew America, we must be bold. We must do what no generation has had to do before. We must invest more in our own people, in their jobs, and in their future, and at the same time cut our massive debt. And we must do so in a world in which we must compete for every opportunity. It will not be easy. It will require sacrifice, but it can be done and done fairly, not choosing sacrifice for its own sake but for our own sake. We must provide for our Nation the way a family provides for its children.

Our Founders saw themselves in the light of posterity. We can do no less. Anyone who has ever watched a child's eyes wander into sleep knows what posterity is. Posterity is the world to come: the world for whom we hold our ideals, from whom we have borrowed our planet, and to whom we bear sacred responsibility. We must do what America does best: offer more opportunity to all and demand more responsibility from all. It is time to break the bad habit of expecting something for nothing from our Government or from each other. Let us all take more responsibility not only for ourselves and our families but for our communities and our country.

To renew America, we must revitalize our democracy. This beautiful Capital, like every capital since the dawn of civilization, is often a place of intrigue and calculation. Powerful people maneuver for position and worry endlessly about who is in and who is out, who is up and who is down, forgetting those people whose toil and sweat sends us here and pays our way. Americans deserve better. And in this city today there are people who want to do better. And so I say to all of you here: Let us resolve to reform our politics so that power and privilege no longer shout down the voice of the people. Let us put aside personal advantage so that we can feel the pain and see the promise of America. Let us resolve to make our Government a place for what Franklin Roosevelt called bold, persistent experimentation, a Government for our tomorrows, not our yesterdays. Let us give this Capital back to the people to whom it belongs.

To renew America, we must meet challenges abroad as well as at home. There is no longer a clear division between what is foreign and what is domestic. The world economy, the world environment, the world AIDS crisis, the world arms race: they affect us all. Today, as an older order passes, the new world is more free but less stable. Communism's collapse has called forth old animosities and new dangers. Clearly, America must continue to lead the world we did so much to make.

While America rebuilds at home, we will not shrink from the challenges nor fail to seize the opportunities of this new world. Together with our friends and allies, we will work to shape change, lest it engulf us. When our vital interests are challenged or the will and conscience of the international community is defied, we will act, with peaceful diplomacy whenever possible, with force when necessary. The brave Americans serving our Nation today in the Persian Gulf in Somalia, and wherever else they stand are testament to our resolve. But our greatest strength is the power of our ideas, which are still new in many lands. Across the world we see them embraced, and we rejoice. Our hopes, our hearts, our hands are with those on every continent who are building democracy and freedom. Their cause is America's cause.

The American people have summoned the change we celebrate today. You have raised your voices in an unmistakable chorus. You have cast your votes in historic numbers. And you have changed the face of Congress, the Presidency, and the political process itself. Yes, you, my fellow Americans, have forced the spring. Now we must do the work the season demands. To that work I now turn with all the authority of my office. I ask the Congress to join with me. But no President, no Congress, no Government can undertake this mission alone.

My fellow Americans, you, too, must play your part in our renewal. I challenge a new generation of young Americans to a season of service: to act on your idealism by helping troubled children, keeping company with those in need, reconnecting our torn communities. There is so much to be done; enough, indeed, for millions of others who are still young in spirit to give of themselves in service, too. In serving, we recognize a simple but powerful truth: We need each other, and we must care for one another.

Today we do more than celebrate America. We rededicate ourselves to the very idea of America, an idea born in revolution and renewed through two centuries of challenge; an idea tempered by the knowledge that, but for fate, we, the fortunate and the unfortunate, might have been each other; an idea ennobled by the faith that our Nation can summon from its myriad diversity the deepest measure of unity; an idea infused with the conviction that America's long, heroic journey must go forever upward.

And so, my fellow Americans, as we stand at the edge of the 21st century, let us begin anew with energy and hope, with faith and discipline. And let us work until our work is done. The Scripture says, "And let us not be weary in well doing: for in due season we shall reap, if we faint not." From this joyful mountaintop of celebration we hear a call to service in the valley. We have heard the trumpets. We have changed the guard. And now, each in our own way and with God's help, we must answer the call.

Thank you, and God bless you all.

President Clinton's Economic Plan

Following is the text of President Clinton's Feb. 17, 1993, address before a joint session of Congress.

Mr. President, Mr. Speaker, Members of the House and the Senate, distinguished Americans here as visitors in this Chamber, as am I. It is nice to have a fresh excuse for giving a long speech.

When Presidents speak to Congress and the Nation from this podium, typically they comment on the full range [of] challenges and opportunities that face the United States. But this is not an ordinary time, and for all the many tasks that require our attention, I believe tonight one calls on us to focus, to unite, and to act. And that is our economy. For more than anything else, our task tonight as Americans is to make our economy thrive again.

Let me begin by saying that it has been too long, at least three decades, since a President has come and challenged Americans to join him on a great national journey, not merely to consume the bounty of today but to invest for a much greater one tomorrow.

Like individuals, nations must ultimately decide how they wish to conduct themselves, how they wish to be thought of by those with whom they live, and later, how they wish to be judged by history. Like every individual, man and woman, nations must decide whether they are prepared to rise to the occasions history presents them.

We have always been a people of youthful energy and daring spirit. And at this historic moment, as communism has fallen, as freedom is spreading around the world, as a global economy is taking shape before our eyes, Americans have called for change. And now it is up to those of us in this room to deliver for them.

Our Nation needs a new direction. Tonight I present to you a comprehensive plan to set our Nation on that new course. I believe we will find our new direction in the basic old values that brought us here over the last two centuries: a commitment to opportunity, to individual responsibility, to community, to work, to family, and to faith. We must now break the habits of both political parties and say there can be no more something for nothing and admit frankly that we are all in this together.

The conditions which brought us as a Nation to this point are well-known: two decades of low productivity, growth, and stagnant wages; persistent unemployment and underemployment; years of huge Government deficits and declining investment in our future; exploding health care costs and lack of coverage for millions of Americans; legions of poor children; education and job training opportunities inadequate to the demands of this tough, global economy. For too long we have drifted without a strong sense of purpose or responsibility or community.

And our political system so often has seemed paralyzed by special interest groups, by partisan bickering, and by the sheer complexity of our problems. I believe we can do better because we remain the greatest nation on Earth, the world's strongest economy, the world's only military superpower. If we have the vision, the will, and the heart to make the changes we must, we can still enter the 21st century with possibilities our parents could not even have imagined and enter it having secured the American dream for ourselves and for future generations.

I well remember 12 years ago President [Ronald] Reagan stood at this very podium and told you and the American people that if our national debt were stacked in thousand-dollar bills, the stack would reach 67 miles into space. Well, today that stack would reach 267 miles. I tell you this not to assign blame for this problem. There is plenty of blame to go around in both branches of the Government and both parties. The time has come for the blame to end. I did not seek this office to place blame. I come here tonight to accept responsibility, and I want you to accept responsibility with me. And if we do right by this country, I do not care who gets the credit for it.

The plan I offer you has four fundamental components. First, it shifts our emphasis in public and private spending from consumption to investment, initially by jump-starting the economy in the short term and investing in our people, their jobs, and their incomes over the long run. Second, it changes the rhetoric of the past into the actions of the present by honoring work and families in every part of our public decisionmaking. Third, it substantially reduces the Federal deficit honestly and credibly by using in the beginning the most conservative estimates of Government revenues, not, as the executive branch has done so often in the past, using the most optimistic ones. And finally, it seeks to earn the trust of the American people by paying for these plans first with cuts in Government waste and efficiency; second, with cuts, not gimmicks, in Government spending; and by fairness, for a change, in the way additional burdens are borne.

Tonight I want to talk with you about what Government can do because I believe Government must do more. But let me say first that the real engine of economic growth in this country is the private sector, and second, that each of us must be an engine of growth and change. The truth is that as Government creates more opportunity in this new and different time, we must also demand more responsibility in turn.

Our immediate priority must be to create jobs, create jobs now. Some people say, "Well, we're in a recovery, and we don't have to do that." Well, we all hope we're in a recovery, but we're sure not creating new jobs. And there's no recovery worth its salt that doesn't put the American people back to work.

To create jobs and guarantee a strong recovery, I call on Congress to enact an immediate package of jobs investments of over $30 billion to put people to work now, to create a half a million jobs: jobs to rebuild our highways and airports, to renovate housing, to bring new life to rural communities, and spread hope and opportunity among our Nation's youth. Especially I want to emphasize, after the events of last year in Los Angeles and the countless stories of despair in our cities and in our poor rural communities, this proposal will create almost 700,000 new summer jobs for displaced, unemployed young people alone this summer. And tonight I invite America's business leaders to join us in this effort so that together we can provide over one million summer jobs in cities and poor rural areas for our young people.

Second, our plan looks beyond today's business cycle because our aspirations extend into the next century. The heart of this plan deals with the long term. It is an investment program designed to increase public and private investment in areas critical to our economic future. And it has a deficit reduction program that will increase the savings available for the private sector to invest, will lower interest rates, will decrease the percentage the Federal budget claimed by interest payments, and decrease the risk of financial market disruptions that could adversely affect our economy.

Over the long run, all this will bring us a higher rate of economic growth, improved productivity, more high-quality jobs, and an improved economic competitive position in the world. In order to accomplish both increased investment and deficit reduction, something no American Government has ever been called upon to do at the same time before, spending must be cut, and taxes must be raised.

The spending cuts I recommend were carefully thought through in a way to minimize any adverse economic impact, to capture the peace dividend for investment purposes, and to switch the balance in the budget from consumption to more investment. The tax increases and the spending cuts were both designed to assure that the cost of this historic program to face and deal with our problems will be borne by those who could readily afford it the most. Our plan is designed, furthermore, and perhaps in some ways most importantly, to improve the health of American business through lower interest rates, more incentives to invest, and better trained workers.

Because small business has created such a high percentage of all the new jobs in our Nation over the last 10 or 15 years, our plan includes the boldest targeted incentives for small business in history. We propose a permanent investment tax credit for the smallest firms in this country, with revenues of under $5 million. That's about 90 percent of the firms in America, employing about 40 percent of the work force but creating a big majority of the net new jobs for more than a decade. And we propose new rewards for entrepreneurs who take new risks. We propose to give small business access to all the new technologies of our time. And we propose to attack this credit crunch which has denied small business the credit they need to flourish and prosper.

With a new network of community development banks and $1 billion to make the dream of enterprise zones real, we propose to bring new hope and new jobs to storefronts and factories from south Boston to south Texas to south central Los Angeles. This plan invests in our roads, our bridges, our transit systems, in high-speed railways, and high-tech information systems. And it provides the most ambitious environmental cleanup in partnership with State and local government of our time, to put people to work and to preserve the environment for our future.

Standing as we are on the edge of a new century, we know that economic growth depends as never before on opening up new markets overseas and expanding the volume of world trade. And so, we will insist on fair trade rules in international markets as a part of a national economic strategy to expand trade, including the successful completion of the latest round of world trade talks and the successful completion of a North American Free Trade Agreement, with appropriate safeguards for our workers and for the environment.

At the same time—and I say this to you in both parties and across America tonight, all the people who are listening—it is not enough to pass a budget or even to have a trade agreement. This world is changing so fast that we must have aggressive, targeted attempts to create the high-wage jobs of the future. That's what all our competitors are doing. We must give special attention to those critical industries that are going to explode in the 21st century but that are in trouble in America today, like aerospace. We must provide special assistance to areas and to workers displaced by cuts in the defense budget and by other unavoidable economic dislocations.

And again I will say we must do this together. I pledge to you that I will do my best to see that business and labor and Government work together for a change.

But all of our efforts to strengthen the economy will fail—let me say this again; I feel so strongly about this—all of our efforts to strengthen the economy will fail unless we also take this year, not next year, not 5 years from now but this year, bold steps to reform our health care system.

In 1992, we spent 14 percent of our income on health care, more than 30 percent more than any other country in the world, and yet we were the only advanced nation that did not provide a basic package of health care benefits to all of its citizens. Unless we change the present pattern, 50 percent of the growth in the deficit between now and the year 2000 will be in health care costs. By the year 2000 almost 20 percent of our income will be in health care. Our families will never be secure, our businesses will never be strong, and our Government will never again be fully solvent until we tackle the health care crisis. We must do it this year.

The combination of the rising cost of care and the lack of care and the fear of losing care are endangering the security and the very lives of millions of our people. And they are weakening our economy every day. Reducing health care costs can liberate literally hundreds of billions of dollars for new investment in growth and jobs. Bringing health costs in line with inflation would do more for the private sector in this country than any tax cut we could give and any spending program we could promote. Reforming health care over the long run is critically essential to reducing not only our deficit but to expanding investment in America.

Later this spring, after the First Lady and the many good people who are helping her all across the country complete their work, I will deliver to Congress a comprehensive plan for health care reform that finally will bring costs under control and provide security to all of our families, so that no one will be denied the coverage they need but so that our economic future will not be compromised either. We'll have to root out fraud and overcharges and make sure that paperwork no longer chokes your doctor. We'll have to maintain the highest American standards and the right to choose in a system that is the world's finest for all those who can access it. But first we must make choices. We must choose to give the American people the quality they demand and deserve with a system that will not bankrupt the country or further drive more Americans into agony.

Let me further say that I want to work with all of you on this. I realize this is a complicated issue. But we must address it. And I believe if there is any chance that Republicans and Democrats who disagree on taxes and spending or anything else could agree on one thing, surely we can all look at these numbers and go home and tell our people the truth. We cannot continue these spending patterns in public or private dollars for health care for less and less and less every year. We can do better. And I will work to do better.

Perhaps the most fundamental change the new direction I propose offers is its focus on the future and its investment which I seek in our children. Each day we delay really making a commitment to our children carries a dear cost. Half of the 2-year-olds in this country today don't receive the immunizations they need against deadly diseases. Our plan will provide them for every eligible child. And we know now that we will save $10 later for every $1 we spend by eliminating preventable childhood diseases. That's a good investment no matter how you measure it.

I recommend that the women, infants, and children's nutrition program be expanded so that every expectant mother who needs the help gets it. We all know that Head Start, a program that prepares children for school, is a success story. We all know that it saves money, but today it just reaches barely over one third of all the eligible children. Under this plan, every eligible child will be able to get a head start. This is not just the right thing to do; it is the smart thing to do. For every dollar we invest today we'll save $3 tomorrow. We have to start thinking about tomorrow. I've heard that somewhere before.

We have to ask more in our schools of our students, our teachers, our principals, our parents. Yes, we must give them the resources they need to meet high standards, but we must also use the authority and the influence and the funding of the Education Department to promote strategies that really work in learning. Money alone is not enough. We have to do what really works to increase learning in our schools.

We have to recognize that all of our high school graduates need some further education in order to be competitive in this global economy. So we have to establish a partnership between businesses and education and the Government for apprenticeship programs in every State in this country to give our people the skills they need. Lifelong learning must benefit not just young high school graduates but workers too, throughout their career. The average 18-year-old today will change jobs seven times in a lifetime. We have done a lot in this country on worker training in the last few years, but the system is too fractured. We must develop a unified, simplified, sensible, streamlined worker training program so that workers receive the training they need regardless of why they lost their jobs or whether they simply need to learn something new to keep them. We have got to do better on this.

And finally, I propose a program that got a great response from the American people all across this country last year: a program of national service to make college loans available to all Americans and to challenge them at the same time to give something back to their country as teachers or police officers or community service workers; to give them the option to pay the loans back, but at tax time so they can't beat the bill, but to encourage them instead to pay it back by making their country stronger and making their country better and giving us the benefit of their knowledge.

A generation ago when President [John F.] Kennedy proposed and the United States Congress embraced the Peace Corps, it defined the character of a whole generation of Americans committed to serving people around the world. In this national service program, we will provide more than twice as many slots for people before they go to college to be in national service than ever served in the Peace Corps. This program could do for this generation of Members of Congress what the land grant college act did and what the GI bill did for former Congressmen. In the future, historians who got their education through the national service loan will look back on you and thank you for giving America a new lease on life, if you meet this challenge.

If we believe in jobs and we believe in learning, we must believe in rewarding work. If we believe in restoring the values that make America special, we must believe that there is dignity in all work, and there must be dignity for all workers. To those who care for our sick, who tend our children, who do our most difficult and tiring jobs, the new direction I propose will make this solemn, simple commitment: By expanding the refundable earned income tax credit, we will make history. We will reward the work of millions of working poor Americans by realizing the principle that if you work 40 hours a week and you've got a child in the house, you will no longer be in poverty.

Later this year, we will offer a plan to end welfare as we know it. I have worked on this issue for the better part of a decade. And I know from personal conversations with many people that no one, no one wants to change the welfare system as badly as those who are trapped in it. I want to offer the people on welfare the education, the training, the child care, the health care they need to get back on their feet, but say after 2 years they must get back to work, too, in private business if possible, in public service if necessary. We have to end welfare as a way of life and make it a path to independence and dignity.

Our next great goal should be to strengthen our families. I compliment the Congress for passing the Family and Medical Leave Act as a good first step, but it is time to do more. This plan will give this country the toughest child support enforcement system it has ever had. It is time to demand that people take responsibility for the children they bring in this world

And I ask you to help to protect our families against the violent crime which terrorizes our people and which tears our communities apart. We must pass a tough crime bill. I support not only the bill which didn't quite make it to the President's desk last year but also an initiative to put 100,000 more police officers on the street, to provide bootcamps for first-time nonviolent offenders for more space for the hardened criminals in jail, and I support an initiative to do what we can to keep guns out of the hands of criminals. Let me say this. I will make you this bargain: If you will pass the Brady bill, I'll sure sign it.

Let me say now, we should move to the harder parts.

I think it is clear to every American, including every Member of Congress of both parties, that the confidence of the people who pay our bills in our institutions in Washington is not high. We must restore it. We must begin again to make Government work for ordinary taxpayers, not simply for organized interest groups. And that beginning must start with real political reform. I am asking the United States Congress to pass a real campaign finance reform bill this year. I ask you to increase the participation of the American people by passing the motor voter bill promptly. I ask you to deal with the undue influence of special interest by passing a bill to end the tax deduction for lobbying and to act quickly to require all the people who lobby you to register as lobbyists by passing the lobbying registration bill.

Believe me, they were cheering that last section at home. I believe lobby reform and campaign finance reform are a sure path to increased popularity for Republicans and Democrats alike because it says to the voters back home, "This is your House. This is your Senate. We're your hired hands, and every penny we draw is your money."

Next, to revolutionize Government we have to ensure that we live within our means, and that should start at the top and with the White House. In the last few days I have announced a cut in the White House staff of 25 percent, saving approximately $10 million. I have ordered administrative cuts in budgets of Agencies and Departments. I have cut the Federal bureaucracy, or will over the next 4 years, by approximately 100,000 positions, for a combined savings of $9 billion. It is time for Government to demonstrate, in the condition we're in, that we can be as frugal as any household in America.

And that's why I also want to congratulate the Congress. I noticed the announcement of the leadership today that Congress is taking similar steps to cut its costs. I think that is important. I think it will send a very clear signal to the American people.

But if we really want to cut spending, we're going to have to do more, and some of it will be difficult. Tonight I call for an across-the-board freeze in Federal Government salaries for one year. And thereafter, during this 4-year period, I recommend that salaries rise at one point lower than the cost of living allowance normally involved in Federal pay increases.

Next, I recommend that we make 150 specific budget cuts, as you know, and that all those who say we should cut more be as specific as I have been.

Finally, let me say to my friends on both sides of the aisle, it is not enough simply to cut Government; we have to rethink the whole way it works. When I became President I was amazed at just the way the White House worked, in ways that added lots of money to what taxpayers had to pay, outmoded ways that didn't take maximum advantage of technology and didn't do things that any business would have done years ago to save taxpayers' money.

So I want to bring a new spirit of innovation into every Government Department. I want to push education reform, as I said, not just to spend more money but to really improve learning. Some things work, and some things don't. We ought to be subsidizing the things that work and discouraging the things that don't. I'd like to use that Superfund to clean up pollution for a change and not just pay lawyers.

In the aftermath of all the difficulties with the savings and loans, we must use Federal bank regulators to protect the security and safety of our financial institutions, but they should not be used to continue the credit crunch and to stop people from making sensible loans.

I'd like for us to not only have welfare reform but to reexamine the whole focus of all of our programs that help people, to shift them from entitlement programs to empowerment programs. In the end we want people not to need us anymore. I think that's important.

But in the end we have to get back to the deficit. For years there's been a lot of talk about it but very few credible efforts to deal with it. And now I understand why, having dealt with the real numbers for 4 weeks. But I believe this plan does; it tackles the budget deficit seriously and over the long term. It puts in place one of the biggest deficit reductions and one of the biggest changes in Federal priorities, from consumption to investment, in the history of this country at the same time over the next 4 years.

Let me say to all the people watching us tonight who will ask me these questions beginning tomorrow as I go around the country and who've asked it in the past: We're not cutting the deficit just because experts say it's the thing to do or because it has some intrinsic merit. We have to cut the deficit because the more we spend paying off the debt, the less tax dollars we have to invest in jobs and education and the future of this country. And the more money we take out of the pool of available savings, the harder it is for people in the private sector to borrow money at affordable interest rates for a college loan for their children, for a home mortgage, or to start a new business.

That's why we've got to reduce the debt, because it is crowding out other activities that we ought to be engaged in and that the American people ought to be engaged in. We cut the deficit so that our children will be able to buy a home, so that our companies can invest in the future and in retraining their workers, so that our Government can make the kinds of investments we need to be a stronger and smarter and safer nation.

If we don't act now, you and I might not even recognize this Government 10 years from now. If we just stay with the same trends of the last 4 years, by the end of the decade the deficit will be $635 billion a year, almost 80 percent of our gross domestic product. And paying interest on that debt will be the costliest Government program of all. We'll still be the world's largest debtor. And when Members of Congress come here, they'll be devoting over 20 cents on the dollar to interest payments, more than half of the budget to health care and to other entitlements. And you'll come here and deliberate and argue over 6 or 7 cents on the dollar, no matter what America's problems are. We will not be able to have the independence we need to chart the future that we must. And we'll be terribly dependent on foreign funds for a large portion of our investment.

This budget plan, by contrast, will by 1997 cut $140 billion in that year alone from the deficit, a real spending cut, a real revenue increase, a real deficit reduction, using the independent numbers of the Congressional Budget Office. Well, you can laugh, my fellow Republicans, but I'll point out that the Congressional Budget Office was normally more conservative in what was going to happen and closer to right than previous Presidents have been.

I did this so that we could argue about priorities with the same set of numbers. I did this so that no one could say I was estimating my way out of this difficulty. I did this because if we can agree together on the most prudent revenues we're likely to get if the recovery stays and we do right things economically, then it will turn out better for the American people than we say. In the last 12 years, because there were differences over the revenue estimates, you and I know that both parties were given greater elbow room for irresponsibility. This is tightening the rein on the Democrats as well as the Republicans. Let's at least argue about the same set of numbers so the American people will think we're shooting straight with them.

As I said earlier, my recommendation makes more than 150 difficult reductions to cut the Federal spending by a total of $246 billion. We are eliminating programs that are no longer needed, such as nuclear power research and development. We're slashing subsidies and canceling wasteful projects. But many of these programs were justified in their time, and a lot of them are difficult for me to recommend reductions in, some really tough ones for me personally. I recommend that we reduce interest subsidies to the Rural Electronic Administration. That's a difficult thing for me to recommend. But I think that I cannot exempt the things that exist in my State or in my experience, if I ask you to deal with things that are difficult for you to deal with. We're going to have to have no sacred cows except the fundamental abiding interest of the American people.

I have to say that we all know our Government has been just great at building programs. The time has come to show the American people that we can limit them too; that we can not only start things, that we can actually stop things.

About the defense budget, I raise a hope and a caution. As we restructure our military forces to meet the new threats of the post-cold war world, it is true that we can responsibly reduce our defense budget. And we may all doubt what that range of reductions is, but let me say that as long as I am President, I will do everything I can to make sure that the men and women who serve under the American flag will remain the best trained, the best prepared, the best equipped fighting force in the world. And every one of you should make that solemn pledge. We still have responsibilities around the world. We are the world's only superpower. This is still a dangerous and uncertain time, and we owe it to the people in uniform to make sure that we adequately provide for the national defense and for their interests and needs. Backed by an effective national defense and a stronger economy, our Nation will be prepared to lead a world challenged as it is everywhere by ethnic conflict, by the proliferation of weapons of mass destruction, by the global democratic revolution, and by challenges to the health of our global environment.

I know this economic plan is ambitious, but I honestly believe it is necessary for the continued greatness of the United States. And I think it is paid for fairly, first by cutting Government, then by asking the most of those who benefited the most in the past, and by asking more Americans to contribute today so that all of us can prosper tomorrow.

 For the wealthiest, those earning more than $180,000 per year, I ask you all who are listening tonight to support a raise in the top rate for Federal income taxes from 31 to 36 percent. We recommend a 10-percent surtax on incomes over $250,000 a year, and we recommend closing some loopholes that let some people get away without paying any tax at all.

For businesses with taxable incomes in excess of $10 million we recommend a raise in the corporate tax rate, also to 36 percent, as well as a cut in the deduction for business entertainment expenses. Our plan seeks to attack tax subsidies that actually reward companies more for shutting their operations down here and moving them overseas than for staying here and reinvesting in America. I say that as someone who believes that American companies should be free to invest around the world and as a former Governor who actively sought investment of foreign companies in my State. But the Tax Code should not express a preference to American companies for moving somewhere else, and it does in particular cases today.

We will seek to ensure that, through effective tax enforcement, foreign corporations who do make money in America simply pay the same taxes that American companies make on the same income.

To middle class Americans who have paid a great deal for the last 12 years and from whom I ask a contribution tonight, I will say again as I did on Monday night: You're not going alone any more, you're certainly not going first, and you're not going to pay more for less as you have too often in the past. I want to emphasize the facts about this plan: 98.8 percent of America's families will have no increase in their income tax rates, only 1.2 percent at the top.

Let me be clear: There will also be no new cuts in benefits for Medicare. As we move toward the 4th year, with the explosion in health care costs, as I said, projected to account for 50 percent of the growth of the deficit between now and the year 2000, there must be planned cuts in payments to providers, to doctors, to hospitals, to labs, as a way of controlling health care costs. But I see these only as a stopgap until we can reform the entire health care system. If you'll help me do that, we can be fair to the providers and to the consumers of health care. Let me repeat this, because I know it matters to a lot of you on both sides of the aisle. This plan does not make a recommendation for new cuts in Medicare benefits for any beneficiary.

Secondly, the only change we are making in Social Security is one that has already been publicized. The plan does ask older Americans with higher incomes, who do not rely solely on Social Security to get by, to contribute more. This plan will not affect the 80 percent of Social Security recipients who do not pay taxes on Social Security now. Those who do not pay tax on Social Security now will not be affected by this plan.

Our plan does include a broad-based tax on energy, and I want to tell you why I selected this and why I think it's a good idea. I recommend that we adopt a BTU tax on the heat content of energy as the best way to provide us with revenue to lower the deficit because it also combats pollution, promotes energy efficiency, promotes the independence, economically, of this country as well as helping to reduce the debt, and because it does not discriminate against any area. Unlike a carbon tax, that's not too hard on the coal States; unlike a gas tax, that's not too tough on people who drive a long way to work; unlike an ad valorem tax, it doesn't increase just when the price of an energy source goes up. And it is environmentally responsible. It will help us in the future as well as in the present with the deficit.

Taken together these measures will cost an American family with an income of about $40,000 a year less than $17 a month. It will cost American families with incomes under $30,000 nothing because of other programs we propose, principally those raising the earned income tax credit.

Because of our publicly stated determination to reduce the deficit, if we do these things, we will see the continuation of what's happened just since the election. Just since the election, since the Secretary of the Treasury, the Director of the Office of Management and Budget, and others who have begun to speak out publicly in favor of a tough deficit reduction plan, interest rates have continued to fall long-term. That means that for the middle class, who will pay something more each month, if they had any credit needs or demands, their increased energy costs will be more than offset by lower interest costs for mortgages, consumer loans, credit cards. This can be a wise investment for them and their country now.

I would also point out what the American people already know, and that is because we're a big, vast country where we drive long distances, we have maintained far lower burdens on energy than any other advanced country. We will still have far lower burdens on energy than any other advanced country. And these will be spread fairly, with real attempts to make sure that no cost is imposed on families with incomes under $30,000 and that the costs are very modest until you get into the higher income groups where the income taxes trigger in.

Now, I ask all of you to consider this: Whatever you think of the tax program, whatever you think of the spending cuts, consider the cost of not changing. Remember the numbers that you all know. If we just keep on doing what we're doing, by the end of the decade we'll have a $650-billion-a-year deficit. If we just keep on doing what we're doing, by the end of the decade 20 percent of our national income will go to health care every year, twice as much as any other country on the face of the globe. If we just keep on doing what we're doing, over 20 cents on the dollar will have to go to service the debt.

Unless we have the courage now to start building our future and stop borrowing from it, we're condemning ourselves to years of stagnation interrupted by occasional recessions, to slow growth in jobs, to no more growth in income, to more debt, to more disappointment. Worse, unless we change, unless we increase investment and reduce the debt to raise productivity so that we can generate both jobs and incomes, we will be condemning our children and our children's children to a lesser life than we enjoyed. Once Americans looked forward to doubling their living standards every 25 years. At present productivity rates, it will take 100 years to double living standards, until our grandchildren's grandchildren are born. I say that is too long to wait.

Tonight the American people know we have to change. But they're also likely to ask me tomorrow and all of you for the weeks and months ahead whether we have the fortitude to make the changes happen in the right way. They know that as soon as I leave this Chamber and you go home, various interest groups will be out in force lobbying against this or that piece of this plan, and that the forces of conventional wisdom will offer a thousand reasons why we well ought to do this but we just can't do it.

Our people will be watching and wondering, not to see whether you disagree with me on a particular issue but just to see whether this is going to be business as usual or a real new day, whether we're all going to conduct ourselves as if we know we're working for them. We must scale the walls of the people's skepticisms, not with our words but with our deeds. After so many years of gridlock and indecision, after so many hopeful beginnings and so few promising results, the American people are going to be harsh in their judgments of all of us if we fail to seize this moment.

This economic plan can't please everybody. If the package is picked apart, there will be something that will anger each of us, won't please anybody. But if it is taken as a whole, it will help all of us. So I ask you all to begin by resisting the temptation to focus only on a particular spending cut you don't like or some particular investment that wasn't made. And nobody likes the tax increases, but let's just face facts. For 20 years, through administrations of both parties, incomes have stalled and debt has exploded and productivity has not grown as it should. We cannot deny the reality of our condition. We have got to play the hand we were dealt and play it as best we can.

My fellow Americans, the test of this plan cannot be what is in it for me. It has got to be what is in it for us. If we work hard and if we work together, if we rededicate ourselves to creating jobs, to rewarding work, to strengthening our families, to reinventing our Government, we can lift our country's fortunes again.

Tonight, I ask everyone in this Chamber and every American to look simply into your heart, to spark your own hopes, to fire your own imagination. There is so much good, so much possibility, so much excitement in this country now that if we act boldly and honestly, as leaders should, our legacy will be one of prosperity and progress. This must be America's new direction. Let us summon the courage to seize it.

Thank you. God bless America.

President Clinton's Remarks on Middle East Peace Accord

Following are remarks by President Clinton Sept. 13, 1993, on the south lawn of the White House in Washington, D.C., at a ceremony for the signing of a "Declaration of Principles," a peace accord between Israel and the Palestine Liberation Organization.

Prime Minister [Yitzhak] Rabin, Chairman [Yasir] Arafat, Foreign Minister [Shimon] Peres, Mr. [Mahmoud] Abbas, President [Jimmy] Carter, President [George] Bush, distinguished guests. On behalf of the United States and Russia, co-sponsors of the Middle East peace process, welcome to this great occasion of history and hope. Today we bear witness to an extraordinary act in one of history's defining dramas—a drama that began in a time of our ancestors when the word went forth from a sliver of land between the River Jordan and the Mediterranean Sea. That hallowed piece of earth, that land of light and revelation, is the home to the memories and dreams of Jews, Muslims and Christians throughout the world.

As we all know, devotion to that land has also been the source of conflict and bloodshed for too long. Throughout this century bitterness between the Palestinian and Jewish people has robbed the entire region of its resources, its potential and too many of its sons and daughters. The land has been so drenched in warfare and hatred, the conflicting claims of history etched so deeply in the souls of the combatants there, that many believe the past would always have the upper hand. Then, 14 years ago, the past began to give way when, at this place and upon this desk, three men of great vision signed their names to the Camp David accords. Today we honor the memories of Menachem Begin and Anwar Sadat. And we salute the wise leadership of President Jimmy Carter.

Then, as now, we heard from those who said that conflict would come again soon, but the peace between Egypt and Israel has endured. Just so this bold new venture today, this brave gamble that the future can be better than the past, must endure.

Two years ago in Madrid another President took a major step on the road to peace by bringing Israel and all her neighbors together to launch direct negotiations, and today we also express our deep thanks for the skillful leadership of President George Bush.

Ever since Harry Truman first recognized Israel, every American President, Democrat and Republican, has worked for peace between Israel and her neighbors. Now the efforts of all who have labored before us bring us to this moment—a moment when we dare to pledge what for so long seemed difficult even to imagine: that the security of the Israeli people will be reconciled with the hopes of the Palestinian people, and there will be more security and more hope for all.

Today the leadership of Israel and the Palestine Liberation Organization will sign a declaration of principles on interim Palestinian self-government. It charts a course toward reconciliation, between two peoples who have both known the bitterness of exile. Now both pledge to put old sorrows and antagonisms behind them and to work for a shared future shaped by the values of the Torah, the Koran and the Bible. Let us salute also today the Government of Norway, for its remarkable role in nurturing this agreement.

But above all, let us today pay tribute to the leaders who had the courage to lead their people toward peace, away from the scars of battle, the wounds and the losses of the past, toward a brighter tomorrow. The world today thanks Prime Minister Rabin, Foreign Minister Peres and Chairman Arafat.

That tenacity and vision has given us the promise of a new beginning. What these leaders have done now must be done by others.

Their achievement must be a catalyst for progress in all aspects of the peace process. And those of us who support them must be there to help in all aspects, for the peace must render the people who make it more secure. A peace of the brave is within our reach. Throughout the Middle East there is a great yearning for the quiet miracle of a normal life. We know a difficult road lies ahead. Every peace has its enemies, those who still prefer the easy habits of hatred to the hard labors of reconciliation, but Prime Minister Rabin has reminded us that you do not have to make peace with your friends, and the Koran teaches that if the enemy inclines toward peace, do thou also incline toward peace.

Therefore, let us resolve that this new mutual recognition will be a continuing process in which the parties transform the very way they see and understand each other. Let the skeptics of this peace recall what once existed among these people. There was a time when the traffic of ideas and commerce and pilgrims flowed uninterrupted among the cities of the fertile crescent. In Spain, in the Middle East, Muslims and Jews once worked together to write brilliant chapters in the history of literature and science. All this can come to pass again.

Mr. Prime Minister, Mr. Chairman, I pledge the active support of the United States of America to the difficult work that lies ahead.

The United States is committed to insuring that the people who are affected by this agreement will be made more secure by it and to leading the world in marshaling the resources necessary to implement the difficult details that will make real the principles to which you commit yourselves today. Together let us imagine what can be accomplished if all the energy and ability the Israelis and the Palestinians have invested into your struggle can now be channeled into cultivating the land and freshening the waters; into ending the boycotts and creating new industry; into building a land as bountiful and peaceful as it is holy. Above all, let us dedicate ourselves today to your region's next generation. In this entire assembly, no one is more important than the group of Israeli and Arab children who are seated here with us today.

Mr. Prime Minister, Mr. Chairman, this day belongs to you. And because of what you have done, tomorrow belongs to them. We must not leave them prey to the politics of extremism and despair, to those who would detail this process because they cannot overcome the fears and hatreds of the past. We must not betray their future.

For too long the young of the Middle East have been caught in a web of hatred not of their own making. For too long they have been taught from the chronicles of war; now we give them the chance to know the season of peace. For them we must realize the prophecy of Isaiah, that the cry of violence shall no more be heard in your land, nor wrack nor ruin within your borders. The children of Abraham, the descendants of Isaac and Ishmael, have embarked together on a bold journey. Together today with all our hearts and all our souls, we bid them Shalom. Salaam. Peace.

President Clinton's Address to the United Nations

Following is the White House text of President Clinton's address to the U.N. General Assembly in New York on Sept. 27, 1993.

Thank you very much. Mr. President, let me first congratulate you on your election as president of this General Assembly.

Mr. Secretary-General, distinguished delegates and guests, it is a great honor for me to address you and to stand in this great chamber which symbolizes so much of the 20th century—its darkest crises and its brightest aspirations.

I come before you as the first American president born after the founding of the United Nations. Like most of the people in the world today, I was not even alive during the convulsive World War that convinced humankind of the need for this organization, nor during the San Francisco Conference [on International Organization] that led to its birth. Yet I have followed the work of the United Nations throughout my life, with admiration for its accomplishments, with sadness for its failures, and conviction that through common effort our generation can take the bold steps needed to redeem the mission entrusted to the United Nations 48 years ago.

I pledge to you that my nation remains committed to helping make the United Nations' vision a reality. The start of this General Assembly offers us an opportunity to take stock of where we are, as common shareholders in the progress of humankind and in the preservation of our planet.

It is clear that we live at a turning point in human history. Immense and promising changes seem to wash over us every day. The Cold War is over. The world is no longer divided into two armed and angry camps. Dozens of new democracies have been born.

It is a moment of miracles. We see Nelson Mandela stand side by side with President [F. W.] De Klerk, proclaiming a date for South Africa's first non-racial election. We see Russia's first popularly elected president, Boris [N.] Yeltsin, leading his nation on its bold democratic journey. We have seen decades of deadlock shattered in the Middle East, as the prime minister of Israel [Yitzhak Rabin] and the chairman of the Palestine Liberation Organization [Yasir Arafat] reached past enmity and suspicion to shake each other's hands and exhilarate the entire world with the hope of peace.

We have begun to see the doomsday weapons of nuclear annihilation dismantled and destroyed. Thirty-two years ago, President [John F.] Kennedy warned this chamber that humanity lived under a nuclear sword of Damocles that hung by the slenderest of threads. Now the United States is working with Russia, Ukraine, Belarus and others to take that sword down, to lock it away in a secure vault where we hope and pray it will remain forever.

It is a new era in this hall as well. The superpower standoff that for so long stymied the United Nations' work almost from its first day has now yielded to a new promise of practical cooperation. Yet today we must all admit that there are two powerful tendencies working from opposite directions to challenge the authority of nation-states everywhere and to undermine the authority of nation-states to work together.

From beyond nations, economic and technological forces all over the globe are compelling the world toward integration. These forces are fueling a welcome explosion of entrepreneurship and political liberalization. But they also threaten to destroy the insularity and independence of national economies, quickening the pace of change and making many of our people feel more insecure.

At the same time, from within nations, the resurgent aspirations of ethnic and religious groups challenge governments on terms that traditional nation-states cannot easily accommodate.

These twin forces lie at the heart of the challenges not only to our national government, but also to all our international institutions. They require all of us in this room to find new ways to work together more effectively in pursuit of our national interests and to think anew about whether our institutions of international cooperation are adequate to this moment.

Thus, as we marvel at this era's promise of new peace, we must also recognize that serious threats remain. Bloody ethnic, religious and civil wars rage from Angola to the Caucasus to Kashmir. As weapons of mass destruction fall into more hands, even small conflicts can threaten to take on murderous proportions. Hunger and disease continue to take a tragic toll, especially among the world's children. The malignant neglect of our global environment threatens our children's health and their very security.

The repression of conscience continues in too many nations. And terrorism, which has taken so many innocent lives, assumes a horrifying immediacy for us here when militant fanatics bombed the World Trade Center and planned to attack even this very hall of peace.

Let me assure you, whether the fathers of those crimes, or the mass murderers who bombed Pan Am Flight 103, my government is determined to see that such terrorists are brought to justice.

As this moment of panoramic change, of vast opportunities and troubling threats, we must all ask ourselves what we can do and what we should do as a community of nations. We must once again dare to dream of what might be, for our dreams may be within our reach. For that to happen, we must all be willing to honestly confront the challenges of the broader world. That has never been easy.

When this organization was founded 48 years ago, the world's nations stood devastated by war or exhausted by its expense. There was little appetite for cooperative efforts among nations. Most people simply wanted to get on with their lives. But a far-sighted generation of leaders from the United States and elsewhere rallied the world. Their efforts built the institutions of postwar security and prosperity.

We are at a similar moment today. The momentum of the Cold War no longer propels us in our daily actions. And with daunting economic and political pressures upon almost every nation represented in this room, many of us are turning to focus greater attention and energy on our domestic needs and problems. And we must. But putting each of our economic houses in order cannot mean that we shut our windows to the world. The pursuit of self-renewal in many of the world's largest and most powerful economies—in Europe, in Japan, in North America—is absolutely crucial because unless the great industrial nations can recapture their robust economic growth, the global economy will languish.

Yet, the industrial nations also need growth elsewhere in order to lift their own. Indeed, prosperity in each of our nations and regions also depends upon active and responsible engagement in a host of shared concerns.

For example, a thriving and democratic Russia not only makes the world safer, it also can help to expand the world's economy. A strong GATT [General Agreement on Tariffs and Trade] agreement will create millions of jobs worldwide. Peace in the Middle East, buttressed as it should be by the repeal of outdated U.N. resolutions, can help to unleash that region's great economic potential and calm a perpetual source of tension in global affairs. And the growing economic power of China, coupled with greater political openness, could bring enormous benefits to all of Asia and to the rest of the world.

We must help our publics to understand this distinction: Domestic renewal is an overdue tonic. But isolationism and protectionism are still poison. We must inspire our people to look beyond their immediate fears toward a broader horizon.

THE PATH OF THE UNITED STATES

Let me start by being clear about where the United States stands. The United States occupies a unique position in world affairs today. We recognize that, and we welcome it. Yet, with the Cold War over, I know many people ask whether the United States plans to retreat or remain active in the world, and if active, to what end. Many people are asking that in our own country as well. Let me answer that question as clearly and plainly as I can.

The United States intends to remain engaged and to lead. We cannot solve every problem, but we must and will serve as a fulcrum for change and a pivot point for peace.

In a new era of peril and opportunity, our overriding purpose must be to expand and strengthen the world's community of market-based democracies. During the Cold War we sought to contain a threat to survival of free institutions. Now we seek to enlarge the circle of nations that live under those free institutions.

For our dream is of a day when the opinions and energies of every person in the world will be given full expression, in a world of thriving democracies that cooperate with each other and live in peace.

With this statement, I do not mean to announce some crusade to force our way of life and doing things on others, or to replicate our institutions, but we now know clearly that throughout the world, from Poland to Eritrea, from Guatemala to South Korea, there is an enormous yearning among people who wish to be the masters of their own economic and political lives. Where it matters most and where we can make the greatest difference, we will, therefore, patiently and firmly align ourselves with that yearning.

Today, there are still those who claim that democracy is simply not applicable to many cultures and that its recent expansion is an aberration, an accident, in history that will soon fade away. But I agree with President [Franklin D.] Roosevelt, who once said, "The democratic aspiration is no mere recent phase of human history. It is human history."

We will work to strengthen the free market democracies, by revitalizing our economy here at home, by opening world trade through the GATT, the North American Free Trade Agreement and other accords, and by updating our shared institutions, asking with you and answering the hard questions about whether they are adequate to the present challenges.

We will support the consolidation of market democracy where it is taking new root, as in the states of the former Soviet Union and all over Latin America. And we seek to foster the practices of good government that distribute the benefits of democracy and economic growth fairly to all people.

We will work to reduce the threat from regimes that are hostile to democracies and to support liberalization of non-democratic states when they are willing to live in peace with the rest of us.

As a country that has over 150 different racial, ethnic and religious groups within our borders, our policy is and must be rooted in a profound respect for all the world's religions and cultures. But we must oppose everywhere extremism that produces terrorism and hate.

And we must pursue our humanitarian goal of reducing suffering, fostering sustainable development, and improving the health and living conditions, particularly for our world's children.

On efforts from export control to trade agreements to peacekeeping, we will often work in partnership with others and through multilateral institutions, such as the United Nations. It is in our national interest to do so. But we must not hesitate to act unilaterally when there is a threat to our core interests or to those of our allies.

The United States believes that an expanded community of market democracies not only serves our own security interests, it also advances the goals enshrined in this body's charter and its Universal Declaration of Human Rights. For broadly based prosperity is clearly the strongest form of preventive diplomacy. And the habits of democracy are the habits of peace.

Democracy is rooted in compromise, not conquest. It rewards tolerance, not hatred. Democracies rarely wage war on one another. They make more reliable partners in trade, in diplomacy and in the stewardship of our global environment. And democracies with the rule of law and respect for political, religious and cultural minorities are more responsive to their own people and to the protection of human rights.

NON-PROLIFERATION

But as we work toward this vision we must confront the storm clouds that may overwhelm our work and darken the march toward freedom. If we do not stem the proliferation of the world's deadliest weapons, no democracy can feel secure. If we do not strengthen the capacity to resolve conflict among and within nations, those conflicts will smother the birth of free institutions, threaten the development of entire regions and continue to take innocent lives.

If we do not nurture our people and our planet through sustainable development, we will deepen conflict and waste the very wonders that make our efforts worth doing.

Let me talk more about what I believe we must do in each of these three categories: non-proliferation, conflict resolution and sustainable development.

One of our most urgent priorities must be attacking the proliferation of weapons of mass destruction, whether they are nuclear, chemical or biological, and the ballistic missiles that can rain them down on populations hundreds of miles away.

We know this is not an idle problem. All of us are still haunted by the pictures of Kurdish women and children cut down by poison gas. We saw Scud missiles dropped during the gulf war that would have been far graver in their consequence if they had carried nuclear weapons. And we know that many nations still believe it is in their interest to develop weapons of mass destruction or to sell them or the necessary technologies to others for financial gain.

More than a score of nations likely possess such weapons, and their number threatens to grow. These weapons destabilize entire regions. They could turn a local conflict into a global human and environmental catastrophe. We simply have got to find ways to control these weapons and to reduce the number of states that possess them by supporting and strengthening the IAEA [International Atomic Energy Agency] and by taking other necessary measures.

I have made non-proliferation one of our nation's highest priorities. We intend to weave it more deeply into the fabric of all of our relationships with the world's nations and institutions. We seek to build a world of increasing pressures for non-proliferation but increasingly open trade and technology for those states that live by accepted international rules.

Today, let me describe several new policies that our government will pursue to stem proliferation. We will pursue new steps to control the materials for nuclear weapons. Growing global stockpiles of plutonium and highly enriched uranium are raising the danger of nuclear terrorism for all nations. We will press for an international agreement that would ban production of these materials for weapons forever.

As we reduce our nuclear stockpiles, the United States has also begun negotiations toward a comprehensive ban on nuclear testing. This summer I declared that to facilitate these negotiations, our nation would suspend our testing if all other nuclear states would do the same. Today, in the face of disturbing signs, I renew my call on the nuclear states to abide by that moratorium as we negotiate to stop nuclear testing for all time.

I am also proposing new efforts to fight the proliferation of biological and chemical weapons. Today, only a handful of nations has ratified the Chemical Weapons Convention. I call on all nations, including my own, to ratify this accord quickly so that it may enter into force by Jan. 13, 1995.

We will also seek to strengthen the Biological Weapons Convention by making every nation's biological activities and facilities open to more international students. I am proposing as well new steps to thwart the proliferation of ballistic missiles. Recently, working with Russia, Argentina, Hungary and South Africa, we have made significant progress toward that goal. Now, we will seek to strengthen the principles of the Missile Technology Control Regime by transforming it from an agreement on technology transfer among just 23 nations to a set of rules that can command universal adherence.

We will also reform our own system of export controls in the United States to reflect the realities of the post-Cold War world, where we seek to enlist the support of our former adversaries in the battle against proliferation.

At the same time that we stop deadly technologies from falling into the wrong hands, we will work with our partners to remove outdated controls that unfairly burden legitimate commerce and unduly restrain growth and opportunity all over the world.

As we work to keep the world's most destructive weapons out of conflict, we must also strengthen the international community's ability to address those conflicts themselves. For as we all now know so painfully, the end of the Cold War did not bring us to the millennium of peace. And, indeed, it simply removed the lid from many cauldrons of ethnic, religious and territorial animosity.

U.N. PEACEKEEPERS

The philosopher Isaiah Berlin has said that a wounded nationalism is like a bent twig forced down so severely that when released it lashes back with fury.

The world today is thick with both bent and recoiling twigs of wounded communal identities.

This scourge of bitter conflict has placed high demands on United Nations peacekeeping forces. Frequently the blue helmets have worked wonders. In Namibia, El Salvador, the Golan Heights and elsewhere, U.N. peacekeepers have helped to stop the fighting, restore civil authority and enable free elections.

In Bosnia, U.N. peacekeepers, against the danger and frustration of that continuing tragedy, [have] maintained a valiant humanitarian effort. And if the parties of that conflict take the hard steps needed to make a real peace, the international community including the United States must be ready to help in its effective implementation.

In Somalia, the United States and the United Nations have worked together to achieve a stunning humanitarian rescue, saving literally hundreds of thousands of lives and restoring the conditions of security for almost the entire country.

U.N. peacekeepers from over two dozen nations remain in Somalia today. And some, including brave Americans, have lost their lives to ensure that we complete our mission and to ensure that anarchy and starvation do not return just as quickly as they were abolished.

Many still criticize U.N. peacekeeping, but those who do should talk to the people of Cambodia, where the U.N.'s operations have helped to turn the killing fields into fertile soil through reconciliation. Last May's elections in Cambodia marked a proud accomplishment for that war-weary nation and for the United Nations. And I am pleased to announce that the United States has recognized Cambodia's new government.

U.N. peacekeeping holds the promise to resolve many of this era's conflicts. The reason we have supported such missions is not, as some critics in the United States have charged, to subcontract American foreign policy, but to strengthen our security, protect our interests, and to share among nations the costs and effort of pursuing peace.

Peacekeeping cannot be a substitute for our own national defense efforts, but it can strongly supplement them.

Today, there is wide recognition that the U.N. peacekeeping ability has not kept pace with the rising responsibilities and challenges. Just six years ago, about 10,000 U.N. peacekeepers were stationed around the world. Today, the United Nations has some 80,000 deployed in 17 operations on four continents.

Yet, until recently, if a peacekeeping commander called in from across the globe when it was nighttime here in New York, there was no one in the peacekeeping office even to answer the call. When lives are on the line, you cannot let the reach of the United Nations exceed its grasp.

As the secretary-general and others have argued, if U.N. peacekeeping is to be a sound security investment for our nation and for other U.N. members, it must adapt to new times. Together we must prepare U.N. peacekeeping for the 21st century. We need to begin by bringing the rigors of military and political analysis to every U.N. peace mission.

In recent weeks in the Security Council, our nation has begun asking harder questions about proposals for new peacekeeping missions: Is there a real threat to international peace? Does the proposed mission have clear objectives? Can an end point be identified for those who will be asked to participate? How much will the mission cost?

From now on, the United Nations should address these and other hard questions for every proposed mission before we vote and before the mission begins.

The United Nations simply cannot become engaged in every one of the world's conflicts. If the American people are to say yes to U.N. peacekeeping, the United Nations must know when to say no. The United Nations must also have the technical means to run a modern world-class peacekeeping operation.

We support the creation of a genuine U.N. peacekeeping headquarters with a planning staff, with access to timely intelligence, with a logistics unit that can be deployed on a moment's notice, and a modern operations center with global communications.

And the United Nations' operations must not only be adequately funded, but also fairly funded. Within the next few weeks, the United States will be current in our peacekeeping bills. I have worked hard with the Congress to get this done.

I believe the United States should lead the way in being timely in its payments, and I will work to continue to see that we pay our bills in full. But I am also committed to work with the United Nations to reduce our nation's assessment for these missions.

The assessment system has not been changed since 1973. And everyone in our country knows that our percentage of the world's economic pie is not as great as it was then. Therefore, I believe our rates should be reduced to reflect the rise of other nations that can now bear more of the financial burden. That will make it easier for me as president to make sure we pay in a timely and full fashion.

Changes in the United Nations' peacekeeping operations must be part of an even broader program of United Nations reform. I say that again not to criticize the United Nations, but to help to improve it. As our Ambassador Madeleine K. Albright has suggested, the United States has always played a twin role to the United Nations-first friend and first critic.

REINVENTING GOVERNMENT

Today corporations all around the world are finding ways to move from the Industrial Age to the Information Age, improving service, reducing bureaucracy and cutting costs.

Here in the United States, our Vice President Al Gore and I have launched an effort to literally reinvent how our government operates. We see this going on in other governments around the world. Now the time has come to reinvent the way the United Nations operates as well.

I applaud the initial steps the secretary general [Boutros Boutros-Ghali] has taken to reduce and to reform the United Nations bureaucracy. Now, we must all do even more to root out waste.

Before this General Assembly is over, let us establish a strong mandate for an office of inspector general so that it can attain a reputation for toughness, for integrity, for effectiveness. Let us build new confidence among our people that the United Nations is changing with the needs of our times.

Ultimately, the key for reforming the United Nations, as in reforming our own government, is to remember why we are here and whom we serve.

It is wise to recall that the first words of the U.N. Charter are not "We, the governments," but, "We, the people of the United Nations." That means in every country the teachers, the workers, the farmers, the professionals, the fathers, the mothers, the children, from the most remote village in the world to the largest metropolis—they are why we gather in this great hall. It is their futures that are at risk when we act or fail to act. It is they who ultimately pay our bills.

As we dream new dreams in this age when miracles now seem possible, let us focus on the lives of those people and especially on the children who will inherit this world.

Let us work with a new urgency and imagine what kind of world we could create for them in the coming generations.

Let us work with new energy to protect the world's people from torture and repression. As Secretary of State [Warren] Christopher stressed at the recent Vienna Conference, human rights are not something conditional, founded by culture, but rather something universal granted by God.

This General Assembly should create, at long last, a high commissioner for human rights. I hope you will do it soon and with vigor and energy and conviction.

Let us also work far more ambitiously to fulfill our obligations as custodians of this planet, not only to improve the quality of life for our citizens and the quality of our air and water and the Earth itself, but also because the roots of conflict are so often entangled with the roots of environmental neglect and the calamity of famine and disease.

During the course of our campaign in the United States last year, Vice President Gore and I promised the American people major changes in our nation's policy toward the global environment. Those were promises to keep, and today the United States is doing so.

GLOBAL COMMITMENTS

Today we are working with other nations to build on the promising work of the United Nations' Commission on Sustainable Development. We are working to make sure that all nations meet their commitments under the Global Climate Convention. We are seeking to complete negotiations on an accord to prevent the world's deserts from further expansion. And we seek to strengthen the World Health Organization's efforts to combat the plague of AIDS, which is not only killing millions, but also exhausting the resources of nations that can least afford it.

Let us make a new commitment to the world's children. It is tragic enough that 1.5 million children died as a result of wars over the past decade. But it is far more unforgivable that in that same period, 40 million children died from diseases completely preventable with simply vaccines or medicine. Every day—this day, as we meet here—over 30,000 of the world's children will die of malnutrition and disease.

Our UNICEF director, Jim Grant, has reminded me that each of those children had a name and a nationality, a family, a personality and a potential. We are compelled to do better by the world's children. Just as our own nation has launched new reforms to ensure that every child has adequate health care, we must do more to get basic vaccines and other treatment for curable diseases to children all over the world. It's the best investment we'll ever make.

We can find new ways to ensure that every child grows up with clean drinkable water, that most precious commodity of life itself. And the United Nations can work even harder to ensure that each child has at least a full primary education—and I mean that opportunity for girls as well as boys.

And to ensure a healthier and more abundant world, we simply must slow the world's explosive growth in population. We cannot afford to see the human waste doubled by the middle of the next century.

Our nation has, at last, renewed its commitment to work with the United Nations to expand the availability of the world's family planning education and services. We must ensure that there is a place at the table for every one of our world's children. And we can do it.

At the birth of this organization 48 years ago, another time of both victory and danger, a generation of gifted leaders from many nations stepped forward to organize the world's efforts in behalf of security and prosperity.

One American leader during that period said this: "It is time we steered by the stars rather than by the light of each passing ship." His generation picked peace, human dignity and freedom. Those are good stars; they should remain the highest in our own firmament.

Now history has granted to us a moment of even greater opportunity, when old dangers and old walls are crumbling; future generations will judge us, every one of us, above all, by what we make of this magic moment.

Let us resolve that we will dream larger, that we will work harder so that they can conclude that we did not merely turn walls to rubble, but instead laid the foundation for great things to come.

Let us ensure that the tide of freedom and democracy is not pushed back by the fierce winds of ethnic hatred. Let us ensure that the world's most dangerous weapons are safely reduced and denied to dangerous hands. Let us ensure that the world we pass to our children is healthier, safer and more abundant than the one we inhabit today.

I believe—I know—that together we can extend this moment of miracles into an age of great work and new wonders. Thank you very much.

President Clinton's Speech on Somalia

Following is the Federal News Service transcript of the Oct. 7, 1993, televised address by President Clinton on the situation in Somalia.

My fellow Americans, today I want to talk with you about our nation's military involvement in Somalia.

A year ago we all watched with horror as Somali children and their families lay dying by the tens of thousands, dying the slow, agonizing death of starvation, a starvation brought on not only by drought but also by the anarchy that then prevailed in that country. This past weekend we all reacted with anger and horror as an armed Somali gang desecrated the bodies of our American soldiers and displayed a captured American pilot, all of them soldiers who were taking part in an international effort to end the starvation of the Somali people themselves.

These tragic events raise hard questions about our effort in Somalia. Why are we still there? What are we trying to accomplish? How did a humanitarian mission turn violent? And when will our people come home? These questions deserve straight answers. Let's start by remembering why our troops went into Somalia in the first place.

We went because only the United States could help stop one of the great human tragedies of this time. A third of a million people had died of starvation and disease. Twice that many more were at risk of dying. Meanwhile, tons of relief supplies piled up in the capital of Mogadishu because a small number of Somalis stopped food from reaching their own countrymen. Our consciences said, "Enough."

In our nation's best tradition, we took action with bipartisan support. President [George] Bush sent in 28,000 American troops as part of the United Nations humanitarian mission. Our troops created a secure environment so that food and medicine could get through. We saved close to 1 million lives. And throughout most of Somalia—everywhere but in Mogadishu—life began returning to normal. Crops are growing. Markets are reopening. So are schools and hospitals. Nearly a million Somalis still depend completely on relief supplies, but at least the starvation is gone. And none of this would have happened without American leadership and America's troops.

Until June things went well with little violence. The United States reduced our troop presence from 28,000 down to less than 5,000, with other nations picking up where we left off.

But then, in June, the people who caused much of the problem in the beginning started attacking American, Pakistani and other troops who were there just to keep the peace. Rather than participate in building the peace with others, these people sought to fight and to disrupt, even if it means returning Somalia to anarchy and mass famine.

And make no mistake about it, if we were to leave Somalia tomorrow, other nations would leave, too. Chaos would resume, the relief effort would stop and starvation soon would return. That knowledge has led us to continue our mission. It is not our job to rebuild Somalia's society or even to create a political process that can allow Somalia's clans to live and work in peace. The Somalis must do that for themselves. The United Nations and many African states are more than willing to help. But we, we in the United States must decide whether we will give them enough time to have a reasonable chance to succeed.

We started this mission for the right reasons, and we're going to finish it in the right way. In a sense, we came to Somalia to rescue innocent people in a burning house. We've nearly put the fire out, but some smoldering embers remain. If we leave them now, those embers will reignite into flames and people will die again. If we stay a short while longer and do the right things, we've got a reasonable chance of cooling off the embers and getting other firefighters to take our place.

We also have to recognize that we cannot leave now and still have all our troops present and accounted for. And I want you to know that I am determined to work for the security of those Americans missing or held captive.

Anyone holding an American right now should understand above all else that we will hold them strictly responsible for our soldiers' well-being. We expect them to be well treated, and we expect them to be released.

So, now, we face a choice. Do we leave when the job gets tough or when the job is well done? Do we invite the return of mass suffering, or do we leave in a way that gives the Somalis a decent chance to survive? Recently, [Joint Chiefs Chairman] Gen. Colin Powell [Jr.] said this about our choices in Somalia: "Because things get difficult, you don't cut and run. You work the problem and try to find a correct solution."

I want to bring our troops home from Somalia. Before the events of this week, as I've said, we had already reduced the number of our troops there from 28,000 to less than 5,000. We must complete that withdrawal soon, and I will. But we must also leave on our terms. We must do it right. And here is what I intend to do.

This past week's events make it clear that even as we prepare to withdraw from Somalia, we need more strength there. We need more armor, more airpower, to ensure that our people are safe and that we can do our job. Today, I have ordered 1,700 additional Army troops and 104 additional armored vehicles to Somalia to protect our troops and to complete our mission. I've also ordered an aircraft carrier and two amphibious groups with 3,600 combat Marines to be stationed offshore. These forces will be under American command. Their mission, what I am asking these young Americans to do, is the following:

First, they are there to protect our troops and our bases. We did not go to Somalia with a military purpose. We never wanted to kill anyone. But those who attack our soldiers must know they will pay a very heavy price.

Second, they are there to keep open and secure the roads, the port and the lines of communications that are essential for the United Nations and the relief workers to keep the flow of food and supplies and people moving freely throughout the country so that starvation and anarchy do not return.

Third, they are there to keep the pressure on those who cut off relief supplies and attack our people, not to personalize the conflict but to prevent a return to anarchy.

Fourth, through their pressure and their presence, our troops will help to make it possible for the Somali people, working with others, to reach agreement among themselves so that they can solve their problems and survive when we leave.

That is our mission. I am proposing this plan because it will let us finish leaving Somalia on our own terms and without destroying all that two administrations have accomplished there, for if we were to leave today, we know what would happen. Within months, Somali children again would be dying in the streets. Our own credibility with friends and allies would be severely damaged. Our leadership in world affairs would be undermined at the very time when people are looking to America to help promote peace and freedom in the post Cold War world. And all around the world, aggressors, thugs and terrorists will conclude that the best way to get us to change our policies is to kill our people. It would be open season on Americans.

That is why I am committed to getting this job done in Somalia not only quickly but also effectively. To do that, I am taking steps to ensure troops from other nations are ready to take the place of our own soldiers. We've already withdrawn some 20,000 troops, and more than that number have replaced them from over two dozen other nations. Now we will intensify efforts to have other countries deploy more troops to Somalia to assure that security will remain when we are gone. And we'll complete the replacement of U.S. military logistics personnel with civilian contractors who can provide the same support to the United Nations.

While we're taking military steps to protect our own people and to help the U.N. maintain a secure environment, we must pursue new diplomatic efforts to help the Somalis find a political solution to their problems. That is the only kind of outcome that can endure, for fundamentally the solution to Somalia's problems is not a military one, it is political.

Leaders of the neighboring African states, such as Ethiopia and Eritrea, have offered to take the lead in efforts to build a settlement among the Somali people that can preserve order and security.

I have directed my representatives to pursue such efforts vigorously, and I've asked Ambassador [Robert B.] Bob Oakley, who served effectively in two administrations as our representative in Somalia, to travel again to the region immediately to advance this process. Obviously, even then there is no guarantee that Somalia will rid itself of violence or suffering, but at least we will have given Somalia a reasonable chance.

This week some 15,000 Somalis took to the streets to express sympathy for our losses, to thank us for our effort. Most Somalis are not hostile to us, but grateful, and they want to use this opportunity to rebuild their country. It is my judgment and that of my military advisers that we may need up to six months to complete these steps and to conduct an orderly withdrawal.

We'll do what we can to complete the mission before then. All American troops will be out of Somalia no later than March 31, [1994,] except for a few hundred support personnel in non-combat roles.

If we take these steps, if we take the time to do the job right, I am convinced we will have lived up to the responsibilities of American leadership in the world, and we will have proved that we are committed to addressing the new problems of a new era. When our troops in Somalia came under fire this last weekend, we witnessed a dramatic example of the heroic ethic of our American military. When the first Blackhawk helicopter was down this weekend, the other American troops didn't retreat, although they could have. Some 90 of them formed a perimeter around the helicopter, and they held that ground under intensely heavy fire. They stayed with their comrades. That's the kind of soldiers they are; that's the kind of people we are.

So let us finish the work we set out to do. Let us demonstrate to the world, as generations of Americans have done before us, that when Americans take on a challenge, they do the job right.

Let me express my thanks, and my gratitude, and my profound sympathy to the families of the young Americans who were killed in Somalia. My message to you is your country is grateful, and so is the rest of the world, and so are the vast majority of the Somali people.

Our mission from this day forward is to increase our strength, do our job, bring our soldiers out and bring them home.

Thank you, and God bless America.

President Clinton's 1994 State of the Union Address

Following is the White House text of President Bill Clinton's State of the Union address, as delivered to a joint session of Congress on Jan. 25, 1994.

Thank you very much. Mr. Speaker, Mr. President, members of the 103rd Congress, my fellow Americans:

I'm not at all sure what speech is in the TelePrompTer tonight—but I hope we can talk about the state of the Union.

I ask you to begin by recalling the memory of the giant who presided over this Chamber with such force and grace. [Former representative] Tip O'Neill liked to call himself "a man of the House." And he surely was that. But, even more, he was a man of the people, a bricklayer's son who helped to build the great American middle class. Tip O'Neill never forgot who he was, where he came from, or who sent him here. Tonight he's smiling down on us for the first time from the Lord's Gallery. But in his honor, may we, too, always remember who we are, where we come from, and who sent us here.

If we do that we will return over and over again to the principle that if we simply give ordinary people equal opportunity, quality education, and a fair shot at the American Dream, they will do extraordinary things.

We gather tonight in a world of changes so profound and rapid that all nations are tested. Our American heritage has always been to master such change, to use it to expand opportunity at home and our leadership abroad. But for too long, and in too many ways, that heritage was abandoned, and our country drifted.

For 30 years, family life in America has been breaking down. For 20 years, the wages of working people have been stagnant or declining. For the 12 years of trickle-down economics, we built a false prosperity on a hollow base as our national debt quadrupled. From 1989 to 1992, we experienced the slowest growth in a half century. For too many families, even when both parents were working, the American Dream has been slipping away.

In 1992, the American people demanded that we change. A year ago I asked all of you to join me in accepting responsibility for the future of our country. Well, we did. We replaced drift and deadlock with renewal and reform. And I want to thank every one of you here who heard the American people, who broke gridlock, who gave them the most successful teamwork between a President and a Congress in 30 years.

This Congress produced a budget that cut the deficit by half a trillion dollars, cut spending and raised income taxes on only the wealthiest Americans. This Congress produced tax relief for millions of low income workers to reward work over welfare. It produced NAFTA [North American Free Trade Agreement]. It produced the Brady bill, now the Brady law. And thank you, Jim Brady, for being here, and God bless you, sir.

This Congress produced tax cuts to reduce the taxes of nine out of 10 small businesses who use the money to invest more and create jobs.

It produced more research and treatment for AIDS, more childhood immunizations, more support for women's health research, more affordable college loans for the middle class; a new national service program for those who want to give something back to their country and their communities for higher education; a dramatic increase in high-tech investments to move us from a defense to a domestic high-tech economy. This Congress produced a new law, the Motor Voter bill, to help millions of people register to vote. It produced Family and Medical Leave.

All passed. All signed into law with not one single veto. These accomplishments were all commitments I made when I sought this office. And, in fairness, they all had to be passed by you in this Congress. But I am persuaded that the real credit belongs to the people who sent us here, who pay our salaries, who hold our feet to the fire.

But what we do here is really beginning to change lives. Let me just give you one example. I will never forget what the Family and Medical Leave law meant to just one father I met early one Sunday morning in the White House.

It was unusual to see a family there touring early Sunday morning, but he had his wife and his three children there, one of them in a wheelchair. I came up, and after we had our picture taken and had a little visit, I was walking off and that man grabbed me by the arm and he said, "Mr. President, let me tell you something. My little girl here is desperately ill. She's probably not going to make it. But because of the Family Leave law, I was able to take time off to spend with her—the most important time I ever spent in my life—without losing my job and hurting the rest of my family. It means more to me than I will ever be able to say. Don't you people up here ever think what you do doesn't make a difference. It does."

Though we are making a difference, our work has just begun. Many Americans still haven't felt the impact of what we've done. The recovery still hasn't touched every community or created enough jobs. Incomes are still stagnant; there's still too much violence and not enough hope in too many places. Abroad, the young democracies we are strongly supporting still face very difficult times and look to us for leadership. And so tonight, let us resolve to continue the journey of renewal; to create more and better jobs; to guarantee health security for all; to reward work over welfare; to promote democracy abroad; and to begin to reclaim our streets from violent crime and drugs and gangs; to renew our own American community.

Last year we began to put our house in order by tackling the budget deficit that was driving us toward bankruptcy. We cut $255 billion in spending, including entitlements, and over 340 separate budget items. We froze domestic spending and used honest budget numbers.

Led by the Vice President, we launched a campaign to reinvent government. We cut staff, cut perks, even trimmed the fleet of federal limousines. After years of leaders whose rhetoric attacked bureaucracy but whose actions expanded it, we will actually reduce it by 252,000 people over the next five years. By the time we have finished, the federal bureaucracy will be at its lowest point in 30 years.

Because the deficit was so large and because they benefited from tax cuts in the 1980s, we did ask the wealthiest Americans to pay more to reduce the deficit. So on April 15th, the American people will discover the truth about what we did last year on taxes. Only the top 1—yes, listen—the top 1.2 percent of Americans, as I said all along, will pay higher income tax rates. Let me repeat—only the wealthiest 1.2 percent of Americans will face higher income tax rates and no one else will. And that is the truth.

Of course, there were, as there always are in politics, naysayers who said this plan wouldn't work. But they were wrong. When I became President the experts predicted that next year's deficit would be $300 billion. But because we acted, those same people now say the deficit is going to be under $180 billion—40 percent lower than was previously predicted.

Our economic program has helped to produce the lowest core inflation rate and the lowest interest rates in 20 years. And because those interest rates are down, business investment and equipment is growing at seven times the rate of the previous four years; auto sales are way up; home sales are at a record high. Millions of Americans have refinanced their homes, and our economy has produced 1.6 million private sector jobs in 1993—more than were created in the previous four years combined.

The people who supported this economic plan should be proud of its early results. Proud. But everyone in this chamber should know and acknowledge that there is more to do.

Next month I will send you one of the toughest budgets ever presented to Congress. It will cut spending in more than 300 programs, eliminate 100 domestic programs, and reform the ways in which governments buy goods and services. This year we must again make the hard choices to live within the hard spending ceilings we have set. We must do it. We have proved we can bring the deficit down without choking off recovery, without punishing seniors or the middle class, and without putting our national security at risk. If you will stick with this plan, we will post three consecutive years of declining deficits for the first time since Harry Truman lived in the White House. And once again, the buck stops here.

Our economic plan also bolsters our strength and our credibility around the world. Once we reduced the deficit and put the steel back into our competitive edge, the world echoed with the sound of falling trade barriers. In one year, with NAFTA, with GATT [General Agreement on Tariffs and Trade], with our efforts in Asia and the National Export Strategy, we did more to open world markets to American products than at any time in the last two generations.

That means more jobs and rising living standards for the American people; low deficits; low inflation; low interest rates; low trade barriers and high investments. These are the building blocks of our recovery. But if we want to take full advantage of the opportunities before us in the global economy, you all know we must do more.

As we reduce defense spending, I ask Congress to invest more in the technologies of tomorrow. Defense conversion will keep us strong militarily and create jobs for our people here at home.

As we protect our environment, we must invest in the environmental technologies of the future which will create jobs. This year we will fight for a revitalized Clean Water Act and a Safe Drinking Water Act and a reformed Superfund program. And the Vice President is right—we must also work with the private sector to connect every classroom, every clinic, every library, every hospital in America into a national information superhighway by the year 2000.

Think of it—instant access to information will increase productivity, will help to educate our children. It will provide better medical care. It will create jobs. And I call on the Congress to pass legislation to establish that information superhighway this year.

As we expand opportunity and create jobs, no one can be left out. We must continue to enforce fair lending and fair housing and all civil rights laws, because America will never be complete in its renewal until everyone shares in its bounty.

But we all know, too, we can do all these things—put our economic house in order, expand world trade, target the jobs of the future, guarantee equal opportunity—but if we're honest, we'll all admit that this strategy still cannot work unless we also give our people the education, training and skills they need to seize the opportunities of tomorrow.

We must set tough, world-class academic and occupational standards for all our children and give our teachers and students the tools they need to meet them. Our Goals 2000 proposal will empower individual school districts to experiment with ideas like chartering their schools to be run by private corporations, or having more public school choice—to do whatever they wish to do as long as we measure every school by one high standard: Are our children learning what they need to know to compete and win in the global economy?

Goals 2000 links world-class standards to grass-roots reforms. And I hope Congress will pass it without delay.

Our School to Work Initiative will for the first time link school to the world of work, providing at least one year of apprenticeship beyond high school. After all, most of the people we're counting on to build our economic future won't graduate from college. It's time to stop ignoring them and start empowering them.

We must literally transform our out-dated unemployment system into a new reemployment system. The old unemployment system just sort of kept you going while you waited for your old job to come back. We're got to have a new system to move people into new and better jobs because most of those old jobs just don't come back. And we know that the only way to have real job security in the future, to get a good job with a growing income, is to have real skills and the ability to learn new ones. So we've got to streamline today's patchwork of training programs and make them a source of new skills for our people who lose their jobs.

Reemployment, not unemployment, must become the centerpiece of our economic renewal. I urge you to pass it in this session of Congress.

And just as we must transform our unemployment system, so must we also revolutionize our welfare system. It doesn't work. It defies our values as a nation. If we value work, we can't justify a system that makes welfare more attractive than work if people are worried about losing their health care. If we value responsibility, we can't ignore the $34 billion in child support absent parents ought to be paying to millions of parents who are taking care of their children. If we value strong families, we can't perpetuate a system that actually penalizes those who stay together.

Can you believe that a child who has a child gets more money from the government for leaving home than for staying home with a parent or a grandparent? That's not just bad policy, it's wrong. And we ought to change it.

I worked on this problem for years before I became President, with other governors and with members of Congress of both parties and with the previous administration of another party. I worked on it with people who were on welfare—lots of them. And I want to say something to everybody here who cares about this issue. The people who most want to change this system are the people who are dependent on it. They want to get off welfare. They want to go back to work. They want to do right by their kids.

I once had a hearing when I was a governor and I brought in people on welfare from all over America who had found their way to work. The woman from my state who testified was asked this question: What's the best thing about being off welfare and in a job? And, without blinking an eye, she looked at 40 governors and she said, "When my boy goes to school and they say what does your mother do for a living, he can give an answer." These people want a better system and we ought to give it to them.

Last year we began this. We gave the states more power to innovate because we know that a lot of great ideas come from outside Washington, and many states are already using it. Then this Congress took a dramatic step. Instead of taxing people with modest incomes into poverty, we helped them to work their way out of poverty by dramatically increasing the earned income tax credit. It will lift 15 million working families out of poverty, rewarding work over welfare, making it possible for people to be successful workers and successful parents. Now that's real welfare reform.

But there is more to be done. This spring I will send you a comprehensive welfare reform bill that builds on the Family Support Act of 1988 and restores the basic values of responsibility. We'll say to teenagers, if you have a child out of wedlock, we will no longer give you a check to set up a separate household. We want families to stay together. Say to absent parents who aren't paying their child support, if you're not providing for your children, we'll garnish your wages, suspend your license, track you across state lines, and if necessary, make some of you work off what you owe.

People who bring children into this world cannot and must not walk away from them. But to all those who depend on welfare, we should offer ultimately a simple compact. We'll provide the support, the job training, the child care you need for up to two years. But after that, anyone who can work must—in the private sector, wherever possible; in community services, if necessary. That's the only way we'll ever make welfare what it ought to be—a second chance, not a way of life.

I know it will be difficult to tackle welfare reform in 1994 at the same time we tackle health care. But let me point out, I think it is inevitable and imperative. It is estimated that one million people are on welfare today because it's the only way they can get health care coverage for their children. Those who choose to leave welfare for jobs without health benefits—and many entry level jobs don't have health benefits—find themselves in the incredible position of paying taxes that help to pay for health care coverage for those who made the other choice to stay on welfare. No wonder people leave work and go back to welfare to get health care coverage. We have got to solve the health care problem to have real welfare reform.

So this year, we will make history by reforming the health care system. And I would say to you, all of you, my fellow public servants, this is another issue where the people are way ahead of the politicians. That may not be popular with either party, but it happens to be the truth.

You know, the First Lady has received now almost a million letters from people all across America and from all walks of life. I'd like to share just one of them with you.

Richard Anderson of Reno, Nevada, lost his job and, with it, his health insurance. Two weeks later, his wife, Judy, suffered a cerebral aneurysm. He rushed her to the hospital, where she stayed in intensive care for 21 days.

The Andersons' bills were over $120,000. Although Judy recovered and Richard went back to work, at $8 an hour, the bills were too much for them and they were literally forced into bankruptcy.

"Mrs. Clinton," he wrote to Hillary, "no one in the United States of America should have to lose everything they've worked for all their lives because they were unfortunate enough to become ill."

It was to help the Richard and Judy Andersons of America that the First Lady and so many others have worked so hard and so long on this health care reform issue. We owe them our thanks and our action.

I know there are people here who say there's no health care crisis. Tell it to Richard and Judy Anderson. Tell it to the 58 million Americans who have no coverage at all for some time each year. Tell it to the 81 million Americans with those preexisting conditions—those folks are paying more or they can't get insurance at all, or they can't ever change their jobs because they or someone in their family has one of those preexisting conditions. Tell it to the small businesses burdened by the skyrocketing cost of insurance. Most small businesses cover their employees, and they pay on average 35 percent more in premiums than big businesses or government. Or tell it to the 76 percent of insured Americans, three out of four whose policies have lifetime limits. And that means they can find themselves without any coverage at all just when they need it the most.

So if any of you believe there's no crisis, you tell it to those people—because I can't.

There are some people who literally do not understand the impact of this problem on people's lives. And all you have to do is go out and listen to them. Just go talk to them anywhere in any congressional district in this country. They're Republicans and Democrats and independents—it doesn't have a lick to do with party.

They think we don't get it. And it's time we show them that we do get it. From the day we began, our health care initiative has been designed to strengthen what is good about our health care system: the world's best health care professionals, cutting edge research and wonderful research institutions, Medicare for older Americans. None of this—none of it should be put at risk.

But we're paying more and more money for less and less care. Every year fewer and fewer Americans even get to choose their doctors. Every year doctors and nurses spend more time on paperwork and less time with patients because of the absolute bureaucratic nightmare the present system has become. This system is riddled with inefficiency, with abuse, with fraud, and everybody knows it.

In today's health care system, insurance companies call the shots. They pick whom they cover and how they cover them. They can cut off your benefits when you need your coverage the most. They are in charge.

What does it mean? It means every night millions of well-insured Americans go to bed just an illness, an accident or a pink slip away from having no coverage or financial ruin. It means every morning millions of Americans go to work without any health insurance at all—something the workers in no other advanced country in the world do. It means that every year, more and more hard-working people are told to pick a new doctor because their boss has had to pick a new plan. And countless others turn down better jobs because they know if they take the better job, they will lose their health insurance.

If we just let the health care system continue to drift, our country will have people with less care, fewer choices and higher bills.

Now, our approach protects the quality of care and people's choices. It builds on what works today in the private sector—to expand employer-based coverage, to guarantee private insurance for every American. And I might say, employer-based private insurance for every American was proposed 20 years ago by President Richard Nixon to the United States Congress. It was a good idea then, and it's a better idea today.

Why do we want guaranteed private insurance? Because right now nine out of 10 people who have insurance get it through their employers. And that should continue. And if your employer is providing good benefits at reasonable prices, that should continue, too. That ought to make the Congress and the President feel better.

Our goal is health insurance everybody can depend on—comprehensive benefits that cover preventive care and prescription drugs; health premiums that don't just explode when you get sick or you get older; the power no matter how small your business is to choose dependable insurance at the same competitive rates governments and big business get today; one simple form for people who are sick; and, most of all, the freedom to choose a plan and the right to choose your own doctor.

Our approach protects older Americans. Every plan before the Congress proposes to slow the growth of Medicare. The difference is this: We believe those savings should be used to improve health care for senior citizens. Medicare must be protected, and it should cover prescription drugs, and we should take the first steps in covering long-term care.

To those who would cut Medicare without protecting seniors, I say the solution to today's squeeze on middle-class working people's health care is not to put the squeeze on middle-class retired people's health care. We can do better than that.

When it's all said and done, it's pretty simple to me. Insurance ought to mean what it used to mean—you pay a fair price for security, and when you get sick, health care's always there, no matter what.

Along with the guarantee of health security, we all have to admit, too, there must be more responsibility on the part of all of us in how we use this system. People have to take their kids to get immunized. We should all take advantage of preventive care. We must all work together to stop the violence that explodes our emergency rooms. We have to practice better health habits, and we can't abuse the system. And those who don't have insurance under our approach will get coverage, but they'll have to pay something for it, too. The minority of businesses that provide no insurance at all, and in so doing, shift the cost of the care of their employees to others, should contribute something. People who smoke should pay more for a pack of cigarettes. Everybody can contribute something if we want to solve the health care crisis. There can't be any more something for nothing. It will not be easy but it can be done.

Now, in the coming months I hope very much to work with both Democrats and Republicans to reform a health care system by using the market to bring down costs and to achieve lasting health security. But if you look at history we see that for 60 years this country has tried to reform health care. President Roosevelt tried. President Truman tried. President Nixon tried. President Carter tried. Every time the special interests were powerful enough to defeat them. But not this time.

I know that facing up to these interests will require courage. It will raise critical questions about the way we finance our campaigns and how lobbyists yield their influence. The work of change, frankly, will never get any easier until we limit the influence of well-financed interests who profit from this current system. So I also must now call on you to finish the job both Houses began last year by passing tough and meaningful campaign finance reform and lobby reform legislation this year.

You know, my fellow Americans, this is really a test for all of us. The American people provide those of us in government service with terrific health care benefits at reasonable costs. We have health care that's always there. I think we need to give every hard-working, taxpaying American the same health care security they have already given to us.

I want to make this very clear. I am open, as I have said repeatedly, to the best ideas of concerned members of both parties. I have no special brief for any specific approach, even in our own bill, except this: If you send me legislation that does not guarantee every American private health insurance that can never be taken away, you will force me to take this pen, veto the legislation, and we'll come right back here and start all over again.

But I don't think that's going to happen. I think we're ready to act now. I believe that you're ready to act now. And if you're ready to guarantee every American the same health care that you have, health care that can never be taken away, now—not next year or the year after—now is the time to stand with the people who sent us here. Now.

As we take these steps together to renew our strength at home, we cannot turn away from our obligation to renew our leadership abroad. This is a promising moment. Because of the agreements we have reached this year, last year, Russia's strategic nuclear missiles soon will no longer be pointed at the United States, nor will we point ours at them. Instead of building weapons in space, Russian scientists will help us to build the international space station.

Of course, there are still dangers in the world—rampant arms proliferation, bitter regional conflicts, ethnic and nationalist tensions in many new democracies, severe environmental degradation the world over, and fanatics who seek to cripple the world's cities with terror. As the world's greatest power, we must, therefore, maintain our defenses and our responsibilities.

This year, we secured indictments against terrorists and sanctions against those who harbor them. We worked to promote environmentally sustainable economic growth. We achieved agreements with Ukraine, with Belarus, with Kazakhstan to eliminate completely their nuclear arsenal. We are working to achieve a Korean Peninsula free of nuclear weapons. We will seek early ratification of a treaty to ban chemical weapons worldwide. And earlier today, we joined with over 30 nations to begin negotiations on a comprehensive ban to stop all nuclear testing.

But nothing, nothing is more important to our security than our nation's armed forces. We honor their contributions, including those who are carrying out the longest humanitarian air lift in history in Bosnia; those who will complete their mission in Somalia this year and their brave comrades who gave their lives there.

Our forces are the finest military our nation has ever had. And I have pledged that as long as I am President, they will remain the best equipped, the best trained and the best prepared fighting force on the face of the Earth.

Last year I proposed a defense plan that maintains our post-Cold War security at a lower cost. This year many people urged me to cut our defense spending further to pay for other government programs. I said no. The budget I send to Congress draws the line against further defense cuts. It protects the readiness and quality of our forces.

Ultimately, the best strategy is to do that. We must not cut defense further. I hope the Congress without regard to party will support that position.

Ultimately, the best strategy to ensure our security and to build a durable peace is to support the advance of democracy elsewhere. Democracies don't attack each other, they make better trading partners and partners in diplomacy. That is why we have supported, you and I, the democratic reformers in Russia and in the other states of the former Soviet bloc. I applaud the bipartisan support this Congress provided last year for our initiatives to help Russia, Ukraine, and the other states through their epic transformations.

Our support of reform must combine patience for the enormity of the task and vigilance for our fundamental interest and values. We will continue to urge Russia and the other states to press ahead with economic reforms. And we will seek to cooperate with Russia to solve regional problems, while insisting that if Russian troops operate in neighboring states, they do so only when those states agree to their presence and in strict accord with international standards.

But we must also remember as these nations chart their own futures—and they must chart their own futures—how much more secure and more prosperous our own people will be if democratic and market reform succeed all across the former communist bloc. Our policy has been to support that move and that has been the policy of the Congress. We should continue it.

That is why I went to Europe earlier this month—to work with our European partners, to help to integrate all the former communist countries into a Europe that has a possibility of becoming unified for the first time in its entire history—its entire history—based on the simple commitments of all nations in Europe to democracy, to free markets and to respect for existing borders.

With our allies we have created a Partnership For Peace that invites states from the former Soviet bloc and other non-NATO members to work with NATO in military cooperation. When I met with Central Europe's leaders, including Lech Walesa and Vaclav Havel, men who put their lives on the line for freedom, I told them that the security of their region is important to our country's security.

This year we must also do more to support democratic renewal and human rights and sustainable development all around the world. We will ask Congress to ratify the new GATT accord. We will continue standing by South Africa as it works its way through its bold and hopeful and difficult transition to democracy. We will convene a summit of the Western Hemisphere's leaders from Canada to the tip of South America. And we will continue to press for the restoration of true democracy in Haiti.

And as we build a more constructive relationship with China, we must continue to insist on clear signs of improvement in that nation's human rights record.

We will also work for new progress toward the Middle East peace. Last year the world watched Yitzhak Rabin and Yasir Arafat at the White House when they had their historic handshake of reconciliation. But there is a long, hard road ahead. And on that road I am determined that I and our administration will do all we can to achieve a comprehensive and lasting peace for all the peoples of the region.

Now, there are some in our country who argue that with the Cold War over, America should turn its back on the rest of the world. Many around the world were afraid we would do just that. But I took this office on a pledge that had no partisan tinge to keep our nation secure by remaining engaged in the rest of the world. And this year, because of our work together—enacting NAFTA, keeping our military strong and prepared, supporting democracy abroad—we have reaffirmed America's leadership, America's engagement. And as a result, the American people are more secure than they were before.

But while Americans are more secure from threats abroad, I think we all know that in many ways we are less secure from threats here at home. Every day the national peace is shattered by crime. In Petaluma, California, an innocent slumber party gives way to agonizing tragedy for the family of Polly Klaas. An ordinary train ride on Long Island ends in a hail of 9-millimeter rounds. A tourist in Florida is nearly burned alive by bigots simply because he is black. Right here in our Nation's Capital, a brave young man named Jason White, a policeman, the son and grandson of policemen, is ruthlessly gunned down. Violent crime and the fear it provokes are crippling our society, limiting personal freedom and fraying the ties that bind us.

The crime bill before Congress gives you a chance to do something about it—a chance to be tough and smart. What does that mean? Let me begin by saying, I care a lot about this issue. Many years ago, when I started out in public life, I was the attorney general of my state. I served as a governor for a dozen years; I know what it's like to sign laws increasing penalties, to build more prison cells, to carry out the death penalty. I understand this issue. And it is not a simple thing.

First, we must recognize that most violent crimes are committed by a small percentage of criminals who too often break the laws even when they are on parole. Now those who commit crimes should be punished. And those who commit repeated, violent crimes should be told, when you commit a third violent crime, you will be put away, and put away for good. Three strikes, and you are out.

Second, we must take serious steps to reduce violence and prevent crime, beginning with more police officers and more community policing. We know right now that police who work the streets, know the folks, have the respect of the neighborhood kids, focus on high crime areas—we know that they are more likely to prevent crime as well as catch criminals. Look at the experience of Houston, where the crime rate dropped 17 percent in one year when that approach was taken.

Here tonight is one of those community policemen—a brave, young detective, Kevin Jett, whose beat is eight square blocks in one of the toughest neighborhoods in New York. Every day he restores some sanity and safety and a sense of values and connections to the people whose lives he protects. I'd like to ask him to stand up and be recognized tonight. Thank you, sir.

You will be given a chance to give the children of this country, the law-abiding working people of this country—and don't forget, in the toughest neighborhoods in this country, in the highest crime neighborhoods in this country, the vast majority of people get up every day and obey the law, pay their taxes, do their best to raise their kids. They deserve people like Kevin Jett. And you're going to be given a chance to give the American people another 100,000 of them well trained. And I urge you to do it.

You have before you crime legislation which also establishes a police corps to encourage young people to get an education and pay it off by serving as police officers; which encourages retiring military personnel to move into police forces, an inordinate resource for our country—one which has a safe schools provision which will give our young people the chance to walk to school in safety and to be in school in safety instead of dodging bullets. These are important things.

The third thing we have to do is to build on the Brady Bill—the Brady Law. To take further steps to keep guns out of the hands of criminals.

I want to say something about this issue. Hunters must always be free to hunt. Law-abiding adults should always be free to own guns to protect their homes. I respect that part of our culture. I grew up in it. But I want to ask the sportsmen and others who lawfully own guns to join us in this campaign to reduce gun violence. I say to you, I know

you didn't create this problem, but we need your help to solve it. There is no sporting purpose on Earth that should stop the United States Congress from banishing assault weapons that out-gun police and cut down children.

Fourth, we must remember that drugs are a factor in an enormous percentage of crimes. Recent studies indicate, sadly, that drug use is on the rise again among our young people. The crime bill contains—all the crime bills contain—more money for drug treatment for criminal addicts, and boot camps for youthful offenders that include incentives to get off drugs and to stay off drugs.

Our administration's budget with all its cuts can paint a large increase in funding for drug treatment and drug education. You must pass them both. We need them desperately.

My fellow Americans, the problem of violence is an American problem. It has no partisan or philosophical element. Therefore, I urge you to find ways as quickly as possible to set aside partisan differences and pass a strong, smart, tough crime bill. But further, I urge you to consider this: As you demand tougher penalties for those who choose violence, let us also remember how we came to this sad point.

In our toughest neighborhoods, on our meanest streets, in our poorest rural areas, we have seen a stunning and simultaneous breakdown of community, family and work—the heart and soul of civilized society. This has created a vast vacuum which has been filled by violence and drugs and gangs. So I ask you to remember that even as we say no to crime, we must give people—especially our young people—something to say yes to.

Many of our initiatives—from job training to welfare reform to health care to national service—will help to rebuild distressed communities, to strengthen families, to provide work. But more needs to be done. That's what our community empowerment agenda is all about—challenging businesses to provide more investment through empowerment zones; ensuring banks will make loans in the same communities their deposits come from; passing legislation to unleash the power of capital through community development banks to create jobs—opportunity and hope where they're needed most.

I think you know that to really solve this problem we'll all have to put our heads together, leave our ideological armor aside and find some new ideas to do even more. And let's be honest; we all know something else too: Our problems go way beyond the reach of government. They're rooted in the loss of values, in the disappearance of work and the breakdown of our families and our communities.

My fellow Americans, we can cut the deficit, create jobs, promote democracy around the world, pass welfare reform and health care, pass the toughest crime bill in history, but still leave too many of our people behind.

The American people have got to want to change from within if we're going to bring back work and family and community. We cannot renew our country when within a decade more than half of the children will be born into families where there has been no marriage. We cannot renew this country when 13-year-old boys get semi-automatic weapons to shoot 9-year-olds for kicks. We can't renew our country when children are having children and the fathers walk away as if the kids don't amount to anything. We can't renew the country when our businesses eagerly look for new investments and new customers abroad, but ignore those people right here at home who would give anything to have their jobs and would gladly buy their products if they had the money to do it.

We can't renew our country unless more of us—I mean all of us—are willing to join the churches and the other good citizens—people like the black ministers I've worked with over the years, or the priests and the nuns I met at Our Lady of Help in East Los Angeles, or my good friend, Tony Campolo in Philadelphia—unless we're willing to work with people like that, people who are saving kids, adopting schools, making streets safer—all of us can do that. We can't renew our country until we realize that governments don't raise children, parents do.

Parents who know their children's teachers and turn off the television and help with the homework and teach their kids right from wrong—those kinds of parents can make all the difference. I know, I had one.

I'm telling you, we have got to stop pointing our fingers at these kids who have no future, and reach our hands out to them. Our country needs it, we need it, and they deserve it.

So I say to you tonight, let's give our children a future. Let us take away their guns and give them books. Let us overcome their despair and replace it with hope. Let us, by our example, teach them to obey the law, respect our neighbors, and cherish our values. Let us weave these sturdy threads into a new American community that can once more stand strong against the forces of despair and evil because everybody has a chance to walk into a better tomorrow.

Oh, there will be naysayers who fear that we won't be equal to the challenges of this time. But they misread our history, our heritage, even today's headlines. All those things tell us we can and we will overcome any challenge.

When the earth shook and fires raged in California, when I saw the Mississippi deluge the farmlands of the Midwest in a 500-year flood, when the century's bitterest cold swept from North Dakota to Newport News, it seemed as though the world itself was coming apart at the seams.

But the American people—they just came together. They rose to the occasion, neighbor helping neighbor, strangers risking life and limb to save total strangers—showing the better angels of our nature.

Let us not reserve the better angels only for natural disasters, leaving our deepest and most profound problems to petty political fighting. Let us instead be true to our spirit—facing facts, coming together, bringing hope and moving forward.

Tonight, my fellow Americans, we are summoned to answer a question as old as the republic itself: What is the state of our union? It is growing stronger, but it must be stronger still. With your help and God's help, it will be.

Thank you and God bless America

President Clinton's Fiscal 1995 Budget Message

Following is the Congressional Record *text of President Clinton's fiscal 1995 budget message sent to Congress Feb. 7, 1994.*

To the Congress of the United States:

The Fiscal Year 1995 budget, which I transmit to you with this message, builds on the strong foundation of deficit reduction, economic growth, and jobs that we established together last year. By encouraging private investment—and undertaking public investment to produce more and higher-paying jobs, and to prepare today's workers and our children to hold these jobs—we are renewing the American dream.

The budget continues to reverse the priorities of the past, carrying on in the new direction we embraced last year.

• It keeps deficits on a downward path;

• It continues our program of investment in long-term economic growth, in fighting crime, and in the skills of our children and our workers; and

• It sets the stage for health care reform, which is critical to our economic and fiscal future.

When I took office a year ago, the budget and economic outlook for our country was bleak. Twelve years of borrow-and-spend budget policies and trickle-down economics had put deficits on a rapid upward trajectory, left the economy struggling to emerge from recession, and given middle class taxpayers the sense that their government had abandoned them.

Perhaps most seriously, the enduring American dream—that each generation passes on a better life to its children—was under siege, threatened by policies and attitudes that stressed today at the expense of tomorrow, speculative profits at the expense of long-term growth, and wasteful spending at the expense of our children's future.

A year later, the picture is brighter. The enactment of my budget plan in 1993, embodying the commitment we have made to invest in our future, has contributed to a strengthening economic recovery, a clear downward trend in budget deficits, and the beginnings of a renewed confidence among our people. We have ended drift and broken the gridlock of the past. A Congress and a President are finally working together to confront our country's problems.

Serious challenges remain. Not all of our people are participating in the recovery; some regions are lagging behind the rest of the country. Layoffs continue as a result of the restructuring taking place in American business and the end of the Cold War.

Rising health care costs remain a major threat to our families and businesses, to the economy, and to our progress on budget deficits. Our welfare system must be transformed to encourage work and responsibility. And our Nation, communities, and families face the ever-increasing threat of crime and violence in our streets, a threat which degrades the quality of life for Americans regardless of their income, regardless of their race, regardless of where they live.

We will confront these challenges this year, by acting on health care reform, welfare reform, and the crime bill now under consideration in the Congress, and by continuing to build on our economic plan, with further progress on deficits, and investments in our people as well as in research, technology, and infrastructure.

WHAT WE INHERITED

When our Administration took office, the budget deficit was high and headed higher—to $302 billion in 1995 and well over $400 billion by the end of the decade.

When our Administration took office, the middle class was feeling the effects of the tax changes of the 1980s, which had radically shifted the Federal tax burden from the wealthy to those less well off. From the late 1970s to 1990, tax rates for the wealthiest Americans had declined, while rates for most other Americans had increased.

When our Administration took office, the economy was still struggling to break out of recession, with few new jobs and continuing high interest rates. In 1992, mortgage rates averaged well over eight percent. Unemployment at the end of 1992 stood at 7.3 percent, and barely a million jobs had been added to the economy in the previous four years. The outlook for the future was slow productivity growth, stagnant wages, and rising inequality—as sagging consumer confidence demonstrated.

A NEW DIRECTION

Today, whether it is the deficit, fairness, or the status of the economy, the situation is much improved.

The budget I am submitting today projects a deficit of $176 billion, a drop of $126 billion from where it would have been without our plan. If the declines we project in the deficits for 1994 and 1995 take place, it will be the first time deficits have declined three years running since Harry Truman occupied the Oval Office.

The disciplines we have put into place are working.

We have frozen discretionary spending. Except in emergencies, we cannot spend an additional dime on any program unless we cut it from another part of the budget. We are reducing low—priority spending to fulfill the promise of deficit reduction as well as to fund limited, targeted investments in our future. Some 340 discretionary programs were cut in 1994, and our new budget cuts a similar number of programs. These are not the kind of cuts where you end up spending more money. These are true cuts, where you actually spend less. Total discretionary spending is lower than the previous year—again, in straight dollar terms, with no allowance for inflation.

As for entitlement spending, the Omnibus Budget Reconciliation Act of 1993 achieved nearly $100 billion in savings from nearly every major entitlement program. Pay-as-you-go rules prevent new entitlement spending that is not paid for, and I have issued an executive order which imposes the first real discipline on unanticipated increases in these programs. For the future, health care reform will address the fastest growing entitlement programs—Medicare and Medicaid—which make up the bulk of spending growth in future budgets, and the Bipartisan Commission on Entitlement Reform, which I have established by executive order, will examine the possibility of additional entitlement savings.

While we have imposed tough disciplines, there is one more needed tool. The modified line-item veto, which would provide Presidents with enhanced rescission authority, has already been adopted by the House as HR1578. If enacted, it will enable Presidents to single out questionable items in appropriations bills and require that they be subject to an up-or-down majority vote in the Congress. I think that makes sense, and it preserves the ability of a majority in Congress to make appropriations decisions.

In addition to budget discipline, we made dramatic changes that restored fairness to the tax code. We made the distribution of the income tax burden far more equitable by raising income tax rates on only the richest 1.2 percent of our people—couples with income over $180,000—and by substantially increasing the Earned Income Tax Credit for 15 million low-income working families. Thus, nearly 99 percent of taxpayers will find out this year that their income tax rates have not been increased.

RESULTS

Finally, the most significant result of our commitment to changing how Washington does business is growing economic confidence. Investment is up—in businesses, in residences, and in consumer durables; real investment in equipment grew seven times as fast in 1993 as over the preceding four years. Mortgage rates are at their lowest level in decades. Nearly two million more Americans are working than were working a year ago, twice as great an increase in one year as was achieved in the previous four years combined; and the rate of unemployment at the end of 1993 was down to 6.4 percent, a drop of nearly a full percentage point.

The fundamentals are solid and strong, and we are building for the future with a steady and sustainable expansion.

THE ECONOMIC PLAN

How did all this happen? Our economic plan had three fundamental components:

Deficit Reduction

First, the introduction and eventual enactment of our $500 billion deficit-reduction plan—the largest in history—brought the deficit down from 4.9 percent of GDP [gross domestic product], where it was in 1992, to a projected 2.5 percent of GDP in 1995 and 2.3 percent of GDP in 1999. This substantially eased pressure on interest rates by reducing the Federal Government's demand for credit and by convincing the markets of our resolve in reducing deficits. Those lower interest rates encouraged businesses to invest, and convinced families to buy new homes and automobiles, along with other durable goods.

Investment

Second, we proposed, and Congress largely provided, a set of fully paid-for measures to encourage private investment (beyond the inducement provided by deficit reduction) and commit public investment to our country's future. The first component was making nine out of ten businesses eligible for tax incentives to invest in future growth—including a major expansion of the expensing allowance for small businesses and a new capital gains incentive for long-term investments in new businesses.

The second component was public investment in the future: in infrastructure, technology, skills, and security. These investments are directed toward preparing today's workers and our children for the new, higher-paying jobs of the modern economy; repairing and expanding our transportation and environment infrastructure; fighting crime; expanding our Nation's technological base; and increasing our health and scientific research.

Among other things, we greatly expanded the very successful Head Start program and WIC nutrition program for pregnant women, infants, and young children; provided a major increase to fulfill the mandate of the Intermodal Surface Transportation Efficiency Act (ISTEA) authorization; provided initial funding for the National Service Act and new funding for educational reforms and other education and training initiatives; began the process of fulfilling my goal of putting another 100,000 police officers on the streets of our cities and towns; and provided additional resources for urban and rural development.

Trade

Finally, our long-term economic strategy depends on the expansion of our international trade markets. In 1993, we did more than at any time in the past two generations to open world markets for American products. The ratification of the North American Free Trade Agreement (NAFTA) establishes the largest market in the world. By lowering tariffs on our exports to Mexico, the agreement is going to increase jobs in this country—and, if previous experience is a guide, they will mostly be high—paying jobs.

We also completed work on the Uruguay Round of the General Agreement on Tariffs and Trade (GATT), a worldwide agreement to reduce tariffs and other trade barriers that will also create high-paying jobs and spur economic growth in this country.

In addition, we established the U.S.-Japan Framework for a New Economic Partnership so that we can work to increase Japanese imports of U.S. goods and services and promote international competitiveness. And to relieve unnecessary burdens on U.S. businesses, we eliminated unneeded export controls on certain technology to encourage exports of U.S. high-technology products.

THE YEAR AHEAD

In 1994, we will build on the strong foundation we laid in 1993.

Fiscal Discipline

We continue to implement the $500 billion in deficit reduction from last year's reconciliation bill. To achieve the required hard freeze in discretionary spending and make needed investments, we propose new cuts in some 300 specific non-defense programs. That includes the termination of more than 100 programs. Many of these savings will be controversial, but we have little choice if we are going to meet our budget goals.

On the other side of the ledger, this budget contains no new tax increases.

New Investment

The investments in this budget continue to target jobs, education, research, technology, infrastructure, health, and crime.

Investing in People First and foremost, the goal of our economic strategy is to provide more and better paying jobs for our people—both today and in the future—and to educate and train them so that they are prepared to do those jobs.

The budget contains a major workforce security initiative to promote job training and reemployment. In the past, government has provided workers who lost their jobs with temporary unemployment benefits to tide them over, and little else. But in this new era, when the fundamental restructuring of our economy is causing permanent layoffs and the virtual shutdown of entire industries, we need to create a reemployment system.

This budget begins the process of establishing that system, which ultimately will give dislocated workers easier access to retraining, job-search, and other services designed not only to help them through a difficult period but also to prepare them to thrive in productive, new jobs.

We also continue to invest in our most precious resource—our children—with proven, effective programs, as well as with new initiatives to confront the problems of a changing society.

We propose to expand funding for the school-to-work program, which will provide apprenticeship training for high school students who do not plan to attend college. And our budget expands the national service program, which gives our young people an opportunity to serve their communities and earn money towards college.

We provide strong support for the Goals 2000 program, which I hope Congress will enact early this year, to help local school systems reform themselves to educate our children for the 21st century. We must set high standards for all of our children, while providing them with the opportunity they deserve to learn.

We also provide major increases for WIC and for Head Start, which we will seek to improve as well. And we significantly expand and better target the Title I program, which focuses on needy children to make sure they can take full advantage of our educational system.

Investing in Know-How America has always sought to be the world's leader in science and technology. In some arenas in recent years, we have lost that status. But in the remainder of this decade and in the 21st century, we must be sure that the United States is on the cutting edge of research and technology advances.

To that end, the 1995 budget proposes critical investments in the National Institute of Standards and Technology's Advanced Technology Program; NASA's research, space, and technology programs; the National Science Foundation; the information superhighway, on which the Vice President has worked so hard; and energy research and development.

In addition, I am determined to continue assisting the industries and communities which have supported our Nation's defense as we continue the defense downsizing that began in the mid-1980's and accelerated in the early 1990's with the end of the Cold War.

I am proposing significant investments in the Technology Reinvestment Project, which will work with the private sector to encourage the development and application of dual-use technologies. And the budget also includes additional resources for the Office of Economic Adjustment, which provides planning grants to communities as they convert their local economies to profitable peacetime endeavors.

Investing in Physical Capital The Nation's capital infrastructure and the economies of too many urban and rural communities have suffered too long from neglect. Last year, we began to address these shortfalls, and in 1995, we propose to continue these initiatives.

We propose, first, to continue full funding of core highway programs within the ISTEA transportation authorization act, as well as a substantial increase in Mass Transit Capital Grants. To help provide this level of funding, the budget proposes rescission of many highway demonstration projects, which frequently are an inefficient allocation of taxpayers' dollars.

In addition, we propose to continue the restoration of our environmental infrastructure with investments in the technologies of the future under the Clean Water Act and other environmental programs.

Last year, we enacted legislation to establish urban and rural Empowerment Zones. This year, we will designate those zones, as well as enterprise communities, to attract investment to neglected communities and provide the kinds of services needed to support economic development.

In this budget, HUD outlays for housing assistance, services to the homeless, and development aid to distressed communities will increase substantially, with aid to the homeless nearly doubling from the previous year. Both housing aid to families and aid to the homeless will be restructured to support transitions to economic independence.

I also propose to continue our rural development initiative, with grants and loans that represent a 35-percent increase over the previous year. This assistance will provide for improved rural infrastructure and services, such as water treatment facilities and rural health clinics, increase rural employment, further diversify rural economics, and provide rural housing opportunities by expanding assistance to allow low- and moderate-income residents to become homeowners.

Investing in Quality of Life This budget continues our efforts to enhance environmental protection and preserve our natural resources.

We propose both to strengthen the stewardship of these resources and improve environmental regulatory and management programs. We increase state revolving funds for clean water and drinking water, and we propose the establishment of four ecosystem management pilot projects. In addition, we are proposing significant improvements and reforms in the Superfund program, as well as important international environmental initiatives.

HEALTH CARE REFORM

Enactment of health care reform, with its focus on controlling health care costs, is the key to making even greater progress on deficits. Indeed, if the Congress adopts the Health Security Act in 1994, we believe that deficits will fall to 2.1 percent of GDP in fiscal year 1999, the lowest since 1979.

Of course, deficit reduction is only one reason for health care reform. Providing health security to every American, with a package of comprehensive benefits through private health insurance that can never be taken away, is critical not only to long-term budget restraint but also to long-term economic growth, to the productivity of our workers and businesses, and to the health and peace of mind of all Americans.

With some 58 million Americans lacking insurance at some time during the year; with the estimated 81 million Americans with preexisting conditions paying more, unable to get insurance, or not changing jobs for fear of losing their insurance; with the small businesses that cover their workers—and a majority do—burdened by the skyrocketing cost of insurance, which is 35 percent higher for them than it is for big business and government; and with 76 percent of Americans carrying policies that contain lifetime limits, which can leave them without coverage when they need it most—this country is facing a health care crisis. And we must confront it now.

In addition to our health care reform effort, the 1995 budget contains key investments in health care and research. We propose the largest increase ever requested in research funds for the National Institutes of Health [NIH]. This national treasure not only keeps our Nation in the forefront of health research but has demonstrably saved millions of lives and improved the quality of millions more. The additional investment we propose will help NIH with its research in many areas, from AIDS to heart problems, from mental health to breast cancer.

WELFARE REFORM

A major initiative for my Administration has been and will continue to be overhauling our welfare system. We must reward work, we must give people the wherewithal to work, and we must demand responsibility.

Welfare reform has already begun. The first step with the expansion of the Earned Income Tax Credit last year. That expansion rewards work by ensuring that families with a full-time worker will not live in poverty.

The second stage of welfare reform is health care reform. Our current health care system often encourages those on welfare to stay there in order to receive health insurance through Medicaid. When we require that every worker be insured, that disincentive to work will disappear.

The next element of welfare reform is personal responsibility. Our welfare reform plan will include initiatives to prevent teen pregnancy, ensure that parents fulfill their child support obligations, and try to keep people from going on welfare in the first place. We must remember this: governments do not raise children, parents do.

The ultimate goal of our reforms is to have our people rely on work, not on welfare. Our plan will build on the Family Support Act by providing education, training, and job search and placement for those who need it; it will require people who can work to do so within two years, either in the private sector or community service; it will restore the basic social contract of providing opportunity and demanding responsibility in return.

CRIME

Enactment of the crime bill now being considered in the Congress is also essential, and it should happen quickly. We simply cannot tolerate what is happening in the streets of our cities and towns today. Crime and violence, the proliferation of handguns and assault weapons, the fear that millions of Americans feel when they emerge from their homes at night—and even in the daytime—must be confronted head-on.

We need to toughen enforcement, and we need to provide our local governments with the resources they need to take on the epidemic of violent crime. The crime bill will provide substantial resources, enough to fulfill my commitment to put 100,000 additional police on our streets. This budget funds major pieces of the crime bill, and I urge the Congress not only to approve the authorizing legislation but to provide the financial resources to back it up.

DEFENSE AND INTERNATIONAL AFFAIRS

Profound shifts are taking place in America's foreign relations and defense requirements. When we came into office, we faced dramatically changed international conditions and problems, but we inherited foreign and defense policies and institutions still geared, in many ways, to the conditions and needs of the Cold War.

This budget reflects the major changes we are carrying out in the content, direction, and institutions which ensure that our interests are defended abroad. We are committed to remaining engaged in a world inextricably linked by trade and global communications. The nature of that engagement is changing, however.

We remain committed to maintaining the best trained, best equipped and best prepared fighting force in the world. Thanks to our 1993 Bottom-Up Review of defense, this force is being reshaped to meet the new challenges of the post-Cold War era. We can maintain our national security with the forces approved in the Bottom-Up Review, but we must hold the line against further defense cuts, in order to protect fully the readiness and quality of our forces.

We have put our economic competitiveness at the heart of our foreign policy, as we must in a global economy. We are following the success of NAFTA and GATT with further market-opening negotiations and intensified focus on the promotion of U.S. exports. We are paying particular attention to the Asian and Pacific markets, which have the most dynamic growth of any region in the world.

We are dedicated to the enlargement of the community of free market democracies, both as a way of ensuring greater security and as a way of expanding economic opportunity. Our programs for the New Independent States of Europe and Central Asia are the centerpiece of this effort.

We are responding aggressively to the new international security challenges that face us: regional conflicts, the proliferation of weapons of mass destruction, the movement of refugees, and the international flow of illegal narcotics. And we are addressing threats to the global environment and rapid population growth with a program to promote sustainable development.

Finally, we are fundamentally reforming and restructuring our international cooperation programs, giving an entirely new post-Cold War structure to our efforts by rewriting the basic legislation that has guided such programs for more than thirty years.

NATIONAL PERFORMANCE REVIEW

The Vice President's National Performance Review (NPR) has paved the way for major reforms of how our government works, which are essential to making government more efficient and responsible. Last year, we began implementing its recommendations. With this budget, that effort shifts into high gear.

First, this budget implements the reduction by 100,000 of Federal positions required by my Executive Order of last year. Indeed, because of discretionary spending constraints, our proposals actually exceed that total by 18,000. In addition, planning has begun on the further downsizing that will be required to implement the remaining portion of the 252,000-position personnel reduction recommended by the NPR. With this downsizing, we will bring the number of Federal employees to the lowest level in thirty years.

To reach these goals, we need to be able to offer incentive packages to those whose positions will be eliminated. This is one of our highest legislative priorities, and it requires attention now. These "buy-out" packages will minimize the need for more costly reductions in force, are less disruptive since they are voluntary, and save the government money in the long run.

The time also has come for swift passage of procurement reform, another of our highest priorities. Streamlining procurement is essential to meeting our personnel downsizing targets. And overhaul of the current, wasteful system can give us significant savings, as well as improved performance by government suppliers.

Further, this budget contains many of the specific programmatic savings proposed by the NPR. These savings have been used in large part to help us meet the discretionary spending freeze.

With my executive order last year, we also began the process of reforming one of the basic functions of government—the regulatory process. Regulations are often necessary to improve the health, safety, environment, and well-being of the American people. Our goal is a more open, more fair, and more honest process that produces smart regulation: rules that impose the least burden and provide the most cost-effective solutions possible.

Finally, all of our departments and agencies have begun to reform their basic operations, including their financial and other administrative practices.

The goal of the NPR is to make government work better and cost less—and to make it more convenient and responsive to those it serves. That is not something that can be completed in one year, in four, or even eight. But we have a responsibility to begin, and that we have done.

CONCLUSION

These are the priorities I seek to pursue in the coming year. Last year, we succeeded in breaking the gridlock that had gripped Washington for far too long. In contrast to past budgets, which lacked credibility, we made sure to use cautious estimates, and we shot straight with the American people.

The results are evident.

We said we would bring the deficit down, and we did. We said we would revitalize the economy, and we did. We said that we would help the private sector to create jobs, and we did. We said that we would reduce the size of the bureaucracy, and we did.

Last year, my Administration and the Congress worked side by side to move our country forward. Let us extend that record of achievement in 1994.

WILLIAM J. CLINTON
THE WHITE HOUSE
February 7, 1994

President Clinton's Announcement of Haitian Agreement

Following is the text of President Clinton's Sept. 18, 1994, televised address to the nation announcing the agreement with Haitian leaders.

My fellow Americans, I want to announce that the military leaders of Haiti have agreed to step down from power. The dictators have recognized that it is in their best interest and in the best interest of the Haitian people to relinquish power peacefully, rather than to face imminent action by the forces of the multinational coalition we are leading.

Our objective over the last three years has been to make sure that the military dictators leave power and that the democratically-elected government is returned. This agreement guarantees both those objectives. It minimizes the risks for American forces and the forces of the 24 nations of the international coalition. And the agreement maximizes the orderly transfer of power to Haiti's democratically-elected government.

This is a good agreement for the United States and for Haiti. The military leaders will leave. The United States and coalition forces will arrive beginning tomorrow. And they'll do so in conditions that are less dangerous, although still not without risk. It will be much easier to preserve human rights. And there is a real chance of a more orderly and less violent transfer of power.

And to the supporters of President [Jean-Bertrand] Aristide, he will be returned. I ask that all Haitians remember what President Aristide said just a couple of days ago: no vengeance, no violence, no retribution. This is a time for peace. That is what the United States is going, along with our coalition partners, to work for.

As all of you know, at my request, President [Jimmy] Carter, General Colin Powell and Sen. Sam Nunn [D-Ga.] went to Haiti to facilitate the dictators' departure just yesterday. I have been in constant contact with them for the last two days. They have worked tirelessly, almost around the clock. And I want to thank them for undertaking this crucial mission on behalf of all of Americans.

Just as important, I want also to thank the men and women of the United States Armed Forces. It was their presence and their preparations that played a pivotal part in this agreement.

Under the agreement, the dictators have agreed to leave power as soon as the Haitian parliament passes an amnesty law, as called for by the Governors Island Agreement, but in any event, no later than Oct. 15. They've agreed to immediate introduction of troops from the international coalition, beginning, as I said, as early as tomorrow. They have also pledged to cooperate fully with the coalition troops during the peaceful transition of power—something we have wanted very much.

I have directed United States forces to begin deployment into Haiti as a part of the U.N. coalition. And [Lt.] General [Henry H.] Shelton, our Commander, will be there tomorrow. The presence of the 15,000-member multinational force will guarantee that the dictators carry out the terms of the agreement. It is clear from our discussions with the delegation that this agreement only came because of the credible and imminent threat of the multinational force. In fact, it was signed after Haiti received evidence that paratroopers from our 82nd Airborne Division, based at Fort Bragg, N.C., had begun to load up to begin the invasion, which I had ordered to start this evening. Indeed, at the time the agreement was reached, 61 American planes were already in the air.

Because of this agreement, the United States and other coalition troops going to Haiti will now be able to go under much more favorable conditions than they would have faced had the generals not decided to leave power.

But let me emphasize that this mission still has its risks, and we must be prepared for them. Haiti is still a troubled country, and there remain possibilities of violence directed at American troops. But this agreement minimizes those risks and maximizes our chance to protect the human rights of all Haitians, both those who support President Aristide and those who oppose him; and to create an environment in which President Aristide can return, as he said, without violence, without vengeance, without retribution.

Under the terms of United Nations Security [Council] Resolution 940, an international coalition from 25 nations will soon go into Haiti to begin the task of restoring democratic government. President Aristide will return to Haiti when the dictators depart.

On Thursday night I told you that the United States must act here to protect our interest, to stop the brutal atrocities that threaten tens of thousands of Haitians, to secure our borders and preserve stability and promote democracy in our hemisphere, to uphold the reliability of commitments we make to others and the commitments others make to us. This agreement furthers all these goals.

From the beginning I have said that the Haitian dictators must go; tonight I can tell you that they will go. And to our troops tonight who are headed to Haiti under less risky conditions, I am confident you will carry out your mission as you already have, effectively and professionally. We depend upon you to do well tomorrow as you have done so very well today; and in the weeks and days before, when you planned this exercise, prepared for it and then began to carry it out.

To all of you I say, thank you, your nation is proud of you.

Good night, and God bless America.

President Clinton's Comments on Midterm Election Results

Following are excerpts from a press conference by President Bill Clinton at the White House on Nov. 9, 1994.

Ladies and gentlemen, last night and again this morning I spoke with both Republicans and Democrats to congratulate those who won and console those who lost their elections. I also called the leaders of the next Congress, Sen. [Bob] Dole and Congressman [Newt] Gingrich, to tell them after this hard-fought campaign that we are ready to work together to serve all the American people in a nonpartisan manner.

The American people sent us here to rebuild the American Dream, to change the way Washington does business, and to make our country work for ordinary citizens again. We've made a good start by cutting the deficit, by reducing the size of the federal government, by reinventing much of our government to do more with less. We have increased our investment in education and expanded trade, and our economy has created more than five million jobs.

We've also made a serious start in the fight against the terrible plague of crime and violence in this country. I remain committed to completing the work we have done. Still, in the course of this work, there has been too much politics as usual in Washington; too much partisan conflict; too little reform of Congress and the political process. And though we have made progress, not enough people have felt more prosperous and more secure, or believe we were meeting their desires for fundamental change in the role of government in their lives.

With the Democrats in control of both the White House and the Congress, we were held accountable yesterday. And I accept my share of the responsibility in the result of the elections.

When the Republican Party assumes leadership in the House and in the Senate, they will also have a larger responsibility for acting in the best interest of the American people. I reach out to them today, and I ask them to join me in this center of the public debate where the best ideas for the next generation of American progress must come.

Democrats and Republicans have often joined together when it was clearly in the national interest. For example, they have often chosen to put international affairs above politics. I urge them to do so again by passing the GATT [General Agreement on Tariffs and Trade] agreement this year. Our prosperity depends upon it, and there can be no compromise when the national interest and the livelihood of American households are at stake.

Last night the voters not only voted for sweeping changes, they demanded that a more equally divided Congress work more closely together with the president for the interest of all the American people. So I hope that we can do that on GATT, and that by doing so, we will pave the way for further cooperation on welfare reform and on health care reform, on a continued investment in our people's educational opportunities, and the continued strength of our economy.

We must also take more steps to restore the people's faith in our political institutions, and agree that, further, in the best tradition of our own foreign policy, that politics will continue to stop at the water's edge.

To those who believe we must keep moving forward, I want to say again, I will do everything in my power to reach out to the leaders and the members of this new Congress. It must be possible to make it a more effective, more functioning institution. It must be possible for us to give our people a government that is smaller, that is more effective, that reflects both our interests and our values.

But to those who would use this election to turn us back, let me say this: I will do all in my power to keep anyone from jeopardizing this economic recovery, by taking us back to the policies that failed us before. I will still work for those things that make America strong—strong families, better education, safer streets, more high-paying jobs, a more prosperous and peaceful world.

There is too much at stake for our children and our future to do anything else. Well, a lot has changed since yesterday. But what hasn't changed is the reason I was sent here and the reason the members of the Congress will be sent here—to restore the American Dream and to make this country work, this government work, this city work for the interest of ordinary Americans again: That is what the American people expect of as.

Last night, they said they were not satisfied with the progress we had made. They said the Democrats had been in control of the White House and the Congress. They said they were going to make a change, and they did make a change. But they still want the same goal. I pledge today to work with all the members of the Congress, and especially the new Republican leadership, to achieve that goal. If they will work with me, and they have pledged to do so today, then we can make great progress for this country. We should be optimistic and we should work to make that optimism real.

Question: Yesterday not a single Republican incumbent lost in any race for governor, House or Senate while the Democratic Party, your party, suffered its worst losses for decades. Do you view this as a repudiation of you, or is there another common denominator in this election that we're missing?

Clinton: Well, I think that I have some responsibility for it. I'm the President. I am the leader of the efforts that we have made in the last two years. And to whatever extent that we didn't do what the people wanted us to do, or they were not aware of what we had done, I must certainly bear my share of responsibility, and I accept that.

You know, a lot of us haven't had a lot of sleep, and we're going to need a few days to digest all these results. There will be a lot of you doing exit surveys, asking the American people what they meant and said. But what I think they said is, they still don't like what they see when they watch us working here. They still haven't felt the positive results of things that have been done here that they agree with when they hear about them, but they don't feel them. They're still not sure that we understand what they expect the role of government to be.

I think they want a smaller government that gives them better value for their dollar, that reflects both their interest and their values, that is not a burden to them, but empowers them. That's what I have tried to do, but I don't think they believe we're there yet—by a long shot. They want us to do more.

I went back today and read my announcement speech for President, and I said in that speech that the job of government was to create opportunity and then to expect citizens to assume the responsibility to make the most of that opportunity. I think that's about where the American people are. They don't think we've done that yet.

And the only thing I think they knew to do yesterday was to try to make a change in the people who were in control and who had been. I regret that some of the people who lost are people who made this a lot better country and who will always, when the history books are written, get the credit they deserve, with hindsight, for helping to make the American people more secure.

I don't believe the American people were saying we're sorry the deficit has been reduced; we're sorry the size of government has been reduced; and we're sorry you've taken the tough stand on crime; we're sorry you're expanding trade. I don't believe that. I don't think they were disagreeing with a lot of the specifics. I do think they still just don't like it when they watch what we do up here, and they haven't felt the positive impact of what has been done. And since I'm the President, I have to take some responsibility for that.

Question: Would you have survived if you had been on the ballot yesterday?

Clinton: Well, some Democrats did. I like to think I would have because I believe that I would have been a ferocious defender of what we have done, and I hope that I could have characterized what the choices were. But I don't know that, and neither does anybody else.

I think it's important to say that yesterday's election, like every election, was fundamentally about the American people. And they looked at us and they said, we want some more changes, and we're going to try this and see if this works. There is a lot of evidence—I've read it in a lot of your reporting—that the American people believe, a majority of them, and have believed for decades now that divided government may work better than united government. As you know, I disagree with that—why I did my best to make it work the other way.

But they didn't agree, and they're in charge. We all work for them, every one of us. And their will, their voice was heard. We got the message. And now we have to think about it, analyze it, rest up and move on. But this country is facing its problems. And what I think they told us was, look, two years ago we made one change; now we made another change. We want you to keep on moving this country forward, and we want you to accelerate the pace of change in the areas that I mentioned.

I do not believe they voted for reversals of economic policy or the positions on crime. I don't think they voted for a reversal of the Brady Bill or the military assault weapons ban. I don't believe that. So—but I do think they sent us a message, and I tried to hear it. And we're going to work together and do the best we can.

Question: Mr. President, did you mean to say here, sir, that the message the voters sent yesterday was basically an extension of the demand for change they made when you were elected in '92, and that you've been going in the right direction, but perhaps made to go farther and faster with the sense of the same agenda?

Clinton: Well, I think they were saying two things to me—or maybe three. . . .

I think they were saying, look, we just don't like what we see when we watch Washington—and you haven't done much about that. You know, we haven't changed the lobbying reform laws. Congress is still not required to live under the same laws that it imposes on private employers. There's still no line item veto. There's still no campaign finance reform. We don't like it when we look at it. It's too partisan, too interest group oriented—things don't get done, too many people up there playing politics. Democrats are in charge; we're holding you ac-

countable. And we hope you hear this, Mr. President. I think they said that.

The second thing I think they said is, look, you may have done all these things, although we haven't heard much of it—we're not sure we believe it. But even if the deficit is down, the government is smaller, more is being invested in education, the crime bill passed, and the economy is growing—we still feel insecure. We don't feel that our incomes are going up, that our jobs are more stable, that our neighborhoods are safer, that the fabric of American life is growing more civilized and more law-abiding.

Then I think the third thing they were saying—and this maybe gets to the point of your question—is there are things we expect government to do, but we don't think government can solve all the problems. And we don't want the Democrats telling us from Washington that they know what is right about everything. We want the government to be smaller. We want it to be more efficient. We want it to create opportunity, to empower us. And we want it to demand responsibility of people who aren't behaving responsibly.

In short, we want it to reflect our interests and our values. And I think what they were saying is that the Republicans did a good job of defining us as the party of government, and that's not a good place to be. I think that was a clear message that they were sending in the election. . . .

President Clinton's 1995 State of the Union Address

Following is the White House text of President Bill Clinton's State of the Union address, as delivered to a joint session of Congress on Jan. 24, 1995.

Mr. President, Mr. Speaker, members of the 104th Congress, my fellow Americans: Again we are here in the sanctuary of democracy, and once again, our democracy has spoken. So let me begin by congratulating all of you here in the 104th Congress, and congratulating you, Mr. Speaker.

If we agree on nothing else tonight, we must agree that the American people certainly voted for change in 1992 and in 1994. And as I look out at you, I know how some of you must have felt in 1992.

I must say that in both years we didn't hear America singing, we heard America shouting. And now all of us, Republicans and Democrats alike, must say: We hear you. We will work together to earn the jobs you have given us. For we are the keepers of the sacred trust, and we must be faithful to it in this new and very demanding era.

Over 200 years ago, our founders changed the entire course of human history by joining together to create a new country based on a single powerful idea: "We hold these truths to be self-evident, that all men are created equal, endowed by their Creator with certain inalienable rights, and among these are life, liberty and the pursuit of happiness."

It has fallen to every generation since then to preserve that idea—the American idea—and to deepen and expand its meaning to new and different times: To Lincoln and his Congress, to preserve the Union and to end slavery. To Theodore Roosevelt and Woodrow Wilson, to restrain the abuses and excesses of the Industrial Revolution, and to assert our leadership in the world. To Franklin Roosevelt, to fight the failure and pain of the Great Depression, and to win our country's great struggle against fascism. And to all our presidents since, to fight the Cold War.

Especially, I recall two who struggled to fight that Cold War in partnership with congresses where the majority was of a different party. To Harry Truman, who summoned us to unparalleled prosperity at home, and who built the architecture of the Cold War. And to Ronald Reagan, whom we wish well tonight, and who exhorted us to carry on until the twilight struggle against communism was won.

In another time of change and challenge, I had the honor to be the first president to be elected in the post-Cold War era, an era marked by the global economy, the information revolution, unparalleled change and opportunity and insecurity for the American people.

I came to this hallowed chamber two years ago on a mission—to restore the American Dream for all our people and to make sure that we move into the 21st century still the strongest force for freedom and democracy in the entire world. I was determined then to tackle the tough problems too long ignored. In this effort I am frank to say that I have made my mistakes, and I have learned again the importance of humility in all human endeavor. But I am also proud to say tonight that our country is stronger than it was two years ago.

Record numbers—record numbers of Americans are succeeding in the new global economy. We are at peace and we are a force for peace and freedom throughout the world. We have almost six million new jobs since I became president, and we have the lowest combined rate of unemployment and inflation in 25 years. Our businesses are more productive and here we have worked to bring the deficit down, to expand trade, to put more police on our streets, to give our citizens more of the tools they need to get an education and to rebuild their own communities.

But the rising tide is not lifting all boats. While our nation is enjoying peace and prosperity, too many of our people are still working harder and harder, for less and less. While our businesses are restructuring and growing more productive and competitive, too many of our people still can't be sure of having a job next year or even next month. And far more than our material riches are threatened; things far more precious to us—our children, our families, our values.

Our civil life is suffering in America today. Citizens are working together less and shouting at each other more. The common bonds of community which have been the great strength of our country from its very beginning are badly frayed. What are we to do about it?

More than 60 years ago, at the dawn of another new era, President Roosevelt told our nation, "New conditions impose new requirements on government and those who conduct government." And from that simple proposition, he shaped the New Deal, which helped to restore our nation to prosperity and define the relationship between our people and their government for half a century.

That approach worked in its time. But we today, we face a very different time and very different conditions. We are moving from an Industrial Age built on gears and sweat to an Information Age demanding skills and learning and flexibility. Our government, once a champion of national purpose, is now seen by many as simply a captive of narrow interests, putting more burdens on our citizens rather than equipping them to get ahead. The values that used to hold us all together seem to be coming apart.

So tonight, we must forge a new social compact to meet the challenges of this time. As we enter a new era, we need a new set of understandings, not just with government, but even more important, with one another as Americans.

That's what I want to talk with you about tonight. I call it the New Covenant. But it's grounded in a very, very old idea—that all Americans have not just a right, but a solid responsibility to rise as far as their God-given talents and determination can take them; and to give something back to their communities and their country in return. Opportunity and responsibility: They go hand in hand. We can't have

one without the other. And our national community can't hold together without both.

Our New Covenant is a new set of understandings for how we can equip our people to meet the challenges of a new economy, how we can change the way our government works to fit a different time, and, above all, how we can repair the damaged bonds in our society and come together behind our common purpose. We must have dramatic change in our economy, our government and ourselves.

My fellow Americans, without regard to party, let us rise to the occasion. Let us put aside partisanship and pettiness and pride. As we embark on this new course, let us put our country first, remembering that regardless of party label, we are all Americans. And let the final test of everything we do be a simple one: Is it good for the American people?

Let me begin by saying that we cannot ask Americans to be better citizens if we are not better servants. You made a good start by passing that law which applies to Congress all the laws you put on the private sector, and I was proud to sign it yesterday.

But we have a lot more to do before people really trust the way things work around here. Three times as many lobbyists are in the streets and corridors of Washington as were here 20 years ago. The American people look at their capital and they see a city where the well-connected and the well-protected can work the system, but the interests of ordinary citizens are often left out.

As the new Congress opened its doors, lobbyists were still doing business as usual—the gifts, the trips, all the things that people are concerned about haven't stopped. Twice this month you missed opportunities to stop these practices. I know there were other considerations in those votes, but I want to use something that I've heard my Republican friends say from time to time—there doesn't have to be a law for everything. So tonight, I ask you to just stop taking the lobbyists' perks. Just stop.

We don't have to wait for legislation to pass to send a strong signal to the American people that things are really changing. But I also hope you will send me the strongest possible lobby reform bill, and I'll sign that, too.

We should require lobbyists to tell the people for whom they work what they're spending, what they want. We should also curb the role of big money in elections by capping the cost of campaigns and limiting the influence of PACs [political action committees].

And as I have said for three years, we should work to open the airwaves so that they can be an instrument of democracy, not a weapon of destruction by giving free TV time to candidates for public office.

When the last Congress killed political reform last year, it was reported in the press that the lobbyists actually stood in the halls of this sacred building and cheered. This year, let's give the folks at home something to cheer about.

More important, I think we all agree that we have to change the way the government works. Let's make it smaller, less costly and smaller—leaner, not meaner.

I just told the Speaker the equal time doctrine is alive and well.

The New Covenant approach to governing is as different from the old bureaucratic way as the computer is from the manual typewriter. The old way of governing around here protected organized interests. We should look out for the interests of ordinary people. The old way divided us by interest, constituency or class. The New Covenant way should unite us behind a common vision of what's best for our country. The old way dispensed services through large, top-down, inflexible bureaucracies. The New Covenant way should shift these resources and decision-making from bureaucrats to citizens, injecting choice and competition and individual responsibility into national policy.

The old way of governing around here actually seemed to reward failure. The New Covenant way should have built-in incentives to reward success. The old way was centralized here in Washington. The New Covenant way must take hold in the communities all across America. And we should help them to do that.

Our job here is to expand opportunity, not bureaucracy; to empower people to make the most of their own lives; and to enhance our security here at home and abroad. We must not ask government to do what we should do for ourselves. We should rely on government as a partner to help us to do more for ourselves and for each other.

I hope very much that as we debate these specific and exciting matters, we can go beyond the sterile discussion between the illusion that there is somehow a program for every problem on the one hand, and the other illusion that the government is a source of every problem we have. Our job is to get rid of yesterday's government so that our own people can meet today's and tomorrow's needs. And we ought to do it together.

You know, for years before I became president, I heard others say they would cut government and how bad it was. But not much happened. We actually did it. We cut over a quarter of a trillion dollars in spending, more than 300 domestic programs, more than 100,000 positions from the federal bureaucracy in the last two years alone. Based on decisions already made, we will have cut a total of more than a quarter of a million positions from the federal government, making it the smallest it has been since John Kennedy was president, by the time I come here again next year.

Under the leadership of Vice President Gore, our initiatives have already saved taxpayers $63 billion. The age of the $500 hammer and the ashtray you can break on David Letterman is gone. Deadwood programs, like mohair subsidies, are gone. We've streamlined the Agriculture Department by reducing it by more than 1,200 offices. We've slashed the small business loan form from an inch thick to a single page. We've thrown away the government's 10,000-page personnel manual. And the government is working better in important ways: FEMA, the Federal Emergency Management Agency, has gone from being a disaster to helping people in disasters.

You can ask the farmers in the Middle West who fought the flood there or the people in California who have dealt with floods and earthquakes and fires, and they'll tell you that. Government workers, working hand in hand with private business, rebuilt Southern California's fractured freeways in record time and under budget. And because the federal government moved fast, all but one of the 5,600 schools damaged in the earthquake are back in business.

Now, there are a lot of other things that I could talk about. I want to just mention one because it will be discussed here in the next few weeks. University administrators all over the country have told me that they are saving weeks and weeks of bureaucratic time now because of our direct college loan program, which makes college loans cheaper and more affordable, with better repayment terms for students, costs the government less, and cuts out paperwork and bureaucracy for the government and for the universities. We shouldn't cap that program. We should give every college in America the opportunity to be a part of it.

Previous government programs gather dust. The reinventing government report is getting results. And we're not through. There's going to be a second round of reinventing government. We propose to cut $130 billion in spending by shrinking departments, extending our freeze on domestic spending, cutting 60 public housing programs down to three, getting rid of over 100 programs we do not need, like the Interstate Commerce Commission and the Helium Reserve Program. And we're working on getting rid of unnecessary regulations and making them more sensible. The programs and regulations that have outlived their usefulness should go. We have to cut yesterday's government to help solve tomorrow's problems.

And we need to get government closer to the people it's meant to serve. We need to help move programs down to the point where states and communities and private citizens in the private sector can do a better job. If they can do it, we ought to let them do it. We should get out of the way and let them do what they can do better.

Taking power away from federal bureaucracies and giving it back to communities and individuals is something everyone should be able to be for. It's time for Congress to stop passing on to the states the cost of decisions we make here in Washington.

I know there are still serious differences over the details of the unfunded mandates legislation, but I want to work with you to make sure we pass a reasonable bill which will protect the national interests and give justified relief where we need to give it.

For years, Congress concealed in the budget scores of pet spending projects. Last year was no different. There was a $1 million to study stress in plants, and $12 million for a tick removal program that didn't work. It's hard to remove ticks; those of us who have had them know. But, I'll tell you something; if you'll give me the line-item veto, I'll remove some of that unnecessary spending.

But I think we should all remember, and almost all of us would agree, that government still has important responsibilities. Our young people—we should think of this when we cut—our young people hold our future in their hands. We still owe a debt to our veterans. And our senior citizens have made us what we are.

Now, my budget cuts a lot. But it protects education, veterans, Social Security and Medicare—and I hope you will do the same thing. You should, and I hope you will.

And when we give more flexibility to the states, let us remember that there are certain fundamental national needs that should be addressed in every state, north and south, east and west—immunization against childhood disease—school lunches in all our schools—Head Start, medical care and nutrition for pregnant women and infants—medical care and nutrition for pregnant women and infants. All these things—all these things are in the national interest.

I applaud your desire to get rid of costly and unnecessary regulations. But when we deregulate, let's remember what national action in the national interest has given us: safer foods for our families, safer toys for our children, safer nursing homes for our parents, safer cars and highways, and safer workplaces, clean air and cleaner water. Do we need common sense and fairness in our regulations? You bet we do. But we can have common sense and still provide for safe drinking water. We can have fairness and still clean up toxic dumps, and we ought to do it.

Should we cut the deficit more? Well, of course, we should. Of course, we should. But we can bring it down in a way that still protects our economic recovery and does not unduly punish people who should not be punished, but instead should be helped.

I know many of you in this chamber support the balanced budget amendment. I certainly want to balance the budget. Our administration has done more to bring the budget down and to save money than any in a very, very long time. If you believe passing this amendment is the right thing to do, then you have to be straight with the American people. They have a right to know what you're going to cut—and how it's going to affect them.

We should be doing things in the open around here. For example, everybody ought to know if this proposal is going to endanger Social Security. I would oppose that, and I think most Americans would.

Nothing is done more to undermine our sense of common responsibility than our failed welfare system. This is one of the problems we have to face here in Washington in our New Covenant. It rewards welfare over work. It undermines family values. It lets millions of parents get away without paying their child support. It keeps a minority, but a significant minority of the people on welfare trapped on it for a very long time.

I worked on this problem for a long time, nearly 15 years now. As a governor I had the honor of working with the Reagan administration to write the last welfare reform bill back in 1988. In the last two years we made a good start in continuing the work of welfare reform. Our administration gave two dozen states the right to slash through federal rules and regulations to reform their own welfare systems, and to try to promote work and responsibility over welfare and dependency.

Last year I introduced the most sweeping welfare reform plan ever presented by an administration. We have to make welfare what it was meant to be—a second chance, not a way of life. We have to help those on welfare move to work as quickly as possible, to provide child care and teach them skills if that's what they need for up to two years. And after that, there ought to be a simple hard rule: anyone who can work must go to work. If a parent isn't paying child support, they should be forced to pay. We should suspend drivers' licenses, track them across state lines, make them work off what they owe. That is what we should do. Governments do not raise children, people do. And the parents must take responsibility for the children they bring into this world.

I want to work with you, with all of you, to pass welfare reform. But our goal must be to liberate people and lift them up, from dependence to independence, from welfare to work, from mere childbearing to responsible parenting. Our goal should not be to punish them because they happen to be poor.

We should—we should require work and mutual responsibility. But we shouldn't cut people off just because they're poor, they're young, or even because they're unmarried. We should promote responsibility by requiring young mothers to live at home with their parents or in other supervised settings, by requiring them to finish school. But we shouldn't put them and their children out on the street.

And I know all the arguments, pro and con, and I have read and thought about this for a long time. I still don't think we can in good conscious punish poor children for the mistakes of their parents. My fellow Americans, every single survey shows that all the American people care about this without regard to party or race or region. So let this be the year we end welfare as we know it. But also let this be the year that we are all able to stop using this issue to divide America.

No one is more eager to end welfare—I may be the only president who has actually had the opportunity to sit in a welfare office, who's actually spent hours and hours talking to people on welfare. And I am telling you, people who are trapped on it know it doesn't work. They also want to get off. So we can promote together education and work and good parenting. I have no problem with punishing bad behavior or the refusal to be a worker or a student, or a responsible parent. I just don't want to punish poverty and past mistakes. All of us have made our mistakes, and none of us can change our yesterdays. But every one of us can change our tomorrows.

And America's best example of that may be Lynn Woolsey, who worked her way off welfare to become a congresswoman from the state of California.

I know the members of this Congress are concerned about crime, as are all the citizens of our country. And I remind you that last year, we passed a very tough crime bill—longer sentences, three strikes and you're out, almost 60 new capital punishment offenses, more prisons, more prevention, 100,000 more police. And we paid for it all by reducing the size of the federal bureaucracy and giving the money back to local communities to lower the crime rate.

There may be other things we can do to be tougher on crime, to be smarter with crime, to help to lower that rate first. Well, if there are, let's talk about them and let's do them. But let's not go back on the things that we did last year that we know work; that we know work because the local law enforcement officers tell us that we did the right things, because local community leaders who have worked for years and years to lower the crime rate tell us that they work.

Let's look at the experience of our cities and our rural areas where the crime rate has gone down and ask the people who did it how they did it. And if what we did last year supports the decline in the crime rate—and I am convinced that it does—let us not go back on it. Let's stick with it, implement it. We've got four more hard years of work to do to do that.

I don't want to destroy the good atmosphere in the room or in the country tonight, but I have to mention one issue that divided this body greatly last year. The last Congress also passed the Brady Bill and, in the crime bill, the ban on 19 assault weapons. I don't think it's a secret to anybody in this room that several members of the last Congress who voted for that aren't here tonight because they voted for it. And I know, therefore, that some of you who are here because they voted for it are under enormous pressure to repeal it. I just have to tell you how I feel about it.

The members of Congress who voted for that bill and I would never do anything to infringe on the right to keep and bear arms to hunt and to engage in other appropriate sporting activities. I've done it since I was a boy, and I'm going to keep right on doing it until I can't do it anymore. But a lot of people laid down their seats in Congress so that police officers and kids wouldn't have to lay down their lives under a hail of assault weapon attack—and I will not let that be repealed. I will not let it be repealed.

I'd like to talk about a couple of other issues we have to deal with. I want us to cut more spending, but I hope we won't cut government programs that help to prepare us for the new economy, promote responsibility and are organized from the grass roots up, not by federal bureaucracy. The very best example of this is the National Service Corps—AmeriCorps.

It passed with strong bipartisan support. And now there are 20,000 Americans, more than ever served in one year in the Peace Corps, working all over this country, helping people person to person in local, grass-roots volunteer groups, solving problems and, in the process, earning some money for their education. This is citizenship at its best. It's good for the AmeriCorps members, but it's good for the rest of us, too. It's the essence of the New Covenant, and we shouldn't stop it.

All Americans, not only in the states most heavily affected, but in every place in this country, are rightly disturbed by the large numbers of illegal aliens entering our country. The jobs they hold might otherwise be held by citizens or legal immigrants. The public services they use impose burdens on our taxpayers. That's why our administration has moved aggressively to secure our borders more by hiring a record number of new border guards, by deporting twice as many criminal aliens as ever before, by cracking down on illegal hiring, by barring welfare benefits to illegal aliens.

In the budget I will present to you we will try to do more to speed the deportation of illegal aliens who are arrested for crimes, to better identify illegal aliens in the workplace as recommended by the commission headed by former Congresswoman Barbara Jordan.

We are a nation of immigrants. But we are also a nation of laws. It is wrong and ultimately self-defeating for a nation of immigrants to permit the kind of abuse of our immigration laws we have seen in recent years, and we must do more to stop it.

The most important job of our government in this new era is to empower the American people to succeed in the global economy. America has always been a land of opportunity, a land where, if you work hard, you can get ahead. We've become a great middle class country. Middle class values sustain us. We must expand that middle class, and shrink the underclass, even as we do everything we can to support the millions of Americans who are already successful in the new economy.

America is once again the world's strongest economic power, almost six million new jobs in the last two years, exports booming, inflation down, high-wage jobs are coming back. A record number of American entrepreneurs are living the American Dream. If we want it to stay that way, those who work and lift our nation must have more of its benefits.

Today, too many of those people are being left out. They're working harder for less. They have less security, less income, less certainty that they can even afford a vacation, much less college for their kids or retirement for themselves. We cannot let this continue.

If we don't act, our economy will probably keep doing what it's been doing since about 1978, when the income growth began to go to those at the very top of our economic scale and the people in the vast middle got very little growth, and people who worked like crazy but were on the bottom then fell even further and further behind in the years afterward—no matter how hard they worked.

We've got to have a government that can be a real partner in making this new economy work for all of our people; a government that helps each and every one of us to get an education, and to have the opportunity to renew our skills. That's why we worked so hard to increase educational opportunities in the last two years—from Head Start to public schools, to apprenticeships for young people who don't go to college, to making college loans more available and more affordable. That's the first thing we have to do. We've got to do something to empower people to improve their skills.

The second thing we ought to do is to help people raise their incomes immediately by lowering their taxes. We took the first step in 1993 with a working family tax cut for 15 million families with incomes under $27,000; a tax cut that this year will average about $1,000 a family. And we also gave tax reductions to most small and new businesses.

Before we could do more than that, we first had to bring down the deficit we inherited, and we had to get economic growth up. Now we've done both. And now we can cut taxes in a more comprehensive way. But tax cuts should reinforce and promote our first obligation—to empower our citizens through education and training to make the most of their own lives.

The spotlight should shine on those who make the right choices for themselves, their families and their communities. I have proposed the Middle Class Bill of Rights, which should properly be called the Bill of Rights and Responsibilities because its provisions only benefit those who are working to educate and raise their children and to educate themselves. It will, therefore, give needed tax relief and raise incomes in both the short run and the long run in a way that benefits all of us.

There are four provisions. First, a tax deduction for all education and training after high school. If you think about it, we permit businesses to deduct their investment, we permit individuals to deduct interest on their home mortgages, but today an education is even more important to the economic well-being of our whole country than even those things are. We should do everything we can to encourage it. And I hope you will support it.

Second, we ought to cut taxes, $500 for families with children under 13.

Third, we ought to foster more savings and personal responsibility

by permitting people to establish an Individual Retirement Account and withdraw from it tax free for the cost of education, health care, first-time home-buying or the care of a parent.

And fourth, we should pass a G.I. Bill for America's workers. We propose to collapse nearly 70 federal programs and not give the money to the states, but give the money directly to the American people; offer vouchers to them so that they, if they're laid off or if they're working for a very low wage, can get a voucher worth $2,600 a year for up to two years to go to their local community colleges or wherever else they want to get the skills they need to improve their lives. Let's empower people in this way. Move it from the government directly to the workers of America.

Now, any one of us can call for a tax cut, but I won't accept one that explodes the deficit or puts our recovery at risk. We ought to pay for our tax cuts fully and honestly.

Just two years ago, it was an open question whether we would find the strength to cut the deficit. Thanks to the courage of the people who were here then, many of whom didn't return, we did cut the deficit. We began to do what others said would not be done. We cut the deficit by over $600 billion, about $10,000 for every family in this country. It's coming down three years in a row for the first time since Mr. Truman was president, and I don't think anybody in America wants us to let it explode again.

In the budget I will send you, the Middle Class Bill of Rights is fully paid for by budget cuts in bureaucracy, cuts in programs, cuts in special interest subsidies. And the spending cuts will more than double the tax cuts. My budget pays for the Middle Class Bill of Rights without any cuts in Medicare. And I will oppose any attempts to pay for tax cuts with Medicare cuts. That's not the right thing to do.

I know that a lot of you have your own ideas about tax relief, and some of them I find quite interesting. I really want to work with all of you. My test for our proposals will be: Will it create jobs and raise incomes? Will it strengthen our families and support our children? Is it paid for? Will it build the middle class and shrink the underclass? If it does, I'll support it. But if it doesn't, I won't.

The goal of building the middle class and shrinking the underclass is also why I believe that you should raise the minimum wage. It rewards work. Two and a half million Americans—2.5 million Americans, often women with children, are working out there today for $4.25 an hour. In terms of real buying power, by next year that minimum wage will be at a 40-year low. That's not my idea of how the new economy ought to work.

Now, I've studied the arguments and the evidence for and against a minimum wage increase. I believe the weight of the evidence is that a modest increase does not cost jobs, and may even lure people back into the job market. But the most important thing is, you can't make a living on $4.25 an hour. Especially if you have children, even with the working families tax cut we passed last year. In the past, the minimum wage has been a bipartisan issue, and I think it should be again. So I want to challenge you to have honest hearings on this; to get together; to find a way to make the minimum wage a living wage.

Members of Congress have been here less than a month, but by the end of the week, 28 days into the new year, every member of Congress will have earned as much in congressional salary as a minimum wage worker makes all year long.

Everybody else here, including the President, has something else that too many Americans do without, and that's health care. Now, last year, we almost came to blows over health care. But we didn't do anything. And the cold, hard fact is that, since last year, since I was here, another 1.1 million Americans in working families have lost their health care. And the cold, hard fact is that many millions more, most of them farmers and small businesspeople and self-employed people, have seen their premiums skyrocket, their co-pays and deductibles go up. There's a whole bunch of people in this country that, in the statistics have health insurance, but really what they've got is a piece of paper that says they won't lose their home if they get sick.

Now, I still believe our country has got to move toward providing health security for every American family. But I know that last year, as the evidence indicates, we bit off more than we could chew. So I'm asking you that we work together. Let's do it step by step. Let's do whatever we have to do to get something done. Let's at least pass meaningful insurance reform so that no American risks losing coverage for facing skyrocketing prices. That nobody loses their coverage because they face high prices or unavailable insurance, when they change jobs and lose a job, or a family member gets sick.

I want to work together with all of you who have an interest in this—with the Democrats who worked on it last time, with the Republican leaders like Senator Dole who has a longtime commitment to health care reform and made some constructive proposals in this area last year. We ought to make sure that self-employed people in small businesses can buy insurance at more affordable rates through voluntary purchasing pools. We ought to help families provide long-term care for a sick parent or a disabled child. We can work to help workers who lose their jobs at least keep their health insurance coverage for a year while they look for work. And we can find a way—it may take some time, but we can find a way—to make sure that our children have health care.

You know, I think everybody in this room, without regard to party, can be proud of the fact that our country was rated as having the world's most productive economy for the first time in nearly a decade. But we can't be proud of the fact that we're the only wealthy country in the world that has a smaller percentage of the work force and their children with health insurance today than we did 10 years ago, the last time we were the most productive economy in the world. So let's work together on this. It is too important for politics as usual.

Much of what the American people are thinking about tonight is what we've already talked about. A lot of people think that the security concerns of America today are entirely internal to our borders. They relate to the security of our jobs and our homes, and our incomes and our children, our streets, our health and protecting those borders. Now that the Cold War has passed, it's tempting to believe that all the security issues, with the possible exception of trade, reside here at home. But it's not so. Our security still depends upon our continued world leadership for peace and freedom and democracy. We still can't be strong at home unless we're strong abroad.

The financial crisis in Mexico is a case in point. I know it's not popular to say it tonight, but we have to act. Not for the Mexican people, but for the sake of the millions of Americans whose livelihoods are tied to Mexico's well-being. If we want to secure American jobs, preserve American exports, safeguard America's borders, then we must pass the stabilization program and help to put Mexico back on track.

Now let me repeat: it's not a loan, it's not foreign aid, it's not a bail out. We will be given a guarantee like co-signing a note with good collateral that will cover our risks. This legislation is the right thing for America. That's why the bipartisan leadership has supported it. And I hope you in Congress will pass it quickly. It is in our interest, and we can explain it to the American people, because we're going to do it in the right way.

You know, tonight, this is the first State of the Union address ever delivered since the beginning of the Cold War when not a single Russian missile is pointed at the children of America. And along with the Russians, we're on the way to destroying the missiles and the bombers that carry 9,000 nuclear warheads. We've come so far so fast in this post-Cold War world that it's easy to take the decline of the nuclear threat for granted. But it's still there, and we aren't finished yet.

This year I'll ask the Senate to approve START II, to eliminate weapons that carry 5,000 more warheads. The United States will lead the charge to extend indefinitely the nuclear Nonproliferation Treaty; to enact a comprehensive nuclear test ban; and to eliminate chemical weapons. To stop and roll back North Korea's potentially deadly nuclear program, we'll continue to implement the agreement we have reached with that nation. It's smart; it's tough; it's a deal based on continuing inspection with safeguards for our allies and ourselves.

This year I'll submit to Congress comprehensive legislation to strengthen our hand in combating terrorists—whether they strike at home or abroad. As the cowards who bombed the World Trade Center found out, this country will hunt down terrorists and bring them to justice.

Just this week, another horrendous terrorist act in Israel killed 19 and injured scores more. On behalf of the American people and all of you, I send our deepest sympathy to the families of the victims. I know that in the face of such evil, it is hard for the people in the Middle East to go forward. But the terrorists represent the past, not the future. We must and we will pursue a comprehensive peace between Israel and all her neighbors in the Middle East.

Accordingly, last night I signed an executive order that will block the assets in the United States of terrorist organizations that threaten to disrupt the peace process. It prohibits financial transactions with these groups. And tonight I call on our allies and peace-loving nations throughout the world to join us with renewed fervor in a global effort to combat terrorism. We cannot permit the future to be marred by terror and fear and paralysis.

From the day I took the oath of office, I pledged that our nation would maintain the best-equipped, best-trained and best-prepared military on Earth. We have, and they are. They have managed the dramatic downsizing of our forces after the Cold War with remarkable skill and spirit. But to make sure our military is ready for action, and to provide the pay and the quality of life the military and their families deserve, I'm asking the Congress to add $25 billion in defense spending over the next six years.

I have visited many bases at home and around the world, since I became president. Tonight, I repeat that request with renewed conviction. We ask a very great deal of our Armed Forces. Now that they are smaller in number, we ask more of them. They go out more often to more different places and stay longer. They are called to service in many, many ways. And we must give them and their families what the times demand and what they have earned.

Just think about what our troops have done in the last year, showing America at its best—helping to save hundreds of thousands of people in Rwanda, moving with lightning speech to head off another threat to Kuwait, giving freedom and democracy back to the people of Haiti.

We have proudly supported peace and prosperity and freedom from South Africa to Northern Ireland, from Central and Eastern Europe to Asia, from Latin America to the Middle East. All these endeavors are good in those places, but they make our future more confident and more secure.

Well, my fellow Americans, that's my agenda for America's future: Expanding opportunity, not bureaucracy; enhancing security at home and abroad; empowering our people to make the most of their own lives. It's ambitious and achievable, but it's not enough. We even need more than new ideas for changing the world or equipping Americans to compete in the new economy; more than a government that's smaller, smarter and wiser; more than all the changes we can make in government and in the private sector from the outside in.

Our fortunes and our posterity also depend upon our ability to answer some questions from within—from the values and voices that speak to our hearts as well as our heads; voices that tell us we have to do more to accept responsibility for ourselves and our families, for our communities, and, yes, for our fellow citizens. We see our families and our communities all over this country coming apart. And we feel the common ground shifting from under us. The PTA, the town hall meeting, the ball park—it's hard for a lot of overworked parents to find the time and space for those things that strengthen the bonds of trust and cooperation. Too many of our children don't even have parents and grandparents who can give them those experiences that they need to build their own character and their sense of identity.

We all know what while we here in this chamber can make a difference on those things, that the real differences will be made by our fellow citizens—where they work and where they live. And it will be made almost without regard to party. When I used to go to the softball park in Little Rock to watch my daughter's league, and people would come up to me, fathers and mothers, and talk to me, I can honestly say I had no idea whether 90 percent of them were Republicans or Democrats. When I visited the relief centers after the floods in California—Northern California—last week, a woman came up to me and did something that very few of you would do—she hugged me and said, "Mr. President, I'm a Republican, but I'm glad you're here."

Now, why? We can't wait for disasters to act the way we used to act every day. Because as we move into this next century, everybody matters; we don't have a person to waste. And a lot of people are losing a lot of chances to do better. That means that we need a New Covenant for everybody.

For our corporate and business leaders, we're going to work here to keep bringing the deficit down, to expand markets, to support their success in every possible way. But they have an obligation when they're doing well to keep jobs in our communities and give their workers a fair share of the prosperity they generate.

For people in the entertainment industry in this country, we applaud your creativity and your world-wide success, and we support your freedom of expression. But you do have a responsibility to assess the impact of your work and to understand the damage that comes from the incessant, repetitive, mindless violence and irresponsible conduct that permeates our media all the time.

We've got to ask our community leaders and all kinds of organizations to help us stop our most serious social problem: the epidemic of teen pregnancies and births where there is no marriage. I have sent to Congress a plan to targets schools all over this country with anti-pregnancy programs that work. But government can only do so much. Tonight, I call on parents and leaders all across this country to join together in a national campaign against teen pregnancy to make a difference. We can do this, and we must.

And I would like to say a special word to our religious leaders. You know, I'm proud of the fact the United States has more houses of worship per capita than any country in the world. These people who lead our houses of worship can ignite their congregations to carry their faith into action; can reach out to all of our children, to all of the people in distress, to those who have been savaged by the breakdown of all we hold dear. Because so much of what we've done must come from the inside out, and our religious leaders and their congregations can make all the difference. They have a role in the New Covenant as well.

There must be more responsibility for all of our citizens. You know, it takes a lot of people to help all the kids in trouble stay off the streets and in school. It takes a lot of people to build the Habitat for Humanity houses that the Speaker celebrates on his lapel pin. It takes a lot of people to provide the people power for all of the civic organizations in this country that made our communities mean so much to most of us when we were kids. It takes every parent to teach the children the difference between right and wrong and to encourage them to learn and grow; and to say no to the wrong things, but also to believe that they can be whatever they want to be.

I know it's hard when you're working harder for less, when you're under great stress to do these things. A lot of our people don't have the time or the emotional stress they think to do the work of citizenship.

Most of us in politics haven't helped very much. For years, we've mostly treated citizens like they were consumers or spectators, sort of political couch potatoes who were supposed to watch the TV ads, either promise them something for nothing or play on their fears and frustrations. And more and more of our citizens now get most of their information in very negative and aggressive ways that are hardly conducive to honest and open conversations. But the truth is, we have got to stop seeing each other as enemies, just because we have different views.

If you go back to the beginning of this country, the great strength of America, as de Tocqueville pointed out when he came here a long time ago, has always been our ability to associate with people who were different from ourselves and to work together to find common ground. And in this day, everybody has a responsibility to do more of that. We simply cannot wait for a tornado, a fire, or a flood to behave like Americans ought to behave in dealing with one another.

I want to finish up here by pointing out some folks that are up with the First Lady that represent what I'm trying to talk about—citizens. I have no idea what their party affiliation is or who they voted for in the last election. But they represent what we ought to be doing.

Cindy Perry teaches second graders to read in AmeriCorps in rural Kentucky. She gains when she gives. She's a mother of four. She says that her service inspired her to get her high school equivalency last year. She was married when she was a teenager. Stand up, Cindy. She was married when she was a teenager. She had four children, but she had time to serve other people, to get her high school equivalency. And she's going to use her AmeriCorps money to go back to college.

Stephen Bishop is the police chief of Kansas City. He's been a national leader. Stand up. He's been a national leader in using more police in community policing, and he's worked with AmeriCorps to do it. And the crime rate in Kansas City has gone down as a result of what he did.

Corporal Gregory Depestre went to Haiti as part of his adopted country's force to help secure democracy in his native land. And I might add, we must be the only country in the world that could have gone to Haiti and taken Haitian-Americans there who could speak the language and talk to the people. And he was one of them, and we're proud of him.

The next two folks I've had the honor of meeting and getting to know a little bit, the Reverend John and the Reverend Diana Cherry of the AME Zion Church in Temple Hills, Maryland. I'd like to ask them to stand. I want to tell you about them. In the early '80s, they left government service and formed a church in a small living room in a small house. Today that church has 17,000 members. It is one of the three or four biggest churches in the entire United States. It grows by 200 a month. They do it together. And the special focus of their ministry is keeping families together.

Two things they did make a big impression on me. I visited their church once, and I learned they were building a new sanctuary closer to the Washington, D.C., line in a higher crime, higher drug rate area because they thought it was part of their ministry to change the lives of the people who needed them.

The second thing I want to say is, that once Reverend Cherry was at a meeting at the White House with some other religious leaders, and he left early to go back to his church to minister to 150 couples that he had brought back to his church from all over America to convince them to come back together, to save their marriages, and to raise their kids. This is the kind of work that citizens are doing in America. We need more of it, and it ought to be lifted up and supported.

The last person I want to introduce is Jack Lucas from Hattiesburg, Mississippi. Jack, would you stand up? Fifty years ago, in the sands of Iwo Jima, Jack Lucas taught and learned the lessons of citizenship. On February 20, 1945, he and three of his buddies encountered the enemy and two grenades at their feet. Jack Lucas threw himself on both of them. In that moment, he saved the lives of his companions, and miraculously in the next instant, a medic saved his life. He gained a foothold for freedom, and at the age of 17, just a year older than his grandson, who is up there with him today, and his son, who is a West Point graduate and a veteran, at 17, Jack Lucas became the youngest Marine in history and the youngest soldier in this century to win the Congressional Medal of Honor.

All these years later, yesterday, here's what he said about that day: "It didn't matter where you were from or who you were, you relied on one another. You did it for your country."

We all gain when we give, and we reap what we sow. That's at the heart of this New Covenant—responsibility, opportunity and citizenship. More than stale chapters in some remote civics book; they're still the virtue by which we can fulfill ourselves and reach our God-given potential and be like them; and also to fulfill the eternal promise of this country—the enduring dream from that first and most sacred covenant.

I believe every person in this country still believes that we are created equal, and given by our Creator, the right to life, liberty and the pursuit of happiness. This is a very, very great country. And our best days are still to come.

Thank you, and God bless you all.

President Clinton's Fiscal 1996 Budget Message

Following is the Congressional Record *text of President Clinton's fiscal 1996 budget message sent to Congress February 6, 1995.*

To the Congress of the United States:

The 1996 Budget, which I am transmitting to you with this message, builds on the Administration's strong record of economic progress during the past two years and seeks to create a brighter future for all Americans.

When I took office two years ago, the economy was suffering from slow growth, inadequate investment, and very low levels of job creation. We moved quickly and vigorously to address these problems. Working with Congress in 1993, we enacted the largest deficit reduction package in history. We cut Federal spending by $255 billion over five years, cut taxes for 40 million low- and moderate-income Americans, and made 90 percent of small business eligible for tax relief, while increasing income tax rates only on the wealthiest 1.2 percent of Americans. And while we placed a tight "freeze" on overall discretionary spending at 1993 levels, we shifted spending toward investments in human and physical capital that will help secure our future.

As we fought for our budget and economic policies, we moved aggressively to open world markets for American goods and services. We negotiated the North American Free Trade Agreement with Canada and Mexico, concluded negotiations over the Uruguay Round of the General Agreement on Tariffs and Trade, and worked with Congress to enact implementing legislation for both.

Our economic plan helped bring the deficit down from $290 billion in 1992, to $203 billion in 1994, to a projected $193 billion this year—providing three straight years of deficit reduction for the first time since Harry Truman was President. Measured as a percentage of our economy—that is, Gross Domestic Product (GDP)—our plan will cut the deficit in half.

By reassuring the financial markets that we were serious about getting our fiscal house in order, our plan also lowered interest rates while holding inflation in check. That helped to stimulate private investment and exports, and sparked the creation of 5.6 million new jobs—more than twice the number in the previous four years.

Now that we have brought the deficit down, we have no intention of turning back. My budget keeps us on the course of fiscal discipline by proposing $81 billion in additional deficit reduction through the year 2000. I am proposing to save $23 billion by reinventing Cabinet departments and two other major agencies, to save $2 billion by ending more than 130 programs altogether, and to provide better service to Americans by consolidating more than 270 other programs. Under my plan, the deficit will continue to fall as a percentage of GDP to 2.1 percent, reaching its lowest level since 1979.

Despite our strong economic record, however, many Americans have not shared in the fruits of recovery. Though these Americans are working harder and harder, their incomes are either stagnant or falling. The problem is particularly acute among those with less education or fewer of the skills needed to compete in an increasingly global economy. To build a more prosperous America, one with rising living standards for all Americans, we must turn our attention to those who have not benefited from the current recovery.

My budget proposes to do that.

PROMOTING A RISING STANDARD OF LIVING FOR ALL AMERICANS

I am proposing a Middle Class Bill of Rights, which will provide tax relief to middle-income Americans. The Middle Class Bill of Rights includes a $500 per child tax credit for middle-income families with children under 13; expands eligibility for Individual Retirement Accounts and allows families to make penalty-free withdrawals for a range of educational, housing, and medical needs; and offers a tax deduction for the costs of college, university, or vocational education. Also as part of my Middle Class Bill of Rights, I am proposing to revamp our confusing array of job training programs by consolidating some 70 of them. In my G.I. Bill for America's Workers, I propose to offer dislocated and low-income workers "Skill grants" through which they can make their own choices about the training they need to find new and better jobs.

The G.I. Bill for America's Workers is the final element of my effort to improve the education and skills of Americans, enabling them to compete in the economy of today and tomorrow. In the last two years, we enacted Goals 2000 to encourage States and localities to reform their education systems; revamped the student loan program to make post-secondary education affordable to more Americans; and pushed successfully for the School-to-Work program that enables young Americans to move more easily from high school to training or more education.

And I am proposing to pay for this Middle Class Bill of Rights with specific spending cuts. In fact, I am proposing enough spending cuts to provide more than twice as much in budget savings—$144 billion—as the tax cuts will cost—$63 billion—over five years.

CREATING OPPORTUNITY AND ENCOURAGING RESPONSIBILITY

By itself, the Federal Government cannot rebuild America's communities. What it can do is give communities some of the tools and resources to address their problems in their own way. My national service program provides incentives for Americans of all ages to volunteer their services in local communities across the country, and earn money for their own education. The budget proposes to invest more in our urban centers as well as in rural areas, and to continue our efforts to build stronger government-to-government relations with American Indian and Alaska Native Tribes. And I will work with Congress to enact comprehensive welfare reform that embodies the principles of work and responsibility for able-bodied recipients, while protecting their children.

My Administration has worked with State and local law enforcement agencies to help retake the streets from the criminals and drug dealers who, in far too many places, now control them. Congress enacted my crime bill last year, finally answering the cries of Americans after too many years of debate and gridlock. We pushed successfully for the "three strikes and you're out" rule for violent criminals, and we are making significant progress on my promise to put 100,000 more police on the street. Congress also passed the long-overdue Brady Bill, which provides for background checks that will keep guns out of the hands of criminals. In this budget, I am proposing new funds with which States and localities can hire more police, build more space in prisons and boot camps, invest in prevention programs for first-time offenders, and provide drug treatment for many more drug users.

My Administration inherited deep-seated problems with the immigration system, and we have gone a long way toward addressing them. This budget proposes the strongest efforts yet, including funds for over 1,000 new Border Patrol agents, inspectors, and support staff. While working to fulfill the Federal Government's responsibility to secure our borders against illegal immigration, the budget also proposes funds to assist States that are unduly burdened with the health, education, and prison-related costs associated with illegal immigrants.

We must redouble our efforts to protect the environment. My Administration has sought more innovative, effective approaches to do so, and this budget would build upon them. In particular, I am proposing to work more with State and local governments, businesses, and environmental groups on collaborative efforts, while seeking more funds for high-priority programs.

Because investments in science and technology pay off in higher productivity and living standards down the road, I am seeking significant new funding for the Advanced Technology Program at the Commerce Department's National Institute of Standards and Technology, NASA's New Technology Investments, the Defense Department's Technology Reinvestment Project, biomedical research at the National Institutes of Health, and research and development at the National Science Foundation. I am also seeking to strengthen our coordinated efforts through the Administration's National Science and Technology Council and to improve the payment system for federally-sponsored research at colleges and universities.

I remain committed to comprehensive health care reform. The problems that prompted me to send Congress the Health Security Act in November 1993 have not gone away. Health care costs have continued to soar for individuals, businesses, and all levels of government. More Americans are losing their health coverage each year, and many others are staying in jobs only out of fear of losing their own coverage. I am asking Congress to work with me on a bipartisan basis, to take the first steps toward guaranteeing health care coverage to every American while containing costs.

PROJECTING AMERICAN LEADERSHIP AROUND THE WORLD

We have begun the post-Cold War era and welcome one of its most significant fruits—the continuing efforts of Russia and the newly-independent states to move toward democracy and economic freedom. We propose to continue our support for this fundamental change that clearly serves the Nation's long-term interests.

My proposals for international affairs also promote and defend this Nation's vital interests in Central Europe, the Middle East, and Asia. The budget supports the important role we play in fostering our historic peace process in the Middle East.

With the global economy offering the prospect of new markets for American goods, we are redoubling our efforts to promote an open trading system in Asia, as well as in Latin America and the rest of the globe. I am, for instance, proposing increased funding for our trade promotion agencies, such as the Export-Import Bank, which strengthen our trade position. I am also asking for continued support for the bilateral and multilateral assistance to less-developed nations that can prevent humanitarian crises, as well as support for a strong American response to these crises.

Our military strength works in synergy with our foreign policy. Our forces defend our interests, deterring potential adversaries and reassuring our friends. My Defense Funding Initiative, a $25 billion increase in defense spending over the next 6 years, marks the third time that I have raised defense spending above my initial funding plan in order to support and maintain the most capable military force in the world. I am determined to ensure a high level of readiness of U.S. military forces, to continue to improve the pay and quality of life for the men and women who serve, and to ensure that our forces are modernized with new systems that will be available near the end of the century.

MAKING GOVERNMENT WORK

None of our efforts can fully succeed unless we make Government work for all Americans. We have made great progress with the National Performance Review (NPR), which I established early in the Administration and which Vice President Gore has so ably run at my direction.

Specifically, departments and agencies across the Government have made substantial progress on each of the NPR's four themes: putting customers first, empowering employees to get results, cutting red tape, and cutting back to basics. The departments and agencies have established customer service standards and streamlined their operations. They also are working with my Office of Management and Budget to focus more on "performance"—what Federal programs actually accomplish. And they are doing all this while we are cutting the Federal workforce by 272,900 positions, bringing it to its smallest size since John Kennedy was President.

We also greatly improved the Federal regulatory system, opening it up more to public scrutiny. We plan to build upon our efforts, to make sure that we are protecting the public while not unduly burdening any one industry or group. We also overhauled the Federal procurement system, cutting mountains of red tape and enabling the Government to buy high-quality goods and services at lower cost.

Despite such progress, however, we are only beginning our efforts. I recently announced a major restructuring of the Departments of

Housing and Urban Development, Energy, and Transportation, the General Services Administration, and the Office of Personnel Management. The budget contains details of these restructurings and our related proposals that affect hundreds of other programs.

In the coming months, the Vice President will lead Phase II of our crusade to reinvent Government—an effort to identify other agencies and programs to restructure or terminate, to sort out responsibilities among the Federal, State, and local levels of government, and to choose functions better performed by the private sector.

CONCLUSION

Our agenda is working. By cutting the budget deficit, investing in our people, and opening world markets, we have begun to lay the foundation for a strong economy for years to come. And by reinventing the Federal Government, cutting red tape and layers of management, we have begun to make Government more responsive to the American people.

This budget seeks to build upon those efforts. It seeks to spread the benefits of our economic recovery to more Americans and give them the tools to build a brighter future for themselves. It also seeks to continue our reinvention efforts—to eliminate or restructure agencies and programs, and to better sort out responsibilities among the Federal, State, and local levels of government.

These proposals will help us to create a stronger economy and more effective Government. I will ask for Congress's help in these efforts.

WILLIAM J. CLINTON
THE WHITE HOUSE
February 6, 1995

President Clinton's Balanced Budget Proposal

Following is the White House transcript of President Clinton's June 13, 1995, televised address to the nation on his balanced budget proposal.

Good evening. Tonight I present to the American people a plan for a balanced federal budget. My plan cuts spending by $1.1 trillion. It does not raise taxes. It won't be easy, but elected leaders of both parties agree with me that we must do this, and we will.

We're at the edge of a new century, living in a period of rapid and profound change. And we must do everything in our power to help our people build good and decent lives for themselves and their children.

These days, working people can't keep up. No matter how hard they work—one, two, even three jobs—without the education to get good jobs, they can't make it in today's America.

I don't want my daughter's generation to be the first generation of Americans to do worse than their parents. Now, balancing our budget can help to change that, if we do it in a way that reflects our values and what we care about the most—our children, our families and what we leave to generations to come.

That's why my budget had five fundamental priorities. First, because our most important mission is to help people make the most of their own lives, don't cut education.

Second, balance the budget by controlling health care costs, strengthening Medicare and saving Medicaid, not by slashing health services for the elderly.

Third, cut taxes for the middle class and not the wealthy. We shouldn't cut education or Medicare just to make room for a tax cut for people who don't really need it.

Fourth, cut welfare, but save enough to protect children, and move able-bodied people from welfare to work.

Fifth, don't put the brakes on so fast that we risk our economic prosperity.

This can be a turning point for us. For 12 years our government—Congress and the White House—ducked the deficit and pretended we could get something for nothing.

In my first two years as president we turned this around and cut the deficit by one-third. Now, let's eliminate it.

It's time to clean up this mess. Here's how:

First, I propose to cut spending in discretionary areas other than defense by an average of 20 percent, except education. I want to increase education, not cut it. We'll continue to cut waste. Under Vice President [Al] Gore's leadership, we're already cutting hundreds of programs and thousands of regulations and 270,000 federal positions. We'll still be able to protect the environment and invest in technology and medical research for things like breast cancer and AIDS. But make no mistake, in other areas there will be big cuts, and they'll hurt.

Second, we should limit tax cuts to middle-income people, not upper-income people, and target the tax cuts to help Americans pay for college—like we did with the G.I. Bill after World War II. Let's help a whole new generation of Americans go to college. That's the way to make more Americans upper-income people in the future.

Third, don't cut Medicare services to the elderly. Instead of cutting benefits, maintain them by lowering costs. Crack down on fraud and abuse, provide more home care, incentives for managed care, respite benefits for families of Alzheimer's patients, and free mammograms.

For all Americans, I propose the freedom to take your insurance with you when you change jobs; to keep it longer after you lose a job; insurance coverage, even if there are preexisting conditions in your family; and lower-cost insurance for groups of self-employed and small-business people. If we don't have tax cuts for upper-income people, as congressional leaders have proposed, we won't need to make harsh cuts in health care or in education.

Finally, balance the budget in 10 years. It took decades to run up this deficit; it's going to take a decade to wipe it out. Now, mind you, we could do it in seven years, as congressional leaders propose. But the pain we'd inflict on our elderly, our students and our economy just isn't worth it. My plan will cut the deficit year after year. It will balance the budget without hurting our future.

This budget proposal is very different from the two passed by the House and the Senate, and there are fundamental differences between Democrats and Republicans about how to balance the budget. But this debate must go beyond partisanship. It must be about what's good for America, and which approach is more likely to bring prosperity and security to our people over the long run.

We ought to approach it in the same spirit of openness and civility which we felt when the Speaker [Newt Gingrich, R-Ga.] and I talked in New Hampshire last Sunday.

There are those who have suggested that it might actually benefit one side or the other politically if we had gridlock and ended this fiscal year without a budget. But that would be bad for our country, and we have to do everything we can to avoid it. If we'll just do what's best for our children, our future and our nation, and forget about who gets the political advantage, we won't go wrong.

Good night. Let's get to work.

President Clinton's Announcement of Normalizing Relations with Vietnam

Following is the text of President Clinton's announcement July 11, 1995, of the establishment of full diplomatic relations between the United States and Vietnam.

. . . Today I am announcing the normalization of diplomatic relationships with Vietnam.

From the beginning of this administration, any improvement in relationships between America and Vietnam has depended upon making progress on the issue of Americans who were missing in action or held as prisoners of war. Last year, I lifted the trade embargo on Vietnam in response to their cooperation and to enhance our efforts to secure the remains of lost Americans and to determine the fate of those whose remains have not been found.

It has worked. In seventeen months, Hanoi has taken important steps to help us resolve many cases. Twenty-nine families have received the remains of their loved ones and at last have been able to give them a proper burial. Hanoi has delivered to us hundreds of pages of documents shedding light on what happened to Americans in Vietnam. And Hanoi has stepped up its cooperation with Laos, where many Americans were lost.

We have reduced the number of so-called discrepancy cases, in which we have had reason to believe that Americans were still alive after they were lost to 55. And we will continue to work to resolve more cases.

Hundreds of dedicated men and women are working on all these cases, often under extreme hardship and real danger in the mountains and jungles of Indochina. On behalf of all Americans, I want to thank them. And I want to pay a special tribute to General John Vessey, who has worked so tirelessly on this issue for Presidents [Ronald] Reagan and [George] Bush and for our administration. He has made a great difference to a great many families. And we as a nation are grateful for his dedication and for his service. Thank you, sir.

I also want to thank the presidential delegation, led by Deputy Secretary of Veterans Affairs Hershel Gober, Winston Lord, James Wold, who have helped us to make so much progress on this issue. And I am especially grateful to the leaders of the families and the veterans organizations who have worked with the delegation and maintained their extraordinary commitment to finding the answers we seek.

Never before in the history of warfare has such an extensive effort been made to resolve the fate of soldiers who did not return. Let me emphasize, normalization of our relations with Vietnam is not the end of our effort. From the early days of this administration I have said to the families and veterans groups what I say again here: We will keep working until we get all the answers we can. Our strategy is working. Normalization of relations is the next appropriate step. With this new relationship, we will be able to make more progress. To that end, I will send another delegation to Vietnam this year. And Vietnam has pledged it will continue to help us find answers. We will hold them to that pledge.

By helping to bring Vietnam into the community of nations, normalization also serves our interest in working for a free and peaceful Vietnam in a stable and peaceful Asia. We will begin to normalize our trade relations with Vietnam, whose economy is now liberalizing and integrating into the economy of the Asia-Pacific region. Our policy will be to implement the appropriate United States government programs to develop trade with Vietnam consistent with U.S. law.

As you know, many of these programs require certifications regarding human rights and labor rights before they can proceed. We have already begun discussing human rights issues with Vietnam, especially issues regarding religious freedom. Now we can expand and strengthen that dialogue. The Secretary of State will go to Vietnam in August where he will discuss all of these issues, beginning with our POW and MIA concerns.

I believe normalization and increased contact between Americans and Vietnamese will advance the cause of freedom in Vietnam, just as it did in Eastern Europe and the former Soviet Union. I strongly believe that engaging the Vietnamese on the broad economic front of economic reform and the broad front of democratic reform will help to honor the sacrifice of those who fought for freedom's sake in Vietnam.

I am proud to be joined in this view by distinguished veterans of the Vietnam War. They served their country bravely. They are of different parties. A generation ago they had different judgments about the war which divided us so deeply. But today they are of a single mind. They agree that the time has come for America to move forward on Vietnam. All Americans should be grateful especially that Senators John McCain [R-Ariz.], John Kerry [D-Mass.], Bob Kerrey [D-Neb.], Chuck Robb [D-Va.], and Representative Pete Peterson [D-Fla.], along with other Vietnam veterans in the Congress, including Senator [Tom] Harkin [D-Iowa], Congressman [Jim] Kolbe [R-Ariz.], and Congressman [Wayne] Gilchrest [R-Md.], who just left, and others who are out here in the audience have kept up their passionate interest in Vietnam but were able to move beyond the haunting and painful past toward finding common ground for the future. Today, they and many other veterans support the normalization of relations, giving the opportunity to Vietnam to fully join the community of nations and being true to what they fought for so many years ago.

Whatever we may think about the political decisions of the Vietnam era, the brave Americans who fought and died there had noble motives. They fought for the freedom and the independence of the Vietnamese people. Today the Vietnamese are independent, and we believe this step will help to extend the reach of freedom in Vietnam and, in so doing, to enable these fine veterans of Vietnam to keep working for that freedom.

This step will also help our own country to move forward on an issue that has separated Americans from one another for too long now. Let the future be our destination. We have so much work ahead of us. This moment offers us the opportunity to bind up our own wounds. They have resisted time for too long. We can now move on to common ground. Whatever divided us before let us consign to the past. Let this moment, in the words of the Scripture, be a time to heal and a time to build.

Thank you all. And God bless America.

President Clinton's Address on Sending Troops to Bosnia

Following is the text of a televised address to the nation by President Clinton on Nov. 27, 1995, concerning U.S. participation in a NATO peacekeeping mission in Bosnia.

Good evening. Last week, the warring factions in Bosnia reached a peace agreement, as a result of our efforts in Dayton, Ohio, and the support of our European and Russian partners. Tonight, I want to speak with you about implementing the Bosnian peace agreement, and why our values and interests as Americans require that we participate.

Let me say at the outset, America's role will not be about fighting a war. It will be about helping the people of Bosnia to secure their own peace agreement. Our mission will be limited, focused and under the command of an American general.

In fulfilling this mission, we will have the chance to help stop the killing of innocent civilians, especially children; and at the same time, to bring stability to Central Europe, a region of the world that is vital to our national interests. It is the right thing to do.

From our birth, America has always been more than just a place. America has embodied an idea that has become the ideal for billions of people throughout the world. Our founders said it best: America is about life, liberty, and the pursuit of happiness.

In this century especially, America has done more than simply stand for these ideals. We have acted on them and sacrificed for them. Our people fought two world wars so that freedom could triumph over tyranny. After World War I, we pulled back from the world, leaving a vacuum that was filled by the forces of hatred. After World War II, we continued to lead the world. We made the commitments that kept the peace, that helped to spread democracy, that created unparalleled prosperity, and that brought victory in the Cold War.

Today, because of our dedication, America's ideals—liberty, democracy and peace—are more and more the aspirations of people everywhere in the world. It is the power of our ideas, even more than our size, our wealth and our military might, that makes America a uniquely trusted nation.

With the Cold War over, some people now question the need for our continued active leadership in the world. They believe that, much like after World War I, America can now step back from the responsibilities of leadership. They argue that to be secure we need only to keep our own borders safe and that the time has come now to leave to others the hard work of leadership beyond our borders. l strongly disagree.

As the Cold War gives way to the global village, our leadership is needed more than ever because problems that start beyond our borders can quickly become problems within them. We're all vulnerable to the organized forces of intolerance and destruction; terrorism; ethnic, religious and regional rivalries; the spread of organized crime and weapons of mass destruction and drug trafficking. Just as surely as fascism and communism, these forces also threaten freedom and democracy, peace and prosperity. And they, too, demand American leadership.

But nowhere has the argument for our leadership been more clearly justified than in the struggle to stop or prevent war and civil violence. From Iraq to Haiti, from South Africa to Korea, from the Middle East to Northern Ireland, we have stood up for peace and freedom because it's in our interest to do so and because it is the right thing to do.

Now, that doesn't mean we can solve every problem. My duty as President is to match the demands for American leadership to our strategic interest and to our ability to make a difference. America cannot and must not be the world's policeman. We cannot stop all war for all time; but we can stop some wars. We cannot save all women and all children; but we can save many of them. We can't do everything; but we must do what we can.

There are times and places where our leadership can mean the difference between peace and war, and where we can defend our fundamental values as a people and serve our most basic, strategic interests. My fellow Americans, in this new era there are still times when America and America alone can and should make the difference for peace.

The terrible war in Bosnia is such a case. Nowhere today is the need for American leadership more stark or more immediate than in Bosnia. For nearly four years a terrible war has torn Bosnia apart. Horrors we prayed had been banished from Europe forever have been seared into our minds again. Skeletal prisoners caged behind barbed-wire fences; women and girls raped as a tool of war; defenseless men and boys shot down into mass graves, evoking visions of World War II concentration camps; and endless lines of refugees marching toward a future of despair.

When I took office, some were urging immediate intervention in the conflict. I decided that American ground troops should not fight a war in Bosnia because the United States could not force peace on Bosnia's warring ethnic groups, the Serbs, Croats, and Muslims. Instead, America has worked with our European allies in searching for peace, stopping the war from spreading, and easing the suffering of the Bosnian people.

We imposed tough economic sanctions on Serbia. We used our air power to conduct the longest humanitarian airlift in history, and to enforce a no-fly zone that took the war out of the skies. We helped to make peace between two of the three warring parties, the Muslims and the Croats. But as the months of war turned into years, it became clear that Europe alone could not end the conflict.

This summer, Bosnian Serb shelling once again turned Bosnia's playgrounds and marketplaces into killing fields. In response, the United States led NATO's heavy and continuous air strikes, many of them flown by skilled and brave American pilots. Those air strikes, together with the renewed determination of our European partners and the Bosnian and Croat gains on the battlefield convinced the Serbs, finally, to start thinking about making peace.

At the same time, the United States initiated an intensive diplomatic effort that forged a Bosnia-wide cease-fire and got the parties to agree to the basic principles of peace. Three dedicated American diplomats—Bob Frazier, Joe Kruzel and Nelson Drew—lost their lives in that effort. Tonight we remember their sacrifice and that of their families. And we will never forget their exceptional service to our nation.

Finally, just three weeks ago, the Muslims, Croats and Serbs came to Dayton, Ohio, in America's heartland, to negotiate a settlement. There, exhausted by war, they made a commitment to peace. They agreed to put down their guns; to preserve Bosnia as a single state; to investigate and prosecute war criminals; to protect the human rights of all citizens; to try to build a peaceful, democratic future. And they asked for America's help as they implement this peace agreement.

America has a responsibility to answer that request, to help to turn this moment of hope into an enduring reality. To do that, troops from our country and around the world would go into Bosnia to give them the confidence and support they need to implement their peace plan. I refuse to send American troops to fight a war in Bosnia, but I believe we must help to secure the Bosnian peace.

I want you to know tonight what is at stake, exactly what our troops will be asked to accomplish, and why we must carry out our responsibility to help implement the peace agreement. Implementing the agreement in Bosnia can end the terrible suffering of the people—the warfare, the mass executions, the ethnic cleansing, the campaigns of rape and terror. Let us never forget a quarter of a million men, women and children have been shelled, shot and tortured to death. Two million people, half of the population, were forced from their homes and into a miserable life as refugees. And these faceless numbers hide millions of real personal tragedies. For each of the war's victims was a mother or daughter, a father or son, a brother or sister.

Now the war is over. American leadership created the chance to build a peace and stop the suffering. Securing peace in Bosnia will also help to build a free and stable Europe. Bosnia lies at the very heart of Europe, next-door to many of its fragile new democracies and some of our closest allies. Generations of Americans have understood that Europe's freedom and Europe's stability is vital to our own national security. That's why we fought two wars in Europe. That's why we launched the Marshall Plan to restore Europe. That's why we created NATO and waged the Cold War. And that's why we must help the nations of Europe to end their worst nightmare since World War II, now.

The only force capable of getting this job done is NATO, the powerful, military alliance of democracies that has guaranteed our security for half a century now. And as NATO's leader and the primary broker of the peace agreement, the United States must be an essential part of the mission. If we're not there, NATO will not be there. The peace will collapse. The war will reignite. The slaughter of innocents will begin again. A conflict that already has claimed so many victims could spread like poison throughout the region, eat away at Europe's stability and erode our partnership with our European allies.

And America's commitment to leadership will be questioned if we refuse to participate in implementing a peace agreement we brokered right here in the United States, especially since the Presidents of Bosnia, Croatia and Serbia all asked us to participate and all pledged their best efforts to the security of our troops.

When America's partnerships are weak and our leadership is in doubt, it undermines our ability to secure our interests and to convince others to work with us. If we do maintain our partnerships and our leadership, we need not act alone. As we saw in the Gulf War and in Haiti, many other nations who share our goals will also share our burdens. But when America does not lead, the consequences can be very grave, not only for others, but eventually for us as well.

As I speak to you, NATO is completing its planning for IFOR—an international force for peace in Bosnia of about 60,000 troops. Already, more than 25 other nations, including our major NATO allies, have pledged to take part. They will contribute about two-thirds of the total implementation force, some 40,000 troops. The United States would contribute the rest, about 20,000 soldiers.

Later this week, the final NATO plan will be submitted to me for review and approval. Let me make clear what I expect it to include, and what it must include, for me to give formal approval to the participation of our Armed Forces.

First, the mission will be precisely defined with clear, realistic goals that can be achieved in a definite period of time. Our troops will make sure that each side withdraws its forces behind the front lines and keeps them there. They will maintain the cease-fire to prevent the war from accidentally starting again. These efforts, in turn, will help to create a secure environment, so that the people of Bosnia can return to their homes, vote in free elections and begin to rebuild their lives. Our Joint Chiefs of Staff have concluded that this mission should and will take about one year.

Second, the risks to our troops will be minimized. American troops will take their orders from the American general who commands NATO. They will be heavily armed and thoroughly trained. By making an overwhelming show of force, they will lessen the need to use force. But unlike the UN forces, they will have the authority to respond immediately, and the training and the equipment to respond with overwhelming force to any threat to their own safety or any violations of the military provisions of the peace agreement.

If the NATO plan meets with my approval, I will immediately send it to Congress and request its support. I will also authorize the participation of a small number of American troops in a NATO advance mission that will lay the groundwork for IFOR, starting sometime next week. They will establish headquarters and set up the so-

phisticated communication systems that must be in place before NATO can send in its troops, tanks and trucks to Bosnia.

The implementation force itself would begin deploying in Bosnia in the days following the formal signature of the peace agreement in mid-December. The international community will help to implement arms control provisions of the agreement so that future hostilities are less likely and armaments are limited, while the world community, the United States and others, will also make sure that the Bosnian Federation has the means to defend itself once IFOR withdraws. IFOR will not be a part of this effort.

Civilian agencies from around the world will begin a separate program of humanitarian relief and reconstruction, principally paid for by our European allies and other interested countries. This effort is also absolutely essential to making the peace endure.

It will bring the people of Bosnia the food, shelter, clothing and medicine so many have been denied for so long. It will help them to rebuild—to rebuild their roads and schools, their power plants and hospitals, their factories and shops. It will reunite children with their parents and families with their homes. It will allow the Bosnians freely to choose their own leaders. It will give all the people of Bosnia a much greater stake in peace than war, so that peace takes on a life and a logic of its own.

In Bosnia we can and will succeed because our mission is clear and limited, and our troops are strong and very well-prepared. But, my fellow Americans, no deployment of American troops is risk-free, and this one may well involve casualties. There may be accidents in the field, or incidents with people who have not given up their hatred. I will take every measure possible to minimize these risks, but we must be prepared for that possibility.

As President my most difficult duty is to put the men and women who volunteer to serve our nation in harm's way when our interests and values demand it. I assume full responsibility for any harm that may come to them. But anyone contemplating any action that would endanger our troops should know this: America protects its own. Anyone—anyone—who takes on our troops will suffer the consequences. We will fight fire with fire—and then some.

After so much bloodshed and loss, after so many outrageous acts of inhuman brutality, it will take an extraordinary effort of will for the people of Bosnia to pull themselves from their past and start building a future of peace. But with our leadership and the commitment of our allies, the people of Bosnia can have the chance to decide their future in peace. They have a chance to remind the world that just a few short years ago the mosques and churches of Sarajevo were a shining symbol of multiethnic tolerance; that Bosnia once found unity in its diversity. Indeed, the cemetery in the center of the city was just a few short years ago a magnificent stadium which hosted the Olympics, our universal symbol of peace and harmony. Bosnia can be that kind of place again. We must not turn our backs on Bosnia now.

And so I ask all Americans, and I ask every member of Congress, Democrat and Republican alike, to make the choice for peace. In the choice between peace and war, America must choose peace.

My fellow Americans, I ask you to think just for a moment about this century that is drawing to a close and the new one that will soon begin. Because previous generations of Americans stood up for freedom and because we continue to do so, the American people are more secure and more prosperous. And all around the world, more people than ever before live in freedom. More people than ever before are treated with dignity. More people than ever before can hope to build a better life. That is what America's leadership is all about.

We know that these are the blessings of freedom. And America has always been freedom's greatest champion. If we continue to do everything we can to share these blessings with people around the world, if we continue to be leaders for peace, then the next century can be the greatest time our nation has ever known.

A few weeks ago, I was privileged to spend some time with His Holiness, Pope John Paul II, when he came to America. At the very end of our meeting, the Pope looked at me and said, "I have lived through most of this century. I remember that it began with a war in Sarajevo. Mr. President, you must not let it end with a war in Sarajevo."

In Bosnia, this terrible war has challenged our interests and troubled our souls. Thankfully, we can do something about it. I say again, our mission will be clear, limited and achievable. The people of Bosnia, our NATO allies, and people all around the world are now looking to America for leadership. So let us lead. That is our responsibility as Americans.

Good night and God bless America.

President Clinton's Veto of the Budget Reconciliation Bill

Following is the text of President Clinton's Dec. 6, 1995, message explaining his veto of the reconciliation bill mandating budget cuts and a balanced budget by fiscal 2002.

TO THE HOUSE OF REPRESENTATIVES:

I am returning herewith without my approval H.R. 2491, the budget reconciliation bill adopted by the Republican majority, which seeks to make extreme cuts and other unacceptable changes in Medicare and Medicaid, and to raise taxes on millions of working Americans.

As I have repeatedly stressed, I want to find common ground with the Congress on a balanced budget plan that will best serve the American people. But, I have profound differences with the extreme approach that the Republican majority has adopted. It would hurt average Americans and help special interests.

My balanced budget plan reflects the values that Americans share—work and family, opportunity and responsibility. It would protect Medicare and retain Medicaid's guarantee of coverage; invest in education and training and other priorities; protect public health and the environment; and provide for a targeted tax cut to help middle-income Americans raise their children, save for the future, and pay for postsecondary education. To reach balance, my plan would eliminate wasteful spending, streamline programs, and end unneeded subsidies; take the first, serious steps toward health care reform; and reform welfare to reward work.

By contrast, H.R. 2491 would cut deeply into Medicare, Medicaid, student loans, and nutrition programs; hurt the environment; raise taxes on millions of working men and women and their families by slashing the Earned Income Tax Credit (EITC); and provide a huge tax cut whose benefits would flow disproportionately to those who are already the most well-off.

Moreover, this bill creates new fiscal pressures. Revenue losses from the tax cuts grow rapidly after 2002, with costs exploding for provisions that primarily benefit upper-income taxpayers. Taken together, the revenue losses for the 3 years after 2002 for the individual retirement account (IRA), capital gains, and estate tax provisions exceed the losses for the preceding 6 years.

Title VIII would cut Medicare by $270 billion over 7 years—by far the largest cut in Medicare's 30-year history. While we need to slow the rate of growth in Medicare spending, I believe Medicare must keep pace with anticipated increases in the costs of medical services and the growing number of elderly Americans. This bill would fall woefully short and would hurt beneficiaries, over half of whom are women. In addition, the bill introduces untested, and highly questionable, Medicare "choices" that could increase risks and costs for the most vulnerable beneficiaries.

Title VII would cut Federal Medicaid payments to States by $163 billion over 7 years and convert the program into a block grant, eliminating guaranteed coverage to millions of Americans and putting States at risk during economic downturns. States would face untenable choices: cutting benefits, dropping coverage for millions of beneficiaries, or reducing provider payments to a level that would undermine quality service to children, people with disabilities, the elderly, pregnant women, and others who depend on Medicaid. I am also concerned that the bill has inadequate quality and income protections for nursing home residents, the developmentally disabled, and their families; and that it would eliminate a program that guarantees immunizations to many children.

Title IV would virtually eliminate the Direct Student Loan Program, reversing its significant progress and ending the participation of over 1,300 schools and hundreds of thousands of students. These actions would hurt middle- and low-income families, make student loan programs less efficient, perpetuate unnecessary red tape, and deny students and schools the free-market choice of guaranteed or direct loans,

Title V would open the Arctic National Wildlife Refuge (ANWR) to oil and gas drilling, threatening a unique, pristine ecosystem, in hopes of generating $1.3 billion in Federal revenues—a revenue estimate based on wishful thinking and outdated analysis. I want to protect this biologically rich wilderness permanently. I am also concerned that the Congress has chosen to use the reconciliation bill as a catch-all for various objectionable natural resource and environmental policies. One would retain the notorious patenting provision whereby the government transfers billions of dollars of publicly owned minerals at little or no charge to private interests; another would transfer Federal land for a low-level radioactive waste site in California without public safeguards.

While making such devastating cuts in Medicare, Medicaid, and other vital programs, this bill would provide huge tax cuts for those who are already the most well-off. Over 47 percent of the tax benefits would go to families with incomes over $100,000—the top 12 percent. The bill would provide unwarranted benefits to corporations and new tax breaks for special interests. At the same time, it would raise taxes, on average, for the poorest one-fifth of all families.

The bill would make capital gains cuts retroactive to January 1, 1995, providing a windfall of $13 billion in about the first 9 months of 1995 alone to taxpayers who already have sold their assets. While my Administration supports limited reform of the alternative minimum tax (AMT), this bill's cuts in the corporate AMT would not adequately ensure that profitable corporations pay at least some Federal tax. The bill also would encourage businesses to avoid taxes by stockpiling foreign earnings in tax havens. And the bill does not include my proposal to close a loophole that allows wealthy Americans to avoid taxes on the gains they accrue by giving up their U.S. citizenship. Instead, it substitutes a provision that would prove ineffective.

While cutting taxes for the well-off, this bill would cut the EITC for almost 13 million working families. It would repeal part of the scheduled 1996 increase for taxpayers with two or more children, and end the credit for workers who do not live with qualifying children. Even after accounting for other tax cuts in this bill, about eight million families would face a net tax increase.

The bill would threaten the retirement benefits of workers and increase the exposure of the Pension Benefit Guaranty Corporation by making it easy for companies to withdraw tax-favored pension assets for nonpension purposes. It also would raise Federal employee retirement contributions, unduly burdening Federal workers. Moreover, the bill would eliminate the low income housing tax credit and the community development corporation tax credit, which address critical housing needs and help rebuild communities. Finally, the bill would repeal the tax credit that encourages economic activity in Puerto Rico. We must not ignore the real needs of our citizens in Puerto Rico, and any legislation must contain effective mechanisms to promote job creation in the islands.

Title XII includes many welfare provisions. I strongly support real welfare reform that strengthens families and encourages work and responsibility. But the provisions in this bill, when added to the EITC cuts, would cut low income programs too deeply. For welfare reform to succeed, savings should result from moving people from welfare to work, not from cutting people off and shifting costs to the States. The cost of excessive program cuts in human terms—to working families, single mothers with small children, abused and neglected children, low-income legal immigrants, and disabled children—would be grave. In addition, this bill threatens the national nutritional safety net by making unwarranted changes in child nutrition programs and the national food stamp program.

The agriculture provisions would eliminate the safety net that farm programs provide for U.S. agriculture. Title I would provide windfall payments to producers when prices are high, but not protect family farm income when prices are low. In addition, it would slash spending for agricultural export assistance and reduce the environmental benefits of the Conservation Reserve Program.

For all of these reasons, and for others detailed in the attachment, this bill is unacceptable.

Nevertheless, while I have major differences with the Congress, I want to work with Members to find a common path to balance the budget in a way that will honor our commitment to senior citizens, help working families, provide a better life for our children, and improve the standard of living of all Americans.

WILLIAM J. CLINTON
THE WHITE HOUSE
December 6, 1995.

President Clinton's 1996 State of the Union Address

Following is the text of President Clinton's State of the Union address as delivered Jan. 23, 1996, provided by the Federal Document Clearing House.

Mr. Speaker [Newt Gingrich], Mr. Vice President [Al Gore], members of the 104th Congress, distinguished guests, my fellow Americans all across our land.

Let me begin by saying to our men and women in uniform around the world, and especially those helping peace take root in Bosnia, and to their families, I thank you. America is very, very proud of you.

My duty tonight is to report on the state of the union, not the state of our government, but of our American community, and to set forth our responsibilities—in the words of our founders—to form a "more perfect union."

The state of the union is strong.

Our economy is the healthiest it has been in three decades. We have the lowest combined rate of unemployment and inflation in 27 years.

We have created nearly 8 million new jobs, over a million of them in basic industries like construction and automobiles. America is selling more cars than Japan for the first time since the 1970s, and for three years in a row we have had a record number of new businesses started in our country.

Our leadership in the world is also strong, bringing hope for new peace. And perhaps most important, we are gaining ground in restoring our fundamental values. The crime rate, the welfare and food stamp rolls, the poverty rate and the teen pregnancy rate are all down. And as they go down, prospects for America's future go up.

"AN AGE OF POSSIBILITY"

We live in an age of possibility. A hundred years ago we moved from farm to factory. Now we move to an age of technology, information and global competition. These changes have opened vast new opportunities for our people, but they have also presented them with stiff challenges. While more Americans are living better lives, too many of our fellow citizens are working harder to just keep up, in search of greater security for their families.

We must answer three fundamental questions: First, how do we make the American dream of opportunity a reality for all Americans who are willing to work for it? Second, how do we preserve our old and enduring values as we move into the future? And third, how do we meet these challenges together, as one America?

We know big government does not have all the answers. We know there's not a program for every problem. We know and we have worked to give the American people a smaller, less bureaucratic government in Washington. And we have to give the American people one that lives within its means. The era of big government is over.

But we cannot go back to the time when our citizens were left to fend for themselves. We must go forward as one America—one nation working together, to meet the challenges we face together. Self-reliance and teamwork are not opposing virtues—we must have both.

I believe our new, smaller government must work in an old-fashioned American way—together with all of our citizens, through state and local governments, in the workplace, in religious, charitable and civic associations. Our goal must be to enable all our people to make the most of their own lives with stronger families, more educational opportunity, economic security, safer streets, a cleaner environment, and a safer world.

To improve the state of our union, we must all ask more of ourselves; we must expect more of each other; and we must face our challenges together.

Here, in this place, our responsibility begins with balancing the budget in a way that is fair to all Americans. There is now broad bipartisan agreement that permanent deficit spending must come to an end.

I compliment the Republican leadership and the membership for the energy and determination you have brought to this task of balancing the budget. And I thank the Democrats for passing the largest deficit-reduction plan in history in 1993, which has already cut the deficit nearly in half in three years.

Since 1993, we have all seen the benefits of deficit reduction: Lower interest rates have made it easier for business to borrow and to invest and create new jobs. Lower interest rates have brought down the cost of home mortgages, car payments and credit card rates to ordinary citizens. Now it is time to finish the job and balance the budget.

Though differences remain among us that are significant, the combined total of the proposed savings common to both plans is more than enough, using the numbers from your Congressional Budget Office, to balance the budget in seven years and to provide a modest tax cut. These cuts are real, they will require sacrifice from everyone. But these cuts do not undermine our obligations to our parents, our children and our future by endangering Medicare, Medicaid, education or the environment, or by raising taxes on working families.

I have said before and I'll say again that many good ideas have come out of our negotiations. I have learned a lot about the way both Republicans and Democrats view the debate before us. I have learned a lot about the good ideas that each side has that we could all embrace. We ought to resolve our remaining differences. I am willing to work to resolve them. I am ready to meet tomorrow. But I ask you to consider that we should at least enact these savings that both plans have in common and give the American people their balanced budget, a tax cut, lower interest rates and a brighter future. We should do that now and make permanent deficits yesterday's legacy.

CHILDREN AND FAMILIES

Now is the time to look to the challenges of today and tomorrow, beyond the burdens of yesterday. The challenges are significant, but our nation was built on challenges. America was built on challenges, not promises. And when we work together, we never fail. That is the key to a more perfect union: Our individual dreams must be realized by our common efforts.

Tonight, I want to speak of the challenges we all face as a people.

Our first challenge is to cherish our children and strengthen American families.

Families are the foundation of American life. If we have stronger families, we will have a stronger America. Before I go on, I'd like to take just a moment to thank my own family, and to thank the person who taught me more than anyone else over 25 years about the importance of families and children. A wonderful wife, a magnificent mother and a great first lady. Thank you Hillary.

All strong families begin with taking more responsibility for our children. I've heard Mrs. Gore say that it's hard to be a parent today, but it's even harder to be a child. So all of us, not just as parents but all of us in our other roles—our businesses, our media, our schools, our teachers, our communities, our churches and synagogues, our businesses, governments—all of us have a responsibility to help children make it, and to make the most of their lives and their God-given capacities.

To the media: I say you should create movies, CDs and television shows you would want your own children and grandchildren to enjoy. I call on Congress to pass the requirement for a "v-chip" in TV sets, so parents can screen out programs they believe are inappropriate for their children.

When parents control what their children see, that's not censorship. That's enabling parents to assume more responsibility for their young children's upbringing. And I urge them to do it. The v-chip requirement is part of the telecommunications bill now pending in this Congress. It has bipartisan support, and I urge you to pass it now.

To make the v-chip work, I challenge the broadcast industry to do what movies have done to identify your programs in ways that help parents protect their children. And I invite the leaders of major media corporations and the entertainment industry to come to the White House next month to work with us in a positive way on concrete ways to improve what our children see on television. I am ready to work with you.

I say to those who produce and market cigarettes: Every year, a million children take up smoking, even though it's against the law; 300,000 of them will have their lives shortened as a result.

Our administration has taken steps to stop the massive marketing campaigns that appeal to our children. We are simply saying: Market your products to adults, if you wish—but draw the line on children.

I say to those on welfare, and especially to those who have been trapped on welfare for a long time: For too long our welfare system has undermined the values of family and work instead of supporting them. The Congress and I are near agreement on sweeping welfare reform. We agree on time limits, tough work requirements and the toughest possible child-support reinforcement. But I believe we must also provide child care so mothers can go to work without worrying about what is happening to their children. I challenge this Congress to send me a bipartisan welfare reform that will really move people from welfare to work and do right by our children. I will sign it immediately.

But let us be candid about this difficult problem. Passing a law, even the best possible law, is only the first step. The next step is to make it work. I challenge people on welfare to make the most of this opportunity for independence. I challenge American business to give people on welfare the chance to move into the workforce. I applaud the work of religious groups and others who care for the poor. More than anything else, they know the true difficulty of this task, and they are in a position to help. Every one of us should join with them. That is the only way we can make welfare reform a reality in the lives of the American people.

To strengthen the family, we must do everything we can to keep the teen pregnancy rate going down. I am gratified, as I'm sure all Americans are, that it has dropped for two years in a row. But we all know it is still far too high. Tonight I am pleased to announce that a group of prominent Americans is responding to that challenge by forming an organization that will support grassroots community efforts all across our country in a national campaign against teen pregnancy. And I challenge all of us and every American to join their efforts.

I call on American men and women in families to respect one another. We must end the deadly scourge of domestic violence in our country. And I challenge America's families to work harder to stay together. For families that stay together not only do better economically, their children do better as well.

In particular, I challenge fathers to love and care for their children. If your family has separated, you must pay your child support. We are doing more than ever to make sure you do, and we are going to do more. But let's admit something about that too: A check will never be a substitute for a father's love and guidance, and only you, only you can make the decision to help raise your children no matter who you are, how low or high your station in life, it is your most basic human duty of every American to do that job to the best of his or her ability.

EDUCATIONAL OPPORTUNITIES

Our second challenge is to provide Americans with the educational opportunities we need for this new century.

In our schools, every classroom in America must be connected to the information superhighway, with computers, good software and well-trained teachers. We are working with the telecommunications industry, educators and parents to connect 20 percent of California's classrooms by this spring, and every classroom and library in the entire United States by the year 2000. I ask Congress to support our education technology initiative so we make sure this national partnership succeeds.

Every diploma ought to mean something. I challenge every community, every school and every state to adopt national standards of excellence to measure whether schools are meeting those standards, to cut bureaucratic red tape so that schools and teachers have more flexibility for grassroots reforms, and hold them accountable for results. That's what our Goals 2000 initiative is all about.

I challenge every state to give all parents the right to choose which public school their children attend and let teachers form new schools with a charter they can keep only if they do a good job.

I challenge all schools to teach character education: to teach good values, and good citizenship. And if it means teen-agers will stop killing each other over designer jackets, then our public schools should be able to require their students to wear school uniforms.

I challenge parents to be their children's first teachers. Turn off the TV. See that the homework is done. And visit your children's classroom. No program, no teacher, no one else can do that for you.

My fellow Americans, higher education is more important today than ever before. We have created a new student loan program that has made it easier to borrow and repay loans; and we have dramatically cut the student loan default rate. That's something we should all be proud of, because it was unconscionably high just a few years ago. Through AmeriCorps, our national service program, this year 25,000 young people will earn college money by serving in their communities to improve the lives of their friends and neighbors. These initiatives are right for America, and we should keep them going.

And we should work hard to open the doors to college even wider. I challenge Congress to expand work study and help 1 million young Americans work their way through college by the year 2000; to provide a $1,000 merit scholarship for the top 5 percent of graduates in every high school in the U.S.; to expand Pell Grant scholarships for deserving and needy students; and to make up to $10,000 a year of college tuition tax deductible. It's a good idea for America.

ECONOMIC SECURITY

Our third challenge is to help every American who is willing to work for it achieve economic security in this new age.

People who work hard still need support to get ahead in the new economy. They need education and training for a lifetime, they need more support for families raising children, they need retirement security, they need access to health care.

More and more Americans are finding that the education of their childhood simply doesn't last a lifetime. So I challenge Congress to consolidate 70 overlapping, antiquated job training programs into a simple voucher worth $2,600 for unemployed or underemployed workers to use as they please for community college tuition or other training. This is a GI Bill for America's Workers we should all be able to agree on.

More and more Americans are working hard without a raise. Congress sets the minimum wage. Within a year, the minimum wage will fall to a 40-year low in purchasing power. $4.25 an hour is no longer a minimum wage. But millions of Americans and their children are trying to live on it. I challenge you to raise their minimum wage.

In 1993, Congress cut the taxes of 15 million hard-pressed working families, to make sure no parents who worked full time would have to raise their children in poverty, and to encourage people to move from welfare to work. This expanded Earned Income Tax Credit is now worth about $1,800 a year to a family of four living on $20,000. The budget bill I vetoed would have reversed this achieve-

ment, and raised taxes on nearly 8 million of those people. We should not do that. We should not do that.

But I also agree that the people who are helped under this initiative are not all those in our country who are working hard to do a good job raising their children and at work. I agree that we need a tax credit for working families with children. That's one thing most of us in this chamber, I hope, can agree on. I know it is strongly supported by the Republican majority and it should be a part of any final budget agreement.

I want to challenge every business that can possibly afford it to provide pensions for your employees, and I challenge Congress to pass a proposal recommended by the White House Conference on Small Business that would make it easier for small businesses and farmers to establish their own pension plans. That is something we should all agree on.

We should also protect existing pension plans. Two years ago, with bipartisan support, it was almost unanimous on both sides of the aisle. We moved to protect the pensions of 8 million working people and to stabilize the pensions of 32 million more. Congress should not now let companies endanger those workers' pension funds. I know the proposal to liberalize the ability of employers to take money out of pension funds for other purposes would raise money for the treasury, but I believe it is false economy. I vetoed that proposal last year, and I would have to do so again.

Finally, if our working families are going to succeed in the new economy, they must be able to buy health insurance policies that they do not lose when they change jobs or when someone in their family gets sick. Over the past two years, over 1 million Americans in working families have lost their health insurance. We have to do more to make health care available to every American. And Congress should start by passing the bipartisan bill sponsored by Senator [Edward M.] Kennedy [D-Mass.] and Senator [Nancy Landon] Kassebaum [R-Kan.] that would require insurance companies to stop dropping people when they switch jobs, and stop denying coverage for pre-existing conditions. Let's all do that.

And even as we enact savings in these programs we must have a common commitment to preserve the basic protections Medicare and Medicaid give, not just to the poor, but people in working families, including children, people with disabilities, people with AIDS, senior citizens in nursing homes. In the past three years we have saved $15 billion just by fighting health care fraud and abuse. We have all agreed to save much more. We have all agreed to stabilize the Medicare trust fund. But we must not abandon our fundamental obligations to the people who need Medicare and Medicaid. America cannot become stronger if they become weaker.

The GI Bill for Workers, tax relief for education and child-rearing, pension availability and protection, access to health care, preservation of Medicare and Medicaid, these things—along with the Family and Medical Leave Act passed in 1993—these things will help responsible hard-working American families to make the most of their own lives.

But employers and employees must do their part as well, as they are in so many of our finest companies, working together, putting long-term prosperity ahead of short-term gain. As workers increase their hours and their productivity, employers should make sure they get the skills they need and share the benefits of the good years as well as the burdens of the bad ones. When companies and workers work as a team, they do better. And so does America.

TAKE BACK THE STREETS

Our fourth great challenge is to take our streets back from crime, gangs and drugs.

At last, we have begun to find the way to reduce crime—forming community partnerships with local police forces to catch criminals and to prevent crime. This strategy, called community policing, is clearly working. Violent crime is coming down all across America.

In New York City, murders are down 25 percent, in St. Louis 18 percent, in Seattle 32 percent. But we still have a long way to go before our streets are safe and our people are free from fear.

The Crime Bill of 1994 is critical to the success of community policing. It provides funds for 100,000 new police in communities of all sizes. We are already a third of the way there. And I challenge the Congress to finish the job. Let us stick with a strategy that's working and keep the crime rate coming down.

Community policing also requires bonds of trust between citizens and our police. I ask all Americans to respect and support our law enforcement officers. And to our police I say: Our children need you as role models and heroes. Don't let them down.

The Brady Bill has stopped 44,000 people with criminal records from buying guns. The assault weapons ban is keeping 19 kinds of assault weapons out of the hands of violent gangs. I challenge the Congress to keep those laws on the books.

Our next step in the fight against crime is to take on gangs the way we once took on the mob. I am directing the FBI and other investigative agencies to target gangs that involve juveniles in violent crime and to seek authority to prosecute as adults teen-agers who maim and kill like adults.

And I challenge local housing authorities and tenant associations: Criminal gang members and drug dealers are destroying the lives of decent tenants. From now on, the rule for residents who commit crimes and peddle drugs should be: One strike and you're out.

I challenge every state to match federal policy: to assure that serious violent criminals serve at least 85 percent of their sentence.

More police and punishment are important, but they're not enough. We have got to keep more of our young people out of trouble, with prevention strategies not dictated by Washington, but developed in communities. I challenge all of our communities, all of our adults, to give our children futures to say yes to. And I challenge Congress not to abandon the crime bill's support of these grassroots prevention efforts.

Finally, to reduce crime and violence, we have to reduce the drug problem. The challenge begins at home, with parents talking to their children openly and firmly. It embraces our churches and synagogues, our youth groups and our schools. I challenge Congress not to cut our support for drug-free schools. People like these DARE [Drug Abuse Resistance Education] officers are making a real impression on grade school children that will give them the strength to say no when the time comes.

Meanwhile, we continue our efforts to cut the flow of drugs into America. For the last two years, one man in particular has been on the front lines of that effort. Tonight I am nominating a hero of the Persian Gulf war and the commander in chief of the U.S. Military's Southern Command, Gen. Barry McCaffrey, as America's new drug czar.

Gen. McCaffrey has earned three Purple Hearts and two Silver Stars fighting for this country. Tonight I ask that he lead our nation's battle against drugs at home and abroad. To succeed, he needs a force far larger than he has ever commanded. He needs all of us. Everyone of us has a role to play on this team. Thank you, Gen. McCaffrey, for agreeing to serve your country one more time.

COMMITMENT TO THE ENVIRONMENT

Our fifth challenge: to leave our environment safe and clean for the next generation.

Because of a generation of bipartisan effort, we do have cleaner water and air. Lead levels in children's blood have been cut by 70 percent and toxic emissions from factories cut in half. Lake Erie was dead. Now it is a thriving resource.

But 10 million children under 12 still live within four miles of a toxic waste dump. A third of us breathe air that endangers our health. And in too many communities, water is not safe to drink. We still have much to do.

Yet Congress has voted to cut environmental enforcement by 25 percent. That means more toxic chemicals in our water, more smog in our air, more pesticides in our food. Lobbyists for the polluters have been allowed to write their own loopholes into bills to weaken laws that protect the health and safety of our children. Some say that the taxpayers should pick up the tab for toxic waste and let polluters who can afford to fix it off the hook.

I challenge Congress to re-examine those policies and to reverse them. I believe . . . This issue has not been a partisan issue. The most significant environmental gains in the last 30 years were made under a Democratic Congress and President Richard Nixon. We can work together. We have to believe some basic things. Do you believe we can expand the economy without hurting the environment? I do. Do you believe we can create more jobs over the long run by cleaning the environment up? I know we can. That should be our commitment.

We must challenge businesses and communities to take more initiative in protecting the environment, and we have to make it easier for them to do it. To businesses, this administration is saying: If you can find a cheaper, more efficient way than government regulations required to meet tough pollution standards, do it—as long as you do it right.

To communities we say: We must strengthen community right-to-know laws requiring polluters to disclose their emissions, but you have to use the information to work with business to cut pollution. People do have a right to know that their air and water are safe.

AMERICAN WORLD LEADERSHIP

Our sixth challenge is to maintain America's leadership in the fight for freedom and peace throughout the world.

Because of American leadership, more people than ever before live free and at peace and Americans have known 50 years of prosperity and security. We owe thanks especially to our veterans of World War II. I would like to say to Senator Bob Dole [R-Kan.] and to all others in this chamber who fought in World War II and to all others on both sides of the aisle who have fought bravely in all our conflicts since, I salute your service and so do the American people.

All over the world, even after the Cold War people still look to us, and trust us to help them seek the blessings of peace and freedom.

But as the Cold War fades into memory, voices of isolation say America should retreat from its responsibilities. I say they are wrong.

The threats we face today as Americans respect no nation's borders—think of them: terrorism, the spread of weapons of mass destruction, organized crime, drug trafficking, ethnic and religious hatred, aggression by rogue states, environmental degradation. If we fail to address these threats today, we will suffer the consequences in all our tomorrows.

Of course we can't be everywhere. Of course we can't do everything. But where our interests and our values are at stake—and where we can make a difference—America must lead. We must not be isolationist; we must not be the world's policeman. But we can and should be the world's very best peacemaker.

By keeping our military strong, by using diplomacy where we can and force where we must, by working with others to share the risk and the cost of our efforts, America is making a difference for people here and around the world.

For the first time since the dawn of the nuclear age, there is not a single Russian missile pointed at America's children. North Korea has now frozen its dangerous nuclear weapons program. In Haiti, the dictators are gone, democracy has a new day, the flow of desperate refugees to our shores has subsided.

Through tougher trade deals for America, over 80 of them, we have opened markets abroad, and now exports are at an all-time high, growing faster than imports and creating good American jobs.

We stood with those taking risks for peace—in Northern Ireland, where Catholic and Protestant children now tell their parents violence must never return, and in the Middle East, where Arabs and Jews, who once seemed destined to fight forever, now share knowledge and resources and even dreams.

And we stood up for peace in Bosnia. Remember the skeletal prisoners, the mass graves, the campaigns of rape and torture, the endless lines of refugees, the threat of a spreading war—all these threats, all these horrors have now begun to give way to the promise of peace.

Now our troops and a strong NATO, together with our new partners from Central Europe and elsewhere, are helping that peace take hold.

As all of you know, I was just there with a bipartisan Congressional group, and I was so proud not only of what our troops were doing but at the pride they evidenced in what they were doing. They knew what America's mission in this world is and they were proud to be carrying it out.

Through these efforts, we have enhanced the security of the American people. But make no mistake about it, important challenges remain. The Start II treaty with Russia will cut our nuclear stockpiles by another 25 percent; I urge the Senate to ratify it—now. We must end the race to create new nuclear weapons by signing a truly comprehensive nuclear test ban treaty—this year. As we remember what happened in the Japanese subway, we can outlaw poison gas forever, if the Senate ratifies the Chemical Weapons Convention—this year. We can intensify the fight against terrorists and organized criminals at home and abroad, if Congress passes the anti-terrorism legislation I proposed after the Oklahoma City bombing—now. We can help more people move from hatred to hope all across the world in our own interest—if Congress gives us the means to remain the world's leader for peace.

RE-INVENTING GOVERNMENT

My fellow Americans, the six challenges I have just discussed are for all of us. Our seventh challenge is really America's challenge to those of us in this hallowed hall tonight—to reinvent our government and make our democracy work for them.

Last year, this Congress applied to itself the laws it applies to everyone else. This Congress banned gifts and meals from lobbyists. This Congress forced lobbyists to disclose who pays them and what legislation they are trying to pass or kill. This Congress did that, and I applaud you for it.

Now I challenge Congress to go further, to curb special interest influence in politics by passing the first truly bipartisan campaign finance reform bill in a generation. You Republicans and Democrats alike can show the American people that we can limit spending and we can open the airwaves to all candidates.

And I also appeal to Congress to pass the line item veto you promised the American people. Our administration is working hard to give the American people a government that works better and costs less. Thanks to the work of Vice President Gore, we are eliminating 16,000 pages of unnecessary rules and regulations and shifting more decision-making out of Washington back to states and communities.

As we move into an era of balanced budgets and smaller government, we must work in new ways to enable people to make the most of their own lives. We are helping America's communities, not with more bureaucracy, but with more opportunities. Through our successful empowerment zones and community development banks we're helping people to find jobs, to start businesses.

And with tax incentives for companies that clean up abandoned industrial property, we can bring jobs back to the places that desperately, desperately need them.

But there are some areas that the federal government should not leave and should address and address strongly. One of these areas is the problem of illegal immigration. After years and years of neglect, this administration has taken a strong stand to stiffen the protection on our borders. We are increasing border patrols by 50 percent. We are increasing inspections to prevent the hiring of illegal immigrants.

And tonight, I announce I will sign an executive order to deny federal contracts to businesses that hire illegal immigrants. Let me be very clear about this: We are still a nation of immigrants, we should be proud of it. We should honor every legal immigrant here working hard to be a good citizen, working hard to become a new citizen. But we are also a nation of laws.

I want to say a special word to those who work for the federal government. Today, the federal work force is 200,000 employees smaller than it was the day I took office as president—our federal government today is the smallest it has been in 30 years, and it's getting smaller every day. Most of our fellow Americans probably don't know that, and there's a good reason, a good reason. The remaining federal work force is composed of Americans who are working harder and working smarter than ever before to make sure that the quality of our services does not decline.

I'd like to give you one example. His name is Richard Dean. He's a 49-year-old Vietnam veteran who's worked for the Social Security Administration for 22 years now. Last year, he was hard at work in the federal building in Oklahoma City when the blast killed 169 people and brought the rubble around him. He re-entered the building four times. He saved the lives of three women. He is here with us this evening, and I want to recognize Richard and applaud both his pubic service and his extraordinary personal heroism.

But Richard Dean's story doesn't end there. This last November, he was forced out of his office when the government shut down. And the second time the government shut down, he continued helping Social Security recipients, but he was working without pay. On behalf of Richard Dean and his family, and all the other people who are out there working every day doing a good job for the American people I challenge all of you in this chamber: Never—ever—shut the federal government down again. On behalf of all Americans, especially those who need their social security payments at the beginning of March, I also challenge Congress to preserve the full faith and credit of the United States, to honor the obligations of this great nation as we have for 220 years, to rise above partisanship and pass a straightforward extension of the debt limit and show the people America keeps its word.

I know that this evening I have asked a lot of Congress and even more from America. But I am confident. When Americans work together in their homes, their schools, their churches, their synagogues their civic groups or their workplace, they can meet any challenge.

TORCH OF CITIZENSHIP

I say again: The era of big government is over. But we can't go back to the era of fending for yourself. We have to go forward, to the era of working together—as a community, as a team, as one America—with all of us reaching across these lines that divide us. The division, the discrimination, the rancor, we have to reach across it to find common ground. We have got to work together if we want America to work.

I want you to meet two more people tonight who do just that. Lucius Wright is a teacher in the Jackson, Miss., public school system. A Vietnam veteran, he has created groups to help inner city children turn away from gangs and build futures they can believe in. And Sgt. Jennifer Rodgers is a police officer in Oklahoma City. Like Richard Dean, she helped to pull her fellow citizens out of the rubble and deal with that awful tragedy. She reminds us that, in their response to that atrocity, the people of Oklahoma City lifted all of us with their basic sense of decency and community.

Lucius Wright and Jennifer Rodgers are special Americans, and I have the honor to announce tonight that they are the very first of several thousand Americans who will be chosen to carry the Olympic torch on its long journey from Los Angeles to the centennial of the modern Olympics in Atlanta this summer—not because they are star athletes, but because they are star citizens, community heroes meeting America's challenges. They are our real champions. Please stand up.

Now each of us must hold high the torch of citizenship in our own lives. None of us can finish the race alone. We can only achieve our destiny together—one hand, one generation, one American connecting to another. There have always been things we could do together, dreams we could make real which we could never have done on our own. We Americans have forged our identity, our very union from the very point of view that we can accommodate every point on the planet, every different opinion, but we must be bound together by a faith more powerful than any doctrine that divides us, by our belief in progress, our love of liberty, and our relentless search for common ground.

America has always sought and always risen to every challenge. Who would say that having come so far together we will not go forward from here? Who would say that this age of possibility is not for all Americans? Our country is and always has been a great and good nation, but the best is yet to come if we all do our part.

Thank you, God bless you, and God bless the United States of America. Thank you.

President Clinton's Fiscal 1997 Budget Message

On February 5, 1996, President Clinton transmitted the fiscal 1997 budget to Congress, noting that "the Office of Management and Budget was not able to provide, by today, all of the material normally contained in the President's budget submission. I anticipate transmitting that material to Congress the week of March 18, 1996." Following is the Congressional Record text of Clinton's fiscal 1997 budget message sent to Congress March 19, 1996.

To the Congress of the United States:

The 1997 Budget, which I am transmitting to you with this message, builds on our strong economic record by balancing the budget in seven years while continuing to invest in the American people.

The budget cuts unnecessary and lower priority spending while protecting senior citizens, working families, and children. It reforms welfare to make work pay and provides tax relief to middle-income Americans and small business.

Three years ago, we inherited an economy that was suffering from short- and long-term problems—problems that were created or exacerbated by the economic and budgetary policies of the previous 12 years.

In the short term, economic growth was slow and job creation was weak. The budget deficit, which had first exploded in size in the early 1980s, was rising to unsustainable levels.

Over the longer term, the growth in productivity had slowed since the early 1970s and, as a result, living standards had stagnated or fallen for most Americans. At the same time, the gap between rich and poor had widened.

Over the last three years, we have put in place budgetary and other economic policies that have fundamentally changed the direction of the economy—for the better. We have produced stronger growth, lower interest rates, stable prices, millions of new jobs, record exports, lower personal and corporate debt burdens, and higher living standards.

Working with the last Congress in 1993, we enacted an economic program that has worked better than even we projected in spurring growth and reducing the deficit. We have cut the deficit nearly in half, from $290 billion in 1992 to $164 billion in 1995. As a share of the Gross Domestic Product, we have cut the deficit by more than half in three years, bringing the deficit to its lowest level since 1979.

While cutting overall discretionary spending, we also shifted resources to investments in our future. With wages increasingly linked to skills, we invested wisely in education and training to help Americans acquire the tools they need for the high-wage jobs of tomorrow. We also invested heavily in science and technology, which has been a strong engine of economic growth throughout the Nation's history.

For Americans struggling to raise their children and make ends meet, we have sought to make work pay. We expanded the Earned Income Tax Credit, providing tax relief for 15 million working families. And we have given 37 States the freedom to test ways to move people from welfare to work while protecting children.

As the economy has become increasingly global, prosperity at home depends heavily on opening foreign markets to American goods and services. With this in mind, we secured legislation to implement the General Agreement on Tariffs and Trade and the North American Free Trade Agreement, and we have completed over 80 other trade agreements. Under our leadership, U.S. exports have grown to an all-time high.

With these policies, we have helped pave the way for a future of sustained economic growth, low interest rates, stable prices, and more opportunity for Americans of all incomes. But our work is not done.

Looking ahead, as I said recently in my State of the Union address, we must answer three fundamental questions: First, how do we make the American dream of opportunity for all a reality for all Americans who are willing to work for it? Second, how do we preserve our old and enduring values as we move into the future? And, third, how do we meet these challenges together, as one America?

This budget addresses those questions.

CREATING AN AGE OF POSSIBILITY

I am committed to finishing the job that we began in 1993 and finally bringing the budget into balance. In our negotiations with congressional leaders, we have made great progress toward reaching an agreement. We have simply come too far to let this opportunity slip away.

A balanced budget would reduce interest rates for all Americans, including the young families across the land who are struggling to buy their first homes. It also would free up funds in the private markets with which businesses could invest in factories and equipment, or in training their workers.

But we have to balance the budget the right way—by cutting unnecessary and lower priority spending; investing in the future; protecting senior citizens, working families, children, and other vulnerable Americans; and providing tax relief for middle-income Americans and small businesses.

My budget does that. It strengthens Medicare and Medicaid, on which millions of senior citizens, people with disabilities, and low-income Americans rely. It reforms welfare. It cuts other entitlements. And it cuts deeply into discretionary spending.

But while cutting overall discretionary spending, my budget invests in education and training, the environment, science and technology, law enforcement, and other priorities to help build a brighter future for all Americans. We should spend more on what we need, less on what we don't.

PROJECTING AMERICAN LEADERSHIP

Across the globe, we live in a time of great opportunity and great challenge. With the end of the Cold War, the world looks to the United States for leadership. Providing it is clearly in our best interest. We must not turn away.

My budget provides the necessary resources to advance America's strategic interests, carry out our foreign policy, open markets abroad, and support U.S. exports. It also provides the resources to confront the emerging global threats that have replaced the Cold War as major concerns—regional, ethnic, and national conflicts; the proliferation of weapons of mass destruction; international terrorism and crime; narcotics trading; and environmental degradation.

On the diplomatic front, our successes have been numerous and heartening, and they have made the world a safer and more stable place. Through our leadership, we are helping to bring peace to Bosnia and the Middle East, and we have spurred progress in Northern Ireland. We also encouraged the movement toward democracy and free markets in Russia and Central Europe, and we led a successful international effort to defuse the nuclear threat from North Korea.

On the military front, we have deployed our forces where we could be effective and where it was in our interest to promote stability by ending bloodshed (such as in Bosnia) and suffering (such as in Rwanda). We also have used the threat of force to ease tensions, such as to unseat an unwelcome dictatorship in Haiti and to stare down Iraq when it threatened again to move against Kuwait.

This budget provides the funds to sustain and modernize the world's strongest, best-trained, best-equipped, and most ready military force. Through it, we continue to support service members and their families with quality-of-life improvements in the short term, while planning to acquire the new technologies that will become available at the turn of this decade.

CREATING OPPORTUNITY AND ENCOURAGING RESPONSIBILITY

The Federal Government cannot—by itself—solve most of the problems and address most of the challenges that we face as a people. In some cases, it must play a lead role—whether to ensure the guarantee of health care for vulnerable Americans, expand access to education and training, invest in science and technology, protect the environment, or make the Tax Code fairer. In other cases, it must play more of a partnership role—working with States, localities, nonprofit groups, churches and synagogues, families, and individuals to strengthen communities, make work pay, protect public safety, and improve the quality of education.

To restore the American community, the budget invests in national service, through which 25,000 Americans this year are helping to solve problems in communities while earning money for postsecondary education or to repay student loans. We want to create more Empowerment Zones and Enterprise Communities to spur economic development and expand opportunities for the residents of distressed urban and rural areas. We want to expand the Community Development Financial Institutions Fund to provide credit and other services to such communities. With the same goal in mind, we want to transform the Department of Housing and Urban Development into an agency that better addresses local needs. And we want to maintain our relationship with, and the important services we provide to, Native Americans.

In health care, our challenge is to improve the existing and largely successful system, not to end the guarantees of coverage on which millions of vulnerable Americans rely. My budget strengthens Medicare and Medicaid, ensuring their continued vitality. For Medicare, it strengthens the Part A trust fund, provides more choice for seniors and people with disabilities, and makes the program more efficient and responsive to beneficiary needs. For Medicaid, it gives States more flexibility to manage their programs while preserving the guarantee of health coverage for the most vulnerable Americans, retains current nursing home quality standards, and continues to protect the spouses of nursing home residents from impoverishment. My budget proposes reforms to make private health care more accessible and affordable, and premium subsidies to help those who lose their jobs pay for private coverage for up to six months. It also invests more in various public health services, such as the Ryan White program to serve people living with AIDS, and research and regulatory activities that promote public health.

Because America's welfare system is broken, we have worked hard to fix those parts of it that we could without congressional action. For instance, we have given 37 States the freedom to test ways to move people from welfare to work while protecting children, and we are collecting record amounts of child support. But now, I need the help of Congress. Together, in 1993 we expanded the Earned Income Tax Credit for 15 million working families, rewarding work over welfare. Now, my budget overhauls welfare by setting a time limit on cash benefits and imposing tough work requirements, and I want us to enact bipartisan legislation that requires work, demands responsibility, protects children, and provides adequate resources to get the job done right—with child care and training, giving recipients the tools they need.

More and more, education and training have become the keys to higher living standards. While Americans clearly want States and localities to play the lead role in education, the Federal Government has an important supporting role to play—from funding pre-school services that prepare children to learn, to expanding access to college and worker retraining. My budget continues the strong investments that we have made to give Americans the skills they need to get good jobs. Along with my ongoing investments, my budget proposes a Technology Literacy Challenge Fund to bring the benefits of technology into the classroom, a $1,000 merit scholarship for the top five percent of graduates in every high school, and more Charter Schools to let parents, teachers, and communities create public schools to meet their own children's needs.

As Americans, we can take pride in cleaning up the environment over the last 25 years, with leadership from Presidents of both parties. But our job is not done—not with so many Americans breathing dirty air or drinking unsafe water. My budget continues our efforts to find solutions to our environmental problems without burdening business or imposing unnecessary regulations. We are providing the necessary funds for the Environmental Protection Agency's operating program, for our national parks and forests, for my plan to restore the Florida Everglades, and for my "brownfields" initiative to clean up abandoned, contaminated industrial sites in distressed urban and rural communities. And we are continuing to reinvent the regulatory process by working collaboratively with business, rather than treating it as an adversary.

With science and technology (S&T) so vital to our economic future, our national security, and the well-being of our people, my budget continues our investments in this crucial area. To maintain our investments, I am asking Congress to fulfill my request for basic research in health sciences at the National Institutes of Health, for basic research and education at the National Science Foundation, for research at other agencies that depend on S&T for their missions, and for cooperative projects with universities and industry, such as the industry partnerships created under the Advanced Technology Program.

To attack crime, the Federal Government must work with States and communities on some problems and lead on others. To help communities, we continue to invest in the Community Oriented Policing Services (COPS) program, which is putting 100,000 more police on the street. We are helping States build more prisons and jail space, better enforce the Brady bill that helps prevent criminals from buying handguns, and better address the problem of youth gangs. At the Federal level, we are leading the fight to stop drugs from entering the country and expand drug treatment efforts, and we are stepping up our efforts to secure the border against illegal immigration while we help to defray State costs for such immigration.

For many families, of course, the first challenge often is just to pay the bills. My budget proposes tax relief for middle-income Americans and small businesses. It provides an income tax credit for each dependent child under 13; a deduction for college tuition and fees; and expanded individual retirement accounts to help families save for future needs and more easily pay for college, buy a first home, pay the bills during times of unemployment, or pay medical or nursing home costs. For small business, it offers more tax benefits to invest, provides estate tax relief, and makes it easier to set up pensions for employees. It also would expand the tax deduction to make health insurance for the self-employed more affordable.

MAKING GOVERNMENT WORK

As we pursue these priorities, we will do so with a Government that is leaner, but not meaner, one that works efficiently, manages resources wisely, focuses on results rather than merely spending money, and provides better service to the American people. Through the National Performance Review, led by Vice President Gore, we are making real progress in creating a Government that "works better and costs less."

We have cut the size of the Federal workforce by over 200,000 people, creating the smallest Federal workforce in 30 years, and the smallest as a share of the total workforce since before the New Deal. We are ahead of schedule to cut the workforce by 272,900 positions, as required by the 1994 Federal Workforce Restructuring Act that I signed into law.

Just as important, the Government is working better. Agencies such as the Social Security Administration, the Customs Service, and the Veterans Affairs Department are providing much better service to their customers. Across the Government, agencies are using information technology to deliver services more efficiently to more people.

We are continuing to reduce the burden of Federal regulation, ensuring that our rules serve a purpose and do not unduly burden businesses or taxpayers. We are eliminating 16,000 pages of regulations across Government, and agencies are improving their rulemaking processes.

In addition, we continue to overhaul Federal procurement so that the Government can buy better products at cheaper prices from the private sector. No longer does the Government pay outrageous prices for hammers, ashtrays, and other small items that it can buy cheaper at local stores.

As we look ahead, we plan to work more closely with States and localities, with businesses and individuals, and with Federal workers to focus our efforts on improving services for the American people. Under the Vice President's leadership, agencies are setting higher and higher standards for delivering faster and better service.

CONCLUSION

Our agenda is working. We have significantly reduced the deficit, strengthened the economy, invested in our future, and cut the size of Government while making it work better for the American people.

Now, we have an opportunity to build on our success by balancing the budget the right way. It is an opportunity we should not miss.

WILLIAM J. CLINTON
March 1996

President Clinton's Reelection Acceptance Speech

Following is a transcript of President Clinton's speech in Little Rock, Ark., early Nov. 6, 1996, after being declared the winner in Nov. 5 balloting, as provided by the Federal Document Clearing House.

My fellow Americans . . . thank you for being here.

Just four years from now, we will enter a new century of great challenge and unlimited possibility. Now, we've got a bridge to build, and I'm ready if you are.

Today the American people have spoken. They have affirmed our course. They have told us to go forward.

America has told every one of us—Democrats, Republicans and independents—loud and clear: It is time to put politics aside, join together and get the job done for America's future.

In the last four years, we've made remarkable progress. But in our schools, our families, our workplaces and our communities, our journey is not done.

My fellow Americans, we have work to do, and that's what this election was all about.

I want to say to all of you here and to all of the American people—no words can convey the gratitude I feel tonight for the honor that has been given to me.

It is an honor that belongs to many. First to my family, to my wonderful wife of 21 years, who from the day I first met her began teaching me that it does take a village to raise our children and build our future.

To our daughter Chelsea for understanding the work we have done together, the burdens it has imposed.

Today, I went down to the train station to vote in the last election in which I will appear on the ballot, and as I have done in every year since she was born, I took Chelsea to the ballot with me. And as we looked at the ballot together and discussed the issues there, I thanked God that I was born an American.

I thank the members of my wonderful family who are here—my stepfather, Dick Kelley, my wonderful mother-in-law Dorothy Rodham and all the others. And I thank my beloved mother, who is smiling up there and said, "I never had a doubt. I always knew it would be this way."

I thank the friends of my lifetime. There are people who have stood with me through thick and thin, who started with me in grade school and junior and senior high school, in college and all across the years since. Friends who knew me and knew my dreams and stood as a powerful force against those who sought to stop America's progress with the politics of personal destruction. Thank you, my friends. Thank you for what you did for America.

I thank the people of my beloved native state. I would not be anywhere else in the world tonight. In front of this wonderful old capital that has seen so much of my own life and our state's history, I thank you for staying with me so long, for never giving up, for always knowing that we could do better.

I thank the finest vice president this country has ever seen. Because of Al Gore, we have a stronger and more secure relationship with the democratic Russia. We are exploring the wonders of new technologies for the benefit of America. We are protecting our environment, and we have reinvented America's government so that it does more with less, thanks to his leadership. It is a legacy unique in the history of this republic.

I thank Tipper [Gore] for her friendship, for her crusades on behalf of our children and the mental health of the American people and for always standing with us along with her children and her family.

I thank the members of our administration, the Cabinet members, the members of the White House staff. . . .

I thank all those who are part of the permanent service to the president at the White House and the medical staff. I thank especially my Secret Service detail that has been so challenged by a president determined not to be isolated from the American people.

I thank the members of our campaign staff, all those who have served in this election and the work you have done.

I thank the leaders of our party in the Congress, in the statehouses. I thank all those who stood for what we believe in in these elections today, those who won and those who did not. You did a service to America by raising the things in which we believe, and I thank you all and wish you Godspeed.

I want to thank the employees of the nation's government. They have had to do a remarkable job. We have reduced the size of our government to its smallest point since President Kennedy served, and yet they have continued to serve the people better, year in and year out.

They had to do it in the face of enormous challenges and outright hatred for momentary periods. They had to live with the horror of Oklahoma City and the difficulties that came along the way. But the people who serve us deserve our thanks—and I thank them.

I thank those who served this administration in our cause who are no longer here tonight and one especially I must thank, my friend and brother, [the late Commerce Secretary] Ron Brown. You're looking down on us, and I know you're smiling too.

On a purely personal note, I must thank my pastor, Rex Horne, who prayed with me before I came out here tonight, and all the ministers and people of God who prayed for me and with me over these last four years. There were a few especially, and they know who they are, who came to the White House time after time in good times and bad.

When the times were bad, they reminded me that God gave Saint Paul a thorn in his flesh, so he would not become exalted in his own eyes, and that certainly was not a problem for me in the bad times.

When the times were good, they reminded me that humility is always in order in the presidency—for in this life we see a glass darkly and we cannot know the whole truth of our circumstances or the motives of those who oppose us. I thank them all for bringing me closer to God and to the eternal wisdom without which a president cannot serve.

I would like to say a special word of thanks to Senator [Bob] Dole, and I ask you to join me in applause for his lifetime of service to the United States.

And I thank Jack Kemp for his service to America and his devotion to the proposition that this is a country in which everyone should have a chance to live free and equal and to have a chance at success.

Let me say . . . I had a good visit with Sen. Dole not too long before he went out to speak. I thanked him for his love of our country, for his years of service.

I applauded the campaign that he fought so bravely to the very last minute. I thanked him for the work we did together to advance the common cause of America. And on behalf of all Americans, I wish him well and Godspeed.

FOUR YEARS AGO

Four years ago, on these very steps, we set forth on a journey to change the course of America for the better, to keep the American dream alive for everyone willing to work for it, to keep America the world's strongest force for peace and freedom and prosperity, to come together as one American community.

The time was one of widespread frustration and doubt about our economic and social problems, about our ability to deal with the vast sweep of change that was all around us. The scope and pace of those changes were threatening to many, and our values seemed to be under attack on all sides.

But, together, you and I vowed to turn our country around, with a strategy to meet our challenges and protect our values, opportunity for all, responsibility from all, an American community of all Americans.

We have worked hard to end the politics of "who's to blame?" and instead to ask, "What are we going to do to make America better?"

Tonight, we proclaim that the vital American center is alive and well. It is a common ground on which we have made our progress. Today, our economy is stronger, our streets are safer, our environment is cleaner, the world is more secure and, thank God, our nation is more united.

To all the men and women across this country who have created our jobs, taught our children, patrolled our streets and kept America safe throughout our world, I say, America's success is your success. This victory is your victory. I thank you from the bottom of my heart.

Now, my fellow Americans, a vast new century lies before us. It will be a time more full of opportunity for people to live out their dreams than any in human history.

We have committed this night to continuing our journey, to doing the hard work that will build our bridge to the 21st century, to give the young people—here and those all across America—the America they deserve, and their children and their children's children.

But we have work to do. We have work to do to keep our economy growing steady and strong, by balancing the budget, while we honor our duties to our families, our parents and our children and our duty to pass on to our children the earth God gave us.

We have work to do to give all of our children the gift of an education, to make sure every 8-year-old can read, every 12-year-old can log on to the Internet and, yes, every single 18-year-old in this country willing to work for it can have a college education.

We have work to do to make the permanent underclass in the country a thing of the past, to lift our fellow citizens who are poor from the degradation of welfare dependency to the pride and dignity of work.

We have work to do to strengthen our families; to help our parents succeed at home and at work; to keep our children safe from harm in their schools, their streets, their homes and their communities; to clean up our environment so that our children grow up next to parks not poison; to tell them that drugs are wrong and illegal and they can kill them; to teach them right from wrong.

My fellow Americans, I will do all I can to advance these causes. But all our citizens must do their part to continue the upsurge of personal responsibility that in the last four years has brought crime to a 10-year low, child support collections to an all-time high, and reduced the welfare rolls.

Will you help me do that? We must do it together.

CAMPAIGN FINANCE REFORM

We must make our democracy stronger by enacting real, bipartisan campaign finance reform. Talk is no longer enough. We must act and act now. And the American people will be watching the leaders of both parties to see who is willing not just to talk but to act. I am willing to act, and I ask others to join me.

And we must keep America the world's indispensable nation. Finishing the unfinished business of the Cold War, meeting the new threats to our security through terrorism and the proliferation of dangerous weapons, and seizing these extraordinary opportunities to extend our values of peace and democracy and prosperity.

Every American here tonight and every American within the sound of my voice can take pride in the fact that in these last few years for the first time in all of human history, a majority of the human beings living on this globe live under democracies where the people rule.

The challenges we face, they're not Democratic or Republican challenges. They're American challenges. What we know from the budget battles of the last two years and from the remarkable success of the last few weeks of this Congress is the lesson we have learned for the last 220 years—what we have achieved as Americans of lasting good, we have achieved by working together. So let me say to the leaders of my Democratic Party and the leaders of the Republican Party, it is time to put country ahead of party.

We do not know the final outcome of the congressional elections but we know this: The races are close. The American people have been closely divided. The Congress, whatever happens, will be closely divided.

They are sending us a message: Work together. Meet our challenges. Put aside the politics of division and build America's community, together.

On this beautiful night when we have shared so much joy and so much music and so much laughter and so much pride, it is hard for me to believe that it was 23 years ago when I first began to go to the people of Arkansas to ask for their support.

The most lasting and important thing that I have learned in all those 23 fleeting years is this: When we are divided, we defeat ourselves. But when we join our hands and build our families and our communities and our country, America always wins.

What we need to do is to do the work of America, the way we seek to do the work of raising our children and doing our work and supporting our religious institutions and our community institutions.

If we would simply be Americans, the way we seek to live in all of our other roles, there is no stopping America. Our best days are still ahead.

And so, I say, when we look into our hearts and simply ask what is right for the American people and the future of our children, when we set aside our differences and build on our shared values of faith and family and work, when we roll up our sleeves and work together, America always wins.

And my fellow Americans, America is going to keep winning these next four years.

Let me say that, as all of you here from my native state know, I believe this and I have tried to live by it because there is no person in America who has been given more gifts than I have. There is no person in America tonight who feels more humble in the face of this victory than I do.

Fifty years ago, when I was born in a summer storm to a widowed mother in a small town in the southwest part of our state, it was unimaginable that someone like me could have ever become president of the greatest country in human history.

It has been, for me, a remarkable journey, not free of failure, but full of adventure and wonder and grace. I have worked hard to serve but I did not get here on my own.

Every step along the way for these last 23 years and long before, there was a teacher, a doctor, a neighbor, a parent, a friend, a wife, a daughter, who always had time to care, who always tried to give me instruction and encouragement and who never gave up.

I got here tonight, my fellow Americans, because America gave me a chance. That is what all the children of America deserve. Our people have to give them the tools to give them not a guarantee, but that real chance to live up to their God-given potential.

And I ask you to join me in that commitment. Every child deserves the main chance that I was given.

And so I say again let us resolve to run our country the way we try to run our lives. Whether you are the party of Thomas Jefferson or the party of Abraham Lincoln, whether you're an independent or unaffiliated, remember that we all belong to the greatest nation in history.

To us, much has been given and much is still expected. We must rise to the challenge of building that bridge to the 21st century. Tonight is a night for joy, not just for us here but for all Americans.

For the 53rd time in our history, our people have made their quiet and deliberate decision. They have come together with their powerful voice and expressed their will.

Tonight we celebrate the miracle of America. Tomorrow we greet the dawn and begin our work anew. I am more grateful than I can say. You have given me an opportunity and a responsibility that comes to few people.

I will do my best, and together we will—we will build that bridge to the 21st century. Thank you. Good night, and God bless America. Thank you.

Political Charts

Victorious Party in Presidential Races, 1860-1996

State	1860	1864	1868	1872	1876	1880	1884	1888	1892	1896	1900	1904	1908	1912	1916	1920	1924	1928	1932	1936	1940	1944	1948	1952	1956	1960	1964	1968	1972	1976	1980	1984	1988	1992	1996	Dem.	Rep.	Other
Ala.	SD	[b]	R	R	D	D	D	D	D	D	D	D	D	D	D	D	D	D	D	D	D	D	SR	D	D[r]	D[s]	R	AI	R	D	R	R	R	R	R	22	9	3
Alaska																										R	D	R	R	R	R	R	R	R	R	1	9	0
Ariz.														D	D	R	R	R	D	D	D	D	D	R	R	R	R	R	R	R	R	R	R	R	D	8	14	0
Ark.	SD	[b]	R	[d]	D	D	D	D	D	D	D	D	D	D	D	D	D	D	D	D	D	D	D	D	AI	R	D	R	R	R	R	R	R	R	D	26	5	2
Calif.	R	R	R	R	R	D[f]	R	R	D[g]	R[l]	R	R	R	PR	D	R	R	R	D	D	D	D	R	R	R	D	D	R	R	R	R	R	R	D	D	11	23	1
Colo.					R	R	R	R	PP	D	D	R	D	R	R	D	R	D	R	R	R	R	R	R	R	R	D	R	R	R	R	R	R	D	D	10	20	1
Conn.	R	R	R	R	D	R	D	D	D	R	R	R	R	D	R	R	R	R	D	D	D	D	R	R	R	D	D	D	R	R	R	R	R	D	D	13	22	0
Del.	SD	D	D	R	D	D	D	D	D	R	R	R	R	D	R	R	R	R	D	D	D	D	R	R	R	D	R	R	D	R	R	R	R	D	D	16	18	1
D.C.																										D	D	D	D	D	D	D	D	D	D	9	0	0
Fla.	SD	[b]	R	R	R	D	D	D	D	D	D	D	D	D	D	D	D	D	D	D	D	D	D	R	R	D	D	R	R	R	R	R	R	R	R	20	13	1
Ga.	SD	[b]	D	D[e]	D	D	D	D	D	D	D	D	D	D	D	D	D	D	D	D	D	D	D	D	D	D	R	AI	R	D	R	R	R	D	R	27	5	2
Hawaii																										D	D	D	R	D	D	D	R	D	D	8	2	0
Idaho									PP	D	D	R	D	R	R	R	D	R	R	R	R	D	D	D	D	R	D	R	R	R	R	R	R	R	D	10	16	1
Ill.	R	R	R	R	R	R	R	R	D	R	R	R	R	D	R	R	R	R	D	D	D	D	R	R	R	D	D	R	R	D	R	R	R	D	D	11	24	0
Ind.	R	R	R	R	D	R	D	R	D	R	R	R	R	D	R	R	R	R	D	R	R	R	R	R	R	D	R	R	R	R	R	R	R	R	R	7	28	0
Iowa	R	R	R	R	R	R	R	R	R	R	R	R	R	D	R	R	R	R	D	R	R	R	R	R	R	D	R	R	R	D	R	R	R	D	D	8	27	0
Kan.		R	R	R	R	R	R	R	PP	D	R	R	R	D	R	R	R	R	D	R	R	R	D	R	R	R	D	R	R	R	R	R	R	R	R	6	27	1
Ky.	CU	D	D	D	D	D	D	D	R[m]	D	D	D	D	D	D	R	R	R	D	D	D	D	D	R	R	D	R	R	R	D	R	R	R	D	D	24	10	1
La.	SD	[b]	D	[d]	R	R	D	D	D	D	D	D	D	D	D	D	D	D	D	D	D	D	SR	D	R	D	R	AI	R	D	R	R	R	D	R	23	7	3
Maine	R	R	R	R	R	R	R	R	R	R	R	R	R	D	R	R	R	R	R	D	R	R	R	R	R	R	R	R	R	D	R	R	R	D	D	5	30	0
Md.	SD	R	D	D	D	D	D	D	D	R	D[n]	D[o]	D	D	R	R	R	R	D	D	D	D	R	R	R	D	D	R	D	D	R	R	R	D	D	22	12	1
Mass.	R	R	R	R	R	R	R	R	R	R	R	R	R	D	R	R	R	D	D	D	D	D	R	R	R	D	D	D	R	D	D	R	D	D	D	15	20	0
Mich.	R	R	R	R	R	R	R	R	R[h]	R	R	R	R	PR	R	R	R	R	D	R	R	R	R	D	R	D	D	R	R	R	R	R	R	D	D	8	26	1
Minn.	R	R	R	R	R	R	R	R	R	R	R	R	R	PR	R	R	R	R	D	D	D	D	R	R	R	D	D	D	D	D	D	D	D	D	D	14	20	1
Miss.	SD	[b]	[c]	R	D	D	D	D	D	D	D	D	D	D	D	D	D	D	D	D	D	D	SR	D	D	[t]	R	AI	R	D	R	R	R	R	R	21	8	3
Mo.	D	R	R	D	D	D	D	D	D	D	D	D	D	R	D	R	R	R	D	D	D	D	R	R	R	D	R	R	R	R	R	R	D	R	D	22	13	0
Mont.									R	D	R	R	R	D	R	D	D	R	R	D	D	R	R	D	R	D	R	R	R	R	R	R	R	R	R	11	16	0
Neb.		R	R	R	R	R	R	R	D	R	R	R	D	R	R	R	D	R	R	R	D	R	R	R	R	R	D	R	R	R	R	R	R	R	R	7	26	1
Nev.		R	R	R	D	R	R	R	PP	D	D	D	R	D	R	D	D	R	R	D	D	R	R	R	D	D	D	R	D	R	R	R	R	R	D	15	18	1
N.H.	R	R	R	R	R	R	R	R	R	R	R	R	R	D	R	R	R	R	D	D	D	D	R	R	R	D	D	D	R	R	R	R	R	D	D	8	27	0
N.J.	R[a]	D	R	R	D	D	D	D	D	R	R	R	R	D	R	R	R	R	D	R	R	R	R	R	R	D	R	R	R	D	R	R	R	D	D	16	19	0
N.M.														D	R	R	R	D	D	D	R	D	D	D	R	D	R	D	D	R	R	R	R	R	D	11	11	0
N.Y.	R	R	D	R	D	R	D	R	D	R	R	R	R	D	R	R	R	D	D	D	D	D	R	R	R	D	D	R	R	D	R	R	R	D	D	16	19	0
N.C.	SD	[b]	R	R	D	D	D	D	D	D	D	D	R	D	D	R	R	R	D	D	D	D	D	R	R	R	R[v]	R	R	D	R	R	R	R	R	23	10	1
N.D.									[i]	R	R	R	D	R	R	R	D	R	R	R	R	D	R	R	R	R	D	R	R	R	R	R	R	R	R	5	21	1
Ohio	R	R	R	R	R	R	R	R	R[j]	R	R	R	R	D	R	R	R	R	D	D	D	D	R	R	R	D	D	R	R	R	R	R	R	D	D	10	25	0
Okla.													D	D	D	R	D	D	R	D	D	D	D	D	R	R	R[u]	D	R	R	R	R	R	R	R	10	13	0
Ore.	R	R	D	R	R	R	R	R	R[k]	R	R	R	R	D	R	R	R	R	D	D	D	D	R	R	R	D	R	R	R	D	D	D	D	D	D	9	25	1
Pa.	R	R	R	R	R	R	R	R	R	R	R	R	R	PR	R	R	R	R	D	D	D	D	R	R	R	D	D	R	R	R	R	R	R	D	D	9	25	1
R.I.	R	R	R	R	R	R	R	R	R	R	R	R	R	D	R	R	R	R	D	D	D	D	R	R	R	D	D	D	R	D	R	D	D	D	D	15	20	0
S.C.	SD	[b]	R	R	D	D	D	D	D	D	D	D	D	D	D	D	D	D	D	D	D	D	SR	D	D	D	R	R	R	D	R	R	R	R	R	21	11	2
S.D.									PP	R	R	R	D	R	R	R	D	R	R	R	R	D	R	R	R	R	R	R	R	R	R	R	R	R	R	4	22	1
Tenn.	CU	[b]	R	D	D	D	D	D	D	D	D	D	D	D	D	R	D	D	D	D	D	D	D	R	R	D	D	R	R	D[q]	R	R	R	R	R	22	10	1
Texas	SD	[b]	[c]	D	D	D	D	D	D	D	D	D	D	D	R	D	D	D	D	D	D	D	D	R	R	D	D	R	R	D	R	R	D	D	D	23	9	1
Utah										D	R	R	R	D	R	R	R	D	R	R	R	D	D	D	D	R	R	R	D	R	R	R	R	R	R	8	18	0
Vt.	R	R	R	R	R	R	R	R	R	R	R	R	R	R	R	R	R	R	R	R	R	R	R	R	R	R	D	R	R	R	R	R	R	D	D	3	32	0
Va.	CU	[b]	[c]	R	D	D	D	D	D	D	D	D	D	D	D	D	D	D	D	D	D	D	D	R	R	R	D	R	R[w]	R	R	R	R	R	D	19	13	1
Wash.									R	D	R	R	R	PR	D	R	R	R	D	D	D	D	R	D	R	D	R	D	R	R[x]	R	D	D	D	D	12	14	1
W.Va.		R	R	R	D	D	D	D	D	R	R	R	R	R[p]	R	R	R	D	D	D	D	D	D	R	D	R	R	D	R	D	R	D[y]	D	D	D	20	14	1
Wis.	R	R	R	R	R	R	R	R	D	R	R	R	R	PR	R	R	R	D	D	D	D	R	R	R	R	R	D	R	D	R	R	R	D	D	D	11	23	1
Wyo.									R	D	R	R	R	D	R	D	R	R	R	R	R	R	R	R	R	R	R	R	R	R	R	R	R	R	R	8	19	0
Winning Party	R	R	R	R	R	R	D	R	D	R	R	R	R	D	D	R	R	R	D	D	D	D	D	R	R	D	D	R	R	D	R	R	R	D	D	14	21	0

NOTE: With the exception of the District of Columbia, blanks indicate states not yet admitted to the Union. The District of Columbia received the presidential vote in 1961.

KEY: AI-American Independent Party; CU-Constitutional Union Party; D-Democratic Party; PP-People's Party; PR-Progressive (Bull Moose) Party; R-Republican Party; SD-Southern Democratic Party; SR-States' Rights Democratic Party.

[a] Four electors voted Republican; three, Democratic.
[b] Confederate states did not vote in 1864.
[c] Did not vote in 1868.
[d] Votes were not counted.
[e] Three votes for Greeley not counted.
[f] Five electors voted Democratic; one, Republican.
[g] Eight electors voted Democratic; one, Republican.
[h] Nine electors voted Republican; five, Democratic.
[i] One vote each for Democratic, Republican and People's parties.
[j] Twenty-two electors voted Republican; one, Democratic.
[k] Three electors voted Republican; one, People's Party.
[l] Eight electors voted Republican; one, Democratic.
[m] Twelve electors voted Republican; one, Democratic.
[n] Seven electors voted Democratic; one, Republican.
[o] Six electors voted Democratic; two, Republican.
[p] Seven electors voted Republican; one, Democratic.
[q] Eleven electors voted Democratic; one, States' Rights.
[r] One elector voted for Walter B. Jones.
[s] Six of eleven electors voted for Harry F. Byrd.
[t] Eight independent electors voted for Byrd.
[u] One vote cast for Byrd
[v] Twelve electors voted Republican; one, American Independent.
[w] One elector voted Libertarian.
[x] One elector voted for Ronald Reagan.
[y] One elector voted for Lloyd Bentsen.

Summary of Presidential Elections, 1789–1996

Year	No. of states	Candidates	Party	Electoral vote	Popular vote
1789[a]	10	**George Washington**	**Fed.**	**69**	—[b]
		John Adams	Fed.	34	
1792[a]	15	**George Washington**	**Fed.**	**132**	—[b]
		John Adams	Fed.	77	
1796[a]	16	**John Adams**	**Fed.**	**71**	—[b]
		Thomas Jefferson	Dem.-Rep.	68	
1800[a]	16	**Thomas Jefferson**	**Dem.-Rep.**	**73**	—[b]
		Aaron Burr	Dem.-Rep.	73	
		John Adams	Fed.	65	
		Charles Cotesworth Pinckney	Fed.	64	
1804	17	**Thomas Jefferson**	**Dem.-Rep.**	**162**	—[b]
		George Clinton			
		Charles Cotesworth Pinckney	Fed.	64	
		Rufus King			
1808	17	**James Madison**	**Dem.-Rep.**	**122**	—[b]
		George Clinton			
		Charles Cotesworth Pinckney	Fed.	64	
		Rufus King			
1812	18	**James Madison**	**Dem.-Rep.**	**128**	—[b]
		Elbridge Gerry			
		George Clinton	Fed.	89	
		Jared Ingersoll			
1816	19	**James Monroe**	**Dem.-Rep.**	**183**	—[b]
		Daniel D. Tompkins			
		Rufus King	Fed.	34	
		John Howard			
1820	24	**James Monroe**	**Dem.-Rep.**	**231**[c]	—[b]
		Daniel D. Tompkins			
1824[d]	24	**John Quincy Adams**	**Dem.-Rep.**	**99**	113,122 (30.9%)
		John C. Calhoun			
		Andrew Jackson	Dem.-Rep.	84	151,271 (41.3%)
		Nathan Sanford			
1828	24	**Andrew Jackson**	**Dem.-Rep.**	**178**	642,553 (56.0%)
		John C. Calhoun			
		John Quincy Adams	Nat.-Rep.	83	500,897 (43.6%)
		Richard Rush			
1832[e]	24	**Andrew Jackson**	**Dem.**	**219**	701,780 (54.2%)
		Martin Van Buren			
		Henry Clay	Nat.-Rep.	49	484,205 (37.4%)
		John Sergeant			
1836[f]	26	**Martin Van Buren**	**Dem.**	**170**	764,176 (50.8%)
		Richard M. Johnson			
		William Henry Harrison	Whig	73	550,816 (36.6%)
		Francis Granger			
1840	26	**William Henry Harrison**	**Whig**	**234**	1,275,390 (52.9%)
		John Tyler			
		Martin Van Buren	Dem.	60	1,128,854 (46.8%)
		Richard M. Johnson			
1844	26	**James K. Polk**	**Dem.**	**170**	1,339,494 (49.5%)
		George M. Dallas			
		Henry Clay	Whig	105	1,300,004 (48.1%)
		Theodore Frelinghuysen			
1848	30	**Zachary Taylor**	**Whig**	**163**	1,361,393 (47.3%)
		Millard Fillmore			
		Lewis Cass	Dem.	127	1,223,460 (42.5%)
		William O. Butler			
1852	31	**Franklin Pierce**	**Dem.**	**254**	1,607,510 (50.8%)
		William R. King			
		Winfield Scott	Whig	42	1,386,942 (43.9%)
		William A. Graham			
1856[g]	31	**James Buchanan**	**Dem.**	**174**	1,836,072 (45.3%)
		John C. Breckinridge			
		John C. Fremont	Rep.	114	1,342,345 (33.1%)
		William L. Dayton			
1860[h]	33	**Abraham Lincoln**	**Rep.**	**180**	1,865,908 (39.8%)
		Hannibal Hamlin			
		Stephen A. Douglas	Dem.	12	1,380,202 (29.5%)
		Herschel V. Johnson			
1864[i]	36	**Abraham Lincoln**	**Rep.**	**212**	2,218,388 (55.0%)
		Andrew Johnson			
		George B. McClellan	Dem.	21	1,812,807 (45.0%)
		George H. Pendleton			
1868[j]	37	**Ulysses S. Grant**	**Rep.**	**214**	3,013,650 (52.7%)
		Schuyler Colfax			
		Horatio Seymour	Dem.	80	2,708,744 (47.3%)
		Francis P. Blair Jr.			
1872	37	**Ulysses S. Grant**	**Rep.**	**286**	3,598,235 (55.6%)
		Henry Wilson			
		Horace Greeley	Dem.	—[k]	2,834,761 (43.8%)
		Benjamin Gratz Brown			
1876	38	**Rutherford B. Hayes**	**Rep.**	**185**	4,034,311 (47.9%)
		William A. Wheeler			
		Samuel J. Tilden	Dem.	184	4,288,546 (51.0%)
		Thomas A. Hendricks			
1880	38	**James A. Garfield**	**Rep.**	**214**	4,446,158 (48.3%)
		Chester A. Arthur			
		Winfield S. Hancock	Dem.	155	4,444,260 (48.2%)
		William H. English			
1884	38	**Grover Cleveland**	**Dem.**	**219**	4,874,621 (48.5%)
		Thomas A. Hendricks			
		James G. Blaine	Rep.	182	4,848,936 (48.2%)
		John A. Logan			

Year	No. of states	Candidates	Party	Electoral vote	Popular vote	Year	No. of states	Candidates	Party	Electoral vote	Popular vote
1888	38	**Benjamin Harrison** *Levi P. Morton*	**Rep.**	**233**	**5,443,892 (47.8%)**	1940	48	**Franklin D. Roosevelt** *Henry A. Wallace*	**Dem.**	**449**	**27,263,448 (54.7%)**
		Grover Cleveland *Allen G. Thurman*	Dem.	168	5,534,488 (48.6%)			Wendell L. Willkie *Charles L. McNary*	Rep.	82	22,336,260 (44.8%)
1892[l]	44	**Grover Cleveland** *Adlai E. Stevenson*	**Dem.**	**277**	**5,551,883 (46.1%)**	1944	48	**Franklin D. Roosevelt** *Harry S. Truman*	**Dem.**	**432**	**25,611,936 (53.4%)**
		Benjamin Harrison *Whitelaw Reid*	Rep.	145	5,179,244 (43.0%)			Thomas E. Dewey *John W. Bricker*	Rep.	99	22,013,372 (45.9%)
1896	45	**William McKinley** *Garret A. Hobart*	**Rep.**	**271**	**7,108,480 (51.0%)**	1948[o]	48	**Harry S. Truman** *Alben W. Barkley*	**Dem.**	**303**	**24,105,587 (49.5%)**
		William J. Bryan *Arthur Sewall*	Dem.	176	6,511,495 (46.7%)			Thomas E. Dewey *Earl Warren*	Rep.	198	21,970,017 (45.1%)
1900	45	**William McKinley** *Theodore Roosevelt*	**Rep.**	**292**	**7,218,039 (51.7%)**	1952	48	**Dwight D. Eisenhower** *Richard M. Nixon*	**Rep.**	**442**	**33,936,137 (55.1%)**
		William J. Bryan *Adlai E. Stevenson*	Dem.	155	6,358,345 (45.5%)			Adlai E. Stevenson II *John J. Sparkman*	Dem.	89	27,314,649 (44.4%)
1904	45	**Theodore Roosevelt** *Charles W. Fairbanks*	**Rep.**	**336**	**7,626,593 (56.4%)**	1956[p]	48	**Dwight D. Eisenhower** *Richard M. Nixon*	**Rep.**	**457**	**35,585,245 (57.4%)**
		Alton B. Parker *Henry G. Davis*	Dem.	140	5,028,898 (37.6%)			Adlai E. Stevenson II *Estes Kefauver*	Dem.	73	26,030,172 (42.0%)
1908	46	**William Howard Taft** *James S. Sherman*	**Rep.**	**321**	**7,676,258 (51.6%)**	1960[q]	50	**John F. Kennedy** *Lyndon B. Johnson*	**Dem.**	**303**	**34,221,344 (49.7%)**
		William J. Bryan *John W. Kern*	Dem.	162	6,406,801 (43.0%)			Richard Nixon *Henry Cabot Lodge*	Rep.	219	34,106,671 (49.5%)
1912[m]	48	**Woodrow Wilson** *Thomas R. Marshall*	**Dem.**	**435**	**6,293,152 (41.8%)**	1964	50*	**Lyndon B. Johnson** *Hubert H. Humphrey*	**Dem.**	**486**	**43,126,584 (61.1%)**
		William Howard Taft *James S. Sherman*	Rep.	8	3,486,333 (23.2%)			Barry Goldwater *William E. Miller*	Rep.	52	27,177,838 (38.5%)
1916	48	**Woodrow Wilson** *Thomas R. Marshall*	**Dem.**	**277**	**9,126,300 (49.2%)**	1968[r]	50*	**Richard Nixon** *Spiro T. Agnew*	**Rep.**	**301**	**31,785,148 (43.4%)**
		Charles E. Hughes *Charles W. Fairbanks*	Rep.	254	8,546,789 (46.1%)			Hubert H. Humphrey *Edmund S. Muskie*	Dem.	191	31,274,503 (42.7%)
1920	48	**Warren G. Harding** *Calvin Coolidge*	**Rep.**	**404**	**16,133,314 (60.3%)**	1972[s]	50*	**Richard Nixon** *Spiro T. Agnew*	**Rep.**	**520**	**47,170,179 (60.7%)**
		James M. Cox *Franklin D. Roosevelt*	Dem.	127	9,140,884 (34.2%)			George McGovern *Sargent Shriver*	Dem.	17	29,171,791 (37.5%)
1924[n]	48	**Calvin Coolidge** *Charles G. Dawes*	**Rep.**	**382**	**15,717,553 (54.1%)**	1976[t]	50*	**Jimmy Carter** *Walter F. Mondale*	**Dem.**	**297**	**40,830,763 (50.1%)**
		John W. Davis *Charles W. Bryan*	Dem.	136	8,386,169 (28.8%)			Gerald R. Ford *Robert Dole*	Rep.	240	39,147,793 (48.0%)
1928	48	**Herbert C. Hoover** *Charles Curtis*	**Rep.**	**444**	**21,411,991 (58.2%)**	1980	50*	**Ronald Reagan** *George Bush*	**Rep.**	**489**	**43,904,153 (50.7%)**
		Alfred E. Smith *Joseph T. Robinson*	Dem.	87	15,000,185 (40.8%)			Jimmy Carter *Walter F. Mondale*	Dem.	49	35,483,883 (41.0%)
1932	48	**Franklin D. Roosevelt** *John N. Garner*	**Dem.**	**472**	**22,825,016 (57.4%)**	1984	50*	**Ronald Reagan** *George Bush*	**Rep.**	**525**	**54,455,074 (58.8%)**
		Herbert C. Hoover *Charles Curtis*	Rep.	59	15,758,397 (39.6%)			Walter F. Mondale *Geraldine Ferraro*	Dem.	13	37,577,137 (40.6%)
1936	48	**Franklin D. Roosevelt** *John N. Garner*	**Dem.**	**523**	**27,747,636 (60.8%)**	1988[u]	50*	**George Bush** *Dan Quayle*	**Rep.**	**426**	**48,881,278 (53.4%)**
		Alfred M. Landon *Frank Knox*	Rep.	8	16,679,543 (36.5%)			Michael S. Dukakis *Lloyd Bentsen*	Dem.	111	41,805,374 (45.6%)

(table continues)

Year	No. of states	Candidates	Party	Electoral vote	Popular vote	Year	No. of states	Candidates	Party	Electoral vote	Popular vote
1992	50*	**Bill Clinton** *Al Gore*	**Dem.**	**370**	**44,908,233 (43.0%)**	1996	50*	**Bill Clinton** *Al Gore*	**Dem.**	**379**	**47,402,357 (49.2%)**
		George Bush *Dan Quayle*	Rep.	168	39,102,282 (37.4%)			Bob Dole *Jack Kemp*	Rep.	159	39,198,755 (40.7%)

SOURCE: Harold W. Stanley and Richard G. Niemi, *Vital Statistics on American Politics,* 5th ed. (Washington, D.C.: CQ Press, 1995), table 3-13.

NOTES: Bold indicates victors. In the elections of 1789, 1792, 1796, and 1800, each candidate ran for the office of president. The candidate with the second highest number of electoral votes became vice president. For elections after 1800, italic indicates vice-presidential candidates. Dem.-Rep.—Democratic-Republican; Fed.—Federalist; Nat.-Rep.—National-Republican; Dem.—Democratic; Rep.—Republican.   a. Elections of 1789–1800 were held under rules that did not allow separate voting for president and vice president.   b. Popular vote returns are not shown before 1824 because consistent, reliable data are not available.   c. Monroe ran unopposed. One electoral vote was cast for John Adams and Richard Stockton, who were not candidates.   d. 1824: All four candidates represented Democratic-Republican factions. William H. Crawford received 41 electoral votes, and Henry Clay received 37 votes. Since no candidate received a majority, the election was decided (in Adams's favor) by the House of Representatives.   e. 1832: Two electoral votes were not cast.   f. 1836: Other Whig candidates receiving electoral votes were Hugh L. White, who received 26 votes, and Daniel Webster, who received 14 votes.   g. 1856: Millard Fillmore, Whig-American, received 8 electoral votes.   h. 1860: John C. Breckinridge, Southern Democrat, received 72 electoral votes. John Bell, Constitutional Union, received 39 electoral votes.   i. 1864: Eighty-one electoral votes were not cast.   j. 1868: Twenty-three electoral votes were not cast.   k. 1872: Horace Greeley, Democrat, died after the election. In the electoral college, Democratic electoral votes went to Thomas Hendricks, 42 votes; Benjamin Gratz Brown, 18 votes; Charles J. Jenkins, 2 votes; and David Davis, 1 vote. Seventeen electoral votes were not cast.   l. 1892: James B. Weaver, People's Party, received 22 electoral votes.   m. 1912: Theodore Roosevelt, Progressive Party, received 86 electoral votes.   n. 1924: Robert M. La Follette, Progressive Party, received 13 electoral votes.   o. 1948: J. Strom Thurmond, States' Rights Party, received 39 electoral votes.   p. 1956: Walter B. Jones, Democrat, received 1 electoral vote.   q. 1960: Harry Flood Byrd, Democrat, received 15 electoral votes.   r. 1968: George C. Wallace, American Independent Party, received 46 electoral votes.   s. 1972: John Hospers, Libertarian Party, received 1 electoral vote.   t. 1976: Ronald Reagan, Republican, received 1 electoral vote.   u. 1988: Lloyd Bentsen, the Democratic vice-presidential nominee, received 1 electoral vote for president.   *Fifty states plus the District of Columbia.

1992 Presidential Election

State	Total vote	Bill Clinton (Democrat)		George Bush (Republican)		Ross Perot (Independent)		Andre V. Marrow (Libertarian)		Other[a]		Plurality	
		Votes	%	Votes	%	Votes	%	Votes	%	Votes	%		
Alabama	1,688,060	690,080	40.9	804,283	47.6	183,109	10.8	5,737	0.3	4,851	0.3	114,203	R
Alaska	258,506	78,294	30.3	102,000	39.5	73,481	28.4	1,378	0.5	3,353	1.3	23,706	R
Arizona	1,486,975	543,050	36.5	572,086	38.5	353,741	23.8	6,759	0.5	11,339	0.8	29,036	R
Arkansas	950,653	505,823	53.2	337,324	35.5	99,132	10.4	1,261	0.1	7,113	0.7	168,499	D
California	11,131,721	5,121,325	46.0	3,630,574	32.6	2,296,006	20.6	48,139	0.4	35,677	0.3	1,490,751	D
Colorado	1,569,180	629,681	40.1	562,850	35.9	366,010	23.3	8,669	0.6	1,970	0.1	66,831	D
Connecticut	1,616,332	682,318	42.2	578,313	35.8	348,771	21.6	5,391	0.3	1,539	0.1	104,005	D
Delaware	289,735	126,054	43.5	102,313	35.3	59,213	20.4	935	0.3	1,220	0.4	23,741	D
Florida	5,314,392	2,072,698	39.0	2,173,310	40.9	1,053,067	19.8	15,079	0.3	238		100,612	R
Georgia	2,321,125	1,008,966	43.5	995,252	42.9	309,657	13.3	7,110	0.3	140		13,714	D
Hawaii	372,842	179,310	48.1	136,822	36.7	53,003	14.2	1,119	0.3	2,588	0.7	42,488	D
Idaho	482,142	137,013	28.4	202,645	42.0	130,395	27.0	1,167	0.2	10,922	2.3	65,632	R
Illinois	5,050,157	2,453,350	48.6	1,734,096	34.3	840,515	16.6	9,218	0.2	12,978	0.3	719,254	D
Indiana	2,305,871	848,420	36.8	989,375	42.9	455,934	19.8	7,936	0.3	4,206	0.2	140,955	D
Iowa	1,354,607	586,353	43.3	504,891	37.3	253,468	18.7	1,076	0.1	8,819	0.7	81,462	D
Kansas	1,157,335	390,434	33.7	449,951	38.9	312,358	27.0	4,314	0.4	278		59,517	R
Kentucky	1,492,900	665,104	44.6	617,178	41.3	203,944	13.7	4,513	0.3	2,161	0.1	47,926	D
Louisiana	1,790,017	815,971	45.6	733,386	41.0	211,478	11.8	3,155	0.2	26,027	1.5	82,585	D
Maine	679,499	263,420	38.8	206,504	30.4	206,820	30.4	1,681	0.2	1,074	0.2	56,600	D
Maryland	1,985,046	988,571	49.8	707,094	35.6	281,414	14.2	4,715	0.2	3,252	0.2	281,477	D
Massachusetts	2,773,700	1,318,662	47.5	805,049	29.0	630,731	22.7	9,024	0.3	10,234	0.4	513,613	D
Michigan	4,274,673	1,871,182	43.8	1,554,940	36.4	824,813	19.3	10,175	0.2	13,563	0.3	316,242	D
Minnesota	2,347,948	1,020,997	43.5	747,841	31.9	562,506	24.0	3,374	0.1	13,230	0.6	273,156	D
Mississippi	981,793	400,258	40.8	487,793	49.7	85,626	8.7	2,154	0.2	5,962	0.6	87,535	R
Missouri	2,391,565	1,053,873	44.1	811,159	33.9	518,741	21.7	7,497	0.3	295		242,714	D
Montana	410,611	154,507	37.6	144,207	35.1	107,225	26.1	986	0.2	3,686	0.9	10,300	D
Nebraska	737,546	216,864	29.4	343,678	46.6	174,104	23.6	1,340	0.2	1,560	0.2	126,814	R
Nevada	506,318	189,148	37.4	175,828	34.7	132,580	26.2	1,835	0.4	6,927	1.4	13,320	D
New Hampshire	537,943	209,040	38.9	202,484	37.6	121,337	22.6	3,548	0.7	1,534	0.3	6,556	D
New Jersey	3,343,594	1,436,206	43.0	1,356,865	40.6	521,829	15.6	6,822	0.2	21,872	0.7	79,341	D
New Mexico	569,986	261,617	45.9	212,824	37.3	91,895	16.1	1,615	0.3	2,035	0.4	48,793	D
New York	6,926,925	3,444,450	49.7	2,346,649	33.9	1,090,721	15.7	13,451	0.2	31,654	0.5	1,097,801	D
North Carolina	2,611,850	1,114,042	42.7	1,134,661	43.4	357,864	13.7	5,171	0.2	112		20,619	R
North Dakota	308,133	99,168	32.2	136,244	44.2	71,084	23.1	416	0.1	1,221	0.4	37,076	R
Ohio	4,939,967	1,984,942	40.2	1,894,310	38.3	1,036,426	21.0	7,252	0.1	17,037	0.3	90,632	D
Oklahoma	1,390,359	473,066	34.0	592,929	42.6	319,878	23.0	4,486	0.3	—		119,863	R
Oregon	1,462,643	621,314	42.5	475,757	32.5	354,091	24.2	4,277	0.3	7,204	0.5	145,557	D
Pennsylvania	4,959,810	2,239,164	45.1	1,791,841	36.1	902,667	18.2	21,477	0.4	4,661	0.1	447,323	D
Rhode Island	453,477	213,299	47.0	131,601	29.0	105,045	23.2	571	0.1	2,961	0.7	81,698	D
South Carolina	1,202,527	479,514	39.9	577,507	48.0	138,872	11.5	2,719	0.2	3,915	0.3	97,993	R
South Dakota	336,254	124,888	37.1	136,718	40.7	73,295	21.8	814	0.2	539	0.2	11,830	R
Tennessee	1,982,638	933,521	47.1	841,300	42.4	199,968	10.1	1,847	0.1	6,002	0.3	92,221	D
Texas	6,154,018	2,281,815	37.1	2,496,071	40.6	1,354,781	22.0	19,699	0.3	1,652		214,256	R
Utah	743,999	183,429	24.7	322,632	43.4	203,400	27.3	1,900	0.3	32,638	4.4	119,232	R
Vermont	289,701	133,592	46.1	88,122	30.4	65,991	22.8	501	0.2	1,495	0.5	45,470	D
Virginia	2,558,665	1,038,650	40.6	1,150,517	45.0	348,639	13.6	5,730	0.2	15,129	0.6	111,867	R
Washington	2,288,230	993,037	43.4	731,234	32.0	541,780	23.7	7,533	0.3	14,646	0.6	261,803	D
West Virginia	683,762	331,001	48.4	241,974	35.4	108,829	15.9	1,873	0.3	85		89,027	D
Wisconsin	2,531,114	1,041,066	41.1	930,855	36.8	544,479	21.5	2,877	0.1	11,837	0.5	110,211	D
Wyoming	200,598	68,160	34.0	79,347	39.6	51,263	25.6	844	0.4	984	0.5	11,187	R
Dist. of Col.	227,572	192,619	84.6	20,698	9.1	9,681	4.3	467	0.2	4,107	1.8	171,921	D
Total	104,425,014	44,909,326	43.0	39,103,882	37.4	19,741,657	18.9	291,627	0.3	378,522	0.4	5,805,444	D

[a]. Others receiving votes: James "Bo" Gritz (Populist), 107,014; Lenora B. Fulani (New Alliance), 73,714; Howard Phillips (U.S. Taxpayers), 43,434; John Hagelin (Natural Law), 39,179; Ron Daniels (Peace and Freedom), 27,961; Lyndon H. LaRouche Jr. (Economic Recovery), 26,333; James Warren (Socialist Workers), 23,096; Drew Bradford (Independent), 4,749; Jack E. Herer (Grassroots), 3,875; J. Quinn Brisben (Socialist), 3,057; Helen Halyard (Workers League), 3,050; John Yiamouyiannas (Take Back America), 2,199; Delbert L. Ehlers (Independent), 1,149; Earl F. Dodge (Prohibition), 961; Jim Boren (Apathy), 956; Eugene A. Hem (Third), 405; Isabell Masters (Looking Back), 339; Robert J. Smith (American), 292; Gloria La Riva (Workers World), 181; "None of these candidates," 2,537; scattered write-ins, 14,041.

1996 Presidential Election

State	Total vote	Bill Clinton (Democrat)		Bob Dole (Republican)		Ross Perot (Reform)		Ralph Nader (Green)		Other[a]		Plurality	
		Votes	%	Votes	%	Votes	%	Votes	%	Votes	%		
Alabama	1,534,349	662,165	43.2	769,044	50.1	92,149	6.0	—		10,991	0.7	106,879	R
Alaska	241,620	80,380	33.3	122,746	50.8	26,333	10.9	7,597	3.1	4,564	1.9	42,366	R
Arizona	1,404,405	653,288	46.5	622,073	44.3	112,072	8.0	2,062	0.1	14,910	1.1	31,215	D
Arkansas	884,262	475,171	53.7	325,416	36.8	69,884	7.9	3,649	0.4	10,142	1.1	149,755	D
California	10,019,484	5,119,835	51.1	3,828,380	38.2	697,847	7.0	237,016	2.4	136,406	1.4	1,291,455	D
Colorado	1,510,704	671,152	44.4	691,848	45.8	99,629	6.6	25,070	1.7	23,005	1.5	20,696	R
Connecticut	1,392,614	735,740	52.8	483,109	34.7	139,523	10.0	24,321	1.7	9,921	0.7	252,631	D
Delaware	271,084	140,355	51.8	99,062	36.5	28,719	10.6	156	0.1	2,792	1.0	41,293	D
Florida	5,303,794	2,546,870	48.0	2,244,536	42.3	483,870	9.1	4,101	0.1	24,417	0.5	302,334	D
Georgia	2,299,071	1,053,849	45.8	1,080,843	47.0	146,337	6.4	—		18,042	0.8	26,994	R
Hawaii	360,120	205,012	56.9	113,943	31.6	27,358	7.6	10,386	2.9	3,421	0.9	91,069	D
Idaho	491,719	165,443	33.6	256,595	52.2	62,518	12.7	—		7,163	1.5	91,152	R
Illinois	4,311,391	2,341,744	54.3	1,587,021	36.8	346,408	8.0	1,447		34,771	0.8	754,723	D
Indiana	2,135,842	887,424	41.5	1,006,693	47.1	224,299	10.5	895		16,531	0.8	119,269	R
Iowa	1,234,075	620,258	50.3	492,644	39.9	105,159	8.5	6,550	0.5	9,464	0.8	127,614	D
Kansas	1,074,300	387,659	36.1	583,245	54.3	92,639	8.6	914	0.1	9,843	0.9	195,586	R
Kentucky	1,388,708	636,614	45.8	623,283	44.9	120,396	8.7	701	0.1	7,714	0.6	13,331	D
Louisiana	1,783,959	927,837	52.0	712,586	39.9	123,293	6.9	4,719	0.3	15,524	0.9	215,251	D
Maine	605,897	312,788	51.6	186,378	30.8	85,970	14.2	15,279	2.5	5,482	0.9	126,410	D
Maryland	1,780,870	966,207	54.3	681,530	38.3	115,812	6.5	2,606	0.1	14,715	0.8	284,677	D
Massachusetts	2,556,785	1,571,763	61.5	718,107	28.1	227,217	8.9	4,565	0.2	35,133	1.4	853,656	D
Michigan	3,848,844	1,989,653	51.7	1,481,212	38.5	336,670	8.7	2,322	0.1	38,987	1.0	508,441	D
Minnesota	2,192,640	1,120,438	51.1	766,476	35.0	257,704	11.8	24,908	1.1	23,114	1.1	353,962	D
Mississippi	893,857	394,022	44.1	439,838	49.2	52,222	5.8	—		7,775	0.9	45,816	R
Missouri	2,158,065	1,025,935	47.5	890,016	41.2	217,188	10.1	534		24,392	1.1	135,919	D
Montana	407,261	167,922	41.2	179,652	44.1	55,229	13.6	—		4,458	1.1	11,730	R
Nebraska	677,415	236,761	35.0	363,467	53.7	71,278	10.5	—		5,909	0.9	126,706	R
Nevada	464,279	203,974	43.9	199,244	42.9	43,986	9.5	4,730	1.0	12,345	2.7	4,730	D
New Hampshire	499,175	246,214	49.3	196,532	39.4	48,390	9.7	—		8,039	1.6	49,682	D
New Jersey	3,075,807	1,652,329	53.7	1,103,078	35.9	262,134	8.5	32,465	1.1	25,801	0.8	549,251	D
New Mexico	556,074	273,495	49.2	232,751	41.9	32,257	5.8	13,218	2.4	4,353	0.8	40,744	D
New York	6,316,129	3,756,177	59.5	1,933,492	30.6	503,458	8.0	75,956	1.2	47,046	0.7	1,822,685	D
North Carolina	2,515,807	1,107,849	44.0	1,225,938	48.7	168,059	6.7	2,108	0.1	11,853	0.4	118,089	R
North Dakota	266,411	106,905	40.1	125,050	46.9	32,515	12.2	—		1,941	0.7	18,145	R
Ohio	4,534,434	2,148,222	47.4	1,859,883	41.0	483,207	10.7	2,962	0.1	40,160	0.9	288,339	D
Oklahoma	1,206,713	488,105	40.4	582,315	48.3	130,788	10.8	—		5,505	0.5	94,210	R
Oregon	1,377,760	649,641	47.2	538,152	39.1	121,221	8.8	49,415	3.6	19,331	1.4	111,489	D
Pennsylvania	4,506,118	2,215,819	49.2	1,801,169	40.0	430,984	9.6	3,086	0.1	55,060	1.2	414,650	D
Rhode Island	390,284	233,050	59.7	104,683	26.8	43,723	11.2	6,040	1.5	2,788	0.7	128,367	D
South Carolina	1,151,689	506,283	44.0	573,458	49.8	64,386	5.6	—		7,562	0.7	67,175	R
South Dakota	323,826	139,333	43.0	150,543	46.5	31,250	9.7	—		2,700	0.8	11,210	R
Tennessee	1,894,105	909,146	48.0	863,530	45.6	105,918	5.6	6,427	0.3	9,084	0.4	45,616	D
Texas	5,611,644	2,459,683	43.8	2,736,167	48.8	378,537	6.7	4,810	0.1	32,447	0.6	276,484	R
Utah	665,629	221,633	33.3	361,911	54.4	66,461	10.0	4,615	0.7	11,009	1.7	140,278	R
Vermont	258,449	137,894	53.4	80,352	31.1	31,024	12.0	5,585	2.2	3,594	1.4	57,542	D
Virginia	2,416,642	1,091,060	45.1	1,138,350	47.1	159,861	6.6	—		27,371	1.1	47,290	R
Washington	2,253,837	1,123,323	49.8	840,712	37.3	201,003	8.9	60,322	2.7	28,477	1.3	282,611	D
West Virginia	636,459	327,812	51.5	233,946	36.8	71,639	11.3	—		3,062	0.5	93,866	D
Wisconsin	2,196,169	1,071,971	48.8	845,029	38.5	227,339	10.4	28,723	1.3	23,107	1.1	226,942	D
Wyoming	211,571	77,934	36.8	105,388	49.8	25,928	12.3	—		2,321	1.1	27,454	R
Dist. of Col.	185,726	158,220	85.2	17,339	9.3	3,611	1.9	4,780	2.6	1,776	1.0	140,881	D
Total	96,277,872	47,402,357	49.2	39,198,755	40.7	8,085,402	8.4	685,040	0.7	906,318	0.9	8,203,602	D

a. Others receiving votes: Harry Browne (Libertarian), 485,798; Howard Phillips (U.S. Taxpayers), 184,658; John Hagelin (Natural Law), 113,668; Monica Moorehead (Workers World), 29,083; Marsha Feinland (Peace and Freedom), 25,332; Charles E. Collins (Independent), 8,930; James E. Harris (Socialist Workers), 8,476; Dennis Peron, (Grassroots) 5,378; Mary Cal Hollis (Socialist), 4,706; Jerome White (Socialist Equality), 2,438; Diane Beall Templin (American), 1,847; Earl F. Dodge (Prohibition), 1,298; A. Peter Crane (Independent Party of Utah), 1,101; Ralph Forbes (America First), 932; John Birrenbach (Independent Grassroots), 787; Isabell Masters (Looking Back), 752; Steve Michael (Independent), 408; "None of These Candidates," 5,608; scattered write-ins, 25,118.

1996 Electoral Votes

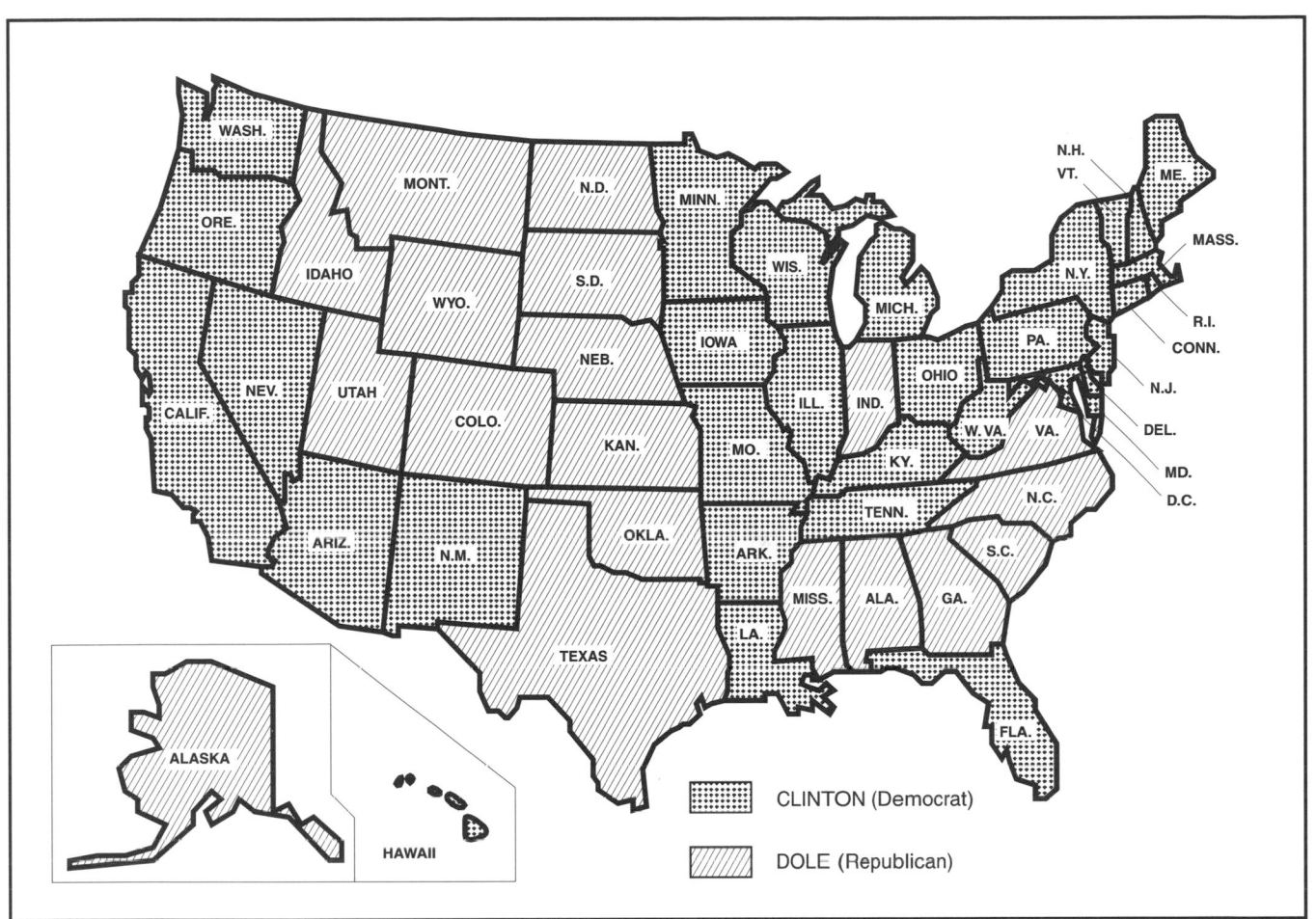

CLINTON (Democrat)

DOLE (Republican)

States	Electoral votes	Clinton	Dole	States	Electoral votes	Clinton	Dole
Alabama	(9)	–	9	Montana	(3)	–	3
Alaska	(3)	–	3	Nebraska	(5)	–	5
Arizona	(8)	8	–	Nevada	(4)	4	–
Arkansas	(6)	6	–	New Hampshire	(4)	4	–
California	(54)	54	–	New Jersey	(15)	15	–
Colorado	(8)	–	8	New Mexico	(5)	5	–
Connecticut	(8)	8	–	New York	(33)	33	–
Delaware	(3)	3	–	North Carolina	(14)	–	14
District of Columbia	(3)	3	–	North Dakota	(3)	–	3
Florida	(25)	25	–	Ohio	(21)	21	–
Georgia	(13)	–	13	Oklahoma	(8)	–	8
Hawaii	(4)	4	–	Oregon	(7)	7	–
Idaho	(4)	–	4	Pennsylvania	(23)	23	–
Illinois	(22)	22	–	Rhode Island	(4)	4	–
Indiana	(12)	–	12	South Carolina	(8)	–	8
Iowa	(7)	7	–	South Dakota	(3)	–	3
Kansas	(6)	–	6	Tennessee	(11)	11	–
Kentucky	(8)	8	–	Texas	(32)	–	32
Louisiana	(9)	9	–	Utah	(5)	–	5
Maine	(4)	4	–	Vermont	(3)	3	–
Maryland	(10)	10	–	Virginia	(13)	–	13
Massachusetts	(12)	12	–	Washington	(11)	11	–
Michigan	(18)	18	–	West Virginia	(5)	5	–
Minnesota	(10)	10	–	Wisconsin	(11)	11	–
Mississippi	(7)	–	7	Wyoming	(3)	–	3
Missouri	(11)	11	–	Totals	(538)	379	159

1996 Republican Convention Balloting

Delegation	Total votes	First presidential ballot[a]	
		Dole	Buchanan
Alabama	40	40	0
Alaska	19	16	0
Arizona	39	37	0
Arkansas	20	16	0
California	165	165	0
Colorado	27	27	0
Connecticut	27	27	0
Delaware	12	12	0
Florida	98	98	0
Georgia	42	42	0
Hawaii	14	14	0
Idaho	23	19	0
Illinois	69	69	0
Indiana	52	52	0
Iowa	25	25	0
Kansas	31	31	0
Kentucky	26	26	0
Louisiana	30	17	10
Maine	15	15	0
Maryland	32	32	0
Massachusetts	37	37	0
Michigan	57	52	5
Minnesota	33	33	0
Mississippi	33	33	0
Missouri	36	24	11
Montana	14	14	0
Nebraska	24	24	0
Nevada	14	14	0
New Hampshire	16	16	0
New Jersey	48	48	0
New Mexico	18	18	0
New York	102	102	0
North Carolina	58	58	0
North Dakota	18	17	0
Ohio	67	67	0
Oklahoma	38	38	0
Oregon	23	18	5
Pennsylvania	73	73	0
Rhode Island	16	16	0
South Carolina	37	37	0
South Dakota	18	18	0
Tennessee	38	37	0
Texas	123	121	2
Utah	28	27	1
Vermont	12	12	0
Virginia	53	53	0
Washington	36	27	9
West Virginia	18	18	0
Wisconsin	36	36	0
Wyoming	20	20	0
District of Columbia	14	14	0
Puerto Rico	14	14	0
Virgin Islands	4	4	0
American Samoa	4	4	0
Guam	4	4	0
Total	1,990	1,928	43

[a] Other candidates: Phil Gramm, 2 (Louisiana); Alan Keyes, 1(Missouri); Robert Bork, 1 (Louisiana); not voting, 15.

1996 Democratic Convention Balloting

Delegation	Total votes	First presidential ballot[a] Clinton
Alabama	66	66
Alaska	19	19
Arizona	59	59
Arkansas	47	47
California	422	416
Colorado	56	56
Connecticut	67	67
Delaware	21	21
Florida	178	178
Georgia	91	91
Hawaii	30	29
Idaho	23	23
Illinois	193	193
Indiana	88	88
Iowa	56	56
Kansas	42	42
Kentucky	61	61
Louisiana	71	71
Maine	32	32
Maryland	88	88
Massachusetts	114	114
Michigan	156	156
Minnesota	92	92
Mississippi	47	47
Missouri	93	93
Montana	24	24
Nebraska	34	34
Nevada	26	26
New Hampshire	26	26
New Jersey	122	122
New Mexico	34	34
New York	289	289
North Carolina	99	99
North Dakota	22	21
Ohio	172	172
Oklahoma	52	52
Oregon	57	54
Pennsylvania	195	195
Rhode Island	32	31
South Carolina	51	51
South Dakota	22	22
Tennessee	80	80
Texas	229	229
Utah	31	31
Vermont	22	22
Virginia	97	97
Washington	90	90
West Virginia	43	43
Wisconsin	93	93
Wyoming	19	19
District of Columbia	33	33
Puerto Rico	58	58
Virgin Islands	4	4
American Samoa	6	6
Guam	6	6
Democrats Abroad	9	9
Total	4,289	4,277

[a] Not voting, 12.

Distribution of House Seats and Electoral Votes

(Based on Censuses of 1950, 1960, 1970, 1980 and 1990)

State	U.S. House seats									Electoral votes				
	1953-1963	1960 Census changes	1963-1973	1970 Census changes	1973-1983	1980 Census changes	1983-1993	1990 Census changes	1993-2003	1952, 1956, 1960	1964, 1968	1972, 1976, 1980	1984, 1988	1992, 1996, 2000
Alabama	9	−1	8	−1	7	—	7	—	7	11	10	9	9	9
Alaska	1	—	1	—	1	—	1	—	1	3	3	3	3	3
Arizona	2	+1	3	+1	4	+1	5	+1	6	4	5	6	7	8
Arkansas	6	−2	4	—	4	—	4	—	4	8	6	6	6	6
California	30	+8	38	+5	43	+2	45	+7	52	32	40	45	47	54
Colorado	4	—	4	+1	5	+1	6	—	6	6	6	7	8	8
Connecticut	6	—	6	—	6	—	6	—	6	8	8	8	8	8
Delaware	1	—	1	—	1	—	1	—	1	3	3	3	3	3
District of Columbia	—	—	—	—	—	—	—	—	—	—	3	3	3	3
Florida	8	+4	12	+3	15	+4	19	+4	23	10	14	17	21	25
Georgia	10	—	10	—	10	—	10	+1	11	12	12	12	12	13
Hawaii	1	+1	2	—	2	—	2	—	2	3	4	4	4	4
Idaho	2	—	2	—	2	—	2	—	2	4	4	4	4	4
Illinois	25	−1	24	—	24	−2	22	−2	20	27	26	26	24	22
Indiana	11	—	11	—	11	−1	10	—	10	13	13	13	12	12
Iowa	8	−1	7	−1	6	—	6	−1	5	10	9	8	8	7
Kansas	6	−1	5	—	5	—	5	−1	4	8	7	7	7	6
Kentucky	8	−1	7	—	7	—	7	−1	6	10	9	9	9	8
Louisiana	8	—	8	—	8	—	8	−1	7	10	10	10	10	9
Maine	3	−1	2	—	2	—	2	—	2	5	4	4	4	4
Maryland	7	+1	8	—	8	—	8	—	8	9	10	10	10	10
Massachusetts	14	−2	12	—	12	−1	11	−1	10	16	14	14	13	12
Michigan	18	+1	19	—	19	−1	18	−2	16	20	21	21	20	18
Minnesota	9	−1	8	—	8	—	8	—	8	11	10	10	10	10
Mississippi	6	−1	5	—	5	—	5	—	5	8	7	7	7	7
Missouri	11	−1	10	—	10	−1	9	—	9	13	12	12	11	11
Montana	2	—	2	—	2	—	2	−1	1	4	4	4	4	3
Nebraska	4	−1	3	—	3	—	3	—	3	6	5	5	5	5
Nevada	1	—	1	—	1	+1	2	—	2	3	3	3	4	4
New Hampshire	2	—	2	—	2	—	2	—	2	4	4	4	4	4
New Jersey	14	+1	15	—	15	−1	14	−1	13	16	17	17	16	15
New Mexico	2	—	2	—	2	+1	3	—	3	4	4	4	5	5
New York	43	−2	41	−2	39	−5	34	−3	31	45	43	41	36	33
North Carolina	12	−1	11	—	11	—	11	+1	12	14	13	13	13	14
North Dakota	2	—	2	−1	1	—	1	—	1	4	4	3	3	3
Ohio	23	+1	24	−1	23	−2	21	−2	19	25	26	25	23	21
Oklahoma	6	—	6	—	6	—	6	—	6	8	8	8	8	8
Oregon	4	—	4	—	4	+1	5	—	5	6	6	6	7	7
Pennsylvania	30	−3	27	−2	25	−2	23	−2	21	32	29	27	25	23
Rhode Island	2	—	2	—	2	—	2	—	2	4	4	4	4	4
South Carolina	6	—	6	—	6	—	6	—	6	8	8	8	8	8
South Dakota	2	—	2	—	2	−1	1	—	1	4	4	4	3	3
Tennessee	9	—	9	−1	8	+1	9	—	9	11	11	10	11	11
Texas	22	+1	23	+1	24	+3	27	+3	30	24	25	26	29	32
Utah	2	—	2	—	2	+1	3	—	3	4	4	4	5	5
Vermont	1	—	1	—	1	—	1	—	1	3	3	3	3	3
Virginia	10	—	10	—	10	—	10	+1	11	12	12	12	12	13
Washington	7	—	7	—	7	+1	8	+1	9	9	9	9	10	11
West Virginia	6	−1	5	−1	4	—	4	−1	3	8	7	6	6	5
Wisconsin	10	—	10	−1	9	—	9	—	9	12	12	11	11	11
Wyoming	1	—	1	—	1	—	1	—	1	3	3	3	3	3

Party Affiliations in Congress and the Presidency, 1789–1997

Year	Congress	House Majority party	House Principal minority party	Senate Majority party	Senate Principal minority party	President
1789-1791	1st	AD-38	Op-26	AD-17	Op-9	F (Washington)
1791-1793	2nd	F-37	DR-33	F-16	DR-13	F (Washington)
1793-1795	3rd	DR-57	F-48	F-17	DR-13	F (Washington)
1795-1797	4th	F-54	DR-52	F-19	DR-13	F (Washington)
1797-1799	5th	F-58	DR-48	F-20	DR-12	F (John Adams)
1799-1801	6th	F-64	DR-42	F-19	DR-13	F (John Adams)
1801-1803	7th	DR-69	F-36	DR-18	F-13	DR (Jefferson)
1803-1805	8th	DR-102	F-39	DR-25	F-9	DR (Jefferson)
1805-1807	9th	DR-116	F-25	DR-27	F-7	DR (Jefferson)
1807-1809	10th	DR-118	F-24	DR-28	F-6	DR (Jefferson)
1809-1811	11th	DR-94	F-48	DR-28	F-6	DR (Madison)
1811-1813	12th	DR-108	F-36	DR-30	F-6	DR (Madison)
1813-1815	13th	DR-112	F-68	DR-27	F-9	DR (Madison)
1815-1817	14th	DR-117	F-65	DR-25	F-11	DR (Madison)
1817-1819	15th	DR-141	F-42	DR-34	F-10	DR (Monroe)
1819-1821	16th	DR-156	F-27	DR-35	F-7	DR (Monroe)
1821-1823	17th	DR-158	F-25	DR-44	F-4	DR (Monroe)
1823-1825	18th	DR-187	F-26	DR-44	F-4	DR (Monroe)
1825-1827	19th	AD-105	J-97	AD-26	J-20	DR (John Q. Adams)
1827-1829	20th	J-119	AD-94	J-28	AD-20	DR (John Q. Adams)
1829-1831	21st	D-139	NR-74	D-26	NR-22	DR (Jackson)
1831-1833	22nd	D-141	NR-58	D-25	NR-21	D (Jackson)
1833-1835	23rd	D-147	AM-53	D-20	NR-20	D (Jackson)
1835-1837	24th	D-145	W-98	D-27	W-25	D (Jackson)
1837-1839	25th	D-108	W-107	D-30	W-18	D (Van Buren)
1839-1841	26th	D-124	W-118	D-28	W-22	D (Van Buren)
1841-1843	27th	W-133	D-102	W-28	D-22	W (W. Harrison) W (Tyler)
1843-1845	28th	D-142	W-79	W-28	D-25	W (Tyler)
1845-1847	29th	D-143	W-77	D-31	W-25	D (Polk)
1847-1849	30th	W-115	D-108	D-36	W-21	D (Polk)
1849-1851	31st	D-112	W-109	D-35	W-25	W (Taylor) W (Fillmore)
1851-1853	32nd	D-140	W-88	D-35	W-24	W (Fillmore)
1853-1855	33rd	D-159	W-71	D-38	W-22	D (Pierce)
1855-1857	34th	R-108	D-83	D-40	R-15	D (Pierce)
1857-1859	35th	D-118	R-92	D-36	R-20	D (Buchanan)
1859-1861	36th	R-114	D-92	D-36	R-26	D (Buchanan)
1861-1863	37th	R-105	D-43	R-31	D-10	R (Lincoln)
1863-1865	38th	R-102	D-75	R-36	D-9	R (Lincoln)
1865-1867	39th	U-149	D-42	U-42	D-10	R (Lincoln) R (A. Johnson)
1867-1869	40th	R-143	D-49	R-42	D-11	R (A. Johnson)
1869-1871	41st	R-149	D-63	R-56	D-11	R (Grant)
1871-1873	42nd	R-134	D-104	R-52	D-17	R (Grant)
1873-1875	43rd	R-194	D-92	R-49	D-19	R (Grant)
1875-1877	44th	D-169	R-109	R-45	D-29	R (Grant)
1877-1879	45th	D-153	R-140	R-39	D-36	R (Hayes)
1879-1881	46th	D-149	R-130	D-42	R-33	R (Hayes)
1881-1883	47th	R-147	D-135	R-37	D-37	R (Garfield) R (Arthur
1883-1885	48th	D-197	R-118	R-38	D-36	R (Arthur)
1885-1887	49th	D-183	R-140	R-43	D-34	D (Cleveland)
1887-1889	50th	D-169	R-152	R-39	D-37	D (Cleveland)
1889-1891	51st	R-166	D-159	R-39	D-37	R (B. Harrison)
1891-1893	52nd	D-235	R-88	R-47	D-39	R (B. Harrison)

(table continues)

Year	Congress	House		Senate		President
		Majority party	Principal minority party	Majority party	Principal minority party	
1893-1895	53rd	D-218	R-127	D-44	R-38	D (Cleveland)
1895-1897	54th	R-244	D-105	R-43	D-39	D (Cleveland)
1897-1899	55th	R-204	D-113	R-47	D-34	R (McKinley)
1899-1901	56th	R-185	D-163	R-53	D-26	R (McKinley)
1901-1903	57th	R-197	D-151	R-55	D-31	R (McKinley)
						R (T. Roosevelt)
1903-1905	58th	R-208	D-178	R-57	D-33	R (T. Roosevelt)
1905-1907	59th	R-250	D-136	R-57	D-33	R (T. Roosevelt)
1907-1909	60th	R-222	D-164	R-61	D-31	R (T. Roosevelt)
1909-1911	61st	R-219	D-172	R-61	D-32	R (Taft)
1911-1913	62nd	D-228	R-161	R-51	D-41	R (Taft)
1913-1915	63rd	D-291	R-127	D-51	R-44	D (Wilson)
1915-1917	64th	D-230	R-196	D-56	R-40	D (Wilson)
1917-1919	65th	D-216	R-210	D-53	R-42	D (Wilson)
1919-1921	66th	R-240	D-190	R-49	D-47	D (Wilson)
1921-1923	67th	R-301	D-131	R-59	D-37	R (Harding)
1923-1925	68th	R-225	D-205	R-51	D-43	R (Coolidge)
1925-1927	69th	R-247	D-183	R-56	D-39	R (Coolidge)
1927-1929	70th	R-237	D-195	R-49	D-46	R (Coolidge)
1929-1931	71st	R-267	D-167	R-56	D-39	R (Hoover)
1931-1933	72nd	D-220	R-214	R-48	D-47	R (Hoover)
1933-1935	73rd	D-310	R-117	D-60	R-35	D (F. Roosevelt)
1935-1937	74th	D-319	R-103	D-69	R-25	D (F. Roosevelt)
1937-1939	75th	D-331	R-89	D-76	R-16	D (F. Roosevelt)
1939-1941	76th	D-261	R-164	D-69	R-23	D (F. Roosevelt)
1941-1943	77th	D-268	R-162	D-66	R-28	D (F. Roosevelt)
1943-1945	78th	D-218	R-208	D-58	R-37	D (F. Roosevelt)
1945-1947	79th	D-242	R-190	D-56	R-38	D (F. Roosevelt)
						D (Truman)
1947-1949	80th	R-245	D-188	R-51	D-45	D (Truman)
1949-1951	81st	D-263	R-171	D-54	R-42	D (Truman)
1951-1953	82nd	D-234	R-199	D-49	R-47	D (Truman)
1953-1955	83rd	R-221	D-211	R-48	D-47	R (Eisenhower)
1955-1957	84th	D-232	R-203	D-48	R-47	R (Eisenhower)
1957-1959	85th	D-233	R-200	D-49	R-47	R (Eisenhower)
1959-1961	86th	D-283	R-153	D-64	R-34	R (Eisenhower)
1961-1963	87th	D-263	R-174	D-65	R-35	D (Kennedy)
1963-1965	88th	D-258	R-177	D-67	R-33	D (Kennedy)
						D (L. Johnson)
1965-1967	89th	D-295	R-140	D-68	R-32	D (L. Johnson)
1967-1969	90th	D-247	R-187	D-64	R-36	D (L. Johnson)
1969-1971	91st	D-243	R-192	D-57	R-43	R (Nixon)
1971-1973	92nd	D-254	R-180	D-54	R-44	R (Nixon)
1973-1975	93rd	D-239	R-192	D-56	R-42	R (Nixon)
						R (Ford)
1975-1977	94th	D-291	R-144	D-60	R-37	R (Ford)
1977-1979	95th	D-292	R-143	D-61	R-38	D (Carter)
1979-1981	96th	D-276	R-157	D-58	R-41	D (Carter)
1981-1983	97th	D-243	R-192	R-53	D-46	R (Reagan)
1983-1985	98th	D-269	R-165	R-54	D-46	R (Reagan)
1985-1987	99th	D-252	R-182	R-53	D-47	R (Reagan)
1987-1989	100th	D-258	R-177	D-55	R-45	R (Reagan)
1989-1991	101st	D-259	R-174	D-55	R-45	R (Bush)
1991-1993	102nd	D-267	R-167	D-56	R-44	R (Bush)
1993-1995	103rd	D-258	R-176	D-57	R-43	D (Clinton)
1995-1997	104th	R-230	D-204	R-53	D-47	D (Clinton)
1997-1999	105th	R-227	D-207	R-55	D-45	D (Clinton)

SOURCES: *Congressional Quarterly Weekly Report,* various issues; U.S. Bureau of the Census, *Historical Statistics of the United States, Colonial Times to 1970* (Washington, D.C.: Government Printing Office, 1975); and U.S. Congress, Joint Committee on Printing, *Official Congressional Directory* (Washington, D.C.: Government Printing Office, 1967–).

NOTE: Figures are for the beginning of the first session of each Congress. Key to abbreviations: AD—Administration; AM—Anti-Masonic; D—Democratic; DR—Democratic-Republican; F—Federalist; J—Jacksonian; NR—National Republican; Op—Opposition; R—Republican; U—Unionist; W—Whig.

103rd Congress Special Elections, 1993 Gubernatorial Returns

1993 Gubernatorial Elections

	Vote total	Percent		Vote total	Percent
New Jersey—Nov. 2, 1993			**Virginia—Nov. 2, 1993**		
Christine Todd Whitman (R)	1,236,124	49.3	George F. Allen (R)	1,045,319	58.3
James J. Florio (D)	1,210,031	48.3	Mary Sue Terry (D)	733,527	40.9

Special House Elections, 103rd Congress

	Vote total	Percent		Vote total	Percent
Mississippi—April 13, 1993			**Michigan—Dec. 7, 1993**		
Bennie Thompson (D)	72,561	55.2	Vernon J. Ehlers (R)	57,484	66.4
Hayes Dent (R)	58,995	44.8	Dale R. Sprik (D)	19,993	23.1
			Dawn Ida Krupp (I)	8,759	10.1
Ohio—May 4, 1993					
Rob Portman (R)	53,020	70.1	**Oklahoma—May 10, 1994**		
Lee Hornberger (D)	22,652	29.9	Frank D. Lucas (R)	71,354	54.2
			Dan Webber Jr. (D)	60,411	45.8
Wisconsin—May 4, 1993					
Peter W. Barca (D)	55,605	49.9	**Kentucky—May 24, 1994**		
Mark W. Neumann (R)	54,930	49.3	Ron Lewis (R)	40,126	55.2
			Joseph E. Prather (D)	32,625	44.8
California—June 8, 1993					
Sam Farr (D)	53,675	51.5			
Bill McCampbell (R)	43,774	42.0			

Special Senate Runoff Election, 103rd Congress

	Vote total	Percent
Texas—June 5, 1993[a]		
Kay Bailey Hutchison (R)	1,188,716	67.3
Bob Krueger (D)	576,538	32.7

NOTE: D—Democrat, I—Independent, R—Republican.

[a] Under Texas law, candidates in special elections for the Senate all run together in an all-party primary. If none receives a majority of the vote, a runoff is held between the top two contenders. Hutchison and Krueger both received 29 percent of the primary vote in a field of five candidates.

Following are the official vote returns for the gubernatorial, Senate and House races compiled by Congressional Quarterly from the figures supplied by the 50 state election boards.

Vote totals are included for all candidates who were listed on the ballot and for write-ins whose votes equaled at least 0.1 percent of the total.

The vote percentages for each race do not always add to 100 due to rounding and the exclusion of scattered write-ins.

An asterisk (*) indicates an incumbent.

An "X" denotes candidates without major-party opposition; no votes were tallied.

An "AL" indicates an at-large district.

	Vote total	Per-cent
Alabama		
Governor		
Fob James Jr. (R)	604,926	50.3
James E. Folsom Jr. (D)*	594,169	49.4
House		
1 Sonny Callahan (R)*	103,431	67.3
Don Womack (D)	50,227	32.7
2 Terry Everett (R)*	124,465	73.6
Brian Dowling (D)	44,694	26.4
3 Glen Browder (D)*	93,924	63.6
Ben Hand (R)	53,757	36.4
4 Tom Bevill (D)*	119,436	98.5
5 Robert E. "Bud" Cramer (D)*	88,693	50.5
Wayne Parker (R)	86,923	49.5
6 Spencer Bachus (R)*	155,047	79.0
Larry Fortenberry (D)	41,030	20.9
7 Earl F. Hilliard (D)*	116,150	76.9
Alfred J. Middleton Sr. (R)	34,814	23.0
Alaska		
Governor		
Tony Knowles (D)	87,693	41.1
James O. "Jim" Campbell (R)	87,157	40.8

	Vote total	Per-cent
John B. "Jack" Coghill (AKI)	27,838	13.0
Jim Sykes (GREEN)	8,727	4.1
Ralph K. Winterrowd II (PP)	1,743	0.8
House		
AL Don Young (R)*	118,537	56.9
Tony Smith (D)	68,172	32.7
Jonni Whitmore (GREEN)	21,277	10.2
Arizona		
Governor		
Fife Symington (R)*	593,492	52.5
Eddie Basha (D)	500,702	44.3
John Buttrick (LIBERT)	35,222	3.1
Senate		
Jon Kyl (R)	600,999	53.7
Sam Coppersmith (D)	442,510	39.5
Scott Grainger (LIBERT)	75,493	6.7
House		
1 Matt Salmon (R)	101,350	56.0
Chuck Blanchard (D)	70,627	39.0
Bob Howarth (LIBERT)	8,890	4.9
2 Ed Pastor (D)*	62,589	62.3
Robert MacDonald (R)	32,797	32.7
James Bertrand (LIBERT)	5,060	5.0
3 Bob Stump (R)*	145,396	70.1
Howard Lee Sprague (D)	61,939	29.9
4 John Shadegg (R)	116,714	60.2
Carol Cure (D)	69,760	36.0

	Vote total	Per-cent
Mark J. Yannone (LIBERT)	7,428	3.8
5 Jim Kolbe (R)*	149,514	67.7
Gary Auerbach (D)	63,436	28.7
Phillip W. Murphy (LIBERT)	7,821	3.5
6 J. D. Hayworth (R)	107,060	54.6
Karan English (D)*	81,321	41.5
Sequoia R. Fuller (LIBERT)	7,687	3.9
Arkansas		
Governor		
Jim Guy Tucker (D)*	428,936	59.8
Sheffield Nelson (R)	287,904	40.2
House		
1 Blanche Lambert (D)*	95,290	53.4
Warren Dupwe (R)	83,147	46.6
2 Ray Thornton (D)*	97,580	57.4
Bill Powell (R)	72,473	42.6
3 Tim Hutchinson (R)*	129,800	67.7
Berta L. Seitz (D)	61,883	32.3
4 Jay Dickey (R)*	87,469	51.8
Jay Bradford (D)	81,370	48.2
California		
Governor		
Pete Wilson (R)*	4,781,766	55.2
Kathleen Brown (D)	3,519,799	40.6
Richard Rider (LIBERT)	149,123	1.7

ABBREVIATIONS FOR PARTY DESIGNATIONS

ACP	A Connecticut Party	GR	Grassroots	NR	Nutritional Rights Alliance
ADEP	A Delaware Party	GREEN	Green	PAC	Politicians Are Crooks
AKI	Alaskan Independence	I	Independent	PAT	Patriot Party
AM	American	IA	Independent American	PFP	Peace and Freedom
AMI	American Independent	IF	Independence Fusion	PHA	Perot Hispano American
ATP	Ax Taxes Party	IFH	Inflation Fighting Housewife	PP	People's Party
BP	Best Party			PV	People of Vermont
C	Conservative	JPR	Jobs, Property Rights	R	Republican
CAP	Capitalist	KAF	Keep America First	RTL	Right to Life
CC	Concerned Citizens	KTAX	Taxpayers Party of Kentucky	SW	Socialist Worker
CONSTL	Constitutional			TAX	Taxpayers
COP	Colorado Prohibition	L	Liberal	TBAGRN	T.B.A. Green
COPP	Concerns of People	LAWR	LaRouche Was Right	TCN	Tax Cut Now
D	Democratic	LIBERT	Libertarian	UNI	United Independents
DDD	Damn Drug Dealers	LIF	Long Island First	USTAX	U.S. Taxpayers
DFL	Democratic Farmer-Labor	LU	Liberty Union	UWS	United We Serve
DIA	Democracy in Action	MSTAX	Mississippi Taxpayers	VG	Vermont Grassroots
FAS	Fascist	NA	New Alliance	WL	Workers League
FUP	Fed Up Party	NJC	N. J. Conservative Party	WTP	We The People
GC	Gun Control Party	NL	Natural Law	WW	Workers World

	Vote total	Percent
Jerome "Jerry" McCready (AMI)	133,734	1.5
Gloria Estela La Riva (PFP)	80,354	0.9

Senate

	Vote total	Percent
Diane Feinstein (D)*	3,979,152	46.7
Michael Huffington (R)	3,817,025	44.8
Elizabeth Cervantes Barron (PFP)	255,036	3.0
Richard Benjamin Boddie (LIBERT)	178,951	2.1
Paul Meeuwenberg (AMI)	142,630	1.7
Barbara Blong (GREEN)	137,710	1.6

House

		Vote total	Percent
1	Frank Riggs (R)	106,870	53.3
	Dan Hamburg (D)*	93,717	46.7
2	Wally Herger (R)*	137,864	64.2
	Mary Jacobs (D)	55,959	26.1
	Devvy Kidd (AMI)	15,569	7.2
	Harry H. "Doc" Pendery (LIBERT)	5,417	2.5
3	Vic Fazio (D)*	97,093	49.8
	Tim Lefever (R)	89,964	46.1
	Ross Crain (LIBERT)	8,100	4.2
4	John T. Doolittle (R)*	144,936	61.3
	Katie Hirning (D)	82,505	34.9
	Damon C. Falconi (LIBERT)	8,882	3.8
5	Robert T. Matsui (D)*	125,042	68.5
	Robert S. Dinsmore (R)	52,905	29.0
	Gordon Mors (AMI)	4,649	2.5
6	Lynn Woolsey (D)*	137,642	58.1
	Michael J. Nugent (R)	88,940	37.6
	Louis Beary (LIBERT)	6,203	2.6
	Ernest K. Jones Jr. (PFP)	4,055	1.7
7	George Miller (D)*	116,105	69.7
	Charles V. Hughes (R)	45,698	27.4
	William A. "Bill" Callison (PFP)	4,798	2.9
8	Nancy Pelosi (D)*	137,642	81.8
	Elsa C. Cheung (R)	30,528	18.2
9	Ronald V. Dellums (D)*	129,233	72.2
	Deborah Wright (R)	40,448	22.6
	Emma Wong Mar (PFP)	9,194	5.1
10	Bill Baker (R)*	138,916	59.3
	Ellen Schwartz (D)	90,523	38.6
	Craig W. Cooper (PFP)	4,802	2.1
11	Richard W. Pombo (R)*	99,302	62.1
	Randy A. Perry (D)	55,794	34.9
	Joseph B. Miller (LIBERT)	4,718	3.0
12	Tom Lantos (D)*	118,408	67.4
	Deborah Wilder (R)	57,228	32.6
13	Pete Stark (D)*	97,344	64.6
	Larry Molton (R)	45,555	30.2
	Robert "Bob" Gough (LIBERT)	7,743	5.1
14	Anna G. Eshoo (D)*	120,713	60.6
	Ben Brink (R)	78,475	39.4
15	Norman Y. Mineta (D)*	119,921	59.9
	Robert Wick (R)	80,266	40.1
16	Zoe Lofgren (D)	74,935	65.0
	Lyle J. Smith (R)	40,409	35.0
17	Sam Farr (D)*	87,222	52.2
	Bill McCampbell (R)	74,380	44.5
	E. Craig Coffin (GREEN)	5,591	3.3
18	Gary A. Condit (D)*	91,105	65.5
	Tom Carter (R)	44,046	31.7
	James B. Morzella (LIBERT)	3,901	2.8
19	George P. Radanovich (R)	104,435	56.8
	Richard H. Lehman (D)*	72,912	39.6

		Vote total	Percent
	Dolores Comstock (LIBERT)	6,579	3.6
20	Cal Dooley (D)*	57,394	56.7
	Paul Young (R)	43,836	43.3
21	Bill Thomas (R)*	116,874	68.1
	John L. Evans (D)	47,517	27.7
	Mike Hodges (LIBERT)	6,899	4.0
	Deborah A. Vollmer (write-in)	339	0.2
22	Andrea Seastrand (R)	102,987	49.3
	Walter Holden Capps (D)	101,424	48.5
	David L. Bersohn (LIBERT)	4,597	2.2
23	Elton Gallegly (R)*	114,043	66.2
	Kevin Ready (D)	47,345	27.5
	Bill Brown (LIBERT)	6,481	3.8
	Robert T. Marston (GREEN)	4,457	2.6
24	Anthony C. Beilenson (D)*	95,342	49.4
	Rich Sybert (R)	91,806	47.5
	John C. Koehler (LIBERT)	6,031	3.1
25	Howard P. "Buck" McKeon (R)*	110,301	64.9
	James H. Gilmartin (D)	53,445	31.4
	Devin Cutler (LIBERT)	6,205	3.7
26	Howard L. Berman (D)*	55,145	62.6
	Gary E. Forsch (R)	28,423	32.2
	Erich D. Miller (LIBERT)	4,570	5.2
27	Carlos J. Moorhead (R)*	88,341	53.0
	Doug Kahn (D)	70,267	42.1
	Bill Gibbs (AMI)	4,328	2.6
	Dennis Decherd (LIBERT)	3,838	2.3
28	David Dreier (R)*	110,179	67.1
	Tommy Randle (D)	50,022	30.4
	Jorj Clayton Baker (LIBERT)	4,069	2.5
29	Henry A. Waxman (D)*	129,413	68.0
	Paul Stepanek (R)	53,801	28.3
	Michael J. Binkley (LIBERT)	7,162	3.8
30	Xavier Becerra (D)*	43,943	66.2
	David A. Ramirez (R)	18,741	28.2
	R. William Weilburg (LIBERT)	3,741	5.6
31	Matthew G. Martinez (D)*	50,541	59.1
	John V. Flores (R)	34,926	40.9
32	Julian C. Dixon (D)*	98,017	77.6
	Ernie A. Farhat (R)	22,190	17.6
	John Honigsfeld (PFP)	6,099	4.8
33	Lucille Roybal-Allard (D)*	33,814	81.5
	Kermit Booker (PFP)	7,694	18.5
34	Esteban E. Torres (D)*	72,439	61.7
	Albert J. Nunez (R)	40,068	34.1
	Carl M. "Marty" Swinney (LIBERT)	4,921	4.2
35	Maxine Waters (D)*	65,688	78.1
	Nate Truman (R)	18,390	21.9
36	Jane Harman (D)*	93,939	48.0
	Susan M. Brooks (R)	93,127	47.6
	Jack Tyler (LIBERT)	4,932	2.5
	Joseph G. "Joe" Fields (AMI)	3,810	1.9
37	Walter R. Tucker III (D)*	64,166	77.4
	Guy Wilson (LIBERT)	18,502	22.3
	Lewis B. Prulitsky (write-in)	263	0.3
38	Steve Horn (R)*	85,225	58.5
	Peter Mathews (D)	53,681	36.8
	Lester W. Mueller (LIBERT)	3,795	2.6
	Richard K. Green (PFP)	2,995	2.1
	John Duke (write-in)	73	0.1
39	Ed Royce (R)*	113,641	66.4
	R. O. "Bob" Davis (D)	49,696	29.0
	Jack Dean (LIBERT)	7,907	4.6
40	Jerry Lewis (R)*	115,728	70.7

		Vote total	Percent
	Donald M. "Don" Rusk (D)	48,003	29.3
41	Jay C. Kim (R)*	82,100	62.1
	Ed Tessier (D)	50,043	37.9
42	George E. Brown Jr. (D)*	58,888	51.1
	Rob Guzman (R)	56,259	48.8
43	Ken Calvert (R)*	84,500	54.7
	Mark A. Takano (D)	59,342	38.4
	Gene L. Berkman (LIBERT)	9,636	6.2
	John Schwab (write-in)	767	0.5
	Velma Hickey (write-in)	141	0.1
44	Sonny Bono (R)	95,521	55.6
	Steve Clute (D)	65,370	38.1
	Donald Cochran (AMI)	10,885	6.3
45	Dana Rohrabacher (R)*	124,875	69.1
	Brett Williamson (D)	55,849	30.9
46	Robert K. Dornan (R)*	50,616	57.1
	Michael Farber (D)	33,004	37.2
	Richard G. Newhous (LIBERT)	5,077	5.7
47	Christopher Cox (R)*	154,071	71.7
	Gary Kingsbury (D)	53,699	25.0
	Victor A. Wagner Jr. (LIBERT)	7,175	3.4
48	Ron Packard (R)*	143,570	73.3
	Andrei Leschick (D)	43,523	22.2
	Donna White (PFP)	8,543	4.4
49	Brian P. Bilbray (R)	90,283	48.5
	Lynn Schenk (D)*	85,597	46.0
	Chris Hoogenboom (LIBERT)	5,288	2.8
	Renate M. Kline (PFP)	4,948	2.7
50	Bob Filner (D)*	59,214	56.7
	Mary Alice Acevedo (R)	36,955	35.4
	Ricardo Duenez (LIBERT)	3,326	3.2
	Guillermo Ramirez (PFP)	3,002	2.9
	Kip Krueger (GREEN)	1,954	1.9
51	Randy "Duke" Cunningham (R)*	138,547	66.9
	Rita K. Tamerius (D)	57,374	27.7
	Bill Holmes (LIBERT)	6,968	3.4
	Miriam E. Clark (PFP)	4,099	2.0
52	Duncan Hunter (R)*	109,201	64.0
	Janet M. Gastil (D)	53,024	31.1
	Joe Shea (LIBERT)	5,240	3.1
	Art Edelman (PFP)	3,221	1.9

Colorado

Governor

	Vote total	Percent
Roy Romer (D)*	619,205	55.5
Bruce Benson (R)	432,042	38.7
Kevin Swanson (TAX)	40,397	3.6
Phillip Hufford (GREEN)	16,956	1.5
Earl F. Dodge (COP)	7,584	0.7

House

		Vote total	Percent
1	Patricia Schroeder (D)*	93,123	60.0
	William Eggert (R)	61,978	39.9
	Gary Cooper (write-in)	154	0.1
2	David E. Skaggs (D)*	105,938	56.8
	Patricia "Pat" Miller (R)	80,723	43.2
3	Scott McInnis (R)*	145,365	69.6
	Linda Powers (D)	63,427	30.4
4	Wayne Allard (R)*	136,251	72.3
	Cathy Kipp (D)	52,202	27.7
5	Joel Hefley (R)*	138,674	100.0
6	Dan Schaefer (R)*	124,079	69.8
	John Hallen (D)	49,701	28.0
	John Heckman (COPP)	2,536	1.4
	Stephen D. Dawson (NL)	1,393	0.8

		Vote total	Per-cent

Connecticut

Governor

	Vote total	Percent
John G. Rowland (R)	415,201	36.2
Bill Curry (D)	375,133	32.7
Eunice Strong Groark (ACP)	216,585	18.9
Tom Scott (I)	130,128	11.3
Joseph A. Zdonczyk (CC)	10,007	0.9

Senate

	Vote total	Percent
Joseph I. Lieberman (D, ACP)*	723,842	67.0
Jerry Labriola (R)	334,833	31.0
Gary R. Garneau (CC)	20,989	1.9

House

		Vote total	Percent
1	Barbara B. Kennelly (D, ACP)*	138,637	73.4
	Douglas T. Putnam (R)	46,865	24.8
	John F. Forry III (CC)	3,405	1.8
2	Sam Gejdenson (D)*	79,188	42.6
	Edward W. Munster (R)	79,167	42.5
	David Bingham (ACP)	27,716	14.9
3	Rosa L. DeLauro (D)*	111,261	63.4
	Susan E. Johnson (R, ACP)	64,094	36.6
4	Christopher Shays (R)*	109,436	74.4
	Jonathan D. Kantrowitz (D)	34,962	23.8
	Irving Sussman (LIBERT)	1,976	1.3
	Terry M. Nevas (NL)	688	0.5
5	Gary A. Franks (R)*	93,471	52.2
	James H. Maloney (D, ACP)	81,523	45.5
	Rosita Rodriguez (CC)	4,059	2.3
6	Nancy L. Johnson (R)*	123,101	63.9
	Charlotte Koskoff (D, ACP)	60,701	31.5
	Patrick J. Danford (CC)	8,915	4.6

Delaware

Senate

	Vote total	Percent
William V. Roth Jr. (R)*	111,088	55.8
Charles M. Oberly (D)	84,554	42.5
John C. Dierickx (LIBERT)	3,387	1.7

House

		Vote total	Percent
AL	Michael N. Castle (R)*	137,960	70.7
	Carol Ann DeSantis (D)	51,803	26.6
	Danny Ray Beaver (LIBERT)	3,869	2.0
	Donald M. Hockmuth (ADEP)	1,405	0.7

Florida

Governor

	Vote total	Percent
Lawton Chiles (D)*	2,135,008	50.8
Jeb Bush (R)	2,071,068	49.2

Senate

	Vote total	Percent
Connie Mack (R)*	2,894,726	70.5
Hugh E. Rodham (D)	1,210,412	29.5

House

		Vote total	Percent
1	Joe Scarborough (R)	112,901	61.6
	Vince Whibbs Jr. (D)	70,389	38.4
	Ralph Boone Jr. (write-in)	106	0.1
2	Pete Peterson (D)*	117,404	61.3
	Carole Griffin (R)	74,011	38.7
3	Corrine Brown (D)*	63,845	57.7
	Marc Little (R)	46,895	42.3
4	Tillie Fowler (R)*	X	X
5	Karen L. Thurman (D)*	125,780	57.2
	"Big Daddy" Don Garlits (R)	94,093	42.8
6	Cliff Stearns (R)*	148,698	99.1
	Phil Denton (write-in)	1,332	0.9
7	John L. Mica (R)*	131,711	73.4
	Edward D. Goddard (D)	47,747	26.6
8	Bill McCollum (R)*	131,376	99.7
	Ron Bedell (write-in)	439	0.3

		Vote total	Percent
9	Michael Bilirakis (R)*	177,253	99.9
	Richard Grayson (write-in)	152	0.1
10	C. W. Bill Young (R)*	X	X
11	Sam M. Gibbons (D)*	76,814	51.6
	Mark Sharpe (R)	72,119	48.4
12	Charles T. Canady (R)*	106,123	65.0
	Robert Connors (D)	57,203	35.0
13	Dan Miller (R)*	X	X
14	Porter J. Goss (R)*	X	X
15	Dave Weldon (R)	117,027	53.7
	Sue Munsey (D)	100,513	46.1
	Jim Owen (write-in)	246	0.1
16	Mark Foley (R)	122,734	58.1
	John Comerford (D)	88,646	41.9
17	Carrie P. Meek (D)*	X	X
18	Ileana Ros-Lehtinen (R)*	X	X
19	Harry A. Johnston (D)*	147,591	66.1
	Peter J. Tsakanikas (R)	75,779	33.9
20	Peter Deutsch (D)*	114,615	61.2
	Beverly "Bev" Kennedy (R)	72,516	38.8
21	Lincoln Diaz-Balart (R)*	X	X
22	E. Clay Shaw Jr. (R)*	119,690	63.4
	Hermine L. Wiener (D)	69,215	36.6
23	Alcee L. Hastings (D)*	X	X

Georgia

Governor

	Vote total	Percent
Zell Miller (D)*	788,926	51.1
Guy Millner (R)	756,371	48.9

House

		Vote total	Percent
1	Jack Kingston (R)*	88,788	76.6
	Raymond Beckworth (D)	27,197	23.4
2	Sanford D. Bishop Jr. (D)*	65,383	66.2
	John Clayton (R)	33,429	33.8
3	Mac Collins (R)*	94,717	65.5
	Fred Overby (D)	49,828	34.5
4	John Linder (R)*	90,063	57.9
	Comer Yates (D)	65,566	42.1
5	John Lewis (D)*	85,094	69.1
	Dale Dixon (R)	37,999	30.9
6	Newt Gingrich (R)*	119,432	64.2
	Ben Jones (D)	66,700	35.8
7	Bob Barr (R)	71,265	51.9
	George "Buddy" Darden (D)*	65,978	48.1
8	Saxby Chambliss (R)	89,591	62.7
	Craig Mathis (D)	53,408	37.3
9	Nathan Deal (D)*	79,145	57.9
	Robert L. Castello (R)	57,568	42.1
10	Charlie Norwood (R)	96,099	65.2
	Don Johnson (D)*	51,192	34.8
11	Cynthia A. McKinney (D)*	71,560	65.6
	Woodrow Lovett (R)	37,533	34.4

Hawaii

Governor

	Vote total	Percent
Benjamin J. Cayetano (D)	134,978	36.6
Frank F. Fasi (BP)	113,158	30.7
Patricia F. Saiki (R)	107,908	29.2
Michael Kioni Dudley (GREEN)	12,969	3.5

Senate

	Vote total	Percent
Daniel K. Akaka (D)*	256,189	71.8
Maria M. Hustace (R)	86,320	24.2
Richard O. Rowland (LIBERT)	14,393	4.0

House

		Vote total	Percent
1	Neil Abercrombie (D)*	94,754	53.6
	Orson Swindle (R)	76,623	43.4
	Alexandra Kaan (BP)	2,815	1.6
	Roger L. Taylor (LIBERT)	2,514	1.4

		Vote total	Percent
2	Patsy T. Mink (D)*	124,431	70.1
	Robert H. Garner (R)	42,891	24.2
	Lawrence R. Bartley (LIBERT)	10,074	5.7

Idaho

Governor

	Vote total	Percent
Phil Batt (R)	216,123	52.3
Larry EchoHawk (D)	181,363	43.9
Ronald B. Rankin (I)	15,793	3.8

House

		Vote total	Percent
1	Helen Chenoweth (R)	111,728	55.4
	Larry LaRocco (D)*	89,826	44.6
2	Michael D. Crapo (R)*	143,593	75.0
	Penny Fletcher (D)	47,936	25.0

Illinois

Governor

	Vote total	Percent
Jim Edgar (R)*	1,984,318	63.9
Dawn Clark Netsch (D)	1,069,850	34.4
David L. Kelley (LIBERT)	52,388	1.7

House

		Vote total	Percent
1	Bobby L. Rush (D)*	112,474	75.7
	William J. Kelly (R)	36,038	24.3
2	Mel Reynolds (D)*	93,998	98.1
	Carl Lanier Bibbs (write-in)	1,565	1.6
	Lionel O. Pittman (write-in)	139	0.1
	John P. Grey (write-in)	83	0.1
3	William O. Lipinski (D)*	92,353	54.2
	Jim Nalepa (R)	78,163	45.8
4	Luis V. Gutierrez (D)*	46,695	75.2
	Steven Valtierra (R)	15,384	24.8
5	Michael Patrick Flanagan (R)	75,328	54.4
	Dan Rostenkowski (D)*	63,065	45.6
6	Henry J. Hyde (R)*	115,664	73.5
	Tom Berry (D)	37,163	23.6
	Robert L. Hogan (LIBERT)	2,633	1.7
	Robert L. Wheat (UNI)	1,918	1.2
7	Cardiss Collins (D)*	93,457	79.6
	Charles "Chuck" Mobley (R)	24,011	20.4
8	Philip M. Crane (R)*	88,225	64.9
	Robert C. Walberg (D)	47,654	35.1
9	Sidney R. Yates (D)*	94,404	66.1
	George Edward Larney (R)	48,419	33.9
10	John Edward Porter (R)*	114,884	75.1
	Andrew M. Krupp (D)	38,191	24.9
11	Gerald C. "Jerry" Weller (R)	97,241	60.6
	Frank Giglio (D)	63,150	39.4
12	Jerry F. Costello (D)*	101,391	65.9
	Jan Morris (R)	52,419	34.1
13	Harris W. Fawell (R)*	124,312	73.1
	William A. Riley (D)	45,709	26.9
14	Dennis Hastert (R)*	110,204	76.5
	Steve Denari (D)	33,891	23.5
15	Thomas W. Ewing (R)*	108,857	68.2
	Paul Alexander (D)	50,874	31.8
16	Donald Manzullo (R)*	117,238	70.6
	Pete Sullivan (D)	48,736	29.4
17	Lane Evans (D)*	95,312	54.5
	Jim Anderson (R)	79,471	45.5
18	Ray LaHood (R)	119,838	60.2
	G. Douglas Stephens (D)	78,332	39.3
	Joyce Harant (write-in)	955	0.5
19	Glenn Poshard (D)*	115,045	58.4
	Brent Winters (R)	81,995	41.6
20	Richard J. Durbin (D)*	108,034	54.8
	Bill Owens (R)	88,964	45.2

		Vote total	Percent

Indiana

Senate

		Vote total	Percent
	Richard G. Lugar (R)*	1,039,625	67.4
	Jim Jontz (D)	470,799	30.5
	Barbara Bourland (LIBERT)	17,343	1.1
	Mary Catherine Barton (NA)	15,801	1.0

House

1	Peter J. Visclosky (D)*	68,612	56.5
	John Larson (R)	52,920	43.5
2	David M. McIntosh (R)	93,592	54.5
	Joseph H. Hogsett (D)	78,241	45.5
3	Tim Roemer (D)*	72,497	55.2
	Richard Burkett (R)	58,878	44.8
4	Mark Edward Souder (R)	88,584	55.4
	Jill L. Long (D)*	71,235	44.6
5	Steve Buyer (R)*	111,031	69.5
	J. D. Beatty (D)	45,224	28.3
	Clayton L. Alfred (I)	3,403	2.1
6	Dan Burton (R)*	136,876	77.0
	Natalie M. Bruner (D)	40,815	23.0
7	John T. Myers (R)*	104,359	65.1
	Michael M. Harmless (D)	55,941	34.9
8	John Hostettler (R)	93,529	52.4
	Frank McCloskey (D)*	84,857	47.6
9	Lee H. Hamilton (D)*	91,459	52.0
	Jean Leising (R)	84,315	48.0
10	Andrew Jacobs Jr. (D)*	58,573	53.5
	Marvin Bailey Scott (R)	50,998	46.5

Iowa

Governor

	Terry E. Branstad (R)*	566,395	56.8
	Bonnie J. Campbell (D)	414,453	41.6
	Richard O'Dell Hughes (I)	5,505	0.6
	Veronica Wells Butler (NL)	3,737	0.4
	Carl E. Olson (LIBERT)	2,772	0.3
	Michael Galati (SW)	770	0.1

House

1	Jim Leach (R)*	110,448	60.2
	Glen Winekauf (D)	69,461	37.9
	Jan J. Zonneveld (I)	2,264	1.2
	Michael Cuddehe (NL)	1,213	0.7
2	Jim Nussle (R)*	111,076	56.0
	Dave Nagle (D)	86,087	43.4
	Albert W. Schoema (LIBERT)	1,281	0.6
3	Jim Ross Lightfoot (R)*	111,862	57.8
	Elaine Baxter (D)	79,310	41.0
	Derrick P. Grimmer (GR)	2,282	1.2
4	Greg Ganske (R)	111,935	52.5
	Neal Smith (D)*	98,824	46.4
	Joshua A. Roberts (NL)	898	0.4
	William C. Oviatt (GR)	803	0.4
	Angela Lariscy (SW)	606	0.3
5	Tom Latham (R)	114,796	60.8
	Sheila McGuire (D)	73,627	39.0

Kansas

Governor

	Bill Graves (R)	526,113	64.1
	Jim Slattery (D)	294,733	35.9

House

1	Pat Roberts (R)*	169,531	77.4
	Terry L. Nichols (D)	49,477	22.6
2	Sam Brownback (R)	135,725	65.6
	John Carlin (D)	71,025	34.4
3	Jan Meyers (R)*	102,218	56.6

		Vote total	Percent
	Judy Hancock (D)	78,401	43.4
4	Todd Tiahrt (R)	111,653	52.9
	Dan Glickman (D)*	99,366	47.1

Kentucky

House

1	Edward Whitfield (R)	64,849	51.0
	Tom Barlow (D)*	62,387	49.0
2	Ron Lewis (R)*	90,535	59.8
	David Adkisson (D)	60,867	40.2
3	Mike Ward (D)	67,663	44.4
	Susan B. Stokes (R)	67,238	44.1
	Richard Lewis (KTAX)	17,591	11.5
4	Jim Bunning (R)*	96,695	74.1
	Sally Harris Skaggs (D)	33,717	25.9
5	Harold Rogers (R)*	82,291	79.4
	Walter "Doc" Blevins (D)	21,318	20.6
6	Scotty Baesler (D)*	70,085	58.8
	Matthew Eric Wills (R)	49,032	41.2

Louisiana

House

1	Robert L. Livingston (R)*	X	X
2	William J. Jefferson (D)*	X	X
3	W. J. "Billy" Tauzin (D)*	X	X
4	Cleo Fields (D)*	X	X
5	Jim McCrery (R)*	X	X
6	Richard H. Baker (R)*	X	X
7	Jimmy Hayes (D)*	X	X

Maine

Governor

	Angus King (I)	180,829	35.4
	Joseph E. Brennan (D)	172,951	33.8
	Susan M. Collins (R)	117,990	23.1
	Jonathan K. Carter (I)	32,695	6.4
	Mark S. Finks (write-in)	6,576	1.3

Senate

	Olympia J. Snowe (R)	308,244	60.3
	Thomas H. Andrews (D)	186,042	36.4
	Plato Truman (I)	17,205	3.4

House

1	James B. Longley Jr. (R)	136,316	51.9
	Dennis L. Dutremble (D)	126,373	48.1
2	John Baldacci (D)	109,615	45.7
	Richard A. Bennett (R)	97,754	40.7
	John M. Michael (I)	21,117	8.8
	Charles FitzGerald (I)	11,353	4.7

Maryland

Governor

	Parris N. Glendening (D)	708,094	50.2
	Ellen R. Sauerbrey (R)	702,101	49.8

Senate

	Paul S. Sarbanes (D)*	809,125	59.1
	William Brock (R)	559,908	40.9

House

1	Wayne T. Gilchrest (R)*	120,975	67.7
	Ralph T. Gies (D)	57,712	32.3
	Wayne Boyle (write-in)	127	0.1
2	Robert L. Ehrlich Jr. (R)	125,162	62.7
	Gerry L. Brewster (D)	74,275	37.2
3	Benjamin L. Cardin (D)*	117,269	71.0
	Robert Ryan Tousey (R)	47,966	29.0
4	Albert R. Wynn (D)*	93,148	75.0
	Michele Dyson (R)	30,999	25.0
5	Steny H. Hoyer (D)*	98,821	58.8
	Donald Devine (R)	69,211	41.2
6	Roscoe G. Bartlett (R)*	122,809	65.9

		Vote total	Percent
	Paul Muldowney (D)	63,411	34.1
7	Kwesi Mfume (D)*	97,016	81.5
	Kenneth Kondner (R)	22,007	18.5
8	Constance A. Morella (R)*	143,449	70.3
	Steven Van Grack (D)	60,660	29.7

Massachusetts

Governor

	William F. Weld (R)*	1,533,430	70.9
	Mark Roosevelt (D)	611,650	28.3
	Dean Cook (LIBERT)	14,698	0.7
	Jeffrey Rebello (LAWR)	3,907	0.2

Senate

	Edward M. Kennedy (D)*	1,266,011	58.1
	W. Mitt Romney (R)	894,005	41.0
	Lauraleigh Dozier (LIBERT)	14,484	0.7
	William Ferguson Jr. (LAWR)	4,776	0.2

House

1	John W. Olver (D)*	150,047	99.4
2	Richard E. Neal (D)*	117,178	58.6
	John M. Briare (R)	72,732	36.3
	Kate Ross (NL)	10,167	5.1
3	Peter I. Blute (R)*	115,810	54.6
	Kevin O'Sullivan (D)	93,689	44.2
	Dale E. Friedgen (NL)	2,375	1.1
4	Barney Frank (D)*	168,942	99.5
5	Martin T. Meehan (D)*	140,725	69.8
	David E. Coleman (R)	60,734	30.1
6	Peter G. Torkildsen (R)*	120,952	50.5
	John F. Tierney (D)	113,481	47.4
	Benjamin A. Gatchell (I)	4,960	2.1
7	Edward J. Markey (D)*	146,246	64.4
	Brad Bailey (R)	80,674	35.5
8	Joseph P. Kennedy II (D)*	113,224	99.0
9	Joe Moakley (D)*	146,287	69.8
	Michael M. Murphy (R)	63,369	30.2
10	Gerry E. Studds (D)*	172,753	68.7
	Keith Jason Hemeon (R)	78,487	31.2

Michigan

Governor

	John Engler (R)*	1,899,101	61.5
	Howard Wolpe (D)	1,188,438	38.5

Senate

	Spencer Abraham (R)	1,578,770	51.9
	Bob Carr (D)	1,300,960	42.7
	Jon Coon (LIBERT)	128,393	4.2
	William Roundtree (WW)	20,010	0.7
	Chris Wege (NL)	14,746	0.5

House

1	Bart Stupak (D)*	121,433	56.9
	Gil Ziegler (R)	89,660	42.0
	Michael McPeak (NL)	2,399	1.1
2	Peter Hoekstra (R)*	146,164	75.3
	Marcus Pete Hoover (D)	46,097	23.7
	Lu Wiggins (NL)	1,892	1.0
3	Vernon J. Ehlers (R)*	136,711	73.9
	Betsy J. Flory (D)	43,580	23.5
	Barrie Leslie Konico (LIBERT)	2,960	1.6
	Susan H. Normandin (NL)	1,815	1.0
4	Dave Camp (R)*	145,176	73.1
	Damion Frasier (D)	50,544	25.5
	Michael Lee (NL)	2,797	1.4
5	James A. Barcia (D)*	126,456	65.5
	William T. Anderson (R)	61,342	31.8

		Vote total	Per-cent
	Larry L. Fairchild (I)	3,022	1.6
	Susan I. Arnold (NL)	2,323	1.2
6	Fred Upton (R)*	121,923	73.5
	David Taylor (D)	42,348	25.5
	E. A. Berker (NL)	1,667	1.0
7	Nick Smith (R)*	115,621	65.1
	Kim McCaughtry (D)	57,326	32.3
	Kenneth L. Proctor (LIBERT)	3,311	1.9
	Scott K. Williamson (NL)	1,223	0.7
8	Dick Chrysler (R)	109,663	51.6
	Bob Mitchell (D)	95,383	44.9
	Gerald Ralph Turcotte Jr. (LIBERT)	4,348	2.0
	Susan Ilene McPeak (NL)	3,076	1.4
9	Dale E. Kildee (D)*	97,096	51.2
	Megan O'Neill (R)	89,148	47.0
	Karen Blasdell (NL)	3,240	1.7
10	David E. Bonior (D)*	121,876	62.2
	Donald J. Lobsinger (R)	73,862	37.7
11	Joe Knollenberg (R)*	154,696	68.2
	Mike Breshgold (D)	69,168	30.5
	John R. Hocking (NL)	2,928	1.3
12	Sander M. Levin (D)*	103,508	52.0
	John Pappageorge (R)	92,762	46.6
	Jerome White (I)	1,386	0.7
	Eric R. Anderson (NL)	1,340	0.7
13	Lynn Nancy Rivers (D)	89,573	51.9
	John A. Schall (R)	77,908	45.1
	Craig L. Seymour (LIBERT)	3,186	1.8
	Helen Halyard (I)	1,388	0.8
	Gail Anne Petrosoff (NL)	606	0.4
14	John Conyers Jr. (D)*	128,463	81.5
	Richard Charles Fornier (R)	26,215	16.6
	Richard R. Miller (NL)	2,953	1.9
15	Barbara-Rose Collins (D)*	119,442	84.1
	John W. Savage II (R)	20,074	14.1
	Cynthia M. Jaquith (I)	987	0.7
	Henry Ogden Clark (NL)	848	0.6
	Larry Roberts (I)	654	0.5
16	John D. Dingell (D)*	105,849	59.1
	Ken Larkin (R)	71,159	39.8
	Noha F. Hamze (NL)	1,968	1.1

Minnesota

Governor

	Vote total	Per-cent
Arne H. Carlson (R)*	1,094,165	62.0
John Marty (DFL)	589,344	33.4
Will Shetterly (GR)	20,785	1.2
Eric Arthur Olson (LIBERT)	15,467	0.9
Leslie Davis (NR)	4,611	0.3
Jon Hillson (SW)	3,022	0.2

Senate

	Vote total	Per-cent
Rod Grams (R)	869,653	49.1
Ann Wynia (DFL)	781,860	44.1
Dean M. Barkley (I)	95,400	5.4
Candice E. Sjostrom (GR)	15,920	0.9
Stephen Johnson (NL)	5,054	0.3
Marea Himelgrin (SW)	2,428	0.1

House

		Vote total	Per-cent
1	Gil Gutknecht (R)	117,613	55.2
	John C. Hottinger (DFL)	95,328	44.7
2	David Minge (DFL)*	114,289	52.0
	Gary B. Revier (R)	98,881	45.0
	Stan Bentz (I)	6,535	3.0
3	Jim Ramstad (R)*	173,223	73.2
	Bob Olson (DFL)	62,211	26.3
4	Bruce F. Vento (DFL)*	115,638	54.9

		Vote total	Per-cent
	Dennis Newinski (R)	88,344	41.9
	Dan R. Vacek (GR)	6,211	2.9
5	Martin Olav Sabo (DFL)*	121,515	61.9
	Dorothy LeGrand (R)	73,258	37.3
6	William P. "Bill" Luther (DFL)	113,740	49.9
	Tad Jude (R)	113,190	49.7
7	Collin C. Peterson (DFL)*	108,023	51.2
	Bernie Omann (R)	102,623	48.6
8	James L. Oberstar (DFL)*	153,161	65.7
	Phil Herwig (R)	79,818	34.2

Mississippi

Senate

	Vote total	Per-cent
Trent Lott (R)*	418,333	68.8
Ken Harper (D)	189,752	31.2

House

		Vote total	Per-cent
1	Roger Wicker (R)	80,553	63.1
	Bill Wheeler (D)	47,192	36.9
2	Bennie Thompson (D)*	68,014	53.7
	Bill Jordan (R)	49,270	38.9
	Vince Thornton (MSTAX)	9,408	7.4
3	G. V. "Sonny" Montgomery (D)*	83,163	67.6
	Dutch Dabbs (R)	39,826	32.4
4	Mike Parker (D)*	82,939	68.5
	Mike Wood (R)	38,200	31.5
5	Gene Taylor (D)*	73,179	60.1
	George Barlos (R)	48,575	39.9

Missouri

Senate

	Vote total	Per-cent
John Ashcroft (R)	1,060,149	59.7
Alan Wheat (D)	633,697	35.7
Bill Johnson (LIBERT)	81,264	4.6

House

		Vote total	Per-cent
1	William L. Clay (D)*	97,061	63.4
	Donald R. Counts (R)	50,303	32.9
	Craig W. Williamson (LIBERT)	5,654	3.7
2	James M. Talent (R)*	154,882	67.3
	Pat Kelly (D)	70,480	30.6
	Jim Higgins (LIBERT)	4,925	2.1
3	Richard A. Gephardt (D)*	117,601	57.7
	Gary Gill (R)	80,977	39.7
	Bradley Ems (LIBERT)	5,362	2.6
4	Ike Skelton (D)*	137,876	67.8
	James A. Noland Jr. (R)	65,616	32.2
5	Karen McCarthy (D)	100,391	56.6
	Ron Freeman (R)	77,120	43.4
6	Pat Danner (D)*	140,108	66.1
	Tina Tucker (R)	71,709	33.9
7	Mel Hancock (R)*	112,228	57.3
	James R. Fossard (D)	77,836	39.7
	Doug Burlison (LIBERT)	5,852	3.0
8	Bill Emerson (R)*	129,320	70.1
	James L. "Jay" Thompson (D)	48,987	26.5
	Greg Tlapek	6,279	3.4
9	Harold L. Volkmer (D)*	103,443	50.5
	Kenny Hulshof (R)	92,301	45.0
	Mitchell Moore	9,198	4.5

Montana

Senate

	Vote total	Per-cent
Conrad Burns (R)*	218,542	62.4
Jack Mudd (D)	131,845	37.6

House

		Vote total	Per-cent
AL	Pat Williams (D)*	171,372	48.7
	Cy Jamison (R)	148,715	42.2
	Steve Kelly (I)	32,046	9.1

Nebraska

Governor

	Vote total	Per-cent
Ben Nelson (D)*	423,270	73.0
Gene Spence (R)	148,230	25.6
Ernie Chambers (write-in)	5,085	0.5

Senate

	Vote total	Per-cent
Bob Kerrey (D)*	317,297	54.8
Jan Stoney (R)	260,668	45.0

House

		Vote total	Per-cent
1	Doug Bereuter (R)*	117,967	62.6
	Patrick Combs (D)	70,369	37.3
2	Jon Christensen (R)	92,516	49.9
	Peter Hoagland (D)*	90,750	49.0
3	Bill Barrett (R)*	154,919	78.7
	Gil Chapin (D)	41,943	21.3

Nevada

Governor

	Vote total	Per-cent
Bob Miller (D)*	200,026	53.9
Jim Gibbons (R)	156,875	42.3
Daniel Hansen (IA)	10,012	2.7
Denis Sholty (LIBERT)	3,978	1.1

Senate

	Vote total	Per-cent
Richard H. Bryan (D)*	193,804	52.7
Hal Furman (R)	156,020	42.4
Anna Nevenich (I)	6,666	1.8
Bob Days (LIBERT)	5,964	1.6
Neal A. Grasteit (IA)	5,450	1.5

House

		Vote total	Per-cent
1	John Ensign (R)	73,769	48.5
	James Bilbray (D)*	72,333	47.5
	Gary Wood (LIBERT)	6,065	4.0
2	Barbara F. Vucanovich (R)*	142,202	63.5
	Janet Greeson (D)	65,390	29.2
	Thomas F. Jefferson (IA)	9,615	4.3
	Lois Avery (NL)	6,725	3.0

New Hampshire

Governor

	Vote total	Per-cent
Stephen Merrill (R)*	218,134	69.9
Wayne D. King (D)	79,686	25.6
Steve Winter (LIBERT)	13,709	4.4

House

		Vote total	Per-cent
1	Bill Zeliff (R)*	97,017	65.6
	Bill Verge (D)	42,481	28.7
	Scott Tosti (I)	4,203	2.8
	Paul Lannon (LIBERT)	3,548	2.4
	Merle Braley (NL)	573	0.4
2	Charles Bass (R)	83,121	51.4
	Dick Swett (D)*	74,243	46.0
	John Lewicke (LIBERT)	2,986	1.8
	Linda Spitzfaden (NL)	1,223	0.8

New Jersey

Senate

	Vote total	Per-cent
Frank R. Lautenberg (D)*	1,033,487	50.3
Garabed "Chuck" Haytaian	966,244	47.0
Michael P. Kelly (KAF)	14,343	0.7
Ben Grindlinger (LIBERT)	14,042	0.7
Richard J. Pezzullo (NJC)	9,387	0.5
Andrea Lippi (JPR)	6,303	0.3
George Patrick Predham (DDD)	4,226	0.2

		Vote total	Per-cent
	Joanne Kuniansky (SW)	3,606	0.2
	Arlene Gold (NL)	3,249	0.2

House

		Vote total	Per-cent
1	Robert E. Andrews (D)*	108,155	72.3
	James N. Hogan (R)	41,505	27.7
3	H. James Saxton (R)*	115,750	66.4
	James Smith (D)	54,441	31.2
2	Frank A. LoBiondo (R)	102,566	64.6
	Louis N. Magazzu (D)	56,151	35.4
	D. James Hill (UWS)	3,015	1.7
	Arthur Fulvio Croce (DIA)	1,122	0.6
4	Christopher H. Smith (R)*	109,818	67.9
	Ralph Walsh (D)	49,537	30.6
	Leonard P. Marshall (NJC)	1,579	1.0
	Arnold Kokans (NL)	833	0.5
5	Marge Roukema (R)*	139,964	74.2
	Bill Auer (D)	41,275	21.9
	William J. Leonard (I)	3,746	2.0
	Roger Bacon (LIBERT)	2,882	1.5
	Helen Hamilton (NL)	638	0.3
6	Frank Pallone Jr. (D)*	88,922	60.4
	Mike Herson (R)	55,287	37.5
	Charles H. Dickson (CAP)	1,774	1.2
	Gary J. Rich (NJC)	800	0.5
	Richard Quinn (NL)	548	0.4
7	Bob Franks (R)*	98,814	59.6
	Karen Carroll (D)	64,231	38.7
	James J. Cleary (LAWR)	2,331	1.4
	Claire Greene (NL)	481	0.3
8	Bill Martini (R)	70,494	49.9
	Herb Klein (D)*	68,661	48.6
	Bernard George (C)	2,213	1.6
9	Robert G. Torricelli (D)*	99,984	62.5
	Peter J. Russo (R)	57,651	36.1
	Gregory Pason (I)	1,490	0.9
	Kenneth Ebel (NL)	763	0.5
10	Donald M. Payne (D)*	74,622	75.9
	Jim Ford (R)	21,524	21.9
	Rose Monyek (IFH)	1,598	1.6
	Maurice Williams (SW)	624	0.6
11	Rodney Frelinghuysen (R)	127,868	71.2
	Frank Herbert (D)	50,211	28.0
	Mary Frueholz (LAWR)	1,065	0.6
	Stuart Bacha (FAS)	436	0.2
12	Dick Zimmer (R)*	125,939	68.3
	Joseph D. Youssouf (D)	55,977	30.4
	Anthony M. Provenzano (NJC)	2,364	1.3
13	Robert Menendez (D)*	67,688	70.9
	Fernando A. Alonso (R)	24,071	25.2
	Frank J. Rubino Jr. (WTP)	1,494	1.6
	Herbert H. Shaw (PAC)	1,319	1.4
	Steven Marshall (SW)	895	0.9

New Mexico

Governor

	Vote total	Per-cent
Gary E. Johnson (R)	232,945	49.8
Bruce King (D)*	186,686	39.9
Roberto Mondragon (GREEN)	47,990	10.3

Senate

	Vote total	Per-cent
Jeff Bingaman (D)*	249,989	54.0
Colin R. McMillan (R)	213,025	46.0

House

		Vote total	Per-cent
1	Steven H. Schiff (R)*	119,996	73.9
	Peter L. Zollinger (D)	42,316	26.1
2	Joe Skeen (R)*	89,966	63.3
	Benjamin Anthony Chavez (D)	45,316	31.9

		Vote total	Per-cent
	Rex Johnson (GREEN)	6,898	4.9
3	Bill Richardson (D)*	99,900	63.6
	F. Gregg Bemis Jr. (R)	53,515	34.1
	Ed Nagel (LIBERT)	3,697	2.4

New York

Governor

	Vote total	Per-cent
George E. Pataki (R, C, TCN)	2,538,702	48.8
Mario M. Cuomo (D, L)*	2,364,904	45.4
Blase T. Golisano (IF)	217,490	4.2
Robert T. Walsh Sr. (RTL)	67,750	1.3
Bob Schulz (LIBERT)	9,506	0.2
Lawrence A. Lane (SW)	5,410	0.1

Senate

	Vote total	Per-cent
Daniel Patrick Moynihan (D, L)	2,646,541	55.2
Bernadette Castro (R, C, TCN)*	1,988,308	41.5
Henry F. Hewes (RTL)	95,954	2.0
Ismael Betancourt Jr. (IF)	26,650	0.6
Norma Segal (LIBERT)	17,991	0.4
Naomi L. Craine (SW)	14,892	0.3

House

		Vote total	Per-cent
1	Michael P. Forbes (R, C, RTL, WTP)	90,491	52.5
	George J. Hochbrueckner (D, LIF)*	80,146	46.5
	Michael Strong (FUP)	1,603	0.9
2	Rick A. Lazio (R, C, WTP)*	100,107	68.2
	James Manfre (D, LIF)	41,102	28.0
	Alice Cort Ross (RTL)	5,567	3.8
3	Peter T. King (R, C)*	115,236	59.2
	Norma Grill (D)	77,774	40.0
	John A. DePrima (L)	1,522	0.8
4	Daniel Frisa (R)	87,815	50.2
	Philip M. Schiliro (D)	65,286	37.3
	David A. Levy (C)*	15,173	8.7
	Vincent P. Garbitelli (RTL)	5,280	3.0
	Robert S. Berkowitz (L)	1,409	0.8
5	Gary Ackerman (D, L)*	93,896	55.0
	Grant M. Lally (R, C)	73,884	43.3
	Edward Elkowitz (RTL)	2,862	1.7
6	Floyd H. Flake (D)*	68,596	80.4
	Denny D. Bhagwandin (R, C)	16,675	19.6
7	Thomas J. Manton (D)*	58,935	87.1
	Robert E. Hurley (C)	8,698	12.9
8	Jerrold Nadler (D, L)*	109,946	82.0
	David I. Askren (R)	21,132	15.8
	Margaret V. Byrnes (C)	3,008	2.2
9	Charles E. Schumer (D, L)*	95,139	72.6
	James McCall (R, C)	35,880	27.4
10	Edolphus Towns (D, L)*	77,026	89.0
	Amelia Smith Parker (R)	7,995	9.2
	Mildred K. Mahoney (C)	1,489	1.7
11	Major R. Owens (D, L)*	61,945	88.9
	Gary S. Popkin (R, LIBERT)	6,605	9.5
	Michael Gaffney (C)	1,150	1.6
12	Nydia M. Velazquez (D, L)*	39,929	92.3
	Genevieve R. Brennan (C)	2,747	6.3
	Eric Ruano-Melendez (PHA)	589	1.4
13	Susan Molinari (R, C)*	96,491	71.4
	Tyrone G. Butler (D, L)	33,937	25.1
	Elisa Disimone (RTL)	4,655	3.4
14	Carolyn B. Maloney (D, I)*	98,479	64.2
	Charles Millard (R, L)	54,277	35.4

		Vote total	Per-cent
	Thomas K. Leighton (TBAGRN)	566	0.4
15	Charles B. Rangel (D, L)*	77,830	96.5
	Jose Suero (RTL, IF)	2,812	3.5
16	Jose E. Serrano (D, L)*	58,572	96.3
	Michael Walters (C)	2,257	3.7
17	Eliot L. Engel (D, L)*	73,321	77.6
	Edward T. Marshall (R)	16,896	17.9
	Kevin Brawley (C)	2,187	2.3
	Ann M. Noonan (RTL)	2,075	2.2
18	Nita M. Lowey (D)*	91,663	57.3
	Andrew C. Hartzell Jr. (R, C)	65,517	40.9
	Florence T. O'Grady (RTL)	2,873	1.8
19	Sue W. Kelly (R)	100,173	52.1
	Hamilton Fish Jr. (D)	70,696	36.8
	Joseph J. DioGuardi (C, RTL)	19,761	10.3
	Catherine Portman-Laux (ATP)	1,679	0.9
20	Benjamin A. Gilman (R)*	120,334	67.5
	Gregory B. Julian (D)	52,345	29.4
	Lois M. Colandrea (RTL)	5,612	3.1
21	Michael R. McNulty (D, C)*	147,804	67.0
	Joseph A. Gomez (R)	68,745	31.2
	Timothy J. Wood (RTL)	4,125	1.9
22	Gerald B. H. Solomon (R, C, RTL)*	157,717	73.4
	L. Robert Lawrence (D)	57,064	26.6
23	Sherwood Boehlert (R)*	124,486	70.5
	Charles W. Skeele Jr. (D)	40,786	23.1
	Donald J. Thomas (RTL)	11,216	6.4
24	John M. McHugh (R, C)*	124,645	78.6
	Danny M. Francis (D)	34,032	21.4
25	James T. Walsh (R, C)*	113,949	57.6
	Rhea Jezer (D, CHGC)	83,853	42.4
26	Maurice D. Hinchey (D, L)*	95,492	49.1
	Bob Moppert (R, C)	94,244	48.5
	Thomas F. Kovach (RTL)	4,772	2.5
27	Bill Paxon (R, C, RTL)*	152,610	74.5
	William A. Long Jr. (D)	52,160	25.5
28	Louise M. Slaughter (D)*	110,987	56.6
	Renee Forgensi Davison (R, C)	78,516	40.1
	John A. Clendenin (IF)	6,464	3.3
29	John J. LaFalce (D, L)*	103,053	55.2
	William E. Miller (R, C)	80,355	43.0
	Patrick Murty (RTL)	3,296	1.8
30	Jack Quinn (R, C)*	124,738	67.0
	David A. Franczyk (D, L)	61,392	33.0
31	Amo Houghton (R, C)*	121,178	84.8
	Gretchen S. McManus (RTL)	21,747	15.2

North Carolina

House

		Vote total	Per-cent
1	Eva Clayton (D)*	66,827	61.1
	Ted Tyler (R)	42,602	38.9
2	David Funderburk (R)	79,207	56.0
	Richard Moore (D)	62,122	44.0
3	Walter B. Jones Jr. (R)	72,464	52.7
	H. Martin Lancaster (D)*	65,013	47.3
4	Frederick Kenneth Heineman (R)	77,773	50.4
	David Price (D)*	76,558	49.6
5	Richard Burr (R)	84,741	57.3
	A. P. "Sandy" Sands (D)	63,194	42.7
6	Howard Coble (R)*	98,355	100.0
7	Charlie Rose (D)*	62,670	51.6

	Vote total	Per-cent
Robert C. Anderson (R)	58,849	48.4
8 W. G. "Bill" Hefner (D)*	62,845	52.4
Sherrill Morgan (R)	57,140	47.6
9 Sue Myrick (R)	82,374	65.0
Rory Blake (D)	44,379	35.0
10 Cass Ballenger (R)*	107,829	71.5
Robert Wayne Avery (D)	42,939	28.5
11 Charles H. Taylor (R)*	115,826	60.1
Maggie Palmer Lauterer (D)	76,862	39.9
12 Melvin Watt (D)*	57,655	65.8
Joseph A. "Joe" Martino (R)	29,933	34.2

North Dakota

	Vote total	Per-cent
Senate		
Kent Conrad (D)*	137,157	58.0
Ben Clayburgh (R)	99,390	42.0
House		
AL Earl Pomeroy (D)*	123,134	52.3
Gary Porter (R)	105,988	45.0
James Germalic (I)	6,267	2.7

Ohio

	Vote total	Per-cent
Governor		
George V. Voinovich (R)*	2,401,572	71.8
Robert L. Burch Jr. (D)	835,849	25.0
Billy R. Inmon (I)	108,745	3.2
Senate		
Mike DeWine (R)	1,836,556	53.4
Joel Hyatt (D)	1,348,213	39.2
Joseph J. Slovenec (I)	252,031	7.3
House		
1 Steve Chabot (R)	92,997	56.1
David Mann (D)*	72,822	43.9
2 Rob Portman (R)*	150,128	77.4
Les Mann (D)	43,730	22.6
3 Tony P. Hall (D)*	105,342	59.3
David A. Westbrock (R)	72,314	40.7
4 Michael G. Oxley (R)*	139,841	100.0
5 Paul E. Gillmor (R)*	135,879	73.4
Jarrod Tudor (D)	49,335	26.6
6 Frank A. Cremeans (R)	91,263	50.9
Ted Strickland (D)*	87,861	49.1
7 David L. Hobson (R)*	140,124	100.0
8 John A. Boehner (R)*	148,338	99.9
Rogers H. Campbell (write-in)	87	0.1
9 Marcy Kaptur (D)*	118,120	75.3
R. Randy Whitman (R)	38,665	24.7
10 Martin R. Hoke (R)*	95,226	51.9
Francis E. Gaul (D)	70,918	38.6
Joseph J. Jacobs Jr. (I)	17,495	9.5
11 Louis Stokes (D)*	114,220	77.2
James J. Sykora (R)	33,705	22.8
12 John R. Kasich (R)*	114,608	66.5
Cynthia L. Ruccia (D)	57,294	33.2
John Yiamouyianni (write-in)	244	0.1
John B. Hurd (write-in)	117	0.1
13 Sherrod Brown (D)*	93,147	49.1
Gregory A. White (R)	86,422	45.5
Howard Mason (I)	7,777	4.1
John Michael Ryan (I)	2,430	1.3
14 Tom Sawyer (D)*	96,274	51.9
Lynn Slaby (R)	89,106	48.1
15 Deborah Pryce (R)*	112,912	70.7
Bill Buckel (D)	46,480	29.1
Ronald D. Dempsey (write-in)	274	0.2
16 Ralph Regula (R)*	137,322	75.0
J. Michael Finn (D)	45,781	25.0
17 James A. Traficant Jr. (D)*	149,004	77.4
Mike G. Meister (R)	43,490	22.6
18 Bob Ney (R)	103,115	54.0
Greg L. DiDonato (D)	87,926	46.0
19 Steven C. LaTourette (R)	99,997	48.5
Eric D. Fingerhut (D)*	89,701	43.5
Ronald E. Young (I)	11,364	5.5
Jerome A. Brentar (I)	5,180	2.5

Oklahoma

	Vote total	Per-cent
Governor		
Frank Keating (R)	466,740	46.9
Jack Mildren (D)	294,936	29.6
Wes Watkins (I)	233,336	23.5
Senate		
James M. Inhofe (R)	542,390	55.2
Dave McCurdy (D)	392,488	40.0
Danny Corn (I)	47,552	4.8
House		
1 Steve Largent (R)	107,085	62.7
Stuart Price (D)	63,753	37.3
2 Tom Coburn (R)	82,479	52.1
Virgil R. Cooper (D)	75,943	47.9
3 Bill Brewster (D)*	115,731	73.8
Darrel Dewayne Tallant (R)	41,147	26.2
4 J. C. Watts (R)	80,251	51.6
David Perryman (D)	67,237	43.3
Bill Tiffee (I)	7,913	5.1
5 Ernest Jim Istook Jr. (R)*	136,877	78.1
Tom Keith (I)	38,270	21.9
6 Frank D. Lucas (R)*	106,961	70.2
Jeffrey S. Tollett (D)	45,399	29.8

Oregon

	Vote total	Per-cent
Governor		
John Kitzhaber (D)	622,083	50.9
Denny Smith (R)	517,874	42.4
Ed Hickam (AM)	58,449	4.8
Danford P. Vander Ploeg (LIBERT)	20,183	1.7
House		
1 Elizabeth Furse (D)*	121,147	47.7
Bill Witt (R)	120,846	47.6
Brewster Gillett (AM)	6,695	2.6
Daniel E. Wilson (LIBERT)	5,161	2.0
2 Wes Cooley (R)	134,255	57.3
Sue C. Kupillas (D)	90,822	38.7
Gary L. Sublett (LIBERT)	9,063	3.9
3 Ron Wyden (D)*	161,624	72.5
Everett Hall (R)	43,211	19.4
Mark Brunelle (I)	13,550	6.1
Gene Nanni (LIBERT)	4,164	1.9
4 Peter A. DeFazio (D)*	158,981	66.8
John D. Newkirk (R)	78,947	33.2
5 Jim Bunn (R)	121,369	49.8
Catherine Webber (D)	114,015	46.8
Jon E. Zimmer (LIBERT)	7,929	3.3

Pennsylvania

	Vote total	Per-cent
Governor		
Tom Ridge (R)	1,627,976	45.4
Mark S. Singel (D)	1,430,099	39.9
Peg Luksik (CONSTL)	460,269	12.8
Patrick Fallon (LIBERT)	33,602	0.9
Timothy E. Holloway (PAT)	33,235	0.9
Senate		
Rick Santorum (R)	1,735,691	49.4
Harris Wofford (D)*	1,648,481	46.9
Diane Blough (PAT)	69,825	2.0
Donald C. Ernsberge (LIBERT)	59,115	1.7
House		
1 Thomas M. Foglietta (D)*	99,669	81.5
Roger F. Gordon (R)	22,595	18.5
2 Chaka Fattah (D)	120,553	85.9
Lawrence R. Watson (R)	19,824	14.1
3 Robert A. Borski (D)*	92,702	62.7
James C. Hasher (R)	55,209	37.3
4 Ron Klink (D)*	119,115	64.2
Ed Peglow (R)	66,509	35.8
5 William F. Clinger (R)*	145,335	99.9
6 Tim Holden (D)*	90,023	56.7
Fred Levering (R)	68,610	43.3
7 Curt Weldon (R)*	137,480	69.7
Sara Nichols (D)	59,845	30.3
8 James C. Greenwood (R)*	110,499	66.1
John P. Murray (D)	44,559	26.7
Jay Russell (LIBERT)	7,925	4.7
Robert J. Cash (I)	4,191	2.5
9 Bud Shuster (R)*	146,688	99.7
10 Joseph M. McDade (R)*	106,992	65.7
Daniel J. Schreffler (D)	50,635	31.1
Albert A. Smith (LIBERT)	5,196	3.2
11 Paul E. Kanjorski (D)*	101,966	66.5
J. Andrew Podolak (R)	51,295	33.5
12 John P. Murtha (D)*	117,825	68.9
Bill Choby (R)	53,147	31.1
13 Jon D. Fox (R)	96,254	49.4
Marjorie Margolies-Mezvinsky (D)*	88,073	45.2
Lee D. Hustead (LIBERT)	7,183	3.7
Frank W. Szabo (I)	3,278	1.7
14 William J. Coyne (D)*	105,310	64.1
John Robert Clark (R)	53,221	32.4
Edward L. Stewart (PAT)	3,826	2.3
Paul Scherrer (WL)	1,819	1.1
15 Paul McHale (D)*	72,073	47.8
Jim Yeager (R)	71,602	47.4
Victor Mazziotti (PAT)	7,227	4.8
16 Robert S. Walker (R)*	109,759	69.7
Bill Chertok (D)	47,680	30.3
17 George W. Gekas (R)*	133,788	99.9
18 Mike Doyle (D)	101,784	54.8
John McCarty (R)	83,881	45.2
19 Bill Goodling (R)*	124,496	99.5
20 Frank R. Mascara (D)	95,251	53.1
Mike McCormick (R)	84,156	46.9
21 Phil English (R)	89,439	49.5
Bill Leavens (D)	84,796	46.9
Arthur E. Drew (I)	6,588	3.6

Rhode Island

	Vote total	Per-cent
Governor		
Lincoln C. Almond (R)	171,194	47.4
Myrth York (D)	157,361	43.5
Robert J. Healey (I)	32,822	9.1
Senate		
John H. Chafee (R)*	222,856	64.5
Linda J. Kushner (D)	122,532	35.5
House		
1 Patrick J. Kennedy (D)	89,832	54.1
Kevin Vigilante (R)	76,069	45.9
2 Jack Reed (D)*	119,659	68.0
A. John Elliot (R)	56,348	32.0

	Vote total	Percent

South Carolina
Governor
David Beasley (R)	470,756	50.4
Nick A. Theodore (D)	447,002	47.9
John Peeples (USTAX)	8,003	0.9
Wayne B. Griffin (NA)	5,875	0.6
Joe Riley (write-in)	557	0.1

House
1 Marshall "Mark" Sanford (R)	97,803	66.3
Robert Barber (D)	47,769	32.4
Robert Paine (LIBERT)	1,836	1.2
2 Floyd D. Spence (R)*	133,307	99.8
3 Lindsey Graham (R)	90,123	60.1
James Bryan (D)	59,932	39.9
4 Bob Inglis (R)*	109,626	73.5
Jerry Fowler (D)	39,396	26.4
5 John M. Spratt Jr. (D)*	77,311	52.1
Larry Bigham (R)	70,967	47.8
6 James E. Clyburn (D)*	88,635	63.8
Gary McLeod (R)	50,259	36.2

South Dakota
Governor
William J. Janklow (R)	172,515	55.4
Jim Beddow (D)	126,273	40.5
Nathan A. Barton (LIBERT)	12,825	4.1

House
AL Tim Johnson (D)*	183,036	59.8
Jan Berkhout (R)	112,054	36.6
Ronald Wieczorek (I)	10,832	3.5

Tennessee
Governor
Don Sundquist (R)	807,104	54.3
Phil Bredesen (D)	664,252	44.7
Stephanie Holt (I)	9,981	0.7
Will Smith (I)	3,365	0.2
Charlie Moffet (I)	2,347	0.2

Senate (Full Term)
Bill Frist (R)	834,226	56.4
Jim Sasser (D)*	623,164	42.1
John Jay Hooker (I)	13,244	0.9
Charles F. Johnson (I)	6,631	0.4
Philip L. Kienlen (I)	3,087	0.2

Senate (Short Term)
Fred Thompson (R)	885,998	60.4
Jim Cooper (D)	565,930	38.6
Charles N. Hancock (I)	4,169	0.3
Charles M. Moore (I)	2,219	0.2
Terry L. Lytle (I)	1,934	0.1
Kerry Martin (I)	1,719	0.1
Jon Walls (I)	1,532	0.1
Hobart Lumpkin (I)	1,184	0.1
Don Schneller (I)	1,150	0.1

House
1 James H. Quillen (R)*	102,947	72.9
J. Carr "Jack" Christian (D)	34,691	24.6
George "Doc" Mauer (I)	3,576	2.5
2 John J. "Jimmy" Duncan Jr. (R)*	128,937	90.5
Randon J. Krieg (I)	6,854	4.8
Greg Samples (I)	6,682	4.7
3 Zach Wamp (R)	84,583	52.3
Randy Button (D)	73,839	45.6
Thomas Ed Morrell (I)	1,929	1.2
Richard M. Sims (I)	1,498	0.9

4 Van Hilleary (R)	81,539	56.6
Jeff Whorley (D)	60,489	42.0
J. Patrick Lyons (I)	1,944	1.4
5 Bob Clement (D)*	95,953	60.2
John Osborne (R)	61,692	38.7
Lloyd Botway (I)	978	0.6
Chuck Lokey (I)	664	0.4
6 Bart Gordon (D)*	90,933	50.6
Steve Gill (R)	88,759	49.4
7 Ed Bryant (R)	102,587	60.2
Harold Byrd (D)	65,851	38.6
Tom Jeanette (I)	1,944	1.1
8 John Tanner (D)*	97,951	63.8
Neal R. Morris (R)	55,573	36.2
9 Harold E. Ford (D)*	94,805	57.8
Rod DeBerry (R)	69,226	42.2

Texas
Governor
George W. Bush (R)	2,350,994	53.5
Ann Richards (D)*	2,016,928	45.9
Keary Ehlers (LIBERT)	28,320	0.6

Senate
Kay Bailey Hutchison (R)*	2,604,218	60.8
Richard Fisher (D)	1,639,615	38.3
Pierre Blondeau (LIBERT)	36,107	0.8

House
1 Jim Chapman (D)*	86,480	55.3
Mike Blankenship (R)	63,911	40.9
Thomas "Jefferson" Mosser (I)	6,001	3.8
2 Charles Wilson (D)*	87,709	57.0
Donna Peterson (R)	66,071	43.0
3 Sam Johnson (R)*	157,011	91.0
Tom Donahue (LIBERT)	15,611	9.0
4 Ralph M. Hall (D)*	99,303	58.8
David L. Bridges (R)	67,267	39.8
Steven Rothacker (LIBERT)	2,377	1.4
5 John Bryant (D)*	61,877	50.1
Pete Sessions (R)	58,521	47.3
Barbara Morgan (I)	1,715	1.4
Noel Kopala (LIBERT)	876	0.7
Regina Arashvand (I)	627	0.5
6 Joe L. Barton (R)*	152,038	75.6
Terry Jesmore (D)	44,286	22.0
Bill Baird (LIBERT)	4,688	2.3
7 Bill Archer (R)*	116,783	100.0
8 Jack Fields (R)*	148,473	92.0
Russ Klecka (I)	12,831	8.0
9 Steve Stockman (R)	81,353	51.9
Jack Brooks (D)*	71,643	45.7
Bill Felton (I)	2,145	1.4
Darla K. Beenau (LIBERT)	1,656	1.1
10 Lloyd Doggett (D)	113,738	56.3
A. Jo Baylor (R)	80,382	39.8
Jeff Hill (LIBERT)	2,953	1.5
Michael L. Brandes (I)	2,579	1.3
Jeff Davis (I)	2,334	1.2
11 Chet Edwards (D)*	76,667	59.2
Jim Broyles (R)	52,876	40.8
12 Pete Geren (D)*	96,372	68.7
Ernest J. Anderson Jr. (R)	43,959	31.3
13 William M. "Mac" Thornberry (R)	79,466	55.4
Bill Sarpalius (D)*	63,923	44.6
14 Greg Laughlin (D)*	86,175	55.6
Jim Deats (R)	68,793	44.4

15 E. "Kika" de la Garza (D)*	61,527	59.0
Tom Haughey (R)	41,119	39.4
John c. c. Hamilton (I)	1,720	1.6
16 Ronald D. Coleman (D)*	49,815	57.1
Bobby Ortiz (R)	37,409	42.9
17 Charles W. Stenholm (D)*	83,497	53.7
Phil Boone (R)	72,108	46.3
18 Sheila Jackson Lee (D)	84,790	73.5
Jerry Burley (R)	28,153	24.4
J. Larry Snellings (I)	1,278	1.1
George M. Hollenbeck (LIBERT)	1,169	1.0
19 Larry Combest (R)*	120,641	100.0
20 Henry B. Gonzalez (D)*	60,114	62.5
Carl Bill Colyer (R)	36,035	37.5
21 Lamar Smith (R)*	165,595	90.0
Kerry Lowry (I)	18,480	10.0
22 Tom DeLay (R)*	120,302	73.7
Scott Douglas Cunningham (D)	38,826	23.8
Gregory D. Pepper (I)	4,016	2.5
23 Henry Bonilla (R)*	73,815	62.6
Rolando L. Rios (D)	44,101	37.4
24 Martin Frost (D)*	65,019	52.8
Ed Harrison (R)	58,062	47.2
25 Ken Bentsen (D)	61,959	52.3
Gene Fontenot (R)	53,321	45.0
Sarah Klein-Tower (I)	2,060	1.7
Robert F. Lockhart (LIBERT)	1,189	1.0
26 Dick Armey (R)*	135,398	76.4
LeEarl Ann Bryant (D)	39,763	22.4
Alfred Adask (LIBERT)	2,030	1.1
27 Solomon P. Ortiz (D)*	65,325	59.4
Erol A. Stone (R)	44,693	40.6
28 Frank Tejeda (D)*	73,986	70.9
David C. Slatter (R)	28,777	27.6
Stephen "Steve" Rothstein (LIBERT)	1,612	1.5
29 Gene Green (D)*	44,102	73.4
Harold "Oilman" Eide (R)	15,952	26.6
30 Eddie Bernice Johnson (D)*	73,166	72.6
Lucy Cain (R)	25,848	25.7
Ken Ashby (LIBERT)	1,728	1.7

Utah
Senate
Orrin G. Hatch (R)*	357,297	68.8
Patrick A. Shea (D)	146,938	28.3
Craig Oliver (I)	9,550	1.8
Gary R. Van Horn (AM)	2,543	0.5
Nelson Gonzalez (SW)	1,514	0.3
Lawrence Rey Topham (IA)	1,462	0.3

House
1 James V. Hansen (R)*	104,954	64.5
Bobbie Coray (D)	57,644	35.5
2 Enid Greene Waldholtz (R)	85,507	45.8
Karen Shepherd (D)*	66,911	35.9
Merrill Cook (I)	34,167	18.3
3 Bill Orton (D)*	91,505	59.0
Dixie Thompson (R)	61,839	39.9
Barbara Greenway (SW)	1,802	1.2

Vermont
Governor
Howard Dean (D)*	145,661	68.7
David Kelley (R)	40,292	19.0
Thomas J. Morse (I)	15,000	7.1
Dennis Lane (VG)	2,118	1.0

	Vote Total	Percent
William "Turkeybill" Brueckner (I)	2,071	1.0
August "Gus" Jaccaci (PV)	2,043	1.0
Richard Gottlieb (LU)	1,733	0.8
Bill Brunelle (NL)	1,668	0.8
Senate		
James M. Jeffords (R)*	106,505	50.3
Jan Backus (D)	85,868	40.6
Gavin T. Mills (I)	12,465	5.9
Matthew S. Mulligan (I)	3,141	1.5
Bob Melamede (VG)	1,416	0.7
Jerry Levy (LU)	1,376	0.7
Joseph Victor Pardo (NL)	709	0.3
House		
AL Bernard Sanders (I)*	105,502	49.9
John Carroll (R)	98,523	46.6
Carole Banus (NL)	2,963	1.4
Jack "Buck" Rogers (VG)	2,664	1.3
Annette Larson (LU)	1,493	0.7

Virginia

	Vote Total	Percent
Senate		
Charles S. Robb (D)*	938,376	45.6
Oliver L. North (R)	882,213	42.9
J. Marshall Coleman (I)	235,324	11.4
House		
1 Herbert H. Bateman (R)*	142,930	74.3
Mary Sinclair (D)	45,173	23.5
Matt B. Voorhees (I)	4,365	2.3
2 Owen Pickett (D)*	81,372	59.0
Jim Chapman (R)	56,375	40.9
3 Robert C. Scott (D)*	108,532	79.4
Tom Ward (R)	28,080	20.6
4 Norman Sisisky (D)*	115,055	61.6
George Sweet (R)	71,678	38.4
5 Lewis F. Payne Jr. (D)*	95,308	53.3
George C. Landrith III (R)	83,555	46.7
6 Robert W. Goodlatte (R)*	126,455	99.9
7 Thomas J. Bliley Jr. (R)*	176,941	84.0
Gerald E. "Jerry" Berg (I)	33,220	15.8
8 James P. Moran (D)*	120,281	59.3
Kyle E. McSlarrow (R)	79,568	39.3
R. Ward Edmonds (I)	1,858	0.9
William C. Jones (I)	868	0.4
9 Rick Boucher (D)*	102,876	58.8
Steve Fast (R)	72,133	41.2
10 Frank R. Wolf (R)*	153,311	87.3
Alan R. Ogden (I)	13,687	7.8
Robert L. "Bob" Rilee (I)	8,267	4.7

	Vote Total	Percent
11 Thomas M. Davis III (R)	98,216	52.9
Leslie L. Byrne (D)*	84,104	45.3
Gordon S. Cruickshank (I)	3,246	1.7

Washington

	Vote Total	Percent
Senate		
Slade Gorton (R)*	947,821	55.7
Ron Sims (D)	752,352	44.3
House		
1 Rick White (R)	100,554	51.7
Maria Cantwell (D)*	94,110	48.3
2 Jack Metcalf (R)	107,430	54.7
Harriet A. Spanel (D)	89,096	45.3
3 Linda Smith (R)	100,188	52.0
Jolene Unsoeld (D)*	85,826	44.6
Caitlin Davis Carlson (GC)	6,620	3.4
4 Doc Hastings (R)	92,828	53.3
Jay Inslee (D)*	81,198	46.7
5 George Nethercutt (R)	110,057	50.9
Thomas S. Foley (D)*	106,074	49.1
6 Norm Dicks (D)*	105,480	58.3
Benjamin Gregg (R)	75,322	41.7
7 Jim McDermott (D)*	148,353	75.1
Keith Harris (R)	49,091	24.9
8 Jennifer Dunn (R)*	140,409	76.1
Jim Wyrick (D)	44,165	23.9
9 Randy Tate (R)	77,833	51.8
Mike Kreidler (D)*	72,451	48.2

West Virginia

	Vote Total	Percent
Senate		
Robert C. Byrd (D)*	290,495	69.0
Stan Klos (R)	130,441	31.0
House		
1 Alan B. Mollohan (D)*	103,177	70.3
Sally Rossy Riley (R)	43,590	29.7
2 Bob Wise (D)*	90,757	63.7
Sam Cravotta (R)	51,691	36.3
3 Nick J. Rahall II (D)*	74,967	63.9
Ben Waldman (R)	42,382	36.1

Wisconsin

	Vote Total	Percent
Governor		
Tommy G. Thompson (R)*	1,051,326	67.2
Chuck Chvala (D)	482,850	30.9

	Vote Total	Percent
David S. Harmon (LIBERT)	11,639	0.7
Edward J. Frami (TAX)	9,188	0.6
Michael J. Mangan (I)	8,150	0.5
Senate		
Herb Kohl (D)*	912,662	58.3
Robert T. Welch (R)	636,989	40.7
James Dean (LIBERT)	15,439	1.0
House		
1 Mark W. Neumann (R)	83,937	49.4
Peter W. Barca (D)*	82,817	48.8
Edward J. Kozak (LIBERT)	3,085	1.8
2 Scott L. Klug (R)*	133,734	69.2
Thomas C. Hecht (D)	55,406	28.7
John J. Stumpf (TAX)	2,676	1.4
Joseph E. Schumacher (I)	1,327	0.7
3 Steve Gunderson (R)*	89,338	55.7
Harvey Stower (D)	65,758	41.0
Chuck Lee (TAX)	2,837	1.8
Mark Weinhold (I)	2,279	1.4
4 Gerald D. Kleczka (D)*	93,789	53.7
Tom Reynolds (R)	78,225	44.8
James Harold Hause (TAX)	2,611	1.5
5 Thomas M. Barrett (D)*	87,806	62.4
Stephen B. Hollingshead (R)	51,145	36.4
David J. Schall (I)	1,576	1.1
6 Tom Petri (R)*	119,384	99.5
7 David R. Obey (D)*	97,184	54.3
Scott West (R)	81,706	45.7
8 Toby Roth (R)*	114,319	63.7
Stan Gruszynski (D)	65,065	36.3
9 F. James Sensenbrenner (R)*	141,617	99.8

Wyoming

	Vote Total	Percent
Governor		
Jim Geringer (R)	118,016	58.7
Kathy Karpan (D)	80,747	40.2
Seaghan Uibreaslain (LIBERT)	2,227	1.1
Senate		
Craig Thomas (R)	118,754	58.9
Mike Sullivan (D)	79,287	39.3
Craig Alan McCune (LIBERT)	3,669	1.8
House		
AL Barbara Cubin (R)	104,426	53.2
Bob Schuster (D)	81,022	41.3
Dave Dawson (LIBERT)	10,749	5.5

104th Congress Special Elections, 1995 Gubernatorial Returns

1995 Gubernatorial Elections

	Vote total	Percent		Vote total	Percent
Kentucky—Nov. 7, 1995			**Louisiana (runoff)—Nov. 18, 1995**		
Paul E. Patton (D)	500,787	50.9	Mike Foster (R)	984,499	63.5
Larry Forgy (R)	479,227	48.7	Cleo Fields (D)	565,861	36.5
Mississippi—Nov. 7, 1995					
Kirk Fordice (R)	455,261	55.6			
Dick Molpus (D)	364,210	44.4			

Special House Elections, 104th Congress

	Vote total	Percent		Vote total	Percent
Illinois—Dec. 12, 1995			**Oregon—May 21, 1996**		
Jesse Jackson Jr. (D)	48,145	76.0	Earl Blumenauer (D)	50,125	69.9
Thomas "T. J." Somer (R)	15,171	24.0	Mark Brunelle (R)	17,085	23.8
California—Dec. 12, 1995			**Missouri—Nov. 5, 1996**		
Tom Campbell (R)	54,372	58.9	Jo Ann Emerson (R)[b]	132,804	63.3
Jerry Estruth (D)	33,051	35.8	Emily Firebaugh (D)	71,625	34.1
Linh Kieu Dao (I)	4,922	5.3			
California Primary—March 26, 1996[a]					
Juanita Millender-McDonald (D)	13,868	27.3			
Willard H. Murray Jr. (D)	10,396	20.4			
Omar Bradley (D)	6,975	13.7			
Paul H. Richards (D)	6,035	11.9			
Robert M. Sausedo (D)	4,495	8.8			
Robin Tucker (D)	3,661	7.2			
Charles Davis (D)	2,555	5.0			
Maryland—April 16, 1996					
Elijah E. Cummings (D)	18,870	80.9			
Kenneth Konder (R)	4,449	19.1			

Special Senate Elections, 104th Congress

	Vote total	Percent
Oregon—Jan. 30, 1996		
Ron Wyden (D)	571,739	48.4
Gordon H. Smith (R)	553,519	46.8

NOTE: D–Democrat, I–Independent, R–Republican

[a] Millender-McDonald was elected. No runoff was held because only Democrats filed for the primary.

[b] Jo Ann Emerson was elected Nov. 5, 1996, as a Republican to complete the remainder of her husband's 104th Congress term; because her husband's death came after Missouri's primary filing deadline, she was listed on the general election ballot for the 105th Congress as an independent. She entered the 105th Congress as a Republican.

Following are the official vote returns for the gubernatorial, Senate and House races compiled by Congressional Quarterly from the figures supplied by the 50 state election boards.

Vote totals are included for all candidates who were listed on the ballot and for write-ins whose votes equaled at least 0.1 percent of the total.

The vote percentages for each race do not always add to 100 due to rounding and the exclusion of scattered write-ins.

An asterisk (*) indicates an incumbent.

An "X" denotes candidates without major-party opposition; no votes were tallied.

An "AL" indicates an at-large district.

		Vote total	Percent
Alabama			
Senate			
	Jeff Sessions (R)	786,436	51.9
	Roger Bedford (D)	681,651	45.7
	Mark Thornton (LIBERT)	21,550	1.8
	Charles Hebner (NL)	9,123	0.6
House			
1	Sonny Callahan (R)*	132,206	64.4
	Don Womack (D)	69,470	33.8
	Bob Burns (LIBERT)	3,311	1.6
2	Terry Everett (R)*	132,563	63.2
	Bob E. Gaines (D)	74,317	35.4
	Michael Probst (LIBERT)	2,653	1.3
3	Bob Riley (R)	98,353	50.9
	T.D. "Ted" Little (D)	92,325	46.9
	Lucy Lawrence (NL)	2,335	1.2
	Ralph "R. E." Stokes (LIBERT)	1,983	1.0
4	Robert B. Aderholt (R)	102,741	50.0
	Robert T. "Bob" Wilson (D)	99,250	48.3
	Alan Barksdale (LIBERT)	3,718	1.7
5	Robert E. "Bud" Cramer (D)*	114,442	55.7
	Wayne Parker (R)	86,727	42.2
	Shirley Madison (NL)	2,484	1.2
	Craig Goodrich (LIBERT)	1,856	0.9
6	Spencer Bachus (R)*	180,781	70.9

		Vote total	Percent
	Mary Lynn Bates (D)	69,592	27.3
	T. Franklin Harris (LIBERT)	2,293	0.9
	Diane Vogel (NL)	2,113	0.8
7	Earl F. Hilliard (D)*	136,651	71.1
	Joe Powell (R)	52,142	27.1
	Ken Hager (LIBERT)	3,157	1.6
Alaska			
Senate			
	Ted Stevens (R)*	177,893	76.7
	Jed Whittaker (GREEN)	29,037	12.5
	Theresa Nangle Obermeyer (D)	23,977	10.3
House			
AL	Don Young (R)*	138,834	59.4
	Georgianna Lincoln (D)	85,114	36.4
	William J. Nemec II (AKI)	5,017	2.1
	John J. G. "Johnny" Grames (GREEN)	4,513	1.9
Arizona			
House			
1	Matt Salmon (R)*	135,634	60.2
	John Cox (D)	89,738	39.8
2	Ed Pastor (D)*	81,982	65.0
	Jim Buster (R)	38,786	30.8
	Alice Bangle (LIBERT)	5,333	4.2

		Vote total	Percent
3	Bob Stump (R)*	175,231	66.5
	Alexander "Big Al" Schneider (D)	88,214	33.5
4	John Shadegg (R)*	150,486	66.8
	Maria Elena Milton (D)	74,857	33.2
5	Jim Kolbe (R)*	179,349	68.7
	Mort Nelson (D)	67,597	25.9
	John C. Zajac (LIBERT)	7,322	2.8
	Ed Finkelstein (REF)	6,630	2.5
6	J.D. Hayworth (R)*	121,431	47.6
	Steve Owens (D)	118,957	46.6
	Robert Anderson (LIBERT)	14,899	5.8
Arkansas			
Senate			
	Tim Hutchinson (R)	445,942	52.7
	Winston Bryant (D)	400,241	47.3
House			
1	Marion Berry (D)	105,280	52.8
	Warren Dupwe (R)	88,436	44.3
	Keith Carle (REF)	5,734	2.9
2	Vic Snyder (D)	114,841	52.3
	Bud Cummins (R)	104,548	47.7
3	Asa Hutchinson (R)	137,093	55.7
	Ann Henry (D)	102,994	41.8
	Tony Joe Huffman (REF)	5,974	2.4
4	Jay Dickey (R)*	125,956	63.5
	Vincent Tolliver (D)	72,391	36.5

ABBREVIATIONS FOR PARTY DESIGNATIONS

AF	America First	IPC	Independent Peoples Coalition	REF	Reform
AKI	Alaskan Independence			RES	Resource Party
AM	American	JPR	Jobs, Property Rights	ROP	Running on Principles
C	Conservative	L	Liberal	RTL	Right to Life
CC	Concerned Citizens	LIBERT	Libertarian	S	Socialist
CONSTL	Constitutional	LU	Liberty Union	SE	Socialist Equality
D	Democratic	NJC	New Jersey Conservative	SM	Save Medicare
FDM	Freedom Party	NJI	New Jersey Independents	SW	Socialist Workers
FN	Future Now Party	NL	Natural Law	TAX	Taxpayers
FWC	Francis Worley Congress	NON	Nonpartisan	TLL	Truth, Life, Liberty
GCP	Green Coalition Party	P	Prohibition	USA	Undauntable Stalwart Allegiance
GR	Grassroots	PAC	Politicians Are Crooks		
GREEN	Green	PACIFIC	Pacific Party	USTAX	U.S. Taxpayers
I	Independent	PF	Protecting Freedom	VG	Vermont Grassroots
IA	Independent American	PFP	Peace and Freedom	VREF	Virginia Reform
IG	Independent Grassroots	PS	Protect Seniors	WC	Working Class
INDC	Independence	PTC	Property Tax Cut	WSN	West Side Neighbors
IP	Independent Party	R	Republican	WW	Workers World

		Vote total	Per- cent

California

House

District	Candidate	Vote total	Percent
1	Frank Riggs (R)*	110,242	49.6
	Michela Alioto (D)	96,522	43.5
	Emil Rossi (LIBERT)	15,354	6.9
2	Wally Herger (R)*	144,913	60.8
	Roberts A. Braden (D)	80,401	33.7
	Patrice Thiessen (NL)	7,253	3.0
	William Brunner (LIBERT)	5,759	2.4
3	Vic Fazio (D)*	118,663	53.5
	Tim LeFever (R)	91,134	41.1
	Timothy R. Erich (REF)	7,701	3.5
	Erin D. Donelle (LIBERT)	4,239	1.9
4	John T. Doolittle (R)*	164,048	60.5
	Katie Hirning (D)	97,948	36.1
	Patrick Lee McHargue (LIBERT)	9,319	3.4
5	Robert T. Matsui (D)*	142,618	70.4
	Robert S. Dinsmore (R)	52,940	26.1
	Joseph B. Miller (LIBERT)	2,548	1.3
	Gordon Mors (AMI)	2,231	1.1
	Charles Kersey (NL)	2,123	1.0
6	Lynn Woolsey (D)*	156,958	61.8
	Duane C. Hughes (R)	86,278	34.0
	Ernest K. Jones Jr. (PFP)	6,459	2.5
	Bruce B. Kendall (NL)	4,141	1.6
7	George Miller (D)*	137,089	71.8
	Norman H. Reece (R)	42,542	22.3
	William C. Thompson (REF)	6,866	3.6
	Bob Liatunick (NL)	4,420	2.3
8	Nancy Pelosi (D)*	175,216	84.3
	Justin Raimondo (R)	25,739	12.4
	David Smithstein (NL)	6,783	3.3
9	Ronald V. Dellums (D)*	154,806	77.0
	Deborah Wright (R)	37,126	18.5
	Tom Condit (PFP)	5,561	2.8
	Jack Forem (NL)	3,475	1.7
10	Ellen O. Tauscher (D)	137,726	48.6
	Bill Baker (R)*	133,633	47.2
	John Place (REF)	6,354	2.2
	Valerie Janlois (NL)	3,047	1.1
	Gregory K. Lyon (LIBERT)	2,423	0.9
11	Richard W. Pombo (R)*	107,477	59.3
	Jason Silva (D)	65,536	36.2
	Kelly Rego (LIBERT)	5,077	2.8
	Selene L. Bush (NL)	3,006	1.7
12	Tom Lantos (D)*	149,052	71.7
	Storm Jenkins (R)	49,278	23.7
	Christopher V.A. Schmidt (LIBERT)	6,111	2.9
	Richard Borg (NL)	3,472	1.7
13	Pete Stark (D)*	114,408	65.2
	James S. Fay (R)	53,385	30.4
	Terry C. Savage (LIBERT)	7,746	4.4
14	Anna G. Eshoo (D)*	149,313	64.9
	Ben Brink (R)	71,573	31.1
	Timothy Thompson (PFP)	3,653	1.6
	Joseph W. Dehn III (LIBERT)	3,492	1.5
	Robert Wells (NL)	2,144	0.9
15	Tom Campbell (R)*	132,737	58.5
	Dick Lane (D)	79,048	34.8
	Valli Sharpe-Geisler (REF)	6,230	2.7
	Ed Wimmers (LIBERT)	5,481	2.4
	Bruce Currivan (NL)	3,372	1.5
16	Zoe Lofgren (D)*	94,020	65.7
	Chuck Wojslaw (R)	43,197	30.2
	David R. Bonino (LIBERT)	4,124	2.9
	Abaan Abu-Shumays (NL)	1,866	1.3
17	Sam Farr (D)*	115,116	58.9
	Jess Brown (R)	73,856	37.8
	John H. Black (NL)	6,573	3.4
18	Gary A. Condit (D)*	108,827	65.7
	Bill Conrad (R)	52,695	31.8
	James B. Morzella (LIBERT)	2,233	1.3
	Page Roth Riskin (NL)	1,831	1.1
19	George P. Radanovich (R)*	137,402	66.6
	Paul Barile (D)	58,452	28.3
	Pamela J. Pescosolido (LIBERT)	6,083	2.9
	David P. Adalian Sr. (NL)	4,442	2.2
20	Cal Dooley (D)*	65,381	56.5
	Trice Harvey (R)	45,276	39.1
	Jonathan Richter (LIBERT)	5,048	4.4
21	Bill Thomas (R)*	125,916	65.8
	Deborah A. Vollmer (D)	50,694	26.5
	John Evans (REF)	8,113	4.2
	Jane Bialosky (NL)	3,380	1.8
	Mike Hodges (LIBERT)	3,049	1.6
	Karen Gentry (write-in)	172	0.1
22	Walter Holden Capps (D)	118,299	48.4
	Andrea Seastrand (R)*	107,987	44.2
	Steven Wheeler (I)	9,845	4.0
	Richard D. "Dick" Porter (REF)	3,975	1.6
	David L. Bersohn (LIBERT)	2,233	0.9
	Dawn Tomastik (NL)	1,847	0.8
23	Elton Gallegly (R)*	118,880	59.6
	Robert R. Unruhe (D)	70,035	35.1
	Gail Lightfoot (LIBERT)	8,346	4.2
	Stephen Hospodar (NL)	2,246	1.1
24	Brad Sherman (D)	106,193	50.4
	Rich Sybert (R)	93,629	42.5
	Ralph Shroyer (PFP)	6,267	3.0
	Erich Miller (LIBERT)	5,691	2.7
	Ron Lawrence (NL)	3,068	1.5
25	Howard P. "Buck" McKeon (R)*	122,428	62.4
	Diane Trautman (D)	65,089	33.2
	Bruce Acker (LIBERT)	6,173	3.1
	Justin Charles Gerber (PFP)	2,513	1.3
26	Howard L. Berman (D)*	67,525	65.9
	Bill Glass (R)	29,332	28.6
	Scott K. Fritschler (LIBERT)	3,539	3.5
	Gary Hearne (NL)	2,119	2.1
27	James E. Rogan (R)	95,310	49.9
	Doug Kahn (D)	82,014	43.4
	Elizabeth Michael (LIBERT)	6,645	3.6
	Walt Contreras Sheasby (GREEN)	4,195	2.2
	Martin Zucker (NL)	1,766	1.0
28	David Dreier (R)*	113,389	60.7
	David Levering (D)	69,037	36.9
	Ken Saurenman (LIBERT)	4,459	2.4
29	Henry A. Waxman (D)*	145,278	67.6
	Paul Stepanek (R)	52,857	24.6
	John Peter Daly (PFP)	8,819	4.1
	Mike Binkley (LIBERT)	4,766	2.2
	Brian Rees (NL)	3,097	1.4
30	Xavier Becerra (D)*	58,283	72.3
	Patricia Jean Parker (R)	15,078	18.7
	Pam Probst (LIBERT)	2,759	3.4
	Shirley Mandel (PFP)	2,499	3.1
	Rosemary Watson-Frith (NL)	1,971	2.4
31	Matthew G. Martinez (D)*	69,285	67.5
	John V. Flores (R)	28,705	28.0
	Michael B. Everling (LIBERT)	4,700	4.6
32	Julian C. Dixon (D)*	124,712	82.4
	Larry Ardito (R)	18,768	12.4
	Neal Donner (LIBERT)	6,390	4.2
	Rashied Jibri (NL)	1,557	1.0
33	Lucille Roybal-Allard (D)*	47,478	82.1
	John P. Leonard (R)	8,147	14.1
	Howard Johnson (LIBERT)	2,203	3.8
34	Esteban E. Torres (D)*	94,730	68.4
	David G. Nunez (R)	36,852	26.6
	J. Walter Scott (AMI)	4,122	3.0
	David Argall (LIBERT)	2,736	2.0
35	Maxine Waters (D)*	92,762	85.5
	Eric Carlson (R)	13,116	12.1
	Gordon Michael Mego (AMI)	2,610	2.4
36	Jane Harman (D)*	117,752	52.5
	Susan Brooks (R)	98,538	43.9
	Bruce Dovner (LIBERT)	4,933	2.2
	Bradley McManus (NL)	3,236	1.4
37	Juanita Millender-McDonald (D)*	87,247	85.0
	Michael E. Voetee (R)	15,399	15.0
38	Steve Horn (R)*	88,136	52.6
	Rick Zbur (D)	71,627	42.7
	William A. Yeager (GREEN)	4,610	2.7
	Paul N. Gautreau (LIBERT)	3,272	2.0
39	Ed Royce (R)*	120,761	62.8
	R.O. "Bob" Davis (D)	61,392	31.9
	Jack Dean (LIBERT)	10,137	5.3
40	Jerry Lewis (R)*	98,821	64.9
	Robert "Bob" Conaway (D)	44,102	29.0
	Hale McGee (AMI)	4,963	3.3
	Joseph T. Kelley (LIBERT)	4,375	2.9
41	Jay C. Kim (R)*	83,934	58.5
	Richard L. Waldron (D)	47,346	33.0
	Richard G. Newhouse (LIBERT)	7,135	5.0
	David F. Kramer (NL)	5,030	3.5
42	George E. Brown Jr. (D)*	52,166	50.5
	Linda M. Wilde (R)	51,170	49.5
43	Ken Calvert (R)*	97,247	54.7
	Guy C. Kimbrough (D)	67,422	37.9
	Annie Wallack (NL)	6,576	3.7
	Kevin Akin (PFP)	3,309	1.9
	Gene L. Berkman (LIBERT)	3,086	1.7
44	Sonny Bono (R)*	110,643	57.7
	Anita Rufus (D)	73,844	38.5
	Donald Cochran (AMI)	3,888	2.0
	Karen Wilkinson (NL)	3,143	1.6
45	Dana Rohrabacher (R)*	125,326	61.0
	Sally J. Alexander (D)	68,312	33.2
	Mark F. Murphy (LIBERT)	8,813	4.3
	Rand McDevitt (NL)	3,071	1.5
46	Loretta Sanchez (D)	47,964	46.8
	Robert K. Dornan (R)*	46,980	45.8
	Lawrence J. Stafford (REF)	3,235	3.2
	Thomas E. Reimer (LIBERT)	2,333	2.3
	J. Carlos Aguirre (NL)	1,972	1.9
47	Christopher Cox (R)*	160,078	65.7
	Tina Louise Laine (D)	70,362	28.9
	Iris Adam (NL)	6,807	2.8
	Victor A. Wagner Jr. (LIBERT)	6,530	2.7
48	Ron Packard (R)*	145,814	65.9
	Dan Farrell (D)	59,558	26.9
	William Dreu (REF)	8,013	3.6
	Sharon K. Miles (NL)	8,006	3.6
49	Brian P. Bilbray (R)*	108,806	52.6
	Peter Navarro (D)	86,657	41.9

		Vote total	Per-cent
	Ernie Lippe (LIBERT)	4,218	2.0
	Kevin Philip Hambsch (REF)	3,773	1.8
	Peter Sterling (NL)	3,314	1.6
50	Bob Filner (D)*	73,200	61.9
	Jim Baize (R)	38,351	32.4
	Dan Clark (REF)	3,253	2.7
	Earl M. Shepard (NL)	2,138	1.8
	Philip Zoebisch (LIBERT)	1,398	1.2
51	Randy "Duke" Cunningham (R)*	149,032	65.1
	Rita Tamerius (D)	66,250	28.9
	Miriam E. Clark (PFP)	5,407	2.4
	J.C. "Jack" Anderson (LIBERT)	5,298	2.3
	Eric Hunter Bourdette (NL)	3,037	1.3
52	Duncan Hunter (R)*	116,746	65.5
	Darity Wesley (D)	53,104	29.8
	Janice Jordan (PFP)	3,649	2.0
	Dante Ridley (LIBERT)	3,329	1.9
	Peter Robert Ballantyne (NL)	1,493	0.8

Colorado

Senate

	Vote total	Per-cent
Wayne Allard (R)	750,325	50.7
Tom Strickland (D)	677,600	46.3
Randy MacKenzie (NL)	41,620	3.0

House

		Vote total	Per-cent
1	Diana DeGette (D)	112,631	56.9
	Joe Rogers (R)	79,540	40.2
	Richard Combs (LIBERT)	5,668	2.9
2	David E. Skaggs (D)*	145,894	57.0
	Pat Miller (R)	97,865	38.3
	Larry E. Johnson (I)	6,304	2.5
	W. Earl Allen (LIBERT)	5,721	2.2
3	Scott McInnis (R)*	183,523	68.9
	Al Gurule (D)	82,953	31.1
4	Bob Schaffer (R)	137,012	56.1
	Guy Kelley (D)	92,837	38.1
	Wes McKinley (AM)	7,428	3.0
	Cynthia Parker (NL)	6,790	2.7
5	Joel Hefley (R)*	188,805	71.9
	Mike Robinson (D)	73,660	28.1
6	Dan Schaefer (R)*	146,018	62.2
	Joan Fitz-Gerald (D)	88,600	37.8

Connecticut

House

		Vote total	Per-cent
1	Barbara B. Kennelly (D, ACP)*	158,222	73.5
	Kent Sleath (R)	53,666	24.9
	John F. Forry III (CC)	2,099	1.0
	Daniel A. Wasielewski (NL)	1,149	0.5
2	Sam Gejdenson (D, ACP)*	115,175	51.6
	Edward W. Munster (R)	100,332	44.9
	Dianne G. Ondusko (INDC)	6,477	2.9
	Thomas E. Hall (NL)	1,263	0.6
3	Rosa DeLauro (D, ACP)*	150,798	71.3
	John Coppola (R)	59,335	28.1
	Gail J. Dalby (NL)	1,219	0.6
4	Christopher Shays (R)*	121,949	60.5
	Bill Finch (D)	75,902	37.6
	Edward H. Tonkin (LIBERT)	2,815	1.4
	Terry M. Nevas (NL)	1,046	0.5
5	Jim Maloney (D, ACP)	111,974	52.0
	Gary A. Franks (R)*	98,782	45.9
	Rosita Rodriguez (CC)	2,983	1.4
	Walter F. Thiessen Jr. (LIBERT)	1,391	0.6

		Vote total	Per-cent
6	Nancy L. Johnson (R)*	113,020	49.6
	Charlotte Koskoff (D, ACP)	111,433	48.9
	Timothy A. Knibbs (CC)	3,303	1.5

Delaware

Governor

	Vote total	Per-cent
Thomas R. Carper (D)*	188,300	69.5
Janet C. Rzewnicki (R)	82,654	30.5

Senate

	Vote total	Per-cent
Joseph R. Biden Jr. (D)*	165,465	60.0
Raymond J. Clatworthy (R)	105,088	38.1
Mark Jones (LIBERT)	3,340	1.2
Jacqueline Kossoff (NL)	1,698	0.6

House

		Vote total	Per-cent
AL	Michael N. Castle (R)*	185,576	69.5
	Dennis E. Williams (D)	73,253	27.5
	George A. Jurgensen (LIBERT)	4,000	1.5
	Felicia B. Johnson (P)	3,009	1.1
	Robert E. "Bob" Mattson (NL)	987	0.4

Florida

House

		Vote total	Per-cent
1	Joe Scarborough (R)*	175,946	72.5
	Kevin Beck (D)	66,495	27.4
2	Allen Boyd (D)	138,151	59.5
	Bill Sutton (R)	94,122	40.5
3	Corrine Brown (D)*	98,085	61.2
	Preston James Fields (R)	62,196	38.8
4	Tillie Fowler (R)*	X	X
5	Karen L. Thurman (D)*	161,050	61.7
	Dave Gentry (R)	100,051	38.5
6	Cliff Stearns (R)*	161,527	67.2
	Newell O'Brien (D)	78,908	32.8
7	John L. Mica (R)*	143,667	62.0
	George Stuart Jr. (D)	87,832	37.9
8	Bill McCollum (R)*	136,515	67.5
	Al Krulick (D)	65,794	32.5
9	Michael Bilirakis (R)*	161,708	68.7
	Jerry Provenzano (D)	73,809	31.3
10	C.W. Bill Young (R)*	114,443	66.6
	Henry Green (D)	57,375	33.4
11	Jim Davis (D)	108,522	57.9
	Mark Sharpe (R)	78,881	42.1
12	Charles T. Canady (R)*	122,584	61.6
	Mike Canady (D)	76,513	38.4
13	Dan Miller (R)*	173,671	64.3
	Sanford Gordon (D)	96,098	35.6
14	Porter J. Goss (R)*	176,992	73.5
	Jim Nolan (D)	63,842	26.5
15	Dave Weldon (R)*	139,014	51.4
	John L. Byron (D)	115,981	42.9
	David Golding (I)	15,349	5.7
16	Mark Foley (R)*	175,714	64.0
	Jim Stuber (D)	98,827	36.0
17	Carrie P. Meek (D)*	114,638	88.8
	Wellington Rolle (R)	14,525	11.2
18	Ileana Ros-Lehtinen (R)*	123,659	100.0
19	Robert Wexler (D)	188,766	65.6
	Beverly "Bev" Kennedy (R)	99,101	34.4
20	Peter Deutsch (D)*	159,256	65.0
	Jim Jacobs (R)	85,777	35.0
21	Lincoln Diaz-Balart (R)*	125,469	100.0
22	E. Clay Shaw Jr. (R)*	137,098	61.9
	Kenneth D. Cooper (D)	84,517	38.1
23	Alcee L. Hastings (D)*	102,161	73.5
	Robert Paul Brown (R)	36,907	26.5

Georgia

Senate

	Vote total	Per-cent
Max Cleland (D)	1,103,993	48.8
Guy Millner (R)	1,073,969	47.6
John Cashin (LIBERT)	81,262	3.6

House

		Vote total	Per-cent
1	Jack Kingston (R)*	108,616	68.2
	Rosemary Kaszans (D)	50,622	31.8
2	Sanford D. Bishop Jr. (D)*	88,256	54.0
	Darrel Ealum (R)	75,282	46.0
3	Mac Collins (R)*	120,251	61.1
	Jim Chafin (D)	76,538	38.9
4	Cynthia A. McKinney (D)*	127,157	57.8
	John Mitnick (R)	92,985	42.2
5	John Lewis (D)*	136,555	100.0
6	Newt Gingrich (R)*	174,155	57.8
	Michael Coles (D)	127,135	42.2
7	Bob Barr (R)*	112,009	57.8
	Charlie Watts (D)	81,765	42.2
8	Saxby Chambliss (R)*	93,619	52.6
	Jim Wiggins (D)	84,506	47.4
9	Nathan Deal (R)*	132,532	65.5
	McCracken "Ken" Poston (D)	69,662	34.5
10	Charlie Norwood (R)*	96,723	52.3
	David Bell (D)	88,054	47.7
11	John Linder (R)*	145,821	64.3
	Tommy Stephenson (D)	80,940	35.7

Hawaii

House

		Vote total	Per-cent
1	Neil Abercrombie (D)*	86,732	50.4
	Orson Swindle (R)	80,053	46.5
	Mark Duering (NON)	4,126	2.4
	Nicholas Bedworth (NL)	1,295	0.8
2	Patsy T. Mink (D)*	109,178	60.3
	Tom Pico Jr. (R)	55,729	30.8
	Nolan Crabbe (NON)	7,723	4.3
	James M. Keefe (LIBERT)	4,769	2.6
	Amanda "Mandy" Toulon (NL)	3,564	2.0

Idaho

Senate

	Vote total	Per-cent
Larry E. Craig (R)*	283,532	57.0
Walt Minnick (D)	198,422	39.9
Mary J. Charbonneau (I)	10,137	2.0
Susan Vegors (NL)	5,142	1.0

House

		Vote total	Per-cent
1	Helen Chenoweth (R)*	132,344	50.0
	Dan Williams (D)	125,899	47.5
	Marion Ellis (NL)	6,535	2.5
2	Michael D. Crapo (R)*	157,646	68.8
	John D. Seidl (D)	67,625	29.5
	John Butler (NL)	3,977	1.7

Illinois

Senate

	Vote total	Per-cent
Richard J. Durbin (D)	2,384,028	55.8
Al Salvi (R)	1,728,824	41.0
Steven H. Perry (REF)	61,023	1.4
Robin J. Miller (LIBERT)	41,218	1.0
Chad Koppie (USTAX)	17,563	0.4
James E. Davis (NL)	13,838	0.3

House

		Vote total	Per-cent
1	Bobby L. Rush (D)*	174,005	85.7
	Noel Naughton (R)	25,659	12.6
	Tim M. Griffin (LIBERT)	3,449	1.7

		Vote total	Per-cent
2	Jesse L. Jackson Jr. (D)*	172,648	94.1
	Frank H. Stratman (LIBERT)	10,880	5.9
3	William O. Lipinski (D)*	137,153	65.3
	Jim Nalepa (R)	67,214	32.0
	George Skaritka (REF)	3,643	1.7
	Robert R. Prazak (LIBERT)	1,906	0.9
4	Luis V. Gutierrez (D)*	85,278	93.6
	William Passmore (LIBERT)	5,857	6.4
5	Rod R. Blagojevich (D)	117,544	64.1
	Michael Patrick Flanagan (R)*	65,768	35.9
6	Henry J. Hyde (R)*	132,401	64.3
	Stephen de la Rosa (D)	68,807	33.4
	George Meyers (LIBERT)	4,746	2.3
7	Danny K. Davis (D)	149,568	82.3
	Randy Borow (R)	27,241	15.3
	Chauncey L. Stroud (I)	1,944	1.1
	Toietta Dixon (LIBERT)	1,571	0.9
	Charles A. Winter (NL)	771	0.4
8	Philip M. Crane (R)*	127,763	62.2
	Elizabeth Ann "Betty Hull" (D)	74,068	36.1
	H. Daniel Druck (LIBERT)	3,474	1.7
9	Sidney R. Yates (D)*	124,319	63.4
	Joseph Walsh (R)	71,763	36.6
10	John Edward Porter (R)*	145,626	69.1
	Philip R. Torf (D)	65,144	30.9
11	Jerry Weller (R)*	109,896	51.8
	Clem Balanoff (D)	102,388	48.2
12	Jerry F. Costello (D)*	150,005	71.6
	Shapley R. Hunter (R)	55,690	26.6
	Geoffrey S. Nathan (LIBERT)	3,824	1.8
13	Harris W. Fawell (R)*	141,651	59.9
	Susan W. Hynes (D)	94,693	40.1
14	Dennis Hastert (R)*	134,432	64.4
	Doug Mains (D)	74,332	35.6
15	Thomas W. Ewing (R)*	121,019	57.3
	Laurel Lunt Prussing (D)	90,065	42.7
16	Donald Manzullo (R)*	137,523	60.3
	Catherine M. Lee (D)	90,575	39.7
17	Lane Evans (D)*	120,008	51.9
	Mark Baker (R)	109,240	47.3
	William J. Herrmann (LIBERT)	1,925	0.8
18	Ray LaHood (R)*	143,110	59.3
	Mike Curran (D)	98,413	40.7
19	Glenn Poshard (D)*	158,668	66.7
	Brent Winters (R)	75,751	31.8
	Patricia Riker (NL)	2,269	1.0
	James R. Lacher (LIBERT)	1,267	0.5
20	John M. Shimkus (R)	120,926	50.3
	Jay C. Hoffman (D)	119,688	49.7

Indiana

Governor

	Vote total	Per-cent
Frank L. O'Bannon (D)	1,087,128	51.5
Stephen Goldsmith (R)	986,982	46.8
Steve Dillon (LIBERT)	35,805	1.7

House

		Vote total	Per-cent
1	Peter J. Visclosky (D)*	133,553	69.2
	Michael Edward Petyo (R)	56,418	29.2
	Michael Crass (LIBERT)	3,142	1.6
2	David M. McIntosh (R)*	123,113	57.8
	R. Marc "Marc" Carmichael (D)	85,105	40.0
	Paul E. Zimmerman (LIBERT)	4,665	2.2
3	Tim Roemer (D)*	114,288	57.9

		Vote total	Per-cent
	Joe Zakas (R)	80,699	40.9
	Bernie Taylor (LIBERT)	2,325	1.2
4	Mark E. Souder (R)*	121,344	58.4
	Gerald L. Houseman (D)	81,740	39.3
	Ken Bisson (LIBERT)	4,796	2.3
5	Steve Buyer (R)*	125,191	64.6
	Douglas L. Clark (D)	63,578	32.8
	Tom Lehman (LIBERT)	5,069	2.6
6	Dan Burton (R)*	193,193	74.9
	Carrie J. Dillard-Trammell (D)	59,661	23.1
	Fred Peterson (LIBERT)	5,003	1.9
7	Ed Pease (R)	130,010	62.0
	Robert F. Hellmann (D)	72,705	34.6
	Barbara Bourland (LIBERT)	7,125	3.4
8	John Hostettler (R)*	109,860	50.0
	Jonathan Weinzapfel (D)	106,201	48.3
	Paul Hager (LIBERT)	3,803	1.7
9	Lee H. Hamilton (D)*	128,123	56.5
	Jean Leising (R)	96,442	42.5
	Diane Feeney (LIBERT)	2,279	1.0
10	Julia Carson (D)	85,965	52.6
	Virginia Blankenbaker (R)	72,796	45.1
	Kurt St. Angelo (LIBERT)	3,605	2.3

Iowa

Senate

	Vote total	Per-cent
Tom Harkin (D)*	634,166	51.8
Jim Ross Lightfoot (R)	571,807	46.7
Sue Atkinson (I)	9,768	0.8
Fred Gratzon (NL)	4,248	0.3
Joe Sulentic (I)	1,941	0.2
Shirley E. Pena (SW)	1,844	0.2

House

		Vote total	Per-cent
1	Jim Leach (R)*	129,242	52.8
	Bob Rush (D)	111,595	45.6
	Thomas W. Isenhour (I)	2,277	0.9
	Michael J. Cuddehe (NL)	1,394	0.6
2	Jim Nussle (R)*	127,827	53.4
	Donna L. Smith (D)	109,731	45.9
	Albert W. Schoema (LIBERT)	901	0.4
	Peter Lamoureaux (NL)	772	0.3
3	Leonard L. Boswell (D)	115,914	49.4
	Mike Mahaffey (R)	111,895	47.6
	Jay B. Marcus (NL)	3,194	1.4
	Edward T. Rusk (WC)	2,534	1.1
	Dick Kruse (LIBERT)	1,261	0.5
4	Greg Ganske (R)*	133,419	52.0
	Connie McBurney (D)	119,790	46.7
	Roger Badgett (NL)	1,206	0.5
	Carl E. Olsen (LIBERT)	1,149	0.4
	Richard McBride (SW)	700	0.3
5	Tom Latham (R)*	147,576	65.5
	MacDonald Smith (D)	75,785	33.6
	Michael C. Dimick (NL)	2,038	0.9

Kansas

Senate

	Vote total	Per-cent
Pat Roberts (R)	652,677	62.0
Sally Thompson (D)	362,380	34.4
Mark S. Marney (REF)	24,145	2.3
Steven Rosile (LIBERT)	13,098	1.2

Senate[a]

	Vote total	Per-cent
Sam Brownback (R)	574,021	53.8
Jill Docking (D)	461,344	43.4
Donald R. Klaassen (REF)	29,351	2.8

House

		Vote total	Per-cent
1	Jerry Moran (R)	191,899	73.5
	John Divine (D)	63,948	24.5
	Bill Earnest (LIBERT)	5,298	2.0
2	Jim Ryun (R)	131,592	52.2
	John Frieden (D)	114,644	45.5
	Art Clack (LIBERT)	5,842	2.3
3	Vince Snowbarger (R)	139,169	49.8
	Judy Hancock (D)	126,848	45.4
	Randy Gardner (REF)	9,495	3.4
	Charles Clack (LIBERT)	3,752	1.3
4	Todd Tiahrt (R)*	128,486	50.1
	Randy Rathbun (D)	119,544	46.6
	Seth L. Warren (LIBERT)	8,361	3.3

Kentucky

Senate

	Vote total	Per-cent
Mitch McConnell (R)*	724,794	55.5
Steven L. Beshear (D)	560,012	42.8
Dennis L. Lacy (LIBERT)	8,595	0.7
Patricia Metten (NL)	8,344	0.6
Mac McElroy (USTAX)	5,284	0.4

House

		Vote total	Per-cent
1	Edward Whitfield (R)*	111,473	53.6
	Dennis L. Null (D)	96,684	46.4
2	Ron Lewis (R)*	125,433	58.1
	Joe Wright (D)	90,483	41.9
3	Anne M. Northup (R)	126,625	50.3
	Mike Ward (D)*	125,326	49.7
4	Jim Bunning (R)*	149,135	68.4
	Denny Bowman (D)	68,939	31.6
5	Harold Rogers (R)*	117,842	100.0
6	Scotty Baesler (D)*	125,999	55.7
	Ernest Fletcher (R)	100,231	44.3

Louisiana

Senate

	Vote total	Per-cent
Mary L. Landrieu (D)	852,945	50.2
Louis "Woody" Jenkins (R)	847,157	49.8

House

		Vote total	Per-cent
1	Robert L. Livingston (R)*	X	X
2	William J. Jefferson (D)*	X	X
3	W.J. "Billy" Tauzin (R)*	X	X
4	Jim McCrery (R)	X	X
5	John Cooksey (R)	135,990	58.3
	Francis Thompson (D)	97,363	41.7
6	Richard H. Baker (R)*	X	X
7	Chris John (D)	128,449	53.1
	Hunter Lundy (D)	113,351	46.9

Maine

Senate

	Vote total	Per-cent
Susan Collins (R)	298,422	49.2
Joseph E. Brennan (D)	266,226	43.9
John C. Rensenbrink (I)	23,441	3.9
William P. Clarke (TAX)	18,618	3.1

House

		Vote total	Per-cent
1	Tom Allen (D)	173,745	55.3
	James B. Longley Jr. (R)*	140,354	44.7
2	John Baldacci (D)*	205,439	71.9
	Paul R. Young (R)	70,856	24.8
	Aldric Saucier (I)	9,294	3.3

Maryland

House

		Vote total	Per-cent
1	Wayne T. Gilchrest (R)*	131,033	61.6
	Steven R. Eastaugh (D)	81,825	38.4
2	Robert L. Ehrlich Jr. (R)*	143,075	61.8

		Vote total	Percent
	Connie Galiazzo DeJuliis (D)	88,344	38.2
3	Benjamin L. Cardin (D)*	130,204	67.3
	Patrick L. McDonough (R)	63,229	32.7
4	Albert R. Wynn (D)*	142,094	85.2
	John B. Kimble (R)	24,700	14.8
5	Steny H. Hoyer (D)*	121,288	56.9
	John S. Morgan (R)	91,806	43.1
6	Roscoe G. Bartlett (R)*	132,853	56.8
	Stephen Crawford (D)	100,910	43.2
7	Elijah E. Cummings (D)*	115,764	83.5
	Kenneth Kondner (R)	22,929	16.5
8	Constance A. Morella (R)*	152,538	61.2
	Don Mooers (D)	96,229	38.6
	Barbara Ann Robson (write-in)	281	0.1

Massachusetts

Senate

	Vote total	Percent
John Kerry (D)*	1,334,345	52.2
William F. Weld (R)	1,142,837	44.7
Susan C. Gallagher (C)	70,007	2.7
Robert C. Snowe (NL)	7,169	0.3

House

		Vote total	Percent
1	John W. Olver (D)*	129,261	52.7
	Jane Swift (R)	115,805	47.2
2	Richard E. Neal (D)*	163,010	71.7
	Mark Steele (R)	49,887	21.9
	Scott Andrichak (I)	9,181	4.0
	Richard Kaynor (NL)	5,124	2.3
3	Jim McGovern (D)	135,047	52.9
	Peter I. Blute (R)*	115,695	45.4
	Dale E. Friedgen (NL)	3,362	1.3
4	Barney Frank (D)*	183,854	71.6
	Jonathan Raymond (R)	72,702	28.3
5	Martin T. Meehan (D)*	183,457	99.1
6	John F. Tierney (D)	133,687	48.1
	Peter G. Torkildsen (R)*	133,315	48.0
	Martin J. McNulty (I)	4,195	1.5
	Randal C. Fritz (C)	2,532	0.9
	Benjamin A. Gatchell (I)	2,043	0.7
	Orrin Smith (NL)	1,371	0.5
7	Edward J. Markey (D)*	177,053	69.8
	Patricia Long (R)	76,407	30.1
8	Joseph P. Kennedy II (D)*	147,246	84.3
	R. Philip Hyde (R)	27,315	15.6
9	Joe Moakley (D)*	172,012	72.2
	Paul Gryska (R)	66,080	27.7
10	Bill Delahunt (D)	160,747	54.5
	Edward Teague (R)	123,523	41.8
	A. Charles Laws (Green)	10,913	3.7

Michigan

Senate

	Vote total	Percent
Carl Levin (D)*	2,195,738	58.4
Ronna Romney (R)	1,500,106	39.9
Kenneth L. Proctor (LIBERT)	36,911	1.0
William Roundtree (WW)	12,235	0.3
Joseph S. Mattingly (NL)	11,306	0.3
Martin P. McLaughlin (SE)	5,975	0.2

House

		Vote total	Percent
1	Bart Stupak (D)*	181,486	70.7
	Bob Carr (R)	69,957	27.2
	Michael C. Oleniczak (LIBERT)	2,830	1.1
	Wendy Conway (NL)	2,465	1.0
2	Peter Hoekstra (R)*	165,608	65.3
	Dan Kruszynski (D)	83,603	33.0

		Vote total	Percent
	Bruce A. Smith (LIBERT)	3,071	1.2
	Henry Ogden Clark (NL)	1,365	0.5
3	Vernon J. Ehlers (R)*	169,466	68.6
	Betsy J. Flory (D)	72,791	29.5
	Erwin J. Haas (LIBERT)	2,994	1.2
	Eric Anderson (NL)	1,739	0.7
4	Dave Camp (R)*	159,561	65.5
	Lisa A. Donaldson (D)	79,691	32.7
	Ben Steele III (LIBERT)	2,410	1.0
	Susan Arnold (NL)	1,928	0.8
5	James A. Barcia (D)*	162,675	70.0
	Lawrence Sims	65,542	28.2
	Mark Owen (LIBERT)	2,906	1.3
	Brian D. Ellison (NL)	1,272	0.5
6	Fred Upton (R)*	146,170	52.0
	Clarence J. Annen (D)	66,243	23.5
	Lawrence H. Sims (R)	65,542	23.3
	Scott Beavers (LIBERT)	3,370	1.2
7	Nick Smith (R)*	120,227	55.0
	Kim H. Tunnicliff (D)	93,725	42.9
	Robert F. Broda Jr. (LIBERT)	3,090	1.4
	Scott K. Williamson (NL)	1,471	0.7
8	Debbie Stabenow (D)	141,086	53.8
	Dick Chrysler (R)*	115,836	44.1
	Doug MacDonald (LIBERT)	3,811	1.5
	Patricia Rayfield Allen (NL)	1,679	0.6
9	Dale E. Kildee (D)*	136,856	59.2
	Patrick M. Nowak (R)	89,733	38.8
	Malcolm Johnson (LIBERT)	3,472	1.5
	Terrence Daryl Shulman (NL)	1,127	0.5
10	David E. Bonior (D)*	132,829	54.4
	Susy Heintz (R)	106,444	43.6
	Stuart E. Scott (LIBERT)	3,747	1.5
	John D. Litle (NL)	1,253	0.5
11	Joe Knollenberg (R)*	169,165	61.2
	Morris Frumin (D)	99,303	35.9
	Dick Gach (LIBERT)	5,059	1.8
	Stuart J. Goldberg (NL)	3,047	1.1
12	Sander M. Levin (D)*	133,436	57.4
	John Pappageorge (R)	94,235	40.5
	Albert J. Titran (LIBERT)	3,101	1.3
	Gail Petrosoff (NL)	1,690	0.7
13	Lynn Rivers (D)*	123,133	56.6
	Joe Fitzsimmons (R)	89,907	41.3
	James F. Montgomery (LIBERT)	3,114	1.4
	Jane Cutter (WW)	976	0.4
	Jim Hartnett (SE)	498	0.2
14	John Conyers Jr. (D)*	157,722	85.9
	William A. Ashe (R)	22,152	12.1
	Scott Boman (LIBERT)	1,705	0.9
	Richard R. Miller (NL)	736	0.4
	Willie M. Reid (I)	717	0.4
	Helen Halyard (SE)	660	0.4
15	Carolyn Cheeks Kilpatrick (D)	143,683	88.4
	Stephen Hume (R)	16,009	9.8
	Raymond H. Warner (LIBERT)	1,357	0.8
	Kevin Carey (WW)	886	0.5
	Gregory F. Smith (NL)	656	0.4
16	John D. Dingell (D)*	136,854	62.0
	James R. DeSana (R)	78,723	35.7
	Bruce W. Cain (LIBERT)	3,155	1.4

	Vote total	Percent
Noha F. Hamze (NL)	1,018	0.5
David Sole (WW)	842	0.4

Minnesota

Senate

	Vote total	Percent
Paul Wellstone (D)*	1,098,493	50.3
Rudy Boschwitz (R)	901,282	41.3
Dean Barkley (REF)	152,333	7.0
Tim Davis (GR)	14,139	0.6
Roy Ezra Carlton (LIBERT)	5,428	0.2
Howard B. Hanson (RES)	4,382	0.2
Steve Johnson (NL)	4,321	0.2
Thomas A. Fiske (SW)	1,554	0.1

House

		Vote total	Percent
1	Gil Gutknecht (R)*	137,545	52.7
	Mary Rieder (D)	123,188	47.2
2	David Minge (D)*	144,083	54.9
	Gary B. Revier (R)	107,807	41.1
	Stan Bentz (REF)	10,283	3.9
3	Jim Ramstad (R)*	205,845	70.1
	Stanley J. Leino (D)	87,359	29.8
4	Bruce F. Vento (D)*	145,831	57.0
	Dennis Newinski (R)	94,110	36.8
	Richard J. Gibbons (REF)	9,323	3.6
	Phil Willkie (GR)	3,615	1.4
	Dan R. Vacek (IG)	2,696	1.1
5	Martin Olav Sabo (D)*	158,275	64.3
	Jack Uldrich (R)	70,115	28.5
	Erika Anderson (GR)	13,102	5.3
	Jennifer Benton (SW)	4,284	1.7
6	William P. "Bill" Luther (D)*	164,921	55.8
	Tad Jude (R)	129,989	44.0
7	Collin C. Peterson (D)*	170,936	67.9
	Darrell McKigney (R)	80,132	31.8
8	James L. Oberstar (D)*	185,333	67.3
	Andy Larson (R)	69,460	25.2
	Stan "The Man" Estes (REF)	16,639	6.0
	Larry Fuhol (LIBERT)	3,688	1.3

Mississippi

Senate

	Vote total	Percent
Thad Cochran (R)*	624,154	71.0
James W. "Bootie" Hunt (D)	240,647	27.4
Ted C. Weill (I)	13,861	1.6

House

		Vote total	Percent
1	Roger Wicker (R)*	123,724	67.6
	Henry Boyd Jr. (D)	55,998	30.6
	John A. "Andy" Rouse (LIBERT)	2,281	1.2
	Luke Lundemo (NL)	963	0.5
2	Bennie Thompson (D)*	102,503	59.6
	Danny Covington (R)	65,263	38.0
	William Chipman III (LIBERT)	4,167	2.4
3	Charles W. "Chip" Pickering Jr. (R)	115,443	61.4
	John Arthur Eaves Jr. (D)	68,658	36.5
	Lamen Clemons (I)	2,502	1.3
	C.T. Scarborough (LIBERT)	1,541	0.8
4	Mike Parker (R)*	112,444	61.2
	Kevin Antoine (D)	66,836	36.4
	Kenneth "K.W." Welch (I)	2,262	1.2
	Eileen Mahoney (NL)	1,164	0.6
	William F. Fausek (LIBERT)	957	0.5

		Vote total	Percent			Vote total	Percent			Vote total	Percent
5	Gene Taylor (D)*	103,415	58.3		John W. DeCamp (LIBERT)	9,483	1.4		David Roger		
	Dennis Dollar (R)	71,114	40.1		Bill Dunn (NL)	4,806	0.7		Headrick (TLL)	1,439	0.7
	Le'Roy C. Carney (I)	1,832	1.0	**House**					Judith Lee Azaren (NL)	1,174	0.5
	Dan Rogers (LIBERT)	483	0.3	1	Doug Bereuter (R)*	157,108	70.0		Andrea Lippi (JPR)	1,084	0.5
	Jordan N. Gollub (I)	429	0.2		Patrick J. Combs (D)	67,152	29.9	3	H. James Saxton (R)*	157,503	64.2
	Philip Mayeux (NL)	172	0.1	2	Jon Christensen (R)*	125,201	56.8		John Leonardi (D)	81,590	33.3
					James Martin Davis (D)	88,447	40.1		Janice Presser (LIBERT)	3,037	1.2

Missouri

Governor

	Vote total	Percent
Mel Carnahan (D)*	1,224,801	57.2
Margaret Kelly (R)	866,268	40.4
J. Mark Oglesby (LIBERT)	51,432	2.4

House

		Vote total	Percent
1	William L. Clay (D)*	131,659	70.2
	Daniel F. O'Sullivan Jr. (R)	51,857	27.6
	Tamara Millay (LIBERT)	4,137	2.2
2	James M. Talent (R)*	165,999	61.3
	Joan Kelly Horn (D)	100,372	37.1
	Anton Charles Stever (LIBERT)	2,737	1.0
	Judith Clessler (NL)	1,618	0.6
3	Richard A. Gephardt (D)*	137,300	59.0
	Deborah Lynn Wheelehan (R)	90,202	38.8
	Michael H. Crist (LIBERT)	3,966	1.7
	James E. Keersemaker (NL)	1,287	0.6
4	Ike Skelton (D)*	153,566	63.8
	Bill Phelps (R)	81,650	33.9
	Edwin "Ed" Hoag (LIBERT)	5,573	2.3
5	Karen McCarthy (D)*	144,223	67.4
	Penny Bennett (R)	61,803	28.9
	Kevin Hertel (LIBERT)	4,110	1.9
	Tom Danaher (NL)	3,835	1.8
6	Pat Danner (D)*	169,006	68.6
	Jeff Bailey (R)	72,064	29.3
	Karl H. Wetzel (LIBERT)	5,212	2.1
7	Roy Blunt (R)	162,558	64.9
	Ruth Bamberger (D)	79,306	31.6
	Mike Harman (LIBERT)	6,543	2.6
	Sharalyn Harris (NL)	2,177	0.9
8	Jo Ann Emerson (I)[b]	112,472	50.5
	Emily Firebaugh (D)	83,084	37.3
	Richard A. Kline (R)	23,477	10.5
	Greg Tlapek (LIBERT)	2,503	1.1
	David R. Zimmer (NL)	1,318	0.6
9	Kenny Hulshof (R)	123,580	49.4
	Harold L. Volkmer (D)*	117,685	47.0
	Mitchell J. Moore (LIBERT)	7,140	2.9
	Douglas Rexford (NL)	1,825	0.7

Montana

Governor

	Vote total	Percent
Marc Racicot (R)*	320,768	79.6
Judy Jacobson (D)	84,407	20.4

Senate

	Vote total	Percent
Max Baucus (D)*	201,935	49.6
Dennis Rehberg (R)	182,111	44.7
Becky Shaw (REF)	19,276	4.7
Stephen Heaton (NL)	4,168	1.0

House

		Vote total	Percent
AL	Rick Hill (R)	211,975	52.4
	Bill Yellowtail (D)	174,516	43.2
	Jim Brooks (NL)	17,935	4.4

Nebraska

Senate

	Vote total	Percent
Chuck Hagel (R)	379,933	56.1
Ben Nelson (D)	281,904	41.7

3 | Bill Barrett (R)* | 167,758 | 77.4
| John Webster (D) | 48,833 | 22.5

Nevada

House

		Vote total	Percent
1	John Ensign (R)*	86,472	50.1
	Bob Coffin (D)	75,081	43.5
	Ted Gunderson (IA)	4,572	2.6
	James Dan (LIBERT)	3,341	1.9
	Richard Eidson (NL)	3,127	1.8
2	Jim Gibbons (R)	162,310	58.6
	Thomas "Spike" Wilson (D)	97,742	35.3
	Dan Hansen (IA)	8,780	3.2
	Lois Avery (NL)	4,628	1.7
	Louis R. Tomburello (LIBERT)	3,732	1.3

New Hampshire

Governor

	Vote total	Percent
Jeanne Shaheen (D)	284,175	57.2
Ovide M. Lamontagne (R)	196,321	39.5
Fred Bramante (I)	10,316	2.1
Robert Kingsbury (LIBERT)	5,944	1.2

Senate

	Vote total	Percent
Robert C. Smith (R)*	242,304	49.2
Dick Swett (D)	227,397	46.2
Ken Blevens (LIBERT)	22,261	4.5

House

		Vote total	Percent
1	John E. Sununu (R)	123,939	50.0
	Joseph F. Keefe (D)	115,462	46.6
	Gary A. Flanders (LIBERT)	8,176	3.3
2	Charles Bass (R)*	123,001	50.5
	Deborah "Arnie" Arnesen (D)	105,867	43.5
	Carole Lamirande (I)	10,753	4.4
	Roy Kendel (IA)	3,726	1.5

New Jersey

Senate

	Vote total	Percent
Robert G. Torricelli (D)	1,519,328	52.7
Dick Zimmer (R)	1,227,817	42.6
Richard J. Pezzullo (NJC)	50,971	1.8
Mary Jo Christian (NL)	23,949	0.8
Paul A. Woomer (GCP)	15,183	0.5
Olga L. Rodriguez (SW)	14,319	0.5
Mark Wise (FN)	13,683	0.5
Wilburt Kornegay (IPC)	11,107	0.4
Steven J. Baeli (PF)	7,749	0.3

House

		Vote total	Percent
1	Robert E. Andrews (D)*	160,415	76.1
	Mel Suplee (R)	44,286	21.0
	Michael Edmondson (LIBERT)	2,668	1.3
	Patricia A. Bily (NL)	1,873	0.9
	Norman E. Wahner (NJC)	1,493	0.7
2	Frank A. LoBiondo (R)*	133,130	60.3
	Ruth Katz (D)	83,912	38.0

		Vote total	Percent
	Agnes A. James (NJC)	1,355	0.6
	Eugene B. Ashworth (NL)	1,134	0.5
	Ken Feduniewicz (AF)	659	0.3
4	Christopher H. Smith (R)*	146,404	63.6
	Kevin John Meara (D)	77,565	33.7
	Robert Figueroa (LIBERT)	3,000	1.3
	J. Morgan Strong (NJC)	2,034	0.9
	Arnold Kokans (NL)	1,111	0.5
5	Marge Roukema (R)*	181,323	71.3
	Bill Auer (D)	62,956	24.8
	Lorraine L. La Neve (NJC)	4,093	1.6
	Dan Karlan (LIBERT)	2,118	0.8
	Helen Hamilton (NL)	1,678	0.7
	Barry Childers (ROP)	1,266	0.5
	E. Gregory Kresge (USA)	899	0.4
6	Frank Pallone Jr. (D)*	124,635	61.3
	Steven J. Corodemus (R)	73,402	36.1
	Keith Quarles (LIBERT)	2,044	1.0
	Richard Sorrentino (NJC)	1,509	0.7
	Susan H. Normandin (NL)	1,247	0.6
	Stepanie C. Trice (SW)	641	0.3
7	Bob Franks (R)*	128,817	55.4
	Larry Lerner (D)	97,283	41.8
	Dorothy De Laura (NJC)	4,076	1.8
	Nicholas W. Gentile (NL)	1,693	0.7
	Robert G. Robertson (SW)	696	0.3
8	Bill J. Pascrell Jr. (D)	98,853	51.2
	Bill Martini (R)*	92,604	48.0
	Jeffrey M. Levine (NL)	1,621	0.8
9	Steve R. Rothman (D)	117,646	55.8
	Kathleen A. Donovan (R)	89,005	42.2
	Arthur B. Rosen (NJI)	2,730	1.3
	Leon Myerson (LIBERT)	1,549	0.7
10	Donald M. Payne (D)*	127,126	84.2
	Vanessa Williams (R)	22,086	14.6
	Harley Tyler (NL)	1,192	0.8
	Toni M. Jackson (SW)	656	0.4
11	Rodney Frelinghuysen (R)*	169,091	66.3
	Chris Evangel (D)	78,742	30.9
	Ed De Mott (NJC)	2,870	1.1
	Austin S. Lett (LIBERT)	2,618	1.0
	Victoria S. Spruiell (NL)	1,837	0.7
12	Michael Pappas (R)	135,811	50.4
	David N. Del Vecchio (D)	125,594	46.7
	Virginia A. Flynn (LIBERT)	3,955	1.5
	Joseph M. Mercurio (NJC)	2,650	1.0
	Phillip G. Cenicola (NL)	1,211	0.4
13	Robert Menendez (D)*	115,457	78.8
	Carlos E. Munoz (R)	25,426	17.4
	Herbert H. Shaw (PAC)	2,136	1.5
	Mike Buoncristiano (LIBERT)	2,094	1.4
	William P. Estrada (I)	720	0.5
	Rupert Ravens (NL)	637	0.4

New Mexico

Senate

	Vote total	Percent
Pete V. Domenici (R)*	357,171	64.7
Art Trujillo (D)	164,356	29.8
Abraham J. Gutmann (GREEN)	24,230	4.4
Bruce M. Bush (LIBERT)	6,064	1.1

Note — Patricia A. Dunn (NL) 4,369 2.0; Phillip E. Torrison (LIBERT) 1,921 0.9 appear under Nebraska House district 2.

	Vote total	Per-cent
House		
1 Steven H. Schiff (R)*	109,290	56.6
John Wertheim (D)	71,635	37.1
John "Jack" Uhrich (GREEN)	7,694	4.0
Betty Turrietta-Koury (I)	4,459	2.3
2 Joe Skeen (R)*	95,091	55.9
E. Shirley Baca (D)	74,915	44.1
3 Bill Richardson (D)*	124,594	67.2
Bill Redmond (R)	56,580	30.5
Ed Nagel (LIBERT)	4,097	2.2

New York

	Vote total	Per-cent
House		
1 Michael P. Forbes (R, C, INDC, RTL)*	116,620	54.6
Nora Bredes (D, SM)	96,496	45.4
2 Rick A. Lazio (R, C)*	112,135	64.2
Kenneth J. Herman (D, INDC)	57,953	33.2
Alice Cort Ross (RTL)	4,506	2.6
3 Peter T. King (R, C, FDM)*	127,972	55.3
Dal LaMagna (D, INDC)	97,518	42.1
John O'Shea (RTL)	4,129	1.8
John A. DePrima (L)	1,807	0.8
4 Carolyn McCarthy (D, INDC)	127,060	57.5
Daniel Frisa (R, C, FDM)*	89,542	40.5
Vincent P. Garbitelli (RTL)	3,252	1.5
Robert S. Berkowitz (L)	1,162	0.5
5 Gary L. Ackerman (D, L, INDC)*	125,918	63.7
Grant M. Lally (R, C, FDM)	69,244	35.0
Andrew J. Duff (RTL)	2,623	1.3
6 Floyd H. Flake (D)*	102,799	84.9
Jorawar Misir (R, C, INDC, FDM)	18,348	15.1
7 Thomas J. Manton (D)*	78,848	71.1
Rose Birtley (R, C, INDC)	32,092	28.9
8 Jerrold Nadler (D, L)*	131,943	82.3
Michael Benjamin (R, FDM)	26,028	16.2
George A. Galip Jr. (C)	2,381	1.5
9 Charles E. Schumer (D, L)*	107,107	74.8
Robert J. Verga (R, INDC, FDM)	30,488	21.3
Michael Mossa (C)	5,618	3.9
10 Edolphus Towns (D, L)*	99,889	91.3
Amelia Smith Parker (R, C, FDM)	8,660	7.9
Julian M. Hill Jr. (RTL)	893	0.8
11 Major R. Owens (D, L)*	89,905	92.0
Claudette Hayle (R, C, INDC, FDM)	7,866	8.0
12 Nydia M. Velazquez (D, L)*	61,913	84.6
Miguel I. Prado (R, C, RTL)	9,978	13.6
Eleanor Garcia (SW)	1,283	1.8
13 Susan Molinari (R, C, FDM)*	94,660	61.6
Tyrone G. Butler (D, L)	53,376	34.7
Kathleen Marciano (RTL)	3,396	2.2
Anita Lerman (INDC)	2,337	1.5
14 Carolyn B. Maloney (D, L)*	130,175	72.4
Jeffrey E. Livingston (R)	42,641	23.7
Thomas K. Leighton (INDC, GREEN)	3,512	2.0
Joseph A. Lavezzo (C)	2,188	1.2
Delco L. Cornett (RTL)	1,221	0.7
15 Charles B. Rangel (D, L)*	113,898	91.3
Edward R. Adams (R)	5,951	4.8

	Vote total	Per-cent
Ruben Dario Vargas (C, INDC)	3,896	3.1
Jose Suero (RTL)	989	0.8
16 Jose E. Serrano (D, L)*	95,568	96.3
Rodney Torres (R)	2,878	2.9
Owen Camp (C)	787	0.8
17 Eliot L. Engel (D, L)*	101,287	85.0
Denis McCarthy (R, C, RTL)	15,892	13.3
Dennis Coleman (INDC)	2,008	1.7
18 Nita M. Lowey (D)*	118,194	63.6
Kerry J. Katsorhis (R, C)	59,487	32.0
Concetta M. Ferrara (INDC)	4,283	2.3
Florence T. O'Grady (RTL)	3,758	2.0
19 Sue W. Kelly (R, FDM)*	102,142	46.3
Richard S. Klein (D, L)	86,926	39.4
Joseph J. DioGuardi (C, RTL)	27,424	12.4
William E. Haase (INDC)	4,104	1.9
20 Benjamin A. Gilman (R)*	122,479	57.1
Yash P. Aggarwal (D, L)	80,761	37.6
Robert F. Garrison (RTL)	6,356	3.0
Ira W. Goodman (INDC)	5,016	2.3
21 Michael R. McNulty (D, C, INDC)*	158,491	66.1
Nancy Norman (R, FDM)	64,471	26.9
Lee H. Wasserman (L)	16,794	7.0
22 Gerald B.H. Solomon (R, C, RTL, FDM)*	144,125	60.5
Steve James (D)	94,192	39.5
23 Sherwood Boehlert (R, FDM)*	124,626	64.3
Bruce W. Hapanowicz (D)	50,436	26.0
Thomas E. Loughlin Jr. (INDC)	10,835	5.6
William Tapley (RTL)	7,790	4.0
24 John M. McHugh (R, C)*	124,240	71.1
Donald Ravenscroft (D)	43,692	25.0
William H. Beaumont (INDC)	6,750	3.9
25 James T. Walsh (R, C, INDC, FDM)*	126,691	55.1
Marty Mack (D)	103,199	44.9
26 Maurice D. Hinchey (D, L)*	122,850	55.2
Sue Wittig (R, C, RTL, FDM)	94,125	42.3
Douglas Walter Drazen (INDC)	5,531	2.5
27 Bill Paxon (R, C, RTL, FDM)*	142,568	59.9
Thomas M. Fricano (D, SM)	95,503	40.1
28 Louise M. Slaughter (D)*	133,084	57.3
Geoffrey Rosenberger (R, C, FDM)	99,366	42.7
29 John J. LaFalce (D, L)*	132,317	62.0
David B. Callard (R, C, RTL, FDM)	81,135	38.0
30 Jack Quinn (R, C, INDC, FDM)*	121,369	54.8
Francis Pordum (D, PS)	100,040	45.2
31 Amo Houghton (R, C, FDM)*	139,734	71.6
Bruce D. MacBain (D)	49,502	25.4
LeRoy Stewart Wilson (RTL)	6,031	3.1

North Carolina

	Vote total	Per-cent
Governor		
James B. Hunt Jr. (D)*	1,436,638	56.0
Robin Hayes (R)	1,097,053	42.8
Scott D. Yost (LIBERT)	17,559	0.7
Julia Van Witt (NL)	14,792	0.6

	Vote total	Per-cent
Senate		
Jesse Helms (R)*	1,345,833	52.6
Harvey B. Gantt (D)	1,173,875	45.9
Ray Ubinger (LIBERT)	25,396	1.0
J. Victor Pardo (NL)	11,209	0.4
House		
1 Eva Clayton (D)*	108,759	65.9
Ted Tyler (R)	54,666	33.1
Todd Murphrey (LIBERT)	1,072	0.6
Joseph Boxerman (NL)	531	0.3
2 Bob Etheridge (D)	113,820	52.5
David Funderburk (R)*	98,951	45.7
Mark D. Jackson (LIBERT)	2,892	1.3
Robert Argy Jr. (NL)	966	0.4
3 Walter B. Jones Jr. (R)*	118,159	62.7
George Parrott (D)	68,887	36.5
Edward Downey (NL)	1,533	0.8
4 David E. Price (D)	157,194	54.4
Fred Heineman (R)*	126,466	43.8
David Allen Walker (LIBERT)	4,132	1.4
Russell Wollman (NL)	1,201	0.4
5 Richard M. Burr (R)*	130,177	62.1
Neil Grist Cashion Jr. (D)	74,320	35.4
Barbara J. Howe (LIBERT)	4,193	2.0
Craig Berg (NL)	1,008	0.5
6 Howard Coble (R)*	167,828	73.4
Mark Costley (D)	58,022	25.4
Gary Goodson (LIBERT)	2,693	1.2
7 Mike McIntyre (D)	87,487	52.9
Bill Caster (R)	75,811	45.8
Chris Nubel (LIBERT)	1,573	0.9
Garrison King Frantz (NL)	569	0.3
8 W.G. "Bill" Hefner (D)*	103,129	55.2
Curtis Blackwood (R)	81,676	43.7
Thomas W. Carlisle (NL)	2,103	1.1
9 Sue Myrick (R)*	147,755	63.0
Michel C. "Mike" Daisley (D)	83,078	35.4
David L. Knight (LIBERT)	2,280	1.0
Jeannine Austin (NL)	1,499	0.6
10 Cass Ballenger (R)*	158,585	70.0
Ben Neill (D)	65,103	28.7
Richard Kahn (NL)	2,909	1.3
11 Charles H. Taylor (R)*	132,860	58.3
James Mark Ferguson (D)	91,257	40.0
Phil McCanless (LIBERT)	2,307	1.0
Milton Burrill (NL)	1,601	0.7
12 Melvin Watt (D)*	124,675	71.5
Joseph A. "Joe" Martino Jr. (R)	46,581	26.7
Roger L. Kohn (LIBERT)	1,874	1.1
Walter Lewis (NL)	1,269	0.7

North Dakota

	Vote total	Per-cent
Governor		
Edward T. Schafer (R)*	174,937	66.2
Lee Kaldor (D)	89,349	33.8
House		
AL Earl Pomeroy (D)*	144,833	55.1
Kevin Cramer (R)	113,684	43.2
Kenneth R. Loughead (I)	4,493	1.7

Ohio

	Vote total	Per-cent
House		
1 Steve Chabot (R)*	118,324	54.2
Mark P. Longabaugh (D)	94,719	43.4
John G. Halley (NL)	5,381	2.5
2 Rob Portman (R)*	186,853	72.0

		Vote total	Per-cent
	Thomas R. Chandler (D)	58,715	22.6
	Kathleen M. McKnight (NL)	13,905	5.4
3	Tony P. Hall (D)*	144,583	63.6
	David A. Westbrock (R)	75,732	33.3
	Dorothy H. Mackey (NL)	5,088	2.2
	James Lawrence (I)	1,800	0.8
4	Michael G. Oxley (R)*	147,608	64.8
	Paul McClain (D)	69,096	30.3
	Michael McCaffery (NL)	11,057	4.9
5	Paul E. Gillmor (R)*	145,692	61.1
	Annie Saunders (D)	81,170	34.1
	David J. Schaffer (NL)	11,461	4.8
6	Ted Strickland (D)	118,003	51.3
	Frank A. Cremeans (R)*	111,907	48.7
7	David L. Hobson (R)*	158,087	67.8
	Richard K. Blain (D)	61,419	26.4
	Dawn Marie Johnson (NL)	13,478	5.8
8	John A. Boehner (R)*	165,815	70.3
	Jeffrey D. Kitchen (D)	61,515	26.1
	William Baker (NL)	8,613	3.7
9	Marcy Kaptur (D)*	170,617	77.1
	Randy Whitman (R)	46,040	20.8
	Elizabeth A. Slotnick (NL)	4,677	2.1
10	Dennis J. Kucinich (D)	110,723	49.1
	Martin R. Hoke (R)*	104,546	46.3
	Robert B. Iverson (NL)	10,415	4.6
11	Louis Stokes (D)*	153,546	81.2
	James J. Sykora (R)	28,821	15.2
	Sonja Glavina (NL)	6,665	3.5
12	John R. Kasich (R)*	151,667	63.9
	Cynthia L. Ruccia (D)	78,762	33.2
	Barbara Ann Edelman (NL)	7,005	3.0
13	Sherrod Brown (D)*	146,690	60.5
	Kenneth C. Blair Jr. (R)	87,108	35.9
	David Kluter (NL)	8,707	3.6
14	Tom Sawyer (D)*	124,136	54.3
	Joyce George (R)	95,307	41.7
	Terry E. Wilkinson (NL)	8,976	3.9
15	Deborah Pryce (R)*	156,776	70.8
	Cliff Arnebeck (D)	64,665	29.2
16	Ralph Regula (R)*	159,314	68.7
	Thomas E. Burkhart (D)	64,902	28.0
	Brad Graef (NL)	7,611	3.3
17	James A. Traficant Jr. (D)*	218,283	91.0
	James M. Cahaney (NL)	21,685	9.0
18	Bob Ney (R)*	117,365	50.2
	Robert L. Burch (D)	108,332	46.3
	Margaret Chitti (NL)	8,146	3.5
19	Steven C. LaTourette (R)*	135,012	54.7
	Tom Coyne Jr. (D)	101,152	41.0
	Thomas A. Martin (NL)	10,655	4.3

Oklahoma

Senate

		Vote total	Per-cent
	James M. Inhofe (R)*	670,610	56.7
	Jim Boren (D)	474,162	40.1
	Bill Maguire (I)	15,092	1.3
	Agnes Marie Regier (LIBERT)	14,595	1.2
	Chris Nedbalek (I)	8,691	0.7

House

		Vote total	Per-cent
1	Steve Largent (R)*	143,415	68.2
	Randolph John Amen (D)	57,996	27.6
	Karla Condray (I)	8,996	4.3
2	Tom Coburn (R)*	112,273	55.5
	Glen D. Johnson (D)	90,120	44.5
3	Wes Watkins (R)	98,526	51.4
	Darryl Roberts (D)	86,647	45.2
	Scott Demaree (I)	6,335	3.3

		Vote total	Per-cent
4	J.C. Watts (R)*	106,923	57.7
	Ed Crocker (D)	73,950	39.9
	Robert T. Murphy (LIBERT)	4,500	2.4
5	Ernest Jim Istook Jr. (R)*	148,362	69.7
	James L. Forsythe (D)	57,594	27.1
	Ava Kennedy (I)	6,835	3.2
6	Frank D. Lucas (R)*	113,499	63.9
	Paul M. Barby (D)	64,173	36.1

Oregon

Senate

		Vote total	Per-cent
	Gordon H. Smith (R)	677,336	49.8
	Tom Bruggere (D)	624,370	45.9
	Brent Thompson (REF)	20,381	1.5
	Gary Kutcher (PACIFIC)	14,193	1.0
	Paul "Stormy" Mohn (LIBERT)	12,697	0.9
	Christopher Phelps (S)	5,426	0.4
	Michael L. Hoyes (NL)	4,425	0.3

House

		Vote total	Per-cent
1	Elizabeth Furse (D)*	144,588	51.9
	Bill Witt (R)	126,146	45.3
	Richard Johnson (LIBERT)	6,310	2.3
	David Princ (S)	1,146	0.4
2	Bob Smith (R)*	164,062	61.7
	Mike Dugan (D)	97,195	36.5
	Frank Wise (LIBERT)	4,581	1.7
3	Earl Blumenauer (D)*	165,922	66.9
	Scott Bruun (R)	65,259	26.3
	Joe Keating (PACIFIC)	9,274	3.7
	Bruce Alexander Knight (LIBERT)	4,474	1.8
	Victoria P. Guillebeau (S)	2,449	1.0
4	Peter A. DeFazio (D)*	177,270	65.7
	John D. Newkirk (R)	76,649	28.4
	Tonie Nathan (LIBERT)	4,919	1.8
	Write-ins	4,374	1.6
	William "Bill" Bonville (REF)	3,960	1.5
	David G. Duemler (S)	1,373	0.5
	Allan Opus (PACIFIC)	1,311	0.5
5	Darlene Hooley (D)	139,521	51.2
	Jim Bunn (R)*	125,409	46.0
	Lawrence Knight Duquesne (LIBERT)	5,191	1.9
	Trey Smith (S)	2,124	0.8

Pennsylvania

House

		Vote total	Per-cent
1	Thomas M. Foglietta (D)*	145,210	87.5
	James D. Cella (R)	20,734	12.5
2	Chaka Fattah (D)*	168,887	88.0
	Larry G. Murphy (R)	23,047	12.0
3	Robert A. Borski (D)*	121,120	68.9
	Joseph M. McColgan (R)	54,681	31.1
4	Ron Klink (D)*	142,621	64.2
	Paul T. Adametz (R)	79,448	35.8
5	John E. Peterson (R)	116,303	60.2
	Ruth C. Rudy (D)	76,627	39.8
6	Tim Holden (D)*	115,193	58.6
	Christian Y. Leinbach (R)	80,061	40.7
	Thomas List (NL)	1,475	0.7
7	Curt Weldon (R)*	165,087	66.9
	John Innelli (D)	79,875	32.4
	John Pronchik (NL)	1,688	0.7
8	James C. Greenwood (R)*	133,749	59.1
	John P. Murray (D)	79,856	35.3

		Vote total	Per-cent
	Richard J. Piotrowski (LIBERT)	6,991	3.1
	David A. Booth (CONSTL)	5,714	2.5
9	Bud Shuster (R)*	142,105	73.7
	Monte Kemmler (D)	50,650	26.3
10	Joseph M. McDade (R)*	124,670	59.8
	Joe Cullen (D)	75,536	36.2
	Thomas J. McLaughlin (REF)	8,311	4.0
11	Paul E. Kanjorski (D)*	128,258	68.0
	Stephen A. Urban (R)	60,339	32.0
12	John P. Murtha (D)*	136,815	70.0
	Bill Choby (R)	58,643	30.0
13	Jon D. Fox (R)*	120,304	48.9
	Joseph M. Hoeffel (D)	120,220	48.9
	Thomas P. Burke (LIBERT)	4,930	2.0
	Bill Ryan (NL)	525	0.2
14	William J. Coyne (D)*	122,922	60.7
	Bill Ravotti (R)	78,921	39.0
	Paul Scherrer (SE)	713	0.4
15	Paul McHale (D)*	109,812	54.8
	Bob Kilbanks (R)	82,803	41.3
	Nicholas R. Sabatine (REF)	6,931	3.5
	Philip E. Faust (NL)	812	0.4
16	Joseph R. Pitts (R)	124,511	59.4
	James G. Blaine (D)	78,598	37.5
	Robert S. Yorczyk (REF)	6,485	3.1
17	George W. Gekas (R)*	150,678	72.2
	Paul Kettl (D)	57,911	27.8
18	Mike Doyle (D)*	120,410	56.0
	David B. Fawcett (R)	86,829	40.4
	Richard Edward Caligiuri (I)	6,859	3.2
	Ralph A. Emmerich (NL)	883	0.4
19	Bill Goodling (R)*	130,716	62.6
	Scott L. Chronister (D)	74,944	35.9
	Francis Worley (FWC)	3,194	1.5
20	Frank R. Mascara (D)*	113,394	53.9
	Mike McCormick (R)	97,004	46.1
21	Phil English (R)*	106,875	50.7
	Ronald A. DiNicola (D)	104,004	49.3

Rhode Island

Senate

		Vote total	Per-cent
	Jack Reed (D)	230,676	63.5
	Nancy J. Mayer (R)	127,368	35.1
	Donald W. Lovejoy (I)	5,327	1.5

House

		Vote total	Per-cent
1	Patrick J. Kennedy (D)*	121,781	69.4
	Giovanni D. Cicione (R)	49,199	28.0
	Michael J. Rollins (I)	1,737	1.0
	Graham R. Schwass (I)	1,408	0.8
	Gregory Raposa (I)	1,300	0.7
2	Bob Weygand (D)	118,827	64.5
	Rick Wild (R)	58,458	31.7
	Thomas J. Ricci (I)	3,139	1.7
	Gail Alison Casman (I)	2,199	1.2
	Jack D. Potter (I)	1,695	0.9

South Carolina

Senate

		Vote total	Per-cent
	Strom Thurmond (R)*	619,859	53.4
	Elliott Close (D)	510,951	44.0
	Richard T. Quillian (LIBERT)	12,988	1.1
	Peter J. Ashy (REF)	9,740	0.8
	Annette C. Estes (NL)	7,691	0.7

House

		Vote total	Per-cent
1	Mark Sanford (R)*	138,467	96.4
	Joseph F. Innella (NL)	5,105	3.6

		Vote total	Per- cent
2	Floyd D. Spence (R)*	158,229	89.8
	Maurice T. Raiford (NL)	17,713	10.0
3	Lindsey Graham (R)*	114,273	60.3
	Debbie Dorn (D)	73,417	38.7
	Linda L. Pennington (NL)	1,835	1.0
4	Bob Inglis (R)*	138,165	70.9
	Darrell E. Curry (D)	54,126	27.8
	C. Faye Walters (NL)	2,501	1.3
5	John M. Spratt Jr. (D)*	97,335	54.1
	Larry L. Bigham (R)	81,455	45.3
	P.G. Joshi (NL)	1,155	0.6
6	James E. Clyburn (D)*	120,132	69.4
	Gary McLeod (R)	51,974	30.0
	Savita P. Joshi (NL)	948	0.5

South Dakota

Senate
	Tim Johnson (D)	166,533	51.3
	Larry Pressler (R)*	157,954	48.7

House
AL	John Thune (R)	186,393	57.7
	Rick Weiland (D)	119,547	37.0
	Stacey Nelson (REF)	10,397	3.2
	Kurt Evans (I)	6,866	2.1

Tennessee

Senate
	Fred Thompson (R)*	1,091,554	61.4
	Houston Gordon (D)	654,937	36.8
	John Jay Hooker (I)	14,401	0.8
	Bruce Gold (I)	5,865	0.3
	Robert O. Watson (I)	5,569	0.3
	Greg Samples (I)	4,104	0.2
	Philip L. Kienlen (I)	2,173	0.1

House
1	Bill Jenkins (R)	117,676	63.9
	Kay C. Smith (D)	58,657	33.2
	Dave Davis (I)	1,947	1.0
	James B. Taylor (I)	1,089	0.6
	Bill Bull Durham (I)	885	0.5
	John Curtis (I)	621	0.4
	Mike Fugate (I)	440	0.2
	Paul Schmidt (I)	367	0.2
2	John J. "Jimmy" Duncan Jr. (R)*	150,953	70.7
	Stephen Smith (D)	61,020	28.6
	Chris G. Dimit (I)	1,306	0.6
	George Njezic (I)	289	0.1
3	Zach Wamp (R)*	113,408	56.4
	Charles "Chuck" Jolly (D)	85,714	42.6
	William A. Cole (I)	1,002	0.5
	Walt "Combat" Ward (I)	718	0.3
	Thomas Ed Morrell (I)	304	0.1
	Richard M. "Dick" Sims (I)	294	0.1
4	Van Hilleary (R)*	103,091	58.0
	Mark Stewart (D)	73,331	41.1
	J. Patrick Lyons (I)	1,075	0.6
	Preston T. Spaulding (I)	561	0.3
5	Bob Clement (D)*	140,264	72.4
	Steven L. Edmondson (R)	46,201	23.8
	Mike Childers (I)	7,318	3.8
6	Bart Gordon (D)*	123,846	54.4
	Steve Gill (R)	94,599	41.6
	Jim Coffer (I)	9,125	4.0
7	Ed Bryant (R)*	136,643	64.1
	Don Trotter (D)	73,629	34.6
	Steven E. Romer (I)	2,803	1.3
8	John Tanner (D)*	123,681	67.3
	Tom Watson (R)	55,024	30.1

		Vote total	Per- cent
	Donna Malone (I)	4,816	2.6
9	Harold E. Ford Jr. (D)	116,345	61.1
	Rod DeBerry (R)	70,951	37.2
	Silky Sullivan (I)	957	1.3
	Mary D. Taylor (I)	498	0.7
	Anthony Burton (I)	424	0.6
	Greg Voehringer (I)	327	0.5
	Tom Jeanette (I)	222	0.3
	Del Gill (I)	199	0.3
	Bill Taylor (I)	179	0.3
	Johhny E. Kelly (I)	156	0.2
	Don Fox (I)	146	0.2

Texas

Senate
	Phil Gramm (R)*	3,027,680	54.8
	Victor M. Morales (D)	2,428,776	43.9
	Michael Bird (LIBERT)	51,516	0.9
	John Huff (NL)	19,469	0.4

House
1	Max Sandlin (D)	102,697	51.6
	Ed Merritt (R)	93,105	46.7
	Margaret A. Palms (NL)	3,368	1.7
2	Jim Turner (D)	102,908	52.4
	Brian Babin (R)	89,838	45.7
	Henry McCullough (I)	2,390	1.2
	David Constant (LIBERT)	1,240	0.6
3	Sam Johnson (R)*	142,325	73.0
	Lee Cole (D)	47,654	24.4
	John Davis (L)	5,045	2.6
4	Ralph M. Hall (D)*	132,126	63.8
	Jerry Ray Hall (R)	71,065	34.3
	Steven Rothacker (LIBERT)	3,172	1.5
	Enos M. Denham Jr. (NL)	814	0.4
5	Pete Sessions (R)	80,196	53.1
	John Pouland (D)	70,922	47.0
6	Joe L. Barton (R)*	160,800	77.1
	Janet Carroll "Skeet" Richardson (I)	26,713	12.8
	Catherine A. Anderson (L)	14,456	6.9
	Doug Williams (USTAX)	6,547	3.1
7	Bill Archer (R)*	152,024	81.4
	Al J.K. Siegmund (D)	28,187	15.1
	Gene Hsiao (I)	3,896	2.1
	Robert R. "Randy" Sims Jr. (I)	2,724	1.5
8	Kevin Brady (R)	80,325	41.5
	Gene Fontenot (R)	75,399	38.9
	Cynthia "C. J." Newman (D)	26,246	13.6
	Robert Musemeche (D)	11,689	6.0
	December 10 runoff		
	Kevin Brady (R)	30,366	59.1
	Gene Fontenot (R)	21,004	40.9
9	Steve Stockman (R)*	88,171	46.4
	Nick Lampson (D)	83,782	44.1
	Geraldine Sam (D)	17,887	9.4
	December 10 runoff		
	Nick Lampson (D)	59,225	52.8
	Steve Stockman (R)*	52,870	47.2
10	Lloyd Doggett (D)*	132,066	56.2
	Teresa Doggett (R)	97,204	41.4
	Gary Johnson (LIBERT)	3,950	1.7
	Steven Klayman (NL)*	1,771	0.8
11	Chet Edwards (D)*	99,990	56.8
	Jay Mathis (R)	74,549	42.4
	Ken Hardin (NL)	1,396	0.8
12	Kay Granger (R)	98,349	57.8
	Hugh Parmer (D)	69,859	41.0
	Heather Proffer (NL)	1,996	1.2

		Vote total	Per- cent
13	William M. "Mac" Thornberry (R)*	116,098	66.9
	Samuel Brown Silverman (D)	56,066	32.3
	Don Harkey (NL)	1,463	0.8
14	Ron Paul (R)	99,961	51.1
	Charles "Lefty" Morris (D)	93,200	47.6
	Ed Fasanella (NL)	2,538	1.3
15	Ruben Hinojosa (D)	86,347	62.3
	Tom Haughey (R)	50,914	36.7
	Rob Wofford (NL)	1,333	1.0
16	Silvestre Reyes (D)	90,260	70.6
	Rick Ledesma (R)	35,271	27.6
	Carl Proffer (NL)	2,253	1.8
17	Charles W. Stenholm (D)*	99,678	51.6
	Rudy Izzard (R)	91,429	47.4
	Richard Caro (NL)	1,887	1.0
18	Sheila Jackson-Lee (D)*	106,111	77.1
	Larry White (R)	13,956	10.1
	Jerry Burley (R)	7,877	5.7
	George A. Young (R)	5,332	3.9
	Mike Lamson (D)	4,412	3.2
19	Larry Combest (R)*	156,910	80.4
	John W. Sawyer (D)	38,316	19.6
20	Henry B. Gonzalez (D)*	88,190	63.7
	James D. Walker (R)	47,616	34.4
	Alejandro "Alex" DePena (LIBERT)	2,156	1.6
	Lyndon Felps (NL)	447	0.3
21	Lamar Smith (R)*	205,830	76.4
	Gordon H. Wharton (D)	60,338	22.4
	Randy Rutenbeck (NL)	3,139	1.2
22	Tom DeLay (R)*	126,056	68.1
	Scott Douglas Cunningham (D)	59,030	31.9
23	Henry Bonilla (R)*	101,332	61.8
	Charles P. Jones (D)	59,596	36.4
	Linda J. Caswell (NL)	2,911	1.8
24	Martin Frost (D)*	77,847	55.7
	Ed Harrison (R)	54,551	39.1
	Marion Jacob (D)	4,656	3.3
	Dale Mouton (I)	2,574	1.8
25	Ken Bentsen (D)*	43,701	34.0
	Dolly Madison McKenna (R)	21,898	17.1
	Beverley Clark (D)	21,699	16.9
	Brent Perry (R)	16,737	13.0
	John Devine (D)	9,070	7.1
	John M. Sanchez (R)	8,984	7.0
	Ken G. Mathis (R)	3,649	2.8
	Ron "RC" Meinke (R)	997	0.8
	Lloyd W. Oliver (R)	827	0.6
	Dotty Quinn Collins (R)	561	0.4
	Jerry Freiwirth (SW)	270	0.2
	December 10th runoff		
	Ken Bentsen (D)*	29,396	57.3
	Dolly Madison McKenna (R)	21,892	42.7
26	Dick Armey (R)*	163,708	73.6
	Jerry Frankel (D)	58,623	26.4
27	Solomon P. Ortiz (D)*	97,350	64.6
	Joe Gardner (R)	50,964	33.8
	Kevin G. Richardson (NL)	2,286	1.5
28	Frank Tejeda (D)*	110,148	75.4
	Mark Lynn Cude (R)	34,191	23.4
	Clifford Finley (NL)	1,796	1.2
29	Gene Green (D)*	61,751	67.5
	Jack Rodriguez (R)	28,381	31.0
	Jack W. Klinger (USTAX)	1,340	1.5

		Vote total	Per- cent
30	Eddie Bernice Johnson (D)*	61,723	54.6
	John Hendry (R)	20,664	18.3
	James L. Sweatt (D)	9,909	8.8
	Marvin E. Crenshaw (D)	7,765	6.9
	Lisa Anne Kitterman (R)	7,761	6.9
	Lisa Hembry (I)	3,501	3.1
	Ada Jane Granado (I)	1,278	1.1
	Stevan A. Hammond (I)	468	0.4

Utah

Governor

	Vote total	Per- cent
Michael O. Leavitt (R)*	503,693	75.0
Jim Bradley (D)	156,616	23.3
Ken Larsen (IA)	4,741	0.7
Dub Richards (IP)	3,845	0.6
Robert C. Lesh (NL)	2,969	0.4

House

		Vote total	Per- cent
1	James V. Hansen (R)*	150,126	68.3
	Gregory J. Sanders (D)	65,866	30.0
	Randall Tolpinrud (NL)	3,787	1.7
2	Merrill Cook (R)	129,963	55.0
	Ross Anderson (D)	100,283	42.4
	Arly H. Pederson (IA)	3,070	1.3
	Catherine Carter (NL)	2,981	1.3
3	Christopher B. Cannon (R)	106,220	51.1
	Bill Orton (D)*	98,178	47.3
	Amy L. Lassen (LIBERT)	2,341	1.1
	Gerald "Bear" Slothower (NON)	706	0.3
	John Phillip Langford (SW)	270	0.1

Vermont

Governor

	Vote total	Per- cent
Howard Dean (D)*	179,544	70.6
John L. Gropper (R)	57,161	22.6
Mary Alice Herbert (LU)	4,156	1.6
Dennis "Denny" Lane (VG)	3,667	1.4
Bill Brunelle (NL)	3,342	1.3
August St. John (I)	3,201	1.2
Neil Randall (LIBERT)	2,916	1.1

House

		Vote total	Per- cent
AL	Bernard Sanders (I)*	140,678	55.2
	Susan Sweetser (R)	83,021	32.6
	Jack Long (D)	23,830	9.4
	Thomas J. Morse (LIBERT)	2,693	1.1
	Peter Diamondstone (LU)	1,965	0.8
	Robert Melamede (VG)	1,350	0.5
	Norio Kushi (NL)	812	0.3

Virginia

Senate

	Vote total	Per- cent
John W. Warner (R)*	1,235,744	52.5
Mark Warner (D)	1,115,982	47.4

House

		Vote total	Per- cent
1	Herbert H. Bateman (R)*	165,574	99.0
2	Owen B. Pickett (D)*	106,215	64.8
	John Tate (R)	57,586	35.1

		Vote total	Per- cent
3	Robert C. Scott (D)*	118,603	82.1
	Elsie Holland (R)	25,781	17.9
4	Norman Sisisky (D)*	160,100	78.6
	A.J. "Tony" Zevgolis (R)	43,516	21.4
5	Virgil H. Goode Jr. (D)	120,323	60.1
	George C. Landrith III (R)	70,869	36.4
	George R. "Tex" Wood (VREF)	6,627	3.5
6	Robert W. Goodlatte (R)*	133,576	67.0
	Jeffrey Grey (D)	61,485	30.8
	Jay P. Rutledge (I)	4,229	2.1
7	Thomas J. Bliley Jr. (R)*	189,644	75.1
	Roderic H. Slayton (D)	51,206	20.3
	Bradley E. Evans (I)	11,527	4.6
8	James P. Moran (D)*	152,334	66.4
	John Otey (R)	64,562	28.1
	R. Ward Edmonds (VREF)	6,243	2.7
	Sarina J. Grosswald (I)	5,239	2.3
	Charles Stanard Severance (I)	740	0.3
9	Rick Boucher (D)*	122,908	65.0
	Patrick Muldoon (R)	58,055	30.7
	Thomas I. "Tom" Roberts (VREF)	8,080	4.3
10	Frank R. Wolf (R)*	169,266	72.0
	Robert L. Weinberg (D)	59,145	25.2
	Gary A. Reams (I)	6,500	2.8
11	Thomas M. Davis III (R)*	138,758	64.1
	Tom Horton (D)	74,701	34.5
	C.W. "Levi" Levy (I)	2,842	1.3

Washington

Governor

	Vote total	Per- cent
Gary Locke (D)	1,296,492	58.0
Ellen Craswell (R)	940,538	42.0

House

		Vote total	Per- cent
1	Rick White (R)*	141,948	53.7
	Jeffrey Coopersmith (D)	122,187	46.3
2	Jack Metcalf (R)*	124,655	48.5
	Kevin Quigley (D)	122,728	47.8
	Karen Leibrant (NL)	9,561	3.7
3	Linda Smith (R)*	123,117	50.2
	Brian Baird (D)	122,230	49.8
4	Richard "Doc" Hastings (R)*	108,647	53.0
	Rick Locke (D)	96,502	47.0
5	George Nethercutt (R)*	131,618	55.6
	Judy Olson (D)	105,166	44.4
6	Norm Dicks (D)*	155,467	65.9
	Bill Tinsley (R)	71,337	30.2
	Ted Haley (I)	5,561	2.4
	Michael Huddleston (NL)	3,545	1.5
7	Jim McDermott (D)*	209,753	81.0
	Frank Kleschen (R)	49,341	19.0
8	Jennifer Dunn (R)*	170,691	65.4
	Dave Little (D)	90,340	34.6

		Vote total	Per- cent
9	Adam Smith (D)	105,236	50.1
	Randy Tate (R)*	99,199	47.3
	David Gruenstein (NL)	5,432	2.6

West Virginia

Governor

	Vote total	Per- cent
Cecil H. Underwood (R)	324,518	51.6
Charlotte Pritt (D)	287,870	45.8
Wallace Johnson (LIBERT)	16,171	2.6

Senate

	Vote total	Per- cent
John D. Rockefeller IV (D)*	456,526	76.6
Betty A. Burks (R)	139,088	23.4

House

		Vote total	Per- cent
1	Alan B. Mollohan (D)*	171,334	100.0
2	Bob Wise (D)*	141,551	68.9
	Greg Morris (R)	63,933	31.1
3	Nick J. Rahall II (D)*	145,550	100.0

Wisconsin

House

		Vote total	Per- cent
1	Mark W. Neumann (R)*	118,408	50.9
	Lydia C. Spottswood (D)	114,148	49.0
2	Scott L. Klug (R)*	154,557	57.4
	Paul R. Soglin (D)	110,467	41.0
	Ben Masel (LIBERT)	4,226	1.6
3	Ron Kind (D)	121,967	52.1
	Jim Harsdorf (R)	112,146	47.9
4	Gerald D. Kleczka (D)*	134,470	57.6
	Tom Reynolds (R)	98,438	42.2
5	Thomas M. Barrett (D)*	141,179	73.3
	Paul D. Melotik (R)	47,384	24.6
	James D. Soderna (TAX)	3,696	1.9
6	Tom Petri (R)*	169,213	73.0
	Alver Lindskoog (D)	55,377	23.9
	James Dean (LIBERT)	4,494	1.9
	Timothy Farness (TAX)	2,532	1.1
7	David R. Obey (D)*	137,428	57.0
	Scott West (R)	103,365	42.9
8	Jay W. Johnson (D)	129,551	52.0
	David T. Prosser Jr. (R)	119,398	48.0
9	F. James Sensenbrenner Jr. (R)*	197,910	74.4
	Floyd Brenholt (D)	67,740	25.5

Wyoming

Senate

	Vote total	Per- cent
Michael B. Enzi (R)	114,116	54.1
Kathy Karpan (D)	89,103	42.2
W. David Herbert (LIBERT)	5,289	2.5
Lloyd Marsden (NL)	2,569	1.2

House

		Vote total	Per- cent
AL	Barbara Cubin (R)*	116,004	55.2
	Pete Maxfield (D)	85,724	40.8
	Dave Dawson (LIBERT)	8,255	3.9

[a] Election to fill the remaining two years of Republican Bob Dole's term.

[b] Jo Ann Emerson was elected Nov. 5, 1996, as a Republican to complete the remainder of her husband's 104th Congress term; because her husband's death came after Missouri's primary filing deadline, she was listed on the general election ballot for the 105th Congress as an independent. She entered the 105th Congress as a Republican.

Results of House Elections, 1946–1996

	1946	1948	1950	1952	1954	1956	1958	1960	1962	1964	1966	1968
National Totals												
Democrats	188	263	235	213	232	234	283	263	259	295	248	243
Republicans	246	171	199	221	203	201	153	174	176	140	187	192
Alabama												
Democrats	9	9	9	9	9	9	9	9	8[1]	3	5	5
Republicans	0	0	0	0	0	0	0	0	0	5	3	3
Alaska												
Democrats	—	—	—	—	—	—	1	1	1	1	0	0
Republicans	—	—	—	—	—	—	0	0	0	0	1	1
Arizona												
Democrats	2	2	2	1	1	1	1	1	2[2]	2	1	1
Republicans	0	0	0	1	1	1	1	1	1	1	2	2
Arkansas												
Democrats	7	7	7	6[1]	6	6	6	6	41	4	3	3
Republicans	0	0	0	0	0	0	0	0	0	0	1	1
California												
Democrats	9	10	10	11[2]	11	13	16	16	25[2,4]	23	21	21
Republicans	14	13	13	19	19	17	14	14	13	15	17	17
Colorado												
Democrats	1	3	2	2	2	2	3	2	2	4	3	3
Republicans	3	1	2	2	2	2	1	2	2	0	1	1
Connecticut												
Democrats	0	3	2	1	1	0	6	4	5	6	5	4
Republicans	6	3	4	5	5	6	0	2	1	0	1	2
Delaware												
Democrats	0	0	0	0	1	0	1	1	1	1	0	0
Republicans	1	1	0	1	0	0	0	0	0	0	1	1
Florida												
Democrats	6	6	6	8[2]	7	7	7	7	10[2]	10	9	9
Republicans	0	0	0	0	1	1	1	1	2	2	3	3
Georgia												
Democrats	10	10	10	10	10	10	10	10	10	9	8	8
Republicans	0	0	0	0	0	0	0	0	0	1	2	2
Hawaii												
Democrats	—	—	—	—	—	—	—	1	2[2]	2	2	2
Republicans	—	—	—	—	—	—	—	0	0	0	0	0
Idaho												
Democrats	0	1	0	1	1	1	1	2	2	1	0	0
Republicans	2	1	2	1	1	1	1	0	0	1	2	2
Illinois												
Democrats	6	12	8	9[1]	12	11	14	14	12[1]	13	12	12
Republicans	20	14	18	16	13	14	11	11	12	11	12	12
Indiana												
Democrats	2	7	2	1	2	2	8	4[3]	4	6	5	4
Republicans	9	4	9	10	9	9	3	7	7	5	6	7
Iowa												
Democrats	0	0	0	0	0	1	4	2	1[1]	6	2	2
Republicans	8	8	8	8	8	7	4	6	6	1	5	5
Kansas												
Democrats	0	0	0	1	0	1	3	1	0[1]	0	0	0
Republicans	6	6	6	5	6	5	3	5	5	5	5	5
Kentucky												
Democrats	6	7	7	6[1]	6	6	7	7	5[1]	6	4	4
Republicans	3	2	2	2	2	2	1	1	2	1	3	3
Louisiana												
Democrats	8	8	8	8	8	8	8	8	8	8	8	8
Republicans	0	0	0	0	0	0	0	0	0	0	0	0
Maine												
Democrats	0	0	0	0	0	1	2	0	0[1]	1	2	2
Republicans	3	3	3	3	3	2	1	3	2	1	0	0
Maryland												
Democrats	4	4	3	3[2]	4	4	7	6	6[2]	6	5	4
Republicans	2	2	3	4	3	3	0	1	2	2	3	4
Massachusetts												
Democrats	5	4	6	6	7	7	8	8	7[1]	7	7	7
Republicans	9	8	8	8	7	7	6	6	5	5	5	5
Michigan												
Democrats	3	5	5	5[2]	7	6	7	7	8[2]	12	7	7
Republicans	14	12	12	13	11	12	11	11	11	7	12	12
Minnesota												
Democrats	1	4	4	4	5	5	4	3	4[1]	4	3	3
Republicans	8	5	5	5	4	4	5	6	4	4	5	5
Mississippi												
Democrats	7	7	7	6[1]	6	6	6	6	5[1]	4	5	5
Republicans	0	0	0	0	0	0	0	0	0	1	0	0
Missouri												
Democrats	4	12	10	7	9	10	10	9	8[1]	8	8	9
Republicans	9	1	3	4	2	1	1	2	2	2	2	1

1970	1972	1974	1976	1978	1980	1982	1984	1986	1988	1990	1992	1994	1996
255	243	291	292	277	243	269	253	258	260	267	258	204	207
180	192	144	143	158	192	166	182	177	175	167	176	230	227
5	4[1]	4	4	4	4	5	5	5	5	5	4	4	2
3	3	3	3	3	3	2	2	2	2	2	3	3	5
1	1[4]	0	0	0	0	0	0	0	0	0	0	0	0
0	0	1	1	1	1	1	1	1	1	1	1	1	1
1	1[2]	1	2	2	2	2[2]	1	1	1	1	3[2]	1	1
2	3	3	2	2	2	3	4	4	4	4	3	5	5
3	3	3	3	2	2	2	3	3	3	3	2	2	2
1	1	1	1	2	2	2	1	1	1	1	2	2	2
20	23[2]	28	29	26	22	28[2]	27	27	27	26	30[2]	27	29
18	20	15	14	17	21	17	18	18	18	19	22	25	23
2	2[2]	3	3	3	3	3[2]	2	3	3	3	2	2	2
2	3	2	2	2	2	3	4	3	3	3	4	4	4
3	3	4	4	5	4	4	3	3	3	3	3	3	4
2	3	2	2	1	2	2	3	3	3	3	3	3	2
0	0	0	0	0	0	1	1	1	1	1	0	0	0
1	1	1	1	1	1	0	0	0	0	0	1	1	1
9	11[2]	10	10	12	11	13[2]	12	12	10	9	10[2]	8	8
3	4	5	5	3	4	6	7	7	9	10	13	15	15
8	9	10	10	9	9	9	8	8	9	9	7[2]	4	3
2	1	0	0	1	1	1	2	2	1	1	4	7	8
2	2	2	2	2	2	2	2	1	1	2	2	2	2
0	0	0	0	0	0	0	0	1	1	0	0	0	0
0	0	0	0	0	0	0	1	1	1	2	1	0	0
2	2	2	2	2	2	2	1	1	1	0	1	2	2
12	10	13	12	11	10	12[1]	13	13	14	15	12[1]	10	10
12	14	11	12	13	14	10	9	9	8	7	8	10	10
5	4	9	8	7	6	5[1]	5[3]	6	6	8	7	4	4
6	7	2	3	4	5	5	5	4	4	2	3	6	6
2	3[1]	5	4	3	3	3	2	2	2	2	1[1]	0	1
5	3	1	2	3	3	3	4	4	4	4	4	5	4
1	1	1	2	1	1	2	2	2	2	2	2[1]	0	0
4	4	4	3	4	4	3	3	3	3	3	2	4	4
5	5	5	5	4	4	4	4	4	4	4	4[1]	2	1
2	2	2	2	3	3	3	3	3	3	3	2	4	5
8	7[4]	6[5]	6	5	6	6	6	5	4	4	4[1]	4	2
0	1	2	2	3	2	2	2	3	4	4	3	3	5
2	1	0	0	0	0	0	0	1	1	1	1	1	2
0	1	2	2	2	2	2	2	1	1	1	1	1	0
5	4	5	5	6	7	7	6	6	6	5	4	4	4
3	4	3	3	2	1	1	2	2	2	3	4	4	4
8	9[6]	10	10	10	10	10[1]	10	10	10	10	8[1]	8	10
4	3	2	2	2	2	1	1	1	1	1	2	2	0
7	7	12	11	13	12	12[1]	11	11	11	11	10[1]	9	10
12	12	7	8	6	7	6	7	7	7	7	6	7	6
4	4	5	5	4	3	5	5	5	5	6	6	6	6
4	4	3	3	4	5	3	3	3	3	2	2	2	2
5	3	3	3	3	3	3	3	4	4	5	5	4	2
0	2	2	2	2	2	2	2	1	1	0	0	1	3
9	9	9	8	8	6	6[1]	6	5	5	6	6	6	5
1	1	1	2	2	4	3	3	4	4	3	3	3	4

s	1946	1948	1950	1952	1954	1956	1958	1960	1962	1964	1966	1968
Montana												
Democrats	1	1	1	1	1	2	2	1	1	1	1	1
Republicans	1	1	1	1	1	0	0	1	1	1	1	1
Nebraska												
Democrats	0	1	0	0	0	0	2	0	0[1]	1	0	0
Republicans	4	3	4	4	4	4	2	4	3	2	3	3
Nevada												
Democrats	0	1	1	0	0	1	1	1	1	1	1	1
Republicans	1	0	0	1	1	0	0	0	0	0	0	0
New Hampshire												
Democrats	0	0	0	0	0	0	0	0	0	1	0	0
Republicans	2	2	2	2	2	2	2	2	2	1	2	2
New Jersey												
Democrats	2	5	5	5	6	4	5	6	7[2]	11	9	9
Republicans	12	9	9	9	8	10	9	8	8	4	6	6
New Mexico												
Democrats	2	2	2	2	2	2	2	2	2	2	2	0
Republicans	0	0	0	0	0	0	0	0	0	0	0	2
New York												
Democrats	16	24	23	16[1]	17	17	19	22	20[1]	27	26	26
Republicans	28	20	22	27	26	26	24	21	21	14	15	15
North Carolina												
Democrats	12	12	12	11	11	11	11	11	91	9	8	7
Republicans	0	0	0	1	1	1	1	1	2	2	3	4
North Dakota												
Democrats	0	0	0	0	0	0	1	0	0	1	0	0
Republicans	2	2	2	2	2	2	1	2	2	1	2	2
Ohio												
Democrats	4	12	7	6	6	6	9	7	6[2]	10	5	6
Republicans	19	11	15	16	17	17	14	16	18	14	19	18
Oklahoma												
Democrats	6	8	6	5[1]	5	5	5	5	5	5	4	4
Republicans	2	0	2	1	1	1	1	1	1	1	2	2
Oregon												
Democrats	0	0	0	0	1	3	3	2	3	3	2	2
Republicans	4	4	4	4	3	1	1	2	1	1	2	2
Pennsylvania												
Democrats	5	16	13	11[1]	14	13	16	14	13[1]	15	14	14
Republicans	28	19	20	19	16	17	14	16	14	12	13	13
Rhode Island												
Democrats	2	2	2	2	2	2	2	2	2	2	2	2
Republicans	0	0	0	0	0	0	0	0	0	0	0	0
South Carolina												
Democrats	6	6	6	6	6	6	6	6	6	6	5	5
Republicans	0	0	0	0	0	0	0	0	0	0	1	1
South Dakota												
Democrats	0	0	0	0	0	1	1	0	0	0	0	0
Republicans	2	2	2	2	2	1	1	2	2	2	2	2
Tennessee												
Democrats	8	8	8	7[1]	7	7	7	7	6	6	5	5
Republicans	2	2	2	2	2	2	2	2	3	3	4	4
Texas												
Democrats	21	21	21	22[2]	21	21	21	21	21[2]	23	21	20
Republicans	0	0	0	0	1	1	1	1	2	0	2	3
Utah												
Democrats	1	2	2	0	0	0	1	2	0	1	0	0
Republicans	1	0	0	2	2	2	1	0	2	1	2	2
Vermont												
Democrats	0	0	0	0	0	0	1	0	0	0	0	0
Republicans	1	1	1	1	1	1	0	1	1	1	1	1
Virginia												
Democrats	9	9	9	7[2]	8	8	8	8	8	8	6	5
Republicans	0	0	0	3	2	2	2	2	2	2	4	5
Washington												
Democrats	1	2	2	1[2]	1	1	1	2	1	5	5	5
Republicans	5	4	4	6	6	6	6	5	6	2	2	2
West Virginia												
Democrats	2	6	6	5	6	4	5	5	4[1]	4	4	5
Republicans	4	0	0	1	0	2	1	1	1	1	1	0
Wisconsin												
Democrats	0	2	1	1	3	3	5	4	4	5	3	3
Republicans	10	8	9	9	7	7	5	6	6	5	7	7
Wyoming												
Democrats	0	0	0	0	0	0	0	0	1	0	0	1
Republicans	1	1	1	1	1	1	1	1	1	0	1	1

1970	1972	1974	1976	1978	1980	1982	1984	1986	1988	1990	1992	1994	1996
1	1	2	1	1	1	1	1	1	1	1	11	1	1
1	1	0	1	1	1	1	1	1	1	1	0	0	0
0	0	0	1	1	0	0	0	0	1	1	1	0	0
3	3	3	2	2	3	3	3	3	2	2	2	3	3
1	0	1	1	1	1	1[2]	1	1	1	1	1	0	0
0	1	0	0	0	0	1	1	1	1	1	1	2	2
0	0	1	1	1	1	1	0	0	0	1	1	0	0
2	2	1	1	1	1	1	2	2	2	1	1	2	2
9	8	12	11	10	8	9[1]	8	8	8	8	7[1]	5	6
6	7	3	4	5	7	5	6	6	6	6	6	8	7
1	1	1	1	1	0	1[2]	1	1	1	1	1	1	1
1	1	1	1	1	2	2	2	2	2	2	2	2	2
24	22[1]	27	28	26	22	20[1]	19	20	21	21	18[1]	17	18
17	17	12	11	13	17	14	15	14	13	13	13	14	13
7	7	9	9	9	7	9	6	8	8	7	8[2]	4	6
4	4	2	2	2	4	2	5	3	3	4	4	8	6
1	0[1]	0	0	0	1	1	1	1	1	1	1	1	1
1	1	1	1	1	0	0	0	0	0	0	0	0	0
7	7[1]	8	10	10	11	10[1]	11	11	11	11	10[1]	6	8
17	16	15	13	13	12	11	10	10	10	10	9	13	11
4	5	6	5	5	5	5	5	4	4	4	4	1	0
2	1	0	1	1	1	1	1	2	2	2	2	5	6
2	2	4	4	4	3	3[2]	3	3	3	4	4	3	4
2	2	0	0	0	1	2	2	2	2	1	1	2	1
14	13[1]	14	17	15	13[6]	13[1]	13	12	12	11	11[1]	11	11
13	12	11	8	10	12	10	10	11	11	12	10	10	10
2	2	2	2	2	1	1	1	1	0	1	1	2	2
0	0	0	0	0	1	1	1	1	2	1	1	0	0
5	4	5	5	4	2	3	3	4	4	4	3	2	2
1	2	1	1	2	4	3	3	2	2	2	3	4	4
2	1	0	0	1	1	1[1]	1	1	1	1	1	1	0
0	1	2	2	1	1	0	0	0	0	0	0	0	1
5	3[1]	5	5	5	5	6[2]	6	6	6	6	6	4	4
4	5	3	3	3	3	3	3	3	3	3	3	5	5
20	20[2]	21	22	20	19	22[2]	17	17	19	19	21[2]	19	17
3	4	3	2	4	5	5	10	10	8	8	9	11	13
1	2	2	1	1	0	0[2]	0	1	1	2	2	1	0
1	0	0	1	1	2	3	3	2	2	1	1	2	3
0	0	0	0	0	0	0	0	0	0	0	0	0	0
1	1	1	1	1	1	1	1	1	1	0	0	0	0
4	3	5	4	4	1	4	4	5	5	6	7[2]	6	6
6	7	5	6	6	9	6	6	5	5	4	4	5	5
6	6	6	6	6	5	5[2]	5	5	5	5	8[2]	2	3
1	1	1	1	1	2	3	3	3	3	3	1	7	6
5	4[1]	4	4	4	2	4	4	4	4	4	3[1]	3	3
0	0	0	0	0	2	0	0	0	0	0	0	0	0
5	5[1]	7	7	6	5	5	5	5	5	4	4	3	5
5	4	2	2	3	4	4	4	4	4	5	5	6	4
1	1	1	0	0	0	0	0	0	0	0	0	0	0
0	0	0	0	1	1	1	1	1	1	1	1	1	1

1. State lost seats due to reapportionment.

2. State gained seats due to reapportionment.

3. Indiana 1960 and Indiana 1984: National and state totals reflect the final outcome of a contested election in which a Republican was first certified the winner, but the House decided to seat the Democrat.

4. California 1962, Alaska 1972 and Louisiana 1972: National and state totals reflect the reelection of a Democrat who died before the election but whose name remained on the ballot.

5. Louisiana 1974: National and state totals reflect the final outcome of a contested election in which no winner was declared, followed by a special election won by the Republican.

6. Massachusetts 1972 and Pennsylvania 1980: National and state Democratic totals reflect the election of an Independent candidate who previously announced he would serve as a Democrat.

NOTE: The above totals do not include "other" representatives elected as independent or third party candidates. Those numbers are California: Progressive 1936 (1). (No formal party. The representative became a Democrat in 1938.) Minnesota: Farmer-Labor 1928 (1), 1930 (1), 1932 (5), 1934 (3), 1936 (5), 1938 (1), 1940 (1) and 1942 (1). (Merged with Democrats in 1944.) New York: American Labor 1938 through 1948 (1). (Party disbanded after 1954.) Ohio: Independent 1950 and 1952 (1). (Defeated by Democrat in 1954.) Wisconsin: Progressive 1934 (7), 1936 (7), 1938 (2), 1940 (3), 1942 (2) and 1944 (1). (Disbanded after 1944. The last Progressive became a Republican in 1946.) Vermont: Independent 1990, 1992, 1994 and 1996 (1). National totals: 1928 (1), 1930 (1), 1932 (5), 1934 (10), 1936 (13), 1938 (4), 1940 (5), 1942 (4), 1944 (2), 1946 through 1952 (1), and 1990 through 1996 (1).

Governors, 1993–1996

Following is a list of governors who served during the period of President Clinton's first term, 1993–1996. All governors serve four-year terms except those representing New Hampshire and Vermont; they serve two-year terms.

Party designations appears in parentheses following the governor's name. The following abbreviations were used: (ALI) Alaskan Independent; (D) Democrat; (I) Independent; (R) Republican. *(Governors, 1981–1984, Congress and the Nation Vol. VI, p. 1122; 1985–1988, Congress and the Nation Vol. VII, p. 1143; 1989–1992, Congress and the Nation Vol. VIII, p. 1259.)*

	Dates of service
Alabama	
Guy Hunt (R)	Jan. 19, 1987–April 22, 1993
James E. Folsom Jr. (D)	April 22, 1993–Jan. 16, 1995
Forrest "Fob" James (R)	Jan. 16, 1995–
Alaska	
Walter J. Hickel (ALI)	Dec. 3, 1990–Dec. 5, 1994
Tony Knowles (D)	Dec. 5, 1994–
Arizona	
Fife Symington (R)	March 6, 1991–
Arkansas	
Jim Guy Tucker (D)	Dec. 12, 1992–July 15, 1996
Mike Huckabee (R)	July 15, 1996–
California	
Pete Wilson (R)	Jan. 7, 1991–
Colorado	
Roy R. Romer (D)	Jan. 13, 1987–
Connecticut	
Lowell P. Weicker Jr. (I)	Jan. 9, 1991–Jan. 4, 1995
John G. Rowland (R)	Jan. 4, 1995–
Delaware	
Dale E. Wolf (R)	Jan. 1, 1993–Jan. 19, 1993
Thomas R. Carper(D)	Jan. 19, 1993–
Florida	
Lawton Chiles (D)	Jan. 8, 1991–
Georgia	
Zell Miller (D)	Jan. 14, 1991–
Hawaii	
John Waihee (D)	Dec. 1, 1986–Dec. 5, 1994
Benjamin J. Cayetano (D)	Dec. 5, 1994–
Idaho	
Cecil D. Andrus (D)	Jan. 4, 1971–Jan. 24, 1977
	Jan. 5, 1987–Jan. 2, 1995
Philip E. Batt (R)	Jan. 2, 1995–
Illinois	
Jim Edgar (R)	Jan. 14, 1991–

	Dates of service
Indiana	
Evan Bayh (D)	Jan. 9, 1989–Jan. 13, 1997
Frank L. O'Bannon (D)	Jan. 13, 1997–
Iowa	
Terry E. Branstad (R)	Jan. 14, 1983–
Kansas	
Joan Finney (D)	Jan. 14, 1991–Jan. 9, 1995
Bill Graves (R)	Jan. 9, 1995–
Kentucky	
Brereton C. Jones (D)	Dec. 10, 1991–Dec. 12, 1995
Paul E. Patton (D)	Dec. 12, 1995–
Louisiana	
Edwin W. Edwards (D)	May 9, 1972–March 10, 1980
	March 12, 1984–March 14, 1988
	Jan. 8, 1992– Jan. 8, 1996
Mike Foster (R)	Jan. 8, 1996–
Maine	
John R. McKernan Jr. (R)	Jan. 7, 1987–Jan. 1995
Angus King Jr. (I)	Jan. 5, 1995–
Maryland	
William D. Schaefer (D)	Jan. 21, 1987–Jan. 18, 1995
Parris N. Glendening (D)	Jan. 18, 1995–
Massachusetts	
William F. Weld (R)	Jan. 3, 1991–
Michigan	
John Engler (R)	Jan. 1, 1991–
Minnesota	
Arne H. Carlson (R)	Jan. 7, 1991–
Mississippi	
Kirk Fordice (R)	Jan. 14, 1992–
Missouri	
John Ashcroft (R)	Jan. 14, 1985–Jan. 11, 1993
Mel Carnahan (D)	Jan. 11, 1993–
Montana	
Marc Racicot (R)	Jan. 4, 1993–

	Dates of service		Dates of service
Nebraska		**Rhode Island**	
Ben Nelson (D)	Jan. 9, 1991–	Bruce Sundlun (D)	Jan. 1, 1991–Jan. 3, 1995
		Lincoln C. Almond (R)	Jan. 3, 1995–
Nevada			
Bob J. Miller (D)	Jan. 3, 1989–	**South Carolina**	
		Carroll Campbell (R)	Jan. 14, 1987–Jan. 11, 1995
New Hampshire		David Beasley (R)	Jan. 11, 1995–
Steve Merrill (R)	Jan. 7, 1993–Jan. 9, 1997		
Jeanne Shaheen (D)	Jan. 9, 1997–	**South Dakota**	
		George S. Mickelson (R)	Jan. 6, 1987–April 19, 1993
New Jersey		Walter D. Miller (R)	April 20, 1993–Jan. 7, 1995
James J. Florio (D)	Jan. 16, 1990–Jan. 18, 1994	William J. Janklow (R)	Jan. 1, 1979–Jan. 6, 1987
Christine Todd Whitman (R)	Jan. 18, 1994–		Jan. 7, 1995–
New Mexico		**Tennessee**	
Bruce King (D)	Jan. 1, 1971–Jan. 1, 1975	Ned R. McWherter (D)	Jan. 17, 1987– Jan. 21, 1995
	Jan. 1, 1979–Jan. 1, 1983	Don Sundquist (R)	Jan. 21, 1995–
	Jan. 1, 1991–Jan. 1, 1995		
Gary E. Johnson (R)	Jan. 1, 1995–	**Texas**	
		Ann W. Richards (D)	Jan. 15, 1991–Jan. 17, 1995
New York		George W. Bush (R)	Jan. 17, 1995–
Mario M. Cuomo (D)	Jan. 1, 1983–Jan. 1, 1995		
George E. Pataki (R)	Jan. 1, 1995–	**Utah**	
		Mike Leavitt (R)	Jan. 3, 1993–
North Carolina			
James B. Hunt Jr. (D)	Jan. 8, 1977–Jan. 5, 1985	**Vermont**	
	Jan. 9, 1993–	Howard Dean (D)	Aug. 14, 1991–
North Dakota		**Virginia**	
Edward T. Schafer (R)	Jan. 5, 1993–	L. Douglas Wilder (D)	Jan. 14, 1990–Jan. 15, 1994
		George F. Allen (R)	Jan. 15, 1994–
Ohio			
George V. Voinovich (R)	Jan. 14, 1991–	**Washington**	
		Mike Lowry (D)	Jan. 13, 1993–Jan. 15, 1997
Oklahoma		Gary Locke (D)	Jan. 15, 1997–
David Walters (D)	Jan. 14, 1991–Jan. 9, 1995		
Frank Keating (R)	Jan. 9, 1995–	**West Virginia**	
		Gaston Caperton (D)	Jan. 16, 1989–Jan. 13, 1997
Oregon		Cecil H. Underwood (R)	Jan. 14, 1957–Jan. 16, 1961
Barbara Roberts (D)	Jan. 14, 1991–Jan. 9, 1995		Jan. 13, 1997–
John Kitzhaber (D)	Jan. 9, 1995–		
		Wisconsin	
Pennsylvania		Tommy G. Thompson (R)	Jan. 5, 1987–
Robert P. Casey (D)	Jan. 20, 1987– Jan. 17, 1995		
Tom Ridge (R)	Jan. 17, 1995–	**Wyoming**	
		Michael J. Sullivan (D)	Jan. 5, 1987–Jan. 2, 1995
		Jim Geringer (R)	Jan. 2, 1995–

Index

Index

Pornography. *See Obscenity and pornography*

Port Hueneme, Calif., Naval Civil Engineering Lab, 290 (table)

Portal-to-Portal Act of 1947, 669

Porter, John Edward, R-Ill.
foreign aid appropriations, 1996, 192
gas tax repeal, 106

Portman, Rob, R-Ohio
election, 7
unfunded mandates, 838, 839

Portsmouth, Va., Naval Electronics Systems Engineering Center, 288

Portugal
reconnaissance overflights, 293
U.S. aid appropriations, 209
U.S. arms transfers, 323

Post Office and Civil Service Committee, House
health care reform, 521
leadership, jurisdiction, 867, 1096
termination, 887

Postal Rate Commission, 806

Postal Service, U.S.
Hatch Act revisions, 805–807
House Post Office scandal, 867
inspector general, 821
retired employees, 48, 816
workplace safety, 818

Postsecondary education. *See Colleges and universities*

Potter, Trevor, 914

Poultry
chilled products, 505
egg marketing promotion, 492
inspection, 848

POW-MIA Affairs, Senate Select Committee on, 214 (box)

Powell, Colin L.,
defense leadership, 259 (box)
defense policy summary, 255
gays in the military, 253, 254, 284–286
Haiti delegation, 196, 941
Republican convention, 20
Somalia action, 323

Prather, Joseph W., 12

Pregnancy. *See also Abortion; Adolescent pregnancy; Birth control; Out-of-wedlock births*
AIDS programs, 568
childbirth hospital stays, 511, 549, 565–566
death penalty stay, 698
drinking water safety, 439, 446
fetal tissue research, 526, 527–528
embryos, 564
infertility research, 529
Medicaid coverage, 559–563, 583
military medical studies, 266
veterans' health care, 599
welfare benefits, 587
food stamp work requirement, 594
illegal immigrants, 591
WIC program, 575

Preschool. *See Head Start*

Presidential election, 1992
China trade status, 173
Clinton candidacy, 929–932
gays in the military, 254, 284
NAFTA, 152, 156
passport records leak, 707
vote by state (table), 1177

Presidential election, 1996
campaign, 24–25
campaign finance scandals, 945–946
Clinton acceptance speech (text), 1168–1170
debates, 24
Democratic nomination, 21–24, 939 (box), 1181
issues
defense policy, 254, 256
immigration, 723
judicial appointments, 758
minimum wage, 667
product liability, 379–380
same-sex marriage, 747–748
summary, 17, 947
telecommunications overhaul, 393
trade, 151, 153, 154
press coverage, 947
Republican nomination, 17–21, 939 (box), 1180
results, 25–26
electoral vote by state (table), 1179
vote by state (table), 1178
summary, 16–17, 946–947

Presidential elections
candidate spending regulations, 914
tax return checkoff financing, 93
victorious party, 1860–1996 (table), 1173
vote summary, 1789–1996 (table), 1174–1176

President's Community Enterprise Board, 640

Presidents, U.S.
radio spectrum auctions, 356
terrorism security, 732

Presidio, 421–422, 461, 462

Presidio Trust, 461

Pressler amendment, 233

Pressler, Larry, R-S.D.
aircraft safety, 336
campaign finance reform, 911
defeat, 26
foreign aid appropriations, 1996, 233
foreign aid authorization, 1994, 203
Kantor Commerce nomination, 331 (box)
nuclear nonproliferation, 233
omnibus science authorization, 852
public broadcasting, 397
radio spectrum auction, 396
school-to-work program, 628
Senate leadership, 863, 884
shipping port fees, 338, 371
telecommunications overhaul, 388–390
trade technical corrections, 183

Preventive medical care, 530

Price, David E., 28

Price Waterhouse, 889 (box)

Primary medical care
health care reform, 514
Medicare cuts, 530, 531, 533, 534
student aid, 546

Primate research centers, 530

Printing industry
federal jobs, 811
vegetable oil ink, 492

Printing, Joint Committee on
leadership, jurisdiction, 1099

Prison labor
China trade status, 173, 179
earned-income tax credit, 172

Prisoners. *See also Sentencing*
drug, alcohol treatment, 684, 688, 697–698
early release, 740
parolee drug testing, 695
escapes, 742, 745
family unity, 696
habeas corpus appeals, 727, 728, 729, 731, 735
illegal immigrants
detention before deportation, 722, 725
prison costs, 684, 688, 692, 695, 735
transfer treaties, 725
job training, 695
juvenile offenders, 700
literacy program, 670
Pell grants, 688, 691, 695
prison conditions lawsuits, 735
release notification, 688, 695
religious freedom, 709
Social Security benefits, 588, 662, 675
TB prevention, treatment, 695
WIC program, 593

Prisons
boot camps, 687, 688, 694
construction aid, 683, 684, 687, 688, 691, 692, 693, 694–695, 733, 734–735
military base conversion, 695
overcrowding
capacity reports, 703
court orders, 688, 695, 734, 735
Supreme Court decisions, 779

Privacy
air pilots background checks, 361
computer hackers, 742
drug testing, 764
encryption, 182 (box)
espionage suspects, 217
federal social surveys, 751–752
immigrant worker verification, 722
medical records, 520, 553
Packwood ethics case, 861, 872–873
telephone companies' information, 395
wiretapping capabilities, 354–355, 395

Private schools, 615, 621

Privatization
airports, 361
college construction loans, 632
Commerce Department elimination, 380–381
fisheries, 426
military maintenance depots, 297, 309, 310 (box), 319–320
multilateral aid fund, 208
public broadcasting, 397
schools, 622
science, space programs, 853
uranium enrichment, 475

Privileged motions, 865

Product liability
aircraft manufacturers, 347
GOP "Contract with America," 885 (box)

lawsuit limits, 328, 346, 359, 376–379
summary, 13

Progress and Freedom Foundation, 876, 899

Progressive Foundation, 480

Project Aries, 530

Property rights
American Heritage areas, 422
appraisals of wilderness designations, 406, 407
clean water bill, 415, 457
Colorado wilderness areas, 422
Conte wildlife refuge, 465
drinking water safety, 408–410
endangered species protection, 416–417, 425, 458–459
environmental protection, 402–403, 404, 405, 436
federal regulation impact, 409
land-use regulation compensation, 408, 419
National Biological Survey, 418–419
regulatory overhaul, 459, 842, 843–844
"superfund" overhaul, 411
Supreme Court decisions, 764, 796
"takings" legislation, 402–403, 426, 842

Property taxes
federal payments in lieu, 822–823

Proposition 187, 745–746

Prosecutors. *See also Attorneys, U.S.; Independent counsels*
crime bill, 679, 681, 687, 700, 701
immigration law revision, 724
terrorism bill, 727, 730, 732
violent crime task forces, 737

Prostate cancer, 529

Protocol on Environmental Protection to the Antarctic Treaty, 470

Prowler planes, 310

Pryce, Deborah, R-Ohio
unfunded mandates, 839

Pryor, David, D-Ark.
balanced-budget amendment, 63
congressional reform, 878
deficit-reduction bill, 1995, 97
health care reform, 510
job discrimination against gays, 748 (box)
Senate leadership, 7 (box), 863, 884, 886
unfunded mandates, 838
welfare reform, 582

Psychologists, 545

Public broadcasting
appropriations, 396–397
National Information Infrastructure, 358

Public Citizen, 905

Public defenders, 687, 701

Public health
drinking water safety, 408–410, 433–446
EPA regulatory authority, 460
health care reform, 519 (box)
unfunded mandates exemptions, 839

Public health pesticides, 451

Public Health Service Act, 536, 540–541